Caribbean Sea

15°N

75°W   60°W

CENTRAL
AMERICA

Maracaibo
Santa Marta
Barranquilla
Cartagena
Cúcuta
Bucaramanga
Medellín
Manizales
Pereira
Cali

Barquisimeto
Coro   Caracas   Barcelona
         Cumaná
Valencia   Maracay
Mérida
San   Barinas
Cristóbal
Tunja
Bogotá
Villavicencio
COLOMBIA
Neiva

Ciudad Guayana
Ciudad
Bolívar
VENEZUELA   GUYANA
         Georgetown
              Paramaribo
         SURINAME   FRENCH
                    GUIANA
                    (France)

ATLANTIC
OCEAN

Gulf of
Panama

Galápagos Islands
(Ecuador)

Orinoco R.

Boa
Vista

Negro R.

Macapá

0°   0°

ECUADOR Quito
Esmeraldas
Pasto
Florencia
Ibarra
Portoviejo   Ambato
Guayaquil   Riobamba
Machala   Cuenca
Loja
Piura   Iquitos

Amazon R.

Manaus   Santarém   Belém
                             São Luis

R.

Tapajós R.
Xingu R.

Fortaleza
Teresina

PACIFIC

OCEAN

Chiclayo   Cajamarca
Trujillo   PERU   Pucallpa
Chimbote   Huánuco
Cerro de Pasco
        Lima   Huancayo
        Ayacucho   Cusco
        Ica

Rio
Branco

Madeira R.

Porto Velho

BRAZIL

Tocantins R.

São Francisco R.

Natal
João
Pessoa
Recife
Maceió
Aracaju
Salvador

15°S

Juliaca
Arequipa   La Paz
Tacna Cochabamba
Arica Oruro
Iquique Potosí

Trinidad
BOLIVIA
Santa
Cruz
Sucre

Paraguay R.

Cuiabá   Brasília
         Goiânia

Uberlândia
Campo Grande

Belo
Horizonte
Vitória

15°S

Tarija

Antofagasta
San
Salvador
de Jujuy
San Miguel
de Tucumán
Copiapó
Catamarca
CHILE
La Serena

Salta
PARAGUAY
Asunción
Pedro Juan
Caballero
Ciudad
del Este

Campinas
Rio de
Janeiro
São Paulo
Niterói
Santos
Curitiba
Florianópolis

Posadas   Encarnación
Resistencia
Santiago   Corrientes
del Estero
La Rioja

Paraná R.

Porto Alegre

30°S

Córdoba   Santa
          Fe
San Juan
Valparaíso   Mendoza
Santiago San Luis   Rosario
Rancagua
Talca

Rivera
Salto
Paysandú
URUGUAY
Buenos   Montevideo
Aires
Río de la Plata

30°S

45°W

Concepción   Chillán
                  ARGENTINA   Bahía
Temuco   Blanca   Mar del Plata
        Neuquén

ATLANTIC

OCEAN

Puerto Montt

Comodoro
Rivadavia

45°S   45°S

Falkland Islands
(Islas Malvinas)
(U.K.)

Strait of
Magellan

Punta Arenas

75°W   60°W

Ushuaia

South America

Elevation in Feet

15,000
10,000
5,000
2,000
1,000
0
Below sea level

Major Cities

⊛ Capital city
■ Over 5,000,000
● 1,000,000–5,000,000
■ 500,000–999,999
● 250,000–499,999
● 100,000–249,999
○ Less than 100,000

0   250   500 mi.

0   250   500 km

ENCYCLOPEDIA OF

LATIN AMERICAN HISTORY AND CULTURE

ENCYCLOPEDIA OF

LATIN AMERICAN HISTORY AND CULTURE

SECOND EDITION

Volume 5

P–S

Jay Kinsbruner

EDITOR IN CHIEF

Erick D. Langer

SENIOR EDITOR

CHARLES SCRIBNER'S SONS
A part of Gale, Cengage Learning

Detroit • New York • San Francisco • New Haven, Conn • Waterville, Maine • London

Encyclopedia of Latin American History and Culture

Jay Kinsbruner, Editor in Chief
Erick D. Langer, Senior Editor

For product information and technology assistance, contact us at
Gale Customer Support, 1-800-877-4253.
For permission to use material from this text or product,
submit all requests online at **www.cengage.com/permissions.**
Further permissions questions can be emailed to
permissionrequest@cengage.com

Library of Congress Cataloging-in-Publication Data

Encyclopedia of Latin American history and culture / Jay Kinsbruner, editor in chief; Erick D. Langer, senior editor. -- 2nd ed.
    p. cm. --
    Includes bibliographical references and index.
    ISBN 978-0-684-31270-5 (set) -- ISBN 978-0-684-31441-9 (vol. 1) -- ISBN 978-0-684-31442-6 (vol. 2) -- ISBN 978-0-684-31443-3 (vol. 3) -- ISBN 978-0-684-31444-0 (vol. 4) -- ISBN 978-0-684-31445-7 (vol. 5) -- ISBN 978-0-684-31598-0 (vol. 6)
    1. Latin America--Encyclopedias. I. Kinsbruner, Jay.

F1406.E53 2008
980.003--dc22   2008003461

Gale
27500 Drake Rd.
Farmington Hills, MI, 48331-3535

978-0-684-31270-5 (set)   0-684-31270-0 (set)
978-0-684-31441-9 (vol. 1)   0-684-31441-X (vol. 1)
978-0-684-31442-6 (vol. 2)   0-684-31442-8 (vol. 2)
978-0-684-31443-3 (vol. 3)   0-684-31443-6 (vol. 3)
978-0-684-31444-0 (vol. 4)   0-684-31444-4 (vol. 4)
978-0-684-31445-7 (vol. 5)   0-684-31445-2 (vol. 5)
978-0-684-31598-0 (vol. 6)   0-684-31598-X (vol. 6)

This title is also available as an e-book.
ISBN-13: 978-0-684-31590-4 ISBN-10: 0-684-31590-4
Contact your Gale, a part of Cengage Learning, sales representative for ordering information.

Printed in the United States of America
1 2 3 4 5 6 7 12 11 10 09 08

CONTENTS

Introduction . . . Volume 1, page ix

Using the Encyclopedia . . . Volume 1, page xiii

List of Contributors . . . Volume 1, page xv

Encyclopedia of Latin American History and
    Culture . . . *1*
    Volume 1: Abadía Méndez, Miguel to Butler,
      Smedley Darlington
    Volume 2: Caaguazú to Dzibilchaltún
    Volume 3: Earthquakes to Izquierdo, María
    Volume 4: Jaar, Alfredo to Oviedo y Valdés,
      Gonzalo Fernández
    Volume 5: Pachacamac to Szyszlo,
      Fernando de
    Volume 6: Tábara, Enrique to Zutuhil

Chronology . . . Volume 6, page 529

*Thematic Outline of Topics . . . Volume 6,
page 551*

*Table of Biographical Subjects by
Profession . . . Volume 6, page 581*

Index . . . Volume 6, page 641

P

PACHACAMAC. Pachacamac, a major deity in the ancient Andean pantheon, whose name translates from Quechua as "creator of the earth." Pachacamac was a pre-Inca deity of enormous prestige dating back at least as early as the Middle Horizon (ca. 540–900). The principal shrine to Pachacamac was a large complex of adobe buildings and pyramids located on a hill above the seashore at the mouth of the Lurín valley, just south of modern Lima. This shrine was one of the most sacred places in all of the Andes. Pilgrims came from everywhere to visit the shrine and to receive prophecies from its oracle. Important people were also brought there for burial. The Spanish described the shrine as a small, fetid, dark chamber on top of a pyramid that contained a wooden idol smeared with the blood of offerings. In order to approach the idol, a supplicant had to be purified through fasts and rituals that were reputed to last a year. Admittance had to be gained through three successive precincts of the temple before one could approach the inner sanctum. There, the idol was addressed through the priestly intermediary, and the Spanish report that even the priests were very much afraid of the idol. The cult of Pachacamac was administered by a large and highly organized priesthood which established branch oracles in other parts of the country. The Incas co-opted this cult into the imperial religion and enlarged and embellished the shrine. The temple of Pachacamac was visited by Hernando Pizarro in January 1533. He and his companions observed the cult, questioned the priests, and finally overthrew the idol in front of the shocked natives.

The ruins of Pachacamac were the site of a pioneering excavation by Max Uhle in 1896. In his classic monograph, published in 1903, Uhle laid the foundations for the basic chronological and culture sequence models of Andean archaeology.

See also **Archaeology; Pizarro, Hernando.**

BIBLIOGRAPHY

John H. Rowe, "Inca Culture at the Time of the Spanish Conquest," in *Handbook of South American Indians*, vol. 2 (1946), pp. 183–330.

Burr Cartwright Brundage, *The Empire of the Inca* (1963) and *The Lords of Cuzco: A History and Description of the Inca People in Their Final Days* (1970). For the archaeology of Pachacamac, see Max Uhle, *Pachacamac* (1903).

Additional Bibliography

Boone, Elizabeth Hill, and Cummins, Tom, eds. *Native Traditions in the Postconquest World: A Symposium at Dumbarton Oaks, 2nd through 4th October 1992.* Washington, DC: Dumbarton Oaks, 1998.

Cantos de Andrade, Rodrígo, and María Rostworowski de Diez Canseco. *El señorío de Pachacamac: el informe de Rodrigo Cantos de Andrade de 1573.* Lima: Instituto de Estudios Peruanos: Banco Central de Reserva del Perú, Fondo Editorial, 1999.

Eeckhout, Peter. *Pachacamac durant l'Intermédiaire récent: Étude d'un site monumental préhispanique de la côte centrale du Pérou.* Oxford: J. and E. Hedges: Distributed by Hadrian Books, 1999.

Rostworowski de Diez Canseco, María. *Pachacamac y el Señor de los Milagros: Una trayectoria milenaria: Señorios indígenas de Lima y Canta.* Lima: Instituto de Estudios Peruanos, 2002.

Urton, Gary. *Inca Myths.* Austin: University of Texas Press, 1999.

GORDON F. MCEWAN

PACHACUTI (c. 1391–c. 1473). Pachacuti (also Pachacuteq; *b.* ca. 1391; *d.* ca. 1473), Inca emperor (ca. 1438–ca. 1471). Pachacuti is regarded as the greatest of the Inca emperors. His name has been translated from the Quechua variously as "Cataclysm," "Earthquake," or literally "You Shake the Earth." The variant Pachacuteq literally means "One Who Shakes the Earth." Pachacuti ascended the throne after defending Cuzco against the Chanca invasion and overthrowing his father, Viracocha Inca, in 1438. He then founded the Inca state and initiated its first great expansion. With his son Topa Inca, Pachacuti conquered a huge territory from Lake Titicaca on the modern Peru-Bolivia border in the south to the city of Quito in modern Ecuador to the north. Among his other achievements were the design and rebuilding of the imperial capital of Cuzco and the construction of Sacsahuaman and other classic Inca monuments including Ollantaytambo and Machu Picchu. Pachacuti is credited with inventing the bureaucratic structure of the Inca state, codifying Inca law, reorganizing and codifying the Inca religion, and developing the institution called the *panaca*, which provided households for the royal mummies. He transformed the Incas from a predatory chiefdom into a highly centralized and stratified state administering a redistributive economy through a monopoly of force and codified law.

Pachacuti was a poet and author of some of the most famous Inca poems: the Sacred Hymns (haillikuna) of the Situa ceremony. These can be found in English translations in *Ancient American Poets* (2005) by John Curl, together with a detailed biography and survey of Inca poetic traditions.

See also **Cuzco; Viracocha.**

BIBLIOGRAPHY

Principal sources on Pachacuti include John H. Rowe, "Inca Culture at the Time of the Spanish Conquest," in *Handbook of South American Indians*, vol. 2 (1946), pp. 183–330; Burr Cartwright Brundage, *The Empire of the Inca* (1963) and *The Lords of Cuzco: A History and Description of the Inca People in Their Final Days* (1967); *The Incas of Pedro de Cieza de León*, translated by Harriet de Onis (1959); and Bernabé Cobo, *History of the Inca Empire*, translated by Roland Hamilton (1979).

Additional Bibliography

Benson, Sonia, and Deborah J. Baker. *Early Civilizations in the Americas.* Detroit, MI: U-X-L, 2005.

Bouysse-Cassagne, Thérèse, and Thierry Saignes. *Saberes y memorias en los Andes: In memoriam Thierry Saignes.* Paris: Institut des hautes études de l'Amérique latine; Lima: Institut français d'études andines, 1997.

Curl, John. *Ancient American Poets.* Tempe, AZ: Bilingual Review Press, 2005.

de Diez Canseco, María Rostworowski. *Pachacutec Inca Yupanqui.* Lima: IEP, Instituto de Estudios Peruanos, 2001.

Espinosa Apolo, Manuel. *Hablan los Incas: Crónicas de Collapiña, Supno, Inca Garcilaso, Felipe Guamán Poma, Titu Cusi y Juan Santacruz Pachacuti.* Quito, Ecuador: Taller de Estudios Andinos, 2000.

Nishi, Dennis. *The Inca Empire.* San Diego, CA: Lucent Books, 2000.

Saunders Nicholas J. *The Inca City of Cuzco.* Milwaukee, WI: World Almanac Library, 2005.

Urbano, Enrique, and Sánchez, Ana. *Antigüedades del Perú.* Madrid: Historia 16, 1992.

GORDON F. McEWAN

PACHAMAMA. Pachamama, the earth mother goddess of the Incas. Pachamama was an agricultural deity worshiped with regard to fertility and the protection of the crops, but little is known of the specifics of her cult as practiced by the Inca. It is still customary in the Andes, when drinking *chica*, to pour a small portion on the ground as an offering to Pachamama.

See also **Incas, The.**

BIBLIOGRAPHY

John H. Rowe, "Inca Culture at the Time of the Spanish Conquest," in *Handbook of South American Indians*, vol. 2 (1946), pp. 183–330. Additional sources include Burr Cartwright Brundage, *The Empire of the Inca* (1963) and *The Lords of Cuzco: A History and Description of the Inca People in Their Final Days* (1967).

Additional Bibliography

Jones, David M. *Mythology of the Incas: Myths and Legends of the Ancient Andes, Western Valleys, Deserts, and Amazonia.* London: Southwater, 2007.

Roza, Greg. *Inca Mythology and Other Myths of the Andes.* New York: Rosen Pub. Group, 2007.

Urton, Gary. *Mitos Incas.* Madrid: Akal, 2003.

GORDON F. McEWAN

PACHECO, GREGORIO (1823–1899).

Gregorio Pacheco (*b.* 4 July 1823; *d.* 20 August 1899), president of Bolivia (1884–1888). Born in Livilivi, Potosí, Pacheco was a merchant who invested in silver mines and later became one of the wealthiest mine owners in the country. He was the first civilian president during the Conservative era (1880–1899), when the southern silver-mining oligarchy, based in Sucre, controlled the destiny of Bolivia. Although he ran on the ticket of the Democratic Party, the Conservative Party's Mariano Baptista became vice president, and Pacheco's organization was later absorbed by Baptista's party. Pacheco's term was unusual for its political tranquility, with no major uprising during his term. Pacheco signed a truce with the Chileans after taking office, officially ending the War of the Pacific. During his tenure, efforts were made to guard the nation's eastern frontiers, and Puerto Pacheco was founded on the Paraguay River. After his presidency, Pacheco returned to managing his silver mines and haciendas, dying just when silver mining had become unprofitable.

See also **Baptista, Mariano; Bolivia: Since 1825.**

BIBLIOGRAPHY

Jaime Mendoza, *Figuras del pasado: Gregorio Pacheco (rasgos biográficos)* (1924), is still the definitive treatment. See also Herbert S. Klein, *Parties and Political Change in Bolivia: 1880–1952* (1969), pp. 19–24, for the political context.

Additional Bibliography

Baptista Gumucio, Mariano. *Chile-Bolivia: La agenda inconclusa.* Santiago, Chile: LOM Ediciones, 1999.

Platt, Tristán. *Historias unidas, memorias escondidas: Las empresas mineras de los hermanos Ortíz y la construcción de las elites nacionales: Salta y Potosí, 1800–1880.* Sucre, Bolivia: Universidad Andina Simón Bolívar, 1998.

ERICK D. LANGER

PACHECO, JOSÉ EMILIO (1939–).

José Emilio Pacheco (*b.* 30 June 1939), Mexican poet, novelist, short-story writer, literary critic, editor, translator, and journalist. Pacheco, a native of Mexico City and a graduate of the National University, stands out for both his creative singularity and the versatility of his cultural activities. Like two distinguished predecessors, Alfonso Reyes and Octavio Paz, he is able to create both highly imaginative works and remarkable scholarly studies.

Pacheco is a poet of desolation, obsessed with the destructive effect of time and moved by apocalyptic flashes, who has gradually abandoned an intimate and introspective poetic voice to acquire, from *No me preguntes cómo pasa el tiempo* (1969), a diction in tune with contemporary sensibilities—conversational, epigrammatic, impersonal, and ironic. He considers writing to be a social act that belongs to no one in particular. Thus, the importance in his poetry of translations ("approximations"), of parodic rewriting of other works, of apocryphal masks, and of intertextuality (the process of creating literature from literature). In many ways his poetry is a palimpsest of readings, a dialogue between his own words and those of others, from which his authentic poetic voice emerges. *Tarde o temprano* (1980) collects his poetry to 1980. His subsequent books of poetry—including *Ciudad de la memoria* (1989) and *An Ark for the Next Millennium* (1993)—show him to be one of the most accomplished poets of our age.

Like his poetry, Pacheco's narrative is tinged by the dominant presence of the passing of time, but it also reveals other dimensions, particularly the betrayal of childhood and innocence, the appearance of the fantastic in daily experiences, and the persistence of cruelty and injustice throughout history. His short-story collections (*El viento distante*, 1963; *El principio del placer*, 1972; and *La sangre de Medusa*, 1990) and his novels (*Morirás lejos*, 1967, and *Las batallas en el desierto*, 1981) exemplify his ability to respond to the many crises of society with innovative literary creations.

He has taught literature at Universidad Nacional Autónoma de México (UNAM) as well as various universities in the United States and the United Kingdom. In addition, he has been awarded various prizes for his poetry including the *Federico García Lorca International Poetry Prize* (2005) and was unanimously elected to the *Academia Mexicana de la Lengua* (2006).

See also **Paz, Octavio; Reyes Ochoa, Alfonso.**

BIBLIOGRAPHY

Yvette Jiménez De Báez, Diana Morán, and Edith Negrín, *Ficción e historia: La narrativa de José Emilio Pacheco* (1979).

Luis Antonio De Villena, *José Emilio Pacheco* (1985).

Hugo J. Verani, ed., *José Emilio Pacheco ante la crítica* (1987; 2d ed., enlarged, 1994).

Additional Bibliography

Friis, Ronald. *José Emilio Pacheco and the Poets of the Shadows.* Lewisburg, PA: Bucknell University Press, 2001.

Monasterios Pérez, Elizabeth. *Dilemas de la poesía del fin del siglo.* La Paz, Bolivia: Plural Editores, 2001.

HUGO J. VERANI

PACHECO, MARIA CRISTINA (1941–).

Cristina Pacheco is one of the outstanding literary journalists of contemporary Mexico. Born on September 13, 1941, in San Felipe Torresmocha, Guanajuato, she studied Hispanic literature at Universidad Nacional de Mexico and began her journalistic work in 1960. In Pacheco's work, as in that of Carlos Monsiváis and Elena Poniatowska, literary writing and journalism are always interconnected. Pacheco has hosted the television program *Aquí nos tocó vivir* since 1980. She has twice won the Premio Nacional de Periodismo (1975, 1985) and has also been awarded the Premio de la Asociación Nacional de Periodistas (1986). Her works include *Para vivir aquí* (1982); *Orozco, iconografía personal* (1983); *Sopita de fideo* (1984); *Testimonios y conversaciones* (1984); *Zona de desastre, Cuarto de azotea,* and *La voz de la tierra* (1986); *La última noche del tigre* (1987); *Luz de México* (1988); and *El corazón de la noche* (1990). Fernando Benítez wrote in the newspaper *La Jornada* that "Cristina Pacheco, without pursuing it, is the best chronicler of the city; she knows more about the city than the members of the city council" (March 25, 1997).

See also **Literature: Spanish America.**

BIBLIOGRAPHY

Cortés, Eladio, ed. *Dictionary of Mexican Literature.* Westport, CT: Greenwood Press, 1992.

Foster, David William. *Handbook of Latin American Literature.* 2nd ed. New York and London: Garland, 1992.

JUAN CARLOS GRIJALVA

PACHECO, MARÍA LUISA (1919–1982).

María Luisa Pacheco (*b.* 22 September 1919; *d.* 21 April 1982), Bolivian artist. Pacheco studied at the National Academy of Fine Arts in her native La Paz with nativists Cecilio Guzmán de Rojas and Jorge de la Reza. She pursued further studies at the Royal Academy of San Fernando in Madrid, and with the Spanish cubist Daniel Vásquez Días (1951–1952). Back in Bolivia, she founded Eight Contemporaries, a modernist group. She expressed her social consciousness in themes such as idol-like figures and women miners (*Idols,* 1956; *Palliri,* 1958), rendering them as fragmented planar structures (1953–1958). In 1956 she moved to New York, where she received a Solomon R. Guggenheim Memorial Foundation fellowship (1958–1960).

After 1959 Pacheco eliminated all figurative and ethnic elements in her painting. Her late style consisted of broad areas of brilliant hues and somber colors, penetrating one another in a constructivist manner. Under the general influence of international expressive abstraction, she emphasized texture and explored some accidental methods of execution (*Anamorphosis,* 1971, and *Catavi,* 1975). Although some have perceived her paintings as interpretations of the Andean environment, she claimed that subjective expression was her primary motivation. She was influential in the acceptance of abstraction in Bolivia. She died in New York City.

See also **Art: The Twentieth Century.**

BIBLIOGRAPHY

Rigoberto Villarroel Claure, *Bolivia: Art in Latin America Today,* translated by Ralph E. Dimmick (1963), pp. 13, 45–49.

Félix Angel, *Tribute to María Luisa Pacheco of Bolivia: 1919–1982* (1986) and "The Latin American Presence," in *The Latin American Spirit: Art and Artists in the United States, 1920–1970,* by Luis R. Cancel et al. (1988), pp. 242–243.

Additional Bibliography

Szmukler, Alicia M. *La ciudad imaginaria: Un análisis sociológico de la pintura contemporánea en Bolivia.* La Paz: PIEB/SINERGIA, 1998.

MARTA GARSD

PACHECO ARECO, JORGE (1920–1998).

Jorge Pacheco Areco (*b.* 8 November 1920; *d.* 29 July 1998), president of Uruguay (1967–1972). A right-wing Colorado Party politician and little-known editor of *El Día*, Pacheco became vice president in 1966. He became president less than a year later upon the death of President Oscar Gestido. A former boxer, Pacheco proved to be a stubborn politician. Faced with rising social unrest, strikes, inflation, and a budding guerrilla movement, he invoked a limited State of Siege (Medidas Prontas de Seguridad) during most of his term as president. As civil liberties became increasingly restricted, opposition voices rose within Congress, but Pacheco would not back down. As the struggle with the Tupamaro guerrillas become more dramatic and bloody, Pacheco actually received more support for his heavy-handed measures and his increased reliance on the military. In 1971, he tried to succeed himself by promoting a change in the constitution. Although this strategy ultimately failed, he was able to pick his successor, an even more conservative rural rancher named Juan María Bordaberry.

Pacheco spent the years after his presidency as an ambassador, first in Spain and later in the United States and Switzerland. He never denounced the military government and appeared to be marginalized as party leaders struggled to restore democracy in the early 1980s. Nevertheless, Pacheco's faction of the Colorado Party, the Colorado and Batllist Union (UCB), did well in the 1984 elections, helping the Colorados to win the presidency. In the 1989 elections Pacheco's faction, with him running for president, received about 50 percent of the Colorado vote in a losing effort.

Pacheco continued to have a surprisingly large following among the urban poor in Montevideo as a no-nonsense law-and-order politician. In 1992 his faction was the only non-Blanco (National Party) group to offer parliamentary support to Blanco president Luis Alberto Lacalle Herrera. In 1994, though in poor health, Pacheco ran again for president and the few votes that he received helped the Colorado Party to defeat the National Party with the election of Julio María Sanguinetti to presidency. After that election Pacheco largely dropped out of politics; soon after he died and was buried with Presidential Honors at the Cementerio Central.

See also **Uruguay, Political Parties: Colorado Party.**

BIBLIOGRAPHY

Martin Weinstein, *Uruguay: The Politics of Failure* (1975).

Edy Kaufman, *Uruguay in Transition: From Civilian to Military Rule* (1979).

Additional Bibliography

Chagas, Jorge. *Pacheco: El trama oculto del poder.* Montevideo, Uruguay: Rumbo Editorial, 2005.

Lepro, Alfredo. *Refrescando la memoria.* Montevideo, Uruguay: 1983.

MARTIN WEINSTEIN

PACHECO DA SILVA, OSVALDO (1918–).

Osvaldo Pacheco da Silva (*b.* 4 September 1918), Brazilian national trade union leader. In 1945, as a candidate of the Communist Party (PCB), Pacheco was elected a federal deputy by the dockworkers of the famous "Red Port" of Santos, São Paulo. Ousted from office in 1948, he served as a national PCB organizer until 1957 when he returned to Santos. Respected for his honesty and courage, Pacheco was elected in 1959 president of the National Federation of Stevedores and in 1961 helped form the Pact of Unity and Action (PUA), which united dockworkers, seamen, and railroad workers. He played a key role in the formation of the General Strike Command that in 1962 became the General Labor Command (CGT), serving as secretary general (1962–1963) and first secretary (1963–1964). After the military coup of 31 March 1964, the CGT and PUa were outlawed. Pacheco was arrested; after his release he went into exile. Returning clandestinely in 1967, he continued his PCB activities until his arrest in April 1975. Sentenced to seven and a half years in prison, he was released in December 1978 and subsequently amnestied.

See also **Brazil, Organizations: General Labor Command (CGT); Communism; Labor Movements.**

BIBLIOGRAPHY

Israel Beloch and Alzira Alves De Abreu, *Dicionário histórico-biográfico brasileiro 1930–1983,* vol. 3 (1984); on the

Santos dockers, see Ingrid Sarti, *Porto vermelho* (1981) and Arlindo Lucena, *"Bagrinhos" e Tubarões* (1964).

Additional Bibliography

Jordão, Rogério Pacheco; Lacerda, Paulo; and Frossard, Denise. *Crime (quase) perfeito: Corrupção e lavagem de dinheiro no Brasil.* São Paulo, SP, Brasil: Editora Fundação Perseu Abramo, 2000.

Ribeiro Gil, Rosangela. *Osvaldo Pacheco; Porto-gente-que-luta.* Rio de Janeiro: Núcleo Piratininga de Comunicacao, 2006.

JOHN D. FRENCH

PACHUCA.

Pachuca, mining center and capital of the state of Hidalgo, Mexico, where silver was first discovered in 1552. Noted as the place where the patio process for silver refining was developed, Pachuca, along with the adjacent Real del Monte workings, was the closest significant mining region to Mexico City. Tributary labor provided by the local sedentary indigenous population was important, but there emerged a large body of free wage laborers, who, beginning in 1766 at Real del Monte, mounted what may be the first strike in Mexican history. Following Mexican independence, mining was taken over by a succession of British, Mexican, and U.S. interests.

See also **Mining: Colonial Spanish America.**

BIBLIOGRAPHY

A monograph-length discussion of Pachuca is Alan Probert, "Silver Quest: Episodes of Mining in New Spain, Nine Readings," *Los Angeles: Journal of the West*, 1975. Real del Monte has received more attention in English: Robert W. Randall, *Real del Monte: A British Mining Venture in Mexico.* Austin: University of Texas Press (1972); Doris M. Ladd, *The Making of a Strike: Mexican Silver Workers' Struggles in Real del Monte, 1766–1775.* Lincoln: University of Nebraska, 1988.

Additional Bibliography

Flores Clair, Eduardo. *Conflictos de trabajo de una empresa minera: Real del Monte y Pachuca, 1872-1877.* México, D.F.: Instituto Nacional de Antropología e Historia, 1991.

Gutiérrez, M. *Caminantes de la tierra ocupada: Emigración campesina de la Huasteca hidalguense a las minas de Pachuca.* México, D.F.: Consejo Nacional para la Cultura y las Artes, 1992.

Lorenzo Monterrubio, Antonio. *Arquitectura, urbanismo, y sociedad en la ciudad de Pachuca durante el porfiriato.* Hidalgo: Sistema de Educación Pública de Hidalgo; Consejo Estatal para la Cultura y las Artes, 1995.

ROBERT HASKETT

PACIFICATION.

The term *pacification* was used in Brazil to describe efforts by agents of the Indian Protection Service (SPI), to establish peaceful relations with indigenous peoples confronted with encroachment and outsiders' expansion into their territories. The term went out of fashion in the 1960s and was replaced by *contact* or *attraction*; these terms describe the same processes that have been implemented by the national Indian foundation (FUNAI), the organization that in 1974 replaced the SPI. Pacification or contact officially sanctions capitalist economic expansion and settlement in indigenous lands. Under General Cândido Rondon, founder (in 1910) and director of the SPI, the organization developed a strategy designed to persuade Indians resisting intrusions that government agents were different from other agents of Brazilian national society (for example, Bandeirantes, settlers, miners). Following this strategy, in the early twenty-first century teams of unarmed Indian agents leave gifts of beads, machetes, mirrors, and clothing in areas frequented by members of the targeted group. The government's stated objectives for these efforts have been to establish relationships with Indians so as to protect them from violent clashes with intruders and thwart devastating epidemics by providing health care and immunizations. Although contact efforts can avert worst-case scenarios, for isolated indigenous peoples these efforts inevitably represent social disruption and territorial limitation. Typically, indigenous peoples assent to government contact efforts when exhausted by violent encounters with intruders or devastated by new contagious diseases to which they have little resistance. In the view of some indigenous peoples, it is in fact they who are "pacifying" outsiders.

See also **Brazil, Organizations: Indian Protection Service (SPI); Brazil, Organizations: National Indian Foundation (FUNAI); Rondon, Cândido Mariano da Silva.**

BIBLIOGRAPHY

Albert, Bruce, and Alcida Rita Ramos. *Pacificando o branco: Cosmologias do contato no Norte-Amazônico.* São Paulo: Imprensa Oficial, 2002.

Davis, Shelton H. *Victims of the Miracle: Development and the Indians of Brazil*. Cambridge, U.K., and New York: Cambridge University Press, 1977.

Garfield, Seth. *Indigenous Struggle at the Heart of Brazil: State Policy, Frontier Expansion, and the Xavante Indians, 1937–1988*. Durham, NC: Duke University Press, 2001.

Graham, Laura R. *Performing Dreams: Discourses of Immortality among the Xavante of Central Brazil*. Austin: University of Texas Press, 1995.

Ribeiro, Darcy. *Os índios e a civilização: A integração das populações indígenas no Brasil moderno*. Petrópolis, Brazil: Editora Vozes, 1977.

Films

Contact: The Yanomami Indians of Brazil, directed by Geoffrey O'Connor. New York: Realis Pictures, 1990.

"In the Ashes of the Forest," directed by Adrian Cowell. Parts 1 and 2 of *The Decade of Destruction*. Oley, PA: Bullfrog Films, 1990.

LAURA R. GRAHAM

PACIFIC MAIL STEAMSHIP NAVIGATION COMPANY (PMSS).

In late 1847, New York entrepreneur William H. Aspinwall expressed interest in establishing a regular mail steamship service over the Isthmus of Panama and up the coast to Oregon. In early 1848, the U.S. government granted the subsidy, but in the meantime California became the end station for Pacific Mail steamers. The PMSS was incorporated in New York in 1848 with Aspinwall as president.

Between 1854 and 1903, PMSS formed a close relationship with the Panama Railroad and the Panama Railroad steamship line, which served the ports on the Pacific coast of Central America. Mexican and Central American exporters and government officials complained often of the poor service of PMSS, especially in the 1870s and 1880s, when it was manipulated by transcontinental railroad interests. At this time, the German Kosmos and Roland lines initiated their competitive service in Central America. The PMSS prospered in the shipping boom of World War I but encountered hard times in the 1920s and the Great Depression, and it went bankrupt in 1938.

See also **Panama Railroad.**

BIBLIOGRAPHY

F. N. Otis, *History of the Panama Railroad; and of the Pacific Mail Steamship Company* (1867).

John Haskell Kemble, *The Panama Route, 1848–1869* (1943).

Raymond A. Rydell, *Cape Horn to the Pacific: The Rise and Demise of an Ocean Highway* (1952).

K. Jack Bauer, *A Maritime History of the United States: The Role of America's Seas and Waterways* (1988).

Additional Bibliography

Schoonover, Thomas David. *The United States in Central America, 1860–1911: Episodes of Social Imperialism and Imperial Rivalry in the World System*. Durham, NC: Duke University Press, 1991.

Wiltsee, Ernest A. *Up the River: Steam Navigation above the Carquinez Strait*. San Francisco: Book Club of California, 2003.

THOMAS SCHOONOVER

PACIFIC NORTHWEST.

Spain first based its claims to Alaska and the Pacific Northwest on Balboa's discovery of the Pacific in 1513 and Juan de Fuca's little-known and barely provable expedition beyond present-day Washington State in search of the Strait of Anián, the so-called Northwest Passage, in 1592. No Spanish expeditions explored Alaska until the 1770s, when authorities became alarmed by reports of Captain James Cook's voyage in 1776–1779 under British colors, which landed at Nootka Sound, on the west side of present-day Vancouver Island, among other sites. In response, Viceroy Antonio María de Bucareli y Ursúa ordered Juan Pérez, commander of the *Santiago,* to sail northward in 1774; he reached what is now Queen Charlotte Island. In 1775 Bruno de Hezeta and Juan de la Bodega y Quadra commanded separate vessels and sailed from Trinidad Bay; this expedition made the first European claim to the Columbia River, mapping and exploring it for nearly twenty miles inland. Bodega y Quadra separated from the expedition, reaching a latitude of 58 degrees north, probably near Sitka. The Hezeta-Bodega expedition enabled Spain to make paper claims to lands in the far northwest of New Spain as an extension of the Alta California coast.

After Ignacio Arteaga and Bodega y Quadra reported no sign of foreigners in the area in 1779,

Spanish activity subsided. However, new reports of foreign trespassers in 1788 forced the resumption of Spanish expeditions to the north. That year, Esteban José Martínez commanded the *Princesa* and the *San Carlos*, which sailed as far as Kodiak and Unalaska Islands to investigate reports of Russians in the Aleutians. Having made contact with the Russians, Martínez learned that they had plans to colonize Nootka Sound. Nootka became the point of contention, and that year Martínez returned to establish a Spanish presence there. When he arrived in Nootka, he found ships under Anglo-American and British command. In the ensuing controversy Martínez captured a British trader, Capt. James Colnett, who boasted he had papers from George III staking claim to the region. Martínez sent Colnett and his two vessels, complete with their crews, to Mexico.

The English responded by demanding indemnity, placing them on the brink of war with Spain. The Spanish, in turn, appealed to their French allies, then occupied by their own revolutionary situation. In October 1790 Spain and England signed the first of the Nootka Sound Conventions whereby Spain agreed to recognize the right of another power to trade freely on the Pacific Coast and to make restitution for the English ships taken by Martínez. England could trade north of California and enter any California port for provisioning, but not for trade unless specified.

Spain made a tremendous effort to preserve its foothold in the Pacific Northwest after 1790 and investigated its ethnography, flora, and fauna as part of the five-year scientific expedition of Alejandro Malaspina. In 1792, Spanish forces sought to extend the northern boundary of California by establishing two short-lived settlements at Nootka Sound and Neah Bay reinforced by the Catalonian Volunteers under Captain Pedro de Alberni, for whom Port Alberni on Vancouver Island is named.

In the summer of 1792, Spanish and English negotiators came to Nootka to work out the details of the convention, and Francisco Bodega y Quadra miraculously managed to win a stalemate from the British. In a settlement arranged in Europe and confirmed in a ceremony at Nootka on 23 March 1795, both sides received trading rights, Spain gave up its claims to the area, and the issue of the California boundary was left unsettled. After the settlement, both parties abandoned the area and Russians took over.

See also **Balboa, Vasco Núñez de; Malaspina, Alejandro; Martínez, Esteban José; Pérez, Juan.**

BIBLIOGRAPHY

Warren L. Cook, *Flood Tide of Empire: Spain and the Pacific Northwest, 1543–1819* (1973).

Joseph P. Sánchez, *Spanish Bluecoats: The Catalonian Volunteers in Northwestern New Spain, 1767–1810* (1990).

Additional Bibliography

Cutter, Donald C. *Malaspina & Galiano: Spanish Voyages to the Northwest Coast, 1791 & 1792*. Vancouver: Douglas & McIntyre; Seattle: University of Washington Press, 1991.

Kendrick, John, Dionisio Alcalá-Galiano, et al. *The Voyage of Sutil and Mexicana, 1792: The Last Spanish Expedition of the Northwest Coast of America*. Spokane, WA: Arthur H. Clark Co., 1991.

San Pío Aladrén, Pilar. *Expediciones españolas del siglo XVIII: El paso del noroeste*. Madrid: Editorial MAPFRE, 1992.

JOSEPH P. SÁNCHEZ

PACT OF SAN JOSÉ DE FLORES. *See* San José de Flores, Pact of.

PACT OF SAN NICOLÁS. *See* San Nicolás, Pact of.

PACT OF THE EMBASSY. Pact of the Embassy is an agreement, also known as the Pact of the Ciudadela, signed in the U.S. Embassy in Mexico City early in the morning of February 19, 1913, that ended the Decena Trágica. After General Victoriano Huerta, commander of the government forces, seized control by deposing President Francisco Madero, U.S. Ambassador Henry Lane Wilson intervened to end the destructive artillery duel in the heart of Mexico City. In the U.S. Embassy Wilson convened and mediated negotiations between Huerta and rebel commander

General Felix Díaz, whose forces remained in control of parts of the capital.

Negotiations lasted several hours, ending at one A.M. on February 19 in an accord between the two rival generals. Under its terms, Díaz recognized Huerta as provisional president, while Huerta allowed Díaz to name his cabinet and pledged to support Díaz in the election that the constitution required within a year. A few hours later the Chamber of Deputies duly accepted the resignations of President Madero and Vice President José María Pino Suárez, and confirmed General Huerta as president.

While not formally part of the pact, Díaz and Huerta orally agreed, at the insistence of Ambassador Wilson, to a number of stipulations, which included joint action between their forces to maintain order in the capital and the release of Madero's cabinet ministers. It conspicuously omitted the president and vice president, who were assassinated on February 22. Various accusations ascribed responsibility to either Huerta or Díaz. Other leaders soon launched the second stage of the Mexican Revolution, leading to a civil war that eventually deposed Huerta in July 1914.

See also **Decena Trágica.**

BIBLIOGRAPHY

Arnáiz y Freg, Arturo. *Madero y Pino Suárez, en el cinquentenario de su sacrificio, 1913–1963. Testimonios históricos seleccionados por Arturo Arnáiz y Freg* (1963).

Grieb, Kenneth J. *The United States and Huerta.* Lincoln: University of Nebraska Press, 1969.

Meyer, Michael C. *Huerta: A Political Portrait.* Lincoln: University of Nebraska Press, 1972.

Ross, Stanley R. *Francisco I. Madero: Apostle of Mexican Democracy.* New York: Columbia University Press, 1955.

KENNETH J. GRIEB

PADILLA, HEBERTO (1932–2000).

Heberto Padilla (*b.* 20 January 1932; *d.* 20 September 2000); one of the greatest Cuban poets and novelists. Padilla was born in Puerta de Golpe in the province of Pinar del Río. He was supportive of the Cuban Revolution of 1959 and enjoyed a favorable position among the cultural elite of his country until 1968, when he won first prize in the prestigious literary contest of the Cuban Writers and Artists Union (UNEAC) for his book of poems *Fuera del juego* (1969). This book, which brought him immediate national and international acclaim as a poet, also made him an object of intense political controversy. Published with a prologue decrying the "counterrevolutionary" nature of some of the poems, the book provoked what came to be known as El Caso Padilla, or the Padilla affair, now seen as a turning point in relations between the Cuban government and intellectuals, Cuban or otherwise. In 1971, Padilla was arrested, tortured, and forced to retract his stand publicly at an assembly of UNEAC. Receiving worldwide attention, his case prompted the drafting of a letter in his defense signed by intellectuals the world over, including Gabriel García Márquez and Simone de Beauvoir. Ultimately Padilla was allowed to emigrate with his wife, the outstanding poet Belkis Cuza Malé, but his case marked the end of a period of relative artistic freedom for Cuban intellectuals. Padilla taught at Princeton, New York University, and eventually settled in Alabama where he taught at Auburn University until his death.

Other works by Padilla include bilingual editions of his poems *Legacies* (1982) and *A Fountain, a House of Stone* (1991). His poetry has been translated into many languages.

See also **Cuba, Revolutions: Cuban Revolution.**

BIBLIOGRAPHY

Lourdes Casal, *El caso Padilla: Literatura y revolución en Cuba: documentos* (1971).

Scott Johnson, ed. and trans., *The Case of the Cuban Poet Heberto Padilla* (1978).

Additional Bibliography

Lezama Lima, José. *Poetas cubanos marginados.* Ferrol: Sociedad de Cultura Valle-Inclán, 1998.

ROBERTO VALERO

PADILLA PEÑALOSA, EZEQUIEL

(1890–1971). Ezequiel Padilla Peñalosa (*b.* 31 December 1890; *d.* 6 September 1971), leading Mexican diplomat and public figure. A native of

Coyuca de Catalán, Guerrero, Padilla graduated from the Sorbonne in constitutional law in 1914 and studied at Columbia University in 1916. A cofounder of the Free Law School in Mexico City, he served in the Revolution under Francisco Villa, leaving Mexico in 1916. On his return to Mexico, he entered politics, becoming a federal deputy in 1922. In 1928 he joined Emilio Portes Gil's cabinet as secretary of education. After his 1930 appointment as minister to Italy, he returned to the Chamber of Deputies in 1932 and to the Senate in 1934. From 1940 to 1945 he was secretary of foreign relations, playing a key role in promoting continental unity during World War II. He provided leadership at the 1942 Rio De Janeiro Conference, a benchmark in wartime inter-American relations. In 1946 he resigned his post to run as the opposition presidential candidate of the Mexican Democratic Party after failing to obtain the nomination of his own party. He remained politically inactive for the next two decades, serving once again as senator shortly before his death.

See also **Mexico: Since 1910.**

BIBLIOGRAPHY

Betty Kirk, *Covering the Mexican Front* (1942).

Josephus Daniels, *Shirt-Sleeve Diplomat* (1947), *New York Times,* 8 September 1971, 48.

Additional Bibliography

Paz Salinas, María Emilia. *Strategy, Security, and Spies: Mexico and the U.S. as Allies in World War II.* University Park: Pennsylvania State University Press, 1997.

RODERIC AI CAMP

PADROADO REAL.

Padroado Real, royal patronage, the right granted by the Holy See to the Portuguese king to introduce clerics to ecclesiastical positions. Only provisional, the appointments were confirmed later by canonical authority. The ruler was allowed to collect the tithe, but, in return, was required to provide for the maintenance and growth of the church in his domain. Despite its medieval origins to foster the Christian reconquest of Muslim territory, the *padroado* did not come under the control of the Portuguese crown until the sixteenth century, when the king also became the Grand Master of the Order of Christ. In Brazil, it lasted from independence in 1822 until it was abolished in 1890.

See also **Patronato Real.**

BIBLIOGRAPHY

Américo Lourenço Jacobina Lacombe and Francisco De Assis Barbosa, *"Padroado,"* in *Enciclopédia Mirador Internacional* vol. 15 (1983), pp. 8397–8400.

Cândido Mendes De Almeida, *Direito civil ecclesiástico brasileiro antigo e moderno em suas relações com o direito canônico* (1866–1873).

Additional Bibliography

Azevedo, Thales de. *Igreja e Estado em tensão e crise: A conquista espiritual e o padroado na Bahia.* São Paulo: Editora Ática, 1978.

Dornas, João. *O padroado e a igreja brasileira.* São Paulo: Companhia editora nacional, 1938.

Quéré, Martin. *Christianity in Sri Lanka under the Portuguese Padroado, 1597-1658.* Colombo: Colombo Catholic Press, 1995.

GUILHERME PEREIRA DAS NEVES

PÁEZ, FEDERICO

(1876–1974). Federico Páez (*b.* 6 June 1876; *d.* 1974), president of Ecuador (nonelected, 1935–1937). Born in Quito and educated at the École Supérieure des Mines in Paris and the École des Hautes Études Sociales in Brussels, Páez served as deputy of Pichincha (1916–1918) and became minister of public works in 1935 when the military named him interim president. During his administration there were reforms in a number of areas, including the organization, administration, and education of the military; the creation of the Institute of Social Security; and the founding of the Inspection of Public Works. These accomplishments were tarnished by restrictions on civil liberties, an expansion of the secret political police, the suppression of dissent, the persecution of leftists, and rumors that the government favored foreign business interests. Public discontent and divisions within the officer corps led to the resignation of Páez in 1937, turning over the office to General Alberto Enríquez Gallo.

See also **Ecuador: Since 1830.**

BIBLIOGRAPHY

Oscar Efren Reyes, *Breve historia general del Ecuador* (1957), esp. pp. 84–89.

Enrique Ayala Mora, ed., *Nueva historia del Ecuador; Epoca republicana VI,* vol. 10 (1983), esp. pp. 100–103.

Additional Bibliography

Febres Cordero, Francisco. *De Flores a flores y miel.* Quito: Ojo de Pez, EDIMPRES, 1996.

LINDA ALEXANDER RODRÍGUEZ

PÁEZ, JOSÉ ANTONIO (1790–1873).

José Antonio Páez (*b.* 13 June 1790; *d.* 6 May 1873), officer in the Venezuelan Liberating Army, president of Venezuela (1831–1835, 1839–1843, and 1861–1863). Páez began his public life in the Liberating Army. He stood out early as a good soldier and attained great popularity among the people of the plains. In 1816, he was named commanding officer of the region, and as such led numerous campaigns which consolidated control of the plains. He met with Simón Bolívar in 1818 and recognized him as supreme commander of the Liberating Army. From the plains, Páez supported the New Granada campaign and took part in the preparations that culminated in the victory at Carabobo in 1821. He was named commander in chief of one of the military districts into which the territory of Venezuela had been divided, and in that position defeated the armed factions that were still operating within Venezuela.

Through his military post and his personal prestige, Páez gradually became a key figure in the political process that evolved in Venezuela after adoption of the Constitution of Gran Colombia in 1821. The conflicting interests and fragile ties that characterized the unstable entity that was Gran Colombia finally led in 1826 to the outbreak of the separatist movement called La Cosiata, whose supporters ignored the authority of the government in Bogotá, recognized Páez as chief civil and military leader of Venezuela, and called for the dissolution of Gran Colombia. From that moment, Páez served as a unifying symbol of independence for the leading groups in Venezuela.

"Vuelvan Cara!" (**"About Face!"**), by nineteenth-century Venezuelan painter Arturo Michelena depicts Páez's early skill as a leader in the Liberating Army. THE GRANGER COLLECTION, NEW YORK

In December 1826 Bolívar returned from Peru and assumed the presidency of Gran Colombia. He traveled to Puerto Cabello, Venezuela, on 1 January 1827 and issued a decree which forgave all those who participated in La Cosiata. Bolívar recognized Páez as military governor of Venezuela and Páez recognized Bolívar as president of Gran Colombia. Between 1827 and 1829, Páez continued consolidating his power, and when separatist sentiment returned among both the elites and the popular classes, Páez was well positioned to take advantage. In November 1829 the Assembly in the San Francisco Convent in Caracas disregarded Bolívar's authority, convened a constituent congress, and handed over all power to Páez, thus completing the dissolution of Gran Colombia.

The Constituent Congress named Páez provisional president of Venezuela, ratified a new constitution, and held an election, which Páez won. His political and military prestige brought a period of consensus during which the bases for the republic were established; the intense process of judicial, political, and economic organization was carried through; and the building of a nation state was initiated. His personal authority did not dissipate at the end of his term in 1835, and his influence continued to be felt in the country's politics. In 1838 he was reelected president. During his second four-year term, differences and confrontations within the ruling elite were becoming more and more evident. In 1846 he supported the election of General José Tadeo Monagas, who afterwards distanced himself from Páez and formed an alliance with the Liberal Party. This caused a rupture in the Conservative Party, with which Páez was associated. In 1847 Páez rose up in arms and was defeated, imprisoned, and exiled.

Páez remained abroad until the overthrow of Monagas in 1858, when he was called back to take charge of the pacification of the country. At the outbreak of the Federal War in 1859, he was appointed chief of operations against the federalists. After a brief absence from the country, he was named supreme chief of Venezuela with dictatorial powers in 1861. The war ended in 1863 with a victory for the federalists. Páez handed over power and again left the country. He spent his later years in the United States, where he wrote his autobiography, published in New York in 1869. He traveled to various Latin American countries, spent three years in Argentina, and then returned to the United States, where he died.

See also **Cosiata, La (1826); Gran Colombia; Monagas, José Tadeo; Venezuela: The Colonial Era; Venezuela: Venezuela since 1830; Venezuela, Political Parties: Conservative Party.**

BIBLIOGRAPHY

José Antonio Páez, *Autobiografía del General José Antonio Páez*, 2 vols. (1869; 1973).

Robert Graham, *José Antonio Páez* (1929).

Jesus Antonio Cova, *El centauro: Vida del General José Antonio Páez, caudillo venezolano y brigadier del ejército argentino* (1947).

Additional Bibliography

Plaza, Elena. *Versiones de la tiranía en Venezuela: El último régimen del General José Antonio Páez, 1861–1863.* Caracas: Facultad de Ciencias Jurídicas y Políticas, Universidad Central de Venezuela, 2000.

Polanco Alcántara, Tomás. *José Antonio Páez, fundador de la República.* Caracas: Ediciones GE, 2000.

INÉS QUINTERO

PAÍS, FRANK

PAÍS, FRANK (1934–1957). Frank País (*b.* 1934; *d.* 30 July 1957), Cuban revolutionary leader during the Batista dictatorship. Born in Santiago de Cuba, País is best remembered as the leader of the 1956 Santiago uprising that coincided with the landing of Fidel Castro and his followers in Oriente Province on 2 December on the boat *Granma*. Under the Batista dictatorship, País built his reputation as a guerrilla fighter and member of Acción Nacional Revolucionaria. In 1955 País and his followers agreed to merge with Castro's Twenty-Sixth of July Movement and to coordinate the Cuban operations with Castro's landing from Mexico. On 30 November 1956, País led an uprising in Santiago that was briefly successful, with the insurrectionists taking control of the city. Stormy weather delayed Castro's landing, however, giving Batista's forces time to quell the País uprising before turning their attention to the landing of the *Granma*. While País escaped capture, he was killed less than a year later, on 30 July 1957, by the Santiago police. País's death was a great blow to the *llano* wing—the lowland and urban wing, as opposed to Castro's Sierra group—of the Cuban revolutionary movement. His role was so important that Ernesto "Che" Guevara asked to take the deceased País's place as leader of the Santiago revolutionary movement.

See also **Batista y Zaldívar, Fulgencio; Castro Ruz, Fidel; Cuba, Twenty-Sixth of July Movement.**

BIBLIOGRAPHY

Peter G. Bourne, *Fidel: A Biography of Fidel Castro* (1986).

Robert Quirk, *Fidel Castro* (1993).

Additional Bibliography

Menéndez Tomassevich, Raúl, and José A. Gárciga Blanco. *Golpes para el triunfo.* Santiago de Cuba: Editorial Oriente, 1998.

Monroy, Juan Antonio. *Frank Pais: Lider evangélico en la Revolución Cubana.* Terrasa, España: Editorial Clie, 2003.

Sweig, Julia E. *Inside the Cuban Revolution: Fidel Castro and the Urban Underground.* Cambridge, MA: Harvard University Press, 2002.

MICHAEL POWELSON

PALACIO, ALFREDO (1939–). Luis Alfredo Palacio González, a cardiologist, became president of Ecuador in April 2005 after Congress voted to remove former president Lucio Gutiérrez. Palacio had served as vice president under Gutierrez (2003–2005), an administration that was widely criticized. After Gutiérrez disbanded the Supreme Court and declared a state of emergency in 2007, Ecuadorean citizens took to the streets to demand his resignation. Upon taking office Palacio promised to restore "a government of the people," but he faced a divided Congress and civil unrest.

Alfredo Palacio was born in Guayaquil on January 22, 1939. He graduated from medical school in Guayaquil (1967) and completed his residency training in cardiology at Case Western Reserve University in Cleveland and hospitals in Missouri (1969–1974). A staunch independent, Palacio has never joined a political party. He served as Minister of Health under Sixto Durán-Bellén from 1994 to 1996.

When Palacio was appointed in 2005 he became Ecuador's eighth president in ten years. In 2006 he was nominated to be director-general of the World Health Organization. Palacio declined the nomination, stating that he wanted to focus on finishing his presidency. During his brief term in office he tried to issue a referendum on constitutional reform, but the electoral court blocked it. He finished his mandate on January 14, 2007, and was succeeded by the economist Rafael Correa.

See also **Argentina, Political Parties: Socialist Party.**

BIBLIOGRAPHY

"Alfredo Palacio González." Fundació Cidob: Centro de Investigación de Relaciones Internacionales y Desarrollo. Available from http://www.cidob.org/es/documentacion/biografias_lideres_politicos/america_del_sur/ecuador/alfredo_palacio_gonzalez.

Gerlach, Allen. *Indians, Oil, and Politics: A Recent History of Ecuador.* Wilmington, DE: Scholarly Resources, 2003.

Weitzman, Hal. "Ruling Could Force Ecuador President Out of Office." *Financial Times,* October 20, 2005.

SUZANNE CASOLARO

PALACIO FAJARDO, MANUEL (1784–1819). Manuel Palacio Fajardo (*b.* 1784; *d.* 8 May 1819), diplomat and political activist in the Venezuelan independence movement. From early on Palacio Fajardo belonged to the independence movement. He was a member of the Constituent Congress of 1811. After the fall of the First Republic in 1812, he traveled to New Granada and was sent on a diplomatic mission to the United States and France. He later passed through London, where he devoted himself to garnering support for the cause of Venezuelan independence. While there, he published his book, *Outline of the Revolution in Spanish America* (1817), which was translated into French and German. He returned to Venezuela in 1818 with men and supplies for the war and was a participant in the Angostura Congress of 1819. On Simón Bolívar's request he revised and made suggestions for the speech that the former would present to that gathering. Palacio Fajardo also collaborated in *El Correo del Orinoco,* a newspaper dedicated to the independence cause, and in 1819 was designated the infant republic's secretary of finance.

See also **Angostura, Congress of; Venezuela: The Colonial Era; Venezuela, Congresses of 1811, 1830, and 1864.**

BIBLIOGRAPHY

Caracciolo Parra-Pérez, *Una misión diplomática venezolana ante Napoleón en 1813* (1953).

José Abel Montilla, *Manuel Palacio Fajardo* (1956).

Amilcar Plaza Delgado, *Manuel Palacio Fajardo* (1975).

Additional Bibliography

Elliott, J. H. *Empires of the Atlantic World: Britain and Spain in the Americas, 1492–1830*. New Haven, CT: Yale University Press, 2006.

Racine, Karen. *Francisco de Miranda: A Transatlantic Life in the Age of Revolution*. Wilmington, DE: Scholarly Resources, 2003.

INÉS QUINTERO

PALACIOS, ALFREDO L. (1880–1965).

Alfredo L. Palacios (*b*. 10 August 1880; *d*. 1965) Argentine Socialist congressman and senator. Born in the city of Buenos Aires, Palacios received his law degree from the local university in 1900. Soon thereafter he joined the Socialist Party, with which he had a long and frequently difficult relationship. Running on the party ticket in the federal capital in 1904, he became the first socialist in the Americas to be elected to a national congress. He served two terms in the Chamber of Deputies (1904–1908 and 1912–1916), during the second of which he was ousted from his party for dueling. He rejoined the party in 1930 and was twice elected to the national senate (1932–1935 and 1935–1944) from the federal capital, at a time when conservatives controlled the national administration. A vigorous opponent of the regime of Juan Perón (1946–1955), he was named ambassador to Uruguay for the two years following Perón's overthrow. After an unsuccessful bid for the presidency in 1958, he won a stunning election to the national Senate from the city of Buenos Aires in 1961 after campaigning as a champion of the Cuban revolution of Fidel Castro.

A charismatic orator and effective legislator, Palacios was a consistent proponent of social justice, especially for women and children, and a vociferous opponent of what he considered the undue influence of foreign investors in the country. He was the author of numerous essays and books, such as *La justicia social* (1954), many of which were collections of his parliamentary speeches.

See also **Argentina, Political Parties: Socialist Party.**

BIBLIOGRAPHY

Víctor O. García Costa, *Alfredo L. Palacios: Un Socialismo argentino y para la Argentina* (1986).

Additional Bibliography

García Costa, Víctor O. *Alfredo Palacios: Entre el clavel y la espada: Una biografía*. Buenos Aires: Planeta, 1997.

González, Liliana C. *Repensando el Dogma socialista de Esteban Echeverría*. Buenos Aires: Instituto Torcuato DiTella, 1994.

RICHARD J. WALTER

PALACIOS, ANTONIA (1915–2001).

Antonia Palacios (*b*. 13 May 1915; *d*. 2001), Venezuelan writer and poet. From a very young age, Palacios was associated with the literary circles of the city. In 1936, she traveled to Europe, where she met César Vallejo, Luis Aragón, and Pablo Neruda. Her account of these contacts is contained in her first work, *París y tres recuerdos* (1945). Upon her return, she joined the Women's Cultural Society and presided at the first Venezuelan Women's Congress. She contributed to the newspaper *El Nacional* and devoted herself to writing *Ana Isabel, una niña decente* (1949), which was declared obligatory reading material for secondary students by the Venezuelan Ministry of Education in 1962. After the publication of *Viaje al frailejón* (1955), Palacios maintained a prolonged silence until *Crónica de las horas* was published in 1964. She pursued her literary activities and in 1976 coordinated the literary workshop at the Rómulo Gallegos Center. That same year she became the first woman to receive the National Literature Prize. In her home she founded the literary workshop Calicanto, a forum for young poets and writers. The results of this experience were published in the magazine *Hojas de Calicanto*. Her career and her work are outstanding components of Venezuelan literary life in the twentieth century.

See also **Neruda, Pablo; Vallejo, César.**

BIBLIOGRAPHY

Juan Liscano, *Panorama de la literatura venezolana actual* (1973).

Julio Miranda, *Proceso a la narrativa venezolana* (1975).

José Ramón Medina, *Ochenta años de literatura venezolana* (1980).

Verónica Jaffé and Dora Dávila, *El relato imposible* (1991).

Additional Bibliography

González Pérez, María Luisa. *Fortaleza del silencio: Aproximación a la poesía de Antonia Palacios.* Caracas, Venezuela: Universidad Católica Andrés Bello, 2001.

Perdomo, Alicia. *Análisis de Ana Isabel, una niña decente.* Caracas, Venezuela: Editorial Panapo, 1998.

INÉS QUINTERO

PALACIOS, PEDRO BONIFACIO. *See* Almafuerte.

PALAFOX Y MENDOZA, JUAN DE
(1600–1659). Juan de Palafox y Mendoza (*b.* 1600; *d.* 1659), bishop of Puebla (1640–1654), visitor-general, and seventeenth viceroy of New Spain. Palafox, born in Fitero, Navarra, was the illegitimate son of an Aragonese noble. After studying law at Salamanca, he rose rapidly in both the church and the royal bureaucracy, serving on the Council of the Indies while still in his thirties. In 1639, he was named visitor-general of New Spain and bishop of Puebla. A moralist with mystical leanings, Palafox believed strongly in the Christian mission of the Hapsburg monarchy and sought to rectify the colonial administration, thereby making it a fit instrument for the reformation of society. He therefore never hesitated to employ the full extent of his authority: Most notably, as bishop he engineered the removal of New Spain's viceroy, the duque d'Escalona, in 1642 because of the latter's supposed pro-Portuguese sympathies. During Palafox's ensuing term as viceroy (June–November 1642), the Inquisition launched a massive persecution of Mexican crypto-Jews

(secret Jews), which culminated in the great autos-da-fé of 1646–1649.

As bishop, Palafox sponsored an impressive program of ecclesiastical construction, building some fifty churches and a seminary (to which he donated his personal library of more than 5,000 volumes), founding the convent of Santa Inés, and completing the imposing Puebla cathedral, which was consecrated in 1649. To strengthen episcopal power, he transferred control of thirty-six parishes from the mendicant orders to the secular clergy. Beginning in 1641, Palafox became embroiled in disputes with the Jesuits concerning tithes on their landed estates and episcopal authority over Jesuit priests. As the conflicts deepened, the new viceroy, García Sarmiento De Sotomayor, conde de Salvatierra, sided with the Jesuits, putting Palafox in an increasingly precarious position. In 1647, to avoid arrest, he fled Puebla and went into hiding until the crown announced its verdict in his favor. However, this triumph was short-lived: In 1649 royal authorities ordered the disputatious bishop back to Spain, where he was named bishop of Osma (in Soria); he was forced to surrender the see of Puebla in 1654. Palafox's ultimate failure, like that of the marqués de Gelves, the reform-minded viceroy who was ousted by a riot in 1624, demonstrated the Spanish crown's inability to challenge entrenched power holders and make significant alterations in the colonial status quo. Palafox died in Osma.

See also **Catholic Church: The Colonial Period; Inquisition: Spanish America; Jesuits; Puebla (City).**

BIBLIOGRAPHY

Charles E. P. Simmons, "Palafox and His Critics: Reappraising a Controversy," in *Hispanic American Historical Review* 46 (November 1966): 394–408.

Jonathan Irvine Israel, *Race, Class, and Politics in Colonial Mexico, 1610–1670* (1975), pp. 190–247.

Genaro García, ed., "Don Juan de Palafox y Mendoza: Su virreinato en la Nueva España...etc.," in *Documentos inéditos o muy raros para la historia de México* (1982), pp. 519–663.

D. A. Brading, *The First America: The Spanish Monarchy, Creole Patriots, and the Liberal State, 1492–1867* (1991), pp. 228–251.

Additional Bibliography

Alvarez de Toledo, Cayetana. *Politics and Reform in Spain and Viceregal Mexico: The Life and Thought of Juan de*

Palafox, 1600–1659. New York: Oxford University Press, 2004.

Torre Villar, Ernesto de la. *Don Juan de Palafox y Mendoza, pensador político.* México: Universidad Nacional Autónoma de México, Instituto de Investigaciones Jurídicas, 1997.

R. DOUGLAS COPE

PALENQUE. Palenque is a principal Classic Maya site on the northern mountain slopes of Chiapas overlooking the coastal plain of the Gulf of Mexico. Palenque was explored in the late eighteenth century by a Spanish expedition, and subsequently was visited and described by John Lloyd Stephens in his *Incidents of Travel in Central America, Chiapas, and Yucatán* in 1841. Other nineteenth-and early twentieth-century archaeologists also recorded the site. The drawings and photographs of these early visitors have greatly benefited more recent scholars because of deterioration that has occurred in the intervening years.

Palenque rose to prominence after 640 under the leadership of Lord Shield Pacal and his son, Chan-Bahlum, and it dominated the western portion of the Maya world during much of the Late Classic period (ca. 600–900). The Temple of the Inscriptions—so named because of the lengthy hieroglyphic panels that adorn the walls—is the funerary monument to Pacal. Pacal's tomb lies deep within the pyramid. The sarcophagus portrays Pacal's fall into the underworld and depicts images of his ancestors.

Palenque is noted for its beautifully crafted inscriptions carved into limestone slabs. In contrast to other Classic Maya sites, where sculpted stone monuments were erected as freestanding stelae, at Palenque the finished tablets were mounted on the interior walls of the temples. Many of the inscriptions are devoted to genealogical affairs, enabling epigraphers to reconstruct a complete dynastic history of Palenque's ruling families. Moreover, with this data, scholars have gained further insight into the timing of military campaigns, alliances, birthdates, and marriages and other rituals.

Palenque is also noted for its innovative architectural style. Architects used techniques such as the mansard (sloped inward) roof design and lattice roof comb to reduce the weight on walls. This enabled them to construct larger and lighter interior vaults in structures. The extensive complex known as the Palace, which is believed to have been an administrative center and residence for elites, utilizes mansard roof design. An astronomical observatory, a unique Mayan structure, rises four stories above.

By 800, Palenque, like other lowland Maya centers, had experienced a serious decline, and construction ceased. The center was abandoned around 820. Archaeological excavations and restorations continue at Palenque, as only a portion of this Maya city's structures have been recovered.

See also **Archaeology; Maya, The; Stephens, John Lloyd.**

BIBLIOGRAPHY

William M. Ferguson in collaboration with John Q. Royce, *Maya Ruins of Mexico in Color* (1977).

Linda Schele and David Freidel, *A Forest of Kings* (1990).

Additional Bibliography

Cobos, Rafael, ed. *Culto funerario en la sociedad maya: Memoria de la Cuarta Mesa Redonda de Palenque.* Mexico City: Instituto Nacional de Antropología e Historia, 2004.

Marken, Damien B., ed. *Palenque: Recent Investigations at the Classic Maya Center.* Lanham, MD: AltaMira Press, 2007.

Navarrete, Carlos. *Palenque, 1784: El inicio de la aventura arqueológica maya.* Mexico City: Centro de Estudios Mayas, Instituto de Investigaciones Filológicas, Instituto de Investigaciones Antropológicas, Universidad Nacional Autónoma de México, 2000.

Robertson, Merle Greene. *The Sculpture of Palenque.* Vols. 1–4. Princeton, NJ: Princeton University Press, 1983–1991.

Schele, Linda, and Peter Mathews. *The Code of Kings: The Language of Seven Sacred Maya Temples and Tombs.* New York: Scribner, 1998.

Stuart, David. *The Inscriptions from Temple XIX at Palenque: A Commentary.* San Francisco, CA: Pre-Columbian Art Research Institute, 2005.

Tiesler, Vera, and Andrea Cucina, eds. *Janaab' Pakal of Palenque: Reconstructing the Life and Death of a Maya Ruler.* Tucson: University of Arizona Press, 2006.

JANINE GASCO

PALENQUE, CARLOS (1944–1997).

The Bolivian businessman and presidential candidate Carlos Palenque (June 28, 1944–March 9, 1997) challenged the political establishment through his party, Conciencia de la Patria (Conscience of the Fatherland, CONDEPA). Palenque was a musician and broadcast announcer before buying Radio Metropolitana and Channel 4 and then forming Radio y Televisión Popular (RTP) in 1985. His entry into politics came after a dispute with the government in which RTP was closed following the broadcast of an interview of Palenque with Roberto Suárez, the country's principal narcotics trafficker. He then founded CONDEPA, which gained substantial support from the indigenous underclass that constituted his main television audience. Alongside Johnny Fernandez's Unidad Cívica Solidaridad (UCS), CONDEPA marked the entry of anti-establishment, personalistic, and populist-style parties into Bolivia's political system and the beginning of a downward trend for the country's traditional parties.

CONDEPA consistently won local elections in the La Paz Department, including the huge yet poor municipality of El Alto, and earned modest results in the national elections of 1989, 1993, and 1997. Palenque's best showing in the presidential contests came in 1997, when he earned 17 percent of the vote in elections that took place shortly after he died of a heart attack. Taking twenty-two seats in the congress, the party formed part of President Hugo Banzer's governing coalition for a short time. However, it suffered without Palenque's charismatic leadership and eventually collapsed in 2002, when it gained no seats at all. Evo Morales's Movimiento al Socialismo (MAS; Movement to Socialism) largely supplanted CONDEPA's appeal to the Aymara indigenous community.

See also **Bolivia, Political Parties: Overview.**

BIBLIOGRAPHY

Gamarra, Eduardo A. "Municipal Elections in Bolivia." In *Urban Elections in Democratic Latin America*, edited by Henry A. Dietz and Gil Shidlo. Wilmington, DE: Scholarly Resources, 1998.

Van Cott, Donna Lee. "From Exclusion to Inclusion: Bolivia's 2002 Elections." *Journal of Latin American Studies* 35 (2003): 751–775.

ROBERT R. BARR

PALÉS MATOS, LUIS (1898–1959).

Luis Palés Matos (*b.* 20 March 1898; *d.* 23 February 1959), Puerto Rican poet, journalist, and essayist. Founding figure of the *negrista* movement and one of its most important exponents within the wider Hispanic Caribbean, Palés Matos is perhaps Puerto Rico's most significant modern poet. He was born in Guayama, the son of poets. A precocious talent, he published his first book of verse, *Azaleas* (1915), under the influence of the romantics, symbolists, and *modernistas*. In his early twenties he served as director of the newspaper *El Pueblo* (1919–1920), and he later became a regular contributor to the newspapers *El Imparcial, El Mundo,* and *La Democracia,* and journals such as *La Semana* and *Puerto Rico Ilustrado*. In 1921 he joined José I. de Diego Padró in inaugurating the short-lived *diepalismo* movement (a term formed from the initial syllables of their patronymics). Its nonconformist insistence on the search for novelty, the need for insular aesthetic renewal, and highlighting of onomatopoeic and musical effects as key elements of poetry were, despite *diepalismo*'s brief moment, suggestive of things to come. In 1918 and 1926 Palés published the first examples of his *negrista* poetry, which culminated in *Tuntún de pasa y grifería: Poemas afroantillanos* (1937). The embodiment of a mestizo middle class's more congregationally inclusive vision of a defining national ethos, this collection reflected an important shift of emphasis in island cultural politics. It pointed to the inevitably syncretic character of Puerto Rican life. Persisting elements of a conventional exoticism and an objectionable racial stereotyping notwithstanding, Palés's Afro-Antillean poems challenged a reigning Hispanophilic disregard of the African ancestor. Palés's metaphorical, thematic, lexical, historical, and powerfully rhythmic invocation of that neglected legacy dramatized its importance and his conviction that "The Antillean is a Spaniard with the manner of a mulatto and the soul of a black." By the 1950s the poet's central image of a *"mulatta antilla"* (mulatto Antilles) had itself become ideologically dominant and Palés was generally regarded as the island's unofficial "national poet." In his later years Palés's poetry, included in *Poesía, 1915–1956* (3d ed., 1968), turned increasingly inward and metaphysical and assumed a less celebratory, more skeptical and intimate tone of existential anguish. Other collections of his works include *Obras, 1914–1959,* 2 vols. (1984), and *Poesía completa y prosa selecta* (1978). Lesser-known works include the unpublished poems of "El palacio en sombras," written in 1919–1920, and "Canciones de la vida media," written between 1922 and 1925, and the novel *Litoral: Reseña de una vida inútil*, an unfinished work published serially in newspapers, mostly in 1949 and 1951.

See also **Literature: Spanish America; Négritude; Puerto Rico.**

BIBLIOGRAPHY

G. R. Courthard, *Race and Color in Caribbean Literature* (1962).

Josefina Rivera De Álvarez, "Luis Palés Matos (1898–1959)," in *Diccionario de literatura puertorriqueña*, vol. 2, pt. 2, 2d ed. (1974).

José Luis Méndez, *Para una sociología de la literatura puertorriqueña* (1982), esp. pp. 119–127.

Arcadio Díaz Quiñones, *El almuerzo en la hierba* (*Llorens Torres, Palés Matos, René Marqués*) (1982), esp. pp. 73–129.

Aníbal González-Pérez, "Luis Palés Matos (1898–1959)," in *Latin American Writers,* vol. 2, edited by Carlos A. Solé (1989).

Additional Bibliography

López-Baralt, Mercedes. *El barco en la botella: La poesía de Luis Palés Matos.* San Juan, PR: Editorial Plaza Mayor, 1997.

Marzán, Julio. *The Numinous Site: The Poetry of Luis Palés Matos.* Madison, NJ: Farleigh Dickinson University Press, 1995.

ROBERTO MÁRQUEZ

PALMA, CLEMENTE (1872–1946).

Clemente Palma is considered the father of the modern Peruvian short story and the initiator of fantastic literature in that country. Born in Lima, on December 3, 1872, the son of the eminent *tradicionista* Ricardo Palma and brother of the noted feminist author Angélica Palma Román, Clemente began his literary career during the modernist movement and was inspired by the fin de siècle ambiance. Although he was a prolific writer whose diverse works include, poetry, novels, short stories, political and sociological essays, and literary theory and criticism, Palma is best remembered for his fiction. He published two collections of short stories, *Cuentos malévolos* (1904, 1913) and *Historietas malignas* (1925), and two novels, *Mors ex vita* (1918) and *XYZ*

(1934). Palma explored the fantastic in eight of his thirty-two short stories, with the finest example being "La Granja Blanca." His first novel also incorporated themes of the fantastic, which may have led to his interest in science fiction that is evident in *XYZ*. Palma died on September 13, 1946.

See also **Literature: Spanish America; Palma, Ricardo; Palma Román, Angélica.**

BIBLIOGRAPHY
Books by Palma

Excursión literaria. Lima, Peru: Imprenta de "El Comercio," 1895.

Dos tesis. Lima, Peru: Imprenta de Torres Aguirre, 1897.

Filosofía y arte. Lima, Peru: Imprenta de Torres Aguirre, 1897.

El porvenir de las razas en el Perú. Lima, Peru: Imprenta de Torres Aguirre, 1897.

El Perú. Barcelona: Librería de Antonio J. Bastinos, Editor, 1898.

Cuentos malévolos. Barcelona: Imprenta Salvat y Cía., 1904. 2nd edition, Paris: Librería Paul Ollendorff, 1913; 3rd edition, Lima, Peru: Editorial Nuevos Rumbos, 1959; 4th edition, Lima, Peru: Ediciones PEISA, 1974. Translated by Guillermo I. Castillo-Feliú as *Malignant Tales.* Lanham, MD: University Press of America, 1988.

La cuestión de Tacna y Arica y la conferencia de Washington. Lima, Peru: Casa Editora M. Moral, 1922.

Mors ex vita. Lima, Peru: Imprenta "Lux," 1923.

Historietas malignas. Lima, Peru: Editorial "Gracilaso," 1925.

XYZ. Lima, Peru: Ediciones Perú Actual, 1934.

Había una vez un hombre . . . Lima, Peru: C.I.P., 1935.

Don Alonso Henríquez de Guzmán y el primer poema sobre la conquista de América. Lima, Peru: C.I.P., 1935.

Writings in Periodicals

"Mi gata Astarté." *Actualidades* 2.85 (21 October 1904): 6–7.

"Una página de mitología." *Actualidades* 3.93 (January 1905): 5–6.

"El quinto Evangelio." *América literaria* 2.36 (20 June 1903): 275–276.

"Imploraciones." *El Ateneo* 1.2 (1899): 195–201.

"¿Ensueño o realidad?" *El Ateneo* 2.11 (1900): 427–444.

"Andrónico." *El Ateneo* 2.14 (1900): 152–159.

"Marionetes." *El Ateneo* 3.17 (1900): 446–452.

"Mensaje de amor." *El Ateneo* 3.18 (1900): 596–601.

"Leyendas de haschischs." *El Ateneo* 6.38 (1905): 2073–2086.

"Vampiros." *El Ateneo* 7.39 (1906): 85–89.

"Datos bibliográficos sobre Clemente Palma." *Boletín de la Biblioteca de la Universidad Mayor de San Marcos* 8.1 (1938): 158–162.

"La nieta del Oidor." *Cultura* 1.1 (1915): 9–20.

"Los canastos." *Cultura peruana* 6, no. 28 (1946): 2–3.

"El último fauno." *Excelsior* 7.118 (December 1942): 31–34.

"Leyendas de haschischs." *Gracilaso* 2, no. 3 (April 1914): 25–28.

"Los faunos viejos." *Ilustración Peruana* 5, no. 1 (1913): 10.

"En el carretón." *Ilustración Peruana* 5, no. 4 (1913): 89–90.

"Anacreonte ebrio." *Ilustración Peruana* 5, no. 7 (1913): 183.

"La nieta del Oidor." *Ilustración Peruana* 5, no. 8 (1913): 205–207.

"El hombre del cigarrillo." *El Mercurio* 4 September 1932, sec. 1, p. 1.

"Aventura del hombre que no nació." *El Mercurio* 8 January 1933, sec. 1, p. 1.

"*Mors ex vita.*" Parts 1, 2. *El Mercurio Peruano* 1, no. 3 and 4 (September, October 1918): 133–142, 190–214.

"Walpurgis." *El Modernismo* 1.10 (1901): 114–116.

"Floreal." *El Modernismo* 1.11 (1901): 121–122.

"Dmitri era un excelente amigo." *El Modernismo* 1, no. 13 (1901): 148–150.

"Dmitri, fantasia malvada." *Monos y monadas* 1, no. 32 (4 August 1906): 4–5.

"En la orgía." *La Neblina* 2, no. 1 (1897): 5.

"Al vuelo." *La Neblina* 2, no. 4 (1897): 91–93.

"Los canastos." *Turismo* 13.123 (January 1938): 9.

"Elogio y diatriba." *Turismo* 13, no. 131 (September 1938): 10.

Secondary Sources

Kason, Nancy. "Elements of the Fantastic in 'La Granja Blanca'." In *The Fantastic in World Literature and the Arts: Selected Papers from the Fifth International Conference on the Fantastic*, edited by Donald E. Morse, pp. 115–121. Westport, CT: Greenwood Press, 1987.

Kason, Nancy. "The Dystopian Vision in *XYZ* by Clemente Palma." *Monographic Review / Revista Monográfica* 3, no. 1–2 (1987): 33–42.

Kason, Nancy. "Société et Mécanisation: *L'Eve Future* de Villiers de L'Isle-Adam et *XYZ* de Clemente Palma." *Bulletin Hispanique* 89 (1987): 359–365.

Kason, Nancy. *Breaking Traditions: The Fiction of Clemente Palma*. Lewisburg, PA: Bucknell University Press, 1988.

NANCY KASON POULSON

PALMA, RICARDO (1833–1919).

Ricardo Palma (*b.* 7 February 1833; *d.* 6 October 1919), Peruvian diplomat, politician, writer, and historian. Born in Lima, Palma was the illegitimate son of Pedro Palma. He began writing as a very young man, as early as 1848. From 1861 to 1863 he lived in Chile. Then in 1864 he journeyed to Europe, living briefly in Paris and traveling to England and Venice.

Upon his return to Peru (1865), Palma served in a number of government posts, including secretary to President José Balta in 1868. In addition he was elected to three terms in the Peruvian Senate. At the same time he worked as assistant librarian of Lima and contributed to the prestigious Buenos Aires newspaper *La Prensa*.

Palma is best remembered, however, for his own written work. He adopted romanticism, which came to Peru from Europe, and became the foremost advocate of that literary movement in his country. He wrote poems and articles but is known primarily for his *Tradiciones peruanas* (Peruvian Traditions, 4 vols., 1893–1896), short stories that combined history with his own imagination. This was a genre of romanticism that Palma acquired from Spain, where it combined the romantic legend with *costumbrismo* (articles about customs). Many of his traditions dealt with Inca themes, and he wrote extensively about colonial Peru, to the point that some critics referred to him as "colonialist Palma." Whatever his subjects, he gained for himself and Peru a wide literary reputation outside the nation and the region.

Palma also popularized history for the reading public. Critics, however, complained that he bound literature so tightly with history that people could not extricate fact from fiction, and that therefore he was deficient as a historian.

Also a political activist, Palma tried to overthrow President Ramón Castilla in 1860, but he failed and was exiled to Chile for two years. When the War of the Pacific with Chile began in 1879, Palma enlisted in the reserves, but the invading Chileans destroyed his personal library of several thousand books and manuscripts. Peru's National Library also suffered looting at the hands of the Chileans. After Palma became director of the library in 1883, he spent the next twenty-eight years rebuilding the collection. He catalogued more than twenty thousand books in less than four years and waged such a tenacious campaign to rebuild the library that he became known as *bibliotecario mendigo* (the begging librarian).

While his library and archival activity was critical to the preservation of Peru's literature, Palma's own written work expanded the historical knowledge of Peru and made the public aware of the nation's past.

See also **Castilla, Ramón; Literature: Spanish America; Peru: Peru Since Independence.**

BIBLIOGRAPHY

Sturgis E. Leavitt, "Ricardo Palma," in *Hispanic American Historical Review* 3 (1920): 63–67.

Harriet De Onís, *The Knights of the Cape, and Thirty-Seven Other Selections from the "Tradiciones peruanas" of Ricardo Palma* (1945).

Sturgis E. Leavitt, "Ricardo Palma and the *Tradiciones peruanas*," in *Hispania* 34 (1951): 349–353.

Shirley L. Arora, *Proverbial Comparisons in Ricardo Palma's* "Tradiciones peruanas" (1966).

Rubén Vargas Ugarte, "Don Ricardo Palma y la historia," in *Journal of Inter-American Studies* 9 (1967): 213–224.

Phyllis Rodríguez-Peralta, "Liberal Undercurrents in Palma's *Tradiciones peruanas*," in *Revista de estudios hispánicos* 15 (1981): 283–297.

José Miguel Oviedo, "Ricardo Palma," in *Latin American Writers,* edited by Carlos A. Solé (1989), vol. 1, pp. 221–228.

Additional Bibliography

Holguín Callo, Oswaldo. *Tiempos de infancia y bohemia: Ricardo Palma, 1833–1860.* Lima: Pontífica Universidad Católica del Perú, Fondo Editorial, 1994.

Santillana Cantella, Tomás Gmo. *Ayacucho en las Tradiciones peruanos de Ricardo Palma.* Lima: Fondo Editorial del Banco Central de Reserva del Perú, 2002.

JACK RAY THOMAS

PALMARES. Palmares, one of the largest and most enduring runaway slave communities (quilombos) in the Americas. Located in the southern part of the captaincy of Pernambuco (in an area which is now part of the northeastern Brazilian state of Alagoas), the *quilombo* of Palmares came into existence at the end of the sixteenth century (the exact date is unknown), approximately fifty years after the beginning of the slave trade to Brazil. It survived until 1694, when it was destroyed by the last of many punitive expeditions undertaken by the Portuguese. Though some of its founding members may have been creoles (Brazilian-born individuals of African descent), it is probable that most were from Bantu-speaking peoples of West Central Africa, the majority of whom were men.

To survive, the *quilombo* had to strike a balance between its need to remain a secluded fortress, protected from external attack, and its reliance on the very society its members had fled. In 1612, for example, Portuguese officials complained of the irksome presence of the runaways, who stole livestock and other goods from settlers. To augment their numbers, *quilombo* raiders kidnapped slaves and settlers, some of whom became hostages subsequently ransomed. Other slaves, however, fled to Palmares of their own accord. Many, for example, took advantage of the disruptions that accompanied the Dutch invasion of Pernambuco in 1630 to escape to the *quilombo*.

In the early 1640s, the Dutch themselves undertook an exploratory mission into the remote, rugged, and densely wooded environs of Palmares to investigate the extent of the community. They found that approximately eleven thousand people lived in several settlements spread over a large territory. It is no wonder, then, that the success of Palmares—its sheer size and longevity—provoked the same contradictory response in the nearby settlements that occurred within the runaway community itself: just as the population of Palmares relied, at times, on nearby settlements, settlers also needed the community of runaways. Even as the government laid out plans to destroy the *quilombo*, local merchants and farmers transacted business with its residents, trading firearms, tools, and other goods for agricultural produce and gold.

The exchange between Palmares and Luso-Brazilian settlers was never enough to discourage the Portuguese (or the Dutch during the time they occupied parts of the northeastern captaincies) from attempting to destroy the *quilombo*. During their failed attempt to defeat Palmares in 1645, for example, the Dutch discovered that the largest of the *quilombo*'s settlements, Macao, was highly organized, with a church, well-constructed houses, blacksmiths, and irrigated fields of corn, cassava, legumes, potatoes, and sugarcane. Each settlement was protectively walled with several rings of sharpened stakes.

By mid-century Palmares was, for all intents and purposes, a centralized state located in Portugal's largest territory. At its head was an elected king who administered justice according to strict laws designed to maintain the integrity and survival of the community. In all, around five generations of kings ruled Palmares, which embraced 20,000–30,000 inhabitants and 1,100 square leagues by the end of the century. Ethnic and cultural differences within the population made governance of the settlement that much more challenging, and encouraged the use of Portuguese as the common language and a syncretic blend of African spiritual beliefs and Roman Catholicism as the religion.

During the period of 1650–1670, Palmares survived a number of attacks, largely because the fighting prowess of its inhabitants, led by the famous general Zumbi, far exceeded that of the government's army, which often found itself surrounded or altogether evaded by the enemy. An especially bloody campaign finally led Ganga-Zumba, the king of Palmares, to sign a peace treaty with the Luso-Brazilians in 1678. His capitulation heightened his rivalry with Zumbi, which led, eventually, to the death of the king and renewed hostility with the government. Between 1680 and 1686, six costly military expeditions failed to defeat Palmares. The final demise would come only after two years of sustained war, from 1692 to 1694, after which Zumbi was captured and beheaded and the remaining five hundred inhabitants sold into slavery.

See also **Quilombo.**

BIBLIOGRAPHY

In English, see R. K. Kent, "Palmares: An African State in Brazil," in Richard Price, ed., *Maroon Societies: Rebel Slave Communities in the Americas*, 2d ed. (1979), pp. 170–190. The best book-length account is Décio Freitas, *Palmares: A guerra dos escravos* (1973).

Additional Bibliography

Funari, Pedro Paulo A., and Aline Vieira de Carvalho. *Palmares, ontem e hoje*. Rio de Janeiro: Jorge Zahar Editor, 2005.

Gomes, Flávio dos Santos. *Palmares: Escravidão e liberdade no Atlântico Sul*. São Paulo: Contexto, 2005.

Reis, João José, and Flávio dos Santos Gomes. *Liberdade por um fio: História dos quilombos no Brasil*. São Paulo: Companhia das Letras, 1996.

                                    JUDITH L. ALLEN

PALMA ROMÁN, ANGÉLICA (1878–1935). Born in Lima on October 25, 1878, and educated at Colegio Fanning, Angélica Palma Román wrote essays and stories in the form of letters, travel accounts, children's stories, novels (historical, psychological, and modernist), and biographies of celebrities. She was the daughter of the Peruvian *tradicionista* Ricardo Palma and the sister of the novelist Clemente Palma. An aesthetic and feminist innovator for her times, she used Hispanic creole and colloquial forms as well as artistic experimentation, and she was skilled at creating characters with psychological depth. She was awarded the International Novel Prize in Buenos Aires in 1921, the Historical Novel Prize in Lima in 1924, and the Commendation of the Order of Alfonso XII in Madrid in 1926.

Palma Román's modernist but moderate views on the status and conditions of women are evident in her novel *Uno de tantos* (1926), in which she criticizes the power of irresponsible fathers, fiancés, and husbands; though she did not support women entering politics, she questioned the ideological constraints that prevented women from having access to education, culture, or mental independence. Her historical novels, *Por senda propia* (1921), *Coloniaje romántico* (1923), and *Tiempos de la Patria vieja* (1926), depict colonial life, Spain's legacy in Peru, and the violent transformations undertaken to establish the democratic republic. All are imbued with her deep love of Peru, which, in *Al azar* (1928), she called a "nuanced, complex and ironic creole society." Palma Román died in Rosario, Argentina, on September 6, 1935.

See also **Literature: Spanish America; Palma, Clemente; Palma, Ricardo.**

BIBLIOGRAPHY

Martínez Gómez, Juana, and Almudena Mejías Alonso. *Hispanoamericanas en Madrid, 1800–1936.* Madrid: Horas y Horas, 1994.

Rojas Benavente, Lady. "Figurando, desfigurando y configurando la feminidad en *La sombra alucinane* (1939) de Angélica Palma." In *Escritura femenina y reivindicación de género en América Latina*, edited by Roland Forgues and Jean-Marie Flores, pp. 87–101. Paris: Thélès, 2004.

Román, Angélica Palma. *Páginas dispersas de la escritora.* 1937. Lima, Peru: Sociedad Amigos de Palma, E. E. B. Sucesor, 1937.

Tamayo Vargas, Augusto. *Literatura peruana*, 3 vols. Lima, Peru: PEISA, 1992–1993.

LADY ROJAS BENAVENTE

PALOU, FRANCISCO (1723–1789).

Francisco Palou (*b.* 22 January 1723; *d.* 6 April 1789), Franciscan missionary in Baja and Alta California. Born in Palma, Mallorca, Palou was a student and lifelong friend of Junipero Serra, the Franciscan architect of the Alta California mission system. Palou went to New Spain in 1749 with Serra, then worked in the California missions under Serra's direction between 1768 and 1784.

Palou, stationed in the Baja California establishments between 1768 and 1773, became the superior of the missions when Serra joined a 1769 expedition that occupied Alta California. When the Franciscans transferred the Baja California missions to the jurisdiction of the Dominicans in 1773, Palou went to Alta California and served in the missions until 1786. During this period, he temporarily served as superior of the Alta California missions in 1784 and 1785, following which he returned to the apostolic college of San Fernando in Mexico City to serve as its superior from 1787 until his death. While there Palou wrote a hagiography of Serra and an important account of the early Franciscan years in Baja California (1768–1773) and Alta California (1769–1786) (*Palou's Historical Memoirs of New California*, trans. and ed. by H. E. Bolton, 4 vols. [1926]).

See also **Franciscans; Missions: Spanish America; Serra, Junipero.**

BIBLIOGRAPHY

Zephyrin Engelhardt, O.F.M., *Missions and Missionaries of California*, 4 vols. (1929–1930).

Maynard J. Geiger, O.F.M., *Franciscan Missionaries in Hispanic California, 1769–1848: A Biographical Dictionary* (1969).

Additional Bibliography

Lightfoot, Kent G. *Indians, Missionaries, and Merchants: The Legacy of Colonial Encounters on the California Frontiers.* Berkeley: University of California Press, 2005.

ROBERT H. JACKSON

PAMPA. Pampa, a vast, rolling plain that stretches through the Río de la Plata from Patagonia in the south to the Andean foothills in the west to the Chaco in the north. In his essay, "La Pampa," the British writer Robert B. Cunninghame Graham rightly described the pampa as "all grass and sky, and sky and grass, and still more sky and grass." Fanning out from the Atlantic coast, the fertile, humid pampa runs several hundred miles inland. Well watered and subject to seasonal flooding, it offers immensely rich agricultural and grazing lands. Beginning in Córdoba province, the pampa becomes drier, the grasslands thinner, and the water sources fewer. Travelers unfamiliar with the vast plains depended on gaucho guides (Baquianos) to lead them. Control of this rich grassland gave the landed elite economic and political power in the Río del la Plata.

See also **Río de la Plata.**

BIBLIOGRAPHY

Enrique Williams Alzaga, *La pampa en la novela argentina* (1955).

John Walker, ed. *The South American Sketches of R. B. Cunninghame Graham* (1978).

Richard W. Slatta, *Gauchos and the Vanishing Frontier* (1983), pp. 17–29.

Richard W. Slatta, *Cowboys of the Americas* (1990), pp. 63–65.

Additional Bibliography

Briones, Claudia, and José Luis Lanta. *Archaeological and Anthropological Perspectives on the Native Peoples of Pampa, Patagonia, and Tierra del Fuego to the Nineteenth Century.* Westport, CT: Bergin & Garvey, 2002.

Etchenique, Jorge. *Pampa libre: Anarquistas en la pampa Argentina*. Buenos Aires: Universidad Nacional de Quilmes: Ediciones Amerindia, 2000.

Fernández Priotti, Carlos Alberto. *El Ferrocarril Oeste Santafecino: Carlos Casada y la colonización del Pampa*. Rosario: CA Fernández Priotti, 2006.

Martínez Estrada, Ezequiel. *X-Ray of the Pampa*. The Texas Pan American Series. Austin: University of Texas Press, 1971.

RICHARD W. SLATTA

PAMPA DE LAS LLAMAS-MOXEKE.

Pampa de las Llamas-Moxeke, a large early site located in the Casma Valley on the north-central coast of Peru. The site, once the center of a larger polity, dates between 1900 BCE and 1400 BCE and covers an area of about 550 acres. All of the site's architecture is built of stone set in mud mortar.

The main axis of the site is formed by two large mounds separated by numerous spacious plazas. The largest mound, Moxeke, was a religious temple for public worship. Along its front face it once had several large anthropomorphic heads and full figures, probably representing deities or mythological beings. These would have been plainly visible to people standing in adjacent plazas. Huaca A, the other large mound, was used as a large warehouse for storing foodstuffs and other commodities. Its symmetrical summit contains seventy-seven large rooms built on different levels and reached by staircases. Access to each room was strictly controlled by the use of wooden bar closures that permitted or prevented entry. The elite class living at the site controlled the access to Huaca A as a means to enforce their authority.

Lining the main plazas of the site are over 110 intermediate-sized mounds that served as administrative structures. Lower-level bureaucrats working within them monitored the flow of goods in and out of Huaca A through the use of ceramic stamp and cylinder seals as symbols of authority. The site also contains hundreds of smaller structures that served as houses for people of different classes and status groups. Two additional small structures have central, ventilated hearths. These structures were once roofed by wood and reeds and probably functioned as private ritual chambers for small groups of people.

See also **Archaeology.**

BIBLIOGRAPHY

Shelia Pozorski and Thomas Pozorski, "Recent Excavations at Pampa de las Llamas-Moxeke," in *Journal of Field Archaeology* 13 (1986): 381–401; *Early Settlement and Subsistence in the Casma Valley, Peru* (1987); and "Storage, Access Control, and Bureaucratic Proliferation: Understanding the Initial Period (1800–900 B.C.) Economy at Pampa de las Llamas-Moxeke, Casma Valley, Peru," in *Research in Economic Anthropology* 13 (1991): 341–371.

Additional Bibliography

Pozorski, Sheila, and Thomas Pozorski. "Multi-dimensional Planning at Pampa de las Llamas-Moxeke on the North Central Coast of Peru," in *Meaningful Architecture: Social Interpretations of Buildings*, edited by Martin Locock. Brookfield: Avebury, 1994.

Pozorski, Thomas, and Sheila Pozorski. "Ventilated Hearth Structures in the Casma Valley, Peru." *Latin American Antiquity* Vol. 7, No. 4 (Dec., 1996): 341–353.

SHELIA POZORSKI
THOMAS POZORSKI

PANAMA.

Panama connects Central America with South America, sharing borders with Costa Rica and Colombia. In 2007 the republic was home to more than 3.24 million people. Although independent for almost a century, Panama has for most of this time been a protectorate and reluctant ally of the United States, which operated a ship canal, railroad, and attendant military bases in the heart of the country. Since the implementation of the 1977 Panama Canal (Carter–Torrijos) treaties, however, the alliance has attenuated, with the transfer of ownership of the canal to Panama on 31 December 1999, and the withdrawal of all U.S. military troops. The nation's political history may be separated into several eras: the protectorate between independence and 1931, when the United States collaborated with elite families to build an effective government; the Arias decade (1931–1941), when Harmodio and Arnulfo Arias Madrid served as presidents; the rise to prominence of the National Guard, culminating in the presidency of commandant José Antonio Remón; the democratic interlude 1955–1968, when three elected

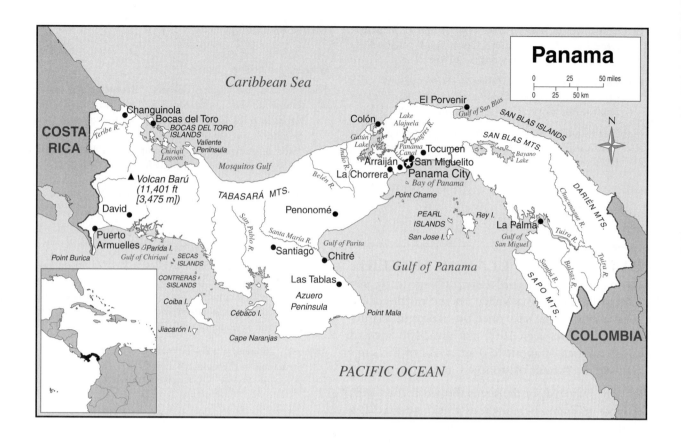

presidents served out terms; the Torrijos era; and the Noriega years (1981–1989). Since the early 1990s, although troubled at first by lack of legitimacy and barracks unrest, Panama has witnessed the development of political stability.

INDEPENDENCE AND PROTECTORATE PERIOD

Panama declared its independence from Colombia as part of a larger plan to give the United States the right to build a canal there and to end its eighty-two-year attachment to Bogotá. Leadership for the plot came from the managers of the Panama Railroad Company, which had run trains across the isthmus since 1855, and from the Conservative Party. The U.S. government played an important part, for the Colombian Senate had just rejected a treaty with the United States authorizing the transfer to it of the excavations and rights of the French-owned Compagnie Nouvelle du Canal de Panama. The company, high U.S. officials, and Panamanian leaders conspired to declare independence and authorize canal construction. Two people deeply responsible for the success of the plan were

Philippe Jean Bunau-Varilla, a former canal engineer unofficially representing the French, and William N. Cromwell, counsel and lobbyist for the railroad and the French company.

The declaration of independence proceeded as expected on 3 November 1903. The conspirators, led by elderly Manuel Amador Guerrero, bought off the Colombian garrison, and railroad officials prevented reinforcements from arriving. U.S. warships on the scene (ostensibly maintaining the peace) protected the rebels, and within three days the United States extended recognition to the Republic of Panama.

During the nineteenth century Panamanians seceded from Colombia on several occasions, usually led by Liberals, only to be brought back into the federation by force. Now the stakes were much higher than in previous revolts. Panamanians had fielded several armies during the War of the Thousand Days (1899–1902) and could not expect favorable treatment from Bogotá. Also they faced the possibility that the United States might abandon them and build a canal in Nicaragua, long the

ENCYCLOPEDIA OF LATIN AMERICAN HISTORY & CULTURE

Panama

Population:	3,242,173 (2007 est.)
Area:	30,193 sq mi
Official language(s):	Spanish
Language(s):	Spanish, English
National currency:	balboa (PAB); US dollar (USD)
Principal religions:	Roman Catholic, 85%; Protestant, 15%
Ethnicity:	mestizo (mixed Amerindian and European), 70%; Amerindian and mixed (West Indian), 14%; European, 10%; Amerindian, 6%
Capital:	Panama City (Panamá) (pop. 930,000, 2005 est.)
Other urban centers:	Colón, David
Annual rainfall:	in Panama City, 70 in; Colón, 129 in
Principal geographic features:	*Mountain Ranges:* Cordillera de San Blas, Serranía de Tabasará, including the Barú volcano (11,401 ft), formerly known as Chiriquí. *Bodies of water:* Tuira River, 300 other rivers, Gulf of Panama *Islands:* Panama has more than 1,600 islands, including the San Blas Islands, Pearls Archipelago (Archipiélago de las Perlas), the penal colony Coiba
Economy:	*GDP per capita:* $8,200 (2006 est.)
Principal products and exports:	*Agriculture:* bananas, rice, corn, coffee, sugarcane, vegetables; livestock; shrimp *Industries:* construction, brewing, cement and other construction materials, sugar milling
Government:	Panama is a republic with executive, judicial, and unicameral legislative branches of government. Both the legislative and executive branches are elected through direct popular vote. The executive branch contains a president and two vice presidents which, after 2009 will be reduced to a president and vice president.
Armed forces:	*National Police Force:* 11,800 members, supported by a maritime service (est. 400) and an air service (400)
Transportation:	In 2002, 7,203 mi of roads, of which about 2,534 mi were paved, including 19 mi of expressways. The principal highway is the National (or Central) Highway, the Panamanian section of the Pan American Highway. As of 2004, there were a total of 220 mi of standard- and narrow-gauge railway lines, all government-run. As of 2004, there were an estimated 105 airports, 47 of which had paved runways as of 2005. The most widely used domestic airline is Compañía Panameña de Aviación (COPA), which also flies throughout Central America. The Panama Canal traverses the isthmus and is 51 mi in length from deepwater to deepwater and is part of Panama's 497 mi of navigable internal waterways. The Bridge of the Americas across the canal at the Pacific entrance unites eastern and western Panama as well as the northern and southern sections of the Pan American Highway.
Media:	In 2004, there was one government-owned educational television station. The same year, there were 8 television stations and 120 radio stations that were privately or institutionally owned. There were five major daily newspapers in 2004. With their estimated circulations, they were: *El Siglo*, 42,000; *Crítica Libre*, 40,000; *La Prensa*, 40,000; *La Estrella de Panama*, NA; and *El Panama America*, 40,000.
Literacy and education:	*Total literacy rate:* 91.9% Education is free for children ages 6 through 15 and the first 6 years are compulsory. Universities include the state-run University of Panama and the Catholic university Santa María la Antigua.

preferred site. Or even if the United States went forward with the Panama canal, most of the contracts and payments would be transferred to Bogotá, as had happened during the French era. From the point of view of most Panamanians, then, independence under the protection of the United States offered more advantages than did continuation as a Colombian province.

Bunau-Varilla, rewarded for his activities with an appointment as Panamanian minister in Washington, and U.S. secretary of state John Hay quickly signed a treaty even more advantageous to the United States than the previous one with Colombia. The Hay–Bunau-Varilla Treaty gave the United States a 10-mile-wide zone through the heart of Panama for the purpose of building, operating, and defending a ship canal. The $10 million paid to Panama represented about 2 percent of the construction cost, or $28 per acre.

Amador Guerrero, chosen president by a constitutional assembly, organized a bureaucracy, promulgated law codes, and disbanded the army. Panama enjoyed the protection of the United States, which was empowered to deal with external and domestic problems alike. The president received counsel from the U.S. minister on all important matters and prevented disruptions in canal construction (1904–1914). Over 150,000 immigrants flooded the country to work on the canal, permanently altering the ethnic, racial, and cultural makeup of the country.

In 1912 the Liberals, led by Belisario Porras, won the elections, inaugurating a twenty-year period of control. Porras celebrated the opening of the canal with an international exposition in 1915. This was a period of nation-building efforts to turn the backwater province into a modern state. Schools, hospitals, railroads, and highways were built, and businessmen created prosperity in the form of banana plantations, logging firms, truck farms, cattle ranches, and urban construction. Panama remained dependent upon canal jobs and transfers, but the republic grew apart from the Canal Zone, which became a self-sufficient compound run by the U.S. government. The governor of the Panama Canal acted as spokesman for U.S. interests in Panama and occasionally sent troops or advisers, or sometimes friendly advice, to the Panamanians. No one doubted that Panama was a protectorate whose existence owed much to the canal that divided it.

THE ARIAS DECADE

Nationalist sentiments arose in the 1920s to protest Panama's subservience, and the secret Acción Comunal (Common Action) group lobbied for better treatment by the United States. It managed to block a treaty governing relations with the zone and eventually took power in a 1931 coup. The brothers Harmodio and Arnulfo Arias Madrid emerged as leaders in the coup, and Harmodio assumed the presidency in 1932–1936. Taking advantage of the noninterventionist policy of Washington, they strengthened the police in order to maintain political control. In 1936 Harmodio oversaw the signing of a new treaty (Hull–Alfaro) that ameliorated some abuses by the canal and adjusted annuity payments, but the depression years created great hardships in a services-dependent economy with little industry or mining and only a modest agriculture. Harmodio tried to improve relations among the country's ethnic groups and founded the University of Panama in 1935. An associate carried on Harmodio's policies during the next presidential term.

Arnulfo Arias won election in 1940, after a violent campaign by his Panameñista Party. He promulgated the nationalist Constitution of 1941 that revoked the citizenship rights of nonwhite immigrants and extended his term to six years. Amazingly energetic, he began a number of initiatives that later bore fruit. His anti-American posturing and harsh treatment of domestic opponents, however, soon generated a coup that overthrew him in favor of a moderate who immediately cooperated with the U.S. defense effort. In jail and then exile, Arnulfo continued to build his populist following among the native poor and children of immigrants, promising to fight exploitation by the United States and to reduce the power wielded by the white elite, the *rabiblancos*.

THE RISE OF THE NATIONAL GUARD

Defense and construction expenditures during the war brought high employment to Panama, but the postwar years saw a collapse in prosperity and rising political conflict. The 1946 Constitution returned the country to democratic procedures, which allowed Arnulfo Arias to mobilize mass support for his nationalistic party. Soon, however, the national police, under the command of José Antonio Remón, assumed the role of political mediator, and it denied Arnulfo's victory in the 1948 election. A confusing period ensued, in which lack of authority exacerbated economic depression. Remón finally allowed Arnulfo to be president in 1949; during his brief second administration Arnulfo stirred up more trouble by feuding with the National Assembly and the Supreme Court, and by attempting to promulgate the 1941 Constitution again. Facing impeachment by the legislature in 1951, he was removed by Remón in a nearly bloodless coup.

Kingmaker by now, Remón (urged by his ambitious wife, Cecilia) decided to run for president in 1952. Elected largely by dint of his power and patronage, he nonetheless tried to be a better president than the country had ever known. He promoted economic development, fiscal responsibility, social reforms, and less dependence on the canal. He renamed the police the National Guard, giving them quasi-military status. He also pushed U.S. president Dwight Eisenhower to sign a new treaty (Eisenhower–Remón) that increased Panama's benefits from the canal. Still, hints of scandal and corruption tainted Remón's presidency, which ended with his gangland assassination in 1955.

DEMOCRATIC INTERLUDE

Efforts by Remón's successors Ernesto de la Guardia (1956–1960) and Roberto Chiari (1960–1964) to improve the economy and strengthen the nation were overshadowed by growing discontent

The Centennial Bridge over the Panama Canal.
The bridge, which opened on the centennial of Panama's independence from Colombia, is one of only two major roadways crossing the Panama Canal. © DANNY LEHMAN/ CORBIS

with U.S. canal policy. Students in particular insisted that Panama's flag be flown in the zone and that the canal's toll profits be shared. They denounced the canal as an instrument of U.S. imperialism, a belief widely shared throughout the hemisphere. Several concessions were wrested from the United States—token flags, equal employee and retirement systems for U.S. and Panamanian canal workers, and some foreign aid—but the basic problem remained unchanged: Panamanians demanded sovereignty over the zone, and the United States would not accede to their demand. The Kennedy administration did, however, agree that the old treaty should be scrapped if and when arrangements could be made to build a sea-level canal. But it was too little too late.

Panamanian frustration erupted in the student-led Flag Riots of 1964, which left two dozen dead and led to suspension of relations between the countries. For the first time, Panama's elite did not go along with suppressing anti-American demonstrations and instead used them for diplomatic pressure. Late that year presidents Marco Aurelio Robles and Lyndon Johnson agreed to negotiate three new treaties to govern the existing canal, to provide for its defense, and to authorize a sea-level canal. Stepped-up aid expenditures helped to relieve unemployment and to stimulate business. Panamanians were optimistic until the treaty drafts were leaked in mid-1967. Robles, already unpopular, avoided impeachment thanks to the military. The draft treaties were met with skepticism—they offered little financial relief, protracted U.S. operation of the canal, and continued the U.S. military presence—and were soon tabled.

THE TORRIJOS ERA

Arnulfo Arias ran for the presidency in 1968 and won a substantial victory, attesting to his staying power with the masses. Wary of the military, which had removed him twice, he made plans to retire or reassign top guard officials. When he did so, eleven days into his administration, a group of officers led by Major Boris Martínez and Colonel Omar Torrijos deposed him. Torrijos, whose senior rank and political skills made him popular among guard officers, shouldered Martínez aside and exiled him in early 1969. The so-called revolutionary government, staffed with intellectuals, brought in representatives of labor, students, and peasants but failed to create a firm coalition. Given these troubles and no support from the United States, Torrijos assumed dictatorial powers, which were enforced by the guard.

In 1972 the Torrijos regime mustered a constituent assembly to give the country a constitution that made "el General" head of state but designated a president for ceremonial purposes. Strong-arm police repression, employing surveillance, censorship, torture, exile, and murder, characterized most of his era. He did, however, enact legislation that favored workers, and his constant attention to agrarian problems brought him acceptance by the rural poor. He also fostered an offshore banking industry whose huge deposits and modern buildings gave the illusion of affluence. These accomplishments, plus his easygoing manner and a steady stream of publicity, helped to ameliorate his dicta-torial methods.

Torrijos reinitiated talks with the United States regarding a new canal treaty in 1974. The 1967 drafts served as a basis for the operating treaty; the sea-level canal no longer beckoned; and the defense treaty gave the United States rights to four military bases through 1999. About two-thirds of the former zone was given back to Panama in a land trust, and Panama received more income from the canal. Torrijos and President Jimmy Carter signed the trea-ties in 1977; the U.S. Senate narrowly approved them in 1978; and they were implemented in 1979.

THE NORIEGA YEARS
Panama was changed by 1980, not so much by the treaties as by the process of achieving them. To appear less autocratic, Torrijos had created the Democratic Revolutionary Party, and after 1978 he increasingly shifted responsibility onto the new president, Aristides Royo. The treaties had not brought great new wealth to the country, and indeed Torrijos's generous spending had left the country with the largest per-capita foreign debt in the world. When Torrijos perished in a plane crash in 1981, signs for the future were already ominous.

Civilian leaders, demoralized by the long dicta-torship, recovered slowly in the 1980s. General Manuel Antonio Noriega, meanwhile, consolidated his control over the guard, which he renamed the Panamanian Defense Force (PDF) in 1983, and behind the scene set policy for the government. For a time there was hope that Nicolás Ardito Barletta, a U.S.-trained economist elected fraudu-lently in 1984, might become a strong president. The United States poured in economic and military aid in hope of separating the two "branches" of government. But Barletta failed to build a strong political base and was forced out by Noriega in 1985. The turmoil of Panamanian affairs stood in marked contrast to the orderly implementation of the 1977 canal treaties.

Noriega, who rose to power from very humble origins, proved cunning and versatile. He exacted unwavering loyalty from his officers, whom he rewarded with money and opportunity for graft. Opponents met with torture and sometimes cruel deaths. Unconcerned with the daily problems of government, left to puppet presidents, Noriega

proceeded octopus-like to engage himself in the most nefarious and farflung enterprises. Since early in his career he had profited from the drug trade, and by the mid-1980s he had become a major link between the Colombian cartels and the U.S. mar-ket. Yet he also produced an occasional drug run-ner or tip for the U.S. Drug Enforcement Agency. He helped the Reagan administration run arms illegally to the Contra forces in Nicaragua, yet he also sold guns to the Salvadoran rebels. During his regime Panama became a regional arms emporium. He multiplied his own forces and equipped them with the best matériel available. He brokered intel-ligence for several governments, even double-crossing the U.S. services. Yet the CIA and the U.S. Army kept him on generous informer payrolls. He arranged for high-tech equipment to be shipped to the Soviet Union, circumventing a U.S. ban on such exports. It was a remarkable record to accumulate in such a short time.

From mid-1986 on, civilian unrest mounted, and U.S. authorities increased their pressure on Noriega to reform his regime or step down. In early 1988 the U.S. Justice Department issued indictments against Noriega for drug crimes, and the Reagan administration enacted economic sanc-tions against Panama, to little avail. For eighteen months the feud went on, including U.S. threats, failed PDF coups, a canceled election, and harass-ment of U.S. servicemen in Panama. Finally, on 20 December 1989, some 12,000 U.S. forces invaded Panama and destroyed PDF headquarters in an effort to capture Noriega, who was eventually taken in custody to Miami, where he stood trial on nar-cotics charges and was sentenced to forty years in prison.

At the time of the Christmas invasion, the United States installed Guillermo Endara as presi-dent, claiming that he had won the canceled elec-tions. Endara, not a strong leader, shared power with two ambitious vice presidents, the U.S. author-ities in Panama, and a new military force built largely out of the remnants of the PDF. His scandal-plagued government presided over reconstruction, funded by a billion dollars in U.S. aid.

In 1994 Panamanians for the first time since 1968 returned to fair elections. They elected Ernesto Pérez Balladares of the Democratic Revolutionary Party (PRD), who won the presidency with a little over 33 percent of the votes. Gilberto Guardia, a Panamanian, took over as administrator of the Panama Canal Commission, guiding the last phase of the 1977 treaty enactment. In 2004 Martín Torrijos also a member of the PRD, and the son of the former dictator Colonel Omar Torrijos, was elected to a five-year term. Panama's government has embarked on an extensive project to expand the canal's capacity, which remains important to the service-oriented economy. Located near the entrance of the canal is the Colón Free Trade Zone, the largest tax-free zone in the Americas and the second-largest in the world, renowned for its modern facilities. It serves as an important conduit for goods between industrialized countries and Latin American markets.

See also **Endara, Guillermo; Noriega Moreno, Manuel Antonio; Panama Canal; Panama Canal, Flag Riots; Panama Canal Treaties of 1977; Porras, Belisario; Torrijos Herrera, Omar.**

BIBLIOGRAPHY

Larry La Rae Pippin, *The Remón Era* (1964).

Gustavo A. Mellander, *United States in Panamanian Politics* (1971).

David Mc Cullough, *The Path Between the Seas* (1977).

Steve C. Ropp, *Panamanian Politics* (1982).

William J. Jorden, *Panama Odyssey* (1984).

Walter La Feber, *The Panama Canal,* rev. ed. (1989); *Panama, a Country Study,* 4th ed. (1989).

Michael L. Conniff, "Panama Since 1903," in *Cambridge History of Latin America* (1990), vol. 7, pp. 603–642.

Michael L. Conniff, *Panama and the United States* (1991).

Additional Bibliography

Avila, Víctor. *Panamá: Luchas sociales y afirmación nacional.* Panamá: Centro de Estudios Latinoamericanos "Justo Arosemena," 1998.

Bonilla, Heraclio, and Gustavo Montañez, eds. *Colombia y Panamá: La metamorfosis de la nación en el siglo XX.* Bogotá: Universidad Nacional de Colombia, 2004.

Center of Military History. *Operation Just Cause: The Incursion into Panama.* Washington, DC: Author, 2004.

Harding, Robert C. *The History of Panama.* Westport, CT: Greenwood Press, 2006.

Howe, James. *A People Who Would Not Kneel: Panama, the United States, and the San Blas Kuna.* Washington, DC: Smithsonian Institution Press, 1998.

O'Reggio, Trevor. *Between Alienation and Citizenship: The Evolution of Black West Indian Society in Panama 1914–1964.* Lanham, MD: University Press of America, 2006.

Pearcy, Thomas L. *We Answer Only to God: Politics and the Military in Panama, 1903–1947.* Albuquerque: University of New Mexico Press, 1998.

Reyes Rivas, Eyra Marcela. *El trabajo de las mujeres en la historia de la construcción del Canal de Panamá, 1881–1914.* Panamá: Universidad de Panamá, Instituto de la Mujer, 2000.

Sánchez, Peter Michael. *Panama Lost?: U.S. Hegemony, Democracy, and the Canal.* Gainesville: University Press of Florida, 2007.

Siu Lok, C. D. *Memories of a Future Home: Diasporic Citizenship of Chinese in Panama.* Stanford, CA: Stanford University Press, 2005.

Szok Peter A. *La última gaviota: Liberalism and Nostalgia in Early Twentieth-Century Panamá.* Westport, CT: Greenwood Press, 2001.

Ward, Christopher. *Imperial Panama: Commerce and Conflict in Isthmian America, 1550–1800.* Albuquerque: University of New Mexico Press, 1993.

MICHAEL L. CONNIFF

PANAMA CANAL.

The Panama Canal is a 51-mile ship canal with six pairs of locks that crosses the Isthmus of Panama and allows vessels to transit between the Caribbean Sea and the Pacific Ocean. Built between 1904 and 1914, the canal shortened maritime voyages considerably. For its first 85 years the canal was operated exclusively by the United States government as an international maritime passage, according to the 1903 Hay–Buneau–Varilla Treaty and the 1977 Carter–Torrijos Treaty that replaced it. Under the latter treaty, the canal was turned over in 1999 to the Republic of Panama, which has operated it ever since.

One of the world's great engineering projects, the canal was controversial because of the method by which the United States gained the concession (by negotiating a treaty with a French shareholder temporarily representing Panama) and its operation of the utility with little regard to the interests of Panama. Panamanian and other critics pointed out that the United States took unfair advantage of the newly independent republic (separated from

Panama Canal construction, 1913. Despite acquiring a piece of land exceptionally well suited to building the canal, the Panama Canal Commission still needed to cut a path through the challenging terrain. Not until 1914 did the first vessels transverse the canal, cutting a 7,800-mile trip around South America to a 51-mile trip through the canal. © UNDERWOOD & UNDERWOOD/CORBIS

Colombia in 1903, with the help of the United States) to impose conditions for near-sovereign ownership; complained that it exceeded its original concession by creating a strategic military complex with fourteen bases and numerous intelligence sites; and asserted that it created a virtual state within a state by establishing public agencies and enterprises in the 500-plus square miles of territory it controlled in the Canal Zone. These controversies were settled by the 1977 treaty, which provided for a twenty-two-year period of U.S. withdrawal and turnover of the canal to Panama.

HISTORY AND DESIGN
The possibility of an interoceanic canal in Central America had been considered since the sixteenth century, but construction had not been feasible until the nineteenth. Ferdinand de Lesseps, organizer of the French company that had built the Suez Canal in the 1860s, gained a concession and undertook to build a canal in Panama in the 1880s, but this effort failed because of design flaws, tropical disease, and mismanagement. The U.S. government began work on a Nicaraguan canal in the 1890s but also desisted. In 1902–1903, however, given the opportunity to build at a more favorable site in Panama, the United States negotiated first with Colombia (of which Panama was a province) and then with Panama for canal rights. The negotiations were unequal and coercive, but guaranteed Panama's independence; the U.S. acquired the rights to build, operate, and protect the canal. This episode confirmed the emergence of U.S. imperialism in the region and helped to project the nation onto the world stage.

Canal construction was carried out by private contractors under the guidance of the U.S. Army Corps of Engineers. Overall authority was exercised by the Interoceanic Canal Commission, which eventually became the Panama Canal Commission. After determining that the French sea-level plan was not feasible, the designers settled on a lock canal that would create an artificial lake in the Chagres River Valley some 85 feet above sea level. The river was dammed a few miles from its mouth to create Gatún Lake, which provided water to operate the locks by gravity flow and allowed ships to complete about half the crossing under their own power. Massive excavation was required to cut through the mountains south of the lake and to create approach channels between the locks and the open sea at either end. It was the largest and costliest engineering project undertaken to that time.

The enormous concrete lock chambers, each measuring 1,000 by 110 feet, receive transiting ships, close their steel gates, and fill with water flowing through underground conduits. Highly trained canal pilots are always in control of the ships while they are in the canal. Three pairs of locks at either end of the canal raise and lower ships 85 feet. Due to close quarters and turbulence, locomotives (called mules) tow and control ships during lockages. All the machinery runs by electric power, a new technology in 1914. Ships proceed under their own power through the lake. The entire transit takes about eight hours, not counting the approach and time spent waiting at anchor to enter the canal. Delays and heavy demand can slow down transit time considerably.

During the U.S. period, the canal served mostly U.S.-owned ships (albeit flying other nations' flags

Panama Canal workers. After one false start by the French and another by the United States, work began on the Panama Canal in 1904, beginning the most expensive public work project of the era. © UNDERWOOD & UNDERWOOD/CORBIS

of convenience) and transported largely bulk cargo. Since the 1980s, however, an increasing percentage of ships, classified as "Panamax" (Panama Canal maximum)—designed specifically to fit the dimensions of the canal locks—are carrying more high-value cargo, mainly containerized.

TRANSFER OF OWNERSHIP

Most of the transition from U.S. to Panamanian management took place in the 1990s, culminating in the turnover of December 31, 1999. Panamanian employees systematically replaced their U.S. counterparts in preparation. Canal managers carried out major capital improvement projects, including widening and dredging the narrowest sections and renewing the heavy equipment inventory. Under legislation passed in the 1990s, two new agencies of the Panamanian government oversaw policymaking for canal operations and the transfer of properties being vacated by the United States. Most challenging was finding productive uses for the former military bases, some of which were hazardous due to toxic chemical wastes and unexploded ordnance. Much vacant land on both sides of the canal was designated as a national park, to prevent development that could threaten the canal watershed and future operations. As part of a general privatization of public enterprises, operation of the contiguous ports of Balboa, Cristobal, and Coco Solo were contracted to private, mainly Asian corporations, and a U.S. company completely rebuilt the Panama railroad to carry containers.

Since the transfer of ownership, canal traffic and revenues have grown with the rise in world trade. The Panama Canal Authority, an independent public agency, has run the canal efficiently and generates considerable profit for the nation. It has also integrated canal business more fully into the national economy.

After several years of debate, the government held a referendum in 2006 on a giant undertaking to build a new set of locks capable of taking much larger ships, dubbed "post-Panamax." These would include supertankers, container vessels from Asian ports, and vehicle transporters. The project, which was approved with over 60 percent of the votes, is expected to cost over five billion dollars.

See also **Hay–Bunau–Varilla Treaty (1903); Lesseps, Ferdinand Marie, Vicomte de; Nicaragua, Organizations:** **Maritime Canal Company of Nicaragua; Panama Canal Company; Panama Canal Tolls Question; Panama Canal Treaties of 1977.**

BIBLIOGRAPHY

Castillero Calvo, Alfredo, ed. *Historia general de Panamá.* Panama: Comité Nacional del Centenario de la República, 2004.

Conniff, Michael L. *Panama and the United States: The Forced Alliance.* 2nd ed. Athens, GA: University of Georgia Press, 2001.

Major, John. *Prize Possession: The United States and the Panama Canal, 1903–1977.* Cambridge, U.K. and New York: Cambridge University Press, 1993.

McCullough, David. *The Path Between the Seas: The Creation of the Panama Canal, 1870–1914.* New York: Simon and Schuster, 1977.

MICHAEL L. CONNIFF

PANAMA CANAL COMPANY. Panama Canal Company, a wholly owned U.S. government corporation that operated the Panama Canal and its auxiliary enterprises (including the Panama Railroad) from 1951 to 1979. Overall policy was established by a board of directors appointed by the U.S. president. The president of the company was also the governor of the Canal Zone. The company was created to replace the Panama Railroad Company, which had performed similar activities since the construction of the canal. The company was succeeded by the Panama Canal Commission, created by the 1977 Panama Canal Treaties and the Panama Canal Act of 1979.

See also **Panama; Panama Canal.**

BIBLIOGRAPHY

John Major, *Prize Possession: The United States and the Panama Canal, 1903–1977* (1993).

Additional Bibliography

Lindsay-Poland, John. *Emperors in the Jungle: The Hidden History of the U.S. in Panama.* Durham, NC: Duke University Press, 2003.

Fitzgerald, Luis. *Historia de las relaciones entre Panamá y los Estados Unidos.* Panamá: Editorial Universitaria, 2001.

MICHAEL L. CONNIFF

PANAMA CANAL, FLAG RIOTS.

Panama Canal Flag Riots, outbursts of violence that occurred several times during the U.S.-Panamanian dispute regarding sovereignty over the Panama Canal.

On 2 May 1958 the Panamanian Union of University Students planted Panamanian flags in the Canal Zone. When U.S. authorities turned the flags over to the Panamanian president, Ernesto de la Guardia, Jr., protests resulted in a prolonged standoff between the Panamanian National Guard and students occupying the university.

Anti-American riots broke out in Panama City on 3 November 1959 during a celebration of Panamanian independence. Mobs attacked the U.S. Embassy, ripping down its flag, and damaged the U.S. Information Agency office and several U.S.-owned businesses. The mob then marched to the Canal Zone, seeking to force entry to plant Panamanian flags in the zone. U.S. troops resisted at the zone frontier, and forty Panamanians were wounded. The United States charged that its flag had been insulted, while Panama alleged that the North Americans used excessive force and dishonored the Panamanian flag. On 17 September 1960, President Dwight D. Eisenhower sought to defuse the issue by directing that the Panamanian flag be flown with the U.S. flag inside the zone. The privileges of U.S. residents of the zone and the Panamanian people continued to fuel sentiments reflecting the ultimate issue of sovereignty.

Riots again broke out when American students at the zone's Balboa High School refused to fly the Panamanian flag with the Stars and Stripes in violation of U.S. policy. On 9 January 1964 a Panamanian protest march into the zone resulted in a confrontation with the high school students and local residents. Rioters in the zone, Panama City, and Colón attacked U.S.-owned businesses and U.S. citizens. The Panamanian National Guard refused to intervene for several days, while U.S. troops fought snipers in pitched battles that resulted in numerous casualties on both sides. Ultimately, the National Guard restored order.

The Panamanian National Guard dispersed several efforts to organize additional protests during 1965. The situation was ameliorated through the gradual elimination of the privileged status of zonians

and was ultimately resolved by the U.S. decision to relinquish control of the Canal Zone (1977).

See also **Panama Canal.**

BIBLIOGRAPHY

Jules Dubois, *Danger over Panama* (1964).

J. Lloyd Mecham, *A Survey of United States–Latin American Relations* (1965).

Lawrence O. Ealy, *Yanqui Politics and the Isthmian Canal* (1971).

Walter La Feber, *The Panama Canal: The Crisis in Historical Perspective* (1978).

Additional Bibliography

McPherson, Alan. "From 'Punks' to Geopoliticians: U.S. and Panamanian Teenagers and the 1964 Canal Zone Riots." *The Americas*, 58:3 (January 2002): 395–418.

Mellander, Gustavo A., and Nelly Maldonado Mellander. *Charles Edward Magoon, the Panama Years.* Río Piedras, Puerto Rico: Editorial Plaza Mayor, 1999.

Méndez, Roberto N. *Panamá, 9 de enero de 1964: Qué pasó y por qué.* Panamá: Universidad de Panamá, 1999.

KENNETH J. GRIEB

PANAMA CANAL TOLLS QUESTION.

Panama Canal Tolls Question, a dispute between the United States and Great Britain regarding charges for use of the Panama Canal.

One of many steps in the lengthy contest between the United States and Great Britain for preeminence in the Caribbean and control of the canal, the U.S. Panama Canal Act of 1912 angered the British government because it exempted U.S. ships engaged in the coastwise trade from canal tolls. As the world's leading shipping nation, Great Britain protested the legislation as a violation of the Hay–Pauncefote Treaties (1900–1901). In accepting exclusive jurisdiction by the United States over the Panama Canal, this accord stipulated that the canal should be open to the ships of all nations on equal terms.

While U.S. President William Howard Taft rejected these protests, President Woodrow Wilson violated his own Democratic Party platform to use the tolls question in the Anglo-American dispute regarding the Mexican regime of General

Victoriano Huerta. The British granted Huerta de facto recognition, seeking stability to continue oil development in view of the impending European conflict. Wilson, who sought to secure the overthrow of Huerta, hinted at concessions if the British were to withdraw support for Huerta. After the British modified their Mexican policy, Wilson proposed repeal of the tolls exemption, which was approved after stormy Senate debate on 15 June 1914.

See also **Huerta, Victoriano; Panama Canal.**

BIBLIOGRAPHY

J. Lloyd Mecham, *A Survey of United States–Latin American Relations* (1965).

Kenneth J. Grieb, *The United States and Huerta* (1969).

Additional Bibliography

Fitzgerald, Luis I. *Historia de las relaciones entre Panamá y los Estados Unidos.* Panamá: Editorial Universitaria, 2001.

Lindsay-Poland, John. *Emperors in the Jungle: The Hidden History of the U.S. in Panama.* Durham, NC: Duke University Press, 2003.

Pearcy, Thomas L. *We Answer Only to God: Politics and the Military in Panama, 1903–1947.* Albuquerque: University of New Mexico Press, 1998.

Kenneth J. Grieb

PANAMA CANAL TREATIES OF 1977.

The Panama Canal Treaties of 1977 (also the Carter–Torrijos Treaties), abrogated prior treaties, established joint administration and defense of the canal, and designated December 31, 1999, as the date the United States would turn the canal over to Panama. The 1977 treaties culminated fourteen years of talks between the two countries. They borrowed operating principles from earlier drafts initialed in 1967. U.S. president Jimmy Carter made treaty revision a priority and lobbied hard for ratification, achieved in 1978 after a long debate and a close vote.

The main treaty created a Panama Canal Commission to replace the Panama Canal Company and Government. The commission is headed by an administrator chosen by the U.S. president. Policy is set by a board of directors made up of five U.S. and four Panamanian members. In 1990 U.S. president George Bush appointed Fernando Manfredo, a Panamanian, to succeed General Dennis "Phil" MacAuliffe, who had served as administrator throughout the 1980s. Soon, however, Manfredo was replaced by a permanent administrator, Gilberto Guardia. In addition, more than 60 percent of the former Canal Zone was returned to Panama, and the remainder was renamed the Panama Canal Area. Most public services there (courts, fire stations, police, sanitation, schools, and post offices) were taken over by Panama during the 1980s. The United States pledged to train Panamanians to assume management of the canal during the course of the treaty.

The second treaty guarantees the neutrality of the canal into the twenty-first century. The United States and Panama share defense responsibilities, while many other countries signed a protocol pledging their agreement.

See also **Panama Canal.**

BIBLIOGRAPHY

Conniff, Michael L. *Panama and the United States.* Athens: University of Georgia Press, 1991.

Farnsworth, David N., and James W. Mc Kenney. *U.S.–Panama Relations, 1903–1978: A Study in Linkage Politics* Boulder, CO: Westview Press, 1983.

Jaén Suárez, Omar. *Las negociaciones sobre el Canal de Panamá, 1964–1970* Bogotá: Grupo Editorial Norma, 2002.

Jorden, William. *Panama Odyssey.* Austin: University of Texas Press, 1984.

Michael L. Conniff

PANAMA CITY.

Panama City, first founded on 15 August 1519 by Pedro Arias de Ávila (2.5 miles east of its present location), lasted for 152 years. Old Panama suffered many adversities: major fires (1539, 1563, twice in 1644, 1671), earthquakes (1541, 1641), rebellions (1544, 1550) and slave revolts (1549, 1554, 1580–1581), and attacks by corsairs Sir Francis Drake (1596) and Henry Morgan (1671). During the Morgan attacks, the retreating forces of Governor Juan Pérez de Guzmán set fire to some buildings, which engulfed the city in a blaze that completely destroyed it.

Between this fire and an epidemic that swept the city that year, 4,000 people died. Of the survivors, all but 300 left the city. An earlier epidemic in 1652 had already killed 1,200 people.

As a transit point to other parts of the Spanish Empire, the old city became an important commercial center. By 1610 it contained five hundred houses and commercial establishments that were distributed in three plazas and eleven streets. It also had six convents and one cathedral. By 1670 it had one thousand houses and ten thousand inhabitants.

On 21 January 1673, Antonio Fernández de Córdoba y Mendoza founded the new Panama City about seven miles west of its previous site. The new city was heavily fortified for defense against pirate attacks. At its founding, Panama City had about 900 inhabitants. With greater commercial activity, the population increased to 1,600 by 1675 and to 20,000 by 1700. However, as the Spanish Empire grew weaker, commercial activity declined. The city also suffered major fires in 1737 ("the big fire"), 1756, and 1781. By 1790 the city's population had declined to 7,000.

After independence and during the years when Panama was a part of Colombia (1821–1903), the city went through two periods of boom and bust. During the California gold rush (1848–1869), Panama City became a transit point between New York City and San Francisco. A railroad was built linking Colón on the Atlantic side to Panama City. The population increased to ten or twelve thousand, and hundreds of thousands more passed through the city to California. The city went through a period of bust until 1881, when a French company began digging an interoceanic canal. This activity stimulated more construction and commercial activity, and the city grew to 24,000. But by 1889, the canal company was bankrupt and the city's fortunes declined again. By the end of the century, Panama City lacked drinking water, a working sewage system, and good schools.

The construction of the Panama Canal under U.S. supervision (1903–1914) revitalized the city. Streets were paved, the sewage system was improved, and garbage was collected. Belisario Porras (president 1912–1916, 1918–1920, 1920–1924) began a period of urban development and renewal. Between independence (1903) and World War II, Panama City became a great urban center, although

it remained essentially a satellite of the Canal Zone. The population grew faster than housing, creating a crisis that led to strikes in 1925 and 1932 protesting high rents and unsanitary conditions.

In 1944 the Bank of Urbanization and Rehabilitation was created to help solve the housing problem. It financed new buildings, renovated old areas, facilitated credit, and undertook the construction of the satellite city of Vista Hermosa. Since the 1960s, Panama City has become one of the world's most important financial centers, due largely to the country's liberal tax and commercial laws. Most of the world's major banks and financial institutions operate branches in the Panamanian capital.

Panama City, which had an estimated population of 829,391 in 2006, is divided into four administrative units, each with its own characteristics. San Felipe, founded in 1673, includes the nucleus. Most of the colonial monuments are found here. The population is mainly white and mestizo. Santa Ana encompasses the area that grew outside the city walls. With El Chorrillo, it is the most densely populated sector. Its population is mostly black and mestizo. El Chorrillo, which dates from the construction of the canal, is the newest area. It is densely populated, mainly by blacks and mestizos. Finally, Calidonia, which also originated with the canal construction and the accompanying arrival of Antillean black laborers, has a mostly black population.

In December 1989 U.S. military forces occupied Panama City. By blaring recordings of Jimi Hendrix in front of the Papal Nuncio where President Manuel Noriega was holed up, they were able to drive him out and install a new Panamanian government.

See also **Noriega Moreno, Manuel Antonio; Panama; Panama Railroad.**

BIBLIOGRAPHY

Angel Rubio, *La Ciudad de Panamá*. Panamá: Banco de Urbanización y Rehabilitación,1950.

John F. Shafroth, *Panamá la vieja*. Panamá: Imprenta Nacional, 1952.

Luis E. García De Paredes, *Mudanza, traslado y reconstrucción de la ciudad de Panamá en 1673*. Panamá: Consejo Municipal de Panamá, 1954.

Benito Reyes Testa, *Panamá la vieja y Panamá la nueva.* Panamá: Sección de Textos Escolares y Material Didáctico del Ministerio de Educación, 1958.

Juan Bautista Sosa, *Panamá la vieja,* 2nd ed. Panamá: Imprenta Nacional, 1959.

Reina T. De Araúz, Marcia A. De Arosemena, and Jorge Conte Porras, eds., *Antología de la Ciudad de Panamá.* Panamá: Instituto Nacional de Cultura de Panamá, 1977.

Additional Bibliography

Dinges, John. *Our Man in Panama: How General Noriega Used the United States and Made Millions in Drugs and Arms.* New York: Random House, 1990.

Furlong, William L. "Panama: The Difficult Transition Towards Democracy." *Journal of Interamerican Studies and World Affairs* 35, no. 3 (Autumn, 1993): 19–64.

LaFeber, Walter. *The Panama Canal: The Crisis in Historical Perspective.* New York: Oxford University Press, 1978.

JUAN MANUEL PÉREZ

PANAMA, COMMUNITY ACTION.

This nationalistic organization was founded in Panama on 19 August 1923 by middle-class professionals. The group promoted nationalism because it feared that Panama would cease to exist as a result of the dominating U.S. presence in the country. Its motto was, "Speak Spanish and count in balboas," Arnulfo Arias Madrid, one of the group's leaders and a president in the 1940s, had sympathies for fascist ideas. The group opposed corruption and incompetence in the government and called for more citizen participation in the affairs of the state. In 1926, Acción Comunal led a successful campaign against the ratification of a new treaty with the United States. In 1931, it led a revolution that overthrew the government. This was the first time since its separation from Colombia that a government was overthrown in Panama.

See also **Arias Madrid, Arnulfo.**

BIBLIOGRAPHY

Víctor Manuel Pérez and Rodrigo Oscar De León Lerma, *El movimiento de Acción Comunal en Panamá* (1964?).

Additional Bibliography

Pearcy, Thomas L. *We Answer Only to God: Politics and the Military in Panama, 1903–1947.* Albuquerque: University of New Mexico Press, 1998.

JUAN MANUEL PÉREZ

PANAMA CONGRESS OF 1826. Pan-

ama Congress of 1826, a gathering called by Simón Bolívar, president of Gran Colombia, in response to the concern that the Holy Alliance (France, Austria, Prussia, and Russia) was encouraging Spain to reclaim its lost possessions in the Americas. In the 1820s the young nations of the Americas had only recently achieved independence. To provide for common security, the congress was held in Panama in June and July 1826. The participants were Gran Colombia, Central America, and Mexico. Great Britain and the Netherlands sent observers. Of the two U.S. delegates sent, one died en route and the other arrived too late. The congress delegates agreed on the need for united defense against reconquest, the utility of an inter-American forum for arbitration of disputes, and the elimination of the slave trade. To this end the members of the conference signed the Treaty of Perpetual Union, League, and Confederation, which was eventually ratified only by Gran Colombia.

Although the Panama Congress of 1826 did not result in a permanent system of cooperation or a sense of American unity, it did serve as a model for future inter-American efforts toward cooperation.

See also **Bolívar, Simón.**

BIBLIOGRAPHY

John J. Johnson, *Simón Bolívar and Spanish American Independence, 1783–1830* (1968).

Antonio Peña y Reyes, *El Congreso de Panamá y algunos otros proyectos de unión hispano-americana,* 2d ed. (1971).

Jesús María Yepes, *Del Congreso de Panamá a la Conferencia de Caracas, 1826–1954* (1976).

Additional Bibliography

Ortega Díaz, Pedro. *El Congreso de Panamá: Y La unidad latinoamericana.* Caracas, Venezuela: Ministro de Comunicación e Información, 2006.

JAMES PATRICK KIERNAN

PANAMA, CONSTITUTIONS.

In December 1903 the Panamanian junta that had declared independence from Colombia conducted elections for a constitutional convention. During January, the assembly concluded its work, establishing a centralized democracy with a popularly elected president. A unicameral legislature (the National Assembly) and presidentially appointed provincial governors streamlined decision making. The three branches of government were to operate separately. The assembly chose three vice presidents to succeed the president. Municipal administrations were elected locally. The most controversial item in the new constitution, Article 136, gave the United States the right to use troops to keep the peace in Panama (as did the Cuban constitution of 1901). The assembly elected Manuel Amador Guerrero as first president and transformed itself into a legislature in order to pass emergency measures and to codify the country's laws. In June it disbanded, leaving Amador free to govern alone until a new legislature was convened.

In 1941 President Arnulfo Arias Madrid promulgated a new constitution, which had been drafted by a select committee of jurists. In the spirit of corporatism, it strengthened the powers of the state to regulate society and charged it with responsibility for the general welfare and economic growth; it also gave the president added authority for a six-year term. Nationalistic to the point of chauvinism, it tightened citizenship requirements so that many thousands of West Indians, Chinese, and Middle Easterners lost their naturalization or even citizenship. Many controversial aspects of the constitution were ignored after Arias was overthrown in late 1941, but it was not formally abrogated until early 1945. Arias attempted to promulgate this constitution again in 1951, but he was removed from power before he was able to do so.

The Constitution of 1946 was very similar to that of 1904, providing for a centralized democracy, with universal suffrage. It separated the governmental branches and protected citizens' civil liberties. The four-year presidential term was restored and reelection forbidden. Two vice presidents were chosen by direct election, governors continued to serve at the pleasure of the president, and the National Assembly was a unicameral legislature. It remained in force until the military coup of 1968.

The 1972 Constitution was written by an assembly of representatives from municipalities (*corregimientos*) convened by the military government of Omar Torrijos. The latter was named "maximum leader" for six years, with broad powers to appoint and remove officials and to conduct foreign relations. This dictatorial authority allowed Torrijos to negotiate and sign the 1977 Carter–Torrijos Treaties. A figurehead president performed ceremonial functions only, and citizens' rights were secondary to the interests of the state.

In 1978 many temporary measures expired, including Torrijos's maximum-leader powers. Torrijos continued to rule from his position as head of the National Guard, yet he delegated more responsibility to the president. The assembly of municipal representatives amended the constitution to provide for elections, parties, political amnesty, and a gradual return to civilian democracy.

In 1983, anticipating presidential elections the following year and the restoration of democracy, the legislature enacted major revisions. The presidency was amended from six to five years, with two vice presidents. Military responsibilities in government were ended legally, and the municipal representatives were replaced by the Legislative Assembly, whose sixty-seven members were directly elected from the provinces. Electoral and judicial procedures were improved, and civil liberties, including habeas corpus, were strengthened. The constitution assigned major social and economic responsibilities to the state. Only briefly honored, these constitutional amendments soon fell into disuse during the regime of Manuel Antonio Noriega, but were restored under Guillermo Endara (1989–1994). Also, in 1994 the Legislative Assembly began to modify the constitution by adding a chapter on the future administration of the Panama Canal.

See also **Amador Guerrero, Manuel; Arias Madrid, Arnulfo; Endara, Guillermo; Noriega Moreno, Manuel Antonio; Torrijos Herrera, Omar.**

BIBLIOGRAPHY

Russell H. Fitzgibbon, ed., *The Constitutions of the Americas* (1948).

Gustavo Mellander, *The United States in Panamanian Politics* (1971); *Panama, a Country Study,* 4th ed. (1989).

Additional Bibliography

Quintero, César. *Evolución constitucional de Panamá.* Panamá: Editorial Portobelo, 1999.

MICHAEL L. CONNIFF

PANAMA, DEMOCRATIC REVOLUTIONARY PARTY (PRD).

The Democratic Revolutionary party (Partido Revolucionario Democratico—PRD) was the progovernment party of the Torrijos and Noriega regimes between 1978 and 1989. Created as part of the liberalization of the late 1970s, the PRD was designed to coordinate political activity among government employees and supporters and to mobilize voters for elections. Operating by means of official patronage, for ten years it managed to retain a majority in the legislature and to dominate most municipal elections. Not a genuine party, it generally espoused the programs and principles of the president in office. It drew on such a wide variety of groups and sectors—labor, peasants, women, young people, civil servants—that it could not generate any ideological unity.

After the U.S. invasion of 1989, the party remained moribund for a time. Squabbling with the government coalition, however, allowed the PRD to rebuild its leadership and image. Civil servants and labor unions, in particular, supported its resurrection in order to protect their jobs. To the surprise of many observers Ernesto Pérez Balladares, the PRD candidate for president in the May 1994 elections, won a plurality and took office on 1 September. The party also won nearly half of the seats in the Legislative Assembly. The PRD's electoral strength has continued into the early twenty-first century. In 2004, the PRD candidate Martín Torrijos won the presidency with nearly 50 percent of the vote.

See also **Noriega Moreno, Manuel Antonio.**

BIBLIOGRAPHY

Steve C. Ropp, *Panamanian Politics: From Guarded Nation to National Guard* (1982); *Panama, a Country Study,* 4th ed. (1989); Margaret E. Scranton, *The Noriega Years* (1991).

Additional Bibliography

Harding, Robert C. "The Military Foundations of Panamanian Politics From the National Police to the PRD and Beyond." Ph.D. diss., University of Miami, 1998.

López Tirone, Humberto, and Omar Torrijos. *Panamá, una revolución democrática.* Lisboa, Portugal: Joan Boldó i Climent, 1995.

MICHAEL L. CONNIFF

PANAMA RAILROAD.

Panama Railroad, the world's first interoceanic railroad. Completed between 1850 and 1855, it linked the Caribbean Sea and the Pacific Ocean by a 47–mile track along the east–west axis of Panama. While the idea of an interoceanic route had existed since the arrival of the Spaniards in the sixteenth century, it was realized only in the mid-nineteenth century as a result of expanding U.S. trade and strategic interests in the world, and, thus, the need for better and faster transportation across the isthmus. Concrete plans for the Panama Railroad began in 1846 with the signing of the Bidlack–Mallarino Treaty, which guaranteed rights of transit to both Colombians and North Americans across Panama, then a Colombian province. Construction of the railroad by the Panama Railway Company (formed in 1847) began in 1850 under the terms of this treaty. Swamps, rivers, rough ground, and Panama's tropical climate made it a challenge for both workers and engineers. Despite this and other problems during the second year, the railway was completed in January 1855, successfully linking the Atlantic port city of Colón with Panama City on the Pacific side.

The Panama Railroad not only facilitated the transit of gold seekers bound for California after 1848 but also stimulated the commercial growth of Panama. The new port city of Colón became a major stopover for travelers and a source of business for merchants. Furthermore, despite completion of the transcontinental railroad in the United States in 1869, the Panama Railroad continued to turn a profit for most of the rest of the century. Because it brought many foreigners into Panama for the first time, the railroad increased tension between foreigners and natives. In 1856, for example, the tragic Watermelon Riot occurred when unruly and armed "forty-niners" clashed with locals, resulting in the deaths of sixteen people. The railroad continues to operate in the mid-1990s, but its importance has been lessened since completion of the Panama Canal in 1914.

See also **Panama; Panama Canal; Watermelon Riot (Panama Riot).**

BIBLIOGRAPHY

Joseph L. Schott, *Rails Across Panama: The Story of the Building of the Panama Railroad, 1849–1855* (1967).

David G. McCullough, *The Path Between the Seas: The Creation of the Panama Canal, 1870–1914* (1977).

Sandra W. Meditz, ed., *Panama: A Country Study* (1989).

Additional Bibliography

Davidson, Frank Paul, and Kathleen Lusk-Brooke. *Building the World: An Encyclopedia of the Great Engineering Projects in History.* Westport, CT: Greenwood Press, 2006.

De Masi, Kenneth F., and R. J. Stahl. *Panama Canal: Building the 8th Wonder of the World.* Amawalk, NY: Jackdaw Publications, 2003.

Morgan, Juan David. *El caballo de oro: La gran aventura de la construcción del ferrocarril de Panamá.* Barcelona, Spain: Ediciones B, 2005.

PAMELA MURRAY

PANAMA, TENANTS' REVOLT.

The Movimiento Inquilinario riots took place in Panama City between October 10 and October 13, 1925 as a result of a strike organized by tenants to protest rising rents and unsanitary conditions in many housing units. Four people died in clashes with the police on Saturday, October 10. By Monday the city was completely shut down as more people joined the strike. That day, at the request of a very nervous Panamanian government, three U.S. Army battalions entered the country. Two people were killed in confrontations with the soldiers. The U.S. troops remained in the country until October 23.

BIBLIOGRAPHY

Alexander Cuevas, "El movimiento inquilinario de 1925," in *Revista lotería* no. 213 (October–November 1973): 133–161.

Additional Bibliography

Castillero Calvo, Alfredo. *Historia general de Panamá.* Panamá: Comité Nacional del Centenario de la República, 2004.

Samudio, César. *El Canal de Panamá, 1903–1955.* Panamá: s.n., 1992.

JUAN MANUEL PÉREZ

PAN-AMERICAN CONFERENCES

This entry includes the following articles:
BOGOTÁ CONFERENCE (1948)
BUENOS AIRES CONFERENCE (1936)
CARACAS CONFERENCE (1954)
HAVANA CONFERENCE (1928)
HAVANA MEETING (1940)
MEXICO CITY CONFERENCE (1945)
MONTEVIDEO CONFERENCE (1933)
PANAMA MEETING (1939)
PUNTA DEL ESTE MEETING (1962)
RIO CONFERENCE (1942)
RIO CONFERENCE (1947)
RIO CONFERENCE (1954)
WASHINGTON CONFERENCE (1889)

BOGOTÁ CONFERENCE (1948)

The Ninth International Conference of American States was held in Bogotá on 30 March 1948. Delegates from twenty-one American republics were in attendance at the Bogotá Conference, including U.S. Secretary of State George C. Marshall. The major achievement of the conference was the adoption of the charter of the Organization of American States, which created a formal structure for the hitherto loosely organized Inter-American System. The delegates also approved a resolution condemning "international communism or any other totalitarian doctrine." In addition, they adopted a treaty on pacific settlement (Pact of Bogotá), which consolidated into a single instrument existing agreements on the prevention of war, but it was never ratified.

Latin American delegates at the conference hoped that the United States would commit itself to greater economic assistance for the region, but U.S. officials gave greater priority to postwar European recovery and stressed the role of private capital in stimulating economic development. The conference was interrupted by the Bogotazo on 9 April but resumed its deliberations on 14 April.

See also **Organization of American States.**

BIBLIOGRAPHY

J. Lloyd Mecham, *The United States and Inter-American Security, 1889–1960* (1961), esp. pp. 301–317.

Additional Bibliography

Shaw, Carolyn M. *Cooperation, Conflict, and Consensus in the Organization of American States.* New York: Palgrave Macmillan, 2004.

Vázquez García, Humberto. *De Chapultepec a la OEA: Apogeo y crisis del panamericanismo.* La Habana: Editorial de Ciencias Sociales, 2001.

HELEN DELPAR

Samuel Guy Inman, *Inter-American Conferences, 1826–1954: History and Problems,* edited by Harold E. Davis (1965), chap. 12.

Graham H. Stuart and James L. Tigner, *Latin America and the United States,* 6th ed. (1975), chap. 2.

Additional Bibliography

Marichal, Carlos. *México y las conferencias panamericanas, 1889-1938: Antecedentes de la globalización.* México: Secretaría de Relaciones Exteriores, 2002.

Sheinin, David. *Beyond the Ideal: Pan Americanism in Inter-American Affairs.* Westport: Greenwood Press, 2000.

LARMAN C. WILSON

BUENOS AIRES CONFERENCE (1936)

Called by the United States, the Buenos Aires Conference of 1936, a Special Conference for the Maintenance of Peace, was held 3–26 December in the capital of Argentina. It was prompted by U.S. concern over the attacks of Japan and Italy on China and Ethiopia, respectively, and the Spanish Civil War and the possibility of global war. A major question was the possibility of neutrality if war resulted. An important Latin American interest was the absolute acceptance of nonintervention by the United States. This was achieved because the latter had continued to implement the Good Neighbor Policy—for example, the occupation of Haiti had ended in 1934.

Secretary of State Cordell Hull headed the U.S. delegation; of great significance to Latin Americans was the presence of President Franklin D. Roosevelt, who addressed the inaugural session. The conference adopted eight conventions, two treaties, and one protocol. One important document provided for consultation if American peace was threatened, and especially important was the Additional Protocol Relative to Non-Intervention (which the United States approved without reservation). Also welcomed by Latin America was the fact that the United States, for the first time, assumed leadership in cultural affairs.

See also **Hull, Cordell; Roosevelt, Franklin Delano.**

BIBLIOGRAPHY

Samuel Flagg Bemis, *The Latin American Policy of the United States: An Historical Interpretation* (1943), chap. 16.

CARACAS CONFERENCE (1954)

The Tenth Inter-American Conference of the Organization of American States (OAS) met in Caracas, Venezuela, from 1 March to 28 March 1954. Although Latin American nations expected economic issues to be the main focus, the United States convinced the organizing committee to place an anticommunist resolution first on the agenda. The Eisenhower administration was worried about the influence of Communists in the elected government of Jacobo Arbenz Guzmán in Guatemala.

Latin Americans were not enthusiastic about this position because they were fearful of U.S. interference in their affairs. Many in the hemisphere were angry that the United States insisted on meeting in Caracas because Marcos Pérez Jiménez was head of state there. Costa Rica refused to attend because of him.

The vote on the anticommunist resolution was seventeen in favor, one against (Guatemala), and two abstentions (Mexico and Argentina). U.S. Secretary of State John Foster Dulles added a statement to the resolution that said the design was to deal with dangers originating outside the hemisphere and not to impair the right of each state to freely choose its own form of government. Failing to obtain support against Arbenz, the United States joined Guatemalan rebels to overthrow him in June 1954.

See also **Arbenz Guzmán, Jacobo; Pérez Jiménez, Marcos.**

BIBLIOGRAPHY

Samuel Guy Inman, *Inter-American Conferences, 1826–1954: History and Problems,* edited by Harold E. Davis (1965), esp. chap. 19.

Richard H. Immerman, *The CIA in Guatemala* (1982).

Stephen G. Rabe, *Eisenhower and Latin America* (1988), esp. chap. 3.

Piero Gleijeses, *Shattered Hope: The Guatemalan Revolution and the United States, 1944–1954* (1991), esp. chap. 12.

Additional Bibliography

Shaw, Carolyn M. *Cooperation, Conflict, and Consensus in the Organization of American States.* New York: Palgrave Macmillan, 2004.

Schmitz, David F. *Thank God They're on Our Side: The United States and Right-wing Dictatorships, 1921-1965.* Westport: Praeger, 2002.

Valdés-Ugalde, José Luis. *Estados Unidos, intervención y poder mesiánico: La Guerra Fría en Guatemala, 1954.* México: Universidad Nacional Autónoma de México, Instituto de Investigaciones Jurídicas: Centro de Investigaciones sobre América del Norte, 2004.

CHARLES CARRERAS

HAVANA CONFERENCE (1928)

Formally known as the Sixth International Conference of American States, this meeting was held in Havana, Cuba, in January and February 1928. It marked a crucial turning point in inter-American relations, the high point of the dominance of the Pan-American Union by the United States, and the intransigence of U.S. interventionist policy in Latin America. The near absolute control of the conference agenda by the United States did not still expressions of frustration and resentment of U.S. policy by the other delegations. While an attempt to wrest control of the Pan-American Union from the United States proved unsuccessful, the conference was singularly productive. Conventions and resolutions were adopted on asylum, consular agents, diplomatic officials, status of aliens, maritime neutrality, duties and rights of states in the event of civil strife, treaties, commercial aviation, literary and artistic copyrights, and private international law.

Public condemnation of the perceived U.S. bullying at the conference and its policy of interventionism eventually had an effect. With a change in administration and the articulation of the Good Neighbor Policy by Franklin Roosevelt, the Seventh International Conference of American States in Montevideo (1933) was able to declare interventionism illegal in the Western Hemisphere.

This new era of understanding was important in setting the stage for greater cooperation during and after World War II.

See also **Inter-American System.**

BIBLIOGRAPHY

Carnegie Endowment For International Peace, Division of International Law, *International Conferences of American States,* vol. 1 (1934).

David Sheinin, *Argentina and the United States at the Sixth Pan American Conference* (1991).

Additional Bibliography

Marichal, Carlos. *México y las conferencias panamericanas, 1889-1938: Antecedentes de la globalización.* México: Secretaría de Relaciones Exteriores, 2002.

Pegueros, Rosemarie. "Flowers without Rain: International Diplomacy and Equality for Women in the Americas at the Sixth Inter-American Conference (January 16-February 20, 1928)." Ph.D. diss., University of California, Los Angeles, 1998.

Solveira, Beatriz Rosario. *La Argentina y la Quinta Conferencia Panamericana.* Córdoba: Centro de Estudios Históricos, 1993.

JAMES PATRICK KIERNAN

HAVANA MEETING (1940)

Formally known as the Second Meeting of Consultation of Ministers of Foreign Affairs, this gathering was held in Havana, Cuba, in July 1940. Its major concerns were the strengthening of the principle of hemispheric solidarity against acts of aggression and reciprocal assistance and cooperation for defense.

With the fall of France and the threatened dominion of Western Europe by Nazi Germany, governments of the American nations were concerned about the fate of the European colonies—particularly those of Great Britain—in the Caribbean. Based on the doctrine that American territories could not be transferred from one European power to another, the meeting declared that the possessions of Britain and any defeated European nations could not become German territory. The meeting adopted the Act of Havana concerning the Provisional Administration of European Colonies and Possessions in the Americas, which provided that the colonies would be controlled and administered by an inter-American force until the war's end, at which time they would become independent or returned to their original status. Exempt from this provision were the Malvinas/ Falkland Islands and British Honduras (Belize). The Act of Havana also stated that "any attempt on the part of a non-American state against the integrity, sovereignty or political independence of an American state shall be considered an act of aggression against the states which sign this declaration." This agreement was the beginning of the mutual defense system that was reinforced by the Act of Chapultepec in 1945 and culminated in the Rio Treaty of 1947, which guaranteed reciprocity in defense, making an attack against one American state equivalent to an attack against all of the Americas. The meeting also adopted a series of resolutions strengthening the inter-American neutrality committee, promoting reciprocal assistance and cooperation for the defense of the American nations, and establishing the agenda for economic and financial cooperation between the American nations during the war.

See also World War II.

BIBLIOGRAPHY

Cordell Hull, Achievements of the Second Meeting of Foreign Ministers of the American Republics (1940).

Pan American Union, The Meetings of Consultation: Their Origin, Significance, and Role in Inter-American Relations (1966).

Inter-American Institute Of International Legal Studies, The Inter-American System (1966).

Additional Bibliography

Leonard, Thomas, and John F. Bratzel. Latin America during World War II. Lanham: Rowman & Littlefield, 2007.

Sheinin, David. Beyond the Ideal: Pan Americanism in Inter-American Affairs. Westport: Greenwood Press, 2000.

Vázquez García, Humberto. De Chapultepec a la OEA: Apogeo y crisis del panamericanismo. La Habana: Editorial de Ciencias Sociales, 2001.

JAMES PATRICK KIERNAN

MEXICO CITY CONFERENCE (1945)

The Inter-American Conference on Problems of War and Peace was held in Chapultepec Castle, Mexico City, from 21 February to 8 March 1945. The conference, which was attended by the U.S. secretary of state and the foreign secretaries of all the Latin American countries except El Salvador and Argentina, established a number of the important principles that shaped inter-American relations in the post–World War II era. Among the most significant was a pronouncement, known as the Act of Chapultepec, by which the governments agreed that any attack by any state against the integrity, sovereignty, territory, or political independence of an American state would be considered an act of aggression against all the other signatories of the declaration.

BIBLIOGRAPHY

Josefina Zoraida Vázquez and Lorenzo Meyer, The United States and Mexico (1985).

Additional Bibliography

Leonard, Thomas, and John F. Bratzel. Latin America during World War II. Lanham: Rowman & Littlefield, 2007.

Sheinin, David. Beyond the Ideal: Pan Americanism in Inter-American Affairs. Westport: Greenwood Press, 2000.

Vázquez García, Humberto. De Chapultepec a la OEA: Apogeo y crisis del panamericanismo. La Habana: Editorial de Ciencias Sociales, 2001.

RODERIC AI CAMP

MONTEVIDEO CONFERENCE (1933)

Convened in the capital of Uruguay 3–28 December, the Montevideo Conference of 1933, the Seventh International Conference of American States, was of great importance because it marked a turning point in U.S.–Latin American relations, with U.S. acceptance of the nonintervention principle. This resulted in a great improvement of relations. The important policy change was in keeping with President Franklin D. Roosevelt's Good Neighbor Policy, proclaimed in his March 1933 inaugural address. Secretary of State Cordell Hull headed the U.S. delegation and voted for the "Convention on the Rights and Duties of States," which declared that "no state has the right to intervene in the internal or external affairs of another." (Although it signed with a reservation, the United States later ratified the convention.) Hull also modified U.S. tariff policy by proposing the reciprocal lowering of customs duties.

See also Hull, Cordell; Roosevelt, Franklin Delano.

BIBLIOGRAPHY

Samuel Flagg Bemis, *The Latin American Policy of the United States: An Historical Interpretation* (1943), chaps. 15 and 16, and Samuel Guy Inman, *Inter-American Conferences, 1826–1954: History and Problems* (1965), chap. 11.

Additional Bibliography

Marichal, Carlos. *México y las conferencias panamericanas, 1889-1938: Antecedentes de la globalización.* México: Secretaría de Relaciones Exteriores, 2002.

Sheinin, David. *Beyond the Ideal: Pan Americanism in Inter-American Affairs.* Westport: Greenwood Press, 2000.

LARMAN C. WILSON

PANAMA MEETING (1939)

The First Meeting of Consultation of Ministers of Foreign Affairs of the American republics (held between 23 September and 3 October) was a response to the declaration of war in Europe. The framework for the meeting of consultation had been established at the Special Inter-American Conference for the Maintenance of Peace (Buenos Aires, 1936) and the Eighth International Conference of American States (Lima, 1938), which provided that if the peace in the Americas was threatened, any member of the Pan-American Union could initiate a meeting of consultation of foreign ministers. The Meeting, as subsequent meetings of consultation in 1940 and 1942, was devoted primarily to the juridical-political and military problems brought on by the war.

The Meeting produced a General Declaration of Neutrality of the American Republics and the Declaration of Panama, which, as a measure of continental self-protection, extended the territorial waters for 300 miles on both sides of the hemisphere. This zone was to be free of hostile acts by any non-American belligerent nation. The Meeting set up an Inter-American Neutrality Committee and an Inter-American Financial and Economic Advisory Committee which allowed Latin American nations to respond to the economic dislocations caused by the war with aid from the United States. In addition, the Meeting approved a resolution permitting ships to change their registry, which allowed U.S. ships to deliver supplies to Allied nations under the flag of Panama, thereby avoiding violation of the United States Neutrality Act. The Panama Conference of 1939 was an example of the effort to strengthen American unity and solidarity as a means of preserving the security of the hemisphere.

See also **Graf Spee; Inter-American System.**

BIBLIOGRAPHY

Carnegie Endowment for International Peace, *International Conferences of American States,* Vol. 2 (1940).

Inter-American Institute of International Legal Studies, *The Inter-American System* (1966).

Jesús María Yepes, *Del Congresso de Panama a la Conferencia de Caracas* (1976).

Additional Bibliography

Leonard, Thomas, and John F. Bratzel. *Latin America during World War II.* Lanham: Rowman & Littlefield, 2007.

Piotti de Lamas, Diosma E., and Alfredo Traversoni. *América Latina y Estados Unidos en el siglo XX: Aspectos políticos, económicos y sociales.* Montevideo: Fundación de Cultura Universitaria, 1996.

Sheinin, David. *Beyond the Ideal: Pan Americanism in Inter-American Affairs.* Westport: Greenwood Press, 2000.

JAMES PATRICK KIERNAN

PUNTA DEL ESTE MEETING (1962)

The eighth meeting of the foreign ministers of the nations belonging to the Organization of American States, held 22–31 January 1962, in Punta del Este, Uruguay. The Punta del Este meeting took place as a direct result of diverging policies among the OAS nations toward the Cuban government led by Fidel Castro. Since gaining power in 1959, Castro had been aligning himself increasingly with Marxist-Leninist ideology and the Soviet Union, a development that led many Latin American nations, particularly those in the Caribbean and Central America, to seek a strong, unified resistance to this perceived threat.

The idea to convene the OAS foreign ministers was first proposed by Peru and Colombia, which sought firm sanctions against Cuba. Other nations, including Argentina, Brazil, and Mexico, were more neutral in their position toward Cuba, while the representatives of the United States, under the Kennedy administration and Secretary of State Dean Rusk, generally took a hard-line stance against

Cuba but disagreed among themselves about the severity of the diplomatic actions to be taken.

Among the provisions issued at the end of the conference was a statement sharply refuting the compatibility of Marxism-Leninism with the Inter-American System. Specific proposals excluding Cuba from participation in the OAS and preventing sales of arms to Cuba were adopted, though suggestions of direct intervention in Cuba, desired by some hard-line nations, did not receive wide support.

In the end, the Punta del Este meeting did not radically alter the course of inter-American relations with Cuba, which already had been determined by Castro's ongoing acceptance of Soviet patronage. The meeting and its resulting compromise did, however, illustrate the difficulty of collective action among the increasingly divergent nations of the OAS.

See also **Castro Ruz, Fidel.**

BIBLIOGRAPHY

F. Parkinson, *Latin America, the Cold War, and the World Powers, 1945–1973* (1974).

Additional Bibliography

Gilderhus, Mark T. *The Second Century: U.S.-Latin American Relations since 1889.* Wilmington: Scholarly Resources, 2000.

Piotti de Lamas, Diosma E. and Alfredo Traversoni. *América Latina y Estados Unidos en el siglo XX: Aspectos políticos, económicos y sociales.* Montevideo: Fundación de Cultura Universitaria, 1996.

Sheinin, David. *Beyond the Ideal: Pan Americanism in Inter-American Affairs.* Westport: Greenwood Press, 2000.

JOHN DUDLEY

RIO CONFERENCE (1942)

The Third Meeting of Consultation of Latin American Ministers of Foreign Affairs (the Rio Conference of 1942) took place in Rio de Janeiro on 15–28 January 1942, in response to the Japanese attack on Pearl Harbor on 7 December 1941. After that attack the United States called for an "emergency consultation" to determine the response of the Pan-American nations to the state of war and the Axis threat to the Western Hemisphere.

The Dominican Republic, Haiti, Cuba, Panama, Costa Rica, Nicaragua, Honduras, El Salvador, and

Guatemala had declared war on the Axis powers prior to this conference, and Mexico, Colombia, and Venezuela had severed diplomatic relations. As a result of the conference, Brazil, Ecuador, Peru, Paraguay, and Uruguay severed diplomatic relations with the Axis powers, and Mexico declared war, in June 1942. Although they agreed to the conference's joint resolutions of cooperation regarding the common defense of the Western Hemisphere, Argentina and Chile did not sever relations until 1943 and 1945, respectively.

Another purpose of this conference was to make plans for the role of Latin American countries as noncombatants allied with the United States. Conference resolutions included calls for the end of economic, financial, and diplomatic relations with the Axis powers; the establishment of an international fund to stabilize currencies; the organization of coordinated censorship; and a unified effort to purge the Western Hemisphere of Axis spies and saboteurs. In addition, representatives from the twenty-one republics were to meet in Washington, D.C., to plan unified defense measures. An Inter-American Defense Board was created to handle defensive measures, and an Emergency Advisory Committee for Political Defense, to organize activities to prevent subversion. The conference also settled a conflict between Peru and Ecuador and endorsed Franklin D. Roosevelt's Good Neighbor Policy.

The United States simultaneously negotiated a series of treaties with various Latin American countries to resupply necessary commodities that were scarce as a result of the interruption of trade. In exchange, the Latin American countries agreed to allow the United States to use strategic sites for naval and air bases, and to sell the United States raw materials totaling more than $25 billion for the defense effort.

See also **World War II.**

BIBLIOGRAPHY

Leonard, Thomas, and John F. Bratzel. *Latin America during World War II.* Lanham: Rowman & Littlefield, 2007.

Sheinin, David. *Beyond the Ideal: Pan Americanism in Inter-American Affairs.* Westport: Greenwood Press, 2000.

Vázquez García, Humberto. *De Chapultepec a la OEA: Apogeo y crisis del panamericanismo.* La Habana: Editorial de Ciencias Sociales, 2001.

LESLEY R. LUSTER

RIO CONFERENCE (1947)

The Inter-American Conference for the Maintenance of Continental Peace and Security, held near Rio de Janeiro from 15 August to 2 September 1947, produced a multilateral mutual defense treaty. This Rio Treaty, or Inter-American Treaty of Reciprocal Assistance, bound the United States and the signatory Latin American republics in a mutual defense system.

Acting under Article 50 of the United Nations Charter, representatives from nineteen of the twenty-one republics of the Western Hemisphere (Nicaragua and Ecuador did not send representatives) declared that an attack on any member state by either an outside force or another member state would obligate all member states to come to the aid of the state under attack. Member states agreed to settle their differences peacefully and to abide by decisions and sanctions imposed by a vote of their foreign ministers.

The Rio Conference of 1947 completed the work begun by the Act of Chapultepec (1945), which had excluded Argentina because of its support of the Axis powers during World War II. But by 1947 the United States, motivated by the fear of active infiltration of Soviet communism moved to secure the Western Hemisphere, electing to strengthen inter-American bonds by filling the gap of an incomplete mutual security pact. The resulting Rio Treaty was the first permanent alliance ratified by the United States that effectively altered the unilateral Monroe Doctrine and created a multilateral commitment to the security of the hemisphere. This Rio Treaty led to the charter of the Organization of American States (OAS), drafted in Bogotá, Colombia, in 1948, which set up a permanent political organization to carry out the terms of the Rio Treaty and end regional disputes before they could explode into open warfare. The Rio Conference and the Bogotá meeting also attempted to mitigate regional hostilities resulting from Latin American desires for political independence and autonomy while sharing a hemisphere with the powerful neighbor to the north.

BIBLIOGRAPHY

Leonard, Thomas, and John F. Bratzel. *Latin America during World War II.* Lanham: Rowman & Littlefield, 2007.

Sheinin, David. *Beyond the Ideal: Pan Americanism in Inter-American Affairs.* Westport: Greenwood Press, 2000.

Vázquez García, Humberto. *De Chapultepec a la OEA: Apogeo y crisis del panamericanismo.* La Habana: Editorial de Ciencias Sociales, 2001.

LESLEY R. LUSTER

RIO CONFERENCE (1954)

The Conference of American Ministers of Finance or Economy (Rio Conference of 1954) was held in Petrópolis (near Rio de Janeiro) for two weeks, beginning 22 November 1954, to discuss economic and trade relations in the Western Hemisphere. In addition to representatives from the twenty-one member states of the Organization of American States (OAS), delegations from Canada, West Germany, Belgium, Spain, France, Great Britain, Italy, Portugal, Japan, and the Netherlands attended.

At the conference Latin American leaders expressed their desire to develop economic integration in the Western Hemisphere and called for increased financial assistance from the U.S. government. João Café Filho, president of Brazil, urged the delegates to discuss such cooperative efforts as a customs union, a single currency, and the establishment of an international American bank, which had first been suggested by the First Inter-American Conference in Washington, D.C., in 1889. Eugenio Gudin, Brazil's minister of finance, expressed deep concerns regarding the Eisenhower administration's emphasis on private rather than public investment as the main thrust of U.S. economic investment in Latin America. Gudin felt that such a policy ignored the severe lack of development in such areas as public utilities, education, and health. However, the U.S. delegation, headed by George M. Humphrey, secretary of the treasury, reiterated the Eisenhower policy and called for the establishment of stable, equitable prices for raw materials, as well as increased developmental capital and technical assistance in the form of private loans and private investments, such as a U.S. $200 million loan that the Bank of Brazil had recently negotiated with a syndicate of nineteen American banks.

Latin American leaders were resentful of U.S. foreign policy that had rebuilt Europe through the Marshall Plan but ignored economic integration and free trade offers from Latin America. In the eyes of some Latin Americans, such policy indicated that Latin America was seen only as a source of tropical foods and raw materials. However, within Latin America many groups supported higher tariffs and tightly regulated foreign investment from the United States. By enacting protectionist measures, Latin American governments hoped to promote the development of domestic industries. The United States would not be ready to discuss free trade in the Western Hemisphere until the late 1980s, when it found itself less able to compete in a global economy. Latin American countries were also more open to free trade in the 1980s after their protectionist industrial policies created unsustainable debts.

See also **North American Free Trade Agreement; Organization of American States (OAS).**

BIBLIOGRAPHY

"Rio Conference (1954)," *New York Times,* 23 November 1954.

Samuel Flagg Bemis, *A Short History of American Foreign Policy and Diplomacy* (1959), pp. 503–516.

Ruhl J. Bartlett, *The Record of American Diplomacy: Documents and Readings in the History of American Foreign Relations* (1964), pp. 730–733.

U.S. Congress, Senate, *Executive II,* 80th Cong. (1969–1970), 1st sess.

Robert F. Smith, ed. *The United States and the Latin American Sphere of Influence* (1981).

Werner J. Feld and Robert S. Jordan with Leon Hurwitz, *International Organizations: A Comparative Approach* (1983), pp. 100–102.

Ann E. Weiss, *Good Neighbors? The United States and Latin America* (1985).

L. Ronald Scheman, *The Inter-American Dilemma: The Search for Inter-American Cooperation at the Centennial of the Inter-American System* (1988).

John J. Johnson, *A Hemisphere Apart: The Foundations of United States Policy Toward Latin America* (1990).

Additional Bibliography

Gilderhus, Mark T. *The Second Century: U.S.-Latin American Relations since 1889.* Wilmington, DE: Scholarly Resources, 2000.

Piotti de Lamas, Diosma E., and Alfredo Traversoni. *América Latina y Estados Unidos en el siglo XX: Aspectos políticos, económicos y sociales.* Montevideo, Uruguay: Fundación de Cultura Universitaria, 1996.

Sheinin, David. *Beyond the Ideal: Pan Americanism in Inter-American Affairs.* Westport, CT: Greenwood Press, 2000.

LESLEY R. LUSTER

WASHINGTON CONFERENCE (1889)

This meeting, the First International Conference of American States, is sometimes known as the first Pan-American Conference. Initiated by the United States and held in Washington, D.C., from 2 October 1889 to 19 April 1890, it marked the institutional beginning of the Inter-American System. Seventeen Latin American states (all but the Dominican Republic) sent delegates. U.S. officials wanted Latin Americans to turn from Europe to the United States for imports and capital. Latin Americans turned down the U.S. proposal for a Pan-American customs union, arguing they would receive few concessions in return for preferences given. The conference approved a treaty of compulsory arbitration for the peaceful settlement of inter-American disputes, but signatories insisted on reservations that eroded its obligatory nature. No state subsequently ratified the treaty, although some of its features were incorporated in later inter-American instruments.

Latin Americans did adopt a resolution (the United States cast the only negative vote), based on the Calvo Doctrine, declaring that resident aliens should not enjoy privileges beyond laws established for citizens and denying outside governments the right to intervene on their behalf. Finally, the conference established the International Union of American Republics as a temporary regional association and the Commercial Bureau of the American Republics (the rudimentary forerunner of the Pan-American Union) as its agency.

See also **Blaine, James Gillespie.**

BIBLIOGRAPHY

Carnegie Endowment For International Peace, *The International Conferences of American States, 1889–1928* (1931).

John Lloyd Mecham, *The United States and Inter-American Security, 1889–1960* (1961), pp. 48–58.

Additional Bibliography

Marichal, Carlos. *México y las conferencias panamericanas, 1889-1938: Antecedentes de la globalización.* México: Secretaría de Relaciones Exteriores, 2002.

Martí, José *En los Estados Unidos: Periodismo de 1881 a 1892.* Roberto Fernández Retamar, and Pedro Pablo Rodríguez. Colección Archivos, 43. Madrid: Allca XX, 2003.

Sheinin, David. *Beyond the Ideal: Pan Americanism in Inter-American Affairs.* Westport: Greenwood Press, 2000.

Ward, Thomas. "Martí y Blaine: Entre la colonialidad tenebrosa y la emancipación inalcanzable." *Cuban Studies* 38 (2007).

G. POPE ATKINS

See also **Darién Gap; Pan-American Conferences: Havana Conference (1928).**

BIBLIOGRAPHY

Koch, Wolfgang. "Beyond the End of the Road." *Americas* 40 (July–August 1988), 44–49.

Koch, Wolfgang. "Across a Gap in Darien." *The Economist* 325 (21 November 1992), 57.

The Pan American Highway System. Washington, DC: General Secretariat, Organization of the American States, 1969.

JAMES PATRICK KIERNAN
VICENTE PALERMO

PAN-AMERICAN HIGHWAY.

Originally conceived as a single road, the Pan-American Highway is a network of roads through fifteen countries that extends from Alaska to Argentina, Brazil, and Chile. Only fifty-four miles remain to be built as of 2007. The idea for a Pan-American highway system originated at the Fifth International Conference of American States in Santiago de Chile in 1923. In 1925 the First Pan-American Highway Conference, held in Buenos Aires, found that the construction of a highway was of immediate importance for the development of the region. In 1928 the Sixth International Conference of American States, held in Havana, issued its approval of a road for longitudinal communication across the continent.

The eventual catalyst for further development of the highway was World War II. Suddenly, adequate land connections between the continents, especially between the United States and the Panama Canal Zone, became crucial for military security. Substantial progress was made, especially in Central America. U.S. assistance was very important.

In the 1950s supporters of the highway convinced the U.S. Congress that a highway and its accompanying economic and social development were an important deterrent to Communist expansion in Latin America. The thoroughfare was finally opened in 1963, except for the Darién Gap, a stretch between northern Colombia and southern Panama. The highway has helped economic development in Mexico and Central America.

PAN-AMERICAN INSTITUTE OF GEOGRAPHY AND HISTORY.

Pan-American Institute of Geography and History (IPGH), an organization created by the Sixth International Conference of American States, which took place in Havana, Cuba, in January 1928, to promote inter-American cooperation in geography, history, and related areas. In 1929 the Mexican government provided the IPGH with the building that has served as its headquarters to the present day. A 1949 accord with the Organization of American States (OAS) established the IPGH as the first specialized body of the OAS. The statutes approved in 1969 continue to guide the organization.

The IPGH contains several agencies of a Pan-American nature: General Assembly, Directing Council, four commissions (cartography, geography, history, and geophysics), and the General Secretariat. In the General Assembly, eight authorities are elected: a president, two vice presidents, four commission presidents, and a secretary general. Also functioning are an Authorities Assembly, an Advisory Committee on Planning and Financial Evaluation, and the committees and task forces of the four commissions. At the national level, there are national departments composed of representatives to the Pan-American commissions and committees. These departments are administered by locally designated authorities.

See also **Pan-American Conferences: Havana Conference (1928).**

BIBLIOGRAPHY

Pan American Institute of Geography and History, *The Pan-American Institute of Geography and History: Its*

Creation, Development, and Current Program, 1929–1954 (1954), and *El Instituto Panamericano de Geografía e Historia: Organismo Especializado de la OEA, 1928–1978* (1978).

Additional Bibliography

Monroy Cabra, Marco Gerardo. *El sistema interamericano.* San José, Costa Rica: Editorial Juricentro, 1993.

Sheinin, David. *The Organization of American States.* New Brunswick, NJ: Transaction Publishers, 1996.

LEOPOLDO F. RODRÍGUEZ

PAN-AMERICANISM. Pan-Americanism is a term that first appeared in the New York City press in the period immediately preceding the 1889–1890 Inter-American Conference held in Washington, D.C. According to Joseph B. Lockey, a leading historian of the movement, Pan-Americanism from that time forward could be described as the cooperative relationship of the sovereign states of the Western Hemisphere, a relationship based upon the principles of law, nonintervention, and equality. Lockey's assessment, of course, represents the Pan-American ideal. Efforts on the part of the American states to achieve these goals in the wake of the Washington Conference were not always successful.

Much the same can be said for the years before 1889 as well. The period from Independence to the late 1880s, depicted in most studies as the "old" Pan-American era, witnessed a series of conferences involving a number of Spanish American nations. Inspired by a fear of foreign aggression, the main objective of these conferences was mutual security. The agreements negotiated at these meetings, however, were never ratified. Moreover, representatives of the United States never attended the conferences. Indeed, these gatherings were at least partially inspired by the Latin American nations' fear of their northern neighbor.

With the convening of the 1889–1890 Washington Conference a second phase of Pan-Americanism began that would last until the early 1930s. The emergence of the United States as a major power provided the opportunity for that country to sponsor this phase of the movement. The agendas for the conferences during this period were carefully orchestrated by North American policymakers to preclude the consideration of so-called "political" topics. Instead, the U.S. government preferred to deal with economic, scientific, and cultural topics that did not lend themselves to confrontation and polemics. The Latin Americans, on the other hand, endeavored to use the Pan-American conferences as vehicles for promoting the concepts of equality, respect for the rule of international law, and adherence to the principles of sovereignty and absolute nonintervention within the hemispheric community.

Ironically, in the years following World War I, when the United States enjoyed seemingly uncontested domination in the Americas, Latin Americans obtained their greatest success in forcing discussion, if not resolution, of political issues at Inter-American meetings. Proposals at Santiago in 1923 for an American League of Nations, an Inter-American court with mandatory arbitration, and the restructuring of the Pan-American Union, combined with the call at Havana in 1928 for the acceptance of the principle of nonintervention, demonstrate the persistence of Latin Americans to develop an Inter-American system governed by the rule of law and bound by the principle of international equality.

The third ("Good Neighbor") phase of the Pan-American movement developed following the 1933 Montevideo Conference. After years of passionate, yet in the final analysis fruitless, advocacy of a wide range of political issues, the Latin Americans were at last able to witness the U.S. government's public adherence to most of these very same principles—the most important, of course, being the principle of nonintervention. The lessening of tensions within the hemispheric community led in turn to the development of solidarity both before and during World War II. The postwar era has formed the latest phase of Pan-Americanism, dating effectively from the signing of the 1947 Rio Treaty and the subsequent 1948 Bogotá Conference. The establishment of the Organization of American States at Bogotá laid the groundwork for the development of the current Inter-American system. Although the postwar conferences initially focused on economic issues, they increasingly turned to anticommunism during the cold war. The end of the cold war in the early 1990s roughly coincided with the rise of democracy in Latin America. Consequently, the OAS began to focus on supporting democratic institutions in the region.

See also **Good Neighbor Policy; Inter-American Organizations; Organization of American States (OAS); Pan-American Conferences: Bogotá Conference (1948); Pan-American Conferences: Montevideo Conference (1933); Pan-American Conferences: Rio Conference (1947); Pan-American Conferences: Washington Conference (1889).**

BIBLIOGRAPHY

For the origins of Pan-Americanism, see Joseph B. Lockey, *Pan-Americanism: Its Beginnings* (1970) and *Essays in Pan-Americanism* (1967). Periodization of the movement is well developed in John Lloyd Mecham, *The United States and Inter-American Security, 1889–1960* (1961). Analysis of the important Santiago and Havana Conferences can be found in Richard V. Salisbury, *Anti-Imperialism and International Competition in Central America, 1920–1929* (1989). For a Latin American perspective on the movement, see Alonso Aguilar Monteverde, *Pan-Americanism from Monroe to the Present: A View from the Other Side* (1968).

Additional Bibliography

Bouvier, Virginia Marie. *The Globalization of U.S.-Latin American Relations: Democracy, Intervention, and Human Rights.* Westport, CT: Praeger, 2002.

Cooper, Andrew Fenton, and Thomas Legler. *Intervention without Intervening?: The OAS Defense and Promotion of Democracy in the Americas.* New York: Palgrave Macmillan, 2006.

Marichal, Carlos. *México y las conferencias panamericanas, 1889–1938: Antecedentes de la globalización.* México: Secretaría de Relaciones Exteriores, 2002.

Sheinin, David. *Beyond the Ideal: Pan Americanism in Inter-American Affairs.* Westport, CT: Greenwood Press, 2000.

RICHARD V. SALISBURY

man who fought in the War of the Pacific (1879–1884) and later explored the Bolivian Amazon region for the government. Astutely allying himself with the La Paz Federalists and the Aymara Indian communities in 1898, Pando managed to overthrow the Conservative administration of Sévero Fernández Alonso in 1899. After the Conservative defeat, Pando turned against both the Federalists and the Indians, thereby establishing the dominance of the Liberal Party for the next two decades. In 1903, Pando led Bolivian forces in the Acre campaign in the rubber-rich Bolivian Amazon against Brazilian-supported separatists. Bolivia lost and had to cede the region to Brazil the same year. Pando was assassinated under mysterious circumstances in 1917.

See also **Bolivia, Political Parties: Liberal Party; War of the Pacific.**

BIBLIOGRAPHY

There is neither a biography of Pando nor a detailed account of his administration. His role in the Federalist War is treated in Ramiro Condarco Morales, *Zárate, el "Temible" Willka: Historia de la rebelión indígena de 1899*, 2d ed. (1983). See also Enrique Finot, *Nueva historia de Bolivia: Ensayo de interpretación sociológica de Tiwanaku a 1930* (1980), pp. 337–346.

Additional Bibliography

Antezana Salvatierra, Alejandro Vladimir. *Los liberales y el problema agrario de Bolivia, 1899–1920.* La Paz: Plural Editores, 1996.

Irurozqui, Marta. *La armonía de las desigualdades: Elites y conflictos de poder en Bolivia, 1880–1920.* Madrid: Consejo Superior de Investigaciones Científicas, 1994.

ERICK D. LANGER

PANDO, JOSÉ MANUEL (1848–1917). José Manuel Pando (*b.* 25 December 1848; *d.* 15 June 1917), president of Bolivia (1899–1904). Born in Araca, La Paz, Major General José Manuel Pando was the military leader of the Liberal and Federalist forces during the Federalist War (1898–1899). He became the first president of the era of Liberal Party dominance (1899–1920), which coincided with the beginning of the tin-export boom. Pando was a professional military

PANE, IGNACIO ALBERTO (1883–1920). Ignacio Alberto Pane (*b.* 1883; *d.* 1920), Paraguayan sociologist, literary critic, and politician. Born in Asunción, Pane was part of an intellectual movement dedicated to the revindication of Francisco Solano López, the dictator who had taken the country into the War of the Triple Alliance (1864–1870), and whose memory had been reviled by liberal Paraguayans ever since. Pane's polemic on the López era graced the pages of several Asunción newspapers and put him in the company of Juan O'Leary and other nationalist writers. He introduced sociology to Paraguay as a separate university discipline, and wrote many volumes of poetry, geography, social theory, and conservative polemics. Several of his works were published under the pseudonym Matías Centella. Pane died in Asunción.

See also **López, Francisco Solano; Sociology.**

BIBLIOGRAPHY

Carlos Zubizarreta, *Cien vidas paraguayas,* 2d ed. (1985).

Additional Bibliography

Cunninghame Graham, R. B. *Retrato de un dictador: Francisco Solano López: Paraguay, 1865–1870.* Buenos Aires: El Elefante Blanco, 2001.

THOMAS L. WHIGHAM

PANIAGUA, VALENTÍN (1936–2006).

Valentín Paniagua was born in the city of Cuzco, Peru, on September 23, 1936. Early in his political career he joined the Partido Democrata Cristiano (PDC, Christian Democratic Party) and in 1963 was elected deputy of the party. He abandoned the PDC because of its support for the military regime (1968–1980), and joined Acción Popular (AP, Popular Action) in 1974. With Peru's return to civilian rule in 1980, Paniagua was reelected to congress. For most of the next two decades he occupied prominent positions in the legislature. In the wake of the political crisis that led to the removal of President Alberto Fujimori (1990–2000) from office, Paniagua, who was acting president of the congress, became interim president of Peru in November 2000. His main goal during his short presidency was to heal the wounds created by the Fujimori regime. He appointed a broad-based cabinet that included prominent figures of the center-right and center-left, headed by former U.N. secretary general Javier Pérez de Cuellar. Military officials implicated in corruption activities were removed, harsh and controversial antiterrorist legislation was repealed, and state officials and media owners involved in illegal activities associated with Fujimori's controversial 2000 reelection were prosecuted. Paniagua also established the

Truth and Reconciliation Commission to investigate abuses perpetrated by guerrilla groups and the Peruvian state in the 1980s and 1990s. After leaving office, Paniagua became AP's secretary general and ran unsuccessfully for the presidency in 2006. He died in Lima on October 16, 2006.

See also **Fujimori, Alberto Keinya.**

BIBLIOGRAPHY

"Valentín Paniagua." Mundo Andino/The Andean World. Available from http://www.mundoandino.com/Peru/Valentin-Paniagua.

"Valentín Paniagua, 69, Leader of Peru after Fall of Fujimori, Dies." *New York Times.* October 18, 2006.

JULIO CARRION

PANIAGUA Y VASQUES, CENOBIO

(1821–1882). Cenobio Paniagua y Vasques (*b.* 30 October 1821; *d.* 2 November 1882), Mexican composer. Born in Tlalpujahua, Paniagua began his musical career as a violinist in the orchestra of the Morelia cathedral, under the direction of his uncle. He later joined the orchestra of the Mexico City cathedral, where he made contact with European musicians who had settled in Mexico, such as the Italian double-bass virtuoso Giovanni Bottesini, who also conducted opera in several cities of the New World. With Bottesini's help, Paniagua's first opera, with Italian libretto, premiered in September 1859. *Catalina de Guisa* (1845), the first opera written and staged in Mexico, created an appreciation for opera in the country. Paniagua's second opera, *Pietro d'Abano,* premiered in 1863, around the time Paniagua organized an opera company to tour the country. The enterprise failed, and in 1868, Paniagua moved to the city of Córdoba, Veracruz, where he composed religious works, among them the cantata *Siete palabras* (1869), the oratorio *Tobías* (1870), a requiem (1882), and about seventy masses. He died in Córdoba.

See also **Music: Art Music.**

BIBLIOGRAPHY

Robert Stevenson, *Music in Mexico* (1952; 2d ed., 1971); *New Grove Dictionary of Music and Musicians,* vol. 14 (1980).

Additional Bibliography

Casares, Emilio, and Alvaro Torrente, eds. *La opera en España e Hispanoamérica: Actas del Congreso Internacional La Opera en España e Hispanoamérica, una Creación Propia: Madrid, 29. XI-3. XII de 1999.* Madrid: Ediciones del ICCMU, 2001.

SUSANA SALGADO

PANI ARTEAGA, ALBERTO J. (1878–1955).

Alberto J. Pani Arteaga (*b.* 12 June 1878; *d.* 25 August 1955), Mexican public figure and entrepreneur. He is considered to have been a critical influence on government financial policies as secretary of the treasury in the postrevolutionary era. As rector of the popular university, he contributed to expanded public education. He held the position of treasury secretary under more presidents than any other Mexican since 1920 and he was an intimate associate of President Plutarco Elías Calles, who recommended him to Congress as one of three candidates for the presidency after Pascual Ortiz Rubio resigned in 1932.

The member of a prominent family from Aguascalientes, Aguascalientes, he married Esther Alba, granddaughter of President Manuel de la Peña y Peña. He is also the uncle of Mario Pani, a notable Mexican architect. Pani graduated from the National School of Engineering in 1902. In 1911, as a teacher there, he founded a student group to support Francisco I. Madero's presidential candidacy and became subsecretary of education in his administration, after which he served as director of public works for the Federal District. A supporter of Venustiano Carranza, he turned down the post of secretary of education in his cabinet but later accepted the post of secretary of industry and commerce in 1917. He also served as Carranza's minister to France (1918–1920), a position he held again from 1927 to 1931. He served as secretary of foreign relations from 1921 to 1923, and became secretary of the treasury, first under President Álvaro Obregón, (1923–1924), and again under Calles (1924–1927 and 1932–1933). He built a number of major buildings in Mexico City with his own construction firm.

See also **Carranza, Venustiano; Mexico: Since 1910.**

BIBLIOGRAPHY

Alberto J. Pani, *Apuntes autobiográficos* (1945), 2d ed. (1950).

John W. F. Dulles, *Yesterday in Mexico: A Chronicle of the Revolution, 1919–1936* (1961).

Enrique Krauze, *Historia de la Revolución mexicana, período 1924–1928* (1977).

Additional Bibliography

Aguirre Anaya, Carmen. *Alberto Pani: evocación de un destino.* Puebla, México: Benemérita Universidad Autónoma de Puebla, 2004.

Aguirre, Carmen, and Alberto Carabarín Gracia, eds. *Tras la huella de personajes mexicanos.* Puebla, México: Universidad Autónoma de Puebla, Instituto de Ciencias Sociales y Humanidades, 2002.

RODERIC AI CAMP

PANTANAL.

Pantanal, the largest expanse of wetlands in the world, is a fluvial flood plain of 55,600 square miles in the states of Mato Grosso and Mato Grosso Do Sul, Brazil. It lies on the east bank of the Paraguay River between Cuiabá and the Bolivian border, and has been referred to as one of the world's greatest wildlife preserves, containing over 600 species of birds and 350 varieties of fish. As of 1990 the Pantanal was 95 percent privately owned, largely by ranchers who pasture cattle and water buffalo there.

Concern has been expressed about the future of the Pantanal, most notably in a 1990 Brazilian prime-time soap opera, because mechanized agriculture and mining continue to outpace scientific studies of the area. Yet it has also been suggested that ranching has not had as negative an impact on the Pantanal as in other regions of Brazil because of its unique ecosystem.

European ranching was introduced in the northern Pantanal during the mid-eighteenth century when former gold miners and merchants began to establish cattle ranches at Poconé and Cáceres with the aid of royal land grants. The anti-Portuguese riots near Cuiabá after Brazil's independence increased migration into the southern Pantanal. During the War of the Triple Alliance (1865–1870) this region suffered extreme disruptions as the ranching population fled toward Cuiabá.

The indigenous wildlife on the Pantanal includes deer, ocelot, puma, boar, anteater, tapir, rhea, capybara, and caiman. The only officially protected areas within the Pantanal include 500,000 acres under the auspices of the Pantanal National Park, and 25,000 acres of the Taiama Ecological Station. The wetlands are accessible by means of the Transpantaneira—a 90-mile dirt road built by military engineers through the northern Pantanal in the 1970s, in hopes of developing the economic potential of the region.

See also **Environmental Movements; War of the Triple Alliance.**

BIBLIOGRAPHY

Vic Banks, *The Pantanal: Brazil's Forgotten Wilderness* (1991).

Additional Bibliography

Brum, Eron, and Regina Frias. *A mídia do Pantanal.* Campo Grande: UNIDERP, 2001.

Pearson, David and Les Beletsky. *Brazil: Amazon and Pantanal.* Northampton, MA: Interlink Books, 2005.

Robert Wilcox, "Cattle and Environment in the Pantanal of Mato Grosso, Brazil, 1870–1970," in *Agricultural History* 66, no. 2 (1992).

Swarts, Frederick. *The Pantanal: Understanding and Preserving the World's Largest Wetland.* New York: Paragon House, 2000.

CAROLYN E. VIEIRA

PANTON, LESLIE, AND COMPANY.

Panton, Leslie, and Company, a trading company in the Floridas (1783–1804). Formed by Loyalists William Panton, John Leslie, and others in St. Augustine in 1783, Panton, Leslie, and Company and its successor firm, John Forbes and Company (1804–1847), played a significant role in the history of the Floridas and the Old Southwest. After 1785, Pensacola became the company headquarters. Aided initially by Alexander McGillivray, the Creek chief, these companies eventually secured a virtual monopoly of the Indian trade. Early on, they successfully opposed U.S. westward expansion. When they recognized the inevitable march of manifest destiny, however, they assisted the United States (and themselves) in acquiring huge land grants from the Indians.

See also **Forbes, John Murray.**

BIBLIOGRAPHY

William S. Coker, *Historical Sketches of Panton, Leslie and Company* (1976); *John Forbes' Description of the Spanish Floridas, 1804,* edited by William S. Coker, translated by Vicki D. Butt et al. (1979).

William S. Coker and Thomas D. Watson, *Indian Traders of the Southeastern Spanish Borderlands: Panton, Leslie, and Company and John Forbes and Company, 1783–1847* (1986).

Research Publications, *The Papers of Panton, Leslie and Co.: Guide to the Microfilm Collection* (1986).

Additional Bibliography

Morris, Michael P. *The Bringing of Wonder: Trade and the Indians of the Southeast, 1700–1783.* Westport, CT: Greenwood Press, 1999.

WILLIAM S. COKER

PÁNUCO RIVER.

Pánuco River, one of the largest river systems in Mexico's Atlantic watershed, is about 365 miles long and drains a basin of approximately 26,500 square miles. Although geographers have debated the location of its headwaters, the Pánuco begins in the storm drains of Mexico City. The Moctezuma, one of its two major tributaries, begins as the Salado, which receives water from the Gran Canal de Desagüe, built during the last half of the nineteenth century to drain water from the Valley of Mexico. The Moctezuma receives other tributaries formed by springs and underground channels in the limestone rocks along its course and cuts through the eastern escarpment of the Sierra Madre Oriental with a deep canyon. It then flows across the Huasteca to be joined by the Tamuín, its other major tributary. The headwaters of the Tamuín have eroded deep into the Mesa Central and have captured many streams that formerly had flowed westward. The river takes the name Pánuco at this juncture and then meanders east toward the coast.

The river's levees, both active and abandoned, show many settlement sites from pre-Columbian times, and Carl Sauer identified the lower Pánuco as the northeastern boundary of the high civilizations of central and southern Mexico (represented by the Huasteca). Hernán Cortés established the first successful Spanish settlement in the region of the Pánuco, Santisteban del Puerto (present-day Pánuco), in 1523. With Nuño de Guzmán's successful introduction of cattle in 1527, the lower Pánuco became a major cattle-producing region during the colonial period.

The port of Tampico is located on the lower Pánuco, about 7 miles upriver from the mouth, where a bar limited traffic until dredging and the construction of jetties in the late nineteenth century allowed ships drawing 25 feet to reach the harbor. The discovery of oil around the turn of the twentieth century transformed the Pánuco region and made it a major oil-producing area.

See also **Papaloapan River.**

BIBLIOGRAPHY

Jorge L. Tamayo, *Geografía general de México*, 2d ed., vol. 2 (1962), pp. 274–296.

Robert Cooper West, ed., *Handbook of Middle American Indians*, vol. 1 (1964), pp. 88, 90–91.

Donald E. Chipman, *Nuño de Guzmán and the Province of Pánuco in New Spain, 1518–1533* (1967).

Additional Bibliography

Blázquez Domínguez, Carmen. *Breve historia de Veracruz.* México: Colegio de México, Fideicomiso Historia de las Américas: Fondo de Cultura Económica, 2000.

Islas Ojeda, Rafael Mario. *Aspectos físicos y recursos naturales del Estado de Veracruz.* Xalapa, Ver., México: Universidad Veracruzana, 1990.

Souto Mantecón, Matilde. *Mar abierto: La política y el comercio del consulado de Veracruz en el sistema imperial.* México: El Colegio de México: Instituto de Investigaciones Dr. José María Luis Mora, 2001.

JOHN J. WINBERRY

PAPALOAPAN RIVER.

Papaloapan River, one of the most important rivers on Mexico's southern Gulf Coast, drains a roughly 15,100-square-mile basin in the states of Veracruz, Oaxaca, and Puebla. Its headwaters are formed by the Salado River in the valley of Tehuacán, Puebla, and by the Tomellín River in the Sierra de Juárez, Oaxaca. The river becomes the Papaloapan near Valle Nacional as it begins to meander across the Gulf coastal plain to discharge into the Laguna de Alvarado. The river's fertile levees were preferred sites for pre-Columbian settlement, and the earliest evidences of civilization in Mexico, that of the Olmecs, are found in the lower floodplain of the Papaloapan and adjacent rivers.

Since colonial times, annual floods and the threat of malaria had limited settlement on the lower Papaloapan to small villages and cattle ranches. In the twentieth century, the floods became more severe, primarily because of the deforestation of the upland basin; the worst floods in history occurred in 1944, killing more than 100 people. In 1947 President Miguel Alemán, a native of the area, established the Comisión del Papaloapan, the first of Mexico's river basin commissions. It was given full planning and construction authority for the integrated development of the region: dam construction, electricity production, channel straightening, swamp clearing, mosquito control, road building, colonization, and the general improvement of social services. Frequently compared to the Tennessee Valley Authority, the Papaloapan project was different in that the commission was always under the federal executive. Completed in 1954, the 250-foot-high Miguel Alemán dam on the Río Tonto near Temascal created a 19,305-square-mile reservoir and provided protection for 77,220 square miles of land that previously had been subject to flood. The Cerro de Oro dam, completed in the early 1980s, protected additional land from flooding and increased the hydroelectric potential of the Alemán dam to 500,000 kilowatts.

See also **Alemán Valdés, Miguel; Energy; Pánuco River.**

BIBLIOGRAPHY

Jorge L. Tamayo, *Geografía general de México,* 2d ed., vol. 2 (1962), pp. 313–325.

Thomas T. Poleman, *The Papaloapan Project* (1964).

Peter T. Ewell and Thomas T. Poleman, *Uxpanapa: Agricultural Development in the Mexican Tropics* (1980).

Robert Cooper West and John P. Augelli, *Middle America: Its Lands and Peoples,* 3d ed. (1989), p. 311.

Additional Bibliography

Lucero, A. *El desarrollo regional en México y su problemática agraria.* México: Departamento de Etnología y Antropología Social, Instituto Nacional de Antropología e Historia, SEP, 1979.

Palacios, Carlos Oguin, Maria del Carmen Alvarez Avila, and Alberto Asiain Hoyos. *Tecnología agroacuícola en la cuenca baja del Río Papaloapan: La experiencia del Campus Veracruz del colegio de posgrados.* México, DF: Red de Gestión Recursos Naturales : Fundación Rockefeller México, 2000.

Villa Rojas, Alfonso. *Los mazatecos y el problema indígena de la cuenca de Papaloapan.* México, Ediciones del Instituto Nacional Indigenista, 1955.

JOHN J. WINBERRY

PAPE, LYGIA (1929–2004). Lygia Pape (*b.* 1929; *d.* 3 May 2004), Brazilian painter, illustrator, engraver. One of the forerunners of the neoconcrete movement, Pape, along with Hélio Oiticica, Lygia Clark, and other Brazilian artists, broke from both the constructivists and the concretes during the 1950s. A member of Grupo Frente from 1953 to 1955, she participated in the national exhibitions of concrete art in 1956 and 1957 and in the first neoconcrete shows in 1959. Pape favored abstraction over the imitation of nature. She began working with xylography, an engraving technique using a wooden block but quickly moved away from the two-dimensional medium and focused her attention on sculpture and other experimental formulas.

Pape is best known for her neoconcrete "book poems" and "box poems." Her *Book of Creation* (1959) serves as a neoconcrete standard-bearer. Geometric shapes serve as pages of a book, each one a metaphor for episodes in the Creation story. Spectators may participate in the experience and test their own creativity by manipulating the forms. Pages from the *Book* were placed around Rio de Janeiro, on benches, on the beach, and on rocks. Interested in working with the different possibilities of light, she put together a film project entitled *Brasília.* In 1967 she joined the New Brazilian Objectivity exhibition at the Museum of Modern Art in Rio, where she exhibited her "box poems" and projects incorporating live insects. In 1968 she took participatory art to its extreme with *The Divider,* which consisted of a huge white sheet cut with holes for people's heads. Spectators became part of the medium, their movements and voices determining the shape and structure of the piece. In 1990 her exhibit of art in metal *Amazoninos* won her the Associação Brasileira de Críticos de Arte award.

See also **Art: The Twentieth Century.**

BIBLIOGRAPHY

Arte no Brasil, vol. 2 (1979), pp. 924–925.

Dawn Ades, *Art in Latin America* (1989), esp. pp. 269–271, 281.

Additional Bibliography

Brett, Guy. *Brasil experimental.* Rio de Janeiro: Contra Capa, 2005.

Mattar, Denise. *Lygia Pape: Intrinsecamente anarquista.* Rio de Janeiro: Relume Dumará, 2003.

CAREN A. MEGHREBLIAN

PAPEL SELLADO. Papel Sellado, a stamped government paper required for all legal and contractual transactions in the Spanish Indies. Initiated first in Spain in 1636, *papel sellado* appeared in the Indies soon after as a crown monopoly. *Papel sellado* needed for dispatches and edicts of viceroys and other royal officials cost twenty-four reales; contracts, wills, and deeds six reales; court documents one real; and legal instruments drawn up for the poor or Indians one-quarter real. The *papel sellado* not only generated income for the crown, but also, since no document was valid unless it had the proper governmental seal, provided the state a method for overseeing all legal activities and property transactions in the Indies. By 1800 sale of *papel sellado* produced an annual net income of approximately 40,000 pesos in Peru and 85,000 pesos in Mexico.

See also **Currency.**

BIBLIOGRAPHY

Recopilacíon de leyes de los Reynos de las Indias, 4 vols. (1681; repr. 1973), libro VIII, título XXIII, ley 18.

Fabían De Fonseca and Carlos De Urrutia, *Historia general de Real Hacienda,* vol. 3 (1850).

Additional Bibliography

Jáuregui, Luis. *The American Finances of the Spanish Empire: Royal Income and Expenditures in Colonial Mexico, Peru, and Bolivia, 1680–1809.* Albuquerque: University of New Mexico Press, 1998.

Marichal, Carlos, and Carlos Rodríguez Venegas. *La bancarrota del virreinato, Nueva España y las finanzas del imperio español, 1780–1810.* México: El Colegio de México, Fideicomiso Historia de las Américas, Fondo de Cultura Económica, 1999.

JOHN JAY TEPASKE

PAPUDO, BATTLE OF.

PAPUDO, BATTLE OF. Battle of Papudo, an important naval engagement in 1865 during Chile's war with Spain. On 26 November 1865, a Chilean vessel, the *Esmeralda,* attacked a Spanish ship, the *Covadonga.* Flying a British ensign as a ruse, the Chilean captain, Juan Williams Rebolledo, was able to approach the *Covadonga,* under the command of Luis Fery. When he came close enough, Williams simultaneously raised the Chilean flag and opened fire on the Spanish ship. Because the two vessels were so close, the Spanish ship's shells passed over the *Esmeralda,* which pounded the *Covadonga.* The Spanish struck their colors and tried to scuttle their ship, but the Chileans managed to board it, close the sea valves, and incorporate the *Covadonga* into their fleet. Capturing this Spanish vessel constituted one of the few high points in Chile's unfortunate war with Spain. The *Covadonga* remained in the Chilean navy until it was sunk during the War of the Pacific.

See also **Chile, War with Spain.**

BIBLIOGRAPHY

W. C. Davis, *The Last Conquistadores: The Spanish Intervention in Peru and Chile, 1863–1866* (1950).

Rodrígo Fuenzalida Bade, *La Armada de Chile: Desde la alborada al sesquicentenario (1813–1968),* vol. 2 (1978), pp. 595–598.

Additional Bibliography

Bethell, Leslie, ed. *Chile since Independence.* New York: Cambridge University Press, 1993.

Campo Rodríguez, Juan del. *Por la República y por la Reina: Una revisión histórica del conflicto de 1864-1871 entre España y la alianza peruano-chilena.* Peru: Asociación de Funcionarios Diplomáticos en Actividad AFDA, 2003.

Rodríguez González, Agustín Ramón. *La Armada Española, la campaña del Pacífico, 1862-1871: España frente a Chile y Perú.* Madrid: Agualarga, 1999.

Tromben Corbalán, Carlos. *La Armada de Chile: Desde la alborada hasta el final del Siglo XX.* Santiago, Chile: Imprenta de la Armada, 2001.

WILLIAM F. SATER

PAQUITA LA DEL BARRIO (1947–).

PAQUITA LA DEL BARRIO (1947–). Paquita la del Barrio (Francisca Víveros Barradas) is a Mexican popular singer. Born on April 2, 1947, in Alto Lucero, Veracruz, Mexico, Paquita began her career in Mexico City in 1970 by singing in night clubs. Her musical style is best described as bridging bolero and ranchera. She has recorded numerous CDs, including *Puro Dolor* (2007), *Para los inútiles* (2005), *Besos callejeros* (2004), *Pierdeme el Respeto* (2001), and *Desquítate conmigo* (1992), but her recognition and fame largely rest on her live performances. Paquita's aggressive lyrics against macho attitudes—"¿Me oyes, inútil?" ("Do you hear me, you useless man?") has become her signature line—and defending a woman's right to be treated with respect are unique in Mexican popular music. In love songs she stresses women's need for emotional and sexual fulfillment and dares men to become true partners. She has achieved iconic status among female audiences but also among males.

See also **Bolero; Music: Popular Music and Dance.**

BIBLIOGRAPHY

Foster, David William. "Paquita la del Barrio: Singing Feminine Rage." *CiberLetras* 2 (2000). Available from http://www.lehman.cuny.edu/ciberletras/index_files/v01n02.htm.

Foster, David William. "Paquita la del Barrio." In *Encyclopedia of Contemporary Latin American and Caribbean Cultures.* London: Routledge, 2000.

CLAUDIA P. RIVAS JIMÉNEZ

PARÁ (GRÃO PARÁ).

PARÁ (GRÃO PARÁ). Pará (Grão Pará), Brazil's second largest state. South of the Amazon Delta, Pará has an area of 482,000 square miles. Based on 2000 census data, Pará has a total population of 6,970,586. The region was densely populated by Native Americans when explored by Europeans in the sixteenth century. Although it was claimed by the Spanish and Portuguese, it was first settled by British, Irish, and Dutch immigrants in the early seventeenth century, as an alternative and rival to colonies in North America.

In the 1620s the Portuguese attacked and drove out the European colonists and used Belém to control access to the Amazon River. From 1626 until 1775, the entire northern region of Brazil was governed as the captaincy of Grão Pará, Maranhão, e Rio Negro, with its capital at São Luís. By the late seventeenth century, however, Belém was de facto capital of the Amazon region and is the state capital today.

Between 1755 and 1778 the Amazon underwent an intensive development effort by a monopoly trading company called the Companhia Geral do Grão Pará e Maranhão. Created by Sebastião José de Carvalho e Melo, Marques de Pombal, the company imported tens of thousands of slaves and exported forest products and cotton. It was dismantled shortly after Pombal's fall from power.

During the late nineteenth century, Belém was the transfer point for rubber exports, one of the great commodity booms in Brazil. The rubber cycle lasted a short time. Seeds of rubber trees were sent to the Far East (Malaysia, Sri Lanka, and other countries), where they adapted well and had the advantage of being cultivated on farms (saving the effort of struggling through the jungle to extract the rubber). The prices of rubber, which reached peaks at the beginning of the twentieth century, saw a sharp drop after the end of World War I. The crash of the New York Stock Exchange affected the entire country.

By 1930, Pará was entering a period of economic stagnation, and attempts to recover the rubber market failed. The economy turned to the exploration of other natural resources. In the 1960s Belém was connected with the highway system of the rest of Brazil and with the Transamazon Highway to the west. The roads were meant to facilitate the movement of people and goods between Belém and other large centers; actual results, however, were far from what had been expected. The small market of the cities, the long distances, the lack of credit, among other factors, prevented the economic development of the region. Over time, roads were abandoned and large parts were reclaimed by the jungle.

In 1966 the federal government created SUDAM (Superintendência para Desenvolvimento da Amazônia), an institution aimed at funding economic projects in the north of Brazil. After several instances of corruption, SUDAM was closed down in 2002.

See also Belém; Brazil, Organizations: Superintendency for the Development of Amazonia (SUDAM); Rubber Industry; Transamazon Highway.

BIBLIOGRAPHY

Antônio Carreira, *A Companhia Geral do Grão-Pará e Maranhão* (1988).

Joyce Lorimer, ed., *English and Irish Settlement on the River Amazon, 1550–1646* (1989).

Marianne Schmink and Charles Wood, *Contested Frontiers in Amazonia* (1992).

Additional Bibliography

Cardoso, Eliana, Ricardo Barros, and André Urani. *Inflation and Unemployment as Determinants of Inequality in Brazil.* Brasilia, D.F.: Instituto de Pesquisa Econômica Aplicada, 1993.

Moguillansky, Graciela. *Factores determinantes de las exportaciones industriales Brasileñas durante la década de 1980.* Brazil: Comisión Económica para América Latina y el Caribe, 1993.

Nimuendajú, Curt, and Marco Antonio Gonçalves. *Etnografia e indigenismo: Sobre os Kaingang, os Ofaié–Xavante e os índios do Pará.* Campinas, Brazil: Editora da Unicamp, 1993.

Scholz, Imme. *Overexploitation or Sustainable Management: Action Patterns of the Tropical Timber Industry: The Case of Pará (Brazil), 1960–1997.* London; Portland, OR: Frank Cass, 2001.

MICHAEL L. CONNIFF

PARACAS. Paracas, a desert peninsula, a textile style, a ceramic style, and a society that emerged on the south coast of Peru with habitation and civic-ceremonial sites distributed most notably in six river valleys (Cañete, Topará, Chincha, Pisco, Ica, and the Río Grande de Nasca drainage area). The culture received its name from the location on the Paracas Peninsula of cemeteries that were used during the last phases of the Paracas period. The arid ecology in this area of the south Peruvian coast is affected by seasonal "Paracas" winds and negligible precipitation, providing among the best natural conditions for preservation of ancient remains.

Paracas culture (c. 800 BCE–100 CE) falls mainly within the Early Horizon (c. 850 BCE–1 CE). The chronology consists of a ten-phase stylistic sequence, but parts of the chronology will remain a source of debate until more radiocarbon dates become available. John H. Rowe suggested that the Early Horizon be defined as the time beginning with the first appearance of pan-regional Chavín influence in the Ica Valley and ending when incised, decorated ceramics (with polychrome paint that was applied after the vessels were fired) were replaced by polychrome slipped painted pottery.

The Early Horizon is best known in the northern highlands and central coast, where excavations have revealed an expansive religious cult tied to the site of Chavín De Huántar and evidence of exchange networks that originated in the preceding Initial Period. On the south coast, the early Paracas period vividly documents the southern quarter of this Chavín religious and ideological sphere of influence. Cotton, painted, Chavín-related textiles have been recovered only within the Paracas culture area, specifically at sites such as Karwa on the coast and Cerrillos in the Andean foothills of the Ica Valley. The Paracas textile tradition became more elaborate over time to include tie-dying, ornamentation with feathers, embroidery, tapestry; twill, gauze, twining, looping, and braiding. The study of these textiles was made possible because large numbers of mummy bundles were recovered from Paracas Peninsula sites, particularly the Wari-Kayan Necropolis, from which we have also gained knowledge on late Paracas garments. Skull deformation was a common aesthetic practice among Paracas peoples, as evidenced from burials, as was cranial surgery, or trephination.

Early Horizon Paracas architecture includes U-shaped and rectangular adobe civic-ceremonial buildings. At least one such building has been excavated at Animas Alta in the Callango sector of the Ica Valley to reveal a U-shaped atrium with an elaborate adobe frieze containing late Paracas iconography. Other similar edifices are visible at this same site and across the Ica River, where numerous Paracas settlements have been recorded. Semi-subterranean adobe structures are typical where stone is less abundant, while stone-faced house structures, as well as residential terraces on hillslopes, are known from the Paracas Peninsula and in the middle and upper reaches of the valleys where Paracas settlements are located. Unlike the patterns described for the northern Chavín sphere, where it is argued that people lived in small, dispersed hamlets away from ceremonial centers, on the south coast, civic-ceremonial buildings are situated in very close proximity or within habitation sites.

See also **Chavín de Huántar.**

BIBLIOGRAPHY

Alfred L. Kroeber and William D. Strong, *The Uhle Pottery Collections from Ica,* with three appendixes by Max Uhle (1924).

John H. Rowe, "Stages and Periods in Archaeological Interpretation," in *Southwestern Journal of Anthropology* 18, no. 1 (1962): 40–54.

Dwight T. Wallace, "Cerrillos, an Early Paracas Site in Ica, Peru," in *American Antiquity* 27, no. 3 (1962): 303–314.

Dorothy Menzel et al., *The Paracas Pottery of Ica: A Study in Style and Time* (1964).

Luis Lumbreras, *The Peoples and Cultures of Ancient Peru* (1974).

Sarah Ann Massey, "Sociopolitical Change in the Upper Ica Valley, B.C. 400 to 400 A.D.: Regional States on the South Coast of Peru" (Ph.D. diss., UCLA, 1986).

Anne Paul, *Paracas Ritual Attire: Symbols of Authority in Ancient Peru* (1990), and ed., *Paracas Art and Architecture* (1991).

Richard Burger, *Chavín and the Origins of Andean Civilization* (1992).

Additional Bibliography

Benson, Elizabeth P., and Anita Gwynn Cook, eds. *Ritual Sacrifice in Ancient Peru.* Austin: University of Texas Press, 2001.

Engle, Frédéric André, Teresa Nicho N., and Edilberto Gutiérrez Ch. *Un desierto en tiempos prehispánicos: Rio Pisco, Paracas, Rio Ica.* Lima: s.n. 2001.

Paul, Anne. "Symmetry on Paracas Necrópolis Textiles." In *Embedded Symmetries: Natural and Cultural,* edited by Dorothy Koster Washburn. Albuquerque: University of New Mexico Press, 2004.

Stone, Rebecca. *Art of the Andes: From Chavín to Inca.* New York: Thames & Hudson, 1996.

ANITA COOK

PARACAS PENINSULAR SITES.

The Paracas period sites on the Paracas Peninsula in the lower Pisco River valley include habitation areas and cemeteries where fine woven and embroidered polychrome textiles have been found. Some burials include decorated ceramics with polychrome paint applied after the vessels were fired; negative-painted pottery; and a technologically superior, thin-walled monochrome ware, referred to as Topará ceramics, that includes various plant and animal vessel forms.

Julio C. Tello and his assistant, Toribio Mejía Xesspe identified Arena Blanca, a habitation site with twelve burial areas (from which 135 funerary bundles were excavated), and the famous Cabeza Larga cemetery, also situated within the Arena Blanca site. About one-half mile south, a second site was excavated on the summit of Cerro Colorado. It was named Paracas Cavernas after the type of bottle-shaped tomb that characterized these burials. By far the most impressive area encountered was the Wari-Kayan Necropolis, situated on the north slopes of Cerro Colorado, from which conically shaped mummy bundles were removed from burial fill.

The cemeteries on the Paracas Peninsula were used from about 300 BCE to 200 CE, and represent at least two burial traditions (Paracas Cavernas and Necropolis-type burials, the latter equated with Topará pottery) that include high-status individuals. The Paracas Cavernas contained individuals wrapped in plain and decorated textiles. The Necropolis burials were in the midden of older, abandoned domestic structures. These individuals were elaborately prepared for the afterlife in the form of mummy bundles and were accompanied by long wooden staves that served as grave markers. A false head was placed on the top of the mummy and adorned with a wig of human hair, headgear, and jewelry. Pottery, weaving utensils, and fishing gear are some of the offerings found within and around the prepared bundle, intended to accompany the deceased into the afterlife.

Trephination (cranial surgery) had been performed on the forty-odd skulls that Tello collected in 1925 from the surface of looted tombs at Cerro Colorado. The surgery, considered to be therapeutic in nature, was performed to release pressure from head wounds and remove broken-bone fragments. The physical remains leave little question that from 300 BCE on there was considerable conflict.

See also **Archaeology; Tello, Julio César.**

BIBLIOGRAPHY

Lumbreras, Luis. *The Peoples and Cultures of Ancient Peru.* Washington, DC: Smithsonian Institution Press, 1974.

Paul, Anne. *Paracas Ritual Attire: Symbols of Authority in Ancient Peru.* Norman: University of Oklahoma Press, 1990.

Paul, Anne, ed. *Paracas Art and Architecture*, 1–34, 240–314. Iowa City: University of Iowa Press, 1991.

Roncal Pretell, César. *Paracas: Flora, fauna e historia de una cultura milenaria.* Lima: G y R Inversiones, 1998.

Sawyer, Alan. *Ancient Peruvian Ceramics: The Nathan Cummings Collection.* New York: Metropolitan Museum of Art, 1966.

Tello, Julio C., and Toribio Mejía Xesspe. *Paracas segunda parte: Cavernas y Necropolis.* Lima: Universidad Nacional Mayor de San Marcos, 1979.

Wallace, Dwight. "Paracas in Chincha and Pisco: A Reappraisal of the Ocucaje Sequence." In *Recent Studies in Andean Prehistory and Protohistory*, edited by D. Peter Kvietok and Daniel H. Sandweiss, 67–94. Ithaca, NY: Latin American Studies Program, Cornell University, 1985.

Wallace, Dwight. "The Topará Tradition: An Overview." In *Perspectives on Andean Prehistory and Protohistory*, edited by D. Peter Kvietok and Daniel H. Sandweiss, 35–47. Ithaca, NY: Latin American Studies Program, Cornell University, 1986.

Weiss, Pedro. *Osteología cultural, prácticas cefálicas.* Lima: Universidad Nacional Mayor de San Marcos, 1958–1961. See especially Part 2, "Tipología de los deformaciones cefálicas—Estudio cultural de los tipos cefálicos y de algunas enfermedades oseas."

ANITA COOK

PARAGUARÍ, BATTLE OF.

Battle of Paraguarí (15 January 1811), a major engagement in the Paraguayan struggle for independence. After their successful seizure of power in May 1810, the insurgents of Buenos Aires expected the rest of the Platine region to quickly accept their authority and to support the cause of independence. Paraguay, however, continued to recognize the legitimacy of

Spanish rule, and rejected the *porteño* appeal. In response, the insurgents dispatched a 700-man army under Manuel Belgrano to bring the Paraguayans to heel.

Belgrano's troops crossed the Alto Paraná at Itapúa in December 1810 and proceeded to penetrate deep into Paraguay, encountering little opposition. Meanwhile, the Spanish governor, Bernardo Velasco, had well prepared the Paraguayans for defending the province, telling them that Belgrano's intention was to press them into service for a war of expansion elsewhere in South America. Since the *porteños* had, in fact, been guilty of this practice, the Paraguayans believed Velasco's claims. The result of Velasco's propaganda was that as Belgrano advanced toward Asunción, the inhabitants fled, leaving behind few cattle or foodstuffs. Desperate for provisions, on 15 January 1811, the *porteños* attacked a Paraguayan force of some 5,000 ill-equipped but well-mounted men just outside the town of Paraguarí. Initially, the battle went in favor of Belgrano, at which point Velasco and most of his *peninsular* staff hastily withdrew to the provincial capital, spreading tales of utter defeat. In fact, the Paraguayans had rallied under militia officers Manuel Atanacio Cavañas, Juan Manuel Gamarra, and Fulgencio Yegros. The *porteños* were driven far back, leaving a number of dead upon the field and 130 prisoners.

The incidents surrounding the Battle of Paraguarí confirmed that the defense of the province was fully in Paraguayan hands.

See also **Belgrano, Manuel.**

BIBLIOGRAPHY

Harris Gaylord Warren, *Paraguay: An Informal History* (1949), pp. 144–147.

John Hoyt Williams, *Rise and Fall of the Paraguayan Republic, 1800–1870* (1979), pp. 24–27.

Additional Bibliography

Ezcurra Medrano, Alberto. *La independencia del Paraguay y otros ensayos.* Buenos Aires: Instituto Nacional de Investigaciones Históricas Juan Manuel de Rosas, 1999.

Giménez, Ovidio. *Vida, época y obra de Manuel Belgrano.* Buenos Aires: Librería "El Ateneo" Editorial, 1993.

THOMAS L. WHIGHAM

PARAGUAY

This entry includes the following articles:
THE COLONIAL PERIOD
THE NINETEENTH CENTURY
SINCE 1900

THE COLONIAL PERIOD

In the territory that became Spanish Paraguay at the time of the Conquest lived 300,000 Native Americans, called Guaranis by the Spaniards, in fourteen Guarás, or regional and ethnic groups. Guaranis were part of the Tupi-Guarani linguistic family and were culturally similar to the Brazilian Tupinamba. Horticulturists who grew manioc, sweet potatoes, maize, and other crops on garden plots, they lived in villages of 1,000 to 3,000 people. They traced descent patrilineally but practiced matrilocalism, that is, couples settled near the wife's family. Their political organization was a chieftainship based on extended families. In the 1530s and 1540s, Guarani traditions of matrilocalism and of formalizing alliances by exchanging women provided the basis for an alliance between Guaranis and Spanish settlers, who brought few women to the upper Río de la Plata. Guarani caciques gave their daughters and nieces to Spaniards in order to formalize Guarani acceptance of Spanish tools, weapons, and military protection, which the Guaranis desired. Spaniards accepted most women as concubines, not wives, but offspring of these unions were the first products of the biological and cultural mixing that gave birth to the modern Paraguayan population.

Early European explorers in the Río de la Plata included Juan Díaz De Solís and Sebastian Cabot. The European founders of Paraguay, however, were the survivors of the expedition led by Pedro de Mendoza in 1535 to Buenos Aires. After indigenous resistance drove Mendoza's subordinates north to Paraguay in 1537, Carios, Guaranis of central Paraguay, befriended Juan de Salazar y Espinosa, who founded the fort of Nuestra Señora de la Asunción. Domingo Martínez de Irala dominated public life in Paraguay's early years. He oversaw the Spanish retreat from Buenos Aires and the founding of the Asunción *cabildo* (city council) in 1541; participated in the overthrow and exile in 1545 of Alvar Nuñez Cabeza De Vaca; and by fathering and recognizing numerous mestizo children, symbolized the ethnic fusion that begat Paraguayans. In 1556 he set a pattern for labor and hierarchy by awarding in encomienda 27,000 tributary Guarani men to 300 Spaniards. The Indians' service ensured Spanish domination.

The Asunción *cabildo* dominated local affairs. It was controlled by the landowners and *encomenderos,* who often ran the province, at times overruling the royally appointed governor, until the late colonial years. The *cabildo* was the arena for the turbulent politics of the province of Paraguay. After the mid-1500s, when trans-Chaco Spanish explorers and Guarani auxiliaries gave up their unsuccessful quest for wealth in Upper Peru, members of the Paraguayan elite lived part of the year on rural estates that exploited Guarani labor and part of the year in Asunción. Guaranis mostly lived in segregated towns and commuted to work on Spanish properties. Spaniards and Guaranis together fought common enemies along the Río Paraguay and in the Gran Chaco. That children of conquerors spoke not Spanish but Guarani at home contributed to the widespread use of the Guarani language, still an integral part of the Paraguayan identity in the 1990s.

Although Paraguay is often identified with the Jesuits, the earliest religious establishments in the province were those of Mercedarians, Jeronymites, and Dominicans. Franciscans founded the first Paraguayan missions. Mission towns, such as Yaguarón, Altos, Tobatí, and Atyrá in the 1500s and Caazapá and Yuty in the 1600s, were founded by Franciscans and Guaranis, and they endured in the 1990s. The Guaranis slowly converted to Catholicism. Outwardly they accepted Catholic ritual quickly, but privately they worshipped in Guarani ways for many decades, as they did in Jesuit missions later.

In Asunción, education for male children of the European elite was entirely by religious masters. Boys from privileged families often obtained their early education from tutors and then attended Franciscan, Mercedarian, and later Jesuit secondary schools. Because Paraguay never had its own institution of higher education, fortunate Paraguayan youths attended the University of Córdoba in what is now Argentina. Education for the Guaranis included instruction in basic literacy for a few and in Catholic religion for the many.

Jesuits first arrived in Asunción in 1588 and began missionary work among the Guaranis in 1609. Governed from Córdoba del Tucumán, the Jesuit province of Paraguay contained only ten of the thirty-two Guarani missions within the boundaries of the present Republic of Paraguay, and most of them avoided colonists and royally appointed bishops and governors as much as they could. Other Jesuit enterprises in colonial Paraguay included a church in Asunción and a *colegio,* or Jesuit chapter house, where many of the boys of the elite were educated. Jesuits also maintained the profitable Paraguarí estate, where in the early 1730s they grazed 30,000 cattle. Produce from this ranch was exchanged in the beef-scarce and largely moneyless province for tobacco and sugar. Jesuit enterprises competed with those of the merchants of Asunción, over whom Jesuits enjoyed several advantages. Spanish landowners, and later Spanish-Portuguese forces, attempted to overthrow and partition the Jesuits' claim to indigenous labor. Only in 1767, when the Jesuits were expelled, did such competition cease.

Colonial Paraguayans faced hostile powers from all sides. From Guaranis, Spanish settlers inherited conflict with Payaguás on the Río Paraguay and from Abipones, Mocobís, and Tobas from the southwestern Chaco. From the north, attacks of the Mbayás pushed back the frontiers of the province in the later 1600s. Hostilities also came from Brazil. In the 1600s, *paulistas* (slave hunters of São Paulo), who coveted Guarani labor, and in the 1700s crown-sponsored Portuguese efforts threatened Paraguay. Brazilian raids in the 1620s and 1630s that desolated Jesuit missions also forced Hispanicized settlers to abandon Guairá, including Ciudad Real and old Villa Rica. Violent conflicts between Paraguayans and Brazilians continued up to the War of the Triple Alliance in the 1860s.

Paraguayan political culture was turbulent, but its rebelliousness resembled that of other Spanish frontier areas. Great turmoil occurred in the 1540s and 1550s among rival conquerors, during the anti-Jesuit uprising led by Bishop Bernardino de Cárdenas in the 1640s and in similarly motivated upheavals led by José de Antequera y Castro in the 1720s and by Paraguayan *comuneros* in the 1730s. This unrest did not express disloyalty to the crown, only violent politics. Until the creation of the Viceroyalty of the Río de la Plata in 1776, Paraguay was far away from superior authorities, specifically, the viceroy in Lima and the Audiencia of Charcas. This distance and neglect encouraged disputes, which normally originated with the men who dominated the municipal council of the capital. They sought special favors and freedom from royal controls, especially wishing to avoid royal laws such as the 1612 Ordinances of Francisco de Alfaro, regulating native labor. The Paraguayan elite also sought lower taxes and the abolition of the privileges that the crown had awarded to competitors. Paraguayans opposed the Jesuit mission province's light tax burden and monopoly of Guarani labor. They also objected to the privileges enjoyed by the city of Santa Fe, which collected taxes on Paraguayan exports to support the war of the *santafecinos* against the indigenous peoples.

The economy of Paraguay for two centuries was largely one of subsistence. Crops included such essential commodities as manioc, sweet potatoes, maize, wheat, citrus fruits, tobacco, and sugar. Paraguayans always raised livestock, although until the last colonial decades, cattle and horses were often in short supply, because the climate, plants, and insects were more hostile to quadrupeds in Paraguay than farther south. In the capital, numerous artisans plied their trades, and in the interior, the Guarani villages of both Jesuit and civil provinces specialized in various crafts.

Until the last decades of the colony, very little money found its way to Paraguay, and barter was the normal means of exchange. Most Paraguayans even paid taxes in kind.

What money there was, chiefly to purchase imported European merchandise, at first came from the exports of yerba maté (*Ilex paraguayensis*), a tea that became popular as far away as Peru. This trade was modest until the last colonial decades, when it expanded rapidly. Specie also came to Paraguay from contraband trade in silver in the 1600s and in tobacco in the 1700s, which Paraguay's border location and crown monopolies encouraged. Jesuits cultivated yerba maté on their own plantations, and these leaves fetched the highest prices. Paraguayan merchants, however, continued to obtain the product from the wild, usually with paid mestizo labor.

In the late colonial years, the Paraguayan economy grew spectacularly, and the supply of money increased. Exports of yerba maté multiplied. Paraguayans also grew tobacco for the royal monopoly, and they exported cattle products, especially second-quality hides, and timber products. As river commerce increased, Asunción became an important regional center of shipbuilding.

Few European immigrants came to Paraguay until the late 1700s, when merchants of Spanish birth began to direct local affairs. Independence in Paraguay came about after citizens in Buenos Aires deposed the viceroy in 1810 and tried to extend their control to Paraguay, where the spirit of localism was strong. Most Paraguayans resented the pretensions of the port city and prepared to resist Argentine demands by force. At Paraguarí on 15 January 1811, Paraguayans routed the *porteño* army of Manuel Belgrano. On 14 and 15 May 1811, led by Dr. José Gaspar Rodríguez de Francia, Captain Pedro Juan Caballero, and others, Paraguayans overthrew Bernardo de Velasco, the last Spanish governor. They declared independence on 12 October 1813.

See also **Asunción; Comunero Revolt (Paraguay, 1730-1735); Guarani Indians; Mendoza, Pedro de.**

BIBLIOGRAPHY

Martin Dobrizhoffer, *An Account of the Abipones: An Equestrian People of Paraguay,* 3 vols., translated by Sara Coleridge (1822; repr. in 1 vol. 1970).

Alfred Métraux, "The Guarani," in *Handbook of South American Indians,* vol. 3, edited by Julian H. Steward (1948).

Harris Gaylord Warren, *Paraguay: An Informal History* (1949).

Elman R. Service, "The *Encomienda* in Paraguay," in *Hispanic American Historical Review* 31, no. 2 (1951): 230–252.

Elman R. Service, *Spanish-Guarani Relations in Early Colonial Paraguay* (1954; repr. 1971).

Philip Raine, *Paraguay* (1956).

Carlos Zubizarreta, *Historia de mi ciudad* (1964).

José L. Mora Mérida, *Historia social del Paraguay, 1600–1650* (1973).

Philip Caraman, *The Lost Paradise: The Jesuit Republic in South America* (1976).

Adalberto López, *The Revolt of the Comuneros, 1721–1735: A Study in the Colonial History of Paraguay* (1976).

Branislava Susnik, *Los aborigenes del Paraguay,* 7 vols. (1978–1987).

James Schofield Saeger, "Survival and Abolition: The Eighteenth-Century Paraguayan *Encomienda*," in *The Americas: A Quarterly Review of Inter-American Cultural History* 38, no. 1 (1981): 59–85.

Jerry W. Cooney, *Economía y sociedad en la intendencia del Paraguay* (1990).

Thomas Whigham, *The Politics of River Trade: Tradition and Development in the Upper Plata, 1780–1877* (1991).

Additional Bibliography

Acevedo, Edberto Oscar. *La Intendencia del Paraguay en el Virreinato del Río de la Plata*. Buenos Aires: Ediciones Ciudad Argentina, 1996.

Boccia Romañach, Alfredo. *Esclavitud en el Paraguay: Vida cotidiana del esclavo en las Indias Meridionales*. Asunción, Paraguay: Centro UNESCO Asunción: Servilibro, 2004.

Ganson, Barbara Anne. *The Guaraní under Spanish Rule in the Río de la Plata*. Stanford, CA: Stanford University Press, 2003.

Quevedo, Roberto, Margarita Durán Estragó, and Alberto Duarte, eds. *Actas capitulares y documentos del Cabildo de Asunción del Paraguay, Siglo XVI*. Asunción, Paraguay: Municipalidad de la Ciudad de Asunción, 2001.

Rivarola Paoli, Juan Bautista. *La Real Hacienda: La fiscalidad colonial, siglos XVI al XIX*. Asunción, Paraguay: Ediciones y Arte, 2005.

Techo, Nicolás del. *Historia de la provincia del Paraguay de la compañía de Jesús*. Translated from Latin into Spanish by Manuel Serrano y Sanz. Asunción, Paraguay: Centro de Estudos Paraguayas Antonio Guasch: FONDEC, 2005.

JAMES SCHOFIELD SAEGER

THE NINETEENTH CENTURY

The history of Paraguay in the nineteenth century can be divided into three periods: 1800–1811, the end of Spanish administration; 1812–1870, the era of independence and dictators; and 1871–1904, the creation of a postwar political and economic system.

SPANISH RULE: 1800–1811

Paraguay was a frontier province in the Spanish Viceroyalty of the Río De La Plata. It had a small Spanish bureaucracy, including a governor, General Bernardo de Velasco y Huidobro, a lieutenant governor, a postmaster, and officials from the royal tobacco monopoly and the treasury. Military officers and judges, usually Paraguayans, were delegated the military-political power to administer local districts. Paraguay's economic expansion between 1770 and 1811 laid the basis for nineteenth-century developments. With the establishment of the Royal Monopoly of Tobacco in 1778, Paraguay in theory produced the crop for the entire viceroyalty. During the era Paraguay annually exported to Buenos Aires over 1 million pounds of tobacco, 40,000 bales of yerba, and significant quantities of timber, sugar, molasses, and rum. It had a favorable trade balance in the eighteenth and nineteenth centuries. Although the nation's foreign trade expanded in this period, most Paraguayans were self-sufficient farmers who cultivated their own land or rented land for that purpose. Indian communities also engaged in agriculture. African and Indian slaves were rare, except as domestics in Asunción or laborers on church lands. Although the market exchange system expanded, barter was widespread. Farmers paid their taxes in yerba or tobacco, and merchants accepted produce for goods. The small Paraguayan mercantile class had difficulty competing with the merchants of Buenos Aires, who offered more credit and dominated the society and economy of Asunción until 1820.

INDEPENDENCE AND DICTATORS: 1812–1870

Paraguay's economic growth under Spanish rule took second place to politics as the colonies shook off imperial authority on 14–15 May 1811. Although Paraguay's Creole population initially supported continued Spanish control, actions by Governor Bernardo de Velasco and Buenos Aires to undermine Paraguayan autonomy encouraged the declaring of independence. After Buenos Aires deposed the Spanish viceroy on 25 May 1810 in the name of Spain's Ferdinand VII, it sought to extend its influence over the entire viceroyalty. Buenos Aires sent troops under General Manuel Belgrano to force Paraguayan compliance. Paraguayan victory and the recognition that Peninsular rule was ending led Velasco to request help from Portuguese Brazil. Once the foreign threats had united the Asunción *cabildo*, Captains Pedro Juan Caballero and Fulgencio Yegros ended Spanish authority.

José Gaspar de Rodríguez de Francia (1814–1840).
After independence, Yegros established a junta, one of whose members, the erratic José Gaspar de Rodríguez de Francia, became the leading Paraguayan nationalist. Having won the confidence of the military, the creole elite, and the general

population, Francia wrote the constitution of Paraguay, which was accepted by a congress in October 1813. Elected perpetual dictator by the Popular Congress in 1816, Francia, known as "El Supremo," became the most powerful and popular politician in Paraguay for the next twenty-four years. The populist government he created benefited the average Paraguayan while decreasing the power of the creoles and *peninsulares* through the control or destruction of elites associated with the Roman Catholic Church, the bureaucracy, the mercantile houses, and the landed estates.

To limit the costs of government, Francia maintained only a small bureaucracy under his direct supervision in Asunción. He divided the nation into twenty regional departments governed by judges or military-political commanders and divided these departments into subdistricts administered by a military commander, tax collector, and judge. Although he abolished the town councils of Asunción and Villa Rica, he allowed smaller towns to elect their officials. Subdelegates administered border regions while three types of judges—ordinary citizens without legal training, individuals with some legal training, and trained judges—enforced order.

Under Francia the government structure was a modification of colonial practices in that it continued the Spanish regional divisions, legal codes, judicial authority, and use of subdelegates. Francia's economic policies included greater utilization of state lands and enterprises, expansion of both external and internal trade, improvements in communication and transportation, and reductions in taxes. Despite trade in the north between Paraguay and Brazil, Francia sought to seal the northern border to prevent raids by the M'bayá Indians. In foreign policy Francia sought autonomy and international recognition. At his death in 1840, Paraguay possessed an independent national economy and a unified political system. Even though the country's military officers and civilians maneuvered for power after his death, the peaceful transfer of authority testified to the strength of Francia's administration.

Carlos Antonio López (1844–1862).

The ineffectual rule of a transitory junta and consulate under Marino Roque Alonso and Carlos Antonio López from 1841 to 1844 provided political opportunities for López. After he drafted a new constitution, delegates to the national assembly elected him president

on 13 March 1844. The Constitution of 1844 established three branches of government: executive, legislative, and judicial. The bicameral legislature consisted of an elected Chamber of Deputies and a Council of State appointed by the president. The new constitution established a powerful president with a ten-year term and the right to promulgate legislation and convene Congress every fifth year to approve it. The constitution codified Francia's system and legitimized López's power. The twenty regional departments of the country remained, but the number of districts in the interior was increased to accommodate population growth. In 1845 there were eighty-five districts, each with a population between 233,000 and 262,000; twenty years later there were ninety-five districts, with populations between 318,000 and 370,000.

López continued Francia's foreign policy, but in domestic affairs he increased funding for education to promote economic development and encouraged foreign trade. After Juan Manuel de Rosas was expelled from Argentina in 1852, the Argentine Confederation recognized Paraguay's independence, upon which Paraguay signed commercial treaties with Great Britain, France, the United States, and Brazil. Having thus obtained international recognition, López increased his efforts to modernize Paraguay's economy. The government bureaucracy grew and taxes increased, but the budget was balanced. The government used additional revenue to strengthen the army, develop a navy to control the rivers, and improve transportation and communication. López ordered a geological survey of the country, established modern medical services, developed industry, promoted technology, and encouraged cultural endeavors. Although his vision for Paraguay was less egalitarian and more self-serving than Francia's, López accepted the Guaraní peasantry as the basis of the Paraguayan economy and society. When López died on 10 September 1862, he left Paraguay a wealthier, more productive country.

Francisco Solano López (1862–1870).

During his administration, Carlos Antonio López worked to ensure the succession of his son, Francisco Solano López, and gave him administrative responsibilities and experience. At the elder López's death, on 16 October 1862, a congress of one hundred members elected his son president of Paraguay for a ten-year term. He was well accepted by the peasantry, who believed their country to be happy, powerful, and well administered. That General López kept the constitution his father had adopted indicated the continuation of economic and administrative policies.

Until 1864 Paraguayan society remained prosperous, suffering little violence or crime. Asunción became socially more vibrant, with regular theater performances and fashionable events. López's encouragement of foreign trade and government loans to Paraguayans for commercial enterprises appealed to the elite, but he also continued to provide benefits to the lower class. He employed more foreign doctors, engineers, teachers, and skilled workers, and he centralized education and economic development. López largely consolidated and reinterpreted the accomplishments of his two predecessors. The orderly government and successful economic development of Paraguay ended violently with the War of the Triple Alliance (1864–1870), which cost the nation lives, territory, and income. The death of General López on 1 March 1870 at Cerro Corá ended the war as well as the age in which Paraguay had shaped its own political and economic destiny.

SOCIAL STRUCTURE

Paraguay's nineteenth-century society was distinct from that of other Latin American nations in that a rural life-style and Guaraní customs and language permeated the nation. Although a small elite copied European styles and spoke Spanish, most men sported the traditional dress of white cotton trousers, embroidered shirt, straw hat, and woolen poncho. The women wore embroidered cotton chemises with muslin skirts and starched petticoats, spoke to their children in Guaraní, and worked in agriculture and industry to alleviate labor shortages. During the war, women provided most of the agricultural labor. Homes, simply furnished, were of adobe with thatched palm roofs. Access to cheap land, public education, and government services assured the rural population of prosperity in a society governed by national regulations. For instance, licenses were required to travel or to hold large parties, and from the age of seventeen to sixty, males were liable for military conscription. The government controlled the Roman Catholic Church by paying clerical salaries, financing church construction, and tolerating religious freedom. The

family rather than religion defined the society's values and served as the basic socioeconomic unit.

African slaves, who made up less than 4 percent of the population in 1846, and unacculturated Indians, lived on the fringe of government influence. At independence the nation assumed responsibility for the Jesuit and Franciscan missions, and in 1842 the National Congress ended the autonomy of the fifteen thousand Indians living in twenty-one missions. Land was divided among those who cooperated. On 7 October 1848 a government decree recognized the indigenous populations of the missions as citizens and transferred much of their land and cattle to the state and to the López family. José Francia and Carlos Antonio López gradually pacified the unacculturated populations and encouraged their participation in national life though barter, trade in salt, marriage, and military service. Paraguayan women outnumbered men because of the assimilation of Indian women into Spanish society through marriage or paid labor. Africans integrated into Paraguayan society through gradual manumission.

THE POSTWAR YEARS: 1871–1904

The duration and demands of the War of the Triple Alliance and the allied military occupation dismantled Paraguay's economy and political system. The reorientation of Paraguay began on 15 August 1869, when the allied powers established a provisional government in Asunción and required Paraguay to create a government that mirrored their own. With some differences, the Paraguayan Constitution of 1870 was modeled on the Argentine Constitution of 1853. The last Brazilian troops evacuated Paraguay in June 1876, but Argentina continued to administer Villa Occidental until 13 November 1878, when U.S. President Rutherford B. Hayes arbitrated a settlement which recognized the area as Paraguayan.

The Colorado and Liberal political parties, formally established in 1887, originated in the struggle for power during the allied occupation. The Liberals, supported by Argentina, initially represented groups of exiles in Buenos Aires that reviled Francisco Solano López and thought that free enterprise, free trade, and free elections would solve Paraguay's problems. Brazil supported the Colorados, nationalists who defended General López. The Colorados dominated Paraguayan politics from 1878 to 1904, when they were ousted by Benigno Ferreira, a Paraguayan general, who invaded from Argentina and established the Liberals in power. Neither party was experienced in democracy, and politics was dominated by factionalism and cronyism.

Despite the Colorados' defense of Francia and the two Lópezes, they did not re-create the old structures. The new Paraguayan state sold and rented state lands to wealthy domestic and foreign entrepreneurs to support basic services and pay debts. Paraguayan industry did not revive until after the 1880s, when it expanded slowly with an influx of foreign capital. Brazilians and Argentines increased their role in the economy by purchasing land and financing exports. Although large foreign private holdings increased, small farms continued to produce food crops such as manioc and maize for local consumption. Tobacco, a cash crop, remained the staple of Paraguayan agriculture.

As in prewar years, much of the country's internal commerce was small business. Argentina was Paraguay's major trading partner, consuming and serving as a middle man for yerba maté, tobacco, hides, cigars, bark for tannin, and hardwoods. By 1887 Great Britain accounted for almost 50 percent of Paraguay's imports. River transport moved most people and goods, while the government extended and operated the railroad and relaid the telegraph lines. The heavy costs of the War of the Triple Alliance and postwar debt payments to Argentina and Brazil slowed the creation of a new monetary and banking system.

The Paraguayan population in the years immediately after the war was economically, culturally, and racially homogeneous. Although between 8 and 18 percent of the population died as a result of the war, Paraguay had a population of 500,000 by the turn of the century. The Guaraní influence continued to dominate in language and folkways. The increasing integration of the Indian populations, the decline of the black population during the war, and the ending of slavery contributed to the homogeneity of the population. As early as 1870 the government reopened the primary public schools and made attendance compulsory. The government had only limited success in encouraging immigration to replace its population losses and promote economic modernization.

See also **Francia, José Gaspar Rodríguez de; López, Carlos Antonio; Paraguay, Political Parties: Colorado Party; Paraguay, Political Parties: Liberal Party; Río de la Plata, Viceroyalty of; War of the Triple Alliance; Women in Paraguay.**

BIBLIOGRAPHY

Printed by the U.S. Government and prepared by the Federal Research Division of the Library of Congress, *Paraguay, a Country Study* (1990) focuses on the twentieth century. Philip Raine, *Paraguay* (1956), although dated, remains the most complete history in English. John Hoyt Williams, *The Rise and Fall of the Paraguayan Republic, 1800–1870* (1979), should be consulted for the nineteenth century, as should Harris Gaylord Warren, *Paraguay and the Triple Alliance: The Postwar Decade, 1869–1978* (1978) and *Rebirth of the Paraguayan Republic: The First Colorado Era, 1878–1904* (1985). Josefina Pla, *The British in Paraguay, 1850–1870* (1976), has also written a variety of other articles and monographs on social history.

The next generation of historians of Paraguay concentrated on articles. Jerry W. Cooney, "Forest Industries and Trade in Late Colonial Paraguay," in *Journal of Forest History* (October 1979): 186–197, researches eighteenth-century economic history. James S. Saeger, "Survival and Abolition: The Eighteenth Century Paraguayan Encomienda," in *The Americas* 38, no. 1 (July 1981): 59–86, writes on indigenous populations of the colonial era. Thomas Lyle Whigham, "The Iron Works of Ybycui: Paraguayan Industrial Development in the Mid-Nineteenth Century," in *The Americas,* 35, no. 2 (October 1978): 201–218, has focused on nineteenth-century economic history. Barbara J. Ganson, "Following Their Children into Battle: Women at War in Paraguay, 1864–1870," in *The Americas* 46, no. 3 (January 1990): 335–371, researches both indigenous populations and women.

Also examine Félix De Azara, *Descripción e historia del Paraguay y del Río de la Plata* (repr. 1896), the result of an official trip in 1785 that deals with the society and economy of colonial Paraguay. Efraim Cardozo, *Paraguay Independiente* (repr. 1987), based on archival research, deals with Paraguayan political history. Atilio García Mellid, *Proceso a los falsificadores de la historia del Paraguay* (1964), is a revisionist approach arising from multi-archival research. Carlos Pastore's *La Lucha por la tierra en el Paraguay* (1972), is a major study on land usage, concentrating on the years from 1870 to 1970.

Additional Bibliography

Cooney, Jerry W., and Thomas L. Whigham., eds. *El Paraguay bajo los López: Algunos ensayos de historia social y política.* Asuncíon, Paraguay: Centro Paraguayo de Estudios Sociológicos, 1994.

Kraay, Hendrik, and Thomas Whigham, eds. *I Die with My Country: Perspectives on the Paraguayan War, 1864–1870.* Lincoln: University of Nebraska Press, 2004.

Leuchars, Chris. *To the Bitter End: Paraguay and the War of the Triple Alliance.* Westport, CT: Greenwood Press, 2002.

Lewis, Paul H. *Political Parties and Generations in Paraguay's Liberal Era, 1869–1940.* Chapel Hill: University of North Carolina Press, 1993.

López-Alves, Fernando. *State Formation and Democracy in Latin America, 1810–1900.* Durham, NC: Duke University Press, 2000.

Maeder, Ernesto J. A. *Misiones del Paraguay: Conflictos y disolución de la sociedad guaraní (1768–1850).* Madrid, Spain: Editorial MAPFRE, 1992.

Ribeiro, Ana. *El Caudillo y el Dictador.* Montevideo, Uruguay: Editorial Planeta, 2003.

Rivarola, Milda. *Vagos, pobres y soldados: La domesticación estatal del trabajo en el Paraguay del siglo XIX.* Asunción, Paraguay: Centro Paraguayo de Estudios Sociológicos, 1994.

Whigham, Thomas. *The Paraguayan War.* Vol. 1. Lincoln: University of Nebraska Press, 2002.

VERA BLINN REBER

THE TWENTIETH CENTURY

The War of the Triple Alliance (1864–1870) still cast a shadow over Paraguay at the beginning of the twentieth century. Though the war had ended thirty years before, the memories of bloody fighting, defeat, military occupation, and subsequent disorder haunted the country's political life. The economy, for its part, had recovered somewhat in the 1880s and 1890s, thanks to the export of yerba maté, tannin, and quebracho wood. European immigration, mostly Italian, Spanish and German, had changed the demographic makeup of the country during these decades, though by no means to the same degree as in neighboring Argentina and Brazil; Paraguay was still a largely mestizo (mixed Guaraní and Spanish) nation. In all, Paraguay remained a poor country with few clear options for the future.

LIBERAL RULE

National politics at the beginning of the century focused on the competition between the Colorado and Liberal Parties. These two organizations, both recently created, shared certain perspectives. Both favored a small state apparatus and a broadly laissez-faire approach to the economy. Both favored a strong diplomatic defense of Paraguayan claims over the disputed Chaco territory. Strong personal and family jealousies, however, as well as differences in social origin, kept the parties at each other's throats. The Liberals, whose influence was felt most keenly in Asunción, had long sought to displace the rural-based Colorados as the dominant force in Paraguay, but internal divisions among the Liberals made this impossible until 1904, when an invasion force of Liberal exiles (aided by Argentine businessmen, the Argentine navy, and the merchant elite of Asunción) succeeded in seizing the reins of power.

Although the Liberals retained control of the government until 1940 (except for brief interludes), their rule was never particularly stable. From 1904 to 1936, for instance, there were twenty-four different presidential administrations as well as dozens of factional revolts within the ruling party. The Colorados, however, were unable to take much advantage of the situation. Instead, they watched while Liberal bosses, such as magnate Eduardo Schaerer (1873–1941), evolved a system that was sympathetic to Paraguayan and foreign business interests, if not especially dedicated to democratic practices. The system brought some economic advantages to Paraguay during World War I, when outside demand for the country's exports was high, but this situation could not last.

The 1920s witnessed growing disillusionment with the Liberal program on the part of students, workers, and intellectuals. The latter group, composed of poets, musicians, historians, and radical polemicists such as Juan Stefanich (1889–1976) and Juan Emiliano O'Leary (1879–1969), had begun to formulate a new interpretation of Paraguayan culture, one that stressed nationalist goals. Specifically, they wanted to reconstruct the image of Francisco Solano López (1826–1870), the defeated leader of Paraguay during the War of the Triple Alliance, as a positive one. No longer satisfied with the vilification of Solano López imposed by the occupiers, Brazil and Argentina, Stefanich and O'Leary worked to rewrite the Paraguayan past. This brought them into regular conflict with the Liberal government.

The peasants, for their part, remained unorganized and outside national politics per se. To be sure, however, they were still the chief victims of the various civil and factional conflicts. In any case, the vagaries of the domestic picture were soon overshadowed by events in the Gran Chaco region.

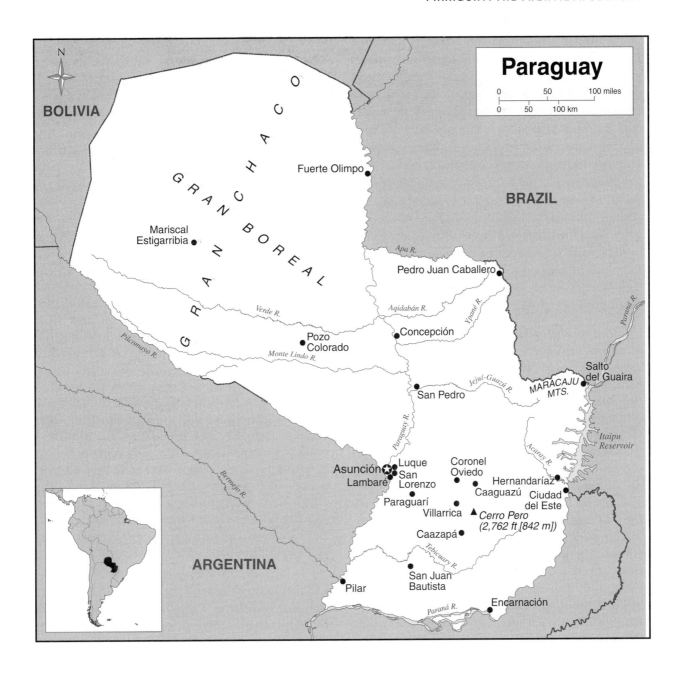

THE CHACO WAR

Ownership of the remote Chaco territory had long been disputed by Paraguay, Bolivia, and Argentina. A vast, semiarid alluvial plain with a tiny population of sometimes fierce Indians, the Chaco had never been of much interest to Europeans during the colonial era. No one bothered to establish clear claim to the land until after the War of the Triple Alliance, when the Paraguayans, perhaps to salvage something in the face of their defeat, chose to challenge Argentine claims to territory north of the Pilcomayo River. An 1878 arbitral award by U.S. president Rutherford B. Hayes upheld the Paraguayan position. The

Argentines stepped back, but this did not end the matter, for the Bolivians, smarting from a military defeat at the hands of Chile in the War of the Pacific (1879–1883), soon began to advance their own claims. Diplomats for both the Bolivians and Paraguayans pored over maps from the Spanish colonial period, attempting to demonstrate where boundaries previously had been drawn. Throughout the 1920s the Paraguayan government attempted to assert control over the region by inviting Canadian and Russian Mennonite immigrants to settle in the region. The first group of Mennonite settlers arrived in the central Chaco in 1926. Throughout the 1930s and

1940s small groups of Mennonite settlers continued to establish new homes in the Chaco. The Paraguayan state also permitted Catholic and Protestant missionaries to establish missions in the region in an attempt to incorporate the inhabitance of the region into the Paraguayan nation-state. The Bolivians were anxious to possess a river route that would give them access to the South Atlantic, particularly because they lost their outlet to the sea to Chile in the War of the Pacific. During the late 1800s they pressed their position only at the negotiating table, but as the new century dawned with no diplomatic resolution in sight, both sides began to establish small forts in the disputed zones. By 1927 about fifty forts faced each other in the Chaco, setting the stage for military confrontation.

Two years after the arrival of the first Mennonite settlers in the Chaco, in December 1928 a bloody incident occurred when Paraguayan major Rafael Franco (1896–1973) led his unit against a fortified Bolivian outpost at Vanguardia, north of Bahía Negra. Franco had hoped to force the reluctant President José Patricio Guggiari (1884–1957) into a general mobilization. In this he was successful, though not quite in the way he had imagined. Fort Vanguardia fell, and Franco took many Bolivians prisoner. The general war that he had hoped to inaugurate failed to materialize, however, when it was discovered that supplies of arms and munitions were woefully limited. The Bolivians, in a similar state of unreadiness, agreed to open negotiations in Washington, D.C., in 1929. Unfortunately for the Paraguayans in 1931, the arbitrators in Washington decided that the Paraguay was the aggressor state and ordered the Paraguayans to rebuild Fort Vanguardia.

The Paraguayan public, however, was in a war-like mood. Major Franco's action had caught the imagination of many in Asunción, and was soon capitalized by those who wished to end Liberal rule. Bolivian encroachments in the Chaco continued unabated, as did the growing anger in the streets of the Paraguayan capital. Following Bolivian raids on Fort Samaklay in September 1931, university students organized strong anti-Guggiari protests. These culminated in a mass demonstration at the presidential palace in October in which troops fired on the students, killing eleven. Major Franco, the Colorados, some trade unionists, and various radicals tried to use this incident to unseat the president, and under threat of impeachment, Guggiari temporarily stepped down. In the process, the Liberal Party was severely weakened, though it did barely manage to retain power.

Both Paraguay and Bolivia had used the uneasy peace to fully arm themselves and to position their forces for combat. A key objective of both sides was control of Lake Pitiantuta, the only permanent source of fresh water in the central Chaco. In June 1932 the Bolivians attacked and occupied Fort Carlos Antonio López at the eastern approach to the lake, thus signaling the beginning of the formal outbreak of the Chaco War.

On paper, the Bolivians had most of the advantages. Their army was larger, somewhat better trained, and far better equipped. The Paraguayans, however, were closer to their homes and more accustomed to the extreme heat of the region. Moreover, they invariably displayed a degree of social cohesion that the men from the Altiplano, with their sharp class and ethnic divisions between officers and men, found quite astonishing. Paraguayan soldiers were able to use their ethnic unity to their advantage. The language of the battlefield quickly became Guaraní, the language spoken in Paraguay prior to Spanish colonization. Colorado writers such as Juan Natalicio González (1897–1966) help to perpetuate a growing sense of the superiority of the *raza Guaraní* (the Guaraní race) and language. His nationalist writings were widely published during and after the Chaco War.

In July 1932 the Bolivians mounted an offensive that in quick order netted them three key forts near the Pilcomayo. The terrain in the Chaco was too difficult to permit an easy advance, however, and the Bolivian movement soon stalled.

In Asunción, Guggiari was replaced by another Liberal, Eusebio Ayala (1875–1942), who emerged as an excellent war leader with good contacts in the armed forces. Ayala organized the home front, gaining the support of all major political groups in Paraguay and gearing the country's economy for war. In the field he turned over command to several experienced officers, the most outstanding of whom was José Félix Estigarribia (1888–1940).

Over the next three years, Estigarribia and his associates transformed the Paraguayan army into a formidable force. In September 1932 the Paraguayans retook Fort Boquerón, then abandoned it in order to reinforce a line of trenchworks around

Paraguay

Population:	6,669,086 (2007 est.)
Area:	157,047 sq mi
Official language(s):	Spanish, Guarani
Language(s):	Spanish, Guarani
National currency:	guarani (PYG)
Principal religions:	Roman Catholic, 89.6%; Protestant and other Christian, 7.3%; other or unspecified, 1.9%; none, 1.1% (2002 census)
Ethnicity:	mestizo (mixed Spanish and Amerindian), 95%; other, 5%
Capital:	Asunción (pop. 1,639,000; 2005 est.)
Other urban centers:	Ciudad del Este, Pedro Juan Encarnación, Caballero, Concepción, Pilar
Annual rainfall:	Rainfall averages about 60 in a year along the eastern frontier with Brazil, gradually diminishing toward the west to an average of 50 in along the Paraguay River and 30 in the Chaco. Asunción has an annual average of about 50 in, which is moderate for its latitude.
Principal geographic features:	*Rivers:* Paraguay River, Pilcomayo River, Paraná River (or Upper [Alto] Paraná), Bermejo River *Other:* Paraná Plateau, Guairá Falls, the Gran Chaco, a vast alluvial plain
Economy:	*GDP per capita:* $4,800 (2006 est.)
Principal products and exports:	*Agriculture:* cotton, sugarcane, soybeans, corn, wheat, tobacco, cassava (tapioca), fruits, vegetables, beef, pork, eggs, milk, timber *Industries:* sugar, cement, textiles, beverages, wood products, steel, metallurgic, electric power
Government:	Paraguay is a republic, with considerable powers conferred on the executive branch. The president is directly elected for a five-year term. There is a bicameral legislature, consisting of the 45-member Senate and the 80-member Chamber of Deputies. Representatives must be at least 25 years of age and are elected for five-year terms. Voting is by secret ballot and is compulsory for all citizens ages 18–60.
Armed forces:	One year of military service is compulsory for all males 18 years of age. There were 10,300 active personnel and 164,500 reservists in 2005. *Army:* 7,600 *Navy:* 1,400 (including 900 Marines and 100 naval aviation personnel) *Air Force:* 1,100 active personnel. The country's paramilitary force consists of the 14,800 member Special Police Service.
Transportation:	Approx. 1,925 mi of domestic waterways provide the chief means of transportation. In 2001, highways totaled an estimated 18,580 mi, only 1,906 mi were paved. As of 2004 there were some 274 mi of standard-gauge rail lines, excluding narrow gauge industrial lines in the Chaco. In 2004, there were an estimated 87 airports and airfields, only 12 of which had paved runways as of 2005. Paraguayan Air Lines (Líneas Aéreas Paraguayas [LAP]) provides both domestic and international service.
Media:	Radio Nacional del Paraguay is the primary state-owned radio station. Other stations for radio and television are privately owned. Newspaper readership in Paraguay is among the lowest in Latin America. There were three major daily papers in circulation in 2004: *Ultima Hora,* 40,000; *Noticias,* 50,000, and *ABC Color,* 35,000 (down from 75,000 in 2002).
Literacy and education:	*Total literacy rate:* 94% Elementary education is compulsory and free for 9 years. In 2001, about 51% of age-eligible students were enrolled in secondary schools. There are at least 12 universities in Paraguay, including the National University of Paraguay and Nuestra Señora de la Asunción Catholic University.

strategically placed Fort Gondra. The Bolivians laid siege to this position for over nine months in 1933. In the meantime, Estigarribia erected yet another trench system, linking Gondra to Nanawa, Arce, Herrera, and Toledo. The Bolivians failed to penetrate these positions despite mounting tremendous frontal attacks on all points.

Estigarribia's troops proved just as successful on the offensive as they had on the defensive. In December 1933, having advanced into the central Chaco, they handily defeated the Bolivians at the battle of Campo Vía. A short-lived truce allowed the Bolivians to regroup under General Enrique Peñaranda (1892–1969), but at the end of January 1934 the Paraguayan advance began again. Despite some reversals (notably a Bolivian victory at Cañada Strongest in May), Estigarribia managed over the next year to reach the foothills of the Andes, and even threatened to capture the oil fields just beyond the Parapití River. In early June 1935 a final Paraguayan victory at Ingavi brought the Bolivians to the negotiating table. A cease-fire was arranged immediately thereafter, followed by a general peace conference that was convened in Buenos Aires from 1935 to 1938. In the end, Paraguay received the lion's share of the disputed territory, though the Bolivians did retain their petroleum lands as well as a tiny outlet high on the Paraguay River.

THE LIBERALS' DECLINE

The factors that facilitated military victory in the Chaco did not assure domestic peace after the war. Although Ayala was personally popular, his old Liberal order—so full of praise for democracy, yet so far removed from the lives of the poor—could no longer really work. Men who had fought in the trenchworks had little sympathy for maintaining an oligarchy. They clamored instead for change, for a national regeneration as comprehensive as possible. Rafael Franco, now a colonel and a war hero, saw this clearly, and as he had done in 1928, set out to galvanize the Paraguayan public.

In February 1936 disaffected military officers associated with Franco overthrew the Ayala regime. They began to forge a revolutionary path for the country that went far beyond the modest programs of earlier Golpistas. To this end, they developed a radical doctrine, Febrerismo, which drew inspiration from an odd combination of European ideologies—Italian fascism, German nazism, Spanish corporatism, and Soviet communism. Representative democracy they rejected as an imperialist sham. Febreristas sought the support of various sectors in Paraguayan society, most notably veterans, through the 100,000-member Asociación Nacional de Ex-Combatientes (Chaco War Veterans Association). The Feberistas also embarked on a crusade to immortalize Solano López. Determined to place their hero into a more respected place in history, they exhumed his body from its resting place in Cerro Corá and placed it in a chapel that had recently been rechristened as the "Pantheon of Heroes" in downtown Asunción.

The practical matter of running the Paraguayan government proved a daunting task for Franco and the Febreristas. Because their experience at administration was nil, they found themselves necessarily cooperating with elements of the old regime. Still more often, they resorted to indiscriminate repression, sending thousands to jail or into exile and censoring every publication, large and small. At the same time, the Febreristas failed to make good on their promised reforms. They did introduce some significant labor legislation and made some minor forays into agrarian reform, but in the end, they were not in power long enough to pursue their innovations. On August 13, 1937, a military coup toppled Franco, and shortly thereafter the Liberals were restored to power.

The Liberals, however, had no way to turn back the clock. Despite their expulsion of Franco, they could not ignore the strong nationalist sentiment that his movement had inaugurated in Paraguay. The Liberal Party now ruled only in tandem with nationalist army officers, who made it clear that they could overthrow the government any time they wanted. For the Liberals, the only solution was to find a strong, influential army leader who was also one of their own. Estigarribia, who was then minister to Washington, D.C., seemed the logical choice. In 1939 he was elected to the presidency without opposition (as the Colorados abstained from voting) and in absentia.

The new president had a strong mandate for change. The heavy human and material cost of the war, as well as the burden imposed by the Great Depression, had combined to create a generation deeply desirous of radical reform. The Febrerista interregnum served as a clarion call. Now the young people of Paraguay—the veterans, some of the radical student and trade-union groups, and the intellectuals—pinned their hopes on Estigarribia the war hero. He, in turn, used their support to bypass his Liberal sponsors and create an authoritarian state.

The instrument for this change was the Constitution of 1940. Although the drafting of this document was entrusted to Cecilio Báez (1862–1941), a conservative, in fact it turned out to be thoroughly corporatist in character. It featured a unicameral legislature, a nonelected council of state, and wide powers for the executive. Armed with these powers, which resembled those granted to Getúlio Vargas in Brazil under the Estado Novo, Estigarribia began to neuter his own political party. He was well on his way to achieving this goal when he died in an airplane crash on September 5, 1940.

THE MORÍNIGO REGIME

The mantle of dictatorship was immediately picked up by War Minister Higínio Morínigo (1897–1985). A relative unknown before the late 1930s, Morínigo transformed the corporatist state of Estigarribia into a personal dictatorship. He crushed an attempted Febrerista revolt in April 1941. A year later he outlawed the Liberal Party.

Ironically, at the same time that he was quashing all opposition at home, he was the object of much coddling abroad. World War II brought to South America a keen competition between those who favored the

Allied cause and those who favored the Axis. The Nazi sympathies of many Paraguayans were already well established. The Americans, for their part, strongly wanted the country support the Allies. The United States poured aid into Paraguay in amounts undreamt of, and tried to woo Morínigo with promises of more to come. In June 1943 he became the first Paraguayan president to visit the United States (where he received an honorary doctorate from Fordham University).

At home, in 1943 Morínigo established a five-year plan for the development of Paraguay. The plan emphasized the construction of roads, the building of electrical and communications networks, and the expansion of clean water facilities. In pursuing these projects, Morínigo frequently used military personnel.

The Allied victory in Europe in 1945 signaled the time for change in Paraguay. For some time Morínigo had been negotiating behind the scenes with various political actors, particularly far–right-wing military officers and representatives of the Colorado Party. Now, under pressure from the United States, he opened the political system widely, legalizing the Liberal, Febrerista, and even the Communist Parties.

CIVIL WAR AND THE BEGINNING OF COLORADO RULE

The sudden liberalization set the stage for civil war. In January 1947 a military putsch ended the blossoming Febrerista influence in the Morínigo government and handed over power exclusively to the right-wing Quionista faction of the Colorado Party. Morínigo retained the presidency, but real control in the government passed to the Quionista leader Juan Natalicio González. On March 7, 1947, Febrerista militants assaulted the central police barracks in Asunción. The following day, junior officers in the northern town of Concepción revolted against the pro-Colorado regime. They were soon joined by armed Febreristas, Communists, and some Liberals. Thousands of people died over the next five months. The Colorados created a peasant militia, the *pynandí* (barefoot ones), which fought a bloody campaign alongside the army. Many of these men were veterans of the Chaco War, when they had forged a strong sense of nationalism. Together they crushed the rebel army by mid-August; they then went on to wreak a terrible revenge on all their political opponents. This initiated Colorado hegemony in

Paraguayan politics, which still prevailed in the mid-1990s.

González replaced the by now powerless Morínigo in August 1948. The Quionista leader was a talented writer and intellectual, but his faction of the Colorados maintained its influence less through a free interchange of ideas than through sheer thuggery. The brutality of his followers antagonized many party members. Perhaps more important, González's nationalism prevented a stronger economic link with Juan Perón's Argentina—a tie that many Paraguayans wanted. In January 1949 González was driven from office by a civilian-military coalition.

In September 1949 the reins of government fell to yet another Colorado, Federico Chaves (1881–1978), the head of the Democrático faction. Apart from bringing a measure of internal peace after so much partisan infighting, the Chaves regime brought Paraguay much closer diplomatically and economically to Argentina. In August 1953 an agreement tantamount to a customs union was signed between the two countries. Though it was never ratified, all indications at the time were that Argentina and Paraguay were closer than they had ever previously been.

THE STROESSNER DICTATORSHIP

Then, in May 1954, another revolt broke out. Led by Colorado politician Epifanio Méndez Fleitas (1917–1985) and General Alfredo Stroessner (1912–2006), the uprising was launched in part to check the increasingly close relationship with Argentina. Then again, it was a typical military coup engineered by an ambitious though little-known officer who was in no way an ideologue. In July Stroessner was elected president. No one at the time could have guessed that this was the beginning of a thirty-four-year dictatorship.

It seemed unlikely that Stroessner would last any longer than his predecessors. An artillery officer from Encarnación who had served in the Chaco War, he had risen slowly through the ranks and had failed to distinguish himself in any clear way. His participation in the 1947 civil war, for instance, had been minimal.

As president, however, Stroessner showed a great aptitude for creating durable alliances among various power brokers, especially between sectors of the military and the Colorado Party. He was also rather lucky in the timing of his presidency. For many years he took advantage of U.S. cold war concerns by portraying himself as a staunch anti-communist and gaining American support in the process. Internally, his government witnessed the longest sustained period of economic growth that Paraguay had seen in a century. This, too, added to the legitimacy of his regime. Stroessner could now hold out to the average Paraguayan real hope for a more prosperous future, while promising his associates many opportunities for advancing their own lot through graft. For those Paraguayans he could not thus co-opt, Stroessner reserved brutally repressive measures.

Consolidating Power. This pattern started early. In October 1955 Stroessner engineered the reunification of the Colorado Party under terms very much to his liking, meaning the concomitant weakening of the Méndez Fleitas faction. One year later he sent his rival into permanent exile, thus ending all effective resistance to Stroessner within the ranks of his own party. He was now free to impose strong anti-inflationary measures that had been opposed by Méndez Fleitas and his "populist" faction. These measures benefited the agro-exporting sector of the country but weakened the small base of organized labor. In 1958 the unionists responded with a general strike, which Stroessner quickly crushed. Over the next three years, he expanded the emergency powers that devolved upon him to deal with protests by students and opposition congressmen, and eventually with guerrilla outbreaks led by pro-Castro insurgents. All these threats to his rule he systematically destroyed.

Foreign Relations. In international matters Stroessner sought early to gain the support of the U.S. government. In this regard, his anticommunist politics paid big dividends. Indeed, through the mid-1970s, the Americans provided Paraguay with economic aid of all kinds—from help with road construction to innovations in animal husbandry to the sending of Peace Corps volunteers. They also provided some military aid.

Stroessner's relations with Argentina were more complicated. Upon first coming to power, he welcomed Juan Perón's support (though not, to be sure, to the same degree that Chaves did).

When the Argentine dictator was ousted in 1955, Stroessner even granted him short-term asylum in Asunción. This friendly attitude toward Perón created a rift with Argentina's new rulers, who canceled several new trade agreements.

Brazil swiftly moved in to take over Argentina's traditional role as Paraguay's patron. In October 1956 Stroessner met with Brazilian president Juscelino Kubitschek at the tiny border town of Foz do Iguaçú, where the two leaders laid the foundation stone for an international bridge to be built over the Paraná River. When the Friendship Bridge was completed in 1965, it linked Paraguay via Brazilian road systems to the Atlantic port of Paranaguá, where Paraguay had enjoyed free-port privileges since 1956.

The Itaipú Hydroelectric Project. Infinitely more important than the Friendship Bridge in terms of economic consequences for Paraguay was the construction of the Itaipú Hydroelectric Project. This binational undertaking, first conceived in the late 1960s, promised to supply most of the electrical needs of southern Brazil's burgeoning industrial base. Since the beginning of the decade many Paraguayan scientists and writers had written articles in scientific journals about the great possibility of hydro power in Paraguay. These nationalist writings helped to drive the Paraguayan imagination about one of the country's great hidden resources. The large dam proposed for Itaipú promised to propel the Paraguayan economy into the modern age by giving employment and training to tens of thousands of poor peasants.

The scale of the Itaipú project was pharaonic. When completed in 1982, the dam was easily the largest in the world (and generated an amount of electricity six times that of Aswan in Egypt). Including its reservoir, the area covered by the project amounted to 540 square miles. New cities—one of which was christened "Puerto Presidente Stroessner"—were built along the frontier to house workers, with concerns over pollution and deforestation put aside. Incredible sums of money flowed into Asunción and into the pockets of everyone associated with the project as well as many who were not.

Itaipú confirmed the rising importance of an urban middle class in Paraguay. The influence of this group had been growing for some time. Highly literate, cosmopolitan, often well-connected, and sometimes chafing under the constraints of the dictatorship, members of the urban bourgeoisie would in time form alliances with those seeking to overthrow the regime. Ironically, then, the success of Stroessner's economic programs spurred the growth of groups that would later oppose him.

Stroessner himself rightly saw the Itaipú project as the pinnacle of his regime. During the 1960s and 1970s he had cemented support by giving his military subordinates a free hand in the smuggling of liquor, cigarettes, automobiles, and eventually drugs. Now, in having joined these military men to Itaipú bankers and financiers, he had created an unbeatable coalition. The message that he constantly reiterated—*Paz y progreso con Stroessner* (Peace and progress with Stroessner)—now seemed tangible to the Paraguayan population. Some people even subscribed to the growing cult of personality surrounding the dictator and decorated their homes with his image. Towns changed their names—Ciudad del Este became "Puerto Stroessner"—and his birthday was reason enough for a yearly pilgrimage to the presidential residence. Furthermore, Stroessner legitimized his regime by portraying himself as the rightful successor to Solano López. The opposition, such as it was, could only bide its time.

Repression and Corruption. In fact, the rosy picture that Stroessner painted was far from accurate. The elections that periodically confirmed his control of the presidential sash were in every way staged. (On only one occasion out of eight did he receive less than 83 percent of the official vote.) The omnipresent secret police, or *pyragüe* (silent-footed one), fostered a climate of terror—to the point where one commentator called Paraguay a "republic of fear." Not even churchmen felt safe. In the countryside, landless peasants increasingly clashed with army units and with armed guards maintained by *latifundistas* (estate owners).

Meanwhile, rather than creating healthy conditions for sustained growth, the Itaipú project actually expanded the degree of corruption in Paraguay. Bribes large and small became a factor in day-to-day life, and some of the most corrupt individuals rose to powerful positions in the government. The completion of Itaipú brought a sharp tapering off of available monies to this group,

which set the stage for a major political shift in the 1980s.

Overthrow of the Dictatorship. Stroessner's control of the Colorado Party had been unchallenged in the country from the late 1950s to the early 1980s. Now, with the old dictator showing some signs of senility, the party split into two factions. Both were nominally loyal to Stroessner. The *tradicionalistas*, who saw themselves as representing a line of Colorado thought dating from before 1954, announced their willingness to be flexible regarding Paraguay's future. In effect, this meant they were willing to consider a political opening. The *militantes* faction, which was composed of Stronista bureaucrats and some high-profile smugglers, argued that loyalty to the general should exceed loyalty to the party. They began to speak openly of Stroessner's son Gustavo as a possible successor to his father. This talk deeply disturbed some key army officers who thought Gustavo, a reported homosexual, a very poor choice for president.

In 1987 the *militantes* managed to seize all the key leadership positions within the party. Stroessner evidently supported this move, although the Paraguayan public regarded it as ominous. As antipathy toward the *militantes* grew, the need to oust Stroessner was recognized not just by the opposition and the *tradicionalistas*, but also by certain sectors of the army. The United States, which had become disenchanted with Stroessner during the Carter administration, also began to press for clear democratic change.

The final act began in January 1989, when the *militantes* attempted to engineer a major reshuffling of the armed forces so as to remove those individuals opposed to Gustavo Stroessner. Before these proposed changes could take effect, however, a coup d'état launched on the night of February 2, 1989, by General Andrés Rodríguez (1923–1997) succeeded in overthrowing Stroessner and the *militantes*.

DEMOCRATIC CHANGE
As commander of the First Cavalry Division, Rodríguez was perhaps the best-known officer in Paraguay aside from Stroessner himself. He had become infamous over the years by involving the army in large-scale smuggling activities (and had become immensely wealthy himself in the process).

It was widely rumored that he had recently turned to drug smuggling. He was also related by marriage to Stroessner. With such a record, almost everyone in Paraguay expected the worst from Rodríguez.

In fact, the new leader immediately initiated democratic reforms. He assumed office as interim president and allowed Stroessner and his son to go into comfortable exile in Brazil. Directly after their departure, Rodríguez repealed the state of siege, eliminated the antisubversive laws, permitted the opening of newspapers closed by the previous government, and began to release political prisoners. His popularity soared.

In May 1989 Rodríguez was elected president on the Colorado ticket. Despite some irregularities in the rural zones, all observers agreed that that he had won the election fairly, and Paraguayans tended to believe his promises to respect democratic norms. And, indeed, his four-year term was marked by increasing liberalization and reform in the political sphere. Many symbols of the old dictatorship were done away with, and on the surface at least, Rodríguez effected a thoroughgoing purge of Stronistas in the Colorado Party. Though they gained some seats in Congress, the Liberal and other opposition parties were unable to challenge the dominant position of the Colorados.

In the economic sphere, Rodríguez proved less committed to change. He inaugurated no programs, for instance, to deal with the problems of the rural poor. Though Rodríguez recognized more than 250 new trade unions, he never left any doubt that he sided with big business. (He was, after all, a businessman himself.) His essentially conservative stance was also reflected in his trade dealings with Brazil, Argentina, Taiwan, South Korea, the United States, and South Africa—dealings that perfectly paralleled the earlier policies of Stroessner.

In 1991 a constitutional convention met in Asunción to rewrite the basic law of the land. When the new constitution was ratified, Rodríguez announced his full support for it, despite the provisions limiting presidents to one five-year term that seemed to have been crafted with him in mind. Over the next year he also gave full support to the democratic process by refraining from interfering in the electioneering efforts of the candidates in the 1993 presidential election.

This did not mean, however, that no interference occurred, especially within the Colorado Party. Despite erratic behavior and some wildly reactionary comments to the press, former foreign minister Luis María Argaña (d. 1999) was nominated to be the Colorado candidate in December 1992. But the military, never far removed from the corridors of power in Paraguay, greatly mistrusted him, and in the end it forced the holding of a new party caucus, which resulted in the nomination of businessman Juan Carlos Wasmosy (b. 1938) as the presidential candidate of the Colorados.

Wasmosy was duly elected in May 1993 with about 40 percent of the vote in a three-way race. He was Paraguay's first civilian president in nearly fifty years. Although his administration initially was regarded with much public sympathy, in private most Paraguayans thought that his was destined to be a weak presidency.

As with Rodríguez before him, Wasmosy made a clear commitment to progressive reform. For instance, he firmly supported the country's entry into a regional free-trade market, Mercosur. Wasmosy could not, however, summon the same degree of influence that Rodríguez had with the armed forces. The army commander Lino Oviedo (b. 1943) was often mentioned as being the éminence grise behind the new government, and outside observers, though unwilling to place Paraguayan democracy in a frankly pessimistic light, nonetheless feared for its future.

Events in Paraguay took a dramatic turn when in April 1996 Oviedo disobeyed orders to step down as commander of the army. Through adept political maneuvering by Wasmosy, he was able to convince Oviedo to resign his command. Nonetheless, this was not the last of Oviedo, who then used his growing political popularity to form his own faction within the Colorado Party. In 1998 Oviedo became the Colorado candidate for president. Wasmosy, acting with presidential authority, placed Oviedo in jail for helping to orchestrate a 1996 failed coup. As a result, the electorate was forced to vote for Oviedo's personal ally, Raúl Cubas (b. 1943), who won the election. Cubas immediately released Oviedo from prison. Outraged over the freeing of Oviedo, the Paraguayan Congress accused Cubas of violating his power, and this split the Colorado Party into two factions: one headed by Cubas and the other by his vice president, Luís

María Argaña. When Argaña was assassinated in March 1998, Oviedo was accused of orchestrating the assassination, and went into exile in Argentina and later in Brazil, only to return in 2004 to seek the presidency in the 2008 election.

Cubas was forced to resign in 1999 because of accusations surrounding the Argaña assassination. The Senate leader Luis González Macchi (b. 1947) then assumed the presidency. Macchi's tenure as president of Paraguay was marked by social and economic instability, culminating in nation-wide peasant-led protests that demanded his resignation in July 2002. These violent protests resulted in two deaths, with hundreds injured or arrested. Macchi's presidency survived these protests until elections were held in 2003, when Nicanor Duarte Frutos (b. 1956), the Colorado candidate, became president. In his July 2003 inaugural address Duarte vowed to fight corruption and organized crime. In the early years of his administration Duarte was extremely popular, but his presidency suffered because of continued economic stagnation, and he was forced to replace various cabinet ministers because of charges of corruption. He also faced charges that he and his family benefitted monetarily from his position as president.

As Paraguay entered the twenty-first century, it was still a country plagued by its own history. It remains the Latin American nation with the most unequal land distributions and a nation haunted by a brutal political system. In 1992 the Archive of Terror in Asunción was established to help historians to better understand the legacies of the Stroessner regime, with its total disregard for human rights and its involvement in Operation Condor, a campaign of political repressions implemented in 1975 by the right-wing dictatorships of the Southern Cone. Although the economy has expanded considerably, it still depends on traditional exports. Duarte's challenges include stabilizing democracy while attempting to promote economic growth and stability. His attempt to amend the constitution to allow a second term in office, was greeted with great hostility by mass protests by 40,000 Paraguayans on March 29, 2006. Leading these protests was the Catholic bishop Fernando Lugo Méndez (b. 1949). His involvement with the anti-reelection campaign against Duarte Frutos launched the former priest into the political spotlight, and he expressed interest in running for president in 2008. This has resulted in Lugo's removal from his clerical position by the church hierarchy. Lugo is the frontrunner in the 2008 elections, which may end the sixty-one-year rule of the Colorado Party in Paraguay if he can face down an intense challenge from the most likely Colorado candidate, the current vice president Luis Alberto Castiglioni Soria (b. 1962).

See also **Ayala, Eusebio; Chaco War; Estigarribia, José Félix; Guggiari, José Patricio; Itaipú Hydroelectric Project; Mestizo; Morínigo, Higínio; Paraguay, Political Parties: Colorado Party; Paraguay, Political Parties: Liberal Party; Rodríguez, Andrés; Stroessner, Alfredo; War of the Triple Alliance.**

BIBLIOGRAPHY

Grow, Michael. *The Good Neighbor Policy and Authoritarianism in Paraguay.* Lawrence: Regents Press of Kansas, 1981.

Lewis, Paul H. "Paraguay from the War of the Triple Alliance to the Chaco War, 1870–1932." In *Cambridge History of Latin America*, vol. 5, edited by Leslie Bethell. Cambridge, U.K.: Cambridge University Press, 1986.

Miranda, Carlos R. *The Stroessner Era: Authoritarian Rule in Paraguay.* Boulder, CO: Westview Press, 1990.

Nickson, R. Andrew. *Historical Dictionary of Paraguay.* 2nd ed. Metuchen, NJ: Scarecrow Press, 1993.

Roett, Riordan. "Paraguay after Stroessner." *Foreign Affairs* 68, no. 2 (1989): 125–142.

Roett, Riordan, and Richard Scott Sacks. *Paraguay: The Personalist Legacy.* Boulder, CO: Westview Press, 1991.

THOMAS L. WHIGHAM

PARAGUAYAN WAR. *See* **War of the Triple Alliance.**

PARAGUAY, CONSTITUTIONS. Paraguay has had six constitutions since gaining independence. The 1813 *Reglamiento de gobierno,* instituted by Dr. José Gaspar de Francia and approved by a general congress, provided for a two-man consular form of government. (The *reglamiento* notwithstanding,

Francia became the sole executive in 1814 and perpetual dictator two years later.)

The Constitution of 1844, also designed by the chief executive and approved by a general congress, established a new state structure for Paraguay after Francia's death. It provided for a presidential republican system with a separate executive, legislature, and judiciary (though in practice the last two branches of government were subservient to the first).

The 1870 Constitution, approved at the time of the allied occupation of Paraguay, drew heavily from Argentine precedents. It established a bicameral legislature and a single four-year presidential term, all set within a centralized, rather than federal, structure. Although this constitution endured for seventy years, it was repeatedly violated in spirit and practice by Colorado and Liberal governments alike.

The Constitution of 1940 was promulgated during the administration of José Félix Estigarribia. Although bearing some similarity to the 1870 document, it also boasted some authoritarian features, including a powerful, nonelected council of state and a wide expansion of executive authority in all areas. It provided for a weak unicameral legislature. The 1940 Constitution facilitated a move toward dictatorship in Paraguay, first under Higínio Morínigo (1940–1946) and then under Alfredo Stroessner (1954–1989).

The 1967 Constitution was designed to permit General Stroessner to rule as president for two more five-year terms. (Ten years later the general pushed through an amendment that allowed him to serve indefinitely.) This constitution also restored a bicameral character to the legislature but retained the council of state.

The Constitution of 1992, written after the fall of Stroessner, was the first essentially democratic constitution for Paraguay. A massive document (291 articles and 20 *artículos transitorias*), it weakened the executive power vis-à-vis the other branches of government; the Council of State was abolished and the choice of Supreme Court justices was left in the hands of the bicameral legislature. Decentralization of authority was also a key feature of the Constitution, with many responsibilities turned over to regions and departmental governors. The 1992 document was highly controversial.

See also **Estigarribia, José Félix; Francia, José Gaspar Rodríguez de; Morínigo, Higínio; Stroessner, Alfredo.**

BIBLIOGRAPHY

Conrado Pappalardo Zaldívar, *Paraguay: Itinerario constitucional* (1991), and R. Andrew Nickson, *Historical Dictionary of Paraguay* (1993), pp. 159–162.

Additional Bibliography

Filártiga Cantero, Fernando Jesús. *Paraguay: Quebradiza institucionalidad*. Asunción, Paragua: F.J. Filártiga Cantero, 2004.

Lambert, Peter, and R. Andrew Nickson. *The Transition to Democracy in Paraguay*. Houndmills, Hampshire [England]: Macmillan Press, 1997.

THOMAS L. WHIGHAM

PARAGUAY, DEMOGRAPHY. The population of Paraguay remained small throughout the colonial period. After the end, around 1600, of the initial influx of *conquistadores*, virtually no further immigration took place until the late eighteenth century. As late as 1700 the population of the province of Paraguay was estimated at no more than 40,000; on the eve of independence in 1811 it was estimated to have risen to 97,460 on the basis of a census carried out in 1796. However, this figure did not include the native population. During the nationalist period, the population is estimated to have grown from around 250,000 in 1828 to 350,000 in 1857.

A 1999 study by Thomas Whigham and Barbara Potthast provides important new evidence on the demographic impact of the War of the Triple Alliance (1865–1870), which many historians have described as genocidal. The authors, who conclude that there was indeed a catastrophic loss of population during the war, analyzed a census from 1870 that in December 1989 was discovered in the ministry of defense. They calculate that the population fell from between 420,000 and 450,000 in 1864 to between 140,000 and 166,000. This represents a loss of 60 to 69 percent of the prewar population, far higher even than previous estimates.

Census data for the period 1887–2002 are shown in Table 1. In 1981 the first census of indigenous peoples revealed a total of 38,703. This rose to

Census data, Paraguay, 1887–2002	
1887	329,645
1899	493,000
1935	992,420
1950	1,328,452
1962	1,819,103
1972	2,357,955
1982	3,029,830
1992	4,152,588
2002	5,163,198

Table 1

87,099 by the time of the second such census in 2002, equivalent to 1.7 percent of the national population.

From 1981 to 1989 the population growth rate was 3.1 percent, one of the highest in Latin America; almost among the highest in the region was the gross fertility rate, at 5.3 live births per woman. By the years 2000 to 2005, the growth rate had fallen to 2.0 percent because of a combination of lower fertility and mortality rates and higher net emigration. Infant mortality has decreased significantly since the 1960s to 39 per 1,000 live births in 1998. Life expectancy at birth is about sixty-five years for men and about seventy years for women. The population is young, with more than half under twenty years of age.

Emigration has been high since the midtwentieth century, especially among men seeking employment in neighboring Argentina and, increasingly, in Spain. About 25 percent of all Paraguayans live outside their country. As a result of emigration from rural areas, migration to cities has been slower than in many Latin American countries. It was not until 1992 that more than half the population (50.3 percent) lived in urban areas, reaching 56.7 percent by 2002. Internal migration is mainly to the Asunción metropolitan area, which has an estimated population of 1.5 million.

According to the latest population census carried out by the Dirección General de Estadística, Encuestas y Censos (DGEEC), the national statistics office, in August 2002 Paraguay had a population of 5.16 million. This was considerably lower than previous official estimates. The DGEEC subsequently adjusted its population estimate to 5,542,886 to correct for under-registration. The estimated population for mid-2006 was 6,009,143.

See also **Paraguay: The Colonial Period; Paraguay: The Nineteenth Century; Paraguay: The Twentieth Century; Paraguay, Immigration; War of the Triple Alliance.**

BIBLIOGRAPHY

Bertoni, Guillermo T., and J. Richard Gorham. "The People of Paraguay: Origins and Numbers." In *Paraguay: Ecological Essays*, ed. J. Richard Gorham, pp. 109–140. Miami, FL: Academy of the Arts and Sciences of the Americas, 1973.

Dirección General de Estadística, Encuestas y Censos. *Paraguay: Resultados Finales: Censo Nacional de Población y Viviendas, Año 2002.* Asunción: DGEEC, 2004.

Mora Mérida, José Luís. "La demografía colonial paraguaya." *Jahrbuch für Geschichte von Staat, Wirtschaft und Gesellschaft Lateinamerikas* (Cologne) 11 (1974): 52–77.

Whigham, Thomas Lyle, and Barbara Potthast. "The Paraguayan Rosetta Stone: New Insights into the Demographics of the Paraguayan War, 1864–1870." *Latin American Research Review* 34, no. 1 (1999): 174–186.

ANDREW NICKSON

PARAGUAY, GEOGRAPHY. Paraguay is a landlocked country located in the heart of South America and is traversed by the Tropic of Capricorn. It is bounded by Brazil to the north and east, Argentina to the south, and Bolivia to the west. With an area of 157,006 square miles (406,752 sq. km.), it is the third smallest of the Latin republics of South America, after Uruguay and Ecuador. Four-fifths of the country's perimeter is traced by the Paraguay, Apa, Paraná, and Pilcomayo rivers. The Paraná forms both the eastern and southern borders of the country. Multiple tributaries of the Paraguay and Paraná cross the eastern and central regions. The Paraná joins the Paraguay River at the country's southwestern corner. The only important tributary flowing from the west is the sluggish Pilcomayo, which joins the Paraguay near Asunción. Rising to the northwest in Bolivia, the Pilcomayo forms the southern border of the Chaco Boreal region and is navigable in its lower reaches by small boats.

The Paraguay River, which runs from north to south, effectively splits the country into two distinct geographic regions. To the west is the Chaco Boreal region, which accounts for 61 percent (or 95,313 square miles) of the total area and is inhabited by only 2.7 percent of the total population. The Chaco is a tract of flat and infertile scrub forest. Along the river banks there are grassy plains and clumps of palms, but the land becomes drier toward the west and is almost desert in the northwest. The Chaco can be divided into three zones: the Low Chaco, with open palm forest and marshes used for extensive cattle ranching; the Middle Chaco scrubland, with a mix of hardwood and cactus; and the High Chaco, with low thorn forest cover and very hot summer temperatures.

In contrast, the Región Oriental to the east of the Paraguay River is fertile, with humid semitropical conditions. With an area of 61,693 square miles, it is an extension of the Brazilian Plateau and varies in elevation from about 165 feet above sea level in the southwest to a few hills that rise to 2,500 feet in the east. The hill ranges of Amambay and Mbaracayú form the watershed between the Paraguay and the Paraná rivers. The highest peak is Mount San Rafael at 2,789 feet, in the Cordillera de San Rafael in southeastern Paraguay. To the east of these hills lies the Paraná River valley. To the west lies the broad valley of the Paraguay River. The area from Encarnación northward to the Brazilian border, comprising one-third of eastern Paraguay, is called the Paraná Plateau and hosts rapidly expanding soybean production.

There has been a swift decline in the forest cover in eastern Paraguay, from 52 percent of the total area in 1950 to 6 percent in 2000. Cleared land is used for cattle ranching and commercial agriculture. Around 4 percent of the national territory is protected as national park land, but enforcement is weak. Paraguay has only two lakes of consequence. The largest, Lake Ypoá, about 40 miles south of Asunción, is drained by channels of the Tebicuary and feeds the marshes of the Ñeembucú plain. The picturesque Lake Ypacaraí, about 30 miles east of Asunción, with summer resorts at San Bernardino and Areguá, has become extremely polluted in recent years.

Paraguay is less urbanized than most Latin American countries. The proportion of the population living in towns rose slowly in the 1990s, reaching 57 percent by the 2002 census. The largest city is the capital, Asunción (population 700,000). Ciudad del Este (formerly Puerto Presidente Stroessner, populataion 250,000) on the eastern border grew rapidly from the 1970s. Other towns are Concepción, Encarnación, Pedro Juan Caballero, Coronel Oviedo, and Villarrica. Brazilians have settled in the Paraná Plateua region in large numbers since the 1970s. There are twenty German-speaking Mennonite colonies in Paraguay, both in the Chaco and the eastern region, with a combined population of 25,000.

Paraguay has a highly centralized form of government. The 1992 constitution introduced seventeen departments as a new intermediate tier of government. Departmental councils and governors are directly elected, but their powers, responsibilities, and financing are still limited. The constitution also guarantees autonomy for the country's 231 municipal districts, but local government responsibilities and finances remain limited.

See also **Paraguay River; Paraná River.**

BIBLIOGRAPHY

Bertoni, Guillermo Tell, and J. Richard Gorham. "The Geography of Paraguay." In *Paraguay: Ecological Essays*, edited by John Richard Gorham. Miami, FL: Academy of the Arts and Sciences of the Americas, 1973.

Palmieri, Juan H., and Juan C. Velásquez. *Geología del Paraguay*. Asunción, Paraguay: Ediciones NAPA, 1982.

Quiroga, Omar, ed. *Geografía ilustrada del Paraguay*, 3rd edition. Buenos Aires: Distribuidora Quevedo de Ediciones, 1998.

Smith, Timothy G. "The Physical Geography of Paraguay." In *The Economy of Paraguay*, edited by Joseph Pincus. New York: Praeger, 1968.

ANDREW NICKSON

PARAGUAY, IMMIGRATION.

Though many countries in Latin America have been shaped by their immigrant populations, Paraguay is unusual in that most of its immigrants have settled in rural agricultural colonies that have been homogeneous ethnic, religious, or ideological enclaves. This pattern was established as early as 1855, when Francisco Solano López, son of the Paraguayan president, arranged for the transport of 400 French colonists to the Gran Chaco region directly across from Asunción. There they expected to receive government help in founding a farming community to be called Nueva Burdeos. In fact, little help was forthcoming, and the colonization effort was abandoned almost at the moment it began.

The War of the Triple Alliance (1864–1870) brought a significant demographic dislocation in Paraguay. Some sources claim the country lost nearly half its population of 400,000, and perhaps as much as 80 percent of its men. Responding to this population loss, in 1881 the Paraguayan government enacted comprehensive legislation to promote immigration. This law authorized the establishment of new agricultural colonies, with grants of land to each colonist, free passage from the point of embarkation, and maintenance for a maximum of one year.

The new legislation brought an immediate response from German colonists, who came in considerable numbers to found a colony at San Bernardino, on the shores of Lake Ypacaraí. The success of San Bernardino attracted immigrants to other areas of Paraguay. New groups of Germans, as well as Italians, French, Swedes, and, in one case, a group of Australian utopian socialists, soon established colonies in various parts of eastern Paraguay.

By far the most successful colonists in Paraguay were German-speaking Mennonites from Canada and Russia who began arriving in 1926. Attracted by government promises to grant them perpetual exemption from military service, the Mennonites founded three colonies—Menno, Fernheim, and Neuland—in some of the most inaccessible areas of the Chaco. These settlements had a combined initial population of 6,143 colonists. Despite the terrible odds against them, the Mennonites managed to tame the harsh environment and created a sizable agricultural and dairy complex in the Chaco. They soon founded new Mennonite colonies in eastern Paraguay. Today the various Mennonite communities are home to thousands of people who still proudly claim a lifestyle and language different from their Paraguayan neighbors.

In addition to the Mennonites, the twentieth century saw the arrival of colonists from many other countries, including Poland, Russia, Ukraine, Slovakia, and Japan, and, after World War II, a new influx of German refugees. It was estimated in 1958 that Paraguay contained 75,000 immigrants out of a total population of 1.8 million, and the number has grown decidedly since then, swollen not only by natural increases but also by the appearance of new immigrants who came individually from Taiwan, Brazil, South Korea, Vietnam, and, since 1990, from the former Soviet Union.

See also **López, Francisco Solano; War of the Triple Alliance.**

BIBLIOGRAPHY

Joseph Winfield Fretz, *Immigrant Group Settlements in Paraguay: A Study in the Sociology of Colonization* (1962).

R. Andrew Nickson, "Brazilian Colonization of the Eastern Border Region of Paraguay," in *Journal of Latin American Studies* 13 (1981): 111–131.

Harris Gaylord Warren, *Rebirth of the Paraguayan Republic: The First Colorado Era, 1878–1904* (1985), pp. 243–271.

Additional Bibliography

Fischer, Sara, Tomás Palau, Noemia Pérez. *Inmigración y emigración en el Paraguay 1870–1960*. Asunción, Paraguay: BASE, Investigaciones Sociales, 1997.

THOMAS L. WHIGHAM

PARAGUAY, ORGANIZATIONS

This entry includes the following articles:
ASOCIACIÓN PARAGUAYA DEL INDÍGENA
CONFEDERACIÓN PARAGUAYA DE TRABAJADORES (CPT)
LEAGUE OF INDEPENDENT YOUTH

ASOCIACIÓN PARAGUAYA DEL INDÍGENA

Although Indian peoples have influenced Paraguayan society since its beginning, the Asociación Paraguaya del Indígena (API), the first representative body for those peoples, came into existence only in 1975. A national organization of Paraguay's seventeen indigenous groups, it drew its initial inspiration from the Proyecto Marandú, an Indian rights group founded by Paraguayan anthropologist Miguel Chase-Sardi. Despite the strong opposition of the Alfredo Stroessner regime to the development of this earlier group, it did receive some important international recognition. After the arrest of Chase-Sardi and other Marandú participants, however, international aid focused on the API, which over the next decade received more than $1 million in funding from the Inter-American Foundation. This support became as much a curse as a boon to the new organization, since it was the object of much bickering between mestizo advisers and Indian caciques. Eventually, the Stroessner government created its own state Indian welfare agency, the Instituto Nacional del Indígena (INDI), which attempted to siphon off a good measure of the foreign support for Paraguay's Indians.

See also **Indigenous Organizations; Indigenous Peoples.**

BIBLIOGRAPHY

R. Andrew Nickson, *Historical Dictionary of Paraguay,* 2d ed. (1993), pp. 44, 295–297, 304–305, and 482.

Additional Bibliography

Bareiro Saguier, Ruben. *La cultura paraguaya y el régimen militar.* Montevideo: Universidad de la República, Facultad de Humanidades y Ciencias de la Educación, Departamento de Publicaciones, 1994.

Horst, René Harder. *The Stroessner Regime and Indigenous Resistance in Paraguay.* Gainesville: University Press of Florida, 2007.

THOMAS L. WHIGHAM

CONFEDERACIÓN PARAGUAYA DE TRABAJADORES (CPT)

The Confederación Paraguaya de Trabajadores (CPT) is one of the principal national trade unions in Paraguay. Trade unionism in Paraguay has always been deeply infused with partisan politics. This tradition remained unbroken with the establishment of the CPT in 1951, which reflected the growing strength of the Chavista/democratic faction within the ruling Colorado Party. As president, Federico Chaves attempted to copy the experience of Perón's Argentina in forging clear links between government and the nascent union movement. The subsequent militancy of the CPT did not, however, always serve its members well. In 1958, in an effort to gain a 29 percent increase in the minimum wage, the union launched a general strike that threatened to paralyze Asunción. General Alfredo Stroessner, who had taken power four years earlier, opted to crush this strike with military force. He subsequently directed that the CPT leadership be sacked in favor of men he could control.

For the next two decades the government exercised the strictest authority in labor questions, and the CPT in effect was an extension of the Ministry of Justice and Labor. In 1979 the U.S.-backed Organización Regional Inter-Americana de Trabajadores removed the CPT from its list of member organizations, a clear signal of the Stroessner regime's growing international isolation. Since the general's fall in 1989 and the return to democracy, the CPT, though still a Colorado Party stronghold, has been eclipsed in influence by rival unions, especially the Central Unitaria de Trabajadores (CUT). During the 1990s the CPT was weakened by internal conflict and the loss of member organizations. However, it has regained viability, winning back its affiliation with the International Trade Union Confederation and joining campaigns with other social organizations, such as raising awareness about and denouncing child labor.

See also **Labor Movements; Paraguay, Political Parties: Colorado Party.**

BIBLIOGRAPHY

R. Andrew Nickson, *Historical Dictionary of Paraguay* (1993), pp. 152, 584–589.

Additional Bibliography

Alexander, Robert Jackson, with Eldon M. Parker. *A History of Organized Labor in Uruguay and Paraguay.* Westport, CT: Praeger, 2005.

Barboza, Ramiro. *Los sindicatos en el Paraguay: Evolución y estructura actual.* Asunción, Paraguay: Centro Interdisciplinario de Derecho Social y Economía Política: Distribuidor exclusivo, Librería El Lector, 1987.

Gaona, Francisco. *Introducción a la historia gremial y social del Paraguay.* 3 vols. Asunción, Paraguay: Editorial Arandú, 1967–1990.

THOMAS L. WHIGHAM

LEAGUE OF INDEPENDENT YOUTH

Founded in 1903, the League was an antipersonalist political movement that favored strict adherence to the Constitution. The League wanted the Paraguayan people to put their aspirations into a party or movement rather than in one man. The leaders believed that a personalist leader ran the risk of taking power into his own hands. They favored constitutional politics over personalism. The movement lasted until the 1908 revolt against the personalist Liberal President Benigno Ferreira, after which the League was dissolved. Many of its members later joined the Liberal Party.

See also **Paraguay, Constitutions; Paraguay, Political Parties: Liberal Party.**

BIBLIOGRAPHY

Efraim Cardozo, *23 de octubre* (1953).

Charles H. Kolinski, *Historical Dictionary of Paraguay* (1973).

Additional Bibliography

Carrón, Juan María. *El régimen liberal, 1870–1930: Sociedad, economía y cultura.* Asunción: Arandurã Editorial, 2004.

Lewis, Paul H. *Political Parties and Generations in Paraguay's Liberal Era, 1869–1940.* Chapel Hill, NC: University of North Carolina Press, 1993.

MIGUEL A. GATTI

PARAGUAY, POLITICAL PARTIES

This entry includes the following articles:
COLORADO PARTY
FEBRERISTA PARTY
LIBERAL PARTY

COLORADO PARTY

This Paraguayan political organization dates to the 1860s and continues to dominate national politics. The Colorado Party (Asociación Nacional Republicana) is a highly centralized, hierarchical organization which encompasses all social groups at all socio-economic levels. General Alfredo Stroessner's unprecedented dominance in Paraguay was largely facilitated by his skillful manipulation of this party.

Along with its perennial rival the Liberal Party, the Colorado Party came into being during the anarchic period following the War of the Triple Alliance (1864–1870). War hero General Bernardino Caballero formally founded the party in 1880 in order to regulate the choice of future presidents and the distribution of spoils to supporters. The Colorados maintained power until 1904, when a coalition of Liberal factions vanquished them in a two-year civil war. A second period of instability resulted in the reestablishment of Colorado rule in 1947, as Stroessner, then an army officer loyal to

President Higinio Morínigo, put down a broad insurrection and consolidated his control over the armed forces. Although Stroessner had little influence over the Colorados at the outset of his rule, the dictator gradually acquired control of the party by placing political debtors and allies in positions of influence within the organization. Following the 1954 coup d'état which established Stroessner as president, the general effected a series of purges which ensured party fealty.

Stroessner perpetuated his hold on power by converting the Colorado Party into a vast network for the distribution of patronage. With successive levels of organization from the central *junta de gobierno* down to neighborhood committees, the party effectively reached all social groups, including professionals, workers, women, students, and farmers. This sophisticated and all-embracing party organization made any anti-government mobilization very difficult.

In spite of Stroessner's ironclad control of the party, dissent within the organization eventually contributed to the dictator's downfall. The conflict between Stroessner's supporters (militants) and political reformers (traditionalists) ended as the expulsion of the reformers from the party convention in 1987. Two years later a traditionalist faction in the military led by General Andrés Rodríguez deposed Stroessner.

The Colorado Party remains an overwhelmingly popular political affiliation in Paraguay. While the post-Stroessner government has effected a limited political liberalization, the tangible benefits of party membership remain persuasive. In the elections of spring 1989, the Colorado presidential candidate (coup leader Rodríguez) secured 72 percent of the vote. In addition to the party's potency as as conduit for patronage benefits, strong family traditions underscore party loyalty, and its long history of hegemony has created a powerful association between the Colorados and the nation itself. Indeed, the strength of the Colorado Party continued into the twenty-first century. The party's candidate Nicanor Duarte Frutos won the presidency in 2003 and the party took a third of the seats in the legislature.

See also **Caballero, Bernardino; Stroessner, Alfredo; War of the Triple Alliance.**

BIBLIOGRAPHY

Byron A. Nichols, "Las espectativas de los partidos políticos en el Paraguay," in *Revista Paraguaya de Sociología* 5, no. 13 (December 1968): 22–61.

U.S. Library Of Congress, *Paraguay, a Country Study* (1990).

Charles D. Ameringer, *Political Parties of the Americas, 1980s to 1990s* (1992).

Additional Bibliography

Lewis, Paul H. *Political Parties and Generations in Paraguay's Liberal Era, 1869-1940.* Chapel Hill: University of North Carolina Press, 1993.

Paredes, Roberto. *Stroessner y el stronismo.* Asunción, Paraguay: Servilibro, 2004.

                                    THOMAS GAROFALO

FEBRERISTA PARTY

The Febrerista Party ended thirty-two years of Liberal rule when it took power in the February 1936 rebellion in Paraguay. Originally controlled by the military under Colonel Rafael Franco, the Febreristas quickly evolved into an assortment of Liberals, nationalists, fascists, social democrats, and Communist sympathizers. The Febrerista government set forth an agrarian reform program that redistributed some land on a relatively small scale. More significantly, Paraguay's first major labor code was passed under Febrerista rule. A combination of ineptitude, party factionalism, and increasingly totalitarian politics led to the end of the Febrerista's rule on August 9, 1937. The Liberals returned to power under General José Félix Estigarribia, hero of the Chaco War, who actually took up many of the labor and agrarian policies of the Febreristas. However, Estigarribia also pushed for a new constitution that expanded executive power.

Years of exile followed, with the Febreristas returning to power in June 1946 in a coalition with the Colorado Party. The dissolution of the alliance in early January 1947 led the Febreristas, remaining with the Liberals and the Communists, to fight a bloody civil war against the Colorados. After being defeated in August 1947, the Febrerista leaders went into exile.

The Febrerista leaders continued to be outlawed under Colorado leader General Alfredo Stroessner, who took power in 1954. When the party was finally legalized in 1967, its popularity stood at less than 3 percent of the electorate.

DEMOCRACIA SOLIDARISTA

The main ideological basis for the party was a political philosophy known as Democracia Solidarista. Its leading exponent was Juan Stefanich, an intellectual who became foreign minister in 1936 under the short-lived Febrerista government. Stefanich based his New Paraguay movement on a combination of liberalism and social democracy as an alternative to the laissez-faire ideology of the epoch. Democratic Solidarity was a centrist political philosophy within the Febrerista Party, flanked on the right by nationalists, many who favored a corporate state, and on the left by radicals, who supported social revolution. Democratic Solidarity was nationalistic and favored a tough bargaining position in the Chaco War peace talks between 1935 and 1938. The movement's followers were also *lopistas,* supporting the resurrection of the nineteenth-century dictator Francisco Solano López's discredited image to the status of patriot. After the Febrerista defeat in the 1947 civil war, many of its members were forced into exile, reducing Democratic Solidarity to the periphery of Paraguayan politics.

See also **Estigarribia, José Félix; Franco, Rafael; Stefanich, Juan.**

BIBLIOGRAPHY

On the Febrerista Party see Paul H. Lewis, *Politics of Exile: Paraguay's Febrerista Party* (1968); *Paraguay: A Country Study,* edited by Dennis Hanratty and Sandra Meditz (1990). On Democratic Solidarity see Juan Stefanich, *Mundo nuevo: Una nueva teoria de la democracia* (1941) and *El Paraguay Nuevo: Por la democracia y la libertad hacia un nuevo ideario americano* (1943); Charles H. Kolinski, *A Historical Dictionary of Paraguay* (1973).

Additional Bibliography

Ashwell, Washington. *Concepción, 1947: Cincuenta años después.* Asunción, Paraguay: W. Ashwell, 1998.

Freire Esteves, Gomes. *Historia contemporánea del Paraguay (1869–1920).* Asunción, Paraguay: Ediciones NAPA, 1983.

Rahi, Arturo. *Franco y la revolución de febrero,* 2nd edition. Asunción, Paraguay: Augusto Gallegos, 2001.

                                    MIGUEL A. GATTI

LIBERAL PARTY

The Liberal Party (Partido Liberal) was one of the two traditional political parties in Paraguay. Arising out of the political confusion of the mid-1880s, the party was originally a small clique of some forty friends, most of them *asunceños*. They had little ideological orientation per se and were chiefly interested in displacing the governing faction led by Bernardino Caballero, Patricio Escobar, and José Segundo Decoud. This latter group, reacting to the establishment of the Liberal Party in 1887, created the Colorado Party during the same year. Thus were mapped out the two contending sides of an enduring political rivalry.

The Liberals got a chance at power in 1891, when they attempted to overthrow the moderate Colorado government of Juan Gualberto González. Their failure led to a split in the party that paralleled a split among the Colorados and led to no end of intrigues over the next decade.

The Liberal Party reunified in 1902, setting the stage for a major revolution two years later that finally gave the Liberals control of the government. The Liberal rule that followed was distinguished by a broad commitment to laissez-faire economic policies and by heavy-handed paternalism in the political realm. The limitations of this model were clear by the mid-1930s, when a combination of factors—the Great Depression, the Chaco War, and the rise of a more radical political alternative—brought about the February Revolution of 1936.

The Liberals, though still relatively unpopular, were briefly restored to power at the end of the decade, but the ancien régime was clearly on the wane. The well-known war hero, General José Félix Estigarribia, promised to "modernize" party doctrine when he became president in 1939. Instead, his death one year later brought about an outright ban on party activities from 1941 to 1946 during the presidency of Higínio Morínigo.

Except for a brief flicker of promise at the time of the 1947 civil war, the Liberal Party has remained in opposition ever since. During the Stronato (1954–1989), the Liberals again split into several factions, with a minority advocating cooperation with General Alfredo Stroessner. Repressive measures enacted against the majority faction, led by Domingo Laino, kept traditional Liberals on their guard until the dictator's fall in 1989. Even with subsequent democratic reforms, however, the party did not regain the strong influence it had once commanded, obtaining only 20 percent of the vote in the 1989

presidential election. As of 2006, the successor of the Liberal Party, the Authentic Radical Liberal Party received approximately 25 percent of the vote in the legislative elections.

See also **Paraguay: The Twentieth Century; Paraguay, Political Parties: Colorado Party.**

BIBLIOGRAPHY

R. Andrew Nickson, *Historical Dictionary of Paraguay* (1993), pp. 452–455.

Additional Bibliography

Freire Esteves, Gomes. *Historia contemporánea del Paraguay.* Asunción, Paraguay: El Lector, 1996.

Lewis, Paul H. *Political Parties and Generations in Paraguay's Liberal Era, 1869-1940.* Chapel Hill: University of North Carolina Press, 1993.

THOMAS L. WHIGHAM

PARAGUAY RIVER. Paraguay River is a major waterway of South America with a watershed of 428,846 square miles and a length of 1,584 miles between its source in Mato Grosso, Brazil, and its confluence with the Paraná River near the Argentine city of Corrientes. A narrowing near Corumbá, Brazil, caused the formation of an enormous swamp—the Gran Pantanal—the largest wildlife refuge of central South America. Flooded from April through June by the high waters of the Paraguay River, it provides nesting grounds for migratory birds and breeding places for the South American alligator, the *jacaré*. However, the growth in the number of Brazilian ranchers has been decreasing the area of this natural refuge.

The river serves as a national boundary between Brazil and Bolivia, Bolivia and Paraguay, and Paraguay and Argentina. During the Conquest and the colonial period, the river was the gate of penetration into the southern edge of the continent's center for conquistadores who were searching for the King of the Silver Mountains, a legendary figure from whom the Río de la Plata derived its name. Spanish settlements sprang up along the river, such as Corumbá, Concepción, Asunción, and Formosa, which achieved greater importance than the Spanish foundations on the middle course of the Paraná River. Today, settlements on the shores of the river are centers of smuggling and drug trafficking, particularly between Bolivia and Brazil. The river is navigable as far as Asunción, as a northward prolongation of the Paraná–Río de la Plata waterway. This makes it an important shipping corridor, as it provides a much-needed Atlantic coast port for Bolivia and Paraguay. Many locals make their living fishing on the river, and its waters irrigate area agricultural ventures.

Since 1997 the Paraguay River has been at the center of an environmental controversy in the region. The area governments sought to develop the Paraguay into an industrial waterway system, and to build hydroelectric dams along the river. However, the Paraguay is an essential part of the Pantanal wetlands, the world's largest tropical wetland ecosystem. The proposed development would significantly lower water levels and damage the complex environment.

See also **Paraná River.**

BIBLIOGRAPHY

Organization of American States, *Cuenca del Río de la Plata. Estudio para su planificación y desarrollo* (1969).

Aníbal Miranda, *Paraguay y las obras hidroeléctricas binacionales* (1975).

Additional Bibliography

Alho, Cleber J. R. *Conservaçao da biodiversidade da bacia do alto Paraguai.* Campo Grande, Brazil: Editora Universidade Para o Desenvolvimento do Estado e da Região do Pantanal, 2003.

Chernoff, Barry, and Phillip W. Willink. *A Biological Assessment of the Aquatic Ecosystems of the Río Paraguay Basin, Alto Paraguay, Paraguay.* Washington, DC: Conservation International, Center for Applied Biodiversity Science, 2001.

Tümpling, Adolfo von. *Río de lágrimas y esperanza: Pasado, presente, y futuro.* Paraguay: El Lector, 2003.

CÉSAR N. CAVIEDES

PARAÍBA. Paraíba (until 1930, Paraíba do Norte), a small northeast Brazilian state with 3,595,886 inhabitants (2000). Paraíba's name derives from the river that is its central geographical feature. On its coast are Cabo Branco, the point in South America closest to Africa, and the first anchorage in Brazil (Baía da Traição, 1501). The Serra do Borborema separates Paraíba's littoral and Agreste from the extensive interior plateau of the *cariri* (a semi-arid zone), which contains the driest Município in Brazil (Cabaceiras) and the highest point in the Northeast (Pico do Jábre). Ninety-five percent of the state lies within the official "drought polygon." Farther west, the more humid far backlands (*alto sertão*), renowned for their tree cotton, reach to Brazil's heartland in the São Francisco Basin. Originally a donatary captaincy (with Itamaracá) whose indigenous Potiguars had sided with French dyewood traders, Paraíba could not be effectively settled until the 1580s, when Spanish soldiers and Portuguese colonists, with their native Tabajara allies, founded Fort Santa Catarina, on the coast, and the capital of Filipéia. Famous for its fertile coastal sugar zone, Paraíba shared in the battle to eject the Dutch (1630s and 1640s) and forge early national consciousness. During the empire, major regional revolts like the Confederation of the Equator (1824) and the Ronco de Abelha (1858) found support in Paraíba, while others, like the Praieira (1848) and the Quebra-Quilos (erupted in Campina Gande in 1874), drew leaders from the province. Paraíba's native sons and daughters include imperial painter Pedro Américo de Almeida; Leandro Gomes de Barros, founder of a Brazilian literature of the Cordel; intellectual and politician José Américo de Almeida, author of the first regionalist novel (*A bagaceira*, 1928); novelist José Lins do Rêgo, whose "sugar cycle" (1930s–1940s) chronicled regional change; President Epitácio Pessoa (1919–1923); economist Celso Furtado (head of the Superintendency for the Development of the Northeast [SUDENE] in the late 1950s and minister of culture in the late 1980s); Luiza Erundina de Sousa, the first woman to be elected mayor of São Paulo; and the seventeenth-century folk heroine Branca Dias (by adoption, as a Portuguese immigrant), martyr to the Inquisition.

See also **Drought Region (Brazil); Pessoa, Epitácio da Silva.**

BIBLIOGRAPHY

Linda Lewin, *Politics and Parentela in Paraíba: A Case Study of Family-Based Oligarchy in Brazil* (1987).

Additional Bibliography

Fanzeres, Anna. *Paraiba: A Challenge in Natural Resources Management.* New Haven, CT: Tropical Resources

Institute, Yale School of Forestry and Environmental Studies, 1990.

Machado, Humberto F. *Esclavos, senhores and café: A crise da cafeicultura esclavista do Vale do Paraíba fluminense, 1860–1888.* Niteroi, Rio de Janeiro: Editora Cromos, 1993.

Oliveira Sobrinho, Reinaldo de. *Anotações para a história da Paraíba Anotações para a história da Paraíba.* João Pessoa, Brazil: Idéia, 2002.

Trigueiro, Osvaldo Meira, and Altimar de Alentar Pimental. *Paraíba.* Recife, Brazil: Editora Massangana, Fundação Joaquim Tabuco, 1996.

LINDA LEWIN

PARAÍBA RIVER.

Paraíba River (Paraíba Do Sol), the southern Paraíba River of Brazil. This river runs 600 miles from just northeast of the city of São Paulo through the state of Rio de Janeiro, at one stretch forming the boundary with the state of Minas Gerais, and empties into the Atlantic Ocean just south of Espírito Santo. Its major tributaries are the Pomba, the Muriaé, the Paraibuna, and the Pirai. While its name signifies "useless river" (from the Tupí *para*, great river, and *aíba*, bad sea), and it is not navigable, it carves out a once-fertile valley that is a major land transport route between Rio de Janeiro and São Paulo, and its waters power two hydroelectric plants. In the mid-nineteenth century the Paraíba Valley was Brazil's major coffee-producing region. Then the land-intensive agricultural techniques used in coffee production wore out the soil, and the coffee frontier moved constantly westward. The exhaustion of the soil, combined with the failure of the planters to modernize their production techniques and labor relations in the face of rising international competition and the imminent abolition of slavery (finally decreed in 1888), ultimately resulted in the decline of the export sector, from which the region has never recovered.

See also **Brazil, Geography; Coffee Industry; Slave Trade, Abolition of: Brazil.**

BIBLIOGRAPHY

Additional Bibliography

Maia, Thereza Regina de Camago, and Tom Maia. *O Vale Paulista da Río Paraíba: História, geografia, fauna, flora, folclore, cidades: guia cultural.* Rio de Janeiro: Documenta Histórica Editora, 2005.

Marcondes, Renado Leite. *A arte de acumular na economia cafeeira: Vale do Paraíba, século XIX.* Lorena: Editora Stiliano, 1998.

Silva, Karla de Carvalho Rocha and Maria da Gloria Lampreia. *Mulheres fluminenses do Vale do Paraíba: Histórias de luta e conquista da cidadania fememnina.* Rio de Janeiro: Conselho Estadual dos Direitos da Mulher, 2001.

SUEANN CAULFIELD

PARAMILITARIES IN LATIN AMERICA.

Paramilitary forces take three forms in Latin America: officially sanctioned forces that supplement the military and police, illegal groups, and private security companies. The privatization of security is a general trend in Latin America, given states' inability to enforce the rule of law, insecurity in rural and urban areas, and often dysfunctional judicial systems. Police are poorly paid, trained, and equipped, and often corrupt. This contributes to the high crime rate in Latin America, where an estimated 15 percent of the gross domestic product is lost to violence annually.

Latin America has numerous examples of legal paramilitary forces. One of the most famous are the *rondas campesinas*, or peasant militias. Based on indigenous communal traditions of providing local security, *rondas* have an important role in Peruvian history. In the nineteenth century *rondas* were employed by General (later president) Andrés Cáceres to fight against Chilean forces during the War of the Pacific (1879–1884). In the 1980s *rondas*, called the Committees of Self Defense, lightly armed and under the control of the Peruvian army, were instrumental in defeating the Sendero Luminoso in the sierra of south central Peru (Junín and Ayacucho) by depriving the Maoists of territorial control. In 2003 President Alejandro Toledo signed legislation that gave the *rondas* extensive legal responsibilities for protecting communal security and resolving conflict.

In El Salvador during the civil war of 1970s and 1980s, the paramilitary Organización Nacional Democrática (ORDEN) was established under the Ministry of Defense. Accordingly, the military organized some 100,000 members at the village and town levels. After developing an unsavory record for human rights violations, ORDEN was disbanded, but some members joined death squads that were totally outside the law.

In the Guatemalan counterinsurgency of the same time, the army expanded the army reserves known as the *comisionados militares* into the Civilian Self-Defense Patrols (Patrullas de Auto-Defensa Civil). Approximately 900,000 peasants were recruited (many forcibly) and rewarded with food, housing, and jobs. Once again, horrendous human rights violations ensued. The patrols were disbanded in 1996. In 2004 the Guatemalan government agreed to pay $600 each to about 700,000 ex-members.

Due to Colombia's chronically weak central authority, absence of effective governance (such as police and military presence, roads, schools, and other infrastructure) in major portions of the national territory, and strong regionalism in a difficult geography, paramilitaries have been prominent in Colombia. They have been used by national, regional, and local political forces. There was even a short-lived experiment at the national level with legal paramilitaries: The CONVIVIR (Vigilance and Private Security Services) system started in 1990 as a neighborhood watch concept in Antioquia, but unlike the *rondas* in Peru, CONVIVIR were allowed to carry only sidearms, and they soon disbanded.

The emergence of Colombia as a producer of cocaine in the early 1980s transformed the simmering internal conflict and helped spawn an immense paramilitary problem. Coca cultivation moved north from Bolivia and Peru into southeastern Colombia, providing a new source of funding for the military operations of the Fuerzas Armadas Revolucionarias de Colombia (FARC) and the smaller Ejército de Liberación Nacional (ELN). By the mid-1990s Colombia had become the largest exporter of cocaine to the United States and the rest of the world. The guerrillas protected and taxed the cultivation, production, and transport of coca. The United States, fearful of the establishment of a narco-state, and fighting drug addiction at home, committed itself to support Colombia via economic and security assistance.

In the 1990s the FARC appeared invincible, stealing livestock and property, forcibly recruiting children to fight, taking over towns, assassinating and kidnapping officials and prominent citizens, defeating the army in battalion-size units, and conducting urban terror operations, all while benefiting from the coca economy. The army, with only 35,000 soldiers available for combat in 2000 and burdened with poor organization, mobility, and intelligence, could not secure territory, protect the population, and defend infrastructure. Thus, a serious security gap emerged, which was filled by some thirty illegal paramilitary groups that came under the umbrella organization Autodefensas Unidas de Colombia (United Self-Defense Forces of Colombia).

In the 1980s cattle ranchers organized self-defense groups to fight Colombia's growing guerrilla threat. As the self-defense groups grew, they meshed with the complex local, regional, and national politics. They also found the lucrative advantage of the coca business: By 2000 some 70 percent of the income of the paramilitaries came from narcotics. The competition with the FARC over territory, coca, and people was intense, resulting in intimidation, killings, massacres, corruption, and more than one million people displaced by the crossfire. Believing that "the enemy of my enemy is my ally," some elements of Colombia's public security forces considered the paramilitaries useful in the fight against the FARC and ELN. This gave rise to the notion that the paramilitaries were the army's "Sixth Division,"—that is, assisting the existing, legitimate five divisions by conducting operations, while the army provided support and intelligence, and then looked the other way. The government was fighting a war on three fronts: against the guerrillas, the narcos, and the paramilitary forces.

By the end of 2006, nearly 32,000 paramilitaries had accepted the government's offer to lay down their guns, demobilize, demilitarize, and reintegrate into society. But there were serious difficulties with reintegration. Moreover, the FARC occupied space vacated by paramilitaries, and corruption engendered by the coca boom reached high political levels. On the plus side, the administrations of Andrés Pastrana Arango (1998–2002) and Álvaro Uribe (2002 to present) undertook a significant expansion of the army and police by, for example, putting policemen in every municipality by 2003. Additionally, Colombia developed variants of legal paramilitary forces, including a national early-warning net composed of private citizens, and the town soldiers (*soldados de mi pueblo*), a local militia under the command of a regular army officer. These measures, combined with a more effective military and sophisticated strategy, improved public security dramatically. But the goal of establishing legitimate state authority across the national territory remained elusive.

See also **Armed Forces; Cáceres, Andrés Avelino; Colombia, Revolutionary Movements: Revolutionary Armed Forces of Colombia (FARC); Colombia, Revolutionary Movements: Army of National Liberation (ELN); Colombia, Revolutionary Movements: United Self-Defense Forces of Colombia (AUC); Peru, Revolutionary Movements: Shining Path; Toledo, Alejandro; War of the Pacific.**

BIBLIOGRAPHY

Brockett, Charles D. *Political Movements and Violence in Central America*. New York: Cambridge University Press, 2005.

Degregori, Carlos Iván. "Reaping the Whirlwind: The Rondas Campesinas and the Defeat of the Sendero Luminoso in Ayacucho." In *Societies of Fear: The Legacy of Civil War and Violence in Latin America*, ed. Kees Koonings and Dirk Krujit. London: Zed Books, 1999.

Human Rights Watch. *The Sixth Division: Military-Paramilitary Ties and U.S. Policy in Colombia*. New York: Author, 2001.

International Crisis Group. "Demobilising the Paramilitaries in Colombia: An Achievable Goal." Latin American Report no. 8. Brussels: Author, 2004.

Kirk, Robin. *More Terrible than Death: Massacres, Drugs, and America's War in Colombia*. New York: Public Affairs, 2003.

Montgomery, Tommie Sue. *Revolution in El Salvador: From Civil Strife to Civil Peace*. Boulder, CO: Westview Press, 1995.

GABRIEL MARCELLA

PARANÁ, HONÔRIO HERMETO CARNEIRO LEÃO, MARQUÉS DE

(1801–1856). Honôrio Hermeto Carneiro Leão, Marqués De Paraná (*b.* 11 January 1801; *d.* 3 September 1856), Brazilian statesman and diplomat—

the preeminent political figure of the 1850s. Because Paraná was a Coimbra-trained magistrate, his ascent as a jurist was rapid but was soon eclipsed by his political success in the early regency. As a *moderado* deputy for Minas Gerais, he was celebrated for turning back Diogo Antônio Feijó's 1832 attempt to reform the Constitution of 1824; though he was quickly taken up by the regents as minister of justice (1832), his party enemies brought him down. In the Chamber of Deputies, however, Paraná worked with Bernardo de Vasconcelos and the Saquaremas to organize a majority and form the Conservative Party in opposition to Feijó's regency (1835–1837); by 1842 he was a member of the Senate and Council of State.

Minister of justice, then minister of foreign affairs, in the Conservative administration of 1843–1844, Paraná also defended Conservative goals in repressing the Liberal revolts of 1842 and the Praieira Revolt of 1848 (as provincial president of Rio de Janeiro and of Pernambuco, respectively) and in effecting the Platine diplomacy that led to the war that toppled Argentina's Juan Manuel de Rosas in 1852. In 1853, Pedro II asked Paraná to lead an administration that would terminate the partisan domestic strife in which Paraná had triumphed. He did so, as prime minister of the Conciliação cabinet, which he composed of willing veterans and able new protégés from both parties. He broke with the Saquarema chieftains to establish a climate of nonpartisan patronage and statism, constructive reform, and more representative elections. He thus closed the era of the monarchy's consolidation.

See also **Feijó, Diogo Antônio; Minas Gerais; Praieira Revolt.**

BIBLIOGRAPHY

Joaquim Nabuco, *Um estadista do império*, vols. 1 and 2 (1898–1899).

Roderick J. Barman, *Brazil: The Forging of a Nation* (1988).

Richard Graham, *Patronage and Politics in Nineteenth-Century Brazil* (1990).

Additional Bibliography

Rohloff de Matos, llamar. *Otempo Saquarema*. São Paulo: Editora Hucitec, 2004.

JEFFREY D. NEEDELL

PARANÁ, ARGENTINA. Paraná, capital city of the Argentine province of Entre Ríos. On the left bank of the Paraná River, it has a population of 235, 931 (2001). Established in 1730 as Bajada de Santa Fé, an outpost of the Santa Fé region to halt the incursions of the Charrúan peoples, the small settlement became a resting station on the route between Buenos Aires and Asunción. In defiance of the primacy of Buenos Aires, General Justo J. de Urquiza declared Paraná the capital of United Provinces of the Río De La Plata in 1853 and it remained so until 1862. After the war against Paraguay, Buenos Aires was reinstated as the national capital. In 1883 Paraná became the capital of Entre Ríos and entered a period of moderate growth based on the raising of cattle and the production of wheat, wood manufactures, and leather products. The port of Bajada Grande is the main outlet for the agrarian and forestry products of Entre Ríos. A railroad line secures connections with Ibicuy and Posadas, and a tunnel passing under the Paraná River leads to the city of Santa Fé. It is the site of the Universidad Nacional de Entre Ríos, a former affiliate of the Universidad Nacional del Litoral in Santa Fé.

See also **Entre Ríos; Livestock.**

BIBLIOGRAPHY

R. E. Reina, *Paraná: Social Boundaries in an Argentine City.* Austin: University of Texas, 1973.

Ofelia Sors, *Paraná: Dos siglos y cuarto de su evolución* (Paraná, 1981).

Additional Bibliography

Rolandi de Perrot, Diana. *Cultura tradicionál del área del Paraná Medio.* Buenos Aires: Fundación F.G. Bracht Editor, 1984.

Pellizzetti, Bruno. *El Paraná y sus hombres: Memorias de un baqueano.* Buenos Aires: Editorial Pleamar, 1991.

CÉSAR N. CAVIEDES

PARANÁ, BRAZIL. Brazil Paraná, southern state whose capital is Curitiba. Paraná covers 79,730 square miles and had a population of 8,443,299 in 1991 and 10,261,256 in 2005. Its boundaries are São Paulo State on the north, Mato Grosso State on the west, Paraguay across the Paraná River, Argentina on the southwest, Santa Catarina State on the south, and the Atlantic Ocean on the east. Settlement of the territory began on the coast at the end of the sixteenth century with the search for indigenous peoples as slave workers and for precious metals. In 1765 the territory of Paraná was absorbed by the captaincy of São Paulo and constituted its fifth county until 1853, when it gained autonomy as the province of Paraná. The population, which was composed of Indians, Europeans, and enslaved and free blacks, registered a greater increase after 1850 through European immigration (mainly Italians, Poles, Ukrainians, and Germans). After the decline of mining, cattle breeding expanded rapidly in the uplands, but it, too, decreased, until by 1820 agriculture production was mainly at the subsistence level. Then yerba maté production was developed, which constituted Brazil's main export until World War I. The coffee growing that was started in 1920 in northern Paraná resulted in Brazil's becoming the world's largest producer. However, after 1960 inadequate economic policies and cold winters diminished the region's crops. Currently, Paraná produces 25 percent of Brazil's soybeans, wheat, beans, potatoes, cotton, ramie, castor beans, barley, oats, and rice—all of which are of economic significance.

See also **Brazil, Geography.**

BIBLIOGRAPHY

Ermelino De Leão, *Dicionario histórico e geográfico do Paraná* (1929).

Altiva Pilatti Balhana, Brasil Pinheiro Machado, and Cecília Maria Westphalen, *História do Paraná* (1969).

Louis Henry and Altiva Pilatti Balhana, "La population du Paraná depuis le XVIII siècle" in *Population, Revue Bimestrielle de l'Institut National d'études Démographiques* (Nov. 1975).

José Francisco Da Rocha Pombo, *O Paraná no centenário: 1500–1900,* 2d ed. (1980).

Márcia Elisa De Campos Graf, "Economia e escravidão no Paraná" in *Boletim do Instituto Histórico, Geográfico e Etnográfico do Paraná* 45 (1987); *Anuário estatístico do Brasil* (1990); *Sinopse preliminar do censo demográfico-1991* (1992).

Additional Bibliography

Albornoz, Miguel. *Biografía del Paraná.* Buenos Aires: El Elefante Blanco, 1997.

Carneiro, David, and Túlio Vargas. *História biográfica da República no Paraná*. Curitibia, Brazil: Banestado, 1994.

Instituto Histórico e Geográfico do Paraná. *Boletim do Instituto Histórico e Geográfico do Paraná*. Curitiba, Paraná, Brasil: O Instituto, 1999.

Saad, Paulo Murad. *Recent Migration in the State of Paraná*. Curitiba, Paraná, Brazil: Paranacidade, 1998.

MÁRCIA ELISA DE CAMPOS GRAF

PARANÁ-PARAGUAY RIVER BASIN.

Ownership of the Paraná and Paraguay River basin is divided among Brazil, Argentina, Paraguay, Bolivia, and Uruguay. Brazil controls the greatest part, which includes portions of the states of Mato Grosso, Goiás, São Paulo, Paraná, Santa Catarina, and Rio Grande do Sul.

The Paraná basin, formed by the Paraná River and its tributaries, includes 1,980,000 square miles and is second in size only to the Amazon Basin in South America. It includes four major waterfalls with hydroelectric potential: Dourada, Santa André, Sete Quedas, and Urubupungá. The Paraná and Paraguay rivers join near the Argentine city of Corrientes. From there the Paraná continues to Buenos Aires and enters the Río De La Plata. The Paraguay River is navigable as far as Asunción by shallow-draft ocean ships, but beyond that only small riverboats reach into Brazil.

The largest subregion of the Paraná-Paraguay basin is the Gran Chaco, a low interior plain formed of sediment from the Andes. In the northern part of the basin, at the junction of Paraguay, Bolivia and Brazil, lies the low and swampy Pantanal. The eastern basin includes the Mato Grosso tropical grasslands. The Paraná Plateau in the southern area of the basin, primarily in the eastern Paraguay and southern Brazil, has rich volcanic soil. Tropical climates dominate in most of the basin; the winter dry period is most severe in the western subregions.

Early minor development by European colonists occurred in the basin in eastern Paraguay and the Misiones province of Argentina, although complaints about the Brazilian Bandeirantes persisted. The Tupi-guarani predominantly inhabited the basin before the Europeans arrived. By the early nineteenth century the basin's economy relied on subsistence agriculture but also included some commercial livestock farms and production facilities in Entre Ríos province of Argentina.

In the twentieth century the basin began to be settled intensively. Extensive cattle grazing became the land's primary economic use, with intensive irrigation introduced into the Gran Chaco region and coffee cultivation (which had started in the 1800s) begun on the Paraná Plateau. Lumbering also became a major industry in the Paraná Plateau's large stand of commercial-grade pines. Minerals played only a minor role in development, in spite of intensive petroleum searches. Poor transportation continued to discourage overdevelopment and often hindered exploitation of the available natural resources.

A number of international conflicts have erupted over the hydroelectric potential of the Paraná and Paraguay rivers. In 1973 Brazil and Paraguay signed the hydroelectric agreement at Itaipú, and hydroelectricity has since been the essential economic focus for developing the basin.

See also **Brazil, Geography; Energy.**

BIBLIOGRAPHY

Thomas Jefferson Page, *La Plata, the Argentine Confederation, and Paraguay* (1859).

J. Eliseo Da Rosa, "Economics, Politics, and Hydroelectric Power: The Paraná River Basin," in *Latin American Research Review* 18, no. 3 (1983): 77–107.

Additional Bibliography

Cordillo, Gastón. *El Gran Chaco: Antropologías e histórias*. Buenos Aires: Prometeo Libros, 2006.

Mendoza Cortez, Omar. *La lucha por la tierra en el Gran Chaco tarijeño*. La Paz: Dirección de Investigación Científica y Tecnológica: Centro Eclesial de Documentación: Centro de Estudios Regionales para el Desarrollo de Tarija: Programa de Investigación Estratégica en Bolivia, 2003.

Redford, Kent Hubbard and Michael Painter. *Natural Alliances between Conservationists and Indigenous Peoples*. Bronx, NY: Wildlife Conservation Society, 2006.

CAROLYN E. VIEIRA

PARANÁ RIVER.

The Paraná River, the world's thirteenth longest, flows through Brazil, Paraguay, Uruguay, and Argentina. At just over 1 million square miles, the basin of the Paraná is the second largest in South America, behind the Amazon River basin. The Paraná empties into the Río de la Plata estuary via a large delta that borders on Greater Buenos Aires at El Tigre. The tributaries of the Paraná flow from the highlands of the Brazilian shield in the east (Paranaíba, Tietê, Paranapanema, Iguaçú), from the Mato Grosso tablelands in the north, and from the eastern slopes of the Andes in the west (Pilcomayo, Bermejo, and Salado). The climatic diversity of its vast drainage basin explains the variations in flow of the Paraná River, which peaks in February and March, during the rainy season, and is at its lowest in October. Seasonal level variations account to 16 feet where the river empties into the Río de la Plata estuary.

Ocean freighters can reach Santa Fé, 150 miles upstream from the delta, and from there barges continue on the Paraguay River to Asunción and Concepción (Paraguay) and to Corumbá (Brazil). Navigation up the Paraná itself is impeded by the Iguaçú waterfalls, a majestic system of cascades located at the boundary of Argentina, Brazil, and Paraguay (25 degrees south latitude). Considered an important waterway into the subtropical interior of South America, the Paraná and its tributaries encompass a system of rivers within Brazil, Argentina, Paraguay, Uruguay, and Bolivia. Stretching as it does into so many counties, this basin has gained in geopolitical importance. The construction of the Itaipú hydroelectric plant, a joint project of Brazil and Paraguay, is a monument to international cooperation. The creation of a navigable waterway along the Pilcomayo River will allow freight from eastern Bolivia to reach international routes via the Argentine ports of Corrientes or Rosario. The river is home to over 350 fish species.

See also **Iguaçu Falls; Itaipú Hydroelectric Project; Río de la Plata.**

BIBLIOGRAPHY

Organization of American States, *Cuenca del Río de la Plata: Estudio para su planificación y desarrollo* (Washington, DC, 1969).

Additional Bibliography

Albornoz, Miguel. *Biografía del Paraná*. Buenos Aires: El Elefante Blanco, 1997.

Elhance, Arun P. *Hydropolitics in the Third World: Conflict and Cooperation in International River Basins.* Washington, DC: United States Institute of Peace Press, 1999.

Giardinellif, Mempo. *Padre rio: Cuentos y poemas del Rio Parana.* Buenos Aires: Ediciones Instituto Movilizador de Fondos Cooperativos, 1997.

Iriondo, Martin, Juan Cesar Pagg, and Maria Julieta Parma. *The Middle Paraná River: Limnology of a Subtropical Wetland.* London: Springer, 2007.

Juzarte, Teotônio José. Souza, Jonas Soares de and Miyoko Makino, eds. *Diário da navegação.* São Paulo: Edusp: Imprensa Oficial SP, 2000.

CÉSAR N. CAVIEDES

PARANHOS, JOSÉ MARIA DA SILVA.
See **Rio Branco, Visconde do.**

■

PARATY. Paraty (Parati), the southernmost *municipio* (county) in the state of Rio de Janeiro, Brazil. Paraty is a fish-hook–shaped, rain-soaked stretch of land hemmed in by the high escarpment of the Serra do Mar, the bay of Ilha Grande, and the Atlantic Ocean. Its original settlement was at the terminus of one of the principal Indian trails linking the coast with the Brazilian interior. Organized as a town in 1667, it remained until the end of the seventeenth century a small trading center with a sparse rural population involved in subsistence agriculture.

With the discovery of gold in Minas Gerais in 1693, Paraty was catapulted into importance; the newly improved mountain trail became the major conduit of men and goods moving from Rio de Janeiro to the mines. With the construction of a more direct route in 1718, however, the boom days for Paraty were over. From the late eighteenth to the latter part of the nineteenth century, Paraty became the principal point of shipment of produce, mainly coffee, from the developing Paraíba Valley to Rio de Janeiro.

Another, smaller, revival for the economy of Paraty came late in the nineteenth century with the production of *cachaça*, which is a sugarcane-derived spirit best known today as the basis for Brazil's most famous drink, the *caipirinha*. The name "Paraty" in that period became synonymous with *cachaça*.

Since Paraty was physically isolated, it did not change for centuries. From the eighteenth century through most of the early twentieth century, Paraty languished, although sugar was grown there, especially to make *aguardente*, and until the 1940s the word *parati* was synonymous with white rum. In 1966 the Brazilian government designated the town of Paraty a historical monument.

In the 1970s, Paraty's fortunes changed when a paved road was built from Rio de Janeiro to Santos, near São Paulo. The city then began a new cycle of activity that transformed a small, almost abandoned town living on very limited economic activity, mainly fishing and agriculture (bananas, manioc, and sugarcane), into what became known as one of the major tourist destinations in Brazil.

See also **Rio de Janeiro (Province and State).**

BIBLIOGRAPHY

J. A. A Pizarro E Araújo et al., *Tricentenário de Parati: Noticias históricas* (1960).

J. Capistrano De Abreu, *Capitulos de historia colonial e os caminhos antigos eo povoamento do Brasil* (1963).

Heitor Grugel Edelweiss Amaral, *Paraty, caminho do ouro* (1973).

Additional Bibliography

Cafi, George Vidor. *Um olhar sobre Angra e Paraty: Povo, cultura e meio ambiente.* Rio de Janeiro, Brazil: Electronuclear, 1999.

Giraldo, Pedro Enrique, and Ivo Pitanguy. *Paraty.* São Paulo, Brazil: Editora Globo, 1992.

Maia, Thereza, and Tom Maia. *Paraty: History, Festivals, Folklore, Monuments.* Rio de Janeiro: Expressão e Cultura, 1991.

Maia, Thereza, and Tom Maia. *Paraty para ti: Guia cultural.* Lorena, Brazil: Editora Stiliano, 2000.

Oliveira Casadei, Thalita de. *Paraty: Uma vida uma saudade.* Rio de Janeiro: Sol Nascente, 1998.

JAMES PATRICK KIERNAN

PARDAVÉ, JOAQUÍN (1900–1955).

Joaquín Pardavé (*b.* 30 September 1900; *d.* 20 July 1955), Mexican film and stage actor, director, and songwriter. Born in Penjamo, Guanajuato, of theatrical parents, from an early age Pardavé displayed a natural talent, composing popular songs and acting in his uncle's theater company. He debuted in a supporting role in the film *Jalisco nunca pierde,* and became a major star with his role in *México de mis recuerdos,* in which he created his most memorable character, Don Susanito Peñafiel y Somellera. One of the most versatile and popular Mexican actors of his time, Pardavé was equally at ease with comedy and drama. In his later career he directed many of his own films. Among his best features are *El baisano Jalil, Ahí está el detalle, Arriba el norte, Yo baile con Don Porfirio, La barca de oro,* and *Los hijos de Don Venancio.* Pardavé also composed such popular songs as "La Panchita," "Caminito de la sierra," "Ventanita morada," and "Negra consentida."

See also **Cinema: From the Silent Film to 1990.**

BIBLIOGRAPHY

Luis Reyes De La Maza, *El cine sonoro en México* (1973).

E. Bradford Burns, *Latin American Cinema: Film and History* (1975).

Carl J. Mora, *Mexican Cinema: Reflections of a Society: 1896–1980* (1982).

John King, *Magical Reels: A History of Cinema in Latin America* (1990).

Additional Bibliography

Carrasco Vásquez, Jorge. *Joaquín Pardavé: Un actor vuelto leyenda.* México, D.F.: Grupo Editorial Tomo, 2004.

Estrada, Josefina. *Joaquín Pardavé: El señor del espectáculo.* México, D.F.: Clio, 1996.

DAVID MACIEL

PARDO. Pardo, a term used throughout Latin America to refer to an individual of mixed racial ancestry. The most common usage of the term is in reference to someone whose brown or tan skin color indicates a racially mixed, black-white ancestry; in that sense, the term is frequently used interchangeably with *mulato.* In contemporary Brazil, the term is often employed as a polite alternative to *negro.*

In those areas of Latin America in which blacks constituted a significant part of the population, *pardos* came to represent the racial and social intermediate group between whites and blacks. Hence, colonial documents in Brazil often used four categories: white, *pardo*, blacks born in Brazil (*crioulo*), and African-born blacks (*negro* or *prêto*). *Pardos* were often seen as politically untrustworthy by imperial authorities, and special efforts were made to control them.

As with mestizos in areas of large indigenous populations, the identification of *pardos* as a separate racial category constituted an important recognition of the results of race mixing. It was also an important part of the sociopolitical process by which relatively small groups of white immigrants were able to preserve their racial homogeneity while racially fragmenting the subject populations and making unified resistance difficult.

See also **African Brazilians, Color Terminology; Africans in Hispanic America.**

BIBLIOGRAPHY

Thomas M. Stephens, *Dictionary of Latin American Racial and Ethnic Terminology* (1989).

Additional Bibliography

Hanchard, Michael George. *Racial Politics in Contemporary Brazil*. Durham, NC: Duke University Press, 1999.

Landers, Jane and Barry Robinson. *Slaves, Subjects, and Subversives: Blacks in Colonial Latin America*. Albuquerque: University of New Mexico Press, 2006.

Santos, Gislene Aparecida dos. *A invenção do "ser negro": Um percusso das idéias que naturalizaram a inferioridade dos negros*. São Paulo: Educ: FAPESP; Rio de Janeiro: Pallas, 2002.

DONALD RAMOS

PARDO, JUAN Juan Pardo, sixteenth-century Spanish soldier. Between 1566 and 1568, Pardo was commissioned by Pedro Menéndez de Avilés, governor of La Florida, to explore and to discover a route to Mexico. He twice led expeditions into the interior of La Florida from the town of Santa Elena (on Parris Island, South Carolina).

On the first journey, Pardo and 125 soldiers marched into western North Carolina. On the second, he followed the same route and then continued farther west, crossing the Appalachian Mountains and reaching Tennessee, probably south of present-day Knoxville. A portion of his route followed that taken by Hernando de Soto in 1540. Pardo established several forts, but they were soon abandoned. Accounts from the expeditions are an important source of information about native societies.

See also **Soto, Hernando de.**

BIBLIOGRAPHY

Chester B. De Pratter, Charles M. Hudson, and Marvin T. Smith, "The Route of Juan Pardo's Explorations in the Interior Southeast," *Florida Historical Quarterly* 62 (1983): 125–158.

Charles Hudson, *The Juan Pardo Expeditions: Exploration of the Carolinas and Tennessee, 1566–1568* (1990).

Additional Bibliography

Clayton, Lawrence. *The De Soto Chronicles: The Expedition of Hernando de Soto to North America in 1539–1543*. Tuscaloosa: University of Alabama Press, 1995.

Thomas, Hugh. *Rivers of Gold: The Rise of the Spanish Empire, from Columbus to Magellan*. New York: Random House Trade Paperbacks, 2005.

JERALD T. MILANICH

PARDO LEAL, JAIME (1941–1987). Jaime Pardo Leal (*b.* 1941; *d.* 11 October 1987), Colombian politician. Born in Ubáque, Cundinamarca, the son of a farmer, Pardo was sent to Bogotá to study. From the age of thirteen, he was involved in student protests and political action. At twenty, while a law student at the National University, he became vice president of the Federation of Colombian Students and was expelled from the university. In 1963, having nearly completed his law studies, he became a court clerk in Bogotá. A university amnesty in 1966 enabled Pardo to receive his law doctorate. He secured a judgeship in 1969. He organized Asonal, the national association of judicial workers in 1974, and led it in several nationwide strikes. From 1979 to 1985, Pardo was a magistrate on Bogotá's Superior Court. As Unión Patriótica's presidential candidate in the March 1986 elections, he polled 4.5 percent of the vote. From 1986 to 1987, more than 450 Unión Patriótica members were killed. Among them was Pardo, who was assassinated at La Mesa, Cundinamarca.

See also **Colombia: Since Independence.**

BIBLIOGRAPHY

Phil Gunson, Andrew Thompson, and Greg Chamberlain, *The Dictionary of Contemporary Politics of South America* (1989), pp. 74–76, 214–215, 248–249.

Jenny Pearse, *Colombia: Inside the Labyrinth* (1990), pp. 227–228, 247, 269–271, 279, 280–283.

Additional Bibliography

Dudley, Steven S. *Walking Ghosts: Murder and Guerrilla Politics in Colombia.* New York: Routledge, 2004.

Matta Aldana, Luis Alberto. *Poder capitalista y violencia política en Colombia: Terrorismo de estado y genocidio contra la Unión Patriótica.* Bogotá, D.C.: Edición Ideas y Soluciones Gráficas, 2002.

J. LEÓN HELGUERA

PARDO Y ALIAGA, FELIPE (1806–1868).

Felipe Pardo y Aliaga (*b.* 1806; *d.* 1868), Peruvian writer. The foremost literary figure of the post-Independence period in Peru, Pardo was a journalist, *costumbrista* (member of a nineteenth-century literary movement that sought to depict local manners and beliefs), poet, and dramatist. He was born into an aristocratic *limeño* family and received a classical Enlightenment education in Spain, returning to Peru in 1828 to become a prominent member of the Conservative Party. His literary work, which had a didactic quality and was European in orientation, satirized the disorders of the new republic, the narrow provincialism of his compatriots, and the generally low level of Peruvian culture. Ideologically his writings expressed a general conservatism and stressed orderly progress through discipline, industry, civic virtue, and respect for culture. The best of his work is represented in the *costumbrista* sketch "El paseo de Amancaes," his play *Frutos de la educación* (1830), and a poem, "El Perú."

See also **Literature: Spanish America.**

BIBLIOGRAPHY

James Higgins, *A History of Peruvian Literature* (1987).

Additional Bibliography

Cornejo Polar, Jorge. *Felipe Pardo y Aliaga: El inconforme.* Lima, Perú: Universidad de Lima, Fondo de Desarrollo Editorial, 2000.

Helg, Aline; Contreras, Carlos; Williams, Derek; and Margarita Garrido de Payan. *Political Cultures in the Andes, 1750–1950.* Edited by Nils Jacobsen and Cristóbal Aljovín de Losada. New York: Duke University Press, 2005.

Varillas, Alberto. *Felipe Pardo y Aliaga.* Lima, Perú: Editorial Brasa, 1995.

PETER F. KLARÉN

PARDO Y BARREDA, JOSÉ (1864–1947).

José Pardo y Barreda (*b.* 1864; *d.* 3 August 1947), president of Peru (1904–1908; 1915–1919). The son of Peru's first full-term civilian president, Manuel Pardo y Lavalle, José Pardo inherited the mantle of leadership of the Civilista Party in 1904 when Manuel Candamo died suddenly in office. Supported by the younger, reform-minded wing of the party, his presidency has been called the golden age of Civilista rule. For the next four years he increased school expenditures by 250 percent, extended major rail lines, and created a merchant marine. He served a second term as president (1915–1919), when, at military urging, the Civilista, Liberal, and Constitutionalist parties supported a common candidate. In his last term, responding to various pressures he unenthusiastically raised the minimum wage for farm workers and supported religious toleration. But the first general strike ever carried out in Peru (1 January 1919), uniting workers and university students, demanded student power in university administration and a universal eight-hour workday. Half-hearted Civilista reforms failed to stem growing student and labor political unrest.

See also **Peru, Political Parties: Civilista Party.**

BIBLIOGRAPHY

Steven Stern, *Populism in Peru: The Emergence of the Masses and the Politics of Social Control* (1980).

Peter Blanchard, *The Origins of the Peruvian Labor Movement, 1883–1919* (1982).

Additional Bibliography

McEvoy, Carmen. *La utopía republicana: Ideales y realidades en la formación de la cultura política peruana,*

1871–919. Lima: Pontifica Universidad Católica del Perú, Fondo Editorial, 1997.

McEvoy, Carmen. *Un proyecto nacional en el siglo XIX: Manuel Pardo y su vision del Perú.* Lima: Pontificia Universidad Católica del Perú, Fondo Editorial, 1994.

VINCENT PELOSO

PARDO Y LAVALLE, MANUEL (1834–1878).

Manuel Pardo y Lavalle (*b.* 9 August 1834; *d.* 16 November 1878), Peru's first full-term civilian president (1872–1876).

Son of the famed conservative writer Felipe Pardo, he was educated in Chile, Lima, and the universities of Barcelona and Paris. He returned to Peru in 1853 to launch a career in commerce and writing. His essays gained him a reputation as a champion of Peruvian nationalism. Already wealthy and well connected from ventures in banking, insurance, and commerce, he served as minister of the treasury in 1866, when guano was controlled by national merchants and the government borrowed heavily in Europe to fight a war with Spain (1864–1866). Two years later he served as president of the prestigious Lima Public Beneficence Society. After a brief, successful term as mayor of Lima (1869–1870), Pardo, a founder of the Civilista Party, was elected president in 1872 by the national electoral college. As president, Pardo sought to institute a program of reduced military expenditure, decentralization of government, restriction of clerical involvement in government, expanded public education, and state-planned economic development.

To carry out these plans under curtailed government spending, Pardo severely cut back the size of government bureaucracy and the army. In the meantime, the government raised taxes and printed paper money. In education, Pardo created public vocational schools, including one for indigenous youth, and founded national colleges to train teachers (men and women), miners, and engineers. New faculties of political and administrative sciences were established at the National University of San Marcos. He also organized a civilian national guard to counterbalance the professional army.

Pardo stepped down in favor of a military candidate in 1876, when party leaders were convinced that political anger was centered on the military; the purpose was to calm the military's fears of political isolation. This tactic did not stem the growing antagonism between the followers of Nicolás de Piérola and the Civilistas. Rebellions by both groups were barely suppressed, and in this tense atmosphere an embittered army sergeant blamed his failure to win a promotion on Pardo. The sergeant assassinated the former president, and his partisans long afterward blamed the assassination on Piérola, who in the days before the murder had delivered a series of bitter anti-Pardo speeches.

See also **Peru, Political Parties: Civilista Party.**

BIBLIOGRAPHY

Alfredo Moreno Mendiguren, *Manuel Pardo y Lavalle* (1961).

Paul Gootenberg, *Imagining Development: Economic Ideas in Peru's "Fictitious Prosperity" of Guano, 1840–1880* (1993).

Alfonso W. Quiroz, *Domestic and Foreign Finance in Modern Peru, 1850–1950: Financing Visions of Development* (1993).

Additional Bibliography

Leiva Viacava, Lourdes. *Nicolás de Piérola.* Lima: Editorial Brasa, 1995.

McEvoy, Carmen. *Un proyecto nacional en el siglo XIX: Manuel Pardo y su vision del Perú.* Lima: Pontificia Universidad Católica del Perú, Fondo Editorial, 1994.

VINCENT PELOSO

PAREDES, MARIANO (c. 1800–1856).

Mariano Paredes (*b.* ca. 1800; *d.* 2 December 1856), president of Guatemala (1849–1851). Paredes began his military career as an officer in the army of Governor Mariano Gálvez and later served with distinction under José Rafael Carrera.

Because he was reputed to be relatively apolitical, the Guatemalan National Assembly named him president of Guatemala after the resignation of Bernardo Escobar on 1 January 1849. He served as a transition between the Liberal revolutionaries of 1848 and the return of Conservative Rafael Carrera as president in 1851. Paredes initially resisted Carrera's return but in June 1849 agreed to it and in August commissioned Carrera as commander of the armed forces. The

Conservative rule that would last until 1871 was thus established under Paredes. He also permitted the Jesuits to return to Guatemala and promulgated a new, conservative constitution, under which Carrera returned to the presidency. General Paredes was a key officer in Carrera's army and commanded the Guatemalan forces in Nicaragua during the National War against William Walker in 1856 until his death from cholera during the siege of Granada.

See also **Carrera, José Rafael; Guatemala.**

BIBLIOGRAPHY

Ralph L. Woodward, Jr., *Rafael Carrera and the Emergence of the Republic of Guatemala, 1821–1871* (1993).

Additional Bibliography

Grandin, Greg. *The Blood of Guatemala: A History of Race and Nation*. Durham, NC: Duke University Press, 2000.

Gudmundson, Lowell, and Héctor Lindo-Fuentes. *Central America, 1821–1871: Liberalism before Liberal Reform*. Tuscaloosa: University of Alabama Press, 1995.

RALPH LEE WOODWARD JR.

PAREDES, TORIBIO DE. *See* Motolinía, Toribio de.

PAREDES Y ARRILLAGA, MARIANO

(1797–1849). Mariano Paredes y Arrillaga (*b.* 6 January 1797; *d.* 7 September 1849), Mexican general and politician. Born in Mexico City, Paredes was briefly president of Mexico in 1846. He had fought for the royalists in the War of Independence and supported Agustín de Iturbide's Plan of Iguala in 1821. A career army officer, he held various military posts in the 1820s but was slow to rise through the ranks. Favored by the regime of Anastasio Bustamante, Paredes was promoted to colonel in 1831 and the following year, at the age of thirty-five, to general. He served as minister of war for a few days in 1838. For the next several years, his base became Guadalajara of which he was made commander general. From 1841, Paredes participated in several rebellions on the side of General Antonio López de Santa Anna, but in 1844 he backed a successful

revolt against him. The next year, he rebelled against President José Joaquín de Herrera and assumed the presidency on 4 January 1846. On 28 July he was forced from office. He participated or was otherwise involved in further revolts until his death in Mexico City.

Paredes, who married into a wealthy Guadalajara family, was both an ardent centralist, supporting the restoration of a monarchy at one point in his career, and a fervent reactionary conservative, once warning Santa Anna of the dangers posed by "los terribles y perniciosos proletarios" (the dreadful and pernicious proletariat). Strongly proclerical, he believed that a liberal democracy and federal structure were inappropriate for Mexico in its then state of development, and that the country could be governed only by the army in alliance with the educated and affluent elite.

See also **Mexico: 1810–1910.**

BIBLIOGRAPHY

See Frank D. Robertson, "The Military and Political Career of Mariano Paredes y Arrillaga, 1797–1849" (Ph.D. diss., University of Texas, 1955).

Additional Bibliography

Andrews, Catherine. *The Political and Military Career of General Anastasio Bustamante (1780–1853)*. St. Andrews, Scotland: C. Andrews, 2001.

Krauze, Enrique. *Mexico: Biography of Power: A History of Modern Mexico, 1810–1996*. New York: Harper Perennial, 1998.

MICHAEL P. COSTELOE

PAREJA DIEZCANSECO, ALFREDO

(1908–1993). Alfredo Pareja Diezcanseco (*b.* 12 October 1908; *d.* 3 May 1993), Ecuadorian novelist and historian. Born in Guayaquil, Pareja had to interrupt his education after primary school because of the untimely death of his father when the young author was just thirteen. Later he attended the University of Quito, after which he became involved in several business activities. Only later did he turn to journalism and literature.

Throughout his long career, Pareja not only wrote extensively both fiction and nonfiction, but he also participated in diplomacy and politics. He represented Ecuador in Mexico, Argentina, and Chile, and he served as the administrator of the United Nations Relief Agency for Central America. In domestic politics, Pareja became elected deputy to the Constituent Assembly of Ecuador in 1944, and a leader in the Democratic National Front in 1956 and 1960. On occasion his impassioned opposition to dictatorial regimes cost him his freedom and forced him into exile.

It is Pareja's written work, however, that built a solid reputation for him within and outside his country. He wrote several realistic novels in the 1930s and 1940s on the harsh life endured by the working Ecuadorian people. Later he turned to biographies and then to histories, culminating in his well-received *Historia del Ecuador* (2 vols., 2d ed. [1958]). His later work *Las pequeñas estaturas* (1970) is renowned for its impact on Hispanic narrative technique. He incorporates various stylistic techniques to exemplify the various assimilations that he saw taking place around him.

See also **Literature: Spanish America.**

BIBLIOGRAPHY

Lilo Linke, "The People's Chronicler: Novelist Alfredo Pareja Writes About His Native Ecuador," in *Américas* 8 (1956): 7–11.

Unión Panamericana, *Diccionario de la literatura latinoamericana: Ecuador* (1962), pp. 144–147.

Agustín Cueva, *La literatura ecuatoriana* (1968), pp. 41, 48–49.

Additional Bibliography

Pérez, Galo René. *Literatura del Ecuador 400 años.* Quito: Ediciones Abya-Yala, 2001.

Rengifo, Alberto. *La narrativa de Alfredo Pareja Diezcanseco.* Quito: Banco Central del Ecuador, 1990.

JACK RAY THOMAS

PARENTELA. Parentela, a term used to describe a large kinship group exceeding the boundaries of a patriarchal family or clan in rural Brazil. It includes not only consanguines and affines, bound through marriage, but also nonrelated dependents linked through godparentage, friendship, and adoption. *Parentela* is most commonly used to refer to political interest groups grounded in family-based clans of the

Brazilian Northeast during the Second Empire (1840–1889) and First Republic (1889–1930). Patronage, government jobs, and subsidies flowed through these extended kinship networks. *Parentela* is also associated with Coronelismo of the First Republic, the oligarchic rule in the Brazilian interior by local bosses who held honorary titles in the National Guard.

See also **Family.**

BIBLIOGRAPHY

Billy Jaymes Chandler, *The Feitosas and the Sertão of Inhamuns: The History of a Family and a Community in Northeastern Brazil, 1700–1930* (1972).

Victor Nunes Leal, *Coronelismo, enxada e voto: O município e o regime representativo no Brasil,* 2d ed. (1975).

Maria Isaura Pereira De Queiroz, *O mandonismo local na vida política brasileira e outros ensaios* (1976).

Linda Lewin, *Politics and Parentela in Paraíba: A Case Study of Family-Based Oligarchy in Brazil* (1987).

Additional Bibliography

Borges, Dain Edward. *The Family in Bahia, Brazil, 1870-1945.* Stanford, CA: Stanford University Press, 1992.

Zephyr, Frank. "Elite Families and Oligarchic Politics on the Brazilian Frontier: Mato Grosso, 1889–1937." *Latin American Research Review.* 36:1 (2001): 49–74.

JUDY BIEBER FREITAS

PARIÁN. Parián, the central marketplace of Mexico City in the eighteenth and early nineteenth centuries. Located in the city's main plaza, the Parián consisted of numerous shops, built of stone to a standardized size and height, and arranged in two concentric rectangles. The market received its name (possibly from Filipino merchants) because of its supposed likeness to an enclosed shopping district in Manila. The construction of the Parián— mandated by a royal Cédula of 30 December 1694—represented a multipurpose response to the Mexico City riot of 1692. The new stone shops, rented to local merchants, provided safer, more durable replacements for the wooden shops (*cajones*) burned in the riot, thereby promoting commerce and restoring an important source of the city's income. The crown also hoped to achieve its long-standing goal of dispersing the petty vendors, beggars, and vagabonds who thronged the plaza. This last aim failed, but the Parián (completed in 1703) did become the most active of Mexico City's markets, selling all manner of goods, elite and plebeian, imported and domestic. Sacked during a popular uprising in 1828, the Parián never recovered; its merchants drifted away, and the increasingly untenanted marketplace came to be an eyesore. Antonio López de Santa Anna ordered its demolition, which took place on 27 July 1843.

See also **Cédula.**

BIBLIOGRAPHY

Manuel Orozco y Berra, *Historia de la ciudad de México desde su fundación hasta 1854.* México: Secretaria de Educación Pública, (1973), pp. 110–118.

John E. Kicza, *Colonial Entrepreneurs: Families and Business in Bourbon Mexico City.* Albuquerque: University of New Mexico Press, 1983.

Silvia M. Arrom, "Popular Politics in Mexico City: The Parián Riot, 1828," in *Hispanic American Historical Review* 68 (1985): 245–270.

Additional Bibliography

Carlos Casas, Bernardo. *El Parián.* Tlaquepaque: H. Ayuntamiento de Tlaquepaque, Dirección de Comunicación Social, 1997.

McFarlane, Anthony. "Popular Politics in Mexico City: The Parián Riot, 1828." In *Riots in the Cities: Popular Politics and the Urban Poor in Latin America, 1765–1910,* eds. Silvia Arrom and Servando Ortoll. Wilmington, DE: Scholarly Resources, 1996.

R. DOUGLAS COPE

PARICUTÍN. Paricutín is the most recently formed volcano in Mexico's 550-mile east-west Cordillera Neovolcánica, which forms the highlands marking the southern boundary of the Mesa Central. Most of the volcanoes in this range were formed during the late Tertiary, but many have been active in historic times. Colima, for instance, erupted in 1913, and Popocatépetl was active in 1920–1924. After two weeks of earth tremors, Paricutín began forming on the northwestern slope of an old volcano, Tancítaro, in the late afternoon of 20 February 1943, actually growing out of the cornfield of a farmer named Dionisio Pullido. The volcano exploded ash and built a cone of about 550 feet within six days. Its lava flows covered 7 square miles and engulfed several towns and villages, including the district capital, San Juan Parangaricutiro, forcing some 5,000 people to relocate. After three years, Paricutín's cone had risen about 1,150 feet above the original vent. Much of the region still bears scars of the eruption, although Paricutín has been dormant since 1952.

See also **Volcanoes.**

BIBLIOGRAPHY

William Foshag and Jenaro Gonzales Reyna, *Birth and Development of Paricutín Volcano, Mexico,* U.S. Geological Survey Bulletin no. 965-D (1956).

Additional Bibliography

Guzmán Villanueva, Raquel. "La erupción del volcán Paricutín: impacto geográfico." *Anuario de Geografía (Mexico)* 26 (1990-1992): 185-192.

Kent, Robert B. *Latin America: Regions and People.* New York: Guilford Press, 2006.

Werner, Luis. "Paricutínn Sparks a Miraculous Pilgrimage." *Américas* 43 (1991): 6–15.

JOHN J. WINBERRY

PARISH, WOODBINE (1796–1882). Woodbine Parish (*b.* 14 September 1796; *d.* 16 August 1882), British diplomat. As Great Britain's consul to the government of the United Provinces of the Río De La Plata in Buenos Aires, Parish served as the embodiment of Foreign Secretary George Canning's policy toward the newly independent former Spanish colonies in the Americas.

Born to a prestigious commercial and political family, Parish served as an aide to Lord Castlereagh in Europe before arriving in Buenos Aires in 1824 as the first European representative to the young republic. During his nine years as consul, Parish was instrumental in convincing the British government to grant full recognition to the United Provinces, and he helped establish the close economic and cultural ties that were to become the hallmark of British-Argentine relations. In 1839 Parish published *Buenos Aires and the Provinces of the Río de la Plata: Their Present State, Debt, and Trade,* a thorough analysis of Argentina during its early years of independence.

Parish became popular with the Argentines, due to his bilingualism and obvious interest in their culture and traditions. Through the efforts of Parish and other like-minded diplomats, Great Britain was able to ensure an economic and political climate favorable to British interests.

See also **Argentina: The Nineteenth Century; British in Argentina; United Provinces of the Río de la Plata.**

BIBLIOGRAPHY

McLean, David. *War, Diplomacy, and the Informal Empire: Britain and the Republics of La Plata, 1836–1853.* London: British Academic Press, 1995.

Solari Yrigoyen, Hipólito. *Malvinas: Lo que no cuentan los ingleses (1833–1982).* Buenos Aires: El Ateneo, 1998.

JOHN DUDLEY

See also **Colombia: Since Independence; Colombia, Political Parties: Radical Olympus; War of the Thousand Days.**

BIBLIOGRAPHY

Helen Delpar, *Red Against Blue: The Liberal Party in Colombian Politics, 1863–1899* (1981).

James William Park, *Rafael Nuñez and the Politics of Colombian Regionalism, 1863–1886* (1985).

Ignacio Arizmendi Posada, *Presidentes de Colombia, 1810–1990* (1990), pp. 147–150.

Additional Bibliography

Rivadeneira Vargas, Antonio José. *Aquileo Parra y la ideología radical.* Bogotá: Editorial Planeta Colombiana, 2001.

RICHARD J. STOLLER

PARRA, AQUILEO (1825–1900). Aquileo Parra (*b.* 12 May 1825; *d.* 4 December 1900), president of Colombia (1876–1878). Born in Barichara, Santander, to a family of modest means, in the 1840s Parra pioneered the jungle route between Vélez and Mompós, slowly accumulating a modest fortune. A reluctant defender of the Radical Liberal regime in Santander, Parra was imprisoned after the Liberal defeat at Oratorio in 1860. In 1874 he was elected president of Santander. In the 1875 elections for the national presidency, Parra represented the establishment Liberal bloc known derisively as the Radical Olympus, and his victory was widely ascribed to fraud. His administration, weakened by budget disputes and renewed conflict with the church, was soon faced with a Conservative rebellion. Despite suppressing the rebellion, Parra left office discredited. In the 1890s Parra attempted to strengthen the vanquished Liberals' organization, hoping to limit the appeal of more bellicose Liberals such as Rafael Uribe Uribe. The outbreak of the War of the Thousand Days in October 1899 represented the failure of this effort; Parra died shortly thereafter. His informative *Memorias* (1912) confirm Parra's ideological place somewhat to the right of his contemporary Salvador Camacho Roldán, but to the left of many other figures of the "Olympus."

PARRA, FÉLIX (1845–1919). Félix Parra (*b.* 1845; *d.* 1919), Mexican painter. In 1861 Parra entered the school of drawing and painting at the College of San Nicolás in Morelia. In 1864 he moved to the Academy of San Carlos in Mexico City, which was occupied by French troops awaiting the arrival of Maximilian. Most of his education was under Mexican masters, since foreigners were not to Maximilian's liking. By this time the academy had already produced a generation of Mexicans trained under Spanish masters.

The themes that Parra presented in different exhibitions demonstrate the changes occurring at the time in the academy as well as in the critical world. In 1871 he presented a tender nude within the theme of the hunter, following the logic of European schools. In 1873 in the school of Padua he presented *Galileo*, which demonstrated the new astronomical theories. This is without a doubt one of his greatest works. In 1875 he unveiled a canvas of great dimensions, *Fray Bartolomé de las Casas*, and in 1877 he presented *La Matanza de Cholula*, whose historical component was taken from the book *Historia general de los Indios* by Fray Bartolomé de Las Casas. In it the Spanish missionary protests to his fellows the massacre of thirty thousand Cholultec Indians. This painting won Parra a scholarship from the academy to study in Europe.

Parra spent four years in France and Italy and returned to Mexico in 1882 as professor of ornamentation at the National School of Fine Arts. Beginning in 1909, another of his occupations was as sketcher at the National Museum, where he developed his skill with watercolor. He retired from his classes in 1915, by which time the school was no longer the center of artistic education.

See also **Art: The Nineteenth Century; Art: The Twentieth Century.**

BIBLIOGRAPHY

Justino Fernández, *El arte del siglo XIX en Mexico,* 3d ed. (1983).

Fausto Ramírez, *La plástica del siglo de la independencia* (1985).

Additional Bibliography

Antiguo Colegio de San Ildefonso. *Arte de las academias: Francia y México, siglos XVII–XIX.* Ciudad de México: Antiguo Colegio de San Ildefonso, 1999.

ESTHER ACEVEDO

PARRA, NICANOR (1914–).

Nicanor Parra (*b.* 5 September 1914), Chilean poet. A former science teacher, Parra, who published his first collection of poems, *Cancionero sin nombre,* in 1937, describes himself, adopting a term coined by Vicente Huidobro, as an antipoet. Like Huidobro, Parra demonstrates in his poems a freedom of experimentation and an irreverence toward traditionally held poetic values. Parra gained immediate popular acclaim with his second collection, *Poemas y antipoemas* (1954). With subsequent books, such as *La cueca larga* (1958), *Versos de salón* (1962), *Artefactos* (1972), *Sermones y prédicas del Cristo de Elqui* (1977), *Hojas de Parra* (1985), *Páginas en blanco* (2001) and *Lear Rey & Mendigo* (2004), Parra received international recognition. His innovative style of poetry combines wordplay, humor, the vernacular, and elements of literary tradition and popular culture to formulate an ironic commentary on human nature and society. Parra avoids personal involvement in his writing; his poems reflect a critical skepticism toward social conformism. A self-styled nihilist, Parra offers no escape from the absurdities and inconsequence of human

values and beliefs. His sobering, if cynical, view of reality and his simple, direct style have made a lasting impact on Hispanic lyrical verse.

See also **Huidobro Fernández, Vicente.**

BIBLIOGRAPHY

Hugo Montes, *Nicanor Parra y la poesía de lo cotidiano* (1970).

Edith Grossman, *The Antipoetry of Nicanor Parra* (1975).

Antonio Skármeta, "Nicanor Parra," in *Latin American Writers,* edited by Carlos A. Solé and Maria Isabel Abreu, vol. 3 (1989), pp. 1195–1200.

Additional Bibliography

Carrasco, Iván. *Para leer a Nicanor Para.* Santiago, Chile: Universidad Nacional Andrés Bello, 1999.

Olivera, Sonia Mereles. *Cumbres poéticas latinoamericanas.* New York, P. Lang, 2003.

Rowe, William. *Poets of Contemporary Latin America.* New York: Oxford University Press, 2000.

S. DAYDÍ TOLSON

PARRA, TERESA DE LA (1890–1936).

Teresa de la Parra (Ana Teresa Parra Sanojo; *b.* 5 October 1890; *d.* 23 April 1936), Venezuelan novelist. She was born in Paris into Venezuela's plantation-owning class. When her father died in 1898, her mother took the family to Spain. As a member of an aristocratic Spanish family, she was sent to a convent to obtain a traditional education. At the age of eighteen, she returned to Caracas and lived in the Hacienda Tazón, where she read constantly. The Caracas society to which she belonged exposed Parra to the prejudice and discrimination that women faced. This awareness of differences in social standing between men and women led her to writing.

Parra's first work was "Mamá X," which later became part of her first novel, *Ifigenia.* This story won her an award that served as an incentive for further development. In 1923, Parra returned to Europe and settled in Paris, where she organized a *salón literario* at which Latin Americans met. Parra was invited to lecture in Cuba and Colombia, but she lived most of her life outside of Venezuela. She died in Madrid. In 1948 her remains were repatriated to her country of origin.

Parra's literary works are *Diario de una señorita que se fastidia,* (1922; Journal of an Upset Young Woman); *Ifigenia: diario de una señorita que escribió porque se fastidiaba* (1924), published in Paris with a preface by Francis de Miomandres; and *Las memorias de la Mamá Blanca* (1929), also published in Paris. Her letters and her unpublished lectures were included in *Obras completas* (1965). Her novels represent life in nineteenth-century Venezuela from the viewpoint of female protagonists, thus constituting a profound reflection on a passing way of life.

See also **Literature: Spanish America.**

BIBLIOGRAPHY

Ramón Díaz Sánchez, *Teresa de la Parra* (1954).

Efraín Subero, Raquel Berlin, et al., eds., *Contribución a la bibliografía de Teresa de la Parra, 1895–1936* (1970).

Mariano Picón Salas et al., *Teresa de la Parra; bibliografía y otros trabajos* (Caracas, 1980).

Additional Bibliography

Guerra-Cunningham, Lucía. "Cuerpo de mujer y rituales del adorno en 'Ifigenia' de Teresa de la Parra." *Letras Femeninas* 30:1 (Summer 2004): 129–140.

Wang, Lih-Lirng Soang. "Power, Language, and Culture: Teresa de la Parra in Latin American Feminism." Ph.D. Dissertation, University of Illinois at Urbana-Champaign, 1995.

MAGDALENA GARCÍA PINTO

PARRA, VIOLETA (1917–1967).

Violeta Parra (*b.* 4 October 1917; *d.* 5 February 1967), Chilean folklorist, singer, and composer. Parra was the mother of the musicians Ángel and Isabel Parra and sister of the poet Nicanor Parra. Born in San Carlos, in the province of Nuble, she moved to Santiago in her teens and scraped together a living by singing in bars, cafes, and restaurants. In the early 1950s she found her vocation as collector and performer of folk songs, and later made some memorable recordings. She soon began writing her own songs in folk idiom as well as developing her talents for weaving, pottery, and painting.

Parra lived for two periods (1954–1956 and 1961–1965) in France. Finally returning to Chile, she recorded her classic "Last Compositions of Violeta Parra," several of whose tracks are of exceptional quality, and established a folklore center in a circus tent in the Santiago suburb of La Reina.

A passionate, direct, sometimes tempestuous woman—she was called by Pablo Neruda "a saint of pure clay"—she shot herself, partly in despair over a broken love affair. The music of this extraordinary woman was a key inspiration for the New Chilean Song movement of the late 1960s and early 1970s.

See also **Music: Popular Music and Dance.**

BIBLIOGRAPHY

Isabel Parra, *El libro mayor de Violeta Parra* (1984).

Carmen Oviedo, *Mentira todo lo cierto: Tras la huella de Violeta Parra* (1990).

Additional Bibliography

Morales T., Leonidas, and Nicanor Parra. *Violeta Parra: La última canción.* Providencia, Santiago de Chile: Editorial Cuarto Propio, 2003.

Sáez, Fernando. *La vida intranquila: Violeta Parra, biografía esencial.* Santiago de Chile: Editorial Sudamericana, 1999.

SIMON COLLIER

PARRAL.

Parral, an important mining center in the Mexican state of Chihuahua. Though prospectors were active in the area as early as the 1560s, it was not until 1631 that the first major silver strike occurred, creating a rush and the foundation of San José del Parral. Because the nonsedentary Chichimecs of the region could not be used as tribute labor, an attempt was made to organize *encomiendas* among the Concho, a semisedentary indigenous group. When this proved unsuccessful, mine operators turned to other sources of labor, including a small number of indigenous people enslaved by war. However, the employment of African slaves and large numbers of free workers of various ethnicities were the norm from almost the beginning. Through the colonial era and beyond, Parral's mines typically experienced numerous booms and busts. The town achieved a different kind of notoriety on 20 July 1923, when Pancho Villa was assassinated there.

See also **Mining: Colonial Spanish America.**

BIBLIOGRAPHY

The basic study remains Robert C. West, *The Mining Community in Northern New Spain: The Parral Mining District*. Berkeley: University of California, 1949. Peter Gerhard, *The North Frontier of New Spain*. Princeton, NJ: Princeton University Press, 1982, pp. 216–219, presents a brief overview of colonial Parral; the town's late colonial social history is investigated in Robert Mc Caa, "Calidad, Clase, and Marriage in Colonial Mexico: The Case of Parral, 1788–90," in *Hispanic American Historical Review* 64 (August 1984): 477–501; and rural labor in colonial Nueva Vizcaya, the greater region surrounding Parral, is examined in Susan M. Deeds, "Rural Work in Nueva Vizcaya: Forms of Labor Coercion on the Periphery," in *Hispanic American Historical Review* 69 (August 1989): 425–449.

Additional Bibliography

Bendesky, León, and Raul Conde Hernández. *Parral, comunidad y desarrollo.* Chihuahua, México: Universidad Autónoma de Chihuahua: Doble Hélice, 2001.

Martínez Meraz, Silvia Margarita. *Educación y género: Docencia femenina en hidalgo del Parral, Chih. (1631-1900.)* Chihuahua: Doble Hélice Ediciones, 2006.

Vargas Valdez, Jesús. *Pedro Alvarado y Virginia Griensen: Una vida, un palacio: Entre la historia y la leyenda.* Gobierno del Estado de Chihuahua, Secretaria de Educación y Cultura, Dirección de Publicaciónes y Proyectos Especiales, 2001.

ROBERT HASKETT

PARRA SANOJO, ANA TERESA DE LA. *See* Parra, Teresa de la.

PARTICIPATORY BUDGETING. Participatory budgeting is a process that provides for citizen input into the allocation of resources by local governments. Originally promoted as a democratizing reform by the Partido dos Trabalhadores (Workers Party or PT) in Brazil, participatory budgeting has been adopted around the world.

Drawing on its tradition of neighbourhood assemblies, Porto Alegre was the first city in Brazil to adopt the arrangement in 1989–1990. Its phased approach to engaging citizens in decision-making combines elements of deliberative and representative democracy. All citizens are eligible to attend district-level assemblies to discuss local needs and budget priorities. In turn, the assemblies elect representatives who serve on a citywide council that formulates budgetary targets and monitors the budgetary process and implementation.

Widely considered to be a successful experiment in promoting citizen participation in Porto Alegre, the practice has spread rapidly throughout Brazil. By 2004, 200 cities in Brazil were using the arrangement, as were hundreds of cities throughout Latin America. Spain, Italy, Canada, Indonesia, South Africa, and India are among the countries that have also adopted variations of participatory budgeting. International organizations from the World Bank to the United Nations have endorsed participatory budgeting as a "best practice" and promote it in their programming. Participatory budgeting is among the most innovative practices in modern democratic government to emerge from contemporary Latin America.

See also **Brazil, Political Parties: Workers Party (PT).**

BIBLIOGRAPHY

Baiocchi, Gianpaolo. *Militants and Citizens: The Politics of Participatory Democracy in Porto Alegre.* Stanford, CA: Stanford University Press, 2005.

Nylen, William. *Participatory Democracy versus Elitist Democracy: Lessons from Brazil.* New York: Palgrave Macmillan, 2003.

CATHERINE CONAGHAN

PARTIDO. *Partido* is the practice of giving mine workers a part of their pay in silver ore. After the worker had extracted a fixed amount of ore from the mine workings, he had the right to half of the additional ore that he could remove from the mine during the shift. In mines where entrepreneurs had no money to pay wages, owner and worker shared the ore. The partido was compensation for the extraordinary dangers of mine work and arose in response to a shortage of free labor as well as a scarcity of capital with which to pay the workers. Even after independence, as mines were developed or acquired by foreign firms that sought to change the work regime, workers continued to press, though increasingly unsuccessfully, for the right of the partido.

See also **Mining: Colonial Spanish America; Mining: Modern.**

BIBLIOGRAPHY

Partido is treated in David A. Brading, *Miners and Merchants in Bourbon Mexico* (1971); Alan Probert," Discord at Real del Monte," in *Journal of the West* 14 (April 1975): 35–50; and in Doris Ladd, *The Making of a Strike: Mexican Silver Workers' Struggles in Real del Monte, 1766–1775* (1988).

Additional Bibliography

Cubillo Moreno, Gilda. *Los dominios de la plata: El precio del auge, el peso del poder: Empresarios y trabajadores en las minas de Pachuca y Zimapán, 1552–1620.* Mexico City: Instituto Nacional de Antropología e Historia, 1991.

Couturier, Edith Boorstein. *The Silver King: The Remarkable Life of the Count of Regla in Colonial Mexico.* Albuquerque: University of New Mexico Press, 2003.

Herrera Canales, Inés, ed. *La Minería mexicana: De la colonia al siglo XX.* Mexico City: Instituto Mora, El Colegio de Michocoán, El Colegio de México, Instituto de Investigaciones Históricas-UNAM, 1998.

EDITH COUTURIER

PASCAL-TROUILLOT, ERTHA (1943–).

Ertha Pascal-Trouillot (*b.* 13 August 1943), provisional president of Haiti (13 March 1990–7 February 1991). A lawyer, Pascal-Trouillot served as a lower court judge, and in 1986 she was the first woman appointed to the Supreme Court. Shortly after General Prosper Avril was forced out as de facto ruler, she was the only one among the twelve court judges who was acceptable or willing to become provisional president, as provided in the 1987 Constitution. When inaugurated, Pascal-Trouillot committed herself to oversee the preparation for a political campaign and national elections and "accepted this heavy task in the name of the Haitian woman." She remained in office—surviving one attempted coup—until the election (December 1990) and inauguration (February 1991) of Father Jean-Bertrand Aristide as president.

See also **Aristide, Jean-Bertrand; Haiti, Constitutions.**

BIBLIOGRAPHY

The New York Times, 13 and 14 March, 16 December 1990.

Additional Bibliography

N'Zengou-Tayo, Marie-José. "'Fanm Se Poto Mitan': Haitian Woman, the Pillar of Society." *Feminist Review* (Summer 1998): 118-142.

Opfell, Olga. *Women Prime Ministers and Presidents.* Jefferson: McFarland & Co., 1993.

LARMAN C. WILSON

PASCOAL, HERMETO (1936–).

The Brazilian composer and multi-instrumentalist Hermeto Pascoal is one of the best-known jazz artists from Latin America. Born on June 22, 1936, in Lagoa da Canoa, a small rural town in the northeastern Brazilian state of Alagoas, Pascoal performs music that is deeply rooted in the folkloric music and ambient sounds of his birthplace. A self-taught musician, Pascoal is a virtuoso pianist who also performs regularly on accordion, flute, saxophone, and various brass, percussion, and string instruments. In addition, he is a prolific composer who by the beginning of the twenty-first century had written well over 2,000 pieces, several of which, including "O Ovo" (The egg), "Chorinho pra Ele" (Chorinho for him), and "Bebê" (Babe) have become standards in the Brazilian jazz repertoire. He often integrates ambient sounds into his compositions —for example, his use of live pigs on "Missa dos Escravos" (Slaves Mass) from his record *Slaves Mass* (1976) and a soccer announcer on "Tiruliruli" from *Lagoa da Canoa Município de Arapiraca* (1984).

Pascoal's musical talent was evident early; by age eleven he was already playing accordion professionally with his father and brother at local dances. In the late 1950s he moved south, first to Rio de Janeiro and eventually to São Paulo, where he worked as a studio musician and played with several influential groups, including the Sambrasa Trio and Quarteto Novo. In 1970 Pascoal traveled to the United States, where he recorded with Miles Davis and Airto Moreira, among others. While there Pascoal also recorded his first solo album, *Hermeto*, before returning to São Paulo to embark on a solo career. In 1977 Pascoal relocated to Rio de Janeiro, where he organized his greatest band, O Grupo (The group). Rehearsing at his home six hours per day, five days per week, the band developed an extensive and varied repertoire that ranged from complex, multilayered works to folklike tunes and free improvisations. From 1980 to 1992 Pascoal enjoyed the most productive phase of his career, touring regularly throughout Europe, the United States, and Asia and releasing a series of influential recordings. Since 1993 his recordings have been more sporadic, but he continues to compose and tour, both as a solo performer and in conjunction with O Grupo. In 1996–1997 he completed a project in which he composed a tune per day for an entire year, the results of which were published in his book *Calendário do Som* (Calendar of sound) (2000).

See also **Music: Popular Music and Dance.**

BIBLIOGRAPHY

Work by Pascoal

Pascoal, Hermeto. *Calendário do Som*. São Paulo, Brazil: Editora Senac, 2000.

Other Works

Connell, Andrew M. "Refiguring the Familiar in Hermeto Pascoal's *Som da Aura*." In *Musical Cultures of Latin America: Global Effects Past and Present*, edited by Steven Loza. Los Angeles: Department of Ethnomusicology and Systematic Musicology, University of California, Los Angeles, 2003. UCLA Selected Reports in Ethnomusicology, vol. 11.

Neto, Luiz Costa Lima. "The Experimental Music of Hermeto Paschoal e Grupo (1981–93): A Musical System in the Making." *British Journal of Ethnomusicology* 9, no. 1 (2000): 119–142.

ANDREW M. CONNELL

PASO, FERNANDO DEL (1935–). Fernando del Paso (*b.* 1 April 1935), Mexican novelist. Born in Mexico City, Paso studied economics and medicine at the Universidad Nacional Autónoma de México. He then worked in advertising and for the BBC in London from 1970 to 1984, and since then has served as cultural attaché, then consul general, to the Mexican embassy in Paris.

Although he has published two volumes of poetry and has gained recognition for his paintings and drawings of whimsical castles and creatures, Paso is best known for his three monumental novels. *José Trigo* (1966) uses experimental techniques to evoke a working-class neighborhood of Mexico City and the railroad workers' movement of 1958. *Palinuro de México* (1977) is the saga of a medical student who, swept up in the student movement of 1968, dies in the government massacre at the Plaza of Tlatelolco. *Noticias del imperio* (1987) is a historical novel about the French Intervention in Mexico, which imposed the Hapsburg monarchy of Maximilian and Carlota (1864–1867); much of it is narrated from the point of view of the mad empress.

Del Paso has been a member of the National College since 1996 and won several international awards prior to that, including the 1985 Best Novel Published in France Award (for Palinurus of Mexico), the 1982 Rómulo Gallegos Prize, the 1976 Mexico Novel Award and the 1966 Xavier Villaurrutia Award. In 2007 the Universidad de Guadalajara (Mexico) honored del Paso by naming its library after him.

See also **Literature: Spanish America.**

BIBLIOGRAPHY

Mónica Mansour, *Los mundos de Palinuro* (1986).

Robbin Fiddian, "Fernando del Paso y el arte de la renovación," in *Revista iberoamericana*, no. 150 (January–March 1990): 143–158.

Cynthia Steele, "The Novel as Pyramid: *Palinuro de México* (1977), by Fernando del Paso," in her *Politics, Gender, and the Mexican Novel, 1968–1988: Beyond the Pyramid* (1992), pp. 66–87.

Additional Bibliography

Corral Peña, Elizabeth. *Recuadros verbales: Imágenes sobre la narrativa de Fernando del Paso*. México, D.F.: Desarrollo Cultural Regional, 1999.

Fiddian, Robin W. *The Novels of Fernando del Paso*. Gainesville: University Press of Florida, 2000.

González, Alfonso. *Voces de la posmodernidad: Seis narradores mexicanos contemporáneos*. México, D.F.: Coordinación de Difusión Cultural, Dirección de Literatura/UNAM, 1998.

Paso, Fernando del. *Palinure de Mexico*. Paris: Seuil, 1991.

Rodríguez Lozano, Miguel G. *José Trigo: El nacimiento discursivo de Fernando del Paso*. Mexico, D.F.: Universidad Nacional Autónoma de México, 1997.

Sáenz, Inés. *Hacia la novela total: Fernando del Paso*. Madrid: Editorial Pliegos, 1994.

Trejo Fuentes, Ignacio. "Fernando del Paso ante la crítica." *Siempre* 44, no. 2317 (November 1997).

CYNTHIA STEELE

PASO, JUAN JOSÉ (1758–1833).

Juan José Paso (*b.* 2 January 1758; *d.* 10 September 1833), Argentine educator, journalist, lawyer, and public official in the Río de la Plata. Born in Buenos Aires, Paso studied law and theology (through 1779) at the universities of Chuquisaca and Córdoba. Returning to his birthplace, Paso taught philosophy at the Colegio de San Carlos (1781–1783). He was a member of the first patriot government of Argentina in 1810. During the early 1800s he edited, with Mariano Moreno, another secretary of the revolutionary junta, *La Gaceta de Buenos Aires,* the official newspaper of the new regime. Paso held the positions of assistant prosecutor of the Royal Treasury in 1803 and advisor to the government during Carlos María de Alvear's directorate in 1815. He also served on the triumvirates of 1811–1812 after the dissolution of the junta and as representative in the Congress of Tucumán in 1816. In addition, Paso was the Santiago-based diplomat of the United Provinces in 1814. Mariano Balcarce, describing him as "the illustrious son of the nation who knew how to provide important services to the cause of independence, skillfully and with talent, and was a jurist known for his integrity and zeal," ordered the construction of a monument in his honor after his death.

See also **Argentina: The Nineteenth Century.**

BIBLIOGRAPHY

José María Saenz Valiente, *Juan José Paso* (1911).

Alberto Rodríguez Varela, *Gobernantes de Mayo* (1960).

Vicente Osvaldo Cutolo, *Nuevo diccionario biográfico argentino,* vol. 5 (1968–1985), pp. 318–322.

Additional Bibliography

Aguirre, Gisela. *Juan José Paso.* Buenos Aires: Planeta, 2001.

Tanzi, Héctor José. *Juan José Paso, el político.* Buenos Aires: Ciudad Argentina, 1998.

FIDEL IGLESIAS

PASO Y TRONCOSO, FRANCISCO DEL (1842–1916).

Francisco Del Paso y Troncoso (*b.* 8 October 1842; *d.* 30 April 1916), Mexican historian. Born in Veracruz, Paso y Troncoso originally studied for a career in business. In 1867 he journeyed to Mexico City in order to pursue a career in medicine, a course of studies which led him to investigate the history of science in Mexico under the Aztecs. He never completed his degree in medicine, turning his attention completely to the study of native history and linguistics. He gathered together major chronicles and other texts and codices on the pre-contact and colonial periods, and mastered Nahuatl, the language of the Aztecs. Appointed director of the National Museum in 1889, he sailed for Europe in 1892 in order to search for documents relating to Mexico. He scoured archives in Spain, England, Russia, Germany, Austria, France, and Italy, where he spent the last period of his life. Though he did not return to Mexico, he was in constant contact with government officials, including President Porfirio Díaz, who were funding his projects. After the outbreak of the Revolution funding became increasingly more difficult.

After his death the repatriation of the documents collected by this major investigator proved problematic, and his complete collection was never fully restored. Nonetheless, as a result of his exhaustive labors he brought to light a corpus of works by the sixteenth-century Franciscan ethnographer Bernardino de Sahagún (ca. 1499–1590). He also prepared a monumental collection of documents known as the *Papeles de Nueva España,* consisting of bibliographies, geography and statistics, histories, letters, and dictionaries of native languages. Such were the volume of his findings and the detail of his inquiry that many of these projects were not published until after his death.

See also **Mexico: The Colonial Period; Sahagún, Bernardino de.**

BIBLIOGRAPHY

Silvio Arturo Zavala, *Francisco del Paso y Troncoso, su misión en Europa, 1892–1916* (1938).

Howard F. Cline, "Selected Nineteenth-Century Mexican Writers on Ethnohistory," in *Handbook of Middle American Indians,* vol. 13 (1973), pp. 370–427.

Additional Bibliography

León Portilla, Miguel. *Bernardino de Sahagún: First Anthropologist.* Norman: University of Oklahoma Press, 2002.

BRIAN C. BELANGER

PASSARINHO, JARBAS GONÇALVES

(1920–). Jarbas Gonçalves Passarinho (*b.* 11 January 1920), Brazilian Military Commander of the Amazon who became a prominent political leader of the military regime that ruled Brazil from 1964 to 1985. Named governor of the state of Pará shortly after the coup in 1964, Passarinho served in that post until 1966. In 1967, after being elected to the Senate (1967–1983), he was appointed minister of labor and social welfare by President Artur da Costa E Silva. In December 1968, Passarinho signed Institutional Act 5, which marked the beginning of Brazil's most repressive phase of military rule. One of the few politicians to enjoy confidence among the competing military factions, he served as minister of education and culture (1970–1973) under President Emilio Garrastazu Médici. Elected to the Senate from Pará in 1975, Passarinho served for eight years. In 1983, Passarinho was appointed minister of welfare and social assistance by President João Baptista Figueiredo. He demonstrated his remarkable resiliency by winning a third eight-year Senate term in 1986, under civilian rule, on the Partido Democrático Social ticket. Appointed minister of justice in 1990 by President Fernando Collor De Mello, Passarinho retained that post until 1992. In 1994 he ran to serve under the government of Pará but lost to Almir Gabriel.

See also **Brazil, Revolutions: Revolution of 1964; Costa e Silva, Artur da.**

BIBLIOGRAPHY

Peter Calvert, ed., *Political and Economic Encyclopedia of South America and the Caribbean* (1991), p. 87.

Additional Bibliography

Houtzager, Peter. "State and Unions in the Transformation of the Brazilian Countryside." *Latin American Research Review.* (1998): 103–142.

SCOTT MAINWARING

PASTA, CARLO ENRICO (1817–1898).

Carlo Enrico Pasta (*b.* 17 November 1817; *d.* 31 August 1898), Italian composer. Born in Milan, Pasta studied there and in Paris. In 1855 he settled in Lima, where he was active in the musical life of the city. A musical pioneer, he composed *zarzuelas* and operas using texts from Peruvian writers; Pasta was the first composer to take as his subject matter Peruvian folklore and Peru's pre-Columbian history. He was a member of the fraternity of Santa Cecilia. His first opera, *I tredici,* premiered in Turin's Teatro Sutera (1851). *La fronda* (1872) and *Una tazza di thé* (1872) premiered in Lima, and *Atahualpa* (1875), based on a libretto by Antonio Ghislanzoni, was first performed at Genoa's Teatro Paganini. *Atahualpa,* based on an Indian theme, received its first performance in America under maestro Francesco Rosa at Lima's Teatro Principal on 1 November 1877. Pasta's *zarzuelas* include *El loco de la guardilla, Rafael Sanzio, El pobre indio,* and *Placeres y dolores,* the last three with libretti by the Peruvian writer Juan Cosio. Pasta's most successful work was the *zarzuela La cola del diablo,* performed at Lima's Teatro Principal in 1865. He died in Milan.

See also **Music: Art Music.**

BIBLIOGRAPHY

Gérard Béhague, *Music in Latin America* (1979); *New Grove Dictionary of Opera,* vol. 3 (1992).

SUSANA SALGADO

PASTO.

Pasto, capital of Colombia's Nariño Department. It was founded in 1539 by Lorenzo de Aldana, among a substantial Indian population. Located astride the main road between Bogotá and Quito, it was a major royalist bastion in the Wars of Independence (1810–1822). Subsequently its elite and masses were severely repressed by the Gran Colombian republic, leaving a power vacuum that non-Pasto leaders like José María Obando and Juan José Flores filled for some twenty years (1823–1842). Once they recovered their power, Pasto's ruling classes and their clients remained extremely conservative and clerically oriented for the next century. A fertile agricultural base and highly skilled artisan industries, including the unique Pasto lacquerware (*barniz de Pasto*), have attracted a population of about 383, 846 (2005.) Pasto is a center of administration and education (two universities, several business and technical colleges, and numerous secondary schools) and a religious hub, the site of several Catholic religious houses.

See also **Wars of Independence, South America.**

BIBLIOGRAPHY

Edgar Bastidas Urresty, *Las guerras de Pasto.* Pasto: Ediciones Testimonio, 1979.

Jaime Álvarez, S.J., *¿Qué es qué en Pasto?* 2d ed. (1985).

Additional Bibliography

Bastidas Urresty, Julián. *Historia urbana de Pasto.* Bogotá: Ediciones Testimonio, 2000.

Montenegro, Armando. *Una historia en contravía: Pasto y Colombia.* Colombia: Malpensante, 2002.

Narvaez Portilla, Silvia. *Evolución urbana: San Juan de Pasto siglo XIX: historia.* Pasto: Fondo Mixto de Cultural Nariño, 1997.

J. León Helguera

PASTORA GÓMEZ, EDÉN   (c. 1937–).

A Nicaraguan revolutionary known as "Commandante Cero," Edén Pastora Gómez led a successful Sandinista raid on the Nicaraguan National Palace on August 22, 1978—an event that proved to be a major catalyst in the Nicaraguan revolution. After the Sandinistas gained power, Pastora became disillusioned with the Sandinista National Liberation Front (FSLN) leadership and was marginalized from the decision-making process within the National Directorate. After resigning from the government in 1981, he resurfaced a year later in Costa Rica, criticizing the FSLN leadership for subverting the revolution. Pastora formed the Revolutionary Sandinista Front (FRS) and joined other dissident groups to form the Revolutionary Democratic Alliance (ARDE). Pastora opposed a formal union with the CIA-backed Honduran-based Contra group Nicaraguan Democratic Forces (FDN), and narrowly escaped assassination at a press conference he called in Costa Rica in 1984. When the ARDE leadership joined with the FDN, Pastora pulled the FRS out. After 1990 Pastora returned to Nicaragua to pursue business interests and political ambitions, running for president with the Alternative for Change (AC) Party in 2006.

See also **Nicaragua, Sandinista National Liberation Front (FSLN).**

BIBLIOGRAPHY

Gilbert, Dennis. *Sandinistas: The Party and the Revolution.* London: Basil Blackwell, 1990.

Kinzer, Stephen. *Blood of Brothers: Life and War in Nicaragua.* Cambridge, MA: Harvard University Press, 2007.

Pardo, Alvaro. *Edén Pastora—Commandante Cero.* 2006. Video.

Walker, Thomas W. *Nicaragua: The Land of Sandino.* 4th edition. Boulder, CO: Westview Press, 2003.

Heather Thiessen-Reily

PASTRANA   BORRERO,   MISAEL

(1923–1997). Misael Pastrana Borrero (*b.* 14 November 1923; *d.* 21 August 1997), president of Colombia (1970–1974). Born to a prominent family in Neiva, Huila, and educated in Bogotá, he took his doctorate in law at Javerian University in 1945. As a teenage Conservative, he was perceived as having a promising future. He served in the Colombian embassy at the Vatican from 1947 to 1949, then was President Mariano Ospina Pérez's secretary (1949–1950) and counselor at the Colombian embassy in Washington, D.C. (1950–1952). Pastrana worked in corporate private finance from 1956 to 1959, then returned to government (1960–1961). He was in the private sector again from 1961 to 1966, and became minister of development, then of public works, and then of finance and credit over sixteen months of the Carlos Lleras Restrepo presidency (1966–1970). In 1968, he returned to Washington, D.C., as Colombia's ambassador. Pastrana was elected president in 1970, after a bitter political campaign, winning by less than 64,000 votes out of 3,250,000 cast. One of the best-prepared, in terms of administrative experience, of any Colombian chief executive of the twentieth century, Pastrana had to overcome virulent opposition before being able to achieve some of his goals in the last two years of his term. These included tax reform, foreign petroleum company buyouts by the government, enlarged social services, and improvements in the infrastructure. Pastrana died in Bogotá one year before his son, Andrés Pastrana Arango, was elected as president (1998–2002).

See also **Colombia, Political Parties: Conservative Party.**

BIBLIOGRAPHY

Rafael Méndez Buendía, *Misael Pastrana Borrero* (1969); *International Who's Who 1992–1993* (1993).

Additional Bibliography

Mendoza, Plinio Apuleyo. *Los retos del poder*. Santa Fe de Bogotá: Intermedio Editores, 1991.

Moreno, Delimiro. *Misael Pastrana Borrero*. Neiva: Instituto Huilense de Cultura, 1997.

J. LEÓN HELGUERA

PASTRY WAR. Pastry War, a conflict between Mexico and France in 1838–1839. Throughout the 1820s and 1830s, Mexico experienced political turmoil and constant rebellions by dissident army officers. Many people, including British, Spanish, U.S., and French residents, suffered losses and damage to their properties and businesses during these revolts and in other incidents of civil disorder. Claims for compensation were made by diplomatic representatives, but with the Mexican treasury virtually empty, no agreement was reached. On 6 February 1838, a French squadron arrived off the coast of Veracruz, and on 26 February, Baron Deffaudis, senior French diplomat in Mexico, issued an ultimatum to the Mexican government that, among other things, demanded 600,000 pesos in partial settlement of the claims of his compatriots. Included in this demand was one from a pastry chef who claimed the enormous sum of 60,000 pesos for alleged damage to his business. The Mexican cabinet rejected the ultimatum, and on 16 April the French responded by breaking off diplomatic relations and blockading the port of Veracruz. Talks between the two sides failed, and on 27 November the French fleet began to bombard Veracruz. The Mexican government declared war three days later.

Veracruz soon fell to the French, and the intermittent skirmishing during the next few weeks was insignificant except for one incident that became notorious in the career of Mexico's leading general, Antonio López de Santa Anna. On 5 December, he suffered a serious leg wound that required amputation. The severed leg was preserved and later placed in a mausoleum, a site of obligatory reverence as long as he was in power but later destroyed.

On 9 March 1839, two treaties were agreed with the French after mediation by British diplomats. These accepted arbitration of several outstanding issues and the payment by Mexico of 600,000 pesos in compensation.

See also **French-Latin American Relations.**

BIBLIOGRAPHY

See Nancy Barker, *The French Experience in Mexico, 1821–1861* (1979)

Additional Bibliography

Aquino Sánchez, Faustino A. *Intervención francesa, 1838-1839: La diplomacia mexicana y el imperialismo del librecambio*. México, D. F.: Instituto Nacional de Antropología e Historia, 1997.

MICHAEL P. COSTELOE

PATAGONES. Patagones (also Fueginos), name given by earliest European explorers in the sixteenth century to indigenous inhabitants north of the Strait of Magellan. Most likely the name referred to the Tehuelches (Aonikenks), or possibly to the Selk'nams or Yamanas. Antonio Pigafetta, the chronicler of Magellan's expedition, first coined the term because of the enormous footprint created by the Guanaco-skin boots worn by the people he observed. The name soon came to allude to the allegedly large feet and gigantism of the people in the region and was incorporated into European cosmological conceptions of the antipodes as a land of opposites. The image of the Patagones as giants persisted into the nineteenth century, when the concept was discredited by scientific measurements of contemporary Tehuelches, who, though perhaps tall, fell within normal height ranges.

See also **Indigenous Peoples; Precontact History: Southern Cone.**

BIBLIOGRAPHY

Antonio Pigafetta, in Giovanni Battista Ramusio, *Delle navigationi et viaggi*, various editions in Venice since 1554.

Benjamin Franklin Bourne, *Life Among the Giants; or the Captive in Patagonia* (1853).

J. Roberto Barcenas, ed. *Culturas indígenas de la Patagonia*. (1990).

KRISTINE L. JONES

PATAGONIA. The word *Patagonia* originated in the accounts, up to the nineteenth century, of seamen circling Cape Horn to reach the Pacific. The origin of the name came from the description of the Indians by the first voyagers, telling that they were extremely tall and with big feet, so they called them "patagones." which was the Spanish word for people with those characteristics. To them the territory beyond the coasts of the Cape region seemed mysterious. Therefore, the region became a land of myth, sighted but unknown.

Patagonia is the southern portion of South America, divided between Argentina and Chile. Its northern border in Argentina is marked by the Colorado River, at about latitude 38 south. In Chile it is the area situated south of Chiloé Island, at latitude 43 south The Andes mountain range lies along the western border, with its low mountains, deeply eroded by glaciers, creating spectacular landscapes. The climate is cold and humid to the west and dry to the east. The mountains are covered with large trees such as araucaria (*Araucaria araucana*) and alerce (*Fitzroya cupressoides*). The eastern portion is an arid, windy plateau, covered by steppelike shrubs. The coastline on the Atlantic side is open, with few natural ports; on the Pacific side the terrain is rugged, with islands, islets, and coves. The hydrography differs with each environment. In the west, the many mountain lakes are a great tourist attraction. Rivers, such as the Negro, flow from them, crossing the plateau and forming deep valleys to empty into the Atlantic. Until the late nineteenth century, Patagonia was inhabited by hunters and gatherers who lived by hunting guanaco (*Llama guanicoe*) and in the south by boat-making groups.

In 1880 Argentina and Chile reached a border agreement and occupied Patagonia after first displacing the indigenous population. The first activity to be taken up was sheep ranching, which extended over the whole plateau, around Punta Arenas, and on the island of Tierra del Fuego. Farmers came as colonists to Argentine Patagonia, first the Welsh at the mouth of the Chubut River in 1865 and years later in the upper Negro River valley to grow apples and pears. When oil was discovered in 1917 the drilling industry spread over the entire plateau, including northern Tierra del Fuego. Tourism came in modern times to take advantage of the natural landscapes. Elite tourism began with the arrival of the railroad around 1920, but it became more popular around 1970, with the completion of a paved road linking Bariloche with Buenos Aires. In Argentina, Patagonia includes the provinces of Río Negro, Neuquén, Chubut, Santa Cruz, and Tierra del Fuego, and in Chile, the eleventh and twelfth regions. The total population numbers around 2 million and is mainly located in Argentina. The larger cities are Neuquén, San Carlos de Bariloche, and Comodoro Rivadavia in Argentina and Punta Arenas in Chile.

See also **Argentina, Geography; Chile, Geography.**

BIBLIOGRAPHY

Bandieri, Susana. *Historia de la Patagonia.* Buenos Aires: Sudamericana, 2005.

Chebez, Juan C. *Patagonia Norte: Guía de las Reservas Naturales de la Argentina.* Buenos Aires: Editorial Albatros, 2005.

Vapñarsky, César. *Pueblos del norte de la Patagonia, 1779–1957.* General Roca, Argentina: Editorial de la Patagonia, 1983.

Williams, Glyn. *The Desert and the Dream: A Study of Welsh Colonization in Chubut, 1865–1915.* Cardiff, U.K.: University of Wales Press, 1975.

CARLOS REBORATTI

PATERSON, WILLIAM (1658–1719). William Paterson (*b.* April 1658; *d.* 2 January 1719), the central figure behind an unsuccessful attempt to establish a Scottish colony at Darién (now Panama) at the end of the seventeenth century.

William Paterson was the key person in an ill-fated effort to establish a great international trading center for future generations, New Caledonia, at Darién from 1698 to 1700. Paterson, the Scot who was the founder of the Bank of England in 1694–1695, and the director of the African Company, was a believer in Scottish unification with England and an advocate of open trade with the Indies. Paterson's leadership of the African Company ensured that by 1696 the Darién project represented the focal point of the company's efforts. The company made two attempts at settlement, both of which failed.

The first settlers landed in New Caledonia in November 1698. These colonists faced poor trading conditions, a lack of leadership, a shortage of supplies, and periodic attacks by the Spanish, who considered them pirates. In June 1699, the first attempt at settlement was abandoned. Paterson protested the colonists' decision but was too ill to prevent their departure. The settlers then went to Belize, New York, and New England, hoping to find temporary refuge.

In November 1699, they returned to Darién in another attempt to establish a colony and found that the Spanish had pillaged their first settlement. Some left for Scotland but many stayed to try and rebuild the colony. They encountered ongoing health problems and a persistent lack of supplies, however. Moreover, Spanish attacks, from 23 February to 17 March 1700, eventually forced the total capitulation of the settlers, who abandoned the colony on 11 April 1700.

Spain never in fact accepted the colonizing group's claims to their small piece of land on the isthmus. And England failed to support the venture because the king wished to forestall the company's settlement of land and instructed colonial governors not to trade with or assist the Darién colony. Paterson thus underestimated the importance of Spain's claims to the territory, and with the forced dissolution of the colony, he lost a substantial sum of his own money. He was later indemnified by the British Parliament.

See also **Caledonia; Darién.**

BIBLIOGRAPHY

J. S. Barbour, *A History of William Paterson and the Darién Company* (1907).

Frances Russell Hart, *The Disaster of Darién: The Story of the Scots Settlement and the Causes of Its Failure, 1699–1701* (1929).

Additional Bibliography

Withers, Charles W. J. *Geography, Science, and National Identity: Scotland since 1520.* New York: Cambridge University Press, 2001.

BLAKE D. PATRIDGE

PATIÑO, JOSÉ DE (1666–1736). José de Patiño, (*b.* 1666/70; *d.* 3 November 1736), secretary of state for the Indies, navy, and treasury (1726–1736) during the reign of Philip V of Spain. Patiño's goal was to restore Spain's power in Europe by strengthening American trade through a strong navy and a fiscal policy designed to stimulate exports. He entered higher administration as intendant of Extremadura (1711) and then Catalonia (1713), where he applied the *Nueva Planta* (a wholesale reorganization of Castilian Spain in order to bring power to the crown of Aragon; 1716) and introduced the *catastro* (a property and income tax). In 1717 he became intendant general of the navy, the superintendant of Seville, and president of the House of Trade, newly located in Cádiz.

A master of bureaucratic compromise who was able to balance the demands of the crown and the needs of the state, Patiño combined expert knowledge of the Indies with administrative talent and proved that careers would be open to talent under the new Bourbon regime. In foreign policy, he took into account the interests of his Italian patron, the queen, Isabella Farnese of Parma, and tried to keep peace with Britain while building up the Spanish navy. In colonial affairs his goal was simply to increase Spain's profits in America and reduce the drain of revenues by British interlopers and American Spaniards.

See also **Spanish Empire.**

BIBLIOGRAPHY

Antonio Rodríguez Villa, *Patiño y Campillo, Reseña histórico-biográfica de estos dos ministros de Felipe V* (1882).

Antonio Béthencourt Massieu, *Patiño en la política internacional de Felipe V* (1954).

John Lynch, *Bourbon Spain, 1700–1808* (1989), esp. pp. 88–100 and 134–139.

Additional Bibliography

Elliott, J. H. *Empires of the Atlantic World: Britain and Spain in the Americas, 1492–1830.* New Haven, CT: Yale University Press, 2006.

Pulido Bueno, Ildefonso. *José Patino: El inicio del gobierno político-económico ilustrado en España.* Huelva, Spain: I. P. Bueno, 1998.

SUZANNE HILES BURKHOLDER

PATIÑO, SIMÓN ITURRI (1860–1947).

Simón Iturri Patiño (*b.* 1 June 1860; *d.* 20 April 1947), Bolivian tin miner. Born in Santivañez, Cochabamba, Patiño spearheaded Bolivia's transition from silver to tin producer and in the process became one of the wealthiest men in the world, powerful enough to influence Bolivian politics greatly in the early twentieth century. Working first for Bolivian and German merchant houses and the Huanchaca Company, Bolivia's foremost silver-mining concern, Patiño purchased his own share of La Salvadora tin mine in 1894. After striking a rich vein in 1900, Patiño continuously modernized mining production and began purchasing other tin mines. He also began buying shares in German and, later, in partnership with U.S. venture capitalists, British tin-smelting operations in Europe. In 1924 he established Patiño Mines and Enterprises in the United States. He also bought into Malaysian tin mines. By the 1920s his Bolivian holdings were only a small fraction of his total business empire, although he continued to produce at least one-third of all Bolivian tin. With his Banco Mercantil, he was one of Bolivia's leading bankers; he also owned a majority share in the Sociedad Agrícola é Ganadera de Cinti, the largest agro-industrial enterprise in Bolivia.

Given his financial clout, Patiño was a major figure in Bolivian politics. His actions led to the splintering of the Liberal Party in 1919 and so aided in the revolution that brought the Republicans to power the following year. The Catavi Massacre in 1942, in which the army killed hundreds of unarmed miners and women and children in a labor dispute with Patiño, raised nationalist fervor against the mine owner. Since Patiño had lived in Europe from the 1920s and controlled so much of the Bolivian economy, many Bolivians resented him. This resentment ultimately led to the expropriation of his mines during the 1952 revolution and the creation of Comibol, the state mining company.

See also **Bolivia, Political Parties: Republican Party; Tin Industry.**

BIBLIOGRAPHY

The best biography of Patiño is Manuel Carrasco, *Simón I. Patiño, un prócer industrial* (1960). See also Herbert S. Klein, "The Creation of the Patiño Tin Empire," in *Inter-American Economic Affairs* 19 (1965): 3–23; Juan Albarracín Millán, *El poder minero en la administración liberal* (1972); and William L. Lofstrom, *Attitudes of an Industrial Pressure Group in Latin America: The Asociación de industriales mineros de Bolivia: 1925–1935* (1968).

Additional Bibliography

Albarracín Millán, Juan. *El poder financiero de la gran minería boliviana.* La Paz: Ediciones AKAPANA, 1995.

García Flores, Pedro Pablo. *La minería en Bolivia.* Bolivia: Observador, 2005.

ERICK D. LANGER

PATO.

Pato, the most popular of the gaucho games. From the colonial era gauchos enjoyed challenging others and showing their courage and skill in a variety of equestrian games. In pato, players sewed a duck (*pato*) into a large rawhide with several leather handles protruding from the outside. At a signal, mounted gauchos tried to grab the duck and ride away. Contestants often covered miles of pampa in this horseback version of "keep away." During the game, gauchos were often injured when pulled from their horses by other riders. The mass of contestants destroyed property and scattered livestock, thereby arousing the ire of plains ranchers. Repeatedly banned from the late eighteenth through the late nineteenth century, pato remained a favorite gaucho contest.

Like many other gaucho activities, pato became embodied in pampa folklore. By the late nineteenth century, however, government officials succeeded in banning or altering many elements of traditional gaucho life. Pato became "civilized," with regulation playing fields, league competitions, and written rules. The modern domesticated game, somewhat akin to polo, retains some of the traditional form but lacks the danger and vitality of the gaucho original.

See also **Gaucho.**

BIBLIOGRAPHY

Richard W. Slatta, *Gauchos and the Vanishing Frontier* (1983), pp. 86–87; and *Cowboys of the Americas* (1990), pp. 137–138.

Additional Bibliography

Assunção, Fernando O. *Historia del gaucho: El gaucho, ser y quehacer.* Buenos Aires: Editorial Claridad, 1999.

Foster, David William, Melissa Fitch Lockhart and Darrell B. Lockhart. *Culture and Customs of Argentina.* Westport, CT: Greenwood Press, 1998.

RICHARD W. SLATTA

PATRIA CHICA.

Patria Chica, literally the "small homeland." The term expresses the sense of affiliation with local entities—villages, regions, ethnic groups—that challenged and sometimes overcame loyalty to the state. Within the Hispanic and Hispanic-American worlds this tension between the immediate and the distant communities created conflicting political and social identities. The expression of loyalty to the *patria chica* and the degree to which local identities predominated varied widely within Spain's American empire, depending on ethnic and class factors, regional political conflicts, economic cycles, and distance from imperial administrative centers. During the independence movements of the early nineteenth century, the concept of *patria chica* played a key role by providing an alternative political identity for Creole elites.

See also **Spanish Empire.**

BIBLIOGRAPHY

Anthony Pagden, "Identity Formation in Spanish America," in *Colonial Identity in the Atlantic World, 1500–1800,* edited by Nicholas Canny and Anthony Pagden (1987).

Additional Bibliography

Brading, D. A. *The First America: The Spanish Monarchy, Creole Patriots, and the Liberal State, 1492–1867.* Cambridge, UK: Cambridge University Press, 1991.

Domínguez Ortiz, Antonio. *La sociedad americana y la corona española en el siglo XVII.* Spain: M. Pons, 1996.

Morgan, Ronald J. *Spanish American Saints and the Rhetoric of Identity, 1600–1810.* Tucson: University of Arizona Press, 2002.

ANN M. WIGHTMAN

PATRIA NUEVA.

Patria Nueva (new homeland), a term applied to the period of Chilean history that began with the battle of Chacabuco on 12 February 1817 and the liberation of the country from Spanish rule by José de San Martín (1777–1850) and his army of the Andes. It is used in contrast with *Patria Vieja,* but, unlike that term, which refers to a very precise four-year period (1810–1814), *Patria Nueva* has no commonly accepted terminal point, and could easily be assumed to have continued to the present day. The expression is used much less frequently than *Patria Vieja.* Insofar as it has a more specific meaning at all, it is probably most applicable to the few years immediately after 1817 and to the heroic events of the first phase of the new Chilean state: the Proclamation of Independence in February 1818, the defeat of the final royalist offensive in April 1818, the creation of the Chilean navy, and the mounting of San Martín's expedition to liberate the Viceroyalty of Peru (1820–1821).

See also **Chacabuco, Battle of; Patria Vieja.**

BIBLIOGRAPHY

Simon Collier, *Ideas and Politics of Chilean Independence, 1808–1833* (1967), chaps. 3 and 6–9.

Additional Bibliography

Díaz Meza, Aurelio. *Patria vieja y patria nueva.* Santiago, Chile: Editorial Antarctica, 1969.

Ibáñez Vergara, Jorge. *O'Higgins, el Libertador.* Santiago, Chile: Instituto O'Higgiano de Chile, 2001.

Villalobos, R. Sergio. *Tradición y reforma en 1810.* Chile: Ril, 2006.

SIMON COLLIER

PATRIA VIEJA.

Patria Vieja (old homeland), the term universally used in Chile to denote the four-year period from the installation of Chile's first national government (18 September 1810) to the battle of Rancagua (1–2 October 1814), which brought about the collapse of patriot Chile and the Spanish reconquest (1814–1817). Politically, this period was marked by dissension within the patriot leadership, including the division between moderates and radicals that was exacerbated by the disastrous family rivalry of the Larraíns and the Carreras. The first national junta gave way in mid-1811 to an elected congress dominated by moderates. This body was dissolved in November 1811 by José Miguel Carrera (1785–1821), who held power until 1813, when the arrival of the first of three successive task forces from the Viceroyalty of Peru (creating royalist armies in the south) forced him to take command of the patriot forces. In his absence the junta in Santiago soon fell under the de facto control of his adversaries, and Carrera himself was relieved of command, which eventually passed to Bernardo O'Higgins (1778–1842). A second vice-regal expedition (1814) then attacked the Central Valley.

On 3 May 1814 a peace treaty between patriots and royalists was negotiated at Lircay, but it was soon repudiated by the viceroy. Meanwhile, Carrera once again seized power (23 July 1814). Conflict between Carrera and O'Higgins was averted only by the arrival of a third viceregal expedition under General Mariano Osorio (1777–1819). Making his last stand at Rancagua, O'Higgins was overwhelmed by Osorio (1–2 October 1814), and the *Patria Vieja* ended. None of its various governments declared independence from Spain.

See also **O'Higgins, Bernardo; Rancagua, Battle of.**

BIBLIOGRAPHY

Simon Collier, *Ideas and Politics of Chilean Independence, 1808–1833* (1967), chaps. 3 and 6–9.

Additional Bibliography

Díaz Meza, Aurelio. *Patria vieja y patria nueva*. Santiago, Chile: Editorial Antarctica, 1969.

Villalobos, R. Sergio. *Historia de los chilenos*. Santiago, Chile: Taurus, 2006.

SIMON COLLIER

PATROCÍNIO, JOSÉ DO (1853–1905).

José do Patrocínio (*b.* 8 October 1853; *d.* 1 February 1905), Brazilian abolitionist, journalist, orator, and poet. The son of a Catholic priest and planter in Rio de Janeiro Province and a black fruit vendor, Patrocínio was brought up in the vicarage of Campos and on a nearby estate, where he acquired an intimate knowledge of slavery. After serving an apprenticeship at Misericórdia Hospital in Rio de Janeiro, he completed the pharmacy course at the Faculty of Medicine. However, lacking funds to establish himself in his profession, he joined the staff of the capital's daily, *Gazeta de Notícias,* and soon gained prominence as an opponent of slavery. In 1881, aided by his wealthy father-in-law, he acquired the *Gazeta de Tarde,* which under his leadership became the principal antislavery journal in Brazil until it was replaced by his equally effective *A Cidade do Rio* in 1887. Patrocínio advanced the antislavery cause as a powerful orator, as author of fiery articles and editorials, as organizer of antislavery groups, as an abolitionist emissary to Europe, and as an effective promoter of regional movements (Ceará in 1882, his native Campos in 1885, and the port of Santos in 1886). With the end of slavery in 1888, he organized the Guarda Negra (Black Guard), an association of black militants dedicated to protecting Princess Isabel, whose succession to the throne was threatened by a growing republican movement. After the military revolt of 1889 and the beginning of the federal republic, Patrocínio suffered persecution from President Floriano Peixoto's government, including exile in 1892 to the state of Amazonas and suspension of his newspaper, *A Cidade do Rio*. He was again active as a journalist at the time of his death.

See also **Amazonas; Brazil: 1808–1889; Slavery: Abolition.**

BIBLIOGRAPHY

Raymundo Magalhães, *A vida turbulenta de José do Patrocínio* (1969).

Robert Brent Toplin, *The Abolition of Slavery in Brazil* (1972).

Robert Edgar Conrad, *Children of God's Fire: A Documentary History of Black Slavery in Brazil* (1983) and *The Destruction of Brazilian Slavery, 1850–1888,* 2d ed., rev. (1992).

Additional Bibliography

Daibert Junior, Robert. *Isabel, a "redentora" dos escravos: Uma historia da princesa entre olhares negros e brancos, 1846–1988*. Bauru, Brazil: FAPESP, EDUSC, 2004.

Fernandes, Maria Fernanda Lombardi, and Eduardo Kugelmas. *A esperança e o desencanto: Silva Jardim e a república*. São Paulo: s.n., 2004.

ROBERT EDGAR CONRAD

PATRONAGE. Patronage, a hierarchically structured relationship of patron and client that defines, most typically, the mutual obligations of a patron and his workers. In rural Latin America patronage is the predominant form of exchanging favors and sustaining loyalty between a *patrón* and the population dependent upon him. This relationship also occurs in urban factories, businesses, and even the state bureaucracy. Patronage in its original form has been in decline as Latin American society has rapidly urbanized and industrialized. It is often replaced by more formal relationships such as contracts, health insurance, social welfare systems, and open electoral processes.

Ranch hands or plantation workers constitute the patron's dependent population, whose obligations as wage laborers and tenant farmers go beyond such daily chores as attending fields of crop and herds of animals. Workers, or clients, and their families are required to labor as household servants in exchange for the right to live on the ranch and perhaps cultivate their own small plots. On occasion the *patrón* calls on a client to provide extracontractual services such as working as a bodyguard, taking his side in family feuds, voting for the *patrón*'s candidate—and even committing murder on behalf of the *patrón* and his family. In return, the *patrón* is expected to look after the well-being of the client and his family.

See also **Coronel, Coronelismo; Fazenda, Fazendeiro; Hacienda.**

BIBLIOGRAPHY

Shepard Forman, *The Brazilian Peasantry* (1975).

Merilee S. Grindle, "Patrons and Clients in the Bureaucracy," in *Latin American Reseach Review* 12, no. 1 (1977): 37–66.

Frances Rothstein, "The Class Basis of Patron–Client Relations," in *Modern Mexico: State, Economy, and Social Conflict,* edited by Nora Hamilton and Timothy F. Harding (1986), pp. 300–312.

Additional Bibliography

Bieber, Judy. *Power, Patronage, and Political Violence: State Building on a Brazilian Frontier, 1822–1889.* Lincoln: University of Nebraska Press, 1999.

Graham, Richard. *Patronage and Politics in Nineteeth-centruy Brazil.* Stanford, CA: Stanford University Press, 1990.

Hagopian, Frances. *Traditional Politics and Regime Change in Brazil.* New York: Cambridge University Press, 1996.

Lemenha, Maria Auxiliadora. *Família, tradição e poder: O(caso) dos coronéis.* São Paulo: Annablume, 1996.

Needell, Jeffrey D. *The Party of Order: The Conservatives, the State, and Slavery in the Brazilian Monarchy, 1831–1871.* Stanford, CA: Stanford University Press, 2006.

Salinas Sánchez, Alejandro. *Parroco y señor: Gamonalismo en Macate (Ancash), 1853–1893.* Lima: Seminario de Historia Rural Andina, Universidad Nacional Mayor de San Marcos, 2005.

Trotta, Miguel E.V. *Las metamorfosis del clientelismo político: Contribución para el análisis institucional.* Buenos Aires: Espacio, 2003.

EUL-SOO PANG

PATRONATO REAL. *Patronato real* (royal patronage; in Portuguese, *padroado real*) is the concept upon which royal control of the Catholic Church in the New World was based. The roots of the *patronato real* can be found in the Reconquest of the Spanish Middle Ages and in early Portuguese explorations of the African coast. Quite simply, in keeping with medieval notions of patronage, the monarchs claimed certain rights of appointment to the churches founded in the newly discovered lands because of their subsidy of the missionary activities.

The *patronato real* was based upon a series of papal bulls and royal decrees of the fifteenth and sixteenth centuries. The most important of these were the *Inter caetera* (1493) and *Eximae devotionis* (1493 and 1501) of Alexander VI and the *Universalis ecclesiae* of Julius II, which essentially granted universal patronage over the church in the New World to the Iberian monarchs, including the right to present candidates for ecclesiastical office and the right to collect the tithe. In response, the Spanish monarchs exercised their authority over the church in two important decrees, the so-called Concordat of Burgos (1512) and the Ordenanza del Patronazgo (1574). In the concordat, the crown returned the tithe to the church, but in the *ordenanza*, the crown regulated the appointment of ecclesiastical officials. The Portuguese *padroado real* was based on privileges given to the Portuguese crown and to the military-religious Order of Christ (Ordem de Cristo). When the leadership of the order was acquired directly by the crown, control over the Portuguese overseas church was centralized in the hands of the monarch.

Under the patronage, the church in the New World administratively became a branch of the royal government. All bishops, archbishops, cathedral chapter members, and parish priests were appointed by the monarch or by other royal officials. There was no direct communication between Rome and the American church, only that through the king and Council of the Indies for the Hispanic Americas and the Mesa da Consciência e Ordens for Brazil. The monarch reserved the right to license the construction of churches and chapels, determine the territorial limits of dioceses and parishes, approve all canons and decrees of local synods and councils, convene those synods and councils, and regulate the travel of clerics to and from the New World.

Once developed in the fifteenth and sixteenth centuries, the patronage did not change dramatically until the eighteenth century, when the monarchs sought greater control over the church. Implicitly excluded from patronage control was the regular clergy, which remained under the authority of its own internal hierarchy directly linked to Rome. The efforts of the Iberian kings to gain greater control over the regulars culminated in the expulsion of the Jesuits from Brazil in 1759 and Spanish America in 1767. The extreme limits of the Spanish patronage were reached in the early nineteenth century, when the monarch amortized outstanding church loans (1804) and rescinded the ecclesiastical *fuero* (1812).

See also **Catholic Church: The Colonial Period.**

BIBLIOGRAPHY

Farriss, Nancy M. *Crown and Clergy in Colonial Mexico, 1759–1812.* London: Athlone P., 1968.

Schwaller, John F. *The Church and Clergy in Sixteenth-Century Mexico.* Albuquerque: University of New Mexico Press, 1987.

Shiels, William E. *King and Church: The Rise and Fall of the Patronato Real.* Chicago: Loyola University Press, 1961.

                                        JOHN F. SCHWALLER

PATRÓN COSTAS, ROBUSTIANO

(1878–1953). Robustiano Patrón Costas (*b.* 5 August 1878; *d.* 1953), Argentine sugar baron and conservative political boss. An old-regime provincial oligarch, Patrón Costas took a law doctorate at the University of Buenos Aires in 1901, then returned to his native Salta to rise through the political ranks to the governorship (1913–1916). In 1916 he was elected as a National Conservative to the federal Senate, where he served from 1916 to 1925 and again from 1932 to 1943; during the latter period he was the Senate's provisional president. Simultaneously he founded and managed the sugar *ingenio* (mill) San Martín del Tabacal at Orán in Salta, which gave him great wealth and power. The *ingenio* was known for its abuse of labor, particularly of Bolivian migrants. In 1943 it was learned that Patrón was the favorite of President Ramón S. Castillo, a provincial politician of similar stripe, to succeed him in office. Patrón was believed to be pro-Allies; his election would have meant a less rigid neutralism than Castillo's. It would also have required the military to supervise the necessary electoral frauds. Patrón's unsavory reputation as a sugar operator and as an exemplar of the corrupt, stagnant politics of the "década infame" (1932–1943) made him unacceptable to broad military and civilian sectors. Thus his nomination by Castillo was a contributing cause to the military coup of 4 June 1943, which ended oligarchic politics in Argentina.

See also **Argentina: The Twentieth Century; Sugar Industry.**

BIBLIOGRAPHY

Ernesto Araoz, *Vida y obra del doctor Patrón Costas* (1966).

Carlos A. Luque Colombres, *Patrón Costas en la historia* (1991).

Additional Bibliography

Sweeney, Ernest S., and A. A. Domínguez Benavides. *Robustiano Patrón Costas: Una leyenda argentina.* Buenos Aires: Emecé Editores, 1998.

                                        RONALD C. NEWTON

PÁTZCUARO, LAKE.

Lake Pátzcuaro, situated in central Michoacán, Mexico. The lake area originally was settled by Nahuatl groups; it was conquered by Tarascans in the twelfth century. The Lake Pátzcuaro area, and specifically the city of Tzintzuntzan, became one of the two centers of

Tarascan civilization. Before the twentieth century, the unique qualities of the many groups living on and around the lake were relatively well preserved, although haciendas always shared the lakeshore and during the Porfiriato (1876–1911) came to dominate the best land. The twentieth-century decline of the relatively shallow lake through pollution, choking vegetation, and natural shrinkage has further exacerbated the already precarious position of the surrounding population, as its chief livelihood, fishing, has become increasingly tenuous. To a certain extent tourism has employed people displaced by the decline of fishing, since despite its deteriorating condition, the lake, in its mountainous setting, remains one of the most beautiful in Mexico.

See also **Janitzio; Tarascans.**

BIBLIOGRAPHY

Pablo G. Macías, *Pátzcuaro* (Morelia, 1978).

Additional Bibliography

Kepecs, Susan and Roni T. Alexander. *The Post-Classic to Spanish Era Transition in Mesoamerica: Archaeological Perspectives.* Albuquerque: University of New Mexico Press, 2005.

Ramos Montes de Oca, Melchor. *La vuelta a Pátzcuaro en 36 fiestas.* Morélia: Morevallo Editores, 2004.

Valencia Oseguera, José, and Ma. Antonio González L. *Cuentos, tradiciones, y leyendas de las comunidades Purhépecha de la región del lago de Pátzcuaro.* Michoacán: Instituto Nacional Indigenista, 2000.

MARGARET CHOWNING

the relative provincialism and slower pace of the inhabitants of the interior from the cosmopolitanism and hard-driving economy and culture of the city.

See also **Bandeiras.**

BIBLIOGRAPHY

Richard M. Morse, *From Community to Metropolis: A Biography of São Paulo.* Gainesville: University of Florida Press, 1958.

Clodomir Vianna Moog, *Bandeirantes and Pioneers,* translated by L. L. Barrett. New York: G. Braziller, 1964, which compares the United States and Brazil; Richard M. Morse, *The Bandeirantes: The Historical Role of the Brazilian Pathfinders.* New York: Knopf, 1974.

Joseph L. Love, *São Paulo in the Brazilian Federation, 1889–1937.* Stanford, CA: Stanford University Press, 1980.

Gilberto Freyre, *The Mansions and the Shanties: The Making of Modern Brazil,* translated and edited by Harriet de Onis. Berkeley: University of California Press, 1986.

Additional Bibliography

Bittencourt, Circe Maria Fernandes. *Patria, civilizacão e trabahlo: O ensino de historía nas escolas paulistas (1917–1939.)* São Paulo: Edicões Loyola, 1990.

Setubal, Maria Alice. *Modos de vida dos paulistas: Identidades, famílias e espacos domésticos.* São Paulo: CENEPEC, Centro de Estudos e Pesquisas em Educacão, Cultura e Acão Comunitária: Imprensa Oficial do Estado, 2004.

Trigo, Maria Helena Bueno. *Os paulistas de quatrocentos anos: Ser e parecer.* São Paulo: Annablume, 2001.

BRIAN OWENSBY

PAULISTAS, PAULISTANOS.

The term *paulistas* refers to inhabitants of the south-central Brazilian state of São Paulo. *Bandeirantes,* referring to the explorers, slave hunters, and gold seekers of seventeenth-century Brazil's westward expansion, can be used as a synonym. *Paulistanos* refers to inhabitants of the city of São Paulo, capital of the state.

The prominent historical role of the two São Paulos, as the home of the *bandeirantes,* the center of political power in nineteenth century Brazil, and the dynamo of the economy in the twentieth century, has fostered an intense regional pride signified by these descriptions. As the city has grown, *paulistanos* use the terms to distinguish what they see as

PAVÓN, BATTLE OF.

The Battle of Pavón was the 17 September 1861 clash between forces of the Argentine Confederation commanded by former president, Entre Rios governor, and Federalist Party head Justo José de Urquiza and those of Buenos Aires Province led by Governor Bartolomé Mitre, leader of the Liberal party. It followed by not quite two years the Battle of Cepeda (23 October 1859), which brought formerly secessionist Buenos Aires back into the Confederation. Both Urquiza and Mitre had played important roles in the province's incorporation into the nation, but relations between provincial and national authorities had broken down again principally over the terms of reunification. When the armies met at Pavón, in southern Santa Fe Province, Urquiza had slightly more men and a particular advantage in cavalry. But the Buenos Aires infantry had superior training and discipline, and when it held firm despite the initial sweep of Confederation cavalry, Urquiza abandoned the field. He was not yet defeated, but he was ill and also preferred not to prolong the bloodshed. In the aftermath of Pavón, the existing Confederation government dissolved itself, and Mitre became provisional president of all Argentina. Although conflict between provincial and national powers continued, Pavón was a landmark for national unification in Argentina.

See also **Mitre, Bartolomé; Urquiza, Justo José de.**

BIBLIOGRAPHY

William H. Jeffrey, *Mitre and Argentina* (1952), chap. 9.

Rosa Farías De Foulkes, *Después de la derrota: Derqui, desde el pacto de San José de Flores hasta la batalla de Pavón (1859–1861)* (1970).

Additional Bibliography

Domínguez Soler, Susana T. P. de, with the collaboration of José Teófilo Goyret et al. *Urquiza: Bibliografía.* Buenos Aires, Argentina: Instituto Urquiza de Estudios Históricos, 1999.

Pasquali, Patricia. *La instauración liberal: Mitre, Urquiza y un estadista olvidado, Nicasio Oroño.* Buenos Aires, Argentina: Planeta, 2003.

Rock, David. *State Building and Political Movements in Argentina, 1860–1916.* Stanford, CA: Stanford University Press, 2002.

Ruiz Moreno, Isidoro J. *El misterio de Pavón: Las operaciones militares y sus consecuencias políticas.* Buenos Aires, Argentina: Claridad, 2005.

DAVID BUSHNELL

PAVÓN AYCINENA, MANUEL FRANCISCO (1798–1855).

Manuel Francisco Pavón Aycinena (*b.* 30 January 1798; *d.* 19 April 1855), leader of the conservative elite that managed the Guatemalan government and developed the corporatist structure of the state during the regime of Rafael Carrera (1839–1865). The son of Manuel José Pavón, a prominent Guatemala City creole, and Maria Micaela Aycinena Nájera, he was closely related to the powerful Aycinena clan. Educated as a lawyer at the University of San Carlos, he served as a lieutenant colonel in the federal army during the civil war of 1826–1829. In exile from 1830 to 1837 in New York, Paris, and Havana, he returned to Guatemala and between 1838 and 1854 served as secretary of the assembly, editor of the government gazette, diplomat, prior of the *consulado,* and minister of finance, foreign relations, war, justice, ecclesiastical affairs, and interior. He formulated major reforms in finance and promoted good relations with Great Britain through his friendship with British Consul Frederick Chatfield (1834–1852). His Ley Pavón of 16 September 1852 gave responsibility for elementary education to parish priests. He played a key role in engineering Carrera's elevation to president for life in 1854.

See also **Carrera, José Rafael; Guatemala.**

BIBLIOGRAPHY

El Tiempo (Guatemala, 1839–1841); *Gaceta oficial* (Guatemala, 1841–1847); *Gaceta de Guatemala* (1847–1855).

Mario Rodríguez, *A Palmerstonian Diplomat in Central America: Frederick Chatfield, Esquire* (1964).

Additional Bibliography

Sullivan-González, Douglass. *Piety, Power, and Politics: Religion and Nation Formation in Guatemala, 1821–1871.* Pittsburgh: University of Pittsburgh Press, 1998.

Woodward, Ralph Lee. *Rafael Carrera y la creación de la República de Guatemala, 1821–1871.* La Antigua, Guatemala: Centro de Investigaciones Regionales de Mesoamérica, 2002.

RALPH LEE WOODWARD JR.

PAYADOR.

Payador, an itinerant troubadour whose skill at musical improvisation earned him the rank of most esteemed gaucho musician. Music and dance played prominent roles in the folklore of the Río De La Plata. It was the *payador,* however, who excelled at singing duels (*payadas*), in which two contestants exchanged witticisms and insults. Singers accompanied themselves on the guitar or *charrango,* a small guitarlike instrument fashioned from the shell of an armadillo. Many famed *payadores* were black.

Two singing duels in particular became celebrated in gauchesco literature. In one, Santos Vega loses a singing duel to the devil in a poem by Rafael Obligado. And in the famous epic by José Hernández, Martín Fierro challenges a black *payador,* then kills him in a knife fight. Leopoldo Lugones titled his influential interpretation of the Hernández poem *El payador* (1916).

See also **Music: Popular Music and Dance.**

BIBLIOGRAPHY

Domingo F. Sarmiento, *Life in the Argentine Republic in the Days of the Tyrants* (1971).

Richard W. Slatta, *Gauchos and the Vanishing Frontier* (1983), pp. 81–82.

Additional Bibliography

Fuente, Alfredo de la. *El payador en la cultura nacional.* Buenos Aires: Corregidor, 1986.

Lugones, Leopoldo. *El payador.* Buenos Aires: Stockero, 2004.

RICHARD W. SLATTA

PAYAGUÁ INDIANS. The Payaguá, a people of the Guaicuruan language family that lived along the Río Paraguay between the modern Corrientes region and the Mato Grosso. Organized in bands that traveled in canoes, the Payaguás, who numbered 6,000 in the early 1500s, are known chiefly from the accounts of enemies and rivals. Although they called themselves Evueví, meaning "people of the water," they were named Payaguá by the Guarani, whom they kept from the river. This designation contributed to the naming of the Paraguay river, province, and nation.

Prior to the arrival of the Spanish in the 1520s, the Payaguá lived by gleaning wild fruits and vegetables along the river, by fishing, and by raiding their Guarani neighbors for crops and captives. After Guaranis allied with Spanish invaders in the 1530s, Spaniards and Spanish goods were often the focus of Payaguá raids. War profits reinforced their aboriginal position as regional brokers who disseminated booty to other Chaco peoples. Southern Payaguá canoe-born bands harassed Spanish river commerce from the 1540s until after 1750. In the 1720s and 1730s, Payaguá attacks cut Brazilian communication between the coast and the settlements of Mato Grosso.

Spanish expeditions against the Payaguás were frequent, but the European strategy of annihilation was never a great success. A relaxation of tension usually followed hostile encounters, and trade with Spaniards allowed Payaguás to adopt Spanish iron for the hooks, needles, and projectile points that made their economy more productive. By the 1740s, groups of southern Payaguás began settling on the outskirts of Asunción. They caught and sold fish to Paraguayans and performed manual labor, but they rejected Christianity. Other Payaguá men worked for the colonial government for wages as couriers or scouts on the river and in military capacities, and Payaguás fought for Paraguay in the War of the Triple Alliance in the 1860s. From 1750 to 1850, Payaguás slowly declined in numbers as they merged into the Guarani-speaking population. The Payaguás had disappeared by the 1940s.

See also **Indigenous Peoples.**

BIBLIOGRAPHY

Alfred Métraux, "Ethnography of the Chaco," in *Handbook of South American Indians,* vol. 1, edited by Julian H. Steward, (1946): 197–370.

Branislava Susnik, *El indio colonial del Paraguay,* vol. 3, *El Chaqueno* (1971).

Barbara Ganson, "The Evueví of Paraguay: Adaptive Strategies and Responses to Colonialism, 1528–1811," in *The Americas: A Quarterly Review of Inter-American Cultural History* 45, no. 4 (1989): 461–488.

JAMES SCHOFIELD SAEGER

PAYNO Y FLORES, MANUEL (1810–1894). Manuel Payno y Flores (*b.* 21 June 1810; *d.* 4 November 1894), Mexican government official and novelist. Son of treasury official Manuel Payno y Bustamante and cousin of President Anastasio Bustamante, Payno y Flores was a native of Mexico City.

As public servant, Payno is most remembered as the treasury minister who negotiated the 1850 settlements of the foreign (14 October) and internal debts (30 November). However, his subsequent service was equally, if not more, significant. Because he was implicated in the coup that overthrew President Ignacio Comonfort in January

1858, Payno never again held the post of treasury minister. He nevertheless remained an active participant in discussions of fiscal matters, particularly those concerning the foreign debt. He wrote major tracts on the debt settlements that provoked the English-French-Spanish invasion of December 1861 and on the internal debt, and produced the only accounting of the expenditures of the imperial government. His views often formed the intellectual rationale for the policies of the Juárez government on those issues.

Beginning in the 1830s, Payno wrote for the daily press. In 1845–1846, he published the first of his two *costumbrista* novels, *El fistol del diablo,* which detailed the everyday life of the period. In the 1870s, he wrote important school texts on Mexican history, geography, and law. Near the end of his life, while consul for the Mexican government in Spain, he published his masterpiece, *Los bandidos del Río Frío* (1889–1891), full of descriptions of local color and famous people. He died in San Ángel, D.F.

See also **Comonfort, Ignacio; Literature: Spanish America; Mexico: 1810–1910.**

BIBLIOGRAPHY

There is to date no major biographical study of Manuel Payno. Readers can find some information on his life in Barbara A. Tenenbaum, "Manuel Payno y los bandidos del erario mexicano," in *Historia Mexicana* 54 (1994). See also Alejandro Villaseñor y Villaseñor, "Preface," in Manuel Payno y Flores, *Novela cortas* (1901).

Additional Bibliography

Glantz, Margo. *Del fistol a la linterna: Homenaje a José Tomás de Cuéllar y Manuel Payno en el centenario de su muerte, 1994.* México: Universidad Nacional Autónoma de México, Coordinación de Humanidades, 1997.

Peloso, Vincent C., and Barbara A. Tenenbaum, eds. *Liberals, Politics, and Power: State Formation in Nineteenth-Century Latin America.* Athens: University of Georgia Press, 1996.

BARBARA A. TENENBAUM

PAYSANDÚ.

Paysandú, capital city of the department of the same name on the Uruguay River (2004 population 73,272), 210 miles northwest of Montevideo. Paysandú was founded by Father Pedro Sandú in 1772 to provide shelter and protection to twelve Guaraní families who had converted to Christianity. Soon after, it developed into an important station where travelers heading for the upper reaches of the Uruguay River changed from fluvial transportation to overland routes. Using to advantage the fact that it was accessible by ship, Paysandú developed rapidly into an agricultural center specializing in grains and, later on, into an industrial city with food processing plants, sugar beet mills, breweries, and packing plants. This balanced commercial and industrial infrastructure allows the city to compete successfully with Salto for the dominant position in Uruguay's western corner.

See also **Uruguay, Geography; Uruguay River.**

BIBLIOGRAPHY

Uruguay González, *Paysandú* (La Paz, 1981).

Additional Bibliography

Barrios Pintos, Aníbal. *Paysandú: Historia general.* Montevideo: Intendencia Municipal de Paysandú, 1989.

Caillabet, Carlos. *Retratos con historias: Paysandú.* Paysandú: Ediciones Carolina, 2003.

Schulkin, Fernando. *Sitiados: La epopeya de Paysandú, 1864-1865.* Montevideo: s.n., 2000.

Tomeo F., Ana Maria. *Suiza En Paysandú: En busca de nuestros abuelos helvéticos.* Montevideo: Ediciones el Galeón, 2004.

CÉSAR N. CAVIEDES

PAZ, JOSÉ MARÍA

(1791–1854). José María Paz (*b.* 9 September 1791; *d.* 22 October 1854), Argentine general and unitarist. Born in Córdoba, Paz abandoned law studies to join the army during the War of Independence. He served in the Army of the North and lost an arm at the battle of Venta y Media. In January 1820, with Juan Bautista Bustos, caudillo of Córdoba, Paz revolted against Buenos Aires. He subsequently declared himself a unitarist and fought to establish a league of provinces under a central government. He was one of a number of military leaders who returned from the war against Brazil (1825–1828) determined to oppose the rise of Federalism. This brought him into conflict with Juan Manuel de Rosas and his allies. Victories over Bustos and Juan Facundo Quiroga in 1829–1830 enabled him to make Córdoba the center of the Liga del Interior with a centralized structure in opposition to federalist Buenos Aires.

For the next two decades Paz combined military and political action. In 1831 he was taken prisoner by Estanislao López, who saved him from the execution ordered by Rosas. As his league collapsed in the interior, he moved his base to Corrientes. But he was frustrated by the political rivalries in the Littoral and the rise of the federalist Justo José de Urquiza. In 1846 he resigned his military command and retired to Brazil. There he remained until 1852, when he returned to Buenos Aires after the defeat of Rosas, in time to take part in the defense of the city against the excesses of its liberator Urquiza. He was briefly minister of war, and in 1854 was elected to the legislature.

Paz was a humane and educated man, regarded by Domingo Sarmiento as a model general and a representative of "civilization" against the barbarism of the caudillos. His *Memorias* are rich in detail and perception, and a prime source for the history of the period.

See also **Argentina: The Nineteenth Century; López, Estanislao; Rosas, Juan Manuel de.**

BIBLIOGRAPHY

José María Paz, *Memorias póstumas*, 2d ed., 3 vols. (1892).

Aurora Rosa Caminos De Artola, *La acción del general Paz en el interior 1829–1831* (1962).

Tulio Halperín Donghi, *Politics, Economics, and Society in Argentina in the Revolutionary Period* (1975).

Additional Bibliography

Raed, José. *Plan para secuestrar al gobernador Juan M. de Rosas: Artigas y Paz exiliados.* Buenos Aires: Ediciones Humus, 1996.

Ruiz Moreno, Isidoro J. *Alianza contra Rosas: Paz-Ferré-Rivera-López.* Buenos Aires: Academia Nacional de la Historia, 1999.

JOHN LYNCH

PAZ, JUAN CARLOS (1897–1972).

Juan Carlos Paz (*b.* 5 August 1897; *d.* 25 August 1972), Argentine composer, teacher, and writer. Paz was born in Buenos Aires, where he studied piano and composition with Alphonse Thibaud and harmony with Constantino Gaito but recognized a main influence in the figure of Eduardo Fornarini, an itinerant Italian musician. Fornarini initiated Paz in the analysis of the works of César Franck, Debussy, and the early works of Schönberg and Stravinsky. In 1924, Paz went to Europe and entered the Schola Cantorum in Paris, where he worked with Vincent d'Indy. In spite of all his studies, Paz considered himself largely self-taught. On returning to Buenos Aires he joined in 1929 with composers Juan José and José María Castro, Gilardo Gilardi, and Jacobo Ficher to create the Renovation Group to promote their music. Later, Paz withdrew from it due to a lack of agreement on the methods to achieve their goals and on aesthetic differences. Soon he began to teach composition privately, and he introduced twelve-tone techniques to his students and to the public at large. In 1937 he created the Agrupación Nueva Música (ANM), which performed in concert featuring works by Schönberg, Webern, Varèse, Cowell, Cage, Messiaen, and many others.

Paz's works were neoclassical well into the mid-1930s, characterized by linear, contrapuntal writing, with some harmonies within an atonal style, as in his *Tres piezas para orquesta* (1931) and Octet for wind instruments (1930). *Tres invenciones a dos voces* (1932), *Tres movimientos de Jazz* (1932) and his Piano Sonatina no. 3 (1933) show his angular, neoclassical writing and jazz influences. The abstract phrasing of these pieces introduced the strict atonal writing that Paz would favor in later years.

In 1934, Paz began to explore twelve-tone writing, a technique he applied in a very personal way in his *Primera composición en los doce tonos* for flute, English horn, and cello (1934); *Segunda composición en los doce tonos* for flute and piano (1934–1935); *Diez piezas sobre una serie de los doce tonos* for piano (1935); *Passacaglia* for orchestra (1936); and *Tercera composición en los doce tonos* for clarinet and piano (1937); and *Cuarta composición en los doce tonos* for solo violin (1938). Paz continued in this phase into the mid-1950s, although he tried something different in his *Rítmica ostinata* for orchestra (1942). In this work, a large toccata in fast tempo with sixteenth- and eighth-note values as a constant figuration, the many pedal points and ostinatos are orchestrated brilliantly. During the 1960s, Paz explored other styles and techniques but favored what he had called the "return to intuition." He wrote only a few works after that, in a free style that offered him a greater freedom of language. During the 1960s he wrote *Continuidad* (1960) for orchestra; *Música* for piano and orchestra (1963); *Invención* for string quartet (1961); *Concreción* for woodwind and brass instruments (1964); *Galaxia* for organ (1964); and the series *Núcleos* for piano (1962–1964). Other important works by Paz include *Dédalus* for flute, clarinet, violin, cello, and piano (1950); *Transformaciones canónicas* (Canonical transformations) for orchestra (1955–1966); and his monumental *Música 1946* for piano (1945–1946).

His books left a mark on many young composers, not only in Argentina but throughout South America and Europe. They included *La música en los Estados Unidos* (1952; revised in 1958); *Introducción a la música de nuestro tiempo* (1955); *Arnold Schoenberg, o el fin de la era tonal* (1958); *Alturas, tensiones, ataques, intensidades* (1972).

See also **Music: Art Music.**

BIBLIOGRAPHY

John Vinton, ed., *Dictionary of Contemporary Music* (1974), p. 557.

J. Romano, *Vidas de Paz* (1976), pp. 7–13, 94–97.

Gérard Béhague, *Music in Latin America: An Introduction* (1979), pp. 245–246, 274–276, 335–336; *Octavo festival internacional de música contemporánea* (1992), pp. 72, 96.

Additional Bibliography

Benarós, León. "Juan Carlos Paz: 'Dodecafonismo o muerte.'" *Todo Es Historia* 35: 408 (July 2001), 30–31.

Scarabino, Guillermo. *El Grupo Renovación (1929–1944) y la "nueva música" en la Argentina del siglo XX.* Buenos Aires: Ediciones de la Universidad Católica Argentina, 2000.

ALCIDES LANZA

PAZ, OCTAVIO (1914–1998). Octavio Paz (*b.* 31 March 1914; *d.* 19 April 1998), Mexican poet and essayist. Recipient of the Nobel Prize for literature in 1990 and one of the leading Mexican poets and intellectuals of the twentieth century, Octavio Paz was born and raised in Mixcoac, now part of Mexico City. His father, Octavio Paz Solórzano, was a political journalist who wrote a biography of Emiliano Zapata and helped found agrarian reform. Paz attended French and English language schools and read widely in the library of his grandfather, the novelist Ireneo Paz, before transferring to public schools, and ultimately the National Preparatory School, where he studied law. He founded the magazine *Barandal* (Balustrade) in 1931–1932, followed by *Cuadernos del Valle de México* (Notebooks from the Valley of Mexico) in 1933–1934. Paz abandoned his legal studies in 1937 to visit Yucatán, where he helped establish a progressive school for workers and discovered Mexico's pre-Columbian past. That same year he went to Republican Spain to attend the Second International Congress of Anti-fascist Writers, where he met most of the great poets writing in Spanish, as well as English and French writers, including André Breton, the founder of surrealism. As a result of this trip, he developed a philosophy of poetry that sought to create language anew, with the dual purpose of revealing human fragmentation and solitude and demonstrating how language prevents the modern world from understanding itself and its "real reality." In this way Paz tried to resolve the tension between pure poetry and art committed to social progress.

In 1938 Paz returned to Mexico and helped found the journal *Taller* (Workshop) to explore his new ideas. When that magazine folded, he helped found *El Hijo Pródigo* (The Prodigal Son) in 1943, a periodical representing the Mexican vanguard, poets who believed that writing had a special mission. In 1944 Paz was awarded a Guggenheim fellowship and spent the next ten years of his life away from Mexico. He went first to San Francisco and then to New York City, where he studied the life and work of José Juan Tablada and published an important critical essay on that poet. Tablada's influence led him to his lifelong fascination with Asian literature and culture. In 1944 he taught at the Middlebury College Spanish Summer School in Vermont, where he met the poet Robert Frost and became reacquainted with Jorge Guillén. In 1945 he joined the Mexican diplomatic service and went to Paris, where he was strongly influenced by the surrealist movement. In 1952 he served as Mexican ambassador in India and Japan, furthering his interests in Eastern art and architecture

Octavio Paz, 1982. Awarded the Nobel Prize for literature in 1990, Mexican-born Paz wrote poetry and essays and is particularly well regarded for his literary criticism, which brought international attention to Mexican authors and culture. STEVE NORTHUP/TIMEPIX/TIME LIFE PICTURES/GETTY IMAGES

and in the classics of Buddhism and Taoism, influences felt subsequently in his poetry. He returned to Mexico in 1953.

Paz's work reached maturity in the late 1940s. Appearing in 1949 was his *Libertad bajo palabra* (Freedom on Parole), championing the Latin American critical avant-garde. In 1950 he published a classic analysis of the Mexican people, *El laberinto de la soledad* (The Labyrinth of Solitude). These works inaugurated his most productive and complex period. He published poetry and essays, lectured on and presented new poets and painters, founded journals and a theatrical group, translated ancient and modern poetry, and participated in literary and political polemics. In 1956 he published

El arco y la lira (The Bow and the Lyre), an important work examining the function of poetry itself. Paz returned to Paris in 1959 and subsequently was renamed ambassador to India in 1962, a post he resigned in 1968 in protest over the 2 October massacre of students in Tlatelolco Square. He displayed his outrage in *Posdata* (1970; Postscript), a critical reevaluation of the *Labyrinth of Solitude*. He expanded on the ideas in this book in *El ogro filantrópico* (1979; The Philanthropic Ogre). During the 1970s, he founded two significant magazines, *Plural* (1971) and *Vuelta* (1977), which he continued to edit in the 1990s, demonstrating his strong commitment to cultural journalism and his anticipation of the "postmodern."

Paz is primarily important as a poet and essayist, but he has also written unpublished short stories and a play. His published works in Spanish include nearly thirty volumes of poetry, over thirty volumes of essays, numerous anthologies of poetry in Spanish, as well as anthologies of poetry in translation from the French, English, Portuguese, Swedish, Chinese, and Japanese. His own poetry and essays have been translated into English, French, Italian, and numerous other languages. Paz is also important as an art critic and promoter.

Paz has taught at major universities in the United States and Europe. He is a member of the Colegio Nacional (Mexico) and the Consejo Superior de Cooperación Iberoamericana (Spain), and has won the International Prize for Poetry (Brussels, 1963), the Cervantes Prize (Spain, 1981), the International Prize for Literature (1982), and the Menéndez Pelayo Prize (Spain, 1987).

In the late twentieth century, Paz remained the leader of the generation that emerged toward the end of the 1930s, which was largely responsible for establishing the outlines of contemporary Mexican literary criticism and cultural thought. His work has been fundamental in bringing the Spanish language and Mexican literature and culture into the modern and postmodern age, as well as in opening them up to other cultures. Further, he has become one of the principal contemporary theorists of Mexican history and what he sees as the crisis of present-day Mexican culture. As he noted when he received the Nobel Prize, a writer has two loyalties, first to literature and second to his native culture.

See also **Literature: Spanish America.**

BIBLIOGRAPHY

Saúl Yurkievich, *Fundadores de la nueva poesía latinoamericana* (1971, 3d ed; 1978).

Rachel Phillips, *The Poetic Modes of Octavio Paz* (1972).

Gordon Brotherston, *Latin American Poetry: Origins and Presence* (1975).

Monique J. Lamaître, *Octavio Paz: Poesía y Poética* (1976).

Carlos H. Magis, *La poesía hermética de Octavio Paz* (1978).

Alfredo Roggiano, ed., *Octavio Paz* (1979).

Pere Gimferrer, *Octavio Paz: El escritor ante la crítica* (1982, reprinted 1989).

John M. Fein, *Toward Octavio Paz: A Reading of His Major Poems, 1957–1976* (1986).

Jason Wilson, *Octavio Paz* (1986).

Maya Schärer-Nussberger, *Octavio Paz: Trayectorias y visiones* (1989).

Manuel Durán, "Octavio Paz: Nobel Laureate in Literature, 1990," in *World Literature Today* (Winter 1991): 5–7.

Additional Bibliography

Bloom, Harold, ed. *Octavio Paz.* Philadelphia: Chelsea House Publishers, 2002.

Grenier, Yvon. *From Art to Politics: Octavio Paz and the Pursuit of Freedom.* Lanham, MD: Rowman & Littlefield, 2001.

Poniatwoska, Elena. *Octavio Paz: Las palabras del árbol.* Barcelona: Plaza Janés, 1998.

KEITH MCDUFFIE

PAZ BARAONA, MIGUEL (1863–1937).

Miguel Paz Baraona (*b.* 1863; *d.* 1937) president of Honduras (1925–1929). Dr. Miguel Paz Baraona, a civilian member of the Nationalist Party, was elected president almost unanimously in 1925 (the Liberals abstained from voting). His election, which marked the final phase of the bloody civil war between multiple bands of rival warlords that had erupted in Honduras in 1924, gradually restored domestic tranquillity to Honduras. Peace enabled the banana companies to resume their expansion, which within a few years made Honduras the premier banana exporter in the world. An even more auspicious breakthrough was the Lyall Plan, which Paz negotiated with the British bondholders association for the reduction and repayment of the country's crippling foreign debt.

See also **Honduras.**

BIBLIOGRAPHY

Lucas Paredes, *Drama político de Honduras* (1958).

Dana G. Munro, *The United States and the Caribbean Republics, 1921–1933* (1974): Richard L. Millett, "Historical Setting," in *Honduras: A Country Study,* edited by James D. Rudolph, 2d. rev. ed., (1984).

Additional Bibliography

O'Brien, Thomas F. *The Revolutionary Mission: American Enterprise in Latin America, 1900–1945.* New York: Cambridge University Press, 1996.

KENNETH V. FINNEY

PAZ DEL RÍO.

Paz del Río, Colombia's first modern integrated steel-production operation. Founded in September 1947 and located along the Chicamocha River in the department of Boyacá, Paz del Río played a key role in Colombian industrialization policy of the 1940s and 1950s. Due to World Bank opposition to the project in the early 1950s, its construction occurred as a result of French financing and technical assistance as well as the nationalist zeal of President Laureano Gómez. Steel production began in 1955. Although Paz del Río became privatized, in contrast to the prevalent pattern of state ownership of steel production in Latin America, it remains a symbol of the country's effort to free itself from dependence on foreign industrial power.

See also **Iron and Steel Industry.**

BIBLIOGRAPHY

Eduardo Wiesner Durán, *Paz del Río* (1963).

René De La Pedraja, *Fedemetal y la industrialización de Colombia* (1986).

Additional Bibliography

Pinto Escobar, Inés. *Progreso, industrialización y utopía en Boyacá: El caso de la siderúrgica de Samacá.* Tunja: Publicaciones del Magister en Historia, Universidad Pedagógica y Tecnológica de Colombia, 1997.

PAMELA MURRAY

PAZ ESTENSSORO, VÍCTOR (1907–2001).

Perhaps Bolivia's most important political leader of the twentieth century, Víctor Paz Estenssoro pursued a populist strategy to gather support from diverse social classes. Born to a well-known landowning family in the southern department of Tarija, he earned a law degree from the national university in La Paz. In 1929 he held the first of numerous government posts and went on to serve as president four times (1952–1956, 1960–1964, 1964, and 1985–1989).

In 1932 Paz Estenssoro joined thousands of Bolivian conscripted soldiers in the ill-fated Chaco War against Paraguay, which resulted in Bolivia's loss of the Chaco territory. After the war he joined prominent middle-class intellectuals in calling for sweeping social and political reform. He was elected deputy to the 1938 constitutional convention that enshrined more active state economic intervention and redress for social grievances in Bolivia's constitution.

In 1941 Paz Estenssoro joined Augusto Céspedes, Carlos Montenegro, Hernán Siles Zuazo, Rafael Otazo, and Walter Guevara Arze to found the Nationalist Revolutionary Movement (MNR). The new party's announced goals stressed "the economic liberation of the Bolivian people" and "the consolidation of the state and the security of the fatherland." As a deputy in Congress, Paz Estenssoro delivered scathing indictments of the military government headed by General Enrique Peñaranda, viewed by the MNR as merely a puppet of the three largest tin-mining companies. Paz's congressional speech condemning the 1942 Catavi massacre of miners and their families by government troops enabled him to rally support for the MNR and forge an alliance with mid-rank officers who advocated taking a more direct role in political affairs. This civil-military alliance installed Major Gualberto Villarroel as president of Bolivia in 1943.

As the minister of finance, Paz Estenssoro undertook Bolivia's first flirtations with strategies of import substitution and state-centered development. In July 1946 a mob incited by both leftist and conservative parties stormed the government palace and lynched President Villarroel. Paz spent the next six years in exile. From Argentina he fought an intense battle to maintain his position at the helm of the MNR while working to broaden the appeal of the party to labor and other social sectors. Paz's characteristic patience, equanimity, and logical analysis of information were well suited to these tasks.

Paz Estenssoro's decisive plurality in the 1951 presidential voting was annulled by the military, but he returned triumphantly to Bolivia following the April 9, 1952, revolution. In two days of street fighting, the militarized police (*carabineros*) had joined the MNR to defeat army rule, launching Bolivia into the era of mass political participation. During his first term as president (1952–1956), Paz nationalized the nation's tin-mining operations, downgraded the military institution, approved a major land-reform decree, and granted universal suffrage to all adult Bolivians. However, the MNR was not able to exert strict discipline over its diverse social coalition, leading (among other consequences) to hyperinflation. Paz endorsed an austere monetary-stabilization plan before leaving office. Returned to power in 1960, and barely reelected in 1964, he was overthrown by a military coup orchestrated by General René Barrientos Ortuño, his own vice president, who had been imposed on the MNR ticket by a restructured military institution.

From exile in Peru, Paz returned to Bolivia in August 1971 to support General Hugo Banzer Suárez's coup against a left-wing military regime. During the next fifteen years, while army-backed governments predominated, Paz restored unity and political prominence to the MNR. In 1985, having placed second in popular balloting, he was elected president by congress in an informal coalition with the Movement of the Revolutionary Left (MIR). On August 29, 1985, he decreed the New Economic Policy (NPE), ending a critical spiral of inflation and declining national income. The new policy diminished the role of state enterprises and enlarged the scope of the private sector. Paz Estenssoro defended the NPE as essential to save the nation, and completed his last term of office with a 70 percent popularity rating.

See also **Bolivia, Political Parties: Nationalist Revolutionary Movement (MNR).**

BIBLIOGRAPHY

Bedregal Gutiérrez, Guillermo. *Víctor Paz Estenssoro, el político: Una semblanza crítica.* Mexico City: Fondo de Cultura Económica, 1999.

Dunkerley, James. *Rebellion in the Veins: Political Struggle in Bolivia, 1952–1982*. London: Verso, 1984.

Fellman Velarde, José. *Víctor Paz Estenssoro: El hombre y la revolución*. La Paz, Bolivia: Editorial Tejerina, 1954.

EDUARDO A. GAMARRA
CHRISTOPHER MITCHELL

PAZ GARCÍA, POLICARPO (1932–1991). Policarpo Paz García (b. 1932; d. 1991), president of Honduras (25 July 1980–27 January 1982). Paz was commander of the armed forces under President Juan Melgar Castro (1975–1978). Leader of the military junta that overthrew Melgar Castro on 7 August 1978, he acted as chief of state and chief of the armed forces until the Constituent Assembly elected him provisional president of Honduras. Under Paz, land reform slowed and external debt accelerated. His government was reputedly corrupt, and rumors persisted of his mafia and drug trafficking ties. The United States liberally supplied aid to Honduras under Paz, considering his government a bulwark against the communist regime in Nicaragua.

See also **Honduras.**

BIBLIOGRAPHY

Mark B. Rosenberg and Philip L. Shepherd, eds., *Honduras Confronts Its Future: Contending Perspectives on Critical Issues* (1986).

Thomas P. Anderson, *Politics in Central America: Guatemala, El Salvador, Honduras, and Nicaragua* (1988).

Additional Bibliography

González de Oliva, Alexis Argentina. *Gobernantes hondureños: Siglos XIX–XX*. Tegucigalpa: Editorial Universitaria, 1996–1997.

Schulz, Donald E., and Deborah Sundloff Schula. *The United States, Honduras, and the Crisis in Central America*. Boulder, CO: Westview Press, 1994.

JOYCE E. NAYLON

PAZ SOLDÁN FAMILY. Paz Soldán family, an aristocratic Peruvian family active in government hroughout much of the nineteenth century. With roots in the early colonial period, the family helped shape the national government and intellectual life in Peru through the major heads of its household. One of the more notable descendants of the line was Mariano Felipe Paz Soldán (1821–1886), who wrote one of the earliest and most caustic histories of the struggle for independence in Peru. In the 1860s he also planned a model prison in Lima, where inmates were to be trained in useful trades. José Gregorio Paz Soldán (1808–1875), a leader among liberals before the era of Ramón Castilla, voiced these views as editor of the newspaper *El Constitucional*, and later he served as rector of the National University of San Marcos. As minister of foreign relations under President Castilla, he organized short courses in international law, protocol, and foreign languages, upgrading Peru's foreign service to one of the most respected in Latin America. Pedro Paz Soldán y Unanue (1839–1895), a poet and essayist, wrote bitterly against obvious signs of ethnic and cultural change, especially the Chinese influence, in an aristocratic Peru he hoped would remain unspoiled. The essay, published under the pseudonym Juan de Arona, appeared as *La inmigración en el Perú* (1891). Other members of the Paz Soldán family also left their mark in letters and public administration.

Edmundo Paz Soldan is a Latin American Literature professor at Cornell (in 1999) and winner of the 1997 Juan Rulfo Short Story Prize.

Mariano Domingo's brother José Gregorio (1808-1875) was senator and prime minister of Perú. He bought the San Isidro hacienda, later a residential district as well as the financial district of Lima.

Mateo (1812–1857) was a mathematician, geographer, astronomer, and mastered ten languages. He wrote books on astronomy and trigonometry and was friend of French mathematician Cauchy. He authored a geographical atlas of Perú, published posthumously by his brother Mariano Felipe.

The younger child of Manuel, Mariano Felipe (1821–1886), wrote a landmark history book *Historia del Perú Independiente* and was minister of justice and education of Peru.

Manuel Rouaud y Paz Soldán (1839–1872) explored the Amazon River. In the first trip he lost a leg due to arrow wounds from a skirmish with natives and in a second exploration trip he died from an infectious disease.

Pedro Paz Soldán y Unanue, also known as Juan de Arona, (1839–1895), was a poet, journalist, traveler and keen observer of his times. He wrote the first dictionary of Peruvian slang *Diccionario de Peruanismos* in 1883.

Francisco Alayza y Paz Soldán (1873–1946) was minister of state for two presidents of Peru.

Luis Alayza y Paz Soldan (b. 1883), was a lawyer, president of the Central Bank of Perú, and minister of justice. He wrote a ten-volume compendium of Peruvian folklore *Mi País*.

Carlos Enrique Paz Soldán y Paz Soldán (1885–1972) was a doctor and pioneer in social medical policy and research. He participated in the organization of the World Health Organization, was a founder of the Peruvian Medicine History Society, and a national chess champion.

Luiz Ortiz de Zevallos Paz Soldán (b. 1910) was a founder of the Urban Studies Institute.

José Pareja Paz Soldán was a professor and director of the Diplomatic Academy of Perú. He wrote many textbooks on diplomacy. He has published books on history, geography, constitutional law and airspace law.

See also **Education: Overview; Literature: Spanish America; Science.**

BIBLIOGRAPHY

Magnus Mörner, *The Andean Past: Land, Societies, and Conflicts* (1985), esp. pp. 120–187.

Paul Gootenberg, *Imagining Development; Economic Ideas in Peru's "Fictitious Prosperity" of Guano, 1840–1880* (1993).

Additional Bibliography

Quiñonez, Ernesto and Paz Soldán, Edmundo. *El vendedor de sueños.* Lima: Santillana USA, 2001.

Sánchez-Blake, Elvira E. and Maria Nowakowska Stycos. *Voces hispanas, siglo XXI: Entrevistas con autores en DVD.* New Haven, CT: Yale University, 2004.

VINCENT PELOSO

PAZ ZAMORA, JAIME (1939–). Jaime Paz Zamora (*b.* 15 April 1939) was president of Bolivia from 1989 to 1993. Born in the department of Cochabamba, Paz Zamora studied for the priesthood at Louvain University in Belgium in the 1960s but changed his course of studies to political science. One of the founders of the Movement of the Revolutionary Left (MIR) in 1971, he was imprisoned in 1974 by General Hugo Banzer Suárez's government for conspiring to overthrow it. He escaped from jail and sought asylum in Venezuela. In 1978 he returned to Bolivia after the democratic opening as one of the founders of the Popular and Democratic Union (UDP) coalition and served as vice president in the government of Hernán Siles Zuazo (1982–1985).

In the mid-1980s the MIR began to attract middle-class intellectuals, professionals, and young voters who were discontented with the traditional parties and politicians. This coalition, dubbed the Nueva Mayoría, and a strategic alliance with General Banzer's Nationalist Democratic Action (Accíon Democrática y Nacionalista—ADN) catapulted Paz Zamora to the presidency in August 1989. Abandoning his party's rhetoric about improving social policy, he concentrated on Bolivia's foreign relations. Domestically, he focused on maintaining the coalition and ensuring compliance with austerity measures. His image with the electorate fell considerably. While the MIR lost its popular appeal, Paz Zamora managed to maintain the confidence of international financial institutions and the United States.

When Paz Zamora stepped down as president in 1993, the general perception was that the MIR and ADN had presided over the largest increase in corruption since 1982. The most serious charge of corruption was the alleged ties of prominent members of the MIR to drug trafficking.

Paz Zamora remained politically active, serving as a member of the international peace commission in Chiapas, Mexico, in 1993. He tried unsuccessfully to return to the presidency in the late 1990s and the early twenty-first century. In 2005 Paz Zamora ran for a gubernatorial post but lost. Many commentators believed that he could not escape the problematic legacy of his presidency.

See also **Bolivia, Political Parties: Movement of the Revolutionary Left (MIR); Drugs and Drug Trade.**

BIBLIOGRAPHY

Eduardo A. Gamarra, "Crafting Political Support for Stabilization: Political Pacts and the New Economic Policy in Brazil," in *Democracy, Markets, and Structural*

Reform in Latin America, edited by William C. Smith, Carlos H. Acuña, and Eduardo A. Gamarra (1994), and "Market-Oriented Reforms and Democratization in Bolivia," in *A Precarious Balance,* edited by Joan M. Nelson, vol. 2 (1994).

Additional Bibliography

Chávez Zamorano, Omar, and Susana Peñaranda de Del Granado. *Jaime Paz Zamora: Un político de raza.* La Paz, Bolivia: S. Peñaranda y O. Chávez, 1997.

EDUARDO A. GAMARRA

PEACE CORPS. The Peace Corps is a U.S. government grass-roots development initiative. President John F. Kennedy created the Peace Corps in 1961 to channel the idealism of American youth toward alleviating the problems of the developing world. One of the first groups went to the island of Saint Lucia in the Caribbean. Soon programs were established in virtually every country in the Western Hemisphere. During the first three decades over 20,000 volunteers were sent for two-year periods of service in the region.

During the 1960s the Peace Corps efforts in Latin America concentrated on community development. The objective was to help poor people solve local problems. Volunteers were expected to live in situations as close as possible to those of the people they served and to learn the local language. The number of volunteers in Latin America peaked in the late 1960s.

During the 1970s and 1980s budget cuts and political factors reduced the program, especially in South America. Nevertheless, a broad range of projects was undertaken in agriculture, education, and health. Skilled technicians in these fields were recruited as volunteers. Community development became a secondary priority. Efforts were made to coordinate the Peace Corps activities with other official U.S. and private assistance programs. Programs were designed in consultation with the recipient countries. However, funding began to increase again in the 1990s. Following the September 11, 2001, terrorist attacks in New York, President George W. Bush proposed doubling the size of the Peace Corps as a way to combat anti-Americanism abroad. With the extra funding, the Peace Corps has begun recruiting more volunteers to meet the president's goal.

The return home of the volunteers increased awareness in the United States of the problems of the poor and dispossessed in Latin America. At the same time the cross-cultural linkages of the program created a better understanding of the United States among the people at the community level in the participating countries.

See also **United States-Latin American Relations.**

BIBLIOGRAPHY

R. Sargent Shriver, "Ambassadors of Good Will, the Peace Corps," in *National Geographic* 126 (September 1964): 297–345.

Robert B. Ridinger, *The Peace Corps* (1989).

Additional Bibliography

Cobbs Hoffman, Elizabeth. *All You Need Is Love: The Peace Corps and the Spirit of the 1960s.* Cambridge, MA: Harvard University Press, 2000.

Fischer, Fritz. *Making Them Like Us: Peace Corps Volunteers in the 1960s.* Washington, DC: Smithsonian Institution Press, 1998.

DAVID L. JICKLING

PEARSON, WEETMAN DICKINSON (1856–1927). Weetman Dickinson Pearson (First Viscount Cowdray; *b.* 15 July 1856; *d.* 1 May 1927), British contractor who headed the construction and engineering firm of S. Pearson and Son, of London. Born at Shelley Woodhouse, Yorkshire, he received a private education at Harrowgate. In 1875 he became a partner in his grandfather's construction firm. Among the projects that made the firm known around the world during the late nineteenth and early twentieth centuries were the Blackwall Tunnel under the Thames River in London (1894), the Hudson River Railroad Tunnel in New York (initiated in 1888, completed ca. 1900), and harbor works and railroads in England, Spain, Mexico, and Chile.

Pearson's firm received several contracts from the government of Mexican General Porfirio Díaz. It initially entered Mexico to construct the Grand Canal, which drained the lake in the Valley of Mexico, ending the perennial flooding of Mexico City. Other projects included the Tehuantepec Railroad (1906–1907) and the Veracruz port facilities (1895–1902).

Pearson formed the Mexican Eagle Oil Company during the oil boom that took place between 1901 and 1920, when Mexico was the fastest-growing oil producer in the world. The company's concessions in Tehuantepec, Tampico, and Veracruz eventually reached a production of 32 million barrels per year. Díaz cautiously split concessions between U.S. and British firms, to retain bargaining power by shifting his favors between them. Pearson's concessions constituted a major source of oil for the British navy during World War I.

The Mexican Revolution rendered the oil firms and their owners controversial as they sought to maintain production and protect their concessions. The resulting political maneuvering caused considerable difficulties between London and Washington. Lord Cowdray was frequently accused of supporting the government of General Victoriano Huerta and opposing the Revolution. Throughout the years that his firm operated in Mexico, Pearson visited the country annually, often spending up to three months, though most of his time was spent directing the firm from London. Mexican Eagle ultimately became part of Royal Dutch Shell.

See also **Díaz, Porfirio; Energy.**

BIBLIOGRAPHY

John A. Spender, *Weetman Pearson: First Viscount Cowdray, 1856–1927* (1930).

Alfred Tischendorf, *Great Britain and Mexico in the Era of Porfirio Díaz* (1961).

Kenneth J. Grieb, *The United States and Huerta* (1969).

Additional Bibliography

Brown, Jonathan C. *Oil and Revolution in Mexico.* Berkeley: University of California Press, 1993.

Connolly, Priscilla. *El contratista de don Porfirio: Obras públicas, deuda y desarrollo desigual.* México, D.F.: El Colegio de Michoacán: Universidad Autónoma Metropolitana-Azcapotzalco: Fondo de Cultura Económica, 1997.

Santiago, Myrna. *The Ecology of Oil: Environment, Labor, and the Mexican Revolution, 1900–1938.* Cambridge: Cambridge University Press, 2006.

                                    KENNETH J. GRIEB

PEASANT LEAGUES. *See* **Brazil, Organizations: Peasant Leagues.**

PEASE, FRANKLIN (1939–1999). A renowned historian and prolific Andean scholar, Franklin Pease García-Yrigoyen (November 28, 1939–November 13, 1999) was born in Lima and educated at the Pontificia Universidad Católica del Perú (Catholic University), receiving a BA in 1964, an LLD in 1965, and a PhD in history in 1967. Pease's main interest was in Andean religion and political form, a departure from the mainly Creole history of the coast. He also became a leading exponent of the new interdisciplinary ethnohistorical approach introduced in the 1970s, which combined archaeology, anthropology, and history. Beginning a long teaching career in 1962 at the Catholic University, he rose to become dean of the humanities department on several occasions.

His first book, *Atahualpa*, appeared in 1964 and was followed soon after by two classics: *Los ultimos incas del Cuzco* (1972) and *El dios creador andino* (1973). He went on to publish and edit numerous books as well as over 125 articles and book chapters. In 1977 he founded the journal *Histórica*, which became the premier historical journal in Peru. Pease received numerous fellowships, including a Guggenheim Fellowship (1982), and served as a visiting professor at institutions including the University of California, Berkeley (1979), the University of Cambridge (1987), and Johns Hopkins University (1989). He also served as director of the National Museum of the Archaeology, Anthropology, and History of Peru from 1969 to 1974 and the Biblioteca Nacional del Perú from 1983 to 1986.

See also **Anthropology; Archaeology; Atahualpa.**

BIBLIOGRAPHY

Works by Franklin Pease G. Y.

Del Tawantinsuyu a la historia del Perú. Lima: Pontificia Universidad Católica del Perú, 1978.

Curacas, reciprocidad y riqueza. Lima: Pontificia Universidad Católica del Perú, 1992.

Las crónicas y los Andes. Lima: Pontificia Universidad Católica del Perú, 1995.

                                    PETER KLARÉN

PEÇANHA, NILO PROCÓPIO (1867–1924). Nilo Procópio Peçanha (*b.* 2 October 1867; *d.* 31 March 1924), president of Brazil

(June 1909–November 1910). Although born to a modest family of the imperial province of Rio de Janeiro, Peçanha enjoyed a rapid rise through the elite-dominated political system of Brazil's First Republic. Peçanha earned political stature while participating in the abolition and republican movements, and in the years following the 1889 Proclamation of the Republic he rose to serve as federal senator (1903) and governor of the state of Rio de Janeiro (1903–1905). He was elected vice president of Brazil in 1906; in 1909 Peçanha assumed the presidency upon the death of President Afonso Pena.

A fiscal conservative, but also a strong advocate of a diversified economy, Peçanha was a noted proponent of the establishment of steel production, technical education, agronomics, and the early repayment of the 1898 funding loan. In spite of his calls for diversification, however, coffee production remained the prime motor of the Brazilian economy throughout Peçanha's political career. As president, Peçanha ordered federal intervention into political crises in Bahia and Amazonas. In 1910 he stepped down from the presidency amid charges that President-elect Marshal Hermes da Fonseca defeated *civilista* candidate Rui Barbosa through electoral fraud. Peçanha remained in politics, serving as governor of Rio (1914–1917), foreign minister (1917–1918), and senator (1918–1924). In 1921 he led the unsuccessful Reação Republicana (Republican Reaction) presidential campaign against Artur da Silva Bernardes.

See also **Brazil, The Empire (First); Rio de Janeiro (Province and State).**

BIBLIOGRAPHY

Brigido Tinoco, *A vida de Nilo Peçanha* (1962).

Robert E. Russell, *Nilo Peçanha and Fluminense Politics, 1889–1917* (1974).

Additional Bibliography

Ferreira, Marieta de Moraes. *Em busca da idade de ouro: As elites políticas fluminenses na Primeira República, 1889–1930*. Rio de Janeiro: Editora UFRJ: Edições Tempo Brasileiro, 1994.

Quaresma, Quélia H. "Electoral Mobilization and the Construction of a Civic Culture in Brazil, 1909–1930." Ph.D. diss., 1998.

Topik, Steven. *The Political Economy of the Brazilian State, 1889–1930*. Austin: University of Texas Press, 1987.

DARYLE WILLIAMS

PEDRA FURADA. The Brazilian archaeological site Pedra Furada is a very large rock shelter located at Serra da Capivara, near the city of São Raimundo Nonato, Piauí, and one of the most controversial sites ever excavated in the Americas. Excavations at Pedra Furada were undertaken by Niède Guidon between 1978 and 1987 and by Fabio Parenti in 1987–1988. Both believe the concentrations of charcoal and fired stone and the lithic assemblage they found, which were radiocarbon dated to about 32,000 years old, are unquestionably the product of human activity. More recent dates obtained by thermoluminescence on some of the burnt stones delimiting the putative hearths reached circa 100,000 years.

Most archeologists do not accept the material evidence presented by Guidon and Parenti as the product of human action. They believe the charcoal fragments could have come from natural fires in front of the shelter and that the lithic material was the product of natural flaking. The sandstone outcrop where the shelter is located is topped by a thick geological layer containing thousands of quartz cobbles of several sizes. The critics suggest the "lithic industry" would be the natural result of cobbles falling from the top of the outcrop and hitting each other in the ground, sometimes repeatedly. This highly dynamic process would have produced natural flakes and simple "stone tools." However simple, some of the putative stone instruments found at Pedra Furada can hardly be dismissed as being the result of human flaking. Similar crude and simple lithic industries in unquestionable archaeological contexts can also be found in several Final Pleistocene/Early Holocene Brazilian sites, including those located at Lagoa Santa.

See also **Archaeology.**

BIBLIOGRAPHY

Meltzer, David J., James M. Adovasio, and Tom D. Dillehay. "On a Pleistocene Human Occupation at Pedra Furada, Brazil." *Antiquity* 68 (1994): 695–714.

Parenti, Fabio, Michel Fontugne, and Claude Guérin. "Pedra Furada in Brazil, and Its 'Presumed' Evidence: Limitations and Potential of the Available Data." *Antiquity* 70 (1996): 416–421.

Parenti, Fabio. *Le gisement quaternaire de Pedra Furada (Piaui, Brésil): Stratigraphie, chronologie, évolucion culturelle*. 2 vols. Paris: Éditions Recherche sur lês Civilisations, 2001.

WALTER A. NEVES

PEDRARIAS. *See* Ávila, Pedro Arias de.

PEDREIRA, ANTONIO S. (1899–1939). Antonio S. Pedreira (*b.* 13 June 1899; *d.* 23 October 1939), Puerto Rican poet. Pedreira's literary works focus on Puerto Rican identity and personality. He proposed the docility thesis of Puerto Ricans and expounded an insular theory of government. Pedreira's travels to Spain brought him into contact with Antonio Machado, Federico García Lorca, Rafael Alberti, Pedro Salinas, and Luis Cernuda. Influenced by Spanish modernism, Pedreira became more protesting and reformist in his writing. Pedreira also analyzed Puerto Rican culture and its intellectual movements.

See also **Literature: Spanish America.**

BIBLIOGRAPHY

Candida Maldonado De Ortíz, *Antonio S. Pedreira: Vida y obra* (1974).

René Marqués, *The Docile Puerto Rican,* translated by Barbara Bockus Aponte (1976).

Additional Bibliography

Díaz, Luis Felipe. *Modernidad literaria puertorriqueña.* San Juan: Editorial Isla Negra: Editorial Cultural, 2005.

Labrador-Rodríguez, Sonia. "Mulatos entre blancos: José Celso Barbosa y Antonio S. Pedreira; lo fronterizo en Puerto Rico al cambio de siglo, 1896–1937." *Revista Iberoamericana* 65:188-189 (July–December 1999): 713–731.

CHRISTOPHER T. BOWEN

PEDRO I OF BRAZIL (1798–1834). Pedro I of Brazil (*b.* 12 October 1798; *d.* 24 September 1834), emperor of Brazil (1822–1831). Born in Queluz palace, Portugal, Prince Pedro de Bragança e Borbón was nine years old when he fled with the Portuguese royal family to Brazil to escape an invading French army. The Braganças settled in Rio de Janeiro in 1808 and Pedro spent the next thirteen years in and around that city. Though he was the elder son and heir of the Portuguese regent, later King João VI (r. 1816–1826), Pedro received little formal education and spent much of his youth hunting, horse racing, bullfighting, brawling, tavern hopping, and wenching—often in the company of the Falstaffian Francisco Gomes da Silva, a native of Portugal commonly known as the *Chalaça* (Joker). Intellectually, the prince was most influenced by the count dos Arcos, former viceroy of Brazil and a proponent of enlightened despotism, and by his tutor and confessor, the liberal Friar António de Arrábida. In his quieter moments, especially after his marriage in 1817 to Princess Leopoldina de Hapsburg, Pedro read extensively in political philosophy.

In February 1821 Pedro persuaded his father to accept publicly in Rio the constitutionalist principles proclaimed by the revolutionary regime in Portugal. Two months later Pedro played a major role in suppressing a movement led by Portuguese-born radicals to set up a revolutionary government in Rio. In April 1821, when King João VI obeyed a summons from the Portuguese Cortes to return to Lisbon, he left Pedro in Rio as regent of Brazil with the advice not to resist Brazilian independence should it seem inevitable but to take control of the separatist movement and make himself king of the new nation.

As regent of Brazil, Pedro disregarded orders from the Cortes that he dismantle his government in Rio and embark for Europe. Fearing the return of Brazil to colonial status if Pedro left, various city and town councils in southern Brazil petitioned him to stay. In Rio in January 1822, Pedro publicly declared "Fico" (I am staying). Following his announcement, Pedro installed a new ministry headed by the Brazilian savant José Bonifácio de Andrada E Silva, and events marched swiftly toward Brazil's declaration of independence, which Pedro issued near São Paulo on 7 September 1822. With the support of José Bonifácio and the major municipalities of the south, Pedro was proclaimed emperor of Brazil in Rio in October 1822.

Overcoming token opposition from the Portuguese garrison in Rio and fierce resistance from Portuguese army and navy units in Bahia province, Pedro's forces extended the emperor's control over virtually all of Portuguese America by the end of 1823. That same year a dispute arose between the emperor and his chief minister over the latter's persecution of his political enemies, which led to José

Bonifácio's resignation from the government. A confrontation between the emperor and a constitutional convention he had summoned ended when Pedro forcibly dissolved the assembly and exiled José Bonifácio. Pedro then produced his own constitution, which he promulgated in March 1824. While in some respects more authoritarian than a draft the convention was considering, Pedro's constitution also was more liberal in providing religious toleration and enumerating civil rights.

The promulgation of Pedro's constitution sparked a major revolt in northeastern Brazil, which imperial forces suppressed in 1824. In the South, however, Pedro's army and navy were unable to prevent the loss of the empire's Cisplatine Province (present-day Uruguay), which was invaded by forces from Buenos Aires in 1825.

The loss of Uruguay (conceded in 1828), the emperor's hostility toward slavery and his attempts to end the African slave trade, his employment of European mercenaries in the Brazilian armed forces, his involvement in Portuguese dynastic affairs, his unconcealed marital infidelities, and his uncouth Portuguese companions contributed to Pedro's growing unpopularity among influential Brazilians. Reconciliation with José Bonifácio and marriage to the admirable Amélia Augusta Leuchtenberg in 1829 (Leopoldina had died in 1826) slowed but did not halt the erosion of his support. In the midst of nativist riots in Rio, Pedro refused to make ministerial changes demanded by the mob and, on 7 April 1831, abdicated the Brazilian throne in favor of his five-year-old son Pedro II.

Pedro returned to Europe and concentrated on removing his reactionary brother Miguel from the Portuguese throne and replacing him with his own daughter, Maria. Shortly after achieving these goals, Pedro died of tuberculosis in Queluz on 24 September 1834.

See also **Andrada, José Bonifácio de.**

BIBLIOGRAPHY

Octávio Tarquínio De Sousa, *A vida de Dom Pedro I,* 3 vols. (1951).

Sérgio Corrêa Da Costa, *Every Inch a King* (1953).

Denyse Dalbian, *Dom Pedro: Empereur du Brésil, roi de Portugal (1798–1834)* (1959).

Brasil Gerson, *A revolução brasileira de Pedro I* (1971).

Neill Macaulay, *Dom Pedro: The Struggle for Liberty in Brazil and Portugal, 1798–1834* (1986).

Additional Bibliography

Barman, Roderick J. *Citizen Emperor: Pedro II and the Making of Brazil, 1825–9.* Stanford, CA: Stanford University Press, 1999.

Ramos, Luís A. de Oliveira. *D. Pedro, imperador e rei: Experiências de um príncipe (1798–1834).* Lisboa: Edições Inapa, 2002.

Silva, Paulo Napoleão Nogueira da. *Pedro I, o português brasileiro.* Rio de Janeiro: Gryphus, 2000.

NEILL MACAULAY

PEDRO II OF BRAZIL (1825–1891).

Pedro II of Brazil (*b.* 2 December 1825; *d.* 5 December 1891), the second and last emperor of Brazil (1831–1889). A central figure in Brazil's development as a nation state, Pedro II was a man of complex personality and considerable abilities. His actions first consolidated and ultimately undermined the monarchical regime. Born in Rio de Janeiro, the son and heir to the emperor Pedro I and the empress Leopoldina, Pedro II was set apart by both ancestry and nurture. Related to almost all the monarchies of Europe, he grew up surrounded by a rigid etiquette and omnipresent deference inherited from the royal court at Lisbon. His destined task was to command, the role of all others to obey. His formal education gave him a love of knowledge and instilled a sense of self-restraint and a devotion to service.

Pedro II's early years were disturbed and psychologically cramping. His mother died before his first birthday, and he lost his father, his beloved stepmother, and his eldest sister when they sailed for Europe following Pedro I's abdication in his favor on 7 April 1831. As guardian of Pedro II from 1831 to 1833, José Bonifácio de Andrada failed to protect his ward's physical and emotional health. An epileptic attack in August 1833 nearly proved fatal. Pedro II's health and conditions of life did improve markedly after José Bonifácio's dismissal, but the psychological pressures remained. Pedro II's approaching adolescence and his intellectual precocity made him credible as a possible savior for Brazil, which was mired in crisis in the late 1830s. Deference and adulation fed his sense of indispensability and

Coronation of Dom Pedro II (1825–1891). Painting (oil on canvas) by Araujo Porto Alegre (19th century). MUSEU HISTORICO NACIONAL, RIO DE JANEIRO, BRAZIL/ INDEX/ THE BRIDGEMAN ART LIBRARY

intensified his isolation from ordinary life. He offered no resistance to the political campaign that prematurely declared him of age, at fourteen years and seven months, on 23 July 1840.

The trappings of authority did not, Pedro II soon discovered, denote real power. Courtiers and politicians cooperated to manipulate his views, exploit his prerogatives, and determine his life, as he realized in October 1843 when the bride chosen for him, Teresa Cristina, proved to be plain and not an intellectual. Coldness, arbitrariness, and brevity of speech increasingly characterized Pedro II's public conduct. In 1845 the birth of a son (to be followed by three more children) and a long tour through the far south of Brazil provided the catalyst that brought maturity and unleashed his capacities as a ruler. By 1850, Pedro II had ended the power of court factions, learned the efficient management of public affairs, and established his public image as a beneficent, highly cultured, and dedicated sovereign. His success as ruler was facilitated both by a boom in coffee production and by an eclipse of radicalism and republicanism following the Praieira Revolt of 1848–1850.

During the 1850s and 1860s, Pedro II embodied, as monarch, the only legitimate source of authority. He exemplified the European civilization that Brazilians desired for their nation. His talents as ruler were formidable: inexhaustible energy, remarkable memory for faces and facts, iron control of speech and action, firmness in purpose, freedom from petty resentments, acute sense of tactics, and utter indifference to the trappings of power. Politicians came and went. He alone remained entrenched at the center of affairs, ultimately determining both the political agenda and the personal characteristics requisite for political success.

Pedro II's skill as ruler played a part in securing long-term political stability for Brazil. He worked tirelessly to promote the development of the nation's infrastructure. Two particular achievements must be mentioned. He pursued the War of the Triple Alliance for five years until Paraguayan President Francisco Solano López was eliminated in 1870. Initiating in 1865 a campaign to force the eventual elimination of slavery, Pedro II brought it to fruition in 1871 with the enactment of the Free Birth Law.

After 1871 new factors—a shift in the intellectual climate toward republicanism, greater confidence among Brazilians in their capacity to rule themselves, and growing resentment against a highly centralized administration—undermined the regime's legitimacy. Pedro II's innate conservatism in thought and behavior, his staleness in mind and body induced by three decades of rule, and his unwillingness to surrender any part of his powers inhibited him from meeting this challenge. He held no intellectual belief in monarchy as such. Both his sons had died in childhood and, much as he loved Isabel as a daughter, he did not perceive her as a credible successor. He therefore felt no duty to assure her future as monarch, an obligation that would have restricted his freedom of action. His antediluvian court, shabby palaces, and distaste for ceremony destroyed the emotional appeal of monarchy.

The growth in the size and complexity of government made Pedro II's insistence on personally supervising every detail of public business a clog on effective administration. His love of knowledge and concern for culture appeared increasingly as superficial, amateur, and antiquated. His dominance of public life and elimination of all competing centers of power produced a vacuum at the heart of the system. Among younger Brazilians his monopoly of power bred feelings of impotence and futility and a resentment against his tutelage.

From the middle of the 1880s diabetes increasingly deprived Pedro II of the qualities that had made him so effective as a ruler. Still respected and even loved, he had ceased to be indispensable or even present in the country. During his prolonged absence in Europe in search of better health (1887–1888), Isabel used her powers as regent to secure the immediate abolition without compensation of slavery (13 May 1888). The disposal of one long-established institution could only suggest similar treatment for another that, for many Brazilians, had become an anachronism.

The army uprising that overthrew the monarchy on 15 November 1889 was as unexpected as it was decisive. Pedro II had no wish nor the ability to contest his dethronement and banishment to Europe. He conducted himself during exile with unwavering dignity, pursuing, as far as ill health would permit, his quest for knowledge. He died in Paris.

See also **Free Birth Law; Praieira Revolt; War of the Triple Alliance.**

BIBLIOGRAPHY

Heitor Lyra, *História de Dom Pedro I (1825–1891)*, 3 vols. (São Paulo, 1938–1940).

Mary Wilhelmine Williams, *Dom Pedro the Magnanimous* (1937).

Pedro Calmon, *História de Dom Pedro II*, 5 vols. (Rio de Janeiro, 1975).

Additional Bibliography

Barman, Roderick J. *Citizen Emperor: Pedro II and the Making of Brazil, 1825–91.* Stanford, CA: Stanford University Press, 1999.

Needell, Jeffrey D. *The Party of Order: The Conservatives, the State, and Slavery in the Brazilian Monarchy, 1831–1871.* Stanford, CA: Stanford University Press, 2006.

Schwarcz, Lilia Moritz. *As barbas do imperador: D. Pedro II, um monarca nos trópicos.* São Paulo: Companhia das Letras: Editora Schwarcz, 1998.

RODERICK J. BARMAN

PEDROSA Y GUERRERO, ANTONIO DE LA

PEDROSA Y GUERRERO, ANTONIO DE LA (c. 1660–). Antonio De La Pedrosa y Guerrero (*b.* ca. 1660; active late seventeenth and early eighteenth centuries), president of the Audiencia of Santa Fe de Bogotá (1718–1719). Pedrosa's public career in New Granada began in the mid-1680s when he served as the *fiscal protector de indios,* an official charged with the oversight of Indian policy, in the Audiencia of Santa Fe. He then rose to high-level metropolitan posts. Pedrosa's chief fame, however, rests on his role as the official sent to New Granada to establish the machinery of viceregal government that followed the royal decision in April 1717 to create a third Spanish American viceroyalty.

Acting with the authority of a viceroy and even called viceroy, Pedrosa largely concerned himself in 1718 and 1719 with administrative affairs, including the decision to establish the viceregal capital in Santa Fe instead of Cartagena, and policy regarding contraband trade. The frugal president clashed with the ostentatious first viceroy, Jorge de Villalonga (1719–1724), and the two remained political enemies even after Pedrosa returned to Spain in 1720.

BIBLIOGRAPHY

Two essential, well-reasoned analyses of the history of the creation of the viceroyalty of New Granada are María Teresa Garrido Conde, *La primera creación del virreinato de Nueva Granada (1717–1723)* (1965); and Sergio Elías Ortiz, *Nuevo Reino de Granada: Real Audiencias y presidentes*, pt. 3, *Presidentes de Capa y Espada (1654–1719)* (1966), which was published as part of vol. 4 of the *Historia extensa de Colombia* (1970). See also the relevant discussion in volume 1 of the *Manual de historia de Colombia*, edited by J. G. Cobo Borda and Santiago Mutis Duran, 3rd ed. (1984).

Additional Bibliography

Grahn, Lance. *Political Corruption and Reform in Cartagena Province, 1700–1740*. Milwaukee: University of Wisconsin-Milwaukee, 1993.

Peñas Galindo and David Ernesto. *La independencia y la mafia colonial: comerciantes, contrabandistas, y traidores*. Bogotá, Colombia: Ediciones Tercer Mundo, 1981.

                                        LANCE R. GRAHN

PEHUENCHES.

Historically, Pehuenches are inhabitants of the eastern and western slopes of the southern Andes in and around the headwaters of the Laja River flowing west to Chile and the Neuquen River flowing east to Argentina. The Pehuenche, literally "the people of the pines," made a living in part by harvesting and trading the large pine nuts from the *Araucania* forests. Since the 1600s the Pehuenche people have been linguistically and culturally part of the larger Mapuche (Araucanian) society, though some argue that the material record shows that at one time the Pehuenche may have been a culturally and linguistically separate entity.

The Pehuenche dominated this critical region of the southern cordillera region of the Andes and resisted and obstructed Spanish attempts to colonize there in the 1500s. A succession of sporadic warfare and battles over territory resulted in a series of formalized treaties that established a relative equilibrium and opportunities for trading and small-scale commerce until late in the nineteenth century. Between 1819 and 1932 the Pehuenche aligned with the bandit Pincheira brothers against encroachments of the emerging Argentine and Chilean states, influencing the course of state-building models, particularly in Chile. A series of military campaigns in Argentina and Chile in the 1880s forcefully imposed the separation of the Pehuenche people. The newly consolidated national armies established national boundaries along a north-south axis, effectively breaking the intercordilleran communication, resistance, and autonomy of the Pehuenche. After the turn of the century the divided Pehuenche eked out a precarious living on separate reservations in Argentina and Chile, following traditional lifestyles. Under the Pinochet regime in the 1980s, collectively held lands in Chile were privatized, which resulted in further disenfranchisement of Pehuenche. In the early twenty-first century this Pehuenche stronghold continues as a center for political resistance against the Chilean state.

See also **Malones.**

BIBLIOGRAPHY

Bengoa, Jose. *Quinquén: Cien años de historia pehuenche*. Santiago: CESOC, 1992.

Casamiquela, Rodolfo. "Notas sobre sitios y piedras rituals del ambito pehuenche austral." In *Congreso de Arqueología Chilena VI, Boletín de Prehistoria* (1972–1973).

Herr, Pilar M. "Indians, Bandits, and the State: Chile's Path toward National Identity, 1819–1833." Ph.D. diss., Indiana University, 2001.

Molina, Raúl, and Martín Correa. *Territorio y comunidades Pehuenches del Alto Bío-Bío*. Santiago: Corporación Nacional de Desarrollo Indígena, 1996.

Morales U., Roberto, et. al. *Ralco: Modernidad o etnocidio en territorio pewenche*. Temuco, Chile: Instituto de Estudios Indígenas, Universidad de la Frontera, 1998.

Villalobos R., Sergio. *Los Pehuenches en la vida fronteriza*. Santiago: Ediciones Universidad Católica de Chile, 1989.

                                        KRISTINE L. JONES

PEIMBERT, MARGARITA

(1795–?). Margarita Peimbert (*b.* 1795; *d.* before 1900), a member of the autonomist secret society Los Guadalupes. Peimbert was the daughter of the lawyer Juan Nazario Peimbert y Hernández, who was also a member of the Guadalupes and who held *tertulias* (gatherings) in his home in Mexico City at which politics was discussed. Margarita was in charge of distributing the group's correspondence. She was betrothed to the lawyer José Ignacio Jiménez, who joined Ignacio Rayón's forces at the beginning of 1812. In May of that year, the royalists captured the correspondence that Rayón had sent to the capital, including letters to Peimbert from various insurgents. She was detained and interrogated in June, but revealed nothing. The same month, the royalists defeated Rayón at Tenango, and Jiménez was killed. Later, Peimbert married José Ignacio Espinosa, another lawyer and member of the Guadalupes.

See also **Guadalupes, Los; Mexico: 1810–1910.**

BIBLIOGRAPHY

Wilbert H. Timmons, "Los Guadalupes," in *Hispanic American Historical Review* 30 (Nov. 1950): 453–479.

Ernesto De La Torre Villar, *Los Guadalupes y la Independencia, con una selección de documentos inéditos* (1985).

Virginia Guedea, *En busca de un gobierno alterno: Los Guadalupes de México* (1992).

VIRGINIA GUEDEA

PEIXE, CÉSAR GUERRA (1914–1993).

César Guerra Peixe (often listed as C. Guerra-Peixe; *b.* 18 March 1914; *d.* 26 November 1993), Brazilian composer, violinist, conductor, and musicologist. Born in Petrópolis, Peixe began to study music theory and solfeggio at the age of nine. Two years later, he enrolled in the Escola de Música Santa Cecília in Petrópolis. After completing studies in theory and solfeggio in 1929, he began to do arranging for instrumental ensembles. He wrote his first piece, a tango, *Otilia*, in 1930 and that same year was appointed professor of violin at the Escola de Música Santa Cecília.

In 1934 Peixe moved to Rio de Janeiro, where ten years later he began the study of composition with Hans Joachim Koellreutter, a former student of Paul Hindemith. Koellreutter introduced him to serial techniques of writing and with Peixe and several other contemporary composers formed the Música Viva group in 1939 to explore serial techniques and promote concerts of recent works by group members and their European counterparts.

Gradually, Peixe became less interested in serial writing and more interested in exploring Brazilian folk traditions and native music. He took a job at a radio station in Recife, a city with rich folk music traditions in the northeastern part of Brazil, where he wrote a series of twenty articles, "A Century of Music in Recife," and a book, *Maracatus do Recife*, a study of a traditional folk festival. Respected for his extensive knowledge of Brazilian folk and traditional music, Peixe has won several awards in Brazil. His Symphony no. 1, a serial composition of 1946, was performed in London by the British Broadcasting Corporation as well as in Brussels, and his Divertimento no. 2 was performed in Zurich in 1947. A set of piano pieces, *Preludios Tropicais*, won the Golfinho de Ouro trophy in 1980.

See also **Music: Art Music; Music: Popular Music and Dance.**

BIBLIOGRAPHY

Gérard Béhague, *Music in Latin America* (1979).

David P. Appleby, *The Music of Brazil* (1983).

Additional Bibliography

Faria, Antonio Guerreiro de. "Guerra-Peixe e a estilização do folclore." *Latin American Music Review* 21:2 (Fall–Winter 2000): 169–189.

Nepomuceno, Rosa. *César Guerra-Peixe: A música sem fronteiras.* Rio de Janeiro: Ministério da Cultura, FUNARTE: Fundação Teatro Municipal do Rio de Janeiro, 2001.

DAVID P. APPLEBY

PEIXOTO, FLORIANO VIEIRA (1839–1895).

Floriano Vieira Peixoto (*b.* 30 April 1839; *d.* 29 June 1895), Brazil's "Iron Marshal" and second head of the Brazilian republic (1891–1894). Born in Alagoas, in Brazil's poor Northeast, Peixoto achieved a distinguished army career, serving in the War of the Triple Alliance (1864–1870), and rising to the rank of brigadier general in 1883.

Peixoto's role in the crucial days prior to the military overthrow of the monarchy and the establishment of the republic on 15 November 1889 has long been a subject of debate. Both sides in the impending clash, republicans and monarchists alike, felt that they could trust this popular army officer who occupied the key post of adjutant general. But the monarchists had misjudged Peixoto. On 15 November he refused to obey repeated orders to fire on the advancing rebels, thus sealing the fate of the monarchy. He then began to serve as a member of the military-dominated provisional republican government established on that same day. In February 1891 the Constituent Congress elected Marshal Deodoro da Fonseca, the so-called Proclaimer of the Republic, president, and Peixoto vice president.

Peixoto, noted for his personal honesty, unpretentiousness, and astuteness, kept out of the squabbles and struggles between President Fonseca and a basically civilian and hostile congress that often protested what it regarded as Fonseca's infringements on civil liberties. But Peixoto played a crucial role in the military movement that overthrew Fonseca following his unconstitutional dissolution of Congress in November 1891, and thereby ensured his own succession to the presidency.

More than any other chief executive of the Old Republic (1889–1930), Peixoto has been held up as a friend of the "people." But his major supporters, middle-class nationalists and army officers, derived far greater benefits from his regime than did the lower classes. His government did much more to aid industry than did his immediate successors. Regarded as a forceful, capable leader by his admirers, he was denounced as a dictator by his opponents. Cleverly using rising anti-Portuguese sentiments to strengthen his own position, Peixoto succeeded in maintaining himself in office despite very difficult times for the infant republic. Not only was a civil war, the Federalist Revolt, raging in Rio Grande do Sul, Brazil's southernmost state, but a naval revolt under the leadership of Admiral Custódio de Melo against Peixoto's army-dominated government broke out in Rio de Janeiro's harbor late in 1893, and took six months to quell. Peixoto's success in restoring order earned him the title "Consolidator of the Republic." Less than a year after he completed his term of office and turned over the presidential palace to his elected civilian successor, Prudente de Morais of São Paulo, Peixoto died, and his funeral drew large crowds.

See also **Brazil: Since 1889.**

BIBLIOGRAPHY

June E. Hahner, *Civilian–Military Relations in Brazil, 1889–1898* (1969); and "Floriano Peixoto, Brazil's 'Iron Marshall': A Re-Evaluation," in *The Americas* 21, no. 3 (1975): 252–271.

Additional Bibliography

Penna, Lincoln de Abreu. *O progresso da ordem: O Florianismo e a construção da República*. Rio de Janeiro: Sette Letras, 1997.

JUNE E. HAHNER

PEIXOTO, JÚLIO AFRÂNIO (1876–1947).

Júlio Afrânio Peixoto (*b.* 17 December 1876; *d.* 12 January 1947), Brazilian author and physician. A polymath whose more than fifty books range from medical texts to regionalist novels to literary studies to history and folklore, he epitomized the spirit of his premodernist generation with the phrase "Literature is the smile of society." His novel *A esfinge* (1911; The Sphinx), written to justify his election to the Brazilian Academy of Letters in 1910, documents life in Rio's high society. Like his other novels, such as *Maria Bonita* (1914), it explores female psychology and the contrasts between city and country life.

Trained in forensic medicine, Peixoto centered his career on health education and public administration. He was director of the national asylum (from 1904), professor of hygiene and legal medicine at the Rio de Janeiro medical school (from 1906) and at the law school (from 1915), director of public education in Rio de Janeiro (from 1916), and professor of the history of education at the Instituto do Rio de Janeiro (from 1932). He represented Bahia as a federal deputy from 1924 to 1930.

See also **Literature: Brazil.**

BIBLIOGRAPHY

Peixoto, *Obras literárias completas* (1944), has twenty-five volumes. Leonídio Ribeiro, ed., *Afrânio Peixoto* (1950), includes a biography, critical studies, and a bibliography. Brito Broca, *A vida literária no Brasil: 1900* (1956), provides a study of Peixoto's milieu.

DAIN BORGES

PELÁEZ, AMELIA (1896–1968).

Amelia Peláez (*b.* 5 January 1896; *d.* 8 April 1968), Cuban painter. The niece of the Cuban symbolist poet Julián del Casal, Amelia Peláez is one of the most respected Cuban artists of the twentieth century. She graduated from the National School of San Alejandro, where she trained in academic impressionism, but she continued to modify her style throughout her life. Peláez studied in Paris under the Russian cubist Alexandra Exter and later experimented with modernist painting, ceramics, and stained glass. Her art evokes the Cuban creole spirit with its values of home, family, and a serene, glorious past. Devoted to her life-style and neighborhood, Peláez remained in Cuba after the revolution. Among her most famous works are *Gundinga* (1931); an illustration for her uncle's poem "The Agony of Petronius" (1935); *Las dos hermanas* (1943); and *Las muchachas* (1943).

See also **Art: The Twentieth Century; Casal, Julián del.**

BIBLIOGRAPHY

Government Of Cuba, *Pintores Cubanos* (1963) and *Pintores Cubanos* (1974).

Giulio V. Blanc, *Amelia Peláez* (1988).

Additional Bibliography

Juan, Adelaida de. "Del silencio al grito: Amelia Peláez, Antonia Eiriz." *Casa de las Américas* 207 (April–June 1997): 133–137.

Martínez, Juan A. *Cuban Art and National Identity: The Vanguardia Painters, 1927–1950.* Gainesville: University Press of Florida, 1994.

KAREN RACINE

PELÉ (1940–).

Pelé (Edson Arantes do Nascimento; *b.* 23 October 1940), Brazilian soccer player. Born in Dico (now Três Corações), Minas Gerais, Pelé grew up mainly in Bauru, São Paulo, where, inspired by the soccer skills of his father, João Ramos do Nascimento (Dondinho), he excelled at versions of street soccer, *peladas,* thus acquiring his future nickname. He played his first professional game with the Santos Football Club on 7 September 1956. The following year he became a member of the Brazilian national team, and in 1958 scored six goals in helping Brazil win its first World Cup. Although Brazil retained its title in 1962, Pelé was hurt and contributed little. In 1966 injuries kept Brazil from reaching the second round, but in his last World Cup (Mexico, 1970) Pelé led a creative team to permanent possession of the Jules Rimet Trophy. Scoring some 1,300 career goals, Pelé also played on clubs that won state and national championships, the Copa Libertadores de América, and the world interclub competition. His style was often more impressive than his numbers.

In 1974 Pelé retired from the Santos club, then surprised the world by joining the New York Cosmos (1975–1977) of the fledgling North American Soccer League. Despite the league's eventual demise, Pelé gained popularity in the United States and inspired a younger generation to try his sport. After leaving competition, Pelé worked in films, music, public relations, journalism, and volunteer coaching. He also coauthored a mystery novel and several pieces about his life and soccer. Through an emotional divorce, temporary economic setbacks, and criticism for failing to denounce Brazil's military regimes, Pelé retained his outward optimism and charm. A unique talent who epitomized the culture and aspirations of his countrymen, "the king" remains for most the world's best soccer player ever and a national hero. Since his retirement he has been an ambassador for football and has also undertaken acting and commercial ventures.

See also **Sports.**

BIBLIOGRAPHY

François Thébaud, *Pelé,* translated by Leo Weinstein (1976).

Joe Marcus, *The World of Pelé* (1976).

Pelé and Robert L. Fish, *Pelé: My Life and the Beautiful Game* (1978).

Joel Millman, "Pelé," in *Sport* 77 (December 1986): 120–123.

Additional Bibliography

Jenkins, Garry, Pedro Redig, and Antonio Pires Soares. *The Beautiful Team.* London: Pocket Books, 1999.

JOSEPH L. ARBENA

PELLACANI, DANTE (1923–1981).

Dante Pellacani (*b.* 6 March 1923; *d.* 6 August 1981), Brazilian trade unionist and president of the

Commando Geral dos Trabalhadores (CGT). Born and educated in São Paulo, Pellacani went to work in a printing plant at age fourteen. Swept up in the political opening of 1944–1946 while in the army, Pellacani led São Paulo's printers in 1948 to demand the end of government intervention in their union. That same year he joined the Brazil Communist Party (PCB) from which he was expelled ten years later. A key figure in the state labor movement, he was elected president of the National Federation of Printing Workers. Allied with the PCB and the Brazilian Labor Party (PTB), Pellacani created a ticket-splitting "Jan-Jan movement" (Jânio Quadros and Jango Goulart) in the 1960 presidential elections. In 1961, he was named to the National Social Welfare Department and served as director general from 1962–1963. Elected president of the CGT in 1963, he simultaneously held office in the National Confederation of Workers in Industry (CNTI). A strong supporter of President Goulart's "basic reforms," he played a key role in the general strikes and popular mobilizations of March 1964. After the 31 March military coup outlawed the CGT, and "intervened" (restricted) the CNTI, Pellacani went into exile in Uruguay. Returning in 1969, he rededicated himself to union and political activities.

See also **Brazil, Organizations: General Labor Command (CGT); Communism; Labor Movements.**

BIBLIOGRAPHY

Israel Beloch and Alzira Alves De Abreu, *Dicionário histórico-biográfico brasileiro 1930–1983,* vol. 3 (1984); for an interesting interview with Pellacani, see Lourenço Dantas Mota, ed., *A historia vivida,* vol. 2 (1981), pp. 283–306.

Additional Bibliography

Alexander, Robert Jackson, and Eldon M. Parker. *A History of Organized Labor in Brazil.* Westport, CT: Praeger, 2003.

French, John D., and Alexandre Fortes. *Urban Labor History in Twentieth Century Brazil.* Albuquerque: Latin American Institute, University of New Mexico, 1998.

Negro, Antonio Luigi. *Linhas de montagem: O industrialismo nacional-desenvolvimentista e a sindicalização dos trabalhadores, 1945–1978.* São Paulo: FAPESP: Boitempo Editorial, 2004.

JOHN D. FRENCH

PELLEGRINI, CARLOS (1846–1906).

Carlos Pellegrini (*b.* 11 October 1846; *d.* 17 July 1906), president of Argentina (1890–1892).

Pellegrini was born in Buenos Aires province to an English mother and an Italian father, a background which exemplifies the cosmopolitan nature of Argentina. He had little interest in religion and was convinced that economic, financial, and political interests were interchangeable. A successful businessman, a veteran of the war with Paraguay, and a skilled orator, Pellegrini fit easily into the upper class. A fervent supporter of European immigration, he made the first of several trips to Europe in 1876. After his election to Congress, he forged an alliance with Julio Argentino Roca. As war minister during Roca's first presidency, Pellegrini played a vital role in establishing Buenos Aires as the national capital. His skill in negotiating foreign loans enabled him to become head of the Partido Autonomista Nacional and vice president (1886). It was no secret that Pellegrini was contemptuous of Miguel Juárez Celman's abilities and policies.

Pellegrini became president in October 1890, after Juárez Celman fled the 1890 revolt. Pellegrini's leadership enabled the elites to keep their opponents out of power while his followers reformed the country. He was Argentina's leading financial representative and a nationalist. He moved to restore fiscal sanity and economic growth. Determined to restore Argentine credit, he began to reduce the foreign debt. The government revived the currency by establishing reserves. When Pellegrini discovered that many banks were fraudulent, he founded a new national bank in 1891. He reduced imports of luxury goods and established the first favorable trade balance in many years. Long a champion of national industries, Pellegrini continued to support the development of sugar, wine, rice, and tobacco. Citizens respected him because he cut waste, frustrated corruption, and prohibited the use of gold in the stock market.

In many ways, Pellegrini challenged the dependency theory that Latin American elites were subservient to U.S. or British influence. He criticized British investments, taxed foreign capital, and clashed repeatedly with the British over the taxation of their businesses and the freezing of the rates that their railroads and tramways could charge in Argentina.

Pellegrini wielded great influence once he left the presidency. He opposed jingoistic calls for war with Chile and opposed an arms race with Brazil. He broke with Roca and urged a better system of labor relations, and until shortly before his death,

Pellegrini continued to attack corruption and campaign for electoral reform. His writings are collected in his five-volume *Obras* (1941), with a two-volume introduction by the editor, Agustín P. Rivero.

See also **Argentina: The Nineteenth Century; Banking: Overview; Buenos Aires.**

BIBLIOGRAPHY

The most recent biography of Pellegrini is Douglas W. Richmond, *Carlos Pellegrini and the Crisis of the Argentine Elites, 1880–1916* (1989). Donna J. Guy, *Argentine Sugar Politics: Tucumán and the Generation of Eighty* (1980), describes Pellegrini's protectionism, as does her "Carlos Pellegrini and the Politics of Early Argentine Industrialization, 1873–1906," in *Journal of Latin American Studies* 11 (May 1979):123–144. John Edward Hodge, has written "Carlos Pellegrini, Argentine Statesman" (Ph.D. diss., University of Illinois, 1963) and two excellent articles: "Carlos Pellegrini and the Financial Crisis of 1890," in *Hispanic American Historical Review* 50 (August 1970): 499–523, and "Julio Roca and Carlos Pellegrini: An Expedient Partnership," in *The Americas* 36 (January 1976): 327–347. For Pellegrini's differences with British diplomats and investors, see Henry Stanley Ferns, *Britain and Argentina in the Nineteenth Century* (1960).

Additional Bibliography

Herz, Enrique Germán. *Pellegrini, ayer y hoy.* Buenos Aires: Editorial Centro de Estudios Unión para la Nueva Mayoría, 1996.

Sanz, Luis Santiago. *La Política exterior durante la presidencia de Pellegrini.* Buenos Aires: Jockey Club, 1996.

DOUGLAS W. RICHMOND

PELLICER CÁMARA, CARLOS (1897–1977). Carlos Pellicer Cámara (*b.* 16 January 1897; *d.* 16 February 1977), Mexican poet. Born in Villahermosa, Tabasco, Pellicer moved with his family to Mexico City in 1908. However, his native state, particularly its tropical scenery and its pre-Hispanic past, was to be a lifetime presence. In 1921 he published his first book of poetry, *Colores en el mar.* Pellicer was a prolific writer, and many more volumes followed. *Hora de junio* (1937), *Subordinaciones* (1949), and *Práctica de vuelo* (1956) are counted among his best. Although he is often grouped with the "Contemporáneos," Pellicer's explicit religiosity, his humor, and his interest in the external world, in nature, and in the epic dimension set him apart. Noteworthy is the incorporation of music and painting into his work, achieved by thematic choices and by transpositions of the techniques and processes of these other arts into poetry.

Besides also writing prose, often on literature and art, Pellicer exercised his acute sense of the visual as a museographer. Particularly significant is the outdoor archaeological-ecological museum of La Venta in Villahermosa, where Olmec sculpture alternates with tropical animals and plants. An admirer of Simón Bolívar and Francis of Assisi, Pellicer was also an active participant in political and humanitarian causes. In 1922 he began his association with José Vasconcelos, which nearly cost him his life in 1930, after the philosopher's unsuccessful bid for the presidency of Mexico. In 1937 Pellicer was one of a group of intellectuals who traveled to Europe to express sympathy for the Spanish Republic, and he visited Cuba on numerous occasions. Between 1943 and 1946 he was the director of what is now the Instituto Nacional de Bellas Artes, and at the time of his death he was senator for the state of Tabasco.

See also **Contemporáneos, Los.**

BIBLIOGRAPHY

Carlos Pellicer, *Obras: Poesía* (1981).

Additional Bibliography

España, Javier. *Los frutos de la voz: Ensayos sobre la obra de Carlos Pellice.* Chimalistac: Consejo Nacional para la Cultura y las Artes, 1997.

Gordon, Samuel, and Fernando Rodríguez. *Tópicos y trópicos pellicerianos: Estudios sobre la vida y obra de Carlos Pellicer.* Villahermosa: Horayveinte, 2005.

CLARA BARGELLINI

PELUCONES. Pelucones (literally "big wigs"), a term first regularly attached to Chilean Conservatives in the 1820s, though it was apparently used earlier, by José Miguel Carrera (1785–1821) and his brothers, to describe the moderate politicians who opposed them in 1811. The expression referred to the Conservatives' use of the large powdered wigs fashionable in later colonial times: These were no longer in use among their Liberal adversaries. Although often applied indiscriminately to nineteenth-century Chilean Conservatives (even at the time), it has the more precise connotation of "traditional" conservative, that is, a proclerical conservative of an old family. Alberto Edwards (1873–1932), writer and politician, sometimes described himself as "the last *pelucón*."

See also **Chile, Political Parties: Conservative Party.**

BIBLIOGRAPHY

Additional Bibliography

Collier, Simon, and William F. Sater. *A History of Chile, 1808–2002.* Cambridge, UK: Cambridge University Press, 2004.

Stuven, Ana María. *La seducción de un orden: Las elites y la construcción de Chile en las polémicas culturales y políticas del siglo XIX.* Santiago, Chile: Ediciones Universidad Católica de Chile, 2000.

                                          SIMON COLLIER

PENA, AFONSO AUGUSTO MOREIRA (1847–1909).

Afonso Augusto Moreira Pena (*b.* 30 November 1847; *d.* 14 June 1909), president of Brazil (1906–1909). Born in Santa Bárbara, Minas Gerais, Pena attended the Lazarist Colégio do Caraça and received a doctorate in law at the University of São Paulo, where he was a colleague of Rodrigues Alves, Rui Barbosa, and Castro Alves. He married Maria Guilhermina de Oliveira, with whom he had one son, Afonso Augusto Moreira Pena Junior.

Pena's political career straddled both the imperial and republican years of Brazil's history. He served as a provincial deputy (1874–1878) and became a national deputy in 1879, serving for four successive legislatures. A novelty at the time, he held the post of minister of war as a civilian (1882–1883). Later, he served as both minister of agriculture in 1883 and minister of justice in 1885. In addition, he served as a member of the Civil Code Commission in 1888 and as a member of the Constitutional Convention from 1890 to 1891. Pena returned to Minas Gerais, where he served as governor from 1892 to 1895. During his administration, he moved the state capital from Ouro Prêto to Belo Horizonte and founded a school of law in the new capital city, where he also taught.

From 1894 to 1898, Pena was the president of the Bank of the Republic. He was elected vice president of Brazil in 1903, and in 1906 he was elected president, an office he held until his death. Among his more noteworthy contributions to the nation were reforms that made possible the exchange of different monetary units, expansion of the national railroad system, and establishment of telegraphic connections between Rio de Janeiro and Acre.

See also **Brazil: 1808–1889; Brazil: Since 1889.**

BIBLIOGRAPHY

Additional Bibliography

Ferreira, Marieta de Moraes. *Em busca da idade de ouro: As elites políticas fluminenses na Primeira República, 1889–1930.* Rio de Janeiro: Editora UFRJ: Edições Tempo Brasileiro, 1994.

Topik, Steven. *The Political Economy of the Brazilian State, 1889-1930.* Austin: University of Texas Press, 1987.

                                    IÊDA SIQUEIRA WIARDA

PEÑA, LÁZARO (1911–1974).

Lázaro Peña (*b.* 29 May 1911; *d.* 11 March 1974), Cuban Communist Party leader and secretary-general of the Cuban Labor Federation. Peña, a black tobacco worker who was born of extremely poor parents but grew up to become a prominent labor leader, became a member of the Communist Party in 1930. Because of his activism, participation in strikes, and denunciation of the Gerardo Machado dictatorship (1925–1933), he was forced to serve a number of jail sentences. When army chief Fulgencio Batista sought for political reasons to woo organized labor as well as gain the support of the Communist Party, Peña was unanimously elected as the first secretary-general of the Confederación de Trabajadores de Cuba (CTC), a new labor confederation established in January 1939. He remained in control of the CTC for some eight years until he was ousted by the anti-Communist government of Ramón Grau San Martín (1944–1948). Peña fled first to Mexico, then to the Soviet Union, returning to Cuba when Fidel Castro Ruz took over in 1959. Although he once again became the leader of the Cuban labor movement, he was merely an instrument chosen by the revolutionary government to implement its policies.

See also **Cuba, Political Parties: Communist Party; Machado y Morales, Gerardo.**

BIBLIOGRAPHY

Lucinda Miranda Fernández, ed., *Lázaro Peña, capitán de la clase obrera cubana* (1984).

Additional Bibliography

Alexander, Robert Jackson. *A History of Organized Labor in Cuba*. Westport, CT: Praeger, 2002.

Córdova, Efrén. *Clase trabajadora y movimiento sindical en Cuba*. Miami: Ediciones Universal, 1995.

JOSÉ M. HERNÁNDEZ

PENA, LUÍS CARLOS MARTINS

(1815–1848). Luís Carlos Martins Pena (*b.* 5 November 1815; *d.* 7 December 1848), considered the founder of Brazilian comedy and cofounder, with Gonçalves de Magalhães, of Brazilian theater. Pena began writing plays as a student in his native Rio de Janeiro between 1832 and 1834. The first to be staged, the comedy *O juiz de paz na roça* (1842; *A Rural Justice of the Peace,* 1948), opened successfully on 4 October 1838. That year Pena received the first of many civil service appointments.

Pena mastered the romantic comedy of manners, initially in rural settings with abundant local color, later in urban settings with an almost helter-skelter movement on stage as his works became more outrightly farcical. His characters are often caricatures but they ring true, especially linguistically. Usually pillorying the lower-middle class, he portrayed penetratingly Brazilian society at the time of King João VI's residency in Brazil (1807–1821).

Enormously popular during his lifetime, Pena wrote prolifically. His known plays include twenty-two comedies—ten new ones in 1845 alone—and six dramas. The former are still played to enthusiastic audiences. The dramas, five of them set outside Brazil, lack authenticity and appeal. He died in Lisbon.

See also **Theater.**

BIBLIOGRAPHY

Pena's works are available in *A Rural Justice of the Peace: Brazilian Comedy in One Act and Four Scenes,* translated by Willis Knapp Jones, in *Poet Lore* 54, no. 2 (Summer 1948): 99–119; and *Teatro de Martins Pena,* edited by Darcy Damasceno and Maria Filgueiras, 2 vols. (1956).

See also Leon F. Lyday, "Satire in the Comedies of Martins Pena," in *Luso-Brazilian Review* 5, no. 2 (December 1968): 63–70.

Claude L. Hulet, *Brazilian Literature,* vol. 1 (1974), pp. 254–261.

Colin M. Pierson, "Martins Pena: A View of Character Types," in *Latin American Theater Review* 11, no. 2 (1978): 41–48.

Nola Kortner Aiex, "Martins Pena: Parodist," in *Luso-Brazilian Review* 18, no. 1 (1981): 155–160.

Additional Bibliography

Heliodora, Barbara. *Martins Pena, uma introdução.* Rio de Janeiro: Academia Brasileira de Letras, 2000.

NORWOOD ANDREWS JR.

PEÑA, MANUEL PEDRO DE (1811–

1867). Manuel Pedro de Peña (*b.* 1811; *d.* 1867), Paraguayan publicist and revolutionary pamphleteer. Although born in Asunción in the first year of his country's independence, Peña chose to live for many years in Buenos Aires, where he moved in expatriate circles that were made up of men and women opposed to the regimes of Carlos Antonio López (1841–1862) and of his son, Francisco Solano López (1862–1879). Peña, who had once worked as a minor official in the government of the elder López in the late 1850s, began acting as spokesman for various Paraguayan revolutionary groups residing in the Argentine capital. He made eloquent, though bitter, attacks on the López family in the Buenos Aires press, especially in the daily *La Tribuna* and in *Nación Argentina.* These attacks appeared all the more poignant because Peña claimed an unproven family relationship with the Lópezes.

Peña's editorial efforts had the greatest impact after the beginning of the War of the Triple Alliance (1864–1870), when he wrote a regular column, "Cartas del ciudadano paraguayo dirijidos a su querido sobrino," that appeared in several newspapers. The men of the Paraguayan Legion who fought in the war under Argentine command, were said to have carried his pamphlets into battle. Peña died in Buenos Aires.

See also López, Carlos Antonio; War of the Triple Alliance.

BIBLIOGRAPHY

Héctor Francisco Decoud, *Los emigrados paraguayos durante la guerra de la Triple alianza* (1930).

Charles J. Kolinski, *Independence or Death! The Story of the Paraguayan War* (1965).

Additional Bibliography

Kraay, Hendrik, and Thomas Whigham. *I Die with My Country: Perspectives on the Paraguayan War, 1864–1870.* Lincoln: University of Nebraska Press, 2004.

Leuchars, Chris. *To the Bitter End: Paraguay and the War of the Triple Alliance.* Westport, CT: Greenwood Press, 2002.

Ramírez Braschi, Dardo. *La Guerra de la Triple Alianza: A través de los periódicos correntinos, 1865–1870.* Corrientes: Moglia Ediciones, 2004.

THOMAS L. WHIGHAM

PEÑA GÓMEZ, JOSÉ FRANCISCO

(1937–1998). José Francisco Peña Gómez (*b.* 6 March 1937; *d.* 10 May 1998), leader of the Dominican Revolutionary Party (PRD) from 1965. The son of Haitian victims of the 1937 massacre, Peña Gómez trained as a lawyer. He was recruited by the PRD and received political training in Venezuela and Peru. His rise to prominence in the party was due to his oratorical skills and charismatic presence. After Juan Bosch's overthrow in 1963, Peña Gómez was responsible for the reorganization of the party and for establishing advantageous contacts in the Dominican military. In 1966 he was elected secretary general of the party, a position he maintained despite pursuing advanced law studies in Paris from 1970 to 1973. His increasing popularity led to conflict with the aging Bosch and to Peña Gómez's resignation as secretary general in August 1973. Bosch, however, overestimated his own popularity and soon found himself resigning from the PRD in light of overwhelming support for Peña Gómez. Peña Gómez regained the position of secretary general and became the driving force behind the party.

Representing the democratic left, Peña Gómez led the PRD to membership in the Socialist International in 1976, and he became a vocal spokesman within the International. His popular base of support among the urban poor made him the bête noir of the Dominican armed forces. Because of his Afro-Haitian parentage, Peña Gómez has often been accused by the traditionally dominant white minority of being anti-Dominican. As illustrated in the 1994 federal elections, the issue of race has played a pivotal role in Dominican politics. Despite the populist and leftist tendencies of his party, Peña Gómez provided a moderating influence on its membership and encouraged a collegial style of leadership, allowing members to rise in the party. In 1978 he was elected mayor of Santo Domingo.

During the 1980s the PRD split in a bitter rivalry between Peña Gómez and Jacobo Majluta. Majluta served as vice president under the first PRD president, Antonio Guzmán (1978–1982). Peña Gómez withdrew from the PRD ticket in 1986 rather than run as Majluta's vice presidential candidate. The conflict between the two men resulted in Majluta splitting from the PRD to form the Independent Revolutionary Party (PRI). Peña Gómez, hoping to be the Dominican Republic's first black president, led the PRD into the 1990 and 1994 federal elections. His presidential aspirations were stymied by the continued domination of the presidency by the aging Joaquín Balaguer. In 1996 Peña won the first round of voting but did not win the majority. Ten days before the mayoral elections of Santo Domingo Peña died in his home from a pulmonary edema.

See also Dominican Republic, Dominican Revolutionary Party (PRD).

BIBLIOGRAPHY

Selden Rodman, *Quisqueya: A History of the Dominican Republic* (1964).

Howard J. Wiarda, *The Dominican Republic: Nation in Transition* (1969).

Ian Bell, *The Dominican Republic* (1981).

Howard J. Wiarda and M. J. Kryzanek, *The Dominican Republic: A Caribbean Crucible* (1982).

James Ferguson, *The Dominican Republic: Beyond the Lighthouse* (1992).

Additional Bibliography

Isa Conde, Narciso. *Comunismo vs. Socialdemocracia: Las ideas de Peña Gómez y el ensayo socialdemócrata dominicano.* Santo Domingo, D.N., República Dominicana, 1981.

Remigio, Diómedes. *Peña Gómez, y su pensamiento político.* Santo Domingo: Editora Victorama, 1994.

HEATHER K. THIESSEN

PEÑALOSA BRICEÑO, DIEGO DIONISIO DE (1621–1687).

Diego Dionisio De Peñalosa Briceño (*b.* 1621/22; *d.* 1687), governor of New Mexico from 1661 to 1664. Born in Lima, Peñalosa held several posts in Peru, Mexico, and Cuba before being appointed governor of New Mexico. Peñalosa was determined to use this office for personal gain, and his scheming strained relations between church and state. At the height of a jurisdictional dispute, Peñalosa arrested the Franciscan superior in Santa Fe. Charged with blasphemy and numerous other offenses by the Inquisition, he was banished from New Spain. Peñalosa traveled to England and France, where he proposed an invasion of New Spain. Although neither country adopted his plans, Peñalosa's intrigues encouraged the 1685 expedition of La Salle to the Gulf coast.

See also **New Mexico.**

BIBLIOGRAPHY

The best account of this era of New Mexican history and of the conflict between church and state is France V. Scholes, *Troublous Times in New Mexico 1659–1670* (1942). Peñalosa's fabricated trip to Quivira, a legend used to entice the English and French, is examined in C. W. Hackett, "New Light on Diego de Peñalosa," in *Mississippi Valley Historical Review* 6, no. 3 (1919–1920): 313–335.

Additional Bibliography

Cutter, Donald C. *España en Nuevo México.* Madrid: Editorial MAPFRE, 1992.

Villagrá, Gaspar Pérez de, and Felipe Echenique March. *Historia de la Nueva México.* México, D.F.: Instituto Nacional de Antropología e Historia, Centro Regional de Baja California, 1993.

SUZANNE B. PASZTOR

PEÑALOZA, ÁNGEL VICENTE (1799–1863).

Ángel Vicente Peñaloza (*b.* 1799; *d.* 12 November 1863), Argentine leader. Peñaloza was born in Guaja, La Rioja, Argentina, and received little education before he enrolled in the militia, where he developed a long-lasting relationship with Juan Facundo Quiroga. He served as a trusted officer during Quiroga's anti-Unitarist campaigns. Popular, especially among the poor, he succeeded Quiroga as a leader after the latter's assassination in 1835. Convinced by the Unitarists that Juan Manuel de Rosas was responsible for the death of Quiroga, Peñaloza turned against Rosas and fought the Federalists in the 1840s. He withdrew to his home once Governor Nazario Benavídez of San Juan promised to protect him. He did not participate in the Acuerdo de San Nicolás, but he was on good terms with Justo José de Urquiza. When Benavídez was assassinated (23 October 1858), Peñaloza invaded San Juan to punish the guilty. In 1862, while Peñaloza was away mediating a dispute between Santiago del Estero and Catamarca, Governor Marcos Paz of Córdoba, a Unitarist, invaded La Rioja, and the governor turned against his followers. The popularity with which Peñaloza was received on his return convinced President Bartolomé Mitre and General Wenceslao Paunero to sign a peace treaty with him on 30 May 1862. Angry Liberal leaders objected and persuaded Mitre to reopen the war.

Peñaloza, allied now with the Federalists, or *"rusos,"* of Córdoba, urged Urquiza to resume leadership of the Federalist party. Mitre wanted the montoneros destroyed, and when Paunero defeated them at Las Playas (28 June 1863), he killed them without mercy. Peñaloza thrice sought peace before surrendering to his pursuers, who killed him despite a promise to spare his life. His body was mutilated; Domingo Sarmiento humiliated and robbed his wife. Mitre officially disapproved of the assassination, but he promoted the assassin.

See also **Argentina, Movements: Federalists; Argentina, Movements: Unitarists; Quiroga, Juan Facundo.**

BIBLIOGRAPHY

Fermín Chávez, *Vida del Chacho: Ángel Vicente Peñaloza, General de la Confederación,* 3d ed. (1974).

Gerardo Pérez Fuentes and Pedro Ignacio Galarza, *Ángel Vicente Peñaloza* (*El Chacho*): *Bosquejo biográfico* (1963).

Leslie Bethell, ed., *Argentina Since Independence* (1933).

Comisión Central De Homenaje A Ángel Vicente Peñaloza, *Ángel Vicente Peñaloza* (1969).

Additional Bibliography

Aguirre, Gisela. *Angel Vicente Peñaloza.* Buenos Aires: Planeta, 1999.

De la Fuente, Ariel. *Children of Facundo: Caudillo and Gaucho Insurgency During the Argentine State-Formation Process (La Rioja, 1853–1870).* Durham, NC: Duke University Press, 2000.

JOSEPH T. CRISCENTI

PEÑARANDA DEL CASTILLO, EN-RIQUE (1892–1969).

Enrique Peñaranda del Castillo (*b.* 17 November 1892; *d.* 8 June 1969), president of Bolivia (April 1940–December 1943). Born in Larecaja, La Paz Province, Peñaranda spent most of his life in the military, where he rose in rank from cadet to full general. During the Chaco War he was supreme commander of the military forces. When the younger and more radical officers seized power in 1937, the next year he took a leave of absence from the military. With their fall from power following the death of President Germán Busch in 1939, Peñaranda emerged rapidly as the main Bolivian leader, first as minister of defense and eventually as elected president. He was overthrown three and a half years later by officers with pro-German sympathies who resented Peñaranda's military accomplishments, his conservatism, and his pro-Allies sympathy during World War II.

Peñaranda's strong pro-U.S. foreign policy brought Bolivia much U.S. attention and aid. During Peñaranda's presidency, democratic reforms were undertaken, the legislative branch was strengthened, and the administration was modernized. He spent his postpresidential years in modest circumstances and died in Cochabamba.

See also **Chaco War; World War II.**

BIBLIOGRAPHY

Quien es quien en Bolivia (1942).

Porfirio Díaz Machicao, *Peñaranda, 1940–1943* (1958).

David H. Zook, Jr., *The Conduct of the Chaco War* (1960).

Additional Bibliography

Farcau, Bruce W. *The Chaco War: Bolivia and Paraguay, 1932–1935.* Westport, CT: Praeger, 1996.

Irurozqui, Marta. *"A bala, piedra y palo": La construcción de la ciudadanía política en Bolivia, 1826–1952.* Seville: Diputación de Sevilla, 2000.

CHARLES W. ARNADE

PEÑA Y PEÑA, MANUEL DE LA (1789–1850).

Manuel de la Peña y Peña (*b.* 1789; *d.* 1850), interim president of Mexico (September 1847–June 1848). The apex of Peña y Peña's career coincided with Mexico's nadir when he, as chief justice of the Supreme Court, succeeded Antonio López de Santa Anna on 16 September 1847. Peña y Peña, a native of Tacuba, maintained a moderate course between radical and reactionary voices from September 1847 to June 1848, during which time the Treaty of Guadalupe Hidalgo was negotiated, signed, and ratified.

Peña y Peña unknowingly spent his life in preparation for this service. He studied civil and ecclesiastic law at the Seminario Conciliar in Mexico City, graduating in December 1811. Two years later he was named *síndico* (receiver) of the Mexico City Municipal Council. In February 1820 Peña y Peña declined an appointment as *oidor* on the *Audiencia* of Quito, in the Viceroyalty of Peru, out of a sense of duty to Mexico at the time of independence. His age, education, experience, and connections brought a succession of public offices, primarily in the Supreme Court. Appointments not in the court included minister of the interior (1837) and minister of foreign relations and government (1845). In 1841 he was concurrently president of the Academia de Jurisprudencia and rector of the Colegio de Abogados. His writings include the four-volume *Lecciones de práctica forense Mexicana* (1835–1839). Ironically, one of the questions treated in this work was the exaggerated pretensions of a foreign power. Peña y Peña died in Mexico City.

See also **Guadalupe Hidalgo, Treaty of (1848).**

BIBLIOGRAPHY

Justo Sierra, *Manuel de la Peña y Peña, 1798–1850: Academia, jurisprudencia y legislación* (1895).

José Rogelio Álvarez, *Enciclopedia de México,* vol. 11 (1988), p. 6293.

Additional Bibliography

DiTella, Torcuato S. *National Popular Politics in Early Independent Mexico, 1820–1847.* Albuquerque: University of New Mexico Press, 1996.

Fowler, Will. *Mexico in the Age of Proposals, 1821–1853.* Westport, CT: Greenwood Press, 1998.

ROBERT HIMMERICH Y VALENCIA

PENINSULAR. Peninsular, a resident of colonial Spanish America born in Spain. More than 400,000 Spaniards immigrated to the New World between 1500 and 1650. Their most important motivation was perceived economic opportunity, and they often followed in the footsteps of established patrons or relatives. Immigrants came from all walks of life, though royal officials and clergymen were heavily overrepresented. Competition for offices in the church and state—particularly the latter, where fewer positions were available— soured relations between the *peninsulares* and Creoles (American-born Spaniards) by the early seventeenth century. The creoles also resented the dominance of overseas trade that *peninsulares* maintained throughout the colonial period.

On the one hand, the development of genuine cultural differences between creoles and *peninsulares,* the emergence of an incipient creole nationalism, and the creation of negative stereotypes on both sides—the indolent creole with suspect racial ancestry opposed to the low-born, avaricious *peninsular*—all contributed to this division. On the other hand, *peninsular* merchants often married creole women and became assimilated into wealthy creole families. However, they typically endowed their children with landed estates while bringing in a relative (usually a nephew) to carry on their business enterprises, thus reinforcing the contrasting economic bases of creole and *peninsular* elites.

In the eighteenth century, several developments provoked a more intense bitterness toward *peninsulares.* Spanish immigration to the colonies increased, and took on a more integrated, familial character; *peninsular* disdain for Americans of all races gained a spurious "scientific" basis; and, most important, royal officials launched a concerted attack on the power of the creole aristocracy. Not surprisingly, *peninsulares* became targets for attack in the uprisings of the late colonial and independence periods. Perhaps the most notorious examples are the depredations of Miguel Hidalgo's army in Mexico and Simón Bolívar's "war to the death" against Spaniards

in Venezuela. The Peruvian novelist Teresa González de Fanning depicted the plight of the *peninsular* in her historical novel, *Roque Moreno.*

See also **Caste and Class Structure in Colonial Spanish America; Creole.**

BIBLIOGRAPHY

D. A. Brading, *Miners and Merchants in Bourbon Mexico, 1763–1810* (1971).

Peter Boyd-Bowman, *Patterns of Spanish Emigration to the New World (1493–1590)* (1973).

James Lockhart and Enrique Otte, trans. and eds., *Letters and People of the Spanish Indies: The Sixteenth Century* (1976).

Ida Altman, *Emigrants and Society: Extremadura and America in the Sixteenth Century* (1989).

Additional Bibliography

González de Fanning, Teresa. *Roque Moreno.* Lima: Tip. de "El Lucero", Unión, 767 [Antes Baquíano, 324], 1904.

Lavallé, Bernard. *Las promesas ambiguas: Ensayos sobre el criollismo colonial en los Andes.* Lima: Pontificia Universidad Católica del Perú, Instituto Riva-Agüero, 1993.

Schmidt-Nowara, Christopher, and John M. Nieto-Phillips. *Interpreting Spanish Colonialism: Empires, Nations, and Legends.* Albuquerque: University of New Mexico Press, 2005.

R. DOUGLAS COPE

PENITENTES. Penitentes (Hermanos Penitentes, Cofradía de Nuestro Padre Jesús Nazareno) are a brotherhood of laymen that appeared in New Mexico during the late colonial period (c. 1790s), dedicated to community service and spiritual devotion to Jesus Christ through acts of penance. Penitente rites include corporal mortification and the reenactment of the passion of Christ during Holy Week. During the late nineteenth century, Protestant missionaries launched an exposé of the New Mexican Penitentes because of their self-flagellation with yucca whips (*disciplinas*) during the Procession of the Cross and their enactment of the Crucifixion by tying a volunteer brother to the cross in emulation of Christ.

The origins of the Penitente brotherhood are a source of continued discussion among scholars. The first historical reference to the brotherhood was made in 1833 by a visiting bishop, who condemned their rites of penance as a distortion of Catholic norms. By this time the Penitente brotherhood was well established and therefore most scholars place their emergence between 1790 and 1820. After three decades of constant warfare with Comanche and Apache raiders and near-isolation from the rest of New Spain, in the 1790s there was a renewal of long-distance trade with the south, the building and refurbishment of churches and chapels, and the geographic expansion of *vecino* (Spanish citizen) communities into areas that had recently been too dangerous to occupy. However, such expansion was not met by an equal expansion of Catholic priests. It is likely that the Penitente brotherhood arose in order to fill this void in clergy representation, and the penitential nature of the brotherhood was probably a response to various influences from within both New Mexico and the wider colony of New Spain.

Early Anglo-American observers attributed the origin of the movement to sixteenth-century Spain and the early Franciscan missionaries to New Mexico. Pointing out the scourging that Juan de Oñate self-administered during Holy Week 1598, they concluded that the Franciscans established the Penitentes in New Mexico as their Third Order of Saint Francis and that it had "degenerated" into the Penitentes and the practices they had witnessed. Recent scholarship accepts a Franciscan influence on the penitential behavior and organizational structure of the Penitentes but places their emergence within a wider context of confraternity (*cofradía*) organization in New Spain. It is likely that New Mexicans adapted the Penitentes during the 1790s from a confraternity already existing elsewhere in northern New Spain. Confraternities of penance came to the colony from Spain during the early colonial period, and penitential societies had long existed in New Spain and the southern Spanish colonies. There is little evidence of a tradition of penitential *cofradías* in New Mexico before the emergence of the Penitentes, so it is likely that such an organization was imported from New Spain and took root there because of the Catholic Church's weak organizational presence. In this context, the Penitente brotherhood brought intense religious devotion into villages that had little regular contact with secular parish clergy.

The Penitentes flourished until 1888, when Archbishop Jean Baptiste Salpointe of Santa Fe

excommunicated them, after warnings from Bishop Zubiría of Durango in 1833 and from Salpointe in 1886. The decline of active Penitente *moradas* (buildings that housed Penitente meetings) was more the result of migration from the northern New Mexican villages, beginning during World War I, than of the efforts of the Roman Catholic Church to stamp out the brotherhood. The 1970s marked the movement of a younger generation of New Mexicans back to "traditional" forms of *vecino* religious devotion, including the renewal of Penitente organizations in northern New Mexican villages, with the active encouragement of the Catholic Church.

See also **Brotherhoods; Catholic Church: The Colonial Period; Cofradía; Franciscans; Zubiría, José Antonio Laureano de.**

BIBLIOGRAPHY

Carroll, Michael P. *The Penitente Brotherhood: Patriarchy and Hispano-Catholicism in New Mexico.* Baltimore: Johns Hopkins University Press, 2002.

Chávez, Fray Angélico. "The Penitentes of New Mexico." *New Mexico Historical Review* 29, no. 2 (1954): 97–123.

Darley, Rev. Alexander M. *Passionists of the Southwest.* Albuquerque, NM: Rio Grande Press: 1968.

López Pulido, Alberto. *The Sacred World of the Penitentes.* Washington, DC: Smithsonian Institution Press, 2000.

Steele, Thomas J., S.J., and Rowena A. Rivera. *Penitente Self-Government: Brotherhoods and Councils, 1797–1947.* Santa Fe, NM: Ancient City Press, 1985.

Weigle, Marta. *Brothers of Light, Brothers of Blood: The Penitentes of the Southwest.* Albuquerque: University of New Mexico Press, 1976.

ROSS H. FRANK
LEAH G. ALLEN

PENSACOLA. Pensacola is the capital of West Florida. Initially investigated by Francisco Maldonado in 1540, Pensacola Bay played a very important role in the history of the Gulf Coast. Tristán de Luna attempted to found a permanent settlement there in 1559, but failed for many reasons. In 1686, during the search for Sieur R. R. C. de La Salle's colony, Ensign Juan Jordán de Reina visited the bay and called it "the best bay I have ever seen in my life." The local Indians he met called the bay Panzacola, Choctaw for "long-haired people." In 1693, Don Carlos de Sigüenza carefully examined the bay and drew an excellent map of it. Finally, in 1698, Spaniards under Andrés de Arriola established a presidio there called San Carlos de Austina. Captured by Mobile-based French in 1719, it was finally regained by Spaniards in 1722. But they moved the presidio to Santa Rosa Island, where it remained until a hurricane devastated the site on 3 November 1752. In 1754, the presidio was relocated to present-day Pensacola and in 1756 the Marqués de las Amarillas, viceroy of New Spain, ordered it moved to the site of Fort San Miguel on the mainland. In 1757 a royal order named it the Presidio San Miguel de Panzacola. In 1763 Spain ceded Florida to the British, and Pensacola became the capital of British West Florida. It remained British until captured by Bernardo de Gálvez's forces in 1781. The British officially returned Pensacola to Spain in 1783. Pensacola remained Spanish until ceded to the United States in 1819 and accepted by Andrew Jackson on 17 July 1821.

When the U.S. Civil War reached the area, Confederate forces invaded the city and remained there until 1862. However, they were never able to capture Fort Pickens, which is located offshore on Santa Rosa Island. In 1914 a naval yard first established in 1821 became a naval air station.

See also **Florida, Spanish West; Maldonado, Francisco Severo.**

BIBLIOGRAPHY

Stanley Faye, "Spanish Fortifications of Pensacola, 1698–1821," in *Pensacola Historical Society Quarterly* 6 (1972): 151–292.

William S. Coker, "The Financial History of Pensacola's Spanish Presidios, 1698–1763," in *Pensacola Historical Society Quarterly* 9 (1979): 1–20 and "Pensacola, 1686–1763," in *Sesquicentennial History of Florida*, edited by Michael V. Gannon (1995).

William S. Coker and G. Douglas Inglis, *The Spanish Censuses of Pensacola, 1784–1820*. Pensacola, FL: Perdido Bay Press, 1980, pp. 1–19.

Additional Bibliography

Bense, Judith Ann. *Archaeology of Colonial Pensacola*. Gainesville: University Press of Florida, 1999.

Bense, Judith Ann. *Presidio Santa Maria de Galve: A Struggle for Survival in Colonial Spanish Pensacola*. Gainesville: University Press of Florida, 2003.

Pearce, George F. *Pensacola during the Civil War: A Thorn in the Side of the Confederacy*. Gainesville: University Press of Florida, 2000.

Petinal, Manuel. *La campaña de Pensacola, 1781*. Madrid, Spain: Almena Ediciones, 2002.

WILLIAM S. COKER

PENSACOLA, BATTLE OF. Battle of Pensacola, part of the conflict between the Spanish and the British over West Florida in 1781. Bernardo de Gálvez reached Pensacola, the British capital of West Florida, with 3,155 troops on 9 March and quickly captured the British battery on Santa Rosa Island. Reinforcements from Mobile and New Orleans soon arrived. After successfully leading the Spanish ships into the bay, Gálvez set up his main encampment on Sutton's Lagoon (Bayou Chico). The British attempted unsuccessfully to stop the Spanish advance. The Spaniards dug entrenchments from their main camp toward the British redoubts and Fort George. Again, the British troops and their indigenous allies failed to stop them. Some 4,700 or more Spanish reinforcements from Cuba, including French troops, reached Pensacola on 19 April, bringing the total to a possible 8,000 on land and about 6,800 on the ships. The Spaniards completed their advanced battery by dawn on 8 May. Then followed a heavy bombardment of the Queen's Redoubt during which the powder magazine exploded, killing many of the British soldiers. The Spaniards quickly occupied the redoubt and bombarded the Prince of Wales Redoubt and Fort George. That afternoon the British proposed a truce. John Campbell formally surrendered on 10 May. Gálvez's three successful campaigns in British West Florida—Baton Rouge (1779), Mobile (1780) and Pensacola (1781)—materially aided the Americans during the Revolution and played an important role in the return of the Floridas to Spain at the end of the war in 1783.

See also **Gálvez, Bernardo de.**

BIBLIOGRAPHY

John Walton Caughey, *Bernardo de Gálvez in Louisiana, 1776–1783* (1934; repr. 1972), pp. 187–214.

Joseph Barton Starr, *Tories, Dons, and Rebels: The American Revolution in West Florida* (1976), pp. 175–215; *YO*

SOLO: The Battle Journal of Bernardo de Gálvez During the American Revolution, translated by A. E. Montemayor (1978).

William S. Coker and Hazel P. Coker, *The Siege of Pensacola, 1781, in Maps* (1981).

Additional Bibliography

Beerman, Eric. *España y la independencia de los Estados Unidos*. Madrid: Editorial MAPFRE, 1992.

Chavez, Thomas E. *Spain and the Independence of the United States: An Intrinsic Gift*. Albuquerque: University of New Mexico Press, 2002.

LaFarelle, Lorenzo G. *Bernardo de Gálvez: Hero of the American Revolution*. Austin, TX: Eakin Press, 1992.

Reparaz, Carmen de. *I Alone: Bernardo de Gálvez and the Taking of Pensacola in 1781: A Spanish Contribution to the Independence of the United States*. Madrid: Ediciones de Cultura Hispánica, 1993.

Valery S, Rafael. *Miranda en Pensacola: Génesis de la independencia hispanoamericana*. Miranda: Biblioteca de Autores y Temas Mirandinos, 1991.

WILLIAM S. COKER

PEONS. Peons are agricultural workers tied to large estates (haciendas). In most cases they live on the haciendas, on land rented from the estate, and in return have to provide labor services to the landlord. In some cases peons live in semi-independent villages close to the estate where they work. Land and labor arrangements vary widely across Latin America, as do the names of peons. For example, they are called *gañanes* in Mexico, *arrenderos* in Bolivia, and *inquilinos* in Chile.

The development of peonage began soon after the Spanish Conquest. Although most Indians lived in independent indigenous communities, the Conquest dislocated many people from their villages. Also, as race mixture became common, some of the mestizos were unable or unwilling to join the communities from whence their mothers had come. When the Spanish began acquiring land, some of these men and women joined the newly founded estates as peons. This was especially the case in the north-central section of Mexico, where the silver mines stimulated the agrarian economy and the Spanish took over lands previously controlled by seminomadic tribal peoples. The sharp demographic decline of the indigenous population in Mesoamerica also freed up land and made other means of capturing Indian labor, such as the state-enforced corvée labor of the *repartimiento* system, less effective than was initially the case. Likewise, in the Andes after the Conquest, migration among Indians became common, with many ending up as peons on haciendas. The feared forced Andean mine labor, called the *mita*, which was required of all Indian community members in a wide swath of the Andes, also encouraged peasants to leave their communities and find protection as peons on the Spanish haciendas.

The rest of Latin America (other than the Caribbean, where the plantations were staffed by slaves) also adopted the hacienda model, which created more peons. By the end of the colonial period (around 1820), peons constituted perhaps a quarter of all rural labor. After independence, the proportion of peons remained relatively steady until the late nineteenth century. At that point, peonage increased as Liberal land reforms brought about the abolition of Indian communities, replaced in many cases by haciendas. Many of the former community members were converted into hacienda peons. By the 1920s, hacienda peons made up perhaps half of the rural population in Latin America.

In some regions, peonage was more restrictive than in others. In areas where there were many opportunities for working in other occupations, such as in northern Mexico close to the U.S. border, peonage was not as severe as elsewhere. Many peons were cowboys and lived relatively independently. In other regions, such as in the Yucatán peninsula and in the Andes, peonage was more exploitative. The landlords ruled over their charges, requiring obeisance, and, as in the Andes, the women were required to work in the masters' households, exposing them to sexual assault. Moreover, in the late nineteenth century debt peonage became more common, in which landlords tied the peons to their estates by indebting them to such an extent that they could never work off what they owed. In some cases, such as for highland Indians, recruiters for estates of the Peruvian coast provided large advances that the workers were unable to pay off. With increased police presence, the landowners were able to enforce these contracts, limiting workers' ability to leave.

Peonage declined by the middle of the twentieth century because of the extensive land reforms in

Latin America. The first of these emerged as a result of the Mexican Revolution (1910–1940), and later reforms in countries including Bolivia (1953), Ecuador (1964), Peru (1969), and Nicaragua (1979) diminished the traditional type of peonage throughout Latin America. Elsewhere, such as in Chile and northern Argentina, the traditional peons disappeared with the modernization of agriculture, creating instead a rural proletariat with no land rights on the estates. In the early twenty-first century there are still peons in certain regions of Latin America, especially in frontier zones such as eastern Bolivia and in Brazil, where local elites are strong and the state is relatively weak.

See also **Debt Peonage.**

BIBLIOGRAPHY

Chevalier, François. *Land and Society in Colonial Mexico: The Great Hacienda.* Translated by Alvin Eustis. Berkeley: University of California Press, 1963.

Peloso, Vincent C. *Peasants on Plantations: Subaltern Strategies of Labor and Resistance in the Pisco Valley, Peru.* Durham, NC: Duke University Press, 1999.

Van Young, Eric. "Mexican Rural History since Chevalier: The Historiography of the Colonial Hacienda." *Latin American Research Review* 18, no. 3 (1983): 5–61.

ERICK D. LANGER

PERALTA, ÁNGELA (1845–1883). Ángela Peralta (*b.* 6 July 1845; *d.* 30 August 1883), Mexican operatic soprano and composer. Born in Mexico City, Peralta showed a natural gift for singing; she is supposed to have impressed the great German soprano Henrietta Sontag in 1854. Thereafter she became a student of Agustín Balderas, who sponsored her debut at fifteen in Verdi's *Il Trovatore* and then took her to Europe, where she made a notable impression. Peralta returned to Mexico during the Second Empire and became a favorite of Maximilian and Carlotta, appearing in the premiere of Melesio Morales's *Ildegonda.*

The decade 1865–1875 was the period of Peralta's greatest activity. She toured Mexico and Europe, with performances in Havana and New York. A celebrated season followed her homecoming in 1871, because she brought with her the famous tenor Enrico Tamberlick and sang with him in another Mexican opera, *Guatimotzín,* by Aniceto

Ortega del Villar. She formed her own opera company and acted as the impresario. Although best known for her bel canto singing, Peralta adopted a more dramatic style when she played the lead in her company's first Mexican production of Verdi's *Aida,* a role closely identified with her. Another facet of her later career was composition of popular songs.

Peralta's husband, Eugenio Castera, died in 1877; Peralta subsequently formed a scandalous liaison with her manager, Julián Montiel y Duarte. Ostracized in Mexico City, she took her company to remote towns, including Mazatlán, where she contracted yellow fever and died at age thirty-eight. In 1937 her remains were moved to the Panteón in Mexico City.

See also **Music: Art Music.**

BIBLIOGRAPHY

A popular biography is Armando De María y Campos, *Angela Peralta: El ruiseñor mexicano* (1944); Ronald H. Dolkart, "Angela Peralta: A Mexican Diva," in *The Human Tradition in Latin America: The Nineteenth Century,* edited by Judith Ewell and William H. Beezley (1989), pp. 161–174.

Additional Bibliography

Alvarez Coral, Juan. *Compositores mexicanos.* México: EDAMEX, 1993.

Sosa M., José Octavio. *Diccionario de la ópera mexicana.* México, D.F.: Consejo Nacional para la Cultura y las Artes, 2005.

RONALD H. DOLKART

PERALTA AZURDIA, ENRIQUE (1908–1997). Enrique Peralta Azurdia (*b.* 17 June 1908; *d.* 18 February 1997), head of government in Guatemala (1963–1966). Born in Guatemala City, Peralta graduated in 1929 from the National Military Academy, which he later headed. He became minister of defense in December 1960 after supporting Miguel Ydígoras Fuentes (1958–1963) against an attempted military coup. However, when Ydígoras allowed former president Juan José Arévalo Bermejo (1945–1951) to return to Guatemala to campaign for the presidency in 1963, Peralta led the coup that overthrew Ydígoras Fuentes.

Peralta, who served as head of government from 1963 to 1966, launched the military-civilian alliance that ruled Guatemala from 1963 to 1986. His administration strengthened military control in the countryside and, through constitutional revisions, reduced the potential power of left-wing parties. Peralta permitted elections to be held in 1966, but the Institutional Democratic Party (PID), which he formed, split, allowing a civilian, Julio César Méndez Montenegro (1966–1970), to capture the presidency.

Peralta remained an active player in Guatemalan politics during the next two decades by organizing the National Unity Front (FUN), originally a coalition between the Christian Democrats and two smaller center-right parties. FUN supported General Ángel Guevara for the presidency in 1982, and his fraudulent election led to the military coup of that year. In 1990 it supported the candidacy of José Efraín Ríos Montt.

See also **Guatemala, Constitutions.**

BIBLIOGRAPHY

Jerry L. Weaver, "The Political Style of the Guatemalan Military Elite," in *Militarism in Developing Countries,* edited by Kenneth Fidel (1975).

Michael Mc Clintock, *The American Connection,* vol. 2: *State Terror and Popular Resistance in Guatemala* (1985).

James Dunkerley, *Power in the Isthmus: A Political History of Modern Central America* (1988).

Additional Bibliography

Booth, John. "A Guatemalan Nightmare: Levels of Political Violence, 1966–1972." *Journal of Interamerican Studies and World Affairs* (May 1980): 195–225.

Loveman, Brian, and Thomas M. Davies. *The Politics of Antipolitics: The Military in Latin America.* Wilmington, DE: Scholarly Resources, 1997.

ROLAND H. EBEL

PERALTA BARNUEVO Y ROCHA, PEDRO DE (1664–1743).

Pedro de Peralta Barnuevo y Rocha (*b.* 26 November 1664; *d.* 30 April 1743), Peruvian polymath. Peralta was born in Lima and educated at the University of San Marcos. An acountant, lawyer, mathematician, and cosmographer who taught mathematics at San Marcos and served as its rector, he was considered by contemporaries to be a "monster of erudition" and was recognized for his learning in both France and Spain.

Poet and historian, Peralta wrote numerous comedies and poems as well as the epic *Lima fundada* (1732). This history of Lima eulogized Francisco Pizarro and underscored the accomplishments of Lima's creole nobility in the offices of church and state.

Several viceroys relied upon Peralta's mathematical abilities and supported his proposal to fortify Callao. The marquis de Castelfuerte (1724–1736), moreover, asked Peralta to prepare his final report. Peralta used the opportunity to argue for maintaining Lima as it had been under Hapsburg rule and to decry the viceroy's loss of authority to name provincial officials and the resulting reduction of Peruvian appointees.

See also **Peru: From the Conquest Through Independence.**

BIBLIOGRAPHY

D. A. Brading, *The First America: The Spanish Monarchy, Creole Patriots, and the Liberal State 1492–1867* (1991), pp. 391–399.

Additional Bibliography

Williams, Jerry M. *Peralta Barnuevo and the Discourse of Loyalty: A Critical Edition of Four Selected Texts.* Tempe: ASU Center for Latin American Studies Press, Arizona State University, 1996.

MARK A. BURKHOLDER

PÉRALTE, CHARLEMAGNE MASSÉNA (1886–1919).

Charlemagne Masséna Péralte (*b.* 10 October 1886; *d.* 30 October 1919), Haitian rebel leader during the 1915–1934 U.S. occupation of Haiti. Charlemagne Masséna Péralte came from a rural, middle-class family in Hinche and was educated at a Catholic secondary school in Port-au-Prince. Afterward, he joined a rebel (Caco) group led by Oreste Zamor, his brother-in-law, who became president in February 1914. Péralte was made commander of Léogane, then of Port-de-Paix (1914).

When the U.S. Marines occupied Haiti, Péralte was forced to leave office. In October 1917, he was implicated in a robbery of the U.S. commander in

Hinche. Péralte was convicted and sentenced to five years hard labor in Cap Haitien but escaped in September 1918.

After Péralte announced his intention to "drive the invaders into the sea and free Haiti," he formed a provisional government in the north, appointed himself its chief, and mobilized several thousand peasant irregulars. He attacked outlying military establishments, and then, on 7 October 1919, Port-au-Prince itself. A Marine order to "get Charlemagne" led Sergeant Herman H. Hanneken to trick Péralte into revealing his whereabouts. Hanneken shot him dead near Sainte Suzanne. When a Péralte associate, Benoît Batraville, was killed on 19 May 1920, armed opposition to the occupation dwindled.

Péralte is the best-known rebel leader of the 1915–1920 Caco Revolt, in which Haitians militarily resisted the occupation (which continued until 1934). Although Péralte did not espouse an economic or social program, his reputation as a Haitian hero and resistance leader has grown since the 1980s. He has appeared on stamps and in popular art, and he figures in political speeches.

See also **Haiti, Caco Revolts.**

BIBLIOGRAPHY

James H. Mc Crocklin, ed., *Garde d'Haïti, 1915–1934* (1956).

Robert Heinl and Nancy Gordon Heinl, *Written in Blood: The Story of the Haitian People 1492–1971* (1978), esp. pp. 451–460.

David Nicholls, *From Dessalines to Duvalier* (1979).

Roger Gaillard, *Les Blancs débarquent*, 2d ed. (1982).

Brian Weinstein and Aaron Segal, *Haiti: The Failure of Politics* (1992), esp. chap. 2.

Additional Bibliography

Michel, George. *Charlemagne Péralte and the First American Occupation of Haiti.* Chapel Hill: University of North Carolina Press, 2001.

Renda, Mary A. *Taking Haiti: Military Occupation and the Culture of U.S. Imperialism, 1915–1940.* Dubuque: Kendall/Hunt Pub. Co., 1996.

ANNE GREENE

PEREDA, SETEMBRINO EZEQUIEL

(1859–1933). Setembrino Pereda was a Uruguayan congressman and historian. He was born in Paysandú, into a family of cattle ranchers. He actively participated in Freemasonry and in politics as a militant of the Constitutional Party until it was dissolved. A lifelong liberal, Pereda continued to be active in politics as a member of the Colorado Party. He served in Congress as a representative of Paysandú for two terms, from 1899 to 1905.

Pereda was also a historian and a publicist. His writings revolved around three main topics: He produced one of the first documented historical works on Paysandú; he wrote biographies of two crucial Uruguayan leaders, José Gervasio Artigas and Fructuoso Rivero; and lastly, from his fascination with the Italian nationalist Garibaldi, who had fought for Uruguay while in exile from his native country, he wrote a massive study of Garibaldi's impact on Uruguayan political life. Almost blind, Pereda completed only three volumes of this work, of a planned six. Because of his commitment to advancing knowledge of local history and culture, the Paysandú city government honored Pereda in several ways: The main street carries his name, as does the public library.

See also **Artigas, José Gervasio; Garibaldi, Giuseppe; Paysandú; Uruguay, Political Parties: Colorado Party; Uruguay: The Twentieth Century.**

BIBLIOGRAPHY

Pereda, Setembrino. *Garibaldi en el Uruguay.* Montevideo: El Siglo Ilustrado, 1914–1916.

Pereda, Setembrino. *Artigas, 1784–1850.* Montevideo: El Siglo Ilustrado, 1930.

Pías, Miguel Angel. *Crónicas sanduceras.* Montevideo: Cámara de Representantes, 2000.

Schulkin, Augusto. *Historia de Paysandú: Diccionario biográfico.* Buenos Aires: Von Roseen, 1967.

VALERIA MANZANO

PEREIRA, JOSÉ CLEMENTE (1786?–

1854). José Clemente Pereira (*b.* 22 February 1786?; *d.* 12 March 1854), Brazilian politician. Pereira was born in Castello Mendo, Portugal, to a humble family. He graduated in law from the University of Coimbra in 1809. In 1815 he arrived in Brazil, where he began his public career as a magistrate. In 1821 he assumed the post of foreign judge in Rio de Janeiro, which provided him a position of influence over events leading up to Brazilian independence. As president of the Senate of Rio de Janeiro, he delegated the representation of that city of Prince Pedro in the famous *Manifesto do fico* of 1822, which requested that the prince disregard the orders of the Cortes and remain in Brazil.

After helping to consolidate independence, Pereira was accused of republicanism because of his being a Mason and his defense of more radical liberal ideas. José Bonifacio had him arrested and deported to France. He returned to Brazil in 1824 and occupied various public posts during the empire, including representative in several legislatures, senator (1842), minister of the empire (1828), minister of war (1841), and adviser of state (1850). Besides his activities as a public figure, he stood out in the area of social assistance founding the Hospital of Mercy and the Peter II Hospice. Through his outstanding role in the struggle for Brazilian independence and his political activities, he became one of the builders of the Brazilian nation.

See also **Brazil: 1808–1889.**

BIBLIOGRAPHY

Antonio De Vasconcelos, *José Clemente Pereira 1786–1854* (1923).

Raul José De Sá Barbosa and Francisco De Assis Barbosa, "José Clemente Pereira," in *Enciclopédia Mirador Internacional*, vol. 16 (1983), pp. 8, 767–768.

Additional Bibliography

Barman, Roderick J. *Citizen Emperor: Pedro II and the Making of Brazil, 1825–9*. Stanford, CA: Stanford University Press, 1999.

Jancsó, István. *Brasil: Formação do estado e da nação*. São Paulo: Editora Hucitec, 2003.

Vainfas, Ronaldo. *Dicionário do Brasil imperial, 1822–1889*. Rio de Janeiro, Brazil: Objetiva, 2002.

LÚCIA M. BASTOS P. NEVES

PEREIRA DE SOUSA. *See* **Luís Pereira de Sousa, Washington.**

PERERA, VÍCTOR (1934–2003). Víctor Perera (*b.* 12 April 1934; *d.* 14 June 2003), Guatemalan writer. Born in Guatemala of Sephardic Jewish parents who had emigrated from Jerusalem, Perera immigrated to the United States at age twelve. Educated at Brooklyn College (B.A., 1956) and the University of Michigan (M.A., 1958), he became a reporter, writer, and editor for the *New Yorker*, the *New York Times Magazine, Atlantic, Harper's*, and many other journals. His articles, short stories, and essays, often dealing with Latin America and Jewish themes, are noted for their sensitivity and perceptiveness. His first novel, *The Conversion* (1970), was followed by works of nonfiction, including *Last Lords of Palenque: The Lacandon Mayas of the Mexican Rain Forest* (with Robert D. Bruce, 1982), *Rites: A Guatemalan Boyhood* (1986), and *Broken Promises: The Guatemalan Tragedy* (1991).

He was awarded the NEA Creative Writing Fellowship (1980), the PEN Syndicated Fiction Prize (1986), and the Lila Wallace-Reader's Digest Fund Writing Award (1992-94). His last project was a book on whales. He suffered from a stroke in 1998 and never fully recovered.

See also **Hispanics in the United States; Journalism.**

BIBLIOGRAPHY

Additional Bibliography

Perera, Victor. *Rites: A Guatemalan Boyhood*. San Francisco: Mercury House, 1994, 1986 1st Mercury House ed.

RALPH LEE WOODWARD JR.

PEREYNS, SIMÓN (c. 1535–1589). Simón Pereyns (*b.* ca. 1535; *d.* 1589), painter. Apparently trained in his native Antwerp in the style of northern mannerism, Pereyns traveled in 1558 to Lisbon, where he worked as a painter, and then to Toledo and Madrid. In 1566 he arrived in New Spain with the viceroy Gastón de Peralta, for whom he painted frescoes of battle scenes (now lost). In 1568 Pereyns was tried before the Inquisition and sentenced to paint at his own expense a retablo of Nuestra Señora de la Merced, which may have been the *Virgen del Perdón*, destroyed by fire in the cathedral of Mexico City in 1967. The records of this trial provide information about the painter's life. Other documents attest to his prolific activity and to his central role in introducing Italianate Flemish mannerism to New Spain. Pereyns executed the paintings of the principal retablo of the cathedral of Mexico City as well as many others. He worked in collaboration with Francisco de Morales, Andrés de la Concha, Luis de Arciniega, and others. His only surviving works, however, are the paintings of the main altar at the Franciscan church in Huejotzingo (1856), possibly done with Concha, and a signed and dated *Saint Christopher* in the cathedral of Mexico City (1588).

See also **New Spain, Viceroyalty of.**

BIBLIOGRAPHY

Manuel Toussaint, *Colonial Art in Mexico* (1967).

José Guadalupe Victoria, "Un pintor flamenco en Nueva España: Simón Pereyns," in *Anales del Instituto de investigaciones estéticas* 55 (1986): 69–83.

Additional Bibliography

Lorenzo Macías, José María. "Una noticia más sobre Simón Pereyns." *Anales del Instituto de Investigaciones Estéticas* 22:76 (Spring 2000): 259–264.

Tovar de Teresa, Guillermo. *Pintura y escultura en Nueva España (1557–1640).* México, D.F.: Grupo Azabache, 1992.

CLARA BARGELLINI

PÉREZ, ALBINO

PÉREZ, ALBINO (?–1837). Albino Pérez (*d.* 9 August 1837), governor of New Mexico from 1835 to 1837. The first Mexican governor of New Mexico, Pérez was appointed by the government of Antonio López de Santa Anna. As part of Mexico's shift away from federalism under Santa Anna, Pérez attempted to impose the authority of the central government through a new system of direct taxation and other measures. The Pérez administration alienated many New Mexicans, and in 1837 the governor's policies sparked a short-lived rebellion of Hispanics and Indians in northern New Mexico. While attempting to end the profederalist, antitaxation revolt, Pérez was captured, executed, and beheaded.

See also **New Mexico.**

BIBLIOGRAPHY

For a detailed account of the 1837 rebellion, see Janet Lecompte, *Rebellion in Río Arriba, 1837* (1985). The administration of Pérez and the 1837 revolt are also discussed in David J. Weber, *The Mexican Frontier, 1821–1846: The American Southwest Under Mexico* (1982), pp. 261–265.

Additional Bibliography

Cutter, Donald C. *España en Nuevo México.* Madrid: Editorial MAPFRE, 1992.

Villagrá, Gaspar Pérez de, and Felipe Echenique March. *Historia de la Nueva México.* México, D.F.: Instituto Nacional de Antropología e Historia, Centro Regional de Baja California, 1993.

SUZANNE B. PASZTOR

PÉREZ, CARLOS ANDRÉS

PÉREZ, CARLOS ANDRÉS (1926–). Carlos Andrés Pérez (*b.* 27 October 1926) was president of Venezuela (1974–1979, 1988–1993). Andrés Pérez was a founder of Venezuela's Democratic Action (AD), inspired by Peru's Popular American Revolutionary Alliance (APRA). During his two presidential terms Pérez completed oil nationalization, was a spokesman for the Third World, and led efforts to influence U.S. policy through the Contadora organization of eight Latin American nations.

Carlos Andrés Pérez was born in Rubio, a Venezuelan Andean village. Dictator Juan Vicente Gómez's repression of *campesinos,* as well as the forced sale of the Pérez family's coffee ranch, led Carlos into populist politics. The protégé of Democratic Action founders Leonardo Ruiz Pineda, Rómulo Gallegos, and Rómulo Betancourt, at eighteen Pérez was a delegate to the party's first convention. After the overthrow of the dictatorship of Eleazar López Contreras in 1945, Pérez became secretary to Betancourt, the president of the revolutionary government junta. The junta was promptly overthrown by a military coup, and Pérez eventually joined Betancourt in Costa Rica, where they published an antimilitary newspaper. At the end of the dictatorship of Marcos Pérez Jiménez in 1958, Pérez returned to Venezuela as Betancourt's minister of the interior.

Pérez, one of Venezuela's most charismatic politicians, is known popularly as "CAP." During his first presidency, he completed the nationalization of Venezuela's petroleum industry and instigated state welfarism, engendered by the rise in international oil prices. Internationally, he championed wealth redistribution to the Third World through commodity power.

When oil prices fell in the 1980s, Pérez pushed austerity moves. In 1988 he was the first president re-elected to a second term after a constitutionally mandated ten-year wait. However, the inability of the conservative coalition to maintain the illusion of easy wealth and permanent subsidized programs led to riots in February 1989. Two unsuccessful coup attempts in 1992 indicated that Pérez's program was no more popular than that of his predecessor, Luis Herrara Campíns. His administration ended in scandal when in 1993 the political opposition accused him of corruption. The Supreme Court validated the charges and the national legislature removed him from office. After spending time in jail, Pérez won a Senate seat in 1998. However, Hugo Chávez, who had led the first coup attempt in 1992, won the presidency in 2000 and dissolved the Senate. Pérez then moved to Miami and became a vocal critic of the Chávez administration.

See also **Chávez, Hugo; Venezuela: Venezuela since 1830; Venezuela, Political Parties: Democratic Action (AD).**

BIBLIOGRAPHY

José Antonio Rangel Barón, *Carlos Andrés Pérez: El hombre, el presidente: Historia viva* (1988).

Paul H. Boeker, *Lost Illusions* (1990).

Additional Bibliography

Méndez, Ana Irene. *Democracia y discurso político: Caldera, Pérez y Chávez.* Caracas, Venezuela: Monte Avila Editores Latinoamericana, 2004.

Tarver, H. Micheal. *The Rise and Fall of Venezuelan President Carlos Andrés Pérez: An Historical Examination.* 2 vols. Lewiston, NY: E. Mellen Press, 2001–2004.

                                        PAT KONRAD

PÉREZ, JUAN (1775). Juan Pérez (*d.* 1775), Spanish explorer. Juan Pérez, a native of Mallorca, was already an experienced pilot when he first sailed as part of the Manila Galleon before participating in the founding of California in 1769. In 1773, Viceroy Antonio María de Bucareli of Mexico ordered him to lead a maritime expedition to explore the northern coast of California to check on Russians rumored to be in the area. Departing from the Pacific coast port of San Blas on the frigate *Santiago* on 24 January 1774, he reached San Lorenzo (present-day Vancouver Island) in August, as well as Nootka Sound and Cerro Nevado de Santa Rosalía (Mount Olympus). His expedition, the first to sail to 55 degrees north latitude, led to the subsequent Spanish exploration of the area as far as the Alaska Peninsula by the 1790s and formed the basis for its claims to that area. Pérez died of scurvy while piloting the *Santiago* along the California coast.

See also **California.**

BIBLIOGRAPHY

Joseph P. Sánchez, *Spanish Bluecoats: The Catalonian Volunteers in Northwestern New Spain, 1767–1810* (1990).

David J. Weber, *The Spanish Frontier in North America* (1992).

Additional Bibliography

San Pío, María Pilar de. *Expediciones españolas del siglo XVIII: El paso del noroeste.* Madrid: Editorial MAPFRE, 1992.

                                JOSEPH P. SÁNCHEZ

PEREZ, TONY (1942–). Tony Perez, born Atanasio Perez Rigal in Ciego de Avila, Cuba, is a baseball player whose accomplishments in the major leagues came both as a player and manager. He gained distinction as a prominent member of the Cincinnati Reds' "Big Red Machine," the team that captured three championships during Perez's tenure there. Perez entered professional baseball in the United States at a time when diplomatic relations with Cuba came to a close. Isolated from his country, Perez rose through the ranks and joined the Reds in 1964 to launch what became a Hall of Fame career. With Cincinnati his best year came in 1970 when he hit 40 home runs, drove in 129 runs, and batted .317. He participated in seven All-Star games and was named Most Valuable Player in the 1967 classic. After playing with three other clubs, the Cuba slugger retired in 1983 with a .279 average, 379 home runs, and 1652 runs batted in. Perez briefly managed the Reds (1993) and Marlins (2001) before Florida employed him as special assistant to the general manager. In 2000 Perez was inducted into the Baseball Hall of Fame.

See also **Sports.**

BIBLIOGRAPHY

Oleksak, Michael M., and Mary Adams Oleksak. *Béisbol: Latin Americans and the Grand Old Game.* Grand Rapids, MI: Masters Press, 1991.

Echevarría, Roberto González. *The Pride of Havana: A History of Cuban Baseball.* New York: Oxford University Press, 1999.

Regalado, Samuel O. *Viva Baseball! Latin Major Leaguers and Their Special Hunger.* Urbana: University of Illinois Press, 1998.

SAMUEL O. REGALADO

PÉREZ ACOSTA, JUAN FRANCISCO (1873–1967).

Juan Francisco Pérez Acosta (*b.* 1873; *d.* 1967), Paraguayan historian. Although his early career was limited to writings published in such opposition newspapers as *La Democracia* and *El Independiente,* Pérez Acosta was eventually recognized as the "dean of contemporary Paraguayan letters." He owed his success to his thorough and painstaking research in primary materials, especially the document collections in Paraguay's national archives. The results, as exemplified in his masterpiece, *Carlos Antonio López: Obrero máximo* (1948), placed him in the first rank of modern scholarship in Paraguay.

After the Liberal Party came to power in 1904, Pérez Acosta accepted various official posts: chief of police, director of the central bank, diplomat, jurist, and educator. He also edited several Asunción newspapers, including *El Diario* and *El Liberal.* With the defeat of the Liberals and the consolidation of Colorado Party rule in the late 1940s, Pérez Acosta retired to private life. Though he continued to write articles, his scholarly work slowly tapered off. He died in Asunción.

See also **Journalism; Paraguay, Political Parties: Colorado Party.**

BIBLIOGRAPHY

Carlos R. Centurión, *Historia de la cultura paraguaya,* 2 vols. (1961).

Harris Gaylord Warren, *Rebirth of the Paraguayan Republic: The First Colorado Era, 1878–1904* (1985), p. 294.

Additional Bibliography

Carrón, Juan María. *El régimen liberal, 1870–1930: Sociedad, economía.* Asunción: Aranduã Editoria, 2004.

Lewis, Paul H. *Political Parties and Generations in Paraguay's Liberal Era, 1869–1940.* Chapel Hill: University of North Carolina Press, 1993.

THOMAS L. WHIGHAM

PÉREZ AGUIRRE, LUIS (1941–2001).

Luis Pérez Aguirre (*b.* 1941; *d.* January 25 2001), Uruguayan human rights activist. Pérez Aguirre was born to a patrician family. He had his primary education at the Richard Anderson School and his secondary education under the Jesuit fathers at Sacred Heart in Montevideo. He later studied civil aviation and in 1959 joined the Jesuits. While becoming a Jesuit priest, he undertook further studies in Chile, Argentina, and Canada in psychology, humanities, philosophy, and theology. He returned to his country in 1970 and threw himself into social work, concentrating primarily on the phenomenon of prostitution, but as the political situation worsened, he became more and more involved in the struggle for human rights.

After he was arrested for "subversive behavior," Pérez Aguirre was forced to leave the country and, under the direction of his superiors, undertook further studies at the University of Comillas in Spain. Returning to Uruguay around the late 1970s, he worked with groups of youths in the city of Las Piedras, in the department of Canelones, where he founded SERPAJ (Service for Peace and Justice) in 1984. This work gained him the support of Adolfo Pérez Esquivel, the Argentine Nobel Peace Prize laureate. From Las Piedras, Pérez Aguirre involved himself in the intense political activity surrounding the plebiscite of 1980, with which began the country's movement toward democracy. With that work complete and a SERPAJ team established in Montevideo, Pérez Aguirre began directing La Huella, a home for abandoned children and young people in Las Piedras. He also publishes books on educational and cultural themes and continues his social work with prostitutes. His work is also associated with liberation theology.

See also **Service for Peace and Justice (SERPAJ).**

BIBLIOGRAPHY

Juan José Mosca, *Derechos humanos* (Montevideo, 1985).

Luis Pérez Aguirre, *Predicaciones en la plaza* (1985), *Anti-confesiones de un cristiano* (1988), and *La iglesia increíble* (1993).

Additional Bibliography

Harper, Charles R. *Impunity, An Ethical Perspective: Six Case Studies from Latin America.* Geneva: WCC Publications, 1996.

Luna, Héctor and Pérez Aguirre, Luis. Huellas de una vida. Montevideo: Trilce, 1997.

Machamer, Gene. *Hispanic American Profiles.* New York: One World, 1996.

Pérez Aguirre, Luis. *La condición femenina.* Montevideo, Uruguay: Ediciones Trilce, 1995.

Pérez Aguirre, Luis. "La penalizacion es injusta inútil e inmoral." *Semanario Brecha,* (March, 2001).

JOSÉ DE TORRES WILSON

PÉREZ DE CUÉLLAR, JAVIER (1920–).

A Peruvian diplomat and politician, Pérez de Cuéllar was the fifth United Nations secretary-general. Born January 19, 1920, he entered Peru's diplomatic service in 1944. He had a long and distinguished career, including ambassadorships to Switzerland, the Soviet Union, Poland, and Venezuela as well as the post of permanent representative to the United Nations (1971–1975). His career included service with the United Nations as special representative in Cyprus from 1975 to 1977 and undersecretary-general for special political affairs from 1979 to 1981. In 1982 Pérez de Cuéllar became the first Latin American UN secretary-general; he was reelected in 1986. In 1995 he ran unsuccessfully for president of Peru, later serving as his country's minister of foreign affairs during the transition government of Valentín Paniagua (2000–2001). His final post was ambassador to France, from which he retired in 2004.

A highlight of his tenure as United Nations secretary-general was supporting efforts to end conflict in Central America by establishing UN peace-keeping missions to Nicaragua, El Salvador, and Guatemala, the first in Latin America. In his last act as secretary-general, he brokered the peace agreement between the government of El Salvador and the Farabundo Martí Liberation Front guerrillas.

Persuaded to run for Peru's presidency in 1995 as the candidate of the Union for Peru (Unión Por el Perú [UPP]), he finished second among fourteen aspirants in the first round but garnered just 35 percent of the votes in the runoff against incumbent Alberto Fujimori. His failure was attributed to a combination of his long absence from Peru, an uncharismatic campaign style, and his opponent's dirty tricks, which included tapping his telephones.

See also **United Nations.**

BIBLIOGRAPHY

Bowen, Sally. *The Fujimori File: Peru and Its President, 1990–2000.* 2000.

Montgomery, Tommie Sue, ed. *Peacemaking and Democratization in the Western Hemisphere.* Coral Gables, FL: North-South Center Press, University of Miami, 2000.

DAVID SCOTT PALMER

PÉREZ DE TOLOSA, JUAN (?–1548).

Juan Pérez de Tolosa (*d.* 1548), governor and captain-general of the province of Venezuela (1546–1548). Pérez de Tolosa was the first governor of the province of Venezuela after the termination of the administration of the Welsers, a group of Germans who were granted permission to settle and exploit the province of Venezuela. Their abuses of native peoples eventually resulted in a rescinding of the original grant and a trial. Pérez de Tolosa was the judge for this trial as well as that of Juan de Carvajal, a Spanish conquistador and colonizer of the Venezuelan interior, who ran afoul of Spanish authorities. He set up his government in the city of El Tocuyo and carried out diverse expeditions to the Andes, placing his brother, Alonso Pérez de Tolosa, and Diego de Losada in charge of them.

During Juan Pérez de Tolosa's rule, the system of the *encomienda* was initiated in Venezuela and the first looms were installed in El Tocuyo. At the end of his two-year mandate, the king extended it indefinitely. However, Pérez de Tolosa died shortly thereafter. His experience as an administrator in Venezuela is recorded in his book *Relación de las tierras y provincias de la gobernación de Venezuela, año 1546.*

See also **Venezuela: The Colonial Era.**

BIBLIOGRAPHY

Letizia Vaccari, *Juicios de residencia en la provincia de Venezuela: Juan Pérez de Tolosa y Juan de Villegas* (1983), and José De Oviedo y Baños, *The Conquest and Settlement of Venezuela,* translated by Jeanette Johnson Varner.

Additional Bibliography

Cunill, Pedro, and Pedro Grases. *Los tres primeros siglos de Venezuela, 1498–1810.* Caracas: Fundación Eugenio Mendoza, 1991.

Gerendas Kiss, Alejandro. *Historia de Venezuela: Narrada año por año: 1410–1640.* Caracas: Edimax, 2005.

INÉS QUINTERO

PÉREZ ESQUIVEL, ADOLFO (1931–).

Adolfo Pérez Esquivel (*b.* 26 November 1931), Argentine sculptor, peace activist, and coordinator of the Service for Peace and Justice (SERPAJ), Latin America's principal organization promoting societal change through nonviolence. In 1980 he received the Nobel Peace Prize for his work with SERPAJ.

Born in Buenos Aires, Pérez Esquivel was educated in Catholic schools and was deeply influenced by the writings of St. Augustine and Thomas Merton, as well as by the pacifist example of Mohandas Gandhi. Trained in sculpture at the National School of Fine Arts, he later taught there for fifteen years. He abandoned his successful career as a sculptor in the early 1970s to promote nonviolence as the most appropriate response to the violence that was afflicting Latin America as a result of increasing pressures for change.

In 1974 Pérez Esquivel joined with other Catholic activists to form SERPAJ, an agency for the dissemination of knowledge of nonviolent strategies and for the promotion of greater observance of human rights, participatory models of economic development, greater political participation especially among the poor, disarmament, and demilitarization. That year Pérez Esquivel became the general coordinator of SERPAJ, traveling throughout Latin America and elsewhere to promote nonviolence. As a result of his work, he was jailed for fourteen months in 1977–1978 by the Argentine military government. Upon his release, he resumed his work promoting nonviolence as the most effective way of creating a democratic and liberating social order. In 1995 he published his book *Walking Together with the People* and beginning in 2003 he became president of the Honorary Council of Service, Latin American Peace and Justice Foundation.

See also **Pérez Aguirre, Luis; Service for Peace and Justice (SERPAJ).**

BIBLIOGRAPHY

Canas, Andrés. *Caminos de nuestra América.* Buenos Aires: Ediciones del Pensamiento Nacional, 1999.

MARGARET E. CRAHAN

PÉREZ GODOY, RICARDO (1905–1982).

Ricardo Pérez Godoy (*b.* 9 June 1905; *d.* 27 July 1982), commander in chief of Peru's armed forces, army general, and senior officer of the four-man junta that governed Peru from 18 July 1962 to 28 July 1963. After inconclusive presidential elections in June 1962 resulted in a virtual three-way tie among the leading contenders, the military took power by an "institutional act" of the armed forces. As commander in chief of Peru's armed forces, Pérez Godoy assumed the ceremonial duties of chief of state.

During the first months of junta government, several reformist initiatives concerning agrarian issues were promulgated. These anticipated the 1968–1980 military government's more sweeping reforms. The junta's reformist phase ended in January 1963 with the countrywide crackdown on Communist organizations and activists. Pérez Godoy was forced to retire in March 1963, amid allegations that he did not share his authority sufficiently with his copresidents. He lived quietly in retirement until his death.

See also **Junta, Spanish America; Peru: Peru Since Independence.**

BIBLIOGRAPHY

Daniel P. Werlich, *Peru: A Short History* (1978).

Daniel M. Masterson, *Militarism and Politics in Latin America: Peru from Sánchez Cerro to Sendero Luminoso* (1991).

Additional Bibliography

Masterson, Daniel M. *Fuerza armada y sociedad en el Perú moderno: Un estudio sobre relaciones civiles militares, 1930–2000*. Lima: Instituto de Estudios Políticos y Estratégicos, 2001.

DAVID SCOTT PALMER

PÉREZ JIMÉNEZ, MARCOS (1914–2001).

Marcos Pérez Jiménez was a Venezuelan professional army officer and president (1942–1958). Pérez Jiménez was the dominant political figure in Venezuela from 1948 to 1958 and was the last of a series of army officers from the state of Táchira who ruled Venezuela in the late nineteenth and early twentieth centuries. A 1934 graduate of the Venezuelan Military Academy, Pérez Jiménez was a central figure in the 1945 overthrow of President Isaías Medina Angarita. Pérez had organized the revolutionary Patriotic Military Union (Unión Patriótica Militar—UPM) in 1944 and when he was arrested on 18 October 1945, the UPM overthrew the government. The junta that emerged the next day, however, headed by Rómulo Betancourt of the Democratic Action Party (Acción Democrática—AD), did not include Pérez Jiménez. Instead, Betancourt sent Pérez Jiménez abroad on an extended diplomatic mission. Alienated, Pérez Jiménez eventually organized the overthrow of the Venezuelan government of Rómulo Gallegos on 24 November 1948, restoring the military to power after three years of civilian rule. Pérez Jiménez was a member of the governing junta through the election of 1952, which appeared to be won by the opposition Democratic Republican Union (Unión Republicana Democrática—URD). Colonel Pérez Jiménez, however, suspended the election and seized power himself. His military dictatorship continued until 23 January 1958, when he was removed in a bloodless coup by other military officers, opening the way for the return of the AD and more democratic rule. Repression, corruption, and electoral fraud characterized his administration. The new government exiled the former dictator to the United States, but in 1963 extradited him and tried him for corruption during his administration. Convicted in a five-year trial during which he was imprisoned, he was once more exiled; he lived in Spain the rest of his life.

Supporters in 1968 organized a political party supporting him. Although he won election as a senator from Caracas, his absence from the country led to his disqualification. His continued popularity, especially in Caracas, led to speculation that he might be a candidate in the 1973 presidential election until a constitutional amendment barred all ex-officeholders who had been convicted of felonies related to their tenure in office from running for any government post. Despite the unfavorable memories much of Venezuela had of his time in office, in 1999 newly elected president Hugo Chávez invited him to attend his inauguration ceremonies. Pérez died on September 20, 2001, in Madrid.

See also **Venezuela: Venezuela since 1830.**

BIBLIOGRAPHY

Tad Szulc, *The Twilight of the Tyrants* (1959).

Judith Ewell, *Indictment of a Dictator: Extradition and Trial of Marcos Pérez Jiménez* (1981).

Antonio Pérez Vivas, *Hegemonía andina (historia) y Pérez Jiménez* (1987).

Carlos Capriles Ayala, *Pérez Jiménez y su tiempo: Biografía del ex-presidente y radiografía de Venezuela en algunas etapas estelares de su historia*, 3d ed. (1988).

Guido Acuña, *Pérez Jiménez, un gendarme innecesario: Libro testimonial de la resistencia, 1948–1958* (1989).

Ocarina Castillo, *Los años del buldozer: Ideología y política, 1948–1958* (1990).

Additional Bibliography

Hernández, Carlos Raúl, and Luis Emilio Rondón. *La democracia traicionada: Grandeza y miseria del Pacto de Punto Fijo (Venezuela 1958–2003)*. Caracas, Venezuela: Rayuela, Taller de Ediciones, 2005.

Neira Fernández, Enrique. *Venezuela: Iva y Va repúblicas (1958–2006)*. Mérida, Venezuela: Publicaciones Vicerrectorado Académico; CDCHT, 2006.

Portillo, Gustavo. *La crisis en tiempo de democracia: 1958–1960 y 1983*. Caracas, Venezuela: Universidad Central de Venezuela, Consejo de Desarrollo Científico y Humanístico, 1998.

RALPH LEE WOODWARD JR.

PÉREZ MASCAYANO, JOSÉ JOAQUÍN (1801–1889).

José Joaquín Pérez Mascayano (*b.* 6 May 1801; *d.* 1 June 1889), president of Chile (1861–1871). Pérez's early manhood was spent largely abroad, in Chile's diplomatic missions in the United States, France, and Argentina. A member of the Chamber of Deputies from 1836 to 1852 and then the Senate (1852–1861 and 1873–1882), Pérez also served as minister of finance (1845–1846) and of the interior (1849–1850). Although he supported the Manuel Montt administration (1851–1861) for its whole duration, his own temperament was averse to Montt's authoritarianism. In 1861, when public opinion fiercely rejected the presidential candidacy of Antonio Varas, Pérez emerged as a suitably conciliatory figure to succeed Montt.

Pérez's presidency marked a genuine turning point in Chilean affairs. His own tolerant, patrician style did much to foster a new, more liberal atmosphere after the upheavals of the 1850s. In July 1862, abandoning Montt's National Party, Pérez invited into the cabinet the opposition Liberal-Conservative Fusion, which supported him for the remainder of his two presidential terms.

Pérez has never been well regarded by the admirers of strong government. Yet a persuasive case can be made for seeing him as *the* vitally important nineteenth-century president, the one head of state who truly consolidated the Chilean "idiosyncrasy" of civilized politics.

See also **Chile, Political Parties: Liberal-Conservative Fusion (Liberal-Conservadora); Chile, Political Parties: National Party.**

BIBLIOGRAPHY

Additional Bibliography

Caistor, Nick. *Chile in Focus: A Guide to the People, Politics, and Culture.* Northampton, MA: Interlink Books, 2002.

Calderón Ruiz de Gamboa, Carlos. *Gobernantes de Chile: De Pedro de Valdivia a Eduardo Frei Ruiz-Tagle.* Santiago de Chile, 1995.

Perera, Victor. *Unfinished Conquest: The Guatemalan Tragedy.* Berkeley: University of California Press, 1993.

SIMON COLLIER

PÉREZ PRADO, DÁMASO (1916–1989).

Dámaso Pérez Prado was one of the great popularizers of the mambo in the 1940s and 1950s. Born in Matanzas, Cuba, on December 11, 1916, he moved to Havana in 1942. A pianist, he played with a number of bands including the Orquesta Casino de la Playa. He relocated to Mexico City in 1948 and remained based there for the rest of his career. In a series of recordings he made there for RCA, he became known for a style that was less demanding though not unsophisticated musically, good for dancing, with a heavy emphasis on brass instruments. Rare are the recordings that do not include his trademark, energetic grunts. Future stars such as singer Beny Moré got their start with him. RCA promoted Pérez Prado heavily, particularly after "Mambo Number Five" became a hit in 1950. Other recordings such as "Cherry Pink and Apple Blossom White" crossed over from the Latin audience and made him popular around the world. Although much maligned by critics then and since, his bands had an influence throughout the Americas and in Europe and Africa as well. He died in Mexico City on September 14, 1989.

See also **Mambo; Moré, Beny.**

BIBLIOGRAPHY

Loza, Steven. *Tito Puente and the Making of Latin Music.* Urbana: University of Illinois Press, 1999.

Orovio, Helio. *Cuban Music from A to Z.* Durham, NC: Duke University Press, 2004.

Roberts, John Storm. *The Latin Tinge: The Impact of Latin American Music on the United States,* 2nd edition. New York: Oxford University Press, 1999.

ANDREW J. KIRKENDALL

PÉREZ SALAS, FRANCISCO ANTONIO (1764–1828).

Francisco Antonio Pérez Salas (*b.* 1764; *d.* 10 November 1828), Chilean patriot politician. Pérez was named municipal *procurador* (attorney) in 1801, and was several times a member of the *cabildo* (municipal government) of Santiago in the last years of the colonial period. He was one of the more obdurate creole opponents of the last Spanish governor, Francisco Antonio García Carrasco (1742–1813). In 1810 he became an adviser of the first national junta, and figured thereafter in a number of public roles.

Pérez played his most important political part in 1813, following the departure of José Miguel Carrera (1785–1821) to take command of the patriot forces in the south at the start of the wars of independence. In April 1813 he was appointed a member of a three-man governing junta, and remained so until September of that year, when, much afflicted by the death of his wife, he withdrew. The junta's reforms during this period included the establishment of a new Instituto Nacional (for secondary and higher education) and the National Library. When Carrera seized power again in July 1813, he confined Pérez to San Felipe de Aconcagua.

During the Spanish reconquest of Chile (1814–1817) he was banished to Juan Fernández (an island prison for exiled political prisoners). After the liberation of Chile in 1817, Pérez served as a member of Bernardo O'Higgins's nominated senate (1818–1822).

See also **Chile: The Nineteenth Century.**

BIBLIOGRAPHY

Additional Bibliography

Collier, Simon, and William F. Sater. *A History of Chile, 1808–1994.* Cambridge: Cambridge University Press, 1996.

Stuven, Ana María. *La seducción de un orden: Las elites y la construcción de Chile en las polémicas culturales y políticas del siglo XIX.* Santiago: Ediciones Universidad Católica de Chile, 2000.

                                    SIMON COLLIER

PERI ROSSI, CRISTINA (1941–).
Cristina Peri Rossi (*b.* 12 November 1941), Uruguayan poet and fiction writer. Born in Montevideo, she studied literature at the University of the Republic in Montevideo. Her first book of short stories, *Viviendo* (Living), was published in 1963. The protagonists are marginal and indecisive female characters, immersed in solitude. In this first collection, Peri Rossi's fictional world began to develop. With the publication in 1969 of *Los museos abandonados,* a collection of short stories, and *El libro de mis primos* (The Book of My Cousins), her first novel, both built on an existentialist vision of reality, Peri Rossi began to be acknowledged as one of the most significant writers of her generation. The

writers she recognizes as "mentors" are Uruguayans Juan Carlos Onetti and Felisberto Hernández together with Jorge Luis Borges, Julio Cortázar, Ray Bradbury, and Dino Buzzati. She explores peculiar aspects of human beings who find themselves in ambiguous situations and in the middle of mysterious happenings. Peri Rossi published *Indicios pánicos* (Frightening Signs) in 1970 and, in 1971, her first book of poems, *Evohé: Poemas eróticos.* Two years later, after being expelled from her country for political reasons, she chose Spain as her home.

Further poetic works include *Descripción de un naufragio* (Description of a Wreck, 1975), *Diáspora* (1976), *Lingüística general* (1979), and *Europa después de la lluvia* (Europe After the Rain, 1987). Between 1976 and 1980, Spanish institutions awarded her three important literary awards. She wrote several works of fiction: *La tarde del dinosaurio* (1976), *La rebelión de los niños* (1980), *Cartas de Abelardo y Heloísa* (1982), *El museo de los esfuerzos inútiles* (The Museum of Useless Efforts, 1983), *La nave de los locos* (The Ship of Fools, 1984), often considered her most important work, and *Una pasión prohibida* (1986), *Cosmoagonías* and *Solitario de amor* (1988), *Acerca de la escritura* (About Writing, 1990), *Babel bárbara* (Barbaric Babel, 1991), *Fantasías eróticas* (1991), and *La última noche de Dostoievski* (1992). A prolific writer, Peri Rossi, like other Romantics, finds her themes in nature and also has become a noteworthy subject in feminist and gender studies due to her incorporation of lesbian eroticism and themes of sexual discovery. Her collection of short stories *Por fin solos* (2004) exemplifies these two themes.

See also **Uruguay: The Twentieth Century.**

BIBLIOGRAPHY

Uberto Stabile, *Cristina Peri Rossi* (1984).

Additional Bibliography

Kaminsky, Amy. *Reading the Body Politic.* Minneapolis: University of Minnesota Press, 1993.

McClennen, Sophia. *The Dialects of Exile: Nation, Time, Language, and Space in Hispanic Literatures.* West Lafayette, IN: Purdue University Press, 2004.

Roffé, Reina. "Homoerotismo y literature. Entrevista con Cristina Peri Rossi." *Esp'eculo: Revista de Estudios Literarios* (2004).

                            MAGDALENA GARCÍA PINTO

PERNAMBUCAN REVOLUTION (1817).

Pernambucan Revolution (1817), an unsuccessful rebellion that started in the town of Recife in Brazil's northeastern state (then captaincy) of Pernambuco on 6 March 1817 and spread to the surrounding area. It represented the most critical challenge to Portuguese authority of any of the late-colonial regional uprisings in Brazil. In addition to declaring Brazil's independence and advocating a republican system of government, the rebellion placed strong emphasis on nationalism and individual freedoms as espoused by Enlightenment philosophy.

The rebellion was planned and carried out by native elites (largely planters) who had become increasingly alienated by the restrictions imposed by colonial control of the economy, and who also had studied and discussed alternative forms of governance in the secret societies, such as the Masonic lodges, that had begun to form throughout Brazil in the late eighteenth century. A monopoly on the trade of cotton and vacillating prices for sugar had slashed profits from the two main crops of Pernambuco for large property owners, among whom were many priests. Taxes and duties charged on imports increased their unhappiness. The poor, who would attempt to place their own mark on the unfolding events, had been severely hurt by a major drought in 1816. Composed largely of individuals of African descent, this particular population had experienced the discrimination common to all such groups in slave societies. The elite conspirators of the rebellion, almost all of whom were white, remained wary of the volatility of this group, especially given the incendiary language of freedom that accompanied many discussions of Enlightenment ideals.

Fighting broke out on 6 March, with Recife easily conquered. The next day provisional government was established, with appointments going to the major planners of the movement, such as Domingos José Martins, the priest João Ubaldo Ribeiro, Manuel Correia de Araújo, and José Luis de Mendonça. From the beginning, philosophical differences divided the members of the provisional government. Though they managed to establish contact with the promoters of a similar movement in Paraíba; with sympathizers in Ceará; and with allies in Buenos Aires, the United States, and England; much of the activity that came after the rebellion suffered from disorganization and a lack of a coherent vision. Furthermore, the response from the government in Rio de Janeiro, which came in the form of overland troops and a blockade of the harbor at Recife, meant that the revolutionaries had to turn their full attention to military preparations.

After a series of negotiations in which the king's military emissary, Admiral Rodrigo Lobo, held the upper hand, the revolutionaries abandoned Recife on 19 May. They were soon captured, and the hanging and dismembering of some of the leaders served as a severe warning to those with dreams of launching a similar challenge to colonial control.

See also **Brazil, Independence Movements; Recife.**

BIBLIOGRAPHY

Very little has been written in English about the Pernambucan Revolution, but there is a good, brief account in Emília Viotti Da Costa, "The Political Emancipation of Brazil," in *From Colony to Nation: Essays on the Independence of Brazil*, edited by A. J. R. Russell-Wood (1975), pp. 43–88. Readers of Portuguese may consult Carlos Guilherme Mota, *Nordeste 1817: Estruturas e argumentos* (1972).

Additional Bibliography

Mello, Evaldo Cabral de. *A outra independencia: O federalsimo pernambuco de 1817 a 1824*. São Paulo: Editora 34, 2004.

Mourão, Concalo de Barros Carvalho e Mello. *A revoluçao de 1817 e a historia do Brasil: Um estudo de historia diplomática*. Belo Horizonte, Brazil: Editora Itatiaia Limitada, 1996.

Silva, Alberto Martins da. *Padre João Baptista da Fonseca, 1787–1831: Revolucionário de 1817*. Brasilia: Thesaurus Editora, 2004.

JUDITH L. ALLEN

PERNAMBUCO.

Pernambuco was historically a key state in the vast Northeast region of Brazil, between the São Francisco and Parnaíba rivers, whose relative political weight in the nation steadily declined over the nineteenth and twentieth centuries. The largest Portuguese colony in Brazil in the sixteenth century, and still the third most populous in 1872, by the mid-twentieth century Pernambuco had slipped behind the modernizing southern and central-southern states. With approximately seven million residents, although the seventh-most populous Brazilian state in 1990, Pernambuco was marginal in many respects to the political, economic, and cultural dynamics of the modern nation.

This profile, however, conceals the vital role Pernambuco has played throughout most of Brazil's history. The first Portuguese colony there was established in 1503 at the expense of the indigenous Tupinambá and Potiguar.

Duarte Coelho Pereira and his sixteenth-century successors exterminated the indigenous people, expelled French challengers, and established a plantation society based on African slavery. By the early seventeenth century Pernambuco was Portugal's most prosperous Brazilian colony and the world's leading sugar region. This primacy ended when Dutch annexation of the northwest coast above the São Francisco River between 1630 and 1654 caused many mill owners (*senhores do engenho*) and planters to relocate to other sugar colonies farther south, and when the eventually dislodged Dutch fostered competitive sugar-growing in the Caribbean. Although sugar continued to provide wealth and status to a few, the society entered a long decline into the characteristic poverty that burdens it today.

Pernambuco is marked by an oligarchical social structure and social attitudes engendered by the plantation system. After the abolition of slavery in 1888, the slow modernization of the sugar industry was not paralleled by a reform of social policies and attitudes. Despite modernization, the sugar industry and the economy of the state continued to decline; and as centralized *usinas* (factories) replaced *engenhos*, land was concentrated in fewer hands, jobs became fewer, and the plight of the rural poor steadily worsened.

As society grew more complex, Pernambuco was divided into three distinct geographic-economic-cultural zones, from the humid coastal sugar zone (*zona da mata*) to the transitional *agreste* farther inland, where diversified agriculture in the twentieth century created flourishing new economic and cultural centers, notably the city of Caruaru. Beyond this, the *sertão* (backlands), a semi-arid region of scant rainfall and xerophilous vegetation, stretches over six hundred miles from the scrubby upland hills (*Borborema*) back to the middle São Francisco River—a region of impoverished subsistence farmers and great cattle barons in sharp distinction to and often in competition with planters and exporters on the sugar coast.

Most Pernambucans remain marginal to the cash-crop economy, and despite the importance of the port of Recife, the state capital, until the late twentieth century most were rural peasants. A century-long trend of migration to the cities has slowly changed the urban-rural ratio, a process sharply accelerated beginning in the 1960s. By 1990, urban residents—many of them recent migrants from the hinterland—outnumbered rural peasants three to one. Demographically, economically, and politically Pernambuco focuses closely on the port of Recife, which, with a population of nearly two million, is home to nearly a third of its inhabitants. Thus, as rural misery continued, it was accompanied by daunting problems in the urban center.

Pernambuco's sense of regional and national leadership, and its relative isolation after 1630 from the political center of Brazil, contributed to a history of political separatism and revolt during the Brazilian independence period at the beginning of the eighteenth century and through the weakly centralized Brazilian empire in the first half of the nineteenth. Having earlier lost political jurisdiction over Paraíba, Rio Grande do Norte, and Ceará to the north, Pernambuco lost Alagoas and the lower São Francisco River in the revolt of 1817, further isolating the interior from the political center at Recife. The political and social history of the state has been characterized by struggles between interior and coast and commercial and planter classes, punctuated by violent episodes from the War of the Mascates in 1710 through the Confederation of the Equator (1824), the Praieira (1848–1849), the Quebra-Quilos revolt (1874–1875), and the Peasant Leagues of the twentieth century. The liberal federalistic and regional rhetoric that frequently defines these ruptures masks a continuous and as yet little-understood participation by the destitute and marginal masses in the history of the state.

Since the 1950s Pernambuco has been the site of an important rural land movement. Midcentury mobilizations among sugar workers were repressed by the military government, but rural trade unions regained strength with the democratic opening in the early 1980s. Although agrarian reform in 1985 promised redistribution and titles, hundreds of thousands in the rural Northeast remained landless. Am economic crisis in the 1990s gave birth to the Rural Landless Workers Movement (Movimento do Trabalhadores Rurais Sem Terra, MST), a political movement based on land redistribution and citizenship. The Pernambucan MST builds on a long history of social mobilization that continues into the twenty-first century.

See also **Brazil: 1808-1889; Brazil: Since 1889; Brazil, Organizations: Peasant Leagues.**

BIBLIOGRAPHY

The best overall guide to an understanding of Pernambuco is Manuel Correia De Andrade, *The Land and People of Northeast Brazil,* translated by Dennis V. Johnson (1980). Gilberto Freyre, *The Masters and the Slaves* (1986) and *The Mansions and the Shanties* (1988), are still indispensable for understanding the nature of and transitions in the colonial patriarchal society. James E. Wadsworth, *Agents of Orthodoxy: Honor, Status, and the Inquisition in Colonial Pernambuco, Brazil* (2007) provides a detailed history of the Inquisition and its effects on colonial Pernambucan society. Peter L. Eisenberg, *The Sugar Industry in Pernambuco: Modernization Without Change, 1840–1910* (1974), and Martha Knisely Huggins, *From Slavery to Vagrancy in Brazil: Crime and Social Control in the Third World* (1985), discuss the social effects of incomplete modernization. Robert M. Levine, *Pernambuco in the Brazilian Federation, 1889–1937* (1978), is a perceptive analysis of the twentieth-century political transitions in Pernambuco. The horrifying social effects of Pernambuco's historical development are made clear in Nancy Scheper-Hughes, *Death Without Weeping: The Violence of Everyday Life in Brazil* (1992). The politics of rural mobilizations from the mid-twentieth century through the start of the twenty-first are analyzed in Angus Wright and Wendy Wolford, *To Inherit the Earth: The Landless Movement and the Struggle for a New Brazil* (2003), and in Anthony W. Pereira, *The End of the Peasantry: The Rural Labor Movement in Northeast Brazil, 1961–1988* (1997).

ROGER CUNNIFF

OKEZI TIFFANI OTOVO

PERÓN, JUAN DOMINGO (1895–1974). Juan Perón, president of Argentina (1946–1955, 1973–1974), was born in Lobos, Buenos Aires *provincia*, on October 8, 1895. He entered the Argentine political stage in June 1943, when, as an infantry colonel, he masterminded a successful military coup. Elected by popular vote in 1946, Perón held the Argentine presidency until 1955, when a military coup forced him to leave the country. After living in exile for more than seventeen years, Perón returned to Argentina in 1973, when voters elected him to a third presidential term that was cut short by his death on July 1, 1974. In office Perón espoused a diverse populist ideology that supported the working class and attacked the elite but also undercut civil liberties.

Perón's political base was primarily in the urban lower and working classes, known as the "shirtless ones" (*descamisados*). Perón's populist rhetoric resonated especially well with organized workers. Furthermore, Perón promoted pro-labor policies, such as higher wages and work-rule enforcement. Labor unions had been important political actors since the early twentieth century, but Perón's actions spurred rapid growth in membership. At the same time, Perón eliminated independent union leadership. Under Perón, the General Labor Confederation (Confederación General de Trabajadores; CGT), which was founded in 1930, became the only official union and grew to be 2 million strong. Eventually the GCT became the backbone of the Peronist Party, later known as the Justicialist Party. Conflicts between the Justicialist Party, opposition parties, and the military created political and economic instability in the second half of the twentieth century. More than three decades after Perón's death, his party continues to be a major political factor. The CGT and the party therefore constitute a major part of Perón's legacy to his nation.

Perón's political genius lay in the fact that he was the first important Argentine leader to perceive labor's potential power and to make it his personal political vehicle. He succeeded so thoroughly in capturing the labor movement that he used its mass voting strength to win three presidential elections. Even while he was living in exile, labor's continuing loyalty to him allowed Perón to undermine every Argentine administration and force his opponents to agree to his return to power.

EARLY LIFE AND RISE TO POWER

Despite his appeal to the lower classes, Perón himself came from a bourgeois background. His paternal grandfather had been a prominent Buenos Aires physician, professor, and public servant. His father,

Mario, however, failed to maintain the family's fortune and social position and was forced to accept a position as the manager of a Patagonian sheep ranch. Perón and his older brother, Mario, were born out of wedlock to a young Indian girl, Juana Sosa Toledo, barely past puberty. Although their parents later married, this branch of the family was socially ostracized.

The young Perón's quick intelligence won the sympathy of his widowed grandmother, whose social connections brought him acceptance into an elite polytechnic boarding school and then into the national military academy. He graduated as an infantry second lieutenant in December 1913, at the age of eighteen. Until 1930 he rose slowly through the ranks. Neither as a cadet nor as a young officer did Perón display any exceptional ability. Sports were his one outstanding area, especially boxing and fencing. An appointment as instructor at a noncommissioned officers' training school finally won Perón some recognition. Growing up on a sheep ranch had made him more at home with the lower classes and given him more of a popular touch than was the case with most army officers. That and his ability at sports made him extremely popular with the sergeants. Glowing reports about his success finally earned him, in 1926, a crucial appointment to the Superior War School. He applied himself to his studies and graduated near the top of his class. His reward was an appointment to General Staff Headquarters in 1929.

In 1930, soon after Perón arrived at his new post, he became deeply involved in a plot led by General José F. Uriburu to overthrow the civilian government headed by President Hipólito Irigoyen, but at the last minute he became convinced it would fail and switched his allegiance to a more broadly based movement led by General José Agustín P. Justo. Uriburu struck first, however, and succeeded. Perón was punished with a stint on the Bolivian frontier, but when Justo's faction got the upper hand in 1931 and began edging out Uriburu, Perón was made an instructor at the Superior War School in Buenos Aires. There he developed into a military intellectual, advocating in a number of books, including *Apuntes de historia militar* (1932) and *Las operaciones en 1870* (2 vols., 1935), the need for national military power, a state-regulated economy, and strong leadership.

From 1936 to 1938 Perón served as military attaché in Chile, where he is reputed to have acted as a spy. Shortly after his return to the Superior War School in 1938, his superiors posted him as military attaché to Rome. For the next two years Perón studied Mussolini's Fascist experiment closely and found that it conformed to his own ideas of good government. He also visited Nazi Germany and described it afterward in glowing terms. Upon his return to Argentina, in January 1941, he involved himself in right-wing nationalist plots to prevent the pro-British conservative government from bringing Argentina into World War II on the Allies' side. He formed the United Officers Group (Grupo de Oficiales Unidos; GOU), composed mostly of colonels and majors, which pulled off the successful coup of June 4, 1943, and helped him become the real power within the government.

Working through figurehead presidents, first General Pedro Ramírez and then General Edelmiro Farrell, Perón concentrated power in his own hands. As undersecretary of war he put his own followers into key army positions. As secretary of labor and social welfare he built up the labor union movement, winning higher pay and better benefits for workers. While working in this position, he met Eva Duarte in 1944 and they married a year later. (His first wife, Aurelia Tizón, whom he had married in 1929, died of cancer in 1938.) Duarte, generally called "Evita" by Argentines, worked in film and radio in the 1930s and 1940s. Through her career and her charitable work, Evita, who had grown up in a poor neighborhood of Junín, became extremely popular with the working class and quickly turned into an important political asset for Perón. During this time Perón moved up to become vice president of the republic. In early October 1945, however, envious army rivals joined together to strip him of his office and place him under arrest. But just as Perón's career seemed at an end, his supporters in the labor movement held a huge rally in downtown Buenos Aires, on October 17, that forced the military men to reverse themselves. A triumphant Perón appeared that evening on the balcony of the Presidential Palace to proclaim himself a candidate for the presidency. Free elections held in February 1946 resulted in a smashing victory for him and his supporters. Peronists controlled both houses of Congress, all provincial governorships, and all the provincial legislatures save one.

Crowds cheer Juan Perón, on the third anniversary of his reversal of his military rivals, Buenos Aires, October 1948. Perón's authoritarian rule did not diminish the idealized image of him held by so many in Argentina. © BETTMANN/CORBIS

THE PRESIDENCY, 1946–1955

Though he had been democratically elected, Perón's rule was increasingly authoritarian. The Supreme Court was purged, as were the lower courts. Congressional opponents faced loss of immunity or arrest if they criticized the government or its policies too vigorously. All radio stations were government owned, and opposition newspapers were closed down. It was necessary to belong to the Peronist Party to get a government job or contract. Opposition parties often saw their rallies broken up by storm troopers from the Peronist "National Liberating Alliance." Peron also supported right-wing dictatorships, especially Francisco Franco's regime in Spain. During the 1940s Perón formed a strong relationship with Franco by providing his regime crucial

agricultural products when his government was under a UN diplomatic boycott. When Perón later went into exile, he lived in one of Franco's houses in Spain. In 1949 Perón rewrote the Constitution to permit his election to a second consecutive term. Two years later he won a second term in elections that were marred by widespread fraud and intimidation.

Perón's aim was a corporate state like Mussolini's, and to this end he sought to force every important social and economic group into a state-controlled organization. All workers had to join the CGT; all businessmen and farmers were in the CGE (General Economic Confederation); all professionals, schoolteachers, and intellectuals were forced into the CGP (General Confederation of Professionals); and all university students and professors had to belong to the CGU (General University Confederation).

Economic policy was aimed at self-sufficiency and the redistribution of wealth in labor's favor. Foreign capital was discouraged, and wages rose faster than productivity. An industrialization program was to be financed by a state monopoly over the export of agricultural products. All went well for the first two years, because Argentina emerged from World War II with large currency reserves, but from 1949 on, the economy rapidly deteriorated. Farmers refused to produce at the government's fixed prices, the currency reserves were squandered on buying obsolete foreign properties such as railroads, trade and budget deficits got out of hand, and inflation negated wage increases. The vast network of bureaucratic regulations and restrictions encouraged widespread corruption.

Growing discontent eventually reached even the military, the labor movement, and the Catholic Church, previously supporters of Perón. Revolts in September 1951 and June 1955 reflected unease among officers at attempts to "Peronize" the military, especially the sergeants. Although Perón initially supported labor, as the economic crisis in the 1950s progressed, he increasingly opposed union demands. Consequently even the working class began to question Perón's leadership. Further, rank-and-file workers, who had always had a strong attachment to Evita, were no longer inclined to support him after her death from cancer in 1952 at the age of thirty-three. The church, alarmed at the personality cult growing up around Perón and Evita, fell out of favor in 1954 when it tried to organize Christian Democratic trade unions independent of the CGT. Perón's escalating war with the Catholic hierarchy, climaxing in the burning of several historic churches in June 1955, hurt him further with the military and gave all of his opponents an issue around which to rally. In September 1955 he was ousted by a military coup.

EXILE AND RETURN TO THE PRESIDENCY

For the next seventeen years Perón was an exile, the guest of right-wing governments in Paraguay, Panama, Venezuela, the Dominican Republic, and Spain. Refusing to admit defeat, he gradually built up a network of contacts, set up an underground operation in Argentina, regained control of the

labor movement, and was able to influence the votes of more than a million Argentines. When terrorist movements appeared in the late 1960s, the most important of them, the Montoneros, placed itself under his orders. Prevented from ruling himself, Perón was able to frustrate every government that tried to succeed him, whether civilian or military. While Perón remained the official leader of the party, his coalition was ideologically diverse, reflecting Perón's mixture of both right-wing and left-wing politics. Groups from all over the political spectrum constructed their own idealized versions of Perón in accordance with their particular political philosophy. Consequently, fractious right-wing, left-wing, and moderate factions of Peronism developed during his exile and each recognized Perón as its leader despite drastically different goals. Nevertheless, the Justicialist Party held together and kept pressure on the state. Finally, in 1972, the military agreed to allow Perón to return from exile and to let his party field candidates in elections the following year. In May 1973 the Justicialist candidate, Héctor Campora, became president, but he soon stepped aside for Perón. New elections in September made Perón president for the third time. Initially Perón had widespread support and popularity, but he died ten months later in 1974, just as mounting social and economic problems deeply divided Argentine society.

During his brief third presidency Perón had to deal with the forces of anarchy he had helped to unleash. He reimposed the same corporate state scheme as before, but failed to reverse the runaway inflation and falling production that had already made a shambles of the economy. The young terrorists who helped him to power were disenchanted by his failure to embrace radical socialism, and resumed their violence. Indeed, Perón firmly sided with the right wing of his movement. Perón, for instance, officially expelled the Montoneros in 1974 from the Justicialist Party. Argentines who had waited so long for their leader's return as a panacea realized that the idealistic image of Perón that had developed during his exile did not meet the reality. Following his death, his third wife, Isabel Martínez de Perón (whom he married in 1961), took over as president, but she also could not contain the growing discontent in Argentina.

With violent activity on the rise, the military in 1976 stepped in and took over. Military rule lasted until 1983, yet Peron's party returned to power in 1989 and controlled the presidency until 1999. Despite internal policy disagreements, the Justicialist Party regained the office in 2003 under the leadership of Néstor Kirchner. In 2007, Christina Fernández De Kirchner, the wife of Néstor, won the presidency representing the Peronists, but also reached out to former members of the radical party as well. Consequently, the Peronist Party remains a powerful force in Argentine politics but also a diverse and divided coalition, reflecting Perón's complicated legacy.

See also **Argentina: The Twentieth Century; Argentina, Organizations: General Labor Confederation (CGT); Argentina, Organizations: United Officers Group (GOU); Perón, María Estela Martínez de; Perón, María Eva Duarte de.**

BIBLIOGRAPHY

Robert J. Alexander, *The Perón Era* (1951).

George Blanksten, *Perón's Argentina* (1953).

Juan D. Perón, with Torcuato Luca De Tena, Luis Calvo, and Esteban Peicovich, *Yo, Juan Domingo Perón: Relato autobiográfico* (1976).

Joseph A. Page, *Perón, a Biography* (1983).

Guido DiTella, *Argentina Under Perón, 1973–76* (1983).

Christian Buchrucker, *Nacionalismo y peronismo* (1987).

Robert Crassweller, *Perón and the Enigmas of Argentina* (1987).

Paul H. Lewis, *The Crisis of Argentine Capitalism* (1990).

Additional Bibliography

Altamirano, Carlos. *Peronismo y cultura de izquierda.* Buenos Aires: Temas Grupo Editorial, 2001.

Brennan, James P. *Peronism and Argentina.* Wilmington, DE: SR Books, 1998.

DiTella, Torcuato S. *Perón y los sindicatos: El inicio de una relación conflictiva.* Buenos Aires: Ariel, 2003.

García Sebastiani, Marcela. *Fascismo y antifascismo, peronismo y antiperonismo: Conflictos políticos e ideológicos en la Argentina (1930–1955).* Madrid: Iberoamericana, 2006.

James, Daniel. *Resistance and Integration: Peronism and the Argentine Working Class, 1946–1976.* Cambridge, U.K.: Cambridge University Press, 1988.

PAUL H. LEWIS

PERÓN, MARÍA ESTELA MARTÍNEZ DE (1931–). María Estela Martínez de Perón (Isabel; *b.* 4 February 1931), third wife of General Juan Domingo Perón and president of Argentina (1974–1976) and vice president (1973–1974). Born in La Rioja, María Estela was the youngest of six children born into a middle-class family. In 1934 the family moved to Buenos Aires, where María Estela attended elementary school. In 1951, when she was twenty, she entered the National School of Dance.

Known as Isabel, a name she adopted when she was a professional dancer with a touring nightclub company, she met the exiled Perón in Panama and became his companion/secretary in December 1955. They were married in Spain in November 1961. Since Perón had been forbidden to return to Argentina, she acted as his emissary on three different occasions. After his return on 17 November 1972, he became a candidate for a third term in office. In an attempt to neutralize Peronist factionalism, he selected Isabel as his running mate. They received 62 percent of the vote in the September 1973 presidential election. As violence among his supporters increased, Perón's economic recovery plan fell apart. On 1 July 1974, he died, and Isabel was sworn in, thus becoming the first female head of state in the Americas. Less than two years later, on 24 March 1976, as the country seemed to drift into anarchy, she was deposed by a military coup. Tried and convicted of corruption charges, she was kept under house arrest until 6 July 1981. After her release, she settled once again in Spain.

In January 2007, a federal judge requested the INTERPOL intervene to capture her because of an investigation of the disappearance of a student in February 1976. On January 12, she was arrested in Villanueva de la Cañada. During the verdict, she went against voluntary extradition and therefore, had to go to the Court Office every other week.

See also **Argentina: The Twentieth Century.**

BIBLIOGRAPHY

Joseph A. Page, *Perón: A Biography* (1983).

Robert D. Crassweller, *Perón and the Enigmas of Argentina* (1987).

Additional Bibliography

Gravovsky, Julian. *Bibliografía sobre María Estela Martínez de Perón*. Buenos Aires: S.J.L., 1987.

Laezman, Rick. *100 Hispanic Americans: Who Changed American History*. Milwaukee, WI: World Almanac Library, 2005.

Martínez, Domingo; Pleguezuelo, Alfonso; and Aranda Bernal, Ana María. *Domingo Martínez en la estela de Murillo: Centro Cultural El Monte, Sevilla, Mayo-Junio 2004*. Sevilla: Fundación El Monte, 2004.

Perón, Isabel. *Mensaje a los trabajadores del mundo: La señora vice presidente María Estela Martínez de Perón habla en la 59a. reunión de la O.I.T.* Buenos Aires: Presidencia de la Nación, Secretaría de Prensa y Difusión, 1974.

Sáenz Quesada, María. *Isabel Perón: La Argentina en los años de María Estela Martínez*. Buenos Aires: Grupo Editorial Planeta, 2003.

MARYSA NAVARRO

PERÓN, MARÍA EVA DUARTE DE

(1919–1952). María Eva Duarte de Perón (Evita; *b.* 7 May 1919; *d.* 26 July 1952), Argentine politician and actress and the second wife of President Juan Domingo Perón during his first term in office (1946–1952). Born on an estate near Los Toldos in Buenos Aires Province, Evita, as she was known, was the fifth illegitimate child of Juana Ibarguren and Juan Duarte, a local landowner. After his death, the family moved to Junín, in eastern Argentina, where Evita attended school and dreamed of becoming an actress. At fifteen, she decided to try her luck in Buenos Aires. Success eluded her in the theater and films, but she was very successful as a soap-opera radio actress. Her life changed substantially after January 1944, when she met Colonel Perón, then undersecretary of war and secretary of labor, and soon-to-be-minister of war and vice president. To the consternation and shock of his fellow

Juan and Evita Perón in a Buenos Aires parade celebrating his second presidential term, June 4, 1952.
Affectionately known as Evita, María Eva Duarte de Perón, was both loved and reviled as Argentina's first lady from 1945 until her death in 1952. She campaigned for women's suffrage and her charity programs won her significant support from the poor and working classes. © BETTMANN/CORBIS

officers and Buenos Aires's sociopolitical elite, not only did Perón and Evita become lovers, but, contrary to accepted norms, they began to live together.

The transformation of the dark-haired young starlet into the elegant, blond, and fiery Evita, the charismatic leader of the *descamisados* (shirtless ones), was a gradual process that began after the 17 October 1945 crisis. On that day, thousands of workers went on strike to demand the release of Perón, who had been forced to resign from his three posts and was imprisoned. Although Peronist and anti-Peronist mythology credits Evita with a leading role in the workers' demonstration, she only tried to obtain a writ of habeas corpus for Perón's release. However, he wrote to her from jail and promised to marry her.

Shortly after their 21 October 1945 wedding, Perón began his campaign for the presidency. In a society where women could not vote and first ladies remained in the background, Evita sat in on strategy meetings and accompanied Perón on his tours of the provinces. After his inauguration, her interest in politics and her influence increased as she began to meet daily with union leaders and represented Perón at numerous functions. Invited by General Francisco Franco to visit Spain in an official capacity, she toured Spain, France, and Italy as if she were a glamorous movie star.

By 1948, Evita was clearly established as an influential member of Perón's government. Until her death, she played a crucial, though informal, role within the Peronist structure. Her only attempt to formalize her activities and become a vice presidential candidate in the 1951 elections generated too much opposition from the military. Officially, she was only Argentina's first lady, but, together with Perón, she was the leader of the *descamisados,* his liaison with organized labor, and his most effective publicist. She was also president of the Eva Perón Foundation, a wealthy social-welfare organization whose funds she used to build hospitals, low-income housing, schools, and youth hotels and to buy thousands of goods that she distributed to the needy. Finally, while her participation in the campaign to obtain women's suffrage was limited, she was instrumental in the massive incorporation of women into the political process and the organization of the women's branch of the Peronist Party. She presided over the party with a firm hand, and though she was already very sick when Perón ran for a second term, he was elected with an overwhelming female vote.

Evita's death transformed her into a powerful myth, but it also shook the stability of the Peronist structure at a time when Perón's economic policies strained the support of the *descamisados.* In September 1955 he was deposed by a military coup and forced into exile. Evita's myth became essential to the survival of Peronism during the following eighteen years and to Perón's own reelection in 1973.

See also **Argentina: The Twentieth Century; Perón, Juan Domingo.**

BIBLIOGRAPHY

Julie Taylor, *Evita: The Myths of a Woman* (1979).

Nicholas Fraser and Marysa Navarro, *Eva Perón* (1980).

Marysa Navarro, *Evita* (1981).

Additional Bibliography

Dujovne Ortiz, Alicia, and Shawn Fields. *Eva Perón.* New York: St. Martin's Press, 1996.

Navarro, Marysa. *Evita: Mitos y representaciones.* México, D.F.: Fondo de Cultura Económica, 2002.

Savigliano, Marta Elena. "Evita: The Globalization of a National Myth." *Latin American Perspectives* 24:6 (November 1997): 156–172.

MARYSA NAVARRO

PERONISM. *See* **Argentina, Political Parties: Justicialist Party.**

PERONIST PARTY. *See* **Argentina, Political Parties: Justicialist Party.**

PERRICHOLI, LA (1739–1819). La Perricholi (Micaela Villegas, Miqueta; *b.* 1739; *d.* 17 May 1819), actress. Immortalized in legend, opera, and film, and reputed for her great beauty, La Perricholi was born in Peru and began her career on the Lima stage in 1760 as a comic actress. The next year she caught the attention of the newly arrived viceroy,

Manuel de Amat y Junient, then over sixty, who brought her to court and provided her with a palatial residence on the Lima Alameda. In 1773, however, they had a falling out. One story is that La Perricholi accepted an offer from a Lima theater manager to return to the stage, but when he criticized her for not learning her lines properly, she stabbed him in a violent rage, scandalizing residents of Lima and forcing Amat to break with her. Another version is that she appeared at the ceremony inducting the viceroy into Charles III's Order of San Jénaro in a golden coach that was exclusively reserved for titled nobility, creating an outcry that forced Amat to give her up. In 1775, however, a year before the viceroy left his post, they reconciled. According to legend, La Perricholi went through a religious change about this time, spending most of the rest of her life until her death dispensing alms and assisting the Carmelites.

Versions of her life story constitute the basis of Jacques Offenbach's opera *La Périchole* and Jean Renoir's film *The Golden Coach*.

See also **Theater.**

BIBLIOGRAPHY

Manuel De Mendiburu, ed., *Apéndice al diccionario histórico-biográfico del Perú*, vol. 4 (1938), pp. 488–494.

Ricardo Palma, *Tradiciones peruanas completas* (1961), pp. 616–620.

Additional Bibliography

Bacacorzo, Gustavo. *La Perricholi: Da. Micaela Villegas: Nulidad y reposición históricas*. Lima: G. Herrera Editores, 1994.

Moraña, Mabel. *Mujer y cultura en la colonia hispanoamerican*. Pittsburgh: Instituto Internacional de Literatura Iberoamericana, University of Pittsburgh, 1996.

JOHN JAY TEPASKE

PERSHING EXPEDITION.

Pershing Expedition U.S. military incursion into Mexico (1916–1917). During the civil war between General Francisco ("Pancho") Villa and First Chief General Venustiano Carranza for control of the Mexican Revolution, Villa sought to draw the United States into the conflict when his defeat became apparent. On 9 March 1916 a force of Villistas crossed the border and raided Columbus, New Mexico, sacking the town and killing a number of U.S. citizens.

The U.S. government dispatched Brigadier General John J. Pershing on an expedition into northern Mexico with a force of 6,600 men to seek out Villa. But operating in a hostile country against an elusive figure who knew the local terrain thoroughly proved difficult, and the army searched in vain despite moving more than 300 miles into Mexico. Reinforcements raising the force to 12,000 men were of little help and inspired strengthened protests from the Carranza government.

Pershing remained in Mexico long after it became clear that he would not find Villa, since the United States did not wish to withdraw the force. On 12 April 1916 a clash with Carrancista forces at Parral raised the possibility of war between the two nations. When Mexico proved unable to control the border and further raids occurred, President Woodrow Wilson mobilized the National Guard, concentrating over one hundred thousand troops on the frontier. At length, the United States realized the futility of the expedition, and Pershing withdrew from Mexico in February 1917.

See also **Villa, Francisco "Pancho."**

BIBLIOGRAPHY

Clarence C. Clendenen, *The United States and Pancho Villa* (1961), and *Blood on the Border* (1969).

Linda B. Hall and Don M. Coerver, *Revolution on the Border: The United States and Mexico, 1910–1920* (1988).

Additional Bibliography

Katz, Friedrich. *The Life and Times of Pancho Villa*. Stanford, CA: Stanford University Press, 1998.

Vanderwood, Paul J., Frank N Samponaro, and Ma Elisa Moreno C. *Los rostros de la batalla: Furia en la frontera México-Estados Unidos, 1910–1917*. México, D.F.: Consejo Nacional para la Cultura y las Artes: Grijalbo, 1993.

Welsome, Eileen. *The General and the Jaguar: Pershing's Hunt for Pancho Villa: A True Story of Revolution and Revenge*. New York: Little, Brown and Co., 2006.

KENNETH J. GRIEB

PERU

This entry includes the following articles:
FROM THE CONQUEST THROUGH INDEPENDENCE
PERU SINCE INDEPENDENCE

FROM THE CONQUEST THROUGH INDEPENDENCE

In November 1532 Atahualpa Inca, victorious in a civil war against his half-brother Huascar, was encamped with his army outside Cajamarca. Drawing his chief support from Quito and the northern part of the Tahuantinsuyu (Inca Empire), Atahualpa was triumphant and confident. He saw little danger in the group of strangers who had trekked inland from Túmbez to Cajamarca. He did not anticipate the cunning and brutality of Francisco Pizarro's Spaniards nor the military advantages of their weapons and horses. Accepting Pizarro's invitation to meet in Cajamarca, the Inca perhaps intended to take the 168 invaders captive. Instead, Pizarro launched the conquest of Peru.

THE CONQUEST, 1532–1538

Accompanied by several thousand warriors armed only with ceremonial weapons, Atahualpa entered the walls of Cajamarca late on the afternoon of 16 November. His anxious men hidden in rooms surrounding the central plaza, Pizarro sent out Friar Vicente de Valverde with an interpreter to require the Incas' submission to Spain and Christianity. After Atahualpa haughtily rejected the friar's presumption, Pizarro and his men stormed into the plaza. The Spaniards massacred many of Atahualpa's entourage, toppled the emperor from his litter, and took him captive. By seizing the god-ruler of the Tahuantinsuyu, Pizarro was consciously following the strategy of Hernán Cortés in capturing Motecuhzoma I and

Painting depicting a Spanish conquerer (perhaps Pizarro) seizing Atahualpa, the last emperor of the Inca, amid a battle of their forces in the 16th century at Cajamarca, Peru. Spanish conquest of Peru was made through manipulating alliances, deceit, and subjugating Incan rulers to their authority. European control remained precarious in ensuing decades, disrupted by native attacks and uprisings. HISTORICAL PICTURES ARCHIVES/CORBIS

ruling the Aztecs through him during the conquest of Mexico.

Aided by divisions among the Andean peoples, the Spaniards spread their grasp to other parts of the Tahuantinsuyu during the following months. Atahualpa attempted to ransom himself with a fabulous treasure of gold and silver artifacts, which the invaders melted down and distributed among themselves, careful to reserve the royal fifth for the king. Pizarro's partner, Diego de Almagro, arrived with 150 or more reinforcements, but Pizarro refused to grant them a share in the spoils. Between January and June, Pizarro dispatched scouts to Pachacamac, the great religious center near modern-day Lima, and to Cuzco, the Inca capital. Fearing the Spaniards might depose him in favor of Huascar, Atahualpa secretly ordered his followers to execute his captive rival. Meanwhile, the Huascar faction looked to the Spaniards as liberators who might rid them of subjugation by Atahualpa's conquering armies. On 26 July 1533, the Spanish executed Atahualpa Inca to remove him as a possible focus of resistance. A few days later they began to move southward toward Cuzco, which Pizarro's main force entered on 15 November 1533. In December they installed a puppet ruler from the Huascar faction, Manco Inca, who seemed anxious to cooperate.

The Spaniards quickly moved to exploit their conquest, and a hybrid Hispano-indigenous society developed. Conquistadores took wives and mistresses from the Inca nobility. From these unions began to emerge the mestizo population of the realm. *Yanaconas* (artisans and servants tied to the indigenous state or aristocracy) became bound instead to individual Spaniards. *Kurakas* (provincial chieftains) sought independence from Inca rule by allying themselves with the Spaniards. During these years, the invaders also founded Spanish cities, laid out in a grid pattern where possible and governed by a *cabildo* (council). Pizarro already had established San Miguel de Piura (1532) when he entered the Tahuantinsuyu. In mid-1534 the Spanish formally established Jauja. On 23 March 1534, Pizarro created the Spanish municipality of Cuzco. Convinced that efficient government required a coastal city to facilitate communications between Cuzco and Panama, Pizarro founded Lima, or the City of the Kings, in January 1535. Its port of Callao soon began to develop.

Nonetheless, Spanish occupation of Cuzco did not bring tranquility. The Quitan faction associated with Atahualpa remained bellicose. Once Manco Inca understood that the Spaniards were exploiters rather than allies, he secretly gathered a huge army of up to 200,000 to lay siege to Cuzco. In May 1536 they attacked, nearly overrunning the 190 Spaniards in the city. Only desperate resistance, the withdrawal of the Andeans for harvest, and the arrival of reinforcements from Lima and Panama relieved the ten-month siege. Manco and some of his forces withdrew to the mountains of Vilcabamba, where they established a neo-Inca state. Meanwhile, a disgruntled Almagro, who had gone off to explore Chile, returned with his expedition and in 1537 seized Cuzco. At the battle of Las Salinas on 26 April 1538, Pizarro's forces defeated Almagro and then tried and executed him in July. Pizarro had conquered Peru, but as royal governor his control of the Andes was insecure.

CIVIL WAR AND REBELLION, 1541–1554

As the first Spanish governor of New Castile (as Peru was also known in the early years), Pizarro had neither the vision nor the ability to establish peace and prosperity, and the realm devolved into brutality and civil strife. Pizarro awarded *encomiendas* (grants of Indian tribute) to his followers, but even had he desired to, he lacked the energy to control their treatment of the Amerindians. Abuses mounted. The Spaniards pillaged shrines, burial sites, and storehouses. They slaughtered llama herds for meat and conscripted thousands of Andeans as porters for little or no pay. Nor did they maintain the infrastructure of the Tahuantinsuyu. Irrigation canals and agricultural terraces fell into disrepair. From their stronghold around Cuzco, Almagro's partisans bitterly plotted to avenge the death of their leader. On 26 July 1541 they assassinated Francisco Pizarro, provoking open hostilities between the two factions. In Vilcabamba, Manco Inca offered refuge to the assassins. As a reward for his hospitality, they treacherously murdered him in 1544 in a futile attempt to curry favor with the crown.

In May 1544 Blasco Núñez Vela, sent by Charles I of Spain to rule as the first viceroy of Peru, arrived in Lima. He established an *audiencia* (high court) to help him enforce the New Laws of 1542, which outlawed almost all indigenous slavery and attacked the *encomienda* system. Spaniards who held such grants could retain them but could not pass them to their heirs. All who had fought in the recent war between Pizarro and Almagro were to forfeit their *encomiendas*. This ruling affected almost all the Peruvian *encomenderos*. Oblivious to the dangers of the situation, Núñez Vela demanded complete obedience, and the *encomenderos* rebelled, led by Gonzalo Pizarro, a member of the Pizarro clan. Abetted by the *audiencia*, the rebels expelled the viceroy from Lima in October 1544 and in January 1546 defeated and killed him at the battle of Añaquito. In control of Peru and Panama, Gonzalo and the rebels could not bring themselves to declare Peru independent of the monarchy. When Pedro de la Gasca arrived in 1547 as president of the *audiencia*, he shrewdly won over many of Gonzalo's supporters with conciliatory promises. Near Cuzco on 9 April 1548, Gasca's royal forces defeated Gonzalo's depleted ranks, and the principal rebels were quickly tried and punished. Some, including Gonzalo, were executed; others were flogged or exiled. Gasca's victory brought temporary respite to the war-ravaged land.

One last rebellion convulsed the colony before the crown brought Spanish Peru under control. Angered when the government prohibited the Spaniards from demanding personal service or forced labor of the Indians, Francisco Hernández Girón led a revolt in November 1553 that lasted for nearly a year before royalist forces defeated and executed him. Vilcabamba still held out as an independent Inca state, although many Inca nobles resided in Cuzco, opting to collaborate with the Spaniards.

CONSOLIDATION OF ROYAL CONTROL AND THE TOLEDAN REFORMS, 1555–1581

With the appointment of the viceroy and the establishment of the *audiencia*, Charles I had prepared the foundations for colonial rule. Peru constituted the core of the viceroyalty, but the viceroy's jurisdiction included the realms of Chile and Charcas (with the Río de la Plata) to the south and Quito, Panama, and New Granada (modern Colombia) to the north. Distance and slow communications made it impossible for the viceroy in Lima to govern the outlying territories effectively. Between 1545 and 1570, the crown created *audiencias* in Bogotá, Quito, Charcas, and Concepción (Chile), although the latter survived only a short time. Settlement of additional territory brought the creation of new provinces (generally called *corregimientos*) and appointment of provincial governors (usually *corregidores*). Branches (*cajas reales*) of the royal treasury opened in the more important cities to collect the crown's revenues.

Spain's economic interest in the colony centered on silver mining. In 1545 Indians revealed to the Spaniards the location of the great silver deposits of Potosí in modern-day Bolivia. So many Spaniards and Indians flocked to Potosí that the settlement of other regions of Peru was slowed down. Mining boomed with the use of indigenous smelting technology. By the 1570s, however, Spanish mine owners were using amalgamation, a process requiring mercury, to refine much of their ore. Mercury came from Huancavelica, southeast of Lima, a source that the Anagaraes people had disclosed to Amador de Cabrera in 1563. The capital requirements of the new process, plus the need for mercury, eliminated most native Andean silver producers.

Christianization of Peru proceeded fitfully. Missionary friars arrived soon after the Conquest, but the civil wars hindered evangelization. In 1546 Lima became the seat of an archdiocese with responsibility for overseeing almost all of Andean South America. In 1570 the Inquisition opened its doors in Lima. One manifestation of growing indigenous resistance to the Spaniards and Catholicism was the emergence of Taki Onqoy, the "dancing disease." It flourished from Lake Titicaca to Huamanga among indigenous converts to Catholicism, who renounced Christianity and were possessed by uncontrollable fits of dancing and shaking. Adherents to Taki Onqoy claimed the *huacas* (deities and other objects of veneration) were angry because the people no longer sacrificed to them. They would rise to drive the Spaniards and their religion out of Peru through floods and plagues of worms. Andeans must abandon Christianity and return to the old gods. The Spaniards discovered the resistance in 1564 and quickly moved to eradicate it. But many clung tenaciously to the old ways.

No individual shaped the colony more than Viceroy Francisco de Toledo y Figueroa (1569–1581), who formally established many policies and institutions that regulated Peruvian life until independence. In particular, Toledo defined the relationship between the Spaniards and the people they conquered. Determined to eliminate the threat and attraction of Vilcabamba, he captured the Inca Túpac Amaru in 1572 and beheaded him in Cuzco. In a propaganda campaign against the Inca state, Toledo commissioned *informaciones* (a series of reports) that stressed the warlike and oppressive character of the Tahuantinsuyu. He personally visited much of the viceroyalty and ordered a census of the indigenous population, in precipitous decline from abuse, war, migration, and Old World diseases. He then undertook a massive resettlement campaign to consolidate Amerindian villages. These *reducciones* (reductions) promoted more effective government supervision of Spanish-Indian relations, facilitated the work of Catholic missionaries, and organized indigenous society for more effective exploitation by the colonial economy. Upon the reductions Toledo imposed tribute assessments, to be collected by *corregidores* rather than *encomenderos,* and established the colonial Mita, a system of rotating forced indigenous labor.

While Toledo's initiatives sought to protect the Andeans from unbridled abuse, his legislation made the viceregal government a partner in the economic exploitation of the native population. For example, the crown was the chief beneficiary of tribute monies. To pay their assessments, conquered peoples often had to work for Spaniards, and tribute thus forced them into the colonial labor market. Anxious both to stimulate and to regulate the flood of silver flowing from Potosí's mines, Toledo expropriated the Huancavelica mines, establishing a crown monopoly over the distribution and sale of the mercury needed to amalgamate silver ores. He also granted the Huancavelica mine operators a *mita* of low-wage, forced labor to produce the mercury, just as he established a *mita* at Potosí. By the time Toledo left Peru in 1581, he had created the legal structures that governed social and economic life well into the eighteenth century.

Toledo left what seemed to Spanish eyes a stable and prosperous viceroyalty, blessed with mineral riches. Although it lay in Upper Peru (modern Bolivia), Potosí was the economic motor that drove much of the viceregal economy. Its official annual production rose from 1 million troy ounces of silver in the early 1570s to more than 5 million during the following decade. No one knows how much silver escaped registration and taxation. At the time, the most important mining district in Lower Peru was Castrovirreina, discovered in 1555. The silver permitted Peru to purchase imported merchandise, and

it monetized the viceregal economy. A royal mint operated irregularly in Lima from 1568 to 1590 and then reopened in 1683. Prior to the latter year, most Peruvian coins came from the Potosí mint, established in 1572.

Other sectors of the domestic economy also adapted to the Spanish presence. Agriculture evolved to meet the conquerors' tastes. While continuing to produce such indigenous staples as maize, potatoes, quinoa, and chile peppers, farmers also cultivated European crops, especially wheat. Vineyards planted near Arequipa, Ica, and Pisco yielded the wine crucial to Catholic ritual and Spanish palates. Coastal plantations produced sugar and olive oil. On the eastern slopes of the mountains, the Andeans continued to harvest coca leaves, chewed by the indigenous population for their narcotic effect, which suppressed hunger and made work tolerable at high altitudes. Seeing profits in coca leaves, Spaniards began to take over the trade. European horses, cattle, pigs, and fowl added diversity to Andean livestock. During the Conquest, Spaniards had used llamas and Amerindians to transport goods. Mules from Tucumán soon dominated transportation because they could carry heavier cargoes.

Peruvian prosperity rested precariously on massive exploitation of indigenous labor, but Peru was in the midst of a precipitous demographic decline. Before contact with Old World diseases, the indigenous population of Peru numbered perhaps as high as 9 million. Even before Pizarro arrived, smallpox had spread from the Caribbean down into the Andes and killed, among others, Huayna Capac, the last great Inca ruler. With no biological immunities to such killers as smallpox, measles, and influenza, millions died. The abuse, malnutrition, and psychological devastation accompanying the Conquest contributed to the impact of such diseases. By 1570 the native population had fallen to 1.3 million. Fifty years later it was only 600,000. Mortality was highest in coastal areas. The indigenous population received another catastrophic blow in the great epidemics of 1717–1720 and then experienced long-term growth. Meanwhile, the number of Spaniards, mestizos, blacks, and mulattoes increased, and competition for indigenous labor intensified.

THE MATURE COLONY AND ITS DECLINE, 1581–1700

For forty or fifty years after Toledo, Peru reigned supreme as the jewel of Spain's American empire,

Peruvian goldsmiths, black and white photo of an engraving from *Americae Tertia Pars VI* by Theodore de Bry (1528–1598). BIBLIOTHEQUE NATIONALE, PARIS, FRANCE/ GIRAUDON/ THE BRIDGEMAN ART LIBRARY

largely due to the riches flowing out of Potosí. Official silver output there peaked in the 1590s at nearly 6.5 million ounces per year. Thereafter, Potosí experienced a gradual decline until registered production was sometimes less than a million ounces per year in the 1710s. Contraband output may have been substantial at times, and large amounts of silver were undoubtedly lost to smuggling via the Río de la Plata or the Pacific coast around Arica. Even so, the wealth of Potosí flowed toward Lima to enrich the government, the church, and entrepreneurs in Peru. A bustling small-scale market of women vendors provided the city with food and supplies. Well into the seventeenth

century, Peru happily depended on Potosí as the motor for its economic life.

Yet Peru's colonial economy developed beyond a simple dependence on silver mining. By the seventeenth century, the vineyards, sugar plantations, and olive groves planted earlier had matured to lend prosperity in some regions. Acquisition of African slaves partially compensated for the decline in indigenous labor in the coastal valleys. Arequipa and Moquegua sold wine to Cuzco, La Paz, and Potosí. The vintners of Nazca and Ica trafficked with Lima and northern Peru. Sugar from Lambayeque found ready customers throughout the viceroyalty. The output of Peruvian *obrajes* (textile workshops) made the colony less dependent on Europe for cloth, although only Quito offered much of a challenge to the higher grades of overseas fabrics. Artisans organized themselves into guilds in the major cities and produced many consumer goods. Around 1600, in fact, Peru's general prosperity led a friar to remark: "All Peru lacks is silk and linens, for they have a surplus of everything else" (Fray Martín de Murua, *Historia general del Perú* [1986], p. 46).

In the late sixteenth century, Creole culture began to flourish in Peru, influenced by its Andean ambience but consciously imitating Spanish standards. Indigenous painters adorned the walls of churches and mansions with religious and mythological themes. The Cuzco School of artists gained fame for its depiction of Renaissance and sacred subjects. El Inca Garcilaso de la Vega, a mestizo son of a conquistador and an Andean princess, employed Renaissance literary techniques to write about the history of his mother's people in *Royal Commentaries* (1609, 1617). In an exotic blend of Spanish, Quechua, and Aymara, Felipe Guamán Poma De Ayala wrote a long letter to the king, *Primer nueva corónica y bueno gobierno* (1936), containing 400 illustrations and a treasure of ethnographic detail. A royal decree of 1551 established the University of San Marcos in Lima, although its doors did not effectively open until the 1570s. Religious orders founded colleges and seminaries in several of the principal cities. While some Peruvians attended Spanish universities, many studied in these Andean schools. Archbishop Toribio de Mogrovejo reformed the Peruvian church and displayed a pastoral zeal rarely seen within the clergy prior to his arrival in 1581. He was later sainted for his efforts, as were Saint Rosa De Lima, a mystical nun, and Saint Martín de Porres, a mulatto whose charitable service won wide respect among Lima's lower classes. Spanish, Creole, and elite indigenous families sought to place their daughters into convents, which also provided a source of borrowed capital throughout society.

Silver enabled Peru to import goods from Europe and, to a lesser extent, from the Far East. Imperial commercial policies provided security for shipping and ensured government fiscal control rather than promoting market mechanisms. In theory an annual fleet (the Galeones) carried merchandise from Spain to Nombre de Dios and later to Portobelo in Panama. There Peruvian merchant houses purchased goods that were then carried overland to the Pacific and embarked on the Armada del Sur (South Seas Fleet). Lima served as the distribution point for most of the viceroyalty. From 1609 the crown generally prohibited trade between Mexico and Peru. Responding in 1613 to petitions from the merchants of Lima, the crown created the *consulado* (merchant guild), thereby sanctioning the virtual monopoly that Lima enjoyed in overseas trade.

Ironically, the Lima *consulado* solidified its control just as the volume of overseas trade started to decline. The tide of imports peaked in the 1630s and then gradually abated. This downturn reflected the flagging output of the silver industry, Spain's own economic and maritime difficulties, and probably the increasing maturity of the Peruvian economy, which had become less dependent on European suppliers for some goods. By the mid-seventeenth century, Spain frequently failed to dispatch the annual fleet to Panama and thus left the Peruvian market unsupplied. Around 1700, several years sometimes passed between fleets, creating great fluctuations in the availability of goods and in prices.

Despite these problems, Peru's reputation for fabulous wealth attracted foreign interlopers. Some were content to trade illegally along the coast, marketing cloth and other goods for silver. To some extent they compensated for Spain's failure to meet Peruvian demand. Of graver concern were those who marauded Peruvian waters, attacking Spanish shipping and occasionally sacking coastal towns. Francis Drake, the most famous of these, plundered the Pacific coast in 1578. Other pirates also ravaged Peru. In the early seventeenth century they were Dutch—later, English and French. To combat the attacks, coastal cities built fortifications, the most imposing of which were at Callao, Lima's port. The government also funded naval forces to combat the marauders at sea. Nonetheless, shipping was sometimes precarious. In the 1680s piracy forced Peru to stop shipping mercury from Huancavelica by sea to Arica and then carrying it inland on mules to Potosí and Oruro and bringing back the royal treasure along the same route. Thereafter, such shipments traveled overland.

As the seventeenth century drew to a close, Spanish Peru faced other crises. Some were geographical. In 1687 a great earthquake devastated central Peru, leaving Lima and Callao in ruins. Such disasters were not rare in the seismically active Andes: Arequipa suffered major tremors, sometimes in conjunction with volcanic eruptions, in 1582, 1600, and 1604. But in addition to the destruction of fortifications, buildings, and human life in Lima and Callao, the 1687 earthquake demolished much of the intricate irrigation systems that watered farmlands around the capital. The ensuing agricultural crisis left Lima dependent on other regions for foodstuffs, especially Chilean wheat.

Labor shortages also afflicted the realm, particularly in provinces subject to the *mitas* of Potosí and Huancavelica. Mining interests complained that the state failed to provide the requisite number of *mita* workers and that *corregidores, kurakas,* and priests interfered out of self-interest with fulfillment of the quotas. Critics of the *mita* alleged that those provinces had experienced serious demographic decline from mortality at the mines or emigration to avoid *mita* service. Melchor de Navarra y Rocaful, duque de la Palata, who was viceroy in 1681–1689, made the last great effort to

reinvigorate the Toledan system. He ordered that a new census of the viceroyalty be conducted on 1 October 1683. It registered more than enough Indians to fill the labor drafts, but many complained the enumeration had artificially inflated the totals. The duke's successor, Melchor Portocarrero, conde de Moncolva, reversed most of Palata's initiative.

From an imperial perspective, Peru presented an increasing challenge. The viceroyalty's registered silver production for 1691–1700 was 42.5 million pesos, slightly more than half of what it had been at its height in 1631–1640. Yet the viceregal fiscal system depended heavily on revenues from mining taxes. Peruvian elites had successfully resisted attempts to broaden the fiscal base and tax their wealth on a permanent basis. After 1660 the Peruvian treasury was no longer able both to meet bureaucratic and military expenses in South America and to remit sizable quantities of revenue to Spain. Until mid-century the Lima treasury, acting as clearinghouse for the viceroyalty, remitted

Ruins of Sacsahuamán fortress overlooking Cuzco, Peru, early 20th century. Andean beliefs and traditions survived and adapted despite Spanish cultural imposition. THE LIBRARY OF CONGRESS

from a third to nearly half of all its income to Spain. For the final thirty years of the century, the average was only 4 percent. By 1700 the viceregal government was badly indebted, encumbered by financial commitments it had no realistic hope of paying.

Spanish control over Peru had weakened. On the negative side, most public officials, including judges on the *audiencia, corregidores,* treasury officials, and members of *cabildos* purchased their offices from the crown. Many officials engaged in venal practices, showing greater devotion to self-interest than to royal justice. The *corregidores* embezzled tribute monies and used the *reparto* to force the colonized people to purchase costly and unwanted merchandise. Provincial treasury officials often failed to send annual reports to the Tribunal of Accounts, and the fleet system sailed so infrequently that officials in Madrid waited years to learn about conditions in Peru. But for the creoles, this debility had a positive side. Spanish control was so weak that they enjoyed more freedom of action than earlier. Spain's inability to enforce its commercial regulations allowed more room for entrepreneurship. Peru, while still a colony, largely avoided Spanish domination in the late 1600s.

IMPOSITION OF THE NEW COLONIALISM, 1700–1808

Spanish Hapsburg rule over Peru ended with the death of Charles II in 1700, but the new Bourbon dynasty had little immediate effect on the viceroyalty. With the support of his grandfather, Louis XIV, Philip of Anjou became king of Spain as Philip V, although the War of the Spanish Succession (1701–1713), in which England and Austria opposed Philip, engulfed the peninsula. To fend off English naval incursions, Philip V allowed the French navy to patrol colonial waters. In compensation for such protection, the king made commercial concessions to the French, allowing them access to colonial markets for the duration of the war. Thus, for Peru the most evident early result of the dynastic change was the presence in Peruvian waters of French shipping, which continued illegally after the war ended. The French siphoned off considerable bullion but supplied Peruvian markets with the merchandise that the decrepit fleet system could not provide.

Peru presented checkered prospects for the Bourbons. Lima still suffered from the effects of the 1687 earthquake. In the north, the sugar-producing regions around Trujillo and Lambayeque prospered during the seventeenth century, but sugar prices had begun to decline by 1700. Viticulture in the southern coastal valleys stood ready to expand through the conversion of excess wine production into brandy. The mining economy languished from depletion of the silver ores at Potosí, the failure to discover new silver districts, corruption, and low mercury output at Huancavelica.

During the eighteenth century, the Bourbons' absolutist state-building eventually imposed severe restraints on Peruvian autonomy, and the government increased its appropriation from the colonial economy. Lima treasury revenues from 1781 to 1785 were double those at the beginning of the century. The increase was much larger for some of the provincial treasury offices. In Arequipa, for instance, the treasury collected nearly sixteen times more revenue in the early 1780s than it had around 1700. The new royal policies led to tensions with creole elites, who saw their privileged status threatened, and with the indigenous and mestizo masses, which bore the brunt of the heightened economic exploitation. Although the crown attempted to stimulate economic growth, it did so primarily to enhance its own revenues and to strengthen imperial defenses rather than to improve the well-being of its Peruvian subjects.

The first period of Bourbon initiatives for Peru lasted until 1766, the year before the initiatives of Charles III began to affect Peru. Creation of the Viceroyalty of New Granada, first attempted in 1717 and permanently established in 1739, stripped territory from Lima's jurisdiction. It foretold the demise of Lima's monopoly over political and economic power in Spanish South America. Abolition of the fleet system in 1739 reduced Lima's power to control overseas trade, as Buenos Aires and Chile received direct shipping from Spain. But the *consulado*'s political and commercial networks enabled it to retain substantial influence. Meanwhile, the crown attempted to invigorate the Peruvian mining industry. To stimulate silver output, the government in 1736 cut the chief mining tax from a *quinto* (fifth) to a *diezmo* (tenth). Production grew, building on a small increase evident during the preceding decade. Headed by Jerónimo de Sola y Fuente, a team of Spanish technicians arrived at Huancavelica in 1737 and achieved a 20 to 30 percent higher level of mercury production. The guild of miners managed to maintain the higher level until 1770 and so assisted the expansion of silver refining.

Bourbon policymakers also tried to curtail the worst examples of abuse and venality in the Peruvian colony. In 1720 they ordered the abolition of the Huancavelica *mita* on humanitarian grounds. But the miners' guild resisted, and the crown allowed itself to be convinced that the measure was impractical, given the need for mercury and the heavy mortality associated with the great epidemics of 1717–1720. The secret report compiled in the 1740s by the naval officers Jorge Juan and Antonio de Ulloa (*Noticias secretas de América* [1826]) indicted the corrupt, exploitative practices of the *corregidores*. To curtail abuses associated with the *repartos,* the government in 1753–1754 stipulated the quantity of goods each governor could dispense. Yet by so doing, the crown gave official sanction to one of the most abusive practices in Peru.

Around mid-century Peru's economy was expanding modestly, although royal policy probably had little to do with the growth. Potosí had begun a noticeable recovery after 1720, and Cerro de Pasco's silver output grew after 1740 until it surpassed Potosí late in the century. Additional bullion entered the economy from Huantajaya, reopened around 1718 in the Atacama Desert, and from Hualgayoc, discovered in 1766. More abundant supplies of overseas merchandise, from both Spanish and contraband sources, probably helped stimulate the mining expansion, as consumers needed silver to purchase the goods. In turn, mining spurred commercial growth. Following the epidemics of 1717–1720, Peru's population increased, both from natural growth and from a wave of Spanish immigrants after 1750. Agricultural output expanded in a number of regions, including Arequipa, Cuzco, and Trujillo, although the price of agricultural products, especially for cash crops such as sugar, wine, and brandy, declined during the 1700s.

During the final third of the century, Peru suffered the imposition of more radical royal initiatives, which threatened the fiber of colonial life dating back to Toledo's time. Charles III and his ministers, especially Secretary of the Indies José de Gálvez, instituted policies designed to make the viceroyalty more economically profitable to Spain. To achieve this end they required greater political control over Peru. The expulsion in 1767 of the powerful and wealthy Jesuit order, too independent-minded for royal absolutists to tolerate, showed that the king was willing to attack privileged groups.

The crown began to undermine Lima's privileges, which had been greater than those of any other Peruvian city. In 1776 the creation of the Viceroyalty of the Río de la Plata deprived Lima of jurisdiction over Upper Peru (including Potosí), Paraguay, and Buenos Aires. Two years later the expansion of free trade to Peru swept away many of the Lima *consulado*'s monopolistic privileges and forced it to compete with goods imported through other ports, including Arica. Despite their loud complaints, the Lima merchants still managed to dominate much of the overseas trade in their reduced orbit.

Imperial pressure reached a peak with the arrival in 1777 of José Antonio de Areche as *visitador general*. Sent by Gálvez to carry out a far-reaching restructuring of Peru, he abolished the Huancavelica guild and turned the mine over to a single operator, who soon died. Thereupon, he placed Huancavelica under royal management, with disastrous results. The cost of its mercury to the state doubled, and in 1786 the top half of the mine collapsed due to the negligence of royal officials. Meanwhile, Areche established royal customhouses throughout the viceroyalty to provide more thorough and efficient collection of commercial taxes. He raised the *alcabala* (sales tax) from 4 to 6 percent and instituted other tariffs. The *visitador* quarreled with Viceroy Manuel de Guirior and secured his dismissal. Areche also planned to carry out a census of the mestizo and mulatto populations, with the intent of making them pay tribute like the Indians.

Social upheavals were nothing new in the Andes. Dozens of village revolts had perturbed the realm. From 1742 to 1752, Juan Santos, under the name Atahualpa, and his Indian followers ravaged the eastern provinces of the Central Andes. Although royal forces failed to defeat them, neither was Juan Santos able to rally the masses to his cause. But combined with the colonial system's long-standing social tensions, Areche's authoritarian policies prepared Peru for explosion.

The result was the Great Andean Rebellion. It endangered Spanish rule more than anything since Manco Inca's revolt in 1536. Indians protested *repartos, mitas,* and *corregidores*. Creoles resented the new taxes and the state's discrimination against them in favor of Spanish immigrants (derisively called *chapetones*). Conspiracies and insurrections flared in several Peruvian provinces, including Arequipa and Cuzco, and news of similar disturbances in Chayanta, La Paz, and Cochabamba added to the turmoil. In November 1780 José Gabriel Condorcanqui, under the name Túpac Amaru, a *kuraka* from Tinta, executed an abusive *corregidor*. Raising an army and appealing to Creoles and mestizos as well as soldiers of pure Andean heritage, he then unsuccessfully besieged Cuzco. By early 1781, much of the southern half of Peru and most of Charcas were in rebellion. Ethnic animosities among the rebels and the leaders' failure to attract Creole support doomed the insurrection. Nonetheless, before it ended in 1783, 100,000 had died.

The Great Rebellion affected Peru for the remainder of the colonial period. Gálvez replaced Areche with a less abrasive Jorge Escobedo, abolished the *repartos* in 1782, and eliminated the *corregidores* in 1784 by instituting the Intendancy System. Consolidating dozens of *corregimientos* were seven intendancies: Lima, Tarma, Trujillo, Arequipa, Cuzco, Huamanga, and Huancavelica (Puno was transferred from the Río de la Plata Viceroyalty to Peru's jurisdiction by a decree of 1795). The intendants curbed some of the worst abuses of the indigenous population and improved public administration. Meanwhile, the *mita* survived, as did Creole resentment against the *chapetones*. But the rebellion's racial violence also chastened the Creoles, many of whom preferred colonial status to the risk of more bloodshed. In 1787 Gálvez created a new *audiencia* in Cuzco to provide better government for the rebellious provinces, thereby diminishing Lima's power still further.

Despite all its problems, Peru still displayed vitality and grandeur as the Bourbon period drew to a close. Aided by the importation of large stocks of European mercury, the silver-mining industry continued to flourish. Liberalized commerce flooded Peruvian markets with so many European goods that prices fell. Enlightenment thought infused the pages of *Mercurio Peruano* (a newspaper founded in 1791) and the writings of José de Baquíjano and Hipólito Unánue. Sponsored by the monarchy in 1778, the botanical expedition of Hipólito Ruiz and José Antonio Pavón spent a decade gathering specimens and drawing Peruvian flora. In 1788 the crown sent the mining mission of Baron Thaddeus von Nordenflicht to raise the technological standards of the Andean industry.

INDEPENDENCE

In 1808 Napoleon invaded Spain, toppled the monarchy of Ferdinand VII, and created a constitutional crisis for the Spanish Empire. Peru and the other American colonies theoretically belonged to the monarchy rather than the Spanish nation. With the king in exile and unable to rule, Peru was left to decide whether or not to obey the *junta* (committee) organized extralegally by Spanish patriots to rule the empire until the French could be expelled. The other options were self-rule in the name of the king and complete independence. Viceroy José Fernando Abascal (1806–1816) worked with vigorous efficiency to preserve Peru for Spain and to roll back the tide of insurrection elsewhere on the continent. Under his able command, Peru became a royalist bastion in South America, and independence finally came to Peru only through liberating armies from outside.

In fact, Peru showed little inclination to break away until 1814. There was considerable discontent with Spanish colonial policies, but the Creoles feared that a war to drive out the *chapetones* might result in even more disastrous racial violence than that of the Great Rebellion of 1780. Creole liberals generally preferred to seek redress for their grievances within the empire rather than pursue the perilous goal of independence. As for the heterogeneous lower classes, they either lacked the political consciousness or saw little advantage to independence if it meant unfettered, oppressive Creole rule.

Abascal's government not only dealt efficiently with signs of rebellion within Peru but put down insurrections outside the viceroyalty. In 1809 royalist forces quashed revolts in Chuquisaca and Quito. Peasant discontent in Huánuco flared into rebellion in late 1811, but its violence alienated Creoles, and the intendant of Tarma soon subdued the rebels. A more serious challenge erupted in 1814, when Creole and Indian dissidents in Cuzco seized the city and named as their leader the mestizo general and *kuraka*, Mateo Pumacahua. Pumacahua had helped the government defeat Túpac Amaru three decades earlier and more recently had provided Abascal with troops to quell unrest in Upper Peru. In 1814, however, he was upset because the Spaniards refused to accept his appointment as president of the Cuzco *audiencia* and because the state showed no sign of improving conditions for indigenous peoples. The Pumacahua Rebellion involved three expeditions: one occupied Puno peacefully and captured La Paz with great bloodshed; another, led by Pumacahua, took Arequipa and killed the intendant; and the third was defeated after liberating Andahuaylas and Huamanga. By mid-1815, royalists had shattered the rebellion.

Despite these successes, the royalist cause was losing strength. Abascal's efforts to block the tide of rebellion had created a financial crisis for his government, and the hostilities sapped the economy. Returned to the throne, Ferdinand VII proved so reactionary that some dismayed creoles went over to the rebels. In 1816 Abascal left office, replaced by General Joaquín de la Pezuela, who was unable to revive Peru's economic base. Neither could he deter the army of Argentine general José de San Martín, who had invaded Chile and defeated a Peruvian force at Maipú on 5 April 1818. Convinced that Argentine independence was not secure as long as Spain held Peru, San Martín launched his campaign against Peru in March 1819, using the ships of the British mercenary Admiral Alfred Lord Cochrane to blockade Callao. San Martín landed forces at Pisco, south of Lima, in September 1820. At nearly the same time Pezuela learned of the Riego Revolt in Spain, which forced Ferdinand VII to reinstate the liberal Constitution of 1812 and enforce its promulgation in Peru. The revolt also meant that Spain could not send a planned expedition against Buenos Aires, which might have undercut San Martín's strategy against Peru. In December 1820 the intendant of Trujillo, José Bernardo Tagle y Portocarrero, pronounced for independence, and most of northern Peru soon followed his lead.

With the royalist cause collapsing, Pezuela retreated from Lima and consolidated his hold over the central and southern highlands. San Martín entered Lima and declared Peru independent on 28 July 1821. Soon thereafter he outlawed personal service such as the *mita* and recognized Indians as citizens. Enthused with French liberalism, creoles blocked San Martín's effort to establish an independent Peruvian monarchy. San Martín presided over the election of Peru's first parliament in 1822 but remained pessimistic about the nation's republican future. At Guayaquil in July 1822, he and Simón Bolívar met to plan the final liberation of Peru. Bolívar brought forces south to reinforce the Peruvians. The final blow to Spanish Peru was struck on 9 December 1824, when General Antonio José de Sucre defeated and captured Viceroy José de la Serna at the Battle of Ayachuco, near Huamanga.

GOVERNORS AND VICEROYS OF PERU

Francisco Pizarro, 1535–1541

Diego de Almagro, 1541–1542

Cristóval Vaca de Castro, 1542–1544

Blasco Núñez Vela, 1544 (first viceroy)

Gonzalo Pizarro, 1544–1547

Pedro de la Gasca, 1547–1550

Antonio de Mendoza, 1550–1552

[Audiencia, 1552–1556]

Andrés Hurtado de Mendoza, Marqués de Cañete, 1556–1561

Diego López de Zúñiga y Velasco, Conde de Nieva, 1561–1564

Lope García de Castro, 1564–1569

Francisco de Toledo y Figueroa, 1569–1581

Martín Enríquez de Almansa, 1581–1583

[Audiencia, 1583–1586]

Fernando de Torres y Portugal, Conde de Villadompardo, 1586–1589

García Hurtado de Mendoza, Marqués de Cañete, 1589–1596

Luis de Velasco, Marquès de Salinas, 1596–1604

Gaspar de Zúñiga Acevedo y Fonseca, Conde de Monterrey, 1604–1607

Juan Manuel de Mendoza, Marqués de Montesclaros, 1607–1615

Francisco de Borja y Aragón, Principe de Esquilache, 1615–1621

Diego Fernández de Córdoba, Marqués de Guadalcázar, 1621–1629

Luis Jerónimo Fernández, Conde de Chinchón, 1629–1639

Pedro de Toledo y Leyva, Marqués de Mancera, 1639–1648

García Sarmiento de Sotomayor, Conde de Salvatierra, 1648–1655

Luis Enríquez de Guzmán, Conde de Alba de Liste, 1655–1661

Diego de Benavides, Conde de Santisteban, 1661–1666

Pedro Antonio Fernández, Conde de Lemos, 1666–1674

Bartolomé de la Cueva Enríquez, Conde de Castellar, 1674–1678

Melchor Liñán de Cisneros, 1678–1681

Melchor de Navarra y Rocaful, Duque de la Palata, 1681–1689

Melchor Portocarrero y Lasso de Vega, Conde de Moncolova, 1689–1705

Manuel Oms, Marqués de Castelldosrius, 1705–1710

Diego Ladrón de Guevara, 1710–1716

Carmine Niccolo Caracciolo, Principe de Santo Buono, 1716–1720

Diego Morcillo, 1720–1724

José de Armendáriz, Marqués de Castelfuerte, 1724–1736

Antonio de Mendoza, Marqués de Villagarcía, 1736–1745

José Antonio Manso de Velasco, Conde de Superunda, 1745–1761

Manuel de Amat y Junient, 1761–1776

Manuel Guirior, Marqués de Guirior, 1776–1780

Agustín de Jáuregui, 1780–1784

Teodoro de Croix, Conde de Croix, 1784–1789

Francisco Gil de Taboada y Lemos, 1790–1796

Ambrosio O'Higgins, 1796–1801

Gabriel Avilés, Marqués de Avilés, 1801–1806

José Fernando Abascal y Souza, Marqués de la Concordia, 1806–1816

Joaquín de la Pezuela, 1816–1821

José de la Serna, 1821–1824

See also **Agriculture; Commercial Policy: Colonial Spanish America; Slavery: Spanish America; Sugar Industry.**

BIBLIOGRAPHY

Arthur Franklin Zimmerman, *Francisco de Toledo: Fifth Viceroy of Peru, 1569–1581* (1938).

John Preston Moore, *The Cabildo in Peru Under the Hapsburgs* (1954), and *The Cabildo in Peru Under the Bourbons* (1966).

James Lockhart, *Spanish Peru, 1532–1560: A Colonial Society* (1968).

John R. Fisher, *Government and Society in Colonial Peru: The Intendant System, 1784–1814* (1970).

John Hemming, *The Conquest of the Incas* (1970).

James Lockhart, *The Men of Cajamarca: A Social and Biographical Study of the First Conquerors of Peru* (1972).

John R. Fisher, *Silver Mines and Silver Miners in Colonial Peru, 1776–1824* (1977).

Nathan Wachtel, *The Vision of the Vanquished: The Spanish Conquest of Peru Through Indian Eyes, 1530–1570,* translated by Ben and Sin Reynolds (1977).

Timothy E. Anna, *The Fall of the Royal Government in Peru* (1979).

Mark A. Burkholder, *Politics of A Colonial Career: José Baquíjano and the Audiencia of Lima* (1980).

Nicholas P. Cushner, *Lords of the Land: Sugar, Wine, and Jesuit Estates of Coastal Peru, 1600–1767* (1980).

Jurgen Gölte, *Repartos y rebeliones: Túpac Amaru y las contradicciones de la economía colonial* (1980).

Noble David Cook, *Demographic Collapse: Indian Peru, 1520–1620* (1981).

Steve J. Stern, *Peru's Indian Peoples and the Challenge of Spanish Conquest: Huamanga to 1640* (1982).

John J. Te Paske and Herbert S. Klein, *The Royal Treasuries of the Spanish Empire in America,* vol. 1, *Peru* (1982).

Keith A. Davies, *Landowners in Colonial Peru* (1984).

Karen Spalding, *Huarochiri: An Andean Society Under Inca and Spanish Rule* (1984).

Kenneth J. Andrien, *Crisis and Decline: The Viceroyalty of Peru in the Seventeenth Century* (1985).

Scarlett O'Phelan Godoy, *Rebellion and Revolts in Eighteenth Century Peru and Upper Peru* (1985).

Kendall W. Brown, *Bourbons and Brandy: Imperial Reform in Eighteenth-Century Arequipa* (1986).

Fray Martín De Murua, *Historia general del Peru* (1986).

Susan E. Ramírez, *Provincial Patriarchs: Land Tenure and the Economics of Power in Colonial Peru* (1986).

Luis Miguel Glave, *Trajinantes: Caminos indígenas en la sociedad colonial, siglos XVI/XVII* (1989).

Ann M. Wightman, *Indigenous Migration and Social Change: The Forasteros of Cuzco, 1520–1720* (1990).

Sabine Mac Cormack, *Religion in the Andes: Vision and Imagination in Early Colonial Peru* (1991).

Additional Bibliography

Adorno, Rolena. *Guáman Poma: Writing and Resistance in Colonial Peru,* 2nd edition. Austin: University of Texas Press, Institute of Latin American Studies, 2000.

Andrien, Kenneth J. *Andean Worlds: Indigenous History, Culture, and Consciousness under Spanish Rule, 1532–1825.* Albuquerque: University of New Mexico Press, 2001.

Archer, Christon I. *The Wars of Independence in Spanish America.* Wilmington, DE: Scholarly Resources, 2000.

Burns, Kathryn. *Colonial Habits: Convents and the Spiritual Economy of Cuzco, Peru.* Durham, NC: Duke University Press, 1999.

Cahill, David Patrick. *From Rebellion to Independence in the Andes: Soundings from Southern Peru, 1750–1830.* Amsterdam: Aksant, 2002.

Dean, Carolyn. *Inka Bodies and the Body of Christ: Corpus Christi in Colonial Cuzco, Peru.* Durham, NC: Duke University Press, 1999.

Fisher, John Robert. *Bourbon Peru, 1750–1824.* Liverpool, U.K.: Liverpool University Press, 2003.

Graubart, Karen B. *With Our Labor and Sweat: Indigenous Women and the Formation of Colonial Society in Peru, 1550–1700.* Stanford, CA: Stanford University Press, 2007.

Mills, Kenneth. *Idolatry and Its Enemies: Colonial Andean Religion and Extirpation, 1640–1750.* Princeton, NJ: Princeton University Press, 1997.

Montoya Rivas, Gustavo. *La independencia del Perú y el fantasma de la revolución.* Lima, Peru: Instituto Francés de Estudios Andinos, Instituto de Estudios Peruanos, 2002.

Morote, Herbert. *El militarismo en el Perú: Un mal comienzo, 1821–1827.* Lima, Peru: Jaime Campodónico Editor, 2003.

Premo, Bianca. *Children of the Father King: Youth, Authority, and Legal Minority in Colonial Lima.* Chapel Hill: University of North Carolina Press, 2005.

Rivara de Tuesta, María Luisa. *Pensamiento prehispánico y filosofía colonial en el Perú.* Lima, Peru: Fondo de Cultura Económica, 2000.

Salas de Coloma, Miriam. *Estructura colonial del poder español en el Perú: Huamanga (Ayacucho) a través de sus obrajes: Siglos XVI–XVIII.* Lima, Peru: Pontificia Universidad Católica del Perú, Fondo Editorial, 1998.

Silverblatt, Irene M. *Modern Inquisitions: Peru and the Colonial Origins of the Civilized World.* Durham, NC: Duke University Press, 2004.

Stavig, Ward. *The World of Túpac Amaru: Conflict, Community, and Identity in Colonial Peru.* Lincoln: University of Nebraska Press, 1999.

Tardieu, Jean-Pierre. *El negro en el Cuzco: Los caminos de la alienación en la segunda mitad del siglo XVII.* Lima, Peru: Pontificia Universidad Católica del Perú, Banco Central de Reserva del Perú, 1998.

Walker, Charles. *Smoldering Ashes: Cuzco and the Creation of Republican Peru, 1780–1840.* Durham, NC: Duke University Press, 1999.

KENDALL W. BROWN

PERU SINCE INDEPENDENCE

In 1780 the great Rebellion of Túpac Amaru shook the Peruvian Viceroyalty to its very foundations, putting Spanish rule in its Andean core in jeopardy. This massive Indian uprising cost up to 100,000 lives, an estimated one-tenth of Peru's population, and reached from Cuzco all the way to La Paz. Despite its defeat by the colonial regime, the revolt set the stage for a series of rebellions over the next decades involving Peru's polyglot population of Spaniards, creoles, mestizos, Indians, and African slaves. Although the specific goals and motives of these rebellions varied, all called into question some aspect of Spanish rule and sought change, ranging from independence to reform of the colonial system to greater political autonomy. The broader context for Andean rebellion was the onset at roughly the same time of the Age of Revolution in the Western World—North American independence (1776), the French Revolution (1789), and the Haitian Revolution (1801).

INDEPENDENCE AND THE ERA OF CAUDILLISMO, 1820–1840

The beginning of the end of Spain in America occurred with Napoleon's invasion and occupation of the Iberian Peninsula in 1808, which led to the abdication of King Ferdinand VII and his replacement by Joseph Bonaparte on the throne of Spain. With Spanish power emasculated by France and Spanish colonies in America isolated and in political limbo, the movements for independence (1810–1825) erupted from Mexico to Argentina. In Peru, the last colony to gain its freedom in South America, the process was slow to materialize, largely because of a widespread fear among creoles in the Viceroyalty that their property, privileges, indeed very lives would be lost in a revolution from below. Moreover, Lima, the main seat of Spanish colonial power in South America for three centuries, contained forces too intimately tied to the metropolis to seriously challenge the colonial system or contemplate experimenting with the new doctrines of republicanism sweeping other parts of the Americas. Therefore, despite internal opposition to

Spanish rule, particularly in the Andean highlands, Peru's independence in 1826 was largely exogenously driven, coming from outside invasion—from the liberation armies led by General José San Martín in the south and by General Simón Bolívar in the north.

The subsequent construction of a new republican government in Lima would prove to be an extremely difficult task, given the three-centuries-long viceregal, monarchical tradition of government, underpinned by a stratified, hierarchical social structure. Mainly conforming to the boundaries of the old viceroyalty, the new Peruvian "nation" was also a sprawling, geographically fractured and regionalized territory containing a large, heterogeneous, preliterate peasant population that was 60 percent Indian. It was not surprising, then, that the task of crafting an entirely new form of government, based largely on republican principals derived from foreign political models, failed to work. Without a consensus, legitimacy, or functional institutions, the weak, fledgling central government was unable to establish its authority in the country, leading to the rise of powerful caudillo strongmen who seized the reigns of power in the interior. These warlords, who emerged to contest power at the local, regional, and eventually national level, were mostly former military figures or landowners who could command a popular following and share the loot of power with their clients and supporters.

In the ensuing economy of scarcity, ravaged by the destructive impact of war, caudillo politics became a means of survival and mobility for large segments of the population while constitutional government lacked the financial means to establish neither law and order or an effective presence in the country. The clashes of individual caudillos and their irregular armies of supporters produced a political panorama of constant civil war and civil turmoil during the first two decades after independence. As a result of this endemic political instability Peru endured, by one count, a total of twenty-four regime changes, an average of one per year between 1821 and 1845, and the constitution was rewritten six times. With the presidency in effect a revolving door and caudillo politics the country's main industry, it is no wonder that the economy showed little growth and development during the immediate postindependence years.

FROM RAGS TO RICHES AND BACK: GUANO, WAR, AND RECONSTRUCTION, 1840–1895

In 1840 the country's political instability and economic stagnation was suddenly reversed when Peruvians discovered large deposits of guano, a natural fertilizer deposited over millennia on nearby islands by sea birds who fed on an abundant supply of fish in the warm Humboldt current along the coast. The ensuing bonanza over the next three decades saw ten million tons of guano "mined" by imported Chinese indentured coolies and shipped to Europe and the United States, where the nineteenth-century agricultural revolution demanded large inputs of fertilizer. It also yielded millions to government coffers, not to mention private entrepreneurs, foreigners, and speculators. This enormous bounty enabled the state to

strengthen and solidify its control over the country by improving communications to the interior and building a modern army capable of routing the petty caudillos from their local and regional fiefdoms. Guano revenue also provided the financing for the state to embark on an ambitious development program that gave priority to the construction of railroads, the symbol at the time of progress throughout the Western World.

The main architects of this era of guano-driven economic progress and political stabilization were General Ramón Castilla (1797–1868), two-time president of the country (1845–1851 and 1854–1862), and Manuel Pardo (1834–1876), a businessman who founded the Civilista Party and was the first civilian president of Peru (1872–1876). Castilla, a pragmatic consensus builder, used the enormous guano bounty to forge a Pax Andina by rooting out local caudillos and extending the power and reach of the government into the interior. He also reined in the power of the church, consolidated the national debt, abolished the onerous Indian head tax, and freed the country's 25,000 or so black slaves (1854) through a program of compensation to their planter overlords. For the latter accomplishment he gained the sobriquet "Emancipator" from his supporters and compatriots.

Manuel Pardo, on the other hand, was an aristocrat, a self-made millionaire and mayor of Lima, who earned his laurels by promoting a program of guano-based economic development and equally important civilian, as opposed to military, governance of the country. Pardo pinned his economic plan to "turning guano into railroads" to stimulate national production and internal markets. He insisted that, without railroads, no real material progress—upon which moral progress depended—would be possible. As a result of his influence Peru embarked on a mammoth railroad-building program, made the more spectacular by its transversal of the steep gorges and mountain divides of the Andes. At the same time, to take advantage of a growing civil society emerging during the century's middle decades, Pardo founded the Civilista Party, designed to purge the country of the military rulers who had monopolized the presidency since Independence. His success was capped when he was elected the first civilian president of Peru in 1872.

Alas, despite Peru's seeming mid-century good fortune, which might have catapulted the country forward in terms of growth and development, the guano boom went bust. The deposits of the

Peru

Population:	28,674,757 (2007 est.)
Area:	496,226 sq mi
Official language(s):	Spanish, Quechua
Language(s):	Spanish, Quechua, Aymara, other Amazonian languages
National currency:	nuevo sol (PEN)
Principal religions:	Roman Catholic, 81%; Seventh Day Adventist, 1.4%; other Christian, 0.7%; other, 0.6%; unspecified or none, 16.3%
Ethnicity:	Amerindian, 45%; mestizo (mixed Amerindian and European), 37%; European, 15%; African, Japanese, Chinese, and other, 3%
Capital:	Lima (pop. 7,899,000; 2005 est.)
Other urban centers:	Trujillo, Arequipa, Chiclayo
Annual rainfall:	75 to 125 in
Principal geographic features:	*Mountains:* Cordillera Occidental, Cordillera Central, Cordillera Oriental ranges of the Andes; Mt. Huascarán, 22,205 ft *Bodies of water:* Lake Titicaca, Marañón River, Huallaga River, Ucayali River, Amazon River
Economy:	*GDP per capita:* $6,600 (2006 est.)
Principal products and exports:	*Agriculture:* asparagus, coffee, cotton, sugarcane, rice, potatoes, corn, plantains, grapes, oranges, coca; poultry, beef, dairy products; fish, guinea pigs *Industries:* mining and refining of minerals; steel, metal fabrication; petroleum extraction and refining, natural gas; fishing and fish processing, textiles, clothing, food processing
Government:	Republic with centralized government. The president is popularly elected for a five-year term and can run for re-election for one additional term. The National Congress consistes of a 60-member Senate and a 180-member Chamber of Deputies; all elected legislators have five-year terms. There are also more than 160 locally elected government councils.
Armed forces:	80,000 active personnel in 2005, supported by 188,000 reservists. *Army:* 40,000 members *Navy:* 25,000 active personnel, including 4,000 Marines, 1,000 Coast Guard members, and 800 naval aviation personnel *Air force:* 15,000 personnel
Transportation:	As of 2004, Peru's railroad system consisted of 2,153 mi of standard and narrow gauge railway lines. In 2002, of the estimated 45,300 mi of existing roads, only 5,406 mi were paved. The two primary routes are the 1,864 mi north-south Pan American Highway and the Trans-Andean Highway, which runs about 500 mi. As of 2004, there were 5,473 mi of waterways, of which 5,349 mi consist of tributaries of the Amazon River and 129 mi on Lake Titicaca. In 2004 there were an estimated 234 airports. In 2005, a total of 54 had paved runways, and there was also one heliport.
Media:	In 2004, there were 65 radio stations and 2 news channels on 2 commercial cable systems in the Lima area. There are many privately owned provincial stations. The government owns one radio station and one television network. The leading Lima dailies are *El Comercio*, 120,000 (2004 circ.), *Ojo* (40,000), and *Expreso* (50,000). Other major papers from Lima include *Aja* (120,000), *El Bocon* (90,000), and *La Republica* (50,000). The official government paper is *El Peruano* (27,000).
Literacy and education:	*Total literacy rate:* 87.7% (2004 est.) Education is compulsory for 12 years, including one year of preprimary education. Peru has a number of universities, including National University of San Marcos of Lima, the National University of Engineering, the National University of Agriculture, and the University of San Cristóbal de Huamanga.

fertilizer, after providing the credit for enormous loans to the state, proved finite; the sudden bonanza of wealth based on guano served only to widen the already considerable gap between rich and poor. Moreover, it opened the country up to an orgy of corruption, speculation, and unnecessary expenditures on luxury goods for the elites rather than productive investment. The business classes were afflicted with a rentier mentality—relying on income from property or holdings—further hindering the economy's progress, and the hugely expensive railroad construction program failed to stimulate the kind of development that Pardo had in mind.

Guano deposits were exhausted by the 1870s, just as Peru was feeling repercussions from the worldwide depression of 1873; the nation defaulted on its national debt in 1876 and then entered an ill-advised war with Chile. Peru lost the War of the Pacific (1879–1883) to its vastly better organized southern rival, whose armies occupied the country, inflicting widespread death and destruction. The war had erupted essentially over undefined boundaries between the two countries and Peru's ally Bolivia, which contained potentially lucrative mineral resources claimed by the combatants.

As a result of the war, which ended in the Treaty of Ancón in 1883, Peru lost the southern province of Tarapaca to Chile and in the provinces of Tacna and Arica was forced to agree to a plebiscite after ten years. Perhaps more significantly, the country was

Plaza Mayor and Cathedral of Arequipa, Peru, 1880s (engraving) by French School (20th century). PRIVATE COLLECTION/ KEN WELSH/ THE BRIDGEMAN ART LIBRARY

thrown back economically and politically to the state of instability and stagnation that had reigned in the country after independence fifty years earlier. The military seized power once again, while the economy slowly recovered. This second period of "militarism" and reconstruction lasted until 1895, a period punctuated by widespread social unrest, Indian uprising, and the humiliating Grace Contract of 1886, which ceded the country's unfinished railway system for sixty-six years to the Peruvian Corporation, made up of foreign bondholders, in return for the cancellation of Peru's foreign debt.

OLIGARCHIC PERU AND POPULIST CHALLENGE, 1895–1968

After losing the war Peru underwent a period of soul searching, led by the biting criticisms of gadfly intellectual Manuel González Prada, who faulted the country's political class for leading Peru into a conflict it was ill-prepared to win. At the same time, the Civilista Party formed again and by the early twentieth century gained control of the presidency, which it held for most of the next two decades. It was now dominated mainly by export-oriented planters, mine owners, and financiers—an oligarchy or plutocracy—who, with the aid of large inflows of foreign capital, reintegrated the country into the industrializing economies of the West. Thanks to expanding production of such commodities as cotton, sugar, silver, copper, ferrous metals, and oil, composing a relatively diversified export sector, the country's GDP advanced smartly, stimulated also by a new manufacturing capacity, particularly textiles, oriented toward an emerging popular domestic market.

The trickle-down effect of this economic growth brought about the emergence of new middle and working classes that by the outbreak of World War I began to have an impact on politics. For example, in 1912 Guillermo Billinghurst, a dissident oligarch and proto-populist, was elected president on a reform platform, momentarily breaking the Civilistas' hold on power, before the armed forces removed him from office in 1914. The Civilistas retook the presidency in elections a year later. Then, in the wake of peasant unrest in the southern highlands, the new working classes struck for the eight-hour day in what came to be known as the Great Strike of 1918–1919, the founding moment of the national labor movement. They were joined by university students who demonstrated alongside the workers and advocated their own University Reform Movement in 1918. Their target was the aristocracy's control of the administration, curriculum, and entrance requirements to higher education, widely considered elitist, old-fashioned, and discriminatory against the new middle sectors. Much of the social unrest of the war years was fueled by popular anger over soaring inflation that sharply reduced the living standards and buying power of the population.

The dissident Civilista Augusto B. Leguía, a self-made businessman and proponent of modernization and Americanization through greater foreign investment and trade, captured the imagination of the new reform-minded popular sectors and was elected president in 1919. At first Leguía initiated a series of progressive social reforms, only to "manage" his reelection in 1924 and assume virtual dictatorial power during the second half of the 1920s. He then became a political victim of the Wall Street crash of 1929 and ensuing Depression: He was overthrown by the army in 1930 as the export-dependent economy virtually collapsed and unemployment soared. The Depression unleashed populist forces in the country, giving expression to the new mass-based political party American Popular Revolutionary Party (APRA), founded in 1923 by Víctor Raúl Haya de la Torre. The charismatic Haya almost captured the presidency in 1931, edged out in the voting by the leader of the coup that had overthrown the unpopular Leguía, Col. Luis M. Sánchez Cerro.

APRA was essentially nationalist and stridently anti-oligarchical, advocating democratization, greater control over foreign capital, state intervention in the economy, agrarian reform, and import-substituting industrialization (ISI). The party took on many of the attributes of the National Revolutionary Party (PNR) in Mexico, where Haya had spent part of a long exile following his leadership of a popular demonstration against Leguía's attempt (ultimately unsuccessful) to dedicate the country and his regime to the Sacred Heart of Jesus in 1923. The Peruvian Communist Party was also founded in this period, in 1928, by journalist-intellectual José Carlos Mariategui, who subsequently became an icon of the Peruvian Left. Although he died a year later, his numerous writings, including a severe critique of APRA, became an inspiration to progressive forces for the rest of the century.

The impact of the Depression was relatively short-lived in Peru, as exports recovered by 1934 and then expanded rapidly through World War II. Politics, however, remained polarized between Left and Right, as APRA forces rebelled in 1932 in Trujillo, Haya's hometown, claiming electoral fraud, and Sánchez Cerro was assassinated a year later by an Aprista militant. The army savagely repressed the rebellion, setting off a vengeful feud between the party and the military that lasted half a century. General Oscar R. Benavides, another military figure, followed Sánchez Cerro in the presidency (1933–1939), establishing a dictatorship. During this period APRA was proscribed by the government and went underground, suffering a period of severe repression that tended to harden its ranks through collective survival and sacrifice. During World War II Peru allied with the United States and profited from wartime sales of critical mineral exports to its ally, while gradually opening up to democratic forces by the end of the war.

A postwar "democratic springtime" brought to power a reformist coalition government that included APRA, holding out the hope of social change and popular political incorporation. However, an inability to cooperate among the coalition partners, excessive demands for radical reforms, and increasing budget deficits collided with the outbreak of the Cold War and Berlin Blockade of 1948. Once again oligarchical forces opposed to change spurred the military to intervene to prevent an alleged Communist undermining of the status quo and conservative interests. General Manuel Odría led the coup, establishing a dictatorship (1948–1956) that again sent APRA underground and Haya into a long political exile in the Colombian embassy in Lima.

The 1950s saw the culmination of an important demographic shift in the country away from the sierra to the coast and from rural to urban areas, as the hacienda system weakened and the cities, where more jobs and government services held out the promise of better living standards, attracted a growing number of rural migrants. Odría's government responded by increasing social benefits to the growing number of shantytown inhabitants around Lima and other urban areas, where government infrastructure and services were overwhelmed by demand. Overall Peru's population had almost quadrupled from 2.6 million in 1876 to almost 10 million in 1961, while the number of inhabitants in Lima had soared to 1.6 million by the same year.

Gradually, a reformist political tide rose again, cresting in the early 1960s. A new progressive political party, Accion Popular (AP), was founded by the charismatic young architect Fernando Belaúnde Terry, posing a severe challenge to APRA. By that time APRA had shifted to a more conservative position after entering into a tacit alliance with the right wing in the 1958 Convivencia pact to support oligarch Manuel Prado for the presidency in return for restoration of the party to political legitimacy. APRA even managed by this maneuver to elect Haya over the newcomer Belaúnde to the presidency in 1962, only to have the army veto the election by a coup. The military junta allowed elections within a year, and this time Belaúnde, advocating agrarian reform and a grassroots development program, won the presidency.

Meanwhile a radical rural insurgency inspired by the Cuban Revolution of 1959 erupted in 1965 in the highlands, where the condition of the peasantry continued to deteriorate as agricultural production declined under the anachronistic hacienda system. In 1961 Peru ranked lowest among fifty-four countries surveyed in the Gini index of land distribution, with an estimated seven hundred estate owners owning approximately one-third of the country's productive land. Belaúnde recognized the urgent need for land reform, but his program was blocked by a congress controlled by the conservative opposition coalition, APRA–UNO (Odría's old party). In the event, Belaúnde called on the armed forces to defeat the insurgency; in the process of doing so, the army was

radicalized, partly under the impact of having to confront its own citizenry militarily. Many officers recognized that the outmoded land tenure system needed major reform, and when a great political scandal erupted over the issue of nationalizing the International Petroleum Company (IPC) so that back taxes owed to the government might be recovered, in 1968 the armed forces, led by General Juan Velasco Alvarado, deposed the Belaúnde government in a coup and seized power.

Unlike previous military takeovers, this one was institutional and not personal (caudillo) in nature. It called for a "revolution" that would modernize the country by ending oligarchical rule, expanding the role of the state, and nationalizing land and industry. Such a restructuring would be tightly controlled from the top in a form of state corporatism with strong populist overtones. Immediately the new government nationalized IPC, forming a new state-run oil agency known as Petroperu, and then took over the sugar plantations of the north coast in a major blow to the historic power of Peru's "forty families." This was followed by a sweeping agrarian reform program, dispossessing hacienda owners of their estates in favor of their peasant workers. Velasco declared in a 1969 speech: "Peasant, the landlord will no longer eat from your poverty." State-run cooperatives and other forms of collective management were implemented in a highly variegated and complex landholding system that included large estates (*latifundio*), small parcels (*minifundios*), and communal Indian holdings.

At the same time, the new regime promoted ISI industrialization, with the state dramatically doubling its share of the GDP to 31 percent, while replacing foreign investment capital with large loans from abroad, which over time exploded the national debt. The regime also promoted worker participation in the management and share of profits of industries. Popular support for the reform program was mobilized in a corporatist fashion with the creation of a state bureaucracy called SINAMOS, composed of cadres of technocrats and militants who guided and controlled a myriad of new state entities all the way down to the community level. Peru's economy was to be "neither capitalist nor socialist," as the government proclaimed; its foreign relations were described as a "third position" between the bipolar international system of democratic West and Communist East.

Although this radical reform program was a well-intentioned effort to redistribute Peru's extremely unequal wealth and income and create a more just social order after centuries of exploitation and oppression, it proved less than successful. Often ill-planned, mismanaged, and overly bureaucratic, it was also undermined by world events such as United State opposition, the impact of the oil embargo of 1973, and a subsequent international recession that saw demand for the country's exports decline sharply. By 1975 the initial popular reaction to the reforms had waned in the context of rising inflation, large government deficits, and an explosion of foreign debt. A more conservative group of generals replaced Velasco and began to reverse and dismantle the reforms while implementing a policy of austerity, during a so-called Second Phase (1975–1980).

Gradually, greater freedom of the media, which had been severely curtailed under Velasco's authoritarian rule, was restored, and by the end of the decade a rising tide of popular democratic sentiment persuaded the military to organize new elections, relinquish power, and return to the barracks, opening the way to a transition to democracy in 1980. The ensuing election results were a surprise, bringing the exiled Belaúnde back as president (1980–1985). He implemented orthodox, free-market, neoliberal economic policies, opening the economy to foreign investment and trade and reducing the size and scope of the state.

RADICAL REFORM, REDEMOCRATIZATION, AND THE SHINING PATH INSURGENCY, 1968–1990

Belaúnde was soon faced with another, more serious insurgency. Over the next decade the Shining Path (Sendero Luminoso; SL) guerrilla group virtually brought the country to its knees. It was led by Abimael Guzmán Reynoso, a charismatic, autocratic professor of philosophy who taught at a remote university in the impoverished and neglected department of Ayacucho in the southern sierra. He managed to recruit a cadre of dedicated student followers, who returned to their peasant communities as teachers to spread a version of violent Marxism and radical change. Many were the first generation from their rural Indian families to attend university and expected that their new degrees would lead to a more prosperous place and respect in the modern world. However, they were frustrated by deep-seated racial discrimination as well as an absence of employment in the stagnant or slow-growing Peruvian economy, particularly in the south.

Beyond Ayacucho, the first Belaúnde government had vastly expanded the number of universities in the country during the 1960s, in the belief that education would lead to progress and development. Nevertheless, the economy did not grow fast enough to absorb thousands of new graduates, who by the 1980s faced a bleak job market and collective disillusionment. Many turned to the Shining Path in hopes of overthrowing the existing system and making a place for themselves in a new Marxist order. As a result the Shining Path movement spread rapidly, beyond its initial stronghold in the southern sierra, gaining supporters and eventually large amounts of drug money to finance their operations from the burgeoning coca industry in the Upper Huallaga Valley. There the guerrillas moved in to protect peasant producers from U.S.-sponsored government eradication programs.

Belaúnde's unpopular neoliberal austerity program, together with the exploding SL insurgency, brought a new social democratic APRA government to power in the presidential elections of 1985. APRA, under its young leader Alan García Pérez (1985–1990), had finally come to power after decades of frustration, but it too proved unable to stem either the country's entrenched social and economic problems or the insurgency. After an initially hopeful start, adopting a heterodox, more socially responsive approach to governing, García made the mistake of abruptly nationalizing the banking system. This rash act quickly undermined confidence in the government by scaring off foreign and domestic capital investment, throwing the economy into turmoil and triggering an inflationary spiral that reached more than 7,000 percent by 1990. Moreover, by this time the decade-long Shining Path insurgency had claimed in excess of 20,000 lives, caused an estimated $15 billion in economic damage, and created more than 200,000 internally displaced refugees.

THE FUJIMORI DEBACLE, 1990–2000

Despite such destabilizing conditions, Peru held regularly scheduled presidential elections in 1990. The surprising winner turned out to be the relatively unknown Alberto Fujimori, the son of Japanese immigrants to Peru who had risen to become rector of Peru's university system. "El Chino," as he became affectionately known, shrewdly played up his immigrant origins, outsider status, and "Oriental" work ethic to edge out the world-renowned writer Mario Vargas Llosa. Many viewed the light-skinned Vargas Llosa as a representative of the discredited traditional "white" elites and their ineffective political parties, who were widely blamed for the country's severe economic and political decline over the previous decade.

Fujimori, who had easily won in the second round of voting, in an abrupt about-face carried out the very proposal of Vargas Llosa's that had most frightened Peruvian voters: He implemented a draconian austerity program that became known as "Fujishock." It succeeded in stemming hyperinflation, encouraging the return of foreign investment, and stabilizing the economy. Riding high in the polls, Fujimori then decided in 1992 to shut down the congress for putting obstacles, as he claimed, in the way of the counterinsurgency campaign of the armed forces against the Shining Path. This "auto-coup" was followed by an extraordinary stroke of good fortune and police work, when SL leader Abimael Guzmán was captured in a Lima safe house, along with computer files identifying a large number of SL leaders. Subsequent police raids succeeded in capturing and imprisoning most of SL's remaining leadership, thereby breaking the back of the insurgency, which in its latter stages had moved into Lima and other cities, posing a serious threat to bring down the state.

Meanwhile, Fujimori secured business and U.S. support by liberalizing the economy. For example, he carried out a radical privatization program, which included mines, banks, telecommunications companies, and utilities, favoring elites and allies with sweetheart deals. The funds garnered from the sell-off of these government-run businesses were directed by the ministry of the presidency into an extensive antipoverty program that would eventually benefit the 70 percent of the population in poverty.

With the socioeconomic panorama of Peru suddenly brightening, Fujimori was able to go to the electorate in the 1995 presidential election with a renewed sense of confidence in the future. Bypassing a constitutional provision against reelection, he had

congress, now restored because of international pressure but controlled by the administration, write a new one and went on to easily win reelection.

Fujimori's second term appeared to many observers an opportunity lost, both politically and economically. With SL defeated and the economy showing signs of life, El Chino could have moved to consolidate democracy and aggressively attack the problem of underdevelopment so as to help the two-thirds of the population mired in poverty. However, his real aims had been very different from the start, as a 1988 "Green Book" produced by the military high command illustrated. Fujimori apparently used this secret document as a blueprint for his new regime in 1990. It called for a long period, perhaps fifteen years, of strong authoritarian government to defeat the insurgency and stabilize the economy, while planting the seeds of authoritarianism, human rights violations, and corruption, which would not come into public view until later. Those tendencies would intensify in the second term, as Fujimori sought to extend his arbitrary personal power, further flaunt government institutions and the political party system, and cement a nefarious relationship with his national security adviser, Vladimiro Montesinos.

An obscure lawyer and former army captain with a murky past who had been cashiered for spying for the CIA, Montesinos was the architect of Fujimori's control over the military whereby promotions and retirements were based not on professional merit but on loyalty to the regime. Put in charge of the National Intelligence Service (SIN) directed against the insurgency, Montesinos turned its covert activities, as SL disintegrated after 1992, against the regime's political enemies. He was later shown to have engaged in extensive bribery of public officials, major disinformation campaigns against enemies of the regime, and widespread manipulation of the media. Even more damaging, he was implicated in some of the most heinous human rights violations perpetrated by members of the armed forces. (As of 2007, Montesinos was in the same prison in which he had incarcerated SL leader Guzmán, facing trial on an array of charges that could keep him there for the rest of his life.)

Through chicanery and fraud, the Fujimori/ Montesinos team managed to engineer a third presidential term in 2000. Their methods included cajoling the judiciary to remove legal barriers to Fujimori's reelection, a monopoly on television coverage the campaign, fake registration signatures so his party could qualify to participate in the elections, and programming of electoral computers to ensure victory. However, only six weeks after his inauguration in what international observers unanimously condemned as fraudulent elections, Fujimori was brought down by the "Vladivideos" broadcast on national television showing Montesinos in the act of bribing a congressman. More compromising videos quickly appeared, leading to street demonstrations led by Alejandro Toledo, who emerged as an outspoken critic of the regime and proponent of democratization. Widespread, popular indignation led Fujimori to resign while out of the country attending an international conference and then into exile in his native Japan. Meanwhile, Montesinos fled to Venezuela, only later to be caught returning to Peru and imprisoned by the new interim government headed by Valentín Paniagua.

One of the first acts of the caretaker government was to appoint a Truth and Reconciliation Commission (CVR) to investigate human rights violations during the Shining Path insurgency. After an exhaustive three-year investigation, the CVR concluded, among other things, that there were almost 70,000 fatalities during the two-decade conflict. This was, according to the CVR final report, the most intense and prolonged period of violence in the entire 182-year history of republican Peru.

New elections called in 2001 brought Alejandro Toledo (2001–2006) to the presidency, the first Peruvian with an indigenous background to gain the high office. Toledo's most enduring achievement was to serve out his presidential term despite inept political behavior, a lack of leadership, and low popular opinion ratings. During the election campaign he had promised to create thousands of new jobs and to make serious progress in reducing poverty. To his credit he did preside over a macroeconomic expansion of the GDP, averaging more than 5 percent per year during his five-year term, but little of this growth trickled down to the general population. As a result popular expectations were dashed and the gap between rich and poor widened. This divide showed up dramatically in the 2006 election results for Toledo's successor, when voting figures graphically illustrated that the

country was split between a relatively more prosperous and modern urban north and the mostly rural, Indian, and impoverished south. Former president and social democrat Alan García Pérez of the APRA party won the election over his nationalist, populist opponent Ollanta Humala, a charismatic, ultranationalist former army officer and staunch opponent of the neoliberal economic program espoused by Toledo. However, despite his defeat Humala's party gained the largest number of seats in congress, promising further political conflict in the years ahead.

See also **Agrarian Reform; Ancón, Treaty of (1883); Belaúnde Terry, Fernando; Bolívar, Simón; Bonaparte, Joseph; Castilla, Ramón; Cuba, Revolutions: Cuban Revolution; Ferdinand VII of Spain; Fujimori, Alberto Keinya; García Pérez, Alan; González Prada, Manuel; González Prada Popular Universities; Grace, W. R., and Company; Guzmán, Abimael; Haya de la Torre, Víctor Raúl; International Petroleum Company (IPC); Leguía, Augusto Bernardino; Mexico, Political Parties: National Revolutionary Party (PNR); Military Dictatorships: 1821-1945; Military Dictatorships: Since 1945; Mining: Modern; Montesinos, Vladimiro; Odría, Manuel Apolinario; Paniagua, Valentín; Pardo y Lavalle, Manuel; Peru, Organizations: National Social Mobilization Support System (Sinamos); Peru, Political Parties: Civilista Party; Peru, Political Parties: Peruvian Aprista Party (PAP/APRA); Peru, Political Parties: Popular Action (AP); Peru, Revolutionary Movements: Shining Path; Peru, Truth Commissions; Plantations; Sánchez Cerro, Luis Manuel; San Martín, José Francisco de; Sugar Industry; Toledo, Alejandro; Túpac Amaru (José Gabriel Condorcanqui); Velasco Alvarado, Juan.**

BIBLIOGRAPHY

Clayton, Lawrence. *Peru and the United States: The Condor and the Eagle.* Athens: University of Georgia Press, 1999.

Conaghan, Catherine M. *Fujimori's Peru: Deception in the Public Sphere.* Pittsburgh: University of Pittsburgh Press, 2005.

Higgins, James. *Lima: A Cultural History.* New York: Oxford University Press, 2005.

Hunefeldt, Christine. *A Brief History of Peru.* New York: Facts on File, 2004.

Klarén, Peter Flindell. *Peru: Society and Nationhood in the Andes.* New York: Oxford University Press, 2000.

Larson, Brooke. *Trials of Nation Making: Liberalism, Race, and Ethnicity in the Andes, 1810–1910.* Cambridge, U.K., and New York: Cambridge University Press, 2004.

McClintock, Cynthia, and Fabian Vallas. *The United States and Peru: Cooperation at a Cost.* New York: Routledge, 2003.

Sheahan, John. *Searching for a Better Society: The Peruvian Economy from 1950.* University Park: Pennsylvania State University Press, 1999.

Starn, Orin, Carlos Iván Degregori, and Robin Kirk, eds. *The Peru Reader: History, Culture, Politics,* 2nd edition. Durham, NC: Duke University Press, 2005.

PETER KLARÉN

PERU–BOLIVIA CONFEDERATION.

Peru–Bolivia Confederation, a short-lived (1837–1839) alliance created by Andrés de Santa Cruz. After he became president of Bolivia in 1829, Santa Cruz began forging the confederation through decisive political and military action. Officially proclaimed on 1 May 1837, it was composed of North and South Peru and Bolivia, each with a separate administration. Santa Cruz was proclaimed the protector for ten years and became the absolute ruler. The confederation was recognized by France and Britain but provoked the military intervention of Argentina and Chile. Argentine forces were repulsed, but after initial success against the Chilean contingents, troops commanded by Santa Cruz were routed on 20 January 1839, at the battle of Yungay. Santa Cruz fled into exile aboard a British frigate. A united Peru and an independent Bolivia emerged.

See also **War of the Peru-Bolivia Confederation.**

BIBLIOGRAPHY

Alfonso Crespo, *Santa Cruz* (1944).

Ernesto Díez Canseco, *Perú y Bolivia: Pueblos gemelos* (1952).

Additional Bibliography

Maquito Colque, Tania Micaela. *La sociedad arequipeña y la Confederación Perú-Boliviana, 1836–1839.* Arequipa: DREMSUR Editores, 2003.

CHARLES W. ARNADE

PERU, CONSTITUTIONS.

Peru has had twelve documents called constitutions since 1823. The first of these was suspended before it went into effect, others were short-lived, and only two have lasted longer than twenty years. Even this claim to longevity may be misleading: The most enduring constitution—that of 1860—was interrupted by a new constitution within seven years (which was in place for only four months), by the War of the Pacific (1879–1883), and by five successful coups d'état before its definitive demise after Augusto B. Leguía's 1919 coup. The second most enduring constitution—that of 1933—lasted through the assassination of President Luis M. Sánchez Cerro within weeks of its promulgation, the unconstitutional three-year extension of President Oscar R. Benavides's term of office from 1936 to 1939, and three major periods of military rule after coups led by Generals Manuel A. Odría, Ricardo Pérez Godoy, and Juan Velasco Alvarado in 1948, 1962, and 1968, respectively. In the context of such constitutional instability, it is noteworthy that the 1993 constitution, written after Alberto Fujimori's self-coup, has outlived its predecessor and has endured longer than most of Peru's political frameworks.

Constitutions recognize rights and organize the distribution of power within the state. The most politically significant set of rights are those related to citizen participation in the political process. In Peru, political participation rights have been limited by age, gender, literacy, property, and professional status. The age of majority oscillated between twenty-five and twenty-one years until 1978, when it was lowered to eighteen years. Women did not vote until 1956; they were first given the right to vote in municipal elections by the 1933 constitution, but no municipal elections were held until after 1955, when women were given the right to vote in all elections. Class and literacy requirements had more complex histories. The 1823 constitution extended political rights to adult males who had property or a profession, and excluded those subject to others as servants or day laborers. It also excluded those who did not know how to read and write, although the literacy requirement was to be suspended until 1840. The 1826 constitution required literacy, but the 1828, 1834, and 1867 constitutions—all short-lived—did not. The 1839 constitution required literacy (except for some indigenous and mestizos) and the payment of a contribution, and the 1856 constitution gave the right of suffrage to adult males who were literate, or workshop chiefs, or real property owners, or legally retired from the army or navy. The 1860 constitution had the same requirements as the 1856 document, but also allowed those who made contributions to the public treasury to vote. The 1860 constitution was modified in 1895 to stipulate only literacy as a requirement for adult male suffrage, a requirement not finally abandoned until 1979.

Despite some promonarchy sentiment, Peru's early constitutions proclaimed Peru's form of government to be popular and representative—even Bolívar's 1826 constitution, in effect for only seven weeks, which called for a president-for-life.

Aside from that, the presidential term has ranged from four to six years with no immediate reelection, but allowing reelection after one term out of office. Only the 1828 and 1993 constitutions allowed for immediate reelection to one additional term, although Leguía's 1920 constitution was twice modified, first to allow for one additional term and then to allow for unlimited reelection. After the fall of Fujimori in 2000, the 1993 constitution was amended to prohibit immediate reelection.

Peru's constitutional regimes have been presidential, but have acquired some characteristics more typical of parliamentary regimes. Congress began calling ministers to account early on, but the 1860 constitution was the first to explicitly oblige ministers to respond to the legislature's interpellations, whereas the 1867 constitution was the first to recognize the right of congress to censure and force the resignation of ministers. To the extent that Peru's constitutions have allowed the legislature to exercise authority over ministerial policy via the power of interpellation and censure, Peru's regime may be described more properly as a mixed regime, even though it has functioned in most other respects as a presidential regime. The repeated breakdown of democracy under the 1933 constitution led to efforts to strengthen the presidency in the 1979 constitution, and the 1993 constitution sought to strengthen the presidency still further. As no regime since independence has lasted without interruption for more than twenty years, Peru's quest for a stable democratic constitutional regime continues.

BIBLIOGRAPHY

García Belaunde, Domingo, and Walter Gutiérrez Camacho. *Las Constituciones del Perú*. Lima: Ministerio de Justicia, 1993.

Pareja Paz-Soldán, José. *Historia de las Constituciones Nacionales (1812–1979)*. Lima: Pontificia Universidad Católica del Perú, 2005.

Planas, Pedro. *Democracia y Tradición Constitucional en el Perú*. Lima: San Marcos, 1998.

CHARLES D. KENNEY

PERU, ORGANIZATIONS

This entry includes the following articles:
CIVIL GUARD
CONFEDERATION OF PERUVIAN WORKERS (CTP)
CONFEDERATION OF WORKERS OF THE PERUVIAN REVOLUTION (CTRP)
GENERAL CONFEDERATION OF PERUVIAN WORKERS (CGTP)
INSTITUTE OF PERUVIAN STUDIES (IEP)
NATIONAL AGRARIAN SOCIETY
NATIONAL CLUB
NATIONAL SOCIAL MOBILIZATION SUPPORT SYSTEM (SINAMOS)
UNION CLUB

CIVIL GUARD

The national police force was established by a Spanish mission to Peru in 1924 and reorganized under the Ministry of the Interior in 1986–1987 as the General Police (Policía General). There are fifty-nine commands in five police regions and a total force of 42,537. The Civil Guard provides patrols and law enforcement, with other police units responsible for prison and border duty. Along with the Security Police (Policía de Seguridad) and the Technical Police (Policía Técnica), it is part of the National Police (Policía Nacional).

BIBLIOGRAPHY

Víctor R. Prado Saldarriaga, *Derecho penal y política: Política penal de la dictadura y la democracia en el Perú* (1990).

Rex Hudson, ed., *Peru: A Country Study,* 4th ed. (1993).

Additional Bibliography

Gonzáles Posada, Luis. *Seguridad ciudadana: Política de estado.* Lima: Fondo Editorial del Congreso del Perú, 2005.

DAVID SCOTT PALMER

CONFEDERATION OF PERUVIAN WORKERS (CTP)

The Confederation of Peruvian Workers (Confederación de Trabajadores Peruanos, or CTP) is a group of labor unions controlled by the Aprista Party in Peru. It developed from the initial formation of the Federation of Sugar Workers (FTA), organized in northern coastal Peru during the regime of President Bustamante y Rivero (1945–1948). At the time, the Aprista Party had considerable official influence. However, under the regime of General Manuel Odría, stern military enemy of the Apristas, the CTP began to lose union affiliations to the Communist-controlled General Confederation of Peruvian Workers (CGTP). By 1968 the CTP's influence on Peruvian unions had been largely supplanted by the CGTP. During the military regime (1968–1980), the CTP lost even more leverage, in part due to its opposition to the military. Although in 1985 and again in 2006 Peruvians elected Alan García of APRA to the presidency, the CTP's role remains relatively diminished. However, the CTP played a part when it joined with the CGTP and CUT in agreeing to support a new Peruvian labor code that includes measures like collective bargaining.

BIBLIOGRAPHY

James Payne, *Labor and Politics in Peru* (1965).

Peter Klarén, *Modernization, Dislocation, and Aprismo* (1973).

Additional Bibliography

Alexander, Robert Jackson, with Eldon M. Parker. *A History of Organized Labor in Peru and Ecuador.* Westport, CT: Praeger, 2007.

Pareja Pflucker, Piedad. *Aprismo y sindicalismo en el Perú, 1943–1948.* Lima: Ediciones Perú, 1980.

Parker, D. S. *The Idea of the Middle Class: White-Collar Workers and Peruvian Society, 1900–1950.* University Park: Pennsylvania State University Press, 1998.

Villanueva, Armando, interviewed by Guillermo Thorndike. *La gran persecución, 1932–1956.* Lima: Empresa Periodística Nacional, 2004.

ALFONSO W. QUIROZ

CONFEDERATION OF WORKERS OF THE PERUVIAN REVOLUTION (CTRP)

The Confederation of Workers of the Peruvian Revolution (Confederación de Trabajadores de la Revolución Peruana, or CTRP) was a blatantly corporatist organization initiated by the military regime in Peru in 1973. This labor institution existed with official government and police support. CTRP leaders and organizers used forceful and corrupt means to control individual unions

and dislodge labor leaders of the radical Left and even the Communist Party, which officially supported the military reformists. The military regime attempted to form a political movement based on the CTRP, but this endeavor floundered because workers preferred affiliation to the Communist-led General Confederation of Peruvian Workers (CGTP) after 1975.

BIBLIOGRAPHY

Denis Sulmont, *Historia del movimiento obrero en el Perú, de 1890 a 1977* (1977).

Alfred Stepan, *The State and Society: Peru in Comparative Perspective* (1978).

Additional Bibliography

Alexander, Robert Jackson, and Eldon M. Parker. *A History of Organized Labor in Peru and Ecuador.* Westport: Praeger, 2007.

Cameron, Maxwell A., and Philip Mauceri. *The Peruvian Labyrinth: Polity, Society, Economy.* University Park: Pennsylvania State University Press, 1997.

Cotler, Julio. *Política y sociedad en el Perú: Cambios y continuidades.* Lima: IEP, 1994.

ALFONSO W. QUIROZ

GENERAL CONFEDERATION OF PERUVIAN WORKERS (CGTP)

The General Confederation of Peruvian Workers (Confederación General de Trabajadores Peruanos, or CGTP) was a group of labor unions under the influence and control of the Peruvian Communist Party. Communist labor organizers had been active in Peru since the late 1920s. However, they were able to considerably expand the formation and control of unions beginning in the 1950s, especially during the regimes of civilians Manuel Prado (1956–1962) and Fernando Belaúnde Terry (1963–1968) and among the modern industrial working sectors. In the 1970s the official Communist Party's policy of "critical support" to the military regime afforded it the political space to continue to expand the labor organization. The CGTP was able to displace both the Aprista-dominated Confederation of Peruvian Workers (CTP) and the corporatist Confederation of Workers of the Peruvian Revolution (CTRP). In 1977 the CGTP successfully staged a general strike that was one of the cornerstones of the popular demand for the return of democracy, which occurred in 1980. Since then, the strength of the CGTP has declined considerably.

See also **Peru, Political Parties: Peruvian Aprista Party (PAP/APRA).**

BIBLIOGRAPHY

David Chaplin, *The Peruvian Industrial Labor Force* (1967).

Denis Sulmont, *Historia del movimiento obrero en el Perú, de 1890 a 1977* (1977).

Additional Bibliography

Alexander, Robert Jackson, and Eldon M. Parker. *A History of Organized Labor in Peru and Ecuador.* Westport: Praeger, 2007.

Cameron, Maxwell A., and Philip Mauceri, eds. *The Peruvian Labyrinth: Polity, Society, Economy.* University Park: Pennsylvania State University Press, 1997.

Lévano, Manuel, Delfín Lévano, César Lévano, and Luis Tejada. *La utopía libertaria en el Perú: Obra completa.* Lima: Fondo Editorial del Congreso del Perú, 2006.

ALFONSO W. QUIROZ

INSTITUTE OF PERUVIAN STUDIES (IEP)

The Institute of Peruvian Studies (Instituto de Estudios Peruanos, IEP) was founded in 1964 by a group of social scientists that included José Maria Arguedas, Alberto Escobar, José Matos Mar, and María Rostworowski. It soon became an important center of modern social research in Peru. Later on, influential scholars such as Julio Cotler, Carlos Ivan Degregori, Efrain Gonzales de Olarte, and Jürgen Golte joined the IEP and cemented its reputation. Since its inception, it has also welcomed foreign scholars as a regular part of its intellectual life. Many of the IEP's publications have become classics of social science and history, and are widely read in Peruvian universities and abroad. The IEP's editorial house is one of the oldest publishers of social science research and one of the most active in Peru today. Analyzing the transformations brought about by the military regime (1968–1980), the IEP published a number of influential studies on land reform, urban sociology, and public policy. It was during this period that the Institute published Julio Cotler's highly influential *Clases, estado y nación en el Perú* (1978). With the transition to democracy, the IEP expanded into new topics: working-class conditions, youth, women, and market reforms. Since the late twentieth century, the IEP has studied the collapse of parties, the transformations of Peruvian society, and the rise of the authoritarian state during the Fujimori years. The IEP has published over 350 books and more than 110 working papers.

See also **Peru: Peru Since Independence.**

BIBLIOGRAPHY

Cotler, Julio. *La cohesión social en la agenda de América Latina y de la Union Europea.* Lima: Institutos de Estudios Peruanos, 2006.

Instituto de Estudios Peruanos. Available from http://www.iep.org.pe/.

JULIO CARRION

NATIONAL AGRARIAN SOCIETY (SNA)

The National Agrarian Society (Sociedad Nacional Agraria, or SNA) was founded in 1876 by a group of coastal planters as a lobbying body called the Sociedad Nacional de Agricultura. Members sought to foster export agricultural interests in the government. The organization collapsed when the War of the Pacific began (1879), but it was revived and renamed by the same planters in the late 1890s. Its reorganization was spearheaded by many of the export planters whose power in government, lending, and commercial circles had been established. The revived lobbying group broadened to include major Andean landowners with outlooks similar to those of coastal planters. Prominent officers included sugar planter Isaac Alzamora, Antero Aspíllaga, and the heads of the wealthy and powerful Boza and Larco families, joined later by sugar planter and publisher Pedro Beltrán and wealthy landowner and cotton planter Miguel Checa. By the mid-1930s the SNA sought legislation to regulate sharecropping and farm labor, to extend its members' control of these important sources of labor. In 1947 the National Assembly passed the Ley de Yanaconaje (Sharecropping Law) that protected sharecroppers by insisting on written contracts and limits on rent. Landowners accepted the legislation as inevitable, but thereafter many switched to wage labor and restricted the number of sharecroppers permitted on their lands.

BIBLIOGRAPHY

Magnus Mörner, *The Andean Past: Land, Societies, and Conflicts* (1985), esp. pp. 188–262.

Paul Gootenberg, *Imagining Development: Economic Ideas in Peru's "Fictitious Prosperity" of Guano, 1840–1880* (1993).

Additional Bibliography

Contreras, Carlos. *El aprendizaje del capitalismo: Estudios de historia económica y social del Perú republicano.* Lima, Perú: IEP, Instituto del Estudios Peruanos, 2004.

VINCENT PELOSO

NATIONAL CLUB

In its heyday, the National Club was an exclusive private institution in Lima where members of the wealthiest and most influential families of coastal Peru met socially. Membership in the club was a business and political asset. Founded in the late nineteenth century, the club achieved its highest position of prestige during the sugar and cotton export booms (1890–1929). The club has been considered by social scientists as a main link among the so-called Peruvian "aristocratic" oligarchy, especially during the military regime's (1968–1980) attack on agro-export interests that temporarily closed down the club in 1969.

BIBLIOGRAPHY

François Bourricaud, *Power and Society in Contemporary Peru* (1970).

Dennis Gilbert, "The Oligarchy and the Old Regime in Peru" (Ph.D. diss., Cornell University, 1977); translated as *La oligarquía peruana: Historia de tres familias* (1982).

Additional Bibliography

Castro Contreras, Jaime. *Violencia política y subversión en el Perú, 1924-1965.* Lima: s.n., 1992.

Huiza, José Luis and José Valdizán Ayala. *Historia del Perú republicano.* Lima: Universidad de Lima, Fondo de Desarrollo Editorial, 1997.

ALFONSO W. QUIROZ

NATIONAL SOCIAL MOBILIZATION SUPPORT SYSTEM (SINAMOS)

The National Social Mobilization Support System (Sistema Nacional de Apoyo a la Mobilización Nacional, or SINAMOS) was an organization created by Peru's military government (1968–1980) in 1971 to stimulate grass roots organizations and support for the regime. From the outset it was divided between those who sought central control and those who supported autonomous, local citizen participation. At its peak it had a national office, ten regional offices, and seventy zonal offices around the country with over 4,000 employees, mostly university-educated social scientists. As the reform momentum of the military government waned in the mid-1970s, local offices became targets for protesters and several were burned down. SINAMOS ceased to function in 1978.

BIBLIOGRAPHY

John A. Booth and Mitchell A. Seligson, eds., *Political Participation in Latin America,* vol. 1 (1978), pp. 189–208.

Cynthia McClintock and Abraham F. Lowenthal, eds., *The Peruvian Experiment Reconsidered* (1983), pp. 275–308.

Additional Bibliography

Dietz, Henry A. *Urban Poverty, Political Participation, and the State: Lima, 1970-1990.* Pittsburgh: University of Pittsburgh Press, 1998.

Kruijt, Dirk. *Revolution by Decree: Peru, 1968-1975.* Amsterdam: Thela Publishers, 1994.

Martín Sánchez, Juan. *La revolución peruana: Ideología y práctica política de un gobierno militar, 1968-1975.* Sevilla: Consejo Superior de Investigaciones Científicas, Escuela de Estudios Hispano-Americanos: Universidad de Sevilla: Diputación de Sevilla, 2002.

Riofrío, Gustavo. *Habilitación urbana con participación popular: Tres casos en Lima, Perú.* Eschborn: Deutsche Gesellschaft für Technische Zusammenarbeit, 1986.

DAVID SCOTT PALMER

UNION CLUB

An elite social club, this organization was founded in 1868. In its heyday, between the late 1800s and the mid-1900s, it could boast that it had "always been the meeting place of the best society." As was the case with the equally exclusive National Club, its membership list was a virtual who's who of Peru's political, economic, and intellectual elite. Many of Peru's most important decisions may well have been made over drinks in the club's elegant salon, located on Lima's Plaza de Armas. In the 1990s the Union Club's membership is predominantly middle class, and its political importance has diminished significantly.

BIBLIOGRAPHY

Cipriano A. Laos, *Lima: La ciudad de los virreyes* (1929), pp. 191–199.

Additional Bibliography

Castro Contreras, Jaime. *Violencia política y subversión en el Perú, 1924-1965.* Lima: s.n., 1992.

Huiza, José Luis and José Valdizán Ayala. *Historia del Perú republicano.* Lima: Universidad de Lima, Fondo de Desarrollo Editorial, 1997.

DAVID S. PARKER

PERUPETRO. *See* **Petroleos del Peru (Petroperu).**

PERU, POLITICAL PARTIES

This entry includes the following articles:

OVERVIEW
CIVILISTA PARTY
MOVEMENT OF THE REVOLUTIONARY LEFT (MIR)
NATIONAL ALLIANCE OF PERU (AN)
NATIONAL DEMOCRATIC FRONT (FDN)
PERUVIAN APRISTA PARTY (PAP/APRA)
POPULAR ACTION (AP)

OVERVIEW

The evolution of Peruvian party politics historically has lagged behind that of many other Latin American states. Not until the 1930s did a mass-based party emerge, and even in the early twenty-first century the nation lacks a full-blown system of well-organized and doctrinally identifiable parties. The most primitive form of parties can be traced back to the nineteenth century, but development has been painfully slow.

The first Peruvian party was the Partido Civilista (PC), created in 1871 by Manuel Pardo in opposition to the military domination of politics. With its leadership characterized for decades as an "oligarchy of talent," the Civilistas remained a potent force well into the twentieth century. During the *oncenio* (1919–1930) of dictatorial rule by Augusto B. Leguía, the party was effectively squashed. By that time the Partido Aprista Peruano (PAP) had come into being as what would become the first party of the so-called democratic Left in

Latin America. Dating from its official founding in Mexico under Víctor Raúl Haya de la Torre in 1924, APRA (Alianza Popular Revolucionaria Americana), as it was then known, became a central actor in twentieth-century Peruvian politics.

At the outset a revolutionary nationalist organization, APRA under the legendary Haya became the main vehicle for all those opposed to oligarchic domination. The party was illegal for much of the time from 1931 to 1956, while Haya and other party leaders experienced harassment and lengthy periods of exile. The party won congressional elections in 1945, when it was permitted to participate, although Haya himself was unable to seek the presidency. Only in 1962 was he finally allowed to become a presidential candidate, the first time in thirty-one years.

Haya narrowly led a three-candidate race but lacked the one-third vote necessary to declare victory. While negotiations with other groups took place, the military intervened and canceled elections. A year later Haya ran second to Fernando Belaúnde Terry, who had founded his own party, Acción Popular (AP) in 1956. Espousing a moderate reformism and presenting a new and fresh face to the public, he defeated Haya when a new round of elections was held in 1963. Winning 39 percent of the vote to Haya's 34 percent, Belaúnde soon found himself opposed in Congress by APRA as well as the former dictator Manuel A. Odría and his personalistic Unión Nacional Odriísta (UNO).

The armed forces ousted Belaúnde in 1968, introducing more than a decade of military authoritarianism. During these years AP withered while APRA sought to maintain its force and prepare for the eventual withdrawal of the military. When military-sponsored elections for a constituent assembly were held in 1978, APRA seized the opportunity to reassert itself. The party won some 35 percent of the vote and dominated the drafting of the Constitution of 1979. Haya presided over the process but died soon after. However, the party was beginning to undergo a renewal of its leadership. Meanwhile, Belaúnde returned home to reorganize AP.

Acción Popular had originally espoused reformist policies, but by 1980 the party had followed its leader to the right of center. After garnering 45 percent of the vote in the presidential elections of

1980, AP declined rapidly as the Belaúnde government fell into disfavor; by 1985 its support dropped to a scant 7 percent. Conversely, APRA regained its primacy. The party's youthful secretary-general, Alán García, formerly a protégé of Haya de la Torre, polled 53 percent of the vote to win his presidential bid. The fate of the party was bound to the García administration, and its fall from public favor, marred by hyperinflation and failed policies, led to a major electoral shift in 1990.

During the 1980s a group of leftist parties amassed popular support. The Izquierda Unida (IU) first emerged as a loose pro-Marxist alliance of mini-groups that won one-third of the vote for the constituent assembly in 1978, and by 1985 its presidential candidate, Alfonso Barrantes Lingán, ran second to García with nearly 25 percent of the vote. The coalition has since fragmented, and its voter appeal has diminished. The rise of the murderous Marxist guerrilla movement Sendero Luminoso (Shining Path) also became a hindrance to left-wing parties. The 1990 elections demonstrated the amorphous nature of the Peruvian party system in the present era. The novelist Mario Vargas Llosa first patched together a group of rightist parties and captured widespread support in criticism of the García administration. Yet his campaign foundered, and at the last minute Alberto Fujimori, a complete unknown, won the presidency with a vague organization known as Cambio 90. Within a year of his inauguration it had virtually disintegrated, and APRA once again became Peru's major national party.

Fujimori's reign has become associated with corruption, although he was reelected in 1995. In 2000 he was challenged by another political dark horse, Alejandro Toledo, who had formed the party Perú Posible. Fujimori was able to stave off Toledo's challenge amid a maelstrom of confusion and suspicion. A year later, in a new election, Toledo won the presidency in a close contest against Alan García's APRA. In 2006 García and APRA narrowly edged Ollanta Humala, whose candidacy was sponsored by the center-left party Unión por el Perú. This reinforces the history of Peruvian politics, which demonstrates few concrete trends. The political process is undoubtedly more personalistic than party-oriented. And increasingly it seems that political parties in Peru, with the exception of APRA, lack dexterity, often disappearing quickly after enjoying popularity with a specific candidate.

See also **Belaúnde Terry, Fernando; Fujimori, Alberto Keinya; García Pérez, Alan; Haya de la Torre, Víctor Raúl; Odría, Manuel Apolinario; Pardo y Lavalle, Manuel; Peru, Revolutionary Movements: Shining Path; Toledo, Alejandro.**

BIBLIOGRAPHY

Gilberg, Trond, ed. *Coalition Strategies of Marxist Parties.* Durham, NC: Duke University Press, 1989.

Kantor, Harry. *The Ideology and Program of the Peruvian Aprista Movement.* New York: Octagon Books, 1953.

Klarén, Peter F. *Modernization, Dislocation, and Aprismo: Origins of the Peruvian Aprista Party, 1870–1932.* Austin: University of Texas Press, 1973.

McDonald, Ronald H., and J. Mark Ruhl. *Party Politics and Elections in Latin America.* Boulder, CO: Westview Press, 1989.

Palmer, David Scott. *Peru: The Authoritarian Tradition.* New York: Praeger, 1980.

Starn, Orin, et al., eds. *The Peru Reader: History, Culture, Politics,* 2nd edition. Durham, NC: Duke University Press, 2005.

JOHN D. MARTZ
SEAN H. GOFORTH

CIVILISTA PARTY

The Partido Civil (Civilista Party) is Peru's first modern political party, in contrast to the ephemeral nineteenth-century electoral clubs organized only at election times. The Partido Civil, founded by Manuel Pardo (1834–1878) in 1871, represented new commercial and financial elites, but drew on middle-class support. Critical of the country's reliance on guano revenues, the Civilistas sought to modernize and diversify Peru's economy through a combination of laissez-faire economics and the development of a strong state. Pardo built a national political network and became the country's first civilian president (1872–1876). After the War of the Pacific (1879–1883), the party reemerged as the country's most powerful political force during the period of the "Aristocratic Republic" (1895–1919). Despite some middle-class support, the Partido Civil continued to be associated primarily with Peru's powerful commercial and financial groups. The new generation of Civilistas included President José Pardo (1904–1908, 1915–1919), son of the party founder, and Augusto B. Leguía during his first presidency (1908–1912). In 1911 a conservative splinter group left the party to form the Partido Civil Independiente. The Partido Civil declined as the era of mass politics began in Peru during the 1920s and 1930s. Throughout its half-century of existence, the party consistently came to power only through electoral means.

BIBLIOGRAPHY

Basadre, Jorge. *Historia de la República del Perú*. Lima: Editorial Universitaria, 1968–1970.

McEvoy Carmen. *Un Proyecto Nacional en el Siglo XIX: Manuel Pardo y su vision del Perú*. Lima: Pontificia Universidad Católica del Perú, 1994.

Muecke, Ulrich. *Political Culture in Nineteenth-Century Peru: The Rise of the Partido Civil*, translated by Katya Andrusz. Pittsburgh, PA: University of Pittsburgh Press, 2004.

IÑIGO GARCÍA-BRYCE

MOVEMENT OF THE REVOLUTIONARY LEFT (MIR)

The Movement of the Revolutionary Left (Movimiento de la Izquierda Revolucionario, or MIR) was a guerrilla organization formed in 1965 by dissident elements of APRA Rebelde that were frustrated by the slow pace of agrarian reform under the government of Fernando Belaúnde Terry (1963–1968). Led by Luis de la Puente Uceda and made up primarily of university students, it was inspired by the Cuban *foco* strategy, articulated by Che Guevara and Régis Debray, of building a rural base of support through armed action. The MIR began operations in September 1965 in the countryside around Cuzco and Junín, but it failed to gain the peasant support it had expected, and the Peruvian army quickly crushed the insurgency. By January 1966, Puente Uceda had been killed and the MIR destroyed.

BIBLIOGRAPHY

Richard Gott, *Rural Guerrillas in Latin America* (1973).

David Scott Palmer, "National Security," in *Peru: A Country Study*, edited by Rex Hudson, 4th ed. (1993).

Additional Bibliography

Brow, Michael F. and Eduardo Fernández. *Guerra de sombras: La lucha por la utopía en la Amazonía peruana*. Peru: CAAAP: CAEA-Conicet, 2001.

DAVID SCOTT PALMER

NATIONAL ALLIANCE OF PERU (AN)

A coalition of four moderate parties formed in 1933 under the leadership of Amadeo de Piérola (son of former President Nicolás de Piérola), the National Alliance of Peru (Alianza Nacional, or AN) opposed the abrupt shift to the right of President Oscar Benavides's cabinet under José de la Riva-Agüero (a descendant of Peru's first president and a leading conservative intellectual). It worked for the acceptance of the American Popular Revolutionary Alliance (APRA) within legal politics, but APRA tactics and military opposition frustrated AN efforts to open up the democratic process in Peru. The AN coalition had dissolved by the end of the Benavides regime in 1939.

BIBLIOGRAPHY

Carleton Beals, *Fire on the Andes* (1934).

David P. Werlich, *Peru: A Short History* (1978).

Additional Bibliography

Anderle, Ádám. *Los movimientos políticos en el Perú entre las dos guerras mundiales: Ensayo*. Ciudad de La Habana: Casa de las Américas, 1985.

Masterson, Daniel M. *Militarism and Politics in Latin America: Peru from Sánchez Cerro to Sendero Luminoso*. New York: Greenwood Press, 1991.

DAVID SCOTT PALMER

NATIONAL DEMOCRATIC FRONT (FDN)

The National Democratic Front (Frente Democrático Nacional, or FDN) was a coalition party organized in 1944 by residents of Arequipa. The party opposed the administration of Manuel Prado (1939–1945) and sought to open up the Peruvian political process to include the American Popular Revolutionary Alliance (APRA), which had been banned in 1932. Its candidate was José Luis Bustamante I Rivero, a native of Arequipa, who won the election in June 1945 but was deposed by a coup in October 1948 after he and the FDN proved unable to control APRA. This marked the end of the FDN as a political force.

BIBLIOGRAPHY

José Luis Bustamante I Rivero, *Tres años de la lucha por la democracia en el Perú* (1949).

David P. Werlich, *Peru: A Short History* (1978).

Additional Bibliography

Ballón Lozada, Héctor. *Cien años de vida política de Arequipa, 1890-1990.* Arequipa: UNSA, 1992-1993.

DAVID SCOTT PALMER

PERUVIAN APRISTA PARTY (PAP/APRA)

In 2006 the venerable Partido Aprista Peruano (Peruvian Aprista Party, PAP), also known as the American Popular Revolutionary Alliance (APRA), won its second presidential election in Peruvian history under the leadership of Alan García Pérez, whose term as president from 1985 to 1990 had left the country in economic ruins. Running on a social democratic platform promising to preserve Peru's free-market economy (honoring a free-trade agreement with the United States), control the deficit, exercise fiscal restraint, and bolster the country's fragile democracy, García decisively defeated his ultra-nationalist opponent, former military officer Ollanta Humala, by 53 to 47 percent of the vote. Despite APRA's no longer being the political powerhouse it had been for much of the twentieth century, a breakdown of the vote by region still showed the party's strength in attracting votes in the modern sector of Peruvian society. The party won an overwhelming majority along the coast—including in Lima, whose population is one-third of the country's total population of 27 million—but lost by two-to-one or more in the heavily indigenous and impoverished central and southern highlands.

APRA was founded in 1923 in Mexico by Víctor Raúl Haya de la Torre, a charismatic young politician who went into exile after making a reputation as a student leader agitating for university reform and an eight-hour workday and against President Augusto B. Leguía's 1923 reelection. He designed the party's five-point program, advocating the political unity of Latin America, nationalization of land and industry, internationalization of the Panama Canal, and solidarity with oppressed people around the world, and resisting Yankee imperialism. Having witnessed the detrimental effects of foreign control over the traditional Peruvian sugar industry, Haya developed a strong anti-imperialist and nationalist outlook. He was also influenced by strong currents of *indigenismo*, a social and intellectual movement in favor of the redemption of the oppressed Indian masses and celebration of the great pre-Colombian civilizations of the past in what he called Indo-America (Meso-America and South American Andes).

In many ways his model for APRA was the new Mexican revolutionary state, his goal to overturn a dominant oligarchy, expand the power and reach of the state, nationalize a predominantly foreign-controlled mining industry, and carry out massive agrarian reform. He also drew on foreign sources, both right and left, during the twenties and thirties, when fascism, socialism, and communism emerged to challenge the liberal Western democracies and capitalism. Because many Latin American intellectuals of the period saw the West as having fallen into decline after World War I and the Depression, they viewed Western states as inappropriate developmental models for Latin America.

Returning to Peru after Leguía was overthrown in a military coup, Haya ran unsuccessfully for the presidency in 1931. Party militants claimed electoral fraud and organized sugar workers near Trujillo, Haya's hometown, to rebel against the government, a revolt that was brutally suppressed by the army. As a result of human rights violations on both sides, APRA became an anathema to the armed forces and the object of a generation-long vendetta to keep the party from power. APRA, declared illegal, went underground during much of the 1930s and early 1940s, when it developed a hierarchical organization, sectarian tendencies, and a psychology of martyrdom that unified the party and enabled it to survive years of persecution by hostile regimes. During these years the Peruvian polity assumed a tripartite shape, in which the military, allied with the ruling oligarchy, sought to control the insurgent popular forces led by APRA.

The victory of the Allies in World War II marked a turning point in the fortunes of the party. A democratic wave washed over Latin America, opening the way for the party's legalization and election in a coalition reform government led by independent José Luis Bustamante y Rivero (1945–1948). By this time, Haya's early radical anti-imperialist and quasi-socialist views had been modified to embrace foreign investment and pro-American, democratic sentiments; this was partly in response to the outcome of the war and partly out of the party's desire to differentiate itself from its rival, the Peruvian Communist Party (PCP), so as to win the allegiance of the country's nascent working classes and labor movement. However, in 1948, in the increasingly tense geopolitical atmosphere of the Cold War, the reform government was overthrown by a military coup, and the subsequent dictatorship of General Manuel Odría (1948–1956) forced APRA once again underground, with Haya taking sanctuary in the Colombian embassy for five years.

Another major turning point for the party's electoral fortunes came with the so-called Convivencia Pact of 1956, in which Haya decided to support his archenemy for the presidency, the oligarch Manuel Prado, in return for the legalization of APRA. This political about-face led to a major rupture in the party and the departure of many long-time party loyalists; nevertheless, it enabled Haya to win election to the presidency in 1962. However, he was denied power once again by the intervention of the armed forces, which still harbored strong anti-Aprista sentiments dating back to the 1932 Trujillo Revolution. Subsequently, APRA and Haya were relegated to the opposition during the reform government of Fernando Belaúnde Terry (1963–1968) and the revolutionary government of the armed forces (1968–1980). Ironically, the latter government up to 1975 carried out many major structural reforms, including the nationalization of land and industry, that Haya and APRA had espoused during the 1930s but largely abandoned after World War II. In 1979 Haya, in his eighties and suffering from cancer, capped his long political career by being selected to lead a constitutional convention, which opened the way for the return of the military to the barracks and the redemocratization of the country beginning in 1980.

Alan García Pérez, Haya's former personal secretary, became his hand-picked successor and in 1985, five years after Haya's death, won the presidency. Under García APRA espoused a social democratic program at a time when the country was engaged in a vicious civil war with the radical Marxist Shining Path guerrilla movement. His five-year term in office was marred by serious human rights violations as well as a financial meltdown, when he impulsively nationalized the banking system, causing the sudden flight of capital and foreign investment and an inflationary spiral of historic proportions. García left office in 1990 under a cloud of government mismanagement and corruption, only to rise phoenix-like from this first-term debacle, after nine years in exile, to become president again in 2006.

See also **García Pérez, Alan; Haya de la Torre, Víctor Raúl; Indigenismo; Peru, Revolutionary Movements: Shining Path.**

BIBLIOGRAPHY

Graham, Carol. *Peru's APRA: Parties, Politics, and the Elusive Quest for Democracy.* Boulder, CO: Lynne Rienner, 1992.

Klarén, Peter F. *Modernization, Dislocation, and Aprismo: Origins of the Peruvian Aprista Party, 1870–1932.* Austin: University of Texas Press, 1973.

Pike, Fredrick B. *The Politics of the Miraculous in Peru: Haya de la Torre and the Spiritualist Tradition.* Lincoln: University of Nebraska Press, 1986.

Planas, Pedro. *Los orígens del APRA: El joven Haya*, 2nd edition. Lima: Okura Editores, 1986.

Stein, Steve. *Populism in Peru: The Emergence of the Masses and the Politics of Social Control.* Madison: University of Wisconsin Press, 1980.

PETER KLARÉN

POPULAR ACTION (AP)

Popular Action (Acción Popular, AP) was founded in 1956 by Fernando Belaúnde and a group of young Peruvian professionals. A reformist alternative to both the oligarchic parties and the increasingly conservative Peruvian Aprista Party (APRA) party, AP quickly established itself as a national organization and serious contender for the presidency. Founded on an amorphous ideology that claimed to have Peru "as a doctrine," AP attracted large segments of the middle class seeking social change within a democratic framework. Belaúnde was elected president in 1963 but was deposed by a military coup in 1968, in the wake of a controversial contract with an American oil company. For most of the 1970s, AP strongly opposed the military government and in 1978 refused to participate in the elections for a constitutional assembly convoked by the regime. This gamble paid off, as Belaúnde won the ensuing 1980 presidential elections. However, AP's second term in office was marked by severe difficulties emanating from growing inflation and mounting political violence. AP became part of the FREDEMO (Frente Democrático) coalition that supported the candidacy of Mario Vargas Llosa for the 1990 elections. (Though he won the first round, Alberto Fujimori won in the runoff.) In the

2000 elections AP's presidential candidate won less than 1 percent of the vote. In 2001 the party did not field a presidential candidate and won only three seats in the 120-seat unicameral congress. In the 2006 presidential elections, AP was part of the alliance Frente de Centro. Its secretary general, former President Valentín Paniagua, won 6 percent of the vote and secured five seats in Congress.

See also **Belaúnde, Víctor Andrés; Paniagua, Valentín; Peru, Political Parties: Peruvian Aprista Party (PAP/APRA); Vargas Llosa, Mario.**

BIBLIOGRAPHY

Matos Mar, José. *Desborde popular y crisis del estado: Veinte años despues.* Lima: Fondo Editorial de Congreso del Perú, 2004.

Parodi Trece, Carlos. *Peru, 1960–2000: Políticas económicas y sociales en entornos cambiantes.* Lima: Universidad del Pacífico, Centro de Investigación, 2000.

JULIO CARRION

PERU, REVOLUTIONARY MOVEMENTS

This entry includes the following articles:
ARMY OF NATIONAL LIBERATION (ELN)
SHINING PATH

ARMY OF NATIONAL LIBERATION (ELN)

The Ejercito de Liberacion Nacional (Army of National Liberation; ELN) was founded by Hector Bejar in the early 1960s in the wake of the Cuban Revolution of 1959. He envisioned the ELN as not just one more leftist political party, but a disciplined military organization that would mobilize the peasant and proletarian classes to overthrow the government. Acting as a revolutionary cadre with ties to the Peruvian Communist Party, the ELN favored a *focista* or vanguard approach modeled after the successful Cuban example. In 1963 the ELN sent a small group of young intellectuals who had been trained in Cuba to assist Hugo Blanco, the leader of a peasant uprising in La Convención province, but they were quickly detected and hunted down by the police. In 1965 Bejar joined with two other revolutionary groups (Movement of the Revolutionary Left and Tupac Amaru), whose headquarters were on the Mesa Pelada not far from La Convención, in an unsuccessful joint guerrilla action.

See also **Movimiento Revolucionario Tupac Amaru (MRTA); Peru, Political Parties: Movement of the Revolutionary Left (MIR); Peru, Revolutionary Movements: Shining Path.**

BIBLIOGRAPHY

Masterson, Daniel M. *Militarism and Politics in Latin America: Peru from Sánchez Cerro to Sendero Luminoso.* Westport, CT: Greenwood Press, 1991.

PETER KLARÉN

SHINING PATH

Sendero Luminoso (Shining Path), a Peruvian insurgent movement following a radical Maoist ideology, began its self-proclaimed "people's war" in May 1980, on the eve of Peru's first presidential elections in seventeen years. Founded and led since its formation in the 1960s by Abimael Guzmán Reynoso, the organization grew initially within the colonial University of San Cristóbal de Huamanga, which was refounded in 1959, in isolated highland Ayacucho, where Guzmán taught between 1962 and 1975. Using his position as director of the teacher training school and later as secretary of the university, after his group won internal elections in 1968, he built a loyal following, from those returning to their peasant communities to teach in local schools to faculty members and cadres of radicalized student activists. Originally part of a wider Maoist movement in Peru following the break between the Soviet Union and China in 1963–1964, Guzmán went his own way between 1968 and 1970 to found the Communist Party of Peru, which became known as Shining Path or PCP-SL.

Adopting the most radical orientation among the factions of China's Cultural Revolution over the course of at least three extended visits between 1965 and 1975, Guzmán was determined to pursue a "true" revolution on his own in Peru after the Chinese radicals lost out in 1976. The isolation and stark poverty of the Ayacucho region and the inadequacy of the agrarian reform pursued there by the military government (1968–1980) contributed to worsening conditions within the local peasantry and gave Shining Path organizers new support for their revolutionary project.

Shining Path violence, 1996. Police inspect the house of a high-ranking government official damaged by a car bomb in Lima, Peru. Shining Path was believed to have been responsible for planting the bomb. AP IMAGES

As quixotic as the initiation of the people's war seemed, just as Peru was returning to elected civilian rule with the full participation of other Marxist parties, governmental indifference for more than two years followed by a repressive and exclusively military response enabled Shining Path to gain support in Ayacucho in the early 1980s and gradually created favorable conditions for generalized political violence that had not previously existed. Not only did government actions worsen the security situation, but misguided policies also produced a major economic crisis by the end of the 1980s that allowed Shining Path to expand its activities throughout the Andean highlands, the Upper Huallaga Valley, and into Lima. By the early 1990s, the guerrillas seemed on the verge of victory.

Shining Path tactics depended on the use of small, highly mobile units that worked to undermine the presence of the central government and other organizations at the local community and neighborhood levels by intimidation, selective attacks, and carefully planned assassinations of key local figures. Operating from a small central committee and six zonal commands nationwide, the strategy was gradually to encircle the cities by expanding operational capacity in the countryside while simultaneously building support groups within the cities. Leaders insisted on complete self-sufficiency: They secured weapons by attacking police and the military, dynamite by raiding mines, and funds by levying "taxes" on drug-trafficking operations in the Upper Huallaga.

But as Guzmán was preparing to launch a "final offensive," to begin in October 1992, he and several other members of the central committee were captured at a Lima safe house, along with the party's master files. This dramatic reversal of fortune was the result of a combination of factors: Shining Path's overconfidence, bordering on hubris; its increasingly repressive actions against the very people that were to be the beneficiaries of its revolution; and, beginning in 1989, major changes in the government's approach, which began to target leaders through a small elite police unit, to train and provide arms to local peasant groups (*rondas*), and to conduct military operations designed to win hearts and minds and to be sensitive to human rights concerns.

Guzmán's capture marked the beginning of the end of Shining Path as a threat to state survival. It was followed by other government initiatives, including rapid trials, a repentance program that reincorporated into Peruvian society some five thousand former militants and sympathizers, and a major microdevelopment program that targeted the poorest rural districts and dramatically reduced extreme poverty by the late 1990s. Even so, the legacy of violence took a huge toll on Peru—seventy thousand deaths (almost half in Ayacucho alone), some $20 billion in direct property and infrastructure damage, more than half a million internal refugees, and the emigration of about a million Peruvians.

Although Shining Path is no longer a threat to the state, it still operates in some parts of Peru and appears to be slowly regaining momentum as a result of ineffective government policies and the return to the field of hundreds of convicted guerrillas who have completed their sentences.

See also **Guerrilla Movements; Guzmán, Abimael; Peru, Truth Commissions.**

BIBLIOGRAPHY

Degregori, Carlos Iván, et al. *Las rondas campesinas y la derrota de Sendero Luminoso.* Lima: IEP Ediciones, 1996.

Palmer, David Scott, ed. *The Shining Path of Peru*, 2nd edition. New York: St. Martin's, 1994.

Stern, Steve J., ed. *Shining and Other Paths: War and Society in Peru, 1980–1995.* Durham, NC: Duke University Press, 1998.

DAVID SCOTT PALMER

PERU, TRUTH COMMISSIONS.

The Peruvian Truth and Reconciliation Commission was created in 2001 to investigate atrocities committed between 1980 and 2000, a period of internal armed conflict between government forces and two insurgent movements, the Maoist Shining Path and the Tupac Amaru Revolutionary Movement (MRTA).

The commission investigated massacres, disappearances, extrajudicial executions, torture, and other atrocities. It was the first truth commission in Latin America to hold public hearings on a variety of themes, including sexual violence against women.

The commission's chairman, Salomón Lerner, former rector of the Catholic University of Peru, presented a final report to President Alejandro Toledo in August 2003. According to the report, 69,280 Peruvians were killed in the conflict and another 6,000 were disappeared; 54 percent of the deaths were attributed to Shining Path, while the armed forces and its proxies were responsible for 37 percent. Three out of four victims of violence were rural Quechua-speaking peasants, the most marginalized and impoverished sector of Peruvian society. The commission proposed institutional reforms, reparations for victims, and criminal trials in forty-three cases of notorious rights abuses.

Critics charged the commission with having a leftist bias, some even accusing it of being pro-terrorist. Defenders say that such criticisms are designed to ensure impunity for rights violators and attest to the integrity of the commission's report and its plan of social repair.

See also **Movimiento Revolucionario Tupac Amaru (MRTA); Guzmán, Abimael; Peru, Revolutionary Movements: Shining Path; Truth Commissions.**

BIBLIOGRAPHY

Amnesty International. *Peru: The Truth and Reconciliation Commission—A First Step Towards a Country without Injustice.* Amnesty International Report (AMR 46/003/2004). August 2004. Available from http://web.amnesty.org/library/index/engamr460032004.

Defensoría del Pueblo del Perú. *A dos años de la Comisión de la Verdad y Reconciliación.* Informe Defensorial no. 97. September 2005. Available from http://www.defensoria.gob.pe/.

Peruvian Truth and Reconciliation Commission. *Final Report.* August 2003. Available from http://www.cverdad.org.pe.

JO-MARIE BURT

PERUVIAN CURRENT. *See* **Humboldt Current.**

PESCAPERÚ.

Pescaperú, Peruvian fishing corporation. The sudden disappearance of the schools of anchovy and other fish off the coast of Peru, due to the invasion of the warm water current called El Niño into the cold waters of the South Pacific in 1972, created a dire situation for the country's extensive fishing industry. In order to rescue the fish meal industry from bankruptcy, the government of Juan Velasco Alvarado nationalized it in May 1973 and created Pescaperú. It became the largest enterprise in Latin America, consisting of the country's 100 fish meal factories and 1,500-boat anchovy fleet. In addition to producing fish meal and oil, Pescaperú also formed joint-venture companies with foreign firms to catch and can other fish, especially tuna.

See also **Fishing Industry.**

BIBLIOGRAPHY

Additional Bibliography

Arévalo Alvarado Zañartu, Alfonso. *Historia y fundamentos de la pesquería del Peru.* Lima: [s.n.], 1995.

PETER F. KLARÉN

PESQUISA, PESQUISADOR.

Pesquisador, Pesquisa, the investigation of a district or minor official. A *pesquisa* was a special investigation of the activities and behavior of a district official, such as a corregidor, alcalde mayor, or other low-ranking functionary, that was initiated by an *audiencia* and its presiding officer after receiving reports of misconduct in office. The commissioned individual conducting a *pesquisa* was known as a *pesquisador* or, at times, *juez de comisión.* Unless he was an *audiencia* judge, the *pesquisador* usually only reported the results to the *audiencia,* which would then resolve the matter. If the official investigated had abused his judicial responsibilities, the *pesquisador* had the authority to suspend or jail him pending final resolution of the case by the *audiencia.*

See also **Audiencia.**

BIBLIOGRAPHY

Recopilación de leyes de los reynos de las Indias, 4 vols. (1681; repr. 1973), *libro* VII, *título* I.

Clarence H. Haring, *The Spanish Empire in America* (1947), pp. 156–157.

Additional Bibliography

Barrios, Feliciano. *El gobierno de un mundo: Virreinatos y audiencias en la América hispánica.* Cuenca: Ediciones de la Universidad de Castilla-La Mancha: Fundación Rafael del Pino, 2004.

Hawkins, Timothy. *José De Bustamante and Central American Independence: Colonial Administration in an Age of Imperial Crisis.* Tuscaloosa: University of Alabama Press, 2004.

Sanciñena Asurmendi, Teresa. *La audiencia en México en el reinado de Carlos III.* México: Universidad Nacional Autónoma de México, 1999.

MARK A. BURKHOLDER

PESSOA, EPITÁCIO DA SILVA

(1865–1942). Epitácio da Silva Pessoa (*b.* 23 May 1865; *d.* 13 February 1942), president of Brazil (July 1919–November 1922). Orphaned son of a Paraíban landowner, Pessoa was raised by relatives in Pernambuco, where he later graduated from the Recife Law Faculty. After his arrival in Rio de Janeiro in 1889, Pessoa steadily rose among the elite of the young republic, serving as minister of justice (1898–1901), Supremo Tribunal Federal justice (1902–1912), and senator (1912–1919). In 1919 Pessoa led Brazil's delegation to the Versailles Peace Conference, winning fame while negotiating German war reparations and participating in the creation of the League of Nations. While in Versailles, Pessoa was chosen to become president of Brazil through a closed-door compromise struck among the political elite of Brazil's most powerful states, Minas Gerais and São Paulo, to fill out the term of deceased president Rodrígues Alves.

As president, Pessoa strongly supported federal investment in roads, railways, electrification, northeastern drought relief, and higher education. Pessoa contended with political discord among northeastern elites and disgruntled members of the Clube Militar. The final year of Pessoa's presidency, 1922, was a watershed in the steady destabilization of the First Republic, as São Paulo's Modern Art Week, the first *tenente* (lieutenant) revolt, and the Centenary Exposition of Brazilian

Independence all challenged the purported vision of republican peace and prosperity. Upon stepping down from the presidency, Pessoa remained active in federal politics, and also served for many years on the International Court of Justice.

See also **Brazil, Independence Movements.**

BIBLIOGRAPHY

E. Bradford Burns, *A History of Brazil* (1970).

Linda Lewin, *Politics and Parentela in Paraíba: A Case Study of Family-Based Oligarchy in Brazil* (1987).

Additional Bibliography

Lewin, Linda. "The Papers of Epitácio Pessoa: An Archival Note and a Personal Comment." *Luso-Brazilian Review* 33:1 (Summer 1996): 1–20

Quaresma, Quélia H. "Electoral Mobilization and the Construction of a Civic Culture in Brazil, 1909–1930," Ph.D. diss., 1998.

Topik, Steven. *The Political Economy of the Brazilian State, 1889–1930.* Austin: University of Texas Press, 1987.

DARYLE WILLIAMS

PESSOA CAVALCANTI DE ALBU-QUERQUE, JOÃO

(1878–1930). João Pessoa Cavalcanti de Albuquerque (*b.* 24 January 1878; *d.* 26 July 1930), Brazilian politician, vice-presidential candidate (1930). Offspring of elite intermarriage in Brazil's northeastern state of Paraíba, Pessoa is best known for his 1930 death by assassination—an event which served as catalyst to the outbreak of the Revolution of 1930. Educated in military school and the Recife Law School, Pessoa moved to Rio de Janeiro in 1909 to begin a career in federal public service. During the 1920s, Pessoa served on various military tribunals, including the courts that judged the rebellious cadets and young officers involved in the decade's *tenente* revolts.

With the support of his uncle, former Brazilian president Epitácio Pessoa, and his home state's Partido Republicano da Paraíba, Pessoa was elected governor (*presidente*) of Paraíba in 1928. The fiscal and administrative reforms undertaken during his governorship often faced stiff opposition, particularly from political bosses (*coronéis*) of the state's interior. Pessoa faced even stronger opposition from the

federal government when he refused to support the official presidential candidacy of Júlio Prestes. Siding with a Rio Grande do Sul-Minas Gerais–supported opposition party, the Aliança Liberal, Pessoa accepted the nomination to run as vice president on the reformist Aliancista ticket headed by Getúlio Vargas.

During the presidential campaign, Paraíban Coronel José Pereira led a regional rebellion, known as the Princesa Revolt, in an effort to undermine Pessoa's regional and national credibility. Soon after the Aliança Liberal's electoral defeat, Pessoa was assassinated by personal and political rival João Dantas. This incident sparked civil and political unrest, as Dantas was linked to factions which supported the Prestes candidacy. Even though Pessoa had declared his opposition to armed insurrection, his assassination became a rallying cry for the defeated Vargas party. With Pessoa's death-cum- martyrdom still fresh in mind, the civil war that would be known as the Revolution of 1930 broke out in early October 1930. The capital of Paraíba was renamed João Pessoa to honor the slain governor.

See also **Brazil, Revolutions: Revolution of 1930.**

BIBLIOGRAPHY

"Pessoa, João," in *Dicionário histórico-biográfico brasileiro,* vol. 4, edited by Israel Beloch and Alzira de Abreu (1984), pp. 2,701–2,705.

Linda Lewin, *Politics and Parentela in Paraíba: A Case Study of Family-Based Oligarchy in Brazil* (1987).

Additional Bibliography

Quaresma, Quélia H. "Electoral Mobilization and the Construction of a Civic Culture in Brazil, 1909–1930," Ph.D. diss., 1998.

Topik, Steven. *The Political Economy of the Brazilian State, 1889–1930.* Austin: University of Texas Press, 1987.

DARYLE WILLIAMS

PETER, MARIAN. *See* **Melville, Thomas and Margarita.**

PETER MARTYR. *See* **Martyr, Peter.**

PETEXBATÚN. Petexbatún, region on the southwestern side of the Petén rain forest of Guatemala centering around Lake Petexbatún and surrounding rivers and swamps. In the Early Classic period of Maya civilization (300– 600 CE) the major Petexbatún centers of Tamarindito and Arroyo de Piedra had excellent architecture and stone stelae. The most important epic of Petexbatún history, however, began in the early seventh century, when outcast princes from the royal dynasty of the great site of Tikal arrived in the region and established a new capital at the site of Dos Pilas. Hieroglyphic stairways and panels at Dos Pilas and throughout the region record the rapid and dramatic saga of this upstart dynasty. In 679 CE, the defeat of the king of Tikal by "Ruler 1" of Dos Pilas brought prestige to the new center. From Dos Pilas, and later from its twin capital at Aguateca, the new rulers used royal marriage, alliance, and warfare to dominate all the Petexbatún region and later most of the adjacent Pasión River valley, one of the most important transport and trade arteries of the Maya world.

Dos Pilas expansionism ended abruptly and tragically in 761 CE when it was besieged, defeated, and abandoned. After that year, the region fragmented into several competing polities that waged intensive wars against each other. Archaeological investigations have shown that this period witnessed a radical shift in the rules of Maya warfare in this region. Massive fortification systems were found by the Vanderbilt University Petexbatún Regional Archaeological Project at many sites, including walled fortresses and moats at the sites of Punta de Chimino, Aguateca, Dos Pilas, Cerro de Cheyo, Cerro de Mariposa, and Quim Chi Hilan. Warfare, disruption of economic activities and trade, and subsequent depopulation appear to have rapidly destroyed Maya civilization in this region. By the beginning of the ninth century, only scattered households are found in the Petexbatún area. Many scholars believe that the early and violent fall of Classic Maya civilization in the Petexbatún holds important clues for understanding the broader enigma of the Classic Maya collapse in other regions.

See also **Maya, The.**

BIBLIOGRAPHY

Arthur Demarest et al., eds., *Petexbatún Regional Archaeological Project Preliminary Report 3* (1991).

Peter Mathews and Gordon R. Willey, "Prehistoric Polities of the Pasión Region," in *Classic Maya Political History,* edited by T. Patrick Culbert (1991), 30–71.

Arthur Demarest et al., eds., *Petexbatún Regional Archaeological Project Preliminary Report 4* (1992).

Arthur A. Demarest, "The Violent Saga of a Maya Kingdom," in *National Geographic* 183, no. 2 (1993): 95–111.

Additional Bibliography

Demarest, Arthur A. *The Petexbatun Regional Archaeological Project: A Multidisciplinary Study of the Maya Collapse.* Nashville: Vanderbilt University Press, 2006.

Emery, Kitty F. *Maya Zooarchaeology: New Directions in Method and Theory.* Los Angeles: Cotsen Institute of Archaeology at University of California, Los Angeles, 2004.

Inomata, Takeshi. *Settlements and Fortifications of Aguateca: Archaeological Maps of a Petexbatun Center.* Nashville: Vanderbilt University Press, 2007.

Masson, Marilyn A., and David A Freidel, eds. *Ancient Maya Political Economies.* Walnut Creek, CA: AltaMira Press, 2002.

Wright, Lori E. *Diet, Health, and Status among the Pasión Maya: A Reappraisal of the Collapse.* Nashville: Vanderbilt University Press, 2006.

ARTHUR A. DEMAREST

PÉTION, ALEXANDRE SABÈS (1770–1818). Alexandre Sabès Pétion (*b.* 2 April 1770; *d.* 29 March 1818), President of Haiti (1807–1818). Born in Port-au-Prince of a mulatto mother and a wealthy French father, Paschal Sabès, Pétion belonged to the *liberto* (free colored) class of Port-au-Prince. He was despised by his father, perhaps partly because of Pétion's dark skin color. It is unclear why he used the name Pétion instead of Sabès. (Pétion is from the patois Pichoun, meaning "my little one," a nickname given to him by a foster mother.) At age eighteen, after serving as an apprentice to a blacksmith, Pétion enlisted in the colonial army. By age twenty-one, he had distinguished himself and risen to the rank of captain. Later, in the ranks of Toussaint L'ouverture, he proved to be a skilled soldier and an excellent leader. In 1791 he joined the mulattoes in the uprising led by Boukman, a fugitive slave from Jamaica, and later was among Toussaint's troops who fought the British.

Pétion's alliance with Toussaint did not last, for he chose to fight in the ranks of General Charles Leclerc, sent by Napoleon in 1802. He soon realized, however, that victory for Leclerc and the French would mean a loss of rights for Haitians, both blacks and mulattoes. It was then that he joined ranks with Jean Jacques Dessalines. He was one of the first to declare the rights of the members of his class, both political and civil equality with the whites, in accordance with the French Constituent Assembly's "Declaration of Rights of Man and Citizen." During the civil war of 1800, Pétion was exiled to France. In 1801, he returned to Haiti, where he began to actively fight for its independence. Pétion and Dessalines are credited with creating the Haitian flag.

In 1806, Pétion founded the Republic of Haiti and was the main force behind the country's constitution. Elected to the presidency by the Haitian Senate in 1807, Pétion was reelected in 1811 and in 1815. He never reconciled himself to the idea of Haiti as a black state. His hope was for a republic governed by an oligarchy of mulattoes. As a result, racial tensions intensified during his presidency. Nevertheless, he is remembered as a great leader of the independence movement and was praised by many of his Latin American contemporaries, including Simón Bolívar, who visited him in 1815–1816. Pétion supplied Bolívar with troops and support for the liberation movement in Venezuela. Pétion is also remembered for his role in the distribution of land to the veterans of the War of Independence. Nonetheless, he did not achieve his economic and political goals. At his death Haiti had gone from the most productive colony in the hemisphere to the poorest.

See also **Louverture, Toussaint.**

BIBLIOGRAPHY

Charles Moran, *Black Triumvirate* (1957).

Cyril L. R. James, *The Black Jacobins* (1963).

Robert D. Heinl, Jr., and Nancy G. Heinl, *Written in Blood: The Story of the Haitian People* (1978).

Additional Bibliography

Dubois, Laurent. *Avengers of the New World: The Story of the Haitian Revolution*. Cambridge, MA: Belknap Press of Harvard University Press, 2004.

Fick, Carolyn. *The Making of Haiti: The Saint Domingue Revolution from Below*. Knoxville: University of Tennessee Press, 1990.

Geggus, David Patrick, ed. *The Impact of the Haitian Revolution in the Atlantic World*. Columbia: University of South Carolina, 2001.

Mézière, Henri. *Le général Leclerc (1772–1802) et l'expédition de Saint-Domingue*. Paris: Tallandier, 1990.

DARIÉN DAVIS

PETROBRÁS. Petróleo Brasileiro S.A., or Petrobrás, is a public-private venture that operates in the oil, natural gas, and power industry within both the Brazilian and international markets. Brazil's oil industry has a long, turbulent history. Up until the 1930s the world's oil market was controlled by a half-dozen U.S. and European companies, leading to concern in Brazil that the country's energy future was at the mercy of this monopoly. The National Petroleum Council (CNP) was set up in 1938 to explore, develop, and market the country's oil resources. Shortly after World War II the country engaged in an intense debate over how to secure oil resources for its future needs. It was generally understood that without a strongly guaranteed supply of energy, industrialization of the Brazilian economy could not be achieved. The armed forces, industrial leaders, and left-leaning factions all considered energy autonomy an imperative for the country's future security and well-being.

Whereas nationalists were in favor of excluding foreign capital and granting rights exclusively to Brazilians for oil exploration, extraction, refining, and marketing, moderate sectors were in support of allowing foreign investment in exploration of these resources, given the country's shortage of capital and technology. President Getúlio Vargas leaned toward the latter view, which the nationalists branded as "selling out" to foreigners. In 1953, amid a far-reaching nationalist campaign around the slogan "It's our oil," Vargas, in his second term of office, instituted a government monopoly on the oil industry and approved the organization of Petrobrás, without foreign investors.

At first Petrobrás was at the center of political disputes, as nationalists and union leaders tried to dictate the company's guidelines. Once the military came to power in 1964, Petrobrás was strengthened considerably, becoming the largest Latin American oil company in terms of sales by 1990, even though Brazil's known reserves at the time were just over 1 billion barrels. Under the military regime, although key management positions were held by officers, the company remained independent of the armed forces and political groups, unlike other Latin American petroleum companies.

In 1983 Petrobrás began discovering large reserves of oil and natural gas, mostly in the continental shelf. In 1997 Brazil's daily output surpassed the one-million-barrel mark. That same year, within the context of liberal reforms and a policy under Fernando Henrique Cardoso's administration (1995–2001) of limiting the government's role, the state oil monopoly was abolished, with the federal government retaining ownership of hydrocarbon reserves. By 2006 two-thirds of shares in Petrobrás were privately held, with 4 percent traded on the New York Stock Exchange. The Brazilian government held 56 percent of the voting capital. In 2006 the country's oil production was nearing self-sufficiency, at 1.92 million barrels per day. Brazil's reserves are estimated at 11.458 billion barrels of oil and natural gas.

Petrobrás operates in twenty-three countries and is a major player in exploration and production in Venezuela, Peru, and Ecuador and in refining in Argentina and Bolivia. In 2006 its overseas output was 230,000 barrels of oil and gas per day. Petrobrás invests in human-resource development and runs a world-class research and development center (CENPES).

See also **Cardoso, Fernando Henrique; State Corporations; Vargas, Getúlio Dornelles.**

BIBLIOGRAPHY

Dias, José Luciano de Mattos, and Maria Ana Quaglino. *A questão do petróleo no Brasil: Uma história da Petrobrás.* Rio de Janeiro: Fundação Getúlio Vargas, 1995.

Kucinski, Bernardo, ed. *Petróleo: Contratos de risco e dependência.* São Paulo: Brasiliense, 1977.

Miranda, Augusta Tibiriçá. *O petróleo é nosso: A luta contra o "entreguismo," pelo monopólio estatal: 1947–1953, 1953–1981.* Petrópolis, Brazil: Vozes, 1983.

Moura, Mariluce, et al. *Petrobrás 50 anos: Uma construção da inteligência brasileira.* Rio de Janeiro: Petrobrás, 2003.

Petrobrás. *Relatório anual 2005.* Rio de Janeiro: Petrobrás, 2006.

Smith, Peter Seaborn. *Oil and Politics in Modern Brazil.* Toronto: Macmillan, 1976.

Wirth, John D. *The Politics of Brazilian Development, 1930–1954.* Stanford, CA: Stanford University Press, 1970.

EUL-SOO PANG
MARIA LETÍCIA CORRÊA

PETROLEOS DEL PERU (PETROPERU).

Petroleos del Peru, or Petroperu, is the state-owned oil company in Peru that was formerly called Empresa Petrolera Fiscal (EPF). The EPF was organized in 1946 but actually goes back to 1934, when the government of Oscar Benavides first established a petroleum department. The department's holdings and operations expanded during the 1930s; by 1938 it constituted the fourth largest oil producer in the country, though it languished under the governments of Manuel Prado and José Luis Bustamente y Rivero in the 1940s. Production eventually picked up, reaching 607,000 barrels by the late 1950s and 1.4 million barrels by the late 1960s. The company was reorganized as Petroperu by the administration of Juan Velasco Alvarado after it seized power in 1968 and nationalized the International Petroleum Company.

From 1968 to 1991 the extraction, refining, and domestic marketing of oil were under the control of Petroperu. The company was the object of widespread criticism during the first administration of Alan Garcia because government patronage had doubled its workforce from 12,000 to 24,000. In August 1993 another state agency, Perupetro, was established to promote, negotiate, and administer exploration and production contracts, for which Petroperu was required to compete with private companies. This measure led to the awarding of several exploration and development rights to private companies such as ARCO and Chevron in 1995. However, attempts to privatize Petroperu have been stalled ever since widespread unrest and rioting in 1997 erupted in opposition to a second wave of privatization announced by the government of Alberto Fujimoro. In effect, large segments of the population consider Petroperu important to the national interest.

See also **Benavides, Oscar Raimundo; Bustamante y Rivero, José Luis; Fujimori, Alberto Keinya; International**

Petroleum Company (IPC); Prado y Ugarteche, Manuel.

BIBLIOGRAPHY

La Esquina del Movimiento. "No Firesale for Petroperu." Available from http://www.gci275.com/log/2003/06/no-firesale-for-petroperu.shtml.

McClintock, Cynthia, and Fabian Vallas. *The United States and Peru: Cooperation at a Cost*. New York: Routledge, 2003.

Thorp, Rosemary, and Geoffrey Bertram. *Peru, 1890–1977: Growth and Policy in an Open Economy*. New York: Columbia University Press, 1978.

U.S. Department of Energy. Office of Energy Statistics. Energy Information Administration. Available from http://www.eia.doe.gov/emeu/pgem/ch3g.html.

PETER KLARÉN

PETRÓLEOS MEXICANOS.

Petróleos Mexicanos (Pemex) is Mexico's national oil company, established in 1938 as the result of expropriation of the oil industry by President Lázaro Cárdenas. Pemex has been the world's largest offshore oil and gas producer for more than a quarter-century, and its reputation lies in its mastery of shallow-water oil and gas production. In recent years it has produced upward of 3.0 million barrels per day of crude oil. But the future for Pemex in this activity—as well as in other areas of refining, chemicals, gas processing, and pipelines—is uncertain. The uncertainty arises from three causes: the decline in output from its main oil field, the Cantarell complex, which reached its peak in October 2004 at 2.4 million barrels per day; the stagnation in the development of infrastructure in the areas of refining, gas, and chemicals; and the future of the financing for Pemex operations and investment. These topics will be addressed in reverse order.

FINANCES

The question of fiscal reform in Mexico goes far beyond matters related to Pemex. Whereas in Latin America on average, taxes as a share of GDP are 20 percent, in Mexico tax revenue is under 10 percent perhaps. Most Mexicans do not pay taxes: The poor often cannot and the rich find loopholes.

The result is that petroleum products are the most reliable way to generate tax revenue for general government services.

Oil-related taxes in a given year contribute 30 to 40 percent of total public revenues. For Pemex, this situation creates an intolerable burden: It forces the company to borrow money for activities and investments that should come from its own operating and capital budgets. Instead, any requirement—from pipeline maintenance to platform construction—can be turned into a "public works project" with contractor financing. This form of invisible debt is known by its acronym "Pidiregas." Pemex executives since the 1990s have argued for fiscal reform that would result in tax relief, but the government seems to be in no position to make up for lower Pemex taxes without restructuring Mexico's entire fiscal system.

INFRASTRUCTURE

No new refinery has been built in Mexico in more than twenty-five years, a period in which demand for petroleum products has risen by 50 percent. Pemex is therefore forced to import petroleum products in volumes approaching 300,000 b/d, about 50 percent more than its pipeline capacity. The result is that Pemex is forced to contract for the hauling services of a fleet of trucks known as *pipas* at a cost estimated at six to nine times that of pipeline transportation. Pemex's chemical unit was hoping for a big injection of private capital and technology in the proposed world-class ethylene plant known as Project Fénix, but negotiations fell apart when the government refused to grant tax relief in the form of discounted prices on energy.

UPSTREAM

Here the situation is made problematic owing to the unique features of Cantarell, Mexico's super-giant oil field. The challenge for Pemex is the replacement of Cantarell's declining output with production from other fields. Candidates are the KMZ complex, Chicontepec, and deepwater. Each of these has its subset of challenges with regard to finance, technology, and manpower. Pemex estimates that there may be as much as 30 billion barrels of oil equivalent (BOE) in the yet unfound deepwater fields. Pemex is seeking solutions that do not include international oil companies (IOCs) as equity partners. An intriguing drama is developing in relation to oil fields that may contain commercial deposits that cross the U.S.-Mexico maritime boundary.

Since inception, Pemex has functioned, and often thrived, despite the tremendous political and economic upheavals that have occurred almost every decade in modern Mexico. In the early twenty-first century, while Pemex faces large problems, it remains a bulwark to the Mexican economy and an integral part of the international energy market. Pemex's future will plausibly remain intertwined with the overall Mexican economy and subject to political calculations, likely encumbering Pemex and highlighting the sticky realities of state-owned enterprises.

See also **Petroleum Industry.**

BIBLIOGRAPHY

Baker, George. "Mexico Ponders Cross-Border Strategy for Deepwater GOM Fields." *World Oil*, August 2007.

Muñoz Leos, Raúl. *PEMEX en la encrucijada*. Mexico: Nuevo Siglo/Aguilar, 2006.

Shields, David. *PEMEX: Un futuro incierto*. Mexico: Planeta, 2003.

GEORGE BAKER
SEAN H. GOFORTH

PETROLEUM EXPROPRIATION OF 1938 (MEXICO).

Petroleum Expropriation of 1938 (Mexico), the takeover of foreign-owned oil properties in Mexico by the government of President Lázaro Cárdenas. This dramatic act climaxed two decades of tense relations between the Mexican government and multinational petroleum companies. These tensions resulted from Article 27 of the Constitution of 1917, through which the Mexican government claimed ownership of subsoil resources including petroleum. Periodic pressures from the United States discouraged the Mexican government's full enforcement of Article 27 until a 1936–1937 labor dispute brought a major confrontation. The oil companies rejected union demands for increased compensation. The workers appealed to the government, which determined that the companies could afford most of the union demands, and

the Mexican Supreme Court soon ordered compliance. The companies, led by Standard Oil, refused, and opened a media assault on the Cárdenas administration. On 18 March, Cárdenas expropriated the oil properties, in part because the companies' defiance threatened to destabilize his government. (He acted under Article 27 and a 1936 law which authorized presidential expropriations.)

The resulting dispute continued for five years. U.S. and British oil companies urged the government of President Franklin D. Roosevelt to pursue an aggressive policy to enforce their claims; however, U.S. Ambassador Josephus Daniels used unorthodox but skillful diplomacy to calm relations between Mexico City and Washington. The Roosevelt State Department wanted to maintain the harmony created by the Good Neighbor Policy as World War II enveloped Europe and the Pacific and threatened the Americas. Finally, in 1943 Mexico agreed to pay the oil companies approximately 30 million dollars, only a fraction of the 400 to 500 million dollars they had originally claimed.

In spite of diplomatic stresses and economic dislocations, Cárdenas enjoyed widespread domestic support for the expropriation. Critics as well as followers regarded his stand against the large oil companies as an act of far-reaching importance in the relations between industrialized powers and nations beginning the process of industrialization.

See also **Cárdenas del Río, Lázaro; Petroleum Industry.**

BIBLIOGRAPHY

Joe C. Ashby, *Organized Labor in the Mexican Revolution Under Lázaro Cárdenas* (1967), explores the role of the oil workers union, esp. pp. 179–271. Lorenzo Meyer traces the evolution of the Mexican government's policies and the foreign pressures it faced in *Mexico and the United States in the Oil Controversy, 1917–1942*, translated by Muriel Vasconcellos (1977). This expropriation is placed in international and comparative contexts in George Philip, *Oil and Politics in Latin America* (1982), esp. pp. 7–82, 201–226, and 329–334.

Cole Blasier, *The Hovering Giant: U.S. Responses to Revolutionary Change in Latin America* (1985). Clayton R. Koppes argues that U.S. diplomats and oil company executives eventually shaped Mexican oil policy in the 1940s in "The Good Neighbor Policy and the Nationalization of Mexican Oil: A Reinterpretation," in *Journal of American History* 69 (1982): 62–81.

Additional Bibliography

Jayne, Catherine E. *Oil, War, and Anglo-American Relations: American and British Reactions to Mexico's Expropriation of Doreign Oil Properties, 1937–1941.* Westport, CT: Greenwood Press, 2001.

Herrera Montelongo, Judith. *Colaboración y conflicto: El sindicato petrolero y el cardenismo.* México: Universidad Autónoma Metropolitana, Azcapotzalco: M.A. Porrúa, 1998.

Santiago, Myrna. *The Ecology of Oil: Environment, Labor, and the Mexican Revolution, 1900–1938.* Cambridge: Cambridge University Press, 2006.

JOHN A. BRITTON

PETROLEUM INDUSTRY. The oil industry is perhaps the only one in Latin America where the most capital-, technology-, and management-intensive industry in the world meets the mercantilist and statist philosophies of sixteenth-century Iberia. During the colonial period the colonies provided raw materials to the mother country, and the commercial exploitation of the natural resources of the colonies could be carried out only with a franchise from the crown. Natural resources such as subsoil wealth were defined as the property of the state.

As with many areas of public policy, an understanding of Latin American issues begins with Mexico, where, in the last quarter of the nineteenth century President Porfirio Díaz opened many areas of the economy to foreign investment. One of these was the recently inaugurated petroleum industry (including crude oil, natural gas, and natural gas liquids). Under Díaz the entrepreneur who took the risk to develop oil-producing properties was entitled to merchandise the production according to his own criteria—paying, of course, the appropriate taxes to the government.

In the first two decades of the twentieth century, British, Dutch, and U.S. entrepreneurs had discovered major oil-producing reservoirs, and by 1919—despite the chaos produced by the Mexican Revolution and World War I—Mexico was second only to the United States as the leading oil exporter in the world. What soured Mexico in the eyes of foreign investors was Article 27 in the Revolutionary Constitution of 1917, which not only reimposed the policy of the colonial period in matters affecting subsoil resources but also prohibited the Mexican state from leasing franchises for the commercial exploitation of those resources.

About ten years of open- and closed-door negotiations considered the question of the extent to which, if at all, the new policy would apply retroactively to properties that had been lawfully acquired by oil companies during the period which the Díaz Mining Codes (as they were called) were valid. The oil companies insisted that Article 27 could not abrogate legally acquired rights to the properties (estimated at 90 percent of their total portfolio) that had been acquired for future exploration and development. Mexican negotiators responded that Article 27 would not apply to properties on which some "positive act" of development had taken place prior to February 5, 1917, the date on which the constitution went into effect.

Mexican negotiators finally proposed that all titles to properties be exchanged for fifty-year leases. Despite the fact that a fifty-year lease was, in effect, title to the property (few wells provide commercial production beyond twenty years), the oil companies objected. They did not want the leaders of other countries to follow Mexico's example of what they regarded as unfair and stultifying regulation. With the policy framework surrounding Mexican investments in doubt, oil companies started looking elsewhere for safe investments. Indirectly, Mexico provided the impetus for the development of the oil industries of Venezuela and Saudi Arabia. With investment and oil production falling in Mexico, relations between the oil companies and the government began a process of polarization that, on March 18, 1938, resulted in the total expropriation of foreign oil companies in Mexico.

For the next fifty years, in varying ways and on varying time schedules (Venezuela nationalized its oil industry only in 1976), Latin America followed at least the rough outline of the Mexican model. In setting up its monopoly state oil company, however, Venezuela tried to avoid creating a clone of the Mexican company, Petréleos Mexicanos (Pemex), that would function as a state within a state; for this reason, three operating companies with a quasi-competitive relationship among them were established.

With the rise in the early 1970s of the Organization of the Petroleum Exporting Countries

(OPEC—the idea for which had been that of a Venezuelan diplomat, Juan Pablo Pérez Alfonso, and the original membership of which had included Venezuela and Ecuador), relations between the international oil companies and Latin American states became more difficult. By the late 1970s, with the world price of oil exceeding $30 per barrel, oil producers such as Mexico and Venezuela borrowed heavily from eager international lenders who wanted to shore up non–Middle East oil reserves. The high price of oil, in turn, stimulated exploration everywhere, and by 1981, substantial new non-OPEC oil production had been achieved in Mexico's Bay of Campeche, the Alaskan North Slope, and the North Sea.

The late 1970s and early 1980s were also years in which increasingly intense efforts were being taken in the First World as well as in the Third World to reduce dependence on imported oil supplies. In Western Europe, Japan, the United States, and Canada, economic growth was registered without a simultaneous increase in hydrocarbon consumption—a relationship that economists previously had thought highly improbable. In Brazil, the state created a new industry dedicated to the production of "gasahol"—an industrial and transportation fuel based on sugar cane alcohol. Meanwhile, oil-producing countries such as Mexico and Venezuela continued, at great cost to the environment, to subsidize motor fuels, believing that economic growth could be induced by offering the public cheap—and low-quality—gasoline and diesel fuel.

As production from non-OPEC sources rose, there was an increasing competition between oil exporters for market share. In 1980 Mexico announced a new energy plan that called for 1.5 million barrels per day (b/d) of crude oil exports, a target that was not price- or profit-sensitive. Within OPEC there was so much cheating by member countries on their oil-export quotas that Saudi Arabia finally decided to punish the others by increasing its oil production, to nearly 10 million b/d, up from a previous level of about 7 million.

By mid-1981 the trend lines of new Saudi and non-OPEC oil production and energy savings symbolically crossed. The result was that for the first time in nearly a decade, the world trading price of crude oil dropped. In many of the producing countries,

notably Mexico, news of the price drop was received skeptically—"just a market fluctuation." Perhaps no one could have foreseen that cargoes of Mexican heavy oil that sold for $32/b in early 1980 would sell for $5/b in mid-1986. Although spokesmen for oil-producing countries such as Mexico and Venezuela denied that their general economic development programs were keyed to oil, the ensuing ten years of economic decline and stagnation—from which, by 1992, Latin America had far from recovered—showed the extent to which leaders of the 1970s had gambled on a single commodity as an economic panacea to underinvestment and widespread rural and urban poverty.

In 1990, the sacrosanct status of the state-as-oil-monopolist began to fade in many parts of Latin America. Privatization as a policy concept was incorporated in government programs in Argentina, Brazil, Peru, Ecuador, and other countries. By late 1992 such countries were reviewing new offers from private industry to participate as direct investors in their oil industry in both upstream and downstream activities. Driving this policy was the realization that property rights by themselves did not translate into efficient oil production, much less into reliable streams of foreign currency from export sales. A second realization was that real fiscal efficiency from the state's point of view lay in its power to tax oil companies' profits from their operations. Contracts were negotiated in which the oil itself remained the property of the host state; the oil company was paid a percentage (typically 20–30 percent) of the market value of total production. Finally, the leaders of some Latin countries realized that a hidden problem with the state-as-oil-producer model was the inherent managerial and technological isolation that it fostered. In some countries the international oil companies were seen in a new light: as a source not so much of risk capital as of managerial and technological expertise that could be bought for an affordable price.

By 1992 Mexico remained the exception to privatization in the industry. Although since 1989 privatization as a policy theme had been touted in Mexico City as much as in other Latin American capitals, the state oil sector was not included in the government's agenda. Despite intense pressure from U.S. and Canadian negotiators in the summer of 1992 during negotiations for the North American Free Trade Agreement (NAFTA), Mexico refused to change any of the basic planks of its nationalistic and monopolistic policies that dated from the 1930s, 1940s, and 1950s. Mexico's view was that Pemex was self-sufficient in technological and managerial skills, and that where it might be deficient, such skills could be acquired through contracts with oilfield services companies. Representatives from integrated oil companies remained skeptical of such a course, and voiced concerns about the future of Mexico's oil production capability. They recalled that in November 1989, Pemex had alerted the administration of President Carlos Salinas de Gortari that unless domestic oil production increased and domestic demand for refined products decreased, Mexico easily could become a net oil importer.

In some countries—again Mexico and Venezuela are good examples—the hidden cost of several decades of subsidized, low-quality motor fuel could be seen by 1992 in the alarming deterioration of air quality in major metropolitan areas. Several policy remedies were being taken in the region: one is the tardy conversion to unleaded gasoline; a second is the reduction of the sulfur content of diesel and residual fuel (in Mexico in the range of 3–4 percent) to acceptable levels (under 0.5 percent); a third is the increased use of natural gas, which has much lower emissions levels than other industrial or transportation fuels. Within Latin America, Mexico, Venezuela, Bolivia, and Argentina have major reserves of natural gas.

The early twenty-first century has been a heyday for much of the petroleum industry in Latin America. The torrid pace of economic growth in emerging markets, especially China and India, has ensured a boom in petroleum exports from the region. Furthermore, as noted by President George W. Bush in his 2006 State of the Union address, the United States remains "addicted to oil." From 2000 to 2006, the price of light crude more than tripled, producing a windfall for many of Latin America's exporters, especially Venezuela. In 2007, Brazil's state-owned oil company, Petrobrás, announced the discovery of enormous oil reserves in the ultra-deep Tupi field. The finding could net as much as 8 billion barrels of light crude, increasing Brazil's oil reserves by 40 percent, and making the nation one of the largest oil exporters in the world. However, these developments are not unqualified

successes for many Latin American economies. Many nations remain hamstrung by their insufficient refining capacity. For example, even Mexico, with its vast reserves of oil, is not necessarily benefiting from soaring oil prices. Recent IMF studies point toward an inverse correlation of oil prices and Mexican economic growth when the price per barrel exceeds a range of $80–$90, a feature attributable to Mexico's reliance on imported refined petroleum products.

Beyond infrastructure shortcomings, Latin American governments have increasingly sought to diversify the nature of their energy exports away from petroleum. Brazil's ethanol industry is generally seen as the most dynamic in the world. This has yet to make a substantial impact on international markets, primarily because the U.S., which would seem to be the ideal importer of Brazil's ethanol, has imposed a more than 40-cent per gallon tariff on it in order to prop up its own corn producers.

The oil industry in Latin America faces a mixed horizon in the twenty-first century. Real technological advances in crucial areas such as deep-water drilling have been made by Brazil; in Argentina, natural gas pipelines and metropolitan distribution systems have been partially privatized. Development of oil and gas production in Peru and Colombia, on the other hand, has been constrained by political unrest, drug-related violence, and the absence of sufficiently attractive regulatory and fiscal frameworks. For most countries, most notably Mexico and Cuba, a sharp limitation under present regulatory frameworks is financing. With the elimination of Soviet oil supplies in 1991, Cuba's energy supplies and hard-currency reserves were severely curtailed. As for Mexico, in 1992 Pemex claimed that it needed funding support for capital investments for the period 1992–1997 of some $22 billion. Pemex's plight has been underscored by the fact that crude production reached it peak in 2004. Most analysts now believe that regardless of technological advancements, Mexico's oil production is undergoing a one-way slide. Furthermore, greater external investment to the oil industry in Latin America is problematic given political instabilities. High-profile nationalization drives undertaken in Ecuador and Venezuela have sent cautionary messages to Western investors. This has been coupled with antagonistic rhetoric from many leaders, chiefly Venezuela president Hugo Chávez, but also Bolivian president Evo Morales and Ecuadoran president Rafael Correa. Chávez has repeatedly sought to tie Venezuela's oil exports to political relations, threatening on several occasions to divert his country's exports to the U.S. to other parts of the world. The combination of infrastructure and financing woes portend continued uncertainty for the oil industry in Latin America as a whole, even before calculations are made considering energy diversification away from petroleum.

See also **Argentina, Organizations: Yacimientos Petrolíferos Fiscales (YPF); Bolivia, Organizations: Bolivian State Petroleum Corporation (YPFB); Economic Development; Ecopetrol; International Petroleum Company (IPC); Petrobrás; Petroleos del Peru (Petroperu); Petróleos Mexicanos (Pemex); Petroleum Expropriation of 1938 (Mexico); State Corporations.**

BIBLIOGRAPHY

Brown, Jonathan C. *Oil and Revolution in Mexico.* Berkeley: University of California Press, 1992.

Koppes, Clayton R. "The Good Neighbor Policy and the Nationalization of Mexican Oil: A Reinterpretation." *Journal of American History* 69:1 (June 1982), 62–81.

Meyer, Lorenzo. *Mexico and the United States in the Oil Controversy, 1917–1942.* Translated by Muriel Vasconcellos. Austin: University of Texas Press, 1977.

Philip, George D. E. *Oil and Politics in Latin America: Nationalist Movements and State Companies.* Cambridge, U.K. and New York: Cambridge University Press, 1982.

Smith, Peter Seaborn. *Oil and Politics in Modern Brazil.* Toronto: Macmillan of Canada, 1976.

Williams, Bob. "Latin American Petroleum Sector at Crossroads." *Oil & Gas Journal* 90:27 (July 6, 1992).

GEORGE BAKER
SEAN H. GOFORTH

PETROPERÚ. *See* **Petroleos del Peru (Petroperu).**

PETRÓPOLIS. Petrópolis, city (estimated population of 310,216 in 2006) in the Organ Mountains 27 miles north of Rio de Janeiro, in the state of Rio de Janeiro. Originally founded in 1745 by Julius Frederick Knoeller, a German immigrant, Petrópolis was adopted by Dom Pedro II in 1843 as a summer residence for the royal court and a refuge from the yellow fever epidemics that ravaged Rio after 1850.

The alpine beauty of the region and its relatively cool climate had attracted the attention of Dom Pedro I, but it was left to his son, Pedro II, to develop the city, which was named in his honor. After the birth of the republic, Petrópolis remained the official summer residence for the presidents and the diplomatic corps until 1962. Although in the mountainous interior, the city hosted two international meetings: the first in 1903, when the Treaty of Petrópolis was signed, and the second in 1947, when the Intercontinental Conference for the Maintenance of Continental Peace and Security met to implement the Act of Chapultepec.

In 1939, the Brazilian government proclaimed the area surrounding Petrópolis a national park. The city itself is a popular tourist spot, since it is connected to Rio by two train lines and a highway. Among its attractions are the Imperial Palace, now used as a museum housing the royal jewels, and the Cathedral of São Pedro de Alcántara, where the remains of Pedro II and his empress, Dona Teresa Cristina, are interred.

See also **Pedro II of Brazil.**

BIBLIOGRAPHY

W. M. Williams, *Dom Pedro the Magnanimous.* New York: Octagon Books, 1937.

T. Lynn Smith, *Brazil: People and Institutions.* Baton Rouge: Louisana State University Press, 1963.

Additional Bibliography

Barman, Roderick. *Citizen Emperor: Pedro II and the Making of Brazil, 1825–91.* Stanford, CA: Stanford University Press, 1999.

Museu Imperial (Brazil); Eletrobrás; Fundacao Roberto Marinho. *Som e luz Petrópolis: Dom Pedro II-Imperador do Brasil.* Petropolis: Acervo Museu Imperial, 2004.

Quevedo, Maria Augusta; Renata Lerina Ferreira Rios. *Petrópolis.* Porto Alegre (Brazil): Unidade Editorial da Secretaria Municipal da Cultura, 2002.

Schwartz, Lilia; John Gledson. *The Emperor's Beard: Dom Pedro II and the Tropical Monarchy of Brazil.* New York: Hill and Wang, 2004.

SHEILA L. HOOKER

PETRÓPOLIS, TREATY OF (1903).

Treaty of Petrópolis (1903), one of the treaties negotiated by the Brazilian José Maria da Silva Paranhos, Jr., Baron of Rio Branco, and other diplomats to settle territorial disputes and open hostility regarding the poorly surveyed interior borders of South America. The Treaty of Petrópolis awarded Acre and its 73,000 square miles of rubber-producing lands to Brazil. Bolivia gained necessary land along the Madeira River for access to the Atlantic, open navigation on the Madeira River, $10 million, and the promise of a Brazilian-financed Madeira-to-Mamore railroad that would permit Bolivia to reach the lower Madeira River, bypassing treacherous rapids.

This settlement ended the hostilities aggravated by the recent economic boom in the rubber industry. Migrant Brazilian rubber tappers resented a Bolivian contract of 1901 to develop Acre in partnership with American capitalists and refused to pay the newly enforced Bolivian taxes demanded of all Brazilians who attempted to transport their goods via the Acre River. Led by José Plácido de Castro, the Brazilians seized the Bolivian customshouse in 1902. Brazil and Bolivia sent troops to the area before the Treaty of Petrópolis ended the threat of war.

See also **Rubber Industry.**

BIBLIOGRAPHY

E. Bradford Burns, *The Unwritten Alliance: Rio-Branco and Brazilian-American Relations* (1966), and *A History of Brazil* (1993), pp. 277–279.

Leslie Bethell, ed., *The Cambridge History of Latin America*, vol. 6 (1984), pp. 346, 565, 570.

Additional Bibliography

Klein, Herbert S. *A Concise History of Bolivia.* Cambridge: Cambridge University Press, 2003.

Tocantins, Leandro. *Formação Histórica do Acre.* Brasília: Senado Federal/Conselho Editorial, 2001.

LESLEY R. LUSTER

PETTORUTI, EMILIO (1892–1971).

Emilio Pettoruti (*b.* 1 October 1892; *d.* 16 October 1971), Argentine painter, pioneer of abstract art in South America, who developed a style incorporating synthetic cubism, futurism and early Renaissance painting. Born in La Plata, Pettoruti was self-taught. In 1913 he went to study in Florence, Italy. Influenced by the futurists and kinetic figuration, Pettoruti painted symbolic abstractions of wind and light (e.g., *Lights in the Landscape,* 1915). From his study of quattrocento painting, he derived a halftone palette, painting quasi-geometrical portraits and landscapes (e.g., *Woman in the Café, Sunshine and Shade,* both 1917). He met Juan Gris in Paris in 1923 and returned to Argentina the following year. He was director of the Museum of Fine Arts, La Plata, from 1930 to 1947. In 1941 he exhibited at the San Francisco Museum of Art. His conception of art polarized traditionalists and avant-gardists. Influenced by cubism, he used dissected forms but did not employ simultaneous presentation of different profiles. In 1953 he moved to Paris, where he lived until his death.

After 1950 Pettoruti returned to pure, dynamic abstractions with a metaphysical bent (e.g., *Quietness of the Beyond,* 1957). Classified by some as an academic cubist, he was considered a classical modernist by others.

See also **Art: The Twentieth Century.**

BIBLIOGRAPHY

Gilbert Chase, *Contemporary Art in Latin America* (1970), pp. 128–133.

Angel Osvaldo Nessi and Jorge Romero Brest, *Pettoruti* (1987).

Nelly Perazzo, "Constructivism and Geometric Abstraction," in *The Latin American Spirit: Art and Artists in the United States, 1920–1970,* by Luis R. Cancel et al. (1988), pp. 118–119.

Additional Bibliography

Fèvre, Fermín. *Emilio Pettoruti.* Buenos Aires: Editorial El Ateneo, 2000.

Sullivan, Edward J., and Nelly Perazzo. *Emilio Pettoruti (1892–1971).* Buenos Aires: Asociación Amigos del Museo Nacional de Bellas Artes, 2005.

MARTA GARSD

PEYOTE. *See* **Drugs and Drug Trade.**

PEZET, JUAN ANTONIO (1809–1879).

Juan Antonio Pezet (*b.* 1809; *d.* 1879), military leader who became president of Peru (1863–1865) upon the death in office of General Miguel de San Román. Born in Lima, Pezet had to confront a difficult international conflict with Spain resulting from the Talambo Affair (August 1863) and the Spanish government's renewed hostility toward its old colonies. The Spanish fleet, off the Peruvian coast at the time, seized the guano-producing islands of Chincha to press a settlement that included an apology for the deaths of two Spanish nationals killed on the Talambo estate, as well as the repayment to Spain of the public debt dating back to 1820. The Pezet government opted for a peaceful solution to the conflict with the signing of the Vivanco-Pareja Treaty (January 1865), which was seen by many Peruvians, including some military leaders, as a submission to Spanish demands. The still influential caudillo Ramón Castilla and Colonel Mariano Ignacio Prado led the opposition to Pezet that caused his ouster in November 1865 and the rejection of the treaty by the new government of Prado. In 1866 the allied forces of Peru, Chile, Ecuador, and Bolivia fought several naval battles with the Spanish fleet, forcing the Spanish contingent to withdraw from the South American Pacific coast. Pezet died in Chorrillos.

See also **Talambo Affair.**

BIBLIOGRAPHY

Jorge Basadre, *Historia de la República del Perú,* vols. 3–4 (1963).

David Werlich, *Peru: A Short History* (1978).

Additional Bibliography

Salinas Sánchez, Alejandro. *Caudillos, partidos políticos y nacionalismo en el Perú, 1850–1879.* Lima: Seminario de Historia Rural Andina, Universidad Nacional Mayor de San Marcos, 2005.

ALFONSO W. QUIROZ

PHELPS, ANTHONY (1928–).

Anthony Phelps (*b.* 25 August 1928), Haitian writer, journalist, photographer, filmmaker, and ceramicist. After finishing his secondary schooling in Haiti, Phelps studied chemistry at Seton Hall University in New Jersey. He then studied plastic arts and photography in Montreal and New York. Together with several fellow writers (Davertige, Serge Legagneur, Roland Morisseau, René Philoctète), Phelps founded a literary group, Haïti Littéraire, and a journal, *Semences* (1962). Phelps was forced to flee Haiti in 1964 because of criticism of the Duvalier regime in his print and radio journalism. In Quebec he worked in television and theater and continued to write. Phelps achieved a level of popular appeal with his live poetry recitals and a number of records. Some of his videos have been broadcast by Radio Québec and in Haiti since the fall of Jean-Claude Duvalier in 1986.

Phelps participated in numerous writers' congresses in Africa and in Latin America and has maintained contacts with Latin American writers. His volume of poetry *Orchidée nègre* (1985, 1987) won the 1985 prize of Casa de las Américas and was first published in Cuba. He continues to publish in multiple genres and is an important figure within the French Canadian context.

See also **Haiti; Journalism.**

BIBLIOGRAPHY

Été (poetry, 1960); *Éclats de silence* (poetry, 1962); *Points cardinaux* (poetry, 1966); *Le conditionnel* (drama, 1968); *Mon pays que voici; suivi de Les dits du Fou-aux-cailloux* (poetry, 1968); *Et moi, je suis une île* (children's stories, 1973); *Moins l'infini* (novel, 1973); *Motifs pour le temps saisonnier* (poetry, 1976); *Mémoire en colin-maillard* (novel, 1976); *La bélière caraïbe* (poetry, 1980); *Même le soleil est nu* (poetry, 1983); and *Haïti! Haïti!* (thriller, with Gary Klang, 1985).

See also Maurice A. Lubin, "Five Haitian Poets," in *Young Poetry of the Americas* (1968); F. Raphaël Berrou and Pradel Pompilus, *Histoire de la littérature haïtienne illustrée par les textes,* vol. 3 (1977), pp. 344–359; Jean Jonassaint, *Le pouvoir des mots, les maux du pouvoir* (1986), pp. 101–128; Max Dominique, *L'arme de la critique littéraire: Littérature et idéologie en Haïti* (1988), pp. 217–229. *Femme Amérique* (2004), *La contrainte de l'inachevé* (2006)

Additional Bibliography

Costantini, Alessandro. *Fantasmi narrative e sovversione linguistica nel romanzo dell'identia in "Mémoire en colin-maillard."* Milano: Cisalpino, Universitario, 2002.

CARROL F. COATES

PHILIP II OF SPAIN (1527–1598).

Philip II of Spain (*b.* 21 May 1527; *d.* 13 September 1598), king of Spain (1556–1598), king of Naples and Sicily (1554–1598), and, as Philip I, king of Portugal (1580–1598).

Philip's priorities were religion, justice, and peace, although circumstances occasionally forced him to subordinate one in pursuit of another. Diplomacy and concern about an heir brought him four marriages: the Portuguese infanta María (1543–1545), who died giving birth to Don Carlos; Mary Tudor of England (1554–1558); Elizabeth of Valois (1559–1568), as part of the Treaty of Cateau-Cambrésis, who bore him two daughters; and his niece Anna of Austria (1570–1580), who bore him one daughter and four sons, only one of whom (Philip III) survived to adulthood.

Very deliberate in making decisions, Philip did much of his own paperwork and was unwilling to delegate authority to ministers whom he did not wholly trust, often with good reason. Nor did he have reason to trust his son and heir, Don Carlos, whom he confined in 1568 until the latter's death six months later.

Foreign policy, the first concern of Philip's government, revolved mainly around the policy toward the Netherlands after the revolt of 1566 when Calvinists overran the cities and desecrated churches. Philip's approach to governing the rebels ranged from reconciliation to brutal military suppression. The efforts consumed vast amounts of imperial revenue, increasing sums of which came from the Indies. On the southern front, Philip was menaced by the Turks and faced a revolt by the Morisco (converted Moors) population in Granada (1568). Spain delivered a resounding defeat to Turkish warships in the Gulf of Lepanto in 1571, one of the few instances when Spain acted in concert with the papacy. Philip's other major military victory was the conquest of Portugal (1580), which led to the union of the Spanish and Portuguese crowns for himself and his heirs.

After the Lepanto victory, Philip again turned his attention to the problem of the Netherlands, recalling the Duke of Alva (Fernando Álvarez de Toledo) in 1573 and instituting a more conciliatory policy. However, in 1576 unpaid troops mutinied and sacked the city of Antwerp. In response, the seventeen northern provinces demanded withdrawal of all foreign troops, but left the religious issue unsettled until 1579, when the rebels and the Catholic estates formed separate unions. Although Spain retook Antwerp, Philip soon realized he would have to come to terms with a major source of Dutch support, and thus prepared the Armada for an invasion of England (1588). In 1599 Philip entrusted the government of the Netherlands to his nephew, Archduke (of Austria) Albert, and the infanta Isabella. Toward the end of his reign Philip put down a short-lived rebellion in Aragon (1590–1591), which linked the liberty of his former secretary, Antonio Pérez, with the liberties of Aragon and in the end allowed a little more royal authority in the kingdom.

Philip's costly foreign policy forced him to declare bankruptcy four times during his reign—in 1557, 1560, 1575, and 1596—despite raising taxes at home and a booming Indies trade. Although his total annual income tripled between 1560 and 1598, it was never enough to cover expenses. The Indies revenue, which included silver from the mines of Potosí (discovered in 1545), never constituted more than a quarter of the crown's total income, but it was especially valuable because it was generally dependable and in the form of hard cash that was internationally negotiable. Drake's destruction of the New Spain fleet in the port of Cádiz (1587), followed by the losses incurred by the Armada expedition (1588), shook the confidence of Spanish merchants, but Spain recovered by reorganizing fortifications and employing smaller and faster ships.

During Philip's reign, the era of conquest in the New World came to an end and bureaucrats increased royal control over the heirs of the conquistadores.

See also **Conquistadores; Mining: Colonial Spanish America.**

BIBLIOGRAPHY

H. G. Koenigsberger, "The Statecraft of Philip II," *European Studies Review* 1, no. 1 (1971): 1–21.

Fernand Braudel, *The Mediterranean and the Mediterranean World in the Age of Philip II,* translated by Sian Reynolds (1972).

Peter Pierson, *Philip II of Spain* (1975).

I. A. A. Thompson, *War and Government in Habsburg Spain, 1560–1620* (1976).

Geoffrey Parker, *Philip II* (1978).

Additional Bibliography

Hilliam, David. *Philip II: King of Spain and Leader of the Counter- Reformation.* New York: Rosen Publishing Group, 2005.

Kamen, Henry. *Philip of Spain.* New Haven, CT: Yale University Press, 1997.

Morales Folguera, José Miguel. *La construcción de la utopía: El proyecto de Felipe II (1556–1598) para Hispanoamérica.* Madrid: Biblioteca Nueva, 2001.

Parker, Geoffrey. *The Grand Strategy of Philip II.* New Haven, CT: Yale University Press, 1998.

Williams, Patrick. *Philip II.* New York: Palgrave, 2000.

SUZANNE HILES BURKHOLDER

PHILIP III OF SPAIN (1578–1621).

Philip III of Spain (*b.* 14 April 1578; *d.* 31 March 1621), king of Spain, Naples, and Sicily (1598–1621) and, as Philip II, king of Portugal (1598–1621).

Philip III was the first king since John II of Castile to begin what was to become a seventeenth-century Hapsburg trend: delegation of power to a chief minister (*valido*). Philip's choice was the politically inexperienced duke of Lerma, Francisco Gómez de Sandoval y Rojas (1553–1623), who used his office to amass a fortune and become the pinnacle of a patronage system riddled with unscrupulous characters. Lerma, however, also steered his practically bankrupt country toward peace with England (1604) and the Dutch (1609). Philip's unwise solution to Spain's budget deficit was to issue and reissue copper coinage. Also unfavorable to Spain's finances was the decision to expel the Moriscos (Moors converted to Christianity) the same day the treaty with the Dutch was signed.

Lerma was succeeded in influence by his son, the duke of Uceda, although after 1618 Philip issued a decree stating that only the king would sign royal orders. Philip was pious like his father but he lacked his father's energy and dedication to affairs of state or empire.

See also **Spanish Empire.**

BIBLIOGRAPHY

Ciriaco Pérez Bustamante, *Felipe III: Semblanza de un monarca y perfiles de una privanza* (1950).

John Lynch, *Spain Under the Habsburgs,* vol. 2, *Spain and America, 1598–1700* (1969), esp. pp. 14–61.

Patrick Williams, "Philip III and the Restoration of Spanish Government, 1598–1603," in *English Historical Review* 88 (1973): 751–769.

Additional Bibliography

Fisas, Carlos. *Historias de reyes y reinas.* Barcelona: Planeta, 1998.

Herrero Sánchez, Manuel. *Las Provincias Unidas y la monarquía hispánica (1588–1702).* Madrid: Arco Libros, 1999.

Kamen, Henry Arthur Francis. *Spain's Road to Empire: The Making of a World Power, 1492–1763.* London: Allen Lane, 2002.

Lynch, John. *The Hispanic World in Crisis and Change, 1598–1700.* Oxford: Blackwell, 1994.

SUZANNE HILES BURKHOLDER

PHILIP IV OF SPAIN (1605–1665).

Philip IV of Spain (*b.* 8 April 1605; *d.* 17 September 1665), king of Spain, Naples, and Sicily (1621–1665) and, as Philip III, Portugal (1621–1640).

Philip inherited from his father (Philip III) a state in decline. Until 1643 Philip's reign was overshadowed by the policies of his favorite, the count-duke of Olivares (1587–1645). Spain was frequently involved in European conflicts financed, in part, by its American empire. Much of Spain's foreign policy and war effort was directed at preserving and defending the Low Countries. Despite seeking peace with England and France, Spain ended up at war with both countries and was menaced overseas by the Dutch, who captured the entire New Spain silver fleet in 1628.

Olivares's attempts at financial and administrative reform met with little success and the crown declared bankruptcy in 1627. His Unión De Armas scheme to get non-Castilian provinces to share the costs of imperial defense ultimately led to the revolt of Catalonia in 1640. This, in turn, encouraged the Portuguese to seek independence and, in December 1640, the Duke of Bragança (1604–1656) was proclaimed John IV of Portugal. After making peace with the Dutch in 1648, Philip signed a treaty with France in 1659 that provided for the marriage of his eldest daughter, María Teresa, to the French king.

Philip, who is known to art history as the patron and frequent subject of the great painter Diego Velázquez (1599–1660), was survived by one sickly son, Charles II (1661–1700). As king, Charles II inherited an empty treasury, a discredited currency, a multitude of new taxes, and very little to show for his father's foreign war expenditure.

See also **Unión de Armas.**

BIBLIOGRAPHY

Antonio Domínguez Ortiz, *Política y hacienda de Felipe IV* (1960).

José Deleito y Piñuela, *El declinar de la monarquía española* (3d ed., 1955).

John Lynch, *Spain Under the Habsburgs,* vol. 2, *Spain and America, 1598–1700* (1969), esp. pp. 62–228.

Jonathan Brown and John H. Elliott, *A Palace for a King: The Buen Retiro and the Court of Philip IV* (1980).

Additional Bibliography

Chamorro, Eduardo. *Felipe IV.* Barcelona: Planeta, 1998.

Fisas, Carlos. *Historias de reyes y reinas.* Barcelona: Planeta, 1998.

Herrero Sánchez, Manuel. *Las Provincias Unidas y la monarquía hispánica (1588–1702).* Madrid: Arco Libros, 1999.

Kamen, Henry Arthur Francis. *Spain's Road to Empire: The Making of a World Power, 1492–1763.* London: Allen Lane, 2002.

Lynch, John. *The Hispanic World in Crisis and Change, 1598–1700.* Oxford: Blackwell, 1994.

SUZANNE HILES BURKHOLDER

PHILIP V OF SPAIN (1683–1746). Philip V of Spain, (*b.* 19 December 1683; *d.* 9 July 1746), king of Spain (1700–1724 and 1724–1746).

Philip V, duke of Anjou and grandson of Louis XIV and María Teresa (daughter of Philip IV of Spain), was the first Bourbon king of Spain. Designated heir to the throne by his Hapsburg predecessor, Charles II, Philip entered Madrid in 1701 with his wife, María Luisa. His claim to the throne, however, was contested by two other candidates, and the first twelve years of his reign witnessed the War of the Spanish Succession (1701–1714). He married Isabella Farnese of Parma in 1714.

As punishment for supporting the rival Austrian claimant, Philip deprived Catalonia, Aragon, and Valencia of most of their autonomous privileges. Subsequent government reforms included the *Nueva Planta* (1716), which replaced viceroys with captains-general and initiated Spain's transformation from a collection of semi-autonomous provinces into a centralized state.

Although foreign policy during Philip's reign was often dictated by his wives or their favorites, after 1726 Philip was well served by a number of able secretaries (who made up an aristocracy of merit rather than privilege) dedicated to strengthening the state and its finances. In order to restore Spain as a great power through the exploitation of empire, the king's ministers modernized the navy and developed trading companies. However, the revitalization of trade awaited the suspension of the fleet system (1740) and its replacement with register ships.

Philip's personal behavior alarmed his subjects, and his sexual compulsions (counterbalanced by religious ones) allowed his wives to manipulate him. He was also the victim of a recurring mental illness that manifested itself in fits of hysteria, complete detachment from reality, profound melancholy, and violent behavior. In order to live a life of retreat in preparation for an afterlife, Philip abdicated in favor of his sixteen-year-old son, Louis, in 1724. However, Louis died eight months later and Philip was persuaded to resume the Spanish throne. Ironically, he died without the presence of a confessor.

See also **War of the Spanish Succession.**

BIBLIOGRAPHY

Alfred Baudrillart, *Philippe V et la Cour de France,* 5 vols. (1890–1900).

Henry Kamen, *The War of Succession in Spain, 1700–1715* (1969).

John Lynch, *Bourbon Spain, 1700–1808* (1989), esp. pp. 22–156.

Additional Bibliography

Garcia Càrcel, Ricard. *Felipe V y los españoles: Una visión periférica del problema de España.* Barcelona: Plaza & Janés, 2002.

González Enciso, Agustín. *Felipe V: La renovación de España: Sociedad y economía en el reinado del primer*

Borbón. Pamplona: Ediciones Universidad de Navarra, 2003.

Kamen, Henry. *Philip V of Spain: The King Who Reigned Twice*. New Haven, CT: Yale University Press, 2001.

SUZANNE HILES BURKHOLDER

PHILIPPINES. The Philippines, officially the Republic of the Philippines (Republika ng Pilipinas; RP), is an island nation located in Southeast Asia, with Manila as its capital city. The Philippine Islands comprise 7,107 islands in the western Pacific Ocean. The country reflects diverse Austronesian cultures from its many islands, as well as European and American influence from Spain, Latin America, and the United States.

Filipinos are mostly of Austronesian descent. Some Filipinos, however, are partly of American, Spanish, Chinese, and Arab ancestry.

Based on the Census of Population and Housing conducted decennially by the National Statistics Office, the total population of the Philippines as of May 1, 2000 was 76,504,077 persons. This was higher by 7,887,541 persons, or about 10.31 percent, from the 1995 census. It was ten times the Philippine population in 1903, when the first census was undertaken.

DISCOVERY AND CONQUEST

In his circumnavigation of the world, Ferdinand Magellan landed at Suluan Island in the Philippines in 1521. Three subsequent Spanish expeditions led by Juan García Jofre de Loaysa (1526), Alvaro de Saavedra Cerón (1528), and Ruy López de Villalobos (1543) tried unsuccessfully to launch a colony in the archipelago. It was not until 1565 that Miguel Lopez De Legazpi succeeded. In 1571 he moved his settlement from Cebu to Manila on Luzon. Except for the British occupation of Manila in 1761–1763, Spain retained its Far Eastern colony bordering China for the next three hundred years.

ADMINISTRATIONS

The colony was governed by a captain-general dependent on the viceroy of Mexico. He possessed legislative, administrative, and, as president of the *audiencia* (court and adviser to the captain-general), judicial control. He was commander of the army (when one existed), upholder of the laws from Spain, vice patron of the church, and finance overseer (until the intendant system was inaugurated in the late eighteenth century). Governors in the Philippines often used their office to increase their own wealth. In the latter half of the eighteenth century, a succession of extraordinarily competent governors (Pedro Manuel de Arandía, 1754–1759; Simón de Anda y Salazar, 1770–1776; and José Basco y Vargas, 1778– 1787) did much to raise the economic level of the colony.

EVANGELIZATION

The first missionaries in the archipelago were the five Augustinians who arrived with Legazpi in 1565. Fifteen Franciscans arrived in 1578, and the Jesuits and Dominicans began mission work in 1581. Augustinian Recollects arrived in 1606. The major motive for retaining the economically unproductive colony was religious. The missionaries appealed to the king's obligation to evangelize the archipelago. The Spaniards arrived just as Islam was making headway in the archipelago and had already converted the southern Philippines. The islands were divided into mission jurisdictions, and missionaries began to evangelize their regions by creating parishes, mission stations, and outlying *vistas*. Missionaries used native languages for instruction rather than Spanish. Within a relatively short period of time, major indigenous groups were Christian. The Dominicans staffed the College of Santo Tomás in Manila, which became a university, and the Jesuits opened the College of Manila (1595) and six others throughout the islands.

TRIBUTE, LABOR, AND COMMERCE

Tribute, either in specie or in kind, was exacted from Filipinos to help defray the costs of colonization and to acknowledge their vassalage to the king of Spain. It was paid to an *encomendero*, who was assigned to accept the payment from a specific town or cluster of villages. In return, the *encomendero* was supposed to protect the inhabitants of his villages and make sure that they were instructed in Christian doctrine. Exemptions were made for age and sex. In 1779, in the archdiocese of Manila, an estimated 68,000 paid tribute while 178,000 did not. Filipinos also provided labor for the shipyards of Cavite, where warships were constructed. Only a few of the famed Manila Galleons were constructed in the Philippines. Most were built in Mexico.

The Manila galleon was a massively large vessel that between 1565 and 1815 made one round trip a year between Manila and Acapulco, Mexico. On the outward trip from Manila, the ship was loaded with silks, spices, and Oriental luxury items. Ports from India through Southeast Asia to China shipped goods to Manila, where they were processed and stored by Manila's Chinese colony, then transshipped by a handful of Spanish merchants who were allotted a specific amount of space each year on the galleon. On the return from Mexico, the galleon carried silver, which paid for the next shipment of luxury items. With these cargoes, the Manila galleon was a sought-after prize of pirates and enemies of Spain, but only one was captured at sea, the *Covadonga,* by George Anson in 1743. He found 1,313,843 pieces of eight aboard, and at Canton a thorough search of the galleon revealed more silver hidden in rinds of cheese, in the ship's timbers, and in other places—clear indication of the smuggling going on.

Taxes were collected on the galleon trade but were never enough to pay for the administration of the colony. A yearly subsidy, called the *situado,* was sent from Spain or Mexico. In the nineteenth century, exports of Manila hemp (used for ships' rigging), sugar, and tobacco spurred the colony's economic development and helped to create an emerging middle class.

INDEPENDENCE
In the latter nineteenth century, Filipinos began to demand assimilation with Spain, representation in the Spanish Cortes, and freedom of speech. Led by José Rizal and Marcelo H. del Pilar, the propaganda movement, as it came to be called, especially attacked the Spanish friars as the visible manifestation of Spanish domination. José Rizal's novel *Noli Me Tangere* (1884) was a biting attack on the Spanish colonial mentality in the Philippines. The movement helped instill a sense of nationalism. Rizal was executed on 30 December 1896 for alleged participation in armed insurrection. In 1897 a war for independence broke out under Filipino General Emilio Aguinaldo. The Filipino revolutionaries signed the

Treaty of Biak-na-Bato, in which they agreed to leave the archipelago in return for 1.5 million pesos. Aguinaldo went to Hong Kong. The Spaniards never paid the full amount, however, so the revolution continued. On 25 April the United States declared war on Spain. On 1 May 1898, Commodore George Dewey left Hong Kong for Manila Bay, where he wrecked the Spanish fleet, blockaded the harbor, and awaited the arrival of American troops. Spanish rule ended in the Philippines with the signing of the Treaty of Paris on 10 December 1898.

Today most Filipinos are aware of their Spanish heritage but few speak Spanish.

See also **Magellan, Ferdinand; Spanish-American War; Spanish Empire.**

BIBLIOGRAPHY

William L. Schurz, *The Manila Galleon* (1939).

John L. Phelan, *The Hispanization of the Philippines* (1959).

Horacio De La Costa, *The Jesuits in the Philippines, 1581–1768* (1961).

León María Guerrero, *The First Filipino: A Biography of José Rizal* (1963).

Edgar Wickberg, *The Chinese in Philippine Life, 1850–1898* (1965).

Nicholas P. Cushner, *Spain in the Philippines: From Conquest to Revolution* (1971).

Norman G. Owen, *Prosperity Without Progress: Manila Hemp and Material Life in the Colonial Philippines* (1984).

Additional Bibliography

Brands, H. W. *Bound to Empire: The United States and the Philippines.* New York: Oxford University Press, 1992.

Dola, Ronald E., ed. *Philippines: A Country Study.* 4th ed. Washington, DC: Federal Research Division, Library of Congress, 1993.

Hamilton-Paterson, James. *America's Boy: A Century of Colonialism in the Philippines.* New York: Henry Holt, 1998.

Oleksy, Walter. *The Philippines.* New York: Children's Press, 2000.

Rodell, Paul A. *Culture and Customs of the Philippines.* Westport, CT: Greenwood Press, 2002.

Zanini, Gianni. *Philippines: From Crisis to Opportunity: Country Assistance Review.* Washington, DC: World Bank, 1999.

NICHOLAS P. CUSHNER

PHILOSOPHY

This entry includes the following articles:
OVERVIEW
FEMINIST PHILOSOPHY

OVERVIEW

The study and teaching of philosophy in Latin America was established early in the period of Iberian colonial rule, when Spain and Portugal established imperial control over the region (sixteenth through the nineteenth century). It therefore occupies an important place in the history of the region, as many of the discipline's central themes developed in close contact with larger issues concerning the history and culture of Latin America. Philosophy not only has enjoyed continuity through five centuries of study and teaching but also has played a significant role in the discussion of contemporary social and political events. Philosophers in different periods have been prominent cultural, educational, social, and political figures. Various political movements, educational experiments, and cultural theories have been rooted in philosophical sources. Therefore, an understanding of the evolution of philosophy in Latin America is essential for the historian.

Although philosophy can and should be seen in the larger context of society, an understanding of the discipline also requires that it be viewed as an enterprise that poses its own methodological problems and questions, maintains a dialogue with issues and thinkers across chronological periods and geographical boundaries, and develops in the rather protected walls of the academy. The student of Latin American philosophy especially confronts a constant tension between the weight that should be given to the significance of philosophy for the larger society and that given to the field's character as a discipline of universal validity.

Another dimension of importance for understanding the evolution of philosophy in Latin America concerns the question of whether there is a philosophy that can be called "Latin American." Since the 1940s scholars have intensely debated whether philosophy can be understood independently of culture or nationality. They have thus utilized the discipline in an attempt to define a Latin American identity that in turn can provide the basis for an original Latin American philosophy. Scholars who understand philosophy as a discipline concerned with thought in its most general sense have strongly rejected any culturally or nationally bound interpretations of philosophical activity. Although this debate has not and probably will not be settled in the near future, it is apparent that philosophy in Latin America has historically engaged intellectuals to a very significant degree.

THE COLONIAL PERIOD

Philosophical studies during the colonial period were primarily the province of clerical institutions. Although the debates between the Dominican friar Bartolomé de las Casas and the theologian Juan Ginés de Sepúlveda in the sixteenth century regarding the humanity of the Indians were by no means disinterested philosophical speculation, their frame of reference was Aristotle and the larger tradition of scholasticism. In Brazil, the Jesuit priest Antônio Vieira put his rigorous training to use in order to defend Indians and slaves, and to oppose the Dutch occupation in the seventeenth century.

Scholasticism, which dominated the thinking of scholars during the colonial period, produced some fairly specialized philosophical treatises. Immersed as they were in a European climate of ideas, texts such as Alonso de la Vera Cruz's *Recognitio summularum* (1554) and *Dialectica resolutio* (1554), and Juan de Espinosa Medrano's *Logica* (1688), are fairly difficult to place in the context of contemporary social and political events in the Iberian colonies. But they demonstrate that philosophy played an important role in the training of civil and ecclesiastical personnel. Philosophy, in fact, was central to the curriculum of the colonial university. Its purpose was to provide students with scholastically inspired methods of thinking. Latin American philosophers discussed medieval scholastics such as Thomas Aquinas (c. 1225–1274) and Duns Scotus (c. 1266–1308), and Iberian commentators such as Francisco de Vitoria, Petrus Fonseca (1528–1599), and Francisco Suárez (1548–1617). In some cases, their intellectual endeavors could be applicable to concrete legal problems and issues concerning Spaniards and Indians, but by and large they were concerned with themes such as individuation and the nature of universals.

Scholasticism had declined somewhat by the 1750s, coinciding with the Bourbon reforms, but its influence on logic and law remained paramount. Reflecting the Bourbon period's emphasis on enlightened thinking and scientific inquiry, Manuel Antonio Talavera's *Triennalis phylosofici cursus* (1792) contains remarkably current discussions on physics. In Brazil, where prominent families sent their children to the University of Coimbra, intellectuals such as José Bonifácio de Andrada absorbed the modernized curriculum introduced by the reforms of Pombal. Some scholars have argued that the roots of independence might be traced to the developing humanism of colonial thinkers, but philosophy overall was at best a contributing factor rather than a primary cause.

THE POSTINDEPENDENCE PERIOD

The process of independence in the early nineteenth century and the steady rise of liberalism as a dominant political force brought about the increasing secularization of society in general, and philosophy in particular. Philosophy, in fact, became a vehicle for the promotion of secular values, in the school curriculum, the periodical press, some literary societies, and even congressional debates. Initially, Latin American thinkers carefully crafted a secular philosophy that was not offensive to Catholic doctrine. While ostensibly confirming the fundamentals of Catholicism, thinkers increasingly incorporated secular authors into their discussions. Prominent among them were Juan Egaña Risco and Ventura Marín (1806-1877) of Chile, the Spanish emigré José Joaquín de Mora (1783-1864), and Félix Varela y Morales of Cuba. The most distinguished philosopher of nineteenth-century Latin America, the Venezuelan Andrés Bello, respectfully nodded to Catholic doctrine, but systematically introduced the work of secular authors such as James Mill (1773–1836) and Jeremy Bentham (1748–1832) in his influential discussions on jurisprudence. He also brought the study of logic and psychology to unprecedented levels of philosophical sophistication, as shown in his posthumously published *Filosofía del entendimiento* (1881).

Other thinkers became increasingly less concerned about the intricacies of philosophical analysis and realized the potential of the discipline for promoting social change. Although not philosophers in the strictest academic sense of the word, intellectuals such as José María Luis Mora, Juan Bautista Alberdi, Domingo Faustino Sarmiento, José Martí, and José Victorino Lastarria often discussed major philosophical movements and authors. Their primary concern, however, was not speculation but social change. Similarly, the emphasis on social change led an entire generation of Latin American thinkers to positivism during the second half of the nineteenth century. Intellectuals openly challenged Catholicism and sought to replace it with the "scientific" premises of positivism. Indeed, Latin American positivism stood for orderly social development and modernization—hence the movement's motto "order and progress." Positivism predominated in Latin America, although not to the exclusion of Catholic doctrines, or spiritualist movements such as Krausismo. Positivism itself was divided between those who followed different aspects of the philosophy of August Comte (1798–1857)—that is, between those who adhered to his scientific social program and those who followed his late religious inclinations and even founded positivist temples. Some positivists developed a form of social Darwinism (which never materialized into a coherent movement) by selectively reading authors such as Herbert Spencer (1820–1903), Ernst Haeckel (1834–1919), and Gustave Le Bon (1841–1931) in order to address racial issues from a generally negative, sociobiological standpoint.

Throughout the period, the study of philosophy was firmly enthroned in the secondary-school curriculum and in higher education. Positivist-oriented "scientific" philosophy became particularly influential in Mexico, Brazil, and Chile, where it informed the educational system, the military, and the platforms of some political parties. Prominent thinkers of a positivist bent were Gabino Barreda and Justo Sierra Méndez of Mexico, Benjamin Constant Botelho de Magalhães and Luis Pereira Barreto (1840–1923) of Brazil, Enrique José Varona y Pera of Cuba, Mariano Cornejo of Peru, José Ingenieros of Argentina, and Valentín Letelier Madariaga of Chile.

THE TWENTIETH CENTURY

The positivist agenda of social and economic modernization remained largely unfulfilled by the 1920s. Latin American intellectuals who became aware of European reactions to positivism launched a movement against the predominance of this school of thought and ushered in philosophical currents that emphasized spiritual development, aesthetic concerns, and a hierarchy of human values in which the allegedly materialistic concerns of the positivists occupied the lowest position. Such anti-materialist concerns were also a response to the rise of mass politics and Marxism. A generation of thinkers between 1920 and 1950 attempted to guide society through philosophy by affirming the centrality of human values. Known as the *funda-dores* because of their knowledge of current European philosophy and to some extent because of the originality of their contributions, these philosophers included Antonio Caso y Andrade and José Vasconcelos Calderón of Mexico, Alceu Amoroso Lima of Brazil, Carlos Vaz Ferreira of Uruguay, Alejandro Korn of Argentina, Enrique Molina Garmendia of Chile, and Alejandro Deustua of Peru. Some of the major themes of Latin American philosophy, such as the human person, values, and cultural identity, are associated with this generation. Although more versed in current trends on philosophy, these thinkers retained some of the traditional social concerns of their predecesors.

In contrast, the new generation that became established in the 1950s fundamentally changed the nature of philosophical activity in the region by emphasizing scholarship and shunning social advocacy. This is the period of professionalization of the discipline, bolstered in important ways by the arrival of several European scholars in the aftermath of the Spanish Civil War and World War II. During this period the first university departments of philosophy were established, philosophical journals appeared, and national and international congresses convened regularly. A strong academic orientation successfully separated philosophy from social and political concerns. Classical philosophy became central to the curriculum, as had been the case in colonial times. Strong emphasis was placed on commentary and textual analysis of traditional philosophical sources. German philosophy as expounded by Max Scheler (1874–1928), Nicolai Hartmann (1882–1950), Edmund Husserl (1859–1938), and Martin Heidegger (1889–1976), and as disseminated by the Spanish philosopher José Ortega y Gasset (1883–1955), dominated the terms of discussion and the writings of Latin American philosophers. Other philosophical currents included existentialism, neoscholasticism, and to a lesser extent, analytical philosophy. The range of subjects of philosophical interest became as wide as it became specialized, although few philosophers achieved recognition beyond their own countries. Those who did tended to emigrate to Europe or the United States, because neither the academic climate nor the resources available in Latin America were conducive to competitive research in the field. Yet the majority of philosophers retained a professionalist emphasis, and continued to look toward Europe and the United States for models of philosophical activity.

The professionalist version of philosophical activity did not go unchallenged. Some philosophers questioned the entire academic philosophical enterprise. Beginning in the 1940s, scholars engaged in discussions concerning the nature and purposes of philosophical activity. The debate polarized between those who, like the Argentines Francisco Romero and Risieri Frondizi, viewed the discipline as a professional field that generated its own epistemological problems, and those who, like Mexico's Leopoldo Zea, argued that philosophy had to be grounded on sociocultural realities. Such debates were reformulated in the 1960s, when Marxism received stronger theoretical attention as a result of the ascendancy of leftist political parties and the continuing Cold War. A critical current of philosophers including Zea, Carlos Astrada (1894–1970) of Argentina, Juan Rivano (b. 1926) of Chile, and Augusto Salazar Bondy (1925–1974) of Peru criticized the detached and antipolitical cultivation of the discipline and called for a stronger emphasis on social and political issues. In the 1970s a movement known as the "philosophy of liberation" developed in response to the perceived need to maintain a specialized disciplinary focus while addressing wider social concerns. Originally developed in Argentina, the movement flourished in Mexico, where many of its major representatives resided.

The fundamental tension between the academic and the critical views of philosophy remains strong. As a result of the wave of military rule that swept Latin America in the 1970s and early 1980s, philosophers discovered to their dismay that philosophical activity could not function as usual in a context of repression and radical economic change. Chilean philosopher Jorge Millas, who had been a major contributor to the establishment of philosophical professionalism, now became a critic of military rule and economic neoliberalism. During this period, philosophy lost not only much of the social stature that allowed philosophers in the past to articulate influential social and political views, but also the means to cultivate the most specialized aspects of the field. The return of most Latin American countries to democratic rule in the last two decades of the twentieth century brought some relief and new opportunities for dialogue among embattled philosophers. With the advent of the twenty-first century, Latin American philosophers are confronting important questions about their social and educational relevance. Although a strong professionalist current persists, thematically, philosophers have shown more willingness to look into a variety of contemporary Latin American problems, including the impact of globalization, human rights, environmental issues, and various demands for the recognition of diversity.

See also **Alberdi, Juan Bautista; Anarchism and Anarchosyndicalism; Andrada, José Bonifácio de; Arguedas, Alcides; Barreda, Gabino; Bello, Andrés; Communism; Cornejo, Mariano H; Egaña Risco, Juan; Frondizi, Risieri; González Prada, Manuel; Hostos y Bonilla, Eugenio María de; Indigenismo; Ingenieros, José; Korn, Alejandro; Krausismo; Las Casas, Bartolomé de; Lastarria, José Victorino; Letelier Madariaga, Valentín; Liberalism; Liberation Theology; Lima, Alceu Amoroso; Martínez Estrada, Ezequiel; Martí y Pérez, José Julián; Millas Jiménez, Jorge; Molina Garmendia, Enrique; Mora, José María Luis; Neoliberalism; Pombaline Reforms; Positivism; Romero, Francisco; Sarmiento, Domingo Faustino; Sepúlveda, Juan Ginés de; Sierra Méndez, Justo; Talavera, Manuel; Varela y Morales, Félix; Varona y Pera, Enrique José; Vasconcelos Calderón, José; Vaz Ferreira, Carlos; Veintemilla, Marietta; Vera Cruz, Alonso de la; Zea Aguilar, Leopoldo.**

BIBLIOGRAPHY

Aldridge, A. Owen, ed. *The Ibero-American Enlightenment.* Urbana: University of Illinois Press, 1971.

Gracia, Jorge J. E., ed. *Latin American Philosophy in the Twentieth Century: Man, Values, and the Search for Philosophical Identity.* Buffalo, NY: Prometheus Books, 1986.

Gracia, Jorge J. E. "Latin American Philosophy Today." *Philosophical Forum* 20, nos. 1–2 (1988–1989): 43–61.

Gracia, Jorge J. E., and Mireya A. Camurati, eds. *Philosophy and Literature in Latin America: A Critical Assessment of the Current Situation.* Albany: State University of New York Press, 1989.

Gracia, Jorge J. E., and Elizabeth Millán-Zaibert, eds. *Latin American Philosophy for the Twenty-first Century: The Human Condition, Values, and the Search for Identity.* Buffalo, NY: Prometheus Books, 2004.

Nuccetelli, Susana. *Latin American Thought: Philosophical Problems and Arguments.* Boulder, CO: Westview Press, 2002.

Recaséns Siches, Luis, et al. *Latin American Legal Philosophy.* Translated by Gordon Ireland. Cambridge, MA: Harvard University Press, 1948.

Salles, Arleen, and Elizabeth Millán-Zaibert, eds. *The Role of History in Latin American Philosophy: Contemporary Perspectives.* Albany: State University of New York Press, 2005.

Sánchez Reulet, Aníbal, ed. *Contemporary Latin American Philosophy.* Albuquerque: University of New Mexico Press, 1954.

Schutte, Ofelia. *Cultural Identity and Social Liberation in Latin American Thought.* Albany: State University of New York Press, 1993.

White, Kevin, ed. *Hispanic Philosophy in the Age of Discovery.* Washington, DC: Catholic University Press, 1997.

Zea, Leopoldo, ed. *Pensamiento positivista latinoamericano,* 2 vols. Caracas: Biblioteca Ayacucho, 1980.

IVÁN JAKSIĆ

FEMINIST

From the middle of the nineteenth century to the 1920s, the early forms of feminism throughout the world advocated equality of rights between women and men. Latin American feminists were no exception, but they distinguished themselves from their European and North American peers by also insisting, from the outset, on fundamental differences between the sexes—a view now mainstream among feminists in the West. Latin American feminism has also been distinctive in its struggle against the Latin culture of *machismo* (from *macho*—literally, "male"). In Latin America, this is the term of choice for the social and cultural tendency to underestimate women's achievements and capabilities and to overrate those of men. Owing to machismo, even women of unquestioned ability, such as Clorinda Matto de Turner (Peruvian, 1852–1909), Alfonsina Storni (Argentinean, 1892–1938), and Frida Kahlo (Mexican, 1907–1954), faced obstacles in their careers.

That this bitter legacy of male dominance affects the lives of nearly all Latina women today is beyond dispute. But the historic roots of this phenomenon can be traced to the Spanish Conquest, which conferred a tacit entitlement on the Iberian invaders in failing to stop their common abusive practices toward native women. The relationship between the Spaniard Hernán Cortés (1495–1547) and Doña Marina or "La Malinche," one of twenty Indian women presented to him as human "gifts," is a notorious example. She traveled with Cortés as his companion and translator of the native languages—thus becoming instrumental in the fall of the Aztecs and ultimately of Mexico itself. The case of Malinche has achieved a certain iconic status among Latin American women, who have been assigned subservient roles for centuries.

Even so, there is in Latin America also a long tradition of women's vigorous defense of equal rights. A pioneer among them was Sor (Sister) Juana Inés de la Cruz (1651–1695). Often referred to today as "the Tenth Muse" and "the Phoenix of Mexico," Sor Juana was a Mexican nun of considerable accomplishments as a poet and playwright. Together with her scientific and philosophical interests, unusual for a woman at the time, these achievements gained her a wide reputation in colonial Mexico. Her erudition, learned conversation, and literary talent impressed the participants of animated *tertulias* (literary social gatherings) which often included prominent intellectuals and leaders of local society. The church's unofficial criticisms of her intellectual activities as inappropriate for a woman were rejected by Sor Juana in her *Reply to Sor Philothea*. This important work is at once a feminist manifesto and also a memoir describing the development of her passion for learning. It is perhaps the earliest modern vindication of women's intellectual competence and rights.

During the struggle for independence and national organization that took place in the nineteenth century, Latin America produced no fully articulated defense of women's rights. Yet some feminist stances are detectable in the writings of women such as Turner. In the late nineteenth century, the first stirrings of modern Latin American feminism began to proliferate, but were manifested in different ways in various Latin countries, sometimes through minor political factions, but more often through social movements and in informal meetings. In the early twentieth century, women's organizations began to emerge across the subcontinent, mostly devoted to obtaining suffrage and cultural, social and economic rights for women— e.g., Club Femenino, Alianza Sufragista and Unión Laborista de Mujeres (Cuba, 1920; 1928); Frente Femenino Anticlerical and Alianza Femenina, and Rosa Luxemburgo (Ecuador 1920; 1922); Agrupación Cultural Femenina (Venezuela 1934); Asociación Feminista Popular (Puerto Rico 1920); Evolución Feminina (Peru 1915); Federación Obrera Femenina de la Paz (Bolivia 1927); Unión Feminista Nacional (Argentina 1918); Consejo Nacional de Mujeres (Chile 1919); Sección Uruguaya and Consejo Nacional de Mujeres (Uruguay 1911, 1919); and Primer Congreso Feminista (Mexico, 1917).

Contemporary Latin American feminists have also struggled tenaciously for equal rights, focusing, through the 1990s, on a strategy of grassroots organizing. But both traditionalist and progressive male political leaders have continued to resist these efforts, the former appealing to conventionalist and religious arguments, the latter holding that feminist concerns are less pressing than other problems facing Latin American society (Álvarez, 1998). Today Latin American feminists pursue a more global, top-down strategy, through nongovernmental organizations (NGOs) and the United Nations. Although considerable progress has been made, independent-minded women in Latin America continue to feel stifled in a *machista* society that ignores their capacity for achievement and restricts them to subservient roles, as attested in the work of Rigoberta Menchú (Quiché Guatemalan, 1959–) and Gloria Anzaldúa (Mexican American, 1942–2004). The repudiation of machismo is also echoed by the "liberation philosophers" Ofelia Schutte, Linda Alcoff, and Enrique Dussel, who hold that there can be no liberation of society without the liberation of women.

See also **Anzaldúa, Gloria; Feminism and Feminist Organizations; Juana Inés de la Cruz, Sor; Malinche; Menchú Tum, Rigoberta; Sexuality: Gender and Sexuality; Women.**

BIBLIOGRAPHY

Alcoff, Linda. *Visible Identities: Race, Gender, and the Self.* New York: Oxford University Press, 2006.

Álvarez, Sonia E. *Engendering Democracy in Brazil: Women's Movements in Transition Politics.* Princeton, NJ: Princeton University Press, 1990.

Álvarez, Sonia E. "Latin American Feminisms 'Go Global': Trends of the 1990s and Challenges for the New Millennium." In *Cultures of Politics/Politics of Cultures,* edited by Sonia E. Álvarez, Evelina Dagnino, and Arturo Escobar. Boulder, CO: Westview Press, 1998.

Álvarez, Sonia E. "Advocating Feminism: The Latin American NGO 'Boom.'" *Global Solidarity Dialogue* (n.d.). Online at http://www.antenna.nl/~waterman/alvarez2.html

Anzaldúa, Gloria E. "La Conciencia de la Mestiza: Towards a New Consciousness." In *Feminist Theory Reader: Local and Global Perspectives,* edited by Carole R. McCann and Seung-Kyung Kim. New York: Routledge, 2003.

Castro-Klarén, Sara, Sylvia Molloy, and Beatriz Sarlo, eds. *Women's Writing in Latin America: An Anthology.* Boulder, CO: Westview Press, 1991.

Dussel, Enrique D. *Ethics and the Theology of Liberation.* Translated by Bernard F. McWilliams. Maryknoll, NY: Orbis, 1978.

Hahner, June E. *Emancipating the Female Sex: The Struggle for Women's Rights in Brazil, 1850–1940.* Durham, NC: Duke University Press, 1990.

Juana Inés de la Cruz, Sor. "Reply to Sor Philothea." In *A Sor Juana Anthology,* edited by Octavio Paz. Translated by Alan S. Trueblood. Cambridge, MA: Harvard University Press, 1988.

Juana Inés de la Cruz, Sor. "Sor Juana: Witness for the Prosecution." In *Sor Juana, or, The Traps of Faith,* by Octavio Paz. Translated by Margaret Sayers Peden. Cambridge, MA: Harvard University Press, 1988.

Juana Inés de la Cruz, Sor. *Sor Juana, Poet, Nun, Feminist, Enigma: Autodefensa Espiritual, A Poet's Translation.* Translated by Alicia Z. Galvan. San Antonio, TX: Galvart Press, 1998.

Lavrin, Asunción, ed. *Latin American Women: Historical Perspectives.* Westport, CT: Greenwood Press, 1978.

Schutte, Ofelia. *Cultural Identity and Social Liberation in Latin American Thought.* Albany: State University of New York Press, 1993.

Townsend, Camilla. *Malintzin's Choices: An Indian Woman in the Conquest of Mexico.* Albuquerque: University of New Mexico Press, 2006.

SUSANA NUCCETELLI

PHOTOGRAPHY

This entry includes the following articles:
THE NINETEENTH CENTURY
1900-1990
SINCE 1990

THE NINETEENTH CENTURY

The first permanent photographic press, perfected by Louis-Jacques-Mandé Daguerre and given to the world by the French Academy in August 1839, came to Latin America with startling rapidity. A visiting French abbot, Louis Comte, produced daguerreotypes of public buildings in Rio de Janeiro in January 1840, and in Montevideo and Buenos Aires a month later. Brazil's fifteen- year-old emperor, Pedro II, already a patron of science and the arts, took personal interest in the invention, and ordered a camera made to Comte's specifications. By 1842, daguerreotypists, all of them European or North American, had set up studios in virtually every major Latin American capital and most large cities. Daguerreotype portraits were instantly popular among those who could afford them; Latin American elite families rushed to have their likenesses preserved. By 1845, daguerreotypists began to venture outdoors, taking their bulky equipment to photograph buildings, static scenic views (for exposure times were still very slow), and landscapes. Traveling daguerreotypists earned as much as the equivalent of U.S. $4,000 a month in the early years of the photographic craze.

By the early 1850s, technological advances had revolutionized photography. Calotypes developed from the Englishman Fox Talbot's process could be duplicated from negatives. Daguerreotypes became obsolete almost overnight, replaced by cameras with fast lenses. Consumers purchased millions of photographic images, from cardboard-backed photographic calling cards to photographs of national heroes (including the Brazilian duke of Caixias, Chile's victorious generals after the War of the Pacific, and Mexico's Benito Juárez). Police officials circulated "wanted" posters made of photographic collages of portraits taken of prisoners at their time of arrest. A new generation of photographic entrepreneurs—mainly German, British, and French— arrived in Latin America offering cheaper wares and willing to travel. Some remained a few years and returned to their home countries, often selling their equipment and businesses to Latin Americans who had worked for them as assistants. Many leading studios continued to be owned by foreigners (for example, A. Pearsall in Caracas; Charles D. Fredricks in Havana; August Stahl, Otto Hees, Benjamin Mulock, William Gaensly, George Leuzinger, and A. Frisch in Brazilian cities; Alexander Witcomb,

Benito Panunzi, and Samuel Boote in Buenos Aires; Eugene Courret in Lima), but as time passed Latin American–born photographers began to compete with the foreigners and ultimately developed prosperous businesses.

There was little difference, however, in the images that photographers produced, whether they were foreign-born or local. Cameramen in Latin America during the nineteenth and early twentieth centuries manufactured images of two kinds: formal portraits, scenic compositions, and photographs of man-made wonders, such as railroads and urban improvements, for sale to local customers, who appreciated poses that made them appear dignified, prosperous, and modern; and photographs of "exotic" scenes (natives in costume, pre-Columbian ruins, jungle rivers, snow-capped mountains) for sale abroad. By the 1860s the cost of studio portraits had dropped so much that even working-class families could pay to dress up in elegant clothing provided by the photographer's studio and preserve their images for posterity. By the time of World War I, many photographers came from middle-class and even lower-class creole backgrounds (Militão de Azevedo in São Paulo; Jorge C. Obando in Colombia, Agustín Víctor Casasola in Mexico, and Martín Chambí in Cuzco, among many others).

Some of the photographers produced masterpieces of documentary photography, although they made their living by manufacturing and selling photographs of everyday subjects posed according to the formal conventions of the day. Marc Ferrez, born in Brazil, produced elegant depictions of urban landscapes in Rio de Janeiro and Recife. The Portuguese-born Christiano Júnior sold portraits of Brazilian slaves, posed to make them look industrious and docile. Francisco Ayerza photographed gauchos on the pampas of Argentina, Meliton Rodríguez in Colombia and Agustín Casasola in Mexico photographed civil strife and warfare. The Spanish-born Juan Gutierrez, working as a war journalist, was the first photographer to be killed at the front, photographing the Brazilian army's assault on Canudos in 1897. The great American photographer Eadweard Muybridge, while working for the Pacific Mail Steamship Company, took elegantly crafted photographs of local life in Guatemala and Panama in 1875. Edward Weston, one of the major figures of twentieth-century photographic art, spent much of the 1920s in Mexico, perfecting his style.

Latin American photographs in the twentieth century did not follow the experimental paths taken by some of their counterparts in North America and Europe. There were too few opportunities to make a living selling compositions that were surreal, jarring, or socially probing. Latin America never developed a muckraking or reformist photographic tradition, seeking to expose the ugly side of life by use of the lens. There was no market for this kind of work; photographers so inclined could only emigrate to Europe. Yet some of the photographers who stayed home managed, through subtle use of mockery too nuanced to be understood by their clientele, to produce images of social commentary. Many of the works of Martín Chambí fall into this category, as well as work by Sebastian Rodríguez from Huancayo, Panama's Sandra Eleta, and the Venezuelan Luis Felipe Toro (Torito).

BIBLIOGRAPHY

Gilberto Ferrez and Weston J. Naef, eds., *Pioneer Photographers of Brazil, 1840–1920* (1976).

Erika Billeter, *Fotografie Lateinamerika von 1860 bis Heute* (1981).

H. L. Hoffenberg, comp., *Nineteenth-Century South America in Photographs* (1982).

Keith McElroy, *Early Peruvian Photography: A Critical Case Study* (1985).

E. Bradford Burns, *Eadweard Muybridge in Guatemala, 1875* (1986).

Robert M. Levine, *Images of History: Nineteenth Century and Early Twentieth Century Latin American Photographs as Documents* (1989), and *Cuba in the 1850s: Through the Lens of Charles D. Fredricks* (1990).

Additional Bibliography

Chambi, Martín. *Martín Chambi, Photographs, 1920-1950.* Washington: Smithsonian Institution Press, 1993.

Debroise, Oliver. *Mexican Suite: A History of Photography in Mexico.* Austin: University of Texas Press, 2001.

Lago, Bia Correo do, and Pedro Correa do Lago. *Os fotógrafos do Imperio: A fotografía brasileira do século XX.* Rio de Janeiro: Capivara, 2005.

Majluf, Natalia, Luis Eduardo Wuffarden, et. al. *La recuperación de la memoria: Peru 1842-1942: El primer siglo de la fotografía.* Lima: Museo de Arte de Lima, 2001.

ROBERT M. LEVINE

1900–1990

The turn of the century did not substantially alter the practice of portrait photography. Studios like those of Alejandro Witcomb (Argentina), Eugene Courret (Peru), and Melitón Rodríguez (Colombia), which had opened in the second half of the 1800s, continued to serve their clientele well into the 1900s. The new century did bring the expectation that an era of progress and material welfare was in the offing. Illustrated periodicals like *Caras y Caretas* (Argentina), *El Cojo Ilustrado* (Venezuela), *Variedades* (Peru), *El Gráfico* (Colombia), and *El Universal Ilustrado* (Mexico) made generous use of photographs of local events taken by photographers who also owned studios. In addition, lucrative government commissions to do visual inventories of the landscape, cities, infrastructure, and culture served as official recognition of their status as accomplished photographers. Some of these photographic surveys were published as luxurious books—Vicente Blasco Ibáñez's *Argentina y sus*

grandezas (1910), *L'état de Rio Grande du Sud* (1916); *El Perú en el primer centenario de su independencia* (1922)—and were given by governments to influential dignitaries or potential investors. Similar books were produced by foreigners following in the romantic steps of earlier travelers. Indeed, the iconography of these three encyclopedic endeavors is strikingly similar even though in the first two it is in printed photographs and in the latter in drawings.

The influence of pictorialism in Latin America must be taken with a grain of salt because its converts are usually camouflaged and its aesthetics mediated by local concerns. Pictorialist literature from all over the world circulated widely in the continent. The magazines *Foto* (Barcelona) and *Foto Magazine* (Buenos Aires) may have been favored because they were in Spanish. These magazines contained critical articles about artistic photography, and information about new techniques and products and about international photo competitions. The pictorialist disregard for

Cuban leader Fidel Castro delivering a speech in Chile, photograph by the Argentine photojournalist Diego Goldberg, 1971.
© DIEGO GOLDBERG/SYGMA/CORBIS

themes like technology and industry did not impress local photographers who were imbued by the spirit of modernity. Carlos and Miguel Vargas of Peru, for example, produced bromoils of romantic nocturnes in which the automobile was featured prominently. Other pictorialists include Hiram Calógero (Argentina), Pedro Ignacio Manrique (Venezuela), and Servio Tulio Barat (Venezuela).

Analogously, the post–World War I pessimism and nihilism of the European artistic avant-garde was never strong in Latin America—perhaps because the latter never experienced the devastation of that conflict but, rather, a period of relative prosperity due to increased exports to the warring nations. The iconoclasm of its own avant-garde came by way of intellectual expectations and social upheaval; most notable was the 1910 Mexican Revolution and the movement for university reform that spread across the continent during the same decade. By the 1920s, Mexican artists understood that they could not continue to do art pleasing to the taste of the regime cast away by the revolution. Agustín Víctor Casasola and his team of photographers exhaustively recorded the unraveling of the Mexican Revolution for over a decade. The epic documentalism characteristic of this work reappeared decades later in the photographic records of the Cuban Revolution, the Chilean denunciation of Augusto Pinochet's repression, the Salvadoran civil war.

Mexico holds a unique place in Latin American photography because its rich image-making tradition has been copiously enhanced by the visit of photographers like Hugo Brehme, Edward Weston, Tina Modotti, Paul Strand, Sergei Eisenstein, and Henri Cartier-Bresson. In the work of Manuel Álvarez Bravo the impact of their influence is as strong as that of his own personality and the cultural idiosyncrasies that molded it. He gained international acclaim in 1938 when André Breton asked Álvarez Bravo for an image (*La buena fama durmiendo*) to illustrate the cover of the catalog for the International Surrealist Exhibition in Mexico City. As an imagemaker and instructor, Álvarez Bravo is partly responsible for the unusual number of first-rate photographers in Mexico today. Immigrant photographers have played important roles in other countries as well. The Bauhaus-trained German photographer Grete Stern and the Frenchman Anatole Sadermann had a considerable influence on the avant-garde photography of Argentina during the 1930s. The Italian Paolo Gasparini has been the most decisive force in Venezuelan photography since the 1950s.

Important features of the early Latin American avant-garde were Pan-Americanism and *indigenismo*. The latter was a movement aimed at reevaluating autochthonous culture—especially Indian—at a time when extremists were proposing a "final solution" for the "Indian problem." The creed of *indigenismo* was expressed in radical 1920s periodicals like Amauta and *Kosko* (Peru), and the epicenter of the movement was Cuzco. The photographic corpus now referred to as the Cuzco school had Martín Chambi as its best-known member; less known are Miguel Chani, Juan Manuel Figueroa Aznar, José Gabriel González, and Crisanto Cabrera. The work of these photographers is modern, socially mordant, and ethnographic. Although Chambi and Álvarez Bravo are considered to be the founding fathers of modern Latin American photography, Chambi's work was unearthed only in the late 1970s—after a quarter- century of oblivion.

The 1978 Primer Coloquio Latinoamericano de Fotografía, held in Mexico City, changed the course of the medium in the Americas. Although its organizers tended to promote a documentary and politically denunciatory type of image, they unified Latin American photography by bringing together people from all over the continent. By touring the exhibit Hecho en Latinoamérica, they internationalized Latin American photography, and by opening new venues of research, publication, and conservation, they cemented it. After 1978 two more colloquia took place, and among subsequent exhibitions were Fotografie Lateinamerika (curated by Erika Billeter in 1981) and FotoFest 92 (curated by Fred Baldwin and Wendy Watriss).

See also **Alvarez Bravo, Manuel; Art: The Nineteenth Century; Art: The Twentieth Century; Chambi, Martín; Photography: The Nineteenth Century.**

BIBLIOGRAPHY

Hecho en Latinoamérica (1978).

Erika Billeter, ed., *Fotografie Lateinamerika von 1860 bis heute* (1981), also in Spanish, *Fotografía latinoamericana: 1860 hasta nuestros días* (1982).

Eduardo Serrano, *Historia de la fotografía en Colombia* (1983), *Colección Río de Luz*, 15 vols. (1984–1987); *Revelaciones: The Art of Manuel Álvarez Bravo* (1990).

María Teresa Boulton, *Anotaciones sobre la fotografía venezolana* (1990) and *Martín Chambi: Fotografía del Perú, 1920–1950* (1990).

FERNANDO CASTRO

SINCE 1990

In the twenty-first century, photography in Latin America reflects the increasingly globalized nature of the art world. Greater interest on the part of curators and collectors in art from the region, the growing number of publications (both in print and on the Web), and the rapid growth and importance of international biennials and art fairs have rapidly altered and extended the theoretical, political, and aesthetic concerns of photographic art. Artists and curators now travel extensively, bringing the work of photographers into the flow of various art-world currents. Graduate-level education for artists has become commonplace, and the Internet has made research and communication much more accessible.

The stylistic distinction of photography in Latin America since the turn of the century is its heterogeneity. There are artists who blur the line between aesthetics and social concerns (Talleres de Fotografía Social, or Social Photography Workshops, of Peru), or photography as art and as photojournalism (Diego Goldberg of Argentina, Sebastião Salgado of Brazil); other artists apply aesthetic concerns to the portrait and contemporary documentary, often blurring the line between art and documentary (Marcos López of Argentina, Miguel Rio Branco of Brazil). Many of the younger practitioners do not define themselves as photographers, but rather as artists who use photographic technologies in their work. They exemplify a larger theoretical, curatorial, and practical trend toward multidisciplinarity. Among such artists are Rosângela Rennó (Brazil), Luis Camnitzer (Uruguay; resides in the United States), Eugenio Dittborn (Chile), and Rubén Ortiz-Torres (Mexico; resides in the United States). Gustavo Artigas (Mexico) often uses photography as an aesthetic and documentary element for his elaborate and risky performances. Artist collectives like Etcetera in Argentina use photography in community-based practices.

Digital information and the Internet have altered the traditional borders that once defined photographic processes. New technology has had a profound impact not only on the amount of communication but also its quality. For example, digital media questions the very foundation of verisimilitude that photography once claimed as its own. The interactive nature of many new media processes brings other issues to the forefront: artists like Alexander Apóstol (Venezuela) and Oscar Muñoz (Colombia) question the veracity of images and the relationship between the image and its referent, technology and the body. Apóstol digitally photographs midcentury Modernist buildings in Caracas and alters their appearance using computers to reveal the discontinuity between official images and their discursive realities.

Artists and photographers of Latin America are revising and combining existing forms and media to push the boundaries of what is understood as photography. Their work resonates with international art audiences as never before.

See also **Photography: 1900–1990; Salgado, Sebastião.**

BIBLIOGRAPHY

Bourriaud, Nicolas. *Postproduction*, 2nd edition. New York: Lukas and Sternberg, 2005.

Bright, Susan, ed. *Art Photography Now*. New York: Aperture, 2005.

Demos, T. J., ed. *Vitamin Ph: New Perspectives in Photography*. New York: Phaidon Press, 2006.

Hansen, Mark B. N. *New Philosophy for New Media*. Cambridge, MA: MIT Press, 2004.

Zamudio-Taylor, Victor, and Elizabeth Armstrong, eds. *Ultra Baroque: Aspects of Post–Latin American Art*. La Jolla, CA: Museum of Contemporary Art, San Diego, 2000.

BILL KELLEY JR.

PIAUÍ. Piauí (formerly Piauhy), a state covering 96,886 square miles on the northeastern coast of Brazil between Ceará and Maranhão. Its capital is Teresina. The majority of its 3,006,885 people (2000 est.) are of mixed European and Indian descent, but there are also some who are part African, particularly in the coastal area.

Settlement of the area began in the 1600s as cattle ranching expanded into the backlands. A subordinate captaincy of Maranhão since 1718,

Piauí became an independent captaincy in 1811, a province of the empire in 1822, and a state of the republic in 1889. Its capital was moved from Oeiras to Teresina in 1852. A major route for cattle drives to the Recôncavo (Bahia) and to Pernambuco passed through the region, contributing to the area's colonial role as a hub of internal communications in northern Brazil.

Ranching continues to play an important part in the state's economy, along with the cultivation and processing of cotton, manioc, wax from carnauba and babassu palm trees, and other agricultural products. Piauí is one of the country's poorest states and suffers from high infant mortality and inadequate medical care.

See also **Brazil, Geography.**

BIBLIOGRAPHY

Carvalho Gonçalves, Wilson. *Roteiro cronológico da história do Piauí: 1535–1995.* Teresina, Brazil: Gráfica e Editora Júnior, 1996.

de Alburqueque Bastos, Cláudio, and Adrião Neto. *Diccionario histórico e geográfico do Estado do Piauí.* Teresina, Brazil: Fundação Cultural Monsenhor Chaves–PMT, 1994.

Sousa Brito, Itamar. *História dos batistas no Piauí 1904–2004: Um século de lutas e vitórias.* Rio de Janeiro: JUERP, 2003.

CARA SHELLY

PIAZZOLLA, ASTOR (1921–1992).

The grandson of Italian immigrants, Astor Piazzola was the outstanding renovator of instrumental tango. He was born March 11, 1921, in Mar del Plata, Argentina. His restless father took him to New York City for much of his early life but gave him a *bandoneon* to reinforce a sense of Argentine identity. The young man learned to speak English with a New York accent and developed a taste for jazz and classical music, as well. The twelve-year-old New Yorker got to know the Argentine singer Carlos Gardel when he was making movies in the area in 1933 and even seems to have accompanied him in private performances. Back in Argentina once again in the late 1930s, Piazzolla devoted himself more seriously to tango. He began to make a name for himself with the ensemble of Aníbal Troilo, as prominent a tango bandleader as there was in the musically vibrant Buenos Aires of the 1940s. Anxious to experiment and move beyond dance music, he formed his own bands beginning in 1944 after five years with Troilo.

By the middle of 1949, frustrated with the life of a *tanguero* as well as with Peronist political pressures, Piazzola stopped performing, devoting much of the next decade to composing and arranging, including film scores and classical pieces. In 1954 he won a scholarship to study in Paris with the renowned music teacher Nadia Boulanger. She encouraged him to explore the musical possibilities of the tango. Returning to his native country in 1955, he formed a new octet to perform a more adventurous style of music. His music drew strong reactions, both positive and negative, with many contending that he was betraying the tango. In the following decade a quintet he led became a symbol of the cultural ferment of the age. His music, with its intense emotions, ferocious drive, daring harmonies, and propulsive rhythms, gained him by age sixty an international following among discerning and adventurous listeners. He left behind a rich legacy of recorded work. Since his death on July 4, 1992, his compositions increasingly have gained a new life in the repertoire of classical music performers.

See also **Music: Popular Music and Dance; Tango.**

BIBLIOGRAPHY

Azzi, María Susana, and Simon Collier. *Le Grand Tango: The Life and Music of Astor Piazzolla.* New York: Oxford University Press, 2000.

Collier, Simon, Richard Martin, Artemis Cooper, and Maria S. Azzi. *Tango!: The Dance, the Song, the Story.* New York: Thames and Hudson, 1995.

Piazzola, Diana. *Astor.* Buenos Aires: Emecé Editores, 1987.

ANDREW J. KIRKENDALL

PICADO MICHALSKI, TEODORO

(1900–1960). Teodoro Picado Michalski (*b.* 10 January 1900; *d.* 1 June 1960), president of Costa Rica (1944–1948), educator, and legislator.

Teodoro Picado Michalski came to the presidency after one of the more violent electoral campaigns in

Costa Rican history. Although he won election by an ample margin, his victory and his presidency were marred by charges of fraud and the consequent questioning of his right to govern.

Picado brought to the presidency a distinguished record as legislator, educator, public servant, and a truly gifted individual. Born in San José, he spent his early years in rural schools. After his graduation from the Liceo de Costa Rica in 1916, he taught high school history; in 1922 he received his law degree from the School of Law in San José. In 1930 he was appointed director of the Instituto de Alajuela, a secondary school. His involvement at all levels of education, from school administrator to law professor, helped in his role as secretary of education under President Ricardo Jiménez Oreamuno (1932–1936). He was elected to Congress in 1936 and served as president of that body from 1941 to 1944.

As the standard bearer of the Victory Bloc (Bloque de la Victoria), the political alliance between the Calderónists and the Communists in the 1944 election, Picado's candidacy was controversial from the beginning. The opposition to his government took many forms, from newspaper attacks to terrorism, and Picado's administration was largely reduced to the task of surviving until the next election.

When Congress nullified the results of the 1948 election, Picado was overthrown by an armed uprising led by José Figueres Ferrer. He remained in exile in Managua, Nicaragua, until his death.

See also **Costa Rica.**

BIBLIOGRAPHY

Alberto Cañas, *Los Ocho Años* (1955).

Ligia Estrada Molina, *Teodoro Picado Michalski: Su aporte a la historiografía* (1967).

John Patrick Bell, *Crisis in Costa Rica* (1971).

Charles D. Ameringer, *Don Pepe* (1978).

Additional Bibliography

LaWare, David Craig. *From Christian Populism to Social Democracy: Workers, Populists, and the State in Costa Rica 1940–1956.* Ph.D. diss., 1996.

Molina Jiménez, Iván. *Urnas de lo inesperado: Fraude electoral y lucha política en Costa Rica (1901–1948).* San José: Editorial de la Universidad de Costa Rica, 1999.

Yashar, Deborah J. *Demanding Democracy: Reform and Reaction in Costa Rica and Guatemala, 1870s–1950s,* Stanford, CA: Stanford University Press, 1997.

JOHN PATRICK BELL

PICHETA. *See* **Gahona, Gabriel Vicente.**

PICHINCHA, BATTLE OF. Battle of Pichincha (23–24 May 1822), a major Andean clash during the Wars of Independence. Although Guayaquil, which had declared independence on 9 October 1820 and established a republic, repeatedly attempted to free the highland provinces of the Audiencia or Kingdom of Quito, it proved unable to dislodge Spanish forces with its limited resources. Therefore, it sought the support of both José de San Martín and Simón Bolívar. While San Martín sent supplies and a few officers, Bolívar, in 1821, dispatched seven hundred men under the command of General Antonio José de Sucre with the charge of annexing the region to Colombia. In the face of local opposition, Sucre only managed to declare Guayaquil a protectorate of Colombia.

After several unsuccessful attempts to liberate the highlands, Sucre raised an army of three thousand, including local forces and Colombians as well as Argentinians, Chileans, and Peruvians from San Martín's army. The patriots fought their way up the Andes in early 1822, reaching the heights west of Quito on the evening of 23 May 1822. After a hard-fought battle of several hours on 24 May, General Melchor Aymerich, the last Spanish president of the Kingdom of Quito, capitulated. Bolívar arrived in June with more Colombian troops and proceeded to incorporate the region into Colombia despite opposition from the ayuntamiento (city council) of Quito. Shortly thereafter, broadsides appeared in the city heralding "The last day of despotism and the first of the same thing."

See also **Wars of Independence, South America.**

BIBLIOGRAPHY

Julio Estrada Ycaza, *La lucha de Guayaquil por el Estado de Quito,* 2 vols. (1984).

Additional Bibliography

Archer, Christon I., ed. *The Wars of Independence in Spanish America*. Wilmington, DE: Scholarly Resources, 2000.

Bolívar, Simón, and Ayala Mora, Enrique. *Simón Bolívar*. Quito: Universidad Andina Simón Bolívar: Corporación Editora Nacional, 2004.

Himiob A., Santos. *Sucre, época & épica, 1795-1995: Bibliografía del general en jefe y gran mariscal de Ayacucho Antonio José de Sucre: Homenaje en el bicentenario de su nacimiento*. Caracas: Biblioteca Nacional, 1995.

Lemus Rojas, Jesús R. *Pichincha: La libertad de Quito*. Caracas, Venezuela: EGE, 1993.

JAIME E. RODRÍGUEZ O.

PICÓN SALAS, MARIANO (1901–1965).

Mariano Picón Salas (*b*. 26 January 1901; *d*. 1 January 1965), Venezuelan essayist, teacher, and diplomat. After publishing his first book, *Buscando el camino* (1920), Picón left the Venezuelan dictatorship of Juan Vicente Gómez in 1923, seeking intellectual freedom in Chile. He completed his education at the University of Chile, where he taught and wrote until Gómez's death. Upon his return to Venezuela in 1936, Picón worked to improve national intellectual life. He held posts in Venezuela's Ministry of Education between 1936 and 1940, founded and directed the *Revista Nacional de Cultura* (1936), founded and was first dean of the Faculty of Philosophy and Letters of the Central University of Venezuela (UCV) (1946), and taught at UCV and in Mexico, Argentina, and the United States. Although he was uncomfortable with political activism, Picón admired and enjoyed a warm friendship with social democrat Rómulo Betancourt, founder of the Democratic Action Party (1941).

In his numerous publications, Picón stressed the importance of spiritual and cultural progress, preferring the universal humanistic values of the eighteenth century to the materialistic tenets of communism or positivism. His historical works, *Pedro Claver, el santo de los esclavos* (1950), *Miranda* (1946), and *De la conquista a la independencia: Tres siglos de historia cultural hispanoamericana* (1944) emphasize humanistic values, as does his autobiographical novel *Viaje al amanecer* (1943). Picón served as Venezuelan ambassador to Colombia, Mexico, Brazil, and UNESCO; as secretary-general in the Venezuelan cabinet (1963–1964); and at the time of his death as president-designate of the National Institute of Culture and Fine Arts.

See also **Gómez, Juan Vicente.**

BIBLIOGRAPHY

Thomas O. Bente, "Man and Circumstance: A Study of Mariano Picón Salas' Work" (Ph.D. diss., UCLA, 1968).

J. M. Siso Martínez and Juan Oropesa, *Mariano Picón Salas* (1977).

Thomas D. Morin, *Mariano Picón Salas* (1979).

Additional Bibliography

Díaz Seijas, Pedro. *Mariano Picón Salas, o, El ámbito universal de una vida y una obra*. Caracas: Universidad Católica Andrés Bello, 2004.

Márquez Rodríguez, Alexis. *Mariano Picón Salas: El arte y la costumbre de pensar*. Caracas: Vadell Hermanos Editores, 2002.

Zambrano, Gregory. *Mariano Picón-Salas y el arte de narrar*. Mérida: Universidad de los Andes, Vicerrectorado Académico, 2003.

JUDITH EWELL

PIEDRAS NEGRAS, GUATEMALA.

Piedras Negras, Guatemala, is a Mayan archaeological site located in the northwestern Petén, on the banks of the Usumacinta River. It is the largest archaeological site in the Sierra del Lacandón National Park, which constitutes 202,865 hectares of the Maya Biosphere Reserve. The earliest permanent occupation of Piedras Negras dates to approximately 500 BCE. The number of inhabitants grew slowly until a ruling dynasty was established, by about 450 CE. Explosive population growth and building followed, and the city quickly grew to house many thousands of people. Piedras Negras reached its apogee in the mid-eighth century CE, when it was at the heart of a kingdom that vied for regional supremacy with nearby centers including Yaxchilán, Palenque, Tonina, and Pomona.

Most of the architecture visible at Piedras Negras today dates to the seventh and eighth centuries CE. Several large plazas are dominated by numerous masonry pyramid-temples, enormous sweatbaths. The Acropolis, a multitiered complex of palace buildings and pyramids, towers over all. These palaces served as the residence and court of the rulers of Piedras Negras from approximately 600 to 800 CE. In 808 CE the last known ruler of Piedras Negras was killed by his rivals upstream at the dynastic center of Yaxchilán, and the site was largely abandoned by the end of the ninth century CE.

French traveler Ludovic Chambon was the first modern visitor to identify the site in print in 1892, naming it after a nearby logging camp. However, it was the explorer and photographer Teobert Maler who brought the site to the attention of other scholars and a wider public. From 1931 to 1939 the University of Pennsylvania Museum supported an archaeological project at Piedras Negras, directed by Linton Satterthwaite Jr. A member of Satterthwaite's research team, Tatiana Proskouriakoff, used hieroglyphic evidence from Piedras Negras to demonstrate for the first time that inscribed Maya monuments contained historical data. A subsequent archaeological project, directed by Stephen Houston and Héctor Escobedo, ran from 1997 to 2000, and again in 2004. In the twenty-first century the site is being developed for ecotourism.

See also **Maya, The; Mayan Alphabet and Orthography; Mayan Epigraphy; Mayan Ethnohistory.**

BIBLIOGRAPHY

Houston, Stephen D., et al. "The Moral Community: Maya Settlement Transformation at Piedras Negras, Guatemala." In *The Social Construction of Ancient Cities*, edited by Monica L. Smith. Washington, DC: Smithsonian Institution Press, 2003.

Martin, Simon, and Nikolai Grube. *Crónica de los reyes y reinas mayas.* Mexico: Planeta, 2002.

Sharer, Robert J. *The Ancient Maya*, 6th ed. Stanford, CA: Stanford University Press, 2006.

Weeks, John M, Jane A. Hill, and Charles W. Golden, eds. *Piedras Negras Archaeology: 1931–1939*. Philadelphia: University of Pennsylvania, Museum of Archaeology and Anthropology, 2005.

CHARLES GOLDEN

PIÉROLA, NICOLÁS DE (1839–1913). Twice president of Peru (1879–1881, 1895–1899), José Nicolás Baltasar Fernández de Piérola y Villena marked the transition between caudillo and modern party politics in Peru. Charismatic and impetuous, he was equally adept at state-building and revolution.

Born in Arequipa on January 5, 1839, he studied theology and law at the santo toribio seminary in Lima from 1853 TO 1861. While working in various commercial establishments, he began his political battles as a Catholic conservative by writing articles for *El Progreso Católico* and editing his own newspaper, *El Tiempo*. At age thirty, as minister of finance under President José Balta, he attracted controversy when he resolved a fiscal crisis by transferring Peru's enormous guano reserves from national contractors to the French financier Auguste Dreyfus, thus getting rid of debt, opening the way for new loans, and earning the enmity of Peru's commercial Civilista elite, his political rivals for the next two decades.

After unsuccessful revolutions against the democratically elected Civilistas, he became de facto president at the outset of the War of the Pacific (1879). During the Chilean invasion of Lima (1881) he led a resistance movement in the central Andes. Following the war he organized the Partido Demócrata. In 1895 a popular revolution returned Piérola to the presidency with the support of his old Civilista rivals. He inaugurated a period of prosperity that returned a civilian elite to power and brought industrialization and investment of national capital. Piérola implemented his vision of a strong central state with reforms including those of the army and the fiscal apparatus. He died June 23, 1913.

See also **Balta, José; Peru, Political Parties: Civilista Party; Peru, Political Parties: Overview.**

BIBLIOGRAPHY

Alexander, Robert J., ed. *Biographical Dictionary of Latin American and Caribbean Political Leaders*. Westport, CT: Greenwood Press, 1988.

Chirinos Soto, Enrique. *Vidas paralelas: Vivanco y Piérola* Lima, 1966.

Congrains Martin, Eduardo. *Desmitificación de Piérola*. Lima: Editorial Ecoma, 1972.

Dulanto Pinillos, Jorge. *Nicolás de Piérola*. Lima: Compañía de Impresiones y Publicidad, 1947.

Ulloa y Sotomayor, Alberto. *Don Nicolás de Piérola: Una época de la historia del Perú*, 2nd edition. Lima: Imprenta Santa María, 1981.

IÑIGO GARCIA-BRYCE

PILCOMAYO RIVER. Pilcomayo River, stream in the northeastern part of Argentina, originating at 13,000 feet in the Andes of Bolivia, south of Sucre, and emptying into the Paraguay River after a 1,000-mile course. Located in an area of great aridity, the river is subject to abrupt seasonal changes: it varies from extreme shallowness in the winter to relatively high waters in the summer that convert some low-lying areas into vast swamps (Estero de Patiño). The river is considered the boundary between the northern and the central Chaco regions, and since 1876 it has served as the border between Argentina and Paraguay. There are no settlements of importance along the river, with the exception of Fuerte Ballivián and Luján, which thrive as centers for smuggling goods into Paraguay and as service centers for scattered cattle ranches. Today the area is home to approximately 1.5 million Bolivians, Argentineans, and Paraguayans. In 2005 a large portion of the watershed was clogged due to pollution and overuse by humans. That year, the governments of Argentina, Bolivia, and Paraguay united, and with financial backing from the European Union, began to study the ecosystem of the watershed and to design a plan to save it.

See also **Argentina, Geography; Paraguay, Geography; Paraguay River.**

BIBLIOGRAPHY

Juan Sosa E., *El Pilcomayo como límite argentino-paraguayo* (Buenos Aires, 1939).

Additional Bibliography

Díaz, José Antonio. *Ibarreta, el último explorador: Tragedia y muerte en su expedición por el río Pilcomayo*. Madrid: Miraguano Ediciones, 2004.

Gordillo, Gastón. *El río y la frontera: Movilizaciones aborígenes, obras públicas y MERCOSUR en el Pilcomayo*. Buenos Aires: Editorial Biblos, 2002.

Vernón, Luis. *Rio rebelde y contumaz: Las exploraciones del Pilcomayo*. Asunción, Paraguay: Embajada Francesa en el Paraguay, 2002.

                                    CÉSAR N. CAVIEDES

PIMERÍA ALTA. Pimería Alta, a desert region in northwest Mexico and southwest United States that spans adjacent portions of the modern states of Sonora (Mexico) and Arizona. Stretching westward from the San Pedro River to the Colorado delta and the Gulf of California, and northward from the Altar-Magdalena drainage to the Gila River in Arizona, Pimería Alta comprises the northern Sonoran Desert and contains some of the desert's most characteristic vegetation. The name symbolizes both the Hispanic and Native American cultural heritage of the region. "The land of the northern Pimas" was so christened by Jesuit missionaries, who began systematic religious conversion activities in the area during the 1690s, building their mission compounds around indigenous settlement patterns. The Pimas were village-dwelling agriculturalists who spoke related dialects belonging to the Uto-Aztecan family of languages.

Since colonization the Piman and Hispanic settlers of Pimería Alta have lived under Spanish, Mexican, and North American rule. The Gadsden Purchase (Treaty of Mesillas) of 1854 divided Pimería Alta between Mexico and the United States. The O'Odham (meaning "people"—the Pima and Papago) of southwest Arizona and northwest Sonora and the Gila River Pimas maintain strong cultural traditions and a binational orientation to Mexico and the United States.

See also **Gadsden Purchase.**

BIBLIOGRAPHY

The authoritative work on political geography is Peter Gerhard, *The North Frontier of New Spain* (1982). Three excellent published primary documents are Juan Nentvig, *Descripción geográfica, natural, y curiosa de la provincia de Sonora*, edited by German Viveros (1971), also in English as *Rudo Ensayo, a Description of Sonora and Arizona in 1764*, edited by Alberto Francisco Pradeau (1980).

Ignaz Pfefferkorn, *Beschreibung der Landschaft Sonora* (1795), also in English as *Sonora: A Description of the Province*, edited by Theodore E. Treutlein (1949).

Diego Bringas De Manzaneda y Encinas, *Friar Bringas Reports to the King: Methods of Indoctrination on the Frontier of New Spain, 1796–1797*, edited by Daniel S. Matson and Bernard L. Fontana (1977). The Bringas report is enhanced by the introduction by Matson and Fontana. Armando Hopkins Durazo, gen. coord., *Historia general de Sonora*, 5 vols. (1985), is an excellent historical synthesis.

Additional Bibliography

Griffiths, James S. *Beliefs and Holy Places: A Spiritual Geography of the Pimería Alta*. Tucson: University of Arizona Press, 1992.

Officer, James E., Bernard L. Fontana, et. al. *The Pimería Alta: Missions & More.* Tucson: Southwestern Mission Research Center, 1996.

Jackson, Robert H. *New Views of Borderlands History.* Albuquerque: University of New Mexico Press, 1998.

CYNTHIA RADDING

PINAL, SILVIA (1931–).

One of the most important actors of Mexican cinema, Silvia Pinal was born on September 12, 1931, in Guaymas, Sonora. Pinal made her first screen appearance in 1948. By the early 1950s she was considered one of Mexico's favorite stars, winning an Ariel for best supporting actress in *Un rincón cerca del cielo* (*A Place Near Heaven*, 1952) and two more for best actress in *Locura pasional* (*Passional Madness*, 1955) and *La dulce enemiga* (*The Sweet Enemy*, 1957). Pinal is known internationally for her work in three films by the Spanish director Luis Buñuel, *Viridiana* (1961), *El ángel exterminador* (*The Exterminating Angel*, 1962), and *Simón del desierto* (*Simon of the Desert*, 1965). By the mid-1970s, Pinal had moved away from cinema and dedicated herself to theater and television. The actress is also well-known for her four marriages, to director Rafael Banquelis, producer Gustavo Alatriste, popular singer Enrique Guzman, and Mexican governor Tulio Hernandez. Since the mid-1990s she has worked in television production; she was also elected to public office while married to Hernandez. Pinal returned to the screen in the film *Ya no los hacen como antes* (*They Don't Make Them Like They Used To*, 2003).

See also **Cinema: From the Silent Film to 1990.**

BIBLIOGRAPHY

García Riera, Emilio. *El cine de Silvia Pinal.* Guadalajara: Universidad de Guadalajara; Mexico: Instituto Mexicano de Cinematografía, 1996.

SOPHIA KOUTSOYANNIS

PINDLING, LYNDEN OSCAR (1930–2000).

Lynden Oscar Pindling, a Bahamian political leader, was born on March 22, 1930, to educated and deeply religious working-class parents in Nassau. After graduating from high school in 1946, he worked as a clerk in Nassau's Post Office Savings Bank. In 1952 he received a law degree from King's College, University of London. Upon returning to the Bahamas he combined his legal practice with active political involvement in the black-based Progressive Liberal Party (PLP). The party had been unsuccessful in displacing the white commercial elite that dominated politics in colonial Bahamas. This changed in 1967 when Pindling led the PLP to a slim electoral victory and became the first black prime minister of the island. His victories after that (in 1968, 1972, 1977, 1982, and 1987) were all by solid majorities. Pindling led the nation to independence from Great Britain in 1973, and in 1983 was knighted by the Queen and made a Privy Councilor. None of the many accusations against him of corruption and receiving monies from drug dealers dulled his popular luster or reputation. His promotion of foreign investments in tourism (such as Paradise Island), offshore banking, and other financial services created jobs and an upwardly mobile black middle class. By the late-1980s several major banking scandals led to a souring of the popular mood, and the PLP lost the 1992 elections. Pindling did win his constituency seat but was now in the opposition. In 1997 he retired from politics. Upon his death on August 26, 2000, he was buried with all honors. Many Bahamians still revere him as "the Father of the Bahamas."

See also **Bahamas, Commonwealth of the.**

BIBLIOGRAPHY

Craton, Michael. *A History of the Bahamas,* 3rd edition. Waterloo, ON, Canada: San Salvador Press, 1986.

ANTHONY P. MAINGOT

PINEDA-DUQUE, ROBERTO (1910–1977).

Roberto Pineda-Duque (*b.* 29 August 1910; *d.* 1977), Colombian composer. Born in Santuario, Antioquia, Pineda-Duque took music courses at Medellín's Institute of Fine Arts under Joaquín Fuster (piano) and Carlos Posada-Amador (harmony). In 1942 he moved to Cali to study with Antonio María Valencia (choral technique). In the early 1950s he studied composition, fugue, counterpoint, instrumentation, and the twelve- tone technique with Carlo Jachino, director of the National Conservatory of the University of Colombia. Two of his major works are the cantata *Edipo Rey* (1959) and the oratorio *Cristo en el seno de Abraham* (1961). His *Concierto para piano* (1960) was awarded the Colombian Sesquicentennial of Independence Prize. In 1961 he became professor of organ, harmony, and composition at the National Conservatory. He has composed primarily church music and has served as *maestro de capilla* at the church of Nuestra Señora de las Nieves in Bogotá. He died in Bogotá.

See also **Music: Art Music.**

BIBLIOGRAPHY

Composers of the Americas, vol. 7 (1961), pp. 68–72; *New Grove Dictionary of Music and Musicians,* vol. 14 (1980).

SUSANA SALGADO

PINEDO, FEDERICO (1895–1971). Federico Pinedo (*b.* 1895; *d.* 1971), Argentine politician and political economist. Born in Buenos Aires, Pinedo graduated from the National University of Buenos Aires in 1915 with a degree in law and social science and then pursued a career in law and politics. He joined the reformist Socialist Party and was later a founder of the Independent Socialist Party. As such he was elected deputy for the Federal Capital in 1920–1922 and again in 1928–1933; he supported the overthrow of President Hipólito Yrigoyen in 1930. A leading figure of the Concordancia, he served as minister of finance under presidents Agustín Pedro Justo (1933–1935) and Ramón S. Castillo (1940–1941). He is best known for the "Pinedo Plan" of 1940, which represented a notable turn away from Argentina's classic economic liberalism. The plan envisioned massive state investment in industry, to be financed by public bonds sold through private banks; an industrial credit bank would make the resultant capital available to industrialists. It emphasized housing construction and envisioned a state agency to purchase surplus primary products for resale overseas as well as state purchase of the British-owned railways, with wartime credits accumulating in London. Radical deputies defeated

the plan in Congress but it won wide political support; Perón later adopted its leading proposals. As a democrat, however, Pinedo opposed Perón and was imprisoned.

Following Perón's overthrow in 1955 Pinedo advocated stern measures to restore the Argentine economy but came to believe that Argentina's problems were political in nature. During 1962 acting president José Maria Guido named him minister of finance. Pinedo believed congressional and judicial authority should be restored but held that the Peronist Party—a totalitarian party, in his view—should remain banned. His stand was unacceptable either to Peronists or to military hardliners, who soon imposed harsh demands on Guido. When the latter acceded to them, Pinedo, the spokesman for moderation, resigned after only two weeks in office. Pinedo had already achieved fame as a journalist and author; his major works include *En tiempos de la república y después* (5 vols., 1946), *El fatal estatismo* (1956), *La CEPAL y la realidad económica en América Latina* (1963), *La Argentina en un cono de sombra* (1968), and *La Argentina* (1971). Pinedo died in Buenos Aires.

See also **Argentina, Political Parties: Independent Socialist Party; Argentina, Political Parties: Socialist Party.**

BIBLIOGRAPHY

Azaretto, Roberto. *Federico Pinedo: Político y economista.* Buenos Aires: Emecé Editores, 1998.

Louro de Ortiz, Amalia A. *El grupo Pinedo-Prebisch y el neoconservadorismo renovador.* Buenos Aires: Grupo Editor Latinoamericano, 1992.

RONALD C. NEWTON

PIÑERA, VIRGILIO (1912–1979). Virgilio Piñera (*b.* 4 August 1912; *d.* 18 October 1979), Cuban poet, playwright, short-story writer, and novelist. Piñera was born in Cárdenas in Matanzas Province. He received a doctorate in philosophy and letters from the University of Havana in 1940. In 1942 he founded and managed the magazine *Poeta.* He lived in Buenos Aires for fourteen years, working on the staff of the Cuban consulate and eventually as a translator for the Argos publishing house. In Buenos Aires he befriended the Polish novelist Witold Gombrowicz, whose 1961 novel *Ferdydurke* he later helped translate into Spanish; he also published in the highly regarded magazine *Sur*. After returning to Cuba in 1955, Piñera and José Rodríguez Feo founded the literary publication *Ciclón*. In 1968 he won first prize in the Casa de las Américas contest for his play *Dos viejos pánicos.*

One of the most original and unique writers in all of Cuban history, Piñera excelled in the genres of poetry, drama, and the short story. His writing style is detached and concise; his work is noted for its black humor and use of the absurd. Piñera was always at odds with the Cuban Revolution, and upon his death many of his unpublished works were confiscated. Of these, two collections of short stories have been published posthumously (*Un fogonazo* and *Muecas para escribientes,* both 1987). Among his best works are *Cuentos fríos* (short stories, 1956), *Dos viejos pánicos* (drama, 1968), *Electra garrigó* (drama, 1960), *La isla en peso* (poem, 1943), *La vida entera* (poetry, 1969), and *Teatro completo* (drama, 1960).

See also **Cuba, Revolutions: Cuban Revolution; Theater.**

BIBLIOGRAPHY

Carmen L. Torres, *La cuentística de Virgilio Piñera* (1989).

Additional Bibliography

Abreu Arcia, Alberto. *Virgilio Piñera: Un hombre, una isla.* El Vedado: Ediciones Unión, 2002.

Anderson, Thomas F. *Everything in Its Place: The Life and Works of Virgilio Piñera.* Lewisburg, PA: Bucknell University Press, 2006.

Valerio-Holguín, Fernando. *Poética de la frialdad: La narrativa de Virgilio Piñera.* Lanham, MD: University Press of America, 1997.

ROBERTO VALERO

PINGRET, ÉDOUARD HENRI THÉOPHILE

(1788–1875). Édouard Henri Théophile Pingret (*b.* 30 December 1788; *d.* 1875), French painter. Pingret was born in Saint-Quentin, France. At the age of fourteen Pingret's father sent him to the studio of Jacques-Louis David, where he excelled as an apprentice. Two years later he went to Rome and frequented the Academy of San Lucas. In 1831 he received his first gold medal at an exhibition, and in 1839 he was awarded the rank of chevalier in the Legion of Honor. He spent time in Tripoli, Morocco, and Algeria, and in 1850, under the advice of Prince Joinville, Pingret traveled to Mexico as a representative of the American Maritime Transportation Company, a French firm, to resell stock belonging to Joinville and the Pignatari family, heirs to the marquisate of Oaxaca. At age sixty-two, Pingret met in Veracruz the printer Ernst Masson, who instilled in him an interest in archaeology. He gathered an interesting collection of pre-Hispanic and colonial pieces, which he later took back with him to Europe.

While in Mexico in 1852, Pingret exhibited for the first time at the Academia de San Carlos a group of paintings with European themes, and the following year demonstrated what he had seen and appreciated in Mexico by exhibiting a series of folkloric works. His scenes of the interiors of kitchens were rapidly copied by his students and exhibited at the academy. Pingret's work also includes landscapes and contemporary historical paintings, making him one of the visual editors of life in the middle part of the nineteenth century. He died in Saint-Quentin.

See also **Art: The Nineteenth Century.**

BIBLIOGRAPHY

Luis Ortiz Macedo, *Édouard Pingret: Un pinto romántico francés que retrató el México del mediar del siglo XIX* (1989).

Additional Bibliography

Ortiz Macedo, Luis. *Édouard Pingret; Pintor románico del siglo XIX.* México, D.F.: CONACULTA, 2004.

ESTHER ACEVEDO

PINHEIRO, JOSÉ FELICIANO FERNANDES

(1774–1847). José Feliciano Fernandes Pinheiro (*b.* 9 May 1774; *d.* 6 July 1847), viscount of São Leopoldo and minister of the Empire of Brazil (1825–1827). Born in Santos of a family of tradesmen, he graduated with a degree in law from the University of Coimbra in 1798. He was employed as a translator at the Arco do Cego

Typography in Lisbon. There, he drew the attention of Rodrigo de Sousa Coutinho, who in 1800 appointed him minister of the colonies, to establish the Customs of Rio Grande de São Pedro do Sul Captaincy. He was elected representative to the Lisbon Cortes for São Paulo in 1821, and in 1823 he became a representative to the Brazilian Constituent Assembly.

Pedro I appointed Pinheiro president of the province of São Pedro do Rio Grande do Sul (1824–1826), where he established the important immigrant colony of São Leopoldo. He was a senator from 1826 until his death and a member of the Council of State in 1827–1830.

Pinheiro played an important part in academic and cultural life. He was one of the founders of the Brazilian Historical and Geographical Institute, and a member of various foreign cultural institutions. He wrote several works, including *Annals of the São Pedro Province,* the first significant history of the region. He contributed to the creation of the Brazilian nation not only as a politician and administrator but as a memorialist and historian as well.

See also **Brazil, The Empire (First).**

BIBLIOGRAPHY

Visconde De São Leopoldo, "Memorias," in *Revista do Instituto Histórico e Geográfico Brasileiro* 37 (1874): 5–69, and 38 (1875): 5–49.

José Feliciano Fernandes Pinheiro, *Anais da Província de São Pedro,* introduction by Viana Moog, biography by Aurelio Porto, 4th ed. (1978).

Additional Bibliography

Lustosa, Isabel. *D. Pedro I.* São Paulo: Companhia das Letras, 2006.

Ramos, Luís A. de Oliveira. *D. Pedro, imperador e rei: Experiências de um príncipe (1798–1834).* Lisboa: Edições Inapa, 2002.

LÚCIA M. BASTOS P. NEVES

PINHEIRO MACHADO, JOSÉ GOMES

(1851–1915). José Gomes Pinheiro Machado (*b.* 1851; *d.* 8 September 1915), the most powerful figure in the Brazilian Senate from 1905 to 1915 and head of the congressional delegation from Rio Grande do Sul. Pinheiro Machado built a national

political machine through which he controlled Brazil's weak northern states, played a key role in presidential successions, and brought his home state to the forefront of national politics. Scion of a ranching family, he graduated from São Paulo Law School, fought in the Paraguayan War (War of the Triple Alliance), joined the Riograndense republican conspiracy against the empire in 1889, rose to the rank of general in the Federalist Revolt (1893), and served continuously in the Constituent Assembly and federal Senate, which elected him vice president (1902–1905, 1912–1915). He wielded his extensive personal power through control of the credentials committee and his national Partido Republicano Conservador, constructed of state political machines in 1910. Armed with his hold over weak President Hermes Rodrigues da Fonseca, he outmaneuvered salvationist army officers who challenged his power in 1911–1912, and he initiated interventions in the smaller states in 1913–1914. Reaction against his corruption, strong-arm tactics, and efforts to control the presidential succession in 1914 led to the breakdown of his political machine and his assassination by an unemployed baker in Rio de Janeiro.

See also **Brazil, Revolutions: Federalist Revolt of 1893.**

BIBLIOGRAPHY

João Da Costa Pôrto, *Pinheiro Machado e seu tempo: Tentativa de interpretação* (1951).

Joseph L. Love, *Rio Grande do Sul and Brazilian Regionalism, 1882–1930* (1971), pp. 136–177.

Additional Bibliography

Borges, Vera Lúcia Bogéa. *Morte na república: Os últimos anos de Pinheiro Machado e a política oligárquica (1909–1915).* Rio de Janeiro: Instituto Histórico e Geográfico Brasileiro, 2004.

Newton, Alvim. *Pinheiro Machado.* Porto Alegre: IEL, 1996.

JOAN BAK

PINHO, JOSÉ WANDERLEY DE ARAÚJO (1890–1967). José Wanderley de Araújo Pinho (*b.* 1890; *d.* 1967), Brazillian historian and politician. Born in Santo Amoro, Pinho graduated from the Faculdade de Direito da Bahia. His career began in local law and proceeded to the

state's judicial hierarchy and politics. He became a minister of the Tribunal de Contas, a federal deputy, and municipal prefect of Salvador. His avocation for history, signaled by a later post at the Universidade da Bahia and his membership in local and national historical institutes, was first evident in early publications related to the career of his great grandfather, the barão de Cotegipe (1815–1889). His work, based on careful archival research, remains important for an understanding of Second Empire politics and elite society in Bahia and Rio.

See also **Brazil, The Empire (Second).**

BIBLIOGRAPHY

Wanderly Pinho's works include *Política e políticos no império* (1930), *Cotegipe e seu tempo* (1937), *Salões e damas do segundo reinado* (1942), and *História de um engenho do recôncavo* (1946).

Additional Bibliography

Castro, Renato Berbert de. *As candidaturas de Almachio Diniz e Wanderley Pinho.* Salvador, Bahia, Brazil: Academia de Letras da Bahia, 1999.

JEFFREY D. NEEDELL

PINILLA, ENRIQUE (1927–1989). Enrique Pinilla (*b.* 3 August 1927; *d.* 1989), Peruvian composer. Pinilla was born in Lima and studied at the National Conservatory until 1946. For the next two years he studied with Nadia Boulanger in Paris. He completed his education at the Royal Conservatory of Music in Madrid where he lived until 1958. He became a student of Boris Blacher at the Berlin School of Music. In 1966–1967, Pinilla studied electronic music at Columbia University under the direction of Vladimir Ussachevsky and Alcides Lanza. Pinilla was the head of the music and film department at the Casa de la Cultura and director of the television and film department at the University of Lima.

Among his principal compositions are Sonatina for flute (1950); *Once canciones populares* for voice and piano (1952); and Six Pieces for strings and woodwinds (1958). A very effective use of shifting meters can be seen in his *Estudio sobre el ritmo de la marinera* for piano (1959). His interest in rhythmic structures evolved further during the 1960s in Four Pieces for fourteen wind instruments (1960);

Three Movements for percussion ensemble (1961); Four Pieces for orchestra (1961); Canto no. 1 for orchestra (1963); Collages nos. 1 and 2 for piano (1966); *Festejo* for orchestra (1966); *Prisma* for tape (1967); Canto no. 2 for orchestra (1968); Piano Concerto (1970); Peruvian Suite for orchestra (1972); *Evoluciones* no. 2 for percussion and orchestra (1976); and *Cinco piezas para percusión* (1977). He also wrote *Tres piezas para guitarra* (1987); *La niña de la lámpara azul* for choir (1981); and *Diez piezas infantiles* for piano (1987).

See also **Music: Art Music.**

BIBLIOGRAPHY

John Vinton, ed., *Dictionary of Contemporary Music* (1974), p. 574.

Gérard Béhague, *Music in Latin America: An Introduction* (1979), pp. 311–312; *New Grove Dictionary of Music and Musicians* (1980).

Additional Bibliography

Valcárcel, Edgar. *Enrique Pinilla: Hombre y artista.* Lima: Universidad de Lima, Fondo de Desarrollo Editorial, 1999.

ALCIDES LANZA

PINOCHET UGARTE, AUGUSTO (1915–2006). Augusto José Ramón Pinochet Ugarte (November 25, 1915–December 10, 2006) was a Chilean army officer and chief of state and president of Chile from 1973 to 1990. Pinochet was born in Valparaíso. He entered the Escuela Militar at the age of seventeen, graduated in 1937, and was promoted to second lieutenant in 1939. He and his wife, Lucía Hiriart, had three daughters and two sons.

Pinochet distinguished himself professionally as a specialist in military geography and geopolitics. His 1968 book *Geopolítica* went through several editions. He held several staff and command posts, and was a member of the Chilean military mission in Washington, D.C., in 1956. He taught at the Escuela Militar Bernardo O'Higgins, at the Academia de Guerra del Ejército, both located in Santiago, and at Ecuador's national war college in the 1950s and 1960s.

By 1970, Pinochet had risen to the rank of division general, and the next year he became commandant of the Santiago garrison, one of the most

Pinochet rides through the streets of Santiago in a parade celebrating the eleventh anniversary of the military coup d'etat, September 1984. Supporters credit Augusto Pinochet with bringing order and economic growth to the country while critics point to the corruption, inequality, and human rights abuses that also characterized his regime. © CARLOS CARRION/SYGMA/CORBIS

sensitive and influential of Chilean army assignments. By his own admission, Pinochet had been very critical of politics in general and Marxism specifically since his days as a junior officer. As Santiago garrison commandant he was profoundly influenced by the social, economic, and political turbulence accompanying the administration of Socialist Salvador Allende Gossens. When the army commander in chief, General Carlos Prats González, became interior minister during a serious trucking strike in late 1972, Pinochet assumed the duties of commander in chief, and held this position on the eve of the putsch of September 11, 1973. Pinochet became president of the military junta, a body composed of military commanders in chief. A year later he became president of the Republic of Chile. His term of office was formally extended later through the adoption of a constitution giving him an eight-year term (1981–1989).

As a result both of Allende's policies and economic pressures applied by foreign interests, especially the administration of U.S. president Richard M. Nixon, and the Chilean political opposition between 1970 and 1973, the country was in an economic depression from late 1973 until late 1976. This was also a period of harsh authoritarian rule, during which Pinochet consolidated his influence over the armed forces and the government. By 1978, however, Chileans, especially those of the middle and upper sectors, and some foreigners were talking of an "economic miracle" based on free enterprise, foreign loans, and "denationalization" of the economy. Pinochet's own popularity peaked in 1978, when a questionably legitimate plebiscite confirmed his leadership and policies. The growing opposition denounced the legitimacy of the exercise. In the early 1980s his popularity plummeted as Chile suffered economic recession, and the government resorted to stricter controls of the press, exile of some dissidents, curfews, and multiple violations of human rights reminiscent of the early stages of Pinochet's rule.

From the beginning of his administration supporters of Pinochet considered him the one figure capable of both controlling the armed forces and politicians and suppressing Marxism. He ultimately also became the figure toward whom the ever-growing opposition, composed of church leaders, labor, politicians, human-rights advocates, centrists, and leftists, would direct its energies. The United States and other foreign governments were cautious in relations with his government until the mid-1980s, when the United States, especially, began to work for a return to democratic government.

In the tenth year of Pinochet's government the opposition organized mass demonstrations against the regime's economic, political, and social programs. Beginning in May of that year, miners, students, workers, and dissident political leaders took to the streets to register their discontent. Pinochet used armed force to quell the demonstrations, then began talks aimed at political compromise. When talks stalled, he again used strong-arm tactics, claiming yet again that politicians and Marxists were to blame for Chile's problems. He employed such tactics for the rest of the decade.

In 1986 Pinochet survived an attempted assassination with only minor injuries. By this time the international outcry against the junta's blatant violations of human rights was growing louder with regularity. Two years later, with the economy once again on the rebound, his bid to remain president of Chile until 1997 was thwarted when a plebiscite (October 5, 1988) repudiated him. He did not run in the presidential election of December 1989 and turned over the sash of office to Patricio Aylwin Azócar in March 1990.

Following his unprecedented sixteen and a half years in office (the longest term of any chief executive in modern Chilean history), Pinochet retained the post of army commander in chief. He made it clear that he would protect the army's (and his own) institutional (and political) interests in this capacity. In late 1998, soon after he retired as commander in chief and assumed an appointive senate seat, Pinochet was placed under house arrest in England, where he had gone for medical treatment. The authorities released him in early 2000, but only after an exhaustive legal process in which a Spanish court requested his extradition to stand trial for violations of human rights of Spanish

citizens in Chile. Back in Santiago he resigned his senate seat and soon became embroiled in a series of legal measures designed to strip him of immunity and bring him to trial on multiple counts of torture, kidnapping, murder, and disappearance of political opponents committed in the wake of the 1973 putsch and throughout his presidency.

Concomitant with court decisions in 1999 and 2000 that the disappearances of members of the opposition were still open cases—many bodies have yet to be found—Pinochet's health failed to a point where it prevented him from ever standing trial for such crimes. In 2004 evidence surfaced confirming long-standing allegations that Pinochet, some military cronies, and members of his family were indeed involved in tax evasion, owned passports under other names, and had established off-shore bank accounts—the most alarming evidence involving the Riggs National Bank, of Washington, D.C. Fifteen years after he left the presidency, Augusto Pinochet Ugarte had become an embarrassment to the army, the subject of endless legal controversy, and the symbol of an epoch that still divides Chileans deeply. He died of complications following surgery after suffering a heart attack in late 2006.

Blunt, normally humorless, and always military in bearing, Augusto Pinochet bequeathed to Chile a legacy that will be hotly debated for years to come: Was he the resolute general who extricated the country from the turbulence and economic collapse of the Allende years, the unrepentant leader who presided over a remarkable (if at times unsteady) economic recovery, the harsh dictator who brooked no opposition to military rule and claimed that nothing happened during his presidency that he did not know of, the corrupt and venal holder of foreign bank accounts and fraudulent passports whose family and friends enriched themselves while his government repeatedly violated the human rights of its and other countries' citizens—or all of the above?

See also **Allende Gossens, Salvador; Aylwin Azócar, Patricio; Chile, The Twentieth Century; Chile, Truth Commissions; Military Dictatorships: Since 1945.**

BIBLIOGRAPHY

Arriagada Herrera, Genaro. *Pinochet: The Politics of Power.* Translated by Nancy Morris, with Vincent Ercolano and Kristen A. Whitney. Boston: Unwin Hyman, 1988.

Constable, Pamela, and Arturo Valenzuela. *A Nation of Enemies: Chile under Pinochet*. New York: Norton, 1991.

Correa, Raquel, and Elizabeth Subercaseaux. *Ego sum Pinochet*. Santiago de Chile: Zig-Zag, 1989.

Dorfman, Ariel. *Exorcising Terror: The Incredible Unending Trial of Augusto Pinochet*. New York: Seven Stories Press, 2002.

Ensalaco, Mark. *Chile under Pinochet: Recovering the Truth*. Philadelphia: University of Pennsylvania Press, 2000.

Haslam, Jonathan. *The Nixon Administration and the Death of Allende's Chile*. New York: Verso, 2005.

Kornbluh, Peter. *The Pinochet File: A Declassified Dossier on Atrocity and Accountability*. New York: New Press, 2003.

Loveman, Brian. *Chile: The Legacy of Hispanic Capitalism*, 3rd edition. New York: Oxford University Press, 2001.

Nunn, Frederick M. "New Thoughts on Military Intervention in Latin American Politics: The Chilean Case, 1973." *Journal of Latin American Studies* 7 (November 1975): 271–304.

Nunn, Frederick M. "One Year in the Life of Augusto Pinochet: Gulag of the Mind." *The Americas* 42 (October 1985): 197–206.

O'Shaughnessy, Hugh. *Pinochet: The Politics of Torture*. New York: New York University Press, 2000.

Pinochet Ugarte, Augusto. *The Crucial Day, September 11, 1973*. Translated by María Teresa Escobar. Santiago de Chile: Editorial Renacimiento, 1982.

Pinochet Ugarte, Augusto. *Política, politiquería, demagogia*. Santiago de Chile: Renacimiento, 1983.

Roht-Arriaza, Naomi. *The Pinochet Effect: Transnational Justice in the Age of Human Rights*. Philadelphia: University of Pennsylvania Press, 2005.

Salinas, Luis Alejandro. *The London Clinic*. Santiago, Chile: Lom Ediciones, 1999.

Valenzuela, J. Samuel, and Arturo Valenzuela, eds. *Military Rule in Chile*. Baltimore, MD: Johns Hopkins University Press, 1986.

Varas, Augusto, Felipe Agüero, and Fernando Bustamante. *Chile, democracia fuerzas armadas*. Santiago, Chile: Facultad Latinoamericana de Ciencias Sociales, 1980.

Weeks, Gregory B. *The Military and Politics in Postauthoritarian Chile*. Tuscaloosa: University of Alabama Press, 2003.

FREDERICK M. NUNN

PIÑOL Y AYCINENA, BERNARDO

(1806–1881). Bernardo Piñol y Aycinena (*b.* 2 November 1806; *d.* 24 June 1881), archbishop of Guatemala (1867– 1881). Born in Guatemala, Piñol entered the Franciscan order and became a priest in 1830. After the suppression of religious associations in the 1830s, he joined the secular clergy. He obtained a doctorate in philosophy from the University of San Carlos, where he held a chair and served as rector during the Rafael Carrera presidency. In 1854 he accepted the bishopric of Nicaragua and served in that post until his appointment as archbishop of Guatemala in 1867. He became embroiled in the church and state conflict after the Liberals assumed power in 1871. His defense of the church against anticlerical writings, his opposition to the government's expulsion of the Jesuits, and his refusal to honor the state's request to issue a pastoral letter calling for an end to Conservative rebellions led to his banishment in 1871 to Havana, Cuba. He remained archbishop of Guatemala until his death, while a series of apostolic administrators governed the archdiocese.

See also **Franciscans; Guatemala.**

BIBLIOGRAPHY

Mary P. Holleran, *Church and State in Guatemala* (1949), esp. pp. 145–166 and 202.

Hubert J. Miller, *La iglesia católica y el estado en Guatemala, 1871–1885* (1976), esp. pp. 72–123 and 317– 326.

Agustín Estrada Monroy, *Datos para la historia de la Iglesia en Guatemala*, vol. 3 (1979), esp. pp. 29–85.

Additional Bibliography

Sullivan-González, Douglass. *Piety, Power, and Politics: Religion and Nation Formation in Guatemala, 1821– 1871*. Pittsburgh: University of Pittsburgh Press, 1998.

Woodward, Ralph Lee. *Rafael Carrera y la creación de la República de Guatemala, 1821–1871*. La Antigua, Guatemala: Centro de Investigaciones Regionales de Mesoamérica, 2002.

HUBERT J. MILLER

PIÑOL Y SALA, JOSÉ (?–c. 1780). José

Piñol y Sala (*d.* ca. 1780), a powerful merchant in late colonial Central America. A native of Barcelona, he emigrated to Guatemala in 1752. There he served as the factor of the Real Asiento de Negros, while conducting trade on behalf of his family's Cádiz firm, dealing primarily in slaves and indigo. In 1760 a vessel belonging to his family's company carried over 200,000 pesos worth of indigo, roughly one-third of Central American indigo exports for the year. Piñol served as *alcalde ordinario* (city magistrate) of Santiago de Guatemala (today Antigua) in 1774, following the devastating earthquakes of 1773, which ultimately prompted the removal of the Central American capital to the present site of Guatemala City. Like many *peninsulares* (natives of Spain) Piñol married into a prominent creole family, the Muñoz clan. His offspring established especially close relations with the powerful Aycinena family—two daughters and a son joined the fellow peninsular clan—and became part of the core of Central America's late colonial and early independence aristocracy.

See also **Indigo.**

BIBLIOGRAPHY

Miles L. Wortman, *Government and Society in Central America, 1680–1840* (1982), p. 123.

Diana Balmori, Stuart F. Voss, and Miles L. Wortman, *Notable Family Networks in Latin America* (1984), pp. 60–61.

Additional Bibliography

Adams, Richard E. W., and Murdo J. MacLeod. *Mesoamerica*. Cambridge, England; New York: Cambridge University Press, 2000.

RICHMOND F. BROWN

PIÑON, NÉLIDA (1935–). Nélida Piñon (*b.* 3 May 1935), Brazilian author. Born in Rio de Janeiro into a family of devout Catholics, Piñon received a traditional education in Catholic schools. These events may have produced a paradoxical effect in her fictional construct, which possesses a mystical atmosphere while simultaneously challenging religious dogma and tradition.

Many of Piñon's life experiences have found their way, if transformed, into her fiction. At an early age she was sent by her family to spend some time in a village in Galicia, Spain, where her father and his parents had been born. That period became indelible in her literary memory and infused itself into the plot of *A república dos sonhos* (1984; *The Republic of Dreams,* 1989). Interested in ballet and opera, she imbues her fiction with the scenic arts, as in *A força do destino* (1978), a parody of the opera *La Forza del Destino,* and in *A doce canção de Caetana* (1987; *Caetana's Sweet Song,* 1992), which takes as its backdrop an itinerant Brazilian theater group.

Piñon tends to focus her work on unconventional topics, and has experimented with the linguistic possibilities of Portuguese. On both fronts, her literary expressiveness is regarded by critics as compelling, innovative, and resourceful. She was the first woman president of the Brazilian Academy of Arts and Letters, a position which she held from 1996 to 1997. In 2005, she won the Prince of Asturias Prize for literature.

See also **Brazilian Academy of Letters; Literature: Brazil.**

BIBLIOGRAPHY

Giovanni Pontiero, "Notes on the Fiction of Nélida Piñon," in *Review* 76, no. 19 (Winter 1976): 67–71, Alan Ryan, "Chronicle of a Brazilian Family: *The Republic of Dreams,*" in *Washington Post Book World* (30 July 1989): 580. Also: Vasda B. Landers, "Interview with Nélida Piñon," in *Belles Lettres* 6 (Winter 1991): 24–25.

Ana Rosa Núñez and Lesbia O. Varona, *The World of Nélida Piñon: Partial Bibliography* (1992).

Additional Bibliography

Kaz, Leonel, and Nigge Piovesan Loddi, eds. *Século XX: A mulher conquista o Brasil.* Rio de Janeiro: Aprazível Edições, 2006.

Piñon, Nélida, and Jorge Orendáin, ed. *Nélida Piñon: 1995.* Guadalajara, Mexico: Editorial Universitaria; Mexico City: Alfaguara, 2006.

Rector, Monica, ed. *Brazilian Writers.* Farmington Hills, MI: Gale, 2005.

REGINA IGEL

PINO SUÁREZ, JOSÉ MARÍA (1869–1913). José María Pino Suárez (*b.* 8 September 1869; *d.* 22 February 1913), vice president of Mexico (1912–1913). Pino Suárez was a prominent prerevolutionary politician and anti-reelectionist who became the only truly popularly elected Mexican vice president, the last individual to occupy that post in the twentieth century. Born on a hacienda in Tenosique, Tabasco, of a modest family, Pino Suárez completed his studies in law in

Mérida, Yucatán, graduating 12 September 1894. In 1904, he founded *El Peninsular,* which he directed. He became active in opposing the government of Porfirio Díaz, and directed the anti-reelectionists in Yucatán, Campeche, and Tabasco. He supported Madero in 1909, and became president of the National Independent Convention of Anti-reelectionist Parties and National Democratic parties in 1910. His role in opposing Díaz was dangerous and caused him to flee the country in 1910–1911. After returning in 1911, he served as a member of Madero's provisional government in Ciudad Juárez and as provisional governor of Yucatán. He served as secretary of public education while vice president. He and President Madero were murdered at the order of Victoriano Huerta.

See also **Huerta, Victoriano; Madero, Francisco Indalecio.**

BIBLIOGRAPHY

Pepe Bulnes, *Pino Suárez, el caballero de la lealtad* (1969); Diego Arenas Guzmán, *José María Pino Suárez,* 2d ed. (1985).

Martha Poblett Miranda, *José María Pino Suárez, semblanza* (1986).

Additional Bibliography

Krauze, Enrique. *Mexico: Biography of Power: A History of Modern Mexico, 1810–1996.* New York: Harper Perennial, 1998.

McLynn, Frank. *Villa and Zapata: A History of the Mexican Revolution.* New York: Carroll and Graf, 2001.

RODERIC AI CAMP

PINTO, JOAQUÍN (1842–1906).

Joaquín Pinto (*b.* 18 August 1842; *d.* 1906), Ecuadorian artist. One of the first Ecuadorian artists to paint local landscapes, Pinto was born in Quito and revealed a talent for art at an early age. He studied with Ramón Vargas, Rafael Vanegas, Andrés Costa, Tomás Camacho, Santos Ceballos, and Nicolás Cabrera. He mastered watercolor technique with Juan Manosalvas, who had studied in Rome. Pinto married fellow artist Eufemia Berrío in 1876; they lived at San Roque, an art colony in Quito.

Pinto painted religious and mythological subjects as well as portraits and scenes from daily life. He favored the small format and was influenced by the French artist Jacques Callot. At the suggestion of Bishop González Suárez, he documented the archaeological treasures of Ecuador. From 1903 to 1904 he was director of the Academy of Painting and Drawing in Cuenca and was a founding member of the New National School of Fine Arts in Quito (1904).

See also **Art: The Nineteenth Century; Art: The Twentieth Century.**

BIBLIOGRAPHY

Arte Ecuatoriano, vol. 2 (1976), pp. 221–226.

Additional Bibliography

Hartup, Cheryl Diane. "Artists and the New Nation: Academic Painting in Quito during the Presidency of Gabriel García Moreno (1861-1875)." M.A. Thesis. University of Texas at Austin, 1997.

MARTA GARSD

PINTO DÍAZ, FRANCISCO ANTONIO

(1775–1858). Francisco Antonio Pinto Díaz (*b.* 1775; *d.* 18 July 1858), patriot general and Liberal president of Chile (1827–1829). An early adherent of the national cause, Pinto Díaz was sent to Buenos Aires in 1811 as Chilean representative and to England in 1813 on a similarly fruitless mission. Once back in South America, he took part in campaigns in Upper Peru and Peru, returning to Chile in 1824 with the rank of brigadier general. Politics swiftly claimed him: after holding ministerial office (1824–1825), he took over from Ramón Freire Serrano as acting president in May 1827.

Pinto's administration saw the most serious attempt yet made in Chile to consolidate a stable, liberal political order. Important administrative changes were instituted, and a new constitution (drafted with the help of Spanish liberal José Joaquín de Mora) went into effect in August 1828. A year later, at a time of mounting political tension, Pinto resigned, on grounds of ill health. Though reelected president in September 1829, he returned to power for no more than two weeks, sensing that there was no way of stopping the Conservative revolt then under way. The victorious Conservative regime in fact cashiered him in May 1830 in a spiteful measure that was only rescinded nine years later. Pinto Díaz was persuaded to run as the

Liberal candidate in the presidential contest of 1841, but there was no chance he would win. In fact, he became largely reconciled to the Conservative regime, during which he served as a senator from 1846 until his death. Both his son-in-law, Manuel Bulnes Prieto, and his son, Aníbal Pinto Garmendia, also served as presidents of Chile.

See also **Bulnes Prieto, Manuel; Chile: The Nineteenth Century; Chile, Political Parties: Liberal Party; Pinto Garmendia, Aníbal.**

BIBLIOGRAPHY

Collier, Simon. *Chile: The Making of a Republic, 1830–1865.* New York: Cambridge University Press, 2003.

SIMON COLLIER

PINTO GARMENDIA, ANÍBAL (1825–1884).

Aníbal Pinto Garmendia (*b.* 15 March 1825; *d.* 9 June 1884), president of Chile (1876–1881). The son of former president Francisco Antonio Pinto Díaz, diplomat and university professor, Pinto served in the Chamber of Deputies, in the Senate, and as minister of war before being elected president in 1876.

Misfortune marked Pinto's tenure in office. Chile's mining economy suffered catastrophic losses because of falling silver and copper prices; alternating drought and floods devastated agriculture; and an overexpansion of credit left all but one of the nation's banks without funds and the country without specie. After traditional methods of resolving the economic crisis proved unsuccessful, Pinto imposed direct taxes on income, gifts, and estates, and changed the tariff law to stimulate the creation of domestic industries.

Economic woes constituted only part of his problems: political infighting as well as conflicts with the Roman Catholic church undermined Pinto's authority. Worse still, in early 1879 a border dispute with Bolivia that was thought to have been settled led to Chile's involvement in the War of the Pacific. Happily, by the time Pinto retired in 1881, the war had turned in Chile's favor. Almost penniless, Pinto spent his last years living on a *fundo* (farm) purchased by public subscription.

See also **Chile: The Nineteenth Century; Pinto Díaz, Francisco Antonio.**

BIBLIOGRAPHY

Cristián A. Zegers, *Aníbal Pinto, historia política de su gobierno* (1969).

William F. Sater, *The Heroic Image in Chile: Arturo Prat, Secular Saint* (1973).

Additional Bibliography

Castillo Fadic, Gabriel. *Las estéticas nocturnas: Ensayo republicano y representación cultural en Chile e Iberoamérica.* Santiago, Chile: Instituto de Estética, Pontificia Universidad Católica de Chile, 2003.

Muñoz Salas, Javier R. *Un monstruo de cien cabezas: La imagen del liberalismo desde al diario El Estandarte Católico, durnate el gobierno de Aníbal Pinto Garmendia (1876–1881).* Ph.D. Thesis. Pontificia Universidad Católica de Chile, 2004.

WILLIAM F. SATER

PINTO SANTA CRUZ, ANÍBAL (1919–1996).

The Chilean economist and journalist Aníbal Pinto Santa Cruz was among the early economists who studied and wrote about underdevelopment in Latin America. The great-grandson of a Chilean president with the same name, he studied law at the University of Chile and economics at the London School of Economics. While in Europe he married the ballerina María Luisa Solari. Upon his return to Chile he founded the journal *Panorama Económico* (which he directed from 1948 to 1956) and taught finance and economics at the Universidad de Chile. In 1960 he joined the United Nations' Economic Commission for Latin America and the Caribbean (CEPAL) as director of its Rio de Janeiro branch, serving in that post until 1965. He returned to Chile as the director of CEPAL's economic development division (1970–1979), and subsequently directed the *Revista de la CEPAL* from 1987 until his death in 1996. Although on the Left, he remained critical of the most extreme proponents of dependency theory and put forth a less deterministic view of underdevelopment that allowed for the possibility that underdeveloped countries could follow in the path of industrialized nations. He published widely on Latin American economic development and was awarded various national and international prizes. He died on January 3, 1996.

See also **Chile: The Twentieth Century; Journalism.**

BIBLIOGRAPHY

Bernal Sahagún, Víctor M. *Pensamiento latinoamericano: CEPAL, R. Prebisch y A. Pinto.* Mexico: Universidad Nacional Autónoma de México, Seminario de Teoría del Desarrollo, Instituto de Investigaciones Económicas, 1980.

Pinto, Aníbal. *La internacionalización de la economía mundial: Una visión latinoamericana.* Madrid: Ediciones Cultura Hispánica del Instituto de Cooperación Iberoamericana, 1980.

IÑIGO GARCIA-BRYCE

PINZÓN, MARTIN ALONSO (mid-1400s–c. 1493).

Martín Alonso Pinzón (*b.* mid-1400s; *d.* ca. 31 March 1493), navigator, captain of the *Pinta*. A shipowner and commercial agent from Palos, on Spain's south Atlantic coast, Martín Alonso and his brother Vicente Yáñez Pinzón proved invaluable to the success of the first expedition of Christopher Columbus. From the mid-1470s he and his brother commanded trading voyages from Palos to the central Mediterranean, the Canaries, and probably the Guinea coast.

Pinzón piloted the *Pinta* on the 1492 expedition and was instrumental in maintaining discipline among the crew of the three ships, especially those on Columbus's flagship, the *Santa María,* as threat of mutiny increased in the days immediately preceding the sighting of land on 12 October. Off the coast of Hispaniola, however, Pinzón broke ranks and sailed ahead, leaving Columbus behind with his brother Vicente Yáñez to face the tragic shipwreck of the *Santa María.* Pinzón rejoined the principal force after many days' absence, reporting gold and other important discoveries. Columbus chafed, planning to charge him for insubordination after safely returning to Spain.

Columbus sailed back to Spain on the *Niña,* along with Vicente Yáñez. The ships were separated during a terrible storm off the Azores. Pinzón reached port at Bayona in Galicia, while Columbus was driven into Lisbon. Pinzón's son and other family members were in Bayona, returning with

goods from Flanders. From there, Pinzón penned a report of the expedition and sent it overland to the Catholic monarchs, then resident in Barcelona. Ill, he set sail for Palos, and by coincidence, arrived the same day (15 March 1493) as Christopher Columbus. Admiral Columbus initiated action against him, but Martín Alonso's death in late March avoided a legal imbroglio. Some suspect that Martín Alonso was one of the first Europeans to fall victim to the New World epidemic—syphilis.

See also **Columbus, Christopher; Pinzón, Vicente Yáñez.**

BIBLIOGRAPHY

Juan Gil, *Marineros y mercaderes en las Indias, 1499–1504* (1985).

Juan Manzano Manzano, *Los Pinzones y el descubrimiento de América,* 3 vols. (1988).

Additional Bibliography

Fernández Duro, Cesáreo. *Los hermanos Pinzón en el descubrimiento de América* Buenos Aires: Emecé Editores, 1944.

Frye, John. *Los otros: Columbus and the Three Who Made His Enterprise of the Indies Succeed.* Lewiston, NY: E. Mellen Press, 1992.

NOBLE DAVID COOK

PINZÓN, VICENTE YÁÑEZ (mid-1400s–c. 1514).

Vicente Yáñez Pinzón (*b.* mid-1400s; *d.* ca. August–September 1514), captain of the *Niña* on the first Columbus expedition, "discoverer" of the Amazon River. A navigator and shipper of the Andalusian port of Palos, Pinzón, along with his brother Martín Alonso Pinzón, conducted trade from the mid-1470s with ports in the central Mediterranean, Canaries, and probably Guinea. He commanded the *Niña* during the first voyage to America in 1492, and after the loss of the *Santa María,* he acted as pilot, returning to Spain with Christopher Columbus. Conflict between Columbus and Pinzón's brother Martín Alonso led to a break in their relations. The untimely death of Martín Alonso probably caused Pinzón to travel separately to Barcelona, after Columbus, to report to the Catholic monarchs on the fleet's discoveries.

In 1499 Pinzón received an agreement (6 June) to explore the coast of South America. He left Seville in mid-November, sailing to the Canaries, then to the Cape Verde Islands. Leaving the island of Santiago on 1 January, he reached the Brazilian coast on 26 January 1500. He named the Cape Santa María de la Consolación, and although exact identification is disputed, it was south of the Amazon River. From here, Pinzón explored northerly, tending west, from the mouths of the Amazon to what is now Venezuela, around the Gulf of Paria, where his small fleet united with Diego de Lepe. He returned via Hispaniola, exploring islands off the north coast before reaching Spain on 30 September 1500. He reported to the monarchs in Granada and in September 1501 was granted governorship of the lands he had discovered, but he was unable to conduct a new expedition that year.

In 1504 Pinzón returned to the Brazilian coast, sailing from roughly Recife to the Gulf of Paria, returning this time via Puerto Rico. In 1505 he attended the famous meeting in Toro with other experienced pilots-cosmographers and was authorized to head an expedition to the Spice Islands (not undertaken). He was named *corregidor* as well as *alcaide* of a fortress of San Juan (Puerto Rico) that was to be constructed. In 1508 he was in service in the Casa de Contratación in Seville and was named a "pilot," along with Juan de la Cosa and Díaz De Solís. In 1508–1509 he sailed with Díaz de Solís from Costa Rica past the Yucatán, and perhaps to the middle Gulf Coast of Mexico. Some dispute the exact route of this venture, while others reject the authenticity of the excursion altogether. Pinzón was ill in Seville in March 1514 and died later that year.

See also **Pinzón, Martín Alonso.**

BIBLIOGRAPHY

Juan Manzano Manzano, *Los Pinzones y el descubrimiento de América* (1988).

Additional Bibliography

Espínola, Rodolfo. *Vicente Pinzón e a descoberta do Brasil.* Rio de Janeiro, RJ: Topbooks, 2001.

Frye, John. *Los Otros: Columbus and the Three Who Made His Enterprise of the Indies Succeed.* Lewiston, NY: E. Mellen Press, 1992.

Szaszdi Nagy, Adam. *Los guías de Guanahaní y la llegada de Pinzón a Puerto Rico.* Valladolid, España: Casa Museo de Colón: Seminario Americanista de la Universidad de Valladolid, 1995.

Washington, Irving. *Voyages and Discoveries of the Dompanions of Columbus.* Escondido, CA: Book Tree, 2000, 1835.

NOBLE DAVID COOK

PIPILES. Pipiles, a Central American people who speak an Uto-Aztecan language. The Pipiles began a series of migrations from Central Mexico to Central America as early as 400 CE, although greater movement occurred between 900 and 1300. Small numbers arrived around 500, during Teotihuacán expansion. Pipiles of Toltec origin established themselves by 801 along the Pacific coast of Central America. The Toltec-influenced Nonoalca group arrived in El Salvador at about 1250–1300.

At the time of the Spanish Conquest, the Pipiles lived along the Pacific coast and slope of Guatemala and El Salvador and in central, northeast, and western Honduras. (William R. Fowler estimates a population of 450,000 Pipiles in Guatemala and El Salvador at this time.) Preconquest Pipil warfare with K'iche' and Kakchikel Mayas in the Late Postclassic Period resulted in a loss of territory on the Pacific coast. However, Pipil migration and warfare extended Nahua culture into Central America, forcibly bringing Mexican religion and science. Pipiles developed states using the *capulli* system, based on descent, to justify power and control resources and a social hierarchy of nobles, commoners, and slaves. Tribute was paid by commoners to nobles, and later by the Pipiles themselves to the Spanish.

Fertile volcanic soils and the use of terracing and irrigation assured abundant agricultural production. Local and long-distance trade of salt, cacao, and cotton were crucial to the Pipil economy to procure obsidian and sacred articles. The Pipil language, in the Uto-Aztecan family, is spoken by Pipiles in El Salvador but is no longer spoken in Guatemala.

See also **Indigenous Peoples; Nahuas.**

BIBLIOGRAPHY

Miguel Armas Molina, *La cultura Pipil de Centro América* (1974).

William R. Fowler, *The Cultural Evolution of the Ancient Nahua Civilizations of Central America: The Precolumbian Pipil-Nicarao* (1989).

LAURA L. WOODWARD

PIPILTÍN. Pipiltín, nobility by birth among the Nahua of central Mesoamerica. Male and female *pipiltín* had many privileges separating them from the Macehualli (commoners), including the rights to own land, receive tribute and labor, and wear richly decorated clothing. *Pipiltín* males received a broad secular and religious education, staffed the bureaucracy, and served as military commanders. After the triumph of Hernán Cortés, the status of the *pipiltín* was recognized by Spanish officials eager to gain the cooperation of influential locals. They maintained certain of their privileges, and staffed the upper ranks of indigenous town government into the late colonial period.

See also **Aztecs; Nahuas.**

BIBLIOGRAPHY

There are many sources dealing with the pre-Hispanic *pipiltín*. Two of the most accessible are Pedro Carrasco, "Social Organization of Ancient Mexico," in *Archaeology of Northern Mesoamerica*. Pt. 1, *Handbook of Middle American Indians*, vol. 10, edited by Gordon F. Ekholm and Ignacio Bernal (1971); Frances Berdan, *The Aztecs of Central Mexico: An Imperial Society* (1982). For the colonial period, see Charles Gibson, *The Aztecs Under Spanish Rule* (1964); Robert Haskett, *Indigenous Rulers: an Ethnohistory of Town Government in Colonial Cuernavaca* (1991); and James Lockhart, *The Nahuas After the Conquest: A Social and Cultural History of the Indians of Central Mexico, Sixteenth Through Eighteenth Centuries* (1992).

ROBERT HASKETT

PIPIOLOS. Pipiolos, the nickname first commonly applied to Chilean Liberals in the 1820s. In conventional Spanish, the word has the connotation of "novices" or "beginners," and also has a slight sense of "men on the make." The local Chilean use is said to have derived from *pío pío*, the noise made by chickens when scratching around for grain. Apparently a similar sound was made by the predominantly Liberal card players who frequented an insalubrious café in Calle Ahumada, Santiago, owned by Spaniard Francisco Barrios. (This café, one of only two or three in Santiago at that time, went out of business in the mid-1820s.) Like many nicknames of this sort (for example, Tories in England), the expression was adopted by those it sought to ridicule. A short-lived newspaper, *El Pipiolo,* published eight issues in 1827. The term is most accurately used to denote the Liberals of the 1820s, 1830s, and 1840s.

See also **Chile, Political Parties: Liberal Party.**

BIBLIOGRAPHY

Collier, Simon. *Chile: The Making of a Republic, 1830-1865: Politics and Ideas.* New York: Cambridge University Press, 2003.

Gazmuri, Cristián; Manuel Loyola; and Sergio Grez Toso. *Los proyectos nacionales en el pensamiento político y social chileno del siglo XIX.* Santiago: Ediciones UCSH, 2002.

Scully, Timothy. *Rethinking the Center: Party Politics in Nineteenth- and Twentieth-century Chile.* Stanford, CA: Stanford University Press, 1992.

SIMON COLLIER

PIQUETEROS. In response to the worsening Argentine economic crisis of 1998–2002, protest groups of impoverished long-term unemployed workers organized *piquetes* (blockades) of strategic roads and bridges to force government officials to include them in relief programs nominally available to all who met certain requirements. In time, the national *piquetero* movement fragmented ideologically among a variety of community-based leftist entities, most loosely affiliated either with nontraditional labor union confederations or with small Marxist political parties. The eventual economic recovery and the growth of employment left a shrinking movement polarized between those now co-opted by the government and those more radical, still challenging government authority.

See also **Argentina: The Twentieth Century.**

BIBLIOGRAPHY

Epstein, Edward. "The Piquetero Movement in Greater Buenos Aires: Political Protests by the Unemployed Poor During the Crisis." In *Broken Promises? The Argentine Crisis and Argentine Democracy*, edited by Edward Epstein and David Pion-Berlin. Lanham, MD: Lexington Books, 2006.

Svampa, Maristella, and Sebastián Pereyra. *Entre la ruta y el barrio: La experiencia de las organizaciones piqueteras.* Buenos Aires: Editorial Biblos, 2003.

EDWARD EPSTEIN

PIRACY. Piracy, robbery and other high crimes committed at sea. A practice as old as navigation, it became common in Latin America as soon as the Spanish began shipping precious metals from Mexico and Peru. The term has often been used to connote all the maritime attacks carried on by privateers, buccaneers, and other freebooters against Spanish and Portuguese commerce from the sixteenth through the eighteenth centuries. For the Spanish, all of these marauders were pirates. Historically, however, the word has had a more narrow definition, excluding from its meaning those who sailed under some guise of legality through letters of marque or patents from European or American governments. True pirates were those who held no commission from any lawful authority and who could legally be attacked and judged by the authorities of any sovereign state.

The buccaneers were very similar to pirates in their operations, but they enjoyed impunity in the non-Iberian colonies. Thus they operated freely from British, French, Dutch, or Swedish ports in the Caribbean and North America. Port Royal, Jamaica, for example, was a frequent hangout for buccaneers until it sank beneath the sea in the earthquake of 1692. Many of the buccaneers held deep religious convictions stemming from their origins in Puritan, Huguenot, or other Calvinist colonies. After 1670, however, these attributes became less common, and buccaneering deteriorated into outright piracy. Caribbean-based buccaneering, in fact, was a transition from the earlier Old World–based privateering (French "corsairs," Dutch "sea beggars," and English "sea dogs") to the "golden age of piracy" in Latin America from about 1680 to 1720, when dangerous pirate fleets operated in the Caribbean and along both the Atlantic and Pacific coasts of the American mainland. Like the buccaneers Henry Morgan and Richard Sawkins, many of these pirates came from Wales, although other nationalities were well represented among them. Sawkins, one of the last of

Henry Morgan and His Pirates Ill-Treating the Citizens of Maracaibo on the Spanish Main in 1669, engraving by English School (17th century). Morgan was a Welsh buccaneer who was allowed to operate freely from non-Spanish ports. However, especially after 1670, the difference between buccaneering and piracy was often difficult to discern, particularly for its victims. PRIVATE COLLECTION/ PETER NEWARK HISTORICAL PICTURES/ THE BRIDGEMAN ART LIBRARY

the buccaneers, is especially representative of the transition from buccaneering to piracy.

A further distinction between pirates and other maritime freebooters of Latin America, although not an absolute one, is that the earlier freebooters preyed primarily on the Spanish and Portuguese, whereas the pirates attacked the commerce of all nations. In the eighteenth century, the maintenance of larger national navies led to the suppression of high crimes on the seas, although sporadic acts of piracy continued to occur throughout the nineteenth and twentieth centuries, especially in politically disturbed areas along Latin American coasts. For example, in the 1980s pirates preyed on yachts and other coastal shipping along the Caribbean shore of Nicaragua.

During the late seventeenth and early eighteenth centuries, the Caribbean was the haven of many notorious pirates who endangered the commerce of many nations. These pirates depended on light, swift, shallow-draft vessels that could overtake heavier cargo vessels or flee from warships. With the rise of the plantation colonies, many of the ports that had offered sanctuary to the buccaneers became hostile to pirate ships. Therefore, the yet unsettled Bahamas became one of the more important bases for pirates, especially the port of Nassau on New Providence Island, although some pirates still frequented ports in New York and New England with relative impunity. The infamous Captain William Kidd was among the most well known. Like other pirates of this age, he sailed not only in Latin American waters, but also along African, Middle Eastern, and Far Eastern coasts as well.

Widespread use of privateers during the War of the Spanish Succession (1701–1714) led to an increase in piracy following the Peace of Utrecht (1714) as many of the suddenly unemployed privateers turned to piracy. New Providence Island became a hotbed of pirate operations. Among the most notable of these pirates was Captain Edward Teach ("Blackbeard"), Edward England, Charles Vane, Edward Low, John Evans, and Bartholomew Roberts (more generally known for his exploits off the African coast). Of considerable notoriety, too, were the female pirates Anne Bonny and Mary Read, who sailed with "Calico Jack" Rackham until they were captured in Jamaica in 1720. Daniel Defoe, writing under the pseudonym of Charles Johnson, popularized these and other pirates of that era in his *General History of the Robberies and Murders of the Most Notorious Pyrates* (1724).

The Nassau pirates were eventually suppressed after the British crown named Captain Woodes Rogers, himself a privateer of great fame, as its governor at Nassau in 1718. He immediately issued a general pardon to those who would abandon piracy and then while still in office (1718–1720, 1729–1732) proceeded to suppress most of the remainder. The emergence of British naval superiority in the eighteenth century was perhaps the major factor in eradicating piracy in American waters. The replacement of much of Spain's commerce by British shipping, especially after the Peace of Utrecht, granted the British the slave *asiento* for thirty years, gave the British a strong incentive to suppress piracy. Many of the pirates who had thrived earlier in the Caribbean or other Latin American waters now moved their operation to African shores, especially the East African coast, where Madagascar became a fabled pirate's nest.

The Napoleonic wars spawned new fleets of privateers, flying the flags of European nations and of the new Latin American republics, some of which were barely outside the definition of piracy. They played an important role in the Latin American struggles for independence between 1815 and 1821, but some degenerated into Caribbean piracy thereafter. Operating from the numerous inlets in Cuba, Hispaniola, and Puerto Rico, as many as 2,000 pirates preyed upon the growing commerce between the Gulf of Mexico and the Atlantic. The United States responded with warships. In a notable encounter off Cape Antonio, Cuba, in 1821, U.S. naval forces captured the notorious Captain Charles Gibbs. When another U.S. force defeated the audacious Cuban pirate "Diabolito" two years later, acts of piracy in the Caribbean dwindled rapidly. The last major act of piracy occurred in September 1832, when the pirate Pedro Gilbert looted and burned the U.S.-registered *Mexican* en route from Salem to Rio de Janeiro.

Piracy was damaging to the commerce of all nations. But Iberian colonial trade suffered the most depredations, since piracy merely continued the assault on it that Spain's rivals had begun in the sixteenth century. British commercial and naval superiority in the eighteenth century led to its suppression, and in modern times naval technology and firepower have greatly reduced its importance in Latin American waters.

See also **Buccaneers and Freebooters.**

BIBLIOGRAPHY

There is a vast popular literature on piracy, much of it dealing with buccaneers and privateers as well as pirates. There are several modern editions of Daniel Defoe's classic *General History of the . . . Pyrates,* including those edited by William Graves (1972) and by Manuel Schonhorn (1972). Especially useful for reference on individual pirates is Philip Gosse, *The History of Piracy* (1932) and his highly useful biographical dictionary of pirates, buccaneers, and other freebooters, *The Pirates' Who's Who* (1924). Among the general works on piracy see Neville Williams, *Captains Outrageous: Seven Centuries of Piracy* (1961), and Douglas Botting, *The Pirates* (1978). Jenifer Marx, *Pirates and Privateers of the Caribbean* (1992), a useful overview of the whole range of foreign interlopers in the Caribbean, also includes several chapters on piracy. George Woodbury, *The Great Days of Piracy in the West Indies* (1951); Hugh F. Rankin, *The Golden Age of Piracy* (1969); Frank Sherry, *Raiders and Rebels: The Golden Age of Piracy* (1986); Clinton V. Black, *Pirates of the West Indies* (1989) (with biographical sketches of leading buccaneers and pirates from Morgan to Nicholas Brown) all focus on the peak period of piratical activity in the Caribbean. Peter T. Bradley's thoroughly documented *The Lure of Peru: Maritime Intrusion into the South Sea, 1598–1701* (1989) is more concerned with buccaneers than pirates, but is useful for its focus on the viceroyalty of Peru. See also the many books on individual pirates.

Additional Bibliography

Corcuera Ibáñez, Mario. *El coraje y el fuego: De piratas y corsarios desde Polícrates a Bouchard*. Buenos Aires: Librería Histórica, 2004.

Lane, Kris E. *Pillaging the Empire: Piracy in the Americas, 1500-1750*. Armonk: M.E. Sharpe, 1998.

Lucena Salmoral, Manuel. *Piratas, bucaneros, filibusteros y corsarios en América: Perros, mendigos y otros malditos del mar*. Madrid: Editorial MAPFRE, 1992.

RALPH LEE WOODWARD JR.

PISCO. Pisco, a seaport town with a population of 77,200 (1990) located about 125 miles south of Lima on the coast of Peru at the mouth of the Pisco River Valley. Founded on the ruins of a village by Spanish invaders in the middle of the seventeenth century, the town lay somewhat to the south of its present location until 1687, when it was leveled by an earthquake. Pisco is the closest major urban center to the famous sites of ancient Peruvian civilizations on the Paracas Peninsula. It was an important stopping point for José de San Martín on his way north in the independence struggle against Spain in 1821. This port town became the railhead of an early railway-building venture of the nineteenth century, linking the wine and cotton center of Ica to a coastal port. Pisco also was the first major target of the invading Chilean army in early 1880, which captured and held the town with relative ease. The Chilean occupation resulted in only minor interference with the local economy, despite the heavy war taxes levied on plantations. Pisco later became a minor tourist attraction for its beach and for a local variant of spicy seafood stew called *parihuela*. After 1900, the town was a major port of exit for cotton shipped overseas, but as a commercial center it never matched Cañete to the north or Ica to the south. After the cotton export boom settled down, Pisco faded into obscurity as a dusty shipping port for baled raw cotton grown on Pisco Valley cooperatives.

See also **Aguardiente de Pisco; Paracas Peninsular Sites.**

BIBLIOGRAPHY

Eugene A. Hammel, *Power in Ica: The Structural History of a Peruvian Community*. Boston: Little, Brown, 1969.

Nicholas P. Cushner, *Lords of the Land: Sugar, Wine, and Jesuit Estates of Coastal Peru, 1600–1767*. Albany: State University of New York Press, 1980.

Additional Bibliography

Caballero, César Angeles. *Peruanidad del Pisco*. Cuarta edición. Lima: Banco Latino, 1995.

Engel, Frédéric André; Theresa Nicho N.; Edilberto Gutiérrez Ch. *Un desierto en tiempos prehispánicos: Río Pisco, Paracas, Río Ica*. Lima: s.n., 1991.

Macera, Pablo. *La ciudad y el tiempo: Pisco, Porras, y Valdelomar*. Lima: Fondo Editorial del Congreso del Perú, 1999.

Peloso, Vincent C. *Peasants on Plantations: Subaltern Strategies of Labor and Resistance in the Pisco Valley, Peru*. Durham, NC: Duke University Press, 1999.

VINCENT PELOSO

PITA RODRÍGUEZ, FÉLIX (1909– 1988). Félix Pita Rodríguez (*b.* 18 February 1909; *d.* 1988), Cuban poet and short-story writer. Pita Rodríguez was born in Bejucal in the province of La Habana. Somewhat of an adventurer, he traveled through Mexico and Guatemala in 1926 and 1927 as an assistant to a snake-oil salesman. In the 1930s, while traveling through France, Italy, Spain, and Morocco, he wrote poems, which he published in *Revista de Avance*. After returning to Cuba in 1940, he joined the staff of *Noticias de Hoy,* the official publication of the Popular Socialist Party. He also wrote scripts for radio novels and in 1943 was voted best dramatic author of the year by the Radio and Press Association. In 1944 his play *El relevo* opened to much acclaim. He also translated Vietnamese literature from French.

After the Cuban Revolution of 1959, Pita Rodríguez became a full-fledged member of the cultural establishment, serving as a juror for some of its most important literary contests, including those of the Casa de las Américas and the Cuban Union of Artists and Writers (UNEAC). He was also president of UNEAC's literature section.

Among Pita Rodríguez's best-known works are *El relevo* (drama, 1944), *El corcel de fuego* (short stories, 1948), and *Tobías* (short stories, 1955). *Cuentos completos* is a collection of his short stories to 1963.

See also **Literature: Spanish America.**

BIBLIOGRAPHY

Félix Pita Rodríguez: The Author and His Work (1973) is very informative and has a good bibliography. See also Aimée González Bolaños, *La narrativa de Félix Pita Rodríguez* (1985).

Additional Bibliography

Howe, Linda S. *Transgression and Conformity: Cuban Writers and Artists after the Revolution.* Madison: University of Wisconsin Press, 2004.

López Lemus, Virgilio. *Oro, crítica y Ulises, o, Creer en la poesía: Figuras clave de la poesía cubana del siglo XX.* Santiago de Cuba: Editorial Oriente, 2004.

ROBERTO VALERO

PITIANTUTA, BATTLES OF.

An isolated freshwater lake in the north-central area of the Gran Chaco territory, Pitiantuta was site of two important battles during the Chaco War of 1932–1935 between Paraguay and Bolivia.

Located some 100 miles north of the Mennonite colonies at Filadelfia, Pitiantuta was only discovered in the early 1930s, when Indians led White Russian general Juan Belaieff to the lake, which was surrounded by thick vegetation. Belaieff, who was then in the Paraguayan service, immediately grasped the strategic significance of this body of water. For much of the year, the Gran Chaco is bone dry, and in such an arid environment, a military force with access to a permanent source of water would have a distinct advantage over any opponent. Belaieff swiftly set up a tiny military post (*fortín*) at a site on the edge of the lake that he grandiloquently christened Mariscal Carlos Antonio López.

This all occurred during a time of considerable tension with Bolivia. Sovereign control over the vast Chaco territory had never been determined, and during the 1920s and early 1930s the La Paz government had established a series of *fortines* in the western Chaco to match the moves made by the Paraguayans in the east. A few violent incidents had taken place between the two sides before 1932, but the establishment of the Paraguayan camp at Pitiantuta upset the rough balance that had previously developed in the region.

Bolivian major Oscar Moscoso had been almost as active as Belaieff in exploring the Chaco and had caught sight of what was probably Lake Pitiantuta in April 1932. He noticed several mud huts that marked the rudimentary Paraguayan *fortín* and returned west with news of his discovery. The Bolivian high command then determined to evict the Paraguayans, making the assumption that this could be accomplished without too much bother. Because of uncertainties as to the location of the lake amidst the thorn forests, however, it was not until June 15 that the Bolivians launched an attack and cut up the tiny Paraguayan garrison. Only two men escaped to tell the tale.

In La Paz, President Daniel Salamanca tried to play down the incident. He claimed that he had done everything possible to avoid the spilling of blood. In retrospect, however, it seems obvious that his officers had misled him as to the state of affairs at Pitiantuta, where the Bolivian army was then busily engaged in the building of trench works, gun emplacements, and a small airstrip.

The Asunción government decided to act without delay, having concluded that all-out war was no longer avoidable. Thus, on June 29 a unit of fifty infantry and thirty horsemen under Paraguayan lieutenant Ernesto Scarone seized a small Bolivian outpost at the south end of the lake but was driven back by Moscoso, who made ample use of automatic weapons. Fifteen days later the Paraguayan commander, Colonel José Félix Estigarribia, dispatched a much larger force to Pitiantuta that included a full battalion of infantry, a cavalry platoon, and a mortar unit, for a total of 350 men under Captain Abdón Palacios. Joining with the forces of Scarone, the Paraguayans attacked and quickly formed a long semicircle around the Bolivian position. Moscoso had prepared ample fieldworks and was well armed with machine guns, but his 200 defenders were unseasoned recruits from the Altiplano with little sense of why they were in the Chaco in the first place.

At noon on July 15, the Paraguayans seized the uncompleted airstrip west of the lake. The next morning, as they started to close the circle, Palacios's mortar crew began to lay down heavy fire on the enemy *fortín*. The Bolivians responded by abandoning their slit trenches and falling back through the thorn forest. Major Moscoso was the last man to leave, following the stragglers all the way to Fortín Camacho. Unaware that he had gone, the Paraguayans kept firing mortar rounds for another hour before they realized that Pitiantuta had fallen entirely into their hands. They had just won the first battle in what promised to be a very bloody war.

See also **Chaco War; Salamanca, Daniel.**

BIBLIOGRAPHY

Farcau, Bruce. *The Chaco War: Bolivia and Paraguay, 1932–1935.* Westport, CT: Praeger, 1996.

Olmedo, Natalicio. *Acciones de Pitiantuta.* Asunción, Paraguay: Casa Editorial Toledo, 1959.

Zook, David H. *The Conduct of the Chaco War.* New York; New Haven, CT: Bookman Associates, 1960.

THOMAS L. WHIGHAM

PITOL, SERGIO (1933–). Sergio Pitol (*b.* 18 March 1933), Mexican writer. Born in Puebla, Pitol has published short stories and novels, beginning with the volume *Victorio Ferri cuenta un cuento* (Victorio Ferri Tells a Tale, 1958). His later works include a collection of short stories that received the Premio Xavier Villaurrutía in 1981, *Nocturno de Bujara* (Bujara Nocturne, 1981), and a trilogy of novels: *El desfile del amor* (Love's Parade, 1984), *Domar a la divina garza* (To Tame the Heavenly Heron, 1988), and *La vida conyugal* (Married Life, 1991). His narrative work is associated with the cosmopolitan writings of Inés Arredondo, Juan García Ponce, Juan Vicente Melo, and José de la Colina, authors who contributed to the *Revista Mexicana de Literatura* in the late 1950s and early 1960s and revealed the influence of such foreign writers as

Henry James, Thomas Mann, Cesare Pavese, Maurice Blanchot, Georges Bataille, and Pierre Klossowski. Pitol has also held diplomatic positions in Rome, Peking, and, most important, in Warsaw. He has translated into Spanish numerous critical and creative works, especially contemporary Polish literature.

His recent works include *El arte de la fuga* (1996), *Pasión por la trama* (1998), *El viaje* (2000), *Todo está en todas las cosas* (2000). His subsequent work is *El mago de Viena* (2005).

In 1999 he was awarded the Premio Juan Rulfo and in 2005 the Cervantes Prize.

See also **Literature: Spanish America.**

BIBLIOGRAPHY

Texto crítico 7, no. 21 (1981), a special issue in honor of Sergio Pitol.

Russell M. Cluff, *Siete acercamientos al relato mexicano actual* (1987), pp. 99–147.

Additional Bibliography

Aguilera Garramuno, Marco Tulio. *Los escritores y la creación en Hispanoamérica.* Madrid: Editorial Castalia, 2004.

Balza, José. *Sergio Pitol, los territorios del viajero.* México: Ediciones era, 2004.

Castro, Maricruz. *Ficción, narración y polifonía: El universo narrativo de Sergio Pitol.* México: Universidad Autónoma del Estado de México, 2000.

DANNY J. ANDERSON

PIURA. Piura, the name of a city, district, province, and department in northern Peru with a population of 325,000 as of the year 2000. The department, which was created by law 30 March 1861, is bounded by Ecuador on the north, the department of Lambayeque on the south, the department of Cajamarca on the east, and the Pacific Ocean on the west. Its territory includes areas of desert as well as fertile lands on the coast and in the Andes Mountains. Its products are tar, petroleum, and such minerals as gold, silver, and copper. Goats, mules, and beef cattle are raised on its ranches.

Piura, the city, is remembered today as the first Spanish city founded (in 1532) on Peruvian territory. More recently Piura is recalled as the birthplace of Luis M. Sánchez Cerro, a president of Peru in the 1930s, and Juan Velasco Alvarado, an army general with a radical reform agenda who came to power following a coup d'état in 1968. It is also the site of a U.S. airbase that was built at Talara during World War II. In 1964 it was the scene of serious peasant unrest, with ten thousand protestors invading and occupying 30,000 acres of land on the coast. In 1969 Opus Dei founded the Universidad de Piura, which has expanded into ten undergraduate faculties and six graduate faculties organized by disciplines.

See also **Sánchez Cerro, Luis Manuel; Spanish Empire; Velasco Alvarado, Juan.**

BIBLIOGRAPHY

Mariano Felipe Paz Soldán, *Diccionario geográfico estadístico del Perú* (1877).

Ruben Vargas Ugarte, *Historia general del Perú,* 2d ed., 10 vols. (1971), especially vols. 1, 2, 5, and 7.

David P. Werlich, *Peru: A Short History* (1978).

Additional Bibliography

Aldana, Susana. *Empresas coloniales: Las tinas de jabón en Piura.* Piura: Centro de Investigación y Promoción del Campesinado; Lima: Instituto Francés de Estudios Andinos, 1989.

Arce Espinoza, Elmer. *La reforma agraria en Piura, 1967/1977.* Lima: Centro de Estudios para el Desarrollo y la Participación, 1983.

Diez Hurtado, Alejandro. *Comunes y haciendas: Procesos de comunización en la Sierra de Piura (siglos XVIII al XX).* Piura: CIPCA: CBC, 1988

Reyes Flores, Alejandro. *Hacendados y comerciantes: Piura, Chachapoyas, Moyobamba, Lamas, Maynas (1770–1820).* Lima: Juan Brito Editor, 1999.

SUSAN E. RAMÍREZ

PIUS IX, POPE (1792–1878). From a noble family with a strong Marian devotion, Giovanni Maria Mastai-Ferretti, possibly an epileptic, needed papal dispensation for his ordination in 1819. He was appointed auditor to the Church mission sent to several emerging South American republics in 1823. His diary reveals that, though he did not oppose independence, he felt that leaders attacked the church to gain power. The trip likely taught Mastai about the Church's presence and importance outside Europe; traced to it are his emphasis on missions, and provisions

for non-Italians to train in Rome and to attend the First Vatican Council (1869–1870), which he had summoned June 29, 1868. His insistence on clerical loyalty also may have been shaped by debate over whether the patronage was transmitted from Spain and Portugal to the new nations or devolved to Rome.

After serving in several positions in the Italian hierarchy, Mastai ascended to the papacy on June 16, 1846, beginning the longest pontificate in history. After an initial period of reform of the papal state's government resulted in revolution, his administration was conservative, emphasized papal power, and expressed antagonism toward liberalism and nationalism. Pius IX enabled non-Italians to study in Rome by founding regional colleges; among the first was the Latin American College (1858). Numerous Latin American hierarchical leaders of the late nineteenth and early twentieth centuries resided there, and many of them manifested an emphasis on loyalty to Rome, meticulous obedience to church doctrine, and intransigent positions on secularization.

Pius IX defined the modern Church and papacy: stripped of political power, it would be absolute in spiritual and moral power, and would demand doctrinal compliance from clergy and laity, and their support and activism to regain influence. In Latin America, as in Europe, this had mixed results at best: Conservatives cited it to support their opposition to the growth of state power and secularization, but liberals took it as proof of Catholicism's destabilization of the nation and its social fabric.

See also **Catholic Church: The Modern Period.**

BIBLIOGRAPHY

Coppa, Frank J. *Pius IX: Crusader in a Secular Age.* Boston: Twayne, 1979.

Pius IX. "Quanta Cura" [Condemning current errors]. December 8, 1864. Available from *Catholic Culture.* Available from http://www.catholicculture.org/library.

Ramírez, Manuel Ceballos. *El catolicismo social: Un tercero en discordia.* Mexico City: Colegio de México, 1991.

KRISTINA A. BOYLAN

PIXINGUINHA (1889–1973). Pixinguinha (Alfredo da Rocha Viana Filho; *b.* 23 April 1889; *d.* 17 February 1973), Brazilian songwriter. Born in the

Rio de Janeiro suburb of Piedade, Pixinguinha, whose name was a blending of two childhood nicknames, grew up in a musical atmosphere encouraged by his stepfather, a flutist and collector of traditional *chôros*. Pixinguinha made his first flute recordings soon after initiating his study of the instrument in 1911, and in 1914 performed at Carnival with the Grupo de Caxangá, organized by João Pernambuco. In 1926 he conducted the Cine Rialto orchestra, which accompanied the Companhia Negra de Revista.

In 1928, with the guitarist Donga, Pixinguinha organized the Orquestra Típica Pixinguinha-Donga and recorded one of his most famous samba *chôros,* "Carinhoso" (Darling). One of the high points of his career came in 1930, when Pixinguinha recorded the *chôros* "Agüenta, seu Fulgêncio" (Suffer, Mr. Fulgêncio) and "Urubu e o gavião" (Vulture and the Falcon). Together with "Segura êle" (Hold Him) by Lourenço Lamartine, these songs demonstrate his clear execution and extraordinary ability to improvise. The following year Pixinguinha organized the Grupo da Guarda Velha, uniting some of the greatest Brazilian instrumentalists of the era. In 1945, Mayor Negrão de Lima honored him by naming a street in Olaria, Rio de Janeiro, the Rua Pixinguinha. When Pixinguinha died in 1973, his body lay in state at the Museum of Image and Sound and was then buried, accompanied by over two thousand mourners singing "Carinhoso."

See also **Samba.**

BIBLIOGRAPHY

Marcos Antônio Marcondes, ed., *Enciclopédia da música brasileira: Erudita folclórica popular* (1977).

Additional Bibliography

Barboza, Marília T., and Arthur L. de Oliveira Filho. *Picinguinha: Filho de ogum bexiguento.* Rio de Janeiro: Gryphus, 1998.

Cabral, Sérgio. *Pixinguinha: Vida e obra.* Rio de Janeiro: Lumiar Editore, 1997.

LISA MARIĆ

PIZARNIK, ALEJANDRA (1936–1972). Alejandra Pizarnik (Flora Alejandra Pizarnik; *b.* 16 April 1936; *d.* 26 September 1972), Argentine poet. Born in Buenos Aires of Russian Jewish origin,

Pizarnik had an intense and difficult life that ended in suicide at age thirty-six. She grew up in Avellaneda, near Buenos Aires, which she left in 1957 to live in Buenos Aires. She studied literature at the University of Buenos Aires, but did not finish. Instead, she began painting under the mentorship of the Argentine artist Juan Battle Planas. Seeking the artistic unity of poetry and painting, she produced in 1955 her first book of poems, *La tierra más ajena,* under the name Flora Alejandra Pizarnik, later to be shortened to Alejandra Pizarnik. *La última inocencia* (1956) included one of her most important compositions, "árbol de Diana." Her third book was *Las aventuras perdidas* (1958). Various feelings of loss (alterity, nostalgia, exile, silence, and orphanhood) became recurring themes in Pizarnik's poetry.

In 1960 Pizarnik moved to Paris, where she lived until 1964. The Parisian experience was hard, both materially and spiritually. She began to fear becoming insane. She confessed in a letter to a friend that she moved between a troubling feeling of wanting to be dead and of wanting to be alive. In 1962 she wrote several critical essays on Antonin Artaud, H. A. Murena, André Breton, Julio Cortázar, Silvina Ocampo, and others in literary magazines of Latin America and Europe: *La Nouvelle Revue Française, Les Lettres Nouvelles, Tempo Presente, Humboldt, Mito, Sur, Diálogos, Temas, Zona Franca, Mundo Nuevo, Imagen,* and *Papeles de Son Armadans.* She also translated poems by Hölderlin, Artaud, Yves Bonnefoy, Aimé Césaire, Léopold-Sédar Senghor, and others.

In 1962 Pizarnik published *Árbol de Diana,* with an introduction by the Mexican poet Octavio Paz. The brief but intense poems illustrate the maturity of her poetic thought as well as her tendency toward condensation. Silence and the night now became constants in her poems, as can be seen in *Los trabajos y las noches* (1965). This book signaled a new height in Pizarnik's poetic development.

Pizarnik's father died in 1966 and this intensified her fear of insanity. *Extracción de la piedra de la locura* (1968; Extraction of the Stone of Madness) was the outcome of this period, with its title taken from the Hieronymous Bosch masterpiece. In 1969 she published a *plaquette* of poems in prose, *Nombres y figuras,* with illustrations by Catalonian Antonio Beneyto. In 1969 she received a grant from the

Guggenheim Foundation, and in 1972 she was granted a Fulbright scholarship to participate in the International Writers Workshop at the University of Iowa, which she decided not to accept. That same year she published the essay *La condesa sangrienta* (1971; The Bleeding Countess), a re-creation of Erzsébet Báthory's life, followed by *Los pequeños cantos* (1971) and *El infierno musical* (1971).

Pizarnik committed suicide by ingesting an overdose of barbiturates. She is considered one of the main poetic voices of Spanish American literature in the twentieth century. Posthumously published works include *El deseo de la palabra* (1975), edited by the author with Antonio Beneyto and Martha I. Moia, and *Textos de sombra y últimos poemas* (1978), edited by Olga Orozco and Ana Becciú.

See also **Literature: Spanish America; Paz, Octavio.**

BIBLIOGRAPHY

Octavio Rossler, *Cantores y trágicos de Buenos Aires* (1981).

Frank Graziano, ed., *Alejandra Pizarnik: A Profile* (1987).

Bernardo Koremblit, *Todas las que ella era* (1991).

Cristina Piña, *Alejandra Pizarnik* (1991).

Additional Bibliography

Bajarlía, Juan-Jacobo. *Alejandra Pizarnik: Anatomía de un recuerdo.* Buenos Aires: Editorial Almagesto, 1998.

Haydi, Susana H. *Alejandra Pizarnik: Evolución de un lenguaje poético.* Washington, DC: Organization of American States, 1996.

Piña, Cristina. *Alejandra Pizarnik: Una biografía.* Buenos Aires: Corregidor, 2005.

MAGDALENA GARCÍA PINTO

PIZARRO, FRANCISCO (c. 1478–1541).

Francisco Pizarro (*b.* ca. 1478; *d.* 26 June 1541), conqueror of Peru. Pizarro was born in Trujillo, in Estremadura, Spain, the illegitimate son of the young hidalgo Gonzalo Pizarro and a peasant woman, Francisca González. Never recognized by his father, Pizarro seems to have grown up in the household of his mother or her relatives, although he did visit frequently the home of his grandfather, Hernando Alonso Pizarro. He never received a formal education. As a youth he probably traveled to Italy, where he may

have served in the Spanish forces. In 1502 he joined the large fleet of fellow Estremaduran Governor Nicolás de Ovando that set sail for Hispaniola.

Pizarro experienced a long apprenticeship in the Caribbean area, serving with Alonso de Ojeda in the exploration of the Gulf of Urabá (1509–1510). He helped found Nuestra Señora la Antigua del Darién with Martín Fernández de Enciso and was a leader of Vasco Núñez de Balboa's 1513 trek across the Isthmus of Panama in search of the South Sea. He was one of the founders of Panama (1519). He served under Governor Pedro Arias de Ávila in other minor expeditions that set out from the isthmus, receiving an *encomienda* for his services to the crown. He acted as lieutenant governor, chief magistrate, and council member of the city of Panama.

Pizarro, along with Diego de Almagro (1480–1538) and cleric Hernando de Luque (*d.* 1532), began to plan the exploration of lands along the west coast of South America, rumored to be rich. He was by then one of the most experienced explorers in the Caribbean region. Largely in control of the enterprise, with Almagro securing supplies and recruiting men and Luque providing additional financial backing, Pizarro moved south on the first expedition in 1524. The group, facing contrary winds and currents, reached as far as the territory controlled by the Cacique de las Piedras, with little success.

The second expedition, beginning in 1526, ended in near disaster at the Isla del Gallo in 1527. Here, some of Pizarro's men returned to Panama for reinforcements, taking along a secret message calling for the rescue of those remaining. When a ship offering to return the men to Panama appeared, Pizarro, according to some, took out his sword and drew a line on the sand, declaring that all who crossed to the south side of the line and stayed with him would be rewarded with vast riches. The famous "thirteen" of the Isla del Gallo who remained with Pizarro ultimately became the heroes of Peru's conquest. They were transferred to the Isla de la Gorgona, and continued exploration southward. When they reached the city of Tumbes, on the edge of the Inca empire, in 1527, they knew then that their quest would bear fruit. After sailing as far south as the Santa River, they returned to Panama to announce the discovery and exhibited gold objects as proof.

Francisco Pizarro leading his men through the Andes to battle the Incan empire, early 16th century. The Spanish conquistador Pizarro conquered the Inca empire and founded the cities of Lima, Peru and Panama City, Panama. © BETTMAN/CORBIS

Francisco Pizarro returned to Spain to secure backers and soldiers, as well as authority to continue as leader. The Agreement of Toledo (26 July 1529) placed Pizarro in full control of the venture and alienated Almagro, whose resentment ignited a civil war in Peru. Pizarro returned from Spain with a fleet and recruits, including half brothers Hernando, Juan, and Gonzalo, and other soldiers mostly from Estremadura. Near the end of 1530 the group left Panama. Sailing southward, they reached the Bay of San Mateo, where some of the men disembarked and marched overland, facing difficult conditions; others continued by sea. By early 1532, they were in the city of Tumbes. From there they continued southward and founded the first Spanish city in Peru, which they named San Miguel. On 24 September 1532 Pizarro and a large group set out from San Miguel for the highland city of Cajamarca, where it was rumored the Inca ruler was staying. Pizarro met the Inca leader Atahualpa at the central plaza of Cajamarca on 16 November 1532. Friar Vicente de Valverde read the *requerimiento* demanding submission to Spain, and the Inca was handed a religious book, which fell or was thrown to the ground. The Spanish, enraged by the insult, rushed out of hiding and massacred thousands of unarmed retainers, capturing Atahualpa.

The Spanish had in their hands a puppet they could manipulate to control an empire. The tactical maneuver was not unlike the taking of Aztec ruler Motecuhzoma by Hernán Cortés a few years earlier. In this case, Atahualpa offered to fill a room with gold and silver as ransom. Pizarro accepted, and for several months a vast treasure was collected from all parts of the realm and later distributed among the Spaniards present at Cajamarca; the crown also received a large portion. Rather than release their captive after the gold and silver was amassed, the Spanish charged Atahualpa with planning a surprise attack and executed the Inca ruler on 26 July 1533. Pizarro then marched toward the Inca capital of Cuzco, fighting several skirmishes along the way. He had named another captive member of the royal family, Tupac Amaru, as Inca, and hoped to rule through him.

There were a number of reasons why a handful of outsiders were able to establish control over a vast empire of up to 14 million people: the recent devastation caused by smallpox; the subsequent civil war between half brothers Atahualpa and Huascar; the many ethnic entities of the Andes who were ready to assert independence from the Incas; the superior weaponry and astute diplomacy of the Spaniards; and the initial hesitation about what type of creatures the outsiders really were (were they gods, Viracocha?). Francisco Pizarro entered the city of Cuzco, established a Spanish municipal corporation, chose officials, and distributed lots and nearby lands to followers. Pizarro also issued grants of Indians (*encomiendas*) as soon as a region was under Spanish control. Cuzco's location, isolated far from the coast at an elevation of about 11,000 feet, made the small number of Spaniards uneasy. An administrative center nearer the north, and the coast, was needed. After a first attempt at highland Jauja, Pizarro founded Lima (18 January 1535) on the central coast. The Spanish conquerors quickly founded other cities and distributed lands, offices, and Indians. Simultaneously, the first Christian missionaries began their work.

In the meantime, the conflict with Diego de Almagro intensified. Almagro reached Cajamarca too late to share in the ransom of Atahualpa. He had received the governorship of New Toledo to the south of Pizarro's jurisdiction, however. Unfortunately, the exact boundaries dividing the territories were imprecise. Almagro was at Cuzco and in 1535 left in search of rumored treasures to the south, in Chile. While the Almagrists were absent, a massive Indian uprising under Manco Inca broke out; the Inca besieged Cuzco, and even the Spanish in the Lima area suffered major Indian resistance. As the uprising faded away in 1537, Almagro and the survivors of the Chilean fiasco returned and wrenched Cuzco from the Pizarrists. This, however, was only a temporary setback. With cunning diplomacy, military victory at Salinas (6 April 1538), and the execution of Diego de Almagro, Francisco Pizarro secured his position.

During the next three years Pizarro traveled extensively, founding several other Spanish cities. The king even made Pizarro a marquis, but on Sunday, 26 June 1541, a group of malcontents, claiming to act in the name of Diego de Almagro the Younger, broke into the house of Francisco Pizarro in Lima and assassinated him. Several others, including Francisco's half brother, Francisco Martín de Alcántara, was killed in the fray. Francisco Pizarro was survived by four mestizo children: doña Francisca and don Gonzalo by doña Inés Yupanqui Huaylas; and don Francisco and don Juan by doña Angelina Yupanqui.

See also **Almagro, Diego de; Luque, Hernando de.**

BIBLIOGRAPHY

José Antonio Del Busto Duthurburu, *Francisco Pizarro, el marqués gobernador* (1966).

James Lockhart, *The Men of Cajamarca* (1972), pp. 135–157.

Additional Bibliography

Lavallé, Bernard. *Francisco Pizarro: Biografía de una conquista*. Lima: Instituto de Estudios Peruanos, Instituto Frances de Estudios Andinos, 2005.

Lavallé, Bernard. *Francisco Pizarro y la conquista del Imperio Inca*. Madrid: Espasa, 2005.

Olaizola, José Luis. *Francisco Pizarro: Crónica de una locura*. Barcelona: Planeta, 1998.

NOBLE DAVID COOK

PIZARRO, GONZALO (c. 1506–1548).

Gonzalo Pizarro (*b.* ca. 1506; *d.* 10 April 1548), conqueror of Peru and leader of the rebellion of *encomenderos*. Gonzalo, illegitimate son of Captain Gonzalo Pizarro and María de Biedma, was the youngest of the Pizarro brothers. He traveled with the third expedition to the Andes in 1531, was literate, and enjoyed the pastimes associated with the hidalgo: he was a good horseman, an excellent lancer, and a fine marksman. His position was minor during the first years of Peru's conquest, probably because of his youth. He was said to have been with De Soto at the interview with Atahualpa and accompanied Hernando Pizarro to Pachacamac, just south of Lima. He did receive a large share of Atahualpa's ransom as Francisco Pizarro's half brother and was named to a seat on the Cuzco council when that Inca city became a Spanish municipality.

Gonzalo's military abilities were first recognized during the Indian siege of Cuzco (1536–1537). Named captain of horse, he gained a reputation for brashness and impetuosity. When Hernando Pizarro left for Spain, Francisco began to groom Gonzalo for leadership in Peru. Commander of the expedition into Charcas and founder of La Plata, he received major *encomiendas* in the districts of Charcas, Arequipa, and Cuzco. In 1540 Francisco appointed him governor of Quito, where he organized and directed the famous search for the "Land of Cinnamon." His second in command, Francisco de Orellana, was the first European to travel the course of the Amazon River to the Atlantic. Gonzalo marched back to Quito from a base camp on one of the tributaries of the Amazon, suffering great hardship and loss of men, but securing fame as a tenacious leader against tremendous odds.

In Quito, Gonzalo learned of his brother's assassination in Lima and the naming of a new governor, Cristóbal Vaca De Castro. Angry and resentful (Francisco had appointed him governor of Peru in his will), Gonzalo retired under protest, by order of Vaca de Castro, to his estates and mines in Charcas. The arrival in 1544 of Peru's first viceroy, Blasco Núñez Vela, an unbending and arrogant administrator dedicated to the literal enforcement of the New Laws that would have destroyed the power base of the Peruvian *encomenderos*, provided Gonzalo the opportunity he needed. Proclaimed captain-general in city after city, he entered Lima in October 1544. The *audiencia* had already imprisoned the viceroy and sent him back to Spain to face numerous charges. But Blasco Núñez Vela had escaped during the voyage and amassed troops loyal to him and the monarch. After a series of maneuvers, loyalist and rebel forces clashed on 18 January 1546 not far from Quito in the battle of Añaquito (Inaquito), in which the viceroy was killed.

Meanwhile, the crown had sent Pedro de la Gasca with authorization to repeal sections of the New Laws and to reestablish royal authority in the rebellious colony. An adept diplomat, Gasca was able to gradually weaken support for Gonzalo and build an army. He effectively played on the fears and dislikes of Francisco de Carvajal, Pizarro's notorious military commander. After a defeat of the royalists at Huarina (21 October 1547), Gonzalo Pizarro established himself in Cuzco and waited for the forces of Gasca, missing, however, several opportunities to block the southward advance of the royalist army. By the time the two forces met on the plain of Jaquijahuana, not far from Cuzco, Gasca not only had gained a superior force, but, with subtle diplomacy, had suborned Pizarro's men. On 9 April 1548, the greater part of Pizarro's army melted away as he watched. Gonzalo Pizarro surrendered, and the following day he, Carvajal, and forty-eight leaders of the rebellion were executed. His body was interred in the Church of la Merced in Cuzco, while his head was sent to Lima to be nailed to a post and at last put to rest in the Franciscan convent there.

Gonzalo was one of the most attractive of the Pizarro brothers. According to James Lockhart, he "was well proportioned and graceful, with a handsome dark face and a beard that grew black and full as he matured." His death brought to an end the most important of the Peruvian civil wars.

See also **Charcas, Audiencia of; Gasca, Pedro de la.**

BIBLIOGRAPHY

José Antonio Del Busto Duthurburu, *Francisco Pizarro, el marqués gobernador* (1966).

James Lockhart, *The Men of Cajamarca* (1972), pp. 175–189.

Alexandra Parma Cook and Noble David Cook, *Good Faith and Truthful Ignorance: A Case of Transatlantic Bigamy* (1991).

Additional Bibliography

Jaramillo, Mario. *Perfiles de conquista: La aventura de España en América*. Bogotá, DC: Universidad Sergio Arboleda, Fondo de Publicaciones, 2003.

Varón Gabai, Rafael. *Francisco Pizarro and His Brothers: The Illusion of Power in Sixteenth-Century Peru*. Norman: University of Oklahoma Press, 1997.

                                        NOBLE DAVID COOK

PIZARRO, HERNANDO (c. 1503–1578).

Hernando Pizarro (*b.* ca. 1503; *d.* 1578), conqueror of Peru. Born in Trujillo, Estremadura, Spain, he was the only legitimate son of Captain Gonzalo Pizarro; his mother was Isabel de Vargas. He received a competent education and entered military service. As a youth he fought alongside his father in the wars in Navarre and then served in Spanish campaigns in Italy. He returned to Spain in 1528 and helped half brother Francisco Pizarro secure from the crown the famous Agreement of Toledo, which placed Francisco fully in charge of the Peruvian venture. In Trujillo, Hernando helped organize the third expedition, in which all four Pizarro brothers participated.

Hernando's difficulties with Francisco's close associate, Diego de Almagro, first began in Panama and would have grave consequences for both Francisco and Almagro. After helping to found the city of San Miguel, Hernando marched into the highlands of Peru with Francisco Pizarro. Hernando was a member of the first delegation to meet Atahualpa at Cajamarca on 6 November 1532, and, after the Inca's imprisonment, he was the one who led the expedition to the shrine of Pachacamac to collect the gold promised as ransom. This first European reconnaissance (5 January to 14 April 1533) of Peru's heartland and the magnificent pyramid of Pachacamac revealed to the outsiders the extent of Inca wealth. Francisco put Hernando in charge of transporting the royal fifth of the treasure from Atahualpa's ransom to Spain, where the wealth of the Incas stimulated the interest of other Europeans. Hernando became a member of the Order of Santiago, and Francisco gained new honors from the crown.

Hernando returned to Peru in 1535 and assumed charge of Cuzco, just as the Native American uprising led by Manco Inca began. Hernando fought with great valor; as the siege at Cuzco was lifted, Diego de Almagro returned from Chile, claimed the city, and jailed Gonzalo and Hernando Pizarro. Gonzalo fled, while Almagro held Hernando captive and negotiated Peru's future with Francisco Pizarro. To win release, Hernando promised to return to Spain, but instead he led an army that destroyed the Almagrists at the battle of Salinas (6 April 1538). Hernando was largely responsible for Almagro's execution in Cuzco.

In July 1539 Hernando returned to Spain via Mexico. He lived briefly in Madrid, then Valladolid, but Almagrists filed charges against him in the Council of the Indies. Ordered imprisoned in the spring of 1540, he was jailed in 1541 in the castle of La Mota in Medina del Campo. He paid heavy fines and remained in prison until 17 May 1561. Throughout his long imprisonment, with the help of able agents, he conducted business in Spain and the Indies. He also maintained ample staff and was allowed female companions. Isabel de Mercado bore him several children, but ultimately he married (1551) his young niece, Francisca (1534–1598), daughter of his brother Francisco and Inca princess I´nes Yupanqui Huaylas. They had three boys and two girls. Hernando built a great palace on the main plaza of Trujillo. Urban and rural properties and investments made the family one of the wealthiest in Estremadura, and in 1578 an entailed estate was established. Between July and August 1578, ill and bedridden, nearly blind, and too weak even to sign, Hernando Pizarro modified his will for the last time and soon died.

See also **Almagro, Diego de; Pizarro, Francisco.**

BIBLIOGRAPHY

José Antonio Del Busto Duthurburu, *Francisco Pizarro: El marqués gobernador* (1966).

James Lockhart, *The Men of Cajamarca* (1972), pp. 157–168.

Rafael Varón Gabai and Auke Pieter Jacobs, "Peruvian Wealth and Spanish Investments: The Pizarro Family During the Sixteenth Century," in *Hispanic American Historical Review* 67 (1987): 657–695.

Maria Rostworowski De Diez Canseco, *Doña Francisca Pizarro* (1989).

Additional Bibliography

Lavallé, Bernard. *Francisco Pizarro: Biografía de una conquista.* Lima: Instituto de Estudios Peruanos, Instituto Frances de Estudios Andinos, 2005.

Varón Gabai, Rafael. *Francisco Pizarro and His Brothers: The Illusion of Power in Sixteenth-Century Peru.* Norman: University of Oklahoma Press, 1997.

NOBLE DAVID COOK

PIZARRO, JOSÉ ALONSO (?–1755). José Alonso Pizarro (Marqués del Villar; *d.* 1755), viceroy of the New Kingdom of Granada (1749–1753). A respected naval officer, Pizarro received the mantle of viceregal authority from Sebastián de Eslava (1740– 1749) in Cartagena de Indias in November 1749. Shortly thereafter, Pizarro fell ill in Santa Fe de Bogotá. Because of inadequate medical care, his condition did not improve over the next several months. Consequently, the viceroy began in 1751 to request that he be replaced. The crown acceded to his request two years later and named José Solís Folch De Cardona (1753–1761) to succeed him.

As an administrator, Pizarro sought to develop the colony and enhance its viability. His policy initiatives focused on developing commerce and mining, colonizing the Magdalena River valley and Santa Marta province, promoting Jesuit evangelization and education, and pacifying the Chimila and Guajiro Indians. He did not leave a *relación de mando* (an official end-of-tenure report). He returned to Spain shortly after stepping down as viceroy.

See also **New Granada, Viceroyalty of.**

BIBLIOGRAPHY

A fine summary of Pizarro's administration appears in Sergio Elías Ortiz, *Nuevo Reino de Granada: El virreynato, 1719– 1753,* in *Historia extensa de Colombia,* vol. 4, (1970). A valuable, though biased, description of both the potential and the problems facing New Granadan leaders at mid-century by a Jesuit connected with the Pizarro administration is Antonio Julián, *La perla de la América: Provincia de Santa Marta* (1951).

Additional Bibliography

Herrera Angel, Martha. *Poder local, población y ordenamiento territorial en la Nueva Granada, siglo XVIII.* Bogotá, D.C.: Arquivo General de la Nación, 1996.

LANCE R. GRAHN

PIZARRO, PEDRO (1515–1587).

A soldier and a chronicler, Pedro Pizarro had an active role in the Spanish Conquest in Peru. Originally from Toledo, he was the cousin of Francisco Pizarro, to whom he referred as "el Marqués." Upon his arrival in Peru in 1530, Pedro Pizarro was only fifteen years old. He fought against Diego de Almagro and won the victory in the battle against Gonzalo Pizarro, Francisco's half-brother, and also helped to frustrate the rebellion of Manco Inca Yupanqui in 1536. He was committed to his mission as conquistador and was granted the encomiendas of Tacna and Arica. Later in his life Pedro Pizarro settled in Arequipa, where in 1571 he completed the *Relacion del descubrimiento y conquista de los reinos del Peru*, one of the most reliable documents about the conquest.

Pizarro's work is not only a narrative of conflict and warfare; it also contains anthropological material about the everyday lives of the Andean people (including the women) and a detailed description of Atahualpa. Pizarro stresses that he is a direct witness of the events he reports, unlike such chroniclers as Pedro de Cieza de León, who writes on what he hears "en una coronica que ha querido hacer de oidas, y creo yo que muy poco de vista" [in a chronicle that he tried to do through hearsay and, I believe, not much by truly seeing] (p. 176). Pizarro consistently provides references to his sources, thus assuring the reader of the accuracy of his information.

See also **Conquistadores; Pizarro, Francisco; Pizarro, Gonzalo.**

BIBLIOGRAPHY

Primary Work

Pizarro, Pedro. *Relación del descubrimiento y conquista de los reinos del Perú y del gobierno y orden que los naturales tenían, y tesoros que en ella se hallaron, y de las demás cosas que en él han subcedido hasta el día de la fecha.* Buenos Aires: Editorial Futuro, 1944.

Secondary Works

Carrillo, Francisco. "Tesis, historia y fábula en la crónica de Pedro Pizarro." *Revista de Critica Literaria Latinoamericana* 20 (1984): 29–43.

Dowling, Lee H. "The Chronicle of Pedro Pizarro." *La Chispa '87: Selected Proceedings*, edited by Gilbert Paolini, 99–105. New Orleans, LA: Tulane University Press, 1987.

Fossa, Lydia. "Los primeros encuentros entre las huestes de Pizarro y los indígenas: Apuntes para una tipología." *Revista de Crítica Literaria Latinoamericana* 60 (2004): 71–98.

Huber, Elena, and Miguel Alberto Guérin. "La crónica de Pedro Pizarro (Arequipa, 1571): El manuscrito de la Huntington Library y su edición (Lima, 1978)." *Filologia* 21, no. 1 (1986): 77–91.

Moses, Bernard. *Spanish Colonial Literature in South America.* London and New York: The Hispanic Society of America, 1922.

YOLANDA CHAVEZ-CAPPELLINI

PLÁ, JOSEFINA (1909–1999).

Josefina Plá (*b.* 1909, *d.* 1999), Paraguayan artist, dramatist, poet, and historian. Plá is generally considered to be the most influential woman in Paraguayan cultural matters in the twentieth century. Yet she was born not in Paraguay but in Spain's Canary Islands and only came to the inland republic in 1927 after having married the noted sculptor Andrés Campos Cervera (better known as Julián de la Herrería), who died ten years later. She gained fame for her earliest poetry, which was part of the *vanguardista* school and included such pieces as "El precio de los sueños" (1934), "La raíz y la aurora," (1960) and "Invención de la muerte" (1964). Her later poetry includes "La muralla robada" (1989) and "Las artesanias en el Paraguay".

During the 1932–1935 Chaco War with Bolivia, she helped operate a radio theater that presented dramas and comedic pieces to soldiers in the field. As part of this effort, she brought together poets and actors who later came to dominate the Paraguayan literary scene after the conclusion of the war.

As a sculptor and plastic artist, Plá has exhibited works all over South America. Several of her murals and mosaics can be seen on important buildings in today's Asunción. Her historical work includes *El barroco Hispano-guaraní* (1975), *Las artes plásticas en el Paraguay* (1967), and *Los britânicos en el Paraguay* (1984).

Plá contributed weekly columns on cultural issues to several Asunción newspapers up until her death in 1999.

See also **Women in Paraguay.**

BIBLIOGRAPHY

Rafael Eladio Velázquez, *Breve historia de la cultura en el Paraguay,* 7th ed. (1980), pp. 251, 256.

Efraím Cardozo, *Apuntes de historia cultural del Paraguay* (1985), pp. 366–374.

Additional Bibliography

Godoy Ziogas, Marylin. *Josefina Plá.* Asunción, Paraguay: Editorial Don Bosco, 1999.

Vallejos, Roque. *Josefina Plá, crítica y antología.* Asunción, Paraguay: La Rural Ediciones, 1995.

Vilarino, Idea. *Antología poética de mujeres hispanoamericanas: siglo XX.* Montevideo, Uruguay: Ediciones de la Banda Oriental, 2001.

MARTA FERNÁNDEZ WHIGHAM

PLÁCIDO. *See* **Valdés, Gabriel de la Concepción.**

PLAN. *See* **Pronunciamiento.**

PLAN INCA. Plan Inca, a secret blueprint of nationalist reforms and measures supposedly authored by the Peruvian general Juan Velasco Alvarado before the military coup of 1968 that ousted president Fernando Belaúnde Terry from office. The plan was made public and published only in 1974, when the military government decided to nationalize the remaining independent press organizations, allegedly as part of the Plan Inca. The plan consisted of thirty-one sections stating the objectives of a revolution whose goal was a modern and more just society. The measures included a series of nationalizations and reforms such as the agrarian reform that had been initiated before 1974. In 1977, during the so-called second phase of the revolution, the Plan Inca was superseded by the Plan Túpac Amaru.

See also **Belaúnde Terry, Fernando; Túpac Amaru; Velasco Alvarado, Juan.**

BIBLIOGRAPHY

E. V. K. Fitzgerald, *The State and Economic Development: Peru Since 1968* (1976).

David Becker, *The New Bourgeoisie and the Limits of Dependency: Mining, Class, and Power in "Revolutionary" Peru* (1983).

Additional Bibliography

Vargas Gavilano, Amílcar. *La revolución de Velasco en cifras.* Lima: Ediciones INPET, 1989.

Zimmermann Zavala, Augusto. *El plan Inca: Objetivo, revolución peruana.* Lima: Empresa Editoral del Diario Oficial el Peruano, 1970.

ALFONSO W. QUIROZ

PLAN OF AGUA PRIETA. On 23 April 1920, generals from the state of Sonora declared the Plan of Agua Prieta, proclaiming themselves in revolt against President Venustiano Carranza. They resented Carranza's insistence on a civilian successor and were infuriated that their candidate, General Alvaro Obregón, had been passed over in favor of colorless Ignacio Bonillas, Mexican ambassador to Washington. Although General Adolfo De La Huerta was named commander of the movement, Obregón soon took control. Within a week the rebellion had won the support of most of the generals throughout the country; President Carranza fled Mexico City on 14 May and was assassinated 21 May. Following his election, Obregón became president on 1 December 1920. Mexico would not have a civilian president until the election of Miguel Alemán in 1946.

See also **Carranza, Venustiano; de la Huerta, Adolfo; Obregón Salido, Álvaro.**

BIBLIOGRAPHY

Edwin Lieuwen, *Mexican Militarism: The Political Rise and Fall of the Revolutionary Army, 1910–1940* (1968).

Linda B. Hall, *Alvaro Obregón: Power and Revolution in Mexico, 1911–1920* (1981).

Additional Bibliography

Bantjes, Adrian A. *As if Jesus Walked on Earth: Cardenismo, Sonora, and the Mexican Revolution*. Lanham, MD: Rowman & Littlefield, 2007.

Gonzalez, Michael J. *The Mexican Revolution, 1910–1940*. Albuquerque: University of New Mexico Press, 2004.

Moguel, Josefina. *Venustiano Carranza*. México: Planeta, 2004.

BARBARA A. TENENBAUM

PLAN OF AYALA.

Plan of Ayala, a declaration written in the fall of 1911 by Emiliano Zapata and a schoolteacher named Otilio Montaño. It was the fundamental text of the Zapatista movement that was centered in the state of Morelos. The plan gave *zapatismo* a national orientation by rejecting the Mexican Revolution's first caudillo, Francisco Madero, as a traitor. It also provided the revolution with a clear and relatively straightforward expression of the popular demand for land reform. For this reason it was one of the key documents of the period, playing an important, if somewhat indirect, role in bringing about the land reform of the 1920s and 1930s.

See also **Madero, Francisco Indalecio; Zapata, Emiliano.**

BIBLIOGRAPHY

John Womack, *Zapata and the Mexican Revolution* (1968), esp. pp. 393–404.

Robert P. Millon, *Zapata: The Ideology of a Peasant Revolutionary* (1969).

Samuel Brunk, *Revolution and Betrayal in Mexico: A Life of Emiliano Zapata* (1995).

Additional Bibliography

López González, Valentín. *El Plan de Ayala, 1911*. Cuernavaca, Mexico: Instituto Estatal de Documentación de Morelos, 2001.

López González, Valentín. *Reforma y ratificación del Plan de Ayala, 1913*. Cuernavaca, Mexico: Instituto Estatal de Documentación de Morelos, 2000.

Tutino, John. *From Insurrection to Revolution in Mexico: The Social Bases of Agrarian Violence, 1750–1940*. Princeton, NJ: Princeton University Press, 1987.

SAMUEL BRUNK

PLAN OF AYUTLA.

Plan of Ayutla, proclaimed at Ayutla de los Libros on 1 March 1854, initiated the Mexican reform. There was little, however, to distinguish this revolutionary plan from its many less significant predecessors. Diverse groups rebelling against president/dictator Antonio López de Santa Anna ultimately followed the leadership of liberal Juan Álvarez. The Plan of Ayutla indicted Santa Anna for selling the Mesilla Valley to the United States in the 1853 Gadsden Purchase, oppressing the people, and eliminating representative government. Its prominent adherents included liberals like Ignacio Comonfort, Melchor Ocampo, and Benito Juárez, who came to dominate the new provisional government following Santa Anna's overthrow in August 1855.

See also **Álvarez, Juan; Comonfort, Ignacio; Gadsden Purchase; Santa Anna, Antonio López de.**

BIBLIOGRAPHY

Richard A. Johnson, *The Mexican Revolution of Ayutla, 1854– 1855* (1939).

Additional Bibliography

Carbajal, Juan Alberto. *La consolidación de México como nación: Benito Juárez, la constitución de 1857, y las leyes de reforma*. México: Editorial Porrua, 2006.

García Ramírez, Sergio. *Plan de Ayutla: Lo de Marzo de 1854*. México: Procuraduría General del República, 1987.

Monsiváis, Carlos. *Las herencias ocultas de la reforma liberal del siglo XIX*. México, DF: Debate, 2006.

ROBERT J. KNOWLTON

PLAN OF CASA MATA.

Plan of Casa Mata, a political proposal leading to the establishment of a federal republic in Mexico. After independence, conflict ensued between the executive and legislative branches of the new government. Emperor Agustín de Iturbide jailed dissenting legislators and ultimately dissolved Congress on 31 October 1822. The generals sent to crush the opposition instead "pronounced" against the emperor, issuing the Plan of Casa Mata on 1 February 1823. The plan, which insisted on the election of a new constituent congress, did not contemplate fundamental change. Indeed, it did not even seek the emperor's removal. But the plan proved revolutionary because it included a provision granting authority to the Provincial Deputation of Veracruz. That offered the provinces an opportunity for home rule, something they pursued immediately. When Iturbide abdicated on 19 March 1823 rather than provoke a civil war, the provinces insisted upon the election of a new congress and ultimately established a federal republic in 1824.

See also **Iturbide, Agustín de; Mexico, Wars and Revolutions: War of Independence.**

BIBLIOGRAPHY

Nettie Lee Benson, "The Plan of Casa Mata," in *Hispanic American Historical Review* 25 (February 1945): 45–56.

William Spence Robertson, *Iturbide of Mexico* (1952), esp. pp. 221–260.

Timothy E. Anna, *The Mexican Empire of Iturbide* (1990), esp. pp. 189–216.

Jaime E. Rodríguez O., "The Struggle for the Nation: The First Centralist-Federalist Conflict in Mexico," in *The Americas* 49 (July 1992): 1–22.

Additional Bibliography

Arenal Fenochio, Jaime del. *Agustín de Iturbide*. México: Editorial Planeta Mexicana, 2004.

Vaile, Rafael Heliodoro. *Iturbide, varón de Dios*. Tegucigalpa, Guatemala: Universidad Pedagógica Nacional Francisco Morazán, 2005.

Vázquez, Josefina Zoriada. *El establecimiento del federalismo en México, 1821–1827*. México, DF: Colegio de México, 2003.

JAIME E. RODRÍGUEZ O.

PLAN OF GUADALUPE. Plan of Guadalupe, a political manifesto dated 26 March 1913, issued by Venustiano Carranza and his followers at the Hacienda de Guadalupe, Coahuila, in northeastern Mexico. The plan was a response to the coup d'état of February 1913 that overthrew the liberal government of Francisco Madero and, following Madero's murder, installed a conservative and increasingly militarist regime under General Victoriano Huerta. Carranza, governor of Coahuila, briefly negotiated with Huerta, then, fearing for his own survival, rose in revolt. At Carranza's instigation (and against the objections of some younger, more radical, rebels) the Plan confined itself to narrowly political goals: the ouster of Huerta and the restoration of constitutional government. Thus, Carranza established himself as "First Chief of the Constitutionalist Army," with a claim to supremacy over all anti-Huerta movements that most northern rebels came to accept.

See also **Carranza, Venustiano; Madero, Francisco Indalecio.**

BIBLIOGRAPHY

Charles C. Cumberland, *The Mexican Revolution: The Constitutionalist Years* (1972), pp. 70–71.

Douglas W. Richmond, *Venustiano Carranza's Nationalist Struggle, 1893–1920* (1983), p. 45.

Enrique Krauze, *Puente entre siglos: Venustiano Carranza* (1987), pp. 35–37.

Additional Bibliography

Dawson, Alexander S. *Indian and Nation in Revolutionary Mexico*. Tucson: University of Arizona Press, 2004.

Moguel, Josefina. *Venustiano Carranza*. México, DF: Editorial Planeta, 2004.

Urquizo, Francisco L. *Carranza: El hombre, el político, el caudillo, el patriota*. Saltillo, Mexico: Gobierno del Estado de Coahuila, 2006.

ALAN KNIGHT

PLAN OF IGUALA. Plan of Iguala, Augustín de Iturbide's pacification program for the reunification of Mexico. By 1820, a decade of revolutionary war against Spain left Mexico divided and exhausted. Royalist forces maintained military strength in the cities and some regions while much of the countryside was occupied by insurgent bands engaged in guerrilla warfare. In late 1820, Viceroy Juan Ruíz de Apodaca appointed Colonel Agustín de Iturbide to take command of the rugged region to the west and south of the capital where entrenched rebel forces opposed the royalists. A most controversial figure and already a focus for creole disaffection, Iturbide clearly accepted the commission with full intentions of terminating the war by overthrowing the existing regime and declaring the autonomy or independence of Mexico.

After meeting with Vicente Guerrero and other insurgent leaders and drawing considerable support from royalist army commanders, on 24 February 1821, at the small town of Iguala, Iturbide issued his Plan of Iguala. Consisting of twenty-three articles, the plan sought to reunify the warring factions and to restore peace to a war-torn nation. The three major initiatives in the program, called the "three guarantees," were Religion, Independence, and Union. Although these three guarantees appear very general in meaning, they possessed deep significance to Mexicans at the time. The Catholic Church was to maintain its dominance, the Mexican nation was to become a constitutional monarchy headed by a Spanish Bourbon, and divisions between different segments of the Mexican population, particularly those between the creole and the European Spaniards, were to be resolved. With a slogan of only three words, Iturbide appeared to solve the deep divisions that prolonged the war. Forming the Army of the Three Guarantees, Iturbide conducted a triumphal march from region to region, as many royalist commanders and their troops embraced the Plan of Iguala. Aided by the irresistible desire for peace throughout the country, Iturbide swept the colonial regime aside and entered Mexico City on 27 September 1821.

See also **Córdoba, Treaty of (1821); Iturbide, Agustín de.**

BIBLIOGRAPHY

William Spence Robertson, *Iturbide of Mexico* (1968).

Jaime E. Rodríguez O., ed., *The Independence of Mexico and the Creation of the New Nation* (1989).

Timothy E. Anna, *The Mexican Empire of Iturbide* (1990).

Additional Bibliography

Benítez González, Florencio. *El plan de Iguala: En la historiografía de su época*. México: Comuna Municipal, 2001.

Caudet Yarza, Francisco. *Agustín de Iturbide*. Madrid, Spain: Dastin, 2003.

Chinchilla, Perla. *Del plan de Iguala a los Tratados de Córdoba*. México DF: Comisión Nacional para las Celebraciones del 175 Aniversario de la Independencia Nacional y 75 Aniversario de la Revolución Mexicana, 1985.

CHRISTON I. ARCHER

PLAN OF LA NORIA. Plan of La Noria, Mexican revolutionary movement of 8 November 1871. The plan's principal goal was to prevent the reelection of Benito Juárez to a fourth term as president. It was aimed at promoting the political fortunes of Porfirio Díaz, Liberal general and defeated presidential candidate in the 1871 elections. Although the plan attracted support from a number of military chieftains, it was unsuccessful due to a lack of leadership and the death of its target, Juárez, in 1872. Juárez's successor—Sebastián Lerdo De Tejada—pardoned the rebels and brought the insurrection to an end. The lessons learned from this unsuccessful plan were used by Díaz to launch his successful Plan of Tuxtepec in January 1876.

See also **Díaz, Porfirio; Juárez, Benito.**

BIBLIOGRAPHY

Daniel Cosío Villegas, *Porfirio Díaz en la revuelta de La Noria* (1953).

Laurens Ballard Perry, *Juárez and Díaz: Machine Politics in Mexico* (1978), esp. chap. 6.

Additional Bibliography

Galeana de Valadés, Patricia. *Juárez en la historia de México*. México: Cámara de Diputados, LIX Legislatura: M. A. Porrúa, 2006.

McNamara, Patrick J. *Sons of the Sierra: Juárez, Díaz, and the People of Ixtlán, Oaxaca, 1855–1920*. Chapel Hill: University of North Carolina Press, 2007.

Villalpando César, José Manuel. *Benito Juárez: Una visión crítica en el bicentario de su nacimiento*. México: Planeta, 2006.

DON M. COERVER

PLAN OF SAN LUIS POTOSÍ. Plan of San Luis Potosí, manifesto by Francisco Madero (6 October 1910) which launched the Mexican Revolution of 1910. Having escaped from prison in the city of San Luis Potosí in early October, Madero wrote and sent out the manifesto from the United States in the days following. It marked the end of Madero's three-year anti-reelectionist movement either to replace the dictatorial regime of Porfirio Díaz through elections or to force concessions. His call to arms nullified the 1910 federal elections, confirmed him as provisional president, reinstituted no reelection, and promised the return of lands illegally taken by the government and courts under Díaz.

See also **Madero, Francisco Indalecio; Mexico, Wars and Revolutions: Mexican Revolution.**

BIBLIOGRAPHY

English translation in U.S. Senate, *Investigation of Mexican Affairs: Report of a Hearing Before a Subcommittee on Foreign Relations,* 66th Cong., 2d Sess., Senate Document 285, vol. 2 (1920), p. 2,631; Stanley Ross, *Francisco I. Madero: Apostle of Mexican Democracy* (1955); Alan Knight, *The Mexican Revolution,* vol. 1 (1986).

Additional Bibliography

González y González, Luís. *La ronda de las generaciones.* México: Clío, 1997.

Katz, Freidrich. *De Díaz a Madero.* México, DF: Ediciones Era, 2004.

Pérez López-Portillo, Raúl, and Juan Gallardo Muñoz. *Madero.* Madrid, Spain: Dastin, 2003.

STUART F. VOSS

PLAN OF TACUBAYA. Proclaimed on December 17, 1857, the Plan of Tacubaya was the political project supporting the military coup of General Félix Zuloaga, commander of Mexico City's garrison. It disowned the recently promulgated Mexican constitution and asked for the convocation of another Congress that would make a new constitution "more in harmony with the will of the Nation." Paradoxically, President Ignacio Comonfort, who had just been sworn in under allegiance to the constitution, backed the Plan. Comonfort, a moderate liberal, had been the provisional president since December 1855. Throughout the time the Congreso Constituyente (1856–1857) had been elaborating the constitution, Comonfort had been faced with the necessity of putting down military insurrections of the Right and of withstanding political pressure of the radical Left, which accused him of being too accommodating. When the constitution finally was proclaimed in February 1857, it was considered far too liberal by the Right

(the Church declared it would excommunicate everyone who swore allegiance to the constitution). For his part, Comonfort, who was very religious, also believed that it did not give sufficient powers to the president to cope with the difficult situation. He therefore decided to back Zuloaga's Plan. Even though Comonfort retracted his support a few days later, he was disowned by both parties and had to go into exile. At this point the Guerra de Reforma (1858–1860) had already started. The Conservative government stayed in Mexico City whereas the liberals established themselves in Veracruz, headed by Benito Juárez who, as president of the Supreme Court of Justice, was the legal successor of the president of the Republic.

See also **Mexico, Constitutions: Constitutions Prior to 1917; Zuloaga, Félix María.**

BIBLIOGRAPHY

Matute, Alvaro. *México en el siglo XIX.* Mexico: Universidad Nacional Autónoma México, 1981. See pp. 296–297.

Nueva historia mínima de México. Mexico: El Colegio de México, 2006. See pp. 172–173.

Pi-Suñer Llorens, Antonia. "Ignacio Comonfort: El hombre de la situación?" In *Gobernantes mexicanos, 1821–2006.* Mexico: Fondo de Cultura Económica, 2007.

ANTONIA PI-SUÑER LLORENS

PLAN OF TUXTEPEC. Plan of Tuxtepec, Mexican revolutionary pronouncement of 1 January 1876. The followers of General Porfirio Díaz protested the effort by incumbent president Sebastián Lerdo De Tejada to seek reelection. Díaz had earlier revolted against the practice of reelection in the unsuccessful Plan of La Noria (8 November 1871). The key provisions of the Plan of Tuxtepec were the prohibition of reelection of the president and state governors and the appointment of Díaz as commander of revolutionary forces. Later reformed by the Plan of Palo Blanco (21 March 1876), the revolutionary movement triumphed at the battle of Tecoac (16 November 1876), ultimately winning Díaz the presidency (1876–1880, 1884–1911).

See also **Díaz, Porfirio.**

BIBLIOGRAPHY

Frank A. Knapp, Jr., *The Life of Sebastián Lerdo de Tejada, 1823–1889* (1951).

Daniel Cosío Villegas, *Historia moderna de México,* vol. 1 (1955), pp. 767–925.

Additional Bibliography

Garner, Paul H. *Porfirio Díaz: Del héroe al dictador, una biografía política.* México: Planeta, 2003.

Katz, Freidrich. *De Díaz a Madero.* México DF: Ediciones Era, 2004.

DON M. COERVER

PLANTATIONS. Plantations, estates established for large-scale agricultural production. The plantation developed in the Americas as part of the region's incorporation into the European world economy beginning in the sixteenth century. A distinctive form of agricultural enterprise, it combined specialized production of tropical and subtropical crops intended for large-scale external markets with the use of various forms of dependent or coerced labor. Over the course of its historical evolution, plantation production transformed tobacco, coffee, bananas, cacao, indigo, cotton, and above all, sugarcane from luxury items into articles of mass consumption. While the development of plantation agriculture was linked to the emergence of world markets for tropical staples, its viability derived from an abundant, cheap, and disciplined labor force secured by direct or indirect compulsion. Slavery, indentured servitude, contract labor, sharecropping, and tenancy concentrated laborers for commercial crop production, reduced their bargaining power, subjected them to lowered standards of living, and imposed upon them a strict labor discipline enforced by a hierarchical staff of supervisors and overseers. A clear distinction obtained between powerful owners, who generally claimed European descent, and a subordinate, and racially and culturally distinct, labor force. The planters' coercive control over the recruitment, allocation, and conditions of labor, guaranteed by the colonial state, established the conditions for profitable, large-scale commodity production in the American plantation zone.

Wherever it took hold, the plantation system disrupted or destroyed preexisting cultural norms and eliminated competing forms of economic and social organization. What anthropologist Charles Wagley termed "plantation America" formed in an area extending from the coastal lowlands of Brazil, through the Guyanas and the coast and islands of the Caribbean, to Chesapeake Bay in the United States, where soil, climate, and ease of transport facilitated the large-scale production of tropical and semitropical crops. The sparse indigenous populations in this region, unaccustomed to settled agriculture and European diseases, provided insufficient labor and were eventually replaced by imported workers. Later, with changes in transportation, in production technologies, and in market patterns, plantation production spread along the coastal lowlands of Peru, Ecuador, and Central America and to inland regions of Mexico, Colombia, and Argentina.

The plantation in the Americas formed as part of a broader political and economic complex within the European world economy. Specialized production of plantation staples depended upon overseas markets for the sale of the crop, while capital, technology, consumer goods, and even labor were imported from abroad. The evolution of the plantation in the Americas was shaped by colonial rivalries between European powers, the expansion and diversification of markets, growing productive capacities, changing sources of labor supply, and shifts in forms of labor organization throughout this international complex and their political and economic consolidation into a world division of labor.

Historically, sugar was the most important plantation crop and the one that developed this productive form to the fullest. Beginning in the eleventh century, growing European demand stimulated the spread of sugar production westward across the Mediterranean to the European Atlantic coast. By 1470 refineries in Venice, Bologna, and Antwerp had established a colonial relationship between producing regions and dominant importers. The adoption of Arab production techniques, especially irrigation, transformed cultivation and enabled intensification of land use. Nonetheless, the sugar industry in the European Mediterranean was characterized by small-scale production and diverse ways of organizing land and labor. This pattern of sugar cultivation was extended to Madeira and the Canary Islands in the

Atlantic. Thus sugar remained a costly luxury product until well into the age of colonization.

During the sixteenth century the emergence in Spanish Hispaniola and, above all, in the Portuguese colony of São Tomé, of large plantations using African slaves to produce cheap, low-quality sugar for metropolitan refiners signaled the transition from Mediterranean polyculture to American sugar monoculture. However, the decisive break with the Mediterranean pattern came in Brazil. There, ideal climate combined with unlimited supplies of fuel, land, and the use at first of indigenous and then of imported African servile labor to create larger-scale operations that established the characteristic pattern of American plantation agriculture. In Pernambuco and the Bahian Recôncavo powerful *senhores de engenho* (mill masters) monopolized access to river courses in order to grind their own cane and that of dependent *lavradores de cana* (cane farmers), who themselves often employed large numbers of slaves. African slavery, the fertile *massapé* soil (a heavy clay soil preferred for sugarcane), and technical innovations in milling and boiling promoted large-scale production. The plantation linked Europe, Africa, and the Americas to form an Atlantic economy. Brazil dominated world production as sugar reached growing numbers of European consumers and became a significant source of wealth in the colonies.

The development of the plantation system in the Americas was tied to intercolonial rivalries between European powers. With the expulsion of the Dutch from Brazil in 1654, the center of the plantation economy shifted to the Caribbean. Rather than directly organizing production, the Dutch now offered slaves, technology, credit, and access to Dutch markets to planters in the British and French Caribbean. Between the mid-seventeenth century and the 1720s, the consolidation of large estates and massive importation of slaves to grow sugar eliminated the preexisting European yeomanry and indentured servants as sources of labor. The West Indies were transformed into "sugar islands," with majority populations of slave workers of African descent.

The eighteenth century was the classic period of sugar and slavery in the Caribbean. The West Indian colonies were the cornerstone of imperial politics and the development of an Atlantic economy. The mercantile policies of France and Britain finally eliminated the Dutch influence and enabled

them to assert control over their respective colonies. Rising demand stimulated by falling prices created a profitable but highly competitive sugar market. In the Caribbean, these conditions resulted in concentrated landownership, intensive cultivation, heavy dependence upon slave labor, and the introduction of various innovations designed to reduce labor costs, improve yields, ameliorate manufacture, and mitigate the effects of deforestation and soil exhaustion. The West Indian sugar plantation was at the heart of the transatlantic commercial complex linking the African slave trade, European manufactures, and North American exports of livestock, lumber, fish, and grain. Perhaps 29 percent of the slaves transported during the course of the entire African slave trade were imported to the British and French Caribbean between 1701 and 1810. In Saint Domingue, the richest colony in the world, nearly half a million slaves produced more wealth than all the British West Indies and enabled France to compete with Britain in international politics and trade.

Between 1790 and 1914 industrialization and urbanization in Europe and North America, slave emancipation, and the end of formal colonialism throughout the hemisphere, together with the expansion and reintegration of markets, led to the decline of the old sugar colonies and the emergence of modern plantation agriculture. Increasing world consumer and industrial demand for sugar, coffee, cotton, cacao, and bananas resulted in the extension and diversification of plantation production. Railroads and steamships opened new areas to cultivation and linked them more firmly to international trade.

By the mid-nineteenth century Cuba was the world's largest sugar producer. Its sugar industry, along with those of Puerto Rico and the Dominican Republic, was totally transformed by massive United States investment during the twentieth century. Peru too emerged as a significant sugar producer, and production for local markets developed in Morelos, Mexico, and Tucumán, Argentina. In new sugar zones, the *usina central* (central refinery), incorporating modern milling and refining technologies, increased the scale of production and transformed the relation between land, labor, and capital in diverse ways. Plantations in the states of Rio de Janeiro, Minas Gerais, and São Paulo made Brazil the world's foremost coffee producer. Coffee was also cultivated as a plantation crop in Colombia, Puerto Rico, Cuba, Guatemala, and El Salvador. Later, after the introduction of the refrigerator ship, bananas became an important plantation crop in Central America, Colombia, and Ecuador.

The abolition of slavery throughout the hemisphere during the nineteenth century, combined with growing demand for plantation products, initiated a search for new sources of labor and new forms of labor control. In the old slave zones, planters and the colonial state struggled, sometimes successfully, sometimes not, to reimpose estate labor on freed populations. In many places state-sponsored immigration, particularly from Asia, provided an alternative source of labor. Contract laborers from India, China, Indochina, Japan, Africa, Madeira, and the Canary Islands were variously distributed to British Guiana, Trinidad, Jamaica, Cuba, Peru, and Brazil. In the Brazilian coffee zone Italian Colonos replaced African slaves. In the tropical lowlands and piedmont areas of the Andes and Central America, labor was recruited from highland peasant communities. The demand for labor sharpened conflicts between plantation owners and smallholders and shaped racial, ethnic, and cultural diversity throughout the American plantation zones.

By the 1920s large-scale international migration had come to an end. A variety of forms of sharecropping, tenancy, contract labor, and wage labor prevailed. Even where workers were juridically free, however, the plantation owners controlled labor by monopolizing resources and eliminating alternative economic activities. Workers were exposed to seasonal employment, and, where local labor was insufficient, especially during planting and harvest times, regional inequalities provided sources of migrant labor. Conversely, by the twentieth century, technical innovation, the growing scale of production and capital investment, and the expansion and integration of markets resulted in a shift to corporate ownership and financing of plantations. Local planter classes were increasingly subordinated to or eliminated by corporate capital as plantation economies were integrated into production, marketing, and financial networks dominated by transnational corporations, particularly

those from the United States. Thus the plantation began to lose its distinctive identity and came to resemble other forms of large-scale capitalist agriculture. Yet pockets of debt peonage still remain in the twenty-first century. In 2007, the Brazilian government freed 1,108 forced workers trapped on a sugar plantation in the state of Para.

See also **Estancia; Hacienda; Slavery: Spanish America; Sugar Industry.**

BIBLIOGRAPHY

Richard B. Sheridan, *Sugar and Slavery: An Economic History of the British West Indies, 1623–1775* (1974).

Manuel Moreno Fragináls, *El ingenio: Complejo económico social cubano del azúcar* (1978).

Francisco A. Scarano, *Sugar and Slavery in Puerto Rico: The Plantation Economy of Ponce, 1800–1850* (1984).

Manuel Moreno Fragináls, Frank Moya Pons, and Stanley L. Engerman, eds., *Between Slavery and Free Labor: The Spanish Speaking Caribbean in the Nineteenth Century* (1985).

Michael J. Gonzales, *Plantation Agriculture and Social Control in Northern Peru, 1875–1933* (1985).

Sidney W. Mintz, *Sweetness and Power: The Place of Sugar in Modern History* (1985).

Stuart B. Schwartz, *Sugar Plantations in the Formation of Brazilian Society: Bahia, 1550–1835* (1985).

Rebecca J. Scott, *Slave Emancipation in Cuba* (1985).

Verena Stolcke, *Coffee Planters, Workers, and Wives: Class Conflict and Gender Relations on São Paulo Plantations, 1850–1980* (1988).

J. H. Galloway, *The Sugar Cane Industry: An Historical Geography from Its Origins to 1914* (1989).

Laird W. Bergad, *Cuban Rural Society in the Nineteenth Century: The Social and Economic History of Monoculture in Matanzas* (1990).

Philip D. Curtin, *The Rise and Fall of the Plantation Complex* (1990).

Additional Bibliography

Barickman, B. J. *A Bahian Counterpoint: Sugar, Tobacco, Cassava, and Slavery in the Recôncavo, 1780–1860.* Stanford, CA: Stanford University Press, 1998.

Wolford, Wendy. "Of Land and Labor: Agrarian Reform on the Sugarcane Plantations of Northeast Brazil." *Latin American Perspectives* 31:2 (March 2004), 147–170.

DALE W. TOMICH

PLATAS ALVAREZ, FERNANDO FAB-RICIO (1973–).

The Mexican diver Fernando Platas does not rank among the world's best in his sport, but his achievements have earned him national acclaim and international respect. Born in Mexico City on March 16, 1973, he has participated in the summer Olympic Games since 1992. In the three-meter springboard event he won a silver medal in 2000 and finished fifth in 2004; he was the standard bearer of the Mexican delegation in both of those years. He has won medals at the Central American and Caribbean Games and the world championships of the International Swimming Federation (FINA). Along with his younger teammate Rommel Pacheco, the charismatic Platas has shown that Mexicans can be competitive in sports not normally considered Mexican strengths.

See also **Sports.**

BIBLIOGRAPHY

"Fernando Platas, Derportista Mexicano." Available from http://www.biosstars-mx.com/f/fernando_platas.htm.

JOSEPH L. ARBENA

PLATT AMENDMENT.

Platt Amendment, an appendix to the Cuban constitution that granted the United States extensive influence in the country, essentially establishing it as a U.S. protectorate. At the conclusion of the Spanish-American War in 1898, the U.S. Army administered Cuba until its adoption of a self-governing constitution. Within the policy parameters that dated to the Monroe Doctrine in 1823, the United States desired to keep its influence on the island and secure it from future European advances. Toward that end, Secretary of War Elihu Root persuaded the U.S. Congress to approve a rider, named after the chairman of the Committee on Relations with Cuba, Senator Orville H. Platt, to the army appropriations bill of 1901. Subsequently, the Cubans reluctantly added the Platt Amendment to their constitution formed in that year and incorporated it in the 1903 treaty with the United States. The Platt Amendment secured U.S. interests but limited Cuba's independence. It restricted Cuba's foreign debt to levels acceptable to the United States and limited its ability to make treaties with foreign nations. It permitted the United States to intervene in order to maintain public order and gave that nation rights to naval stations eventually located at Guantánamo Bay. The United States intervened on several occasions after 1903 to supervise elections and provide for peaceful transfer of presidential administrations. The amendment was abrogated by treaty in 1934.

See also **Cuba, Constitutions; Monroe Doctrine.**

BIBLIOGRAPHY

Manual Márquez Sterling, *Proceso histórico de la Enmienda Platt, 1897–1934* (1941).

Louis A. Pérez, *Cuba Under the Platt Amendment, 1902–1934* (1986), and *The United States and Cuba: Ties of Singular Intimacy* (1990).

Additional Bibliography

Ibarra, Jorge. *Cuba, 1898–1921: Partidos políticos y clases sociales.* La Habana: Editorial de Ciencias Sociales, 1992.

Whitney, Robert. *State and Revolution in Cuba: Mass Mobilization and Political Change, 1920–1940.* Chapel Hill: University of North Carolina Press, 2001.

THOMAS M. LEONARD

PLAZA, VICTORINO DE LA (1840–1919).

Victorino de la Plaza (*b.* 2 November 1840; *d.* 2 October 1919), president of Argentina (1914–1916). De la Plaza, a native of Cachi, Salta, was a University of Buenos Aires–trained lawyer and a financier. He became president upon the death of Roque Sáenz Peña on 9 August 1914. He had been interim president since September 1913 and had also served for several shorter periods because of the president's ill health. He had been chosen for the vice presidency because of his support for the establishment of fair voting procedures, his ties to the political establishment, and his lack of clear identification with political factions. He had been active in government service, serving three presidents as a cabinet minister.

As president, de la Plaza faced two challenges: World War I and the voting reforms of Sáenz Peña. He maintained Argentine neutrality and attempted to meet a growing economic crisis by taking Argentina off the gold standard. Although not enthusiastic about the reformed electoral code or the Radical

Party, he oversaw fair elections that resulted in a Radical victory. De la Plaza died in Buenos Aires.

See also **Argentina: The Twentieth Century.**

BIBLIOGRAPHY

Jorge A. Mitre, "Presidencia de Victorino de la Plaza (su gestión presidencial)," in Academia Nacional De La Historia, *Historia argentina contemporánea,* vol. 1, sec. 2 (1956).

Jimena Sáenz, *Entre dos centenarios, 1910–1916* (1976).

Additional Bibliography

Mayer, Jorge M. *Victorino de la Plaza, 1840–1919: Un eje institucional.* Buenos Aires: Academia Nacional de Derecho y Ciencias Sociales de Buenos Aires, 1995.

Vanossi, Jorge Reinaldo. *Victorino de la Plaza.* Buenos Aires: Consejo Argentino para las Relaciones Internacionales, 2004.

Weinmann, Ricardo. *Argentina en la Primera Guerra Mundial: Neutralidad, transición política y continuismo económico.* Buenos Aires: Editorial Biblos, 1994.

JOEL HOROWITZ

PLAZA GUTIÉRREZ, LEONIDAS

(1865–1932). Leonidas Plaza Gutiérrez (*b.* 18 April 1865; *d.* 18 September 1932), military figure and president of Ecuador (constitutional, 1901–1905 and 1912–1916). Born in Charapoto, Manabí Province, of Colombian parents, Plaza began a military career at age eighteen. After participating in the failed 1883–1884 liberal uprising in Manabí Province, Plaza escaped to Central America. During the next decade, he served in various administrative positions in El Salvador, Costa Rica, and Nicaragua, and earned an international reputation as a liberal revolutionary. He returned to Ecuador to participate in the liberal revolt that triumphed in August 1895. Plaza remained in Ecuador, and subsequently served as a member of the constituent assembly of 1896–1897, military commander of the coastal provinces, and deputy for Tungurahua Province at the 1900 and 1901 congresses, where he was president of the Chamber of Deputies.

At the end of his first presidential term, Eloy Alfaro selected Plaza as the candidate of the Liberal Party, but subsequently withdrew his support. Plaza, who retained substantial support within the military, won the presidency. The division between the two liberal leaders was one of the major causes of the turbulence of the ensuing decade. During his first administration, Plaza encouraged moderate conservatives to participate in his government, prompting his rivals to accuse the president of betraying liberalism. Plaza was a capable administrator who sought to build consensus, foster respect for civil liberties, including freedom of the press, and develop a secular, activist state. He supported Lizardo García for president in 1905.

Plaza was out of the country when Eloy Alfaro ousted García and convened a constituent assembly to ratify his usurpation of power in 1906. Plaza served as minister of finance in the short-lived government of Emilio Estrada. Estrada's death in December 1911 precipitated a struggle between the alfarista and plazista factions of the Liberal Party. The defeat of Alfaro, and his subsequent murder by a Quiteño mob, allowed the election of Plaza to a second presidential term in 1912. As arbiter of national politics between 1912 and 1925, Plaza used his influence to strengthen political institutions and the peaceful transfer of political power.

See also **Ecuador: Since 1830.**

BIBLIOGRAPHY

Linda Alexander Rodríguez, *The Search for Public Policy: Regional Politics and Government Finances in Ecuador, 1830–1940* (1985), esp. pp. 44–52, 123–125.

Frank Mac Donald Spindler, *Nineteenth-Century Ecuador* (1987), esp. pp. 184–192, 205–211.

Additional Bibliography

Cárdenas Reyes, María Cristina. *José Peralta y la trayectoria del liberalismo ecuatoriano.* Quito: Ediciones del Banco Central del Ecuador, 2002.

Díaz Cueva, Miguel, and Fernando Jurado Noboa. *Alfaro y su tiempo.* Quito: Fundación Cultural del Ecuador, 1999.

LINDA ALEXANDER RODRÍGUEZ

PLAZA LASSO, GALO (1906–1987).

Galo Plaza Lasso (*b.* 17 February 1906; *d.* 28 January 1987), president of Ecuador (1948–1952). The son of the former Liberal president Leónidas Plaza Gutiérrez, he received his university education in the United States and was named attaché at the Ecuadorian legation in Washington, D.C., in 1929. Upon later returning to Ecuador, he was active as gentleman farmer, diplomat, and politician. He served as minister of defense (1938–1940), ambassador to the United States (1944–1946), and senator from Pichincha (1946–1948). In 1948 he became the presidential candidate of the Movimiento Cívico Democrático Nacional (MCDN). Backed by the Liberal Party and by a group of independents and young professionals, he defeated the Conservative opposition.

Plaza sought a modernization of the economy and expanded the role of the state. His active promotion of the banana industry led to a boom that provided an important new economic resource. Plaza also devoted constant attention to the nurturing of his nation's fledgling democracy, insisting upon the basic importance of constitutional rule. Despite the unbridled partisanship of domestic opponents and the devastating impact of the worst earthquake in the nation's history, he served out his term—the first time in twenty-eight years any leader had served a full term.

Eight years later Plaza sought a second presidential term, once again putting together a coalition that included moderate reformers and progressives. However, he was soundly defeated in 1960 by José María Velasco Ibarra. Plaza, however, remained one of the nation's most respected figures and was called upon for advice in times of crisis, as when a provisional president had to be named in 1966 following the swift withdrawal of the military junta of the day.

Although his candidacy was marred by a long and cordial relationship with the United States, Plaza was nonetheless chosen as secretary-general of the Organization of American States (OAS); he served two terms before stepping down in 1975. In his later years he was active in such efforts as the Inter-American Dialogue. He continued to espouse the cause of democracy until his death at the age of eighty.

See also **Organization of American States (OAS).**

BIBLIOGRAPHY

Galo Plaza, *Problems of Democracy in Latin America* (1955).

John D. Martz, *Politics and Petroleum in Ecuador* (1987).

Additional Bibliography

Coral Patiño, Héctor. *Galo Plaza Lasso: El hombre de las Américas.* Quito: Letramía, 2003.

Fundación Galo Plaza Lasso. *Galo Plaza Lasso, 1906–2006.* Quito: Fundación Galo Plaza Lasso, 2006.

JOHN D. MARTZ

POBLETE POBLETE DE ESPINOZA, OLGA

(1908–). Olga Poblete Poblete de Espinoza (*b.* 21 May 1908), Chilean women's rights and peace activist and historian. Poblete received her degree in history, geography, and civic education from the Instituto Pedagógico de la Universidad de Chile in 1929 and held the chair in contemporary history at the Universidad de Chile in 1952–1970. She was active in national and international summer school programs, including the one at Columbia Teachers College, New York, in 1945. Poblete traveled widely on behalf of her work in the international peace movement, cofounded the Movimiento Chileno de Partidarios de la Paz (1949), served as Latin American representative to the World Council of Peace from 1960 to 1966, and was president of the Chilean Peace Committee until 1973. In 1962 she received the Lenin Peace Prize and in 1988 was awarded the Eugenie Cotton Medal from the International Democratic Federation of Women. A member of the Movimiento Pro-Emancipación de la Mujer Chilena (MEMCH), Poblete took over leadership of that organization in 1947. In the early 1980s she joined the efforts of MEMCH83 to coordinate protest against the Pinochet regime.

See also **Feminism and Feminist Organizations.**

BIBLIOGRAPHY

Olga Poblete Poblete De Espinoza, *Historia contemporanea, 1914–1964* (1968), *La guerra, la paz, y los pueblos* (1990), and *Una mujer: Elena Caffarena* (1993).

Corinne Antezana-Pernet, "Peace in the World and Democracy at Home: The Chilean Women's Movement in the 1940s," in *Latin America in the 1940s: War and Post-War Transitions,* edited by David Rock (1994).

Additional Bibliography

Aliaga Rojas, Fernando. "Aporte pastoral de la mujer en el siglo XIX." *Anuario de la Historia de la Iglesia en Chile,* 13 (1995): 67–78.

Caffarena de Jiles, Elena. *Un capítulo en la historia del feminismo: Las sufragistas inglesas.* Santiago: Ediciones del Memch, 1952.

Klimpel Alvarado, Felícitas. *La mujer chilena: El aporte femenino al progreso de Chile, 1910–1960.* Santiago de Chile: Editorial Andrés Bello, 1962.

Poblete de Espinoza, Olga. *Una mujer, Elena Caffarena.* Santiago de Chile: Cuarto Propio, 1993.

Poblete de Espinoza, Olga y otros. *La Enseñanza Moderna de las Ciencias Sociales.* Chile: Editorial Universitaria, 1971.

CORINNE ANTEZANA-PERNET FRANCESCA MILLER

POCHO. Pocho, a culturally Americanized Mexican residing in the United States. The Mexican term (literally, "discolored" or "faded") refers to a Mexican who has adopted North American values, traditions, and language at the expense of his Mexican heritage. The term was widely used in Mexico from the 1920s on; the extent of its use was directly related to the immigration to the United States of thousands of Mexicans in the aftermath of the Mexican Revolution of 1910, and the resentment that this immigration generated. "Pocho" can also refer to a process or a condition of assimilation. The word became institutionalized as a pejorative denomination for Mexicans residing in the United States until the term *Chicano* began to replace it in the late 1960s. As of 2005, 26.8 million Mexican-Americans resided in the United States.

See also **Mexico, Wars and Revolutions: Mexican Revolution.**

BIBLIOGRAPHY

Richardson, Chad. *Batos, bolillos, pochos, & pelados: Class and culture on the South Texas border.* Austin: University of Texas Press, 1999.

Paz, Octavio. "El pachuco y otros extremos." In *El laberinto de la soledad.* México: Fondo de Cultura Económica, 1959.

Valenzuela Arce, José Manuel. "Fronteras y representaciones sociales: La figura del pocho como estereotipa del chicano." *Aztlán.* 30:6 (Spring 2004): 125–133.

Wilson, William E. "A Note on 'Pochismo.'" *The Modern Language Journal.* 30:6 (October 1946): 345–346.

DAVID MACIEL

POCHTECA. Pochteca, hereditary merchants of central Mesoamerica, especially associated with imperial Tenochtitlán-Tlatelolco. Though some operated locally, they are best known as long-distance traders who led caravans of *tlameme* (bearers) through sometimes hostile territory, not uncommonly acting as spies or even conquerors. From the Chaco Canyon area of New Mexico to Guatemala, *pochteca* exchanged processed goods for precious feathers, stones, and other items which fueled Nahua artisan production. Internally stratified, residing in their own districts, and organized in a guildlike fashion, they acquired enough wealth to rival that of the nobility. Although privileged to own property, have their own law codes, and sacrifice captives, as commoners they were nonetheless restricted in the display of their wealth, normally flaunting their riches only in the sumptuous interiors of their outwardly humble dwellings. Following the Conquest, *pochteca* continued to operate, disappearing as a distinct group only in the later sixteenth century with the advent of more intense Spanish competition.

See also **Nahuas; Tlatelolco.**

BIBLIOGRAPHY

The best recent discussion of *pochteca* in English is in Ross Hassig, *Trade, Tribute, and Transportation: The Sixteenth-Century Political Economy of the Valley of Mexico* (1985). Frances Berdan, *The Aztecs of Central Mexico: An Imperial Society* (1982), also provides a very useful account.

Additional Bibliography

López-Austin, Alfredo and Leonardo López-Luján. *El pasado indígena.* México: Colegio de México, Fideicomiso Historia de las Américas: Fondo de Cultura Económica, 1996.

ROBERT HASKETT

POINSETT, JOEL ROBERTS (1779–1851). Joel Roberts Poinsett (*b.* 2 March 1779; *d.* 12 December 1851), first U.S. ambassador to

Mexico (1825–1829). In 1822, Poinsett, a native of Charleston, South Carolina, accepted a commission as special agent to Mexico, then ruled by Emperor Agustín de Iturbide. He returned to Mexico in May 1825 as U.S. minister plenipotentiary. During these missions he sought, without success, to acquire northern Mexican territory for the United States.

The struggles for influence in Mexico between the U.S. and British ministers were acrimonious. To provide a counterweight to the Scottish Rite Masonic lodges linked to the British ambassador, Henry George Ward, Poinsett helped to establish and regularize York Rite Masonic lodges in Mexico. After the York Rite Masons organized a successful revolt led by Vicente Guerrero, Mexican public opinion could no longer tolerate the U.S. ambassador's blatant interference in Mexico's internal affairs. President Guerrero requested that Poinsett be replaced as U.S. minister, and in January 1830 Poinsett returned to the United States.

He was elected U.S. senator in 1836 and named President Martin Van Buren's secretary of war in 1837. He supported the independence and annexation of Texas but opposed the war of 1846–1847. He introduced the Mexican plant called *nochebuena* to the United States, where it is popularly known as poinsettia.

See also **Masonic Orders; United States-Mexico Border; Yorkinos.**

BIBLIOGRAPHY

Joel Roberts Poinsett, *Notes on Mexico, Made in the Autumn of 1822, Accompanied by an Historical Sketch of the Revolution* (1825; repr. 1969); *Diccionario Porrúa de historia, biografía y geografía de México*, 5th ed. (1986).

Stanley C. Green, *The Mexican Republic: The First Decade, 1823–1832* (1987), pp. 45, 89, 91–93, 148–149, 158, 167.

Additional Bibliography

Feliú Cruz, Guillermo, and Rafael Sagredo Baeza. *La primer misión de los Estados Unidos de América en Chile.* Santiago, Chile: Centro de Investigaciones Diego Barros Arana, Universidad de Chile, 2000.

Rich, P.J., and Guillermo de los Reyes. *Joel Poinsett: The First Gringo in Mexico.* Stanford, CA: Hoover Institution, Stanford University, 1995.

D. F. STEVENS

POLAY CAMPOS, VÍCTOR (1951–).

Víctor Polay Campos is a founding member of the Movimiento Revolucionario Túpac Amaru (Tupac Amaru Revolutionary Movement, MRTA), a Peruvian guerrilla movement. Born April 6, 1951, in Callao, the son of Víctor Polay Risco, a prominent leader and former deputy of the Peruvian Aprista Party (APRA), Polay Campos grew up in a family affected by frequent paternal absences caused by political persecution. A member of APRA since his preteen years, Polay Campos rose rapidly through its ranks. In the early 1970s he studied in Paris (where his roommate was Alan García, a fellow APRA member and future Peruvian president) and Madrid; during this stay in Europe he abandoned APRA and adopted a left-wing ideology. Polay Campos contributed to the creation of the MRTA in 1982. In February 1989 he was captured by the Peruvian police but escaped from prison in July 1990 with dozens of other MRTA leaders. He was recaptured in June 1992 and in April 1993 was sentenced to life in prison. Polay Campos is now incarcerated in the Callao Naval Base.

See also **Movimiento Revolucionario Tupac Amaru (MRTA); Peru, Political Parties: Peruvian Aprista Party (PAP/APRA).**

BIBLIOGRAPHY

Jiménez Bacca, Benedicto. *Inicio, desarrollo y ocaso del terrorismo en el Perú: El ABC de Sendero Luminoso y el MRTA ampliado y comentado.* Peru: Impr. Sanki, 2000.

McCormick, Gordon H. *Sharp Dressed Men: Peru's Túpac Amaru Revolutionary Movement.* Santa Monica, CA: RAND, 1993.

JULIO CARRION

POLÍTICA DOS GOVERNADORES.

Política dos Governadores, practice employed during Brazil's Old Republic (1889–1930) that enabled the president and certain powerful governors to make important decisions without any "outside" interference. In a broader sense, it was the policy whereby all government incumbents sought to maintain each other in power indefinitely.

In early 1900 President Manuel Campos Sales instituted the *política* as a means of ensuring that the president would always have a majority in the Chamber of Deputies. To achieve this end, he pushed two procedural changes through the chamber. One effectively gave the president control of the chamber's credentials committee. The second required that a majority of county councils in each congressional district certify the winner's vote. Since the establishment party at the state level supported local politicians and vice versa, this was another safeguard against the entry of noncompliant deputies into congress.

Campos Sales introduced the *política* to guarantee congressional support for fiscal and monetary policies required for the Rothschild funding loan (1898), which consolidated Brazil's external debt. These included such unpopular measures as raising taxes, decreasing both the currency in circulation and government expenditures, and placing a lien for Rothschild on customs collections. Thus the *política* was an adaptation of formal democratic structures to political conditions in a neocolonial economy.

The practice of mutual support by incumbents continued throughout the Old Republic and was associated with the domination of politics by the president and the governors of Minas Gerais and São Paulo. The inability of opposition groups to obtain office except by revolution, coupled with the exclusion of urban middle and working classes from power through rural bossism (Coronelismo), contributed to the demise of the 1891 Constitution in 1930.

See also **Brazil: Since 1889; Campos Sales, Manuel Ferraz de.**

BIBLIOGRAPHY

Manuel Ferraz De Campos Salles, *Da propaganda à presidência* (1908), pp. 236–250.

Francisco De Assis Barbosa, "A Presidência Campos Sales," in *Luso-Brazilian Review*, 5, no. 1 (1968): 3–26.

Joseph L. Love, *Rio Grande do Sul and Brazilian Regionalism, 1882–1930* (1971), pp. 95–96, 109–124.

Boris Fausto, "Brazil: Social and Political Structure, 1889–1930," in *The Cambridge History of Latin America*, vol. 5, edited by Leslie Bethell (1986), pp. 779–829.

Additional Bibliography

Villa, Marco Antonio. *O nascimento da República no Brasil: A primeira década do novo regime.* São Paulo: Editora Ática, 1997.

JOSEPH L. LOVE

POLITICAL PARTIES. *See* **under individual countries.**

POLK, JAMES KNOX (1795–1849). James Knox Polk (*b*. 2 November 1795; *d*. 15 June 1849), president of the United States during the Mexican War. Born in North Carolina and raised in Tennessee, Polk distinguished himself as a lawyer, state legislator, and congressman. He was a Democrat and an ardent supporter of President Andrew Jackson's policies, including western expansion and the acquisition of Mexican territories. When he was elected president in 1844, Polk vowed to acquire Mexican California. The following year he sent John Slidell to Mexico with an offer to pay fifteen to twenty million dollars for the territory, but this proposal was rejected. Simultaneously Polk had sent Captain John C. Frémont to California, where he assisted in the Bear Flag Revolt and the conquest of that territory.

For this and the dispatch of Zachary Taylor to the Rio Grande in 1846, Polk was criticized by his political opponents for manipulating events to justify a war against Mexico in order to acquire territory. New England Whigs opposed him because of his proslavery stance. He opposed the Wilmont Proviso, which would have excluded slavery from the newly acquired Mexican territories. Due to controversies thus engendered, his party lost the 1848 election.

See also **United States-Latin American Relations.**

BIBLIOGRAPHY

Eugene I. Mc Cormac, *James K. Polk: A Political Biography* (1922).

Allan Nevins, ed., *The Diary of a President, 1845–1849*, 2 vols. (1929; repr. 1952).

Charles A. Mc Coy, *Polk and the Presidency* (1960).

Additional Bibliography

Haynes, Sam W., and Oscar Handlin. *James K. Polk and the Expansionist Impulse.* New York: Longman, 1997.

Leonard, Thomas M. *James K. Polk: A Clear and Unquestionable Destiny.* Wilmington, DE: S.R. Books, 2001.

Seigenthaler, John. *James K. Polk.* New York: Times Books, 2004.

RICHARD GRISWOLD DEL CASTILLO

POMA DE AYALA. *See* **Guaman Poma de Ayala, Felipe.**

POMBAL, MARQUÊS DE (SEBASTIÃO JOSÉ DE CARVALHO E MELLO)

(1699–1782). Marquês de Pombal (Sebastião José de Carvalho e Mello; *b.* 13 May 1699; *d.* 8 May 1782), Portuguese diplomat and initiator of reforms in Brazil. Pombal, the eldest of twelve children, came from a family of modest gentry who had served as soldiers, priests, and state functionaries within Portugal and occasionally in its extensive overseas empire. He studied law at Coimbra University and served as ambassador to England (1739–1745) and envoy to Austria (1745–1749). His father had served in both the army and the navy, and had been an officer of the court cavalry. An uncle, an archpriest of the Lisbon patriarchy, managed an entailed estate consisting of a mansion on the present-day Rua do Sécolo in Lisbon (Pombal's birthplace) and an estate in Oeiras, a small town overlooking the Tagus estuary near Lisbon. Pombal inherited both properties; and it was at Oeiras, after his return from diplomatic service in Vienna in 1750, that he built an impressive country house and accumulated further landholdings.

Pombal's noble status was not hereditary but a reward for service to the monarch and to the Portuguese state. His background was neither as grand as his title might imply nor as modest as his enemies claimed. In fact, it was much like that of many ministers the absolutist monarchs chose to strengthen their power and enhance that of the state. His honors came late in life: he was made count of Oeiras in 1759 and was granted the title of Marquês de Pombal in 1769. During that time he was secretary of state and foreign affairs (1750–1776), which meant he virtually ruled Portugal. In 1777, however, Queen Maria I stripped him of all power.

His brothers Paulo and Francisco were close collaborators in his administration. Paulo, a priest, was elevated to cardinal by Pope Clement XIV and subsequently became inquisitor general and president of the Municipal Council of Lisbon (a post to which Pombal later appointed his eldest son, Henrique, following the death of Paulo). Francisco served as governor and captain general of the

Brazilian provinces of Grão Pará and Maranhão (an area that essentially covered the vast Amazon Basin); later, in Lisbon, Pombal appointed him secretary of state for the overseas dominions. Since neither Francisco nor Paulo married, they pooled their financial resources and property in Pombal's interest.

See also **Maria I of Portugal; Pombaline Reforms.**

BIBLIOGRAPHY

Kenneth Maxwell, *Pombal: Paradox of the Enlightenment* (1995).

Additional Bibliography

Brito, Ferreira de. *Cantigas de escárnio e mal-dizer do Marquês de Pombal, ou, A crónica rimada da Viradeira.* Porto: Associação de Jornalistas e Homens de Letras do Porto, 1990.

Lopes, António. *O Marquês de Pombal e a Companhia de Jesus: Correspondência inédita ao longo de 115 cartas (de 1743 a 1751).* Cascais: Principia, 1999.

Lopes, António. *Enigma Pombal: Nova documentação, tentativa de interpretação.* Lisboa: Roma editora, 2002.

Santos, J. J. Carvalhão. *Literatura e política: Pombalismo e antipombalismo.* Coimbra: Livraria Minerva, 1991.

Theilemann, Werner. *Século XVIII: Século das luzes: Século de Pombal.* Frankfurt am Main: TFM, 2001.

KENNETH MAXWELL

POMBALINE REFORMS.

The Marqués de Pombal, the Portuguese statesman who was brought to power when José I came to the throne in 1750, changed the administrative organization of Brazil and the demographic, economic, social, and cultural policies of the entire Portuguese Empire.

In response to military and diplomatic operations, Pombal decided to promote settlement in the unoccupied north and west of Brazil: the Estado do Maranhão and the captaincy of Mato Grosso. Settlers from the Azores and Madeira islands were given assistance in order to populate and labor in these unexploited regions. New towns, planned according to eighteenth-century rationality and sense of regularity, were created in the hinterland.

Pombal revised policies toward Indians during his administration. He believed that whites and Indians should mingle. Marriages between white men and Indian women were encouraged by giving white men access to some public offices. In order to better integrate Indians into white society, the Jesuit *aldeias* (villages) were converted into parishes or even *villas* (small towns). As in the north and west of the country, Azorean immigration and settlement also were promoted in southern Brazil, in Rio Grande de São Pedro and Santa Catarina; vagrants in the captaincy of São Paulo were ordered to settle in towns. Indian villages were dealt with in the same way as those of the northern regions.

Parallel changes in the administrative organization of Brazil were undertaken through the creation of new captaincies and the incorporation to the crown of the last private captaincies, which went back to the earliest colonization of Brazil. The seat of the viceroyalty was transferred from Bahia to Rio de Janeiro in 1763. The creation of new administrative bodies, such as the Junta do Comércio (Board of Trade) in 1755 and the Erário Régio (Royal Treasury) in 1761, also changed the administration of Brazil.

Beginning in 1767, as the result of the new financial institutions, the local finances of each captaincy were administered by a Junta da Fazenda (Board of Treasury) comprised of five or six members, including the already existing *provedor da fazenda,* with the governor as its president. Accountable only to the Royal Treasury in Lisbon, these local juntas were responsible for collecting and distributing royal income. Some specialized institutions were also created: the Mesas de Inspeção de Açúcar e Tabaco (Boards for the Inspection of Sugar and Tobacco) in Bahia, Recife, Rio de Janeiro, and São Luís do Maranhão (1751); and the Intendentes da Marinha e Armazéns Reais (Intendants for the Navy and Royal Warehouses) in Bahia, Rio de Janeiro, and Recife.

To speed up justice, a second Relação (High Court) was created in Rio de Janeiro in 1751. It assumed responsibilities of the Relação da Bahia for the southern captaincies. Other judicial changes were the Juntas de Justiça (Boards of Justice), which were established first in Pará and Pernambuco in 1758 and then throughout Brazil in 1765. More significantly, secular magistrates were no longer allowed to base their decisions on canon law, and Roman law was abandoned. Only the laws of the country (*ordenações*

and subsidiary laws) along with custom and well-established practices would be followed.

The military reorganization was less successful in Brazil than it had been in Portugal, but some efforts were made to reinforce the southern frontier, and military recruitment became easier when Pombal ordered a census of inhabitants in each captaincy. Henceforth, it became more difficult for the male population to escape from military enlistment.

From the social point of view, Pombal's administration was marked by a deep change in the Portuguese system of inheritance, especially concerning entailed property. After the law of 9 September 1769, it became impossible to create *capelas* (chapels) with the obligation of masses *ad perpetuum* at a high cost for the heirs; and the law of 3 August 1770 prevented the abuses of entailing property (*morgados*).

The expulsion of the Jesuits in 1759 resulted in wide-ranging changes in the educational system. Jesuit methodology was abandoned, and Aulas Régias (Royal Classes) were created in most towns and townships of Brazil. They were funded by a new tax, the *subsídio literário*. The reform of the University of Coimbra also contributed to the secularization of culture and the formation of a Brazilian-born elite.

See also **Pombal, Marquês de (Sebastião José de Carvalho e Melo).**

BIBLIOGRAPHY

Marcos Carneiro De Mendonça, *O marqués de Pombal e o Brasil* (1960).

António Alberto Banha De Andrade, *A reforma pombalina dos estudos secundários no Brasil* (1978).

Biblioteca Nacional De Lisboa, *Marqués de Pombal: Catálogo bibliográfico e iconográfico* (1982).

António Carreira, *As companhias pombalinas: De Grão-Pará e Maranhão e Pernambuco e Paraíba* (1983).

Alvaro Teixeira Soares, *O marqués de Pombal* (1983).

Leslie Bethell, ed., *Colonial Brazil* (1987).

Additional Bibliography

Maxwell, Kenneth. *Pombal, Paradox of the Enlightenment.* Cambridge: Cambridge University Press, 1995.

Maria Beatriz Nizza da Silva

POMBERO. Pombero is a fantastic creature whose existence is widely believed in by many Paraguayans, especially rural dwellers. Pombero is said to be short, hairy, and robust, but is seldom seen as he is also able to make himself invisible. His presence is known by the noises he makes, such as whistling or imitating birds, or by the mischief he causes, braiding horses' manes or letting loose domestic animals. He is a creature of the night, sometimes called *kara'i pyharé* (*señor* of the night, in Guaraní), so as not to evoke his real name. When angered, he can cause accidents or cause people traveling at night to lose their way, and he can impregnate women with his touch. He can be appeased by leaving him gifts of cigars, honey, and rum.

Pombero appears to be a post-conquest myth. Gustavo González attributes the name to the Portuguese surname *pombeiro*, in reference either to the *bandeirantes* (raiders) from São Paulo who hunted Guaraní for slaves, or to spies. Dionisio González Torres says the creature does not appear in early texts describing the Guaraní at the time of contact. Milciades Giménez argues that Pombero's hairy body is a sign of virility in European, not Amerindian, culture.

See also **Guarani Indians.**

BIBLIOGRAPHY

Giménez, Milciades. *Tenondeté: Mitos, leyendas y tradiciones del area Tupi-Guaraní.* N.p.: Editorial El Foro, n.d.

González, Gustavo. "Mitos, leyendas y supersticiones guaranties del Paraguay." *Suplemento Antropológico del la Revista del Ateneo Paraguayo* 2, no. 7 (1967).

González Torres, Dionisio M. *Folklore del Paraguay.* Asunción: ServiLibro, 2003.

BRIAN TURNER

POMPÉIA, RAÚL (1863–1895). Raúl Pompéia (*b.* 12 April 1863; *d.* 25 December 1895), Brazilian writer. Pompéia was born in Angra dos Reis, in Rio de Janeiro State. He lived a very solitary and repressed life, having to yield constantly to his parents' strict and exigent ways. A kind soul, he also possessed a depressed and morbid personality, having gone through many existential conflicts throughout his entire life. He committed suicide, by shooting himself in the heart, at the age of thirty-two.

Upon his family's relocation to the city of Rio de Janeiro, Pompéia was sent to the Abílio Boarding School, run by the baron of Macaubus, where he experienced neglect and abuse at the hands of school officials and classmates. Most of his critics agree, however, that while attending this school Pompéia found the inspiration to write his realist-naturalist, existentialist masterpiece *O Ateneu,* published in 1888. This novel inspired authors from all over the world, including Sartre in his *Huis-clos* (1944; *No Exit,* 1947). Through his limited literary production, Pompéia captured the psychological agonies of modern man and expressed them in a literary discourse that was universal in nature. His other works include *Uma tragédia no Amazonas* (1880), his first novelistic essay, published in the newspaper *Gazeta de Notícias; Canções sem metro* (1881), prose poems; and *As jóias da coroa* (1883), also published in *Gazeta de Notícias* in 1882.

See also **Literature: Brazil.**

BIBLIOGRAPHY

Claude Hulet, *Brazilian Literature,* vol. 2 (1974).

Additional Bibliography

Capaz, Camil. *Raul Pompéia: Biografia.* Rio de Janeiro: Gryphus, 2001.

Prado, Antonio Arnoni, et al. *Raul Pompéia.* Campinas, São Paulo, Brazil: UNICAMP, Departamento de Teoria Literária, 1995.

ROSÂNGELA MARIA VIEIRA

PONCE, MANUEL (1886–1948). Manuel Ponce (*b.* 8 December 1886; *d.* 14 April 1948), composer and pianist, born in Fresnillo, Mexico. Ponce studied at the National Conservatory in Mexico City, at Liceo Rossini in Bologna, and the Stern Conservatory in Berlin. He taught piano at the Mexican Conservatory (1909–1915 and 1917–1922), founded the periodical *Revista Musical de México* (1919), and directed the National Symphony Orchestra briefly in 1917. He spent a year as professor of folk music at the National Free University of Mexico (1933–1934), promoting Mexican criollo and mestizo music and the native Cuban music he absorbed during his stay there from 1915 to 1917. In Paris (1925–1933) he worked with Paul Dukas and founded the music journal *Gaceta Musical;* after returning to Mexico he published the journal *Cultura Musical.* He served brief terms as director of the National Conservatory and of the music department of the Free University. Ponce's music reveals, in addition to native influences, leanings toward the impressionism of Debussy, Ravel, and Dukas. His best-known composition remains the popular song "Estrellita," but he is also known for his Mexican symphonic poem *Chapúltepec* (1921), a violin concerto, and salon pieces for solo piano.

See also **Music: Art Music.**

BIBLIOGRAPHY

Robert Stevenson, *Music in Mexico: A Historical Survey* (1952).

Additional Bibliography

Barrón Corvera, Jorge. *Manuel María Ponce: A Bio-Bibliography.* Westport, CT: Praeger, 2004.

Miranda, Ricardo. *Manuel M. Ponce: Ensayo sobre su vida y obra.* México: Consejo Nacional para la Cultura y las Artes, 1998.

ROBERT L. PARKER

PONCE DE LÉON, FIDELIO (1895–1949).

Fidelio Ponce de Léon (*b.* 24 January 1895; *d.* 19 February 1949), Cuban painter. Born in Camagüey, Ponce attended the National School of San Alejandro, where he fell under the influence of Leopoldo Romañach. Ponce had an artist's temperament and refused to work on subjects that did not interest him. He disappeared from public record in 1918 but reappeared in 1923 in Havana, where he lived cheaply and gave art lessons to poor children. As part of the burgeoning Cuban vanguard movement in the 1930s, Ponce began to exhibit his works and won a prize at the national salon of 1935 for his painting *Las beatas.* Typical of Ponce's style are pale colors, a fascination with light, and melancholy reflection on the animalistic nature of the human race. Unfortunately, his work suffers from deterioration and age and has lost much of its original brilliance.

See also **Art: The Twentieth Century.**

BIBLIOGRAPHY

Loló De La Torriente, *Estudio de las artes plásticas en Cuba* (1954).

Government Of Cuba, *Pintores cubanos* (1963) and *Pintores cubanos* (1974).

Additional Bibliography

Bermúdez, Carmen Paula. "Fidelio Ponce de León." *Art Nexus* 39 (Feb.–Apr. 2001): 64–69.

KAREN RACINE

PONCE DE LEÓN, JUAN (c. 1460–1521).

Juan Ponce de León (*b.* ca. 1460; *d.* July 1521). Spanish soldier, governor of San Juan, and leader of the first Spanish expedition to La Florida. He explored the island colony of San Juan (Puerto Rico) beginning in 1508 and served as its governor in 1509–1511.

Ponce de León was born in San Tervás del Compo, Valladolid, Spain. In 1512 he received a royal charter to explore and settle Bimini, an island rumored to be north of the Lucayos (Bahamas). He set sail from Puerto Rico in March 1513 on a course through the Bahamas that took him to the east coast of Florida. Because his arrival coincided with the Feast of Flowers (Easter Holy Week), he named the land La Florida. Ponce then sailed southward past Cape Canaveral and what is now Miami before rounding the Florida Keys and traveling up the Gulf coast to Charlotte Harbor and perhaps beyond. His was the first sanctioned Spanish voyage to the mainland of the United States.

In 1521 Ponce returned to Florida to establish a colony. That attempt failed when the Spaniards were driven off by native peoples and Ponce received a fatal wound.

See also **Explorers and Exploration: Spanish America; Florida.**

BIBLIOGRAPHY

T. Frederick Davis, "Juan Ponce de León's Voyages to Florida," *Florida Historical Quarterly,* 14 (July 1935): 5–70.

Samuel Eliot Morison, *The European Discovery of America: The Southern Voyages, A.D. 1492–1616* (1974), esp. pp. 499–516.

Robert S. Weddle, *Spanish Sea: The Gulf of Mexico in North American Discovery, 1500–1685* (1985), esp. pp. 38–54.

Additional Bibliography

Fuson, Robert Henderson. *Juan Ponce de León and the Spanish Discovery of Puerto Rico and Florida.* Blacksburg, VA: McDonald & Woodward, 2000.

JERALD T. MILANICH

PONCE ENRÍQUEZ, CAMILO (1912–1976).

Camilo Ponce Enríquez (*b.* 31 January 1912; *d.* 14 September 1976), president of Ecuador (1956–1960). A member of a traditional highland family, Ponce received his law degree from the Central University in Quito in 1938 and soon combined politics with his legal career. Conservative in outlook, he founded the Movimiento Social Cristiano (MSC) in 1951. It was to be his personal political vehicle for the next three decades.

After serving as the key minister to José María Velasco Ibarra during the latter's third term as president (1952–1956), Ponce became the rightist candidate in 1956 and won a disputed victory by a bare 3,000 votes. The first Conservative president since 1895, Ponce survived his term despite a weak political base, economic difficulties, and bitter opposition from labor, which was subdued by stern police action. Eight years after leaving office Ponce sought his second term, running under the Alianza Popular label at the head of a rightist coalition. He finished third in a tight race that was won by Velasco.

Ponce remained influential as an elder statesman in later years and never relinquished hopes of returning to office once again. However, the intrusion of the military into politics in 1972 helped thwart these hopes. He gradually withdrew from politics, and by the time of his death in 1976 his personalist party had reorganized as the Partido Social Cristiano.

See also **Ecuador, Political Parties: Overview.**

BIBLIOGRAPHY

John D. Martz, *Ecuador: Conflicting Political Culture and the Quest for Progress* (1972).

Additional Bibliography

Alexander, Robert Jackson, and Eldon M. Parker. *A History of Organized Labor in Peru and Ecuador.* Westport, CT: Praeger, 2006.

Lara Guzmán, Marco. *Camino y significación del Partido Social Cristiano.* Quito: Corporación Editora Nacional, 2005.

JOHN D. MARTZ

PONIATOWSKA, ELENA (1932–).

The Mexican writer and journalist Elena Poniatowska is an advocate for dispossessed segments of Mexican society and of the democratic movement in Mexico. Born on May 19, 1932, in Paris, she moved to Mexico in 1942 with her father, Estanislao Poniatowski, a direct descendant of the last king of Poland, and her aristocratic Mexican-born mother. She began work in 1953 as a journalist for the Mexican newspaper *Excelsior* and rapidly gained recognition for her interviews and political and social chronicles.

She joined the ranks of Mexico's leading contemporary writers with the publication of *Hasta no verte, Jesús mío* (1969), a fictional narrative based on the oral history of Josefina Bórquez, a washerwoman who participated in the Mexican Revolution and then struggled to survive in the shantytowns of Mexico City. Poniatowska refused the Mexican literary Prize Xavier Villaurrutia for *La noche de Tlatelolco* (1971), an oral-history collage of the 1968 student movement and its brutal repression, because, as she said, "who will award the dead?" Her many writings include *Nada, nadie: Las voces del temblor* (1988), a testimonial narrative of the 1985 Mexico City earthquake; *Tinísima* (1992), a fictionalized biography of photographer Tina Modotti, on which she worked for ten years; *Todo México*, a compilation in several volumes of her interviews; and *El tren pasa primero* (2005), a novel.

Since the 1970s Poniatowska has led a writer's workshop from which several women writers have emerged. She was the first woman to receive the Mexican National Award for Journalism (1979) and remains the only woman to be awarded a title by the French Legion of Honor (2003). Among her many other awards is the Courage in Journalism Lifetime Achievement Award from the International Women's Media Foundation (2006).

See also **Journalism; Journalism in Mexico.**

BIBLIOGRAPHY

Works by the Author

Lilus Kikus. Mexico City: Los Presentes, 1954.

Massacre in Mexico. Translation by Helen R. Lane of *La noche del Tlatelolco* [1971]. New York: Viking Press, 1975.

Fuerte es el silencio. Mexico City: Era, 1982.

Dear Diego. Translation by Katherine Silver of *Querido Diego, te abraza Quiela* [1978]. New York: Pantheon, 1986.

La Flor de Lis. Mexico City: Era, 1988.

Luz y luna, las lunitas. Mexico City: Era, 1994.

Tinisima. Translation by Katherine Silver of *Tinísima* [1992]. New York: Farrar, Straus, and Giroux, 1996.

Here's to You, Jesusa! Translation by Deanna Heikkinen of *Hasta no verte, Jesús mío* [1969]. New York: Farrar, Straus, and Giroux, 2001.

Las siete cabritasi. Mexico City: Era, 2000.

The Skin of the Sky. Translation by Deanna Heikkinen of *La piel del cielo* [2001]. New York: Farrar, Straus, and Giroux, 2004.

Works on the Author

Monsiváis, Carlos. "'Mira, para que no comas olvido'...: Las precisiones de Elena Poniatowska." *La Cultura en México: Suplemento de Siempre!* (July 15, 1981): 2–5.

Schuessler, Michael K. *Elena Poniatowska: An Intimate Biography.* Tucson: University of Arizona Press, 2007.

Steele, Cynthia. "Gender, Genre, and Authority: *Hasta no verte Jesús mío* (1969), by Elena Poniatowska." In her *Politics, Gender, and the Mexican Novel, 1968–1988: Beyond the Pyramid,* pp. 28–65. Austin: University of Texas Press, 1992.

CLAIRE JOYSMITH

PONTA PORÃ (FEDERAL TERRITORY).
Ponta Porã, a federal territory in southwest Brazil from 1943 to 1945. Ponta Porã was created by the Getúlio Vargas administration in what is now the southern portion of the state of Mato Grosso do Sul to strengthen government control over an area that was a major center of resistance to Vargas's regime. The district was bordered to the east by the Paraná River and to the west and south by Paraguay. The northern border was at approximately 23 degrees south latitude. It was a sparsely populated region whose closest city was Campo Grande, now the capital of Mato Grosso do Sul. In present-day Brazil, Ponta Porã is a small city on the Paraguayan border, in Mato Grosso do Sul, with a population of 68,317 in 2006.

See also **Vargas, Getúlio Dornelles.**

BIBLIOGRAPHY

Roy Nash, *The Conquest of Brazil* (1926).

John W. Dulles, *Vargas of Brazil* (1967).

Thomas E. Skidmore, *Politics in Brazil, 1930–1964: An Experiment in Democracy* (1967).

Additional Bibliography

do Valle Pereira, Jacira Helena, and Roseli Fischmann. *Educação e fronteira: Processos identitários de migrantes de diferentes etnias.* São Paulo, Brazil: Thesis, 2002.

Torrecilha, Maria Lucia, and Heliana Comin Vargas. *A Fronteira, as cidades e a linha.* Sao Paulo, Brazil: Thesis, 2003.

MICHAEL J. BROYLES

POPAYÁN.
Popayán, a city in southwestern Colombia and capital of the department of Cauca. The city was a major administrative and commercial center during the colonial period, but it declined in importance after 1850 and had an estimated population of only 239,087 in 2005.

Located in the foothills of the Central Cordillera at an altitude of 5,700 feet, Popayán was founded in 1537 by Sebastián de Belalcázar. In 1540 Belalcázar was named governor of the province of Popayán, which included the Cauca Valley as well as the region to the west bordering the Pacific Ocean. The indigenous inhabitants of the province, who were divided into numerous chiefdoms, resisted the Spanish fiercely and were never completely subdued, though their numbers declined drastically. Gold mining became the province's most important economic activity, made possible by the forced labor of Indians and later Africans.

The city of Popayán was the birthplace of numerous statesmen and intellectuals of the early national period, such as the scientist Francisco José de Caldas (1768–1816), and President Tomás Cipriano de Mosquera (1798–1878), and it became the capital of the huge state (later department) of Cauca. It was gradually superseded economically, however, by Cali. In addition, Cauca lost most of its territory as new departments, such as Nariño (1905) and Valle (1910), were carved out of it. Popayán remained important for its colonial art and architecture and its Holy Week processions. A severe earthquake on 31 March 1983 destroyed or badly damaged more than 5,000 buildings, but subsequent restoration work preserved Popayán's colonial character.

See also **Cauca Valley.**

BIBLIOGRAPHY

Andrew H. Whiteford, *An Andean City at Mid-Century: A Traditional Urban Society.* East Lansing: Michigan State University, 1977.

Peter Marzahl, *Town in the Empire: Government, Politics, and Society in Seventeenth-Century Popayán.* Austin: University of Texas Press, 1978.

Additional Bibliography

Cieza de León, Pedro de. *Crónica del Perú: primera parte* Lima: Pontificia Universidad Católica del Perú, 1996.

Colmenares, German. *Historia económica y social de Colombia.* Santafé de Bogotá: TM, 1997.

Díaz de Zuluaga, Zamira. *Oro, sociedad, y economía: El sistema colonial en la Gobernación de Popayán, 1533–1733.* Santafe de Bogotá: Banco de la República, 1994.

Ramos Gómez, Oscar Gerardo. *Sebastián de Benalcázar: Conquistador de Quito y Popayán.* Madrid: Anaya, 1988.

Whiteford, Andrew Hunter. *Two Cities of Latin America: A Comparative Description of Social Classes.* Prospect Heights, IL: Waveland Press, 1991.

HELEN DELPAR

POPENOE, FREDERICK WILSON

(1892–1975). Frederick Wilson Popenoe (*b.* 9 March 1892; *d.* 20 June 1975), Honduran agriculturalist. Born in Topeka, Kansas, Wilson Popenoe accompanied his father at an early age to Central America and had a long career in the scientific development of the region's agricultural resources. Early in the twentieth century he was instrumental in promoting U.S. avocado production from Mexican budwood. From 1913 to 1925 he was a plant explorer in Latin America for the U.S. Department of Agriculture. Beginning in 1925 he established the United Fruit Company's Agricultural Research Station and botanical garden at Lancetilla, near Tela, Honduras. In 1941 he founded, in collaboration with Samuel Zemurray and the United Fruit Company, the Escuela Agrícola Panamericana at

Zamorano, Honduras, which Popenoe directed until his retirement in 1957.

Popenoe was also an active promoter of Central American culture, and was, for example, responsible for bringing the great Honduran primitivist painter José Antonio Valásquez to world attention. He and his wife also restored a beautiful colonial house in Antigua, Guatemala, the Casa Popenoe, which is still a major tourist attraction there. Popenoe published extensively on tropical horticulture and other subjects from 1911 to 1971.

See also **Agriculture; Antigua; United Fruit Company; Zemurray, Samuel.**

BIBLIOGRAPHY

Frederic Rosengarten, Jr., has written a fine biography of Popenoe: *Wilson Popenoe: Agricultural explorer, educator, and friend of Latin America* (1991).

Additional Bibliography

Claasen, Cheryl. *Women in Archaeology.* Philadelphia: University of Pennsylvania Press, 1994.

O'Brien, Thomas F. *The Revolutionary Mission: American Enterprise in Latin America, 1900–1945.* Cambridge: Cambridge University Press, 1996.

RALPH LEE WOODWARD JR.

POPHAM, HOME RIGGS (1762–

1820). Home Riggs Popham (*b.* 12 October 1762; *d.* 10 September 1820), British admiral who led an ill-fated invasion of the Río de la Plata region by British troops in 1806. The son of a diplomat, Popham was born in Morocco and attended Cambridge University before joining the British navy in 1778. He served in the Napoleonic wars and the colonial government in India as well as in Parliament. While in Capetown, South Africa, Popham became aware of growing discontent toward the Spanish throne among the people of the viceroyalty of Río de la Plata. Though lacking official orders, he left Africa in 1806, along with about fifteen hundred men under the command of William Carr Beresford, with the intention of capitalizing on the rebelliousness of the Spanish colonies in Latin America.

For two years, British troops mounted invasions of the Río de la Plata, Montevideo, and Buenos Aires before being driven from the region by the Spanish, whose rebelliousness he had seriously misjudged. Popham returned to England to stand trial for mounting the invasion without prior approval. He was cleared of all charges and continued his naval career, achieving the rank of rear admiral in 1814.

See also **British in Argentina; Río de la Plata, Viceroyalty of.**

BIBLIOGRAPHY

Henry S. Ferns, *Britain and Argentina in the Nineteenth Century* (1960).

Additional Bibliography

Elliott, J. H. *Empires of the Atlantic World: Britain and Spain in the Americas, 1492–1830.* New Haven, CT: Yale University Press, 2006.

JOHN DUDLEY

POPOL VUH. The Quiche (K'iche') Maya of the west central Guatemalan highlands produced (*ca.* 1555) one of the more impressive works of literature written to date by a Native American author or authors (it is not known whether its creation was an individual or collective effort). Often called the "American Bible," it is a Mayan description of the creation and evolution of the world; in Quiche it is called the *Popol Vuh* (Counsel Book).

The work presents the history of the universe in Mayan terms. There are four Mayan cycles of creation, in each of which the gods attempt to produce worshippers for themselves. When they finally succeed, they find they have made man.

The mythology of the Quiche Maya was greatly influenced by their neighbors, and quite particularly by the Nahuatl-speaking peoples, from about the twelfth century on, when the Nahuas infiltrated Guatemala. The resulting *Popol Vuh* was thus a multicultural product.

The work is nonetheless clearly cognate with the emerging dynastic histories of the Classic Maya on stone monuments, depicting a patrilineal monarchy remarkably similar to that of the ancient Near East and its European successors.

The last creation and, particularly, the last few pages of the *Popol Vuh* are historical. They constitute a genealogy of the Quiche kings from the thirteenth to the sixteenth century, and they allude to (but do not always circumstantially describe) prevailing customs of that period.

The *Popol Vuh* is the single most important *native* source for interpreting the history and culture of pre-Columbian America. This text, which was not published until the nineteenth century, has aroused the interest of ethnographers, historians, novelists, and practitioners of New Age spirituality. Of special note is the ethnographic work of the Nobel laureate Miguel Angel Asturias on the *Popol Vuh* and Guatemala in the 1920s and 1930s, which inspired his award-winning novel *Hombres de maiz* (1949; *Men of Maize*, 1975).

See also **Annals of the Cakchiquels; Ball Game, Pre-Columbian; Chilam Balam; K'iche'; Maya, The; Mayan Epigraphy.**

BIBLIOGRAPHY

Munro S. Edmonson, *The Book of Counsel: The Popol Vuh of the Quiche Maya of Guatemala* (1971).

Dennis J. Tedlock, *The Popol Vuh* (1985).

Additional Bibliography

Chávez, Adrián I. *Pop Wuj: Libro de acontecimientos: Traducción directa del manuscrito del padre Jiménez.* Mexico City [?]: Ediciones de la Casa Chata, 1979.

Powell, Timothy B. "Recovering Precolonial American Literary History: 'The Origin of Stories' and the *Popul Vuh.* In *A Companion to the Literatures of Colonial America*, edited by Susan Castillo and Ivy Schweitzer. Malden, MA and Oxford: Blackwell, 2005.

Preble-Niemi, Oralia. "The *Popol-Vuh* and the Heroic Cycle in *Men of Maize*." In *The Image of the Hero in Literature, Media, and Society.* Edited by Will Wright and Steven Kaplan. Pueblo: Society for the Interdisciplinary Study of Social Imagery, Colorado State University–Pueblo, 2004.

Recinos, Adrián. *Popul vuh: Las antiguas historias del Quiché.* Mexico City: Fondo de Cultura Económica, 1947.

Uzquiza, José Ignacio. "Relato del *Popol Vuh*, libro mágico de los mayas-quiché." In *La palabra recuperada: Mitos prehispánicos en la literatura latinoamericana.* Edited by Helena Usandizaga. Madrid: Iberoamericana; Frankfurt: Vervuert, 2006.

Ward, Thomas. "Expanding Ethnicity in Sixteenth-Century Anahuac: Ideologies of Ethnicity and Gender in the Nation-Building Process." *MLN* 116:2 (March 2001), 419–452.

MUNRO S. EDMONSON

POPULATION

This entry includes the following articles:
BRAZIL
SPANISH AMERICA

BRAZIL

The history of Brazilian population in the colonial period was shaped by the arrival of Portuguese settlers, the reduction and retreat of indigenous tribes, and the importation of African slaves. In 1500 the entire Atlantic coast was occupied by scattered tribes, mostly of the Tupi-Guarani language group, totaling about 2.5 million. Portuguese military campaigns in the 1560s and 1570s sometimes resulted in the annihilation of whole tribes; the survivors were commonly enslaved. By 1585, African slaves had substantially replaced Indian slaves on the sugar plantations of the northeast. However, in the interior and in the Amazon region, enslaved Indians continued to predominate as the labor force through the seventeenth century. In Maranhão the emerging cacao trade after 1720 finally prompted the greater use of African slaves.

Slavery was the dominant form of labor in colonial and nineteenth-century Brazil. Estimates for Brazilian slave imports from 1551 to 1870 vary from 2.5 million to 4.3 million. More than 80 percent of all African slaves entered Brazil after 1700, the vast majority through Rio de Janeiro to the mines of Minas Gerais in the period 1700–1780 or to the sugar and coffee plantations in the period 1780–1850. Proportions of slaves in the populations of various Brazilian municipalities in the eighteenth century varied from 39 to 52 percent, while in the sugar zones often as much as 70 percent of the population was slave. The slave population had an abnormally low fertility rate and a high death rate; the rate of natural increase was almost always negative. Slavery was also important in urban skilled and unskilled occupations in the early nineteenth century; slaves sometimes provided more than half the urban labor force, a situation that was facilitated by the location of most production in artisan households.

The European population grew from about 20,000 in 1570 to approximately 100,000 in 1700, and to about 2 million in 1798. Brazil had a

Population increase in Brazil		
	Millions	Rate of increase (per annum)
1800	3.33	
1850	7.23	1.56
1870	9.80	
1900	17.98	1.85
1920	27.40	
1940	41.24	
1950	51.94	2.12
1970	92.34	2.92
1985	133.36	2.24
2005	183.88	1.43

SOURCE: Thomas W. Merrick and Douglas H. Graham, *Population and Economic Development in Brazil, 1800 to the Present* (Baltimore: Johns Hopkins University Press, 1979), p. 31.

Table 1

population of between 3 and 4 million at the end of the eighteenth century and began the nineteenth century with a moderate growth rate, succeeded in the twentieth century by one of the highest growth rates in the world. For the period from 1850 to 1900, Giorgio Mortara estimated a gradual increase in rate of growth from 1.6 percent per annum from 1850 to 1870, to 2.4 percent from 1890 to 1900. The crude death rate declined to about 28 to 29 per thousand and immigration accounted for almost one-third of population growth between 1891 and 1900. This was the peak period of the impact on population of European immigration, with the growth from immigration declining to about 8 percent for each of the next four decades.

The ethnic and racial composition of the Brazilian population changed significantly during the nineteenth century. The free population of color, which was only 20 percent of the total colored population in 1800, had ballooned to 74 percent by 1872. It was the fastest-growing population group in the nineteenth century, constituting 58 percent of the total population of Brazil in 1872. However, the free colored population was a much more important proportion of the population in the Northeast than in the Southeast, and the white population continued to predominate in the urban areas. In the twentieth century the *parda*, or racially mixed, population continued to expand relative to both the white and the black populations, increasing from 21 percent of the population in 1940 to 39 percent in 2006. In the same period the *preta*, or black, population declined from 15 to 6 percent of the population.

The Brazilian slave population declined from 1,715,000 in 1864 to 1,240,806 in 1883, with the remaining slaves concentrated in the coffee-producing south. The expansion of commercialized export activities in the late nineteenth century resulted in a substantial transfer of slaves from urban areas back into rural cash-crop activities. Although industrial occupations characterized only a small part of the slave population, 11 percent of manual and mechanical industrial workers in Brazil in 1872 were slaves, as were more than 25 percent of the total industrial labor force in the province of Rio de Janeiro.

Recent research on the slave family in Brazil suggests that—in spite of a strongly unbalanced sex ratio—between 50 and 80 percent of the rural Paulista slave population had the experience of living within a family context, that is, either with a marital partner or with one or two parents. On large Paulista plantations, couple-headed households were the norm. Many households in smallholdings were composed of a slave mother and her children. The frequency of the slave family was also much higher on older plantations, whose slaves tended to be native-born (creoles). Little is known about the frequency with which such unions were broken up by sale or inheritance or about their duration, but other studies reveal that levels of slave marriage and family life were very low, particularly on small plantations and in urban areas.

The relationship between the abolition of slavery and the immigration program in Brazil is complicated. Thomas Holloway demonstrates that the decline in available slaves relative to labor needs by 1887 necessitated a transition to a new labor system in São Paulo. Planters viewed abolition as necessary if free immigrant labor was to be attracted.

In the period between 1880 and 1930, more than 4 million immigrants entered Brazil, with almost 60 percent settling in the state of São Paulo. The foreign-born proportion of the Brazilian population increased from about 4 percent in 1872 to a peak of 7 percent in 1900. From 1908 to 1941 almost 200,000 Japanese immigrated to Brazil; another 50,000 Japanese immigrated after World War II. Most Japanese entered as farm laborers and

settled in São Paulo. In addition, German, Polish, and Italian immigrant entrepreneurs played a significant role as small farmers or pioneers in industrial activity in Santa Catarina, Rio Grande do Sul, and São Paulo.

In the early twentieth century, population growth tapered off, primarily because of the decline in immigration to 7 to 8 percent per year of population growth from 1900 to 1930. Mortality declined slightly, probably due to the abolition of slavery and increased public health measures, especially the eradication of yellow fever. From 1918 to 1966, infant mortality—whose primary cause was inadequate diet—declined dramatically. Mortality declined about 50 percent from 1920 to 1960, but the continued strong birth rate resulted in the most rapid population increase in Brazilian history (3 percent per year) for the decade 1950 to 1960. In the 1960s Brazil experienced the first marked decline in its crude birth rate, from 43 to 44 per thousand in the period 1940–1960 to near 40 per thousand in the period 1960–1970. By 1990, the birth rate had declined dramatically to 27 per thousand and fell further by 2006 to 16.56 per thousand. Although this rate of growth continues to be high by international standards, there has been a substantial fertility change. It has occurred in spite of only modest economic growth.

Internal migration is one of the dominant population characteristics of twentieth-century Brazil. From a rate of 3 percent per year in the period 1890–1900, the net rate of internal migration increased to 5.5 percent for the period 1950–1960. Rural–urban migration was not significantly related to macroeconomic processes until about 1920. For the period 1890–1930 international migration was more important demographically than internal migration and essentially preempted internal migration as a source of labor in the south and the east. After 1930 internal migration became more significant. This pattern is particularly apparent in São Paulo, the most important region for both internal and foreign migration in the twentieth century. While migration in the period 1890–1950 was focused on moves between rural labor markets and the opening of new land on the frontiers, the migration patterns since 1960 have been predominantly rural–urban and urban–urban migration. Urban population, which composed only 16 percent of total population in 1940, increased to 40 percent of total population by 1970, to 67 percent by 1980, and to 80 percent by 2005.

After 1890 the demographic center of Brazil shifted southward (particularly with the massive arrival of European and Japanese immigrants); by 1950, the state of São Paulo was the largest state in the republic, with 18 percent of the total population. Since the 1940s, the frontier regions in Brazil have grown most rapidly, with the old agricultural regions in relative decline. Urbanization became pronounced in the south in the latter part of the nineteenth century, stimulating the growth of internal markets. Since the 1960s, cities in all regions have expanded dramatically, exceeding 4 percent population growth per annum. During this period Brazil shifted from an essentially rural nation (75 percent rural in 1940) to an urban one (80 percent urban in 2005). In 2005 Brazil had a total estimated population of 183.88 million.

Thomas Merrick and Douglas Graham explain the intense migration to rural destinations in the period after 1930 by the growing push factors of increased capital-intensive sugar production in the northeast as well as the increased labor demand in São Paulo. They suggest four patterns of rural frontier settlement: (1) the Paulista plantation immigrant pattern of 1885–1930, based on a rural oligarchy and leading to economic mobility and sustained economic growth; (2) the Paraná small-to-medium farmer pattern of the 1940s and 1950s; (3) settlement in central Goiás and Mato Grosso, focused on cattle in the 1950s and 1960s, including many low-income migrants from the northeast; and (4) Amazon colonization projects in the 1970s, which gave way to corporate estates as colonization by small farmers failed.

Recent urbanization has taken the form of increasing growth of the larger cities (over 250,000 population), especially the metropolitan areas of São Paulo, Rio de Janeiro, Belo Horizonte, Recife, Salvador, Pôrto Alegre, Belém, Curitiba, and Fortaleza, primarily as a result of migration from the Northeast. The growth rates in small and medium cities have generally been slowing and the southeastern urban areas continue to dominate. Migration has involved people from all socioeconomic levels, but since about 1970 migrants have increasingly come from lower-income groups. Nevertheless, although migration is often associated with urban poverty, migrants as a

whole (based on income, occupational, and labor-force participation data) compare favorably to non-migrants, and they constituted 60 to 70 percent of the urban labor force in the center-south and about 45 percent in northeastern cities in 1975. Even more telling, in terms of an evaluation of migration as a strategy for social mobility, is the fact that the greatest poverty is found among very recent migrants. Female migrants are also less favored than male migrants, with a large proportion of women in domestic service and the informal employment sector as compared to men.

The Brazilian population in the twenty-first century continues to display many of its historical characteristics. Racial and cultural diversity, along with a somewhat insidious racism, was visible in the structure of occupations and in residential patterns. Personalistic modes of economic and political organization, along with an "urban peasantry" attitude toward multiple, often subsistence-based occupations, lent a rural flavor to urban life. The informal sector of the economy supported about 40 percent of the population, and income distribution was among the most polarized in the world. While mortality has diminished substantially, levels of child abandonment in urban areas were astounding, and malnutrition was still a major cause of death. Fertility levels, particularly among educated working women, have begun to decline, but "motherhood" was still reported to be "the essence of woman," and child labor continued to be significant to lower-class household income, a factor that encourages fertility. Public education was vastly underfunded on the primary level; most upper-class and middle-class children went to private schools. The secondary level of education was private and university education was free, essentially providing a subsidy for the elite. The system did not encourage lower-class families to restrict births and educate children for a better life. Future population trends are clearly dependent on changes in fertility, but the social and economic structure was hardly propitious for fertility decline in the near future.

See also **Brazil: The Colonial Era, 1500-1808; Brazil: 1808-1889; Brazil: Since 1889; Slavery: Brazil.**

BIBLIOGRAPHY

For historical studies of colonial and nineteenth-century Brazilian population see John Hemming, *Red Gold:*

The Conquest of the Brazilian Indians (1978), and Herbert Klein, "The Trade in African Slaves to Rio de Janeiro, 1795–1811: Estimates of Mortality and Patterns of Voyages," in *Journal of African History* 10, no. 4 (1969): 533–550. Work on the slave population in the nineteenth century is best represented by Robert Slenes, "The Demography and Economics of Brazilian Slavery: 1850–1888" (Ph.D. diss., Stanford University, 1976). The best and most comprehensive study on Brazilian population since the late nineteenth century is Thomas W. Merrick and Douglas H. Graham, *Population and Economic Development in Brazil, 1800 to the Present* (1979). Other works are Giorgio Mortara, *Contribuição para o estudo de demografia no Brasil* (1970), and Thomas Holloway, "Creating the Reserve Army: The Immigration Program of São Paulo, 1886–1930," in *International Migration Review* 12, no. 2 (Summer 1978): 187–209.

Additional Bibliography

Bergad, Laird W. *Slavery and the Demographic and Economic History of Minas Gerais, Brazil, 1720–1888.* New York: Cambridge University Press, 1999.

Instituto Brasileiro de Geografia e Estatística, Centro de Documentação e Disseminação de Informações. *Brasil, 500 anos de povoamento.* Rio de Janiero: Author, 2000.

Marcilio, Maria Luiza. *Crescimento demográfico e evolução agrária paulista, 1700–1836.* São Paulo: Editora Hucitec, Edusp, 2000.

Oliveira, Maria Coleta. *Demografia da exclusão social: Temas e abordagens.* Campinas, São Paulo: Editora da UNICAMP, 2001.

Pagliaro, Heloísa, Marta Maria Azevedo, and Ricardo Ventura Santos. *Demografia dos povos indígenas no Brasil.* Rio de Janeiro: Editora Fiocruz; and Campinas, Brazil: Associação Brasileira de Estudos Populacionais, 2005.

ELIZABETH ANNE KUZNESOF

SPANISH AMERICA

Over the past thirty thousand years in the region now called Latin America, six great stages in peopling this area can be identified: (1) initial settlement from Asia; (2) emergence of agriculture and urban civilization; (3) the catastrophe of European conquest; (4) stabilization and recovery; (5) the growth of national populations in the nineteenth century; and (6) demographic transition in the twentieth. A seventh, postmodern phase, in which births and deaths are nearly in balance, emerged in Cuba, Uruguay, Argentina, and Chile in the 1980s and is spreading rapidly in urban areas throughout the region. In 1990 the population of a single urban megalopolis, Mexico City, surpassed the population of the whole of Spanish America as recently as 1810 (14 million, with Brazil accounting for an additional one-third). Over the nineteenth century the population of Latin America more than tripled to reach 60 million, then surged an astonishing eightfold, topping 512 million at the end of the twentieth. By 2050 a peak of 800 million will be reached. According to projections of the United Nations, the demographic surge will then subside and stabilize at 700 million before 2100. Figure 1 traces the trajectory of population change for twenty Latin American nations over the twentieth century and projections for a couple of decades beyond.

PRE-COLUMBIAN POPULATIONS

In the first settling, from perhaps 30,000 to as recently as 10,000 years ago, when the last Asian connections disappeared, humans infiltrated from Asia to the Americas via Arctic routes. With as many as a thousand generations in the North of the region but as few as several hundred in the South, nine-tenths of the demographic history of this region is a matter of settlement by fishers and foragers. About 10,000 years ago, overhunting and climatic change led to the extinction of large mammalian species and the beginnings of cultivation. Seed crops date from 9,000 BP (before the present) in south-central Mexico (Tehuacán Valley), preceding root cultures in the Andes by three to four millennia. Around 7,000 BP, pastoralism began in the central Andes with the domestication of the llama. About 3,000 BP, irrigation gradually emerged, followed closely by the appearance of fortified towns and then cities. With the unhurried emergence of agriculture, there occurred an almost imperceptible increase in population growth rates, eventually leading to the emergence of sophisticated urban cultures in Mesoamerica and the Andes. Accelerated growth was facilitated by high fertility with early, universal coupling, counterbalanced by high mortality. More technologically advanced sedentary populations doubled in size as often as once per century, unless checked by climate change, seismic disruptions, famine, war, or administrative decay.

Ironically, the monotonous diets and greater demographic densities of agricultural settlements probably caused life chances to worsen. The great famine of the 1450s in central Mexico is a thoroughly documented example of a prehistoric Malthusian crisis in the Americas. It caused great hardship, including widespread human sacrifice, a sharp rise in slavery, and extreme mortality. According to one native account, fathers "sold their families, their children one by one, for a bit of corn and two tamales, and for the wife, one tamale, and finished by selling themselves." Yet, on the whole, the Native American population balance sheet remained positive as dense settlement improved the chances of mating, thereby boosting fertility. By the year 1500, thickly ensconced populations had emerged in Central Mexico and along a swath in the Andean Highlands. Core cities in these regions, Tenochtitlan and Cuzco, exceeded 100,000 inhabitants. (Some scholars would double or triple these figures.) Meanwhile, on the peripheries—Patagonia, the pampas, densely forested tropical lowlands, and the desert-like plains of northern Mexico—low population densities were the rule.

Although in the popular imagination ancient America is often seen as a paradise, "demographic hell" may be the more accurate characterization. The Mexica (Aztec) pantheon, with its large number of deities devoted to sickness and death, hints at oppressions endured for health's sake. Pre-Columbian skeletal evidence, even from the Inca paradise Machu Picchu, suggests that high population densities and a steady diet of maize, with its severe iron and protein deficiencies, were associated with a multitude of afflictions from worms and parasites to life-threatening dental caries, tuberculosis, porotic hyperostosis (a manifestation of severe iron deficiency anemia), and a syphilis-like treponema (a sexually transmitted spirochete) as well as famine. Among the Aztecs, almost everything edible was eaten, from algae to insects, suggesting a diet that was frugal to an extreme. Short stature and the youthfulness of skeletal samples leave little doubt that mortality was high. Even for the lucky minority surviving to puberty, barely twenty additional years of life remained on the average adolescent's biological clock.

Thus, the riddle of *why* some great civilizations, such as the Maya, disappeared should, according to some bioarchaeologists, be rephrased to ask *how*

they persisted for so long, given the enormous stresses from hard labor and high mortality evident everywhere in the skeletal record. A partial answer is that demographic accounts were kept positive by the Amerindian mode of reproduction. Marriage at puberty was nearly universal, as in much of Asia, but in the Americas reproductive potential was heightened through polygamy, rapid remarriage of widows, and shortened birth intervals (due to weaning around three years of age instead of four, as was common in Ancient Asia and Africa). With few social constraints on fertility, the Amerindian mode of reproduction maximized population growth within an intensely high-pressure demographic regime.

CATASTROPHE OF CONQUEST

Beginning in 1492, demographic catastrophe struck and continued for at least a century, the consequence of conquest, colonization, and disease. The debate over the size of Amerindian populations, the degree of catastrophe, and the precise mix of causes is as lively now as it was in Bartolomé de Las Casas's time almost five centuries ago. Disease explains the catastrophe for many historians, but a compelling new study argues for more nuanced, regionally specific explanations: the primacy of plunder, enslavement, and overwork in the Caribbean; disease, famine, and heavy tributes in Central Mexico; conquest, war, and forced migration in the Andes, and so on. The case of Mexico is illustrative. For Central Mexico, a region of some 200,000 square miles, the maximalists Sherburne F. Cook and Woodrow Borah propose a contact population ranging from 18 to 30 million. (This range honors the cautions and caveats with which Cook and Borah report their results, although their point estimate of 25.2 million is now an academic talisman for many.) Maximalists register the catastrophe at 90 to 97 percent over wide areas, with extinction in tropical lowlands and throughout much of the Caribbean. Minimalists, such as Angel Rosenblat, favor a figure of 4.5 million for Central Mexico in 1519 and a demographic collapse of "only" 20 percent.

Both schools agree that a demographic catastrophe occurred and identify the principal causes as the "normalcy of conquest" (Livi-Bacci, 2007)—war, overwork, forced resettlement, exploitation, and ecological disruption—as well as the appearance of

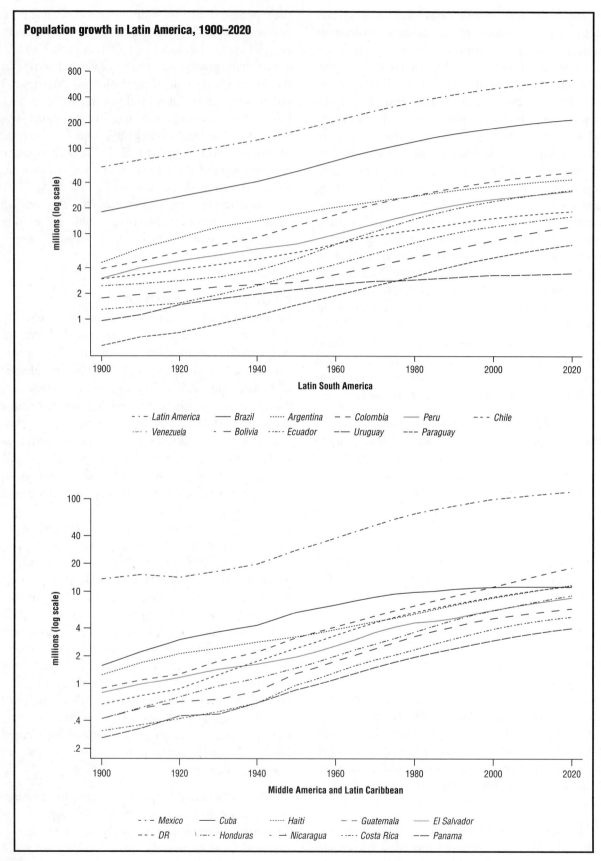

Figure 1

extra-hemispheric diseases, particularly smallpox, measles, influenza, and, later, malaria and yellow fever. Virgin-soil epidemics were severe, although not because of some supposed genetic inferiority. There is no convincing evidence that Europeans ever acquired genetic advantages against any of the crowd diseases exported to the Americas. Mortality differences were matters of first, morbidity—in Europe measles, smallpox, and the like were limited to children—and second, care—in Europe mothers and fathers, having acquired immunities in childhood, were the caregivers, readily providing water, food, and succor to infected children. In the Americas, as native chroniclers testify, when contagious disease struck for the first time, almost the entire population became ill. With everyone ailing all at once there was no one to provide food, water, shelter, or the will to live. As the intervals between outbreaks shortened, death rates soared uncontrollably at irregular, but increasingly shorter, intervals. Nevertheless, diseasologists easily exaggerate the frequency and devastation of disease, particularly for large areas.

STABILIZATION AND RECOVERY

The fourth phase, demographic recovery, began for densely settled Amerindians about a century after sustained contact with Europeans. The process consisted of renewed reproductive vitality, cultural amalgamation, and *mestizaje*, the mixing of races and ethnicities, including Europeans, Africans, and even Asians, as well as the first Americans.

Through more than three centuries of Spanish rule, there were Christian protectors of the Indians, who strove mightily to shield converts from secular corruption and unremitting toil. But Indian survival and demographic recovery had more to do with economics or ecology than theology. Indeed, missions often proved to be deathtraps, notwithstanding the charitable motives of the missionaries. Unless wholly isolated from European colonialists, such as the Jesuit-run Guarní settlements in Paraguay, most missions were demographically unsustainable without continued infusions of fresh conscripts from outside. It was precisely the concentration of scattered native populations into missions that doomed them to extinction. Yet, in remote Amazonian rain forests and the seemingly hostile highlands of Patagonia or Mexico's Sierra Madre Occidental, many Amerindian groups—the Mapuche, Aymara, Lacandón,

Tarahumara, and others—recovered their numbers in two, three, or four centuries, as they clung to their languages and cultures.

In densely settled regions, material benefits of Spanish colonization aided recovery. *Relaciones geográficas* from the 1570s and 1580s (surveys of 44 questions authored by Spanish royal cosmographer Juan López de Velasco distributed throughout the Spanish controlled portions of the Americas as part of a larger effort to extensively map the region) testify to the austerity of pre-Conquest life and the greater abundance and ease that ensued for commoners because of the availability of new plants and animals. Nevertheless, until well beyond the end of Spanish colonial rule, famine, epidemics, and political strife caused annual death rates to double or even quadruple, killing from 10 to 25 percent of the population during the worst years. Wherever indigenous languages and cultural traits survived, pre-contact Amerindian family patterns thrived in the form of early, universal coupling, moderate birth intervals (30–36 months), and timely remarriage.

Tracking the evolution of Amerindian population size is an unending guessing game, confounded by the lack of reliable censuses and by the fact that identities, whether racial or ethnic, are sociopolitical constructs. Rosenblat estimates that in 1825 cultural Amerindians numbered some 9 million, or from one-half to two-thirds of the total population of Spanish America. By 1950 their numbers rose to 15 million, yet their growth rate was only a fraction of that for non-Indians. By 2000, Amerindians had increased to some 30 million, concentrated in the Andean and Mesoamerican highlands, but they amounted to slightly less than 9 percent of a total Spanish American population exceeding 330 million. Secular education in the twentieth century proved to be as great a threat to Amerindian populations as virgin-soil epidemics in the sixteenth.

Demographic recovery, then, was the result both of an increasingly positive population balance sheet for Native Americans and the transformation of peoples through acculturation, immigration, and racial mixing. One historian has called the Conquest a conquest of women. In colonial times, Spanish immigration to the Americas scarcely averaged 3,000-4,000 annually, with Spanish males outnumbering females five or ten to one. This enormous gender squeeze meant that if Spaniards were to reproduce, a great deal of ethnic mixing was necessary. Immense inequalities in wealth, privilege, and power fueled sexual conquest. Concubinage, widely practiced for a century or more after first contact, had its defenders, as suggested by the well-known refrain "mejor estar bien amancebado que mal casado" (better to be well fixed with a concubine than badly married). While this heretical utterance excited the wrath of the Inquisition, the practice of rampant violations of the marital sacrament was universally ignored. Half of all children in Hispanic towns and cities were illegitimate or abandoned, according to Catholic baptismal registers. To the solitary woman—orphaned, single, widowed, or simply abandoned—urban places offered refuge, sustenance, and shelter, if not honor. They were simmering cauldrons of ethnic mixing and racial passing where women always greatly outnumbered adult men. In the countryside, *mestizaje* and migration were almost as frequent as in the cities. Microscopic studies of rural spaces—villages, hamlets, haciendas, ranchos, and mines—reveal a vast transiency, geographic as well as social. Thus, from a base of several hundred thousand immigrants from the Iberian Peninsula over three centuries, the "Spanish kind of people" (*de calidad español*) amounted to several million by the beginning of the nineteenth century, one-fifth to one-third of the total population in the most densely settled regions of Spanish America.

Africans played a significant role in the peopling of the hemisphere, although African slavery in continental Spanish America was less important demographically than in Brazil. Of some 10 million slaves entering the Atlantic traffic over almost four centuries, roughly one in six was destined for a Spanish port, primarily for Cuba. The demographic viability of black populations was weakened by unbalanced sex ratios. Whether this was due to conditions of supply in Africa or demand in the Americas remains something of a puzzle. But the biggest threat to Africans in America was plantation and mining slavery, not unbalanced sex ratios (which often were more nearly in balance for blacks than for whites). Slavery in Latin America was doomed by a

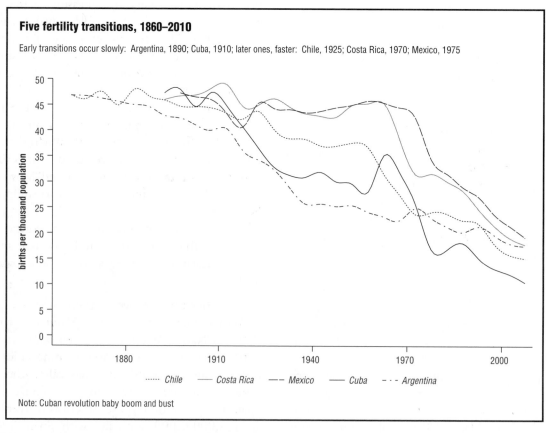

Five fertility transitions, 1860–2010

Early transitions occur slowly: Argentina, 1890; Cuba, 1910; later ones, faster: Chile, 1925; Costa Rica, 1970; Mexico, 1975

births per thousand population

······ Chile   —— Costa Rica   – – Mexico   —— Cuba   - - - Argentina

Note: Cuban revolution baby boom and bust

Figure 2

slaveholders' demographic regime that generally favored buying over "breeding." The new social history emphasizes that even under plantation slavery African family life thrived. Yet the life cycle of individual African American families faced a triple threat, from the mortality of slaveholders as well as the excess mortality of adult slaves and their children. For blacks as well as Indians, *mestizaje* offered something of an escape hatch: liberation both from slavery and from an oppressive demographic system. Ironically, the greatest threats to African identities and demography came with political independence, the destruction of slavery, and the abolition of laws underpinning the *sistema de castas*. Beyond the regions of plantation agriculture and the coastal lowlands, Spanish-speaking blacks became amalgamated into the broader population.

GROWTH OF NATIONAL POPULATIONS

The fifth phase of demographic change, the long nineteenth century, began with independence movements in 1808 and ended in 1929 with the onset of the Great Depression. During this period demographic growth rates accelerated with early improvements in education, sanitation, and food supply. At the same time population patterns grew ever more diverse as Spanish America fragmented into nation states. Yet, there ruled almost everywhere a single demographic ideology of growth—pronatalist and pro-immigration. The slogan *gobernar es poblar* (to govern is to populate), coined in 1853 by the Argentine political theorist Juan Bautista Alberdi, retained its appeal into the 1970s. Between 1880 and 1935, more than 5 million European immigrants flocked to Spanish America, mainly to Argentina (3.4 million), Uruguay (600,000), and after independence in 1898, to Cuba (800,000). In these countries immigrants and their children accounted for half or more of the total demographic growth during this period. Everywhere ruling elites decried the shortage of labor. But immigrants could be enticed only to places where prevailing wages were higher than in their homelands—unless, as in the case of Asians to Peru (87,000) and Cuba (132,000), they were shanghaied through ill-conceived forms of slavery. Thus barely a trickle of immigrants reached Mexico, Central America, the Andean republics, or even Chile. The overwhelming predominance of male immigrants ensured their rapid amalgamation, even where they constituted almost a majority of the population, as in Buenos Aires and Montevideo.

The native rural poor were rarely offered enticements to settle new areas, but their rates of growth probably accelerated after independence, thanks to improvements in mortality. Life expectancy at birth, which as late as 1850 averaged only twenty-five years (colonial estimates are too few for comparison), rose gradually to thirty-four years by 1930. While improvements were greatest where public education and health measures advanced most rapidly, as in Costa Rica, Chile, Cuba, Argentina, and Uruguay, rates of natural increase probably quickened for all of Spanish America. The gradual replacement of the Amerindian mode of reproduction by a mestizo pattern delayed by a year or two the onset of procreation (whether within a legal marriage or an informal union), but fertility remained high and uncontrolled. From age twenty-five to menopause the mestizo pattern matched the "natural" historical fertility of peasant women in France and England. (There are no reliable figures for early modern Spain.) What is remarkable about the mestizo pattern of reproduction is the higher fertility rates at early ages (fifteen to twenty-four) and the much larger fraction of young girls entering unions at those ages than for western European populations. Under such conditions, a total fertility rate of eight children was the norm, which provided enormous demographic momentum to Latin America.

DEMOGRAPHIC TRANSITIONS

The sixth turning point in the peopling of the region occurred after 1930, when the modern demographic transition pushed death rates to unprecedentedly low levels and, after some delay, birth rates as well. From 1930 to 1960, life expectancy at birth improved by twenty-two years—a remarkable achievement—followed by an additional fifteen years from 1960 to 2000. At the beginning of the twentieth century, only three countries had life expectancies greater than thirty-five years (Argentina, Uruguay, and perhaps Panama). By 1935 the list had grown to nine, as conditions improved in Chile, Costa Rica, Colombia, Cuba, and Mexico. At mid-century only Haiti remained below this threshold. By 2000 the mean for all of Latin America was 72.2 years. Only Haiti and Bolivia lagged with life expectancies at birth less than sixty-five years, while the figure exceeded seventy-four years for eight countries: Argentina, Chile, Costa Rica, Cuba, Ecuador, Mexico, Panama, and Uruguay.

The causes of these improvements are well known, although the importance of factors varied over time. In the first phase (before 1930), improved nutrition, public education, and sanitation were most salient. In the middle phase (1930-1960), medicine and medical technology effects were most closely associated with improving life expectancy. In recent decades, socioeconomic conditions have become increasingly critical. In addition to inequalities of dying by ethnicity and class are those of age and gender. The mortality transition in Latin America has been kinder to females and the young than to males and the elderly.

The enormous demographic growth that occurred in the twentieth century is highlighted in Figure 1. The graph also reveals the great national diversity in the timing of transitions. The fact that the population lines in this graph are not parallel shows how different growth rates were in the various countries. In the 1950s, the region's rate of natural increase stood at 2.8 percent, the highest in the world. To the experts, it seemed that birth rates might never fall, but the decline was already underway in several countries, although hidden by persisting high rates in others. The fertility transition in Spanish America began before 1900 in Argentina and Uruguay, then continued decades later in Cuba, Puerto Rico, Chile, and Costa Rica, and even more recently in Colombia, Venezuela, Mexico, Peru, and Paraguay. Beginning in 1960, birth rates for Latin America as a whole fell by almost one-half in a generation, from 41 to 21 per thousand population. No coun-try registered a rate as high as 31, whereas four decades earlier, only two countries—Argentina and Uruguay—had rates lower than 35. The total fertility rate, which declined from six children in 1960 to 2.5 in 2000, is expected to reach replacement level (2.0) in 2020. This is an amazing transformation.

Figure 2 illustrates three distinct patterns of fertility transition in Latin America: early (Argentina), intermediate (Cuba, Chile), and late (Costa Rica, Mexico). For the first, decline was slow and gradual, beginning almost a century ago in countries with higher educational standards and large contingents of European immigrants. In Argentina, the crude birth rate fell from 45 births per thousand population in 1880 to less than 30 in 1930, when average completed family size dropped below 3.0 children.

In Chile and Cuba, decline can also be traced to the nineteenth century, but the descent was interrupted in 1930 and did not resume until the 1960s. The most common pattern of fertility transition in Latin America was the third, in which crude birth rates remained high to 1960 (exceeding 40 births per thousand population), then fell swiftly to the mid-20s, a twenty-point drop in less than three decades. At the beginning of the twentieth century, the crude birth rate was above 40 in every nation except Argentina. In 1980 the region-wide average stood at 30 and continued its decline to 20 in 2005.

Spanish American fertility is also responsive to short-term conditions as illustrated in Figure 2. The sharp plunge in Mexican birth rates during the civil war (1910–1920) is not surprising; but it is unexpected that, as strikingly revealed by the graph, birth curves in the past were not simply high and flat. Once again, instead of parallel lines, the historical fertility record shows a surprising degree of fluctuation and change.

POSTMODERN TRENDS

The future course of Spanish America may be foreshadowed by the Cuban experience of a baby boom in the first years after the 1959 revolution followed by a baby bust as conditions worsened in the 1970s and 1980s. Fertility in Spanish America is responsive to economic and social conditions. Deteriorating conditions as well as changing ideas about what constitutes the ideal family may lead to even more dramatic shifts in fertility and growth rates. The postmodern mode of reproduction in Europe, with its very late age at marriage (or union) and extremely low fertility, pushes reproduction rates at or below replacement levels. If Spanish America is to follow the path of Cuba, Europe, and especially Spain (whose intrinsic growth rate is among the lowest in the world)—or, more likely, simply escape the Malthusian threat of rising death rates—fertility must continue its downward course. If so, by the middle of the century, the Latin America will stabilize at approximately three-quarters of a billion people, more than ten times the total in 1900. In the twenty-first century the cities, the customary escape valves for "excess" (rural) population, no longer suffice for the enormous volume of migrants.

Political strife and economic stagflation, along with the allures of affluence elsewhere, are generating a floodtide of emigration, washing away national borders and crossing continental barriers into North America and western Europe.

See also **Cities and Urbanization; Diseases; Indigenous Peoples; Medicine: The Modern Era; Public Health.**

BIBLIOGRAPHY

Arrom, Silvia Marina. *The Women of Mexico City, 1790-1857.* Stanford, CA: Stanford University Press, 1985.

Centro Latinoamericano y Caribeño de Demografía. "Total Population of the Region by Countries, 1970-2050." Available from http://www.eclac.cl/celade/proyecciones/htm/LATpobTO.html.

Cook, Noble David. *Born to Die: Disease and New World Conquest, 1492-1650.* Cambridge, U.K., and New York: Cambridge University Press 1998.

Denevan, William M., ed. *The Native Population of the Americas in 1492,* 2nd edition. Madison: University of Wisconsin Press, 1992.

Guzmán, José Miguel, Jorge Rodríguez, Jorge Martínez, et al. "The Demography of Latin America and the Caribbean since 1950." *Population* (English ed.) 61 (2006): 519-576.

Hackel, Steven W. *Children of Coyote, Missionaries of Saint Francis: Indian-Spanish Relations in Colonial California, 1769-1850.* Chapel Hill: Omohundro Institute of Early American History and Culture, University of North Carolina Press, 2005.

Haines, Michael R., and Richard H. Steckel, eds. *A Population History of North America.* Cambridge, U.K., and New York: Cambridge University Press, 2000.

Livi-Bacci, Massimo. *Conquest: The Destruction of the American Indios.* Cambridge, U.K.: Polity Press, 2007.

McCaa, Robert. *Marriage and Fertility in Chile: Demographic Turning Points in the Petorca Valley, 1840-1976.* Boulder, CO: Westview Press, 1983.

McCaa, Robert. "Revisioning Smallpox in Mexico Tenochtitlán, 1520-1950: What Difference Did Charity, Quarantine, Inoculation and Vaccination Make?" In *"Vivere in Citta / Living in the City," Poverty, Charity and the City,* ed. Eugenio Sonnino. Rome: University of Rome, 2004.

Minnesota Population Center. IPUMS-Latin America, 2004. Available from http://international.ipums.org.

Nugent, Walter. *Crossings: The Great Transatlantic Migrations, 1870-1914.* Bloomington: Indiana University Press, 1992.

Rabell Romero, Cecilia Andrea. *La población novohispana a la luz de los registros parroquiales.* Mexico: Instituto de Investigaciones Sociales, Universidad Nacional Autónoma de México, 1990.

Sánchez Albornoz, Nicolás. *The Population of Latin America: A History,* trans. W. A. R. Richardson. Berkeley: University of California Press, 1974; rev. Spanish ed., 1994.

Steckel, Richard H., and Jerome C. Rose, eds. *The Backbone of History: Health and Nutrition in the Western Hemisphere.* Cambridge, U.K., and New York: Cambridge University Press, 2002.

Storey, Rebecca. *Life & Death in the Ancient City of Teotihuacan: A Modern Paleodemographic Synthesis.* Tuscaloosa: University of Alabama Press, 1992.

Verano, John W., and Douglas H. Ubelaker, eds. *Disease and Demography in the Americas.* Washington, DC: Smithsonian Institution Press, 1992.

ROBERT MCCAA

POQOMAM. Poqomam (Pocomam/Pokomam), one of the twenty-nine extant Mayan languages of Guatemala, Mexico, Belize, and Honduras. It is spoken in Guatemala in scattered areas from the city of Guatemala eastward and southward, principally in the townships of Mixco and Chinautla in the department of Guatemala, in Palín in the department of Escuintla, and in San Luís Jilotepeque in Jalapa. There may still be some speakers in San Pedro Pinula and San Carlos Alzatate in Jalapa. Poqomam belongs to the K'ichean (Quichean) branch of the Eastern Division of Mayan languages and is most closely related to Poqomchi' (Pocomchí/Pokomchí), spoken in Baja Verapaz, Alta Verapaz, and El Quiché.

At the time of European contact, Poqomam and Poqomchi' were at most separate dialects of the same language. With about 30,000 speakers, Poqomam is by no means the smallest of the Mayan languages, but it has suffered considerable loss and is in danger of extinction. It once was spoken in a much larger territory in the east of Guatemala; the Poqomam-speaking population is shrinking in townships where it still exists. There are few monolingual speakers of Poqomam. The Poqom subgroup of K'ichean languages separated from them about 2,600 years ago.

See also **Maya, The.**

BIBLIOGRAPHY

Additional Bibliography

Feldman, Lawrence H. *A Dictionary of Poqom Maya in the Colonial Era*. Lancaster, CA: Labyrinthos, 2004.

McArthur, Carolina de, and Ricardo McArthur. *Diccionario pocomam y español*. Guatemala: Instituto Lingüístico de Verano de Centroamérica, 1995.

NORA C. ENGLAND

PORFIRIATO. Porfiriato, a term used to designate the period of Porfirio Díaz's presidency. Díaz came to power in 1876 but was succeeded by Manuel González (1880–1884). The Porfiriato refers generally to the period from 1876 until his fall in 1911, but especially to the successive administrations from 1884 to 1911. It has come to symbolize the dominance of a single, strong figure, political order and stability, centralized authority, a period during which Mexico achieved considerable (but badly distributed) economic growth, and an era of serious social ills, ranging from child labor to peasant indebtedness and exploitation. The Porfiriato sums up those ills—social, economic, and political—that produced the 1910 Revolution.

See also **Díaz, Porfirio; Mexico, Wars and Revolutions: Mexican Revolution.**

BIBLIOGRAPHY

Daniel Cosío Villegas, *Historia moderna de México*, 8 vols. (1955–1972).

Thomas Benjamin and Marcial Ocasio- Meléndez, "Organizing the Memory of Modern Mexico: Porfirian Historiography in Perspective, 1880s–1890s," in *Hispanic American Historical Review* 64 (1984): 323–364.

Additional Bibliography

Tenorio Trillo, Mauricio, and Aurora Gómez Galvarriato. *El porfiriato*. México, D.F.: Fondo de Cultura Económica, 2006.

RODERIC AI CAMP

PORRAS, BELISARIO (1856–1942). Belisario Porras (*b.* 1856; *d.* 1942), Panamanian politician and three-time president (1912–1916, 1918– 1920, 1920–1924). One of the most popular figures in Panama's history, Porras was born in Las Tablas. He headed the Liberal revolution in 1901, but he opposed Panamanian independence in 1903 under U.S. auspices, fearing that Panama would become a colony of the United States. As a result, he was stripped of his citizenship for one year (15 November 1905–13 September 1906).

He remained in Panama City for a while, but as his enemies made his life more and more difficult, he moved to Colón and later to his ranch in his native Las Tablas, where he remained until his rights were reinstated. He was first elected president in 1912. In 1918, with the death of his successor, Ramón Maximiliano Valdés, Porras, as first vice president, assumed the presidency once again to finish Valdés's term amid charges of fraud. The United States intervened to maintain order. In 1920 he was elected to another term.

Porras was a populist leader with both an urban and a rural following. He maintained his leadership through the system of *compadrazgo*. It was believed that he had as many as 757 *compadres* throughout the country.

Porras helped to build modern Panama. He organized a civil registry, the national archives, and the national bank; built the Chiriquí Railroad; and nationalized the lottery. On 6 November 1913, Porras had organized a national commission for the drafting of a Panamanian legal code. Prior to his election, the country was still governed by Colombian law. The commission included people like Carlos Antonio Mendoza, Harmodio Arias, and Ricardo J. Alfaro. Its work was completed in 1916 when by Law 1 of 22 August 1916, the Administrative Code was approved. Law 2 of 22 August 1917 approved the penal, commercial, mining, civil, and judicial codes.

See also **Panama; Panama Railroad.**

BIBLIOGRAPHY

Manuel Octavio Sisnet, *Belisario Porras o la vocación de la nacionalidad* (1972).

Additional Bibliography

Araúz, Celestino Andrés. *Belisario Porras y las relaciones de Panamá con los Estados Unidos*. Panama: Editorial Portobelo, 1998.

Conte Porras, J., and Belisario Porras. *Belisario Porras: Pensamiento y acción*. Panama: Fundación Belisario Porras, 1996.

JUAN MANUEL PÉREZ

PORRAS, DIEGO (1677–1741).

Diego Porras (also Porres; *b.* 19 November 1677; *d.* 25 September 1741), Guatemalan architect. The most important architect in the kingdom of Guatemala during the first half of the eighteenth century, Porras won renown for designing and building the monastery and church of the Escuela de Cristo, the Santa Clara convent and church, the Archbishop's Palace, the Royal Mint, the San Alejo Hospital, and the City Hall, all monuments in Antigua, Guatemala. He helped design the following churches: Los Remedios, San Agustín, the Cathedral, la Recolección, Santa Teresa, and la Compañía de Jesús in Antigua, and the well-known church of Esquipulas, the Church of Concepción in Ciudad Vieja, and the churches in Patzicía and Escuintla.

Porras also was in charge of hydraulic engineering and planning. Under his direction, water was brought to the towns of San Bernardino Patzún and to San Juan Comalapa. He was the architect for the famous siren fountain in the central plaza in Antigua. In addition, he is credited with being the first architect in Guatemala to use the serliana balustered pilaster.

See also **Architecture: Architecture to 1900.**

BIBLIOGRAPHY

José A. Mobil, *100 personajes históricos de Guatemala* (1979), pp. 72–74.

Luis Luján Muñoz, *El arquitecto mayor Diego de Porres 1677–1741* (1982).

Elizabeth Bell and Trevor Long, *Antigua Guatemala* (1991), pp. 93–94.

Additional Bibliography

Luján Muñoz, Luis. *Diego de Porres*. Guatemala: Consejo Nacional para la Protección de La Antigua Guatemala, 2001.

Luján Muñoz, Luis. *Síntesis biográfica del Maestro Mayor de Arquitectura Diego de Porres: 1741–1991*. Guatemala: Consejo Nacional para la Protección de la Antigua Guatemala, 1990.

JANE EDDY SWEZEY

PORRAS, JOSÉ BASILIO (1794–1861).

José Basilio Porras (*b.* 14 June 1794; *d.* 9 November 1861), Guatemalan politician. Born in Guatemala City, Porras was the illegitimate son of Micaela Porras, from a notable creole family, and Mario Álvarez de las Asturias y Arroyve. A prosperous indigo merchant and owner of a printing business, he also rose to the rank of colonel in the army. Porras was a leading proponent of independence from Spain in 1821, and he thereafter served in both federal and state legislatures and in several other government positions, and briefly as minister of war in 1848–1849. Although a liberal ideologically, he served both liberal and conservative governments until 1849, when he retired from public life. Unlike many liberal politicians, Porras remained in Guatemala throughout the Carrera dictatorship.

See also **Guatemala.**

BIBLIOGRAPHY

Carlos C. Haeussler Yela, *Diccionario general de Guatemala*, vol. 3 (1983), pp. 1264–1273.

Additional Bibliography

Woodward, Ralph Lee. *Rafael Carrera y la creación de la República de Guatemala, 1821–1871*. La Antigua, Guatemala: Centro de Investigaciones Regionales de Mesoamérica, 2002.

RALPH LEE WOODWARD JR.

PORRAS BARRENECHEA, RAÚL

(1897–1960). Raúl Porras Barrenechea was an important historian of colonial Peru, a literary critic, and a diplomat. Born in Pisco on March 23, 1897, Porras studied at the University of San Marcos, earning a law degree in 1922 and a doctorate in 1928. He was one of the leaders of the Student University Reform Movement (1919). From 1922 to 1926 he was librarian at the Ministry of Foreign Relations. Interested in Peru's boundary disputes with Bolivia, he published many documents in defense of his nation's claims.

As a historian Porras focused his attention on the primary accounts of the early Andean world, the chroniclers, the biography of Francisco Pizarro, the Quechua legacy, the era of the Spanish conquest, and liberalism in the early republic. In 1945 his *Los cronistas del Perú* won the Inca Garcilaso de la Vega Prize for history, and it has since been used by generations of Peruvianists.

Porras was elected senator in 1956 and had a distinguished diplomatic career in Europe, serving as Peru's representative to the League of Nations (1936–1938), its ambassador to Spain (1948–1949), and its foreign minister (1958–1960). On August 18, 1960, he gave a memorable speech to the Organization of American States against the U.S. blockade of Cuba. Porras died a little more than month later, on September 27.

A research institute at the University of San Marcos honors Porras's name. His most important writings include *Historia de los límites del Perú* (1926); *El Congreso de Panamá, 1826* (1930); *El testamento de Pizarro* (1936); *Las relaciones primitivas de la conquista del Perú* (1937); *Cedulario del Perú (1529–1534)*, (2 vols., 1944 and 1948); *El Inca Garcilaso de la Vega (1539–1616)* (1946); *Crónicas perdidas, presuntas y olvidadas sobre la conquista del Perú* (1951); *Fuentes históricas peruanas* (1954); *El Inca Garcilaso en Montilla (1561–1614)* (1955); and *Cartas del Perú (1524–1543)* (1959).

See also **Liberalism; Pizarro, Francisco; Quechua; Spanish Empire.**

BIBLIOGRAPHY

Primary Work

Los cronistas del Perú (1528– 1650) y otros ensayos. Edited by Franklin Pease G.Y. Lima: Banco de Crédito del Perú: Ministerio de Educación, 1986.

Secondary Works

Homenaje a Raúl Porras Barrenechea. Lima: Universidad Nacional Mayor de San Marcos, 1984.

López y Sebastián, Lorenzo Eladio. "Raúl Porras Barrenechea en el centenario de su nacimiento." *Revista Complutense de Historia de América* 23 (1997): 303–309.

NOBLE DAVID COOK
KENDALL W. BROWN

PORRES, MARTÍN DE (1579–1639).

Martín De Porres (*b.* 9 December 1579; *d.* 3 November 1639), Peruvian saint. Porres was the son of a union between Juan de Porres, knight of the Order of Calatrava, and Ana Velázquez, his black servant from Panama. At first the father failed to recognize his son or daughter Juana. He did so later, and took Martín to Guayaquil to be educated. When Juan de Porres was named governor of Panama, he returned with his children to Lima to get orders from the viceroy. There, the young Martín was confirmed by Archbishop Alfonso de Toribio de Mogrovejo. Juan de Porres left the boy in the care of his mother when he traveled to Panama to assume office.

Apprenticed to a surgeon at the age of twelve, Martín learned the basics of healing. He worked in the store of Mateo Pastor, who sold spices and medicinal herbs, and served the barber-bleeder Marcelo Rivero. Entering the Dominican convent in Lima at age fifteen as lay helper, he professed as a lay brother of the Dominican order on 2 June 1603. He experienced visions and ecstasies, did penance, and at the same time achieved renown for his healing powers and ability to control animals. Moreover, he gained fame for charity and humility. According to one observer, there was "a flood of beggars always awaiting him at the entrance of the convent."

Martín's funeral was attended by a mass of people; the archbishop and viceroy carried his bier. In 1668 there began a long apostolic process that would ultimately lead to canonization. In 1763 his virtues were declared "heroic." He was beatified in 1837, and finally, on 6 May 1962, Pope John XXIII canonized him. The popular festival of San Martín de Porres is celebrated on 3 November.

See also **Dominicans; Rosa de Lima.**

BIBLIOGRAPHY

Giuliana Cavallini, *St. Martín de Porres: Apostle of Charity* (1963).

Additional Bibliography

Forcada Comíns, Vicente. *San Martín de Porres: Martír de la caridad.* Burgos: Monte Carmelo, 2002.

NOBLE DAVID COOK

PORTAL, MAGDA (1900–1989).

Born in Lima, Peru, on May 27, 1900, Magda Portal was a poet who won the Floral Games in poetry convened by the National State University of San Marcos in

Lima in 1923. She was known as a political militant and cofounder of the American Popular Revolutionary Party (Alianza Popular Revolucionaria Americana, or APRA) in 1924 with Raúl Haya de la Torre, and of the Apra Party of Peru (1928).

Through her actions and writings she opposed the dictatorial pro-oligarchic governments of her time. She was deported and jailed. She denounced the conditions that resulted from the colonization of nations on the American continent and supported radical changes in the nations' politics and economies. She debated the socialist ideology of José Carlos Mariátegui. To both writers, the revolution represented a commitment to the creation of a new society that would not only improve the standard of living of Peru's poor but would also enable them to experience intellectual growth through the arts and sciences and allow their spiritual development. In 1948 she resigned from the Apra Party because it would not allow women to be executive members.

Portal promoted literature as an aesthetic practice with social and intellectual functions, and her work spanned several genres. Her poetry includes *Ánima absorta* (1925), *Vidrios de amor* (1925), *Una esperanza y el mar* (1927), *Costa Sur* (1945), and *Constancia del ser* (1965). Nonfiction works include the essays *El nuevo poema i su orientación hacia una estética económica* (1928), *Frente al imperialismo y defensa de la Revolución Mexicana* (1931), *Hacia la mujer nueva* (1933), *Flora Tristán, la precursora* (1946), and *La mujer en el Partido del Pueblo* (1948). She also wrote fiction: the short story collection *El derecho de matar* (1925), and one novel, *La trampa* (1956) In her poem "Palabras a Micaela Bástidas " (in *Constanccia del ser*, 1965, pp. 200–203), Portal portrays the prototype of "the new woman," an "immortal warrior" who plays a historical role in the name of liberty. For her conviction in the power of letters, Mexico named her Writer of the Americas in 1981. She died on July 11, 1989.

See also **Literature: Spanish America; Mariátegui, José Carlos; Peru, Political Parties: Overview; Peru, Political Parties: Peruvian Aprista Party (PAP/ APRA).**

BIBLIOGRAPHY

Andradi, Esther, and Ana María Portugal, eds. *Ser mujer en el Perú*. Lima: Ediciones Mujer y Autonomía (1978): 209–232.

Arrington, Melvin S., Jr. "Magda Portal: Vanguard Critic." In *Reinterpreting the Spanish American Essay: Women Writers of the 19th and 20th Centuries*, edited by Doris Meyer, pp. 148–156. Austin: University of Texas Press, 1995.

Bermúdez Gallegos, Marta. "Magda Portal, la eterna rebelde." In *Las desobedientes*, edited and introduced by Betty Osorio de Negret and María Mercedes Jaramillo, pp. 298–308. Bogota: Panamericana Editorial, 1997.

Bustamante, Cecilia. "Magda Portal y sus poderes." *Ciberayllu*, November 16, 2003. Available from http://www.andes.-missouri.edu/andes/Cronicas/CB_ MagdaPortal.htm.

Castañeda Vielakamen, Esther. *El vanguardismo literario en el Perú: Estudio y selección de la revista Flechas (1924)*. La Victoria, Peru: Amaru Editores, 1989.

Forgues, Roland. "Magda Portal: Nací para luchar." In *Palabra Viva Las Poetas se Desnudan*, pp. 51–62. Lima: El Quijote, (1991).

Grünfeld, Mihai. "Voces femeninas de la vanguardia: El compromiso de Magda Portal." *Revista de Crítica Literaria Latinoamericana* 51 (2000): 67–82.

Guardia, Sara Beatriz. *Mujeres peruanas: El otro lado de la historia*. Lima: Mineva, 2002.

Mariátegui, José Carlos. "Magda Portal." *7 Ensayos de interpretación de la realidad peruana*. Lima: Biblioteca Amauta, 1928.

Reedy, Daniel R. *Magda Portal: La pasionaria peruana; Biografía intelectual*. Lima: Ediciones Flora Tristán, 2000.

Rojas Benavente, Lady. "Mujeres y movimientos sociales en América Latina: Ángela Ramos and Magda Portal, escritoras políticas de pie en la historia del Perú." Available from http://www.flora.org.pe/DEBATE.htm.

Santisteban, Rocío Silva. "Cuidado zona de deslizamientos: La cuestión de la estética y el poder en la recepción de los debates sobre 'literatura femenina' en el Perú." In *Repensando la violencia y el patriarcado frente al nuevo milenio: Nuevas perspectivas en el mundo hispánico y germánico*, edited by Fernando de Diego and Ágata Schwartz, pp. 219–242. Ottawa, ON: University of Ottawa, 2002.

Smith, Myriam. "Re-Thinking the Vanguardia: The Poetry and Politics of Magda Portal." PhD diss., University of California, Santa Barbara, 2001.

Unruh, Vicky. "Las rearticulaciones inesperadas de las intelectuales de Amauta: Magda Portal and María Wiesse." In *Narrativa femenina en América Latina: Prácticas y perspectivas teóricas* [Latin American women's narrative: Practices and theoretical perspectives], edited by Sara Castro-Klarén, 93–110. Princeton, NJ: M. Wiener, 2003.

Weaver, Kathleen. "Magda Portal: Translation-in-Progress." *Translation Review* 32–33 (1990): 41–43.

LADY ROJAS BENAVENTE

PORTALES PALAZUELOS, DIEGO JOSÉ PEDRO VÍCTOR (1793–1837).

Diego José Pedro Víctor Portales Palazuelos (*b.* 15 June 1793; *d.* 6 June 1837), Chilean political leader and architect of his nation's political stability. Portales was one of more than twenty-three children of a Spanish colonial official who directed the mint. Originally destined for the church, he switched to more secular pursuits. A graduate of the University of San Felipe, he abandoned the study of law to become an assayer in the mint.

Both of Portales's parents participated in the struggle for independence and suffered for their political beliefs: His father was exiled to the Pacific island of Juan Fernández and his mother incarcerated. In 1819, Portales married his first cousin, Josefa Portales y Larraín, who died two years later. Her death, as well as that of his infant son, deeply affected Portales, who went through a religious crisis, vowing never to marry again. Although Portales's religious fervor subsequently subsided, he never did remarry. Still, while he eschewed matrimony, it is clear that he did not lead a celibate life.

After these events, Portales moved to Peru, where in 1821 and 1822 he established a business in partnership with José Manuel Cea. This experience apparently was pivotal in shaping Portales's political philosophy. Peru's political environment became so chaotic that Portales had to close his business, at great personal cost. In 1824 he returned to Chile, where he and Cea purchased from the government a concession giving them the exclusive right to sell tobacco, playing cards, and liquor. However, the same problems that had plagued Portales in Peru dogged his footsteps in Chile: Domestic violence made it impossible for him to make a profit from his government concession. For a second time, political turmoil cost Portales his investment.

Portales concluded that because Latin America's citizens lacked the requisite civic culture or education, its countries could not function under democracy. He felt that years would pass before the Latin nations would be ready for this form of government. Not surprisingly, Portales concluded that Chile desperately needed internal order if it were to survive and prosper. Hence, he became involved in a political bloc called the *estanqueros*, which advocated the creation of a strong central government that would guarantee property rights and restore domestic stability. Portales allied himself with the Conservatives, who defeated the Liberal forces at the 1830 battle of Lircay. This victory provided Portales with the opportunity to implement his ideas.

Portales feared and loathed the prospect of political instability. Consequently, he worked strenuously to ensure that the government possessed the necessary political powers. He backed the 1833 Constitution, which virtually delivered control of the nation's political system to the oligarchy. Moreover, he moved to eradicate his political opposition, depriving the supporters of Bernardo O'Higgins and the old Liberals of their power and, in some cases, their lives. Portales also purged the army of any officers who might possibly threaten the government, founded a military academy to train professional—and, hopefully, apolitical—subalterns, and created a national guard, which could, in an emergency, subdue military conspirators. Although he was not religious, he gave the Catholic Church a privileged position, even requiring government officials to attend mass in return for the Church's support of his regime.

Portales struck a Faustian bargain with the nation's oligarchy: The same constitution that granted the aristocrats control of the government also expected them to obey the laws they had enacted. Once established, this principle, backed up by the government's bayonets, ensured order, out of which perhaps prosperity might come. Though the constitution seemed democratic, the high voting restrictions made Portales a virtual dictator.

Consistent with Portales's ideas was his desire to limit partisan activity to a minimum, not because he personally lusted for power but because, like Henry VIII, he saw bending the rules as a means of guaranteeing political order. Presidential campaigns, Portales rightly believed, revived vendettas, which the recently established republic could not withstand. Hence, he insisted that President Joaquín Prieto remain in office rather than subject Chile to a campaign which, he correctly feared, would plunge the nation into the maelstrom of civil war.

Although Portales wielded enormous power, he never held elective office, preferring to be

Prieto's *éminence grise*. He did serve in various capacities, including minister of the interior, the second most important position after president, and as minister of war, navy, and foreign relations, as well as governor of Valparaíso. Portales never actively sought office. Indeed, in 1833 he quit public service to retire to his hacienda, *El Rayado*. There he remained in touch with the government, which often consulted him.

In September 1835, when a struggle between ministers Joaquín Tocornal and Manuel Rengifo threatened to disrupt the national political balance, Portales reentered public life, first as minister of war and the navy and then as minister of the interior and foreign relations. For all intents and purposes, Portales was running Chile. But as before, he preferred to remain outside the seat of power, from where he choreographed Prieto's reelection to the presidency.

While he was politically innovative, Portales did not deviate substantially from his predecessors' economic policies. Fortunately for Chile, the War for Independence did not damage the nation's mines, located in the north. Consequently, this most valuable of Chile's natural resources continued to contribute mightily to the economy. Gold production slowed, but silver mining, fueled by discoveries at Chañarcillo, increased by 60 percent in the period of 1830 to 1840, while the output of copper almost doubled. The mining of these metals attracted substantial foreign investment, which provided the state with substantial revenues.

In conjunction with the minister of Hacienda Pública, Manuel Rengifo, Portales developed Valparaíso into the hemisphere's premier port on the Pacific. In order to attract international shipping en route to the Orient and the Pacific coast of the Western Hemisphere, the state spent large sums improving Valparaíso's facilities, building new wharfs as well as secure warehouses. An 1832 law permitted the storage of cargoes in Valparaíso, at very low tax rates, for up to three years. A combination of innovative laws and modern facilities made Valparaíso the ideal place for merchant vessels to drydock for repairs and to revictual. The government also modernized the ports of Coquimbo and Huasco. In addition, it promulgated a new *aduana* (customs) code, which attempted to encourage the creation of a merchant marine and reserved coastal traffic to Chilean nationals.

If not an economic innovator, Portales did forge new foreign policy goals for Chile. Officially, he stated that Chile, while zealously defending its sovereignty, would remain aloof from hemispheric squabbling. In fact, however, Portales seemed willing to impose Chile's will on its neighbors, as its national motto stipulated, either "by reason or force." Fundamentally, Portales sought to ensure that no hemispheric nation could threaten Chile's territorial integrity. Consequently, he disdained the United States and its Monroe Doctrine, warning all his Hispanic neighbors to beware of Washington's evil intentions.

The creation of the Peru–Bolivia Confederation in 1836 by Bolivia's General Andrés Santa Cruz threatened Portales's vision of the Pacific. Clearly, this new nation, whose combined land mass and population dwarfed that of Chile, posed a potential military threat to the government in Santiago. Moreover, the confederation early on demonstrated an unhealthy independence, one example of which was the Santa Cruz government's abrogation of an 1835 treaty granting Chilean wheat access to Peru's markets. Worse still was Santa Cruz's wish to restore the port of Callao to its colonial preeminence. In pursuit of this goal he imposed special taxes on all imports entering the confederation via Valparaíso. Clearly, the Bolivian leader, whom Portales deprecated for being an "Indian," was challenging Valparaíso's attempt to secure commercial hegemony. Fearful that Chile's northern neighbor might eventually turn on it, Portales launched a preemptive war in December 1836 to destroy the confederation before it could jeopardize Chile's economic and political domination of the region.

The onset of this unpopular conflict—the masses did not want to serve in the army and had to be impressed into the military—threatened to destroy Portales's government. Political conspirators hoped to take advantage of the popular discontent to overthrow the government of Joaquín Prieto. Portales responded by organizing flying courts-martial, which tried and executed individuals suspected of plotting against the regime. This tactic had only limited success. A mutinous army unit captured Portales after he had come to visit the garrison at Quillota. The rebels took Portales to Valparaíso, where they hoped to entice other military units to join in a revolt. When the loyal garrison refused, the rebels murdered Portales, mutilating his body with more than thirty stab wounds and stripping him of his clothes, which they divided among themselves.

The political system that he established survived Portales's death. Though harsh, this form of government imposed the order necessary for economic development and progress. Thus, while other Latin American nations seemed convulsed in internal upheavals, Chile, largely thanks to Diego Portales, prospered.

Interestingly, his remains, missing since his assassination, were found on March 2005 in Santiago's Metropolitan Cathedral during renovations.

See also **Chile, Political Parties: Conservative Party; Peru-Bolivia Confederation.**

BIBLIOGRAPHY

Luis Galdames, *A History of Chile* (1941), pp. 236–240, 255– 256, 262–263, 265–270.

Simon Collier, *Ideas and Politics of Chilean Independence, 1808–1833* (1967), pp. 133–134, 295–296, 321– 332, 334–335, 339, 342–345, 353–360.

Jay Kinsbruner, *Diego Portales: Interpretative Essays on the Man and Times* (1967).

Roberto Hernández Ponce, *Diego Portales, vida y tiempo* (1974).

Bernardino Bravo Lira, ed., *Portales, el hombre y su obra: La consolidación del gobierno civil* (1989).

Sergio Villalobos R., *Portales, una falsificación histórica* (1989).

Additional Bibliography

Barba, Fernando. *Argentina y Chile en la época de Rosas y Portales.* La Plata: Editorial de la Universidad de La Plata, 1997.

Bravo Lira, Bernadino. *El Absolutismo ilustrado en Hispanoamérica.* Santiago de Chile: Editorial Universitaria, 1994.

WILLIAM F. SATER

PORT-AU-PRINCE.

Port-au-Prince, capital of Haiti. Established as the new colonial capital of Saint Domingue in 1749 (the first had been Cap Haitien), it was the leading port of the western region and had the advantage of a protected and deep harbor. Soon after independence it dominated politics. The city also served as the stronghold of the mulatto elite, which controlled the political, economic, and, later, cultural life of Haiti. One major result of the U.S. occupation (1915–1934) was the centralization of governmental, political, economic, and military power there. The capital became the locus of national politics, for the candidates winning there won nationally. This was especially true as the city rapidly grew in population and universal suffrage went into effect in 1957.

After World War II, two presidents helped improve the quality of Port-au-Prince. President Dumarsais Estimé (1946–1950) spent $6 million in organizing its bicentennial in 1949 and President Paul Magloire (1950–1956) improved housing opportunities by the construction of his Cité Magloire. Although President François Duvalier (1957–1971) engaged in some housing projects and removed some slums, mainly for public-relations purposes, during his regime and that of his son, Jean-Claude (1971–1986), the city deteriorated, as did the quality of services.

When François Duvalier established his absolute rule, he further centralized economic, military, and political authority and power in the capital. He pursued policies that intentionally weakened provincial Haiti and the secondary cities and ports by refusing to improve or even maintain roads, airports, and harbors. This had the desired effect of maintaining and enhancing the capital's economic primacy in the export and import trade. In 1990, Port-au-Prince accounted for around 90 percent of Haiti's exports and about 60 percent of its imports. Two other indicators of the city's central role are government expenditures and population. About 80 percent of the national expenditures were spent on and in the city itself in 1990. As of 1995, the city of Port-au-Prince had an estimated population of 846,247, and the greater metropolitan area was home to 1,425,594 individuals. Almost 20 percent of Haiti's population of 7,180,294 lived in the Port-au-Prince metropolitan area at this time.

See also **Duvalier, François; Estimé, Dumarsais; Haiti.**

BIBLIOGRAPHY

James G. Leyburn, *The Haitian People* (1941), esp. pp. 244– 245, 274–277.

Selden Rodman, *Haiti, the Black Republic: The Complete Story and Guide* (1961), esp. pp. 45–46, 54–55, 91–92, 106–115.

Robert D. Heinl, Jr., and Nancy G. Heinl, *Written in Blood: The Story of the Haitian People, 1492–1971* (1978).

Brian Weinstein and Aaron Segal, *Haiti: Political Failures, Cultural Successes* (1984), pp. 17–18, 24–25, 83–85, 92–93.

Michel-Rolph Trouillot, *Haiti, State Against Nation: The Origins and Legacy of Duvalierism* (1990), esp. pp. 104–105, 141–142, 182–184.

Additional Bibliography

Dubois, Laurent. *Avengers of the New World: The Story of the Haitian Revolution.* Cambridge, MA: Belknap Press of Harvard University Press, 2004.

Kovats-Bernat, J. Christopher. *Sleeping Rough in Port-au-Prince: An Ethnography of Street Children and Violence in Haiti.* Gainesville: University Press of Florida, 2006.

Portes, Alejandro, and Mario Lungo, eds. *Urbanización en el Caribe.* San José: FLACSO, 1992.

Renda, Mary A. *Taking Haiti: Military Occupation and the Culture of U.S. Imperialism, 1915–1940.* Chapel Hill: University of North Carolina Press, 2001.

LARMAN C. WILSON

PORTEÑO.

Porteño, inhabitant of the city of Buenos Aires. Referring to Buenos Aires's being the chief port for the Río de la Plata drainage basin, the word *porteño* came to symbolize the city's commercial, financial, and political dominance over the region. By the late colonial era *porteños* boasted a self-confident and distinctive culture, strongly influenced by European mores and political ideas. They were among the first to declare independence from Spain, but their presumptions soon alienated rural dwellers of the littoral and the interior. Much of the political and social conflict of the nineteenth century reflected long-standing grievances against *porteño* ambitions. By the twentieth century, Buenos Aires's hegemony was unchallenged. Since the late nineteenth century, between a quarter and a third of the country's population has lived in the city and its environs, and Argentina's principal cultural, social, and economic activities have clustered in Buenos Aires. This has often earned *porteños* the reputation of arrogance and willful neglect of the rest of the country.

See also **Buenos Aires; Río de la Plata.**

BIBLIOGRAPHY

Bertoni, Lilia Ana. *Patriotas, cosmopolitas y nacionalistas: La construcción de la nacionalidad argentina a fines del siglo XIX.* Buenos Aires: Fondo de cultura económica, 2001.

Casdevall, Domingo F. *El carácter porteño.* Buenos Aires: Centro Editor de América Latina, 1970.

Wilson, Jason. *Buenos Aires: A Cultural and Literary Companion.* New York: Interlink Books, 2000.

JEREMY ADELMAN

PORTER, DAVID

(1780–1843). David Porter (*b.* 1 February 1780; *d.* 3 March 1843), commander of Mexican navy of independence. An officer in the U.S. Navy, Captain Porter captured the first British ship during the War of 1812. In 1813, he led the first U.S. naval cruise to the Pacific, preying on British shipping off the South American coast and cruising the Marquesas until losing his ship in a battle at Valparaíso, Chile. As commander of the West Indies squadron in 1823, Porter displayed a degree of aggressiveness in Puerto Rico with the Spanish officials that resulted in his court-martial, conviction, and resignation. In 1826, he became commander in chief of the Mexican navy of independence, a post he filled for three years with moderate success. He later filled U.S. diplomatic posts in the Mediterranean until his death.

See also **Puerto Rico.**

BIBLIOGRAPHY

David F. Long, *Nothing Too Daring: A Biography of Commodore David Porter, 1780–1843* (1970).

David Porter, *Journal of a Cruise Made to the Pacific Ocean,* edited by R. D. Madison and Karen Hamon (1986).

E. JEFFREY STANN

PORTER, LILIANA

(1941–2000). Liliana Porter (*b.* 6 October 1941; *d.* 2000), Argentine artist. Beginning in the late 1960s, Porter created prints, paintings, and wall installations in which she explores the relationships between illusion, artistic representation, and reality—a theme that has captivated many Argentine artists and writers. (Her major influences included the writer Jorge Luis Borges and the artist René Ma-gritte.) Born in Buenos Aires, she studied printmaking at the Universidad Iberoamericana, Mexico City, in 1960; she graduated from the Escuela Nacional de Bellas Artes, Buenos Aires, in 1963. A year later Porter moved to New York City, where she attended the Pratt Graphic Art Center. In 1965 she, Luis Camnitzer, and José Guillermo Castillo founded the New York Graphic Workshop, where she began to create prints utilizing the techniques of photoetching and photo–silk screen. She simultaneously became a member of the conceptual art movement. Always a prolific printmaker, Porter produced numerous mixed-media paintings beginning in the early 1980s. In the early 2000s, Porter began taking still photographs of small toys and objects. For example, her work "Kiss" is a paparazzi-influenced photograph of a Minnie Mouse figurine kissing an image of Che Guevara. This series of work was shown at the Hosfelt Gallery in San Francisco.

See also **Art: The Twentieth Century; Borges, Jorge Luis.**

BIBLIOGRAPHY

Liliana Porter: Obra gráfica, 1964–1990 (1990).

Mari Carmen Ramírez and Charles Merewether, *Liliana Porter: Fragments of the Journey* (1992).

Charles Merewether, "Displacement and the Reinvention of Identity," in *Latin American Artists of the Twentieth Century* (1993).

Additional Bibliography

Porter, Liliana, and Inés Katzenstein. *Liliana Porter: Fotografía y ficción.* Buenos Aires: Centro Cultural Recoleta y Malba–Colección Costantini, 2003.

Porter, Liliana, and Virginia Pérez-Ratton. *Liliana Porter: Una "puesta en imágenes."* San José: TEOR/Ética, 2003.

JOHN ALAN FARMER

PORTES GIL, EMILIO (1890–1978).

Emilio Portes Gil was president of Mexico from 1928 to 1930, the youngest person to become the country's president in the twentieth century. Born on October 3, 1890, in Ciudad Victoria, Tamaulipas, he graduated from the local normal school in 1910 and then taught elementary school. He attended the National University before joining with fellow students to form the Free School of Law in 1912, from which he graduated in 1915. He worked for the Department of Military Justice as a civilian employee before serving as a member of congress from 1917 to 1918, a post he held again in 1920 and 1924. Portes Gil did not participate in the 1910 Revolution. He became governor of his home state in 1925. (He would continue to influence politics there well into the 1950s, similar to other presidents in their home states, notably Lázaro Cárdenas in Michoacán.) Under President Plutarco Elías Calles, he briefly served as secretary of government before assuming the presidency in 1928.

Portes Gil was the first of three Mexicans to serve out the six-year term presidential term won by General Álvaro Obregón, who was assassinated before he could take office in 1928. A favorite of Calles, Portes Gil was selected by Congress to serve as interim president while new elections were held in 1929. He was the only civilian to hold the presidential office between 1920 and 1946. Although many historians consider him to have been subservient to Calles during his brief administration, he pursued many of his own policies. He is best remembered for having settled a university strike that led to the autonomy of the National University in 1929, and even more so for secretly negotiating the resolution of the violent civil war between church and state known as the Cristero Rebellion, thereby paving the way for the church-state relationship that lasted until the 1992.

During the administrations of his two successors, Portes Gil served as ambassador to France and to the League of Nations in 1931–1932 and then became attorney general of Mexico. When Lázaro Cárdenas became president in 1934, Portes Gil served in his first cabinet as secretary of foreign relations. An important leader of the National Revolutionary Party, he served twice as its president, initially in 1930 and then in 1935–1936. He held a number of minor administrative and ambassadorial posts until 1970, having achieved the stature of a senior statesman. He died in Mexico City on December 10, 1978.

See also **Calles, Plutarco Elías; Cárdenas del Río, Lázaro; Mexico: Since 1910; Mexico, Political Parties:**

National Revolutionary Party (PNR); Obregón Salido, Álvaro.

BIBLIOGRAPHY

Alvarado Mendoza, Arturo. *El portesgilismo en Tamaulipas.* Mexico: Colegio de México, 1992.

Dulles, John W. F. *Yesterday in Mexico: A Chronicle of the Revolution, 1919–1936.* Austin: University of Texas Press, 1961.

Meyer, Lorenzo. *Historia de la revolución mexicana, periodo 1928–1934.* Mexico: Colegio de México, 1978.

RODERIC AI CAMP

PORTINARI, CÂNDIDO TORQUATO

(1903–1962). Cândido Torquato Portinari (*b.* 29 December 1903; *d.* 6 February 1962), Brazilian genre painter. Born in Bródosqui, São Paulo, the second of twelve children of Italian immigrants, Portinari was raised in an impoverished working-class environment. His experiences as a youth on coffee and cotton plantations made him aware of the harshness of plantation work.

Considered by many to be the only Latin American painter outside Mexico able to create a national epic through his work, Portinari revealed an interest in painting at an early age, while assisting in the decoration of a local church. At fifteen, he began study at the National School of Fine Arts in Rio de Janeiro. In 1928, he received an award from the National Salon that enabled him to travel and study in Europe, where he was influenced by the works of Pablo Picasso, Marc Chagall, and Joan Miró.

In the 1930s Portinari, known as a social realist painter, was involved in an art movement in which Latin American social themes and a rejection of European forms predominated. Using both mural and easel painting, he concentrated on depicting the harsh working conditions and poverty of the coffee plantation workers and miners. His first international recognition came in 1935 with the exhibition of a painting titled *Coffee* at the Carnegie International Exhibition in Pittsburgh. Having won second prize at the exhibition, the painting established Portinari in the art world. Combining traditionalism, lyricism, realism, and nationalism, his portraits of both common people (like *The Mestizo*) and Brazilian celebrities (like poet Olegário Mariano) reflected a keen awareness of the ethnic diversity in Brazilian society.

In 1941 he was commissioned by the Hispanic Foundation of the U.S. Library of Congress to produce four murals titled *Discovery of the New World.* The individual murals were *Discovery of the Land, the Entry into the Forest, the Teaching of the Indians,* and *The Mining of Gold.* Two of his most significant projects were completed in 1945: the *Way of the Cross* murals for Brazil's first modern church, the Church of São Francisco in Pampulha, and the *Epic of Brazil* murals for the Ministry of Education and Health Building in Rio de Janeiro, which depicted the cultivation of sugarcane, tobacco, cotton, coffee, and rubber; cattle raising; and gold prospecting. He completed the *War and Peace* murals for the United Nations Building in New York City in 1953, and in 1957, he received the Guggenheim National Award. In 1961 he returned to Rio de Janeiro, where he died the following year from paint poisoning.

See also **Art: The Twentieth Century; Coffee Industry.**

BIBLIOGRAPHY

Murals by Cândido Portinari in the Hispanic Foundation of the Library of Congress (1943).

Cândido Portinari, *Portinari* (1943).

Gilbert Chase, *Contemporary Art in Latin America* (1970).

Carlos Lemos, *The Art of Brazil* (1983).

Dawn Ades, *Art in Latin America* (1989).

Sarah Lemmon, "Cândido Portinari, the Protest Period," in *Latin American Art* 3 (Winter 1991): 31–34.

Additional Bibliography

Giunta, Andrea, ed. *Candido Portinari y el sentido social del arte.* Buenos Aires: Siglo Veintiuno Editores Argentina, 2005.

Moreira, Marcos. *Cândido Portinari.* São Paulo: Grupo de Comunicação Três, 2001.

MARY JO MILES

PÔRTO ALEGRE.

Pôrto Alegre, Brazil's tenth largest city (estimated 2006 population, 1,440,939), fourth largest industrial center, and capital of the state of Rio Grande do Sul. On the Guaíba estuary, with access to the region's navigable central rivers and, through the Lagoa dos Patos, to the sea, Pôrto Alegre is the natural entrepôt to the agricultural economy of northern and central Rio Grande do Sul. Its history, dating to 1732, was shaped by divisions between the region's agricultural north and pastoral south.

Formerly Pôrto do Viamão and Pôrto dos Casais, it was renamed Pôrto Alegre after the capital moved there in 1773. By 1814 exports from local Azorean wheat farms boosted population to 6,000, but after 1820 the collapse of the wheat trade and growth of a cattle economy shifted the region's economic balance south. The city was held by imperial forces for most of the Farroupilha Revolt (1835–1845), in opposition to the rebel south. In the late nineteenth century, when the pastoral economy stalled, the region's economic center moved north again, and the city regained importance, first as an outlet for the agricultural production of immigrant farms that spread across its hinterland, then, after 1890, as their supplier of industrial goods. Population growth peaked from 1900 to 1910. German and Italian immigrants played leading roles in the city's growth, leaving a distinctive imprint. By 1920 the population topped 100,000, and Pôrto Alegre consolidated its position as the state's industrial center and point of articulation for its two distinct subregions.

In subsequent decades, economic decline in its agricultural hinterland due to loss of markets, soil exhaustion, and subdivision of small farms undermined the city's economic base, slowed its industrial growth, and swelled its population with migrants from the countryside. Pôrto Alegre maintained its position of commercial and industrial preeminence within the state but saw its share of Brazilian industry much reduced as São Paulo consolidated national industrial dominance.

See also **Brazil, Geography; Rio Grande do Sul.**

BIBLIOGRAPHY

Francisco Riopardense De Macedo, *Pôrto Alegre: Origem e crescimento.* Porto Alegre: Liv Sulina, 1968.

Paul Singer, *Desenvolvimento econômico e evolução urbana: Análise da evolução econômica de São Paulo, Blumenau, Pôrto Alegre, Belo Horizonte e Recife* (1968).

Additional Bibliography

Baiocchi, Gianpolo. *Militants and Citizens: the Politics of Participatory Democracy in Porto Alegre.* Stanford, CA: Stanford University Press, 2005.

Kittleson, Roger Alan. *The Practice of Politics in Postcolonial Brazil: Porto Alegre, 1845-1895.* Pittsburgh: University of Pittsburgh Press, 2006.

Lazarri, Alexandre. *Coisas para povo náo fazer: Carnaval em Porto Alegre (1870-1915.)* Campinas, SP, Brazil: Editora de UNICAMP: CECULT, 2001.

Lourieiro, Isabel Maria; José Corréa Leite; Maria Elisa Cevasco. *O espírito de Porto Alegre.* Sáo Paulo: Paz e Terra, 2002.

JOAN BAK

PÔRTO ALEGRE, MANUEL ARAÚJO

(1806–1879). Manuel Araújo Pôrto Alegre (*b.* 29 November 1806; *d.* 29 December 1879), Brazilian painter, poet, and playwright. In 1827, soon after arriving in Rio de Janeiro from his home province of Rio Pardo, Pôrto Alegre enrolled in the Brazilian Imperial Academy of Fine Arts. He studied under the French history painter Jean-Baptiste Debret, who had come to Brazil in 1816 as part of the French artistic mission. After studying painting in Paris for five years, Pôrto Alegre returned to Rio de Janeiro, where he was appointed the academy's professor of history painting.

In 1840, the year of Pedro II's acclamation, Pôrto Alegre was named official court painter and produced court portraits and canvases depicting important imperial events. In 1854 Pôrto Alegre was appointed the academy's fifth—and first Brazilian-born—director. That same year, as part of Pedro II's program to encourage nationalism and overhaul imperial cultural and economic institutions, the emperor asked his new director to carry out a thorough reform of the academy. But in 1857, with a new organizational structure in place, Pôrto Alegre resigned. He blamed irreconcilable differences with the academic faculty and imperial ministers. He spent the last years of his life as a foreign diplomat.

In addition to his artistic contributions, Pôrto Alegre was also a celebrated poet, journalist, and playwright. His most important literary work was a poem about the discovery of America, entitled *Columbo.* Emperor Pedro II conferred on him the title of *barão* in 1874.

See also **Art: The Nineteenth Century; Literature: Brazil; Pedro II of Brazil.**

BIBLIOGRAPHY

Dioclécio De Paranhos Antunes, *O pintor do romantismo: Vida e obra de Manoel de Araujo Pôrto Alegre* (1943).

Alfredo Galvão, "Manuel de Araújo Pôrto Alegre—Sua influencia na Academia imperial das belas artes e no meio artístico de Rio de Janeiro," in *Revista do Serviço do patrimonio histórico nacional* 14 (1959): 19–120.

Caren Meghreblian, "Art, Politics, and Historical Perception in Imperial Brazil, 1854–1884" (Ph.D. diss., UCLA, 1990).

Additional Bibliography

Squeff, Letícia. *O Brasil nas letras de um pintor: Manuel de Araújo Porto Alegre (1806–1879)*. Campinas, SP, Brazil: Editora da UNICAMP, 2004.

CAREN A. MEGHREBLIAN

PORTO BELLO (PORTOBELO).

Porto Bello (Portobelo), home of a large Spanish fair in the New World from the late 1500s through the mid-eighteenth century. Founded as a settlement in 1510, Porto Bello is located along the northern (Caribbean) shore of modern-day Panama. It became important because of its strategic location. As the entrepôt for Spanish trade with the viceroyalty of Peru, the port also became a regular target for pirates and buccaneers.

Originally a shanty port, after 1584 Porto Bello replaced Columbus's earlier colony of Nombre de Dios as the Spanish center of trade on the isthmus. The crown had ordered the abandonment of Nombre de Dios because of its unhealthiness, poor climate, and general indefensibility. Thus, Porto Bello became the central location for trans-Atlantic trade with Peru, rivaling the great fairs of Cartagena and Veracruz. Thousands of sailors, merchants, officials, and soldiers regularly traveled through it.

After 1597, Porto Bello became the central trading post for most South American goods. There, merchandise from Spain was exchanged for Peruvian silver and other South American precious metals and raw materials. The fair was open for forty days originally but was later shortened to ten or twelve days, from a growing lack of commodities and silver. Throughout the period of the fair, mule trains trudged daily through Panama to the town, trading their goods to Spanish merchants for items from continental Europe and elsewhere. Meanwhile, the Spanish Flota, or merchant marine, came bearing goods from South America, hoping to attain a profitable exchange for them. Food and shelter were costly; the town's sanitation poor. The level of trading decreased over time until by the mid-eighteenth century the fair had become much smaller.

Throughout the period of heaviest trading, Porto Bello was a regular target for pirates and buccaneers. Although the Spanish defeated an English fleet led by Drake and Hawkins in 1595, Porto Bello fell prey to a brutal raid by Henry Morgan in 1668. Overall, however, the port was strategically located and thus fairly defensible, for which reason it generally prospered well into the eighteenth century, when the Spanish abandoned the annual *flota* system.

See also **Drake, Francis; Morgan, Henry.**

BIBLIOGRAPHY

Sir Julian S. Corbett, *Drake and the Tudor Navy: With a History of the Rise of England as a Maritime Power*, 2 vols. (new edition. Cranbury, NJ: Scholar's Bookshelf, 2005.

C. H. Haring, *The Buccaneers in the West Indies in the XVII Century*. Hamden, CT: Archon Books, 1910.

J. H. Parry, et al., *A Short History of the West Indies*, 4th ed. New York: St. Martin's Press, 1987.

Additional Bibliography

Castillero Calvo, Alfredo. *Arquitectúra, urbanismo y sociedad: La vivienda colonial en Panamá: historia de un sueño.* República de Panamá: Fondo de Promoción Cultural Shell, 1994.

Gutiérrez, Ramón. *Panamá viejo y Portobelo: La huella de la historia*. Madrid: Dirección General de Relaciónes Culturales y Científicas, 2004.

McGehee, Patricia. *Portobelo chronicles*. Colón (Panamá): P.A. McGehee, 2005.

BLAKE D. PATRIDGE

PORTOCARRERO, RENÉ (1912–1986).

René Portocarrero (*b.* 24 February 1912; *d.* 7 April 1986), Cuban artist. Born on the outskirts of Havana, Portocarrero was a child prodigy, mostly self-taught, except for a brief period of study at the Academy of San Alejandro in Havana. Initially he painted domestic interiors, later incorporating images of Cuban festivities and religious practices. Socially conscious, he taught drawing to prison inmates and claimed to have been influenced by them. Critics characterized Portocarrero's style as "baroque" for its exuberant ornamentation and multiple-foci compositions, characteristics that reached a peak in his painting between 1946 and 1947. In 1956 he worked on a series of imaginary urbanscapes reminiscent of Havana, and won the national prize for painting at the Eighth National Salon of Painting and Sculpture in Cuba. Four years later he helped found the National Union of Sculptors and Artists of Cuba. He worked on *The Color of Cuba*, scenes of Carnival celebrations on the island (1962–1963), for which he received the International Samba Prize at the Seventh Biennial in São Paulo, Brazil, in 1963. He painted a series called *Portraits of Flora*, emblematic images of a Cuban woman (1966) and executed several murals in public buildings throughout Cuba.

Portocarrero received the Félix Varela Order from the Cuban government in 1981 and was awarded the Aztec Eagle from the Mexican government the following year. He illustrated several of José Lezama Lima's books as well as publications such as *Orígenes, Carteles, Bohemia, Revolución y cultura, Signos, Islas, La gaceta de Cuba,* and *Juventud rebelde.*

See also **Art: The Twentieth Century.**

BIBLIOGRAPHY

José Lezama Lima et al., *René Portocarrero: Exposición Antológica* (1984).

Marta Traba, *Museum of Modern Art of Latin America: Selections from the Permanent Collection* (1985), pp. 46–47.

Additional Bibliography

Mosquera, Gerardo. "René Portocarrero." *Art Nexus* 19 (Jan.–Mar. 1996): 76-80.

Piñera, Virgilio. "La pintura de Portocarrero." *Caravelle* 80 (2003): 237–244.

MARTA GARSD

PORTOCARRERO Y LASSO DE LA VEGA, MELCHOR. Melchor Portocarrero y Lasso de la Vega (the count of Monclova),

viceroy of Peru (1689–1705). As successor to the controversial duke of Palata, Monclova sought to increase the revenue base and labor pool of the colony without increasing the colonists' resentment and Indian resistance. Monclova enacted various measures that reversed earlier decrees: He reduced the number of Indians assigned to *mita* service (forced labor) at the silver mines of Potosí, he encouraged the use of wage labor, and he issued a new labor code that superseded the Palata regulations. In spite of persistent problems with tax collection and *mita* quotas, Monclova also reaffirmed the primacy of the Toledo *reducción* (resettlement) system, avoiding a fundamental reorganization of Peru's Indian community. His reversal of the Palata reforms postponed but could not prevent the major labor crises of the eighteenth century.

See also **Navarra y Rocaful, Melchor de; Repartimiento.**

BIBLIOGRAPHY

Jeffrey A. Cole, *The Potosí Mita, 1573–1700: Compulsory Indian Labor in the Andes* (1985).

Ann M. Wightman, *Indigenous Migration and Social Change: The Forasteros of Cuzco, 1570– 1720* (1990), esp. pp. 9–44.

Additional Bibliography

Fernández Ariza, Guadalupe. *Literatura hispanoamericana del siglo XX: Historia y maravilla.* Málaga, Spain: Universidad de Málaga, 2004.

Lavalle, J. A. and Domingo de Vivero. *Galería de retratos de los gobernadores y virreyes del Perú (1532–1824).* Barcelona, Spain: Tip. de la casa editorial Maucci, 1909.

Moreyra Paz Soldán, Manuel and Grover Antonio Espinoza Ruiz. *Estudios históricos.* Lima: Pontificia Universidad Católica del Perú, Instituto Riva-Agüero, 1994–1995.

Torres Arancivia, Eduardo. *Corte de virreyes: El entorno del poder en el Perú en el siglo XVII.* Lima: Pontificia Universidad Católica del Perú, Fondo Editorial, 2006.

ANN M. WIGHTMAN

PORTOLÁ, GASPAR DE (c. 1717– 1786). Gaspar De Portolá (*b.* ca. 1717; *d.* 10 October 1786), commandant-governor of the Californias. A native of Balaguer, Cataluña, Portolá rose from infantry ensign (1734) to lieutenant (1743), and to captain

(1764). After serving in campaigns in Italy and Portugal, he arrived in New Spain in 1764. Three years later he was sent to Baja California to effect the expulsion of the Jesuits. In 1768 Portolá was commander of the Catalan Volunteers and led the expedition to settle Alta California that had been ordered by Visitor General José de Gálvez. With the Franciscan Junípero Serra he marched overland from Loreto to San Diego, where he aided in the founding of the mission and presidio (3 July 1768). On 14 July 1769 he led an expedition in search of Monterey; he discovered San Francisco Bay in November of that year, and returned to San Diego in January 1770. By that August, Portolá was back in San Blas, and as a lieutenant colonel of dragoons he returned to Spain later that year. As a colonel, he served as governor of Puebla de los Angeles, New Spain, from 1777 to 1785. In the latter year he returned to Spain in the Numancia regiment of dragoons. In February 1786 Portolá was named royal lieutenant of the city and castles of Lérida. He died in Lérida.

See also **Catalonian Volunteers; Franciscans; Jesuits; Missions: Spanish America; Serra, Junipero.**

BIBLIOGRAPHY

Francisco Palóu, *Historical Memoirs of New California,* translated by Herbert E. Bolton, 4 vols. (1926).

Fernando Boneu Campanys, *Don Gaspar de Portolá, Explorer and Founder of California,* translated and revised by Alan K. Brown (1983).

Additional Bibliography

Kessell, John L. *Spain in the Southwest: A Narrative History of Colonial New Mexico, Arizona, Texas, and California.* Norman: University of Oklahoma Press, 2002.

W. MICHAEL MATHES

PÔRTO SEGURO. Pôrto Seguro, port town on the Brazilian coast. Pôrto Seguro, Bahia, has been called the cradle of post-indigenous Brazil, and it was here that Pedro Cabral landed on his voyage of discovery in 1500. Impressed by the physical beauty of the region as well as by the Tupi people, the Portuguese claimed the new territory as rightfully theirs in accordance with the Treaty of Tordesillas (1494). In what he called the Land of the Holy Cross, Cabral left behind a number of *degredados* (Portuguese undesirables, mainly criminals); a scant year later reinforcements arrived, including members of the clergy. It was in Pôrto Seguro that the first extractive industry of Brazil began, based on cutting stands of brazilwood (*pau brasil*) or dyewood (*pau da tinta*). The red dye from the wood yielded a profitable commodity eagerly sought by the European textile market. Ironically, Pôrto Seguro today has one of the few stands of coastal forest left along the Brazilian littoral. In the eighteenth century, the Comarca of Pôrto Seguro, in the shadow of more developed Salvador da Bahia, was revitalized with a town-building program. Even more regimented than the Pombaline towns of the Amazon region, the Pôrto Seguro townships of Vila Viçosa, Portalegre, and Prado (with both Indian and European colonists) formed the backbone of a trade network that shipped cotton, grain, and fish to Bahian sugar planters. Declared a historic city, Pôrto Seguro is now a popular tourist attraction in Brazil.

See also **Brazil, Geography; Forests.**

BIBLIOGRAPHY

Odália, Nilo. *As formas do mesmo: Ensaiso sobre o pensamento historiográfico de Varnhagen e Oliviera Vianna.* São Paulo: Editora UNESP Fundacão, 1997.

Ortega Fontes, Armando. *Bibliografia de Varnhagen.* Rio de Janeiro: Ministerio de relacões exteriores, 1945.

Telles, Vera; Sergio Telles. *Porto Seguro: História estórias.* Rio de Janeiro: L. Christiano Editorial, 1987.

ROBERTA M. DELSON

PORTUGAL. From 1400 to 1700 Portugal played a pivotal role in European expansion into the non-Western world. Its salient location, relatively homogeneous society, and unified monarchy facilitated Portuguese efforts toward exploration and empire. Crown motives for expansion included strategic considerations, hopes for economic gain, and promotion of the Catholic faith. During the fifteenth century, Portuguese mariners discovered many of the Atlantic islands, explored the African coast, and sailed past the Cape of Good Hope into the Indian Ocean. In 1500, while sailing to India, Pedro Cabral landed in Brazil and claimed it for Portugal. By the mid-sixteenth century the Portuguese had reached Japan. Meanwhile, the great but ill-fated Portuguese navigator Ferdinand Magellan led a Spanish expedition westward around Cape Horn, in 1521 reaching the Philippine Islands, where he died.

Portugal complemented these seaborne expeditions by exploring the African and South American continents. After 1600, Brazilian settlers, later known as *bandeirantes,* extended Portuguese territory far beyond that demarcated by the Treaty of Tordesillas, signed with Spain in 1494.

In Africa, India, and the Far East, Portuguese holdings were usually little more than commercial outposts where slaves, commodities, and finished goods were procured. But in Brazil the emergence of a great sugar plantation culture stimulated a huge demand for African slaves. During the colonial era, more than 4 million blacks were shipped across the Atlantic to labor on the plantations, mines, and port cities of Brazil.

After 1500 the wealth flowing into Portugal from its imperial outposts helped give rise to a golden age in this small Iberian power. During the first half of the sixteenth century, Portugal, with a population of only one million, held sway as one of the great seafaring powers in the world. Its navigators and shipbuilders stood in the forefront of European technical advancement. Lisbon became an opulent, bustling commercial entrepôt. Manuel I (1495–1521) reigned over the richest monarchy in Europe. The wealth coming from Portugal's African and Eastern enclaves buoyed artistic and cultural achievement.

But by the time Luís de Camões's great epic poem, *The Lusiads,* was published in 1572, Portugal had fallen into decline. Much of the inflowing wealth had been absorbed by the feudalistic privileged classes, who spent vast sums on ornate churches and European finished goods. The Counter-Reformation allowed the Inquisition to tighten its intolerant grip. Portugal's small merchant class, many of Jewish descent, faced increasing persecution. And the costs of an overextended empire weakened a domestic economy dependent on a backward agrarian sector. In 1560 financial difficulties led the crown to declare bankruptcy. Twenty years later dynastic control of the Portuguese world passed to the Spanish Hapsburgs, who held sway until 1640. During those sixty years other powers, particularly the Dutch, captured numerous Portuguese possessions.

By the mid-seventeenth century, what remained of Portugal's eastern empire was in decay, but expansion of the Brazilian economy helped sustain Portugal through the tumultuous middle decades of that century. And, after a lengthy struggle, from 1640 to 1668, the Portuguese finally defeated Spanish attempts to reassert dynastic control. The reform-minded reign of Pedro II (1683–1706) brought stability and economic growth. After 1700 prosperity reminiscent of that of the early sixteenth century returned, this time borne primarily by the domestic wine trade as well as Brazilian sugar, tobacco, and gold.

See also **Slave Trade; Sugar Industry.**

BIBLIOGRAPHY

Frédéric Mauro, *Le Portugal, le Brasil et l'Atlantique au XVIIe siècle (1570–1670)* (1960).

Charles R. Boxer, *The Portuguese Seaborne Empire: 1415–1825* (1969; repr. 1991).

Antônio Henrique De Oliveira Marques, *History of Portugal,* rev. ed. (1976).

Bailey W. Diffie and George D. Winius, *Foundations of the Portuguese Empire, 1415–1580* (1977).

James Lang, *Portuguese Brazil: The King's Plantation* (1979).

Carl A. Hanson, *Economy and Society in Baroque Portugal, 1668–1703* (1981).

Stuart B. Schwartz, *Sugar Plantations in the Formation of Brazilian Society: Bahia, 1550–1835* (1985).

Additional Bibliography

Cervo, Amado Luiz, José Calvet de Magalhães and Dário Moreira de Castro Alves. *Depois das caravelas: As relações entre Portugal e Brasil, 1808–2000.* Brasília: IBRI: Editora UnB, 2000.

Malerba, Jurandir. *A corte no exílio: Civilização e poder no Brasil às vésperas da Independência, 1808 a 1821.* São Paulo, Brazil: Companhia das Letras, 2000.

Metcalf, Alida C. *Go-betweens and the Colonization of Brazil, 1500–1600.* Austin: University of Texas Press, 2005.

Miller, Shawn William. *Fruitless Trees: Portuguese Conservation and Brazil's Colonial Timber.* Stanford, CA: Stanford University Press, 2000.

Schultz, Kirsten. *Tropical Versailles: Empire, Monarchy, and the Portuguese Royal Court in Rio de Janeiro, 1808–1821.* New York: Routledge, 2001.

Viana Pedreira, Jose Miguel. "From Growth to Collapse: Portugal, Brazil, and the Breakdown of the Old Colonial System (1750–1830)." *Hispanic American Historical Review*. 80:4, Special Issues: Colonial Brazil: Foundations, Issues, and Legacies (November 2000): 839–864.

CARL A. HANSON

BIBLIOGRAPHY

Enciclopédia da música brasileira (1977); *New Grove Dictionary of Music and Musicians* (1980).

Additional Bibliography

Schultz, Kirsten. *Tropical Versailles: Empire, Monarchy, and the Portuguese Royal Court in Rio de Janeiro, 1808–1821*. New York: Routledge, 2001.

DAVID P. APPLEBY

PORTUGAL, MARCOS ANTÔNIO DA FONSECA (1762–1830).

Marcos Antônio da Fonseca Portugal (*b.* 24 March 1762; *d.* 7 February 1830), Portuguese composer and conductor. Born in Lisbon, Marcos Antônio, as he was called in Portugal, was admitted at the age of nine to Lisbon's Seminário Patriarchal, where he studied composition with João Souza de Carvalho. His first composition, a *Miserere*, was written at the age of fourteen. On 23 July 1783 he was admitted to the fraternity of musicians, the Brotherhood of Saint Cecilia, and between the years 1785 and 1792 wrote six comic operas.

A royal grant in 1792 made it possible for him to go to Italy, where he wrote twenty-one operas. Performances of his more successful operas in Italy, Germany, Austria, Spain, France, England, and Russia established Marcos Antônio Portugal, as he called himself at this time, as a prestigious composer with an international reputation. Appointed in 1800 as *mestre de capela* of the royal chapel and director of the São Carlos opera in Lisbon, he produced his own operas as well as adaptations of Italian operas.

When Napoleon invaded Portugal and the royal court fled to Brazil in 1807, Marcos Antônio Portugal remained in Lisbon and composed a work honoring Napoleon on his birthday, which earned him the title of "turncoat." After the French left Lisbon, Marcos Antônio Portugal sailed to Brazil and received an appointment as *mestre de capela* of the royal chapel in Rio de Janeiro. He contributed to the rich musical life of the city during the period preceding Brazilian independence in 1822, after which the economic problems of the new nation severely limited funds for musical activities. Portugal died in Rio de Janeiro in 1830, the same year as Padre José Maurício Nunes Garcia, the Brazilian composer who had also served as *mestre de capela*.

See also **Music: Art Music; Napoleon I.**

PORTUGAL, RESTORATION OF 1640.

The revolt of December 1640 resulted in the acclamation of João IV, duke of Bragança, as king, bringing to an end sixty years of Spanish rule. Philip II had seized control of Portugal two years after the death of the unmarried King Sebastian at the battle of Alcacer Quibir in 1578. Prior to 1620, most of the opposition to the Hapsburgs came from the Portuguese masses, who were driven by economic hardship and by Sebastianism—the belief that King Sebastian, whose body was never recovered from the battlefield, would return to reclaim his throne. Portuguese elites voiced few protests during the early years of Spanish rule, which allowed a relatively high degree of administrative autonomy to the Portuguese and coincided with the rapid expansion of both the Brazil trade and contraband traffic with Spanish America. The Portuguese nobility and the church hierarchy generally accepted the Iberian union as a means of controlling the masses during a period of crisis in the domestic economy, and many Portuguese merchants (particularly New Christians, who faced persecution by the Inquisition) gained economic and social benefits from Spanish rule.

The independence movement gained ground rapidly after 1620 as a result of mounting domestic unrest and of military and economic threats to the Portuguese empire. As high taxation and increasing poverty among the masses led to a large-scale revolt in Évora (1637) and more limited rebellions elsewhere, the Dutch seized territory from the Portuguese in northeastern Brazil and West Africa, and gained dominance of the spice trade in Asia. The failure of the Spanish to mount an adequate counterattack in Brazil or to take steps to protect the Portuguese imperial economy strengthened Portuguese opposition to Philip IV.

The gradual erosion of Portuguese political autonomy and the increasing provincialization of the nobility at the Vila Viçosa court of the Braganças (and at the courts of other leading families) added to the hostility of the Portuguese nobility toward the Spanish, as did the comparatively favorable position of New Christian merchants under the Hapsburgs.

The Restoration of 1640 is generally considered to have been conservative in character, a move to redress the grievances of the nobility and to forestall more widespread popular unrest of the kind that had occurred during the decade preceding independence. Portuguese jurists and clergymen produced an extensive literature that sought to legitimize the new dynasty, arguing that the people had a right to rebel against unjust rulers and that the Hapsburgs had usurped a crown that rightfully belonged to the Braganças. The war that followed the Restoration ended with the recognition by Spain of Portuguese independence in the peace treaty of 1668.

See also **João IV of Portugal.**

BIBLIOGRAPHY

Eduardo D'oliveira França, *Portugal na época da Restauração* (1951).

Charles R. Boxer, *Salvador Correia de Sá and the Struggle for Brazil and Angola, 1602–1686* (1952).

Vitorino Magalhães Godinho, "Portugal and Her Empire, 1648–1688," in *The New Cambridge Modern History,* vol. 5 (1961).

James C. Boyajian, *Portuguese Bankers at the Court of Spain, 1626–1650* (1983).

Additional Bibliography

Stella, Roseli Santaella. *Brasil durante el gobierno español, 1580–1640.* Madrid: Fundación Histórica Tavera, 2000.

THOMAS M. COHEN

PORTUGUESE EMPIRE. Portuguese expansion, beginning in 1415 with the conquest of Ceuta, through 1999 with the independence of Timor, is known for its durability in comparison to other empires of the Modern Age. In Portugal, the liberal historiography of the nineteenth century regarded the Portugal of the past as a centralizing power. In this view, King João I (r. 1385–1433) demonstrated the precociousness of the Portuguese state, free from war and ready for great navigations. In 1879 Oliveira Martins wrote about this metaphysical sense that guided the nation's destiny. King João II (r. 1481–1495) was, then, the "Perfect Prince" upon establishing control over half the world in Tordesillas (the city in which, in 1494, an important treaty was signed by the kings of Portugal and Spain dividing the Earth in two with an imaginary line). From 1926 to 1974 academic output was influenced by Salazarism, a period of dictatorship whose principal leader was António Salazar and later Marcelo Caetano. Damião Peres's collected works became a symbol of New State historiography. It aimed at strengthening the national state, enemy of Spain, ruler of a vast colonial empire. Magalhães Godinho's work, focused on discoveries and produced in France, was a distinct example of this official approach. Abroad, the British author Charles Boxer stood out when in 1969 he examined the Portuguese empire based on its circumstantial and characteristic vicissitudes, with inaccuracies that do not diminish the work's value as an analysis of the whole.

In Brazil, the historical process of living with the Portuguese court from 1808 and an independent empire since 1822 seems to have influenced an analysis that tended toward bipolarity (Portugal x Brazil) when discussing relations with Portugal. In the mid-nineteenth century Francisco Varnhagen described conflicts between the *mazombos* (Portuguese born in Brazil) and the *reinóis* (those born in the kingdom) with a xenophobic tone, but one in favor of continuing the reigning dynasty of Bragança, whose emperor, Pedro II (r. 1831–1889), was a descendant of the Portuguese Monarchy. In 1942 the Marxist author Caio Prado Júnior introduced a study model that made a major impact on Brazilian historiography, in which the "meaning of colonization" emerged from the purposes of European expansion, configuring commercial exploration and dependence on the mother country. This analysis became more sophisticated in Fernando Novais's 1973 thesis, when the former colonial system was defined by trade exclusivity and slavery, aspects that bound Portugal to its colony.

This dichotomy between Portugal and Brazil was revisited in Felipe de Alencastro's thesis, published in 2000, regarding the importance of the slave trade in relations among Africa, Brazil, and Portugal. The origination of the European Union and globalization occurred at the same time of the five-hundred-year anniversary of Portuguese discoveries. In this context, other authors began emphasizing the decentralization of the Portuguese Empire. A world with various micro powers involved in the concession of positions and deals among parts of this Empire. These new historians began to notice the negotiations and political pacts, and the importance of clientele and familial networks within the imperial dynamic. This dynamic occurred in various lands in America, Africa, and Asia, in particular during the sixteenth and seventeenth centuries. João Fragoso, Maria Fernanda Bicalho, and Maria de Fátima Gouvêa, in a collection of studies published in 2001, apply certain cultural and political values of a European ancien régime society in their study of the Portuguese empire's distant provinces, without overlooking the specifics of slavery and other issues. Among numerous papers inspired by this new perspective, the most notable are by António Hespanha regarding Portugal history, Francisco Bethencourt and Kirti Chaudhuri regarding the cultural history of the Portuguese expansion, Evaldo Cabral de Mello regarding Pernambuco's special political vassalage, and Luís Filipe Thomaz's analysis of the noble ethos in the expansion from Ceuta to Timor.

See also **Dutch in Colonial Brazil; Explorers and Exploration: Brazil; João I of Portugal; João II of Portugal; Pedro II of Brazil.**

BIBLIOGRAPHY

Alencastro, Luiz Felipe de. *O trato dos viventes: Formação do Brasil no Atlântico Sul.* São Paulo: Companhia das Letras, 2000.

Bethencourt, Francisco, and Kirti Chaudhuri, eds. and principal writers. *História da expansão portuguesa,* 3 vols. Lisbon: Círculo dos Leitores, 1997.

Boxer, Charles. *O Império marítimo português: 1415–1825.* São Paulo: Companhia das Letras, 2002.

Fragoso, João, Maria Fernanda Bicalho, and Maria de Fátima Gouvêa, eds. and principal writers. *O Antigo Regime nos trópicos: A dinâmica imperial portuguesa (séculos XVI–XVIII).* Rio de Janeiro: Civilização Brasileira, 2001.

Godinho, Vitorino Magalhães. *Os descobrimentos e a economia mundial,* 2nd edition, 4 vols. Lisbon: Presença, 1981–1983.

Martins, J. P. Oliveira. *História de Portugal.* Lisbon: Imprensa Nacional/Casa da Moeda, 1988.

Mattoso, José, ed. *História de Portugal.* Vol. 4: *O Antigo Regime,* edited by António Manuel Hespanha. Lisbon: Estampa, 1993.

Mello, Evaldo Cabral de. *A Fronda dos mazombos: Nobres contra mascates Pernambuco 1666–1715.* São Paulo: Companhia das Letras, 1995.

Monteiro, Rodrigo Bentes. *O rei no espelho: A monarquia portuguesa e a colonização da América, 1640–1720.* São Paulo: Hucitec, 2002.

Novais, Fernando A. *Portugal e Brasil na crise do antigo sistema colonial (1777–1808).* São Paulo: Hucitec, 1983.

Peres, Damião. *História de Portugal,* vols. 5–6. Barcelos, Portugal: Portucalense, 1984.

Prado Júnior, Caio. *Formação do Brasil contemporâneo.* São Paulo: Brasiliense, 1987.

Thomaz, Luís Filipe F. R. *De Ceuta a Timor.* Lisbon: DIFEL, 1994.

Varnhagen, Francisco Adolfo de. *História geral do Brasil,* 10th edition, 3 vols. São Paulo and Belo Horizonte: Editora da Universidade da São Paulo/Itatiaia, 1981.

RODRIGO BENTES MONTEIRO

PORTUGUESE IN LATIN AMERICA.

The Portuguese have migrated from continental Portugal and the Atlantic Islands (Madeira and Azores) to Latin America from the sixteenth century to the twenty-first century. The political and economic context, however, has changed through the centuries, and the migrants' destinations have varied. Most migrants chose Brazil as their favorite region after the independence of the colony and it was not until the late 1970s that Venezuela would compete as a destination. Recent studies reveal some exceptions to this trend. By the middle of the nineteenth century, Madeiran migrants went mainly to the West Indies (86 percent), and Brazil received only 12 percent of the islanders, far behind British Guiana (Guyana) and even Hawaii.

Research on Portuguese emigration to Brazil in colonial times has just begun under the supervision of Robert Rowland, whose first draft was presented during the XVIIth International Congress of Historical Sciences (Madrid, 1990). Historians have studied Portuguese emigration of the second half of the nineteenth century more thoroughly than that which took place after independence in

1822. We know, however, from official Portuguese reports as well as from the foreigners' registers in Brazil that in this first period the migratory flow was directed toward commercial rather than agricultural activities.

Between 1822 and 1838 the Register Books for Foreigners in the Brazilian National Archive reveal 2,987 Portuguese in Rio de Janeiro, 13.7 percent of whom arrived in 1836. This was a male immigration on the whole: only three women registered. The highest percent of immigrants (54.6 percent) was of young men between the ages of fifteen and twenty–four. These figures suggest that they were escaping conscription in the Portuguese army, which began at age fourteen. Of these men, only 10.7 percent were married and most of them traveled alone, leaving their wives in Portugal. Surprisingly, 85.5 percent could sign their name in the register book even if they were not fully literate. These Portuguese declared a great variety of occupations with a predominance of commercial clerks (*caixeiros*, 56.6 percent), followed by merchants (17.9 percent).

It is difficult sometimes to ascertain the place of birth (*naturalidade*) because some immigrants indicated it in a vague way: Portugal, northern Portugal, and so forth. We have precise indications that 32.2 percent were born in Oporto and 14 percent in Viana do Castello, towns located in northern Portugal, while 9.7 percent indicated the Atlantic Islands as their place of birth. In response to the question, "Where do you come from?" 59.9 percent answered "Oporto," meaning that they had embarked in this port, even if they lived in other northern towns. It is, however, interesting to notice that 16.1 percent of those who arrived in Rio de Janeiro had embarked in other Brazilian ports. Sometimes these immigrants registered only two or more years after their arrival in Brazil. Between 1822 and 1838, most immigrants arrived without a work contract.

In the mid–nineteenth century, the decline and extinction of the slave trade to Brazil led to a change in Brazilian policies toward immigration. As early as 1835 a deputy named Baptista Caetano de Almeida defended the immigration of Azorean colonists to the southern provinces of the empire; and the Brazilian consuls in Portugal as well as the Azorean merchants actively cooperated in the colonization project. Between 1836 and 1842, 3,681 emigrants left the islands of São Miguel and Faial, and also, though on a smaller scale, from Graciosa and Terceira. Their destinations included Pernambuco, Bahia, and Rio de Janeiro, and not the southern provinces, as Caetano de Almeida had proposed. The immigrants were badly needed in agriculture and Portuguese officials and consuls complained that "white slavery" had begun. In these years, work contracts were mostly verbal. However, a written contract from Pernambuco reveals that one immigrant arrived with a debt of 107,253 *réis* because of the travel costs. He was bound to a sugar–mill owner, who was going to pay him 100,000 *réis* per year, and he had to work for him until his debt was fully paid.

In the province of São Paulo, the Portuguese worked in agricultural "colonies" along with immigrants from other European countries. In an official report presented to the Provincial Assembly in 1858, Portuguese individuals and families were working in the following colonies: "Senador Vergueiro" (313 workers); "Cresciumal" (17); "Boa Vista" (74); "Morro Azul" (44); another "Boa Vista" (47); "São João do Morro Grande" (28); "Tatu" (135); "Capitão Diniz" (13); still another "Boa Vista" (22); and "Sítio Novo" (23). Even if this 1858 list is not complete, coffee planters had already imported 716 Portuguese workers, most of them under a special form of contract called *de parceria* (sharecropping). When the coffee was sold, half of the net amount of money obtained from the sale belonged to the planter and the other half to the colonist.

Agricultural immigration from the Azorean islands and also from mainland Portugal followed the first immigration that was related to commercial activities. However, both coexisted in the second half of the nineteenth century. In the 1880s a systematic policy of subsidies directed the Portuguese migratory flow to the coffee plantations in São Paulo, but even then the Portuguese continued to seek destinations ouside the coffee areas, taking up traditional forms of employment as artisans and merchants. Less related to Brazilian economic cycles, Portuguese immigration continued to spread all over the country; unlike other European immigrations, it did not concentrate exclusively in the southern states.

As the Portuguese immigrants were predominantly male, few studies have concentrated on female immigrants, except those that focus on prostitution and domestic service. Data from the Portuguese consulates in the 1870s reveal that in Rio de Janeiro in 1872, 35,740 men registered and only 4,280 women; in Bahia, in the same year, women represented only 4.2 percent of the registered immigrants. Without giving any specific numbers, the consul in Pará thought that female immigration was only 2 percent of male immigration. The women who emigrated alone in the second half of the nineteenth century were employed as servants or were classified as prostitutes in the consular reports. By the end of the nineteenth century, the number of female immigrants had risen due to increased family immigration and new opportunities for female work in cities such as Rio de Janeiro. According to the 1920 census, the percentage of Portuguese women in Brazil had risen to 32.8 percent of the Portuguese. Most of them were living in the Federal District, the city of Rio de Janeiro (54,734), and in the state of São Paulo (65,283).

Such statistics may be unreliable since Portuguese officials only recorded authorized emigrants, and many Portuguese emigrated illegally through Spain, especially from the port of Vigo in Galicia. Sometimes they traveled with a Spanish passport and were included, on their arrival, in the Spanish group. The discrepancies between the Portuguese and the Brazilian data have been pointed out by June Hahner (1986), who presents a useful table of Portuguese immigrants entering Brazil from 1884 to 1923.

The Portuguese emigration to Venezuela only began in the 1940s, and by the 1980s around 300,000 Portuguese immigrants lived in that country. Most of them resided in Caracas, and most of them participated in commercial affairs.

See also **Portugal.**

BIBLIOGRAPHY

Marcelo J. Borges, "Características residenciales de los inmigrantes portugueses en Buenos Aires en la segunda mitad de siglo XIX," in *Estudios Migratorios Latino–Americanos* 6, no. 18 (1991): 223–247.

Marcelo J. Borges, "Historia y memoria en una comunidad rural de inmigrantes portugueses: Las fuentes orales en los estudios migratorios," in *Estudios de Historia Rural* 7 (1991): 131–155.

José Guerreiro, "Análise tendencial da emigração portuguesa nos Últimos anos," in *Estudos sobre a emigração portuguesa,* edited by Maria Beatriz Rocha Trindade (1981).

June E. Hahner, "Jacobinos versus Galegos: Urban Radicals versus Portuguese Immigrants in Rio de Janeiro in the 1890s," in *Journal of Interamerican Studies and World Affairs* 18, no. 2 (1976): 125–154.

Miriam Halpern Pereira, "O rico 'brasileiro' ou o dinheiro dos emigrantes," in *Seara Nova* 1485 (1969): 242–244.

David Higgs, ed., *Portuguese Migration in Global Perspective* (1990).

Maria Beatriz Nizza Da Silva, *Filantropia e imigração: A Caixa de Socorros D. Pedro V* (1990).

Maria Beatriz Nizza Da Silva, *Documentos para a história da imigração portuguesa no Brasil, 1850–1938* (1991).

Manuel J. Pinto Dos Santos, "Subsídios para o estudo da emigração açoriana para o Brasil," in *Revista da Sociedade Brasileira de Pesquisa Histórica* 3 (1986–1987): 47–73.

Maria Beatriz Rocha Trindade, "Refluxos culturais da emigração portuguesa para o Brasil," in *Cadernos Luso–Brasileiros* 1 (1987): 35–52.

Additional Bibliography

Lobo, Eulália Maria Lahmeyer. *Portugueses en Brasil en el siglo XX.* Madrid: Editorial MAPFRE, 1994.

MARIA BEATRIZ NIZZA DA SILVA

PORTUGUESE LANGUAGE.

In Brazil, as in other American countries, the European settlements were created by people from all parts of the mother country. The varieties of speech that existed, and still exist, in Portugal were mixed and combined into a more or less general speech in the colony. There was, of course, in the early colonial period, a speech characteristic of a limited class, which was, or tried to be, similar to that of the Portuguese court. But the speech of the ordinary folk of each region of the colony became more or less uniform. Certain differences developed among the various regions; these still persist to some extent, although within the last generation there has been a strong tendency toward uniformity.

After Brazil became independent, the influence of formal education and the continuance of the class system for a long time perpetuated a considerable difference between the speech of the upper levels of society and that of the lower ones. But during the twentieth century a new middle class arose in considerable numbers and brought with it its own manner of speaking, so that the special language of the former upper classes generally disappeared.

The area in which this speech is largely based is the city of Rio de Janeiro. Like that of all other regions, the speech here is characterized principally by certain features of pronunciation, such as palatalization of *t* and *d* before *e* and *i* (*tʃ* and *dʒ*), some of them peculiar to the city itself, others common to the entire area. The region may be defined roughly as consisting of the states of Rio de Janeiro, Espírito Santo, and most of Minas Gerais. The southwestern part of Minas, roughly the part known as the Zona Sul, shows great similarity of speech to the state of São Paulo. The slang of Rio de Janeiro, extraordinarily rich and varied, is universal in the speech of the area, to the extent that the boundaries between slang and more formal language have been practically obliterated. Some slang has long penetrated even serious literature, the lectures of university professors, and even the pulpit. As elsewhere, some types are specialized—used by students, the military, certain professions, or the underworld. Slang does not often affect the structure of the language but is confined largely to unusual use of words, or to phrases that have special meanings in the context in which they are used.

One of the most notable developments in the speech of Brazil in the last quarter of the twentieth century was the rapid expansion of the typical speech of Rio de Janeiro through a large part of the country. There are several reasons for this. The city's cultural prestige and the influence of radio and television played considerable roles. Many network programs originate in Rio, and well-known personalities of radio and television often have ties to the city and its local speech. In addition, the educational system of the country has adopted the speech of Rio as the standard of language for the schools. While this fact undoubtedly enhances the prestige of *carioca* speech, the influence of other factors is probably much greater. The most important factor in the spread of the speech of Rio is probably the mystique of the "Marvelous City" itself. However, as the financial center of Latin America, São Paulo's influence cannot be underestimated. In the interior of the state of São Paulo there are cities in

which the *caipira* dialect has been handed down from early colonial times. Northeastern residents likewise have distinctive accents.

In the twenty-first century, Portuguese is spoken throughout the world, and the Lusophone nations of Europe, South America, Africa, and Asia continue to develop diplomatic, cultural, and linguistic ties. After an intense period of decolonialization during the 1970s, these nations include Brazil, Portugal, Mozambique, Angola, São Tomé and Príncipe, Cape Verde, Guinea-Bissau, and East Timor, as well as a small region each in China (Macau) and India (Goa). The Lusophone nations that are independent are bound together by the *Comunidade dos Países de Língua Portuguesa*, the Community of Portuguese Language Countries.

See also **Portugal; Rio de Janeiro (City).**

BIBLIOGRAPHY

Earl W. Thomas, *A Grammar of Spoken Brazilian Portuguese* (1974).

Additional Bibliography

Castro, Yeda Pessoa de. *Falares africanos na Bahia: Um vocabulário afro-brasileiro*. Rio de Janeiro: Academia Brasileira de Letras, Topbooks, 2001.

Cristóvão, Fernando Alves; Maria de Lourdes A. Ferraz; and Alberto Carvalho. *Nacionalismo e regionalismo nas literaturas lusófonas*. Lisbon: Edições Cosmos, 1997.

Dietrich, Wolf, and Volker Noll. *O português do Brasil: Perspectivas da pesquisa atual*. Madrid: Iberoamericana; Frankfurt am Main: Vevuert, 2004.

Louceiro, Clenir; Emília Ferreira; and Elizabeth Ceita Vera Cruz. *7 vozes: Léxico coloquial do português luso-afro-brasileiro: Aproximações*. Lisbon: LIDEL, 1997.

Machado Filho, Américo Venâncio Lopes, and Sônia Bastos Borba Costa. *Do português arcaico ao português Brasileiro*. Salvador, Bahia, Brazil: EDUFBA, 2004.

Megenney, William W. *A Bahian Heritage: An Ethnolinguistic Study of African Influences on Bahian Portuguese*. Chapel Hill: UNC Department of Romance Languages, University of North Carolina Press, 1978.

Pessoa, Marlos de Barros. *Formação de uma variedade urbana e semi-oralidade: O caso do Recife, Brasil*. Tübingen, Germany: Niemeyer, 2003.

Rodríguez-Seda de Laguna, Asela. *Global Impact of the Portuguese Language*. New Brunswick, NJ: Transaction, 2001.

Roncarati, Cláudia, and Jussara Abraçado. *Português brasileiro: Contato lingüístico, heterogeneidade e história*. Rio de Janeiro, Brazil: 7 Letras, 2003.

                                    RICHARD A. MAZZARA

PORTUGUESE OVERSEAS ADMINISTRATION.

Portuguese Overseas Administration (Casa da India and Conselho da India). Within two decades after the Portuguese conquest of Ceuta in 1415, a Casa de Ceuta was established in Lisbon to arm and provision Portuguese North Africa. Later in that century, as the Portuguese worked their way southward along the coast of Africa, similar institutions were established. By 1445, in the Algarve seaport of Lagos, an agency had been established for the trade with Arguim. A few years later, another was created in Lagos for trade with the Guinea coast. The latter, called the Casa da Guiné, was eventually transferred to Lisbon. Early in the reign of King João II (1481–1495), as the crown sought to tighten its control over exploration and mercantile activity along the west coast of Africa, its title and jurisdiction were enlarged to include Mina on the Gold Coast. By late 1501, after the return from India of the expeditions of Vasco Da Gama and Pedro Álvares Cabral, a Casa da India was established in Lisbon.

As the sixteenth century progressed, the Casa da India became the main institution for administering overseas activity. The history of all those administrative entities was marked by frequent reorganizations and a variety of additional designations, such as the sixteenth-century ones of Casa da Guiné e India, the Casa da Mina e Indias, and the Casa da Guiné, Mina e India. The Casa da India served many functions: it was a customhouse; the crown's private trading agency; the superintendent of such crown monopolies as gold, spices, and brazilwood; and a supply house for all the crown's overseas expeditions. By the early sixteenth century the casa was located on the ground floor of the royal palace on the Lisbon waterfront.

In 1486 a Casa dos Escravos with its own officials was established and attached to the Casa da Guiné e Mina. Staffed by different personnel, but working closely with the Casa da Guiné e Mina and eventually with the Casa da India, was the Armazém da Guiné, later known as the Armazém da Mina e India. Headed by a *provedor*, the Armazém was responsible for the construction, outfitting, and manning of overseas shipping. The same *provedor* was also in charge of the nearby Armazém dos Mantimentos and the Armazém das Armas, which provisioned and armed shipping destined for the Portuguese overseas. A judicial official, the *juiz da Guiné e India* (judge of Guinea and India), had jurisdiction over the Casa and the Armazém.

In 1509, the agencies supervising overseas activity (which now included Portuguese America) were reorganized and granted a new *regimento*, or set of standing orders. In 1516, King Manuel I (r. 1495–1521) enacted major financial reforms and named three *vedores da fazenda* (overseers of the treasury). Among their many responsibilities were overseas finances and the careful supervision of overseas trade. In 1527, King João III (r. 1521–1557) increased the number of *vedores da fazenda* to four. During that monarch's reign, three *mesas* (boards) and tribunals of finance (one of which was responsible for India, Mina, Guinea, and Brazil) evolved. Under King Sebastian (r. 1557–1578), the three individual *mesas* were united under one *mesa da fazenda* with a separate department for Portugal's holdings overseas. In 1584, the new Hapsburg monarch of Portugal, King Philip II (r. 1580–1598), divided the *mesa da fazenda* into three, with one of the *mesas* having jurisdiction over India, Mina, Guinea, and Brazil. Seven years later, a second major financial reform was instituted. By a decree dated 20 November 1591, Philip II created a Conselho da Fazenda (Treasury Council) for Portugal. Initially headed by a *vedor da fazenda* who served as president, the council also had four councillors (two of whom were *letrados* with law degrees) and four secretaries. The council's jurisdiction was divided into four *repartições*, with one of these covering India, Mina, Guinea, Brazil, and the islands of São Tomé and Cape Verde. During the next five decades the Conselho da Fazenda underwent a number of organizational modifications.

The most important change took place in 1604, when many of its overseas responsibilities were transferred to a new tribunal, the Conselho da India (Council of India). With its *regimento* dated 25 July 1604, the new council was established to govern the Portuguese overseas empire. The Council of India had a president, four councillors (two military men and two *letrados,* one of whom held a degree in canon law), and two secretaries. Though the Conselho da India had broad powers, the Conselho da Fazenda retained control of a number of its earlier responsibilities. Bitter rivalries with the Portuguese Conselho da Fazenda, the Desembargo do Paço, and the Mesa da Consciência e Ordens doomed the Conselho da India to a short lifetime. On 21 May 1614, King Philip III ordered its extinction. Within several months the Conselho da India's responsibilities were restored to the tribunals that earlier had held them. Most of the functions of the Conselho da India were taken over by the Conselho da Fazenda until 1643. In December of that year, the newly created Conselho Ultramarino (Overseas Council) took responsibility for all the overseas matters previously under the jurisdiction of the Conselho da Fazenda and the Conselho da India.

See also **Conselho da Fazenda; Portuguese Empire.**

BIBLIOGRAPHY

A survey of Portuguese overseas administration with a focus on the Council of India is found in Francisco Paulo Mendes Da Luz, *O Conselho da India* (1952). Very useful is the doctoral dissertation of Joseph Newcombe Joyce, Jr., "Spanish Influence on Portuguese Administration: A Study of the Conselho da Fazenda and Habsburg Brazil, 1580–1640" (University of Southern California, 1974). A brief summary of the history of the precursors of the Overseas Council is found in Marcello Caetano, *O Conselho Ultramarino: Esboço da sua história* (1967). Also valuable are the three articles by Maria Emília Cordeiro Ferreira in the *Dicionário de história de Portugal* entitled "India, Armazém da"; "India, Casa da"; and "Mina, Casa da." For discussion of the sixteenth-century economic reforms, see Virginia Rau, *A Casa dos Contos* (1951). The text of the 1509 reorganization and subsequent reforms is found in Damião Peres, ed., *Regimento das Cazas das Indias e Mina* (1947). A revision of the Regimento da Casa da India was prepared ca. 1630. A transcription of the manuscript (from Spain's Archivo General de Simancas) and an introduction can be found in Francisco Mendes Da Luz, *Regimento da Casa da India,* 2d ed. (1992). John Vogt, *Portuguese Rule on the Gold Coast, 1469–1682* (1979), provides a good description of how the Casa da Guiné e Mina operated.

Additional Bibliography

Bethencourt, Francisco, and Diogo Ramada Curto. *Portuguese Oceanic Expansion, 1400–1800.* Cambridge, UK: Cambridge University Press, 2007.

Fragoso, João Luís Ribeiro, Maria Fernanda Bicalho, and Maria de Fátima Gouvêa. *O Antigo Regime nos trópicos: A dinâmica imperial portuguesa, séculos XVI–XVIII.* Rio de Janeiro: Civilização Brasileira, 2001.

FRANCIS A. DUTRA

PORTUGUESE TRADE AND INTERNATIONAL RELATIONS.

Portugal was the major European commercial power in the Far East in the sixteenth century, and its Estado da India trading company operated throughout the Indian Ocean basin. Increased competition in the region, combined with vastly profitable sugarcane cultivation in Brazil led to Portugal's redoubled efforts in Brazil and a subsequent significant withdrawal from India in the period from 1580 to 1620. Consequently, the Portuguese reorganized the empire as their commercial and maritime power waned in the East; the East, however, never ceased growing in economic strength.

Portugal established the capital of its Asian empire at Goa, an ancient Hindu port on the Arabian Sea, in 1510. The Portuguese aim was to control the pepper trade of south India, the spice trade of the Moluccas, the sandalwood trade of Timor, and the coastal trade of western India and the northern areas of the Indian Ocean via the *cartaz* passport system, whereby Asian traders were forced to call at Portuguese ports to pay duties and to trade. Controlling trade enabled the Portuguese to seriously weaken the Muslim monopoly of spices. Asian products went from Goa to Lisbon, where the goods cleared the Casa da India (the institution controlling duties, running warehouses, and directing overseas voyages). Control of Asian commerce rested on Portuguese supremacy at Daman, Diu, Hormuz, and Aden, as well as at Malacca and the Spice Islands. Portugal failed to control Aden in 1551 and lost Hormuz in 1622; Holland seized the Moluccas in 1612, Malacca in 1641, Sri Lanka in 1658, and Cochin in 1663; and England gained Bombay via a royal dowry to Charles II in 1661. The Marathas conquered most Portuguese northern Indian provinces in 1739. Moreover, the Hindu Saraswat Brahmans in Goa and the Banyans throughout Portuguese India easily dominated economic life from early in the sixteenth century. Consequently, Portuguese trade declined sharply in the East after 1620.

In the eighteenth century, Goa, Daman, and Diu maintained close commercial ties with Mozambique through exports of Indian cotton cloth and imports of ivory, gold, and slaves. From 1759, when the captain-generalship of Mozambique was established, until 1818, the area was under the jurisdiction of Goa. The slave trade from Mozambique to Portuguese India ended in the 1830s. Slavers, however, found expanding markets in Brazil to 1850, and in the French islands of the Indian Ocean until the 1880s.

The annual ship linking Lisbon and Goa often stopped in Bahia between the early sixteenth century and the 1830s. After 1783, there was a commercial renaissance because of the crown's semifree trade policy between selected Indian Ocean ports and Lisbon and because of Portuguese neutrality in the Anglo–French conflicts from the 1790s to 1815. After 1808, ships sailed directly to Brazil from the East. Brazilian gold and tobacco and reexported Spanish silver went from Brazil to Goa, while Indian cotton textiles entered Europe, Brazil, La Plata, and Africa. This Indo–Brazilian trade ended in the late 1820s. During the Napoleonic conflicts the British stationed troops in all Portuguese–Asian enclaves except Timor, for varying periods from 1799 to 1815. In addition, a conflict between the Catholic Saraswat Brahmans and the Portuguese over the issues of social position and racial prejudice in Goa flared in the Pinto Revolt of 1787. Forty-seven Goans died and many went to prison or exile. This revolt influenced crown administrators to adopt enlightened policies toward the rebels in the uprising in Minas Gerais, Brazil, in 1789. Declining Indian textile exports were offset by increased sales of opium to the Far East and silver from Guangdong (Canton) and Macau going to India.

Macau served as the transfer agent for Chinese silks and Japanese silver from 1560 to the 1630s. Prior to 1770, silk and porcelain went from Macau and China via Manila to Acapulco for Mexican silver. From the 1780s to the 1830s significant quantities of silver entered Macau from the Philippines but there are few indications of silk and porcelain exports to Manila; consequently, there probably existed direct trade from Guangdong to Manila. Impressive quantities of silver also entered India from China due to the opium trade. Opium exports from India to Macau were largely from Calcutta prior to 1805. After 1815, western India, especially Bombay and Daman, sent the bulk of the opium, called "malwa," to Macau and Guangdong. Legal opium shipments peaked at six thousand chests in 1836. The opium trade on Portuguese ships to Macau was controlled by Hindus, Muslims, Sindis, and Parsees, while only a small percentage was Portuguese. Portuguese India also sent raw cotton, sandalwood, and pepper to the Far East. Trade and commerce in the Portuguese eastern empire was perhaps 50 percent of Luso–Brazilian trade from 1780 to 1822.

British interests continued to dominate Portuguese–Indian foreign trade after 1800. Trade between India and Brazil declined precipitously in the 1820s. The substitution of Virginia for Bahia in supplying the tobacco monopoly of Portuguese India signified the closing of commercial links between Brazil and Goa in the 1830s. Trade between India and Latin America has been severely limited in the twentieth century. Since World War II, Goan ore exports have competed with Latin American suppliers. However, the levels of trade between India and Brazil picked up dramatically at the end of the twentieth century. In 2000 trade was valued at $488 million but jumped to $2 billion by 2006. Moreover, India has begun negotiations to create free trade areas with South American countries.

See also **Goa and Portuguese Asia; Portugal; Portuguese Empire; Portuguese in Latin America.**

BIBLIOGRAPHY

Charles R. Boxer, *Fidalgos in the Far East: 1550–1770* (1968), and *Four Centuries of Portuguese Expansion, 1415–1825: A Succinct Survey* (1969).

Anthony R. Disney, *Twilight of the Pepper Empire: Portuguese Trade in Southwest India in the Early Seventeenth Century* (1978).

Teotonio R. De Souza, *Medieval Goa: A Socio-Economic History* (1979).

Charles R. Boxer, *Portuguese India in the Mid-Seventeenth Century* (1980).

Rudy Bauss, "A Legacy of British Free Trade Policies: The End of Trade and Commerce Between India and the Portuguese Empire, 1780–1830," in *Calcutta Historical Journal* 6, no. 2 (1982): 81–115.

Michael N. Pearson, *The Portuguese in India,* vol. 1 of *The New Cambridge History of India* (1988).

Sanjay Subrahmanyam, *The Political Economy of Commerce: Southern India, 1500–1650* (1990), and *The Portuguese Empire in Asia, 1500–1700: A Political and Economic History* (1993).

Additional Bibliography

Ahmed, Afzal. *Portuguese Trade and Socio-Economic Changes on the Western Coast of India, 1600-1663.* Delhi: Originals, 2000.

Miller, Shawn William. *Fruitless Trees: Portuguese Conservation and Brazil's Colonial Timber.* Stanford, CA: Stanford University Press, 2000.

Pedreira, Jorge Miguel Viana. *Estrutura industrial e mercado colonial: Portugal e Brasil (1780–1830).* Lisbon: DIFEL, 1994.

Topik, Steven; Carlos Marichal; and Zephyr Frank, eds. *From Silver to Cocaine: Latin American Commodity Chains and the Building of the World Economy, 1500–2000.* Durham, NC: Duke University Press, 2006.

RUDY BAUSS

POSADA, JOSÉ GUADALUPE (1852–1913).

José Guadalupe Posada (*b.* 2 February 1852; *d.* 20 January 1913), Mexican printmaker. Posada grew up in Aguascalientes, Mexico, where he attended drawing classes for a short time. Otherwise, he was a self-taught artist. In 1868 he joined the local lithography shop of José Tinidad Pedroza, where the opposition newspaper *El Jicote* was printed. In 1872 Posada and Pedroza moved to León to open a print shop, and there they produced illustrations for documents, cigar wrappers, religious images, caricatures, and the like. Posada moved to Mexico City in 1888 and soon joined forces with editor Antonio Vanegas Arroyo, with whom he would work until his death. By this time Posada had begun to work in the simple, free-flowing style for which he would posthumously become known. He also changed medium, to a kind of print that could be quickly created and easily combined with text.

Posada illustrated flyers, sensational news stories, books of magic tricks, new songs, recipes, and numerous other items for the popular penny press, many of which were printed on colored tissue paper and haphazardly hand tinted. The images

for which Posada is now best known are the *calaveras* (skeletons) he created for the Day of the Dead celebrations. Though he produced well over twenty thousand images in print, in his lifetime Posada was not well known. He considered himself a printmaker and craftsman, not an artist. Posada died in Mexico City and was buried in a pauper's grave. Later, his works were discovered by the Mexican muralists, who made him their artistic mentor and teacher (though he had had little, if any, contact with them) and a political hero (though there is no evidence that he had any particular political affiliation). Posada made prints that satirized everyone and did not single out any one group. His prints do reflect the everyday life and concerns of the people of his time.

See also **Art: The Nineteenth Century; Art: The Twentieth Century.**

BIBLIOGRAPHY

Roberto Berdecio and Stanley Appelbaum, eds., *Posada's Popular Mexican Prints: 273 Cuts by José Guadalupe Posada* (1972).

José Guadalupe Posada, *José Guadalupe Posada Aguilar: [Exhibition] Commemorating the 75th Anniversary of His Death* (1988).

Julian Rothenstein, ed., *Posada: Messenger of Mortality* (1989).

Additional Bibliography

Frank, Patrick. *Posada's Broadsheets: Mexican Popular Imagery, 1890–1910.* Albuquerque: University of New Mexico Press, 1998.

Topete del Valle, Alejandro. *José Guadalupe Posada: Prócer de la gráfica popular mexicana.* México: Seminario de Cultura Mexicana, 2002.

KATHERINE CLARK HUDGENS

POSADAS, GERVASIO ANTONIO DE (1757–1833).

Gervasio Antonio de Posadas (*b.* 19 June 1757; *d.* 2 July 1833), Argentine political leader of the independence period. Born in Buenos Aires to Felipe Santiago de Posadas and María Antonia Dávila, Posadas studied languages, philosophy, and theology in the Franciscan convent of that city. Despite his initial ambivalence about the revolutionary cause, an uncertainty that landed him in jail in 1811, Posadas eventually held various high-level positions in the patriot regime. They included membership in the general assembly and the triumvirate in 1813 and the supreme directorate the following year. Bartolomé Mitre described him as an "objective observer with common sense in whom seriousness and humor were combined." Posadas was not seen in that light, however, by his enemies. In 1815 he was exiled for almost six years after the revolt against Carlos María de Alvear, his relative and a political ally. His autobiography was completed before his death. An 1833 order for a monument honoring Posadas to be erected in the Recoleta Cemetery of the capital has yet to be implemented.

See also **Argentina: The Nineteenth Century.**

BIBLIOGRAPHY

Carlos Alberto Silva, *El Poder Legislativo y la Nación Argentina* (1937).

Jacinto R. Yaben, *Biografías argentinas y sudamericanas,* vol. 4 (1938–1940), pp. 701–704.

Arturo Capdevila, *Vidas de grandes argentinos,* vol. 2 (1966), pp. 381–385.

Additional Bibliography

Szuchman, Mark D., and Jonathan C. Brown. *Revolution and Restoration: The Rearrangement of Power in Argentina, 1776–1860.* Lincoln: University of Nebraska Press, 1994.

FIDEL IGLESIAS

POSADAS OCAMPO, JUAN JESÚS

(1926–1993). Cardinal archbishop of Guadalajara, Mexico, Posadas Ocampo was born on November 10, 1926, in Salvatierra, Guanajuato, and completed his seminary studies in Morelia in 1943. A product of the anticlerical environment in the 1930s, Ocampo Posadas began his career as a parish priest in Patzcuaro, Michoacán, in 1950, after which he became a professor at his alma mater until 1969. He was then selected as bishop of Tijuana and served there from 1970 to 1982. The following year he became bishop of Cuernavaca, Morelos, where he actively countered the liberal liberation influence of his predecessor. He held many posts in the Mexican Episcopate and became archbishop of Guadalajara, one of Mexico's most influential dioceses, in 1987.

An outspoken critic of the government, he was mistakenly murdered on May 24, 1993, by gang members from Tijuana, allegedly hired to kill a drug kingpin. His assassination contributed significantly to an environment of political instability in Mexico.

See also **Catholic Church: The Modern Period.**

BIBLIOGRAPHY

Carpizo, Jorge, and Julián Andrade. *Asesinato de un Cardenal: Ganancia de pescadores.* Mexico: Nuevo Siglo Aguilar, 2002.

Moreno Valencia, Héctor, and José Alberto Villasana. *Sangre de mayo: El homocidio del cardinal Posadas Ocampo.* Mexico: Océano, 2002.

RODERIC AI CAMP

POSITIVISM. Positivism is a philosophy developed in France by Auguste Comte (1798–1857), who set out his views in the six-volume *Cours de philosophie positive* (1830–1842). Comte identified three stages of human thought: (1) the theological, (2) the metaphysical, and (3) the positive, this last being the culminating stage, when reliance on supernatural and abstract entities is replaced by empirical, scientific explanation. In his classification of the sciences, Comte placed sociology in a supreme position (modern sociologists do in fact regard him as one of the great pioneers in their field), whereas in his study of "social dynamics" he sought to analyze the conditions of progress. Reason, order, and progress were key terms in the Comtean lexicon. Later on, Comte tried to ground his theories in a paradoxical "religion of humanity," with ceremonies reminiscent of those of Catholicism. In Europe one of the writers most strongly influenced by positivism was Herbert Spencer (1820–1903), who combined it with insights drawn from Darwinian evolutionism.

In Latin America positivist influence was at its height in the last quarter of the nineteenth century. It was a major intellectual trend in the region, best seen in the context of the attempts made from the 1870s onward to modernize and rationalize the Latin American states, at precisely the moment when the region was being drawn more closely into the international division of labor that was a feature of the burgeoning world capitalist economy. Positivist ideas (not least their emphasis on order, science, and progress) proved attractive to several generations of Latin American intellectuals, who were eager to overcome the still tenacious social legacy of the colonial period and to stimulate the kind of progress they perceived as taking place in western Europe and North America. Several countries are clearly associated with the impact of positivism. In each, however, the results were somewhat different.

In Brazil, given the persistence of monarchy, positivism took a distinctively republican slant, and positivists were in the forefront of the movement to overthrow the Empire in 1889. Miguel Lemos (1854–1917) and Raimundo Teixeira Mendes (1855–1927) developed Comte's "religious" tendency and founded a Positivist Church in Rio (1881). Another major focus of positivist teaching was the Military School of Rio de Janeiro. Benjamin Constant Botelho de Magalhães (1836–1891), one of the school's instructors, made aggressive contributions to politicizing Brazilian positivism.

In Mexico the chief agent of positivism was Gabino Barreda, educational reformer of the Benito Juárez period and director of the Escuela Nacional Preparatoria (1867). Barreda left as his legacy the group of advisers to Porfirio Díaz known (after 1892) as the "científicos." This group advanced an interpretation of positivism that was both elitist and informed by concerns with race. Members included Justo Sierra (1848–1912), Francisco Bulnes (1847–1924), and José Yves Limantour (1854–1935).

In Argentina, positivism was compatible with the highly influential thought of Domingo Faustino Sarmiento (1811–1888). Comte's ideas provided him with new tools for developing the more subtle racialist contents of his early work. His book *Conflicto y armonías de las razas en América* (1883; Conflict and harmonies of races in the Americas) was defined by Sarmiento himself as a scientific and well-documented rewriting of his "too literary" masterpiece *Facundo* (1845). The "whitening" of Argentina also factored as a major concern for positivists such as Carlos Octavio Bunge (1875–1918) and José Ingenieros (1877–1925).

In Chile intellectuals developed two positivist currents. One, a strongly "religious" faction, was led by the Lagarrigue brothers, Juan (1852–1927), Jorge (1854–1894), and Luis (1864–1949). A second, more heterodox faction, advanced predominantly democratic readings of Comte, such as those of José Victorino Lastarria (1817–1888). Valentín Letelier (1852–1919), another heterodox, was a member of the Radical Party and rector of the University of Chile.

Latin American positivism was flexible in its appeal. The Puerto Rican pedagogue and sociologist Eugenio María de Hostos (1839–1903) used it to fight for a full decolonization of the Hispanic Caribbean, whereas Peruvian writers such as Manuel González Prada (1848–1918) and Mercedes Cabello de Carbonera (1845–1909) used it to criticize ethnic and/or gender discrimination. Conversely, the Venezuelan sociologist Laureano Vallenilla Lanz (1870–1936) described dictatorship as an unavoidable consequence of Latin America's history and ethnic makeup, and the Bolivian writer Alcides Arguedas (1879–1946) asserted in *Pueblo enfermo* (1909; A sick people) that native cultures and interracial breeding posed overwhelming obstacles for progress. Although the label becomes less useful after about 1920, traces of "positivist" thought can be found in a number of twentieth-century literary, philosophical, and political movements.

See also **Bulnes, Francisco; Bunge, Carlos Octavio; González Prada, Manuel; Ingenieros, José; Limantour, José Yves; Philosophy: Overview.**

BIBLIOGRAPHY

Hale, Charles A. *The Transformation of Liberalism in Late Nineteenth-Century Mexico*. Princeton, NJ: Princeton University Press, 1989.

Martí, Oscar. *The Revolt against Positivism in Latin America*. Ph.D. diss., City University of New York, 1978.

Mead, Karen. "Gendering the Obstacles to Progress in Positivist Argentina, 1880–1920." *Hispanic American Historical Review* 77, no. 4 (1997): 645–675.

Woodward, Ralph L., ed. *Positivism in Latin America, 1850–1900*. Lexington, MA: Heath, 1971.

Zea, Leopoldo. *Positivism in Mexico*. Austin: University of Texas Press, 1974.

Zea, Leopoldo, ed. *Pensamiento positivista latinoamericano*, 2 vols. Caracas: Biblioteca Ayacucho, 1980.

SIMON COLLIER
MIGUEL GOMES

POSITIVIST CHURCH OF BRAZIL.

Positivist Church of Brazil, a politically influential civic-religious organization founded on the tenets of Auguste Comte (1798–1857), the French philosopher and political theorist who founded the school of positivism. After studying in Paris from 1877 to 1881, Miguel Lemos returned to his native Brazil to promote the writings of Comte. In 1881 Lemos founded the church in Rio de Janeiro in order to cultivate positivism in Brazilian public and private life. The Positivist church's institutional mission reflected the later, more spiritual tenets of Comte's views on the value of positivist thinking and practice in social organization. Thus, the Positivist church developed elaborate ecclesiastical structures and religious rituals that were not to be found in the more political-technical redoubts of positivism, such as the Escola Politécnica and military academies, or among the disciples of a Brazilian positivist as prominent as Lemos—Benjamin Constant Botelho De Magalhães.

Active in the political and rhetorical jockeying that followed the fall of the monarchy on 15 November 1889, as well as later in the republican period, members of the Igreja Positivista (orthodox positivists, as opposed to the heterodox positivists who never became active church members) were vocal advocates of public education, literacy, social harmony, and cultural nationalism. Although still functioning in the twenty-first century, the church has experienced a steadily declining influence in the intellectual and cultural formation of Brazil's social and political elite.

See also **Positivism.**

BIBLIOGRAPHY

Miguel Lemos, *Resumo histórico do movimento positivista no Brasil* (1882; 1981).

Robert G. Nachman, "Brazilian Positivism as a Source of Middle Sector Ideology" (Ph.D. diss., University of California at Los Angeles, 1972).

José Murilo De Carvalho, *A formação das almas: O imaginário da república no Brasil* (1990), pp. 129–140.

Additional Bibliography

Moussatché, Iara, Maria Isabel Gomes de Sant'Anna, and Regina Célia Alves. *Igreja Positivista do Brasil: Acervo bibliográfico.* 2nd ed. Rio de Janeiro: Museu da República, 1994.

Soares, Mozart Pereira. *O positivismo no Brasil: 200 anos de Augusto Comte.* Porto Alegre: AGE Editora: Editora da Universidade, Universidade Federal do Rio Grande do Sul, 1998.

DARYLE WILLIAMS

POST, FRANS JANSZ (1612–1680).

Frans Jansz Post was a Dutch painter known for his Brazilian landscapes. Born in Haarlem in the Netherlands, Post was the nephew of the noted architect Pieter Post, famous for his work on the Mauritshuis at The Hague. Post was part of Johan Maurits's artistic entourage and most probably accompanied the governor-general of Dutch Brazil when he arrived in America in 1637. Post traveled widely in Brazil and accompanied Maurits on a number of military campaigns. One of Post's main tasks in Brazil seems to have been preparing sketches of a variety of fortifications and buildings. His first dated work in Brazil was a view of Itamaracá, north of Pernambuco, in 1637. His last dated work (1640) was the island of Antônio Vaz, renamed Mauritsstad, which became the capital of Dutch Brazil and in the early twenty-first century is part of downtown Recife. However, a drawing of Mauritsstad with Vrijburg (the name Maurits gave to his palace on the island) reveals Post's presence in Pernambuco in early 1644 because of the inclusion of a bridge connecting the island to Recife.

Post seems to have left Brazil shortly after completing this drawing and before Maurits departed in May 1644. Many experts believe that Post visited Dutch-controlled parts of West Africa on his return to Europe and later contributed a number of drawings (dated 1645) of Elmina, Luanda, and São Tomé that were the basis of engravings for Caspar Barlaeus's *Rerum per octennium in Brasilia* (1647). However, some other authors, pointing to the absence of African landscapes by Post, argue that the artist could have based the drawings on the work of another.

Post made many sketches in Brazil, but only a relatively small number of his known paintings seem to have been completed there. The great majority of his landscapes were painted in the Netherlands after his return. In these works he occasionally regrouped buildings or had them facing in the wrong direction. These paintings include many architectural details of forts, town houses, palaces, sugar mills, sheds, churches (often in ruin), convents, chapels, monasteries, plantation houses and their outbuildings, and thatched huts. The landscapes also show many aspects of daily life, especially that of the region's many African slaves. Because of Post's eye for detail, his paintings and sketches have been invaluable to a wide variety of scholars of seventeenth-century Brazil. Good examples are his drawings of both water- and animal-powered sugar mills and their labor forces. His last dated landscape portrayed Pernambuco's *várzea*, or sugar-producing region (1669).

The remaining years of his life were ones of decline. In 1679 Post was described by Jacob Cohen, banker and agent of Maurits, as "covertly degraded by drink and trembling" (Whitehead, p. 180). The following year Post died in Haarlem, where he had reestablished his residence in 1646 after returning from Brazil.

See also **Art: The Colonial Era; Brazil: The Colonial Era, 1500–1808; Maurits, Johan.**

BIBLIOGRAPHY

Joppien, Rudigier. "The Dutch Vision of Brazil: Johan Maurits and His Artists." In *Johan Maurits van Nassau-Siegen, 1604–1679*, edited by E. van den Boogaart, pp. 297–376. The Hague: Johan Maurits van Nassau Stichting, 1979.

Larsen, Erik. *Frans Post, interprète du Brésil*. Amsterdam: Colibris Editora, 1962.

Smith, Robert C., Jr. "The Brazilian Landscapes of Frans Post." *Art Quarterly* 1, no. 4 (1938): 238–267.

Sousa Leão, Joaquim de. *Frans Post, 1612–1680*. Amsterdam: A. L. van Gendt, 1973.

Whitehead, Peter J. P., and Marinus Boeseman. *A Portrait of Dutch 17th Century Brazil: Animals, Plants, and People by the Artists of Johan Maurits of Nassau*. Amsterdam and New York: North-Holland, 1989.

FRANCIS A. DUTRA

POTATO. The high Andes Mountains were the first area of domestication for the potato, the most important root crop in the world. The potato supported many pre-Columbian Andean civilizations, culminating with the Incas. Originally cultivated as a cool-weather crop, it was an important contributor to the agricultural and industrial revolutions of Europe. Today, the potato is increasingly relied upon in the tropics as a staple for underdeveloped countries.

The potato is a member of the *Solanaceae* family, which includes several other New World domesticates such as tomatoes, tobacco, and Chile peppers. The genus *Solanum* is one of many tuber-bearing species found in the Andes. Biologists recognize eight cultivated species within the genus. Like many other cultivated plants, potatoes can be segregated according to the number of chromosomes, and four chromosome groups, diploid to pentaploid, are cultivated in the Andes. Outside of their home, however, only the tetraploids are common. Thousands of distinct types of potatoes are grown in the Andes, distinguished by color, shape, number and depth of "eyes," and other plant characteristics. The International Potato Center in Lima, Peru, has a collection of over 3,600 potato varieties.

EARLY CULTIVATION

The potato was one of several root crops to be domesticated in the Andes, but it is by far the most important. The earliest plant remains of domesticated potatoes occur around 5000 BCE. The tubers were modeled in ancient Peruvian ceramics, starting with the Nazca culture after about CE 1 and subsequently throughout the pre-European period. The Incas facilitated empire building by feeding their armies with freeze-dried potatoes. Several South American Indian names exist for potato, but the Quechua term *papa* was universally adopted in Latin America after its diffusion by the Spaniards in the sixteenth century. There is no evidence of potato cultivation outside of the Andes before 1500.

The Andean tuber first arrived in Europe in Spain (1570) and then England (1588). The actual origin of the European potato is disputed. Genetic evidence suggests that European varieties came from Chile, where the plant was adapted to long days similar to those found in northern Europe. The trip between Chile and Europe in the sixteenth century was long and arduous, and Chilean tubers might not have survived the journey. Moreover, the first potatoes to become established in Europe

Harvesting potatoes, Cuzco, Peru, 2004. © KAZUYOSHI NOMACHI/CORBIS

did better in the shorter days of southern Europe, suggesting that they perhaps came from the central or northern Andes.

The potato was slow to become established in Europe, but once established it played a major role in revolutionizing northern European agriculture. For nearly two centuries following its introduction into Europe, the potato was a curiosity, often regarded with skepticism. In several countries, its cultivation was prohibited because of its resemblance to deadly nightshade and because the plant was believed to cause diseases such as leprosy and tuberculosis. General acceptance of the potato occurred after 1785, following the efforts of the French chemist Parmentier, who suggested that King Louis XVI promote the crop by pretending to guard a mature field with soldiers who were withdrawn at night so the valuable tubers could be stolen.

Potatoes were especially important in increasing the productivity of land in more northerly areas where cereals had been the staple. The tubers produce two or three times as many calories as wheat or rye on the same amount of land, although they require more labor than the cereals. Ireland experienced the first conversion to potatoes as the major staple, and the island's increase in population in the eighteenth century was due to the tuber's productivity. Steadily rising cereal prices in Europe after 1750 led to increased potato cultivation throughout northern Europe.

One of history's worst famines followed the outbreak of a potato fungus disease, late blight (*Phytophthora infestans*), in Ireland in 1845. More than a million of Ireland's 8 million people died, and more than 1.5 million emigrated. While late blight continues to be a major problem for potato growers everywhere, it is now effectively controlled by varietal resistance and fungicides.

MODERN CULTIVATION
Andean farmers, especially in Peru and Bolivia, continue to grow a vast diversity of potatoes. Part

of their crop is bitter potatoes of two Andean species that are frost resistant and can be produced in very high altitudes, up to 13,000 feet above sea level. These bitter tubers are processed by freeze-drying them into *chuño*. While the tuber remains important to Andean people, per capita consumption is higher in Poland, Germany, and Belgium than in Peru. Argentina, Colombia, and Guatemala are the primary potato exporters in Latin America, and their main markets are in their neighboring countries, rather than overseas.

Potatoes are produced under many different farming conditions and for different uses. Farmers in the Netherlands harvest an average of over 42 metric tons per acre, while in Peru and Bolivia the average yield is less than 10 tons per acre. Russia has more area sown to potatoes than any other country, and it leads the world in per capita consumption of the tubers. Andean farmers cultivate a dozen or more varieties on a small plot of land, while the variety Russet Burbank, first developed in 1874, is grown on tens of thousands of acres in North America. Potatoes are helping to satisfy human hunger in nonindustrial countries where population growth is high. Of the major staples in developing countries, potatoes have shown the greatest increase in production since 1961. Less-developed countries are discovering the same advantage of potatoes that was recognized in Europe 200 years ago. As land resources become increasingly scarce, potatoes deliver higher carbohydrate returns per acre than most other major food crops. Potatoes also contain a good protein-to-calorie ratio and high amounts of vitamins B and C.

The constraints on increased use of potatoes to feed the world include its high water content at harvest (80 percent), difficulty in storing and transporting fresh tubers, and difficulty in multiplying the seed of new varieties. The last problem is being overcome in some areas by the use of true botanical seed rather than tubers as seed.

See also **Agriculture.**

BIBLIOGRAPHY

John S. Niederhauser and William C. Cobb, "The Late Blight of Potatoes," in *Scientific American* 200 (May 1959): 100– 112.

Donovan S. Correll, *The Potato and Its Wild Relatives* (1962).

Cecil Woodham-Smith, *The Great Hunger: Ireland, 1845–1849* (1962).

W. G. Burton, *The Potato: A Survey of Its History and Factors Influencing Its Yield, Nutritive Value, Quality, and Storage* (1966).

Donald Ugent, "The Potato," in *Science* 170 (11 December 1970): 1161–1166.

Stephen B. Brush, Heath J. Carney, and Zozimo Huaman, "Dynamics of Andean Potato Agriculture," in *Economic Botany* 35 (1981): 70–85.

International Potato Center, *Potatoes for the Developing World* (1984).

E. J. Kahn, "Potatoes: Man Is What He Eats," in *The Staffs of Life* (1985).

Redcliffe Salaman, *The History and Social Influence of the Potato,* rev. ed. (1985).

Douglas Horton, *Underground Crops: Long-Term Trends in Production of Roots and Tubers* (1988).

J. G. Hawkes, *The Potato: Evolution, Biodiversity, and Genetic Resources* (1990).

Timothy Johns, *With Bitter Herbs They Shall Eat It: Chemical Ecology and the Origins of Human Diet and Medicine* (1990).

Carlos Ochoa, *The Potatoes of South America: Bolivia* (1990).

Additional Bibliography

Biarnès, Anne; Jean Philippe Colin; and Ma. de Jesús Santiago Cruz; eds. *Agroeconomía de la papa en México.* Mexico City: ORSTOM, Colegio de Postgraduados, 1995.

Ochoa, Carlos M., and Franz Frey. *Las papas de Sudamérica: Peru.* Lima: Centro Internacional de la Papa, 1999.

STEPHEN B. BRUSH

POTIGUAR. Potiguar, or Potiguara, a Tupi-speaking tribe of northeastern Brazil. According to an unnamed contemporary Jesuit, the Potiguar were the "largest and most united" of the coastal Tupi in sixteenth-century Brazil. Early trade relations with the French and traditional rivalry with the Tobajara made the Potiguar natural enemies of the Portuguese, who waged a long war against them in the conquest of Paraíba (1574–1599). Defeated, several Potiguar groups were placed in Jesuit missions, while others fought alongside the Portuguese against the Aimoré of southern Bahia and the Tupinambá of Maranhão and Pará. Potiguar factions became deeply involved in the

Luso-Dutch War (1645–1654) on both sides, with the native chief Felipe Camarão playing an especially critical role. A few small Potiguar groups, numbering just over 10,000, live today in Paraíba, at Traição Bay. In the twenty-first century the Potiguara were awaiting a federal Supreme Court decision in their struggle for land rights in Monte Mor and Jacaré de São Domingos.

See also **Indigenous Peoples; Tupi.**

BIBLIOGRAPHY

John Hemming, *Red Gold* (1978), provides the most complete account in English. The conquest of Paraíba is chronicled expertly in Frei Vicente Do Salvador, *História do Brasil* (1627). Charles Ralph Boxer, *Salvador da Sá and the Struggle for Brazil and Angola* (1992), covers the Luso–Dutch War in detail.

Additional Bibliography

Gurgel, Deífilo. *Espaço e tempo do folclore potiguar: Folclore geral, folclore Brasileiro.* Natal, Brazil: Governo do Estado do Rio Grande d Norte, Departamento Estadual de Imprensa, 2001.

Maia, Luciano Mariz, and Francisco Moonen, eds. *Etnohistória dos índios potiguara.* João Pessoa, Brazil: Secretaria da Educação e Cultura do Estado da Paraíba, 1992.

Pinto, Lenine, and Gerardo Pereira. *A integração do Rio Grande do Norte e do Amazônas à província do Brasil.* Natal, Brazil: RN Econômica, 1998.

JOHN M. MONTEIRO

POTOSÍ. Potosí, a city and region that was the most famous silver-mining center of the Spanish Empire. The *Villa Imperial* (Imperial Town) of Potosí was the envy of Spain's rivals throughout the colonial era. It perches high (ca. 13,100 feet) in the eastern range of the Andes in southern Bolivia, inland from the altiplano. Mining dates from the discovery of silver ores in the upper reaches of the Cerro Rico (Rich Hill) in 1545. The town developed rapidly, with a characteristic Spanish colonial gridiron plan, on a sloping site some two miles north of the summit of the cerro.

This site was one of the largest deposits of silver ore ever found by the Spanish in America and certainly the most concentrated rich deposit. The ore from the topmost few hundred feet of the Cerro made Potosí (with some help from district mines after 1600) the source of roughly half Spanish America's silver output up to 1650. Officially registered production to that date amounted to some 450 million ounces. Actual production was surely higher. Output boomed particularly in the last quarter of the sixteenth century, after the introduction in 1571 of a method of refining the ores with mercury (the amalgamation process). The decade from 1575 to 1585 was the most extraordinary in Potosí's history, with output quintupling. The highest-yielding year ever was 1592, when some 7.1 million ounces of silver were declared at the treasury office in the town. This immense quantity of metal was refined in eighty mills extending along the *Ribera* (water course) descending through Potosí. The noise of their water-driven stamps and the fumes coming from furnaces roasting ores must have made this seem an industrial city—as indeed it was, the first in colonial Spanish America.

By 1600, however, much of the easily accessible ore in the summit of the Cerro had been mined. Plenty of ore remained lower in the hill, but it was less rich and, because deeper, more expensive to extract. This high cost was the main reason for production leveling off around 1600 and then slowly declining for more than a century. During this time, various lesser deposits scattered over the highlands around Potosí were discovered; they became important for periods ranging from a few years to a few decades. The most productive of them (after Oruro, which was the center of a separate district) was probably San Antonio del Nuevo Mundo, 170 miles south-southwest of Potosí, active from about 1647 until the 1690s. San Antonio was worked to especially good effect by Antonio López De Quiroga. Although these district mines occasionally yielded as much silver as the Cerro itself, they generally flared but briefly, and their bonanzas served only to interrupt the downward trend of total production. The year of lowest output in the entire colonial period was 1712, with some 915,000 ounces registered from the Cerro and the district together. By this time Potosí was being overtaken in production by northern Mexican mines such as Zacatecas (1546) and Guanajuato (1550), which dominated Spanish-American silver output for the rest of the colonial period.

After some thirty years of flat output, the Potosí district staged a recovery from 1750 to 1800, though barely reaching half the production levels

Pack Train of Llamas Laden with Silver from Potosí Mines of Peru. From *Americae,* 1602 by Jacques Le Moyne (de Morgues) (d. 1587/88) after an engraving by Theodore de Bry (1528–1598). LIBRARY OF CONGRESS, WASHINGTON D.C., USA/ THE BRIDGEMAN ART LIBRARY

of two centuries earlier. The reasons for the recovery include higher demand for silver early in the eighteenth century, a reduction of the royalty tax in 1736 from a fifth to a tenth of gross production, great pressure on draft laborers to raise their productivity after about 1750, and possibly the expanding use of blasting to reach and remove ore.

Potosí suffered greatly, as did all silver-mining centers in Spanish America, during the Wars of Independence. Refining plants were destroyed, maintenance of mines was neglected, and, after the wars, capital for restoration of productive capacity was scarce and dear. The Cerro itself, however, still yielded about half Bolivia's silver in 1846. And in the last quarter of the century Potosí mining again saw substantial recovery, though it was largely the doing of district mines, such as Huanchaca, 75 miles southwest of the town, which in 1895 yielded just over 1 million ounces. Bolivian silver mining had benefited in general from the availability of cheaper mercury once large amounts began to be produced in California in 1850. This price cut for the prime raw material needed for amalgamation encouraged investment in silver mining by Bolivians for the first time since Independence. Foreign engineers were also brought in to advise on technical renovation. The outcome, at Huanchaca, was enlarged ore-crushing capacity, especially once steam-driven mills were installed in 1878, and improved methods of amalgamation. Potosí also benefited from the advice of foreign experts.

In the late 1890s a drop in the world price of silver severely depressed Bolivian silver mining. But at the same time world demand for tin was rising fast, a need that Bolivia, and particularly Potosí, was well endowed to meet. The department of Potosí proved to hold large and rich tin deposits, among the most famous of which was Uncía, 100 miles northwest of Potosí. Mining was developed there by Simón Iturri Patiño, the most famous of the Bolivian "tin barons," from 1897. Potosí shared in the tin boom, partly through extraction of tin ores from the Cerro Rico and partly through reprocessing of tailings (wastes) from silver refining, which proved rich in tin. Many tailings in Potosí have in fact been processed several times. Since the Bolivian Revolution of 1952, which nationalized the major tin companies, the large mines in the Cerro have been worked by the state mining company, Comibol (Mining Corporation of Bolivia), mainly for tin, though with some subsidiary product of silver. Enormous amounts of silver ore still remain in the Cerro, but they could be exploited profitably only by open-cast mining.

The great silver industry of colonial Potosí required many workers. From the late sixteen century on, about a half of these were wage laborers—Indians who found permanent employment in mines and refineries at a relatively high wage more desirable than other possible livelihoods. The other half, though, were native draftees, forced to work in mining and refining by the demands of the notorious Mita ("time" or "turn" in Quechua) set up in the 1570s by Don Francisco de Toledo, fifth viceroy of Peru. According to this system, some 13,400 adult male Indians came to Potosí each year from a highland catchment area reaching almost as far north as Cuzco. Each of them performed forced work in silver production for four of his twelve months' presence in Potosí. Many of these *mitayos* brought wives and children with them. These families often stayed on after the year was up, both men and women finding work in Potosí in a variety of possible jobs preferable to the long journey home. In this way, and because Potosí from the start offered much employment for Indians wanting to earn money for their tribute payments (among other things), the town's population grew fast. By 1600, it was very probably over 100,000. In the space of about fifty years, Potosí had become one of the world's most populous cities.

Most of this population was Indian, living in *rancherías* (native quarters) encircling the Spanish town center, with a particular concentration on the south side of the town beneath the Cerro. The sixteenth-century street plan of the center has changed little to the present. A rectangular pattern of streets, oriented north-south and east-west, extended out from the main plaza for three or four blocks in each direction. Mine and refinery owners, merchants, officials of the treasury and mint, town councillors, and priests lived here. Facing onto the central square were the main parish church of Potosí, the town hall, the mint, and the royal treasury offices.

Potosí had an estimated population of 768,203 as of 2005. Contrary to reports of its being a "ghost town," it is in fact an active administrative, marketing, and mining center. It is the capital of the department of Potosí, an area quite similar to the colonial mining district of which the *Villa Imperial* was the center. The department consists of parts of the western and eastern ranges of the Andes, with peaks approaching 20,000 feet, and the southern altiplano between them, at about 12,000 feet. It forms the southwestern corner of Bolivia, bordering on Argentina to the south and on Chile to the west. Apart from tin and silver, the department contains ores of bismuth, lead, copper, zinc, antimony, tungsten, and wolfram, some of which are worked.

See also **Bolivia: The Colonial Period; Mining: Colonial Spanish America.**

BIBLIOGRAPHY

Edmond Temple, *Travels in Various Parts of Peru, Including a Year's Residence in Potosí* (1830; repr. 1833, 1971). Philadelphia: E.E. Carey & A. Hart.

Lewis Hanke, *The Imperial City of Potosí*. The Hague: Nijhoff, 1956.

Cornelius H. Zondag, *The Bolivian Economy, 1952–1965; the Revolution and its Aftermath*. New York: Praeger, 1966.

Salomón Rivas and Raúl Carrasco, *Geología y yacimientos minerales de la región de Potosí* (1968).

Orlando Capriles Villazón, *Historia de la minería boliviana* La Paz: Banco Minero de Bolivia, 1977. Rose Marie Buechler, *The Mining Society of Potosí, 1776–1810*. Ann Arbor, MI: Published for Dept. of Geography, Syracuse University, by University Microfilms International, 1981.

Antonio Mitre, *Los patricarcas de la plata: Estructura socio-económica de la minería boliviana en el siglo XIX* (1981).

Enrique Tandeter, "Forced and Free Labour in Late Colonial Potosí," in *Past and Present* 93 (1981): 98–136.

Peter Bakewell, *Miners of the Red Mountain: Indian Labor in Potosí, 1545–1650*. Albuquerque: University of New Mexico Press, 1984.

Jeffrey A. Cole, *The Potosí Mita, 1573–1700: Cumpulsory Indian Labor in the Andes*. Stanford, CA: Stanford University Press, 1985.

Gastón Arduz Eguía, *Ensayos sobre la historia de la minería altoperuana*. Madrid: Editorial Paraninfo, 1985.

Enrique Tandeter, *Coercion and Market: Silver Mining in Colonial Potosí, 1692–1826*. Albuquerque: University of New Mexico Press, 1993.

Additional Bibliography

Klein, Herbert. *A Concise History of Bolivia*. New York: Cambridge University Press, 2003.

Mangan, Jane E. *Trading Roles: Gender, Ethnicity, and the Urban Economy in Colonial Potosí*. Durham, NC: Duke University Press, 2005.

PETER BAKEWELL

POYAIS.   Poyais, a loosely defined geographic area drained by the Black River (Río Tinto) on the Caribbean coast of Honduras. The name derives from the original inhabitants of the region, the Poyas Indians (usually spelled Payas, sometimes Poyers or Pawyers). The undeveloped area, historically important as the western extremity of British Mosquito Coast, spawned several speculative colonization projects, beginning with the "Albera Poyer" scheme of James Lawrie and William Pitt in 1770, peaking with the highly publicized venture of Gregor Mac Gregor, the self-styled "Prince of Poyais," in 1820, and terminating with the failure to resurrect the Poyais artifice in 1837. By that time the name Poyais had become synonymous with fraud.

See also **Honduras.**

BIBLIOGRAPHY

Robert A. Naylor, *Penny Ante Imperialism: The Mosquito Shore and the Bay of Honduras, 1600–1914* (1989).

Additional Bibliography

Bonta, Mark. *Seven Names for the Bellbird: Conservation Geography in Honduras*. College Station: Texas A&M University Press, 2003.

Pineda Portillo, Noe. *Geografía de Honduras*. Tegucigalpa: Editorial Guaymuras, 1997.

Shields, Charles J. and James D. Henderson *Honduras*. Philadelphia: Mason Crest Publishers, 2003.

ROBERT A. NAYLOR

PRADO, JOÃO FERNANDO DE ALMEIDA (1898–1987). João Fernando de Almeida Prado ("Yan"; *b*. 8 December 1898; *d*. 23 October 1987), Brazilian historian and essayist. Born in Rio Claro in the state of São Paulo, Prado studied music and composition in Paris and Italy under several teachers, and took a degree at the São Paulo Law School. He also participated in the Brazilian modernist movement of the 1920s, an aesthetic and cultural reaction against European cultural dominance. Between 1928 and 1938 he wrote for major newspapers and literary magazines, among them *O Estado do São Paulo*, *Diário da Noite*, and *Correio da Manhã*; the literary magazines *Klaxon* and *Antropofagia*; and foreign publications such as *Recueil Sirey* and *Revue de synthèse*.

Prado was a lifelong student of Brazilian colonial history, one of the first to systematically study that era. His many published works, considered obligatory for students of colonial Brazil, are known primarily for their inclusion of important documents from the period. In the course of his life Prado amassed an enormous and important collection of Braziliana, including many rare books written by European travelers in Brazil. This collection as well as his personal library of 30,000 volumes are now housed at São Paulo University's Instituto de Estudos Brasileiros (Brazilian Studies Institute).

Prado's works include *Primeiros povoadores do Brasil* (1935); *Pernambuco e as capitanias do norte do Brasil* (1939); *O Brasil e o colonialismo europeu* (1955); *A Bahia e as capitanias do centro do Brasil* (1964); *Historia da formação da sociedade brasileira: D. João VI e o início da classe dirigente do Brasil* (1968).

See also **Brazil: The Colonial Era, 1500–1808; Modernism, Brazil.**

BIBLIOGRAPHY

Camargos, Marcia. *Semana de 22: Entre vaias e aplausos*. São Paulo: Boitempo, 2002.

Pesavento, Sandra Jatahy. *Escrita, linguagem, objetos: Leituras de história cultural*. Bauru, SP, Brazil: Editora da Universidade do Sagrado Coração, 2004.

BRIAN OWENSBY

PRADO, MARIANO IGNACIO (1826–1901).

Mariano Ignacio Prado (*b.* 1826; *d.* 1901), a general in the Peruvian military. Early in his career he was exiled for his opposition to the government of José Echenique but jumped ship, swam to freedom, and returned to Peru in 1854 to help overthrow his enemies. As dictator in 1866, he declared war on Spain and stood off a Spanish invasion. Later he oversaw a far-reaching program of constitutional reform aimed at curbing the power of the Roman Catholic church and the army. He halted dissident military rebellions against his rule, but then, in 1868, he decided to retire, leaving the field to the liberals. Eight years later civilians persuaded him to return to politics as the candidate of the Civilista Party. As president he disliked political maneuvering, and his enemies constantly plotted uprisings against him. When the economy deteriorated in the late 1870s, he fueled inflation by printing worthless paper money. At that point Peruvian diplomats feared for Peru's nitrate fields in the south, and the country headed toward war with Chile. In the early stage of the War of the Pacific (1879–1883), he watched as Peru's navy was destroyed by Chile. Losing confidence in his ability to rule, Prado sailed for exile in Europe in 1879.

See also **Peru: Peru Since Independence; Peru, Political Parties: Civilista Party; War of the Pacific.**

BIBLIOGRAPHY

William F. Sater, *Chile and the War of the Pacific* (1986).

Paul Gootenberg, *Imagining Development: Economic Ideas in Peru's "Fictitious Prosperity" of Guano, 1840–1880* (1993).

Additional Bibliography

McEvoy, Carmen. *La utopía republicana: Ideales y realidades en la formación de la cultura política peruana, 1871–1919*. Lima: Pontífica Universidad Católica del Perú, Fondo Editorial, 1997.

VINCENT PELOSO

PRADO, PAULO (1869–1943).

Paulo Prado (*b.* 20 May 1869; *d.* 3 October 1943), Brazilian businessman and historian. Scion of an influential coffee-planting family, Paulo Prado was a native of São Paulo and the son of Antônio Prado, one of the last ministers of agriculture under the monarchy. He graduated from the São Paulo law school two weeks before the fall of the empire, in November 1889, and soon departed his uncertain homeland for a grand tour of Europe. Returning to Brazil during the period of Paulista ascendancy, he joined the family coffee-exporting firm and, in 1897, became its president. Under his direction, the company attained new levels of wealth and power. Prado served briefly as president of the National Coffee Council after the 1930 Revolution.

A patron of arts and letters, Prado made large donations to the São Paulo Municipal Library and supported the 1922 Modern Art Week celebration. He befriended some of the most talented Brazilian historians of his time and facilitated their work. His own major publications consist of two collections of historical essays: *Paulística* (São Paulo–like, 1925), in which the theme is regional, and the broader *Retrato do Brasil* (Portrait of Brazil, 1928). Prado's historical writings are strongly influenced by the work of João Capistrano de Abreu.

See also **Brazil: Since 1889; Capistrano de Abreu, João; Coffee Industry.**

BIBLIOGRAPHY

Geraldo Ferraz, "Paulo Prado e duas reedições," in *Província y nação*, edited by Paulo Prado (1972).

Additional Bibliography

Berriel, Carlos Eduardo Ornelas. *Tietê, Tejo, e Sena: A obra de Paulo Prado*. Campinas, SP, Brazil: Papirus Editora, 2000.

Levi, Darrell E. *The Prados of São Paulo, Brazil: An Elite Family and Social Change, 1840–1930*. Athens: University of Georgia Press, 1987.

NEILL MACAULAY

PRADO, PEDRO (1886–1952).

Pedro Prado (*b.* 8 October 1886; *d.* 31 January 1952), Chilean writer. His earlier poetic work, beginning with *Flores de cardo* (1908; Thistle Flowers) and *El llamado del mundo* (1913; The Beckoning World) established a departure from modernism in vogue in Chile that marked the inauguration of free verse, the poem in prose, and antirationalist experimentation in the poetic endeavor. In his later poetry, *Camino de las horas* (1934; Path of the Hours), *Otoño en las dunas* (1940; Autumn in the Dunes), *Esta bella ciudad envenenada* (1945; This Beautiful Poisoned City), and *No más que una rosa* (1946; Only a Rose), he adopted the sonnet as a preferred form of esthetic expression.

Santiago-born Prado published three novels, *La reina de Rapa-Nui* (1914; The Queen of Rapa Nui), *Alsino* (1920), and *Un juez rural* (1924; A Country Judge). His masterpiece *Alsino*, an allegorical novel about a hunchback boy who wants to fly, has attracted much critical attention as well as continuous editorial success. In 1949 he was awarded the National Prize for literature in recognition of his overall creative production. He died in Viña del Mar.

See also **Literature: Spanish America.**

BIBLIOGRAPHY

Hernán Díaz Arrieta, *Los cuatro grandes de la literatura chilena curante el siglo XX* (1963), pp. 55–118.

Raúl Silva Castro, *Pedro Prado* (1965).

John R. Kelly, *Pedro Prado* (1974).

Lucía Guerra-Cunningham, "La aventura del héroe como representación de la visión de mundo en *Alsino* de Pedro Prado," in *Hispania* 66, no. 1 (1983): 32–39.

Hernán Castellano-Girón, "Signos de modernidad en las novelas de Pedro Prado," in *Hispamérica* 18, no. 52 (1989): 31–47.

Additional Bibliography

Martín, Marina. "'Asino' y la novela modernista: Pedro Prado, pintor de cadencias." *Revista Iberoamericana* 62:174 (Jan.–Mar. 1996): 71–84.

J. A. EPPLE

PRADO, VASCO (1914–1998). Vasco Prado (*b.* 16 April 1914; *d.* 9 December 1998), Brazilian sculptor and engraver. Born in Rio Grande do Sul, Prado received a grant from the French government that allowed him to study in Paris under the French painters Fernand Léger and Étienne Hadju. Upon his return to Brazil in 1950, Prado, along with Carlos Scliar, Glenio Bianchetti, Danúbio Gonçalves, and Glauco Rodrigues, founded the Clube de Gravura (Engraving Club) in Pôrto Alegre in 1950. This group supported social realism, an artistic movement rejecting romanticized and idealized subject matter and favoring an unadorned art with a political content.

Prado's repertory draws heavily from regional themes, focusing primarily on the life and customs of the gaucho from the southern state of Rio Grande do Sul. One of his best-known engravings, *Dead Soldier,* was executed for the Third Gaucho Congress in Defense of Peace (1951). In 1962 he won first prize in a competition for a monument to the composer Heitor Villa-Lobos. In 1965 there was a one-man exhibition of his sculpture at the Galería de Arte in São Paulo.

See also **Art: The Twentieth Century.**

BIBLIOGRAPHY

Arte no Brasil, vol. 2 (1979), pp. 842–845.

Dawn Ades, *Art in Latin America* (1989), p. 354.

Additional Bibliography

Baldino, Angela. *Vasco Prado escultor.* Porto Alegre, Brazil: Organização Odebrecht, 2001.

Masina, Léa. *A geração de 30 no Rio Grande do Sul* Porto Alegre, Brazil: Editora da Universidade Federal do Rio Grande do Sul, 2000.

CAREN A. MEGHREBLIAN

PRADO DA SILVA JÚNIOR, CAIO (1907–1990). Caio Prado da Silva Júnior (*b.* 11 February 1907; *d.* 23 November 1990), Brazilian writer and editor. Caio Prado da Silva Júnior, a pioneer in historical materialist interpretation in Brazil, was born in São Paulo. He was a founder of the Partido Democrático (1926) and received a law degree from the University of São Paulo (1928). He joined the Communist Party in 1931, and Marxism guided both his life and his work. He expressed his political views in his first book, *Evolução política do Brasil* (1933), a summary of Brazilian history, and in his masterpiece, *Formação do Brasil contemporâneo* (1942), he analyzed the colonial period, especially at the turn of the nineteenth century. The enlargement of the latter book resulted in *História econômica do Brasil* (1945), which, with Roberto Simonsen's *História econômica do Brasil* (1937) and Celso Furtado's *Formação econômica do Brasil* (1959), led to emphasis on economic factors in Brazilian history.

Prado Júnior also wrote books on economics, philosophy, and politics. He was editor of the *Revista Brasiliense* (1955–1964) and founder of the traditional publishing firms Gráfica Urupês and Editôra Brasiliense.

Prado Junior combined intense political activity with profound intellectual work for which he suffered political repression. He was imprisoned twice (1935–1937 and 1971) and went into exile in France for two years (1937–1939). He died in São Paulo, where his family continued to have an important cultural role.

See also **Brazil: The Colonial Era, 1500–1808; Brazil, Political Parties: Brazilian Communist Party (PCB).**

BIBLIOGRAPHY

Luís Correia De Melo, *Dicionário de autores paulistas* (1954).

Francisco Iglésias, *Caio Prado Júnior* (1982).

Additional Bibliography

Rêgo, Rubem Murilo Leão. *Sentimento do Brasil: Caio Prado Júnior, continuidades e mudanças no desenvolvimento da sociedade brasileira.* Campinas, SP, Brazil: Editora da UNICAMP, 2000.

Ricupero, Bernardo. *Caio Prado Jr. e a nacionalização do marxismo no Brasil.* São Paulo: Departamento de Ciência Política da USP, FAPESP, Editora 34, 2000.

Santos, Raimundo. *Caio Prado Júnior na cultura política brasileira.* Rio de Janeiro: Mauad, FAPERJ, 2001.

ELIANA MARIA REA GOLDSCHMIDT

PRADO Y UGARTECHE, JAVIER

(1871–1921). Javier Pradoy Ugarteche (*b.* 1871; *d.* 25 July 1921), a Peruvian sociologist with extremely anti-indigenous, pro-European cultural views. In *Estado social del Perú durante la dominación española* (1894), he argued that drunkenness and coca leaf addiction were signs of the cultural inferiority of the indigenous population of the country. He saw such practices as an outgrowth of frustration at not being able to rise to the level of Europeans. He attributed to Afro-Peruvians the genetic qualities of thievery and lasciviousness, traits he argued they had inherited from Africans. The son of former president Mariano Ignacio Prado, Prado finished a doctoral dissertation at age twenty and in public competition won a chair of modern philosophy at the National University of San Marcos. He condemned the Spanish past of Peru for its deleterious effect upon the masses of people. To counter these ills, he argued that the national educational system should teach Peruvians a sense of social solidarity, civic virtue, and technical awareness. These qualities would awaken a desire in the citizen to acquire material wealth and thus would benefit the entire nation. Like many social scientists of his day, he was largely unaware of the local sources of investment and banking that had begun to tap the economic potential of Peru.

See also **Indigenous Peoples; Race and Ethnicity; Sociology.**

BIBLIOGRAPHY

Thomas M. Davies, Jr., *Indian Integration in Peru: A Half Century of Experience, 1900–1948* (1974).

Alfonso W. Quiroz, *Domestic and Foreign Finance in Modern Peru, 1850–1950: Financing Visions of Development* (1993).

Additional Bibliography

Wade, Peter. *Race and Ethnicity in Latin America.* London: Pluto Press, 1997.

VINCENT PELOSO

PRADO Y UGARTECHE, JORGE

(1887–1970). Jorge Pradoy Ugarteche (*b.* 1887; *d.* 29 July 1970), Peruvian politician. Exiling himself early in the dictatorship of Augusto Leguía as a protest against tyranny, he was a Civilista and son of past president Mariano Ignacio Prado. He opposed President Guillermo Billinghurst in 1914. In 1933 he served briefly as prime minister to Oscar Benavides and formed a cabinet that sought to conciliate opponents. Politically moderate with democratic views, Prado wooed both socialists and fascists at various times. By 1936 it seemed that Benavides had chosen him as successor. During his presidency, Benavides formed the Frente Nacional to voice his views and banned the rival Aprista Party (APRA) from political activity. Fragmentation weakened other groups, yet in the election of 1936 Prado came in third behind the candidates of reform. Benavides nullified the election and extended his own term as president until 1939. He was succeeded by Jorge Prado's brother, Manuel. Jorge faded into obscurity. His candidacy symbolized the political malaise that gripped Peru when a dictatorship banned APRA from politics for fear of its ability to carry out popular economic reforms.

See also **Benavides, Oscar Raimundo; Peru: Peru Since Independence; Peru, Political Parties: Civilista Party.**

BIBLIOGRAPHY

Magnus Mörner, *The Andean Past: Land, Societies, and Conflicts* (1985).

Fredrick B. Pike, *The Politics of the Miraculous in Peru: Haya de la Torre and the Spiritualist Tradition* (1986).

Additional Bibliography

Portocarrero S, Felipe. *El imperio Prado, 1890–1970.* Lima: Universidad del Pacífico, 1995.

VINCENT PELOSO

balance of payments. The numbers of wealthy and well off increased in these years, but with Peru experiencing a population increase, the numbers of poor also increased dramatically. Demands for new housing and land reform went unmet. To blunt criticism from the wealthy, Prado appointed Pedro Beltrán, the sharply critical editor of the influential *La Prensa,* as prime minister. Beltrán unsuccessfully sought to meet government needs through indirect taxes on oil products. Meanwhile, the legalization of APRa after 1956 allowed the leaders of that party to increase their popular support by campaigning against Beltrán and in favor of land reform. Prado had nearly completed his second term when military officers, fearing the rise to power of APRa through a deal among presidential contenders, seized control just after the 1962 vote count.

See also **Peru: Peru Since Independence.**

BIBLIOGRAPHY

Fredrick B. Pike, *The Modern History of Peru* (1967), pp. 282– 320.

François Bourricaud, *Power and Society in Contemporary Peru,* translated by Paul Stevenson (1970).

Additional Bibliography

Portocarrero S, Felipe. *El imperio Prado, 1890–1970.* Lima: Universidad del Pacífico, 1995.

VINCENT PELOSO

PRADO Y UGARTECHE, MANUEL

(1889–1967). Manuel Prado y Ugarteche (*b.* 1889; *d.* 14 August 1967), son of former president Mariano Ignacio Prado, president of Peru (1939–1945; 1956–1962). During his first term Prado completed many projects begun under the preceding dictatorship of Oscar Benavides, including the national census of 1940, only the second in the country's history. His budgetary management encouraged a literacy campaign that led to the building of many schools and the training of new teachers, the establishment of a social security system, new medical facilities, and the extension of roads by 2,400 miles. During his second term Prado raised new public funds through indirect taxes on gasoline and other oil products. After 1955 Peruvian products found new markets abroad and the country imported more goods. Indeed, imports outweighed exports, adversely affecting the

PRADO Y UGARTECHE, MARIANO IGNACIO

(1870–1946). Mariano Ignacio Prado y Ugarteche (*b.* 1870; *d.* 1946), owner of the Santa Catalina textile mill in Lima at the turn of the twentieth century. As a member of the Civilista Party elected to the Chamber of Deputies to represent Lima, in 1906 he staunchly opposed the demands of labor for a workmen's compensation law. Despite his stubborn opposition, a law finally passed when the crowd observing the proceedings grew so large that the balcony railing broke, spilling spectators onto the house floor.

Between 1900 and 1914 some locals, like Prado y Ugarteche, believed it was in the best interest of the country to collaborate with foreign investors. He became the general manager of Empresas Eléctricas Asociadas (EE.EE.AA.), the oligopolistic provider of electrical power and rail service to Peru for much of the twentieth century. The Empresas Eléctricas was formed by a highly speculative 1907 merger of the major providers of rail and electrical power to Peru. Although the EE.EE.AA. and its creditors lost heavily when world markets collapsed at the start of World War I, by war's end the energy enterprise was producing over 47 million kilowatts of electricity per hour. In 1929 it had nearly doubled its capacity. By the 1930s the Banco Italiano, which in 1931 became a national bank, controlled its finances.

See also **Economic Development; Energy; Labor Movements; Peru: Peru Since Independence.**

BIBLIOGRAPHY

Rosemary Thorp and Geoff Bertram, *Peru 1890–1977: Growth and Policy in an Open Economy* (1978).

Peter Blanchard, *The Origins of the Peruvian Labor Movement, 1883–1919* (1982).

Additional Bibliography

Portocarrero S, Felipe. *El imperio Prado, 1890–1970*. Lima: Universidad del Pacífico, 1995.

VINCENT PELOSO

PRAIEIRA REVOLT.

PRAIEIRA REVOLT. Praieira Revolt, Brazilian political movement in the northeastern province of Pernambuco. The revolt was led by the Praia, a faction of the Liberal Party named after the Rua da Praia, where the group's printing press was located. In 1842 this faction emerged when a schism developed between two politically powerful Pernambucan families. Comprising a group of urban professionals and some marginalized farmers from the interior, the Praia faction was supported in Rio de Janeiro by congressmen from Pernambuco. The Praia promoted land reform in the interior and access to employment opportunities then monopolized by Portuguese retailers, moneylenders, clerks, and artisans in the city of Recife. The revolt involved more than two thousand free farmers, former National Guard soldiers and police, artisans, and unemployed freemen. Slaves were not involved in the movement.

In its initial stages the Praieira revolt was led by planters protesting changes resulting from the replacement of the Liberal Party by the Conservatives in the imperial government on 19 September 1848. On the provincial level in Pernambuco, these changes brought back to power planters and their dependents whose policies were not compatible with those of the Praia faction, which had governed Pernambuco since 1845. The return of the Conservative Party to the central and provincial governments also led to a reshuffling of the police and National Guard as well as the replacement of Praia partisans in the provincial security forces by personal and political rivals. This not only cost many poor freemen their jobs but also set off a rearrangement of the local power structure in the province.

Many Praia supporters were indebted planters who, attracted by recent higher international prices for sugar, had converted from cotton to sugar production and were then adversely affected by the decline in international sugar prices that occurred in the mid-1840s. Other Praia supporters were unemployed skilled workers protesting Portuguese retailers and artisans who were monopolizing coveted positions in the commercial sector, thereby marginalizing the indigenous labor force in the process. In response to rescue appeals following the hostilities of the Brazilians against Portuguese citizens, known as the Mata Marinheiro street riots of 1847 and 1848, the Portuguese government sent ships to transport its citizens from Pernambuco to southern Angola, where they established a settlement in the port of Moçâmedes.

See also **Brazil, Liberal Movements; Brazil, Political Parties: Liberal Party.**

BIBLIOGRAPHY

Nancy Priscilla Smith Naro, "The 1848 Praieira Revolt in Brazil" (Ph.D. diss., University of Chicago, 1981).

Additional Bibliography

Barman, Roderick J. *Citizen Emperor: Pedro II and the Making of Brazil, 1825–1891*. Stanford, CA: Stanford University Press, 1999.

Beattie, Peter M. *The Human Tradition in Modern Brazil*. Wilmington, DE: SR Books, 2004.

Jancsó, István. *Brasil: Formação do estado e da nação*. São Paulo: Editora Hucitec; Ijuí: Editora Unijuí; [São Paulo]: FAPESP, 2003.

Vainfas, Ronaldo. *Dicionário do Brasil imperial, 1822–1889*. Rio de Janeiro: Objetiva, 2002.

NANCY PRISCILLA SMITH NARO

PRAT, ARTURO (1848–1879). Arturo Prat (April 3, 1848–May 21, 1879) was a Chilean naval officer and his nation's preeminent hero. In reduced economic circumstances following his father's premature death, Prat entered the Naval Academy in 1858. While serving with the fleet, Prat distinguished himself first as a line officer and then as an intelligence officer. Although on active duty, Prat studied for and obtained a legal degree from the University of Chile; he also taught at the Benjamin Franklin School, an institution dedicated to educating the poor of Valparaíso.

Admiral Juan Williams Rebolledo, commander of Chile's navy at the onset of the War of the Pacific (1879–1884), apparently disliked Prat, who had acquired a reputation for being an intellectual and someone who would question his superiors. Thus Williams did not assign him to command a warship until May 1879, when he appointed Prat to the *Esmeralda*, one of the fleet's most decrepit vessels. In mid May, when Williams led most of his naval force north to attack Callao, Prat and his subordinate, Carlos Condell, captain of the *Covadonga*, remained to continue the blockade of the Peruvian nitrate port of Iquique.

Early on May 21, the Peruvian ironclads *Huáscar* and the *Independencia* attacked the two Chilean vessels. Prat held off his more powerful foe until the *Huáscar* rammed his vessel three times. Before his ship sank, however, Prat boarded the *Huáscar*, trying to capture it. Although the Peruvians killed him before he could achieve his mission, Prat emerged as an example of heroic sacrifice which has served as a standard of conduct for subsequent generations of Chileans.

See also **Chile: The Nineteenth Century; War of the Pacific.**

BIBLIOGRAPHY

Sater, William F. *The Heroic Image in Chile: Arturo Prat, Secular Saint.* Berkeley: University of California Press, 1973.

WILLIAM F. SATER

PRAT ECHAURREN, JORGE (1918–1971). Jorge Prat Echaurren (*b.* 24 April 1918; *d.* 1971), Chilean politician and well-known

Conservative. Prat, the grandson of Chile's supreme naval hero Arturo Prat, never sat in Congress, though he served as minister of finance (1954–1955). A man of strong nationalist convictions, he mounted a campaign for the presidency in 1964, for which he formed his own party, the Acción Nacional (November 1963), but later withdrew his candidacy. Failing to win election to the Senate in March 1965, he subsequently led the Acción Nacional into the newly formed National Party in June 1966.

See also **Chile, Political Parties: Conservative Party; Chile, Political Parties: National Party; Prat, Arturo.**

BIBLIOGRAPHY

Arancibia Clavel, Patricia. *Los orígenes de la violencia política en Chile, 1960–1973.* Santiago: Universidad Finis Terrae, CIDOC: Libetad y Desarrollo, 2001.

Gamonal R, J Germán. *Historia de las elecciones en Chile.* Santiago: Ercilla, 2005.

SIMON COLLIER

PRATS GONZÁLEZ, CARLOS (1915–1974). Carlos Prats González (February 2, 1915–September 30, 1974) was a Chilean general and government minister under Salvador Allende. Prats, who attended Chile's Escuela Militar and Academia de Guerra plus the U.S. Army Command and General Staff College at Fort Leavenworth, enjoyed a successful military career, becoming a general in 1968. Appointed commander of the army following the 1970 assassination of General René Schneider, Prats also served as President Salvador Allende's minister of interior, the second most important political post in Chile, as well as holding other ministerial portfolios in a vain attempt to shore up the Allende government.

Prats backed Allende initially because the constitution required it and increasingly because he supported some of the Unidad Popular's political and economic goals. Unfortunately, the more the public perceived him as an Allende supporter, the more he lost the support of numerous civilians and also of his fellow army officers. Indeed, the general became the target of public insults and some vulgar displays of disdain. Eventually the pressure became too great: In August 1973, Prats resigned his commission, but not before recommending that Allende appoint General Augusto Pinochet as his replacement.

Following the 1973 coup, Prats and his wife fled to Buenos Aires, Argentina. Fearing that he might become the leader of an anti-junta cabal, Pinochet authorized his murder. Operatives of the Chilean secret police, including Michael Townley, an American citizen, used a car bomb to kill Prats and his wife. Their death illustrated the length to which the junta would go to remain in power. Prats remains a symbol of loyalty to Chile's constitution.

See also **Allende Gossens, Salvador; Chile: The Twentieth Century; Pinochet Ugarte, Augusto.**

BIBLIOGRAPHY

Prats González, Carlos. *Memorias Testimonio de un soldado.* Santiago, Chile: Pehuén, 1985.

Additional Bibliography

Carrió, Alejandro. *Los crímenes del Cóndor: El caso Prats y la trama de conspiraciones entre los servicios de inteligencia del Cono Sur.* Buenos Aires: Sudamericana, 2005.

Haslam, Jonathan. *The Nixon Administration and the Death of Allende's Chile: A Case of Assisted Suicide.* London: Verson, 2005.

WILLIAM F. SATER

PREBISCH, RAÚL (1901–1986). Argentine Raúl Prebisch was the most influential Latin American economist of the twentieth century. As theorist, statesman, and policymaker, he had a major impact on Argentina, Latin America, and the Third World generally.

Born in Tucumán in 1901, Prebisch studied at the University of Buenos Aires. The young economist quickly gained favor with political leaders, organizing research in the government bank, and then heading the country's first central bank, beginning in 1935 and ending in 1943, following a military coup.

Thereafter, Prebisch's principal instrument for developing his ideas was the United Nations (UN)

Economic Commission for Latin America (ECLA), which he directed from 1949 to 1962. The most famous ECLA thesis appeared in *Economic Development of Latin America and Its Principal Problems* (1949; English edition 1950), of which Prebisch was the sole author. In this work, Prebisch sought to explain the secular deterioration of the relative prices of primary goods in the world market, a trend documented in a UN study in 1948. Prebisch argued that the world was organized into an industrial center and an agricultural periphery, and that gains in productivity for the half century before World War II had been greater in industrial than in primary products. He held that such gains were absorbed by the center during recessions, when labor contracts kept wages high; meanwhile, wages fell in the periphery, where agricultural labor remained unorganized. Prebisch also pointed to monopolistic pricing for industrial goods at the center as a cause of unequal exchange.

Prebisch's analysis pointed to negative features in the periphery's economy: structural unemployment, external disequilibrium, and deteriorating terms of trade—all of which a properly implemented policy of industrialization would help eliminate. Industrialization could be achieved by substituting domestic manufactures for previously imported goods. A storm of criticism arose quickly about the terms-of-trade argument, and the debate about its validity has lasted fifty years. In the early twenty-first century, the export profiles of the more advanced Latin American countries are largely composed of industrial goods, making the terms-of-trade argument increasingly less relevant. Nonetheless, this thesis was a point of departure for a "structuralist" school of development studies that emphasized macroeconomics, the role of institutions (especially the state), interdisciplinary approaches, and long-term changes. Meanwhile, Prebisch took a direct hand in promoting Latin American economic integration, and in creating the UN Conference on Trade and Development (UNCTAD), of which he was the first secretary general (1964–1969).

Dependency theory arose in the mid-1960s to address the problems that industrialization by import substitution had engendered or exacerbated. In particular, stagnation in per capita incomes was associated with the increasing capital imports needed to continue industrial development. Secondly, income concentration was accompanying industrialization. Finally, manufacturing was absorbing less labor than ECLA had anticipated.

In *Capitalismo periférico* (Peripheral capitalism, 1981), Prebisch offered a non-Marxist interpretation of dependency. He contended that the structural features of peripheral countries prevented the full development of capitalism, owing to the share of income appropriated by the privileged classes, "unequal exchange" with industrial countries, and extramarket "power relations" between center and periphery.

See also **Dependency Theory; Economic Commission for Latin America and the Caribbean (ECLAC); Economic Development.**

BIBLIOGRAPHY

Prebisch, Raúl. *Capitalismo periférico: crisis y transformación.* Mexico City: Fondo de Cultura Económica, 1981.

Prebisch, Raúl. "Five Stages in My Thinking on Development." In *Pioneers in Development*, edited by Gerald M. Meier and Dudley Seers. New York: Oxford University Press, 1984.

Love, Joseph L. "Economic Ideas and Ideologies in Latin America since 1930." In *Ideas and Ideologies in Twentieth Century Latin America since 1870*, edited by Leslie Bethell. Cambridge, U.K., and New York: Cambridge University Press, 1996.

United Nations Economic Commission for Latin America. *The Economic Development of Latin America and its Principal Problems.* Lake Success, NY: United Nations Department of Economic Affairs, 1950.

Additional Bibliography

Grinspun, Pablo Ariel. *Crisis argentina y globalización: La vigencia de Raúl Prebisch.* Buenos Aires: Nuevohacer, Grupo Editor Latinoamericano, 2003.

Iglesias, Enrique V. *The Legacy of Raúl Prebisch.* Washington, DC: Inter-American Development Bank, 1994.

Love, Joseph L. *Crafting the Third World: Theorizing Underdevelopment in Rumania and Brazil.* Stanford, CA: Stanford University Press, 1996.

Piñeiro Iñiguez, Carlos. *Herejías periféricas: Raúl Prebisch, vigencia de su pensamiento.* Buenos Aires: Nuevohacer, Grupo Editor Latinoamericano, 2003.

JOSEPH LOVE

PRECONTACT HISTORY

This entry includes the following articles:
LATIN AMERICA IN THE PRECONTACT PERIOD
EMERGENCE OF COMPLEX SOCIETY
MESOAMERICA
AMAZONIA
ANDEAN REGION
SOUTHERN CONE

LATIN AMERICA IN THE PRECONTACT PERIOD

It is fair to say that very little is known about the vast contingents of indigenous peoples who populated the territory of what is now called Latin America, which is not a geographic entity but a geopolitical construct. In part, this is because the ideological impact of the first European chronicles of the territory and the peoples who populated it is still strong: Present-day impressions of both are still influenced by the impressions of the first explorers and settlers. These chronicles tend to present the land they are describing as a territory populated by "primitive" peoples who did not modify their environment significantly.

It is with the "discovery" of the great states—the Mexica and the Inca—and their wealth, in the third decade of the sixteenth century, that the invaders started to produce accounts that described highly complex societies. This may explain why the peoples about whom more is known are those who built cities and states and were located in the Andean and Mesoamerican regions. The Inca, the Maya, and the Mexica (including the Aztec) to name the best known of them, caught the West's fancy from the moment they were "discovered." Both the chroniclers of the colonial period and the investigations of scholars in disciplines such as archaeology and ethnohistory (to name just two of the most influential ones), affirm that these peoples showed a highly complex organization in the realms of culture, society, religion, and economics.

One of the characteristics of the Maya, the Mexica, and the Inca is that their subsistence patterns were based on the exploitation of the land known as agriculture. In order to feed the large populations of the cities and the countryside, those Amerindian states needed great numbers of agricultural workers; a very significant labor force that had to be organized from above—by the state, the chiefdom, the local lords, and/or other intermediate authorities. Another important trait of these societies is their penchant for monumentality: The ruins of their impressive stone buildings have long attracted the attention of scholars and the general public and indeed have been the first things noticed by Western eyes. These structures (temples, palaces, and other buildings) and public works (irrigation systems, terraces, plazas, etc.) recall the more familiar monumentality of the ruins of classical antiquity.

The resemblance, in more than one respect, of these highly complex societies and their institutions to modern Western societies might explain the interest and admiration that contemporary Western publics show for them. They had, in some cases, a complex bureaucracy, a regular army, institutions of education, commerce, complex systems of belief, and other forms of social organization. Another factor that may account for Western fascination with these indigenous peoples is a certain evolutionist prejudice that pervades contemporary standards and values. According to this prejudice, human societies progressed or advanced from a basic level of minimal social organization to what the developed world has become in the early twenty-first century. The implicit (and sometimes very explicit, as in the case of Hegelian philosophy) narrative is a teleology according to which humans become more complex over time and therefore better than they were at the beginning of their existence on the planet.

Yet, counter to this teleology, it is an undeniable fact that those complex societies coexisted with others who chose to organize themselves in different ways—and by the fact that even today there are many indigenous peoples who prefer not to embrace the Western way of life and their institutions and organizational principles. The other societies that populated the geopolitical region that came to be known as Latin America were numerous and constitute a significant percentage of the total precontact indigenous population. They organized themselves in myriad ways that include the subsistence patterns of hunter-gatherers, foragers, and early agriculturalists. The peoples who gave themselves these different forms of social organization inhabited not only the territories dominated by the great states, but also other areas of the continent:

among them, the Amazon basin, the plains of present-day Argentina, Uruguay, Venezuela, and Brazil, and the cold regions of Argentinean Patagonia and southern Chile.

One of the peoples who existed in great numbers in different parts of the continent are the Guaraní, who inhabited a significant portion of present-day Brazil, Paraguay, and other areas. The agricultural practices of this ethnic group were very different from the ones predominant in the states and chiefdoms: They did not require huge numbers of people and they were not organized from above. On the contrary, the exploitation of the land they practiced did not require a state or a chiefdom to organize and control the production of food. As Clark Erickson and others have proved in the case of the Llanos de Moxos in present-day Bolivia, subsistence agriculture does not require a great number of workers organized by institutions above the kinship units. It can be developed and sustained by small contingents of people tightly organized at the extended family level.

Hunter-gatherers, traditionally presented as ecologically unsound peoples who depleted the territories they inhabited, were (and are) more successful than traditionally thought in the exploitation of the land. The level of complexity of their societies is, in many cases, significant. The same can be said of optimal foragers, who combine a series of practices that result in subsistence patterns much more successful and ecologically sound than predicted by the evolutionist narratives still predominant in the West. Lack of agriculture does not mean lack of complexity, as the studies by José López Mazz and others on the Archaic period of the eastern region of modern-day Uruguay show: Peoples are able to subsist as foragers and still have time and energy to produce a series of monuments related to their belief system. That is, they were able to have a complex society (with incipient social stratification, a complex system of beliefs, and a significant production of monumentality) without needing recourse to agriculture.

The farther one goes back in time, the less is known about the peoples who preceded those Amerindians encountered by Europeans at the time of contact. The human landscape of the continent looks even more diverse: The "great" civilizations were not even close to materializing and the relationships between different groups were much weaker. Archaeological production from the late twentieth century into the twenty-first shows a growing interest among researchers in precontact societies of the continent. Much work will be necessary to recover a more complete picture of human life in the several millennia before the arrival of Europeans in the Americas. Even more work is needed to understand the conflictive moment known as the peopling of the Americas; since the 1990s a growing number of archaeologists, paleo-ethnobotanists, geologists, and other scholars have shown interest in this topic.

Some of the cultures that flourished in the Andes before the Inca and in Mesoamerica before the peak of the great civilizations have received much more attention than the hunter-gatherers or foragers that populated much of the continent. Scholars have studied cultures such as the Moche, the Chimu, and Chavin de Huantar, and the body of research on those peoples is still growing. Scholars of Mesoamerica have also shown a growing interest in the Olmec, Toltec, and other cultures. However, most of these peoples are generally seen (consciously or not) as steps toward the narrative that leads to the peak of either Inca or Mexica civilizations. Again, there is still much to learn about other human groups that do not fit these narratives or that developed in different areas of the continent—human groups that, in many cases, have not even been given a name by scholars.

The peoples from the great states were colonized by Europeans in different ways, but overall it can be said that their subsistence patterns were, at the beginning, left relatively untouched. The newcomers did not know anything about the local crops and the kinds of agricultural practices needed for their cultivation. For this reason, the productive machine was respected to a point. The incorporation of these societies into a new form of social organization based on European models was relatively smooth in comparison to what happened in areas populated by hunter-gatherers and foragers, who were less prone to adapt to social structures that were completely alien to them. For subjects of a state or chiefdom, for dwellers of a city, things were, to a point, less incomprehensible than for those peoples who lived in different environments and for whom the idea of a city was either irrelevant

or repugnant. One of the consequences of these differences among indigenous peoples is that those Amerindians who inhabited the peripheral areas of the great states were more difficult to colonize—that is to say, to incorporate into Western models of social organization. These were, according to the chronicles, the *indios infieles* ("infidel Indians"), whose subjugation took, in some cases, more than three centuries.

See also **Aztecs; Chavín de Huántar; Chichimecs; Chimú; Incas, The; Maya, The; Moche; Olmecs; Toltecs.**

BIBLIOGRAPHY

Bracco, Roberto. "Dataciones 14C en sitios con elevación." *Revista Antropología* 1, no. 1 (1990): 11–17.

Burger, Richard L. *Chavin and the Origins of Andean Civilization*. London: Thames and Hudson, 1992.

Coe, Michael D. *The Maya*, 7th edition. New York: Thames and Hudson. 2005.

Coe, Michael D., and Rex Coontz. *Mexico: From the Olmecs to the Aztecs*, 5th edition. New York: Thames and Hudson, 2002.

Dillehay, Thomas D. *The Settlement of the Americas: A New Prehistory*. New York: Basic Books, 2000.

Erickson, Clark. "The Social Organization of Prehispanic Raised Field Agriculture in the Lake Titicaca Basin." In *Economic Aspects of Water Management in the Prehispanic New World: Research in Economic Anthropology*, Supplement 7, ed. Vernon L. Scarborough and Barry L. Isaac, pp. 369–426. Greenwich, CT, and London: Jai Press, 1993.

Lockhart, James. *The Nahuas after the Conquest: A Social and Cultural History of the Indians of Central Mexico, Sixteenth through Eighteenth Centuries*. Stanford, CA: Stanford University Press, 1992.

López Mazz, José María. "El fósil que no guía y la formación de los sitios costeros." "Aproximación al territorio de los 'constructores de cerritos'." In *Arqueología en el Uruguay: VIII Congreso Nacional de Arqueología Uruguaya*, ed. Mario Consens, José María López Mazz, and María del Carmen Curbelo, pp. 92–105; 65–78. Montevideo: Banco Comercial, 1995.

Lumbreras, Luis G. *The Peoples and Cultures of Ancient Peru*, trans. Betty J. Meggers. Washington DC: Smithsonian Institution Press, 1974.

Malpass, Michael, ed. *Provincial Inca: Archaeological and Ethnohistorical Assessment of the Impact of the Inca State*. Iowa City: University of Iowa Press, 1993.

Spalding, Karen. *Huarochirí: An Andean Society under Inca and Spanish Rule*. Stanford, CA: Stanford University Press, 1984.

GUSTAVO VERDESIO

EMERGENCE OF COMPLEX SOCIETY

Andean South America and Mexico are the two New World centers for the independent development of complex society leading to major civilizations. Although the concept of "civilization" has been defined in many different ways, it is taken to apply to those few exceptional cultures that develop urban centers, formal institutions of government (sometimes referred to as the "state"), organized religion and art, monumental construction projects, marked social stratification, and a highly productive agricultural economy. The first signs of a distinctive Andean civilization appear in the Norte Chico region of the Pacific Coast in the third millennium BCE, and the first signs of a distinctive Mesoamerican civilization are seen in the second millennium BCE Olmec culture on the Veracruz coast of Mexico. In both areas, surplus production was transformed by economic processes of trade and craft production along with social processes of leadership and ritual to build monumental architecture. Three characteristics mark the shift toward social complexity in both the Andes and in the Olmec region: the lack of prior antecedents, the rapid pace of early monument-building, and the long-term continuity of complex systems once begun.

NORTE CHICO

On the Peruvian coast, about 200 kilometers north of present-day Lima, is a cluster of four small valleys, Huaura, Supe, Pativilca and Fortaleza, that make up what is known locally as the Norte Chico, or "Little North." This region of approximately 1,800 square kilometers witnessed a stable and qualitative change in the years between about 3100 and 2500 BCE. This evolutionary transformation resulted in a significant and permanent increase in cultural complexity with more parts to the overall cultural system and significantly more roles being played by interacting human agents. In contrast to the rest of the Andean region, the third millennium BCE Norte Chico witnessed the appearance of large ceremonial/residential centers with permanent monumental architecture and a complex regional economy based on a combination of maritime exploitation and irrigation-based agriculture. This pattern was accompanied by the emergence of locally (as opposed to regionally) centralized decision making, new kinds of relationships between respondent populations and power-holding elites, and distinct differences in status and rank. The transformation of the Norte Chico cultural system at the turn of the third millennium BCE took place in a politically "pristine" situation. Although there was certainly contact and some form of interaction between the Norte Chico and outside areas, there are no indications that an outside polity existed that was more complex and exerted influence over the evolution of the Norte Chico system.

Change was relatively rapid. In other world areas, the development of similar levels of cultural complexity took place over millennia, whereas in the Norte Chico it took only a few centuries. There are no signs of large, organized urban/ceremonial centers with monumental communal architecture anywhere on the Peruvian landscape prior to about 3100 BCE. Yet by no later than 2800 BCE in the Norte Chico, there were multiple large sites with monumental platform mounds and circular plazas. By about 2300 BCE there were more than thirty large sites with significant monumental architecture and extensive residential architecture. Extensive radiocarbon dates from a sample of eighteen of these sites confirm that the area was occupied continuously and intensively between 3100 and 1800 BCE. In the entire Andean region, the Norte Chico Late Archaic occupation is distinct historically and processually. While there are individual Late Archaic sites outside the region, such as La Galgada to the north and El Paraiso to the south, with comparable monumental architecture, these sites are isolated and have date ranges that fall toward the end of the Late Archaic rather than the beginning. The Norte Chico Late Archaic occupation is not identifiably centralized on any given site or any given valley. When site sizes and the respective volumes of communal structures at the different sites are compared, they produce a relatively continuous curve from small to large across the region. From a pan-regional perspective, however, the Norte Chico as a whole does constitute a dominant center of both power and productivity during this time.

This social, economic and religious transformation in the Norte Chico began in the early third millennium BCE with a shift from hunting and gathering to intensified exploitation of marine resources and the introduction of irrigation-based agriculture. Ephemeral campsites and small fishing villages were replaced by permanent residential and ceremonial centers. A simple system of irrigation was initiated, and they adopted plants already domesticated in other areas, including maize, beans, squash, and cotton. A completely new economic regime was quickly established. These inland innovators gained power based on control over the production of both cotton, critical for the fishing nets needed for the effective exploitation of marine resources, and domesticated plant foodstuffs, critical for a nutritionally balanced diet.

The effective exploitation of marine resources up and down the Peruvian coast, in turn, was also inextricably related to the production of cotton at the inland sites concentrated in the Norte Chico region. All Late Archaic coastal sites excavated to date were using cotton for textiles and nets used for the exploitation of abundant populations of anchovies and sardines. All of these sites also have the full suite of domesticated plant resources that were being grown at the inland sites in the Norte Chico. At the same time, the inland sites in the Norte Chico relied heavily on anchovies and sardines as their source of protein, though fishing implements and nets are rare to absent. The scarcity of nets and other fishing apparatus at inland sites also indicates that the residents were not doing their own maritime harvesting but getting their marine resources from fishermen living right on the coast. In turn, the majority of maritime sites are well removed from arable land, and what land is nearby tends to be saline. By combining the total maritime output of numerous coastal villages up and down the coast with the domesticated plant output of the cluster of sites in the Norte Chico, a regionally balanced economy developed and thrived throughout the third millennium BCE.

The population/labor base for the construction of all the monumental architecture at the numerous inland sites in the Norte Chico also appears to have combined the forces of the maritime coastal sites with the agricultural inland sites. Although the inland sites are quite large in terms of total area occupied, comparatively little of this space is taken up by permanent residential architecture. Caballete, a site with major monumental architecture in the Fortaleza Valley, has about the largest area given over to residential architecture, and even here the residential architecture covers no more than 20 percent of the site area. Permanent residential housing appears unlikely to have accommodated more than a few hundred people at most. However, there are indications that people from coastal fishing communities were coming to the inland sites on a temporary basis and building more ephemeral structures. Mound excavation data show that many mounds were remodeled and resurfaced repeatedly, indicating numerous construction events over many years. There are also indications that feasting may have been an integral part of seasonal ceremonialism and construction activities, with food remains and fire-altered rock from cooking pits being incorporated into the construction of all the platform mounds. Thus a relatively small resident population at inland sites appears to have been augmented by visitors from the string of maritime sites up and down the coast coming in to stay for short times at the Norte Chico sites, contributing to monument building and remodeling, and participating in associated ceremonial activities and feasting. Presumably these seasonal visits would also have provided the occasion for the regular exchange of dried anchovies from the maritime people for cotton and other domesticates from the inland agricultural people.

The emergent social system in the Norte Chico proved not to be an episodic phenomenon but a lasting transformation that put the Andean region on the evolutionary pathway to subsequent civilizations. Cultural development with very similar terraced platform mounds and sunken plazas to the north and south on the coast as well as to the east in the highlands can be directly traced back to Norte Chico antecedents. Such platform mounds with associated sunken plazas, for example, appeared in the Initial Period (1800–1000 BCE) in the Casma Valley to the north and the Lurín Valley to the south. The same pattern is also a dominant element in the site layout of the Early Horizon (1000 to 200 BCE) highland center of Chavín de Huántar just to the northeast of the Norte Chico region as well as at the contemporary site of Chiripa in the southern highlands. Thus the beginnings of a distinctive Andean civilization can be traced directly to the third millennium BCE occupation of the Norte Chico.

OLMEC CULTURE

The emergence of complex society in Mesoamerica is quite different from that of South America. The first monumental construction, accompanied by monumental sculptures and a highly distinctive art style, appeared in the Olmec culture in the second millennium BCE in the current state of Veracruz. In the period from about 1500 to 400 BCE in an area of approximately 9,000 square kilometers, a small number of large ceremonial centers rose and fell in the Olmec heartland. The first of these was the well-known site of San Lorenzo, which has yielded Olmec-type iconography dating from as early as 1500 BCE and where the distinctive Olmec culture was well established by 1200 BCE. San Lorenzo appears to have fallen as a major Olmec center in around 900 BCE, just as another major center, La Venta, was being constructed 90 kilometers to the northeast. La Venta is a much more formally organized site with a central cone-shaped pyramidal mound 33 meters high, with a large associated complex of formally arranged public architecture. La Venta thrived as a major ceremonial center for 500 years, going into steep decline in around 400 BCE. There were additional large Olmec ceremonial centers with monumental architecture at Tres Zapotes and Laguna de los Cerros.

The complexity and centralization of Olmec society is manifested in the monumental architecture as well as in the transportation and carving of numerous large stone monuments. Of particular importance are the monumental carved heads for which the Olmec culture is justly famous. These heads have been interpreted as representing a succession of Olmec rulers. Other sculptures depict priests, warriors, and specialists. The stone for these sculptures, weighing as much as 40 tons, was transported to sites throughout the Olmec heartland from sources in the Tuxtla Mountains as much as 120 kilometers away from the major sites of San Lorenzo and La Venta. Additional evidence of craft specialization can be seen in the exquisitely made ceramics and fine jade carvings.

The Olmec diet was based on domesticated plants, augmented by freshwater fishing and hunting. Maize, beans, squash, and tubers formed the bulk of the diet. The arable land in the Olmec region is quite variable, and it has been argued that the highly productive river levee lands in the immediate vicinity around San Lorenzo encouraged significant population growth. These same levee lands also would have provided the foundation for

leaders to tap into a wealth of agricultural surplus to support craft specialists and command the construction of monumental architecture. Though social inequality may initially have resulted from differential agricultural yields, monumental architecture and sculpture, labor-intensive buried offerings, and distinctive iconography effectively rationalized and institutionalized distinct roles and high status for religious practitioners and an elite class in Olmec society.

Like the Norte Chico, the Olmec developed independently and had a broad and lasting impact on subsequent Mesoamerican civilizations. The nature of the impact of the Olmec on later cultures such as the Maya, Zapotecs, or Teotihuacán is the subject of much debate. However, there is evidence that parts of Olmec ceremonialism and iconography are indeed found in the form of ceramics and imagery in the earliest complex polities to arise in other locations such as Oaxaca, the Maya area, and Central Mexico.

See also **Caral; Chavín de Huántar; La Venta; Norte Chico (Peru); Olmecs; San Lorenzo.**

BIBLIOGRAPHY

Burger, Richard. *Chavin and the Origins of Andean Civilization*. New York: Thames and Hudson, 1992.

Hass, Jonathan. *The Evolution of the Prehistoric State*. New York: Columbia University Press, 1982.

Haas, Jonathan, and Winifred Creamer. "The Crucible of Andean Civilization." *Current Anthropology* 47 (2006): 745–775.

Hass, Jonathan, and Winifred Creamer. "The Late Archaic in Andean Prehistory: 3000–1800 BC." In *Andean Archaeology*, edited by Helaine Silverman, pp. 35–50. Malden, MA: Blackwell, 2004.

Hass, Jonathan, Winifred Creamer, and Alvaro Ruiz. "Dating the Late Archaic occupation of the Norte Chico Region of Peru." *Nature* 432 (2004): 1020–1023.

Hass, Jonathan, Winifred Creamer, and Alvaro Ruiz. "Power and the Emergence of Complex Polities in the Peruvian Preceramic." In *Foundations of Power in the Prehispanic Andes*, edited by Kevin Vaughn, Dennis Ogburn and Christina Conlee, pp. 37–52. Arlington, VA: American Anthropological Association, 2005.

Hass, Jonathan, Thomas Pozorski, and Sheila Pozorski. *The Origin and Development of the Andean State*. Cambridge, U.K., and New York: Cambridge University Press, 1987.

Kembel, Silvia Rodriguez, and John W. Rick. "Building Authority at Chavín de Huantar: Models of Social Organization and Development in the Initial Period and Early Horizon." In *Andean Archaeology*, edited by Helaine Silverman, pp. 51–76. Malden, MA: Blackwell, 2004.

Pozorski, Sheila, and Thomas Pozorski. "Reexamining the Critical Preceramic/Ceramic Period Transition: New Data from Coastal Peru." *American Anthropologist* 92 (1990): 481–491.

WINIFRED CREAMER
JONATHAN HAAS

MESOAMERICA

Mesoamerica is the name given to the culture area that includes most of Mexico and Central America. The concept was originally defined by Paul Kirchhoff in 1943 on the basis of the geographical distribution of hundreds of cultural traits shared by the many civilized societies from northern Mexico to western Costa Rica at the time of the Spanish Conquest. The traits included virtually all cultural aspects of life, such as agriculture (the use of the digging stick; cultigens such as maize, beans, squash, chili peppers, avocados, and cotton), food preparation (the use of grinding stones and clay griddles; tortillas, tamales), domestic animals (dogs and turkeys), beverages (pulque, chocolate), clothing (cotton tunics for the nobility, loincloths for commoners), architecture (terraced platform temples arranged in plazas, ball courts), economy (regional markets; the use and exchange of obsidian, cacao, and jade), and religion (pan-Mesoamerican deities such as Tlaloc and Quetzalcoatl that were more or less parallel in different societies, ancestor worship, hieroglyphic writing, the Mesoamerican calendar, painted bark paper manuscripts, human sacrifice, and an institutionalized priesthood). Most of these traits were present throughout the Mesoamerican culture area at the time of the Conquest, but they developed gradually in different regions and spread among different societies as a result of interregional contacts from the time the area was first inhabited.

THE PRECERAMIC PERIOD

Biologically modern humans, the ancestors of modern American Indians, first entered the Americas by crossing the Bering Strait from northeast Asia more than 15,000 years ago. At this time a broad landmass, known as Beringia, which was exposed when large amounts of water were locked up in the glaciers, offered passage to these early migrants from eastern Siberia to Alaska. The earliest date of their arrival in the Americas is disputed by specialists, but by the end of the Pleistocene epoch (12,000–9,000 years ago) a very distinctive form of projectile point, known by the type names Clovis and Folsom, was widespread from Alaska and Canada to Tierra del Fuego. These are large, lanceolate points with fluted or channeled bases to facilitate hafting. They were used in hunting big game such as mammoths, mastodons, camelids, and giant sloths, and the remains of such Pleistocene megafauna are often found in association with fluted points at ancient hunting camps and kill sites throughout North, Central, and South America. These sites were the settlements of small social groups of nomadic hunters and gatherers. One such site in Mexico is Tlapacoya, in the Valley of Mexico, which has yielded evidence suggestive of human presence more than 20,000 years ago.

As the last great ice age came to an end and the large mammals became extinct, the adaptations of the earliest Mesoamericans shifted to a mixed economy emphasizing hunting of small game and gathering of wild plant foods. These changes characterize the Archaic period (9000–2000 BCE), during which there was an adaptive shift from hunting and gathering to full-time agriculture supporting sedentary villages. The earliest known evidence of plant domestication occurs in arid highland valleys such as the Tehuacán Valley of Puebla and the Valley of Oaxaca, where a number of excavated sites provide a glimpse of the gradual course of plant domestication in Mesoamerica. Research from these sites has demonstrated that the process was not uniform throughout the area. Different crops were domesticated at different times in widely separated regions.

During the long course of the Archaic period, maize, beans, and squash became the basis of the Mesoamerican diet. Other important cultigens that were domesticated during the period include the bottle gourd, chilies, avocados, and cotton. The evidence from Tehuacán and the Valley of Oaxaca indicates that most of these crops were domesticated between 5000 and 3000 BCE.

Social groupings at this time consisted of small, semisedentary, egalitarian bands that coalesced during times of abundance to form seasonal macrobands. In richer environments, such as the Basin of Mexico and the fertile coastal regions, where fish and shellfish were always available in abundance, sedentism and larger, permanent social groups may have developed earlier. Mesoamerican religious ceremonialism also began to develop during the Archaic. Tehuacán has provided possible evidence of human sacrifice and ritual cannibalism dating to 7000–5000 BCE, and Gheo-Shih, a site in the eastern Valley of Oaxaca dated to about 5000 BCE, has a cleared space lined by stones that may have been a dance ground or possibly a very early ball court.

THE FORMATIVE, OR PRECLASSIC, PERIOD

By about 2000 BCE almost all of Mesoamerica was inhabited by full-time agriculturalists who lived in small villages of wattle-and-daub houses. These villages were generally small communities, usually containing no more than about a dozen houses with associated cooking sheds and storage pits. Social and political organization was generally egalitarian and kinship-oriented. Status differences were based strictly on age, sex, and personal achievement. Agricultural tasks, craft production, and trading activities were probably organized by extended-family households.

As population increased in most regions during the Early Preclassic, or Formative, period (1500–900 BCE), some of these small villages grew in size and importance, becoming centers of political, economic, and religious activities. These sites were larger than most contemporary settlements, and they were characterized by nonresidential civic-ceremonial structures. Social inequality, political hierarchies, and tributary economies developed during the latter part of this period. These changes are reflected in differences in grave goods and residential form and construction, and differential distributions of imported goods (such as ceramics, marine shells, jade, and obsidian).

One of the most complex societies in Formative Mesoamerica was the Olmecs of the Gulf Coast region of Mexico. They emerged during the latter part of the Early Formative, and their power and influence continued into the Middle Formative period (900–400 BCE). Sometimes considered to be Mesoamerica's first civilization, the Olmecs built sumptuous monumental centers, such as San Lorenzo, Tenochtitlán (not to be confused with the Aztec capital), and La Venta, in the lush tropical lowlands of southern Veracruz and Tabasco. The heartland Olmecs maintained social and economic relations with contemporaneous societies all over Mesoamerica, from Chalcatzingo, Morelos, in the west, to Chalchuapa, El Salvador, in the southeast. These connections are revealed by the presence of distinctive Olmec iconography, such as the so-called flaming eyebrow and the jaguar paw-wing motifs of the fire serpent and were-jaguar, in ceramics and on stone monuments in these distant centers. The widespread distribution of these symbols reflects interlocking exchange and interaction networks, and probably also the existence of a pan-Mesoamerican belief system.

By the Late Preclassic period (400 BCE–CE 200), Olmec influence had waned in Mesoamerica, but population continued to increase and great centers of a different kind arose throughout the highlands and the lowlands. Monte Albán, perhaps the earliest urban center in the Americas, was established by the Zapotecs on a mountaintop in the center of the Valley of Oaxaca at about 500 BCE. In the highlands of central Mexico, Cuicuilco in the south and Teotihuacán in the north became prominent centers of political, economic, and ritual activity with populations of approximately 20,000 each at the beginning of the Christian era.

In the Maya lowlands, a population increase on the order of 300 percent from the Middle to the Late Preclassic is suggested by settlement pattern studies. During this time, the distinctive hallmarks that would later characterize Classic Lowland Maya culture (elaborately carved stelae and altars, hieroglyphic writing, masonry structures with corbeled arches, and so on) were developed. Sites such as El Mirador, Tikal, Cerros, Becan, and Dzibilchaltún became the centers of complex, hierarchical chiefdoms with very large populations. Large temple platforms and spacious plazas attested to the power and authority of rulers. Ritualized warfare was conducted on a large scale as an aspect of interregional elite competition. Widespread uniformity in Lowland Maya ceramics during the Late Preclassic indicates a high degree of craft specialization and strong interregional economic ties throughout the area that transcended political hostilities. Exchange networks linked the lowland centers with the great

Highland Maya capital of Kaminaljuyú, on what is now the western edge of Guatemala City, and Izapa, on the Pacific coast of Chiapas, which shared a common sculptural style.

THE CLASSIC PERIOD

By about CE 250–300, major transformations occurred in Mesoamerican culture and society. The Classic period (CE 250–900) witnessed the development of macroregional state-level political organization with hierarchical class divisions, an internally stratified ruling class, full-time craft and agricultural specialization, tributary economies, and often large market systems. By CE 500, Teotihuacán had become a city of perhaps 200,000 people; most of them were farmers, but a large number were craft specialists. The capital of a hegemonic empire, Teotihuacán had a powerful, centrally organized government. It maintained colonies at distant centers such as Matacapan, Veracruz, and Kaminaljuyú for the control of trade in luxury goods such as jade, cacao, animal pelts, and tropical bird feathers. Teotihuacán maintained a special diplomatic relationship with Monte Albán (a group of Oaxacans lived in a special ward of the city), and its influence was felt as far away as Tikal.

The southern Maya lowlands were dominated during the Classic by a number of state-level polities. Major centers included Palenque, Piedras Negras, Yaxchilan, Altar De Sacrificios, Seibal, Dos Pilas, Tikal, Uaxactún, Altún Ha, Caracol, Quiriguá, and Copán. These city-states claimed a regional territory that included a number of secondary and tertiary centers paying tribute to rulers in the primary centers. These kings erected monuments with hieroglyphic inscriptions legitimizing their authority and glorifying their royal ancestry. The major centers possessed a complex division of labor that included craft specialists such as potters, obsidian and chert knappers, weavers, feather workers, leather workers, basket makers, architects, stonemasons, manuscript painters, and monument carvers. The population in the southern lowlands was very large, at least as high as 10 million in the Late Classic period (CE 600–900).

At the end of the Classic the population suffered a precipitous decline. Monument erection and other elite activities ceased in all of the major centers of the southern lowlands between about 800 and 900. Various causes have been suggested for this collapse: ecological deterioration, demographic pressure, endemic warfare, and disease. Whatever the causes, the collapse profoundly altered the balance of power in eastern Mesoamerica. The northern lowlands maintained a large and growing population, and centers such as Chichén Itzá and Cobá experienced florescence rather than decline.

Teotihuacán collapsed as a major economic and political power about 750, an event that undoubtedly had a ripple effect in the decline of Classic Lowland Maya civilization. The population of Teotihuacán had fallen to as low as 30,000 by the end of the Classic. The heart of the civic-ceremonial zone was burned and looted in a massive act of political destruction and desanctification. In the wake of the collapse, fortified centers of long-distance trade such as Xochicalco and Cacaxtla rose to power, filling the economic vacuum left when the Teotihuacán empire contracted.

THE POSTCLASSIC PERIOD

The Postclassic marks the advent of history in central Mexico. The salient theme is the rise of the Toltec capital, Tollan, founded by the legendary leader Quetzalcoatl at the site of present-day Tula, Hidalgo, in the tenth century. Tollan, which had a strong centralized government, was the center of a multiethnic trading empire within which Nahuatl speakers enjoyed political and probably numerical superiority. The population of Tollan at its peak was around 60,000.

Toltec influence spread throughout Mesoamerica during the Early Postclassic (900–1200). Unmistakable evidence of Toltec art and architecture appears as far away as Chichén Itzá, Yucatán, and Cihuatan, El Salvador. Nahuatl speakers known as Pipils began to migrate to Central America at this time. Toltecs from both Tollan and Chichén Itzá apparently had close ties with El Tajín, on the north coast of Veracruz.

Toltec dominance ended in the late twelfth century, when Tollan began to experience a long decline caused by drought, famine, rebellion, and Chichimec invasions from the north. After the collapse of Tollan there were no more great centers in central Mexico until the rise of the Mexica Aztecs at Tenochtitlán in 1427. Within less than a century they controlled the greatest empire yet in Mesoamerica, incorporating earlier city-states established in the Valley of Mexico such as Tetzcoco, Atzcapotzalco, and Tlatelolco, and extending their hegemony from Veracruz to the Pacific Ocean and from central Mexico to southern Chiapas. The population of Tenochtitlán at its peak was 150,000–200,000, and the population of the entire Valley of Mexico in the early sixteenth century was as high as 1 million.

Elsewhere in Postclassic Mesoamerica, the Valley of Oaxaca disintegrated economically and politically with the long decline of Monte Albán, which began around 700. A number of small trading centers, such as Lambityeco, arose at this time. Mixtec warloads from the highland and coastal regions of western Oaxaca began a series of conquests that even took them into the valley. Principal Zapotec centers of the valley at the time of the Conquest included Zaachila, Yagul, and Mitla. In Veracruz, El Tajín collapsed around 1200, and the Totonacs first encountered the Spaniards at Cempoala in 1519.

In Yucatán, Chichén Itzá, which had been the center of a large tributary state from about 850 to 1224, was overthrown by Mayapán. In the latter, a small, fortified center, a confederation of three elite lineages unified Yucatán from about 1224 to 1441. This unity eventually gave way to an estimated sixteen to twenty-four highly competitive, small city-states. Tulum, a major trading port on the east coast, was sighted in 1517 by Spanish explorers who mistakenly described it as being larger than Seville. In highland Guatemala, the Kaqchiquels at Iximché, the Quichés (K'iche') at Utatlan, and the Zutuhils at Chuitinamit, all of whom were ruled by warrior aristocrats claiming Toltec heritage, were conquered by the Spanish in 1524.

See also **Aztecs; Indigenous Peoples; Maya, The; Nahuas.**

BIBLIOGRAPHY

General surveys include Richard E. W. Adams, *Prehistoric Mesoamerica*, rev. ed. (1991); Michael D. Coe, *Mexico*, 4th ed. (1994); Muriel Porter Weaver, *The Aztecs, Maya, and Their Predecessors*, 3d ed. (1993). More theoretically oriented treatments are Richard E. Blanton, Stephen A. Kowalewski, Gary Feinman, and Jill Appel, *Ancient Mesoamerica: A Comparison of Change in Three Regions*, 2d ed. (1993), and William T. Sanders and Barbara J. Price, *Mesoamerica: The Evolution of a Civilization* (1968). The results of the Tehuacán Valley research are summarized by general editor Richard S. MacNeish in *The Prehistory of the Tehuacán Valley*, vol. 5, *Excavations and Reconnaissance*, by Richard S. MacNeish, Melvin L. Fowler, Angel García Cook, Frederick A. Peterson, Antoinette Nelken-Turner, and James A. Neely (1972). A good overview of the Formative is Kent V. Flannery, ed., *The Early Mesoamerican Village* (1976). A detailed settlement history of the pre-Columbian Valley of Mexico is William T. Sanders, Jeffrey R. Parsons, and Robert S. Santley, *The Basin of Mexico: Ecological Processes in the Evolution of a Civilization* (1979). For Oaxaca, see Richard E. Blanton, *Monte Albán: Settlement Patterns at the Ancient Zapotec Capital* (1978); Kent V. Flannery and Joyce Marcus, eds., *The Cloud People: The Divergent Evolution of the Zapotec and Mixtec Civilizations* (1983); John Paddock, ed., *Ancient Oaxaca* (1966); Ronald Spores, *The Mixtec Kings and Their People* (1967); Joseph W. Whitecotton, *The Zapotecs: Princes, Priests, and Peasants* (1977); and Ernesto González-Licón, *Zapotecas y mixtecas: Tres mil años de civilización precolombina* (1992). Several excellent books are available on the pre-Columbian Maya civilization: Richard E. W. Adams, ed., *The Origins of Maya Civilization* (1977); Michael D. Coe, *The Maya*, 5th ed. (1993); Robert M. Carmack, *The Quiche Mayas of Utatlan: The Evolution of a Highland Guatemala Kingdom* (1981); John W. Fox, *Maya Postclassic State Formation* (1987); Norman Hammond, *Ancient Maya Civilization* (1982); John S. Henderson, *The World of the Ancient Maya* (1981); Robert J. Sharer, *The Ancient Maya*, 5th ed. (1994); and Mercedes de la Garza and Gerardo Bustos *Los Mayas: Su tiempo antiguo* (1996). For the Pipils of Central America, see William R. Fowler, Jr., *The Cultural Evolution of Ancient Nahua Civilizations: The Pipil–Nicarao of Central America* (1989). On the Toltecs, see Richard A. Diehl, *Tula: The Toltec Capital of Ancient Mexico* (1983); Dan M. Healan, *Tula of the Toltecs* (1989); Nigel Davies, *The Toltec Heritage: From the Fall of Tula to the Rise of Tenochtitlán* (1980). On the Aztecs, consult Frances Berdan, *The Aztecs of Central Mexico: An Imperial Society* (1982); Ross Hassig, *Trade, Tribute, and Transportation: The Sixteenth-Century Political Economy of the Valley of Mexico* (1985), and *Aztec Warfare: Imperial Expansion and Political Control* (1988); Nigel Davies, *The Aztecs: A History* (1973), and *The Aztec Empire: The Toltec Resurgence* (1987); Susan D. Gillespie, *The Aztec Kings: The Construction of Rulership in Mexica History* (1989) and Silvia Trejo *Dioses, mitos y ritos del México antiguo* (2000).

WILLIAM R. FOWLER

AMAZONIA

Covering well over 2 million square miles, the humid tropical forests of the Amazon and Orinoco basins remain relatively unstudied from the standpoint of scientific archaeology. Complete cultural sequences are few and widely scattered. Perhaps because of the paucity of data, Amazonian prehistory has been the subject of much debate. The region has been seen as an immense and uniform tract of tropical forest cleaved by mighty rivers but otherwise only occasionally broken by the small clearings of native agricultural fields. It has been characterized as a stable and unchanging environment—the largest remaining vestige of a forest primeval, a virginal land largely untouched by human endeavor until the coming of Europeans. In the eyes of some nineteenth-century naturalists, it was portrayed as an incredibly rich land with unlimited agricultural potential and teeming with fish and game. Under the gaze of twentieth-century anthropologists, this charitable view has been challenged. From a Paradise Lost, Amazonia has been recast as a counterfeit paradise, one beset by environmental limiting factors such as poor soils that constrain agriculture or by scant and dispersed faunal resources that limit protein intake. These polar verdicts, whether leaning toward the paradisiacal or toward the bleak view of a reluctantly giving nature, are imported caricatures and, as such, are unlikely to be correct.

As the custodian of the long stretches of time during which Amazonian societies diversified and evolved, archaeology has a privileged role in evaluating the mercurial vogues that have been brought to bear on the nature of Amazonia as a stage for cultural development. Although archaeological work in the lowland tropics is scant in comparison with most other parts of the world, it constitutes a large and growing body of evidence that forces this overview to be selective and to focus on three central issues: (1) the existence and nature of a pre-ceramic and perhaps pre-agricultural or foraging way of life; (2) the development of pottery and agriculture; and (3) the emergence of complex societies.

FORAGING IN THE FOREST
A current debate centers on the feasibility of subsisting in the tropical forest through hunting and gathering (foraging) alone. Some see the tropical forest as a poor environment for foragers. Game tends to be dispersed, nocturnal, or arboreal, and wild flora is often deficient in energy-yielding carbohydrate. In support of this argument, it is pointed out that most recent foraging populations in the tropical forest have regularized exchange relations with nearby farmers. It does not follow, however, that because recent foragers have links with farmers, an independent foraging way of life was impossible in the past.

Archaeological discoveries indicate that there *were* pre-agricultural foragers in greater Amazonia. On the middle Orinoco, an area where tropical forest and savanna interface, a long pre-ceramic sequence beginning by at least 7000 BCE has been identified. Early artifacts include pitted stones (presumably for the cracking of palm nuts), ground stone axes, scrapers made of local quartz, and stemmed points made from non-local chert. Certainly these stone artifacts are but the durable part of a more complex material culture based on perishable wood and other organic materials. Twelve hundred miles to the south, on the upper Madeira, the beginnings of a long archaeological sequence have been dated to the tenth millennium BCE in deposits buried deep beneath later pottery-bearing occupations. On the lower Amazon, near Santarém, stone tools at the base of a stratified rock shelter date as early as 9000 BCE. On the basis of this evidence, it would seem that the time depth of Amazonian culture history is fully in line with that known for other parts of the Americas, namely a terminal Pleistocene occupation by Paleo-Indians that reached from the Arctic to Tierra del Fuego. Although the nature of these pioneering adaptations to diverse habitats spanning two continents remains poorly understood, archaeological fact clearly indicates that Amazonia was hardly a no-man's land avoided by early foragers.

POTTERY AND PLANTS
To outsiders, the archaeologist's apparent infatuation with pottery may seem mysterious; however, there are good reasons for this obsession. Pottery is a relatively non biodegradable, and therefore abundant, residue of human behavior. As plastic art, it solidifies decorative and formal information that can reveal much about the past. From a technological perspective, pottery represents a breakthrough that facilitated the boiling of foods. Boiling, in turn, is an effective means of detoxifying many plant foods and opens up the new culinary possibilities of stews, porridges, and, perhaps above all, beer. Beer, brewed from manioc, maize, or other plants, is an ancient staple and social lubricant in much of Amazonia.

With respect to pottery, Amazonia is precocious. Seven thousand-year-old ceramics have been reported from the Taperinha shell midden at

Santarém. If confirmed by further research, the Taperinha finds represent the oldest pottery yet identified in the Americas. At the mouth of the Amazon, pottery of the Mina style is dated to the fourth millennium BCE. In northwestern South America, in environments that some have viewed as Amazonian extensions, several cases of fourth millennium BCE ceramics are well documented. In terms of pottery, lowland South America, including the Amazon, has a decided jump on the rest of the Americas. These Amazonian data also bring into question the long-held notion that pottery and agriculture necessarily go together. In some areas of Amazonia such as the upper Madeira, agriculture would appear to have preceded pottery, whereas the Santarém evidence suggests the opposite. Or perhaps our notions of what constitutes "agriculture," based as they are on temperate-latitude models, need to be rethought to be applicable to the tropical forest, where the arboriculture of useful palms and other species is a widespread and presumably ancient practice. The peach palm (*Guiliema gasipaes*) is a case in point. It produces a biannual harvest of nutritious fruit, an edible heart, and an extremely hard wood widely used in house construction and for clubs and bows. The peach palm qualifies as a cultigen. Supposed wild specimens are probably feral, and a cluster of useful palms, anywhere in Amazonia, often marks the former presence of meddlesome humans.

In terms of the more familiar cultigens that fueled the American Neolithic, Amazonia would also seem to play a pivotal role. Maize is attested for the Ecuadorian and Colombian Amazon by the fourth millennium BCE, and a suite of cultivated plants including achira, soursop, canavalia beans, and manioc had a variable presence along the Peruvian and Ecuadorian coasts by 2000 BCE. On botanical grounds, many of these plants are likely to have a prior history of cultivation in the humid lowlands east of the Andes. Although sparse, these data suggest that Amazonia was a participant in the emergence of early agriculture.

COURSES TOWARD COMPLEXITY

Far-flung similarities in pottery styles indicate that Amazonia constituted a vast network of interacting societies at least by the first millennium BCE. This network was based on canoe travel along riverine highways that connected local farming and fishing economies on the fertile floodplains of major waterways. In the first millennium of our era, complex societal configurations that anthropologists call chiefdoms emerged throughout Amazonia. Recent research indicates that Marajoara culture at the mouth of the Amazon, long renowned for its fancy polychrome ceramics, mortuary elaboration, and monumental earthworks, was indeed an autochthonous development with local roots extending back to the first centuries of our era. It can no longer be viewed as an import from the Andes that, over time, withered away under the rigors of an inhospitable environment.

Marajoara is not unique in the scale of its earthen monuments. At the fringes of Amazonia, where gallery forests penetrate seasonally flooded savannas, extensive networks of raised agricultural fields, causeways, and house mounds were erected by pre-Colombian populations. Ethnohistorically these sophisticated systems of hydraulic engineering were associated with complex chiefdoms such as the Mojos; archaeological work indicates that their construction began in the first millennium CE in both Bolivian and Venezuelan lowlands. In the upper Amazon abutting the Ecuadorian Andes, the site of Sangay provides another impressive case of prehistoric construction. This site contains dozens of earthen mounds, some arranged in geoglyphic patterns. Midden is deep over an area about 0.5 square miles. Although the radiocarbon dates span several millennia, most of the ceramic debris at Sangay appear to date after 500 BCE.

In the 1540s, the expedition led by Francisco de Orellana reported extensive and expansive polities stretching along the Napo and Amazon. Settlements were large; subsistence entailed intensive agriculture and the tending of river turtles in artificial corrals; and chiefs were able to mobilize sizable forces to defend their territories. The archaeological record testifies that these polities were the culmination of a long in-place development, one rather abruptly truncated under the assault of European colonial expansion and introduced diseases.

See also **Archaeology; Indigenous Peoples.**

BIBLIOGRAPHY

Basic introductions are Donald Lathrap, *The Upper Amazon* (1970) and Betty Meggers, *Amazonia: Man and*

Culture in a Counterfeit Paradise (1971). Overviews of more recent work include J. Scott Raymond, "A View from the Tropical Forest," in *Peruvian Prehistory,* edited by Richard Keatinge (1988); and Anna C. Roosevelt, "Resource Management in Amazonia Before the Conquest: Beyond Ethnographic Projection," in *Resource Management in Amazonia,* edited by D. Posey and W. Balée (1989). On the foraging debate, see the special issue "Human Foragers in Tropical Rain Forests," *Human Ecology* 19, no. 2 (1991). Also consult William Barse, "Preceramic Occupations in the Orinoco River Valley," *Science,* 250 (1990): 1388–1390; Eurico Miller et al., *Archeology in the Hydroelectric Projects of Eletronorte* (1992). The issue of early ceramics is covered in John W. Hoopes, "Ford Revisited: A Critical Review of the Chronology and Relationships of the Earliest Ceramic Complexes in the New World, 6000–1500 B.C.," in *Journal of World Prehistory* 8, no. 1 (1994): 1–49. On the historiography of complex societies in prehistoric Amazonia, see Thomas Myers, "Agricultural Limitations on the Amazon in Theory and Practice," in *World Archaeology* 24, no. 1 (1992): 82–97. For Marajoara, check Anna C. Roosevelt, *Moundbuilders of the Amazon* (1991); and the review by Betty Meggers in *Journal of Field Archaeology* 19, no. 3 (1992): 399–404. An accessible introduction to Sangay is Pedro Porras, "Investigations at the Sangay Mound Complex, Eastern Ecuador," in *National Geographic Research* 5, no. 3 (1989): 374–381.

Additional Bibliography

Mann, Charles C. *1491: New Revelations of the Americas Before Columbus.* New York: Knopf, 2005.

WARREN DEBOER

ANDEAN REGION

The history of the Andean region before the Spanish Conquest is long, complex, and poorly understood. In the absence of indigenous alphabetic writing systems, and with the art of the *quilcacamayoc* and the *quipucamayoc* (textile and quipu interpreters, respectively) lost to colonialist practices, most information on the subject comes from archaeology, and in many regions little, if any, archaeological research has been conducted. Descriptive chronicles, government administrative records, and other written evidence left by the sixteenth- and seventeenth-century Spanish regimes shed some light on the centuries immediately prior to the Iberian invasion, but have limited value for understanding the many millennia that preceded it. Recently, anthropologists have looked for clues to the pre-Hispanic past in contemporary oral tradition.

Unlike Mesoamerica, the Andes never constituted a single area of cultural development. In a comprehensive archaeological synthesis by Gordon Willey, four archaeological culture areas were recognized in South America: the Intermediate (or northern Andean) area, which includes much of the present-day Venezuela, Colombia, and Ecuador; the Peruvian (or central Andean) area, which consists of the Andean portions of present-day Peru and northernmost Bolivia; the South Andean area, which includes portions of Bolivia, northern Chile, and northwest Argentina; and the Fuegian area, which encompasses southern Chile. There was limited contact between the different Andean archaeological areas, and some communication occurred with areas outside the South American continent.

The situation changed dramatically when the Incas of Cuzco created an empire that grew well beyond their homeland in the southern Peruvian highlands and expanded to incorporate portions of what are now Bolivia, Ecuador, Argentina, and Chile. With the Inca military and administrative expansion came the introduction of an imperial language (Quechua) and cultural elements native to the central Andes. However, the veneer of similarity left by the short-lived Inca presence never fully obscured the fundamental cultural diversity that characterized the pre-Columbian Andes.

THE SETTLEMENT OF SOUTH AMERICA

South America was unoccupied by human populations before the arrival of small bands of hunters and gatherers during the Late Pleistocene. These groups entered the New World from northeasternmost Asia by crossing a now largely submerged landmass known as Beringia. Small nomadic groups following animal herds moved into the rich hunting lands of Alaska and eventually down through North America into the Andes. There is little consensus concerning the exact timing of entry into either North or South America, but groups already had dispersed into a variety of Andean habitats by 12,000 years ago.

Due to the limitations of preservation in the archaeological record, most of these groups are known mainly through their stone tools. By 10,000 years ago there was already considerable diversity in the unifacial and bifacial lithic assemblages that they employed. One striking exception to the widespread variability was the production of bifacial tools known as "fishtail points" because of their characteristic shape. Fishtail points have been found at sites in Panama, Ecuador, Peru, Uruguay, and Chile in early contexts, and the frequent presence of fluting on these points, as well as their early date, has led some to see a relation between them and the famous Clovis points of North America.

Evidence of the perishable structures in which these early Andean peoples lived is rare. However, at Monte Verde in Chile, excavations unearthed a settlement of small rectangular huts built of wood and skin; the dwellings are dated to around 11,000 BCE. Although there is evidence that early Andean peoples occasionally hunted large mammals such as mastodon, smaller animals and a variety of wild plant species comprised the core of the daily diet.

With the end of the Pleistocene, the variety of utilizable habitats increased sharply, and many environments that had been glaciated became available for occupation. Human populations expanded both numerically and geographically. Groups focused on a broad range of resources, from the rich marine stocks of the Pacific to the high plains of the central Andes. Over the subsequent millennia, subsistence strategies increasingly focused on stable, localized resources. For example, at rock shelters such as Uchkumachay in Peru there was a shift from a generalized strategy of hunting to a more specialized pattern of wild camelid exploitation, and ultimately, by 3500 BCE, to the development of llama herding. During this time, many groups began to manipulate flora to enhance the qualities or the environmental range of food or industrial plants. This process ultimately resulted in domesticated crops such as potatoes, sweet potatoes, quinoa, peanuts, squash, cotton, and coca that made pre-Columbian civilizations possible, and which remain one of the most enduring contributions of the ancient Andes to the modern world. Although these plants initially supplemented the core of gathered foods and hunted game, they steadily increased in importance and eventually made possible the shift to a sedentary lifestyle.

A well-documented expression of differing preceramic cultural patterns exists in the sphere of mortuary ritual. The oldest example of New World mummification was developed by the Chinchorro Tradition in what is now northern Chile and southernmost Peru. Between 5500 BCE and 2000 BCE

these coastal peoples introduced artificial treatment of the dead that included desiccation, evisceration, and reconstitution of the body through the use of fillers, clay modeling, and wigs. These elaborate practices contrasted with those of other areas, such as the simple pit-burials placed beneath the floors of houses in the early Peruvian coastal village of Paloma, and the carefully arranged secondary burials of disarticulated human bones by the Las Vegas culture of southern Ecuador.

SEDENTARY LIFE AND THE BEGINNINGS OF ANDEAN CIVILIZATION

In the Andes, as in the rest of the world, the adoption of a sedentary lifestyle resulted in population increases, and these demographic pressures ultimately reinforced a dependence on the raising of food crops and, where appropriate, on the breeding of livestock or the exploitation of year-round maritime resources. Sedentary farming villages appeared first in the northern Andes of Ecuador and Colombia sometime before 3000 BCE. At sites such as Valdivia and Puerto Hormiga these early agriculturists introduced the first ceramic vessels for the preparation and storage of the new dietary staples.

Along the coast of the central Andes, at roughly the same time, large shoreline settlements focused on the rich fishing and shellfish resources of the Humboldt Current. This maritime emphasis was made possible by the cultivation of cotton for fishing line and bottle gourds for floats. Some domesticated food plants also were consumed, and there were strong ties between the fisherfolk and the inland valley farmers. Communal activity was central to group subsistence and identity, and these coastal cultures were responsible for erecting some of the oldest monumental architecture in the New World. At shoreline sites such as Aspero and Bandurria and inland sites such as El Paraíso and Chupacigarro, stepped pyramids were built as settings for public ceremonies and religious rituals and as the focus for community life.

Archaeological investigation has discovered what might very well be the oldest municipal center in the New World, the city of Caral. This urban center was organized some four and one-half millennia before the Incas, making it coeval with ancient civilizations in the Old World.

In the adjacent highlands in the third millennium BCE, dispersed farming populations began to construct public buildings with central hearths for the presentation of burnt offerings. Although these ceremonial structures were small, their repeated burial and re-creation at higher levels gradually resulted in the growth of large pyramid-platforms at sites such as Kotosh on the eastern Andean slopes and La Galgada in the entrenched western Andean valleys.

Agricultural expansion and intensification characterize the second millennium BCE in much of the central Andes. Through the creation of gravity canals, the cultivable lands of the Peruvian coastal desert were greatly expanded, and new centers with monumental architecture were established throughout the central and northern coast. Some find it a paradox that although this period produced some of the largest public constructions in Andean history—such as Sechín Alto in Casma and Garagay in Rímac—there is only limited evidence for sharp differences in economic and political power; hence the suggestion that the scale of these constructions may be a function of communal solidarity and cultural continuity rather than an expression of coercive political power by an overbearing elite.

Near the end of the first millennium BCE, most of these coastal centers were abandoned, whereas coeval settlements in the adjacent highlands continued to flourish. One of these highland centers, Chavín De Huántar, achieved special prominence by 500 BCE because of the pan-regional importance of its temple, as well as its role in an expanding sphere of long-distance exchange. Its ceremonial center became the focus of pilgrims from distant areas, and branches of the center's religious cult were established elsewhere in the highlands and coast. Distinctive coastal cultures such as Paracas on the south coast and Cupisnique on the north coast were drawn into this sphere of interaction, but maintained their independence and cultural distinctiveness.

It is within this context that we find the first indisputable evidence for sharp hierarchical differences in socioeconomic status. Elaborate elite burials have been found at sites such as Kuntur Wasi and Chongoyape. Innovations in textile manufacture and metallurgy were used to represent the symbols of the Chavín cult, in some cases on clothing or jewelry worn by elites. Although *Spondylus* and *Strombus* shells from the shores of Ecuador were imported for use in the central Andes, northern Andean agricultural villages of the first millennia BCE, such as Cotocollao near Quito, appear largely free of influence from the central Andes, and do not show a degree of social complexity or cultural accomplishment comparable to that of the Cupisnique or Chavín cultures.

With the collapse of the Chavín sphere of interaction at the end of the first millennium BCE, local identity reasserted itself in the form of distinctive local styles. Nevertheless, the existence of social inequality remained as a legacy of the preceding period. For example, on Peru's south coast the large Paracas mummy bundles from Cerro Colorado contained many layers of multicolored cloth mantles embroidered with highland alpaca wool, and dozens of other objects, whereas burials at a nearby coeval cemetery had few, if any, grave goods. Defensive architecture became widespread in the central Andes for the first time as small-scale political units and short-lived confederations engaged in fluctuating cycles of warfare and alliance.

In the lands surrounding Lake Titicaca, a trajectory of local development toward more complex societies occurred during the first millennium BCE. With an economy focusing on camelid herding, lacustrine resources, and high-altitude agriculture, large sedentary populations developed and began to produce major centers for civic and ceremonial activities. At centers such as Chiripá in northern Bolivia, highland populations erected public architecture decorated with distinctive stone sculpture in what has been called the Yaya Mama Religious Tradition. By the end of the first millennium BCE, Pucará culture and the other heirs to the Yaya Mama Tradition flourished and became increasingly involved with the groups and resources at lower elevations of the Chilean western slopes and coast.

CONQUEST STATES AND URBANISM

Over the next five centuries, there were repeated attempts by small polities to expand into neighboring territories and establish multivalley states. One of the first attempts was by the Gallinazo culture (CE 100–300), which expanded from the Viru Valley on Peru's north coast into several of the adjacent valleys, including Moche. The capital of this short-lived state was the Gallinazo Group, an urban center that covered 1.5 to 2 square miles. Between CE 300 and 500, the center of power shifted to the neighboring valley of Moche, where a capital was established at Cerro Blanco. Large adobe pyramids were built for religious and civic activities, and substantial residential populations, including specialized artisans, were present. The naturalistic ceramics of the Moche give a vivid picture of a warlike people whose leaders identified with the mythical supernaturals of their cosmology. In 1987 intact tombs of Moche elite dressed in the costume of mythical figures and buried with enormous qualities of fine gold and silver artifacts were discovered at Sipán in the Lambayeque drainage. The Moche culture stretched over 250 miles from the Huarmey to Lambayeque, and materials of the Moche culture have been found still farther north, alongside Guangala materials from southern Ecuador and local cultural materials known as Vicús.

The emergence of elites in the northern Andean area can be traced through the presence of elaborate shaft tombs, such as those of La Florida near Quito and Las Cruzes in southern Colombia. The presence of elites is also suggested by the growth of large public centers, such as La Tolita and Cochasquí, and the artistic sophistication of the ceramics of northern Andean cultures such as the Jama-Coaque, the fine goldwork of the Quimbaya and Tairona, and the stone tomb sculptures at San Agustín. Nevertheless, none of these northern Andean cultures seems to have established a multivalley state comparable to that of the Gallinazo or Moche. Unlike their neighbors to the south, these northern Andean societies appear to have remained small in scale, nonurban in character, and politically balkanized.

Yet, even in the central Andes, some well-known contemporaries of the Moche, such as the Nasca culture of the Peruvian south coast, apparently lacked urban centers. Investigations at Cahuachi, the largest known Nasca site, failed to reveal evidence of large resident populations. The ceremonial center at Cahuachi, along with the nearby geometric and figurative geoglyphs known as the Nasca Lines, apparently provided the religious focus for an otherwise decentralized agrarian society.

PRE-HISPANIC ANDEAN EMPIRES AND THEIR COLLAPSE

The earliest large highland state apparently developed out of the cultural tradition represented by Pucara and the older Yaya Mama Religious Tradition. Its capital was located in highland Bolivia at the site of Tiwanaku. Large constructions were under way there by CE 100, and the center reached its apogee by CE 600, when it covered more than 3.5 square miles. Tiwanaku controlled much of the land surrounding Lake Titicaca, and its authority extended into neighboring valleys to the east and west. Vast tracts of ridged fields were created on the high plains, and government centers were built to administer these lands. Long-distance exchange linked the Tiwanaku heartland to distant resource areas such as the desert coast of northern Chile and the tropical montane forests of Bolivia.

In southern Peru, an equally formidable urban center developed in Ayacucho during the sixth century. Drawing upon elements of the same religious tradition as Tiwanaku, Huari developed its own distinctive architectural and artistic style. From its urban core of roughly 1.5 square miles, the Huari state expanded into neighboring highland and coastal lands, subjugating other cultures and constructing distinctive rectangular multistory administrative structures. Huari expansion eventually reached into the northern and southern highlands of the central Andes. Moreover, burials of the Huari administrators and Huari religious offerings have been found in centers on the south and central coasts of Peru. The Huari Empire provides a clear antecedent for the later Inca Empire in its unification of diverse coastal and highland cultures under the control of a highland center. It also foreshadowed the Inca in many respects, including its maintenance of road systems, its standardization of government architecture and dress, its emphasis on terracing and maize agriculture, and its use of *quipus* (coded cords that served as recording and accounting devices).

In most areas, the collapse of the Huari Empire around CE 800 and of the Tiwanaku state around CE 1000 led to increased political fragmentation and the reemergence of extreme cultural diversity. On the north coast of Peru, legends tell of the arrival by sea of a cultural hero who established a new dynasty. Archaeologists have tried to link this legend to the appearance of a new culture, known as Sicán, and to equate Chotuna, one of its early centers, with the founding settlement mentioned in the myth. Batán Grande is the largest center of this culture, and it contains vast cemeteries and more than a dozen adobe pyramids. By CE 1100 the center of power on the north coast had shifted again to the Moche Valley, where the urban center of Chan Chan gained ascendency as the capital of the Chimor, or Chimú, Empire, a conquest state that spanned all of Peru's north coast and part of its central coast. A host of other distinctive cultures, such as Chancay on the central coast and Ica on the south coast, coexisted with Chimor, and some of these societies had centers, such as La Centinela in Chincha, that were very impressive.

In the fifteenth century the Inca, a small and rather undistinguished highland ethnic group, successfully resisted defeat by larger cultures to the north and south. Under the leadership of a remarkable king known as Pachacuti, they began a succession of conquests and alliances that ultimately united much of the Andes. Few aspects of Inca culture were innovative, and indeed, their success was made possible by the millennia of Andean cultural achievements that preceded their rise. The Inca built hundreds of state administrative centers throughout their empire. Among the most impressive of these is Sacsahuaman, a temple-fortress that overlooks the Inca capital of Cuzco, and Machu Picchu, a royal estate built within the montane forests of the eastern Andean slopes. An effort was made to transform the Andes into a coherent political unit through a multitude of cultural, social, and economic strategies. Yet, like the preceding empires and states, this attempt was short-lived, lasting less than a century. In 1532, weakened by European diseases, civil war, and internal rebellions by defeated ethnic groups, the empire of the Incas crumbled before an invading force led by Francisco Pizarro.

See also **Caral; Chan Chan; Chavín; Chimú; Huari; Incas, The; Moche; Nasca; Paracas; Quimbaya; Tairona; Tiwanaku; Valdivia Culture.**

BIBLIOGRAPHY

Bauer, Brian S. *The Sacred Landscape of the Inca: The Cusco Ceque System.* Austin: University of Texas Press, 1998.

Brokaw, Galen. "The Poetics of Khipu Historiography: Felip Guaman Poma De Ayala and the Khipukamayuqs from Pacariqtambo." *Latin American Research Review* 38, no. 3 (2003): 111–147.

Brokaw, Galen. "Toward Deciphering the Khipu." *Journal of Interdisciplinary History* 35, no. 4 (2005): 571–590.

Bruhns, Karen. *Ancient South America.* Cambridge, U.K.: Cambridge University Press, 1994.

Burger, Richard L. *Chavin and the Origins of Andean Civilization.* London: Thames and Hudson, 1992.

Cieza de León, Pedro de, Alexandra Parma Cook, and Noble David Cook. *The Discovery and Conquest of Peru Chronicles of the New World Encounter.* Durham, NC: Duke University Press, 1998.

Guamán Poma de Ayala, Felipe. *El primer nueva corónica y buen gobierno.* Edited John V. Murra, Rolena Adorno, and Jorge Urioste. México, D.F.: Siglo Veintiuno, 1980.

Hidalgo, Jorge, ed. *Culturas de Chile: Prehistoria desde sus origenes hasta los albores de la conquista.* Santiago: Editorial Andrés Bello, 1989.

Lumbreras, Luis. *Arqueología de la américa andina.* Lima: Editorial Milla Batres, 1981.

Meggers, Betty. *Ecuador.* New York: Praeger, 1966.

Moseley, Michael. *The Incas and Their Ancestors.* London: Thames and Hudson, 1992.

Quilter, Jeffrey, and Gary Urton. *Narrative Threads Accounting and Recounting in Andean Khipu.* Austin: University of Texas Press, 2002.

Ravines, Rogger. *Panorama de la arqueología andina.* Lima: Insituto de Estudios Peruanos, 1982.

Reichel-Dolmatoff, Gerardo. *Colombia.* London: Thames and Hudson, 1965.

Reichel-Dolmatoff, Gerardo. *Arqueología de Colombia: Un texto introductorio.* Bogotá: Banco Popular, 1986.

Schobinger, Juan. *Prehistoria de Sudamérica.* Madrid: Editorial Alianza, 1988.

Shady Solís, Ruth. *Caral Supe, Perú la civilización de Caral-Supe: 5000 años de identidad cultural en el Perú.* Lima: Instituto Nacional de Cultura, Proyecto Especial Arqueológico Caral-Supe, 2005.

Silverblatt, Irene Marsha. *Moon, Sun, and Witches: Gender Ideologies and Class in Inca and Colonial Peru.* Princeton, NJ: Princeton University Press, 1987.

Urton, Gary. *Signs of the Inka Khipu: Binary Coding in the Andean Knotted-String Records.* Austin: University of Texas Press, 2003.

Vega, Garcilaso de la. *Comentarios reales de los incas.* Edited by Ángel Rosenblat. Buenos Aires: Emecé Editores, 1943.

Willey, Gordon. *An Introduction to American Archaeology,* Vol. 2: *South America.* Englewood Cliffs, NJ: Prentice Hall, 1971.

RICHARD L. BURGER

SOUTHERN CONE

The southern cone of South America, with its tip pointed towards Antarctica, is a region of over 1.5 million square miles (more than 4 million square kilometers) that includes territory in the republics of Uruguay, Paraguay, Argentina, and Chile. The Tropic of Capricorn crosses it in the north. By virtue of its position, it contains high western lands and low eastern lands of middle latitudes, with a marked influence of the Atlantic Ocean and a succession of tropical to cold climates in the extreme south. In the west rises the imposing Andean mountain range and associated mountain ranges. The cold waters of the Pacific bathe the coasts of Chile, forming deserts. The climatic and regional diversity provided abundant resources and various alternatives for the development of native societies, including both nomads and peoples in various degrees of sedentary lifestyles and social complexity.

The territory was first populated 13,000 years ago, at the end of the Pleistocene, the time when archaeology records the initial occupations by groups of hunter-gatherers in the Chilean-Argentine Andean area, Patagonia, and Pampa. Some of these sites have yielded the remains of extinct wildlife, as in Tagua Tagua, Cueva del Medio, Fell, Las Buitreras, Los Toldos, and Arroyo Seco; in others there are primarily remains of today's wildlife such as cervids, camelids, and rodents. Types of stone tools vary, but there were projectiles with "fishtail"-type points, used in different regions of Chile (Querero) and Patagonia (Fell, Piedra Museo) and even at La China, Sombrero, and Los Pinos, Buenos Aires.

As different environments came under the colonization process, they underwent changes in their types of occupation, ways in which the dead were buried (as in Arroyo Seco), and in stone technology. As hunter-gatherer groups incorporated milling stones and ceramic containers some 2,500 years ago (as at Cueva Tixi, La Guillerma, and Zanjón Seco), they were able to expand the range of foods they consumed. Rocky overhangs and walls with friezes of cave paintings reveal a rich symbolic life. These can be seen at Cueva de las Manos Pintadas and Los Toldos in Santa Cruz, Argentina. Bands of hunters and fishers survived in Tierra del Fuego and neighboring islands until the eighteenth century, when the harsh encounter with the Europeans occurred.

On the Atlantic coast, at the Uruguay and Paraná rivers, hunter-fisher societies existed as far back as ten thousand years ago. With a typical habitat of mounds raised above flood level, their construction displays the first signs of social complexity in the lowlands at Laguna Merín, Uruguay, 2,000 years ago. Around the tenth century CE, population growth and intensive use of river resources took place among the Goya-Malabrigo peoples along the Paraná River basin. A few centuries before the arrival of Europeans, the Guaraní tribes expanded from the upper Paraná River basin, navigating the river and leaving signs of their occupation at various points including Martín García Island, in the estuary of Río de la Plata.

The area of Gran Chaco comprises two sectors: the Chaco Boreal in Paraguay and Bolivia and the Chaco Austral in Argentina. The elevated mounds in the flood-prone areas of the Bermejo and Pilcomayo rivers were the characteristic settlement. There are vestiges of hunting and fishing, fires, pottery, and carved stone axes. Worship of the dead included burial in large vessels or urns decorated with impressions of cords and claws, as at Lomas de Olmedo, Quirquincho, Naranjo, Pozo de Maza, and Las Lomitas. Preserved in Pocitos are long lines of artificial mounds, which might have been used as housing and as elevated agricultural fields. This way of life—based on hunting, fishing, and gathering—prevailed between 500 and 1500 CE. Similar ways of life spread through the Chaco of Santiago, but these were more predominantly based on farming practices. Cultures that raised llamas and other livestock developed in the region of Sierras Centrales, Argentina, and in central Chile between 1 CE and the Spanish Conquest.

In the Andes, several millennia of nomadic life left vestiges in caves such as Inca Cueva, Huachichocana, Yavi, Quebrada Seca (Argentina), Tuina, Hakenasa, Tojo-Tojone, Tulán, and San Lorenzo and in open sites such as Puripica (Chile). The exploitation of marine resources was common at sites on the Pacific coast (Camarones 14, El Morro, Quiani, Punta Pichalo, Las Conchas), where at Chinchorro there developed the tradition of preserving the dead through mummification (7,000 to 4,000 years ago). Between the fifth and fourth millennium BCE, there was a move toward food production with the domestication of the llama and the exploitation of basic plant species such as corn, beans, *ají* peppers, and pumpkins observable at Tiliviche, Pichasca, Los Morrillos, and other sites. Around 1000 BCE, sedentary life was emerging in villages of farmers and herders that utilized fertile portions of the high plateau and the valleys, such as at Azapa, Caserones, Guatacondo, Chiu Chiu, Toconao, Tilocalar, and Tulor in Chile and Campo Colorado, Candelaria, San Francisco, Ciénaga, and Punta del Barro in the Argentine northwest. In the sixth century CE, socioeconomic changes took place among the peoples of Alamito, Ambato, and Ciénaga, which led to new, hierarchically differentiated social organizations and an autonomous religious system called La Aguada, while influences were being felt from the Tiwanaku state in the far north of Chile (Cabuza, Loreto, Pica, Topater, Quitor, and Coyo) and Argentina (Doncellas, Volcán).

The decomposition of these systems marked the rise, four centuries later, of the Regional Development period, during which population increased and was concentrated in centers on strategic hills (*pukara*) such as Huaihuarani, Saxamar, Tangani, Lasana, and Turi in Chile and Yacoraite, Los Amarillos, Tastil, Quilmes, Rincón Chico, and Hualfin in the Argentine northwest. Subsistence was based on irrigation agriculture and the raising of camelids. There was a marked specialization in artisan work, especially in metalwork and the weaving of wool. Many chiefdoms arose, some more powerful than others, as in Arica, Toconce, Lasana, Atacama, and Copiapó in Chile and Humahuaca, Tilcara, Tastil, Calchaquí, Yocavil, and Belén in the Argentine northwest. There were also dynamic networks of exchange from El Chaco to the Pacific. Disputes and wars occurred over control of farmlands and water sources. In the mid-fifteenth century the Incas arrived on the scene, gaining dominance over the various chiefdoms and making them Inca provinces: Atacama, Jujuy, Chicoana, Quirequire, and Copayapo. A complex road and administrative system was established with focal points at Mendoza, Argentina, and Santiago, Chile. The Spanish incursion began in 1536, bringing on a marked opposition from the indigenous peoples and generating the Calchaqui Wars (1560–1666). By the mid-seventeenth century, the Spanish colonial era had fully begun in the valleys of the Argentina northwest.

See also **Argentina, Geography; Chile, Geography; Paraguay, Geography; Uruguay, Geography.**

BIBLIOGRAPHY

Berberián, Eduardo E., and Axel E. Nielsen. 2 vols. *Historia Argentina Prehispánica*. Córdoba, Argentina: Editorial Brujas, 2001.

Durán Coirolo, Alicia, and Roberto Bracco Boksar, eds. *Arqueología de las tierras bajas*. Montevideo: Ministerio de Educación y Cultura, Comisión Nacional de Arqueología, 2000.

Hidalgo, J., V. Schiappacasse, H. Niemeyer, A. Aldunate, and I. Solimano, eds. *Culturas de Chile: Prehistoria desde sus orígenes hasta los albores de la conquista*. Santiago: Editorial Andrés Bello, 1989.

Lavallée, Danièle. *The First South Americans: The Peopling of a Continent from the Earliest Evidence to High Culture*. Translated by Paul G. Bahn. Salt Lake City: University of Utah Press, 2000.

Miotti, Laura, Monica Salemme, and Nora Flegenheimer, eds. *Where the South Winds Blow: Ancient Evidence of Paleo South Americans*. Dexter: The Center for the Study of the First Americans, Texas A&M University, 2003.

Rojas Rabiela, T., and J. V. Murra, eds. *Las sociedades originarias*. Vol. 1: *Historia General de América Latina*. Paris: UNESCO, Historia 1999.

Tarragó, Myriam N., ed. *Los pueblos originarios y la conquista*. Vol. 1: *Nueva Historia Argentina*. Buenos Aires: Sudamericana, 2000.

MYRIAM N. TARRAGÓ

PRENSA, LA (DE NICARAGUA).

La Prensa (de Nicaragua), Nicaragua's leading daily newspaper for three-quarters of a century. Established in 1926 by Pedro Joaquín Chamorro Zelaya (1891–1952), a noted lawyer and publicist from Granada, *La Prensa* became the primary critic of the Somoza dynasty.

After his father's death, Pedro Joaquín Chamorro Cardenal assumed direction of Nicaragua's most widely circulated newspaper. As editor, Chamorro Cardenal reaffirmed the conservative tradition of *La Prensa*. However, under his guidance the paper became more political than ever before. In 1959 Chamorro participated in an unsuccessful revolt against the regime of Luis Somoza Debayle. Throughout the 1960s the paper espoused a steady dose of pro-Christian, anti-Marxist, conservative views that are most clearly articulated in a series of editorials called "5 P.M." in 1967.

The turning point for *La Prensa*, the Chamorro family, and Nicaragua occurred in 1972, when the Central American nation suffered a severe earthquake that destroyed much of the capital, Managua. In the aftermath of the quake, *La Prensa* repeatedly embarrassed the Somoza regime by exposing unsavory official behavior, the diversion of international earthquake aid to private interests, and government incompetence.

Chamarro's increasing political clout and his highly critical daily commentaries provoked intensified attacks on the paper. On various occasions in the mid-1970s unidentified assailants fired automatic weapons at *La Prensa*'s plant. In 1974 the Somoza government declared a state of siege, implemented strict press censorship, banned criticism of the government, and restricted reports of insurgent activities. At the same time, attacks against individual *La Prensa* reporters became common. In 1977 the newspaper published a story that accused a business owned by individuals close to the Somoza family of exporting badly needed blood plasma for profit. In retaliation, the company's owners reportedly hired the assassins who murdered Chamorro Cardenal on 10 January 1978.

Following this murder, the slain editor's widow, Violeta Barrios De Chamorro, assumed direction of the paper. She helped mobilize massive demonstrations that condemned the actions of the assailants and she publicized her belief that the government was directly linked to her husband's assassination. *La Prensa* thereafter was at the forefront of the movement that overthrew the Somoza regime in 1979.

Nonetheless, the coalition against the Somozas that the Chamorro family and *La Prensa* helped to consolidate following the death of the paper's editor was only temporary. Although the paper originally supported Nicaragua's 1979 revolutionary government, by 1981 *La Prensa* became a bitter opponent of the Sandinista regime. After declaring a state of emergency in 1982, the government reinstituted censorship. Although the paper continued to publish, it did so under severe restrictions. In the mid- and late 1980s publication of *La Prensa* was suspended on several occasions by the government. Despite these interruptions, under the editorship of Violeta Barrios de Chamorro's son, Pedro Joaquín Chamorro Barrios, the newspaper opposed the swing to the left under Sandinista leadership and remained the focus of political resistance to the regime throughout the 1980s.

See also **Chamorro Cardenal, Pedro Joaquín; Journalism; Somoza Debayle, Luis.**

BIBLIOGRAPHY

Pedro Joaquín Chamorro Cardenal, *Estripe sangrienta: Los Somozas* (1957), and *Diario de un preso* (1963).

John A. Booth, *The End and the Beginning: The Nicaraguan Revolution*, 2d ed. (1985).

Ralph L. Woodward, Jr., *Central America: A Nation Divided*, 2d ed. (1985).

James Dunkerley, *Power in the Isthmus: A Political History of Modern Central America* (1988).

Additional Bibliography

Kodrich, Kris *Tradition and Change in the Nicaraguan Press: Newspapers and Journalists in a New Democratic Era* (2002).

Rockwell, Rick J. and Noreene Janus. *Media Power in Central America* (2003).

WADE A. KIT

PRESCOTT, WILLIAM HICKLING

(1796–1859). William Hickling Prescott (*b.* 14 May 1796; *d.* 28 January 1859), American historian and man of letters. William Hickling Prescott was born in Salem, Massachusetts, into a prosperous, old-line family. Blinded in the left eye while a student at Harvard, soon after graduation he also suffered serious problems in his right eye that turned him from the study of law to letters. Forced to depend on a special writing case that enabled him to write without seeing, Prescott relied upon a secretary to turn his scrawls into readable form.

Prescott learned several European languages, including Spanish, and in the mid-1820s he decided to write the three-volume *History of the Reign of Ferdinand and Isabella the Catholic* (1837). This narrative history, based upon numerous books and manuscripts received from Spain and read to him by his secretary, won Prescott considerable fame and long remained the standard work on the Catholic kings.

His early acclaim and several well-placed friends bought Prescott election to the Royal Academy of History in Madrid and access, through copyists, to numerous documentary collections. From these and published sources, Prescott wrote his finest works, *A*

History of the Conquest of Mexico (3 vols., 1843) and *A History of the Conquest of Peru* (2 vols., 1847).

Although the histories of both conquests begin with discussions of the native civilizations that preceded the arrival of the Spaniards, Prescott's true interest lay in the conquests themselves. His histories present flowing narratives of epic events based on a rigorous devotion to facts. While they have been supplemented by subsequent economic, political, social, and intellectual studies, the histories remain classics unsurpassed in their ability to capture the imagination and engage the reader.

See also **Ferdinand II of Aragon; Isabella I of Castile; Spanish Empire.**

BIBLIOGRAPHY

Robin A. Humphreys, "William Hickling Prescott: The Man and the Historian," *Hispanic American Historical Review* 39, no. 1 (1959): 1–19.

C. Harvey Gardiner, *William Hickling Prescott: A Biography* (1969).

Additional Bibliography

Costeloe, Michael P. "Prescott's 'History of the Conquest' and Calderón de la Barca's 'Life in Mexico': Mexican Reaction, 1843–1844." *The Americas* 47:3 (January 1991): 337–348.

Eipper, John E. "The Canonizer De-Canonized: The Case of William H. Prescott." *Hispania* 68:200 (September 2000): 416–427.

Krauze, Enrique. "Mister Prescott y Lord Thomas." *Vuelta* 18:216 (November 1994): 25–31.

MARK A. BURKHOLDER

PRESIDENTIALISM/PRESIDENTIAL SYSTEMS.

The preponderance of presidential systems is one of the distinctive political features of the Latin American region. After independence from Spain and Portugal in the nineteenth century, most of the new republics that emerged in South and Central America and Mexico adopted political institutions modeled on the 1787 Constitution of the United States. Parliamentary constitutions based on the British model are found almost exclusively in the Commonwealth Caribbean. Because Latin American presidential systems have tended to be unstable, a major controversy has focused on the link between types of constitutions and regime durability.

A constitution is presidential if the executive and legislative branches of government are elected separately for fixed terms. In parliamentary systems, the executive (typically led by a prime minister) is selected from among the members of the legislature and may be removed through a vote of no confidence. The difference between these types of democratic constitutions hinges, therefore, on two distinctions. First, in a presidential system, candidates compete for seats in the legislature or for executive office by running in separate elections. In a parliamentary system, candidates run for seats in the legislature, and then form a government based on the ability of a party or coalition to win the confidence of a majority of the members of parliament. Second, presidential systems follow fixed electoral calendars. Once elected, the president and the congress typically hold office for a specified term. In parliamentary systems, the government's term can be brought to an end at any time by a vote of no confidence or an act of dissolution.

Not all constitutions can be neatly classified into purely presidential or parliamentary categories. Mixed constitutions combine features of both. In the French semipresidential system, for example, the president is directly elected for a fixed term, but executive power is shared with a head of government responsible to the legislature. In Bolivia the president is chosen by congress if no presidential candidate wins an absolute majority of the popular vote. Within presidential systems there is considerable variation in presidential veto powers, legislative prerogatives, decree authority, powers of dissolution, and influence over budgetary processes. Nevertheless, most of the world's democracies can be classified as presidential, parliamentary, or mixed, and nearly all Latin American states, in contrast to the English-speaking Caribbean, fall unambiguously into the presidential category. Each pure system shares traits sufficiently distinctive to make it possible for them to be differentiated and compared.

Indeed, one of the most robust generalizations in comparative politics is that presidential systems are more prone to breakdown than parliamentary systems. This finding was first published by Alfred Stepan and Cindy Skach in their 1993 essay "Constitutional

Frameworks and Democratic Consolidation: Parliamentarism versus Presidentialism." Although there has been no subsequent disagreement over the validity of this finding, sharply different explanations have been advanced and the ensuing debate has divided scholars into two main camps. One traces the instability of presidentialism to problems inherent in constitutional design, while the other attributes it to serendipity. Presidentialism, in the latter view, has been adopted in places such as Latin America where political systems are unstable for other reasons.

In "Presidential or Parliamentary Democracy: Does It Make a Difference?" Juan J. Linz famously argued that presidentialism creates a problem of "dual legitimacy" (6–8). Directly elected presidents can make a claim to democratic legitimacy separate from that of legislators, and they hold executive power regardless of the composition of the legislature. Prime ministerial survival depends on the confidence of the legislature; in parliamentary systems the executive has no separate claim to legitimacy. The plebiscitary tendencies inherent in all mass democracies—the risk that politicians with neither legislative experience nor party attachments will gain executive office and seek to bypass the legislature or govern at the margins of the constitution—are exacerbated by presidentialism.

Linz also argued that fixed terms introduce rigidity into presidential constitutions. In parliamentary systems elections can be called after a vote of no confidence or an act of dissolution; in a presidential system the executive and members of congress are normally elected for a period of time that cannot easily be adjusted. Fixed electoral calendars allow presidents and members of congress to refuse to cooperate without consequently having to face an election. Although minority and coalition governments are possible in both systems, parliamentarism has a built-in mechanism for changing a government that no longer enjoys the confidence of a legislative majority.

Skeptics argue that the brittleness of presidentialism is best explained by its popularity among states that are unstable for reasons other than the intrinsic features of their constitutions. In Latin America, presidential institutions were grafted onto countries with social and political conditions different from those in the model state, the United States. The brittleness of constitutional order in Latin American is due to long-standing patterns of inequality and social exclusion, weak states, an uneven rule of law, and the propensity of the military to intervene in politics. In this view, the adoption of presidentialism by Latin American states makes this type of constitution appear to be more prone to instability than it really is.

As a result of the decline of regime instability caused by direct military interference in politics since the transitions to democracy in the 1980s, the debate on presidentialism has shifted to the system's more subtle effects on the quality of democratic governance. Although coup attempts have been rare since the 1980s (examples include Venezuela in 1992 and 2002), there have been serious constitutional crises in Peru (1992, 2000), Guatemala (1993), Paraguay (1996, 1999), Ecuador (2000, 2005), Bolivia (2003), Nicaragua (2005), and Venezuela (1999–2000; 2002–2004). A key lesson from these crises is that democratically elected leaders may use conflicts—occasionally arising from dual legitimacies—as a pretext to unconstitutionally interrupt the tenure in office of other elected officials, to arbitrarily or illegally appoint or remove members of the judiciary or electoral bodies, or to aid and abet in the interference by the military in the jurisdiction of elected officials.

Presidentialism alone is neither a necessary nor a sufficient condition for democratic instability. Presidential constitutions, because they are designed to create checks and balances by pitting one branch of government against another, may set in motion characteristic patterns of political struggle involving sharp disputes over the powers of the president, the legislature, and the courts when other forces trigger a crisis. How much presidentialism itself contributes to instability relative to broader social and political conditions or mechanisms, and whether it is more or less conducive to settling political differences within the framework of the rule of law and constitutional government, remain matters for continuing scholarly debate.

See also **Democracy.**

BIBLIOGRAPHY

Cheibub, José Antonio. *Presidentialism, Parliamentarism, and Democracy.* New York: Cambridge University Press, 2007.

Linz, Juan J. "Presidential or Parliamentary Democracy: Does It Make a Difference?" In *The Failure of Presidential Democracy: Comparative Perspectives*, edited by Juan J. Linz and Arturo Valenzuela. Baltimore and London: Johns Hopkins University Press, 1994.

Shugart, Matthew Soberg, and John M. Carey. *Presidents and Assemblies: Constitutional Design and Electoral Dynamics.* New York: Cambridge University Press, 1992.

Stepan, Alfred, and Cindy Skach. "Constitutional Frameworks and Democratic Consolidation: Parliamentarism versus Presidentialism." *World Politics* 46:1 (1993), 1–22.

Valenzuela, Arturo. "Latin American Presidencies Interrupted." *Journal of Democracy* 15:4 (2004), 5–19.

MAXWELL A. CAMERON

PRESIDIO. Presidio, a term used to describe military garrisons, particularly in frontier areas and ports. Established in the New World by the middle of the sixteenth century, the presidio was one of the fundamental institutions of Spanish colonization. These defensive military establishments were found from Chile to the Philippines to the northern frontier of New Spain. Coastal presidios, often stationed in heavily armed fortifications, such as the fortresses of El Morro and La Punta in Havana, protected maritime trade routes against pirates. Their presidial complements could be more than one hundred men. By contrast, the modal frontier presidio was a small, rectangular, walled fort with towers. The presidios of the interior guarded mines and defended against hostile Indians. The earliest frontier presidios consisted of a handful of armed men under the command of a low-ranking officer. These presidios grew in size and complexity as Native Americans adjusted to the military challenge of European weaponry and became a more serious threat. While need determined the size of a presidial company, by the late seventeenth century, a captain and his subalterns commonly commanded twenty-five to fifty active-duty soldiers and on rare occasions as many as a hundred or more.

Frequently, no permanent structure was erected, and the presidio was located wherever need dictated. In times of extreme danger, soldiers could be assigned to posts away from the presidio and additional men from local communities added to the force. Liberal land grants were made to presidial soldiers and their families and to settlers around the presidio to establish self-sufficient communities that would consolidate the Spanish presence.

See also **Forts and Fortifications, Spanish America.**

BIBLIOGRAPHY

Max L. Moorhead, *The Presidio: Bastion of the Spanish Borderlands* (1975).

Thomas H. Naylor and Charles W. Polzer, *The Presidio and Militia on the Northern Frontier of New Spain, 1570–1700* (1986), esp. pp. 15–29.

Additional Bibliography

Weber, David J., and Jorge Ferreiro. *La frontera española en América del Norte.* Sección de obras de historia. México: Fondo de Cultura Económica, 2000.

RICK HENDRICKS

PRESTES, LUÍS CARLOS (1898–1990). Luís Carlos Prestes (*b.* 3 January 1898; *d.* 7 March 1990), secretary-general of the Brazilian Communist Party (PCB) (1943–1980). Prestes was born in Porto Alegre, Rio Grande do Sul. He was in Rio de Janeiro in 1908 when his father, an army captain, died, leaving the family (Prestes had four sisters) with an insufficient pension. Prestes's mother gave lessons in French and music. Later Prestes occasionally tutored classmates in mathematics while attending the military school in Rio de Janeiro and the military academy, where, as an outstanding student, he earned a degree in engineering.

Prestes achieved fame in 1925–1927 as chief of staff of the revolutionary column that made what became known as the Long March in the interior. However, Prestes, the "Cavalier of Hope," condemned as insufficiently radical the objectives of the 1930 revolution that brought Getúlio Vargas to power. After working with Dmitri Manuilski in the Comintern in Russia, Prestes returned clandestinely to Brazil, where he helped prepare the uprising of 1935. Its failure was followed by anticommunist repression and torture. Prestes was arrested in 1936 and sentenced to 16.5 years of prison for having led the uprising. In 1940 the sentence was extended by 30 years because he was found guilty of having persuaded Communist leaders, before his arrest, to murder Elza Fernandes, a young woman accused by Communists of aiding the police. Olga Benário, a German Jewish Communist whom Prestes had married while abroad, was deported from Brazil to Germany, where she died, a prisoner of the Nazis, after giving birth to their daughter, Anita Leocádia.

A prisoner in Rio de Janeiro, Prestes supported the war effort of President Vargas. His "alliance with Vargas," which arose after his release in April 1945, was accompanied by Communist penetration of labor unions. The growing PCB espoused a moderate program and became legal until outlawed during a new presidential administration at the beginning of the cold war. Prestes then lost his Senate seat. From hiding he issued thunderous manifestos calling for uprisings.

During the administration of Juscelino Kubitschek, whom the Communists helped elect in 1955, Prestes emerged from hiding and campaigned for candidates who purchased PCB support in the local elections of 1958. Adhering to the Moscow line, he welcomed any ally who would oppose "United States imperialism." In the early 1960s, Prestes sought legality for the PCB and advocated achieving socialism by a peaceful path. But the very strength of the PCB in labor and student organizations, combined with the activities of violence- minded leftists, provided public support for the 1964 military coup that deposed left-leaning President João Goulart.

Prestes, forced again into hiding, was criticized by those advocating violent struggle against the new military regime. Following a party schism and the emergence of guerrilla groups and minor Communist parties, he denounced terrorism and went abroad. An amnesty decree of 1979 allowed Prestes to return to Brazil, where he accused PCB leaders of betraying the working class by cooperating with the government in the quest to legalize the party. He lost his post of secretary-general and sought, unsuccessfully, to have another party name him its senatorial candidate. Separated from the PCB, he spent his last days supporting the political aspirations of Leonel Brizola.

See also **Brazil: Since 1889; Brazil, Political Parties: Brazilian Communist Party (PCB); Lacerda, Maurício Pavia de.**

BIBLIOGRAPHY

Dulles, John W. F. *Brazilian Communism, 1935–1945: Repression during World Upheaval*. Austin: University of Texas Press, 1983.

O Velho: A Historia de Luis Carlos Prestes (film), directed by Toni Venturi (1997).

Prestes, Anita Leocádia. *Luiz Carlos Prestes e a Aliança Nacional Libertadora: Os caminhos da luta antifascista no Brasil*. Petrópolis: Editora Vozes, 1998.

Vianna, Marly de Almeida Gomes. *Revolucionários de 35: Sonho e realidade*. São Paulo: Companhia das Letras, 1992.

JOHN W. F. DULLES

PRESTES COLUMN. Prestes Column, military brigade fueling the political discontent in Brazil that played a role in the Revolution of 1930. Late in 1924 former army captain Luís Carlos Prestes led 800 rebels from Rio Grande do Sul to Paraná to join the São Paulo Column that had revolted in July against President Artur Bernardes and the political fraud that they felt had helped make him president in 1922. Fleeing superior federal forces in Paraná, the Prestes and São Paulo columns marched through Paraguay in April 1925 and, in Mato Grosso, organized themselves into one column of 1,200 revolutionaries headed by Miguel Costa (a former major in the São Paulo state troop), with Prestes as chief of staff and Juarez Távora as assistant chief of staff and with four detachments led by Oswaldo Cordeiro de Farias, João Alberto Lins de Barros, Antônio de Siqueira Campos, and Djalma Soares Dutra.

Prestes provided the Long March of more than 15,000 miles with the leadership needed to prevail in the face of malaria, unfavorable terrain, federal and state troops, and ruffians (*jagunços*), armed by the Bernardes government. After the column moved from the north to Brazil's northeast bulge, it had to battle continuously and failed to obtain allies. In February 1926, Costa and Prestes issued a manifesto decrying Brazil's administrative dishonesty, fraudulent elections, press censorship, and lack of social legislation and justice. While government troop commanders bickered, the column reached Bahia's interior, where the thirsty, hungry revolutionaries, many suffering from malaria, plodded on foot, carrying the wounded. But on the circuitous return to Mato Grosso, they replaced lost horses and warded off savage attacks by *jagunços,* led by backland "colonels." Early in 1927 the men supported Costa's recommendation to disband, undefeated by Bernardes, whose term had ended. Prestes, made popular by the anti-Bernardes press, took 620 men into Bolivia and found road-building jobs for many. The last 65 to disband entered Paraguay with Siqueira Campos in March 1927.

See also **Brazil, Revolutions: Revolution of 1930; Coronel, Coronelismo.**

BIBLIOGRAPHY

Lourenço Moreira Lima, *A Coluna Prestes* (1934).

Neill Macaulay, *The Prestes Column* (1974).

Anita L. Prestes, *A Coluna Prestes* (1990).

Additional Bibliography

Barros, João Alberto Lins de. *A marcha da coluna*. Rio de Janeiro: Biblioteca do Exército Editora, 1997.

Camillo Filho, José. *A Coluna Prestes no Piauí*. Teresina, Piauí, Brazil: UFPI, 1996.

Meirelles, Domingos. *As noites das grandes fogueiras: Uma história da Coluna Presta*. Rio de Janeiro: Editora Record, 1995.

JOHN W. F. DULLES

PRESTES DE ALBUQUERQUE, JULIO

(1882–1946). Julio Prestes de Albuquerque (*b*. 15 March 1882; *d*. 9 February 1946), president-elect of Brazil at the time of the 1930 coup that brought Getúlio Vargas to power. Son of a traditional São Paulo family, Prestes served in both the state legislature and the national Congress before being elected governor of the state of São Paulo in 1927. As majority leader in the Chamber of Deputies at the start of Washington Luís Pereira De Sousa's presidential term (1926), Prestes won the confidence of the president, who selected him to run as his successor in the 1930 election. This decision ignored the "governor's politics," whereby the governor of the state of Minas Gerais should have been the preferred candidate for the presidency in 1930. Disgruntled *mineiros* joined the Liberal Alliance supporting the candidacy of Getúlio Vargas. In the meantime, the 1929 stock market crash highlighted the president's inability to mitigate his supporters' economic troubles. Although official election results confirmed Prestes as Brazil's new president, the widespread disenchantment with Pereira's final year in office cemented the success of Vargas's challenge. The armies of the Northeast and of the South marched on Rio de Janeiro and deposed Pereira, who went into exile as did Prestes. Upon his return from exile, Prestes retired to his ranch in the interior of the state of São Paulo, no longer interested in politics.

See also **Brazil, Revolutions: Revolution of 1930; Vargas, Getúlio Dornelles.**

BIBLIOGRAPHY

José Maria Bello, *A History of Modern Brazil, 1889–1964*, translated by James L. Taylor (1966), esp. p. 261.

E. Bradford Burns, *A History of Brazil*, 2d ed. (1980), esp. pp. 395–397.

Additional Bibliography

Casalecchi, José Enio. *O Partido Republicano Paulista: Política e poder (1889–1926)*. São Paulo: Editora Brasiliense, 1987.

JOAN MEZNAR

PRÊTO. *See* **African Brazilians, Color Terminology.**

PRICE, GEORGE

(1919–). George Cadle Price (b. January 15, 1919) was prime minister of Belize from 1981 to 1984 and 1989 to 1993. Acclaimed as the Father of the Nation, Price was the dominant figure in Belizean politics in the second half of the twentieth century. From 1954, when universal adult suffrage was first granted to British Hondurans, through independence in 1981, his People's United Party won every election, remaining undefeated until 1984.

Of Scottish and Mayan extraction, Price was born in Belize City, the third of eleven children of William and Irene Price. His father was an auctioneer and justice of the peace. After primary school he enrolled in the Jesuit-run St. John's High School of Belize. He narrowly escaped death in the floodwaters of a 1931 hurricane. After graduating in 1935 he enrolled in St. Augustine's College in Bay St. Louis, Mississippi, to pursue a religious vocation. Graduating in 1940, he planned to go to Rome but was prevented by World War II. He returned home to work for a year before entering the diocesan seminary in Guatemala in 1941. His father's illness in 1942 forced him to end his studies and return to Belize. For the next thirteen years he served as a private secretary to Robert Sydney Turton, a Creole chicle millionaire and member of the colonial legislative council. Price accompanied Turton on frequent trips to New York, Chicago, and Washington, D.C.

At the urging of Turton, Price entered politics in 1943 and lost his first bid for the Belize town board, or city council. In 1947 he won the first of his many political victories in his second bid for the council, on which he served until 1965, also serving as mayor of Belize City from 1958 to 1962. On the national front, Price was a founding member of the People's United Party (PUP) in 1950 and served successively as party secretary, party leader, member of the Legislative Council, member of the House of Representatives, first minister, and premier from 1965 to 1981.

Price survived charges of sedition by the British in 1957 when as part of a delegation to London he attended meetings with the Guatemalan ambassador. For his independent foreign policies, he has also withstood the opposition's charges of pro-socialist views. There have been charges of corruption against members of his cabinet as well as numerous factional splits and defections within his own party.

Price was the chief architect of Belizean independence, secured in 1981. An ascetic, charismatic bachelor who attended 6:00 AM mass every morning, he seemed to know virtually every family in Belize—familiarity born of dozens of trips around the country in his personal Land Rover and years of citizens' day meetings each Wednesday in Belize City, where any citizen could discuss problems personally with the prime minister. He wrote poetry and musical theater, read voraciously, and was very knowledgeable about foreign affairs.

Severe economic problems, internal party wrangling, and the feeling by a majority of Belizeans that it was time for a change contributed to a landslide victory by the opposition United Democratic Party (UDP) in the national elections of 1984. Price lost his own seat, Belize North. Out of office for the first time in thirty-seven years, he spent the next five years rebuilding the PUP and the *Belize Times*, the party-dominated weekly newspaper. In the national

elections of 1989 he lead the PUP to a narrow victory, winning fifteen of twenty-eight seats, and reassumed the office of prime minister.

Price wisely chose to continue some of the successful economic policies of his predecessor, Manuel Esquivel. However, in contrast to the large-scale foreign investment policies of his predecessor, the PUP Manifesto for 1989–1994 promoted smaller-scale investments by Belizeans in the tourist and agricultural sectors.

Following a by-election victory in January 1993 and landslide victories in local elections in April 1993, Price decided to call for an early election on 30 June 1993. However, a series of events beyond his control contributed to his government's defeat. These included a May decision by Great Britain to pull all troops out of Belize by January 1994 followed by a coup in Guatemala on May 25, which reawakened Belizean fears of Guatemalan intervention. Promising suspension of a Maritime Areas Act granting Guatemala access to the Atlantic Ocean through Belizean territory, the UDP won sixteen seats to thirteen seats for Price's PUP. Price retained his Belize City constituency and became leader of the opposition in the new parliament.

In 1996 Price handed over leadership of the PUP to his former minister of education, Said Musa, who led the PUP to a resounding electoral victory in the national elections of August 27, 1998, winning 26 of 29 seats in the House of Representatives. Price became senior minister, a post he retained until retiring from politics in 2003.

Price became Belize's very first National Hero when he was presented the Order of Belize Award in 2000. In 2001 he was honored with the Order of Caricom for his outstanding contributions to the political, social, and cultural development of the Caribbean community. On Belizean independence day, September 21, 2002, Prime Minister Musa inaugurated the new George Price Center for Peace and Development in Belmopan. Price's May 2004 nationwide tour of the country to promote national pride included teaching 1,200 students assembled in a stadium in Corozal the proper singing of the Belizean national anthem. "It's a march," he said.

See also **Belize; Musa, Said.**

BIBLIOGRAPHY

Benske, John L. "George Price and Belize: The Creation of a Nation." MA thesis, University of Florida, 1990.

George Price: Father of the Nation Belize. Belize: ION Media, 2000. Available from http://gpcbelize.com.

BRIAN E. COUTTS

PRICE-MARS, JEAN (1876–1969).

Jean Price-Mars (*b.* 15 October 1876; *d.* 1 March 1969), Haitian teacher, diplomat, writer, and ethnographer. Price-Mars served as secretary of the Haitian legation in Washington (1909) and as chargé d'affaires in Paris (1915–1917). In 1922 he completed medical studies that he had given up for lack of a scholarship. After withdrawing as a candidate for the presidency of Haiti in favor of Stenio Vincent in 1930, Price-Mars led Senate opposition to the new president and was forced out of politics. In 1941, he was again elected to the Senate. He was secretary of state for external relations in 1946 and, later, ambassador to the Dominican Republic. In his eighties, he continued service as Haitian ambassador at the United Nations and ambassador to France.

Through his lectures and writing, Price-Mars brought popular culture, the Creole language, and the religion of Vodun into respectable focus. He laid the groundwork for the formation of the Indigenist movement and the important literary journals, *La revue indigène* and *Les griots*. Among his important doctrines was his opposition to the concept of "race" applied to human beings. He returned to the very sources of Haitian folklore in demonstrating parallels and resemblances with other early cultures (European and African). Berrou and Pompilus wrote that *Ainsi parla l'oncle* (1928) was "the condemnation of the bovarysm of the Haitian middle class." Depestre criticized Price-Mars for not early repudiating François Duvalier, but Hoffman takes a more balanced view, that Price-Mars maintained a distance from Duvalier and the "Griots."

See also **Haiti; Négritude; Vodun, Voodoo, Vaudun.**

BIBLIOGRAPHY

Other works include *La vocation de l'élite* (1919); *Ainsi parla l'oncle* (1928), translated with critical introduction by Magdaline W. Shannon as *So Spoke the Uncle* (1983); *Une étape de l'évolution haïtienne* (1929); *Formation ethnique, folklore et culture du peuple haïtien* (1939); *La République d'Haïti et la République dominicaine* (1953); *De Saint-Domingue à Haïti* (1959).

See also F. Raphaël Berrou and Pradel Pompilus, *Histoire de la littérature haïtienne illustrée par les textes,* vol. 3 (1977), pp. 716–747; René Depestre, "La négritude de Jean Price-Mars," in his *Bonjour et adieu à la négritude* (1980), pp. 43–57; Léon- François Hoffman, "Price-Mars et les Griots," in his *Haïti: couleurs, croyances, créole* (1990), pp. 183–197.

Additional Bibliography

Shannon, Magdaline W. *Jean Price-Mars, the Haitian Elite and the American Occupation, 1915–1935.* New York: St. Martin's Press, 1996.

CARROL F. COATES

PRIETO, GUILLERMO (1818–1897).

Guillermo Prieto (*b.* 1818; *d.* 1897), Mexican cabinet minister, poet, dramatist, and author. Born in Mexico City, Prieto lived at Molino del Rey, near Chapultepec, where his father managed the mill and a bakery. When his father died in 1831 and his mother lost her sanity, Prieto worked in a clothing store until his poetry attracted the attention of Andrés Quintana Roo, who got him a post in the customs house and enrolled him in the Colegio de San Juan de Letrán.

Prieto's first poems were published when he was nineteen. The same year, President Anastasio Bustamante named Prieto his personal secretary and brought him to the presidential palace to live. Prieto's first theatrical work, *El alférez,* was produced in 1840, and others followed in 1842 and 1843. Prieto edited the *Diario Oficial* until Santa Anna overthrew Bustamante in 1841. He then wrote for *El Siglo XIX* and *El Monitor Republicano,* and in 1845 founded *Don Simplicio* with Ignacio Ramírez. He was elected to the national legislature in 1848, 1850, and 1852.

Prieto published his analysis of Mexico's fiscal circumstances, *Indicaciones...,* in 1850, and President Mariano Arista appointed him minister of finance in 1852. Although he recorded in his memoirs that he had sought attention and ostentation, Prieto also envisioned himself as a reformer. He favored lifting prohibitions on trade and reducing the costs of administration.

Arista's administration was soon overthrown, however, and Prieto was subjected to house arrest on orders from Antonio López de Santa Anna. A supporter of the Revolution of Ayutla, Prieto was appointed minister of finance by President Juan Álvarez. Prieto was a delegate to the Constitutional Convention of 1856–1857 and served on the finance committee. Benito Juárez, who assumed the presidency in 1858, selected Prieto as his first finance minister. In March 1858, when conservative troops captured Juárez in Guadalajara during the War of the Reform, Prieto's eloquence saved the president from a firing squad. Prieto again headed the finance ministry in 1859 and 1861, but he broke with Juárez when the president refused to turn power over to Jesús González Ortega in 1865.

Prieto remained active in politics, however, favoring congressional authority over that of the executive. He supported the efforts of José María Iglesias against President Sebastián Lerdo De Tejada's abuse of executive authority in the 1876 elections and served as Iglesias's minister of government for several months before Iglesias was overthrown by Porfirio Díaz. Prieto remained a popular poet and continued publishing on such subjects as travel, history, and political economy. His *Memorias de mis tiempos* (1906) records his impressions of the years from 1828 to 1853.

See also **Arista, Mariano; Bustamante, Anastasio; Iglesias, José María; Juárez, Benito; Literature: Spanish America; Mexico: 1810–1910.**

BIBLIOGRAPHY

Walter V. Scholes, *Mexican Politics During the Juárez Regime, 1855–1872* (1957), pp. 26–27, 60–65, 70.

Moisés González Navarro, *Anatomía del poder en México, 1848–1853* (1977), pp. 173–175.

Richard N. Sinkin, *The Mexican Reform, 1855–1876: A Study in Liberal Nation-Building* (1979), pp. 49–50, 80, 85, 136–137.

Barbara A. Tenenbaum, *The Politics of Penury: Debts and Taxes in Mexico, 1821–1856* (1986), pp. 115–116; *Diccionario Porrúa de historia, biografía y geografía de México,* 5th ed. (1986).

Additional Bibliography

Castro, Miguel Ángel. *Poliantea periodística: Homenaje a Guillermo Prieto.* México, D.F.: Universidad Nacional Autónoma de México, 1997.

McLean, Malcolm Dallas. *Vida y obra de Guillermo Prieto.* México, D.F.: El Colegio de México, 1998.

D. F. STEVENS

PRIETO FIGUEROA, LUIS BELTRÁN

(1902–1978). Luis Beltrán Prieto Figueroa (*b.* 1902; *d.* after 1978), Venezuelan political leader. Founder and head of the Venezuelan Teachers Federation, Prieto subsequently was one of the founders and principal leaders of Democratic Action (Acción Democrática, AD). A leader of the revolution that overthrew President Isaías Medina Angarita (1945), he later was a member of the revolutionary junta, serving as education minister. In exile during the military dictatorship (1948–1958), Prieto returned to Venezuela to become, first, secretary-general and, later, president of AD. He also held a Senate seat. In 1968 he left AD to form the Electoral Movement of the People. He lost bids for the presidency in 1968, 1973, and 1978.

See also **Venezuela, Political Parties: Democratic Action (AD).**

BIBLIOGRAPHY

Robert J. Alexander, ed., *Biographical Dictionary of Latin American and Caribbean Political Leaders* (1988).

Joaquín Soler Serrano, *Venezolanos a fondo* (1990); pp. 193–206.

Additional Bibliography

Luque, Guillermo. *Prieto Figueroa, maestro de América: Su labor pedagógica y gremial por la Escuela Nueva en Venezuela.* Caracas: Fondo Editorial de la Facultad de Humanidades y Educación, Universidad Central de Venezuela, 2002.

Subero, Efraín. *Historia de un maestro que quiso ser: Vida y obra de Luis Beltrán Prieto Figueroa.* Caracas: Universidad Pedagógica Experimental Libertador, 2001.

WINFIELD J. BURGGRAAFF

PRIETO RODRÍGUEZ, SOTERO

(1884–1935). Sotero Prieto Rodríguez (*b.* 25 December 1884; *d.* 22 May 1935), Mexican mathematician and scientist. Son of engineer Raúl Prieto and nephew of writer Isabel Prieto, Sotero Prieto came from a prominent intellectual family in Guadalajara,

Jalisco, where he completed his primary and secondary studies. He graduated from the National School of Engineering with a specialty in mathematics, and in 1912 began teaching mathematics and geometry at the National University, where many future political and intellectual leaders were his students. He founded and directed the mathematics section of the Antonio Alzate Science Society from 1932 to 1935, and contributed significantly to the expansion of science in general in Mexico. He also influenced the progress of mathematics research in Mexico, and is remembered for his expertise in the Spanish language.

See also **Engineering; Science.**

BIBLIOGRAPHY

Enciclopedia de México, vol. 10, p. 432.

RODERIC AI CAMP

PRIETO VIAL, JOAQUÍN (1786–1854).

Joaquín Prieto Vial (*b.* 20 August 1786; *d.* 22 November 1854), president of Chile (1831–1841). Born in Concepción, and a soldier from his youth onward, Prieto was sent as a patriot auxiliary to Buenos Aires in 1811, but returned to fight in Chile's wars of independence (1813–1814). After exile in Argentina during the Spanish reconquest (1814–1817), he took part in the battles of Chacabuco (12 February 1817) and Maipú (5 April 1818), following which he took charge of patriot operations in the south. A member of several of the congresses of the 1820s, he was appointed commander of the army in the south in 1828. In 1829–1830 he led the successful Conservative rebellion in the hope (soon frustrated) of securing the restoration of Bernardo O'Higgins (1778–1842). He commanded the Conservative troops at the battle of Lircay in April 1830.

Diego Portales (1793–1837) persuaded Prieto to assume the presidency from September 1831. During his two consecutive terms, he saw the stabilization of Chile, the Constitution of 1833, the war against the Peru-Bolivia Confederation, the murder of Diego Portales, and, at the end of the decade, political relaxation.

Prieto was a pious, rather serious figure. Portales used to make fun of him, calling him "Isidro Ayestas"—the name of a deranged man who wandered the streets of Santiago during that time.

See also **Chile: Foundations Through Independence; Chile, Constitutions; Portales Palazuelos, Diego José Pedro Víctor.**

BIBLIOGRAPHY

Ramón Sotomayor Valdés, *Historia de Chile bajo el gobierno del general don Joaquín Prieto,* 4 vols. (1900–1903).

Additional Bibliography

Cardoso Ruíz, Patricio. *Formación y desarrollo del estado nacional de Chile: De la independencia hasta 1930.* Toluca: Universidad Autónoma del Estado de México, 2000.

Stuven, Ana María. *La seducción de un orden: Las elites y la construcción de Chile en las polémicas culturales y políticas del siglo XIX.* Santiago: Ediciones Universidad Católica de Chile, 2000.

SIMON COLLIER

PRIMO DE VERDAD Y RAMOS, FRANCISCO (1760–1808).

Francisco Primo de Verdad y Ramos (*b.* 19 June 1760; *d.* 4 October 1808), lawyer and early martyr of the Mexican independence movement. Born in Ciénega del Rincón, Aguascalientes, Primo de Verdad studied law in Mexico City, where he became a representative in the *cabildo.* The *cabildo* was a stronghold of nationalist sentiment in New Spain and a leading institution in the independence movement. Shortly after Napoleon invaded Spain and forced the abdication of the Bourbon king, Ferdinand VII, Primo de Verdad called for a meeting of New Spain's regional *cabildos* and other authorities in July 1808. Acting as spokesman for the criollos, he delivered a speech that effectively called for New Spain's autonomy. The region's loyalty, he reasoned, was never to Spain or the Spanish people but rather to the monarchy and the legitimate king, Ferdinand VII. In the king's absence, civil authority reverted to the Mexican people. His speech failed to convince powerful peninsular interests, whose sentiments still rested with Spain. In September 1808, Primo de Verdad was thrown into jail, where he died under questionable circumstances. Had Primo de Verdad and the other criollo leaders succeeded, Mexican independence could have occurred as early as 1808.

See also **Ferdinand VII of Spain; Mexico, Wars and Revolutions: Coup d'État of 1808.**

BIBLIOGRAPHY

Enrique Lafuente Ferrari, *El Virrey Iturrigaray y los orígenes de la independencia de Méjico* (1941).

O. Carlos Stoetzer, *The Scholastic Roots of the Spanish American Revolution* (1979).

J. DAVID DRESSING

PRÍO SOCARRÁS, CARLOS (1903–

1977). Carlos Prío Socarrás (*b.* 1903; *d.* 1977), Cuban lawyer and politician, president of Cuba (1948–1952). From a middle-class family outside Havana, Prío Socarrás moved to the capital city to further his education and quickly became embroiled in the university reform movement of the 1920s. As a student of law, he upheld constitutionality and led the student protest when Gerardo Machado decided to run for a second term as president in 1927. In response, Machado abolished the student federation and briefly closed the university itself. Prío and other student leaders were banned from campus, but Ramón Grau San Martín, a professor-activist and future Auténtico president, permitted Prío to read his manifesto out loud in Grau's class; this was the beginning of a close political relationship between the two men.

In 1930 Cuban students organized opposition to dictator Machado, with Prío serving as a leader of the student Directorio. The generation of 1930 viewed themselves as the heirs of José Martí and the legitimate representatives of the Cuban national will. Its members were young, middle-class idealists, usually from rural regions where people naively thought all Cuba's ills could be solved merely by removing Machado. In August 1933 their wish was fulfilled when a military coup and general strike forced Machado into exile. Prío, as a Directorio leader, wielded great power and supported the civilian-dominated Pentarchy of Grau over the military elements during the subsequent struggle for control. Grau's reform experiment lasted only four months before, he, too, was ousted by the military under Fulgencio Batista y Zalvídar. In February 1934 Prío and like-minded Cubans founded the Auténtico Party and named Grau, now in exile, its leader.

Their platform pledged economic and political nationalism, social justice, civil liberties, and greater Cuban control of the island's natural resources. Prío attended the Constitutional Convention of 1940 as a delegate and won recognition for university autonomy, a long-held student goal.

Carlos Prío Socarrás served in many government positions during the 1940s. He was a senator from 1940 to 1948, prime minister from 1945 to 1947, and labor minister under Grau from 1947 to 1948. In 1948 the electorate chose Prío as president, and he continued the moderate reformist policies of his Auténtico mentor, Grau San Martín. Prío managed to reduce political gangsterism, but his administration was plagued by charges of corruption and ineptitude. The 1940s were afterward generally seen as the high-water mark of constitutional liberalism in Cuba, although they failed to legitimize politics or entrench a system of loyal opposition and regular transfers of power. The Cuban public increasingly lost confidence in politicians, and the ensuing instability led Batista to oust Prío in a coup on 10 March 1952, less than three months before elections were to be held.

See also **Cuba: The Republic (1898–1959); Grau San Martín, Ramón; Machado y Morales, Gerardo.**

BIBLIOGRAPHY

Jaime Suchlicki, *University Students and Revolution in Cuba, 1920–1968* (1969).

Luis Aguilar, *Cuba 1933: Prologue to Revolution* (1972).

Samuel Farber, *Revolution and Reaction in Cuba, 1933–1960* (1976).

Louis A. Pérez, Jr., *Cuba: Between Reform and Revolution* (1988).

Additional Bibliography

Whitney, Robert. *State and Revolution in Cuba: Mass Mobilization and Political Change, 1920–1940.* Chapel Hill: University of North Carolina Press, 2001.

KAREN RACINE

PRIVATEERS. See **Buccaneers and Privateers; Piracy.**

PRIVATIZATION.

Privatization is a term used to describe any activity that reduces a government's ownership in or control over a state enterprise, or that results in the liquidation and sale of assets of a state enterprise.

Since independence, Latin American public policy has been shaped by two, often loosely defined but overall, highly distinct political-economy traditions. In both traditions, property, who owns it, and how it is used plays a central role in determining economic production efficiency, accumulation, distribution, poverty, inequality, and the path to well-being and good life. These traditions, and the origins and consequences of the corresponding public policies, are here examined within the political economy and collective markets framework, approach, and theory (Mamalakis 2005a, 2005b). These traditions have distinct goals, and propose often polar-opposite collective-market actions and configurations.

According to the liberal tradition, individuals can attain a good life if they use the power of the state to create and sustain liberal commanding heights within the Latin American collective markets. These consist of the recognition and satisfaction of the moral collective needs for political and economic freedom; for sanctity of life, private property, and environment; for equal treatment by government; and for social harmony. All these elements are emphasized to different degrees by different parties, governments, and authors, at different periods, in various Latin American countries. A variation of the liberal approach, the "Washington Consensus," which was first formulated in 1989 by John Williamson, includes among its ten recommendations four focusing on privatization: privatization of state enterprises, legal security for property rights, fiscal policy discipline, and liberalization of inward foreign direct investment. It also singles out the importance of economic freedoms (e.g., market deregulation, trade liberalization, interest and exchange-rate determination under free and competitive market conditions), equal treatment by government (e.g., elimination of indiscriminate and regressive subsidies, broadening the tax base, and adopting moderate marginal tax rates), and social harmony (e.g., redirection of public investment towards pro-growth, pro-poor services such as primary education, health care, and infrastructure investment). There is a conspicuous absence in the Washington Consensus (which has been widely criticized) of any mention of the importance of satisfying the collective moral need for political freedom. Collective market success is defined by the existence and control of *liberal* commanding heights.

According to the interventionist tradition (e.g., statist, populist, Marxist, dependency, structuralist, dirigista versions), the commanding heights of the economy—which need to be created and controlled by the state if good life is to be attained—are the recognition and satisfaction of the collective needs for state property (ownership of the means of production by the state); controlled rather than free input and output markets, both internally and internationally (protectionist trade policies); dominance of fiscal over monetary policy and authority (a central bank controlled by and subservient to central government); unequal treatment of activities (generally, promotion of industry via import-substituting industrialization, education, and health, and neglect-discrimination of agriculture, exports, and unproductive services); and subordination or subservience of the individual to the state, which has the coercive power and decides how to use it. Collective market success is defined by the dominant existence and control of "interventionist" commanding heights. Government intervention is seen as the ideal engine for modernization and economic growth.

Latin America is characterized by the existence of highly heterogeneous collective markets. All are dynamic and in a constant state of flux. They are different in terms of place, culture, ecology, and economic structure. There are spatially unequal degrees of satisfaction of all seven moral collective needs, and of their interactions with the privatization processes. The transformation of the collective market recognizing and satisfying the collective needs for public (state-owned) versus private ownership is not uniform. The impact of privatization on economic growth and democracy has been highly uneven, first, because of the different degrees of divestiture and, second, because of nonuniform degress of collective action in the six complementary collective markets.

SATISFACTION OF THE MORAL COLLECTIVE NEED FOR SAFETY, SECURITY, AND PROTECTION OF PRIVATE PROPERTY

Privatization, in Latin America and elsewhere, implies, reflects, and is based upon a transformation of collective markets from a type where the commanding heights embody the principle of state sovereignty and supremacy (wherein institutional units and sectors—individuals—exist to serve the state) to a type where the commanding heights are inspired by the axiom of individual sovereignty and supremacy (wherein the state exists to serve the individual-institutional units and sectors). Thus, privatization is characterized by an increased recognition and satisfaction of the collective need for private property, and by a transfer of state-owned assets, enterprises, and corporations to national or foreign private owners. As a consequence of the sale or transfer of the ownership titles of state-owned enterprises to all citizens (creation of a minicapitalist class), labor (labor capitalism), and other private investors, the size of the state-owned enterprise component of the public sector and of the public sector itself has shrunk precipitously. This process began in 1973 in Chile, and at a galloping degree after 1980 and 1990 in the majority of the Latin American countries, with the exception of Cuba. The triangular relationship between general government (promoting the public-sector component of industrial and other state-owned enterprises), the central bank (covering general government and public-sector deficits with inflationary credit), and industry (all state-owned enterprises) was dissolved. State-owned enterprises were privatized and had to become profitable. Production of commodities was guided by the preferences of individual institutional units and sectors (consumer sovereignty) rather than government fiat (state sovereignty). The central bank became autonomous of general government and fiscal policy. Its goal was price stability (monetarism) as a pillar of private property and free and competitive market forces. Its redistributive role was eliminated. The central and general governments returned to their traditional role of producing primarily liberal collective services.

According to the World Bank, proceeds from privatization in Latin America from 1990 to 1999 were US $177,839 million, or 56.32 percent of the total privatization proceeds of US $315,720 million in all developing countries (Chong and López-de-Silanes 2005, p. 5). Since 2000, proceeds from privatization transactions in Latin America and the Caribbean declined precipitously: US $12,321 million (2000), US $3,141 million (2001), US $303 million (2002), US $410 million (2003), US $2,189 million (2004), and US $922 million (2005) (World Bank 2007).

The privatization process started in Chile in the 1970s. More than 500 firms, the majority of which had been nationalized during the Allende presidency, were privatized between 1974 and 1978. The 1982 banking crisis led to a short period of renationalization. By 1992, however, 96 percent of all Chilean state-owned enterprises had been privatized (Morley, Machado, and Pettinato 1999).

The privatization boom in Latin America in the 1980s and 1990s followed upon a long period of stagnation, hyperinflation, and dissatisfaction with the performance of state enterprises, the collapse of centrally planned economies, and overall frustration with interventionism. It received support from the unprecedented dynamism of Chile's private-sector–based economy. In Mexico, a measure of popular support for privatization was created by the earmarking of a portion of the proceeds for antipoverty programs. An early, successful privatization program took place in Chile during the military dictatorship of General Augusto Pinochet (1973–1990); later initiatives were implemented by democratic governments, such as those of Carlos Salinas in Mexico, wherein the number of state-owned enterprises was reduced from 1,155 to fewer than 80 by the end of his presidency (Morley, Machado, and Pettinato 1999), and of Carlos Saúl Menem in Argentina.

By the mid-1990s, Latin America had privatized a larger share of its state enterprises than any other region in the developing world. Between 1985 and 1992, more than 2,000 state enterprises were privatized, including major public utilities, insurance companies, airlines, banks, highways, and ports. Chile had privatized 90 percent of its state enterprises by the late 1980s. In the decade after 1983, Mexico raised $22 billion through privatization of almost 90 percent of its state enterprises, the largest revenues derived from privatization of any developing country.

Privatization programs also raised large amounts of revenue in Argentina ($19 billion) from 1989 to 1994; in Brazil ($6.5 billion) between 1990 and 1993 from the sales of state enterprises in steel, petrochemicals, and fertilizers; and in Venezuela ($2.5 billion) from the sale of eighteen state enterprises. Other significant privatization programs of the 1980s and 1990s were implemented in Peru, where twenty state enterprises, including those in mining and petroleum, were returned to the private

Proceeds from privatization transactions per year

(in US$ millions)

Region/country	2000	2001	2002	2003	2004	2005
Latin America and Caribbean						
Argentina	12	12	—	—	—	—
Belize	—	50	38	—	—	—
Bolivia	11	—	—	—	—	—
Brazil	11,078	2,566	4	—	648	74
Chile	282	235	—	306	782	—
Colombia	483	—	—	70	—	462
Costa Rica	—	—	—	—	—	34
El Salvador	—	—	—	—	295	—
Jamaica	—	201	—	—	—	—
Mexico	190	—	—	—	—	352
Nicaragua	115	43	—	—	49	—
Peru	—	—	262	—	397	—
Uruguay	151	34	—	34	18	—

SOURCE: World Bank Privatization Database. Available at https://rru.worldbank.org/Privatization/.

Table 1

---

sector; in Colombia, where four formerly nationalized banks and twenty-one other concerns were sold off; and in Bolivia, Nicaragua, Trinidad and Tobago, Belize, and Jamaica. Small privatization programs were also implemented in Grenada, Panama, Puerto Rico, and Uruguay. Cuba announced a privatization program in 1994 involving the sale of its telecommunications enterprise to Mexican investors.

Some of the largest privatizations in Latin America involved banks (in Mexico, Chile, and Colombia). Argentina, Chile, Mexico, and Venezuela privatized many giant, monopolistic enterprises in infrastructure sectors previously off-limits to privatization. In Argentina and Mexico, privatization of large firms proceeded at previously unthinkable speed, within two years of the first public announcement. In some countries, such as Mexico and Venezuela, foreign investment accelerated the speed of the sell-off.

Natural resource enterprise remained largely immune to privatization in Chile (copper), Mexico (oil), and Venezuela (oil) because of its strategic importance as a source of foreign exchange and tax revenues, some of which were earmarked specifically for the military, as in Chile. Throughout Latin America, privatization has contributed to the reduction of fiscal deficits and foreign debt. It has also attracted foreign investment and the return of fugitive capital. In Argentina, Chile, and Peru,

privatization has led to a loss of jobs because of organizational restructuring.

PRIVATIZATION AND ECONOMIC FREEDOM
Privatization has been introduced to replace state ownership, partly in order to eliminate preprivatization monopolistic and oligopolitic practices and create a postprivatization climate of freedom of choice and competition. This has been difficult, especially when natural monopolies in electricity, gas, and water were privatized. Few, if any, governments in Latin America had the expertise to create a postprivatization regulatory framework that balanced the interests of the producers and the consumers. In addition, governments privatized deficit-ridden, subsidized enterprises in an effort to reduce their own deficits. The resulting adjustments in absolute and relative prices were necessary, but required enormous political skill and perserverance.

Latin American privatization experiments were widely emulated. Overall, they were successful in achieving a more efficient allocation of resources and improved public-sector management; early mistakes and weaknesses (as in Chile from 1973 to 1979) were corrected. Their success has created a consensus in Latin America that privatization is a necessary, but not sufficient, step toward solving the pervasive problems of poverty and inequality in the region.

PRIVATIZATION LINKS TO THE SATISFACTION OF THE COLLECTIVE NEED FOR POLITICAL FREEDOM

There has existed no clear positive or negative link between, on the one hand, statization (state ownership) or privatization (private ownership), and on the other hand, political freedom in Latin America from 1800 until 2007. Liberal and interventionist commanding heights have alternated in collective markets controlled by democratic as well as authoritarian political regimes. There are exceptions. In Castro's Cuba, a Marxist dictatorship (i.e., suppression of the collective need for political freedom) coincides with the satisfaction of the collective need for state ownership of the means of production and complete suppression of the moral collective need for sanctity of private property—a rare global Marxist holdout. In contrast, in Pinochet's Chile, an initially brutal repression of the moral collective need for political freedom coincided with an historically and globally unprecedented satisfaction of the moral collective need for private property and economic freedom in almost all markets. Furthermore, since the 1980s and 1990s, Latin American governments of all political persuasions abandoned their earlier "interventionist commanding heights" preferences, which were embodied in statization and nationalization strategies, and jointly embarked on building collective markets with "liberal commanding heights." This led to the privatization (destatization and denationalization) stampede of the 1980s and 1990s, which was globally unparalled in its magnitude. Latin America's siren call of privatization found an unforeseen, dramatic resonance in China, Russia, and elsewhere.

Not unexpectedly, in recent years, because of a perceived inability of the liberal model to solve the continent's persistent postcolonial structural defects, there has resurfaced an antiliberal, antiprivatization, antidemocratic, neosocialist movement spearheaded by presidents Hugo Chavez of Venezuela, Evo Morales of Bolivia, and Rafael Correa of Ecuador. Their aim is to replace the prevailing, allegedly failed, collective market liberal commanding heights order with interventionist ones—to largely restore the pre-1973 economic order. Deprivatization, renationalization, and restatization are advocated and implemented as embodying a desperately needed, more people- and poor-friendly, problem-solving, interventionist collective action. In Argentina, newly elected president Cristina

Fernández de Kirchner also may continue the populist, interventionist policies of her ex-president husband, Néstor Kirchner.

PRIVATIZATION AND EQUAL TREATMENT BY GOVERNMENT

In few areas was the power of the state used as pervasively, during the 1935 to 1973 era of interventionism, as in the determination of prices of all goods, services, inputs, and outputs. A systematic pattern of unequal treatment imposed by government replaced (or at least attempted to replace) the free-market determination of prices. All processes of production, allocation, primary, secondary, and tertiary distribution, accumulation, and use were controlled and directed by government. Despite, or because of, all these largely well-intentioned policies, Latin America fell behind the rest of the world in terms of prosperity (income), labor productivity, equality, mobility, and political, social and economic progress. The powerful commanding height of unequal treatment of all institutional units and sectors was all-pervasive and dominant. State ownership of enterprises and controls went hand in hand. Black (or free but illegal) markets became widespread. Hyperinflation, stagnation, unemployment and underemployment, inequality, and poverty became endemic despite extremely important industrial growth in Argentina, Brazil, Mexico, Colombia, Chile, Peru, Venezuela, and almost everywhere else in Latin America. The massive distortions resulting from ever more complex regulatory, coercive, ineffective, interventionist, and regulatory regimes strengthened rather than removed many of the inherited postcolonial structural defects plaguing production, income distribution, and capital accumulation. Deprivation of the fundamental freedom from governmental discrimination sapped and misdirected the energies of almost all institutional units and sectors.

PRIVATIZATION AND SOCIAL HARMONY

The post-1973 urge of Latin American governments to privatize was, to a large extent, created by intensifying social disharmony during the 1935 to 1973 period of state interventionism and state property ownership. Similarly, the tirades by Chavez in Venezuela, Morales in Bolivia, and Correa in Ecuador against the liberalization, privatization, and stabilization policies enacted by previous administrations with the advice of the World Bank, the International Monetary Fund, and the U.S. government resonate favorably among the majority of the population, which lives in poverty, exclusion, misery, and hopelessness. Privatization can be seen as a necessary condition for sustainable democracy and growth, but so can social harmony. Nowhere in post-independence Latin America has the complementary moral collective need for social harmony been satisfied to the minimum degree required for sustainable peace and prosperity. Even Pinochet's otherwise remarkable liberal commanding heights of Chile's collective markets from 1973 to 1980 failed to create pillars of political freedom and social harmony, which are the irreplaceable for procedural democracy and civil society. Chile's post-1980 democratic governments have recognized the umbilical link between (satisfaction of the moral collective need for) private property and (satisfaction of the moral collective need for) social harmony, and they have strengthened both pillars. Chile, however, remains an exception in Latin America. The challenge of expanding private property to all and advancing social harmony remains formidable. According to the Washington office of the United Nations Economic Commission for Latin America and the Caribbean (CEPAL), as of 2006, some 36.5 percent of the population (194 million people) of Latin America and the Caribbean were poor; 13.4 percent (71 million) were extremely poor. For the first time since 1990, the total number of people living in poverty dropped below 200 million. Throughout Latin America, privatization in the production and delivery of primary, secondary, vocational, and university education, social security, health, water, gas, electricity, and telecommunication services has complemented or replaced state and not-for-profit services as part of an increased focus on the delivery of economic and social services to the poor and indigent. An extremely low degree of recognition and satisfaction of the moral collective need for social harmony, which has historically plagued the region, remains a major bottleneck to the acceptance of privatization and private property as tools and preconditions for social harmony itself. Social harmony has suffered whenever the privatization process was rigged in favor of the old guard of state employees.

PRIVATIZATION AND THE SANCTITY OF LIFE

Since precolonial times, the vast majority of the region's inhabitants had no private property, and little or no protection of their lives. Most of the land and other property were in the hands of a small colonial elite and the Catholic Church. Even in 2007, half of the total population of 541 million, including approximately 165 million poor and indigent, have little land or other financial and nonfinancial property. Their lives are often as precarious as those of their ancestors centuries ago. The Latin American post-1973 privatization policies have led to a spectacular increase in productive capacity, real and financial wealth accumulation, and economic security and independence for hundreds of millions. Hundreds of millions are, however, still without property and security. Unless they can also become property owners through a rapid increase in their participation in an ever larger production process—that is, a deepening (more wealth) and widening (increasing share of property owners in the population)—privatization will lead to a destabilizing distance, inequality, and separation between the haves and have nots. The excluded ones will, and indeed already do, provide fertile ground to the opponents of liberal development strategies, including privatization.

PRIVATIZATION LINKAGES TO THE ENVIRONMENT

The substantial increase in production as a consequence of privatization-facilitated growth has taken its toll on the environment in rural (Amazon) areas in Brazil, in marine resources in Peru and Chile, air, land and water pollution throughout Latin America and so forth. The vital interactions between privatization, environmental degradation, and growth-poverty issues pose major, difficult, dilemmas and unresolved choices to all institutional units and sectors.

Privatization, as a networking process, links the seven fundamental components of the Latin American collective markets. It serves as a precondition for the recognition and satisfaction of the other six collective needs, which are vital pillars of accelerated labor productivity and income growth, and, ultimately, sustainable democracy and growth. In turn, their satisfaction has reinforced privatization and private property, as, especially, in Chile, but also, increasingly, in Mexico, Brazil, much of Central America, Uruguay and Peru. Complementary satisfaction of these moral collective needs provides the checks and balances of the centripetal growth processes also observed in Asia and Europe. Failure of privatization, political and economic freedom, sanctity of life, equal treatment by government and social harmony, has fed the volcanic centrifugal political, economic and social forces observed in the past in all Latin American countries as well as, currently, in Venezuela, Ecuador and Bolivia.

See also **Banking: Overview; Banking: Since 1990; Democracy; Dependency Theory; Economic Development; Foreign Investment; International Monetary Fund (IMF); World Bank.**

BIBLIOGRAPHY

Basanes, Federico, Evamaria Uribe, and Robert Willig, eds. *Can Privatization Deliver? Infrastructure for Latin America.* Washington, DC: Inter-American Development Bank, 1999.

Basanes, Federico, and Robert Willig, eds. *Second-Generation Reforms in Infrastructure Services.* Washington, DC: Inter-American Development Bank, 2002.

Bear, Werner, and Melissa H. Birch, eds. *Privatization in Latin America: New Roles for the Public and Private Sectors.* Westport, CT: Praeger Publishers, 1994.

Birch, Melissa H., and Jerry Haar, eds. *The Impact of Privatization in the Americas.* Coral Gables, FL: University of Miami North-South Center Press, 2000.

Chase, Jacquelyn, ed. *The Spaces of Neoliberalism: Land, Place, and Family in Latin America.* Bloomfield, CT: Kumarian Press, 2002.

Chong, Alberto, and Florencio López-de-Silanes, eds. *Privatization in Latin America: Myths and Reality.* Palo Alto, CA: Stanford University Press and the World Bank, 2005.

Glade, William, ed. *State Shrinking.* Austin: University of Texas Press, 1986.

Glade, William, ed. *Privatization of Public Enterprises in Latin America.* San Francisco, CA: Institute of Contemporary Studies Press, 1991.

Glade, William, with Rosanna Corona, eds. *Bigger Economies, Smaller Governments: Privatization in Latin America.* Boulder, CO: Westview Press, 1996.

Hachette, Dominique, and Rolf Lüders. *Privatization in Chile: An Economic Appraisal.* San Francisco, CA: Institute of Contemporary Studies Press, 1993.

Hemming, Richard, and Ali M. Mansoor. *Privatization of Public Enterprises in Latin America.* San Francisco, CA: Institute for Contemporary Studies Press, 1988.

Lawton, Jorge A. *Privatization amidst Poverty: Contemporary Challenges in Latin American Political Economy.* Coral Gables, FL: University of Miami North-South Center Press, 1995.

"Lessons of Privatization in Latin America." Conference Proceedings, Committee on Inter-American Affairs of the Association of the Bar of the City of New York, June 5, 1991.

Madrid, Raul L. *Retiring the State: The Politics of Pension Privatization in Latin America and Beyond.* Stanford, CA: Stanford University Press, 2003.

Mamalakis, Markos. *Historical Statistics of Chile.* Westport, CT: Greenwood Press, 1989.

Mamalakis, Markos J. "Social Justice in a Global Environment: A Theory of Natural Law and Social Justice." In *The Quest for Social Justice III: The Morris Fromkin Memorial Lectures 1992–2002,* edited by Peter G. Watson-Boone. Milwaukee: UWM Libraries, University of Wisconsin–Milwaukee, 2005a.

Mamalakis, Markos J. "Sustainable Democracy and the Golden Rules." *Global Currents* 1, no. 2 (Spring 2005b): 18–19.

Manzetti, Luigi. *Privatization and Regulation: Lessons from Argentina and Chile.* Coral Gables, FL: University of Miami North-South Center Agenda Papers, 1997.

Manzetti, Luigi. *Privatization South American Style.* New York: Oxford University Press, 1999.

Manzetti, Luigi, ed. *Regulatory Policy in Latin America: Post-Privatization Realities.* Coral Gables, FL: University of Miami North-South Center Press, 2000.

Morley, Samuel A., Roberto Machado, and Stefano Pettinato. *Indexes of Structural Reform in Latin America.* Santiago, Chile: Economic Commission for Latin America, 1999.

Ramamurti, Ravi. "The Impact of Privatization on the Latin American Debt Problem." *Journal of Interamerican Studies and World Affairs* 34 (Summer 1992): 93–125.

Ramamurti, Ravi, ed. *Privatizing Monopolies: Lessons for the Telecommunications and Transport Sectors in Latin America.* Baltimore: Johns Hopkins University Press, 1996.

Sanchez, Manuel, and Rosanna Corona, eds. *Privatization in Latin America.* Washington, DC: Inter-American Bank, 1993.

Schamis, Hector E. *Re-Forming the State: The Politics of Privatization in Latin America and Europe.* Ann Arbor: University of Michigan Press, 2002.

Sinha, Tapen. *Pension Reform in Latin America and Its Lessons for International Policy Makers.* Boston: Kluwer Academic, 2000.

Teichman, Judith A. *Privatization and Political Change in Mexico.* Pittsburgh, PA: University of Pittsburgh Press, 1995.

Ugaz, Cecilia, and Catherine Waddams Price, eds. *Utility Privatization and Regulation: A Fair Deal with Consumers?* Cheltenham, U.K.: Edward Elgar, 2003.

World Bank. Privatizations by Region: Latin America and Caribbean. Privatization Database, 2007. Available from https://www.doingbusiness.org/Privatization/.

MARKOS J. MAMALAKIS

PROAÑO VILLALBA, LEONIDAS EDUARDO (BISHOP) (1910–1988).

Known as the "Bishop of the Indians," Leonidas Eduardo Proaño Villalba represented a strand of liberation theology that advocated for the rights of impoverished people in Ecuador. Proaño was born on January 19, 1910, to a mestizo family in the northern Ecuadorian community of San Antonio de Ibarra. In 1936 he was ordained as a priest and for the next eighteen years served in Ibarra. In 1954 he was named bishop of Riobamba in the central highland province of Chimborazo. As bishop Proaño gained acclaim for dressing in a poncho and visiting rural communities. In 1962 he founded radio schools to broadcast literacy and educational programs. In 1964, when the military government passed an agrarian reform law, Proaño gave the land of Monjas Corral and Zula, two estates that belonged to his dioceses, to indigenous workers. At Monjas Corral he created the Tepeyac Institute to train indigenous leaders.

Because of Proaño's advocacy of indigenous issues, the wealthy elite accused him of stirring up dissent. In August 1976 the military dictatorship raided an international pastoral meeting in Riobamba, arresting seventeen bishops, priests, and religious workers and interrogating Proaño. Although accused of subversion, Proaño sought to present Catholic alternatives to leftist political organizing in indigenous communities. Upon his retirement in 1985, in recognition of his lifetime of work Pope John Paul II named Proaño "Bishop of the Indians." Shortly before his death on August 31, 1988, he founded the Fundación Pueblo Indio del Ecuador (Indian peoples foundation of Ecuador) to educate and defend the rights of indigenous peoples.

See also **Indigenismo; Indigenous Organizations; John Paul II, Pope; Liberation Theology.**

BIBLIOGRAPHY

Proaño Villalba, Leonidas E. *Creo en el hombre y en la comunidad: Autobiografía.* Quito, Ecuador: Corporación Editora Nacional, 2001.

MARC BECKER

PRONUNCIAMIENTO. Pronunciamiento,

the revolt that occurred in Mexico when a group rebelled against the Mexican government and issued a plan. The plan was a continuation and adaptation of a technique used during the independence wars in which its author espoused ideas for the organization of a future Mexican state. After the acceptance of the Plan of Iguala, Mexicans understood the "plan" as a document designed to "build the nation, give it foundations, [and] protect its institutions." Following independence, the plan became a protest document through which military officers, local political officials, or both asked for ratification from other groups around the country; each group had its own plan that adopted the guiding plan's message, and rose up in its support.

The first plan, issued on 23 January 1824 by José María Lobato, received six adherences but failed to topple the government. The Plan of Jalapa, issued by General Anastasio Bustamante on 4 December 1829, received an equivalent number and took power. The most famous period of *pronunciamientos* occurred when Antonio López de Santa Anna left the government in the hands of liberal Vice President Valentín Gómez Farías, on 1 April 1833. By May 26 the troops in Morelia had "pronounced." For the next year Mexico was flooded with plans and, even though Santa Anna dismissed Gómez Farías in April 1834, they continued. During a two-week period in May 1834, citizens in Cuernavaca, Toluca, and Jalapa issued three separate plans that were seconded by an additional 112 throughout the country. They indicate that during that month, Mexicans gathered in juntas, studied the *pronunciamientos,* and decided to support an already articulated plan, adapting its language and demands to meet their own particular situation. Nevertheless, the plans should not be seen as an example of democracy in action; rather, they reflect the wishes of the local notables seconded by those nearby. Although various leaders of the Mexican Revolution issued plans, by then the idea of the *pronunciamiento* had disappeared, having given way to the more sophisticated concept of revolution.

See also **Cuartelazo; Gómez Farías, Valentín; Plan of Iguala; Santa Anna, Antonio López de.**

BIBLIOGRAPHY

Guadalupe Jiménez Codinach, coord., *Planes de la nación mexicana,* 11 vols. (1988).

Barbara A. Tenenbaum, "'They Went Thataway': The Pronunciamiento During the Centralist Period, 1836–1847," in *Patterns of Contention in Mexican History,* edited by Jaime E. Rodríguez O. (1992).

Additional Bibliography

Benítez González, Florencio. *El plan de Iguala: En la historiografía de su época.* México: Comuna Municipal, 2001.

Vázquez, Josefina Zoriada. *El establecimiento del federalismo en México, 1821–1827.* México, DF: Colegio de México, 2003.

BARBARA A. TENENBAUM

PROTESTANTISM.

For much of its history, Protestantism, long associated with the people and society of North America and northern Europe, has been a foreign religion in Latin America. In colonial times, Protestants (called *evangélicos* or "evangelicals," regardless of denomination) in Spanish America were subject to prosecution by the Spanish Inquisition. Long after the Inquisition was abolished, Latin Americans continued to think of Protestantism as alien and hostile to their own faith and culture. It is only in recent decades that this perception has ceased to be a factor in Protestant church growth in the region.

After most of Latin America gained its independence in the 1820s, the liberal leadership of the new nations legalized religious pluralism, but most nations retained Roman Catholicism as the state religion. In the early years of the nineteenth century, Protestantism in Latin America remained confined to the foreign population. The Anglican church established a stronghold along the Atlantic ("Mosquito") coast of Central America, from what was then British Honduras to Costa Rica. With its diocesan seat in Jamaica, the Anglican church served British Protestants who lived and worked in the Mosquito area and in Belize, which were both claimed by Britain at that time. The Anglican church was also established in Argentina, Chile, and Brazil during this period for British subjects who were engaged in commercial and consular activities in these countries. Likewise, the Prussian Evangelical church was established in Brazil and Chile for German immigrants to those nations. Neither the Anglican church nor the German churches proselytized the native Roman Catholics, and their influence was little felt outside the foreign communities.

Spurred by the growth of the Methodist movement, a new spirit of evangelism spread through Britain and the United States in the last years of the eighteenth century. By the early 1800s, this enthusiasm had translated into mission work. The British and Foreign Bible Society and the Society for the Propagation of the Gospel, two English agencies, first sent Bible sellers, known as *colporteurs,* to Latin America to evangelize actively in the 1820s. The first agent was a Scot named James Thompson, who in 1821 went to Argentina, where he established a school. Thompson was invited to Chile by Bernardo O'Higgins, and he eventually also worked in Peru. Thompson was succeeded by another agent of the society, Allan Gardiner, who attempted without success to convert the Indians living in Argentina's Patagonia.

In northern Latin America, Francisco Penzotti, an agent of the British and Foreign Bible Society, sold Bibles throughout the Central American isthmus from 1839 until the mid-1840s. Another of the society's agents, Frederick Crowe, was active in British Honduras and Guatemala until his efforts attracted the attention of the pro-Catholic Conservative leader of Guatemala, Rafael Carrera, who expelled Crowe from the country in 1846. Due to private and public opposition to their work, the impact of these early *colporteurs* was minimal.

It was not until the last decades of the nineteenth century that foreign missionaries came to Latin America on a permanent basis. Some of the earliest missionaries to the region were members of the German Pietist sect, the Church of the United Brethren (Moravians), who came to the Atlantic coast of Nicaragua in 1849 to evangelize the non-Christian Miskito Indians. Elsewhere, traditional denominations in the United States such as the Methodists, the Presbyterians, and the Congregationalists sent missionaries to work among Spanish-speaking Catholics

An evangelical Christian group performs on Quito church steps in late 20th century Ecuador. Protestant faiths, particularly Pentecostal denominations, have grown significantly throughout Latin America since the 1960s. © OWEN FRANKEN/ CORBIS

and, less commonly, among non–Spanish-speaking indigenous groups. They were later joined by non-denominational mission agencies such as the Central American Mission, which was active primarily in Guatemala, Honduras, and Nicaragua, and the Christian Missionary Alliance, which worked in the Southern Cone. In addition to founding churches, the missionaries established schools, hospitals, vocational training institutes, and translation projects. The impact of these efforts was most apparent in those countries where the missionaries worked with the tacit approval of the nation's government, such as in Guatemala, Chile, and Brazil.

In many countries, the liberal governments that came to power in the 1860s, 1870s, and 1880s generally endorsed Protestant work. Liberal leaders such as Guatemala's Justo Rufino Barrios encouraged Presbyterian missions in that country in the

hope that they would engender a work ethic in the nation's people, inspire economic development, and act as a political counterweight to the Catholic majority, which generally opposed liberal reforms. Nowhere was the political link between Protestantism and liberalism so apparent as in Mexico, where Benito Juárez endorsed the creation of a Mexican innovation known as the Church of Jesus. This was a "reformed" Catholic Church, where supporters of Juárez's Reforma could seek a spiritual home outside of the conservative Roman Catholic Church.

Despite the government support that Protestant work received in some countries of Latin America, Protestantism remained on the fringe of Latin American society and attracted relatively few native converts until the 1960s. As recently as 1970, the Latin American nation with the largest Protestant population was Uruguay, which then claimed an evangelical population of slightly less than 6 percent.

Beginning in the early 1960s, Latin perceptions of Protestantism changed, and the conversion rate in the region increased dramatically. This stemmed in part from the emergence of "national" denominations, which had no ties to the old mission system. Protestant churches also benefited from changes within the Catholic Church resulting from the Second Vatican Council (1962–1965), which precipitated the exodus of many Latin Americans from the Church. Scholars suggest that social and economic factors, including urban migration, civil strife, unemployment, the decline of the traditional peasant community, and the breakdown of customary kinship networks in Latin America have all been influential in turning Latin Americans toward Protestant churches.

By far, the greatest trend in Protestant growth has been the rise of Pentecostal denominations, which emphasize the manifestations of the "gifts of the Holy Spirit," such as faith healing and speaking in tongues. In virtually all countries with a sizable Protestant population (including Guatemala, where Protestants count for an estimated one-third of the national population), the vast majority of churches are Pentecostal. Between 1960 and 1990, Protestant membership doubled in Chile, Paraguay, Venezuela, Panama, and Haiti. In the same time period, the evangelical population tripled in Argentina, Nicaragua, and the Dominican Republic, and quadrupled in Brazil and Puerto Rico. The most significant growth has been in El Salvador, Costa Rica, Peru, and Bolivia, where the percentage of Protestants has quintupled since 1960, and in Ecuador, Colombia, and Honduras, where the converted population in 1990 was six times what it was in 1960.

See also **Catholic Church: The Colonial Period; Moravian Church.**

BIBLIOGRAPHY

Emilio Willems, *Followers of the New Faith* (1967).

Christian Lalive D'epinay, *The Refuge of the Masses* (1969).

Wilton M. Nelson, *El Protestantismo en Centro América* (1982).

David Stoll, *Fishers of Men or Founders of Empire? The Wycliffe Bible Translators in Latin America* (1982).

Jean-Pierre Bastian, *Breve historia del protestantismo en América Latina* (1986).

Sheldon Annis, *God and Production in a Guatemalan Town* (1987).

Deborah J. Baldwin, *Protestants and the Mexican Revolution* (1990).

David Martin, *Tongues of Fire: The Explosion of Protestantism in Latin America* (1990).

David Stoll, *Is Latin America Turning Protestant?* (1990).

Additional Bibliography

Bastian, Jean Pierre. *Protestantismos y modernidad latinoamericana: Historia de unas minorías religiosas activas en América Latina.* México: Fondo de Cultura Económica, 1994.

Bowen, Kurt. *Evangelism and Apostasy: The Evolution and Impact of Evangelicals in Modern Mexico.* Montréal; Buffalo, NY: McGill-Queen's University Press, 1996.

Brusco, Elizabeth. *The Reformation of Machismo: Evangelical Conversion and Gender in Colombia.* Austin: University of Texas Press, 1995.

Chesnut, R. Andrew. *Born Again in Brazil: The Pentecostal Boom and the Pathogens of Poverty.* New Brunswick, NJ: Rutgers University Press, 1997.

Garrard-Burnett, Virginia. *Protestantism in Guatemala: Living in the New Jerusalem.* Austin: University of Texas Press, 1998.

Garrard-Burnett, Virginia. *On Earth as It Is in Heaven: Religion in Modern Latin America.* Wilmington, DE: Scholarly Resources, 2000.

Martínez-Fernández, Luis. *Protestantism and Political Conflict in the Nineteenth-century Hispanic Caribbean.* New Brunswick, NJ: Rutgers University Press, 2002.

Mondragón, Carlos. *Leudar la masa: El pensamiento social de los protestantes en América Latina, 1920–1950.* Buenos Aires: Kairos Editiones, 2005.

Rivera, Paulo Barrera. *Tradição, transmissão e emoção religiosa: Sociologia do protestantismo contemporâneo na América Latina.* São Paulo: Olho d'Água, 2001.

Steigenga, Timothy J. *The Politics of the Spirit: The Political Implications of Pentecostalized Religion in Costa Rica and Guatemala.* Lanham, MD: Lexington Books, 2001.

Yaremko, Jason M. *U.S. Protestant Missions in Cuba: From Independence to Castro.* Gainesville: University of Florida Press, 2000.

VIRGINIA GARRARD- BURNETT

PROTESTANTISMO EN MÉXICO.

Although Mexico is a Catholic country, the 2000 census revealed that approximately 8 percent of the population practices a faith other than Catholicism—principally Protestant Evangelical Christianity. Religious diversity has been evident in Mexico since the sixteenth century. Mexican Protestantism, represented by seventeen different denominations, was established between 1872 and 1912 in some regions of the north, center, and south-southeast of the country, through churches, schools, periodical publications, and social centers. This trend led to the development of a socioreligious movement identified with radical liberalism. Protestantism contributed to the modernization of values and attitudes within society as some of its members participated in popular workers' and peasant movements at the beginning of the Mexican Revolution. The antichurch provisions in the 1917 Constitution robbed the movement of much of its social impact. Between 1940 and 1950 Protestantism suffered persecution fostered by the Roman Catholic hierarchy. Nevertheless, soon after that it gained new strength in the form of Pentecostalism, which accelerated its growth, especially between 1970 and 1990. In 1992 constitutional reforms in the area of religion opened new opportunities for the social legitimization of Protestantism.

See also **Juárez, Benito; Mexico, Constitutions: Constitution of 1917; Protestantism; Religion in Mexico, Catholic Church and Beyond; Salinas de Gortari, Carlos.**

BIBLIOGRAPHY

Baldwin, Deborah J. *Protestants and the Mexican Revolution: Missionaries, Ministers, and Social Change.* Urbana: University of Illinois Press, 1990.

Bastian, Jean Pierre. *Los Disidentes.* México: Fondo de Cultura Econömica, 1989.

Bowen, Kurt Derek. *Evangelism and Apostasy: The Evolution and Impact of Evangelicals in Modern Mexico.* Montreal, Québec; Buffalo: McGill-Queen's University Press, 1996.

Ruiz Guerra, Rubén. *Hombres Nuevos.* México: Casa Unida de Publicaciones, 1995.

RUBÉN RUIZ GUERRA

PROTOMEDICATO. Protomedicato, a board of physicians in the Spanish Indies responsible for regulating medical practitioners and inspecting apothecary shops. Established in Spain in the fourteenth century, the *protomedicato* evolved very slowly in the Indies. Initially, regulation and licensing of physicians fell to city councils (Cabildos), which tried to verify the legitimacy of medical practitioners, inspect apothecary shops, and provide medical care for the local jails and the indigent. Then in 1570 Philip II took steps to bring the protomedicato to the Indies by appointing the physician-botanist Francisco Hernández as *protomédico general* of the Indies with instructions not only to regulate medical practice but also to investigate New World medicinal herbs, seeds, trees, and curatives. Since Hernández proved far more interested in the latter task, the Cabildo continued to be responsible for examining and licensing physicians.

In 1646, however, Philip IV finally ordered establishment of protomedicatos in the major cities of the Indies. Made up of three physicians (*protomédicos*), the protomedicato consisted of the most distinguished chair in medicine (*prima*) at the local university, the senior professor of the medical faculty, and a third physician appointed by the viceroy. Salaries for this board came from fees collected for examination and licensing of physicians, surgeons, phlebotomists (blood-letters), midwives, and other practitioners and from inspections of apothecary shops. Jurisdiction of the protomedicato was never resolved. Anxious to collect more fees, the protomédicos hoped to extend their jurisdiction beyond the city where they exercised their authority, but practitioners and pharmacists outside the major cities strongly resisted their attempts in order to avoid the onerous fees and to remain independent of the meddlesome protomedicato.

Establishment of the protomedicato manifested the belief of Spanish authorities that the state must assume some responsibility for regulating medical practice, and in many respects, the institution was successful, particularly in the larger cities. Through both a rigorous oral questioning in the halls of the protomedicato and a practical examination in a hospital, *protomédicos* made certain that those entering medical practice in the Indies were adequately trained. The board also exposed those who practiced without a medical degree—or with a forged one—and helped to ensure that apothecary shops maintained a proper stock of drugs that conformed to the standard pharmacopoeia.

On the other hand, the protomedicato was less successful in regulating medical practitioners in the provinces, where unlicensed doctors, surgeons, midwives, and local healers (Curanderos) went about their business unchecked. In fact, in Mexico the medical board licensed only two midwives in all the colonial period, and this at the very end. Moreover, certain surgeons (not trained in Latin), barbers, and phlebotomists consistently avoided examination— and payment of fees—even in the large cities. Strangely, too, the protomedicato proved less interested than the viceroy, local authorities, and professors at the universities in promoting public health policies, new medical techniques, and measures to stop the spread of epidemics, particularly the use of inoculation and vaccination against smallpox in the last half of the eighteenth century. The view of most *protomédicos* was that well-being and health of the community could be best maintained if trained, licensed doctors practiced medicine in the Indies.

See also **Medicine: Colonial Spanish America; Philip II of Spain; Philip IV of Spain.**

BIBLIOGRAPHY

John Tate Lanning, *The Royal Protomedicato: The Regulation of Medical Practitioners in the Spanish Empire,* edited by John Jay TePaske (1986).

Additional Bibliography

Astrain Gallart, Mikel. *Barberos, cirujanos y gente de mar: La sanidad naval y la profesión quirúrgica en la España ilustrada.* Madrid: Ministerio de Defensa, 1996.

Fajardo Ortiz, Guillermo. *Los caminos de la medicina colonial en Iberoamérica y las Filipinas.* México: Universidad Nacional Autónoma de México, Coordinación de Humanidades, Facultad de Medicina, 1996.

Hernández Sáenz, Luz María. *Learning to Heal: The Medical Profession in Colonial Mexico, 1767–1831.* New York: Peter Lang, 1997.

Sánchez, Raúl Francisco. *Del protomedicato al Colegio de Médicos y Cirujanos: 145 años de historia.* San José: Editorial Porvenir, 2002.

JOHN JAY TePASKE

PROVEDOR MOR DA FAZENDA.

Provedor Mor da Fazenda, the superintendent of the treasury who, together with the governor-general and superior crown magistrate *(ouvidor geral),* formed one of the three highest administrative positions in colonial Brazil. It remains, however, the least studied of all the major governmental or administrative colonial offices. The *regimentos* (statutes) of 17 December 1548 summarized the duties of the *provedor mor* and the officers who served under him. They included organizing Brazil's primary *alfândega* (customhouse) in Bahia, supervising crown monopolies and tax farms, maintaining account books pertaining to crown revenues and expenditures, and overseeing treasury officials in Brazil's other captaincies. In the colony's early history, a single individual frequently held both the offices of *provedor mor* and *ouvidor geral,* but conflicting responsibilities ended such practices. Ambiguous jurisdictions brought the *provedor mor* into recurring controversy with other high officials. In addition to his treasury duties, the *provedor mor* became part of the government in the absence of the governor-general. Brazil's vast size together with the office's extensive responsibilities presented *provedores mor* with insolvable problems and kept the colonial treasury in constant disarray.

By the early eighteenth century, lower-ranking *provedores* had gained considerable independence from the *provedor mor,* causing problems for the royal government. In 1731, for example, the *provedor mor* of Maranhão absconded with treasury funds. The marquês de Pombal's administrative reforms substantially reduced the office's power and prestige by creating *juntas da fazenda* (treasury boards) that reported directly to Portuguese administrators and by installing *junta* presidents who outranked the *provedor mor.*

See also **Brazil: The Colonial Era, 1500–1808.**

BIBLIOGRAPHY

The 1548 *regimentos* are in Marcos Carneiro De Mendonça, ed., *Raizes de formação administrativa do Brasil,* vol. 1 (1972). See also Rodolpho Garcia, *Ensaio sôbre a historia política e administrativa do Brasil, 1500–1810* (1956), pp. 187–190; Dauril Alden, *Royal Government in Colonial Brazil* (1968); Stuart B. Schwartz, *Sovereignty and Society of Colonial Brazil: The High Court of Bahia and Its Judges, 1609–1751* (1973).

Additional Bibliography

Fragoso, João Luís Ribeiro, Maria Fernanda Bicalho, and Maria de Fátima Gouvêa. *O Antigo Regime nos trópicos: A dinâmica imperial portuguesa, séculos XVI-XVIII.* Rio de Janeiro: Civilização Brasileira, 2001.

WILLIAM DONOVAN

PROVIDENCIA. Providencia (Providence Island; Old Providence), western Caribbean island, about 440 miles northwest of Cartagena, Colombia, and 110 miles east of Nicaragua. English Puritans of the Providence Company began settling the island in 1629. At first they cultivated tobacco and sugar, but soon many turned to buccaneering. A Spanish fleet expelled the settlers in 1641, but some returned, and it continued to be a buccaneering and privateering base, its population increased by black slaves brought from Jamaica. The Convention of London (1786) recognized Spain's claim to the island, but Providence again became a haven for privateers during the wars for independence, especially for Louis-Michel Aury (1818–1821), when he operated under the flag of Buenos Aires. Colombia claimed the island after independence, and it became a part of the intendancy of San Andrés and Providencia. Its modern economy is based principally on subsistence agriculture and tourism.

See also **Aury, Louis-Michel; Buccaneers and Privateers.**

BIBLIOGRAPHY

Arthur Percival Newton, *The Colonising Activities of the English Puritans* (1914).

James J. Parsons. *San Andrés y Providencia: Una geografía histórica de las islas colombianas del mar Caribe occidental* (1964).

Cecilia De Los Ríos, *San Andrés y Providencia, aspectos geográficos* (1986).

Additional Bibliography

Lozano Simonelli, Alberto. *San Andrés y Providencia, la amenza de Nicaragua: Aspectos jurídicos y políticos de la posición de Colombia.* Bogota: Universidad de Bogotá Jorge Tadeo Lozano, 2002.

Rouillard, Patrick, and Walwin G. Peterson B. *San Andrés y Providencia.* Medellin, Colombia: Editorial Colina, 1990.

Vollmer, Loraine. *The History of the Settling Process of the Archipelago of San Andres, Old Providence and St. Catherine.* San Andrés, Isla: Ediciones Archipielago, 1997.

Zamora R., Augusto. *Intereses territoriales de Nicaragua: San Andrés y Providencia, Cayos, Golfo de Fonseca, Río San Juan.* Managua: Fondo Editorial de lo Jurídico, 1995.

RALPH LEE WOODWARD JR.

PROVINCIAL DEPUTATION. When Napoleonic armies occupied Spain in 1808, patriots appointed provincial juntas to govern the country in the name of deposed King Ferdinand VII and to help in its defense. On 28 March 1811, the juntas declared that each of their numbers would include a captain-general, intendant, and nine members. No provision, however, was made for Spanish America, whose residents spontaneously had formed juntas of their own. On 23 October 1811, a delegate to the Cortes of Cádiz representing New Spain, José Miguel Ramos Arizpe, proposed that such a junta, which he later dubbed "provincial deputation," be established in Saltillo, the capital of the Eastern Interior Provinces of New Spain.

The Spanish Constitution of 1812 ultimately established six locally elected provincial deputations in Mexico and one in Guatemala. Their function was to execute and oversee government orders concerning military recruits, taxation, the census, education, and state jobs. They were located in Mexico City (including México, Veracruz, Puebla, Oaxaca, Michoacán, Querétaro, and Tlaxcala), San Luis Potosí (comprising San Luis Potosí and Guanajuato), Guadalajara (New Galicia and Zacatecas), Mérida (Yucatán, Tabasco, and Campeche), Monterrey (Nuevo León, Coahuila, Nuevo Santander, and Texas), and Durango (Durango, Chihuahua, Sonora, Sinaloa, and the Californias). This decision, together with several others, combined to transform the way Spain would govern its empire and gave the former colonies some measure of home rule. At the same time, the Cortes abolished the viceroyalty, made the audiencia into a high court, and prepared to govern each American province directly and individually.

The elections for provincial deputation, although indirect, gave residents in New Spain their first experience with popular democracy and autonomy from control by both Spain and Mexico City. Soon the original seven groupings divided into provinces, jurisdictional entities that would continue into the early years of independence. Selection of the provincial deputations helped pave the way for self-rule. In the words of their foremost scholar, Nettie Lee Benson, "the people had been awakened to citizenship through the numerous elections held annually in the parishes to elect deputies for the various positions in the municipalities, Cortes, and Provincial Deputations, and they were enlightened politically in preparation for a new system." (*The Provincial Deputation*, p. 129).

See also **Benson, Nettie Lee; Spain, Constitution of 1812.**

BIBLIOGRAPHY

Nettie Lee Benson, ed., *Mexico and the Spanish Cortes* (1966), and *The Provincial Deputation in Mexico: Harbinger of Provincial Autonomy, Independence, and Federalism* (1992).

Additional Bibliography

Medina Peña, Luis. *Invención del sistema político mexicano: Forma de gobierno y gobernabilidad en México en el siglo XIX*. México, D.F.: Fondo de Cultura Económica, 2004.

Vázquez, Josefina Zoraida. *El establecimiento del federalismo en México, 1821-1827*. México, D.F.: Colegio de México, 2003.

CARMEN RAMOS-ESCANDÓN

PROVINCIAS INTERNAS.

PROVINCIAS INTERNAS. Provincias Internas, a *comandancia general* (1776–1823) created for northern New Spain as part of the Bourbon Reforms to revitalize Spain's military and economic control of its New World colonies. The Provincias Internas included, at various times, the Californias, Sonora, Sinaloa, Nueva Vizcaya (modern Durango and Chihuahua), Nuevo México, Texas, Coahuila, Nuevo León, and Nuevo Santander (modern Tamaulipas). Conceived by José de Gálvez during his *visita* to the north (1768–1770), the Provincias Internas took form when he became minister of the Indies in 1776. In an attempt to reverse a long history of piecemeal, ad hoc efforts to defend the northern periphery of Spain's empire against foreign intrusions and indigenous peoples who resisted incorporation, Gálvez designed an administrative entity to integrate the north along an east-west axis from Texas to California. To remedy the disjointed and inefficient pattern of articulation between the northern frontier and Mexico City along several north-south routes, the new jurisdiction at first reported directly to the king, bypassing viceregal control.

Gálvez and the many local architects of the Provincias Internas formulated bold policies to establish peace and security. French and British trading and colonizing east of the Mississippi River and the introduction of the horse had gradually produced territorial dislocations among Plains and southwestern Indian groups, resulting in increasing pressure from the Comanches and Apaches on the sparsely settled northern frontier. The Spanish sought to reduce administrative and defensive costs by bringing frontier groups under Spanish control and using them as buffers against foreign intrusions. The resulting relative peace would, it was hoped, attract settlers. In Alta California, where Spain had never established a sustained presence in the face of Russian and English encroachments, Gálvez brought the indigenous people under the control of missions and presidios in the 1770s, despite the blow dealt to missions in more established areas by the 1767 expulsion of the Jesuits. Missionary work among nonsedentary groups such as Comanches, Apaches, and Navajos, however, proved unsuccessful.

Shifts in policy and administrative organization occurred frequently in the Provincias Internas. The first *comandante general*, Teodoro de Croix (1776–1783), built the infrastructure to implement Gálvez's goals and modified the earlier presidential reform implemented after the Marqués de Rubí's inspection, but achieved no stunning success. The theoretical detachment of the Provincias Internas from the viceroyalty prevailed during Croix's tenure and again from 1792 to 1811, although independence was primarily military rather than administrative and judicial. During the rest of the period, the Provincias Internas were subject to viceregal control. Top-level shifts, complicated by subdivisions of the Provincias Internas into eastern and western provinces (1787–1792 and 1811–1823) and by overlapping military and civil jurisdictions within the provinces and later intendancies, assured continuous bureaucratic turmoil. In 1788 the seat of government moved from Arizpe, Sonora, to Chihuahua, which remained an important administrative and commercial center despite short-lived capitals in Arizpe, Durango, and Monterrey.

A common thread running through the chaotic shifts in policy and administrative organization was the use of diplomacy rather than force, a strategy most effectively developed by Viceroy Bernardo de

Gálvez (1785–1786). Called "peace by deceit" or "peace by subsidy," the policy of using trade to make the natives dependent on colonial powers (embodied in the Instructions of 1786) encouraged the extensive use of trade and gifts (defective firearms, alcohol, horses, and other commodities). Conciliation and negotiation pursued by Comandante General Jacobo Ugarte y Loyola (1786–1790) and New Mexico Governor Juan Bautista de Anza (1778–1788) produced the most successful results with Comanches. The two men also fashioned a balance of power with Navajos, Utes, and Apaches while encouraging alliances with Pueblos and other northern groups. When diplomacy failed, force—even extermination—remained an option.

Also, a different culture dynamic existed in the northern frontier. In Chihuahua, for instance, the small Spanish elite tried to establish a rigid racial hierarchy. However, labor scarcity, in addition to limited resources on the frontier, gave the local working class and poor leverage to demand rights and respect within the social order. Hence, scholars have suggested that political authority was more fluid on the northern frontier than in the rest of New Spain.

Although bureaucratic wrangling ultimately subverted the implementation of overall goals, Spain's late colonial focus on the north did engender relative peace and stemmed European (if not U.S.) advances. During the period of the Provincias Internas, the population more than doubled; non-Indians tripled in numbers, and the indigenous population began to recover from its 1750 nadir. Mining, agriculture, and commerce expanded modestly in the more established areas of Nueva Vizcaya, Nuevo México, and Sonora.

See also **Bourbon Reforms; Croix, Teodoro de; Gálvez, José de.**

BIBLIOGRAPHY

Alfred B. Thomas, ed. and trans., *Teodoro de Croix and the Northern Frontier of New Spain, 1776–1783* (1941).

Bernardo De Gálvez, *Instructions for Governing the Interior Provinces of New Spain, 1786,* edited and translated by Donald E. Worcester (1951).

Luis Navarro García, *Don José de Galvez y la comandancia general de las Provincias Internas del norte de Nueva España* (1964).

María Del Carmen Velázquez Chávez, *Establecimiento y pérdida del septentrión de Nueva España* (1974).

Elizabeth A. H. John, *Storms Brewed in Other Men's Worlds: The Confrontation of Indians, Spanish, and French in the Southwest, 1540–1795* (1975).

Peter Gerhard, *The North Frontier of New Spain* (1982).

Thomas D. Hall, *Social Change in the Southwest, 1350–1880* (1989).

David J. Weber, *The Spanish Frontier in North America* (1992).

Additional Bibliography

Martin, Cheryl English. *Governance and Society in Colonial Mexico: Chihuahua in the Eighteenth Century.* Stanford, CA: Stanford University Press, 1996.

Río, Ignacio del. *La aplicación regional de las reformas borbónicas en Nueva España: Sonora y Sinaloa, 1768–1787.* México: Universidad Nacional Autónoma de México, Instituto de Investigaciones Históricas, 1994.

SUSAN M. DEEDS

PROYECTISTAS. According to the classic 1955 definition of José Muñoz Pérez, the phenomenom of *proyectismo* (the writing of long-term plans) manifested itself in Spain and Spanish America in the eighteenth century as a sophisticated version of the *arbitrismo* (expediency) of the seventeenth century. Both were derived from the economic crisis experienced by the Spanish monarchy from the early seventeenth century, which was characterized, particularly during the reigns of Philip IV and Charles II, by inflation, industrial decline, falling taxation yields, a declining Indies trade, and repeated state bankruptcies, famines, and epidemics.

While each Arbitrista tended to reduce these complex problems to a single causal factor, capable of being remedied by a simple expedient (*arbitrio*), the *proyectistas* of the eighteenth century moved away from panaceas toward the production of more complex treatises, which suggested concrete programs of long-term reform, often derived from their authors' experience of government service. In the imperial sphere, one of the most influential *proyectistas* was José del Campillo y Cossío (1693–1744), minister of finance in the reign of Philip V, who in his *Nuevo sistema de gobierno económico para la América,* written in 1743, turned his attention from the economic problems of the peninsula—in 1741 he had produced an important work on the domestic economy entitled *Lo que hay de más y de menos en España*—to the empire, which he saw as an undeveloped market for Spanish manufactures and as an unexploited source of raw materials for Spanish industry. His main proposals: for a series of general inspections, or *visitas generales;* the creation of intendancies; and the introduction of free trade, became the basis for the imperial reform program implemented by Charles III and his ministers beginning in 1763.

Other influential *proyectistas*, who also held important government posts, included Gerónimo de Uztáriz (1670–1732), Bernardo Ward (*d.* 1762/63), Pedro Rodríguez de Campomanes (1723–1803), and Gaspar de Jovellanos (1744–1811).

See also **Arbitristas; Charles II of Spain.**

BIBLIOGRAPHY

José Muñoz Pérez, "Los proyectos sobre España e Indias en el siglo XVIII: El proyectismo como género," in *Revista de Estudios Políticos* 81 (1955): 169–195.

Jean Vilar, *Literatura y economía: La figura satírica del arbitrista en el Siglo de Oro* (1973).

Sara Almarza, "El comercio en el siglo XVIII: Arbitrios a las autoridades," in *Revista de Indias* 45, no. 175 (1985): 13–26.

María Luisa Martínez De Salinas Alonso, "Contribución al estudio sobre los arbitristas. Nuevos arbitrios para las Indias a principios del siglo XVII," in *Revista de Indias* 50, no. 188 (1990): 161–169.

Additional Bibliography

Blanco, Mónica and Ma Eugenia Romero Sotelo. *Tres siglos de economía novohispana, 1521–1821.* México: Universidad Nacional Autónoma de México: Editorial Jus, 2000.

Campillo y Cosío, José del and Dolores Mateos Dorado. *Dos escritos politicos.* Oviedo: Junta General del Principado de Asturias, 1993.

Marichal, Carlos Daniela Marino and Ana Lidia García. *De colonia a nación: Impuestos y política en México, 1750–1860.* México: El Colegio de México, Centro de Estudios Históricos, 2001.

Sánchez Santiró, Ernest, Luis Jáuregui and Antonio Ibarra. *Finanzas y política en el mundo iberoamericano: Del antiguo régimen a las naciones independientes, 1754–1850.* México, D.F.: Universidad Autónoma de México, Facultad de Economía: Instituto de Investigaciones Mora, 2001.

JOHN R. FISHER

PUBLIC HEALTH. Providing public health care has long been a special challenge for Latin America. Because much of the region lies in the tropics, Latin America is home to many microorganisms that can bring illness and death to human hosts. Economic underdevelopment has impeded governments' efforts to provide clean water, proper sewage disposal, vaccinations, and care for the sick. And because many people in Latin America are poor and malnourished, they have weak or compromised immune systems, depriving them of the best defense against illness. Only in the twentieth century have significant strides been made in improving public health care in Latin America, but this progress has been very uneven.

COLONIAL ERA

Until the arrival of the Europeans in the late fifteenth century, the Western Hemisphere had enjoyed complete isolation from some global disease pools. The conquerors and their African slaves introduced into the Americas many deadly epidemic diseases from which the natives had no natural immunities to protect them. Smallpox, measles, influenza, typhus, and many other afflictions ravaged the New World; its population fell by roughly 90 percent in the first 110 years after the Conquest. Almost nothing could have been done to halt this disaster, and certainly little was tried. At the time, about the only public health measure taken was sometimes to quarantine incoming ships and isolate their crews during the worst epidemics.

European notions about the origin and spread of disease generally focused on *miasmas* (Greek for "pollution" or "stain"), which were believed to be foul, disease-bearing airs that arose from putrefying organic waste. Traditional medicine stressed the need to rid the body of poisons and recommended frequent bleedings, induced vomiting, sweating, and repeated enemas. One stood a better chance of recuperating if a doctor's ministrations could be avoided. During the era of the Spanish Bourbon Reforms, especially under King Charles III (1759–1788), enlightened colonial officials began to take more aggressive public sanitation measures to rid communities of the sources of miasmas. The clean-up campaigns served to make urban settings less foul but could do little to prevent or halt most epidemics.

THE NINETEENTH AND TWENTIETH CENTURIES

Beginning in the closing decades of the nineteenth century, several critical advances led to the rise of the modern era of public health in Latin America. The economy of Latin America rose swiftly in these years on the strength of increased primary product exports to the developed world. In the cities that served as the focal points for this expanding trade, control of epidemics became an urgent business concern, for quarantines halted commerce. Fortunately, these socioeconomic developments coincided with some stunning scientific breakthroughs in the field of medicine. In Europe the work of Robert Koch, Louis Pasteur, and others established the germ theory of disease. Their work, along with that of many others—including Latin Americans Oswaldo Cruz, Carlos Chagas, and Carlos J. Finlay—provided a sound theoretical basis for attacking the spread of infectious diseases.

Accordingly, by the late nineteenth and early twentieth centuries Latin American cities underwent significant sanitary reforms, including the construction of their first mass potable water systems and underground sewers (greatly reducing the risk of cholera, typhoid fever, and other waterborne diseases). They established vaccination programs against smallpox (which was quite effective) and bubonic plague (less so); developed mosquito abatement programs (greatly reducing the risk of yellow fever and malaria); began to inspect and regulate the sale of food, especially milk and meat; and opened modern laboratories to test foods and drugs for purity. They also built many new hospital facilities, incorporating modern medical methods developed in Western Europe and the United States, in particular better diagnostic and surgical techniques (including anesthesia and asepsis) and more specialized training of physicians. Doctors typically received their advanced training in France, although some good schools were established in the leading Latin American cities. National health departments were also formed across Latin America, beginning in Argentina and Uruguay.

These advances in medical treatment and urban sanitation contributed to an overall lowering of death rates in Latin America, which followed from a reduced incidence of infectious diseases such as yellow fever, cholera, typhoid fever, bubonic plague, smallpox, typhus, and tetanus. But other factors may actually have played a larger role. Scholars disagree as to what best explains the transition from lower overall death rates to rapid population growth. Some believe that microorganisms were gradually changing, becoming less deadly. Certainly there would be an evolutionary tendency for microorganisms to move in that direction: if they killed their hosts, they, too, died. Another possible factor for Latin America may have been the end to the African slave trade by the 1860s, which halted the steady importation of people from other disease environments. Perhaps most important of all was a general improvement in diet and housing conditions, although measuring such progress is difficult.

Certain political circumstances made government action in the field of public health more likely. Health care reforms came fastest in those nations where the urban middle class and the trade union movement first grew strong. As they pushed for incorporation into the political system, they also advanced a social agenda that included health concerns. Where skilled export workers occupied a strategic bottleneck position in the economy, they could sometimes join with privileged middle-class employees and press effectively for reforms. The elites responded by co-opting these groups with the creation of health programs to serve them, even as the health needs of those with less political leverage were ignored. Social programs to provide medical insurance for the middle class and favored sectors of the urban working class were enacted in Argentina, Brazil, Chile, Cuba, and Uruguay as early as the 1910s and 1920s.

In some circumstances, imperialism led directly to sanitation and public health reform. The United States occupation of Cuba, Haiti, the Dominican Republic, and Panama and, likewise, British control of Jamaica, meant stationing officials and troops in unhealthy tropical zones. Responding to this threat to their own citizens, the United States and Great Britain carried out massive public works projects in their colonial holdings, including effective mosquito abatement measures and the construction of hospitals, potable water systems, and underground sewers, thereby greatly reducing public health risks for all.

TWENTIETH-CENTURY PROGRESS

During the twentieth century international organizations played an important role in the advancement

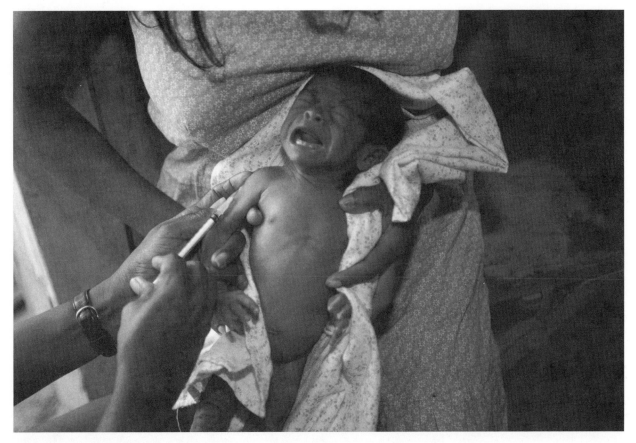

Infant being vaccinated for tuberculosis on the Wai-Wai Indian Reservation, Brazil, 1993. Since the mid-twentieth century vaccination programs have greatly reduced the incidence of major infectious illnesses in Latin America. © KAREN KASMAUSKI/CORBIS

of Latin American public health care. Based in the United States, the Rockefeller Foundation's International Health Division (created in 1913) took an active role, launching campaigns against malaria, yellow fever, and hookworm. The programs against yellow fever and malaria proved quite effective, even if the hookworm campaign did not. Overall, however, the foundation's usual practice of retaining direct control over policies and funding often rankled public officials in host nations.

The Pan American Health Organization (PAHO) also played a key role in Latin American public health progress in the twentieth century. The first Pan American Sanitary Conference met in 1902, under the aegis of the Pan American Union (now the Organization of American States). This small organization was actually run and staffed through the Surgeon General's Office of the U.S. Public Health Service. By 1924 the organization had

drawn up the Pan American Sanitary Code, adopted everywhere in the Americas by 1936. In 1947 the Pan American Sanitary Bureau (PAHO since 1958) finally obtained its own building in Washington, D.C., and added more personnel. In 1949 this bureau became a Latin American regional organization under the newly created World Health Organization. PAHO came to play an important role in the eradication of infectious diseases such as smallpox, malaria, and yellow fever.

Over the course of the twentieth century life expectancy doubled in Latin America, with most of the gain coming from the lowering of infant mortality rates (the number of deaths ages 0–1 per 1,000 live births). (The infant mortality rate for Latin America fell from 125 in the five years from 1950 to 1955 to 36 in the five years from 1995 to 2000.) But whereas prior to 1930 most Latin American public health care advances could be

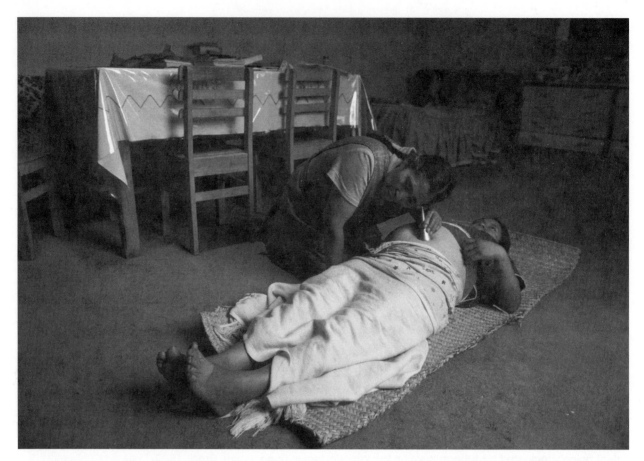

A midwife examines an expectant mother in rural Mexico, late 20th century. STEPHANIE MAZE/NATIONAL GEOGRAPHIC IMAGE COLLECTION

linked to the improved economic circumstances, after 1930 the gains stemmed principally from the importation of new sanitation and medical technologies from the United States and the rest of the developed world.

One key development was the mass spraying of the insecticide DDT. In the late 1950s PAHO undertook massive effort to wipe out the mosquitoes that serve as vectors for yellow fever, malaria, and dengue (or "breakbone") fever. The program was an enormous success, and illness and death from most mosquito-vectored diseases were all but eliminated. However, the overuse of DDT, especially in commercial agriculture, in time reduced its effectiveness against mosquitoes. Concerns in the 1960s over the possible harmful implications of introducing massive amounts of DDT into the environment brought an end to the program.

Other public health efforts included the chlorination of potable water; better sewage disposal and treatment; expanded vaccination; and the widespread introduction of new antibiotics (which proved especially effective in reducing the number of deaths due to pneumonia and tuberculosis). These steps, in the words of Nicolás Sánchez-Albornoz, were "grafts from other civilizations" (*The Population of Latin America*, p. 5). Through them, the risk from nearly all major infectious illnesses in Latin America was eliminated or greatly reduced, at least for a time.

POVERTY, EQUITY, AND HEALTH
In the largest sense, the economic context most determines success in providing for public health. Two macro-measures are most significant: per capita gross domestic product (GDP) and distribution of income. As a rule, the more advanced the economy, the better the overall public health situation. Because economic growth usually brings a reduction of poverty, it usually results in improvement in the public health situation.

Although historically this general relationship among economic performance, reduction of poverty, and improvement in public health has held true in Latin America, since the 1990s it has no longer been the case. When the region's economy grew in the 1960s and 1970s, the number of families living in poverty fell; the deep economic decline of the 1980s brought a sharp increase in poverty levels. (During the 1980s, workers' real wages across Latin America fell by about one-quarter.) However, when economic growth eventually returned in the 1990s, albeit at a much slower pace than in the 1960s and 1970s, the percentage of those living in poverty did *not* decrease. Indeed, in the late 1990s the percentage of Latin Americans living in extreme poverty (earning less than a dollar a day) began to grow again. In the twenty-first century, in Nicaragua and Haiti over half of the population lives on less than a dollar a day. More than half of the population of Bolivia, Colombia, Ecuador, Guatemala, and Paraguay live in poverty (less than two dollars a day). In Haiti, Nicaragua, and Honduras more than seven out of ten people live in poverty. In Latin America as a whole, six of every ten children live in poverty.

The problem is that Latin America has the most unequal distribution of income of any region in the world, a situation that has significantly worsened since the 1990s. From 1990 to 1995, a time of economic recovery and growth, the income share received by to the bottom 10 percent of the population *fell* 15 percent. If Latin America's income were only as unevenly distributed as that of Eastern Europe or South Asia, its economic growth since the 1990s would have all but eliminated poverty (reducing poverty to around 3 percent of the population). In Latin America income is so unequally distributed that economic growth cannot reduce poverty. This has enormous implications for Latin America's public health.

The poor are more likely to become ill, less likely to receive medical attention when they become ill, and more likely to suffer premature death. Infant mortality is especially associated with poverty. In Peru, for example, the infant mortality rates for the poorest one-fifth of the population is five times higher than that of the wealthiest one-fifth. In Bolivia the infant mortality rate of the poorest one-fifth of the population is 107 while that of the

wealthiest one fifth is 26. Moreover, in Latin America racial and ethnic minorities are more likely to live in poverty, and these groups suffer worse public health conditions as a result. In Brazil, for example, the infant mortality rate for whites is 37, but for people of color it is 62. In Mexico, childhood mortality (ages 5 or younger) is two and a half times higher for indigenous than nonindigenous people.

Improvement in public health is much more strongly linked to income equity than to economic growth: the more even the distribution of income, the better the overall public health situation. To illustrate, the per capita GNPs of Haiti and Cuba are roughly equal (ranking at the bottom of all Latin American nations), but in Haiti income is very unevenly distributed whereas in Cuba it is very evenly distributed. As a result, by almost any measure Haiti has the worst public health situation in Latin America and Cuba has the best. Life expectancy in Haiti is 60 years; in Cuba it is 82. Most contemporary public health experts therefore regard social inequality as the leading source of deficiencies in public health care in contemporary Latin America.

HEALTH INSURANCE
Beginning in the 1930s, many Latin American nations developed national health insurance programs, although these systems tended to cover only salaried employees. Consequently, even by the late 1960s only one of six Latin Americans was covered by a social health insurance program. In the early 1980s Chile, as part of its conversion to free market (or neoliberal) economic policies under the Augusto Pinochet dictatorship (1973–1990) privatized its public health care system. Soon many other Latin American nations followed, establishing private, for-profit health insurance systems. This policy direction continues to be actively supported by the United States, acting through the Inter-American Development Bank and the World Bank. The reforms are patterned after the U.S. health care system, even though it is the most expensive per capita in the world and ranks behind most developed nations in nearly all leading public health indicators.

A key concern with the privatization of public health care in Latin America is that for-profit health insurance companies seek naturally to enroll those individuals who are both in excellent health and can afford to pay high premiums. Moreover, providing health care through private insurance systems works best in urban areas among workers employed in the formal sector, but works far less well for peasants and urban informal sector workers. For Latin America the difficulty is that these latter two categories make up the bulk of the economically active population. During the 1990s and to 2005 at least seven of every ten new jobs created was in poorly paid informal sector. In Latin America today more than three-quarters of the population has no health insurance of any kind.

Women have been especially disadvantaged by the changes to the health care system. The new private health insurance systems are tied to employment in the formal sector, with payment coming in the form of paycheck withholding. Women who do not work for pay (half of the working age population of females in Latin America) or work in the informal sector and are paid less than men (Latin American women earn on average three-quarters of what men earn) are extremely unlikely to be able to afford the cost of private health insurance. Compounding this are the special health care needs of women. Beyond the health burdens of childbirth (a woman's risk of dying from maternal causes was 1 in 160 in Latin America, but 1 in 3,500 in the United States and Canada), women tend to live longer and suffer higher rates of morbidity and disability than do men. Reflecting this reality, health insurance premiums are higher for women than for men. In Chile, for example, health insurance premiums cost on average two and a half times more for women than men.

TRENDS IN SCHOLARSHIP

Public health care officials have long recognized the link between poverty and problems in public health, but historically most treated poverty as a given, focusing their efforts instead on measures that seek to ameliorate the social conditions that stem from poverty. But by the 1930s an influential minority of Latin American public health researchers and physicians began to push beyond just noting the health implications of poverty, taking a more activist political stance. These "social medicine" critics sought to diagnose the etiology of poverty itself, offering socioeconomic and political prescriptions: government-provided food, clothing, and shelter, and above all, income redistribution. The writings of Salvador Allende Gossens, especially *La realidad médico-social*

chilena (The Chilean medico-social reality, published in 1939, when he was Chile's minister of health), stimulated increasing interest in the "social medicine" approach. Elected to the presidency in 1970, Allende sought to put in place some of the leading precepts of social medicine. Since the late twentieth century, a host of new studies and specialized journals have come to focus on research into the relationship between social inequities and health care problems in Latin America.

PRESENT CHALLENGES

There has been some heartening progress in public health care in Latin America, most notably in the area of vaccination coverage. Routine childhood vaccinations against diphtheria, whooping cough, and tetanus have dramatically reduced the incidence of these afflictions across Latin America. Vaccination programs have also succeeded in eradicating both polio and measles in Latin America, even as these diseases continue to disable and kill people, especially children, elsewhere in the developing world.

Yet in several key areas Latin America has failed to progress in the provisioning of public health. Whereas life expectancy in Latin America was five years longer than in East Asia in the mid-1960s, by the mid-1990s Latin America had fallen behind by 1.2 years. Contemporary neoliberal economic policy has stressed the need to reduce the role of government, favoring instead free market solutions to social concerns. However, reductions in public spending on both potable water and sewers has had serious public health implications. Beginning in 1991 contaminated water supplies led to a widespread Latin American outbreak of cholera, a disease that had been unseen in the region for nearly a hundred years. Nevertheless, today roughly two-thirds of Latin American cities make no attempt to treat their raw sewage before dumping it into nearby rivers or the sea. In several nations only half of the population has in-home potable water, and its purity is by no means guaranteed. Across Latin America, only about a quarter of piped water is routinely checked for contaminants. These deficiencies represent a substantial failure in the provisioning of public health needs in Latin America, for with each percentage point increase in potable water coverage for the population, the infant mortality rate drops 1 person per 1,000 births.

Another serious concern is rising antibiotic resistance, a result of massive overuse and/or inappropriate use of antibiotics. Fully two-thirds of all pharmaceutical drugs used in Latin America are purchased without a doctor's prescription. Today a wide array of antibiotics have been rendered partly or completely ineffective, and lethal strains of multi-drug-resistant tuberculosis have appeared in Peru and Haiti. Their spread to the rest of the world is but a plane ride away.

Although maternal mortality is rare in the developed world, in Latin America it remains the main cause of death for women aged 20 to 34. A leading cause of maternal mortality in Latin America is complications from abortions. Abortion is generally illegal in Latin America, except in Cuba. (In Cuba the number of abortions has dropped sharply because of widespread availability and use of contraception.) Nevertheless, about half of all pregnancies in Latin America end in abortion. Another leading cause of female mortality is cervical cancer, especially in poorer nations where women are unlikely to undergo periodic Pap smears.

Another concern is HIV/AIDS, which now infects at least 2.4 million people in Latin America. The Caribbean region has been especially hard hit, and prevalence there is higher than any other region in the world except sub-Sahara Africa. In the Caribbean HIV/AIDS is the leading cause of death for people aged 15 to 49. All told, at least half a million people have died from AIDS in Latin America. Education remains a problem: a third of Latin American adolescents do not understand how to protect themselves from the disease.

Several mosquito-borne diseases, once thought to be eradicated, have now either come back or are on the verge of doing so. Lapses in mosquito control have led to the reemergence of dengue fever (a debilitating and painful affliction) and dengue hemorrhagic fever (a less frequently occurring but lethal counterpart) across much of the Caribbean. There is no vaccine, no cure, and no effective treatment for dengue. Urban yellow fever, driven from all Latin American cities in the early twentieth century, now appears poised to return. The reinfestation of the mosquito vector, *aedes aegypti*, and the advance of human settlements into the Amazon where jungle yellow fever is endemic among some species of monkeys, raises the risk of reintroduction of yellow fever into urban areas.

Despite continuing and serious public health concerns, today most spending on health in Latin America goes for modern, expensive, curative measures and for private physicians serving the more privileged in society, while less-expensive, mass preventive measures are not usually well funded. Critics argue that the existing system misallocates scarce public health spending, for preventive programs could help attack the health concerns of poorer, especially rural regions, and diseases that especially affect children. To critics, Latin America's pattern of spending on health represents a massive shift of resources from the poor to the rich and from the young to the old.

See also **Acquired Immune Deficiency Syndrome (AIDS); Cities and Urbanization; Diseases; Medicine: Colonial Spanish America; Medicine: The Modern Era; Population: Brazil; Population: Spanish America.**

BIBLIOGRAPHY

Abel, Christopher. *Health, Hygiene and Sanitation in Latin America c. 1870 to c. 1950.* London: Institute of Latin American Studies, 1996. Provides a historical sketch of public health care history in Latin America.

Barrientos, Armando, and Peter Lloyd-Sherlock, "Health Insurance Reforms in Latin America: Cream Skimming, Equity and Cost-Containment," in *Social Policy Reform and Market Governance in Latin America*, edited by Louise Haagh and Camilla T. Helgø. New York: Palgrave Macmillan, 2002.

Casas, Juan Antonio, J. Norberto W. Dachs, and Alexandra Bambas. "Health Disparities in Latin America and the Caribbean: The Role of Social and Economic Determinants." In *Equity and Health: Views from the Pan American Sanitary Bureau.* Washington, DC: Pan American Health Organization, 2001. Provides a summary of equity issues.

Pineo, Ronn. "Misery and Death in the Pearl of the Pacific: Health Care in Guayaquil, Ecuador, 1870–1925," in *Hispanic American Historical Review* 70, no. 4 (1990): 609–637. Discusses public health care at the turn of the twentieth century.

Kiple, Kenneth F., ed. *Cambridge World History of Human Disease.* Cambridge, U.K., and New York: Cambridge University Press, 1993. The best place to begin a study of the history of Latin American public health.

Londoño, Juan Luis, and Miguel Székely. "Persistent Poverty and Excess Inequality: Latin America, 1970–1995," *Journal of Applied Economic*, 3, no. 1 (2000): 93–134, Supplies numbers on economic growth and inequality.

Pan American Health Organization. *Health in the Americas*, vols. 1 and 2. Washington, DC: Pan American Health Organization, 2002.

Sánchez-Albornoz, Nicolás. *The Population of Latin America: A History*, translated by W. A. R. Richardson. Berkeley: University of California Press, 1974. Demography and public health.

United Nations. *The Millennium Development Goals: A Latin American and Caribbean Perspective*. Santiago, Chile: United Nations, 2005. Provides a full overview of existing conditions.

RONN PINEO

PUBLIC SECTOR AND TAXATION.

The *public sector* is a term used to describe the three entities—general government, nonfinancial public enterprises, and public financial institutions—through which governments carry out public policy. General government, made up of central, state (provincial, regional), local (municipalities, school boards), and supranational authorities, and social security schemes, forms the core of the public sector and has been the most important entity used by Latin American governments to formulate and implement public policy. Through its branches of public administration and defense, general government has directly determined the nature and transformation of collective, semicollective, and, indirectly, individual commodities (goods and services) produced in each Latin American country.

PUBLIC SECTOR FORMATION IN POSTCOLONIAL LATIN AMERICA

Collective Services. Collective services satisfy the collective (public) needs for public order and safety, defense and conduct of foreign affairs, protection of life and private and public property, political and economic freedom, equal treatment by government, and social harmony and environmental protection. These services guarantee to citizens the enjoyment of fundamental human, political, and economic rights, and free and equal participation in governance, production, and exchange. Collective services are said to be nonrival and nonexcludable in consumption: Consumption of collective services by one agent (person) does not reduce the availability of such services to someone else.

In the aftermath of independence, from 1820 to 1930, the primary task for governments was national reconstruction—the establishment of a postcolonial institutional framework that would enable the production of collective services. Much of the nineteenth century was taken up in the pursuit of this elusive goal. Endemic violence between 1830 and 1850, especially in the small Central American countries and Colombia; boundary disputes; and internal conflicts between competing factions delayed establishment of independent and democratic legislative, executive, and judiciary branches, which constituted the vital foundations of procedural democracy and civil society. With the exception of Chile, control of government remained largely in the hands of military dictatorships, which did not produce services satisfying these collective needs.

Semicollective Services. From 1820 to 1930 all Latin American governments made major efforts to increase the supply of semicollective services—education, health and sanitation, social security and welfare, and recreation and culture. Governments raised educational standards and made education available to more people at all levels—primary, secondary, vocational, and university. Mortality rates began declining, especially among infants. Argentina and Uruguay led the way in providing such services. In other countries, success was achieved mostly in urban areas and among the upper and middle classes and organized labor. The distribution of publicly and privately produced semicollective services remained highly unequal. More than a century after independence, the poorest 60 percent of households in Brazil, Bolivia, Guatemala, Mexico, Peru, Honduras, Ecuador, Venezuela, and elsewhere still had minimal or no access to educational, health, welfare, and other semicollective services.

Individual Commodities. Individual (or rival) services are defined as commodities whose consumption by one agent precludes consumption of the same unit by another. Individual commodities, which satisfy individual needs for food, clothing, shelter, and so forth, are normally produced by private- or state-owned enterprises in agriculture, manufacturing, mining, or services (personal, business) for sale in a market at a price expected to cover their cost of production.

Spending by the consolidated nonfinancial public sector as a percentage of gross domestic product, selected Latin American countries, 1970–1985

	Argentina	Brazil	Chile	Mexico	Peru	Venezuela
1970	38.62	35.92	41.27	22.30	24.50	28.70
1971	37.76	34.44	49.93	20.50	27.10	29.20
1972	37.00	35.19	56.05	23.00	31.20	33.50
1973	40.52	33.96	49.39	25.70	38.60	32.80
1974	47.06	38.81	43.17	27.00	45.10	29.50
1975	46.40	42.74	40.44	31.90	46.10	38.90
1976	43.46	44.17	37.82	32.00	45.80	44.00
1977	43.01	42.04	40.74	30.30	48.40	50.50
1978	48.92	47.56	34.57	31.40	47.60	52.60
1979	45.88	54.45	31.65	33.00	48.40	49.40
1980	49.06	52.66	31.58	35.00	60.10	53.30
1981	53.30	42.70	34.11	41.40	57.40	54.00
1982	49.16	46.06	39.84	46.40	60.20	57.60
1983	55.79	44.44	38.31	42.80	66.30	47.00
1984	51.86	43.10	39.66	40.30	55.50	42.90
1985	52.09	48.26	39.92	40.70	56.90	43.60

SOURCE: Felipe Larraín and Marcelo Selowsky, eds., *The Public Sector and the Latin American Crisis* (1991), p. 2.

Table 1

In addition to relying on central, state, and local authorities, Latin American governments have always utilized government-owned or government-controlled (i.e., public) corporate and quasi-corporate, nonfinancial enterprises as instruments for the formulation and execution of public policy. Following independence, national governments continued to use such government monopolies as tobacco, salt, liquor, matches, the post office, mining, and agricultural products, which were inherited from the Spanish and Portuguese crowns and their followers, to generate revenues to support the production of collective services by the public administration and defense activities. Between 1820 and 1860 many of these enterprises were privatized, that is, ownership and control were transferred from the state to private entities, in an effort to raise revenues, reward the leaders of the wars of independence, fulfill popular liberal philosophies, or simply to benefit those in power. State ownership or control and privatization were not always implemented to promote the common good; fraud and outright theft were not uncommon.

Following the consolidation of political power and establishment of political stability, Latin American governments increasingly ventured into production of individual commodities. They assumed ownership and control of enterprises in public utilities, such as gas, water, and electricity, in an effort to satisfy the needs of growing urban populations. They often assumed ownership of railroads to facilitate public transportation or to maintain employment when the railroads were abandoned by private owners. They also relied on monopolies to raise revenues.

Although the nonfinancial enterprise segment of the public sector was important, even before 1930, in public utilities, including transportation, and selected monopolies, it rarely played a leading or dominant role in industry, agriculture, mining, trade, and construction. Furthermore, public policy, as defined by the collective services produced by general government, was generally friendly to private enterprise, foreign capital, and free trade. Overall, there was a high degree of recognition and satisfaction of the collective needs for freedom of internal and external trade, and safety, security and protection of national and foreign private property

Monetary and Financial Institutions. Monetary and financial institutions constitute the third major pillar of the public sector. Following independence, governments made concerted efforts to develop and control the first segment of monetary institutions, or institutions whose liabilities are money: the monetary authorities. These consisted of monetary agencies, currency authorities, and, since the 1920s, central banks. Governments also actively promoted, although generally they did not own and control, the second segment of monetary institutions: banks whose liabilities include deposits payable and transferable on demand, often referred to as deposit money banks. Governments attempted to create and expand the money and capital markets to advance private property and the efficient use of resources.

Public Sector Finances. Public sector finances were precarious in much of Latin America between 1820 and 1930. More often than not, public sector expenditures exceeded ordinary revenues. Current expenditures, which included wages and salaries of government employees, purchases of supplies, and transfers, rose significantly; they exploded during periods of external or internal conflict. Capital expenditures on public buildings, ports, railroads, canals, roads, schools, and so forth increased. Public sector revenues also increased, often spectacularly.

Public sectors generated both ordinary and extraordinary revenues. Following independence, general government in all Latin American countries relied heavily on such ordinary revenues as customhouse duties, land, property and excise taxes, trade and professional license receipts, tithes, bridge tolls, mint receipts, and surpluses generated by state monopolies selling tobacco, salt, liquor, and even opium (in Peru). As international trade expanded between 1860 and 1930, export and import duties increasingly became a major, even primary, source of tax revenues. Whenever trade-based taxes declined, sales and income taxes were introduced. During crisis periods, such as war, severe depressions, and trade collapse, general government relied heavily on such extraordinary revenues as government issue of paper money, sale of bonds in domestic and international capital markets, issue of treasury notes, and sales of public land and properties confiscated from the crown and its followers. Increasingly, governments also relied on inflationary finance (printing of money) from monetary authorities and deposit money banks to cover public sector deficits.

Rising, often rigid, expenditures, including subsidies to state railroads and public utilities, on the one hand, and excessive dependence on volatile, foreign-trade-based taxes and lack of broad-based, progressive income taxes, on the other hand, weakened the capacity of most governments to pursue the public

Government consumption as a percentage of GDP, 1990 and 1997

Latin America & Caribbean	Purchasing power parity prices 1990	Domestic prices 1990	Domestic prices 1997
Antigua and Barbuda	—	18.0	20.6
Bahamas	—	13.6	15.8[e]
Barbados	—	20.2	21.4
Belize	18.7	14.4	16.9
Bolivia	16.2	11.8	13.7
Brazil	16.9	19.1	18.1
Chile	16.4	9.8	10.0
Colombia	13.5	10.3	16.1[f]
Costa Rica	19.4	18.2	16.7
Dominican Republic	3.0	2.9	7.7
Ecuador	16.1	8.6	11.6
El Salvador	24.1	9.9	9.1
Grenada	11.4	21.6	16.0[b]
Guatemala	11.1	6.8	5.1
Guyana	24.7	13.6	20.5
Honduras	16.2	12.9	8.3
Jamaica	14.5	14.0	14.4[f]
Mexico	9.8	9.1[a, c]	8.4
Nicaragua	33.9	32.5	14.6
Panama (exc. Canal Zone)	25.5	18.1	16.1
Paraguay	12.3	6.2	8.1[b]
Peru	17.4	6.1	8.4
St. Kitts-Nevis-Anguilla	21.6	18.4	18.2[f]
Saint Vincent and the Grenadines	—	17.5	26.3[f]
Suriname	—	25.2	16.9[a, d]
Trinidad and Tobago	14.9	16.2	14.6
Uruguay	17.4	13.9	13.7
Venezuela	16.2	8.4	6.4[b]

Note: Statistics in domestic prices estimated from UNESIS data base of United Nations DESA unless otherwise noted. Statistics in PPP prices estimated by adjusted domestic price data by the relative price of government consumption, as reported in Penn World Table, version 5.6a.
[a] from IMF, International Financial Statistics, February 1999
[b] Provisional or preliminary estimate
[c] 1991
[d] 1993
[e] 1995
[f] 1997

SOURCE: United Nations Online Network in Public Administration and Finance (UNPAN), UNPAN Statistical Database, *International Statistical Databases & the World Reports*, 2007, Basic Data on Government Expenditure and Taxation (1990–2002), Appendix Table 1, p. 26.

Table 2

policies needed to achieve economic, social, and political development. Instead, public policies between 1860 and 1930 either reinforced or created unsustainable and inequitable middle- and upper-class entitlements. Collective, semipublic, and even individual goods and services were produced by the state largely, often exclusively, for the minority middle and upper socioeconomic groups. In addition, often massive but volatile tax revenues from agriculture, mining, and foreign trade were used to reduce taxes and prices paid by the privileged minorities rather than to deliver more and better services to the underprivileged, needy, poor, rural, indigenous majorities.

Despite significant progress by 1930, Latin American governments and collective markets had not delivered the critical mass of collective services that could satisfy the complementary collective needs for political freedom (the foundation of electoral democracy); safety, security, and protection of life (the quintessential pillar of civil society); universal safety, security, and protection of private property (the precondition for efficient allocation of resources through free and competitive markets); equal treatment by government; social harmony; and environmental protection. They had not produced the collective (political, social, and economic modernization and justice, efficient markets, price stability) and semipublic (education, health, and welfare) services needed to achieve sustainable growth and equitable distribution. According to many, public sector policies and the complex forces that shaped them, have been largely responsible for the failure to transform the transitory, often fabulous, eras of prosperity between 1860 and 1930 into permanent ones.

AFTER 1930: EXPANSION OF THE PUBLIC SECTOR AND THE INTERVENTIONIST TRANSFORMATION OF COLLECTIVE MARKETS

The Great Depression of the 1930s, which precipitated a collapse in foreign trade, capital inflows, and immigration, had an immediate, profound impact on the public policy goals of Latin American governments and the instruments used to pursue them. The public sector, which was already large and complex in many countries before 1930, became larger and assumed even greater strategic significance in shaping the political, social, and economic evolution of Latin America.

Since 1930, Latin American governments have continued to face the formidable task of producing collective services recognizing and satisfying the seven complementary collective needs for political and economic freedom; safety, security, and protection of life and private property, equal treatment by government; social harmony; and environmental protection. Satisfaction of these needs would guarantee basic human, political, and economic

rights and freedoms on a sustainable and equal basis to all citizens. However, beginning with the Great Depression of the 1930s, recognition and satisfaction of the collective need for freedom of external as well as domestic trade was increasingly reduced by a recognition and satisfaction of the collective need for barriers to internal and external trade. Progress in the satisfaction of the collective needs for political freedom and social harmony was achieved whenever democratic governments were in power. Basic political rights and freedoms were neglected, even suppressed, however, during the prolonged reign of dictatorial political regimes in Argentina, Bolivia, Brazil, Chile, Cuba, the Dominican Republic, Ecuador, El Salvador, Guatemala, Haiti, Honduras, Nicaragua, Panama, Peru, Uruguay, and Venezuela. Satisfaction of the collective need for political freedom was reduced, often to minimal levels. Stable, sustainable democracies have been rare and largely overshadowed by prolonged dictatorships. With the exception of Cuba, however, the production of collective services satisfying the seven fundamental collective needs that underlie procedural democracy and civil society, thus promoting basic rights and freedoms, improved considerably whenever parliamentary democracies were restored. Even in procedural democracies, however, provision of the collective services that satisfy the aforementioned seven collective needs, thus advancing the basic political, social, human, and economic rights and freedoms of the poor, both urban and rural, often indigenous populations, has left much to be desired. Endemic political and economic crises undoubtedly weakened the ability of governments to produce enlightened collective services for the poor and needy.

Despite improvements in semipublic services after 1930, with resultant population increases (from 103 million in 1930 to 436 million in 1990 and 556 million in 2006), public and private delivery of semipublic services has frequently been inadequate, and distribution of these services has remained highly unequal. Middle and upper socioeconomic groups and organized labor have benefited greatly, but delivery of services to the rural and urban poor and the indigenous populations in Bolivia, Brazil, El Salvador, Guatemala, Honduras, Peru, and elsewhere has been minimal to nonexistent. In most of

Central government expenditure as a percentage of GDP

(domestic prices, 1990 and 1997)

	Year	Ratio (%)	Year	Ratio (%)
Argentina	1990	10.6	1996	14.1
Bahamas	1990	18.3	1993	20.5
Barbados	1989	33.2	—	—
Bolivia	1990	16.4	1997	23.1
Brazil	1990	35.0	1994	33.8
Belize[b, c, d]	1991	31.4	1997	29.2
Chile	1990	20.4	1997	20.7
Colombia	1990	11.6	1993	8.8
Costa Rica	1990	25.6	1996	30.1
Dominican Republic	1990	11.7	1996	15.6
Ecuador	1990	14.5	1994	15.7
El Salvador[c]	1990	10.9	1997	12.3
Grenada[c]	1991	30.7	1995	28.1
Guatemala	1990	10.0	1997	9.7
Mexico	1990	19.2	1996	15.5
Netherlands Antilles[a]	1990	16.7	1995	15.4
Nicaragua	1990	7.2	1994	32.3
Panama (exc. Canal Zone)	1990	23.7	1996	27.7
Paraguay	1990	9.4	—	—
St. Kitts-Nevis-Anguilla	—	—	—	—
Saint Vincent and the Grenadines[e]	1990	32.9	1997	42.7
Trinidad and Tobago	1993	29.4	1995	28.2
Uruguay	1990	26.0	1997	31.7
Venezuela	1990	20.7	1997	20.6

[a]GDP source: UNDESA, based on national statistical information
[b]1997 value based on estimated GDP figures
[c]Budgetary Central Government expenditures
[d]Fiscal year ending March, GDP accordingly adjusted
[e]Fiscal year ending June for 1990 figure, and December for 1997 figure, GDP adj.

SOURCE: United Nations Online Network in Public Administration and Finance (UNPAN), UNPAN Statistical Database, *International Statistical Databases & the World Reports,* 2007, Basic Data on Government Expenditure and Taxation (1990–2002), Appendix Table 2.

Table 3

Latin America, public policies have failed to eradicate endemic poverty and inequality. As a consequence, in 1989, according to World Bank statistics, 131 million people, or 31 percent of Latin America's population, lived in poverty, with incomes of less than $60 per month.

After the Great Depression, Latin American governments implemented a radical shift in public policy goals. As a result, the size of the public sector and of government involvement (participation) in economic affairs increased. The governments' immediate goal was restoration of income and employment to pre-Depression levels, with parallel goals of economic development, full employment, balance-of-payments equilibrium, and economic independence. Argentina, Brazil, Chile, Colombia, Cuba, Jamaica, Mexico, Peru, Nicaragua, Venezuela, and other countries transformed the nature of collective services produced by public administration and defense (i.e., the mesoeconomics of government) by increasing the direct use of nonfinancial state enterprises and public financial institutions in carrying out public policy; at the same time, they initiated an unparalleled increase in government intervention in production, exchange, and distribution.

Public Production of Individual Commodities. The component of collective services promoting the role of the state as lender to and owner, operator, and manager of enterprises increased, often sharply. The public sector grew, in many countries spectacularly, as the state expanded its direct involvement in the production of individual commodities beyond public utilities, railroads, and revenue-generating monopolies, into agriculture, industry, mining, communications, banking, commerce, and health. Nonfinancial public enterprises emerged not only in industry, mining, and construction, but also in agriculture, forestry, fishing, transport, communications (newspapers, magazines, radio, TV stations), wholesale and retail trade, hotels, restaurants, real estate, and business services.

Governments established public enterprises to pursue a multiplicity of policy goals. Expulsion of foreign capitalists from Chile under Salvador Allende, from Cuba under Fidel Castro, and from Nicaragua under the Sandinistas, aimed at wresting sectors, even economies, from actual or perceived foreign control. Land reform, including expropriation of large estates, and widespread nationalization of banks, mines, factories, newspapers, radio stations, and other large-scale private enterprises aimed at severing the national, private elites from their economic base and creating a new, sometimes Marxist, political, social, and economic order. State ownership and control of enterprises was also motivated by the desire to save jobs, stem capital outflow, rescue failing firms, and increase saving, or was simply accidental.

A further change in the nature of the public sector materialized after 1930 as governments increasingly relied on public financial institutions to finance the budget deficits of the nonfinancial public sector, that is, of general government and state-owned enterprises. From 1930 to 1980 financial institutions, especially central banks, in Argentina, Brazil, Bolivia, Mexico, Peru, Nicaragua, Uruguay, Venezuela, and elsewhere were assigned the role of transferring enough resources from the private sector to cover the deficits of the public nonfinancial sector. Shortages of domestic and foreign savings forced central banks to print money to finance skyrocketing deficits. The ensuing galloping inflation, which, according to the Economic Commission for Latin America and the Caribbean, reached an annual rate of 1,185.2 percent in 1990 and 416.8 percent in 1992, caused profound political, social, and economic damage and chaos. In an attempt to control destructive hyperinflation, beginning with Chile in the 1970s, most governments reassigned to financial authorities, in particular the central bank, the role of maintaining price stability and a sound, private financial system. Central banks were even constitutionally prohibited, as in Chile, from printing money to cover public sector deficits. By 1995 aggressive control of inflation was evident.

Increased Regulation. In pursuing their public policy goals, Latin American governments also increasingly relied on pervasive regulation and interventionist institutions. During the 1950s and 1960s, the complex web of rent, food, fuel, foreign exchange, interest, credit, and other price controls and regulations coincided with accelerated growth. By the 1970s and 1980s, however, the picture had changed. The implicit taxes associated with these controls had discouraged production, trade, and formal activities. The implicit subsidies established by these controls had created entitlements that the privileged public sector employees, the urban middle classes, and organized labor refused to give up. Efforts to establish a level playing field through deregulation, liberalization, and privatization were largely successful in Chile and Argentina but encountered stiff resistance in Venezuela, Brazil, and Ecuador.

The size of the public sector increased between 1930 and 1990, whether measured in terms of the magnitude of its expenditures or revenues. Its formidable size and growth from 1970 to 1985 is revealed by the time series statistics of spending by the consolidated nonfinancial public sector as a percentage of gross domestic product (GDP) in Argentina, Brazil, Chile, Peru, and Venezuela (see table). The nonfinancial public sector was also very large in Cuba, the Dominican Republic, Nicaragua, Uruguay, and elsewhere. The total public sector, which includes the public financial institutions, was even larger.

As the size of the public sector increased almost continuously between 1930 and 1990, the aggregate deficit of the public sector also reached, in some periods and countries, unprecedented levels. The nominal deficits of the nonfinancial public sector rose (to, for example, 83 percent of GDP in Brazil in 1989) because its expenditures, including those on interest due to rising public debt, were flexible upward but rigid downward, and generally significantly higher than its unstable, even declining, current revenues. The nominal deficits of the financial public sector also increased, as a result of numerous fiscal expenditures, such as the assumption of private debt, that these institutions, in particular the central banks, had to take upon themselves.

For the most part, the public sector revenues structure has remained highly inflexible and regressive since 1930. General government revenues, which consisted primarily of regressive indirect taxes and social security contributions, and only marginally of progressive income taxes, were adversely affected by rampant tax evasion, accelerating inflation, capital flight, and informalization of economies. Sales, the primary revenue of state enterprises, suffered as price controls turned these enterprises into distributors of implicit consumer subsidies. Finally, heavy dependence on revenues from internal and external borrowing increased expenditures on interest and the debt burden of all segments of the public sector. It also contributed to inflation by forcing central banks to print money and, ultimately, precipitated the widespread suspension of debt payments in the 1980s. The fundamental collective need for safety, security, and protection of private property was neither sufficiently appreciated nor adequately satisfied by the majority of Latin American governments.

With the exception of oil-exporting countries, indirect taxes have been the primary source of central and general government revenues since 1930. Within the indirect tax category, production and

Central government tax revenue as percentage of GDP, 1990 and 1997

Latin America & Caribbean	year 1	year 2	Total tax revenue		Trade taxes		Sales and VAT		Social Security		Income & wealth		Other taxes	
			1990	1997	1990	1997	1990	1997	1990	1997	1990	1997	1990	1997
Argentina	1990	1996	9.37	11.05	1.48	0.78	2.06	4.69	4.53	3.57	0.77	1.98	0.53	0.03
Bahamas	1990	1993	14.63	17.02	10.57	11.11	2.08	2.18	0.00	0.00	0.63	0.70	1.34	3.04
Belize[b, c, d]	1991	1997	20.67	20.23	12.67	7.17	2.25	8.15	0.00	0.00	5.31	4.33	0.44	0.58
Bolivia	1990	1997	8.60	15.98	0.94	1.15	4.30	8.95	1.20	3.18	1.68	2.65	0.49	0.05
Brazil	1990	1994	19.11	20.12	0.48	0.52	5.54	6.57	8.41	9.38	4.69	3.65	0.00	0.00
Chile	1990	1997	16.26	18.94	2.41	1.87	8.95	10.45	1.73	1.39	2.57	4.03	0.60	1.20
Colombia	1990	1994	10.24	13.63	2.51	1.40	3.84	6.65	0.00	0.00	3.73	5.57	0.17	0.02
Costa Rica	1990	1996	20.81	23.12	5.30	2.22	6.29	10.51	6.62	7.14	2.40	2.84	0.20	0.40
Dominican Republic	1990	1996	10.84	13.88	4.86	5.55	2.71	5.09	0.54	0.62	2.67	2.58	0.06	0.03
Ecuador	1990	1994	17.80	13.87	2.41	1.77	3.94	4.05	0.00	0.00	11.36	8.05	0.09	0.04
El Salvador[c]	1990	1997	8.90	10.51	2.00	1.34	4.16	6.03	0.00	0.00	2.62	3.10	0.12	0.04
Grenada[c]	1991	1995	23.05	23.08	6.22	4.61	11.67	11.43	0.00	0.00	4.69	6.38	0.46	0.66
Guatemala[c]	1990	1997	6.87	8.69	1.54	1.42	3.31	4.97	0.00	0.00	1.61	2.14	0.40	0.16
Mexico	1990	1996	17.72	15.64	1.03	0.59	9.25	8.73	2.19	1.93	5.05	4.08	0.20	0.32
Netherlands Antilles[a]	1990	1995	10.78	7.62	3.44	4.26	3.20	2.84	3.64	0.00	0.19	0.39	0.31	0.14
Nicaragua	1990	1995	2.93	23.88	0.62	5.31	1.16	10.89	0.30	3.30	0.70	2.81	0.14	1.56
Panama (exc. Canal Zone)	1990	1994	17.72	17.96	3.07	2.71	4.38	4.37	5.11	5.53	4.85	4.88	0.31	0.47
Paraguay	1990	1993	9.17	9.08	2.46	1.75	2.60	5.03	0.11	0.16	2.21	2.00	1.78	0.13
Peru	1990	1997	10.49	14.83	1.77	1.35	5.34	7.79	0.78	1.94	1.35	3.29	1.24	0.46
St. Kitts-Nevis-Anguilla	1990	1994	22.52	23.57	12.58	11.21	1.48	3.32	2.85	3.25	5.12	4.81	0.48	0.98
St. Lucia[a, d]	1990	—	27.72		8.74		10.56		0.00	—	7.87		0.55	
St. Vincent and the Grenadines	1991	1997	25.03	28.16	11.99	13.32	3.05	3.78	1.52	1.83	7.77	7.81	0.70	1.42
Trinidad and Tobago	1993	1995	24.00	23.34	2.57	1.56	8.63	7.13	0.74	0.57	11.93	13.91	0.14	0.18
Uruguay	1990	1997	24.20	26.84	2.60	1.15	9.53	10.35	7.30	7.99	3.19	5.56	1.59	1.79
Venezuela	1990	1997	18.41	18.34	1.61	1.61	0.75	7.16	0.89	0.37	15.16	9.20	0.00	0.00

[a]GDP source: UNDESA, based on national statistical information
[b]1997 value based on estimated GDP figures
[c]Budgetary Central Government expenditures
[d]Fiscal year ending March, GDP accordingly adjusted

SOURCE: United Nations Online Network in Public Administration and Finance (UNPAN), UNPAN Statistical Database, *International Statistical Databases & the World Reports, 2007*. Basic Data on Government Expenditure and Taxation (1990–2002), Appendix Table 3.

Table 4

sales taxes, which include all general sales, value added, and turnover taxes, and all other taxes and duties levied on the production, extraction, sale, leasing, and delivery of goods and rendering of services were the main sources of central government revenues (again, except in oil-exporting countries). During prolonged periods, indirect taxes contributed more than two-thirds of central government current revenues in the Bahamas, Bolivia, Costa Rica, El Salvador, Guatemala, Haiti, and Honduras. In much of Latin America, within the indirect tax category international trade taxes—which include all taxes on international trade and commercial transactions in the form of both specific and ad valorem import and export duties raised for purposes of revenue mobilization and for protectionism—have been the second-most important source of central government current revenues.

Nontax revenues, which have comprised noncompulsory current revenues arising from government ownership of property, enterprises, financial assets, land, and intangible holdings, in the form of dividends, interest, rents, royalties, and entrepreneurial income, have been an important source of central or general government current revenues since 1930 in Argentina, Chile, the Dominican Republic, Haiti, Mexico, Panama, Paraguay, Suriname, and Venezuela.

AFTER THE 1970s: REDUCTIONS IN THE PUBLIC SECTOR AND LIBERAL TRANSFORMATION OF COLLECTIVE MARKETS

Since the 1970s governments in Argentina, Brazil, Chile, Jamaica, Mexico, Peru, and elsewhere have once again drastically transformed their public administration and defense. The component of collective services promoting the role of the state as lender to and owner, operator, manager, and controller of enterprises was sharply curtailed. Increasingly, most governments recognized and tried to satisfy the collective needs of their populations, though often failing to ensure political freedom. The public sector shrank, especially in the 1990s, as state-owned enterprises in agriculture, industry, telecommunications, newspapers, and transportation (railroads, airlines) were privatized, often at unprecedented speed. Government regulation also was drastically curtailed. The component of collective services facilitating private enterprise; free, competitive, and efficient markets;

overall price stability; and free trade was increased drastically. This phenomenal withdrawal of governments from ownership and control of enterprises engaged in production of individual commodities was motivated by a desire to reduce huge public sector deficits, harness skyrocketing inflation, improve efficiency of production, increase foreign trade, repatriate capital, and, above all, use the limited resources and energies of the state in the production of better and more equitable collective and semipublic services.

Traditional indicators of the economic impact of government include, first, its claim on GDP as measured by general government consumption as a percentage of GDP (see Table 2) or by central government expenditure as a percentage of GDP (see Table 3). General government consumption has ranged between a low of 2.9 (Dominican Republic, 1990, domestic prices) and a high of 33.9 (Nicaragua, 1990, purchasing power parity [PPP] prices, which take into account differences in price levels among countries) (see Table 2). Central government expenditure as a percentage of GDP ranges between 7.2 (Nicaragua, 1990) and 42.7 (Saint Vincent and the Grenadines, 1990) (see Table 3). The second indicator is the amount of taxes collected by different levels of government. As shown in Table 4, central government tax revenues as a percentage of GDP ranged between a low 2.93 (Nicaragua, 1990) and a high 27.72 (St. Lucia, 1990). The third and fourth indicators of government impact on the economy are regulation and state ownership of corporations. These have greatly varied over time among Latin American countries.

To achieve price stability and satisfy the collective need for safety, security and protection of private property, governments increasingly offered constitutional guarantees for the institutional independence of central banks. Furthermore, since 1980 production by general government, through collective markets, of the collective services satisfying the collective needs for economic freedom, social harmony, and environmental protection also has significantly increased. It remains to be seen, however, whether Latin American governments can, on a long-term basis, achieve sustainable democracy and economic growth. Venezuela under President Hugo Chavez and Bolivia under

President Evo Morales have been subjected to significant curtailments of political and economic freedoms, suggesting that great difficulties lie ahead in turning the Latin American economic failure into a success through the establishment of both sustainable democracy and economic growth. The public sector must become both smaller and much more efficient if the policy goals of sustained development and improved distribution are to be achieved. In the face of persistent poverty and inequality, the need for a leaner and better public sector grows ever more urgent.

See also **Economic Development; Income Distribution; Privatization; Public Health; Service Sector.**

BIBLIOGRAPHY

Góngora, Mario *Ensayo histórico sobre de noción de estado en Chile en los siglos XIX y XX.* Santiago: Eds. la Ciudad, 1981.

Inter-American Development Bank. *Economic and Social Progress in Latin America.* Annual reports.

International Monetary Fund. *Government Finance Statistics Yearbook.* Annual reports.

International Monetary Fund. *A Manual on Government Finance Statistics.* 1986.

Larraín, Felipe, and Marcelo Selowsky, eds. *The Public Sector and the Latin American Crisis.* San Francisco: ICS Press, 1991.

Latin America and the Caribbean: Selected Economic and Social Data. Washington, DC: United States Agency for International Development, (USAID), Bureau for Latin America and the Caribbean, 20523. September 2006.

Mamalakis, Marko J. "Public Policy and Sectoral Development: A Case Study of Chile, 1940–1958." In *Essays on the Chilean Economy* (1965), edited by Markos J. Mamalakis and Clark Winton Reynolds, pp. 3–200.

Mamalakis, Markos J. "The Notion of the State in Chile: Six Topics." *Historia* 22 (1987): 107–115.

Mamalakis, Markos J., comp. *Historical Statistics of Chile: Government Services and Public Sector and a Theory of Services.* Vol. 6. Westport, CT: Greenwood Press, 1989.

Mamalakis, Markos J. "Las reglas doradas." *Diario Financiero, Supplemento Anniversario 16 años,* Santiago, Chile, Monday, 29 November 2004, p. 133. Reprinted in Spanish and also published in English as "Sustainable Democracy and the Golden Rules." *Global Currents* 1, no. 2 (2005): pp.18–19.

Mamalakis, Markos J. "Social Justice in a Global Environment: A Theory of Natural Law and Social Justice." In *The Quest for Social Justice III: The Morris Fromkin Memorial Lectures 1992–2002,* edited by Peter G. Watson-Boone, pp. 227–304. Milwaukee, Wisconsin: University of Wisconsin–Milwaukee, 2005. A detailed examination of the role collective needs, outputs and markets in determining poverty, inequality, civil society, procedural as well as sustainable democracy and growth in Latin America.

Mesa-Lago, Carmelo. "Social Security in Latin America Pension and Health Care Reforms in the Last Quarter Century." *Latin American Research Review* 42, no. 2 (2007): 181–201.

Ramos, Joseph. *Neoconservative Economics in the Southern Cone of Latin America, 1973–1983.* Baltimore: Johns Hopkins University Press, 1986.

Saulniers, Alfred H. *Public Enterprises in Peru: Public Sector Growth and Reform.* Boulder, CO: Westview Press, 1988.

United Nations Commission for Latin America and Caribbean (ECLAC). *Statistical Yearbook for Latin America and the Caribbean.* 2006.

United Nations, Economic Commission for Latin America and the Caribbean. *Public Finances in Latin America in the 1980s.* 1992, pp. 1–96.

United Nations. *Classification of the Functions of Government.* 1980.

World Bank. *World Development Report 1988: Opportunities and Risks in Managing the World Economy, Public Finance Development, World Development Indicators.* 1988.

MARKOS J. MAMALAKIS

PUCARÁ. Pucará, a central Andean archaeological culture and style, named after a site in the department of Puno, Peru. Pucará sites are concentrated in the northern Lake Titicaca Basin of southern Peru, but Pucará contact or influence extends as far north as Cuzco, to the west in the coastal Moquegua Valley, and to the southwest in the area of Tiwanaku, Bolivia. Radiocarbon dates center between 100 BCE and 100 CE, and stylistically Pucará appears contemporary with early Nasca on the coast.

Pucará, the largest site and the religious center of a powerful polity, covering about 371 acres, is situated at 12,800 feet and overlooks the Pucará River, which flows into Lake Titicaca some fifty miles to the southeast. At the base of a huge cliff are monumental stone-faced terraces on which at least six temples were built. On the plain below are mounds and a large, low, public platform, with adjoining rooms, where about 100 human skull fragments were concentrated.

The U-shaped temples, oriented east facing the river, consist of adjoining rooms of finely-cut stone blocks around a square, slab-lined sunken court. The rooms have internal compartments, likely used for storage, and the court has a grave chamber in the center of each wall. While some have argued Pucará was a city, habitation areas within the site remain unclear, and much of the refuse may be explained as the result of periodic pilgrimage.

Herding of llama and alpaca, hunting of deer and birds, fishing, and use of dogs and guinea pigs were complemented by agriculture, probably involving local grains and tubers such as quinoa and potato, respectively. Raised fields intensified production on lake margins, while *qocha* (artificial depressions containing raised fields) were perhaps used inland.

The Pucará pottery style represents a standardized, explicit expression of a powerful religion manipulated by an elite at a major production center, but it is not yet known whether the Pucará polity was a state. Pucará continues many aspects of the Yaya Mama Religious Tradition (c. 600–100 BCE), including details of the temple- storage architectural complexes (including the use of the double jamb with double stepfret that persisted into Tiwanku and Inca times), sculpture, trumpets, and aspects of iconography (felines, frogs and toads, serpents, checkered crosses, rings, heads with rayed appendages, divided eyes, and "tear" bands). The earlier complex at Chiripá, or others like it, served as a direct model for those at Pucará; little is known of the earlier temple at Pucará. Pucará was suddenly abandoned and power in the basin shifted to Tiwanaku (400–1000 CE). Although the Tiwanaku corporate style, and that of the Huari state in Peru (600–800 CE) influenced by Tiwanaku, draws heavily and specifically on the crystallized Pucará religious iconography, it is still unclear how that process occurred, especially since a substantial Pucará occupation in the southern basin has yet to be documented.

See also **Agriculture.**

BIBLIOGRAPHY

Elías Mujica, "Altiplano-Coast Relationships in the South-Central Andes: From Indirect to Direct Complementarity," in *Andean Ecology and Civilization: An Interdisciplinary Perspective on Andean Ecological Complementarity,* edited by Shozo Masuda, Izumi Shimada, and Craig Morris, pp. 103–140.

Karen L. Mohr Chávez, "The Significance of Chiripa in Lake Titicaca Basin Developments," in *Expedition* 30, no. 3 (1988): 17–26.

Clark L. Erickson, "Raised Field Agriculture in the Lake Titicaca Basin: Putting Ancient Agriculture Back to Work," in *Expedition* 30, no. 3 (1988): 8–16.

Sergio J. Chávez, "The Conventionalized Rules in Pucará Pottery Technology and Iconography: The Nature of Pucará Pottery in the Northern Lake Titicaca Basin" (Ph.D. diss., Michigan State University, 1992).

Additional Bibliography

Isbell, William H., and and Helaine Silverman, eds. *Andean Archaeology.* 2 v. New York: Kluwer Academic/Plenum Publishers, 2002-

Stanish, Charles. *Ancient Titicaca: The Evolution of Complex Society in Southern Peru and Northern Bolivia.* Berkeley: University of California Press, 2003.

Young-Sánchez, Margaret, ed. *Tiwanaku: Ancestors of the Inca.* Denver: Denver Art Museum; Lincoln: University of Nebraska Press, 2004.

KAREN L. MOHR CHÁVEZ

PUEBLA, BATTLE AND SIEGE OF.

Battle and Siege of Puebla, military disaster of the French Intervention (1862–1867) that took place at Puebla, Mexico's second city. This 5 May 1862 defeat delayed the French capture of Mexico City by one year. Brigadier General Charles Latrille, comte de Lorencez, advanced inland from the city of Veracruz with 4,000 men in late April 1862. At the fort of Cerro de Guadalupe, above the city of Puebla, General Ignacio Zaragoza with 6,000 men defeated the French, inflicting heavy losses. Lorencez withdrew to Orizaba, Veracruz. Napoleon III sent General Élie-Frédéric Forey, veteran of the Crimean and Italian campaigns, to avenge the defeat. With 30,000 veteran French troops, Forey established his headquarters at Amozoc and on 9 March 1863 opened the siege of Puebla in conjunction with Marshall François Bazaine. Trenches around the city prevented relief or escape. Artillery battered the Guadalupe and Loreto forts. General Jesús González Ortega surrendered on 17 May 1863. Forey took over 17,000 prisoners and 150 pieces of artillery.

Although González Ortega escaped, the French captured generals Mariano Escobedo and Porfirio Díaz. Officers were sent to France or Martinique for internment. Nearly 6,000 men joined the division led by Conservative General Leonardo Márquez, a leading supporter of the empire. The rest were mainly put to work on the construction of the Veracruz railroad. Forey entered Puebla on 19 May 1863.

The fifth of May is celebrated throughout Mexico as one of the principal national days—along with 16 September (Independence Day) and 20 November (outbreak of the 1910 Revolution).

See also **Cinco de Mayo; Maximilian; Railroads.**

BIBLIOGRAPHY

Jack Autry Dabbs, *The French Army in Mexico, 1861–1867* (1963).

Additional Bibliography

Cabello-Argandoña, Roberto, and Luis A Torres. *Cinco de Mayo: A Symbol of Mexican Resistance.* Encino, CA: Floricanto Press, 1992.

García Cantú, Gastón. *La intervención francesa en México.* México: Clío, 1998.

Hamnett, Brian R. *Juárez.* New York: Longman, 1994.

Ridley, Jasper Godwin. *Maximilian and Juárez.* New York: Ticknor & Fields, 1992.

BRIAN HAMNETT

PUEBLA (CITY).

Puebla (City), the capital city of the Mexican state of the same name. With a population of 1,271,673 (2000), it is situated in a large, volcano-rimmed valley at an altitude of 7,096 feet, 80 miles southeast of Mexico City. The climate is mild, with distinct rainy (May–October) and dry seasons.

Founded on 16 April 1531 as Puebla de los Ángeles by the Spaniards, the city remained the second largest commercial and population center in Mexico until the twentieth century. Although the city has experienced numerous strong earthquakes, many original colonial era structures survive, especially in the city's historic center, which was designated a UNESCO World Heritage Site in 1987. Puebla's Cathedral of the Immaculate Conception is one of the country's largest and most renowned churches. With its colonial architecture and many churches and museums, Puebla attracts large numbers of tourists.

Puebla has played an important historical role in Mexico. As the principal city between the national capital and the key port of Veracruz, it has been the target of many domestic and foreign armies bent on control of the nation. U.S. General Winfield Scott held the city in 1847, during the Mexican–American War. Mexican forces under General Ignacio Zaragoza defeated the invading French army at Puebla on 5 May 1862, thus establishing the Cinco De Mayo holiday and gaining for Puebla a new official name, Puebla de Zaragoza.

With the establishment of textile manufacturing in the early nineteenth century, Puebla became one of Mexico's earliest industrial areas. Although now the country's fourth largest city, Puebla is still a major business and industrial center known for its cotton and woolen goods, automobiles, steel, chemicals, pharmaceuticals, food processing, onyx, pottery, tiles, candies, and leather goods. The state government apparatus and the seat of the archdiocese are located there. The city has several institutions of higher learning, including one of Mexico's principal state universities, the Universidad Autónoma de Puebla. It is also home to various cultural institutions, such as the Regional Museum of Puebla State, the Museum of Religious Art (housed in the Santa Monica convent, built in the seventeenth century), and the José Luis Bello y González Art Museum.

Despite its proximity to Mexico City and its rapidly growing population, Puebla remains a politically and socially conservative city. The Catholic church and old-line Spanish and Lebanese commercial and industrial interests wield a great deal of influence. Familial and long-time personal connections continue to be the principal entrées to society. In recent years the major conservative party, the Partido de Acción Nacional (National Action Party—PAN) has enjoyed substantial backing.

See also **Mexico, Political Parties: National Action Party (PAN); Mexico, Wars and Revolutions: Mexican-American War; Puebla, Battle and Siege of; Puebla (State).**

BIBLIOGRAPHY

Antonio Carrión, *Historia de la ciudad de Puebla de los Ángeles,* 2 vols. Puebla, Mexico: Editorial J. M. Cajica, Jr., (1897; 1970).

Carlos Contreras Cruz, comp., *Espacio y perfiles: Historia regional mexicana del siglo XIX.* Puebla, Mexico:

Universidad Autónoma de Puebla, Instituto de Ciencias, Centro de Investigaciónes Historicas y Sociales, 1989.

Centro De Investigaciones Históricas y Sociales, Instituto De Ciencias De La Universidad Autónoma De Puebla, *Puebla en el siglo XIX: Contribución al estudio de su historia*.1983 and *Puebla en la colonia a la revolución: Estudio de historia regional* (1987).

Guy P. C. Thomson, *Puebla de los Ángeles: Industry and Society in a Mexican City, 1700–1850*. Boulder, CO: Westview Press, 1989.

Reinhard Liehr, *Ayuntamiento y oligarquía en Puebla, 1787–1810*, 2 vols. Mexico: Secretaría de educación pública, (1976).

Additional Bibliography

Altman, Ida.*Transatlantic Ties in the Spanish Empire: Brihuega, Spain and Puebla, Mexico, 1560–1620*. Stanford, CA: Stanford University Press, 2000.

Henderson, Timothy J. *The Worm in the Wheat: Rosalie Evans and the Agrarian Struggle in the Puebla-Tlaxcala Valley of Mexico, 1906–1927*. Durham, NC: Duke University Press, 1988.

LaFrance, David G. *Revolution in Mexico's Heartland: Politics, War, and State Building in Puebla, 1913–1920*. Wilmington, DE: SR Books, 2003.

Thomson, Guy P. C. *Patriotism, Politics, and Popular Liberalism in Nineteenth-Century Mexico: Juan Francisco Lucas and the Puebla Sierra*. Wilmington, DE: Scholarly Resources, 1999.

Vaughan, Mary Kay. *Cultural Politics in Revolution: Teachers, Peasants, and Schools in Mexico, 1930–1940*. Tucson: University of Arizona Press, 1997.

DAVID G. LAFRANCE

PUEBLA (STATE).

PUEBLA (STATE). Located on the central plateau southeast of Mexico City, Puebla covers 13,096 square miles and contains 5,076,686 (2000) inhabitants. It has a generally mild climate with distinct rainy (May to October) and dry seasons.

Puebla is divided into three major regions. The Sierra (northern region) consists of a high plateau and mountains. It is the most isolated area of the state and contains the highest percentage of indigenous peoples. Its largest city is Teziutlán. The central region, ringed by four volcanoes, all with elevations over 14,600 feet, consists of rolling plains that are cut by low, rugged mountains. It is the most industrialized region, and its population is the largest, densist, and most urbanized. It includes the capital and largest city, Puebla City. The southern region, with an average altitude under 6,000 feet, is characterized by dry mountains and verdant river valleys. Its two most important cities are Tehuacán and Atlixco.

What is today called the state of Puebla has always played an important role in Mexican history. The Tehuacán Valley, for example, is the site of some of the oldest peoples in Mesoamerica. Cholula was one of the principal religious centers of pre-Columbian civilization. With the establishment of the Aztec Empire in the fifteenth century, the area assumed a strategic location between the Aztec capital, Tenochtitlán (now Mexico City), and southeastern Mexico. This pattern continued after the Spanish conquest in the early sixteenth century, as Puebla straddled the main routes between Mexico City and the major port, Veracruz, on the Gulf of Mexico.

The state has always been important economically. The production of coffee, fruit, and lumber in the north, cereals in the center, and sugarcane in the south, as well as livestock in all three regions, have been significant. Hydroelectric generation in the north, at times, has supplied much of central Mexico with energy. A cotton and woolen textile industry, the nation's earliest and largest, began in the 1830s. Other nineteenth-century economic activities, including the manufacture of tobacco products and craftwork such as pottery, were subsequently complemented in the twentieth century by processed foodstuffs, steel, pharmaceuticals, chemicals, and automobiles. Puebla City was the second largest population and commercial center in Mexico from its founding in 1532 until the twentieth century.

The state of Puebla, formed at the time of Mexican independence from Spain (1821), was created out of the much larger colonial viceregal intendancy of Puebla. Like much of Mexico, the political factionalism of the nineteenth century affected Puebla. Dominated by the proclerical and traditional Puebla City–Cholula area, the state, except for parts of the Sierra, generally sided with the Conservatives against the Liberals.

Because of its strategic and economic importance, then, competing domestic factions vied for control of Puebla from Independence through the regime of Porfirio Díaz (1876–1880; 1884–1911). Foreigners, too, realized the importance of the state; the U.S. army occupied portions of it during the Mexican War (1846–1848), and the French military did the same during the French Intervention (1862–1867).

Following the relative stability of the Porfiriato, factionalism and violence again dominated the state's politics during the 1910s and 1920s as a result of the Mexican Revolution of 1910. Since the 1930s, Puebla has been under the aegis of the official party, which, through the brokerage of powerful families such as the Avila Camachos of Teziutlán, has been able to mediate the political divisions and modernize the state's economic sector.

See also **Díaz, Porfirio; French Intervention (Mexico); Mexico State; Mexico, Wars and Revolutions: Mexican-American War; Mexico, Wars and Revolutions: Mexican Revolution; Puebla, Battle and Siege of; Puebla (City).**

BIBLIOGRAPHY

Jack A. Licate, *Creation of a Mexican Landscape: Territorial Organization and Settlement in the Eastern Puebla Basin, 1520–1605* (1981).

David G. LaFrance, *The Mexican Revolution in Puebla, 1908–1913: The Maderista Movement and the Failure of Liberal Reform* (1989).

Wil G. Pansters, *Politics and Power in Puebla: The Political History of a Mexican State, 1937–1987* (1990).

Additional Bibliography

Grosso, Juan Carlos, and Juan Carlos Garavaglia. *La región de Puebla y la economía novohispana: Las alcabalas en la Nueva España, 1776–1821.* Puebla, Mexico: Benemérita Universidad Autónoma de Puebla: Instituto de Ciencias Sociales y Humanidades, 1996.

LaFrance, David G. *Revolution in Mexico's Heartland: Politics, War, and State Building in Puebla, 1913–1920.* Wilmington, DE: SR Books, 2003.

Lomelí, Leonardo. *Breve historia de Puebla.* México: Colegio de México, Fideicomiso Historia de las Américas: Fondo de Cultura Económica, 2001.

Pansters, W. G. *Politics and Power in Puebla: The Political History of a Mexican State, 1937–1987.* Amsterdam: CEDLA, 1990.

Tecuanhuey Sandoval, Alicia. *Los conflictos electorales de la elite política en una época revolucionaria, Puebla, 1910–1917.* México: Instituto Nacional de Estudios Históricos de la Revolución Mexicana, 2001.

DAVID LAFRANCE

PUEBLO INDIANS. Pueblo Indians, Native Americans of New Mexico and northern Arizona. The modern Pueblos are descendants of the prehistoric Anasazi, who inhabited the Four Corners area. About 700 CE the Anasazi underwent a complete transition to agriculture and sedentary life, ushering in the Pueblo cultural period, which continues to this day. With the arrival of the Spaniards in New Mexico during the sixteenth century, most of the Pueblo Indians were settled along the Rio Grande and its tributaries. Encountering people of a common culture living in multistoried stone and mud apartments, the Spaniards dubbed these native peoples "Pueblos" (from the Spanish word for village). Although the Spanish crown promulgated laws designed to protect the Pueblos, they were forced to pay tribute and provide personal services for the Spaniards. Spanish abuses, including the efforts of Franciscan missionaries to eliminate native religion, eventually led to a revolt in 1680. In a rare show of unity, the various Pueblo groups threw the Spaniards out of New Mexico. Twelve years later the Spaniards reconquered New Mexico, but rule over the Pueblos was now tempered. After Mexico's independence, the Pueblos of the Southwest were largely neglected by political officials, although in theory they became full citizens of Mexico.

See also **New Mexico.**

BIBLIOGRAPHY

An extensive treatment of Pueblo history and culture may be found in Alfonso Ortiz, ed., *Handbook of North American Indians,* vol. 9, *Southwest* (1979). A general survey is provided by Edward P. Dozier, *The Pueblo Indians of North America* (1983). For an account of the Pueblos' interaction with Europeans and Anglo-Americans, see Edward H. Spicer, *Cycles of Conquest: The Impact of Spain, Mexico, and the United States on the Indians of the Southwest, 1533–1960* (1962). An interesting anthropological study of one group of Pueblos is contained in Alfonso Ortiz, *The Tewa World* (1969).

SUZANNE B. PASZTER

PUEBLO REBELLION. Pueblo Rebellion (1680–1692), the single most significant event in the history of the Spanish colony of New Mexico. Breaking nearly a century of Spanish control, it preserved the religious and cultural autonomy of the Pueblo Indians of New Mexico from Spanish attempts to destroy native lifeways, and entirely reoriented the social relations between the two peoples after the Spanish reconquest.

The Spanish colonial system, established in New Mexico by the early seventeenth century, sought to join a mission system, converting and "civilizing" the Pueblo Indians under the control of the Franciscans, with a secular government under a royal governor. The economic burden of tribute—the labor demanded by the missionaries, *encomenderos,* and Spanish officials—and episodic epidemics reduced the Pueblo population. Severe smallpox epidemics broke out in the Pueblo region in the 1640s and again during the 1660s; starvation often weakened immunity and intensified the effects of disease. During one period of drought (1665–1668), a sizable portion of the population of the Humanas Pueblo starved, and its inhabitants abandoned the pueblo and its surrounding area. However, by the 1660s, there was a gradual resurgence of native ceremony and leaders in opposition to Spanish occupation and Franciscan cultural domination.

The Pueblo Rebellion began 10 August 1680, when Governor Antonio de Otermín's discovery of the plot forced its speedy execution. Spanish officials credit Popé, a Tewa Indian of San Juan Pueblo, with leading the general rebellion, whereas Pueblo tradition identifies leaders in individual pueblos who united the group in revolt. Spanish missionaries and settlers were overwhelmed by the fury of the general uprising; in a few days the combined Pueblo forces had killed 21 of the 32 Franciscans and over 380 Spanish colonists and officials. Governor Otermín and the few hundred remaining settlers fled to Santa Fe, under siege from Pueblo warriors beginning August 15. Six days later, after the Pueblos had cut off their water supply, Otermín and approximately 1,000 refugees fled to present-day El Paso, along with more than 2,000 from the Piro and Tompiro pueblos. Pueblo sources maintain that they deliberately allowed the remaining Spanish to escape with their lives.

News of the success of the Pueblo Rebellion in New Mexico spread quickly to other native groups in Sonora and Nueva Vizcaya. The Suma Indians of the Río de los Janos mission rebelled at the end of August 1680, following news from the north. In 1682, the Opatas of Sonora rebelled; the Sumas rose up in 1684 when Spanish officials discovered a conspiracy among the Mansos and Janos in the El Paso area, people who had suffered displacement because of the refugees from New Mexico.

During the next twelve years, the Pueblo Indians reestablished their religious and cultural traditions. Pueblo witnesses testified later that the victorious people destroyed the churches and virtually all materials of Spanish origin, purified themselves ritualistically from the stain of baptism, and rejoined, according to Pueblo rite, couples whom the missionaries had married.

In 1692 Diego de Vargas led a successful reconquest expedition and reestablished Spanish authority in the area. However, the Franciscans no longer controlled the internal hierarchy of the pueblos, and continued attempts to campaign against the Pueblo religion met with firm resistance from within and general lack of cooperation from provincial officials and settlers. The Pueblos of New Mexico today firmly believe that they owe their survival as a people to the Pueblo Rebellion.

See also **Colonialism; New Mexico; Pueblo Indians; Spanish Empire; Vargas, Diego de.**

BIBLIOGRAPHY

Charles W. Hackett and Charmion C. Shelby, *Revolt of the Pueblo Indians and Otermín's Attempted Reconquest, 1680–1682* (1942).

Joe S. Sando, *Pueblo Nations: Eight Centuries of Pueblo Indian History* (1991).

David J. Weber, *The Spanish Frontier in North America* (1992).

Additional Bibliography

Barrett, Elinore M. *Conquest and Catastrophe: Changing Rio Grande Pueblo Settlement Patterns in the Sixteenth and Seventeenth Centuries.* Albuquerque: University of New Mexico Press, 2002.

Fulsom, Harry. *Los gobernadores y los franciscanos en Nuevo México, 1589–1693.* New Mexico: H. Fulsom, 2004.

Pruecel, Robert W. *Archaeologies of the Pueblo Revolt: Identity, Meaning, and Renewal in the Pueblo World.* Albuquerque: University of New Mexico Press, 2007.

Roberts, David. *The Pueblo Revolt: The Secret Rebellion that Drove the Spaniards out of the Southwest.* New York: Simon & Schuster, 2004.

ROSS H. FRANK

PUEBLOS DE INDIOS. The Pueblos de Indios were the Indian towns established by the Spanish Crown early in the colonial period to protect the native population from exploitation by Spanish and racially mixed colonists. The towns, structured much like those of the Spanish colonial towns, were laid out in a grid pattern with a central square dominated by the church and to a lesser degree the municipal buildings. The Pueblos de Indios were governed by their own town councils, with native *alcaldes* (chief magistrates and administrative officers), law enforcement, and other officials. The Pueblos de Indios served to incorporate the native populations into the Spanish imperial system, but they served also as a means of imperial control. Spanish colonial cities and towns with large Indian populations were required to set aside separate barrios for the Indians, and these too were administered by town councils with the traditional array of officials.

The purity of the system did not last long. From the beginning of the colonization, whites, Indians, and people of African descent mixed racially, and racially mixed spouses and children sometimes resided in the Indian towns. Over decades many of these supposedly segregated towns had become integrated, and in a way that did not always favor the needs and desires of the native population. After independence many countries abolished racial classification, and eventually the Indian towns were no longer racially exclusive habitats. Because of racial mixing, this already had become the norm in many places.

See also **Alcalde; Alcalde Mayor.**

BIBLIOGRAPHY

Kinsbruner, Jay. *The Colonial Spanish-American City: Urban Life in the Age of Atlantic Capitalism.* Austin: University of Texas Press, 2005.

Mörner, Magnus. *La Corona española y los foráneos en los pueblos de indios de América*, 2nd edition. Madrid: Agencia Española de Cooperacíon Internacional, Ediciones de Cultura Hispánica, 1999.

JAY KINSBRUNER

PUENTE, TITO (1923–2000). Ernest Anthony "Tito" Puente was one of the most important bandleaders, arrangers, percussionists, and recording artists (he made more than a hundred albums) in Latin dance music of the twentieth century. Puente was born in New York City to Puerto Rican parents. At an early age he studied ballroom dancing as well as piano and percussion. His earliest professional engagements in Latin popular music date from 1939 to 1942, when he was a member of the Noro Morales and Machito orchestras. After serving in the U.S. Navy during World War II, Puente returned to New York and eventually established his first group, the Picadilly Boys, in 1949. Soon after he became one of the three most important and popular mambo bandleaders in New York. Representative recordings from this period include "Ran Kan Kan" (1949) and "Mambo Diablo" (c. 1951) and the albums *Cuban Carnival* (1956) and *Dance Mania* (1957). His career in the following decades is marked by his influential recording "Oye Como Va" (1962), which was later made famous by Carlos Santana; his first Grammy Award, for *Homenaje a Beny* (1978); and his numerous Latin jazz recordings, which date from the early 1980s until his death in 2000. From the beginning of his career as a bandleader and recording artist, Puente incorporated arranging techniques, including voicings and chord progressions from the jazz big band repertoire, while remaining rooted in the musical aesthetics of Cuban music. Such fusions continue to shape the musical language of Latin jazz, which, as musicians and arrangers working in the genre agree, Puente helped to initiate.

See also **Machito; Mambo; Music: Popular Music and Dance; Samba; Santana, Carlos.**

BIBLIOGRAPHY

Loza, Steven. *Tito Puente and the Making of Latin Music.* Urbana: University of Illinois Press, 1999.

DAVID F. GARCIA

PUENTE UCEDA, LUIS DE LA (?–1965). Luis de la Puente Uceda (*d.* 1965), radical politician in Peru, founder of the Rebel APRa and the Movement of the Revolutionary Left (MIR) in the early 1960s. Puente Uceda, a former student leader, led a group of Aprista dissidents who were disillusioned with the increasingly conservative character of the Populist Party, especially after the establishment in 1962 of a political alliance with the former dictator Manuel A. Odría. In 1965 the MIR launched a seriously flawed armed insurrection in the interior provinces of Cuzco and Junín. Lacking a sound strategy and coordination with other guerrilla movements, such as the Army of National Liberation led by Héctor Béjar, the MIR was defeated and its main leaders, Puente Uceda and Ernesto Lobatón, killed by counterinsurgency forces of the Peruvian military.

See also **Peru, Political Parties: Movement of the Revolutionary Left (MIR); Peru, Political Parties: Peruvian Aprista Party (PAP/APRA).**

BIBLIOGRAPHY

Héctor Béjar, *Peru 1965: Notes on a Guerrilla Experience* (1970).

Daniel Masterson, *Militarism and Politics in Latin America: Peru from Sánchez Cerro to "Sendero Luminoso"* (1991).

Additional Bibliography

Rénique C., José Luis. "De la traición aprista al gesto heroico: Luis de la Puente y la guerrilla del MIR." *Estudios Interdisciplinarios de América Latina y el Caribe* 15:1 (January–June 2004): 89–114.

ALFONSO W. QUIROZ

PUERTO BARRIOS.

Puerto Barrios, seaport of Guatemala. Located on one of the finest deep-water harbors on Central America's Atlantic coast, Puerto Barrios (estimated 2002 population 81,078) was officially founded by the Guatemalan government in 1895 as the northern terminus and principal port for the Northern Railroad project. In 1904, when the Guatemalan Railway Company (owned by United States interests) received the rights to complete the line between Guatemala City and Puerto Barrios, it was also granted ownership of the port's steel pier. The United Fruit Company was the major user and developer of the port during the first half of the twentieth century, during which it became one of the busiest banana ports in Central America. After the inauguration in 1955 of a modern new port at nearby Santo Tomás de Castilla, Puerto Barrios languished, especially after the earthquake of 1976 severely damaged its wharf. The wharf was finally restored to use in 1990 by Cobigua, the Guatemalan banana company, in collaboration with United Brands, or

Chiquita, successor to United Fruit. Puerto Barrios began to show some signs of rejuvenation in the 1990s.

See also **Railroads; United Fruit Company.**

BIBLIOGRAPHY

Wayne F. Anderson, "The Development of Export Transportation in Liberal Guatemala, 1871–1920 (Ph.D. diss., Tulane, 1985), pp. 321–406.

Paul Glassman, *Guatemala Guide,* 4th ed. Dallas: Passport Press, 1990, pp. 260–264.

Additional Bibliography

Chang Sagastume, Germán Rolando. *Guía de historia y geografía del Departamento de Izabal.* Guatemala: s.n., 1995.

Pinto Rodríguez, Lisandro. *Primera monografía de Puerto Barrios, cabecero del Departamento de Izabal.* Ciudad de Puerto Barrios: L. Pinto Rodríguez, 1995.

Pinto Rodríguez, Lisandro. *Tercera monografía del Departamento de Izabal y sus cinco municipios.* Puerto Barrios: s.n., 1997.

DIANE STANLEY

PUERTO HORMIGA.

Puerto Hormiga (modern Puerto Badel) is an archaeological shell midden that gives its name to the earliest pottery tradition found in the Americas. The pottery is characterized by the presence of fiber temper (fibers of grasses mixed with clay) and is distributed in the lowlands of northern Colombia. The Puerto Hormiga site was excavated by Gerardo Reichel Dolmatoff and Alicia Dussan de Reichel in 1961 and 1963. It is located 1,100 feet from a natural channel (Canal del Dique) in the high part of an alluvial terrace. The shell midden had a ring shape with a diameter between 258 and 281 feet and a height of 3.9 feet. The excavated artifacts are mainly fragments of fiber-temper pottery (70 percent); the rest is pottery with a sand temper (30 percent). The lithic material consists predominantly of tools for scraping, grinding, and pounding.

The shell midden is composed of shells from the genera *Pitar* (75 percent) and *Ostrea* (25 percent). The site was directly influenced by the sea; it may have been on the shore of a deep bay or large lagoon formed after a sea-level transgression. The chronology of the site falls between 3100 BCE and 2500 BCE Other sites that form part of this tradition include the shell middens of Bucarelia and Puerto Chacho; the riverine site of El Pozón; and the inland sites of El Bongal, El Guamo, San Jacinto 2, and San Jacinto 1. San Jacinto 1 is currently the oldest and most extensively excavated of these. It dates from between 4000 BCE and 3750 BCE

See also **Archaeology.**

BIBLIOGRAPHY

Gerardo Reichel Dolmatoff, *Arqueología de Colombia* (1986).

John W. Hoopes, "Ford Revisited: A Critical Review of the Chronology and Relationships of the Earliest Ceramic Complexes in the New World, 6000–1500 B.C.," in *Journal of World Prehistory* 8, no. 1 (1994): 1–49.

Additional Bibliography

Langebaek, Carl Henrik, and Alejandro Dever. *Arqueología en el Bajo Magdalena: Un estudio de los primeros agricultores del Caribe colombiano.* Bogotá: Departamento de Antropología, Universidad de los Andes, 2000.

Reichel-Dolmatoff, Gerardo. *Arqueología de Colombia: Un texto introductorio.* 2nd Ed. Bogotá: Magistra Editores: Asesoría Editorial, 1997.

Reichel-Dolmatoff, Gerardo, Augusto Oyuela-Caycedo, and J. Scott Raymond, Eds. *Recent Advances in the Archaeology of the Northern Andes: In Memory of Gerardo Reichel-Dolmatoff.* Los Angeles: Institute of Archaeology, University of California, Los Angeles, 1998.

AUGUSTO OYUELA-CAYCEDO

PUERTO PRESIDENTE STROESS-NER. *See* **Ciudad del Este.**

PUERTO RICO.

Puerto Rico, the smallest island of the Greater Antilles, has an area of 3,435 square miles and a 2007 population of 3,944,259. Christopher Columbus landed on Puerto Rico on November 19, 1493, claimed the island for Spain, and named it San Juan Bautista. At that time, the island had a population of approximately 30,000 Tainos, the last of several Native American cultures, who had begun living on the island in the first century CE. The Tainos called the island *Boriquén,* "land of the brave lord," and this word and others of the Taino language survive in the idiomatic expressions used in Puerto Rico.

SPANISH RULE

Juan Ponce De León led colonization of the island in 1508, arriving with forty-two settlers and founding the town of Caparra, near the site of present-day San Juan. Dissension soon arose over control of the island, and in 1511 the Consejo de Castilla, the highest court in Spain, granted Diego Columbus the right to govern the colony. Until 1536, when he sold his rights to the Crown, he controlled appointments to and administration of the island. The policies assigning native labor to colonists coupled with European diseases, rebellions, and desertions led to a decimation of the Taino population. From 1545 to 1581 the Crown named civilians as governors of the island but in 1582 elevated the island to a captaincy, administered by a captain-general.

Spain's rivals, angered by the Treaty of Tordesillas (1494) and desiring the wealth found in the New World, coveted the colony as a gateway to Spain's empire. The French, English, and Dutch began military and economic incursions, attempting to break the Spanish trade monopoly. With the wealth found on the mainland, Spain gave meager attention to Puerto Rico, and between 1595 and 1625 San Juan suffered attacks from privateers. Although the residents repelled an attack by the forces of Francis Drake in 1595, the city was occupied and burned by George Clifford, third Earl of Cumberland, in 1598, and again by the Dutch under Boudewün Hendrickszoon in 1625. After the Clifford attack, defenses for the city of San Juan were strengthened, though not adequately, and after the Dutch siege, the crown ordered construction of a wall around San Juan. Neither the fortifications nor the wall were completed until the last half of the eighteenth century. The crown ordered payment of a *situado,* a yearly amount to be paid for support of defenses, from New Spain (Mexico) in 1586, and despite its irregular delivery, it became the primary source of income for the colony through the next two centuries.

Early on, the colony depended on gold placer deposits, but these were exhausted by the late

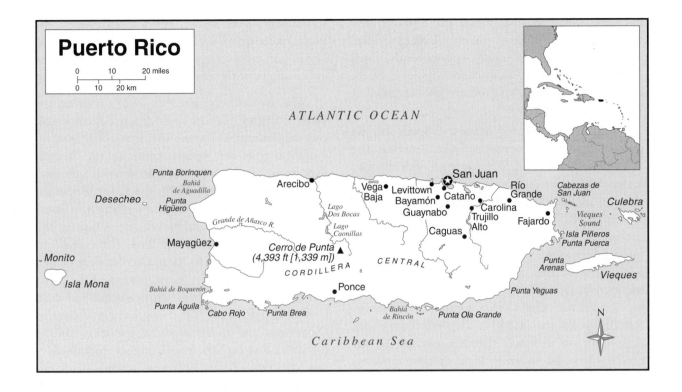

Puerto Rico

0   10   20 miles
0   10   20 km

ATLANTIC OCEAN

Punta Borinquen
Bahía de Aguadilla
Desecheo
Punta Higüero
Arecibo
Vega Baja
Levittown
San Juan
Río Grande
Cabezas de San Juan
Culebra
Bayamón
Cataño
Catano
Carolina
Guaynabo
Trujillo Alto
Fajardo
Vieques Sound
Grande de Añasco R.
Lago Dos Bocas
Caguas
Isla Piñeros
Punta Puerca
Lago Caonillas
Mayagüez
Cerro de Punta
(4,393 ft [1,339 m])
CORDILLERA
CENTRAL
Punta Arenas
Monito
Vieques
Isla Mona
Bahía de Boquerón
Ponce
Punta Yeguas
Punta Águila
Cabo Rojo
Punta Brea
Bahía de Rincón
Punta Ola Grande
N

Caribbean Sea

1530s and the island moved to a subsistence economy. Although sugar was introduced in 1512 and the first mill was in operation by 1523, the meager resources of the residents did not allow for expansive development. Since they could not compete in the global market, planters moved to production of ginger, despite objections by the Crown, and to tobacco and cacao by the seventeenth century. Coffee, introduced in 1736, made a contribution to the island's economy by 1765 but did not reach importance until the nineteenth century.

By the eighteenth century Puerto Rico had a strong agricultural base, but Spain refused to see her as anything but a military outpost. Because of contraband trade, island-based privateers plied her waters and harassed all shipping. The program of reforms under the Bourbon kings after 1700 did not reach Puerto Rico until 1755 when the Crown authorized the Compañía de Barcelona, a trading company created to control the flow of goods between Spain and Puerto Rico. The company existed until 1784 but sent few ships to the island, and its officials abandoned the legal system to join in the lucrative contraband trade.

After the fall of Havana to the British and its return to the Spanish in 1762, Charles III took major steps to centralize his authority, to improve the defenses of the empire, and to enhance profitability. He sent Field Marshal Alejandro O'Reilly to examine the military conditions on Puerto Rico, but, realizing the social conditions inherent to the decay of the military, he reported on all facets of Puerto Rico life. He found, among other things, the need for immediate improvement of defenses and training of soldiers and the pervasiveness of contraband trade. His census showed a total population of 44,883, consisting of 39,846 free persons (white and of color) and 5,037 slaves. He made suggestions to improve the island and efforts began to implement his recommendations. The 1775 census showed settlement projects and slightly improved conditions increased the total population to 70,210 and by 1787 to 103,581. However, the island and her mother country were soon to enter a century of upheaval.

The Haitian revolution of 1792 sent immigrants throughout the Caribbean, though only a few settled in Puerto Rico. Lacking large amounts of capital and with a small slave population, the island was again unable to expand her sugar industry. Spain entered wars against France and then England in the 1790s. Thanks to the improved defenses, San Juan repelled a siege by the British in 1797. Due to disruptions in shipping, the Crown initiated trade with the United States. This trade remained open intermittently until 1819, when it became permanent under a treaty allowing the United States to purchase almost all of Puerto Rico's sugar output.

With the Napoleonic invasion of Spain and the independence movements in Latin America, the face of the island changed. Growing Creole identity fostered a nationalistic movement evident in the election of Ramón Power y Giralt to the Spanish Cortes in 1810 and in the demands presented for the island. Power succeeded in obtaining abrogation of discretionary powers given to the governor, a response to the growing independence movements, and the creation of a separate intendancy for the island. The Cortes appointed Alejandro Ramírez y Blanco in 1811. He found an island dependent on a *situado* that had not arrived for eleven years and suffering from extreme poverty. He revitalized the tax and trade systems and, by the time he departed in 1816, turned the island into a self-sufficient colony. In 1815 Ferdinand VII issued the Real Cédula de Gracias, honoring the improvements in Puerto Rico and liberalizing immigration, taxation, trade, and naturalization laws. Under this decree, the first official representative of the U.S. government, John Warner, arrived in Puerto Rico to regulate trade matters between the island and the United States. U.S. government officials began to talk of the value of the island to their country.

With the independence movements in other parts of Latin America, revolutionaries hounded Spanish shipping, causing severe economic problems for Puerto Rico that were exacerbated by the influx of loyalists escaping the war-torn countries. These immigrants changed the tone of the political situation on the island because their numbers bolstered the conservative faction supporting the status quo. A second faction supported liberal reforms within the Spanish system and a third favored independence.

Many of the reforms and gains earned under Ramírez disappeared with the changes on the island. Unenlightened captains-general, seeing conspiracies in all corners, repressed the population to maintain a forced loyalty to the Crown. Plots for slave revolts were uncovered from 1822 onward and their leaders were executed. To facilitate the administration of justice, the Crown created the Real Audiencia Territorial de Puerto Rico in 1831, but events in Spain continued to intervene in the affairs of the island.

The Cortes, convened in 1837, rewrote the 1812 Constitution, declaring Puerto Rico, Cuba, and the Philippines to be under special laws and no longer eligible for representation in the Spanish Parliament. Revolts in the garrison of San Juan occurred in 1835 and 1838, the latter supported by civilians, both mirroring the sentiment in Spain for a return of the liberal movement. Although the Special Laws were never applied, from 1837 to 1864, the liberal Puerto Rican Creoles were denied a voice in island matters. Governors used the garrison uprisings as an excuse to persecute and exile Creole leaders, especially those vocal members of abolitionist and *independentista* societies. Among these was Ramón Emeterio Betances. Initially fleeing to New York, Betances settled in Santo Domingo to plan an armed revolt for independence. Led by the juntas from Mayagüez and Lares, the rebels, led by Manuel Rojas, took the town of Lares on September 23, 1868, declared the Republic of Puerto Rico, and set up a provisional government. A column then moved toward San Sebastián, where it was defeated with relative ease by the Spanish opposition. The rebels' proclamation, the Grito De Lares, became the symbol for independence of Puerto Rico under both Spanish and United States sovereignty.

The rebellion, coupled with the ongoing war in Cuba, thwarted the hopes and plans of the island's Creoles for many years. As a result, however, the Spanish government authorized the restoration of the *diputación provincial* (a provincial government) in 1870, the same year the first political parties were formed on the island. In 1873 slavery was abolished with little effect on the island.

The liberals working for reform within the Spanish framework then called for autonomous government. In 1887 Román Baldorioty De Castro formed the Autonomist Party. Almost simultaneous with the creation of the party was the founding of an organization to protect Creoles from Spanish reactionary policies. The conservatives and the governor saw these as covert actions for independence and began a regime of torture and persecution known

Puerto Rico

Population:	3,944,259 (2007 est.)
Area:	3,435 sq mi
Language(s):	Spanish, English
National currency:	US dollar (USD)
Principal religions:	Roman Catholic 85%, Protestant and other 15%
Ethnicity:	white (mostly Spanish origin) 80.5%; mixed race and other 10.9%; black 8%: Amerindian 0.4%; Asian 0.2%
Capital:	San Juan (pop. 428,591; 2005 est.)
Other urban centers:	Bayamon, Carolina, Ponce, Caguas
Annual rainfall:	South coast, 32 in; highlands, 108 in; rain forest, 183 in. San Juan's average annual rainfall is 54 in, the rainiest months being May through November.
Principal geographic features:	*Mountains:* Cordillera Central range, includes the island's highest peak, Cerro de Punta (4,389 ft); Luquillo Mountains, including El Yunque (3,496 ft). *Islands:* Vieques, 51 sq mi; Culebra, 24 sq mi; Mona Island (uninhabited),19 sq mi. *Bodies of water:* Rio de la Plata, Dos Bocas (artificial lake), Phosphorescent Bay.
Principal products and exports:	*Agriculture:* sugarcane, coffee, pineapples, plantains, bananas; livestock products, chickens *Industries:* pharmaceuticals, electronics, apparel, food products, tourism
Government:	Became commonwealth of the United States 25 July 1952.
Armed forces:	No local armed forces; defense the responsibility of the United States.
Transportation:	Airports: 29 (2007); 17 with paved runways; railways: 60 mi; roadways: total: 15,991 mi; 15,132 mi paved (includes 265 mi of expressways); ports and terminals: Las Mareas, Mayaguez, San Juan.
Literacy and education:	*Total literacy rate:* 94.1% The main state-supported institution of higher learning is the University of Puerto Rico.

as Los Compontes that struck strongly at the region around Ponce.

Baldorioty died in 1889 and party leadership fell to Luis Muñoz Rivera, who joined in a coalition with the Spanish Liberal Party. Its leader, Práxedes Mateo Sagasta, agreed to grant autonomy when he attained power, which he did in 1897, immediately granting the Autonomic Charter. The charter created a bicameral legislature, elected by secret ballot by an expanded electorate. Headed by a governor-general, who appointed a five-member cabinet, the island moved to form its provincial assembly and elect representatives to the Spanish Parliament. Muñoz Rivera won the election for governor-general and prepared to take office in May 1898. However, on April 21, the Spanish government broke relations with the United States in response to an April 19 recognition by the United States of Cuban independence. On May 12, a U.S. fleet bombarded San Juan for four hours.

On July 17 the autonomous parliament called its first session to order, and on July 24 Luis Muñoz Rivera assumed the post of governor-general. Four days later, acting on information about the anti-Spanish sentiment in Ponce caused by the Compontes, U.S. troops took the city without firing a shot, raised the U.S. flag, and issued a proclamation that they were bringing freedom from Spanish rule. At the peace conference, the U.S. demanded the cession of Puerto Rico; thus, the experiment in autonomous government never really began. On December 10, Puerto Rico passed from the control of Spain to the sovereignty of the United States.

U.S. RULE

The military government installed on the island had no experience in administrative matters and, blinded by anti-Spanish rhetoric in the United States, saw little value in the Puerto Rican people. Some Puerto Ricans agreed that they had little foundation for democracy and needed a period of tutelage, but the new government gave no indication that self-government was in the foreseeable future. Nevertheless, after a two-year campaign for elimination of the military government and citizenship for island residents, the U.S. Congress passed the Foraker Act, establishing a civil government for the island. All officials, from the governor to judges, were to be appointed by the U.S. president. A thirty-five-member Chamber of Deputies and a commissioner to the United States were to be elected directly by the islanders. The U.S.

Congress reserved the right to annul any legislation passed by the Chamber and to legislate for the island. Subsequently installed civil governors were no more enlightened than their military predecessors, and none would call for direct election of the governor until Rexford Tugwell in 1948.

Officials ruling the island understood little about Puerto Rican culture or values. Assuming the imperialistic attitude of American superiority, governors attempted to legislate "americanization" of the residents. For example, they decreed that all education be conducted in English, despite the fact that Spanish was the language of popular choice. After years of dispute, the Puerto Ricans settled the issue in 1991 when they voted Spanish their official language.

Political parties calling for statehood began internal and external campaigns. In 1917, under the Jones Act, Puerto Ricans were granted U.S. citizenship, and in June of the same year island males became eligible for the military draft.

Economically the island benefited little from U.S. administration. A 1900 census showed a total population of 953,243, with a density equal to that of New Jersey. Only 21.4 percent lived in urban centers, while the remainder was rural. Of that rural population, absentee ownership comprised only 7 percent of the total area under cultivation. Most of the sugar plantations were owned by whites, but the coffee industry was more ethnically diversified and family oriented. By 1930 the population stood at 1,869,000, with 70 percent still in agriculture, but 59 percent of the island's wealth was controlled by three absentee sugar corporations. Free incorporation into the U.S. system did not occur immediately, and tariffs were placed on Puerto Rican goods entering the United States, thwarting the desires of many of the Creoles. During the tumultuous period of the 1920s and 1930s, a resurgence of independence support occurred while the worldwide depression dropped per capita income to $86 in 1932. Two major political movements emerged in this period. One, led by Pedro Albizu Campos, called for independence; the other, led by Luis Muñoz Marín, son of Muñoz Rivera, called for reform within the system. Under Albizu Campos, the Nationalist Party adopted violent means, and the tumult came to a head in 1937 when the police opened fire on a Nationalist Party parade in Ponce, killing 21 and wounding over 150, including

spectators. Albizu Campos was tried and convicted for conspiring against the United States, and the party declined with its leader imprisoned. An investigation determined the fault to lie with the governor of the island and with the police who opened fire without provocation.

In 1938 Muñoz Marín founded the Popular Democratic Party (PPD) and assumed control of Puerto Rican politics for the next three decades. Muñoz Marín is seen as a true reformer by some historians and by others as the man who led Puerto Rico firmly into the U.S. fold. He implemented a policy of reform and industrialization that increased per capita income from $121 in 1940 to $900 in 1965. Illiteracy dropped from 41.5 percent to 15.1 percent while college enrollment grew nearly eight times in the same period.

In 1949 Luis Muñoz Marín became the first Puerto Rican governor of the island. In 1950 the U.S. Congress passed Public Law 600. It required a referendum to choose between continuing the status quo or creating a commonwealth government on the British model. The people chose the latter. They elected officials to write, and then voted approval of, a constitution. On approval by the U.S. Congress, Muñoz Marín declared the Estado Libre Asociado (Associated Free State) on July 25, 1952. Relations between the United States and Puerto Rico are governed by the United States–Puerto Rico Federal Relations Act, comprised of three sections of the Jones Act not repealed by P.L. 600. Puerto Rico has full autonomy in internal affairs and shares a common currency, defense, market, and citizenship. In 1953 the General Assembly of the United Nations declared Puerto Rico no longer a dependent territory but in 1972 resolved for Puerto Rico's right to become independent.

Muñoz Marín chose not to seek reelection in 1965, naming his own successor, whose defeat in 1968 was the first PPD defeat in nearly three decades. A referendum in 1967 voted for continuation of commonwealth status, though actions by the *independentistas* to boycott the election resulted in 33.7 percent of the 1,067,349 registered voters abstaining from the election. In the U.S. election campaign of 1988, the Republican candidate George H. W. Bush called for a plebiscite to determine the status of Puerto Rico. To date it has not been held, mainly because of the conditions placed on the various options. Puerto Ricans were given the choice of either continuing the tax and industrial incentives under the status quo, losing all if they chose statehood, or else attempting self-government with independence. While a majority seem to desire some affiliation with the United States, there is an active independence movement on the island. Political consensus has disappeared as leaders after Muñoz Marín have failed to form the necessary coalitions or popular followings. The electorate is affected by personalities and by the economic conditions on the island. There are two main parties that lock horns consistently. Puerto Ricans are torn by U.S. officials pushing for statehood and UN representatives advising independence.

Operation Bootstrap, formed in the 1940s to industrialize the island, was weakened during the 1970s and 1980s. The population grew to over 3.1 million in 1980 and to over 3.5 million by 1990. Federal aid disbursements increased dramatically during this period, partly because of inclusion of Puerto Rico in the food stamp and other assistance programs. Recent island governments adopted programs leaning toward more rather than less federal assistance.

Job programs instituted during World War II promoting Puerto Rican employment in U.S. industries on the mainland as well as other economic factors have led to a mass migration and traffic between Puerto Rico and the United States. Large Puerto Rican populations exist in eastern metropolitan centers, and travel between the two areas is common. Economic difficulties in the United States have further exacerbated the problems of assimilation into mainland society, and some Puerto Ricans have returned to the island.

Although Presidents Ronald Reagan and George H. W. Bush formed commissions to resolve the problems of Puerto Rico, no long-range planning has laid a foundation for development or improvement on the island. Factional interests within the United States debate the Puerto Rico issue as strongly as it is debated on the island. At this point, Puerto Rico's economic future and political status remain unanswered questions. The full impact of the elimination in 1996 of Section 936 of the IRS code that granted tax incentives to U.S. firms operating in Puerto Rico is still to be felt. As of 2001, however, the per capita income of Puerto Ricans living on the island was $11,200, which was about 30 percent of that of the U.S. mainland. Puerto Rico's double-digit unemployment rate is twice that of its North American metropolis.

CULTURE, CULTURAL AFFIRMATION, AND THE QUEST FOR SELF-DETERMINATION

Puerto Rican culture reflects the contributions of the island's Taino, European, and African heritage. The European element stems largely but not exclusively from the Spanish explorers, military men, convicts, and immigrants who put down roots in the Antillean colony at various points after 1493. Newcomers from other Old World origins, most notably from Portugal, France, Italy, and Ireland, also added to the white population of the island, especially after the promulgation of the 1815 Cédula de Gracias. Early on, Iberians were concentrated in a few urban centers, such as San Juan and San Germán, where they enforced Catholicism and its liturgical calendar, communicated in Castilian, experimented with imported European animals and plants, and developed housing, centers of worship, defensive bulwarks, and a communications infrastructure consonant with their Spanish background and imperial objectives. Their attempts to extend this activity to out-of-the-way parts of the island peopled by fugitive Amerindians and Africans, deserters, and religious dissidents had to wait until the urbanizing and commercializing thrust set in motion by the Bourbon reforms.

Following their steep decline, the Amerindians were all but written off the official historical records. However, the listing of about two thousand "indios" as a distinct category in the censuses of the late eighteenth century suggests that some may have survived the Spanish Conquest or that others imported from elsewhere in the Americas remained in the island. Whatever the case may be, nineteenth-century creoles seeking to construct a Puerto Rican nation revived the indigenous legacy. As a result, both *Borinquén* and *Boricua* began to resurface with some frequency in their literary and political projects. For instance, an early 1820s conspiracy called for the creation of a República Boricua. *Borínquen* appears in the subtitle of a novel penned by Ramón Emeterio Betances in 1853. A decade later, "La Borinqueña" became Puerto Rico's national anthem. Numerous Taino/Arawak terms can also be found in the island's cuisine, flora and fauna, music, religion, and folklore and in the names of towns, rivers, mountains, and communities.

Wolofs, Mandingas, Fulas, Fantis, Ashantis, Yorubas, and Congolese, among others, represent the ethnic origins of Africans that became part of Puerto Rican culture. Whether enslaved or free, they filled just about every occupation in the coastal areas, hilly outback, and sea-lanes that connected Puerto Rico to the Atlantic world. Far from passive victims, those who had been brought across the Atlantic in chains asserted their right to be free, as exemplified by the Maroon town of San Mateo de Cangrejos. They partook in the day-to-day forms of resistance that undermined the system of slavery and figured prominently in the abolitionist and revolutionary events that periodically shook the white-controlled colonial society. Various crops (such as plantains and their unique preparations in *mofongos, tostones* and *pasteles*), religions (Santería), dances (*bomba, plena*), and percussion instruments (congas, bongos) reveal the island's unmistakable ties to the African diaspora.

During the five hundred years of colonialism, countless Puerto Rican men and women have sought to carve a niche for themselves or make meaningful contributions to the world around them. The carpenter of Jewish extraction Alonso Ramírez may have been the first Puerto Rican to travel to Asia. The *letrado* Francisco Ayerra y Santa María (1630–1708) distinguished himself as a poet and administrator in Mexico. Popular folklore has immortalized José "Pepe" Díaz, who died heroically during the 1797 British siege of San Juan. The watercolorist, sketcher, and painter José Campeche (1751–1809) stands among the best visual artists of eighteenth-century Latin America. María Mercedes Barbudo and Mariana Bracetti took leading roles in the struggle to gain independence from Spain in the nineteenth century. Schoolchildren in Puerto Rico are reminded of "El Maestro" Rafael Cordero, a humble teacher who plied his trade without pay. The freedom fighter Betances (1827–1898) was also a noted physician with scientific and humanities interests in ophthalmology, public health, botany, agronomy, journalism, history, and literature. The essayist and educator Eugenio María de Hostos (1839–1903) condemned slavery and Spanish colonialism. Antonia Pantoja spearheaded the establishment of several educational programs and community agencies in the mainland United States. The singers Ismael Rivera and Héctor Lavoe helped to popularize Puerto Rican musical rhythms around the globe. The outfielder Roberto Clemente became the first Puerto Rican player inducted into the Baseball Hall of Fame.

History reveals that, whether fashioning a Maroon-like lifestyle in the remote interior, engaging in acts of civil disobedience, crafting their own artistic expressions and organizations, or immersing themselves in protracted electoral politics, Puerto Ricans both on the island and in the United States share the values of nationalism and cultural affirmation. The popular outcry over the U.S. Navy's use of the island municipality of Vieques for live-bombing training—which in April 1999 resulted in the death of a security guard, David Sanes Rodríguez, and the wounding of four civilians—sparked widespread protests. The case even galvanized support for the release of eleven Puerto Rican political prisoners, who were offered clemency in August 1999 and were released the following month. Between 1999 and 2003 key members of all three major political parties, the Catholic Church, college students and faculty, organized labor, and Puerto Ricans in the United States mobilized to stop the naval maneuvers. Another nationalist wave surged in response to the FBI's 2005 killing of Filiberto Ojeda Ríos, leader of the *Macheteros*, or Ejército Popular Boricua.

See also **Taínos; United States-Latin American Relations; Vieques Protests.**

BIBLIOGRAPHY

On pre-Spanish culture see Sven Lovén, *Origins of the Tainan Culture, West Indies* (1979). Good overviews are Arturo Morales Carrión, ed., *Puerto Rico: A Political and Cultural History* (1983), and his *Puerto Rico and the Non-Hispanic Caribbean* (1972). A thorough, but alternative, view from an *independentista* standpoint is Manuel Maldonado-Denis, *Puerto Rico: A Socio-Historic Interpretation* (1972). A good reference work is Federico Ribes Tovar, *A Chronological History of Puerto Rico* (1973). For an overview of the tumult of the nineteenth century, see Lidio Cruz Monclova, *Historia de Puerto Rico en el siglo XIX* (1962). Its effect on the predominant agricultural society is detailed in Fernando Pico, *Cafetal adentro: Una historia de los trabajadores agrícolas en el Puerto Rico del siglo 19* (1986). Fernando Bayrón Toro, *Elecciones y partidos políticos de Puerto Rico 1809–1976* (1988), provides a good overview of the twentieth century. The migration to and from the United States has a growing bibliography, notably National Puerto Rican Forum, *The Next Step Toward Equality: A Comprehensive Study of Puerto Ricans in the United States Mainland* (1980), and Celia Cintrón and Pedro Vales, *A Pilot Study: Return Migration to Puerto Rico* (1974); and Luz M. Torruellas and José L. Vázquez, *Los puertorriqueños que regresaron: Un analisis de su participación laboral* (1984).

Additional Bibliography

Barreto, Amílcar Antonio. *Vieques, the Navy, and Puerto Rican Politics.* Gainesville: University Press of Florida, 2002.

Malavet, Pedro A. *America's Colony: The Political and Cultural Conflict between the United States and Puerto Rico.* New York: New York University Press, 2004.

García Passalacqua, Juan Manuel. *Afirmación nacional: Verdadera historia de los puertorriqueños.* San Juan: Editorial Cultural, 2001.

JACQUELYN BRIGGS KENT
JORGE CHINEA

PUERTO RICO, GEOGRAPHY. Puerto Rico is the easternmost point of the Greater Antilles with an area covering 3,435 square miles. Located to the east of the Dominican Republic, north of Venezuela, and west of the Virgin Islands, its jurisdiction includes the largest island, properly known as Puerto Rico (which is also the smallest of the Greater Antilles); two adjacent islands to the east, Vieques and Culebra; three other islands to the west, Mona, Monito, and Desecheo; and small surrounding islands and keys. Belonging to the Virgin Island chain, Vieques and Culebra are known as the Spanish or Puerto Rican Virgin Islands and are located in close proximity to the U.S. Virgin Islands. The territory is bordered to the south by the Caribbean Sea and to the north by the Atlantic Ocean. Puerto Rico's inhabitants numbered 3,927,776 (2006 est.) with a population density of more than 1,100 people per square mile. More than 4 million Puerto Ricans reside in the mainland United States.

Since the sixteenth century, the geographical location of Puerto Rico at the center of the Antillean arch has made its territory a valuable and strategic military zone. U.S. military bases once occupied most of the territory of the islands of Vieques and Culebra.

Three elements compose the island of Puerto Rico's physical surface: mountains, coastal plains, and valleys. The Central Cordillera runs from east to west, shaping three-fourths of the island as hills and mountains. The Sierra de Cayey and Sierra de Luquillo are two small mountain ranges respectively to the east and northeast of the Central Cordillera. Cerro de Punta is Puerto Rico's highest peak, at 4,390 feet. The highest points of the cordillera contrast with the lowest levels along the island's coasts.

Most of the industrial activity of the main island is on the coastal plains surrounding the cordillera. The major cities are San Juan (the capital), Ponce, Mayagüez, Arecibo, and Fajardo, all connected by a highway system. In the center-eastern part of the island, the city of Caguas occupies an extensive valley. Although unnavigably narrow, Puerto Rico's rivers (including Río Grande de Loíza, Río Bayamón, Río Grande de Arecibo, and Río La Plata) have been used as a source of hydroelectric power.

Puerto Rico's average temperatures fluctuate between 75°F and 80°F. Divided into two zones according to altitude, the climate shows slight differences in temperature between the "moderate" (higher parts of the mountains) and the "hot" (plains and low hills) areas. These climatic zone differences are accompanied by rainfall variations, ranging from averages of 200 inches a year in the rain forests to less than 30 inches in some of the urban coastal sections.

The main island's rain forests include Luquillo, Carite, Toro Negro, and Maricao. To the east, Luquillo, the largest of these reserves, hosts the Yunque peak at 3,494 feet and is home to the Puerto Rican parrot, an endangered species. At the island's center, shaped by the Usabón River, is the San Cristóbal Canyon, whose walls rise between 495 and 660 feet high. Endemic to Puerto Rico's fauna is the *coquí* (of which there are sixteen species), a petite member of the frog family that sings its name. Trees such as the *flamboyán* and the *maga* adorn Puerto Rico's vistas.

See also **Caribbean Sea; Virgin Islands.**

BIBLIOGRAPHY

Arana-Soto, Salvador. *Diccionario geográfico de Puerto Rico.* San Juan: n.p., 1978.

Blanco De Galiñanes, Maria Teresa, ed. *Geovisión de Puerto Rico: Aportaciones recientes al estudio de la geografía.* Río Piedras: Editorial Universitaria, Universidad de Puerto Rico, 1977.

Cadilla, José Francisco, et al. *Elementos de geografía de Puerto Rico.* San Juan: Editorial Librotex, 1988.

MARÍA DEL ROSARIO RAMOS GONZÁLEZ
ISMAEL GARCÍA COLÓN

PUERTO RICO, POLITICAL PARTIES

This entry includes the following articles:
OVERVIEW
POPULAR DEMOCRATIC PARTY (PPD)

OVERVIEW

Puerto Rican political parties traditionally fall into three categories, defined according to the ideological alternatives of the island's political relationship with the United States: autonomist, annexationist, and separatist. Most autonomists approve of Puerto Rico's present status as a commonwealth of the United States, whereas others advocate for more local powers, and free association according to United Nations resolutions. The annexationists support complete integration as a state of the union. The separatists call for political independence from the United States. Following this political taxonomy, the main parties in Puerto Rico are the Popular Democratic Party (Partido Popular Democrático, PPD), the New Progressive Party (Partido Nuevo Progresista, PNP), and the Puerto Rican Pro-Independence Party (Partido Independentista Puertorriqueño, PIP).

The PPD was founded by Luis Muñoz Marín in 1938. With the Puerto Rican peasant straw hat as its symbol and the slogan *pan, tierra y libertad* ("bread, land, and liberty"), the PPD launched a plan of social and economic reform that included industrialization, agrarian reform, and population control. The PPD controlled most of the legislative and municipal government offices from 1940 to 1968. In 1948 Muñoz Marín became the first elected governor of Puerto Rico, a post he held until 1964. A party split caused its first electoral defeat in 1968, but the PPD came back to power in the years from 1972 to 1976 and 1984 to 1992 under the leadership of Rafael Hernández Colón. After losing the elections of 1992 and 1996, the PPD candidate Sila María Calderón became the first Puerto Rican woman governor in 2000, and Aníbal Acevedo Vilá, former resident commissioner, was elected governor in 2004. Since 1952 the PPD has become the principal supporter of local autonomy through the constitution of the Commonwealth of Puerto Rico, also known as Free Associated State (Estado Libre Asociado de Puerto Rico). Despite countless efforts, the PPD has failed to obtain the federal support necessary to transform the commonwealth status into a more autonomous entity within the United States.

The PNP evolved from the Pro-Statehood Republican Party (Partido Estadista Republicano, PER), founded in 1948. The PER dissolved in 1968 after most of its rank and file joined the PNP. Established in 1967 by Luis A. Ferré, the PNP won the gubernatorial elections of 1968, 1976, 1980, 1992, and 1996. Three PNP leaders have been elected to the governorship: Luis A. Ferré, Carlos Romero Barceló, and Pedro Roselló Gonzalez. Roselló Gonzalez, whose administration was marked by many corruption scandals, lost the elections of 2004 and faces competition for control of the party from Luis G. Fortuño Burset, PNP's resident commissioner. Committed to statehood, the PNP argues that commonwealth status makes Puerto Ricans second-class citizens and perpetuates an ambiguous colonial relationship with the United States. Despite numerous efforts, the PNP has not been able to achieve majority support within the Puerto Rican electorate for formal petition of statehood to the U.S. Congress. However, party membership and statehood support has increased substantially since the late 1980s.

The PIP, founded in 1946 by Gilberto Concepción de Gracia, is the main pro-independence group on the island. Contrary to the Nationalist Party (Partido Nacionalista) during the 1930s and 1940s, or the Puerto Rican Socialist Party (Partido Socialista Puertorriqueño, PSP) during the 1970s and 1980s, the PIP follows a moderate leftist ideology in the quest for Puerto Rican independence; it advocates political independence through a negotiated settlement with the U. S. government. Since 1948 the PIP has participated in every election, representing less than 5 percent of the electorate. Its main leader, Rubén Berríos Martínez, has emphasized democratic socialism and close ties with the international social democratic movement. After losing its electoral franchise briefly in 2004, the PIP has renewed its leadership by nominating Edwin Irizarry Mora as its candidate for governor in 2008. María de Lourdes Santiago, a senator, and Victor García San Inocencio, a house representative, are its principal elected officials.

The PPD and PNP dominate the political system. Together, the parties represent over 90 percent of the voters, share similar domestic agendas, and differ only with respect to their stands on Puerto Rico's status. Since the 1980s there has been increasing cross-voting among the electorate, making it difficult to predict winners along party lines for candidates at the local and central levels. The same holds true for the status issue: although the pro-statehood PNP won the 1992 elections, the statehood option lost to the commonwealth status in a 1993 plebiscite.

At the turn of the twenty-first century, Puerto Ricans' increasing dissatisfaction with these three traditional parties led to the creation of new political organizations. The most prominent new political parties are the Partido Acción Civil (Civil Action Party, PAC) and the Partido Puertorriqueños por Puerto Rico (Puerto Ricans for Puerto Rico Party, PPR). The PAC, under the leadership of Nelson Rosario, promotes free association and has been unable to gain an electoral franchise. In 2007 the PPR obtained official recognition, becoming the fourth electoral party for the 2008 elections. Rogelio Figueroa is the PPR's candidate for governor.

See also **Calderon, Sila María; United States-Latin American Relations.**

BIBLIOGRAPHY

Anderson, Robert W. *Gobierno y partidos políticos de Puerto Rico.* Madrid: Editorial Tecnos, 1970.

Bayrón Toro, Fernando. *Elecciones y Partidos Políticos de Puerto Rico,* 6th ed. Mayagüez, P.R.: Editorial Isla, 2003.

Carr, Raymond. *Puerto Rico: A Colonial Experiment.* New York: Vintage Books, 1984.

Morales Carrión, Arturo, ed. *Puerto Rico: A Political and Cultural History.* New York: Norton, 1983.

Pagán, Bolívar. *Historia de los partidos políticos puertorriqueños, 1898–1956.* 2 vols. San Juan: Librería Campos, 1972.

Scarano, Francisco A. *Puerto Rico: Cinco siglos de historia.* San Juan: McGraw-Hill, 1993.

Trías Monge, José. *Puerto Rico: The Trials of the Oldest Colony in the World.* New Haven, CT: Yale University Press, 1997.

MARISABEL BRÁS
ISMAEL GARCÍA COLÓN

POPULAR DEMOCRATIC PARTY (PPD)

Under the leadership of Luis Muñoz Marín, the Popular Democratic Party (Partido Popular Democrático, PPD) was established in 1938 from a splinter group of the Liberal Party. The PPD's emblem is the silhouetted head of a Puerto Rican peasant wearing a straw hat, with the slogan *pan, tierra y libertad* ("bread, land, and liberty"). The party leaders, combining elements of Latin American populism with New Deal policies on a platform of social justice, supported a program of industrialization, agrarian reform, and population control aimed at transforming the rural and agricultural Puerto Rico of the 1940s into an urban and industrial society.

The PPD maintained almost absolute control of most elected offices from 1940 through 1968, while benefiting from local autonomy granted by the U.S. government. The first elections for the governorship took place in 1948, when Muñoz Marín became governor. Muñoz Marín also led an elected assembly that drafted the constitution of the Estado Libre Asociado de Puerto Rico (Commonwealth of Puerto Rico), coming into effect in 1952. After Muñoz Marín's retirement in 1964, Roberto Sánchez Vilella assumed the leadership of the PPD and became governor. In 1968 internal party conflicts and personal scandals forced Sánchez Vilella to abandon the PPD, resulting in the first election loss for the party.

Rafael Hernández Colón assumed PPD's leadership and reorganization and was elected governor in 1972. After losing the elections of 1976 and 1980, he regained the office in 1984 and was reelected in 1988. Another leadership transition proved difficult for the PPD, which lost the elections of 1992 and 1996. In 2000 Sila María

Calderón, the PPD's candidate, became the first Puerto Rican woman governor. In 2004 Aníbal Acevedo Vilá, the party's former U.S. resident commissioner, was elected governor by a slight margin. Despite failed attempts to obtain more autonomy from the United States, the PPD has favored the continuation of Puerto Rico's commonwealth status with the hope of achieving future autonomy. Some minority sectors within the PPD support free association as defined by international law and UN resolutions.

See also **Calderon, Sila María; Puerto Rico.**

BIBLIOGRAPHY

Bayrón Toro, Fernando. *Elecciones y Partidos Políticos de Puerto Rico, 1809–2000*, 6th ed. Mayagüez, P.R.: Editorial Isla, 2003.

Morales Carrión, Arturo, ed. *Puerto Rico: A Political and Cultural History.* New York: Norton, 1983.

Trías Monge, José. *Puerto Rico: The Trials of the Oldest Colony in the World.* New Haven, CT: Yale University Press, 1997.

ISMAEL GARCÍA COLÓN

PUEYRREDÓN, CARLOS ALBERTO

(1887–1962). Politician, historian and financier Carlos Alberto Pueyrredón was born in Buenos Aires on July 18, 1887, into a prominent Argentine family. Nephew of Radical Party politician Honorio Pueyrredón, he accompanied Marcelo T. de Alvear as delegate to the League of Nations in 1920. Pueyrredón nonetheless supported the September 1930 military ouster of Radical President Hipólito Yrigoyen. In 1932 Pueyrredón was elected national deputy for the province of Buenos Aires as a member of the conservative Partido Demócrata Nacional. Later that year he introduced legislation designating the colonial-era cabildo building a national historical monument, thus protecting the Buenos Aires landmark from destruction. In December 1940 President Ramón Castillo appointed Pueyrredón intendente (mayor) of Buenos Aires, a position he held until displaced by the military shortly after the June 1943 coup. His brief tenure as intendente put the conservative Pueyrredón at odds with a city council largely controlled by the opposition Radical and Socialist Parties.

In addition to his political activity, Pueyrredón served on the boards of directors of the Banco Popular Argentino and several agricultural insurance and financial organizations. Pueyrredón was a member of the Academia Nacional de Historia, and author of several works focusing primarily on the process of independence. He died on June 16, 1962.

See also **Alvear, Carlos María de; Argentina, Political Parties: Radical Party (UCR); Buenos Aires; Castilla, Ramón; Irigoyen, Hipólito; Pueyrredón, Honorio.**

BIBLIOGRAPHY

Pueyrredón, Carlos Alberto. *En tiempos de los virreyes: Miranda y la gestación de nuestra independencia.* Buenos Aires: Rosso Editor, 1932.

Pueyrredón, Carlos Alberto. *La campaña de los Andes.* Buenos Aires: Emecé Editores, 1944.

Pueyrredón, Carlos Alberto. *1810: La Revolución de Mayo según amplia documentación de la época.* Buenos Aires: Ediciones Peuser, 1953.

Walter, Richard J. *Politics and Urban Growth in Buenos Aires, 1910–1942.* Cambridge, U.K., and New York: Cambridge University Press, 1993.

JAMES CANE

PUEYRREDÓN, HONORIO (1876–1945).

Honorio Pueyrredón (*b.* 9 July 1876; *d.* 23 September 1945), Argentine lawyer, university professor, political leader, and diplomat. Born into a prominent Argentine landholding family, Pueyrredón studied and taught law at the University of Buenos Aires before winning a political appointment in 1916. In recognition of Pueyrredón's strong support for the recently formed Unión Cívica Radical, newly elected president Hipólito Yrigoyen named him agriculture minister

Pueyrredón served as foreign minister between 1917 and 1922, during which time he led his government's diplomatic efforts to chart a leadership role for Argentina in Latin America. Under Pueyrredón's stewardship, Argentina remained neutral after 1916 despite mounting U.S. pressures on Yrigoyen to enter the war. In addition, the foreign minister tried to organize an association of Latin American neutrals, which directly challenged U.S. political influence in the region.

In domestic politics Pueyrredón represented the interests of cattle raisers and other elites within the multiclass-based Unión Cívica. When the movement split in 1922, Pueyrredón sided with the more conservative antipersonalists and was named ambassador to the United States in the administration of President Marcelo T. de Alvear. During the 1920s Pueyrredón abandoned his antagonism toward Washington. He encouraged the growth of U.S. commercial interests in Argentina and offered to assist Washington in negotiating a favorable peace in Nicaragua.

In 1928, however, Pueyrredón did an about-face. As Argentine delegation chief to the Sixth Pan-American Conference, he gained international fame by contravening his government's instructions and publicly attacking U.S. intervention in Latin America. As a result, Pueyrredón was recalled to Buenos Aires. He remained active in politics and private legal practice during the 1930s.

See also **Argentina: The Twentieth Century; Argentina, Political Parties: Radical Party (UCR).**

BIBLIOGRAPHY

Luis Alén Lascano, *Yrigoyen, Sandino, y el panamericanismo* (1986).

Joseph S. Tulchin, *Argentina and the United States: A Conflicted Relationship* (1990).

David Sheinin, *Argentina and the United States at the Sixth Pan-American Conference (Havana 1928)* (1991).

Additional Bibliography

Lanús, Juan Archibaldo. *Aquel apogeo: Política internacional argentina, 1910–1939.* Buenos Aires: Emecé Editores, 2001.

DAVID M. K. SHEININ

PUEYRREDÓN, JUAN MARTÍN DE

(1777–1850). Juan Martín de Pueyrredón (*b.* 18 December 1777; *d.* 13 March 1850), one of the most important figures in Argentina's wars of independence. Pueyrredón was born in Buenos Aires of French and Spanish ancestry and became one of the leaders in the defense of Buenos Aires against the British invasion in 1806. He played an important role in recruiting men and matériel for the defense effort, and his own squad of Hussars fought brilliantly. Santiago de Liniers, then the military governor, promoted him to lieutenant colonel. After the British were driven out, secure in the prestige and influence that he enjoyed, Pueyrredón demanded that the *cabildo* remove Viceroy Rafael de Sobremonte and replace him with Liniers. In recognition of his contributions, the *cabildo* sent Pueyrredón to Madrid.

He was in Spain when the French invaded the Iberian peninsula in 1808, and seeing what was happening, he became convinced that Argentine independence was necessary to prevent the country from being dominated by a Spanish junta or by the French. Disillusioned with the turn of events, Pueyrredón wrote to the *cabildo* advising it not to accept the appointments of viceroys that any junta would probably make. This act was considered treasonable, and when he returned to Argentina in 1809, he was arrested. He soon escaped to Brazil with the help of Manuel Belgrano and others.

Pueyrredón returned to Argentina after the May 1810 revolution and was appointed governor of Córdoba. In January 1811, he was sent to the northern regions as governor and president of the Audiencia of Charcas. In 1812, Pueyrredón was elected to the first triumvirate to govern the United Provinces of Río de la Plata. He was overthrown in the October revolution and moved to San Luís.

In 1816, Pueyrredón was elected supreme director of the United Provinces. His tenure brought stability, which enabled him to concentrate on the war effort against Spain. His total support for José de San Martín's expedition to Chile was crucial to its success. Pueyrredón favored a centralized form of government dominated by Buenos Aires, for which he often faced rebellions by the provinces. He resigned in June 1819 and soon left for Europe, where he remained for most of the next thirty years. He went home to Buenos Aires in 1850, where he died.

See also **Argentina: The Nineteenth Century; British in Argentina; Wars of Independence, South America.**

BIBLIOGRAPHY

Adrián Beccar Varela, *Juan Martín de Pueyrredón* (1924).

Hialmar Edmundo Gammalsson, *Juan Martín de Pueyrredón* (1968).

Additional Bibliography

Halperin Donghi, Tulio. *Revolución y guerra: Formación de una elite dirigente en la Argentina criolla.* Buenos Aires: Siglo XXI Editores Argentina, 2002.

Herrero, Fabián, and Klaus Gallo. *Revolución, política e ideas en el Río de la Plata durante la década de 1810.* Buenos Aires: Ediciones Cooperativas, 2004.

Szuchman, Mark D., and Jonathan C. Brown, eds. *Revolution and Restoration: The Rearrangement of Power in Argentina, 1776–1860.* Lincoln: University of Nebraska Press, 1994.

JUAN MANUEL PÉREZ

PUEYRREDÓN, PRILIDIANO (1823–1870).

Prilidiano Pueyrredón (*b.* 24 January 1823; *d.* 3 November 1870), Argentine painter and architect. Pueyrredón was born in Buenos Aires, the son of the former Supreme Director Juan Martín de Pueyrredón. From the time he finished grammar school at age twelve until 1849, he spent more time in Europe than in Argentina. He earned an engineering degree from the Institut Polytechnique in Paris and began his painting career during his early European travels.

As an architect, Pueyrredón designed both public and private structures, including the mansion that is now the presidential residence at Olivos in the suburbs of Buenos Aires. He also undertook projects of architectural restoration. However, he was above all a portraitist in the neoclassical tradition. He has left portraits of Manuelita Rosas and his own father, as well as of other politically or socially prominent figures. Pueyrredón also painted landscapes and realistic country scenes, in both oil and watercolor. Like the portraits, these have documentary value over and above their artistic merit (which is probably greater in the watercolors). He is remembered as Argentina's outstanding nineteenth-century painter.

See also **Architecture: Architecture to 1900; Art: The Nineteenth Century.**

BIBLIOGRAPHY

J. L. Pagano, *Prilidiano Pueyrredón* (1945).

Bernard S. Myers, ed., *McGraw-Hill Dictionary of Art* (1969), vol. 4, p. 453.

Bonifacio Del Carril, *Prilidiano Pueyrredón (1823–1870)* (1970).

Additional Bibliography

Chianelli, Trinidad Delia. "Prilidiano Pueyrredón, pionero de la pintura argentina." *Todo Es Historia* 35:410 (September 2001): 38–42.

DAVID BUSHNELL

PUGA, MARÍA LUISA (1944–2004).

María Luisa Puga (*b.* 3 February 1944; *d.* 25 December 2004), Mexican writer. Born in Mexico City, Puga has published literary criticism, essays, short stories, and novels. She is most widely known for her first novel, *Las posibilidades del odio* (The Possibilities of Hate, 1978), about Kenyan society, and for *Pánico o peligro* (Panic or Danger, 1983). The latter novel, which received the Premio Xavier Villaurrutía in 1983, explores social relations in contemporary Mexico City through the experiences of a middle-class secretary. Puga's other works include three collections of short stories, *Inmovil sol secreto* (Immobile Secret Sun, 1979), *Accidentes* (Accidents, 1981), and *Intentos* (Attempts, 1987), and four other novels, *Cuando el aire es azul* (When the Air Is Blue, 1980), *La forma del silencio* (The Form of Silence, 1987), *Antonia* (1989), and *Las razones del lago* (The Reasons of the Lake, 1991). Puga's concern with the implications of racial, class, and gender differences constitutes the basis of her social criticism. Her critical view of Mexican society is shared by a generation of Mexican writers marked by the tragic results of the Mexican student movement in 1968.

See also **Literature: Spanish America.**

BIBLIOGRAPHY

Fabienne Bradu, "Todos los otros, el otro," in *Señas particulares: Escritora* (1987), pp. 118–135.

Danny J. Anderson, "Cultural Conversation and Constructions of Reality: Mexican Narrative and Literary Theories after 1968," in *Siglo XX/20th Century* 8 (1990–1991): 11–30.

Additional Bibliography

De Beer, Gabriella. *Contemporary Mexican Women Writers: Five Voices.* Austin: University of Texas Press, 1996.

Ibsen, Kristine. *The Other Mirror: Women's Narrative in Mexico, 1980–1995.* Westport, CT: Greenwood Press, 1997.

López, Irma M. *Historia, escritura e identidad: la novelística de María Luisa Puga.* New York: P. Lang, 1996.

Ortega, Julio and Carlos Fuentes. *The Vintage Book of Latin American Stories.* New York: Vintage Books, 2000.

Poniatowska, Elena. "Réquiem por María Luisa Puga, a un año de su muerte." *La Jornada* (2005).

DANNY J. ANDERSON

PUIG, MANUEL

PUIG, MANUEL (1932–1990). Manuel Puig (*b.* 28 December 1932; *d.* 22 July 1990), Argentine novelist. Born in General Villegas, Buenos Aires Province, he was educated at a U.S. boarding school in Buenos Aires. Puig had such a childhood passion for American movies that he learned English in 1942 to enjoy them more thoroughly. He also was very interested in French and Italian movies and studied filmmaking in Italy on a scholarship during the mid- 1950s. Returning to Argentina in 1960, Puig began writing film scripts and working as an assistant director in the Argentine film industry. He then moved to New York City to devote himself to writing.

Under the disguise of pop literature, Puig built a complex narrative oeuvre, in which, paradoxically, he used film techniques. Both *La traición de Rita Hayworth* (1968; *Betrayed by Rita Hayworth,* 1971) and *Boquitas pintadas* (1969; *Heartbreak Tango,* 1973) examine the narrow world of alienated human beings who find refuge in the massive consumption of movies and soap operas. These initial novels, together with the rest of his production, including *The Buenos Aires Affair* (1973) and *El beso de la mujer araña* (1976; *Kiss of the Spider Woman,* 1979), implicitly attack the stratified and conventional realism of the traditional novel and the cultural foundations of the experimental and vanguardist novel, and they demystify modern Argentine conventions. He used sexual frustration as a literary tool for his task of demolition both at the individual and social levels.

One of the major interests of Puig's books resides in the kind of clichéd speech used by his characters, a speech canonized by the mass media. It is a euphemistic language that reveals the aberrant character of the linguistic codes of the mass culture, which confers a "subversive" dimension to his literature. He published a total of eight novels, two plays, and two movie scripts. He received the Curzio Malaparte Award (Italy) in 1986 for his novel *Sangre de amor correspondido* (1983; *Blood of Requited Love,* 1984).

See also **Cinema: From the Silent Film to 1990.**

BIBLIOGRAPHY

Alfred Macadam, "Manuel Puig: Things as They Are," in *Modern Latin American Narratives: The Dreams of Reason* (1977): 91–101.

Naomi Lindstrom, "The Problem of Pop Culture in the Novels of Manuel Puig," in *The American Hispanist* 4 (1978): 28–31.

Frances Wyers Weber, "Manuel Puig at the Movies," in *Hispanic Review* 49, no. 2 (1981): 163–181.

David W. Foster, "Latin American Documentary Narrative," in *PMLA* 99, no. 1 (1984): 41–55.

Lucille Kerr, *Suspended Fictions: Reading Novels by Manuel Puig* (1987).

Additional Bibliography

Craig, Linda. *Juan Carlos Onetti, Manuel Puig and Luisa Valenzuela: Marginality and Gender.* Rochester, UK: Tamesis, 2005.

Giordano, Alberto. *Manuel Puig: La conversación infinita.* Buenos Aires: Beatriz Viterbo Editora, 2001.

Levine, Suzanne Jill. *Manuel Puig and the Spider Woman: His Life and Fictions.* New York: Farrar, Straus and Giroux, 2000.

Logie, Ilse. *La omnipresencia de la mímesis en la obra de Manuel Puig: Análisis de cuatro novelas.* Amsterdam; New York: Rodopi, 2001.

ANGELA B. DELLEPIANE

PUIG CASAURANC, JOSÉ MANUEL

PUIG CASAURANC, JOSÉ MANUEL (1888–1939). José Manuel Puig Casauranc (*b.* 31 January 1888; *d.* 9 May 1939), Mexican politician-diplomat of the 1920s and 1930s. Born in Campeche and educated as a physician, Puig emerged in national politics as manager of Plutarco Elías Calles's successful presidential campaign in 1924. Calles appointed him to head the prestigious Ministry of Education in his cabinet. In the uncertainty following the 1928 assassination of Álvaro Obregón, Puig was a leading power broker and a presidential contender. The apogee of his public career was his confrontation with U.S. Secretary of State Cordell Hull at the 1933 Pan-American Conference in Montevideo, Uruguay. Cognizant of the leftward shift in Mexican politics, Puig criticized international bankers and U.S. dominance of the Mexican economy. In spite of his political adaptability, Puig became a peripheral figure during the Lázaro Cárdenas presidency.

See also **Calles, Plutarco Elías; Hull, Cordell; Mexico: Since 1910; Pan-American Conferences: Montevideo Conference (1933).**

BIBLIOGRAPHY

José Manuel Puig Casauranc, *Galatea rebelde a varios pigmaliones* (1938).

John W. F. Dulles, *Yesterday in Mexico: A Chronicle of the Revolution, 1919–1936,* esp. pp. 404–436, 481–549.

Additional Bibliography

Buchenau, Jürgen. *Plutarco Elías Calles and the Mexican Revolution.* Lanham, MD: Rowman & Littlefield, 2006.

JOHN A. BRITTON

PUIGGRÓS, RODOLFO (1906–1980).

Rodolfo Puiggrós, born in Buenos Aires on November 19, 1906, was an Argentine journalist, historian, and intellectual with Marxist leanings. A militant in the Argentine Communist Party, he was thrown out in 1946 for backing Peronism. He became a prominent intellectual referent in the relationship between the Argentine left and Peronism and a bridge between leftist political and intellectual sectors and university students and other young people who moved toward or joined Peronism from the late 1960s onward. His principal works—not actually original contributions but rather a synthesis of Latin American Marxism and the historiographical school of Argentine historical revisionism—include *De la colonia a la revolución* (1940), *Historia económica del Río de la Plata* (1945), *Historia crítica de los partidos políticos argentinos* (1956), and *Las Izquierdas y el problema nacional* (1966).

When the Perónist government took over the University of Buenos Aires in 1973, it appointed Puiggrós rector and renamed the school Universidad Nacional y Popular de Buenos Aires. But with violence increasing between the left and the Perónist right and the ousting of Héctor José Cámpora from the presidency, Puiggrós was forced to move to Mexico in 1974. He founded the Committee for Solidarity with the Argentine People and, in exile, was an active opponent of the military dictatorship established in 1976. He died on November 12, 1980, in Havana, Cuba.

See also **Argentina: The Twentieth Century; Cámpora, Héctor José; Perón, Juan Domingo.**

BIBLIOGRAPHY

Altamirano, Carlos. *Peronismo y cultura de izquierda.* Buenos Aires: Temas, 2001.

Romero, José Luis. *Las ideas políticas en Argentina.* Buenos Aires: FCE, 2001.

VICENTE PALERMO

PULPEROS. *Pulperos* were retail grocers in the colonial period of Spanish America. Their stores, *pulperías,* were normally small in size and inventory and located mostly in the towns and cities, though some were in rural regions and on farms and haciendas. *Pulperos* constituted the largest group of fixed entrepreneurial storekeepers in the towns and cities. Artisan guilds had many stores, but they could be opened and operated only by trained artisans. The urban grocers were licensed and supervised by the town councils. In some places councils regulated what they could sell as well as where they could make their purchases.

Some towns limited grocery-store licenses to poor widows, and at times, as in Mexico City in the mid-eighteenth century, neither free people of color nor Indians were permitted to operate such stores. Nevertheless, the small retail grocery stores could be established in many urban centers with only modest capital investment. Much and sometimes all of their inventories could be acquired through credit extended by their suppliers, which again enabled people of limited means to enter the entrepreneurial sector of the economy. The vast majority of *pulperos* were men; some male grocers, and some of the few women grocers also, owned more than one grocery store. Functioning in the commercial marketplace was not without its risks, and only a few grocers endured in business over the long term.

Pulperos supplied basic food items, among other goods, to a large segment of the population, and they did so at times by extending credit. When they were required by law to accept pawns in return for food items, as in Mexico City from the mid-eighteenth century, they were again extending food items for credit. Where the grocers were permitted to sell alcoholic beverages, as in Buenos Aires, their stores were part grocery and part tavern.

After independence retail grocery stores continued to exist, but by the later nineteenth century they often became indistinguishable from *bodegas*, which during the colonial period had sold a different category of goods. During the twentieth century the typical neighborhood retail grocery store in many cities of Spanish America were known simply as bodegas.

See also **Spanish Empire.**

BIBLIOGRAPHY

Kinsbruner, Jay. *Petty Capitalism in Spanish America: The Pulperos of Puebla, Mexico City, Caracas, and Buenos Aires.* Boulder, CO: Westview Press, 1987.

Mayo, Carlos, ed. *Pulperos y Pulperías de Buenos Aires, 1740–1830.* Mar del Plata, Argentina: Universidad Nacional de Mar del Plata, 1997.

JAY KINSBRUNER

PULQUE. *See* **Alcoholic Beverages.**

PUMA. The puma (*Felis concolor*) takes its name from the Quechua language and is also known as cougar, mountain lion, or panther. Solitary and territorial, the puma is present in all types of habitat in Argentina, Belize, Bolivia, Brazil, Canada, Chile, Colombia, Costa Rica, Ecuador, El Salvador, Honduras, Guatemala, Guyana, Mexico, Nicaragua, Panama, Paraguay, Peru, Surinam, the United States, and Venezuela. Its coloring is yellow-brown above and pale underneath. The length of its head and body ranges from 40 to 64 inches, with a tail up to 32 inches; it can weigh up to 225 pounds. Females are usually smaller.

After a gestation period of ninety to ninety-six days, usually two or three (or as many as six) cubs are born with a speckled coat and a ringed tail. These markings disappear with time. In the adults, only black markings remain on the head and near the mouth.

Pumas are expert hunters, preying on most species of mammals, especially deer. Active both day and night, they have become nocturnal in areas inhabited by humans, their sole enemy. Once extensively hunted, pumas are strictly protected throughout most of their range.

In the Andes the feline deity appeared as early as 850 BCE and has been venerated by various mountain and coastal cultures. The Moche painted the puma on their ceramics, most certainly considering it a deity. The Inca worshiped the puma, and it was noted by Manuel Chávez Ballón during the twentieth century that their imperial capital had been constructed in the shape of a puma, although the actual form is not perfectly delineated. Among the Nahua of Central Mexico, the puma has been associated with Mixcoatl. In the United States, the Winnebago, Cheyenne, and Apache peoples have held the puma or cougar in high metaphysical esteem.

Previously among the largest and most populous American mammals, pumas have declined steadily in number due to overhunting, reduced deer populations (its primary food source), and human development. The Florida, Central American, and eastern North American subspecies are listed in Appendix I of the Convention on International Trade in Endangered Species of Wild Fauna and Flora, which denotes them as threatened with extinction. As such, trade in specimens of these subspecies is permitted only in exceptional circumstances. Additionally, the Mexican, Mayan, and Missoula subspecies are listed in Appendix II, indicating that they are not necessarily threatened with extinction, but that trade in them must be controlled.

BIBLIOGRAPHY

Luigi Boitani and Stefania Bartoli, *Simon and Schuster's Guide to Mammals* (1982), p. 310.

Erwin Patzelt, *Fauna del Ecuador* (1989), pp. 83–84.

Additional Bibliography

CITES (Convention on International Trade in Endangered Species of Wild Fauna and Flora). 2001. United

Nations Environment Programme. Available from http://www.cites.org/.

Gasparini, Graziano, and Luise Margolies. *Inca Architecture.* Translated by Patricia J. Lyon. Bloomington: Indiana University Press, 1980.

RAÚL CUCALÓN

PUMACAHUA REBELLION.

Pumacahua Rebellion, an anticolonial uprising in 1814–1816 that spread from its base in Cuzco, Peru, in the southern Andes, to central Peru and to what is today Bolivia. In late 1813 and early 1814, tensions in Cuzco between the *audiencia,* the high court and the focal point of Spanish interests, and the more liberal, creole *cabildo,* the city council, erupted when the former had prominent members of the *cabildo* imprisoned. On 2 August 1814, the prisoners escaped, imprisoned many Spaniards, and demanded the implementation of the liberal 1812 Spanish constitution. They were led by middle- class Cuzco residents José and Vicente Angulo and Gabriel Béjar. The rebellion has been named, somewhat erroneously, after one of its military leaders, Mateo Pumacahua, a *curaca* (an Indian local official).

The rebels advanced quickly to Huamanga and Huancavelica in the north and to La Paz and Arequipa in the south. Their numbers were in the tens of thousands, primarily indigenous peasants and the urban lower classes. They allied with Río de la Plata rebels who were besieging Upper Peru. Yet by the end of 1814, colonial forces had largely defeated the rebels, who had not counted on the rapid demise of their Río de la Plata allies. The return of Ferdinand to the throne of Spain also bolstered royalist efforts in Peru. Finally, divisions between the creole leadership and the Indian masses weakened the rebels.

Although the repression of the rebels was brutal, sparks of the revolt continued to flicker in distant provinces. Nonetheless, with the rebellion's defeat and the subsequent concentration of colonial forces in Cuzco, the southern Andes of Peru thereafter played a minor role in the struggle for independence in Peru.

See also **Audiencia; Cuzco; Peru: From the Conquest Through Independence; Spain, Constitution of 1812.**

BIBLIOGRAPHY

Jorge Cornejo Bouroncle, *Pumacahua: La revolución del Cuzco de 1814. Estudio documentado* (1956).

John Lynch, *The Spanish-American Revolutions 1808–1826* (1973), pp. 117–126, 164–171.

David Cahill and Scarlett O'Phelan Godoy, "Forging Their Own History: Indian Insurgency in the Southern Peruvian Sierra, 1815," in *Bulletin of Latin American Research* 11, no. 2 (1992): 125–167.

Additional Bibliography

Andrien, Kenneth. *Andean Worlds: Indigenous history, Culture, and Consciousness under Spanish Rule, 1532–1825.* Albuquerque: University of New Mexico Press, 2001.

Fisher, John. *Bourbon Peru, 1750–1824.* Liverpool, England: Liverpool University Press, 2003.

Walker, Charles C. *Smoldering Ashes: Cuzco and the Creation of Republican Peru, 1780–1840.* Durham, NC: Duke University Press, 1999.

CHARLES F. WALKER

PUNÁ ISLAND.

Puná Island is located in the Gulf of Guayaquil at the mouth of western South America's largest river system, which drains the fertile Guayas River basin. The island, 350 square miles in area, is characterized by extensive mangrove estuaries and a seasonally dry tropical forest which has been decimated since the colonial period.

Because La Puná is remote from modern population centers, few of its archaeological sites have been excavated, but evidence indicates that the island was occupied over 5,000 years ago by preceramic people who exploited wild resources. After about 2000 BCE people at El Encanto left a giant, annular mound of shell containing shards of a regional variant of Valdivia pottery. These Valdivians were agriculturists and navigators of the open sea who may have visited the island seasonally or settled there permanently to exploit the resources of the forest, mangrove swamps, and marine waters as part of a broad-based economy. Some scholars have suggested, however, that the preceramic and early ceramic people developed a specialized estuarine-marine economy focused on the productive mangrove habitat.

Between 650 and 250 BCE the Bellavista people were permanently settled in a large village on the northwest coast of Puná, where they practiced agriculture in combination with fishing and shell fishing. They made distinct pottery related to the Chorrera (Guayaquil phase), Engoroy, and Pechiche styles of the adjacent mainland areas and northern Peru. Later (250 BCE–800 CE?) people using Jambelí pottery occupied some large village sites as well as small sites in many coastal locations. On the mainland to the east of Puná, Jambelí towns were located in river valleys away from the coast where people emphasized agriculture, formed groups governed by central authorities, and had extensive trade relations with Peru. People using Guangala pottery, characteristic of the mainland to the northwest, also may have occupied sites on Puná in this period.

Between 1000 and 1532 CE people making Manteño- style pottery occupied large sites where archaeologists have found evidence of sociopolitical, technological, and artistic complexity: monumental stone sculptures in the form of animals; the foundations of large buildings; gold, silver, and copper artifacts; quantities of spindle whorls indicating specialized production of cotton textiles; and elaborate burials. A large Contact Period cemetery has been found on Puná, but most of what is known of ethnohistoric Punáes comes from colonial documents.

At the time of Spanish contact in 1531 the Punáes were organized in an independent polity that was not under Inca control. A wealthy chief controlled seven subchiefs. The Punáes were renowned warriors, metalsmiths, productive farmers, fishermen, and merchants. It is widely repeated that the ancient Ecuadorians of the coast participated in a mercantile system that included societies from Peru to Mexico and involved the exchange of valuables such as metal artifacts, textiles, and Spondylus beads (thorny oyster shell) at ports of trade and pilgrimage centers like La Tolita and La Plata Island. Exotic Chimu vessels from Peru have been found in Punáe graves.

Because of the wealth and importance of La Puná it was made a *repartimiento* of the Crown and was amply described in colonial records. The Punáes continued to resist colonial domination until about 1543, and they allegedly killed and ate the Dominican friar Vicente de Valverde during the Peruvian civil war in 1541. Ships bound from Lima to Panama regularly stopped at the port of Puná, an important market and manufacturing center and commissary, in whose *astilleros* the first galley in South America was completed in 1557.

Early in the colonial period some Indians became prosperous entrepreneurs, supplying the Spaniards with labor for shipbuilding, as well as salt, timber, and maritime transport. One native *cacique*, Don Diego Tomalá, was so wealthy that his house was sacked by English pirates in 1587. Gradually the island became economically marginalized as Guayaquil developed, and by the eighteenth century the Indian population had disappeared and La Puná was deserted.

See also **Archaeology; Indigenous Peoples; Precontact History: Mesoamerica.**

BIBLIOGRAPHY

Emilio Estrada, *Los Huancavilcas: Últimas civilizaciones pre-históricas de la costa del Guayas* (1957).

Emilio Estrada, Betty J. Meggers, and Clifford Evans, "The Jambelí Culture of South Coastal Ecuador," in *Pro-ceedings of the United States National Museum* 115 (1964): 483–558.

Pedro I. Porras G., *El Encanto, isla de la Puná, Guayas: La fase valdivia en conchero anular* (1973).

Adam Szászdi, "D. Diego Tomalá, cacique de la isla de La Puná: Un caso de aculturación socioeconómica," in *Estudios sobre política indigenista española en América* 3 (1977): 157–183.

Thomas Frank Aleto, *The Guayaquil Phase Ceramic Complex: The Late Formative Period in the Gulf of Guayaquil, Ecuador* (Ph.D. diss., Univ. of Illinois, 1988).

Jenny Estrada, comp. and ed., *La balsa en lá historia de la navegación ecuatoriana: Compilación de crónicas, estudios, gráficas y testimonios* (Guayaquil, 1988).

Additional Bibliography

Almeida Reyes, Eduardo. *Culturas prehispánicas del Ecuador*. Quito: Viajes Chasquiñan, 2000.

Di Capua, Constanza. *De la imagen al icono: Estudios de arqueología e historia del Ecuador*. Quito: Ediciones Abya-Yala, 2002.

Madsen, Jens E., Robert Mix, and Henrik Balslev. *Flora of Puná Island: Plant Resources on a Neotropical Island*. Aarhus, Denmark; Oakville: Aarhus University Press, 2001.

Pearsall, Deborah M. *Plants and People in Ancient Ecuador: The Ethnobotany of the Jama River Valley.* Belmont, CA: Wadsworth/Thompson Learning, 2004.

KAREN E. STOTHERT

PUNO. Puno, the fourth largest of Peru's twenty-four departments. Puno covers about 28,000 square miles of mainly high Andean plains on the shores of Lake Titicaca, on Peru's southeastern border with Bolivia. As recent as 2005, Puno had 1,245,508 inhabitants as compared to about 900,000 in 1987, of whom 200,000 resided in the departmental capital of the same name. The majority of Puno's inhabitants are poor Quechua- and Aymará-speaking peasants engaged in pastoral and agricultural activities.

Throughout its history the Puno region has been integrated into the regional economy of southern Peru and northern Bolivia as a supplier of wool and foodstuffs. Under Spanish rule (1533–1824), Puno's indigenous communities provided cloth, meat, and labor to the silver mines at Potosí. In the mid-nineteenth century they sold alpaca wool to British merchants based in Arequipa. In the early twentieth century large cattle and sheep estates began to displace traditional producers. Extreme concentration of landowning has contributed to making Puno a center of peasant mobilization and rural conflict.

See also **Peru: From the Conquest Through Independence; Titicaca, Lake.**

BIBLIOGRAPHY

Edward Dew, *Politics in the Altiplano: The Dynamics of Change in Rural Peru* (1969).

Alberto Flores-Galindo, *Arequipa y el sur andino: Ensayo de historia regional (siglos XVIII–XX) (1977);* David Guillet, *Agrarian Reform and Peasant Economy in Southern Peru* (1979).

Nils Jacobsen, *Mirages of Transition: The Peruvian Altiplano, 1780–1930* (1993).

Additional Bibliography

Pineda, Ignacio Frisancho. *La Catedral de Puno: Historia documentada.* Lima: CONCYTEC, Consejo Nacional de Ciencia y Tecnología, 1994.

Poole, Deborah. *Unruly Order: Violence, Power, and Cultural Identity in the High Provinces of Southern Peru.* Boulder, CO: Westview Press, 1994.

Rénique C., José Luis. *La batalla por Puno: Conflicto agrario y nación en los Andes peruanos 1866–1995.* Lima: IEP: SUR: CEPES, 2004.

San Cristóbal Sebastián, Antonio, and Daniel Giannoni. *Puno: Esplendor de la arquitectura virreinal.* San Isidro, Lima: PEISA, 2004.

Zambrano, Augusto Ramos. *Fundación de Puno y otros ensayos históricos.* Arequipa, Peru: Instituto de Estudios Históricos Pukara, 2004.

STEVEN J. HIRSCH

PUNTA ARENAS. In 1520, Ferdinand Magellan was the first European to cross the strait that now bears his name, but it was Pedro Sarmiento de Gamboa, in 1583, who first attempted to settle the area. The settlement, Rey don Felipe, failed, and it would not be until 1843 that the government of Manuel Bulnes established a claim over the region with the founding of Fuerte Bulnes. In 1848 the city of Punta Arenas proper was founded some 38 miles (50 kilometers) from the fort. It was primarily used as a penal colony until 1877, when a mutiny destroyed much of the town. At that time, sheep brought from the Falkland (Malvinas) Islands provided the foundations for a prosperous pastoral economy.

Soon a significant number of immigrants from Great Britain, Italy, and Croatia, as well as other parts of Chile, provided a population base that ensured the long-term development of the city. Oil was discovered in 1945, and by 1970 Punta Arenas was also the center of a thriving fishing industry. Beginning in 1987 the area became a leading producer of coal. Formerly the capital of Magallanes Province, the city was long considered the southernmost city in the world. Since 1974, Punta Arenas has been the capital of the Magallanes y la Antártica Chilena region. The population, according to the 2002 census, numbers 119,496 inhabitants.

See also **Bulnes Prieto, Manuel; Chile, Geography; Magellan, Ferdinand; Sarmiento de Gamboa, Pedro.**

BIBLIOGRAPHY

Collier, Simon, and William F. Sater. *A History of Chile, 1808–2002.* 2nd edition. New York: Cambridge University Press, 2004.

Martinic Beros, Mateo. *Historia del Estrecho de Magallanes.* Santiago, Chile: Editorial Andrés Bello, 1977.

IVÁN JAKSIĆ

PUNTA DEL ESTE.   Punta del Este is a peninsular beach resort city in Uruguay's Department of Maldonado with a year-round population of approximately 9,000 (2007 est.). Francisco Aguilar, a shipowner, landowner, and merchant, founded what was first called Villa Ituzaingó in 1829. More than 300 years earlier, the Spanish explorer Juan Díaz de Solís had named the area Cabo Santa María. Aguilar was the small settlement's economic and political boss and went on to serve as senator in the national government before his death in 1840. Situated on the country's southeastern coast, where the Río de la Plata meets the Atlantic Ocean, Punta del Este was a valuable whaling settlement and a base for sea lion hunters, among other things, during the nineteenth century. It was an appendage of the city of Maldonado, of which Aguilar was mayor in 1829–1830, until residents and local leaders officially founded the municipality of Punta del Este in 1907. The littoral city remained small and relatively underdeveloped until it emerged as one of South America's most popular vacation destinations during the 1940s.

In the 1960s Punta del Este hosted two significant international meetings. The first, in 1961, was a meeting of the Inter-American Economic and Social Council, which brought together representatives from the United States and 22 Latin American countries and established the Charter of Punta del Este, the founding document of the U.S.-led Alliance for Progress. The following year, in a meeting of the Organization of American States, a majority of governments voted with the United States to exclude Cuba from the organization and condemn communism. Today Punta del Este boasts five-star hotels, casinos, and fine dining, and its striking port is a favorite of boaters and sailors.

See also **Maldonado; Uruguay, Geography.**

BIBLIOGRAPHY

Barreda, Felipe. *Punta del Este: Historia, vida, destino.* Buenos Aires: Cristol, 1965.

Fischer, Diego, and Silvia Pisani. *100 años de Punta del Este.* Montevideo: Aguilar, 2007.

PATRICK BARR-MELEJ

PUNTA DEL ESTE MEETING (1961). *See* **Pan-American Conferences: Punta del Este Meeting (1962).**

PURÉPECHA.   *See* **Tarascans.**

PUROS.   *Puros,* a name given to radical, anticlerical liberals in nineteenth-century Mexico. The term *puro,* meaning "the pure ones," apparently dates from divisions that resulted from Valentín Gómez Farías's attempt to use church property to pay for the war against the United States in 1846–1847. Moderate liberals (Moderados) supported a revolt (known as the Rebellion of the Polkos) that forced both the withdrawal of a decree using church property to finance the war against the United States, and the removal of Gómez Farías as president. *Puros* opposed the Treaty of Guadalupe Hidalgo, which the *moderados* had negotiated to end the war. Despite disagreements and tensions, the *puros* often allied themselves with the conservative dictator Antonio López de Santa Anna. The two factions of liberals eventually reunited against the conservatives in 1854. Still, this ideological split continued through the era of the reform and the French Intervention, with the *puros* pushing for more rapid reduction of the church's wealth and power, and the retention of republican government. Liberals believed in individual liberties in theory, but *puros* were unsuccessful in including explicit religious toleration in the Constitution of 1857. *Puros* were more troubled by the inequities of Mexican society and more insistent on the reduction of the power and wealth of the church. Most also regarded the communal land tenure of Indian villages as an oppressive institution. Liberty and equality were, for *puros,* goals that could be reached only by the transformation of Mexican society through the use of state power. The *puros* found that the struggle to disestablish the church required greater power for the state, higher taxes and expropriations, and ever larger armies. Ponciano Arriaga, Melchor Ocampo, Ignacio Ramírez, Manuel Crescencio Rejón, and Francisco Zarco, among others, were considered *puros.*

See also **Gómez Farías, Valentín; Guadalupe Hidalgo, Treaty of (1848); Santa Anna, Antonio López de.**

BIBLIOGRAPHY

Walter V. Scholes, *Mexican Politics During the Juárez Regime, 1855–1872* (1957).

Jesús Reyes Heroles, *El liberalismo mexicano,* 3 vols. (1957–1961).

Charles A. Hale, *Mexican Liberalism in the Age of Mora, 1821–1853* (1968).

Richard N. Sinkin, *The Mexican Reform, 1855–1876: A Study in Liberal Nation-Building* (1979).

Donald F. Stevens, *Origins of Instability in Early Republican Mexico* (1991).

Additional Bibliography

Fowler, Will. *Mexico in the Age of Proposals, 1821–1853.* Westport, CT: Greenwood Press, 1998.

Santoni, Pedro. *Mexicans at Arms: Puro Federalists and the Politics of War, 1845–1848.* Fort Worth, TX: Texas Christian University Press, 1996.

Villegas Revueltas, Silvestre. *El liberalismo moderado en México, 1852–1864.* México, D.F.: Universidad Nacional Autónoma de México, 1997.

D. F. STEVENS

QUADROS, JÂNIO DA SILVA (1917–1992).

Jânio da Silva Quadros (*b.* 25 January 1917; *d.* 16 February 1992), president of Brazil (1961), mayor (1953–1954, 1986–1988) and governor (1955–1959) of São Paulo. Born in Mato Grosso, Quadros soon moved with his family to Paraná, where his father practiced medicine and dabbled in politics. In 1930 the family moved to São Paulo, where Quadros completed his education and received a law degree. While practicing law and teaching, he became active in local politics. As a campaigner and later as a councilman, he gained a reputation as a bohemian, unpredictable, and quixotic figure.

In 1950 Quadros won a seat in the state legislature, and his notoriety grew because of his constant questioning of officials and demands for rectitude. In 1953, with the backing of Paulista influentials, he ran for mayor on a platform that stressed cleaning up graft and curbing expenditures. He adopted the broom as a campaign symbol. His victory over veteran politicians brought national attention, and the following year he took on Adhemar de Barros in the gubernatorial election. Promising to "sweep out corruption," he used unorthodox appeals that won broad support from the working and middle classes. His victory confirmed his image as a dragon slayer and quintessential populist.

From the moment of his election, Quadros turned his attention to the presidential succession, maneuvering for influence and federal patronage. São Paulo prospered from business expansion, and Quadros plowed growing taxes into infrastructure.

São Paulo surpassed Rio in population as it became an industrial megalopolis.

In 1959 Quadros began campaigning for president, accepting the nomination of the National Democratic Union (UDN). His fresh image, unusual methods, and promises of national prosperity attracted a plurality of the voters, who also returned João Goulart to the vice presidency. As the first president inaugurated in Brasília, Quadros made headlines in early 1961 with an ambitious program of reforms while retaining his reputation for moralism and eccentricity. He pursued fiscal austerity, an activist and neutral foreign policy, closer relations with the third world, and industrial growth. Soon, however, relations between the president and Congress soured, and in August Quadros abruptly resigned. He hoped to be recalled because Goulart was unpalatable to conservatives and the military, but Congress accepted his resignation and Goulart eventually succeeded him.

Failing to make a comeback as governor of São Paulo in 1962 and again in 1982, Quadros remained on the sidelines throughout the military years. Then he surprised critics by winning the mayoralty of São Paulo in 1985. His decision not to run for president in 1989 marked the end of his active career.

See also **Barros, Adhemar de; Brazil, Political Parties: National Democratic Union of Brazil (UDN); São Paulo (City).**

BIBLIOGRAPHY

Thomas E. Skidmore, *Politics in Brazil* (1967).

John W. F. Dulles, *Unrest in Brazil* (1970).

Maria Victoria Benavides, *O governo Jânio Quadros* (1981).

Jânio da Silva Quadros, 1960. Moving his way up the political hierarchy, as mayor and governor Quadros transformed São Paolo into a major industrial city and state in Brazil before he gained the national presidency in 1961. FRANK SCHERSCHEL/TIME LIFE PICTURES/GETTY IMAGES

Israel Beloch and Alzira Alves De Abreu, comps., *Dicionário histórico-biográfico brasileiro, 1930–1983* (1984).

Edgard Carone, *A república liberal* (1985).

Additional Bibliography

Benevides, María Victoria. *O Governo Jânio Quadros.* São Paulo: Brasilense, 1999.

Chaia, Vera. *A Liderança Política de Jânio Quadros.* Ibitinga: Humanidades, 1992.

MICHAEL L. CONNIFF

QUEBRACHO COLORADO. Quebracho Colorado (*Schinopsis lorentzii*). The name derives from the Spanish *quiebra-hacha* (axe-breaker), alluding to the hardwood properties of this useful and much-storied tree of northern Argentina and Paraguay. Colorado ("red" in Spanish) refers to the wood's color. The strong, durable wood is useful in buildings and for railway ties. Tannin, essential to the important hides industry, is extracted from the tree. The tree's juice produces a serious skin irritation (called *paaj* in Santiago del Estero). According to one legend, a woodsman tied his vain, flirtatious wife beneath a *quebracho* tree. After becoming covered with disfiguring eruptions, she promised to change her ways. Like the Ceibo and Ombú, other native South American trees, the *quebracho* has inspired wonder and fear, and it figures in folklore. It is also widely used in folk medicine to lower fevers and treat respiratory ailments.

See also **Ceibo; Ombú.**

BIBLIOGRAPHY

Félix Coluccio, *Diccionario folklórico argentino,* vol. 2 (1964), pp. 342, 392.

RICHARD W. SLATTA

QUECHUA. Quechua was the language of the Incas, though it originated prior to the rise of the Inca Empire in the fifteenth century. The people of the Chincha nation were likely the primary source of the particular dialect of Southern Quechua that was instituted as the official language of the Incan state. The Chincha were located on the coast, enjoying vast maritime wealth, a critical component for the promotion of pan-Andean trade. When the Inca subjugated the Chincha, they adopted their language and then spread it throughout large swaths of South America as they conquered other tribes and assimilated various ethnic groups. Quechua was co-opted by the Spanish in the sixteenth century, and was used for a time by Spanish priests in their proselytizing missions, even expanding its usage beyond the realm of the Inca.

Quechua facilitates the expression of affection in interpersonal relations. It is also a living language that aids in literary creations from ancestral voices being retained in the collective memory. Quechua shares about one-third of its vocabulary with Aymara, and its words often substitute for Spanish locutions, even in parts of Peru and Bolivia where Spanish is almost exclusively spoken.

The Quechua language is certainly extant, despite lacking a written form until after the Spanish conquest. Scholars typically categorize a handful of dialects, while recognizing more hybrid dialects exist. The most popular dialect of the language, Southern Quechua, is spoken throughout southern Peru, Bolivia, Chile, and even parts of Argentina. Another dialect, Northern Quechua, is spoken in parts of Colombia and Ecuador. A third dialect, known as *Waywash*, is spoken in parts of Peru's central highlands. The fourth main dialect, *Yunkey*, is spoken in pockets of the Peruvian highlands.

Quechua is an official language in both Bolivia and Peru. Censuses in Andean countries have tried to gauge the number of Quechua speakers, though the results suffer from underreporting. It is generally estimated that there were between 8 and 11 million Quechua speakers in South America in the early twenty-first century.

See also **Aymara; Chincha; Indigenous Languages.**

BIBLIOGRAPHY

Alvarez, Luis R. *Las lenguas aborigines: Testimonio de nuestra raices.* Cordoba: Alcion Editora, 2003.

Campbell, Lyle. *American Indian Languages: The Historical Linguistics of Native America.* New York: Oxford University Press, 1997.

WILFREDO KAPSOLI
SEAN H. GOFORTH

QUEIRÓS COUTINHO MATOSO DA CÂMERA, EUSÉBIO DE (1812–1868).

Eusébio de Queirós Coutinho Matoso da Câmera (*b.* 27 December 1812; *d.* 7 May 1868), Brazilian statesman. Born in São Paulo Luanda, Angola, Queirós was the son of a Portuguese magistrate who rose to the highest Brazilian judicial elite. He took his law degree at Olinda in 1832 and was immediately appointed a judge. Shortly thereafter, he became chief of police in Rio de Janeiro (1833–1844). Queirós's fierce defense of order, underwritten by marriage into a powerful merchant and political family (1835), helps explain his rise in the Conservative Party (1837). With

Joaquim José Rodrigues Torres and Paulino José Soares de Sousa, Eusébio formed the *trindade saquarema*, the party's most powerful, reactionary leadership. Eusébio took up crucial political responsibilities early on: provincial deputy in Rio de Janeiro (1838); national deputy for that province (1842–1844, 1848–1854); *desembargador da relação* in Rio (1842–1848); minister of justice (1848–1852); senator for Rio de Janeiro Province (1854); and member of the Council of State (1855). Responsible for developing the Código Comercial of 1850, he is better known for suppressing the African slave trade (1850) when he was minister of justice and for maintaining the power of the *saquarema* "oligarchy" in the Senate.

See also **Brazil: 1808–1889; Slavery: Abolition.**

BIBLIOGRAPHY

Leslie Bethell, *Abolition of the Brazilian Slave Trade* (1970).

Joaquim Nabuco, *Um estadista do império* (1975).

Ilmar Rohloff De Mattos, *O tempo saquarema* (1987).

Additional Bibliography

Curto, José C., and Renee Soulodre-LaFrance. *Africa and the Americas: Interconnections during the Slave Trade.* Trenton, NJ: Africa World Press, 2005.

Drescher, Seymour. *From Slavery to Freedom: Comparative Studies in the Rise and Fall of Atlantic Slavery.* New York: New York University Press, 1999.

Gonçalves, Maria José; Eusébio, António; and Maria de Fatima Nunes. *A illustre casa Ramires de Eça de Queirós.* Mem Martins, Portugal: Publicações Europa-América, 1987.

Johnson, Walter. *The Chattel Principle: Internal Slave Trades in the Americas.* New Haven, CT: Yale University Press, 2004.

Needell, Jeffrey. *The Party of Order: The Conservatives, the State, and Slavery in the Brazilian Monarchy, 1831–1871.* New York: Stanford University Press, 2006.

JEFFREY D. NEEDELL

QUEIRÓS LAW.

Queirós Law (named for Minister of Justice Eusébio de Queirós), an enactment passed in 1850 by the Brazilian Parliament that effectively put an end to the transatlantic slave trade between Africa and Brazil. Although a similar law had existed since 1831, making all Africans who entered Brazil after that date technically free persons, within Brazil it had been ignored. Planters, especially those in the rich coffee-producing areas of Rio de Janeiro, had continued to import slaves in record numbers despite their sharply rising prices. Such practices became less tenable after the British passed the Aberdeen Act in 1845, thereby declaring the slave trade equivalent to piracy and claiming the authority to search and seize slave cargoes even from ships in Brazilian ports. The Queirós Law assigned stiff penalties against both sellers and buyers of contraband slaves and declared null and void all debts owed for past purchases from illegal slave traders. Enforcement of the Queirós Law caused the trade in slaves to dwindle to a trickle within a few years, although as late as 1859 a few wealthy planters continued to import contraband slaves for their up-country coffee fazendas. Both contemporaries and later scholars have debated whether British pressure or Brazilian initiative accounts for the end of the trade. All would have to agree, however, that without enforcement by Brazilian authorities the trade could not have been suppressed.

See also **Coffee Industry; Queirós Coutinho Matoso da Câmera, Eusébio de; Slavery: Brazil; Slave Trade, Abolition of: Brazil.**

BIBLIOGRAPHY

Leslie Bethell, *The Abolition of the Brazilian Slave Trade: Britain, Brazil, and the Slave Trade Question, 1807–1869* (1970).

Additional Bibliography

Leite, Alfredo Carlos Teixeira. *O tráfico negreiro e a diplomacia britânica.* Caxias do Sul: EDUCS, 1998.

Tavares, Luís Henrique Dias. *Comércio proibido de escravos.* São Paulo: Editora Atica em co-ed. com o Conselho Nacional de Desenvolvimento Científico e Tecnológico, 1988.

SANDRA LAUDERDALE GRAHAM

QUEIROZ, DINAH SILVEIRA DE

(1910–1983). Dinah Silveira de Queiroz (*b.* 9 November 1910; *d.* 1983), Brazilian fiction writer. From the 1940s to the 1960s Queiroz was one of Brazil's most popular novelists. She was the second woman to be elected to the Brazilian Academy of Letters (1980). From a São Paulo literary family,

Queiroz was a diplomat and a diplomat's wife; she lived for a time in Europe and in Russia. A journalist, she wrote technically skillful and sensitive stories, thus helping innovate Brazilian fiction. She also wrote *crônicas* (sketches), drama, children's literature, and science fiction. Queiroz received important literary prizes, including the Academy's Machado de Assis Prize for her complete works in 1954. Her fame, however, derived from novel serializations in popular magazines. Her novels *Floradas na serra* (1939; Blossoms on the Mountain) and *A muralha* (1954; The Wall) also became successful cinema and television vehicles.

See also **Literature: Brazil.**

BIBLIOGRAPHY

Additional works by Queiroz are *Margarida La Rocque* (1949) and *Eu, venho* (1974), translated as *I, Christ, I'm Coming* (1977). *A muralha* was translated by Roberta King as *The Women of Brazil* (1980). A critical view of her work is Maria Teresa Leal, "Dinah Silveira de Queiroz: An Innovator in Brazilian Literature," in *Rice University Studies* 66 (1980): 81–88.

MARIA ANGÉLICA LOPES

QUEIROZ, RACHEL DE (1910–2003).

Rachel de Queiroz (*b.* 17 November 1910; *d.* 4 November 2003), Brazilian novelist and journalist. Born in Fortaleza, Ceará, and reared on her father's ranch in the *sertão*, Rachel de Queiroz returns to the Northeastern region of Brazil in her literature. Educated in a convent school to be a teacher, she became a journalist in 1927 and has written for several newspapers and magazines. Her career as a novelist began when she published *O quinze* (1930) at age twenty. Although she is also a dramatist, chronicler, translator, and writer of children's literature, *O quinze* remains her most noted work. It placed her in the mainstream of the Northeastern regional novelists who documented the human, social, and geographical complexity of the Brazilian *sertão*. *O quinze* is a realistic drama told through one family's struggle to survive the disastrous consequences of the drought of 1915, which had in fact caused Queiroz's family to flee to Rio de Janeiro.

Other novels include *João Miguel* (1932), *Caminho de pedras* (1937), *As três Marias* (1939; The Three Marias, 1963), *Dôra, Doralina* (1975; Dora, Doralina, 1984), and *Memorial de Maria Moura* (1992). Much of Queiroz's fiction addresses social problems associated with banditry and religious fanaticism in the *sertão,* such as in the dramas *Lampião* (1953) and *A beata Maria do Egito* (1958). Towards the end of her career she co-authored two texts with her sister Maria Luiza *Tantos anos* (1996)a book of memories and *Não me Deixes—Suas histórias e sua cozinha* (2000). Her special talent is illustrated in her portrayals of feminine characters who question their traditional roles in society and the family, but these sociological aspects form only a backdrop to situations and individual characters. Her literature incorporates simplicity of style and language.

Her limited political activity included a diplomatic mission to the United Nations on the Commission for Human Rights in 1966. Throughout her journalistic career, Queiroz continued to write *crónicas* (short prose pieces), published in several collections. In 1957 she received the Machado de Assis award for her body of work, and she was the first woman to be admitted to the Brazilian Academy of Letters, in 1977. Upon her death in 2003 she left the book *Visoes: Maurício Albano e Rachel de Queiroz* pending publication.

See also **Journalism; Literature: Brazil; Sertão, Sertanejo.**

BIBLIOGRAPHY

Almir De Andrade, *Aspetos da cultura brasileira* (1939), pp. 107–121.

Fred P. Ellison, "Rachel de Queiroz," in *Brazil's New Novel: Four Northeastern Masters* (1954), and "Introduction" in Queiroz's *The Three Marias* (1963).

Adonias Filho, "Rachel de Queiroz," in *O romance brasileiro de 30* (1969).

Additional Bibliography

Acioli, Socorro. *Rachel de Queiroz.* Fortaleza, Brazil: Edições Demócrita Rocha, 2003.

Barbosa, María de Lourdes Dias Leite. *Protagonistas de Rachel de Queiroz: Caminhos e descaminhos.* Campinas: Pontes, 1999.

Nery, Hermes Rodriguez. *Presenca de Rachel: Conversas informais com a escritora Rachel de Queiroz.* São Paulo: FUNPEC Editora, 2002.

LORI MADDEN

QUELEPA. Quelepa, meaning "jaguar of rock" in the ancient Potón language is a major pre-Hispanic site in the eastern portion of the Mesoamerican culture area (outside and to the east of the Maya area). It lies in the eastern third of modern El Salvador, about 25 miles from the Pacific coast, on the banks of the Río San Esteban, a tributary of the Río Grande de San Miguel. Forty structures divided into two groups, east and west, by a small stream stretch along a little over one-half mile of the riverbank.

Major structures (in the east group), dated to the Early Classic Period, consist of large, 30-foot-high, stepped truncated pyramids with front ramps, built upon terraces that leveled areas of the sloped terrain. Terrace walls are of well-cut horizontally laid stones. There is a Late Classic I-shaped ball court at the site, and there are numerous low house mounds.

Quelepa was first occupied in the Late Formative Period (400–300 BCE), and ceramic evidence, of the style called Usulutan, links it with the southeastern Maya area as far away as highland Guatemala. An early jaguar altar is stylistically related to sculpture from Izapa, Abaj Takalik, and Kaminaljuyú. *Manos, metates* (both used in grinding grain), and *comals* from the lowest levels of archaeological test excavations indicate early maize cultivation. The large terraced areas of Quelepa date to the Early Classic Period, and architecture includes the use of massive blocks of volcanic bedrock. The unusual arrangement of structures along terrace edges has been found at only two other sites.

In the Late Classic, about 600 CE, foreigners and governors related to Veracruz arrived, possibly by sea, and left their mark on both the ceramics and the architecture (west group) at Quelepa, where they built smaller structures, more tightly grouped, and of more coarse construction. About 900 CE, the site was finally abandoned. Quelepa's archaeological importance derives from the knowledge it supplies of the culture chronology of the easternmost part of Mesoamerica.

See also **Archaeology; Precontact History: Mesoamerica.**

BIBLIOGRAPHY

Further reading: Edward Wyllys Andrews, *The Archaeology of Quelepa, El Salvador,* publication 42 of the Middle American Research Institute, Tulane University, New Orleans (1976).

Additional Bibliography

Cobos, Rafael. *Síntesis de la arqueología de El Salvador (1850–1991)*. San Salvador: Dirección General de Publicaciones e Impresos, Consejo Nacional para la Cultura y Arte, Dirección General del Patrimonio Cultural, 1994.

Fowler, William R., and Federico Trujillo. *El Salvador: Antiguas civilizaciones*. San Salvador: Banco Agrícola Comercial de El Salvador, 1995.

Lange, Frederick W. *Paths to Central American Prehistory*. Niwot: University Press of Colorado, 1996.

WALTER R. T. WITSCHEY

QUERANDÍES.

Querandíes, name used by Spanish colonists to refer to the people who attacked and impeded the first settlement of Buenos Aires. Little is known about the origins of the Querandíes or their subsequent history. Some scholars suggest that the Querandíes disappeared perhaps because of a combination of disease, intertribal warfare, and migrations north up the Paraná River. The more common interpretation, however, is that the Querandíes were part of the larger Pampas linguistic group (*Gunun a kena*) who originally inhabited the region between the Río Carcarañá in the north and the Río Salado in the south and who later migrated south, away from the littoral, to escape disease and intertribal warfare.

See also **Indigenous Peoples; Paraná River.**

BIBLIOGRAPHY

Rodolfo M. Casamiquela, *Un nuevo panorama etnológico del area pan-pampeana y patagónica adyacente* (1969).

Additional Bibliography

Conlazo, Daniel, María Marta Lucero, and Teresa Authié. *Los querandíes: Tras las huellas de su cultura*. Buenos Aires: Galerna, 2006.

KRISTINE L. JONES

QUEREMISTAS.

Queremistas, members of the Brazilian popular movement that emerged in 1945 seeking to retain Getúlio Vargas as president. Their name came from their slogan, "Nos queremos Getúlio!" (We want Getúlio). Under growing pressure to liberalize the Estado Novo, in February 1945 Vargas announced that a date for general elections would be established within ninety days. The following month a nascent movement seeking to maintain Vargas in office began to organize in São Paulo, and by May leading Vargas supporters in Rio de Janeiro had launched the Movimento Queremista. As their primary goal, the *queremistas* sought to delay elections and instead to organize a constituent assembly. Failing that, they would support Vargas's candidacy for the presidency. The movement employed the mass media and staged large public rallies at the presidential palace. The movement ended on 29 October 1945 with the coup that overthrew Vargas.

See also **Vargas, Getúlio Dornelles.**

BIBLIOGRAPHY

Thomas E. Skidmore, *Politics in Brazil* (1967).

Israel Beloch and Alzira Alves De Abreu, eds., *Dicionário histórico-biográfico brasileiro, 1930–1983* (1984).

Additional Bibliography

Levine, Robert M. *Father of the Poor? Vargas and his Era*. Cambridge: Cambridge University Press, 1998.

Nascimento, Benedicto Heloiz. *A ordem nacionalista brasileira: O nacionalismo como política de desenvolvimento durante o Governo Vargas, 1930–1945*. São Paulo, SP, Brasil: Humanitas, FFLCH/USP: USP, IEB, Instituto de Estudos Brasileiros, 2002.

Rose, R. S. *One of the Forgotten Things: Getúlio Vargas and Brazilian Social Control, 1930–1954*. Westport, CT: Greenwood Press, 2000.

WILLIAM SUMMERHILL

QUERÉTARO (CITY).

Querétaro (City), capital of the modern state of Querétaro in Mexico. The town was founded in 1531 by combined Spanish and Indian forces, led by Hernán Pérez de Bocanegra and Hernando de Tapia. Querétaro achieved the status of a city in 1656, and by 1810 it was one of the largest cities of the realm, with an estimated population of 58,000. The population climbed to 88,424 by 1910 and was estimated at 734,139 in 2005.

The city of Querétaro was the commercial center for an active trade in cereals and wool products, which were shipped to the emerging mining towns of the north and the established cities of the south. *Obrajes* and the smaller *trapiches* were the typical sites of production for textiles. By the end of the eighteenth century, the city was one of the leading producers of textiles in the Americas. Cotton production increased in the nineteenth century, but overall textile production occupied a less prominent position in the local economy. In addition to textiles, the city contained a large royal tobacco factory in the eighteenth century. The modern period of industrial growth began after World War II, and by the 1960s Querétaro was producing automobile parts, farm implements, and food products for national and international markets.

With its size and wealth during the colonial period, the city supported the construction of many chapels, convents, and churches. Missionary efforts in the rugged northeastern mountains of the state, as well as in Texas and the Californias, relied on the religious institutions of the city for support. Junípero Serra and Francisco Palóu, both later to achieve fame in California, labored in the mission fields of northern Querétaro in the 1750s.

Querétaro has figured prominently in the political history of Mexico, beginning with the independence movement of 1808. It was the capital of Mexico in 1847 and 1848 during the Mexican-American War, the headquarters of Benito Juárez during La Reforma (the War of the Reform), the location of the capture and execution of Maximilian in 1867, and the site for the writing of the Mexican Constitution of 1917.

See also **Mexico: The Colonial Period; Mexico: 1810– 1910; Mexico, Wars and Revolutions: The Reform.**

BIBLIOGRAPHY

For the early history of the city, see John C. Super, *La vida en Querétaro durante la Colonia, 1531–1810.* Mexico: Fondo de Cultura Economica, 1983. Andrew Hunter Whiteford analyzes social change in Querétaro in *Two Cities of Latin America: A Comparative Description of Social Classes.* Garden City, NY: Doubleday, 1964.

Additional Bibliography

Couturier, Edith Boorstein. *The Silver King: The Remarkable Life of the Count of Regla in Mexico.* Albuquerque: University of New Mexico Press, 2003.

García Ugarte, Marta Eugenia. *Breve historia de Querétaro.* México: Colegio de México: Fideicomismo Historia de las Américas: Fondo de Cultura Económica, 1999.

García Ugarte, Marta Eugenia. *Génesis del porvenir: Sociedad y política en Querétaro (1913–1940.)* México: Instituto de Investigaciones Sociales/UNAM: Gobierno del Estado de Querétaro: Fondo de Cultura Económica, 1997.

Gunnarsdóttir, Ellen. *Mexican Karismata: The Baroque Vocation of Francisca de Los Angeles, 1674–1744.* Lincoln, NE: University of Nebraska Press, 2004.

JOHN C. SUPER

QUERÉTARO (STATE). Querétaro (State), one of the smallest Mexican states, today encompassing 4,544 square miles. The estimated population in 1990 was 1,044,200. It is located in central Mexico, bounded on the south by the states of Mexico and Michoacán, on the west by Guanajuato, the east by Hidalgo, and the north by San Luis Potosí. The western section of the state extends into the Bajío, the rich agricultural region long important in the history of Mexico. Rugged mountain ranges dominate much of the landscape of the state. Bordering the city of Querétaro are the Sierra Queretana to the south and the Sierra del Zamorano to the north. In the northeast is the Sierra Gorda, for centuries an obstacle to colonization. The highest point in the state is the Cerro de la Calentura, reaching 11,647 feet above sea level in the Sierra Gorda.

Long the home of Otomí-speaking peoples, the early history of the region experienced the influence of Tarascans and Aztecs from the south. With the arrival of Europeans in 1531, Querétaro became a political and religious province, administered by the city of the same name. Administrative reorganization in the eighteenth century created the intendancy of Mexico, which included the *corregimiento* (jurisdiction) of Querétaro, which in turn included the three large municipal divisions of Querétaro, Cadereyta, and San Juan del Río. With the independence of Mexico, Querétaro formally became a state in 1824 with the official name of Querétaro de Arteaga.

Traditionally, the wealth of the state came from a combination of agriculture, manufacturing, and trade. Already by the end of the sixteenth century, the region was known for its abundant harvests of maize and wheat and its large numbers of sheep, cattle, and horses. Large sheep *estancias* (ranches) spread to the west and north of the province as Spaniards laid claim to the land. Wool provided the raw material necessary for Obrajes, the textile factories that dominated the urban economy in the eighteenth century. The location of the city and state of Querétaro between the mines of the north and the densely populated regions of the south stimulated agricultural and industrial production and commerce. Mining, including that of turquoise and opals, around which artisan activities developed, provided another source of economic activity, increasing in significance in the nineteenth and twentieth centuries.

By the end of the colonial period, the population of the region was a modest 126,000. Growth in the nineteenth century was slow and sporadic, reaching 232,289 in 1900. After the reversals of the Mexican Revolution of 1910, the population began to expand more rapidly, totaling 355,045 in 1960. Since that time, as with the rest of Mexico, the state experienced very rapid population growth.

See also **Agriculture; Mexico, Wars and Revolutions: Mexican Revolution; Mining: Colonial Spanish America; Mining: Modern; Otomí.**

BIBLIOGRAPHY

Septién y Septién, *Historia de Querétaro* (1966).

John C. Super, "The Agricultural Near North: Querétaro in the Seventeenth Century," in *Provinces of Early Mexico,* edited by Ida Altman and James Lockhart (1976), pp. 231–251, and *La vida en Querétaro durante la Colonia, 1531–1810* (1983).

Additional Bibliography

Cabello, Gaspar Real. *El campo queretano en transición.* La Jolla, CA: Ejido Reform Research Project, Center for United States; Mexican Studies, University of California, San Diego, 1997.

Coerver, Don M; Pasztor, Suzanne B., and Buffington, Robert. *Mexico: An Encyclopedia of Contemporary Culture and History.* Santa Barbara, CA: ABC-CLIO, 2004.

Crespo, Ana María; Brambila Paz, Rosa, and Pastrana, Alejandro. *Querétaro prehispánico.* México, D.F.: Instituto Nacional de Antropología e Historia, 1991.

García Ugarte, Marta Eugenia. *Génesis del porvenir: Sociedad y política en Querétaro (1913–1940).* México: Instituto de Investigaciones Sociales/UNAM: Gobierno del Estado de Querétaro: Fondo de Cultura Económica, 1997.

García Ugarte, Marta Eugenia. *Breve historia de Querétaro.* México: Colegio de México: Fideicomiso Historia de las Américas: Fondo de Cultura Económica, 1999.

Gilly, Adolfo. *The Mexican Revolution.* New York: New Press: Distributed by W.W. Norton & Company, 2005.

Monsiváis, Carlos; del Paso, Fernando, and Pacheco, José Emilio. *Belleza y poesía en el arte popular mexicano: Guerrero, Hidalgo, Estado de México, Morelos, Oaxaca, Querétaro, Tlaxcala, Veracruz.* México: Circuito Artístico Regional Zona Centro, 1996.

Niemeyer, Victor. *Revolution at Querétaro: the Mexican Constitutional Convention of 1916–1917.* Austin: Published for the Institute of Latin American Studies by the University of Texas Press, 1991.

Pahissa, Angela Moyano. *Querétaro en la Guerra con los Estados Unidos, 1846–1848.* Santiago de Querétaro, Qro. [Mexico]: Gobierno del Estado de Querétaro, Oficialía Mayor, Archivo Histórico, 1998.

Tostado, Conrado and Aldana, Guillermo. *The State of Querétaro, México.* Mexico, 1997.

JOHN C. SUPER

QUERINO, MANOEL RAIMUNDO

(1851–1923). Manoel Raimundo Querino (Manuel; *b.* 28 July 1851; *d.* 14 February 1923), Brazilian folklorist and reformer. His essays on religious cults, artists and artisans, cuisine, folk customs, and other topics celebrated skilled artisans and the Afro-Brazilian achievement.

Querino's works challenged racism by means of objective documentation. Those collected posthumously in *Costumes africanos no Brasil* (1938; African Customs in Brazil) and *A raça africana e os seus costumes* (1955; The African Race and Its Customs) assemble a gallery of black heroes and assess the African contribution to colonial Brazil. They describe Bahia's Candomblé religion without the social Darwinist theorizing of his contemporary, Raimundo Nina Rodrigues.

Querino championed the arts and skilled trades in Bahia. He was founder (1872) and teacher at the Liceu de Artes e Ofícios, a vocational arts school, and founder (1877) of the Escola de Belas Artes. He represented Salvador's workers in cooperatives, at the 1892 Rio labor congress, and on the city council.

See also **Art: Folk Art; Bahia; Race and Ethnicity.**

BIBLIOGRAPHY

J. Teixeira Barros, in the preface to Manoel Raimundo Querino, *A Bahia de outr'ora* (1922), offers a biographical sketch. E. Bradford Burns, "Manuel Querino's Interpretation of the African Contribution to Brazil," in *Journal of Negro History* 59, no. 1 (1974): 78–86, analyzes Querino's thought. Jorge Amado, *Tent of Miracles,* translated by Barbara Shelley (1978), is a novel based on Querino's life. See also Manuel Querino, *The African Contribution to Brazilian Culture,* translated by E. Bradford Burns (1978).

Additional Bibliography

Leite, José Roberto Teixeira. *Pintores negros do oitocentos.* São Paulo: Edições K: Motores MWM Brasil, 1988.

DAIN BORGES

QUESADA, ERNESTO (1858–1934).

Ernesto Quesada (*b.* 1 June 1858; *d.* 7 February 1934), Argentine scholar and diplomat. Quesada, the son of Vicente G. Quesada and Elvira Medina, was born in Buenos Aires. He studied at the Colegio San José, then went to Europe to continue his education. Upon his return, he enrolled in the Colegio Nacional, and from there went to the University of Buenos Aires, where he received a law degree in 1882. Quesada taught foreign literature at the Colegio Nacional from 1881 to 1884. When his father was Argentine ambassador to the United States (1885–1892), Quesada and his wife, Eleonora Pacheco, spent most of 1885 sightseeing there, and he studied American literature before leaving for Europe at the end of the year.

Quesada was devoted to his father, accompanying him on his numerous trips abroad and often serving as his interpreter and secretary. Father and son collaborated on many publications; thus, the works of each contain references to those of the other. Quesada's articles on contemporary intellectuals relied on notes made after hearing them at informal gatherings. He helped his father publish *Virreinato del Río de la Plata, 1776–1810* (1881), and together they edited the *Nueva revista de Buenos Aires* (1881–1885). The son was not active in politics, but he briefly was a supporter of Miguel Juárez Celman before joining the Unión Cívica Radical. From 1893 to 1895 he was editor of the newspaper *El Tiempo,* in which many of his essays first appeared.

Quesada was not only a journalist and polemicist but also a distinguished lawyer and public servant. A strong supporter of Pan-Americanism, he was elected president of the Argentine delegation to the Pan-American Scientific Congress in 1915. That year Harvard University appointed him professor of history and Latin American economy, beginning in 1916, but for an unexplained reason he never appeared in Cambridge. He became professor of international law and treaties at the University of Buenos Aires in 1919.

From 1904 to 1923 Quesada was professor of sociology at the University of Buenos Aires. In 1907 he was named professor of political economy at the Law Faculty of the University of La Plata. In his lectures he stressed the need for social legislation and an examination of labor conditions. In 1908, at the request of the Law Faculty, he examined the methods of faculty promotion and history teaching at twenty-two German universities. During this investigation he met Karl Lamprecht, head of the Institute of World History and Civilization at the University of Leipzig. Lamprecht's institute probably was Quesada's model for the Institute of Historical Investigations, which he helped establish at the University of Buenos Aires. Quesada's second wife, Leonore Niessen Deilers, undoubtedly was instrumental in his decision to give his library—consisting of 60,000 books, 18,000 manuscripts, and the thirty unpublished volumes of his father's memoirs—to the University of Berlin. The university created the Ibero-American Institute to house it, and began publishing a journal, *Ibero-Amerikanische Archiv.* Quesada retired to Spiez, Switzerland, where he spent the rest of his life.

See also **Argentina: The Nineteenth Century; Argentina: The Twentieth Century; Pan-Americanism; Sociology.**

BIBLIOGRAPHY

This biographical sketch is based primarily on Juan Canter, "Bio-Bibliografía de Ernesto Quesada," in the University of Buenos Aires's *Boletín del Instituto de investigaciones históricas* 20, nos. 67–68 (January–June 1936): 343–722. The bibliographical essay, with many annotated entries, begins on 551. See also Rómulo D. Carbia, *Historia crítica de la historiografía argentina (desde sus orígenes en el siglo XVI)* (1940).

Additional Bibliography

Lanús, Juan Archibaldo. *Aquel apogeo: Política internacional argentina, 1910–1939*. Buenos Aires: Emecé Editores, 2001.

Zimmermann, Eduardo A. *Los liberales reformistas: La cuestión social en la Argentina, 1890–1916*. Buenos Aires: Editorial Sudamericana: Universidad de San Andrés, 1995.

JOSEPH T. CRISCENTI

QUESADA, VICENTE GREGORIO

(1830–1913). An Argentine legal adviser, essayist, and politician, Vicente Quesada was born on April 5, 1830, in Buenos Aires and moved to the province of Corrientes in 1853. In that year Buenos Aires backed down from the commitment made by all Argentine provinces, in the Pact of San Nicolás, to ratify a new national constitution. In 1856 Quesada was elected deputy to the Paraná congress for the province of Corrientes, and he also worked as a journalist. In 1871 President Domingo F. Sarmiento appointed him director of the Buenos Aires Public Library, which later became the National Library.

In 1875, following a trip to Europe, he published his controversial book, *La Patagonia y las tierras australes del continente Americano*, which made the claim, against that of Chile, that Argentina was the exclusive heir to Patagonia. In 1877 he was appointed minister of government for the province of Buenos Aires and in 1878 was elected deputy to the National Congress. In 1881 he published *El vierreinato del Río de la Plata, 1776–1819*, again motivated by the border disputes between Argentina and Chile. In this book he forcefully developed the legend of the Viceroyalty of La Plata as a great nation conceived by Charles III of Spain and forever lost by the actions of incompetent Argentine governments. This legend was to create a school within Argentina's liberal or revisionist territorial nationalism. In 1883 President Julio Argentino Roca appointed Quesada to be a special envoy to the empire of Brazil. He continued diplomatic life in the United States, Mexico, France, Spain, and Germany until 1904. On his return to Argentina, he chaired the Academy of Philosophy and Letters at the University of Buenos Aires. In 1910 Quesada published his renowned work, *La vida intelectual en la América española durante los siglos XVI, XVII y XVIII*. He died in Argentina on September 19, 1913.

See also **Argentina: The Nineteenth Century; Sarmiento, Domingo Faustino.**

BIBLIOGRAPHY

Cavaleri, Paulo. *La restauración del Virreinato: Orígenes del nacionalismo territorial argentino*. Buenos Aires: Universidad Nacional de Quilmes, 2004.

Halperín Donghi, Tulio. *Una nación para el desierto argentino*. Buenos Aires: Centro Editor de América Latina, 1995.

Quesada, Vicente G. [under the name Víctor Gálvez]. *Memorias de un viejo* [1888]. Buenos Aires: Academia Argentina de Letras, 1990.

VICENTE PALERMO

QUETZAL.

A beautiful, climbing bird (*Pharomachrus mocinno mocinno*), green with a red breast. The male has a long tail. Its name comes from the Nahuatl *quetzaltototl* (bird with esteemed green feathers). The quetzal cannot live in captivity. For this reason, it is a symbol of liberty and the national bird of Guatemala. The bird can be found in the mountainous cloud forests of Costa Rica, El Salvador, Guatemala, Honduras, Mexico, Nicaragua, and as far south as Panama. While the population continues to decline due to deforestation, it is officially protected in order to slow or prevent its extinction.

Quetzal is also the name of the Guatemalan monetary unit established in 1925. Until 1984 the quetzal maintained parity with the U.S. dollar.

See also **Guatemala.**

BIBLIOGRAPHY

Victor Wolfgang Von Hagen, *Quetzal Quest* (1939).

Carlos Samayoa Chinchilla, *El Quetzal* (1974).

Additional Bibliography

Stattersfield, Alison, and David Capper, eds. *Threatened Birds of the World: The Official Source for Birds on the IUCN Red List*. Cambridge, UK: BirdLife International, 2000.

FERNANDO GONZÁLEZ DAVISON

QUETZALCOATL. Quetzalcoatl, the name of one of the most important Mesoamerican deities, also borne as a title by a semilegendary Toltec ruler. Although at the time of the Conquest the two Quetzalcoatls were to some degree merged, it is convenient to distinguish them by designating the former as Ehecatl Quetzalcoatl and the latter as Topiltzín Quetzalcoatl of Tollán. "Quetzalcoatl," in Nahuatl, literally means "quetzal-feather (*quetzalli*) snake (*coatl*)," and the icon that symbolized the god consisted of a rattlesnake with scales covered by the long green feathers of the quetzal bird. The usual interpretation of this fusion of avian and reptilian features is a contrastive dualism signifying the union of sky and earth, embodying a creative concept. Quetzalcoatl does play a major demiurgic role in the central Mexican cosmogonies and, when additionally designated as Ehecatl (wind), expressed the fundamental fertility theme with particular emphasis on the fructifying aspect of the wind (in the sense of breath).

The feathered-serpent icon is quite ancient in Mesoamerica. It is strikingly manifested in Early Classic Teotihuacán in the sculptured friezes of the Temple of the Feathered Serpent, datable to the beginning of our era, and in related painted images. It evolves through the subsequent Xochicalco, Cacaxtla, and Toltec iconographic traditions, particularly flowering in that of the Aztecs, where it frequently was depicted in relief and three-dimensional stone sculpture. When conceived as Ehecatl Quetzalcoatl, the deity wears a projecting mask covering the lower face through which he was believed to blow the wind. Quetzalcoatl was the special patron deity of the great mercantile and religious pilgrimage center of Cholollan (modern Cholula, Puebla). Deities analogous to Quetzalcoatl were present in the Mixteca of western Oaxaca (9 Wind), highland Guatemala (Gucumatz), and northern Yucatán (Kukulcan).

Topiltzín (Our Esteemed Lord) Quetzalcoatl of Tollán was featured prominently in the native histories of central Mexico. Ruling at Tollán (modern Tula, Hidalgo) during a golden age of Toltec power and dominance, he seems to have espoused the cult of the ancient fertility/ wind/creator deity, Quetzalcoatl, whose name he bore as a title. He introduced various sacerdotal rituals, especially sanguinary auto-sacrifice, and was considered the

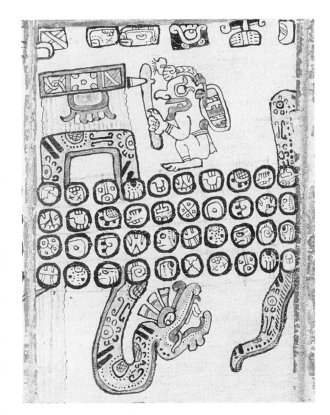

Quetzalcoatl depicted as a feathered serpent. From a pre-Conquest Mayan codex, early 15th century. THE ART ARCHIVE/MUSEO DE AMERICA MADRID/DAGLI ORTI. REPRODUCED BY PERMISSION OF THE PICTURE DESK INC.

archetype of the post-Toltec priesthood. Due to circumstances that are somewhat obscure but may have involved opposition to his religious doctrines, he was forced to abandon Tollán. He traveled east, to the Gulf Coast, where he either disappeared or died, his soul ascending to heaven, transformed into the planet Venus.

Topiltzín Quetzalcoatl was also considered to have established the basis for legitimate political power in western Mesoamerica—and, to some extent, in eastern Mesoamerica (highland Guatemala, northern Yucatán) as well. Nearly all of the ruling dynasts of the leading city-states of Late Postclassic central Mexico claimed political legitimacy through their connections with the royal house of Tollán. Motecuhzoma II, ninth member of the ruling dynasty of Mexico Tenochtitlán—master, with its allies, Tetzcoco and Tlacopán, of the most extensive polity in North America—claimed direct dynastic descent from Topiltzín Quetzalcoatl. The evidence for a widespread belief in Topiltzín Quetzalcoatl's eventual return to reclaim his royal dignity, which significantly influenced Motecuhzoma in his initial dealings with Hernán Cortés, is very strong.

See also **Cortés, Hernán; Quetzal; Toltecs.**

BIBLIOGRAPHY

Pedro Armillas, "La serpiente emplumada: Quetzalcoatl y Tlaloc," in *Cuadernos Americanos* 31, no. 1 (1947): 161–178.

Alfredo López-Austin, *Hombre-Dios: Religión y política en el mundo Náhuatl* (1973).

Gordon R. Willey, "Mesoamerican Civilization and the Idea of Transcendence," in *Antiquity* 50, nos. 199–200 (1976): 205–215.

H. B. Nicholson, "The Deity 9 Wind 'Ehecatl-Quetzalcoatl' in the Mixteca Pictorials," in *Journal of Latin American Lore* 4, no. 1 (1978): 61–92, and "Ehecatl Quetzalcoatl vs. Topiltzín Quetzalcoatl of Tollán: A Problem in Mesoamerican Religion and History," in *Actes du XLIIe Congrès international des américanistes, Paris, 2–9 septembre 1976*, vol. 6 (1979), pp. 35–47.

Eloise Quiñones Keber, "The Aztec Image of Topiltzín Quetzalcoatl," in *Smoke and Mist: Mesoamerican Studies in Memory of Thelma D. Sullivan*, edited by J. Kathryn Josserand and Karen Dakin (1988), pp. 329–343.

Additional Bibliography

Carrasco, David. *Quetzacoatl and the Irony of Empire: Myths and Prophecies in the Aztec Tradition*. Rev. ed. Boulder, CO: University Press of Colorado, 2000.

Florescano, Enrique. *The Myth of Quetzalcoatl*. Trans. Lysa Hochroth. Baltimore, MD: Johns Hopkins University Press, 1999.

Nicholson, H. B. *Topiltzin Quetzacoatl: The Once and Future Lord of the Toltecs*. Boulder, CO: University Press of Colorado, 2001.

Read, Kay Almere and Jason J. Gonzáles. *Handbook of Mesoamerican Mythology*. Santa Barbara, CA: ABC-CLIO, 2000.

Sugiyama, Saburo. *Human Sacrifice, Militarism, and Rulership: Materialization of State Ideology at the Feathered Serpent Pyramid, Teotihuacan*. New York: Cambridge University Press, 2005.

H. B. NICHOLSON

QUETZALTENANGO. Quetzaltenango, second largest city of Guatemala (2002 est. pop. 127,569) and the most important of Los Altos, the western highlands region. It occupies a wide and fertile valley at 7,654 feet above sea level, surrounded by a group of high mountains and volcanoes, one of which, the Santa María, destroyed the city in 1902.

In pre-Columbian times, Quetzaltenango was an important Maya-K'iche' center, known as Xelajú; it still has a sizable Indian population. It is near the site of the battle in which the Spanish army under Pedro de Alvarado defeated the legendary Tecúnumán and his Quiché warriors in 1524. This encounter marked the beginning of the Spanish conquest of the area. A backwater of the Kingdom of Guatemala for most of the colonial period, Quetzaltenango finally obtained the rank of city in 1825. As early as the latter half of the eighteenth century, however, the city had developed into the chief commercial center of Los Altos, home to a sizable Spanish and ladino population.

In the early nineteenth century its principal citizens led Los Altos in a determined campaign to win greater economic and political autonomy from the capital, Guatemala City. This regionalist movement bore fruit for a brief period (1838–1840) when Quetzaltenango became the capital of the state of Los Altos, the sixth of the Central American Federation. The federation collapsed, however, and the region was forcefully reincorporated into Guatemala by the Conservative dictator Rafael Carrera in 1840.

Under the Liberal regimes (1873–1944), Quetzaltenango quickly developed into the financial and marketing center of the expanding coffee industry. The inauguration of the electric railway in 1930 and its dismantling shortly afterward signaled the end of the coffee boom and the onset of less prosperous times for the city. Today Quetzaltenango is a marketing and manufacturing center and the seat of two university faculties.

See also **Guatemala.**

BIBLIOGRAPHY

Julio De La Roca, *Biografía de un pueblo* (1971).

Jorge H. González, "Una historia de Los Altos, el sexto estado de la Federación Centroamericana," M.A. thesis, Tulane University, 1989.

Additional Bibliography

Grandin, Greg. "Everyday Forms of State Decomposition: Quetzaltenango, Guatemala, 1954." *Bulletin of Latin American Research* (July 2000): 303–320.

Grandin, Greg. "Can the Subaltern Be Seen?: Photography and the Affects of Nationalism." *Hispanic American Historical Review* (February 2004): 83–111.

JORGE H. GONZÁLEZ

QUICHÉ. *See* **K'iche'**.

QUIJANO, CARLOS (1900–1984).

Carlos Quijano (*b.* 1900; *d.* 10 June 1984), Uruguayan journalist, writer, and political activist born in Montevideo, where he received a degree in law in 1923. He left Uruguay to study economics and political science at the Sorbonne in Paris. There he acted as a correspondent for the Uruguayan newspaper *El País* and cofounded the General Association of Latin American Students (AGELA). Intellectually, he came under the influence of the theoretical socialism of thinkers such as Gramsci, Sorel, and Croce, which greatly motivated his subsequent political committment when he returned to Uruguay in 1928. After returning to Uruguay, he was elected to Congress as a member of the National (or Blanco) Party from 1928 to 1931.

But Quijano's greatest influence on Uruguayan culture was through his role as founder and director of the weekly *Marcha*, through which he truly became mentor to a generation. For thirty-five years (1939–1974) *Marcha* served as a cultural reference throughout Latin America and a forum for writers and thinkers of different countries. In its pages appeared the work of Juan Carlos Onetti, Angel Rama, Emir Rodríguez Monegal, Carlos Real De Azúa, Idea Vilariño, Joaquín Torres García, Arturo Ardao, Mario Benedetti, Mercedes Rein, Cristina Peri Rossi, and Jorge Ruffinelli, among many others. In 1974, *Marcha* was shut down by the dictatorship, and after a brief period of imprisonment, Quijano left for Mexico along with other members of the weekly's staff. In exile he continued to work incessantly until his death, editing *Cuadernos de Marcha* and teaching classes at the National Autonomous University in Mexico City.

See also **Journalism; Uruguay: The Twentieth Century; Uruguay, Political Parties: Blanco Party.**

BIBLIOGRAPHY

Hugo R. Alfaro, *Navegar es necesario: Quijano y el Semanario "Marcha"* (1984).

Gerardo Caetano and José Pedro Rilla, *El joven Quijano, 1900–1933: Izquierda nacional y conciencia crítica* (1986).

Pablo Rocca, *35 años en MARCHA* (1992).

Additional Bibliography

Traversoni, Alfredo, and Diosma Piotti. *Historia del Uruguay siglo XX*. Montevideo: Ediciones de la Plaza, 1993.

MARÍA INÉS DE TORRES

QUILOMBO.

Quilombo, a refuge for runaway slaves (*quilombolas* or *calhambolas*) in Brazil. *Quilombos* ranged from small hideouts in which several slaves concealed themselves from their masters to vast, organized communities that housed and protected thousands of runaway captives. *Quilombos* typically were located in isolated, inaccessible places, but they also existed at the edges of plantations and towns where runaways relied on the occasional theft of food and weapons, on trade, and on alliances with sympathetic free people or other slaves.

Whether they were the *quilombos* or *mocambos* of Brazil, the Palenques of Spanish America, or the Maroon villages of the British Caribbean, runaway communities represented a vital means of collective slave resistance and a persistent feature of slave societies. In Brazil they appeared in the late sixteenth century and remained a constant irritation to authorities until slavery was abolished in 1888. Their presence was a visible reminder of the brutality of the slave regime, a factor that contributed to the army's unceasing efforts to hunt and destroy them.

While many *quilombos* fell to the superior firepower of the military, some survived for decades and others were never destroyed. The larger ones developed a range of strategies to deal with constant embattlement, including guerrilla tactics, spying networks, and even occasional cooperation with authorities—agreeing to return new runaways to the army, for example—to ensure continued existence. Some long-established settlements developed into sophisticated fortresses capable of withstanding attack, and these protected not only the runaways but the crops and livestock necessary to sustain the community.

Quilombo organization depended on successful cooperation among members, a task which was sometimes complicated by the diverse cultural backgrounds of the runaways. Many who fled captive life were African but of different "nations," while others were *crioulos* (Brazilian-born slaves of African parentage) or of African-European descent. Adding occasionally to this mixture were free people, including whites and Amerindians. While some runaways seized the chance to express aspects of their African heritage, the variety of backgrounds among the members meant that adaptation and innovation marked cultural life in the *quilombos* much as they did elsewhere in Brazilian society.

See also **Palmares; Slavery: Brazil.**

BIBLIOGRAPHY

The best source on runaway slave societies throughout the Americas is Richard Price, ed., *Maroon Societies: Rebel Slave Communities in the Americas,* 2d ed. (1979). See especially the three articles on the Brazilian *quilombos* by R. K. Kent, Roger Bastide, and Stuart B. Schwartz, on pp. 169–226. Katia M. De Queirós Mattoso also discusses *quilombos* in her *To Be a Slave in Brazil, 1550–1888,* translated by Arthur Goldhammer (1986), which provides a brief history of several of the well-known runaway settlements in Northeastern Brazil. See also Waldemar De Almeida Barbosa, *Negros y quilombos em Minas Gerais* (1972).

Additional Bibliography

Gomes, Flávio dos Santos. *A hidra e os pântanos: Mocambos, quilombos e comunidades de fugitivos no Brasil (séculos XVII–XIX).* São Paulo: UNESP, 2005.

Reis, João José and Flávio dos Santos Gomes. *Liberdade por um fio: História dos quilombos no Brasil.* São Paulo: Companhia das Letras, 1996.

JUDITH L. ALLEN

QUIMBAYA.
Quimbaya, the name given to various ethnic groups inhabiting the Middle Cauca River valley of Colombia (departments of Quindío, Risaralda, Caldas, and Antioquia) in the sixteenth century, as well as to an immense complex of archaeological artifacts, dating from approximately 1000 to 1500 CE, that were found in the same region. Quimbaya ceramics of the Caldas complex (1000–1400) are characterized by red resist ware, and the

Middle Cauca complex (1050–1500) includes stirrup vessels and anthropomorphic figurines. Gold artifacts associated with cremation burials of elite individuals are documented from the area.

The ethnic communities associated with the archaeological complex maintained a high population density supported by maize agriculture. These groups, which exhibited features of the chiefdom level of sociopolitical integration, were characterized by accentuated social hierarchy, hereditary political leaders, and an economic system based on the redistribution of subsistence products. The ethnohistorical record emphasizes Quimbaya religious practices, including human sacrifice and the flaying of slain enemies, as a means of acquiring their power.

The Quimbaya of the Conquest period are known for their fierce resistance to Spanish domination, which culminated in a series of mid-sixteenth-century rebellions against the *encomienda* system. Resistance to Spanish rule continued with attacks on towns on the mining frontier well into the seventeenth century.

See also **Archaeology; Encomienda; Precontact History: Andean Region.**

BIBLIOGRAPHY

Juan Friede, *Los Quimbayas bajo la dominación española* (1963).

Luis Duque Gómez, *Los Quimbayas: Reseña etno-histórica y arqueológica* (1970).

Armand Labbé, *Colombia Before Columbus* (1986).

Alonso Valencia, *Resistencia indígena a la colonización española* (1991).

Additional Bibliography

Arango Cano, Jesús. *La gran cultura quimbaya.* Armenia: Editorial QuinGráficas, 1994.

Gamboa Hinestrosa, Pablo. *El tesoro de los Quimbayas: Historia, identidad y patrimonio.* Bogotá: Planeta, 2002.

McEwan, Colin. *Precolumbian Gold: Technology, Style and Iconography.* Chicago: Fitzroy Dearborn Publishers, 2000.

JOANNE RAPPAPORT

QUININE.
Quinine, an extract from the bark of the chinchona tree found in Peru, Ecuador, and Bolivia. Indigenous peoples had long used ground

chinchona bark to treat fever and cold and the name *quinine* comes from the Quechua term "quina" or "quinquina" meaning "bark" or "holy bark". Europeans in seventeenth-century South America came to recognize the native use, and in utilizing it found quinine to be effective in treating malaria. Samples were sent to Europe where chinchona bark's antimalarial value and demand grew. The Jesuits were particularly effective in organizing the early trade, and chinchona bark also came to be known as "Jesuits' bark." Thus quinine became the major antimalarial drug of the eighteenth and nineteenth centuries. Synthetic antimalarial drugs such as Atabrine, so important to the Allies during World War II, lessened but did not eliminate the reliance on quinine. Once quinine was a valuable commodity shipped from Peru to Europe, but its commercial value has been far less significant in world history than its medical value. With quinine, Europeans had a new weapon against the fevers of the tropics. Demographic and settlement patterns for Europeans and indigenous peoples changed as quinine brought malaria under control.

See also **Diseases; Jesuits; Medicinal Plants; Medicine: Colonial Spanish America.**

BIBLIOGRAPHY

Henry Hobhouse, *Seeds of Change: Five Plants that Transformed Mankind* (1985).

Additional Bibliography

Appel, John Wilton. *Francisco José de Caldas: A Scientist at Work in Nueva Granada*. Philadelphia: American Philosophical Society, 1994.

Jarcho, Saul, and Francesco Torti. *Quinine's Predecessor: Francesco Torti and the Early History of Cinchona*. Baltimore, MD: Johns Hopkins University Press, 1993.

Puerto Sarmiento, F. Javier. *La ilusión quebrada: Botánica, sanidad y política científica en la España ilustrada*. Barcelona: Serbal; Madrid: CSIC, 1988.

Rocco, Fiammetta. *The Miraculous Fever Tree: Malaria and the Quest for a Cure that Changed the World*. New York: HarperCollins, 2003.

Zárate, Carlos G. *Extracción de quina: La configuración del espacio andino-amazónico de fines del siglo XIX*. Bogotá: Universidad Nacional de Colombia, Sede Leticia, Instituto Amazónico de Investigaciones, 2001.

JOHN C. SUPER

QUINN, ANTHONY (1915–2001). Anthony Quinn's personal story is as legendary as many of the roles he played on film. He was born Antonio Rudolfo Oaxaca Quinn in Chihuahua, Mexico, on May 21, 1915. His Mexican-Indian mother, Manuela Oaxaca, and half-Irish father, Frank Quinn, both followed Pancho Villa's forces in the Mexican Revolution. The confusion of the war caused his parents to become separated when Antonio was only eight months old, after which his mother escaped to El Paso, Texas, and did not reconnect with her husband until nearly three years later. The Quinn family made the trek to Southern California, settling in the Boyle Heights and Echo Park neighborhoods of Los Angeles. Quinn grew up tough but also had experiences that tapped into his many talents. He began sculpting at age nine and later won a competition for a bust of Abraham Lincoln. He studied under Frank Lloyd Wright after winning a prize for architectural design during his junior year in high school. He would continue his artistic pursuits for the rest of his life, and in his later years he became rather well known as a painter and sculptor.

One of Quinn's early films, *The Plainsman* (1936), also forecast his future. He played a Native American, anticipating his frequent casting as swarthy ethnic "others." Additionally, the film was directed by Cecil B. DeMille, whose daughter, Katherine, Quinn married in 1937. Their nearly thirty-year union produced five children and also allowed Quinn to move in the upper echelons of Hollywood society. He did not become a naturalized U.S. citizen until 1947, so he did not fight in World War II, which opened up his acting prospects as he was available to work when others were off serving in the military.

Besides DeMille, Quinn worked with many important directors, including Elia Kazan and Federico Fellini. In 1953 he won an Oscar for Best Supporting Actor for *Viva Zapata!* (1952), the first Mexican American actor to receive an Academy Award, and another in 1957 for *Lust for Life* (1956). He was also nominated for Oscars for Best Lead Actor for *Wild Is the Wind* (1957) and *Alexis Zorbas* (a.k.a. *Zorba the Greek*, 1964) During the 1960s he made a number of films in Europe, mainly spaghetti westerns, and in the 1990s, when he was already in his eighties, he still had an active career, mainly in television. He died on June 3, 2001. Quinn's career spanned an amazing sixty-six years with the posthumous release of *Avenging Angelo* (2002).

See also **Cinema: From the Silent Film to 1990; Mexico, Wars and Revolutions: Mexican Revolution; Villa, Francisco "Pancho".**

BIBLIOGRAPHY

Cárdenas, Jaime, Jr. "Brusque and Exotic: Anthony Quinn, National Identity, and Masculinity, 1951–1966." *Southern Quarterly* 39, no. 4 (2001): 175–188.

García Jerez, Silvia, and Miguel Juan Payán. *Anthony Quinn*. Las Rozas, Madrid: Dastin, 2003.

CARYN C. CONNELLY

QUIÑONES MOLINA, ALFONSO

(1873–1950). Alfonso Quiñones Molina (*b.* 1873; *d.* 1950), president of El Salvador (1914–1915, 1918–1919, and 1923–1927). Alfonso Quiñones Molina belonged to the Quiñones–Meléndez Family dynasty that controlled the presidency of El Salvador. Members of the dominant civilian landowning elite, these families used rigged elections to maintain governmental control from the 1890s until the Great Depression brought military control in 1931. The landowners facilitated the emergence of coffee as the dominant agricultural crop during an era characterized by peace, prosperity, and the concentration of land ownership among a few families.

Quiñones Molina held the presidency three times. He governed briefly in 1914 during the election that installed his brother-in-law, Carlos Meléndez (acting president, 1913–1914). After organizing the first official party, the Liga Roja (Red League) in 1918, he again held office during a transition that allowed the election of Jorge Meléndez (president 1919–1923). Quiñones Molina became president in his own right in 1923, serving until 1927. His controversial foreign borrowing to secure funds for street paving in San Salvador caused a rejection of external debt by the populace, a situation that was exploited by later military regimes, particularly that of General Maximiliano Hernández Martínez.

See also **El Salvador; Meléndez Family.**

BIBLIOGRAPHY

There are no detailed studies of this era. A laudatory contemporary account can be found in Juan Ramón Uriarte, *La esfinge de Cuzcatlán (el Presidente Quiñones)* (1929); a brief general discussion in English can be found in Alastair White, *El Salvador* (1973).

Additional Bibliography

Ching, Erik Kristofer. "From Clientelism to Militarism: The State, Politics and Authoritarianism in El Salvador, 1840–1940." Ph.D. diss., 1997.

Soto Gómez, Arturo. *Todos los presidentes, 1821–2004: Elecciones presidenciales en El Salvador*. San Salvador: Insta Prints, 2005.

KENNETH J. GRIEB

QUINQUELA MARTÍN, BENITO

(1890–1977). Benito Quinquela Martín (*b.* 1 March 1890; *d.* 28 January 1977), Argentine painter and muralist. Quinquela Martín was born in Buenos Aires and adopted by a humble family. He attended a night drawing academy in La Boca, a picturesque Italian neighborhood on the outskirts of Buenos Aires, and was fond of painting the harbor by the Riachuelo bank. He was discovered by Master Pío Collivadino, who decided to support him in his career. In 1920 he received second prize in the National Salon of Buenos Aires; the same year he had his first individual exhibition in Rio de Janeiro with great success. He visited Europe and the United States and exhibited in Paris, Madrid, Rome, London, and New York. In 1970 he was invited to Cuba, where he had a one-man show in Havana.

On large canvases, Quinquela Martín painted views of the port and dockyards, showing the bustling life of La Boca in scenes that are a hymn to human effort. He was a colorist of exceptional talent, creating high contrasts with strong spatula strokes. His masterpieces are in the great American and European museums. He is the founder of the Fine Arts School and Museum of La Boca. The National Museum of Fine Arts had a retrospective of his works in 1990.

See also **Art: The Twentieth Century.**

BIBLIOGRAPHY

Vicente Gesualdo, Aldo Biglione, and Rodolfo Santos, *Diccionario de artistas plásticos en la Argentina* (1988).

Additional Bibliography

Sánchez Pórfido, Elisabet. *Cándido López, Florencio Molina Campos y Benito Quinquela Martín como paradigmas de la plástica argentina.* La Plata: Editorial de la Universidad Nacional de La Plata, 1995.

AMALIA CORTINA ARAVENA

QUINTANA, MANUEL (1835–1906).

Manuel Quintana (*b.* 19 October 1835; *d.* 12 March 1906), president of Argentina (1904–1906). Born in Buenos Aires, Quintana received his law degree from the University of Buenos Aires in 1858. He entered public service and in 1860 was elected a deputy in the Buenos Aires provincial Congress. He rose rapidly, representing Buenos Aires Province first as a national deputy (1862–1864 and 1867–1870) and then as a senator (1870–1874). In 1889, Quintana represented Argentina at the first Pan-American Conference in Washington, D.C. Soon after, in 1892, he served as President Luis Sáenz Peña's (1892–1895) minister of the interior. In the years that followed, Quintana became an important opponent of the reformist Radical Civic Union Party. In the wake of the Radicals' 1893 "revolution," he served as federal interventor in Tucumán, Santiago del Estero, and Santa Fe Provinces. In 1904, he succeeded Julio Roca (1880–1886, 1898–1904) as president. During his administration, Quintana maintained his conservative stand against the Radicals, who rebelled again unsuccessfully in 1905. He died in office and was succeeded by José Figueroa Alcorta.

See also **Argentina: The Nineteenth Century; Argentina: The Twentieth Century; Figueroas Alcorta, José.**

BIBLIOGRAPHY

David Rock, *Politics in Argentina, 1890–1930: The Rise and Fall of Radicalism* (1975).

Natalio R. Botano, *El orden conservador: La política argentina entre 1880 y 1916*, 2d ed. (1985).

Additional Bibliography

López, Mario Justo. *De la república oligárquica a la república democrática: Estudio sobre la reforma política de Roque Sáenz Peña.* Argentina: Lumiere, 2005.

DANIEL LEWIS

QUINTANAR, HÉCTOR (1936–).

Héctor Quintanar (*b.* 15 April 1936), Mexican composer, conductor, and founder of the first electronic music studio in Mexico (1970). He studied composition with Rodolfo Halffter and Carlos Chávez and assumed leadership of Chávez's composition workshop at the National Conservatory in 1965. His experimental interests took him to New York for electronic music study and Paris to explore *musique concrète* (the use of nonmusical recorded sounds in music scores). He has also pursued other styles such as nonrepetition, twelve-tone pointillism, and new sounds derived from traditional instruments. Quintanar has conducted the orchestras of the Free University of Mexico and the city of Morelia. He is a founding member in both Colegio de Compositores Latinoamericanos de Música y de Arte and Academia Guanajuatense de Arte y Cultura, and in 2000 he was named a member of the Sistema Nacional de Creadores.

See also **Music: Art Music.**

BIBLIOGRAPHY

José Antonio Alcaraz et al., *Período contemporáneo,* in *La música de México,* edited by Julio Estrada, vol. 1, pt. 5 (1984).

Additional Bibliography

Véjar Pérez-Rubio, Carlos. *Contrapuntos: Colegio de Compositores Latinoamericanos de Música de Arte, su nacimiento.* México: Archipiélago, 2000.

ROBERT L. PARKER

QUINTANA ROO, ANDRÉS (1787–1851).

Andrés Quintana Roo (*b.* 30 November 1787; *d.* 15 April 1851), Mexican political theorist and statesman, who helped lay the groundwork for Mexico's nineteenth-century liberal reforms. Born in Mérida, on the Yucatán Peninsula, Quintana Roo moved to Mexico City in 1808 to complete his education. In 1812 he joined the insurgent struggle for Mexican Independence. His future wife, Leona Vicario, whom he had met in Mexico City, joined him in 1813. Not a military man, Quintana Roo provided intellectual leadership, writing for the rebel newspapers *El Ilustrador Americano* and the

Semanario Patriótico Americano and serving in the Congress of Chilpancingo.

For several decades following Independence in 1821, Quintana Roo held executive posts under federalist governments, such as minister of justice in 1833. During centralist-conservative regimes, he played an important role as an opposition legislator. Throughout the era, he continued his work as a trenchant political commentator, most notably in the 1830s for the periodicals *El Federalista* and *El Correo de la Federación*.

See also **Journalism; Mexico, Wars and Revolutions: War of Independence.**

BIBLIOGRAPHY

Charles A. Hale, *Mexican Liberalism in the Age of Mora, 1821–1853* (1968).

Ana Carolina Ibarra, ed., *Andrés Quintana Roo* (1987).

Jesús Reyes Heroles, *El liberalismo mexicano,* 3 vols., 3d ed. (1988).

Additional Bibliography

Arnold, Linda. *Política y justicia: La Suprema Corte mexicana (1824–1855).* México, D.F.: Universidad Nacional Autónoma de México, Instituto de Investigaciones Jurídicas, 1996.

Fowler, Wil. *Mexico in the Age of Proposals, 1821–1853.* Westport, CT: Greenwood Press, 1998.

RICHARD WARREN

QUINTERO, ÁNGEL (1805–1866).

Ángel Quintero (*b.* 1805; *d.* 2 August 1866), Venezuelan politician. Quintero earned a doctorate in law from the University of Caracas in 1835. He began his political activity as a member of the Constituent Congress of 1830. Associated with the Conservative Party, he became secretary of the interior and of justice in 1839. Quintero opposed the government of José Tadeo Monagas, founded the periodical *El Espectador,* and joined José Antonio Páez in his revolution against Monagas. The revolution defeated, he was seized and expelled from the country. Quintero returned shortly after the outbreak of the Federal War (1859–1863) and again joined Páez, but when Páez proclaimed his dictatorship, Quintero again left the country. He returned after the war and remained at the margin of political activity until his death.

See also **Venezuela: Venezuela since 1830.**

BIBLIOGRAPHY

Francisco González Guinán, *Historia contemporánea de Venezuela,* vol. 4 (1954).

Additional Bibliography

Carvallo, Gastón. *Próceres, caudillos y rebeldes: Crisis del sistema de dominación en Venezuela, 1830-1908.* Caracas: Grijalbo, 1994.

Zahler, Reuben. *Honor, Corruption, and Legitimacy: Liberal Projects in the Early Venezualan Republic, 1821–50.* Ph.D. diss., University of Chicago, 2005.

INÉS QUINTERO

QUINTO REAL.

The "royal fifth" on gold and silver mined in Spanish America had its origins in medieval Castile, where the royalty ranged as high as two-thirds of bullion and a fifth of booty. To encourage mining output in America, however, a decree of 1504 established the royalty on bullion at one-fifth.

Gold washing in the Caribbean yielded some quinto revenue, but with the discovery of the great silver-mining districts of Mexico and Peru in the mid-1500s, the quinto became a significant and dependable source of revenue for the royal treasury. When miners presented silver or gold for taxation, treasury officials first collected an assay charge of 1–1.5 percent and then calculated the quinto on the remaining bullion.

Declining ore quality and lower profits led the crown to rescind the quinto on silver and to levy a lower royalty, the tenth (*diezmo*). The government temporarily halved the Mexican quinto in 1548 for the refiners, although bullion merchants were to continue paying one-fifth. But the concession to the mine operators soon became permanent, and treasury officials found the distinction between producers and merchants impossible to enforce. By the mid-1600s, the quinto on Mexican silver had practically disappeared, replaced by the *diezmo*. The Peruvian quinto remained in force until 1736, when Andean silver producers also began to pay the tenth.

As to gold, mined in much smaller quantities, the crown maintained the quinto longer: until 1723 for Mexico; 1738 for Guatemala; and 1778 for the Andes. In 1778 the crown imposed a uniform rate of 3 percent on colonial gold production.

It is impossible to know how much silver and gold escaped paying the royal fifth, but the quinto yielded large sums for the treasury: for example, more than 1.5 million pesos per year during the 1630s from the viceroyalty of Peru. The quinto and diezmo data in colonial tax records have enabled economic historians to calculate the amount of bullion legally produced in the colonies.

Brazilian gold producers also paid a quinto on their output to the Portuguese crown. As in the case of the Spanish colonies, Brazilians found the quinto a serious disincentive to production and reportedly engaged in massive smuggling to avoid the royalty.

See also **Mining: Colonial Spanish America.**

BIBLIOGRAPHY

Clarence H. Haring, "The Early Spanish Colonial Exchequer," in *American Historical Review* 23, no. 4 (1918): 779–796.

Ismael Sánchez-Bella, *La organización financiera de las Indias (siglo XVI)* (1968).

John Jay Te Paske, *La Real Hacienda de Nueva España: La Real Caja de México, 1576–1816* (1976).

John Jay Te Paske and Herbert S. Klein, *Ingresos y egresos de la Real Hacienda de Nueva España*, 2 vols. (1986), and *The Royal Treasuries of the Spanish Empire in America*, 4 vols. (1982–1990).

Additional Bibliography

Bordo, Michael D. Bordo, and Roberto Cortés Conde, eds. *Transferring Wealth and Power from the Old to the New World: Monetary and Fiscal Institutions in the 17th through the 19th Century.* New York: Cambridge University Press, 2001.

Hausberger, Bernd. *La Nueva España y sus metales preciosos: La industria minera colonial a través de los libros de cargo y data de la Real Hacienda, 1761–1767.* Frankfurt am Main; Vervuert; Madrid: Iberoamericana, 1997.

Pijning, Ernst. *Passive Resistance: Portuguese Diplomacy of Contraband Trade during King John V's Reign (1706–1750).* [S.l.]: Ponta Delgada, 1997.

Sluiter, Engel. *The Gold and Silver of Spanish America, c. 1572–1648: Tables Showing Bullion Declared for Taxation in Colonial Royal Treasuries, Remittances to Spain, and Expenditures for Defense of Empire.* Berkeley: University of California, Bancroft Library, 1998.

KENDALL W. BROWN

QUIPU.

The term *quipu*, from the Quechua word *khipu*, meaning "knot," refers to an accounting system used by Inca officials. A mnemonic system of cords of cotton or camelid fiber, a quipu consisted of a central or main cord positioned horizontally, from which hung other, secondary cords with knots tied in them to symbolize quantities. These cords varied in size, color, thickness, and type of braiding. Colonial documents describe a system of quipus to keep accounting records of people, livestock, and goods, and to gather information and send messages. The system continued to be used into the early years of Spanish colonial rule.

The quipus found to date display a great variety and complexity, the majority of them from the Inca era (1400 to 1532 CE). However, evidence from archaeological excavations indicates that the Incas did not invent the system. Quipus have been found from pre-Inca cultures such as the Caral (2,750 BCE), the Wari (sixth to thirteenth centuries; Spanish, Huari), and the Chachapoyas (ninth to fifteenth centuries). The Incas perfected and made extensive use of this system, with specialists called *quipukamayuq*.

See also **Caral; Huari; Incas, The.**

BIBLIOGRAPHY

Ascher, Marcia, and Robert Ascher. *Mathematics of the Incas: Code of the Quipu.* Mineola, NY: Dover Publications, 1997.

Urton, Gary. *The Social Life of Numbers: A Quechua Ontology of Numbers and Philosophy of Arithmetic.* Austin: University of Texas Press, 1997.

CARMEN ESCALANTE

QUIRIGUA.

Quirigua, a modest Classic Period Maya site, is strategically located in the lower Motagua River valley in Guatemala, near the Honduran border, 40 miles from the Caribbean. The site is closely linked with Copán, 30 miles south, and stone inscriptions at Quirigua record the success of a raiding party that captured Waxaklahuun Ub'aah K'awiil (18 Rabbit), ruler of Copán in 738 CE. Masonry structures date from the Early Classic Period. Dated inscriptions span 8.19.10.17 (426 CE) on Zoomorph P to 9.19.0.0.0 (810 CE) on Structure 1B-1, constructed by Jade Sky, the last recorded ruler of Quirigua.

The site center is adjacent to an earlier bed of the Motagua River; and evidence indicates that, during the century following 737 CE, Quirigua controlled river trade of jade and obsidian passing down the Motagua and then northward along the Caribbean coast to Yucatán.

The Great Plaza of Quirigua is studded with enormous stelae and zoomorphic stone sculptures with inscriptions. Most portray Waxaklahuun Ub'aah K'awiil, the ruler whose war party captured K'ak Tiliw Chan Yopaat and began Quirigua's domination of the area. To the south of the plaza is a ball court surrounded on three sides by terraces and steps. Behind these and further south is a large acropolis of ceremonial and elite residential structures built over an earlier ball court. Much of this architectural plan was realized after 737 CE and may have been a deliberate attempt by K'ak Tiliw Chan Yopaat to imitate (and surpass) the ceremonial precinct of his greatest conquest, Copán.

Modest activity continued into the Terminal Classic Period, and early metallurgy is documented by copper disks and cast copper bells. Following the possible arrival of settlers from Central Mexico, Quirigua was ultimately abandoned before the close of the Early Postclassic Period.

See also **Archaeology; Maya, The.**

BIBLIOGRAPHY

Quirigua Reports, Vol. 1, ed. Wendy Ashmore. Philadelphia: University Museum Monograph No. 37, University of Pennsylvania 1979.

Quirigua Reports, Vol. 2, ed. Edward Mark Schortman and Patricia Urban. Philadelphia, PA: University of Philadelphia, 1983.

Quirigua Reports, Vol. 3, ed. Edward Mark Schortman. Philadelphia: University Museum Monograph No. 80, University of Pennsylvania, 1993.

Looper, Matt. "New Perspectives on the Late Classic Political History of Quirigua, Guatemala." *Ancient Mesoamerica* 10 (1999): 263–280.

WALTER R.T. WITSCHEY

QUIROGA, HORACIO (1878–1937).

Horacio Quiroga (*b.* 31 December 1878; *d.* 19 February 1937), Uruguayan writer and one of Spanish America's greatest narrators. Quiroga was born in Salto; his father died in a hunting accident when he was three months old. Quiroga's life had more than its share of violent personal tragedies—his stepfather and one of his two wives committed suicide and Quiroga killed one of his best friends in a gun accident—which explains his interest in death and the monstrous. His earliest literary influence was Edgar Allan Poe.

Quiroga attended the University of Montevideo for a short time. In 1903 he went to Misiones, the following year to the Argentine Chaco. When the farming venture failed, he went to Buenos Aires, taught school, and married. In 1915 his wife committed suicide. During the ensuing decade, he wrote some of his best stories, including *Cuentos de amor, de locura y de muerte* (1917), the haunting *Cuentos de la selva* (1918; *South American Jungle Tales*, 1941), and *Los desterrados* (1926); he also published in the journal *Caras y Caretas*.

To make ends meet, he served as Uruguay's consul in Buenos Aires from 1917 to 1926, and he married again in 1927. In 1932 he returned to San Ignacio, Misiones, with his second wife and children as Uruguay's consul. When the consulate closed, Quiroga returned to Buenos Aires, plagued by lifelong asthma and neurasthenia. He was diagnosed with cancer and in 1937 took his own life. Many of his more than 200 powerful stories, written with great economy of style, are set in the spectacular Argentine wilderness—the jungle, the plantations, the powerful Paraná River. Although his early writings tend to deal more with the extraordinary, the monstrous, and talking animals, his later production drew more on his own rich experience with people. *The Exiles and Other Stories* (1987) and *The Decapitated Chicken and Other Stories* (1976) represent some of his best writings translated into English.

See also **Literature: Spanish America.**

BIBLIOGRAPHY

Emir Rodriguez Monegal, *El desterrado: Vida y obra de Horacio Quiroga* (1968).

Angel Flores, ed., *Aproximaciones a Horacio Quiroga* (1976).

George D. Schade, "Horacio Quiroga," in *Latin American Writers*, edited by Carlos A. Solé and M. I. Abreu, vol. 2 (1989), pp. 551–558.

Additional Bibliography

French, Jennifer. *Nature, Neo-Colonialism, and the Spanish American Regional Writers*. Hanover, NH: Dartmouth College Press, 2005.

Orgambide, Pedro G. *Horacio Quiroga: una historia de vida*. Buenos Aires: Planeta, 1994.

Pasteknik, Elsa Leonor. *El Mito en la obra de Horacio Quiroga*. Buenos Aires: Editorial Plus Ultra, 1997.

GEORGETTE MAGASSY DORN

QUIROGA, JORGE

QUIROGA, JORGE (1960–). The youngest vice president in Bolivia's history, Jorge Quiroga held the presidency for one year in 2001–2002 after the resignation of the ailing Hugo Banzer Suárez. Born May 5, 1960, in Cochabamba, Quiroga spent substantial time in the United States as a student of industrial engineering at Texas A&M University in College Station and business administration at Saint Edwards University in Austin, Texas. Prior to entering politics, he worked in the private sector in the United States and in Bolivia upon returning in 1988. He became an undersecretary in the Ministry of Planning in 1989 and rose to finance minister in 1992.

In 1993 Quiroga managed Banzer's unsuccessful bid for the presidency and later served as a deputy chief for the Acción Democrática Nacionalista (ADN; Nationalist democratic action) Party. Banzer chose him as running mate in their successful 1997 campaign. The World Economic Forum in Davos, Switzerland, honored the young vice president with its World Leader of Tomorrow award. In August 2001 Banzer was forced to resign and hand the presidency to Quiroga, who served out the remainder of Banzer's term until August 2002.

Quiroga continued Banzer's market orientation and controversial zero coca eradication policy, which helped fuel Bolivia's rising social discontent. After leaving office, he was scholar in residence at the Woodrow Wilson Center in Washington, D.C., and chaired the Unión de Partidos Latinoamericanos (UPLA, Union of Latin American Parties). Quiroga sought the presidency in 2005 as the PODEMOS (Poder Democrático y Social; Democratic and social power) party candidate, losing to leftist Evo Morales in the first round. Many voters considered him too conservative and too connected to the political establishment. He subsequently became president of the nongovernmental foundation, FUNDEMOS.

See also Banzer Suárez, Hugo; Bolivia: Bolivia Since 1825; Bolivia, Political Parties: Nationalist Democratic Action (ADN); Bolivia, Political Parties: Overview.

BIBLIOGRAPHY

Van Cott, Donna Lee. "From Exclusion to Inclusion: Bolivia's 2002 Elections." *Journal of Latin American Studies* 35 (2003): 751–775.

ROBERT R. BARR

QUIROGA, JUAN FACUNDO

QUIROGA, JUAN FACUNDO (1788–1835). Juan Facundo Quiroga (*b.* 1788; *d.* 16 February 1835), Argentine caudillo known as "The Tiger of the Llanos." Born in La Rioja to a family of landowners and regional officials, Quiroga began his own ascent in 1816 as a militia officer, serving the revolutionary government in Buenos Aires by mobilizing men and supplies for the Army of the North. As delegate of the center, he added military and political credentials to his landed power, and from this it was a short step to independent authority. In 1820 La Rioja proclaimed its "provisional independence" of neighboring Córdoba and became in effect a personal fiefdom of Quiroga. From this power base he waged war on Bernardino Rivadavia's centralized constitution, and in spite of defeat at the hands of General Gregorio Aráoz de La Madrid, he went on to extend his control over the provinces of the west and northwest from Catamarca to Mendoza. Recovering from losses to General José María Paz in 1829 and 1830, he furthered his reputation as a federalist by defeating the unitarist forces under Aráoz de La Madrid in 1831. Thus, as Juan Manuel de Rosas was establishing his power in Buenos Aires, Quiroga was consolidating his control in the interior. But Quiroga went further. He moved to Buenos Aires and attempted to secure the calling of a constituent congress to give Argentina a federal republic, a proposal which was anathema to Rosas. He further challenged the idea of Rosas by demanding that the customs revenue of Buenos Aires be nationalized. In 1834 Quiroga was sent by the government of Buenos Aires on a peace mission to the northwest, in the hope that his influence could prevent a threatened civil war between Salta and Tucumán. Returning from successful negotiations, he was ambushed and assassinated at Barranca Yaco on 16 February 1835. The death of Quiroga removed a challenge to Buenos Aires and an irritant to Rosas, and among the possible assassins Rosas himself was suspected. The official judgment, probably correct, convicted the caudillos of Córdoba, all four Reinafé brothers, and their henchmen.

Quiroga, whom Juan Bautista Alberdi regarded as an obscure guerrilla and a common killer, survives in history largely through the exposure he received in Domingo Sarmiento's *Facundo* (1938), a classic of Argentine literature. There he not only was described as a tyrant and a terrorist but also was elevated to a thesis—the conflict between civilization and barbarism—which was widely invoked to explain the state of Latin America. He was the model of the provincial caudillo, his life a series of outrages, his rule the epitome of personal power.

See also **Argentina: The Nineteenth Century; Rosas, Juan Manuel de; Sarmiento, Domingo Faustino.**

BIBLIOGRAPHY

Domingo Faustino Sarmiento, *Facundo* (1938), and *Life in the Argentine Republic in the Days of the Tyrants, or Civilization and Barbarism* (1961).

David Peña, *Juan Facundo Quiroga*, 2d ed. (1971).

Instituto De Historia Argentina y Americana, "Doctor Emilio Ravignani," *Archivo del brigadier general Juan Facundo Quiroga*, 4 vols. (1957–1988).

John Lynch, *Caudillos in Spanish America 1800–1850* (1992).

Additional Bibliography

Cárdenas de Monner Sans, María Inés. *Juan Facundo Quiroga: otra civilización.* Buenos Aires: Libreria Histórica, 2004.

De la Fuente, Ariel. *Children of Facundo: Caudillo and Gaucho Insurgency during the Argentine State-Formation Process (La Rioja, 1853–1870).* Durham, NC: Duke University Press, 2000.

JOHN LYNCH

QUIROGA, VASCO DE (c. 1477–1565). Vasco de Quiroga (*b.* ca. 1477/79; *d.* February/March 1565), judge of the second *audiencia* of Mexico (1530) and consecrated as the first bishop of Michoacán (1538). Born in Madrigal de las Altas Torres, Spain, Quiroga was sent by the Spanish crown to Mexico where, as both judge and bishop,

he devoted most of his energy and resources to bringing an idealized, European lifestyle to the indigenous people. He organized utopian communities emphasizing religious instruction, encouraging the development of crafts, and promoting agricultural self-sufficiency, self-government, and care for the sick and needy, including an unusual plan for an infirmary for each town. Quiroga also brought indigenous youths raised in monasteries to his towns to help priests instruct other Indians in the Christian doctrine. One observer referred to Santa Fe de la Laguna, Michoacán, as a monastery. Quiroga's communities have also been called pueblo-hospitals and hospital-schools.

Most scholars agree that the utopian vision of "Tata Vasco," as his admirers called him, was influenced by St. Thomas More, but some controversy lingers regarding questions about Quiroga's communal intent and his perspectives on conquest. Sixteenth-century critics included some Indians who charged him with unremunerated labor and neighboring Spaniards who were jealous of his land and his residents' exemption from tributes and labor drafts. Both groups complained about his harboring of runaway slaves. Quiroga spent his last years making pastoral visits to the rural communities of Michoacán.

See also **Mexico: The Colonial Period; Michoacán.**

BIBLIOGRAPHY

Silvio Arturo Zavala, *Sir Thomas More in New Spain* (1955).

Paul L. Callens, S.J., *Tata Vasco, a Great Reformer of the Sixteenth Century* (1959).

Fintan B. Warren, O.F.M., *Vasco de Quiroga and His Pueblo-Hospitals of Santa Fé* (1963).

Additional Bibliography

Cattana, Edgard Fabián. *La utopía humanista en Vasco de Quiroga.* Córdoba: Editorial de la Universidad Católica de Córdoba, 2004.

Gómez, Fernando. *Good Places and Non-Places in Colonial Mexico: The Figure of Vasco de Quiroga (1470–1565).* Lanham, MD: University Press of America, 2001.

Verástique, Bernardino. *Michoacán and Eden: Vasco de Quiroga and the Evangelization of Western Mexico.* Austin: University of Texas Press, 2000.

STEPHANIE WOOD

QUIROGA SANTA CRUZ, MARCELO

(1931–1980). Marcelo Quiroga Santa Cruz (*b.* 13 March 1931; *d.* 17 July 1980), founder and leader of the Socialist Party-One (PSU). Born in Cochabamba, Quiroga Santa Cruz was the intellectual leader of the Bolivian Left from 1970 until his death. In the 1960s he switched from the right-wing Bolivian Socialist Falange (FSB) to the socialist cause, becoming leader of the PSU in 1971. As minister of hydrocarbons, he effected the nationalization in 1970 of the Bolivian holdings of Gulf Oil Company. In 1979, Quiroga Santa Cruz began a congressional inquiry into the responsibility for human rights abuses during the General Hugo Banzer regime (1971–1978). He was assassinated in 1980 on the first day of the infamous "cocaine coup," in which General Luis García Meza (1980–1981) took power.

The most effective public speaker of his generation, Quiroga Santa Cruz was unable to translate his personal popularity into a popular political base. Nevertheless, he served as an important political gadfly and the conscience of the Bolivian Left during his lifetime.

See also **Bolivia: Bolivia Since 1825; Drugs and Drug Trade.**

BIBLIOGRAPHY

There is no biography of Quiroga Santa Cruz. The best political narrative of the period in which Quiroga Santa Cruz was active is contained in James Dunkerley, *Rebellion in the Veins: Political Struggle in Bolivia: 1952–1982* (1984).

Additional Bibliography

Cortez Romero, Enrique. *Marcelo Quiroga Santa Cruz: pensamiento político: Estado dependiente, FF.AA. y golpe militar en Bolivia.* Santa Cruz de la Sierra: Universidad Autónoma "Gabriel René Moreno," 1992.

Lavaud, Jean-Pierre. *El embrollo boliviano: Turbulencias sociales y desplazamientos políticos, 1952–1982.* Lima: Hisbol, 1998.

ERICK D. LANGER

QUIRÓS, CESÁREO BERNALDO DE

(1881–1968). Cesáreo Bernaldo de Quirós (*b.* 29 May 1881; *d.* 29 May 1968), Argentine painter. Quirós was born in Gualeguay, Entre Ríos Province, and began to paint while very young. In 1899 he received the Prix de Rome, and the following year he won a scholarship and traveled to Italy. In 1901 he won a prize at the Venice Biennale. He also traveled in Spain, Italy, and Sardinia. In 1906 he returned to Argentina, where he had his first one-man show at the Salon Costa. The Modern Art Museum in Barcelona bought one of his paintings. He won the grand prize and the gold medal at the international art exhibition held in Buenos Aires in 1910. That year he returned to Europe, where he lived until 1915. Back in Argentina, he lived in his native province until 1927, working on a series of paintings dealing with gaucho life, which were later exhibited in Europe and North America. Quirós was a professor at the National Academy of Decorative Arts and chairman of the National Academy of Fine Arts. In 1963 he made an endowment of his works to the National Museum. In 1981 the Museo Pedro Martínez, in Paraná, Entre Ríos, inaugurated a hall in his honor, and in 1991 the Salas Nacionales de Exposiciones in Buenos Aires exhibited more than 150 of his paintings.

See also **Art: The Twentieth Century.**

BIBLIOGRAPHY

Vicente Gesualdo, Aldo Biglione, and Rodolfo Santos, *Diccionario de artistas plásticos en la Argentina* (1988).

Additional Bibliography

Funes, Ofelia A., Pablo Rolando Marianetti, and Marta Gómez de Rodríguez Britos. *Arte argentino del siglo XX.* Buenos Aires: Telefónica: Fundación para la Investigación del Arte Argentino, 1999.

Gutiérrez Viñuales, Rodrigo. *La pintura argentina: Identidad nacional e hispanismo (1900–1930).* Granada: Editorial Universidad de Granada, 2003.

San Martín, María Laura. *Breve historia de la pintura argentina contemporánea.* Buenos Aires: Editorial Claridad, 1993.

AMALIA CORTINA ARAVENA

QUISPE, FELIPE

(1942–). An outspoken indigenous leader and presidential candidate known as "El Mallku" (the chief), Felipe Quispe has been an instrumental player in Bolivia's social movements. An Aymara Indian from Ajllata Grande in the La Paz Department, Quispe helped found the

Movimiento Indio Túpac Katari (MITKA; Túpac Katari Indian Movement), an ethno-nationalist party and part of the so-called Katarist indigenous movement, in 1978. A decade later he founded the Ejército Guerrillero Túpac Katari (EGTK; Túpac Katari Guerrilla Army), the armed actions of which led to a five-year jail sentence for Quispe in 1992. After his release, he was elected head of a peasant labor organization, the Confederación Sindical Única de Trabajadores Campesinos de Bolivia (CSUTCB; Unitary Syndical Confederation of Peasant Workers of Bolivia). From this position Quispe mobilized thousands of supporters on numerous occasions in the social protests that rocked Bolivia in the first few years of the twenty-first century, including those that forced President Carlos Mesa from office in 2005. In 2000 Quispe created a new political party, the Movimiento Indígena Pachakuti (MIP; Pachakuti Indigenous Movement), and competed in the 2002 presidential elections on an Aymara separatist platform. Although he was unsuccessful, earning just over 6 percent of the vote, the results did give him a seat as a representative from the La Paz Department. His campaign in 2005 was also unsuccessful; with only 2.16 percent of the vote, he lost his party's legal registration.

See also **Indigenous Organizations.**

BIBLIOGRAPHY

Van Cott, Donna Lee. *From Movements to Parties in Latin America: The Evolution of Ethnic Politics.* Cambridge, U.K.: Cambridge University Press, 2005.

ROBERT R. BARR

QUISQUEYA. Quisqueya, one of two names given by the Tainos to the island that Christopher Columbus was to call Hispaniola. In addition to Quisqueya (Mother of the Earth), the Tainos referred to their island as Haiti (Land of Mountains). Quisqueya was divided into five parts: the central region, Maguá; the western section, Jaragua; the northwest, Marién; the east, Higüey; and the south, Maguana. The Tainos belonged to the family of Arawaks, who, over the course of centuries, had migrated from what is now Venezuela, across the Lesser Antilles, to Puerto Rico, Hispaniola, and Cuba. The arrival of the Spaniards proved disastrous to the Tainos. It is estimated that they numbered 400,000

when Columbus reached Quisqueya in 1492. By 1568, there were thirteen left.

See also **Columbus, Christopher; Hispaniola.**

BIBLIOGRAPHY

Roberto Cassa, *Los Tainos en la Española* (1975).

Frank Moya Pons, "The Tainos of Hispaniola: The Island's First Inhabitants," in *Caribbean Review* 13, no. 4 (1984): 20–23, 47.

Juan Tomás Tavares K., *Los Indios de Quisqueya* (1988).

Additional Bibliography

Cambeira, Alan. *Quisqueya La Bella: the Dominican Republic in Historical and Cultural Perspective.* Armonk, NY: M.E. Sharpe, 1997.

Deagan, Kathleen A and José Maria Cruxent. *Columbus's Outpost among the Tainos: Spain and America at La Isabela, 1493-1498.* New Haven, CT: Yale University Press, 2002.

Maya Pons, Frank. *Manual de historia dominicana.* Santo Domingo: Cribbean Publishers, 1997.

KAI P. SCHOENHALS

QUITO. Quito is the capital of Ecuador, with a population of 1.4 million (2001 census). Founded by Spanish conquistador Diego de Almagro in 1534, it is located in the northern sierra of Ecuador, 9,350 feet (2,805 meters) above sea level. The city sits at the foot of the active Pichincha volcano, which last erupted in October 1999. Quito claims credit for the first cry of independence in South America, on August 10, 1809, giving the city the nickname "Light of America."

Quito served as the northern Inca capital for Huayna Capac (c. 1493–1527) and as the capital for the half of his kingdom left to his son Atahualpa (c. 1527–1533). When the conquistador Sebastián de Benalcázar approached in 1534, Rumiñahui, Atahualpa's leading general, destroyed the city. The Spanish focused their sixteenth-century colonizing efforts in Ecuador in the sierra because of its gold reserves and large population of sedentary Indians, who were compelled to work on haciendas in the surrounding verdant valleys. Quito became the leading residence for absentee Spanish landowners, the beneficiaries of forced Indian labor. In 1563 the crown named the city the seat of the newly created Audiencia of Quito.

Because of epidemic diseases introduced by the Spanish, the population of the Quito area fell from between 750,000 and 1,000,000 in 1534 to about 95,000 in 1590, a loss of 85 to 90 percent. However, the region soon enjoyed an uncommonly strong demographic recovery, doubling in population between 1590 and 1670; this increase has led scholars to surmise that some of Quito's sixteenth-century losses may have been due to migration. The growth of the workforce contributed greatly to the emergence of a successful textile industry in the seventeenth century after gold mining declined. Using forced labor, Quito produced ponchos and blankets for export to the silver-mining districts of Peru. However, in 1691 and 1695 a series of epidemics struck the region again: The sierra population fell by 25 to 50 percent, and the population of the city of Quito fell from about 50,000 in the mid-seventeenth century to 21,700 by 1830. The loss of workers and of the Potosí market crippled local textile production, which never recovered; demographic and economic stagnation continued until the twentieth century.

During the colonial period Quito acquired a reputation it still retains for particular devotion to the Catholic faith. Indeed, to critics Quito became a priest-ridden city. The church helped Quito earn acclaim for advances in the arts. Some of the best expressions of Spanish colonial art came out of the Quito School, notably the sculptures of Bernardo de Legarda (for example, his *Nuestra Señora de Quito*) and the work of painters Miguel de Santiago, Hernando de la Cruz, José Javier de Goríbar, and Manuel de Santiago.

Ecuador is a nation cut in half by the towering Andes, and thus profound regional differences, culturally and politically, have developed naturally. Quito and the coastal commercial center of Guayaquil have been the two principal rivals since the eighteenth-century rise of Guayaquil's cacao economy. Each has often regarded the other with contempt and suspicion. This cultural feud has also punctuated Ecuadoran politics. Import and export taxes collected at the port of Guayaquil have nearly always been the sole important source of government revenue, with the funds controlled by the national government in Quito. The two cities recurrently clashed over this system, but because the sierra historically had a much larger population than did the coast, Quito prevailed.

After World War II the advent of mass urbanization in Guayaquil, coupled with the banana export boom, began to tilt the political advantage to the coast, a development reflected in the rise of populist leaders such as José María Velasco Ibarra and Assad Bucaram. In the late twentieth century, however, the flood of tax revenue from the export of Oriente oil freed Quito from its economic dependence on Guayaquil. The city has drastically expanded, quintupling in population between 1947 and 2001, even as its public image remains that of a cloistered capital. In 1978 Quito was the first city to be named a World Heritage Site by UNESCO. This has led to increased municipal and national attention to rehabilitation of the colonial core and a corresponding increase in Quito's tourist economy.

See also **Ecuador: Conquest through Independence; Ecuador: Since 1830; Guayaquil; Incas, The; Sierra (Ecuador).**

BIBLIOGRAPHY

Gauderman, Kimberly. *Women's Lives in Colonial Quito: Gender, Law, and Economy in Spanish America*. Austin: University of Texas Press, 2003.

Kingman Garcés, Eduardo. *La ciudad y los otros, Quito 1860–1940: Higienismo, ornato y policía*. Quito: FLACSO Sede Ecuador/Universidad Rovira e Virgili, 2006.

Lane, Kris. *Quito 1599: City and Colony in Transition*. Albuquerque: University of New Mexico Press, 2002.

Salvador Lara, Jorge. *Quito*. Madrid: Editorial Mapfre, 1992.

ERNESTO CAPELLO

QUITO, AUDIENCIA (PRESIDENCY) OF.

Audiencia (Presidency) of Quito, governing body for the administrative division of the Spanish Empire in the New World that encompassed roughly the area of modern Ecuador. The term *audiencia* is also used sometimes to refer to the district governed by the audiencia. After having overthrown Inca rule in the north Andes by 1534, the Spanish invaders first governed the region by distributing the Amerindian towns in grants of encomienda. These protectorates allowed the Europeans to collect taxes and exact labor from the Andean villagers in return for providing military protection and religious instruction. To centralize Spanish control over these *encomenderos*, Francisco Pizarro established a governorship in 1534 over the region extending from Popayán in the north to Loja in the south and from the highlands to the coastal city of Guayaquil. Nevertheless, periodic civil wars among the conquistadores impeded the consolidation of Spanish rule until 1563, when the crown formed an *audiencia* (high court) in the city of Quito to head the imperial bureaucracy. By then, a more stable government had begun to form in the region, extending Spanish control over the Native American peoples and helping to establish a viable colonial socioeconomic order.

The new Audiencia of Quito exercised jurisdiction over the region encompassed by the old governorship established by Pizarro and later extended its control over the frontier provinces of Atacames (in the northwest) and Quijos, Macas, Mainas, and Yaguarzongo (east of the Andes). The audiencia district was further divided into smaller provincial units, called either *corregimientos* (magistracies) or *gobiernos* (governorships). The first *corregimiento* was established in the city of Quito in 1548. By the eighteenth century, such provincial magistracies were also located in Guayaquil, Cuenca, Loja-Zamora, Chimbo-Guaranda, Latacunga, Otavalo, Ibarra, Riobamba, and Pasto. The governorships were usually situated in more isolated regions such as Popayán, Atacames, Quijos-Macas, Mainas, and Yaguarzongo (later Jaén de Bracamoros). *Cabildos* (city councils) in the major cities and indigenous village councils in rural areas formed the lowest echelon of the royal bureaucracy in the audiencia district.

The viceroy of Peru initially exercised political, military, and administrative powers over the Audiencia of Quito, but in practice he delegated effective control over most local affairs to the tribunal. The audiencia administered civil and criminal cases, enforced royal and viceregal edicts, and issued laws to govern the realm. The exact size of the audiencia varied during the colonial period, but the crown usually maintained a chief justice (president), two to four *oidores* (civil justices), two *alcaldes del crimen* (criminal judges), and one or two *fiscales* (crown attorneys).

By the seventeenth century, competing elite political factions had gained considerable control over the audiencia. Strong-willed presidents such as Antonio de Morga (1615–1636) asserted the prerogatives of the court at the expense of the viceroy. In addition, as the crown began selling audiencia appointments from 1687, local partisan groups bought the posts and exercised direct political power through the tribunal. By the first half of the eighteenth century, the court had a well-deserved reputation for representing local factions rather than imperial interests.

This decline of royal power culminated in the overthrow of the audiencia in 1765. In that year, Viceroy Pedro de Messía De La Cerda transferred the administration of the *alcabala* (sales tax) and the *aguardiente* (cane liquor) monopoly from local tax farmers to direct royal control. Fearing opposition from the audiencia justices, he dispatched a special commissioner from Bogotá, Juan Díaz de Herrera, to implement the policy.

The growing assertiveness of local partisan interests led the Bourbon monarchs to make numerous administrative changes over the course of the eighteenth century, all aimed at increasing royal control in the audiencia district. To this end, officials in Madrid experimented briefly in 1718 with suppressing the Audiencia of Quito and placing the region under the jurisdiction of the newly created Viceroyalty of New Granada (Colombia). The Madrid government reestablished the tribunal in 1720 and suppressed the new viceroyalty in 1722, placing the tribunal once again under the jurisdiction of the Viceroyalty of Peru. This arrangement lasted until 1739, when the crown reestablished the Viceroyalty of New Granada and put the Audiencia of Quito under its control permanently. Metropolitan authorities later restricted the power of local partisan groups by ending the sale of audiencia judgeships in Quito—and elsewhere—by 1750.

After mid-century, the demographic and economic expansion of the southern highlands and the coast also prompted crown authorities to upgrade the *corregimiento* of Guayaquil to a governorship in 1763 and that of Cuenca to an intendancy in 1770. Local opposition to royal control prompted the Quito Revolt of 1765. A popular coalition government suspended the audiencia and ruled over the district until royal troops from Guayaquil restored the justices to power in September 1766. In the aftermath of the revolt, the crown dispatched officials to conduct *visita general* (special inspection) in 1778. It was under the control of the new audiencia president-regent (a newly created post of presiding officer) José García de León y Pizarro, and was charged with increasing revenues and heightening administrative control over the region. During his tenure as president-regent, García Pizarro and his royalist allies gained firm control over the audiencia and local politics.

Despite the crown's successes in reasserting its authority over the audiencia district of Quito, popular discontent erupted again in 1809 after the abdication of Charles IV and his son, Ferdinand VII. A *junta* (provisional government) controlled by *quiteño* elites disbanded the audiencia in that year and tried to extend its own control throughout the district. Although the *junta* fell in 1812 and the audiencia regained control, royal power remained tenuous. Finally, after the insurgent armies of General Antonio José de Sucre defeated the royalist forces in 1822 at the Battle of Pichincha, the victors permanently suppressed the Audiencia of Quito.

See also **Quito; Quito Revolt of 1765; Spanish Empire.**

BIBLIOGRAPHY

Recent treatments are John Leddy Phelan, *The Kingdom of Quito in the Seventeenth Century: Bureaucratic Politics in the Spanish Empire* (1967); Alfredo Pareja y Diez Canseco, *Las instituciones y la administración de la Real Audiencia de Quito* (1975); Christiana Borchart De Moreno, "El periódo colonial," in *Pichincha: Monografía histórica de la región nuclear Ecuatoriana*, edited by Segundo Moreno Yánez (1981), pp. 195–274; Jean Paul Deler, N. Gómez, and M. Portais, *El manejo del espacio en el Ecuador–Etapas claves* (1983). For the audiencia judges in an imperial context see Mark A. Burkholder and D. S. Chandler, *From Impotence to Authority: The Spanish Crown and the American Audiencias, 1687–1808* (1977).

Additional Bibliography

Andrien, Kenneth J. *The Kingdom of Quito, 1690-1830: The State and Regional Development.* Cambridge: Cambridge University Press, 1995.

Borchart de Moreno, Christiana Renate. *La Audiencia de Quito: Aspectos económicos y sociales (siglos XVI–XVIII).* Quito, Ecuador: Ediciones del Banco Central del Ecuador, 1998.

KENNETH J. ANDRIEN

QUITO REVOLT OF 1765. Quito Revolt of 1765, rebellion by the populace of Quito, Eucador, in protest against the imposition of new taxes. It proved to be one of the most serious threats to Spanish authority in the colonial period. In its wake, a popular coalition expelled the peninsular (European-born) residents of the city, suspended royal government, and ruled the city until viceregal troops reestablished royal authority more than a year later.

The viceroy of New Grenada, Pedro Messía De La Cerda, had first provoked popular hostility by transfering control over the *aguardiente* (cane liquor) monopoly and the *alcabala* (sales tax) from local tax farmers to the *caja real* (royal treasury). This reform threatened to raise taxes at a time when the region's important textile industry was in decline. From the late seventeenth century on, a demographic crisis in the Ecuadorian highlands, declining demand in Peru for Quito's rough woolens, and, most important, the influx of cheap, high-quality European cloth had undermined the textile industry of the province.

Many influential landowners tried to compensate for declining profits in textile manufacturing by growing sugarcane and processing it into *aguardiente*. In addition, Quito's middle- and lower-class groups, left unemployed as the textile mills closed, found jobs in a burgeoning underground economy—operating small grocery stores, butcher or leather shops, and bootleg stills and bars, and growing foodstuffs on small holdings in the city's suburban parishes. The new sales tax administration threatened to raise levies on rural haciendas and small farms. In addition, the administration of taxes on *aguardiente* jeopardized the profits of both the elite and the plebians who produced and sold the liquor. In short, the reforms of the *alcabala* and *aguardiente* administrations promised to undermine the material welfare of a broad segment of *quiteño* society amid an economic depression, creating an ominous and potentially explosive situation.

After the outbreak of these revolts of May and June 1765, a broad-based popular coalition effectively disbanded the royal government and ruled the city and its hinterland. The coalition took power in June, but political differences soon emerged, particularly when plebeian leaders sought a wider political role in the region. Within the next year the latent ethnic, class, and political tensions within *quiteño* society had undermined the unity of the coalition and hastened the return to royal control. On 1 September 1766, when a viceregal army entered the city under the command of the conciliatory governor of Guayaquil, Antonio de Zelaya, the divided citizenry offered no effective resistance.

See also **Quito; Spanish Empire.**

BIBLIOGRAPHY

Despite its obvious importance, the Quito Revolt has attracted little scholarly attention until recently. Older accounts are Federíco González Suárez, *Historia general de la República del Ecuador* (1970), pp. 1126–1139, and Juan De Velasco, *Historia del reino de Quito en la America meridional,* vol. 1 (1971), pp. 136–149. The best discussion of the roots of the Quito Revolt is Kenneth J. Andrien, "Economic Crisis, Taxes, and the Quito Insurrection of 1765," in *Past and Present* 129 (November 1990): 104–131. For an account of the protesters see Anthony Mc Farlane, "The 'Rebellion of the Barrios': Urban Insurrection in Bourbon Quito," in *Hispanic American Historical Review* 69, no. 2 (May 1989): 283–330.

Additional Bibliography

Arrom, Silvia and Servando Ortoll. *Riots in the Cities: Popular Politics and the Urban Poor in America, 1765–1910.* Wilmington, DE: Scholarly Resources, 1996.

Milton, Cynthia E. *The Many Meanings of Poverty: Colonialism, Social Compacts, and Assistance in Eighteenth-century Ecuador.* Stanford, CA: Stanford University Press, 2007.

Powers, Karen Viera. *Andean Journeys: Migration, Ethnogenesis, and the State in Colonial Quito.* Albuquerque: University of New Mexico Press, 1995.

Sevilla Larrea, Carmen. *Vida y muerte en Quito: Raíces del sujeto moderno en la colonia temprana.* Quito: Ediciones Abya-Yala, 2003.

KENNETH J. ANDRIEN

QUITO REVOLT OF 1809. The collapse of the Spanish monarchy in 1808 and the revolt of the Spanish people on 2 May created a constitutional crisis in the Spanish Empire. In America, as in Spain, local leaders argued that in the absence of the king, sovereignty reverted to the people and therefore sought to form governing juntas.

In Quito, the elite established a Sovereign Junta on 9 August 1809 to govern in the name of the imprisoned king, with the Marqués de Selva Alegre as president and the bishop, José Cuero y Caicedo, as vice president. The movement found little support in other regions of the kingdom and considerable opposition from the viceroys of Peru and New Granada, eventually collapsing on 28 October 1809. Many participants were imprisoned by the authorities. A popular attempt to free them on 2 August 1810 failed when troops from Peru massacred more than seventy patriots in their cells.

The situation changed shortly thereafter when Carlos Montúfar, a Quiteño, arrived from Spain with instructions to resolve local issues. As a native, he sided with those who favored autonomy and reorganized the Quito junta in September 1810. The second junta established the "free" state of Quito, but, nonetheless, recognized the sovereignty of the king of Spain. The body drafted a constitution that was promulgated in February 1812. The new government still considered itself part of the Spanish commonwealth. But the forces of the viceroy of Peru eventually overwhelmed the second junta, restoring the area to "royal" authority in December 1812. Ecuadorians, however, consider the movement their first step toward independence.

See also **Wars of Independence, South America.**

BIBLIOGRAPHY

Torre Reyes, Carlos De La, *La Revolución de Quito del 10 de agosto de 1809* (1961).

José Gabriel Navarro, *La Revolución de Quito del 10 de agosto de 1809* (1962).

Michael T. Hamerly, "Selva Alegre, President of the *Quiteña* Junta of 1809: Traitor or Patriot?" in *Hispanic American Historical Review* 48 (November 1968): 642–653.

Additional Bibliography

Chacón Izurieta, Galo E. *Las guerras de Quito, por su independencia: orígenes del estado ecuatoriano y su ejército.* Quito: Centro de Estudios Históricos del Ejército, 2002.

Chiriboga, Angel I. *El coronel Carlos Montúfar y Larrea: Prócer de la independencia ecuatoriana.* Quito: Centro de Estudios Históricos del Ejército, 2003.

Garaicoa Ortiz, Xavier. *Hacia la cumbre de la libertad: Abdón Calderón Garaicoa y la independencia quiteña.* Guayaquil: Departamento de Publicaciones de la Facultad de Jurisprudencia y Ciencias Sociales y Políticas de la Universidad de Guayaquil, 2003.

Rodríguez O., Jaime E. *La revolución política durante la época de la independencia: El reino de Quito, 1808–1822.* Quito: Universidad Andina Simón Bolívar: Corporación Editora Nacional, 2006.

JAIME E. RODRÍGUEZ O.

Hernán Crespo Toral, Filoteo Samaniego Salazar, José María Vargas, O.P., eds., *Arte ecuatoriano*, vol. 2 (1976), esp. pp. 87–128.

José María Vargas, O.P., et al., "El arte durante la colonia," in *Historia del Ecuador*, vol. 4 (1988), pp. 233–262.

Additional Bibliography

Arte en la historia de Santo Domingo. Quito: Ediciones Banco de los Andes, 1994.

Vargas, José Maria. *El arte quiteño en los siglos XVI, XVII, y XVIII.* Quito: Impr. Romero, 1949.

LINDA ALEXANDER RODRÍGUEZ

QUITO SCHOOL OF ART.

Quito School of Art, the first school of its kind established in the Audiencia of Quito. The school was founded in 1552 at El Colegio de San Andrés. From its inauguration, the school attracted a number of talented Indians and Mestizos who studied painting, manuscript illumination, and sculpture. In the last quarter of the sixteenth century, Fray Pedro Bedón, who had studied painting in Lima with the Italian Jesuit Bernardo Bitti, was the most influential patron of indigenous popular religious art; his support became the basis for the Quito School of Art.

Arte Quiteño merged Catholic religious imagery with indigenous symbols and composition, producing a unique mixture of European baroque and plateresque style with the rigid, static composition of indigenous art. The Virgin may be painted with European features, but clothed in a feathered robe and holding a child dressed in indigenous fashion. Quito artists and artisans quickly made European techniques of oil painting and polychrome sculpture their own. The city's monastaries and convents became major centers of religious art production for South America. Although most of the artists are anonymous, a few, like the painter Miguel de Santiago and the sculptors Bernardo de Legarda, Caspicara, Padre Carlos, and Diego de Olmos, produced identifiable bodies of work.

See also **Art: The Colonial Era; Catholic Church: The Colonial Period.**

BIBLIOGRAPHY

José Gabriel Navarro, *El arte en la provincia de Quito* (1960).

QUITO SCHOOL OF SCULPTURE.

The history of the Quito School of Sculpture begins in 1535 with the establishment of the first art school in America. The Flemish friar Jodoco Ricke, the Franciscan friar responsible for the school's foundation, brought artists from Spain in an effort to instruct Creoles, mestizos, and Indians in the arts of painting, sculpture, and music. Although the art school was originally adjunct to the convent of San Francisco, by 1551 it became known as the school of San Andrés. Here Ecuadorian artists quickly mastered the techniques of Spanish polychrome wood sculptures. The school produced sculptures and paintings for Ecuador and the rest of the Spanish empire throughout the colonial era.

These artifacts were crafted by native artists who imitated the polychrome wood statues, the old master etchings, and the large scale paintings by Flemish, Italian, and French artists which the early colonists and friars had brought with them to decorate both churches and private houses. Technically they imitated influential Andalusian sculptors like Alonso Cano and Pedro de Mena, continuing the Spanish tradition of pathos and an almost theatrical expressivity. This intense realism included inlaid glass eyes, the use of gold and silver plates to decorate the intricate brocade of the figures robes; and by the eighteenth century the use of real hair, fingernails, and teeth. Most scholars use the art history terms "baroque" and "rococo" to describe the historical development of polychrome sculpture in Quito.

When peninsular sculpture declined, however, Quito entered its "golden age," which coincided with the ascension of the Bourbon monarchs. By

1741 guilds of artists operated independently of the Catholic church and produced for an economically prosperous consumer society composed mainly of lower-class mestizos. These guilds produced Quito's most eminent and well-documented sculptors, Bernardo Legarda and Manuel Chili (Caspicara).

Legarda (1727–1792) is the attributed creator of the ubiquitous Virgin of Quito, which stems iconographically from St. John's Apocalypse. As patroness of the Franciscan Order, she was given a local identity in the early colonial period, and today she is Quito's favorite icon. Legarda sculpted other American imagery, including Santa Rosa De Lima, the first creole saint. The delicacy of her sculpted image is a stylistic approximation of the effeminate qualities of the Caspicara school.

Although much research is needed to prove the numerous attributions made to Caspicara, he is known for his sculptural groups, such as the Assumption of Mary in the church of San Francisco. His work personifies the heightened baroque spirituality. Caspicara's statue of San Pedro de Alcántara, the confessor of Santa Teresa, exudes the austerity, poverty, and contemplative nature of the Spanish mystic.

Due to the lack of primary sources and signed work, more investigation is needed to correctly identify and catalog the vast body of sculpture in colonial Quito. Unfortunately only the names of major artists appear in the scanty records, leaving hundreds of statues anonymous. However, the Quito School continues to the present day with artists who still employ the traditional modes of polychrome sculpture which the early colonists imported centuries ago. The commercial production of sculptures like these reflects free enterprise, private patronage, and the stalwart presence of the Catholic church.

See also **Art: The Colonial Era.**

BIBLIOGRAPHY

José Gabriel Navarro, *La escultura en el Ecuador* (Madrid, 1929).

Gabrielle G. Palmer, *Sculpture in the Kingdom of Quito* (1987).

Ximena Escudero De Terán, *América y España en la escultura colonial quiteña: Historia de un sincretismo* (1992).

Additional Bibliography

Gallegos de Donoso, Magdalena. *The Development of Sculpture in the Quito School.* Washington, DC: Inter-American Development Bank, Cultural Center, 1994.

Vargas, José María. *El arte quiteño en los siglos XVI, XVII, y XVIII.* Quito: Impr. Romero, 1949.

VERÓNICA PESANTES-VALLEJO

QUITU. The term *Quitu-Cara* refers to the legendary pre-Hispanic founders of the Kingdom of Quito, in the modern state of Ecuador. The source is the Jesuit Juan de Velasco's 1789 *Historia del Reino de Quito en la América meridional*, which bases his account on three documents that are unavailable to modern scholars: *Las dos líneas de los Incas y de los Scyris, señores del Cuzco, y del Quito*, by Fray Marcos de Niza, a Franciscan who accompanied Sebastián Benalcázar's conquest of Quito in 1533; *Las antigüedades del Perú*, by Melchor Bravo de Saravia, an *oidor* (judge) of Lima; and *Guerras civiles del Inca Atahualpa con su hermano Atoco, llamado comúnmente Huáscar-Inca*, by Jacinto Collahuaso, an eighteenth-century cacique of Ibarra (north of Quito).

According to Velasco, the Caras, also known as the Scyris after the title of their sovereign (Scyri means "Lord of all"), arrived on the western coast of what is now Ecuador in approximately 700 or 800 CE and founded a town there called Cara, named after their first ruler, Carán Scyri. They had navigated from across the sea on balsa wood rafts. Finding the coastal region unhealthy, they migrated up to the Andean region, where in 980 CE they defeated the barbarous native Quitus, ruled by King Quitu, and adopted his name as the name of their kingdom. Velasco asserts that the Scyris reached heights in governing, religion, the arts and sciences. For example, they excelled at carving precious stones, especially emeralds, the stone worn by the Scyri leader and later adopted by the conquering Incas. According to Velasco, their customs and achievements included the right to private property and inheritance of both goods and lands, proper burials away from population centers, a kind of writing system made of stones for preserving their deeds, and, most notably, pure religious practices, which they cleansed of fables by introducing the worship of the sun and the moon. Their state was expansionist, conquering or confederating with other polities in the region, always establishing a town with a central plaza and ceremonial buildings.

The Inca conquest led by Huayna Cápac in the late fifteenth century was actually a reunion, because the Incas and Scyris shared the same overseas origin, according to Velasco. Huayna Cápac married the last Scryi's daughter, Paccha. Their son, Atahualpa, struggled with the Cuzqueño Inca Huáscar for control of the empire, after Huayna Cápac split the empire in two. The Quitu-Scyri legacy has had long-lasting effects on Ecuadorian nationalist thought. Debates have ensued among Velasco's "defenders" and "detractors," though contemporary scholars have found no physical remains or other convincing proof of their existence.

See also **Ecuador: Conquest Through Independence; Incas, The; Quito; Tinajero Martínez de Allen, Eugenia; Velasco, Juan de.**

BIBLIOGRAPHY

Jaramillo Alvarado, Pío. *El indio ecuatoriano*, 4th edition. Quito, Ecuador: Casa de la Cultura Ecuatoriana, 1954.

Jijón y Caamaño, Jacinto. *Antropología prehispánica del Ecuador*, 2nd edition. Quito, Ecuador: Museo Jacinto Jijón y Caamaño, 1997.

Salazar, Ernesto. *Entre mitos y fábulas: El Ecuador aborigen*, 5th edition. Biblioteca General de Cultura, vol. 4. Quito, Ecuador: Corporación Editora Nacional, 2000.

Salomon, Frank. *Native Lords of Quito in the Age of the Incas: The Political Economy of North-Andean Chiefdoms.* Cambridge, U.K., and New York: Cambridge University Press, 1986.

Silva, Erika. *Los mitos de la Ecuatorianidad.* Quito, Ecuador: Abya-Yala, 1992.

Velasco, Juan de. *Historia del Reino de Quito en la América meridional*, edited by Alfredo Pareja Diezcanseco. Caracas, Venezuala: Biblioteca Ayacucho, 1981.

EILEEN M. WILLINGHAM

QUIVIRA. Quivira, a legendary wealthy city on the Great Plains of North America that captured the imagination of conquistadors. The story of Quivira emerged during the 1540–1542 Coronado expedition when an Indian known as "the Turk" enticed the Spaniards onto the Great Plains in search of a land rich in gold and silver. Coronado and his men reached "Quivira," in what is today central Kansas, in the spring of 1541. Finding nothing of value, the Spaniards executed the Turk for his deception and abandoned the area. Only Fray Juan de Padilla stayed there to establish a mission for the local population but was soon martyred on the Plains. Despite Coronado's disappointing search, the legend of Quivira endured, serving as an impetus for further exploration.

See also **Conquistadores.**

BIBLIOGRAPHY

Herbert Eugene Bolton, *Coronado on the Turquoise Trail: Knight of Pueblos and Plains* (1949).

William Brandon, *Quivira: Europeans in the Region of the Santa Fe Trail, 1540–1820* (1990).

Additional Bibliography

Vigil, Ralph H.; Frances W. Kaye; and John R. Wunder. *Spain and the Plains: Myths and Realities of Spanish Exploration and Settlement on the Great Plains.* Niwot: University Press of Colorado, 1994.

SUZANNE B. PASZTOR

RABASA, EMILIO (1856–1930). Emilio Rabasa (*b.* 22 May 1856; *d.* 25 April 1930), Mexican novelist. Rabasa, a native of Ocozocuatla, Chiapas, studied law at the Instituto de Ciencias y Artes in Oaxaca and began his career as a deputy in the state legislature in 1881. In 1886 he went to Mexico City, returned to Chiapas as governor from 1891 to 1894, and then served as its senator from 1894 to 1913. He represented the government of Victoriano Huerta at the Niagara Falls Conference in Canada (20 May–15 July 1914), alongside the envoys of Venustiano Carranza, to discuss the U.S. occupation of Veracruz and the incident at Tampico. Huerta fell in 1914, and Rabasa and his family remained in New York City until 1920.

Rabasa was known as one of Mexico's outstanding constitutional lawyers. He also distinguished himself as a novelist and journalist. In 1887 he cofounded *El Universal*, still in publication. In that year and the following one, he published four novels using the pseudonym of Sancho Polo, *La bola, La gran ciencia, El cuarto poder,* and *Moneda falsa.* A novel, *La guerra de tres años,* published serially in *El Universal* in 1891, appeared in 1931. Rabasa has been hailed as the father of "Mexican realism," and his work is frequently compared with that of his Spanish contemporary, Benito Pérez Galdós.

See also **Literature: Spanish America.**

BIBLIOGRAPHY

Alfonso De Lascurain, *Influencia de don Emilio Rabasa en la constitución de 1917* (1956).

Marcia A. Hakala, *Emilio Rabasa, novelista innovador mexicano en el siglo XIX* (1974).

Lorum H. Stratton, *Emilio Rabasa: Life and Works* (1974).

Elliot S. Glass, *Mexico en las obras de Emilio Rabasa,* translated by Nicolas Pizarro Suárez (1975).

Additional Bibliography

Cortazar, Alejandro. *Reforma, novela y nación: México en el siglo XIX.* Puebla: Benemérita Universidad Auntónoma de Puebla, Dirección de Fomento Editorial, 2006.

Hale, Charles A. "The Civil Law Tradition and Constitutionalism in Twentieth Century Mexico: The Legacy of Emilio Rabasa." *Law and History Review* 18:2 (Summer 2000): 257–279.

BARBARA A. TENENBAUM

RABINAL ACHÍ. The *Rabinal Achí* (Man of Rabinal) is a Maya play that predates the arrival of the Spanish to the New World. Little is known about its origins. Through dialogue, music, and dance it recounts events of Maya history that culminate in the early fifteenth century. During the colonial period the *Rabinal Achí* was eventually transcribed using alphabetic script; the date of the first transcription remains unknown. The play was published in 1862 as a French translation of a copy that Father Charles Étienne Brasseur de Bourbourg made of an earlier manuscript that was read to him while serving as parish priest in the town of Rabinal. All current publications are based on Brasseur's French translation or on his original Maya script, which Manuel Pérez copied in 1913. Translators who have worked directly from the Maya text include Georges Raynaud, Alain Breton, and Dennis Tedlock. For his English translation, Tedlock also used a video recording he had made of performances in Rabinal in 1998 under the direction of José León Coloch.

Although the play may have acquired European stylistic influences over the centuries—in the design of masks, for instance—its style and delivery put the *Rabinal Achí* in a class of its own. Its repetitive and static dynamics are unparalleled in colonial drama. The play dramatizes the trial of Cawek, a renegade Quiché Maya warrior who fought against the neighboring Mayas of Rabinal and was captured. Cawek, the Man of Quiché, emerges as the main character in the drama. He is allowed to explain his actions, defend himself against accusations, and freely express his wishes until his inevitable execution concludes the drama.

Tedlock stresses in his translation that the execution of Cawek is not a heart sacrifice as earlier translations had rendered it, but a beheading. This removes from the play an inaccurate bit of Aztec exoticism that may have been introduced by Brasseur de Bourbourg in his nineteenth-century translation. The death of Cawek is not a ceremonial sacrifice but a quick execution preserving his dignity as a warrior, which his enemies profoundly respect. Paradoxically, the play is a celebration of valor and mutual respect among peoples. Laws of warfare and death, although inevitable, appear trivial in comparison with the underlying sense of humanity and self-respect that the play ultimately conveys. In 2005 UNESCO proclaimed the *Rabinal Achí* one of the Masterpieces of the Oral and Intangible Heritage of Humanity.

See also **Maya, The; Theater.**

BIBLIOGRAPHY

Tedlock, Dennis. *Rabinal Achi: A Mayan Drama of War and Sacrifice.* New York: Oxford University Press, 2005.

LUIS O. ARATA

RACE AND ETHNICITY.

The concept of race emerged with modernity and European expansion. Race was entrenched by the nineteenth century as a scientific category, only to have its validity questioned in the twentieth century. Scholars in the early twenty-first century widely view race as a social construct. Race (*raza* in Spanish, *raça* in Portuguese) has been used throughout the Americas to mark human difference with reference to geographical origin and to inherited bodily and cultural traits. Yet traits commonly used to differentiate among racial groups (such as skin color, cultural attributes, or facial features) are not used consistently. The boundaries between racial groups are not universally agreed upon; nor is it always evident how to categorize any specific individual. Indeed, Latin America is known for the complexity and fluidity of its racial categories, especially in comparison to the more racially rigid United States.

Ethnicity is another concept that is also used to mark differences among human groups. Like race, ethnicity often makes reference to geographic origin and is also passed on through the generations. Ethnicity tends to emphasize language and cultural heritage, and is often used as a subset of broader racial categories. But ethnicity and race are sometimes used interchangeably. No single definition of either race or ethnicity suffices to encompass their historical uses.

This essay encompasses both Brazil and Spanish America. Specialists tend to treat them separately when studying race, and indeed, there are some important historical differences between the areas colonized by the Spanish and the Portuguese empires. But these differences are not necessarily greater than the historical variations within those areas. Similar historical patterns of colonization and exploitation have shaped race and ethnicity across Brazil and Spanish America.

Racial hierarchy is rooted historically in the European conquest of the Americas and the unequal development of global capitalism. In the colonial period, dominant ideologies of rigid segregation and hierarchy coexisted with dynamic processes of racial mixture. Since independence, ideologies of racial equality, harmony, and national unity have coexisted with ongoing discrimination, exploitation, violence, and prejudice along racial and ethnic lines. Time and again, revolutions have proclaimed the end of racism, yet every time the proclamation has proved premature.

Despite their status as social constructions that lack "fixed referents" (Wade, p. 5), race and ethnicity nonetheless affect the lives of Latin Americans. Across

Latin America, racial and ethnic labels have varied widely from country to country, and from one era to the next. Yet an underlying pattern has persisted until the present: Latin Americans labeled as "black" or "Indian" have tended to inhabit the lowest socioeconomic strata of their respective societies. They are found disproportionately among the poor and they are underrepresented among the middle and elite classes. Race and class hierarchies, while not perfectly correlating, have been conjointly constructed.

ORIGINS, THEORIES, AND EVOLVING DEFINITIONS

Contemporary historians often use modern understandings of race and ethnicity, and variations on these terms (e.g., "racialization," "ethnic group," "racial hierarchy") as analytical terms to apply to places and historical periods when those terms were not explicitly used in the modern sense. Thus one can detect evidence of what is now called racism throughout world history. The specific terms "race" and "ethnicity," however, have their own histories, which are worth reviewing. These histories were initially shaped by European expansion and colonization.

"Race" first appeared in European languages during the early sixteenth century. The term referred simply to lineage, and was not widely used until the end of the eighteenth century. At the dawn of the Early Modern era, religion was paramount in the definition of Europe's emerging identity. Non-Christians were increasingly expelled or otherwise marginalized. Religion, not skin color, defined who belonged in Christendom. There was, however, already evidence of what in the early twenty-first century would be called "racial thought," whereby Europeans defined the Other with reference to bodily traits. Thus, Europeans called Africans—whom they were importing as slaves—"black." In the Iberian Peninsula, in particular, religion and lineage conjoined. With the forced conversion of Jews and Muslims in the Iberian Reconquest, "Old Christians" differentiated themselves from "New Christians" by claiming to have "clean blood" (*limpieza de sangre* in Spanish, *limpeça de sangue* in Portuguese) free of the "stain" of Jewish or Muslim ancestry.

As early modern Europeans explored and conquered ever more distant lands, they encountered peoples whose diversity they sought to explain. The resulting theories, not surprisingly, tended to favor European superiority and expansionism. Climate was thought to determine human appearance, temperament, and intellect. The course of civilization in each region was attributed to the environment's effects on its inhabitants. According to the predominant school of thought, the overly humid and astrologically ill-fated New World climate had negative effects on the bodies, minds, and civilizations of its inhabitants. Most explanations of human difference did acknowledge that individual traits were passed on from one generation to another, yet such traits were also viewed as mutable, even within an individual's lifetime. Skin color, for example, could presumably be changed by prolonged exposure to a different climate, or even spontaneously by maternal disposition during conception. Thus, Europeans living in the tropics would be transformed by their environments.

Historian Jorge Cañizares-Esguerra has shown that as early as the seventeenth century, Spanish-American colonists viewed the difference between themselves and the other inhabitants of the Americas in what would considered present-day racial terms. Bristling at European assumptions of American inferiority, American-born (creole) Europeans did not view themselves as inferior simply because they had spent a lifetime in the tropics. They preferred to explain their physical and moral traits as resulting from lineage rather than environmental influences. Spanish creoles viewed themselves as bodily distinct from the indigenous peoples they colonized and the African peoples they imported. Thus the creole colonists racialized and justified the relationship between themselves and the peoples they exploited.

In the late eighteenth century, the pioneering Enlightenment naturalist Carolus Linneaus and his disciple Johann Friedrich Blumenbach divided humanity into varieties by geographical origin, color, posture, and temperament. The Blumenbach scheme divided the species into Caucasians, Mongolians, Ethiopians, Americans, and Malays. Thus he provided the lasting template for modern-day racial categories of White, East Asian, Black, American Indian, and Southeast Asian/Pacific Islander.

By the nineteenth century, physical traits were widely understood to be inherited, and the Enlightenment's broad racial categories were accepted as biological facts that formed the basis for racial science. Scientific racists in Europe and North America elaborated theories that justified white supremacy, slavery, and colonialism. Influential racial theorists such as Gustave Le Bon and Joseph-Arthur de Gobineau viewed the "mongrel" races of Latin America with especial horror. Promiscuous racial mixture in the tropical zones, they believed, had caused racial "degeneration." Latin American intellectuals, such as the Brazilian Nina Rodrigues, made use of these theories, adapting them to their national context. Rodrigues drew on Cesare Lombroso's racial theories of criminality to recommend different criminal penalties for individuals of different races. Racial science culminated toward the end of the century with the emergence of eugenics, the science of racial improvement, founded by Francis Galton.

Eugenicists split between "hard" eugenics that emphasized the immutability of races (especially popular in North America and Britain) and "soft" or "Neo-Lamarckian" eugenics (more popular in Latin America and parts of Continental Europe), that posited the "inheritance of acquired characteristics." According to the latter school of thought, environmental influences (such as climate, hygiene, nutrition, and education) could "improve" a race from one generation to the next. The hard eugenicists, drawing on the early genetic theories of Gregor Mendel, believed that races were immutable. The boundaries between hard and soft eugenics were themselves permeable, with many theorists borrowing freely from both. Eugenics peaked in the 1930s and then declined, largely discredited by the extremes to which the Nazis took it in World War II. Neo-Lamarckian theories regarding acquired characteristics were invalidated by Darwinian evolution and the modern science of genetics. The assumptions behind eugenics did not, however, disappear from popular thought or even entirely from scientific practice.

Enlightenment racial typologies persist in the early 2000s, and are used by doctors, demographers, bureaucrats, and rights activists—not to mention ordinary people in daily life—although scholars increasingly agree that "biologically speaking, races do not exist" (Wade, p. 13). Contemporary geneticists have found that genetic inheritance patterns are far more complex than simple overarching divisions according to continental origin would imply.

Despite the predominance of the Enlightenment five-race scheme, additional usages and definitions of race have continued to operate in Latin America and elsewhere. In the mid-1850s, intellectuals from several Latin American republics started using the terms "Latin race" (*raza latina*) and "Latin America." Concerned with nineteenth-century U.S. expansionism and filibusterism, the Colombian writer José María Torres Caicedo defined the Latin race in explicit opposition to the "Saxon race." In a poem of 1856 he wrote: "The race of Latin America / Finds itself confronted by the Saxon Race" (Aims McGuinness, in Appelbaum, et al., p. 99). His Panamanian contemporary Justo Arosemena, angry about U.S. actions on the Isthmus of Panamá, referred to his northern neighbors as *la raza Yankee*, which he described as a conquering and materialistic race. Spanish Americans commonly refer to October 12 as "The Day of the Race" (*el día de la raza*). Race has also been used with reference to much smaller geographical entities: to denote the people of a particular republic (e.g. *la raza chilena*, of Chile), region (*la raza antioqueña*, of the Colombian province of Antioquia), town, or even neighborhood.

In these various usages, race has encompassed ideas about biology, blood, culture, nation, morality, phenotype, or even spirituality. It has sometimes referred to skin color, although Latin Americans have often conceptually separated race from color (thus, the "Brazilian race" is made up of many colors). Underlying the various Latin American definitions of race has been a reference to geography and an assumption that "essential" traits, whether physical or moral, are passed on from one generation to the next.

"Ethnic" is a closely related concept which has often been used as a synonym for racial type. Ethnography emerged as a field of research on "primitive" or "uncivilized" peoples in the nineteenth century (ethnicity was thus a foundational component of the emerging social science of anthropology). The use of "ethnic groups" to refer to minority identities within a given country, however, dates largely to the mid-twentieth century. This usage gained in popularity with the discrediting of racial science after World War II and the codification of minority rights in international treaties. In Latin America, ethnicity (*etnia* in Spanish, *etnicidade* in Portuguese) is most often used to refer to the multitude of groups that maintain an "indigenous" (Indian) cultural identity, or sometimes to differentiate among peoples of African or

European origin, or to refer to immigrants from Asia or the Middle East. In recent decades, Afro-Latin American activists have sometimes referred to themselves as an "etnia," because ethnicity has fewer negative historical connotations than race.

Scholars have, since the latter part of the twentieth century, emphasized the creative and innovative aspects of ethnicity formation, showing how individuals and groups reshape and revise their identities rather than simply passing them along unchanged from generation to generation. The final decades of the twentieth century saw a renaissance of indigenous identities in Latin America, such as the pan-Mayan movement in Mesoamerica. Indigenous communities that had long stopped identifying as "Indian" have reconstituted themselves throughout the Americas, putting forth land claims and grappling with complex issues over who should or should not be considered truly indigenous.

The boundaries between different races and ethnicities vary from one country to the next. For example, many Latin Americans who have viewed themselves as white have traveled to the United States or Europe only to discover themselves labeled "black," "Indian," or "of color." A *pardo* ("brown" or of mixed ancestry) in Brazil might be "black" in the United States. The traditional U.S. "one-drop rule," whereby anyone with any trace of African ancestry is considered black, is exceptional in the larger context of the Americas; likewise the "blood quantum" used to measure "percentage" of Indian, black, or other "blood" is more common in the United States. In most of the Americas, whiteness tends to be a more inclusive category, though just how inclusive varies widely; in areas that experienced a significant influx of European immigration in the late nineteenth and early twentieth centuries (such as southern Brazil, Argentina, and Uruguay) whiteness tends to be a prerogative of people who consider themselves to be of exclusively European lineage. Whiteness can be more inclusive in a country such as the Dominican Republic or Costa Rica, which did not experience such large-scale immigration.

Even within one country, such definitions can vary from one region to the next. A person considered in his native highland Andean community to be *mestizo* (mixed), might be viewed as Indian when he migrates to Lima, by virtue of his *sierra* origins, mother tongue, clothing, and other cultural habits.

Anthropologist Marisol de la Cadena, a native of Lima, reported in the 1990s that her young informants in the highland Peruvian city of Cuzco viewed her as white and themselves as indigenous, despite her observation that her phenotype was very similar to theirs. The Cuzco informants differentiated themselves from her in part because she did not practice indigenous cultural rituals. Also important in the differentiation of de la Cadena from her informants was the fact that she was from Lima, not the highlands, illustrating that race and region in Latin America are often conflated. Even more intriguingly, the *cuzqueños* viewed themselves as simultaneously indigenous and mestizo, because as urban students they were more cultured and educated than poor rural Indians from surrounding villages.

What constitutes a distinct race or ethnicity in Latin America is a hotly contested political and cultural question. It is a very personal issue for many individuals grappling with how best to define themselves in rapidly changing societies that value both tradition and modernity. Definitions of race and ethnicity have varied over time and space and have been fluid and contested. Yet an examination of Latin American history demonstrates that, regardless of such fluidity, beliefs about racial hierarchy and ethnic identity have had a profound impact on people's lives.

CONQUEST AND THE CREATION OF COLONIAL HIERARCHY

At the time of the Iberian conquest, the Americas were inhabited by a plethora of peoples with their own languages and collective identities. Although the traditional view of pre-Columbian America has been one of stasis, more recent scholarship has shown that the political and cultural landscape was quite dynamic. Sophisticated imperial states such as the Inca and Mexica empires had emerged during the century before the Conquest, absorbing the technological innovations of previous empires and conquering their neighbors. As political entities rose and fell, and as peoples migrated from one region to another, new identities emerged and others disappeared.

The Conquest brought Old-World pathogens, which, in combination with violence and exploitation, triggered a catastrophic demographic decline in the New World. Many of the indigenous identities that had existed in 1500 were gone by the mid-sixteenth century. New communities and new identities emerged out of the mixture and relocation of survivors of older communities. Frank Salomon and Stuart B. Schwartz have referred to this process of mixture as "intra-indigenous *mestizaje*" (p. 460) and to the emergence of new ethnicities as "ethno genesis" (p. 443).

Sedentary indigenous groups in core areas of Spanish America, mainly in the Andes and Mesoamerica, reconstituted their identities and cultural practices in local communities, blending pre-Columbian institutions with Iberian ones, while providing labor to their conquerors. Many of them were accustomed to providing labor for pre-Columbian empires. Over the centuries, their communal lands, villages, and communal councils—institutions created by the Spanish state to facilitate evangelization and tribute collection—became integral elements of "traditional" indigenous culture that indigenous communities would struggle to conserve.

Brazil lacked these sedentary indigenous societies. Much of its indigenous population was semi-sedentary, living in relatively small autonomous units rather than large kingdoms or empires. In contrast to Spanish America, the state did not seriously attempt to segregate the Indian population from settlers. Portugal was even less effective than Spain in prohibiting Indian slavery, and until about 1600, Portuguese settlers relied heavily on the enslavement of Indians for their labor force.

Nonsedentary indigenous groups in peripheral regions of both the Spanish and Portuguese empires remained relatively autonomous, but most of them also experienced dramatic changes. They selectively adapted some European technology for their own purposes. In some cases, Europeans raided these communities for slaves. Indigenous groups that successfully resisted colonization attracted new members, including members of other Indian communities as well as runaway African and Indian slaves, forming new ethnic identities in the process. Some of these new entities, such as the Miskito nation of Central America, survived in part by taking advantage of the territorial competition between European colonial powers, allying with one or the other as circumstances dictated (the Miskitos, for example, allied with the British).

"White" was not commonly used to identify people of European extraction until the late colonial period, but "Indian" and "black" provided central organizing concepts for the organization of colonial labor regimes from the outset (historians nonetheless often translate the terms *español* and *portugués* in colonial documents as "white"). Beginning with Columbus, Iberian colonizers collapsed the diverse indigenous identities into the category of *indio*, which, according to Salomon and Schwartz "quickly evolved from a cursory overgeneralization to an innovative juridical category ... and then, more slowly and ambivalently, to a sign by which peoples identified themselves" (p. 446). Even as they increasingly identified as Indian, many indigenous peoples maintained strong ethnic identities of their own.

A similar process of ethnic homogenization was imposed upon the Africans forcibly brought to the New World. The diverse peoples of Africa were lumped together as "black," a term often used as synonymous with "slave." Africans were torn from their communities of origin by African slavers, sold to Europeans, and imported to the New World in notoriously inhumane conditions. The survivors of this ordeal were scattered throughout the plantations, mines, and cities of the Americas. Ethnic divisions between groups from different regions of Africa persisted, especially in areas with large concentrations of slaves from specific areas, but the boundaries were also often blurred by dispersal and intermixture. Throughout the African Diaspora, Africans and their descendants reconstituted and reinvented African cultural practices, combining elements from various regions of Africa with European customs. As was also the case for Indians, Africans blended their original religious beliefs and rituals with Christianity.

In Spanish America, colonial administrators sought to keep Indians separate from Europeans and newly imported African slaves, but to little avail: From the beginning the conquerors had children with indigenous and African women. Such mixing was likely even more widespread in Brazil. New categories emerged to describe the results: In Spanish America, "mestizo" initially referred to the child of an Indian and a European, *mulato* to the child of a European and African, *zambo* to the child of an Indian and African. *Castizo*, which had originally suggested purity, came to mean the child of a mestizo and an español. The Portuguese adapted an Ottoman military term to call the children of Portuguese-Indian unions *mamelucos*. Additional "castes" proliferated to denote the offspring of people of mixed background, and colloquial terms particular to various regions also took hold. The term *ladino*, for example, came to refer to mestizos and later to all non-Indians in parts of Central America; the term *cholo* was used for a kind of mestizo in parts of the Andes.

This process of mestizaje, which resulted in proliferating caste categories, was diagrammed with some apparent irony by eighteenth-century Spanish-American artists in a genre known as *casta*. Casta paintings, originating mainly in Mexico City but also in the Andes, consisted of series of captioned images, each showing a family unit of a father and mother, each of a different caste, and a child of another caste resulting from that mixture. The family groups were usually placed in a local context of home or work, and usually organized in sets of sixteen. Each set of images would begin with an image such as "Spaniard and Indian beget Mestizo" and then go on to document a series of mixtures, which by the end would degenerate into absurdities: "from a Spaniard and an Albino comes a Black Turn-Backwards."

COLONIAL CASTE SOCIETY: ADAPTATION AND CONTESTATION

Over generations, casta paintings notwithstanding, the intermediate casta categories tended to collapse into mestizo and mulato. The term "pardo," in Brazil and many regions of Spanish America, was widely used by the late colonial period to denote some degree of African ancestry. Creoles struggled to maintain their own privilege and control over this demographically complex society; they emphasized their own "pure" ancestry as separating themselves from the subordinate castas. Colonists had imported the ideal of purity of bloodlines from Iberia. In the Indies, "limpieza de sangre" came to include the absence of African or Indian "blood." But the Creoles' purity was suspect in European eyes. Some Peninsula-born Iberian bureaucrats and commentators derided Creole elites as polluted by the climate, unacknowledged non-European ancestors, and even "bad milk" (because many Creoles had been suckled by indigenous or African wet nurses; "milk" was also a metaphor for nurture).

The notion of clean bloodlines was closely related to the Iberian concept of honor. Honor was used to justify and explain colonial hierarchies; individuals and families insisted that their honor be publicly recognized and thus their place in the colonial hierarchy assured. The elite, in particular, associated honor with birth status and limpieza de sangre. Families sought to preserve their honor by policing the sexuality and marital choices of their members. Parents especially tried to guard the virginity of their daughters. Male offspring were generally allowed greater latitude to mix with and sexually exploit women of the lower orders, as long as such informal unions did not end in marriage. The state, and more ambiguously the church, colluded with parents in guarding family honor. In the 1770s, the Spanish state promulgated the Royal Pragmatic on marriage, which allowed white parents (and later those of other castes) to prevent their children from choosing marital partners deemed socially or racially inferior, in an effort to preserve a hierarchical social order.

People born into lower castes often emphasized their own honorable behavior in an effort to claim honor for themselves, but elites and officials tended to assume that people of higher birth status behaved more honorably. Thus, as historians have shown, an elite unmarried Creole woman was assumed to be a virgin unless she flagrantly and publicly flouted the norms of sexual modesty. A poor market woman or a slave woman, meanwhile, was generally assumed not to be virtuous; her station in life was assumed to leave her unprotected from sexual assault and seduction and her "nature," if she were not white, predisposed her to dishonorable acts. Such assumptions were manifest in legal rulings that discriminated by caste. The transcript of a 1688 Mexico City Inquisition case, studied by the historian R. Douglas Cope, epitomizes this tendency. A poor mulata named Josefa and her roommate, an española named Mariana, were accused of harassing another woman. Although the accused were of similar economic means, one inquisitor placed full blame on "the sad mulata, Josefa," whom he found "gravely suspect because of her status, her way of life, and her nature and caste; and although a similar presumption could be made of Mariana ... because Mariana is married and is an española, such a presumption would not have much force" (Cope, p. 40). Josefa was assumed to be guilty because of her intrinsic nature as a member of a subordinate caste, in addition to the fact that she was an unattached female without a male authority figure to protect and control her.

The colonial legal order determined different privileges, duties, and legal sanctions for each caste, ranging from allowable clothing to admission to educational institutions, suitable occupations, taxes owed, and appropriate punishments for crimes. "Clean blood" was a requirement for admittance to universities, honorable professions, most government positions, religious orders, and the secular priesthood. The military was off-limits to nonwhites, with the exception of segregated militias. Yet, despite seemingly rigid legal discrimination and caste labeling, the caste hierarchy was nonetheless somewhat fluid. Individuals of mixed heritage did enter prohibited institutions and professions, either by obtaining royal dispensation for their ancestral "defect" or by circumventing the law. Exceptionally intrepid and fortunate individuals and families could ascend the hierarchy by migrating out of their birth communities, becoming wealthier, dressing differently, and obtaining higher-status marital partners. Such ascension was usually incremental: A black might become a mulatto, a mulatto might become a white. The same individual might be labeled "india" on her baptismal record and "mestiza" in her marriage document. Escaping from the category of Indian or mulatto could be a way of escaping the burden of tribute imposed on those castes. Economic class affected caste affiliation; money whitened. Public recognition of one's caste status mattered more than actual ancestry. The state tried to visibly mark off one group from another through sumptuary laws, but numerous court cases attest to the difficulty with which these laws were enforced; likewise, numerous court cases in which individuals' caste identities were the subject of competing sworn depositions also demonstrate the fluid and contested nature of caste. Mestizaje was as much a cultural and socioeconomic process as a genetic one.

"Whitening" was not the only tendency. A mestizo might redefine himself as indio and thus gain access to Indian lands. One way to do this was through marriage. For example, in 1664 some indigenous officials in the Puna area in the southern Andes denounced their *cacique* (chief or leader), Francisco Castillo, an originally non-Indian man who had married into the community (Salomon and Schwartz, p. 485). The great eighteenth-century indigenous rebel leader Tupac Amaru II, according to some historians, was a mestizo before he assumed the identity of heir to the Inca Empire.

At the top of the hierarchy, Creole elites in Brazil and Spanish America selectively allowed wealthy individuals of mixed ancestry into their midst. But they did not tend to look favorably on upwardly mobile subordinate groups. Spanish American elites disdained pardo militiamen. The colonial state antagonized some Creole leaders when it offered meritorious pardos the option of purchasing exemptions from their subordinate caste status—effectively of purchasing whiteness. Although very few pardos throughout the empire took advantage of this opportunity, it was controversial, especially in a city such as Caracas, where pardos had come to dominate several key sectors of the urban economy, much to the chagrin of the elite. In a famous 1796 letter to the crown, Creole councilmen complained that pardo impudence threatened the social hierarchies upon which the colonial economy was based. Even the Caracas leaders implied, however, that an occasional exceptional person of mixed ancestry might receive dispensation. The councilmen suggested that they, not royal officials, should decide who merited such an honor.

Within a few decades, the colonial order would crumble and the caste hierarchy would come under attack by a new generation of leaders. The colonial order had been characterized by tension between institutional caste rigidity and discrimination, on the one hand, and mestizaje and individual mobility on the other. Subsequently, the national era would be characterized by racial tensions of its own.

RACIAL EQUALITY AND RACISM IN REPUBLICAN LATIN AMERICA

In the early nineteenth century, a radical liberal republican ideal of racial equality and unity among all male citizens gained adherents across Spanish America and even in imperial Brazil. The egalitarianism of this ideology was in constant tension, however, with panicky fears of "race war" and elite desires to safeguard privilege. Despite the rhetoric of republican citizenship, racial division and discrimination remained part of everyday life.

In stark contrast to the United States, the other newly independent American nations abolished caste distinctions and enshrined equality in their constitutions for all free and native-born men, regardless of color or ancestry. This about-face on the part of the Creole elite had several causes. Enlightenment liberal philosophy played a part, as did the Spanish Americans' efforts to increase their political representation in the liberal Spanish parliament of 1812 in Cádiz, by claiming political rights for men of African descent. If men of African descent were granted political representation, the Spanish American representatives would vastly outnumber peninsular Spaniards. Spanish intransigence in Cádiz allowed the Creoles to claim that they, not the Spaniards, were the true champions of racial equality.

Possibly the most important factor contributing to identify patriotism with racial equality was the crucial military role played by the subordinate castes in the independence wars. Without the participation of Indians, free castas, and even slaves, independence would have been impossible. In South America, the Creole patriot leaders Simón Bolívar, in the north, and José de San Martín, in the south, needed the mixed-race expert horsemen of their respective interior grasslands to fight on their side in the military struggles for independence. In Mexico, meanwhile, the first movement for independence, the Hidalgo Revolt in 1810, was largely composed of Indians, mestizos, and mulattos, inspiring more revulsion than support among the creole population. Mexico waited a decade for the creole military commander of the Spanish forces to ally with the patriot guerrilla leader Vicente Guerrero to push for independence. A few nonwhite men who had emerged from humble beginnings, such as Guerrero, became presidents and power brokers in the new republics.

The independence wars eroded the institution of slavery. The plantation sectors of war-torn regions were devastated and many slaves gained freedom in the conflict, which they did not want to give up when the fighting ended. Yet, despite the racially egalitarian, anticolonial ideology of the independence movements and the "free-womb" laws that several new republics enacted, slavery did linger on for several more decades. In some areas, the gradual termination of slavery included transitional forms of bondage, referred to with euphemistic terms such as "apprenticeship." Even with such setbacks, within a generation slavery disappeared from the Spanish-American republics, in part because of pressure from below by the slaves themselves, who took every opportunity to extricate themselves from bondage. Slavery lasted until the last quarter of the century, however, in the remaining Spanish colonies of Cuba and Puerto Rico and in the Brazilian Empire, which did not experience the disruptions of the early nineteenth-century independence wars. The continuation of slavery in these areas was accompanied by institutionalized segregation, discrimination, and repression targeted at free people of color as well as at slaves.

Throughout Latin America, a discourse of racial harmony was adopted, yet racial discrimination remained part of everyday life. Any efforts by members of subordinate groups to demand real equality sparked accusations of racism and sedition against the individuals who brought the complaints. Recent research on early nineteenth-century Colombia suggests that individuals of African descent who protested discrimination were more likely to be punished by the courts than vindicated. Rumors of Haitian-style "race war" proliferated. As long as slavery persisted, moreover, any plots or rumored plots of slave rebellion were brutally repressed.

As national politics divided along Liberal-Conservative lines, Liberal leaders viewed former slaves and other free blacks and mulattos as potential constituents. Thus, in some regions, midcentury Liberals actively promoted manumission and emancipation, making sure to portray themselves publicly as the champions of freedom and equality, in contrast to Conservatives. In these regions, blacks and mulattos flocked to the Liberal cause. In the province of Cauca, Colombia, for example, blacks and mulattos were heavily recruited into radical Liberal political clubs known as Democratic Societies in the 1850s and 1860s; they participated avidly in civil strife and wars against Conservative landowners who had tried to prolong slavery. These "popular" Liberals of Cauca reframed Liberal ideals of equality and citizenship to suit their own needs, pressuring for access to land and the end of hated taxes and government monopolies on liquor production. Ultimately, by the 1870s, many upper-class Liberals recoiled in horror at the assertiveness and violence of the popular Liberals and allied with Conservatives to bring an end to the era of Afro-Colombian Liberal mobilization. Universal male suffrage, which Colombian men had enjoyed since the 1850s, was revoked in 1886, at a time when Latin American governments were generally becoming more authoritarian and distancing themselves from the egalitarian ideals of radical Liberalism. Economic restrictions on suffrage effectively excluded most blacks and Indians from the full rights of male citizenship in many countries.

Regarding Indians, the republican elite was also ambivalent. The ideologues of national progress drew on the legacy of pre-Columbian empires as a source of national pride, while disparaging the contemporary Indian descendants of the people who created those empires. With the end of the colonial caste system, Indians were rechristened with the less derogatory label "indigenous" (*indígena*), but in several countries they continued to pay a special Indian tribute well into the nineteenth century. Republican leaders, particularly those who believed in liberal ideals of individualism and private property, argued that indígenas should be educated and assimilated into the modern national citizenry and labor force. Liberals sought to privatize Indian landholdings, as part of a larger assault on corporate privileges and colonial institutions. As a result, many Indians lost their communal lands and self-governing institutions. With these losses, they often lost their identities as indigenous; the members of many former communities and their descendents became known as mestizos, even if other citizens continued to refer them pejoratively as indios. Some community members benefited from the partition of their communal lands and formed rural middle classes, others lost their land and became laborers or poor tenant farmers. This process of land privatization and concomitant cultural mestizaje intensified during the late nineteenth-century export boom.

Some indigenous communities protected the integrity of their communal landholdings by allying with Conservative or Liberal elites in the factional strife that roiled Spanish America. Conservative elites, who were less critical of colonial hierarchies than were Liberals, often looked more favorably on communal indigenous land holdings than did Liberals, but ideology was mitigated by expediency. Generally, both Liberal and Conservative leaders sought to privatize and alienate indigenous lands whenever they deemed it in their best economic interests, for example when Indian lands were coveted for coffee or other export crops. Leaders in both parties, meanwhile, were more willing to protect communal lands when they needed indigenous military or electoral support. Moreover, impoverished indigenous communities were sometimes useful to the elite; poor Indian villages provided nearby elite-owned *haciendas* and mines (often located on former communal lands) with a convenient seasonal labor force. When Indians resisted working for private enterprises or on public works projects such as roads and railroads, moreover, the state would respond with forced labor drafts and harsh vagrancy laws. Thus, the integration of nineteenth-century Latin American republics into the capitalist world economy was facilitated in part by coerced labor organized along racial lines as well as the privatization of communal lands.

Nineteenth-century elite intellectuals in the fragile new republics associated human diversity with a frightening disunity. They hoped that their motley populations would be replaced by unitary national races. Colombian liberal intellectual and diplomat Manuel Ancízar, writing in the early 1850s (when Colombia was called New Granada) predicted optimistically that "when the absorption of the indigenous race by the European has been completed ... a homogenous, vigorous and well formed race will be left, the character of which will be half way between the impetuousness of the Spaniard and the calm and patience of the Chibcha Indian" (Ancízar, p. 120). While he clearly viewed race as the product of inherited stereotypical traits, he also stated "today the indigenous race is being substituted by the Granadan race, diverse from the first in character, in intelligence, and in moral necessities, and, moreover, galvanized by democratic institutions and modified in its way of life by liberty of industry and of movement" (p. 121). Thus, race was not only inherited, it was also shaped by the social and political environment. This dualism echoed the debates of the Early Modern era and foreshadowed the twentieth-century discourse of mestizo nationalism (discussed below) whereby mestizaje and social improvements were supposed to produce a superior national race. Ancízar and his contemporaries construed the existence of Indians and Afro-Latin Americans as a problem that would be overcome in the process of national progress and unification.

That Ancízar wrote these lines while reporting on his travels as part of a national mapping commission underscores the extent to which the goal of racial unification was identified with the goal of territorial integration. Nineteenth-century writers, geographers, naturalists, and illustrators—both Creole and foreign—explored, mapped, and illustrated the flora and fauna of the national landscapes. Their expeditions chronicled the diversity of national populations and topographies. By identifying particular races of humans with particular environmental niches, geographers organized each nation conceptually into discrete regions with particular racial characteristics. Ancízar briefly joined Colombia's Chorographic Commission, which in the 1850s produced maps, paintings, and texts that portrayed particular regional and racial "types"—the blacks, whites, Indians, mestizos, and mulattos particular to each area of the country—with their particular modes of dress, occupation, and complexion. He was also part of the *costumbrista* literary movement that produced stories and travel narratives that highlighted the customs and racial characteristics of each locality. The new technology of photography and the new science of anthropology contributed to the proliferation of images of regional racial types linked to particular places.

By the end of the nineteenth century, the conflation of regional and racial identities was firmly entrenched in national imaginaries. Argentine Liberals such as Domingo Faustino Sarmiento portrayed their interior plains as a place of racial savagery, inhabited by "barbarous" Indians and mixed-race *gauchos*. But the *pampa* was also, these writers hoped, the future home for waves of "civilized" European immigrants who would bring progress to their nation. The Colombian and Venezuelan frontier plains known as the *llanos* occupied a similar symbolic place in the aspirations of elite writers in those countries. In Brazil, the northeastern "backlands" region was described as populated by mixed-race hordes, most notably in Euclides da Cunha's 1902 classic *Os sertões* (*Rebellion in the Backlands*).

Over the nineteenth century, the elites had to grapple with European and North American racial theories that emphasized white supremacy. By the last quarter of the century, as Latin American elites became wealthy through the export of primary commodities to industrialized countries, they increasingly disdained their mixed-race populations; the elites associated modernity with whiteness. Policymakers viewed European immigration as the panacea for a host of racial and social ills. European immigrants, it was hoped, would not only bring their reputedly superior work ethic and educational level; they would

intermarry with the native population and thus supposedly improve it. European traits would predominate over African and indigenous in this intermixture, intellectuals argued, and thus the population would whiten.

European immigration accelerated rapidly in fast-growing late nineteenth-century economies on the Atlantic seaboard, such as Argentina, southern Brazil, and Cuba. European immigrants were accompanied by less-celebrated and more controversial immigrant waves from the Caribbean, the Middle East, and East Asia that further complicated Latin America's racial and ethnic landscape. But most Latin American countries, even as their export economies grew, were not successful in attracting European immigrants. The leaders of these countries had to turn to alternative means—coerced labor drafts, for example, or non-European immigration—to generate a low-cost labor force for their growing export sectors and infrastructures. They also turned to alternative theories for "improving" their national races, such as neo-Lamarckism.

As eugenics swept the Atlantic world around the turn of the twentieth century, Latin Americans tended to embrace the neo-Lamarckian school of eugenics that assumed the inheritability of acquired characteristics. Echoing Ancízar's emphasis on institutions, this "optimistic" or "soft" eugenics allowed for the promise of racial improvement through societal improvements—education, nutrition, hygiene, urban planning—as well as beneficial breeding. As in Europe and North America, eugenics constituted both a science and a social movement. Eugenics proliferated through scholarly conferences and local eugenics clubs. It influenced jurists, legislators, educators, doctors, and social reformers on both right and left. Social reformers targeted poor women, in particular, for reform and surveillance. Reformers sought to promote motherhood, improve maternal and child health and nutrition, and stop the spread of venereal disease in order to improve the national race.

RACIAL DEMOCRACY AND MESTIZO NATIONALISM IN THE TWENTIETH CENTURY

In the first half of the twentieth century, the oligarchic "white republic" of "progress and order" gave way to mestizo nationalism and "racial democracy." In much of Latin America, revolutionaries and reformists swept out the old oligarchic orders of the late nineteenth century. Populist leaders tapped into the newly emerging sectors of the urban working and middle classes to build more inclusive (though not necessarily democratic) political movements. Leading intellectuals, ranging from Gilberto Freyre in Brazil to José Vasconcelos in Mexico, viewed cultural and genetic melding as the basis of national identity. The national race, the *pueblo*, was a mestizo race. This putatively inclusive ideology had exclusive aspects. It was usually predicated on uniformity and the bleaching out of unwanted racial stains rather than a full acceptance of ethnic or racial diversity.

The role of Indians in the mestizo nation remained ambivalent. In Mexico, the new bureaucracy produced by the Mexican Revolution (1910–1917) justified the revolution as having redeemed the Indians. A new agency was staffed by Indian advocates, mainly anthropologists, who were known as *indigenistas*. These official indigenists promoted various projects to benefit Indian communities, such as bilingual education, at the same time that the Mexican state was redistributing massive amounts of land into communal landholdings. The first international indigenist congress was held in Mexico City in 1940 and indigenista organizations sprang up around the Latin America. But a strong paternalist strain ran through the indigenistas' agenda of Indian redemption; despite a conscious effort on the part of indigenists to reject racism, they still tended to view Indians as culturally (and even physically) deficient, in need of improvement and tutelage.

Indigenous ethnicity was increasingly celebrated by non-Indians in the Andes and Mesoamerica, but, at the same time, Indian cultural practices were relegated to the realm of folklore, outside of the national cultural mainstream. Indian markets, crafts, and rituals became tourist attractions, but most indigenous communities remained mired in poverty, with precarious access to land. In the Amazon basin, in particular, development and deforestation eroded the resource base of Amazonian indigenous groups. In Brazil the ideology of racial democracy and the imperatives of national integration precluded any concerted national effort to fully include remaining Indian groups or to protect their environmental niche. As the state built roads and cities in the Amazon in the mid-twentieth century, several remaining Amazonian indigenous groups were displaced; some

disappeared altogether or saw their numbers tragically reduced. The government agency charged with protecting Indians collaborated in their displacement. Indians were largely ignored, and in fact the census—which categorized Brazilians as black, brown, and white—had no category for "indigenous" during most of the twentieth century. Until 1991, Indians were simply lumped into the "pardo" category.

The place of blacks and black identity in the nation was even more problematic. The ideologues of racial democracy such as Freyre acknowledged and even celebrated African contributions to the cultural heritage and gene pool of their nations. This was a radical change from the nineteenth century, but elite proponents of racial democracy still tended to see the presence of blacks as a problem that would be overcome through interracial whitening; white traits would prevail over black and Indian in the formation of the mestizo nation. Afro-Latin American cultural and religious practices, moreover, were often viewed, even by successful mulattos and blacks, as barbaric and uncivilized, with little place in the modern nation outside of anthropology museum exhibits. This was true even in Cuba, where the writings of celebrated Cuban nationalist José Martí, among others, had identified Cuban patriotism with racial fraternity and inclusion. Afro-Cubans had participated notably in the late-nineteenth-century independence struggles; Antonio Maceo, the great independence military leader, was remembered as a national hero even though he was mulatto. Nonetheless, the upper and middle classes in early twentieth-century Cuba were uncomfortable with Cuba's vibrant Afro-Cuban cultural practices; they feared and persecuted black "witchcraft" practiced by believers in Afro-Cuban religions. Cubans of noticeable African descent were often excluded from restaurants, hotels, schools, beaches, clubs, and parks, as they had been under the Spanish Empire, even though the new constitution provided for full equality and universal male suffrage.

By the 1920s and 1930s, sanitized and Europeanized versions of Afro-Latin American music, dance, and celebrations were incorporated into the national imaginaries of countries with significant populations of African descent. Populist politicians promoted popular cultural manifestations such as Carnival; avant-garde literary figures looked to African and indigenous culture for inspiration. The emerging recording industry, radio, and traveling bands popularized African-influenced dance music, which the middle classes embraced and made respectable. Yet, to emphasize one's black identity in a country such as Brazil or Cuba, or to organize an ethnic- or race-based autonomous social movement anywhere in Latin America, was still to open oneself to accusations of antipatriotism and even racism.

Mestizo nationalism and racial democracy had a violent side. Ironically, some of the worst episodes of large-scale, racially motivated or racially tinged violence occurred in the early twentieth century, the era of mestizo nationalism: the massacre of black Cubans in 1912; the massacres and expulsions of Chinese immigrants from post-Revolutionary Mexico; the 1932 *matanza* of indigenous peasants in El Salvador; and the massacre of ethnic Haitians along the Dominican-Haitian border in 1937. Violence against Indians continued in frontier areas of countries such as Brazil and Colombia. These atrocities claimed thousands of lives. Buenos Aires even saw pogrom-like violence against its Jewish inhabitants. The perpetrators of such violence were not only immune to prosecution, they were celebrated, in some cases, for carrying out their patriotic duty by helping to purge their nations of unwanted, putatively unassimilated racial elements. Nonetheless, forced sterilization as a means of racial improvement never caught on in Latin America.

Despite the continent-wide celebration of mestizaje, some nations have continued to identify as white. In a country such as Argentina, this white identity is largely based on the massive European immigration it experienced in the late nineteenth and early twentieth centuries. The image of the white nation obscures the continued existence of Afro-Argentines, Indians, and mestizos. A population's whiteness can also be a relational concept; Costa Ricans and Dominicans tend to define themselves as white in contrast to the inhabitants of neighboring countries. And within countries, inhabitants of some regions—such as Antioquia and Santander in Colombia, Sonora in Mexico, or São Paulo in Brazil, to name a few—pride themselves on their whiteness in comparison to neighboring regions. Whether on a regional or national level, however, the notion of a homogeneous people elides internal diversity.

CONTEMPORARY MULTICULTURALISM

The last three decades of the twentieth century brought both gains and suffering to people of African and indigenous heritage. National myths of racial homogeneity were questioned. National identities were redefined. New racial and ethnic-rights movements emerged, but Indians and blacks suffered disproportionately from political violence and social strife.

Guerrilla warfare and brutal counterinsurgency campaigns profoundly affected indigenous and rural black communities. Marxist guerrilla movements often proclaimed themselves the champions of oppressed indigenous peasants, among whom they recruited. But the guerrillas were largely unable to protect these communities from devastating scorched-earth counterinsurgency campaigns. In Guatemala and Peru, in particular, tens of thousands of Indians died in the 1980s; in Guatemala, most of the deaths were at the hands of state forces, while in Peru, both the Maoist Sendero Luminoso (Shining Path) and the state brutalized indigenous communities. Such violence was both political and racially tinged; the Guatemalan and Peruvian elites disdained and feared the indigenous masses, and they indoctrinated their troops—many of whom had been born in Indian communities— with this disdain. In Colombia, indigenous leaders have been salient among the thousands of political leaders assassinated by right-wing paramilitaries; neither the Colombian Marxist guerrillas nor the anticommunist paramilitaries have much respect for the Indians' insistence on their own political autonomy. Thousands of black Colombians from isolated coastal regions, meanwhile, have fled the violence and flooded into dismal refugee camps and urban slums.

The last several decades have seen the emergence of national and continent-wide ethnic-rights movements proudly espousing black and indigenous identities. The contemporary indigenous movement, which emerged in the 1970s and mushroomed in the 1980s and 1990s, has been particularly successful. In alliance with leftists, international nonprofit organizations, celebrities, and activist academics, indigenous activists have achieved considerable political gains. They have lobbied successfully for constitutional reform. By the dawn of the twenty-first century, most Latin American countries had enacted constitutional reforms that recognized the existence of indigenous ethnicities and the rights of Indian communities to their own lands, culture, and institutions. New constitutions have redefined nations such as Colombia or Bolivia as "multiethnic."

Indians have become powerful political forces in several countries, most notably Bolivia and Ecuador, where they have succeeded in making or breaking presidencies. Indians have become mayors, congressional representatives, provincial governors, and presidents, most notably Evo Morales, an Aymara Indian who became president of Bolivia in 2006. In Guatemala, after bearing the brunt of the atrocious counterinsurgency repression of the early 1980s, indigenous Mayans have formed a pan-Mayan movement.

The black movement has been somewhat less successful, even in countries such as Colombia or Brazil where people of African descent far outnumber people who identify as Indian. In part, this has to do with the lack of any unifying racial or ethnic identity among most people with African heritage; they tend to identify with their region, their social class, their neighborhood, or their political party. For decades, black Brazilian activist leaders have explicitly decried Brazil's vaunted racial democracy, and the idealization of *mestiçagem*, as a facade for the continued racial discrimination that has been amply documented at every level of Brazilian society. Brazilian black activists have campaigned to convince more Brazilians to identify as black on the national census, but little more than 5 percent of Brazilians do so; most prefer to mark "pardo." Affirmative action is a subject of much controversy in Brazil in the early twenty-first century.

Throughout Latin America, the new state-endorsed multiculturalism has been resisted by those who fear that national unity will be fragmented. Local political bosses do not tend to look favorably on autonomous indigenous governing institutions that threaten entrenched patronage networks. The recognition of indigenous landholdings is resisted by private property owners and impeded by social strife. Official multiculturalism has also been criticized of glossing over class inequalities and of conceptually dividing national populations into overly discrete, reified ethnic components.

Social scientists have since the 1950s consistently demonstrated that, to an alarming degree, race continues to correlate roughly with social class. The correlation is of course not complete: Numerous individuals defy the odds and challenge the prevailing stereotypes by obtaining professional success. Nonetheless, disproportionate numbers of people who consider themselves, or are considered by others, to be indigenous or black live in abject poverty. They tend to be overrepresented in the lowest paid sectors of the economy: domestic service and agricultural labor. For example, half the Afro-Brazilian (*preto* or pardo) workforce in 1987 worked in agriculture or the service industry, mainly domestic service; at that time, one fourth of Afro-Brazilian workers "earned monthly incomes of US$20 or less; another one-quarter earned between $20 and $40"; 60 percent of Afro-Brazilian women worked in agriculture or domestic service (Andrews, p. 173). As this last statistic reflects, the situation is especially dire for women, and thus for their children.

In 1997 a study showed that half of Afro-Uruguayan women surveyed worked as domestic servants, while a 1980 study in Brazil showed that black male earnings exceeded black female earnings by 70 percent or more (Andrews, p. 176). Interpretation of such numbers must be contextualized, however, by the blurriness of racial categories and, moreover, the general association of blackness and Indianness with poverty. When successful individuals and families do succeed in rising out of poverty, they are less likely to be counted as black or Indian and more likely to be labeled "brown"; money tends to whiten. Nonetheless, it is often these rising middle classes of color that feel the sting of racism most explicitly, when they come up against racial discrimination on the part of lighter-complexioned compatriots who habitually deem darker-looking people—or people who hail from a particular province or who speak an indigenous language—inappropriate for professional promotion. Limpieza de sangre, or the cleanliness of the blood, has long ceased serving as a prerequisite for entry into high-status professions, but light complexions are often still favored.

Race and ethnicity are thus variable social constructs with enormous social impact. Historically emerging out of imperialism, beliefs about race and ethnicity have structured Latin American labor systems, social hierarchies, and political alliances ever since the Conquest. Racial and ethnic discrimination have at times been institutionalized through the legal system, but even during those periods when discriminatory regimes were overthrown and equality was embraced, informal discrimination and prejudice continued. Racial and ethnic boundaries can be blurry; they have been drawn differently from one nation to the next, and even from one neighborhood to the next. Despite (or perhaps because of) their fluidity and flexibility, race and ethnicity are tenacious in their persistence. Although the lines of demarcation continually shift, race and ethnicity continue to shape people's lives in profound ways.

See also **African Brazilians, Color Terminology; Africans in Hispanic America; Arosemena, Justo; Caste and Class Structure in Colonial Spanish America; Creole; Family; Freyre, Gilberto (de Mello); Gaucho; Indigenous Peoples; Liberalism; Martí y Pérez, José Julián; Mestizo; Morales, Evo; Pardo; Slavery: Brazil; Slavery: Spanish America; Vasconcelos Calderón, José.**

BIBLIOGRAPHY

Aguirre Beltrán, Gonzalo, *La Población negra de México: estudio etnohistórico*, 3rd edition. México City: Fondo de Cultura Económica, 1990.

Ancízar, Manuel. *Peregrinación de Alpha*. 2 vols. Bogotá: Biblioteca Banco Popular, 1984 (1853).

Andrews, George Reid. *Afro-Latin America, 1800–2000*. Oxford and New York: Oxford University Press, 2004.

Appelbaum, Nancy P. *Muddied Waters: Race, Region, and Local History in Colombia, 1846–1948*. Durham, NC: Duke University Press, 2003.

Appelbaum, Nancy P., Anne S. Macpherson, and Karin Alejandra Rosemblatt, eds. *Race and Nation in Modern Latin America*. Chapel Hill: University of North Carolina Press, 2003.

Azevedo, Célia Maria Marinho de. *Onda negra, medo branco: O negro no imaginário das elites—século XIX*. Rio de Janeiro: Paz e Terra, 1987.

Banton, Michael. *Racial Theories*, 2nd edition. Cambridge, U.K. and New York: Cambridge University Press, 1998.

Cañizares-Esguerra, José. "New World, New Stars: Patriotic Astrology and the Invention of Indian and Creole Bodies in Colonial Spanish America, 1600–1650." *Hispanic American Historical Review* 104, no. 1 (February 1999), 33–68.

Castro, Hebe Maria Mattos de. *Escravidão e cidadania no Brasil monárquico*. Rio de Janeiro: Jorge Zahar, 2000.

Cooper, Frederick, Thomas C. Holt, and Rebecca J. Scott. *Beyond Slavery: Explorations of Race, Labor, and Citizenship in Postemancipation Societies*. Chapel Hill: University of North Carolina Press, 2000.

Cope, R. Douglas. *The Limits of Racial Domination: Plebeian Society in Colonial Mexico City, 1660–1720*. Madison: University of Wisconsin Press, 1994.

Costa, Emília Viotti da. *The Brazilian Empire: Myths and Histories*. Rev. edition. Chapel Hill: University of North Carolina Press, 2000.

Cunha, Euclides da. *Os Sertões*, 15th edition. Rio de Janeiro: Livraria Francisco Alves, P. de Azevedo & c., 1940 (1902).

Cunha, Euclides da. *Rebellion in the Backlands (Os sertões)*, trans. Samuel Putnam. Chicago: University of Chicago Press, 1964.

De la Cadena, Marisol. *Indigenous Mestizos: The Politics of Race and Culture in Cuzco, Peru, 1919–1991*. Durham, NC: Duke University Press, 2000.

De la Fuente, Alejandro. *A Nation for All: Race, Inequality, and Politics in Twentieth-Century Cuba*. Chapel Hill: University of North Carolina Press, 2001.

Fernandes, Florestan. *A integração do negro na sociedade de classes*, 2 vols. São Paulo: Dominus Editôra, 1965.

Freyre, Gilberto. *Casa-grande & senzala: Formação da família brasileira sob o regime de economia patriarchal*, 4th edition, 2 vols. Rio de Janeiro: J. Olympio, 1943.

Freyre, Gilberto. *Brazil: An Interpretation*. New York: Alfred A. Knopf, 1945.

Gamio, Manuel. *Forjando patria*, 3rd edition. Mexico City: Editorial Porrúa, 1982.

González Casanova, Pablo and Marcos Roitman Rosenmann, eds. *Democracia y estado multiétnico en América Latina*. México City: La Jornada Ediciones, 1996.

Gould, Jeffrey L. *To Die in This Way: Nicaraguan Indians and the Myth of Mestizaje, 1880–1965*. Durham, NC: Duke University Press, 1995.

Graham, Richard, ed. *The Idea of Race in Latin America, 1870–1940*. Austin: University of Texas Press, 1990.

Hanchard, Michael George. *Orpheus and Power: The Movimento Negro of Rio de Janeiro and São Paulo, Brazil, 1945–1988*. Princeton, NJ: Princeton University Press, 1994.

Helg, Aline. *Our Rightful Share: The Afro-Cuban Struggle For Equality, 1886–1912*. Chapel Hill: University of North Carolina Press, 1995.

Johnson, Lyman L., and Sonya Lipsett-Rivera, eds. *The Faces of Honor: Sex, Shame, and Violence in Colonial*

Latin America. Albuquerque: University of New Mexico Press, 1998.

Kinsbruner, Jay. *Not of Pure Blood: The Free People of Color and Racial Prejudice in Nineteenth-Century Puerto Rico*. Durham, NC: Duke University Press, 1996.

Larson, Brooke. *Trials of Nation Making: Liberalism, Race, and Ethnicity in the Andes, 1810–1910*. Cambridge, U.K. and New York: Cambridge University Press, 2004.

Lasso, Marixa. *Myths of Harmony: Race and Republicanism during the Age of Revolution: Colombia, 1795–1831*. Pittsburgh, PA: University of Pittsburgh Press, 2007.

Lesser, Jeffrey. *Negotiating National Identity: Immigrants, Minorities, and the Struggle for Ethnicity in Brazil*. Durham, NC: Duke University Press, 1999.

Lovell, Peggy A., ed. *Desigualdade racial no Brasil contemporâneo*. Belo Horizonte, Brazil: CEDEPLAR, FACE, UFMG, 1991.

Lynch, John, ed. *Latin American Revolutions, 1808–1826: Old and New World Origins*. Norman: University of Oklahoma Press, 1994.

Martí, José. *Obras completas*, 28 vols. Havana: Editorial Nacional de Cuba, 1963–1973.

Mörner, Magnus. *Race Mixture in the History of Latin America*. Boston: Little, Brown, 1967.

Múnera, Alfonso. *El fracaso de la nación: Región, clase y raza en el Caribe colombiano (1717–1821)*. Bogotá: Banco de la República and Ancora Editores, 1998.

Nazzari, Muriel. "Concubinage in Colonial Brazil: The Inequalities of Race, Class and Gender." *Journal of Family History* 21:2 (1996), 107–24.

Nobles, Melissa. *Shades of Citizenship: Race and the Census in Modern Politics*. Stanford, CA: Stanford University Press, 2000.

Robaína Fernández, Tomás. *El negro en Cuba, 1902–1958: Apuntes para la historia de la lucha contra la discriminación racial*. Havana: Editorial de Ciencias Sociales, 1990.

Rosemblatt, Karin Alejandra. "Sexuality and Biopower in Chile and Latin America." *Political Power and Social Theory* 15 (2001), 315–372.

Safford, Frank. "Race, Integration, and Progress: Elite Attitudes and the Indian in Colombia, 1750–1870." *Hispanic American Historical Review* 71, no. 1 (February 1991): 1–33.

Salomon, Frank, and Stuart B. Schwartz. "New Peoples and New Kinds of People: Adaptation, Readjustment, and Ethnogenesis in South American Indigenous Societies (Colonial Era)." In *The Cambridge History of the Native Peoples of the Americas*, Vol. 3: *South America*, part 2, edited by Frank Salomon and Stuart B. Schwartz. Cambridge, U.K. and New York: Cambridge University Press, 1999.

Sanders, James E. *Contentious Republicans: Popular Politics, Race, and Class in Nineteenth-Century Colombia*. Durham, NC: Duke University Press, 2004.

Sarmiento, Domingo Faustino. *Facundo: Civilización y Barbarie*. Garden City, NY: Doubleday, 1961.

Serje, Margarita. *El revés de la nación: Territorios salvajes, fronteras y tierras de nadie*. Bogotá: Universidad de los Andes, Facultad de Ciencias Sociales, 2005.

Stepan, Nancy Leys. *"The Hour of Eugenics": Race, Gender, and Nation in Latin America*. Ithaca, NY: Cornell University Press, 1991.

Turits, Richard. "A World Destroyed, A Nation Imposed: The 1937 Haitian Massacre in the Dominican Republic." *Hispanic American Historical Review* 82, no. 3 (August 2002), 589–635.

Twinam, Ann. "Racial Passing: Informal and Official 'Whiteness' in Colonial Spanish America." In *New World Orders: Violence, Sanction, and Authority in the Colonial Americas*, ed. John Smolenski and Thomas J. Humphrey. Philadelphia: University of Pennsylvania Press, 2005.

Van Cott, Donna Lee. *The Friendly Liquidation of the Past: The Politics of Diversity in Latin America*. Pittsburgh, PA: University of Pittsburgh Press, 2000.

Vasconcelos, José. *The Cosmic Race/La raza cósmica*. Baltimore, MD: Johns Hopkins University Press, 1997.

Vinson, Ben III. *Bearing Arms for His Majesty: The Free-Colored Militia in Colonial Mexico*. Stanford, CA: Stanford University Press, 2001.

Wade, Peter. *Race and Ethnicity in Latin America*. London: Pluto Press, 1997.

Warren, Kay B., and Jean E. Jackson, eds. *Indigenous Movements, Self-Representation, and the State in Latin America*. Austin: University of Texas Press, 2002.

NANCY P. APPELBAUM

RADA, MANUEL DE JESÚS

Manuel de Jesús Rada (early 1800s), priest, politician, and author. Rada was pastor of the parish of Villa de Santa Cruz de la Cañada, northwest of Santa Fe, New Mexico, in 1821. Santa Cruz, the seat of regional government, incorporated the Indian pueblos of Santa Clara, San Ildefonso, Pojoaque, Nambé, San Juan, Taos, Picuris, and Abiquiú, with a population of just over 6,500. As the community leader, Rada delivered a trapping license from Governor Bartolomé Baca to William Becknell, establisher of the Sante Fe Trail, on 29 October 1824.

Rada was pastor of San Juan pueblo and vicar of Río Arriba from 1826 to 1828. He was elected as a deputy to the national Congress in October 1828; his report to New Mexico constituents in Chihuahua, dated 13 November 1828 and printed in Zacatecas, was later used by Deputy Diego Archuleta in 1845 to promote development of New Mexico. In January 1829, Rada presented *Proposición hecha al Soberano congreso general de la unión,* which called for increased spending on defense and education; development of industry; foreign investment; efficient, qualified government; abolition of taxes on tobacco and gunpowder; and abolition of tithes.

See also **New Mexico; Pueblo Indians.**

BIBLIOGRAPHY

David J. Weber, ed., *Northern Mexico on the Eve of the United States Invasion* (1976).

David J. Weber, *The Mexican Frontier, 1821–1846* (1982).

Additional Bibliography

Esquibel, José Antonio. *Seeds of Struggle, Harvest of Faith.* Albuquerque, NM: LPD Press, 1998.

W. MICHAEL MATHES

RADICAL OLYMPUS. *See* **Colombia, Political Parties: Radical Olympus.**

RADIO AND TELEVISION. Radio and television are the main channels for the transmission of culture and information in Latin America. They are largely privately owned, used primarily for entertainment, and funded primarily by advertising. Television ownership is highly concentrated: four major media groups control (on regional average) more than 70 percent of the advertising revenues and audience. These revenues are bolstered by program exports to countries outside the region, most notably in the form of *telenovelas* (prime-time soap operas), which in 2003 was a $2 billion industry in exports to one hundred countries in fifty languages and dialects.

Radio and television reach far more people in most Latin American countries than do print media and the Internet. Except perhaps in Argentina and Uruguay, leading print media are largely for those in the middle and upper classes; working-class people turn more to radio and television. Television and radio advertisements tend to feature products for mass consumption, although elite consumer items are advertised as well.

RADIO

Outside of a few indigenous communities and isolated rural areas, exposure to radio is almost ubiquitous. In major cities, formats on both AM and FM bands are increasingly specialized and their audiences segmented by social class, taste in music, informational needs and interests, and political and cultural orientation. Although radio is largely an entertainment medium in Latin America, it is also the primary source of news for many people. Television usurped this role for national news, but radio is still the primary medium for local news. Being a cheaper medium to produce, radio also reflects more diverse interests and approaches than does television. Over time, commercial radio stations owned by major media groups tend to change the stations' names and formats in accordance with market trends: for example, *reggaeton* and *cumbia* are preferred in some Peruvian radio stations where salsa was previously the main musical genre.

From the 1930s through the 1960s, many radio stations carried programs that have since moved primarily to television. These included *radionovelas,* serial radio programs related to soap operas. These were originally produced in Cuba by Colgate-Palmolive, based on the firm's successful marketing experience with radio soap operas in the United States. Also prominent on early Latin American radio were variety shows, dramas, sports, talk shows, and news.

In recent decades, as radio has accommodated to television, Latin American radio programming has concentrated more on music along with news, talk shows, and sports. Typically AM stations carry news, talk, and local popular music; they frequently reflect the interests of regional cultures and language groups outside the Spanish/Portuguese mainstream. In the 1970s a new phenomenon was that several Lima stations featured ethnic music in Quechua or Aymara for immigrants from the highlands. In the 1980s eighty programs aired Andean folk music and *chicha* (a combination of Andean and tropical music that uses electric musical instruments), which was very popular among new migrants and the sons and daughters of the first wave of Andean migration. In 2007 two illegal (pirate) radio stations programmed this kind of music and genres of Andean origin on FM in Lima (where a paid hour in commercial stations is expensive), and there are the preferred genres for many radio stations in rural areas, where it is still common to air early-morning programs oriented to farmers.

FM stations tend to carry more music-oriented formats, either national popular music or international music. Foreign popular music audiences tend to be younger and more affluent, whereas national popular music audiences tend to be somewhat older and more working-class. Network radio, especially in news formats, is important in some countries, particularly in the Andean region, but most radio stations are locally programmed.

Major AM and FM news radio networks include CBN (Cadena Brasileira de Noticias) in Brazil, Radio Monitor in Mexico, Caracol in Colombia, and RPP (Radio Programas del Perú) in Peru. All of these have Web sites with live online transmission, so the audience can listen to the programs or follow updates of the news on the screen.

CBN in Brazil is a good example of quality journalism in radio: It has a team of experts in economics, politics, and sports, along with experienced commentators and reporters. A notable program is *Los Chistosos* (The Fun Guys), a political humor program that began in 1999 on RPP in Peru and is aired from Monday to Friday in the afternoon. The program was an example of democratic struggle against the government of President Alberto Fujimori from 1999 to 2000, when most radio and TV news programs were controlled and censored by corrupt media owners and journalists who supported a government that distributed money to them in an attempt to get reelected.

Latin America is home to hundreds of community radio stations and community-based broadcasters: the World Association of Community Radio Broadcasters (Asociación Mundial de Radios Comunitarias de América Latina y el Caribe, AMARC) has three thousand members, and almost a third are Latin American. Some community radio stations are also part of the Asociación Latinoamericana de Educación

Radiofónica (ALER; Latin American Association of Radio Education), in which one satellite system is shared by 117 affiliates in Argentina, Bolivia, Colombia, Costa Rica, Chile, Ecuador, El Salvador, Guatemala, Honduras, Mexico, Nicaragua, Panama, Paraguay, Peru, Dominican Republic, Uruguay, and Venezuela. Most of these are Catholic or educational stations.

Radio also carries more political discussion and educational programs than does television. Several religious- or government-backed radio stations in Colombia, the Dominican Republic, and Ecuador, for example, have been very successful in delivering formal primary school education to rural areas. In Peru, radio has been the voice against abuses by international mining companies and governmental corruption. Radio stations such as those operated by Bolivian miners have added diverse political points of view. However, efforts in some countries, such as Brazil, to get more licenses for community, religious, and labor groups have been repressed by military governments and ignored by civilian governments in favor of allocating broadcast licenses as political patronage. Among political and development activists, radio is seen as a locally responsive, affordable, and flexible medium of choice.

TELEVISION

Television is, by contrast, more centralized and entertainment-oriented. For some years after the beginning of Latin American television in the 1950s, TV was restricted to urban and middle-class audiences. Since the 1960s it has increasingly become a truly mass medium. Estimates for Brazil and Mexico are that 85 to 90 percent of the population has some access to television fairly regularly. In urban areas, more than 80 percent of households have television; the proportion in rural areas is lower but growing. Many rural, small-town, and low-income people still see television primarily at friends' homes and in public places. The ubiquity of television advanced in the 1980s, as satellite dishes linked to repeater transmitters brought television to more and more small towns.

Most countries have developed at least two or three commercial television networks and often a government or educational channel, although the latter stations are usually underfunded and produce relatively little, except in Brazil, Chile, and Mexico, where state stations have larger budgets than others in the region.

Television networks have tended to dominate the landscape because of the high costs of production, which require the economies of scale made possible by centralized program production and network distribution. In the 1980s and 1990s the number of networks and independent stations, and the number of their productions, increased because of a reduction in the cost of production technology, an increase in trained personnel, and the development of program genres.

There are four major media groups in Latin America, considered monopolies by most academics and experts: Televisa (Mexico), Globo (Brazil), Cisneros (Venezuela), and Clarín (Argentina). In Mexico, Televisa's main competitor is Televisión Azteca. In 1996, reforms made in the Mexican Federal Law of Radio and Television and the Federal Law of Telecommunications favored Televisa so much that it became known as the "Ley Televisa" (Televisa Law).

Televisa is the major Spanish-language media company in the region, producing about fifty thousand hours of transmission per year. It has participation in Univision, the main Latino network in the United States. In 2001 Televisa signed a contract to provide content to Univision until 2017, but they want to cancel it; the judiciary will decide in 2008.

Globo, Brazil's largest TV and radio content producer, has more than a million cable TV clients and owns part of the satellite operator SkyLA. The international cable signal of Globo advertises U.S.-based firms that serve the Brazilian population living in this country.

The Cisneros Group holds the Venevisión network in Venezuela but also some others such as Chilevisión (Chile) and Caracol (Colombia). The group is a large shareholder of Univision and Galavisión (Spain) and is a partner of DirecTV (satellite TV) and AOL Latin America.

In 2007, Venezuela's opposition TV channel Radio Caracas Televisión (RCTV) was denied the renewal of its license, its equipment was seized, and RCTV journalists lost their jobs because they refused to support the Hugo Chávez government. Months later, RCTV reappeared as a cable news channel, but the government responded with plans to stop these transmissions too by changing some laws.

The Argentinean Clarín Group publishes *Clarín*, one of the country's two leading newspapers. The group owns Radio Mitre, Canal 13, and Multicanal, the main cable operator in the country, with more than 1.5 million clients.

In terms of programming, *telenovelas* remain the best known of Latin America's characteristic program genres, which also include live variety shows, live regional music, and solo and ensemble comedies. *Telenovelas* appeared after the 1950s in several countries, which developed different forms of the genre. Mexican *telenovelas* are considered to be relatively more melodramatic and romantic; Brazilian *telenovelas* are somewhat more realistic, cinematic, trendy, and social-issue-oriented; and Colombian *telenovelas* have tended to use historical themes.

Since the mid-1990s, however, a number of *telenovelas* have moved beyond the genre's traditional formulas. For example, *Ugly Betty*, a Sony Entertainment TV series produced in the United States in 2007, was inspired by *Yo soy Betty la fea*, a Colombian *telenovela* that triumphed in several Latin American countries after being a ratings success in Colombia in 1999. The traditional stereotype of the nice, submissive young girl usually featured in a *telenovela* was broken with Betty—an intelligent girl who knows how to deal with numbers, paperwork, and business decisions but lacks a sense of fashion. The Mexican version of the story was produced by Televisa in 2006.

In Brazil, *Senhora do Destino* (Mistress of Destiny), which aired there in 2004–2005, obtained the best ratings of any program in the early 2000s; for the final episode, 83 percent of Brazil's televisions switched on were tuned in. It was the first *telenovela* in history to show two homosexual women sleeping together and to show the family's acceptance of this kind of relationship. *Senhora do Destino* was based on a true story that occurred during the military dictatorship in Brazil, and it included some scenes that revisited the riots and repression against civilians in the streets.

Variety shows are also characteristic of Latin American television. These are usually presented live, before a studio or theater audience. They rely on the pattern and interaction of the host (*animador*) with the audience. Key elements are games, music, comedy, amateur performances, contests, and discussion.

Particularly notable is the marathon version, two to eight hours in length, which generally appears on Sunday afternoon and in the evening; an example is *Siempre en domingo* (Always on Sunday), which was broadcast in Mexico from 1969 until 1998. *Domingão do Faustão* (Big Fausto's Big Sunday), a three-hour program on the Brazilian network Globo, debuted in 1989 and is still on the air.

Talk shows became popular in the 1990s. Some famous hosts have included Cristina Saralegui (the *Cristina* show), Jaime Bayly (*El Show Jaime Bayly*, "Jaime Bayly's Show"), Marcelo Tinelli (*Videomatch*) and Laura Bozzo (*Laura en América*, a reality show). Most of Bozzo's programs were known for using false facts that were dramatized by common people. Even so, her show was popular among low-income urban people in times of low-level content in Peruvian television. In Brazil the leading late-night show is Globo's *Programa do Jô*, hosted by Jô Soares, who from 1988 to 1999 had an interview show on SBT. Soares has reportedly interviewed ten thousand people for his Globo show between 2000 and 2007.

BIBLIOGRAPHY

Alisky, Marvin. *Latin American Media: Guidance and Censorship.* Aimes: Iowa University Press, 1982.

Bresnahan, Rosalind. "The Media and the Neoliberal Transition in Chile." *Latin American Perspectives* 30, (2003): 30, 39–68.

Fox, Elizabeth, ed. *Medios de comunicación y política en América Latina: La lucha por la democracia.* Barcelona: Gustavo Gili, 1989.

Fox, Elizabeth, and Silvio Waisbord, eds. *Latin Politics, Global Media.* Austin: University of Texas Press, 2002.

Fowks, Jacqueline. *Suma y resta de la realidad: Los medios de comunicación y las elecciones generales 2000 en el Perú.* Lima: Fundación Friedrich Ebert, 2000.

Fuenzalida, Valerio. *Televisión abierta y audiencia en América Latina.* Buenos Aires: Editorial Norma, 2002.

Getino, Octavio. *Cine y televisión en América Latina: Producción y mercados.* Santiago de Chile: LOM Ediciones-Universidad ARCIS, 1998.

Kottak, Conrad. *Prime Time Society.* Belmont, CA: Wadsworth, 1990.

Mastrini, Guillermo, and Martín Becerra. *Periodistas y magnates: Estructura y concentración de las industrias culturales.* Buenos Aires: Prometeo Libros, 2006.

Mattelart, Michele, and Armand Mattelart. *The Carnival of Images*, trans. David Buxton. New York: Bergin and Garvey, 1990.

Orozco, Guillermo, coord. *Historias de la televisión en América Latina.* Barcelona: Gedisa Editorial, 2002.

Sánchez de Armas, Miguel Angel, and Pilar Ramírez Morales, coords. *Apuntes para una Historia de la Televisión Mexicana I y II.* Mexico: Revista Mexicana de Comunicación, Espacio 98 y Televisa, 1998.

Vilches, Lorenzo. *Culturas y mercados de la ficción televisiva en Iberoamérica: Anuario Obitel 2007.* Barcelona: Gedisa Editorial, 2007.

Vink, Nino. *The Telenovela and Emancipation: A Study on Television and Social Change in Brazil.* Amsterdam: Royal Tropical Institute, 1988.

JOSEPH STRAUBHAAR
JACQUELINE FOWKS

RAILROADS. Latin American leaders of the mid- to late nineteenth century, committed to modernization through technological advance, welcomed the advent of the railroad. Along with the promise of progress and national integration, however, there developed a host of challenges and problems associated with a new industry vast in both scale and impact. Financing, structure and management, developmental questions, and relations with labor and consumers were among the concerns that had to be addressed.

The railroad era dawned in Mexico in 1837 when work began on the Mexico City–Veracruz line. By 1860 only short segments totaling about 93 miles had been constructed. During the rule of the emperor Maximilian (1864–1866), concession rights were controlled by the London-registered Imperial Mexican Railway Company. Construction directed by British engineers progressed over tremendously difficult terrain but was forced to a halt in 1866 because costs had nearly bankrupted the company. A subsidy provided by the government of Benito Juárez allowed work to resume on the line, renamed the Ferrocarril Mexicano, and service was inaugurated in 1873. Other lines were built in rapid succession and by 1911 Mexico had 15,000 miles of track.

The province of Buenos Aires early in 1854 enacted Argentina's first railroad legislation, which created the provincially owned Western Railroad. By 1914 the Argentine rail network had grown to

Railroad bridge, La Oroyo, Peru, c. 1920s. During the second half of the nineteenth century, public and private sectors invested heavily in building a network of railroads in Latin America. While British and French companies initially provided much of the capital needed to construct a rail system, most governments in Latin America eventually took control of the lines in the early part of the twentieth century. © MICHAEL MASLAN HISTORIC PHOTOGRAPHS/CORBIS

20,857 miles, with about 70 percent under British ownership. Four large British-owned lines, the Buenos Aires Great Southern, the Buenos Aires Western, the Buenos Aires and Pacific, and the Central Argentine controlled about half of the network, with the remainder in the hands of smaller British, French, or government-owned lines.

Brazil's early railroads were largely the achievement of Irineu Evangelista de Sousa (Viscount de Mauá). The first, inaugurated in 1854, ran just nine miles from Rio de Janeiro to the foot of the escarpment just below Petrópolis. Its purpose was to facilitate passenger travel between the winter and summer capitals of the empire. The first major line, the Companhia Paulista de Estradas de Ferro, incorporated in

São Paulo in 1868, served the coffee export economy. These and most other lines in Brazil were linked to English capital, directors, engineers, and equipment. By 1900 Brazil could count 9,517 miles of track.

Chile's most important railroads were owned by the state. The early lines were built in the populous northern Central Valley. One, the Ferrocarril de Santiago a Valparaíso, was completed in 1863, and another, the Ferrocarril del Sur, was completed in 1875 after twenty years of construction.

Peru began the construction of its railway system in 1869 when contracts were signed between the government and the North American entrepreneur Henry Meiggs. The two most important systems were the Central Railway of Peru, Ltd., and the Southern

Railway of Peru, Ltd., both of which linked the coast with the interior. By 1920 the republic had 1,718 miles of track.

Colombia's need to transport coffee stimulated a modest extension of that nation's rudimentary rail system in the early nineteenth century. In 1885 there were only 126 miles in use; this gradually grew to 2,026 miles in 1934, a relatively unimpressive network relative to much of the rest of Latin America.

In the 1850s and 1860s Latin American railroads were backed by a combination of domestic private and government funding, with additional modest amounts coming from abroad. Denationalization of rail networks occurred in the 1870s and 1880s, once the profitability of the lines, the stability of host governments, and concomitant risk reduction convinced investors of the safety of their capital. Latin American governments pragmatically divested themselves of railroads, having provided the initial pump-priming investment and guaranteeing themselves certain levels of profitability. Foreign investment bore the costs of further expansion and modernization. Denationalization did not result in loss of control by host governments. Legislation in all countries, enacted from the 1870s to the turn of the century, articulated regulations concerning personnel, train schedules, rights of way, acquisition of new equipment, extension of networks, rates, and capitalization.

With the growth of nationalism in Latin America in the twentieth century, foreign-owned or managed railroads were returned to state control. In Mexico the government, through the purchase of the majority of shares in the lines, effectively controlled the foreign-owned railroads by 1911. British managers were kept in positions of responsibility until 1937, when the administration of Lázaro Cárdenas completed the process of nationalization. In Peru, although the state owned the railways, from 1890 the lines were operated by the London-based Peruvian Corporation under a lease agreement. Colombia nationalized its railroads in the 1930s and Argentina followed in 1947.

There was much diversity among lines in the management of railroads. For every well-run company, such as the Buenos Aires Great Southern, there was the poor leadership of the Ferrocarril Mexicano or the Central Railway of Peru. Successful companies grew confident with assured markets and traffic. Once

Latin American governments, in the closing decades of the nineteenth century, made the decision to push hard for modernization and the development of their infrastructures, railroad management responded aggressively to new opportunities.

Zonal amalgamation, pooling agreements, developmental rates policies, and vertical diversification of the industry were typical managerial responses to an auspicious business climate. Managers reduced rates for long-distance hauls to promote increased economic activity; bureaucracies were streamlined; and, in Argentina, agricultural experiment stations were established by the railroads to improve crop yields and livestock quality. Companies in 1910 jointly invested in the exploitation of Argentine oil fields, with an eye to substituting cheap petroleum for expensive Welsh coal.

Mergers and amalgamation improved efficiency and helped local economies. Between 1901 and 1914 the Argentine Great Western merged with the Trasandino and the Buenos Aires and Pacific railways. As a result, the Great Western was able to build new branch lines, double the track of its main line, and expand station facilities. Merging with the Pacific gave the Great Western access to needed rolling stock and working capital. The subsequent economic boom in the province of Mendoza was underwritten by the improved capability of the railway to serve the province.

The railroads made pooling agreements to prevent ruinous rate-cutting competition. In Mexico in 1909 the British-owned Ferrocarril Mexicano agreed with the government-owned Ferrocarriles Nacionales de Mexico to pool all freight and passenger traffic between Veracruz and Mexico City and not to compete for traffic. Critics contended that such agreements conspired to maintain high prices for moving freight. In Chile, where all trunk lines were state owned, it was the government that directed the construction and operation of the railroads and set artificially low rates for freight, which by 1911 had resulted in perennial deficits. At times, in Argentina and Brazil, governments stimulated conservative foreign railroad management to extend their networks with threats of state competition through the construction of parallel lines.

Railroads were in many cases the largest employers of Latin American industrial workers, from the unskilled laborer, which included Chinese coolies in

Chile, Peru, and Mexico, to the highly qualified engine drivers and machine-shop personnel. The labor policies of Latin American railroads were shaped by many factors, including the emergence of independent unions beginning in the 1880s, management responses to labor unrest and workers' demands, and the impact of those demands on the policies of Latin American governments. Labor policies involved far more than matters of an economic character. Rather, social, economic, political, and cultural elements interacted in a complex manner.

As a rule, management's relations with labor were highly paternalistic regardless of the ownership of the railroad. Chilean managers treated laborers in much the same way that rural laborers were treated and control over their lives was stringent. On British lines paternalism was used to foster staff loyalty and thwart unionization. Benefits and services were offered to workers on an individual basis in exchange for their loyalty to the company. By the 1930s and 1940s Latin American governments such as Argentina under Juan Perón, Brazil under Getúlio Vargas, and Mexico under Lázaro Cárdenas, had won the support of the rail workers.

By the 1990s the use of railroads in countries such as Argentina and Peru was declining. Instead, riders turned more to bus routes.

See also **Coffee Industry; Economic Development; Engineering; Mauá, Visconde de.**

BIBLIOGRAPHY

Richard Graham, *Britain and the Onset of Modernization in Brazil, 1850–1914* (1968).

Eduardo A. Zalduendo, *Libras y rieles: Las inversions británicas para el desarrollo de los ferrocarriles en Argentina, Brazíl, Canadá e India durante el siglo XIX* (1975).

John H. Coatsworth, *Growth Against Development: The Economic Impact of Railroads in Porfirian Mexico* (1981).

Colin M. Lewis, *British Railways in Argentina, 1857–1914: A Case Study of Foreign Investment* (1983).

Arthur Schmidt, *The Social and Economic Effect of the Railroad in Puebla and Veracruz, Mexico, 1867–1911* (1987).

Additional Bibliography

Kogan, Jorge H. *Rieles con futuro: Desafíos para los ferrocarriles de América del Sur.* Caracas: Corporación Andina de Fomento, 2004.

Rowe, D. Trevor. *The Railways of South America.* London: Locomotives International, 2001.

Thomson, Ian. *Integración en el sector transporte en el Cono Sur: Los ferrocariles y su contribución al comercio internacional.* Buenos Aires: Banco Interamericano de Desarrollo, Instituto para la Integración de América Latina y el Caribe, 1997.

PAUL B. GOODWIN JR.

RAIN FORESTS. *See* **Forests.**

RAMA, ANGEL (1926–1983). Born in Montevideo on April 30, 1926, to Spanish immigrants, Angel Rama was an indefatigable Uruguayan literary scholar, journalist, publisher, and educator. Through his teaching and research in Uruguay, Venezuela, Puerto Rico, and the United States, he became one of the most acute cultural critics of Latin America. From the 1960s to his untimely death in a 1983 plane crash near Madrid, and from then to this day, his interdisciplinary work, enthusiasm for teaching, and broad vision of Latin America have inspired generations of younger scholars.

Rama was part of the Uruguayan "Generation of 1945." While studying humanities at the Universidad de la República he worked for Agence France Presse (1945). In 1950 he and Carlos Maggi founded the publishing house Fábula, which brought out Rama's first two books. He married the poet Ida Vitale in 1950 and later joined the influential journal *Marcha*, directed by Carlos Quijano, remaining a regular contributor until Uruguay's dictatorship closed it down in 1974. Rama was director of the Biblioteca Artigas (1951–1958) and editor of twenty-eight volumes in its collection of Clásicos Uruguayos, and he managed the journal *Entregas de la Licorne* (1953–1956). With his brother Germán he established the publishing house Arca in 1962. Rama wrote for the Uruguayan newspaper *El País* and held posts at the National Library of Uruguay (1949–1965). He taught in high school, at the Instituto de Profesores Artigas, and at the Universidad de la República (1966–1974), where he served as head of the Department of Hispanic American literature. He was on the editorial board of the Cuban publication *Casa de las Américas* from

1964 to 1971, when he resigned over the political trial of the Cuban poet Heberto Padilla. Having divorced Vitale, Rama married Argentine art critic and essayist Marta Traba in 1969 and moved to Puerto Rico, beginning his life in exile. In 1974 they went to Caracas, where he directed the publication of Latin American classics under the general title Biblioteca Ayacucho, and taught at the Universidad Central de Venezuela. He became a tenured professor at the University of Maryland in 1981. Rama died November 27, 1983.

In thirty books and numerous articles, Rama examined literature and cultural topics from all periods of Latin American history. In addition to his work on gaucho poetry, he also wrote about José Martí, Rubén Darío, Horacio Quiroga, Juan Carlos Onetti, and Gabriel García Márquez. His major works include *Rubén Darío y el modernismo* (1970), *Los gauchipolíticos rioplatenses* (1976), *Transculturación narrativa en América Latina* (1982), and the posthumous *La ciudad letrada* (1984, translated as *The Lettered City*, 1996).

See also **Darío, Rubén; García Márquez, Gabriel; Onetti, Juan Carlos; Quijano, Carlos; Uruguay: The Twentieth Century.**

BIBLIOGRAPHY

Angel Rama, 1926–1983: Bibliografía sumaria. College Park: Department of Spanish and Portuguese, University of Maryland, College Park, 1984.

Benedetti, Mario, et al. "Angel Rama, presencia que no acaba." *Casa de las Américas* 34:192 (July–September 1993): 3–63.

Blixen, Carina, and Alvaro Barros-Lémez. *Cronología y bibliografía de Angel Rama.* Montevideo, Uruguay: Fundación Angel Rama, 1986.

Moraña, Mabel. *Angel Rama y los estudios latinoamericanos.* 2nd ed. Pittsburgh, PA: Instituto Internacional de Literatura Iberoamericana, University of Pittsburgh, 2006.

Rama, Angel. *Rubén Darío y el modernismo (circunstancia socioeconómica de un arte americano).* Caracas: Ediciones de la Biblioteca de la Universidad Central de Venezuela, 1970.

Rama, Angel. *Los gauchipolíticos rioplatenses: Literatura y sociedad.* Buenos Aires: Calicanto Editorial, 1976.

Rama, Angel. *Transculturación narrativa en América Latina.* México, D.F.: Siglo Veintiuno Editores, 1982.

Rama, Angel. *La ciudad letrada.* With a prologue by Hugo Achugar. Hanover, NH: Ediciones del Norte, 1984; Montevideo, Uruguay: Arca, 1998.

Rama, Angel. *Las máscaras democráticas del modernismo.* Montevideo, Uruguay: Fundación Angel Rama; Arca, 1985.

Rama, Angel. *The Lettered City.* Translated and edited by John Charles Chasteen. Durham, NC: Duke University Press, 1996.

SAÚL SOSNOWSKI
WILLIAM G. ACREE JR.

RAMALHO, JOÃO (c. 1490–c. 1580).

João Ramalho (*b.* c. 1490; *d.* c. 1580), earliest permanent Portuguese resident of southern Brazil. Born in Vouzela, Portugal, Ramalho was stranded on the coast near São Vicente around 1513 and lived for many years among the Tupinikin, marrying Chief Tibiriçá's daughter Bartira. Wielding extraordinary influence among the Indians, Ramalho "could assemble five thousand warriors in a single day," according to contemporary traveler Ulrich Schmidl. With these attributes of an Indian headman, Ramalho played a central role in guaranteeing the European occupation of São Vicente, as he persuaded his indigenous relatives to form an alliance with the Portuguese against their mortal enemies, the Tupinambá (Tamoio). Ramalho's village on the interior plateau was one of the nuclei that later formed São Paulo, where he died.

See also **Brazil: The Colonial Era, 1500–1808; Indigenous Peoples; São Vicente.**

BIBLIOGRAPHY

The role of Portuguese castaways in early relations with the Indians is discussed summarily in Alexander Marchant, *From Barter to Slavery* (1942), and in James Lockhart and Stuart Schwartz, *Early Latin America* (1983), chap. 6. On the early formation of São Paulo, Richard Morse, *From Community to Metropolis* (1958), provides an excellent starting point.

Additional Bibliography

Dos Santos, Vasco. *João Ramalho: Memórias dum povoador.* Lisboa, Portugal: Universitária Editora, 2001.

JOHN M. MONTEIRO

RAMÍREZ, FRANCISCO (1786–1821).

Francisco Ramírez (*b.* 13 March 1786; *d.* 10 July 1821), Argentine caudillo of Entre Ríos and leader of provincial federalism against Buenos Aires. Born in Concepción del Uruguay, into the colonial elite of land and office, he joined the independence movement in 1810. The following year he supported José Gervasio Artigas against the Spanish regime in Uruguay, and in 1816 against Portuguese invaders from Brazil. But Ramírez represented the interests of the *estancieros* of Entre Ríos and distanced himself from the agrarian populism of Artigas. He also resisted the centralism of Buenos Aires and its demands for resources. In 1819 he joined the caudillo Estanislao López of Santa Fe, and in 1820 he led a force of federalist *montoneros* (gaucho cavalry) to victory over Buenos Aires at the battle of Cepeda; Buenos Aires was forced to agree to the Treaty of Pilar (23 February 1820), which recognized the jurisdiction of the provinces in a loose federal structure. In a decree of 29 September 1820 Ramírez styled himself *jefe supremo* of the Republic of Entre Ríos. The caudillo alliance was short-lived. Disputes between Ramírez and López over political leadership in the Littoral and strategy toward the Portuguese in Uruguay caused violent conflict which culminated in the defeat of Ramírez at Río Seco in July 1821. Returning to rescue his woman, the legendary Delfina, who had fallen into the hands of the enemy, Ramírez was killed. His head was exhibited in public by López.

See also **Buenos Aires; Entre Ríos.**

BIBLIOGRAPHY

Tulio Halperín Donghi, *Politics, Economics, and Society in Argentina in the Revolutionary Period* (1975).

John Lynch, *Caudillos in Spanish America 1800–1850* (1992).

Additional Bibliography

Salduna, Horacio. *La muerte romántica del general Ramírez.* Buenos Aires: Corregidor, 1998.

JOHN LYNCH

RAMÍREZ, IGNACIO (1818–1879).

Ignacio Ramírez (*b.* 1818; *d.* 1879), Mexican journalist and cabinet minister. Ramírez was born in San Miguel de Allende, Guanajuato, and educated in Querétaro and Mexico City, where he received his degree in law. In 1845, with Guillermo Prieto and Vicente Segura, he began publishing the satirical journal *Don Simplicio*. Using the pseudonym "El Nigromante" (The Necromancer), Ramírez denounced the wealthy and the church with a wicked sense of humor. For example, El Nigromante proposed that "The Ten Commandments shall be retained in all their vigor, except the seventh, as long as citizens lack another honorable means to maintain their subsistence." Ramírez extended this social analysis more directly in other articles: "We the workers say to the hacendados: Why without the sweat of your brows do you eat bread, or toss it to your prostitutes and lackeys? If you say because God made you rich, show us the deeds."

Ramírez may have been the most radical journalist and politician of his day and Mexico's most prominent atheist. Elected to the Constitutional Congress of 1856–1857, he advocated religious toleration. He argued that juridical equality was not sufficient and would not improve the standard of living for the majority of Mexico's people. Ramírez was critical of the Ley Lerdo because it would make property available only to the middle class and the wealthy, who already owned some property and had the money to buy more.

President Benito Juárez selected Ramírez to serve as minister of justice (21 January 1861–9 May 1861) and minister of development (18 March 1861–3 April 1861). Ramírez believed that the Constitution of 1857 gave Congress supremacy over the presidency and came to regard Juárez as a dictator. He spent much of the second empire in exile in California. After the restoration of the republic, Ramírez returned to Mexico and served as a justice of the Supreme Court from 1868 to 1879. He supported Porfirio Díaz's Plan of Tuxtepec and served as Díaz's first minister of justice (29 November 1876–7 May 1877).

See also **Journalism; Ley Lerdo; Mexico: 1810–1910.**

BIBLIOGRAPHY

Walter V. Scholes, *Mexican Politics During the Juárez Regime, 1855–1872* (1957), pp. 8–9, 16, 60, 152.

Jesús Reyes Heroles, *El liberalismo mexicano,* 3 vols. (1957–1961), vol. 3, pp. 656–675.

Richard N. Sinkin, *The Mexican Reform, 1855–1876: A Study in Liberal Nation-Building* (1979), pp. 37, 41–42, 49,

126; *Diccionario Porrúa de historia, biografía y geografía de México*, 5th ed. (1986).

Additional Bibliography

Fowler, Wil. *Mexico in the Age of Proposals, 1821–1853.* Westport, CT: Greenwood Press, 1998.

Villegas Revueltas, Silvestre. *El liberalismo moderado en México, 1852–1864.* México, D.F.: Universidad Nacional Autónoma de México, 1997.

D. F. STEVENS

RAMÍREZ, JOSÉ FERNANDO (1804–

1871). José Fernando Ramírez (*b.* 5 May 1804; *d.* 4 March 1871), Mexican political figure. Although born in Hidalgo del Parral, Chihuahua, Ramírez represented Durango in the federal Congress in 1833–1834 and was rector of the State College of Lawyers. He helped formulate the Bases Orgánicas of 1843 and served as secretary of foreign relations three times: December 1846–January 1847, September 1851–March 1852, and June 1864–October 1865 under the empire. A moderate Liberal, he rallied to the Plan of Ayutla in 1854. In Europe from mid-1855 until spring 1856, he continued research, which he had begun in the previous decade, on the pre-Columbian era. He declined to participate in the Assembly of Notables of 1864, but served on Maximilian's Council of State until March 1866. Tainted by collaboration with the empire, he died in exile in Bonn.

A collector of rare books and manuscripts, Ramírez championed the idea of a national library. His *Vida de Fray Toribio de Motolinía* (1858) formed volume one of Joaquín García Icazbalceta's *Colección de documentos para la historia de México.*

See also **Mexico: 1810–1910; Plan of Ayutla.**

BIBLIOGRAPHY

Additional Bibliography

Duncan, Robert. "For the Good of the Country: State and Nation Building during Maximilian's Mexican Empire, 1864–67." Ph.D. diss., 2001.

Fowler, Wil. *Mexico in the Age of Proposals, 1821–1853.* Westport, CT: Greenwood Press, 1998.

Rodríguez O, Jaime E. *The Divine Charter: Constitutionalism and Liberalism in Nineteenth-Century Mexico.* Lanham, MD: Rowman & Littlefield Publishers, 2005.

Villegas Revueltas, Silvestre. *El liberalismo moderado en México, 1852–1864.* México, D.F.: Universidad Nacional Autónoma de México, 1997.

BRIAN HAMNETT

RAMÍREZ, PEDRO PABLO (1884–

1962). Pedro Pablo Ramírez was the de facto president of Argentina for nine months in 1943–1944. Born in La Paz, Entre Ríos, Ramírez became president on June 6, 1943, in the wake of the June 4 coup that overthrew conservative President Ramón Castillo, who was determined to maintain the oligarchic character of the political regime and to end Argentine neutrality in the World War II. A major general, Ramírez had been minister of war in Castillo's administration. Ramírez's first cabinet was sharply divided on World War II, and while pledging to eliminate corruption and restore democracy, it severely harassed Communists and restricted unions. Beginning in October 1943, ultra-rightists dominated the government and repression increased drastically; Communist organizations went underground; political parties were abolished; Catholic education was mandatory in public schools; and the press was strictly censored.

Ramírez lacked a strong personality and clear opinions. Into this vacuum stepped a military lodge, the United Officers Group (Grupo Obra de Unificación, or GOU), controlled by nationalist colonels, admirers of the Nazi regime, among whom was Juan Domingo Perón. This group quickly began to push its own objectives: the enlargement of the social and political support of the regime, the prevention of any progress by communism, and the preservation of neutrality. Perón became the head of the Department of Labor and gained labor union support by means of cooptation.

Using Argentine involvement in a Bolivian coup and an aborted weapons deal with Germany as leverage, the United States pressed Ramírez to break relations with Germany and Japan, which he did on January 26, 1944. Furious officers called for Ramírez's resignation. But when he tried to do so on February 24, 1944, Ramírez was persuaded instead to delegate his authority to his vice president, Edelmiro Farrell, because of fears that his resignation would complicate diplomatic recognition. Ramírez ultimately resigned on March 9.

See also **Argentina: The Twentieth Century; Argentina, Organizations: United Officers Group (GOU); Castillo, Ramón; Perón, Juan Domingo.**

BIBLIOGRAPHY

Potash, Robert A. *The Army and Politics in Argentina.* Vol. 1: *1928–1945: Irigoyen to Perón.* Stanford, CA: Stanford University Press, 1969.

Rouquié, Alain. *Poder militar y sociedad política en la Argentina.* 2 vols. Translated by Arturo Iglesias Echegaray. Buenos Aires: Emecé, 1982.

JOEL HOROWITZ
VICENTE PALERMO

RAMÍREZ MERCADO, SERGIO (1942–).

Sergio Ramírez Mercado is a Nicaraguan writer who served as vice president of Nicaragua from 1984 to 1990 in the Sandinista government. In the early twenty-first century Ramírez is a harsh critic of the Frente Sandinista de Liberación Nacional (Sandinista National Liberation Front, FSLN). He was born in the town of Masatepe, where his father was a coffee planter and a member of the Somoza family's National Liberal Party. Ramírez helped form the Student Revolutionary Front in 1961 while at the National Autonomous University of Nicaragua. In 1964 he started a literary career with the journal *Ventana*. He attended the University of Kansas and studied in West Berlin between 1972 and 1975. He went to Costa Rica to serve on the Central American Council of Universities. There he completed an essay about the Nicaraguan revolutionary Augusto César Sandino that appeared in a collection on Sandino's life and thought. In 1988 Ramírez revitalized his literary career with his most celebrated novel *Castigo Divino* (Divine punishment).

After the FSLN's electoral defeat in February 1990, Ramírez joined the Sandinista National Directorate. However, powerful Sandinista commanders expelled him in July 1994 due to serious disagreements about the future of the revolutionary movement. He founded the dissident Movimiento de Renovación Sandinista (Sandinista Renewal Movement) in 1995. Since that time, he has published several award-winning novels and short stories and a memoir of his revolutionary experiences. Though he no longer runs as a candidate for national political office, he maintains an active role in the Sandinista renewal movement.

See also **Nicaragua, Sandinista National Liberation Front (FSLN); Sandino, Augusto César; Somoza Debayle, Anastasio.**

BIBLIOGRAPHY

Ramírez, Sergio. *Castigo Divino.* Madrid: Mondadori, 1988.

Ramírez, Sergio. *Margarita, está linda la mar.* Madrid: Alfaguara, 1998.

Ramírez, Sergio. *Adiós Muchachos: Una Memoria de la revolución sandinista.* México City: El País; Madrid: Aguilar, 1999.

Ramírez, Sergio. "La revolución que no fue." *La Jornada* (México City), July 18, 2004.

Ramírez, Sergio, ed. *El pensamiento vivo de Sandino.* San José, Costa Rica: EDUCA, 1975; Managua: Editorial Nueva Nicaragua, 1984.

MARK EVERINGHAM

RAMÍREZ VÁZQUEZ, PEDRO (1919–).

Pedro Ramírez Vázquez (*b.* 16 April 1919), leading Mexican architect and public figure. Internationally renowned for his architectural designs of private residences and public buildings, he designed Mexico's Secretariat of Foreign Relations and Aztec Stadium. But he is best known outside of Mexico for the imaginative and modern National Museum of Anthropology. A native of Mexico City, Ramírez Vázquez graduated from the National University with a degree in architecture in 1943 and taught architectural composition and urbanism at the National School of Architecture for fifteen years. A long-time public servant, Ramírez Vázquez began his career as head of building conservation in the educational secretariat and worked many years in the school building program. He became president of the Olympic Games Organizing Committee in 1966 and served as secretary of public works from 1976 to 1982. He then returned to private practice.

See also **Architecture: Modern Architecture.**

BIBLIOGRAPHY

Pedro Ramírez Vázquez, un architecte mexicain (1979).

Additional Bibliography

Doumato, Lamia. *Mexican Architecture and Pedro Ramirez Vazquez*. Monticello, IL: Vance Bibliographies, 1990.

González de León, Teodoro. *Obras y proyectos: Arquitectura contemporánea mexicana*. México: Central de Publicaciones, 1969.

Vargas, Ramón. *Pabellones y museos de Pedro Ramírez Vázquez*. México: Noriega Editores, 1995.

RODERIC AI CAMP

RAMÍREZ VILLAMIZAR, EDUARDO

(1923–2004). Eduardo Ramírez Villamizar (*b*. 1923, *d*. 2004), Colombian sculptor. Ramírez studied architecture and fine art at the National University in Bogotá. Upon graduation in 1945, he began his career as a painter. His later work amalgamated architecture, painting, and sculpture. From 1949 to 1952 and 1954 to 1956, he lived in Paris. While there, he abandoned expressionism and began to create paintings, murals, and sculptures based on the abstract geometric principles of constructivism. His later forms, however, are increasingly inspired by the pre-Columbian art of Mexico and Peru.

In 1956 Ramírez had his first one-man show at the Pan-American Union, and the Museum of Modern Art purchased his painting *Blanco y Negro*. In 1971 he participated in the International Sculpture Symposium at the University of Vermont, where he showed his first monumental sculptures (*Cuatro Torres*). When the Kennedy Center opened in 1973, Colombia presented as its gift Ramírez's *De Colombia a John Kennedy*.

In 1990 the Colombian government established the Ramírez Villamizar Museum of Modern Art in Pamplona, his birthplace.

See also **Art: The Twentieth Century.**

BIBLIOGRAPHY

Eduardo Ramírez Villamizar—Exposición retrospectiva 1958–1972, text by Ida Ely Rubin (Bogotá, 1972).

Germán Rubiano Caballero, *Escultura colombiana del siglo XX* (1983); *Ramírez Villamizar*, text by Frederico Morais (Bogotá, 1984); *Ramírez Villamizar: Obra reciente* (1987); *Eduardo Ramírez Villamizar—Homenaje a los artífices pre-colombinos* (Caracas, 1993).

Additional Bibliography

Herzog, Hans-Michael, and Nadin Ospina. *Cantos cuentos colombianos arte colombiano contemporáneo = Contemporary Colombian Art*. Zürich, Switzerland: Daros-Latinamerica, 2004.

Mutis Durán, Santiago, and Eduardo Ramírez Villamizar. *Eduardo Ramírez Villamizar la belleza del pensamiento*. Colombia: Ediciones Jaime Vargas, 2000.

IDA ELY RUBIN

RAMÍREZ Y BLANCO, ALEJANDRO

(1777–1821). Alejandro Ramírezy Blanco (*b*. 25 February 1777; *d*. 20 May 1821), Intendant of Puerto Rico (1813–1816) and of Cuba (1816–1821). Born in Alaejos, Spain, and educated in Valladolid and at the University of Alcalá de Henares, Ramírez immigrated to Guatemala in 1795. He became secretary to the consulado in 1798 and to the captain-general in 1802. For his work as a member of the economic society and as editor of its newspaper, he was the only Latin American of his time named a member of the American Philosophical Society.

In Havana on 14 December 1812, he took the oath as intendant of Puerto Rico. He found a bankrupt colony and began reformation of its tax structure and diversification of its economy. He retired an inflationary issue of paper money, founded an economic society and edited its newspaper, and opened vocational schools for women and night schools for artisans. Despite efforts from peninsular officials to thwart his reforms, the island became self-sufficient during his tenure.

On 3 July 1816, he became superintendent of Cuba and intendant of Havana and pursued his policies of economic diversification and tax reform, doubling royal revenues by 1820. Recognizing the problems of monoculture, he introduced new crops to be utilized by small landowners. He obtained abolition of the tobacco monopoly, thus invigorating the industry. He also created a school of chemistry and a botanical garden and school of botany, and his efforts led to public education programs and support of charitable institutions for women and orphans. Due to opposition from sugar interests and peninsular Spaniards, he became the first colonial official to utilize the press to defend his actions. In early 1821, he accepted appointment as *jefe político* of Guatemala, but he died before leaving Cuba.

Ramírez showed that a liberal official, cooperating with creole interests, initiated outstanding successes utilizing Bourbon Reform policies. His legacy was the economic success in the colonies he served and a reputation for outstanding honesty.

See also **Cuba: The Colonial Era (1492–1898); Puerto Rico; Tobacco Industry; Tobacco Monopoly.**

BIBLIOGRAPHY

A brief overview of Ramírez's career can be found in Luis González Vales, "Towards a Plantation Society," in *Puerto Rico: A Political and Cultural History,* edited by Arturo Morales Carrión (1983). For a more thorough examination, see Luis González Vales, *Alejandro Ramírez y su tiempo* (1978), and M. Isidro Méndez, *El Intendente Ramírez* (1944).

JACQUELYN BRIGGS KENT

RAMOS, ARTUR (1903–1949).

Artur Ramos (Arthur Ramos; *b.* July 1903; *d.* 31 October 1949), Brazilian anthropologist, psychiatrist, and educator. Trained as a physician, Ramos first wrote psychiatric studies. In 1934 he moved to Rio de Janeiro to establish the psychiatric service of the Department of Education. That year he published *O negro brasileiro,* primarily a study of religion, and in 1935, *O folk-lore negro do Brasil: Demopsychologia e psychanalyse,* a study of dance, music, religion, and folktales. These studies explore psychoanalytical interpretations of Afro-Brazilian culture, but his later works emphasize processes of acculturation.

During World War II, Ramos's public career turned toward the application of anthropological research to antiracist propaganda. He founded the Brazilian Society of Anthropology and Ethnology in 1941 and became professor of anthropology at the Faculdade Nacional de Filosofia in Rio de Janeiro in 1946. Ramos died in 1949 while serving as director of the social science department of UNESCO in Paris, where he promoted the postwar UNESCO study of race relations.

See also **Anthropology.**

BIBLIOGRAPHY

Artur Ramos, *O negro brasileiro: Ethnographia, religiosa e psychanalyse*...(1934), translated by Richard Pattee, under the title *The Negro in Brazil* (1939).

Marilu Gusmão, *Artur Ramos: O homem e a obra* (1974), a biographical sketch.

Thomas Skidmore, *Black into White: Race and Nationality in Brazilian Thought* (1974).

Additional Bibliography

Barros, Luitgarde Oliveira Cavalcanti. *Arthur Ramos e as dinâmicas sociais de seu tempo.* Macció: Universidade Federal de Alagoas, 2000.

Campos, Maria José. *Arthur Ramos, luz e sombra na antropologia brasileira: Uma versão da democracia racial no Brasil nas décadas de 1930 e 1940.* Rio de Janeiro: Edições Biblioteca Nacional, 2004.

Sapucaia, Antonio. *Relembrando Arthur Ramos.* Maceió: EDUFAL, 2003.

DAIN BORGES

RAMOS, GRACILIANO (1892–1953).

Graciliano Ramos (*b.* 27 October 1892; *d.* 20 March 1953), Brazilian novelist. A member of the literary generation of 1930, Ramos is one of Brazil's most eminent writers. His works have been widely translated and have received international critical acclaim. Three of his narratives have been made into highly successful films.

Ramos was born into a modest family in a small town in Alagoas and spent much of his childhood on a farm in the *sertão* (backlands) of Pernambuco. There he witnessed the poverty and misery caused by unequal patterns of land ownership and by the periodic droughts that afflict the region, all of which would later be incorporated into his narratives with masterful artistry. Ramos never finished secondary school and began his adult life working in, and subsequently managing, his father's dry goods store. In 1928 he was elected mayor of the small Alagoan town of Palmeira dos Índios, following which he held numerous appointed posts in the state bureaucracy, notably as director of the government printing office and head of the Department of Education.

In March 1936, following the unsuccessful revolt of the Aliança Nacional Libertadora, a popular front organization, Ramos was arrested because he was suspected of being a Communist, and thereafter was held in various prisons until February 1937. Formal charges were never brought against him. Ramos recounted the humiliation and degradation of this experience in *Memórias do cárcere* (1953), one of the most eloquent condemnations of authoritarianism written by a Brazilian.

In "Os bichos do subterrâneo," Antônio Candido suggests that the actual events of 1936–1937, plus their subsequent fictional elaboration, made Ramos go from a view of the world as a prison to one of prison as the world. All of Ramos's major fictional works focus on his characters' inability to escape from or transcend the limitations imposed by their own psychological makeup and social situation. His first three novels offer a complex exploration of the dark corners of the human psyche, which has led some critics to see Ramos primarily as a psychological writer. Yet his characters are always portrayed in terms of the social situation of the Brazilian Northeast in a period characterized by the onset of modernization, a technique that identifies him as a social novelist. Ramos thus combines psychological and social analysis as few other Brazilian writers since Machado de Assis have been able to do.

The first three novels, all written in the first person, take the form of fictional memoirs. Set largely in a boardinghouse in a small town, *Caetés* (1933) deals with self-interest and the relativity of human moral values. The narrator-protagonist, João Valério, seduces his boss's wife, an act that eventually drives his boss to suicide. Valério is writing a novel about the Caeté Indians, who, through explicit comparison, serve as a metaphor for humanity's underlying primitive, egotistical, and barbarous self. Ramos's second novel, *São Bernardo* (1934), is structured as the memoirs of Paulo Honório, who has risen from worker to owner of a large *fazenda*. The story of his violent rise to wealth and power is also the story of his fall as a human being, for his ultimate financial, ethical, and psychological failure exposes the reification of human beings under capitalism, then rapidly expanding in Brazil. In its dense soundings, reminiscent of Dostoyevsky, Ramos's third novel, *Angústia* (1936), published while he was in prison, reconstructs the psychological disintegration of petit-bourgeois intellectual Luís da Silva, the scion of a decadent fraction of a previously dominant class of rural landowners. Together, these three novels constitute a complex portrait of what Valentim Facioli has called the contradictory and chaotic dynamism of a dependent capitalist Brazil.

Many critics see *Vidas secas* (1938), Ramos's only novel written in the third person, as the high point of his career. The novel, circular in structure, portrays the suffering of an impoverished family during a period of drought. Through their strength and determination in the face of overwhelming odds, the family—composed of the cowherd Fabiano, his wife Vitória, their two sons, and the memorable dog Baleia—reveals a level of human dignity that is largely absent from Ramos's previous work. With his economical, harsh style, in a literary tour de force Ramos manages to penetrate the minds of his illiterate characters, and even of Baleia the dog, providing a haunting and moving portrait of the personal impact of environment and social tragedy.

With the exception of a few short stories, after *Vidas secas,* Ramos turned almost exclusively to journalistic and memorialistic writing.

See also **Literature: Brazil.**

BIBLIOGRAPHY

Fred P. Ellison, "Graciliano Ramos," in his *Brazil's New Novel: Four Northeastern Masters* (1954).

Antônio Candido, *Ficção e confissão* (1956).

Russell Hamilton, "Character and Idea in Ramos's *Vidas secas,*" in *Luso-Brazilian Review* 1 (June 1968): 86–92.

Richard A. Mazzara, *Graciliano Ramos* (1974).

Antônio Candido, "Os bichos do subterrâneo," in his *Tese e antítese*, 3d ed. (1978).

Randal Johnson, "*Vidas secas* and the Politics of Filmic Adaptation," in *Ideologies and Literature* 3, no. 15 (1981): 3–18.

Valentim Facioli, "Um homem bruto da terra (Biografia intelectual)," in *Graciliano Ramos,* edited by Valentim Facioli et al. (1987), pp. 23–106.

Additional Bibliography

Leitão, Cláudio. *Líquido e incerto: Memória e exílio em Graciliano Ramos.* Niterói: EdUFF, Editora da Universidade Federal Fluminense, 2003.

Rezende, Marcelo. *Literatura brasileira: Machado de Assis, Graciliano Ramos, Guimarães Rosa.* São Paulo: Editora Bregantini, 2004.

Santos, Vasco dos. *Graciliano Ramos: Vida e obra.* São Paulo: Editora Nova Aldeia, 2003.

RANDAL JOHNSON

CLASS, RACE, AND SOCIETY

Tango demonstration on the streets of Buenos Aires, Argentina. The tango, which emerged from the poor neighborhoods and brothels of Buenos Aires, has spread to all levels of society and become Argentina's national dance.
ROBERT FRERCK/STONE/GETTY IMAGES

A Mulatto Woman with Her White Daughter, Visited by Negro Women in the Their House in Martinique (1775)
by the Flemish painter Le Masurier, showing the social and racial diversity of the West Indies in the eighteenth century.

RIGHT: A father and child beg on the streets of a Buenos Aires shopping district, 2002. The financial crises hitting Argentina at the turn of the early twenty-first century took their toll on those already living below the poverty line. © REUTERS/CORBIS

OPPOSITE: A food stand in Mexico City. Stands such as these are a ubiquitous sight in Latin America. As part of the informal sector of the economy, this fruit stand owner likely does not pay taxes and thus receives no government benefits. STEPHANIE MAZE/NATIONAL GEOGRAPHIC IMAGE COLLECTION

BELOW: A teenager watches tourists on Sosúa beach in the Dominican Republic, 2002. Adolescent vagrancy and prostitution have become significant problems in the Dominican Republic. Luxurious all-inclusive resorts located in areas of overwhelming poverty are an irresistible lure for poor children seeking to make even a little bit of money. AP IMAGES

ABOVE: **Wedding day in Quito, Ecuador.** A bride waits for the start of her wedding as townspeople look on in interest. © Pablo Corral Vega/Corbis

LEFT: **An indigenous child on the streets of La Paz, Bolivia.** Bolivia is one of South America's poorest countries and poverty is particularly severe among its indigenous people, the majority of the population. The rural poor come to the city in the hopes of finding some way to make a living. Spencer Platt/Getty Images

RAMOS ARIZPE, JOSÉ MIGUEL (1775–1843).

José Miguel Ramos Arizpe (*b.* 1775; *d.* 1843), Mexican political theorist and politician. Born in Valle de San Nicolás, Coahuila, Ramos was ordained in 1803 and subsequently became professor of canon and civil law in Monterrey. Elected deputy to the Spanish Cortes in 1810, he became a leading champion of American rights and was the architect of the provincial deputation, an organization that provided home rule to the provinces. Arrested in 1814, when Ferdinand VII returned from France and abolished the constitutional system, he remained in prison until 1820, when the constitution was restored. Elected to the Cortes once again, he, together with other American deputies, proposed commonwealth status for the New World. After Independence Ramos returned to Mexico in 1822 in time to join the opposition to Iturbide; he was instrumental in mobilizing the provinces and in drafting the Plan of Casa Mata. Elected to the Second Constituent Congress, he was an advocate of moderate federalism and the principal author of the Constitution of 1824.

One of the founders of the Yorkino Masonic lodges in 1825, Ramos sided with the moderates in opposing the expulsion of the Spaniards and in supporting the presidency of Manuel Gómez Pedraza in 1828. He served as minister of justice and ecclesiastic affairs in the Victoria and Gómez Farías administrations, distinguishing himself as a champion of national control of the church, while also continuing his clerical career, becoming dean of the cathedral chapter of Puebla. He was elected delegate from Puebla to the 1842 Congress shortly before he died.

See also **Masonic Orders; Mexico: 1810–1910.**

BIBLIOGRAPHY

Nettie Lee Benson, ed. and trans., *Report That Dr. Miguel Ramos de Arizpe, Priest of Borbon and Deputy to the General and Special Cortes of Spain for the Province of Coahuila . . . Presents to the August Congress* (1950); *La Diputación Provincial y el federalismo mexicano* (1955); and her *Mexico and the Spanish Cortes, 1810–1822* (1966).

Jaime E. Rodríguez O., "La Constitución de 1824 y la formación del Estado mexicano," *Historia Mexicana* 40, pt. 3 (1991): 507–535, and his "Intellectuals and the Constitution of 1824," in Roderic A. Camp, Charles A. Hale, and Josefina Z. Vázquez, eds., *Los intelectuales y el poder en México* (1991), pp. 63–74.

Additional Bibliography

Fowler, Wil. *Mexico in the Age of Proposals, 1821–1853.* Westport, CT: Greenwood Press, 1998.

González Salas, Carlos. *Miguel Ramos Arizpe.* Montemorelos: Publicaciones Interamericanas Pacific Press de México, 1990.

Toro, Alfonso. *Don Miguel Ramos Arizpe, "Padre del Federalismo Mexicano": Biografía.* Saltillo: Coordinación General de Extensión Univesitaria y Difusión Cultural, 1992.

                                        JAIME E. RODRÍGUEZ O.

RAMOS MEJÍA, EZEQUIEL (1853–1935).

Ezequiel Ramos Mejía (*b.* 15 December 1853; *d.* 7 November 1935), Argentine politician who actively participated in the removal of President Julio Argentino Roca's political machinery from power during the first decade of the twentieth century. Elected a provincial deputy in Buenos Aires in 1880, and a national deputy in 1900, Ramos Mejía was appointed minister of agriculture by President Roca in 1901. A native of Buenos Aires, he was aligned politically with Carlos Pellegrini rather than the provincial forces led by Roca. When Roca and Pellegrini parted ways in 1901, Ramos Mejía resigned and became a member of the growing opposition within the liberal-conservative forces. Under President José Figueroa Alcorta (1906–1910) he served as minister of agriculture and minister of public works, continuing in the latter office under President Roque Sáenz Peña until 1913. He was, therefore, at the forefront in the battle for power that developed during the Figueroa Alcorta administration between *roquistas* and the group of former *juaristas* (followers of former president Miguel Juárez Celman), such as Roque Sáenz Peña and Estanislao Zeballos, who supported the president. His memoirs thus provide an invaluable source for the analysis of the political conflicts of the period.

Ideologically, Ramos Mejía evolved from a moderate nationalism to a growing disillusionment with democratic institutions. By the 1930s, influenced by his first-hand knowledge of the fascist experiment in Italy, where he served as ambassador between 1933 until his death, he was advocating the abandonment of the classical model of liberal democracy for a new type of political and economic organization.

See also **Argentina: The Twentieth Century; Figueroa Alcorta, José; Roca, Julio Argentino.**

BIBLIOGRAPHY

Ezequiel Ramos Mejía, *Mis memorias, 1853–1935* (1936).

Donald M. Peck, "Las presidencias de Manuel Quintana y José Figueroa Alcorta, 1904–1910," in *La Argentina del ochenta al centenario,* compiled by Gustavo Ferrari and Ezequiel Gallo (1980).

Additional Bibliography

Deutsch, Sandra McGee. *Las Derechas: The Extreme Right in Argentina, Brazil, and Chile, 1890–1939.* Stanford, CA: Stanford University Press, 1999.

Zimmermann, Eduardo A. *Los liberales reformistas: La cuestión social en la Argentina, 1890–1916.* Buenos Aires: Editorial Sudamericana: Universidad de San Andrés, 1995.

EDUARDO A. ZIMMERMANN

RAMOS MEJÍA, JOSÉ MARÍA (1849–
1914).

José María Ramos Mejía (*b.* 24 December 1849; *d.* 19 June 1914), Argentine physician, statesman, and intellectual. After studying medicine at the University of Buenos Aires, from which he graduated in 1879, Ramos Mejía promoted the creation of the Asistencia Pública de Buenos Aires, a municipal system of medical care for the needy, becoming its first director in 1883. Appointed professor at the Medical School at the University of Buenos Aires, he specialized in the study of mental pathologies, becoming one of the precursors of scientific psychiatry in Argentina. His first works reflected this interest: *Las neurosis de los hombres célebres en la historia argentina* (1878–1882); *Estudios de patología nerviosa y mental* (1893); and *La locura en la historia* (1895). Elected to Congress, he served as a national deputy (1888–1892) and was subsequently appointed director of the National Department of Health (1893–1908).

The profound social transformations that were taking place in early-twentieth-century Argentina awakened Ramos Mejía's interest in social psychology, as reflected in his works *Las multitudes argentinas* (1899), influenced by the work of Gustave Le Bon, and *Los simuladores del talento* (1904). Between 1908 and 1913 Ramos Mejía was in charge of the Consejo Nacional de Educación, where he launched an aggressive campaign to introduce the concept of "patriotic education" (emphasis on civics) in the schools, as a means of strengthening what he thought was a weakened sense of national identity, threatened by the impact of massive immigration.

See also **Argentina: The Twentieth Century; Medicine: The Modern Era.**

BIBLIOGRAPHY

Hugo Vezzetti, *La locura en la Argentina* (1985).

Oscar Terán, ed., *Positivismo y nación en la Argentina* (1987).

Carlos Escudé, *El fracaso del proyecto argentino. Educación e ideología* (1990).

Additional Bibliography

Plotkin, Mariano Ben. *Argentina on the Couch: Psychiatry, State, and Society, 1880 to the Present.* Albuquerque: University of New Mexico Press, 2003.

EDUARDO A. ZIMMERMANN

RAMOS Y MAGAÑA, SAMUEL (1897–
1959).

Samuel Ramos y Magaña (*b.* 8 June 1897; *d.* 20 June 1959), Mexican intellectual and educator. A student of Antonio Caso and collaborator of José Vasconcelos and Pedro Henríquez Ureña, Samuel Ramos wrote a seminal work of Mexican philosophy and culture, *Profile of Man and Culture in Mexico* (1934), in the "lo mexicano" line of intellectual thought, continued by Octavio Paz in the 1960s. Although criticized for its lack of "empirical" evidence, this work continues to provoke significant discussion in the intellectual community.

Growing up in Michoacán, where he attended the Colegio de San Nicolás in Morelia, Ramos attended medical school before switching to philosophy his third year. He studied in Rome and in Paris, at the Sorbonne. He taught logic and the history of philosophy at the National Preparatory School and the National University. Ramos founded and edited *Ulises,* and managed José Vasconcelos's intellectual journal *Antorcha.* He entered public life briefly as *oficial mayor* of public education (1931–1932) under his friend Narciso Bassols, and in the 1940s represented Mexico at UNESCO. He was appointed a member of the National College in 1952.

See also **Caso y Andrade, Antonio; Philosophy: Overview.**

BIBLIOGRAPHY

Samuel Ramos, *Profile of Man and Culture in Mexico,* translated by Peter G. Earle (1962).

Henry C. Schmidt, *The Roots of* Lo Mexicano: *Self and Society in Mexican Thought, 1900–1934* (1978).

Juan Hernández Luna, *Samuel Ramos: Etapas de su formación espiritual* (1982).

Additional Bibliography

Arreola Cortés, Raúl. *Samuel Ramos: La pasión por la cultura.* Morelia, México: Universidad Michoacana de San Nicolás de Hidalgo, 1997.

RODERIC AI CAMP

RANCAGUA, BATTLE OF.

Battle of Rancagua, the October 1814 conflict that temporarily derailed Chile's attempt to free itself from Spain. The Chilean independence leader Bernardo O'Higgins sought to defend the city of Rancagua, near Santiago, against advancing Spanish forces under the command of General Mariano Osorio. Outnumbered by Madrid's superior forces, O'Higgins and his men managed to hold the city, but without the assistance of Chile's other independence figure, José Miguel Carrera, who apparently resented O'Higgins's popularity, O'Higgins was defeated and put to flight. Although Osorio's victory ended Chile's period of independence (1810–1814), known as the Patria Vieja, it did not stop the Chileans from regrouping and launching a second war, which ultimately freed them from Spanish rule.

See also **Wars of Independence, South America.**

BIBLIOGRAPHY

Luis Galdames, *A History of Chile* (1941), pp. 183–184.

Simon Collier, *Ideas and Politics of Chilean Independence, 1808–1833* (1967), pp. 101–102.

Additional Bibliography

Archer, Christon I., ed. *The Wars of Independence in Spanish America.* Wilmington, DE: Scholarly Resources, 2000.

Ibáñez Vergara, Jorge. *O'Higgins, el Libertador.* Santiago: Instituto O'Higginiano de Chile, 2001.

López Rubio, Sergio E. *Los vengadores de Rancagua.* Santiago: Fundación Alberto Blest Gana, 1987.

WILLIAM F. SATER

RANGEL, ALBERTO (1871–1945). Rangel was a prolific and versatile Brazilian writer of regional Amazonian literature, stories, chronicles, historical novels, literary essays, and political histories. He was born on May 29, 1871, in Recife but lived in São Paulo, Rio Grande do Sul, and Rio de Janeiro through his adolescence. He attended the Military Academy in Rio de Janeiro during the transition from the Empire to the Republic and graduated with a degree in science, surveying, and engineering. In 1900 he relocated to Belém do Pará, but, disillusioned with Republican rule and his military career, he left the army and published *Fora de forma*, an antimilitary pamphlet. Previously he had published a few stories in the Symbolist magazine *Cenaculo* (Curitiba, 1895). Upon leaving the army he made his way to Manaus, where he lived until 1907. As secretary of lands, mines, navigation, and colonization of the Amazonas State Government, he traveled throughout the entire region. These experiences are recounted in his books *Inferno verde* (1908; Green Hell, with a preface by Euclides da Cunha) and *Sombras n'água* (1913; Shadows in the Water), two collections of his stories, chronicles, and tales of the Amazon.

From 1907 to 1942, because of his adoption of anti-republican ideas, he lived in self-imposed exile, in Europe, with short trips to Brazil. He took up residence in France, with long stays in Italy, Switzerland, and England. He was one of the few Brazilian writers to be an eyewitness to both world wars in Europe: From World War I came the book *Quinzenas de campo e guerra* (1915; A fortnight of battlefield and warfare); from World War II, he wrote recollections in the introduction to his unpublished memoirs, *Águas revessas* (Backwaters), written between 1937 and 1942 (National Archive, 5 vols). Fleeing that war, he returned to Brazil in 1942 to live in Rio de Janeiro and Nova Friburgo, where he died on December 14, 1945. His other books include *Dom Pedro I e a Marquesa de Santos*

(1916; Dom Pedro I and the Marquis of Santos), *Quando o Brasil amanhecia* (1919; When Brazil Awoke), *Livro de figuras* (1921; Book of Figures), *Lume e cinza* (1924; Fire and Ash), *Papéis pintados* (1929; Colored Papers), and Gastão de Orléans (1935).

See also **Literature: Brazil.**

BIBLIOGRAPHY

Filgueiras, Philomena. "Cronologia biobibliográfica" and "Notícias da obra de Alberto Rangel." In *Quando o Brasil amanhecia: Fantasia e passado*, by Alberto Rangel. Rio de Janeiro: Instituto Nacional do Livro, 1971.

Hardman, Francisco Foot. "Visões da guerra: O Brasil na crise da civilização." In *Discurso histórico e narrativa literária*, edited by Jacques Leenhardt and Sandra Pesavento. Campinas: Unicamp, 1998.

FRANCISCO FOOT HARDMAN

RANQUELES.

Ranqueles, a coalition of Mapuches, Pehuenches, and creole military deserters who settled in the Argentine pampas south of Córdoba in the late 1700s and who followed the leadership of Yanquetruz in the mid- to late nineteenth century. The Ranqueles are best known from Lucio V. Mansilla's description in *Una excursión a los indios ranqueles* (Buenos Aires, 1966), which provides a view of a rural intercultural frontier society. As a unique frontier society with its own forms of social relations that characterized and formalized Indian-creole military and diplomatic interactions, the Ranqueles enjoyed relative autonomy until the Argentine military expeditions of conquest and subjugation in the 1880s.

See also **Creole; Frontiers in Latin America; Malones; Mansilla, Lucio Victorio; Mapuche; Pehuenches.**

BIBLIOGRAPHY

Kristine L. Jones, "Conflict and Adaptation in the Argentine Pampas" (Ph.D. diss., University of Chicago, 1984).

Additional Bibliography

Hanway, Nancy. *Embodying Argentina: Body, Space, and Nation in 19th Century Narrative.* Jefferson, NC: McFarland & Co. Publishers, 2003.

Mansilla, Lucio Victorio. *An Expedition to the Ranquel Indians.* Trans. Mark McCaffrey. Texas Pan American series. Austin: University of Texas Press, 1997.

Weber, David J. *Bárbaros: Spaniards and Their Savages in the Age of Enlightenment.* New Haven, CT: Yale University Press, 2005.

KRISTINE L. JONES

RAOUSSET-BOULBON, GASTON RAUL DE

(1817–1854). Gaston Raul de Raousset-Boulbon (*b.* 2 December 1817; *d.* 12 August 1854), French filibuster. Scion of a French noble family, adventurer in the new colony of Algeria, and supporter of the 1848 Revolution, Raousset saw in the California gold rush the next opportunity to make his fortune. But the ambitions of most French immigrants there were frustrated. Encouraged by Mexican officials who sought European colonists on the northern frontier as an impediment to further U.S. expansion, three expeditions of French colonists from California to Sonora were attempted in the early 1850s, the last and most audacious led by Raousset. It was caught up in the struggle between two powerful foreign banking houses for the right to exploit the fabled mines of Arizona, on the present northwest border of Sonora. Raousset was the colonizing partner of Jecker de la Torre y Cia; state officials supported Barron, Forbes and Company. When Raousset ignored state regulations and the company cut off his supplies, he tried to foment an independence movement on the frontier. Defeated by state forces, he was deported. Undaunted, he returned two years later. Xenophobic feelings were now growing and Raousset's expedition of 400 men was met and defeated at the port of Guaymas on 13 July 1854. He was executed; his men were deported.

See also **Explorers and Exploration: Spanish America; Filibustering.**

BIBLIOGRAPHY

Rufus K. Wyllys, *The French in Sonora, 1850–1854* (1932).

Horacio Sobarzo, *Crónica de la aventura de Raousset Boulbon en Sonora* (1959).

Hypolite Coppey, *El Conde Raousset Boulbon en Sonora*, translated from the French ed. (1855) by Alberto Cubillas (1962).

Margo Glantz, *Un folletín realizado: La aventura del Conde Raousset Boulbon en Sonora* (1973).

Additional Bibliography

Bonaparte-Wyse, Louis-Napoléon, and Marie-Christine d' Aragon. *Gaston Ier: Le rêve mexicain du comte de Raousset-Boulbon.* Paris: France-Empire, 2000.

STUART F. VOSS

RASTAFARIANS. The Rastafarian movement largely emanates from the influence of the Jamaican Marcus Mosiah Garvey (1887–1940), founder of the African Orthodox Church and the Universal Negro Improvement Association (UNIA) in the 1920s. Garvey believed in the unification of black people(s) in the Americas toward a physical return to the African continent for economic, political, and social reasons. With the crowning of Ras ("Prince" or "Lord") Tafari Makonnen as Emperor Haile Selassie I (his baptismal name, meaning "Power of the Holy Trinity") of Ethiopia on November 2, 1930, the socioreligious movement of the Rastafarians was born. Basing their beliefs on Garvey's premise that an African king would signal redemption for black people, followers of this philosophy began to regard Haile Selassie I as the Black Messiah, the leader of black people worldwide in their quest for freedom and respectability. Although Garvey did not embrace this belief in Haile Selassie I as the leader of black people, his basic comments on the origins of a leader for black people were catalytic and fueled interest, support, and involvement for both his enterprise—the UNIA—and the rise of Rastafarianism. The Jamaican Leonard P. Howell purportedly was the first to declare Garvey a prophet and Ras Tafari as the incarnation of the Second Coming. Haile Selassie I was not instrumental in organizing or promoting the Rastafarian movement. In fact, he was a devout member of the Ethiopian Orthodox Church, which was a prerequisite in his political position in Ethiopia. During his 1966 visit to Jamaica told the Rastafarian community that they should refrain from immigrating to Ethiopia until they had liberated the people of Jamaica.

The Rastafarian faith system is an evolutionary one, which adds to its mystique and mythology with seven "original" and basic tenets of the faith: (1) Black people were exiled to the West Indies because of their moral transgressions; (2) the wicked white man is inferior to black people; 3) the Caribbean situation is hopeless; (4) Ethiopia is heaven; (5) Haile Selassie is the Living God; (6) the emperor of Ethiopia will arrange for all expatriated persons of African descent to return to their true homeland; and (7) Black people will get revenge by compelling white people to serve them. Contemporary Rastas worldwide focus on various but not all elements of the basic tenets in their faith systems. Rastafarians often cite the *Holy Piby*, written in 1913 and consisting of portions of the Hebrew and Christian Bibles, as the Rastafarian scriptural text. Strong adherents of the faith believe in a life of simplicity with an avoidance of excessive materialism and the embrace of a diet of "I-tal" foods, those that are pure and free of chemical additives. One who is "dread" is considered Jah (God)-fearing. The famous dreadlocks that identify many proponents of the faith system stem from the Rastafarian prohibition against cutting or using chemical products on the hair. *Ganja* (marijuana) is used by adherents of the faith as a sacrament that accelerates the awakening of the "I in I," the true will and form of Jah. The impact of the Rastafarian faith system is felt throughout the world and with an emphasis throughout the Caribbean and countries in both North and South America.

See also **African-Latin American Religions: Overview; Garvey, Marcus.**

BIBLIOGRAPHY

Campbell, Horace. *Rasta and Resistance: From Marcus Garvey to Walter Rodney.* Trenton, NJ: Africa World Press, 1987.

Lee, Hélène. *The First Rasta—Leonard Howell and the Rise of Rastafarianism.* Translated by Lily Davis and edited by Stephen Davis. Chicago: Lawrence Hill Books, 2003.

Murrell, Nathaniel Samuel, et al., eds. *Chanting Down Babylon: The Rastafari Reader.* Philadelphia: Temple University Press, 1998.

Pollard, Velma. *Dread Talk: The Language of Rastafari.* 2nd ed. Montreal and Kingston, ON: McGill-Queens University Press, 2000.

Rogers, Shepherd Robert Athlyi. *The Holy Piby.* Research Associates School Times Publication, 2000.

EMILY ALLEN WILLIAMS

RAVIGNANI, EMILIO (1886–1954).

Emilio Ravignani (*b.* 15 January 1886; *d.* 8 March 1954), the founder of modern historical studies in Argentina. He was known for his objectivity and impartiality, his minute analysis of a document, his rejection of the anecdote, and his insistence on the complete and accurate publication of a document. He was a born teacher, always ready to help native and foreign students who sought his guidance.

A native of Buenos Aires, Ravignani attended the National University of Buenos Aires, where he received a law degree in 1906 and joined its recently created but short-lived history section. At the time, interest in historical studies was reviving, and scholars like Juan Agustín García, Ernesto Quesada, and Clemente L. Frageiro were demanding that previously ignored documents on the post-Rosas period, especially those in the provinces, be located and consulted. Ravignani was a founding member and head of a second history section in 1915 and then the director of the newly organized Institute of Historical Investigations, which replaced it in 1921. Under the energetic and erudite Ravignani, the institute became a model for other Latin American countries. It collected documents found in national, provincial, foreign, and private archives on a wide variety of subjects, for Ravignani believed a historian should be deeply grounded in the documents and spirit of the period he studied. It published scholarly monographs and assumed editorial responsibility for *Documentos para la historia Argentina,* a rich source of documents pertaining to before 1824.

Ravignani himself wrote numerous works but is most remembered for his *Historia constitucional de la República Argentina* (1926; 2d ed., 1930) and *Asambleas constituyentes argentina* (1937–1939). He had a remarkable ability to obtain congressional funding for the institute. In 1950 he organized the Institute of Historical Investigations in Montevideo. He was the dean of the Faculty of Philosophy and Letters at the National University of Buenos Aires from 1927 to 1931 and 1940 to 1943. Politically, he was an influential member of the Radical Civic Union and a national deputy for the Federal Capital (1936–1942, 1946–1947, and 1952–1953).

See also **Argentina: The Nineteenth Century; Argentina: The Twentieth Century.**

BIBLIOGRAPHY

Ricardo R. Caillet-Bois, "Emilio Ravignani," "Bibliografía del doctor Emilio Ravignani," and Ricardo Levene, "Homenaje a la memoria del historiador doctor Emilio Ravignani," in *Boletín del Instituto de Historia "Emilio Ravignani,"* 2, nos. 4–6 (1957).

Additional Bibliography

Buchbinder, Pablo. "La historiografía académica ante la irrupción del primer peronismo: Una perspectiva a partir de la obra de Emilio Ravignani." *Investigaciones y Ensayos* 51 (January–December 2001): 139–168.

Chávez, Fermín. *El pensamiento nacional: Breviario e itinerario.* Buenos Aires: Nueva Generación, 1999.

Girbal de Blacha, Noemí M. "Emilio Ravignani: Entre la convivencia y compromiso; 'verdad histórica' y acción política." *Investigaciones y Ensayos* 46 (January–December 1996): 207–234.

JOSEPH T. CRISCENTI

RAWSON, GUILLERMO (1821–1890).

Guillermo Rawson (*b.* 25 June 1821; *d.* 2 February 1890), Argentine medical doctor and statesman. The son of a New England physician who settled in Argentina during the Independence era, Guillermo Rawson was born in San Juan. He practiced medicine in his native city and later Buenos Aires, ultimately becoming a professor of medicine at the University of Buenos Aires. He took a special interest in matters of public health and in 1880 was the principal founder of the Argentine Red Cross.

Rawson's political career began in the 1840s in San Juan, where as a member of the legislature he took a cautious yet public stand against the dictatorship of Juan Manuel de Rosas. Privately he worked for the overthrow of Rosas, in cooperation with his fellow *sanjuanino* Domingo Sarmiento (from whom he subsequently became estranged despite their shared liberal ideology). After the fall of Rosas, Rawson served in the Congress and held other positions, of which the most important was minister of the interior during the presidency of Bartolomé Mitre (1862–1868). As minister he coped with a rash of provincial uprisings, and worked vigorously to promote immigration and infrastructure development.

See also **Argentina: The Nineteenth Century; Mitre, Bartolomé; Rosas, Juan Manuel de.**

BIBLIOGRAPHY

Vidas de grandes argentinos, 2d ed., vol. 3 (1963), pp. 51–54.

Antonio Aguilar, *Hombres de San Juan: El Dr. Guillermo Rawson* (1971).

Additional Bibliography

Maurín Navarro, Emilio. *Tres maestros de la medicina argentina: Rawson, Quiroga y Navarro.* San Juan: Academia Provincial de la Historia, 1972.

Villaverde, Juan. "Guillermo Rawson's Idealistic Vision of the United States." *Américas* 23:8 (August 1971): 25–35.

DAVID BUSHNELL

RAYÓN, IGNACIO (1773–1832).

Ignacio Rayón (Ignacio [López] Rayón; *b.* 1773; *d.* 2 February 1832), Mexican insurgent leader. Born in Tlalpujahua, he studied at Valladolid, and became a lawyer in 1796. He joined Miguel Hidalgo y Costilla (1753–1811) in Maravatío in October 1810 and became his private secretary. In Guadalajara, Hidalgo named him secretary of state. In March 1811, in Saltillo, he was named acting chief of the army while Hidalgo traveled to the United States and became the principal leader after the first insurgent chiefs died. Rayón reorganized his troops in Zitácuaro and, in August 1811, formed a government, the Suprema Junta Nacional Americana, which he headed. He drafted a plan for a constitution and attempted several times to establish relations with the United States.

Insurgent defeats and divisions among the members of the Suprema Junta cost him the leadership of the movement. Against his wishes, José María Morelos y Pavón (1765–1815) then convened a congress (El Supremo Congreso Nacional Americano), in September 1813, in which Rayón represented Michoacán. So ordered by Congress, he took charge of the province of Oaxaca. After the loss of its capital to the royalists, he moved on to Puebla, and in Zacatlán suffered a serious defeat in September 1814. He joined his brother Ramón (1775–1839) in Cerro del Cóporo, where he helped in its defense and where he stayed until September 1816. When he disavowed the insurgent government of the Junta de Jaujilla, the junta ordered his arrest, and Rayón was taken prisoner by

Nicolás Bravo. In December 1817 he was captured by the royalists and condemned to death, but he requested amnesty and won his freedom in 1820. After independence, Rayón served as treasurer of San Luis Potosí, commanding general of Jalisco, and president of the Military Tribunal. He died in Mexico City.

See also **Chilpancingo, Congress of; Mexico: 1810–1910.**

BIBLIOGRAPHY

José María Miquel I Vergés, *Diccionario de insurgentes* (1969), pp. 338–341.

Ignacio Oyarzábal and Ignacio Rayón, *La independencia según Ignacio Rayón* (1985).

Additional Bibliography

Herrejón Peredo, Carlos, and Ignacio López Rayón. *Morelos: Documentos inéditos de vida revolucionaria.* Zamora: Colegio de Michoacán, 1987.

Pérez Escutia, Ramón Alonso. *Ignacio López Rayón: Militar y político de la Independencia.* Morelia: Comité Editorial del Gobierno de Michoacán, 1985.

VIRGINIA GUEDEA

READ, MARY (late 1600s–c. 1720).

Mary Read (*b.* late 1600s; *d.* c. 1720), early-eighteenth-century pirate. Read was born out of wedlock in England in the late seventeenth century. Her mother had been married to a sailor who either died or abandoned her and their young son while at sea. Shortly thereafter, the son died and Read was born. As a ruse to receive financial support from her deceased son's grandmother, Read's mother disguised the young girl as a boy and claimed that the imposter was the sailor's offspring. Such trickery proved successful and would become Read's modus operandi throughout her life. She went on to serve in the British army in the Low Countries and married a fellow trooper.

When Read's husband died, she resumed her masquerade as a man and joined a Dutch vessel bound for the West Indies. Pirates raided the ship and took on Read, still in disguise, as a fellow pirate. Read and her companions took advantage of the king's proclamation of 1717, which offered amnesty to pirates who turned themselves in. They later joined the British privateering ship *Griffin* with the intention of raiding the Spanish. However, Read and her crewmates mutinied and resumed their piracy under the leadership of Captain "Calico Jack" Rackam. During this period, Read and Anne Bonny met and began a close friendship.

By all accounts, Read displayed enthusiasm, skill, and fortitude in her trade. In one incident, she dueled to the death with another pirate who had threatened her lover. Read was brought to trial in 1720, but escaped the hangman's noose because she was pregnant. Shortly thereafter, fever overtook Read and she died in prison.

See also **Bonny, Anne; Piracy.**

BIBLIOGRAPHY

Charles Johnson, *A General History of the Robberies and Murders of the Most Notorious Pirates from Their First Rise and Settlement in the Island of Providence to the Present Year,* edited by Arthur L. Hayward (1926).

George Woodbury, *The Great Days of Piracy in the West Indies* (1951).

Rafael Abella, *Los piratas del Nuevo Mundo* (1989).

Additional Bibliography

Pennell, C. R. *Bandits at Sea: A Pirates Reader.* New York: New York University, 2001.

                                    JOHN J. CROCITTI

REAL ALTO. Real Alto, a large village site of the Early Formative Valdivia Culture of coastal Guayas Province, Ecuador. It is located near the modern town and estuary of Chanduy, on a low ridgetop between the seashore and the floodplain of the Verde River. Excavations conducted there in 1974–1975 by archaeologist Donald Lathrap and colleagues, and by the latter during the 1980s, helped transform the understanding of Valdivia society in terms of chronology and social change, community plan and settlement pattern evolution, and agricultural production.

Stratigraphic excavation of cultural features permitted the identification of discrete occupations within the village configuration and confirmed the validity of the eight-phase ceramic sequence developed by Betsy Hill. Although the phase-1 occupation may have conformed to the earlier view of Valdivia as a small-scale egalitarian society of fishermen and shellfish gatherers, phases 2 through 7 exhibit progressive shifts toward greater population density and social complexity. Archaeological indicators of social ranking and status inequality suggest that a complex "big man" political system may have existed as early as Middle Valdivia times.

The Early Valdivia village was laid out in a horseshoe shape with small, flimsy dwellings (probably housing a small nuclear family) forming a ring around a small open plaza. At the opening of the U-shaped plan is evidence of ritual activity, presumably of a communal nature. By phase 3, the Real Alto village had grown to a maximum size of 31 acres through a doubling of the previous U-shaped configuration into an elliptical plan measuring 440 yards x 330 yards. Dwellings again formed a dense ring around a long plaza, but the house structures were much larger and more permanent in their construction, probably housing larger extended families of eight to twelve people. At the center of the new configuration were two small opposing mounds, each supporting a ceremonial structure. To the west was a funerary facility or charnel house, while the eastern mound supported a communal structure that, judging from its internal midden refuse, had ritual functions. By Late Valdivia times (phase 6–7), the habitation area had become reduced within the village as small satellite settlements appeared adjacent to floodplain agricultural plots and the ceremonial precinct began to serve a wider local area. Mortuary patterning at Real Alto and other Valdivia sites suggests a central political and/or ritual role for high-status females from phase 3 through phase 8.

Although exploitation of maritime resources in a constant, agriculture formed an integral part of the Real Alto economy throughout the sequence, as shown by the presence of large grinding stones, corn kernel impressions in pottery, and direct botanical evidence. Research by archaeobotanist Deborah Pearsall and associates has documented a variety of plant cultigens, including two varieties of maize, canavalia beans, root crops (including manioc, arrowroot, lleren, and canna), cotton, and chili peppers.

The phase 3 town configuration may have been laid out as a "cosmogram" with a distinct intercardinal orientation and alignments toward heliacal risings that signaled fixed points in the planting season as well as the Valdivia ritual calendar.

See also **Valdivia Culture; Valdivia, Ecuador.**

BIBLIOGRAPHY

Emilio Estrada, *Valdivia: Un sitio arqueológico formativo en la provincia del Guayas, Ecuador* (1956).

Betsy D. Hill, "A New Chronology of the Valdivia Ceramic Complex from the Coastal Zone of Guayas Province, Ecuador," in *Ñawpa Pacha* 10–12 (1972–1974): 1–32.

Donald W. Lathrap et al., *Ancient Ecuador: Culture, Clay, and Creativity, 3000–300 B.C.* (1975).

Donald W. Lathrap et al., "Real Alto: An Ancient Ceremonial Center," in *Archaeology* 30, no. 1 (1977): 2–13.

Deborah M. Pearsall, "An Overview of Formative Period Subsistence in Ecuador: Paleoethnobotanical Data and Perspectives," in *Diet and Subsistence: Current Archaeological Perspectives* (1988).

James A. Zeidler, "Maritime Exchange in the Early Formative Period of Ecuador: Geo-Political Origins of Uneven Development," in *Research in Economic Anthropology,* edited by Barry L. Isaac, vol. 13 (1991), pp. 247–268.

Additional Bibliography

Chandler-Ezell, Karol, Deborah M. Pearsall, and James A. Zeidler. "Root and Tuber Phytoliths and Starch Grains Document Manioc (*Manihot esculenta*), Arrowroot (*Maranta arundinacea*), and Llerén (*Calathea* sp.) at the Real Alto Site, Ecuador." *Economic Botany* 60, no. 2 (2006): 103–120.

Marcos, Jorge G. *Real Alto: La historia de un centro ceremonial Valdivia.* 2 vols. Quito, Ecuador: Corporación Editora Nacional, 1988.

Marcos, Jorge G. *Los pueblos navegantes del Ecuador prehispánico.* Quito, Ecuador: Ediciones Abya-Yala, 2005.

Meggers, Betty J., Clifford Evans, and Emilio Estrada. *Early Formative Period of Coastal Ecuador: The Valdivia and Machalilla Phases.* Washington, DC: Smithsonian Institution, 1965.

Pearsall, Deborah M., Karol Chandler-Ezell, and James A. Zeidler. "Maize in Ancient Ecuador: Results of Residue Analysis of Stone Tools from the Real Alto Site." *Journal of Archaeological Science* 31, no. 4 (2004): 423–442.

Perry, Linda, Ruth Dickau, Sonia Zarrillo, et al. "Starch Fossils and the Domestication and Dispersal of Chili Peppers (*Capsicum* spp. L.) in the Americas." *Science* 315, no. 5814 (16 February 2007): 986–988.

Zeidler, James A. "Cosmology and Community Plan in Early Formative Ecuador: Some Lessons from Tropical Ethnoastronomy." *Additional Studies Presented to Reiner Tom Zuidema on the Occasion of His 70th Birthday. Journal of the Steward Anthropological Society* 26, nos. 1–2 (1998): 37–68.

Zeidler, James A. "Gender, Status, and Community in Early Formative Valdivia Society." In *The Archaeology of Communities: A New World Perspective,* edited by Marcello A. Canuto and Jason Yaeger, 161–181. London: Routledge, 2000.

JAMES A. ZEIDLER

REAL CONSULADO DE CARACAS.

The Real Consulado de Caracas was a late-eighteenth- and early-nineteenth-century Venezuelan tribunal for mercantile affairs and the promotion and protection of commerce. The consulship was created by a royal decree of June 3, 1793, and was established in Caracas with jurisdiction over the entire captaincy-general of Venezuela. To facilitate the merchant guild's operation, representatives were also established in Puerto Cabello, Coro, Guiana, Maracaibo, Cumaná, and the islands of Margarita and Trinidad. Because of its autonomy, the institution rapidly became a recourse and center of power for the elite of Caracas, who took control of it. Its functions included exposing and solving maritime crimes, increasing commerce and agricultural production, improving lines of communication, introducing new cultivation techniques, and maintaining a pool of skilled labor. During independence, the guild became a point of conflict as its members were somewhat divided over trade. Planters and landholders, many of whom were creoles, sought free trade, whereas the mainly Spanish merchants preferred a continuation of Spain's monopoly trade arrangement. After independence in 1810, it functioned sporadically until it was eliminated in 1821.

See also **Commercial Policy: Colonial Spanish America; Judicial Systems: Spanish America.**

BIBLIOGRAPHY

Mercedes M. Álvarez F., *El tribunal del Real Consulado de Caracas: Contribución al estudio de nuestras instituciones,* 2 vols. (1967).

Humberto Tandron, *The Consulado of Caracas and Venezuela's Overseas Commerce, 1793–1811* (Ph.D. diss., Columbia University, 1970).

Additional Bibliography

McKinley, P. Michael. *Pre-Revolutionary Caracas: Politics, Economy, and Society, 1777–1811.* Cambridge, U.K., and New York: Cambridge University Press, 1985.

Tarver Denova, H. Micheal, and Julia C. Frederick. *The History of Venezuela*. Westport, CT: Greenwood Press, 2005.

INÉS QUINTERO

REAL CUERPO DE MINERÍA.

Real Cuerpo de Minería, the guild of mine operators and refiners formally created in late-eighteenth-century Mexico and Peru. Impetus for this reform came in 1771 from the inspector general of New Spain, don José de Gálvez, probably as a result of his conversations with Mexican mine operators. Gálvez complained that the miners of Spanish America lacked the organizational structure to regulate the industry or improve its technological standards.

In 1776, Mexican mine operators received royal permission to establish a formal guild. The decree ordered the *cuerpo* to form a tribunal for adjudication of mining cases, with the tribunal drawing up mining ordinances to regulate the industry. Charles III approved the revised ordinances in 1783. Through a small tax on each mark of silver produced, the guild paid the costs of the tribunal and of the mining school, which opened in 1792.

As Secretary of the Indies, Gálvez created similar guilds in the Peruvian and Río de la Plata viceroyalties, with the Mexican mining code adapted to fit local circumstances. The Peruvian guild began functioning in Lima in 1787, although it failed to establish a mining school. After considerable delay, the Potosí tribunal opened officially in 1794.

The guilds gave miners an institutional voice, which they used to obtain tax reductions and other concessions from the crown, but they were less successful as instruments of technological change within the industry.

See also **Mining: Colonial Spanish America; Potosí.**

BIBLIOGRAPHY

Walter Howe, *The Mining Guild of New Spain and Its Tribunal General, 1770–1821* (1949).

J. R. Fisher, *Silver Mines and Silver Miners in Colonial Peru, 1776–1824* (1977).

Rose Marie Buechler, *The Mining Society of Potosí, 1776–1810* (1981), esp. chap. 3.

Miguel Molina Martínez, *El Real Tribunal de Minería de Lima (1785–1821)* (1986).

Additional Bibliography

Brading, David. A. *Miners and Merchants in Bourbon Mexico, 1763–1810*. Cambridge: Cambridge University Press, 1971.

Castillo Martos, Manuel, ed. *Minería y metalurgia: Intercambio tecnológico y cultural entre América y Europa durante el período colonial español*. Sevilla: Muñoz Montoya y Montraveta Editores, 1994.

Falcón Gutiérrez, José Tomás. *Guanajuato, minería, comercio y poder: Los criollos en el desarrollo económico y político del Guanajuato de las postrimerías del siglo XVIII*. Guanajuato: La Rana, 1998.

KENDALL W. BROWN

REAL DE AZÚA, CARLOS (1916–1977).

Carlos Real de Azúa (*b.* 15 March 1916; *d.* 16 July 1977), Uruguayan intellectual, historian, and essayist. Real de Azua was one of the most brilliant essayists of the so-called Generation of '45. His work consists of over 180 publications and in its breadth is typical of this avidly intellectual and political generation. Writings on travel, literature, Spanish-American culture, political science, history, and historiographical criticism are only some of the areas included in his multifaceted intellectual life. His works are essential references to understanding the spiritual trends in the arts during the nineteenth century: romanticism, classicism, and modernism. Through his first book, *España de cerca y de lejos* (1943) and his critique of the work of José Enrique Rodó, he contributed to the debate over Spain's legacy in Latin America and especially Uruguay. His work is a fundamental part of the political science of Uruguay. *El patriciado uruguayo* (1961), perhaps his most successful book, analyzes what was a recurring preoccupation of his work: the formation of the Uruguayan nation-state and the role of the elite. Other works include *El impulso y su freno* (1964), *La clase dirigente* (1969), *Uruguay: Una sociedad amortiguadora?* (1984), and "Política, poder y partidos" in Luis Benvenuto et al., *Uruguay Hoy* (1971). Real de Azua was a professor at the University of the Republic, where he taught a variety of courses.

See also **Journalism; Uruguay: The Twentieth Century.**

BIBLIOGRAPHY

Vigencia de Carlos Real de Azúa (1987).

Additional Bibliography

Cotelo, Rubén. *Carlos Real de Azúa de cerca y de lejos: Diez bocetos sobre su personalidad.* Montevideo: Ediciones del Nuevo Mundo, 1987.

Vázquez Franco, Guillermo. *La historia y sus mitos: A propósito de un libro de Real de Azúa, comentarios, digresiones, reflexiones.* Montevideo: Cal y Canto: Distribuye Gussi, 1994.

CARLOS FILGUEIRA

REAL HACIENDA. The *real hacienda* (royal treasury) encompassed all state fiscal activities in the Spanish Indies: collection of taxes, disbursement of funds to meet colonial needs, remission of surplus revenues to Castile, accounting and auditing (Contaduría), and all other functions involved in the oversight, protection, and promotion of royal fiscal interests. From the time of discovery late in the fifteenth century, state treasury officials were on the spot to ensure the Catholic monarchs their proper share of the fruits of conquest. As Spain extended its domination over the Indies, the Hapsburgs sent more fiscal officials and established formal royal treasury districts (*cajas*) to implant the fiscal authority of the state in bustling port cities, mining centers, administrative market centers, key military outposts, and areas with large indigenous populations. These *cajas* and the officials serving in them—accountants (*contadores*), treasurers (*tesoreros*), factors or business managers (*factores*), quartermasters (*proveedores*), and paymasters (*pagadores*)—constituted an integral part of Spanish colonial administration.

The royal treasury system in Spanish America was far more rational and efficient than its metropolitan counterpart. In Spain treasury jurisdictions overlapped and semiautonomous institutions collected taxes, a function which in a modern state properly belonged to the crown. Moreover, medieval privileges (fueros) giving the church, various kingdoms, institutions, and individuals exemptions from taxes, prevented establishment of a uniform tax and fiscal system for early modern Spain. In the Indies, however, the crown, perhaps because of the fragmented, unequal system at home, established a far more unified, rational, and efficient system than the complex, labyrinthine framework which had developed in late medieval and early modern Spain.

Spain set up treasury districts in virtually every area of the Indies. In the Caribbean formal *cajas* replaced supervisory treasury officials at the beginning of the sixteenth century in Española, Puerto Rico, Cuba, and Jamaica. Mexican accountants began keeping their first ledgers in 1521, the year of the final conquest of Tenochtitlán. In Peru both Lima and Cuzco had royal treasuries by the mid-1530s, and in New Granada, Santa Fe de Bogotá had a *caja* by 1538. In Upper Peru the mining center of Potosí became a royal treasury district in 1549, four years after the discovery of the silver-rich Cerro de Potosí. As the Spanish presence in the Indies grew, new treasuries emerged in the sixteenth and seventeenth centuries to create a fiscal network of *cajas* linked closely to the matrix treasuries in the viceregal capitals of Lima and Mexico City.

Royal *cajas* functioned in very much the same manner in most areas of the Indies. In larger, heavily populated districts an accountant or comptroller (Contador) kept the books, entered all collections and disbursements of tax revenues, certified all treasury transactions, and held one of the three keys to the royal strongbox (*caja*), hence the term *caja*. A treasurer personally collected taxes, physically deposited the specie in the *caja*, disbursed it as needed, and also held one of the three keys. A factor served as business manager for the treasury, negotiated with factors in other districts, and safeguarded the supplies, arms, and munitions in royal warehouses. A fourth official, initially the *veedor*, supervised the weighing and smelting of gold and silver and all activities relating to mining and minting, but in the seventeenth century the *veedor* gave way to an assayer (*ensayador*) and a bullion-smelting expert (*fundador*). In major treasuries myriad accountants, bookkeepers, and minor functionaries assisted the chief accountant and treasurer or royal officials (*oficiales reales*), as they were called. In minor *cajas* no coterie of bureaucrats was necessary, and oftentimes one official took on all treasury duties.

The crown rigidly prescribed the conduct of royal treasury officials. They could not deposit or disburse funds from the *caja* unless all three keyholders were present, usually the accountant, treasurer, and factor. They had to keep both a daily record of receipts and disbursements (*libro manual*) and a ledger (*libro mayor*) listing tax collections and disbursements by tax category (*ramo*), both subject to a sudden audit by royal inspectors and, after 1605, by one of the three auditing bureaus (Tribunales De Cuentas) in Mexico City, Lima, and Bogotá. These tribunals were set up specifically to audit and close all the *caja* district accounts and special ledgers before sending them off to Spain for still another audit by the Central Accounting Bureau of the Council of the Indies.

Officials of the *real hacienda* collected all sorts of revenues including sales taxes (Alcabalas), import-export imposts (Almojarifazgos), thc royal fifth (quintos real) or tenth (Diezmo) levied on silver and gold production, tithes allocated exclusively to the crown (*novenos*), and the sale of certain colonial offices (*oficios vendibles*). They also took in salary taxes imposed on both secular officials (Medias Anatas) and clergy taking posts in the Indies (Mesadas Eclesiásticas or *medias anatas eclesiásticas*). Collecting revenues from royal monopolies such as snow (for drinks and iced foods), playing cards, stamped legal paper, lotteries, tobacco, and mercury, usually paid by a private contract holder, was also their responsibility. Store or bar license fees (*pulperías*), payments for legalization of land titles or validation of residence (Composiciones), and, late in the eighteenth century, pension-fund collections from various public and military officials (Montepíos) all fell under the purview of treasury officials. Moreover, they took in tribute, the major contribution of the indigenous population exempt from most other taxes, as well as contributions for the Indians' legal protectors and hospitals.

Royal officials disbursed funds for a variety of purposes: administrative salaries and expenses, military and naval stipends, war supplies, fortifications, militias, and military subsidies (*situados*) sent to remote areas of the empire such as Florida or Concepción in Chile, where military garrisons defended Spanish interests. At the same time, the treasury expended tax revenue for parish and mission work, hospitals, poorhouses, orphanages, seminaries, colleges, and universities and for other charitable, educational, and philanthropic endeavors.

Record keeping was a simple task, with accountants keeping ledgers of revenues (*cargo*) and expenditures (*data*) as they were deposited or expended.

In 1787, however, Charles III ordered a change to a double-entry system to obtain a clearer picture of the fiscal realities in imperial treasury districts. He also dictated the establishment of separate categories within the royal treasury: one allocated for the general operating funds of the district (*ramos de real hacienda*), another reserved especially for the crown (*ramos particulares*), and still another to be set aside for specific crown or institutional purposes (*ramos agenos*). The move to the double-entry system never worked out, however, and by 1790 accountants were again keeping their ledgers in the old manner, except for Lima, where bookkeepers learned the new methods prescribed by the crown.

The large number of *cajas* in Spanish America by the end of the eighteenth century testifies to the growth and strength of the Real Hacienda in the Indies. New Spain (Mexico) had twenty-three treasuries: Acapulco, Arispe, Bolaños, Campeche, Chihuahua, Durango, Guadalajara, Guanajuato, Mérida, Michoacán, Mexico, Oaxaca, Pachuca, Presidio del Carmen, Puebla de los Ángeles, Rosario, Saltillo, San Luis Potosí, Sombrerete, Tabasco, Veracruz, Zacatecas, and Zimapán along with some lesser subtreasuries. Lower Peru had seven: Arequipa, Cuzco, Huamanga, Lima, Puno, Trujillo, and Vico y Pasco. Upper Peru (present-day Bolivia) had nine, including Arica, Carangas, Charcas, Chucuito, Cochabamba, La Paz, Oruro, Potosí, and Santa Cruz de la Sierra.

A whole host of new treasuries were set up in the last half of the eighteenth century in the Río de la Plata, which had thirteen in all at the close of the colonial epoch: Buenos Aires, Catamarca, Córdoba de Tucumán, Corrientes, La Rioja, Maldonado, Montevideo, Paraguay, Salta, San Juan, Santa Fe de Veracruz, Santiago del Estero, and Tucumán. In 1800 five treasuries were functioning in Chile at Chiloé, Concepción, Mendoza, Santiago, and Valdivia, while farther north in Ecuador treasury officials in the three *cajas* of Cuenca, Guayaquil, and Quito watched over royal fiscal interests. At least ten treasuries fell within the orbit of the treasury of Santa Fe de Bogotá in New Granada, including Antioquia, Cartagena, Cartago, Honda, Medellín, Novitas, Pamplona, Panamá, Popayán, and Río Negro. By 1800 eight *cajas* functioned in Venezuela, in Caracas, Coro, Barinas, La Guaira, Puerto Cabello,

Cumaná, Guayana, and Maracaibo. At least eight had cropped up in Central America, including Portobelo, Chiapas, Guatemala, León de Nicaragua, Trujillo, Sosanante, San Salvador, and Trujillo. In the Caribbean, Española, Puerto Rico, and Trinidad all had *cajas,* while more than thirty were functioning in Cuba at the beginning of the nineteenth century. The distant Philippines also had its *caja.*

These treasuries of the *real hacienda* thus bound the Spanish Indies together into regional groupings, gave the state a significant degree of fiscal control over the Indies, and ensured the crown at least a share of the tax revenues being generated in the empire. The breakup of this system during the Wars of Independence severely affected state-building in many areas of Spanish America in the nineteenth century.

See also **Potosí; Spanish Empire.**

BIBLIOGRAPHY

Fabián De Fonseca and Carlos De Urrutia, *Historia general de Real Hacienda,* 6 vols. (1845–1853).

Gaspar De Escalona Agüero, *Gazofilacio real del Perú,* 4th ed. (1941).

John J. Te Paske and Herbert S. Klein, *The Royal Treasuries of the Spanish Empire,* 3 vols. (1981).

Additional Bibliography

Jáuregui, Luis. *La real hacienda de Nueva España: Su administración en la época de los intendentes, 1786–1821.* México: Universidad Nacional Autónoma de México, Facultad de Economía, 1999.

Maniau, Joaquín. *Compendio de la historia de la real hacienda de Nueva España.* México: Universidad Nacional Autónoma de México, Instituto de Investigaciones Jurídicas, 1995.

Rodríguez Vicente, Encarnación. *Economía, sociedad y real hacienda en las Indias españolas.* Madrid: Alhambra, 1987.

TePaske, John J., Herbert S. Klein, Kendall W. Brown, and Alvaro Jara. *The Royal Treasuries of the Spanish Empire in America.* 4 vols. Durham, NC: Duke University Press, 1982–1990.

JOHN JAY TEPASKE

REBELIÓN DE SAN MARTÍN TEXMELUCAN, PUEBLA 1879.

On April 22, 1879, the peasant farmers of the town of San Martín Texmelucan, Puebla, rose up in arms,

inspired by the ideology of the Community Central Committee formed on August 15, 1877, and by "La Ley del Pueblo" ("The People's Law") a manifesto written by Alberto Santa Fe (1839–1904). The peasants first took the San Rafael hacienda, adjacent to Texmelucan, to recover the lands that the hacienda had appropriated from them. They then set out for Cholula and Atlixco, where they attacked haciendas, merchants, and roads. The uprising ended when army troops captured the movement's leader, Santa Fe, on May 8.

Santa Fe and Manuel Serdán founded the Socialist Party on July 15, 1878, and published the newspaper *La Revolución Social,* which carried Santa Fe's famous manifesto, "La Ley del Pueblo. The manifesto, which was inspired by the ideas of the French philosopher Charles Fourier (1772–1837), whom Santa Fe knew through Fourier's disciple, Victor Considerant (1808–1893), is an agrarian and nationalistic manifesto proposing redistribution of the lands of the large haciendas, the development of a national industry, the replacement of the army with a people's militia, and the establishment of free, compulsory education. Santa Fe had developed these ideas while serving in the army during the war of reform and the French intervention. Santa Fe was freed two years after the uprising of San Martín Texmelucan and rejoined the army, but he was separated from the peasant movement.

See also **Chalco Agrarian Rebellion of 1868; Díaz, Porfirio; Movimiento Chamula 1869; Tomochic Rebellion.**

JOSÉ R. PANTOJA REYES

REBELIÓN SIERRA GORDA.
During the U.S. intervention in Mexico (1847–1848), Eleuterio Quiroz led an indigenous uprising in Sierra Gorda, a region in the state of Querétaro.

In 1847 and 1848 members of the Mexican military critical of how the government was conducting the war against the United States hid out in the Sierra Gorda mountains, where they organized and trained indigenous people and some hacienda owners to help fight their cause. The indigenous people joined the struggle because the dissident military leaders Tomás Mejía (1820–1867) and Mariano Paredes (1797–1849) suspended the government's unpopular wartime measures—a military draft, special taxes, and expropriation of community lands. The indigenous Jonase and Pame of the region had an economy complemented by the cultivation of leased lands and access to forest resources (firewood, coal, hunting, gathering), and the hacienda owners' restrictions on those resources threatened their way of life The Nahuatl and Otomi Indians joined the uprising because they opposed the government's expropriation of their community lands to pay the costs of the war.

In late 1848 and early 1849, indigenous rebels led by Quiroz waged a guerrilla war against the hacienda owners and towns in the region until they formed an army that threatened the towns of Río Verde and San Luis Potosí. They were inspired by the Sierra Gorda Political and Regeneration Plan of March 4, 1849, which opposed the peace treaties between Mexico and the United States, and also sought to reestablish the rights of indigenous peasants to the forests, distribute fallow lands, abolish the perquisites of churches, and eliminate forced labor. The uprising ended with the capture of Quiroz on October 3, 1849 and his execution in December of the same year.

See also **Chalco Agrarian Rebellion of 1868; Guanajuato; Mexico, Wars and Revolutions: Mexican-American War; Mexico, Wars and Revolutions: Mexican Revolution; Movimiento Chamula 1869; Querétaro (State); Rebelión de San Martín Texmelucan, Puebla 1879; San Luis Potosí; Tomochic Rebellion.**

JOSÉ R. PANTOJA REYES

REBOUÇAS, ANDRÉ (1838–1898).

André Rebouças (*b.* 13 January 1838; *d.* 9 May 1898), Brazilian abolitionist, engineer, teacher, and advocate of land reform. A mulatto, Rebouças was the son of Antônio Pereira Rebouças, a national deputy from Bahia. Educated at the military school in Rio de Janeiro as a mathematician and engineer, he became a close friend and adviser to many influential Brazilians, including Emperor Dom Pedro II. After travel and study in Europe in the early 1860s, he returned to Brazil in time to play an important role in the War of the Triple Alliance (1864–1870) as an adviser and strategist. Later, having supervised major engineering projects, including the construction of railroads and docks in Rio de Janeiro, he became a teacher at the Polytechnical School, where

he influenced many students. As an abolitionist in the 1880s he wrote articles, pamphlets, and manifestos; helped create immigrationist and antislavery organizations; advised fellow reformers; and donated his wealth to the cause. With slavery's collapse in 1888, Rebouças and other major abolitionists worked for additional reforms, including popular education and a program of land reform he called "rural democracy." Forced to leave Brazil during the military revolt of 1889, he accompanied the imperial family into exile. He spent the rest of his life in Europe, Africa, and on the island of Madeira, where he died mysteriously ten years to the day after the Brazilian Chamber of Deputies voted to end slavery. Rebouças was the author of many polemical articles, an informative diary, and *Agricultura nacional* (1883), an antislavery work calling for the democratization of Brazil's agriculture for the benefit of ex-slaves, immigrants, and the rural poor.

See also **Slave Trade, Abolition of: Brazil; War of the Triple Alliance.**

BIBLIOGRAPHY

Inácio José Veríssimo, ed., *André Rebouças através de sua auto-biografia* (1939).

Robert Brent Toplin, *The Abolition of Slavery in Brazil* (1972).

Robert Edgar Conrad, *The Destruction of Brazilian Slavery, 1850–1888,* 2d ed., rev. (1992).

Additional Bibliography

Carvalho, Maria Alice Rezende de. *O quinto século: André Rebouças e a construção do Brasil.* Rio de Janeiro: Editora Revan, and IUPERJ, Univ. Candido Mendes, 1998.

Pessanha, Andréa Santos. *Da abolição da escravatura à abolição da miséria: A vida e as idéias de André Rebouças.* Rio de Janeiro: Quartet; and Belford Roxo: UNIABEU, 2005.

Santos, Sydney M. G. dos. *André Rebouças e seu tempo.* Petrópolis: Editora Vozes, 1985.

Spitzer, Leo. *Lives In Between: Assimilation and Marginality in Austria, Brazil, West Africa, 1780–1945.* Cambridge: Cambridge University Press, 1989.

ROBERT EDGAR CONRAD

RECABARREN SERRANO, LUIS EMILIO (1876–1924).

Luis Emilio Recabarren Serrano (*b.* 6 July 1876; *d.* 19 December 1924),

Chilean labor leader, newspaper editor, and politician. Born into modest circumstances in Valparaíso, Recabarren began work as a printer, which provided him with the means to educate himself. A newspaper editor of numerous journals, he also organized workers in the north, particularly the nitrate miners, to protest their horrible living and unsafe working conditions. His organizing efforts, as well as his newspaper editorials, led to his arrest and incarceration for sedition.

Recabarren joined the Democratic Party, then Chile's most left-wing party. Although he was twice elected to the Chamber of Deputies, the opposition refused to seat him, arguing that he advocated ideas that would lead to social discord. After serving more than a year in jail for inciting a strike of railroad and dock workers in 1906, he left for Argentina and Europe.

After denouncing the Democratic Party for its willingness to compromise and to support reformist tactics, in 1912 Recabarren created the Partido Obrero Socialista (POS), a working-class party dedicated to bringing socialism to Chile. Extremely puritanical, Recabarren preached a combination of personal morality, opposing alcoholism and prostitution and emphasizing individual hygiene and education, and dedication to the class struggle as a means of uplifting the masses. Recabarren traveled throughout Chile, personally preaching this message and founding countless newspapers.

Disenchanted with Europe's Social Democratic parties because they had supported their nations' participation in World War I, Recabarren became an early supporter of the Communist revolution. Elected a deputy in 1921, he led the Partido Obrero Socialista to join the Third Communist International. After visiting the Soviet Union in 1922, he returned to Chile to continue his legislative battle to improve the lot of the working class and to oppose the incumbent bourgeois government. Recabarren refused to run for a second congressional term. Apparently despondent over infighting within the Communist Party, in ill health, and perhaps depressed over a failed love affair, Recabarren committed suicide in 1924.

See also **Chile, Political Parties: Communist Party; Journalism; Labor Movements.**

BIBLIOGRAPHY

Paul W. Drake, *Socialism and Populism in Chile, 1932–52* (1978), pp. 44–45, 50, 52, 54, 58, 65, 101, 134–139.

Peter De Shazo, *Urban Workers and Labor Unions in Chile, 1902–1927* (1983), pp. 91, 99, 110–111, 120–122, 135, 141, 187, 221–222, 229, 235.

Additional Bibliography

Arnaiz, María del Carmen, and Michael Monteón. *Movimientos sociales en la Argentina, Brasil y Chile, 1880–1930.* Buenos Aires: Editorial Biblos: Fundación Simón Rodríguez, 1995.

Silva, Miguel. *Recabarren y el socialismo.* Santiago: M. Silva, 1992.

Varas, Augusto. *La formación del pensamiento político de Recabarren: Hipótesis para una investigación histórica.* Santiago de Chile: FLACSO, 1983.

WILLIAM F. SATER

RECIFE. Recife, the capital of the state of Pernambuco, is Brazil's seventh-largest city, with a population of 1.5 million (2007). Although its regional economic primacy was challenged in the late twentieth century by Fortaleza and to a lesser degree by the growing cities of its own *agreste* hinterland, Recife remains the economic, cultural, and political center of the vast Northeast region between the São Francisco and Parnaíba rivers. In the sixteenth century Recife was the country's largest city and the commercial center of the most important sugar region in the world. Its strategic location at the confluence of the Capibaribe and Beberibe rivers on the sugar coast drew attacks by the French in 1561 and by English pirates in 1578, and between 1630 and 1654 occupation by the Dutch, under whom it took the name of Mauritzstad after its governor, Count Johann Mauritz of Nassau. Although Recife's sugar hinterland lost primacy to Bahia after the Dutch invasion, Recife's commercial and foreign-oriented classes gradually overshadowed the traditional planter aristocracy at nearby Olinda, a transition marked by the War of the Mascates (1710–1711) and finally sealed by the city's emergence as provincial capital in 1823, after Brazilian independence.

Its regional pride, peripheral position, and sustained contact with foreign ideas made Recife the center of several nineteenth-century regionalist revolts, notably in 1817, 1824 (Confederation of the Equator), 1831 (*Setembrizada*), 1832 (*Abrilada*), and 1848–1849 (Praieira), a resistance to centralized authority that emerged again briefly in 1911 and 1930. Recife's intellectual leadership continues to be exerted throughout the Northeast and beyond by the Recife Law School, the newspaper *Diário de Pernambuco*, the philosophical and literary Germanism of the "Recife School," and the Federal University of Pernambuco. Dominating a network of smaller towns and subregions throughout the area, Recife reached a population of 100,000 by 1872, and grew steadily by absorbing migrants and rural laborers from the remote backlands and by centralization of the sugar industry. A decaying colonial city in the late nineteenth century, Recife's surges of modernization during the twentieth century gave it a more European look than most Brazilian cities but did not resolve the economic misery, poor health, and illiteracy that characterize the majority of its inhabitants. The social contrasts and tensions underlying the revolts that have punctuated the city's history continue to typify Recife today.

Home to the first Afro-Brazilian Congress (1934), broad programs of urban reform in the Vargas period, and the rise of union activism following the military dictatorship, Recife reflected tensions over citizenship and progress in the twentieth century. These sociopolitical transformations, despite a history of patronage and unequal social relations, exemplify broader Brazilian trends of conservative modernization.

See also **African-Brazilian Cultural and Political Organizations; Agreste; Confederation of the Equator; Maurits, Johan; Pernambuco; Praieira Revolt; War of the Mascates.**

BIBLIOGRAPHY

C. R. Boxer, *The Golden Age of Brazil, 1695–1750* (1962) and *The Dutch in Brazil, 1624–1654* (1957), provide reliable and readable accounts of colonial Recife and environs. Gilberto Freyre, *The Mansions and the Shanties* (1986), and Vamireh Chacon, *A Capibaribe e o Recife: Historia social e sentimental de um rio* (1989), describe the color and variety of the city in the nineteenth and twentieth centuries. For an introduction to Recife as an intellectual center, see João Cruz Costa, *A History of Ideas in Brazil* (1989). Martha Knisely Huggins, *From Slavery to Vagrancy in Brazil: Crime and Social Control in the Third World* (1985), details the relationship between the disintegrating plantation economy and the class structure of Recife, while Robert M. Levine, *Pernambuco in the Brazilian Federation* (1978), integrates the political history of Recife with the history of the Northeast region and Brazil as a whole. The politics of rural mobilizations from the mid-twentieth century through the start of the twenty-first are analyzed in Angus Wright and Wendy Wolford, *To Inherit the Earth: The Landless Movement and the Struggle for a New Brazil* (2003), and in Anthony W. Pereira, *The End of the Peasantry: The Rural Labor Movement in Northeast Brazil, 1961–1988* (1997). Joel Outtes, *O Recife: Gênese do urbanismo, 1927–1943* (1997), explores citizenship, urbanity, and modernization in twentieth-century Recife. For contemporary issues of industrial labor and unionism, see Maurício Rands Barros, *Labour Relations and the New Unionism in Contemporary Brazil* (1999).

ROGER CUNNIFF
OKEZI TIFFANI OTOVO

RECOLETA. Recoleta is an affluent neighborhood in the northern district of Buenos Aires. In the early eighteenth century, the French Franciscan order of the Padres Recoletos built a chapel and convent in the area. The chapel became the Basilica Nuestra Señora del Pilar, completed in 1732. In 1822 the order was dissolved and the woods it owned near the basilica became the Northern Cemetery, or Cementerio de la Recoleta. The cemetery contains the mausoleums of prominent men and women, including Bartolome Mitre, Domingo Faustino Sarmiento, and Eva Perón.

Recoleta became more heavily populated after the 1871 yellow fever epidemic, when the well-off fled from the more affected southern neighborhoods of the city. By the late nineteenth century many French-style palaces and villas had been built in the area, especially on Avenida Alvear. The University of Buenos Aires Law School, an institution crucial to the maintenance of Argentina's elite, was built close to the Basilica del Pilar. In 1910 the intendant Joaquin de Anchorena ordered the redesigning of the neighborhood's plazas and squares and the building of the Palais de Glace, originally an ice rink and ballroom for elite social affairs, which serves as an art gallery in the early twenty-first century. In 1932 the Hotel Alvear opened, for decades the most expensive five-star hotel in Latin America. In 1968 the Jockey Club, a club of wealthy horse breeders, moved to Recoleta as well.

Since the 1960s the verdant areas that surround the cemetery and the basilica, known as Plaza Francia, host an artisans' market and numerous street artists. In 1980 architects Clorindo Testa, Jacques Bedel, and Luis Benedit remodeled an eighteenth-century building that had belonged to the Franciscans to build the Recoleta Cultural Center. The Buenos Aires Design Center was opened in the early 1990s. Especially on weekends, the Plaza Francia and its cultural spaces and activities attract thousands of people, who also patronize the varied cafes and restaurants of the area.

See also **Argentina: The Twentieth Century; Buenos Aires.**

BIBLIOGRAPHY

Cutolo, Vicente. *Historia de los barrios de Buenos Aires.* Buenos Aires: Elche, 1998.

Lafuente Marchain, Ricardo. *El barrio de la Recoleta.* Buenos Aires: Municipalidad de la Ciudad de Buenos Aires, 1973.

Luque Lagleyze, Julio. *Apuntes sobre el barrio de la Recoleta.* Buenos Aires: Cuadernos del Águila, 1990.

Nogués, Germinal. *Buenos Aires, ciudad secreta.* Buenos Aires: Sudamericana, 1996.

VALERIA MANZANO

RECÔNCAVO. Recôncavo, literally "bay shore," a semitropical area of the state of Bahia in Brazil surrounding the Bay of All Saints and extending inland approximately 25 miles. Heavy, black, fertile soil called *massapê* covers the landscape of rolling fields and shallow valleys, and navigable estuaries of several rivers emptying into the bay penetrate the Recôncavo. These waterways facilitated rapid Portuguese development of the area in the mid-1500s, and the Recôncavo soon became Brazil's most densely populated region and an important producer of sugar, tobacco, and manioc.

Sugar production in the Recôncavo—particularly in the northeastern section—began in the 1530s. Under the Portuguese, the Recôncavo produced much of the world's sugar. Sugar and tobacco formed the basis of a slaveholding plantation society headed by a largely endogamous rural oligarchy. This planter aristocracy, by virtue of both its wealth and its proximity to Salvador, dominated the economic, social, and political life of the colony.

See also **Bahia; Plantations; Slavery: Brazil; Sugar Industry; Tobacco Industry.**

BIBLIOGRAPHY

Harry William Hutchinson, *Village and Plantation Life in Northeastern Brazil* (1957).

Paul V. A. Williams, *Primitive Religion and Healing: A Study of Folk Medicine in North-East Brazil* (1979).

Esterzilda Bernstein De Azevedo, *Arquitectura do acúcar: Engenhos do Recôncavo Baiano no período colonial* (1990).

Additional Bibliography

Alves, Aristedes. *Areas de proteçao ambiental da Bahia.* Salvador: Centro de Recursos Ambientais, 2000.

Barickman, B.J. *A Bahian Counterpoint: Sugar, Tobacco, Cassava, and Slavery in the Reconcavo, 1780–1860.* Stanford, CA: Stanford University Press, 1998.

Oliveira, Waldir Freitas. *A crise da economia açucareira do Reconcavo na segunda metade do século XIX.* Salvador: Universidade Federal da Bahia, Centro de Estudos Baianos: Fundação Casa de Jorge Amado, 1999.

CARA SHELLY

RECOPILACIÓN DE LEYES DE LAS INDIAS. *Recopilación de Leyes de las Indias,* compilation of legislation related to the New World. The *Recopilación de leyes de los reynos de las Indias,* published in Madrid in 1681, is a four-volume collection of laws relating to the Indies. Initiated by order of the Council of the Indies in 1624, it tried to systematize laws promulgated since Columbus's exploration of the New World. Antonio de León Pinelo was the principal author of the work, but Juan de Solórzano Pereira's contribution in settling the final form of the collection also deserves recognition. The draft was completed in 1636, but several successive financial crises prevented its publication for decades. Finally, 3,300 copies were printed in 1681. In addition to organizing more than eleven thousand laws for imperial officials, the *Recopilación,* in D. A. Brading's words, "demonstrated the justice and legitimacy of Spanish rule in the New World."

The *Recopilación* consists of nine parts (*libros*) which ordered legislation related to the following major topics: the church, clerics, educational institutions, and publishing (I); councils, audiencias, and related staff associated with the provision of justice (II); viceroys, presidents, the military, and lesser offices (III); discovery, conquest, settlement, local government and services, and mines and commerce (IV); district administration, the supervision of the medical profession, judicial procedures, residencias (V); the native population and its treatment and financial and labor obligations, encomiendas and repartimientos (VI); special investigations, the black and mulatto population, jails and judicial sentences (VII); taxes and their collection, the sale of offices, treasury and accounting offices and their responsibilities (VIII); the House of Trade, oversight of trade to and from the Indies, naval personnel, travel and travelers to and from the Indies, the merchant guilds of Mexico City and Lima (IX). Fortunately, the *Recopilación* contains a detailed index.

Described by Clarence H. Haring as "one of the most humane, and one of the most comprehensive, codes published for any colonial empire," the *Recopilación* contains legislation that illuminates much of the colonies' institutional structure and procedure. Nearly all of its prescriptions should, however, be read as statements of good intentions rather than actual statutes that were enforced.

See also **Council of the Indies; Judicial Systems: Spanish America; Solórzano Pereira, Juan de; Spanish Empire.**

BIBLIOGRAPHY

Recopilación de leyes de los reynos de las Indias, 4 vols. (1681; repr. 1973).

Clarence H. Haring, *The Spanish Empire in America* (1947), pp. 110–114.

D. A. Brading, *The First America: The Spanish Monarchy, Creole Patriots, and the Liberal State 1492–1867* (1991), pp. 213–215.

Additional Bibliography

Domínguez Ortiz, Antonio. *La sociedad americana y la corona española en el siglo XVII.* Spain: M. Pons, 1996.

Mark A. Burkholder

RECUAY. Recuay, style of pottery named for the province from which it was principally collected in the nineteenth century and closely identified with the intermontane Callejón De Huaylas of north-central Peru (department of Ancash). Recuay, defined largely on the basis of ornate funerary vessels of fine white kaolin clay, highly decorated by both modeling and slip painting in red, brown, and black, and by the use of postfiring negative, or resist, techniques, was in use between about A.D. 200 and 600, and has been found in coastal and highland valleys adjacent to the Callejón, but also as far away as Ecuador.

Recuay vessel forms are highly variable and include several different forms, among which are necked bottles, effigy vessels, pots, and bowls. The necked ovate bottles with flaring or flat disk rims sometimes have geometrical designs, or symmetrical humans or animals, painted or modeled in low relief but with corresponding heads in full relief. Effigy vessels of humans or animals, modeled with varying degrees of representativeness, usually with flaring collars or flat disk rims around the vessel apertures, often have an additional horizontal cylindrical pouring spout. Individual males with unique headdresses and earspools are the most common figures; individual females are portrayed with cinched waists and flowing cloth *manta* head coverings, sometimes holding infants in outstretched arms. Highly modeled males sometimes carry shields, play musical instruments, or hold llamas on ropes; unaccompanied llamas or felines also are depicted. Squat, flat-topped, sometimes square pots have modeled scenes of hierarchically arranged human figures, some situated in detailed architectural settings. Hemispherical bowls with pedestal ring bases are painted with simple geometric patterns or with humans or animals. Long-handled spoons, water dippers, and popcorn "poppers" are also known.

Almost half of the some 2,000 known Recuay pots are accounted for from nineteenth-century tomb lootings; thus scanty provenience information severely hampers efforts to define a chronological sequence within the Recuay style. Although subterranean stone-lined and stone-roofed tombs are clearly associated with the funerary wares, little information from modern excavations correlates the distinctive white, red, and black Recuay pottery with a society that produced and used it. The pots reiterate themes of a locally emergent sociopolitical hierarchy, probably newly asserted, which is evident in the portrayals of wealth and position on effigy vessels and in the depictions of pomp and ceremony on architectural vessels, as well as in the few known

Recuay burials that concentrate pots, gold and copper adornments, lathed stone cups, and other labor-intensive artifacts in graves as at Pashash. The presumably commissioned artistry of Recuay ceramics suggests a specialized and stratified sociopolitical order.

See also **Archaeology; Art: Pre-Columbian Art of South America.**

BIBLIOGRAPHY

Wendell Clark Bennett, "The North Highlands of Peru: Excavations in the Callejón de Huaylas and at Chavín de Huantar," *Anthropological Papers of the American Museum of Natural History,* vol. 39, pt. 1 (1944).

Raphael X. Reichert, "The Recuay Ceramic Style: A Re-Evaluation" (Ph.D. diss., UCLA, 1977).

Terence Grieder, *The Art and Archaeology of Pashash* (1978).

Dieter Eisleb, *Altperuanische Kulturer,* vol. 4, *Recuay* (1987).

Additional Bibliography

Kauffmann Doig, Federico. *Mochica, Nazca, Recuay en la arqueología peruana.* Lima: Universidad Nacional Mayor de San Marcos, 1966.

Klein, Cecilia F. *Gender in Pre-Hispanic America.* Washington, DC: Dumbarton Oaks, 2001.

Lau, George F. "The Recuay Culture of Peru's North-Central Highlands: A Reappraisal of Chronology and Its Implications." *Journal of Field Archaeology* 29, no. 1–2 (Spring 2002): 177–202.

Makowski, Krzysztof, ed. *Los dioses del antiguo Perú.* Lima: Banco de Crédito del Perú, 2000.

Zanabria Zamudio, Rómulo. *Visión castrense del antiguo Perú.* Qosqo: Municipalidad del Qosqo, 1994.

JOAN GERO

REDUCCIONES. See **Missions: Jesuit Missions (Reducciones).**

REED, WALTER (1851–1902). Walter Reed (*b.* 13 September 1851; *d.* 23 November 1902), an American military physician. After studying medicine at the University of Virginia and the Bellevue Hospital Medical College in New York City, Reed entered the U.S. Army in 1875. In 1893 he was named curator of the Army Medical Museum and professor of bacteriology at the Army Medical School in Washington, D.C. During the Spanish-American War, Reed directed a study on the origin and spread of typhoid fever that proved mosquitos were the most important carriers of the infection and that dust and uncleanliness helped spread the disease. In 1900, Reed led a commission to investigate a yellow fever epidemic among U.S. Army troops in Cuba. Applying the theories of Cuban physician Carlos Juan Finlay, Reed conducted a series of daring experiments that included the deliberate infection of volunteers to verify that the mosquito transmitted yellow fever. His discovery led to the extermination of mosquito-breeding sites in Cuba and subsequently in Panama, an important step that paved the way for the construction of the Panama Canal. Walter Reed Army Medical Center in Washington, D.C., is named for him.

See also **Diseases; Finlay, Carlos Juan; Medicine: The Modern Era; Panama Canal.**

BIBLIOGRAPHY

L. O. Howard, *The Yellow Fever Mosquito* (1913).

James H. Hitchman, *Leonard Wood and Cuban Independence, 1898–1902* (1971).

William B. Bean, *Walter Reed: A Biography* (1982).

Additional Bibliography

Espinosa, Mariola. "Epidemic Invasions: Yellow Fever, Public Health, and the Limits of Cuban Independence, 1878 through the Early Republic." Ph.D. diss., University of North Carolina at Chapel Hill, 2003.

Espinosa, Mariola. "The Threat from Havana: Southern Public Health, Yellow Fever, and the U.S. Intervention in the Cuban Struggle for Independence." *Journal of Southern History* 72:3 (August 2006): 541–568.

Pierce, John R., and Jim Writer. *Yellow Jack: How Yellow Fever Ravaged America and Walter Reed Discovered Its Deadly Secrets.* Hoboken, NJ: J. Wiley, 2005.

THOMAS M. LEONARD

REEVE, HENRY M. (1850–1876). Henry M. Reeve (*b.* 4 April 1850; *d.* 4 August 1876), cavalry commander in Cuba's Ten Years' War of independence. Cubans dubbed Reeve, the Brooklyn-born son of a preacher, "El Inglesito" because he was tall, blond, and, at first, spoke no Spanish. He came to Cuba in 1869 in an expedition commanded by the former Confederate general Thomas Jordan. Having been taken prisoner shortly after the landing, he soon found himself facing a Spanish firing squad. Having miraculously survived the experience, he joined the forces of the insurgent leader Ignacio Agramonte, who came to hold him in high esteem. Because of his bravery and prowess, Reeve rose rapidly through the ranks, and eventually succeeded Agramonte as chief of Camagüey (1874). When the Cubans began a march toward the west, invading the province of Las Villas, Reeve was appointed to spearhead the offensive. He had gone beyond Las Villas and reached the rich sugar region of Colón, in the neighboring province of Matanzas, when he was killed near Yaguarma, fighting against superior Spanish forces. By then he had participated in about 400 war actions, been wounded ten times, and had lost the use of one of his legs.

See also **Agramonte y Loynaz, Ignacio; Ten Years' War.**

BIBLIOGRAPHY

The best biography of Reeve is Gilberto Toste Ballart, *Reeve: El Inglesito* (1978).

JOSÉ M. HERNÁNDEZ

million hectares were given to about 866,000 peasant families and communities. During the administration of Lázaro Cárdenas (1934–1940), land reform was given a boost when the government organized the peasants into the National Peasant Confederation, which became a pillar of subsequent administrations and formed part of the Partido Revolucionario Institucional (PRI, or Institutional Revolutionary Party) that governed Mexico for nearly seventy years, until 2000. During Cárdenas's administration, almost 19 million hectares were redistributed, of which almost one million were lands with irrigation. Agrarian reform slowed considerably between 1940 and 1964, but gathered pace once again during the administrations of Gustavo Díaz Ordaz (1964–1970) and Luis Echeverría (1970–1976). In those years 37.5 million hectares were distributed to almost half a million agrarian groups. Land distribution dropped markedly during subsequent administrations until 1992, when President Carlos Salinas (1988–1994) had Article 27 of the Constitution amended to modernize and capitalize the legal system governing cooperative ownership.

See also **Cárdenas del Río, Lázaro; Ejidos; Mexico, Constitutions: Constitution of 1917; Mexico, Organizations: National Peasant Federation (CNC); Mexico, Wars and Revolutions: Mexican Revolution.**

FELIPE AVILA

REFORMA AGRARIA, REVOLUTION.

The Mexican Revolution (1910–1917) was predominantly agrarian in nature, which is why the new, postrevolutionary state installed in 1917 made the commitment to distribute the land to the peasants as a means of social justice. This also legitimized the regime and gained it the political support of the peasant beneficiaries.

The agrarian reform is defined by Article 27 of the Mexican Constitution, which establishes that the nation owns the lands and waters and transfers them to the private citizens under its rule, and that the land thus becomes private property. One of the forms of property ownership is cooperative ownership.

The agrarian reform had different phases during the twentieth century. In the years following the Revolution there was only a moderate amount of land redistribution: From 1915 to 1934, 11.6

REFUGEES. *See* **Asylum.**

REGALADO, TOMÁS (1861–1906).

Tomás Regalado (*b.* 7 November 1861; *d.* 11 July 1906), president of El Salvador (1898–1903). As president of El Salvador, the flamboyant Tomás Regalado withdrew El Salvador from the Republic of Central America, effectively terminating that union. He also involved his country in numerous plots and skirmishes.

Regalado, a native of Santa Ana, seized the presidency in November 1898 after a period of political chaos and economic decline. He reduced the national debt, adjusted the tariff structure to help commercial agriculture, and expanded the railroad and port system. Through strong executive authority he ended the threats of invasion by political exiles and restored domestic peace, often suppressing individual liberties. Regalado opposed President Manuel Estrada Cabrera of Guatemala, leading a military campaign against him in 1899 and aiding Guatemalan exiles throughout his presidency. President José Santos Zelaya of Nicaragua, in turn, supported Regalado's enemies.

Regalado is criticized for favoring the coffee oligarchy, of which he was a member. In 1903, for the first time in twenty-six years, El Salvador inaugurated an elected president. Nevertheless, Regalado exercised strong influence over his successor. General Pedro José Escalón, whom Regalado selected because he could be easily controlled.

In 1906 Regalado encouraged Guatemalan expatriates to organize a military campaign against Manual Estrada Cabrera from Salvadoran territory. Hoping to install his own man as the Guatemalan president, Regalado apparently also provided the rebels with arms and personally led the attack on Guatemala. His death occurred during this invasion, near Yupiltepeque, Guatemala.

See also **El Salvador; Guatemala.**

BIBLIOGRAPHY

J. Lizardo Díaz O., *Estrada Cabrera, Barillas y Regalado* (1962).

Patricia Antell Andrews, "Tomás Regalado and El Salvador, 1895–1906" (M.A. thesis, Louisiana State Univ., New Orleans, 1971).

Derek N. Kerr, "The Role of the Coffee Industry in the History of El Salvador, 1840–1906" (M.A. thesis, Univ. of Calgary, 1977).

Additional Bibliography

Flores de Escalante, Aída, and Enrique Kuny Mena. *Tomás Regalado: El último caudillo de Cuscatlán.* San Salvador: Editorial R.H. Dimas, 2004.

PATRICIA A. ANDREWS

REGENERACIÓN. *Regeneración*, a weekly newspaper that attacked the regime of Porfirio Díaz for corruption, elitism, and failure to defend the people's interests. Founded in 1900 by Ricardo, Jesús, and Enrique Flores Magón and others, it continued to be published irregularly until 1918, despite unceasing repression.

While it began by denouncing corruption more than economic oppression, *Regeneración* became a leading force for anarchist ideas in Mexico and was influential in the uprising at the mines of Cananea, Sonora, in 1906. In 1904 it had to move its place of publication to San Antonio, Texas, changing location again in 1905 to Saint Louis, Missouri, to escape border harassment by the Mexican government.

See also **Díaz, Porfirio; Flores Magón, Ricardo; Journalism.**

BIBLIOGRAPHY

James D. Cockcroft, *Intellectual Precursors of the Mexican Revolution, 1900–1913* (1968).

William Dirk Raat, *Revoltosos: Mexico's Rebels in the United States, 1903–1923* (1984).

Additional Bibliography

Albro, Ward. *Always a Rebel: Ricardo Flores Magón and the Mexican Revolution* (1992).

Escobedo-Cetina, Humberto *Ricardo Flores Magón: Semblanza biográfica* (1997).

CARMEN RAMOS-ESCANDÓN

REGIDOR. Regidor, alderman of a city council. The *regidores* were the backbone of a city council (Cabildo). Even small towns had at least four aldermen; the largest cities had many more.

Originally *regidores* were elected to one-year terms by a municipality's property owners, but Charles V soon began to appoint aldermen for life (*regidores perpetuos*). Philip II approved the systematic sale of the post of *regidor* in 1591, and in 1606 Philip III confirmed that purchasers held their positions in full propriety and enjoyed full rights of transferring the positions in perpetuity upon the payment of taxes. This guaranteed that local families would dominate the city councils generation after generation, benefiting financially from decisions the councils made.

Originally highly prized, the post of *regidor* lost its luster as *cabildos* lost authority to royal bureaucrats. From the early seventeenth century to the late eighteenth century, positions of *regidor* in many towns remained vacant for years.

See also **Philip II of Spain; Spanish Empire.**

BIBLIOGRAPHY

Clarence H. Haring, *The Spanish Empire in America* (1947).

Peter Marzahl, *Town in the Empire: Government, Politics, and Society in Seventeenth-Century Popayán* (1978).

Additional Bibliography

Baskes, Jeremy. *Indians, Merchants, and Markets: A Reinterpretation of the Repartimiento and Spanish-Indian Economic Relations in colonial Oaxaca, 1750–1821.* Stanford, CA: Stanford University Press, 2000.

Burkholder, Mark A., ed. *Administrators of Empire.* Brookfield, VT: Ashgate, 1998.

Domínguez Ortiz, Antonio. *La sociedad americana y la corona española en el siglo XVII.* Spain: M. Pons: Asociación Francisco López de Gómara, 1996.

Dym, Jordana and Christophe Belaubre. *Politics, Economy, and Society in Bourbon Central America, 1759–1821.* Boulder: University Press of Colorado, 2007.

Irles Vicente, María del Carmen. *Al servicio de los Borbones: Los regidores valencianos en el siglo XVIII.* València: Edicions Alfons el Magnànim, Institució Valenciana d'Estudis i Investigació: Generalitat Valenciana, Diputació Provincial de València, 1996.

Mariluz Urquijo, José María. *El agente de la administración pública en Indias.* Buenos Aires: Instituto Internacional de Historia del Derecho Indiano: Instituto de Investigaciones de Historia del Derecho, 1998.

MARK A. BURKHOLDER

REGINA, ELIS (1945–1982). Elis Regina was the major female singer of the second wave of bossa nova in the 1960s. Born March 17, 1945, in the slums of Porto Alegre, Rio Grande do Sul, the daughter of a glazier, she appeared on television and radio from the time she was twelve and began recording ballads and boleros for Continental Records in her hometown in 1961 for a teenage audience. She was originally dismissed as a hick by none other than Antonio Carlos Jobim upon her arrival in Rio de Janeiro at the age of nineteen. There her repertoire improved, as she began to sing the music of pianist Edu Lobo and to perform with percussionist Dom um Romão. She soon became widely admired for her powerful voice, boundless energy, and her distinctive way of whirling her arms as if she were swimming while performing. It was her performances in São Paulo, however, that made her a star, particularly her television appearances on the hit show *O Fino da Bossa,* which aired for the first time in 1965. In the same year she paired with singer Jair Rodrigues to make a series of successful recordings, including "Dois na Bossa," said to have been the most popular Brazilian record ever released up to that time.

By 1967 bossa nova was in decline in its native country. Regina had a stormy marriage with composer and record producer Ronaldo Bôscoli from 1967 to 1972. She got into trouble with the military regime for publicly criticizing it while touring abroad, and later was threatened with prison if she did not sing the national anthem at an Independence Day celebration held by the military. In Los Angeles in 1974, she and Jobim recorded *Elis & Tom,* which most consider the best album of her career. Her recordings of music by Milton Nascimento and Gilberto Gil in the 1960s and João Bosco in the 1970s introduced them to national audiences. One of Bosco's songs that she recorded became associated with the campaign for amnesty for those Brazilians forced to live in exile from the 1960s military dictatorship. Unfortunately, Regina's abuse of drugs and alcohol led to her early death on January 19, 1982. Maria Rita Camargo, a daughter of Regina's second marriage to the musician César Camargo Mariano, has since become a star of Brazilian popular music.

See also **Bossa Nova; Gil, Gilberto; Jobim, Antônio Carlos "Tom"; Nascimento, Milton.**

BIBLIOGRAPHY

Castro, Ruy. *Bossa Nova: The Story of the Brazilian Music that Seduced the World.* Chicago: A Capella Books, 2000.

Echeverria, Regina. *Furacao Elis.* Rio de Janeiro: Nordica, 1985.

Perrone, Charles A. *Masters of Contemporary Brazilian Song: MPB 1965–1985.* Austin: University of Texas Press, 1989.

ANDREW J. KIRKENDALL

REGIONALISM. Regionalism can be defined as a sense of place that distinguishes it from other areas within a country. Typically, residents of the region often feel they are not getting their fair share of government revenues, power, or respect. Regionalism is a problem in virtually all countries of Latin America, and is based on perceived climatic, geographical, and ethnic differences, as well as historical factors. In particular, the division of Spanish and Portuguese colonies into separate nation-states followed logics that lumped together disparate regions that had little in common.

Examples abound. The residents of Brazil's northeast, which is located in the tropics and contains more descendants from Africa, felt disconnected from the more temperate center-south of Rio de Janeiro and São Paulo. Indeed, in Pernambuco and in four other provinces an independence movement emerged in 1824 as the Confederation of the Equator, but it was crushed by the central government. Likewise, during the *Revolução Farroupilha* (1836–1845), centered in Brazil's far south, leaders demanded independence, but in the end lost to imperial troops. Because these movements were unsuccessful, they are now termed *regional revolts*.

Regionalism led to the breakup of many Spanish American states. In 1823 Central America declared independence after the first Mexican Empire broke up. The Central American Federation itself disintegrated in 1838, and as a result, the countries of Guatemala, El Salvador, Honduras, Nicaragua, and Costa Rica emerged. Guatemala held off further disintegration in the late 1830s by annexing the state of Los Altos (in present-day western Guatemala), though Los Altos revolted several times in the 1840s. Similarly, Gran Colombia, founded by Simón Bolívar in 1819, separated into the republics of Ecuador, Venezuela, and New Granada (today's Colombia) in 1830. A regional revolt in Texas led to the establishment of a new country in 1836 and annexation into the United States in 1845. The Dominican Republic separated itself from Haiti in 1844. The last successful regional revolt that led to the establishment of a new country was the separation of Panama from Colombia in 1903 under U.S. auspices.

Regional sentiments existed and continue to exist in many other countries as well. In Bolivia, the population of the eastern lowland Santa Cruz department saw themselves as different from the highlanders of La Paz and Sucre. The *cruceños* were virtually ignored during the nineteenth century. In 1876 the *cruceño*

Andrés Ibañez revolted and tried to force the government to accept a federalist regime that gave more autonomy to Santa Cruz. Bolivian troops suffocated the movement, and Ibañez was executed in 1876. Massive migration from the highlands to Santa Cruz has transformed the ethnic composition of the city, but even today Santa Cruz, which provides about 30 percent of Bolivia's GNP, continues to press for greater autonomy from the central government.

Likewise, in Venezuela the city of Maracaibo (the capital of Zulia state) was long isolated from the rest of the country because it was located on the other side of Lake Maracaibo; indeed, it had much easier communication with adjacent Colombia. Regional sentiment was strong because the Zulianos felt that they contributed an inordinate amount to the country's wealth without receiving their fair share of tax revenue. In the nineteenth century this was because of Maracaibo's role as earner of customs duties for coffee exports, and in the twentieth century because of their petroleum fields.

In many countries, negative stereotypes of inhabitants of certain regions persist. People from the Brazilian northeast often feel discriminated against by those in the south because of their darker skin color. In Peru, people from the capital city of Lima look down on the heavily indigenous people from the southern Andean highlands. In Argentina, citizens of Buenos Aires feel superior to the often poor migrants from the northern interior, insulting them as *cabecitas negras* ("little black heads").

The strong sense of regionalism in many countries of Latin America attests to the tenuousness of nation-states and the artificiality of many boundaries. Regionalism has both negative and positive consequences. In the postcolonial period it led to revolts and the division of states into smaller units. However, regional pride can also be a positive force, providing incentives for regions to compete, and leading to greater development.

See also **Indigenous Peoples; Migration and Migrations; Nationhood and the Imagination; Race and Ethnicity.**

BIBLIOGRAPHY

Bushnell, David, and Neill Macaulay. *The Emergence of Latin America in the Nineteenth Century.* 2nd ed. New York: Oxford University Press, 1994.

Cardozo Galué, Germán. *Historia zuliana: Economía, política, y vida intelectual en el siglo XIX.* Maracaibo, Venezuela: Universidad del Zulia, 1998.

Love, Joseph L. *Rio Grande do Sul and Brazilian Regionalism, 1882–1930.* Stanford, CA: Stanford University. Press, 1971.

Palacios, Marco. *La Unidad nacional en América Latina: Del regionalismo a la nacionalidad.* México: El Colegio de México, 1983.

ERICK LANGER

REGO MONTEIRO, VICENTE DO

(1899–1970). Vicente Do Rego Monteiro (*b.* 1899; *d.* 1970), Brazilian painter and poet. Born in Recife into a family of artists, Rego Monteiro manifested artistic talent at an early age. He began his training at the age of twelve at the Académie Julien in Paris. Two years later, in 1913, he exhibited in the Salon des Indépendants. In 1919, two years after returning to Brazil, he had his first exhibition. He returned to Paris in 1922. Before his departure, he left the poet and art critic Ronaldo de Carvalho with ten of his paintings for inclusion in the 1922 Semana de Arte Moderna (Modern Art Week).

Rego Monteiro's work remained virtually unknown in Brazil until the mid-1960s, because of his long absences from Brazil and a devastating fire in the late 1920s that destroyed most of his best works. When he returned to Brazil in 1964, he became closely identified with the modernist movement. National and biblical themes predominate in his paintings. At the same time, eclectic artistic influences punctuate his repertory: futurism, cubism, Japanese prints, black art, the School of Paris, Brazilian baroque, and especially Amerindian art from the island of Marajó.

In addition to painting, Rego Montiero devoted his talents to other cultural pursuits. In the 1950s he organized the First International Congress of Poetry in Paris and founded a literary magazine in Recife entitled *Renovação.*

See also **Art: The Twentieth Century; Literature: Brazil.**

BIBLIOGRAPHY

Arte no Brasil, vol. 2 (1979), p. 686.

Walmir Ayala, "Um precursor de modernismo," in *Arte Brasileira Hoje,* edited by Ferreira Gullar (1973), pp. 193–204.

Additional Bibliography

Atik, Maria Luiza Guarnieri. *Vicente do Rego Monteiro: Um brasileiro de França.* São Paulo: Editora Mackenzie, 2003.

Atik, Maria Luiza Guarnieri. "Vicente do Rego Monteiro: O percurso de um pintor-poeta." In *Aquém e além mar: Relações culturais: Brasil e França,* Sandra Nitrini, editor. São Paulo: Editora Hucitec, 2000.

Oiticica Filho, Francisco. *Vincent Monteiro, poeta cordial: Marcas textuais de sociabilidade literária: Paris, 1946–1960.* Maceió: Edufal, 2004.

Zanini, Walter. *Vicente do Rego Monteiro: Artista e poeta.* São Paulo: Empresa das Artes: Marigo Editora, 1997.

CAREN A. MEGHREBLIAN

REINÓIS.

Reinóis, Portuguese-born residents of Brazil. Corresponding to the peninsulares in the Spanish colonies, the *reinóis* maintained their loyalty to the crown and filled high-level positions above that of the municipality. They also dominated the hierarchy of the Catholic Church and, as powerful merchants, they controlled international trade. Resentment against their political and economic prerogatives fueled Brazilian nationalism in the early nineteenth century.

See also **Peninsular.**

BIBLIOGRAPHY
Additional Bibliography

Diffie, Bailey W. and Edwin J Perkins. *A History of Colonial Brazil, 1500–1792.* Malabar: R.E. Krieger Pub. Co., 1987.

Furtado, Joaci Pereira and Cecília de Lara. *O viver em colônia: Cultura e sociedade no Brasil colonial.* São Paulo: Universidade de São Paulo, Instituto de Estudos Brasileiros, 1999.

Russell-Wood, A. J. R. *Society and Government in Colonial Brazil, 1500–1822.* Brookfield, VT: Variorum, 1992.

SHEILA L. HOOKER

REJÓN, MANUEL CRESCENCIO

(1799–1849). Manuel Crescencio Rejón (*b.* 1799; *d.* 1849), Mexican politician and cabinet minister, creator of the writ of *amparo* (protection). Rejón was born into a poor family in Bolonchenticul,

Yucatán, and educated in Mérida. At an early age he entered politics and agitated for independence. Elected to the national legislature in 1822, Rejón spoke against Iturbide and for liberalism, federalism, and republicanism. Iturbide dissolved Congress and jailed Rejón in 1822. After the fall of Iturbide, Rejón served in the Constituent Congress and was one of the authors of the Constitution of 1824. Repeatedly elected to represent Yucatán in Congress from 1827 to 1834, he attempted to organize popular resistance to Bustamante's overthrow of Guerrero, and was jailed again.

Rejón returned to Yucatán in 1840 and wrote a constitution that included guarantees of individual rights and a writ of *amparo* to protect them. Soon afterward he returned to Mexico City, where he was first arrested and then named to a diplomatic post in Caracas. Rejón served as minister of domestic and foreign relations in 1844 and 1846 before he was exiled and fled to New Orleans. Upon returning to Mexico, he attempted to organize resistance to the United States annexation of Texas and opposed the Treaty of Guadalupe Hidalgo. Rejón served his final term in Congress in 1848 and died the following year.

See also **Amparo, Writ of; Mexico: 1810–1910; Yucatán.**

BIBLIOGRAPHY

Carlos A. Echánove Trujillo, *La vida pasional e inquieta de D. Crescencio Rejón* (1941); *Diccionario Porrúa de historia, biografía y geografía de México,* 5th ed. (1986).

Additional Bibliography

Lerín Valenzuela, Jorge. *Antologia de Manuel Crecencio Rejón: Pionero del juicio de amparo Mexicano, en su esencia,* 2nd edition. Puebla: O.G.S. Editores, S.A.de C.V., 2000.

Moreno, Daniel A. *Manuel Crescencio Rejón, pensamiento político.* Mexico City: Secretaría de Educación Pública, Cultura, 1986.

D. F. STEVENS

RELACIONES GEOGRÁFICAS.

Relaciones Geográficas, a large body of manuscripts and maps or paintings from the sixteenth and eighteenth centuries that were commissioned by the Spanish crown to gain information on the Spanish American colonies. The most unusual and greatest volume of data is found in the 1577 series (actually made in 1578–1589), which, in response to a fifty-chapter questionnaire, details the nature of Spanish and indigenous towns, their origins, pre-Conquest histories, experiences during the Conquest, cultures, and subsequent political and social administration, economic, and military concerns. The greatest number of responses came from New Spain and the Andean region, the wealthiest and most populous colonies.

See also **Colonialism; Spanish Empire.**

BIBLIOGRAPHY

The general nature of the "RGs," as some scholars refer to them, their bibliographical history, and an important study of indigenous languages described in them comprises much of *Handbook of Middle American Indians,* vol. 12, pt. 1, edited by Howard F. Cline (1972), pp. 183–449. See also René Acuña, ed., *Relaciones geográficas del siglo XVI: México* (1985–1986).

Additional Bibliography

Mignolo, Walter D. "El mandato y la ofrenda: La Descripción de la ciudad y provincia de Tlaxcala de Diego Muñoz Camargo, y las relaciones de Indias." *Nueva Revista de Filología Hispanica* 35, no. 2 (1987): 451–484.

Mignolo, Walter D. "La grafía, la voz y el silencio: Las relaciones geográficas de Indias en el contexto de las letras virreinales." *Revista de Letras y Ciencias Humanas (Insula)* 45, no. 522 (June 1990): 11–12.

Mundy, Barbara E. *The Mapping of New Spain: Indigenous Cartography and the Maps of the Relaciones Geográficas.* Chicago: University of Chicago Press, 1996.

STEPHANIE WOOD

RELAÇÕES.

High Courts of Appeal that served as the supreme tribunal in colonial Brazil. Relações were at the top of the colonial administrative structure and exercised broad administrative and political powers in the colonies. There were two Relações in colonial Brazil. The first was in Salvador, Bahia, while the second, created in Rio de Janeiro in 1751, served the southern captaincies. Each Relação consisted of about thirty officials, including *agravistas* (appeals judges), *procuradores* (procurators), and *juizes da coroa* (crown judges). The governor-general or viceroy presided over the

Relação. The Crown considered Relações as reliable sources of information in the colonies. In Brazil the Relação often served as an advisory council on fiscal, economic, and common-welfare matters. Relações also reviewed performances of officials in captaincies following tours of duty.

See also **Judicial Systems: Brazil.**

BIBLIOGRAPHY

Caio Prado, Jr., *The Colonial Background of Modern Brazil* (1967).

Stuart B. Schwartz, *Sovereignty and Society of Colonial Brazil* (1973).

Additional Bibliography

Wehling, Arno, and Maria José C. de M. Wehling. *Direito e justiça no Brasil Colonial: O Tribunal da Relação do Rio de Janeiro, 1751–1808.* Rio de Janeiro: Renovar, 2004.

ROSS WILKINSON

RELIGION IN MEXICO, CATHOLIC CHURCH AND BEYOND. One of the most profound and farthest-reaching effects of Spain's Conquest of the New World was the introduction—especially in Mexico—of the Catholic religion and the institution of the Catholic Church. As church scholars readily point out, the Spaniards left more than the Catholic religion; they left a Catholic culture as well. The degree of Catholic influence on various regions within Mexico depended on the value the individual conquistador placed on religion—for example, Cortés, the person most responsible for the initial conquest of New Spain, considered it of primary importance—and the presence of large native populations for whom organized, formal religion was already an essential aspect of their culture.

The relationship between church and state is of signal importance in understanding the role of religion in Mexico. The origins of the church-state relationship in Mexico goes back to the time of the Conquest, the result of papal bulls or pronouncements known at the time as the *patronato real.* These agreements assigned a number of privileges and roles to the Catholic Church both in the Conquest itself and in the colonization process. In return for its religious monopoly over New Spain, the church also conceded certain administrative rights and decisions to the state. Thus Mexico did not enjoy freedom of religion: the church established a principle of collaboration with the state, rather than pursuing the concept of separation of church and state as in the United States. Given this framework, both the Spanish Crown and its representative, the Viceroy of New Spain, and the Catholic leadership, functioned under hierarchical, authoritarian institutional cultures.

This symbiotic relationship functioned fairly well during the three centuries of colonial rule. Clergy performed a significant role, through the establishment of mission towns, in the expansion of the frontiers, extending into what is today New Mexico, Arizona, and California. Many of the major cities in these states, including San Francisco, Los Angeles, San Diego, Albuquerque, and Tucson, were founded as mission towns. The clergy also performed a political task for civil authorities, acting as Inquisition officials overseeing the censoring of books and other forms of publications promoting revolutionary ideas. Carrying out these traditionally nonreligious tasks often produced conflicts within the church or between religious and civil officials.

The Catholic Church became the privileged church—in effect, the state religion, the only religion legally permitted and financially supported by the Crown. The church helped the state to govern, maintaining its own privileged position with special legal rights for more than three hundred years. Most important, by the early nineteenth century its acquisition of land made it the wealthiest institution in Mexico.

The church's wealth, multiplied through centuries of gifts from its laity, made it a significant economic actor. Because of its privileged institutional position, it became deeply involved in Mexican politics after the country's independence from Spain in 1824. As Mexico evolved into two major political currents in the nineteenth century, liberals and conservatives, the church allied itself with conservative interests, hoping to protect its privileged status. By mid-century the liberals had achieved superiority over their conservative opponents, and after the War of the Reform (1858–1861) they imposed restrictions on the church, forcing it to sell most of its property. These restrictions were eventually incorporated into

Praying for the Pope's health, Basilica of Guadalupe, Mexico City, 2005. A woman holds a portrait of Pope John Paul II during a Mass for the pontiff's worsening health. Despite the growing popularity of evangelical Protestantism, twenty-first-century Mexico remains a largely Catholic country. © ANDREW WINNING/REUTERS/CORBIS

the 1857 constitution. In response, conservatives and their religious allies sought assistance from outside Mexico to impose a European monarch on the populace, resulting in a lengthy civil war that ended in 1867.

When Porfirio Díaz came to power in 1876, the former liberal negotiated an understanding with the Catholic leadership that retained the 1857 constitutional provisions but did not actively enforce them. During the 1910 Revolution, the church leadership once again allied itself with the status quo and was severely punished by the victors through more severe restrictions in the 1917 constitution, which did not recognize the Catholic Church or its small Protestant counterparts as legal entities. The active enforcement of these restrictions led to the unsuccessful Cristero Rebellion (1926–1929), fueled by resistance among clergy and the religious faithful in rural Mexico. In 1992 some of the 1917 provisions were eliminated, and the church regained legal status.

Given this history, the Catholic Church in the latter half of the twentieth century confined itself to teaching religious dogma and focusing on spiritual and family issues. Protestantism, originally confined to small, traditional groups such as the Methodists, came to be dominated by Evangelicals and began to attract more adherents in the 1970s, growing rapidly in the 1980s and 1990s. Despite this dramatic growth, particularly in rural areas, Mexico remains approximately 85 percent Catholic. Religion, and respect for religious institutions, is of great importance in the lives of Mexicans. In survey after survey, Mexicans overwhelmingly report that they believe in God, that religion is important in their lives, and that a majority attend religious services regularly. Mexicans have more confidence in religious institutions than in all other institutions, with the exception of education. The advent of electoral democracy, the 1992 constitutional revisions, and civic respect for clergy have encouraged many clergy to articulate non-religious concerns publicly, including criticisms of human rights violations, exploitation of indigenous cultures, and failures to address economic inequality and poverty. The Catholic leadership played a crucial role in the 1994 and 2000 presidential elections, actively encouraging citizens to participate in the election as both a Christian and civic responsibility. A large minority of laity in Mexico expect their religious leaders to explore broader social and political issues that go beyond traditional religious concerns.

See also **Catholic Church: The Colonial Period; Catholic Church: The Modern Period; Cristero Rebellion; Díaz, Porfirio; Pernambuco; Protestantism; Protestantismo en México.**

BIBLIOGRAPHY

Blancarte, Roberto. *Historia de la Iglesia Católica en México.* Mexico: Colegio Mexiquense, Fondo de Cultura Económica, 1992.

Camp, Roderic Ai. *Crossing Swords: Politics and Religion in Mexico.* New York: Oxford University Press, 1997.

Legorreta Zepeda, José de Jesús. *Cambio religioso y modernidad en México.* Mexico: Universidad Iberoamericana, 2003.

"Religiosity in Mexicans and Americans." *World Values Surveys 1990, 2000.* Available from http://www.worldvaluessurvey.org/.

Tangeman, Michael. *Mexico at the Crossroads: Politics, the Church, and the Poor.* Maryknoll, NY: Orbis Books, 1995.

RODERIC AI CAMP

REMESAS AND DIVISAS.

Remesa (remittance) is the term used to describe the money that migrants set aside from their wages to send back to friends or family in their home communities. Often from Latin America, *remesas* are sent in the *divisa* (currency) of U.S. dollars. Studies conclude that remittances sent to Latin America, specifically Mexico, Central America, and the Caribbean, constitute a significant contribution to those countries' national incomes (see Table 1). In fact, in 2004 an estimated $45 billion was sent in remittances to Latin America and the Caribbean, exceeding the amount of all foreign aid to the region. However, remittances are not unique to Latin American migrants: In 2004 workers all over the world sent more than $175 billion in remittances to their home countries.

Remittances as percentage of GDP, 2000			
	1980	1990	1999
Dominican Republic	2.5	5	15
Mexico	1	2	2.5
El Salvador	1	6	17
Nicaragua	N/A	4	25
Honduras	N/A	1	5
Cuba	N/A	1	4.5
Guatemala	N/A	2	4

SOURCE: World Bank, *The 2000 World Development Indicators*, CD-ROM (Washington, D.C.: World Bank, 2002).

Table 1

Since 1970, migration out of Latin America and the Caribbean has increased significantly, and that increase in migration has produced greater amounts of money remitted back to Latin America. Consequently, remittances have become one of the most significant links between migrants and their home countries. The majority of remittances are sent through money-transfer companies, which typically charge a transaction fee of 10 percent. Less commonly, remittances are transmitted via couriers or travelers, as well as through banks and the mail. Overwhelmingly, remittances are utilized by receivers for daily expenses such as food, clothing, and medicine. Remittances can also assist in increasing quality of life, making investments, establishing savings, and attaining educational pursuits.

Typically, those sending remittances are family members, most often the siblings or children of family members back in the home country. The majority of those sending remittances to Latin America from the United States are undocumented workers or legal residents of the United States whose annual incomes were less than $20,000 in 2004. Scholars have noted the number of Hometown Associations (social organizations of migrants from the same local towns) that collectively send money to their hometowns in Latin America. With increased migration, the number and size of such groups continues to grow.

Increased migration has become an essential factor of the global economy, and family remittances have contributed to bringing Latin America into this context. The money brought into Latin America through family remittances plays a significant role in the national economies of many Latin

American countries. In Nicaragua remittances constitute a quarter of the country's income. In El Salvador remittances have at times exceeded the amount made through exports. Overall, they are becoming a more significant percentage of the overall gross domestic product of many Latin American countries (Table 1).

There is some debate about the positive and negative impacts of remittances on Latin America. On the one hand, they are seen as improving the standards of living and quality of life of many families, as well as stimulating development and the economies of Latin America. On the other hand, case studies allude to the fact that they do little to solve the economic problems of Latin America because they fail to halt migration, which depletes Latin America of its working-aged population and decreases the likelihood of investment by foreign investors or national governments. Some critics point to the unpredictable nature of remittances, which create dependency in recipients and, conversely, for nonrecipients, leads to income inequality.

See also **Economic Development; Migration and Migrations.**

BIBLIOGRAPHY

De la Garza, Rodolfo O., and Briant Lindsay Lowell, eds. *Sending Money Home: Hispanic Remittances and Community Development.* New York: Rowman and Littlefield, 2002.

Despipio, Louis. *Sending Money Home . . . For Now: Remittances and Immgirant Adaptation in the United States.* Los Angeles: Tomás Rivera Policy Institute, 2000.

Lowell, Briant L., and Rodolfo de la Garza. *The Developmental Role of Remittances in Latino Communities and in Latin American Countries.* Los Angeles: Tomás Rivera Policy Institute, 2000.

Orozco, Manuel. "Globalization and Migration: The Impact of Family Remittances in Latin America." *Latin American Politics and Society* 14, no. 2 (Summer 2002): 41–66.

Terry, Donald F., and Steven R. Wilson, eds. *Beyond Small Change: Making Migrant Remittances Count.* Washington, DC: Inter-American Development Bank, 2005.

Waller Meyers, Deborah. "Migrant Remittances to Latin America." In *Sending Money Home: Hispanic Remittances and Community Development*, edited by Rodolfo O. de la Garza and Briant Lindsay Lowell. New York: Rowman and Littlefield, 2002.

ANDREA VICENTE

REMÓN CANTERA, JOSÉ ANTONIO

(1908–1955). José Antonio Remón Cantera (*b.* 1 June 1908; *d.* 2 January 1955), president of Panama (1952–1955). Born into a prominent Panamanian family, Remón received a scholarship to attend the Military Academy in Mexico. After graduating third in his class in 1931, he returned to Panama and was made a captain in the National Police. Remón's attempts to reform and modernize the force were well received, and in 1947 he was made commandant. Under Remón, the National Police became the arbiter of Panama's political fate, making or breaking presidents at the will of the commandant.

In 1951, Remón made a bid for the presidency and, endorsed by a party of his own creation, won the 1952 elections with nearly half the votes. He immediately began a domestic campaign to bring order and prosperity to the country. During Remón's administration there were advances in education, health care, and commerce, but severe restrictions on political parties and labor unions earned him the reputation of dictator. Remón's greatest achievement while in office was the renegotiation of the 1903 Hay–Bunau-Varilla Treaty. The result of his efforts was the Eisenhower–Remón Treaty (1955), which gave Panama additional rights to Canal Zone revenues, ended discriminatory wage practices in the zone, and increased the annuity paid by the United States for the canal. Remón was assassinated in Panama City before the treaty was finalized.

See also **Eisenhower-Remón Treaty (1955); Hay-Bunau-Varilla Treaty (1903); Panama; Panama Canal.**

BIBLIOGRAPHY

Larry La Rae Pippin, *The Remón Era* (1964).

Manuel María Alba C., *Cronología de los gobernantes de Panamá, 1510–1967* (1967).

Additional Bibliography

Romeu, José Vicente. *Del caso Remón-Guizado.* Panama City: Instituto Nacional de Cultura, Editorial Mariano Arosemena, 2000.

SARA FLEMING

RENGIFO CÁRDENAS, MANUEL

(1793–1846). Manuel Rengifo Cárdenas (*b.* 29 December 1793; *d.* 16 March 1846), Chilean trader and politician. At the age of fifteen he went to work for a Spanish trading house in Santiago, later undertaking numerous commercial ventures of his own. In the late 1820s he became a close associate of trader and politician Diego Portales (1793–1837). With the Conservative triumph in 1830, he served as the new regime's finance minister (1830–1835). Rengifo systematically reorganized Chilean finances and implemented policies to promote the commercial predominance of Valparaíso in the Pacific. His presidential aspirations were ruthlessly checkmated by Portales in 1835. Rengifo returned to the finance ministry for a second period (1841–1844), during which his main achievement was the settlement of the long-standing debt arising from the London loan of 1822. His brother Ramón Rengifo (1795–1861) was the author of the still-popular patriotic "Canción de Yungay" (Song of Yungay).

See also **Chile: The Nineteenth Century; Portales Palazuelos, Diego José Pedro Víctor.**

BIBLIOGRAPHY

Osvaldo Rengifo, *Don Manuel Rengifo, su vida y su obra* (1983).

Additional Bibliography

Sagredo B., Rafael. "Chile, 1823–1831: El desafío de la administración y organización de la hacienda pública." *Historia* 30 (1997): 287–312.

SIMON COLLIER

REPARTIMIENTO. Repartimiento (labor levy), the system of forced labor demanded of indigenous communities by the colonial state. In the Andes, the system was also known as the Mita, a Spanish adaptation of the Inca term *mita* and labor service in the mining zone was known as the *mita de minas*. Usually one-seventh of a community's male population between the ages of eighteen and fifty-five was required to be in service to employers who had been assigned Indian labor by the state. Eligibility criteria could vary according to local regulations. For example, in some communities widows within this age group were required to serve, and individuals or entire communities could claim exemption based on some special service that they or their ancestors had performed for the state. In theory, individual men served two to four months of *repartimiento* labor and were then exempt for a year. In practice, however, excessive labor assessments based on outdated community censuses meant that individuals served with greater frequency, and this increased obligation contributed to a further population decline, chiefly through migration, which only intensified labor demands.

Repartimiento labor could be performed on the estates of local elites, but workers also could be assigned to distant work sites, and those who were often stayed at those sites after their *repartimiento* term had expired, sometimes abused by local employers and sometimes earning higher wages for the same, previously *repartimiento,* labor. *Repartimiento* labor was brutal and debilitating, particularly in mercury mines and coca fields, and *repartimiento* obligations caused Indians to flee communities subject to these services, so that rather than stabilizing the indigenous labor force, the *repartimiento* contributed to its dispersal. The system was plagued by the unwillingness and inability of local communities to meet labor quotas and a variety of alternative labor relationships arose, including wage labor and debt peonage.

See also **Encomienda; Mita; Naboría.**

BIBLIOGRAPHY

See the general discussion of indigenous labor in Mark A. Burkholder and Lyman L. Johnson, *Colonial Latin America* (1990). For a detailed study of mining labor see Peter Bakewell, *Miners of the Red Mountain: Indian Labor in Potosí, 1545–1650* (1984).

Additional Bibliography

Baskes, Jeremy. *Indians, Merchants, and Markets: A Reinterpretation of the Repartimiento and Spanish-Indian Economic Relations in Colonial Oaxaca, 1750–1821.* Stanford, CA: Stanford University Press, 2000.

Contreras Sánchez, Alicia del C. *Capital comercial y colorantes en la Nueva España, segunda mitad del siglo XVIII.* Zamora: El Colegio de Michoacán: Universidad Autónoma de Yucatán, 1996.

Menegus Bornemann, Margarita. *El repartimiento forzoso de mercancías en México, Perú y Filipinas.* México, D.F.: Instituto de Investigaciones, Dr. José María Luis Mora: Centro de Estudios sobre la Universidad-UNAM, 2001.

Mira Caballos, Esteban. *El indio antillano: Repartimiento, encomienda y esclavitud (1492–1542).* Sevilla: Múñoz Moya Editor, 1997.

Solís Robleda, Gabriela. *Bajo el signo de la compulsión: El trabajo forzoso indígena en el sistema colonial yucateco, 1540–1730.* México: CIESAS: ICY, Instituto de Cultura de Yucatán: M.A. Porrúa Grupo Editorial: Conaculta, INAH, 2003.

Stavig, Ward. *The World of Túpac Amaru: Conflict, Community, and Identity in Colonial Peru.* Lincoln: University of Nebraska Press, 1999.

Tandeter, Enrique. *Coercion and Market: Silver Mining in Colonial Potosí, 1692–1826.* Albuquerque: University of New Mexico Press, 1993.

ANN M. WIGHTMAN

REPARTIMIENTO DE MERCAN-CÍAS.

Repartimiento de mercancías (distribution of goods), also known as *repartimiento de bienes,* an obligation on indigenous peoples and their communities to purchase goods they neither wanted nor could afford. Merchants, colonial officials, and, at times, community leaders profited from an arrangement in which surplus goods were forced upon the local population that was obligated to pay for these "purchases" with labor service, land, or cash. The goods involved, frequently luxury items, were sometimes never even delivered but were repeatedly resold on paper to other "buyers." This abusive system arose in the seventeenth century and became particularly acute in the eighteenth, when the volume of goods illegally entering colonial markets exceeded the volume imported through the formal Consulado (merchant guild) system, whose merchant members were left with excess stock.

The *repartimiento de mercancías* was a major factor in the depletion of indigenous community resources, in the growth of debt peonage labor, and in indigenous revolts against colonial authority. Sporadic efforts to reform this system, including legalization and heightened regulation of the *repartimiento de mercancías* during the mid-eighteenth-century Bourbon Reforms, failed to curb the worst abuses.

See also **Debt Peonage; Repartimiento.**

BIBLIOGRAPHY

Karen Spalding, *Huarochirí: An Andean Society Under Inca and Spanish Rule* (1984), esp. pp. 188–190, 200–204.

Additional Bibliography

Baskes, Jeremy. *Indians, Merchants, and Markets: A Reinterpretation of the Repartimiento and Spanish-Indian Economic Relations in Colonial Oaxaca, 1750–1821.* Stanford, CA: Stanford University Press, 2000.

Menegus Bornemann, Margarita. *El repartimiento forzoso de mercancías en México, Perú y Filipinas.* México, D.F.: Instituto de Investigaciones Dr José María Luís Mora: Centro de Estudios sobre la Universidad-UNAM, 2000.

ANN M. WIGHTMAN

REPILADO, FRANCISCO.   *See* Compay Segundo.

REPÚBLICA DE TULE.

República de Tule (1925), the name given by the Kuna people on the San Blas Islands off of Panama's Atlantic coast to their short-lived independence in 1925. Since colonial days the Kuna had always lived isolated from the rest of Panama, refusing to accept white rule. In February 1925, instigated by the former chargé d'affaires at the American legation in Panama, Richard O. March, they rose in rebellion against Panama and declared the region an independent republic. In the process many Panamanian police stationed in the area were killed. The government of Rodolfo Chiari quelled the rebellion, and a peace treaty was signed on 3 March 1925. March was declared persona non grata and expelled from the country.

See also **Indigenous Peoples.**

BIBLIOGRAPHY

Ernesto De Jesús Castillero Reyes, *Historia de Panamá,* 7th ed. (1962).

Additional Bibliography

Howe, James. *A People Who Would Not Kneel: Panama, the United States, and the San Blas Kuna.* Washington, DC: Smithsonian Institution Press, 1998.

JUAN MANUEL PÉREZ

REPUBLIQUETAS.

Republiquetas, partisan enclaves that were formed during the Bolivian War of Independence. The War of Independence in

Bolivia (Upper Peru) lasted from 1809 to 1825. Loyalist forces prevailed most of the time; until 1816 the anti-Spanish cause was kept alive mainly in the countryside by partisan forces. Some guerrilla leaders became local *caudillos,* organizing *republiquetas* (small republics). Of the six that can be clearly identified, five were named after their leaders: Juan Antonio Alvarez de Arenales, Vicente Carmargo, Ildefonso de las Muñecas (a priest), Manuel Ascencio Padilla, and Ignacio Warnes. The other *republiqueta,* Ayopaya, was the most enduring, and its leader, José Miguel Lanza, survived and later assumed leadership in the Bolivian army until his death in 1828. Arenales also lived to see independence, eventually becoming governor of Salta, in Argentina. The guerrilla Padilla shared power and combat with his wife, Juana Azurduy, who is a legendary heroine in Bolivia.

Besides the six major *republiquetas,* others existed intermittently with equally daring but less well-known leaders. The *republiquetas* lacked coordination and a definite purpose. They did, however, have a common goal—opposition to Spanish rule. Only in 1824 did the concept of an independent Upper Peru (Bolivia) take root with the urban elite, who until then had supported the status quo.

See also **Caudillismo, Caudillo; Wars of Independence, South America.**

BIBLIOGRAPHY

Julio Díaz Arguedas, *Los generales de Bolivia* (1929).

Additional Bibliography

Acosta Rentería, Hilarión. *La evolución de Bolivia: Chuquisaca insurgente 25 de Mayo 1809.* Sucre, Bolivia: Cotes, 2006.

Gandarilla Guardia, Niño. *Libertadores cruceños.* Santa Cruz de la Sierra, Bolivia: Comité Pro Santa Cruz, 2003.

Ríos de Reyes, Evelyn. *Antecedentes de la revolución del 16 de Junio de 1809 en La Paz.* La Paz, Bolivia: Plural Editores, 2002.

CHARLES W. ARNADE

REQUERIMIENTO.

Requerimiento, a legal document ("requirement") drawn up in 1513, to be read before initiation of the conquest of Amerindians. The famous 1511 sermon of the Dominican friar Antonio de Montesinos raising the question of Spanish mistreatment of the native peoples of the island of Hispaniola led to a review of whether or not conquest of the New World was justified, and if so, under what conditions. Spanish jurist Juan López de Palacios Rubios articulated the rationale for Spanish action in a treatise *Of the Ocean Isles* (1513). He argued, as did Bishop Hostiensis earlier, that the pope could annul political jurisdictions of heathens and transfer them to Christian princes, as Pope Alexander VI had done for the Spanish in the Bulls of Donation of 1493.

The *requerimiento* summarized just title in the hands of the pope and recognized his authority to transfer jurisdiction to the Spanish monarchs. Before combat could begin, the native peoples were to be told that if they acceded, they could become loyal vassals; if they resisted, they would be deprived of both liberty and property. The ceremony was probably first performed in the Indies on 14 June 1514. Historian Gonzalo Fernández de Oviedo y Valdés, who as notary had frequent occasion to administer the oath, lamented that "it appears to me that these Indians will not listen to the theology of this Requirement, and that you have no one who can make them understand it; would Your Honor be pleased to keep it until we have some of these Indians in a cage, in order that he may learn it at his leisure and my Lord Bishop may explain it to him?" (Lewis Hanke, *The Spanish Struggle,* pp. 33–34).

See also **Indigenous Peoples; Slavery: Spanish America.**

BIBLIOGRAPHY

Lewis Hanke, *The Spanish Struggle for Justice in the Conquest of the New World* (1949).

Lyle N. Mc Alister, *Spain and Portugal in the New World: 1492–1700* (1984).

Additional Bibliography

De Cesare, Michele. *El debate sobre el "indio" y las instituciones españolas en el Nuevo Mundo.* Salerno: Edizioni del paguro, 1999.

Mackenthun, Gesa. *Metaphors of Dispossession: American Beginnings and the Translation of Empire, 1492–1637.* Norman: University of Oklahoma Press, 1997.

Pérez, Joseph, ed. *La época de los descubrimientos y las conquistas (1400–1570).* Madrid: Espasa Calpe, 1998.

Roa–de–la-Carrera, Cristián Andrés. *Histories of Infamy: Francisco López de Gómara and the Ethics of Spanish Imperialism.* Boulder: University Press of Colorado, 2005.

Thomas, Hugh. *Rivers of Gold: The Rise of the Spanish Empire, from Columbus to Magellan.* New York: Random House, 2003.

NOBLE DAVID COOK

RESGATE. Resgate, the "ransoming" of indigenous peoples held as captives in the interior of Brazil during the colonial period. Portuguese law banned the direct enslaving of native Brazilians by colonists but allowed Indians already held as slaves by other Indians or those slated for death in tribal rituals to become the slaves of colonists. The exchange of such captives between tribes and colonists was seen by the Portuguese as "ransoming," for the colonists liberated the captives who in turn repaid their deliverers with lifetime service. Widely abused, *resgate* provided a thin legal patina for the illegal enslavement of native peoples in colonial Brazil

See also **Slavery: Brazil.**

BIBLIOGRAPHY

Alexander Marchant, *From Barter to Slavery: The Economic Relations of Portuguese and Indians in the Settlement of Brazil, 1500–1580* (1966).

John Hemming, *Red Gold: The Conquest of the Brazilian Indians* (1978).

ALIDA C. METCALF

RESGUARDO. Resguardo, a Colombian institution regulating indigenous landholdings. The *resguardo* is a territorial unit comprising communal and inalienable lands administered by native authorities and legitimized by colonial titles granted to indigenous communities. *Resguardos* were carved out of more extensive aboriginal territories by the colonial administration in order to isolate indigenous populations from surrounding ethnic groups and to free remaining aboriginal lands for exploitation by non-Indians. By the eighteenth century, however, the *resguardo* served as a

vehicle for expanding native holdings and for legitimizing new forms of indigenous authority.

During the Republican period, the Colombian state enacted legislation to privatize *resguardo* lands but was only partially successful; alliances between regional elites and indigenous communities under the federalist system succeeded in maintaining the institution, especially in the southern highlands. A return to centralized political authority in the last decade of the nineteenth century brought a more protectionist Indian policy that codified the existence of the *resguardo* as a small and politically weak unit dependent upon municipal authorities.

Notwithstanding protectionist legislation, state policy in the twentieth century continued to foster the privatization of *resguardo* lands. Some extinguished *resguardos,* however, succeeded in revalidating their communal status during the 1980s, and existing ones expanded their territorial base by occupying usurped lands. Indigenous communal landholdings received more extensive protection under the 1991 Constitution, which transcended existing *resguardo* legislation, granting native communities the right to define modes of territorial organization.

See also **Encomienda; Pueblos de indios; Repartimiento.**

BIBLIOGRAPHY

Juan Friede, *El indio en lucha por la tierra,* 2d ed. (1972).

Margarita González, *El resguardo en el Nuevo Reino de Granada,* 2d ed. (1979).

Adolfo Triana, *Legislación indígena nacional* (1980).

Myriam Jimeno and Adolfo Triana, *Estado y minorías étnicas en Colombia* (1985).

Joanne Rappaport, *The Politics of Memory: Native Historical Interpretation in the Colombian Andes* (1990).

Additional Bibliography

Bohórquez M., Carmen L. *El resguardo en la Nueva Granada: Proteccionismo o despojo?* Bogotá: Editorial Nueva América, 1997.

Castro Blanco, Elias. *La extinción de los resguardos indígenas de Colombaima y Paquilo en Ambalema en el siglo XIX.* Bogotá: CRIT: Notaría de Ambalema, 1999.

Gros, Christian. *Políticas de la etnicidad: Identidad, estado y modernidad.* Bogotá: Instituto Colombiano de Antropología e Historia, 2001.

Holguín Sarria, Armando. *Los indígenas en la Constitución colombiana.* Bogotá: G. Rivas Moreno, 1997.

Maybury-Lewis, David. *The Politics of Ethnicity: Indigenous Peoples in Latin American States.* Cambridge, MA: Harvard University David Rockefeller Center for Latin American Studies: Distributed by Harvard University Press, 2002.

JOANNE RAPPAPORT

RESIDENCIA.

Residencia, judicial review of an official's actions in office conducted at the conclusion of his tenure. The *residencia* had Castilian precedents and was extended to the New World as early as 1501, as part of the crown's effort to establish control over its officials there. *Residencias* were subsequently employed for viceroys, audiencia ministers, district administrators such as Corregidores, and a variety of other officials. Although they were used throughout the colonial period, their effectiveness was often nil. Nonetheless, the information collected during these reviews is an important source for historians.

In conducting a *residencia,* a specially appointed judge (*juez de residencia*), often an *audiencia* minister or, for district officials, an incumbent's successor, posted the time and place where he would be available to receive accusations about the behavior of the official in question. After gathering the information and hearing the official's defense, the judge prepared a formal report, pronounced sentence, and sent the relevant documentation to the local *audiencia* or, for senior officials, to the Council of the Indies.

The penalties levied for abuse of office, and especially for malfeasance, included fines, prohibition from further royal service, loss of property, and imprisonment. Appeals, however, were commonplace, and rarely did the sentenced official have to suffer the full punishment originally specified.

Residencias, like *visitas* and *pesquisas,* represented the Spanish crown's deep and frequently justified suspicion that colonial officials could not be trusted to implement its will. The myriad, often conflicting legislation promulgated for the Indies, moreover, meant that officials invariably violated some laws. Nonetheless, as a major administrative tool to keep colonial officials true to their responsibilities, the *residencia* never fully met royal expectations. Despite its threat, officials typically balanced local pressures and personal objectives against royal intentions, and rarely suffered permanently from this form of imperial surveillance.

See also **Judicial Systems: Spanish America; Pesquisa, Pesquisador; Visita, Visitador.**

BIBLIOGRAPHY

Recopilación de leyes de los reynos de las Indias, 4 vols. (1681; repr. 1973), *libro* V, *título* XV.

Clarence H. Haring, *The Spanish Empire in America* (1947), pp. 148–153.

Additional Bibliography

Alvarez de Toledo, Cayetana. *Politics and Reform in Spain and Viceregal Mexico: The Life and Thought of Juan de Palafox, 1600–1659.* New York: Oxford University Press, 2004.

Barrios, Feliciano. *El gobierno de un mundo: Virreinatos y audiencias en la América hispánica.* Cuenca: Ediciones de la Universidad de Castilla-La Mancha: Fundación Rafael del Pino, 2004.

Burkholder, Mark A., ed. *Administrators of Empire.* Brookfield, VT: Ashgate, 1998.

Dym, Jordana and Christophe Belaubre. *Politics, Economy, and Society in Bourbon Central America, 1759–1821.* Boulder: University Press of Colorado, 2007.

MARK A. BURKHOLDER

RESORTES, ADALBERTO MARTÍNEZ

(1916–2003). Adalberto Martínez Resortes, known also by the nickname "Resortes Resortin de la Resortera," was a prominent figure in the Mexican entertainment industry, working primarily as a comedian but also as an actor and dancer for over seventy years. Resortes was born Adalberto Martínez Chávez on January 25, 1916, in Mexico City, and began his artistic career at the age of fifteen at the city's Teatro Hidalgo. He soon discovered his talent for tap dance and formed a duo, Los Espontáneos ("the spontaneous ones"), with fellow dancer and friend Juan Flores. When the partnership ended, his love for entertaining expanded into cinema. His first film role came in the 1946 feature *Voces de primavera* (Spring Voices) and was immediately followed by parts in

Yo dormí con un fantasma (I Want to be an Artist; 1947), *El rey de México* (The Mexican King; 1955), *Quiero ser artista* (I Slept with a Ghost; 1957), and *La chamaca* (The Kid; 1960), among others. In 1992 he began a career in television, with a role on the telenovela *El Abuelo y yo* (The Grandfather and I). In 1987, he was honored by Mexico's Instituto Nacional de Bellas Artes for his exceptional career in the arts, and in 1994 he received a Golden Ariel (the Mexican equivalent of the Academy Awards) for his lifetime contributions to the industry. He died on April 4, 2003.

BIBLIOGRAPHY

"Falleció anoche el comediarte Adalberto Martínez Resortes." *La Jornada Virtual.* April 3, 2003. http://www.jornada.unam.mx.

STACY LUTSCH

RESTREPO, CARLOS EUGENIO

(1867–1947). Carlos Eugenio Restrepo (*b.* 12 September 1867; *d.* 6 July 1947), president of Colombia (1910–1914). Born into a prestigious but poor family in Medellín, he studied law in his hometown. Restrepo began a bureaucratic career in his early twenties. His diligence and honesty brought him important posts. He served in the War of the Thousand Days, then returned home to the rectorship of the University of Antioquia (1901–1902). Later he became professor of constitutional law there. Elected as a Conservative to the Congress of 1909, Restrepo strongly opposed the dictatorship of Rafael Reyes. These personal and political credentials won him election to the presidency in 1910—the first Antioquian to hold the office for a full term. His term coincided with a boom in coffee exports that made possible expansion in educational and transportation infrastructure, legal codification, and pensions for schoolteachers. Colombia's territories were also reorganized, and the Thomson–Urrutia Treaty with the United States was negotiated in 1914. Restrepo's Unión Republicana, an effort at bipartisanship, ceased to exist after he left office. Back in Antioquia, he became a spokesperson for the region's interests and, in 1930, for the presidential candidacy of the Liberal Enrique Olaya Herrera. Restrepo

served Olaya as minister of interior (1930) and as ambassador to the Holy See (1931–1934). He died in Medellín.

See also **Antioquia; Colombia: Since Independence.**

BIBLIOGRAPHY

Ivan Duque Escobar, *Perfil y huella de Carlos E. Restrepo* (1982).

Ignacio Arizmendi Posada, *Presidentes de Colombia, 1810–1990* (1989), pp. 205–208.

Additional Bibliography

Brugman, Catalina. "El fracaso del republicanismo en Colombia, 1910–1914." *Historia Crítica* 21 (January–June 2001): 91–110.

J. LEÓN HELGUERA

RESTREPO, JOSÉ MANUEL (1781–1863).

José Manuel Restrepo (*b.* 30 December 1781; *d.* 1 April 1863), Colombian public official and historian. Born in Envigado in the province of Antioquia, Restrepo studied law in Bogotá and participated in the scientific and intellectual ferment of the late colonial period. He was active in the independence movement, for example, as secretary to the dictator Juan del Corral in his native province. During the Spanish reconquest he was allowed to stay in Antioquia as a tithe official (*juez de diezmos*), but fearing reprisals, he fled to Jamaica (1816) and then the United States (1817). After the victory at Boyacá he returned to New Granada, where he served as governor of Antioquia and deputy to the Congress of Cúcuta.

Restrepo's highest official position was minister of the interior of Gran Colombia (1821–1830). He assisted Vice President Francisco de Paula Santander while he was acting chief executive, and then Simón Bolívar once he assumed the presidency. As a political moderate, Restrepo exercised a restraining influence on the two leaders when a bitter feud arose between them. After the breakup of Gran Colombia, he held various positions in independent New Granada, most notably that of director of the Bogotá mint.

The lasting importance of Restrepo is due above all to his stature as the classic historian of Colombian independence. With unrivaled access to official documentation and personal knowledge of people and events, he produced the ten-volume *Historia de la revolución de la República de Colombia,* published in Paris in 1827. An expanded second edition appeared in 1858. A sequel, the two-volume *Historia de la Nueva Granada,* was published posthumously (1952–1963). He also left a four-volume *Diario político y militar* (1954) relating all manner of developments in Gran Colombia and New Granada. Though Restrepo eschewed blatant partisanship, his perspective is clearly conservative, distrustful of rapid innovation, and disdainful of the lower social orders.

See also **Antioquia; Colombia: From the Conquest Through Independence; Colombia: Since Independence; Gran Colombia; New Granada, United Provinces.**

BIBLIOGRAPHY

Frank Safford, *The Ideal of the Practical: Colombia's Struggle to Form a Technical Elite* (1976).

Juan Botero Restrepo, *El prócer historiador, José Manuel Restrepo (1781–1863),* 2 vols. (1982).

Germán Colmenares, "La 'Historia de la revolución,' por José Manuel Restrepo: Una prisión historiográfica," in Germán Colmenares, Zamira Díaz De Zuluaga, José Escorcia, and Francisco Zuluaga, *La independencia: Ensayos de historia social* (1986).

Additional Bibliography

Adelman, Jeremy. "Colonialism and National Histories: José Manuel Restrepo and Bartolomé Mitre." In *Interpreting Spanish Colonialism: Empires, Nations, and Legends,* Christopher Schmidt-Nowara and John M. Nieto-Phillips, editors. Albuquerque: University of New Mexico Press, 2005.

Múnera, Alfonso. "El Caribe colombiano en la república andina: Identidad y autonomía política en el siglo XIX." *Boletín Cultural y Bibliográfico* 33:41 (1996): 29–49.

Tovar Zambrano, Bernardo. *La colonia en la historiografía colombiana.* Bogotá: Carreta, 1984.

DAVID BUSHNELL

RETABLOS AND EX-VOTOS.

Retablos and ex-votos, religious images whose production has had great flowering in provincial areas of Mexico as well as Peru, where they are sometimes known as *santero* boxes. Retablo art continues to be made in each of these countries. Before 1800 *retablo* referred only to the carved, gilded, and painted screens behind (*retro*) the altars (*tabula*) of churches. In the nineteenth century the term also meant a small painting of a cult image hung on home altars for private devotion. Subjects included scenes from the life of Christ, the saints, and other venerated persons from the rich Catholic hagiography.

Carried as protection on arduous journeys, *retablos* reached remote regions of Peru with muleteers and tradesman. Local people began to utilize and create these religious images during animal brandings, healing ceremonies and everyday life.

While the wealthy could commission or import elegant and expensive paintings on copper or canvas, the poor had to be content with more humble works on wood or coarse material. But by the 1820s, the new process of applying tin to thin sheets of iron made paintings on metal cheaper and more available to the common people.

The folk artists (*retableros*) who painted the images were mostly self-taught, with little or no formal training. Unaware of sophisticated metropolitan movements like neoclassicism or romanticism, they often imitated in naive fashion the seventeenth- and eighteenth-century painting they saw in churches around them. The retablo style derived from copying, often from copies of copies. Details lovingly painted but not always understood were sometimes lost or became merely decorative. Thus the baroque tradition was perpetuated by retablo artists into the twentieth century. Because of their often rustic style and uneven quality characteristic of folk art, retablos can be difficult to date precisely.

The ex-voto (from Latin *votum,* vow) is a particular kind of retablo, a votive painting of a miracle (*milagro*). It shows a recovery from an illness, accident, or other misfortune, and was painted either by the person miraculously saved or by a folk artist to hang in the church near the image of Christ or the interceding saint. Since ex-votos usually tell a story, they almost always bear a text that recounts the event and often locates and dates it as well. Because an ex-voto is not based on something copied, the artist could give free rein to his creativity.

Many ex-votos give insight into the customs of the time, for they are full of significant ethnohistorical data: occupations and trades of ordinary people; costumes, furniture, and architecture; popular religion and its cult images; droughts, diseases, conflicts, and accidents—all appear in vivid and refreshing pictures of life among the common people. These genre paintings also give much information on the painters and the donors.

The condition of many retablos and ex-votos leaves much to be desired. Rust and ordinary wear and tear have taken their toll, and numerous nail holes show they have been rehung many times. The desire for newer images has resulted in many ending up in antique stores or flea markets, and churches have had to clear out older votive paintings (thereby making them *ex*-votos) to make room for the new.

The development of color lithography and other mechanical ways of reproducing images greatly lessened the demand for the *retablero*'s handiwork, though new work reflecting contemporary themes continues to resonate. One of Mexico's greatest and most popular turn-of-the-century artists, José Guadalupe Posada, mass-produced prints of retablos (even showing the nail holes); he also illustrated miracles and disasters just as the ex-voto artists had. The modern art movements of Mexico certainly had their roots in this kind of painting. Frida Kahlo's style was influenced by ex-voto painting, and Diego Rivera was so inspired by the freshness and naive charm of this art that in the 1920s he wrote articles on folk or popular art in *Mexican Folkways* and other magazines. Typical Peruvian *retablos* of the twentieth century have three scenes, one depicting Christ's birth, one the harvest, and one the blood festival depicting the Andean condor locked in struggle with the Iberian bull. Nicario Jimenez Quispe is a popular Peruvian *retablero* artist from Arequipa. In the San Blas neighborhood of Cuzco, the Mendívil family workshop established by Hilario Mendívil (1929-77) continues producing fine works of art during the new millennium.

See also **Kahlo, Frida; Rivera, Diego.**

BIBLIOGRAPHY

Roberto Montenegro, *Retablos de México: Mexican Votive Paintings,* translated by Irene Nicholson (1950); "Retablos mexicanos," in *Artes de México* 106 (1968).

Gloria Kay Giffords, *Mexican Folk Retablos: Masterpieces on Tin* (1974).

Martha B. Robertson, *Magic, Miracles, and Mystery* (1984).

Gloria Fraser Giffords et al., *The Art of Private Devotion: Retablo Painting of Mexico* (1991).

Additional Bibliography

Centro Cultural/Arte Contemporáneo (Mexico); Fundación Cultural Televisa (Mexico). *Dones y promesas: 500 años de arte ofrenda (exvotos mexicanos).* México, D.F.: Centro Cultural/Arte Contemporáneo: Fundación Cultural Televisa, 1996.

Durand, Jorge, and Douglas S. Massey. *Miracles on the Border: Retablos of Mexican Migrants to the United States.* Tucson: University of Arizona Press, 1995.

Giffords, Gloria Fraser. *Mexican Folk Retablos.* Albuquerque: University of New Mexico Press, 1992.

San Cristóbal Sebastián, Antonio. *Esplendor del barroco en Ayacucho: Retablos y arquitectura religiosa en Huamanga.* Lima: Banco Latino: Ediciones Peisa, 1998.

Toledo Brückmann, Ernesto. *Retablos de Ayacucho: Testimonio de violencia.* Lima: Editorial San Marcos, 2003.

Zarur, Elizabeth Netto Calil, and Charles M. Lovell. *Art and Faith in Mexico: The Nineteenth-Century Retablo Tradition.* Albuquerque: University of New Mexico Press, 2001.

MARTHA BARTON ROBERTSON

RETIRANTE. Retirante, a term used to identify the *sertanejos* fleeing from the droughts that periodically scourge the backlands (Sertão) of northeastern Brazil. It came into wide usage during the Great Drought of 1877–1880, during which hundreds of thousands of backlanders migrated in search of shelter and subsistence, most of them to the coastal areas of the region. Substantial numbers, however, wound up leaving the Northeast and never returned. A short–lived newspaper with that name advocated the cause of these displaced people. *Os flagellados,* literally the "Beaten Ones," is another term applied to drought refugees. Despite a succession of government measures against drought beginning in the early twentieth century, these migrations still occur during major regional droughts.

See also **Drought Region (Brazil).**

BIBLIOGRAPHY

Gileno Dé Carli, *Séculos de secas* (1984).

Gerald Michael Greenfield, "The Great Drought and Elite Discourse in Imperial Brazil," in *Hispanic American Historical Review* 72, no. 3 (1992): 375–400.

GERALD MICHAEL GREENFIELD

REVERÓN, ARMANDO (1889–1954).

Armando Reverón (*b.* 10 May 1889; *d.* 18 September 1954), Venezuelan artist. Reverón was a delicate child raised by a foster family in Valencia, near Caracas, and his health was permanently damaged by an attack of typhoid contracted in his youth. His formal education began at home and he received art lessons from his maternal uncle, Ricardo Montilla. In 1908 he went to Caracas and entered the Academy of Fine Arts, where he began painting still lifes. He was expelled from school for participating in a strike against the director, the painter Antonio Herrera Toro. But he returned the following year and in 1911 graduated with distinction as well as with a scholarship to Europe. That same year after his first exhibition, Reverón went to Spain to study at the Academy of San Fernando in Madrid. During his stay in Europe, he became interested in impressionism, pointillism, and the paintings of Francisco Goya. Upon his return to Caracas in 1915, he joined the Fine Arts Circle, a group of landscape painters strongly influenced by the Russian artist Nicolas Ferdinandov, who organized an exhibition of Reverón's work at the Academy of Fine Arts in 1919. Ferdinandov also encouraged Reverón to move to the coastal village of Macuto near Caracas, where the painter constructed a *castillete* ("little castle") that served as his home for the rest of his life. There he began his seascapes, which capture the bright light of the sun heating the sea.

His work falls into three periods. First, the blue period (1919–1924), featuring street scenes, portraits of common people, urban landscapes, and seascapes. Then the white period (1925–1929), which includes near monochrome white paintings of the sea, portraits of his friends, his Muse Juanita, and life-size rag dolls. Finally, his sepia period (1936–1949), in which his painting of female nudes and seascapes becomes much more transparent. In 1940 he won the first prize at the Official Salon of Venezuelan Art. After 1950 his mental health deteriorated and he entered the Sanatoria San Jorge in 1953, where he died the following year. His work found a much greater audience after his death.

See also **Art: The Twentieth Century.**

BIBLIOGRAPHY

Roldán Esteva Grillet, *Siete artistas venezolanos siglo XX: Rafael Monasterios, Armando Reverón, Héctor Poleo, Alejandro Otero, Carlos Cruz Diez, Jesús Soto y Jacobo Borges* (1984).

Alfredo Boulton, *Mirar a Reverón* (1990).

Additional Bibliography

Arráiz Lucca, Rafael. *Los oficios de la luz.* Caracas: Fondo Editorial 60 Años, Contraloría General de la República, 1998.

Calzadilla, Juan. *Voces y demonios de Armando Reverón: Cuentos, anecdotas, pensamientos.* Caracas: Alfadil Ediciones, 1990.

Huizi, María Elena. *Armando Reverón: guia de estudio.* Caracas: Asociacion Civil Proyecto Armando Reveron (PAR), 2005.

Salcedo Miliani, Antonio. *Armando Reverón y su época.* Mérida: Dirección General de Cultura y Extensión, Universidad de Los Andes; and Caracas: Fundación Museo Armando Reverón, 2000.

BÉLGICA RODRÍGUEZ

REVILLAGIGEDO, CONDE DE (1740–1799).

Conde de Revillagigedo (Juan Vicente de Güemes-Pacheco y Padilla; *b.* 1740; *d.* 1799), one of New Spain's greatest viceroys. Born in Havana, Revillagigedo gained firsthand knowledge of Mexico as a youth, during the viceregal administration of his father (1746–1755). Appointed viceroy himself in 1789, he initiated many new projects and reforms, including a large-scale road-building program, the development of more efficient and regular mail service, the construction of many primary schools, the founding of the Archivo General, and the marked improvement of public facilities in Mexico City, making the capital cleaner, healthier, and better policed. He also sponsored artistic, scientific, and scholarly endeavors, providing patronage to the Academy of San Carlos and inaugurating the Museum of Natural History in 1793.

The epitome of an enlightened Bourbon administrator, Revillagigedo sought to bring New Spain under more efficient bureaucratic control and to increase its yield to the crown. Toward these ends, he established a new system of intendancies, initiated an overhaul of the treasury department, and reorganized and reduced Mexican militia units. He also attempted, with less success, to weaken the power of the church, the Audiencia of Mexico, and the Mexico City merchants' guild. Though many of his reforms were undermined by entrenched bureaucratic opposition, or by later viceroys, Revillagigedo demonstrated what could be accomplished by a government leader who combined energy, scope, and attention to detail in planning with pragmatism and flexibility in execution. He died in Madrid.

See also **New Spain, Viceroyalty of; Spanish Empire.**

BIBLIOGRAPHY

Ignacio J. Rubio Mañe, "Síntesis histórica de la vida del II conde de Revillagigedo, virrey de Nueva España," in *Anuario de Estudios Americanos* 6 (1949): 451–496.

D. A. Brading, *Miners and Merchants in Bourbon Mexico, 1763–1810* (1971), pp. 33–92.

Additional Bibliography

Brading, D. A. *El ocaso novohispano: Testimonios documentales.* Mexico City: INAH: Dirección General de Publicaciones del Consejo Nacional para la Cultura y las Artes, 1996.

González Echegaray, María del Carmen. *El Virrey Revillagigedo y sus orígenes.* Santander: Diputación Regional de Cantabria, 1990.

R. DOUGLAS COPE

REVOLTOSOS. Revoltosos, insurgents and political refugees, both rightist and leftist, who used the United States as a base for revolution in Mexico from 1900 to the early 1920s. As exiles in revolt, the *revoltosos* were the object of suppression by both American and Mexican authorities.

Mexico's *revoltosos* were a varied group, often appearing to be an incoherent conglomeration of rival elements. Ideologically they ranged from the socialist

and anarchist followers of Ricardo Flores Magón (*magonistas*, members of the Mexican Liberal Party) to the reactionary, proclerical proponents of Porfirio Díaz's nephew, Félix Díaz (*felicistas*). At various points along the spectrum were Pizaña "seditionists," *orozquistas, zapatistas, obregonistas, reyistas, maderistas, maytorenistas, vazquistas, villistas, carrancistas, huertistas, científicos,* and other assorted groups of the Right and Left. The *magonistas* and the "seditionists" of south Texas were the most consistently radical. All of these groups made alliances with their rivals. The characteristics they shared were hostility toward the established Mexican government and a desire to use the United States as a revolutionary (or counterrevolutionary) base.

See also **Díaz, Félix, Jr; Flores Magón, Ricardo; Mexico, Wars and Revolutions: Mexican Revolution.**

BIBLIOGRAPHY

Most of the existing literature treats specific *revoltoso* groups. The only general study is W. Dirk Raat, *Revoltosos: Mexico's Rebels in the United States, 1903–1923* (1981). For printed documents see Manuel González Ramírez, ed., *Epistolario y textos de Ricardo Flores Magón* (1973).

Additional Bibliography

Balderrama, Francisco E., and Raymond Rodriguez. *Decade of Betrayal: Mexican Repatriation in the 1930s.* Albuquerque: University of New Mexico Press, 2006.

Rosales, Francisco A. *Pobre raza!: Violence, Justice, and Mobilization among México Lindo Immigrants, 1900–1936.* Austin: University of Texas Press, 1999.

Ruíz, Vicki, and John R. Chávez. *Memories and Migrations: Mapping Boricua and Chicana Histories.* Urbana: University of Illinois Press, 2007.

W. DIRK RAAT

REVOLUTION ON THE MARCH. *See* López Michelsen, Alfonso.

REVUELTAS, JOSÉ (1914–1976). José Revueltas (*b.* 20 November 1914; *d.* 14 April 1976), Mexican writer and activist. Revueltas was born in the state of Durango to an exceptional family in which all the children were outstanding artists: Silvestre, a musician; Fermin, a painter; and Rosaura, an actress. José mastered the novel and the short story like few others. *El luto humano* (1943), *Los errores* (1964), and *El apando* (1969) are outstanding works in Mexican and Latin American literature due to their rigorous style and uncommon ambition as well as their austere, anecdotal expression of the great ideological conflicts of our time. He also wrote dramas and screenplays and some of the most important essays in twentieth-century Mexico.

But Revueltas's work cannot be reduced merely to his literary production. He was also one of the most intense, honest, and contradictory personalities in twentieth-century Mexico. A militant Marxist from adolescence until death, Revueltas was imprisoned several times for his ideas. The last time, from 1968 to 1971, was for his role as a leader of the student movement of 1968 that resulted in the massacre of Tlatelolco. Even his very funeral was an unforgettably moving political act. At the cemetery the mostly young crowd sang "The International" and other revolutionary songs. When the minister of education tried to speak, he was shouted down and forced to leave—very much in keeping with Revueltas's opposition to hypocrisy and illegitimate power.

Revueltas's work is a vast drama in which is represented the struggle to make public and private life, art and the exercise of thought, one singular and great undertaking of redemption and sacrifice for those oppressed in "this somber period in history," as he himself called our era. With such a messianic sensibility, it is not strange that his dramas combine the biblical and the mundane, the prophetic and the grotesque, the degraded and the sublime. He considered his life and his writing to be examples, nothing more and nothing less, of the simple destiny of a human being.

See also **Literature: Spanish America; Tlatelolco.**

BIBLIOGRAPHY

Sam Slick, *José Revueltas* (1983).

Additional Bibliography

Arias Urrutia, Angel. *Entre la cruz y la sospecha: Los cristeros de Revueltas, Yáñez y Rulfo.* Madrid: Iberoamericana; and Frankfurt am Main: Vervuert, 2005.

Cheron, Philippe. *El árbol de oro: José Revueltas y el pesimismo ardiente.* Ciudad Juárez: Universidad Autónoma de Ciudad Juárez, 2003.

Cluff, Russell M. *Cuento mexicano moderno.* Mexico City: Universidad Nacional Autónoma de México, and Xalapa: Universidad Veracruzana: Editorial Aldus, 2000.

Durán, Javier. *José Revueltas: Una poética de la disidencia.* Xalapa: Universidad Veracruzana, 2002.

Fuentes Morua, Jorge. *José Revueltas: Una biografía intelectual.* Mexico City: Universidad Autónoma Metropolitana, Unidad Iztapalapa: M.A. Porrúa, 2001.

JORGE AGUILAR MORA

REVUELTAS, SILVESTRE (1899–1940).

Silvestre Revueltas (*b.* 31 December 1899; *d.* 5 October 1940), Mexican violinist, composer, and conductor from Santiago Papasquiaro, Durango. He started violin lessons at age eight in Colima, and continued in Mexico City in 1913. His high school years at St. Edwards College in Austin, Texas (1916–1918), were followed with advanced training at the Chicago Music College (1918–1920; 1922–1924). He worked as a freelance violinist and conductor in the United States and Mexico before settling permanently in Mexico City, where he was appointed Carlos Chávez's assistant conductor of the Symphony Orchestra of Mexico in 1928. Revueltas also taught violin and chamber music at the National Conservatory, serving as its interim director briefly in 1933. In 1937 Revueltas went to Spain to join the Loyalists in the Civil War.

Revueltas's compositions embody the Mexican spirit in their vigorous, indigenous rhythms and bracing dissonances, taking on in some instances the character of musical landscapes (*Janitzio,* 1933). He was one of the first in Mexico to compose for films in the emerging sound cinema industry (*Redes,* 1935). His substantial and colorful output and its universal appeal have made him perhaps the most revered Mexican composer of the twentieth century.

See also **Chávez, Carlos; Music: Art Music.**

BIBLIOGRAPHY

Robert Stevenson, *Music in Mexico: A Historical Survey* (1952).

Additional Bibliography

Bitran, Yael, and Ricardo Miranda. *Diálogo de resplandores: Carlos Chávez y Silvestre Revueltas* Mexico City: INBA, 2002.

Contreras Soto, Eduardo. *Silvestre Revueltas: Baile, duelo y son.* Mexico City: Consejo Nacional para la Cultura y las Artes, Dirección General de Publicaciones, Instituto Nacional de Bellas Artes, 2000.

Cortez M., Luis Jaime. *Favor de no disparar sobre el pianista: Una vida de Silvestre Revueltas.* Mexico City: Consejo Nacional para la Cultura y las Artes, Instituto Nacional de Bellas Artes y Literatura, Dirección General de Publacions, 2000.

Kolb, Roberto. *Silvestre Revueltas (1899–1940): Catálogo de sus obras.* Coyoacán: Universidad Nacional Autónoma de México, Escuela Nacional de Música, 1998.

Sanchez-Gutierrez, Carlos. "The Cooked and the Raw: Syncretism in the Music of Silvestre Revueltas." Ph.D. diss., Princeton University, 1996.

ROBERT L. PARKER

REYES, LUCHA (1906–1944).

Lucha Reyes was a Mexican mariachi-ranchera singer of the 1930s and 1940s. She was born Maria de la Luz Flores Aceves on May 23, 1906, into a lower-class family in Guadalajara, Jalisco. She later moved with her mother to Mexico City where she worked in *carpa* (tent) theaters from a young age. There she developed her singing talents as an operatic-style soprano. She spent time in Los Angeles in the early 1920s and gained popularity among the Mexican American population; there is a statue of her in East Los Angeles. Before becoming a solo artist she performed in the Trío Reyes-Ascencio and the Cuarteto Anáhuac. Reyes's voice changed after a respiratory illness she contracted while touring in Europe in the late 1920s. This caused her to lose her voice for a period of time, after which it was deeper and hoarser, thus lending itself to the ranchera style. "Guadalajara" was one of her first solo hits.

Reyes was a pioneer in mariachi music and in Mexican culture in general, as women did not typically sing in mariachi bands. Her distinct singing style, *el estilo bravío* (the rebellious or ferocious style) was an attack on dominant social norms, including sexist treatment of women. She appeared in many classic *comedias rancheras* (musical melodramas set in the countryside), such as *¡Ay Jalisco, no te rajes!* (1941) and *Flor silvestre* (1943). She suffered from alcoholism and depression and died on June 25, 1944, from a lethal combination of alcohol and barbiturates.

See also **Mariachi; Music: Popular Music and Dance.**

BIBLIOGRAPHY

Garcia-Orozco, Antonia. "El estilo bravío de Lucha Reyes y la canción." *Nerter: Revista Dedicada a la Literatura, el Arte y el Conocimiento* 5–6 (Spring–Summer 2003): 72–76.

Garcia-Orozco, Antonia. "*Cucurrucucu palomas.* The *estilo bravío* of Lucha Reyes and the Creation of Feminist Consciousness via the *canción ranchera*." Ph.D. diss., Claremont Graduate University, 2005.

CARYN C. CONNELLY

REYES, OSCAR EFRÉN (1894–1966).

The Ecuadoran pedagogue, journalist, and historian Oscar Efrén Reyes was born June 13, 1894, in Baños, Tungurahua Province, one year before the Liberals came to power. He died in Quito several decades after the Liberal Radical Party had ceased to be a major force in national politics. Reyes, however, remained a Liberal all his life. An influential pedagogue—his disciples are legion—he began his teaching career in Ambato. Subsequently he also taught in Guayaquil before establishing permanent residency in Quito, where he taught at several of the capital's more prestigious high schools and normal schools and at the Universidad Central, where he was associate dean of the Facultad de Pedagogía y Letras. Reyes was also a newspaperman and a quasiprofessional, albeit self-taught, historian. As a journalist he contributed to the Quito dailies *El Guante, El Universo, El Ecuatoriano,* and *La Nación.* His first major book was *Los últimos siete años* (The Last Seven Years, 1933), a classic eyewitness account of the July Revolution of 1925 and the Isidro Ayora years (1926–1931). His most important books, however, are his *Vida de Juan Montalvo* (Life of Juan Montalvo, 1935) and his *Breve historia general del Ecuador* (Brief General History of Ecuador, originally published in 1938 and which has since appeared in multiple editions and printings).

Reyes's general history of Ecuador was the standard high school text in the country for many years. It was also used at the university level, for want of anything more appropriate at the time. And his life of Montalvo is one of the better biographies of the would-be assassin of Gabriel García Moreno. Reyes's other books include the posthumously published *Baños del Tungurahua desde sus orígenes al cabildo* (2001), and with Francisco Terán, *Historia y geografía del Oriente ecuatoriano* (1939). Reyes died December 1, 1966.

See also **Ayora Cueva, Isidro; Ecuador, Political Parties: Radical Liberal Party (PLR); Ecuador, Revolutions: Revolution of 1925; García Moreno, Gabriel.**

BIBLIOGRAPHY

Castillo Jácome, Julio. *Oscar Efrén Reyes: Historiador y maestro.* Ambato, Ecuador: Casa de la Cultura Ecuatoriana, Núcleo de Tungurahua, 1995.

Pazos Barrera, Julio, ed. *Acercamiento a la obra de Oscar Efrén Reyes, 1896–1996.* Guayaquil, Ecuador: Casa de la Cultura Ecuatoriana, Núcleo de Guayas, 1997.

Reyes, Oscar Efrén. *Los últimos siete años.* Quito: Talleres gráficos nacionales, 1933.

Reyes, Oscar Efrén. *Vida de Juan Montalvo.* Quito: Talleres gráficos nacionales, 1935.

Reyes, Oscar Efrén. *Breve historia general del Ecuador*, 12th edition. Quito: Maurilia Mendoza de Jiménez, 1982.

Reyes, Oscar Efrén. *Baños del Tungurahua desde sus orígenes al cabildo.* Ambato, Ecuador: Casa de la Cultura Ecuatoriana, Núcleo de Tungurahua, 2001.

Reyes, Oscar Efrén, and Francisco Terán. *Historia y geografía del Oriente ecuatoriano.* Quito: Talleres gráficos de educación, 1939.

Reyes Torres, Marta. *Oscar Efrén Reyes: Testigo de la historia: Biografía.* Quito: Banco Central del Ecuador, 2004.

MICHAEL T. HAMERLY

REYES, RAFAEL (1849–1921). Rafael Reyes (*b.* 5 December 1849; *d.* 18 February 1921), president of Colombia (1904–1909). A native of Boyacá, Reyes made a fortune in the quinine boom of the 1870s, and later explored the Putumayo region. His prominence within the Conservative Party began with the civil war of 1885, and peaked in 1895 when he led government forces at Enciso, Santander. Reyes opposed the governing Nationalist wing of the Conservatives in the 1890s, and sat out the War of the Thousand Days (1899–1902) abroad. In 1904 Reyes won the presidency in a tight election plagued by fraud. His administration, known as the *quinquenio,* reformed public administration and fostered economic recovery through tariff protection and amortization of paper money; his generous policy toward the defeated Liberals won him widespread support from that party. But his authoritarian style, particularly his dissolution of Congress in 1905, eventually alienated political elites of both parties. In June 1909, following street demonstrations in Bogotá, Reyes secretly boarded a ship for Europe, to the surprise of guests expecting him at a Santa Marta dinner.

See also **Colombia: Since Independence; War of the Thousand Days.**

BIBLIOGRAPHY

Eduardo Lemaitre Román, *Rafael Reyes* (1967).

Charles W. Bergquist, *Coffee and Conflict in Colombia, 1886–1910* (1978), pp. 220–246.

Ignacio Arizmendi Posada, *Presidentes de Colombia 1810–1990* (1989), pp. 195–198.

Additional Bibliography

Motta Vargas, Ricardo, and Jaime Castro. *Ordenamiento territorial en el quinquenio de Rafael Reyes.* Bogotá: Ediciones Doctrina y Ley Ltda., 2005.

Olano Correa, Carmenza. *Rafael Reyes y la apertura.* Boyacá: Thalassa Editores, 1991.

Santisteban Gómez, Flaminio. *Ideas políticas y realizaciones de Rafael Reyes.* Bogotá: Cámara de Representantes, Congreso Nacional de Colombia, 1996.

RICHARD J. STOLLER

REYES HEROLES, JESÚS (1921–1985). A prominent Mexican political figure and intellectual, Reyes Heroles was born in Veracruz on April 3, 1921. He graduated from the National School of Law in 1944 and taught there for two decades, mentoring an influential generation of politicians. He held a number of minor government posts before serving as a member of congress (1961–1964). President Gustavo Díaz Ordaz appointed him director of the national petroleum company, where he served from 1964 to 1970. He was president of the Partido Revolucionario Institucional (PRI) from 1972 to 1975, during which time he attempted to institute major reforms. He served as secretary of government in 1976 and secretary of public education from 1982 to 1985.

See also **Díaz Ordaz, Gustavo; Mexico, Political Parties: Institutional Revolutionary Party (PRI).**

BIBLIOGRAPHY

Reyes Heroles, Jesús. *Obras completas.* Mexico City: Fondo de Cultura Económica, 1995.

Reyes Heroles, Jesús. *Jesús Reyes Heroles y el petróleo.* Mexico City: Fondo de Cultura Económica, 1992.

RODERIC AI CAMP

REYES OCHOA, ALFONSO (1889–1959).

Alfonso Reyes Ochoa (*b.* 17 May 1889; *d.* 27 December 1959), Mexican essayist and intellectual. The son of prominent nineteenth-century politician General Bernardo Reyes, Alfonso studied in Mexico City. In 1909 he cofounded the famous Ateneo de la Juventud, an intellectual society, and in 1913 he graduated from the National University, where he had served as secretary of the graduate school and where he later became a founding professor of Spanish language and literature. To survive financially as a writer, Reyes pursued a career in the foreign service, occupying posts in France, Spain, Argentina, and Brazil, and spent most of his life abroad, at one time working under José Ortega y Gasset. Although lacking a political or ideological focus, his writing helped develop the intellectually inward concentration on Mexican identity continued by Samuel Ramos and Octavio Paz. He was a candidate for the Nobel Prize in literature, and was awarded Mexico's National Prize of Arts and Sciences in 1945. Reyes contributed to Mexican intellectual institutional development as first president of the Colegio de México (1939–1959). He presided over Mexico's prestigious Academy of Language shortly before his death.

See also **Ateneo de la Juventud (Athenaeum of Youth); Colegio de México.**

BIBLIOGRAPHY

Alfonso Reyes, *Obras completas,* 24 vols. (1955–1990).

Universidad De Nuevo León, *Páginas sobre Alfonso Reyes* (1955).

Alfonso Reyes, *"Mexico in a Nutshell" and Other Essays* (1964).

James Robb, *El estilo de Alfonso Reyes* (1965).

Barbara B. Aponte, *Alfonso Reyes and Spain* (1972).

Pedro Henríquez Ureña and Alfonso Reyes, *Epistolario íntimo, 1906–1946* (1981–1983).

Additional Bibliography

Arenas Monreal, Rogelio. *Alfonso Reyes y los hados de febrero.* Mexicali: Universidad Autónoma de Baja California; and Mexico City: Universidad Nacional Autónoma de México, 2004.

Enríquez Perea, Alberto, compiler. *Alfonso Reyes en la casa de España en México (1939 y 1940).* Mexico City: El Colegio Nacional, 2005.

Enríquez Perea, Alberto, compiler. *Días de exilio: Correspondencia entre María Zambrano y Alfonso Reyes, 1939–1959 y textos de María Zambrano sobre Alfonso Reyes, 1960–1989.* Mexico City: Taurus: El Colegio de México, 2005.

Gutiérrez Girardot, Rafael. *Tradición y ruptura.* Bogotá: Debate: Random House Mondadori, 2006.

Pineda Franco, Adela Eugenia and Ignacio M. Sánchez Prado, editors. *Alfonso Reyes y los estudios latinoamericanos.* Pittsburgh, PA: Instituto Internacional de Literatura Iberoamericana, Universidad de Pittsburgh, 2004.

Popovic Karic, Pol, Fidel Chávez Pérez and Paulette Patout, editors. *Alfonso Reyes, perspectivas críticas: Ensayos inéditos.* Monterrey: Tecnológico de Monterrey: Feria Internacional del Libro; and Mexico City: Centro de Investigaciones Humanísticas: Plaza y Valdés, 2004.

RODERIC AI CAMP

REYES OGAZÓN, BERNARDO (1850–1913).

Bernardo Reyes Ogazón (*b.* 30 August 1850; *d.* 9 February 1913), Mexican military officer and politician. Bernado Reyes, governor of the important northern state of Nuevo León and a leading contemporary of Porfirio Díaz, began campaigning for the presidency in 1909 to replace Díaz. Forced to leave the country, he lived in exile from 1909 to 1911. He returned in 1911, and, in 1913, with Félix Díaz, led a counter-revolutionary movement against President Madero known as the Tragic Ten Days, during which he was killed leading an attack on the national palace.

Born in Guadalajara, Jalisco, he was the father of Alfonso Reyes, a notable poet, and Rodolfo Reyes, a public figure. In 1865 he left school to fight against the French, becoming an aide to General Ramón Corona. He remained loyal to President Sebastián Lerdo De Tejada in 1877 but continued his military career under Porfirio Díaz, rising to chief of military operations in Nuevo León and, ultimately, to secretary of war. He later served as governor of Nuevo Léon from 1889 to 1900 and from 1902 to 1909. Reyes had reached the rank of division general (three stars) in 1900.

See also **Díaz, Félix, Jr; Díaz, Porfirio; Nuevo León.**

BIBLIOGRAPHY

El Norte, *Constructores de Monterrey* (1945).

Anthony T. Bryan, "Mexican Politics in Transition, 1900–1913: The Role of General Bernardo Reyes," Ph.D. diss., University of Nebraska (1970).

Peter V. N. Henderson, *Félix Díaz, the Porfirians, and the Mexican Revolution* (1981).

Additional Bibliography

Arellano, Josefina González de. *Bernardo Reyes y el movimiento reyista en México.* Mexico City: Instituto Nacional de Antropología e Historia, Programa de Historia Indigena, 1982.

Benavides H., Artemio. *El general Bernardo Reyes: Vida de un liberal porfirista.* Monterrey: Ediciones Castillo, 1998.

Piñera Ramírez, David. *El Gobernador Bernardo Reyes: Y sus homólogos de la frontera norte.* Monterrey: Fondo Editorial de Nuevo León, 1991.

RODERIC AI CAMP

REYES VILLA, MANFRED (1956–). Bolivian politician Manfred Reyes, running as an outsider, lost the 2002 presidential elections by less than 2 percent. Born in La Paz, he served in the military before entering politics. He was mayor of Cochabamba from 1993 to 2002, formed the New Republican Force (NFR) in 1995, and sparked the "water wars" of 2000. He entered a governing coalition with the Nationalist Revolutionary Movement (MNR), but his withdrawal in 2003 precipitated the president's resignation. Rather than run again in 2005, he

supported Jorge Quiroga for president and successfully ran for the Cochabamba prefecture.

See also **Bolivia, Political Parties: Nationalist Revolutionary Movement (MNR); Bolivia, Political Parties: Overview; Cochabamba.**

BIBLIOGRAPHY

Mayorga, Fernando. "Neopopulismo y Democracia en Bolivia." *Revista de Ciencia Política* 23, no. 3 (2003): 99–118.

ROBERT R. BARR

REYNA BARRIOS, JOSÉ MARÍA

(1854–1898). José María Reyna Barrios (*b.* 24 December 1854; *d.* 8 February 1898), president of Guatemala (1892–1898). Born in San Marcos, he was a nephew of the revered father of Guatemalan Liberalism, Justo Rufino Barrios (1873–1885). At the age of seventeen, he joined his uncle and father in the Liberal Revolt of 1871. He studied at the Escuela Politécnica, the Guatemalan military college. After reaching the rank of general, Reyna Barrios easily defeated his Conservative opponent in the 1892 presidential election. The republic's incipient coffee elite expected the new president to capitalize on the successes of the nation's rapidly expanding agricultural exports in order to secure continued prosperity and enlightened government indefinitely. During the first four years of his administration, several contemporary Guatemalan authors described Reyna Barrios as a "young military officer, filled with prestige, educated in the Liberal School, [a] brave son of the 1871 [Liberal] revolution," "a sincere republican," "fully democratic," and "committed to sustaining the Reforma inaugurated in 1871."

These glowing accounts of the Liberal virtues of Reyna Barrios and his administration ended in the summer of 1897. Increasingly dictatorial in nature and under assault from a significant fraction of the nation's coffee planters, Reyna Barrios responded by ruthlessly crushing a regional Liberal revolt in the fall of 1897 that was led by caudillos in Los Altos. Faced with a severe economic and monetary crisis and increasingly assailed by the criticisms of coffee growers from the highlands, Reyna Barrios received the support necessary from the National Assembly to extend his government until 15 March 1902—four years beyond his constitutionally recognized tenure. Nonetheless, for Reyna

Barrios, this proved to be an empty victory. On 8 February 1898, he was assassinated in the capital by a mysterious single gunman. On that same evening, the cabinet met and acknowledged Manuel Estrada Cabrera's (1898–1920) constitutional claim to the presidency as first designate.

See also **Guatemala.**

BIBLIOGRAPHY

Barbaroux [pseud.], *El 9 de febrero de 1898 en Guatemala* (1899).

José Lizardo Díaz O., *De la democracia a la dictadura: La revolución de 1897 en occidente, sus motivos, sus hombres, su fracaso* (1946).

James Bingham, "Guatemalan Agriculture During the Administration of President Manuel Estrada Cabrera, 1898–1920" (Master's thesis, Tulane Univ., 1974).

Mary Catherine Rendon, "Manuel Estrada Cabrera, Guatemalan President, 1898–1920" (Ph.D. diss., Oxford Univ., 1988).

WADE A. KIT

RHEA.

Rhea, a flightless bird smaller than the ostrich. The two species of rhea are the only examples of ratites (running birds with a flat- rather than keel-shaped breastbone) in the New World. The greater rhea (*R. americana*) lives on the Pampa (fertile, grassy plain) that runs from Paraguay to Patagonia. It is an herbivorous bird that lives in flocks of about twenty or so and breeds polygamously. The females in the harem lay their eggs in a communal nest that is incubated by the lone male. The Puna rhea (*R. pennata*) is found in Peru, Bolivia, and Chile. In parts of its range it is considered an endangered species because of excessive hunting for its meat and skin (mostly exported to Japan and the United States) and egg poaching. The rhea is also commonly known in Bolivia as the *piyo*, in Quechua-speaking regions as the *surí*, in the Guaraní language as *ñandú guasú* ("big spider," referring to the spread of the bird's feathers when they run), and the *ema* in Portuguese.

See also **Pampa.**

BIBLIOGRAPHY

Rodolphe Meyer De Schauensee, *The Species of Birds of South America* (1966).

Additional Bibliography

Folch, A. "Rheidai/Rhea." In vol. 1 of *Handbook of the Birds of the World* , edited by Josep del Hoyo, Andrew Elliot, Jordi Sargatal, José Cabot et al. Barcelona: Lynx Edicions, 1992.

SHEILA L. HOOKER

RIACHUELO, BATTLE OF THE.

The Battle of the Riachuelo of June 11, 1865, was a decisive naval engagement of the Triple Alliance War (1864–1870). As part of his invasion of northeastern Argentina, Paraguay's marshal-president Francisco Solano López needed to clear the Paraná River of Brazilian and Argentine naval vessels. To this end, he formulated a plan that called for a surprise attack at dawn against an Allied fleet of eleven steamers anchored just south of the port of Corrientes near its confluence with the Riachuelo River. But various delays prevented the arrival of Paraguayan admiral Ignacio Meza's flotilla until 11 a.m.

Having thus lost the element of surprise, the Paraguayans proceeded to lose every chance for effective maneuver against the better-armed Brazilian steamers. For the next six hours, the two forces seesawed back and forth across the waters. During this time the Allies generally turned their superiority in firepower to good effect. Brazilian admiral Francisco Manoel Barroso managed to direct his flagship, the *Amazonas*, in a wide arc to attack several of Meza's warships in succession. In the end, the Paraguayans were forced to retreat upriver, having lost four of their nine steamers (with all the rest badly damaged). The Brazilians lost two steamers of their own, the *Belmonte* and the *Jequitinhonha*, the latter of which ran aground where it was destroyed by Paraguayan shore batteries. Casualties were high on both sides, with Meza dying from wounds the next day. The Allied victory at the Riachuelo denied to the Paraguayans any hope of an unchallenged advance southward into Argentina. Within weeks, López ordered his land forces to withdraw back into Paraguay, thus assuring an entirely defensive campaign from that point forward.

See also **López, Francisco Solano; Paraná River; War of the Triple Alliance.**

BIBLIOGRAPHY

Whigham, Thomas L. *The Paraguayan War*, Vol. 1: *Causes and Early Conduct*. Lincoln: University of Nebraska, 2002.

THOMAS L. WHIGHAM

Additional Bibliography

Paula, Hilda Rezende and Nilo de Araújo Campos. *Clodesmidt Riani: Trajetória*. Juiz de Fora, Rio de Janeiro: FUNALFA Edições, 2005.

JOHN D. FRENCH

RIANI, CLODSMITH (1920–). Clodsmith Riani (*b.* 15 October 1920), Brazilian trade unionist and president of the National Confederation of Workers in Industry (CNTI) and of the Commando Geral dos Trabalhadores (CGT). Born in Minas Gerais, Riani went to work as an apprentice electrician in 1936 for a utility company in Juiz de Fora, where he emerged in 1949 as a key labor leader. He forged close ties with João "Jango" Goulart, the national leader of the Brazilian Labor Party (PTB), and was elected PTB state deputy several times between 1954 and 1964. Joining the CNTI, Riani led the opposition to its conservative president whom he defeated in an upset election in 1961. Elected vice president of the CGT in 1962 and president in 1963, Riani played a central role in the tumultuous struggles prior to the military coup of 31 March 1964. With the CGT dissolved and the CNTI taken over by the government, he was arrested and sentenced to a total of nineteen years in prison, of which he served six. After his release, he returned to his original job in Juiz de Fora, finished secondary school, and went on to earn a law degree. In 1982, Riani was elected state deputy of the Party of the Brazilian Democratic Movement (PMDB), thus continuing the fight, in Riani's words, for "democratic, progressive, and nationalist ideals."

See also **Brazil, Organizations: General Labor Command (CGT); Brazil, Political Parties: Brazilian Democratic Movement (MDB); Communism; Labor Movements.**

BIBLIOGRAPHY

Israel Beloch and Alzira Alves De Abreu, *Dicionário histórico-biográfico brasileiro 1930–1983*, vol. 4 (1984); on labor in Juiz de Fora, see Maria Andrea Loyola, *Os Sindicatos e o PTB: Estudo de um caso em Minas Gerais* (1980); Riani was interviewed extensively by Lucília De Almeida Neves Delgado in *O Comando Geral dos Trabalhadores no Brasil 1961–1964* (1981) and *PTB: Do Getulismo ao Reformismo (1945–1964)* (1989).

RIAÑO Y BÁRCENA, JUAN ANTONIO (1757–1810). Juan Antonio Riaño y Bárcena (*b.* 1757; *d.* 28 September 1810), intendant of Guanajuato and defender of the Alhóndiga in the Hidalgo revolt (1810). A native of Santander, Spain, Riaño served as a frigate captain in the Spanish navy. In 1792, he was appointed intendant of the important Mexican mining province of Guanajuato, a position he held until his death in defense of the *alhóndiga* (granary) against the rebel forces of Father Miguel Hidalgo. A true product of the Spanish Enlightenment, Riáno studied mathematics, astronomy, literature, languages, drawing, and architecture. Unlike many other intendants, he surveyed his province thoroughly and sought to introduce new industries and agricultural crops. He stimulated the planting of olive groves and vineyards.

Despite his popularity and recognized honesty, Riaño was ineffective in defending Guanajuato against Hidalgo's Indian and mestizo rebels. Convinced that the city was indefensible, he moved valuables and members of the Spanish elite into the fortified granary. The populace felt abandoned, and many from the lower classes joined the rebel assault. When Riaño was killed by a musket ball, the defenses collapsed and the garrison of the granary was massacred.

See also **Guanajuato.**

BIBLIOGRAPHY

Lucas Alamán, *Historia de México desde los primeros movimientos que prepararon su independencia en el año de 1808 hasta la época presente*, 5 vols. (1849–1852; repr. 1942).

José María Luis Mora, *México y sus revoluciones*, 3 vols. (1965).

Hugh M. Hamill, *The Hidalgo Revolt: Prelude to Mexican Independence* (1966).

Additional Bibliography

Rionda Arreguín, Isauro. *Hidalgo en la intendencia de Guanajuato.* Guanajuato: Archivo General del Gobierno del Estado de Guanajuato, 2003.

CHRISTON I. ARCHER

RIBAS, JOSÉ FÉLIX

RIBAS, JOSÉ FÉLIX (1775–1815). José Félix Ribas (*b.* 19 September 1775; *d.* 31 January 1815), officer in the Venezuelan Liberating Army. Ribas was connected to Simón Bolívar's family by his marriage to the Liberator's aunt. He was an outstanding participant in the declaration of a *cabildo abierto* and in the ouster of the Spanish governor, Emparán, on 19 April 1810 in Caracas. Ribas was a member of the Junta Suprema de Caracas and participated in the military campaign in defense of the republic under the orders of Francisco de Miranda. When the First Republic fell, he traveled to New Granada in 1813 and then returned with Bolívar as a troop commander in the Admirable Campaign. Bolívar appointed Ribas military chief of Caracas and commander of the province of Caracas. Ribas was successful in various military campaigns in the central area of the republic. With the fall of the Second Republic and the defeat of the republican forces, he was captured and executed by the royalist troops. His head was sent to Caracas and placed in a cage at the entrance to the city as a warning.

See also **Bolívar, Simón; Cabildo, Cabildo Abierto; Junta Suprema de Caracas.**

BIBLIOGRAPHY

Juan Vicente González, *Biografía de José Félix Ribas* (1956).

Miguel Ángel Mudarra, *Biografía de José Félix Ribas* (1975).

César Chirinos y Ender Cepeda, *José Félix Ribas: Rebelde de la juventud* (1980).

INÉS QUINTERO

RIBEIRO, DARCY

RIBEIRO, DARCY (1922–1997). Darcy Ribeiro (*b.* 26 November 1922; *d.* 17 February 1997), Brazilian anthropologist. Born in Montes Claros, Minas Gerais, Ribeiro did fieldwork among Indians in Amazonas and central Brazil. He also studied Indian acculturation with the support of UNESCO and organized the Indian Museum in Rio de Janeiro (1953). Interested in public education, Ribeiro became the first rector of the Universidade de Brasília (1961–1962) and served as minister of education and culture (1962–1963) during João Goulart's presidency. When the military seized power in 1964, Ribeiro, who was a member of the Executive Office of President Goulart, went into exile in Montevideo, Uruguay, where he taught anthropology at the Universidad de la República Oriental del Uruguay. He returned to Brazil in 1974 and resumed his political activity. From 1983 to 1987 he was governor of the state of Rio de Janeiro. His works on cultural anthropology treat the differences between American societies and the effects of civilization on Indian populations. During his last year of his life he dedicated himself to creating a distance education program for adults, *Escola Normal Superior*, in order to educate more teachers.

Among the most notable are *Religião e mitologia Kadiwéu* (1950), *Línguas e culturas indígenas no Brasil* (1957), *A política indigenista brasileira* (1962), *O processo civilizatório* (1968), *As Américas e a civilização* (1970), *Os índios e a civilização* (1970), *Os brasileiros* (1972), *O dilema da América latina* (1978), *O povo brasileiro* (1995). He wrote also several novels, *Maíra* (1977), *O mulo* (1981), and *Migo* (1988).

See also **Anthropology; Education: Overview; Education: Nonformal Education.**

BIBLIOGRAPHY

Egon Shaden, *Aculturação indígena* (1969).

John W. F. Dulles, *Unrest in Brazil: Political-Military Crisis 1955–1964* (1970).

Additional Bibliography

Bodley, John. *Tribal Peoples and Development Issues.* Mountain View, CA: Mayfield Publishing Co., 1988.

Bomeny, Helena. *Darcy Ribeiro: Sociologia de um indisciplinado.* Belo Horizonte, Brazil: Editora UFMG, 2001.

ELIANA MARIA REA GOLDSCHMIDT

RIBEIRO, JOÃO UBALDO

RIBEIRO, JOÃO UBALDO (1941–). João Ubaldo Ribeiro (*b.* 1941), Brazilian author. Born on the island of Itaparica, off the coast of

Bahia, Ribeiro spent his childhood in the state of Sergipe. Though he graduated from law school, he never pursued a legal career, becoming a journalist before turning to writing full time. A man of the world, he has lived in Bahia, as a university professor and editor of the *Tribuna da Bahia;* in Rio de Janeiro, as a journalist; in the United States, where he earned a master's degree in political sciences from the University of Southern California; in Portugal, as a recipient of a Gulbenkian scholarship; and in Germany, as a fellow of the Deutscher Akademicher Austranschdiens. Upon returning to Brazil shortly after celebrating his fortieth birthday, and feeling pressured by urban life, he moved back to his hometown in Itaparica, where he found the spiritual peace he craved to continue writing his books.

At age twenty-one Ribeiro published *Semana da Pátria* (National Week, 1962), which was followed by *Sargento Getúlio* (1971), the novel that earned him not only Brazilian fame but also world recognition. Its subject focuses on the paradoxical personality and isolation of a "strongman." With more than ten editions, the novel was the theme of a motion picture in Brazil and has been translated into more than six languages. Ribeiro's later books also received critical acclaim and high public praise: *Viva o povo brasileiro* (1984; *An Invincible Memory,* 1989) and *O sorriso do lagarto* (1989; The Iguana's Smile), which became a television miniseries in Brazil, *A Casa dos Budas Ditosos* (1999), *Miséria e grandeza do amor de Benedita,* (2000), which was the first electronic novel to be published in Brazil, and *Diário do Farol* (2002). In addition to his many novels, Ribeiro publishes frequently in the daily newspaper *O Globo.*

See also **Journalism; Literature: Brazil.**

BIBLIOGRAPHY

Cremilda De Araújo Medina, "João Ubaldo Ribeiro," in *A posse da terra: Escritor Brasileiro hoje* (1983), pp. 371–372.

Thomas Colchie, "João Ubaldo Ribeiro," in *A Hammock Beneath the Mangoes: Stories from Latin America* (1992), pp. 184–185.

Additional Bibliography

Coutinho, Wilson. *João Ubaldo Ribeiro: Um estilo da seducao.* Rio de Janeiro: Relume Dumará, 1998.

Domínguez, Mignon. *Historia, ficción y metaficción en la novela latinoamericana contemporánea.* Buenos Aires: Corregidor, 1996.

REGINA IGEL

RIBERA Y ESPINOSA, LÁZARO DE

(?–1824). Lázaro de Ribera y Espinosa (*d.* 1824), penultimate colonial governor of Paraguay. This Spanish-born hidalgo, soldier, and engineer, served as *gobernador-intendente* of Paraguay from 1795 to 1806. A prolix memorialist, contentious, and touchy about his "honor," he nonetheless was representative of the best type of authoritarian, efficient Bourbon administrator. During his eleven-year service he conducted a census of the province, improved public education, encouraged shipbuilding, and energetically promoted the export commerce of the province.

The War of Oranges with Portugal in the first years of the century caught Ribera in the midst of a reorganization of Paraguay's militia. He led an unsuccessful expedition up the Paraguay River to eject the Portuguese from Coimbra. Around the same time Ribera incurred the wrath of the viceroy, the Marqués de Avilés, by objecting to the military exemption for growers who contracted with the Real Renta de Tabacos in Paraguay and opposing the extinction of the communal property system in the Guaraní missions. In both cases Ribera was correct, but his contentious nature was noted in Spain and in 1806 he was relieved of his post. In 1812 he was appointed intendant of Huancavelica.

See also **Hidalgo.**

BIBLIOGRAPHY

John Lynch, *Spanish Colonial Administration, 1782–1810: The Intendant System in the Viceroyalty of the Río de la Plata* (1958).

Jerry W. Cooney, *Economía y sociedad en la Intendencia del Paraguay* (1990).

Additional Bibliography

Palau Baquero, Mercedes, and Blanca Sáiz, editors. *Moxos: Descripciones exactas e historia fiel de los indios, animales y plantas de la provincia de Moxos en el virreinato del Perú.* Madrid: Ministerio de Agricultura, Pesca y Alimentación, ICONA-INSPV: Ediciones El Viso, 1989.

JERRY W. COONEY

RIBEYRO, JULIO RAMÓN (1929–1994).

Julio Ramón Ribeyro (*b.* 31 August 1929; *d.* 4 December 1994), Peruvian fiction writer. Ribeyro is known for his short stories, more than one hundred in all, most of which have been published collectively in four volumes, *La palabra del mudo* (1972–1992). He also wrote successful novels, plays, and literary criticism. Ribeyro especially captured a unique perspective on contemporary life in *Prosas apátridas* (1975; 3d ed., 1986), a combination of pithy but ironic philosophical vignettes, intimate diary, and brief thought pieces. Ribeyro began writing in 1952; he moved to Europe, where he lived thereafter. His fiction reflects this separation from Peru, and writing from a marginalized position of self-imposed exile, Ribeyro's sharp observation and minute detail bring biting irony to his social commentary and give it life by enveloping his characters in fantastic elements—enigma, the double, the eccentric, and the bizarre. His characters suffer the anonymity of urban life in Lima or Paris, where their simple lives are played out in private and public places. Ribeyro probed his characters' psyches from a position of compassionate skepticism; hence, the stories have a tone of melancholic pessimism that captures in ironic fashion the banality, absurdity, and anguish of a fake bourgeoisie that lacks any history, future, or identity. The subtle combination of social commentary and fantasy in Ribeyro's narrative is what makes the stories distinct, readable, and contemporary. In 1994, the year that Ribeyro died, he was awarded the *Premio Juan Rulfo de Literatura Latinoamericana y del Caribe*.

See also **Literature: Spanish America.**

BIBLIOGRAPHY

Dick Gerdes, "Julio Ramón Ribeyro: Un análisis de sus cuentos," *Kentucky Romance Quarterly* 26, no. 1 (1979): 51–110.

Julio Ortega, "Los cuentos de Ribeyro," *Cuadernos Hispanoamericanos* 417 (1985): 128–145.

José Miguel Oviedo, Introduction to his *Julio Ramón Ribeyro: Silvio in the Rose Garden*, translated by Maria Rosa Fort and Frank Graziano (1989).

James Higgins, *Cambio social y constantes humanos: La narrativa corta de Ribeyro* (1991).

Additional Bibliography

Elmore, Peter. *El perfil de la palabra: La obra de Julio Ramón Ribeyro*. Lima, Peru: Fondo de Cultura Económica, 2002.

Navascués, Javier de. *Los refugios de La memoria: Un studio espacial sobre Julio Ramón Ribeyro*. Madrid: Verveurt, 2004.

Weiss, Jason. *The Lights of Home: A Century of Latin American Writers in Paris*. New York: Routledge, 2003.

DICK GERDES

RICCHIERI, PABLO (1859–1936).

Pablo Ricchieri (*b.* 1859; *d.* 1936), Argentine military leader. Born in Santa Fe Province, Argentina, Ricchieri was the son of Italian immigrants. He studied in the Franciscan College, San Lorenzo, and entered the Military Academy, graduating in 1879. Between 1883 and 1886 Ricchieri studied at the Belgium War College. He was then assigned to the Argentine military legation in Germany. He returned to Argentina in 1886 and served on the general staff. Between 1890 and 1898 Ricchieri made numerous trips to Europe to purchase arms. Returning to Argentina, he was designated director general of arsenals and later chief of staff of the army. In 1900 he was named minister of war and on 12 October 1904 he was designated director of the Military Academy.

Ricchieri is credited for having modernized the Argentine army. In 1901 he approved Law 4301 (known as the Ricchieri Law), which created obligatory military service (conscription). He divided Argentina into seven military districts and reorganized the War Department. In 1910 Ricchieri was promoted to division general and in 1916 commissioned as an observer to the fighting on the Western Front. On 7 August 1922 he retired with the rank of lieutenant general. After retiring, General Ricchieri served on numerous commissions.

See also **Argentina: The Nineteenth Century; Armed Forces.**

BIBLIOGRAPHY

Reseña historica y organica del ejercito argentino, 3 vols. (1972); *Ejercito argentino: Cronología militar argentina, 1806–1980* (1982).

Additional Bibliography

Forte, Ricardo. *Fuerzas armadas, cultura política y seguridad interna: Orígenes y consolidación del poder militar en Argentina, 1853–1943.* Mexico City: R. Fonte, 2001.

ROBERT SCHEINA

RICE INDUSTRY. A basic foodstuff of Latin America, rice is grown in nearly every country, primarily for domestic consumption, under varying ecological conditions: as a rain-fed ("upland" or "dryland") crop or as "wet rice" in coastal lowlands, river deltas, interior swamps, and savannas. Native varieties, semiaquatic plants similar to the "wild rice" of North America, exist, but *Oryza sativa,* the customary white rice of Asian origin, which had been brought to the Mediterranean and Africa by the Arabs, reached Latin America through the Atlantic migrations of Europeans and Africans. Its introduction is relatively obscure, eclipsed by indigenous staples and the development of large-scale plantation export crops.

Scarcely developed in Spain and Portugal in the sixteenth century, rice was extended to settlements in the Americas at the time of their founding. Rice shoots from the Cape Verde Islands were furnished to Portuguese colonists at Salvador, Bahia, in the 1550s. The contribution of African slaves, whose ethnic and regional origins were the rice-growing groups of the Upper Guinea coast, was undoubtedly significant to the diffusion of rice. The history of rice in Guyana has been traced to communities of runaway slaves. By the mid-seventeenth century, rice agriculture was common on marginal lands of the great plantations in Brazilian colonies and was probably well established in Spanish America as well. Rice surpluses from the Lambayeque River valley in Peru were exported to the Isthmus of Panama.

Loading rice onto a riverboat, Santarém, Brazil. Brazil is the largest producer of rice in Latin America and the Caribbean and also a major importer. **PHOTOGRAPH BY SUSAN D. ROCK. REPRODUCED BY PERMISSION**

From humble origins in the provision plots of slaves and sailors' rations, rice consumption has been linked since the eighteenth century to demand from expanding populations for nutritionally varied and efficiently stored comestibles. In imitation of the successful plantation production of rice in the British American colonies, Portugal looked to Brazilian rice to reduce its trade balances, introducing "Carolina rice" seed in the Amazon Delta (Maranhão and Pará) in the 1750s and granting monopoly licenses to rice millers there and in Rio de Janeiro. (The millers were responsible for threshing, dehusking, and polishing the "paddy," or unprocessed grain in the husk.) State-led development afterward languished as a result of South Atlantic trade disruptions during the Napoleonic Wars and an emphasis on export staples after independence. With the spread of mechanized agriculture and increased migration to the cities late in the eighteenth century, large landholders sought tariff protection that benefited domestic crops such as rice.

Rice is now a crop of the modern frontier. Interim rice plantings transform land cleared by indiscriminate burning into cattle pasture. Traditional production is mostly of the upland variety by small farmers who interplant it with other crops and straddle the subsistence sector with occasional surpluses for cash. In some microregions, such as Brazil, where three-quarters of Latin America's total rice acreage is concentrated (most of it of the upland variety), irrigated rice is exploited by large-scale commercial agriculture. Rice is grown as well in Argentina, Colombia, Ecuador, Peru, and Uruguay. The higher-yielding irrigated rice has been the focus of "green revolution" efforts to expand production through the introduction of hybrid varieties, increased mechanization, and the application of chemical fertilizers. Indeed, rice production has become significantly more efficient. In South America, between the 1980s and 2002, the area used to produce rice decreased 25 percent, but overall production increased by 59 percent. This greater efficiency has generally brought down prices, which has helped the poor, who spend a disproportionate amount of their income on food. By 2006, rice contributed more to the average Latin American's diet than wheat, maize, or potatoes.

See also **Agriculture; Slavery: Spanish America.**

BIBLIOGRAPHY

Edward Albes, "Rice in the Americas," *Bulletin of the Pan American Union* 44, no. 2 (February 1917): 137–160.

Paul I. Mandell, "A expansão da moderna rizicultura brasileira—crescimento da oferta numa economia dinâmica," *Revista brasileira de economia* 26, no. 3 (1972): 169–236.

Corsino Medeiros Dos Santos, "Cultura, indústria e comérccio de arroz no Brasil colonial," *Revista do Instituto Histórico e Geográfico brasileiro* 318 (1978): 36–61.

Additional Bibliography

Lang, James. *Feeding a Hungry Planet: Rice, Research and Development in Asia and Latin America.* Chapel Hill: University of North Carolina Press, 1996.

CATHERINE LUGAR

RIEGO Y NÚÑEZ, RAFAEL DEL

(1785–1823). Rafael del Riego y Núñez (*b.* 24 October 1785; *d.* 7 November 1823), leader of a revolt (*pronunciamiento*) against Ferdinand VII (1820) and president of the Cortes (1822–1823) in Spain. Riego y Núñez was an army officer stationed in Cádiz on the eve of Spain's Great Expedition to quell rebellion in the New World. Disaffected with Ferdinand's treatment of the army and the proposed American campaign, Riego y Núñez and his troops proclaimed their support for the Constitution of 1812 on 1 January 1820. In February, the military uprising spread to royal armies stationed at La Coruña, Saragossa, and Barcelona. Ferdinand accepted the constitutional restoration in March and, for the next three years, presided over increasingly liberal governments led by men he had persecuted in 1814.

In Spain, the revolt established a pattern for future liberal revolutions, which would begin with an army revolt followed by provincial support and, finally, government response in Madrid. In the New World, the revolt signified the end of any chance of sending a large army to reinforce royalist forces and practically guaranteed independence for the various colonies.

See also **Ferdinand VII of Spain; Spain, Constitution of 1812.**

BIBLIOGRAPHY

José Luis Comellas, *Los primeros pronunciamientos en España, 1814–1820* (1958).

Margaret L. Woodward, "The Spanish Army and the Loss of America, 1810–1824," in *Hispanic American Historical Review* 48, no. 4 (1968): 586–607.

Timothy E. Anna, *Spain and the Loss of America* (1983), esp. pp. 189–294.

Additional Bibliography

Pérez López-Portillo, Raúl. *La España de Riego*. Madrid: Sílex, 2005.

SUZANNE HILES BURKHOLDER

RIESCO, LAURA (1940–). Laura Riesco is a Peruvian-born writer who lived in the United States after 1959. After studies in Michigan and Kentucky, Riesco taught Spanish-American literature at the University of Maine at Orono from 1969 until her retirement in 2005. Her experimental novel *El truco de los ojos* was published in 1978. Her second novel, *Ximena de dos caminos* (*Ximena at the Crossroads*), published in 1994, won many awards, including the designation "best novel of the year" in Peru and the 1995 Latino Literature Prize of the New York Latin American Writers' Institute. The novel is an innovative depiction of a Peruvian white middle-class child who examines the Indian and European cultures that surround her. Riesco has published literary articles and numerous short stories, many of which have been translated into English.

See also **Literature: Spanish America.**

BIBLIOGRAPHY

Riesco, Laura. *El truco de los ojos*. Lima: Editorial Milla Batres, 1978.

Riesco, Laura. *Ximena de dos caminos*. Lima: PEISA, 1994. Translated by Mary G. Berg as *Ximena at the Crossroads*. Fredonia, NY: White Pine Press, 1998.

MARY G. BERG

RIESCO ERRÁZURIZ, GERMÁN (1854–1916). Germán Riesco Errázuriz (*b*. 18 May 1854; *d*. 8 December 1916), president of Chile (1901–1906). A lawyer and professional bureaucrat, Riesco served for almost twenty years as a judge before entering the Senate. Apparently selected as a presidential candidate because he did

not threaten the political order, Riesco fulfilled his backers' expectations by essentially doing nothing. His inactivity proved grievous, because the nation suffered from mounting social unrest as well as bitter labor disputes during his tenure. His government's response was to crush outbreaks brutally.

Although Riesco's internal policies lacked both compassion and vision, he did manage to end an extremely costly naval arms race and to avoid war with Argentina by seeking a negotiated settlement to a long-festering border problem. In 1902 he signed the May Pacts (Pactos de Mayo), which, while limiting Chile's sphere of influence to the Southern Hemisphere's Pacific Coast, ended open hostility with Buenos Aires. Riesco's government also negotiated a peace treaty with Bolivia in 1904 which granted Chile the Atacama region but obliged Santiago to finance a railroad from Arica, where the Bolivians would enjoy a duty-free zone, to La Paz.

See also **Chile: The Twentieth Century; May Pacts (1902).**

BIBLIOGRAPHY

Germán Riesco, *Presidencia de Riesco, 1901–1906* (1950).

Luis Galdames, *A History of Chile* (1941), pp. 437, 510–511.

Additional Bibliography

Errázuriz Guilisasti, Octavio, and Germán Carrasco Domínguez. *Las relaciones chileno-argentinas durante la presidencia de Riesco, 1901–1906*. Santiago de Chile: Editorial Andrés Bello, 1968.

WILLIAM F. SATER

RIGAUD, ANDRÉ (1761–1811). André Rigaud (*b*. 1761; *d*. 18 September 1811), Haitian general. A mulatto born in Les Cayes, Haiti, and educated in Bordeaux, France, Rigaud trained as a goldsmith and began his military career serving the French during the American Revolution. At the height of the Haitian Revolution, he was appointed commander in the South, where he reestablished prosperity and gained mulatto support through harsh but effective rule. His superiors in Port-au-Prince found him resistant to their direction, but depended heavily on his control over mulattoes and his excellent military skills against the British. In

1799 he entered into a power struggle with the black leader and national hero Toussaint Louverture that resulted in Rigaud's defeat and exile to France. He returned to Haiti in 1810.

See also **Haiti.**

BIBLIOGRAPHY

Theodore Lothrop Stoddard, *The French Revolution in San Domingo* (1914).

Cyril L. R. James, *The Black Jacobins: Toussaint L'Ouverture and the San Domingo Revolution,* 2d ed. (1963).

Ralph Korngold, *Citizen Toussaint* (1965).

Victor Schoelcher, *Vie de Toussaint Louverture* (1982).

Robert Louis Stein, *Léger Félicité Sonthonax. The Lost Sentinel of the Republic* (1985).

Additional Bibliography

Heinl, Robert Debs, Nancy Gordon Heinl, and Michael Heinl. *Written in Blood: The Story of the Haitian People, 1492–1995.* Lanham, MD: University Press of America, 2005.

Nicholls, David. *From Dessalines to Duvalier: Race, Colour, and National Independence in Haiti.* New Brunswick, NJ: Rutgers University Press, 1996.

PHILIPPE L. SEILER

RÍMAC RIVER.

Rímac River, a waterway in coastal Peru flowing east-west from the central highlands to the Pacific Ocean. The Rímac joins the Santa Eulalia River to form the main valley of the Peruvian capital city, Lima. The water supply of this river depends mainly on seasonal highland rains. On the coast during the dry months of June to October, the Rímac's water flow is reduced to a trickle. Old Lima was founded by the Spaniard Francisco Pizarro in 1535 along the southern banks of the Rímac. By the eighteenth century the Lima district of Rímac had developed on the northern side of the river, connected to Old Lima through bridges. The town of Chosica, just north of Lima, is another urban settlement in the Rímac Valley.

See also **Lima.**

BIBLIOGRAPHY

Manuel A. Fuentes, *Lima, apuntes históricos, descriptivos, estadísticos y de costumbres* (1867).

Additional Bibliography

Atlas ambiental popular del cuenca alta del Río Rímac. Lima: OACA: Christian Aid, UK, 2003.

Hunefeldt, Christine. *A Brief History of Peru.* New York: Facts on File, 2004.

Tello, Julio C. *Arqueología del valle de Lima.* Lima: Museo de Arqueología y Antropología, Universidad Nacional Mayor de San Marcos, 1999.

ALFONSO W. QUIROZ

RINCONCITO, TREATY OF (1838).

The Treaty of (1838) Rinconcito was an accord signed at Rinconcito, Guatemala, near Jutiapa, on December 23, 1838, between the rebel caudillo Rafael Carrera and General Agustín Guzmán of Totonicapán. Carrera agreed to lay down his arms and recognize the Guatemalan government in return for his restoration as military commander of Mita. Although he had to turn over several hundred rifles to Guzmán, the treaty allowed Carrera time to reorganize his forces at a point when he was in desperate straits. When federal President Francisco Morazán deposed Mariano Rivera Paz, the conservative governor of Guatemala, Carrera resumed his revolution on March 24, 1839. On April 13 he took Guatemala City and restored Rivera Paz.

See also **Carrera, José Rafael.**

BIBLIOGRAPHY

Tobar Cruz, Pedro. *Los montañeses,* 2nd edition. Guatemala: Ministerio de Educación Pública, 1959.

Woodward, Jr., Ralph Lee. "Social Revolution in Guatemala: The Carrera Revolt." *Applied Enlightenment: Nineteenth Century Liberalism.* Middle American Research Institute, Tulane University, 23 (1972), pp. 45–70.

Zamora Castellanos, Pedro. *Vida militar de Centro América.* Guatemala: Editorial del Ejército, 1966.

RALPH LEE WOODWARD JR.

RIO, JOÃO DO (1880–1921).

João Do Rio (pseudonym of Paulo Barreto; (*b.* 5 August 1880; *d.* 23 June 1921), Brazilian writer. João do Rio—reporter, short story writer, and man about town—enjoyed a tremendous reputation during his brief lifetime; he was regarded as the personification of Brazilian culture at the turn of the century and was elected to the Brazilian Academy of Letters before he reached age thirty. While one or two of his short stories (particularly the grotesque carnival tale "O bebê de Tarlatana Rosa") are still anthologized, his fame dissipated within a few years after his death. That fame depended, in large measure, upon his public persona, which João do Rio carefully modeled on Oscar Wilde; the persona is also the focus of much of the bibliography on his life and work, although few biographers and critics have directly addressed the central issue of his homosexuality. His stories and nonfiction accounts of Rio de Janeiro, such as *A alma encantadora das ruas* (1908), are now read primarily as social documents, for they provide more or less realistic descriptions of the city's underworld of brothels and cabarets, a world in which perversion, cruelty, disease, and suffering reigned.

See also **Homosexuality and Bisexuality in Literature; Literature: Brazil.**

BIBLIOGRAPHY

I. De L. Neves Manta, *A arte e a neurose de João do Rio,* 5th ed. (1976).

R. Magalhães Júnior, *A vida vertiginosa de João do Rio* (1978).

Julie Jones, "Paulo Barreto's 'O bebê de tarlatana rosa': A Carnival Adventure," in *Luso-Brazilian Review* 24, no. 1 (1987): 27–33.

Raúl Antelo, *João do Rio: O dândi e a especulação* (1989).

Additional Bibliography

Gomes, Renato Cordeiro. *João do Rio: Vielas do vício, ruas da graça.* Rio de Janeiro: Relume Dumará: Rio Arte, 1996.

Rodrigues, Antonio Edmilson Martins. *João do Rio, a cidade e o poeta: O olhar de flâneur na belle époque tropical.* Rio de Janeiro: Editora FGV, 2000.

Rodrigues, João Carlos. *João do Rio: Uma biografia.* Rio de Janeiro: Topbooks, 1996.

DAVID T. HABERLY

RÍO AZUL. Río Azul, a Maya archaeological site in the extreme northeastern part of Guatemala, on the river of the same name. The zone was occupied from about 900 BCE to 880 CE. Pioneer farmers and, later, early aristocrats organized the zone into a line of villages, temples, and large platforms along the east bank of the river. About 380 CE, the zone was conquered by Tikal and the native elite executed. Tikal then established a new city, which had the functions of protecting the state's northwestern frontier, controlling trade to the Caribbean, and administering the region. Río Azul was defensible and probably fortified. In about 150 years, 729 buildings were constructed and one of the largest Early Classic temples in the Maya lowlands was built (Str. A–3).

In the fifth century CE the rulers of Tikal sent a member of the family to Río Azul as governor. He was accompanied by two advisers who were most likely foreigners from Teotihuacán in central Mexico. Eventually, the governor died and was buried in the most elaborate painted tomb ever found in the Maya lowlands. A series of painted tombs for other governors and their family members was created during this period. Elaborate temples were built over the tombs. During the sixth century CE Río Azul was devastated by burning and other destruction and abandoned for about 120 years. It later became a military outpost, but about 840 CE was taken again and burned in a raid by northern Maya. The zone was abandoned in the general collapse of southern Maya civilization by 900 CE.

See also **Archaeology; Maya, the.**

BIBLIOGRAPHY

Richard E. W. Adams, "Río Azul, Lost City of the Maya," in *National Geographic* 169, no. 4 (1986): 420–451, and "Archaeological Research at the Lowland Maya City of Río Azul," in *Latin American Antiquity* 1, no. 1 (1990): 23–41.

Richard E. W. Adams and Hubert R. Robichaux, "Tombs of Río Azul, Guatemala," in *National Geographic Research and Exploration* 8, no. 4 (1992): 412–427.

Additional Bibliography

Adams, Richard E. W. *Río Azul: An Ancient Maya City.* Norman: University of Oklahoma Press, 1999.

Atran, Scott, Ximena Lois, and Edilberto Ucan Ek. *Plants of the Petén Itza' Maya = Plantas de los maya itza' del Petén.* Ann Arbor: Museum of Anthropology, University of Michigan, 2004.

Evans, Susan Toby. *Ancient Mexico & Central America: Aarchaeology and Culture History*. London: Thames & Hudson, 2004.

R. E. W. ADAMS

RIOBAMBA.

Riobamba, sierra city (2001 population est. 124,807), the capital of Chimborazo province in the central sierra of Ecuador. Riobamba, the "Sultan of the Andes," was founded in 1534 by Spanish conquistador Sebastián de Belalcázar. Earlier an important Inca center, Riobamba under Spanish colonialism developed as a relatively prosperous textile manufacturing center. Obrajes produced woolen ponchos and blankets for export to Peru's silver-mining districts. However, a series of epidemics hit the sierra in 1692–1695, reducing the population by from a quarter to half. The loss of the labor force crippled Riobamba's textile industry. It never recovered, and demographic and economic stagnation continued until the present century.

Continuing exploitation of the natives by the Europeans during the colonial period and after gave the Riobamba region a certain notoriety for frequent Indian revolts. The most serious occurred in 1764, when Indians rose up in response to the imposition of higher taxes. In this revolt, as in all others, authorities settled the issue by killing an untold number of Indians. Earthquakes have also repeatedly brought disaster to Riobamba. That of 1645 was particularly severe. The earthquake of 1797 destroyed the city, forcing city fathers to relocate Riobamba on the plain of Tapi.

Riobamba played an important role in Ecuador's separation from Gran Colombia, serving as the site for the Constituent Congress of May 1830 that drew up the nation's declaration of independence and its first constitution.

On August 16, 2006, Riobamba's inhabitants were imperiled when a volcano 80 miles south of Quito known as Tungurahua erupted and rained down rocks and ash in the city.

See also **Belalcázar, Sebastián de; Earthquakes; Textile Industry: The Colonial Era; Volcanoes.**

BIBLIOGRAPHY

For a summary of sierra history and culture, see Thomas Weil et al., *Area Handbook for Ecuador* (1973).

Additional Bibliography

Campaña, Victor. *Fiesta y poder: La celebración de Rey de Reyes en Riobamba*. Quito: AbyaYala, 1991.

Morales Mejía, Juan Carlos. *Riobamba: Del luterano al terremoto*. Riobamba, Ecuador: Diario de la Prensa, 1998.

Pazmiño, Rocio; Nidia Gómez; Rocío Rueda N.; and Rosemarie Teran. *La antigua Riobamba: Historia oculta de una ciudad colonial*. Riobamba, Ecuador: Municipio de Riobamba; Quito: Abya-Yala, 2000.

RONN F. PINEO

RÍO BLANCO STRIKE.

Río Blanco Strike, an incident that started at the Río Blanco Cotton Mill near Río Blanco, Veracruz, in January 1907. In December 1906 textile factory workers in the neighboring state of Puebla went on strike to protest the owners' implementation of a new, unified set of regulations that affected all aspects of mill hands' lives. Laborers in Veracruz, including those at Río Blanco, aided their striking colleagues in Puebla through donations of monies and foodstuffs. In retaliation, owners in Veracruz implemented a lockout to prevent the flow of aid and to break the local labor organization, the Gran Confederación de Obreros Libres (Grand Confederation of Free Workers—GCOL).

In early January 1907, unprecedented mediation by President Porfirio Díaz (1876–1880, 1884–1911) resulted in an agreement to end the conflict. Nevertheless, at Río Blanco, many workers rejected the pact and determined not to return to work. Meanwhile, resentment over the actions of the French-owned company store, which had refused credit during the lockout, grew. Many families were without food, and payday was a full week away. When laborers converged on the store, shots were fired from inside, prompting its sacking and burning. Violence soon spread to the whole Orizaba region, and rural and regular federal troops hunted down protesters, executing many on the spot. Over a three-day period, 7–9 January 1907, at least fifty to seventy workers died. Subsequently, the Río Blanco strike, although strictly speaking not a strike but a revolt, became a nationalist symbol representing the long historical struggles for social justice and for the economic independence of the Mexican nation.

See also **Cotton; Labor Movements.**

BIBLIOGRAPHY

Rodney D. Anderson, *Outcasts in Their Own Land: Mexican Industrial Workers, 1906–1911* (1976), pp. 137–171.

John M. Hart, *Anarchism & the Mexican Working Class, 1860–1931* (1978), pp. 93–100.

Ciro F. S. Cardoso, Francisco G. Hermosillo, and Salvador Hernández, *La clase obrera en la historia de México* (1980), pp. 139–186.

Additional Bibliography

García Díaz, Bernardo. *Textiles del valle de Orizaba (1880–1925): Cinco ensayos de historia sindical y social.* Xalapa: Universidad Veracruzana, Centro de Investigaciones Históricas, 1990.

Koth, Karl B. *Waking the Dictator: Veracuz, the Struggle for Federalism and the Mexican Revolution, 1870–1927.* Calgary: University of Calgary Press, 2002.

DAVID G. LAFRANCE

RIO BRANCO. *See* **Roraima.**

RIO BRANCO, BARÃO DO (1845–1912). Barão do Rio Branco (José Maria da Silva Paranhos Junior; *b.* 20 April 1845; *d.* 9 February 1912), Brazilian foreign minister. Rio Branco's prestige was founded on his successful settlement of frontier disputes. He was influenced forcefully by his father and namesake, the Viscount do Rio Branco, who was a noted diplomat and Conservative statesman. As a law student at São Paulo (1862) and Recife (1866) as secretary to his father during delicate diplomacy in the Río de la Plata (1869, 1870–1871), Rio Branco acquired a taste for diplomatic and military history not only of that area but of Brazil generally. He cultivated this taste over decades, first as a political journalist and deputy, then in his quiet diplomatic routine as consul in Liverpool (1876–1893). He pursued his studies and bibliophilia in the Parisian home he maintained for his family.

Rio Branco's erudition gradually became well known among cognoscenti; when a representative for the arbitration with Argentina over the Missions area was required, Rio Branco was remembered. His celebrated commitment to painstaking research and analysis was first remarked in this case (1893–1895). Victory dispelled obscurity; first named to a more prestigious European post, he was then sent to contest Gallic claims associated with French Guiana (1898–1900). A second victory was rewarded with the ministerial position in Berlin (1900–1902), after which he became the minister of foreign affairs in the dynamic administration of Rodrigues Alves (1902–1906).

Rio Branco was a member of that administration and those that followed for an unprecedented ten years, comprising the golden age of Brazil's diplomatic prestige. From Itamaratí Palace, Rio Branco continued to orchestrate the peaceful settlement of various frontier disputes from Dutch Guiana to Uruguay. He is noted, for example, for negotiating the end to the confrontation over the upper-Amazon sources of natural rubber, a negotiation that led to the origins of the present state of Acre (1904). Rio Branco also oversaw Brazil's developing relationship with the United States. He raised the diplomatic status of Brazil's representation in Washington, D.C., and he appointed Joaquim Nabuco as the first ambassador (1905–1910) to signal appreciation of the relationship's importance.

While Argentina saw itself as a hemispheric rival of the United States, Brazil preferred the role of junior partner. Brazil supported the Pan-American movement, whose Third Conference was held in Rio de Janeiro in 1906. Rio Branco is famed for his successful projection of Brazil's image as a "civilized" nation during this era of Eurocentric imperialism. He did this by attracting the nation's cultivated elite to diplomacy, by ensuring Brazil's inclusion at international meetings, by encouraging celebrated foreigners to travel to Brazil, and by promoting positive reports of the country and its past. His triumphs brought him a singular popularity which, like his books and maps, surrounded him in the cluttered Itamaratí apartment in which he died.

See also **Acre; Pan-Americanism.**

BIBLIOGRAPHY

Raul Do Rio-Branco, *Reminiscencias do Barão do Rio-Branco* (1942).

Álvaro Lins, *Rio Branco* (1945).

Carolina Nabuco, *The Life of Joaquim Nabuco* (1950).

Luís Viana, *A vida do Barão do Rio Branco* (1959).

E. Bradford Burns, *The Unwritten Alliance* (1966).

Additional Bibliography

Lins, Alvaro. *Rio Branco, o Barão do Rio Branco: Biografia pessoal e história política: texto completo.* São Paulo: Editora Alfa Omega, 1996.

Moura, Cristina Patriota de. *Rio Branco, a monarquía e a república.* Rio de Janeiro: FGV, 2003.

Ricupero, Rubens. *Rio Branco: O Brasil no mundo.* Rio de Janeiro: Petrobrás, 2000.

JEFFREY D. NEEDELL

RIO BRANCO, VISCONDE DO (1819–1880).

Visconde do Rio Branco (José Maria da Silva Paranhos; *b.* 16 March 1819; *d.* 1 November 1880), Brazilian statesman and diplomat. Paranhos, father of the Barão do Rio Branco, was a foremost statesman of the monarchy (1822–1889), celebrated for his Platine diplomacy and the Free Birth Law (1871), the first direct attack on Brazilian slave holding.

Born in Bahia and orphaned early, Paranhos escaped poverty through scholarship at Rio's navy and army academies, where he studied and then taught. Literary skill brought him early prominence as a journalist and as a Liberal deputy (1848). He caught the attention of Honório Hermeto Carneiro Leão, later Marquês de Paraná, a powerful chief of the Conservative Party. Leão was entrusted by his old ally, Paulino José Soares de Sousa, later Visconde do Uruguai, with the diplomacy in Uruguay that would lead to the victorious alliance against Argentina's Juan Manuel de Rosas in 1850. In Paranhos, Leão hoped for an able lieutenant, and he was vindicated. Both Soares de Sousa and Leão were impressed enough to champion Paranhos's entry into the Conservative Party and his election as Conservative deputy for Rio de Janeiro province in 1853.

Paranhos, despite his relative youth, was next appointed a minister in the celebrated *Conciliação* (Conciliation) Cabinet organized by Paraná in 1853. He served in several posts from 1853 to 1871, including minister of foreign affairs. Other portfolios followed in the 1850s and 1860s, as did the presidency of Rio de Janeiro Province (1858), ascension to the Senate (for Mato Grosso in 1862) and to the Council of State (1866), and several controversial missions to the Río de la Plata republics (1857, 1864–1865, 1869–1870, and 1870–1871), involving negotiations leading up to and ending the War of the Triple Alliance.

In 1871 the emperor picked him as prime minister to organize a cabinet to address the question of slavery. Rio Branco did so, at the beginning of the longest ministry (1871–1875) of the monarchy. He also defended the crown's prerogatives vis-à-vis the church in the Religious Question, a dispute sparked by two bishops' decision to condemn the participation of Brazilian Catholics in freemasonry. And he introduced many reforms on elections, education, justice, and the infrastructure. But his greatest accomplishment was the passage of the Free Birth Law in 1871, which, like earlier Spanish and English colonial legislation, declared all children of slave mothers free upon majority and provided for self-manumission and apprenticeship. A consummate politician and orator, Rio Branco successfully isolated and then dominated the fierce and able resistance to slavery's reform, led by the namesake and son of his old protector, Paulino José Soares de Sousa. Although its ultimate failure figured in the struggle for complete abolition begun less than a decade later, Rio Branco's legislation was a hard-won and politically crucial step and thus remains his great claim upon posterity.

See also **Brazil, Political Parties: Conservative Party; Slave Trade, Abolition of: Brazil.**

BIBLIOGRAPHY

Visconde De Taunay, *O Visconde do Rio Branco* (1930).

Lidia Besouchet, *José Maria Paranhos* (1945).

Barão Do Rio Branco, *Biografías* (1947).

Robert E. Conrad, *The Destruction of Brazilian Slavery, 1850–1888* (1972).

Joaquim Nabuco, *Um estadista do império* (1975).

José Murilo De Carvalho, *Teatro de sombras* (1988).

Additional Bibliography

José, Oiliam. *Visconde do Rio Branco: Terra, povo, história.* Belo Horizonte: Impr. Oficial de Minas Gerais, 1982.

Vieira, Hermes. *A vida e a época do Visconde do Rio Branco*. São Paulo: T.A. Queiroz, Editor, 1992.

JEFFREY D. NEEDELL

RIO BRANCO INSTITUTE.

Rio Branco Institute, an advanced school of diplomacy that provides the professional training required of all candidates for service in the Brazilian diplomatic corps. Founded 18 April 1945, on the centenary of the birth of the "father of Brazilian diplomacy," the Barão do Rio Branco, the institute operates in coordination with federal and state universities in twelve regional locations (Belém, Belo Horizonte, Campo Grande, Curitiba, Florianópolis, Fortaleza, Manaus, Porto Alegre, Recife, Rio de Janeiro, Salvador, and São Paulo). For the Foreign Service Preparation Course (Curso de Preparação à Carreira de Diplomata), the institute accepts qualified candidates from other developing nations as well, preparing them to serve in their own nations' diplomatic corps. Incoming candidates must have completed university, speak Portuguese and French or English, and pass a rigorous entrance exam before beginning study. In addition to training new recruits, the school provides advanced training to serving diplomats. The institute is the only school authorized to recruit and train Brazilian diplomats, and is one reason why the foreign ministry is considered to be among the most effective in the government as well as a leader in the field throughout the developing world.

See also **Rio Branco, Barão do.**

BIBLIOGRAPHY

Ministério Das Relações Exteriores, *Relatório* (1985) and "Guia de Estudos para o Concurso de Admissão ao Curso de Preparação à Carreira de Diplomata do Instituto Rio Branco" (1995).

U.S. Library of Congress, *Brazil, a country study* (1983).

Additional Bibliography

Ministério das Relações Exteriores. *Instituto Rio-Branco, 50 anos*. Rio de Janeiro: Ministério das Relações Exteriores, 1996.

THOMAS GAROFALO

RIO BRANCO LAW. *See* **Free Birth Law.**

RIO CONFERENCE. *See* **Pan-American Conferences: Rio Conference (1942); Pan-American Conferences: Rio Conference (1947); Pan-American Conferences: Rio Conference (1954).**

RIO DE JANEIRO (CITY).

Founded in 1565, Rio de Janeiro first served as a port for some local sugar and as the effectively autonomous capital for its hinterland and the southern captaincies. As such the city was eclipsed by others on the northern coast of the state of Brazil, such as Recife, Olinda, and Salvador, the capital—all wealthy places associated with more lucrative trade in sugar, African captives, and European luxuries.

COLONIAL METAMORPHOSES: 1565–1822

Rio's ascension came with the discovery of gold and diamonds in Minas Gerais in 1690s and with the eighteenth-century Río de la Plata conflicts. As Minas's port and the capital closest to the disputes with Spain, Rio was made viceregal seat in 1763, supplanting Salvador. New building, wealth, mercantile and official elites, and amenities followed; Rio grew west between its old hills, filling its marshlands. By 1799, its population was about 43,000, of which one-third were slaves. Still, the city remained small and backward by European notions when the Portuguese court sought refuge from Napoléon there (1808–1820). João VI brought with him a numerous, refined court population as well as commercial obligations to British allies. These, and Rio's new imperial role, effected radical change. Restrictions on trade, industry, education, and printing ended; political supremacy, advanced schooling, foreign merchants, and economic incentives were established. By 1821, with a population of about 112,000, half of it slaves, Rio was a thriving, more cosmopolitan city.

NATIONAL PRIMACY: 1822–1930

Coffee, brought inland from Rio by the late eighteenth century, quickly prospered in the city's hinterland; by the 1830s, its export value surpassed that of sugar. Rio flourished with coffee and the court, and its elite enjoyed new wealth and European luxuries. The city's population reached 186,000 (half slave) by 1850 and 235,000 by 1870. Life was marked by a slow acquisition of amenities. European-style urban transportation, sewage, lighting, new docks to the north, and the first important railhead were established between 1830 and 1870. Other trends included new epidemic diseases; crowded, wretched housing for the masses; and new residential class distinctions. By 1850, elite urban homes were increasingly built in the South Zone. The poor survived near the shops, port, and workshops in the Old City; on the hills near the northern dockside (where the first Favelas, hillside shantytowns, emerged by the late 1800s); and on the filled-in marshlands leading north. Mass-consumption manufacturing began around 1850, when investors in the suppressed African slave trade were forced to seek new possibilities for their capital. The role of manufacturing, however, was relatively insignificant; Rio's grandeur derived from commercial, financial, political, and cultural supremacy. Publishing, cafés, and luxury trade were concentrated on the Rua do Ouvidor, the francophile realm of Machado De Assis, and the home of the empire's literature, art, politics, and high society.

The Old Republic (1889–1930) witnessed only the beginning of a gradual transition from Rio's overwhelming primacy. In fact, the Republic undertook Rio's Parisian reforms and modern port to demonstrate national civilization and progress (1902–1910). Despite decentralization, regional oligarchies cut deals and disputed policies in Rio. Hinterland agriculture survived and diversified after the decline of the late 1800s; manufacturing, spurred by the abolition of slavery in 1888, demographic growth (from about 523,000 in 1890 to 811,000 in 1900), and the 1890s boom (*Encilhamento*), continued. Financial and commercial strength endured, and São Paulo's export superiority, industrial surge, and Modern Art Week (1922) only suggested the coming threat to national supremacy.

STRUGGLE AGAINST DECLINE: 1930–1990

Rivalry for national primacy with São Paulo has nineteenth-century roots; decline, twentieth-century origins. By the 1880s, *paulista* coffee led Brazilian exports; by the 1900s, it dominated the world coffee market. The wealth was poured into railways, wages, services, and manufacturing. São Paulo achieved industrial, if not demographic, superiority by the 1920s. Rio's population grew (1,188,000 by 1920; nearly twice the 570,000 of São Paulo, which outstripped Rio in 1960), along with industry, but without São Paulo's speed and within a more regional market. Despite these limitations, growth has consistently outpaced services and housing. By the end of the Estado Nôvo (1938–1945), with a population of about 2.3 million, Rio was presiding over a metropolitan empire of wretched industrial suburbs to the northwest and satellite cities across Guanabara Bay, with *favelas* throughout, encroaching on every hillside close to work. Although dramatic new landfills, highways, and architecture continued through the 1950s, and construction continues, the process of deterioration has been overwhelming.

Beginning in the 1950s, suburbs grew to the north and west of the city zone, and these are the most rapidly expanding areas of the city. Most of these neighborhoods are poor, with little modern infrastructure.

The creation of a new capital at Brasília (1960) and post-1964 administrations have exacerbated Rio's problems. Much federal aid, employment, investment, and attention have been shifted to Brasília or have been naturally diverted to the *paulista* dynamo. However, Rio still is a major financial center, and home to headquarters of many multinational corporations. The greater Rio area has one of the highest per-capita incomes of anywhere in Brazil.

In 2007 Rio was equally notorious for the filth, inefficiency, violence, and hopeless poverty which its 11.2 million metropolitan inhabitants confront. Yet, Rio's popular music remains unchallenged. Letters, arts, and sciences still flourish in traditional and new institutions. Finally, the Carioca lifestyle, distinguished by a matchless setting in which the elite's refined pleasures mingle with the common leisure of long-celebrated beaches, continues to compel envy and participation.

See also **Carioca; Coffee Industry; João VI of Portugal; Minas Gerais; São Paulo (City); Slavery: Brazil.**

BIBLIOGRAPHY

Socioeconomic statistics and analysis tracing Rio's development make Eulália Maria Lahmeyer Lobo, *História do Rio de Janeiro*, Rio de Janeiro: Access Editora, 1978, indispensable. A useful collection of essays can be found in Fernando Nascimento Silva, ed., *Rio de*

Janeiro em seus cuatrocentos anos. Rio de Janeiro: Distribuidora Récord, 1965. For a broad exploration of the Côrte, see the encyclopedic study of Adolfo Morales De Los Rios, *O Rio de Janeiro imperial,* Rio de Janeiro: A Noite, 1946. Mary C. Karasch uncovers the vital and painful Afro-Brazilian experience in *Slave Life in Rio de Janeiro, 1808–1850,* Princeton, NJ: Princeton University Press, 1987. Jeffrey D. Needell analyzes elite sociocultural trends from about 1808 to 1914 in *A Tropical Belle Époque,* Cambridge, U.K.: Cambridge University, 1987. Wilson Cano provides a comparative study of industrial development in *Raizes da concentração em São Paulo,* Rio de Janeiro: Difel, 1977. Michael L. Conniff sketches the establishment of Carioca populism in *Urban Politics in Brazil,* Pittsburgh, PA: University of Pittsburgh, 1981.

Additional Bibliography

Esteves, Martha de Abreu. *O império do divino: Festas religiosas e cultura popular no Rio de Janeiro, 1830–1900.* Rio de Janeiro: Editora Nova Fronteira, 1999.

Frank, Zephyr. *Dutra's World: Wealth and Family in Nineteenth-Century Rio de Janeiro.* Albuquerque: University of New Mexico Press, 2004.

Gomes, Angela Maria de Castro. *Histórias de imigrantes e imigraciao no Rio de Janeiro.* Rio de Janeiro: 7 Letras, 2000.

Schultz, Kirsten. *Tropical Versailles: Empire, Monarchy, and the Portuguese Royal Court in Rio de Janeiro, 1808–1821.* New York: Routledge, 2001.

JEFFREY D. NEEDELL

RIO DE JANEIRO (PROVINCE AND STATE).

The present state of Rio de Janeiro was settled in the sixteenth century by Frenchmen who traded with the indigenous Tupinambá. In 1565 the city of Rio de Janeiro was founded. Two years later, after the Portuguese defeated the French, the coast and inland became the royal captaincy of Rio de Janeiro. As in the Northeast, but on a smaller scale, its economy was based on the production of sugar with slave labor. In the late seventeenth century the captaincy's proximity to the new mining region of Minas Gerais and the emergence of the city of Rio de Janeiro as Brazil's primary southern port gave it strategic importance. In the eighteenth century the captaincy's economy grew, and in 1780 its population was recorded to be 167,760.

The captaincy of Rio de Janeiro became a province in 1815, when Brazil was raised to the status of "kingdom." In 1835, after the city of Rio (now the capital of independent Brazil) and its hinterland were separated from the province, Niterói was named provincial capital. In 1889, with the proclamation of the republic, the province became a state.

Throughout the nineteenth century coffee cultivation expanded in the Paraíba Valley, giving Rio's landowning elite an important role in national politics. In the 1880s, however, Rio de Janeiro's economic and political prominence waned. São Paulo surpassed Rio as the leading producer of coffee. In the twentieth century, the state developed as one of several important agricultural and industrial centers.

In 1975, with Brasília as the federal capital, the city of Rio and its hinterland (the state of Guanabara) were merged with the state of Rio de Janeiro, and the city of Rio became the state capital. Currently, the state's economy is based on agriculture, manufacturing, commerce, and services. In 1991, most of the state's almost 12.6 million inhabitants live in the city of Rio. As a consequence, the city's politics and economy dominate those of the state.

See also **Captaincy System; Coffee Industry; Tupinambá.**

BIBLIOGRAPHY

Jean De Léry, *History of a Voyage to the Land of Brazil* (1577), translated and introduced by Janet Whatley (1990).

Auguste De Saint-Hilaire, *Viagem pelas províncias do Rio de Janeiro e Minas Gerais* (1830), translated by Vivaldi Moreira (1975).

Dauril Alden, *Royal Government in Colonial Brazil* (1968).

Stanley Stein, *Vassouras, a Brazilian Coffee County, 1850–1900* (1985).

Additional Bibliography

Arias, Enrique Desmond. *Drugs & Democracy in Rio de Janeiro: Trafficking, Social Networks, & Public Security.* Chapel Hill: University of North Carolina Press, 2006.

Castro, Ruy, and John Gledson. *Rio de Janeiro: Carnival under Fire.* Translated by John Gledson. New York: Bloomsbury, 2004.

De A Abreu, Mauricio. *Rio de Janeiro: Formas, movimentos, representações: Estudos de geografia histórica carioca.* Rio de Janeiro, Brazil: Da Fonseca Comunicação, 2005.

Kent, Deborah. *Rio de Janeiro.* New York: Children's Press, 1996.

Kreimer, Alcira. *Towards a Sustainable Urban Environment: The Rio de Janeiro Study.* Washington, DC: World Bank, 1993.

St Louis, Regis. *Rio de Janeiro.* Oakland, CA: Lonely Planet, 2006.

KIRSTEN SCHULTZ

RÍO DE LA PLATA.   Río de la Plata (River Plate). Not properly a "river," the estuary of the Paraná and Uruguay rivers has been thus named since early discovery times. The Paraná, which in the Charrúa language means "like the sea," was first sailed in 1516 by Juan Díaz de Solís, who believed it was a passage to a western ocean leading to the Indies. Spaniards and Portuguese called the estuary Mar Dulce; later on, as the legend of the King of the Mountains of Silver (*plata*) evolved, the estuary was commonly referred to as Río de la Plata.

The two major river systems that empty into the estuary have a total drainage basin of more than 1.5 million square miles, which comprises 100 percent of Paraguay, 80 percent of Uruguay, 32 percent of Argentina, 19 percent of Bolivia, and 17 percent of Brazil. The estuary starts out at a width of 25 miles and upon entering the Atlantic Ocean widens to 138 miles. Its depth lies between 10 and 13 feet, which makes dredging a necessity for safe navigation. While the northern shore is relatively steep, reaching 150 feet of elevation in some places, the southern shore is rather flat and partly made up of riverine swamps. The saltwater estuary is home to the small La Plata dolphin, known as *La Franciscana* in Spanish and the *Cachimbo* in Portuguese. Overfishing, pollution, and invasive exotic species threaten the health of the aquatic communities and habitats in this important river basin.

Since its discovery and early colonization, the Río de la Plata has been a place of converging territorial interests. While initially the estuary was considered a point of entry for Spanish conquerors into the continent's interior, the strife between Asunción and Buenos Aires for primacy in the region divided the Spanish power. The Portuguese profited from the disunion and attempted to establish a foothold in the region by founding the enclave of Colônia do Sacramento in 1680. In response to this invasion,

the Spanish crown decided not only to evict the Portuguese forcibly but also to build a military-civil base in Montevideo (1724). Even when the entire northern shore of the estuary was recognized as Spanish territory in the Treaty of San Ildefonso (1777), the intentions of the British to establish an outpost in the Río de la Plata led to unsuccessful sieges of Buenos Aires in 1806 and 1807 and to the temporary seizure of Montevideo by the British in 1807. At the time of independence, the growing nationalistic feelings of the Montevideans led to separation from Buenos Aires and the creation of an autonomous province in 1814. Brazilians made use of the temporary split to invade Uruguay and stayed there until 1828, when they were dislodged by Uruguayan and Argentine militias.

See also **Colonialism.**

BIBLIOGRAPHY

Horacio Difrieri, *El virreynato del Río de la Plata: Ensayo de geografía histórica* (Buenos Aires, 1980).

Additional Bibliography

Biswas, Asit K. *Management of Latin American River Basins Amazon, Plata, and São Francisco.* Tokyo: United Nations University Press, 1998.

Kroeber, Clifton B. *The Growth of the Shipping Industry in the Río de la Plata Region, 1794–1860.* Madison: University of Wisconsin Press, 1957.

Rela, Walter. *España en el Río de la Plata: Descubrimiento y poblamientos, 1516–1588.* Montevideo: Club Español, 2001.

Whigham, Thomas. *The Politics of River Trade: Tradition and Development in the Upper Plata, 1780–1870.* Albuquerque: University of New Mexico Press, 1991.

CÉSAR N. CAVIEDES

RÍO DE LA PLATA, VICEROYALTY OF.   Viceroyalty of Río de La Plata, the colonial political jurisdiction embracing current-day Argentina, Paraguay, Uruguay, and Bolivia until the outbreak of the Independence Wars in 1810. This was the last viceregal unit of the Spanish Empire, and was supposed to become the showcase of Bourbon Reforms. Divided into seven provinces (Buenos Aires, Tucumán, Paraguay, Potosí, Santa Cruz de la Sierra, Charcas, and Cuyo), the Río de la Plata came to embody the advances and contradictions of the crumbling hold over Spanish America. Thus it became the first of the colonies effectively to secede.

Created in 1776 as part of Charles III's attempt to invigorate the fiscal and commercial machinery of empire, the new viceroyalty was split from Peru. It was so distant from Lima that contraband and fiscal evasion in Buenos Aires had become a costly drain on the empire. By making Buenos Aires the capital of the new entity, trade and taxation could be more easily monitored.

The Bourbons introduced a bureaucratic apparatus that was essentially traditional but incorporated a group of innovations. Without an entrenched aristocracy or bureaucracy, as in Mexico or Lima, Spanish authorities could experiment in the Río de la Plata. They vested conventional executive authority in the viceroy, giving him sweeping powers over taxation through the Real Hacienda (Treasury Department), the customhouse, tobacco monopoly, and communications, and made him the supreme military commander over the district. As the king's personal envoy, the viceroy also possessed religious authority. In 1783, judicial power was vested in the audiencia, in part to check the power of the viceroy and in part as a concession to local demands for more responsive administration. As in the rest of the empire, this dual power system generated more tension and conflict than balanced administration.

The Río de la Plata became the arena for half-hearted innovation. The Bourbons introduced a French model of the intendancy (despite its inability to cope with tensions that exploded in the French Revolution) in 1783. Appointed to rationalize and more closely monitor the powers of the exchequer (Tribunal De Cuentas), the superintendent openly challenged the power of the viceroy. He oversaw multiple intendancies and took control of justice, general administration, war, and most important, finance. Rather than increasing revenues, the innovation led to internal squabbling between the intendants and viceroys, the *audiencias* and cabildos; the experiment was rescinded in 1788. Fiscal control returned to the viceroy.

Frustrated by the region's failure to channel funds to the thirsty coffers of empire, and burdened by the costs of war in Europe, Charles IV sent Diego de la Vega as *visitador general* to review all the branches of

the Real Hacienda. His report prompted Charles to reintroduce the intendancy system in 1804, albeit with a narrower mandate. The viceroy (Fernando Rafael de Sobremonte) remained supreme.

Buenos Aires, however, was still a marginal outpost of the empire, and thus never a favored position for officials sent from Spain. Consequently, high officers of the crown seldom remained for long, and their competency left much to be desired. From 1776 to 1810, eleven viceroys and three intendants served the crown. Much of the day-to-day work fell to middle-rank bureaucrats who were underpaid and unrespected. Their upward mobility through the ranks of the imperial state was snail-paced, and the bureaucracy soon became a breeding ground for resentment of the crown. When creole merchants and artisans eventually declared their open opposition to the Spanish government in May 1810, much of the vice-regal bureaucracy affiliated with the patriots.

Local representation expressed itself through municipal *cabildos,* where merchants and notables kept up a steady fire of demands on the viceroy and audiencia. Cabildos served as councils for local notables (*vecinos*) and controlled local judges. The *alcaldes ordinarios* (mayors) of these municipalities covered basic civil criminal laws. Disputed cases were appealed to the *audiencia.* The *alcaldes ordinarios* supervised district judges, *alcaldes de barrio.* There was a parallel set of courts governing military justice (*fueros de guerra*), taxes and public debts (*fueros de hacienda*), and the church (*fueros eclesiásticos*).

For reasons that remain unclear, the crown did not create a Consulado for merchants until 1794. Agitation for the creation of the Consulado began in the early 1780s. As a semiofficial organ, the Consulado served as the judicial body for merchants, to reconcile disputes according to the revised Ordenanzas de Bilbao. The Consulado was controlled by wholesale merchants whose power rested on their grip over Buenos Aires's import-export business.

Two years after the viceroyalty's creation, Madrid declared "free" trade in 1778, both as a concession to creole demands for greater commercial freedom and as a measure to promote more exchange with the mother country. More than any other region of the empire, the Río de la Plata flourished. Licensed ships replaced imperial fleets, and Porteño merchants could enjoy direct links with peninsular ports. Once based on the trade in contraband and specie flow, a booming merchant community in Buenos Aires turned to the trade in hides and jerked beef for slave consumption in Cuba and Brazil. These became the first staples of the emerging pampas economy. Reforms also helped integrate different regions around the port: yerba maté was produced in Paraguay, woolen textiles in Córdoba, wine and *aguardiente* in Cuyo. Buenos Aires increasingly became the trade hub for the region.

Potential for trade attracted merchants from Spain, France, England, and elsewhere in Europe, and brought commercial links to foreign ports and financiers. Buenos Aires was the first major Spanish American port to diversify its trade links beyond peninsular exchange. Merchants also extended their credit and sales networks through agents in the interior. From internal and foreign trade emerged a strong class of wholesale merchants based in the viceregal capital, many of whom grew from quite modest beginnings. Their wealth soon allowed them to extend their enterprises into landholding and export staple production.

Commercial wealth made merchants the financiers of colonial administration, as contributors of the largest portion of revenues to the exchequer and as the source of loans. This strength might have given them indirect control over the reins of political power, but crown authorities were not always sensitive to local commercial concerns. Frequently, as in the 1799 order to suspend all shipping of goods in neutral vessels, merchants vented their umbrage at the viceroy. Crown insensitivity soon led to the accumulation of grievances that spilled out in 1810, when the Spanish Cortes intensified fiscal demands. The bulk of Buenos Aires merchants stood behind the cabildos' open declaration of revolt in May 1810.

A list of Viceroys follows.

Juan José Vértiz y Salcedo, 1778–1784

Francisco Cristóbal del Campo, Marqués de Loreto, 1784–1789

Nicolás de Arredondo, 1789–1795

Pedro Melo de Portugal y Vilhena, 1795–1797

Antonio Olaguer y Feliú Heredia y Donec, 1797–1799

Gabriel de Avilés y del Fierro, Marqués de Avilés, 1799–1801

Joaquín del Pino y Rosas Romero Negrete, 1801–1804

Fernando Rafael de Sobremonte, Marqués de Sobremonte, 1804–1807

Pascual Ruíz Huidobro, 1807

Santiago Antonio María de Liniers y Bremont, 1807–1809

Baltasar Hidalgo de Cisneros y la Torre, 1809–1810

See also **Alcalde; Audiencia; Bourbon Reforms; Cabildo, Cabildo Abierto; Consulado; Fueros; Intendancy System; Spanish Empire; Viceroyalty, Viceroy.**

BIBLIOGRAPHY

John Lynch, *Spanish Colonial Administration, 1782–1810: The Intendant System in the Viceroyalty of the Río de la Plata* (1958).

Ricardo Zorraquín Becú, *La organización política argentina en el período hispánico* (1959).

Herbert S. Klein, "Structure and Profitability of Royal Finance in the Viceroyalty of the Río de la Plata in 1790," in *Hispanic American Historical Review* 53 (August 1973): 440–469.

Susan M. Socolow, *The Merchants of Buenos Aires, 1778–1810: Family and Commerce* (1978).

Ricardo Zorraquín Becú, *La organización judicial argentina en el período hispánico* (1981).

David Rock, *Argentina, 1516–1982: From Spanish Colonization to the Falklands War* (1985; rev. ed. 1987), esp. pp 59–66.

Samuel Amaral, "Rural Production and Labour in the Late Colonial Buenos Aires," in *Journal of Latin American Studies*, 19, no. 2 (1987): 235–278.

Susan M. Socolow, *The Bureaucrats of Buenos Aires, 1769–1810: Amor al real servicio* (1987).

Additional Bibliography

Acevedo, Edberto Oscar. *Funcionamiento y quiebra del sistema virreinal: Investigaciones.* Buenos Aires: Ciudad Argentina, 2004.

JEREMY ADELMAN

RIO GRANDE. Rio Grande, a river that rises in the San Juan Mountains of southwestern Colorado and flows south past Santa Fe and Albuquerque as it bisects New Mexico. Near El Paso/Ciudad Juarez, it gradually bends and begins a southeasterly flow toward Brownsville, Texas, and, finally, to its mouth in the Gulf of Mexico. The 1845 annexation of Texas by the United States precipitated a boundary dispute with Mexico, in which Mexico maintained that the Nuences River (to the north of the Rio Grande) formed the southern border of Texas. Both sides amassed troops to defend their claims, and the 24 April 1846 clash at Carricitos convinced the U.S. Congress to vote for war (the Mexican-American War). Today, the river forms the boundary between Mexico, where it is known as Río Bravo, and the United States, between El Paso and the Gulf of Mexico.

Although it extends 1,885 miles and drains an immense region, the Rio Grande has become a mere trickle in some places, or is entirely dry. Irrigation demands and the needs of increasing populations along its banks have siphoned off any excess flow. The upper Rio Grande in New Mexico was settled by the Spanish as early as the seventeenth century. In recent years, the populations of cities along the Mexican side of the river have mushroomed as manufacturers take advantage of low Mexican wages and proximity to U.S. markets to set up Maquiladoras (assembling plants). In the past several decades, the Rio Grande has been the final obstacle for hundreds of thousands of Mexican and Central American immigrants looking for work in the United States or fleeing war and poverty in their own countries.

See also **Chamizal Conflict; United States-Mexico Border.**

BIBLIOGRAPHY

Paul Horgan, *Great River: The Rio Grande in North American History,* 2 vols. (1954).

Pat Kelley, *River of Lost Dreams: Navigation on the Rio Grande* (1986).

Additional Bibliography

Kearney, Milo, and Anthony K. Knopp *Studies in Rio Grande Valley History.* Brownsville: University of Texas at Brownsville and Texas Southmost College, 2005.

Los Caminos del Río: the Roads of the River: Legacies of the Borderlands. Austin: Texas Department of Transportation and Texas Historical Commission, 2004.

Westerhoff, Paul. *The U.S.-Mexican Border Environment: Water Issues along the U.S.-Mexican Border.* San Diego, CA: San Diego State University Press; Tempe AZ: Herberger Center for Design Excellence, College of Architecture and Environmental Design, Arizona State University, 2000.

J. DAVID DRESSING

RIO GRANDE DO NORTE. Rio Grande do Norte, one of the easternmost states of Brazil, covers 20,470 square miles and has a population of 2.7 million (2000 estimate). The capital is Natal. The socioeconomic conditions of the state are poor; 92 percent of the state is semi-arid. The interior is devoted to livestock, cotton, and other agricultural enterprises. Salt marshes near Natal and southward produce much of Brazil's crude and refined salt. Mining yields tungsten, gypsum, limestone, marble, gold, and beryl.

The Portuguese began settling the region in the late 1500s, although the territory was contested, not only by the local Potiguar people but also by the French. The Portuguese consolidated their hold on the region in the early part of the seventeenth century but lost it again in 1633 to the Dutch, who controlled much of the northeast until 1654. The colonial economy centered on sugar, but cotton, introduced in the 1700s, quickly became a leading crop. Originally a dependency of Pernambuco, Rio Grande do Norte became a province of the empire in 1824 and a state of the republic in 1889.

In the spring of 1817 Rio Grande do Norte, Alagoas, Paraíba, and Pernambuco, displaying nationalistic tendencies, attempted unsuccessfully to establish a northeastern republic. Rio Grande do Norte supported another such movement in the mid-1820s. The state's geographic position lent it strategic importance during World War II, when the United States maintained a key air base near Natal.

In the 1950s Bishop Eugênio Sales, auxiliary bishop of Natal, attempting to ameliorate conditions in the interior, launched the Rural Assistance Service (SAR). Explicitly anticommunist and disavowing any desire for radical socioeconomic change, the SAR set out to provide medical and educational services, protect peasants' basic legal rights, organize unions of rural workers, and work for mild land reform. Although only moderately successful, this "Movement of Natal" became a model for similar activities elsewhere in northeastern Brazil.

By the early 1960s, radio literacy programs sponsored by the SAR and similar organizations burgeoned into the government-sponsored national Movement for Basic Education (MEB). The United States made the state under Governor Aluízio Alves a centerpiece of its Alliance for Progress program. Paulo Freire came to national prominence with an Alliance-funded literacy campaign in Alves's home town of Angicos. After the military coup in 1964, however, the MEB and other social reform movements and programs became targets of brutal repression. In recent decades, as in most northeastern states, there has been an attempt to encourage the development of tourism.

See also **Alagoas; Education: Overview; Freire, Paulo; Literacy; Natal; Paraíba; Pernambuco; Sales, Eugênio de Araújo.**

BIBLIOGRAPHY

Alves, Aluizio. *O Que Eu Não Esqueci: Reminscências Políticas 1933–2001.* Rio de Janeiro: Léo Christiano Editorial, 2001.

Camara Cascudo, Luis da. *História do Rio Grande do Norte.* Rio de Janeiro: Ministério de Educação e Cultura, 1955.

De Kadt, Emanuel. *Catholic Radicals in Brazil.* London: Royal Institute of International Affairs, 1970.

Fernandes, Calazans and Antonio Terra. *40 Horas de Esperança: Política e Pedagogia na Experiência de Angicos.* São Paulo: Editora Ática, 1994.

Hemming, John. *Red Gold: The Conquest of the Brazilian Indians.* London: Macmillan, 1978.

Ireland, Rowan. "The Catholic Church and Social Change in Brazil: An Evaluation." In *Brazil in the Sixties,* edited by Riordan Roett. Nashville, TN: Vanderbilt University Press, 1972.

Page, Joseph A. *The Revolution That Never Was: Northeast Brazil, 1955–1964.* New York: Grossman, 1972.

ANDREW J. KIRKENDALL

RIO GRANDE DO SUL.

Rio Grande do Sul, Brazil's southernmost state, fifth largest in population (2005 population, 10,854,343), fourth in industrial production. Long remote from the national center of power and a recurrent source of instability, Rio Grande do Sol has had a disproportionate impact on Brazilian history due to its strategic position bordering Uruguay and Argentina, its influence as headquarters of the powerful Third Army, and the exceptional list of national leaders it has produced, including seven presidents.

The state's historical development has been shaped by strong regionalism, an economy dependent on Brazil's internal market, and divisions between its pastoral south, linked by geography and customs to the Río de la Plata, and its agricultural center and northern plateau. Spanish Jesuits first settled its northwest, founding the Sete Povos missions in 1687. With the first Portuguese settlement in 1737, it became a contested border zone between Spanish and Portuguese empires. The captaincy of Rio Grande do São Pedro was created in 1760; the captaincy-general of Rio Grande do Sul in 1807. Caught up in the continual strife of the La Plata region, its inhabitants, often called *gaúchos,* formed strong military traditions. They proclaimed an independent republic in the Farroupilha Revolt (1835–1845), the longest of the regional revolts that threatened the unity of the empire during the regency.

In the late nineteenth century, German and Italian immigrants spread small family farms across the northern plateau, challenging the dominance of the southern cattle economy. During the Old Republic, the state was distinctive in its positivist constitution, authoritarian presidential structure, and strong two-party system. The region was plunged into bloody civil war in 1893 by the Federalist Revolt (1893), the first serious threat to the republic, but by 1910 Rio Grande do Sul had taken its place beside Minas Gerais and São Paulo as one of the three dominant states and coarbiter of presidential successions. In the 1920s it was a focus of *tenente* revolts.

Rio Grande do Sul took a leading part in the 1930 revolution that put its governor, Getúlio Vargas, in the presidency and began a period of major Riograndense influence in national politics. Its support of Vargas condemned the 1932 Paulista Revolt to failure, and it played a critical role in securing the succession of *gaúcho* João Goulart to the presidency in 1961. Once the traditional breadbasket of the country, land shortages and soil exhaustion weakened the state economy, accelerating out-migration and land conflict. Diversification in telecommunications and energy has yielded new growth in the industrial sector, which accounts for more than 40 percent of the state's economy.

See also **Farroupilha Revolt; Minas Gerais; Río de la Plata; São Paulo (State).**

BIBLIOGRAPHY

Joseph L. Love, *Rio Grande do Sul and Brazilian Regionalism, 1882–1930* (1971).

Carlos E. Cortés, *Gaúcho Politics in Brazil* (1974).

Additional Bibliography

Baiocchi, Gianpaolo. *Militants and Citizens: The Politics of Participatory Democracy in Porto Alegre.* Stanford, CA: Stanford University Press, 2005.

Bell, Stephen. *Campanha gaúcha: A Brazilian Ranching System, 1850–1920.* Stanford, CA: Stanford University Press, 1998.

César, Guilhermino. *História do Rio Grande do Sul.* Pôrto Alegre, Brazil: Editôra Globo, 1970.

Chasteen, John Charles. *Heroes on Horseback: A Life and Times of the Last Gaucho Caudillos.* Albuquerque: University of New Mexico Press, 1995.

Conde d'Eu, Gastão de Orléans, and Max Fleiuss. *Viagem militar ao Rio Grande do Sul (agosto a novembro de 1865).* São Paulo: Companhia editora nacional, 1936.

Kittleson, Roger Alan. *The Practice of Politics in Postcolonial Brazil: Porto Alegre, 1845–1895.* Pittsburgh, PA: University of Pittsburgh Press, 2006.

Koonings, Kees. *Industrialization, Industrialists, and Regional Development in Brazil: Rio Grande do Sul in Comparative Perspective.* Amsterdam: Thela Publishers, 1994.

Oliven, Ruben George. *Tradition Matters: Modern Gaúcho Identity in Brazil.* New York: Columbia University Press, 1996.

Wright, Angus Lindsay, and Wendy Wolford. *To Inherit the Earth: The Landless Movement and the Struggle for a New Brazil.* Oakland, CA: Food First Books, 2003.

JOAN BAK

which corresponds to the present-day Colombian state of La Guajira, remained an underdeveloped frontier for most of the colonial period, its pearl beds and strategic location notwithstanding. Likewise, the port of Riohacha, established in 1545, seldom approached the status of Santa Marta to the southwest. Poor and isolated from Cartagena de Indias by prevailing currents and winds, the town became an easy target for pirates.

In the late 1600s and the 1700s, English and Dutch smugglers and Guajiro Indians dominated economic life in the area and posed a military threat to the port. Successive viceregal governments attempted to impose Spanish power on the peninsula, but they largely failed. The city's mention in Gabriel García Márquez's novel *One Hundred Years of Solitude* (1967) brought Riohacha international fame.

See also **Colombia: From the Conquest Through Independence; Colombia: Since Independence; García Márquez, Gabriel.**

BIBLIOGRAPHY

Grahn, Lance R. "Guajiro Culture and Capuchin Evangelization: Missionary Failure on the Riohacha Frontier." In *The New Latin American Mission History*, eds. Erick Detlef Langer and Robert H. Jackson. Lincoln: University of Nebraska Press, 1995.

Kuethe, Allan J. "The Pacification Campaign on the Riohacha Frontier." *Hispanic American Historical Review* 50 (1970): 467–481.

Perrin, Michel. *The Way of the Dead Indians: Guajiro Myths and Symbols*, trans. Michael Fineberg with the author. Austin: University of Texas Press, 1987.

Tirado, Ernesto Restrepo. *Historia de la provincia de Santa Marta*, 2 vols. Bogotá: Ministerio de Educación Nacional, Ediciones de la Revista Bolívar, 1953.

Weston, Julian A. *The Cactus Eaters.* London: H. F. & G. Witherby, 1937.

Wilbert, Johannes. *Survivors of Eldorado: Four Indian Cultures of South America.* New York: Praeger, 1972.

LANCE R. GRAHN

RIOHACHA. Riohacha is a town and provincial jurisdiction (also known as Río de la Hacha) on Colombia's Caribbean coast, in the Audiencia of Santa Fe de Bogotá and, in the eighteenth century, the Viceroyalty of the New Kingdom of Granada. Spanish mariners first sailed past the Guajira peninsula in 1499. The region, however,

RÍOS MONTT, JOSÉ EFRAÍN (1926–). José Efraín Ríos Montt (*b.* 16 June 1926), president of Guatemala (23 March 1982–9 August 1983). General Ríos Montt came to power in the 23 March 1982 coup that overthrew then president General Fernando Romeo Lucas García. The military-instigated coup named a three-man junta consisting of Ríos Montt, General Horatio Maldonado Schad, and Colonel Francisco Gordillo to head the government. In June 1982, Ríos Montt dismissed his fellow junta members and named himself president of the republic.

At the time Ríos Montt took office, significant portions of the western highlands, particularly in the department of El Quiché and the northern Transversal along the Mexican border, were controlled by or sympathetic to Guatemala's armed resistance, which had united in 1980 to form the Guatemalan National Revolutionary Unity (URNG). Ríos Montt launched a massive counterinsurgency campaign, known as "rifles and beans," to drive the insurgents from the largely Indian highlands. This effort was a military success in that it greatly reduced rebel power; but thousands of civilian lives were lost, and the United Nations estimated that as many as 1 million Guatemalans were forced into exile during this period.

From 1 July 1982 until 23 March 1983, Ríos Montt declared a nationwide state of siege, banning all union and political activity, granting arresting powers to the armed forces, nullifying guarantees of privacy, eliminating writs of habeas corpus, and enforcing strict press censorship. Ríos Montt also established "special tribunals" in which suspected guerrillas and criminals were prosecuted without trial by jury.

Ríos Montt attracted a great deal of attention outside of Guatemala during his term of office, in part because he was an evangelical Protestant and publicly associated himself with his church, the Church of the Word (*Verbo*), which had its home office in California. Ríos Montt's strong reliance on advisers from his church displeased the Guatemalan military, which forced his ouster in 1983. Other reasons for the military's dissatisfaction with Ríos Montt included his failure to shore up the nation's faltering economy, and his reluctance to set a date for new national presidential elections.

On 9 August 1983, Ríos Montt was overthrown in a military coup led by his own minister of defense, Oscar Humberto Mejía Victores. After the military removed him, Ríos Montt returned to Guatemalan politics in 1989, when he founded the Guatemalan Republican Front (FRG). While the government banned him from running for the presidency, he served as a deputy in Guatemala's national legislature between 1990 and 2004. In 2003, he received permission to run for the presidency but obtained only 11 percent of the popular vote in that year's election.

See also **Guatemala; Guatemala, Political Parties: National Guatemalan Revolutionary Unity (URNG); Mejía Victores, Oscar Humberto.**

BIBLIOGRAPHY

Joseph Anfuso and David Sczepanski, *He Gives, He Takes Away: Efraín Ríos Montt, Servant or Dictator?* (1983).

Peter Calvert, *Guatemala: A Nation in Turmoil* (1985).

Jean-Marie Simon, *Guatemala: Eternal Spring, Eternal Tyranny* (1987).

Additional Bibliography

Asturias Montenegro, G. *Los 504 días de Ríos Montt.* Guatemala: Gamma, 1995.

Soto Rosales, Carlos Rafael. *El sueño encadenado: El proceso político guatemalteco, 1944–1999.* Guatemala: Tipografía Nacional, 2002.

                                VIRGINIA GARRARD BURNETT

RÍOS MORALES, JUAN ANTONIO

(1888–1946). Juan Antonio Ríos Morales (*b.* 1888; *d.* 27 June 1946), president of Chile (1942–1946). In 1924, Ríos, a lawyer and businessman, won his first election to Congress, where he quickly became a leading member of the Radical party and a contender for the party's presidential nomination in 1938. With the death of Radical president Pedro Aguirre Cerda in November 1941, Ríos was elected his successor with 56 percent of the vote. He continued Aguirre Cerda's policies but focused on the principal issue of the time, Chile's neutrality in World War II. Chile finally broke off relations with the Axis in January 1943. Ríos subsequently became the first Chilean president to make an official visit to the United States (October 1945). His health, however, was failing, and, like his predecessor, he died before the end of his term.

See also **Chile: The Twentieth Century; Chile, Political Parties: Radical Party.**

BIBLIOGRAPHY

R. A. Humphreys, *Latin America and the Second World War,* vol. 2 (1982), pp. 105–119.

Additional Bibliography

Moulian, Tomás, and Isabel Torres Dujisin. *Las candidaturas presidenciales de la derecha: Ross e Ibáñez.* Santiago de Chile: Programa FLACSO, 1986.

SIMON COLLIER

RIO TREATY (1947). The Rio Treaty (1947) was an agreement binding the republics of the Western Hemisphere together in a mutual defense system. Also called the Rio Pact or the Inter-American Treaty of Reciprocal Assistance, the treaty became effective on December 3, 1948, when two-thirds of the member states had ratified it.

The treaty provided for mutual assistance if an act of aggression threatened the peace of the Western Hemisphere. An act of aggression against one member state was considered an act against all the signatory states, which were obligated to provide assistance and aid. The state or states directly attacked were authorized to determine emergency measures of self-defense that would be examined by a special meeting of foreign ministers, known as the Organ of Consultation, which would meet and agree on collective action. In addition, the Organ of Consultation was authorized to impose sanctions and the use of military force if approved by two-thirds of the ministers.

The Rio Treaty reiterated the principles of the Act of Chapultepec of 1945, but its inclusion of Argentina, which had been purposely excluded in 1945 because of its support of the Axis powers during World War II, reflected the United States's motivation to restructure the Monroe Doctrine into a multilateral defense organization. The principles of the Rio Treaty became the basis of the Pact of Bogotá (1948), which established the Organization of American States (OAS). The Rio Treaty also became a prototype for the formation of the North Atlantic Alliance of 1949. The treaty was used many times during the cold war, notably during the Cuban Missile Crisis.

The treaty lost its influence in 1982 when the United States supported the United Kingdom in its war with Argentina over the Falkland Islands. Yet, the United States invoked the treaty in the aftermath of the September 11, 2001, terrorist attacks on New York City and Washington, D.C., and tried to enlist Latin American countries in its War on Terror. Latin American nations voiced their support for the United States and the Rio Treaty at an OAS meeting after the attacks, but many countries did not join the United States's subsequent wars in Afghanistan and Iraq. In 2002 Mexico left the treaty, arguing that a new agreement needed to be produced.

See also **Organization of American States (OAS).**

BIBLIOGRAPHY

Cargnelutti, Hugo Luis. *Seguridad interamericana un subsistema del sistema interamericano?* Buenos Aires: Editorial Centro de Estudios Unión para la Nueva Mayoría, 1992.

Smith, Peter H. *Talons of the Eagle Dynamics of U.S.–Latin American Relations.* New York: Oxford University Press, 1996.

LESLEY R. LUSTER

RIPSTEIN, ARTURO (1943–). Arturo Ripstein (*b.* 13 December 1943), Mexican film director. Ripstein studied law, art, and Mexican history at the National University of Mexico, the Universidad Iberoamericana, and El Colegio de México. He made his directorial debut at the age of twenty-one with the film *Tiempo de morir* (1965), which he followed with a number of noted films in the 1970s. He is one of the most respected directors of the post-1968 generation. Almost all his films have been financed by the state. Many of his best films are adaptations of literary works. His favorite cinematic themes are moral decay and social crises; he is also known for unique character studies. Among his critical successes are *El castillo de la pureza* (1972), *La viuda negra* (1977), *La tía Alejandra* (1978), *El lugar sin límites* (1977), *El otro* (1984), *El imperio de la fortuna* (1985), and *Mentiras piadosas* (1988), *La reina de la noche* (1994), *Profundo carmesí* (1996), *La perdición de los hombres* (2000), *La virgin de la lujuria* (2002), and *Carnaval de Sodoma* (2006). Ripstein received the Ariel for best direction from the Mexican film academy for *Cadena perpetua* and *El imperio de la fortuna*. His film *Profundo Carmesí* (Deep Crimson) has become one of his most celebrated films. It deals with the real-life "Lonely Hearts Murders" that took place in Mexico during the late 1940s. Ripstein is the only Mexican filmmaker aside from Buñuel to receive the National Prize for the Arts, which he was awarded in 1997.

See also **Buñuel, Luis; Cinema: From the Silent Film to 1990; Cinema: Since 1990.**

BIBLIOGRAPHY

Luis Reyes De La Maza, *El cine sonoro en México* (1973).

E. Bradford Burns, *Latin American Cinema: Film and History* (1975).

Carl J. Mora, *Mexican Cinema: Reflections of a Society: 1896–1980* (1982).

John King, *Magical Reels: A History of Cinema in Latin America* (1990).

Additional Bibliography

Aldama, Arturo. *Violence and the Body: Race, Gender, and the State.* Bloomington: Indiana University Press, 2003.

Mora, Sergio de la. *Cinemachismo: Masculinities and Sexuality in Mexican Film.* Austin: University of Texas Press, 2006.

Paranaguá, Paulo Antonio. *Arturo Ripstein: La espiral de la identidad.* Madrid: Cátedra, 1997.

DAVID MACIEL

RIQUELME, DANIEL (1855?–1912).
Daniel Riquelme was born in Santiago, Chile; his birth year is given variously as 1853, 1854, 1855, and 1857. Son of a stenographer and a teacher, he became a prominent figure in Chilean letters. During the War of the Pacific Riquelme served as a correspondent for the Valparaiso newspaper *El Heraldo* and accompanied Chilean forces on their excursions into Peru and their capture of Lima. Many of his articles on the War of the Pacific, often written under the pseudonym Inocencio Conchalí, were later published by the Chilean government under the title *La campaña del ejército chilena en Lima*; others appeared in his *Chascarrillos militares*, which appeared in 1885 and was reissued in expanded form in 1888 as perhaps his best-known work, *Bajo la tienda*.

Riquelme's descriptive, often humorous, and very human sketches of common soldiers and, later, Santiago's workers and bohemians—sometimes amalgamated into a single type, *el roto*—garnered him high praise as a chronicler of Chilean popular culture and the everyday life of central Santiago. Riquelme sought treatment for tuberculosis in Lausanne, Switzerland, and died there on August 9, 1912; an obituarist noted that "perhaps no one has penetrated so deeply into the popular soul as has Daniel Riquelme."

See also **Journalism.**

BIBLIOGRAPHY

Works by Daniel Riquelme

Chascarrillos militares [Humoristic Military Sketches]. 1885.

Bajo la tienda, recuerdos de la campaña al Perú y Bolivia, 1879–1884 [1888] [Under the Tent: Reminiscences of the Peruvian and Bolivian Campaigns, 1879–1884]. Santiago: Zig-Zag, 1937.

La revolución del 20 de abril de 1851 [1893] [The Revolution of April 20, 1851]. Santiago: Editorial Andrés Bello, 1966.

El incendio de la iglesia de la Compañía el 8 de diciembre de 1863 [The Conflagration of the Church of the Society, December 8, 1863]. 1893.

Compendio de Historia de Chile [A Condensed History of Chile]. 1899.

El terremoto del Señor de Mayo [The Earthquake of Senor de Mayo]. 1905.

Secondary Work

Castro, Raúl Silva. "Introducción Biográfica." In *La revolución del 20 de abril de 1851*, by Daniel Riquelme. Santiago: Editorial Andrés Bello, 1966.

RAYMOND B. CRAIB

RIUS (1934–). Rius (pen name of Eduardo del Río; b. 20 July 1934), Mexican comic-book writer and cartoonist. Eduardo del Río, more popularly known to millions of his readers by his pen name Rius, is the creator of the most explicitly political comic books and illustrated books in Mexico and perhaps in all of Latin America. As a young man he worked briefly as a cartoonist for the Mexico City newspaper *Ovaciones,* but was dismissed because of the controversial nature of his political cartoons. During the 1950s and early 1960s, he alternately was unemployed and worked for several Mexico City publications. He soon became known to his readers for his outspoken criticism of social customs and prominent political figures, including the Mexican president.

In 1966, Rius made the switch from cartoonist to comic-book writer with the creation of his first comic book, *Los supermachos,* for Editorial Meridiano. Unable to tolerate the censorship of his publisher, he abandoned that series. In 1968, Rius created a second comic book, *Los agachados,* which he continued to write and illustrate until 1977. Since the early 1970s he has also written and illustrated over thirty-five books.

Rius's overtly political criticism of Mexican institutions has frequently angered government officials, even to the point of threatening his life. Nonetheless, he has continued to issue sharply satirical attacks against some of Mexico's most sacrosanct beliefs and institutions: the Catholic Church, the Revolution, and machismo. Rius is an unabashed admirer of socialism and has devoted many comic-book issues and books to instructing his readers about its basic tenets.

See also **Cartoons in Latin America; Journalism.**

BIBLIOGRAPHY

Paula K. Speck, "Rius for Beginners: A Study in Comic-book Satire," in *Studies in Latin American Popular Culture* 1 (1982): 113–124.

Harold E. Hinds, Jr., and Charles M. Tatum, *Not Just for Children: The Mexican Comic Book in the Late-1960s and 1970s* (1992).

Additional Bibliography

García Flores, Margarita. "Embalsamo vivos: Entrevista con Eduardo del Río (Ruis)." *Entorno: Revista Cultural del la Universidad Autónoma de Ciudad Juárez,* (Winter 1993): 30-31.

Proctor, Phyllis Ann Wiegand. *Mexico's Supermachos: Satire and Social Revolution in Comics by Ruis.* Austin: University of Texas, 1973.

CHARLES TATUM

RIVA AGÜERO Y OSMA, JOSÉ DE LA

(1885–1944). José de la Riva Agüero y Osma (*b.* 26 February 1885; *d.* 26 October 1944), Peruvian historian, literary scholar, and politician. Born in Lima, Riva Agüero attended schools in his native city, receiving degrees in literature and law at the University of Lima. In 1907 he advocated military service for Peruvian students,

and he himself enlisted when war with Ecuador and Bolivia appeared imminent. He then wrote an article in which he demanded amnesty for all political prisoners, a work for which he himself was imprisoned. Students rallied on his behalf, and he and all other prisoners were released.

Riva Agüero traveled widely in Latin America and Europe and in the process attended historical and literary conferences. In 1915 he returned to political activity and helped establish the National Democratic Party. Later he was elected mayor of Lima. As the young democrat aged, however, his political philosophy became more conservative. Eventually, he concluded that an enlightened elite should lead the nation rather than trust control to the masses, a belief that eventually led him to accept Fascism in the 1930s.

Riva Agüero focused his historical work on the general history of Peru and on the growth of the Inca Empire in the pre-Hispanic period. Historiographically, he advocated careful research and evaluation of sources. He also believed that history could be used to expand patriotism.

See also **Peru.**

BIBLIOGRAPHY

William Belmont Parker, *Peruvians of Today* (1919), pp. 59–63.

Fred Bonner, "José de la Riva Agüero (1885–1944)," in *Hispanic American Historical Review* 36 (1956): 490–502.

Charles Arnade, "The Historiography of Colonial and Modern Bolivia," in *Hispanic American Historical Review* 42 (1962):333–384.

Jack Ray Thomas, *Biographical Dictionary of Latin American Historians and Historiography* (1984), pp. 305–306.

Additional Bibliography

Martínez Riaza, Ascensión. *La construcción de la identidad iberoamericana textos históricos.* Madrid: Fundación Histórica Tavera: DIGIBIS: Mapfre Mutualidad, 1999.

Sánchez, Luis Alberto. *Conservador, no, reaccionario, sí: Notas sobre la vida, obra y proyecciones de don José de la Riva Agüero y Osma, marqués de Montealegre y Aulestia (26/II/1885-25/VI/1944) seguidas de su correspondencia con el autor.* Lima: Mosca Azul Editores, 1985.

Vidal Martínez, Leopoldo. *José de la Riva Agüero y Osma y José Carlos Mariátegui: Son "generaciones" distintas? Distantes? Hay "generaciones"?* Lima: Generali Perú; and Miraflores: Minerva, 1997.

JACK RAY THOMAS

RIVADAVIA, BERNARDINO (1780–1845).

Bernardino Rivadavia (*b.* 20 May 1780; *d.* 2 September 1845), Argentine statesman, liberal, and unitarist. Born in Buenos Aires, son of a wealthy Spanish merchant, Rivadavia was educated at the Real Colegio de San Carlos; subsequently he married the daughter of Viceroy Joaquín del Pino. He served as an officer in the Galician Corps, which fought against the British invaders in 1806–1807. An active supporter of the Revolution of May 1810, Rivadavia thenceforth made his career as a professional politician of independence. After some vacillation, he supported the Liberal side of the independence movement. As secretary of the First Triumvirate (1811–1812), he was the driving force behind its liberal policies in education, civil rights, and the slave trade. He also showed his commitment to strong central government, marginalizing the agents and agencies of provincial representation, and provoking opposition from federalists and the military. The First Triumvirate was overthrown in October 1812, and Argentina entered a period of acute instability, as unitarists and federalists fought for control.

Rivadavia was a distant observer of these events, being absent on a diplomatic mission in Europe from 1814 to 1820. His own interest lay in the transfer of ideas and resources. In London he visited Jeremy Bentham and became one of his leading disciples. Rivadavia saw that utilitarianism offered a new philosophy in the aftermath of independence and could give liberal republicanism a moral legitimacy in the gap left by the Spanish crown and church. Liberal institutions in turn would be the framework of economic growth, in which British capital, shipping, goods, and immigrants would play an indispensable part.

Rivadavia seized his opportunity in July 1821, when he became chief minister in the government of Martín Rodríguez in Buenos Aires and gave an instant display of applied liberalism. Drawing on previous planning, he established the University of Buenos Aires. He curtailed the temporal power of the church, extended religious freedom, abolished the ecclesiastical *fuero* and the tithe, and suppressed some religious orders. His plan of modernization included the promotion of a mining industry and improvement of transport; the federalization of Buenos Aires and its customhouse; the expansion of agriculture through immigration and land distribution; and a plan of colonization which he promoted in London. Economic development depended on British capital, trade, and markets, and Rivadavia offered his partners generous terms in Argentina. To Argentines themselves, outside the merchant and landed groups, he offered little; vagrants were pursued with ruthless disregard for traditional usages and swept into the army or labor gangs.

Rivadavia sought to extend modernization beyond the province of Buenos Aires and to create a united and centralized Argentina; on 7 February 1826 he was named president of the United Provinces of the Río de la Plata. But his policy was premature and in many respects ineffective. He alienated traditional interest groups, and these came together under Juan Manuel de Rosas to force his resignation in July 1827. He retired to his country estate and then, in 1829, to Spain. He attempted to return in 1834 but was not permitted to disembark. He died in modest circumstances in Cádiz.

See also **Argentina, Movements: Unitarists; Río de la Plata, Viceroyalty of; Slavery: Spanish America.**

BIBLIOGRAPHY

Ricardo Piccirilli, *Rivadavia y su tiempo*, 2d ed., 3 vols. (1960).

Sergio Bagú, *El plan económico del grupo Rivadaviano 1811–1827* (1966).

John Lynch, *The Spanish American Revolutions 1808–1826*, 2d ed. (1986).

Additional Bibliography

Areces, Nidia R., and Edgardo Ossana. *Rivadavia y su tiempo*. Buenos Aires: Centro Editor de América Latina, 1984.

Gallo, Klaus. *The Struggle for an Enlightened Republic: Buenos Aires and Rivadavia*. London: Institute for the Study of the Americas, 2007.

Paz, Carlos. *Poder, negocios y corrupción en la época de Rivadavia*. Buenos Aires: Ediciones De Alejandría, 2001.

Segreti, Carlos S. A., and Patricia Pasquali. *Bernardino Rivadavia: Hombre de Buenos Aires, ciudadano argentino*. Buenos Aires: Planeta, 2000.

JOHN LYNCH

RIVA PALACIO, VICENTE (1832–1896).

Vicente Riva Palacio (*b.* 16 October 1832; *d.* 22 November 1896), Mexican military, political, and literary figure. Born in Mexico City, the son of Mariano Riva Palacio, governor of the state of Mexico, Riva Palacio was educated at the Literary Institute in Toluca and qualified in law in 1854. He was a Liberal deputy in the Constituent Congress of 1856–1857. Though a civilian, he commanded a section of the Liberal army during the Civil War of the Reform (1858–1861). It was in 1861, while a deputy in the federal Congress, that Riva Palacio became known as a skillful satirist and a playwright. His literary proclivities notwithstanding, he fought under Ignacio Zaragoza at the battle of Puebla in May 1862. He remained loyal to President Benito Juaréz, whom he followed to San Luis Potosí in 1863. As governor of Mexico and later of Michoacán (1865) under Juaréz, he became known for his generous treatment of enemy prisoners, and in 1867 took part in the capture of Querétaro.

After election to the Supreme Court of Justice (1868–1870), he dedicated himself increasingly to writing. With his friend Ignacio Altamirano, Riva Palacio stood for the creation of a national literature. From 1888 he oversaw the publication of the multivolume *Mexico a través de los siglos.* He founded *El Ahuizote* (1874–1876), a satirical newspaper, which attacked the administration of President Sebastián Lerdo De Tejada (1872–1876). He supported Portfirio Díaz's Plan of Tuxtepec in 1876 and served as secretary for development from 1877 to 1880. For attacks in the Chamber of Deputies on the administration of General Manuel González (1880–1884), he was sent to the Santiago Tlatelolco Military Prison in 1883. Upon returning to power in 1884, Porfirio Díaz sent him in 1886 as minister plenipotentiary to Spain and Portugal. Riva Palacio died in Madrid; his remains were brought back to Mexico in 1936.

See also **Mexico: 1810–1910; Mexico, Wars and Revolutions: The Reform.**

BIBLIOGRAPHY

Daniel Cosío Villegas, *Historia moderna de México,* 8 vols. (1955–1972).

Eduardo Ruíz, *Historia de la guerra de intervención en Michoacán* (1975).

Additional Bibliography

Algaba Martínez, Leticia. *Las licencias del novelista y las máscaras del crítico.* México: Universidad Autonoma Metropolitana: Azcapotzalco, 1997.

Díaz y de Ovando, Clementina. *Las ilusiones perdidas del general Vicente Riva Palacio: La Exposición International Mexicana, 1880 y otras utopias.* Mexico City: Universidad Nacional Autónoma de México, 2002.

Ortiz Monasterio, José. *México eternamente: Vicente Riva Palacio ante la escritura de la historia.* Mexico City: Instituto de Investigaciones Dr. José María Luis Mora: Fondo de Cultura Económica, 2004.

BRIAN HAMNETT

RIVAROLA, CIRILO ANTONIO (1836–1879).

Cirilo Antonio Rivarola (*b.* 1836; *d.* 31 December 1879), Paraguayan president (1870–1871). Born into a distinguished elite family, Rivarola began his career as an attorney in Asunción in the period just before the War of the Triple Alliance (1864–1870). He soon ran afoul of the autocratic regime of Francisco Solano López for daring to advocate liberal reform, and was briefly imprisoned. Early in the war, López had him sent to the front as a sergeant. Rivarola acquitted himself well in battle, but after his capture by the Allies in 1869, he cooperated with his captors, who discovered in him the perfect puppet.

With Carlos Loizaga and José Díaz de Bedoya, Rivarola was named to preside over a provisional administration in Asunción that favored Brazilian interests. This government abolished slavery, fostered freedom of the press, arranged for loans from Britain, and held a convention in 1870 to establish a new constitution. By then, Rivarola's two colleagues had resigned, and he stayed on as president. His base of popular support, however, was extremely weak, and he antagonized many of the politicians around him. He went so far as to close Congress in October 1870. A year later his congressional opponents forced him to step down in favor of his vice president, Salvador Jovellanos.

Over the next seven years, Rivarola figured in many political intrigues in a vain effort to recapture the presidential sash (and with it, he hoped, the support of Brazil's minister in Asunción). He continued to be involved in various conspiracies after the Brazilian army evacuated Paraguay in 1876, which brought him still more enemies. He was assassinated on the street in Asunción, in full view of many passersby.

See also **López, Francisco Solano.**

BIBLIOGRAPHY

Harris Gaylord Warren, *Paraguay and the Triple Alliance: The Postwar Decade, 1869–1878* (1978), and *Rebirth of the Paraguayan Republic: The First Colorado Era, 1878–1904* (1985).

Carlos Zubizarreta, *Cien vidas paraguayas,* 2d ed. (1985).

Additional Bibliography

Lewis, Paul H. *Political Parties and Generations in Paraguay's Liberal Era, 1869–1940.* Chapel Hill: University of North Carolina Press, 1992.

THOMAS L. WHIGHAM

RIVAROLA, RODOLFO (1857–1942).

Rodolfo Rivarola (*b.* 18 December 1857; *d.* 10 November 1942), Argentine jurist and intellectual. Founder in 1910 of the influential *Revista Argentina de Ciencias Políticas,* Rivarola was a strong advocate of political reform in pre–World War I Argentina. After studying law at the University of Buenos Aires, he specialized in criminal law; he was one of the precursors of the Italian school of positivist criminology in Argentina. In 1888, with José Nicolás Matienzo and José María Ramos Mejía, among others, Rivarola founded the Sociedad de Antropología Jurídica, following the teachings of the Italian psychiatrist Cesare Lombroso.

Rivarola wrote extensively on Argentine judicial institutions: *Orígenes y evolución del derecho penal argentino* (1900) and *Proyecto de Código penal para la República Argentina* (1891), a project for a code drafted in collaboration with Norberto Piñero and Matienzo, deal with criminal law. *Instituciones del derecho civil argentino* (1901) deals with civil law.

In politics, Rivarola became an advocate of centralization against the federalist system, as can be seen in his *Partidos políticos unitario y federal* (1905) and especially in *Del régimen federativo al unitario* (1908). But he was mostly concerned, as exemplified in his writings for the *Revista,* with the reform of the political practices of the liberal-conservative regime that governed the country between 1880 and 1916.

See also **Judicial Systems: Spanish America.**

BIBLIOGRAPHY

Natalio Botana, *El orden conservador: La política argentina entre 1880 y 1916* (1979).

Enrique Marí, "El marco jurídico," in *El movimiento positivista argentino,* compiled by Hugo E. Biagini (1985).

Additional Bibliography

Ancarola, Gerardo. *Las ideas políticas de Rodolfo Rivarola.* Buenos Aires: Ediciones Marymar, 1975.

EDUARDO A. ZIMMERMANN

RIVAS, PATRICIO.

Patricio Rivas, provisional president of Nicaragua (October 1855–1857). Although he had served in several governmental capacities, including senator, interim chief of state (1838), and customs officer, Rivas is most remembered for his role in Nicaragua's National War. In October 1855, the American filibuster William Walker chose Rivas as his president, under the assumption that he could control the relatively inexperienced old man. In February 1856, Rivas signed Walker's revocation of the Accessory Transit Company's canal charter, a popular action, but protested the next day when Walker presented him with a charter for the Morgan and Garrison Company. The terms of this contract gave away much more than had its predecessor, and Rivas would not sign it without modifying its worst clauses. In June 1856, Rivas defected from the Walker government altogether to join the patriot forces that had opposed the foreign invasion. Although he was known to his contemporaries as "Patas Arriba" ("Feet-Up" or "Topsy-Turvy") for his supposed lack of mettle, subsequent generations have come to regard Rivas as a courageous patriot. He is buried in a place of honor in the cemetery in León.

See also **National War; Nicaragua; Walker, William.**

BIBLIOGRAPHY

William Walker, *The War in Nicaragua* (1860; repr. 1985).

Sara L. Barquero, *Gobernantes de Nicaragua, 1825–1947* (1945).

Albert Z. Carr, *The World and William Walker* (1963).

Karl Bermann, *Under the Big Stick: Nicaragua and the U.S. Since 1848* (1986).

Additional Bibliography

Díaz Lacayo, Aldo. *Gobernantes de Nicaragua (1821–1956): guía para el estudio de sus biografías políticas.* Managua, Nicaragua: Aldilá Editor, 1996.

Plunkett, Hazel. *Nicaragua in Focus: A Guide to the People, Politics and Culture.* New York: Latin America Bureau, 1999.

KAREN RACINE

RIVERA, DIEGO

RIVERA, DIEGO (1886–1957). Diego Rivera (*b.* 13 December 1886; *d.* 24 November 1957), Mexican artist, known primarily for the many murals he painted in Mexico and the United States from the early 1920s through the early 1950s. Over a period of more than fifty years Rivera also produced an extraordinary number of easel paintings, drawings, watercolors, illustrations for books and other publications, and designs for theater productions. A number of his easel paintings and murals, dating from every period of his life, stand out for their artistic quality and thematic coherence.

Rivera was born in Guanajuato. During his formative years in Paris from 1911 to 1921, he experimented with a number of styles before returning to Mexico in 1921 to begin his muralist career. Among the many exemplary works dating from his stay in Paris are *Zapatista Landscape—The Guerrilla* (1915) and *The Mathematician* (1918). Rivera expressed his feeling for his native land in the *Zapatista Landscape,* a major cubist work, by including references to the mountains surrounding the Valley of Mexico, the Revolution of 1910 (a sombrero, a serape, and a rifle), and traditional Spanish and Mexican painting (with the realistic depiction of a small piece of paper identifying the subject "nailed" to the lower right of the canvas). *The Mathematician* represents Rivera's deep involvement and assimilation of the work of Paul Cézanne. Rivera depicted a lone figure seated at a small table on which are placed two books. The sitter appears lost in thought. The artist defined

Mexican artist Diego Rivera, 1948. Best known for his distinctive murals and easel paintings, Rivera often incorporated subjects from his Mexican heritage throughout his work. HULTON ARCHIVE/GETTY IMAGES

every part of the picture with intersecting lines and angles that correspond to several eye levels consistent with Cézanne's approach to painting. He used all of these in a series of linear connections to create a spare yet visually cohesive composition.

One of the most important easel paintings dating from Rivera's mature period is the portrait *Lupe Marín* (1938), which demonstrates his continuing interest in formal and spatial problems. Marín is shown seated on a backless Mexican chair in a corner of the artist's studio. There is a mirror propped up against the wall behind her, in which she and the window she faces are reflected. Rivera paid homage to several artists he admired in this portrait: El Greco, in the exaggerated proportions and pose of the sitter; Velázquez, in the mirrored image; and Cézanne, in the complex structure of the composition.

Rivera's great artistic achievement is also seen in a few mural panels that form part of larger programs and in several mural cycles that have to be considered as a unit. Among the single panel masterpieces are *The Deliverance of the Peon* (1926), from the Ministry of Education in Mexico City (1923–1928); *Germination,* from the Chapingo Chapel mural cycle *The Land Liberated* (1926–1927); and *Production of Automobile Bodies and Final Assembly,* from the mural *Detroit Industry* (1932–1933), in the Detroit Institute of Arts. Each of these encapsulates the artist's deep involvement with formalist as well as thematic concerns.

Rivera used the Christian theme of the descent from the cross for *The Deliverance of the Peon,* in which the dead figure echoes the lowering of the figure of Christ onto a shroud. The scene is filled with tenderness and compassion. It is also a powerful image of a martyr of the Revolution.

Germination has a number of beautifully rendered nude figures that represent various stages from gestation to near birth. It is one of four panels on the right wall of the chapel that focus on the forces of nature. The process begins with chaos and ends with fruition. Comparable forces in society leading to revolutionary action are represented in four panels on the left wall. A synthesis of these forces is represented on the end wall with man at the center in control of nature for the benefit of humankind.

Rivera carried his positive view of technology further in his Detroit mural cycle, in which he devised a complex iconographic program to extoll its virtues. He merged U.S. technology with Mexican mythology on the south wall (*Production of Automobile Bodies and Final Assembly*) by including a reference to the Aztec earth goddess Coatlicue as a fender-stamping machine. The deity, not immediately discernible, is seen to the right of the men working on the assembly line with an automotive chassis. The Coatlicue-like machine retains the silhouette of the deity but not its component parts. The artist's belief in material progress and the benefits to be derived from technology are evident in this panel and the many others that comprise the entire mural cycle. The other panels include the origins of human life and technology on the east wall; the industries of the air (aviation) and water (shipping) on the west wall; the production, manufacture, and assembly of the automobile, and the other industries of Detroit (medical, chemical, and pharmaceutical) on the north and south walls.

Rivera's roles as a political activist, lecturer, and writer pitted him against other artists, art critics, the Communist Party (which expelled him several times), his biographers, Frida Kahlo and his other three wives, and the general public. At the core of these many battles were his views regarding the essence, purpose, and function of art; his views on politics; his love of the Mexican Indian; and his belief that the pre-Columbian past had to be accepted before a true Mexican art and identity could be attained. These battles and controversies, as well as his art, have provided material for numerous articles, monographs, books, exhibition catalogues, and other publications by biographers, journalists, art critics, art historians, and others.

See also **Art: The Twentieth Century; Kahlo, Frida.**

BIBLIOGRAPHY

Jacinto Quirarte, "The Coatlicue in Modern Mexican Painting," in *Research Center for the Arts and Humanities Review* (1982): 5–12, and *Mexico: Splendors of Thirty Centuries* (1990), pp. 617–618, 633–634.

Ramón Favela, *Diego Rivera: The Cubist Years* (1984); *Diego Rivera: A Retrospective* (1986), esp. articles by Stanton Catlin, Laurance P. Hurlburt, and Francis O'Connor.

Laurance P. Hurlburt, *The Mexican Muralists in the United States* (1989).

Additional Bibliography

Cardoza y Aragón, Luis. *La nube y el reloj: Pintura mexicana contemporanea.* México: UNAM, Instituto de Investigaciones Estéticas: Landucci, 2003.

Lara Elizondo, Lupina. *Referencias de Picasso en México: Ocho pintores (1900–1950): Angel Zárraga, Diego Rivera, Carlos Mérida, Manuel Rodríguez Lozano, Alfonso Michel, Rufino Tamayo, Francisco Gutiérrez, Federico Cantú.* Mexico City: Qualitas Compañía de Seguros, 2005.

Tibol, Raquel. *Los murales de Diego Rivera: Universidad Autónoma Chapingo.* Chapingo: Universidad Autónoma Chapingo, 2002.

Vaughan, Mary K., and Stephen E. Lewis. *The Eagle and the Virgin: Nation and Cultural Revolution in Mexico, 1920–1940.* Durham, NC: Duke University Press, 2006.

JACINTO QUIRARTE

RIVERA, FRUCTUOSO (c. 1784–1854).

Fructuoso Rivera (*b.* ca. 1784; *d.* 13 January 1854), president of Uruguay (1830–1835 and 1839–

1843), around whom the Colorado Party, one of the two traditional parties in the country, was formed. When the movement for independence began in 1810, he joined immediately and soon became one of José Gervasio Artigas's most trusted lieutenants, supporting him against the attempts of Buenos Aires to control the region. Rivera played a key role in the fight against Portuguese domination (1816–1820), holding out until March 1820, when he was defeated. As a result of his defeat, he came to terms with the Portuguese invaders and signed the charter of incorporation of Uruguay into the United Kingdom of Portugal and Brazil. In 1822, as a result of Brazil's declaration of independence, Rivera joined the Brazilians against the Portuguese in Uruguay. The Brazilian emperor, Dom Pedro I, promoted him to brigadier general, and in 1824 he was named commander of all the forces in the countryside. However, when Juan Antonio Lavalleja, a leading Uruguayan independence leader and an old friend and collaborator, invaded in 1825, he was captured by Lavalleja's troops, apparently in agreement with Lavalleja himself, and soon became his second in command. But in 1826, he broke off with Lavalleja and moved to Santa Fe, Argentina. While in Santa Fe, with the help of Estanislao López, a prominent regional military leader, Rivera prepared and launched an invasion against the Brazilian territory of Misiones in February 1828. This military feat increased his prestige.

On 28 August 1829, Rivera became minister of war of the provisional government, and on 24 October 1830, he became the first elected president of independent Uruguay. As president, Rivera did not carry out a specific program and was very disorganized, acting more like a caudillo than a president of a country and paying no attention to the affairs of government. Rivera helped General Manuel Oribe get elected president in 1835 with the hope that he could influence him, but when Oribe wanted to pass a series of laws that affected the interior, which Rivera considered his fiefdom, he rose in revolt on 16 July 1836, forcing Oribe's resignation on 23 October 1838. Rivera was then elected president. His second presidential term was disastrous for the country, for he turned an internal political dispute into a regional conflict with his alliances and intrigues with Argentine Unitarians and the Brazilian *farrapos* (ragamuffins). The affair

became an international conflict when France and England intervened in favor of Rivera's Colorados and Argentine Unitarians.

Ten days after he had begun his second term (1839–1843), Rivera declared war on Juan Manuel de Rosas of Argentina, who had given asylum to Oribe, and plunged Uruguay into a conflict that did not end until 1852. Rivera did have some initial success, but between 1842 and 1845, Oribe and the Argentines had the upper hand. In 1845, Rivera sought refuge in Brazil and in 1846 went back to Uruguay and organized an unsuccessful campaign. He was removed from his command on 3 October 1847 because he had started secret negotiations with Oribe. Sentenced to four years in exile, he left for Brazil. In 1851, when the ban was lifted, he tried to go back to Uruguay. However, the Brazilian government blocked his return and kept him a virtual prisoner. He was not allowed to leave Brazil until 20 January 1853. On his way back to Uruguay, he learned that he had been named as a member of a triumvirate, but he died en route.

See also **Farroupilha Revolt; Uruguay: Before 1900.**

BIBLIOGRAPHY

Telmo Manacorda, *Fructuoso Rivera: El perpetuo defensor de la República Oriental* (1933).

José Luciano Martínez, *Brigadier General Fructuoso Rivera* (1961).

Marta Canessa De Sanguinetti, *Rivera: Un oriental liso y llano* (1976).

Additional Bibliography

Giménez Rodríguez, Alejandro. *El libro de los presidentes uruguayos: De Fructuoso Rivera a Jorge Batlle (1830–2004)*. Montevideo: Linardi y Risso, 2004.

Lepro, Alfredo. *Fructuoso Rivera: Hombre del pueblo, sentido revolucionario De su vida y de su acción*, 2 vols. Montevideo: República Oriental del Uruguay, Cámara de Representantes, 1993.

JUAN MANUEL PÉREZ

RIVERA, JOAQUÍN (1796–1845). Joaquín Rivera (*b.* 26 July 1796; *d.* 6 February 1845), head of state of Honduras (1833–1836). Born in Tegucigalpa, Rivera was elected head of state of Honduras in 1830 but declined the office because it was not the result of a popular election. Elected again in 1832, this time in a popular election, he accepted the position. Rivera concentrated on improving the educational system, reducing the debt, and developing commerce and industry. He was particularly concerned with maintaining the relationship between Honduras and the other members of the Central American Federation and was a close ally of Francisco Morazán. Rivera's term of office ended in 1836.

Rivera returned to private life but was forced to leave the country when his former "vice president" and main political detractor, Francisco Ferrera, rose to power. While in exile in El Salvador, Rivera aided Morazán in his efforts to restore the disintegrated Central American Federation. In 1844, Rivera was captured in Danlí while leading a rebellion against Ferrera. He was condemned to death and was executed.

See also **Central America, United Provinces of; Ferrera, Francisco.**

BIBLIOGRAPHY

Victor Caceres Lara, *Gobernantes de Honduras en el siglo 19* (1978), pp. 29–37.

José Ángel Zúñiga Huete, *Presidentes de Honduras, desde José Gregorio Tinoco de Contreras hasta José María Medina* (1987), pp. 87–99.

Additional Bibliography

Durón, Rómulo E. *Don Joaquín Rivera y su tiempo.* Tegucigalpa: Ministerio de Educación Pública, 1965.

SARA FLEMING

RIVERA, JOSÉ EUSTASIO (1888–1928).

José Eustasio Rivera (*b.* 1888; *d.* 1 December 1928), Colombian poet and novelist. Born of a poor family in Neiva, in southeastern Colombia, Rivera was a difficult child both at home and at school. Expelled from three schools, he made his family's economic situation yet more precarious. But he had a natural inclination for literature, and during his best days at school, he was called upon to give speeches, recitals, and even poetry improvisations.

Rivera studied to become a teacher at the Escuela Normal in Bogotá, attending an extra year to apply for the position of school inspector. In 1910 he was finally appointed inspector of Tolima, a province in central Colombia. Rivera took up his work zealously and conscientiously, but was frustrated at having to slow down and accept routine procedures and traditional methods. On top of this frustration came the sudden death of his sister at seventeen years of age. Rivera's life was marked by suffering that was both personal and a reflection of Colombia's condition at the end of the nineteenth and beginning of the twentieth centuries, when the country was in the midst of civil war and beset by rancorous party politics.

Despite his surroundings, this poor, unknown Colombian became a renowned Latin American figure as a poet and a novelist. In poetry, laurels were bestowed on his volume *Tierra de promisión* (1921), and he achieved his right to sit among the great novelists of America for *La vorágine* (1924; *The Vortex*, 1935). The former, a collection of fifty-five sonnets, won him the stature of national poet; the latter made him famous even outside the boundaries of the Hispanic world when it was published in other countries in translation. In fact, *The Vortex* is a breathtaking romantic vision of the Colombian llanos (plains), a bold encounter with the "green inferno," an exhilarating display of the beauty of the tropics. But most of all, it is a tragic document of the dehumanizing influence of the jungle and *caucherías* (rubber-collecting sites) on the souls and lives of those lured by the promise of fast wealth, who were doomed to endless suffering and often merciless death by the savagery of the *enganchador* (recruiting man). Only five years after the publication of his novel, Rivera died in Bogotá.

See also **Literature: Spanish America.**

BIBLIOGRAPHY

J. David Suárez-Torres, "José Eustasio Rivera," in *Latin American Writers,* edited by Carlos A. Solé and Maria Isabel Abreu, vol. 2 (1989), pp. 671–675.

Additional Bibliography

Morales T., Leonidas. *Figuras literarias, rupturas culturales: Modernidad e identidades culturales tradicionales.* Santiago de Chile: Pehuén, 1993.

Ramírez, Liliana. *La vorágine, José Eustasio Rivera: Estudio literario.* Bogotá: Panamericana Editorial, 2001.

Walker, John. *Rivera, La vorágine.* London: Grant & Cutler in association with Tamesis, 1988.

J. DAVID SUÁREZ-TORRES

RIVERA, MARIANO (1969–). One day, the right-handed relief pitcher Mariano "Mo" Rivera will likely join Rodney Carew as the only Panamanians in Cooperstown, New York's Baseball Hall of Fame. The son of a fisherman, Rivera played baseball on the streets of Panama City with a cardboard glove till age ten. He showed enough talent playing with the Panamá Oeste team to sign with the New York Yankees in 1990. After his Major League debut as a Yankee in 1995, he moved from starter to set-up man to closer by 1997. Since then, relying on his dominant cut fastball, he has established himself in many minds as the greatest closer in Major League history and the best pitcher in the history of postseason baseball.

These claims reflect his statistics and many awards through the 2006 season: fourth all-time in career saves (413), lowest career earned run average (ERA) of closers in top fifty of career saves (2.29), most postseason saves of all-time (34), lowest postseason ERA of all-time (0.80), most appearances in postseason history (72), most saves in World Series play (9), only player named American League Championship Series Most Valuable Player (2003) and World Series Most Valuable Player (1999), eight-time All-Star, and record for converting twenty-three consecutive postseason saves. For this, he has won the Rolaids Relief Man of the Year Award four times, the DHL Delivery Man of the Year Award twice, the *Sporting News* Reliever of the Year Award five times, MLB.com's Closer of the Year Award three times, and New York Yankee Player of the Year once (2005). When summoned, he strolls to the mound to the heavy-metal band Metallica's "Enter Sandman," the source of another of his nicknames.

See also **Sports.**

BIBLIOGRAPHY

Kernan, Kevin, ed. *Mariano Rivera: Panama Express.* Topeka, KS: Tandem Library, 2000.

Mondore, Scot E. "Mariano Rivera." In *Latino and African American Athletes Today: A Biographical Dictionary,* edited by David L. Porter. Westport, CT: Greenwood Press, 2004.

Russo, Christopher, and Allen St. John. *The Mad Dog Hall of Fame: The Ultimate Top Ten Rankings of the Best in Sports.* New York: Doubleday, 2006.

JOSEPH L. ARBENA

RIVERA, PEDRO DE (?–1744). Pedro De Rivera (*d.* 1744), reformer of Mexico's northern frontier military system. In 1724 Pedro de Rivera was the commander of the garrison of San Juan de Ulua, the fort that guarded the port of Veracruz. In that year Viceroy Juan de Acuña Casafuerte commissioned Rivera to inspect the twenty-three presidios in northern New Spain and in particular to report on fiscal irregularities in their administration. The members of presidio garrisons received a flat salary from which they had to buy their own horses, equipment, and uniforms. The administration in Mexico City had been receiving reports of graft by presidio commanders. The commanders were charging inflated prices not only for the three types of necessities mentioned but also for other items.

Rivera inspected the presidios in 1724 and submitted suggestions that were implemented in 1729 as a comprehensive *reglamento* for the garrisons. The new set of rules reduced the number of presidios from 23 to 19, and the size of the garrisons from 1,006 to 734 soldiers. The *reglamento* also lowered the salary of most common soldiers. The reduction in the number of presidios and soldiers decreased the government's expenditures for frontier defense from 444,883 pesos prior to Rivera's inspection to 381,930 pesos following it. However, his reforms did not improve frontier security, and in the face of continued hostility from tribes beyond Spanish control, the number of presidios and soldiers and the amount of government expenditures grew during the eighteenth century.

See also **New Spain, Colonization of the Northern Frontier; Presidio.**

BIBLIOGRAPHY

Max L. Moorhead, *The Presidio: Bastion of the Spanish Borderlands* (1975).

Additional Bibliography

Naylor, Thomas H., and Charles W. Polzer, compilers and editors. *Pedro de Rivera and the Military Regulations for Northern New Spain, 1724–1729: A Documentary History of His Frontier Inspection and the Reglamento de 1729.* Tucson: University of Arizona Press, 1988.

Smith, Fay Jackson. *Captain of the Phantom Presidio: A History of the Presidio of Fronteras, Sonora, New Spain, 1686–1735, Including the Inspection by Brigadier Pedro de Rivera, 1726.* Spokane, WA: A. H. Clark, 1993.

ROBERT H. JACKSON

RIVERA CABEZAS, ANTONIO (1784–

1851). Antonio Rivera Cabezas (*b.* 1784; *d.* 8 May 1851), a radical liberal leader in early independent Central America. Born in Guatemala City to a prominent creole family, Rivera was a lawyer by profession. He also served as an officer in the colonial militia and as a member of the *diputación provincial* (regional council) established by the Cortes of Cádiz in 1812. A signer of the declaration of Guatemalan independence on 15 September 1821, Rivera was allied politically with radical liberals (*fiebres*) Pedro Molina and José Francisco Barrundia and was a member of the Mexican Congress during Agustín de Iturbide's empire.

After Central America separated from Mexico (1 July 1823), Rivera became a member (substituting for Manuel José Arce, who was in the United States), with Molina and Juan Vicente Villacorta, of the triumvirate that directed the United Provinces of Central America. He was its provisional president from 9 July to 4 October 1823, served as *jefe político* of Guatemala in 1824, and then held the post of intendant of El Salvador. Known for his witty political satire in the press, he edited *El Melitón* in 1825. Elected lieutenant governor of Guatemala in 1829, Rivera became its governor from 9 March 1830 to 10 February 1831 after the legislature pressured Governor Pedro Molina to resign. During his brief administration, he launched anticlerical reforms, established schools (including Lancastrian model schools in Quezaltenango and Guatemala City), worked for judicial reform, and established a highway department. Francisco Morazán defeated him in the 1830 Central American presidential election, but he served as Morazán's finance minister in 1835 and as a district judge in 1832 and 1837. After the

1839 conservative victory, he went into exile and conspired with Pedro Molina against the Guatemalan conservatives.

See also **Barrundia, José Francisco; Central America, United Provinces of; Iturbide, Agustín de; Molina, Pedro; Morazán, Francisco.**

BIBLIOGRAPHY

Ernesto Bienvenido Jiménez, *Ellos, los presidentes* (1981), includes a detailed biographical sketch. See also Manuel José Arce, *Memoria* (1831); Alejandro Marure, *Efemérides de los hechos notables acaecidos en la República de Centro-América desde el año 1821 hasta el de 1842*, 2d ed. (1895); and Julio C. Pinto Soria, *Centroamérica, de la colonia al estado nacional* (*1800–1840*) (1986).

Additional Bibliography

Bardales B., Rafael. *Morazán, defensor de la unión de Centroamérica*. Tegucigalpa: Editorial Universitaria, 1983.

RALPH LEE WOODWARD JR.

RIVERA CARBALLO, JULIO ADALBERTO (1921–1973). Julio Adalberto

Rivera Carballo (*b.* 1921; *d.* 29 July 1973), army officer and president of El Salvador (1962–1967). Lieutenant Colonel Rivera headed the provisional government established on 25 January 1961, when a military coup d'état overthrew a leftist junta that had been in power since October 1960. Later, he resigned in order to assume leadership of the National Conciliation Party (PCN). In 1962, he was elected to the presidency as the PCN candidate, following a campaign boycotted by the opposition parties.

Although an outspoken anti-Communist, Rivera appeared to accept the Kennedy administration's argument that the best way to defeat communism was to attack poverty, injustice, and tyranny at home. An enthusiastic supporter of the Alliance for Progress, Rivera initiated a number of significant reforms in El Salvador, including a rural minimum wage. He also liberalized the political system, a policy that encouraged the development of opposition parties. In pushing reforms over conservative objections, Rivera benefited from the country's rapid economic growth in the early 1960s. Later, however, a downturn caused problems for his hand-picked successor, Colonel Fidel Sánchez Hernández

(1967–1972). Rivera was serving as ambassador to the United States at the time of his death.

See also **El Salvador, Political Parties: National Conciliation Party (PCN).**

BIBLIOGRAPHY

On Salvadoran politics in the 1960s, see Stephen Webre, *José Napoleón Duarte and the Christian Democratic Party in Salvadoran Politics, 1960–1972* (1979); James Dunkerley, *Power in the Isthmus: A Political History of Modern Central America* (1988); and Sara Gordon Rapoport, *Crisis política y guerra en El Salvador* (1989).

Additional Bibliography

Domínguez, Carlos Armando. *Datos para una biografía del ex Presidente de la República Julio Adalberto Rivera.* San Salvador: Taller Gráfico UCA, 1998.

STEPHEN WEBRE

RIVERA DAMAS, ARTURO (1923–1994).

Arturo Rivera Damas (*b.* 30 September 1923; *d.* San Salvador, El Salvador, 26 November 1994), archbishop of San Salvador. Born in San Esteban Catarina and ordained a Salesian priest in 1953, Rivera, who held a degree in canon law, was consecrated auxiliary bishop of San Salvador in 1960. His support of progressive clergy soon gained him the enmity of the conservative oligarchy, especially when, in January 1970, he refused to leave the Ministry of Defense building until the government released Father José Alas, who had been arrested for advocating land reform.

When Oscar Romero was named archbishop of San Salvador in 1977, Rivera was made bishop of Santiago de María, Usulután. He was the only Salvadoran bishop to back Romero consistently in his struggle against government-sponsored repression and in his actions on behalf of Christian base communities.

After Romero's assassination in March 1980, the Vatican named Rivera apostolic administrator. Nearly three years later, he was made archbishop. As leader of the Salvadoran church, Rivera did not totally follow in his predecessor's footsteps. Although he consistently denounced the brutalities of the security forces and opposed U.S. military aid, he was less sympathetic than Romero to

popular organizations. He tried to take a neutral position in the civil war, calling for dialogue and a negotiated solution, while sometimes acting as a mediator.

In 1989, Rivera faced a difficult period when six Jesuits priests were assassinated at the Universidad Centroamericana "José Simeón Cañas" (UCA) by the Fuerza Armada de El Salvador's group. In this massacre died Ignacio Ellacuría, S. J., adviser and friend of Rivera. In 1992, he mediated the final peace accords negotiation that ended the civil war.

In the year preceding his death, Rivera worked tirelessly for the canonization of Oscar Romero, who was assassinated and considered a martyr of the Church.

See also **Catholic Church: The Modern Period; Jesuits; Romero, Oscar Arnulfo; San Salvador.**

BIBLIOGRAPHY

Tommie Sue Montgomery, "The Church in the Salvadoran Revolution," in *Latin American Perspectives* 10, no. 1 (1983): 62–87.

Phillip Berryman, *The Religious Roots of Rebellion: Christians in Central American Revolutions* (1984), pp. 100–161.

Additional Bibliography

Rivera Damas, Arturo. *Dar desde nuestra pobreza: Segunda exhortación pastoral.* San Salvador: Arzobispado, 1995.

Rivera Damas, Arturo. *La palabra queda. Vida de Monseñor Oscar A. Romero.* Archdiocese of San Salvador: Arzobispado de San Salvador, 1983.

EDWARD T. BRETT

RIVERA MAESTRE, MIGUEL (1806–1888).

Miguel Rivera Maestre (*b.* 1806; *d.* 1888), prominent architect in nineteenth-century Guatemala. Together with his brother, Julián Rivera Maestre, also an architect, or individually, the two designed and planned most of the major public buildings of the era, including the Sociedad Económica building, which later became the home of the national congress. Miguel was in charge of the planning and construction of the Teatro Carrera, the national theater in Guatemala City, until he resigned for political reasons and was replaced by the German architect José Beckers. Miguel also drew the first detailed maps of Guatemala City and was responsible for the country's first atlas, *Atlas del Estado de Guatemala* (1832).

See also **Architecture: Architecture to 1900; Guatemala City.**

BIBLIOGRAPHY

Carlos C. Haeussler Yela, *Diccionario General de Guatemala*, vol. 3 (1983), p. 1379.

Additional Bibliography

Claxton, Robert H. "Miguel Rivera Maestre: Guatemalan Scientist-Engineer." *Technology and Culture* 14 (July 1973): 384–403.

SUE DAWN MCGRADY

RIVERA PAZ, MARIANO (1804–
1849). Mariano Rivera Paz. (*b.* 24 September 1804; *d.* 22 February 1849), chief of state of Guatemala (1838–1839, 1839–1841, 1842–1844). The son of a creole family of modest means, Rivera rose to the rank of lieutenant colonel in the federal army during the civil war of 1826–1829. After the army's defeat by Francisco Morazán, Rivera went to Cobán, and during the administration of Mariano Gálvez (1831–1838) he represented Verapaz in the legislature and acquired considerable property. Rivera was an active member of the conservative faction led by Juan José de Aycinena, and following Rafael Carrera's overthrow of Gálvez in 1838, served as chief of state of Guatemala for most of the subsequent five years. In collaboration with Carrera, he presided over restoration of Hispanic values and institutions in Guatemala. Rivera later served as alcalde of Guatemala City, director of the Sociedad Económica, and corregidor of the Department of Guatemala. In 1849 President Mariano Paredes named him *corregidor* of Jutiapa, with orders to pacify that rebellious *montaña* department. Guerrillas ambushed and killed him as he traveled to his new post.

See also **Central America; Guatemala.**

BIBLIOGRAPHY

Edgar Escobar Medrano, *Mariano Rivera Paz y su época* (1982).

Additional Bibliography

Pinto Soria, Julio César. *Nación, caudillismo y conflicto étnico en Guatemala (1821–1854).* Guatemala: Instituto de Investigaciones Políticas y Sociales, Escuela de Ciencia Política, Universidad de San Carlos de Guatemala, 1996.

Sullivan-González, Douglass. *Piety, Power, and Politics: Religion and Nation Formation in Guatemala, 1821–1871.* Pittsburgh, PA: University of Pittsburgh Press, 1998.

RALPH LEE WOODWARD JR.

RIVERA Y MONCADA, FERNANDO DE (1711–1781). Fernando de Riveray Moncada (*b.* 1711; *d.* 18 July 1781), Spanish commandant of the Californias. Rivera y Moncada, a native of Compostela, Nayarit, served in the military at Loreto, Baja California, in 1742. He explored the Bahía de Sebastián Vizcaíno with the Jesuit Fernando Consag in 1751. As commandant, he aided in the founding of missions at Santa Gertrudis (1752) and San Francisco Borja (1762). With the Jesuit Wenceslaus Linck, Rivera y Moncada explored as far as the Sierra San Pedro Mártir in 1766. In January 1768 he aided Gaspar de Portolá in the expulsion of the Jesuits from California, and in May of that year he and the Franciscan Juan Crespí led the first land party to San Diego. With Portolá he explored as far as San Francisco and Monterey from July 1769 to January 1770, and from Baja California he supplied Alta California in 1770–1771. Rivera y Moncada retired to Guadalajara in 1772, but by 1774 he was back in service as military commandant of Alta California, where he put down the San Diego revolt in 1775. He was commandant of Loreto from 1777 to 1779, and in 1781 he led Sonoran colonists to Alta California. He was massacred in an uprising by the Yuma Indians near La Concepción on the Colorado River.

See also **Baja California; Jesuits.**

BIBLIOGRAPHY

Francisco Palóu, *Historical Memoirs of New California*, translated by Herbert E. Bolton, 4 vols. (1926).

Ernest J. Burrus, ed., *Diario del capitán comandante Fernando de Rivera y Moncada*, 2 vols. (1967).

Additional Bibliography

Gustafson, Janie L. "Never to Turn Back: The Controversy Between Junipero Serra, OFM, Fermin Francisco de Lasuen, OFM, and Commander Fernando de Rivera y Moncada and its Effects on the Evangelization/Acculturation of the California Indians at Missions San Diego de Alcala and San Carlos Borromeo de Carmelo in the Years 1774–1777." Ph.D. diss. Graduate Theological Union, 1986.

Rodríguez Sala de Gomezgil, María Luisa, and Pedro López González. *Exploraciones en Baja y Alta California, 1769–1775: Escenarios y personajes.* Mexico City: UNAM, Instituto de Investigaciones Sociales: Amat, 2002.

W. MICHAEL MATHES

ROA BÁRCENA, JOSÉ MARÍA (1827–1908).

An impassioned romantic at the beginning of his literary career (1849), José María Roa Bárcena became the originator of Mexico's modern short story with his series of tales in *Noche al raso* (1865). With "Lanchitas" (1877), rooted in oral tradition, he consolidated the fantasy genre in Mexico. His novel of ideas, *La Quinta Modelo* (1857), was an attempt to ridicule liberalism. Roa Bárcena supported the establishment of the Second Empire under Maximilian (1864–1867). His traumatic experience of the U.S. invasion of Mexico brought about *Recuerdos de la invasion norteamericana* (1883), which at the time was the best documented work on that era of history. During his long, prolific career, Roa Bárcena wrote in various genres: journalism, poetry, fiction, history, and criticism.

See also **French Intervention (Mexico); Journalism in Mexico; Literature: Spanish America; Mexico, Wars and Revolutions: Mexican-American War.**

RAFAEL OLEA FRANCO

ROA BASTOS, AUGUSTO (1917–2005).

Paraguay's most renowned novelist, Augusto Roa Bastos was born in Asunción on June 12, 1917, and grew up in the small town of Iturbe, far from a large metropolitan center. His writing, like that of José Maria Arguedas and Juan Ruffo, brings together cultural forms rooted in Latin America's rural spaces (such as oral storytelling and indigenous languages) with literary techniques and trends associated with high modernism. Although Roa Bastos spent many years in exile, Paraguay is central to all his work. He left in 1947 because of political pressures, living first in Buenos Aires and later France after the military coup in Argentina in 1976. He taught Latin American literature and the Guaraní language at the University of Toulouse. Roa Bastos returned to Paraguay only with the fall of the Alfredo Stroessner dictatorship in 1989.

Roa Bastos's best-known works are his short stories and novels, but he also wrote plays and poems. His two masterpieces, the novels *Hijo de hombre* (1960) and *Yo el Supremo* (1972), are part of what he called his trilogy on the monotheism of power. "The meditation on power," he once declared in an interview, "is the guiding thread of all my work" (Meliá, p. 130). This meditation on power addresses not only Paraguay's tradition of authoritarian rule—José Gaspar Rodríguez de Francia (1814–1840) and Alfredo Stroessner (1954–1989) were two of the most powerful and longest-governing dictators in Latin American history—but also its ruinous experiences in two of the most important hemispheric wars, the War of the Triple Alliance (1864–1870) and the Chaco War (1932–1935), and the legacy of colonialism in the uneasy coexistence of the Spanish and Guaraní languages in Paraguayan public and private life. Thus much of Roa Bastos's writing revolves around the exploration of popular spaces that have withstood colonialism, war, and dictatorship.

In *Yo el Supremo* Francia, the dying dictator, occupies the center of the novel as he recounts his projects for Paraguay and justifies his actions to his assistant and scribe. The novel exposes the failings of absolute power in the discrepancy between the dictator's dreams and reality by presenting other discourses that contradict these "statements of the state." *Hijo de hombre*, a fragmented text that has at times been described as a series of short stories, studies power not at its source but by examining its effects on the people. These stories lay out a series of reflections on the conflict between a popular peasant strata and the ruling order. Popular resistance does not take place through open rebellion but through more oblique forms. In fact, the only instance of rebellion is an absolute failure and ends in an explosion that kills most of the rebels and opens a crater that acts as an emblem of the multiple disasters of Paraguayan history. Roa Bastos died in Asunción on April 26, 2005.

See also **Arguedas, José María; Chaco War; Stroessner, Alfredo; War of the Triple Alliance.**

BIBLIOGRAPHY

Works by the Author: Short-Story Collections

El trueno entre las hojas. Buenos Aires: Editorial Losada, 1953.

El Baldío. Buenos Aires: Editorial Losada, 1966.

Madera quemada [1967]. Asunción: El Lector, 1983.

Moriencia [1969]. Caracas, Venezuela: Monte Avila Editores, 1979.

Lucha hasta el alba. Asunción: Editorial Arte Nuevo, 1979.

Contar un cuento y otros relatos. Buenos Aires: Editorial Kapelusz, 1984.

Novels

Hijo de hombre [1960]. Buenos Aires: Editorial Sudamericana, 1990.

Yo el Supremo [1972]. Translated by Helen Lane as *I, the Supreme.* New York: Vintage, 1986.

El fiscal. Madrid: Alfaguara, 1994.

Contravida. Asunción: El Lector, 1994.

Vigilia del Almirante. Asunción: RP Ediciones, 1992.

Madama Sui. Asunción: El Lector, 1995.

Interview

Meliá, Bartomeu. "Entrevista con Augusto Roa Bastos." In *El Paraguay Inventado.* Asunción: Centro de Estudios Paraguayos Antonio Guasch, 1997.

ADRIANA MICHÉLE CAMPOS JOHNSON

ROBERTSON, JOHN PARISH, AND WILLIAM PARISH.

The Robertson brothers (John Parish Robertson, 1792–1843, and William Parish Robertson, 1795–?), born in Scotland, became successful businessmen in South America, lost their fortune, returned to Britain, and published chronicles of their experiences. They were active in trade between Great Britain and Paraguay, Argentina, Chile, and Peru from 1813 to 1830. The letters between them provide a personal insight into business, finance, and politics.

John Robertson first visited the River Plate region in 1806. At twenty-one, he set himself up in Asunción as a mercantile agent. The future was so promising that his brother William joined him.

Their partnership thrived until the financial crisis of 1826, when they lost their fortune.

During the years that their firm thrived they were active on many fronts: commercial, financial, social, and political. The immediacy and intimacy of their correspondence provides a revealing account of life when these countries were becoming institutionally viable.

After their auspicious start in Asunción, the dictator José Gaspar Francia expelled them from Paraguay in 1815. Still in their twenties, they moved their operations to Corrientes. In 1817, John returned to London to consolidate connections in the financial world, returning to Argentina in 1820, when he established an agricultural colony for Scottish immigrants on 6,500 hectares of prime land in Monte Grande in Buenos Aires Province. The initiative was authorized by Bernardino Rivadavia, governor of the province, in a decree signed on March 11, 1824. Fifteen months later, more than two hundred Scottish settlers arrived from Scotland. The colony failed in 1829.

The riskiest project the brothers undertook was syndicating loans for the governments of Peru and Buenos Aires Province. John convinced Alexander Baring that the profitability of loans to Latin American governments outweighed the risks involved. Baring Brothers' loan to Argentina set a precedent for Argentina's future erratic handling of international loans and public finance. The brothers' books on their experiences in South America were entertaining and sold well in their different editions.

See also **Baring Brothers; Francia, José Gaspar Rodríguez de; Paraguay: The Nineteenth Century; Rivadavia, Bernardino.**

BIBLIOGRAPHY

Robertson, John Parish. *Solomon Seesaw.* Philadelphia: Lea & Blanchard, 1839.

Robertson, J. P. and W. P. *Letters on Paraguay, Comprising an Account of a Four Years' Residence in That Republic.* 2 vols. London: John Murray, 1838, 1839.

Robertson, J. P. and W. P. *Francia's Reign of Terror, Being the Continuation of Letters on Paraguay.* Vol. III. London: John Murray, 1839.

Robertson, J. P. and W. P. *Letters on South America, Comprising Travels on the Banks of the Parana and the Rio de la Plata.* London: John Murray, 1843.

Robertson, J. P. and W. P. *Cartas del Paraguay (1838–1839)*. Translated by Carlos A. Aldao. Buenos Aires: La Cultura Argentina, 1920.

Robertson, J. P. and W. P. *Cartas de Sud-América: Andanzas por el litoral argentino*. Translated by José Luis Busaniche. Buenos Aires: Editorial Nova, 1946.

Robertson, J. P. and W. P. *Cartas de Sud-América*. 3 vols. Translated by José Luis Busaniche. Buenos Aires: Emecé Editores, 1950.

Robertson, J. P. and W. P. *Cartas de Sudamérica*. Buenos Aires: Emecé Editores, 2000.

Robertson, William Parish. *Visit to Mexico*, 2 vols. London: Simpkin Marshall, 1853.

EDWARD L. SHAW

ROBLES, FRANCISCO (1811–1893).

Francisco Robles (*b.* 5 May 1811; *d.* 11 March 1893), president of Ecuador (1856–1859). Robles, born in Guayaquil, served as deputy from Manabí Province (1852) and as governor of Guayas Province (1854–1856) prior to assuming the presidency, the successor selected by departing president José María Urbina (1851–1856). In 1857 Robles moved to abolish Indian tribute but took no steps to make up for lost revenues. As a result, government revenues fell sharply. Not a strong leader, his presidency was further compromised by his serious illness in 1858. Later that year Peru threatened to invade Ecuador, and opponents in Congress, led by the Conservative Gabriel García Moreno and the Liberal Pedro Moncayo y Esparsa, refused to cooperate in establishing necessary defenses. Peru blockaded Guayaquil in 1858 and invaded in 1859, effectively cutting off Ecuador from its sole remaining source of revenue, the Guayaquil customs house. The nation quickly disintegrated into civil war: Loja and Cuenca declared their independence, Guayaquil annexed itself to Peru, and in Quito, Gabriel García Moreno selected former president Juan José Flores to battle Robles. Flores won, and Robles fled into exile in Peru. He died in Guayaquil.

See also **Ecuador: Since 1830; Flores, Juan José.**

BIBLIOGRAPHY

On nineteenth-Century Ecuadorian politics, see Mark J. Van Aken's splendid study, *King of the Night: Juan José Flores and Ecuador, 1824–1864* (1989); or consult Frank MacDonald Spindler's descriptive narrative, *Nineteenth Century Ecuador: An Historical Introduction* (1987).

Additional Bibliography

Febres Cordero, Francisco. *De Flores a flores y miel*. Quito: Ojo de Pez, EDIMPRES, 1996.

RONN F. PINEO

ROBLES, MARCOS AURELIO (1905–1990).

Marcos Aurelio Robles (*b.* 8 November 1905; *d.* 29 April 1990), president of Panama (1964–1968). A native of Aguadulce, Robles was an active National Liberal Party (PLN) legislator and was appointed minister of the interior and justice in 1960. After being elected to the presidency as the candidate of the National Opposition Union (UNO), composed of the PLN and seven smaller parties, Robles took office 1 October 1964.

Robles, a banker, represented the business-planter elite that had dominated Panama since independence and, in many ways, since the Spanish conquest. He sought new economic development and especially promoted Panama as a Latin American banking center. He encouraged partial incorporation of Panama into the Central American Common Market, but his moderate efforts at tax reform and agrarian reform divided the Liberal Party. His unsuccessful attempt to secure a better treaty with the United States vis-à-vis the Panama Canal following the 1964 flag riots, charges of corruption, and failure to represent a wider constituency led to his impeachment by the National Assembly in 1968. Although the Supreme Court overturned the impeachment, Robles had become unpopular. After his coalition lost the 1968 election to Arnulfo Arias, Robles went into voluntary exile in the United States.

See also **Central American Common Market (CACM); Economic Development; Panama.**

BIBLIOGRAPHY

Richard F. Nyrop, ed., *Panama: A Country Study* (1980), pp. 37–43.

Additional Bibliography

Palmarola J., Verónica A. and Yamileth Z. Robles V. *El proceso de reversión del Canal de Panamá y las áreas civiles y militares en el marco del Tratado del Canal de Panamá de 1977.* Panamá: Editorial Universitaria (EUPAN), 1999.

Schneider, Ronald M. *Latin American Political History: Patterns And Personalities.* New York: Westview Press, 2006.

RALPH LEE WOODWARD JR.

ROBLES, WENCESLAO (?–1866).

Wenceslao Robles (*d.* January 1866), Paraguayan general. At the outbreak of the War of the Triple Alliance in 1864, Robles was a ranking army officer stationed at the fortress of Humaitá, in southern Paraguay. Less than a year later, he was chosen by President Francisco Solano López to command a large force sent to invade the neighboring Argentine province of Corrientes. After the surprise capture of the port of Corrientes on 13 April 1865, Robles disembarked with 3,000 men and immediately pushed southward along the east bank of the Paraná. Reinforcements amounting to another 22,000 men reached Robles en route, and permitted him to advance as far as Goya.

Diversionary attacks by the Argentines in late May and the disastrous naval engagement at Riachuelo in June caused Robles to falter, however, and by the end of the year, the Paraguayans had evacuated Corrientes, leaving much destruction behind. Robles had been relieved of command in July. López later had him arrested and charged with dereliction of duty and possible collusion with the enemy. Despite the lack of evidence against him, a military court found Robles guilty, and he was executed at Humaitá.

See also **War of the Triple Alliance.**

BIBLIOGRAPHY

Charles J. Kolinski, *Independence or Death! The Story of the Paraguayan War* (1965).

Leandro Aponte Benítez, *Hombres ... armas ... y batallas de la epopeya de los siglos* (1971), pp. 168–170.

Additional Bibliography

Whigham, Thomas. *The Paraguayan War. Volume 1.* Lincoln: University of Nebraska Press, 2002.

THOMAS L. WHIGHAM

ROBLES BERLANGA, ROSARIO

(1956–). A prominent Mexican politician and party leader, Rosario Robles Berlanga was a native of the Federal District. She attended National Preparatory School No. 4, graduated from the National University of Mexico with an economics degree, and earned an MA in rural development from the Autonomous Metropolitan University. She entered politics as a member of the executive committee of the National Autonomous University Workers Union (1988–1993). A cofounder of the PRD (Democratic Revolutionary Party), she served in Congress from the Federal District from 1994 to 1997 and as secretary of organization of the PRD in 1996–1997. In 1997 Cuauhtémoc Cárdenas appointed her as secretary general of the Federal District, the first opposition party member to hold that post. When Cárdenas resigned as governor to run a third time for the presidency, she replaced him in 1999, serving out the remainder of his term, the first woman to hold that post. In 2002 she became president of the PRD but resigned in 2004 amid corruption scandals.

See also **Cárdenas Solorzano, Cuauhtémoc; Mexico, Political Parties: Democratic Revolutionary Party (PRD).**

BIBLIOGRAPHY

Carlsen, Laura. "Renegade Regente." *Latin Trade* 8, no. 4 (April 2000): 22.

Welch, Liz. "Rosario Robles." *Ms. Magazine* 11, no. 2 (February–March 2001): 14–17.

RODERIC AI CAMP

ROCA, BLAS (1898–1987).

Blas Roca (Francisco Calderío; *b.* 1898; *d.* 1987), Cuban union organizer and politician. Roca was born in Manzanillo, Oriente Province. A shoemaker by trade, he changed his name to Blas Roca and fought to unionize his fellow workers before joining the Cuban Communist Party in 1929. Five years later he was elected secretary general of the party. Roca held many important positions in the party and government. He helped form the new Cuban Communist Party (PCC) in 1965, served on the central committee, politburo, council of state, and in the National Assembly, of which he was president from 1976 to 1981. Roca played a decisive role in consolidating and institutionalizing the control of the Communist Party. His writings include *The Fundamental Principles of Socialism in Cuba* (1962) and *The Cuban Revolution: Report to the Eighth National Congress of the Popular Socialist Party of Cuba* (1961).

See also **Castro Ruz, Fidel; Cuba, Political Parties: Communist Party.**

BIBLIOGRAPHY

Hugh Thomas, *Cuba: The Pursuit of Freedom* (1971).

Additional Bibliography

Batlle, Lucilo, and Blas Roca Calderío. *Blas Roca, continuador de la obra de Baliño y Mella.* La Habana: Editorial de Ciencias Sociales, 2005.

Whitney, Robert. *State and Revolution in Cuba: Mass Mobilization and Political Change, 1920–1940.* Chapel Hill, NC: University of North Carolina Press, 2001.

TODD LITTLE- SIEBOLD

ROCA, JULIO ARGENTINO (1843–1914).

Julio Argentino Roca (*b.* 1843; *d.* 20 October 1914), president of Argentina (1880–1886, 1898–1904). Roca, a clever politician who dominated Argentina from 1880 to 1904, represents the predominance of rural landowners. He presided over a period of political order as well as spectacular economic growth until overtaken by reformist opponents.

Roca's rise to power began in the army. As an officer from Tucumán, Roca viewed the army as an agent of national unification. At the age of sixteen, he completed his formal education at the Colegio Nacional de Concepción del Uruguay. He then participated in the battle of Cepeda as a lieutenant in José de Urquiza's army. Roca became popular after successfully completing his military campaigns along the pampas. He won the support of cattlemen, politicians, and farmers in the interior because he protected and enriched them. Through his military career, Roca broadened his understanding of Argentina and of the provincial upper class.

Roca began to consider himself a viable presidential candidate during the Avellaneda regime, in

which he served as minister of war. In 1879, he began his desert campaign against the Ranqueles Indians. The government transferred 35 percent of the national territory from the Indians to local caudillos between 1876 and 1893. The provincial *estancieros* (hacienda owners) became part of a capitalistic oligarchy. Land speculation increased as landowners borrowed on the basis of higher land values. Many of these landowners urged Roca to seize power. By January 1880, he had selected candidates and discussed the possibility of their election to the presidency.

Turmoil surrounding the 1880 presidential election enabled Roca to become chief executive. When Carlos Tejedor became the Autonomist leader of Buenos Aires province, he provoked the conservative interior because he was a representative of the liberal tradition of Bartolomé Mitre. Roca articulated provincial resentment at the unfair distribution of tariff revenues by officials in Buenos Aires, demanding that the city be federalized as the national capital. The interior wanted to operate the port in order to benefit the other provinces. With friendly governors behind him throughout Argentina, Roca defeated Tejedor in the presidential balloting. Avellaneda lost his nerve when Tejedor revolted in June 1880, but Roca's popularity in the army enabled him to crush the dissidents.

Roca's first regime was generally successful. His program of order appealed to many because Argentina needed economic growth. Landed interests appreciated Roca's railroad construction. Anticlericals within the Partido Autonomista Nacional approved of his secular outlook. Roca was not an idealist and had few scruples about his cynical use of power. A shrewd politician known as "the fox," he used his authority to ensure peace in the interior. Well organized and a prolific correspondent with local supporters, he allowed few details to escape his attention.

The economic boom of the 1880s established Roca's authority. Exports grew tremendously, to the point that Argentina eventually became the world's leading corn exporter and second in wheat exports. Wool, mutton, sheepskin, and beef exports enabled the pastoral sector to retain a slim lead over agriculture. Roca also supported the sugar industry and presided over the best railroad system in Latin America. Foreign capital poured in, to the extent that

The Visit to the River Negro, by General Julio Argentino Roca (1843–1914) and his army (oil on canvas) by Juan Manuel Blanes (1830–1901). MUSEO MUNICIPAL JUAN MANUEL BLANES, MONTEVIDEO, URUGUAY/ INDEX/ THE BRIDGEMAN ART LIBRARY

by 1889, British capital in Argentina represented about half of British overseas investments. Unwisely, however, Roca allowed mortgage banks to sell notes using land as collateral. Meanwhile, the Roca regime encouraged massive European immigration to Argentina despite its lack of a consistent land policy. Fine shops, a wonderful opera theater, and pleasant surroundings led Buenos Aires to become known as the Paris of the Americas.

Roca played a strong role in the Pellegrini government. He controlled the countryside as interior minister. At this time Roca formulated a famous *acuerdo* with Mitre and the moderate faction of the Unión Cívica. As Roca probably anticipated, a radical faction of the Unión Cívica split off in protest. Hipólito Yrigoyen began a long struggle to unseat Pellegrini's and subsequent governments until he triumphed in 1916.

Roca established several local regimes that were improvements over preceding administrations. Elected as head of the national Senate, he imposed Luis Sáenz Peña as Argentina's next president in 1892. Once again, Roca controlled politics. When Sáenz Peña would not allow him to dominate his government, however, Roca and Mitre turned Congress against the president. Using his network, Roca was reelected president in 1898.

Roca's second regime was unsatisfying. He nearly went to war with Chile. Anarchists and socialists established powerful working-class movements. Therefore Roca attempted to repatriate critical immigrants by means of a foreigners' residence law. Economic growth continued, but the foreign debt remained high. For the first time in two decades, Roca discovered that he could not mandate who would become president. Manuel Quintana, Roca's successor, was a compromise selection. But the vice president, José Figueroa Alcorta, was Carlos Pellegrini's choice. When the elderly Quintana died in 1906, Roca quickly lost influence.

After retiring from politics, Roca regretted the imbalance of wealth and power between Buenos Aires and the rest of the country. Although he was the symbol of provincial resentments, he became a classic elite figure. Roca spent many of his later years in Europe and died in Buenos Aires.

See also **Argentina: The Nineteenth Century; Pellegrini, Carlos.**

BIBLIOGRAPHY

The most compelling biography is Félix Luna, *Soy Roca* (1989). A thorough study of the first Roca regime is Bruce Lee Kress, "Julio Roca and Argentina, 1880–

1886. A Political and Economic Study" (Ph.D. diss., Columbia University, 1972). Douglas W. Richmond, *Carlos Pellegrini and the Crisis of the Argentine Elites, 1880–1916* (1989), contains data for the 1880s and 1890s. A solid overview of the latter period is David Rock, *Politics in Argentina, 1890–1930: The Rise and Fall of Radicalism* (1975). Richard J. Walter, *The Socialist Party of Argentina, 1890–1930* (1977), provides the background on labor. The early section of Guido Di Tella and D. C. M. Platt, *The Political Economy of Argentina, 1880–1946* (1986), covers the economic context. Alfred Díaz De Molina, *José Figueroa Alcorta: De la oligarquía a la democracia, 1898–1928* (1979), illustrates Roca's bitter political decline. Also see A. G. Ford, *The Gold Standard, 1880–1914: Britain and Argentina* (1962); and Carl E. Solberg, *Immigration and Nationalism: Argentina and Chile, 1890–1914* (1970).

Additional Bibliography

Fraga, Rosendo. *Roca y el Brasil.* Buenos Aires: Editorial Centro de Estudios Unión para la Nueva Mayoría, 1994.

Fraga, Rosendo. *Roca y Chile.* Buenos Aires: Editorial Centro de Estudios Unión para la Nueva Mayoría, 1996.

Luna, Félix. *La época de Roca.* Buenos Aires: Planeta, 1998.

DOUGLAS W. RICHMOND

ROCAFUERTE, VICENTE (1783–1847).

Vicente Rocafuerte (*b.* 1 May 1783; *d.* 16 May 1847), Ecuadorian independence leader, diplomat, and statesman. Born in Guayaquil to one of the region's wealthiest families, Rocafuerte studied at the Colegio de Nobles Americanos in Granada, Spain, and at the Collège de Saint Germain-en-Laye in France. Returning to Guayaquil in 1807, he devoted himself to family affairs; three years later he was elected *alcalde ordinario* (city magistrate) of Guayaquil. In 1812 he traveled to England, then to the Continent as far as Russia. Elected to the Cortes, he arrived in Madrid in April 1814 in time to witness the abolition of that parliament. Thereafter, he devoted his efforts and his fortune to the interests of the new American nations, serving Colombia, Cuba, and Mexico during 1820–1824.

An advocate of republicanism, Rocafuerte wrote extensively on its behalf and opposed the Mexican empire of Iturbide. From 1824 to 1830, he served as Mexico's representative to England and continental Europe. Returning to Mexico in 1830, he advocated social reforms and religious freedom as well as opposition to the conservative regime of Anastasio Bustamante. Upon his return to Guayaquil in 1833, he joined the opposition to President Juan José Flores, was elected to Congress, and led a revolt against the president. After reaching an understanding with Flores, however, he later served as president (1835–1839) and then as governor of Guayas (1839–1843), while Flores served another term. But when the president sought to retain power, Rocafuerte opposed him. After Flores's ouster in 1845, Rocafuerte served as president of the Senate in 1846 and accepted a diplomatic mission to Lima, where he died.

In addition to his political and diplomatic activities, Rocafuerte's writings on political systems, social reform, religious toleration, and economic development had significant influence on liberals in several Spanish American nations.

See also **Bustamante, Anastasio; Flores, Juan José.**

BIBLIOGRAPHY

Jaime E. Rodríguez O., *The Emergence of Spanish America: Vicente Rocafuerte and Spanish Americanism, 1808–1832* (1975) and *Estudios sobre Vicente Rocafuerte* (1975).

Kent B. Mecum, *Vicente Rocafuerte: El prócer andante* (1983).

Mark J. Van Aken, *King of the Night: Juan José Flores and Ecuador, 1824–1864* (1989).

Additional Bibliography

Cordero Aroca, Alberto P. *Transcendencia histórica de don Vicente Rocafuerte.* Guayaquil, Ecuador: Archivo Histórico del Guayas, 1997–1998.

Febres Cordero, Francisco. *De Flores a flores y miel.* Quito: Ojo de Pez, EDIMPRES, 1996.

JAIME E. RODRÍGUEZ O.

ROCA RODRÍGUEZ, VICENTE RAMÓN (1792–1858).

Vicente Ramón Roca Rodríguez (*b.* 2 September 1792; *d.* 23 February 1858), member of ruling triumvirate (March 1845–October 1845), president of Ecuador (1846–1849). A coastal businessman born in Guayaquil, Roca helped lead the 9 October 1820 uprising that brought independence to Guayaquil. He served as a deputy to the Riobamba convention of 1830 that separated Ecuador from Gran Colombia. Roca held several posts in the new government: vice president of the Congress (1833), governor of Guayas (1835), and senator from Guayas (1837–1839). Roca played a leading role in the 6 March 1845 overthrow of President Juan José Flores. The subsequent Roca administration faced serious financial problems and repeated coup attempts.

As Congress was pondering impeachment in 1846, news arrived of a planned invasion by former president Flores, backed by 30 million pesos from the Spanish government. South America rallied to Ecuador's side, and Spain withdrew its support for Flores. But if the Spanish threat had temporarily united Ecuador, the cost of building defenses had diverted scarce resources away from urgent domestic concerns, thus weakening the young nation in the long run. Roca raised money through forced contributions and the advance collection of the Indian tribute, both extremely unpopular measures. When Roca left office in 1849, Ecuador fell into fractious dispute, and drifted into a disastrous civil war. He died in Guayaquil.

See also **Flores, Juan José.**

BIBLIOGRAPHY

On nineteenth-century Ecuadorian politics, see Mark J. Van Aken's splendid study, *King of the Night: Juan José Flores and Ecuador, 1824–1864* (1989). Also consult Frank MacDonald Spindler's descriptive narrative, *Nineteenth Century Ecuador: An Historical Introduction* (1987).

Additional Bibliography

Febres Cordero, Francisco. *De Flores a flores y miel.* Quito: Ojo de Pez, EDIMPRES, 1996.

Ortíz M., José Luis. *Guayaquil: Historia y futuro.* Ecuador: Fundación Vicente Rocafuerta, 2000.

RONN F. PINEO

ROCA–RUNCIMAN PACT (1933). The

Roca–Runciman Pact (1933) was an Anglo-Argentine trade agreement that gave Britain sweeping concessions. Since 1825 Anglo-Argentine trade had been conducted on the most-favored-nation principle, except for a brief suspension during World War I

(1914–1918) and an increasing number of sometimes successful attempts at circumvention from the late 1920s. The Argentine leadership feared that the rise of British imperial preference implied the reduction if not abolition of Anglo-Argentine trade. Britain's government, in contrast, saw it as a means to deal with Argentina more harshly by buying less Argentine farm produce and selling more British manufactured goods to help British industry out of the depression. The negotiations for Argentina were conducted by Vice President Julio A. Roca, Ángel Cárcano, and Raúl Prebisch. The British were led by Walter Runciman, the president of the Board of Trade. Meat and foreign-exchange issues were dealt with in London and Argentine tariff policy in Buenos Aires. The outcome was judged so unfavorable to Argentina that the pact, which some argued was a failure, has generated fierce controversy ever since.

See also **British-Latin American Relations.**

BIBLIOGRAPHY

Fodor, Jorge G., and Arturo A. O'Connell. "La Argentina y la economía atlántica en la primera mitad del siglo XX." *Desarrollo económico* 49 (April–June, 1973)

Gravil, Roger. *The Anglo-Argentine Connection, 1900–1939.* Boulder: Westview Press, 1985.

Additional Bibliography

Mauro Pipino, Ovidio. *Tratado Roca-Runciman y el desarrollo industrial en la década del treinta.* Buenos Aires: Editorial Galerna, 1988.

ROGER GRAVIL

ROCHA, DARDO (1838–1921). Dardo

Rocha (*b.* 1 September 1838; *d.* 6 September 1921), Argentine jurist and politician. Born in Buenos Aires, Rocha obtained a doctorate in law at the university in 1863. Gravitating to politics, he became known as an orator. He was elected to the Chamber of Deputies in 1873 and to the Senate in 1874, becoming its presiding officer in 1877. In 1881 he was elected governor of the province of Buenos Aires. In that post he is best remembered as the founder of La Plata, designed to be the provincial capital city following the federalization of the city of Buenos Aires in 1882, when the latter became the national capital. Following his unsuccessful bid for the national presidency in 1884, Rocha served on the national Supreme Court and the Superior Court of Buenos Aires Province.

See also **La Plata.**

BIBLIOGRAPHY

Blasi, Hebe Judith. *Dardo Rocha, un exponente de la generación de 1880.* Buenos Aires: Editorial Dunken, 2004.

RONALD C. NEWTON

ROCHA, GLAUBER PEDRO DE ANDRADE

ROCHA, GLAUBER PEDRO DE ANDRADE (1939–1981). The Brazilian filmmaker and critic Glauber Rocha was born in Vitória da Conquista, in inland Bahia, on March 14, 1939. He took an early interest in the performing arts, writing his first play at age ten. As a teenager he worked in radio, joined amateur theater and cinema groups, and participated in the students' union. At age eighteen he was accepted at the University of Bahia to study law. He released his first short film, *Pátio*, in 1958 and shortly thereafter left the university, devoting himself to film production and criticism.

In 1962 he relocated to Rio de Janeiro, attracted by the Cinema Novo (New Cinema) movement, which prioritized human, existential, and social contradictions. He proposed a more realistic, more politicized, and less costly type of filmmaking. His 1963 book *Revisão crítica do cinema brasileiro* (Critical review of Brazilian cinema), discussed fundamental historical aspects of the country's cinema. At the same time, he filmed *Deus e o diablo na terra do sol* (Black god, white devil), released in 1964, considered an icon of Brazilian identity.

Rocha was promoting his film at international festivals when the military coup occurred in Brazil. He remained abroad, and in January 1965 he published a manifesto, A Estética da Fome (The aesthetics of hunger) in which he explained his aesthetic and political foundations for Cinema Novo. Upon returning to Brazil, he was arrested in November 1965 during a protest against the military. Well-known European filmmakers headed up a petition for his release, which occurred twenty-three days later.

Rocha's 1967 film *Terra em transe* (Earth entranced; also released as *Land in Anguish*) won the Critics' Award at the Cannes Film Festival. His next film, *O Dragão da Maldade contra o Santo Guerreiro* earned him the Best Director Award at Cannes in 1969 and was his most famous and widely seen creation. Shortly thereafter he filmed *Cabezas cortadas* (1970; *Severed Heads*).

Faced with an increasingly harsh military regime, Rocha went into exile in 1971. Three years later he sent a letter to a Brazilian journalist praising the recently installed military government. The letter raised the hackles of the Left, which until then had supported him.

Claro, a feature-length drama filmed in Italy in 1975, ended a five-year hiatus from filmmaking. After returning to Brazil in mid-1976, he was involved in yet another controversy by October: He filmed the funeral of the famous painter Emiliano Di Cavalcanti without consent from the family, who subsequently blocked public screenings of the documentary.

In 1978 Rocha began shooting *A idade da terra* (*The Age of the Earth*; released 1980), and the following year he interviewed guests on a provocative television series, *Abertura*. While in Europe to promote *The Age of the Earth* in 1981, he fell severely ill and was hospitalized. He was rushed back to Brazil, where he died two days later, on August 22.

See also **Cinema: From the Silent Film to 1990; Cinema Novo.**

BIBLIOGRAPHY

Bandeira, Roberto. *Pequeno dicionário crítico do cinema brasileiro.* Rio de Janeiro: Shogun Arte, 1983.

Bentes, Ivana. *Cartas ao mundo/Glauber Rocha.* São Paulo: Companhia das Letras, 1997.

Miranda, Felipe, and Ramos, Fernão Ramos, eds. *Enciclopédia do cinema brasileiro.* São Paulo: SENAC, 2000.

CARMEN LUCIA DE AZEVEDO

ROCHA, JUSTINIANO JOSÉ DA

ROCHA, JUSTINIANO JOSÉ DA (1812–1862). Justiniano José Da Rocha (*b.* 8 November 1812; *d.* 10 July 1862), Brazilian political journalist, litterateur, and Conservative polemicist.

Born in Rio de Janeiro, Rocha, a mulatto, was schooled in France and at the São Paulo faculty of law. He taught at the Colégio Pedro II and the military school in Rio, and represented Minas Gerais thrice in the Chamber of Deputies (1843–1844, 1850–1852, 1853–1856). He was also the first in Brazil to write and translate serial novels as a minor figure in the first Romantic generation. His greatness, however, lay in being the heir (and counterpoise) to the political journalism tradition associated with Evaristo da Veiga (1799–1837), the liberal who had dominated so many of the First Empire and Regency debates.

Rocha wrote polemics with a celebrated clarity and facility as the servant of the Conservative Party from its beginnings, writing or editing in the Rio press as the party's voice until the era of the Conciliação. He presided over *O Chronista* (1836–1839), *O Brasil* (1840–1852), as well as a number of more ephemeral periodicals, and from 1839 to 1862 he took the Conservative's part in pieces for the *Jornal do Commércio*. Protégé and partisan of Bernardo Pereira de Vasconcelos (1795–1850) and partisan of the saguarema reactionary leadership of the party in its years of struggle, Rocha is most justly remembered for his incisive analysis in the pamphlet "Ação; reação; transação" (1855).

See also **Brazil, The Empire (First); Brazil, The Regency; Literature: Brazil.**

BIBLIOGRAPHY

José Antônio Soares De Sousa, *A vida do visconde do Uruguai* (1944).

Raimundo Magalhães, Jr., *Tres panfletários do segundo reinado* (1956).

Ilmar Rohloff De Mattos, *O tempo saguarema* (1987).

Leslie Bethell and José Murilo De Carvalho, "Brazil from Independence to the Middle of the Nineteenth Century," in *Brazil: Empire and Republic, 1822–1930,* edited by Leslie Bethell (1989).

Additional Bibliography

Needell, Jeffrey D. *The Party of Order: The Conservatives, The State, and Slavery in the Brazilian Monarchy, 1831–1871.* Stanford, CA: Stanford University Press, 2006.

Vasconcelos, Bernardo Pereira de. José Murilo de Carvalho. *Bernardo Pereira de Vasconcelos.* São Paulo: Editora 34, 1999.

JEFFREY D. NEEDELL

ROCHA, MANOEL RIBEIRO (1687–1745). Little is known about the life of Manoel Ribeiro Rocha. He was born in Lisbon, and after completing his studies at the University of Coimbra in Portugal, he moved to the Captaincy of Bahia in Brazil, where he became a priest, jurist and prominent lawyer. In 1742 the powerful Bahian brotherhood of the Santa Casa da Misericórdia appointed him as its lawyer for civil cases.

Father Rocha wrote one of the first in-depth treatises on slavery in Brazil and on the Luso-Brazilian traffic in African slaves. It was a theological, juridical discourse titled *Etíope resgatado, empenhado, sustentado, corrigido, instruído, e libertado* (1758; The Ethiopian ransomed, indentured, sustained, corrected, educated, and liberated), and in it Rocha expressed his criticism of slavery. He is considered a forerunner of the nineteenth-century abolitionists because he admonished slave owners against cruel punishments and condemned as a mortal sin the trade of unjustly enslaved Africans.

Rocha's main concern, however, was to harmonize compulsory labor with Christian morals and civil justice. As an alternative to slavery and its complete abolition, *Etíope resgatado* suggests a third way in the form of indentured labor lasting for up to twenty years. He believed that unjust slavery—the enslavement not respectful of the code of Bellum justum—was unfair and sinful, though it was the trafficker's fault, not the buyer's. Therefore if a person buys someone unjustly enslaved, this person is in fact ransoming the slave, and for this benefice acquires a right of indemnification. Rocha suggested that indentured work for up to twenty years would be acceptable as indemnification. After that the slave, if he or she should survive, would be liberated from bondage.

Rocha stated that traffickers might continue pursuing their trade "licitly and with no burden of conscience" if with this activity they do "no more than ransom the slaves, acquiring over them only a right of pledge and retention. Such rights could be bought and sold, but not the property of anyone's freedom (although the owner of a slave would still have the right of pledge ("iure pignoris") and retention over him or her. In this way of putting it, the freedom of a man or woman is not "commodified."

Rocha's works were published posthumously in Lisbon during 1758. In addition to *Etíope resgatado*, he wrote *Socorro dos fiéis* (Believer's resource) and *Nova prática dos oratórios particulares* (The new practice of private oratories).

See also **Slavery: Brazil.**

BIBLIOGRAPHY

Work by Rocha

Rocha, Manuel Ribeiro. *Etíope resgatado, empenhado, sustentado, corrigido, instruído, e libertado*. 1758. Petrópolis, Brazil: Vozes, 1992.

Other Works

Azevedo, Celia M. "Rocha's 'The Ethiopian Redeemed' and the Circulation of Anti-Slavery Ideas." *Slavery & Abolition* 24, no. 1 (April 2003): 101–126.

Carvalho, José Murilo de. *Pontos e bordados: Escritos de história e política*. Belo Horizonte, Brazil: UFMG, 1998.

ELIANA MARIA REA GOLDSCHMIDT
SÉRGIO ALCIDES

ROCHAMBEAU, DONATIEN MARIE JOSEPH DE VIMEUR DE (1755–1813).

Donatien Marie Joseph de Vimeur de Rochambeau (*b.* 7 April 1755; *d.* 20 October 1813), French general and last colonial governor of Saint-Domingue. Born at the Rochambeau estate near Vendôme, Rochambeau entered the army at fourteen and accompanied his father, Jean Baptiste de Vimeur de Rochambeau, commander of French troops, to America during the War of Independence. In the early 1790s he was commandant of the Windward Islands and in 1793 was in Martinique. From January to May 1796, he was governor-general of Saint-Domingue. He returned to Saint-Domingue, serving as captain-general from January to November 1803, during which time he helped to put down the revolt led by Toussaint Louverture.

On the return voyage to France, Rochambeau's ship was seized by the British, who imprisoned him until 1811. He then resumed his military career. He died of wounds suffered at the Battle of Leipzig.

See also **Louverture, Toussaint; Windward Islands.**

BIBLIOGRAPHY

Jean-Edmond Weelen, *Rochambeau, Father and Son: A Life of the Maréchal de Rochambeau*, translated by Lawrence Lee (1936).

James Breck Perkins, *France in the American Revolution* (1971).

David P. Geggus, *Unexploited Sources for the History of the Haitian Revolution* (1983).

Additional Bibliography

Brown, Gordon S. *Toussaint's Cause: The Founding Fathers and the Haitian Revolution*. Jackson: University Press of Mississippi, 2005.

Haynsworth, James Lafayette. "The Early Career of Lieutenant General Donatien Rochambeau and the French Campaigns in the Caribbean, 1792–1794." Ph.D. thesis. Florida State University, 2003.

ANNE GREENE

ROCHA PITA, SEBASTIÃO (1660–1738).

Sebastião Rocha Pita (*b.* 3 May 1660; *d.* 2 November 1738), Brazilian historian and member of the Royal Academy of Portuguese History. Born in Bahia, Rocha Pita wrote *Tratado, político* around 1715, but it remained unpublished until 1972. Best known to historians but seldom quoted is his *História da América portuguesa, desde ano de 1500 do seu descobrimento até o de 1724*, published in 1730. The author's purpose was to narrate the events that had taken place in Brazil with the help of "truthful reports" and "modern information" given by those who had traveled in the vast Brazilian territory. This was the only history of Brazil available to his contemporaries, since most of the others composed in the first two centuries of colonization remained in manuscript until the nineteenth century.

According to the model then followed by historians, Rocha Pita wrote a political and natural history, where human events took the same place and aroused the same interest as the description of the productions of nature. Sugarcane, tobacco, manioc, rice, and medicinal plants occupy a large place in the book, and the information on them is mostly the result of direct observation. Although Rocha Pita pays little attention to the academic discussion of the origin of America's inhabitants, the Indians of Portuguese and Spanish America are compared.

See also **Brazil: The Colonial Era, 1500–1808.**

BIBLIOGRAPHY

José Honório Rodrigues, *História da história do Brasil.* Vol. 1, *Historiografia colonial* (1979).

Massaud Moisés, *História da literatura brasileira,* vol. 1, *Origens, barroco, arcadismo* (1983).

Additional Bibliography

Novais, Fernando A. *Aproximações: Estudos de história e historiografia.* São Paulo: CosacNaify, 2005.

                    MARIA BEATRIZ NIZZA DA SILVA

ROCKEFELLER, NELSON ALDRICH

(1908–1979). Nelson Aldrich Rockefeller (*b.* 8 July 1908; *d.* 27 January 1979), businessman, governor of New York (1958–1974), vice president of the United States (1974–1977).

In 1969, President Richard Nixon selected Governor Nelson Rockefeller to tour Latin America and report his findings. Rockefeller's Latin American involvement had begun in 1935 when he became a director of the Venezuelan Creole Petroleum Corporation, an affiliate of Standard Oil of New Jersey. On a trip in 1939, he encountered bitter anti-Americanism, which provoked him to establish an advisory group to study U.S. relations with Latin America. A resulting memorandum addressed business, diplomatic, and cultural issues, and concluded that the government should place someone in charge of improving relations. In August 1940, President Franklin D. Roosevelt appointed Rockefeller to head the newly created Office of the Coordinator of Inter-American Affairs.

In 1944, Rockefeller recommended upgrading the Department of State position that dealt with Latin America. When this was done, he was given the position, assistant secretary of state for Latin America. He later served sixteen years as governor of New York before being appointed to the vice presidency by Gerald Ford in 1974.

See also **Petroleum Industry; United States-Latin American Relations.**

BIBLIOGRAPHY

Michael S. Kramer and Sam Roberts, *"I Never Wanted to Be Vice-President of Anything!" An Investigative Biography of Nelson Rockefeller* (1976).

Joseph E. Persico, *The Imperial Rockefeller: A Biography of Nelson A. Rockefeller* (1982).

Additional Bibliography

Colby, Gerard, and Charlotte Dennett. *Thy Will Be Done: The Conquest of the Amazon: Nelson Rockefeller and Evangelism in the Age of Oil.* New York: HarperCollins, 1995.

Reich, Cary. *The Life of Nelson A. Rockefeller: Worlds to Conquer, 1908–1958.* New York: Doubleday, 1996.

Rivas, Darlene. *Missionary Capitalist: Nelson Rockefeller in Venezuela.* Chapel Hill: University of North Carolina Press, 2002.

Tota, Antônio Pedro. *O imperialismo sedutor: A americanização do Brasil na época da Segunda Guerra.* São Paulo: Companhia das Letras, 2000.

                    CHARLES CARRERAS

ROCK MUSIC. Known variously as Latin rock, *rock en español* (rock in Spanish), *rock nacional* (national rock), and *rock en tu idioma* (rock in your language), rock music is an integral part of popular culture throughout the Americas. Yet rock's history in Latin America has been contentious, involving issues of cultural imperialism, modernity, and national identity. In part this is because the term "rock" is itself somewhat problematic, referring as it does not only to a broad range of musical styles (rock and roll, metal, progressive, punk, rap) but also to ideas about youth, fashion, politics, and social identity.

Beginning in the late 1950s, recordings by Elvis Presley, Chuck Berry, and others made their way south and had a tremendous impact, especially among middle- and upper-class urban listeners for whom rock represented a direct connection to international modernity. In contrast, critics of rock tended to view it as just the latest example of U.S. cultural imperialism, a form of capitalist consumerism with little connection to local, more "authentic" musical practices. This view was supported by the fact that much of the early rock produced in Latin America was little more than a direct copy of U.S. models. In Mexico, early 1960s bands such as Los Teen Tops, Los Locos del Ritmo, and others produced a style known as *refrito* (refried)—Spanish language versions of American hits—while in Brazil, artists associated with the *jovem guarda* (youth guard) movement popularized a clean-cut style of pop music known as *iê-iê-iê* (from the Portuguese transliteration of the Beatles-inspired "yeah, yeah, yeah").

In addition to critical attacks, in a number of places the state attempted to limit rock's influence by imposing tariffs on record imports (as Mexico did in 1961) or ban it outright (Cuba prohibited the broadcast of English-language rock on radio and television from 1964 to 1966). Ironically, these and other steps to protect indigenous music often led to the development of local rock scenes, many featuring artists who wrote their own material, which, like that of their North American counterparts, engaged in a political and social critique of middle-class life. By the 1970s Latin American rock musicians were mixing blues and other U.S. rock forms with local and regional styles to create sophisticated pop music that moved away from slavish imitation and toward a more distinctively indigenous creation.

In the 1980s and 1990s, authenticity in rock throughout Latin America came to be defined as much by the individual artist's attitude and political stance as by musical form and instrumentation. Rock groups such as Mexico's Café Tacuba, Colombia's Aterciopelados, and Argentina's Los Fabulosos Cadillacs freely mixed rock, ska, reggae, punk, *cumbia*, tango, bolero, and hip-hop. For an ever more diverse fan base throughout the region, international styles such as punk and rap are now seen as universal, hybrid musical styles that embody a wide range of social identities. Artists such as those mentioned above enjoy international careers and a critical reception that no longer views rock in Latin America as simply a music based on U.S. and English models but instead as a collection of distinctively national musical genres.

See also **Music: Popular Music and Dance.**

BIBLIOGRAPHY

Brewer, Roy. "The Use of Habanera Rhythm in Rockabilly Music." *American Music* 17, no. 3 (Autumn 1999): 300–317.

Esterrich, Carmelo, and Javier H. Murillo. "Rock with Punk with Pop with Folklore: Transformations and Renewal in Aterciopelados and Café Tacuba." *Latin American Music Review* 21, no. 1 (Spring–Summer, 2000): 31–44.

Hernandez, Deborah Pacini, Héctor Fernández L'Hoeste, and Eric Zolov, eds. *Rockin' Las Américas: The Global Politics of Rock in Latin/o America.* Pittsburgh: University of Pittsburgh Press, 2004.

Loza, Steven. *Barrio Rhythm: Mexican American Music in Los Angeles.* Urbana and Chicago: University of Illinois Press, 1993.

Magaldi, Cristina. "Adopting Imports: New Images and Alliances in Brazilian Popular Music of the 1990s." *Popular Music* 18, no. 3 (1999): 309–329.

Vila, Pablo. "Argentina's 'Rock Nacional': The Struggle for Meaning." *Latin American Music Review* 10, no. 1 (Spring–Summer 1989): 1–28.

ANDREW M. CONNELL

RODAS ALVARADO, MODESTO

(1921–c. 1978). Modesto Rodas Alvarado (*b.* 16 March 1921; *d.* c. 1978), a charismatic Honduran political leader. The Liberal Party in Honduras had been out of power since 1932 when its leader, Ramón Villeda Morales, became president in 1957. Rodas Alvarado, who had been provisional secretary of the Liberal Party in 1954, was president of the National Congress during Villeda Morales's period in office (1957–1963). Rodas Alvarado became the Liberal candidate to replace Villeda Morales in the election of 1963. All signs pointed toward his probable victory. During the campaign he talked about ending the military's budget autonomy and restricting its ability to nominate candidates for the position of chief of staff. Had he been elected he probably would have carried forward the land reforms and other measures opposed by landholders, fruit companies, and conservative military elements.

A few days before the scheduled election, the military under General Oswaldo López Arellano took over. U.S. President John F. Kennedy refused to recognize the new government, but in December 1963 President Lyndon B. Johnson granted it recognition. In retrospect, the 1963 coup was a major setback for Honduran political development. After the coup, Rodas dropped completely out of public life. His contribution was symbolically recognized by the continuation of the Rodista Liberal Movement, the faction of the Liberal Party led by President Roberto Suazo Córdova in the 1980s.

See also **Honduras; López Arellano, Oswaldo; United States-Latin American Relations; Villeda Morales, Ramón.**

BIBLIOGRAPHY

"Military Forces Under López Overthrow Villeda Government," *New York Times,* October 4, 1963.

Thomas P. Anderson, *Politics in Central America,* rev. ed. (1988).

Additional Bibliography

Caballero Zeitún, Elsa Lily, and Marcos Carías Chaverri. *Crisis y política social en Centroamérica: Tendencias y perspectivas: el caso de Honduras.* Tegucigalpa, D.C., Honduras, C.A.: Universidad Nacional Autónoma de Honduras, Editorial Universitaria, 1990.

Salomón, Leticia. *Política y militares en Honduras.* Tegucigalpa, Honduras: Centro de Documentación de Honduras, 1992.

DAVID L. JICKLING

RODNEY, CAESAR AUGUSTUS (1772–1824).

Caesar Augustus Rodney (*b.* 4 January 1772; *d.* 10 June 1824), U.S. senator, congressman, statesman, diplomat, and first minister plenipotentiary to Argentina. Rodney was born in Dover, Delaware, to a distinguished family. His father was a farmer, merchant, Revolutionary War soldier, jurist, and statesman. At the age of seventeen he graduated from the University of Pennsylvania and proceeded to study law with Philadelphia lawyer Joseph McKean, a signer of the Declaration of Independence. After several years of legal practice, Rodney entered politics and earned respect in the Delaware House of Representatives, the U.S. House of Representatives, and as U.S. attorney general from 1807 to 1811. In 1817 the U.S. government appointed Rodney to a three-man commission with directions to assemble information about the South American independence movements on which to base an official diplomatic policy. Rodney and a comember of the commission, John Graham, traveled to Argentina in 1817, remaining until April 1818. The report he submitted to Congress overviews the colonial history of Spanish America and describes in detail the political situation, natural resources, commerce, industry, society, and religion of Argentina. Rodney presented Argentina in a very favorable light and encouraged recognition of its independence. The report remains a valuable source on Argentina's early revolutionary period and provides an idea of the development of U.S. diplomatic policy toward Latin America before the elaboration of the Monroe Doctrine.

Rodney returned to political life, serving briefly in the U.S. Senate. In 1823 President Monroe offered him the post of first U.S. minister plenipotentiary to the Argentine Republic. This act of official U.S. recognition pleased the Argentine government, and Rodney arrived in Buenos Aires to assume his post in November 1823. Shortly thereafter he became ill and died. He was eulogized by Bernardino Rivadavia, and the Argentine government built a marble monument over his burial site in Buenos Aires.

See also **United States-Latin American Relations.**

BIBLIOGRAPHY

Caesar Augustus Rodney and John Graham, *The Reports on the Present State of the United Provinces of South America* (1819). The Praeger edition (1969) of this report has an informative biographical introduction on both Rodney and Graham written by Charles Wilgus.

Additional Bibliography

American National Biography. New York: Oxford University Press, 1999.

J. DAVID DRESSING

RODÓ, JOSÉ ENRIQUE (1871–1917).

José Enrique Rodó (*b.* 15 July 1871; *d.* 1 May 1917), Uruguayan writer and literary critic. Rodó was born in Montevideo. In secondary school and at the University of Montevideo he was weak in the sciences but excelled in literature and history. As professor of literature at the University of Montevideo (1898–1902), deputy in Congress for the Colorado Party (1902–1905, 1908–1914), and essayist, he was the spokesman for intellectual motivation, moderation, and good taste—in public life as well as in literature. His principal books are *Ariel* (1900), his first and best-known work; the much longer and less-structured spiritual quest

Motivos de Proteo (1909; *The Motives of Proteus*, 1928); and a collection of essays, vignettes, and literary criticism, *El mirador de Próspero* (1913; Prospero's Balcony). His writings are collected in *Obras completas,* edited by Emir Rodríguez Monegal, 2d ed. (1967).

Like José Martí in Cuba and Rubén Darío in Nicaragua, Rodó was a leading exponent of modernism in Hispanic American literature in the late nineteenth and early twentieth centuries. As the symbolic name Proteus in one of his titles suggests, change was a fundamental virtue for Rodó: "To change is to live," the first sentence of *The Motives of Proteus,* reflects the indirect but vital influence of Charles Darwin's and Herbert Spencer's evolutionary thought on Rodó's essentially aesthetic view of the world.

Ariel and most of the rest of Rodó's work were composed with clearly didactic intentions and in a refined rhetorical manner. Writing for him was a vocation more than a profession, a quiet endeavor that seemed to symbolize his solitary and meditative way of life. In *The Motives of Proteus* the author extends and elaborates on the encouragement of individualism, expounded before in *Ariel,* and underscores the energy of youth and the importance of self-education and self-knowledge. In his repeated mention of the need for intellectual heroism, which he divides into "wisdom," "art," and "action," he shows agreement with some ideas of Carlyle, Emerson, and Nietzsche.

Rodó was writing in an era of transition for Latin America. The war of 1898 between the United States and Spain awoke a new Latin American consciousness of cultural ties to Spain and sharpened awareness of North American hegemony in the Western Hemisphere. In those circumstances he called consistently for a reaffirmation of Hispanic American "spiritual" values as distinct from allegedly more pragmatic North American values. All his written work was an elegant elaboration of that point of view.

See also **Darío, Rubén; Literature: Spanish America.**

BIBLIOGRAPHY

Víctor Pérez Petit, *Rodó: Su vida, su obra,* 2d ed. (1937).

Medardo Vitier, "El mensaje de Rodó," in his *Del ensayo americano* (1945).

Mario Benedetti, *Genio y figura de José Enrique Rodó* (1966).

Peter G. Earle, "José Enrique Rodó," in *Latin American Writers,* vol. 2 (1989).

Additional Bibliography

Brading, D.A. *Marmoreal Olympus: José Enrique Rodó and Spanish American Nationalism.* Cambridge: Center for Latin American Studies, University of Cambridge, 1998.

Rocca, Pablo. *Enseñanza y teoría de la literatura en José Enrique Rodó.* Montevideo: Ediciones de la Banda Oriental, 2001.

Suiffet, Norma. *José Enrique Rodó: Su vida, su obra, su pensamiento.* Montevideo: Ediciones de la Urpila, 1995.

PETER G. EARLE

RODRIGUES, JOSÉ HONÓRIO (1913–1987).

José Honório Rodrigues (*b.* 20 September 1913; *d.* 6 April 1987), Brazilian historian. Soon after graduating from the National Law School in his native city of Rio de Janeiro in 1937, José Honório Rodrigues embarked on his chosen career as a historian. His first major work, *Civilização holandesa no Brasil* (Dutch Civilization in Brazil) was written in collaboration with Joaquím Ribeiro and appeared in 1940, before Rodrigues had received any academic training in historical methodology. A fellowship from the Rockefeller Foundation enabled him to study historical theory and methods at Columbia University in 1943–1944 and put him in touch with the main currents of world historiography. Returning to Brazil, he promoted the use of advanced techniques in the researching and writing of Brazilian history, urged the creation of graduate programs in history at Brazilian universities, campaigned for the opening of government archives to scholars and for the publication of important source material, and developed his own *visão* (perception) of Brazilian history.

As curator of rare books at the Brazilian National Library (1946–1958) and director of the National Archives (1958–1964), Rodrigues made these institutions more responsive to the needs of professional historians. Removed from his directorship as a result of the military coup of 1964, he had more time for writing and lecturing at Brazilian and foreign universities. For Rodrigues, a committed liberal and acute observer of the contemporary scene, writing history was more important than political activism. In his landmark *Independência: revolução e contrarevolução* (5 vols., 1975–1976), he argues that a traditionalist elite has consistently thwarted liberal movements in Brazil and crushed the aspirations of the Brazilian people. In historiographical works like *História da história do Brasil* (4 vols., 1979–1988), Rodrigues exposes the biases of conservative historians who, he charges, have served the ruling class and perpetuated its myths of "nonviolence" and "conciliation." Rodrigues's works translated into English include *Brazil and Africa* (1965) and *The Brazilians: Their Character and Aspirations* (1967).

See also **Brazil: Since 1889.**

BIBLIOGRAPHY

John D. Wirth, "An Interview with José Honório Rodrigues," in *Hispanic American Historical Review* 64, no. 2 (1984): 217–232.

Stanley J. Stein, "José Honório Rodrigues (1913–1987)," in *Hispanic American Historical Review* 68, no. 3 (1988): 573–576.

Additional Bibliography

Iglésias, Francisco. *Historiadores do Brasil: Capítulos de historiografia brasileira.* Rio de Janeiro: Editora Nova Fronteira, 2000.

Rodrigues, Lêda Boechat, and José Octávio. *José Honório Rodrigues: Um historiador na trincheira.* Rio de Janeiro: Civilização Brasileira, 1994.

NEILL MACAULAY

RODRIGUES, NELSON (1912–1980).

Nelson Rodrigues (*b.* 23 August 1912; *d.* 22 December 1980), Brazilian dramatist and journalist. Rodrigues's plays deal with the lives of the bourgeoisie and the lower classes—including slum dwellers and prostitutes—who see themselves as victims of oppression. He described his dramas as "pestilent," fetid" and his characters as "monsters." His exaggerated preoccupations with Brazilian machismo and sex brought him great popularity. His plays were brought to the stage by Brazil's leading directors, including Zbigniew Ziembinski and Antunes Filho. Artistically, Rodrigues

singlehandedly brought Brazilian drama into the twentieth century with *O vestido de noiva* (1943; *The Wedding Dress,* 1980), an innovative play for its time owing to its complex narrative levels: the past, the present, and the plane of hallucinations. Other works include *O Beijo no Asfalto* (1961) and *Toda nudez será castigada* (1965).

See also **Journalism; Theater.**

BIBLIOGRAPHY

See Fred M. Clark's introduction to his translation of *The Wedding Dress* (Valencia, 1980); and Randal Johnson, "Nelson Rodrigues as Filmed by Arnaldo Jabor," in *Latin American Theater Review* (Fall 1982): 15–28.

Additional Bibliography

Cafezeiro, Edwaldo, and Carmem Gadelha. *História do teatro brasileira: Um percurso de Anchieta a Nelson Rodrigues.* Rio de Janeiro: Editora UFRJ, 1996.

Fraga, Eudinyr. *Nelson Rodrigues expressionista.* Cotia, SP, Brazil: Ateliê Editorial, 1998.

IRWIN STERN

RODRIGUES, RAIMUNDO NINA

(1862–1906). Raimundo Nina Rodrigues (*b.* 4 December 1862; *d.* 17 July 1906), founder of Afro-Brazilian studies and anthropology. Trained in Bahia as a physician, he began around 1888 to study Brazilian blacks from the perspective of criminological psychiatry. His work diagnosed Afro-Brazilian culture as the manifestation of racial evolutionary backwardness, yet it pioneered the empirical study of that culture.

His most important contribution was *O animismo fetichista dos negros bahianos* (1896; The Fetishist Animism of Bahian Blacks). This book describes the divinities and rituals of the Candomblé religion and classifies its beliefs as animism, higher on the evolutionary scale than fetishism. *Os africanos no Brasil* (1932; Africans in Brazil), a posthumous collection of articles, includes studies on the regional origins of African slaves in Brazil and on the history of slavery.

Nina Rodrigues's ethnological research was always an adjunct to his primary interest in criminology. His major work was *As raças humanas e a responsabilidade penal no Brasil* (1894; Human Races and Criminal Accountability), but he also published on such diverse topics as the diagnoses of wounds and the nature of criminal crowds. Rodrigues trained or influenced many of the next generation of physician-anthropologists, including Afrânio Peixoto and Artur Ramos. His disciples continued the study of Afro-Brazilian culture but repudiated his racial theories.

See also **Slavery: Brazil.**

BIBLIOGRAPHY

Afrânio Peixoto, "A vida e a obra de Nina Rodrigues," in Raimundo Nina Rodrigues, *As raças humanas e a responsabilidade penal no Brasil,* 3d ed. (1938), pp. 11–26, a biographical sketch.

Henrique L. Alves, *Nina Rodrigues e o negro no Brasil* (1962), critical and biographical essays.

Thomas Skidmore, *Black into White: Race and Nationality in Brazilian Thought* (1974), a general study of racial ideology.

Additional Bibliography

Corrêa, Mariza. *As ilusões da liberdade: A Escola Nina Rodrigues e a antropologia no Brasil.* Bragança Paulista, Brazil: Instituto Franciscano de Antropologia, Universidade São Francisco, 1998.

DAIN BORGES

RODRIGUES ALVES, FRANCISCO DE PAULA

(1848–1919). Francisco de Paula Rodrigues Alves (*b.* 7 July 1848; *d.* 16 January 1919), president of Brazil (1902–1906). Allied by birth and through marriage with the coffee-producing elites of São Paulo, Rodrigues Alves graduated from São Paulo Law School in 1870. A Conservative in his youth, he joined the Republican Party after the 1889 overthrow of the monarchy and helped to write the 1891 constitution. He later served as senator, minister of finance, and governor of São Paulo.

Rodrigues Alves's presidency exemplified both positive and negative aspects of the Brazilian drive for "order and progress." A sound treasury and the appointment of men of ability to office enabled a successful campaign to transform Rio de Janeiro into a beautiful and healthful capital. A central boulevard and new municipal buildings, including the Municipal Theater and National Library, were built. Port facilities and rail lines were modernized. Oswaldo Cruz, director of public health, waged a vigorous campaign to improve sanitation and eradicate pestilence; by 1906 yellow fever deaths had dropped to zero in the city.

Resistance to the sanitation and reconstruction campaigns, in which poor inhabitants of the central city were displaced, was reinforced by the regime's political opponents. In November 1904 the issue of compulsory vaccination for smallpox precipitated riots. Several hundred people suspected of participating in the riots were summarily rounded up and sent to the new Brazilian territory of Acre. Opposition leaders and students from the Praia Vermelha Military School who were involved were arrested but later granted amnesty.

Brazil enjoyed increased international prestige during Rodrigues Alves's administration. In 1903 Foreign Minister Barão do Rio Branco resolved the dispute with Bolivia over the territory of Acre in Brazil's favor; in 1905 the first cardinal in Latin America was appointed to Rio de Janeiro; and the Third International Conference of American States convened there in 1906. After leaving the presidency, Rodrigues Alves served again as governor of São Paulo (1912–1916), and in 1918 he was reelected to the presidency, but was too ill to assume office.

See also **Diseases; Petrópolis.**

BIBLIOGRAPHY

José Maria Bello, *A History of Modern Brazil 1889–1964* (1966).

Gilberto Freyre, *Order and Progress: Brazil from Monarchy to Republic* (1970).

Additional Bibliography

Arinos de Melo Franco, Afonso. *Rodrigues Alves: Apogeu e declínio do presidencialismo.* Brasília: Senado Federal, 2001.

Meade, Teresa A. *"Civilizing" Rio: Reform and Resistance in a Brazilian City, 1889–1930.* University Park: Pennsylvania State University Press, 1997.

FRANCESCA MILLER

RODRÍGUEZ, ANDRÉS (1923–1997).

Andrés Rodríguez (*b.* 19 June 1923; *d.* 21 April 1997), Paraguayan president (1989–1993). Born in the small town of San Salvador de Guairá, Rodríguez entered the army at an early age. He participated in the 1947 civil war, but came into prominence only after the rise to power of his mentor, General Alfredo Stroessner, in 1954. Seven years later, Rodríguez was promoted to full colonel and given command of the Cavalry Division, after which he became a general and head of the First Army Corps.

Rodríguez prospered tremendously under the corrupt Stroessner dictatorship. Long the number-two man in the army, Rodríguez cemented his relationship with the president when his daughter Marta married Stroessner's youngest son. In turn, this loyalty was rewarded with many concessions. Rodríguez built up major interests in banking and currency exchange, flour milling, brewing, real estate, ranching, and construction—not to mention near-monopoly control of cigarette, liquor, and luxury car imports. By the late 1980s, his personal fortune was estimated at over $1 billion.

At this time, however, the Stroessner regime was visibly weakening. Fairly open arguments concerning who would succeed the old president broke out among his various henchmen, and Rodríguez decided not to wait any longer. On the night of 2 February 1989, he launched a coup d'état that toppled the thirty-five-year dictatorship. Rodríguez announced that the new government would abandon the old ways in favor of a political democracy. Much to the surprise of many, he did precisely that, freeing the press, permitting the return of exiles, removing the most corrupt and brutal of Stroessner's associates, even saddling a few with long prison terms. In May 1989, a presidential election—arguably the fairest ever held in Paraguay—placed Rodríguez in the presidential palace for a four-year term with 75 percent of the popular vote.

Skeptics still doubted his commitment to democracy, but Rodríguez's liberalization program was nonetheless applauded by the majority of Paraguayans.

See also **Paraguay: The Twentieth Century; Stroessner, Alfredo.**

BIBLIOGRAPHY

Paul H. Lewis, *Paraguay Under Stroessner* (1980), pp. 136–138.

Riordan Roett and Richard Scott Sacks, *Paraguay: The Personalist Legacy* (1991), pp. 1–3, 78–82, 131–134.

Additional Bibliography

Rivarola, Milda. *Marzo Paraguayo: Una lección de democracia.* Asunción, Paraguay: Ultima hora, 2001.

                              THOMAS L. WHIGHAM

RODRIGUEZ, ARSENIO (1911–1970).

Arsenio Rodriguez, as a bandleader and composer, transformed Cuban music in the 1940s. He was born on August 30, 1911, into a family in rural Güira de Macarijes that took pride in its African ancestry. This pride led him later to write songs such as "Soy de Africa" ("I am from Africa"). Many facts regarding his life are in dispute. At the age of six or so (some sources say thirteen), he was blinded when a mule (or a horse) struck him in the face. Rodriguez is often given credit for making the conga drum a regular part of the rhythm section in Afro-Cuban dance music, as well as for adding the piano and trumpets. He was a master of the *tres*, although he also played a wide variety of other string, as well as percussion, instruments.

In the 1930s Rodriguez began to experiment with traditional *son* sound and instrumentation. He introduced many elements of African music, as well as North American jazz, as well as lyrics which employed Congolese words and Afro-Cuban slang, into the mainstream of Cuban music. He initially was barred from playing on some Cuban radio stations and in upscale nightclubs. His band helped set the stage for the mambo, which developed out of his "son montuno." In the 1940s and early 1950s, many leading Cuban musicians played in his bands. He relocated to New York City around 1953 and recorded for a wide variety of record labels in his years in the United States. Unfortunately his career gradually petered out, and he was relatively unknown when he died after a number of years in Los Angeles on December 31, 1970.

See also **Mambo; Music: Popular Music and Dance; Musical Instruments; Son.**

BIBLIOGRAPHY

Collazo, Bobby. *La Última Noche que Pasé Contigo: 40 Años de la Farándula Cubana.* San Juan: Editorial Cubanacán, 1987.

Díaz Ayala, Cristóbal. *Música Cubana del Areyeto a la Nueva Trova.* San Juan: Editorial Cubanacán, 1981.

Loza, Steven. *Tito Puente and the Making of Latin Music.* Urbana: University of Illinois Press, 1999.

Moore, Robin. *Nationalizing Blackness: Afrocubanismo and Artistic Revolution in Havana, 1920–1940.* Pittsburgh, PA: University of Pittsburgh Press, 1997.

Orovia, Helio. *Cuban Music from A to Z.* Durham, NC: Duke University Press, 2004.

ANDREW J. KIRKENDALL

RODRÍGUEZ, CARLOS RAFAEL

(1913–1997). Carlos Rafael Rodríguez (*b.* 23 May 1913), Cuban revolutionist. Born in Cienfuegos, Cuba, Rodríguez became actively involved in 1930 with the student movement against Gerardo Machado, soon heading the student movement in Cienfuegos. At this time he began meeting with a small nucleus of Communists. For the next two decades, he remained active in political affairs, becoming a member of the Popular Socialist Party (PSP) and editing numerous political publications. In 1958, along with the PSP, he allied with Fidel Castro. In postrevolutionary Cuba, Rodríguez devised agrarian reforms and published the official socialist periodical *Hoy.* He often represented Cuba at international meetings. In 1976, the Cuban government named him to several ministries, where he played a vital role in establishing Cuba's foreign policy.

By the early 1980s, Rodríguez ranked behind only Fidel and Raúl Castro within the Cuban hierarchy. He also held numerous administrative posts, including fourth secretary of the Cuban Communist Party. In 1990, he won the special Raul Prebisch Prize given by the Latin American and Caribbean Economists Association. In 1991, he was given an honorary doctorate in international relations from the Cuban Instituto Superior de Relaciones Internacionales. He died on December 8, 1997 in Havana.

See also **Cuba, Revolutions: Cuban Revolution; Machado y Morales, Gerardo.**

BIBLIOGRAPHY

Araceli García-Carranza and Josefina García-Carranza, *Biobibliografía de Carlos Rafael Rodríguez* (1987).

Additional Bibliography

Guevara, Ernesto. *El gran debate: Sobre la economía en Cuba, 1963–1964.* 2nd ed. Havana: Editorial de Ciencias Sociales, 2004.

Hernández Rodríguez, Rafael, and John H. Coatsworth, eds. *Culturas encontradas: Cuba y los Estados Unidos.* Havana: Centro de Investigación y Desarrollo de la Cultura Cubana Juan Marinello; Cambridge, MA: David Rockefeller Center for Latin American Studies, Harvard Univesity, 2001.

Miranda Francisca, Olivia. *Carlos Rafael Rodríguez: Tradición y universalidad.* Havana: Editora Política, 1997.

ALLAN S. R. SUMNALL

RODRÍGUEZ, LORENZO (1704–1774).

Lorenzo Rodríguez (*b.* 1704; *d.* 1774), innovative colonial architect. Born in Gaudix, Andalusia, Rodríguez was in New Spain in 1731 and was examined as an architect in Mexico City in 1740. Despite competition from native architects, his career advanced. In 1744 he was an inspector of the architects' guild, and between 1749 and 1768 he was the architect of the Sagrario Metropolitano of Mexico City Cathedral, a very important commission, which is the basis of his reputation. In 1758 he was also named *maestro mayor* (chief architect) of the Royal Palace, a post he held until his death. During the last years of his life, Rodríguez wrote an architectural treatise, only recently discovered, in which he stresses the importance of mathematics for his profession.

Rodríguez is considered to have been responsible for introducing the *estípite* (architectural support whose main element is an elongated inverted pyramid) on church exteriors in New Spain. Previously, the *estípite* had been used only in retablos. At the Sagrario, Rodríguez combined a sober, centralized plan and classicistic interior with elaborate *estípite* portals full of figures. Most *estípite* façades in and near Mexico City have been attributed to him in the past, although later these attributions were rejected or considered doubtful. He died in Mexico City.

See also **Architecture: Architecture to 1900.**

BIBLIOGRAPHY

Margaret Collier, "New Documents on Lorenzo Rodríguez and his Style," in *Acts of the Twentieth International Congress of the History of Art* (1963), pp. 203–218.

Additional Bibliography

Weismann, Elizabeth Wilder, and Judith Hancock de Sandoval. *Art and Time in Mexico: Architecture and Sculpture in Colonial Mexico.* New York: Icons Editions, 1995.

CLARA BARGELLINI

RODRÍGUEZ, PEDRO. *See* **Campomanes, Pedro Rodríguez, Conde de.**

RODRIGUEZ, RICHARD (1944–).
Richard Rodriguez is a writer, journalist, television commentator, and public speaker who writes primarily about U.S. culture. His views have stirred lively discussions among readers, academics, and critics. Born on July 31, 1944, of Mexican parents in San Francisco, Rodriguez received a BA from Stanford University and an MA from Columbia University; he then attended the University of California–Berkeley, where he did doctoral work in English Renaissance literature. His *Hunger of Memory: The Education of Richard Rodriguez* (1982) generated numerous reviews, some praising the book, others denouncing it. Chicano studies scholars criticized it for implicitly challenging the Chicano/Chicana movement's understanding of Mexican American politics and culture, especially Rodriguez's open embrace of assimilation and opposition to affirmative action and bilingual education. His other two books, 1992's *Days of Obligation: An Argument with My Mexican Father* (where he disclosed his homosexuality) and *Brown: The Last Discovery of America* (2002) focus particularly on issues of ethnicity, sexuality, and race.

See also **Hispanics in the United States.**

BIBLIOGRAPHY

Alarcón, Norma. "Tropology of Hunger: The 'Miseducation' of Richard Rodriguez." In *The Ethnic Canon:* *Histories, Institutions, and Interventions,* ed. David Palumbo-Liu, pp. 140–152. Minneapolis: University of Minnesota Press, 1995.

Aldama, Frederick Luis. "Arturo Islas's and Richard Rodriguez's Ethnosexual Re-architexturing of Metropolitan Space." In his *Brown on Brown: Chicano/a Representations of Gender, Sexuality, and Ethnicity,* pp. 73–88. Austin: University of Texas Press, 2005.

Romero, Rolando J. "Richard Rodriguez." In *Latino and Latina Writers,* ed. Alan West-Durán, María Herrera-Sobek, and César A. Salgado, vol. 1, pp. 455–474. New York: Scribners, 2004.

MARK A. HERNÁNDEZ

RODRÍGUEZ, SIMÓN (1769–1854).
Simón Rodríguez (*b.* 28 October 1769; *d.* 28 February 1854), Venezuelan educator and teacher of Simón Bolívar. Rodríguez began life in Caracas as a foundling. He became well educated largely through his own efforts. From an early age Rodríguez was teaching and articulating an educational philosophy that stressed the need for practical studies as well as for making education available to all sectors of society, including women. In his belief in human perfectibility through schooling, he was undoubtedly influenced by Rousseau, but his ideas also bore the stamp of his own highly original personality.

Rodríguez's most famous pupil was Bolívar, who at one time lived with Rodríguez, with the latter serving as guardian, and who conceived a deep admiration for his teacher's "genius." About 1796, Rodríguez left Caracas, traveling first to the United States (where he worked for a time in Baltimore as a printer) and then to France, where he taught and traveled widely. In 1804, in Paris, he renewed his relationship with Bolívar, and he was with him at Rome the next year when Bolívar took an oath to liberate Spanish America.

Rodríguez returned to America in 1823, intending to help in the construction of a republican new order. In Peru he again joined Bolívar, who gave him the task of organizing schools there and, later, in Bolivia. However, his insistence on mixing youths from different social backgrounds and teaching useful crafts to all in his model school at Chuquisaca (later Sucre) aroused much strong criticism, as did his disregard for personal appearance and social conventions.

After a falling out with Bolivia's first president, Antonio José de Sucre, Rodríguez moved on. For the next three decades he divided his time among Peru, Chile, Ecuador, and Colombia. In all of these nations he was a teacher who won warm admiration from some and harsh rejection from others. He continually publicized his educational ideas, his social egalitarianism, and such pet causes as the simplification of Spanish spelling. Best known of his writings is *Sociedades americanas en 1828*, first published in Arequipa (1840) and then in an expanded version in Lima (1842). He died in Amotape, Peru.

See also **Bolívar, Simón.**

BIBLIOGRAPHY

Pedro Grases, comp., Simón Rodríguez, *Escritos,* 3 vols. (1954–1958).

Mercedes M. Álvarez F., *Simón Rodríguez tal cual fué* (1966).

Gerhard Masur, Simón Bolívar, rev. ed. (1969), esp. pp. 40–41.

Germán Carrera Damas, *Simón Rodríguez, hombre de tres siglos* (1971).

Jorge López Palma, *Simón Rodríguez: Utopía y socialismo* (1989).

Gustavo Adolfo Ruiz, *Simón Rodríguez: Maestro de primeras letras* (1990).

Additional Bibliography

Orgambide, Pedro G. *El maestro de Bolívar: Simón Rodríguez, el utopista.* Buenos Aires: Editorial Sudamericana, 2002.

Ramírez Fierro, María del Rayo. *Simón Rodríguez y su utopia para América.* Mexico City: Universidad Nacional Autónoma de México, 1994.

DAVID BUSHNELL

RODRIGUEZ, TITO (1923–1973). Tito Rodriguez was one of the great singers and bandleaders of the mambo era in the 1940s and 1950s. Born on January 4, 1923, in San Juan, Puerto Rico, of Dominican and Cuban parentage, he moved to New York City as a teenager. He had served in the U.S. Army and sung with Xavier Cugat and Nora Morales before he got his musical break in 1946 when he joined the band of Cuban pianist José Curbelo. Curbelo is often given credit for originating the New York mambo sound. In the following year Rodriguez left to form his own Mambo Devils, which recorded for Tico Records and which soon expanded from a small group into a big band, later known as the Lobos del Mambo. He later also recorded for RCA and United Artists. His bands, along with those of Machito and Puente, dominated the mambo scene at the Palladium Ballroom in New York in the early 1950s.

Although there was much made of Rodriguez's alleged rivalry with timbale player and bandleader Tito Puente, they had actually been friends since the 1930s, and both had gotten their start with Curbelo. His band, like Puente's and Machito's, was more influenced by jazz and incorporated more Afro-Cuban elements than the more commercial style of Pérez Prado. In 1962, Rodriguez had three number one hits in Puerto Rico with "Vuela la Paloma," "Cuando, Cuando," and "Cara de Payaso." As a singer, he excelled whether improvising at top speed or slowing down for a romantic ballad. His versatility is demonstrated by the fact that in 1963 he recorded with jazz greats Zoot Sims and Clark Terry on the album *Live at Birdland*, whereas in the same year he also had a hit with a bolero version of "Inolvidable" ("Unforgettable"), which sold more than a million copies. He disbanded in 1965 and moved to Puerto Rico, where he had a television program for a year or two. Over the next few years, he moved back and forth among New York, Florida, and Puerto Rico. Illness plagued the last five years of his life, and he died of leukemia in New York on February 28, 1973.

See also **Cugat, Xavier; Machito; Mambo; Music: Popular Music and Dance; Pérez Prado; Puente, Tito.**

BIBLIOGRAPHY

Loza, Steven. *Tito Puente and the Making of Latin Music.* Urbana: University of Illinois Press, 1999.

Roberts, John Storm. *Latin Jazz: The First of the Fusions, 1880s to Today.* New York: Schirmer Books, 1999.

"Tito Rodriguez." In *The Encyclopedia of Popular Music,* 3rd edition, edited by Colin Larkin. London: Muze, 1998.

ANDREW J. KIRKENDALL

RODRÍGUEZ-ALCALÁ, HUGO (1917–).

Hugo Rodríguez-Alcalá (*b.* 25 November 1917), Paraguayan poet, short story writer, and literary critic. Rodríguez-Alcalá is the son of José Rodríguez Alcalá and Teresa Lamas Carísimo, both established writers. Born in Asunción, Hugo studied at the National College and obtained a doctorate from the National University. His *Poemas* appeared in 1938, followed by *Estampas de la guerra,* based on his experiences in the Chaco War, in 1939. In 1947 he moved to the United States and earned a second Ph.D., after which he taught literature at several universities, most notably the University of California at Riverside. He has directed and advised many literary journals, including *Hispanic Review* and *Revista Iberoamericana.*

Rodríguez-Alcalá is perhaps best known for his poetry and his numerous studies in the area of literary criticism. Most of his poetry and short stories revolve around the theme of childhood innocence and contain nostalgic and vivid images in the manner of the Spanish poet Antonio Machado and other members of the Generation of 1898, of which he was a specialist. Rodríguez-Alcalá's critical studies include stylistic analyses of the works of Juan Rulfo and Roa Bastos. His *Historia de la literatura paraguaya* (1970) has become a standard reference manual.

Other works include *Abril, que cruza el mundo* (1960); *El arte de Juan Rulfo* (1965); *Relatos de norte al sur* (1985); and *Augusto Roa Bastos, Premio Cervantes 1989* (1990).

See also **Literature: Spanish America.**

BIBLIOGRAPHY

Vallejos, Roque. *La literatura paraguaya, como expresión de la realidad nacional.* Asunción: Editorial Don Bosco, 1971.

THOMAS E. CASE

RODRÍGUEZ CABRILLO, JUAN (?–1543).

Juan Rodríguez Cabrillo (*b. ca.* 1498; *d.* 3 January 1543), first European explorer to reach California. Rodríguez Cabrillo, probably born in Seville, Spain, participated in the conquest of Cuba and served in the conquest of Mexico as a crossbowman and sailor under Hernán Cortés (1485–1547) in 1519. He joined Pedro de Alvarado (ca. 1485–1541) in the conquest of Guatemala in 1523. After settling there as a mine owner and *encomendero,* he traveled to Seville to marry Beatríz Sánchez de Ortega about 1532. Subsequently, Rodríguez Cabrillo ran a shipyard and led an expedition of three ships to the North Pacific on 27 June 1542. After exploring the Baja California coast, he entered the present bay of San Diego on 28 September 1542 and named it San Miguel. He claimed the area for Spain and later explored the coastal areas of California. He died on one of the Santa Barbara Channel Islands as a result of complications from a broken bone.

See also **California; Cortés, Hernán.**

BIBLIOGRAPHY

The most complete biographical study is Harry Kelsey, *Juan Rodríguez Cabrillo* (1986). For arguments claiming Portugal as Cabrillo's nationality, see Celestino Soares, *California and the Portuguese* (1939); João Antonio de Mascarenhas Logoa, *João Rodrigues Cabrilho, achegas para a sua biografia* (1958).

Additional Bibliography

Mattox, Jake. *Explorers of the New World.* San Diego, CA: Greenhaven Press, 2004.

Nauman, James D. *An Account of the Voyage of Juan Rodríguez Cabrillo.* San Diego, CA: Cabrillo National Monument Foundation, 1999.

IRIS H. W. ENGSTRAND

RODRÍGUEZ CERNA, JOSÉ (1885–1952).

José Rodríguez Cerna (*b.* 18 September 1885; *d.* 20 July 1952), Guatemalan novelist, poet, and journalist. Rodríguez is considered the first Guatemalan modernist poet and novelist. He graduated from the University of San Carlos with a legal degree in 1904 but never practiced law professionally. Among his literary works are *El poema de la Antigua* (1915), *Tierra de sol y de montaña* (1930), and *Bajo las alas del águila* (1942). Rodríguez's career in journalism included service as the editor-in-chief of the newspaper *La*

República and the magazine *Centro América*. He was a contributing writer for other Guatemalan and Salvadoran newspapers. Rodríguez at times wrote under the pseudonyms Hernani, Barba Azul, Martín Paz, Casa Roja, and Juan Chapin.

See also **Literature: Spanish America.**

BIBLIOGRAPHY

Catalina Barrios y Barrios, "José Rodríguez Cerna," in *Alero* 4 (December 1980): 29–40.

Francisco Albizúrez Palma and Catalina Barrios y Barrios, *Historia de la literatura guatemalteca*, vol. 2 (1982), pp. 85–96.

STEVEN S. GILLICK

RODRÍGUEZ DEMORIZI, EMILIO

(1908–1986). Emilio Rodríguez Demorizi (*b*. 14 April 1908; *d*. 27 June 1986), Dominican historian. Rodríguez earned a law degree at the University of Santo Domingo and served as ambassador to Colombia, Spain, and Italy as well as in government positions. He was secretary of state, secretary of state for education and fine arts, rector of the Universidad Autónoma de Santo Domingo, and director of the National Archive. He was president of the Academia Dominicana de la Historia beginning in 1965. While director of the National Archive, he made his greatest contribution in terms of collecting and editing Dominican historical documents. Many of the documents were made available for the first time, and many were found when Rodríguez visited all the major European archives. The series *Documentos para la historia de la República Dominicana* and *Relaciones históricas de Santo Domingo* exceeded 100 volumes. Rodríguez also wrote *Fábulas dominicanas* (1946), *El cancionero de Lilís: Poesía, dictadura y libertad* (1962), and several works on Columbus.

See also **Dominica.**

BIBLIOGRAPHY

sFrank Moya Pons, *Quién es quién en la República Dominicana*, 2d ed. (1978), p. 236, and *El pasado dominicano* (1986), p. 257.

LARMAN C. WILSON

RODRÍGUEZ DE VELASCO Y OSORIO BARBA, MARÍA IGNACIA (1778–1851).

María Ignacia Rodríguez de Velasco y Osorio Barba (*b*. 20 November 1778; *d*. 29 October 1851). Born in Mexico City, "La Güera Rodríguez" (Rodríguez the Blond) was a member of a distinguished aristocratic family of New Spain and a partisan of the insurgents who became notorious for her great beauty as well as for her several love affairs. Rodríguez was a friend of important personages of the era, among them Baron Alexander von Humboldt and Agustín de Iturbide, with whom she was said to have had a love affair. During the struggle for independence, La Güera corresponded with the insurgents and sent them money and other forms of aid. Two of her haciendas were in the hands of the insurgent chiefs José Sixto Verduzco and José María Liceaga from the beginning of 1813, but no harm came to her properties. She died in Mexico City.

See also **Humboldt, Alexander von; Iturbide, Agustín de.**

BIBLIOGRAPHY

Artemio Del Valle Arizpe, *La Güera Rodríguez* (1950); and *Diccionario Porrúa de historia, geografía y biografía de México*, 5th ed. (1986).

Additional Bibliography

Arrioja Vizcaíno, Adolfo. *El águila en la alcoba: La güera Rodríguez en los tiempos de la independencia nacional.* México, D.F.: Grijalbo, 2005.

Oropeza Martínez, Roberto. *Artemio de Valle-Arizpe: La güera Rodríguez: Con introducción y antecedentes, aspectos generales, sinopsis, comentario y análisis guiado, autoevaluación, bibliografía.* México, D.F.: Fernández editores, 1990.

Valle-Arizpe, Artemio de. *La Güera Rodríguez.* México: Planeta de Agostini: CONACULTA, 2004.

VIRGINIA GUEDEA

RODRÍGUEZ ERDOIZA, MANUEL

(1785–1818). Manuel Rodríguez Erdoiza (*b*. 25 February 1785; *d*. 26 May 1818), legendary Chilean guerrilla chief. A lawyer by training and a fervent partisan of José Miguel Carrera during the Chilean *Patria Vieja* (the period, 1810–1814, before the Spanish reconquest), Rodríguez fled to Argentina after the collapse of Chilean independence in October 1814. He soon recrossed the mountains at the head of a guerrilla band. His audacious comings and goings were an irritant to the Spanish forces and won Rodríguez a place in Chilean folk memory that he has never lost. For Chileans he is the guerrilla. Unfortunately, the Bernardo O'Higgins–José Miguel Carrera feud meant that Chile, ruled after 1817 by Bernardo O'Higgins, was a less than safe place for the guerrilla hero. Though he rallied the panic-stricken citizenry of Santiago magnificently after the royalist victory at the second battle of Cancha Rayada (19 March 1818) and fought at the battle of Maipú (5 April 1818), he could not escape imprisonment. While on his way to Valparaíso, ostensibly to be sent into exile, he was treacherously murdered at Tiltil, whether on O'Higgins's direct orders or not was later debated.

See also **Carrera, José Miguel; Chile: Foundations Through Independence.**

BIBLIOGRAPHY

Additional Bibliography

Reyno Gutiérrez, Manuel. *José Miguel Carrera*. Santiago de Chile: Edit. Andujar, 2003.

SIMON COLLIER

RODRÍGUEZ FREILE, JUAN (1566– c. 1642).

Juan Rodríguez Freile (*b.* 15 April 1566; *d.* ca. 1642), Colombian chronicler. The son of a conquistador, Rodríguez Freile studied for the priesthood in his native Bogotá, learning Chibcha as well as Latin and attaining minor orders by 1585. Abandoning clerical life, he took service in an *oidor*'s household and spent the years 1585–1569 as a soldier/clerk in Spain and various parts of the Indies. Back in Bogotá, Freile married Francisca Rodríguez, a mestiza, about 1600, and in 1608 fought against Indians in the Neiva Valley; thereafter he settled as a farmer near Bogotá. Between 1636 and 1638, he wrote his masterpiece, *El carnero,* a racy, sprightly (occasionally fictionalized) firsthand account of colonial Colombia's first century. Considered too salacious for publication, *El carnero* circulated in manuscript. The original was lost after 1850, but a later copy served as the basis for the first printed version (1859).

See also **Literature: Spanish America; New Granada, Viceroyalty of.**

BIBLIOGRAPHY

The Conquest of New Granada by Juan Rodríguez Freile, translated by William C. Atkinson (1961).

José Restrepo Posada, "La familia del cronista Rodríguez Freile," in *Boletín de historia y Antigüedades* 53 (April– May 1966): 227–230.

Mario Germán Romero, "Autobiografía de Juan Rodríguez Freile," in his edition of Rodríguez Freile's *El carnero* (1984), pp. xiii–xxii.

Additional Bibliography

Bruno, Charles J. *(Re)writing History in Juan Rodríguez Freile's Conquista Y Descubrimiento del Nuevo Reino de Granada: Myth, Irony, Satire.* Madison: University of Wisconsin, 1990.

Freyle, Juan, and Mario Germán Romero. *El carnero: Según el manuscrito de Yerbabuena.* Bogotá: Instituto Caro y Cuervo, 1984, 1997.

Hernandez-Torres, Ivette N. *El contrabando de lo secreto: La escritura de la historia en El Carnero de Juan Rodríguez Freile.* Santiago: Editorial Cuarto Propic, 2004.

J. LEÓN HELGUERA

RODRÍGUEZ JUÁREZ, JUAN (1675– 1728).

Juan Rodríguez Juárez (*b.* 1675; *d.* 1728), Mexican painter. Grandson of José Juárez, son of Antonio Rodríguez, and brother of Nicolás Rodríguez Juárez, Juan Rodríguez Juárez is the principal artist of the transition from the Zurbaranesque baroque tradition of Villalpando and Correa to eighteenth-century baroque and rococo tendencies in New Spain. His first known work was done in 1694. In 1719 he was given a major commission, the canvases for the Retablo de los Reyes of the cathedral of Mexico City. In his works one sees the softer coloring, more spacious compositions, and gentler expressions of Bartolomé Murillo. Besides his religious paintings, Rodríguez Juárez produced excellent portraits and an extraordinary self-portrait, symptomatic of the changing role of the artist in the colony in the eighteenth century.

See also **Art: The Colonial Era.**

BIBLIOGRAPHY

Manuel Toussaint, *Colonial Art in Mexico* (1967).

María Concepción García Saiz, *La pintura colonial en el Museo de América*, vol. 1 (1980).

Additional Bibliography

Andrade, Carmen. "Los hermanos Nícolas y Juan Rodríguez Juárez: siglo XVII." *Artes de México* 22:188 (n.d.): 41–44.

Katzew, Ilona. *Casta Painting: Images of Race in Eighteenth-Century Mexico.* New Haven, CT: Yale University Press, 2004.

CLARA BARGELLINI

RODRÍGUEZ JULIÁ, EDGARDO

(1946–). Among the most gifted and versatile voices of his historically revisionist generation in Puerto Rico is the novelist and essayist Edgardo Rodríguez Juliá. His early novels—*La renuncia del héroe Baltasar* (1974; *The Renunciation*, 1997) and *La noche oscura del Niño Avilés* (1984)—skillfully blend, with considerable narrative verve and formal ingenuity, elements of fact and fiction, realism and myth, revelation and coverup, past and present. Each evokes the baroque ambiance of colonial Puerto Rico as it reveals the political, social, and cultural drama of the era and, offering a revised view of island history, proposes that dilemmas of race, caste, and class inherited from that formative period are still powerful, if calculatedly elided, features of Puerto Rico's contemporary reality. *El camino de Yyaloide* (1993) extends his chronicle of the fictive Nueva Venecia begun with *La noche oscura del Niño Avilés*, and so completes its author's eighteenth-century trilogy of novels.

The short stories of *Cortejos fúnebres* (1997) and novels *Sol de medianoche* (1995), *Cartagena* (1997), and *Mujer con sombrero Panamá* (2004) all have a more contemporary locale and focus, but are as adventurous creatively as the earlier work, and equally devoted to Rodríguez Juliá's continuing critical assessment of his society's most pressing, if often concealed or evaded, realities. Equally prolific as the island's most accomplished and popular practitioner of the essay-cum-cultural chronicle, Rodríguez Juliá has produced meditations on the contradictory distinctiveness and vivacity of Puerto Rican art, history, politics, literature, photography, popular culture, thought, and feeling in *Las tribulaciones de Jonás* (1981), *El entierro de Cortijo* (1983; *Cortijo's Wake*, 2004), *Campeche o los diablejos de la melancolía* (1986), *Una noche con Iris Chacón* (1986), *El cruce de la bahía de Guánica* (1989), *Puertorriqueños: Album de la sagrada familia puertorriqueña a partir de 1898* (1989), *Cámara secreta* (1994), *Peloteros* (1997), *Mapa de una pasión literaria* (2003), *Musarañas de domingo* (2004), and *San Juan, ciudad soñada* (2005; *San Juan; Memoir of a City* (2007).

See also **Literature: Spanish America; Puerto Rico.**

BIBLIOGRAPHY

Duchesne Winter, Juan, ed. *Las tribulaciones de Juliá.* San Juan: Instituto de Cultura Puertorriqueña, 1992.

González, Rubén. *La historia puertorriqueña de Rodríguez Juliá.* Río Piedras: Editorial de la Universidad de Puerto Rico, 1997.

ROBERTO MÁRQUEZ

RODRÍGUEZ LARA, GUILLERMO

(1923–1988). Guillermo Rodríguez Lara (*b.* 4 November 1923; *d.* 1988), president of Ecuador (1972–1976). Born of a modest family in the provincial town of Pujilí, Rodríguez Lara became a career army officer; his training included study at Fort Leavenworth, Kansas, as well as military courses in Argentina and Colombia. During thirty-three years of service he rose to become director of the Army War Academy and eventually commanding general of the army in April of 1971. When a series of events provoked the ouster of José María Velasco Ibarra on 15 February 1972, Rodríguez Lara became head of the new, self-styled "national revolutionary government."

At the outset of his administration, an explicit program for socioeconomic reform and modernization was outlined, but the military leadership was somewhat ambivalent. Traditionalists fought to block agrarian and tax reforms while opposing a nationalistic policy toward the new petroleum industry. Other officers fought for such measures, while Rodríguez Lara sought with increasing difficulty to maintain a position of compromise. Not a persuasive or crowd-pleasing personality, he lacked a popular movement of his own. In September 1975 an uprising by rightist officers was put down, but Rodríguez's position had been fatally damaged. He was forced to resign on 11 January 1976 and was succeeded by a three-man military junta that eventually returned Ecuador to elected government. Rodríguez Lara retired to his farm outside Pujilí and lived there quietly until his death.

See also **Ecuador: Since 1830.**

BIBLIOGRAPHY

John Samuel Fitch, *The Military Coup d'état as a Political Process: Ecuador, 1948–1966* (1977).

John D. Martz, *The Military in Ecuador: Policies and Politics of Authoritarian Rule* (1988).

Additional Bibliography

Febres Cordero, Francisco. *De Flores a flores y miel*. Quito: Ojo de Pez, 1996.

Jaramillo Palacio, José María. *Velasco Ibarra: Presidente idealista: Medio siglo de história en el Ecuador, 1930–1980*. Quito: Delta, 1995.

JOHN D. MARTZ

RODRÍGUEZ LUJÁN, ABELARDO

(1889–1967). Abelardo Rodríguez Luján (*b.* 12 May 1889; *d.* 13 February 1967), president of Mexico (1932–1934). Last of the troika of presidents during the 1928–1934 administration, General Rodríguez replaced Pascual Ortiz Rubio when he resigned. As chief executive, he is generally considered to have been a caretaker, subordinate to his mentor, General Plutarco Elías Calles. He was a major stockholder in many incipient Mexican industries, including Portland Cement and La Suiza.

From a humble family in Guaymas, Sonora, and with little formal education, Rodríguez worked at many unskilled jobs before joining the Constitutionalists in 1913. He made the military his career, rising through the ranks to division general (three stars) in 1928. He became governor and military commander of Baja California del Norte (1923–1929), a post he used to develop his personal financial holdings in the fishing and packing industries. Rodríguez held several cabinet posts, including secretary of industry and commerce (1932) and secretary of war and the navy (1932). He served as a regional military commander during World War II and as governor of his home state (1943–1948).

See also **Mexico: Since 1910.**

BIBLIOGRAPHY

Francisco J. Gaxiola, *El Presidente Rodríguez* (1938).

John W. F. Dulles, *Yesterday in Mexico: A Chronicle of the Revolution, 1919–1936* (1961).

Lorenzo Meyer, *Historia de la revolución mexicana, período 1928–1934* (1978).

Additional Bibliography

Gómez Estrada, José Alfredo. *Gobierno y casinos: Origin de la riqueza de Abelardo L. Rodríguez*. Mexicali, Baja California, México: Universidad Autónoma da Baja California, 2002.

Moncada, Carlos. *Aquel hombre: Abelardo L. Rodríguez*. Hermosillo, Sonora, México: Fondo Editorial el Libro Sonorense, 1997.

RODERIC AI CAMP

RODRÍGUEZ MONEGAL, EMIR

(1921–1985). Emir Rodríguez Monegal (*b.* 28 July 1921; *d.* 14 November 1985), Uruguayan literary critic. Rodríguez Monegal was a prodigious literary critic, author of forty books and countless articles, and "maker of writers," whose controversial career spanned five decades and three continents. He began publishing in 1943 in *Marcha*, a Uruguayan magazine for which he wrote until 1959. Some of his early pieces appear in *Narradores de esta América*, a collection of his essays published in 1969 (2d ed., 2 vols., 1974). A writer of books as well as articles, he published *El juicio de los parricidas: La nueva generación argentina y sus maestros* in 1956, a work that demonstrated Jorge Luis Borges's importance and also identified themes that would dominate literary debate in Latin America for the next thirty years. Other book-length studies include works on Andrés Bello, Pablo Neruda, José Enrique Rodó, and Horacio Quiroga. After an acrimonious separation from *Marcha*, Rodríguez Monegal left Uruguay for Paris, where in 1966 he founded *Mundo Nuevo*, a magazine credited with initiating the so-called boom that brought world attention to such writers as Borges, Julio Cortázar, Gabriel García Márquez, Carlos Fuentes, and Mario Vargas Llosa. Despite the magazine's extraordinary effectiveness, its Ford Foundation support led pro-Castro intellectuals to accuse Rodríguez Monegal of fronting for the U.S. Central Intelligence Agency. After a bitter exchange with his accusers, he resigned his position with *Mundo Nuevo,* thus hastening the demise of the magazine, and accepted an influential position at Yale University in 1968. In 1984 he finally returned to Uruguay, where he received a presidential award for his intellectual contributions. He died and is buried in New Haven, Connecticut.

See also **Literature: Spanish America.**

BIBLIOGRAPHY

John P. Dwyer et al., *Homenaje a Emir Rodríguez Monegal* (1986).

Additional Bibliography

Moraña, Mabel, and Horacio Machín, eds. *Marcha y América Latina.* Pittsburgh, PA: Instituto Internacional de Literatura Iberoamericana, Universidad de Pittsburgh, 2003.

NICOLAS SHUMWAY

RODRÍGUEZ SAÁ, ADOLFO (1947–).

Adolfo Rodríguez Saá, an Argentine politician born on July 25, 1947, was governor of the province of San Luis for from 1983 to 2001, and interim president of the republic for seven days in 2001. Known as "the Adolf," he began his career as a member of the Peronist ranks in 1969. In 1971 he passed the bar and became an attorney. In the 1973 elections, he was elected as deputy to the Argentine Congress for his native province and was president of the Justicialista bloc in the lower chamber until the military coup of 1976.

With the return of democracy in 1983, he was elected governor of the province of San Luis and consecutively reelected for five more terms. His populist style of government and efficient administration of the province's fiscal revenues allowed him to consolidate his power in the province. During this period, however, the governor was denounced for his antidemocratic practices and for alleged illicit self-enrichment.

In 2001, after the sudden resignation of President Fernando de la Rúa, the congress asked Rodríguez Saá to serve as interim president.

During his one-week administration, payment of the foreign debt was suspended. Pressured by the Peronist governors worried about the extravagant nature of his administration and because they feared losing all control over it, he was forced to resign.

See also **Argentina: The Twentieth Century; Argentina, Political Parties: Justicialist Party; Rúa, Fernando de la.**

BIBLIOGRAPHY

Camarasa, Jorge. *Días de Furia: Historia oculta de la Argentina desde la caída de De la Rúa hasta la asunción de Duhalde.* Buenos Aires: Sudamericana, 2002.

Novaro, Marcos. *Historia de la Argentina contemporánea: De Perón a Kirchner.* Buenos Aires: EDHASA, 2006.

VICENTE PALERMO

RODRÍGUEZ SANDOVAL, LUIS ARSENIO (1898–1977). Luis Arsenio

Rodríguez Sandoval (*b.* 21 June 1898; *d.* 21 November 1977), Ecuadoran military officer and defender of Ecuador during the Peruvian invasion of 1941. Born into a prominent conservative highland family, Rodríguez was among the early graduates of Ecuador's military academy. In October 1924 he and other lieutenants formed a military league to reform the nation. On 9 July 1925 the officers overthrew the government of Gonzalo Córdova, thereby initiating a period of social change designed to modernize the nation. When the military installed the progressive dictator Isidro Ayora Cueva to carry out reforms, Rodríguez was named aide-de-camp.

Disillusioned by politicization of the military and the failure of reform, Rodríguez thereafter became a supporter of the constitutional order. During the 1930s he opposed military intervention in national politics and supported the government. During those years, he devoted himself to the improvement of the armed forces, publishing several pamphlets on the future of the army and the need for professionalization. Rodríguez was one of the founders of the air corps and one of the highest-ranking army officers when Peru invaded Ecuador in July 1941. He voluntarily left command of the military zone of Guayaquil to defend the nation with small frontier garrisons while the regular army moved to the border. The government, however, failed to send forces, and the nation suffered a crushing defeat.

Abandoned in the jungle, Rodríguez became a "nonperson" until 1944, when a revolt overthrew the government. He was imprisoned for the national defeat, but was ultimately exonerated. Nevertheless, Rodríguez was blackballed for many years, finding it difficult to obtain employment. With the passage of time and the publication of the second edition of his book *La invasión peruana* (1955), public opinion changed. In particular the new military leaders came to admire his patriotism. His book was studied at the War College. In recognition of his earlier service, he was appointed to the High Court of Military Justice, where he served from 1963 to 1965. In 1965 the military government awarded him the Order of Abdón Calderón in recognition of his actions in 1941.

Rodríguez devoted his later years to helping organize the archives of the army and to historical research on the military. Of the many important works he published during his life, the most significant for him was his account of the 1941 conflict.

See also **Ecuador-Peru Boundary Disputes.**

BIBLIOGRAPHY

Luis A. Rodríguez S., *La agresión peruana documentada* (1948).

Linda Alexander Rodríguez, "The Liberal Crisis and the Revolution of 1925 in Ecuador" (M.A. thesis, Univ. of Texas, Austin, 1972).

Additional Bibliography

Salvador Lara, Jorge. *Breve historia contemporánea del Ecuador*. México: Fondo de Cultura Económica, 1994.

JAIME E. RODRÍGUEZ O.

ROGATIS, PASCUAL DE (1880–1980).

Pascual de Rogatis (*b.* 17 May 1880; *d.* 2 April 1980), Argentine composer. Born in Teora, Italy, Rogatis came to Argentina when he was very young. He began his musical studies at the National Conservatory in Buenos Aires, where he studied under Pietro Melani and Rafael Díaz Albertini (violin) and Alberto

Williams (composition). During his studies he was awarded the gold medal in violin (1899), first prize in ensemble performance (1902), and the first award in composition (1906). He was a nationalist composer, attracted by the exotic and mythical stories of the indigenous peoples of America. His first works included piano pieces, songs, and orchestral compositions. Among them were the *Suite árabe* (1902) for strings, and three symphonic poems, *Marko y el hada* (1905), *Belkiss en la selva* (1906), and *Zupay* (1910). His opera *Anfión y Zeto*, a Greek tragedy, premiered at the Teatro Colón in Buenos Aires with the Gustavo Salvini Company and the celebrated baritone Titta Ruffo (1877–1953) in 1915. Two orchestral works, *Atipac* (1931) and *Estampas Argentinas* (1942), were awarded, respectively, the Municipal Prize and the National Award for Composition. In his seventies, he produced three works for piano: one in 1952; two in 1957.

Rogatis's best-known work is his opera *Huemac*, based on a Mexican legend; it premiered at the Teatro Colón in 1916 and was conducted by the composer. It was later performed in Rome at the Teatro Costanzi. *Huemac* was awarded the Municipal Prize of Buenos Aires in 1916. Another opera, *La Novia del hereje*, was performed in 1935 in Buenos Aires. Rogatis was professor of chamber music at the National Conservatory and a member of the Argentine Commission of Fine Arts. He died in Buenos Aires.

See also **Music: Art Music.**

BIBLIOGRAPHY

Composers of the Americas, vol. 12 (1966), pp. 131–135.

Rodolfo Arizaga, *Enciclopedia de la música argentina* (1971); *New Grove Dictionary of Music and Musicians* (1980).

Additional Bibliography

Kuss, Malena. "'Huemac' by Pascual de Rogatis: Native Identity in the Argentine Lyric Theatre." *Anuario Interamericano de Investigación Musical* 10 (1974): 68–87.

SUSANA SALGADO

ROIG DE LEUCHSENRING, EMILIO

(1889–1964). Emilio Roig de Leuchsenring (*b.* 23 August 1889; *d.* 8 August 1964), Cuban journalist and historian. Roig, a native of Havana, is best known as one of the founders and leaders of the Cuban revisionist school of historians, a group of writers and scholars, some of them Marxists, who distinguished themselves by their negative appraisal of U.S. influence on Cuban affairs. His work began to reflect this view as early as 1922. In 1933 he was appointed historian of the city of Havana, a position that he used to launch the journal *Cuadernos de historia habanera*. In 1940 he was instrumental in forming the Cuban Society of Historical and International Studies, and two years later he began to promote, with the help of the society, a series of National Historic Congresses, the thirteenth of which met in 1960. Among Roig's favorite theses were that the Cuban struggle for independence was not a series of wars but one continuous war that lasted thirty years, and that U.S. entry into the struggle in 1898 was not necessary for Cuban victory.

See also **Cuba: Cuba Since 1959; Cuba: The Republic (1898–1959).**

BIBLIOGRAPHY

See Duvon C. Corbitt, "Cuban Revisionist Interpretations of Cuba's Struggle for Independence," *Hispanic American Historical Review* 43 (August 1963): 395–404. A list of Roig's considerable literary and historical output and a chronology of his life appear in Araceli García-Carranza, *Biobibliografía de Emilio Roig de Leuchsenring* (1986).

Additional Bibliography

Pérez, Louis A. *The War of 1898: The United States and Cuba in Historiography.* Chapel Hill: University of North Carolina Press, 1998.

Whitney, Robert. *State and Revolution in Cuba: Mass Mobilization and Political Change, 1920–1940.* Chapel Hill: University of North Carolina Press, 2001.

JOSÉ M. HERNÁNDEZ

ROJAS, ARÍSTIDES (1826–1894). A physician by training, Arístides Rojas is best known for his outstanding contributions to history and natural science research in Venezuela. He wrote prolifically on geology, botany, seismology, geography, pedagogy, literary criticism, and especially on national history and folklore. His impressive collection of print, art, and archaeological objects of Venezuela's past became the core of the Bolivarian Collection now housed at the John Boulton Foundation in Caracas.

Rojas, born on November 5, 1826, was educated with the children of the political elite and was a pupil of Fermín Toro, the renowned educator. Rojas's father's bookstore served as a cultural hub for the most important intellectual and political figures of his time. Rojas started publishing on Venezuelan customs and folklore as a university student during the mid-1840s. He studied medicine at the University of Caracas, graduating in 1852, and began practicing in rural areas. After additional training in the United States and France, Rojas practiced medicine in Puerto Rico, before returning permanently to Venezuela in 1864. While maintaining his medical practice, Rojas published treatises on botany, seismology, and geography and helped establish the Venezuelan Society for Physical and Natural Sciences and created the Bibliography Society.

Upon the death of his wife, he abandoned medicine to dedicate himself fulltime to scholarship. Two of his works—*El elemento vasco en la historia de Venezuela* (1874) and *Estudios indígenas: Contribución a la historia Antigua de Venezuela* (1878)—earned important awards in Venezuela. He helped organize the Venezuelan exhibit for the World's Columbian Exposition of 1893 held in Chicago. A government contract granted in 1890 to gather his entire historical works in a multi-volume set was cut short by his death on March 4, 1894. Rojas enjoyed international recognition and was a member of the Zoological Society of France and of the Academy of Physical and Natural Sciences of Havana; he was an honorary member of the Chilean Academy of Letters. For these accomplishments, Arístides Rojas has been called the founder of professional historical research in Venezuela.

See also **Venezuela: Venezuela since 1830.**

BIBLIOGRAPHY

Grases, Pedro. *Cuatro varones venezolanos: Valentín Espinal, Arístides Rojas, Manuel Segundo Sánchez, Vicente Lecuna.* Caracas, 1953.

Grases, Pedro. *Bibliografía de don Arístides Rojas, 1826–1894,* 2nd ed. Caracas: Fundacíon para el Rescate del Acervo Documental Venezolano, 1977.

LUIS A. GONZÁLEZ

ROJAS, ISAAC

(1906–1993). Isaac Rojas, born in Buenos Aires on December 3, 1906, was an Argentine naval officer. He advanced in his career as a loyal Peronist while the Perón regime was at its zenith (the Peronist Loyalty Medal was bestowed upon him by Eva Perón). Although he was a latecomer to the conspiracy, Rojas was one of the organizers of the 1955 coup d'état that overthrew Perón and became a staunch anti-Peronist. His threat that the navy would bombard oil storage facilities in Buenos Aires and the national oil refinery in La Plata contributed greatly to the success of the uprising.

Made a full admiral of the navy in 1955, Rojas was prominent in Argentine public life from 1955 to 1958, when he served as vice president in the governments of both Eduardo Lonardi and Pedro Aramburu and became renowned for the ferocity of his hard-line anti-Peronist sentiments. Rojas dealt harshly with the participants of the abortive June 1956 uprising of military officers sympathetic to Perón, and supported the execution of its leader, Major General Juan José Valle, and some twenty-six coconspirators. He supported unconditionally the permanent exclusion of Peronists from Argentine politics. He died April 12, 1993.

See also **Aramburu, Pedro Eugenio; Argentina: The Twentieth Century; Lonardi, Eduardo; Perón, Juan Domingo; Perón, María Eva Duarte de.**

BIBLIOGRAPHY

Potash, Robert A. *The Army and Politics in Argentina.* Vol. 2: *1945–1962: Perón to Frondizi.* Stanford, CA: Stanford University Press, 1980.

Rouquié, Alain. *Poder militar y sociedad política en la Argentina.* 2 vols. Translated by Arturo Iglesias Echegaray. Buenos Aires: Emecé, 1982.

JAMES P. BRENNAN
VICENTE PALERMO

ROJAS, MANUEL

(1896–1973). Manuel Rojas (*b.* 8 January 1896; *d.* 11 March 1973), Chilean novelist. The most important storyteller and novelist of his generation, Rojas received the National Award of Literature in 1957. His early work pays tribute to Latin American regionalism, but from the beginning his narratives reveal an anarchist view of the world and demonstrate an awareness of the literary avant garde. The values and experience of laborers and outcasts are represented in Rojas's fiction in terms of pristine anarchism and emotive humanism that are difficult to find in the works of any of his contemporaries. *Lanchas en la bahía* (1932) is the story of a young man's initiation into adult life. Rojas's most important novel is *Hijo de ladrón* (1951), a masterwork of Latin American narrative. It is part of a tetralogy formed by *Mejor que el vino* (1958), *Sombras contra el muro* (1964), and *La oscura vida radiante* (1971), which traces four steps in the life of one man, exploring both personal and social struggles. Rojas also wrote *La ciudad de los Césares* (1936), based on a legend of a Spanish utopia in southern Chile, and *Punta de rieles* (1960), a counterpoint of two defeated men told in thoughts and speech. Among his short stories, closer to Horacio Quiroga's than to Jorge Luis Borges's, are the collections *Hombres del sur* (1926), *El delincuente* (1929), and *Travesía* (1934). Rojas also wrote poetry and numerous essays.

See also **Literature: Spanish America.**

BIBLIOGRAPHY

Myron I. Lichtblau, "Ironic Devices in Manuel Rojas' *Hijo de ladrón,*" in *Symposium* 19, no. 3 (1965): 214–225. Cedomil Goic, "Manuel Rojas," in *Latin American Writers,* edited by Carlos A. Solé and María Isabel Abreu, vol. 2 (1989), pp. 815–820.

Additional Bibliography

Nómez, Naín, and Emmanuel Tornés Reyes, eds. *Manuel Rojas: Estudios críticos.* Santiago de Chile: Editorial Universidad de Santiago, 2005.

Pérez, Floridor. *Manuel Rojas: La novelesca vida de un novelista.* Santiago: Zig-Zag, 1994.

CEDOMIL GOIC

ROJAS, PEDRO JOSÉ

(1818–1874). Pedro José Rojas (*b.* 1818; *d.* 1874), Venezuelan politician and journalist. Rojas began his journalistic career as an editor for the weekly *El Manzanares* (1843–1845). He traveled to Caracas in 1846 and was chosen representative to Congress from Cumaná in 1848. He opposed President José Tadeo Monagas and left the country for the United States, where he connected with General José Antonio Páez, whom he served as personal secretary. With the fall of Monagas in 1858, Rojas returned to Venezuela. After another period of exile, he returned during the days of the Federal War (1859–1863). Rojas promoted the dictatorship of General Páez and, together with Antonio Guzmán Blanco, was one of the principal protagonists of the 1863 Treaty of Coche, which ended the Federal War. After yet another period of exile in the United States and Europe, he returned to Venezuela, where he was imprisoned in 1871 by Guzmán Blanco and later expelled from the country once again. He died in exile.

See also **Federal War (Venezuela 1859–1863); Monagas, José Tadeo.**

BIBLIOGRAPHY

See Pedro José Rojas, *Pedro José Rojas o una pasión al servicio de la política* (1966). A selection of Pedro José Rojas's writings can be found in Congress of the Republic in Venezuela, *Pensamiento político venezolano del siglo XIX,* vols. 7 and 8, *Pedro José Rojas* (1983).

Additional Bibliography

Machado Guzmán, Gustavo. *Historia gráfica de la Guerra Federal de Venezuela: Período de la federación.* Caracas: s.n., 2002.

INÉS QUINTERO

ROJAS, RICARDO (1882–1957).

Ricardo Rojas (*b.* 16 September 1882; *d.* 29 July 1957), Argentine intellectual, historian, and educator. Born in the northern provincial city of Tucumán, Rojas came to Buenos Aires in 1899 to study law, as did many other provincial intellectuals of his generation. He never completed his studies at law school but began to devote himself exclusively to literature, publishing his first poems in 1903.

The patriarch of Argentine letters, Rojas cultivated all literary genres, with the grandeur and uniqueness of the Americas as a common thread. Yet it is as a humanist that he made his most lasting contribution to an understanding of Argentina at the deepest intellectual and cultural levels. The spirit of *argentinidad,* or awareness of a national identity within the wider context of the Americas as a civilization, dominated his thinking. In such works as *Blasón de plata* (Silver Blazon, 1912) and *Eurindia* (1924), Rojas proclaimed the essential greatness of Argentina and all Hispanic America as deriving from a symbiosis of European and indigenous cultures.

In 1912 Rojas became the first professor of Argentine literature at the University of Buenos Aires. Then, in 1922, he founded the Instituto de Literatura Argentina, and for twenty-five years was its inspiration and guiding force. He served as chancellor of the university from 1926 to 1930. Between 1917 and 1921, Rojas published his monumental *Historia de la literatura Argentina,* which is as much an exegesis of Argentine culture as a remarkable account of Argentine literature from colonial times to the modern period.

Rojas also played an important role in Argentine politics. It was through his efforts to form a new political party that the Liga Patriótica was formed in 1919. In 1930, with the fall of President Hipólito Yrigoyen, Rojas supported the Unión Cívica Radical (Popular Radical Party) in its struggle against the power of the oligarchy. As a consequence of his outspoken opposition to the Juan Perón regime (1946–1955), Rojas suffered persecution and the loss of his university position.

See also **Argentina, Political Parties: Radical Party (UCR); Literature: Spanish America.**

BIBLIOGRAPHY

Ismael Moya, *Ricardo Rojas* (1961).

Earl T. Glauert, "Ricardo Rojas and the Emergence of Argentine Cultural Nationalism," in *Hispanic American Historical Review* 43, no. 1 (1963): 1–13.

Alfredo De La Guardia, *Ricardo Rojas, 1882–1957* (1967).

Martin S. Stabb, *In Quest of Identity: Patterns in the Spanish American Essay of Ideas, 1890–1960* (1967), pp. 61–63, 147–149.

Additional Bibliography

Castillo, Horacio. *Ricardo Rojas.* Buenos Aires: Academia Argentina de Letras, 1999.

MYRON I. LICHTBLAU

ROJAS PAÚL, JUAN PABLO (1829–1905).

Juan Pablo Rojas Paúl (*b.* 1829; *d.* 1905), Liberal president of Venezuela (1888–1890). Following a failed coup attempt by General Joaquín Crespo, Rojas Paúl was selected as the presidential candidate by former dictator Antonio Guzmán Blanco. Rojas Paúl took office heading a divided Liberal Party and facing serious civil strife in Venezuela. Nevertheless, his progressive attitudes and generosity soon won over even former enemies, including Crespo. Rojas Paúl reinstated freedom of the press, resurrected the idea of responsible government, and created the National Academy of History in 1888. His efforts to achieve a modicum of liberal democracy were rewarded in 1890 when he successfully and peacefully transferred power to Raimundo Andueza Palacio. He then served as a senator but was exiled by Andueza in 1891.

See also **Andueza Palacio, Raimundo; Guzmán Blanco, Antonio Leocadio; Venezuela: Venezuela since 1830.**

BIBLIOGRAPHY

Francisco González Guinan, *Episodio histórico: Historia del gobierno del doctor Juan Pablo Rojas Paúl* (1925).

Hugo Lequízamon, *Breve historia de Venezuela, 1810–1979* (1980).

John V. Lombardi, *Venezuela: The Search for Order, the Dream of Progress* (1982).

Additional Bibliography

Tavera-Marcano, Carlos Julio. *El gobierno civil de Juan Pablo Rojas Paúl y el guzmanicismo, 1888–1890.* Caracas: Impr. Universitaria, 2004.

KAREN RACINE

ROJAS PINILLA, GUSTAVO (1900–1975).

Gustavo Rojas Pinilla, president of Colombia (1953–1957), was born in Tunja, Boyacá. Rojas attended the Colombian military academy in Bogotá and later studied engineering in the United States. After a stint as a road engineer, he rejoined the Colombian army during the war with Peru in 1932, rising to the rank of lieutenant general by 1949. Despite his Conservative sympathies, on June 13, 1953, Rojas deposed Laureano Gómez in a bloodless coup; his pledge to end the disastrous *violencia* and establish political peace was initially well received by both traditional parties. However by 1956 renewed violence, an economic downturn, and bipartisan opposition to Rojas's own political ambitions had weakened his position both within the armed forces and among the civilian political elites of both parties, and on May 10, 1957, he was forced out by his fellow senior officers.

In 1959 Rojas was convicted of abuses of power by the Colombian Senate, but throughout the 1960s his hazily populist and highly personalist National Popular Alliance (ANAPO) was a thorn in the side of the bipartisan National Front. In April 1970 Rojas narrowly lost the presidential election against the Front candidate, Misael Pastrana Borrero, after a controversial suspension of vote counting by the outgoing president, Carlos Lleras Restrepo. Although ANAPO declined in the 1970s and 1980s under the leadership of Rojas's daughter, María Eugenia Rojas (b. 1932), an armed splinter group developed into the "M–19" or "April 19 movement," named after the date of the alleged electoral fraud against Rojas.

See also **Colombia: Since Independence; Colombia, Political Parties: National Popular Alliance (ANAPO).**

BIBLIOGRAPHY

Martz, John. *Colombia: A Contemporary Political Survey.* Chapel Hill: University of North Carolina Press, 1962.

Berry, R. Albert, et al, eds. *Politics of Compromise: Coalition Government in Colombia.* New Brunswick, NJ: Transaction Books, 1980.

RICHARD STOLLER

ROJAS URTUGUREN, JOSÉ ANTONIO DE (1732–1817).

José Antonio de Rojas Urtuguren (*b.* 1732; *d.* 1817), a precursor of Chilean independence. Educated at the University of San Felipe in Santiago, Rojas spent the 1770s in Spain, where he eagerly imbibed the ideas of the Enlightenment. His involvement in a desultory plot against Spanish rule in Chile in 1780 was never proved, but he remained suspect, and in 1810 was arrested and deported to Peru. Too old to play much of a part in the independence governments of 1810–1814, Rojas, nonetheless, was one of those imprisoned on the Juan Fernández Islands in the South Pacific during the restored colonial regime (1814–1817), which hastened his death.

See also **Chile: Foundations Through Independence.**

BIBLIOGRAPHY

Additional Bibliography

Elliott, J. H. *Empires of the Atlantic World: Britain and Spain in the Americas, 1492–1830.* New Haven, CT: Yale University Press, 2006.

SIMON COLLIER

ROJO, MARÍA   (1946–). María Rojo (*b.* 15 August 1946), Mexican actress. As a child, Rojo debuted in the film *Besos prohibidos.* She later studied acting at the University of Veracruz. Her first starring role was in the film *El apando.* Among her other important feature performances are: *Naufragio, Bajo la metralla, María de mi corazón, Confesiones, Las Poquianchis, Lo que importa es vivir, Rojo amanecer, La tarea, Danzón, Salón México, El callejón de los Milagros, Demasiado Amor,* and *El misterio de los almendros.* Her acting style lends itself to a wide range of roles. One of the finest dramatic actresses in Mexico, Rojo has received more film awards than any actress in the history of the Mexican cinema.

See also **Cinema: From the Silent Film to 1990; Cinema: Since 1990.**

BIBLIOGRAPHY

Luis Reyes De La Maza, *El cine sonoro en México* (1973).

E. Bradford Burns, *Latin American Cinema: Film and History* (1975).

Carl J. Mora, *Mexican Cinema: Reflections of a Society: 1896–1980* (1982).

John King, *Magical Reels: A History of Cinema in Latin America* (1990).

Additional Bibliography

Chon, Noriega. *Visible Nations: Latin American Cinema and Video.* Minneapolis: Univeristy of Minnesota Press, 2000.

Moseley, Rachel. *Fashioning Film Stars: Dress, Culture, Identity.* London: BFI, 2005.

DAVID MACIEL

ROJO, VICENTE   (1932–). Vicente Rojo (*b.* 1932), Spanish painter working in Mexico. Born in Barcelona, Rojo moved in 1949 to Mexico, where he has lived ever since. He is one of the most important exponents of geometric art in Mexico. He studied painting at the Escuela de Pintura y Escultura (La Esmeralda) in Mexico City, and privately with Arturo Souto. He also worked as an assistant for the exiled Spanish artist Miguel Prieto. Rojo's works are in series. From 1966 to 1981 he created the series *Señales* (Signs), *Negaciones* (Negations), *Recuerdos* (Memories), and *Mexico bajo la lluvia* (Mexico Under the Rain). From the late 1980s dates the series *Códices* (Codices), in which Rojo incorporates symbols used in pre-Columbian writing. *Escenas* (Scenes), a series that draws on pre-Columbian imagery, dates from 1992–1993. Rojo's work has been featured in numerous group and solo exhibitions in Mexico, the United States, and Europe. In 1997, he had an exhibition at the Reina Sofia Museum in Madrid. In 1998, he was elected a member of Mexico's Colegio Nacional.

See also **Art: The Twentieth Century; Indigenous Languages.**

BIBLIOGRAPHY

Juan García Ponce, *Vicente Rojo* (1971).

Jorge Alberto Manrique, Ida Rodríguez Prampolini, Juan Ache, Xavier Moyssén, and Teresa Del Conde, *El geometrismo mexicano* (1977).

Museo De Arte Moderno De México, *Vicente Rojo,* (1981).

Additional Bibliography

Dreben, Lelia. *Vicente Rojo: El arte de las variaciones sutiles.* Mexico City: Consejo Nacional para la Cultura y las Artes, Dirección General de Publicaciones, 1996.

Rojo, Vicente. *Vicente Rojo: Dos estaciones.* Monterrey, Mexico: Universidad Autónoma de Nuevo León, 2006.

ILONA KATZEW

ROKHA, PABLO DE (1894–1968). Pablo de Rokha (*b.* 17 October 1894; *d.* 10 September 1968), Chilean poet. Born Carlos Díaz Loyola but taking the pen name Pablo de Rokha, this writer is seen by some critics as one of the main figures of the Chilean avantgarde. He had a tempestuous personality that put him in frequent conflict with Vicente

Huidobro and Pablo Neruda (*Neruda y yo* [1955]). Rokha's poetic voice was one of ideological and socialist bias; his inordinate epic tone encompassed both the revolutionary facts and figures of world history and the daily life of the local peasant. The hypertrophic "I" of his poetry takes on Nietzschean dimensions in its Dionysian exultation and sensual enjoyment. His poetic diction has its distinct features in verbal violence, lexical creativity, prosaism, and materialist images; Rokha's verse is full of vital gestures and Pantagruelian rural meals. A Marxist, Rokha never accepted the party discipline or espoused any official party line. His huge number of works include *Los quemidos* (1922), *Escritura de Raimondo Contreras* (1929), *Jesucristo* (1933), *Gran temperatura* (1937), *Morfología del espanto* (1942), *Canto al ejército rojo* (1944), *Fuego negro* (1953), and *Canto de fuego a China Popular* (1963). Although addressed to the popular reader, his works, due to their baroque poetic diction and mixture of cosmopolitanism and popular culture, were largely inaccessible to the masses. In 1965 he received the National Literary Award. Two years later, he shot himself.

See also **Literature: Spanish America; Neruda, Pablo.**

BIBLIOGRAPHY

Fernando Lamberg, *Vida y obra de Pablo de Rokha* (1965).

Mario Ferrero, *Pablo de Rokha, guerrillero de la poesía* (1967).

Naim Nómez, *Pablo de Rokha, una escritura en movimiento* (1988).

Additional Bibliography

Zerán, Faride. *La guerrilla literaria: Huidobro, de Rokha, Neruda.* Providencia, Santiago, Chile: Editorial Sudamericana, 1997.

CEDOMIL GOIC

ROKHA, WINÉTT DE (1894–1951).

Winétt de Rokha (*b.* 7 July 1894; *d.* 7 August 1951), Chilean poet. Born Luisa Anabalón Sanderson, de Rokha published her first poetic works under the pseudonym Juana Inés de la Cruz, a seventeenth-century Mexican poet. After her marriage to the poet Pablo de Rokha, she adopted the literary name Winétt de Rokha. Her poetic works include, in a romantic first stage, *Lo que me dijo el silencio* (1915) and *Horas*

de sol (1915). In a second stage, she appropriated the Spanish-American avant garde's poetic diction, as shown in *Formas del sueño* (1927). A new stage began with *Cantoral* (1936), followed by *Oniromancia* (1945), *El valle pierde su atmósfera* (1949), which was included in Pablo de Rokha's *Arenga sobre el arte,* and *Suma y destino* (1951). *Antología* (1953) is a selection of her poetry published posthumously. The main characteristic of de Rokha's poetry in its final form is the adoption of a social and revolutionary hyperbolic tone, in permanent dialogue with Pablo de Rokha.

See also **Literature: Spanish America.**

BIBLIOGRAPHY

Oreste Plath, *Poetas y poesía de Chile* (1941), pp. 51–62.

Antonio De Undurraga, *Atlas de la poesía de Chile, 1900–1957* (1958), pp. 253–256.

Additional Bibliography

Villegas Morales, Juan. "El discurso lírico de Winett de Rokha: la otra cara de la mujer poeta." *Hispamérica* 18:53–54 (Aug.–Dec. 1989): 75–87.

CEDOMIL GOIC

ROLDÁN, AMADEO (1900–1939).

Amadeo Roldán (*b.* 12 July 1900; *d.* 2 March 1939), Cuban composer, conductor, and violinist. Born in Paris of Cuban parents, Roldán settled in Havana in 1921 after studying with A. F. Bordas and Conrado del Campo in Spain. He continued his studies with Pedro Sanjuan in Cuba and established the Society of Chamber Music in 1921. First appointed concertmaster of the Havana Philharmonic Orchestra in 1924, he rose to conductor in 1932. He served as director and taught at the Havana Conservatory from 1934 until his death.

Among the first to bring elements of African Cuban folklore to the concert hall, his works are filled with African Cuban mythology and his collaboration with Alejo Carpentier brought forth the first African Cuban ballet on the island. Associated with the group of intellectuals who invigorated Cuban artistic life in the 1920s and 1930s, he was a guiding spirit for the younger generation of Cuban composers.

See also **Music: Art Music.**

BIBLIOGRAPHY

Roldán's best-known works are *Overture on Cuban Themes* (1925) and *Motivos de son* (1934). For information on his life, see *Composers of the Americas,* edited by Pan American Union (1955), p. 77; L. Argeliers, "Las obras para piano de Amadeo Roldán," in *Revista de música* i/4 (Havana, n.d.): 112; Oscar Thompson, ed., *International Cyclopedia of Musicians and Music,* 11th ed. (1985).

Additional Bibliography

Carpentier, Alejo. *La música en Cuba.* La Habana: Letras Cubanas, 2004.

Henríquez, María Antonieta, and José Piñeiro Díaz. *Amadeo Roldán: Testimonios.* La Habana: Letras Cubanas, 2001.

JACQUELYN BRIGGS KENT

ROLDÁN, FRANCISCO (?–1502).

Francisco Roldán (*d.* 1502), a native of Donjimeno, Spain; appointed *alcalde mayor* (chief justice) in Hispaniola by Christopher Columbus. Poverty and the harsh, inept government of Bartholomew and Diego Columbus led to discontent among the Spanish settlers. In 1497 they rallied to the sympathetic Roldán, who rebelled with some ninety men, a number perhaps greater than those reliably loyal to the Columbus brothers. Withdrawing to the interior of the island, the rebels pursued lives of idleness, rape, and pillage. When Christopher Columbus returned to Hispaniola in 1498, having been absent for two years, he found the colony in chaos; after weighing the gravity of the situation, he acceded to the rebels' demands in 1499. In addition to amnesty, each was to have an allotment of Indian labor, which, with some modifications, became known as a *repartimiento* and, eventually, as *encomienda.* Roldán, once again loyal to Columbus, assisted in subduing other revolts. He was lost at sea in 1502.

See also **Columbus, Christopher; Hispaniola.**

BIBLIOGRAPHY

Roldán's activities are covered in Troy Floyd, *The Columbus Dynasty in the Caribbean, 1492–1526* (1973). See also Hubert Howe Bancroft, *History of Central America,* vol. 1 (1882); and Carl Ortwin Sauer, *The Early Spanish Main* (1966).

Additional Bibliography

Deagan, Kathleen A., and José María Cruxent. *Columbus' Outpost among the Taínos: Spain and America at La Isabela, 1493–1498.* New Haven, CT: Yale University Press, 2002.

WILLIAM L. SHERMAN

ROLDÓS AGUILERA, JAIME (1940–1981).

Jaime Roldós Aguilera (*b.* 5 November 1940; *d.* 24 May 1981), president of Ecuador (1979–1981). While a student at the University of Guayaquil, Roldós became a political activist. After completing a law degree, he entered private practice, taught at the University of Guayaquil, and was active in the Concentration of Popular Forces (CFP) led by Asaad Bucaram. Elected deputy from Guayas in 1968 and 1970, he became a member of the Comisión Legislativa Permanente and headed a second commission appointed by the military government in 1978 to prepare for the return to civilian rule. That same year the CFP selected him to run for the presidency after the party's leader, Asaad Bucaram, was disqualified as a candidate by the military.

Roldós represented a new generation of political leaders who were committed to significant social and economic reform. The reformist program was doomed, however, when the CFP split into factions supporting Roldós and his former mentor Asaad Bucaram. Bucaram used his position as president of the Chamber of Representatives to block presidential initiatives to implement structural change, to maintain fiscal restraint, and to adopt a development program that subordinated regional demands to national objectives. Public support for the government eroded as a result of the legislative impasse. Even the renewed threat of a border conflict with Peru in January 1981 failed to provide the administration sustained public support. Growing economic problems resulting from declines in the world-market price for petroleum, budget deficits, and rising international interest rates forced the government to adopt austerity measures that alienated large segments of the public. The administration was facing growing challenges to its authority when Jaime Roldós died in the crash of a military plane while touring the contested border with Peru.

See also **Bucaram Elmhalin, Asaad; Ecuador: Since 1830; Ecuador-Peru Boundary Disputes.**

BIBLIOGRAPHY

Howard Handelman, "The Dilemma of Ecuadorian Democracy. Part I, Jaime Roldós and the Politics of Deadlock," in *UFSI Reports* 34 (1984).

David W. Schodt, *Ecuador: An Andean Enigma* (1987), esp. pp. 129–144.

John D. Martz, *Politics and Petroleum in Ecuador* (1987), esp. pp. 224–303.

Additional Bibliography

Febres Cordero, Francisco. *De Flores a flores y miel.* Quito: Ojo de Pez, 1996.

Galarza Zavala, Jaime. *Operación Gavilan.* Cuenca, Ecuador: Ninacuru, 1995.

LINDA ALEXANDER RODRÍGUEZ

ROLÓN, RAIMUNDO (1903–1981).

Raimundo Rolón (*b.* 1903; *d.* 1981), a prominent Paraguayan soldier and politician. During the Chaco War (1932–1935), he served as General José Félix Estigarribia's chief of operations. Following the February Revolution (17 February 1936) he retired from the army. With the overthrow of Rafael Franco by a conservative military faction on 13 August 1937, Rolón was reinstated as the chief of staff. During 1949 he served as the ambassador to Brazil and as the minister of defense. Between 30 January and 27 February 1949 he was the provisional president of Paraguay. Rolón wrote numerous books on the Chaco War, the most important being *La guerra del Chaco, campaña de 1934,* 2 vols. (1962–1963).

See also **Chaco War; Estigarribia, Antonio de la Cruz; Paraguay: The Twentieth Century.**

ROBERT SCHEINA

ROMÁN DE NÚÑEZ, SOLEDAD

(1835–1924). Soledad Román de Núñez (*b.* 6 October 1835; *d.* 19 October 1924), second wife of Colombian president Rafael Núñez. Román became a controversial figure in strongly Catholic Colombia because she married Núñez in a civil ceremony in 1877 while his first wife was still alive. She is also believed to have influenced his political opinions.

A native of Cartagena like Núñez, Román was the daughter of a prominent pharmacist. She became acquainted with Núñez as a girl and renewed the friendship upon his return to Colombia in 1874 after a long absence abroad. Because Núñez was divorced from Dolores Gallego, whom he had wed in a Catholic ceremony in 1851, Catholics could not regard his marriage to Román as valid, and some women boycotted her when she traveled to Bogotá as first lady in 1884. After Gallego's death in 1889, she and Núñez were remarried in a religious ceremony. A staunch Conservative, Román is credited with encouraging Núñez, a Liberal, to move toward an accommodation with the Conservative Party.

See also **Núñez Moledo, Rafael.**

BIBLIOGRAPHY

Juan Pablo Llinás, *Soledad Román* (1986).

Helen Delpar, "Soledad Román de Núñez: A President's Wife," in *The Human Tradition in Latin America: The Nineteenth Century,* edited by Judith Ewell and William H. Beezeley (1989), pp. 128–140.

Additional Bibliography

Pombo Román, Marcela de. *A Rafael Núñez y Soledad Román.* Cartagena de Indias, Colombia: Centro de Editorial Fondo Rotatorio, 2000.

Liévano Aguirre, Indalecio. *Rafael Núñez.* Bogotá: Intermedio, 2002.

HELEN DELPAR

ROMAY Y VALDÉS CHACÓN, TOMÁS (1764–1849).

Tomás Romay y Valdés Chacón (*b.* 21 December 1764; *d.* 30 March 1849), Cuban physician and scientist. Romay, a native of Havana, achieved prominence in Cuba between 1790 and 1830, a period of transition during which Cubans discovered their own national identity. A writer, orator, and poet, he was one of the founders in 1790 of *Papel Periódico,* the first Cuban newspaper. He was also a professor of philosophy at the University of Havana and a mentor of students and patron of the arts. Probably Romay's greatest achievement was to introduce in Cuba the vaccine against smallpox and to initiate early investigations into the causes of yellow fever. He was also a founding member of the Sociedad Patriótica, one of the key institutions in the development of colonial Cuba. In a very real sense he was the initiator of the scientific movement in Cuba. Romay died in Havana.

See also **Diseases; Medicine: The Modern Era; Science.**

BIBLIOGRAPHY

José López Sánchez, *Tomás Romay y el origen de la ciencia en Cuba*, 2d rev. ed. (1964).

Additional Bibliography

López Sánchez, José. *Vida y obra del sabio médico habanero Tomás Romay Chacón.* La Habana: Editorial Científico-Técnica, 2004.

JOSÉ M. HERNÁNDEZ

ROMERO, CARLOS HUMBERTO

(1924–). Carlos Humberto Romero (*b.* 1924), president of El Salvador (1977–1979). Educated at the National Military Academy, Romero rose through the ranks to become minister of defense during the presidency of Arturo Armando Molina (1972–1977). He resigned that post to become the military-backed PCN (Partido de Conciliación Nacional) candidate in 1977.

Aligned with the agro-exporting wing of the PCN, Romero ended the mild reformism of the Julio A. Rivera, Fidel Sánchez Hernández and Arturo Armando Molina administrations (1960–1977), thereby galvanizing the guerrilla and urban popular organizations into mass action. Responding to appeals by business and agro-export groups to curb the agitation, Romero's repressive policies alienated both the Roman Catholic Church (producing the so-called war of the Romeros—a reference to the struggle between President Romero and Oscar Arnulfo Romero, archbishop of El Salvador, who was assassinated by a right-wing death squad in 1980) and the Jimmy Carter administration (1977–1981). With the tacit approval of the United States, he was overthrown by a group of progressive officers on 15 October 1979 and went into exile to Guatemala.

See also **El Salvador; Molina, Arturo Armando; Romero, Oscar Arnulfo.**

BIBLIOGRAPHY

Enrique Baloyra, *El Salvador in Transition* (1982).

James Dunkerley, *The Long War: Dictatorship and Revolution in El Salvador* (1982).

Steffen W. Schmidt, *El Salvador: America's Next Vietnam?* (1983).

Additional Bibliography

Brockett, Charles D. *Political Movements and Violence in Central America.* Cambridge, UK; New York: Cambridge University Press, 2005.

Francisco Lazo M. *El sistema político salvadoreño y sus perspectivas: Notas para la discusión.* San Salvador, El Salvador: CINAS, 1992.

Latin America Bureau. *El Salvador under General Romero: An Analysis of the First Nine Months of the Regime of President Romero.* London: Latin America Bureau, 1979.

Rico-Martínez, Francisco. *Ideología y sociedad: El Salvador, 1975–1983.* México, D.F.: Edición Taller de Arte e Ideología, 1990.

ROLAND H. EBEL

ROMERO, EMILIO (1899–1993). Emilio

Romero (*b.* 16 February 1899; *d.* 1993), Peruvian geographer, economist, lawyer, and writer. Born in Puno, Romero was the son of Eladio and Honorata Padilla Romero. He studied at schools in Arequipa and Lima, receiving his doctorate at the National University of Arequipa in 1932. Between 1920 and 1933, Romero taught school at the secondary and university levels and, beginning in the 1930s, began a government career while continuing to hold academic positions. After holding a ministerial post as chief of the Bureau of Colonization and Mountain Lands, he was elected deputy to the Constituent Congress in 1932–1933. In 1939, he became director of commerce and finance and continued his political career as a senator from Puno from 1945 to 1948.

In the 1950s, Romero wrote essays on the Indian practice of chewing coca leaves, claiming that the Indian use of the hallucinogen coca was similar to, but no more damaging than, the North American practice of chewing gum or smoking cigarettes. In a 1955 book, *Perú por los senderos de América,* he also praised the Incas for their religion and way of life, insisting that their idea of love and marriage surpassed that of the Spaniards who had conquered them.

See also **Incas, The.**

BIBLIOGRAPHY

Percy Alvin Martin, *Who's Who in Latin America* (1940).

Fredrick B. Pike, *The Modern History of Peru* (1967) p. 10.

Marvin Alisky, *Historical Dictionary of Peru* (1979), p. 91.

Additional Bibliography

Luque Talaván, Miguel. "Bibliografía del Doctor Emilio Romero Padilla (Puno 1899–Lima 1993)." *Revista complutense de historia de América* 28 (2002): 213–216.

Padilla, Feliciano. *Antología comentada de la literatura puneña*. Peru: Fondo Editorial Cultura Peruana, 2005.

JACK RAY THOMAS

ROMERO, FRANCISCO (1891–1962).

Francisco Romero (*b*. 19 June 1891; *d*. 7 October 1962), Argentine philosopher who is recognized as one of the most important philosophers in Latin America and the Spanish-speaking world in general. Romero was born in Seville, Spain, and attended a military school in Argentina. He became a disciple of Alejandro Korn, and was professor of philosophy at the Universities of Buenos Aires and La Plata. The German philosophy that flourished during the first three decades of the twentieth century, represented in the writings of Wilhelm Dilthey, Edmund Husserl, Nicolai Hartmann, and Max Scheler, had a great influence on the maturation of Romero's philosophical thought. Within this framework, he made original contributions in his chief work, *Theory of Man* (1964), a philosophical anthropology based on the concept of "intentionality" as a characteristic distinguishing the human psyche from that of animals. *Theory of Man* is also the outline of a metaphysics founded on the idea of the spirit as an absolute transcendence.

Part of Romero's work concerned itself with the diffusion—as well as the interpretation—of philosophy from the Renaissance to the twentieth century. Unlike most other Latin American philosophers, he was interested in the history and structure of philosophy, as can be seen in *Sobre la historia de la filosofía* (1943) and *La estructura de la historia de la*

filosofía y otros ensayos (1967). Through his writings and personal activities, he became one of the great inspirations to the development of professional philosophy in Latin American and to the study of Latin American thought.

See also **Korn, Alejandro; Philosophy: Overview.**

BIBLIOGRAPHY

Majorie Silliman Harris, *Franciso Romero on Problems of Philosophy* (1960).

Universidad De Buenos Aires, *Homenaje a Francisco Romero* (1964).

Arturo Ardao et al., *Francisco Romero, maestro de la filosofía latinoamericana* (1983).

Additional Bibliography

Speroni, José Luis, and Jorge Victoriano Alonso. *El pensamiento de Francisco Romero: Retrato de un filósofo argentine del siglo XX*. Buenos Aires: Edivérn, 2001.

JUAN CARLOS TORCHIA ESTRADA

ROMERO, JOSÉ LUIS (1909–1977).

José Luis Romero (*b*. 24 March 1909; *d*. 2 March 1977), Argentine historian. Romero was born in Buenos Aires and earned a doctorate in history at the University of La Plata. His work developed in the areas of social history and the history of culture and ideas. As a medievalist, he studied the formation and development of the bourgeoisie in *La revolución burguesa en el mundo feudal* (1967) and *Crisis y orden en el mundo feudoburgués* (1980). He also wrote works interpreting Latin American and Argentine history, the most important of which is *Latinoamérica: Las ciudades y las ideas* (1976). In this book, he tries to understand the role urban societies played in the Latin American historical process from colonial days to the twentieth century. He pursued the relationships between ideologies and historical reality in Latin America in *El pensamiento político de la derecha latinoamericana* (1970) and *Latinoamérica: Situaciones e ideologías* (1967).

Romero's classic work on Argentina is *A History of Argentine Political Thought* (1963), an accurate and widely read synthesis. He investigated ideas in relation to societal changes in *El desarrollo de las ideas en la sociedad argentina del siglo XX* (1965).

Possessed of a great talent for historical interpretation, Romero also considered the history of historiography itself in *De Herodoto a Pobilio* (1952) and *Maquiavelo historiador,* 3d ed. (1986). In *La historia y la vida* (1945), he expressed his views on the theory of history.

See also **Anthropology; Argentina: The Colonial Period.**

BIBLIOGRAPHY

Félix Luna, *Conversaciones con José Luis Romero sobre una Argentina con historia, política y democracia* (1976).

Tulio Halperín Donghi, "José Luis Romero y su lugar en la historiografía argentina," in *Desarrollo Económico* 20 (1980):78.

Sergio Bagú et al., *De historia e historiadores: Homenaje a José Luis Romero* (1982).

Additional Bibliography

Betancourt Mendieta, Alexander. *Historia, ciudad e ideas: La obra de José Luis Romero.* México: Universidad Nacional Autónoma de México, 2001.

Iturrieta, Aníbel, and Antonio Lago Carballo. *El pensamiento político argentino contemporáneo.* Buenos Aires: Grupo Editor Latinoamericano, 1994.

JUAN CARLOS TORCHIA ESTRADA

ROMERO, JOSÉ RUBÉN (1890–1952).

José Rubén Romero (*b.* 25 September 1890; *d.* 4 July 1952), Mexican writer. Although Romero wrote poetry and served as a diplomat, his reputation rests upon his achievements as a novelist of the Mexican Revolution. Born in Cotija, Michoacán, Romero took a nostalgic, humorous, and often satirical view of provincial life during the early decades of the twentieth century. He is most famous for a picaresque novel, *La vida inútil de Pito Pérez* (The Futile Life of Pito Pérez, 1938). In addition, two autobiographical novels, *Apuntes de un lugareño* (Notes of a Villager, 1932) and *Desbandada* (Disbandment, 1934), recount Romero's experience of the Mexican Revolution as it arrived in small provincial towns, and serve as vehicles for his trademark irony as a social critic. He was named to the Mexican Academy of Language in 1941. Romero died in Mexico City.

See also **Mexico, Wars and Revolutions: Mexican Revolution.**

BIBLIOGRAPHY

Raúl Arreola Cortés, *José Rubén Romero: Vida y obra* (1946, 1990).

David William Foster and Virginia Ramos Foster, eds., *Modern Latin American Literature,* vol. 2 (1975), pp. 277–282.

Luis Leal, "José Rubén Romero," in *Latin American Writers,* vol. 2, edited by Carlos A. Solé and Maria Isabel Abreu (1989), pp. 711–715.

Additional Bibliography

Cárdenas Fernández, Blanca. *Influencias e ideología en la obra de Rubén Romero.* Morelia, Michoacán, México: Universidad Michoacana de San Nicolás de Hidalgo, 1995.

Martínez, José Luis. *José Rubén Romero: Vida y obra.* México: Universidad Nacional Autónoma de México, 2001.

DANNY J. ANDERSON

ROMERO, MATÍAS (1837–1898).

Matías Romero (*b.* 24 February 1837; *d.* 30 December 1898), Mexican politician and diplomat. Romero was born in Oaxaca, in southwestern Mexico, the birthplace of fellow Mexican liberal leaders Benito Pablo Juárez, Porfirio Díaz, and Ignacio Mariscal. Romero filled important posts in the Mexican government for thirty-eight years of his life, beginning with the Foreign Relations Ministry in 1857. Romero's service included a total of twenty-six years as secretary of the legation, chargé, or minister to the United States (1859–1868, 1882–1892, 1893–1898), a total of about seven years as secretary of the treasury (1868–1872, 1877–1879, 1892–1893), and two years in the Mexican Senate (1875–1877).

Educated as a lawyer, Romero joined the Liberal government under President Benito Juárez during La Reforma (1857–1861). As a protégé of Juárez, he served some time as an unpaid employee in the Ministry of Foreign Relations before being given a salaried post. When the outbreak of the American Civil War thrust considerable responsibility upon the twenty-four-year-old Romero, he already had acquired two years of experience in the United States as secretary of the legation and chargé d'affaires. During the American Civil War and early Reconstruction, he labored tirelessly in establishing personal contacts with U.S. political, military, and business leaders such as Montgomery Blair, Benjamin Wade, Henry Winter Davis, Ulysses S. Grant, and John Schofield. Romero returned to Mexico briefly in late 1867, but was picked to negotiate the U.S.–Mexican Claims Agreement of 1868 in order to facilitate Mexico's credit rating with potential American investors. He married Lucretia Allen on 16 July 1868 just before becoming, at thirty-one, Juárez's secretary of the treasury.

Juárez's decision to seek reelection in 1872 displeased Romero, who resigned to pursue coffee culture in southern Mexico. This activity lasted only three years, in part because of the hostility of the Guatemalan president, Justo Rufino Barrios, and in part because Romero was elected to the Mexican Senate in 1875. After serving two years as senator, he became Porfirio Díaz's secretary of the treasury.

In 1879 failing health compelled Romero to resign. Battling recurring stomach problems, which had plagued him since his youth, he traveled to the United States to consult medical specialists. In 1880 and 1881, while recuperating, he was involved in several railroad schemes with former U.S. president Ulysses S. Grant, Albert K. Owen, Hiram Barney, and others. Then, from 1882 until his death, Romero served as minister to the United States, except for a short period from mid-1892 until early 1893, when he returned to Mexico for his third period as secretary of the treasury. He died in Washington on 30 December 1898, after an attack of appendicitis.

See also **Díaz, Porfirio; Juárez, Benito.**

BIBLIOGRAPHY

Correspondencia de la legación mexicana en Washington durante la intervención extranjera, 10 vols. (1870–1892).

Emma Cosío Villegas, ed., *Diario Personal (1855–1865)* (1960), pp. vii–xx.

Guadalupe Monroy Huitrón, ed., *Archivo histórico de Matías Romero*, vol. 1 (1965) pp. vii–xx.

Harry Bernstein, *Matías Romero, 1837–1898* (1973).

Thomas Schoonover, *Dollars over Dominion: The Triumph of Liberalism in Mexican–United States Relations, 1861–1867* (1978).

Thomas Schoonover, ed., *Mexican Lobby: Matías Romero in Washington, 1861–1867* (1986), and *A Mexican View of America in the 1860s: A Foreign Diplomat Describes the Civil War and Reconstruction* (1991).

Additional Bibliography

Márquez, Graciela. *La administración hacendaria de Matías Romero*. México: Centro de Estudios Económicos, El Colegio de México, 1999.

Torrent y Díaz, Eduardo. *Epistolario liberal: En el archivo histórico del Banco de México, Benito Juárez, Matías Romero, correspondencia 1856–1872*. México: Banco de México, 2003.

THOMAS SCHOONOVER

ROMERO, OSCAR ARNULFO (1917–1980). Oscar Arnulfo Romero (*b*. 15 August 1917; *d*. 24 March 1980), archbishop of El Salvador (1977–1980). Romero was born in Ciudad Barrios and originally apprenticed as a carpenter, but his early religious inclinations won him over and in 1931 he enrolled in San Miguel seminary. In 1937 he progressed to the National Seminary, then proceeded to Rome to study at the Gregorian University. He was ordained in 1942 and began a doctorate in ascetic theology, but World War II curtailed his studies. He returned to El Salvador and served his home parish until he was elevated to monsignor in 1967. Shortly thereafter, Romero was appointed to the National Bishops' Conference and quickly earned additional responsibilities, including auxiliary bishop (1970), editor of the archdiocesan newspaper *Orientación* (1971), bishop of Santiago de María (1974), and membership on the Pontifical Commission for Latin America (1975). Even at this late date, Romero still clung to a moderate, traditional interpretation of Catholic doctrines. He warned against the dangers of a politicized priesthood and instead advocated the higher ideals of brotherhood, faith, and charity. Although he frequently quoted the teachings of the Second Vatican Council, he refrained from mentioning those of the more radical conference of Catholic bishops at Medellín in 1968.

To the surprise of many, Romero was chosen over the equally qualified Arturo Rivera y Damas as archbishop of El Salvador in February 1977. The

Mourners at Archbishop Romero's funeral, San Salvador, March 30, 1980. Army sharpshooters opened fire on the crowd of thousands who had gathered for Romero's funeral mass. Approximately forty people died in the ensuing panic. PHOTO BY HARRY MATTISON

shy, retiring new archbishop faced growing tensions between church and state, and within the church itself. Shortly after his installation, Romero's close friend Father Rutilio Grande was murdered on his way to visit parishioners. When the government failed to investigate and instead stepped up its attacks on the Church by expelling several priests, Archbishop Romero withdrew his support for the government and refused to attend the presidential inauguration of Carlos Humberto Romero (no relation) in 1977. Despite the rising tide of violence, Romero still tried to distance the Church from the new liberation theology and denied the priests permission to participate in political organizations. As the situation deteriorated, Romero's position became untenable and the moderate archbishop metamorphosed into an impassioned crusader against the violation of human rights in El Salvador. He used his sermons to preach the equality and dignity of all peoples and set up a commission to monitor and document the abuses of power by governmental authorities.

For Romero's efforts the British Parliament nominated him for the Nobel Peace Prize. In February 1980 Romero angered the Vatican by speaking out against U.S. military aid to El Salvador, which he claimed would lead to further human rights abuses. On 24 March he was assassinated while saying evening mass. His death removed a powerful voice for peace in El Salvador and contributed to the bitterness of the struggle. Archbishop Romero remains a powerful symbol of the new direction of the Catholic Church in Latin America.

See also **Catholic Church: The Modern Period.**

BIBLIOGRAPHY

Plácido Erdozain, *Archbishop Romero: Martyr of Salvador* (1981).

James R. Brockman, *The Word Remains: A Life of Oscar Romero* (1982).

Jesús Delgado, *Oscar A. Romero: Biografía* (1986).

Jon Sobrino, *Archbishop Romero: Memories and Reflections* (1960).

Additional Bibliography

Dennis, Marie, Renny Golden, and Scott Wright. *Oscar Romero: Reflections on His Life and Writings*. Maryknoll, NY: Orbis Books, 2000.

Pelton, Robert S., Robert L. Ball, and Kyle Markham. *Monsignor Romero: A Bishop for the Third Millennium*. Notre Dame, IN: University of Notre Dame Press, 2004.

KAREN RACINE

ROMERO, SÍLVIO (1851–1914). Sílvio Romero (*b.* 21 April 1851; *d.* 18 June 1914), Brazilian critic and historian of literature. Silvio Vasconcelos da Silveira Ramos Romero was born in Lagarto, Sergipe, and began his intellectual life in Recife, Pernambuco, where he was the leader, with Tobias Barreto, of the Escola de Recife, a group advocating a change from romanticism to realism. Romero criticized Antônio Federico de Castro Alves, one of the most important Brazilian romantic poets; he debated Joaquin Maria Machado De Assis, the great novelist of realism; and he opposed José Veríssimo, who studied Brazilian literature from the artistic point of view. Romero followed the sociological method in his literary criticism and was one of the most significant members of the Brazilian naturalistic movement, searching in social life for the source of literary creation.

Romero's books include *Cantos do fim do século* (1878), poetry; *Introdução à história da literatura brasileira* (1882) and *Estudos de literatura contemporânea* (1885), criticism; *Contos populares do Brasil* (1883) and *Estudos sobre a poesia popular no Brasil* (1888), folklore; and *Doutrina contra doutrina: O evolucionismo e o positivismo no Brasil* (1894) and *As oligarquias e sua classificação* (1908), sociological meditation. His most important book

as a critic is *História da literatura brasileira* (1888), the first systematization of Brazilian literature. He died in Rio de Janeiro, where he had lived since 1876.

See also **Literature: Brazil.**

BIBLIOGRAPHY

Antônio Cândido De Melo E Souza, *Introdução ao método crítico de Sílvio Romero* (1945).

Ari Machado Guimarães, *Sílvio Romero* (1951).

Additional Bibliography

Matos, Cláudia. *A poesia popular na república das letras: Sílvio Romero folclorista*. Rio de Janeiro: Editora UFRJ, 1994.

Mota, Maria Aparecida Rezende. *Sílvio Romero: Dilemmas e combates no Brasil da virada do século XX*. Rio de Janeiro: FGV Editora, 2000.

ELIANA MARIA REA GOLDSCHMIDT

ROMERO BARCELÓ, CARLOS (1932–). Carlos Romero Barceló (*b.* 4 September 1932), governor of Puerto Rico (1977–1980; 1981–1984). Romero Barceló was educated at Phillips Exeter Academy and at Yale University. He earned a law degree from the University of Puerto Rico in 1956. Romero Barceló helped found the nonpartisan coalition *Ciudadanos Pro Estada 51* (Citizens for State 51), and in 1968 he was elected mayor of San Juan. First elected governor in 1976, he was an advocate of statehood for Puerto Rico. He believed that Puerto Rico as a commonwealth could not compete for federal funds, equal citizenship, and security from the United States government.

On 25 July 1978, Commonwealth Day, two dissidents were assassinated by police, and five years later a cover-up of the incident was exposed. Romero Barceló lost the 1984 elections in the aftermath of the investigations. From 1993 to 2001 he served as resident commissioner of Puerto Rico and took up residency in Washington D.C. He was not re-elected for a third term, being defeated by Luis Fortuno, but he remained active in the Progressive Party of Puerto Rico (PNP).

See also **Puerto Rico, Political Parties: Overview.**

BIBLIOGRAPHY

Carlos Romero Barceló, *Statehood Is for the Poor* (1974).

Antonio Quiñones Calderón, *El Libro de Puerto Rico* (1983), pp. 58–59.

Manuel Suárez, *Requiem on Cerro Maravilla: The Police Murders in Puerto Rico and the U.S. Government Coverup* (1987).

Additional Bibliography

Barbosa Muñiz, José. *El fracaso de la administración de Carlos Romero Barceló*. Rio Piedras: Barbosa Muñiz, 1988.

CHRISTOPHER T. BOWEN

ROMERO DE TERREROS, PEDRO

(1710–1781). Pedro Romero de Terreros (*b.* 28 June 1710; *d.* 27 November 1781), mining entrepreneur. One of the outstanding miners of eighteenth-century New Spain, Pedro Terreros was born in western Andalucia (modern Huelva) in Spain and before 1733 migrated to the Mexican city of Querétaro, where he became a manager of the business of a maternal uncle. In 1735, upon the death of his uncle, Terreros expanded this already substantial wholesale-retail business. By 1741 he had become the financier (*aviador*) and then the partner in a silver mine near Pachuca. When his partner, José Alejandro Bustamante, died in 1750, Terreros inherited the mines, and within fifteen years, became the principal entrepreneur in the region. When miners were unable to repay loans from Terreros, he became the owner of their mines. Beyond his abundant financial resources and managerial skills, he displayed considerable talent in the construction of refining haciendas and the planning of drainage works that permitted the exploitation of rich veins of ore. His success as an entrepreneur was soured by troubled relations with workers in the mines and refining haciendas.

In 1775 Terreros founded in Mexico City the first Monte de Piedad—a credit institution that loaned money for pawned articles. As early as the 1750s, donations of dowries for nuns and the financing of the missions of San Saba in Texas (1756–1758) and many other Franciscan projects established his reputation as a generous supporter of eccelesiastical projects. His contributions to the government included money to construct warships and loans to establish a lottery. He also purchased the former Jesuit haciendas that had belonged to the novitiate of Tepozotlán and the Colegio de San Pedro y San Pablo, which made him one of the leading landowners in New Spain. He died in San Miguel Regla.

See also **Avio; Mining: Colonial Spanish America.**

BIBLIOGRAPHY

A biography written by his descendant, Manuel Romero De Terreros is entitled *El Conde de Regla: Creso de Nueva España* (1943). David A. Brading's *Miners and Merchants in Bourbon Mexico* (1971) has considerable information about Terreros. Edith Couturier, "The Philanthropic Activities of Pedro Romero de Terreros: First Count of Regla," in *The Americas* 32, no. 1 (July 1975): 13–29, and Doris Ladd, *The Making of a Strike: Mexican Silver Workers' Struggles in Real del Monte, 1766–1775* (1988), explore different aspects of his life. Alan Probert, "Pedro Romero de Terreros: The Genius of the Vizcaina Vein," in *Journal of the West* 14, no. 2 (April 1975): 51–78, is also of interest.

Additional Bibliography

Couturier, Edith Boorstein. *The Silver King: The Remarkable Life of the Count of Regla in Colonial Mexico*. Albuquerque: University of New Mexico Press, 2003.

Guido, John F., and Lawrence R. Stark. *The Regla Papers: An Indexed Guide to the Papers of the Romero de Terreros Family and Other Colonial and Early National Mexican Families*. Pullman: Washington State University Press, 1994.

EDITH COUTURIER

ROMERO ROSA, RAMÓN (1863–1907). Ramón Romero Rosa (R. de Romeral; *b.* 30 August 1863; *d.* 25 April 1907), Puerto Rican labor organizer, essayist, and dramatist. Romero Rosa was a leading spokesman of the movement to create a national labor union in the years between 1896 and 1907, which led eventually to the formation and political centrality of Santiago Iglesias Pantin's Federación Libre de Trabajadores (Free Federation of Labor) from 1899 to 1930. A typesetter by trade, he served as president of the San Juan Union of Typographers and cofounded the

pioneering weekly *Ensayo Obrero* (1897). A charter member of the Federación Regional de los Trabajadores (Regional Federation of Workers, 1897–1899) and a firm supporter of Santiago Iglesias, he was twice (1904 and 1906) elected to the Puerto Rican House of Delegates. Affirming "no homeland but the workplace and no religion but labor," as the masthead of *Ensayo Obrero* expressed it, Romero was equally certain that "the triumph of the cause of labor will be the triumph of the *homeland* in Puerto Rico." (Angel G. Quintero Rivera, *Patricios y plebeyos,* p. 258).

Occasionally writing under the pseudonym R. de Romeral, his incisive commentaries on the class structure and exploitative character of Puerto Rican society embodied a novel, anarchist-influenced, and socialist-oriented analytical break with a patrician-dominated discourse as well as the most broadly inclusive expression of the period's emerging working-class consciousness. In addition to writing articles for such periodicals as *El Porvenir Social* (1898–1899), *La Miseria* (1901), and *El Pan del Pobre* (1901), his published works include *La cuestión social en Puerto Rico* (1904), *Musarañas* (1904), *Catecismo Socialista* (1905), *Entre Broma y Vera* (1906), and the allegorical play *La emancipación del obrero* (1903).

See also **Iglesias Pantin, Santiago; Labor Movements.**

BIBLIOGRAPHY

Angel G. Quintero Rivera, *Lucha obrera en Puerto Rico* (1972), esp. pp. 14–32, and *Patricios y plebeyos: Burgueses, hacendados, artesanos, y obreros: Las relaciones de clase en el Puerto Rico de cambio de siglo* (1988), esp. pp. 252–279.

Amilcar Tirado Áviles, "Ramón Romero Rosa, su participación en las luchas obreras (1896–1906)," in *Caribe* 2, nos. 2–3 (1977): 3–25.

Additional Bibliography

Bird Carmona, Arturo. *A lima y machete: La huelga cañera de 1915 y la fundación del Partido Socialista.* Rio Pedras, P.R.: Huracán, 2001.

ROBERTO MÁRQUEZ

ROMERO RUBIO, MANUEL (1828–1895). Manuel Romero Rubio (*b.* 1828; *d.* 3 October 1895), Mexican Liberal and public figure. A native of Mexico City, Romero Rubio attended the Conciliar Seminary before completing his legal studies at the Colegio de San Gregorio. He began his career as a practicing lawyer before becoming an active supporter of Benito Juárez during the Revolution of Ayutla (1855). He served as a constitutional deputy from Puebla in the 1856–1857 convention and became governor of Mexico City in 1857. During the French invasion, he was captured and exiled to France (1863). In 1876, he supported Sebastián Lerdo De Tejada for the presidency and subsequently became his secretary of foreign relations. Although exiled after Porfirio Díaz's rebellion, he returned to establish an opposition newspaper and became a senator from the state of Tabasco from 1880 to 1895. He eventually collaborated with his former political opponent by serving in the key post of secretary of government (1884–1895). During these years he became financially and politically prominent, establishing personal and economic ties with other leading figures. His daughter, Carmen, married Díaz in 1881.

See also **Díaz, Porfirio; Juárez, Benito; Lerdo de Tejada, Sebastián.**

BIBLIOGRAPHY

Alfonso Luis Velasco, *Manuel Romero Rubio, estudio biográfico* (1892).

Andrés Clemente Vázquez, *El ilustre mexicano Manuel Romero Rubio* (1896).

Additional Bibliography

Fowler, Wil. *Mexico in the Age of Proposals, 1821–1853.* Westport, CT: Greenwood Press, 1998.

Rodríguez O, Jaime E. *The Divine Charter: Constitutionalism and Liberalism in Nineteenth-Century Mexico.* Lanham, MD: Rowman & Littlefield Publishers, 2005.

Villegas Revueltas, Silvestre. *El liberalismo moderado en México, 1852–1864.* México, D.F.: Universidad Nacional Autónoma de México, 1997.

RODERIC AI CAMP

RONDEAU, JOSÉ (1773–1844). José Rondeau (*b.* 4 March 1773; *d.* 18 November 1844), military and political leader of the independence period in Argentina and Uruguay. Born in Buenos Aires, Rondeau was educated in Montevideo, where he spent his early years. His military career included appointments as commander in chief of the Argentine patriot army that fought against Upper Peru (1814), inspector general of Argentine troops (1820), and minister of the navy and of war in Uruguay in 1839. He also held numerous political offices, such as supreme director (1819–1820) in Buenos Aires and captain-general and governor (1828–1830) in Montevideo during the period of Uruguay's transition to independent statehood. Rondeau was thus instrumental in Platine independence and early nation building. Viewed as a native and patriot on both banks of the Río de la Plata, his remains were eventually entombed in the National Pantheon in the Uruguayan capital after negotiations with the Argentines. Rondeau was eulogized as a perfect gentleman by General José María Paz and as a just and honest man by Bartolomé Mitre.

See also **Wars of Independence, South America.**

BIBLIOGRAPHY

León Rebollo Paz, ed., *Varones de su tiempo, vistos por José María Paz* (1969).

Vicente Osvaldo Cutolo, *Nuevo diccionario biográfico argentino,* vol. 6 (1968–1985), pp. 402–404.

Additional Bibliography

Ferrer, Jorge A. *Brigadier general don José Casimiro Rondeau: Boceto biográfico.* Buenos Aires: Ediciones Ciudad Argentina, 1997.

FIDEL IGLESIAS

RONDON, CÂNDIDO MARIANO DA SILVA

(1865–1958). Cândido Mariano da Silva Rondon (*b.* 5 May 1865; *d.* 19 January 1958), Brazilian general and first director of the Indian Protection Service (SPI). At the beginning of the twentieth century, when the Brazilian government was considering large-scale army intervention to halt episodes of violence between settlers and native peoples along frontiers, Rondon was a principal spokesman for adoption of a humanistic attitude toward indigenous peoples. Influenced by the positivist writings of Auguste Comte, Rondon believed that indigenous peoples were neither savage nor barbarian. He advanced the theory that their societies represented an earlier stage in the development of human civilization and, therefore, deserved governmental protection against exploitation and destruction caused by expansion. Together with a number of other young army officers who shared his philosophy, Rondon successfully convinced the government to establish a special agency to protect Brazil's native peoples and in 1910 the government founded the Indian Protection Service. Rondon maintained that Indian peoples would eventually become members of the national society.

Since 1890 Rondon had headed a governmental commission charged with conducting military and scientific expeditions in Brazil's unexplored interior. The Rondon Commission laid over 1,362 miles of telegraph lines, mapped more than 20,000 square miles of land, and discovered twelve new rivers in the Amazon and Mato Grosso regions. During these expeditions Rondon contacted the Bororo, Nambikuara, and Paresí Indians and developed the strategy for peacefully contacting "hostile" groups that was employed by the SPI and later by National Indian Foundation (FUNAI) pacification teams. In 1913–1914 Rondon also accompanied Theodore Roosevelt on his geographical expedition throughout the Brazilian interior.

See also **Brazil, Organizations: Indian Protection Service (IPS).**

BIBLIOGRAPHY

Vincenzo Petrullo, "General Cândido Mariano da Silva Rondon: 'Sertanista' and Indianist," *America Indígena* 2, no. 1 (1942): 81–83.

Darcy Ribeiro, "A Obra Indigenista de Rondon," *America Indígena* 19, no. 2, (1959): 85–113.

Shelton H. Davis, *Victims of the Miracle: Development and the Indians of Brazil* (1977), esp. pp. 1–4.

Additional Bibliography

Bigio, Elias dos Santos. *Cândido Rondon, a integração nacional.* Rio de Janeiro: PETROBRAS: NUSEG: Contraponto, 2000.

Diacon, Todd A. *Stringing Together a Nation: Candido Mariano da Silva Rondon and the Construction of a Modern Brazil, 1906–1930.* Durham, NC: Duke University Press, 2004.

LAURA GRAHAM

RONDÔNIA.

Rondônia is a state, about the size of Arizona, in the western Amazon Basin of Brazil. Rondônia borders Bolivia to its west and south, and the Brazilian states of Mato Grosso to its east, Amazonas to its north, and Acre to its northwest.

Rondônia was part of the state of Amazonas until 1943, when it became the territory of Guaporé, named for the river that separates it from Bolivia. It was renamed Rondônia in 1956 to honor Cândido Rondon (1865–1958), the Indian protector and explorer. In 1981 Rondônia became Brazil's twenty-sixth and final state.

Before 1900 the region was occupied mainly by indigenous groups that included the Urueu-Wau-Wau, the Wayoró, and the Tuparí. As the automobile industry grew, demand for rubber led settlers to the region to harvest latex from *hevea brasiliensis* trees. The settlers, called *seringueiros*, tapped trees dispersed along trails through the tropical rain forest. A complex, river-based trade system that brought the rubber to Manaus and Belém was interrupted by a series of waterfalls on the Rio Madeira. The city of Porto Velho, which eventually became Rondônia's capital, was established around 1907 when U.S. and British investors built the Madeira–Mamoré Railroad to circumvent the waterfalls. The rubber boom ended when plantation-grown rubber was established in Asia.

Only 70,000 people lived in Rondônia in 1960, when the Brazilian government began the POLONOROESTE project (Northeastern Brazil Integration Development Program) to promote agriculture in the region. As part of the program, an old telegraph road was paved and named BR-364, connecting Porto Velho to Cuiabá, Mato Grosso, and service centers were created near some of the old telegraph stations. Intended to attract 10,000 settlers, the paving of the road attracted nearly a half million migrants seeking farmland and gold. Crop yields from the tropical soils were low, leading many settlers to clear vast tracts of land before eventually abandoning farming attempts. Violence sometimes attended the consolidation of small farms into large ranches, and Rondônia suffered the highest rates of tropical deforestation in the world.

Beginning in the 1990s, service employment and inexpensive urban land continued to attract migrants to Rondônia. A majority of Rondônia's 1.4 million people now live in cities and towns. Electricity is provided by imported diesel fuel and a large hydroelectric plant along the Rio Candeis. Proposals for additional hydroelectric plants on the

Rio Madeira have led to renewed environmental concerns at the international level.

See also **Brazil: Since 1889; Railroads.**

BIBLIOGRAPHY

Browder, John O., and Brian J. Godfrey. *Rainforest Cities: Urbanization, Development, and Globalization of the Brazilian Amazon.* New York: Columbia University Press, 1997.

Ellis, William. "Rondônia's Settlers Invade Brazil's Imperiled Rain Forest." *National Geographic* 174, no. 6 (December 1988): 772–799.

Hayes-Bohanan, James. Rondônia Web. Available from http://webhost.bridgew.edu/jhayesboh/ rondonia.htm.

Hemming, John. *Amazon Frontier: The Defeat of the Brazilian Indians.* Cambridge, MA: Harvard University Press, 1987.

Martine, George. "Rondônia and the Fate of Small Producers." In *The Future of Amazonia: Destruction or Sustainable Development?*, edited by David Goodman and Anthony Hall. London: Macmillan, 1990.

Mendes, Chico. *Fight for the Forest: Chico Mendes in His Own Words.* London: Latin American Bureau, 1990.

                                        JAMES HAYES-BOHANAN

ROOSEVELT, FRANKLIN DELANO

(1882–1945). Franklin Delano Roosevelt (*b.* 30 January 1882; *d.* 12 April 1945), president of the United States (1933–1945). Roosevelt presided over the most harmonious period of United States–Latin American relations in the twentieth century. His Good Neighbor Policy, which emphasized cooperation rather than confrontation, marked a significant departure from the strong-arm approach that many of his predecessors had taken.

When Roosevelt became president in 1933, he seemed unlikely to inaugurate an era of good feelings with his country's hemispheric neighbors. After all, his great hero was his fifth cousin (and his wife's uncle), Theodore Roosevelt, whose heavy-handed efforts to secure a route for the Panama Canal Franklin Roosevelt had applauded. Moreover, as assistant secretary of the navy under Woodrow Wilson, Roosevelt had enthusiastically supported American military intervention in Mexico and elsewhere in Latin America. Even Roosevelt's initial use of the phrase "good neighbor" in his first inaugural address had less to do with Latin America than with Europe.

But the Good Neighbor Policy, with exclusive reference to Latin America, gradually took shape in response to the two overriding realities that confronted Roosevelt: the Great Depression of the 1930s and the coming of World War II. In hopes of stimulating the economy, Roosevelt and his advisers sought to expand trade with Latin America. But to expand trade they needed to improve diplomatic relations. International considerations figured even more prominently in Roosevelt's calculations. Fearful that Nazi Germany might one day menace the Western Hemisphere, Roosevelt hoped to draw the Americas into a protective alliance. He even believed that if the United States and Latin America provided an example of friendly cooperation, they might inspire the nations of Europe to pull back from the brink of war.

In practice, the Good Neighbor Policy took many forms. After an initial display of saber-rattling in Cuba, the Roosevelt administration endorsed the principle of nonintervention in the affairs of Latin American nations, lowered trade barriers, terminated U.S. military occupation of Haiti, abrogated the Platt Amendment of 1902, which previous administrations had used to justify military intervention in Cuba, and entered into collective security arrangements with most of the U.S.'s hemispheric neighbors. Roosevelt's goodwill approach reached its symbolic high point in 1936 when he visited Brazil and Argentina and received warm welcomes. The Good Neighbor Policy survived its stiffest challenge in 1938 when Roosevelt resisted pressure from U.S. oil companies to send troops to Mexico to protect their interests.

Certain aspects of Roosevelt's policies remain controversial. Some experts have argued that Roosevelt deserves less credit for inaugurating a new approach to Latin America than do his immediate Republican predecessors, Calvin Coolidge and Herbert Hoover. Others contend that the Good Neighbor Policy, far from representing a new departure, was simply a more benign form of U.S. imperialism. Still others note that Roosevelt's policy of nonintervention may have meant less overt meddling in Latin American affairs but it also meant turning a blind eye to the rise of repressive regimes—so long, that is, as those regimes backed the United States.

See also **Good Neighbor Policy; United States-Latin American Relations.**

BIBLIOGRAPHY

Useful and largely favorable accounts of Roosevelt's Latin American policies are Edward O. Guerrant, *Roosevelt's Good Neighbor Policy* (1950); Donald M. Dozer, *Are We Good Neighbors? Three Decades of Inter-American Relations, 1930–1960* (1961); Bryce Wood, *The Making of the Good Neighbor Policy* (1961). A critical account emphasizing U.S. economic motives is David Green, *The Containment of Latin America: A History of the Myths and Realities of the Good Neighbor Policy* (1971). Two other fine works are Randall Bennett Woods, *The Roosevelt Foreign-Policy Establishment and the Good Neighbor: The United States and Argentina, 1941–1945* (1979); and Irwin F. Gellman, *Good Neighbor Diplomacy: United States Policies in Latin America, 1933–1945* (1979). See also Robert Dallek, *Franklin D. Roosevelt and American Foreign Policy, 1932–1945* (1979).

Additional Bibliography

Friedman, Max Paul. *Nazis and Good Neighbors: The United States Campaign against the Germans of Latin America in World War II.* Cambridge: Cambridge University Press, 2003.

Joseph, G. M., Catherine LeGrand, and Ricardo Donato Salvatore. *Close Encounters of Empire: Writing the Cultural History of U.S.-Latin American Relations.* Durham, NC: Duke University Press, 1998.

Pike, Fredrick B. *FDR's Good Neighbor Policy: Sixty Years of Generally Gentle Chaos.* Austin: University of Texas Press, 1995.

PATRICK J. MANEY

ROOSEVELT, THEODORE (1858–1919).

Theodore Roosevelt (*b.* 27 October 1858; *d.* 6 January 1919), president of the United States (1901–1909), who had a profound and lasting impact on U.S. policy toward Latin America.

In his presidency Roosevelt charted a new and ambitious policy in Latin America. His principal concerns were strategic, though his policies were often couched in bombastic and hortatory rhetoric, and often described as the policy of the Big Stick. His criticism of the U.S.–British canal treaty in 1901 (which had not provided for a fortified waterway) led to revision of the treaty. He played a critical role in shifting congressional sentiment away from a Nicaraguan to a Panamanian canal. When a proposed canal treaty with Colombia (Panama was a Colombian province until November 1903) faltered under Colombian political opposition in August 1903, Roosevelt quietly lent his support to the Panamanian independence movement. When the revolution broke out on 3 November 1903, Roosevelt dispatched U.S. warships to prevent Colombian forces from suppressing it. (He argued that an 1846 U.S.–Colombian commercial treaty, which permitted the U.S. government to guarantee the isthmian transit, justified his action in preventing Colombia from intervening in 1903.) Though harshly criticized in Latin America and by many North Americans, Roosevelt always contended that the need to build the Panama Canal was paramount.

In May 1902 the U.S. military withdrew from Cuba, but a Cuban protectorate was created through the Platt Amendment. Four years later, Roosevelt cited the breakdown of public order in Cuba as grounds for the second U.S. occupation of the island. He confronted Britain, Germany, and Italy when these governments jointly blockaded Venezuela in 1902–1903 for nonpayment of its debt. In 1905 he used the Venezuelan example to justify the creation of a customs receivership in the debt-plagued Dominican Republic. In December 1904 he declared in the Roosevelt Corollary to the Monroe Doctrine that in order to prevent European intervention in the Western Hemisphere, the United States might have to be a reluctant policeman, especially in the Caribbean. In 1906–1907, Roosevelt and Secretary of State Elihu Root used U.S. diplomatic and military power in Central America, then going through a cycle of debilitating interstate conflicts. One result was the Central American treaties of 1907, which were designed to provide for peaceful settlement of disputes and to discourage the seizure of power by revolutionary means.

Roosevelt articulated the U.S. imperial role in Latin America, thus reviving Latin American suspicions of U.S. intentions in the hemisphere. Curiously, despite his Big Stick diplomacy, Roosevelt was less of an interventionist than President Woodrow Wilson (1913–1921).

See also **Big Stick Policy; Platt Amendment; United States-Latin American Relations; Wilson, Woodrow.**

BIBLIOGRAPHY

Dana G. Munro, *Intervention and Dollar Diplomacy in the Caribbean, 1900–1921* (1964).

Lester D. Langley, *The Banana Wars: U.S. Intervention in the Caribbean, 1900–1934* (1983).

David Healy, *Drive to Hegemony: The United States in the Caribbean, 1898–1917* (1988).

Richard Collin, *Theodore Roosevelt's Caribbean: The Panama Canal, the Monroe Doctrine, and the Latin American Context* (1990).

Additional Bibliography

Joseph, G. M., Catherine LeGrand, and Ricardo Donato Salvatore. *Close Encounters of Empire: Writing the Cultural History of U.S.-Latin American Relations.* Durham, NC: Duke University Press, 1998.

                                    LESTER D. LANGLEY

ROOSEVELT COROLLARY. Roosevelt Corollary, a statement by President Theodore Roosevelt in December 1904 that "chronic wrongdoing" by a Latin American government might require the United States to carry out the role of "international policeman" of the Western Hemisphere in order to uphold the Monroe Doctrine (1823).

Roosevelt sympathized with European leaders involved in disputes with nationalistic governments in Latin America—governments that refused to pay their debts to foreign creditors or ill-treated foreign nationals. But two crises in the Caribbean prompted him to change his mind. The first occurred when Great Britain, Germany, and Italy blockaded Venezuela in 1902–1903 over a debt imbroglio; the second, when European creditors made it clear to Roosevelt that they were expecting their governments to confront the problem of collecting the large debt of the Dominican Republic. Roosevelt understood the danger to U.S. security in the hemisphere if those European governments followed a nineteenth-century practice of using forceful means to deal with recalcitrant Latin American governments. The Roosevelt Corollary offered a compromise whereby the United States would be able to maintain its domination of Latin America yet obtain Europe's acquiescence because the United States, not Europe, would "police" the hemisphere.

Using the Roosevelt Corollary as a pretext for defending the Monroe Doctrine, the United States greatly expanded its policing role in Latin America, especially in the Caribbean. It established a financial protectorate in the Dominican Republic in 1905, occupied Cuba in 1906, intervened continuously in Central America from 1906 until 1933, and created de facto military governments in Haiti and the Dominican Republic in 1915 and 1916, respectively.

See also **Big Stick Policy; Clark Memorandum; United States-Latin American Relations.**

BIBLIOGRAPHY

Dexter Perkins, *A History of the Monroe Doctrine* (1963).

Dana G. Munro, *Intervention and Dollar Diplomacy in the Caribbean, 1900–1921* (1964).

Lester D. Langley, *The United States and the Caribbean in the Twentieth Century,* 4th ed. (1989).

Richard Collin, *Theodore Roosevelt's Caribbean: The Panama Canal, the Monroe Doctrine, and the Latin American Context* (1990).

Additional Bibliography

Dent, David W. *The Legacy of the Monroe Doctrine: A Reference Guide to U.S. Involvement in Latin America and the Caribbean.* Westport, CT: Greenwood Press, 1999.

Hilton, Sylvia-Lyn. "La "nueva" doctrina Monroe de 1895 y sus implicaciones para el Caribe español: Algunas interpretaciones coetáneas españolas." *Anuario de Estudios Americanos.* 55:1 (January–June 1998): 125–151.

Rosenberg, Emily S. *Financial Missionaries to the World: The Politics and Culture of Dollar Diplomacy, 1900–1930.* Cambridge, MA: Harvard University Press, 1999.

LESTER D. LANGLEY

RORAIMA. Roraima, Brazilian state that shares its foreign borders with Venezuela and Guyana and its domestic borders with Pará and Amazonas. Roraima was part of the vast state of Amazonas until 1943, when the Brazilian government created the Federal Territory of Rio Branco out of this 88,000-square-mile region. To avoid confusing it with Rio Branco, the capital of Acre, Brazilian officials renamed it "Territorio de Roraima" in honor of Mount Roraima in Venezuela in 1964. Roraima became a state in 1988. By 2000 the population was 324,397 inhabitants.

Roraima contains distinct topographical divisions. The bottom third of the state, part of the Amazon basin, is a tropical rain forest; the middle portion is a savannah; and the northern portion is a hilly, rocky terrain that leads into the Guiana Highlands. The whitish-watered Rio Branco, tributary of the Río Negro, has always dominated Roraima, even though it can only be used for transportation during the rainy season.

Indigeneous peoples, such as the Yanomami, Makuxi, and the Wapixana, were the only inhabitants of Roraima until 1773, when Europeans permanently settled on the Rio Branco. The settlers eventually introduced cattle, which became part of Roraima's economy. Diamonds, uranium, and cassiterite (tin ore) are twentieth-century discoveries in the area. In the 1980s gold prospectors (*garimpeiros*) flooded the area, extracting what may have been $1 billion worth of gold between 1987 and 1990. These soldiers of fortune, however, encroached on the indigenous lands of the surviving 10,000 Yanomami people, so that by 1990, environmentalists were pressuring the Brazilian government to protect them. President Collor de Mello appointed the "sheriff of the emergency," Romeu Tuma, to head Operation Yanomami and remove illegal gold prospectors from Yanomami lands.

See also **Brazil, Geography; Indigenous Peoples; Mining: Colonial Brazil; Yanomami.**

BIBLIOGRAPHY

Peter Riviere, *The Forgotten Frontier: Ranchers of North Brazil* (1972).

David Cleary, *Anatomy of the Amazon Gold Rush* (1990).

John Hemming, "How Brazil Acquired Roraima," in *Hispanic American Historic Review* 70, no. 2 (1990): 295–325.

Andrew Hurrell, "The Politics of Amazonian Deforestation," in *Journal of Latin American Studies* 23, no. 1 (1991): 197–215.

Additional Bibliography

Cortez Crocia de Barros, Nilson. *Roraima: Paisagens e tempo na Amazônia setentrional: Estudo de ocupação pioneira na América do Sul.* Recife, Brasil: Editora Universitária, 1994.

Furley, Peter A. *The Forest Frontier: Settlement and Change in Brazilian Roraima.* London; New York: Routledge, 1994.

Hemming, John. *Roraima: Brazil's Northernmost Frontier.* London: Institute of Latin American Studies, 1990.

Koch–Grünberg, Theodor, and Alberts–Franco, Cristina. *Do Roraima ao Orinoco*. São Paulo: Editora UNESP, 2005.

Menezes Braga, Ramayana. *Cavalo lavradeiro em Roraima: Aspectos históricos, ecológicos e de conservação*. Brasília, DF: Embrapa, 2000.

CAROLYN JOSTOCK

ROSA, JOÃO GUIMARÃES (1908–1967).

João Guimarães Rosa was a Brazilian fiction writer, medical doctor, and diplomat. Born on June 27, 1908, in the rural town of Cordisburgo in he central Brazilian state of Minas Gerais, Guimarães Rosa enjoyed a multifaceted career and gained international renown with the volumes *Sagarana* (1946; *Sagarana* 1966), *Corpo de baile* (1956), *Grande sertão: Veredas* (1956; *Devil to Pay in the Backlands*, 1963), *Primeiras estórias* (1962; *Third Bank of the River and Other Stories*, 1968), *Tutaméia* (1967), *Estas estórias* (1969), and *Ave, palavra!* (1970). He was elected to the Brazilian Academy of Letters in 1961.

Guimarães Rosa appeared on the Brazilian literary scene as an independent successor to the modernist Mário de Andrade. The short-story collection *Sagarana*, his first published volume, challenged the Brazilian tradition, established in the 1930s, of regionalist fiction based on pictorial re-creation of rural life around a crude theoretical framework. Rosa flouted such stereotypes while remaining faithful to the most ancient and enduring qualities of regionalism. Early commentators likened him to Herman Melville because of his simultaneous treatment of inner and outer realities; he was also compared to James Joyce in his use of neologisms, lexical borrowings from classical and modern languages, syntactic inversions, the introduction of an apocopated "telegraphic" syntax, and the preference for an orally based storytelling style reminiscent of medieval archetypes conveying simultaneously a popular and an epic tone.

The nine stories in *Sagarana*, all set in the backlands of central Brazil, depict a primitive level of existence: Protagonists include a small donkey, a prodigal husband, two old friends dying of malaria, a witch doctor and his "educated" neighbor, a town bully, a pair of vengeful men in a love triangle, a timid rival who emerges victorious with the help of a spell, talking oxen, and a bully-turned-saint. The author's empathy for his characters is evident, as is his use of what may be called redemptive analogy in the Judeo-Christian tradition. In *Corpo de baile*, a series of seven novelettes of varying lengths, Rosa skillfully renders childhood, with its particular perceptions and world-view, in terms adult readers can appreciate without condescension. With great psychological insight he explores fantasies, fears, forebodings, tenderness, suspense, and erotic tensions in an atmosphere bordering on the surrealistic.

Grande sertão: veredas, an epic novel in first-person monologue, is considered the author's masterpiece. The plot of this metaphysical *chanson de geste* in the backlands of Brazil involves warring bandits, a possible homoerotic relationship and pact with the Devil, a democratic kangaroo court, Herculean trials and travels, and the triumph of Good over Evil. By contrast, The *Primeiras estórias* is made up of twenty-one brief short stories, and *Tutaméia* of forty narratives so brief as to be minuscule. The first of this pair structures most of its episodes around epiphanies in the lives of children and other marginal or powerless members of society; the second is a series of "anecdotes of abstraction" interspersed with four longer essays of a theoretical, though fanciful, nature.

Guimarães Rosa's two posthumous works echo the style of *Sagarana* but incorporate a more cosmopolitan cast of characters and concerns. The oral quality diminishes over the author's thirty-five-year literary career, although all his works may be read from a tripartite perspective: form/sound, semantic value, and metaphysical meaning. He died of a heart attack in Rio de Janeiro on November 19, 1967.

See also **Andrade, Mário de; Brazil: Since 1889; Literature: Brazil.**

BIBLIOGRAPHY

Duarte, Lélia Parreira, and Maria Theresa Abelha Alves, eds. *Outras margens: Estudos da obra de Guimarães Rosa*. Belo Horizonte, Brazil: Autêntica, 2001.

Hansen, João Adolfo. *O o: A ficção da literatura em Grande Sertão: Veredas*. São Paulo: Hedra, 2000.

Sperber, Suzi Frankl. *Caos e cosmos: Leituras de Guimarães Rosa.* São Paulo: Livraria Duas Cidades, 1976.

Vincent, Jon S. *João Guimarães Rosa.* Boston: Twayne Publishers, 1978.

MARY L. DANIEL

Rosa, José María. *Historia argentina*, 13 vols. Buenos Aires: Oriente, 1970.

Rosa, José María. *Defensa y pérdida de nuestra independencia económica.* Buenos Aires: Peña Lillo, 1986.

VALERIA MANZANO

ROSA, JOSÉ MARÍA (1906–1991).

José María Rosa, born August 20, 1906, was an Argentine lawyer and a well-known revisionist historian. In the 1930s, Rosa taught Argentine history at the University of Litoral, in Santa Fe. He founded the Instituto de Estudios Federalistas, which was crucial for articulating the contemporary historical revisionist movement that sought to "revise" Argentine history from a nationalist and anti-liberal perspective. Rosa's historical work is a prime example of that perspective: He conceives of Argentine history as a permanent struggle between two immobile blocs, the liberal pro-imperialist and the national and popular.

In 1945 Rosa became a Peronista. During the regime of Juan Domingo Perón (1945–1955), he was a professor at the University of La Plata; after Perón's fall, he was briefly imprisoned and then went into exile in Uruguay and Spain. Back in Argentina in 1958, Rosa directed the Instituto de Investigaciones Históricas Juan Manuel de Rosas (named for the nineteenth-century nationalist dictator). His thirteen-volume *Historia argentina* (1970) was critical for modeling the historical imagination of young Peronistas. During the third Peronist government (1973–1976), Rosa was appointed ambassador to Paraguay and to Greece. Rosa returned to Argentina in the late 1970s and found that the dictatorship had banned his books. From the early 1980s to his death on July 2, 1991, he directed a magazine called *Línea*.

See also **Argentina: The Twentieth Century; Argentina, Political Parties: Justicialist Party; Perón, Juan Domingo.**

BIBLIOGRAPHY

Galasso, Norberto. *Las luchas de los argentinos: Y cómo la cuentan diversas corrientes históricas.* Buenos Aires: Pensamiento Nacional, 1995.

Halperin Donghi, Tulio. *El revisionismo histórico argentino.* Buenos Aires: Siglo XXI, 1970.

ROSA, NOEL (1910–1937).

Noel Rosa (Noel de Medeiros Rosa; *b.* 11 December 1910; *d.* 4 May 1937), Brazilian songwriter. Rosa was born in Rio de Janeiro; complications at birth left him disfigured and partly paralyzed. Raised in the neighborhood of Vila Isabel in São Paulo, Rosa began to play the mandolin by ear at the age of thirteen and later took up the guitar. Together with friends from his high school, Colégio Batista, Rosa formed the band Flor do Tempo. Invited to record in 1929, the group renamed themselves the Bando de Tangarás. That same year, Rosa composed his first pieces, "Minha viola" (My Viola) and "Festa no céu" (Party in the Sky), both of which he recorded in 1930.

Rosa's first hit came in 1930 with the samba "Com qué roupa?" (With What Clothes?), featuring humorous observations of life in Rio de Janeiro that would characterize his future work. He was a prolific songwriter; in 1933, his best year, he recorded more than thirty pieces. Beyond the successes of Carnival such as "Até amanhã" (Until Tomorrow) and "Fita amarela" (Yellow Ribbon), other major works of that year included the sambas "Onde está a honestidade?" (Where Is the Honesty?), "O orvalho vem caindo" (The Dew Is Falling), and "Três apitos" (Three Whistles).

Rosa's bohemian lifestyle and his frequenting of bars and nightclubs had a deleterious effect on his health. After years of intense composing, performing, and traveling, Rosa died in 1937 at the age of twenty-six. Since 1950, when his music was rediscovered through the recordings of singer Araci de Almeida, Rosa is always included in any retrospective collections of Brazilian popular music.

See also **Music: Popular Music and Dance.**

BIBLIOGRAPHY

Marcos Antônio Marcondes, ed., *Enciclopédia da música brasileira: Erudita folclórica popular* (1977).

Additional Bibliography

Fernandes, Juvenal. *História da música brasileira: Com tópicos da história do Brasil (1500–2000)*. São Paulo: EDICON, 2004.

Máximo, João. *Noel Rosa: Uma biografia*. Brasília: Linha Gráfica Editora: Editora UnB, 1990.

LISA MARÍC

ROSA, RAMÓN (1848–1893).

Ramón Rosa (*b.* 1848; *d.* 1893), Honduran statesman. Born in Tegucigalpa, Rosa studied law at the University of San Carlos in Guatemala and began his law career in 1869. He took part in the military victory over the Conservatives in 1871.

Rosa is known for his participation in Honduran political and intellectual life during the late nineteenth century. He was a member of the Council of Ministers, exercising executive authority from 10 June 1880 to 30 July 1880. More importantly, Rosa reflected the positivist intellectual currents of his time. This intellectual trend manifested itself throughout Latin America as political leaders sought to develop their societies through a combination of education, training, and agro-export economies. Rosa wrote on the effects of positivism in Honduras, emphasizing the need for material progress and scientific education. He and Honduran president Marco Aurelio Soto were protégés of Guatemalan intellectuals at the University of San Carlos and of the Guatemalan dictator Justo Rufino Barrios. Together, these Liberal "positivists" transformed Honduran society from one characterized by isolation and Liberal-Conservative rivalry to one more open to international commerce and, eventually, the banana trade.

See also **Honduras; Soto, Marco Aurelio.**

BIBLIOGRAPHY

Ramón Rosa, "Social Constitution of Honduras," in Ralph Lee Woodward, Jr., ed., *Positivism in Latin America, 1850–1900: Are Order and Progress Reconcilable?* (1971).

Luis Mariñas Otero, *Honduras*, 2d ed. (1983).

Additional Bibliography

Cortés, Carlos R. *Obra educativa relevente del Dr. José Ramón Rosa*. Tegucigalpa: Editorial Cultura, 2000.

Perdomo Interiano, Claudio Roberto. *Pensamiento positivista y liberal de Ramón Rosa*. Tegucigalpa: Mejores Ideas, 1994.

Zelaya, Gustavo. *El legado de la Reforma Liberal*. Tegucigalpa: Editorial Guaymuras, 1996.

JEFFREY D. SAMUELS

ROSA DE LIMA (1586–1617).

Santa Rosa de Lima was baptized Isabel Flores de Oliva in Lima. Hagiography holds that her indigenous nursemaid declared her as beautiful as a rose and that she was called Rosa thereafter. Archbishop Toribio de Mogrovejo confirmed her as "Rosa" in 1597 in rural Quives, where her noble but impecunious family lived briefly; her presence did not, as hagiographers claim, ameliorate the local indigenous people's hostility toward him. Some accounts of Rosa's childhood describe it as humble, some as abusive. An admirer of Catherine of Siena, she responded to compliments by cutting her hair and disfiguring her skin. She refused to marry, though she at first declined to join a convent because of poverty and her mother's opposition. She withdrew to a shack in her family's garden, engaging in prayer and often painful penitential acts that scholars interpret as, if not masochistic, one of the few means she had to control her own life.

Rosa became a Dominican tertiary at twenty and continued her prayer and charitable work. She also supplemented the family income by taking in needlework (some of which, along with writings and drawings, is preserved). Although religious authorities prosecuted other *beatas* of colonial Lima, Rosa escaped criticism. Later biographies recount her friendship with Dominican tertiary Martin de Porres (little evidence of it exists), and her charity extending to poor women, the indigenous, and Afro-Peruvians. Reported miracles of her lifetime include healings, mystical visions (interpreted by some as erotic, by others as challenging institutional hierarchy), and the sudden deliverance of Lima-Callao from a Dutch attack in 1615 after she prayed for such an outcome at the Church of Nuestra Señora del Rosario.

At her funeral in 1617, onlookers clamored for relics and called for her canonization. Posthumous testimonies describe the preservation of her corpse, the use of her relics to cure the sick, and appearances to petitioners. Her beatification was proposed in 1630 and completed in 1664, when she was named patroness of Lima and Peru. Church leaders recognized the necessity of local devotions for securing the loyalty of New World Christians, thus hastening the process of her beatification, as did Creole ambitions to prove American worth. Her following first surged in Mexico, antedating approval of devotion to the Virgin of Guadalupe. Peruvians' enthusiasm grew over time, with eighteenth-century indigenous rebels adopting her as their standard, as did both royalists and patriots during the independence wars. With canonization in 1671, she became First Patron of the Americas, the Philippines, and the Indies. Although this may have "domesticated" extra-hierarchical female claims to religious revelation, it made sainthood a possibility for the New World.

See also **Guadalupe, Virgin of; Mogrovejo, Toribio Alfonso de; Porres, Martín de; Solano, Francisco.**

BIBLIOGRAPHY

Glave, Luis Miguel. *De Rosa y espinas: Economía, sociedad y mentalidades andinas, siglo XVII*. Lima: Instituto de Estudios Peruanos, 1998.

Graziano, Frank. *Wounds of Love: The Mystical Marriage of Saint Rose of Lima*. New York and Oxford: Oxford University Press, 2004.

Hampe Martínez, Teodoro. *Santidad e identidad criolla: Estudio del proceso de canonización de Santa Rosa*. Cuzco, Peru: Centro de Estudios Regionales Andinos Bartolomé de las Casas, 1998.

Hansen, Leonardus. *Vida admirable de Sta Rosa de Lima Patrona del Nuevo Mundo* [1664–1668], trans. Jacinto Parra, OP (reformada por el Zuavo Pontificio Sevilla, Caballero de Pío IX), 2nd edition. Vergara: Edit. "El Santísimo Rosario," 1929.

Millones, Luis. *Una partecita del cielo: La vida de Santa Rosa de Lima narrada por Dn. Gonzalo de la Maza a quien ella llamaba padre*. Lima: Editorial Horizonte, 1993.

Múgica Pinilla, Ramón. *Rosa limensis: Mística, política e iconografía en torno a la patrona de América*. Lima: IFEA, 2001.

KRISTINA A. BOYLAN

ROSÁINS, JUAN NEPOMUCENO

(1782–1830). Juan Nepomuceno Rosáins (*b.* 13 February 1782, *d.* 27 September 1830), Mexican insurgent leader. Born in San Juan de los Llanos, Rosáins was a lawyer who joined the insurgency in 1812 and eventually became the auditor general of the army. After Mariano Matamoros (1770–1814) was captured, José María Morelos y Pavón (1765–1815) named Rosáins his second in command (1814). From the outset, Rosáins had conflicts with other insurgents and acted arbitrarily. Defeated and imprisoned by his companions in the Barranca de Jamapa, he escaped and won amnesty from the colonial regime. In 1815, he presented the viceroy, Félix María Calleja Del Rey, with a report on the insurgency with recommendations for defeating it. In 1821 he supported the Plan of Iguala promulgated by Agustín de Iturbide (1783–1824), and in 1824 he was elected senator from Puebla. He later conspired against President Anastasio Bustamante (1780–1853) and was shot as a traitor.

See also **Matamoros y Guridi, Mariano; Mexico: The Colonial Period.**

BIBLIOGRAPHY

Alejandro Villaseñor y Villaseñor, *Biografías de los héroes y caudillos de la Independencia*, vol. 2 (1910), pp. 271–278.

José María Miquel I Vergés, *Diccionario de insurgentes* (1969), pp. 512–514.

Additional Bibliography

Archer, Christon. *The Birth of Modern Mexico, 1780–1824*. Wilmington, DE: Scholarly Resources Inc., 2003.

Rodríguez O, Jaime E. *The Origins of Mexican National Politics, 1808–1847*. Wilmington, DE: Scholarly Resources Inc., 1997.

VIRGINIA GUEDEA

ROSARIO.

Rosario, fourth-largest city of Argentina (906,004 as of 2001 census), located on the bank of the Paraná River, 190 miles upstream from Buenos Aires. It has been the major city of the province of Santa Fe since 1852. Established in 1689 by Luis Romero de Pineda as a fortification against the Indians, it was no more than a port of export for mules and tobacco in colonial times. During the struggle for independence and the wars fought in its aftermath, Rosario was severely affected by the strife between federalists and unitarians. Although it was almost totally destroyed in 1829 by gunboats from Buenos Aires, Rosario opposed the rule of Manuel de Rosas and sent troops to battle the dictator at Caseros (1852). During the presidency of Bartolomé Mitre, the Central Railroad was built between Rosario and Córdoba, which along with fluvial navigation facilitated the migration of many foreign immigrants from Buenos Aires to Rosario. The city rapidly developed as an exporter of grain and beef, and metal industries, breweries, grain mills, leather-processing establishments, textile industries, and chemical works widened the industrial base of the city. In 1919 the National University of the Littoral was founded there.

The city of Rosario expands along the western bank of the river for nearly 25 miles and reaches its greatest extension at the intersection of the highway (connecting Buenos Aires and Córdoba with that leading to Santa Fe). Railway lines of the Bartolomé Mitre system secure communications with Buenos Aires, Santa Fe, and Córdoba, making Rosario not only a fluvial center but also a hub of overland communications. The Fisherton airport has several daily flights to Buenos Aires and to Posadas, Corrientes, and Resistencia.

See also **Argentina, Geography.**

BIBLIOGRAPHY

Consejo Municipal, *Rosario: Esa ciudad*. Rosario: Editorial Biblioteca, 1970.

María M. Enríquez, *El puerto de Rosario*. Buenos Aires: Imprenta de la Facultad de Filosofía y Letras, 1979.

Additional Bibliography

Dalla Corte, Gabriela; Piacenza,Paola. *A las puertas del Hogar: Madres, niños, y damas de Caridad en el hogar del huérfano de Rosario, 1870–1920*. Rosario: Prehistoria ediciones, 2006.

Karush, Matthew B. *Workers or Citizens: Democracy and Identity in Rosario, Argentina (1912–1930.)* Albuquerque: University of New Mexico Press, 2002.

CÉSAR N. CAVIEDES

ROSAS, JUAN MANUEL DE (1793–1877).
Juan Manuel de Rosas (*b*. 30 March 1793; *d*. 14 March 1877), Argentine dictator.

ROAD TO POWER
Rosas was born in Buenos Aires to a creole family of landowners and officeholders, a characteristic beginning for an Argentine caudillo. He himself was a landowner and military commander. He acquired his education mainly on his parents' *estancia* before striking out on his own account, first in the meat-salting industry, then in the accumulation of land in the south of the province of Buenos Aires, where he developed his principal cattle *estancias* and those of his cousins, the Anchorenas. Rosas was thus at the leading edge of Argentina's new frontier of settlement and helped to promote the transition of Buenos Aires from viceregal capital to export center. It was on the *estancia* that he first practiced his principles of government. There, on an anarchic population of peons, gauchos, Indians, and vagrants Rosas imposed respect for authority, social order, and private property; by a mixture of discipline and example he exacted subordination and created a work force and a following. In 1820 he turned his peons into patriots and led a cavalry force to rescue Buenos Aires from the caudillos of the interior, a further victory over anarchy and another tribute to the military power of the southern caudillo.

The next objective was to raise his political profile. From his *estancia* Rosas observed the course of government in Buenos Aires with growing concern. In February 1826 Bernardino Rivadavia was appointed president of the United Provinces of the Río de la Plata, and came to power with a unitarist constitution and a modernizing program. The entire package was rejected by Rosas and his associates, who represented a more primitive economy—cattle production for export of hides and salt meat—and objected to sharing their provincial resources with a greater Argentina. In the latter half of 1826, at the head of a network of friends, relations, and clients, Rosas allied himself to the federalist party. Rivadavia bowed to the combined force of his opponents and resigned, and in August 1827 the veteran federalist, Manuel Dorrego, was elected governor. Federalist government in itself was not the political solution sought by Rosas. To secure the hegemony of the *estancia*, the dominance of the export economy, security on the frontier and in the countryside, it was necessary to establish direct control of policy: the time had come for those who possessed economic power, the *estancieros,* to displace the professional politicians of independence and take possession of government through their representative Rosas.

As militia commander, frontiersman, and rancher, Rosas had unique qualifications to assume leadership. He was already a caudillo in his own right with access to land, men, and resources, and the ability to mobilize them for armed action. The opportunity came in 1828, when a unitarist coup engineered by General Juan Lavalle overthrew and assassinated Dorrego, leaving a gap in the federalist leadership which was instantly filled by Rosas. He had the support of militiamen, *estancieros,* and friendly Indians. He also had a power base among the popular forces of the countryside who looked to him as their *patrón* and protector. In the course of 1829 he waged a guerrilla war on his unitarist enemies and defeated the regular army of Lavalle; on 3 November he entered Buenos Aires at the head of a force which only he could control, and virtually dictated his own terms. On 6 December 1829 he was elected governor of Buenos Aires with absolute powers (*facultades extraordinarias*). From these beginnings he dominated Argentina for the next two decades and beyond.

CONSERVATIVE DICTATOR

Rosas divided society into those who commanded and those who obeyed. He abhorred democracy and liberalism, and the reason why he detested unitarists was not that they wanted a united Argentina but that they were liberals who believed in humanism and progress. The constitutional doctrines of the two parties did not interest him, and he was never a true federalist. He thought and ruled as a centralist, and he insisted on the supremacy of Buenos Aires. This was *rosismo,* and there was nothing quite like it anywhere else in Spanish America. Its power base was the *estancia,* a focus of economic resources and a system of social control.

The domination of the economy by the *estancia* was continued and completed under Rosas. He stood for a policy of territorial settlement and expansion, conquering land from the Indians, rewarding his followers with land, selling public land and eventually giving it away. The trend of his regime was toward greater concentration of property in the hands of a small elite. The *estancia* gave Rosas the sinews of war, the alliance of fellow *estancieros,* and the means of recruiting an army of

peons, gauchos, and vagrants. In December 1829 he claimed that, unlike his predecessors, he had cultivated the common people, and had become a gaucho himself in order to control them. To identify with gaucho culture was not necessarily to represent the gauchos or to receive their spontaneous support. The core of Rosas's forces were his own peons and dependents, who were obliged to follow him in war as they worked for him in peace.

Rural uprisings occurred in times of exceptional crisis, such as in 1829 and 1835, when Rosas deliberately raised popular forces in order to counter his unitarist enemies. The gaucho forces lasted only as long as Rosas needed them; once he controlled the bureaucracy, the police, the death squads, and the regular army, his rural followers had to return to their *estancias*. Finally, in many cases these informal troops were mobilized not directly by Rosas but by their own *patrón,* who was usually commander of the local militia; this meant that Rosas received his support not from free gaucho hordes but from other *estancieros* leading their peon conscripts.

Another popular sector, the artisans of Buenos Aires and the interior, also looked to Rosas for protection, in this case against the competition of foreign imports. In the Customs Law of December 1835 he introduced higher import duties, giving greater protection to more vulnerable products, and actually prohibiting the import of a large number of articles such as textiles, hardware, and, depending on the domestic price, wheat. The tariff was designed to relieve distress in the industrial and farming sectors without subverting the livestock export economy. In any event, national industries failed to respond, and within five years Rosas was forced to relax protection in the interests of consumers.

TERRORIST STATE

Rosas ruled from 1829 to 1832 with absolute power. After an interregnum during which anarchy once more raised its head, he returned to the governorship in March 1835 and ruled for the next seventeen years with total and unlimited power. The House of Representatives remained a creature of the governor, whom it formally "elected." It consisted of forty-four deputies, half of whom were annually renewed by election. But only a small minority of the electorate participated, and it was the duty of the justices of the peace to deliver these votes to the regime. The Assembly, lacking legislative function and financial control, was largely an exercise in public relations for the benefit of foreign and domestic audiences.

Propaganda was an essential ingredient of *rosismo*, and conformity in dress, language, and behavior was imposed. The church rallied to the cause, supported the dictator, and extolled the federal system. But the ultimate sanction of the regime was force, controlled by Rosas and applied by the military and the police. The enemy within, conflict with other provinces and with foreign powers, and the obligation to support his allies in the interior caused Rosas to maintain a large defense budget, to recruit a large standing army, and to press the rural areas to increase their militias. One way or another, the people were forced to conform, at every level of society and in every aspect of life. There was a totalitarian character to the regime, untypical of contemporary Spanish America. The government of Rosas responded in some degree to conditions inherent in Argentine society. He offered an escape from anarchy and a promise of peace, on condition that he was granted total power.

To exercise his sovereignty, Rosas personally administered justice and kept the bureaucracy, the military, and the police under close control. Even so, there was resistance. Internally he faced an ideological opposition, partly from unitarists and partly from younger reformists; this came to a head in an abortive conspiracy in 1839 and continued to function throughout the regime from its base in Montevideo. A second focus of opposition formed among the landowners of the south; they were particularly hit by the French blockade which cut off their export outlets and for which they blamed Rosas. But their rebellion of 1839 did not synchronize with the political conspiracy, and they, too, were crushed. Finally, there was external opposition, partly from other provinces and partly from foreign powers. If the external opposition could link up with internal dissidents, Rosas would be in real danger.

Rosas therefore held in reserve another weapon, terror. He used it as an instrument of government, to eliminate enemies and control his own supporters. The special agent of terrorism was the Sociedad Popular Restauradora (Popular Society of the Restorer), a political club and a paramilitary organization. The Society had an armed wing, commonly called the *mazorca*, whose members were the terrorists on the streets. The incidence of terrorism varied according to the pressures on the regime, rising to a peak in 1839–1842, when French intervention, internal rebellion, and unitarist invasion threatened to destroy the Rosas state and produced violent countermeasures. The use of state terrorism was an essential and unique feature of the Rosas regime.

DECLINE AND FALL

The system gave Rosas hegemony in Buenos Aires for over twenty years. But he could not apply the same strategy in the whole of Argentina. He did not govern "Argentina." The thirteen provinces governed themselves independently, though they were grouped in one general Confederation of the United Provinces of the Río de la Plata. Even without a constitution and formal union, however, the provinces were forced to delegate certain common matters to the government of Buenos Aires, partly to secure a broad base for economic and foreign policy and partly to acquire a national dimension for the regime. Rosas tamed the interior in the years between 1831 and 1841 by a mixture of diplomacy and coercion, establishing a series of client caudillos who recognized his informal sovereignty.

But Rosas could not impose these methods on the Littoral provinces, where economic grievances coincided with powerful foreign interests. These provinces wanted trading rights for the river ports of the Paraná and the Uruguay; they wanted a share in customs revenue; and they wanted local autonomy. With outside assistance they could become the Achilles' heel of Rosas. Brazil had its own account to settle with the dictator. Determined to prevent satellites of Buenos Aires from becoming entrenched in Uruguay and the Littoral, and anxious to secure free navigation of the river complex from Matto Grosso to the sea, Brazil was ready to move. An ally was at hand in Entre Ríos, where Justo José de Urquiza, a powerful *estanciero* and caudillo, placed himself at the head of provincial interests, liberal exiles, and Uruguayan patriots, in an alliance backed by enough Brazilian money and naval force to tip the balance against Rosas. The Triple Alliance of Entre Ríos, Brazil, and Montevideo went into action in May 1851.

In Buenos Aires itself enthusiasm for the regime waned. The economy was no longer dominated exclusively by Rosas's allies, the cattle *estancieros,* but now also contained sheep farms, whose owners were less militarized and less committed to the regime. Rosas had taxed and conscripted more than the *estancieros* could bear. And by his terrorist methods he had depoliticized Buenos Aires, destroying in the process whatever existed of "popular" support for the government. When the army of the Triple Alliance invaded, his troops fled and the people in the town and country did not rise in his support. On 3 February 1852, at Monte Caseros, he was defeated. He rode alone from the field of battle, took refuge in the house of the British minister, boarded a British vessel, and sailed for England and exile. He died in Southampton in 1877, in his eighty-fourth year.

See also **Argentina: The Nineteenth Century; Argentina, Federalist Pacts (1831, 1852); Argentina, Movements: Federalists; Caudillismo, Caudillo; Estancia; Gaucho; Lavalle, Juan Galo.**

BIBLIOGRAPHY

Carlos Ibarguren, *Juan Manuel de Rosas: Su vida, su drama, su tiempo* (1961).

Ernesto H. Celesia, *Rosas: Aportes para su historia*, 2d ed., 2 vols. (1968).

Tulio Halperín Donghi, *Argentina: De la revolución de independencia a la confederación rosista* (1972).

John Lynch, *Argentine Dictator: Juan Manuel de Rosas 1829–1852* (1981), and *Caudillos in Spanish America 1800–1850* (1992).

Additional Bibliography

Adelman, Jeremy. *Republic of Capital: Buenos Aires and the Legal Transformation of the Atlantic World.* Stanford, CA: Stanford University Press, 1999.

Barba, Fernando E., Carlos A Mayo, and Carlos S A Segreti. *Argentina y Chile en la época de Rosas y Portales.* La Plata: Editorial de la Universidad Nacional de La Plata, 1997.

Gálvez, Manuel. *Vida de Juan Manuel de Rosas.* Buenos Aires: Claridad, 1997.

JOHN LYNCH

ROSAS, JUVENTINO (1868–1894).

Juventino Rosas (*b.* 23 or 25 January 1868; *d.* 13 July 1894), Mexican (Otomi Indian) violinist and composer. At age six Rosas's father brought him and two brothers from their native Santa Cruz de Galeana to Mexico City to perform as a family quartet. He later joined the orchestra of San Sebastian church and toured with the orchestra of legendary opera singer Angela Peralta. He died in Cuba while on tour with a traveling zarzuela company. Best known for his set of waltzes entitled *Sobre las olas,* he also composed numerous other waltzes, mazurkas, and schottisches, many of them published.

See also **Music: Art Music.**

BIBLIOGRAPHY

Robert Stevenson, *Music in Mexico: A Historical Survey* (1952).

Additional Bibliography

Brenner, Helmut. *Juventino Rosas: His Life, His Work, His Time.* Warren, MI: Harmonie Park Press, 2000.

ROBERT L. PARKER

ROSAS DE TERRERO, MANUELA

(1817–1898). Manuela Rosas de Terrero (*b.* 24 May 1817; *d.* 17 September 1898), daughter of Argentine dictator Juan Manuel de Rosas and Encarnación Ezcurra de Rosas. After her mother's death in 1838, "Manuelita" served as her father's hostess and confidante. Poorly educated and socially awkward, she was ridiculed as provincial by the liberal intellectuals of Buenos Aires, but as English merchant William MacCann wrote, "For all who appealed to General Rosas in an extrajudicial character, his daughter Doña Manuelita was the universal intercessor." According to John Lynch "she was an intermediary between client and patron, a channel of grace and favor." In 1852 she accompanied her father into exile in England, where she married longtime suitor Máximo Terrero on 23 October 1852. Her father considered her marriage a betrayal and attempted to sever relations with Manuela; for Manuela the marriage was what she described as "an emancipation."

See also **Rosas, Juan Manuel de.**

BIBLIOGRAPHY

Lily Sosa De Newton, *Diccionario Biográfico de Mujeres Argentinas* (1980).

John Lynch, *Argentine Dictator: Juan Manuel de Rosas, 1839–1852* (1981).

Additional Bibliography

Gálvez, Manuel. *Vida de Juan Manuel de Rosas*. Buenos Aires: Claridad, 1997.

FRANCESCA MILLER

ROSCIO, JUAN GERMÁN (1763–1821).

Juan Germán Roscio (*b.* 27 May 1763; *d.* 10 March 1821), Venezuelan political activist and ideologue in the movement for independence. Roscio earned doctorates in canonical and civil law from the University of Caracas, where he was later a professor, and held the post of provisional treasurer in the Audiencia of Caracas. He played a role in the declaration of a *cabildo abierto* and in the ouster of the Spanish governor on 19 April 1810 in Caracas and was a member of the Junta Suprema de Caracas, secretary of foreign affairs, and representative to the Constituent Congress of 1811. Roscio helped draw up the Declaration of Independence and the Constitution of 1811, distinguishing himself as one of the foremost publicists regarding the American right to independence.

With the fall of the First Republic in 1812, Roscio was sent to the military prison in Ceuta, Africa. When released, he traveled to Jamaica in 1816 and later to Philadelphia, where he published his principal work, *El triunfo de la libertad sobre el despotismo* (1817). In 1818 he returned to Venezuela, became editor of *El Correo del Orinoco*, presided at the Congress of Angostura in 1819, and was appointed vice president of the department of Venezuela. Later that year, when Gran Colombia was formed (17 December 1819), he was appointed vice president of that new republic.

See also **Caracas, Audiencia of.**

BIBLIOGRAPHY

Benito Raúl Losada, *Juan Germán Roscio, 1763–1821* (1953).

Juan Germán Roscio, *Obras,* 3 vols. (1953).

Pedro Grases, *El catecismo religioso político del Doctor Juan Germán Roscio* (1964).

Additional Bibliography

Ruiz, Nydia M. *El pensamiento teológico-político de Juan Germán Roscio*. Caracas: Ediciones La Casa de Bell, 1992.

Ugalde, Luis. *Las confesiones de un pecador arrepentido: Juan Germán Roscio y los orígenes del discurso liberal venezolano*. Caracas: Fondo Editorial Tropykos/Facultad de Ciencias Económicas y Sociales, 1996.

INÉS QUINTERO

ROSENBLUETH, ARTURO STEARNS (1900–1970).

Arturo Stearns Rosenblueth (*b.* 2 October 1900; *d.* 19 September 1970), Mexican educator and physiologist. Born in Chihuahua, Chihuahua, Rosenblueth studied in Monterrey and Mexico City, where he graduated from the National School of Medicine in 1921. He did advanced work in Berlin and at the University of Paris before returning to the National University to teach in 1927. He obtained a Guggenheim fellowship to study under Walter Cannon at Harvard (1930–1932) and stayed to teach physiology until 1944, earning in the process an international reputation in neurophysiology. His work was published by the Massachusetts Institute of Technology, and on his return to Mexico, he mentored a select group of prominent future scientists. He was chief of the department of physiology at the National Polytechnic Institute and directed the physiology laboratory under Ignacio Chávez at the National Institute of Cardiology (1944–1960). He became a member of the National College in 1947, and received Mexico's National Prize in Sciences in 1966.

See also **Medicine: The Modern Era; Science.**

BIBLIOGRAPHY

Colegio Nacional, *Memoria,* vol. 7 (1973), pp. 159–165; *Tres científicos mexicanos* (1981).

RODERIC AI CAMP

ROSE OF LIMA. *See* Rosa de Lima.

ROSSELL Y ARELLANO, MARIANO (1894–1964).

Mariano Rossell y Arellano (*b.* 18 July 1894; *d.* 10 December 1964), archbishop of Guatemala (1939–1964). A native Guatemalan, Rossell y Arellano became a priest in 1918. He served as the private secretary of Archbishop Luis Javier Muñoz y Capurón and held the posts of secretary and chancellor in the metropolitan curia. In 1935 he became vicar-general under archbishop Luis Durou y Sure, upon whose death in 1939, Rossell became archbishop. The arrival of foreign missionaries and Rossell's active promotion of the lay apostolate helped to relieve a long-standing clerical shortage in Guatemala.

During the administrations of Juan José Arévalo and Jacobo Arbenz, the archbishop and lay Catholic leaders promoted social-justice teachings and criticized the government for its failure to stem the growth of communism. Their anticommunist crusade played a role in the downfall of Arbenz in 1954. Under the conservative leadership of president Carlos Castillo Armas, Rossell worked for the reversal of nineteenth-century liberal anticlerical laws, the repeal of which was achieved in the constitutions of 1956 and 1965.

See also **Catholic Church: The Modern Period; Guatemala.**

BIBLIOGRAPHY

Bruce J. Calder, *Crecimiento y cambio de la iglesia católica guatemalteca, 1944–1966* (1970).

José Luis Chea, *Guatemala: La cruz fragmentada* (1988), esp. pp. 67–100.

Ralph Lee Woodward, Jr., ed., *Central America: Historical Perspectives on the Contemporary Crises* (1988), esp. 85–105.

Additional Bibliography

Pattridge, Blake D. "The Catholic Church and the Closed Corporate Community during the Guatemalan Revolution, 1944–1955." *America* 52:1 (July 1995): 25–42.

HUBERT J. MILLER

ROSS SANTA MARÍA, GUSTAVO

(1879–1961). Gustavo Ross Santa María (*b.* June 1879; *d.* 5 April 1961), Chilean financier, businessman, and government minister. Born in Valparaíso, Ross, who supported the efforts to depose President Carlos Ibáñez Del Campo, served as minister of finance during Arturo Alessandri Palma's second term of office. Through a variety of sometimes controversial methods, he successfully renegotiated Chile's foreign debt. He also engineered Chile's economic recovery during the Great Depression by stimulating local industries, asserting state control over certain utilities as well as the nitrate industry, and restricting the profits of foreign businesses, particularly the American-owned copper mines. Singularly uncharismatic and identified with the nation's most conservative elements, Ross sought the presidency in 1938. Only the abortive Nazi putsch, which led to Ibáñez's support of Pedro Aguirre Cerda, prevented him from winning the Moneda.

See also **Chile: The Twentieth Century; Nazis.**

BIBLIOGRAPHY

John Reese Stevenson, *The Chilean Popular Front* (1942).

Ernst Halperin, *Nationalism and Communism in Chile* (1965).

Additional Bibliography

Fermandois H, Joaquín. *Abismo y cimiento: Gustavo Ross y las relaciones entre Chile y Estados Unidos, 1932–1938*. Santiago: Ediciones Universidad Católica de Chile, 1997.

WILLIAM F. SATER

ROTO. Roto, depreciative word used in Chile to refer to people of the "lower" classes. The word carries negative connotations regarding rural Mestizos in the south of Chile, although it is sometimes used informally in a more affectionate context. The term may have been used for the first time during the sixteenth century to refer to the Conquistador Pedro de Valdivia who on his return to Peru, was dressed in rags, a *roto*. The roto also has been a recurring figure in Chilean literature since the nineteenth century. Joaquín Edwards Bello's *El Roto* published in 1920 looks at the criminal life of the roto, but also suggests that this figure has good qualities and can be redeemed with proper education.

See also **Caste and Class Structure in Colonial Spanish America; Conquistadores.**

BIBLIOGRAPHY

Rodolfo Lenz, *Diccionario etimológico* (1910).

Additional Bibliography

Stephens, Thomas M. *Dictionary of Latin American Racial and Ethnic Terminology*. Gainesville: University of Florida Press, 1989.

Vergara-Mery, Alvaro R. "Espacio, marginalidad, disidencia y homosociabilidad del roto en la narrativa chilena." Ph.D. diss., Arizona State University, 2001.

KRISTINE L. JONES

ROUMAIN, JACQUES (1907–1944).

Jacques Jean-Baptiste Roumain, the Haitian poet, novelist, essayist, ethnographer, political activist, and diplomat, was one of the major literary and political figures of his generation and arguably the most lastingly influential of Haiti's early twentieth-century writers and intellectuals. Roumain early emerged as a powerful voice of the local indigenous cultural movement and of the *négritude* and nationalist populism for which *La Revue Indigène* (1927) and *La Trouée* (1927), both of which he helped to found, and *Le Petit Impartial: Journal de la Masse* (1928), of which he was editor-in-chief, spoke during the American occupation of Haiti (1915–1934). Educated in Switzerland and Spain, he had traveled in Belgium, France, and Germany, and brought a broadly cosmopolitan perspective and a radically revisionist sweep to his understanding of the national crisis precipitated by the U.S. occupation and its revelation of the Haitian elite's political insolvency. His rejection of the values and politics of the mulatto aristocracy into which he had been born eventually led him to the founding, in 1934, of the Haitian Communist Party. In his *L'Analysis schématique, 1932–1934*, the Party's inaugural document, and in his equally significant meditation on "Le Grief de l'homme noir" (1939), Roumain analyzes colonialism, racism, class conflict, intraracial contradiction, and the looming political dangers of a too narrowly *noiriste* cultural nationalism, effectively anticipating elements of later, better known critiques of these phenomena by his compatriot René Depestre, by the Martinican Frantz Fanon, and the Guyanese Walter Rodney, among others.

Joining with Jean Price-Mars to create a national Bureau d'Ethnologie in 1941, Roumain became its first director. His signature collection of poetry, *Bois d'ébène* (1939) and his much-acclaimed posthumous novel *Gouverneurs de la rosée* (1944) epitomize the synthesis of négritude, Marxist internationalism, lyrical realism, and the figurative evocation of voodoo ritual, popular belief, vernacular inflection, and a general human solidarity typical of his most accomplished verse and fiction. Revealing their unexplored narrative, thematic, and formal possibilities, Roumain's crafting and cultivation of the peasant or proletarian novel proved at once precursory and a provocative stimulus to the "marvelous realism" (Alexis 1956) of later generations of Haitian writers, including Jacques Stéphen Alexis, Pierre Clitandre, and, more recently, Edwidge Denticat. Lesser known works include the short stories of *La Proie et l'ombre* (1930) and *Les Fantoches* (1931), and the novels *La Montagne ensorcelée* (1931) and the as yet unpublished *Le Champ de Potier*. During World War II, Roumain served as the Haitian embassy's chargé d'affaires in Mexico. Suffering a fatal heart attack in 1944, he died at the height of his powers, while still only in his thirties.

See also **Alexis, Jacques Stéphen; Depestre, René; Haiti; Price-Mars, Jean.**

BIBLIOGRAPHY

Alexis, Jacques Stephan. "Of the Marvelous Realism of the Haitians." *Presence Africaine* (June–November 1956): 249–275.

Fowler, Carolyn. *A Knot in the Thread: The Life of Jacques Roumain.* Washington, DC: Howard University Press, 1980.

Roumain, Jacques. *When the Tom-Tom Beats.* Translated by Joanne Fungaroli and Ronald Sauer. Washington, DC: Azul Editions, 1995.

Roumain, Jacques. *Oeuvres complètes.* Edition critique coordonnée par León-François Hoffmann. Madrid et Nanterre: Allca XX, 2003.

ROBERTO MÁRQUEZ

ROY, EUGÈNE (?–1939).

Eugène Roy (*d.* 27 October 1939), president of Haiti (15 May–18 November 1930). In 1918, President Philippe Sudre Dartiguenave (1915–1922) appointed Roy to several government positions. Because of the high esteem in which many held Roy, who was by profession an exchange broker and a member of the elite, he was selected in April 1930 as provisional president. He was then elected by the council of state as the neutral, interim president who then arranged and presided over the election of the legislative chambers, which then elected the new president. This arrangement was designed to carry out the recommendations of U.S. president Herbert Hoover's Forbes Commission, which had investigated the unpopular U.S. occupation (1915–1934), which was forced upon the Louis Borno government (1922–1930) and its opposition. The opposition's landslide victory in the legislature resulted in the election in November 1930 of Sténio Vincent as president (1930–1941).

See also **Haiti.**

BIBLIOGRAPHY

Henry P. Fletcher, "Quo Vadis, Haiti?," in *Foreign Affairs* 8, no. 4 (1930): 533–548.

Harold Palmer Davis, *Black Democracy: The Story of Haiti*, rev. ed. (1967), pp. 61–65.

Robert D. Heinl, Jr., and Nancy G. Heinl, *Written in Blood: The Story of the Haitian People, 1492–1971* (1978), pp. 446, 501, 505–506.

Additional Bibliography

Renda, Mary A. *Taking Haiti: Military Occupation and the Culture of U.S. Imperialism, 1915–1940.* Chapel Hill: University of North Carolina Press, 2001.

LARMAN C. WILSON

RÚA, FERNANDO DE LA (1937–).

This Argentine politician served as president from 1999 to 2001. Born in Córdoba on September 15, 1937, de la Rúa attended secondary school at the General Paz Military School and graduated in law from the National University. A practicing Catholic, he was active as a young man in the Radical Civil Union Party.

He began his political career as adviser to the Ministry of the Interior during the administration of Arturo Illia (1963–1966). In April 1973 he was elected to the national senate for the city of Buenos Aires. That year he also backed Ricardo Balbín in his run for president of the Radical Civil Union Party. At the end of the military dictatorship in 1983, de la Rúa wanted to run for president but had to give way to Raúl Alfonsín's overwhelming triumph as the party's choice. He was again elected as senator for Buenos

Aires. In 1989 he won the popular vote for this position but the Peronistas and liberals worked together to defeat him in the electoral college. In 1991 he became a deputy and two years later returned to the senate. He left his position in 1996 when he was elected the mayor of Buenos Aires.

In 1997 the Radical Civil Union Party, in alliance with the Front for a Country in Solidarity (FREPASO), regained the nationwide majority thanks to tensions within the Peronist party and criticism of the Menem administration for corruption and unemployment. With de la Rúa as candidate, the alliance won the presidency in December 1999. But the economic situation continued to deteriorate, with 18 percent unemployment and successive failures in various adjustment measures. The last of them was the *corralito*, which partially froze bank accounts and savings, bringing on a crisis for the coalition and increasing discontent. By late 2001 protests by the unemployed and account holders became widespread, while rival parties were organizing looting on the periphery of the large cities. A declaration of a state of siege and an order to suppress protests left twenty-seven dead throughout the country. This marked the end of de la Rúa's administration, and he was forced to resign on December 20.

See also **Alfonsín, Raúl Ricardo; Argentina: The Twentieth Century; Argentina, Political Parties: Personalist Radical Civic Union.**

BIBLIOGRAPHY

Morales Solá, Joaquín. *El sueño eterno: Ascenso y caída de la Alianza.* Buenos Aires: Planeta, 2001.

Novaro, Marcos. *Historia de la Argentina contemporánea.* Buenos Aires: Edhasa, 2006.

Semán, Ernesto. *Educando a Fernando.* Buenos Aires: Planeta, 1999.

MARCOS NOVARO

RUBBER GATHERERS' UNIONS.

Rubber Gatherers' Unions, groups of Amazonian rubber tappers who unite to address financial, social, and environmental issues. Formation began in 1974, when the Confederacão dos Trabalhadores na Agricultura (CONTAG), a government agency controlled by the minister of labor, sent its field delegate, João Maia, to Acre to establish workers' unions. Maia founded the first union in Sena Madureira, Acre. Later that year, a more powerful union was developed in the small border town of Brasiléia, Acre. Elias Roseno was the first leader of the Brasiléia union. He was succeeded by Wilson Pinheiro, who headed the Brasiléia union until his assassination in 1980. Chico Mendes founded the Xapuri Rural Workers' Union in 1977. His leadership, and later, his assassination by a rancher in December 1988, brought international attention to the rubber tappers because his union addressed Brazilian environmental and social problems. An extractive reserve of nearly one million hectares was later designated in his honor.

In 1978, local unions in Acre, led by Chico Mendes, organized FETACRE (*Federacão dos Sindicatos dos Trabalhadores Rurais do Acre*) at a state level, and by 1990 it had 30,000 members. Rubber gatherers' unions extended to Rondônia, Amazonas, Amapá, and the few remaining areas in Pará where tappers extract latex from rubber trees. In 1985, Mary Allegretti, an anthropologist who worked for the Instituto de Estudos Sócio-Econômicos, helped these unions form the Conselho Nacional dos Seringueiros (CNS), which meets semiannually in Brasília. The CNS sets up schools, health-care posts, and cooperatives that enable members to buy products at reasonable prices as well as to market their rubber.

In the 1980s, conflicts between cattle ranchers, who wanted to cut down the forest to create pasture, and the populations who live from the forests and collect their products, became acute. With financial backing from OXFAM, the Ford Foundation, and various Brazilian organizations, rubber tappers focused international attention on their fight to save the rain forest through their tactic of *empate* (nonviolent standoff) to halt clear cutting. International environmentalists and CNS also formulated and promoted the concept of extractive reserves (federal lands based on traditional land tenure structure on which workers live and from which they extract goods, like latex, fruit, and nuts, but which they do not destroy). As of 2005, the Brazilian government had established twenty-five extractive reserves encompassing 3.8 million hectares in the Amazon.

Since winning recognition for their struggle, rubber tappers have entered the political arena. The cofounder of the union movement in Acre, Marina Silva, was elected to the the federal senate, and forester Jorge Viana was elected governor of the state.

See also **Environmental Movements; Forests; Labor Movements; Rubber Industry.**

BIBLIOGRAPHY

Chico Mendes, with additional material by Tony Gross, *Fight for the Forest: Chico Mendes in His Own Words* (1989).

Augusta Dwyer, *Into the Amazon: The Struggle for the Rain Forest* (1990).

Susanna Hecht and Alexander Cockburn, *The Fate of the Forest: Developers, Destroyers, and Defenders of the Amazon* (1990).

Andrew Revkin, *The Burning Season* (1990).

Additional Bibliography

Almeida Neto, Domingos José de. *"Aos trancos e barrancos": Identidade, cultura e resistência seringueira na periferia de Rio Branco-AC, 1970–1980.* Rio Branco, Brazil: EDUFAC, 2004.

Cardoso, Catarina A. S. *Extractive Reserves in Brazilian Amazonia: Local Resource Management and the Global Political Economy.* Aldershot, U.K., and Burlington, VT: Ashgate, 2002.

Costa, Francisco Pereira. *Seringueiros, patrões e a justiça no Acre Federal, 1904–1918.* Rio Branco: EDUFAC, 2005.

Martins, Edilson. *Chico Mendes: Um povo da floresta.* Rio de Janeiro: Garamond, 1998.

O'Dwyer, Eliane Cantarino. *Seringueiros da Amazônia: Dramas sociais e o olhar antropológico.* Niterói, Brazil: Editora da Universidade Federal Fluminense, 1998.

Posey, Darrell A., and Michael J. Balick, eds. *Human Impacts on Amazonia: The Role of Traditional Ecological Knowledge in Conservation and Development.* New York: Columbia University Press, 2006.

Rodrigues, Gomercindo. *Walking the Forest with Chico Mendes: Struggle for Justice in the Amazon.* Edited and translated by Linda Rabben. Austin: University of Texas Press, 2007.

Souza, Márcio. *Chico Mendes.* São Paulo: Callis Editora, 2005.

Teixeira, Carlos Corrêa. *Visões da natureza: Seringueiros e colonos em Rondônia.* São Paulo: Educ: FAPESP, 1999.

Wolff, Cristina Scheibe. *Mulheres da floresta: Uma história: Alto Juruá, Acre, 1890–1945.* São Paulo: Editora Hucitec, 1999.

CAROLYN JOSTOCK

RUBBER INDUSTRY.

Latin America was once the source of most of the world's natural rubber. It was gathered in the wild from various latex-bearing plants, principally *Hevea brasiliensis,* a tree native to the Amazon Basin. This species was transferred to Southeast Asia and, by 1913, when plantations there had begun production, the Amazon gathering trade largely collapsed, surviving in Brazil to the present only because of government subsidies. Factories for the production of tires and other rubber products have been in operation in several Latin American countries since the 1930s. Latin America now depends on synthetic rubber for most of its requirements. Synthetic rubber manufacturing plants were installed in Mexico, Brazil, and Argentina by the 1950s.

Natural rubber is a product derived from latex, a milky white fluid produced by a number of plant species, probably as a protection against insects. Among those plants commercially exploited, the most important is Pará rubber (*Hevea brasiliensis*), a tree whose natural habitat is the lowland tropical rainforest of the southern tributaries of the Amazon River. Less important is caucho (*Castilla elastica*), a tree that grows from Central America to the western part of the Amazon basin. Another is guayule (*Parthenium argentatum*), a northern Mexican desert shrub that has been the object of fifty years of desultory experimentation.

The indigenous peoples of the Amazon knew of the elastic properties of latex. They had learned how to coagulate it by "smoking" it over an open fire, and they made various objects from it. By the late eighteenth

Workers planting rubber trees at the Ford plantation in Para, Brazil, 1942. The Amazon economy boomed from natural rubber exports in the late nineteenth century but was soon overtaken cultivated rubber in Asia. Efforts by government and private entities to develop rubber plantations in Brazil have largely been thwarted by resistant fungus and leaf diseases. © BETTMANN/ CORBIS

century Portuguese colonial authorities were ordering waterproof boots and other articles of latex for their army. The trade in rubber was unimportant, however, until the late 1830s, when it was discovered simultaneously in Great Britain and the United States that rubber could be made to retain its elasticity by mixing it with sulphur and heating it. Numerous applications were quickly found for vulcanized rubber, from gaskets for steam engines to bumpers for railway cars, and demand grew immensely with the invention of the bicycle and of the automobile and with its use in electrical insulation.

Rubber trees, like other tropical species, grow extremely scattered in the forest. It was usual to strip the caucho tree of its bark to obtain the latex, a practice that resulted in a highly itinerant trade that brutalized its workers. The Pará rubber tree's bark was incised, or "tapped," to extract the latex. This practice may be continued for many years, but often the trees were damaged in haste or greed; as a result, rubber gathering spread rapidly ever further up the rivers. Steamboats, supplies, and labor recruiters, all financed in Belém and, ultimately, in London, accompanied this expansion. In 1876, however, the Royal Botanic Gardens at Kew obtained a shipment of rubber seeds, which it planted and sent on to Ceylon (Sri Lanka) and Malaya (Malaysia). Through the efforts of a few dedicated colonial service botanists, by the turn of the century a vast plantation industry had been launched.

There were numerous attempts in Brazil and the Guianas to plant rubber, just as other native plants, such as cacao, had been domesticated there. All were failures, including the large plantations of the Ford Motor Company at Fordlândia and Belterra, founded near Santarém in the 1920s and abandoned in 1945. The Pará rubber tree, grown in close stands in its native habitat, is vulnerable to South American leaf blight, caused by the fungus *Microcyclus ulei,* and to other leaf diseases, none of which have found their way to Southeast Asia. Unfortunately, no wild specimen or cultivated clone has been found that combines high latex yield and high resistance.

During World War II the U.S. government, desperate to replace lost Southeast Asian sources of supply, tried to stimulate wild rubber gathering in the Western Hemisphere. Despite large investments in transport, public health, and labor recruitment, only a trifling increase in exports was achieved, at the further cost of disorganizing the trade in other extracted products. The war effort did institute in Brazil a policy that was continued for nearly fifty years—a guaranteed price for natural rubber. Brazilian rubber manufacturers were obliged to pay a price double or triple that charged in the world market. This policy, however, failed to stimulate the gathering trade, and by 1951 Brazil was obliged to import rubber from Southeast Asia. The investment during World War II still resonates in the early twenty-first century because the 1988 Brazilian constitution stated that World War II rubber workers should receive a state pension. However, in 2006, many workers still have not received anything due to the difficulty of finding documentation.

Later attempts to cultivate the Pará rubber tree in the Western Hemisphere have mostly failed to overcome the parasitic problem, but rubber planting has developed on a modest scale in Brazil. Recent efforts to establish "extractive reserves" in the Amazon gave new life to rubber gathering, which was moribund, but the ending of Brazil's rubber price guarantee has rendered these reserves much more problematic.

Rubber tire manufacture began in the larger countries of Latin America before World War II. In the early 1960s, synthetic rubber plants were installed in Brazil, Argentina, and Mexico. By 1989, the Latin American countries were producing only 60,000 tons of natural rubber, while they were obliged to import 225,000 tons from Southeast Asia. In Latin America, synthetics equal 66 percent of consumption; by comparison, India, a developing country that grows all of its natural rubber, is able to restrict its use of environmentally less desirable synthetic rubbers to 21 percent of consumption.

From the late 1970s through the late 1980s, considerable planting of Pará rubber was carried out in Brazil in various non-Amazonian states, in the hope that the leaf blight fungus would not appear in cooler, drier regions. Although rubber trees were surviving on Brazilian plantations in the 1990s, more time was needed to evaluate their long-term resistance to plant disease.

As of the early twenty-first century, Brazil has had only limited success in regenerating natural rubber production. However, the project still receives support from environmental groups, who see natural rubber gathering as a less environmentally damaging form of development.

See also **Forests; Plantations; World War II.**

BIBLIOGRAPHY

Walter E. Hardenburg, *The Putumayo: The Devil's Paradise* (1912).

Dudley M. Phelps, *Rubber Developments in Latin America* (1957).

Loren G. Polhamus, *Rubber: Botany, Cultivation, and Utilization* (1962).

Roberto Santos, *História econômica da Amazônia (1800–1920)* (1980).

Barbara Weinstein, *The Amazon Rubber Boom, 1850–1920* (1983).

Nelson Prado Alves Pinto, *A política da borracha no Brasil* (1984).

Paul Holliday and K. H. Chee, *South American Leaf Blight of Hevea Rubber* (1986).

Warren Dean, *Brazil and the Struggle for Rubber* (1987).

Additional Bibliography

Barham, Brad, and O. T. Coomes. *Prosperity's Promise: The Amazon Rubber Boom and Distorted Economic Development.* Boulder, CO: Westview Press, 1996.

Stanfield, Michael Edward. *Red Rubber, Bleeding Trees: Violence, Slavery, and Empire in Northwest Amazonia, 1850–1933.* Albuquerque: University of New Mexico Press, 1998.

WARREN DEAN

RUBÍ, MARQUÉS DE Marqués de Rubí (Cayetano María Pignatelli Rubí Corbera y San Climent), Spanish inspector (*visitador*). Rubí arrived in New Spain in November 1764 as part of the Juan de Villalba military mission charged with reorganizing New Spain's defenses. Rubí's assignment was to inspect New Spain's northern presidio system. He left Mexico City in March 1766 with a small entourage that included the expedition's diarist and cartographer, Nicolás de Lafora and draftsman José de Urrutia. Over the next twenty-three months the expedition traveled 7,500 miles from Louisiana to California and visited twenty-three presidio companies. Rubí's report revealed the lamentable condition of the presidio system. His proposals included a realignment of the presidio defenses to reflect New Spain's actual territory rather than its imagined domain. Rubí suggested the creation of a line of fifteen presidios across the frontier with only Santa Fe and San Antonio beyond the line. He also suggested that the danger of Comanche attacks in Texas could best be eliminated by creating alliances with them against the Apache tribes in the area. In response, the king issued the Reglamento of 1772, which incorporated most of Rubí's recommendations.

See also **New Spain, Colonization of the Northern Frontier; Presidio.**

BIBLIOGRAPHY

Max L. Moorhead, *The Presidio: Bastion of the Spanish Borderlands* (1975), chap. 3.

Luis Navarro García, "The North of New Spain as a Political Problem in the Eighteenth Century," in David J. Weber, ed., *New Spain's Far Northern Frontier: Essays on Spain in the American West, 1540–1821* (1979), pp. 201–216.

Oakah Jones, *Nueva Vizcaya: Heartland of the Spanish Frontier* (1988), pp. 158–161, 169–170.

Additional Bibliography

Chipman, Donald E, and Denise Joseph Harriett. *Explorers and Settlers of Spanish Texas.* Austin: University of Texas Press, 2001.

Pedro de Rivera, Cayetano, María Pignatelli, Rubí Corbera, Marques de, Jack Jackson, and William C. Foster. *Imaginary Kingdom: Texas as Seen by the Rivera and Rubí Military Expeditions, 1727 and 1767.* Austin: Texas State Historical Association, 1995.

AARON PAINE MAHR

RUBIÃO, MURILO (1916–1991). Murilo Rubião (*b.* 1 July 1916; *d.* 16 September 1991), Brazilian author. Born in Carmo, Minas Gerais, Rubião earned a degree in law and in 1939 became an editor at the newspaper *Folha de Minas.* One year later, with the publication of his short story "Elvira e outros mistérios" (Elvira and Other Mysteries), he initiated his literary career, which was to be interrupted several times by his many other activities. He became a cabinet officer for Juscelino Kubitschek at the time the future president of Brazil was governor of Minas Gerais. In 1947 Rubião published his first book of short stories, *O ex-mágico* (The Ex-Magician); after six years a second book appeared, *A estrela vermelha* (The Red Star). Subsequent publications followed at extended intervals. Among the reasons given by the author for the sparsity of his creative output was his own dissatisfaction with his work; he apparently destroyed many pieces before they were sent to print.

In 1956 Rubião was nominated cultural attaché for the Brazilian embassy in Madrid, where he served for four years. Returning to Brazil, he resumed his duties with the state government, and in 1966 became editor in chief of the literary supplement to the newspaper *Minas Gerais*. Rubião published a total of six books during his lifetime. The most prominent was *O pirotécnico Zacarias* (Zacarias, the Fireworks Maker, 1974). Rubião's work contains elements of the surreal and the fantastic. His fictional construct leans to a great extent upon dreams and hallucinations; his characters are most often presented as victims of insanity. Through portrayals of extreme isolation, his work conveys a critical sense of life's absurdities.

See also **Literature: Brazil.**

BIBLIOGRAPHY

Davi Arrigucci, Jr., Preface to *O pirotécnico Zacarias* (1974).

Jorge Schwartz, "Obra muriliana—Do fantástico como máscara" (preface to *O convidado*) (1974), and *Murilo Rubião: A poética do uroboro* (1981).

Additional Bibliography

Bastos, Hermenegildo. *Literatura e colonialismo: Rotas de navegação e comércio no fantástico de Murilo Rubião*. Brasília: Editora Universidade de Brasília: Editora Plano: Oficina Editorial, Instituto de Letras, 2001.

REGINA IGEL

RUEDA, MANUEL (1921–1999). Manuel Rueda (*b*. 27 August 1921; *d*. 1999), Dominican musician, playwright, folklorist, and poet. Born in Montecristi, Rueda has received his country's National Book Award four times, and in 1994 he won the Fundación Corripio's National Prize in Literature for a life's work, the highest literary distinction in the Dominican Republic. Associated in the 1940s and 1950s with the Poesía Sorprendida movement, Rueda also spent 14 years studying music in Chile, where he began publishing his work and befriended Vicente Huidobro, Chilean poet and theorist. From his first book, *Las noches* (1949), Rueda has demonstrated a commitment to enhancing the possibilities of his craft through formal explorations.

In February 1974, he presented a lecture, "Claves para una poesía plural," whereby he launched an aesthetic creed called *pluralismo*, which sought to liberate the poetic text by turning it into an interactive, open artifact for both the poet and the reader. His text *Con el tambor de las islas* (1975) exemplifies the aesthetics of *pluralismo*, which, despite the uproar it provoked initially, did not produce notable followers. His mature poetic work appears in *Por los mares de la dama: Poesía 1970–1975* (1976), *Las edades del viento: Poesía inédita 1947–1979* (1979), and *Congregación del cuerpo único: Poesía 1980–1989* (1989). Rueda has also received numerous honors for his musical accomplishments, including the directorship of his country's National Conservatory of Music. On six different occasions he won the *Premio Anual de Literatura* for his poetry, theater and fiction. In addition, in 1994 he earned the *Premio Nacional de Literatura*.

See also **Huidobro Fernández, Vicente; Literatura: Spanish America.**

BIBLIOGRAPHY

José Alcántara Almánzar, *Estudios de poesía dominicana* (1979).

Guillermo Piña Contreras, *Doce en la literatura dominicana* (1982).

José Alcantara Almánzar, *Los escritores dominicanos y la cultura* (1990).

Additional Bibliography

Veloz Maggiolo, Marcio. *Santo Domingo en la novela dominicana*. Santo Domingo: Comisión Permanente de la Feria del Libro, 2002.

SILVIO TORRES- SAILLANT

RUELAS, JULIO (1870–1907). Julio Ruelas (*b*. 21 June 1870; *d*. 16 September 1907), Mexican artist. Born in Zacatecas, Ruelas is one of the precursors of modernism in Mexico and the most important representative of symbolism in that country. In 1885 he enrolled at the National School of Fine Arts in Mexico City, where he received an academic training. In 1892 he traveled to Germany and studied at the Academy of Arts in Karlsruhe, where he became interested in the works of Arnold Boeklin. After his return to Mexico in 1895, Ruelas published his works in the *Revista moderna,* founded by the poet Jesús E. Valenzuela; this publication was extremely influential in disseminating the aesthetic of Latin American symbolists. In 1904 Ruelas went to Paris to perfect his etching technique. He also traveled to Belgium, where he may have seen the works of Félicien Rops. Although Ruelas created a number of paintings, he is basically known as an engraver and draftsman. He died in Paris, having produced a small but highly inventive body of work.

See also **Art: The Twentieth Century.**

BIBLIOGRAPHY

Justino Fernández, *El arte en el siglo XIX en México* (1967), esp. pp. 146–147.

Teresa Del Conde, *Julio Ruelas* (1976).

Additional Bibliography

Rodríguez Lobat, Marisela. *Julio Ruelas ... siempre vestido de huraña melancolía: Temática y comentario a la obra ilustrativa de Julio Ruelas en la Revista moderna, 1898–1911.* México: Universidad Iberoamericana, Departamento de Art, 1998.

ILONA KATZEW

RUFFO APPEL, ERNESTO (1952–).

The Mexican politician and opposition leader Ernesto Ruffo was born on June 25, 1952, in San Diego, California, the son of a fish packer. Ruffo received most of his education in Ensenada, Baja California, graduating in business administration and accounting from the Technological Institute of Higher Studies of Monterrey in 1975. He began a long career in the Zapata Fishing Company, beginning as the personnel manager and including fleet and operations manager, before becoming general manager in 1982.

After joining the National Action Party (PAN) in 1983, Ruffo became president of Coparmex, a politically active business organization in Ensenada, and was elected the municipality's mayor in 1986. He won the governorship of Baja California in the benchmark election of 1989, becoming the first Mexican politician outside the PRI to win a governorship. His victory set off a pattern of PAN victories against the incumbent party, contributing significantly to the democratization of the electoral system that led to the presidential victory of Vicente Fox in 2000. After completing his term as governor in 1995, Ruffo ran unsuccessfully for the presidency of his party. President Fox subsequently appointed him as coordinator of migration affairs for the Northern Border, a position he held from 2000 to 2003.

See also **Fox Quesada, Vicente; Mexico: Since 1910; Mexico, Political Parties: National Action Party (PAN).**

BIBLIOGRAPHY

Diccionario biográfico del gobierno federal, 1992. Mexico: Presidencia, 1992.

Mizrahi, Yemile. *From Martyrdom to Power: The Partido Acción Nacional in México.* Notre Dame, IN: Notre Dame University Press, 2003.

RODERIC AI CAMP

RUGENDAS, JOHANN MORITZ

(1802–1858). Johann Moritz Rugendas (*b.* 29 March 1802; *d.* 29 May 1858), German landscape painter who completed more than 5,000 paintings and drawings of the landscapes and peoples of Latin America between 1821 and 1847. He was not only an artist but also a historian, a scientist, and a geographer.

By far the most varied and important of the European artists to visit Latin America, Rugendas, a native of Augsburg, first journeyed there when he accompanied an expedition into the interior of Brazil led in 1821 by the Russian consul-general in Rio de Janeiro, Baron Georg Heinrich von Langsdorff. Rugendas left the expedition and traversed the Brazilian countryside for the next two years, drawing the landscapes, people, animals, and plants of Minas Gerais, Mato Grosso, Espírito Santo, and Bahia. In 1823 he returned to Europe, and from 1827 to 1835, he published a four-part collection of lithographs from over 500 of these drawings of Brazil, *Pictorial Journey Through Brazil.*

In 1831, Rugendas returned to Latin America to complete drawings and watercolors of the people and countryside of the Mexican states of Morelia and Guerrero, and the regions near Teotihuacán, Xochimilco, and Cuernavaca. In 1833 he traveled to Chile, where he remained until 1845, drawing the countryside and people. He visited Argentina from 1837 to 1838, and from 1842 to 1844, Peru and Bolivia. In 1845 Rugendas moved on to Montevideo and Buenos Aires, Argentina. Two years later, after visiting Rio de Janeiro, he returned to Germany. He died in Weilheim, Germany.

See also **Germans in Latin America.**

BIBLIOGRAPHY

Leopoldo Castedo, *A History of Latin American Art and Architecture,* translated by Phyllis Freeman (1969).

Johann Moritz Rugendas, *Viagem pitoresca através do Brasil,* translated by Sergio Milliet (1972).

Carlos Lemos, *The Art of Brazil* (1983).

Dawn Ades, *Art in Latin America* (1989).

Additional Bibliography

Diener, Pablo. *Rugendas: 1802–1858.* Augsburg: Wissner, 1998.

Taunay, Aimé-Adrien, and Hercules Florence. *Expedição Langsdorff ao Brasil, 1821–1829: Rugendas, Taunay, Florence.* Rio de Janeiro: Edições Alumbramento: Livroarte Editora, 1998.

                                        MARY JO MILES

RUIZ, ANTONIO (1897–1964). Antonio Ruiz (*b.* 1897; *d.* 9 October 1964), Mexican painter, muralist, theater and movie set designer, art teacher, and arts administrator. Ruiz was born in Texcoco and studied at the National School of Fine Arts in Mexico City. In 1926 he went to Hollywood to study set design, and he assisted in painting four murals for Pacific House, in San Francisco. Returning to Mexico in 1929, in 1932 he founded the first workshop on technical maquettes at the School of Engineering and Architecture. In 1938 he became professor of set design and perspective in the National School of the Plastic Arts. From 1942 to 1954 he designed sets for Mexico City theaters, a film company, and some ballets. He died in Mexico City.

Ruiz is known for his very small, carefully composed, and meticulously painted pictures. Each is full of details that add to the meaning of the subjects portrayed. His use of perspective in some of his pictures to create illusions of great depth demonstrates his knowledge of architecture and stage design. As a painter of the Mexican School, he depicted the people of Mexico at work, at leisure, window shopping, performing, courting, and commemorating national holidays. In some cases, the Mexicans are presented as part of a complex world in which the modern mingles with the past. Ruiz also satirized, in a humorous way, the failings of those who cannot overcome their limitations, for example, the nouveau riche who acquire worldly possessions but not good taste, an aspiring opera singer without talent, and an orator without an audience or a message to deliver.

See also **Cinema: From the Silent Film to 1990; Theater.**

BIBLIOGRAPHY

Exposición homenaje Antonio M. Ruiz (1966).

Jacinto Quirarte, "Mexican and Mexican American Artists in the United States: 1920–1970," in *The Latin American Spirit: Art and Artists in the United States, 1920–1970,* catalogue of The Bronx Museum of the Arts (1988), pp. 38–39, and *Mexico: Splendors of Thirty Centuries* (1990), pp. 651–661.

Additional Bibliography

Folgarait, Leonard. *Mural Painting and Social Revolution in Mexico, 1920–1940: Art of the New Order.* Cambridge: Cambridge University Press, 1998.

Pellicer, Carlos, and Rafael Carrillo Azpéitia. *La Pintura mural de la Revolución Mexicana.* México: Fondo Editorial de la Plástica Mexicana, 1998.

                                        JACINTO QUIRARTE

RUÍZ, HENRY (1940–). A former member of the Sandinista National Directorate, Henry Ruíz joined the movement in 1967 and supported prolonged popular war under the code name "Modesto." In December 1974 he participated in a Christmastime raid on the house of a cotton exporter. In July 1979 he became minister of planning and designed a mixed economy. In 1985 he became minister of external cooperation and traveled widely in Europe and Africa.

See also **Nicaragua, Sandinista National Liberation Front (FSLN).**

BIBLIOGRAPHY

Primary Work

"La montaña era como un crisol donde se forjaban los mejores cuadros." *Nicaráuac* 1 (1980): 17–18.

Secondary Work

García Márquez, Gabriel, ed. *Los Sandinistas.* Bogotá, Colombia, Editorial Oveja Negra, 1979.

MARK EVERINGHAM

RUIZ, SAMUEL (1924–). Samuel Ruiz was appointed bishop of San Cristóbal de Las Casas, Chiapas, in 1959. He participated in the Second Vatican Council, and in 1968 was appointed president of the Latin American Episcopal Conference (CELAM) for Indigenous People and delegated to participate in the CELAM in Medellín, Colombia. He promoted the 1974 Indigenous Congress, which set guidelines for hearing the social and religious demands of indigenous people. Ruiz helped to defend the refugees from the war in Guatemala, and founded the Fray Bartolomé de Las Casas Human Rights Center in conjunction with the Dominicans in the diocese. He promoted indigenous deaconship, and was a mediator between the Mexican government and the Zapatista Army of National Liberation (EZLN). In 1994 he created the National Commission for Intermediation (CONAI) to seek a political solution to the armed conflict. UNESCO awarded him its Simon Bolívar International Prize in 2000 for his human-rights efforts.

See also **Chiapas; Colombia: Since Independence; Guatemala; Human Rights; Las Casas, Bartolomé de; Medellín; Mexico, Organizations: Zapatista Army of National Liberation; Religion in Mexico, Catholic Church and Beyond; Salinas de Gortari, Carlos; San Cristóbal de las Casas.**

BIBLIOGRAPHY

Ruiz García, Samuel. *Mi trabajo Pastoral, en la diócesis de San Cristóbal de Las Casas. Principios teológicos.* México: San Pablo, 1999.

Ruiz García, Samuel, and Carles Torner. *Comment les Indiens m'ont converti.* Paris: Atelier, 2002.

PABLO ROMO

RUIZ, TOMÁS (1777–c. 1820). Tomás Ruiz (*b.* 10 January 1777; *d.* ca. 1820), Central American priest and patriot. An Indian born in Chinandega, Nicaragua, Tomás Ruiz received a doctoral degree in canon law from the University of San Carlos in Guatemala in 1804. He was the only Indian in Central America to receive this degree. Ruiz was a founder of the University of León in Nicaragua. He taught there and served as vice-rector of the seminary where he himself had studied.

Tomás Ruiz was active in modernizing the curriculum of the University of León; Ruiz stressed mathematics, which he taught. He became involved in disputes and rivalries, and was denied the position of *canongía* (a professorship of holy law) in León in 1807 and then at Comayagua, Honduras, a year later. Racial prejudice and nepotism seem to have been the reasons. His frustration at having suffered discrimination as an Indian probably led to his involvement in the conspiracy at the Belén monastery in Guatemala in December 1813, which anticipated an armed revolt for independence from Spain.

The Belén Conspiracy was quashed; Padre Ruiz was arrested and spent a number of years in confinement. He remained a part of the reformist faction as independence loomed. His main biographer, the Nicaraguan Jorge Eduardo Arellano, argues that Ruiz should be regarded as his country's primary *prócer* (founding father), rather than the conservative Miguel Larreynaga, who signed the independence document. Padre Ruiz may have gone to Chiapas, Mexico, after his release in 1819, but there is no further record of his activities beyond that point.

See also **Belén Conspiracy; Central America, Independence of.**

BIBLIOGRAPHY

Jorge Eduardo Arellano, *El padre-indio Tomás Ruiz, prócer de Centroamérica* (1979).

Gene A. Müller, "La formación de un revolucionario del siglo XIX: El doctor Tomás Ruiz de Centroamérica," in *Revista del Pensamiento Centroamericano* 154 (January–March 1977): 22–32.

GARY G. KUHN

RUIZ CORTINES, ADOLFO (1890–1973).

Adolfo Ruiz Cortines (*b.* 30 December 1890; *d.* 3 December 1973), president of Mexico (1952–1958). The administration of Ruiz Cortines is best known for the stabilizing effect it produced in the wake of the political and economic excesses of his predecessor, Miguel Alemán. In terms of political leadership, Ruiz Cortines provided the last hurrah for the revolutionary generation, of which he himself was part. His selection as president, in fact, represented a generational reversal of political trends after Alemán. Socially, like Lázaro Cárdenas, he served as an apt personal model of presidential integrity, nationalizing the properties of some of Alemán's more corrupt collaborators. His administration offered no major political innovations but provided a transition for economic growth known as the "stabilizing period."

From a modest family, Ruiz Cortines left school at an early age in the port city of Veracruz to help support his widowed mother. After holding a series of unskilled jobs, he joined the Revolution in 1914 as a second captain during the U.S. invasion of Veracruz, during which he served as an assistant to two major revolutionary figures, generals Heriberto Jara and Jacinto B. Treviño. After holding a number of minor administrative posts in the military, he joined the office of social statistics in the 1920s.

His political career did not prosper until 1934, when he became secretary general of his home state of Veracruz, after which he served as the *oficial mayor* of the Department of the Federal District (1934–1937). In 1937, he represented his home state in the Chamber of Deputies. During the late 1930s, he became friends with Miguel Alemán, who, based on Ruiz's reputation for integrity, appointed him treasurer of Manuel Ávila Camacho's presidential campaign in 1945. When Alemán, his political mentor, was appointed secretary of government in 1940, he brought Ruiz Cortines with him as his *oficial mayor* (1940–1944). In 1944, Ruiz Cortines left the executive branch to serve as governor of his home state of Veracruz. After serving four years, Alemán brought him back into the cabinet as his secretary of government, a position he served in until his candidacy as president was announced in 1952.

Alemán's designation of Ruiz Cortines as the government party's (PRI) candidate provoked the last major political opposition from a group of revolutionary generals disappointed in the direction of Mexico's leadership. Their removal from decision-making authority led to the formation of an intense opposition campaign under the leadership of General Miguel Henríquez Guzmán and the lowest reported vote tallies for a government presidential candidate in many years. After his election, Ruiz Cortines did succeed in mollifying those elements and in restoring unity to his party. After leaving office in 1958, he lived modestly in Veracruz, serving as a minor consultant to the government.

See also **Alemán Valdés, Miguel.**

BIBLIOGRAPHY

Frank R. Brandenburg, *The Making of Modern Mexico* (1964).

Manuel García Purón, *México y sus gobernantes, biografías* (1964).

Olga Pellicer De Brody, *El afianzamiento de la estabilidad política: Historia de la Revolución mexicana, 1952–1960* (1978).

Olga Pellicer De Brody and Esteban L. Mancilla, *El entendimiento con los Estados Unidos y la gestación del desarrollo estabilizador: Historia de la Revolución mexicana, 1952–1960* (1978).

Additional Bibliography

Alemán Velasco, Miguel. *No siembro para mí: Biografía de Adolfo Ruiz Cortines.* México: Editorial Diana, 1997.

Krauze, Enrique. *Mexico: Biography of Power: A History of Modern Mexico, 1810–1996.* New York: HarperPerennial, 1998.

RODERIC AI CAMP

RUIZ DE ALARCÓN Y MENDOZA, JUAN (1581?–1639).

Juan Ruiz de Alarcón y Mendoza (*b.* 1581?; *d.* 4 August 1639), one of the four great dramatists of the Spanish Golden Age, which reached its peak in the first half of the seventeenth century. Born in Mexico City to an illustrious family, Ruiz de Alarcón studied canon and civil law at the Royal Pontifical University of Mexico (1596–1600) and at the University of Salamanca in Spain (1600–1605). As a lawyer, Alarcón served as assistant to the *corregidor* (mayor) in Mexico City and advisor to the city council. He litigated at the royal court in Madrid and the Audiencia of Mexico, sought and obtained public offices, was financial adviser to those in debt, and in 1610 investigating judge in Veracruz, Mexico. He crossed the Atlantic three times, but he lived most of his life in Spain. He died in Madrid.

Alarcón wrote drama mainly for his own enjoyment, but it was lucrative. *Las paredes oyen* was first performed in 1617. Envious of the success of his plays, his rivals ridiculed him for his physical deformity as a hunchback with bow legs. The Spanish critic Mendéndez y Pelayo described Alarcón as the classic dramatist of a romantic theater. His plays are humorous, subdued, and clever and illustrate moral truths. *La verdad sospechosa* (1619) condemns lying, *Las paredes oyen* (1617) illustrates the evils of slander, and *Mudarse para mejorarse* (1622) deals with inconstancy in love. Alarcón wrote twenty-four plays published under *Parte primera de las comedias de don Juan Ruiz de Alarcón y Mendoza* (1628) and *Parte segunda de las comedias del Licenciado Don Juan Ruiz de Alarcón* (1634). *La prueba de las promesas* is considered by many to be Alarcón's masterpiece, along with *Las paredes oyen* and *La verdad sospechosa*. Alarcón's plays influenced Corneille, Molière, and Goldoni.

See also **Theater.**

BIBLIOGRAPHY

Agustín Millares Carlo, ed., *Obras completas de Don Juan Ruiz de Alarcón*, 3 vols. (1957).

Walter Poesse, *Juan Ruiz de Alarcón* (1972).

Margarita Peña, *Juan Ruiz de Alarcón, semejante asi mismo* (1992).

Cynthia Leone Halpern, *The Political Theatre of Seventeenth-Century Spain, with Special Reference to Juan Ruiz de Alarcón* (1993).

Additional Bibliography

Josa, Lola. *El arte dramático de Juan Ruiz de Alarcón.* Kassel: Edition Reichenberger, 2002.

Revueltas, Eugenia. *El discurso de Juan Ruiz de Alarcón: Texto y representación.* Zamora: Colegio de Michoacán, 1999.

Whicker, Jules. *The Plays of Juan Ruiz de Alarcón.* Rochester, U.K.: Tamesis, 2003.

GEORGETTE MAGASSY DORN

RUÍZ DE APODACA, JUAN, CONDE DE VENADITO (1754–1835). Juan Ruíz de Apodaca, Conde de Venadito, (*b.* 3 February 1754; *d.* 11 January 1835), viceroy of New Spain (1816–1821). Born in Cádiz, Apodaca joined the Spanish navy in 1767 and distinguished himself during wartime service against Great Britain and France. When France invaded Spain in 1808, Apodaca commanded a squadron of five warships. During the government of the Junta Central, he served in London as the Spanish plenipotentiary until 1811, then returned to Cádiz. In 1812, he was appointed captain-general of Cuba, a post he held with success until 1816.

Named viceroy of New Spain in 1816, Apodaca renewed and expanded amnesty programs, granting insurgent leaders and their followers resettlement and entry into royalist military forces. Although these policies restored the appearance of peace in some Mexican regions and the invasion of Javier Mina was crushed in 1817, Apodaca understood that victory against the dispersed guerrilla forces was not complete. By 1820, burdensome wartime taxation and the exhaustion of the Mexican royalists made the war impossible to sustain. The restoration of the Spanish constitution and Apodaca's appointment of Agustín de Iturbide to quell the guerrilla activities of Vicente Guerrero and other insurgents destroyed the will of the royalists. Iturbide's rebellion and Plan of Iguala attracted many royalist army officers, and Mexicans invoked the constitution to suspend onerous taxes that supported the counterinsurgency system. During 1821, loyalist officers in Mexico City deposed the viceroy.

King Ferdinand VII granted Apodaca recognition, honors, and high offices. He was named viceroy of Navarre and later was appointed to the Council of State and as captain-general of the

Spanish navy. Under Queen Isabel II, Apodaca served as the senior member of the Council of War.

See also **New Spain, Viceroyalty of.**

BIBLIOGRAPHY

Lucas Alamán, *Historia de México desde los primeros movimientos que prepararon su independencia en el año de 1808 hasta la época presente,* 5 vols. (1849–1852; repr. 1942).

William S. Robertson, *Iturbide of Mexico* (1952).

Carlos María De Bustamante, *Cuadro histórico de la Revolución Mexicana,* 3 vols. (1961).

Timothy E. Anna, *The Fall of the Royal Government in Mexico City* (1978).

Additional Bibliography

Archer, Christon, ed. *The Wars of Independence in Spanish America.* Wilmington, DE: Scholarly Resources Inc., 2000.

CHRISTON I. ARCHER

RUIZ DE MONTOYA, ANTONIO

(1583–1653). Antonio Ruiz de Montoya (*b.* 11 November 1583; *d.* 11 April 1653), Jesuit missionary who worked among the Guaraní Indians. Ruiz was born in Lima, Peru, and entered the Society of Jesus in 1606. He completed his novitiate in Córdoba, Argentina, two years later. After ordination he was sent to the Guaraní missions along the Paraná River and was superior there from 1623 to 1637. He was deeply involved in opposing the Paulista raids on the missions. His writings include the *Conquista espiritual* (1639), which describes the natural features and peoples of the mission area; the *Tesoro de la lengua guaraní* (1639), a catechism and grammar of the Guaraní language; and *Arte y vocabulario de la lengua guaraní* (1640). Ruiz died in Lima and was buried in the reduction of Loreto.

See also **Missions: Jesuit Missions (Reducciones).**

BIBLIOGRAPHY

Raúl Alvarez et al., *El P. Antonio Ruiz de Montoya: Su vida y su obra* (1974).

Carlos Teschauer, *Vida e obras do preclaro Pe. Ruiz de Montoya, apóstolo do Guairá e do Tape* (São Paulo, 1980).

Additional Bibliography

Coronado Aguilar, Jurandir. *Conquista espiritual: A história da evangelização na Província Guairána obra de Antônio Ruiz de Montoya, S.I. (1585–1652).* Roma: Pontificia università gregoriana, 2002.

Rouillón, José Luis. *Antonio Ruiz de Montoya y las reducciones del Paraguay.* Asunción: Centro de Estuidos Paraguayos "Antonio Guasch", 1997.

NICHOLAS P. CUSHNER

RUÍZ TAGLE PORTALES, FRANCISCO

(?–1860). Francisco Ruíz Tagle Portales (*d.* 23 March 1860), Chilean political figure. A prominent creole landowner, Ruíz Tagle played several public roles as a patriot during the Chilean *Patria Vieja* (the period, 1810–1814, before the Spanish reconquest). He nevertheless found no difficulty accepting municipal office under the restored Spanish colonial regime (1814–1817), although his collaborationism won him a 12,000-peso fine after the liberation of Chile. In the 1820s, easily adapting to the new order, he served as a member of the legislature and as a minister during the presidency of Francisco Antonio Pinto. When the Conservatives seized power in 1829–1830, Ruíz Tagle became interim president of Chile (18 February 1830). But his ruthless cousin Diego Portales, leader of the Conservative regime, found him insufficiently zealous and forced him to resign only a few weeks after he assumed office (31 March 1830). Ruíz Tagle's days as a trimmer were over: he played no further public role.

See also **Pinto Díaz, Francisco Antonio.**

BIBLIOGRAPHY
Additional Bibliography

Cardoso Ruíz, Patricio. *Formación y desarrollo del estado nacional de Chile: De la independencia hasta 1930.* Toluca: Universidad Autónoma del Estado de México, 2000.

Collier, Simon, and William F. Sater. *A History of Chile, 1808–1994.* Cambridge: Cambridge University Press, 1996.

Stuven, Ana María. *La seducción de un orden: Las elites y la construcción de Chile en las polémicas culturales y políticas del siglo XIX.* Santiago: Ediciones Universidad Católica de Chile, 2000.

SIMON COLLIER

RULFO, JUAN   (1918–1986).

Juan Rulfo (*b*. 16 May 1918; *d*. 7 January 1986), Mexican writer. Born in Sayula, Jalisco, Rulfo was a man of vast culture and a writer of extreme economy, despite the fact that his literary aptitude became apparent during childhood. His first works were published while he was still very young in a literary magazine in his native province, where he met Juan José Arreola. Arreola and Rulfo became friends as well as representatives of the two most influential styles—both opposing and complementary—in the 1950s and 1960s in Mexico. In 1934, Rulfo moved to Mexico City, where he lived until his death, although in his varied career he traveled throughout the entire country. He came to know intimately the local dialects of many rural areas, which he put to brilliant use in his works. In a period of two years, Rulfo published his only two books: the collection of short stores *El llano en llamas* in 1953 and the novel *Pedro Páramo* in 1955. The revised edition (1970) of the former consists of seventeen stories. All the stories are set in rural Mexico, and in all of them the most diverse possibilities of the genre, ranging from narration in the first person to the objective and impersonal, are developed to perfection.

Pedro Páramo makes use of brief passages of extremely diverse narrative techniques in a disconcerting arrangement. It describes a world in which appear all aspects of human life and death, a world that is at the same time merely a town. This town, in the author's own words, "is dying of itself." It is the symbol of a country and of the myth of paradise lost (Pedro Páramo is the overlord of a paradise-in-reverse called Comala, and it is also desolation, devastation, the desert).

In his works Rulfo also displayed the best of the large, complex tradition of realist prose in Mexico, one phase of which is known as Mexican Revolution novels. At the same time, since their publication, his works have been enormously influential, not only in Mexico but in all of Latin America. Rulfo knew how to portray with linguistic precision the radiant universality that dwelled within the lives of the poorest, most anonymous campesinos as well as within the most renowned leaders. Through the most mundane acts, each of Rulfo's characters embodies and expresses the essential truths and myths of humanity.

A father carries his agonizing son, reproducing an inverted version of the myth of Saint Christopher; a son travels in search of his father, who has never left the place of his birth, and repeats in reverse the story of Telemachus and Ulysses. Rulfo's world is a world in reverse, where extremes touch. Thus, the silence in his work is always murmuring and the dead never stop manifesting their vitality. Rulfo never forgot that in order to be authentic the universality of his imagination had to be rooted in the most profound interconnections of Mexican reality.

Several things stand out about these interconnections: the discreet omnipotence of language which, without great fanfare and with simple, fleeting metaphors, gets to the bottom of the daily miracles of life; the complicity between humankind and nature, which, in Rulfo's eyes, makes the rustic Mexican world an environment full of movement, of animism, where each object and act provides a unique means of seeing the universe; and the vitality that makes his protagonists unforgettable because they are not moved by psychological motives but rather by intense, sanguine convictions. This transforms his characters into human beings whose singular "Mexicanness" is startling, whose fondness for the earthy forces of passion, obsession, and vengeance is disturbing to many foreign readers. With his vision, Rulfo was able to influence Mexican as well as Latin American literature. He created the basic characteristics of "magic realism" and has become a primary source of the universal modern narrative.

See also **Literature: Spanish America; Mexico: Since 1910.**

BIBLIOGRAPHY

Rose S. Minc, *Lo fantástico y lo real en la narrativa de Juan Rulfo y Guadalupe Dueñas* (1977).

Luis Leal, *Juan Rulfo* (in English) (1983).

Luis Fernando Veas Mercado, *Los modos narrativos en los cuentos en primera persona de Juan Rulfo: Los relatos considerados como una metáfora de una visión del mundo* (1984).

Francisco Antolín, *Los espacios en Juan Rulfo* (1991).

Gustavo C. Fares, *Imaginar Comala: El espacio en la obra de Juan Rulfo* (1991).

Additional Bibliography

Arias Urrutia, Angel. *Entre la cruz y la sospecha: Los cristeros de Revueltas, Yáñez y Rulfo*. Madrid: Vervuert, 2005.

Campbell, Federico. *La ficción de la memoria: Juan Rulfo ante la crítica*. México, D.F.: Ediciones Era, 2005.

Estrada Cárdenas, Alba Sovietina. *Estructura y discurso de género en Pedro Páramo de Juan Rulfo*. México, D.F.: Eón: Universidad Michoacana de San Nicolás de Hidalgo, 2005.

Ortega, María Luisa. *Mito y poesía en la obra de Juan Rulfo*. Bogotá: Siglo del Hombre Editores, 2004.

JORGE AGUILAR MORA

RUM. *See* **Alcoholic Beverages.**

RUMI MAQUI REVOLT. Rumi Maqui Revolt, a peasant uprising in the Lake Titicaca region of the Peruvian southern Andes (1915–1916). On 1 December 1915, a group of several hundred peasants attacked two haciendas owned by prominent landowners in the province of Azángaro. Although the rebels were turned back, with dozens of them shot in the attack or subsequently hunted down, they continued to act throughout 1916. The rebellion gained notoriety in part because of the leadership of an outsider, Teodomiro Gutiérrez Cuevas, a military officer. He was called Rumi Maqui, "Hand of Stone" in Quechua.

The rebels opposed the growth of estates owned by non-Indians. They also expressed their discontent with the monopolization of regional politics by corrupt non-Indians and the undue power of some local authorities. The movement cast its ideology in terms of Incan restoration versus feudalism, thus catching the attention of intellectuals and other Indian rebels in the 1920s.

BIBLIOGRAPHY

Augusto Ramos Zambrano, *Movimientos campesinos de Azángaro* (Puno), *Rumi Maqui* (1985).

Nils Jacobsen, *Mirages of Transition: The Peruvian Altiplano, 1780–1930* (1993), esp. pp. 337–345.

Additional Bibliography

Conteras, Carlos. *Historia del Perú contemporáneo*. Lima: Red Para el Desarrollo de las Ciencias Sociales en el Perú, 1999.

CHARLES F. WALKER

RURALES. Rurales, Mexico's Rural Police Force. The Rurales gained notoriety as one of the world's finest constabularies during the dictatorship of Porfirio Díaz (1885–1911). Uniformed as dandies in bolero jackets, leg-hugging pants trimmed with silver buttons, and wide-brimmed sombreros, some 3,000 Rurales patrolled major transportation routes and symbolized the government's intention to impose public order. Their frequently slovenly and ill-disciplined field performance contrasted sharply with the image of the corps deliberately tailored to fit them by the government. In fact, relatively few Rurales were good horsemen or decent marksmen; they deserted in droves and often failed to catch their man. However, in police work, the image counts, and the Rurales were romanticized in the public's mind even beyond the myths associated with the Texas Rangers.

Using Spain's Guardia Civil as a model, Benito Juárez founded the constabulary in 1861. Initial recruits included some known bandits; their recruitment was one of the ways in which Juárez bought loyalty for his regime. Although Díaz nourished the legend of bandit-turned-lawman, he purged brigands from the constabulary. During his tenure, ten rural police corps of approximately 300 men each were periodically rotated to potential trouble spots, especially those most visible to foreign investors. As proletarians became organized in unions, more Rurales were stationed in factory towns. A sizable core remained close to the dictator in Mexico City.

When revolution erupted in 1910, the constabulary by and large remained loyal to Díaz. His successor, Francisco Madero, not only retained the Porfirian Rurales but also tripled the size of the organization with men who had joined his rebellion. When Victoriano Huerta assumed power in 1913, he reorganized and reformed the corps, but when his government fell, the constabulary was disbanded; many of its officers later turned up in the ranks of Venustiano Carranza. Throughout the nineteenth century and into the twentieth, many states and municipalities, even private individuals, organized constabularies called "rurales." Hence the occasional overlap and confusion in the historical record and public mind concerning the deeds and image of the national police force and its regional and local counterparts.

See also **Juárez, Benito.**

BIBLIOGRAPHY

Paul J. Vanderwood, *Los rurales mexicanos* (1982), and *Disorder and Progress: Bandits, Police, and Mexican Development* (1992).

Additional Bibliography

Hart, Paul. *Bitter Harvest: The Social Transformation of Morelos, Mexico, and the Origins of the Zapatista Revolution, 1840–1910.* Albuquerque: University of New Mexico Press, 2006.

Reina, Leticia. *Las rebeliones campesinas en México, 1819-1906.* México, D.F.: Siglo Veintiuno Editores, 1998.

PAUL J. VANDERWOOD

See also **Herrera, Luis Alberto de; Nardone, Benito; Uruguay, Organizations: Rural Association; Uruguay, Political Parties: Blanco Party.**

BIBLIOGRAPHY

Philip B. Taylor, *Government and Politics of Uruguay* (1960).

Raúl Jacob, *Benito Nardone: El ruralismo hacía el poder, 1945–1958* (1981).

Additional Bibliography

Costa Bonino, Luis. *La crisis del sistema político uruguayo: Partidos políticos y democracia hasta 1973.* Montevideo, Uruguay: Fundación de Cultura Universitaria, 1995.

HENRY FINCH

RURALISMO.

Ruralismo, a political movement in Uruguay that gave rise to the Federal League of Ruralist Action (LFAR). Originating in the early 1940s, the LFAR achieved considerable significance in the 1950s, but disappeared in the 1960s. The movement was founded by a conservative landowner, Domingo Bordaberry, but its principal personality and leader was Benito Nardone, who broke with Bordaberry in 1951. Broadcasting on Radio Rural during the 1950s as "Chicotazo" ("Whiplash"), Nardone delivered strident and scurrilous attacks on communism, anticlericalism, government policy, and the corruption of urban politicians. Nardone's demagogy was designed to appeal to small farmers and rural producers who were inadequately represented by the established rural associations dominated by large landowners. In the elections of 1954, Nardone supported the Colorado faction of Luis Batlle, but switched to form an uneasy alliance with Luis Alberto de Herrera, caudillo of the Blanco Party, a move crucial to the victory of Herrera's faction of the Blancos in the 1958 elections. Following Herrera's death in 1959, Nardone formed the Herrerist-Ruralist Alliance with the Blanco leader Martín Echegoyen to contest the 1962 elections, another move by Nardone that was probably crucial to the Blanco victory.

In spite of its electoral significance, ruralismo had little impact on government policy. Nardone died in 1964, and the movement as an effective political force died with him.

RUSSELL, JOHN H.

(1872–1947). John H. Russell (*b.* 14 November 1872; *d.* 6 March 1947), military figure and diplomat. Born in Mare Island, California, Russell attended the U. S. Naval Academy, graduating in 1892. As brigadier general in the U.S. Marines, he served in Haiti throughout the U.S. occupation of that nation (1922–1934) holding the title U.S. high commissioner in Haiti, which combined military and diplomatic functions, from 1922 to 1930. As high commissioner, he reported directly to the U.S. State Department.

Russell was heavily involved in Haitian politics and development projects, drawing criticism for his suppression of revolts and maintenance of segregationist policies, even though he was considered an advocate of a diplomatic approach to solving Haiti's internal affairs and ending U.S. occupation. He was responsible for the gradual reduction of U.S. marines in Haiti and the training of the Haitian Garde, a local force designed to assume police duties in the interior. Both constituted important steps leading toward the eventual end of the occupation in 1934.

See also **Haiti.**

BIBLIOGRAPHY

Hans Schmidt, *The United States and the Occupation of Haiti, 1915–1934* (1971).

Kenneth J. Grieb, *The Latin American Policy of Warren G. Harding* (1976).

Additional Bibliography

Renda, Mary A. *Taking Haiti: Military Occupation and the Culture of U.S. Imperialism, 1915–1940.* Chapel Hill: University of North Carolina Press, 2001.

KENNETH J. GRIEB

RUSSIAN–LATIN AMERICAN RELATIONS.

Russia's diplomatic relations with Latin American began in 1828 with imperial Brazil. This was followed, in the mid-nineteenth century, by relations with Venezuela, Uruguay, and Central America. Ties were not officially established with Argentina until 1885, and with Mexico in 1890.

Between 1810 and 1820, under Czar Alexander and in restoration alliances with Europe, Russia helped stifle revolutionary processes in America. But Russian influence on the continent was countered by the more prudent stance taken by Great Britain, which had an increasing commercial presence in Latin America and was wary of any attempt by European powers to extend their influence over the American continent. Given the delicate balance of power among the great European nations, Russia could do little to cross that threshold. Furthermore, in 1823, with the Monroe Doctrine, the United States had proclaimed that European powers should not intervene in the internal affairs of American nations. Russia's relations with Latin America thus remained weak and intermittent.

The effects of World War I (in which Latin American nations chose to remain neutral), the collapse of Czarist Russia, the Bolshevik Revolution in 1917, and the creation of the League of Nations in 1919 altered the world stage. Most Latin American governments joined the League of Nations, from which the USSR was excluded until 1934.

THE COMINTERN

Latin American delegates began participating in the Communist International (Comintern) at its Fourth Congress, held in Moscow in 1922. The evolution of the ideas held by the Comintern leaders exercised a decisive influence over American Communist parties and their strategies, but their refusal to consider the diverse local conditions created resistance among Latin American leftists. Under the directors of Joseph Stalin, before the height of German Nazism in the mid-1930s, Latin American Communist parties promoted the creation of broad national fronts. The strategy of alliances with "reformist" and "progressive" political forces would be maintained during and after World War II.

THE COLD WAR AND THE CUBAN REVOLUTION

In the postwar bipolar division of the world, Latin America remained under the influence of the United States and its foreign policy conditioned on economic and military aid provided by the United States. The Inter-American Treaty of Reciprocal Assistance (1947), sponsored by the United States and signed by the majority of Latin American nations, established that the continent would defend itself collectively. Communist parties were repressed and generally not allowed representation in governments. Nevertheless, the USSR maintained trade relations with many Latin American nations (even with those governed by anti-Communist military dictatorships). The Cuban Revolution (1959–1962) had a strong impact on foreign and domestic policy in the region. Excluded from the Organization of American States (OAS), Cuba, with Soviet financial backing, supported Communist guerrilla groups (mainly in Bolivia, Colombia, and Peru), while the United States gave its military and economic support to military dictatorships willing to contain potential Communist advances (as in the overthrow of Jacobo Arbenz in Guatemala). In 1962 the Soviets installed long-range missiles in Cuba, provoking the Cuban missile crisis; the United States, with Latin American backing, cut off the island from international affairs and forced the withdrawal of the missiles while promising not to invade the island. With the exception of Mexico, no Latin American nation renewed official relations with Cuba until 1970. In the late twentieth century some Latin American nations experienced strong swings to the left, but the Soviet Union did not always have a direct influence on events. The Soviets did provide military aid to the Sandinistas in Nicaragua following their overthrow of the government in 1979.

With perestroika, the Soviet economic restructuring begun by Mikhail Gorbachev, relations weakened between the USSR and Cuba. The dissolution of the Soviet Union, bringing the end of the cold war, redefined Russian-Latin American ties. In 1992 the Russian Federation was granted permanent observer status in the OAS. It has also established contacts with Mercosur, the regional trade association of Brazil, Argentina, Uruguay, and Paraguay, and with the Andean Community. Cuba, Brazil, Argentina, and Chile continue to be Russia's principal trade partners in the region.

See also **Communism; League of Nations; Mercosur; Monroe Doctrine; Nicaragua, Sandinista National Liberation Front (FSLN); Organization of American States (OAS); Soviet-Latin American Relations.**

BIBLIOGRAPHY

Bartley, Russell H. *Imperial Russia and the Struggle for Latin American Independence, 1808–1828.* Austin: University of Texas Press, 1978.

Cisneros, Andrés, and Carlos Escudé, eds. *Historia general de las relaciones exteriores de la República Argentina*, 4 vols. Buenos Aires: Grupo Editor Latinoamericano, 1998–2003.

Gilbert, Isidoro. *El oro de Moscú: La historia secreta de las relaciones argentino-soviéticas.* Buenos Aires: Planeta, 1994.

Lafeber, Walter. *America, Russia, and the Cold War, 1945–2002*, 9th edition. Boston: McGraw-Hill, 2004.

Miller, Nicola. *Soviet Relations with Latin America, 1959–1987.* Cambridge, MA: Cambridge University Press, 1989.

Russell, Roberto, ed. *Nuevos rumbos en la relación Unión Soviética/América Latina* Buenos Aires: Grupo Editor Latinoamericano/FLACSO, 1990.

VICENTE PALERMO

RUTINEROS. *See* **Sanjuanistas.**

S

SÁ, ESTÁCIO DE (c. 1520–1567). Está-
cio de Sá (*b.* c. 1520; *d.* 20 February 1567), nephew
of Mem de Sá, Brazil's third governor-general, who
had initially expelled French intruders from Guanabara Bay. In January 1565, Estácio sailed from Bahia
de Todos os Santos to Guanabara Bay, where he
found that the French had returned and were too
strongly entrenched to be dislodged by his forces.
Accordingly, he withdrew to Santos to await reinforcements. Upon his return to Guanabara Bay in
March 1565, he founded a fortified outpost near the
base of Sugar Loaf Hill, the nucleus of the future city
of Rio de Janeiro. A year later Sá was wounded while
leading his forces on Glória Hill. He died of his
wounds just as Mem de Sá was refounding the city
on Castle Hill, opposite the island of Villegaignon.

BIBLIOGRAPHY

Luis Norton, *A dinastia dos Sás no Brasil* (1953).

Herbert Ewaldo Wetzel, *Mem de Sá: Terceiro governador
geral (1557–1572)* (1972).

Additional Bibliography

Vainfas, Ronaldo. *Dicionário do Brasil colonial, 1500–1808.*
Rio de Janeiro: Objetiva, 2000.

DAURIL ALDEN

SÁ, MEM DE (c. 1500–1572). Mem de Sá
(*b. ca.* 1500; *d.* 1572), Brazilian high magistrate.
Nominated third governor-general of Brazil, he
arrived in Salvador, Bahia, on 28 December 1557.
During his administration he fought the usury of
merchants who sold slaves on credit with a gain of
100 percent a year, controlled the excessive enslavement of the Indians by the Portuguese colonists,
and expanded the number of Jesuit *aldeias* (villages)
from two or three to around eleven. Mem de Sá
helped the chief-captain of Espirito Santo, Vasco
Fernandes Coutinho, and the settlers of the captaincy of São Vicente in wars with the Indians. He
attacked the French of the so-called Antarctic France
who had built the Coligny fort on an island in Rio
de Janeiro Bay. The fortress was taken in 1560,
but the French took shelter in some Indian villages around the bay. As Sá lacked men to occupy
the fort, it was abandoned, and a second attack on
the French survivors was led by Sá's nephew,
Estácio de Sá (ca. 1526–1567), who established
a military base at the foot of Sugarloaf Mountain
in 1565. The primitive settlement was transferred
to its current site in 1567 by Mem de Sá, who, in a
letter to the king, considered himself the true
founder of Rio de Janeiro. In 1569 he asked to
be replaced as governor-general; he died in
Salvador.

See also **Sá, Estácio de.**

BIBLIOGRAPHY

Herbert Ewaldo Wetzel, *Mem de Sá: Terceiro governador
geral, 1557–1572* (1972).

Francisco Adolfo De Varnhagen, *História geral do Brasil,*
9th ed. (1975).

Additional Bibliography

Vainfas, Ronaldo. *Dicionário do Brasil colonial, 1500–1808.* Rio de Janeiro: Objetiva, 2000.

MARIA BEATRIZ NIZZA DA SILVA

SAAVEDRA, CORNELIO DE (1759–1829). Cornelio de Saavedra (*b.* 15 September 1759; *d.* 29 March 1829), landowner and merchant who played a leading role in the first phase of Argentine independence. Born in Potosí of creole parents, Saavedra moved with his family to Buenos Aires, where he was educated at the Real Colegio de San Carlos. Alongside his merchant career he gained experience in public office, serving on the cabildo and as grain administrator during the last decade of Spanish rule. He also demonstrated military leadership when he organized a creole militia unit, the Patricios, and commanded them in action against the British invaders in 1807. From his military power base Saavedra intervened decisively in the events of May 1810, voted for a change of government, and became president of the patriotic junta which prepared the way for full independence. Saavedra led the conservative wing of the movement, favoring gradual change and representation of the provinces, against Mariano Moreno and the radical reformists who wanted to impose instant revolution and sought a unified as well as an independent Argentina.

The conservatives ousted the radicals in April 1811 but were themselves weakened by internal opposition and military defeat in Upper Peru. Saavedra went personally to reorganize the Army of the North, but while absent from Buenos Aires (September 1811) he was ousted from government and deprived of his army command. He then suffered political persecution and periods of exile, until in 1818 the national Congress cleared his name and the Supreme Director, Juan Martín de Pueyrredón, restored his military rank and appointed him chief of staff. He spent the year of anarchy (1820) in Montevideo but returned to Buenos Aires during the government of Martín Rodríguez. He retired to private life and died in Buenos Aires.

BIBLIOGRAPHY

Enrique Ruíz Guiñazú, *El Presidente Saavedra y el pueblo soberano de 1810* (1960).

John Lynch, *The Spanish American Revolutions 1808–1826,* 2d ed. (1986).

Additional Bibliography

Muñoz Moraleda, Ernesto. *Los grupos políticos españoles y su influencia en los sucesos rioplatenses (1809–1820).* Argentina: s.n., 1993.

JOHN LYNCH

SAAVEDRA LAMAS, CARLOS (1878–1959). Carlos Saavedra Lamas (*b.* 1 November 1878; *d.* 5 May 1959), statesman and Nobel Prize–winning Argentine diplomat. Born in Buenos Aires, Saavedra Lamas received a law degree from the University of Buenos Aires in 1903. He began his career as a professor, but he turned to politics in 1912. As a national deputy he authored the tariff law that protected Argentina's sugar industry in Salta Province. In 1915, he served as President Victorino de la Plaza's (1914–1916) minister of the interior and as minister of justice and public instruction.

It was as a member of the Concordancia that he achieved international prominence. Between 1932 and 1938 he served under President Agustín P. Justo (1932–1938) as minister of foreign affairs. Conservative and nationalistic, he represented Argentina at numerous international conferences. In particular, he challenged efforts to establish the hegemony of the United States in hemispheric affairs. He was instrumental in obtaining Latin American support for the Anti-War Pact (1933). His efforts to find a negotiated settlement to the Chaco War (1932–1935) between Bolivia and Paraguay earned him the Nobel Peace Prize in 1936. Although he remained active in national affairs, Saavedra Lamas retired from public service after 1938. He returned to teaching and became the rector of the University of Buenos Aires in 1941.

See also **Concordancia.**

BIBLIOGRAPHY

Harold F. Peterson, *Argentina and the United States, 1810–1960* (1964).

Alberto A. Conil Paz and Gustavo Ferrari, *Argentina's Foreign Policy, 1930–1962* (1966).

Additional Bibliography

Farcau, Bruce W. *The Chaco War: Bolivia and Paraguay, 1932–1935.* Westport, CT: Praeger, 1996.

Fraga, Rosendo, and Raúl Alberto Gatica. *Carlos Saavedra Lamas: Estudio preliminar.* Buenos Aires: Editorial Centro de Estudios Unión para la Nueva Mayoría, 1991.

DANIEL LEWIS

SAAVEDRA MALLEA, BAUTISTA

(1870–1939). Bautista Saavedra Mallea (*b.* 30 August 1870; *d.* 1 March 1939), president of Bolivia (January 1921–September 1925). Born in Sorata, La Paz Province, Saavedra was a lawyer, journalist, and author. Following a peaceful palace revolt that ended several decades of government by the Liberal Party and installed the Republican Party, which appealed more to the literate, lower middle class, Saavedra became head of a governing junta in July 1920. In January 1921 he was elected president. He is considered one of the strongest civilian presidents of Bolivia, having captured the leadership of his party from the venerable Daniel Salamanca.

Although Saavedra's presidency was stormy, it also boasted solid achievements, including the first social and labor legislation and construction of direct rail links to Argentina. Saavedra left office in September 1925, turning it over to the president of the Senate, Felipe Segundo Guzmán. A year later, annoyed at postelection statements by the president-elect, Gabino Villanueva, Saavedra had the election annulled on a technicality and imposed Hernando Siles Reyes as his successor in the presidency. Saavedra died in Santiago, Chile.

See also **Bolivia, Political Parties: Republican Party.**

BIBLIOGRAPHY

Porfirio Díaz Machicao, *Saavedra, 1920–1925* (1954).

Additional Bibliography

Irurozqui, Marta. *"A bala, piedra y palo": La construcción de la ciudadanía política en Bolivia, 1826–1952.* Seville: Diputación de Sevilla, 2000.

CHARLES W. ARNADE

SABAT ERCASTY, CARLOS (1887–

1982). Carlos Sabat Ercasty (*b.* 1887; *d.* 1982), Uruguayan poet, literary critic, and educator. Before teaching literature and mathematics in Montevideo and serving as administrator of the Young Women's Teachers College, he worked as a reporter for *El Día* and *La Razón,* both in Montevideo. Sabat Ercasty's prolific poetic production includes more than forty published collections. Early verses—such as the eight volumes of *Poemas del hombre* (1921–1958)—were characterized by Wagnerian thematic shifts from sensuality to mysticism, with traces of pantheistic musings. Later poetry, dramatic and fluid, treated philosophical issues and Oriental myths; at times a sense of abstract and conceptual stoicism predominated.

Works by Sabat Ercasty that were inspired by historical themes include *El charrúa* (1957) and *Himno a Artigas e Himno de mayo* (1964). His major works of poetry are *Sonetos de las agonías y los extásis* (1977), *Parábolas* (1978), *Cánticos a Euridice* (2 vols., 1978–1980), and *Antología* (2 vols., 1982). His major works of literary criticism are *Retratos del fuego: José Zorrilla de San Martín* (1958), *Retratos del fuego: Carlos Vaz Ferreira* (1958), and *Retratos del fuego: María Eugenia Vaz Ferreira* (1953).

See also **Literature: Spanish America.**

BIBLIOGRAPHY

Sarah Bollo, *Literatura uruguaya, 1807–1965,* vol. 2 (1965).

Gary Lewis Haws, *El Prometeo uruguayo: Carlos Sabat Ercasty* (1968).

Isabel Sesto Gilardoni, *Memoria y sed de Dios en la poesía de Carlos Sabat Ercasty* (1983).

Additional Bibliography

García Orallo, María Antonia. *La obra poética de Carlos Sabat Ercasty.* Burgos: Universidad de Burgos, 2002.

WILLIAM H. KATRA

SABATINI, GABRIELA (1970–). The

Argentine tennis player Gabriela Beatriz Sabatini was born May 16, 1970 in Buenos Aires. Sabatini took up tennis at age six, won her first tournament at eight, rose to be the world's number-one ranked junior player in

1984, and turned professional the next year, when she became the youngest woman ever to reach the singles semifinals of the French Open. Before her retirement in October 1996, she collected twenty-seven singles titles, including the U.S. Open in 1990, and twelve doubles titles, rose to the number three world ranking, and amassed almost $9 million in winnings. Energetic, attractive, and popular, Sabatini was inducted into the International Tennis Hall of Fame in 2006. Her focus during the late 1990s and early 2000s was her expanding line of perfumes.

See also **Sports.**

BIBLIOGRAPHY

"Gabriela Sabatini." *Sports Illustrated*, July 2, 2001, 130–131.

Luy, Vicente. *La sexualidad de Gabriela Sabatini*. Córdoba, Argentina: Ediciones de Boulevard, 2006.

Morelli, Liliana. *Mujeres deportistas*. Buenos Aires: Planeta, 1990.

Sabatini, Gabriela. *My Story*. University Park, IL: Avatar General, 1994.

JOSEPH L. ARBENA

SÁBATO, ERNESTO (1911–). Ernesto Sábato (*b*. 24 June 1911), Argentine novelist, essayist, and thinker. The years during which Sábato studied at the University of La Plata, where he received a Ph.D. in physics, were crucial in the political life of Argentina. Since he felt great concern for the social problems of his country, Sábato embraced communism for five years, and as a spokesman for the party he suffered personal persecution. In 1934 he traveled secretly to Europe as a representative of the Argentine Communist Youth Organization to attend an antifascist congress in Brussels. However, after suffering a spiritual and ideological crisis, he severed his relationship with the party, refusing a trip to Moscow for indoctrination. In 1938, on a fellowship at the Joliot-Curie Laboratory in Paris, he became acquainted with the surrealists and began writing. This was a turning point in his life since, at that moment, Sábato understood his deeply felt interest in and aptitude for literature.

After a stay at MIT (1939), he taught at the University of La Plata and in Buenos Aires, and contributed to the newspaper *La Nación* and the literary journal *Sur*. At the end of 1945, with the Perón government securely in power, Sábato was fired from both of his teaching jobs because he was

an enemy of the dictatorship and dared to proclaim this publicly. This precipitated a second crisis that ended his career in the sciences. Thus was born Sábato-the-writer and his public persona. For the next ten years he earned his livelihood with articles and conferences and as a consultant for the publishing houses Raigal, Codex, and Emecé. In 1947 he worked for two months as an assistant officer of the executive committee of UNESCO in Paris and Rome. In 1955, after Perón's fall and with a de facto government in power, Sábato showed his idealistic nature by accepting the directorship of the important weekly *Mundo Argentino*. But the relationship was short-lived when he resigned for not acquiescing to press censorship. Between 1958 and 1959 he served as director of cultural relations at the Foreign Ministry.

Sábato's scientific education together with his literary passion created an Apollonian and Dionysian personality. Like Sartre, Sábato is a thinker who uses fiction to fully express his ideas. To him, today's novel is closer to metaphysics than to literature. His novels and essays revolve around obsessive ideas that have conditioned his works and his social conduct: a deep existential preoccupation with humanity, literary creation, and his country. In some essays, Sábato emphasized that a writer should be at the service of truth and freedom. Of his three novels, the first, *El túnel* (1948; *The Tunnel*, 1988), could be considered a psychological, existential thriller. The second, *Sobre héroes y tumbas* (1961; *On Heroes and Tombs*, 1981), remains a veritable fresco of modern Argentina, a synthesis of his surrealistic imagination and speculative thinking. The third, *Abaddón, el Exterminador* (1974; *The Angel of Darkness*, 1991), is a "gnostic eschatology" showing that the prophecies of Apocalypse 9:11 are about to become a reality: our materialistic civilization will end and the human race will be renewed on the basis of a new principle that will reestablish the divine order.

The ideas that are the foundation of Sábato's fiction are expressed in five books of essays that must be read to fully understand him. He has also written numerous articles and has presided over the compilation of one of the most heinous texts in the letters of his country and of the world: *Nunca más* (1984), which was the report, based on the testimony of survivors and relatives, of the commission that he chaired to investigate the tragedy of the

Argentine *desaparecidos* ("disappeared" persons). Sábato's texts are full of antidogmatic, testimonial, and denunciatory passages, which have revitalized Argentine letters. He has received numerous international awards and honors. At home Sábato was given the prestigious Prize of National Consecration for making the greatest contribution to the enrichment of Argentina's cultural heritage. In 1984 Sábato was a major contributor to a groundbreaking report on human rights violations in Argentina, and later that year he won the Cervantes Prize, the highest award in Hispanic literature. In 1987 the French government awarded him the decoration of the Legion of Honor. In 1997, he won the Premio Internacional Menéndez Pelayo, awarded by the Universidad Internacional Menéndez Pelayo in Spain. He also published several nonfiction works, including *Informe sobre ciegos* (Report on Blind People) in 1994 and *España en los diarios de mi vejez* (Spain in the Newspapers of My Old Age) in 2004.

See also **Argentina, Political Parties: Socialist Party.**

BIBLIOGRAPHY

Angela B. Dellepiane, *Sábato: Un análisis de su narrativa* (1970).

H. D. Oberhelman, *Ernesto Sábato* (1970).

William Kennedy, "Sábato's *Tombs and Heroes*," in *Review* 29 (1981): 6–9.

Earl M. Aldrich, Jr., "Esthetic, Moral, and Philosophic Concerns in *Sobre héroes y tumbas*," in *Romance Literary Studies, Homage to Harvey L. Johnson*, edited by Marie A. Wellington and Martha O'Nan (1983), pp. 3–14.

Additional Bibliography

Catania, Carlos. *Genio y figura de Ernesto Sábato*. Buenos Aires: Editorial Universitaria de Buenos Aires, 1987.

Constenla, Julia. *Sábato, el hombre: Una biografía*. Buenos Aires: Seix Barral, 1997.

Petrea, Mariana D. *Ernesto Sábato: La nada y la metafísica de la esperanza*. Madrid: Ediciones J. Porrúa Turanzas, 1986.

Sábato, Ernesto. *The Writer in the Catastrophe of Our Time*. Tulsa, OK: Council Oak Books, 1990.

ANGELA B. DELLEPIANE

SABATO, JORGE ALBERTO (1924–1983).

Jorge Alberto Sabato (June 4, 1924–November 16, 1983) was a physicist and thinker with a long public career promoting technological development in Latin America. He was an exponent of the Latin American current of thought on science, technology production, development, and dependency along with Helio Jaguaribe (Brazil), Osvaldo Sunkel (Chile), Miguel Wionczek (Mexico), Francisco Sagasti (Venezuela) and Máximo Halty (Uruguay).

Sabato began his career as a physics professor high school teacher and, with Alberto Maiztegui, coauthored a physics textbook that was widely used in Latin America: *FÍSICA I* and *FÍSICA II* (first editions 1951 and 1955, respectively). In 1955 he joined Argentina's National Atomic Energy Commission (Comisión Nacional de Energía Atómica), and later became head of its technology department. Comisión with Carlos Martínez Vidal he founded the metallurgical laboratory, a seedbed for researchers that provided a starting point for the Comisión's involvement in technology production through its Technical Assistance Service for Industry (Servicio de Asistencia Técnica a la Industria). These initiatives resulted in the participation of Argentine industry in the construction of nuclear power plants. The laboratory was also the hub of the Pan American Metallurgy Course (Curso Panamericano de Metalurgia) that has been a fundamental academic agency for the field of metallurgy in Latin America.

Sabato wrote hundreds of articles, among them the notable "La ciencia y la tecnología en el desarrollo futuro de América Latina" (1968), which proposes "the triangle model," articulating the scientific and technological system, government policies, and the production system. He wrote and edited several books, including *La producción de tecnología* (1982) and *El pensamiento latinoamericano en la problemática ciencia-tecnología-desarrollo- dependencia* (1975).

He was a guest researcher at the universities of Birmingham (United Kingdom), Stanford (United States), Sussex (United Kingdom), and Montreal (Canada), and with the Woodrow Wilson International Center for Scholars in Washington, D.C. Sabato participated in the creation of the Bariloche Foundation (Fundación Bariloche) and the Bariloche Physics Institute (Instituto de Física) in Bariloche, Argentina, with José Balseiro and Fidel Alsina. He was a scientific journalist, promoter of the arts, acerbic political humorist, and active defender of public freedoms.

See also **Jaguaribe Gomes de Matos, Hélio; Science.**

BIBLIOGRAPHY

Dagnino, Renato. *As trajetórias dos Estudos sobre Ciência, Tecnologia e Sociedade e da Política Científica e Tecnológica na Ibero-América, Proceedings.* 1ª Conferencia Argentina de Estudios Sociales de la Ciencia y Tecnología. Julio de 2007, Universidad Nacional de Quilmes, Argentina.

Jorge A. Sabato: Ensayos en campera. Edited by Juarez. 1970; 2nd edition, Bernal: Universidad Nacional de Quilmes Editorial, 2004.

Libanatti, Nelly A. de, and Jorge A. Sabato. "Conferencia Interamericana sobre Tecnología de Materiales." In *El Curso Panamericano de Metalurgia: Una experiencia de postgraduado.* New York: South West Research Institute/ASME, 1968.

Maiztegui, Alberto, and Jorge A. Sabato. *Física I.* Buenos Aires: Editorial Kapelusz, 1951.

Maiztegui, Alberto, and Jorge A. Sabato. *Física II.* Buenos Aires: Editorial Kapelusz, 1955.

Sabato, Jorge A., ed. *El pensamiento latinoamericano en la problemática ciencia-tecnología-desarrollo-dependencia.* Buenos Aires: Editorial Paidos, 1975.

Sabato, Jorge A., and Natalio Botana. "*La ciencia y la tecnología en el desarrollo futuro de América Latina.*" Buenos Aires: Revista De La Integración, 1968.

Sabato, Jorge A., and Michael Mackenzie. *La producción de tecnología: ¿Autónoma o transnacional?* Mexico City: Editorial Nueva Imagen, 1982.

CARLOS GARCÍA BLAYA

SABINADA REVOLT. Sabinada Revolt, the rebellion that led to the seizure of Brazil's second-largest city, Salvador (capital of the northeastern province of Bahia), from 17 November 1837 to 16 March 1838. Occurring during the tumultuous and experimental years of Brazil's Regency period (1834–1840), the Sabinada was initiated by radical liberals and republicans, the most famous of whom, Francisco Sabino Álvares da Rocha Vieira (or Sabino), gave the rebellion its name.

The movement began with the revolt of the soldiers of the Third Artillery Battalion, garrisoned in the Fort of São Pedro. Leading them were several civilians, including Sabino, a doctor and editor of the radical *Novo Diário*. Within hours, the city's Third Infantry Battalion had joined; ultimately, only the marines and part of the National Guard would remain loyal to the government. Soldiers and civilian adherents soon occupied the city and declared the province's independence from the central government in Rio de Janeiro.

At the onset of the Sabinada, many civilians, especially Portuguese merchants whose privileged position with the Rio government rendered them the source of widespread antipathy, fled to the Recôncavo (the nearby sugar-producing region), where large property owners had begun to organize the resistance forces known as the Restorationist Army. By the end of November, they had 1,900 men, mostly National Guardsmen, on the outskirts of Salvador. With land routes already cut off, the arrival of warships from Rio assured that the capital would also be without water-borne cargoes. By December, Salvador felt the first pangs of hunger resulting from the blockade.

Reinforcements from neighboring provinces swelled the Restoration Army to nearly 5,000, and on 12 March the siege to retake Salvador began. In what was easily one of the most violent periods in the city's history, hundreds of rebels and innocent bystanders were massacred within two days after the battle began. Surrender came quickly, on 16 March. A week later the government captured Sabino, and after lengthy court hearings, exiled him to remote Goiás. Thousands of others were condemned to hard labor on the island of Fernando de Noronha.

Scholars have interpreted the Sabinada in a number of ways: as the result of battles between liberal separatists and conservatives who supported greater centralization within Brazil's monarchy; as a reaction to the narrow scope of political options that followed independence in 1822; or as a conflict fueled by discontent within the army and the militia over a series of military reforms in the early 1830s.

Most recently scholars have explored the rebellion in social terms, highlighting the ways in which questions of race and class challenged the dominant political arrangements from "below." As the Sabinada ran its course, the goals of its poor mulatto and black adherents became far more radical than those of the men who initiated the rebellion. The latter group, for example, supported the monarchy and only grudgingly freed Brazilian-born slaves (on 19 February 1838) after vast numbers of them escaped bondage by joining the rebel army. Given this comparatively conservative stance, the lower classes had no choice but to take matters into their own hands: this they did by burning the houses of their enemies. As a result, mulatto and black rebels suffered the harshest punishments once the rebellion was over, and more vigorous government surveillance of the lower groups ensued. It would be decades before federalist and republican sentiments were so boldly expressed, and individual rather than collective acts would characterize the resistance of the poor to a system that continued to discriminate on the basis of skin color and to maintain humans in bondage.

See also **Brazil, The Regency.**

BIBLIOGRAPHY

Paulo Cesar Souza, *A Sabinada: A revolta separatista da Bahia* (*1837*) (1987), and Hendrik Kraay, " 'As Terrifying as Unexpected': The Bahian Sabinada, 1837–1838," in *Hispanic America Historical Review* 72, no. 4 (1992): 501–527.

Additional Bibliography

Morel, Marco. *As transformações dos espaços públicos: Imprensa, atores políticos e sociabilidades na cidade imperial, 1820–1840.* São Paulo: Hucitec, 2005.

Vainfas, Ronaldo. *Dicionário do Brasil imperial, 1822–1889.* Rio de Janeiro: Objetiva, 2002.

JUDITH L. ALLEN

SABOGAL, JOSÉ (1888–1956). José Arnaldo Sabogal Dieguez, born in Cajabamba, Cajamarca, on March 19, 1888, was a Peruvian painter and printmaker who portrayed Peru's cultural and regional diversity in his depictions of indigenous figures and themes. In this his art resembled the work of Peruvian writers Ciro Alegría and José María Arguedas. His work is characterized by the use of strong color, expressive brushwork, and delineated forms. Sabogal's emphasis on Indian figures placed him at the center of Peruvian *indigenismo* during the 1920s. He contributed to José Carlos Mariátegui's vanguard magazine *Amauta* and taught at the Escuela Nacional de Bellas Artes, where his art was integral to the institution's role in defining an *arte nacional*, as well as to President Augusto B. Leguía's moderniaing ideology of the *patria nueva*.

Under Sabogal's tutelage, first as teacher and later as director of the art school, a group of *indigenista* artists—Camilo Blas, Enrique Camino Brent, Teresa Carvallo, and Julia Codesido—were to ensure *indigenismo*'s lasting influence on Peruvian art. During his career Sabogal painted a number of murals and was important in reviving interest in popular art forms in Peru. He died in Lima on December 15, 1956.

See also **Art: The Twentieth Century.**

BIBLIOGRAPHY

Antrobus, Pauline. *Peruvian Art of the Patria Nueva, 1919–1930.* Ph.D. dissertation, University of Essex, 1997.

Falcón, Jorge. *Simplemente Sabogal: Centenario de su nacimiento 1888–1988.* Lima: Ediciones Hora del Hombre, 1988.

Lauer, Mirko. "La pintura indigenista peruana: Una vision de los años noventa!" In *Voces de Ultramar: Arte en América Latina, 1910–1960,* pp.73–79. Las Palmas de Gran Canaria, Spain: Centro Atlántico Arte Moderno, 1992.

Torres Bohl, José. *Apuntes sobre José Sabogal: Vida y obra.* Lima: Banco Central de Reserva del Peru, Fondo Editorial, 1989.

PAULINE ANTROBUS

SACASA, JUAN BAUTISTA (1874–1946). Juan Bautista Sacasa (*b.* 21 December 1874; *d.* 17 April 1946), president of Nicaragua (1933–1936). Born in León, Sacasa rose to prominence in the volatile politics of Nicaragua as a leading member of the Liberal Party during the early twentieth century. He served as vice president in Carlos Solorzano's shaky coalition government in 1926 but was ousted after a coup by discontented Conservatives led by Emilano Chamorro Vargas. Sacasa became the leader of Liberal opposition and along with General José María Moncada led subsequent Liberal uprisings. The U.S. government opposed Sacasa's claim to the Nicaraguan presidency because of his ties with the Liberal Party and his support from Mexican president Plutarco Elías Calles. The United States placed Adolfo Díaz, a Conservative, in the presidency and backed him up with marines. After successfully splitting the Liberal forces of Sacasa and Moncada, the United States supervised the 1928 elections. Moncada became president and Sacasa served as Nicaraguan minister to Washington, D.C. Sacasa ultimately came to power in 1932, in the midst of guerrilla commander Augusto César Sandino's war against the U.S. Marines. During this period, the United States established the Nicaraguan National Guard and placed Anastasio Somoza García in its command. Sacasa attempted to negotiate a peace accord with Sandino in good faith, but Sandino was assassinated by the National Guard, leaving Sacasa locked in a power struggle with Somoza (his nephew-in-law). The increasing power and influence of Somoza and his National Guard soon decreased the de facto power of the president. Somoza forced Sacasa to resign from the presidency in June 1936, at which time he went into exile in the United States. He died in Los Angeles.

See also **Moncada, José María.**

BIBLIOGRAPHY

Richard Millet, *Guardians of the Dynasty* (1977).

Eduardo D. Crawley, *Dictators Never Die* (1979).

Thomas Walker, *Nicaragua: The Land of Sandino* (1986).

David Close, *Nicaragua: Politics, Economics, and Society* (1988).

Additional Bibliography

Arellano, Jorge Eduard. *La Pax americana en Nicaragua: (1910–1932)*. Managua: Academia de Geografía e Historia de Nicaragua: Fondo Editorial CIRA, 2004.

Crawley, Andrew. *Somoza and Roosevelt: Good Neighbour Diplomacy in Nicaragua, 1933–1945*. Oxford: Oxford University Press, 2007.

HEATHER K. THIESSEN

SACHS, JEFFREY (1944–).

Jeffrey Sachs is an American economist whose proposals as an international adviser on all continents have been controversial, earning both high praise and sharp criticism. Credited for ending hyperinflation in Bolivia in 1985, he later advised postsocialist countries on the transition to capitalism. Sachs argued for debt cancellation in crisis-stricken countries. Committed to the increase of international aid to reduce poverty and disease, he launched the Global Fund to Fight AIDS, Tuberculosis, and Malaria, and published the best-selling *The End of Poverty* (2005). Although he was at one time a believer in market orthodoxy, he later came to advocate "clinical economics," crafting solutions specific to circumstances, including climate and geography.

Since 2002 he has served as director of the Earth Institute at Columbia University, where he also teaches sustainable development and health policy and management.

See also **Chicago Boys; Neoliberalism.**

BIBLIOGRAPHY

Conaghan, Catherine M. "Reconsidering Jeffrey Sachs and the Bolivian Economic Experiment." In *Money Doctors, Foreign Debts, and Economic Reforms in Latin America from the 1890s to the Present*, edited by Paul W. Drake. Wilmington, DE: Scholarly Resources, 1994.

Sachs, Jeffrey. *The End of Poverty: Economic Possibilities for Our Time*. New York: Penguin, 2005.

Sachs, Jeffrey. "Investing in Development: A Practical Plan to Achieve the Millennium Development Goals." 2005. Available from http://www.unmillenniumproject.org/reports/index.htm.

VERONICA MONTECINOS

SACO, JOSÉ ANTONIO (1797–1879).

José Antonio Saco (*b.* 7 May 1797; *d.* 26 September 1879), Cuban writer, editor, and statesman. Born in Bayamo, Cuba, Saco studied philosophy and politics and became a professor of philosophy at the San Carlos Seminary in Havana. In 1828 he traveled to New York, where he founded the *Mensajero Quincenal* (Quarterly Messenger), a liberal publication that stressed the evils of slavery. Four years later, back in Havana, Saco founded a similar publication, the *Revista Bimestre Cubana* (Cuban Bimonthly Review). In 1830 Saco wrote *Memoria sobre la vagancia* (On Vagrancy), a subtle attack on many aspects of Cuban government and society, which was still under Spanish colonial rule. In 1834 Saco was exiled to Trinidad for writing *Justa defensa de la Academia Cubana de literatura*, a piece that marked his emergence as one of the leading spokespersons for the progressive Cuban creoles. Two years later Saco returned from exile and was named the Cuban representative in the Spanish Cortes. He traveled throughout Europe and while in Paris published an article arguing for U.S. annexation of Cuba. His greatest literary work was his monumental *Historia de la esclavitud* (History of Slavery) (2 vols., 1875–1879). Saco died in Barcelona, Spain.

BIBLIOGRAPHY

Richard B. Kimball, *Cuba, and the Cubans* (1850).

José Antonio Saco, *Historia de la esclavitud de la raza africana* (1938).

Robert M. Levine, comp., *Cuba in the 1850s: Through the Lens of Charles DeForest Fredericks* (1990).

Additional Bibliography

Aguilera Manzano, José María. *La formación de la identidad cubana (el debate Saco-La Sagra)*. Sevilla: Consejo Superior de Investigaciones Científicas, Escuela de Estudios Hispano-Americano, 2005.

Portuondo Zúñiga, Olga. *José Antonio Saco: Eternamente polémico*. Santiago de Cuba: Editorial Oriente, 2005.

MICHAEL POWELSON

SACRAMENTO, COLONIA DEL. Colonia del Sacramento, a city in Uruguay on the north bank of the Río de la Plata, began as a settlement that became the focus of a territorial dispute between Portugal and Spain until the end of the eighteenth century. According to the Treaty of Tordesillas (1494), the region was Spanish, and during the period when Portugal and Spain were united in one kingdom (1580–1640), a profitable commercial activity in meat, leather, and silver from Potosí in Upper Peru developed there. The king of Portugal, for geopolitical reasons, decided to establish a settlement in the area, and toward that end he influenced the Catholic Church to include the area in the bishopric of Rio de Janeiro, created in 1676. The king sent two expeditions to take possession of the river port and establish a settlement: the first attempt, led by Jorge Soares de Macedo, failed; the second, under the command of Manuel Lobos, was more successful, and in January 1680 he established the Portuguese settlement of Colônia do Sacramento. Soon after, José de Garro, then governor of Buenos Aires, ordered an attack on Colônia by 250 soldiers and 3,000 Indians. Lobo and his colonists surrendered later that year.

The hostilities were accompanied by intense diplomatic negotiations. The Treaty of Lisbon (1700) specified that the colony, reoccupied in 1683, belonged to the Portuguese kingdom. Four years later the colony reverted to Spain, but the Treaty of Utrecht (1713) returned it to Portugal. The Treaty of Madrid (1750) once again restored Colonia to Spain. Finally the Treaty of San Ildefonso (1777)

fixed Lagoa Mirim, and not the Río de la Plata, as the southern border of Brazil. Because of this, Colônia returned to being a Spanish colony.

After thriving as an alternative port to Buenos Aires in the colonial period, Colonia del Sacramento became, through the efforts of Spanish colonists, a commercial center for a rich agricultural and live-stock-raising region. The town prospered in the nineteenth century, becoming the capital of the Department of Colonia, one of the richest in the republic of Uruguay. In the early twentieth century, Colonia became a tourist attraction for *porteños* willing to take the twenty-five-mile boat trip across the Río de la Plata. Argentine investors built a hotel with a casino, a bullring, and a small railway connected to the port, but the project failed because the Argentine government imposed a heavy tax on all passengers disembarking in Colonia. An American resident, who brought the first electricity-generating plant and the first telephone to the region, planned a bridge to Buenos Aires. That project is periodically updated and revived, but the bridge has never been built. A plan for a bridge was approved by both the Argentine and Uruguayan governments in the late 1990s, but a regional financial crisis caused the project to be abandoned. In the 1960s Argentines began to buy properties in the marginal Barrio Histórico and restore houses dating back to the eighteenth century, and a new hotel-casino was built for international visitors. Colonia del Sacramento, with dozens of hotels and restaurants, is now the third-most-active center for tourism in Uruguay, attracting weekend visitors and vacationers. Its population is approximately 20,000.

See also **Río de la Plata; San Ildefonso, Treaty of (1777); Tordesillas, Treaty of (1494); Uruguay: The Twentieth Century.**

BIBLIOGRAPHY

Almeida, Luís Ferrand de. *A Colônia do Sacramento na época da sucessão de Espanha*. Coimbra, Portugal: Universidade de Coimbra, 1973.

Vianna, Hélio. *História diplomática do Brasil*. São Paulo, Brazil: Edições Melhoramentos, 1958.

EDWARD L. SHAW

SACRISTAN, QUESTION OF THE. Question of the Sacristan, a complex legal case that grew into a highly contentious political issue in

1856 in Chile. It began in January 1856 with the dismissal of a servant by the senior sacristan of Santiago cathedral. Two canons of the cathedral, seeking to overturn this action, appealed to the secular Supreme Court, a procedure disliked by many ecclesiastics, who felt that matters of ecclesiastical discipline should be dealt with by the church alone. The combative archbishop of Santiago, Rafael Valentín Valdivieso (1804–1878), denied the supreme court's competence in the affair. Backed by the government of President Manual Montt (1809–1880), the court eventually ruled in favor of the two canons, and later threatened the archbishop with exile.

Deep passions were aroused by the issue. With fears of a political upheaval (which was almost certainly being plotted), the principals reached a compromise. The aftereffects of the "question" were serious: the powerful proclerical wing of the ruling Conservative Party, alienated by Montt's Erastian attitude, was prompted to defect and join forces with the Liberal opposition in the Liberal-Conservative Fusion (1858). This effectively undermined the Conservative hegemony in Chile and opened the way to greater political competition.

BIBLIOGRAPHY

Bravo Lira, Bernardino. *El Absolutismo ilustrado en Hispanoamérica: Chile (1760–1860) de Carlos III a Portales y Montt.* Santiago, Chile: Editorial Universitaria, 1994.

Collier, Simon. *Chile: The Making of a Republic, 1830–1865: Politics and Ideas.* New York: Cambridge University Press, 2003.

SIMON COLLIER

SACSAHUAMAN. Sacsahuaman, the hill overlooking the city of Cuzco, Peru, from the northwest. An important *Huaca* or oratory in Inca times, Sacsahuaman, which in Quechua means "hill of the hawk," was believed to represent the head of the puma that was reproduced in the ground plan of Inca Cuzco. Elaborate construction projects, probably beginning in the time of Pachacuti, transformed Sacsahuaman into the largest megalithic structure in the ancient Americas. The most impressive portion of the ruins that still stand is composed of three walls of zigzag design laid in Inca polygonal stonework. Some of the individual stones in this wall have been calculated to weigh as much as 60 tons. Above these walls, on the crest of the hill, originally stood three towers that were razed by the Spanish during the Conquest. The function of Sacsahuaman has never been definitely established. Probably it served multiple functions during Inca times, including religious, military, and royal residence. It also symbolized Inca resistance to the Spanish invaders until it fell to Juan Pizarro in 1536. Today it still holds meaning for Cuzco's current residents. Near this site, Inti Raymi, the Inca festival in honor of the winter solstice, is celebrated annually on June 24th.

See also **Archaeology; Incas, The.**

BIBLIOGRAPHY

Sources on Sacsahuaman include Graziano Gasparini and Luise Margolies, *Inca Architecture* (1980); and Vincent R. Lee, "The Building of Sacsahuaman," in *Nawpa Pacha* 24 (1986): 49–56.

Additional Bibliography

Angles Vargas, Víctor. *Sacsayhuaman, portento arquitectónico.* Lima: INDUSTRIALgráfica, 1990.

Hemming, John; photos by Edward Ranney. *Monuments of the Incas.* Albuquerque: University of New Mexico Press, 1990.

Palomino Díaz, Julio. *Intiwatanas y números: Ciencia del pasado andino.* Cuzco: Municipalidad del Qosqo, 1994.

GORDON F. McEWAN

SÁ E BENAVIDES, SALVADOR CORREIA DE (1602–1681). Salvador Correia de Sá e Benavides (*b.* 1602; *d.* 1 January 1681), one of the most important figures in the seventeenth-century Portuguese South Atlantic Empire. Born in Cádiz, Spain, Salvador Correia de Sá e Benavides was the son of Martim de Sá, governor of Rio de Janeiro in 1602–1608 and 1623–1632.

In 1615 Salvador sailed with his father to Brazil for the first time. Back in the Iberian Peninsula by early 1618, he was again in Brazil with his father by the end of the year, searching for minerals in Bahia and Rio de Janeiro. Salvador returned to Portugal about 1623 and sailed to Brazil for the third time in 1624 to help defend it against the Dutch in Espírito Santo and Bahia.

Sá returned to Europe and in 1627 received the title of Admiral of the Southern Coast and Rio de la Plata. He was back in Rio de Janeiro by 1628. In the early 1630s, Sá pacified Payaguá and Guaicurú Indians in the Paraguayan Chaco and Calchaquis Indians in Tucumán Province in Argentina. Sá returned to Portugal and in 1637 was appointed governor and *capitão-mor* of Rio de Janeiro, where he fought attempts by the colonists to expel the Jesuits. Two years later he succeeded his grandfather as administrator of the mines of São Paulo and Santos. Sá returned to Portugal in 1643 and the next year was appointed to the Overseas Council. In 1645 he began leading convoys to and from Portuguese America.

Named governor and captain-general of Angola in 1647, Sá was given the task of driving the Dutch from that captaincy. In November 1647 Sá sailed from Lisbon. After picking up additional men and supplies in Rio de Janeiro, he arrived off the coast of Angola in July 1648. Dutch authorities in Luanda surrendered to him on 21 August 1648 and Benguela fell soon after. To contemporaries, his successes in Angola were Sá's greatest achievements.

In 1652 Sá left Luanda for Brazil but soon returned to Portugal. He was put in charge of the defense of the port of Lisbon in 1654. In September 1658 he was named governor and captain general of the Repartição do Sul—Rio de Janeiro and the captaincies to the south plus Espírito Santo to the north. Sá put down a revolt in 1661 but was relieved of his governorship in 1662 for his harshness in doing so. Returning to Portugal, Sá fell in and out of favor with the crown between 1663 and 1669, until he finally was restored to the good graces of the court in the latter year.

See also **Explorers and Exploration: Brazil.**

BIBLIOGRAPHY

The best biography to date in any language is Charles R. Boxer, *Salvador de Sá and the Struggle for Brazil and Angola, 1602–1686* (1952). Also useful are Luis Ferrand De Almeida, "A data da morte de Salvador Correia de Sá," in *Revista Portuguesa de História* 8 (1959): 327–330; Charles R. Boxer, *Dicionário de História de Portugal*, vol. 3 (n.d.), pp. 702–703; Manoel Cardozo, "Notes for a Biography of Salvador Correia de Sá e Benavides, 1594–1688," in *The Americas* 7, no. 2 (1950): 135–170. Three useful Portuguese accounts, the latter two of which include a number of documents on Sá's life and career, are Clado Ribeiro De Lessa, *Salvador Correia de Sá e Benavides: Vida e feitos, principalmente no Brasil* (1940); Bertha Leite, "Salvador de Sá e Benavides," in *Anais do IV Congresso de História Nacional, 1949*, vol. 12 (1951), pp. 261–559; Luis Norton, *A dinastia dos Sás no Brasil, 1558–1662*, 2d ed. (1965).

Additional Bibliography

Monteiro, Rodrigo Bentes. *O rei no espelho: A monarquia portuguesa e a colonizacão da América, 1640–1720.* São Paulo: Editora Hucitec, 2002.

Vainfas, Ronaldo. *Dicionário do Brasil colonial, 1500–1808.* Rio de Janeiro: Objetiva, 2000.

FRANCIS A. DUTRA

SÁENZ, JAIME (1921–1986). Jaime Sáenz (*b.* 8 October 1921; *d.* 1986), Bolivian poet and novelist. Sáenz is one of the most original poets of contemporary Bolivia. Oblivious to common sense, his works reject the construction of clear and well-defined meanings. Syllogistic, closer to concept than to image, Sáenz's poetry is made up of syntactic torsions, paradoxes, and tautologies. From *El escalpelo* (1955), *Muerte por el tacto* (1957), *Aniversario de una visión* (1960), and *Visitante profundo* (1963) to *El frío* (1967), *Recorrer esta distancia* (1973), and *Bruckner: Las tinieblas* (1978), this poetic universe follows a spiral movement, in search of the unity of being. This search, which places Sáenz within the tradition of German romanticism, is markedly subjective. For Sáenz, the human body, the corporeal, is merely an "instrument of living" with little influence on the routines of everyday life. This eccentric view of the world is also present in his novel, *Felipe Delgado* (1979), a challenging exploration of the modern grotesque.

See also **Literature: Spanish America.**

BIBLIOGRAPHY

The most comprehensive analysis of Sáenz's poetry is Blanca Wiethüchter, "Las estructuras de lo imaginario en la obra poética de Jaime Sáenz," in *Obra poética de Jaime Sáenz* (1975). Two other major contributions are Luis H. Antezana, "Hacer y cuidar" in *Ensayos y lecturas* (1986), and Eduardo Mitre, *El árbol y la piedra: Poetas contemporáneos de Bolivia* (1988). In English, see Javier Sanjinés C., "Jaime Sáenz," in *Dictionary of Literary Biography: Modern Latin American Fiction Writers,* edited by William Luis and Ann González (1993).

Additional Bibliography

Blanco Mamani, Elías. *Jaime Sáenz, el ángel solitario y jubiloso de la noche: Apuntes para una historia de vida.* La Paz, Bolivia: Casa de la Cultura "Franz Tamayo," 1998.

Monasterios Pérez, Elizabeth. *Dilemas de la poesía de fin de siglo: José Emilio Pacheco y Jaime Saenz.* La Paz, Bolivia: Plural Editores: Carrera de Literatura, Facultad de Humanidades, Universidad Mayor de San Andrés, 2001.

JAVIER SANJINÉS C.

SÁENZ, MOISÉS (1888–1941).

Moisés Sáenz (*b.* 1888; *d.* 1941), Mexican educator. Sáenz was born in Monterrey and studied at a Presbyterian preparatory school in Coyoacán. He received his teaching degree from the Escuela Normal of Jalapa, studied at the Sorbonne, and completed his graduate studies at Columbia Teachers College in New York, where he became a disciple of John Dewey. He was influential in Mexican revolutionary education when, as undersecretary of education in the Plutarco Elías Calles government (1924–1928), he fleshed out a program of rural education based on Dewey's notions of action education. The Casa del Pueblo, as the rural school was called by the then *secretaría de educación pública,* was designed to teach farming, hygiene, horticulture, apiculture, aviculture, and civics through student-operated gardens, beehives, orchards, chicken coops, and producer and consumer cooperatives. Sáenz was a strong advocate of indigenous and rural integration into a modernizing, Western society.

Sáenz was known for promoting North American ideas in Mexican education and was singled out by some Catholics as a propagandist for Protestantism. Nonetheless, after José Vasconcelos, no other Mexican has had as much influence on rural education. Sáenz was also influential in the creation of Mexico's system of secondary schools and the Casa de Estudiante Indígena. He held many educational posts in Mexico, organized the Primer Congreso Indigenista Interamericano, and served as Mexican ambassador to Denmark, Ecuador, and Peru, where he died in 1941. He was the author of several books, including *Sobre el indio peruano y su incorporación al medio nacional* (Mexico, 1933); *Carapán: Bosquejo de una experiencia* (Lima, 1936); *México íntegro* (Lima, 1939); and, with Herbert J. Priestley, *Some Mexican Problems* (Chicago, 1926).

See also **Education: Overview.**

BIBLIOGRAPHY

Ramón Eduardo Ruíz, *Mexico: The Challenge of Poverty and Illiteracy* (1963).

John Britton, "Moisés Sáenz, nacionalista mexicano," in *Historia Mexicana* 22 (July–September 1972): 77–98.

Mary Kay Vaughan, *The State, Education, and Social Class in Mexico, 1880–1928* (1982).

Additional Bibliography

Pedraza Salinas, Jorge, and Manuel Pérez Ramos. *Moisés Sáenz, educador vigente.* Apodaca: Presidencia Municipal de Apodaca, N.L., 2001.

Vaughan, Mary K. *Cultural Politics in Revolution: Teachers, Peasants, and Schools in Mexico, 1930–1940.* Tucson: University of Arizona Press, 1997.

MARY KAY VAUGHAN

SÁENZ DE THORNE, MANUELA (1797–1856).

Manuela Sáenz de Thorne (*b.* 1797; *d.* 23 November 1856), best known as the lover of Simón Bolívar, but also a political figure in her own right. Though she was of illegitimate birth, her parents belonged to the upper class of late colonial Quito. At age twenty she was given in an arranged marriage to an English merchant, James Thorne. However, the enduring passion of her life was for Bolívar, whom she met in 1822 when he first came to Ecuador.

Abandoning her husband, Sáenz followed Bolívar to Peru. She was with him on campaign and subsequently in Lima, where she assumed a prominent role in social and political life. But her most controversial role was in Bogotá, where she arrived in late 1827. There she showed uninhibited vigor in defending Bolívar against his opponents, especially the faction of Vice President Francisco de Paula Santander, at one point having Santander shot in effigy. When an attempt was made on Bolívar's life in September 1828, she was in the palace with him and helped him escape.

Sáenz remained in Bogotá after the final departure of Bolívar in 1830. She continued to be active in politics on behalf of the Bolivarian party and was implicated in a conspiracy against her old enemy Santander after he became president of New Granada. Exiled in 1833, she eventually settled in Paita, on the Peruvian coast, where she lived until her death.

See also **Bolívar, Simón.**

BIBLIOGRAPHY

Alfonso Rumazo González, *Manuela Sáenz, la libertadora del Libertador* (1944).

Victor W. Von Hagen and Christine Von Hagen, *The Four Seasons of Manuela: A Biography* (1952).

Additional Bibliography

Cacua Prada, Antonio. *Manuelita Sáenz: Mujer de América.* Quito: Fondo Editorial CCE, 2002.

Mogollón Cobo, María, and Ximena Narváez Yar. *Manuela Sáenz: Presencia y polémica en la historia.* Quito: Corporación Editora Nacional, 1997.

Padrón, Leonardo. *Manuela Sáenz: Guión original.* Caracas: AlterLibris Ediciones, 2001.

                                    DAVID BUSHNELL

SÁENZ GARZA, AARÓN (1891–1983).

Aarón Sáenz Garza (*b.* 1 June 1891; *d.* 26 February 1983), Mexican politician and entrepreneur. A native of Monterrey, Nuevo León, Sáenz was trained as a lawyer at the National University. He joined the revolutionary army of General Álvaro Obregón in 1913 and thereafter steadily rose in national politics. He was minister of foreign relations from 1924 to 1927, manager of Obregón's successful presidential campaign in 1928, a founder of the National Revolutionary Party in 1928–1929, and minister of public education in 1930. A powerful ally of Obregón (who was assassinated after his election in 1928), Sáenz was a prime contender for the presidential nomination of the National Revolutionary Party in 1929 but lost it to Pascual Ortiz Rubio. Although he remained active in politics, Sáenz focused on his business ventures, particularly a multimillion-dollar system of sugar mills. With the help of his sons he expanded the family business interests into paper manufacturing and aviation during the 1950s and 1960s to become one of the nation's leading entrepreneurs.

See also **Mexico, Political Parties: National Revolutionary Party (PNR).**

BIBLIOGRAPHY

James C. Hefley, *Aarón Sáenz: Mexico's Revolutionary Capitalist* (1970), is a laudatory biography. Aarón Sáenz, *La política internacional de la Revolución: Estudios y documentos* (1961), covers the author's work in diplomacy in the 1920s.

Additional Bibliography

Salmerón Sanginés, Pedro. *Aarón Sáenz Garza: Militar, diplomático, político, empresario.* México: M.A. Porrúa, 2001.

                                    JOHN A. BRITTON

SÁENZ PEÑA, LUIS (1822–1907).

Luis Sáenz Peña (*b.* 2 April 1822; *d.* 4 December 1907), Argentine politician. Born and raised in Buenos Aires, Sáenz Peña received his law degree from the University of Buenos Aires in 1845. He entered politics in 1860 as a deputy to the Constitutional Convention, thereafter serving in both Buenos Aires provincial assemblies and the national assembly. He also held posts in the provincial Supreme Court, the Provincial Bank, and the General Council on Education. In the wake of the 1890 uprising of the Civic Union and the stock market crash, Sáenz Peña became the compromise candidate for president in 1892. In that post he served the interests of the National Autonomist Party of Julio A. Roca and Carlos Pellegrini, but he never succeeded in emerging from their shadows. Afflicted by ill health and an indecisive temper, Sáenz Peña served a two-year term marred by strong opposition in Congress, an uprising by the new Radical Civic Union led by Leandro Alem and future president Hipólito Irigoyen, and a worsening economic situation after the Baring Brothers crisis. He submitted his resignation in January 1895 and was replaced by the equally ill-fated José Evaristo Uriburu. Argentine politics did not settle down until Roca reassumed the presidency in 1898. Sáenz Peña's son, Roque, followed in his father's footsteps. Elected in 1910, he was best known for the electoral reform law of 1912.

BIBLIOGRAPHY

Natalio Botana, *El orden conservador: La política argentina entre 1880 y 1916* (1985).

Ezequiel Gallo, "Argentina: Society and Politics, 1880–1916," translated by Richard Southern, in *The Cambridge History of Latin America,* edited by Leslie Bethell, vol. 5 (1986), pp. 359–391.

Paula Alonso, "Politics and Elections in Buenos Aires, 1890–1898: The Performance of the Radical Party," in *Journal of Latin American Studies* 25 (October 1993): 465–487.

Additional Bibliography

Rock, David. *State Building and Political Movements in Argentina, 1860–1916.* Stanford, CA: Stanford University Press, 2002.

Zimmermann, Eduardo A. *Los liberales reformistas: La cuestión social en la Argentina, 1890–1916.* Buenos Aires: Editorial Sudamericana: Universidad de San Andrés, 1995.

JEREMY ADELMAN

SÁENZ PEÑA, ROQUE (1851–1914).

Roque Sáenz Peña (*b.* 19 March 1851; *d.* 9 August 1914), president of Argentina (1910–1914) who in 1912 initiated an electoral reform law that made voting compulsory and provided for the secret ballot and minority political representation in Congress. The law is known as the Sáenz Peña Law. Sáenz Peña belonged to the Argentine upper class. His father, Luis, was president of Argentina (1892–1895). Roque Sáenz Peña studied law at the University of Buenos Aires, but in 1874 he discontinued his studies for a brief period to join the forces that were suppressing a rebellion led by former President Bartolomé Mitre. He graduated in 1875 and a year later was elected to the Buenos Aires legislature representing the Partido Autonomista Nacional. When the War of the Pacific broke out in 1879, Sáenz Peña moved to Lima and joined the alliance of Peru and Bolivia against Chile. He became known for his bravery and participated in the battles of San Francisco and Tarapacá and also in the heroic defense of Arica, where he was taken prisoner in 1880.

After his return to Argentina, he was named undersecretary of the Ministry of Foreign Relations. In August 1887 he was appointed special envoy and minister plenipotentiary to Uruguay. In 1888 he served as a member of the delegation representing Argentina at the South American Conference of Private International Law held in Montevideo. A year later, he participated in the Pan-American Conference in Washington, D.C. In 1890, he served briefly as minister of foreign relations, having to resign as a consequence of the revolution of 26 July 1890. In 1891, Sáenz Peña became a presidential candidate but withdrew when Julio A. Roca and Bartolomé Mitre engineered his own father's candidacy. He resigned from the Senate in December 1892 to avoid a confrontation with his father and retired for three years to an *estancia* in the province of Entre Ríos. He returned to Buenos Aires in 1895 after his father's resignation. From that moment on he began attacking the corrupt, personalistic political system. The Reformista faction of the Partido Autonomista Nacional, headed by Carlos Pellegrini until his death in 1906, supported Sáenz Peña in the congressional elections of 1906 and 1908. In 1910, he was elected president.

See also **Sáenz Peña Law.**

BIBLIOGRAPHY

Fermín Vicente Arenas Luque, *Roque Sáenz Peña: El presidente del sufragio libre* (1951).

Felipe Barreda y Laos, *Roque Sáenz Peña* (1954).

Miguel Angel Cárcano, *Sáenz Peña: La revolución por los comicios,* 2d ed. (1977).

Additional Bibliography

López, Mario Justo. *De la república oligárquica a la república democrática: Estudio sobre la reforma política de Roque Sáenz Peña.* Argentina: Lumiere, 2005.

Rock, David. *State Building and Political Movements in Argentina, 1860–1916.* Stanford, CA: Stanford University Press, 2002.

Zimmermann, Eduardo A. *Los liberales reformistas: La cuestión social en la Argentina, 1890–1916.* Buenos Aires: Editorial Sudamericana: Universidad de San Andrés, 1995.

JUAN MANUEL PÉREZ

SÁENZ PEÑA LAW.

Sáenz Peña Law, measure initiated by Argentine President Roque Sáenz Peña, also known as the Law of 1912, which provided for the secret ballot and minority party representation in Congress. It also made voting compulsory for all native and naturalized Argentine men over the age of 18. The electoral roll was to be based on the military's conscription lists. The military was also given policing duties during electoral periods to ensure a peaceful and orderly process. The law, which altered the political process, was passed after a protracted congressional debate stemming from Conservative opposition to it.

The minority representation was to be established through the incomplete list, a process by which it was possible to give one-third of the seats available in each electoral district to the party with the second-highest number of votes.

This law radically changed Argentine politics. For example, voter turnout in the elections increased to between 70 and 80 percent of eligible voters, while before its passage, about a third of eligible voters turned out. As a result of the law, the number of eligible voters increased to 1 million in 1912. Also as a result of these changes, the Unión Cívica Radical, part of the opposition since the late nineteenth century, won the presidential election of 1916, and its leader, Hipólito Irigoyen, became the first president who did not come from the traditional ruling class. The Radicals remained in control until they were overthrown by a military coup in 1930.

See also **Sáenz Peña, Roque.**

BIBLIOGRAPHY

Miguel Angel Cárcano, *Sáenz Peña: La revolución por los comicios*, 2d ed. (1977).

Honorio Alberto Diaz, *Ley Sáenz Peña: Pro y contra* (1983).

David Rock, *Argentina, 1516–1982* (1985).

Additional Bibliography

Giacobone, Carlos Alberto. *Sáenz Peña "salió la nueva ley!": Elecciones en la ciudad de Buenos Aires, 1912.* Buenos Aires: Instituto de Investigaciones Históricas Cruz del Sur, 2003.

López, Mario Justo. *De la república oligárquica a la república democrática: Estudio sobre la reforma política de Roque Sáenz Peña.* Buenos Aires: Lumiere, 2005.

JUAN MANUEL PÉREZ

SAER, JUAN JOSÉ (1937–2005). Juan José Saer is considered one of Argentina's finest fiction writers. Born on June 28, 1937, in Serodino, in the province of Santa Fe, Saer was a professor at the School of Film at the Universidad Nacional del Litoral. In 1968 he moved to France, where he taught Latin American literature at the University of Rennes. His first novels, such as *Responso* (1964) and *La vuelta completa* (1966; The Complete Return), and his collections of short stories, *En la zona* (1960; In the Zone), *Palo y hueso* (1965; Wood and Bone), and *Unidad de lugar* (1967; Unit of Place), are in the realist vein, with elements of American regionalism. The stories in *Cicatrices* (1969; Scars) and the novels *El limonero real* (1974; The Real Lemon Tree), *Nadie nada nunca* (1980; translated as *Nobody Nothing Never*, 1993), *El entenado* (1983; The Entenado), *Glosa* (1985; It Glosses), *La ocasión* (1986; The Occasion), and *Lo imborrable* (1992; The Imborrable) display the influence of objectivism on the new French novel. His poetic works are collected in *El arte de narrar* (1977; The Art of Narration), a paradoxical title that reflects his persistent attempt to combine poetry and fiction. His work has been translated into French, English, German, Italian, and Portuguese. In 1987 he won the Nadal Prize for Literature. Saer died June 11, 2005, in Paris. His last novel, *La Grande* (2005; The Great One), was published posthumously.

See also **Argentina: The Twentieth Century; Literature: Spanish America.**

BIBLIOGRAPHY

Corbatta, Jorgelina. *Juan José Saer, arte poética y práctica literaria.* Buenos Aires: Corregidor, 2005.

Riera, Gabriel. *Littoral of the Letter: Saer's Art of Narration.* Lewisburg, PA: Bucknell University Press, 2006.

ELENA MOREIRA

SAGRA, RAMÓN DE LA (1798–1871). Ramón de la Sagra (*b.* 1798; *d.* 1871), Spanish naturalist and economist. De la Sagra studied agriculture in Madrid until 1820; subsequently he was appointed director of the botanical gardens in Havana, where he arrived in 1823. While there he also served as professor of agricultural botany at the university and studied the plant life of the island to assess its potential productivity. In 1828 he began to contribute to the new journal *Anales de la ciencia* and kept in close touch with academics abroad. In 1831 he published *Historia económica, política y estadística de la Isla de Cuba*. De la Sagra relocated to Paris in 1835 and there published an expanded version as *Histoire physique, politique et naturelle de L'Ile de Cuba* (1842–1857). The latter, considered his masterwork, describes all aspects of the lives of the Cuban people and their environment. In his later years de la Sagra fell under the influence of the French socialist Pierre-Joseph Proudhon and wrote on social and economic issues.

BIBLIOGRAPHY

Fermín Peraza Sarauza, *Diccionario biográfico cubano* (1951–).

Dawn Ades, *Art in Latin America: The Modern Era, 1820–1980* (1989).

KAREN RACINE

SAHAGÚN, BERNARDINO DE (c.

1499/1500–1590). Bernardino de Sahagún, a Franciscan missionary, arrived in New Spain in 1529 and began a prolific career of evangelization of the Nahua peoples to Christianity. Born Bernardino de Rivera in Sahagún, Spain, he was trained in Latin, history, philosophy, and theology at the University of Salamanca and became a Franciscan around 1527. He spent his first years in the New World in Tlalmanalco (1530–1532) and as guardian of the Xochimilco Convent. In 1537, Sahagún began teaching Latin at the newly established Colegio de Santa Cruz in Tlatelolco. At the college, indigenous *pipiltin* (sons of nobles) were trained in the Renaissance humanist tradition of missionary teachers and became the painters, sculptors, scribes, interpreters, and historians of the New World. Sahagún also worked as missionary to the convents of Xochimilco, Huejotzingo, and Cholula, and fulfilled various ecclesiastical duties in the Puebla, Tula, and Tepeapulco and Michoacán regions. From 1547 until his death, and with the help of several youths from the Tlatelolco college, he gathered testimony and information on Nahua life and history. The material collected, analyzed, and presented in Spanish and Nahuatl in three manuscripts is known as the *General History of the Things of New Spain*. For this work, he is often considered the first ethnographer

of the New World. In addition to the *Historia*, Sahagún wrote several other studies of the Nahuatl language as well as doctrinal works, only one of which, *Psalmodía Cristiana* (1583), was published in his lifetime.

See also **Franciscans; Missions: Spanish America.**

BIBLIOGRAPHY

Klor de Alva, J. Jorge; H. B. Nicholson; and Eloise Quiñones Keber. *The Work of Bernardino de Sahagún: Pioneer Ethnographer of Sixteenth-Century Aztec Mexico*. Albany: Institute for Mesoamerican Studies, University at Albany, State University of New York, 1988.

León Portilla, Miguel. *Bernardino de Sahagún, First Anthropologist*. Translated by Mauricio J. Mixco. Norman: University of Oklahoma Press, 2002.

Nicolau d'Olwer, Luis. *Fray Bernardino de Sahagún, 1499–1590*. Translated by Mauricio J. Mixco. Salt Lake City: University of Utah Press, 1987.

Sahagún, Bernardino de. *General History of the Things of New Spain: Florentine Codex*. 13 vols. Edited and translated by Arthur J. O. Anderson and Charles E. Dibble. Santa Fe, NM: School of American Research, and Salt Lake City: University of Utah, 1950–1982.

STEPHANIE WOOD
COLLEEN EBACHER

SAINT AUGUSTINE. Saint Augustine,

Spanish capital of Florida and East Florida, 2004 estimated population 12,157. Saint Augustine, the earliest permanent city of European origin in the United States, was an afterthought. Pedro Menéndez De Avilés, charged by Philip II in 1565 with cleansing the Florida coast of French interlopers, hurried across the Atlantic to destroy Fort Caroline, a French fort in the mouth of the Saint Johns River, only to find it reinforced by a fleet under Jean Ribault. Menéndez fell back to the nearest harbor and took possession of it in the king's name, commandeering and fortifying an Indian village. In honor of the patron saint of Avilés, he named the camp Saint Augustine. From there, he marched on during a hurricane and took Fort Caroline. Ribault's ships were wrecked in the storm, and the castaways received short shrift as pirates. Having cleared the land of intruders, Menéndez moved to strengthen Spain's hold on the Southeast by founding forts and settlements at every deep water port and far into the interior. But this expansion was premature. Famines, mutinies, and Indian warfare gradually reduced the Spanish presence to Saint Augustine and the capital of Santa Elena, on Parris Island.

Sir Francis Drake stopped by Saint Augustine in 1586 to burn the houses and cut down the fruit trees. Governor Pedro Menéndez Márquez reacted by abandoning Santa Elena to consolidate his forces. In 1599 the city was again devastated, this time by a fire and a hurricane. After some debate over whether to abandon the flood-prone port, with its shallow bar and sandy soil, the Spanish rebuilt Saint Augustine where it was.

As Florida's one Spanish municipality, formally titled "the noble and loyal city," Saint Augustine was the seat of all branches of government. The two officials of the royal treasury were also *regidores* (governors) of the *cabildo*. The royal governor doubled as captain-general. Florida was a presidial colony, with officers, warehouses, and quarters for convicts and slaves. Of the 300 to 350 soldiers stationed there, a portion was always on detachment at secondary garrisons or on coast guard and supply vessels. A creole elite of *floridanos* drew pay as reserve officers while tending to their personal trading ventures and ranches in the provinces. Indian chiefs stalked through town, delivering Spanish-imposed labor levies and burdened with food and other products from the provinces.

Saint Augustine was also a religious center. The parish priest exercised a monopoly on sacramental services for non-Indians and supervised the confraternities. The friary, headquarters of the Franciscan province of Santa Elena, which took in both Florida and Cuba and at full strength numbered seventy missionaries, provided the community with a grammar school and a locus for political opposition.

In 1668 Jamaican privateers raided Saint Augustine in the dead of night, killing sixty people in the streets. Their captain, Robert Searles, allowed his Spanish prisoners to be ransomed but kept all the Indians, free blacks, and mestizos to sell as slaves. This raid, followed by the founding of Charleston in 1670, persuaded the Council of the Indies to grant Florida a larger share of the defense budget. The Castillo de San Marcos, begun in 1672 and completed in 1695, fortified the center

of the settlement at the expense of the peripheries. Provincial defenses were neglected and food reserves fell to dangerous lows as extra laborers and maize were channeled toward the capital.

The *castillo* quickly proved its worth as a place of refuge from pirates. Later governors added a seawall to protect the city from storms. The Christian Indians, however, were left exposed not only to pirates but also to their native enemies equipped with firearms to take slaves for the English. The demoralized provinces collapsed during Queen Anne's War, and by 1706, Saint Augustine had lost its hinterland.

Twice in the eighteenth century English invaders besieged the *castillo* without success. After 1702, when they watched Colonel James Moore of Carolina destroy their homes, the fifteen hundred or so inhabitants rebuilt Saint Augustine as a walled city, with earthworks and a fort, Mose, to defend the only road out of town. In 1740, when General James Oglethorpe of Georgia came to lay siege, the city was saved. However, the Indian refugees living in pueblos outside the walls were not as fortunate. When the Spanish refused to come to their aid during Colonel William Palmer's attack in 1728, many of them left Florida for good. The last remnants of the missions were secularized and the Franciscans, bereft of purpose, split into factions.

As military expenditures escalated during the wars for empire, Saint Augustine's presidio and population grew, and with them opportunities for illicit trade and smuggling. Florida's newly appointed auxiliary bishop reported English ships in the harbor and English traders walking about town. Southeastern Indians were demanding—and getting—English goods as gifts from a Spanish governor. It was time again to consolidate. In 1763, after the Seven Years' War, Spain exchanged Florida for British-held Havana. Approximately three thousand soldiers, friars, *floridanos*, and slaves, in company with eighty-three Indians, pulled up stakes and left, mostly for Cuba.

Twenty years later the British returned Florida to Spain. From 1784 to 1821, Saint Augustine was the capital of East Florida, a colony much changed in character. Few of the expatriates returned. The populace was a cosmopolitan mixture of Minorcans and others from the Mediterranean, assorted Europeans, Canary Islanders, Scots, English, Americans, and

Africans. The soldiers of several companies from Cuba were mulattoes or free blacks and the Hibernian Regiment was Irish, as were two of the governors. A distinctive style of domestic architecture developed featuring two-story houses of coquina with a loggia, an outside stairway, and a balcony facing the street. The public buildings erected included a parish church, a school, a hospital, and barracks.

Plans for further progress were interrupted when the Napoleonic invasion of Spain created a vacuum in metropolitan government. To commemorate Spain's Constitution of 1812 local liberals erected a monument on the plaza that stood there undisturbed through royal reversals, distant wars for independence, transient republics, and Jacksonian invasions. By the time the United States annexed East Florida in 1821, Saint Augustine was Spanish chiefly in name.

See also **Menéndez de Avilés, Pedro.**

BIBLIOGRAPHY

Charles W. Arnade, *The Siege of St. Augustine in 1702* (1959).

Albert C. Manucy, *The Houses of St. Augustine, 1565–1821* (1962; repr. 1992).

Luis Rafael Arana and Albert Manucy, *The Building of Castillo de San Marcos* (1977).

Amy Turner Bushnell, *The King's Coffer: Proprietors of the Spanish Florida Treasury, 1565–1702* (1981).

Kathleen Deagan, *Spanish St. Augustine: The Archaeology of a Colonial Creole Community* (1983).

Jean Parker Waterbury, ed., *The Oldest City: St. Augustine, Saga of Survival* (1983).

Additional Bibliography

Feldman, Lawrence H. *The Last Days of British Saint Augustine, 1784-1785: A Spanish Census of the English Colony of East Florida.* Baltimore, MD: Clearfield, 2003.

Kapitzke, Robert L. *Religion, Power, and Politics in Colonial St. Augustine.* Gainesville: University Press of Florida, 2001.

Manucy, Albert C. *Sixteenth-Century St. Augustine: The People and Their Homes.* Gainesville: University Press of Florida, 1997.

AMY TURNER BUSHNELL

SAINT BARTHÉLEMY. Saint Barthélemy (also Saint Barts). In 1493 Christopher Columbus named the island after his brother Bartolomeo. Now part of the French department of Guadeloupe, French West Indies, it encompasses 8.3 square miles and has 3,500 inhabitants, almost all white, the descendants of fishermen from Brittany, Normandy, and Poitou. Strategically located between the Dutch and English Leeward Islands, the daily language is English. It was held by Sweden from 1784 to 1877, then was bought back by France.

French from Saint Kitts (Leeward Islands) settled before 1648, and the Knights of Malta assumed ownership in 1656. The Caribs forced them to leave, only to have the French reoccupy Saint Barts in 1674 and establish a fishing economy. The knights were evacuated to reinforce the French at Saint Kitts in 1689, but a remnant returned to their devastated island after the Treaty of Ryswick (1697).

Saint Barts was briefly occupied by Great Britain during the Seven Years' War (1756–1763). The French traded the island to the Swedes in return for concessions on the Baltic island of Gotland. The Swedish renamed the port of Saint Barts Gustavia, and its free trade status rivaled that of nearby Danish Saint Thomas during the remaining Caribbean wars.

After 1877, the French maintained Gustavia's free port status. Swedish/French architecture and Swedish/French road signs attest to the island's mixed heritage. Manioc, cotton, pineapple, and cattle and goat herding complement fishing. A controlled and exclusive tourism is based on its isolated beaches, French cuisine, and "unspoiled" rustic atmosphere.

See also **French-Latin American Relations.**

BIBLIOGRAPHY

Sir Alan Burns, *History of the British West Indies* (1965).

Robert L. Breedan, ed., *Isles of the Caribbean* (1980).

Franklin W. Knight, *The Caribbean* (1990).

Additional Bibliography

Aub-Buscher, Gertrud, and Beverley Ormerod Noakes. *The Francophone Caribbean Today: Literature, Language, Culture.* Barbados: University of the West Indies Press, 2003.

Didcott, Charles, and Christine Didcott. *St. Barth, French West Indies.* Waitsfield, VT: Concepts Publishers, 1997.

O'Shaughnessy, Andrew Jackson. *An Empire Divided: The American Revolution and the British Caribbean.* Philadelphia: University of Pennsylvania Press, 2000.

PAT KONRAD

SAINT CHRISTOPHER (SAINT KITTS).

Saint Christopher (Saint Kitts), an island in the Lesser Antilles that was of strategic importance in colonial times. Saint Christopher is a Caribbean island just west and a bit north of Antigua, and east and slightly south of Puerto Rico. It represented the earliest nucleus of French and English colonization in the area. Thomas Warner, an Englishman, first settled the island in 1623.

Having stopped off there briefly in 1620, Warner went to England, secured capital, returned to Saint Christopher with forty to fifty companions, and quickly commenced planting tobacco. Difficulties arose with the native Carib tribe, however, and in order to secure assistance Warner agreed to the division of the island with some French settlers who had arrived shortly after he had. According to the terms of the agreement, the French would occupy the northern and southern extremities, and the English, the middle coastal strips.

In 1625 Warner obtained from the crown its letters patent, meaning that the English government officially recognized his settlement. Later, however, while in England, Warner received the news that on 7 September 1629 a Spanish fleet had taken Saint Christopher and expelled most of the French and English inhabitants. Nevertheless, after the Spanish departed some fugitives reestablished a provisional government and Warner returned.

A serious depression resulting from an oversupply of tobacco, and the growing conversion to sugar cultivation after 1630 led some colonists from Saint Kitts to move to Tortuga Island and numerous others to become buccaneers. Saint Christopher became an important buccaneering base during this era.

Although French Bourbons briefly conquered Saint Christopher early in 1782, the Treaty of Versailles later that year returned the island to Great Britain. Slave trading was abolished in 1807, and the Emancipation Act followed in 1833; Saint Christopher, however, remained predominantly a sugar producer until well into the twentieth century.

By the mid-twentieth century, many British West Indian colonies were clamoring for autonomy, and in the early 1960s these efforts accelerated. Thus, in May 1962 the British Parliament dissolved the Federation of the West Indies. In August of that year Jamaica and Trinidad and Tobago achieved independence. The eight remaining states of the federation, including Saint Christopher, entered into negotiations with the United Kingdom to form a smaller federation within the empire. By 1965 the negotiations had proved fruitless, and Barbados declared independence in 1966.

Trinidad and Tobago offered the remaining seven countries statehood, but they instead chose to pursue new negotiations with Great Britain. They wanted to be self-governing while maintaining their eligibility for financial assistance from their mother country. In the course of the discussions, it was agreed in 1966 that each of the seven states would enter into a free, voluntary association with Britain. Each island-state would be fully self-governing internally, and either side could terminate the agreement at any time. Thus, in 1967, when Saint Christopher joined this association, it simultaneously became fully self-governing internally for the first time in its history. On September 19, 1983, Saint Kitts became an independent commonwealth. Though the island of Anguilla seceded in 1971, Nevis still struggles for separation.

The volcanic island has a tropical climate, and the population of 39,349 (2007 estimate) relied on sugar production into the late twentieth century. Yet, by the 1970s, economic growth in this sector fell precipitously owing to low market prices and rising costs. The government shut down the state-run sugar industry after the 2005 harvest and implemented economic diversification efforts. Though hard hit by hurricanes and tropical storms, tourism is now the economic engine of the island's economy. Export manufacturing and offshore banking also are growing sectors.

See also **Piracy; Slave Trade.**

BIBLIOGRAPHY

Browne, W. T. *From Commoner to King: Robert L. Bradshaw, Crusader for Dignity and Justice in the Caribbean* (1992).

Cox, Edward L. *Free Coloreds in the Slave Societies of St. Kitts and Grenada, 1763–1833.* Knoxville: University of Tennessee Press, 1984.

Crouse, N. M. *The French Struggle for the West Indies, 1665–1713* (1943).

Dyde, Brian. *Out of the Crowded Vagueness: A History of the Islands of St. Kitts, Nevis, and Anguilla.* Oxford, U.K.: Macmillan Caribbean, 2005.

Hubbard, Vincent K. *A History of St. Kitts: The Sweet Trade.* Oxford, U.K.: Macmillan, 2002.

Merrill, G. C. *The Historical Geography of St. Kitts and Nevis* (1958).

Moll, V. P. *St. Kitts–Nevis.* Santa Barbara, CA: Clio Press, 1995.

Parry, J. H., et al. *A Short History of the West Indies,* 4th ed. (1987).

BLAKE D. PATRIDGE

SAINT LUCIA. Saint Lucia, one of the Windward Islands of the eastern Caribbean archipelago chain stretching from Antigua and Barbuda in the north to Trinidad and Tobago in the south, gained its independence from the United Kingdom in 1979, after a long period of interchange between the French and the British empires. Its population was estimated at 166,100 in 2006, with about of third of that number located in the capital city, Castries, and its environs in the northwest of the island.

Saint Lucia's Parliament, based on the British Westminister parliamentary system, consists of a seventeen-seat elected House of Assembly and an eleven-seat nominated Senate. In general elections held in 2006, the United Workers Party (UWP) led by Sir John Compton (a former prime minister) won an 11–6 victory in House of Assembly, defeating the incumbent Saint Lucia Labour Party (SLP) led by Dr. Kenny Anthony. Sir John died shortly afterward and was succeeded by Stephenson King, formerly chairman of the UWP.

Together with other states in the island chain, Saint Lucia is part of the Organisation of Eastern Caribbean States, whose Eastern Caribbean Central Bank is responsible for a currency union managing the Eastern Caribbean dollar (US$1 = EC$2.7). Saint Lucia is also a member of the Caribbean Community and Common Market (CARICOM), formed in 1973 as a successor institution to the Caribbean Free Trade Area (CARIFTA).

The modern history of this volcanic island is one of movement from a largely agricultural economy based on sugar grown on large plantations to one dominated after the mid-1950s by the export of bananas through the British company Geest under a British protectionist preference arrangement. This was subsequently transformed, after the United Kingdom's entry into the European Community/Union, into the Lomé/Cotonou Conventions organized between the EC and the African, Caribbean, and Pacific (ACP) countries in 1975. Banana exports came to be dominated by small farm producers, marking a transition from estate-based labor to a more independent peasantry.

However, the subordination of the EU-ACP regime to the requirements of the World Trade Organization's (WTO) liberalized trading and production rules at the beginning of the 1990s has led to a relatively rapid decline of the banana production and exports that formerly dominated the economy. These constituted 41 percent of the country's export revenues in 2004 but fell to 21 percent in 2006. Although substantial diplomacy has been devoted to negotiating a system of partial protection acceptable to the WTO, the prospects are for further decline of the industry, now under substantial challenge from U.S.-dominated Latin American exports to the EU. Adverse climatic conditions (hurricanes) during these years have aggravated this situation.

Attempts during the 1970s and 1980s to introduce foreign investment–induced manufactures for export both to the United States and under the protected Caribbean Common Market have also, in some measure, fallen victim to the new global liberalized regime. For while these exports benefited from the establishment by the United States of the Caribbean Basin Initiative (CBI) in 1983, the establishment of the North American Free Trade Agreement (NAFTA) in 1994 led to a subsequent decline. In this context, and partially anticipating the necessity to extend the bases of the economy, the Saint Lucian government encouraged the growth of tourism and related services based on the global informatics and telecommunications revolution. These areas saw substantial growth in the 1990s, with tourism replacing agricultural exports as the main foreign-exchange earner, and with Saint

Lucia dominating the industry in the Windward Islands. Tourism activity is divided between visitors from cruise ships (an estimated 320,000 between January and May 2007, the main tourism season) and hotel visitors (125,998 over the same period).

In the early 2000s the tourism industry has been subject to adverse climatic conditions, increased competition from other destinations, and changing air-transport arrangements. But it has also facilitated an increase in construction activity, thus limiting the decline in unemployment that has been a consequence of the decline of the banana industry.

See also **Caribbean Sea, Commonwealth States.**

BIBLIOGRAPHY

Eastern Caribbean Central Bank. *Economic and Financial Review* 27, no. 2 (2007).

Economist Intelligence Unit Limited. *Country Report 2007.* London: EIU.

Payne, Anthony, and Paul Sutton. *Repositioning the Caribbean within Globalisation.* Caribbean Paper No. 1. Waterloo, ON: Centre for International Governance Innovation, 2007. Available from http://www.cigionline.org.

VAUGHAN A. LEWIS

SAINT VINCENT.

SAINT VINCENT. Saint Vincent, one of the Windward Islands in the Lesser Antilles. Kingstown is its major city and capital. The self-governing state of Saint Vincent, with a total area of 150 square miles, comprises the island of Saint Vincent and dozens of the northern Grenadine islands (including Union and Bequia).

In 2005 the population of Saint Vincent and the Grenadines numbered 119,100. About 66 percent of the population is of African descent, 19 percent of mixed origin, 6 percent West Indian, 2 percent Carib Indian, and 7 percent of other or non-specified origin. Although English is the official language, French and a French patois are still spoken. About 47 percent of the population are Anglican, 28 percent are Methodist, 13 percent are Roman Catholics, and 12 percent are of other Protestant denominations, Seventh-Day Adventist, Hindu, and Afro–Caribbean faiths.

The first known inhabitants were Arawak and Carib Amerindians. Although Christopher Columbus reached the island on 22 January 1498, Saint Vincent was not settled by Europeans for another two and a half centuries. Without European interference, the native population prospered. In addition, runaway and shipwrecked African slaves intermarried with the native population, creating a distinct ethnic group known as Black Caribs. Except when France governed the island from 1779–1783, the British occupied Saint Vincent from 1762 until independence on 27 October 1979.

In the twenty-first century the British monarch remains the nominal head of government, represented on the island by a governor general. But executive power is vested in the island's prime minister and cabinet. There is a twenty-one-seat unicameral legislature.

Agriculture is the mainstay of the island's economy, producing bananas, vegetables, coconuts, spices, and sugar. Tourism is another important industry. In 2005 the per capita income on the island was estimated at US$3,600.

Saint Vincent is home to the volcano "La Soufriere" (sulphur outlet), which rises 1,219 meters. It erupted in 1902, killing close to 2,000 people. No people were killed but devastation to agricultural crops, the economic mainstays, occurred when La Soufriere erupted again in 1979. Hurricanes and tropical storms since the 1980s have also levied destruction, wiping out coconut and banana crops. Hurricane Lenny in 1999 inflicted severe damage to the island's western coast.

See also **Caribbean Sea, Commonwealth States.**

BIBLIOGRAPHY

Anderson, John. *Between Slavery and Freedom: Special Magistrate John Anderson's Journal of St. Vincent during the Apprenticeship.* Edited by Roderick A. McDonald. Philadelphia: University of Pennsylvania Press, 2001.

Grossman, Lawrence S. *The Political Ecology of Bananas: Contract Farming, Peasants, and Agrarian Change in the Eastern Caribbean.* Chapel Hill: University of North Carolina Press, 1998.

Knight, Franklin W. *The Caribbean: The Genesis of a Fragmented Nationalism,* 2d ed. (1990).

Potter, Robert B. *St. Vincent and the Grenadines.* Santa Barbara, CA: Clio Press, 1992.

Richardson, Bonham C. *The Caribbean in the Wider World, 1492–1992: A Regional Geography* (1992).

Young, Virginia Heyer. *Becoming West Indian: Culture, Self, and Nation in St. Vincent.* Washington, DC: Smithsonian Institution Press, 1993.

Zane, Wallace W. *Journeys to the Spiritual Lands: The Natural History of a West Indian Religion.* New York: Oxford University Press, 1999.

STEPHEN E. HILL

SÁINZ, GUSTAVO (1940–).

Gustavo Sáinz (*b.* 13 July 1940), Mexican fiction writer and critic. Born in Mexico City, Sáinz is known as a writer of Mexican "urban picaresque." *Gazapo* (1965), *Obsesivos días circulares* (1969), *La princesa del Palacio de Hierro* (1974), and *Compadre Lobo* (1977) are his best-known novels. Other works include *Fantasmas aztecas* (1982), *Paseo en trapecio* (1985), and *Muchacho en llamas* (1988). Together with José Agustín, Sáinz is associated with the generation of "La Onda," a group of young Mexican writers who published in the 1960s and 1970s and whose literature was characterized by attention to an urban adolescent subculture, the use of colloquial language and the oral quality of the text, and the characters' self-centered, nonconformist attitudes toward established social codes. In Sáinz's fiction Mexico City is a constant, autobiographically based reference, a voracious space intimately experienced by his characters, where language acts, in his words, "as the major protagonist of history." In 2003 his *A troche y moche* (2002) won the Colima Prize for best novel of the year in Mexico. When it was published in French, it won the best novel of the year award in Quebec. In 2006 his *El juego de las sensaciónes elementales: Autobiografía a cuatro dedos* was published.

See also **Literature: Spanish America.**

BIBLIOGRAPHY

Batis, Humberto, comp. *Crítica bajo presión: Prosa mexicana, 1964–1985.* Mexico: Universidad Nacional Autónoma de México, Coordinación de Humanidades, Programa Editorial, 2004.

LAURA GARCÍA-MORENO

SALADERO.

Saladero, a slaughterhouse and meat-salting plant. During much of the colonial era, gauchos slaughtered wild cattle on the pampa for their hides and tallow. During the eighteenth century, dried meat, exported to feed slaves in Cuba and Brazil, became another important product. During the late eighteenth and early nineteenth centuries, the slaughtering and meat-drying operations were moved from the Estancia to the *saladero.* Quick, substantial profits attracted many investors, including young Juan Manuel de Rosas, who later gained infamy as a ruthless despot.

These primitive factories depended more on manpower than on technology. Discarded meat, bones, and blood drew scavengers, emitted a stench, and created health hazards, including water pollution. Despite such primitive methods, *saladeros* south of Buenos Aires were processing some 250,000 cattle per year by about 1850. In Uruguay and the Brazilian state of Rio Grande do Sul, the traditional *saladeros* remained important livestock markets into the twentieth century. Buenos Aires, however, modernized its cattle-processing industry, and Frigoríficos (cold-storage plants) largely supplanted *saladeros* in the late nineteenth century.

See also **Rosas, Juan Manuel de.**

BIBLIOGRAPHY

Alfredo Montoya, *Historia de los saladeros argentinos* (1956; repr. 1970).

Jonathan C. Brown, *A Socioeconomic History of Argentina, 1776–1860* (1979), pp. 109–114.

Additional Bibliography

Barsky, Osvaldo, and Jorge Gelman. *Historia del agro argentino: Desde la conquista hasta fines del siglo XX.* Buenos Aires, Argentina: Grijalbo Mondadori, 2001.

RICHARD W. SLATTA

SALADO RIVER.

Salado River, also known as Río Salado del Norte to differentiate it from the Río Salado that flows south of San Luis and the Río Salado that serves as the boundary to the province of Buenos Aires in Argentina. The river springs from the Nevado del Acay (near Salta) and after 1,200 miles empties into the Paraná River at Santa Fe. Europeans became aware of the Río Salado in 1573 when Juan de Garay discovered it. The river was an active border between the southern Chaco and the province of Córdoba during colonial times.

On its banks the Army of the North commanded by Manuel Belgrano swore allegiance to the confederation of the United Provinces of the Río De La Plata in 1813.

See also **Garay, Juan de.**

BIBLIOGRAPHY

Diccionario biográfico, histórico, y geográfico argentino El Ateneo. Buenos Aires: El Ateneo, 1997.

Lobato, Mira Zaida, and Juan Suriano. *Nueva historia Argentina. Atlas histórico de la Argentina.* Buenos Aires: Editorial Sudamericana, 2000.

Schroh, María Beatríz. *Argentina futura: Geografía y atlas de la República Argentina: Desarrollo económico, humano, ecológico, y turístico.* Buenos Aires: J.K. Akian, 1998.

CÉSAR N. CAVIEDES

SALAMANCA, DANIEL (1868–1935).

Daniel Salamanca (*b.* 8 July 1868; *d.* 17 July 1935), president of Bolivia (1931–1934). Blamed for Bolivia's defeat by Paraguay in the Chaco War (1932–1935), Salamanca may be the most controversial figure of twentieth-century Bolivian history. A wealthy Cochabamba landowner and eloquent congressional deputy and senator for thirty years, he served as secretary of treasury in the cabinet of President José Manuel Pando (1899–1904). In 1914 he broke with the conservative Liberal Party and helped found the Republican Party, only to break away again in 1921 to form the Genuine Republican Party. Hailed as the "new messiah" and *hombre símbolo* (human symbol) because of his fierce nationalism and scrupulous integrity in an era of political corruption, Salamanca was the establishment's popular choice for president in March 1931. However, his economic austerity, political repression of the opposition (particularly leftists and Communists), and failed Chaco policy soon left him one of the most unpopular of Bolivian presidents. In November 1934, while he was visiting the Chaco command in Villa Montes, the military seized and deposed him.

See also **Chaco War.**

BIBLIOGRAPHY

Julio Díaz Arguedas, *Como fue derrocado el hombre símbolo, Salamanca* (1957).

David Alvéstegui, *Salamanca, su gravitación sobre el destino de Bolivia,* 4 vols. (1962).

Herbert S. Klein, *Parties and Political Change in Bolivia, 1880–1952* (1969).

Augusto Céspedes, *Salamanca: O el metafísico del fracaso* (1973).

Additional Bibliography

Farcau, Bruce W. *The Chaco War: Bolivia and Paraguay, 1932–1935.* Westport, CT: Praeger, 1996.

Pereira Fiorilo, Juan. *Historia secreta de la guerra del Chaco: Bolivia frente al P.* La Paz: H. Cámara de Diputados, Federación de Entidades Empresariales Privadas de Cochabamba, 1999.

WALTRAUD QUEISER MORALES

SALARRUÉ. *See* **Salazar Arrué, Salvador Efraín.**

SALAS, MANUEL DE (1754–1841).

Manuel de Salas (*b.* 19 June 1754; *d.* 28 November 1841), Chilean reformer and patriot, and one of the best-loved Chileans of his time. From a rich creole family, Salas studied law at the University of San Marcos, Lima, from which he graduated in 1774. In the later 1770s he paid a long visit to Spain, taking great interest in economic reforms and education. Superintendent of public works under the governorship of Ambrosio O'Higgins, he was named a member of the newly founded *consulado* (merchant guild) of Santiago in 1795. The following year he wrote a classic report on the economy and society of Chile for the Spanish finance minister. In 1798 he founded the Academia de San Luis, a college which aimed to introduce stronger technical education in Chile. He also played an active part in introducing vaccination into the colony in 1806.

Salas's early hopes for reform rested in the Spanish crown, but from 1810 onward he was a patriot, a member of the first national congress (1811), and, briefly, foreign minister (1812–1813). He was exiled to Juan Fernández (an island prison for exiled political prisoners) during the Spanish reconquest (1814–1817). The first director of Chile's National Library, Salas retained a strong interest in educational matters, often visiting schools and advising them.

BIBLIOGRAPHY

Miguel Luis Amunátegui, *Don Manuel de Salas,* 3 vols. (1895); *Escritos de don Manuel de Salas y documentos relativos a él y a su familia,* 3 vols. (1910–1914).

Additional Bibliography

Cardoso Ruíz, Patricio. *Formación y desarrollo del estado nacional de Chile: De la independencia hasta 1930.* Toluca: Universidad Autónoma del Estado de México, 2000.

Collier, Simon, and William F. Sater. *A History of Chile, 1808-1994.* Cambridge, U.K.: Cambridge University Press, 1996.

Stuven, Ana María. *La seducción de un orden: Las elites y la construcción de Chile en las polémicas culturales y políticas del siglo XIX.* Santiago: Ediciones Universidad Católica de Chile, 2000.

SIMON COLLIER

SALAVARRIETA, POLICARPA (1795–1817).

Policarpa Salavarrieta (*b.* 26 January 1795; *d.* 14 November 1817), heroine of Colombian independence. Born into a respectable creole family, Policarpa Salavarrieta ("La Pola") grew up in Guaduas, a way station between Bogotá and the Magdalena River. When the independence movement started, she became a strong sympathizer, and the flow of traffic through her town kept her well informed. With the Spanish reconquest of New Granada in 1816, Salavarrieta began providing information and other assistance to the patriot underground, first in Guaduas and then in Bogotá, where it was easier for her to remain inconspicuous. Nevertheless, her key role in the urban network of the resistance was discovered, and she was condemned to death. She went to her execution shouting a tirade against Spanish oppression. Salavarrieta's place in the pantheon of patriot martyrs is indicated by the fact that she was the first Latin American woman commemorated on a postage stamp, one of Colombia's 1910 independence-centennial issue.

See also **Women.**

BIBLIOGRAPHY

Oswaldo Díaz Díaz, *Los Almeydas: Episodios de la resistencia patriota contra el ejército pacificador de Tierra Firme* (1962).

James D. Henderson and Linda Roddy Henderson, *Ten Notable Women of Latin America* (1978), chap. 5.

Additional Bibliography

Alvarez Guerrero, Rafael. *Policarpa: Úna heroína genio–?.* Guaduas: Centro de Historia de la Villa, 1995.

Anseume, William, editor. *El drama en Venezuela durante los primeros cincuenta años del siglo XIX: Antología comentada.* Caracas: CELCIT, 1998.

DAVID BUSHNELL

SALAVERRY, FELIPE SANTIAGO (1805–1836).

Felipe Santiago Salaverry (*b.* 6 March 1805; *d.* 18 February 1836), Conservative caudillo who became president of Peru (1835–1836). A participant in the final battles against the Spanish in 1824, Salaverry, a native of Lima, was promoted to general by President Luis José Orbegoso in 1834. In February 1835, however, the twenty-nine-year-old Salaverry denounced the government of the Liberal Orbegoso and took power in Lima. By the middle of the year, he had allied with Agustín Gamarra against General Andrés de Santa Cruz and Orbegoso, who still claimed the presidency. Salaverry imposed an authoritarian government that gained broad support in Lima and along the coast. In February 1836, his forces finally squared off against those of Santa Cruz. Salaverry was taken prisoner in the battle of Socabaya and, in an unusual action for the period, was executed at Arequipa, setting the stage for the Peru-Bolivia Confederation.

See also **Gamarra, Agustín.**

BIBLIOGRAPHY

Manuel Bilbao, *Historia del General Salaverry,* 3d ed. (1936).

Fredrick B. Pike, *The Modern History of Peru* (1967), pp. 76–81.

Jorge Basadre, *Historia de la República del Perú,* 7th ed., vol. 2 (1983), pp. 27–51.

Additional Bibliography

Guerra, Margarita. *Felipe Santiago Salaverry.* Lima: Editorial Brasa, 1996.

CHARLES F. WALKER

SALAZAR, MATÍAS (1828–1872).

Matías Salazar (*b.* 1828; *d.* 17 May 1872), Venezuelan caudillo. Salazar participated in the Federal War (1859–1863) as a military chief of the central region. After the Federalist triumph he fought in several local armed controversies. When President Juan Crisóstomo Falcón was deposed in 1868, Salazar joined the April Revolution of 1870 led by Antonio Guzmán Blanco, becoming an important military leader for Yellow Liberalism, second only to Guzmán. When Guzmán took control of the government, Salazar was named second appointee to the presidency of the republic and later president of the state of Carabobo. He gradually distanced himself from Guzmán and organized a conspiracy against the government but was discovered and expelled from the country. From abroad Salazar instigated a new armed movement in 1872. He was defeated, tried by the War Council, convicted of treason, and sentenced to death by firing squad.

See also **Federal War (Venezuela 1859-1863); Guzmán Blanco, Antonio Leocadio.**

BIBLIOGRAPHY

Felipe Larrazábal, *Asesinato del General Salazar* (1873), and José Carrillo Moreno, *Matías Salazar, historia venezolana* (1954).

Additional Bibliography

Barnola Q., Isaías. *Matías Salazar: Un caudillo del siglo XIX venezolano.* Caracas: Fundarte, Alcaldía de Caracas, 1993.

INÉS QUINTERO

SALAZAR ARRUÉ, SALVADOR EFRAÍN (SALARRUÉ) (1899–1975).

Salvador Efraín (Salarrué) Salazar Arrué (*b.* 22 October 1899; *d.* 27 November 1975), Salvadoran writer and painter who used the pseudonym Salarrué. A native of Sonsonate, he became the most popular literary figure of mid-twentieth-century El Salvador. After education in San Salvador and at the Corcoran Art Academy in Washington, D.C. (1917–1919), Salazar produced short stories, novels, poems, and paintings that reflected the Salvadoran common people; helped to preserve Salvadoran folk culture; and awakened a social consciousness in the country. In the late 1920s he was an important contributor to Alberto Masferrer's *Patria,* and he continued to be an influential writer and intellectual force in El Salvador until his death in 1975. Rural Salvadoran themes dominate Salazar's major novel, *El señor de la burbuja* (1927), and his classic collection of stories, *Cuentos de barro* (1933).

See also **Literature: Spanish America.**

BIBLIOGRAPHY

Luis Gallegos Valdés, *Panorama de la literatura salvadoreña del período precolombino a 1980* (1987), esp. pp. 239–258.

Ramón L. Acevedo, "Salvador (Salarrué) Salazar Arrué," in *Latin American Writers,* edited by Carlos A. Solé and Maria Isabel Abren, vol. 2 (1989), pp. 875–879.

John Beverley and Marc Zimmerman, *Literature and Politics in the Central American Revolutions* (1990), p. 119.

Additional Bibliography

Monterroso, Augusto and Bárbara Jacobs, eds. *Antología del cuento triste.* Madrid: Punto de Lectura, 2005.

Salazar Arrue, Salvador. *Cuentos de barro.* San José: Editorial Legado, 2000.

Salazar Arrue, Salvador. *La lumbra y otros textos. El Salvador.* Madrid: Cultura Hispánica, 1999.

RALPH LEE WOODWARD JR.

SALAZAR BONDY, SEBASTIÁN

(1924–1965). Sebastián Salazar Bondy (*b.* 4 February 1924; *d.* 4 July 1965), Peruvian writer and journalist. Salazar Bondy, born in Lima, began publishing his poetry while studying literature at San Marcos University. His artistic interest led him to work in Buenos Aires (1948–1951) and study in Paris (1956–1957). Twice he received the Peruvian national prize for theater (1948, 1952) and once the national prize for journalism (1958). Although he earned his living as a newspaperman, briefly directed the Institute of National Art, and participated in politics as an activist member of the Movimiento Social Progresista (Social Progressionist Movement) he had helped to found, Salazar Bondy devoted most of his time to creative writing, purportedly divested of social and ideological content. He is remembered for his strong opposition to pro-Indianist literary trends and advocacy of art for art's sake. His play *Amor, gran laberinto* (1948), his short stories *Pobre gente de París* (1958), and his essay *Lima la horrible* (1964) are among his best books. In collaboration with other writers, he edited *La poesía contemporánea del Perú* (1946), *Antología general de la poesía peruana* (1957), and *Cuentos infantiles peruanos* (1958).

See also **Literature: Spanish America.**

BIBLIOGRAPHY

Manuel Salazar Bondy, *Obras* (1967).

Luis Alberto Sánchez, *La literatura peruana,* vol. 5 (1975), pp. 1580–1581, 1607–1609.

Maurilio Arriola Grande, *Diccionario literario del Perú,* vol. 2 (1982), pp. 256–259.

Pedro Shimose, *Diccionario de autores hispanoamericanos* (1982), p. 385.

Additional Bibliography

Hirschhorn, Gerald. *Sebastián Salazar Bondy: Pasión por la cultura.* Lima: Fondo editorial de la UNMSM and Embajada de Francia: IFEA Instituto francés de estudios andinos.

Salazar Bondy, Sebastián, and Mario Vargas Llosa. *Escritos políticos y morales: Perú, 1954–1965.* Lima: Fondo Editorial, Universidad Nacional Mayor de San Marcos, 2003.

EUGENIO CHANG-RODRÍGUEZ

SALDANHA DA GAMA, LUÍS FELIPE DE (1846–1895).

Luís Felipe de Saldanha da Gama (*b.* 7 April 1846; *d.* 24 June 1895), Brazilian admiral and principal figure in a revolt of the fleet during the civil war of 1893. Gama had been the navy's chief representative in the court of Dom Pedro I because he was cultured, brave, well traveled, and of noble ancestry. Although a monarchist by preference, he acknowledged the republic as an accomplished fact.

Gama and two other Brazilian admirals, Custódio José de Melo and Eduardo Wandenkolk, became unhappy over the way that the new government had placed the army over the navy in terms of prestige and material benefits. Wandenkolk wasted his prestige in aborted political adventures. Melo, having successfully led a naval revolt against President Deodoro da Fonseca, then tried the same maneuver against Vice President Floriano Peixoto,

but without success. Gama opposed Melo's revolt and declared his neutrality. Then head of the Naval Academy, Gama was offered the vacated position of minister of the navy, which he refused. He felt that once the fighting was over his mission would be to rebuild the navy using the Naval Academy. His position of neutrality eventually became unbearable since he could not declare loyalty to Peixoto. Finally, despite the evidence that the Federalist and naval revolts would fail, Gama joined the losing cause, and, along with Federalist leader Gaspar da Silveira Martins, called for a plebiscite on the issue of the restoration of the monarchy. That stand ensured their defeat, since the pro-Republican forces by then were strong enough to win the war. Gama was killed in fighting while trying to reach neutral territory (Uruguay).

See also **Brazil: 1808–1889.**

BIBLIOGRAPHY

Raul Oliveria Rodrigues, *Um militar contra o militarismo: A vida de Saldanha da Gama* (1959).

José Maria Bello, *A History of Modern Brazil,* translated by James L. Taylor (1966), pp. 119–129, 134–145.

June E. Hahner, *Civilian-Military Relations in Brazil, 1889–1898* (1969), pp. 63–66, 71–72.

Additional Bibliography

Corrêa da Costa, Sérgio. *A diplomacia no Marechal: Intervenção estrangeira na revolta da Armada.* 2nd ed. Rio de Janeiro: Tempo Brasileiro, 1979.

ROBERT A. HAYES

SALDÍAS, ADOLFO (1849–1914).

Adolfo Saldías, born September 6, 1849, was an Argentine lawyer, politician, diplomat, journalist, and historian. In 1875 Saldías graduated from the University of Buenos Aires Law School with an honors thesis devoted to civil marriage, sixteen years before it was legalized in Argentina. In 1876 he became a deputy in the national legislature, representing the Partido Autonomista de Buenos Aires, led by Adolfo Alsina. He joined the military and fought in the battles over the federalization of Buenos Aires in 1880. The following year Saldías was appointed to a diplomatic position in London. In England, he had access to Juan Manuel de Rosas's personal archive, which he drew on extensively in writing his three-volume *Historia de Rosas*, published between 1881 and 1887, which provoked heated debates among liberal historians, such as Bartolomé Mitre. Saldias promoted a more nuanced understanding on the Rosas' regime (1829–1852) by focusing on issues relating to nationalism and economic development.

In 1891 Saldías was one of founders of the political party Unión Cívica Radical (UCR). In the early 1890s he participated in several armed revolts carried out by the new party and was sent to prison in Ushuaia and into exile in Uruguay. Back in Argentina in 1896, Saldías was appointed minister of public works in Buenos Aires Province in 1898, where he was elected vice governor in 1902. Saldías also actively participated in and wrote about Freemasonry.

See also **Alsina, Adolfo; Argentina: The Twentieth Century; Argentina, Political Parties: Radical Party (UCR); Mitre, Bartolomé; Rosas, Juan Manuel de.**

BIBLIOGRAPHY

Irazusta, Julio. *Adolfo Saldías.* Buenos Aires: Ediciones Culturales Argentinas, 1964.

Gorostiaga Saldías, Leonor. *Adolfo Saldías: Leal servidor de la República.* Buenos Aires: Corregidor, 1999.

Saldías, Adolfo. *Páginas políticas.* Buenos Aires: La Facultad, 1912.

Saldías, Adolfo. *Historia de la Confederación Argentina*, 3 vols. Buenos Aires: Hyspamérica, 1987.

VALERIA MANZANO

SALES, EUGÊNIO DE ARAÚJO

(1920–). Eugênio de Araújo Sales (*b.* 8 November 1920), archbishop and cardinal of Rio de Janeiro. For decades, Sales has been one of the most important and visible leaders of the Brazilian Catholic Church. Ordained as a priest in 1942, Sales became bishop of Natal, Rio Grande do Norte, in 1954. In the 1950s and 1960s, he was known as a leader of the moderately progressive faction within the Brazilian church. As archbishop of Natal, he promoted radio schools as a means of working with the poor, and he supported the creation of the Basic Education Movement in 1958 and of rural Catholic unions in the late 1950s and early 1960s. Both

initiatives became important within the Brazilian church and in national politics.

After the coup in 1964, Sales was less critical of the military government and more willing to work with it than most other prominent church leaders. For this reason, he became identified as a leader of the moderately conservative faction of the Brazilian hierarchy. He was named archbishop of Salvador in 1968 and of Rio de Janeiro in 1971. As archbishop of Rio, convinced that the church needed to focus on religious issues, he became one of Brazil's most prominent critics of liberation theology. His theological and ecclesiastical positions made him a favorite of Pope John Paul II after 1978. He was involved in numerous assemblies and conferences, including the Assembly of the World Synod of Bishops at Vatican City in 1980, the Second Plenary Assembly of the Sacred College of Cardinals (also at Vatican City) in 1982, and the Fourth General Conference of the Latin American Episcopate in the Dominican Republic in 1992. In 1997, he served as president delegate of the Special Assembly for America of the World Synod of Bishops. When he turned 80 in November 2000, he lost his right to participate in the Assembly. In 2001, he resigned his governance of the archbishopric of Rio de Janeiro. However, he was still able to serve as a special papal envoy to various celebrations in Brazil in 2004. After the death of Pope John Paul II in 2005, he presided over most of the funeral masses during the nine days of official mourning.

See also **Catholic Church: The Modern Period.**

BIBLIOGRAPHY

Sales, Eugenio de Araújo. *Viver é fé: Em um mundo a construir.* Rio de Janeiro: Marques Saraiva, 1991.

SCOTT MAINWARING

SALESIANS.

The Society of Saint Francis de Sales is a male religious order of the Roman Catholic Church founded in 1859 in Turin, Italy, by Giovanni Bosco (1815–1888), who was canonized as a saint in 1934. An innovative educator, Don Bosco began his charitable works in 1841 by helping poor and abandoned youngsters. The Vatican formally approved the constitution of the Pious Society of Saint Francis de Sales in 1874. The order's purpose was to educate the poor and the lower classes by establishing vocational education programs, day and boarding schools, and orphanages. The order also fostered adult education and the formation of groups of families who needed help (the Salesian "family" remains a goal in the 1990s). More than other religious orders of the time, the Salesians relied on "coadjutors," or religious brothers, who were not ordained priests. These lay brothers were craftsmen and teachers whose role was to educate youngsters and assist in missionary activities. A parallel order of female religious, the Salesians Figlie di Maria Ausiliatrice (Daughters of Mary, Help of Christians), was established to complement the order and to help support the education of the poor.

The Salesians looked beyond Europe and undertook ambitious programs of missionary activities in other lands. Argentina attracted Don Bosco's attention because of its burgeoning Italian population. Italian Giovanni Cagliero (1838–1926), the first Salesian priest who became a bishop and later a cardinal, and a group of his brethren arrived in Argentina in 1875. They established schools and parishes for Italian immigrants in the slums of Barracas, Boca, and Avellaneda near Buenos Aires. The Salesians founded industrial and agricultural schools, teacher training schools, and business colleges, many of which provided subsistence for boarders. Many of these schools still function today.

In 1875 intrepid Salesian missionaries set out to evangelize the Amerindians from the vast territory of Patagonia to the far reaches of Tierra del Fuego. Santiago Costamagna, a Salesian priest, accompanied General Julio A. Roca's campaign of 1879 to subdue the Amerindian populations of southern Argentina. Ceferino Namuncurá, revered as a saint by the Roman Catholic Church since 1905, was a product of Salesian schools. Salesians played a prominent role in incorporating the Amerindians of Patagonia into national life. They established agricultural and technical schools for settlers and Amerindians in the northwestern region of Argentina, and they trained people to work in Mendoza. By the end of the century, their institutions were present throughout Argentina.

The Salesian missions and schools in Chile were mainly geared toward the southern part of the country. The first Salesian schools were established in Concepción, Punta Arenas, and Talca, all in 1887. Bishop Cagliero then sent Father Santiago Costamagna to establish missions and schools in the Andean highlands of Peru, Bolivia, and Ecuador from 1888 to 1890. Technical schools, secondary institutes, orphanages, and parishes were established in the *altiplano* and in the lowlands of the Beni in Bolivia.

Salesians worked with Amerindians throughout Latin America teaching and converting them to Christianity, forming communities, and often recording and documenting their ways of life, which were being lost to industrialization and urbanization. The Salesians working in the Paraguayan Chaco and in Ecuador are good examples. In Ecuador, Salesian Father Juan Bottasso established the Ediciones Abya-Yala and the Latin American Center of Indigenist Documentation in Quito, which preserves invaluable ethnographic records of the Shuar and other tribes. The Salesians also made an impact on the educational and social systems in Brazil. In 1988 there were 123 Salesian institutions in Brazil, 47 in Mexico, 33 in Venezuela, 36 in Colombia, 14 in Bolivia, 11 in Paraguay, 25 in Chile, 24 in Uruguay, and 114 in Argentina. The Salesians' hands-on activities, their technical schools, and their printing presses helped shape infrastructures throughout Latin America. Salesians also trained many political and professional leaders.

BIBLIOGRAPHY

Raúl A. Entraigas, *Los Salesianos en la Argentina*, 5 vols. (1918–1989).

José De Alarcón y Canedo and Ricardo Pittini, *El chaco paraguayo y sus tribus* (1924).

Lorenzo Massa, *Monografía de Magallanes: 60 años de acción Salesiana en el sur, 1886–1946* (1946).

Pascual Paesa, *El Patiru Domingo: La cruz en el ocaso Mapuche* (1964).

Lorenzo Massa, *Historia de las misiones Salesianas de la Pampa* (1968).

Osvaldo Venturuzzo, *Bandeirantes, atuais* (1969).

Alberto Aramayo, *Los Salesianos en Bolivia*, 2 vols. (1976–1988).

Juan Esteban Belza, *La expedición al desierto y los Salesianos, 1879* (1979).

Riolando Azzi, *Os Salesianos no Rio de Janeiro*, 4 vols. (1982–1984).

Juan Bottasso, *Los Shuar y las misiones: Entre la hostilidad y el diálogo* (1982); Ernesto Szanto, *Los Salesianos en el país de los Césares* (1982).

Riolando Azzi, *Os Salesianos no Brasil: A luz da historia* (1983).

Simón Kuzmanich Buvinic, *Presencia Salesiana en Chile: 100 años en Chile. Los inicios* (1987).

Carlos Valverde Romero, ed., *Presencia Salesiana en el Ecuador* (1987).

Cayetano Bruno, *Los Salesianos y las Hijas de María Auxiliadora en la Argentina,* 4 vols. (1989).

Additional Bibliography

Bottasso, Juan. *Los Salesianos y la amazonía.* Quito-Ecuador: Abya-Yala, 1993.

Castilho, Maria Augusta de. *Os índios Bororo e os Salesianos na Missão dos Tachos.* Campo Grande: Editora UCDB, 2000.

Castillo Lara, Lucas G. *La raigambre salesiana en Venezuela: Cien años de la primera siembra.* Caracas: Academia Nacional de la Historia, 1995.

Chovelon, Hipólito, Francisco Fernandes, and Pedro Sbardellotto. *Do primeiro encontro com os Xavante à demarcação de suas reserves.* Campo Grande: Missão Salesiana de Mato Grosso, 1996.

Guerriero, Antonio, and Pedro Creamer. *Un siglo de presencia salesiana en el Ecuador: El proceso histórico, 1888-1988.* Quito: s.n, 1997.

Novaes, Sylvia Caiuby. *The Play of Mirrors: The Representation of Self as Mirrored in the Other.* Austin: University of Texas Press, 1997.

Rodríguez, Jorge. *Elena Arellano, los salesianos en Centroamérica y la Casa de Granada, Nicaragua.* Managua: MED, 1992.

Salamone, Frank A. *Who Speaks for Yanomami?* Williamsburg: Dept. of Anthropology, College of William and Mary, 1996.

Sopeña, Germán. *Monseñor Patagonia: Vida y viajes de Alberto de Agostini, el sacerdote salesiano y explorador.* Buenos Aires: El Elefante Blanco, 2001.

GEORGETTE MAGASSY DORN

SALGADO, JOSÉ (c. 1775–1845).

José Salgado and his wife Pascuala Rivas were the founders of Lobos, a town in Buenos Aires Province, Argentina. Originally a merchant from Buenos Aires, in the late 1790s Salgado received a grant of land from the viceroy, José Vertiz. The land was located seventy miles from the Buenos Aires port and two miles north of the fort called San Pedro de los Lobos constructed in 1779 to secure the region from Indian attacks. Salgado and Rivas traveled to San Pedro de los Lobos and began to work on their land. They were fervent Catholics, and had to travel for days to find the chapel closest to their new home. In 1802 the Salgados, although among the poorest families in the region, used their savings to have a humble chapel built, which they called Nuestra Señora del Carmen. It officially opened in 1803, and became the social center of the thinly populated countryside around the fort. Until the 1820s the chapel's priest and the Salgados, recognized as the founders of the town of Lobos, were the only residents. In the decades that followed Salgado's death, Lobos became one of the most important agricultural centers in Buenos Aires Province. Lobos was also the town in which Juan Domingo Perón was born in 1895.

See also **Argentina: The Colonial Period; Perón, Juan Domingo.**

BIBLIOGRAPHY

Angueira, Juan R. *El pago de los Lobos: Noticias y apuntes.* La Plata, Argentina: Taller de impresiones oficiales, 1937.

Levene, Ricardo. *Historia de la provincia de Buenos Aires y la formación de sus pueblos.* Buenos Aires: Archivo Histórico de la Provincia de Buenos Aires, 1941.

VALERIA MANZANO

SALGADO, PLINIO (1895–1975).

Plinio Salgado (*b.* 22 January 1895; *d.* 7 December 1975), Brazilian politician and journalist. Salgado was born in São Bento de Sapucaí, São Paulo and died in São Paulo. As a youth, he began his long and prolific career as a writer when he founded the hometown paper *O Correio de São Bento.* After moving to the state capital, Salgado began contributing regularly to nationwide newspapers and magazines. In 1931, he launched an integralist campaign and made himself the movement's supreme authority. One year later, the writer and politician founded the Ação Integralista Brasileira. On May 10, 1937, a group of anti-Vargas and integralist demonstrators attacked the presidential palace in Rio de Janeiro. The attack was repulsed and Salgado was exiled to Portugal until 1945. After returning to Brazil, he founded the Partido de

Representação Popular (PRP) and became its presidential candidate in 1955. From 1958 to 1966, he served as a federal deputy representing the PRP and, later, the ARENA party from 1966 to 1974.

Salgado was a member of the Academia Paulista de Letras and authored numerous political, fictional, and poetic works such as *Tabor, O estrangeiro, O cavaleiro de Itararé, Literatura e política, a psicologia da revolução, O que é integralismo, Cartas aos camisas-verdes, a doutrina do sigma, O conceito cristão da democracia, Extremismo e democracia, Direitos e Deveres do homem,* and *Espírito de burguesia.* His integralist movement (or *camisas verdes*—green shirts) envisaged an integral state under a single authoritarian head of government patterned after European corporatist movements. Using the motto "God, country, and family," the movement sought to enlist the middle classes who feared communism.

See also **Vargas, Getúlio Dornelles.**

BIBLIOGRAPHY

Araújo, Ricardo Benzaquen de. *Totalitarismo e revolução: O integralismo de Plínio Salgado.* Rio de Janeiro: J. Zahar Editor, 1988.

Cavalari, Rosa Maria Feiteiro. *Integralismo: Ideologia e organização de um partido de massa no Brasil, 1932–1937.* Bauru: Editora da Universidade do Sagrado Coração, 1999.

Dorea, Augusta Garcia. *Plínio Salgado: Um apóstol brasileiro em terras de Portugal e Espanha.* São Paulo: Edições GRD, 1999.

                                        IÊDA SIQUEIRA WIARDA

SALGADO, SEBASTIÃO

SALGADO, SEBASTIÃO (1944–). Sebastião Salgado (*b.* 8 February 1944), Brazilian photographer. Born in Minas Gerais, Salgado was the only son among eight children of the owners of a large cattle farm. In 1963, he began studying law, and later switched to economics. Around this time, he married the architect Lélia Deluiz Wanick; they had two children. In 1968, Salgado obtained two master's degrees in economics: one from São Paulo University, and one from Vanderbilt University; in 1971, he received a doctorate in agricultural economy from the Sorbonne. Immediately thereafter he went to work in Africa for the London-based International Coffee Organization. In 1973, Salgado changed careers once again and became a freelance photojournalist documenting the drought in the Sahel region of Africa for the World Council of Churches. The following year he joined the Paris-based Sygma agency and covered the coup in Portugal and the revolutions in its colonies of Mozambique and Angola. In 1975, he switched to the Gamma agency, covering stories in Africa, Europe, and Latin America. He began the work on peasants that was featured in his 1986 book *Other Americas* started around this time. Three years later, Salgado joined Magnum, a cooperative agency founded in 1947 by Henri Cartier-Bresson, Robert Capa, and others. In 1982 he received the W. Eugene Smith grant in humanistic photography and an award from the French Ministry of Culture to continue his work in Latin America. Working with a French humanitarian aid group, Médecins sans Frontières, he returned to the Sahel to photograph the calamitous effects of famine in 1984. After the publication of his book *Sahel: L'homme en détresse,* Salgado was internationally recognized as a leading photojournalist. In 1991, he and his wife, Lélia Deluiz Wanick, began to work to save a small portion of the Atlantic forest in Brazil. In 1998, this land officially became a nature preserve, as well as home to an environmental educational center known as Instituto Terra. His most ambitious project, on workers and the end of manual labor, was completed in 1992 and published as *Workers: An Archeology of the Industrial Age* (1993). In 1993 the Tokyo National Museum of Modern Art mounted a retrospective of Salgado's work, titled "In Human Effort." In 1994, he founded his own press agency, Amazonas Images, to represent him and his work. In 1997, his *Terra: Struggles of the Landless* was published to wide critical acclaim. His compilation of photographs taken of displaced people in thirty–five countries throughout the 1990s was published in 2000 in a work titled *Migrations: Humanity in Transition.* He currently lives in Paris. Salgado's work has gone beyond the printed page and onto the walls of galleries and museums. Controversy has arisen over the alleged "beautification of tragedy" in his work, and in an attempt to understand it, critics have variously labeled it "lyric documents," "mannerist documents," or "documentary photography."

See also **Photography: 1900-1990.**

BIBLIOGRAPHY

Collections of Salgado's photographs also include *An Uncertain Grace,* with essays by Eduardo Galeano and Fred Ritchin (1990). Articles on Salgado include

Liba Taylor, "Sebastião Salgado," in *British Journal of Photography*, 12 November 1987; Ingrid Sischy, "Good Intentions," in *The New Yorker*, 9 September 1991; and Henry Allen, "Of Beatitudes and Burdens," in *The Washington Post*, 19 January 1992.

Costa, Flavia. "Beautiful Misery: The Travels of Sebastião Salgado—An Interview with Julio Ramos." *Journal of Latin American Cultural Studies* 2 (August 2003): 215–227.

Harris, Mark Edward. *Faces of the Twentieth Century: Master Photographers and Their Work*. New York: Abbeville Press, 1998.

Mraz, John. "Sebastião Salgado's Latin America." *Estudios Interdisciplinarios de América Latina y el Caribe* 9 (January–June 1998): 27–37.

FERNANDO CASTRO

SALGAR, EUSTORGIO (1831–1885).

Eustorgio Salgar (*b.* 1 November 1831; *d.* 25 November 1885), president of Colombia (1870–1872). Scion of prominent Santander families, he was born in Bogotá, where he received his law doctorate in 1851. Salgar's talents and Liberal affiliation brought him responsible posts in Cundinamarca. He went on to govern portions of Santander (1853–1855, 1856–1857), was elected a senator (1858–1859), was governor of Cundinamarca (1859), and was a delegate to the Rionegro Convention (1863). He served as Colombian minister in Washington, D.C. (1865–1866), and was elected president in 1870 (nominated in part to attract votes away from General Tomás Cipriano Mosquera). A devout Catholic and friend of Archbishop Vincente Arbeláez, Salgar won easily. His administration sponsored educational expansion at the primary and secondary levels and established normal schools. Other notable achievements during Salgar's presidency were the chartering of the Banco de Bogotá, Colombia's first successful bank (1870); a reduction of the army by 29 percent; and the construction of roads and of asylums for the insane and leprous. Salgar's elegant personal style and courtesy won him plaudits from both parties. After his term as president, he was governor of Cundinamarca (1874–1876), minister of war (1876), minister of foreign affairs (1878), and minister of the interior (1884). Salgar died in Bogotá.

See also **Colombia, Political Parties: Liberal Party; Parra, Aquileo.**

BIBLIOGRAPHY

Antonio Pérez Aguirre, *Los radicales y la regeneración* (1941), pp. 87–97.

Helen Delpar, *Red Against Blue* (1981), pp. 67ff.

Arizmendi Ignacio Posada, *Presidentes de Colombia, 1810–1990* (1989), pp. 137–141.

J. LEÓN HELGUERA

SALINAS DE GORTARI, CARLOS

(1948–). As president of Mexico from 1988 to 1994, Carlos Salinas established himself as a major figure in contemporary Mexican presidential history. He was born on April 3, 1948, in Mexico City, the son of Raúl Salinas Lozano, a former cabinet secretary, and Margarita de Gortari Carvajal, a teacher. Salinas studied in public schools in Mexico City, completing his pre-college work at the National Preparatory School No. 1, where he was active in student politics. He pursued an economics degree at the National University (1966–1969) with an important generation of future politicians, studying under Miguel de la Madrid and again participating in student politics. After graduating in 1971 he earned three degrees from Harvard: two MA degrees in public administration (1973) and political economy (1976) and a PhD in political economy and government (1978). His professors there included Otto Eckstein and Karl Deutsch. In 1966 he began his political career in the PRI (Institutional Revolutionary Party) under Gonzalo Martínez Corbalá, but he quickly entered the public financial sector on completion of his first master's degree. After serving in several posts in the 1970s, including the Department of Financial Studies and International Affairs in the Treasury Secretariat, the source of many of his future collaborators, Salinas became director general of social and economic policy under de la Madrid in the Secretariat of Planning and Budgeting (1979–1981). When de la Madrid was selected as the PRI presidential candidate, he asked Salinas to serve as director of the PRI's Institute of Political, Economic, and Social Studies during the campaign of 1981–1982. He also served as de la Madrid's secretary of budgeting and planning, following in his mentor's footsteps, until his own designation as the PRI candidate for president in 1987.

Elected in the most disputed presidential campaign since the PRI's formation in 1929, Salinas came into office with barely a simple majority of the officially tallied vote, the lowest figure ever in a successful presidential campaign. With little legitimacy, outside of or within his own party, he took charge of the presidency in a dynamic, decisive manner. The major leitmotif of his ideology was economic liberalization and political modernization. Building on the legacy of his predecessor de la Madrid, Salinas sought to engineer a reversal of the growing role of the state in Mexican economic life. His administration sold off hundreds of state-owned enterprises, allowed North American firms to participate in the exploration of oil for the first time since 1938, significantly denationalized the banking industry, and advocated the establishment of a regional free trade block among Mexico, the United States, and Canada, thereby significantly reducing many of Mexico's traditional trade barriers. He continued to renegotiate the debt, while keeping up payments, and implemented policies to attract large amounts of foreign capital. While those policies contributed to economic growth beginning in the late 1990s, by 2007 they had yet to succeed in bringing economic benefits to most members of the working and lower middle classes, who saw their standard of living decline markedly after 1980.

Salinas's promises of political modernization were not fulfilled. Although some structural reforms were implemented during the 1990 PRI convention, and the government successfully legislated political reform through Congress in 1989, elections were characterized by excessive fraud and political violence. The government pursued a political strategy of co-opting the traditional Right, represented by the National Action Party (PAN), and implementing an uncompromising, repressive policy toward the new center Left, represented by Cuauhtémoc Cárdenas and the Democratic Revolutionary Party (PRD). This strategy was reflected in the 1989 and 1990 state and local elections, in which the National Action Party won its first gubernatorial race since 1929, but in which the PRD fared badly in every contest. This failure of political reform was a factor in the sudden emergence of a revolutionary peasant movement (the Zapatista Army of National Liberation) in Chiapas at the start of 1994. That uprising, together with a series of political assassinations (including that of the PRI's presidential candidate, Luis Donaldo Colosio), dominated the troubled close of the Salinas administration. When economic collapse ensued in December 1994 and Salinas's own brother, Raúl, was implicated in one of the assassinations, Carlos Salinas left Mexico with his reputation in considerable disarray. His ambition to become an important actor in the international community was destroyed. He lived in Ireland during the Ernesto Zedillo administration, and returned to Mexico after Vicente Fox became president. Salinas began to be active behind the scenes in PRI politics, but a widely held negative image in the media and among the citizenry prevented him from exerting a statesman's role as an ex-president.

Salinas also adopted a controversial policy toward the Catholic Church, appointing an official representative to the Vatican, consulting the hierarchy on numerous matters, inviting clergy to his inauguration, and welcoming Pope John Paul II to Mexico in 1990. Human rights organizations, including Americas Watch and Amnesty International, severely criticized his administration for the increase in human rights violations and abuses. In response, the government established a new Human Rights Commission in the summer of 1990, reinforcing the activities of nongovernmental human rights groups. On other bilateral fronts, especially in drug eradication, Salinas increased cooperation with the United States and took a hard-nosed approach toward this problem within Mexico.

The divisiveness of Salinas's presidency proved to have lasting effects on PRI's viability. His designation as president, and the economic policies he represented, helped provoke the split within the PRI in which Cárdenas and Porfirio Muñoz Ledo bolted the organization to form their own political movement in support of political reforms and more populist economic policies. Another group of reformers, calling themselves the "Critical Current," remained within the party, adopting a new structure in 1990, in hopes of exerting further pressure favoring internal reforms. Salinas's failure to decentralize and allow for greater political pluralization contributed to further divisions within his own party and the growth of political opposition in Mexico, culminating in the presidential electoral victory of the National Action Party in 2000.

See also Cárdenas Solorzano, Cuauhtémoc; Colosio Murrieta, Luis Donaldo; Fox Quesada, Vicente; John Paul II, Pope; Mexico: Since 1910; Mexico, Political Parties: Institutional Revolutionary Party (PRI); Mexico, Political Parties: National Action Party (PAN); Mexico, Zapatista Army of National Liberation; Muñoz Ledo Lazo de la Vega, Porfirio; Salinas de Gortari, Raul.

BIBLIOGRAPHY

Primary Work

Salinas de Gortari, Carlos. *México: Un paso difícil a la modernidad*. Mexico City: Plaza y Janés, 2000.

Secondary Works

Ayala Anguiano, Armando. *Salinas y su México*. Mexico City: Grijalbo, 1995.

Chand, Vikram K. *Mexico's Political Awakening*. Notre Dame, IN: University of Notre Dame Press, 2001.

Domínguez, Jorge I. *Democratizing Mexico: Public Opinion and Electoral Choices*. Baltimore, MD: Johns Hopkins University Press, 1996.

Levy, Daniel C., and Kathleen Bruhn. *Mexico: The Struggle for Democratic Development*. Berkeley: University of California Press, 2006.

Roett, Riodan, ed. *The Challenge of Institutional Reform in Mexico*. Boulder, CO: Lynne Rienner, 1995.

RODERIC AI CAMP

SALINAS DE GORTARI, RAÚL (1946–).

Salinas is the oldest son of Raúl Salinas Lozano and Margarita de Gortari and older brother to the former president of Mexico Carlos Salinas de Gortari. He studied civil engineering at the National Autonomous University of Mexico (1965–1969) and earned two master's degrees in France (1972–1974). After 1977 he held various public positions. In private business he was a planning assistant with the civil engineering company Ingenieros Civiles Asociados (1970–1972). During his brother's presidential administration (1988–1994) there were rumors that Raúl would run for an elected position, but instead he was accused of masterminding the murder of the leading political figure and former president of the PRI, José Francisco Ruiz Massieu (brother-in-law of Carlos Salinas), and of illicit personal enrichment. He was incarcerated in a high security prison on February 28, 1995.

The investigations and public debate about his rampant corruption intensified on November 15, 1995, when his wife, Paulina Castañón, was arrested in Switzerland trying to withdraw millions of dollars from Raúl's secret accounts, using a false passport. She was freed, but the $130 million in their accounts was frozen and then investigated by Swiss authorities, who suspected potential money laundering from drug trafficking. The Mexican Congress also held hearings on Raúl's shady dealings when he was an official in government institutions addressing food poverty (Conasupo and Diconsa).

The Swiss authorities concluded that part of the money had come from drug trafficking and confiscated $90 million. In addition, the federal government of Mexico determined that former President Salinas had transferred some $38 million to accounts under various pseudonyms of his brother Raúl. The investigations lurched along until January 21, 1999, when a federal judge declared Raúl guilty and sentenced him to fifty years in prison for the murder of Ruiz Massieu. The sentence was later reduced to twenty-seven years and Salinas was released on bail on July 14, 2005.

See also **Salinas de Gortari, Carlos.**

BIBLIOGRAPHY

Bruce, Ian. "Mexico Frees Ex-Leader's Brother." BBC News, June 10, 2005. Available from http://news.bbc.co.uk/2/hi/americas/4079372.stm.

Hernández, Ignacio. *El clan Salinas; o, La persistencia en el poder*. Mexico: Col. Héroes de Padierna, Seri Editores y Distribuidores, 2000.

Oppenheimer, Andres. *Bordering on Chaos: Guerrillas, Stockbrokers, Politicians, and Mexico's Road to Prosperity*. Boston: Little, Brown, 1996.

Trueba Lara, José Luis. *Raúl Salinas de Gortari: El abuso del poder*. Mexico: Grupo Editorial Planeta, 1996.

ENCISCO FROYLÁN

SALLES, WALTER (1956–).

An internationally known Brazilian film director, Walter Salles grew up in France and the United States as the son of a millionaire banker who was the Brazilian ambassador to those countries. Salles directed documentaries for ten years before making feature films. In 1995 he codirected *Terra Estrangeira* (*Foreign Land*) with Daniela Thomas. It is a black-and-white thriller depicting the reverse migration of a couple from Brazil to Portugal. *Central do Brasil* (*Central Station*, 1998) catapulted his career. It revolves around a retired school teacher who meets a young boy in search of his father. An allegory of Brazil's development, it is a road movie about self-discovery. Set in Rio and the Northeastern *sertão* (hinterland), the film pays homage to the *Cinema Novo* film movement from the 1960s. It won the top prize at the Berlin film festival and was nominated for two Oscars.

Salles is known for creating beautiful imagery, despite the apparent poverty faced by his characters. His other films include *Diarios de motocicleta* (*The Motorcycle Diaries*, 2004) based on the writings and life of Ernesto "Che" Guevara. Salles traversed Che's 5,000-mile motorcycle route three times in preparation for the film. There he met the people who served as actors in the film (he also employed nonprofessional actors in *Central do Brasil*). This technique follows from Salles's impulse to portray naturalistic Latin American people, and shows the clear influence on him of Italian neorealism. The film solidified his status as a world-renowned *auteur*.

See also **Cinema: From the Silent Film to 1990; Cinema: Since 1990; Cinema Novo.**

BIBLIOGRAPHY

Films by Salles

Socorro Nobre [*Life Somewhere Else*], 1995

Terra Estrangeira [*Foreign Land*], 1996

Central do Brasil [*Central Station*], 1998

O *Primeiro Dia* [*Midnight*], 1998

Somos Todos Filhos da Terra [We Are All Children of the Land], 1998

Abril Despedaçado [*Behind the Sun*], 2001)

Armas E Paz [*Guns and Peace*], 2002)

Castanha e Caju Contra o Encouraçado Titanic [Chestnut and Cashews against the Battleship Titanic] (SHORT), 2002

Diarios de motocicleta [*The Motorcycle Diaries*], 2004

Dark Water (2005)

Secondary Sources

Andrew, Geoff. "Walter Salles." *Guardian* (London), August 26, 2004.

D'Avila, Roberto. *Os cineastas: Conversas com Roberto D'Avila*. Rio de Janeiro: Bom Texto, 2002.

Falicov, Tamara L. "Central Do Brasil." In *International Dictionary of Films and Filmmakers*, edited by Sara and Tom Pendergast. New York: St. James Press, 2000. Also available at http://www.filmreference.com/Films-Ca-Chr/Central-do-Brasil.html.

Kaufman, Anthony. "Sentimental Journey as National Allegory: An Interview with Walter Salles." *Cineaste* 24, no.1 (1998), 19–21.

Nagib, Lucia, ed. *The New Brazilian Cinema*. London: I. B. Taurus, 2003.

Shaw, Deborah. *Contemporary Cinema of Latin America: Ten Key Films*. London and New York: Continuum, 2003.

TAMARA L. FALICOV

SALNAVE, SYLVAIN (1827–1870).

Sylvain Salnave (*b.* 1827; *d.* 15 January 1870), president of Haiti (1867–1869). Sylvain Salnave's presidency was marked by civil unrest that threatened to tear the country apart and tempted foreign powers to intervene, once again, in Haitian affairs. Tensions produced in part by the collapse of cotton exports to the United States contributed to the problems Salnave faced. Yet, Salnave's seizure of power through a military rebellion backed by U.S. and Dominican elements also provoked angry reactions from other Haitian leaders. Salnave faced a general uprising in the countryside as various chieftains from the provinces refused to recognize his regime. This led to a state of chronic civil war in which the country became divided into the northern, southern, and central regions. While Salnave faced opposition from armed peasants in the North, the Cacos, and peasant bands in the South, the *piquets*, most of his support came from the center, especially the capital. Salnave became quite popular among the black urban masses, who appreciated his populist economic policies, including the establishment of state-run food stores where basic goods could be bought at low prices. Because of this black support and despite his status as a mulatto, he has been viewed as a founder of Haiti's National Party, which has claimed to speak for the interests of the ordinary black Haitian.

See also **Haiti.**

BIBLIOGRAPHY

Frank Moya Pons, "Haiti and Santo Domingo, 1790–ca. 1870," in *The Cambridge History of Latin America*, vol. 3, edited by Leslie Bethell (1985), pp. 237–275.

Michel-Rolph Trouillot, *Haiti: State Against Nation* (1990).

Additional Bibliography

Nicholls, David. *From Dessalines to Duvalier: Race, Colour, and National Independence in Haiti.* New Brunswick, NJ: Rutgers University Press, 1996.

PAMELA MURRAY

SALOMON, LOUIS ÉTIENNE LYSIUS FÉLICITÉ (1820–1888).

Louis Étienne Lysius Félicité Salomon (*b.* 1820; *d.* 1888), Haitian president (1879–1888) and polemicist. He was born to an elite black landowning family in Les Cayes, and after a brief period in the army, turned while still young to politics. He became known as a *noiriste,* an advocate of black dominance, and an opponent of the mulatto elite.

Salomon served as minister of finance and commerce under Faustin Soulouque (1785–1867) and tried to emphasize state ownership of coffee exports. When Fabre Nicolas Geffrard (1806–1878) overthrew Soulouque, Salomon left for Jamaica, and from there he bitterly opposed Geffrard.

After his election to the presidency in 1879, many Liberals were exiled or fled. In 1880 Salomon founded the National Bank with foreign capitalization. Some have argued that he thus opened the way for foreign interference and, perhaps, the nineteen-year U.S. occupation that began in 1915. He gave some state land to the peasantry, but he was permissive toward foreign ownership. He was overthrown by a northern coalition in 1888, and he died soon after in exile.

BIBLIOGRAPHY

Berloquin-Chassany, Pascale. *Haïti, une démocratie compromise, 1890-1911.* Paris: Harmattan, 2004.

Gaillard, Roger. *La république exterminatrice.* Port-au-Prince: R. Gaillard, 1984.

Gaillard, Roger. *Une modernisation manqueé (1880–1896).* Port-au-Prince: R. Gaillard, 1995.

MURDO J. MACLEOD

SALOMÓN–LOZANO TREATY (1922).

The Salomón–Lozano Treaty (1922) was a controversial agreement that settled a border dispute between Peru and Colombia. The treaty ceded Colombia a narrow corridor of land between the Putumayo and Amazon rivers (and thus granted it long-desired access to the Amazon River) that included the port of Leticia. In return, Peru received land south of the Putamayo River that Colombia had received from Ecuador in 1916. The latter served Peru's interest by undermining Ecuadorian claims in the Oriente. The treaty was strongly criticized by the Ecuadorian government, which suddenly found itself confronting an antagonist where it had previously had an ally (Colombia).

BIBLIOGRAPHY

St. John, Ronald Bruce. *The Foreign Policy of Peru* Boulder, CO: L. Rienner Publishers, 1992.

Additional Bibliography

Valverde, Carlos A. *Por la paz de América: El tratado de límites Salomón-Lozano entre el Perú y Colombia. La actitud del Ecuador / Análisis del tratado y artículos del diputado nacional por Huallaga.* Lima: Talleres de La Prensa, 1928.

PETER F. KLARÉN

SALTA.

Salta, capital of the province of the same name in northwestern Argentina, located at an elevation of 3,893 feet and 140 miles north of Tucumán (2001 population of 464,678). Founded at its present site in 1582 by Hernando de Lerma, it was intended, along with other settlements in northwestern Argentina, to secure the presence of the Spaniards in Río de la Plata against territorial claims of advancing conquerors from Peru. During colonial times it gained notoriety for blending Spanish and Indian traditions in its religious art and as the site of the Intendancy of Salta. However, constant attacks from Calchaquí Indians and devastating earthquakes halted an otherwise sustained development based on agriculture (maize, wheat, alfalfa) and the export of mules for the silver mines of Potosí in Bolivia. Near Salta, General Manuel Belgrano defeated the Spanish royalists in 1813 and brought this conservative province over to the independents. The novelist Juana Manuela Gorriti, who was born in Salta and described the city in many of her works, offered colorful *costumbrista* portraits of nineteenth–century life in the church and in the home. Today the city is an active center of communications; railway lines lead to Antofagasta (Chile) and to La Paz (Bolivia) via La Quiaca, and there is a motorway to Potosí,

Oruro, and La Paz. The city's industries are restricted to cement factories and ironworks in the Chachapoyas district.

See also **Argentina, Geography.**

BIBLIOGRAPHY

Gorriti, Juana Manuela. *Peregrinaciones de una alma triste.* Edited by Mary G Berg. Buenos Aires: Stockcero, 2006.

Mata de López, Sara. *Persistencias y cambios: Salta y el noroeste argentino, 1770–1840.* Rosario, Argentina: Prohistoria & Manuel Suárez–Editor, 1999.

Poderti, Alicia. *Palabra e historia en los Andes: La rebelión del inca Túpac Amaru y el noroeste argentino.* Buenos Aires: Corregidor, 1997.

Scobie, James R. *Secondary Cities of Argentina: The Social History of Corrientes, Salta, and Mendoza, 1850–1910* (1988).

Vinuales, Graciela M. *La ciudad de Salta y su región* (Buenos Aires, 1983).

César N. Caviedes

SALTO. Salto, capital of the department of the same name in Uruguay on the eastern margins of the Uruguay River, 260 miles from Montevideo, and second-largest individual city of Uruguay, with 80,823 inhabitants (1985). One of the oldest settlements in the country, Salto was founded in 1756 as a military post not far from the noted Salto Grande waterfalls and rapids, which made upstream navigation impossible. It was originally meant to be a mission, but the foundation of Paysandú in 1772 diminished its significance as a center of evangelism. The proper city was founded in 1817, and the department of the same name in 1837. Mainly a service hub for the numerous sheep ranches of the region, it is the most important administrative center of Uruguay's Littoral. In 1974 the governments of Uruguay and Argentina began construction on the Salto Grande Dam, which spans the Uruguay River between Salto and two Argentinean cities: Entre Ríos and Concordia. Built with hydroelectric capacity, the dam began generating power in 1979. The fourteen Kaplan turbines that power the dam's generators are capable of producing 1,890 megawatts of power.

BIBLIOGRAPHY

Conti, Susana. *Salto.* Montevideo, Uruguay: Editorial Fin de Siglo, 2000.

Fá Robaína, Juan Carlos. *Reminiscencias salteñas.* Montevideo, Uruguay: Editorial Fin del Siglo, 1996.

Giuffra, Elzear. *La República del Uruguay* (Montevideo, 1935).

Kleinpenning, Jan M. G. *Peopling the Purple Land: A Historical Geography of Rural Uruguay, 1500–1915.* Amsterdam: Centre for Latin American Research and Documentation, 1995.

César N. Caviedes

SALT TRADE

This entry includes the following articles:
ANDEAN REGION
BRAZIL
MESOAMERICA
RÍO DE LA PLATA

ANDEAN REGION

The pre-Columbian agricultural peoples of the Andes and the adjacent coastal valleys considered salt an essential component of their cuisine. In the northern Andes of Ecuador and Colombia, where salt was relatively scarce, its production and trade granted economic power to the peoples that controlled access to it. Northern Andean salt was traded for gold, emeralds, cotton, hot pepper, and dried fish from the coast. Relatively abundant in the southern and central Andes and the adjacent coast, salt constituted a fundamental product to which the states maintained access.

Andean peoples preferred cooked salt loaves, processed at salt springs by full-time specialists, typically women. In Ecuador, this preference had a medicinal basis—salt loaves contained the iodine needed to prevent goiters and cretinism. However, salt was also gathered from salt outcrops and dried salt lake beds—the latter abundant in the Andes of Bolivia, Chile, and Argentina.

Sea salt was produced by solar evaporation in the populated coastal valleys of Peru and at Puná Island (Ecuador) and the mouth of the Magdalena River (Colombia). Sea salt from Puná Island and Paita (Peru) was transported long distances north along the coasts of Ecuador and Colombia and reached much of the Ecuadorian highlands.

In the northern Andes, commoners and trade specialists (*mindalaes*) participated in the distribution of salt within and between ethnic nations. In Inca areas, salt specialists (*cachicamayoc*) from diverse ethnic groups shared the saline waters at the major sites, each providing for the salt needs of her or his group.

During colonial times, Spanish entrepreneurs and holders of crown grants took control over much of the native salt production, often to the detriment of native peoples. Mule teams replaced human carriers in the northern Andes, facilitating Spanish trade there. The production of salt loaves continued during colonial times but was eclipsed by that of sea salt and lake bed salt, which were abundant and easily obtained.

See also **Spices and Herbs.**

BIBLIOGRAPHY

A good primary source for the sixteenth century is Marcos Jiménez De La Espada, ed., *Relaciones geográficas de Indias* (1965). Brief overviews of salt trade and production are Marianne Cardale-Schrimpff, "Salt Production in the Eastern Cordillera of Colombia Before and After the Spanish Conquest—A Preliminary Survey," in *Actas del XLI Congreso internacional de americanistas*, vol. 2 (1976), pp. 419–428; and Cheryl Pomeroy, "The Salt of Highland Ecuador: Precious Product of a Female Domain," in *Ethnohistory* 35, no. 2 (1988): 131–160.

Additional Bibliography

Malpass, Michael Andrew. *Daily Life in the Inca Empire.* Westport, CT: Greenwood Press, 1996.

CHERYL POMEROY

BRAZIL

The salt trade in Brazil lasted from 1631 to 1801, during which time the Portuguese crown kept salt as a royal monopoly, forbidding colonists to develop it locally or to sell it freely. Salt was shipped to Brazil from Portugal and distributed by those who had purchased monopoly contracts (usually for three years) in Lisbon. Because of its fundamental dietary importance for humans and domesticated animals, and its use as a food preservative, salt was one of the most prominent and controversial monopolies in colonial Brazil. Although the salt trade furnished lucrative revenues for the crown, it created artificially high prices and intermittent

shortages for colonists, producing widespread complaints and periodic riots over its imposition.

See also **Foreign Trade.**

BIBLIOGRAPHY

Myriam Ellis, *O monopólio do sal no estado do Brasil (1631–1801)* (1955).

Joel Serrão, ed., *Dicionário de história de Portugal*, 6 vols. (1979).

Additional Bibliography

Giffoni, José Marcello. *Sal: Um outro tempero ao Império, 1801–1850.* Rio de Janeiro: Arquivo Público do Estado do Rio de Janeiro, 2000.

WILLIAM DONOVAN

MESOAMERICA

Salt sources are found throughout Mesoamerica, though their uneven distribution, coupled with high levels of dietary demand, have made salt a strategic trade commodity. The largest production areas are located in the Central Highlands of Mexico and along the north coast of the Yucatán peninsula. Other production areas include the highlands and Pacific coasts of El Salvador, Guatemala, Chiapas and Oaxaca states in Mexico, and Mexico's west coast. Traditional native production techniques vary. Coastal salt is obtained by solar evaporation (*sal solar*) or by the cooking of saline estuarine waters, sometimes leached through salt-impregnated soils (*sal cocida*); most highland salt is produced by the cooking of salt from wells that tap underground brine springs, or by a process that combines soil leaching and the cooking of the resulting saline residue.

At the beginning of the Late Formative period (ca. 300 BCE), trade networks originating in the main production areas supplied most of Mesoamerica with salt. The trade was a prominent part of the economy of pre-Hispanic Classic (first millennium CE) and Postclassic (ca. 1000 to the Conquest) states of Central Mexico and the Valley of Oaxaca; salt from northern Yucatán was exported throughout the Maya lowlands, and was a key economic factor in the growth of political complexity in the north. The trade of salt continued under Spanish control during the colonial period, and demand increased with its use in the cattle, tanning, and silver mining industries. Today, most table salt is manufactured by large coastal solar producers; it is heavily used in the food preparation and chemical industries.

See also **Mining: Colonial Spanish America.**

BIBLIOGRAPHY

Miguel Othon De Mendizábal, *Influencia de la sal en la distribución geográfica de los grupos indígenas de México* (1929, 1944).

Raúl Lozano García, *Estudio tecnológico de la industria de la sal en México* (1946).

Anthony P. Andrews, *Maya Salt Production and Trade* (1983).

Ursula Ewald, *The Mexican Salt Industry, 1560–1980: A Study in Change* (1985); Anthony P. Andrews, "Las salinas de El Salvador: Bosquejo histórico, etnográfico y arqueológico," in *Mesoamérica* 21 (1991): 71–93.

Additional Bibliography

Ewald, Ursula and Jorge Ferreiro. *La industria salinera de México, 1560–1994*. México: Fondo de Cultura Económica, 1997.

Parsons, Jeffrey R. *The Last Saltmakers of Nexquipayac, Mexico: An Archaeological Ethnography*. Ann Arbor: Museum of Anthropology, University of Michigan, 2001.

ANTHONY P. ANDREWS

RÍO DE LA PLATA

Increasing exports of hides and dried beef from the Río De La Plata after 1770 required large quantities of salt. Shipments of those commodities, first from the Banda Oriental and later from Buenos Aires, relied mainly on salt carried overland from the Salinas Grandes (large salt flats), located approximately 240 miles southwest of Buenos Aires, in the unsettled Pampas. Large escorted caravans (*tropas*), consisting of hundreds of carts drawn by thousands of oxen, made annual trips to the *salinas* to obtain sufficient supplies of salt for the hide processors and *frigoríficos* (packing houses) of Buenos Aires. The *cabildo* of Buenos Aires organized this trade, reserving for itself the exclusive right to market the salt brought back.

Pampas peoples extracted tariffs from the *tropas*. The many different caciques demanded constant negotiations and repeated payments in *aguardiente,* tobacco, yerba maté, bread, and meat. By 1809, in an effort to alleviate recurrent shortages and inconvenient negotiations, many in Buenos Aires called for agreements with the Pehuenche and Ranquele Indians to mine salt and supply the city's *tropas*. Periodic shortages of salt forced suppliers to turn to alternative sources, which included the Río Negro, the Bahía de San Julián, imports from La Rioja and Tucumán, and occasional shipments from Cádiz. Despite the difficulties of bringing enough salt to Buenos Aires, the export of hides and beef continued to grow during the viceregal era and made the Río de la Plata an important region of Bourbon Spain's empire.

See also **Foreign Trade; Hides Industry; Spices and Herbs.**

BIBLIOGRAPHY

Alfredo J. Montoya, *Historia de los saladeros argentinos* (1956).

Pedro Andrés García, *Viajes a Salinas Grandes* (1969).

Jonathan C. Brown, *A Socioeconomic History of Argentina* (1979).

Additional Bibliography

Barsky, Osvaldo. *Historia del capitalismo agrario pampeano*. Buenos AirsL Siglo XXI Editores, 2003.

JEREMY STAHL

SALVACIONISMO. Salvacionismo, movement by Brazilian military officers to "redeem" their home states from control by local oligarchies (1910–1914). When the 1910 election divided the dominant state parties of São Paulo and Minas Gerais, Rio Grande do Sul's Republican Party and the army emerged as the dominant political forces, and Marshal Hermes Rodrigues da Fonseca became the first soldier to attain the presidency in sixteen years. In these circumstances, officers sought to overthrow oligarchies in state governments through military force and "clean" elections. Localized anarchy followed, as garrisons used cannon to achieve power. By 1912 army officers had taken the governorships in four northeastern states—Ceará, Alagoas, Pernambuco, and Sergipe—in contests marked by military intervention.

By 1914 *salvacionismo* was spent, because of compromises with local elites, military dissension, a new Minas–São Paulo alliance, and lack of support from Hermes, who was dominated by Riograndense

Senator José Gomes Pinheiro Machado. The *salvacionistas* broke with Pinheiro, who consequently helped local oligarchs overthrow Ceará's *salvacionista* governor.

Pinheiro was assassinated in 1915, but *salvacionismo* had already dissipated when a new president, supported by Mineiros and Paulistas, took office in 1914. Nonetheless, the myth of military "redemption" remained alive, influencing the Tenentes (lieutenants) a decade later.

See also **Armed Forces.**

BIBLIOGRAPHY

Emygdio Dantas Barreto, *Conspirações* (1917).

Fernando Setembrino De Carvalho, *Memórias: Dados para a história do Brasil* (1950), pp. 87–126.

Edgard Carone, *A república velha (evolução política)* (1971), pp. 255–296.

Joseph L. Love, *Rio Grande do Sul and Brazilian Regionalism, 1882–1930* (1971), chap. 6.

Additional Bibliography

Carvalho, José Murilo de. *Forças armadas e política no Brasil*. Rio de Janeiro: Jorge Zahar Editor, 2005.

Castro, Celso. *Os militares e a república: Um estudo sobre cultura e ação política*. São Paulo: Rio de Janeiro: J. Zahar Editor, 1995.

JOSEPH L. LOVE

SALVADOR. Salvador, capital of Bahia State, Brazil, with an estimated population of 2.65 million in 2006. Located on a hilly promontory overlooking the large Bay of All Saints, the city of Salvador (also known during much of its history as Bahia) was founded in 1549 by Tomé de Sousa, the first governor-general of Brazil, near the site of an earlier Portuguese settlement destroyed by Indian attacks in 1545. Serving from its foundation as the seat of royal government in Brazil, the city housed, after 1609, the colony's first high court. After the 1763 transfer of the viceregal government to Rio De Janeiro, the city remained the capital of the captaincy (later province and, after 1889, state) of Bahia. Made the seat of Brazil's first bishopric in 1551, the city became an archepiscopal see in 1676.

Salvador ranked, throughout the colonial period, as one of the wealthiest and largest cities in Brazil, claiming perhaps 15,000 inhabitants by the 1680s and more than 50,000 by the start of the nineteenth century. Visitors were impressed not only by its spectacular location straddling a high bluff along the bay, but also by its dozens of churches and chapels, several convents and monasteries, and public buildings. Although it lost its Jesuit college after 1759, the city gained a public library in 1811, a theater in 1812, and Brazil's second medical school in 1813.

Salvador owed its colonial prosperity to the rich slave-based agricultural export economy of the Recôncavo, the city's immediate hinterland, which early on had emerged as a major sugar-producing region and, from the start of the seventeenth century, also as the chief center of tobacco production in colonial Brazil. The demand for slave labor in sugar and tobacco production in turn made Salvador a principal port in the transatlantic slave trade and helped establish strong and lasting cultural links between the city and West Africa. Moreover, throughout Salvador's history, the population of African descent has always outnumbered by a wide margin its white inhabitants. Even in the early nineteenth century, slaves made up somewhere between one-third and two-fifths of the city's population.

Social and political turmoil, beginning with the Inconfidência Dos Alfaiates (1798), an early and quickly crushed independence movement, characterized Salvador's history in the first decades of the nineteenth century. Held by forces loyal to the Portuguese crown, the city suffered a nine-month siege in 1822–1823 during Brazil's brief war for independence. After 1823 Salvador witnessed revolts, numerous anti-Portuguese riots, and barracks uprisings, culminating in 1837–1838 in the Sabinada, a federalist rebellion, during which the city again was besieged. The city and the neighboring Recôncavo also experienced a spectacular series of slave revolts between 1809 and 1835, including the 1835 Malê revolt, led by Muslim urban slaves and freed slaves of West African origin, which was perhaps the best-planned slave rising in Brazilian history.

In the late nineteenth and early twentieth centuries, Salvador continued to grow (reaching a population of 283,422 by 1920) but suffered with the decline in sugar production in the Recôncavo and the stagnation of the Bahian export economy.

Petroleum production in the city's hinterland and the later development of a petrochemical industry gave the city new dynamism from the 1960s onward. Today, Salvador ranks as a major industrial and commercial center and also carries enormous weight in cultural matters—contributing disproportionately to innovative trends in popular music and serving as the country's principal center of Afro–Brazilian culture. It is home to the highest proportion of people of African descent in Brazil. In 1985 UNESCO declared the historical center of Salvador, also known as the Pelourinho, a World Heritage Site.

See also **Brazil, Geography.**

BIBLIOGRAPHY

Butler, Kim D. *Freedoms Given, Freedoms Won: Afro–Brazilians in Post–Abolition São Paulo and Salvador.* New Brunswick, NJ: Rutgers University Press, 1998.

De Azevedo, Thales. *Povoamento da cidade do Salvador* (1969).

De Queirós Mattoso, Katia M. *Bahia: A cidade do Salvador e seu mercado* (1978).

Reis, João José. *Slave Rebellion in Brazil: The Muslim Uprising of 1835 in Bahia* (1993).

Reis, João José. *Death Is a Festival: Funeral Rites and Rebellion in Nineteenth–Century Brazil.* Chapel Hill: University of North Carolina Press, 2003.

Schwartz, Stuart B. *Sugar Plantations in the Formation of Brazilian Society: Bahia, 1550–1835* (1985), and *Bahia, século XIX: Uma provincia no Império* (1992).

Vainfas, Ronaldo. *Confissões da Bahia: Santo Ofício da Inquisição de Lisboa.* São Paulo: Companhia das Letras, 1997.

Verger, Pierre. *Flux et reflux de la traite des nègres entre le Golfe de Bénin et Bahia de Todos os Santos, du dix-septième au dix-neuvième siècle* (1968).

B. J. BARICKMAN

SALVADOR, VICENTE DO (1564–1639).

Vicente do Salvador (*b.* 1564; *d.* 1639), Portuguese historian and member of the Franciscan order. At the age of sixty-three he wrote a *History of Brazil* that was more concerned with human events than with Brazilian fauna and flora as had been the case with his sixteenth-century predecessors. The first chapter was still devoted to nature and to Brazil's original inhabitants, but all the others narrated the main events of Portuguese colonization in America from 1500 until 1627. In his dedication to the Portuguese scholar Manuel Severim de Faria, the author wrote that he expected his work to be printed at this patron's expense. However, his *History* remained unpublished until the nineteenth century, and some chapters were lost.

Written in Bahia, Salvador's opus is a general history, rather than a local one. The Franciscan does not reveal his sources, but João Capistrano de Abreu, the nineteenth-century historian, proved that Frei Vicente had read Simão Estácio da Silveira's *Relação sumária das cousas do Maranhão* (1624) and Pero de Magalhaes Gandavo's *História da Província de Santa Cruz* (1576). Wars against the Indians, the French pirate attacks, and the Dutch invasions are narrated. Military actions of governors-general attract his attention more than the colonists and their agricultural and mercantile activities.

BIBLIOGRAPHY

João Capistrano De Abreu, *Ensaios e estuados: Crítica e história* (2d ser. 1976).

José Honório Rodrigues, *História da história do Brasil,* vol. 1, *Historiografia colonial* (1979).

Additional Bibliography

Vieira, Nelson H. *Brasil e Portugal—A imagem recíproca (O mito e a realidade na expressão literária).* Lisbon: Ministério de Educação, Cultura e Língua Portuguesa, 1993.

MARIA BEATRIZ NIZZA DA SILVA

SALVATIERRA, CONDE DE. *See* Sarmiento de Sotomayor, García.

SALVATIONISM. *See* Salvacionismo.

SAM, JEAN VILBRUN GUILLAUME (?–1915).

Jean Vilbrun Guillaume Sam (*d.* 28 July 1915), president of Haiti (March–July 1915). Sam's presidency was marked by mounting chaos and violence that resulted in the occupation of the country by U.S. Marines. While responding to U.S. pressures to arrange a customs receivership similar to the one the Americans had created for the Dominican Republic,

Sam spent most of his time fighting his political enemies, who were led by the virulently anti-American Rosalvo Bobo. Sam ordered the execution of 167 prisoners, many of them Bobo's supporters. In retaliation, on 28 July 1915, he was lynched and butchered by a mob in Port-au-Prince. Shortly thereafter, the U.S. Marines occupied Haiti.

See also **Bobo, Rosalvo.**

BIBLIOGRAPHY

Rayford W. Logan, *Haiti and the Dominican Republic* (1968).

Lester D. Langley, *The Banana Wars: United States Intervention in the Caribbean, 1898–1934,* rev. ed. (1988).

Michel-Rolph Trouillot, *Haiti: State Against Nation* (1990).

Additional Bibliography

Heinl, Robert Debs, Nancy Gordon Heinl, and Michael Heinl. *Written in Blood: The Story of the Haitian People, 1492–1995.* Lanham, MD: University Press of America, 2005.

Renda, Mary A. *Taking Haiti: Military Occupation and the Culture of U.S. Imperialism, 1915–1940.* Chapel Hill: University of North Carolina Press, 2001.

PAMELA MURRAY

SAM, TIRÉSIAS AUGUSTIN SIMON

(1835–1916). Tirésias Augustin Simon Sam (*b.* 15 May 1835; *d.* 1916), president of Haiti (31 March 1896–12 May 1902). Military potentate of his native North, minister of war and marine under the presidency of Lysius Salomon (1879–1888), Sam had strong ties within the then dominant dark-skinned faction of the oligarchy. He offered the Haitian elites the combination of force and compromise they expected. With limited formal training, he used his contacts to bring competence to the service of government. He encouraged the construction of railroads around Cap Haïtien and Port-au-Prince. Financial scandals, factionalism, and the renewed bullying of Haiti by foreign powers, notably Germany, France, and the United States, distracted him from an already loose agenda. Forced out of power when he tried to prolong his constitutional mandate, he predicted an endless civil war: "I am the last president of Haiti." In 1915, his son, Jean Vilbrun Guillaume Sam, was briefly the president of Haiti from February until his assassination on July 27.

See also **Haiti.**

BIBLIOGRAPHY

Brenda G. Plummer, *Haiti and the Great Powers, 1902–1915* (1988).

Additional Bibliography

Auguste, Yves L. *Haïti et les Etats-Unis: 1862-1900.* Port-au-Prince, Haiti: Impr. H. Deschamps, 1987.

Berloquin-Chassany, Pascale. *Haïti, une démocratie compromise, 1890-1911.* Paris: Harmattan, 2004.

Gaillard, Roger. *L'état vassal (1896-1902).* Port-au-Prince, Haiti: R. Gaillard, 1988.

Jolibois, Annie Hilaire. *Démocrates et démocratie.* Port-au-Prince, Haiti: s.n., 1994.

MICHEL-ROLPH TROUILLOT

SAMANÁ BAY. Samaná Bay, harbor on the Samaná Peninsula, at the northeasternmost point of the Dominican Republic. Facing the Mona Passage, the key exit channel of the Caribbean for warships, oil tankers, and civilian passenger vessels, Samaná Bay is the Caribbean's best natural harbor. During the second half of the nineteenth century, U.S. presidents Ulysses Grant, James Buchanan, and Andrew Johnson, Dominican presidents Buenaventura Báez and Pedro Santana, naval strategists, and diplomats all made efforts to purchase or lease Samaná Bay and the peninsula on which it is located. At the same time, the United States was eager to keep the area out of the control of its European rivals, England, France, and Germany.

BIBLIOGRAPHY

Frank Moya Pons, *Manual de historia dominicana,* 7th ed. (1983), esp. pp. 376–377, 380.

Michael J. Kryzanek and Howard J. Wiarda, *The Politics of External Influence in the Dominican Republic* (1988), esp. pp. 5, 27, 29–30, 153.

Additional Bibliography

Moya Pons, Frank. *The Dominican Republic: A National History.* Princeton, NJ: Markus Wiener Publishers, 1998.

Sang, Lena, and Rosa Lamelas. *Línea costera de la Bahía de Samaná: Desde Punta la Palometa hasta Punta Yabón.* Santo Domingo, República Dominicana: Centro para la Conservación y Ecodesarrollo de la Bahía de Samaná y su Entorno, 1995.

Turits, Richard Lee. *Foundations of Despotism: Peasants, the Trujillo Regime, and Modernity in Dominican History.* Stanford, CA: Stanford University Press, 2003.

KAI P. SCHOENHALS

SAMANEZ OCAMPO, DAVID (1866–1947).

David Samanez Ocampo (*b.* 1866; *d.* 1947), landowner, provincial leader of Nicolás de Piérola's Democratic Party, and president of a provisional government in Peru between March and December 1931. Born in Huambo, Samanez Ocampo was elected deputy of the province of Antabamba, Apurímac. In 1909 he rebelled against the first government of Augusto B. Leguía and later supported President Guillermo Billinghurst (1912–1914). In political retirement by the time Colonel Luis M. Sánchez Cerro was forced to resign as de facto president in March 1931, Samanez Ocampo was selected to head a transitional government that held presidential and congressional elections in October 1931. Samanez Ocampo's government partially adopted some of adviser Edwin W. Kemmerer's economic recommendations. Samanez Ocampo retired again from national politics when Sánchez Cerro assumed power after the contested elections of 1931.

See also **Peru: Since Independence.**

BIBLIOGRAPHY

Steve Stein, *Populism in Peru: The Emergence of the Masses and the Politics of Social Control* (1980).

Additional Bibliography

Drake, Paul W. *Kemmerer en los Andes: La mision Kemmerer, 1923–1933.* Quito, Ecuador: Banco Central del Ecuador, 1995.

ALFONSO W. QUIROZ

SAMAYOA CHINCHILLA, CARLOS (1898–1973).

Carlos Samayoa Chinchilla (*b.* 10 December 1898; *d.* 14 February 1973), Guatemalan writer. A member of the same generation as Miguel Ángel Asturias and Luis Cardoza y Aragón, he is especially famous for his nativist short stories collected in *Madre Milpa* (1934).

Born in Guatemala City, the son of wealthy landowners, Samayoa traveled extensively throughout Europe in the 1920s. Forced to return to his native country after the stock market crash of 1929, he served as a minor bureaucrat in the Jorge Ubico administration (1931–1944). While traveling with the dictator throughout the country, he developed his ideas for *Madre Milpa*. The Ubico dictatorship collapsed in 1944, and Samayoa published a book of memoirs about his experience working with the most feared man in the country, *El dictador y yo* (1945). During the 1940s he was director of the National Library and was active in founding several museums. As the new democratic administration became more liberal, Monterroso became a bitter critic of its progressive tendencies and joined in red-baiting the Arbenz government (1951–1954). In his later years he published books of short stories, but none were as accomplished as his original success. Other books by Samayoa are *Cuatro suertes* (1936); *Estampas de la costa grande* (1954); *El quetzal no es rojo* (1956); and *Chapines de ayer* (1957).

See also **Literature: Spanish America.**

BIBLIOGRAPHY

Francisco Albizúrez Palma and Catalina Barrios y Barrios, *Historia de la literatura guatemalteca,* vol. 3 (1987), pp. 38–52.

Additional Bibliography

Barraza Arriola, Marco Antonio. *Antología de escritores del istmo centroamericano.* San Tecla: Clásicos Roxsil, 2003.

ARTURO ARIAS

SAMBA.

Samba, the most famous Brazilian musical form and dance. Musically, samba is characterized by a 2/4 meter with the heaviest accent on the second beat and features pronounced syncopation, a stanza-and-refrain structure, responsorial singing, and many interlocking rhythmic parts. Samba has African roots, but its exact origins are unknown. Samba's true parent may have been the *lundu* song and circle dance, featuring the *umbigada* navel-touching movement, which came to Brazil from Angola. A primitive type of samba may have developed in Bahia from African musical elements and then brought to Rio de Janeiro by slaves and former slaves in the late 1800s.

Samba began to crystallize into its modern form in the early 1900s at the homes of Bahian matriarchs such as Tia Ciata, who lived near Rio's Praça Onze. There, musicians like Pixinguinha, Donga, João da Baiana, and Sinhô developed the budding form and added influences from the *maxixe* and *marcha* styles. The first recorded samba was "Pelo telefone" (On the Phone), composed by several musicians (but registered to Donga) and performed by the Banda Odeon in 1917.

Near Praça Onze was Estácio, the neighborhood of the sambistas Ismael Silva, Nilton Bastos, and Armando Marçal, who added longer notes, two-bar phrasing, and a slower tempo to samba, and solidified what would be samba's standard form for decades (later called, in the 1950s, *samba de morro*). It was they who also founded Deixa Falar, the first *escola de samba* (samba school), in 1928. Later important samba composers include: Noel Rosa, Caninha, Heitor dos Prazeres, Ataulfo Alves, Assis Valente, Geraldo Pereira, Lamartine Babo, Ary Barroso, Braguinha, Dorival Caymmi, Martinho da Vila, and Paulinho da Viola.

Samba's primary rhythm and its cross-rhythms can be carried by drum and percussion playing (the *batucada*) involving numerous instruments such as *surdo* (three different sizes), *caixa, repique, tamborim, pandeiro, prato, cuíca, frigideira, agogô, reco-reco,* and *chocalho*. Samba is also typically accompanied by guitar, four-string *cavaquinho*, and—less frequently—brass instruments.

Different styles of samba include *samba-canção* (a slower, more sophisticated style with more emphasis on melody and harmony than on the rhythm); *samba de breque* (a samba that features a "break" in which the singer dramatizes the story told in the lyrics); *samba de gafieira* (a dance-hall type of samba, usually instrumental, with horn arrangements influenced by American big-band jazz); *samba de roda* (a circle-dance samba, accompanied by hand clapping and *batucada*); *samba-enredo* (a "theme" samba, performed by samba schools during Carnaval in Rio); *pagode samba* (a "street"-type of samba popularized in the 1980s by

composers from Rio's Ramos neighborhood, who added *tan-tan* and banjo to the instrumentation); and *samba-reggae*. In addition, bossa nova mixed simplified samba rhythms with harmonies influenced by American West Coast "cool" jazz and classical music.

See also **Bossa Nova; Samba Schools.**

BIBLIOGRAPHY

Sergio Cabral, *As escolas de samba* (1974).

Rita Caurio, ed., *Brasil musical* (1988).

João Maximo and Carlos Didier, *Noel Rosa: Uma biografia* (1990).

Chris Mc Gowan and Ricardo Pessanha, *The Brazilian Sound: Samba, Bossa Nova, and the Popular Music of Brazil* (1991).

Additional Bibliography

Chasteen, John Charles. *National Rhythms, African Roots: The Deep History of Latin American Popular Dance.* Albuquerque: University of New Mexico Press, 2004.

Guillermoprieto, Alma. *Samba.* New York: Knopf: Distributed by Random House, 1990.

McCann, Bryan. *Hello, Hello Brazil: Popular Music in the Making of Modern Brazil.* Durham, NC: Duke University Press, 2004.

Naves, Santuza Cambraia. *O violão azul: Modernismo e música popular.* Rio de Janeiro: Fundação Getulio Vargas Editora, 1998.

Shaw, Lisa. *The Social History of the Brazilian Samba.* Brookfield: Ashgate, 1999.

Vianna, Hermano. *The Mystery of Samba: Popular Music & National Identity in Brazil.* Trans. John Charles Chasteen. Chapel Hill: University of North Carolina Press, 1999.

CHRIS McGOWAN

SAMBAQUI. Sambaqui, word of Tupi origin (*tãba'ki*) designating shell mounds, archaeological sites found in Brazilian seashore paleo-environments near rivers, lagoons, and mangroves. These shell mounds consist mainly of large accumulations of mollusk shells, remains of crustaceans, and fish bones from seasonal campsites of small prehistoric groups of coastal fishermen and collectors. In spite of the similar sources of subsistence of these groups, adaptive variations characterize the *sambaqui*. Different types resulted from successive or simultaneous phases of intense collecting of mollusks and phases of intense gathering of crustaceans and/or catching of fish, followed by hunting as well as fruit collecting. *Sambaquis* offer clues into past shorelines, changes in sea-level, and marine life. The term *sambaqui* has synonyms: in São Paulo and Santa Catarina shell mounds are *casqueiro, concheira,* or *ostreira;* in Pará, *cernambi* or *sarnambi;* in other places, *samauqui, caieira,* or *caleira* and even "island of shell." In English, it is a "shell" or "kitchen-midden."

See also **Archaeology.**

BIBLIOGRAPHY

Lina Maria Kneip et al., *Pesquisas arqueológicas no litoral de Itaipú* (1981), and *Coletores e pescadores pré-históricos de Guaratiba* (1985).

Additional Bibliography

Barbosa, Márcia, and Maria Dulce Gaspar. *Bibliografia brasileira sobre pescadores, coletores e caçacores pré-históricos litoráneos e ribeirinhos.* Rio de Janeiro: Museu Nacional, 1998.

Gaspar, Madu. *Sambaqui: Arquelogia do litoral Brasileiro.* Rio de Janeiro: Jorge Zahar Editor, 2000.

Johnson, Lucille Lewis, and Melanie Stright, eds. *Paleoshorelines and Prehistory: An Investigation of Method.* Boca Raton: CRC Press, 1992.

CHARLOTTE EMMERICH

SAMBA SCHOOLS. Samba schools, Brazilian organizations (*escolas de samba*) that plan and stage samba parades during Carnaval. Based for the most part in Rio de Janeiro, they often perform other social functions and may serve as community centers in poorer neighborhoods. For decades they have served as a source of pride, identity, and creativity for working-class Brazilian blacks and mulattoes, who make up the majority of members of each samba school.

As of 2007, there were eighty four officially registered *escolas de samba* in Rio and dozens more in other cities throughout Brazil. There is a hierarchy among the schools, and each year they compete for top ranking. The top fourteen "special" schools (*Grupo Especial*) parade on the Sunday and Monday of Carnaval week, seven each night. The rest of the schools are divided in descending rank into Groups A, B, C, D, and E. Each year, however, a school is downgraded from the Special to the Access Group, or Group A. The seven schools of the Special Group with the best scores march again at the Champion's Parade the following Saturday. The bigger ones, such as Mangueira, typically parade with four to five thousand singers and dancers, and three hundred-member percussion section. Every *escola*'s parade has a theme, an *enredo,* for that year's performance, which often focuses on Brazilian culture, history, or politics. This theme is explored in the lyrics of a *samba-enredo* chosen for that year, and these songs are often written by some of Brazil's top samba composers. The *enredo* is also illustrated in the ornamented floats and the lavish costumes of the participants, who are divided into several dozen different wings (*alas*), each of which features a distinct costume. The *carnavalesco* is the art director who coordinates the visual aspects of the floats (*carros alegóricos*) and the *alas* in order to elaborate upon the theme. The *puxador* is the lead singer of the *escola,* and the *mestre de bateria* is the percussion director who conducts the musicians playing a dozen or more different drum and percussion instruments. The latter typically include the *surdo* (three different sizes), *caixa, repique, tamborim, pandeiro, prato, cuíca, frigideira, agogô, reco-reco,* and *chocalho.*

The first *escola,* Deixa Falar, was founded on 12 August 1928 in Rio's Estácio neighborhood by the famed samba musicians Ismael Silva, Bide, Armando Marçal, and Nilton Bastos. Deixa Falar was defunct by 1933, but other schools rose up to take its place, such as Mangueira (founded in 1929) and Portela (1935). At the beginning, the government repressed manifestations of Afro-Brazilian culture and discouraged blacks and mulattoes from parading. But, with official recognition by the Getúlio Vargas administration in 1935, the festivities moved to the wide avenues of downtown Rio and then in 1984 to the Passarela do Samba (or Sambódromo), designed by architect Oscar Niemeyer. From the 1960s on, the *escola de samba* parades have been broadcast live on national television, which has firmly established their importance and also made them into a major tourist attraction.

By the 1970s there were complaints that the *escolas* and the parade had become too large and overly commercialized; many poorer members had to save all year to pay for their parade costumes, and the huge budgets of certain schools were often bankrolled by drug dealers or the *bicheiros* who ran illegal lotteries. Many musicians left the larger *escolas* and formed smaller groups independent of the televised festivities in the Sambodromo. One example was Quilombo, founded in 1975 by samba singer-songwriter Paulinho da Viola and composer Candeia.

Among Rio's biggest and most important *escolas* in the early 2000s were the aforementioned Mangueira and Portela, as well as Império Serrano, Salgueiro, Imperatriz Leopoldinense, Império da Tijuca, Unidos do Cabaçu, Beija-Flor, Mocidade Independente de Padre Miguel, and Vila Isabel, Unidos da Viradouro, and São Clemente.

See also **Carnival; Music: Popular Music and Dance; Samba.**

BIBLIOGRAPHY

Cabral, Sérgio. *As Escolas de Samba* (1974).

Caurio, Rita, ed. *Brasil musical* (1988).

Fernandes, Nelson da Nobrega. *Escolas de samba: Sujeitos celebrantes e objetos celebrados, Rio de Janeiro, 1928–1949*. Rio de Janeiro: Prefeitura da Cidade do Rio de Janeiro, Secretaria das Culturas, 2001.

Guillermoprieto, Alma. *Samba*. New York: Alfred A. Knopf, 1990.

McGowan, Chris, and Ricardo Pessanha. *The Brazilian Sound: Samba, Bossa Nova, and the Popular Music of Brazil* (1991).

Shaw, Lisa. *The Social History of the Brazilian Samba*. Aldershot, U.K. and Brookfield, VT: Ashgate, 1999.

CHRIS MCGOWAN

SAMBUCETTI, LUIS (NICOLÁS)

(1860–1926). Luis (Nicolás) Sambucetti (*b*. 29 July 1860; *d*. 7 September 1926), Uruguayan composer, conductor, violinist, and teacher. Born in Montevideo, Sambucetti first studied with his father, a musician, and later with Luigi Preti, who instructed him in violin, and José Strigelli, in counterpoint. He enrolled at the National Conservatory in Paris in 1885, where he studied violin with Hubert Léonard, harmony with Théodore Dubois, and composition under Ernest Guiraud, Jules Massenet, and Léo Delibes for three years. For two years

he was the concertmaster of the Chatelet Théâtre Orchestra under the baton of Édouard Colonne. In 1890 he returned to Montevideo, where he founded the Instituto Verdi, one of the major conservatories of Uruguay. He also started three chamber groups: the Cuarteto Sambucetti (1891), a second Cuarteto Sambucetti (1900), and the Sociedad de Conciertos (1911). As founder, organizer, and conductor of the Orquesta Nacional (1908), he introduced to Montevideo the contemporary symphonic repertoire, especially that of the French impressionists.

As a composer Sambucetti is considered the master of early Uruguayan symphonism. Besides his lyric poem, *San Francesco d'Assisi*, winner of a first prize and gold medal at the Milan International Fair Competition (1906), his *Suite d'orchestre*—a symphonic triptych performed at the Teatro Solís on 29 September 1899—has unique shades of orchestral color, particularly in the use of woodwind instruments. It is considered the best Uruguayan symphonic work of the nineteenth century. As a teacher and educator Sambucetti guided a whole generation of Uruguayan composers in the early twentieth century. He also wrote three operettas, orchestral and chamber music, and works for voice and piano and for violin. With his wife, the pianist María Verninck, he translated Reber-Dubois's *Harmony Treatise* and other didactic music books into Spanish. He died in Montevideo.

See also **Music: Art Music.**

BIBLIOGRAPHY

Lauro Ayestarán, *Luis Sambucetti: Vida y obra* (1956); *Composers of the Americas*, vol. 14 (1968), pp. 140–146.

Susana Salgado, *Breve historia de la música culta en el Uruguay*, 2d ed. (1980).

Additional Bibliography

Manzino, Leonardo. "La Música Uruguaya en los Festejos de 1892 con Motivo del IV Centenario del Encuentro de Dos Mundos." *Latin American Music Review/Revista de Música Latinoamericana* 14:1 (Spring, 1993): 102–130.

SUSANA SALGADO

SAME-SEX BEHAVIOR IN LATIN AMERICA. *See* Sexuality: Same-sex Behavior in Latin America, Pre-Conquest to Independence; Sexuality: Same-sex Behavior in Latin America, Modern Period.

SAMORA, JULIAN (1920–1996).

A pioneering scholar in Mexican American Studies, U.S.-Mexican border studies, and immigration studies, Samora was born on March 1, 1920, in Pagosa Springs, Colorado. He graduated from Adams State College in 1942 and in 1953 became the first Mexican American known to earn a doctorate in sociology (Washington University in St. Louis). In 1959 Samora joined the Department of Sociology at the University of Notre Dame and within a few years became a nationally recognized researcher in Mexican American studies as editor of *La Raza: Forgotten Americans* (1966), a collection of scholarly papers. His seminal 1971 study of undocumented Mexican immigration, *Los Mojados: The Wetback Story*, was the first book-length study of the phenomenon. Around the same time, Samora established the Mexican American Graduate Studies Program, the largest program of its kind in the 1970s. Samora also developed a major publication series in Mexican American Studies at Notre Dame Press. He served as board member and consultant for a number of organizations and was one of the founders of the National Council of La Raza. After his retirement in 1985 he continued to do research on Mexican American history and *mestizaje* in the American Southwest until his death on February 2, 1996.

See also **Hispanics in the United States; Migration and Migrations; United States-Mexico Border.**

BIBLIOGRAPHY

Primary Works

National Study of the Spanish-Speaking People. Washington, DC: United States Commission for Civil Rights, 1961.

As editor. *La Raza: Forgotten Americans.* Notre Dame, IN: University of Notre Dame Press, 1966.

With Ernesto Galarza and Herman Gallegos. *Mexican-Americans in the Southwest.* Santa Barbara, CA: McNally & Loftin, 1969.

With assistance of Jorge Bustamante Fernández and Gilbert Cárdenas. *Los Mojados: The Wetback Story.* Notre Dame, IN: University of Notre Dame Press, 1971.

With Patricia Vandel Simon. *A History of the Mexican-American People.* Notre Dame, IN: University of Notre Dame Press, 1977.

BARBARA DRISCOLL DE ALVARADO

SAMPER, JOSÉ MARÍA (1828–1888).

José María Samper (*b.* 31 March 1828; *d.* 22 July 1888), Colombian writer. Samper came from a mercantile family of Honda, Tolima. He received his law doctorate in Bogotá, in 1846, and plunged into politics. In his early years a Liberal with romantic socialist ideas, he began, after his second marriage (1855), to move toward more traditional political views, culminating in his return to Catholicism in 1865. Samper's abandonment of his earlier principles (added to a difficult personality) resulted in his effective exclusion from major political office until a decade before his death. It also meant that he had to earn a living by writing. His production was enormous. Poetry, drama, essays, editorials, novels, travel accounts, history, and legal treatises flowed from his pen. His autobiography, *Historia de un alma…1834 a 1881* (1881), remains a classic; so does his play *Un alcalde a la antigua y dos primos a la moderna* (1856). His reportage, *El sitio de Cartagena de 1885* (1885), and his *Ensayos sobre las revoluciones políticas de las repúblicas colombianas* (1861) are Colombian literary treasures. Samper represented Colombia in the Netherlands and Belgium (1858–1863) and in Argentina (1884). He also served several terms as a congressman. He died in Anapaima, Cundinamarca.

See also **Literature: Spanish America; López, José Hilario.**

BIBLIOGRAPHY

Frank M. Duffey, *The Early Cuadro de Costumbres in Colombia* (1956), pp. 102–106.

Harold E. Hinds, Jr., "José María Samper: The Thought of a Nineteenth-Century New Granadan during His Radical-Liberal Years (1845–1865)" (Ph.D. diss., Vanderbilt University, 1976).

Helen Delpar, *Red Against Blue* (1981), pp. 47–48, 59–60, 62–63.

Additional Bibliography

Manrique, Marco Antonio, and Alvaro Ucrós M. "Apuntes sobre el pensamiento filosófico-político de José Ma. Samper." *Franciscanum* 31:93 (September–December 1989): 237-258.

Vásquez Carrizoza, Alfredo. "José María Samper: Su vida de escritor y la Regeneración dirigida por Rafael Núñez en 1886." *Boletín de Historia y Antigüedades* 86:807 (October–December 1999): 1037–1062.

J. LEÓN HELGUERA

SAMPER AGUDELO, MIGUEL (1825–1899).

Miguel Samper Agudelo (*b.* 24 October 1825; *d.* 16 March 1899), Colombian Liberal economist and politician. Samper's devotion to liberal economic principles distinguishes him as one of Colombia's leading nineteenth-century Liberals. Born to a modest family in Guaduas, Cundinamarca, Samper was trained as a lawyer at San Bartolomé College in Bogotá. He dedicated his energies to business rather than politics and invested profitably in tobacco production and trade in the Magdalena Valley during the 1850s. His brothers, José María, Silvestre, Antonio, and Manuel, were also active in politics and commerce. Samper's liberalism is apparent in his noted social commentary *La miseria en Bogotá* (1867), his fervent support of lower tariff rates (1880), and his staunch opposition to the monetary policies of the Regeneration. Despite his economic beliefs, his social conservatism is evident in his increased devotion to Catholicism later in his life. Samper's political roles included positions in the national congress, minister of finance under two administrations, and the Liberal presidential candidate in 1897.

See also **Colombia: Since Independence.**

BIBLIOGRAPHY

Miguel Samper, *Escritos político-económicos*, 4 vols. (1925–1927), and *La miseria en Bogotá y otros escritos* (1969).

Jaime Jaramillo Uribe, *El pensamiento colombiano en el siglo XIX* (1969).

Additional Bibliography

Samper, Armando. *Miguel Samper: Su personalidad y su pensamiento.* Colombia: Tres Culturas Editores, 1994.

DAVID SOWELL

SAMUDIO, JUAN A. (1879–1936).

Juan A. Samudio (*b.* 21 April 1879; *d.* 1936), Paraguayan artist. Often considered the finest Paraguayan painter of the twentieth century, Samudio was a native-born Asunceño. Though he received his early education in the capital city, he was irresistibly drawn to painting—an interest that he could little hope to pursue if he stayed in Paraguay. Thanks to a scholarship, he went to Rome in 1903 for five years of study.

In Italy, Samudio developed a painting style characterized by a careful interplay of shadows. He limited himself to traditional subjects and avoided the avant garde, but his work nonetheless received a measure of acclaim. He was already winning prizes while still a student in Rome. In 1910 he exhibited two canvasses at the International Exposition of Art in Buenos Aires. One of these, entitled *Noche de luna*, brought the artist a bronze medal and was later acquired by the National Museum in Asunción.

After his return to Paraguay, Samudio dedicated himself as much to teaching and to artistic theory as to painting. He became director of the Paraguayan Academy of Fine Arts, a position he held throughout the 1920s. He also cooperated with the municipal government of Asunción in the design of public parks and gardens.

See also **Art: The Nineteenth Century.**

BIBLIOGRAPHY

William Belmont Parker, *Paraguayans of To-Day* (1921), pp. 134–136.

Rafael Eladio Velázquez, *Breve historia de la cultura en el Paraguay* (1984), p. 246.

THOMAS L. WHIGHAM

SANABRIA MARTÍNEZ, VÍCTOR M. (1898–1952).

Víctor M. Sanabria Martínez (*b.* 17 January 1898; *d.* 8 June 1952), archbishop of San José, Costa Rica (1940–1952).

Archbishop Sanabria's advocacy of social justice and his political role in the 1940s make him the most famous, popular, and controversial twentieth-century Costa Rican prelate. He rose from humble beginnings to become a well-educated, "people's" priest who addressed the issues that moved his nation during the tumultuous decade 1940–1950. As the established leader of the Costa Rican church, he committed his institution to the social reforms called for in the papal encyclical *Rerum Novarum*. He studied civil and canon law in Rome and returned to San José with an earned doctorate in canon law.

Sanabria wrote extensively on church history. He also produced a multivolume genealogy of

Cartago that elicited almost as much controversy as his social activism because it brought to light so many details that the residents of that patriarchal city wished to maintain in obscurity.

Sanabria was appointed the second archbishop of San José in March 1940, the same year in which his friend Dr. Rafael Ángel Calderón Guardia (1940–1944) was inaugurated. These two young leaders shared the deep conviction that their nation needed profound social change based on church teachings in order to ensure social justice and progress. Somewhat the older, Sanabria came to political prominence as a mentor to the president. Together they worked to pass a sweeping program of legislation that culminated in the amendment of the constitution to include social guarantees, such as social security insurance, an eight-hour workday, minimum wage, the right to organize trade unions and to form cooperatives, and the basic right to human dignity.

Sanabria publicly advocated the government's reform program and indirectly sanctioned its political alliance with the Popular Vanguard Party (PVP), a communist party. Sanabria was criticized by conservative Catholics at home, and he was denied entry to Guatemala because of his political orientation. He played an active role in organizing Catholic labor unions to rival those organized by the communists.

Sanabria tried valiantly but in vain to mediate the political crisis following the 1948 election. He helped protect president-elect Otilio Ulate Blanco (1949–1953) and he participated in the mediations that led to the cessation of the armed conflict.

His active role in a time of change and conflict made Sanabria a towering but controversial personage. His accomplishments were recognized after his death, when he was named Benemérito de la Patria by the national congress in 1959.

See also **Costa Rica.**

BIBLIOGRAPHY

Ricardo Blanco Segura, *Monseñor Sanabria* (1962).

Franklin D. Parker, *The Central American Republics* (1964).

John Patrick Bell, *Crisis in Costa Rica* (1971).

Richard Biesanz, Karen Zubris Biesanz, and Mavis Hiltunen Biesanz, *The Costa Ricans* (1982; rev. ed. 1988).

Additional Bibliography

Creedman, Theodore S. *El gran cambio: De León Cortés a Calderón Guardia*. San José: Editorial Costa Rica, 1996.

Rosales Blandino, José Francisco. *Los laicos en el magisterio eclesiológico de Monseñor Victor Manuel Sanabria Martínez Arzobispo de San José de Costa Rica (1940–1952)*. Rome: Pontificia Studiorum Universitas a S. Thoma Aq in Urbe, 2004.

Solís, Javier. *La herencia de Sanabria: Análisis político de la iglesia costarricense*. San José: Departmento Ecuménico de Investigaciones, 1983.

JOHN PATRICK BELL

SAN AGUSTÍN. San Agustín, archaeological region located at the headwaters of the Magdalena River in southern Colombia. Containing evidence of statuary and artificial mounds, San Agustín and neighboring areas have been the focus of intensive archaeological research. Human occupation of the area probably dates back to before 1000 BCE, but evidence is still scarce. In the Valle de la Plata, to the south of where the construction of the most impressive statues and mounds took place, archaeological research has allowed the reconstruction of three periods of pre-Columbian development. Since ceramic materials found in La Plata and in San Agustín are similar, and chronological periodization is comparable, results from La Plata help to reconstruct patterns of social evolution in the Upper Magdalena in general.

By the Early Period (1000 BCE–1 CE) the population was concentrated in areas of fertile soil where conditions favored agriculture with simple technologies. The population density was low. Little is known in terms of social organization and trade activities. During the Middle Period (1–850 CE) there was strong population growth; the total number of people in the area doubled. Two concentrations of population correspond to areas where monumental sculpture and barrows were found, suggesting increasing political centralization. This period also marks the peak of sculpture in San Agustín. Pollen analysis indicates that maize, potato, sweet potato, quinoa, and beans were cultivated at this time. There is also evidence of gold trade, and probably of gold adornments production, but at a small scale when compared with other southern Colombian societies such as Calima.

The Late Period (850–1530 CE) represents a continuation of population growth. At one of the large sites that emerged during the previous period, funerary monuments were found. The monuments investigated are less impressive than those of the Middle Period, inasmuch as the tombs are now deep narrow shafts. Pottery and goldwork of this time are simpler than that of previous periods. At the time of the Spanish Conquest, populations of the region are described as small chiefdoms with little political centralization compared with other societies in northern South America, such as the Muisca. As of yet, it is not clear if processes of social change implied the decadence of regional elites before the Conquest. It is just as possible that chiefly status in the region was displayed by means other than the construction of splendid monuments.

See also **Archaeology.**

BIBLIOGRAPHY

Luis Duque and Julio César Cubillos, *Arqueología de San Agustín: Alto de Lavapatas* (1988). Also see Gerardo Reichel-Dolmatoff, *San Agustín: A Culture of Colombia* (1972). For research conducted in the Valle de la Plata see Robert Drennan, "Regional Dynamics of Chiefdoms in the Valle de la Plata," in *Journal of Field Archaeology* (1991).

Additional Bibliography

Duque Gómez, Luis. *San Agustín, Colombia: Patrimonio de la humanidad.* Bogotá: Editorial Arco, 2000.

Duque Gómez, Luis, and Julio César Cubillos. *Arqueología de San Agustín: Exploraciones arqueológicas realizadas en el Alto de las Piedras (1975-1976.)* Bogotá: Fundación de Investigaciones Arqueológicas Nacionales, Banco de la República, 1993.

Pinto Nolla, María, and Héctor Llanos Vargas. *Las industrias líticas de San Agustín.* Bogotá: Fundación de Investigaciones Arqueológicas Nacionales, Banco de la República, 1997.

CARL HENRIK LANGEBAEK R.

SAN ANDRÉS.

San Andrés (Campana San Andrés), the primary regional center for the Zapotitán Valley in central El Salvador during the Late Classic period (650–900 CE). The site is located west of San Salvador, in the eastern part of the Zapotitán Valley, along the upper Río Sucio drainage. San Andrés covers approximately six square miles and includes about sixty mounds. Over 200 mounds are clustered around the site center.

San Andrés was first settled in the Preclassic period (400 BCE–250 CE). Little is known about this initial occupation. The Ilopango volcano, just east of San Salvador, erupted violently about 250 CE, depositing a thick layer of ash over the site that rendered the area uninhabitable.

During the Late Classic, San Andrés was reoccupied and reached its zenith in size and power. Stylistically it is most strongly associated with the major Maya center of Copán, in southwestern Honduras, and with Tazumal, in the Chalchuapa region of western El Salvador. Artifacts such as Copador polychrome ceramics, pyrite mirrors, and finely carved jadeite suggest connections with these major Maya centers. The architectural plan of San Andrés is comparable to that of Copán, especially in its plaza-acropolis arrangement. The balustraded stairways at San Andrés are reminiscent of those at Tazumal and Copán.

Mound construction is of two types: adobe block cores, with wall facings and floors covered with mortar, as at Tazumal, and talpetate masonry walls covered with mortar. San Andrés structures included terraced pyramidal temples, residences, and walled courts. The majority of construction took place during the Late Classic period.

Postclassic (900–1400 CE) occupation of San Andrés, evinced by artifacts such as Nicoya polychrome ceramics, was sparse. Thus, it appears that San Andrés was heavily occupied for only the brief span of the Late Classic period, then was largely abandoned.

See also **Archaeology.**

BIBLIOGRAPHY

Maurice Ries, "First Season's Archaeological Work at Campana–San Andrés, El Salvador," in *American Anthropologist* 42 (1940): 712–713.

John M. Dimick, "Notes on Excavations at Campana–San Andrés, El Salvador," in *Carnegie Institution of Washington Yearbook* 40 (1941): 298–300.

Stanley H. Boggs, "Notas sobre las excavaciones en la hacienda 'San Andres,' departmento de La Libertad," in *Tzumpame* 3, no. 1 (1943): 104–126.

John M. Longyear III, "Archaeological Survey of El Salvador," in *Handbook of Middle American Indians,*

Vol. 4, *Archaeological Frontiers and External Connections,* edited by Gordon Ekholm and Gordon Willey (1966).

Additional Bibliography

Fowler, William R., and Stanley A. South. *Arqueología histórica de la Villa de San Salvador, El Salvador: Informe de las excavaciones (1996–2003.)* Columbia: South Carolina Institute of Archaeology and Anthropology, 2006.

Sheets, Payson D. *Before the Volcano Erupted: The Ancient Cerén Village in Central America.* Austin: University of Texas, 2002.

Sheets, Payson D. *The Cerén Site: An Ancient Village Buried by Volcanic Ash in Central America.* Belmont, CA: Thomson Higher Education, 2006.

KATHRYN SAMPECK

SAN ANDRÉS ISLAND.

San Andrés is the largest and most populous of the islands comprising the Colombian department of San Andrés y Providencia, located slightly more than a hundred miles east of Nicaragua and about four hundred miles northwest of Cartagena, Colombia. There was no permanent colonization of San Andrés until the eighteenth century, when settlers arrived from Jamaica, closely connecting the island to other British settlements on the Mosquito Coast of Nicaragua. Spanish claims to the islands were recognized in the Convention of London in 1786, but a strong African-English cultural and economic influence remains. Colombia claimed the islands in 1810, although Nicaragua maintains a claim.

San Andrés was declared a free port in 1953, greatly increasing its economic activity, and an airport was built in 1955. San Andrés' population has grown slowly from about 3,000 in 1900 to over 100,000 in 2006. Over 60 percent are Spanish-speaking Colombians.

See also **Drugs and Drug Trade; Nicaragua.**

BIBLIOGRAPHY

Morren, R. C. "Creole-Based Trilingual Education in the Caribbean Archipelago of San Andre's, Providence and Santa Catalina," *Journal of Multilingual and Multicultural Development,* 22:3 (2002): 227–241.

ANTHONY P. MAINGOT

SAN ANTONIO.

San Antonio, a presidio–mission-town complex founded in 1718, as a way station between Spanish settlements on the Río Grande and the recently founded Spanish outpost on the French Louisiana frontier. Originally composed of Presidio San Antonio de Béxar and Misión San Antonio de Valero (now the Alamo), the settlement was enlarged in 1720 with the addition of a second Franciscan mission, San José y San Miguel de Aguayo, and in 1731 by the relocation of three other missions, Nuestra Señora de la Purísima Concepción, San Juan Capistrano, and San Francisco de la Espada. That same year Canary Islands colonists, holding a royal charter, founded Villa San Fernando de Béxar adjacent to the presidio and Misión San Antonio.

San Antonio grew slowly through the 1760s because of chronic Indian warfare, an absence of mineral wealth, and remoteness from colonial population centers. Throughout the colonial and Mexican periods the economy depended on cattle ranching, subsistence agriculture, and the furnishing of services to the presidio. In the 1770s, as part of a reform of New Spain's frontier defenses, the garrison was strengthened and the population augmented by the resettlement of settlers from the extinguished East Texas presidio of Los Adaes. In 1773 San Antonio became the capital of Texas, a position it maintained until its status was reduced to departmental seat of government following the union of Texas with Coahuila under the Mexican constitution of 1824.

During the Mexican War of Independence the city experienced outbreaks of violence and brief insurrectionary governments in 1811 and 1813. In the 1820s secularization of the missions, which had begun in 1793, was completed. The presidio went out of existence in the spring of 1836, following the successful Texan revolt against Mexico, but the town survived as the largest Texas city for much of the nineteenth century.

Today San Antonio is the second-largest city in Texas with a 2005 population of over 1.2 million. The city is home to a number of military bases, including Fort Sam Houston and Lackland Air Force Base. Almost 20 million tourists visit San Antonio each year, drawn by its Tejano culture, the Alamo, Riverwalk, and the Marion Koogler McNay Art Museum.

See also **Alamo, Battle of the; Texas.**

BIBLIOGRAPHY

Castañeda, Carlos E. *Our Catholic Heritage in Texas,* 7 vols. (1936–1958).

Crisp, James E. *Sleuthing the Alamo: Davy Crockett's Last Stand and Other Mysteries of the Texas Revolution.* New York: Oxford University Press, 2005.

De La Teja, Jesús F. *San Antonio de Béxar: A Community on New Spain's Frontier* (1995).

Matovina, Timothy M. *Tejano Religion and Ethnicity: San Antonio, 1821–1860.* Austin: University of Texas Press, 1995.

JESÚS F. DE LA TEJA

SAN CARLOS DE GUATEMALA, UNIVERSITY OF.

The University of San Carlos de Guatemala was begun with a legacy left by Francisco Marroquín, first bishop of Guatemala, who endowed the College of Saint Thomas, attached to the Dominican convent in Guatemala City. The town council at once tried to raise the college to the status of a university, but encountered financial problems and bureaucratic delays. In 1622, the Jesuits secured the right to confer degrees in their own college, further complicating the town council's efforts. It was only in 1676 that a combination of a fortunate legacy and patient maneuvering finally induced the crown to authorize a public university, named for the then reigning Charles II.

The new foundation followed the pattern used at the University of Salamanca by confiding governance to the body of doctors and masters in residence (called the Cloister) led by a rector elected annually from its members. Both were subject to crown authority through the captain-general. Faculty positions were filled by *oposiciones,* contests of specimen lectures, given before a body of judges. Winners of the *oposiciones* filled junior chairs for a term of years, and senior (proprietary) posts were held for life. The faculty consisted of nine to twelve professors at a time. Between 1625 and 1821 2,006 students received bachelor's degrees and 504 earned advanced degrees.

The university's economic base was always fragile. Guatemala was a poor area, and the crown adamantly resisted using any of its monies for education. In addition, relations between the University and the Jesuits remained delicate. Until their expulsion in 1767, the Jesuits continued to grant degrees and enjoyed a high reputation for their instruction.

San Carlos, like other Hispanic universities, exemplified and exalted the neoscholastic learning of sixteenth-century Spain. But again in common with others, the curriculum had become stale and routine by the first decades of the eighteenth century, and demands for reform emerged.

In 1784 a Dominican professor, newly arrived from Spain, officially accused his colleagues of laxity and backwardness. The responses to these charges showed that quiet changes had been going on for a decade or more. For example, the Franciscan José Antonio Goicoechea had taught experimental physics since about 1770. Goicoechea and others submitted plans of reform, and over the next three decades there was a ferment of new projects and ideas. These included incorporating mathematics and up-to-date geography and cosmography in the curriculum, introducing experimental (Newtonian) physics, and shifting the theology curriculum to emphasize scripture study, dogmatic theology, and moral philosophy at the expense of speculative scholasticism. A strong regalist impulse was imposed on law studies, with great emphasis on the power and authority of the crown and the importance of Spanish law. Finally, the study of medicine was made current by new texts, anatomical studies, and training in botany and chemistry.

These reforms in the university were encouraged and paralleled by the actions of a coterie of government officials, professors, clerics, students, and prominent citizens who clustered around the Sociedad Económica De Amigos Del País and wrote in the Gazeta De Guatemala. They clearly had access to new books and benefited from contact with two visiting scientific expeditions. The *Gazeta* discussed such questions as the wisdom of replacing Latin with Spanish as the language of the schools, advocated sensationalist psychology, and considered various plans to improve the lot of the Indians as well as numerous other economic questions.

The political and intellectual significance of the university and the impact of the intellectual changes made after 1780 is best indicated by the fact that nine of the thirteen signers of the 1821 declaration of Guatemalan independence were graduates of San Carlos.

See also **Dominicans; Enlightenment, The; Universities: Colonial Spanish America.**

BIBLIOGRAPHY

The definitive study is John Tate Lanning's twin volumes, *The University in the Kingdom of Guatemala* (1955) and *The Eighteenth-Century Enlightenment in the University of San Carlos de Guatemala* (1956). Lanning's *Academic Culture in the Spanish Colonies* (1940) provides a general comparative picture.

Additional Bibliography

Cazali Avila, Augusto. *Historia de la Universidad de San Carlos de Guatemala, época republicana (1821-1994)*. 3 vols. Guatemala: Editorial Universitaria, Universidad de San Carlos de Guatemala, 1997.

Kobrak, Paul. *Organizing and Repression in the University of San Carlos, Guatemala, 1944-1996*. Washington, DC: American Association for the Advancement of Science: Centro Internacional para Investigaciones en Derechos Humanos, 1999.

Pattridge, Blake D. *Institution Building and State Formation in Nineteenth-Century Latin America: The University of San Carlos, Guatemala*. New York: P. Lang, 2004.

GEORGE M. ADDY

SÁNCHEZ, CUCO (1921–2000).

Refugio "Cuco" Sánchez was a popular and prolific Mexican songwriter as well as a singer and actor. One of his most famous songs is "Mi Chata" (My sweetheart), which he composed at the age of eight. Born in Altamira, Tamaulipas, on May 3, 1921, he went to Mexico City as a young man and began a career as a singer-songwriter and actor, appearing in many movies during the 1950s and 1960s. Sánchez's famous bolero "Fallaste Corazón" (Broken heart), first released in 1954, continues to be performed and recorded by Mexican and Latino singers. Several of his *rancheras* were also popular hits of the 1950s. In the 1960s Sánchez continued to have success with several songs, including his original and famous composition of 1964, "Anillo de Compromiso" (Engagement ring). His last year as a composer was 1970, with "Arbol Seco" (Dry tree), "La Herfanita" (The little orphan), "Me Desgracié" (I'm disgraced), and "Nuestro Gran Amor" (Our great love). He appeared in several TV shows from the 1970s through the 1990s. In addition to his status as a beloved performer, Sánchez is the Mexican composer with the greatest number of songs used in cinema. He died in Mexico City on October 5, 2000.

See also **Music: Popular Music and Dance.**

PETER GARCIA

SÁNCHEZ, FLORENCIO (1875–1910).

Florencio Sánchez (*b.* 17 January 1875; *d.* 2 November 1910), Uruguayan playwright. Born in Montevideo and raised in the interior, Sánchez, one of eleven children, left high school to help support his family. He worked as a clerk, wrote theater reviews and articles for small-town newspapers, and acted in amateur plays. He fought with the caudillo Aparicio Saravia against President Juan Idiarte Borda, an experience that inspired his work *El caudillaje criminal en Sudamérica* (Criminal Caudillo Rule in South America [1914]). Disillusioned with traditional politics, Sánchez became interested in the anarchist movement; his earliest plays were presented in anarchist recreation centers.

Working for newspapers such as *La República* in Rosario, Argentina, Sánchez attained recognition with his muckraking play *El canillita* (The Newspaperboy), which was performed on 2 October 1904. He lost his job as a result of his anarchist activities. In ill health, he accepted a friend's invitation to spend time in the Argentine countryside. The sojourn inspired Sánchez's famous rural plays *La gringa* (The Immigrant Girl [1904]), *M'hijo el dotor* (My Son the Lawyer [1903]), and *Barranca abajo* (Down the Gully [1905]). He then moved to Buenos Aires, where he worked feverishly on a succession of plays and married, but he continued his bohemian life of much drinking and little sleep.

With a sharp ear for dialogue, Sánchez's plays depicted racial antagonism between the native *criollos* and the immigrants. A social activist, Sánchez used theater as a vehicle to educate the public about poverty and the plight of people in urban tenements. His play, *Nuestros hijos* (Our Children [1907]), influenced progressive legislation enacted in Uruguay. On the verge of bankruptcy and struggling with depression and tuberculosis, Sánchez received a grant from the Uruguayan government to survey Italian theater. He died in Milan shortly after his arrival.

See also **Anarchism and Anarchosyndicalism; Theater.**

BIBLIOGRAPHY

Roberto Fernando Giusti, *Florencio Sánchez: Su vida y su obra* (1920).

Ruth Richardson, *Florencio Sánchez and the Argentine Theater* (1933).

Karl Eastman Shedd, *Florencio Sánchez's Debt to Eugène Brieux* (1936).

Fernando García Esteban, *Vida de Florencio Sánchez: Con cartas inéditas del insigne dramaturgo* (1939).

Florencio Sánchez, *Representative Plays of Florencio Sánchez,* translated by Willis Knapp Jones (1961).

Walter Rela, *Florencio Sánchez: Persona y teatro* (1967).

Vladimirio Muñoz, *Florencio Sánchez: A Chronology,* translated by Scott Jacobesen (1980).

Additional Bibliography

Castro, Griselda. *Sainetes: Análisis de obras de Florencio Sánchez y Armando Discépolo.* Montevideo: Editorial Técnica, 1988.

Detoca, Anastasia. *Estética e ideología en el teatro de Florencio Sánchez.* Montevideo: Ediciones del CEHU, 2003.

Pellettieri, Osvaldo, and Roger Mirza. *Florencio Sánchez entre las dos orillas.* Buenos Aires: Galerna, 1998.

Rosso, Ignacio. *Anatomía de un genio: Florencio Sánchez.* Montevideo: Ediciones de la Casa del Estudiante, 1988.

GEORGETTE MAGASSY DORN

SÁNCHEZ, LUIS ALBERTO (1900–1994).

Luis Alberto Sánchez (*b.* 12 October 1900; *d.* 6 February 1994), Peruvian literary historian and politician. Sánchez received doctorates in literature (1922) and law (1925) from the University of San Marcos, where he taught Latin American literature for forty years and served three times as president (1946–1949, 1961–1963, 1966–1969). After joining the Peruvian Aprista Party in 1931, he was elected to two Constituent Assemblies (1932, 1978–1979), the Chamber of Deputies (1945–1948), the Senate (1963–1968, 1980–1992), and the vice presidency

of the Republic (1985–1990), and served as acting president of the country on several occasions from 1985 to 1990. During two decades as a political exile, Sánchez was literary editor of *Ercilla* in Chile and visiting professor in several universities, including Columbia and the Sorbonne. In 1980 he was elected a member of the Peruvian Academy of the Spanish Language and corresponding member of the Spanish Royal Academy. Sánchez, one of the most prolific Peruvian writers of his time, wrote more than sixty books, including *La literatura peruana* (5 vols., 1982), *Historia comparada de las literaturas americanas* (4 vols., 1973–1976), and *Perú: Nuevo retrato de un país adolescente* (Lima, 1981). He died in Lima.

See also **Literature: Spanish America.**

BIBLIOGRAPHY

Eugenio Chang-Rodríguez, "¿Tuvimos maestros en nuestra América?" in *Hispania* 40 (1957): 251–253; *Homenaje a Luis Alberto Sánchez* (1960).

Donald C. Henderson and Grace R. Pérez, eds., *Literature and Politics in Latin America* (1982); *Homenaje a Luis Alberto Sánchez* (1983).

Additional Bibliography

Alva Castro, Luis, et al. *Cien años de Luis Alberto Sánchez: Homenaje del Congreso de la República.* Lima: Fondo Editorial del Congreso del Perú, 2001.

Alva Castro, Luis, editor. *Múltiples miradas de Luis Alberto Sánchez sobre el Perú contemporáneo.* Lima: Fondo Editorial del Congreso del Perú, 2002.

Benavides Correa, Alfonso. *Luis Alberto Sánchez, el oncenio de Leguía.* Lima: 1994.

EUGENIO CHANG-RODRÍGUEZ

SÁNCHEZ, LUIS RAFAEL (1936–).

Luis Rafael Sánchez (*b.* 1936), Puerto Rican playwright, story writer, essayist, and novelist. Born in Humacao and educated at the University of Puerto Rico (B.A., 1960), Columbia University (M.A., 1963), and the Central University of Mexico (Ph.D., 1966), Sánchez was recognized as a talented young actor and playwright in the late 1950s and early 1960s. He emerged shortly thereafter, the first major voice of a new literary generation, as an equally inventive and critically probing fictional observer of contemporary

Puerto Rican life and experience. Beginning with *La espera* (1958; The Wait), *Los ángeles se han fatigado* (1960; The Angels Have Become Weary), *La hiel nuestra de cada día* (1962; Our Daily Bile), and more recently, with *Quíntuples* (1985), he examines the insular and more broadly Hispanic American predicament of a dependent society confronted by an often fraudulent and lethal "modernity" as well as the delusions, poses, moral complicity, and uncertain personas assumed by different participants in a poignant national drama. His most widely celebrated play, *La pasión según Antígona Pérez: Crónica americana en dos actos* (1968), reimagines the classical Greek heroine as a twenty five year old mestiza condemned to death by the dictator of a paradigmatic Latin American republic for her dissenting ideas and identification with "those of us growing up in a harsh America, a bitter America, a captured America" (*La pasión según Antígona Pérez* [1973], p. 14).

Sánchez's first collection of stories, *En cuerpo de camisa* (1966), demonstrates his singularly keen ear and eye for the various inflections and social and psychological textures of island life. He especially captures the furtive, taboo worlds of the delinquent, socially alienated, sexually outcast, misfit, and derelict that are produced by a still-colonial society, its failed social policies, clash of classes, prudishness, crude machismo, and pretentious mimicry. *La guaracha del Macho Camacho* (1976) and *La importancia de llamarse Daniel Santos* (1989), his only published novels to date, confirm their author's analytical acuity, thematic daring, and linguistic and formal virtuosity. Powerful repositories of his characters' universe of meaning and an irrepressible popular ethos, language and music ultimately emerge as organizing metaphors for a miscegenated, culturally syncretic creole sensibility of stubborn ubiquity and resilience, despite both internal and external assault. Empathetic recognition of this defining resilience in the "commuting" experience and shifting spaces of Puerto Rican (im)migrants to (and from) the United States is more evident in his later than in his earlier essays and short fiction.

A member of the faculty of the University of Puerto Rico and the most celebrated Puerto Rican writer of his generation, Sánchez has produced many other works, including the plays *Farsa del amor compradito* (1960), *Sol 13, interior* (1961),

and *O casi el alma* (1969); the popular short story "La guagua aérea," (1983) (made into an equally popular film in the early 1990s); *Ventana interior*, an unpublished book of verse; the monograph *Fabulación e ideología en la cuentística de Emilio S. Belaval* (1979); and a collection of selected essays, commentaries, and reviews also entitled *La guagua aérea* (1994). He is a professor emeritus at the University of Puerto Rico and at the City University of New York. Sánchez has also been politically active. In January 2006, along with other internationally known Latin Americans, such as Gabriel García Márquez, Eduardo Galeano, and Pablo Milanés, he demanded sovereignty for Puerto Rico by signing the Proclamation for the Independence of Puerto Rico.

See also **Literature: Spanish America; Theater.**

BIBLIOGRAPHY

Barradas, Efraín. *Para leer en puertorriqueño: Acercamiento a la obra de Luis Rafael Sánchez* (1981).

Colón Zayas, Eliseo R. *El teatro de Luis Rafael Sánchez* (1985).

Figueroa, Alvin Joaquín. *La prosa de Rafael Sánchez: Texto y contexto*. New York: P. Lang, 1989.

Hernández Vargas, Nélida, and Daisy Caraballo Abréu. *Luis Rafael Sánchez, crítica y bibliografía*. Río Piedras: Editorial de la Universidad de Puerto Rico, 1985.

Nouhaud, Dorita. *Luis Rafael Sánchez: Dramaturge, romancier, et essayiste porto–ricain*. Paris: L'Harmattan, 2001.

Perivolaris, John Dimitri. *Puerto Rican Cultural Identity and the Work of Luis Rafael Sanchez*. Chapel Hill: University of North Carolina, Department of Romance Languages, 2000.

ROBERTO MÁRQUEZ

SÁNCHEZ, PRISCILIANO (1783–1826).

Prisciliano Sánchez (*b*. 4 January 1783; *d*. 30 December 1826), Mexican federalist leader and first governor of Jalisco. Born in the village of Ahuacatlán, Nueva Galicia province, Sánchez's parents died when he was young. After largely educating himself, Sánchez entered Guadalajara's Conciliary Seminary (1804). He briefly took the Franciscan habit, later studying law. During Hidalgo's revolution (1810), Sánchez served in various municipal positions in Compostela, where he was known to sympathize with the insurgent cause.

After independence Sánchez helped make Jalisco a federalist center. He served in the first Mexican congress (Iturbide period) and in 1823 published his influential Federal Pact (Pacto Federal de Anáhuac). In the Constitutional Congress (1823–1824) and as Jalisco's governor (1826), Sánchez helped frame federalist measures, notably the personal contribution tax and Article 7, which made Catholicism the state religion.

See also **Mexico: 1810–1910.**

BIBLIOGRAPHY

Luis Perez Verdía, *Biografías: Fray Antonio Alcalde, Priscilliano Sánchez* (1981).

Additional Bibliography

Cuevas Contreras, Marco Antonio. *Reivindicación de don Prisciliano Sánchez: Precursor del federalismo mexicano y fundador del estado de Jalisco.* Guadalajara: Ayuntamiento Constitucional de Guadalajara, 2003.

STANLEY GREEN

SÁNCHEZ CERRO, LUIS MANUEL

(1889–1933). Luis Manuel Sánchez Cerro (*b.* 1889; *d.* 1933), military officer and president of Peru (1930–1931, 1931–1933). The politically ambitious Sánchez Cerro, who was born in Piura, participated in three military uprisings between 1914 and 1931. The first ousted President Guillermo Billinghurst. The second, in 1922, was an unsuccessful rebellion against President Augusto Leguía in Cuzco. Imprisoned for his participation, Sánchez Cerro later was allowed to serve in the Ministry of War and to advance his training in Spain. Finally, Lieutenant Colonel Sánchez Cerro led the military putsch that ousted Leguía in August 1930. Opposition within the armed forces, however, forced Sánchez Cerro to resign in March 1931. Back from exile and embracing the support of the fascist Revolutionary Union, he claimed victory after the general elections of October 1931. As constitutional president he unleashed a harsh political and military repression of the opposition Aprista Party led by Víctor Raúl Haya De La Torre. Aprista members

conspired to assassinate Sánchez Cerro, failing in 1932 and succeeding in Lima in 1933.

See also **Peru: Since Independence.**

BIBLIOGRAPHY

Carlos Miró Quesada Laos, *Sánchez Cerro y su tiempo* (1947).

Daniel Masterson, *Militarism and Politics in Latin America: Peru from Sánchez Cerro to "Sendero Luminoso"* (1991).

Additional Bibliography

Adrianzén, Alberto, editor. *Pensamiento político peruano, 1930–1968.* Lima: DESCO, 1990.

González Calleja, Eduardo. "La derecha latinoamericana en busca de un modelo fascista: La limitada influencia del falangismo en el Perú, 1936–1945." *Revista Complutense de Historia de América* 20 (1994): 229–255.

ALFONSO W. QUIROZ

SÁNCHEZ DE BUSTAMANTE Y SIRVEN, ANTONIO

(1865–1951). Antonio Sánchez de Bustamante y Sirven (*b.* 13 April 1865; *d.* 24 August 1951), Cuban jurist and politician. A professor of international law at the University of Havana, Bustamante achieved widespread prestige and distinction as an orator and the author of numerous scholarly books that were translated into many languages, including Turkish and modern Greek. Upon the inauguration of the Cuban republic in 1902, he was elected to the Cuban Senate, serving several terms. In 1922 he was chosen as one of the first eleven justices who sat on the Permanent Court of International Justice established at The Hague, and in 1929 he was chosen for a second term. His most celebrated contribution to international law, however, was the Code of International Private Law (known as the Bustamante Code), approved by the Sixth International Conference of American States that met in Havana in 1928 and subsequently ratified by fifteen member states. Accused of supporting the Machado dictatorship (1925–1933), he was exonerated and continued to teach international law until his death.

See also **Pan-American Conferences: Havana Conference (1928).**

BIBLIOGRAPHY

For a short biography of Bustamante see José I. Lasaga, *Cuban Lives: Pages from Cuban History,* vol. 2 (1988), pp. 397–409; also, Otto Schoenrich, "Dr. Antonio Sánchez de Bustamante," in *The American Journal of International Law* 45 (1951): 746–749.

JOSÉ W. HERNÁNDEZ

SÁNCHEZ DE LOZADA BUSTAMANTE, GONZALO (1930–).

Twice elected president, Gonzalo Sánchez de Lozada engineered Bolivia's modern economic reforms but resigned his office when faced with intransigent public opposition in 2003. Nicknamed "Goni," he was born in La Paz but raised and educated in the United States. After receiving a degree from the University of Chicago, he returned to Bolivia and started several enterprises during his business career. Most successful among them was COMSUR, a mining company that made him a millionaire. He began his political career during Bolivia's tortured transition to democracy, running for the lower house in 1979 with Victor Paz Estenssoro's Nationalist Revolutionary Movement (MNR) party. Political instability prevented the members from taking their seats until 1982, but thereafter Sánchez de Lozada established himself as an outspoken opposition leader. In 1985 he was elected senator, chosen to be chamber president, and then named minister of planning and coordination in the Paz government. He was one of the architects of Paz's neoliberal New Economic Policy, including decree 21060, the "shock therapy" program of economic stabilization. Despite the controversial change in the MNR's historic economic platform, the program ended Bolivia's hyperinflation, and Sánchez de Lozada was rewarded with the MNR's nomination for president in 1989. Although he edged out a plurality in the first round, an agreement between two opposing parties gave the second-round vote in congress to Jaime Paz Zamora. Sánchez de Lozada became leader of the MNR in 1990 and ran again as its candidate in 1993, this time winning a third of the popular vote and the second-round vote in congress. His administration's centerpiece was the "Plan for Everyone," which implemented a form of privatization that gave citizens shares in newly private enterprises ("capitalization") and an extensive decentralization program that included citizen oversight mechanisms ("popular participation"). Constitutionally limited to nonconsecutive terms, he could not compete in 1997 but did so in 2002, campaigning with television journalist and political independent Carlos Diego Mesa Gisbert. The vote was extremely close, with Sánchez de Lozada beating by less than 2 percent radical coca growers' leader Evo Morales, who in turn barely edged out populist Manfred Reyes Villa. Although the former presidentwon the second round, the rising popularity of Morales represented a problem for Sánchez de Lozada. By this point, public opinion had turned against the neoliberal economic model that he helped implement. Facing pressure from Washington, moreover, he pledged to continue his predecessors' coca eradication programs, thus earning him the animosity of Morales's followers. Furthermore, proposals to allow foreign corporations to exploit Bolivia's enormous natural gas reserves and export it through Chile sparked widespread protests in September and October of 2003. These culminated in clashes with security forces that left scores dead. As a result, he lost the support of his vice president and his coalition fell apart. Severely weakened, Sánchez de Lozada resigned on October 17, 2003, and went to live in the United States. He faces numerous indictments in Bolivia issued by the Morales government.

See also **Bolivia, Political Parties: Nationalist Revolutionary Movement (MNR); Morales, Evo; Paz Zamora, Jaime; Reyes Villa, Manfred.**

BIBLIOGRAPHY

Barr, Robert R. "Bolivia: Another Uncompleted Revolution?" *Latin American Politics and Society* 47, no. 3 (2005): 69–90.

Gray-Molina, George, Ernesto Pérez de Rada, and Ernest Yañez. *La economía política de reformas institucionales en Bolivia.* Working Paper R-350. Washington, DC: Inter-American Development Bank, 1999.

Grindle, Merilee S. "Shadowing the Past? Policy Reform in Bolivia, 1985–2002." In *Proclaiming Revolution: Bolivia in Comparative Perspective,* edited by Merliee S. Grindle and Pilar Domingo. Cambridge, MA: David Rockefeller Center for Latin American Studies, Harvard University, 2003.

ROBERT R. BARR

SÁNCHEZ DE TAGLE, FRANCISCO MANUEL (1782–1847).

Francisco Manuel Sánchez de Tagle (*b.* 11 January 1782; *d.* 17 December 1847), a politician. In 1794 Sánchez, a native of Valladolid, entered the Colegio de San Juan de Letrán in Mexico City. He received a bachelor's degree in philosophy and theology and was appointed to the chair of philosophy in 1803. He was active in politics, becoming *regidor perpetuo* of the Ayuntamiento of Mexico from 1805 to 1812 and from 1815 to 1820. Because of his autonomist leanings, Sánchez became a member of the secret society Los Guadalupes, and he participated in the elections resulting from the Constitution of Cádiz; he was elected constitutional *regidor* in 1813 and in 1820. In 1821 he signed the Declaration of Independence, and he was a member of the Provisional Governing Junta. Sánchez remained active in politics after independence; he was elected deputy on various occasions as well as senator, vice governor of the state of Mexico, governor of the state of Michoacán, and secretary of the Supreme Conservative Power. In addition, he was one of the best-known members of the *escocés* (Scottish-rite Masons) party. At his death, he was director of the national pawnbrokerage.

See also **Guadalupes, Los.**

BIBLIOGRAPHY

Jose María Miguel I Vergés, *Diccionario de insurgentes* (1969), pp. 537–538; *Diccionario Porrúa de historia, geografía y biografía de México,* 5th ed. (1986), vol. 3, p. 2,642.

Virginia Guedea, *En busca de un gobierno alterno: Los Guadalupes de México* (1992).

Additional Bibliography

Andrade Castro, Manuel. *De la patria y sus héroes: Antología de la poesía cívica de México.* Mexico City: Planeta, 2000.

VIRGINIA GUEDEA

SÁNCHEZ DE THOMPSON, MARÍA

(1786–1868). María Sánchez de Thompson (*b.* 1 November 1786; *d.* 23 October 1868), author, social reformer. "Mariquita" Sánchez de Thompson was born in Buenos Aires, the daughter of a prominent local merchant. As a young woman she showed herself to be headstrong and independent, going as far as marrying the man of her choice, Martín J. Thompson y López Cárdenas, over parental objections in 1805. Thompson, a career naval officer, died in 1817, while returning from a diplomatic mission to the United States. A widow with five small children, Mariquita soon remarried (1820); her second husband was the young French consul in Buenos Aires, Jean-Baptiste Washington de Mendeville.

Her position in society secure, Mariquita then formed a salon that served as a meeting place for liberal politicians, poets, and other literary figures such as her friends Bernardino Rivadavia, Juan María Gutiérrez, Esteban Echeverría, and Juan Bautista Alberdi. A leading member of *porteño* society, Mariquita took a commanding role in the founding of the Sociedad de Beneficencia, and served as the organization's secretary and president. She pressed for elementary education for girls, founding schools in Buenos Aires and the surrounding towns.

Although her second husband was forced from his diplomatic post by Juan Manuel de Rosas and returned to France in 1835, Mariquita continued to live in Buenos Aires, serving as a magnet for the defeated *unitarios.* An outspoken foe of her childhood friend Rosas, Mariquita was alternately forced into exile in Montevideo and allowed to return to Buenos Aires between 1836 and 1852. After Rosas's downfall, Mariquita once again established herself in Buenos Aires, befriending a new generation of reformers, such as Domingo Sarmiento. She died in Buenos Aires just short of her eighty-second birthday.

Throughout her life Mariquita had been an avid letter writer, and her published letters, *Cartas de Mariquita Sánchez* (1952), provide an interesting view of daily life, politics, and society under Rosas. Her reminiscences of life in preindependence Buenos Aires, *Recuerdos de Buenos Aires virreynal* (1953), give a valuable albeit pointed view of late colonial society.

See also **Literature: Spanish America; Women.**

BIBLIOGRAPHY

Jorge A. Zavalía Lagos, *Mariquita Sánchez y su tiempo* (1986).

Additional Bibliography

Rodríguez, Teresa V. *Mariquita Sánchez y Martín Thompson: Un himno a la independencia y al amor.* Buenos Aires: Planeta, 2000.

Sáenz Quesada, María. *Mariquita Sánchez: Vida política y sentimental.* Buenos Aires: Editorial Sudamericana, 1995.

Sánchez, Mariquita. *Intimidad y política: Diario, cartas y recuerdos,* compiled by María Gabriela Mizraje. Buenos Aires: A. Hidalgo, 2003.

SUSAN M. SOCOLOW

SÁNCHEZ HERNÁNDEZ, FIDEL

(1917–2003). Fidel Sánchez Hernández (*b.* 1917; *d.* 28 February 2003), president of El Salvador (1967–1972). Born in San Miguel, Sánchez Hernández graduated from the National Military Academy. He was minister of the interior when he was tapped by outgoing president Julio A. Rivera (1962–1967), to be the candidate of the military-backed National Conciliation Party (PCN) in 1967. Although winning easily nationwide, the PCN won only 41 percent of the votes in San Salvador. As a result, Sánchez Hernández felt pressed to continue the mild reformism of his predecessor, pushing through a rural minimum-wage law.

Falling coffee and cotton prices in 1968 stimulated trade union militancy and the congressional elections brought the opposition parties within two seats of the PCN. However, success in fighting in the 1969 "Football War" with Honduras (a conflict over borders, trade relations, and immigration policy triggered by the actions of unruly fans at two preliminary World Cup soccer matches held in Tegucigalpa and San Salvador in June 1969) restored the popularity of the government. He died of a heart attack on February 28, 2003.

See also **El Salvador, Political Parties: National Conciliation Party (PCN).**

BIBLIOGRAPHY

Thomas P. Anderson, *The War of the Dispossessed: Honduras and El Salvador, 1969* (1981).

Kenneth L. Johnson, "Parties, Union and the State: An Historical-Structural Interpretation of the Salvadoran Crisis, 1948–1982." (M.A. thesis, Tulane University, 1988).

Additional Bibliography

Domínguez, Carlos Armando. *La representación proporcional y la apertura política en el período del Presidente Rivera (1962–1967).* San Salvador, El Salvador: Tribunal Supremo Electoral, 1997.

Ellacuria, Ignacio. *Veinte años de historia en El Salvador (1969–1989): Escritos políticos.* San Salvador, El Salvador: UCA Editores, 1993.

Montgomery, Tommy Sue. *Revolution in El Salvador: From Civil Strife to Civil Peace.* Boulder, CO: Westview Press, 1995.

ROLAND H. EBEL

SÁNCHEZ MANDULEY, CELIA (1920–

1980). Celia Sánchez Manduley (*b.* 1920; *d.* 11 January 1980), Cuban revolutionary and adviser to Fidel Castro. A dentist's daughter born in Oriente Province, Celia Sánchez Manduley was a leader of the Twenty-Sixth of July Movement. She helped to organize the shipment of arms and material to the forces fighting against Fulgencio Batista in the Sierra Maestra. At El Uvero (a battle fought on 28 May 1957), she became the first woman combatant in the revolutionary army; subsequently she formed the Mariana Granjales Platoon for women. She held the position of secretary of the Council of State, and she was a member of both the Communist Party Central Committee and the National Assembly. Her most influential position was as secretary and lifelong companion to Fidel Castro. After her death from cancer, she was given a state funeral and buried in the Mausoleum of the Revolutionary Armed Forces.

See also **Batista y Zaldívar, Fulgencio; Castro Ruz, Fidel.**

BIBLIOGRAPHY

Hugh Thomas, *Cuba: The Pursuit of Freedom* (1971).

Carlos Franqui, *Diary of the Cuban Revolution,* translated by Georgette Felix, et al. (1980); "Celia Sánchez Manduley," in *Cuba Update* 1, no. 1 (1980): 6–7.

Tad Szulc, *Fidel: A Critical Portrait* (1986).

Additional Bibliography

Alvarez Tabío, Pedro. *Celia, ensayo para una biografía.* Havana: Oficina de Publicaciones del Consejo de Estado, 2003.

Béquer Céspedes, Adelaida. *Celia: La flor más autóctona de la Revolución.* Havana: Editorial de Ciencias Sociales, 1999.

DANIEL P. DWYERO. F. M.

SÁNCHEZ NAVARRO, JUAN (1913–2006).

A Mexican entrepreneur, lawyer, university professor, and journalist, Juan Sánchez Navarro was considered the ideologist of the Mexican private sector. He was the son of Carlos Sánchez Navarro and Guadalupe Peón and descendant of one of the richest families in Mexico before 1867. His grandfather lost most of his fortune after supporting Maximiliano of Hapsburg during the French occupation of Mexico. His family subsequently moved to Mexico City, where Sánchez Navarro was born on April 24, 1913. After studying at the Universidad Nacional Autonoma de México, Sánchez Navarro started his career as journalist in Mexico City's newspaper *Novedades*. He also had a modest role in the foundation of the Mexican Partido Acción Nacional (PAN) before abandoning his editorial and political activities to start a successful career in the Mexican private sector. He started at Cervecería Cuauhtemoc and in 1942 moved to Grupo Modelo, where he became vice president in 1960. During his tenure, Grupo Modelo went from a medium-size local company to an important competitor in international beer markets.

However, what made Sánchez Navarro especially prominent among Mexican businessman was his role in employers' organizations such as CONCANACO, CONCAMIN, and the Mexican Council of Businessmen. This involvement made him a natural interlocutor for the Mexican government and workers' organizations. It is this influential role and the relevance of his political and economic positions that made his reputation as the ideologist of the Mexican private sector. He died on April 12, 2006.

See also **Mexico, Political Parties: National Action Party (PAN).**

BIBLIOGRAPHY

Camp, Roderic Ai. *Entrepreneurs and Politics in Twentieth-Century Mexico.* New York: Oxford University Press, 1989.

Harris, Charles H., III. *A Mexican Family Empire, the Latifundio of the Sánchez Navarros, 1765–1867.* Austin: University of Texas Press, 1975.

Ortiz Rivera, Alicia. *Juan Sánchez Navarro: Biografía de un testigo del México del siglo XX.* Mexico: Grijalbo, 1997.

SERGIO SILVA-CASTAÑEDA

SÁNCHEZ VILELLA, ROBERTO (1913–1997).

Roberto Sánchez Vilella (*b.* 19 February 1913; *d.* 25 March 1997), governor of Puerto Rico (1965–1969). Born in Ponce, Sánchez Vilella studied civil engineering at Ohio State University, graduating in 1934. He was one of the founders of the Partido Democrático Popular (PDP). From 1940 on, he occupied important posts in the public administration of Puerto Rico. Sánchez became governor in 1965 and interpreted his victory as a mandate for change. Because of his governing style, however, he soon ran into problems with the old guard of the party. Although for personal reasons he announced that he would retire from politics upon completing his term as governor in 1969, he nevertheless sought reelection in 1968. When he was unsuccessful, however, he left the PDP and joined the Partido del Pueblo (PP). Because of the PP's inability to become a registered party, Sánchez failed to be elected a member of the legislature in 1972. After he retired from politics, he became a professor in the School of Public Administration of the University of Puerto Rico. In 1997, he was diagnosed with cancer, and he died later that year.

See also **Puerto Rico, Political Parties: Overview.**

BIBLIOGRAPHY

Acevedo, Héctor Luís. *Los administradores en la modernización de Puerto Rico.* Puerto Rico: Universidad Interamericana de Puerto Rico, Recinto Metropolitano, 2004.

Muñoz Marín, Luis, Nestor R. Duprey Salgado, and Juan R. Fernández. *Conversaciónes en el bohío: Luis Muñoz Marín y Roberto Sánchez Vilella en sus propias palabras.* San Juan, P.R: Fundación Luís Muñoz Marín, 2005.

Sánchez Vilella, Roberto, and Mario Negrón Portillo. *Roberto Sánchez Vilella: Servidor público por excelencia: Documentos para la historia.* Río Piedras, P.R.: Escuela Graduada de Administración Pública, Universidad de Puerto Rico, 1998.

OSCAR G. PELÁEZ ALMENGOR

SANCHO DE HOZ, PEDRO (?–1547).

Pedro Sancho de Hoz (also Pero; *d.* December 1547), Spanish conquistador, secretary to Francisco Pizarro, and author (at Pizarro's request) of a valuable account of the first phase of the conquest of Peru. He secured from Emperor Charles V the right to conquer territory south of the Strait of Magellan, which conflicted with the claim to Chile then being made by Pedro de Valdivia. At Cuzco, in December 1539, Pizarro persuaded the two men to jointly undertake the conquest of Chile. Sancho de Hoz, frustrated in an effort to assassinate Valdivia in the Atacama Desert, was permitted to remain with the expedition, with the Cuzco agreement rescinded. A plot to seize control of the newly established Chilean colony (1547) was also treated leniently. A third plot, soon thereafter, when Valdivia had left Santiago for Peru, caused Valdivia's lieutenant, Francisco de Villagra, to have Sancho de Hoz beheaded without trial.

See also **Conquistadores; Pizarro, Francisco.**

BIBLIOGRAPHY

H. R. S. Pocock, *The Conquest of Chile* (1967).

Additional Bibliography

Páez, José Roberto. *Cronistas coloniales.* Quito: Corporación de Estudios y Publicaciones, 1989.

SIMON COLLIER

SAN CRISTÓBAL DE LAS CASAS.

San Cristóbal de las Casas, the preeminent city (2005 population of 142,000) of the central highlands of the southernmost Mexican state of Chiapas. Founded in 1524 by Luis Marín, it was originally called La Chiapa de los Indios and renamed Ciudad Real de Chiapa in 1527. As the provincial capital of isolated Chiapas, Ciudad Real fell within the jurisdiction of the Kingdom of Guatemala of the Viceroyalty of New Spain. It served as the diocesan center of Chiapas until 1744 despite the fact that its Spanish population never exceeded 250 during the seventeenth century.

When Chiapas joined the Mexican federation in 1824, this city became the state capital. During the nineteenth century its name changed from San Cristóbal (1829) to San Cristóbal de las Casas (1844), in honor of Chiapas' first bishop, Bartolomé de Las Casas. During the mid-nineteenth-century struggle between Liberals and Conservatives, San Cristóbal was the bastion of provincial Conservatives. As a delayed consequence of Liberal ascendancy in Chiapas, the powers of the state government were

transferred definitively to Tuxtla Gutiérrez in 1892. Cristobalense malcontents attempted without success to exploit the national revolution of 1910–1911 by initiating a rebellion against the government in Tuxtla Gutiérrez in order to reestablish San Cristóbal as the state capital.

The political and economic marginalization of the city in the twentieth century has contributed to the preservation of the city's numerous colonial-era architectural monuments. Its colonial and Indian ambience has made it a popular tourist attraction in recent decades. In January 1994 the city was briefly seized by the Ejército Zapatista de Liberación Nacional (EZLN) during a regional uprising of Indians and peasants. In 2006 the EZLN launched its "Other Campaign" from San Cristóbal.

See also **Chiapas.**

BIBLIOGRAPHY

Aubry, Andrés. *San Cristóbal de las Casas: Su historia urbana, demográfica y monumental, 1528–1990* (1991).

De Vos, Jan. *San Cristóbal ciudad colonial* (1986).

Guillén, Diana. *Chiapas: Una modernidad inconclusa.* Mexico: Instituto Mora, 1995.

Meyer, Jean A., Federico Anaya Gallardo, and Julio Ríos. *Samuel Ruiz en San Cristóbal, 1960–2000.* Mexico: Tusquets Editores, 2000.

Womack, John. *Chiapas, el Obispo de San Cristóbal y la revuelta zapatista.* Mexico: Cal y Arena, 1998.

THOMAS BENJAMIN
VIRGINIA GARRARD-BURNETT

SANDI, LUIS (1905–). Luis Sandi (*b.* 22 February 1905), Mexican composer, music teacher, administrator, and critic. When Carlos Chávez was appointed director of the National Conservatory in 1929, he named Sandi head of choral activities. Sandi also assisted Chávez in reforming public music education within the department of fine arts of the Ministry of Public Education in 1933. He was later chief music administrator in the Ministry of Public Education (1946–1951) and the National Institute of Fine Arts (1959–1963). His *Yaqui Music* for Mexican orchestra, performed at the Museum of Modern Art in New York in 1940, brought him international attention. Other works include the opera *Carlotta,* about the wife of Emperor Maximilian; the Mayan ballet *Bonampak;* and a number of didactic and critical writings.

See also **Chávez, Carlos.**

BIBLIOGRAPHY

Gérard Béhague, *Music in Latin America: An Introduction* (1979).

ROBERT L. PARKER

SANDINISTAS. *See* **Nicaragua, Sandinista National Liberation Front (FSLN).**

SANDINO, AUGUSTO CÉSAR (1895–1934).

Augusto César Sandino (*b.* 18 May 1895; *d.* 21 February 1934), general of guerrilla liberation army and Nicaraguan hero. Sandino was the illegitimate son of Gregorio Sandino, a small businessman, and Margarita Calderón, a coffee picker, in the town of Niquinohomo. From an early age he was exposed to bitter human experiences and poverty. At the age of ten, he witnessed his mother's miscarriage while she was imprisoned for debt. He also toiled in the coffee fields with his mother before returning to live with his father in Niquinohomo in 1906. However, his life was not much better with his father. His half brother Socrates received all the attention and benefits while Augusto worked and ate with the servants. He began to question the fairness of society, life, and God. In school, he learned the principles of capitalism and the meaning of exploitation. His education ended in 1910, when he was forced to work in his father's grain business.

In 1916, Sandino left Nicaragua to work as a mechanic in Costa Rica, then returned three years later to start his own grain business. Despite some success, he had to abandon the enterprise after shooting a man during an argument. Between 1920 and 1923, he worked odd jobs until he found employment as a mechanic with the Southern Pennsylvania Oil Company in Tampico, Mexico. There he acquired an eclectic political and spiritual philosophy and an understanding of social revolution

POLITICAL THOUGHT AND LIBERAL REVOLT

In Mexico, Sandino absorbed a wide range of political ideologies in the midst of revolutionary change. Anarchism, socialism, and communism competed in the workers' unions in the oil fields of Tampico and Veracruz. Sandino grasped the unconditional opposition of government, church, and capitalist institutions advanced by the anarchists; he learned the importance of strategies of social change from the socialists; and he endorsed the Communists' demand for proletarian revolution. In addition, Sandino immersed himself in theological doctrines that attempted to explain the human relationship to God. Mexican Freemasonry and spiritualism penetrated his thinking by 1926, when he returned to Nicaragua to join the Liberal opposition to the Conservative government. Sandino's expectations upon his arrival on the Atlantic coast, to join the constitutionalist army of General José María Moncada, are conjecture. Moncada espoused classical liberal values of law, property, and limited government.

At the behest of the U.S. government, Emiliano Chamorro yielded the presidency to his Conservative colleague Adolfo Díaz at the end of 1926. Concurrently, the Liberals formed a provisional government in Puerto Cabezas. Sandino continued to press Moncada for stronger and faster action. Moncada rejected Sandino's request for arms in their only face-to-face meeting in late December. When U.S. Marines landed at the Pacific coast port of Corinto in January 1927, Sandino decided to go to San Juan del Norte in the northern mountains and establish his own military command.

The Liberal-Conservative conflict continued until May 1927, when U.S. envoy Henry Stimson arranged a truce between Moncada and Díaz. Both agreed that Díaz would serve until the 1928 election. The Liberal troops voluntarily disarmed, and the U.S. Marine Corps took control of the Nicaraguan National Guard on 16 May 1927. Moncada sent a telegram to Sandino, asking him to give up the fight. Sandino responded bluntly: "Now I want you to come and disarm me.... You will not make me cede by any other means. I am not for sale. I do not give up. You will have to defeat me" (Ramírez, p. 85).

In September 1927, in the village of El Chipote, Sandino promulgated the Articles of Incorporation of the Defending Army of the National Sovereignty

Augusto César Sandino and staff, 1929. As he worked in the oil fields of Mexico, Nicaraguan guerrilla general Sandino was exposed to a wide array of differing ideologies, including socialism, anarchism, and communism. When he returned to his native Nicaragua, Sandino fought against U.S. interference, leading rebel forces against the U.S. Marines. TIME LIFE PICTURES/US MARINE CORPS/NATIONAL ARCHIVES/TIME LIFE PICTURES/GETTY IMAGES

of Nicaragua. The Chilean poet Gabriela Mistral later called Sandino's guerrilla band "the crazy little army." The army launched attacks against the marines and the Conservative government, each time retreating to El Chipote. Gradually, the general achieved a mystical quality in Latin America, the United States, and Europe. The marines constantly searched for El Chipote, often interrogating uncooperative peasants in the dense jungle of Las Segovias. The secret camp was discovered in January 1928 by air reconnaissance. Intense bombings began immediately, and the marines entered El Chipote on 3 February, to find only stuffed "soldiers."

Over the next few years, Sandino rejected compromises with the Liberal government that came to power in 1928. His army achieved many small victories, such as downing a U.S. bomber. Carleton Beals of *The Nation* provided an inside look at Sandino's life for the North American public. However, a review of recent literature does not reveal a consensus on Sandino's political thought and revolutionary intentions. The eclectic mix of socialism, nationalism, and theosophy has created disagreement about Sandino's intelligence and ability to apply abstract ideas to the Nicaraguan reality. He insisted on social justice for workers and peasants, often using deeply philosophical and sometimes confusing language to explain his motivation.

TRUCE AND DEATH

In 1932, political conditions in the United States and Nicaragua changed. Franklin D. Roosevelt succeeded the conservative Herbert Hoover. Roosevelt promulgated the Good Neighbor Policy, which redirected resources away from U.S. political adventures abroad. And Liberal candidate Juan Batista Sacasa triumphed over Adolfo Díaz in the 1932 presidential election. Thus, the U.S. Department of State laid the groundwork for the withdrawal of the marines and the installation of the National Guard with Anastasio Somoza García as chief. One of Sacasa's first actions was to send a peace delegation to San Rafael del Norte, to negotiate a truce with Sandino. On 23 January 1933, an agreement was reached that facilitated the departure of the marines on 1 February. Three weeks later, the Defending Army was disarmed.

From this point Sandino's life took a severe turn for the worse. In June 1933 his wife, Blanca, died giving birth to their daughter; in August the National Guard attacked Sandinistas in Las Segovias, which prompted Sandino to request that President Sacasa declare the Guard unconstitutional. Sacasa invited Sandino to come to Managua in late February 1934. Sandino met with Sacasa and Somoza on the evening of 21 February. Upon leaving the presidential house, apparently satisfied with the result, Sandino, his brother Socrates, and two Sandinista generals were kidnapped by the National Guard. They were murdered in an open field. Sandino's remains have never been found.

See also **Communism; Nicaragua; United States-Latin American Relations.**

BIBLIOGRAPHY

Neill Macaulay, *The Sandino Affair* (1967).

Gregorio Selser, *Sandino: General de los hombres libres* (1979).

Sergio Ramírez, *El pensamiento vivo de Sandino*, 5th ed. (1979).

Miguel Jesús Blandón, *Entre Sandino y Fonseca Amador* (1980).

Carlos Fonseca, *Ideario político de Augusto César Sandino* (1984).

David Nolan, *The Ideology of the Sandinistas and the Nicaraguan Revolution* (1984).

Donald Hodges, *The Intellectual Foundations of the Nicaraguan Revolution* (1986).

Steven Palmer, "Carlos Fonseca and the Construction of Sandinismo in Nicaragua," in *Latin American Research Review* 23, no. 1 (1989): 91–109.

Wayne G. Bragg, trans., *Sandino in the Streets* (1991).

Additional Bibliography

Bendaña, Alejandro. *La mística de Sandino*. Managua: Centro de Estudios Internacionales, 1994.

Bolaños Geyer, Alejandro. *Sandino*. Masaya: A. Bolaños Geyer, 2002.

Isaguirre, R. R., and Adrián Martínez Rodríguez. *Sandino y los U.S. Marines: Reportes de los agregados militares y comandantes marines en acción*. Tegucigalpa: Omni Editores, 2000.

Tirado, Víctor. *Sandino y la doctrina de liberación nacional*. Managua: Editorial Vanguardia, 1989.

Wünderich, Volker. *Sandino, una biografía política*. Managua: Editorial Nueva Nicaragua, 1995.

MARK EVERINGHAM

SAN DOMINGO IMPROVEMENT COMPANY.

San Domingo Improvement Company, a group of U.S. investors (including many high government officials) who, in 1893, bought up the Dominican interests of the bankrupt Westendorp Company of Amsterdam. Beginning in 1888, Westendorp had made several large loans to Dominican President Ulises Heureaux (1882–1899). The San Domingo Improvement Company assumed the financial interests of Westendorp in the Dominican Republic at a time when Heureaux was secretly negotiating with Washington over the leasing of the Samaná Peninsula to the United States. In return for being permitted to assume the Westendorp interests, the San Domingo Improvement Company loaned Heureaux U.S. $1,250,000 and £2,035,000 to enable him to cover the internal debt of the country. Like Westendorp, the San Domingo Improvement Company took control of the Dominican Republic's customhouse in order to ensure that the loans would be repaid. The activities of the San Domingo Improvement Company symbolized the increasing power of U.S. interests in the economic and political spheres of the Dominican Republic and the simultaneous decline of European influence, which had been paramount at Santo Domingo during the nineteenth century.

See also **Dominican Republic.**

BIBLIOGRAPHY

Frank Moya Pons, *Manual de historia dominicana*, 7th ed. (1983), esp. pp. 416–427, 429–431, 436.

Additional Bibliography

Veeser, Cyrus. *A World Safe for Capitalism: Dollar Diplomacy and America's Rise to Global Power.* New York: Columbia University Press, 2002.

KAI P. SCHOENHALS

SANDOVAL, JOSÉ LEÓN (1789–1854).

José León Sandoval (*b.* 1789, *d.* October 1854), supreme director (chief of state) of Nicaragua (4 April 1845–24 July 1846). A mestizo descendant of the conquistador Gonzalo de Sandoval, Sandoval was a justice of the peace at the close of the colonial period in his native Granada, but he also worked in transporting goods on Lake Nicaragua and the Río San Juan. Resentful of the privileges of Spanish officials and wealthier creoles, Sandoval supported independence from Spain and then opposed Nicaraguan incorporation into Iturbide's Mexican Empire. In 1825 he became *jefe político* of Granada and later served in other government positions while rising in military rank.

A fervent unionist, he also served Francisco Morazán's federal government in San Salvador. He was supreme director of Nicaragua during the violent struggles among the caudillos Francisco Malespín, José María Valle, José Trinidad Muñoz, and Bernabé Somoza. Although a liberal, Sandoval remained loyal to the elected governments, and under the conservative Fruto Chamorro, he directed Granada's defense against the siege begun in May 1854 by Máximo Jérez. Brigadier General Sandoval died in this defense and was buried in Granada.

See also **Nicaragua.**

BIBLIOGRAPHY

Emilio Álvarez, *Ensayo biográfico del prócer José León Sandoval* (1947).

RALPH LEE WOODWARD JR.

SANDOVAL VALLARTA, MANUEL

(1899–1977). Manuel Sandoval Vallarta (*b.* 11 February 1899; *d.* 18 April 1977), Mexican physicist and educator. A graduate of the Massachusetts Institute of Technology in 1921, Sandoval Vallarta later became a disciple of Albert Einstein and other scientists of that time, as well as a costudent and collaborator of Robert Oppenheimer. He received a Guggenheim fellowship to study in Berlin in 1927–1928 and was an exchange professor at Louvain University, Belgium. He began teaching at MIT in 1926 and left his position in 1943 to return to Mexico, where he became director of the National Polytechnic Institute in 1944 and assistant secretary of education in 1953. An internationally recognized physicist, he produced many students who formed the next generation of important Mexican scientists, including Carlos Graef Fernández. The Mexican government selected him as one of the original members of the National College and awarded him its National Prize in Sciences in 1959.

See also **Grenada; Mestizo; Morazán, Francisco; Nicaragua; San Salvador.**

BIBLIOGRAPHY

Manuel Sandoval Vallarta, "Reminiscencias," in *Naturaleza* 4 (1973): 178; *Proceso,* 23 April 1977, 28.

Additional Bibliography

Mendoza Avila, Eusebio. *Semblanza del doctor Manuel Sandoval Vallarta: Ex-director del Instituto Politécnico Nacional.* Mexico City: Editorial Instituto Politécnico Nacional, 1995.

Moshinsky, Marcos. "Manuel Sandoval Vallarta." *Vuelta* 2:24 (November 1978): 46–50.

RODERIC AI CAMP

SAN FERNANDO DEL VALLE DE CATAMARCA. *See* **Catamarca.**

SANFUENTES ANDONAEGUI, JUAN LUIS (1858–1930).

Juan Luis Sanfuentes Andonaegui (*b.* 27 December 1858; *d.* 1930), president of Chile (1915–1920). The younger brother of Enrique Sanfuentes (whom President José Manuel Balmaceda Fernández had tapped as his successor in 1891), Juan Luis Sanfuentes was a supporter of Balmaceda in the civil war of 1891 and later led the Liberal Democratic Party, which nominally espoused Balmaceda's principles. Sanfuentes held several ministerial posts and was a prominent figure during the "parliamentary republic" period in Chile. His main achievement was to uphold Chile's neutrality in World War I. His administration marked the end of the oligarchic era in Chilean politics.

See also **Balmaceda Fernández, José Manuel; Chile, Political Parties: Liberal Party; Chile, Revolutions: Revolution of 1891.**

BIBLIOGRAPHY

Rivas Vicuña, Manuel. *Historia política y parlamentaria de Chile: Ordenada según diversos manuscritos del autor, con varios apéndices relativos a dicha "Historia," a los sucesos de 1920 a 1934 y documentos concernientes a Rivas Vicuña*, 3 vols., Guillermo Feliú Cruz, editor. Santiago de Chile: Ediciones de la Biblioteca Nacional, 1964.

SIMON COLLIER

SAN GIL.

San Gil, a town in northeastern Colombia, 186 miles northeast of Bogotá, 1990 estimated population 40,000. Site of an Indian parish from the 1620s, San Gil was founded as a town in 1689, becoming the seat for a large, initially desolate region south of the Río Chicamocha. The growth of other towns in the jurisdiction, especially the artisanal and commercial center of Socorro, gave rise to endless struggles for municipal status, culminating in the separation of Socorro in 1776 and of Barichara in 1803. Bitterness produced by these losses may have inspired the San Gil elite's opposition to the Comunero Revolt of 1781, and indifference to the Independence struggle, both movements which had their epicenter in the northeast. In the early republican period, San Gil achieved relative prosperity as an educational, bureaucratic, and urban artisanal center. Its merchant-landholder elite combined economic liberalism and social conservatism, the tensions of which led them to switch from Liberal to Conservative affiliation in the 1850s, making the town a Conservative redoubt for the rest of the nineteenth century. In the twentieth century San Gil retained its regional economic supremacy, particularly as a road transportation center, but its political importance declined.

BIBLIOGRAPHY

Rito Rueda, *Presencia de un pueblo* (1968).

John L. Phelan, *The People and the King* (1978).

Isaías Ardila Díaz, *Historia de San Gil en sus 300 años* (1990).

Additional Bibliography

Palacios, Marco. *Between Legitimacy and Violence: A History of Colombia, 1875-2002.* Durham, NC: Duke University Press, 2006.

Safford, Frank and Marco Palacios. *Colombia: Fragmented Land, Divided Society.* New York: Oxford University Press, 2002.

Uribe Urban, Victor. *Honorable Lives: Lawyers, Family, and Politics in Colombia, 1750-1850.* Pittsburgh: University of Pittsburgh Press, 2000.

RICHARD J. STOLLER

SANGUINETTI, JULIO MARÍA (1936–).

Julio María Sanguinetti (*b.* 1936), president of Uruguay (1985–1989). Sanguinetti was the first president to be elected following the 1973 coup. A forty-eight-year-old lawyer at the time of his election, he had thirty years of experience in the Colorado Party. He was elected to the Chamber of Deputies in 1962 and reelected in 1966 and 1971. He served as minister of education and culture under President Juan María Bordaberry in 1972 but resigned in early 1973 in protest over the increasing political role of the military. An erudite speaker and skilled negotiator, Sanguinetti was general secretary of the Colorado Party during the negotiations in 1983 and 1984 that led to the Pact of the Naval Club, which paved the way for the November 1984 elections. Building on the success of his newspaper, *Correo de los Viernes*, Sanguinetti ran a skillful campaign for president, putting several young newcomers on his ticket and making effective use of television. His party received 41 percent of the vote to 35 percent for the Blancos (National Party).

Sanguinetti inherited a country mired in recession and still traumatized by the repression and torture that were the hallmarks of military rule. He immediately released the remaining political prisoners and restored all constitutional rights. He made the economist and diplomat Enrique Iglesias his minister of foreign affairs and gave him the leeway to develop an active trade policy. The years 1986 and 1987 were a period of economic recovery but growing political controversy. The stated refusal of the military to participate in any civilian trials concerning human-rights abuses led the government to sponsor and pass an amnesty law. This law was challenged in 1989 by a plebiscite that divided the country. Although the vote ultimately upheld the amnesty for the military, it cost the government much political goodwill.

A stagnant economy in the last two years of his administration and a bitter struggle for the presidential nomination of the Batllist wing of the party, with Jorge Batlle prevailing over Sanguinetti's choice, vice president Enrique Tarigo, led to a Colorado defeat in the November 1989 elections. Sanguinetti, who could not succeed himself, was eligible to run for president in future elections. Head of the Colorado faction known as the Batllist Forum and the major Colorado presidential candidate, Sanguinetti won the election of 1994. He was elected again for the 1995 through 2000 term. He was an outspoken critic of the 2006 arrest of former president Juan María Bordaberry. In 2007 he was awarded the Lifetime Achievement Award from the prestigious Spanish *Fundación Cristobal Gabbaron*.

See also **Uruguay, Political Parties: Colorado Party.**

BIBLIOGRAPHY

Martin Weinstein, *Uruguay: Democracy at the Crossroads* (1988).

Charles Gillespie, *Negotiating Democracy: Politicians and Generals in Uruguay* (1991).

Additional Bibliography

Esquibel, Daniel. *Sanguinetti: Sexo, sombreros, y silencio.* Montevideo, Uruguay: Editorial Fin del Siglo, 1997.

Liscano, Carlos. *Ejercicio de impunidad: Sanguinetti y Battle contra Gelman.* Montevideo, Uruguay: Ediciones del Caballo Perdido, 2004.

Sanguinetti, Julio Maria. *El doctor Figari.* Montevideo, Uruguay: Aguilar: Fundación Bank Boston, 2002.

MARTIN WEINSTEIN

SAN ILDEFONSO, TREATY OF (1777).

The Treaty of San Ildefonso (1777) was one in a series of agreements aimed at settling territorial disputes between Portugal and Spain regarding the interior of South America. On October 1, 1777, the Treaty of San Ildefonso ended fifteen years of irregular open fighting. The Portuguese regained Santa Catarina, seized by Spain in 1777, and the coastal Rio Grande area but acknowledged Spanish control of Colônia do Sacramento, a center of Portuguese contraband trade and an access to the silver mines of Potosí; the Seven Missions territory, occupied by seven Jesuit missions and thirty thousand Guaraní Indians; and the Banda Oriental (present-day Uruguay). Although neither power achieved its objective of complete control of what was known as the Debatable Lands, secret treaty provisions provided Spanish access to the Portuguese islands of Principe and São Tomé for the purpose of purchasing African slaves. Thus the Spanish gained direct access to the African slave market and circumvented the necessity of relying on foreign middlemen.

The Treaty of San Ildefonso was significant because it satisfactorily implemented the practical solution of recognizing that possession is the legal basis of territorial settlement (*uti possidetis*). This principle was originally agreed upon in the Treaty of Madrid (1750), but practical implementation of territorial allocation had been ignored since that treaty was nullified by the Treaty of El Pardo (1761).

In 1776 a Spanish expedition crossed the Río de la Plata and forcibly claimed a portion of what now is the southernmost territory of Brazil. The Treaty of San Ildefonso then recognized Spanish claims based on *uti possidetis* and inadvertently confirmed Portuguese claims to the Amazon basin, which was accepted as Brazilian territory because the Portuguese had explored, charted, and established permanent outposts there. The Spanish invasion of Portugal in 1801 prompted the Brazilian reconquest of portions of the contested area and reestablished the Chui River as Brazil's southern boundary. This was confirmed by the Treaty of Badajoz (1801), but the remainder of Brazil's territorial boundaries would not be settled until the twentieth century.

See also **Madrid, Treaty of (1750).**

BIBLIOGRAPHY

Dauril Alden, *Royal Government in Colonial Brazil* (1968), pp. 262–267, 474.

Geoffrey J. Walker, *Spanish Politics and Imperial Trade, 1700–1789* (1979).

E. Bradford Burns, *A History of Brazil* (1980), pp. 70–72, 107, 146.

Peggy K. Liss, *Atlantic Empires: The Network of Trade and Revolution, 1713–1826* (1983); *The Cambridge History* of Latin America, edited by Leslie Bethell, vol. 1 (1984), pp. 401, 473, 612.

Additional Bibliography

Torres, Simei Maria de Souza. Dominios y fronteras en la Amazonia colonial: El Tratado de San Ildefonso, 1777–1790. *Fronteras de la Historia* 8 (2003): 195–226.

SUZANNE HILES BURKHOLDER
LESLEY R. LUSTER

Hardin, Stephen L. *Texian Iliad: A Military History of the Texas Revolution, 1835-1836.* Austin: University of Texas Press, 1994.

Moore, Stephen L. *Eighteen Minutes: The Battle of San Jacinto and the Texas Independence Campaign.* Dallas: Republic of Texas Press: Distributed by National Book Network, 2004.

Vázquez, Josefina Zoraida, and Andreas Reichstein. *De la rebelión de Texas a la guerra del 47.* México D.F.: Nueva Imagen, 1994.

MICHAEL R. GREEN

SAN JACINTO, BATTLE OF.

Battle of San Jacinto (21 April 1836), the final military action of the Texas Revolution. On 13 March 1836 the Texan forces under General Sam Houston began a retreat eastward to Louisiana, joined by hundreds of families dispossessed by the advancing Mexican army. The retreat continued until 17 April, when General Houston ordered a movement to meet the enemy. Two days later, the Texans arrived at Buffalo Bayou, where the Mexican army under President Antonio López de Santa Anna intended to pass en route to the coast. On 20 April the Texan cavalry fought a brief skirmish with Santa Anna's advance guard, while the main body of the Mexican army encamped on the plains between Buffalo Bayou and San Jacinto Bay. On the morning of 21 April the Mexican army was reinforced, and General Houston ordered the destruction of Vince's Bridge, preventing the further reinforcement or retreat of either army. That afternoon, while the Mexicans were taking their siesta, the Texans attacked. The conflict lasted only eighteen minutes but resulted in the decimation of the Mexican force and the capture of Santa Anna. Moreover, the battle secured Texas independence and nearly a million square miles of territory.

See also **Houston, Sam; Santa Anna, Antonio López de.**

BIBLIOGRAPHY

Frank X. Tolbert, *The Day of San Jacinto* (1959).

James W. Pohl, *The Battle of San Jacinto* (1989).

Additional Bibliography

Brands, H. W. *Lone Star Nation: How a Ragged Army of Volunteers Won the Battle for Texas Independence, and Changed America.* New York: Doubleday, 2004.

SAN JOSÉ, COSTA RICA.

San José, capital city of Costa Rica. The most populous city in San José Province, with a population of 344,747 in 2006, it is the governmental, educational, business, banking, and manufacturing center of the country.

San José was first settled during the second quarter of the eighteenth century, principally by immigrants from Cartago. It takes its name from Saint Joseph, the patron saint of the first parish established in the Asserí Valley. For some time the settlement was referred to as Villa Nueva to distinguish it from the earlier settlement at Villa Vieja (present-day Heredia).

The village grew more rapidly than Cartago for the rest of the colonial period and by the time of independence, San José challenged the colonial capital for hegemony in the sparsely populated new nation. San José had prospered in the second half of the eighteenth century as a commercial center from a significant amount of contraband trade as well as from legitimate tobacco production.

The final shift in power from Cartago to San José came in 1823 in a short, violent clash in which armed bands from the four centers of population in the central valley fought to determine whether Costa Rica would be part of Agustín Iturbide's Mexican empire (Cartago and Heredia's position) or would join the Central American Federation (San José and Alajuela's position). San José's victory marked the beginning of its ascension as the great city of Costa Rica. San José defeated a combined force from the other three cities in 1835 (The War of the League) to assure its position. Throughout the rest of the nineteenth century and into the early twentieth century the city grew more rapidly than its rivals.

With the rapid modernization that has taken place since 1940, San José has grown prodigiously and has become ever more dominant in power and population. Its growth has been so dynamic that the distinctions among the four cities of the central valley have been blurred in functional terms as they begin to blend into one great central megapolis that embraces almost one-half of the nation's population (over one million inhabitants). San José is the unquestioned hub of politics, business, culture, education, transportation, and industry; San José province remains a major agricultural producer.

See also **Cartago; Costa Rica; Heredia.**

BIBLIOGRAPHY

Carolyn Hall, *Costa Rica: A Geographical Interpretation in Historical Perspective* (1985).

Carlos Monge Alfaro, "The Development of the Central Valley," in *The Costa Rica Reader,* edited by Marc Edelman And Joanne Kenen (1989), pp. 1–9.

Additional Bibliography

Paige, Jeffery M. *Coffee and Power: Revolution and the Rise of Democracy in Central America.* Cambridge, MA: Harvard University Press, 1997.

Palmer, Steven Paul, and Iván Molina Jiménez. *The Costa Rica Reader: History, Culture, Politics.* Durham, NC: Duke University Press, 2004.

JOHN PATRICK BELL

SAN JOSÉ CONFERENCE OF 1906.

As stipulated in the 20 July 1906 Marblehead Pact, representatives of El Salvador, Guatemala, and Honduras met in September 1906 in San José, Costa Rica. Nicaragua was invited to attend the conference, but President José Santos Zelaya declined the invitation. Most observers agreed that Zelaya's refusal was a protest against what he considered to be the excessive interference of the United States in isthmian affairs. The Conference produced an impressive series of treaties and conventions designed to promote isthmian peace and stability. The promise of the San José accords, however, was not immediately fulfilled, for within a matter of months a new round of hostilities erupted in Central America that led to the 1907 Washington Conference.

See also **Marblehead Pact (1906).**

BIBLIOGRAPHY

Papers Relating to the Foreign Relations of the United States, 1906 (1909), esp. pp. 853–866.

Dana G. Munro, *Intervention and Dollar Diplomacy in the Caribbean, 1900–1921* (1964), esp. pp. 146–147.

Additional Bibliography

Buchenau, Jürgen. *In the Shadow of the Giant: The Making of Mexico's Central America Policy, 1876-1930.* Tuscaloosa: University of Alabama Press, 1996.

RICHARD. V. SALISBURY

SAN JOSÉ DE FLORES, PACT OF.

The Pact of San José de Flores was a peace agreement signed on November 11, 1859, between the Argentine Confederation and the state of Buenos Aires. After Buenos Aires seceded from the rest of the Confederation, in 1852, relations between the two governments worsened and preparations were made for armed conflict. In October 1859 the Buenos Aires forces under General Bartolomé Mitre were defeated on the fields of Cepeda by those commanded by Justo José de Urquiza. In the peace agreement, Buenos Aires agreed to join the Confederation after a revision of the National Constitution of 1853. The revision was entrusted to a Provincial Convention. If this convention were to propose reforms, the national government was to send them to Congress, which would also form a convention—with Buenos Aires represented in proportion to its inhabitants—to study the reforms. The Buenos Aires customs—one of the most controversial issues—was to come under national control while the government of the Confederation guaranteed the province of Buenos Aires its revenues for the five years following its reunion with the Confederation. Although this pact sought to end the secession of Buenos Aires, national unification did not come until two years later.

See also **Argentine Confederation; Mitre, Bartolomé; Urquiza, Justo José de.**

BIBLIOGRAPHY

Gorostegui de Torres, Haydée. *La organización nacional.* Colección Historia Argentina, 4. Buenos Aires: Paidós, 2000.

Oszlak, Oscar. *La formación del Estado argentino: Orden, progreso y organización Nacional.* Buenos Aires: Planeta, 1997.

Marcela Ternavasio

SAN JUAN, ARGENTINA.

San Juan, capital city (112,778 inhabitants in 2001) of the province of the same name in western Argentina (population over 450,000). The city of San Juan de la Frontera was founded in 1562 by Captain Juan de Jofré under orders from Francisco de Villagra, governor of Chile, and moved to its present location in 1593 to avoid the floods caused by the high waters of the San Juan River. In 1776 it passed to the Viceroyalty of Río de la Plata, and in 1813 it joined Mendoza and San Luis in the intendancy of Cuyo. After the repulsion of the British invasions of Buenos Aires in 1806 and 1807, English prisoners were interned in San Juan, and several decided to settle there. The city is known as the birthplace of the political leader and future president Domingo Faustino Sarmiento, who depicted it in many of his writings. After the passage of laws encouraging foreign immigration in 1860, there was a great influx of Italian and German families, who planted vineyards in the area. The city was destroyed by several earthquakes, the most damaging being those of 1894 and 1944. Clean, hospitable, and progressive, San Juan is a showcase of the agricultural development achieved by western Argentina under European colonization.

See also **Argentina, Geography.**

BIBLIOGRAPHY

López, Celia. *Con la cruz y con el dinero: Los Jesuitas del San Juan colonial.* San Juan, Argentina: Universidad Nacional de San Juan, 2001.

Sarmiento, Domingo F. *Mi vida.* 2 Vols. Buenos Aires: Angel Estrada, 1938. See especially Vol. 1, pp. 3–54.

Sarmiento, Domingo F. *Recuerdos de provincia.* Edited by Jorge Luís Borges. Buenos Aires: Emecé Editores, 1998.

César N. Caviedes

SAN JUAN DEL NORTE.
See **Greytown (San Juan del Norte).**

SAN JUAN DE ULÚA.

San Juan de Ulúa, a fortress on La Gallega Island, a coral key facing the Mexican port of Veracruz. Juan de Grijalva gave it this name on his first expedition in 1518. Cortés landed there in 1519. Until the beginning of the seventeenth century, it was the port where the Spanish fleets moored and from where silver and gold were shipped. In the late 1500s, Juan Bautista Antonelli began its fortification, which was completed by Jaime Franck in 1692. John Hawkins and Francis Drake attacked San Juan de Ulúa in 1568. In 1683 it was taken by Lorencillo (Lorenzo Jácome), who also captured and sacked Veracruz. It was the last stronghold of the Spanish on the continent and resisted a siege from 1821 until 1825. Occupied by French troops in 1838 and American forces in 1847, the fortress was the presidential residence of Benito Juárez (1859–1860) during the war of the Reform and of Carranza in the Revolution (1915). That same year it ceased being used as a prison. Its narrow cells, made dank by the sea, were known as *las tinajas* (large earthen jugs). The Jesuits expelled in 1767 were imprisoned there, as were supporters of independence and some opponents of Porfirio Díaz.

When the modern port of Veracruz was completed in 1902, the key on which the fortress stands was connected to the mainland by a breakwater. All but abandoned for many years, San Juan de Ulúa was restored in 1991. It is preserved as a historic monument, the site of much Mexican and American history throughout four centuries.

See also **Grijalva, Juan de.**

BIBLIOGRAPHY

Francisco Santiago Cruz, *San Juan de Ulúa: Biografía de un presidio* (1966).

Leonardo Pasquel, *San Juan de Ulúa: Fortaleza, presidio, residencia presidencial* (1969).

Bernardo García Díaz, *Puerto de Veracruz* (1992).

Additional Bibliography

Lane, Kris E. *Pillaging the Empire: Piracy in the Americas, 1500–1750.* Armonk, NY: M.E. Sharpe, 1998.

Montero, Pablo. *Ulúa, puente intercontinental en el siglo XVII.* Mexico: Instituto Nacional de Antropología e Historia: Internacional de Contenedores Asociados de Veracruz, 1997.

Muñoz Espejo, Francisco Martín. *La construcción de la fortaleza de San Juan de Ulúa*. México: Instituto Nacional de Antropología e História, 2005.

J. E. PACHECO

SANJUANISTAS.

Sanjuanistas, a group of individuals gathered at the Hermitage of San Juan Bautista in Mérida, Yucatán, to discuss religious and social questions, particularly the conditions of Indian servitude. They were under the direction of the hermitage's chaplain, Father Vicente María Velázquez. The imperial crisis of 1808 turned their discussions to political issues. Avowed autonomists, the Sanjuanistas supported the liberal reforms introduced by the Cortes and were determined partisans of the Constitution of 1812. When the first printing press was brought to Mérida in 1813, the Sanjuanistas battled the *rutineros,* the partisans of absolutism, through newspapers and pamphlets.

The Sanjuanistas included Lorenzo de Zavala, José Matías Quintana—father of Andrés Quintana Roo—and Francisco Bates. When the constitutional system was abolished in 1814, the Sanjuanistas were persecuted and some of them were imprisoned. Zavala, Quintana, and Bates were sent to San Juan de Ulúa, where they remained imprisoned until 1817. Encouraged by Zavala, the former Sanjuanistas reorganized the society when the constitution was restored in 1820, and numerous Masons joined the new organization. The Junta de San Juan ultimately changed its name to the Confederación Patriótica, which managed to force the swearing in of the constitution once again, even though the authorities opposed it. Shortly afterward the group deposed both the governor and the captain-general of Yucatán.

See also **Zavala, Lorenzo de.**

BIBLIOGRAPHY

Ignacio Rubio Mañé, "Los sanjuanistas de Yucatán I. Manuel Jiménez Solís, el padre Justis," in *Boletín del Archivo general de la nación,* 2nd ser., 8, nos. 3–4 (1967): 1,211–1,234, 9, nos. 1–2 (1968): 193–243, and nos. 3–4 (1968): 401–508, 10, nos. 1–2 (1969): 127–252.

Virginia Guedea, "Las sociedades secretas durante el movimiento de independencia," in *The Independence of Mexico and the Creation of the New Nation,* edited by Jaime E. Rodríguez O. (1989), pp. 45–62.

Additional Bibliography

Antochiw, Michel. *Los primeros años de la imprenta en Yucatán: El período colonial, 1813-1821*. Mérida: Centro de Apoyo a la Investigación Histórica de Yucatán: Instituto de Cultura de Yucatán, 1994.

Rodríguez O, Jaime E. *The Origins of Mexican National Politics, 1808-1847*. Wilmington, DE: SR Books, 1997.

VIRGINIA GUEDEA

SAN JUAN, PUERTO RICO.

The capital of San Juan (2006 pop. 426,618) has throughout its history been at the center of Puerto Rico's political, economic, and cultural life. Although the island was discovered in 1493, Spain did not establish a permanent foothold there until 1509, when Juan Ponce de León founded Caparra on the western rim of San Juan Bay. In 1521 colonists resettled on the islet on the bay, the city's present site, naming the town Puerto Rico. Over time the harbor city and country traded names, with the island coming to be called Puerto Rico and the city San Juan.

A key node in the Caribbean imperial defensive system, San Juan developed as a military garrison facing the menace of foreign hostility. The city experienced four major attacks, three by the British (1595, 1598, and 1797), and a particularly devastating one, in which most of San Juan was destroyed by fire, by the Dutch (1625).

San Juan remained sparsely populated and economically stagnant until the mid- to late-1700s, when Puerto Rico reaped the benefits of trade liberalization, growing international demand for sugar, and extensive new military construction projects. With negligible manufacturing, mining, and agriculture, the city focused on commerce. As the sugar trade expanded, the city became a leading commercial center as well as a hub for the Caribbean slave trade. Military construction injected capital into the city, attracting new businesses and services, additional military personnel, and an influx of free, slave, and penal laborers. In this period women were the city's largest population group, with many poor females of color performing domestic work and street vending activities. This economic boom also fueled the rise of a wealthy merchant class with investments in sugar haciendas.

During the 1800s San Juan's population increased fourfold, from 7,800 civilians and military personnel in 1803 to nearly 32,000 people in 1899. A well-defined hierarchy characterized this urban society: an upper class of royal and military officers, planters, and merchants; a middle class of professionals; and, representing the largest percentage of nonwhite residents, the laboring classes and the urban poor. After the mid-1850s, military and public policies forced working-class neighborhoods to relocate outside the city walls, transforming San Juan's social, racial, and spatial configuration. In 1897 a segment of the defensive wall was torn down to allow urban sprawl to the east of the historic colonial district.

Historically, the interplay between the needs of the military and civilian populations shaped the city's urban development. From 1898 through the early 1960s, San Juan was strategically important for the United States' hemispheric defense. During World War II the city served as the Caribbean control center for U.S. naval and air operations. In the early 1960s the U.S. military closed its bases in Old San Juan, transferring control of the colonial-era fortifications to the U.S. National Park Service and other facilities to the Commonwealth of Puerto Rico.

As one of the oldest European settlements in the Americas, San Juan exhibits distinctive Spanish colonial and neoclassical architecture. Since its creation in 1955, the Institute of Puerto Rican Culture has restored and preserved invaluable religious, military, government, and residential structures, including Casa Blanca (1521), residence of Ponce de León's descendants; the Dominican monastery (1523), a superb example of colonial Spanish monastic architecture; San José Church (1523), a rare instance of gothic architecture in the Americas; and several eighteenth- and nineteenth-century private dwellings that now house exhibits of art, architecture, history, ethnology, and rare books. The Columbus Quincentennial of 1992 sparked a new wave of projects in Old San Juan, comprising restoration of the Ballajá army barracks, which later housed the Museum of the Americas; La Princesa, a nineteenth-century prison, then home to the Puerto Rico Tourism Company; and Paseo de la Princesa, a promenade on the waterfront of San Juan. This successful restoration program has refreshed public understanding of the national past and has revitalized Old San Juan as a vibrant residential, commercial, and cultural center, strengthening San Juan's position as a leading tourism destination in the Caribbean.

See also **Ponce de León, Juan; Puerto Rico.**

BIBLIOGRAPHY

Hernández, Carmen Dolores. *Ricardo Alegría: Una vida.* San Juan: Editorial Plaza Mayor, 2002.

Hostos, Adolfo de. *Ciudad murada: Ensayo acerca del proceso de la civilización en la ciudad española de San Juan Bautista de Puerto Rico, 1521–1898.* Havana: Editorial Lex, 1948. Reprinted as *Historia de San Juan, ciudad murada: Ensayo acerca del proceso de la civilización en la ciudad española de San Juan Bautista de Puerto Rico, 1521–1898.* San Juan, P. R.: Instituto de Cultura Puertorriqueña, 1983.

Martínez-Vergne, Teresita. *Shaping the Discourse on Space: Charity and Its Wards in Nineteenth-century San Juan, Puerto Rico.* Austin: University of Texas Press, 1999.

Matos Rodríguez, Félix V. *Women and Urban Change in San Juan, Puerto Rico, 1820–1868.* Gainesville: University Press of Florida, 1999.

ALLAN S. R. SUMNALL
LUIS A. GONZÁLEZ

SAN LORENZO. San Lorenzo, the premier Early Formative Olmec capital, overlooks the tropical lowlands of southern Veracruz, Mexico, from a privileged vantage point bounded by meandering water courses of the Coatzacoalcos river system. Initial occupation from about 1500 BCE was followed by its florescence, dated between 1200 and 850 BCE. For more than three centuries this political center charged with cosmological significance was the heart of the Olmec world. As it waned after 850 BCE, La Venta emerged as the capital.

San Lorenzo's complex organization is attested by immense earthen architecture and numerous monolithic stone monuments totaling about 500 tons. The site core, a plateau ringed by multiple levels of terraces, is the product of massive artificial modification of the natural landscape. Its 129 stone monuments, including ten colossal heads and several sovereigns' thrones, bear witness to the power of Olmec lords who organized the long-distance transport of the weighty sculptures from the Tuxtla Mountains. Recent (1990–1996) findings at the site include the ostentatious residence of an Olmec noble, a recycling workshop where sculptures were transformed into new forms, a buried architectural complex composed of low earthen platforms surrounding a sunken patio, and numerous sculptures, such as the tenth colossal head, which is displayed in the community museum of Tenochtitlán, Veracruz.

See also **Archaeology; Olmecs.**

BIBLIOGRAPHY

Cyphers, Ann. "Reconstructing Olmec Life at San Lorenzo." In *Olmec Art of Ancient Mexico*, edited by Elizabeth P. Benson and Beatriz de la Fuente, 61–72. Washington, DC: National Gallery of Art/Harry N. Abrams, 1996.

Cyphers, Ann. "From Stone to Symbols: Olmec Art in Social Context at San Lorenzo Tenochtitlán." In *Social Patterns in Pre-Classic Mesoamerica*, edited by David C. Grove and Rosemary A. Joyce, 155–182. Washington, DC: Dumbarton Oaks, 1999.

Cyphers, Ann, ed. *Población, subsistencia y medio ambiente en San Lorenzo Tenochtitlán*. Mexico City: Universidad Nacional Autónoma de México, Instituto de Investigaciones Antropológicas, 1997.

Cyphers, Ann, and Mario Arturo Ortiz. "Geomorphology and Ancient Cultural Landscapes of Southern Veracruz." In *Mounds, Modoc, and Mesoamerica: Papers in Honor of Melvin L. Fowler*, edited by Steven R. Ahler, pp. 99–110. Springfield: Illinois State Museum, 2000.

Cyphers, Ann, and Mario Arturo Ortiz. *Escultura olmeca de San Lorenzo Tenochtitlán*. Mexico City: Universidad Nacional Autónoma de México, Instituto de Investigaciones Antropológicas, 2004.

Cyphers, Ann, and Mario Arturo Ortiz. "The Olmec." In *The Aztec Empire*, edited by Felipe Solis, pp. 110–113. New York: Guggenheim Museum, 2004.

Symonds, Stacey, Ann Cyphers, and Roberto Lunagómez. *Asentamiento prehispánico en San Lorenzo Tenochtitlán*. Vol. 2, Serie San Lorenzo. Mexico City: Universidad Nacional Autónoma de México, Instituto de Investigaciones Antropológicas, 2002.

ANN CYPHERS

SAN LORENZO, BATTLE OF.

Battle of San Lorenzo, fought on 3 February 1813 between Spanish loyalists ascending the Paraná River and Argentine revolutionaries led by José de San Martín. This was the first engagement in which San Martín commanded the patriot forces following his return to Argentina from Spain in 1812.

The site was a monastery not far from Rosario, on the west bank of the Paraná. Troops from a Spanish flotilla landed and began to move inland, only to be surprised and routed by the mounted grenadiers whom San Martín had concealed behind the building. Though few men were involved, the victory helped secure the river for the patriots and gave an important boost to morale.

See also **Wars of Independence, South America.**

BIBLIOGRAPHY

J. C. J. Metford, *San Martín the Liberator* (1950), pp. 36–38.

Ricardo Rojas, *San Martín, Knight of the Andes*, translated by Herschel Brickell and Carlos Videla (1967), pp. 31–35.

Additional Bibliography

Luna, Félix. *La emancipación argentina y americana*. Buenos Aires: Planeta, 1998.

Pasquali, Patricia. *San Martín: La fuerza de la misión y la soledad de la gloria: Biografía*. Buenos Aires: Planeta, 1999.

Ruiz Moreno, Isidoro J. *Campañas militares argentinas: La política y la Guerra*. v. 1–2. Buenos Aires: Emecé, 2005.

Szuchman, Mark D., and Jonathan C. Brown. *Revolution and Restoration: The Rearrangement of Power in Argentina, 1776–1860*. Lincoln: University of Nebraska Press, 1994.

DAVID BUSHNELL

SAN LUIS.

San Luis, capital city (153,322 inhabitants in 2001) of the homonymous province (2001 population 367,933) in western Argentina. San Luis was founded in 1594 near Punta de los Venados by Spanish forces from Chile commanded by Juan de Jofré. The natives of San Luis are still referred to as *puntanos*. Rebuilt in 1596, after its destruction by Indians, the city was continually attacked by Indians throughout colonial times as it developed into a prosperous cattle-raising center. In 1711 and 1750 punitive action was taken against the Tehuelche Indians. In 1776 the city became part of the Viceroyalty of Río de la Plata, and in 1782 it was incorporated into the Intendancy of Córdoba. Finally, in 1813, it returned to the Intendancy of Mendoza, as part of the Cuyo region. Cattle and durum wheat are the main products of the province. Since the 1940s the region has been progressively losing inhabitants to the dynamic and prosperous city of Mendoza.

See also **Argentina, Geography.**

BIBLIOGRAPHY

Follari, Rodolfo S. *El noventa en San Luis: Autonomistas y radicales en 1890.* Buenos Aires: Ediciones Ciudad Argentina, 1995.

CÉSAR N. CAVIEDES

SAN LUIS POTOSÍ. San Luis Potosí, north-central Mexican state and its capital city, historically connected to the revolutionary Plan of San Luis Potosí (1910) of Francisco I. Madero. In the sixteenth century, the region was settled by Spaniards seeking to protect Zacatecas from Indian attacks. The town of San Luis Potosí, named after Upper Peru's Potosí, was founded in 1591 or 1592 in the wake of silver strikes. Mining remained an important part of the colonial economy, invigorated by the discovery of the rich Catorce veins in 1778. In the arid lands surrounding the mines there were stock-raising estates, and to the east were some agricultural properties, on which lived much of the working rural population.

During the independence struggle, leaders of San Luis city and rural village residents supported Miguel Hidalgo, while estate owners and their workers were loyalists; a militia drawn from this latter group was largely responsible for Hidalgo's shattering defeat at Aculco in 1811. Following independence, the new state of San Luis Potosí's mining economy was disrupted, not recovering until late in the century. Stock raising and agriculture improved, sparked by the advent of rail service, but deteriorating conditions for the rural majority led to a number of uprisings. Dissatisfaction with the Porfirio Díaz regime in San Luis city led to the formation of Ricardo Flores Magón's radical Mexican Liberal Party (Partido Liberal Mexicano) in 1900, and after Francisco Madero's call for revolution, the countryside erupted under the leadership of a Zapata-like figure, Saturnino Cedillo Martínez. San Luis weathered the storm of revolution, and its importance as a communications, industrial, and agricultural center was enhanced.

In 2005, the population of the city of San Luis Potosi had reached 730,950.

See also **Mining: Colonial Spanish America.**

BIBLIOGRAPHY

The rural history and revolutionary connections of San Luis Potosí are featured in Jan Bazant, *Cinco haciendas mexicanas: Tres siglos de vida rural en San Luis Potosí (1600–1910)* (1975); Bazant also has some information on sixteenth-century San Luis and the development of mining there. Dudley Ankerson, *Agrarian Warlord: Saturnino Cedillo and the Mexican Revolution in San Luis Potosí* (1984); and John Tutino, *From Insurrection to Revolution in Mexico: Social Bases of Agrarian Violence, 1750–1940* (1986). Scattered information is provided in David A. Brading, *Miners and Merchants in Bourbon Mexico, 1763–1810* (1971).

Additional Bibliography

Monroy, María Isabel, and Tomás Calvillo Unna. *Breve historia de San Luis Potosí.* México: El Colegio de México, Fideicomiso Historia de las Américas, 1997.

Gámez, Moisés. *De negro brillante a blanco plateado: La empresa minera mexicana a finales del siglo XIX.* San Luis Potosí: Colegio de San Luis, 2001.

ROBERT HASKETT

SAN MARCOS, UNIVERSITY OF. University of San Marcos, premier university of colonial South America. Because Spanish colonists in Peru wanted their sons to be eligible for positions that required a university education, the city council of Lima petitioned for a university. Authorized in 1551 by Charles V, the Royal and Pontifical University of San Marcos finally became an endowed secular institution with sixteen academic chairs in the 1570s.

Modeled on the University of Salamanca, the University of San Marcos boasted the five faculties necessary to be a major university: arts (philosophy), theology, medicine, civil law, and canon law. In addition, it initially offered instruction in Quechua, and in 1678 it added a chair of mathematics. The religious orders also sponsored chairs offering instruction in the writings of their most venerated theologians—for example, St. Thomas Aquinas and St. Augustine. At its peak, San Marcos had about thirty-five academic chairs. Although religious institutions in Lima offered college-level instruction, only San Marcos was authorized to confer baccalaureate, master's, licentiate, and doctoral degrees.

The faculty of San Marcos long used prescribed texts employed throughout the Hispanic world. In the late eighteenth century, however, some more contemporary authors' works were incorporated into the curriculum as the university sought to regain its former glory after suffering a period of decline.

The intellectual elite of colonial Lima passed through the halls of San Marcos and often taught there. As a focus of intellectual life for much of the viceregal era, the university fulfilled its charge of educating men for service in the clergy or bureaucracy.

In the twenty-first century, the university continues to be considered the most prestigious and selective in Peruvian higher education.

See also **Universities: Colonial Spanish America.**

BIBLIOGRAPHY

John Tate Lanning, *Academic Culture in the Spanish Colonies* (1940), chap. 1.

Additional Bibliography

Aparicio Quispe, Severo. *Los mercedarios en la Universidad San Marcos de Lima*. Lima: [s.n.], 1999.

Buford, Nick. *The University of San Marcos of Lima in the Eighteenth Century*. Baton Rouge: Louisiana State University, 1969.

Valcárcel, Carlos Daniel. *San Marcos, universidad decana de América*. Lima, [s.n.], 1968.

Williams, Jerry M., ed. *Peralta Barnuevo and the Discourse of Loyalty: A Critical Edition of Four Selected Texts*. Tempe: ASU Center for Latin American Studies Press, Arizona State University, 1996.

MARK A. BURKHOLDER

SAN MARTÍN, JOSÉ FRANCISCO DE

(1778–1850). José Francisco de San Martín (*b.* 25 February 1778; *d.* 17 August 1850), the liberator of three South American countries who aspired to create the United States of South America. San Martín was born in Yapeyú, in the province of Corrientes, Argentina. His Spanish parents took him to Spain in 1784, where he studied at the Seminary of Nobles in Madrid. In 1789 he joined the Murcia Regiment as a cadet, and later participated in military campaigns in Africa, the Iberian Peninsula, and France. His first combat experience was at Oran (25 June 1791), where he fought the Moors. In 1793 he served under General Ricardos, the tactician who had led his troops across the Pyrenees to attack the French enemies of

José Francisco de San Martín (1778–1850), on horseback. A national hero of Argentina, General San Martín was integral in the country's struggle for independence from Spain, which was declared in 1816. He went on to lead revolutionary movements in Peru and Chile. BETTMANN/CORBIS

Louis XVI. At Bailén he fought under General Castaños and later was an aide to the Marquess of Coupigny.

In 1811, San Martín retired from the army without a pension, and although authorized to go to Lima, he sailed instead for London. Before leaving Spain, however, San Martín was initiated into the Caballeros Racionales No. 3, which sought the independence of South America. He later joined a similarly inspired secret organization, the Great American Assembly of Francisco de Miranda in London, where he met the Venezuelan Andrés Bello and the Argentines Manuel Moreno and Tomás Guido. Bello was the teacher of General Simón Bolívar, and Moreno and Guido were the brother and secretary, respectively, of Mariano Moreno, a prominent leader of the independence movement in Buenos Aires. In January 1812, San Martín sailed for Buenos Aires aboard the British frigate *George Canning,* with fellow passengers Carlos de Alvear and his young wife, José Zapiola, and Francisco Chilavert.

In Buenos Aires, Alvear introduced San Martín to the most influential members of *porteño* society. The ruling triumvirate recognized his Spanish military grade of lieutenant colonel and asked him to organize the Regimiento de Granaderos a Caballo (Mounted Grenadier Regiment). Alvear was second in command. Its personnel eventually consisted of veteran officers of the revolutionary war, young men drawn from the leading families of the city of Buenos Aires, and the provinces of La Rioja, Córdoba, Banda Oriental del Uruguay, and the Guaraní of Corrientes. San Martín taught them military tactics and the use of different weapons. The grenadiers became a model for other regiments.

On 12 September 1812, with Alvear and his wife, María del Carmen Quintanilla, as witnesses, San Martín married fifteen-year-old María de los Remedios de Escalada de la Quintana, daughter of a wealthy Spanish merchant. On 8 October, he and his regiment participated in the military movement that replaced the existing triumvirate with another. This revolution bolstered the independence movement. Four months later he commanded the troops that repulsed superior Spanish numbers seeking to land at San Lorenzo.

In December 1813, San Martín replaced Manuel Belgrano as commander of the Expeditionary Force to liberate Upper Peru at Posta de Yatasto. In March 1814 he proposed that the best way to win independence was to take Lima by way of Chile, not Bolivia, believing that a small, well trained army invading Chile from Mendoza would prevail in ending Spanish rule on the continent. At his request Supreme Director Gervasio Antonio de Posadas appointed him intendant governor of the province of Cuyo (14 August 1814), with an annual salary of 300 pesos and instructions to prepare the defenses of Mendoza against any possible Spanish invasion. San Martín established himself at Plumerillo, outside Mendoza, and took steps to provide smallpox vaccinations for all the inhabitants of Cuyo, to help Chilean émigrés arriving after Rancagua, and to persuade those not in militia units to join one or be called traitors to the fatherland. Among the Chilean émigrés were Bernardo O'Higgins and the Carrera brothers. In February 1815 he declined promotion to major

colonel in the Armies of the United Provinces of the Río de la Plata, saying that he expected to withdraw from military service once independence was won, and the order relieving him of his command was revoked at the request of the local *cabildo.*

In 1816, San Martín informed the Supreme Director that he needed an army of 4,000 to invade Chile, and with the aid of the Cuyo deputies, and especially of Tomás Godoy Cruz, he obtained from the Tucumán Congress a declaration of the independence of the United Provinces of South America. On 21 July 1816 he and the new Supreme Director Juan Martín de Pueyrredón met in Córdoba, completing arrangements for the liberation of Chile. Pueyrredón agreed to send him more men, armaments, and supplies, and he appointed San Martín commanding general of the Army of the Andes. The army then took an oath to defend the independence of the United Provinces of South America. San Martín now trained his troops and the local militia in basic military tactics and maneuvers, personally instructed the officers in military subjects, and invited neutral foreigners to join him. One of his students was José María Paz, later a prominent leader in Argentine civil wars. The local people freed their slaves on the condition that they enlist in the army. They supplied San Martín with provisions and transported military goods without charge. The labor guilds took up voluntary contributions, and women offered their jewels. San Martín levied forced loans on the royalists and extracted extraordinary contributions from wealthy natives. The Army of the Andes made its own armaments, ammunition, guns, gunpowder, saddles, bayonets, cannons, and cannonballs. The provincial women sewed military uniforms without charge.

San Martín was named captain-general so that he could have both military and political authority, but he delegated the political functions to Colonel Toribio Luzuriaga, who was ably assisted by the lieutenant governors of San Juan and San Luis. The commander of the general staff was Brigadier General Miguel Estanislao Soler, and the battalion commanders were Juan Gregorio de Las Heras, Rudecindo Alvarado, Pedro Conde, and Ambrosio Crámer. The five squadrons of the Granaderos a Caballo were under Mariano Necochea, and among its officers were Juan Lavalle, Federico de Brandzen, Manuel Medina y Escalada, and Domingo Arcos. The Patriotic Legion of the South was formed primarily by Chilean émigrés who supported O'Higgins. Another Chilean émigré, José Ignacio Zenteno, was the military secretary.

San Martín inaugurated the so-called *guerra de zapa* by placing spies in the enemy camps, spreading false rumors, sending secret emissaries to collect information throughout Chile, and encouraging uprisings. Field Marshal Francisco Marcó del Pont, in charge of the Chilean government, reacted by increasing political repression and stationing his forces at possible invasion points along the Andes. Replying to his request for military and political guidance, Supreme Director Pueyrredón sent San Martín his instructions on 24 December 1816, setting forth in fifty-nine articles how he was to conduct the war, deal with political parties and governments, and pay all expenses of the expeditionary force. The sole purpose of the campaign, he emphasized, was to secure American independence and the glory of the United Provinces. San Martín was to avoid favoring any of the political groups dividing Chile, to seek to improve the condition of the people, and to negotiate a perpetual alliance between the two nations.

Once the Army of the Andes was fully organized and trained, San Martín named the Virgin of Carmen del Cuyo as its patron and gave it a flag that his wife and other patriots embroidered. He also provided it with a printing press, which was to spread revolutionary ideas and publish battle bulletins. At San Martín's suggestion Brigadier O'Higgins was to become the temporary governor of Chile once Santiago was free.

The Army of the Andes that moved out of Mendoza on 18–19 January 1817 consisted of 4,000 soldiers, over 1,000 militiamen to transport munitions and a twenty-day supply of provisions, muleteers, and laborers to repair the roads. The Andean passes had been surveyed in advance by the engineer Álvarez Condarco. The bulk of the army, under San Martín, used Los Patos pass to cross the Andes to the valley of Putaendo, in the province of Aconcagua. An army division under General Soler formed the vanguard; O'Higgins commanded the reserve division. A column of 800 men under Las Heras used the Uspallata Pass to Chile. It had the ammunition train, the dismounted artillery, and the arsenal, with workers armed with long poles and ropes so that they could suspend the cannons on litters. Once across the peak of the Andes,

they defeated the royalists at Guardia Vieja and took Santa Rosa de los Andes. A northern column under Commandant Cabot, crossing the Andes in fourteen days, defeated the royalists at Salala, and took the province of Coquimbo, while a detachment from La Rioja took Copiapó. A southern column under the Chilean Captain Freyre used the Planchón pass to cross the Andes, defeated the royalists at Vega del Campeo, and entered Talca. All the soldiers were mounted on mules, and moved slowly according to the availability of pasture, water, and wood.

The entire army reached San Felipe, from which it dominated the valley of Aconcagua, and its forward units made contact with the royalists at Chacabuco. The Spanish army of 2,500 under Brigadier Rafael Maroto occupied advantageous positions on the hill of Chacabuco, which blocked the road to Santiago. When his army was assembled, San Martín attacked in two corps: the one on the left, under O'Higgins, was to distract the enemy until the corps on the right, under Soler, could attack the enemy from the rear. O'Higgins advanced without waiting for Soler to complete his maneuver, but reinforced by cavalry troops under Zapiola and Necochea, he was able to destroy the royalist squadrons. The retreating Spaniards were routed by Soler. The patriots captured all the enemy artillery, its ammunition train, and 600 prisoners. The battle of Chacabuco (12 February) marked the beginning of the patriot offensive.

On 14 February, the patriot army entered Santiago. An assembly convoked by San Martín elected him governor of Chile, a position he declined, and it then named O'Higgins. Marcó del Pont and other Spanish leaders were captured and sent to San Luis. On 10 March, the Santiago *cabildo* presented San Martín with 10,000 gold pesos, which he donated for the establishment of the national library. An overjoyed directorate in Buenos Aires rewarded him the title of brigadier general of the Armies of the Fatherland (26 February 1817), which he did not accept. San Martín went to Buenos Aires with his aide, John T. O'Brien, to settle military problems and to obtain the resources needed to organize the expedition to Peru. He entered the city disguised, hoping to avoid a public demonstration, but he was detected, and the *cabildo* honored him on 9 April 1817. San Martín discussed the forthcoming campaign to liberate Peru with Pueyrredón, and then left for Santiago.

On 20 June, O'Higgins appointed San Martín as commanding general of the Chilean army, and on 12 February 1818, he and San Martín proclaimed the independence of Chile. Meanwhile, the Spanish forces under Colonel José Ordóñez, which had not been involved in any battle, gathered in the plaza of Talcahuano. Las Heras and O'Higgins unsuccessfully attacked the town fortifications. General Mariano Osorio then arrived with 3,000 men, stationing them in the town of Talca. San Martín went to help O'Higgins, and while he was repositioning the troops, he was attacked on 19 March at Cancha Rayada by Ordóñez, and was forced to retreat. Las Heras alone kept his division intact. The patriots regrouped and, 5,000 strong, attacked and defeated the royalists under Osorio at Maipú (5 April). San Martín was compelled to use his reserves in the battle. Osorio and his escort abandoned the battlefield, leaving Ordóñez to negotiate surrender. One thousand Spaniards were killed and 3,000 taken prisoners. Victory established the independence of Chile, and provided for Argentina's security by giving it a base of operations on the Pacific. Argentina and Chile concluded an alliance to liberate Peru, while San Martín asked Great Britain to persuade Spain to grant independence to South America.

With the Spaniards now on the defensive, San Martín left for Buenos Aires to obtain the support needed for invading Peru. On 4 May, Congress congratulated O'Higgins, awarded a prize to San Martín and the army, and authorized a loan of 500,000 pesos to finance the expedition to Peru and the formation of a naval unit. It also ordered the erection of a statue to commemorate Chacabuco and Maipú and recognized the officers and soldiers of the Army of the Andes as "heroic defenders of the nation." San Martín asked Congress to prevent Pueyrredón from promoting him, saying that the army alone deserved praise for the victories. On 14 May, Congress appointed him Brigadier of the Armies of the Fatherland. Three days later Congress celebrated in extraordinary session the victories of Chacabuco and Maipú. After Congress authorized a personal coat of arms for him on 20 October, San Martín left for Santiago de Chile. The Buenos Aires government later informed him that it was unable to fulfill its promise of aid.

At the end of 1818, Commandant Manuel Blanco Encalada, an Argentine serving Chile, doubled the size of the Chilean navy by capturing first a Spanish frigate in the Bay of Talcahuano and then five Spanish transports with 700 men bound for the city with abundant military supplies. He relinquished command of the fleet to Lord Thomas Alexander Cochrane, who had signed a contract in London with the agents of O'Higgins and San Martín. In January 1819, Cochrane attacked the Spanish fleet in Callao, but he was unable to destroy it. Early in 1820, San Martín refused the request of Director José Rondeau to concentrate his troops in Buenos Aires in order to fight the caudillos. However, he did send a division to Mendoza and San Juan, but he soon withdrew half of it for his campaign to liberate Peru. San Martín went to Mendoza to recover his health, returning to Chile in a litter in January, still expecting to unite Argentina, Chile, and Peru as one nation. On 20 August 1820 the liberating expedition of 2,300 Argentines and 2,100 Chileans sailed from Valparaiso. Most of the officers were Argentines. The fleet consisted of eight warships and sixteen troop transports with a crew of 1,600 men under Cochrane. The cargo of the transports consisted of rifles, swords, cannons, ammunition, artillery shells, grenades, gunpowder, and horses with their feed. San Martín commanded the expedition as captain-general, and he informed the *cabildo* of Buenos Aires of his departure for Peru.

The royal armies San Martín faced consisted of 23,000 men in Upper and Lower Peru. San Martín disembarked in the port of Paracas and established his headquarters at Pisco. His aim was to avoid battle and to provoke rebellions among the people and desertions in the Spanish troops by spreading revolutionary propaganda. Desertions among Spanish commanders and officers did increase, and an entire battalion surrendered. He moved to Ancón, then to Huaura, and finally to Huamanga, from which he could dominate the valley of Huancayo. He negotiated an armistice of short duration with Viceroy Pezuela at Miraflores (26 September). He assured the success of the expedition when he defeated Brigadier Alejandro O'Reilly at Cerro de Pasco (6 December 1820), and captured both O'Reilly and Mayor Andrés de Santa Cruz. On 2 June 1821, San Martín met Viceroy Pezuela at Punchauca and asked him to recognize Peru as a sovereign nation, to approve a junta which would write a temporary constitution, and to join him in naming a commission that would ask Ferdinand VII to select a son to become king of

Peru after accepting a constitution. The vacillating viceroy agreed only to another armistice. On 19 July, San Martín entered Lima and called a council of notables, which voted for independence. Peruvian independence was declared on 28 July.

San Martín assumed political and military command of the new nation as "protector of a free Peru." He thus prevented Simón Bolívar from seizing Peru. Then, through his secretary, Dr. Bernardo Monteagudo, he abolished the personal service of the Indians (the tributes, the *mitas*, and *encomiendas*); declared the freedom of the newborn children of slaves; established a free press and the sanctity of the home; and ended torture in judicial proceedings. He fought gambling and maintained security and order in town. On 21 November, Lima awarded 500,000 pesos to the officers and commissioned officers of the liberating army. The reward was distributed by lot among the twenty officers named by San Martín. The officers who were ignored probably participated in the conspiracy that led to the downfall of San Martín.

With the bulk of the royalist army, Canterac was in the valley of Jauja, controlling the sierra and suppressing Indian revolts supporting the revolution. Bolívar sent General Antonio José de Sucre with a division to liberate Quito Province. This inadequate force sought reinforcements from San Martín, who sent Santa Cruz with 1,000 men. The war ended when the Argentine granaderos under Lavalle destroyed the Spanish cavalry at Riobamba and Sucre and the Argentine Manuel de Olazábal defeated the royalists at Pichincha (24 May 1822). By that time the port of Guayaquil had declared its independence, and Peru wanted to annex it. On 13 July, Bolívar placed the port under the protection of Colombia.

San Martín landed at Guayaquil on 25 July, and held three interviews with Bolívar. What transpired at these meetings is still disputed, but the two men evidently discussed the form of government the new nations should have and the military operations required to end the war. San Martín favored a constitutional monarchy for South America, Bolívar a republic. Both men sought the formation of something like the United States of America, a goal which would be reached by first uniting the former viceroyalties, now republics, in a South American Confederation and then fusing them in a federation,

the United States of South America. With too meager a force to end the war alone, San Martín asked for help and reminded Bolívar of the aid he had given to Sucre. Bolívar declined to place a substantial Colombian force under his command, and refused San Martín's offer to serve under him. San Martín returned to Lima, and at the meeting of the Constituent Congress on 20 September 1822 he resigned as Protector. He then sailed for Chile, where he was no longer popular, and crossed the Andes to his small farm in Mendoza. In late 1823 he learned that his ailing wife had died on 3 August.

San Martín enjoyed the support of the federalists and the provincial governors, especially that of Governor Estanislao López of Santa Fe, but Bernardino Rivadavia was his enemy. He left for Buenos Aires in November to see Rivadavia, who already had negotiated a preliminary peace treaty with Spain (4 July 1823). On 7 February he sailed with his daughter Mercedes for Le Havre and from there to Southampton, England, finally settling in Brussels. In 1828 San Martín briefly returned to Buenos Aires, but he never landed and instead stayed for two months in Montevideo. He declined an invitation from Juan Lavalle to assume command of the government and army of Buenos Aires. He returned to Brussels. In 1834 the wealthy Spaniard Alejandro Aguado helped San Martín purchase a house in Grand Bourges. In 1838, when France was blockading Buenos Aires, San Martín offered his services to Juan Manuel de Rosas, who declined. Attacks against him appeared in the Buenos Aires press, but Domingo F. Sarmiento and later Bartolomé Mitre rose to his defense. He was restored to his former rank of captain-general, and Chile awarded him a lifelong pension in 1842.

San Martín died in Boulogne-sur-Mer. He bequeathed his sword to Rosas. At the suggestion of Sarmiento a statue in his honor was erected in Buenos Aires in 1862. In 1880 his remains were moved from the cemetery in Brunoy to the cathedral in Buenos Aires.

See also **Bolívar, Simón; Caballeros Racionales, Sociedad de; Wars of Independence, South America.**

BIBLIOGRAPHY

Bartolomé Mitre, *Historia de San Martín y de la emancipación sudamericana*, 3 vols. (1887–1888).

Museo Mitre, *Documentos del Archivo de San Martín*, 12 vols. (1910–1911).

José Pacífico Otero, *Historia del Libertador don José de San Martín*, 4 vols. (1932).

Jacinto R. Yaben, *Biografías argentinas y sudamericanas*, vol. 5 (1940), pp. 507–528.

Ricardo Rojas, *San Martín, Knight of the Andes,* translated by Herschel Brickell and Carlos Videla (1945).

José Luis Busaniche, *San Martín vivo* (1950), J. C. J. Metford, *San Martín the Liberator* (1950).

Instituto Nacional Sanmartiniano, *Documentos para la historia del libertador general San Martín*, 12 vols. (1953–).

Ricardo Piccirilli, *San Martín y la polítca de los pueblos* (1957).

José Luis Romero, *A History of Argentine Political Thought*, translated by Thomas F. McGann (1963).

Harold F. Peterson, *Argentina and the United States, 1810–1960* (1964).

Enrique De Gandía, *San Martín: Su pensamiento político* (1964).

Cristián García-Godoy, ed., *The San Martín Papers*, translated by Barbara Huntley and Pilar Liria (1988).

Additional Bibliography

Chumbita, Hugo. *Hijos del país: San Martín, Yrigoyen, Perón*. Buenos Aires: Emecé Editores, 2004.

Guzmán, Carlos Alberto. *San Martín ante la historia*. Buenos Aires: Academia Argentina de la Historia, 2000.

Kohan, Martín. *Narrar a San Martín*. Buenos Aires: Adriana Hidalgo Editora, 2005.

Nascimbene, Mario C. *San Martín en el olimpo nacional: Nacimiento y apogeo de los mitos argentinos*. Buenos Aires: Editorial Biblos, 2002.

Pasquali, Patricia. *San Martín: La fuerza de la misión y la soledad de la gloria: Biografía*. Buenos Aires: Planeta, 1999.

Ramos Pérez, Demetrio. *San Martín: El libertador del Sur*. Madrid: Anaya, 1988.

Uzal, Francisco Hipólito. *San Martín contraataca*. Buenos Aires: Ediciones Theoría, 2002.

JOSEPH T. CRISCENTI

SAN NICOLÁS, ACUERDO DE (1852).

Acuerdo de San Nicolás (1852), an agreement reached on 31 May 1852 by representatives of the United Provinces of the Río De La Plata at a small town on the Arroyo del Medio, the brook that forms the boundary between the provinces of Buenos Aires and Sante Fe. The three provinces whose governors arrived late—Salto, Jujuy, and Córdoba—later approved the accord. Justo José de Urquiza, representing Entre Ríos and Catamarca, called the meeting to organize the nation. The governor of Buenos Aires was authorized by the provincial legislature only to attend the meetings, while the others received instructions from their provincial legislatures. The accord declared that the Treaty of the Littoral (1831)—an alliance between the provinces of Buenos Aires, Corrientes, Entre Ríos, and Santa Fe—was the fundamental law of the nation, and asked each province to send two deputies without restrictions to a constituent congress. A majority vote would suffice to approve a constitution. Urquiza was appointed temporary director of the Argentine Confederation. Free trade was approved and transit duties abolished. Each province was to contribute to the administrative expenses in proportion to its customhouse revenues. The provincial legislature of Buenos Aires rejected the accord.

See also **Urquiza, Justo José de.**

BIBLIOGRAPHY

David Rock, *Argentina, 1516–1987: From Spanish Colonization to Alfonsín*, rev. ed. (1987).

Joseph T. Criscenti, ed., *Sarmiento and His Argentina* (1993).

Additional Bibliography

Laferrère, Alfonso de. *El Acuerdo de San Nicolás y su polítca*. Buenos Aires: Instituto Urquiza de Estudios Históricos, 2002.

Szuchman, Mark D., and Jonathan C. Brown, eds. *Revolution and Restoration: The Rearrangement of Power in Argentina, 1776-1860*. Lincoln: University of Nebraska Press, 1994.

JOSEPH T. CRISCENTI

SAN NICOLÁS, PACT OF. The Pact of

San Nicolás was signed in San Nicolás, Argentina, on May 31, 1852, by all the governors of the Argentine Confederation for the purpose of convening a Constituent Congress and organizing the country's institutions. The pact provided for each province to send two deputies to the Congress. It was also decided to create a provisional government under Justo José de Urquiza, the governor of Entre Ríos, who had removed Juan Manuel de Rosas from power. Also, under the terms of the pact, Urquiza was given command of all the military forces, placed in charge of foreign affairs and regulation of rivers inland, and given the authority to execute all provisions of the Federal Pact of 1831. The opposition of the Buenos Aires government to the pact was aroused by the fact that representation in the Congress was not to be in proportion to the population of the provinces and that enormous powers were conferred on the provisional government. In what came to be called the "June meetings," after the Chamber of Representatives of the Province of Buenos Aires heatedly debated the agreement, the governor of Buenos Aires, Vicente López y Planes, announced his resignation, and Urquiza dissolved the Chamber to assume provisionally the leadership of the government of Buenos Aires.

See also **Argentine Confederation; Rosas, Juan Manuel de; Urquiza, Justo José de.**

BIBLIOGRAPHY

Gorostegui de Torres, Haydée. *La organización nacional.* Colección Historia Argentina, vol. 4. Buenos Aires: Paidós, 2000.

Oszlak, Oscar. *La formación del estado argentino: Orden, progreso, y organización Nacional.* Buenos Aires: Planeta, 1997.

MARCELA TERNAVASIO

SAN PASCUAL, BATTLE OF. During the Mexican-American War (1846–1848), the U.S. invasion and occupation of California was met with local resistance. One of the many battles fought there was the battle of San Pascual, near San Diego. The Mexican forces had recaptured Los Angeles from the U.S. army, and in December 1846 General Andrés Pico (1810–1876) along with about 100 men were sent to the Indian *ranchería* of San Pascual to prevent the Americans from reinforcing their garrison in San Diego. Meanwhile, Colonel Stephen W. Kearny with about 150 men marched overland from Santa Fe, New Mexico, and entered the area

near the present-day city of Ramona, in the Santa Maria valley.

Early in the morning of December 6 the two forces discovered each other and engaged in a running battle. After intense hand-to-hand combat, twenty American soldiers were killed. The Californios had eleven wounded. Neither side surrendered.

Later, Kearny wrote that the battle of December 6 had been a "victory" and that the Californios had "fled from the field." But the Navy officers, headed by Commodore Robert Stockton (1795–1866), labeled the battle of San Pascual a defeat for the U.S. Army. Of course, the Californios considered this engagement a victory, and news of it spread throughout the district.

The battle of San Pascual proved that despite internal dissention and division, many Californios were willing to die to defend their homeland from the U.S. invasion. A month after the battle, the U.S. forces recaptured Los Angeles and forced the Mexican governor to sign a treaty ending the hostilities.

See also **Kearny, Stephen W.; Mexico, Wars and Revolutions: Mexican-American War.**

BIBLIOGRAPHY

Griswold del Castillo, Richard. "The Mexican War in San Diego: Loyalty and Resistance." *Journal of San Diego History* 49, no. 1 (2003): 15–29.

Jones, Salley Caval. "The Battle of San Pascual." Master's Thesis, University of San Diego, 1973.

RICHARD GRISWOLD DEL CASTILLO

SAN PATRICIO. During the Mexican-American War of 1846–1848, Irish, German, and other Catholic soldiers deserted the U.S. Army and joined the Mexican side. In November 1846, following the orders of General Antonio López de Santa Anna, hundreds of deserters joined a new artillery company, initially called Voluntarios Irlandeses, organized by John Riley (known as Juan O'Reilly in Mexico), an experienced officer born in Clifden, County Galway. Riley had served in the British army as a noncommissioned officer and in 1843 emigrated to Canada and then to the United

States. Two years later he enrolled in the Fifth U.S. Infantry together with several other Irish soldiers.

From the beginning of the conflict, the Mexican army actively induced U.S. Catholic soldiers to defect to the enemy, characterizing the war as a religious struggle between Catholics and Protestants. Pamphlets circulated among the Irish and German soldiers that included a promise of promotions and land grants. Bigotry against Catholic soldiers was common among nativist U.S. officers, an attitude that further encouraged desertion, though of the 4,811 Irish-born soldiers serving in the U.S. Army, only 200–800 joined the San Patricios.

As a battery of artillery, the San Patricios first fought from September 19 to 24, 1846, in the Battle of Monterrey. The Mexican forces were defeated, but the San Patricios were granted safe passage to Saltillo by the U.S. commander, Zachary Taylor. On February 23, 1847, the battalion fiercely engaged at the Battle of Buena Vista, where it served with distinction under a banner of green silk with the image of St. Patrick. Santa Anna ordered a general retreat and the San Patricios marched to San Luis Potosí. They also distinguished themselves at Cerro Gordo (April 17 and 18, 1847) and at the decisive Battle of Churubusco (August 20, 1847), where they were decimated and the survivors made prisoners.

Between September 12 and 18, 1847, forty-seven were hanged and fifteen were whipped and branded with the letter "D" as deserters, including the leader, John Riley. The remainder of the San Patricio battalion was dispersed in 1848 by the Mexican president, José Joaquín de Herrera. The story of the San Patricios generated a significant amount of historical and fictional narratives in the form of books and films. Riley and his men were considered heroes in Ireland and in Mexico, where a street in Churubusco was named Mártires Irlandeses, but the battalion's existence put Irish Americans in an uncomfortable position within the larger society in the United States.

See also **Mexico, Wars and Revolutions: Mexican-American War; Santa Anna, Antonio López de; Taylor, Zachary.**

BIBLIOGRAPHY

Cox, Patricia. *Batallón de San Patricio*. Mexico City: Editorial Stylo, 1954.

Hogan, Michael. *The Irish Soldiers of Mexico*. Mexico City: Fondo Editorial Universitario, 1997.

Miller, Robert Ryal. *Shamrock and Sword: The Saint Patrick's Battalion in the U.S.-Mexican War*. Norman: University Press of Oklahoma, 1989.

Murray, Edmundo. "The San Patricio Battalion: A Bibliography." Irish Migration Studies in Latin America, 2006. Available from http://www.irlandeses.org/sanpatriciosbiblio.htm.

Stevens, Peter F. *The Rogue's March: John Riley and the St. Patrick's Battalion*. Washington, DC: Brassey's, 1999.

Wynn, Dennis J. *The San Patricio Soldiers: Mexico's Foreign Legion*. Southwestern Studies, monograph 74. El Paso: Texas Western Press, University of Texas at El Paso, 1984.

EDMUNDO MURRAY

SAN RAFAEL. San Rafael, city of over 170,000 inhabitants (2001) located 125 miles south of Mendoza in Argentina. The settlement emerged at the northern margin of the Diamante River as a trading place for cattle drivers taking their herds across the Andes to Chile. A fort was built in 1770 to keep Indians at bay, and in 1777 punitive actions against the raiders were taken from this stronghold. In 1805 commander Teles Meneses founded the fort of San Rafael, as well as a permanent settlement, to establish a Spanish presence in the region. As a well-irrigated oasis, San Rafael attracted French and Italian families who from 1870 to 1890 began to cultivate grapes in well-irrigated vineyards. San Rafael produces one of the finest white wines of Argentina. Situated in the agrarian province of Mendoza, it is the last major city on the border of the desert south of the Atuel River.

See also **Argentina, Geography.**

BIBLIOGRAPHY

Izuel, María Elena. *Compendio de historia de San Rafael y del sur Mendocino*. Mendoza, Argentina: Editorial Ciencias y Artes, 1995.

CÉSAR N. CAVIEDES

SAN SALVADOR. San Salvador, name given in the colonial period to both the approximate territory of present-day El Salvador and the city that historically presided over it. The territory was an *alcaldía mayor* until 1785, when it became an *intendencia*. During the Central American Federation (1824–1839) it was one of the five constituent states. When the state left the federation and was renamed El Salvador, the name San Salvador was reserved for one of its subdivisions. Today it is one of fourteen departments of the country (2005 est. pop. 2.2 million). It is located in the central region with an area of 354 square miles. Its most prominent geographical features are the San Salvador volcano and Lake Ilopango.

The city (2001 est. pop. 485,847), now capital of El Salvador, was founded in 1525, probably by Diego de Alvarado. Twenty years later it moved to its present location, a valley 2,200 feet above sea level, 19.3 miles north of the Pacific coast. The valley is called "Valley of the Hammocks" because of the frequency of earthquakes. San Salvador is linked with the other major cities of the country and the capitals of Central America by the Pan-American Highway, and has easy access to an international airport located on the coast.

Historically the city has been the uncontested administrative, economic, cultural, and educational center of the country. In 1811, San Salvador's city notables, a group of creole indigo producers, led the first stage of Central American independence and thereafter played a prominent role in the movement. Francisco Morazán made it capital of the Central American Federation from 1834 until 1839. After an earthquake in 1854 the capital was moved east to Cojutepeque until 1859, when it returned to San Salvador. The most recent earthquake was in 1986, when important buildings, including the largest children's hospital and the American embassy, were seriously damaged and about a thousand people died. The city witnessed some of the most dramatic moments of the 1979–1992 civil war, including the murders of Archbishop Oscar Arnulfo Romero in 1980 and of six Jesuit priests nine years later, and the emotional celebration of the end of the civil war in January 1992.

Thanks to its central location, good communications, and access to government and financial services, San Salvador and its metropolitan area have become the heart of the industrial sector. According to the 1979 industrial census, almost half of the manufactures of the country were produced in the

area. Migration from the countryside increased in the 1960s and accelerated after the outbreak of the civil war, when thousands of peasants abandoned their land and sought refuge in the capital. More than one-fifth of the total population of the country lives within San Salvador's metropolitan area (2001 est. pop. 1.4 million) and San Salvador is the second-largest city in Central America. In the early twenty-first century gangs and gang-related crime plague parts of the city. The rise in gang violence is often portrayed as a result of the deportation of thousands of Salvadorans from the United States in the mid-1990s, the same Salvadorans and their descendants who had to flee from the civil war violence of the 1980s.

See also **El Salvador.**

BIBLIOGRAPHY

For the early history of the city, see Rodolfo Barón Castro, *La población de El Salvador* (1942) and *Reseña histórica de la villa de San Salvador* (1950). For recent population and economic data, see República De El Salvador, *Indicadores económicos y sociales, 1987–1989* (1989).

Lauria-Santiago, Aldo, and Leigh Binford. *Landscapes of Struggle: Politics, Society, and Community in El Salvador.* Pittsburgh, PA: University of Pittsburgh Press, 2004.

Rodríguez Herrera, América. *San Salvador: Historia urbana, 1900–1940.* San Salvador: Dirección de Publicaciones e Impresos, CONACULTURA, 2002.

HÉCTOR LINDO-FUENTES

SAN SIMÓN. *See* **Maximón.**

SANTA ANNA, ANTONIO LÓPEZ DE (1794–1876). Antonio López de Santa Anna (*b.* 21 February 1794; *d.* 21 June 1876), president of Mexico (nine times, 1833–1855). Santa Anna was the most important political figure in Mexico between 1821 and 1855. He was in many ways a quintessential caudillo, one of the regional military leaders who played such important roles in nineteenth-century Latin America. With a strong base in the Veracruz region in eastern Mexico, Santa Anna was consistently

Ever Memorable Battle of Buena Vista, Fought on 22nd and 23rd February 1847, between U.S. General Zachary Taylor and Santa Anna. Black and white photo of an engraving by American School (19th century). LIBRARY OF CONGRESS, WASHINGTON D.C., USA/ THE BRIDGEMAN ART LIBRARY

able to recruit and finance an army, which brought him to national power nine times. He never remained in the capital long, however, and often abdicated his authority soon after gaining executive office, only to return. Over the course of his career, Santa Anna became increasingly conservative. His first ascension to the presidency was as an ostensible federalist, his last as an ostentatious dictator. He was known as an untrustworthy but sometimes necessary political ally and a military tactician with an uncanny knack for survival.

Santa Anna was born in Jalapa, Veracruz, and began his military career in 1810 with the Fixed Infantry Regiment of Veracruz. During most of the War of Independence, he was involved in royalist

counterinsurgency. However, in March 1821, the young lieutenant colonel switched sides in support of Agustín de Iturbide's plan to achieve independence. Upon Iturbide's victory, Santa Anna was awarded a political-military position in his native region.

Santa Anna, whose relationship with Iturbide quickly soured, was instrumental in overthrowing the infant monarchy in 1823. For the rest of the decade, he played an intermittent role in national politics from his Veracruz stronghold, but it was not until the very end of the decade that the first of several military engagements with foreign troops greatly elevated his national stature.

In 1829 Spanish troops made an ill-fated attempt to reconquer Mexico. Santa Anna's victory against the invasion force at Tampico earned him popular approval and a certain cachet as a nationalist and military strategist. He would capitalize on this reputation often in the following twenty-five years.

Santa Anna gained the presidency for the first time on 1 April 1833, in a coalition with federalists who needed his military support to oust a conservative regime. However, he quickly turned the government over to his vice president, the ardent reformer Valentín Gómez Farías. At this point in his career, Santa Anna's political affiliations turned away from the federalist-liberal camp. Conservative leaders convinced him to oust Gómez Farías, whose proposed reforms were deemed a threat to both the Catholic Church and the military. Santa Anna thus began his next presidential term in April 1834 on the opposite end of the political spectrum from his first.

In the last half of the 1830s, Santa Anna's career was almost ended, and then resurrected, by international conflicts. He chose to lead the Mexican army sent to squelch the Texas Revolution. In 1836, after a number of early victories, including the infamous battle at the Alamo, Santa Anna was captured. He conceded Texas independence and then retired in defeat from public life. However, in 1838, French troops invaded Mexico to collect indemnities from the government. Santa Anna lost a leg in battle against the French and was once again proclaimed a hero. His role in national politics resumed when he was declared president in March 1839, and in the early 1840s his now familiar oscillation between power (1841, 1843, 1844) and exile was repeated.

Santa Anna's conduct during the Mexican-American War formed another controversial episode in the general's life. Although in exile when the war broke out in 1846, he managed to slip through a U.S. naval blockade, an act that spurred accusations he had secretly agreed to peace terms with the United States. Once back in Mexico, however, Santa Anna took up arms, was appointed president by the congress in December 1846, and for a time bravely led his troops before experiencing defeat and exile once again.

The war with the United States brought Mexico to the brink of disintegration. The political situation in the late 1840s and early 1850s was more chaotic than ever. Santa Anna was in and out of office in 1847. Finally, in 1853 a fragile conservative coalition formed to bring him back to Mexico, and he was granted extraordinary powers in the hope that he might somehow hold the nation together. From 1853 to 1855, as a military dictator he ruled imperiously, the coalition that had brought him to power disintegrated, and he was forced yet again into exile by the liberal leaders of the Revolution of Ayutla. From 1855 until his death in 1876, Santa Anna played only a marginal role in Mexican politics.

What are we to make of the "age of Santa Anna's revolutions"? The traditional view of Mexican history portrays his greed and fickleness as one of the main causes of the nation's instability. However, Santa Anna's role must be placed within the broader context of Mexican society during this era. He was an important military leader at a time when military power was the key to political control in Mexico. His unique asset was his ability to present himself as a necessary ally to extraordinarily different political factions. Ultimately, though, his career was more a symptom of Mexico's deeper political, social, and economic problems than the cause of them.

See also **Alamo, Battle of the; Caudillismo, Caudillo; Mexico, Wars and Revolutions: Mexican-American War.**

BIBLIOGRAPHY

A truly satisfying biography of Santa Anna remains to be written, though several have been attempted in English. Two dramatic portraits were produced in the 1930s: Wilfrid Hardy Callcott, *Santa Anna: The Story of an Enigma Who Once Was Mexico* (1936), and Frank C. Hanighen, *Santa Anna: The Napoleon of the West* (1934). A third biography is Oakah L. Jones, *Santa Anna* (1968). Santa Anna's autobiography is an interesting attempt by the general himself to justify his checkered career and answer his critics: Antonio López De Santa Anna, *The Eagle: The Autobiography of Santa Anna,* translated and edited by Ann Fears Crawford (1988). An influential study of *caudillismo* that compares Santa Anna and Juan Álvarez is Fernando Díaz Díaz, *Caudillos y caciques: Antonio López de Santa Anna y Juan Álvarez* (1972). Two recent attempts to reevaluate Santa Anna are Christon I. Archer, "The Young Antonio López de Santa Anna: Veracruz Counterinsurgent and Incipient Caudillo," in *The Human Tradition in Latin America: Nineteenth Century,* edited by William Beezley and Judith Ewell (1989), which examines Santa Anna's emergence as a political actor during the Independence wars.

Carmen Vázquez Mantecón, *Santa Anna y la encrucijada del estado: La dictadura (1853–55)* (1986), a fine analysis of Santa Anna's last years as ruler of Mexico.

Additional Bibliography

Blanco Moheno, Roberto. *Iturbide y Santa Anna: Los años terribles de la infancia nacional*. Mexico City: Editorial Diana, 1991.

Costeloe, Michael P. *La República central en México, 1835-1846: "Hombres de bien" en la época de Santa Anna*. Mexico City: Fondo de Cultura Económica, 2000.

Díaz Zermeño, Héctor. *La culminación de las traiciones de Santa Anna*. Mexico City: Nueva Imagen, 2000.

González Pedrero, Enrique. *País de un solo hombre: El México de Santa Anna*. Mexico City: Fondo de Cultura Económica, 1993.

Veraza Urtuzuástegui, Jorge. *Santa Anna en la historiografía y el en sentido común*. Mexico City: Editorial Itaca, 2000.

Yáñez, Agustín. *Santa Anna, espectro de una sociedad*. Mexico City: Fondo de Cultura Económica, 1993.

RICHARD WARREN

SANTA CATARINA.

Santa Catarina, state in southern Brazil bordered on the east by the Atlantic Ocean, on the west by Argentina, and along the south by the Pelotas and Uruguay rivers. The interior region of Santa Catarina lagged significantly behind the coast in population and economic development until the twentieth century, even as Santa Catarina as a whole was overshadowed by states in Brazil such as São Paulo and Rio Grande do Sul. Lages, the largest city in its interior, was founded in 1770 by cattle ranchers who gradually expanded land development west and north toward Paraná.

Until the expansion of the Brazil Railway Company into Santa Catarina after 1906, and its subsequent lumbering, sawmill, and colonization enterprises, landowners largely depended upon sharecropping to attract workers to the interior. One of Santa Catarina's most famous historical figures was José Maria, whose millenarian movement within the Contestado called for a restoration of the monarchy in opposition to the capitalist transformations of the beginning of the twentieth century. The railroad expansion and subsequent land boom had led to a convergence of national, international, and private interests in the removal of subsistence peasants or "squatters." To defeat the 15,000 peasant followers of José Maria after his death, the Brazilian army utilized nearly half its forces and $250,000 from 1912 to 1916.

In 2000 Santa Catarina had a population of 5,356,360. Since 1823 its capital city has been Florianópolis (originally Destêrro; renamed for President Floriano Peixoto in 1893). At present Santa Catarina's economy depends on cattle raising, coal mining, food processing, textiles, and petrochemical production. It has one of the best economies of any Brazilian state, and its inhabitants enjoy a relatively high standard of living. It is also a popular tourist destination, as its coastline boasts more than 500 beaches, including the famous beach resort Balneário Camboriú, where the two main beaches are linked by a cable car.

See also **Brazil, Geography.**

BIBLIOGRAPHY

Diacon, Todd A. "Peasants, Prophets, and the Power of a Millenarian Vision in Twentieth-Century Brazil," in *Comparative Studies in Society and History* 32 (1990): 488–514.

Diacon, Todd A. *Millenarian Vision, Capitalist Reality: Brazil's Contestado Rebellion, 1912–1916*. Durham, NC: Duke University Press, 1991.

Lenard, Alexander. *The Valley of the Latin Bear* (1965).

Mello, Amilcar d'Avila de. *Expedições: Santa Catarina na era dos descobrimientos geográficos*. Florianópolis, Brazil: Editora Expressão, 2005.

Otto, Claricia. *Catolicidades e itallianidades: Tramas e poder em Santa Catarina (1875–1930)*. Florianópolis, Brazil: Editora Insular, 2006.

Piazza, Walter F. *Santa Catarina: Sua historia* (1983).

Ribiero, Edaléa Maria. *Movimientos sociais em tempos de democracia e globalizaçao em Santa Catarina: Os años 90*. Florianópolis, Brazil: Fundaçao Boiteaux, 2005.

CAROLYN E. VIEIRA

SANTA CRUZ.

Santa Cruz is the principal city in eastern Bolivia and a national department. Founded in 1561, Santa Cruz changed both its name and its location several times before definitively establishing itself in 1595 as Santa Cruz de la Sierra at a location near its current site. Until the mid-twentieth century, Santa Cruz was separated from the highland cities that governed it by some 350 kilometers of rain forest and high mountains. Geographical isolation has produced a self-perception of Santa Cruz as a distinctive region within the nation and a rivalry between its people (*cambas*) those of the highlands (*coyas*).

Recent research on the early history of Santa Cruz has shown that Spanish colonists, who explored the region in search of El Dorado, ultimately assumed a hardscrabble existence on the eastern frontier of the empire. Cowhides and sugar became the principal exports to the highland economy, and the latter product became a medium of exchange locally. Although the city never grew beyond a few thousand *vecinos* (Europeans) as the only consequential Spanish settlement east of the Andes, Santa Cruz exercised regional influence beyond its size, as exemplified by its becoming a bishopric in 1605.

The colonial period also saw the establishment of two mission systems in the region. In Mojos (present-day Bolivia's Beni department), Jesuits based in Lima founded two dozen mission centers stretching north along the Mamoré River basin. Another Jesuit mission in Chiquitos began near Santa Cruz and extended eastward toward Brazil. Spanish colonial law prohibited non-clerical and non-Indian contact with the missions, a proscription resented and furtively violated by *cruceños*, who saw the Jesuits as interlopers and the Indian neophytes as both a market and a labor supply. Jesuit banishment from the Spanish colonies in 1767 removed the priests and partially opened the former mission centers to commerce from Santa Cruz. For the last fifty years of the colonial period Santa Cruz maintained its bishopric but saw its former political authority curtailed in its subordination to the intendant of Cochabamba.

With Bolivian independence in 1825, Santa Cruz became de facto capital of the nation east of the Andes, which restored its political influence but did little to decrease its isolation. Two events in the middle of the nineteenth century marked the beginning of Santa Cruz's integration into the Bolivian nation. The first was the War of the Pacific, which produced a patriotic response to the nation's call for volunteers to fight against the Chilean army. The second came with a heightened demand for tropical products by the industrializing world. A brief involvement in the gathering of cinchona (a tree with bark containing a substance that could be used in malaria treatment) from 1840 to 1860 was followed by a longer-lived rubber boom. Rubber became the El Dorado that *cruceños* had long sought, and a few of the city's sons, especially Nicolás Suárez, reaped large fortunes in gathering and transporting latex to Europe and the United States. Santa Cruz also became the commercial center for provisioning those who extracted rubber from Bolivian forests. The discovery of oil in the Andean foothills, the completion of an auto road to Cochabamba, and the Chaco War (1932–1935) strengthened Santa Cruz's ties with the Bolivian nation. But these developments did not stifle desire for autonomy. Santa Cruz would declare itself a federal state in 1876 and sponsor brief federalist rebellions in 1891 and 1957.

After World War II, Santa Cruz became the focus of national development planning. Fueled by loans from the U.S. Agency for International Development and the World Bank, several Bolivian governments invested in building industry and a transport infrastructure that, along with petroleum revenues, made Santa Cruz the most prosperous region of the country and a magnet for internal migration. The city grew from 42,764 inhabitants in 1950 to 254,682 in 1976 to more than a million in 2000. The department's share of GDP is currently nearly half of the nation's aggregate.

In the early twenty-first century Santa Cruz is Bolivia's most cosmopolitan region. But even as increasing numbers of highlanders migrate there, *cruceños* insist on their uniqueness. The contemporary "autonomies movement," a demand for greater self-government and greater regional control of natural resources, expresses the continuation of a historic *camba–coya* rivalry.

See also **Bolivia: The Colonial Period; Bolivia: Since 1825; Chaco War; El Dorado; Jesuits; War of the Pacific.**

BIBLIOGRAPHY

García Recio, José María. *Análisis de una sociedad de frontera: Santa Cruz de la Sierra en los siglos XVI y XVIII.* Sevilla, Spain: Diputación Provincial de Sevilla, 1988.

"Santa Cruz de la Sierra, ciudad de." In *Diccionario histórico de Bolivia*, vol. 2, pp. 861–862. Sucre: Grupo de Editores Históricos, 2002.

DAVID BLOCK

SANTA CRUZ, ANDRÉS DE (1792–1865).

Andrés de Santa Cruz (*b.* 30 November 1792; *d.* 25 September 1865), president of Peru (1827), president of Bolivia (1829–1836), and president of the Peru-Bolivia Confederation (1836–1839).

A royalist officer who switched to the patriot side in 1820, Santa Cruz distinguished himself in the Wars of Independence and later became one of the longest lasting and most able presidents of Bolivia. His reorganization of governmental institutions on the Napoleonic model provided the basis for republican government for over a century. However, his attempt in 1836 to reunite Peru and Bolivia engendered a Chilean invasion that led to his downfall in 1839.

The son of a minor Spanish colonial official and the wealthy heiress of an Indian chieftainship, Santa Cruz was born in La Paz to wealth and received a good education in Cuzco, though he left school before graduating. He first joined his father's regiment in 1811, and in 1817 fought against the invading Argentine armies. Taken prisoner the same year, Santa Cruz was sent to a prison close to Buenos Aires but managed to escape and return to Peru. Recaptured in 1820, he decided to become a patriot. In 1822, Santa Cruz distinguished himself in the battle of Pichincha, Ecuador, under Antonio José de Sucre, achieving the rank of brigadier general in both the Colombian and Peruvian patriot armies. Despite a victory in Zepita over the Spanish army (for which he was promoted to grand marshal), Santa Cruz was unable to liberate his home territory.

After Peru and Bolivia achieved independence, Santa Cruz briefly became president of Peru in 1827 under the auspices of Simón Bolívar. Voted out in the anti-Bolivarian reactions of 1827, Santa Cruz went to Chile on a diplomatic mission. Wanting to reunite Peru and Bolivia, Santa Cruz was convinced that Antonio José de Sucre should be ousted from the Bolivian presidency because his presence made the reunification impossible. In 1828, in the wake of Agustín Gamarra's invasion of Bolivia, Sucre resigned and Santa Cruz was elected president. He took power in 1829.

Santa Cruz was a mercantilist and favored domestic industries, particularly textiles, over foreign products. Nevertheless, he developed the port of Cobija on the Pacific coast by building a road and providing import tax relief as a way of achieving sovereignty over this sparsely populated desert region.

Santa Cruz also lowered mining taxes, but this action did not stimulate silver mining sufficiently to provide enough government revenues. In 1830 he resorted to minting debased silver currency as a way of covering the fiscal deficit, thereby setting a pattern that would continue into the 1860s and provide a relatively high indirect tariff that protected domestic production from foreign competition.

Recognizing the lack of government revenue and forever a pragmatist, Santa Cruz formally reinstituted the payment of Indian tribute in return for which the state guaranteed the Indians' possession of community lands for ten years. Although this went against the president's otherwise Bolivarian ideas (Bolívar had abolished tribute payments in 1824 and 1825), Santa Cruz recognized the crucial economic role of the Indian communities' economies and the benefits of a regular and substantial income for the fiscally strapped government.

This legislation also provided resources and a stable home base for his other projects, most notably the reunification of Peru and Bolivia. In 1836, Santa Cruz briefly tried to take advantage of the political chaos in Argentina and attempted unsuccessfully to annex Jujuy to Bolivia. More successful, at least temporarily, were Santa Cruz's expansionist plans toward Peru. In 1835 he moved against the divided Peruvian leadership and was able to defeat his rival, Agustín Gamarra, and by 1836 the Peruvian president, Felipe Santiago Salaverry.

Once Santa Cruz had conquered Peru, he reorganized the two states into three units, Northern Peru, Southern Peru, and Bolivia. Each unit elected its own president, and Santa Cruz named himself the confederation's protector. As a result, Santa Cruz dropped his efforts at developing the port of Cobija and encouraged trade between the more easily accessible southern Peruvian ports of Arica and Tacna.

Both Chile and Argentina feared a powerful northern neighbor and did everything in their power to eliminate the confederation. While Argentina was suffering from its own internal problems, Chile actively aided Peruvian dissidents, finally invading the confederation in 1838. In 1839 the Chileans won a major battle outside Lima, and Santa Cruz fled into exile in Ecuador. However, in 1841 pro-Santa

Cruz forces overthrew the Bolivian president, General José Miguel de Velasco, precipitating the invasion of Peruvian General Agustín Gamarra. When it became clear that Gamarra intended to annex parts of Bolivia to Peru, Bolivian forces united under the anti-Santa Cruz General José Ballivián and, in the battle of Ingaví in 1841, defeated the Peruvian army and killed the Peruvian leader. As a result, Santa Cruz was prevented from returning to Bolivia. More important, the battle of Ingaví signaled the end of overt Peruvian and Bolivian intervention into each other's affairs and the end of Bolivia's dominance as a regional power. Santa Cruz was exiled for life and died in Nantes, France.

See also **Gamarra, Agustín; Jujuy.**

BIBLIOGRAPHY

A standard popular biography is Alfonso Crespo Rodas, *Santa Cruz, el cóndor indio* (1944). The best recent work is Philip Parkerson, *Andrés de Santa Cruz y la Confederación Perú-Boliviana 1835–1839* (1984), a Spanish translation of his Ph.D. dissertation, "Sub-Regional Integration in Nineteenth Century South America: Andrés de Santa Cruz and the Peru-Bolivia Confederation, 1835–39" (Univ. of Florida, 1979). A good brief summary of the Santa Cruz period is contained in Herbert S. Klein, *Bolivia: The Evolution of a Multi-Ethnic Society* (1982), pp. 112–119.

Additional Bibliography

Fajardo Sainz, Humberto. *Andrés de Santa Cruz y la Unión Latino Americana.* Santa Cruz de la Sierra: H. Fajardo Sainz, 2003.

Guardia, Amelia. *El personalismo político de Andrés de Santa Cruz: Un voluntarismo al serivicio de la integración.* Caracas: Facultad de Ciencias Económicas y Sociales, Universidad Central de Venezuela, 2000.

Martínez Azcui, Hernán. *Mariscal Andrés de Santa Cruz: Síntesis biográfica: Homenaje del Comando General del Ejército.* La Paz: Editorial El Siglo, 1992.

Saavedra Arce, René. *El condor andino: Biografía del mariscal de Zepita, Andrés de Santa Cruz.* La Paz: Publicidad e Impresión Génesis, 2003.

ERICK D. LANGER

the city of Rio de Janeiro. The fortifications constructed over the centuries on this site, christened Santa Cruz in 1632, command an enviable artillery position. In the colonial period the fort easily repelled several pirating expeditions, allowing Rio de Janeiro to develop in relative peace. The fort's cold gray granite environs also surrounded one of Brazil's largest and oldest prisons. It held both military and civilian convicts, including such notable figures as Tiradentes, Plínio Salgado, and Juarez Távora. The prison's conditions were harsh, some cells being so small and crowded that inmates had to squat once inside. These cruel conditions encouraged rebellions.

The revolt in 1892 of Sergeant Silvino Honório de Macedo, a promonarchist noncommissioned officer, threatened to topple President Floriano Peixoto's republican government. Silvino plotted a successful mutiny in Santa Cruz, armed the prisoners there, and subverted other garrisons around the bay. It required a full-scale army assault on Santa Cruz finally to overwhelm the insurgent inmates. No longer a prison but still an army barracks, Santa Cruz now also serves as a historical museum.

See also **Forts and Fortifications, Spanish America; Rio de Janeiro (City).**

BIBLIOGRAPHY

Sources on Santa Cruz's history are sparse, even in Portuguese. Augusto Fausto De Souza provides a brief history of the fort in "Fortificações no Brazil," in *Revista do Instituto Histórico, Geográphico e Ethnográphico do Brazil* 48 (1885): 5–140. General Dermeval Peixoto provides a description of conditions in Santa Cruz at the turn of the century in *Memórias de um velho soldado* (1960).

Additional Bibliography

Barman, Roderick J. *Citizen Emperor: Pedro II and the Making of Brazil, 1825–1891.* Stanford, CA: Stanford University, 1999.

Vaiinfas, Ronaldo. *Dicionário do Brasil imperial, 1822–1889.* Rio de Janeiro: Objetivo, 2002.

PETER M. BEATTIE

SANTA CRUZ, FORTALEZA DE.
Fortaleza de Santa Cruz, a fort at the northeastern lip of Guanabara Bay's narrow mouth, which since the sixteenth century functioned as the first line of land-based defense against enemy naval attack on

SANTA CRUZ PACHACUTI YAMQUI SALCAMAYGUA, JOAN DE Joan
de Santa Cruz Pachacuti Yamqui Salcamaygua, writer. Not much is known about the life of Santa Cruz Pachacuti other than that he lived in the first part of

the seventeenth century in the region between Cuzco and Lake Titicaca in Peru. But his importance grows day by day because of the information contained in his work *Relación de la antigüedades de este reyno del Pirú* (1613; An Account of the Antiquities of Peru), one of the most interesting views of the Inca world. The text includes several drawings that have served as clues to the interpretation of the Quechua cosmological view of the world. At the time, Spanish culture, which emphasized writing as its privileged system of recording and as the mark of civilization, coexisted with Quechua culture, based on oral and visual systems of signification. Santa Cruz Pachacuti attempts to explain his native religion in the framework of the Christianity brought by the Spaniards, and in doing so he discovers that language is limited and must employ visual images. From this tension emerges the force of the *Relación*. Together with the works of El Inca Garcilaso De La Vega and Felipe Guamán Poma De Ayala, that of Santa Cruz Pachacuti is one of the most important indigenous sources of Inca society as well as of the conflicts of acculturation during the colonial period in the Andean region.

See also **Literature: Spanish America.**

BIBLIOGRAPHY

Gary Urton, *At the Crossroads of the Earth and the Sky: An Andean Cosmology* (1981).

Regina Harrison, "Modes of Discourse: *Relación de antigüedades de este reyno del Pirú* by Joan Santa Cruz Pachacuti Yamqui Salcamaygua," in *From Oral to Written Expression: Native Andean Chronicles of the Early Colonial Period*, edited by Rolena Adorno (1982), pp. 65–100.

Regina Harrison, "Script and Sketch: A Semiotics of Knowledge in Santa Cruz Pachacuti Yamqui's *Relación*," in her *Signs, Songs, and Memory in the Andes* (1989), pp. 55–84.

Additional Bibliography

MacCormack, Sabine. "Pachacuti: Miracles, Punishments, and Last Judgement: Visionary Past and Prophetic Future in Early Colonial Peru." *American Historical Review* 93 (Oct. 1998): 960–1006.

Urbano, Henrique, and Ana Sánchez. *Antigüedades del Peru*. Madrid: Historia 16, 1992.

LEONARDO GARCÍA PABÓN

SANTA CRUZ Y ESPEJO, FRANCISCO JAVIER EUGENIO DE (1747–1795).

Francisco Javier Eugenio de Santa Cruz y Espejo (*b.* 21 February 1747; *d.* 27 December 1795), Ecuadorian writer. Born in Quito to a Quechua father and a mulatto mother, Espejo rose from humble origins to become one of Ecuador's leading intellects. Although mostly self-taught through first-hand observation at a women's hospital, he received the degree of doctor of medicine in July 1767 from the Colegio de San Fernando, and later obtained degrees in civil and canon law.

Espejo became most widely known for his diverse writings on economics, medicine, pedagogy, politics, sociology, and theology. In a frequently satirical tone he criticized the clergy and Ecuador's backwardness. His most famous works are *El nuevo Luciano o despertador de ingenios* (1779), which aimed at educational reform, and *Reflexiones … acerca de un método seguro para preservar a los pueblos de las viruelas* (1785), which proposed ways to prevent smallpox and received international recognition.

In 1788 Espejo successfully defended himself in Bogotá against charges of having written and circulated *El retrato de Golilla,* which ridiculed both Charles III and José de Gálvez, minister of the Indies. While in Bogotá, Espejo met such New Granadan firebrands as Antonio Nariño and Francisco Antonio Zea, who radicalized his thought. Upon returning to Quito, he helped establish the Sociedad Patriótica de Amigos del País de Quito on 30 November 1791. He also edited the society's newspaper, Ecuador's first, the short-lived *Primicias de la Cultura de Quito* in 1792. At the same time he became director of Ecuador's first public library and was founder of the National Library.

Espejo was tried and imprisoned on charges of sedition in January 1795. He became ill while in jail and died shortly after being released.

See also **Libraries in Latin America; Nariño, Antonio.**

BIBLIOGRAPHY

Francisco Javier Eugenio Santa Cruz y Espejo, *Escritos del doctor Francisco Javier Eugenio Santa Cruz y Espejo,* edited by Federico González Suárez (1912).

Philip L. Astuto, "Eugenio Espejo: A Man of the Enlightenment in Ecuador," in *Revista de historia de América* (1957): 369–391.

Additional Bibliography

Albornoz Peralta, Osvaldo. *Eugenio Espejo: El espírtu más progresista del siglo XVIII.* Quito: 1997.

Breilh, Jaime. *Eugenio Espejo: La otra memoria: Nueva lectura de la historia de las ideas científicas.* Cuenca: Universidad de Cuenca, Facultad de Ciencias Médicas; Centro de Estudios y Asesoría en Salud; Consejo Internacional de Salud de los Pueblos, 2001.

Cacua Prada, Antonio. *Antonio Nariño y Eugenio Espejo: Dos adelantados de la libertad.* Guayaquil: Archivo Histórico del Guayas, 2000.

Freile Granizo, Carlos. *Eugenio Espejo, precursor de la independencia: (Documentos 1794–1797).* Quito: ABYA-YALA, 2001.

PHILIPPE L. SEILER

SANTA ELENA.

Santa Elena, city in Spanish colonial Florida, founded in 1566 by Pedro Menéndez De Avilés on Parris Island in present-day South Carolina. Its garrison manned three successive forts. In 1569, 193 settlers came to Santa Elena, bringing with them many of the trades, crafts, and professions of Spain. Secondary to Saint Augustine until 1571, Santa Elena became the capital of Florida in that year when Menéndez moved his wife and household there. Menéndez hoped to establish his royal land grant in the upland piedmont, at Guatari, near present-day Charlotte, North Carolina. He imported many rich household goods, and began the fur trade with the Native Americans. Other economic enterprises included the raising of corn and hogs, the export of sassafras root and lumber, and the building of two small ships. Jesuit and Franciscan missionaries came to Santa Elena but failed to make many converts among the Native Americans. After Menéndez's death at Santander, Spain, in 1574, relations with the Indians deteriorated, and a confederation of neighboring Caciques forced the Spaniards to evacuate Santa Elena in 1576. The city was rebuilt the following year and was finally abandoned in 1587.

See also **Menéndez de Avilés, Pedro.**

BIBLIOGRAPHY

Eugene Lyon, *Santa Elena: A Brief History of the Colony, 1566–1587* (1984).

Stanley South, Russell K. Skowronek, and Richard E. Johnson, with contributions by Eugene Lyon, Richard Polhemus, William Radisch, and Carl Steen, *Spanish Artifacts from Santa Elena* (1988).

Additional Bibliography

Gallegos, Eloy J. *Santa Elena: Spanish Settlements on the Atlantic Seaboard from Florida to Virginia, 1513 to 1607.* Knoxville, TN: Villagra Press, 1998.

EUGENE LYON

SANTA FE, ARGENTINA.

Argentina Santa Fe, administrative province and historical region of Argentina significant for its size (with 3,000,701 inhabitants in 2001, it has the third-largest provincial population) and for its economic output. The region around the city of Sante Fe was pioneered by Juan de Garay in 1573 and comprised within its jurisdiction the present provinces of Santa Fe, Entre Ríos, and northern Buenos Aires. Sante Fe was an important port on the fluvial route to Asunción. It exported salted meat, hides, and wood products, as well as yerba maté and wheat.

As an active supporter of the federalists struggling in the wake of independence against the centralism of Buenos Aires, Santa Fe paid dearly as it became a theater of action for federalist and unitarian warlords. The wars continued until the fall of Manuel de Rosas in 1852. Right after approval of the federalist constitution, signed in Santa Fe, the first attempts were made at establishing farming colonies with foreign immigrants in Argentina. Thus Esperanza was founded in 1854, and other agricultural colonies multiplied in the northern part of the Pampa, growing grain and raising cattle. Today Santa Fe province produces 35 percent of Argentina's wheat as well as more than half of the country's sunflower seeds. Other agricultural commodities include flax, lentils, soybeans, and potatoes. The main population centers in the province are Greater Rosario, Santa Fe, Esperanza, La Paz, Villa Federal, and San Lorenzo.

BIBLIOGRAPHY

Leoncio Gianello, *Historia de Sante Fe* (Buenos Aires, 1978).

Ezequiel Gallo, *La Pampa gringa: La colonización agrícola de Santa Fé (1870–1895)* (Buenos Aires, 1983).

Additional Bibliography

Barriera, Dario, and Juan Nobile. *Nueva historia de Santa Fe.* Rosario, Argentina: Prohistoria Ediciones, 2006.

CÉSAR N. CAVIEDES

SANTA FE DE BOGOTÁ. *See* **Bogotá, Santa Fe de.**

SANTA FE, NEW MEXICO.

Santa Fe, capital of New Mexico founded about 1609 by governor Pedro de Peralta (*ca.* 1584–1666). The villa stood close to the banks of the upper Rio Grande at the southernmost tip of the Sangre de Cristo mountains; to the east were the plains; to the west, the pueblos. To the southwest were the river communities and the Camino Real (Royal Road) that tied New Mexico to the rest of New Spain and the world beyond.

Santa Fe played a crucial role in the Pueblo Rebellion of 1680. In August the pueblos, briefly united in their hatred of the injustices of the colonial system, laid siege to the capital and forced the Spaniards to flee, first to Isleta, some 70 miles to the south, and then to El Paso. Thirteen years later, Diego de Vargas (*d.* 1704) led a recolonizing force into New Mexico. In the Battle of Santa Fe (29 December 1693), he retook the capital with the help of Pecos Pueblo auxiliaries who had grown disillusioned with pueblo rule. This was the last major battle in Santa Fe history, and by 1697 Vargas had subdued the last of the rebellious pueblos and completed the reconquest of New Mexico.

Santa Fe developed into a unique Hispanic frontier community in the eighteenth century. Although a presidio town that lived under the constant threat of attack from Navajo and Ute Indians, Santa Fe was not walled and its settlement pattern was notably decentralized. It hardly resembled other fortified presidios nor did it have the strict gridlike pattern of most other Hispanic cities. Santa Fe was an agricultural community of 2,542 people in 1790. Other than the occasional trade caravan that came up the Royal Road from Chihuahua with luxury items, New Mexico and its capital lived in isolation and became nearly self-sufficient.

New Mexico's role in the fight for independence from Spain was small; of more importance to the isolated community was the end of the Spaniards' monopoly on trade. In 1821 William Becknell brought a small trade caravan from Missouri to Santa Fe and found a ready market for his goods. The opening of the Santa Fe Trail that tied New Mexico to the United States affected the frontier community immediately. Calicos and gingham fabrics were found in most houses; American styles and furniture became commonplace on the streets and in homes. The duties collected from the traders supplemented the town's meager income.

In the New Mexico Revolution of 1837, the rebels from the northern communities held Santa Fe for a short time until the capital was retaken by former and future governor Manuel Armijo. And in 1846 General Stephen W. Kearny marched into the town without bloodshed and established U.S. rule. Santa Fe remained the capital when New Mexico became a U.S. Territory in 1850 and when statehood was achieved in 1912.

Today Santa Fe draws large numbers of tourists for its climate, culture, and history. In 2005 the estimated population was 70,631, making Santa Fe the third-largest city in New Mexico.

See also **New Mexico; Pueblo Rebellion.**

BIBLIOGRAPHY

Dary, David. *The Santa Fe Trail: Its History, Legends, and Lore.* New York: Knopf, 2000.

Gregg, Josiah. *Commerce of the Prairies,* edited by Max L. Moorehead (1954).

Hazen-Hammond, Susan. *A Short History of Santa Fe* (1988).

Horgan, Paul. *The Centuries of Santa Fe* (1976).

Noble, David Grant, ed. *Santa Fe: History of an Ancient City* (1989).

Pérez de Villagrá, Gaspar. *A History of New Mexico.* Chicago: Rio Grande Press, 1962.

Simmons, Marc. *Yesterday in Santa Fe: Episodes in a Turbulent History* (1969).

Tobias, Henry Jack, and Charles E. Woodhouse. *Santa Fe: A Modern History, 1880–1990.* Albuquerque: University of New Mexico Press, 2001.

AARON PAINE MAHR

SANTA LUISA.

Santa Luisa, a major archaeological site with one of the longest culture chronologies in coastal Mexico, dating from about 6,000 BCE to the present. Covering a 6.2-square-mile area of alluvial terraces between the modern towns of

Gutiérrez Zamora and Tecolutla, in the state of Veracruz, this significant ancient site along the Tecolutla River has extremely abundant cultural remains. Its strategic location at the convergence of diverse riverine, estuarine, forest, and savannah zones with plentiful food resources made it attractive for long-term human occupation. At nearby La Conchita, a small, closely related site, there are remains of extinct Pleistocene fauna as well as later campsites radiocarbon-dated to 5,600 BCE.

The population peak at Santa Luisa, which corresponds with the construction of numerous temple structures and extensive irrigated field systems for intensive agriculture, occurred during the Classic period (about 300–900 CE) and the locally defined Epi-Classic period (about 900–1100 CE). At that time the site was dominated by and heavily reflected the regional culture, whose major expression was the city of El Tajín, some 21 miles distant.

Extensive explorations of Santa Luisa were undertaken between 1968 and 1979 by this writer in the effort to define a workable culture chronology for the north-central region of Veracruz. The resulting nearly continuous evidence of human presence, currently divided into seventeen archaeological phases, has been most useful for interpreting the processes of cultural evolution throughout the region since the time of Early Archaic hunter-gatherers. One of the unanticipated conclusions of these excavations was that, in this traditional Totonac area, the oldest identifiable ethnic evidence appears to be Huastec.

Other important discoveries at Santa Luisa include evidence of preceramic villages on deltaic islands, early ceramics, Olmec-inspired artifacts, vestiges of various forms of intensive agriculture, rare in situ examples of ritual ball-game sculptures called yokes and *palmas,* painted stucco fragments, and architectural remains.

See also **Archaeology; Huasteca, The; Totonacs.**

BIBLIOGRAPHY

S. Jeffrey K. Wilkerson, *Ethnogenesis of the Huastecs and Totonacs* (1973); "Pre-Agricultural Village Life: The Late Preceramic Period in Veracruz," in *Contributions of the University of California Archaeological Research Facility,* edited by John A. Graham, no. 27 (1975): 111–122; "Man's Eighty Centuries in Veracruz," in *National Geographic Magazine* 158, no. 2 (August 1980): 202–231; "The Northern Olmec and Pre-Olmec Frontier on the Gulf Coast," in *The Olmec and Their Neighbors: Essays in Memory of Matthew W. Sterling,* edited by Michael D. Coe and David Grove (1981), pp. 181–194.

Additional Bibliography

Clark, John E., and Mary E. Pye. *Olmec Art and Archaeology in Mesoamerica.* Washington, DC: National Gallery of Art; New Haven, CT: Distributed by Yale University Press, 2000.

White, Nancy M. *Gulf Coast Archaeology: The Southeastern United States and Mexico.* Gainesville: University Press of Florida, 2005.

Winfield Capitaine, Fernando. *Bibliografía arqueológica de Veracruz.* Xalapa: Universidad Veracruzana, 1997.

S. JEFFREY K. WILKERSON

SANTA MARÍA, ANDRÉS DE (1860–1945). Andrés de Santa María (*b.* 10 December 1860; *d.* 29 April 1945), Colombian artist. Born to a wealthy family that left Colombia for Europe during the civil war of 1862, Santa María spent most of his life in Europe. In 1882 he studied at the École des Beaux Arts in Paris and in 1887 his work *Seine Laundresses* was exhibited at the Salon des Artistes Français and the Salon des Tuileries. He returned to Bogotá in 1893 and was appointed professor of landscape painting at the School of Fine Arts the following year. He went back to Europe in 1901, but returned to Colombia in 1904 and was appointed director of the School of Fine Arts. He generally painted landscapes and scenes of daily life in an impressionist style. His work was shown at the School of Fine Arts, the Teatro Colón (1906), and the Exposición del Centenario (1910). Criticism of his work at the School of Fine Arts prompted his return to Brussels, where he lived for the rest of his life.

His paintings were shown in Paris, Brussels, and Bogotá. In 1923 the French government made him a chevalier of the Legion of Honor and in 1930 he was named academic correspondent of the Academy of San Fernando in Madrid. His later work had richer colors as well as chiaroscuro. Santa María had retrospective exhibitions in Bogotá (1931), Brussels (1936), and London (1937). In 1971 the Museum of Modern Art in Bogotá honored him with a posthumous exhibition of 126 works.

See also **Art: The Nineteenth Century; Art: The Twentieth Century.**

BIBLIOGRAPHY

Gabriel Giraldo Jaramillo, *La miniatura, la pintura y el grabado en Colombia* (1980).

Eduardo Serrano, *Andres de Santa María* (1988).

Additional Bibliography

Serrano, Eduardo, Andrés de Santa María, and Myriam Acevedo. *Andrés de Santa María: Pintor colombiano de resonancia universal.* Bogotá: Museo de Arte Moderno de Bogotá: Novus Ediciones, 1991.

BÉLGICA RODRÍGUEZ

SANTAMARÍA, HAYDÉE (1927–1980).

Haydée Santamaría (*b.* 1927; *d.* 26 July 1980), Cuban revolutionary and cultural director. Haydée Santamaría was one of two women who participated in the 1953 attack on Cuba's Moncada army barracks in Santiago. Arrested and imprisoned, she was released on 20 February 1954. She met with Fidel Castro in Mexico, and then returned to Cuba to organize resistance to the Batista government in Santiago. Santamaría was a founding member of the national directorate of the Twenty-Sixth of July Movement. She was a member of the Central Committee of the Cuban Communist Party, and the director of the Casa de las Américas, an institution for the study of popular culture. Santamaría was married to Minister of Education Armando Hart. She died from a self-inflicted gunshot wound.

See also **Castro Ruz, Fidel; Cuba, Political Parties: Communist Party; Cuba, Twenty-Sixth of July Movement.**

BIBLIOGRAPHY

Carlos Franqui, *Diary of the Cuban Revolution,* translated by Georgette Felix, et al. (1980); "Haydée Santamaría, Director of Casa de las Américas Dies," in *Cuba Update* 1, no. 3 (1980): 16.

Tad Szulc, *Fidel: A Critical Portrait* (1986).

Ernesto Guevara, *Che Guevara and the Cuban Revolution: Writings and Speeches of Ernesto Che Guevara,* edited by David Deutschmann (1987).

Additional Bibliography

Fernández Retamar, Roberto. *Cuba defendida.* Buenos Aires: Nuestra América, 2004.

Hart Santamaría, Celia. *Haydée: Del Moncada a casa.* Buenos Aires: Nuestra America, 2005.

Maclean, Betsy. *Haydée Santamaría.* Melbourne and New York: Ocean Press, 2003.

DANIEL P. DWYER O.F.M.

SANTA MARÍA GONZÁLEZ, DOMINGO (1825–1889).

Domingo Santa María González (*b.* 4 August 1825; *d.* 18 July 1889), president of Chile (1881–1886). The early political activities of this attorney, professor, and civil servant twice forced him into exile. Following his second return to Chile in 1862, he served numerous terms in both houses of the legislature and as a justice of the Supreme Court, a cabinet minister, and a diplomat. Elected president in 1881, he led the nation to triumph over Peru and Bolivia in the War of the Pacific.

Apparently a haughty, if not arrogant, man, Santa María launched his own *Kulturkampf,* forcing the legislature to remove the cemeteries from the control of the Roman Catholic Church, make marriage a civil contract, and have the state—not the church—keep the civil registry. Violently anticlerical, Santa María supposedly improved the political environment by limiting the power of provincial officials, increasing individual freedoms, and extending suffrage by ceasing to demand that voters possess property. Paradoxically, he shamelessly manipulated the 1882 congressional and 1886 presidential elections.

Ending the War of the Pacific constituted Santa María's greatest achievement. Chile had to withstand pressure from the United States to abandon its demands for territorial concessions and wage a prolonged guerrilla war before forcing Peru to cede to Chile the province of Tarapacá. The following year, in 1884, Bolivia agreed to an armistice.

Santa María concluded his term by pacifying the Araucanian Indians in the south. By 1886, when he left office, Chile had increased its size by approximately a third, controlled the world's supply of nitrates, and dominated the Southern Hemisphere's Pacific coast.

See also **Chile: The Nineteenth Century; Chile, Organizations: Chilean Nitrate Company (COSACH).**

BIBLIOGRAPHY

Luis Galdames, *A History of Chile* (1941), pp. 336–340.

William F. Sater, *Chile and the War of the Pacific* (1986), pp. 60–61, 184–189, 192–195, 206–207, 211–222.

Additional Bibliography

Villalobos R., Sergio. *Chile y Perú: La historia que nos une y nos separa, 1535-1883.* Santiago de Chile: Editorial Universitaria, 2002.

WILLIAM F. SATER

SANTA MARTA.

Santa Marta, a city and province in northern New Granada (Audiencia of Santa Fe de Bogotá and, in the eighteenth century, the Viceroyalty of the New Kingdom of Granada). Founded by Rodrigo de Bastidas in 1525, twenty-five years after Spanish mariners first sighted its location, the town of Santa Marta played an important role in the history of New Granada during the Conquest. For a short time it was the capital of Tierra Firme and the port of call for the galleons. It was also the first bishopric see established in present-day Colombia (1531) and the location from which Gonzalo Jiménez De Quesada launched his conquest of the Chibcha Indians.

The prominence of the port faded with the founding of Cartagena de Indias in 1533. Political, commercial, ecclesiastical, and military focus shifted westward, leaving Santa Marta relatively undeveloped and thus more susceptible to political corruption, repeated foreign attacks, and Indian hostilities throughout the eighteenth century. Santa Marta province extended from the Magdalena River to the Sierra de Perijá and from the Caribbean southward to Ocaña.

See also **Jiménez de Quesada, Gonzalo; New Granada, Viceroyalty of.**

BIBLIOGRAPHY

A straightforward history of Santa Marta can be found in Ernesto Restrepo Tirado, *Historia de la Provincia de Santa Marta*, 2 vols. (1953). A useful, though biased, contemporary description of the region is Antonio Julián, *La perla de la América: Provincia de Santa Marta* (1951). For the military and architectural history of the port of Santa Marta see Juan Manuel Zapatero, *Historia de las fortalezas de Santa Marta y estudio asesor para su restauración* (1980). For an overview of the province see also James R. Krogzemis, *A Historical Geography of the Santa Marta Area, Colombia* (1967).

Additional Bibliography

Colajanni, A. *El pueblo de la montaña sagrada: Tradición y cambio.* Santa Marta: Organización Indigena Gonawindúa Tayrona: Ricerca e Cooperazione de Colombia: Comisión de Asuntos Indígenas, 1997.

Ospino Valiente, Alvaro. *El drama urbano de Santa Marta durante la dominación española: Cartografía e historia en tres actos.* Bogotá: Ministerio de Cultura, 2002.

Posada Carbó, Eduardo. *The Colombian Caribbean: A Regional History, 1870-1950.* New York: Clarendon Press, 1996.

Romero Jaramillo, Dolcey. *Esclavitud en la provincia de Santa Marta, 1791-1851.* Santa Marta: Fondo de Publicaciones de Autores Magdalenenses, Instituto de Cultura y Turismo del Magdalena, 1997.

Viloria de la Hoz, Joaquín. *Empresas y empresarios de Santa Marta durante el siglo XIX: El caso de la familia de Mier.* Bogotá: Publicaciones-Facultad de Administración, Universidad de los Andes, 2002.

LANCE R. GRAHN

SANTANA, CARLOS

(1947–). Known for his distinctive guitar sound and melodic improvisational style, Carlos Santana is a pioneer of Latin rock and one of the most influential guitarists of his time. Born in Autlán de Navarro, Mexico, on July 20, 1947, he moved to San Francisco as a teenager. He formed the Santana Blues Band in 1966 (eventually dropping the "Blues Band" moniker), and the group's combination of rock, Latin percussion, and Afro-Cuban rhythms made it a popular draw in northern California clubs. Santana's performance at the 1969 Woodstock Festival (and on the subsequent film and LP set documenting the event) propelled the band into the national spotlight. The group's first three records, *Santana* (1969), *Abraxas* (1970), and *Santana III* (1971), all went platinum and yielded a number of hit singles, including "Evil Ways," "Black Magic Woman," and "Oye como va." Despite extensive personnel changes throughout the 1970s and 1980s, Carlos Santana's guitar playing provided a consistent central focus of the band's sound. His growing interest in jazz and spirituality led to collaborations with artists such as John McLaughlin (*Love Devotion Surrender, 1973*) and Alice Coltrane (*Illuminations*, 1974). While remaining a popular live act, Santana did not return to the pop charts until

1999, when he released the multi-platinum-selling CD *Supernatural*. The album yielded two number one hits ("Smooth" and "Maria Maria") and earned nine Grammy Awards including awards for album, record, and song of the year.

See also **Music: Popular Music and Dance.**

BIBLIOGRAPHY

Heath, Chris. "The Epic Life of Carlos Santana." *Rolling Stone*, March 16, 2000, pp. 38–42, 45–46, 48, 86–89.

Leng, Simon. *Soul Sacrifice: The Santana Story*. London: Firefly Publishing, 2000.

Saidon, Gabriela. "Entrevista con Carlos Santana: El regreso del chamán." *Clarín Contenidos* (Argentina), March 5, 2006. Available from http://www.clarin.com/diario/2006/03/05/espectaculos/c-00601.htm.

ANDREW M. CONNELL

SANTANA, PEDRO (1801–1864).

Pedro Santana (*b*. 29 June 1801; *d*. 14 June 1864), cattle rancher, general, and president of the Dominican Republic (1844–1848, 1853–1856, and 1857–1861). Santana was a wealthy landowner from the eastern part of Hispaniola known as El Seibo, where he organized the armed forces at the time of the Dominican Republic's declaration of independence from Haiti on 27 February 1844. Heading the victorious Dominican troops during the battle of 19 March 1844 at Azua, he emerged as one of the heroes of the war of liberation against Haiti as well as the commander in chief of the liberation forces.

After becoming the first president of the Dominican Republic, Santana ruled as a caudillo with an iron hand, suppressing all opposition and exiling many of his former associates, including the "father of the Dominican Republic," Juan Pablo Duarte. Santana executed many Dominican patriots, including María Trinidad Sánchez, who had sewn the first Dominican flag; the brothers José Joaquín and Gabiño Puello, who had distinguished themselves in the war against Haiti; General Antonio Duvergé, victor of many battles against the Haitians; and the national hero, Francisco del Rosario Sánchez, who along with Duarte and Ramón Matias Mella is regarded as one of the three founding fathers of the Dominican Republic.

Throughout his terms as president, Santana faced Haitian invasions that were organized by the Haitian ruler Faustin Soulouque. In the battles of Santomé (1845), Las Carreras (1845), Cambronal (1855), and Sabana Larga (1856), Santana nullified all Haitian attempts to reconquer the Dominican Republic. However, the frequent Haitian incursions convinced Santana that his country should be annexed by a larger nation. His efforts to persuade France or the United States to annex the Dominican Republic proved futile.

In 1861, Santana made arrangements with the government of Queen Isabel II for the reannexation of the Dominican Republic by Spain and was rewarded with the title of Marqués de Las Carreras. The majority of Dominicans opposed the renewal of Spanish control and fought the successful War of Restoration (1863–1865) against Spain. By the time Santana died at Santo Domingo in 1864, he was no longer regarded by most Dominicans as the hero of the fight against Haiti but as the traitor in the War of Restoration against Spain. His reburial in the Pantheon of Dominican Heroes by order of President Joaquín Balaguer stirred up the controversy over Santana's ambivalent role in the history of his country.

See also **Caudillismo, Caudillo; Dominican Republic; Duarte, Juan Pablo.**

BIBLIOGRAPHY

Emilio Rodríguez Demorizi, *El General Pedro Santana* (1982).

Additional Bibliography

Cassá, Roberto. *Pedro Santana: Autócrata y anexionista*. Santo Domingo: Tobogan, 2000.

KAI P. SCHOENHALS

SANTANDER, FRANCISCO DE PAULA (1792–1840).

Francisco de Paula Santander (*b*. 2 April 1792; *d*. 6 May 1840), vice president of Gran Colombia and later president of New Granada. Born at Cúcuta, on the New Granada–Venezuela border, to a locally prominent family of cacao planters, Santander was sent at age thirteen to Bogotá to complete his education. He studied for a law degree, but after the independence movement began, he enlisted in the armed forces of the revolution without completing his studies.

In the civil warfare that soon broke out between centralists in Bogotá and the federalist United Provinces of New Granada, Santander, a junior officer, sided with the latter and in 1813 joined the patriot army defending northeastern New Granada against the royalists. Victory alternated with defeat until the patriots suffered a crushing setback at the battle of Cachirí in February 1816. Santander was among the survivors who made their way to relative safety on the eastern llanos, the lowland plains stretching from the foothills of the Andes to the Orinoco Basin.

Santander helped defend the llanos against royalist incursions, ultimately winning promotion to general. It was also in the llanos that he first displayed his talents as an administrator by organizing the province of Casanare as a base of patriot resistance. His success in this effort was one reason Simón Bolívar decided in 1819 to strike westward from the llanos of Venezuela into the heart of New Granada. He picked Santander to lead the vanguard of his army as he invaded the Andean highlands and won the decisive battle of Boyacá on 7 August.

Although Santander played an important part in that victory, Boyacá was the last battle he fought, for Bolívar placed him in charge of organizing all the liberated territories of New Granada. Santander put government on a sound footing and raised troops and supplies for the armies still fighting. When, in 1821, Gran Colombia was formally constituted by the Congress of Cúcuta, Santander was elected vice president. Since the president, Bolívar, was still leading the military struggle against Spain, Santander became acting chief executive and as such again provided an effective administrator. He also endeavored to implement the liberal reforms adopted by the Congress of Cúcuta and subsequent legislatures, which ranged from a free-birth law to tax reforms and various measures curbing the traditional wealth and power of the church.

The government of Santander faced growing disaffection especially in Venezuela, which resented subordination to authorities in Bogotá. These feelings came to a head with the revolt of José Antonio Páez in 1826, just as Bolívar prepared to return home from Peru. Santander was disappointed when Bolívar proceeded to pardon Páez and to work toward revamping the new nation's institutions as a way of preventing future upheavals. Bolívar wanted a moratorium on liberal reform and strengthening

of the national executive, policies that, combined with personal and factional rivalry, produced an open split with Santander. Following an unsuccessful attempt at constitutional reform, Bolívar assumed dictatorial powers and stripped Santander of the vice presidency. When liberal supporters of the latter attempted to assassinate Bolívar in September 1828, Santander himself was charged with complicity. Although the charge was never substantiated, the former vice president was exiled.

From 1829 to 1832 Santander traveled in Europe and the United States. He was still in exile at the final breakup of Gran Colombia and the reorganization of its central core as the Republic of New Granada. He returned in 1832 to become the first elected president of New Granada, a position he held until 1837. Once again exercising his administrative talents, he consolidated public order and even produced a balanced budget. Now more cautious than before, he did not push for sweeping reforms, although he did work hard to expand public education.

Santander was succeeded as president by José Ignacio de Márquez, a one-time collaborator of Santander who had forged an alliance with his main political adversaries, the former supporters of Bolívar. As ex-president, Santander won election to the Chamber of Representatives, where he was a leader of congressional opposition to Márquez until his death in 1840.

Santander has been revered as "Man of Laws" and "Civil Founder of the Republic" in token of his lasting commitment to constitutional government. He received special honor from members of Colombia's Liberal Party, whose principal founders had been among his strongest supporters. Proclerical conservatives were less enthusiastic, and in recent years they have been joined by new detractors on the left who depict Santander as a spokesman for creole oligarchs and friend to the United States. Nevertheless, among the founders of the Colombian nation he has no close rival apart from Bolívar himself.

See also **Cacao Industry; Gran Colombia; Llanos (Colombia); Llanos (Venezuela).**

BIBLIOGRAPHY

David Bushnell, *The Santander Regime in Gran Colombia* (1954; repr. 1970).

José Manuel Restrepo, *Diario político y militar*, 4 vols. (1954).

Indalecio Liévano Aguirre, *Razones socio-económicas de la conspiración de septiembre contra el Libertador* (1968).

Gilberto Salazar Parada, *El pensamiento político de Santander* (1969).

Eugene R. Huck, "Economic Experimentation in a Newly Independent Nation: Colombia Under Francisco de Paula Santander, 1821–1840," *The Americas* 29, no. 1 (1972):17–29.

Horacio Rodríguez Plata, *Santander en el exilio* (1976).

Pilar Moreno De Ángel, *Santander* (1989).

Additional Bibliography

Forero Benavides, Abelardo. *Francisco de Paula Santander: El hombre de las leyes.* Madrid: Ediciones Anaya, 1988.

Reales Orozco, Antonio. *Santander, fundador del estado colombiano.* Bogotá: Tercer Mundo Editores, 1994.

Riaño Cano, Germán. *El gran calumniado: Réplica a la leyenda negra de Santander.* Bogotá: Planeta, 2001.

Sant Roz, José. *Sandemonio: Así se jodieron Colombia y Venezuela.* Mérida, Venezuela: Kari'ña Editores, 1995.

DAVID BUSHNELL

SANTARÉM. Santarém, one of the largest cities in the Brazilian Amazon (2000 population 262,538). It is located halfway between Belém and Manaus on the southern bank of the Amazon River where it meets the Tapajós River in the state of Pará. It was founded in 1661 as a Jesuit Aldeia (large mission settlement), in which many Indians were enslaved and exposed to Portuguese diseases to which they had no immunities. On 9 January 1799, Governor Sousa Coutinho officially declared it an assembly town, where Indians were collected for redistribution as a labor supply. Although Indians and Caboclos captured Santarém during the Cabanagem rebellion in the 1830s, the government reclaimed it with the help of Munduruku warriors, who had been pacified in the eighteenth century. In the 1850s, rubber gatherers began extracting latex from the Tapajós River region, which they exported on steamships that serviced Santarém from 1853.

After the collapse of the rubber boom, Santarém experienced a slump. Subsequently, it has begun to thrive as a jumping-off point for gold prospectors and miners. Commercial Santarém fishermen extract sizable catches from the Amazon; Santarém also has a large timber and bauxite industry. The town, with its white, sandy beaches and Indian artifacts, also attracts some tourists. The advanced pottery of a pre-Columbian civilization was discovered in its streets in 1922 and was named for the town.

See also **Amazon River.**

BIBLIOGRAPHY

John Hemming, *Red Gold: The Conquest of the Brazilian Indians, 1500–1760* (1978); and his *Amazon Frontier: The Defeat of the Brazilian Indians* (1987).

Additional Bibliography

Amorim, Antonia Terezinha dos Santos. *Santarém: Uma síntese histórica.* Canoas, RS: Editora da ULBRA, 2000.

CAROLYN JOSTOCK

SANTARÉM CULTURE. East of the Andes there was an elaborate late prehistoric culture, known to historians through its pottery, called the incised and punctate horizon. (In archaeology, a "horizon" is an area in which roughly contemporary and clearly similar artifacts have been found, defining the geographical limits of a culture or complex of related cultures. "Incised and punctuate" refers to decorative characteristics of some pottery.) Santarém culture, whose dates are roughly 1000 to 1550 CE, in the Brazilian lower Amazon near the city of Santarém, is the most elaborate culture of the horizon, although whether it was at the center of the horizon is not certain because there are few radiocarbon dates available. So far, the earliest dates for the horizon are approximately 1000 years BP (before the present), from the middle Orinoco region. The few Santarém radiocarbon dates suggest that the culture existed there by 500 years before the European conquest of the Amazon and died out soon after the Conquest. This finding contrasts with the expectations of earlier scholars that it was an ethnohistoric culture.

Santarém culture is distinguished by elaborate pottery decorated with modeled animal and human images and incised or polychrome geometric designs. (A related but bolder pottery style in the area is called "Kondurí.") There are vessels with scenes from creation myths that survive among South American lowland Indians. Also found are terra cotta sculptures of nude humans (mostly female) with long, slit earlobes. Some of the figures are life size.

In addition to the pottery, carved jade pendants, stone scepters, ground rock mace heads, and projectile points have been found. The jades are shaped like frogs and other animals, such as insects. The scepters depict alter ego figures of humans or animals with animals perched on their shoulders.

Known sites of the Santarém culture are numerous, varied, and widespread within the lower Amazon, indicating a complex settlement system. Many major sites are located in defensible locations on cliffs high above the Amazon flood plain. Roads and round wells have been reported in the area of such sites. Santarém city, with many acres of low archaeological mounds containing ritual caches, hearths, and middens, may have been the capital. Pottery found in domestic contexts was simple and washed with red paint. Stone tools were limited mostly to small flint flakes and sandstone abraders. Ceremonial areas had fancy incised, punctate, and polychrome vessels and decorated stone artifacts such as spindle whorls and tools to make artifacts. Food remains also varied, depending on their site context. In domestic house floors, the bones of small fish and palm fruits are common. In ritual caches and activity areas, in contrast, larger fish, some game, and cultivated fruits and rare maize kernels were found. The isotopic chemistry of the carbon-dated specimens is suggestive of open, disturbed forest.

In a hinterland cave occupation of the period, dry maize cobs were recovered in a large pole-and-thatch structure, along with a wide range of fruits and faunal remains from closed-canopy tropical rainforest. At this cave site, richly decorated ceremonial pottery is lacking and simple, redwashed pottery is common.

Conquest documents mention a warlike chiefdom called Tapajó, a ranked society with a paramount chief over lower chiefs, some of whom were women. The chief was said to be descended from the sun and from a woman culture hero, in whose name maize tribute was given for beer for ceremonies. Cultivation and fishing furnished subsistence, and there was extensive trade. Large war parties with poisoned arrows resisted the Europeans but eventually were defeated, and the Tapajó merged into the racially mixed population of the region.

See also **Archaeology; Precontact History: Amazonia; Santarém.**

BIBLIOGRAPHY

Harrison, Regina. "The Order of Things: An Analysis of the Ceramics of Santarém." *Journal of the Steward Anthropological Society* 4 (Fall 1972), 39–57.

Palmatary, Helen Constance. *The Archaeology of the Lower Tapajós Valley, Brazil.* Philadelphia: American Philosophical Society, 1960.

ANNA CURTENIUS ROOSEVELT

SANTERÍA.   Santería, the Spanish name for a system of religious practices of African origin brought to Cuba in the late eighteenth and early nineteenth centuries. In that period hundreds of thousands of Africans were enslaved to work in the thriving sugar industries of the island. A plurality of these arrivals shared a similar culture and language called Yoruba by English ethnographers and Lucumí in Cuba. Since they came in such large numbers in such a short period of time, the Lucumí were able to maintain and adapt many of their cultural institutions, not the least of which were the complex theology and liturgies for a pantheon of spirits called *orishas* (Orixás). The Lucumí found correspondences between their *orishas* and the saints of popular Cuban Catholic piety, often masking their secret and suppressed traditions with the public faces of the saints. Thus, the tradition came to be known as *Santería,* the way of the saints.

The name *Santería* is not always acceptable to many present-day practitioners, since it has so long borne, like the North American use of "voodoo," the misrepresentations of outsiders. By its reference to the Catholic saints, the name also implies an admixture of Catholic elements to African traditions that present-day practitioners would argue are purely African. Alternatives such as *la regla de ocha* (the order of the *orishas*), *la religión Lucumí,* or simply "Lucumí" or "Orisha" are used.

The core of the Cuban *orisha* tradition is the development of an intimate relationship between a human being and his or her patron spirit, or *orisha.* The relationship often begins when an individual is so troubled by problems such as ill health or lack of money that he or she will consult a priest or priestess of the *orishas*. The priest and priestess will have been trained as diviners and, depending on their rank, they will utilize a variety of means to determine the spiritual source of and solutions to the seeker's problem. All priests and priestesses are empowered to divine solutions with sixteen cowrie shells called *dilogun*. The heads-or-tails patterns that result from the fall of the shells reveal the path of action for the seeker to take to resolve his or her problem. A related but more complex system of divination called *ifa* is reserved for a special male priest called the *babalawo*, the "father of the mystery." In either system the diagnosis of the problem will lie in the seeker's neglect of his or her patron *orisha*. The divination will tentatively determine the *orisha*'s identity, and a resolution of the problem will be found in a series of ritual actions culminating in a sacrifice to the *orisha*.

This opening sacrifice leads toward a growing, reciprocal relationship with the *orisha* as a human being offers respect, praise, and ritual food while the *orisha* reciprocates with gifts of power, blessings, and wisdom. As the relationship matures, divination will determine that the *orisha* seeks a permanent relationship, a kind of marriage in which the human being will become an *iyawo*, a bride to the spirit. In a lengthy and costly series of ceremonies, the initiate will have the *orisha* "seated" in his or her "head," thus marking the permanent presence of the spirit within the consciousness of the human being. This *asiento* (seating) initiation marks the entry of the individual into the *orisha* priesthood, and he or she is to be called a *babalorisha* (father in the *orisha*) or *iyalorisha* (mother in the *orisha*). Often enough the Spanish terms *santero* and *santera* are applied to this level of priesthood.

The most dramatic encounters with the *orishas* are found in communal drum and dance ceremonies called *bembés*. Here, amid elaborate polyrhythms and complex choreography, certain *orishas* are called to "mount" the heads of their initiates so that they lose consciousness while the *orishas* use their bodies to join in the ceremony. Manifested in the bodies of their "horses," the *orishas* sing and dance with the community, offer advice and warnings, and gladden the hearts of their devotees.

Since the Cuban Revolution of 1959, nearly 1 million Cubans have left the island to form communities, primarily on the U.S. mainland and in Puerto Rico and Venezuela. Carried by Cuban *babalorishas* and *iyalorishas*, the *orisha* tradition has undergone a second diaspora, adapting itself to these new environments. Just as it is likely that there are more *orisha* devotees in the New World than in the Old, so there are probably more in the Cuban diaspora than in Cuba itself. Since every community is autonomous, it is impossible to determine the numbers of practitioners of the tradition. It has grown well beyond its original Cuban community to include Latin Americans of all nationalities and ethnicities, as well as North American blacks and whites.

See also **African-Latin American Religions: Overview; Syncretism.**

BIBLIOGRAPHY

William R. Bascom, "The Focus of Cuban Santería," in *Southwestern Journal of Anthropology* 6, no. 1 (1950): 64–68.

Fernando Ortíz, *Los bailes y el teatro de los negros en el folklore de Cuba* (1951).

Mercedes Cros Sandoval, *La religión afrocubana* (1975).

Julio Sánchez, *La religión de los orichas* (Hato Rey, Puerto Rico: Colección Estudios Afrocaribeños, 1978).

Lydia Cabrera, *Koeko iyawó, aprende novicia: Pequeño tratado de regla Lucumí* (1980).

Joseph M. Murphy, *Santería: An African Religion in America* (1988).

Migene González-Wippler, *Santería: The Religion* (1989).

George Brandon, *Santería from Africa to the New World: The Dead Sell Memories* (1993).

Additional Bibliography

Ayorinde, Christine. *Afro-Cuban Religiosity, Revolution, and National Identity.* Gainesville: University Press of Florida, 2004.

Brown, David H. *Santería Enthroned: Art, Ritual, and Innovation in an Afro-Cuban Religion.* Chicago: University of Chicago Press, 2003.

Cros Sandoval, Mercedes. *Worldview, the Orichas, and Santería: Africa to Cuba and Beyond.* Gainesville: University Press of Florida, 2006.

Fernández Olmos, Margarite, and Lizabeth Paravisini-Gebert. *Creole Religions of the Caribbean: An Introduction from Vodou and Santería to Obeah and Espiritismo.* New York: New York University Press, 2003.

Hagedorn, Katherine J. *Divine Utterances: The Performance of Afro-Cuban Santería*. Washington, DC: Smithsonian Institution Press, 2001.

Pérez Medina, Tomás. *La santería cubana: El camino de Osha: Ceremonias, ritos, y secretos*. Madrid: Biblioteca Nueva, 1998.

Wedel, Johan. *Santería Healing: A Journey into the Afro-Cuban World of Divinities, Spirits, and Sorcery*. Gainesville: University Press of Florida, 2004.

JOSEPH M. MURPHY

SANTIAGO, ESMERALDA (1948–).

Peabody Award–winning screenwriter, essayist, and novelist Esmeralda Santiago is the best-selling author of three memoirs, *When I Was Puerto Rican* (1993), *Almost a Woman* (1998), and *The Turkish Lover* (2004), as well as the novel *América's Dream* (1996).

The oldest of eleven children, Santiago was born in Puerto Rico and immigrated to the United States in 1961. She attended junior high school in Brooklyn, then went on to the Performing Arts High School in New York City, where she majored in drama and dance. Santiago studied film production at Harvard University, graduating magna cum laude in 1976. She has also earned a Master of Fine Arts degree from Sarah Lawrence College, and she holds honorary doctoral degrees from Trinity University (Texas), Pace University, Metropolitan College of New York, and the University of Puerto Rico, Recinto Mayagüez.

Shortly after graduation from Harvard, Santiago married Frank Cantor, with whom she founded Cantomedia, a film and media production company that has won numerous awards for excellence in documentary filmmaking. Indeed, it is from her work as a documentary film writer that her career as an essayist and novelist has evolved.

Critics of Santiago's work often praise her moving portraits of the Puerto Rican immigrant experience, which are peppered with Spanish in order to more accurately depict the bilingual and bicultural realities of her community.

As of the early 2000s Santiago lives with her husband in Westchester County, New York, where she continues to translate her life story into print and film, contributing a powerful voice and commentary on the immigrant experience in the United States.

See also **Feminism and Feminist Organizations; Puerto Rico; Women.**

BIBLIOGRAPHY

Primary Works

When I Was Puerto Rican. New York: Perseus, 1993.

América's Dream. New York: HarperCollins, 1996.

Almost a Woman. New York: Perseus, 1998.

Las Christmas: Favorite Latino Authors Share Their Holiday Memories. Edited with Joie Davidow. New York: Knopf, 1998.

Las Mamis: Favorite Latino Authors Remember Their Mothers. Edited with Joie Davidow. New York: Knopf, 2000.

The Turkish Lover. Boston: Merloyd Lawrence, 2004.

A Doll for Navidades. New York: Scholastic, 2005.

Secondary Works

Copeland, Libby Ingrid. "Cultural Go-Between: Author Esmeralda Santiago's Two Languages and Two Lives." *Washington Post*. November 12, 1998.

Muñiz, Ismael. "Bildungsroman Written by Puerto Rican Women in the United States: Nicholasa Mohr's *Nilda: A Novel* and Esmeralda Santiago's *When I Was Puerto Rican*." *Atenea* 19, no. 1–2 (1999): 79–101.

Sprouse, Keith Alan. "Between Bilingüe and Nilingüe: Language and the Translation of Identity in Esmeralda Santiago's Memoirs." *American Studies in Scandinavia* 32, no. 1 (2000): 107–116.

ETHRIAM CASH BRAMMER

SANTIAGO, CHILE.

Santiago is the capital of Chile, the center of the metropolitan region, and home to one third of the country's inhabitants (5,623,000 of 16,185,000, according to the UN's *World Urbanization Prospects: The 2003 Revision*). The city is located in a closed basin between the Andes and the Coastal Range (Cordillera de la Costa). The only natural openings are the Maipo River valley and the narrow passage of the Angostura de Paine that leads into the Central Valley. Founded in February of 1541 by Pedro de Valdivia, who had been appointed *adelantado* (governor) of Chile by Francisco Pizarro, governor of Peru, it developed at the site of a small indigenous settlement located between the southern bank of the Mapocho River and the Santa Lucía hill. During colonial times it was only one of several Spanish administrative and cultural centers. Its position was contested by the outpost of Concepción, where much of the military was massed against the Mapuche population (known to the Spaniards as *Araucanos*, or Araucanians) and pirates, and by La Serena, then the center of commerce and communications. An inland town, Santiago was served by the port city of Valparaíso, 85 miles to the west. Other cities continued to challenge Santiago's primacy over the emerging country, but the political, cultural, and economic power of Santiago's colonial elite prevailed and established the strongly centralized tradition of government that continues to characterize Chile.

The basin of Santiago stretches out at the foot of the Andes, which serve as a majestic backdrop to the city. High above the bustling metropolis, four major ski resorts provide a snowy playground to wealthy *Santiaguinos* and many foreign visitors. Well ventilated by the mountain winds, the eastern section of the city—the Barrio Alto—is the preferred place of residence of the wealthy: boasting numerous parks and traversed by wide avenues, the municipalities of Providencia, Vitacura, Valdivia, Los Leones, Los Condes, and La Reina serve as home to the city's financial sector, the largest malls, the residences of diplomats, the military academy, and the medical school. The original site of Santiago, between the Mapocho River and the Avenida de las Delicias, today known as La Alameda (renamed Avenida Libertador Bernardo O'Higgins and Avenida 11 de septiembre in different sectors of the city), is still the core of the city and lodges ministries, major banks, embassies, large department stores, theaters, and cultural institutions. The presidential palace, Casa de la Moneda (the colonial Mint House), sits prominently on La Alameda, but Chile's legislative bodies meet in Valparaíso. This sector is also the cultural center of the city. Sites include a new cultural center under la Moneda, the extensive collection at the Pre-Colombian Art Museum, and the Fine Art Museum and Contemporary Art Museum, both housed in the "palace of fine arts" within Parque Forestal. Surrounding neighborhoods, including Barrio Brasil, Barrio Bellavista, and Bellas Artes, are home to filmhouses, theater companies, and art galleries.

To the north of the city, at the foot of the lofty San Cristóbal hill, spread the popular neighborhoods of El Salto, Conchali, and Huechuraba. Also to the north lie the plains of Colina and Pudahuel, site of the Arturo Merino Benítez International Airport. To the west lay more populous boroughs interspersed with industrial establishments—Renca, Quinta Normal, Los Pajaritos, and Maipú. Nearby lies the industrial park at Los Cerrillos at the former site of the international airport of Santiago. Toward the south, and readily accessible by subway and the wide southern segment of the Pan-American Highway, are middle-class boroughs such as San Miguel and San Bernardo, and extensive *poblaciones*, or populous neighbohoods, such as La Cisterna, Espejo, and Cardenal Caro. Slums are located in the southwest: it was in La Florida that the the forces of General Augusto Pinochet met with popular resistance during his rule (1973–1989). These municipalities are only a few of the thirty-seven which make up Greater Santiago, the 64,140-hectare (as of 2002) conurbation comprised of Santiago, San Bernardo (which lies in Maipo province), and Puente Alto (in Cordillera province).

Santiago is the final station of a major railway to the south of the country and of another from the port city of Valparaíso. The city is also the connecting point of the northern and southern segments of the Pan-American Highway.

Enhancing the centralized character of the capital city was the decision of past administrations to bolster the industrial clout of Santiago by allowing the establishment of manufacturing plants in the capital, which now account for over half of the country's total. The city generates 45 percent of the nation's GDP, notable in an economy that continues to be dominated by mining and agriculture. In addition, the leading papers, television stations, the stock exchange, three major universities (Universidad de Chile, Universidad Católica de Chile, and the technical school Universidad de Santiago), the Air Force Academy, and the Officers School of Carabineros (the national police), as well as international institutions such as ECLAC (the United Nations Economic Commission for Latin America and the Caribbean), are established in Santiago.

In February 2007 the city launched Transantiago, revamping the city's transportation system with the hope of introducing more people to the

Metro and of making the bus system more efficient. However, the transition to the new system backfired as patrons confused by a new fare card system and different bus routes vied for space in overloaded metro cars and suffered long waits due to a decreased bus fleet and malfunctioning GPS devices.

The city's position in a valley creates meteorological conditions in which warm air holds colder air close to ground. Combined with the emissions of automobiles and industry, this phenomenon results in smog that sometimes becomes dense enough to blot out the mountains on the horizon. This pollution, in addition to the contamination of the Mapocho River, have accelerated the exodus of the affluent toward the slopes of the Andes, thus accentuating the socioeconomic divide evident in the city's geography.

This socioeconomic divide manifested itself in massive student protests which shut down the city's schools in May of 2006. Students rallied in the streets and took over their schools in protest of the resource and performance gaps between public schools and private ones. Dubbed the Revolution of the Penguins for the students' appearance in their grey and blue uniforms, the protests won concessions from the government, but students have continued to protest what they perceive as the slow response to educational inequality.

See also **Chile, Geography; Economic Commission for Latin America and the Caribbean (ECLAC); Mapocho River; Valparaíso.**

BIBLIOGRAPHY

Galetovic, Alexander, ed. *Santiago: Dónde estamos y hacia dónde vamos.* Santiago: Centro de Estudios Públicos, 2006.

Vicuña-Mackenna, Benjamín. *Historia de Santiago.* Santiago: Universidad de Chile, 1938.

Walter, Richard J. *Politics and Urban Growth in Santiago, Chile, 1891–1941.* Stanford, CA: Stanford University Press, 2005.

CÉSAR N. CAVIEDES
KATY BERGLUND SCHLESINGER

SANTIAGO DE CUBA. Santiago de Cuba, the second city of Cuba from colonial through modern times and capital of Oriente Province.

With a 2004 population of 490,849, it is located on the southeastern side of the island. Founded in 1514 by Diego de Velázquez, it quickly became an ecclesiastical and administrative center as well as an active international port. Following the British seizure of nearby Jamaica in 1655 and an influx of refugees and contraband, Santiago's economy flourished—a situation similar to that of the French planters during the Haitian Revolution in the 1790s. The harbor and region around Santiago were sites of numerous military engagements between Spain and its rivals in the eighteenth century, of considerable anticolonial activities during the Ten Years' War (1868–1878), of a decisive naval battle between the United States and Spain in 1898, and of early revolutionary operations involving Fidel Castro. The city has long been an industrial and commercial center; the original home of Bacardi rum, it boasts the oldest chamber of commerce in Cuba (1885).

See also **Ten Years' War; Velásquez, Diego de.**

BIBLIOGRAPHY

Emilio Bacardí Moreau, *Crónicas de Santiago de Cuba,* 10 vols. (1972–1973).

Vicente Báez, ed., *La Enciclopedia de Cuba: Municipios, Oriente,* vol. 12 (1974).

Leví Marrero, *Cuba: Economía y sociedad,* 15 vols. (1974–1992).

Additional Bibliography

Duharte Jiménez, Rafael. *El negro en la sociedad colonial.* Santiago de Cuba: Editorial Oriente, 1988.

Duharte Jiménez, Rafael and Elizabet Recio Lobaina, Eds. *Santiago de Cuba siglo XX: Cronistas y viajeros miran la ciudad.* Santiago de Cuba: Editorial Oriente, 2005.

Gott, Richard. *Cuba: A New History.* New Haven, CT: Yale University Press, 2004.

LINDA K. SALVUCCI

SANTIAGO DE LOS CABALLEROS. Santiago de los Caballeros, the second largest city in the Dominican Republic (after Santo Domingo), with a population of 622,101 in 2006. It is the capital and considered the most Spanish city in the province of Santiago. The city gets its name from the thirty Spanish gentlemen who settled there in 1504; in Dominican history it is the city of earthquakes and uprisings. Earthquakes struck the city in 1775, 1783, 1842, and 1946. Santiago is the economic center and historical rival of Santo Domingo, the political center, less than 85 miles to the southeast. It is 23 miles from the main port on the north coast, Puerto Plata. The city lies in the rich Cibao Valley, the country's breadbasket.

Santiago is the home of a prosperous, enlightened conservative elite. These *cibaeños* are the landed aristocracy, the best educated and most cosmopolitan and cultured citizens. A score of related families have dominated business, and their wealth is based on land, cattle, sugar and rum, tobacco, coffee, cacao, and rice. The business community and the Conference of Dominican Bishops together established the Universidad Católica Madre y Maestra in 1962 as an alternative to the public Universidad Autónoma de Santo Domingo. It was modeled after the U.S. style of university in terms of curriculum, pedagogy, and organization. The Universidad Tecnológica de Santiago followed in 1974.

BIBLIOGRAPHY

Brown, Isabel Zakrzewski. *Culture and Customs of the Dominican Republic.* Westport, CT: Greenwood Press, 1999.

Espinal Hernández, Edwin. *Historia social de Santiago de los Caballeros, 1863–1900.* Santo Domingo, Dominican Republic: Fundación Manuel de Jesús Tavares Portes, 2005.

Martin, John Bartlow. *Overtaken by Events: The Dominican Crisis from the Fall of Trujillo to the Civil War* (1966), chap. 6.

Moya Pons, Frank. *El pasado dominicano* (1986).

Rosario, Esteban. *La oligarquía de Santiago.* 2nd Edition. Santiago de los Caballeros, Dominican Republic: Editora Central, 1997.

Wiarda, Howard J., and Michael J. Kryzanek. *The Dominican Republic: A Caribbean Crucible,* 2d ed. (1992).

LARMAN C. WILSON

SANTO, SANTA. Santo and Santa are terms that may refer to a saint or holy person in Roman Catholicism or, by extension, to a representation of such a person in sculpted or flat format. The term is the basis for *santero,* a maker of religious images, and Santería, a folk religion of African origin. Historical records also refer to a holy image as *imagen*, but the modern use of the term may emphasize material form over spiritual content. *Santo* often referred to a smaller domestic representation while *imagen* was used for a larger, church sculpture defined as *de talla* if carved or *de bulto* if also dressed in clothing.

In popular Catholicism and Caribbean *santería,* folk religious images of Puerto Rico, the Dominican Republic, Venezuela, and New Mexico are known as *santos.* In the United States, many non-Hispanic dealers and collectors use the term to promote the artistic and monetary value of *santos* while *Hispano* and Chicano artisans use the term to enforce the ethnic and cultural identity of the images and themselves.

See also **Catholic Church: The Modern Period.**

BIBLIOGRAPHY

E. Boyd, *Popular Arts of Spanish New Mexico* (1974).

Yvonne Lange, " 'Santos': The Household Saints of Puerto Rico" (Ph.D. diss., University of Pennsylvania, 1975).

William Wroth, *Christian Images in Hispanic New Mexico* (1982).

Teodoro Vidal, *Los espada: Escultores sangermeños* (1994).

Additional Bibliography

Colón, Doreen. *Los santos de Puerto Rico: Estudio de la imaginería popular.* Hong Kong: Asia Pacific, 2003.

Farago, Claire J., Donna Pierce, et al. *Transforming Images: New Mexican Santos In-Between Worlds.* University Park: Pennsylvania State University Press, 2006.

Freites, Natividad. *Recetario santero.* Caracas: Editorial Panapo, 1999.

Vélez, María Teresa. *Drumming for the Gods: The Life and Times of Felipe García Villamil, Santero, Palero, and Abakuá.* Philadelphia: Temple University Press, 2000.

RICHARD E. AHLBORN

SANTO DOMINGO. Santo Domingo, capital of the Dominican Republic, situated on the southern shore of the island of Hispaniola along the Ozama River. Since earliest Spanish colonial times, Santo Domingo has been the largest and most important urban settlement in the Dominican Republic. Its role as administrative, trade, and industrial center helped to make it the largest urban agglomeration of the entire Caribbean. As of 2007, 2.25 million people, almost a quarter of the country's population of about 9.2 million, resides in the 60 square miles of this city, which is home to 47 percent of the urban population, 55 percent of all industrial workers, and 63 percent of all white-collar workers of the Dominican Republic. The population can be divided into four major social groups: (1) the largest group, constituting 48 to 50 percent of all households, consists of poor and marginal slum dwellers who reside in some of the worst barrios of the Caribbean; (2) the second largest group (30–35 percent) consists of those who have overcome extreme poverty and live in relatively stable economic conditions; (3) a heterogeneous middle class constitutes 12 to 15 percent of the population; and (4) a very wealthy elite makes up 2 percent of the populace.

The city of Santo Domingo was founded on 4 August 1496 by Bartolomé Colón, brother of Christopher Columbus. It became the capital of the Spanish colonial realm in the Americas, and it was from here that Spanish conquistadores (Hernán Cortés, Diego de Velásquez, Juan Ponce de León) launched their conquests of other parts of the Americas. The city's buildings were originally made of wood, but after a violent hurricane in 1502, many stone buildings were erected, among them the first cathedral (Catedral Primada de India), first university, first hospital, and first paved street in the Americas. In 1586 the city was pillaged and partially destroyed by Francis Drake.

With the rapid expansion of Spanish colonial rule in the Americas and the discovery of gold in Mexico and Peru, Santo Domingo, along with the rest of the country, became a backwater of the Spanish colonial empire. Natural catastrophes, Haitian invasions, and civil wars prevented the growth and expansion of the city during the next three centuries. The census of 1908 registered a mere 19,000 inhabitants.

After a devastating hurricane destroyed most of the capital in September 1930, Santo Domingo had to be reconstructed. The only buildings that withstood the storm were the stone buildings dating from colonial times. It was not until the reign of dictator Rafael Leónidas Trujillo Molina (1930–1961) that Santo Domingo—named Ciudad Trujillo from 1936 to 1961—underwent a large public building program consisting of massive neoclassical edifices such as the Presidential Palace, the Palace of Fine Arts, and buildings at "La Feria" (the fair). In 1966, the government established a national university there. In 1990 UNESCO made the city a World Heritage site.

See also **Dominican Republic.**

BIBLIOGRAPHY

Joaquín Balaguer, *Guía emocional de la ciudad romántica* (1969).

Additional Bibliography

Hoffnung-Garskof, Jesse. *A Tale of Two Cities: Santo Domingo and New York after 1950*. Princeton, NJ: Princeton University Press, 2008.

Pérez Montás, Eugenio. *La ciudad del Ozama: 500 años de historia urbana*. 2nd ed. Santo Domingo: Patronato de la Cuidad Colonial de Santo Domingo, 1999.

Kai P. Schoenhals

SANTO DOMINGO, AUDIENCIA OF.

Audiencia of Santo Domingo, the first appeals court in the New World, it heard civil and criminal appeals from Spain's Caribbean colonies and had original jurisdiction over matters involving the royal treasury (including auditing the accounts). From its creation in 1511 until 1799 it was convened in the city of Santo Domingo, Hispaniola, and from 1799 to 1861 in Puerto Príncipe, Cuba. The audencia returned to Santo Domingo in 1861 when the Dominican Republic was again made part of the Spanish Empire. That episode, and the audiencia's existence, ended in 1865.

A royal decree of 5 October 1511 created this three-judge appeals court, ostensibly to save litigants the delay and expense of appeals to courts in Spain. The unstated purpose was to limit the judicial and administrative powers that Diego Colón, son and heir of Christopher Columbus, had won in his lawsuit against the crown over the validity of the privileges granted to his father in the Capitulation of Santa Fe (1492) and later reaffirmed by royal decrees of 1493 and 1497. According to the judgment, Colón had the right as governor to appoint the judges of first instance (*justicias*) and the district judges (*justicias mayores*, so named to distinguish them from royally appointed Alcaldes Mayores, even though their duties were the same) on Hispaniola, Puerto Rico, and Jamaica. As viceroy and governor of Hispaniola, he had extensive administrative powers there and in Puerto Rico.

The audiencia's area of jurisdiction included all of the Spanish conquests until 1527, when New Spain was given its own audiencia with a district that ran from the Cape of Honduras to Cape Sable, Florida. In subsequent decades, the on-going conquest temporarily added parts of Central America, New Granada (Colombia), and Venezuela and (in theory) Peru, Ecuador, and even Chile to the Santo Domingo district. Central America, Colombia, Peru, and all Spanish territories along the Pacific coast were transferred to the new Audiencia of Panama (created in 1538) when it began operation in 1540 and then to other audiencias as they were created. This left the Audiencia of Santo Domingo with jurisdiction over Maracaibo, Venezuela, Cumaná, Margarita, Guiana, and the Caribbean islands. The conquest of Florida in 1565 added that area to the district. The district remained stable except for the addition of Trinidad and the loss of the Lesser Antilles, Haiti, and Jamaica during the seventeenth century.

In the eighteenth century, the audiencia's district underwent many changes. Florida was transferred to the British for a time (1763–1783) and Louisiana was added (1763), although most of Louisiana's appeals went to a special court at Havana. The provinces of the northern coast of South America from Maracaibo east were withdrawn from the district in 1717–1723 and again in 1739–1777 and assigned to the Audiencia of Santa Fe de Bogotá as part of the creation of the Viceroyalty of New Granada. The province of Venezuela was returned to Santo Domingo's jurisdiction in 1742 and the others in 1777. These territories were again withdrawn in 1786 when the Audiencia of Caracas was founded. Finally, the Spanish part of Hispaniola was ceded to France in 1795, and the audiencia moved to Puerto Príncipe, Cuba, in 1799. Thereafter, its jurisdiction was confined to Cuba, Hispaniola (until the Haitian conquest of 1821), Puerto Rico, Florida (to 1821), and Louisiana (to 1803).

The Audiencia of Santo Domingo played its greatest historical role during the first thirty or so years of its existence. Not only did it help reduce Colón's power, it also attempted to mediate the early conquistadores' conflicts over territory, for example, those between Hernán Cortés and Diego de Velázquez over New Spain (1520) and among the various claimers of Honduras. The court also helped formulate and implement policies of various kinds because its original mandate included instructions to meet with Colón and the royal treasury officials for a meeting called the *real acuerdo* to open royal letters and formulate policies for implementing orders. This function grew during the 1520s, becoming the characteristic political advisory role later exercised by other audiencias, especially those in the viceregal capitals. The audiencia was not active in the protection of the Indians. The private interests of its early judges in the trade in Indian slaves and in *encomiendas* caused them to make common cause with other Spaniards in the Caribbean, at least until the 1540s, when the disappearance of Indians on the islands and the New Laws changed attitudes.

After Colón's final return to Spain in 1523, the Audiencia of Santo Domingo assumed the additional duties of governor of the island. The arrival of the first president of the tribunal, Bishop Sebastián Ramírez de Fuenleal, in 1529 began a pattern of conflict between the judges and the president, each claiming the right to govern as well as administer justice. In theory, they were to govern the island jointly. This conflict was never fully resolved, although in 1583 the crown borrowed from the practice in other audiencias and added the title of governor to those held by the president and spelled out his duties as chief administrative officer. During the 1530s the president began to exercise the military functions of a captain-general, an office formerly added to his titles in 1577.

During the second half of the sixteenth century, the audiencia judges became notorious for their inspection tours of the northern and western districts of Hispaniola. The public purposes were to gather current information about the districts and to see that royal laws were being enforced. The latter especially meant arresting smugglers and confiscating their goods. However, many contemporaries charged that the judges used the tours to enrich themselves and the staff that accompanied them by claiming shares of the confiscated goods and by charging high per-diem fees, which the residents of the visited areas had to pay. In 1605 the crown ordered the northern and western coasts depopulated because of smuggling and evidence that Protestants had given Spanish Bibles to the residents. Baltasar López de Castro, an official from Santo Domingo, was a key figure in lobbying for this action. Judicial visits continued to the remaining districts of the island.

With the reduction of the audiencia's district as other audiencias were created, and the gradual decline of the economy of Hispaniola, the audiencia's prestige and influence also declined. By 1600 it serviced mostly Hispaniola, Puerto Rico, and the Venezuelan settlements. As often as not, Cuban appeals went to Spain because that journey was no more difficult than the one to Santo Domingo. This declining area of effective jurisdiction and the general decline of Santo Domingo meant that by the last quarter of the sixteenth century the Audiencia of Santo Domingo was considered the lowest ranking of the audiencias, the normal point of entrance for jurists hoping to work their way up the ladder of appointments to the more prestigious audiencias of Lima and, especially, Mexico City. The rank and prestige of the court were further diminished in 1786 when it lost jurisdiction over the northern coast of South America and was reduced from four judges to three, and again in 1861, when it returned to Santo Domingo, where it became a territorial audiencia like all those in Spain's other provinces.

See also **Audiencia.**

BIBLIOGRAPHY

There is no comprehensive study of this audiencia, but parts of its history can be found in Clarence H. Haring, *The Spanish Empire in America* (1947), esp. pp. 84–86; Fernando Muro Romero, *Las presidencias-gobernaciones en Indias (siglo XVI)* (1975), pp. 73–84; Javier Malagón Barcelo, *El distrito de la Audiencia de Santo Domingo en los siglos XV a XIX,* 2d ed. (1977). Information on the judges and *fiscales* who served on the court from 1687 to 1808 is in Mark A. Burkholder and D. S. Chandler, *From Impotence to Authority: The Spanish Crown and the American Audiencias, 1687–1808* (1977). Frank Moya Pons, *Historia colonial de Santo Domingo* (1974), provides general context. Details of particular periods are in Américo Lugo, *Historia de Santo Domingo desde el 1556 hasta el 1608* (1952); María Rosario Sevilla Soler, *Santo Domingo: Tierra de frontera, 1750–1800* (1980); and Juana Gilbermejo García, *La española: Anotaciones históricas, 1600–1650* (1983).

Additional Bibliography

Barrios, Feliciano. *El gobierno de un mundo: Virreinatos y audiencias en la América hispánica.* Cuenca: Ediciones de la Universidad de Castilla-La Mancha, 2004.

PAUL E. HOFFMAN

SANTORO, CLAUDIO (1919–1989).

Claudio Santoro (*b.* 23 November 1919; *d.* 27 March 1989), Brazilian composer, conductor, violinist, and teacher. Santoro studied composition with Hans Joachim Koellreutter, a pupil of Paul Hindemith. Through his studies with Koellreutter, he was introduced to serial compositional techniques, which, according to Santoro, were the most significant single influence on the works he produced between 1939–1947. His *Impressions of a Steel Mill* (1943), an orchestral composition, won a competition sponsored by the Orquestra Sinfônica Brasileira, and his First String Quartet won the Chamber Music Guild Award, Washington, D.C.

From 1950 to 1960 Santoro focused on national subjects for his compositions. The period after 1960 represents a return to serialism and the beginnings of electro-acoustical writing. In 1962 Santoro became director of the department of music of the University of Brasília, a post he held until 1964, when political changes in the government resulted in resignations at the university. Following his departure from Brasília, Santoro went to Germany, where he did research in Heidelberg on electronic music and experiments in aleatoric sketches combining painting and aleatoric sound.

Santoro returned to Brazil in 1978 as professor of composition at the University of Brasília. He founded the Orquestra Sinfônica do Teatro Nacional and worked tirelessly to establish a national center for theater. Santoro's final Symphony no. 14, first performed eight months after his death, is one of his best works.

See also **Music: Art Music; Musical Instruments.**

BIBLIOGRAPHY

The New Grove Dictionary of Music and Musicians (1980).

David P. Appleby, *The Music of Brazil* (1983).

Additional Bibliography

Gandelman, Saloméa. *36 compositores brasileiros: Obras para piano (1950-1988)*. Rio de Janeiro: Ministério da Cultura, Funarte: Relume Dumará, 1997.

Mariz, Vasco. *Cláudio Santoro*. Rio de Janeiro: Civilização Brasileira, 1994.

DAVID P. APPLEBY

SANTOS. Santos, one of the most important of Brazil's deep-water ports. First in Brazil in exports and second only to Rio de Janeiro in imports, Santos is the world's largest coffee-exporting port. The neighboring countries of Bolivia and Paraguay have free ports at Santos.

Located in the state of São Paulo, Santos is approximately 30 miles southeast of São Paulo, Brazil's largest city, and 200 miles southwest of Rio de Janeiro. The city itself is 3 miles from the Atlantic Ocean on São Vicente Island, in a tidal inlet called the Santos River. Its modern dock and warehouse facilities, the largest in Latin America, now handle over 40 percent (by value) of Brazil's imports and over half its exports, which include bananas, beef, oranges, and hides, in addition to coffee. The suburb Guarujá is one of Brazil's principal seaside resorts.

Modern-day Santos stands near the site of Brazil's first permanent European settlement, São Vicente, which was founded in 1532. The city of Santos itself was settled between 1543 and 1546. Linked to the city of São Paulo by railroad, Santos became the fastest-growing port in Brazil by the late nineteenth century as coffee cultivation developed in the interior of the state of São Paulo. Its population grew from 30,000 in 1900 to 295,000 in 1960 and to 429,000 in 1990.

Just outside Santos is one of Brazil's major industrial areas that houses oil refineries, chemical plants, and the hydroelectric plant at Cubatão. Severe pollution resulted in the area being called the "Valley of Death" by the local populace. However, a loan from the World Bank facilitated the reduction of pollution from petrochemical and fertilizer plants to a fraction of their previous levels.

As a result of changes in world shipping after September 11, 2001, the port of Santos has begun to upgrade its security system entering in an agreement with Verint Systems of New York to enhance security with wire and wireless networks for video monitoring. These upgrades will bring Santos in line with the new International Ship and Port Facility Security (ISPS) Code regulations for surveillance.

See also **Coffee Industry.**

BIBLIOGRAPHY

Burns, E. Bradford. *A History of Brazil* (1970).

Honorato, Cezar Teixeira. *O polvo e o porto: A Cia: Docas de Santos, 1888–1914*. São Paulo: Editora Hucitec; Santos, Brazil: Prefeitura Municipal de Santos, 1996.

Poppino, Rollie E. *Brazil: The Land and People* (1968).

MARY JO MILES

SANTOS, EDUARDO (1888–1974). Eduardo Santos was president of Colombia from 1938 to 1942. A lawyer by training, Santos entered Liberal politics through journalism; in the 1920s he built Bogotá's *El Tiempo*, which he owned and directed, into one of the continent's most important newspapers and a force in the Liberal Party. In 1938 he succeeded Alfonso López Pumarejo in the presidency, abandoning his predecessor's vocal reformism but laying the institutional basis for much of Colombia's modern economic structure. The Industrial Development Institute, the Municipal Development Institute, and the Territorial Credit Institute, among others, were created during his administration.

During World War II Santos was among the most pro-U.S. leaders of Latin America, for which he was attacked by the pro-Axis Conservative leader Laureano Gómez. During his administration the Conservatives returned to Congress after four years' absence, and political life was relatively normal. Santos's battles to publish *El Tiempo* during the military regime of the mid-1950s attracted world attention, and the newspaper's editorials carried enormous weight as an expression of elite opinion during the bipartisan National Front years (1958–1974) and thereafter. The newspaper has remained in Santos's extended family, and in the early twenty-first century it is the heart of a large media group, the Casa Editorial El Tiempo (CEET), with a variety of print and online publications. For several decades family members involved with the newspaper declined government appointments, but in 2002 Francisco Santos was elected vice president as the running mate of Álvaro Uribe, to the rumored consternation of many in the family.

See also **Colombia: Since Independence; Gómez Castro, Laureano.**

BIBLIOGRAPHY

Bushnell, David. *Eduardo Santos and the Good Neighbor, 1938–1942.* Gainesville: University of Florida Press, 1967.

Dix, Robert. *Colombia: The Political Dimensions of Change.* New Haven, CT: Yale University Press, 1967.

RICHARD STOLLER

SANTOS, JUAN. *See* Atahualpa (Juan Santos).

SANTOS, MARQUESA DE (1797–1867).

Marquesa de Santos (Domitila de Castro Canto e Melo; *b.* March 1797; *d.* 13 November 1867), Emperor Pedro I's Brazilian mistress. Domitila was Pedro I's lover from 1822 to 1831. She was one of many Castro women who were chosen to be the mistresses of Pedro I of Castile and Pedro II of Portugal. A striking beauty with ivory skin and dark hair, the marquesa was married at age fourteen. She bore three children during her first marriage. Unknown to her spouse, they were actually Pedro's. Eventually, her deranged and jealous husband drove her out of their home. Pedro I arranged an ecclesiastical divorce for his lover. Domitila and the emperor had four children during this often stormy love affair. After Pedro left Brazil, the marquesa married for a second time. She was one of the richest women in Brazil when she died, leaving a fortune of over 1 million *milréis,* the equivalent of $1 million U.S.

See also **Pedro I of Brazil; Pedro II of Brazil.**

BIBLIOGRAPHY

Sergio Correa Da Costa, *Every Inch a King: A Biography of Dom Pedro I, First Emperor of Brazil* (1950).

Alberto Rangel, *Dom Pedro I e a Marquesa de Santos á vista de cartas íntimas e de outros documentos públicos e particulares,* 3d ed. (1969), and *Marginados: Anotações e as cartas de D Pedro I a D Domitila* (1974).

Eul-Soo Pang, *In Pursuit of Honor and Power: Noblemen of the Southern Cross in Nineteenth-Century Brazil* (1988).

Additional Bibliography

Pinheiro Neto, João. *Pedro e Domitila: Amor em tempo de paixão.* Rio de Janeiro: Mauad, 2002.

EUL-SOO PANG

SANTOS, NELSON PEREIRA DOS

(1928–). Brazilian filmmaker Nelson Pereira dos Santos, best-known for his "generous presiding spirit" and for serving as the "conscience" of the country's Cinema Novo (New cinema) movement, was born on October 22, 1928, in São Paulo. His first feature films, *Rio 40 Graus* (1955; Rio 40 Degrees) and *Rio Zona Norte* (1957; Rio Northern Zone), which drew attention to the plight of poor urban dwellers, are considered stylistic and thematic precursors to the Cinema Novo movement. In contrast, his 1963 masterpiece, *Vidas Secas* (Barren Lives), an adaptation of the novel by Graciliano Ramos, shows the difficult conditions of rural Brazilian life in the *sertão* (Brazilian northeast desert). The film represents what fellow filmmaker Glauber Rocha would later call the *estética da fome* (esthetic of hunger), using a bare bones style of filming to reflect the dismal, barren condition of the characters. Although the story takes place from 1940 to 1942, many have observed that the film critiques the political and social problems of the 1960s. In 1971 he made *Como era gostoso o meu francés* (How Tasty Was My Little Frenchman), part of the Tropicália (Tropicalist) movement, which was followed by noteworthy films such as *O Amuleto de Ogum* (1974; The Amulet of Ogum) and *Memórias do Cárcere* (1984; Memories of prison). He has maintained a strong presence in the film community with more recent endeavors such as *Raízes do Brasil* (2004; The Roots of Brazil) and *Brasília 18%* (2006).

BIBLIOGRAPHY

Johnson, Randal, and Robert Stam, eds. *Brazilian Cinema,* expanded ed. New York: Columbia University Press, 1995.

STACY LUTSCH

SANTOS, SÍLVIO (1931–).

Sílvio Santos (Senhor Abravanel; *b.* 1931), Brazilian television variety show host, network owner, and 1989 presidential candidate, represents one of the major rags-to-riches stories of Brazil. He started as a street peddler (*camelô*) and developed a Sunday afternoon television variety show that is still one of the most popular in Brazil, featuring games, amateur performances, music, and sensational interviews, such as an adaptation of *Queen for a Day,* in which poor women vie to tell the most pathetic life story. In 1976, he purchased TV Record (São Paulo), and in 1978, TV Rio. In 1981, Santos was awarded four licenses for Rio de Janeiro, São Paulo, Belém, and Pôrto Alegre that belonged to TV Tupi, the earliest Brazilian network, which had gone bankrupt. Within two years, his SBT/TVS network had twenty-one affiliates and roughly 25 percent of the audience, ranking second after TV Globo, which often had 60 to 80 percent of the audience. The network followed the pattern of Santos's own programs, emphasizing four or five live variety shows, lowbrow comedies, imported series and films from the United States, and *telenovelas* and comedies from Mexico. Santos's programming aimed at a popular (lower-middle-class to lower-class) audience and was very successful. He briefly tried to compete for a broader audience with more news and his own *telenovelas,* but returned to popular programming. In 1989, after creating an empire of over forty businesses, including some in agriculture, real estate, and sales, Santos made a late entry into the 1989 Brazilian presidential race. His personal popularity put him high in polls, but the party that nominated him was found to be improperly registered and his candidacy was quickly canceled.

He has influenced Brazilian television in many ways, particularly by producing Brazilian versions of popular American shows such as *Câmera Escondida* (*Candid Camera*), *Show do Milhão* (*Who Wants To Be a Millionaire*), *O Grande Perdedor* (*The Biggest Loser*), *Roda a Roda* (*Wheel of Fortune*), *Topa ou Não Topa* (*Deal or No Deal*) and *Ídolos* (*The Idol series*).

See also **Radio and Television.**

BIBLIOGRAPHY

Joseph Straubhaar, "Brazilian Television Variety Shows," in *Studies of Latin American Popular Culture* 2 (1983): 71–78.

Additional Bibliography

Arlindo Silva. *Fantástica História de Silvio Santos.* Brazil: IMES Noticias, Diario online.

                                    JOSEPH STRAUBHAAR

SANTOS-DUMONT, ALBERTO (1873–1932).

Alberto Santos-Dumont (*b.* 20 July 1873; *d.* 23 July 1932), pioneer aviator, inventor, and engineer. Known internationally as the "father of aviation," Santos-Dumont was born on his family's coffee plantation in Palmira (now Santos Dumont), Minas Gerais, Brazil. His engineer father encouraged the young man's passion for mechanics and interest in flying machines, and supported his move in 1891 to Paris, where Santos-Dumont joined an international coterie of aviators experimenting with all manner of aircraft.

During the next three decades Santos-Dumont won international renown for his achievements. He was the first person to turn the internal combustion engine to practical use for aviation (1897). In 1901, flying a dirigible of his own design, he won the coveted Deutsch Prize for being the first to navigate a set-time course, from Saint-Cloud, around the Eiffel Tower, and back. He subsequently turned his attention to the development of heavier-than-air machines and in 1906 piloted his *14-Bis* to claim the Archdeacon Award. The European press proclaimed him the first man to conquer the air, a title immediately disputed by the Wright Brothers, who were conducting their experiments in secrecy in North Carolina. Santos-Dumont, who believed that his designs belonged to the world, began work on a new model. In 1908 he constructed a waterplane, the *Santos Dumont 18,* that is regarded as the precursor of the hydroplane. His *Demoiselle,* completed in 1909, became the world's first successful monoplane, the prototype of the modern airplane.

Santos-Dumont's interests and inventions were broad. He designed the model from which the French jeweler Cartier constructed the first wristwatch, and he wrote three books: *A Conquista do ar* (1901), *Os meus balões* (1903), and *O que eu vi o que nós veremos* (1918). At the outbreak of World War I, he denounced the employment of aircraft for the purposes of war. The Allied governments accused him of espionage, and the French government stripped him of the Legion of Honor it had awarded him in 1909. In poor health, he returned to São Paulo in 1928. During the 1932 Constitutional Revolt, the federal government of Brazil sent planes to bomb the city of São Paulo. Horrified that bombs were being dropped by Brazilians on their fellow countrymen, Santos-Dumont committed suicide.

See also **Aviation.**

BIBLIOGRAPHY

Alexandre Brigole, *Santos-Dumont: The Air Pioneer* (1943); *Santos-Dumont: Cinquecentenario de primero vôo do mais pesado que o ar* (1956).

Peter Wykeham, *Santos-Dumont: A Study in Obsession* (1962).

Francesca Miller, "Alberto Santos-Dumont," in *Biographical Dictionary of Modern Peace Leaders,* edited by Harold Josephson (1984).

Additional Bibliography

Barros, Henrique Lins de. *Santos-Dumont e a invenção do vôo.* Rio de Janeiro: Jorge Zahar, 2003.

Domenico, Guca, and Lauret Godoy. *O jovem Santos-Dumont.* São Paulo: Editora Nova Alexandria, 2005.

Hoffman, Paul. *Wings of Madness: Alberto Santos-Dumont and the Invention of Flight.* New York: Theia, 2003.

FRANCESCA MILLER

SANTO TOMÁS. *See* **Belgian Colonization Company.**

SANTO TORIBIO. *See* **Mogrovejo, Toribio Alfonso de.**

SÃO FRANCISCO RIVER. São Francisco River, waterway that rises in the Brazilian highlands and flows north and east through the semiarid backlands of the Northeast of Brazil for approximately 1,988 miles. About 44 percent of the population of Brazil (as of 1990) lives in the São Francisco River region.

Known as "the river of national unity," the São Francisco River is famed for the political, social, and economic union of northeastern and southern Brazil. André Joaõ Antonil spoke in 1711 of over five hundred large ranches in the vicinity of the São Francisco River. Since then the river has provided the water necessary for pastures and irrigated farmlands as well as a transportation system for the cattle ranches that dot the river region. It is also a major source of hydroelectric power in the Northeast. In its lower reaches the river drops abruptly over the Itapárica and Paulo Afonso falls. In 1955 the Paulo Afonso power plant, with a generating capacity of more than 1 million kilowatts, was constructed. Another large dam was built far inland at Três Marias in 1960.

See also **Brazil, Geography.**

BIBLIOGRAPHY

Robert M. Levine, *Historical Dictionary of Brazil* (1979), pp. 192–193.

Christopher Richard, *Brazil* (1991), p. 20.

Additional Bibliography

Abrantes, José Israel. *São Francisco: Rio abaixo.* Belo Horizonte: Conceito, 2005.

Porto, Katia Cavalcanti, and Jarcilene S. de Almeida-Cortez. *Diversidades biológica e conservaçao da floresta atlantica ao norte do Rio São Francisco.* Brasília, DF: Ministério do Meio Ambiente, 2006.

Rocha, Geraldo. *O rio São Francisco: Fator precípuo da existencia do Brasil.* São Paulo: Companhia Editora Nacional, 2004.

ORLANDO R. ARAGONA

SÃO LUÍS. São Luís, capital of the state of Maranhão, Brazil (population 870,028 as of 2000), and island on which the city is located (originally called *Upaon-açu* [Big Island] by the native Tupinambá). The Frenchman Daniel de La Touche founded the city on 8 September 1612, naming it in honor of King Louis XIII. The Portuguese drove out the French in 1615; the Dutch occupied the city from 1641 to 1644, when they, too, were expelled.

São Luís became the capital of the vast colonial state of Maranhão in 1626. With the growth of Maranhão's slave-based economy in the seventeenth and eighteenth centuries, significant quantities of sugar, cotton, and rice were exported through São Luís. The city maintained direct relations with the Court in Lisbon. Sons of the elite, educated in Coimbra, held key court positions and received noble titles. São Luís was known as the "Athens of Brazil" owing to the remarkable number of its authors, poets, playwrights, scientists, journalists, and politicians who were nationally known during the 1800s. Modern writers, including Josué Montello and Ferreira Gullar, continue to give Maranhão national literary prominence.

São Luís was the first city in northern Brazil to feature public gas illumination, a trolley system, and public fountains with piped water. More than 4,000 buildings still remain from the seventeenth, eighteenth, and nineteenth centuries, many with facades of colorful tiles brought as ballast from Portugal, along with the cobblestones that pave the narrow streets of the historical district. Brazilian independence and the abolition of slavery, followed by declining markets for agricultural exports, initiated a period of economic decline that continued through the early 1990s, despite the metallurgical industries and port facilities that were built in the 1980s.

See also **Brazil, Geography.**

BIBLIOGRAPHY

César Augusto Marques, *Dicionário histórico-geográfico da Provincia do Maranhão*, 2d ed. (1970).

Ivan Sarney Costa, *São Luís: Nature's Island of Loveliness* (1989).

Jomar Da Silva Moraes, *Guia de São Luís do Maranhão* (1989).

Additional Bibliography

Andrés, Luiz Phelipe de Carvalho Castro, et al. *Centro histórico de São Luís Maranhão: Patrimonio mundial.* Sao Paulo: Audichromo Editora, 1998.

Santos, Maria do Rosário Carvalho. *Caminho das matriarcas Jeje-Nago: Uma contribuicão para história da religião Afro Maranhão.* São Paulo: Imprensa Oficial, 2005.

GAYLE WAGGONER LOPES

SÃO PAULO (CITY). Located on a plateau over the sierra about 30 miles from the coastal port of Santos, the city of São Paulo was founded in 1554 by a group of Jesuit priests who decided to build a school to proselytize among Indians who lived in the region. Through most of the colonial period São Paulo remained an isolated, impoverished town with no more than a few thousand inhabitants. It was the base from which the famous *bandeiras*—slave-hunting expeditions into the unexplored interior—were launched during the seventeenth century. During the eighteenth century the city lived off the gold trade of Minas Gerais. With the decline of mining, São Paulo became a modest commercial entrepôt for trade in mules, cotton cloth, and sugar.

In the nineteenth century São Paulo underwent a dramatic transformation as it became the center of the world's largest coffee exporting economy. Early in the century, with a population approaching 20,000, its primary product was tea, won with great effort from the infertile land surrounding the city. At mid-century it was a thriving if modest city of 25,000, with a prominent law school and a number of colleges. By the 1860s proliferating coffee plantations in the northwest of the state were fueling the growth of São Paulo, as all export shipments had to pass through the city on their way to the port at Santos. This relationship was strengthened in the 1870s and 1880s as coffee surpassed sugar and cotton in Brazil's export portfolio and as railroads were built to transport coffee from the hinterland to São Paulo and then on to Santos.

After mid-century São Paulo's importance also grew in other ways. The law school, founded in 1827, was by the 1870s a cynosure of intellectual and political thought, and turned out a substantial number of Bacharéis, many of whom were destined for careers in politics or the government bureaucracy. With an eye turned toward European political currents, Paulistano landowners founded a republican party in the early 1870s that espoused the end of monarchic rule. By the 1880s the city was the headquarters of the São Paulo State Republican Party, the largest and most important republican organization in Brazil.

Also in the 1870s, a new group of professionals and military officers began to discuss the ideas of positivism, a doctrine of "progress" in human affairs derived from the writings of the Frenchman Auguste Comte (1798–1857). São Paulo also became a center of the abolitionist movement in the 1880s. By the late 1880s *paulistano* abolitionists were able to persuade the Republican Party to condemn slavery outright, which it had been unwilling to do initially because so many Republicans were themselves slave owners. When slavery was abolished in 1888 and the Republic was declared in 1889, members of the *Paulista* coffee elite, many of whom lived in the city of São Paulo, were poised to take control of the nation's political apparatus. They established a political alliance with their wealthy counterparts in Minas Gerais. Their shared dominion lasted for the next forty years, during which time São Paulo underwent yet another remarkable transformation.

The character of the city changed dramatically in the three decades after the turn of the century. Between 1890 and 1920 its population mushroomed from 65,000 to nearly 600,000. Much of this growth was due to the arrival of immigrants from Italy, Portugal, Spain, Japan, and the Middle East. Industry made enormous strides during the period, financed by coffee magnates who were willing to invest because of a continuing price-production crisis in coffee. The growth of industry created a true urban working class, which in 1917–1920 launched a series of general strikes that were brutally repressed by the government, and a population of nonmanual employees who formed the embryo of a salaried, white-collar middle class.

After the Revolution of 1930, which removed the *paulista* oligarchy from power, economic momentum in São Paulo passed from coffee to industry. Between 1920 and 1940 the number of industrial firms increased from 4,000 to over 11,500. The city's population exploded from roughly 600,000 to nearly 2 million. In the 1950s the pace of change accelerated even further, and São Paulo became the engine of Brazil's modernizing economy, producing textiles, shoes, furniture, chemicals, pharmaceuticals, automobiles, and electrical equipment. As a part of this process, São Paulo industrialists became a political force unto themselves, industrial workers organized into powerful unions, and a salaried middle class was incorporated into political life and enjoyed the benefits of a consumer economy.

In the years after 1960 São Paulo attained the status of a megalopolis. In 2006 it was the fifth most populous metropolitan area in the world, with an estimated population of 19.7 million. Population growth in the last two decades has been the result primarily of rural–urban migration that has made São Paulo a focus of the country's social and economic ills.

Like many other cities in Brazil, São Paulo is full of contrasts. Although São Paulo is famous for hosting cultural events that attract visitors from all over the world, such as the twice–yearly São Paulo Fashion Week and the São Paulo Art Biennial, 55.4 percent of its population in 2000 lived in poor conditions.

See also **Brazil, Political Parties: Republican Party (PR); Brazil, Revolutions: Revolution of 1930; Mining: Colonial Brazil; Slavery: Brazil.**

BIBLIOGRAPHY

Richard Morse, *From Community to Metropolis: A Biography of São Paulo, Brazil* (1974), is a standard work on the growth of the city and the culture of urbanization. The collection of essays *Manchester and São Paulo: Problems of Rapid Urban Growth* (1978), edited by John D. Wirth and Robert L. Jones, provides a comparative perspective. Warren Dean, *The Industrialization of São Paulo, 1880–1945* (1969), is the standard text on the early period of industrialization. See also Joseph Love, *São Paulo in the Brazilian Federation, 1889–1937* (1980), for a study of regional politics. A very personal vision of São Paulo's poorest can be had from Carolina Maria De Jesus, *Child of the Dark,* translated by David St. Clair (1962).

Azevedo, Elciene. *Orfeu de carapinha: A trajetória de Luiz Gama na imperial cidade de São Paulo.* Campinas, Brazil: Editora da UNICAMP (State University of Campinas), 1999.

Lesser, Jeff. *Negotiating National Identity: Immigrants, Minorities, and the Struggle for Ethnicity in Brazil.* Durham, NC: Duke University Press, 1999.

Owensby, Brian Philip. *Intimate Ironies: Modernity and the Making of Middle–Class Lives in Brazil.* Stanford, CA: Stanford University Press, 1999.

Porta, Paula, et al. *História da cidade de São Paulo.* São Paulo, Brazil: Paz e Terra, 2004.

BRIAN OWENSBY

SÃO PAULO (STATE).

The first settlement in what is today the south-central state of São Paulo was established at the coastal island of São Vicente in 1532 by the explorer Martim Afonso de Sousa. Until mid-century settlements hugged the coast, producing a thriving enclave based on exports of sugar, brazilwood, and agricultural products second in prosperity only to the captaincy of Pernambuco in Northeastern Brazil. The interior was officially settled in 1554, when Jesuit priests climbed the steep sierra to the inland plateau and founded São Paulo do Campo de Piratininga as a base for proselytizing among the indigeneous. For the remainder of the sixteenth century, the captaincy was subject to attacks by the Tamóio people in league with the French from "Antarctic France" (today Rio de Janeiro) and by foreign raiders along the coast.

In the first half of the seventeenth century, explorers from the town of São Paulo made expeditions, known as *bandeiras*, into the unexplored interior, drawn by the chance to enslave Amerindians and by persistent rumors of gold deposits. The Jesuits of São Paulo condemned slave-hunting raids against the Tupi-Guaranís of the Jesuit missions in the southwest (today Paraguay), and were forced to leave the São Vicente captaincy by a citizen uprising in 1640.

The discovery of gold in what became Minas Gerais resulted in a frantic gold rush, led by long-time São Vicente residents, who abandoned the sugar mills along the coast, and swelled by European fortune seekers who flocked to Brazil. *Paulistas* lost control of the gold fields to Portuguese foreigners in the War of the Emboabas (1708–1709). Now displaced, *paulistas* pushed deeper into the interior, opening up new areas for exploration. Mining and population growth led the government to create the captaincy of São Paulo and Minas Gerais in 1710. Gold exports during this period shored up Portugal's sagging economy and contributed to Great Britain's industrialization. Mining declined through the eighteenth century, however, and the captaincy of São Paulo was thrown back on commerce in mules, cotton cloth, and sugar.

The modern chapter of the state's history dates from the early nineteenth century, as coffee cultivation gradually replaced sugar cultivation. After mid-century, coffee wealth and republican sentiment grew in tandem, such that São Paulo's upper class led the opposition to the emperor. By the 1880s São Paulo had the strongest Republican Party in Brazil. With the advent of the Republic in 1890, the *paulistas* formed the "coffee with cream" political alliance with Minas Gerais (so called because of São Paulo's coffee and Minas's

dairy products) that dominated Brazilian politics until 1930. The *paulista* oligarchy was ousted from national power by the Revolution of 1930, though it still retained considerable political clout.

The period after 1930 was defined by continued coffee exports, greater agricultural diversification, and the coffee-financed industrialization that had begun around 1900. Together these made the state of São Paulo the dynamo of Brazil's modernizing economy until the present day.

The importance of the state of São Paulo in Brazilian history cannot be underestimated. The *bandeirantes* expanded Portuguese territorial claims well beyond the line separating Portuguese from Spanish America (established by the Treaty of Tordesillas in 1494), and were the basis of the Brazilian myth of rugged individualism that lives on to this day. The rise of *paulista* republicanism, colored by patriarchy and exclusionary political practices, was at the center of Brazilian politics between the mid-nineteenth century and 1930. Finally, São Paulo has been a driving economic force in the twentieth century.

The state of São Paulo comprises an area of approximately 248,800 square kilometers (95,700 square miles). It had a population of around forty million (21.5% of the population of Brazil) in 2006, making it the most populous country subdivision in the Western Hemisphere.

See also **Brazil, Political Parties: Republican Party (PR); Brazil, Revolutions: Revolution of 1930; Mining: Colonial Brazil; Slavery: Brazil.**

BIBLIOGRAPHY

A good background is available from Richard Morse, *From Community to Metropolis: A Biography of São Paulo, Brazil* (1974). Morse also has a useful book on the *bandeirantes, The Historical Rule of the Brazilian Pathfinders* (1965). Clodomir Vianna Moog has an interesting comparative study of the United States and Brazil in *Bandeirantes and Pioneers* (1964), focusing on Brazilian and U.S. national character. Joseph Love, *São Paulo in the Brazilian Federation, 1889–1937* (1980), is the standard study of regional political history. Warren Dean, *Rio Claro: A Brazilian Plantation System, 1820–1920* (1976), usefully details a São Paulo coffee community and its incorporation into an export economy.

Additional Bibliography

Andrews, George Reid. *Blacks & Whites in São Paulo, Brazil, 1888–1988.* Madison, WI: University of Wisconsin Press, 1991.

Domínguez, Jorge I., ed. *Race and Ethnicity in Latin America*. New York: Garland Publishing, 1994.

Fausto, Boris. *Historiografia da imigração para São Paulo*. São Paulo, Brazil: IDESP, Editora Sumaré, 1991.

Monteiro, John M. *Negros da terra: Índios e bandeirantes nas origens de São Paulo*. São Paulo, Brazil: Companhia das Letras, 1994.

Moura, Carlos Eugênio Marcondes de. *Vida cotidiana em São Paulo no século XIX: Memórias, depoimentos, evocações*. Cotia, Brazil: Ateliê Editorial, 1999.

Romeu Landi, Francisco. *Science, Technology, & Innovation Indicators in the State of São Paul, Brazil 2004*. São Paulo, Brazil: FAPESP, 2005.

BRIAN OWENSBY

SÃO TOMÉ.

SÃO TOMÉ. São Tomé, an island with a population of 132,000 (1994 estimate), 190 miles off the west coast of Africa. São Tomé was uninhabited when the first Portuguese navigators arrived in the early 1470s. It became a base for trade with the adjacent coast of west and central Africa and a plantation colony. Its original colonists were convicts and exiled Jews from Portugal as well as enslaved Africans. By the mid-sixteenth century it had become a leading producer of sugar. The hostile climate of the island made it difficult for Europeans to settle there, and the sugar planters were largely the racially mixed offspring of Portuguese settlers and African women (mestizos) and free Africans, some of noble birth and others who had obtained freedom and became prominent. São Tomé was unusual in the Portuguese Empire in that local official positions were not subject to a color bar. However, it did experience a major slave revolt at the end of the sixteenth century and the establishment of a maroon community (the Angolars) in the mountains.

Although its role as a sugar producer was soon surpassed by Brazil, the island remained an important base for Portuguese activities in Africa, especially the slave trade. Its economic functions were revived in the late nineteenth century when cacao planting became prominent, utilizing British capital and contract labor, especially from Nigeria and Angola.

Although the island did not develop a major dissident movement in the 1960s, the republic of São Tomé and Príncipe achieved independence in 1975 as a result of Portugal's disengagement from Africa.

See also **Portuguese Empire.**

BIBLIOGRAPHY

Garfield, Robert. *A History of Sao Tome Island, 1470-1655: The Key to Guinea*. San Francisco: Mellen Research University Press, 1992.

Lloyd-Jones, Stewart, and António Costa Pinto. *The Last Empire: Thirty Years of Portuguese Decolonization*. Portland: Intellect, 2003.

Seibert, Gerhard. *Comrades, Clients, and Cousins: Colonialism, Socialism, and Democratization in São Tomé and Príncipe*. Leiden, the Netherlands: Research School of Asian, African, and Amerindian Studies, Leiden University, 2000.

JOHN THORNTON

SÃO VICENTE.

SÃO VICENTE. São Vicente, Portugal's first permanent settlement in Brazil. São Vicente was founded by Martim Afonso de Sousa in 1532 as was the much larger captaincy of the same name which dominated the settlement of southern Brazil. The settlement of São Vicente survived while other settlements failed because of the good relations the Portuguese established with nearby Indians. The Jesuit Order played an important role in São Vicente by building missions, churches, and schools for the Indians and by opposing the widespread use of Indian slavery. By the second half of the sixteenth century the sugar mills of Bahia and Pernambuco had rapidly overshadowed those of São Vicente, so that in the seventeenth century, the colonists of São Vicente turned inward, toward the wilderness. Claiming large tracts of virgin land, they created wheat farms and ranches worked by Indian slaves brought by the Bandeiras to the major towns, such as São Paulo.

In the early eighteenth century, after the discovery of gold in the interior, the captaincy of São Vicente reverted to the crown. It was renamed "São Paulo and the Mines of Gold," after its largest and most prosperous town. Thereafter, the name São Vicente referred only to the small coastal town, site of Brazil's first settlement.

See also **Slavery: Brazil.**

BIBLIOGRAPHY

Alida C. Metcalf, *Family and Frontier in Colonial Brazil* (1992).

Additional Bibliography

Stella, Roseli Santaella. *Sobre a capitania de São Vicente: Séc. XVI-XVII.* São Paulo: Academia Lusíada de Ciencias, Letras e Artes, 1999.

ALIDA C. METCALF

Additional Bibliography

Franca, Mário Ferreira. *O reconhecimiento da independencia do Paraguia pelo Império: A Missão Pimenta Bueno.* Rio de Janeiro: Imprensa Naval, Ministerio da Marinha, 1953.

São Viente, José Antonio Pimenta Bueno, Marques de. *José Antonio Pimenta Bueno, Marques de São Vicente.* São Paulo: Editora 34, 2002.

JEFFREY D. NEEDELL

SÃO VICENTE, JOSÉ ANTÔNIO PIMENTA BUENO, MARQUÊS DE

(1803–1878). José Antônio Pimenta Bueno, Marquês de São Vicente (*b.* 4 December 1803; *d.* 19 February 1878), Brazilian jurist and statesman. Born in São Paulo, São Vicente earned a doctorate from the São Paulo faculty of law and went on to judicial appointments in that province. He represented São Paulo in the Chamber of Deputies (after 1845), the Senate (after 1853), and served on the Council of State (after 1859). There, with José Tomás Nabuco de Araújo (1813–1878), he shared the task imposed by Pedro II of researching and writing (1866–1868) a legislative project to effect the gradual abolition of slavery. His political career included portfolios for foreign affairs and justice in the Liberal cabinets of 1847 and 1848 and the provincial presidencies of Mato Grosso (1836) and Rio Grande do Sul (1850); he also dabbled in Paraguayan diplomacy in the 1840s. His most important position, however, was as prime minister of a moderate Conservative cabinet in 1870, when he tried, and failed, to marshal the political support for the abolitionist legislation he had helped author in the Council of State; it was the Visconde do Rio Branco (1819–1880), a consummate politician, who realized the project instead in 1871. São Vicente's greatest legacy is his widely read discussion of the monarchy's charter: *Direito publico brazileiro e analise da Constituição do Império* (1857).

See also **Brazil, Political Parties: Conservative Party; Brazil, Political Parties: Liberal Party; Paulistas, Paulistanos; Slave Trade, Abolition of: Brazil.**

BIBLIOGRAPHY

Joaquim Nabuco, *Um estadisto do império,* vol. 3 (1899).

SAQUAREMAS. *See* Brazil, Political Parties: Conservative Party.

SARAIVA, JOSÉ ANTÔNIO (1823–1895). José Antônio Saraiva (*b.* 1 March 1823; *d.* 23 July 1895), prime minister of Brazil (1880–1882, 1885). After beginning his political career in the judiciary and the provincial legislature of his native Bahia, Saraiva quickly rose to national prominence in the Liberal Party. Between 1850 and 1858 he served as president of the provinces of Piauí, Alagoas, São Paulo, and Pernambuco. In the first of these he ordered the construction of a new capital city, Teresina. In the same years he won election to the national Chamber of Deputies. His success continued in the Congress; in 1857 and in 1865 he held cabinet posts in Liberal ministries.

Saraiva's greatest fame came during his tenure as prime minister. Showing tremendous political skills, he oversaw the passage of important reform laws in both of his administrations. In 1880 he proposed an electoral reform bill that became known as the Saraiva Law after its passage the following year. By mandating direct elections for the two houses of Congress and easing income criteria for voters, this law ostensibly expanded suffrage. Its provisions dealing with how voters were to prove their qualifications were, however, restrictive. In practice, the law ensured that the wealthy and politically powerful would retain control of Brazil's electoral politics.

When Saraiva became prime minister in 1885, after the fall of the Manuel Dantas regime, he once more proposed a key reform bill. This bill was a more conservative version of Dantas's proposal to free all slaves over sixty years of age and to increase the effectiveness of the system of buying slaves' emancipation. In Saraiva's legislation, only slaves aged sixty-five or over would receive freedom immediately; those between sixty and sixty-five would have to continue in their masters' service for up to three more years. By making such concessions to slaveholding interests, Saraiva managed to have his bill passed by the Chamber of Deputies. In the partisan confusion that this reform provoked, approval by the Senate seemed in doubt. In response, Saraiva dissolved his cabinet, thus clearing the way for the Conservative Cotegipe ministry to achieve final passage of the bill, now known as the Saraiva–Cotegipe Law (Sexagenarian Law), in the Senate.

After the advent of the republic in 1889, Saraiva withdrew from politics for two years. He was elected to the new regime's first Senate in 1891, but soon resigned from office.

See also **Brazil, Liberal Movements; Dantas, Manuel Pinto de Souza; Slave Trade, Abolition of: Brazil.**

BIBLIOGRAPHY

Robert E. Conrad, *The Destruction of Brazilian Slavery, 1850–1888* (1972); *José Antônio Saraiva: Discursos parlamentares,* edited by Álvaro Valle (1978).

Richard Graham, *Patronage and Politics in Nineteenth-Century Brazil* (1990).

ROGER A. KITTLESON

SARAIVA-COTEGIPE LAW. *See* Sexagenarian Law.

SARALEGUI, CRISTINA (1948–).

Cristina Saralegui is widely known as the "Latina Oprah." Her family left Cuba, as did many upper-class families in the early waves of exile migrations, and moved to Miami, Florida, in 1960. In Cuba her family had been well established in the publishing business and owned and operated several Cuban magazines. Saralegui attended the University of Miami and majored in communications, with intentions of following in the family business. After college she worked for women's magazines and eventually became editor-in-chief of *Cosmopolitan en Español.* In 1989 she became the executive producer and host of her own talk show, "El Show de Cristina." The show has become known for dealing with controversial subjects, and early on it received criticism from sectors of the Latino population in the United States and Latin America. Despite her critics, the show has become an entertainment success, ranking among the top Spanish-language programs in the United States and winning an Emmy award in 1991. The popularity of the show spiked in the 1990s, and it has drawn many famous Latino guests. Overall, Saralegui is considered an important figure within the Latino community, and she sees her role as helping to address and deal with the problems of the Latino population in the United States.

See also **Hispanics in the United States; Radio and Television.**

BIBLIOGRAPHY

Telgen, Diane, and Jim Kamp, eds. *Latinas! Women of Achievement.* Detroit, MI: Visible Ink Press, 1996.

ANDREA VICENTE

SARAMAKA.

The Saramaka are one of six tribes of Maroons (also known as Refugee Blacks or Bush Negroes), descendents of African slaves brought to Suriname as plantation laborers in the late seventeenth century. In the years before emancipation, large groups of slaves escaped from the plantations, and the Saramaka settled in the central, upper part of the Suriname River Basin. After escaping, the former slave groups carried out small-scale raids on the plantations, searching for food, women, equipment, and weapons, or acting to liberate kinsmen. Fearing the military threat of the escaped slaves, a peace treaty was signed between the Dutch colonists and the Saramaka in 1762. At this time the Saramaka numbered between 2,500 and 3,000. The peace treaty guaranteed the Saramaka territorial integrity, periodic tribute, and recognition of tribal leaders, in exchange for refraining from aggression against the plantation colony.

In 1863, true emancipation occurred. While the Saramaka held onto an isolationist worldview, they could not escape incursions from the outside world. This was particularly evident during the 1960s when the American company Alcoa joined forces with the Suriname government to build a hydroelectric dam. The dam, built to power a bauxite refinery, flooded almost half of tribal territory and pushed 6,000 Saramaka to relocate their villages below the lake.

Despite the conditions of the peace treaty, the Suriname government has done little to recognize the land rights of the Saramaka. This forestland, however, is key to the Saramaka's economic, spiritual, and cultural survival. In the 1990s, after facing international pressure to end logging and mining concessions in Saramaka territory, the Surinamese government created the Central Suriname Nature Reserve, the largest area of protected tropical forest in the world. Despite years of relocation and conflict with the government, the Saramaka remain one of the largest Maroon tribes, with 20,000 people living in more than seventy villages along the Suriname River.

See also **Maroons (Cimarrones); Suriname and the Dutch in the Caribbean.**

BIBLIOGRAPHY

Price, Richard. *Saramaka Social Structure: Analysis of a Maroon Society in Surinam.* Río Piedras: Institute of Caribbean Studies, University of Puerto Rico, 1975.

Price, Richard, and Sally Price. *Two Evenings in Saramaka.* Chicago: University of Chicago Press, 1991.

ALISON FIELDS

SARAVIA, APARICIO (1856–1904). Aparicio Saravia (*b.* 1856; *d.* 1 September 1904), leader of the last of Uruguay's many uprisings of mounted insurgents. Born near Santa Clara de Olimar in northern Uruguay, the son of a Brazilian-born landowner, Saravia was not a member of the country's traditional ruling groups. Most Brazilian-born landowning families in northern Uruguay maintained social and political contacts in Brazil, which explains the Saravias' involvement in the Brazilian civil war of 1893–1895. Aparicio's oldest brother, Gumercindo Saravia, rose to the rank of general during the fighting, and Aparicio won fame leading the charges of his brother's horsemen. At Gumercindo's death in 1894, Aparicio inherited his army. Meanwhile, the Blancos (National Party) of Uruguay had begun to reorganize after many years of proscription. When Saravia returned

from the Brazilian war with the rank of general, many young Blancos saw in him the leader they awaited. An "armed demonstration" led by Saravia in 1896 galvanized Blancos all over the country to rebel in 1897, and Saravia was acclaimed the party's new caudillo. Unable to subdue them, the government made some power-sharing concessions to the Blancos, and Saravia emerged from the war a symbol of Blanco unity and pride. Within a few years, the Colorado government tried to withdraw the concessions, and Saravia mobilized the Blanco militia again in 1903 and 1904. Though bloodier and on a larger scale, this second period of fighting might have resulted in another standoff if not for Saravia's death in Masoller.

See also **Caudillismo, Caudillo; Uruguay, Political Parties: Blanco Party.**

BIBLIOGRAPHY

Enrique Mena Segarra, *Aparicio Saravia: Las últimas patriadas* (1981).

Additional Bibliography

Chasteen, John Charles. *Heroes on Horseback: A Life and Times of the Last Gaucho Caudillos.* Albuquerque: University of New Mexico Press, 1995.

Pelúas, Daniel. *El ocaso del caudillo.* Montevideo: Arca, 2004.

JOHN CHARLES CHASTEEN

SARDÁ, JOSÉ (?–1834). José Sardá (*d.* 22 October 1834), Colombian military officer and conspirator. Born in Catalonia (or possibly Navarra), José Sardá fought in the Napoleonic Wars in Europe and later joined the 1817 expedition of Francisco Javier Mina in the fight for Mexican independence. Escaping from capture, he eventually joined the patriots in Gran Colombia, where he was a strong supporter of Simón Bolívar and of the short dictatorship of Rafael Urdaneta. With the latter's fall in 1831, liberal supporters of Francisco de Paula Santander purged Sardá from the army. After Santander became president of New Granada in 1832, Sardá and other malcontents turned to plotting against him, but they were discovered and Sardá, along with other ringleaders, was condemned to death. He again escaped but was tracked down and killed by loyal officers, whose alleged "assassination" of Sardá gave rise to bitter criticism of Santander.

See also **Bolívar, Simón; Santander, Francisco de Paula.**

BIBLIOGRAPHY

Marco Aurelio Vila, *Josep Sardá, un general catalá en le independéncia d'América* (1980).

Pilar Moreno De Ángel, *Santander* (1989), pp. 585–608.

Additional Bibliography

Miramón, Alberto. *Biografía de Sardá y cronicon del Nuevo Reyno*. Bogotá: Imprenta Nacional de Colombia, 1997.

DAVID BUSHNELL

SARDANETA Y LLORENTE, JOSÉ MARIANO DE (1761–1835).

José Mariano de Sardaneta y Llorente (Second Marqués de San Juan de Rayas; *b.* 1761; *d.* 1835), a politician. Sardaneta was a rich miner and landowner from Guanajuato, who served as *regidor* (alderman), magistrate, and administrator in Guanajuato, as well as administrator of mining in Mexico City. In 1808 he favored the establishment of a governing junta in New Spain. After the coup d'état of that year, Sardaneta, who was a friend of the deposed viceroy José de Iturrigaray, tried to vindicate him. A well-known autonomist, he was denounced in 1809 as disaffected with the colonial regime, but nothing was proved against him. In 1811 he was accused of corresponding with the insurgent leader Ignacio Allende, and he was listed as an accomplice of the conspiracy in April of that year. As a member of the secret society of Los Guadalupes, Sardaneta corresponded with José María Morelos and with Carlos María de Bustamante and participated in the arrangements to buy a printing press for Morelos. In 1813 he was elected to the Cortes, although he did not occupy his seat. That same year he voted for Morelos as generalísimo in the insurgent elections. Imprisoned by the authorities in February 1816, Sardaneta was sentenced to be deported to Spain, but after reaching Veracruz, he was able to remain. He was one of the signers of the Declaration of Independence in 1821 and a member of the Provisional Governing Junta. He was elected to the Constituent Congress in 1822, and became a member of the Junta Nacional Instituyente during 1822 and 1823. Sardaneta died in Guanajuato.

See also **Guanajuato.**

BIBLIOGRAPHY

Wilbert H. Timmons, "Los Guadalupes: A Secret Society in the Mexican Revolution for Independence," in *Hispanic American Historical Review* 30, no. 4 (Nov. 1950): 453–479.

Doris Ladd, *The Mexican Nobility at Independence, 1780–1826* (1976).

Ernesto De La Torre Villar, *Los Guadalupes y la independencia, con una selección de documentos inéditos* (1985).

Virginia Guedea, *En busca de un gobierno alterno: Los Guadalupes de México* (1992).

Additional Bibliography

Jáuregui de Cervantes, Aurora. *Los marqueses de Rayas: Promotores del desarrollo económico y social de Guanajuato*. México: Ediciones La Rana, 1998.

VIRGINIA GUEDEA

SARDUY, SEVERO (1937–1993).

Severo Sarduy (*b.* 25 February 1937; *d.* 8 June 1993), Cuban novelist, poet, and essayist. Sarduy was born in Camagüey. In 1956 he moved to Havana, where he came in contact with the vital community of writers associated with the literary magazine *Ciclón* and where he began to publish poetry. He studied medicine for two years at the University of Havana, but left to concentrate on writing. After the Cuban Revolution of 1959, he became a contributor to *Lunes de Revolución*, a literary weekly edited by Guillermo Cabrera Infante.

In 1960 Sarduy left for France to study art history at the École du Louvre. From 1964 to 1967 he continued his studies in Paris and became a member of two influential literary groups associated with the publications *Mundo Nuevo*, edited by the critic Emir Rodríguez Monegal, and *Tel quel*, the most influential French publication of the 1960s and 1970s, where he collaborated with Roland Barthes. As editor of the Latin American collection of Éditions du Seuil since 1966, Sarduy has been responsible for launching the writers Gabriel García Márquez, José Lezama Lima, Jorge Luis Borges, and Guillermo Cabrera Infante into the French arena. In 1971 he was awarded the Prix Paul Gilson for his radio play *La playa* (The Beach). The following year his novel *Cobra* received the prestigious Prix Médici, and another radio play, *Relato,* won the Prix Italia.

Sarduy's work has received enormous critical acclaim, as he is one of the most innovative of Latin American writers. An aesthetic heir of Cuban master José Lezama Lima, for whom he professes great admiration, he uses a rich, elaborately baroque style to combine such seemingly disparate elements as Cuban folklore and music and the art, philosophy, and religion of the Far East. His work has been translated into many languages.

Sarduy's best-known works are *De dónde son los cantantes* (From Cuba with a Song [novel, 1967]), *La playa* (play, 1971), *Cobra* (novel, 1972), *Relato* (play, 1972), and *Maitreya* (novel, 1980; trans. 1987). He died of AIDS in Paris.

See also **Borges, Jorge Luis; García Márquez, Gabriel; Havana; Literature: Spanish America.**

BIBLIOGRAPHY

Julia Alexis Kushigian deals extensively with Sarduy in *Orientalism in the Hispanic Literary Tradition* (1991). The most authoritative source on Sarduy's work is Roberto González Echevarría, *La ruta de Severo Sarduy* (1986).

See also Jorge Aguilar Mora, *Severo Sarduy* (1976); Adriana Méndez Ródenas, *Severo Sarduy: El neobarroco de la transgresión* (1983); Oscar Montero, *The Name Game: The Semiotic Intertext of "De dónde son los cantantes"* (1988).

Additional Bibliography

Fernández, Nancy, and Ignacio Iriarte. *Fumarolas de jade: Las poéticas neobarrocas de Severo Sarduy y Antonio Carrera.* Mar del Plata: E. Balder, 2002.

González, Oneyda. *Severo Sarduy: Escrito sobre un rostro.* Camagüey: Editorial Ácana, 2003.

Gotera, Johan. *Severo Sarduy: Alcances de una novelística y otros ensayos.* Caracas: Monte Avila Editores Latinoamericana, 2005.

Machover, Jacobo. *La memoria frente al poder: Escritores cubanos del exilio: Guillermo Cabrera Infante, Severo Sarduy, Reinaldo Arenas.* Valencia: Universitat de València, 2001.

ROBERTO VALERO

SARMIENTO, DOMINGO FAUSTINO (1811–1888).

Domingo Faustino Sarmiento (*b.* 15 February 1811; *d.* 11 September 1888), writer, educator, journalist, historian, linguist, and president of Argentina (1868–1874). According to Mary Peabody Mann, Sarmiento was "not a man but a nation." Born in the frontier city of San Juan, near the Andes, he was the son of a soldier who fought in the wars of independence and a mother who supported the family by weaving. An early intellectual influence was a maternal uncle and private tutor, the priest José de Oro. Steeped in the classics, the Bible, Latin, and French, Sarmiento began teaching elementary school in his teens. Post-Independence chaos and anarchy awakened his interest in orderly government. By 1829 he fought with the unitarists against caudillo rule. When the federalists gained control of San Juan, he fled to Chile to the town of Los Andes, where he taught school and worked in a store. Upon returning to San Juan in 1836, he started the newspaper, *El Zonda,* in which he expounded his ideas about education, agriculture, and modernization. Ahead of his time, Sarmiento advocated educating women. In 1839 he founded a secondary school for girls in San Juan (Colegio de Santa Rosa de América), for which he wrote the by-laws. Facing jail because of political activities against tyrant Juan Manuel de Rosas, Sarmiento fled to Chile in 1840.

In contrast to Argentina, Chile was developing peacefully under a government framework organized by Diego Portales. In Santiago, Sarmiento rose to a position of prestige and influence; he befriended educator and writer Andrés Bello, director of education (and later president of Chile) Manuel Montt, historian José Victorino Lastarria, and political activist Francisco Bilbao. Sarmiento pursued his twin interests—education and journalism—and he contributed articles to the influential newspapers *El Mercurio, El Nacional,* and *El Progreso.* He believed that Argentina's problems were "rooted in barbarism," and he said that he "only dreamed of founding schools and teaching the masses to read." For him, universal education was the key to defeating backwardness, and he thought he could transform the gaucho. In 1845 he serialized and also published in book form the work for which he is best known: *Civilización i barbarie: Vida de Juan Facundo Quiroga. I aspecto físico, costumbres, i ámbitos de la República Argentina* (translated by Mary Mann as *Life in the Argentine Republic in the Days of the Tyrants; or, Civilization and Barbarism* [1868]). In this work, also known as *Facundo,* Sarmiento expounded penetrating observations about the Argentine countryside and gaucho life and about the depredations caused by caudillo warfare, and he described the career of the federalist caudillo Juan Facundo Quiroga. The book represented a passionate indictment of Rosas, which the tyrant perceived as a threat.

In Santiago, Sarmiento served as the head of a new normal school (teacher training institute). He prepared textbooks, school programs, and curricula. Many of his progressive ideas were adopted in Chilean elementary and secondary education. Following the lead of preeminent thinker and educator Andrés Bello, Sarmiento tried to simplify Spanish orthography and render it more phonetic. He published *Memoria sobre ortografía americana* (Compendium of American Orthography [1843]), and all his writings used the new phonetic spelling. He tirelessly advocated universal education—the cornerstone of a true democracy—believing that an educated electorate is the best antidote to anarchy and tyranny.

Rosas dispatched a diplomatic mission to Chile to secure the extradition of the man who wrote *Facundo.* Coincidentally, the Chilean government sent Sarmiento to Europe and the United States to survey various educational methods. Disappointed in the rigid social class system, the lack of democratic governments, and the stultifying educational methods he saw in Spain, France, Germany, Holland, and Switzerland, Sarmiento did not think the fledgling American republics should emulate European models. In England, Sarmiento chanced upon a report written by Horace Mann to the Massachusetts Board of Education. During his stay in the United States, he met in Boston with educators Horace Mann and Mary Peabody Mann, who influenced his ideas about public education. His visit to the Boston area and other parts of the United States convinced Sarmiento of the importance of strong, representative, local government for a meaningful democracy on the national level. He also visited public libraries; elementary, secondary, and normal schools; and universities.

Upon returning to Chile he married his common-law wife Benita Martínez (1848), and he wrote *Viajes en Europa, Africa, i América, 1845–1847* (2 vols., 1849–1851). The portion relating to the United States was translated by Michael Rockland as *Sarmiento's Travels in the United States in 1847* (1970). Like Alexis de Tocqueville before him, Sarmiento perceptively analyzed life in the United States. His *Travels* remains a timeless classic. In addition to his two popular works, *Facundo* and *Travels,* Sarmiento also produced the romantic prose masterpiece *Recuerdos de provincia* (Provincial recollections [1850]); *De la educación popular* (About public education [1849]), which was revised as *Memoria sobre educación común* (Report on public education [1856]); and *Las escuelas: Base de prosperidad i de la república en los Estados Unidos* (Schools as the basis of prosperity and republican government in the United States [1866]).

When General Justo José de Urquiza successfully rallied the remaining caudillos against Rosas in 1851, Sarmiento traveled to Montevideo to join the armed struggle. After the defeat of Rosas at the Battle of Caseros (1852), and as a result of disagreements with Urquiza, Sarmiento returned to Chile. He moved permanently to Argentina in 1855, where he became the director of the department of education in Buenos Aires Province and threw himself into reforming education with his accustomed energy. Juana Manso de Noronha, an Argentine educator, became his closest assistant and confidante. He founded the journal *Anales de la educación común* (Annals of public education) in 1858; he wrote for the newspaper *El Nacional;* and he continued to promulgate ideas about universal public education with a modern curriculum that included science, practical learning, and gymnastics for both men and women. The proposed reforms met the stiff resistance of the Sociedad de la Beneficiencia (Society for Charity), which had been in charge of women's education since the 1820s. Sarmiento was prevented from reforming women's education. Between 1856 and 1861 Sarmiento founded thirty-four new schools, and he ordered the publication of new textbooks.

Following national unification in 1882, Sarmiento played an important role in bringing peace and order to the provinces. He served as senator and later as governor of San Juan Province (1862–1864), where he tried to implement programs of education reforms and economic development; he also continued writing for newspapers. His projects for land reform were relentlessly opposed by the caudillo Angel Vicente Peñaloza (El Chacho). Federal forces defeated El Chacho on 12 November 1863, and his severed head was displayed on a pike, as was the custom of the times.

By 1862 Sarmiento had separated from his wife Benita and was engaged in a long-term liaison with Aurelia Vélez. In 1864 he became minister plenipotentiary first to Peru, then to the United States. Finding Washington provincial, Sarmiento settled in New York, where he saw greater opportunities to learn about educational innovations and business practices. He reacquainted himself with Mary Mann (Horace Mann died in 1859) and other educators and intellectuals he had met during his previous trip. He visited teachers' colleges and universities in Boston, New York, and Chicago, always helped by Mary Mann. He lectured on North and South America to the Rhode Island Historical Society (1865). The talk was translated into English by the young Bartolomé Mitre, the Argentine president's son. In 1866 Sarmiento's only son, twenty-year-old Dominguito, was killed in the Battle of Curupaití in the War of the Triple Alliance.

In 1868 Sarmiento was elected the second president of a newly unified Argentina. His presidency was the culmination of his tireless struggle to transform Argentina into a modern nation. As president he vigorously promoted economic, social, and cultural development. Following the ideas of Juan Bautista Alberdi and Bartolomé Mitre, Sarmiento fostered European immigration and encouraged the establishment of agricultural colonies. He worked to expand railways and roads; he promoted shipping, commerce, and advances in public health; and he modernized and beautified the city of Buenos Aires. To further educational reforms, he established public libraries throughout the country, and he recruited North American schoolteachers. More than eighty-eight teachers came to Argentina between 1867 and 1889. In 1869 he mandated the establishment of a normal-school network. He introduced advanced teaching techniques, added foreign languages to curricula, and founded kindergartens. Many of the reforms were implemented by Sarmiento's successor, President Nicolás Avellaneda. As a result of their efforts, Argentine schools became the best in Latin America. Sarmiento ordered the first national census of Argentina in 1869; he founded the Colegio Militar (National Military Academy), the first astronomical observatory, and trade and technical schools; he fostered the modernization of agriculture, mining, and industry; and he established the Sociedad Rural to improve livestock breeds.

After leaving the presidency, Sarmiento served in the Senate (1875–1880), held the office of interior minister, visited Chile, was once again superintendent of education of Buenos Aires Province (1879–1882), and founded the journal *La educación común* (Public Education) in 1876 and the newspaper *El Censor* in 1885. Quite ill during the last three years of his life, he died in Asunción, Paraguay.

Political and historical writings of Sarmiento include: *Comentarios de la constitución de la Confederación Argentina* (1853), *Arjirópolis: O la capital de los estados confederados del Río de la Plata* (1850), *Discursos parlamentarios* (2 vols. [1933]), *Emigración alemana al Río de la Plata* (1851), *Condición del extranjero en América* (The Foreigner's Condition in the Americas [1888]), and studies about the War of the Triple Alliance.

Published correspondence includes: *Sarmiento-Mitre: Correspondencia, 1846–1868* (1911), *Epistolario íntimo* (1963), and Julia Ottolenghi's *Sarmiento a través de un epistolario* (Sarmiento Through His Correspondence [1940]). Sarmiento's last publication was *La vida de Dominguito* (1886), which mourned his son Domingo Fidel. Posterity harshly criticized him for the 1883 book *Conflicto y armonías de las razas* (Conflict and Harmony in the Races), in which he largely repeats the prevalent theories about race mixing and racial purity. His *Obras completas* in fifty-three volumes were published in 1888.

During his presidency, Sarmiento dealt with the last of the caudillos. Despite his lifelong opposition to caudillo rule, Sarmiento governed as a personalist and strengthened the power of the executive. As president he used the central government's power to crush political opposition in the interior provinces, and he imposed sieges to quell uprisings. When the law seemed inadequate, he ruled by decree. Viewed by some of his contemporaries as an egotist ("don Yo" or "Mr. Me"), Sarmiento nevertheless looms as a protean figure: a visionary, an educator, a writer, and a seminal nation-builder.

See also **Bello, Andrés; Caudillismo, Caudillo; Rosas, Juan Manuel de.**

BIBLIOGRAPHY

Watt Stewart and William M. French, "Influence of Horace Mann on the Educational Ideas of Domingo Faustino

Sarmiento," in *Hispanic American Historical Review* 20 (1940): 12–31.

Ricardo Rojas, *El profeta de la pampa* (1945).

Allison Williams Bunkley, *The Life of Sarmiento* (1952; repr. 1969).

Alberto Palcos, *Sarmiento: La vida, la obra, las ideas, el genio,* 4th ed. (1962), and "La presidencia de Sarmiento," in *Historia argentina contemporaranea,* vol. 1, ed. Academia Nacional de Historia (1963), pp. 89–148.

Paul Verdevoye, *Domingo Faustino Sarmiento: Educateur et publiciste, 1839–1852* (1964).

Ezequiel Martínez Estrada, *Meditaciones sarmientinas* (1968).

Frances G. Crowley, *Domingo Faustino Sarmiento* (1972).

Elda Clayton Patton, *Sarmiento in the United States* (1976).

Aníbal Ponce, *Sarmiento: Constructor de la nueva Argentina* (1976).

Manuel Gálvez, *Vida de Sarmiento* (1979).

Noé Jitrik, *Muerte y resurrección del Facundo* (1983).

Natalio Botana, *Alberdi, Sarmiento, y las ideas políticas de su tiempo* (1984).

Gabriel Brizuela, *Bibliografía sarmientina* (1989).

Dardos Pérez Guilhou, *Sarmiento y la constitución: Sus ideas políticas* (1989).

Joseph T. Criscenti, ed., *Sarmiento and His Argentina* (1993).

Additional Bibliography

Bellotta, Araceli, and Nora Fusillo. *Sarmiento: Maestro del éxito.* Buenos Aires: Grupo Editorial Norma, 2000.

Botana, Natalio R. *Domingo Faustino Sarmiento.* Buenos Aires: Fondo de Cultura Económica, 1996.

Feinmann, José Pablo. *Filosofía y nación: Estudios sobre el pensamiento argentino.* Buenos Aires: Seix Barral, 2004.

Gárate, Miriam V. *Civilização e barbárie n'os Sertões: Entre Domingo Faustino Sarmiento e Euclides da Cunha.* São Paulo: Fapesp, and Campinas: Mercado de Letras, 2001.

Sorensen, Diana. *El Facundo y la construcción de la cultura argentina.* Rosario: Beatriz Viterbo Editora, 1998.

Tacca, Oscar Ernesto. *Los umbrales de Facundo: Y otros textos sarmientinos.* Buenos Aires: Academia Argentina de Letras, 2000.

GEORGETTE MAGASSY DORN

---

of South America. Born in Pontevedra, in northwestern Spain, Sarmiento served in the navy of Philip II, reaching the rank of admiral. Combining his maritime profession with the writing of history, he researched the history of the Incas before the Conquest, pursuing his work on *Historia índica* (History of the Incas, 1572) while Viceroy Francisco de Toledo ruled Peru. He voyaged to the Strait of Magellan, becoming the first to enter from the west, and attempted to found a colony there. Lacking the enthusiastic backing of the king, the colony failed and its inhabitants perished while Sarmiento was imprisoned in Europe. He described his experience in *Derrotero al Estrecho de Magallanes* (Voyage to the Straits of Magellan, 1580).

Among the chroniclers of sixteenth-century Peru, Sarmiento stands out for these two works. The *Historia* is an example of the efforts of Viceroy Toledo and those around him to establish a historiographic record that would confirm the justification for Spanish dominance of the Andean peoples. Arguing against the claims of native Andeans to self-government, chroniclers such as Sarmiento promoted a providentialist view of Spain's role as Christianizer of the New World.

See also **Philip II of Spain; Providencia.**

BIBLIOGRAPHY

Clements R. Markham translated the *Narratives of the Voyages of Pedro Sarmiento de Gamboa to the Straits of Magellan* into English (1895). A biography in Spanish is that by Ernesto Morales, *Sarmiento de Gamboa, un navegante español del siglo XVI* (1932).

Additional Bibliography

Benites, María Jesús. *Con la lanza y con la pluma: La escritura de Pedro Sarmiento de Gamboa.* San Miguel de Tucumán: Instituto Interdisciplinario de Estudios Latinoamericanos, Facultad de Filosofía y Letras, Universidad Nacional de Tucumán, 2005.

Carrillo, Francisco. *Cronistas del Perú antiguo.* Lima: Editorial Horizonte, 1989.

KATHLEEN ROSS

SARMIENTO DE GAMBOA, PEDRO
(c. 1530–1608). Pedro Sarmiento de Gamboa (*b.* ca. 1530; *d.* 1608), Spanish admiral and chronicler

SARMIENTO DE SOTOMAYOR, GARCÍA
García Sarmiento de Sotomayor (count of Salvatierra), viceroy of Peru (1648–1654). Faced with the continuing decline in crown revenues,

Salvatierra initiated various policies to increase state income. Citing weaknesses in the official trade system of the *consulado* (merchant guild), Salvatierra proposed altering that system to reduce smuggling and collect more taxes. Salvatierra wanted to increase Indian tribute payments as well, but his inconsistent policies, including initiating and then suspending a census of the Indian community, failed. Although not as effective as his predecessor, the marquis of Mancera, Salvatierra did raise some crown revenues through *composiciones de tierras,* the practice of declaring Indian lands depopulated or abandoned and thus the property of the crown, subject to sale to private investors. His efforts to tighten control over the regional treasuries were less successful.

See also **Peru: From the Conquest through Independence.**

BIBLIOGRAPHY

Kenneth J. Andrien, *Crisis and Decline: The Viceroyalty of Peru in the Seventeenth Century* (1985).

Ann M. Wightman, *Indigenous Migration and Social Change: The Forasteros of Cuzco, 1570–1720* (1990).

Additional Bibliography

Osorio, Alejandra. "The King in Lima: Simulacra, Ritual, and Rule in Seventeenth-Century Peru." *The Hispanic American Historical Review* 84 (Aug 2004): 447–474.

San Cristobal Sebastian, Antonio. *La casa virreinal limeña de 1570 a 1687.* Lima: Fondo Editorial del Congreso del Peru, 2003.

Torres Arancivia, Eduardo. *Corte de virreyes: El entorno del poder en el Perú en el siglo XVII.* Lima: Pontifica Universidad Católica del Perú, Fondo Editorial, 2006.

ANN M. WIGHTMAN

SARMIENTOS DE LEÓN, JORGE ALVARO

(1933–). Jorge Alvaro Sarmientos de León (*b.* 1933), Guatemalan composer, conductor, and percussionist. Born in San Antonio Suchitepéquez, Sarmientos began his training at the National Conservatory of Music in Guatemala City under Ricardo Castillo, José Arévalo Guerra, and other distinguished Guatemalan musicians. He continued his studies in Paris and later at the Instituto Torcuato di Tella in Buenos Aires. Sarmientos returned to Guatemala, where he taught at the National Conservatory and served as musical and artistic director of the National Symphony Orchestra. He has composed over sixty works, among them film scores, chamber music, orchestral works, and a ballet. His music often features indigenous themes, as in his *Las estampas del Popol Vuh.* He has received prizes from several international cultural organizations, including the Japanese International Concert Association, the Guatemalan Order of the Quetzal, and the Government of Venezuela. In May 1999, he organized the Tenth Caribbean Composers Forum, which brought together 23 composers from the Caribbean, Central, and South America. Since 2002, he has been a board member of the College of Latin American Composers of Art Music.

See also **Music: Art Music.**

BIBLIOGRAPHY

Ronald R. Sider, "Central America and Its Composers," in *Inter-American Music Bulletin,* no. 77 (May 1970): 10–16.

Enrique Anleu Díaz, *Esbozo histórico-social de la música en Guatemala* (1978), pp. 107–108.

Additional Bibliography

Anleu Diaz, Enrique. *Historia crítica de la música en Guatemala.* Guatemala: Artemis, 1991.

Sarmientos, Jorge. "Raíces y futuro de la música en Guatemala y Latinoamérica." *Revista Musical Chilena,* 33 (Oct–Dec 1979): 58–65.

STEVEN S. GILLICK

SARNEY, JOSÉ

(1930–). José Sarney was the president of Brazil from 1985 to 1990. He was born José Ribamar Ferreira Araújo Costa in Pinheiro, Maranhão on April 24, 1930, and received a law degree in 1953. From childhood he was referred to as Zé do Sarney. For electoral purposes, in 1958 he adopted the name José Sarney and legally changed his name to José Sarney da Costa in 1965.

Sarney began his political career in 1954 as an alternate federal deputy from the National Democratic Union (UDN) and assumed the deputy position in 1956. He was reelected in 1958 and 1962. Although part of the reformist and nationalist wing of the UDN, he made his peace with the military government established in 1964. In 1965 he became the governor of his home state on the Arena ticket, the same party that brought him to the federal senate in 1970 and 1978. He was a founder of the Social Democratic Party (PDS) and twice its president and a loyal supporter of the military government. Asked by President João Figueiredo to coordinate the presidential succession with the goal of finding a national union candidate within the PDS, Sarney failed and renounced the party presidency at that time. He refused to back the PDS candidate Paulo Maluf, and subsequently ran for vice president on the opposition Democratic Alliance ticket of the PMDB-PFL (Brazilian Democratic Movement Party-Liberal Front Party) in the indirect elections won easily by Tancredo Neves in January 1985.

When Neves fell ill on the eve of his inauguration in March 1985, Sarney became interim president and reaffirmed the ministerial choices made by Neves. With the death of Neves in April, Sarney was sworn in as president and governed until March 1990. He helped to lead the country toward direct elections and a new constitution in 1988, but his time in office was marred by extremely high inflation rates. In November 1990 he was elected senator from Amapá, which had achieved statehood during his presidency. His attempts to become a presidential candidate in 1994 were frustrated even though polls indicated he still retained a small but solid following. He has remained a flexible and powerful politician, illustrated by his role as head of the Senate. His children have also pursued successful political careers.

Sarney became a member of the Brazilian Academy of Letters in 1980. He has written several books, including *Norte das Águas* (1969), *Marimbondos de fogo* (1980), *Brejaldos Guajas* (1985), and *Sentimento do Mundo* (1985).

See also **Brazil: Since 1889; Brazil, Political Parties: Brazilian Democratic Movement (MDB); Brazil, Political Parties: Liberal Party; Brazil, Political Parties: National Democratic Union of Brazil (UDN); Brazil, Revolutions: Revolution of 1964; Figueiredo, João Baptista de Oliveira; Neves, Tancredo de Almeida.**

BIBLIOGRAPHY

Noblat, Ricardo. *Ceu dos Favoritos: O Brasil de Sarney a Collor*. Rio de Janeiro: Rio Fundo Editora, 1990.

Skidmore, Thomas E. *The Politics of Military Rule in Brazil, 1964–85*. New York: Oxford University Press, 1988.

ANDREW J. KIRKENDALL

SARRATEA, MANUEL DE (1774–1849).

Manuel de Sarratea (*b.* 13 August 1774; *d.* 21 September 1849), Argentine statesman of the independence and early national periods. Born in Buenos Aires into a distinguished family that eventually included Santiago de Liniers y Bremond as his brother-in-law, Sarratea spent much of his early life in Spain but returned in time to take part in the independence movement. Though Sarratea received important government positions (such as president of the First Triumvirate in 1811 and captain-general and governor of Buenos Aires Province in 1820), he seldom retained any post for long. Some authors have focused on these career changes and his friendship with British merchants to dismiss him as an intriguer, yet he made numerous contributions during three decades of public service. During the second regime of Juan Manuel de Rosas, for example, Sarratea was named special envoy and minister plenipotentiary to Brazil (in 1838) and France (in 1841). He died in Limoges and his remains were transported to Buenos Aires in 1850.

See also **Buenos Aires; Rosas de Terrero, Manuela.**

BIBLIOGRAPHY

Jacinto R. Yaben, *Biografías argentinas y sudamericanas* vol. 5 (1938–1940), pp. 591–593.

Oreste Carlos Ales, *D. Manuel de Sarratea: Ensayo histórico* (1975).

Additional Bibliography

Halperin Donghi, Tulio. *Revolución y guerra: Formación de una elite dirigente en la Argentina criolla*. Buenos Aires: Siglo XXI Editores Argentina, 2002.

Herrero, Fabián, and Klaus Gallo. *Revolución, política e ideas en el Río de la Plata durante la década de 1810*. Buenos Aires: Ediciones Cooperativas, 2004.

Szuchman, Mark D., and Jonathan C. Brown, eds. *Revolution and Restoration: The Rearrangement of Power in Argentina, 1776–1860*. Lincoln: University of Nebraska Press, 1994.

FIDEL IGLESIAS

SAS, ANDRÉS

SAS, ANDRÉS (1900–1967). Andrés Sas (*b*. 6 April 1900; *d*. 26 August 1967), Peruvian musicologist and composer. Born in Paris, Sas grew up in Brussels, where from 1918 to 1923 he studied at the Royal Conservatory under Fernand Bauvais (theory), Alfred Marchot (violin), Paul Miry (chamber music), and Ernest Closson (music history). He took private lessons in fugue and counterpoint with Maurice Imbert. In 1920 he began studies in harmony at the Anderlecht Academy in Brussels. Soon afterward he started a teaching career as a violin instructor at the Forest Music School in Brussels. In 1924 the Peruvian government invited him to direct violin classes and chamber music concerts at the National Academy of Music in Lima. The following year he was appointed an instructor in music history at the academy. He returned to Belgium, where he founded and directed the Municipal School of Music in Ninove (1928–1929). Again in Lima, he established the Sas–Rosay Academy with his wife, the pianist Lily Rosay, in 1930. With María Wiesse de Sabogal, he started the *Antara/Revista Musical* (1935). Sas was director of Lima's Bach Institute (1931–1933) and vice president of the Lima Orchestral Society (1932).

Sas was known for his studies of pre-Columbian instruments such as the clay syrinx of the Nazca tribe; his numerous writings on the music of the Nazca and other indigenous groups made him a leading authority on the history of Peruvian music. In addition to his research, Sas was active as an editor of music magazines, lecturer, conductor, recitalist, and teacher. Sas composed symphonic pieces (*Recuerdos* for violin or piano and orchestra [1927]) and choral works (the triptych *Ollantai* [1933]), ballets (*Sueño de Zamba* [1943]), music for the stage, chamber music (*Cuarteto de cuerdas* [1938]) and songs (*Seis canciones indias del Perú* [1946]). Although some of his songs used French texts, most of his works were inspired by Indian themes and display the pentatonic melodies of the Andean region, but were written with an almost impressionist technique. He died in Lima.

See also **Music: Art Music; Sabogal, José.**

BIBLIOGRAPHY

Composers of the Americas, vol. 2 (1956), pp. 116–125; "Andrés Sas (1900–1967)" in *Revista Musical Chilena*, no. 101 (1967): 123–125; *New Grove Dictionary of Music and Musicians*, vol. 16 (1980).

Additional Bibliography

Romero, Raúl R. *Debating the Past: Music, Memory, and Identity in the Andes.* New York: Oxford University Press, 2001.

SUSANA SALGADO

SAYAÑA

SAYAÑA. Sayaña, a plot of land in the Bolivian altiplano and in the valleys to which the holder and his family have exclusive access. A *sayaña* may consist of a single plot, but it is often fragmented because of inheritance patterns and additional land acquired by the *sayañero*. Sayañas range in size from less than 2.5 acres to 75 acres or more. *Sayañas* probably existed during pre-Columbian times, and on the northern altiplano present-day house plots may still correspond to their boundaries.

Prior to the agrarian reform of 1953, both the free peasant and the peon on the hacienda had *sayañas* that they could cultivate as they desired. However, the *colono* had to work (as much as five days weekly) without pay on hacienda lands in exchange for usufruct rights on the *sayaña*.

The agrarian reform did not drastically change land categories. It gave legal titles to all peasants for the land they had previously occupied and worked for their own benefit. It did not break up large *sayañas* but increased the number of *sayañas* by converting some *aynokas* (large sections of land cultivated in a strict pattern of rotation).

See also **Agrarian Reform.**

BIBLIOGRAPHY

William E. Carter, *Aymara Communities and the Bolivian Agrarian Reform* (1964).

Dwight B. Heath, Charles J. Erasmus, and Hans C. Buechler, *Land Reform and Social Revolution in Bolivia* (1969).

Additional Bibliography

Antezana Ergueta, Luis. *La política agraria en la primera etapa nacional boliviana.* La Paz, Bolivia: Plural Editores, 2006.

Vargas Vega, John D. *La reforma agraria desde las regiones: Tierra y territorio.* La Paz, Bolivia: CIDES-UMSA, 2004.

MARIA LUISE WAGNER

SAYIL. Sayil, an ancient Maya city located in what has been called the "breadbasket" of Yucatán that flourished in the Terminal Classic period (800–1000 CE). Sayil rose to prominence in the hilly Puuc region following the collapse of the southern dynastic centers of the Maya in the Petén during the ninth century. At its height Sayil covered more than 1.5 square miles and housed from eight to ten thousand people. Research has shown that this thriving urban center might best be described as having been a "garden" city where urban and agricultural space were mixed in a pattern well adapted to the food needs of the people and to the health of a forested environment.

Picking up the fallen standard of Classic Maya civilization, Sayil and other Terminal Classic centers of the Puuc represent some of the finest examples of monumental architecture anywhere in the ancient world. The elaborate decorative motifs of the Puuc style, which dominate the façade of the three-story palace at Sayil, commemorate the major Maya deities, including the peculiar "diving god," who ruled over honey and beekeeping, as well as curly-nosed Chac, the god of rain. Ancient Sayileños did well to honor Chac, for surface streams are nonexistent and water was at a premium in this dry, karstic landscape. To assure a good supply of drinking water, the Maya of Sayil excavated water cisterns (*chultunes*) in the soft, limestone substrate. Around the *chultunes* they piled rubble into large platforms upon which they erected massive cut-stone buildings that survive to this day in the Yucatán forest. Recently completed maps of this site represent one of the most detailed records available for any ancient urban center in the Maya world and provide a blueprint for research in the years to come.

See also **Mesoamerica.**

BIBLIOGRAPHY

Harry E. D. Pollock, *The Puuc: An Architectural Survey of the Hill Country of Yucatán and Northern Campeche, Mexico* (1980).

Thomas W. Killion, et al., "Intensive Surface Collection of Residential Clusters at Terminal Classic Sayil, Yucatán, Mexico," in *Journal of Field Archaeology* 16 (1989): 273–294.

Jeremy A. Sabloff and Gair Tourtellot, *The Ancient Maya City of Sayil: The Mapping of a Puuc Region Center* (1991).

Additional Bibliography

Andrews, George F. *Pyramids and Palaces, Monsters and Masks: The Golden Age of Maya Architecture: The Collected Works of George F. Andrews.* 3 v. Lancaster, CA: Labyrinthos, 1995-1999.

Demarest, Arthur A., Prudence M. Rice, and Don S. Rice. *The Terminal Classic in the Maya Lowlands: Collapse, Transition, and Transformation.* Boulder, CO: University Press of Colorado, 2004.

Michelet, Dominique, Pierre Becquelin, and Marie-Charlotte Arnauld. *Mayas del Puuc: Arqueología de la región de Xculoc, Campeche.* México: Centre Français d'études mexicaines et centraméricaines: Gobierno del Estado de Campeche, 2000.

THOMAS W. KILLION

SCALABRINI ORTIZ, RAÚL (1898–1959). Raúl Scalabrini Ortiz (*b.* 14 April 1898; *d.* 30 May 1959), Argentine nationalist writer and historian. Although trained in the physical sciences, Scalabrini early showed literary talent in his collection of short stories, *La manga* (1923). In 1931 he published a famous analysis of the Argentine mindset *El hombre que está solo y espera,* from which emerge two key ideas. First, echoing nationalist thinkers from Johann Gottfried von Herder to Charles Maurras, Scalabrini holds that authentic Argentines uncontaminated by foreign ideas find their real identity in "the spirit of the land." Second, he argues that nineteenth-century Argentine liberalism, by failing to understand the country's true spirit, had built a country at cross-purposes with its true destiny. Scalabrini's increasing nationalist militance eventually produced two famous revisionist studies, *Política británica en el Río de la Plata* (1940) and *Historia de los ferrocarriles argentinos* (1940), which argue that British imperialists in cahoots with Argentine liberals had dispossessed Argentines of their rightful patrimony. Distrusting the British, Scalabrini supported Argentine neutrality during World War II, a position that led to charges of pro-Nazi sympathies. While he never became a Peronist functionary, his rhetoric and ideas became staples of Peronist thinking. Scalabrini's sympathy for Peronism emerges most powerfully in his book of poetry, *Tierra sin nada, tierra de profetas* (1946). His other writings include *Historia del primer empréstito* (1939), *Cuatro verdades sobre* *nuestras crisis* (1948; 2d ed. 1985), and *Bases para la reconstrucción nacional* (1965). After Juan Perón's ouster in 1955, Scalabrini fought until his death for the president's return and vindication.

See also **Nazis.**

BIBLIOGRAPHY

Vicente C. Tripoli, *Raúl Scalabrini Ortiz* (1943).

Norberto Galasso, *Scalabrini Ortiz* (1975).

René Orsi, *Jauretche y Scalabrini Ortiz* (1985).

Additional Bibliography

Galasso, Norberto. *La búsqueda de la identidad nacional en Jorge Luis Borges y Raúl Scalabrini Ortiz*. Rosario: Homo Sapiens Ediciones, 1998.

Shumway, Nicolas. *La imaginación tribal: Raúl Scalabrini Ortiz y su reconstrucción de la tribu argentina que nunca fue*. São Paulo: Universidade de São Paulo, Faculdade de Filosofia, Letras e Ciências Humanas, Departamento de Letras Modernas, 1997.

NICOLAS SHUMWAY

SCHAERER, EDUARDO (1873–1941).

Eduardo Schaerer (*b*. 2 December 1873; *d*. 12 November 1941), Paraguayan statesman and president (1912–1916). Schaerer was related to German colonists who came to Paraguay in the wake of the disastrous War of the Triple Alliance. Though he was born in Caazapá, a small hamlet in the Paraguayan interior, Schaerer displayed distinctly urban ambitions and efficiency, which stood him in good stead at the Colegio Nacional and ultimately in his business affairs.

Politically, Schaerer was a Liberal, and after the Liberal Party came to power after the 1904 revolution, he held a variety of important government posts, including director general of the Customs House, mayor of Asunción, and interior minister. Schaerer's business acumen had already made him a wealthy man, and he used his money to promote his candidacy for president. During his administration, considerable progress was made in the modernization of Asunción, an undertaking highlighted by the inauguration of a tramway system. In foreign relations, he kept Paraguay neutral during World War I.

Schaerer remained influential in Liberal circles after his term of office had expired. For a time he was a national senator and eventually became president of the Senate. He provided financial backing for various Liberal newspapers and remained an important force in the party into the 1930s.

See also **Paraguay, Political Parties: Liberal Party; War of the Triple Alliance.**

BIBLIOGRAPHY

William Belmont Parker, *Paraguayans of To-Day* (1921), pp. 161–162.

Harris Gaylord Warren, *Rebirth of the Paraguayan Republic: The First Colorado Era, 1878–1904* (1985), pp. 125–126.

Additional Bibliography

Amaral, Raúl, and Roberto Paredes. *Los presidentes del Paraguay*. Asunción: Servilibro, 2005.

Carrón, Juan María. *El régimen liberal, 1870-1930: Sociedad, economía*. Asunción: Arandurã Editorial, 2004.

Lewis, Paul H. *Political Parties and Generations in Paraguay's Liberal Era, 1869-1940*. Chapel Hill: University of North Carolina Press, 1993.

THOMAS L. WHIGHAM

SCHENDEL, MIRA (1919–1988).

Mira Schendel (*b*. 1919; *d*. 1988), graphic artist, painter, and sculptor. Swiss-born Schendel lived in Italy until age thirty, when she emigrated to Brazil. Abstract art with minimalist overtone dominated her repertory until the 1960s, when her work took on constructivist influences, with a monumentality of void characterizing her graphic works. In one piece, simply titled *Drawing,* for example, linguistic and mathematical signs and scratches are drawn on inked glass and are then transferred onto delicate Japanese paper. The visual result recalls Chinese painting. In 1964 Schendel represented Brazil in the Second Biennial of American Art of Córdoba, Argentina, She had solo exhibitions at the Museum of Modern Art in São Paulo in 1964, at a London gallery in 1965, and in 1971 at the Brazilian-American Cultural Institute in Washington, D.C. In 1975 she was one of twelve artists selected to participate in a nationally sponsored traveling exhibition and discussion series.

See also **Art: The Twentieth Century.**

BIBLIOGRAPHY

Fundação Nacional De Arte, *Pinacoteca do Estado—São Paulo* (1982), p. 174.

Dawn Ades, *Art in Latin America: The Modern Era, 1820–1980* (1989), pp. 275–276.

Additional Bibliography

Carvajal, Rina, Alma Ruiz, and Susan Martin. *The Experimental Exercise of Freedom: Lygia Clark, Gego, Mathias Goeritz, Hélio Oiticica, Mira Schendel.* Los Angeles: Museum of Contemporary Art, 1999.

Marques, Maria Eduarda Castro Magalhães. *Mira Schendel.* São Paulo: Cosac & Naify Edições, 2001.

Zegher, M. Catherine de. *Inside the Visible: An Elliptical Traverse of 20th Century Art in, of, and from the Feminine.* Cambridge, MA: MIT Press, 1996.

CAREN A. MEGHREBLIAN

SCHERER GARCÍA, JULIO (1926–).

The Mexican journalist Julio Scherer was born on April 7, 1926. At age twenty he was hired by the newspaper *Excélsior* and served as its editor from 1968 to 1976. Within a national press almost entirely aligned with the government, this paper offered professionalism and pluralism. Scherer was ultimately forced off the paper by some of its cooperativists who, according to some, were manipulated by the government of Luis Echeverría. With other journalists who left *Excélsior*, in November 1976 he founded the weekly *Proceso*, which he headed for twenty years. The investigative journalism displayed in the paper, especially concerning corruption in the government, heralded the country's transition to democracy in the late twentieth century. Scherer authored several books, including *Siqueiros: La piel y la entraña* (1965), *Los presidentes* (1986), *Cárceles* (1998, and *Parte de guerra* (co-authored with Carlos Monsiváis, 1999). Scherer, who had studied law and philosophy, was also a professor of journalism at the National Autonomous University of Mexico. In 2001 he received CEMEX-FNPI's New Journalism Prize and in 2005 the University of Guadalajara awarded him an honorary doctorate. Commenting on his trade, Scherer stated: "Journalism, like surgery, extracts what it finds. Journalism must be as precise as the scalpel."

See also **Excélsior (Mexico City); Journalism in Mexico.**

RAUL TREJO

SCHICK GUTIÉRREZ, RENÉ (1909–1966). René Schick Gutiérrez (*b.* 1909; *d.* 1966), president of Nicaragua from 1963 to 1966. A close associate of the Somoza family, Schick served as Anastasio Somoza García's personal secretary and was named minister of education and of foreign relations during the presidency of Luis Somoza Debayle. Long portrayed as a quiet "yes-man" and Somoza puppet, Schick proved to be more independent. His term in office was relatively peaceful and he followed Luis Somoza's lead in liberalizing Nicaragua. The Nicaraguan state and economy boomed as government expenditure and entrepreneurial activity increased. Schick, who died in office, was succeeded by Vice President Lorenzo Guerrero Gutiérrez.

See also **Nicaragua; Somoza Debayle, Anastasio.**

BIBLIOGRAPHY

Eduardo Crawley, *Dictators Never Die* (1979).

Claribel Alegría and D. J. Flakoll, *Nicaragua: La revolución Sandinista, una crónica política, 1855–1979* (1982).

Thomas Walker, *Nicaragua: The Land of Sandino* (1986).

Additional Bibliography

Gambone, Michael D. *Capturing the Revolution: The United States, Central America, and Nicaragua, 1961–1972.* Westport, CT: Praeger, 2001.

HEATHER K. THIESSEN

SCHNEIDER, RENE (1913–1970). Rene Schneider, born December 31, 1913, was a Chilean army officer. A graduate of the Escuela Militar, he became commander of the army after the government forced the resignation of General Camilo Valenzuela, for failing to prevent a coup launched by General Roberto Viaux of the Tacna Artillery Regiment in 1969. This incident became known as the Tacnazo in reference to the rebellious unit.

Schneider became important following the presidential election of 1970. Because none of the three candidates, Salvador Allende, Jorge Alessandri, or Radomiro Tomic, a Christian Democrat, had won a majority of the votes cast, the Constitution called for the Congress to select the winner. Chilean political tradition had stipulated that the legislature would elect the candidate who had won a plurality, in this case, Allende, a socialist.

Right-wing elements hoped to convince the legislature to elect Alessandri, who would immediately resign, thus allowing Eduardo Frei, president from 1964 to 1970, to seek the presidency again. Failing that, they were prepared to launch a coup. Schneider had earlier stated that he saw the army as the guarantor of the Constitution of 1925, making it clear that the military would not meddle in the election. Consequently, General Viaux ordered some of his followers to kidnap Schneider and whisk him out of Chile until Frei could be reelected. The kidnappers, however, mistakenly mortally wounded Schneider, thereby unifying the nation behind Allende.

See also **Alessandri Rodríguez, Jorge; Allende Gossens, Salvador; Chile: The Twentieth Century; Chile, Constitutions; Frei Montalva, Eduardo; Tomic, Radomiro.**

BIBLIOGRAPHY

Davis, Nathaniel. *The Last Two Years of Salvador Allende.* Ithaca, NY: Cornell University Press, 1985.

WILLIAM SATER

SCHOMBURG, ARTURO ALFONSO

(1874–1938). Bibliophile, curator, Pan-Africanist, black nationalist, and vindicationist historian.

Arturo Alfonso Schomburg was a Puerto Rican of African ancestry. He was born in San Juan on January 24, 1874, to Mary Joseph, from Saint Croix, and Federico Schomburg, a German-born merchant who lived in San Juan. As a primary school student in Puerto Rico, Schomburg was exposed to racial and class prejudice when his fifth grade teacher told the young Schomburg that black people had no history. The teacher's remark sparked Schomburg's intellectual curiosity, which eventually led him to document the experience of the African Diaspora around the world.

In April 17, 1891, Schomburg arrived in New York, where he joined the Hispanic Caribbean community by serving as secretary of the Las Dos Antillas, an organization that fought for the independence of Cuba and Puerto Rico. He married Elizabeth "Bessie" Hatcher of Staunton, Virginia, in 1895;

they had three sons. After Bessie Schomburg died in 1900, Schomburg married Elizabeth Morrow Taylor in 1902. She died early, leaving two young sons. In 1914 Schomburg took a third wife, Elizabeth Green. They had three children.

While living in Harlem, Schomburg strengthened his ties with the African American and Afro-Caribbean communities. He joined the Prince Hall Lodge, becoming the master of the lodge in 1911 and the grand secretary of the Grand Lodge of the State of New York in 1918. As a key contributor to the Harlem Renaissance, Schomburg became friends of Alain Locke and Langston Hughes. Schomburg's civic and intellectual life was driven by his mission to teach, enlighten, and instruct black people about their own history and achievements. He embarked on the task of collecting books, artworks, manuscripts, rare books, slave narratives, and other artifacts of black history. He wrote numerous articles and essays. His essay "The Negro Digs Up His Past," which was published in the *Survey Graphic* of Harlem in March 1925, influenced thousands of students and scholars, including the noted historian Dr. John Henrik Clarke, who sought out Schomburg to further his studies in African history. During 1931 and 1932 Schomburg served as curator of the Negro Collection at the library of Fisk University in Nashville, Tennessee.

Schomburg's personal collection consisted of artworks, manuscripts, rare books, slave narratives, and other documents. The New York Public Library regarded Schomburg's collection so highly that the Library managed to acquire it through the Carnegie Corporation for $10,000. The collection became the cornerstone of the Library's Division of Negro History's branch at 135th Street in Harlem. In 1940 the branch was renamed the Schomburg Center for Research in Black Culture. Following a dental surgery, Schomburg became ill and died in Madison Park Hospital, Brooklyn, New York, on June 10, 1938; he was buried in Cypress Hills Cemetery in Brooklyn. Schomburg is regarded as a pioneer of African Diaspora studies and a leading advocate of Black Nationalism.

See also **Hispanics in the United States.**

BIBLIOGRAPHY

Asukile, Thabiti. "Arthur Alfonso Schomburg (1874–1938): Embracing Black Motherhood Experience in

Love of Black Peoples." *Afro-Americans in New York Life and History* 30, no. 2 (2006): 69–97.

Piñeiro de Rivera, Flor. *Arturo Schomburg, un puertorriqueño descubre el legado histórico del negro: Sus escritos anotados y apéndices.* San Juan, Puerto Rico: Centro de Estudios Avanzados de Puerto Rico y el Caribe, 1989.

Sinnette, Elinor Des Verney. *Arthur Alfonso Schomburg, Black Bibliophile and Collector: A Biography.* New York: New York Public Library, 1989.

MILAGROS DENIS

SCHWARZ-BART, SIMONE (1938–).

Simone Schwarz-Bart (*b.* 8 January 1938), Guadeloupean novelist and dramatist. Schwarz-Bart was born in Charente-Maritime, where her father was serving in the army. Her mother returned to Guadeloupe with her daughter, whose early schooling took place in Trois-Rivières. Schwarz-Bart began the lycée in Point-à-Pitre and finished in Paris. Married in Paris, Simone and André Schwarz-Bart spent a year in Dakar, and then settled in Switzerland, where Simone began writing short stories. Returning to Guadeloupe, she was instrumental in editing the encyclopedic *Hommage à la femme noire*, 6 vols. (1988–1989).

Schwarz-Bart has been compared with writers as diverse as Antonine Maillet and Toni Morrison. Through her presentation of various insular experiences (a Haitian sugarcane worker, an elderly Martinican woman in a French hospice) she would seem to be in the process of creating a Caribbean mythology in her dramatic and fictional writing. In 1973, she won the Grand Prize of the magazine *Elle* for her novel *Pluie et vent sur Télumée-Miracle* (1972)/*The Bridge of Beyond* (1982). All of her individually authored works have appeared in English. In 1992, the English translation of *Between Two Worlds* was published in English and Spanish. Between 2001 and 2004, the University of Wisconsin Press published four volumes of *In Praise of Black Women* in English translation. Schwarz-Bart currently lives in Lausanne, France, and Guadeloupe.

See also **Literature: Spanish America.**

BIBLIOGRAPHY

Un plat de porc aux bananes vertes (novel, with Andre Schwarz-Bart, 1967); *Ti-Jean l'horizon* (novel, 1979), translated as *Between Two Worlds* (1981); and *Ton beau capitaine* (play, 1987), translated as *Your Handsome Captain* (1989).

See also Ronnie Scharfman, "Mirroring and Mothering in Simone Schwarz-Bart's *Pluie et vent sur Télumée-Miracle* and Jean Rhys's *Wide Sargasso Sea*," in *Yale French Studies* 62 (1981): 88–106; Fanta Toureh, *L'imaginaire dans l'oeuvre de Simone Schwarz-Bart: Approche d'une mythologie antillaise* (1986); Elizabeth Mudimbe-Boyi, "*Pluie et vent sur Télumée-Miracle,*" in *Continental, Latin American, and Francophone Women Writers,* edited by Ginette Adamson et al., vol. 2 (1987), pp. 155–164; Monique Bouchard, *Une lecture de "Pluie et vent sur Télumée-Miracle..."* (1990); Marie-Denis Shelton, "Literature Extracted: A Poetic of Daily Life," in *Callaloo* 15, no. 1 (1992): 167–178.

Additional Bibliography

Aub-Buscher, Gertrude, and Beverly Ormerod Noakes. *The Francophone Caribbean Today: Literature, Language, Culture.* Barbados: University of West Indies Press, 2003.

Campbell, Elaine, and Pierette M. Frickey. *The Whistling Bird: Women Writers of the Caribbean.* Boulder, CO: Lynne Reiner Publishers, 1998.

Higonnet, Margaret R., and Joan Templeton. *Reconfigured Spheres: Feminist Explorations of Literary Space.* Amherst: University of Massachusetts Press, 1994.

CARROL F. COATES

SCIENCE.

The European encounter with the New World begun in 1492 stimulated a rush of new information about the natural environment without parallel in human history, kindling the fire of scientific empiricism in Europe. The Spanish Empire thus became a source of scientific information diffused through the new print technology and evaluated by Europeans in the context of the received view of the natural world, highly colored by the works of classical antiquity. Thus Columbus's discovery stimulated the comparative study of Old World and New World nature. Works such as Gonzalo Fernández de Oviedo y Valdés's *Historia general de las Indias* (1535), itself conceptually dependent on ancient authors such as Pliny, made available data that eventually led to the overthrow of classical authority. The reflection of exploration in cartography, for example, had by the end of the sixteenth century destroyed the standard geometrized Ptolemaic view of the Earth's surface.

COLONIAL ERA

The Spanish crown, eager to learn of economically useful minerals and plants, dispatched an expedition led by Francisco Hernández in 1570–1577, mainly to investigate the flora of New Spain. Hernández was a typical Renaissance figure both steeped in ancient science and endowed with an empirical cast of mind. He sought both to describe and codify Aztec *materia medica* and also to test their properties in colonial hospitals. The avalanche of new medicinal and other species from the Americas overwhelmed the cramped little garden of classical natural history, ultimately creating a demand for a viable system of classification.

The scientific revolution of the seventeenth century was observed, if not accepted, in the Spanish Empire. Galileo's astronomical writings were read and appreciated by Diego Rodríguez and Carlos Sigüenza y Góngora in New Spain, although the two failed to push Galileo's critique of classical cosmology to its ultimate limits. New World naturalists of Galileo's generation and later shared Europe's passion for observing comets; indeed, the Spanish crown stimulated such research by collecting observational data from various sites in its empire.

The eighteenth century saw a fully developed colonial science system characterized by militarization and centralization. Like their French cousins, the Spanish Bourbons believed that investment in science was both a way of associating the crown with a prestigious activity and a utilitarian pursuit that promised economic benefits to the entire empire. As early as the 1750s, the crown was devoting around 0.5 percent of its annual budget to scientific activities, a very large investment in science among European nations of the day. The real science budget was even larger because numerous scientific activities were hidden in the military budget. The Spanish navy accommodated officers attracted to the new Newtonian science and gave them commissions that exploited their interest in cosmology while carrying out strategically important "hydrographical" activities, such as the mapping of the coastlines of Latin America and service on numerous boundary commissions. The navy procured the best scientific instruments produced in London and Paris and made them available to colonial men of science, in contrast to the restrictive practices of the British in their American colonies. The problem with the militarization of science was that its net effect was to delay the emergence of science as a profession and to discourage the open discussion or publication of scientific results, which were frequently viewed as state secrets. Thus a concomitant of militarization was a scientific system that was highly centralized. All results were communicated to the relevant officials in Madrid rather than published directly by the scientist. This meant that the independent-minded botanist José Celestino Mutis (1732–1808), for example, incurred the wrath of his superiors in Madrid when he corresponded directly with Carl Linnaeus.

The two areas that most attracted those who wished to associate themselves with modern science were Newtonian physics and Linnaean taxonomy. In an intellectual world that had officially rejected the views of Copernicus, heliocentrism was diffused and accepted through the circulation of books popularizing Newtonian physics. In Lima, Cosme Bueno disseminated Newtonian ideas from his chair of Galenic medicine (which he used as a platform to attack outmoded medical concepts), and theses on Newtonian subjects were produced at the University of San Marcos. In Bogotá, Mutis lectured on Newton at the Colegio Mayor de Nuestra Señora del Rosario and prepared a partial translation of the *Principia*, the first in Spanish. In these capitals and in Mexico City roughly the same proportion of Newtonian works circulated in relation to population as in any European center. The notion of the empire as a scientific backwater must be rejected, or at least carefully qualified.

The broad acceptance of Linnaean taxonomy permitted the numerous botanists working in colonial Latin America to participate in a vast international network of botanical information gathered by disciples dispatched to various parts of the world by Linnaeus himself or by institutions that adopted his system. Linnaeus's man in South America was to have been Pehr Loefling, whom he sent in 1751 to Madrid and in 1754 to New Granada, where he died. Mutis, who began to correspond with Linnaeus in 1764, believed he had inherited Loefling's mantle. All botanists who were subjects of the crown worked as dependents of the Madrid Botanical Garden, which had become a Linnaean stronghold in the 1770s. Because of this tight centralization, budding nationalists in New Spain, led by José Antonio de Alzate y Ramírez, rejected the

Linnaean system while attempting to revive Aztec taxonomy, mainly for nationalistic reasons. When the Linnaeans of the Malaspina expedition arrived in New Spain in 1791, they became embroiled in a dispute over taxonomy with botanists influenced by Alzate. At this time there were so many naturalists working in New Spain in official capacities that one of them complained to the crown that botanists were tripping over each other in the jungle.

The two most characteristic forms of centralized scientific institutions in the eighteenth century were botanical expeditions and boundary commissions. The first important expedition of the century, the La Condamine expedition (1735–1745), was a geophysical enterprise, although botanists were included. Although the expedition was French-led, two Spanish military officers, Jorge Juan y Santacilia and Antonio de Ulloa, were attached to it. The purposes of the expedition were to establish a value for an arc of the meridian in equatorial South America and to corroborate Newton's prediction regarding the flattening of the Earth's poles and consequent shortening of the degree of longitude near the equator. Thus Spain entered Enlightenment science in Newtonian guise. For their efforts, Ulloa was elected a fellow of the Royal Society and Juan a member of the French Academy of Sciences, whereas in Spain their careers were wholly military.

Botany, focused on the search for economically useful plants, was something like a national craze. The crown both dispatched expeditions and undertook to gather information indirectly by surveys directed through the colonial bureaucracy. The three great botanical expeditions (among nearly forty) were to New Granada, Peru, and New Spain. Only the first, conducted in 1782–1810, was established in the colonies rather than by Madrid directly; it also became, under Mutis's direction, a full-fledged scientific institution, establishing an astronomical observatory (1803) and conducting research in zoology and mineralogy as well as botany. The Peruvian expedition (1777–1788), led by Hipólito Ruiz and José Antonio Pavón, was more narrowly botanical, its major focus being the species of quinine-producing cinchona. The expedition to New Spain (1787–1804), led by the Spaniard Martín de Sessé and the Creole José Mociño, made a systematic study of Mexican flora and established a botanical garden in Mexico City.

The greatest and most productive expedition of the period was that led by the Italian Alejandro Malaspina (1789–1794). The Malaspina expedition, inspired by Captain James Cook's second voyage, collected data and natural history specimens from Uruguay up the Pacific coast of South and North America as far as Alaska, as well as from the Philippines, New Zealand, and Australia. The last great expedition of the colonial period, the royal vaccination expedition (1803–1806), led by Francisco Balmis, was a public health venture designed to inoculate as many subjects of the empire as possible with the Jenner smallpox vaccine.

Europeans such as the French naturalist Georges Buffon held that the environment and biota of the New World were degenerate and inferior with respect to their European counterparts, and Enlightenment naturalists in the Americas rigorously countered such claims. In this "dispute of the New World," José Hipólito Unanue in Peru and Alzate in Mexico (and Thomas Jefferson in the United States) presented data to demonstrate the falsity of the original proposition. This polemic provided scientific input to a Creole ideology already building justifications for independence. In Bogotá, Francisco José de Caldas, in whose work resentment of Creole dependence on European science was a constant theme, asserted that America was not in need of any second discovery by foreign expeditions.

In the area of technology and technical education, two first-class institutions emerged in eighteenth-century Mexico City. One was the Colegio de Minería, where mining engineers were trained by a gifted staff using the advanced European science and technology. The mineralogy professor, Andrés del Río, who had studied with Antoine Lavoisier in Paris, discovered vanadium, while the chemist and botanist Vicente Cervantes produced the first translation of Lavoisier's *Elements of Chemistry* in the New World. The other institution was the mint (Casa de Moneda), which became an important center for technological, particularly mechanical, innovation. Thus, by the end of the colonial period a foundation had been laid for scientific as well as political independence, a promise that the dislocation of the wars of independence completely frustrated.

The fate of science in colonial Brazil was largely determined by the absence of universities there.

There were a few individual naturalists of high quality, such as the botanist José Mariano de Conceição Vellozo, a Linnaean whose *Florae fluminensis*, a description of the flora of Rio de Janeiro province completed in 1790 (published in 1825), is considered the best representative of Enlightenment science in Brazil. An attempt to found a Brazilian university is associated with José Bonifácio Andrada e Silva, a native of Santos who studied chemistry and mineralogy in Paris and Freiburg in the 1790s. His conception of science was highly utilitarian, for its core was the study of the mineral wealth of the vast nation.

INDEPENDENCE PERIOD

In the former countries of the Spanish Empire, science had been integrated into a tightly centralized institutional and economic system in which scientific communication within the empire was not encouraged and all information flowed to and from Madrid. This meant that when Madrid's patronage and tutelage were removed, the infrastructure that had supported scientific achievement in Mexico, Colombia, and Peru disappeared. So did many of the practitioners of Enlightenment science—either killed in the revolutionary upheaval (as in Colombia) or co-opted by the new state bureaucracies (as in Peru). Brazilian science was spared such an upheaval but had started from a lower level. Then too, Creole elites, which before independence had seen science as a symbol of intellectual and political freedom, set their sights on the more pressing problem of maintaining and consolidating power in the new nations. If the military was the surest road to success, then parents would not encourage their children to take up scholarly careers. Medicine, military engineering, surveying, and a few other fields for which there was constant demand constituted exceptions. Science, therefore, may be pictured as having taken refuge in the most proximate fields available in these years of severe deinstitutionalization: During the first half of the nineteenth century, biology was cultivated by medical doctors; mathematics and physics by military engineers.

The fate of colonial scientific institutions is exemplified by the Royal College of Mining in Mexico City and the Astronomical Observatory of Bogotá: Both lingered on in impoverished conditions after independence. The former was officially abolished in 1833 and reorganized as a general science faculty; the latter suffered long periods of inactivity, notably between 1851 and 1858, after the death of the director, F. J. Matiz, the last survivor of Mutis's expedition. Brazil fared better than the Spanish viceroyalties during the first half of the nineteenth century owing to the foundation in 1810 of a central technical institution, the Royal Military Academy, which had a rigorous four-year course of mathematics that preceded military training.

LATER NINETEENTH CENTURY

The second half of the century was marked by the introduction of positivist philosophy and a general movement of institutionalization, particularly of applied sciences. Positivism describes the followers of Auguste Comte and Herbert Spencer, who developed philosophies of "positive" (that is, objective) knowledge, which was supposed to replace outmoded forms of human thought, notably religion. In Europe, positivism was developed as a kind of philosophical synthesis of scientific method, based on secure knowledge and appreciation of the success of the scientific revolution. Inasmuch as Latin American science was stagnant, positivism there tended to be programmatic. Positivists founded almost all the important scientific institutions of the second half of the century: In Brazil the Polytechnic School was founded in 1874 in open imitation of the French engineering school of the same name; the following year the Mining School of Ouro Preto was established to train technicians to develop the country's ample mineral resources. Toward the end of the century the Brazilian Ministry of Agriculture became a center of practical positivist programs in technology and applied sciences, including the Geological and Mineralogical Service; it even ran the old Imperial Observatory (created in 1827, active from 1845), which had an important meteorological section.

In Mexico a number of important institutions were organized under the banner of positivism, including the National Preparatory School (1868), the Mexican Society of Natural History (1868), the Geographical and Exploration Commission (established in 1877 by the Darwinian industry minister, Vicente Riva Palacio), the Geological Commission, and the National Medical Institute (both in 1888). In Uruguay, under the regime of the positivist Lorenzo Latorre, the entire educational system was controlled by positivists who overhauled the educational establishment from the primary grades through university, promoting positivist norms of science education.

Latin American science was noted for highly visible participation of foreigners, particularly Americans, in scientific enterprises, especially in geology. Thus in Brazil, the Imperial Geological Commission (1875–1877) was headed by Charles F. Hartt. His disciple Orville A. Derby was director of the Geographical and Geological Commission of the state of São Paulo from 1886 to 1906, when he resigned to head the making of the geological map of the state of Bahia. Derby was head of the Brazilian Geological and Mineralogical Service in from 1907 to 1915, and trained a generation of Brazilian geologists. In Brazil, Peru, Chile, and elsewhere, the U.S. Geological Service provided a model for professional geology from the late nineteenth century well into the twentieth, particularly in the design and execution of geological maps and surveys of mineral resources.

As the practice of science revived, Latin Americans sought training abroad, with different disciplinary groups showing partiality for distinctive European traditions. Thus, Brazilian engineers preferred to study in Belgium, Mexican chemists in Germany, Argentine mathematicians in Italy, and Mexicans in the United States.

Besides positivism, a number of important European scientific ideas had powerful repercussions in Latin America. Darwinism was widely debated in all Latin American countries except for Paraguay. In general, Comtean positivists opposed Darwinism, occasionally forming tenuous alliances with Catholics to defeat evolutionary ideas, whereas Spencerians supported it. However, in those countries where Comteans were strong (Brazil, Mexico, Venezuela), later generations of Spencerians introduced Darwin's ideas once the Comteans had left the educational stage. Thus in Brazil, the Polytechnic School, which had been a Comtean stronghold, became a focus of Darwinian debate in the 1880s. In Mexico, Gabino Barreda, the Comtean founder of the Preparatory School, was anti-Darwinian, whereas the next generation of positivists, led by Porfirio Parra, was evolutionist.

In some countries Darwinism became elevated to the rank of national ideology. In Brazil, a Darwinian stronghold, Republican medical doctors elaborated a Darwinian worldview mixed with polygenism, the notion that humankind emerged from several ancestral racial lines, a doctrine designed to support racial stratification. Brazil's Museo Nacional, under the directorship of Ladislao Neto, became a node of Darwinian research. Neto employed the German evolutionary zoologist Fritz Müller as a roving naturalist. In Uruguay, even cattlemen discussed Darwinism in the 1870s and 1880s. They divided into two factions that debated whether and how to improve the herds of creole cattle (the descendants of cattle brought by the Spanish in the sixteenth century). One group, comprising the wealthier cattlemen, wanted to cross creole cows with expensive Durham bulls imported from England. The other group, citing Darwin, claimed that natural selection had already acted on the creole herd, adapting it admirably to the local pastures. Argentine governments, for nationalist reasons, supported the paleontologist Florentino Ameghino's claim that *Homo sapiens* had emerged in Argentina, making it the cradle of the human race.

Another European scientific idea with tremendous transcendence in late-nineteenth-century Latin America was the germ theory of Louis Pasteur. In Paris, Pasteur had founded an institute where he imparted his views of epidemiology as well as the techniques according to which preventive serum could be produced. Numerous Latin Americans studied there, including the Brazilian Oswaldo Cruz, who later founded a Pasteur-type institute at Manguinhos, near Rio de Janeiro, that developed into the premier biomedical research institute in Latin America during the first half of the twentieth century (Oswaldo Cruz Institute). There Carlos Chagas solved the riddle of American sleeping sickness (trypanosomiasis), now called Chagas disease, and made it one of the most studied pathologies in the history of medicine. Other Pasteur-style institutes were founded in São Paulo, Caracas, Maracaibo, and Asunción, all before 1900.

TWENTIETH CENTURY TO THE PRESENT

Around 1900, yellow fever was the most urgent medical problem. As early as 1881 a Cuban, Carlos Finlay, had identified the vector of disease, the mosquito *Aedes aegypti*, but his hypothesis was not confirmed until after the Spanish-American War of 1898, when the U.S. Public Health Service effectively wiped out the disease both in Cuba and in Panama. When the Rockefeller Foundation (RF)

Engineering student, Universidad Tecnológica de Querétaro, Mexico, 2006. Despite lapses during periods of political unrest, Latin American countries have contributed much to the world of science, particularly in the fields of physics, medical research, and genetics. © KEITH DANNE-MILLER/CORBIS

was established in 1913, it made the eradication of yellow fever a high priority, going so far as to have the Peruvian government name an RF doctor as director of public health in 1919–1922.

Almost from its inception, the RF assumed an active role in the promotion of science in Latin America. It was opposed to what it called "didactic science"—that is, university science instruction that was limited to classroom lectures and textbooks and lacked a laboratory component. The RF also favored full-time teaching or research positions rather than the part-time positions standard in all Latin American universities, which had the effect of forcing scientists to support themselves with multiple jobs. Finally, the RF, seeking to "make the peaks higher,"

tried to identify the best scientific minds in the region and to support those individuals. With these objectives in mind, the RF surveyed medical education in virtually all Latin American countries between 1916 and the late 1920s. Out of these reports emerged a roster of biomedical scientists that the RF supported over the next several decades, including the Argentine physiologist Bernardo Houssay, who won the Nobel Prize in 1947 for research on the role of the pituitary gland in the metabolism of carbohydrates. Latin America's second Nobel Prize was won in 1970 by a disciple of Houssay, Luis Leloir, for work on the biochemistry of carbohydrates. Thus the region's first two Nobel Prizes were in part the result of the RF's support for research. In Peru, another group of physiologists, led by Carlos Monge, built a successful research program that concentrated on problems related to the high altitudes of the Andean region.

Classical genetics had an early start in Argentina, where the rediscovery of Mendel's theories was recognized as early as 1908 by the biologist Angel Gallardo. At the University of La Plata, German-trained Miguel Hernández began teaching Mendelian genetics in 1915. Hernández trained Salomón Horovitz and Francisco Alberto Sáez, whose research centered on plant genetics and cytogenetics, respectively. Sáez was coauthor of a general cytology textbook that was widely adopted in the English-speaking world. Population genetics was introduced in Brazil by Theodosius Dobzhansky, a Russian-born biologist trained in the United States by Thomas Hunt Morgan. Dobzhansky had studied wild populations of the fruit fly *Drosophila* in temperate climates and came to Brazil to study a tropical population. In the fifteen years that Dobzhansky pursued Brazilian research (intermittently from 1943 to 1958), he trained a generation of geneticists in seminars held at the University of São Paulo (USP). This research was not only backed in large part by the RF; USP had been founded in part to meet RF specifications regarding full-time research and teaching appointments. Dobzhansky's group discovered that tropical populations of *Drosophila* display considerably more variation and genetic plasticity than their temperate cousins do, in response to the greater variety of ecological niches available in the tropics. The second generation of Dobzhansky's Brazilian students founded a strong group in human genetics that worked mainly with models derived from population genetics.

The third major scientific discipline in Latin America was physics. In the nineteenth century Latin

European Southern Observatory, La Silla Mountain, Chile, 1993. Scientists in Latin America and Europe frequently collaborate on projects, exchanging researchers and ideas to advance learning. © ROGER RESSMEYER/CORBIS

America was as much as a century behind Europe in mathematics and physics. In order to raise the level of discipline quickly, the Argentine government contracted with a number of German professors to found a modern Institute of Physics at the University of La Plata in 1909. The institute's longtime director, Richard Gans, trained the first generations of Argentine physicists, including a group of relativists who welcomed Albert Einstein during his Latin American visit in 1925. In Latin America, Einstein was viewed as a symbol of modernization, or rather the will to modernize, because—it was said—a country could not hope to modernize if its mathematicians and physicists could not master the theory of relativity. Inasmuch as Maxwellian physics had been scantily diffused in Argentina (and the other countries of the region), there was no entrenched scientific resistance to Einstein anywhere, except for a small group of Comtean mathematicians in Brazil. In the three countries he visited (Argentina, Uruguay, and Brazil), Einstein's trip stimulated an outpouring of books on relativity and a general public debate on the role of science in modern society. In Argentina two physicists trained at La Plata, Ramón Enrique Gaviola and Enrique Loedel, published papers on relativity in the 1920s. In Brazil Einstein's visit caused a debate in the Brazilian Academy of Sciences. A younger generation led by the mathematician Manoel Amoroso Costa and the engineer Roberto Marinho, with relativity as their battle cry, won control of the Academy, ousting the positivists led by the Comtean mathematician Vicente Licínio Cardoso.

Brazil became a leader in experimental physics after the arrival, in the 1930s, of the German Jewish refugee Bernard Gross and the Italo-Russian Gleb Wataghin. Gross's group, in Rio de Janeiro, and Wataghin's, in São Paulo, performed research on cosmic rays. Gross measured the intensity of cosmic rays in an ionization chamber, and his student Joaquim Costa Ribeiro discovered the thermodielectric effect in 1944. Wataghin's group studied cosmic ray showers, and two of his disciples, Marcello Damy de Souza and Paulus Aulus Pompéia, discovered the penetrating or "hard" component of cosmic radiation. A third disciple, Mário Shenberg, collaborated with George Gamow on the neutrino theory of stellar collapse, and a fourth, Cesar Lattes was part of an international team that discovered the pi-meson (pion) at the Bolivian astrophysical laboratory at Chacaltaya in 1947.

Nuclear physics was introduced after World War II. In Brazil the American Richard Feynman collaborated with José Leite Lopes on weak particle interactions, and the São Paulo group under Damy de Souza acquired a particle accelerator and worked on elementary particles. Argentine physics had a parallel history: first came cosmic radiation studies and then atomic physics. In 1949 Juan Perón hired a German physical chemist named Ronald Richter to perform experiments on nuclear fusion. Richter proved to be a charlatan who was able to fool Perón's generals by exploding hydrogen in a voltaic arc, but even though he was exposed, his laboratory at Bariloche became the center of advanced nuclear physics research, and cyclotrons purchased to support his group were used to train a new generation of physicists.

In Mexico, MIT-trained Manuel Sandoval Vallarta (one of Feynman's professors, incidentally) introduced cosmic radiation studies, especially the effect of the Earth's magnetic field on the rays. Sandoval and some of his students also did research in theoretical physics and were especially interested in George Birkhoff's notion of gravitation in flat space-time, a relativistic model that avoided certain difficulties related to the curvilinear nature of Einstein's general theory.

By the 1940s there was sufficient scientific activity in Argentina, Brazil, Venezuela, Mexico, Uruguay, and a few other nations to stimulate scientists to organize themselves into self-consciously national scientific communities. Thus in 1948 the Brazilian Association for the Progress of Science was organized, in 1950 a similar association in Venezuela, and so forth. These societies viewed their roles as both professional and political. They wanted to stimulate a positive climate of public and governmental interest in science and pressed for the formation of national research councils, which were established in most Latin American countries between 1958 and 1979. These

institutions all had similar objectives and helped channel government money into scientific projects. In spite of these efforts the scientifically advanced countries experienced severe "brain drains" from the 1950s through the 1970s. The 1966 coup led by Juan Carlos Onganía in Argentina decimated the Faculty of Exact Sciences at the University of Buenos Aires, which lost 215 members. Entire research groups emigrated at the same time, mainly to Chile, Venezuela, and the United States. Mexico was one of the few Latin American countries that did not lose scientists in the 1960s because of the capacity of the National Autonomous University (UNAM) to absorb them.

The period between the late 1960s and mid-1980s witnessed a general debate over the role of science in Latin American society. Of particular concern has been the issue of whether a developing country can afford to invest money in "pure" (that is, basic) science when it is desperately in need of utilitarian, practical projects that will aid in the country's modernization and improve its standard of living. According to dependency theory, national science communities should concentrate on the specific social and economic needs of their country. Applied scientists soon discovered, however, that they were unable to pursue complex projects without the aid of basic science.

Since the time of Perón, science and scientists have repeatedly fallen victim to the whims of authoritarian repressive regimens. In Brazil, soon after the military regime came to power in 1964, threats were directed at the Oswaldo Cruz Institute. Finally, in 1970, ten researchers were fired by the government and the Institute's research program was severely compromised. In Argentina in 1978, a provincial governor attempted to outlaw the "new math," finding set theory to be subversive of Western values, at the same time that the generals in Buenos Aires were denouncing Freud and Einstein, along with Marx.

Toward the end of the century, the pace of integration of Latin American science into the international science system accelerated, with increased investment in research and development and a growing pool of national scientists. The number of articles on science and engineering published by Latin American authors rose by nearly 200 percent between 1988 and 2001. The increase was concentrated in four countries: Argentina, Brazil, Chile and Mexico, where the output quadrupled. These countries, together with three in the next tier (Costa Rica, Colombia, and Venezuela) accounted for 95 percent of the region's scientific articles in 2001. Growth was most marked in biomedicine and physics. In the same period, the number of citations to Latin American science literature tripled.

See also **Alzate y Ramírez, José Antonio de; Ameghino, Florentino; Astronomy; Barreda, Gabino; Cruz, Oswaldo Gonçalves; Diseases; Hernández (Fernández) de Córdoba, Francisco; Malaspina, Alejandro; Mutis, José Celestino; Positivism; Sigüenza y Góngora, Carlos de; Technology.**

BIBLIOGRAPHY

Colonial Science

Amaya, José Antonio. *Mutis, apóstol de Linneo*, 2 vols. Bogotá: ICAHN, 2005.

Barrera-Osorio, Antonio. *Experiencing Nature: The Spanish American Empire and the Early Scientific Revolution*. Austin: University of Texas Press, 2006.

Cañizares-Esguerra, Jorge. "Iberian Colonial Science." *Isis* 96 (2005): 64–70.

Engstrand, Iris H. W. *Spanish Scientists in the New World: The Eighteenth-Century Expeditions*. Seattle: University of Washington Press, 1981.

Gerbi, Antonello. *Nature in the New World from Christopher Columbus to Gonzalo Fernández de Oviedo*. Pittsburgh, PA: University of Pittsburgh Press, 1985.

González Claverán, Virginia. *La expedición científica de Malaspina en Nueva España, 1789–1794*. Mexico City: Colegio de México, 1988.

Nieto Olarte, Mauricio. *Remedios para el Imperio: La apropiación del Nuevo Mundo*. Bogotá: Instituto Colombiano de Antropología e Historia, 2000.

Sellés, Manuel, José Luis Peset, and Antonio Lafuente, eds. *Carlos III y la ciencia de la ilustración*. Madrid: Alianza, 1988.

Steele, Arthur R. *Flowers for the King: The Expedition of Ruiz and Pavón and the Flora of Peru*. Durham, NC: Duke University Press, 1964.

Varey, Simon, Rafael Chabrán, and Dora B. Wiener, eds. *Searching for the Secrets of Nature: The Life and Works of Dr. Francisco Hernández*. Stanford, CA: Stanford University Press, 2000.

Wilton Appel, John. *Francisco José de Caldas: A Scientist at Work in Nueva Granada*. Philadelphia: American Philosophical Society, 1994.

Nineteenth Century

Glick, Thomas F., Miguel Angel Puig-Samper, and Rosaura Ruiz, eds. *The Reception of Darwinism in the Iberian World*. Dordrecht and Boston: Kluwer, 2001.

Lopes, Maria Margaret. *O Brasil descobre a pesquisa científica: Os museus e as ciências naturais no sécolo XIX*. São Paulo: Hucitec, 1997.

Twentieth Century

Glick, Thomas F. "Science and Society in Twentieth-Century Latin America." In *The Cambridge History of Latin America*, vol. 6, pt. 1, 463–535. Cambridge, U.K.: Cambridge University Press, 1993.

Hill, Derek L. "Latin America Shows Rapid Rise in S&E Articles." National Science Foundation *InfoBrief* 04-336. Washington, DC, August 2004.

Mariscotti, Mario. *El secreto atómico de Huemul*, 3rd edition. Buenos Aires: Estudio Sigma, 1996.

Montserrat, Marcelo, ed. *La ciencia en la Argentina entre siglos*. Buenos Aires: Manantial, 2000.

Quevedo, Emilio, ed. *Historia social de la ciencia en Colombia*, 10 vols. Bogotá: Colciencias, 1993–1996.

Ribeiro de Andrade, Ana Maria. *Físicos, mesons e política*. São Paulo and Rio de Janeiro: Hucitec, 1998.

Schwartzman, Simon. *A Space for Science: The Development of the Scientific Community in Brazil*. University Park: Pennsylvania State University Press, 1991.

Vessuri, Hebe M. C., ed. *La ciencia académica en la Venezuela moderna*. Caracas: Acta Científica Venzolana, 1984.

THOMAS F. GLICK

SCIENCE FICTION IN LATIN AMERICA.

Science fiction (SF) is not a literary form native to the region, but many Latin American writers have utilized its creative freedom to reflect local settings and concerns. The definition of science fiction is particularly fluid in Latin America, where it overlaps considerably with horror, mystery, fantasy, and other genres.

BEGINNINGS TO THE 1950S

The eighteenth and nineteenth century precursors to modern Latin American SF used the latest technological advances, scientific theories, and speculative future possibilities, such as hot air balloons, eugenics, mesmerism, and space travel, as a framework for tales that served as vehicles for social commentary. The earliest known example is a philosophical tale of a lunar journey published in 1775 by Manuel Antonio de Rivas, a Mexican friar. The few proto-SF works published over the next century, especially in Brazil, Mexico, Argentina, and Chile, were usually styled after the scientific adventures of Verne and Flammarion and reflect a positivist faith in human perfectibility through the judicious application of science and technology.

Latin American modernism, social realism, and the avant-garde movements that bridged the nineteenth and twentieth centuries encouraged greater stylistic experimentation, and regional SF writers no longer had to look exclusively abroad for inspiration. Latin American authors who tried their hand at science fiction writing and who, by their example, emphasized literary quality and introduced horror and the fantastic to the genre include Horacio Quiroga, Amado Nervo, José Asunción Silva, Leopoldo Lugones, Clemente Palma, and Adolfo Bioy Casares.

By the late 1920s, foreign pulp magazines such as the U.S. *Amazing Stories* were becoming known in Latin America; similar local publications soon emerged, such as the Mexican *Emoción* (1934–1936) and *Los cuentos fantásticos* (1948–1953). The pulps catered to a taste for exotic locales and stirring adventure tales, but current events also provided a wealth of somber themes for stories, which far outnumbered novels, as Latin American SF writers responded to the rapid social changes brought on by industrialization and urbanization and to global events such as the Depression and the two World Wars. Authors like Jerônimo Monteiro in Brazil examined issues of national sovereignty and cultural identity in the face of continued U.S. and European hegemony. Scientific and technological advances were seen alternately as humanity's salvation (as in Francisco Urquizo's *Mi tío Juan* [1934]) and as modernization's sinister companion (Ernesto Silva Román's "El astro de la muerte" [1929]).

1950S TO THE PRESENT

SF production in Latin America remained sporadic through the first half of the twentieth century due to the dominance of realism in literature, the paucity of commercial opportunities for authors, and readers' unfamiliarity with the genre. Starting in the 1950s, however, the situation improved dramatically with the launch of several magazines (of variable quality and duration) devoted exclusively to science fiction. These publications, such as *Más Allá* (Argentina, 1953–1957) and *Fantastic* (Brazil, 1955–1960), featured translations of some of the best foreign SF alongside works by local authors. Other factors contributed to this first flourishing of Latin American SF: Gumercindo Rocha Dórea in Brazil and Marcial Souto in Argentina, visionary editors at the small SF presses GRD and Minotauro, respectively, cultivated emerging talent. The Cold War space race kindled interest in the genre, and fans began to form clubs and organize reading groups, writing workshops and conventions. SF prizes such as the David in Cuba, the Más Allá in Argentina, and the Puebla in Mexico encouraged new authors and set higher standards for the genre. Some writers, like Chile's Hugo Correa, published stories abroad. And Anglophone SF, always a strong influence on Latin American writers, was opening up to stories grounded in the humanities and social sciences, disciplines with a longer tradition in Latin American letters than the physical sciences.

Although SF output declined somewhat in the late 1980s as the publishing industry reacted to economic recessions and authoritarian regimes, there was a significant renaissance in the 1990s that continues unabated to this day. The Internet and desktop publishing allow for the cheaper and wider dissemination of texts and ideas and enable greater communication among writers and fans. More novels are being published, and some have been published abroad by major presses. Mexico, Brazil, and Argentina continue to lead the field in terms of output and consumption, followed by Cuba and Chile, but there are SF writers and organizations in every country in the region and increased activity overall.

Much of Latin American SF treats universal themes of science and society, but with a distinct regional flavor. (This was especially true both of the early social extrapolation novels and of contemporary SF, but was less the case during the "boom" of the 1960s–1980s, when there was a strong desire to follow U.S. and European models.) In conceptualizing the future, for example, Latin American utopian and dystopian works have addressed agrarian reform, race and ethnicity, local politics, religious practices, the environment, and other concerns. Alternate histories have reimagined the outcome of the European conquest and the War of the Triple Alliance. Settings range from the Amazon jungle to the Andes to the great metropolises. In Castro's Cuba, SF was actively supported by the state as a way of promoting socialist ideals. And both during and after military regimes, SF has provided ideal camouflage for critiquing authoritarianism and imagining freedoms not enjoyed in the real world.

Women are a growing presence in the field and figure among the genre's earliest practitioners. During the 1970s and 1980s, two of the most prolific and celebrated SF writers were women, Angélica Gorodischer (Argentina) and Daína Chaviano (Cuba). Although it is early to speak of a feminist movement, some Latinas (and Latinos) are challenging gender stereotypes through their SF writing.

SF criticism by scholars in Latin America is still rare, as the academy does not hold the genre in high esteem. Most critical studies have been published by academics working in the U.S. and Europe. Occasionally, a mainstream periodical will cover a local SF event or profile a writer. Many of the best histories and reviews are written by fans and independent scholars who publish on websites or in fanzines.

The vast majority of SF in Latin America is short prose; comics are also popular, and there is some poetry. Although few films can be classified as science fiction, numerous Mexican movies have mingled SF iconography with vampires and masked wrestlers. Some recent films that incorporate SF themes include Argentina's *Hombre mirando al sudeste* (Eliseo Subiela, 1986), *Moebius* (Gustavo Mosquera, 1996) and *La sonámbula* (Fernando Spiner, 1998), and Chile's *El huésped* (Coke Hidalgo, 2005).

See also **Bioy Casares, Adolfo; Gorodischer, Angélica; Literature: Brazil; Literature: Spanish America; Lugones, Leopoldo; Nervo, Amado; Palma, Clemente; Quiroga, Horacio; Silva, José Asunción.**

BIBLIOGRAPHY

Axxón: *Ciencia Ficción en Bits*. Online at http://axxon.com. ar/axxon.htm.

Baradit, Jorge. *Ygdrasil*. Santiago: Ediciones B, 2005.

Bell, Andrea L., and Yolanda Molina-Gavilán. "Introduction." In *Cosmos Latinos: An Anthology of Science Fiction from Latin America and Spain*, edited by Andrea L. Bell and Yolanda Molina-Gavilán. Middletown, CT: Wesleyan University Press, 2003.

Bioy Casares, Adolfo. *La invención de Morel*. Buenos Aires: Losada, 1940.

Causo, Roberto de Sousa. *Terra verde*. São Paulo: Cone Sul, 1999.

Chaviano, Daína. *Fábulas de una abuela extraterrestre*. Mexico City: Editorial Océano, 2002.

Ciencia Ficción Mexicana. Online at www.ciencia-ficcion. com.mx.

Fernández Delgado, Miguel Ángel, ed. *Visiones periféricas: Antología de la ciencia ficción mexicana*. Buenos Aires and Mexico City: Grupo Editorial Lumen, 2001.

Ginway, M. Elizabeth. *Brazilian Science Fiction: Cultural Myths and Nationhood in the Land of the Future*. Lewisburg, PA: Bucknell University Press, 2004.

Goorden, Bernard, and A. E. Van Vogt, eds. *Lo mejor de la ciencia ficción latinoamericana*. Barcelona: Ediciones Martínez Roca, 1982.

Molina-Gavilán, Yolanda. *Ciencia ficción en español: Una mitología ante el cambio*. Lewiston, NY: Edwin Mellen, 2002.

Monteiro, Jerônimo. *3 meses no século 81*. Rio de Janeiro: Livraria do Globo, 1947.

Porcayo, Gerardo Horacio. *La primera calle de la soledad*. Chimalistac, D.F., Mexico: Consejo Nacional para la Cultura y las Artes, 1993.

Rivas, Fray Manuel Antonio de. "Sizigias y cuadraturas lunares" [1775]. Manuscript transcribed by Miguel Ángel Fernández Delgado. *Ciencia Ficción Mexicana*, 2001. Online at www.ciencia-ficcion.com.mx/?uid=4&sec=textos.

Rocha Dórea, Gumercindo, ed. *Antologia brasileira de ficção científica*. Rio de Janeiro: Edições GRD, 1961.

Rojas, Agustín de. *El año 200*. Havana: Editorial Letras Cubanas, 1990.

Silva Román, Ernesto. "El astro de la muerte." In *El dueño de los astros*. Santiago: La Novela Nueva, 1929.

Toledano, Juan Carlos. "Ciencia-ficción cubana: El proyecto nacional del hombre nuevo socialista." Ph.D. diss., University of Miami, 2002.

Urquizo, Francisco L. *Mi tío Juan: Novela fantástica*. Mexico City: Editorial Claret, 1934.

ANDREA L. BELL

SCLIAR, MOACYR

SCLIAR, MOACYR (1937–). Moacyr Scliar (*b*. 23 March 1937), Brazilian author. Born in Pôrto Alegre, Rio Grande do Sul, Scliar studied medicine and has worked in the public health field for most of his life. As a fiction writer, he has published more than twenty books, including novels, collections of short stories, and chronicles. Many of his works have been translated into English and other languages. He has also written stories for children and short novels for young adults. A descendant of Russian Jews, Scliar is internationally recognized as having raised Jewish consciousness in Latin American fiction, focusing on the Jewish immigrant in Brazil. Scliar's writings are characterized by a subtle irony; his short stories have been widely anthologized. He has received prestigious prizes for his fiction in Brazil and elsewhere, and is known as a gifted lecturer. Scliar's works include *O carnaval dos animais* (1968; *The Carnival of Animals,* 1985); *A guerra do Bom Fim* (1972); *O exército de um homem só* (1973); *Os deuses de Raquel* (1975; *The Gods of Raquel,* 1986); *O ciclo das águas* (1977); *Mês de cães danados* (1977); *O centauro no jardim* (1980; *The Centaur in the Garden,* 1985); *A estranha nação de Rafael Mendes* (1983; *The Strange Nation of Rafael Mendes,* 1988); and *Cenas da vida minúscula* (1991). In 1998 he published a collection of short stories titled *O amante de madonna e outras histórias.* In 2002 and 2003 he was involved in a controversy with Canadian author Yann Martel, author of the Booker Prize–winning novel, *Life of Pi.* Martel claimed he was inspired to create a similar premise after reading a review of Scliar's work, *Max and the Cats* (1990). Scliar claimed Martel had abused his intellectual property rights, but he and his publishers decided not to press charges after Martel reiterated that he had been inspired by the premise only and had not actually read the book. In 2003, Scliar was named to the Brazilian Academy of Letters.

See also **Literature: Brazil.**

BIBLIOGRAPHY

Barr, Lois Baer. *Isaac Unbound: Patriarchal Traditions in the Latin American Jewish Novel.* Tempe, AZ: ASU Center for Latin American Studies, Arizona State University, 1995.

DiAntonio, Robert. "The Brazilianization of the Yiddishkeit Tradition," in *Latin American Literary Review* 17, no. 34 (July–December 1989): 40–51.

DiAntonio, Robert E., and Nora Glickman, eds. *Tradition and Innovation: Reflections on Latin American Jewish Writing.* Albany: State University of New York Press, 1993.

Glickman, Nora. "Os Voluntários: A Jewish-Brazilian Pilgrimage," in *Modern Jewish Studies* Annual 4 (1982).

Mota, Lourenço Dantas, and Benjamin Abdala Juniór. *Personae: Grandes personagens da literatura brasileira.* São Paulo: Editora SENAC, 2001.

Szklo, Gilda Salem. *O bom fim do shtetl: Moacyr Scliar* (1990).

Vieira, Nelson. "Judaic Fiction in Brazil: To Be and Not to Be Jewish," in *Latin American Literary Review* 14, no. 28 (July–December 1986): 31–45.

REGINA IGEL

SCOTT, WINFIELD

SCOTT, WINFIELD (1786–1866). Winfield Scott (*b.* 13 June 1786; *d.* 29 May 1866), U.S. army general who led the invasion and occupation of central Mexico in 1847. Scott ordered the largest amphibious landing yet attempted south of Veracruz on 9 March 1847. His troops thus avoided the fortress of San Juan de Ulúa guarding the harbor. Scott ordered his artillery to surround and bombard the city, ignoring the pleas of foreign diplomats to allow women, children, and other noncombatants to escape. He would accept no truce without unconditional surrender. By the time the city surrendered on 27 March, there were twice as many civilian as military casualties.

After Scott's army outmaneuvered General Santa Anna's troops at Cerro Gordo, the city of Puebla surrendered without opposition. The defense of Mexico City was poorly coordinated, but soldiers under Pedro María Anaya at Churubusco and young cadets defending Chapultepec fought valiantly. During the occupation of Mexico City, civilians threw stones and sniped at U.S. troops until Scott threatened to turn his artillery on the city. Word of the destruction of Veracruz was so widespread that the disturbances stopped. The Duke of Wellington considered Scott's campaign against Mexico City the most brilliant in modern warfare.

The Whig Party, which had opposed the war with Mexico, chose Scott as its candidate for president in the election of 1852, but he lost to the Democratic candidate, Franklin Pierce. Scott was later general-in-chief under President Abraham Lincoln. He is buried at West Point.

See also **Mexico, Wars and Revolutions: Mexican-American War.**

BIBLIOGRAPHY

Charles L. Dufour, *The Mexican War: A Compact History* (1968).

K. Jack Bauer, *The Mexican War, 1846–1848* (1974).

John S. D. Eisenhower, *So Far from God: The U.S. War with Mexico, 1846–1848* (1989).

Additional Bibliography

Eisenhower, John S. D. *Agent of Destiny: The Life and Times of General Winfield Scott.* New York: Free Press, 1997.

Frazier, Donald S. *The United States and Mexico at War: Nineteenth-Century Expansionism and Conflict.* New York: Macmillan Reference USA, 1998.

Levinson, Irving W. *Wars within War: Mexican Guerrillas, Domestic Elites, and the United States of America, 1846–1848.* Fort Worth: TCU Press, 2005.

Libura, Krystyna, Luis Gerardo Morales Moreno, and Jesús Velasco Márquez. *Ecos de la guerra entre México y los Estados Unidos.* Toronto: Libros Tigrillo, 2004.

D. F. STEVENS

SEAGA, EDWARD

SEAGA, EDWARD (1930–). Edward Seaga, a Jamaican politician, served as prime minister from 1980 to 1989. Born on May 28, 1930, in Boston, Massachusetts, to Jamaican parents of Christian Lebanese and Scottish origin, he received his primary and secondary education at Wolmer's Boy's School in Kingston. In 1952 he graduated with a Bachelor of Arts in social sciences from Harvard University. Upon returning to Jamaica he took up a research post at the University of the West Indies, devoting his attention to folk music and revivalist religions. He founded his own record label that produced albums of Jamaican folk and popular music. In 1959 he was nominated to the still colonial legislative council. When Jamaica became independent in 1962, he began militating in the Jamaican Labour Party (JLP) led by Alexander Bustamante. That same year he was elected member of parliament (MP) for West Kingston and became the JLP government's minister of labour and development. It was from that position that he converted the slums of West Kingston into a planned working-class community, Tivoli Gardens. This became his, and the JLP's, most loyal stronghold and guaranteed Seaga's reelection as the MP for that "garrison community" for the length of this political career.

As MP and minister of finance (1967–1972), Seaga promoted and expanded the private sector and put state organizations—the Jamaican Stock Exchange, the National Development Bank, the Agricultural Credit Bank and the Jamaican National Investment Promotion (JAMPRO) Corporation—behind this effort to encourage direct foreign and domestic investments. In the 1972 general elections, Seaga lost to Michael Manley and the People's National Party (PNP). As leader of the opposition, Seaga vehemently opposed Manley's sharp turn to the left and his increasingly close relationship with the Cuban revolutionary government. In 1980 Seaga led the JLP to a resounding defeat of the PNP and as prime minister tightened his political and economic ties to Washington. Drawing on his lifelong interest in folk music and culture, he created the Jamaica Festival, which introduced the musical styles ska and later reggae to the world. In 1989 Michael Manley, having become much more moderate, defeated Seaga and the JLP, and the PNP has held power ever since. After failing in three consecutive electoral contests, Seaga retired from active politics in 2005. That year he was appointed to a distinguished professorship at the University of the West Indies.

See also **Jamaica.**

BIBLIOGRAPHY

Munroe, Trevor. *Renewing Democracy into the Millennium: The Jamaican Experience in Perspective.* Barbados: University of the West Indies Press, 1999.

Seaga, Edward. "Revival Cults in Jamaica: Notes Towards a Sociology of Religion." *Jamaica Journal* 3, no. 2 (1969): 3–13.

Stone, Carl, and Aggrey Brown, eds. *Essays on Power and Change in Jamaica.* Kingston: Jamaica Publishing House, 1977.

ANTHONY P. MAINGOT

SEBASTIANISMO

SEBASTIANISMO. Sebastianismo, the popular beliefs surrounding the figure of the Portuguese king Sebastian (1557–1578). Even before his birth, Sebastian was heralded as *O Encoberto,* "the hidden-one," the mythical ruler who was to establish a powerful Portuguese empire. The popular reinterpretation of an apocalyptic poem, the "Trovas do Bandarra," confirmed his divine commission. The dismal outcome of his reign—his untimely death in battle, the failure of his troops to recover his body, and the loss of the Portuguese throne to the Spanish in 1580—gave rise to Sebastianist legends in Portugal and later Brazil. While some claimed that he had merely vanished to perform penances for his failures, and others that he had died but would be resurrected, supporters agreed that Sebastian would yet inaugurate the *Quinto Império,* or Fifth Empire.

Reports of his return began soon after his death, and at least four claimants appeared between 1580 and 1610. Portuguese folktales still eulogize their lost leader. Brazilian Sebastianists connected the legends with their New World experiences, and three messianic movements, in 1817, the 1830s, and the 1890s, linked their rebellions to the long-awaited king. Predictions of his return (in the year 2000) still recur in songs and popular publications.

See also **Messianic Movements: Brazil.**

BIBLIOGRAPHY

João Lúcio De Azevedo, *A evolução do sebastianismo,* 2d ed. (1947).

Mary Elizabeth Brooks, *A King for Portugal* (1964).

António Machado Pires, *D. Sebastião e o Encoberto* (1971).

Carole A. Myscofski, "Messianic Themes in Portuguese and Brazilian Literature in the Sixteenth and Seventeenth Centuries," in *Luso-Brazilian Review* 28 (1991): 77–94.

Additional Bibliography

Godoy, Marcio Honorio de. *Dom Sebastião no Brasil: Fatos da cultura e da comunicação em tempo/espaço.* São Paulo: FAPESP, 2005.

CAROLE A. MYSCOFSKI

SEBASTIAN (SEBASTIÃO) OF PORTUGAL

(1554–1578). Sebastian (Sebastião) of Portugal (*b.* 20 January 1554; *d.* 4 August 1578), king of Portugal. Camões called him "the well-born hope" of the Portuguese; his nation remembers him as "O Desejado," the Desired One; yet Sebastian also became a symbol of the disgrace the Portuguese dreaded most: loss of their independence.

Sebastian succeeded his grandfather, Dom João III of Portugal, in 1557, and assumed his powers as ruler in 1568. Educated by the Jesuits, Sebastian had acquired a taste for religion; had developed the belief that he was to be Christ's soldier; and had dedicated himself to the goal of leading a crusade to rid North Africa of the Muslims. A succession dispute in Morocco that pitted Abd-al-Malik against his nephew Sultan Al-Mutawakki provided Sebastian with the pretext for launching his crusade. After collecting a force of Portuguese, Spanish, German, and Italian mercenaries, Sebastian invaded North Africa in June 1578. On 4 August, at Al-Ksar-al-Kabir in Morocco, in what became known as the Battle of the Three Kings, Sebastian's army was crushed by a vastly superior Moroccan force. During this battle, three "kings" lost their lives: Al-Mutawakki, Abd-al-Malik, and Sebastian. Sebastian was childless; after his death the Portuguese crown passed to his aged great-uncle, Cardinal Henry, the last monarch of the house of Aviz. After Henry died in 1580, the crown passed to Philip II of Spain, who was acclaimed king of Portugal in 1581; Portugal did not regain its independence until 1640.

The death of King Sebastian left a vacuum in the Portuguese soul that was filled by the illusion that the king was not really dead and that he would return to claim his throne and initiate a new golden age. "Sebastianismo" is the longing for the return of King Sebastian, a longing that crossed the ocean to Brazil and became part of that country's popular culture.

See also **Portuguese Empire; Sebastianismo.**

BIBLIOGRAPHY

José Maria De Queirós Veloso, *D. Sebastiao, 1554–1578* (1945).

José Timóteo Montalvão Machado, *Causas da morte dos reis portugueses* (1974).

Joaquim Verissimo Serrão, *História de Portugal,* 12 vols. (1978–1990).

A. H. De Oliveira Marques, *História de Portugal,* 3 vols. (1981–1983).

M. El Fasi, "Morocco," in *Africa from the Sixteenth to the Eighteenth Century,* edited by B. A. Ogot, vol. 5 of the *UNESCO General History of Africa* (1992).

Additional Bibliography

Villacorta Baños, Antonio. *Don Sebastián, Rey de Portugal.* Barcelona: Editorial Ariel, 2001.

TOMÉ N. MBUIA JOÃO

SECHÍN ALTO.

Sechín Alto, a large complex of sites located in the Casma Valley on the north-central coast of Peru. The complex, probably once the center of a larger polity in the valley, covers 4.2 square miles and consists of four sites: Sechín Alto proper, Sechín Bajo, Taukachi-Konkán, and Cerro Sechín. The group of sites dates between 1900 and 1200 BCE All construction at the sites is stone set in mud mortar.

The main mound at Sechín Alto is the largest monumental construction for its time period in the New World, measuring 990 feet by 825 feet by 145 feet tall. Off its front face is a series of four rectangular plazas that extend 4,620 feet to the northeast. Within these rectangular plazas are three sunken circular courts. The mound and its associated plazas and courts were probably used for a variety of public ceremonial activities.

Sechín Bajo and Taukachi-Konkán contain numerous mounds, plazas, and circular courts. Some of these structures may have been used as warehouses to store commodities or as administrative buildings to monitor the movement of goods in and out of the complex. This would be a situation similar to that documented for the site of Pampa De Las Llamas-moxeke, located only a few miles to the south. Despite the similarities, the differences between the sites attest to the sophistication of early Casma Valley society. The Mound of Columns at Taukachi-Konkán features a roof, a unique feature most likely utilized for elite privacy.

Cerro Sechín is the best known of the four sites that comprise the Sechín Alto complex. Extensive excavation there has revealed a moderate-sized square building, some 175 feet on a side that is decorated on all four exterior faces with carved stones set in mud mortar. The stones, carved in a simple, realistic style, depict the results of a military engagement in which warrior figures, holding large clubs or axes, stand triumphantly over victims who have been decapitated or whose bodies have been cut into various pieces.

See also **Archaeology.**

BIBLIOGRAPHY

Burger, Richard L. *Chavin and the Origins of Andean Civilization*. London and New York: Thames & Hudson, 1992.

Maldonado, Elena. *Arqueología de Cerro Sechín*. Lima: Pontificia Universidad Católica del Perú; Fundación Volkswagenwerk, 1992.

Pozorski, Shelia, and Thomas Pozorski. *Early Settlement and Subsistence in the Casma Valley, Peru* (1987).

Pozorski, Shelia. "Theocracy vs. Militarism: The Significance of the Casma Valley in Understanding Early State Formation," in *The Origins and Development of the Andean State,* edited by Jonathan Haas et al. (1987), pp. 15–30.

Samaniego Román, Lorenzo. "El arte escultórico de Sechín, monumento arqueológico de Casma, Ancash, Perú." Ph.D. diss. Lima: Universidad Nacional Mayor de San Marcos, 1996.

SHELIA POZORSKI
THOMAS POZORSKI

SEDEÑO, ANTONIO DE (?–1539).

Antonio de Sedeño (*d.* 1539), conquistador of Tierra Firme, *adelantado* of Trinidad. In 1531 Sedeño, a *contador* of San Juan, Puerto Rico, was granted the title of *adelantado* for the island of Trinidad. Sedeño's original assault of the island with eighty men was repulsed by hostile Arawaks. In spite of the tenacity of the island's native population, a second attempt by Sedeño to conquer the island proved successful. Drawn to the wealth of the South American mainland, Sedeño proceeded to the Gulf of Paria, where he competed with Jerónimo de Alderete and Martín Nieto for conquest of the coastal region in open rebellion of the legitimate governor, Jerónimo de Ortal. The Audiencia of Santo Domingo sent its *fiscal* Juan de Frías to bring Sedeño to trial, but Sedeño captured the royal official and proceeded inland along the Orinoco River. During his escape, Sedeño was poisoned by one of his own men.

See also **Adelantado.**

BIBLIOGRAPHY

Pierre G. L. Borde, *The History of Trinidad Under Spanish Government,* vol. 1, translated by James Alva Bain (1982), esp. pp. 92–124.

Michael Anthony, *First in Trinidad* (1985), pp. 5–7.

José De Oviedo y Baños, *The Conquest and Settlement of Venezuela,* translated by Jeannette Johnson Varner (1987), esp. pp. 59–60.

MICHAEL A. POLUSHIN

SEGALL, LASAR (1891–1957).

Lasar Segall (*b.* 1891; *d.* 2 August 1957), Brazilian painter considered the pioneer of expressionism in Brazil. Born in Vilna, Lithuania, Segall moved to Berlin at the age of fifteen and studied at the Imperial Academy of Fine Arts from 1907 to 1909, the year he was expelled for participating in the Freie Sezession, an exhibition by artists opposed to official aesthetics. In 1910 he moved to Dresden to study at the Meisterschüle (Art Academy). A year later he joined the German expressionist movement, and in 1912 made his first trip to Brazil.

In Brazil from 1912 to 1914, Segall prompted controversy over expressionism when his work was displayed in 1913 at solo exhibitions in São Paulo and Campinas. In 1923 he returned to Brazil and became a citizen. His paintings of Brazilian themes (1923–1926) were exhibited in 1926 in Dresden, Stuttgart, and Berlin. From 1928 to 1932 he lived in Paris. Segall returned once again to Brazil in 1932, when he cofounded the São Paulo Society of Modern Art.

In 1935, Segall completed a series of Campos de Jordão landscape paintings of Brazil and his *Portraits of Lucy* series. From 1936 to 1950, he produced paintings like *Concentration Camp* (1945) that focused on such social themes as the suffering and plight of Jews in Europe. He also participated in the Brazilian People's Graphics Workshop, a collective work center for artists founded first in Mexico in 1937, producing a series of linocut and woodcut prints published in an album entitled *Mangue* (1944), in which he depicted the theme of prostitution. In 1938, he represented Brazil at the International Congress of Independent Arts (Paris) and had a solo exhibition at the Renou et Colle Gallery in Paris. In the 1940s, his work was exhibited in New York and Rio de Janeiro, and in 1951 and 1953, he had special exhibitions at the São Paulo Biennial. He died in São Paulo.

See also **Art: The Twentieth Century.**

BIBLIOGRAPHY

Pietro Maria Bardi, *Lasar Segall* (1959).

Leopoldo Castedo, *A History of Latin American Art and Architecture* (1969).

Gilbert Chase, *Contemporary Art in Latin America* (1970).

Carlos Lemos, *The Art of Brazil* (1983).

Dawn Ades, *Art in Latin America* (1989).

Additional Bibliography

Carneiro, Maria Luiza Tucci, and Celso Lafer. *Judeus e judaísmo na obra de Lasar Segall.* Cotia: Ateliê Editorial, 2004.

D'Alessandro, Stephanie, Reinhold Heller, and Vera d'Horta Beccari. *Still More Distant Journeys: The Artistic Emigrations of Lasar Segall.* Chicago: David and Alfred Smart Museum of Art, 1997.

Mattos, Cláudia Valladão de. *Lasar Segall.* São Paulo: EDUS, 1997.

MARY JO MILES

SEGUÍN, JUAN JOSÉ MARÍA ERASMO (1782–1857).

Juan José María Erasmo Seguín (*b.* 26 May 1782; *d.* 30 October 1857), Texas political figure. A merchant, farmer, and rancher, Seguín served as San Antonio postmaster and held other municipal posts in the 1810s and 1820s. During the Mexican War of Independence he apparently remained loyal to Spain.

Seguín undertook special assignments for the government. In 1821 the governor of Texas sent him to inform Moses Austin of approval of the latter's colonization plan. Elected Texas representative to the Constituent Congress of 1823–1824, Seguín spent much time in Mexico City advocating Anglo immigration to Texas.

Closely identified with the Anglos, Seguín was removed from government office at the outbreak of the Texas rebellion in 1835. Following the war he served briefly as county judge. He soon retired to rebuild his farm and ranch, where he died.

See also **Texas.**

BIBLIOGRAPHY

Jesús F. De La Teja, ed., *A Revolution Remembered: The Memoirs and Selected Correspondence of Juan N. Seguín* (1991).

Additional Bibliography

Jackson, Jack. *Los tejanos.* Stamford, CT: Fantagraphics Books, 1982.

Teja, Jesús F. de la, ed. *A Revolution Remembered: The Memoirs and Selected Correspondence of Juan N. Seguín*. Austin: State House Press, 1991.

Woods, J.M. *Don Erasmo Seguín: A Spanish Aristocrat, a Trusted Agent of Governor Martinez, a Counselor of Stephen F. Austin, and Able Deputy of the Mexican State of Texas to the National Congress, a Patriot of the Republic of Texas and a Loyal Citizen of the American Commonwealth*. San Antonio: s.n.; 1900.

JESÚS F. DE LA TEJA

Jesús F. De La Teja, ed., *A Revolution Remembered: The Memoirs and Selected Correspondence of Juan N. Seguín* (1991).

Additional Bibliography

Frazier, Donald S. *The United States and Mexico at War: Nineteenth-Century Expansionism and Conflict*. New York: Macmillan Reference USA, 1998.

Winders, Richard Bruce. *Crisis in the Southwest: The United States, Mexico, and the Struggle over Texas*. Wilmington, DE: SR Books, 2002.

JESÚS F. DE LA TEJA

SEGUÍN, JUAN NEPOMUCENO

(1806–1890). Juan Nepomuceno Seguín (*b.* 27 October 1806; *d.* 27 August 1890), Texas political and military figure. Son of the politically prominent Erasmo Seguín, he served in a number of political posts between 1829 and 1835, including *alcalde* and interim *jefe político* in 1834. Like his father, he was a strong supporter of Anglo settlement.

Seguín, a federalist, involved himself in the 1834–1835 dispute with the centralists over control of the state government. At the outbreak of the Texas revolt, he was commissioned a captain of the Texas forces, and he led the only Mexican-Texan company at the Battle of San Jacinto, 21 April 1836. In the late 1830s Seguín served as senator from Bexar County in the Texas Congress and as mayor of San Antonio.

Compromised by political enemies in early 1842, Seguín was forced to flee to Mexico, where he apparently was given a choice of joining the army or going to prison. He participated in General Adrián Woll's invasion of Texas later that year and remained in the Mexican service through the end of the Mexican-American War. He subsequently returned to San Antonio, and again entered politics in the 1850s, serving as a justice of the peace and as one of the founders of the Bexar County Democratic Party. Increasingly alienated by conditions in Texas, Seguín took his family to Nuevo Laredo, Mexico, where he lived with one of his sons until his death.

See also **Mexico, Wars and Revolutions: Mexican-American War; San Jacinto, Battle of; Texas; Texas Revolution.**

BIBLIOGRAPHY

Ida Vernon, "Activities of the Seguíns in Early Texas History," in *West Texas Historical Association Year Book* 25 (1949): 11–38.

SEGUNDO, COMPAY. *See* Compay Segundo.

SEIBAL.

Seibal, Maya archaeological site located at the great bend of the Pasión River, near the southwestern corner of Guatemala's Petén rain forest. Extensive investigations by Harvard University archaeologists from 1964 to 1968 revealed an occupation history of approximately 2,000 years, considerably older and longer than that of most Maya sites. The site's initial occupation during the Xe phase (900–600 BCE) of the early Middle Preclassic period is represented by distinctive ceramics and the remains of simple houses. The emergence of an incipient sociopolitical hierarchy (600–300 BCE), reflected in the construction of small public works, was followed during the Late Preclassic (300 BCE–150 CE) by dramatic population increases and the construction of imposing public structures, when the Seibal people developed many of the hallmarks of Maya civilization (monumental architecture, hieroglyphic inscriptions, elaborate pottery). This era of florescence was interrupted by an abrupt 150-year "hiatus" (450–600 CE), when the site was largely abandoned.

During the Late Classic period (600–771 CE) Seibal reemerged as a powerful political center, a process halted in November 735, when Ruler 3 of the Petexbatún polity, centered at the nearby site of Dos Pilas, captured the Seibal ruler Yich'ak Balam, or "Jaguar Paw," and killed him. When the Petexbatún polity broke apart during the mid-eighth century, the newly independent Seibal enjoyed unprecedented prosperity. Between 771 and 950 CE, after Maya civilization collapsed and most Maya centers were abandoned, Seibal thrived under the rulership of probable outsiders, sometimes identified as Putun Maya invaders, whose presence is marked by fine paste pottery, an art style not fully in the Classic Maya tradition, and by distinctive skeletal attributes. Yet the Maya collapse isolated Seibal politically and economically, and sometime in the late eleventh century the site was abandoned.

See also **Archaeology; Maya, The.**

BIBLIOGRAPHY

Richard E. W. Adams, "Maya Collapse: Transformation and Termination in the Ceramic Sequence at Altar de Sacrificios," in *The Classic Maya Collapse,* edited by T. Patrick Culbert (1973), pp. 133–163.

Jeremy A. Sabloff, *Excavations at Seibal, Department of Petén, Guatemala: Ceramics* (Memoirs of the Peabody Museum, Harvard University, 1975) vol. 13, no. 2.

Gordon R. Willey, "The Rise of Classic Maya Civilization: A Pasión Valley Perspective," in *The Origins of Maya Civilization,* edited by Richard E. W. Adams (1977), pp. 133–157.

Gordon R. Willey, ed., "General Summary and Conclusions," *Excavations at Seibal, Department of Petén, Guatemala* (Memoirs of the Peabody Museum, Harvard University, 1990), vol. 17, no. 4, pp. 175–276.

Additional Bibliography

Demarest, Arthur A., Prudence M. Rice, and Don S. Rice. *The Terminal Classic in the Maya Lowlands: Collapse, Transition, and Transformation.* Boulder: University Press of Colorado, 2004.

Schele, Linda, and Peter Mathews. *The Code of Kings: The Language of Seven Sacred Maya Temples and Tombs.* New York: Simon & Schuster, 1999.

KEVIN JOHNSTON

SELENA

(1971–1995). Selena (her full name was Selena Quintanilla-Pérez), a Mexican-American singer who was murdered at the age of twenty-three, had great popular success in introducing a female style to the Tejano, or Tex-Mex, musical genre. Born in Lake Jackson, Texas, on April 16, 1971, she debuted as a singer at the age of eight. She grew up in Corpus Christi, speaking only English, although her father taught her to sing in Spanish. In 1990 she and her band, Los Dinos, signed a contract with the EMI Latin company and recorded the albums *Ven Conmigo* and *Entre a mi mundo.* In 1993 they recorded a live concert that became the album *Selena Live!,* which earned Selena a Grammy Award for best Mexican-American album. In 1992 she married Chris Pérez, her band's guitarist. In February 1995 she performed at the Houston Astrodome for a crowd of fifty thousand. A few days later, on March 31, 1995, in Corpus Christi, she was shot to death by the president of her fan club. Thousands attended her funeral. Her album in English, *Dreaming of You,* released a few months after her death, sold more than two million copies in two months. *Selena,* a 1997 film based on her life, starring Jennifer Lopez, was a popular hit.

See also **Hispanics in the United States; Music: Popular Music and Dance.**

BIBLIOGRAPHY

Kantrowitz, Barbara. "A Year after Her Death, Family and Fans Are Still Haunted by Memories of Selena." *People Weekly* 45, no. 13 (April 1, 1996): 110–112.

Novas, Himilce, and Rosemary Silva. *Remembering Selena.* New York: St. Martin's Press, 1995.

ELENA MOREIRA

SELK'NAMS.

Selk'nams (also referred to as Onas) are indigenous inhabitants of the northern and eastern regions of Tierra del Fuego. The first recorded sightings of the Selk'nams indicate that they occupied the northern steppes and southern forests of the island of Tierra del Fuego, surviving on the fruits of the hunt for Guanaco, rodents, and other small mammals, as well as wild fruits, mushrooms, and mollusks gathered along the coasts. The archeological record leads anthropologists to suggest that Selk'nam occupation of Tierra del Fuego predates the separation of the island from the continent more than 11,000 years ago.

Terrestrial hunters and gatherers arrived in the Patagonian region by land during the Paleoindian phase (c. 9000 BCE), when the climactic conditions of the last Pleistocene glaciation permitted. They hunted the now extinct American horse and mylodon, as well as guanaco, puma, fox, rodents, and nandu (rhea). Between 8,500 and 6,000 years ago, during the temperate Altithermal epoch, they began to employ more specialized tools, including spears and *boleadoras,* as well as the bow and arrow.

About 5,000 to 4,500 years ago, when the Altithermal period ended and the Neoglacial period began, less favorable climatic conditions precipitated cultural changes. The wider demographic distribution and more numerous groups of hunters in the region encouraged more intensive exploitation of specific ecological zones to hunt and gather the different species available. Around 1000 CE the separation, both geographically as well as culturally, of the Selk'nams from the Tehuelches was complete.

The Selk'nams subsisted on hunting (by foot) and gathering (exclusive of maritime navigation), although they did take advantage of sources of coastal shellfish and the bounty provided by beached whales and other large sea creatures. The Selk'nams in the northern regions of the island specialized in the hunt of guanaco and rodents; those in the southeast hunted marine animals off the rocky coast; and those in the south hunted guanaco. Organized in small family groups with defined territorial limits, the northern Selk'nams found shelter around fires in lean-tos constructed from posts and skins, while their relatives in the colder southern regions lived in conical huts reinforced with earth as protection from the bitingly cold winds. Each local group claimed specific hunting territories and respected the rights of others.

Early European expeditioners commented on the notable lack of protective clothing, apart from occasional skin mantles (constructed to leave the right shoulder free) with the fur on the outside. While some anthropologists note a similarity between Selk'nam ceremonial and familial structures and those of the maritime Fuegian peoples (Alakalufs or Yamanas), their exclusively terrestrial orientation as well as linguistic similarity support a stronger relationship to the Tehuelches or Patagones of continental Patagonia.

When colonization of Tierra del Fuego began in the late nineteenth century, the Selk'nams numbered around 4,000; as of 1990 fewer than 50—some say only 2—of their descendants remained as a result of massive deportations, sport hunting, massacres, diseases, and other little-studied factors.

See also **Indigenous Peoples.**

BIBLIOGRAPHY

Osvaldo Silva G., *Culturas y pueblos de Chile prehispano* (1980).

Anne Chapman, *Drama and Power in a Hunting Society: The Selk'nam of Tierra del Fuego* (1982) and *Los Selk'nam: La vida de los Ona* (1986).

Museo Chileno De Arte Precolombino, *Hombres del sur: Aonikenk, Selknam, Yamana, Kaweshkar* (1987).

Additional Bibliography

Borrero, Luis Alberto. *Los selk'nam (onas): Evolución cultural en la Isla Grande de Tierra del Fuego.* Buenos Aires: Búsqueda-Yuchán, 1991.

Inda, Enrique S. *El exterminio de los Onas.* Buenos Aires: Cefomar Editora, 2005.

KRISTINE L. JONES

SELVA (ECUADOR). Selva (Ecuador), the forest regions of Ecuador. The *selva* of the coast has long been of great economic importance to Ecuador. In the early national period the *selvas* were open public zones in which mixed-blood freemen, known in Ecuador as *montuvios* (part Amerindian, African, and European), collected a variety of wild plants: *tagua* (vegetable ivory), *paja* (straw, used for weaving "Panama hats"), rubber, quinine, and cinnamon. In the late nineteenth century, great cacao estates appeared on the open lands. The labor force gravitated to cacao production, and the export of wild forest products all but ceased.

See also **Costa (Ecuador); Sierra (Ecuador).**

BIBLIOGRAPHY

Details on Ecuador's geography can be found in Preston James, *Latin America* (1986). For information on the natives of Ecuador's *selvas,* see *Handbook of South American Indians,* vol. 2, *The Andean Civilizations,* edited by Julian H. Steward (1963).

Additional Bibliography

Cerón Sularte, Benhur. *Los awa-kwaiker: Un grupo indígena de la selva pluvial del Pacífico Nariñense y el Nor-Occidente Ecuatoriano.* Quito: ABYA-YALA, 2000.

Silva, Erika. *Mushuk allpa: La experiencia de los indígenas de Pastaza en la conservación de la selva amazónica.* Quito, Ecuador: COMUNIDEC Fundación: I. AMAZANGA [Instituto Ambiental Amazónico de Ciencia y Tecnologa], 2002.

Varea, Anamaría. *Ecologismo ecuatorial*. Quito: ABYA-YALA, 1997.

RONN F. PINEO

SELVA (PERU).

SELVA (PERU). Selva (Peru), one of the three principal geographic regions of Peru, with the costa and sierra. The selva, or tropical rain forest, is located east of the Andes in an area that comprises fully two thirds of the country's total landmass, but contains only 11 percent of the population. Most of its cultivatable land and population is located in the *ceja de montaña* (eyebrow of the jungle), a subregion of broad tropical valleys along the eastern Andean foothills. Although sparsely populated, mostly by Amerindians, the selva has long loomed large in the imagination of policymakers, who historically envisioned its resources and vast space as a potential panacea for resolving the nation's chronic underdevelopment.

See also **Costa (Peru); Sierra (Peru).**

BIBLIOGRAPHY

Santos-Granero, Fernando and Frederica Barclay. *Selva Central: History, Economy, and Land Use in Peruvian Amazonia*. Washington, DC: Smithsonian Institution Press, 1998.

Schellerjup, Inge. *Los valles olvidados: Pasado y presente en la utilización de recursos en la Ceja de Selva, Perú*. Copenhagen: National Museum of Denmark, 2003.

Schellerjup, Inge. *Redescubriendo el Valle de los Chilcos: Condiciones de vida en la Ceja de Selva, Perú*. Copenhagen: National Museum of Denmark, 2005.

PETER F. KLARÉN

SEMANA DE ARTE MODERNA.

SEMANA DE ARTE MODERNA. *See* **Modern Art Week.**

SEMANA ROJA.

SEMANA ROJA. Semana Roja, a riot which swept Santiago, Chile, from 22 to 25 October 1905. Upset by the high price of food, a mass of about 20,000 to 30,000 of Santiago's poorer urban residents, including women and children, demonstrated to demand that the government rescind an import tax on Argentine meat. Some of the protestors, who had initially behaved peacefully, became unruly. When various demonstrators began to loot, the local authorities overreacted by opening fire and charging the crowds. It soon became clear that the police could not calm the situation. With the army away on maneuvers, Santiago's officials created a "white guard," consisting of members of the upper class and some of the foreign community, who brutally repressed the demonstrators until the army could return and restore order. Death toll estimates reached 250. Although this riot should have forced the upper class to recognize that it had to address the needs of the lower classes, the elites instead tended to blame the demonstration on foreigners, anarchists, and unspecified troublemakers. Conversely, the riot galvanized the working class and encouraged the formation of unions.

See also **Peru: Peru Since Independence.**

BIBLIOGRAPHY

De Shazo, Peter. *Urban Workers and Labor Unions in Chile 1902–1927* (1983), pp. 124–126.

Garcés, Mario. *Crisis social y motines populares en el 1900*. 2nd Edition. Santiago: LOM Ediciones, 2003.

Izquierdo, Gonzalo. "Octubre de 1905: Un episodio en la historia chilena," in *Historia* 13 (1976): 55–96.

Ortiz Letalier, Fernando. *El movimiento obrero en Chile, 1891–1919*. Santiago: LOM Ediciones, 2005.

WILLIAM F. SATER

SEMANA TRÁGICA.

SEMANA TRÁGICA. Semana Trágica, a period of labor unrest that shook Argentina in early January 1919. The Semana Trágica (Tragic Week) was the result of a conflict that had been brewing for quite some time. Since the Radicals had come to power in 1916, they had been courting labor for its support. This courtship created resentment among conservative and business circles. Employers were allied against the Radicals' labor policies and in 1918 even created a strikebreaking body called the Asociación Nacional de Trabajo. Discontent among workers increased in part also as a result of the poor economic situation after World War I.

The problems began outside the metallurgical plant of Talleres Metalúrgicos Pedro Vasena, where workers had been on strike since 2 December

1918. At 4:00 P.M. on 7 January, as a truck under armed guard made its way into the plant, shots were fired, and a confrontation took place between security forces and strikers. Two hours later four people were dead, and thirty were wounded. Two days later a general strike was called by FORA IX (Federación Obrera Regional Argentina) in solidarity with the metallurgical workers. The workers took to the streets very early, and clashes with security forces soon ensued, such as the one that began in a cemetery at the burial of one of the victims of the fighting on 7 January. Many were killed. In desperation, President Hipólito Irigoyen called in the army to restore order, perhaps the first time the army had been used to quell social unrest. Thousands were arrested. After the strike was crushed, civilian vigilante groups patrolled the streets for several days in a sort of witch hunt against those suspected of having instigated the strike. Among their targets were Russian Jews, who were accused of planning a Communist uprising. There are no definite figures as to the casualties. Government sources put the figures at about forty dead and several hundred wounded. On the other hand, labor sources put the death toll at over 100. The strike reflected the long-standing antagonism between labor and business.

See also **Argentina: The Twentieth Century.**

BIBLIOGRAPHY

Julio Godio, *La Semana Trágica de enero de 1919* (1972).

Edgardo J. Bilsky, *La Semana Trágica* (1981).

Enrique Díaz Araujo, *La Semana Trágica de 1919: Precedida de un estudio de los antecedentes de la inmigración y la rebelión social*, 2 vols. (1988).

Additional Bibliography

Alexander, Robert Jackson. *A History of Organized Labor in Argentina*. Westport, CT: Praeger, 2003.

Deutsch, Sandra McGee. *Las Derechas: The Extreme Right in Argentina, Brazil, and Chile, 1890-1939*. Stanford, CA: Stanford University Press, 1999.

Lvovich, Daniel. *Nacionalismo y antisemitismo en la Argentina*. Buenos Aires: Javier Vergara, Grupo Zeta, 2003.

Munck, Ronaldo, Ricardo Falcón, and Bernardo Galitelli. *Argentina: From Anarchism to Peronism: Workers, Unions, and Politics, 1855-1985*. Atlantic Highlands: Zed Books, 1987.

Rock, David. *Authoritarian Argentina: The Nationalist Movement, Its History, and Its Impact*. Berkeley: University of California Press, 1993.

Seibel, Beatriz. *Crónicas de la semana trágica: Enero de 1919*. Buenos Aires: Corregidor, 1999.

JUAN MANUEL PÉREZ

SENADO DA CÂMARA. Senado da Câmara, town council. In colonial Brazil municipal government was in the hands of the *senado da câmara*. Elected by the propertied men of status (*homens bons*), it was the smallest and most independent unit of local self-government. Similar to the Spanish *cabildo*, it was an arena where local elites fought with the Portuguese-born royal officials for control of local affairs. The first town councillors (*vereadores*) were chosen by the governor rather than elected by the people. Even when elected, the number of electors was restricted to local propertied elites and landowners. The town council was composed of the following: a president or presiding judge, an ordinary judge or a crown judge, two justices of the peace (*juiz de paz*), three aldermen (*vereadores*), and one procurator (*procurador*). The ordinary judge (*juiz ordinário*) was elected by the other councillors, but the crown judge (*juiz de fora*) was sent by the crown. The justices of the peace, aldermen, and procurators were elected once every three years by an indirect system of election, whereby local electors composed of propertied men drew up names of qualified candidates.

The town council was in charge of local justice, land disputes, and implementation of royal laws and collection of municipal taxes. The *senado da câmara* had its seat in a town or city but exercised jurisdiction over the county. The town council met in session twice weekly every Wednesday and Saturday. It had its own source of revenue and patrimony independent of public funds or the royal treasury. Rent on land and local taxes were its chief sources of income.

In important cities like São Luís de Maranhão, Rio de Janeiro, and Salvador, the town councils challenged the governor's power and succeeded in having him removed from office. During the colonial period, the town councils increased their power and independence. In emergencies the *senado da câmara* was responsible for calling upon the people to meet together to draw up local bylaws and rule on cases of petty theft, land disputes, verbal abuse, and disputes over rights of way. The crown judges meddled in municipal affairs by confirming appointments to the local *senado da câmara*. The crown judge decided who was eligible for local office, and attended council meetings and special sessions. The governors also intervened in municipal affairs by controlling nominations to government office, extending terms of office, and initiating public works.

The town councils acted as local executive agents of the government by enforcing royal laws, thus functioning as an agency of the central government. Although the governors held the town councillors responsible for the execution of their written orders, the town council was also responsible to the local elite interests for transmitting their complaints to the higher authorities. Municipal government survived the colonial period and was actively involved in the independence movement.

See also **Judicial Systems: Brazil.**

BIBLIOGRAPHY

Charles R. Boxer, *Portuguese Society in the Tropics: The Municipal Councils of Goa, Macao, Bahia, and Luanda, 1510–1800* (1965).

Caio Prado, Jr., *The Colonial Background of Modern Brazil* (1971).

Additional Bibliography

Fragoso, João Luís Ribeiro, Maria Fernanda Bicalho, and Maria de Fátima Gouvêa. *Antigo Regime nos trópicos: A dinâmica imperial portuguesa, séculos XVI-XVIII.* Rio de Janeiro: Civilização Brasileira, 2001.

PATRICIA MULVEY

SENDERO LUMINOSO. *See* **Peru, Revolutionary Movements: Shining Path.**

SENDIC, RAÚL (1925–1989). Raúl Sendic (*b.* 1925; *d.* 28 April 1989), Uruguayan politician and guerrilla leader. As a prominent young socialist, Sendic worked as a legal adviser for rural labor unions in the northern region of Uruguay during the late 1950s. In 1961, he participated in the foundation of the sugarcane workers' union.

Due to the lack of response from political institutions to the workers' request for land distribution, Sendic became disappointed with legal procedures as a means to achieve social justice. Starting in 1962, Sendic and other members of the Uruguayan left formed the National Liberation Movement, Tupamaros, one of Latin America's most important urban guerrilla organizations. As a Tupamaro leader, Sendic was captured in December 1964, released, and captured again in 1970. In September 1971 he escaped in a massive jail break. In September 1972, Sendic was shot in the face and captured and the Tupamaros were destroyed by the armed forces. For twelve years Sendic was imprisoned and tortured at various military units. In 1985 Sendic and other Tupamaro leaders were freed by an amnesty granted by the new democratic government. After 1985, Sendic remained a leader of the Tupamaros, as they reentered the political arena on peaceful and legal terms. As a consequence of his torture, Sendic became sick with Charcot's disease and died in France in 1989. While in prison he wrote *Cartes desde la prisión* (1984) and *Reflexiones sobre política económica: Apuntes desde la prisión* (1984).

See also **Guerrilla Movements.**

BIBLIOGRAPHY

Arturo C. Porzecanski, *Uruguay's Tupamaros: The Urban Guerrilla* (1973).

Luis Costa Bonino, *Crisis de los partidos tradicionales y movimiento revolucionario en el Uruguay* (1985).

Additional Bibliography

Blixen, Samuel. *Sendic.* Montevideo: Ediciones Trilce, 2000.

ASTRID ARRARÁ

SENZALA. Senzala, the slave quarters on Brazilian plantations during the colonial period and the Empire. Typically a long, one-story building, the *senzala* was divided into a series of separate units, each housing four or five individual slaves or an entire slave family. The *senzala* frequently formed one side of a rectangular compound of buildings that included workshops, a waterwheel or mill, storage sheds, and even the Casa Grande of the plantation owner. In this way, the planter or his foreman could readily observe slaves and their daily comings and goings; proximity made clandestine activity or flight more difficult. On large plantations on which a single *senzala* could not house all the slaves, additional slave quarters were built outside but near the central compound. Some descriptions indicate that many slaves were housed dormitory-style, with single women and men separately housed in two large rooms. One practical nineteenth-century coffee planter urged building a veranda the length of the *senzala* so that slaves could visit one another in rainy weather without getting soaked and risking illness.

See also **Fazenda, Fazendeiro.**

BIBLIOGRAPHY

Francisco Peixoto De Lacerda Werneck, *Memória sobre a fundação de uma fazenda na província do Rio de Janeiro,* edited by Eduardo Silva (1847; 1985).

Stuart B. Schwartz, *Sugar Plantations in the Formation of Brazilian Society: Bahia, 1550–1835* (1985), esp. pp. 135–136.

Stanley J. Stein, *Vassouras: A Brazilian Coffee Country, 1850–1900* (1985).

Additional Bibliography

Araújo, Ricardo Benzaquen de. *Guerra e paz: Casa-Grande & Senzala e a obra de Gilberto Freyre nos anos 30.* Rio de Janeiro: Editora 34, 1994.

Slenes, Robert W. *Na senzala, uma flor: Esperanças e recordações na formação da família escrava: Brasil Sudeste, século XIX.* Rio de Janeiro: Editora Nova Fronteira, 1999.

SANDRA LAUDERDALE GRAHAM

SEOANE, MANUEL (1900–1963). Manuel Seoane (*b.* 1900; *d.* 10 September 1963), Peruvian journalist, author, and politician, one of the most conspicuous leaders of the Aprista Party. Born in Lima, Seoane was educated in a Jesuit school and at San Marcos University. In 1922 he was elected vice president of the Student Federation led by Víctor Raúl Haya De La Torre. In 1924, President Augusto B. Leguía deported Seoane to Buenos Aires, where he engaged in journalism. After the fall of Leguía, Seoane returned to Lima to found the newspaper *La Tribuna* and to activate the Aprista political campaign for the 1931 elections. Elected deputy for the Constituent Assembly, he was forced into exile by President Luis M. Sánchez Cerro in 1932.

Seoane lived mostly in exile until 1945, when he was elected senator for Lima and vice president of the Chamber of Senators. General Manuel Odría exiled him again after the 1948 coup against President Bustamante y Rivero, who had governed with initial Aprista support. Although Seoane criticized Haya on several ideological and political points in 1954 and 1957, he participated once more as first vice-presidential candidate in the nullified elections of 1962. Retired from politics, he died in Washington, D.C., while working for the Alliance for Progress.

See also **Peru, Political Parties: Peruvian Aprista Party (PAP/APRA).**

BIBLIOGRAPHY

Manuel Seoane, *Nuestros fines* (1931).

Frederick Pike, *The Politics of the Miraculous in Peru: Haya de la Torre and the Spiritualist Tradition* (1986).

Additional Bibliography

Castro Contreras, Jaime. *Violencia política y subversión en el Perú, 1924–1965.* Lima: Editorial "San Marcos," 1992.

ALFONSO W. QUIROZ

SEPP, ANTON (1655–1733). Anton Sepp (*b.* 21 November 1655; *d.* 13 January 1733), Tyrolean-born Jesuit active in the missions of Paraguay. Of noble birth, Sepp dedicated himself early to various scholarly pursuits. For a time, he taught rhetoric at Augsburg. Then, in 1674, he entered the Society of Jesus, hoping to be sent to missionary fields in South America. Being a non-Spaniard, however, Sepp encountered many obstacles in securing permission to travel in the New World. Only in 1690 was permission finally granted.

A cloud of unwarranted suspicion followed Sepp throughout his labors. He spent forty-one years in the Jesuit *reducciones* of Paraguay, yet he never held high office, nor was his ordination as priest ever confirmed. Still, he had a claim on being the most important cleric in the lives of thousands of Guaraní Indians. His talent and energy seemed boundless. He founded one major mission, San Juan Bautista, in 1698. He designed buildings for several more missions, and organized workshops for the manufacture of musical instruments. He wrote poetry, sermons, and musical compositions that became well known in the region. The schools that he operated at Yapeyú gave the Indians access to many aspects of Western culture. The Indians, in turn, made the Jesuit missions so prosperous and so famous that Voltaire later described them as a sort of Utopia in his classic, *Candide*.

Sepp's own role in giving life to this image was revealed in a series of copious letters he wrote to European relatives. These were published in two volumes between 1696 and 1709, and still constitute a key source for historians studying the Jesuit missions. Sepp died at San José, in what later became the Argentine Misiones.

See also **Missions: Jesuit Missions (Reducciones).**

BIBLIOGRAPHY

Efraím Cardozo, *Historiografía paraguaya* (1959), pp. 263–270.

Philip Caraman, *The Lost Paradise* (1976), pp. 120–122, 134–136, 140–143, 150–155, and *passim*.

Additional Bibliography

Abou, Sélim. *The Jesuit "Republic" of the Guaranís (1609-1768) and Its Heritage.* New York: Crossroad Pub. Co., 1997.

Reiter, Frederick J. *They Built Utopia: The Jesuit Missions in Paraguay, 1610–1768.* Potomac: Scripta Humanistica, 1995.

Techo, Nicholás del, Manuel Serrano y Sanz, and Bartomeu Meliá. *Historia de la provincia del Paraguay de la compañía de Jesús.* Asunción: Centro de Estudos Paraguayas Antonio Guasch: FONDEC, 2005.

THOMAS L. WHIGHAM

SEPÚLVEDA, JUAN GINÉS DE

(c. 1490–1573). Juan Ginés de Sepúlveda (*b.* ca. 1490; *d.* 1573), Spanish humanist. "The most strident champion of Spanish imperialism," to quote Anthony Pagden, Sepúlveda translated Aristotle, supported the idea of universal monarchy, and wrote a number of works, including *Democrates alter* (or *secundus*, published 1780), which strongly defended the rights of the Castilian crown in the New World. He is best known for his opposition to the Dominican friar Bartolomé de Las Casas in "the Spanish struggle for justice" in the mid-sixteenth century. In contrast with Las Casas and the theologians of Salamanca,

Sepúlveda believed that the Aristotelian doctrine of natural aristocracy and natural servitude justified the Spanish conquest of the Indies and wars against the native populations. He also believed that the conquest of the natives was an act of charity, for it brought them the benefits of civilization, religion, and trade with Spain. The colonists' exploitation of native labor, thus, was justified. Not surprisingly, the conquistadores and early settlers considered Sepúlveda their champion.

See also **Slavery: Indian Slavery and Forced Labor.**

BIBLIOGRAPHY

Lewis Hanke, *All Mankind Is One: A Study of the Disputation Between Bartolomé de Las Casas and Juan Ginés de Sepúlveda in 1550 on the Intellectual and Religious Capacity of the American Indians* (1974).

Anthony Pagden, *Spanish Imperialism and the Political Imagination: Studies in European and Spanish-American Social and Political Theory 1513–1830* (1990).

Additional Bibliography

Castañeda, Felipe. *El indio, entre el bárbaro y el cristiano: Ensayos sobre filosofía de la conquista en Las Casas, Sepúlveda y Acosta.* Bogotá: Ediciones Uniandes, Departamento de Filosofía: Alfaomega Colombiana, 2002.

MARK A. BURKHOLDER

SERDÁN, AQUILES

(1876–1910). Aquiles Serdán Alatriste, an early agitator in the Mexican Revolution, was born in Puebla on November 2, 1876. His father was Manuel Serdán Guanes, founder of the Mexican Socialist Party and co-author of Ley del Pueblo (The People's Law), and his grandfather was Miguel Cástulo Alatriste, governor of Puebla, an attorney, and a distinguished military man. Both father and grandfather were liberals and fought the invading French army in 1862.

Beginning in mid-1909 Serdán, a follower of the revolutionary Francisco I. Madero, actively opposed the reelection of Porfirio Díaz. He enlisted large contingents of workers, peasants, and students for the cause; because of these activities he was persecuted and held for a time in prison. When Madero was captured and Díaz consequently reelected, the opposition called for revolution. Serdán participated by directing preparations in his native state. He prepared a plan of attack and obtained an arsenal but was discovered; he died on November 19, 1910, defending his center of operations. Serdán was one of the first victims of the revolutionary cause.

See also **Díaz, Porfirio; Madero, Francisco Indalecio; Mexico, Wars and Revolutions: Mexican Revolution.**

BIBLIOGRAPHY

Frías Olvera, Manuel. *Aquiles de México.* Mexico: Biblioteca del Instituto Nacional de Estudios Históricos de la Revolución Mexicana, 1978

Gilly, Adolfo. *The Mexican Revolution,* expanded and rev. edition, trans. Patrick Camiller. New York: New Press, 2005.

LAURA ROJAS HERNÁNDEZ

SEREBRIER, JOSÉ (1938–). José Serebrier (*b.* 3 December 1938), Uruguayan composer and conductor. Of Russian and Polish descent, Serebrier was born in Montevideo, where he studied violin with Juan Fabbri. At Montevideo's Municipal School of Music his instructors were Miguel Pritsch (violin) and Vicente Ascone (harmony). He also took lessons in composition, fugue, and counterpoint with Guido Santórsola, and piano with Sarah Bourdillon. After attending counterpoint and composition classes at the National Conservatory with Carlos Estrada, he moved to the United States to enter the Curtis Institute in Philadelphia (1956), where he studied composition under Vittorio Giannini. He has resided in the United States ever since. Serebrier attended Aaron Copland's classes at Tanglewood, and Antal Dorati and Pierre Monteux coached him in conducting. When he was only seventeen he was chosen by Leopold Stokowski to be associate conductor of the American Symphony Orchestra (1962–1967). He received scholarships and grants from the Organization of American States, and the Guggenheim, Rockefeller, and Koussevitsky foundations. Serebrier served as conductor of the Utica Symphony (1960–1962) and composer-in-residence with the Cleveland Orchestra (1968–1971). At eighteen Serebrier composed his *Leyenda de Fausto Overture,* which won the Uruguayan National Award. He experimented with mixed media, adding lighting to his works, as in *Colores mágicos,* premiered by him at the Fifth Inter-American Music Festival in Washington, D.C., in 1971. In his later works, he explored more advanced composition techniques.

Since 1989 Serebrier has conducted the Scottish Chamber Orchestra and frequently has been guest conductor of the Royal Philharmonic. Many of his compositions have been performed, among them Concerto for Violin and Orchestra (Winter), which premiered March 1994 in New York and which he later recorded with the Royal Philharmonic. In addition to his recordings, Serebrier also has numerous film scores to his credit. In 1984 he founded the Miami Music Festival. He is the recipient of the Alice Ditson Award for his achievements in contemporary music. In 1995 his violin concerto, *Winter,* premiered in New York. It received wide critical acclaim and has since been performed in London and Madrid. In 2001 French music critic Michel Faure published a new biography about his life and work. In 2004 he received a Grammy nomination for Best New Composition with his *Symphonie Mystique.* That same year, his arrangement of Bizet's music into the *Carmen* symphony won the Latin Grammy for Best Classical Album. In 2005, he released his first recording with the New York Philharmonic Orchestra. He conducts and records frequently in the United States and London.

See also **Music: Art Music.**

BIBLIOGRAPHY

Faure, Michel. *José Serebrier: Un chef d'orchestre et compositeur a l'aube du XXIéme siecle: Propos et textes receueillis, traduits et annotés, discographie complete.* Paris: L'Harmattan, 2001.

Salgado, Susan. *Breve historia de la música culta en el Uruguay,* 2d ed. (1980).

Vinton, John, ed. *Dictionary of Contemporary Music* (1974); *New Grove Dictionary of Music and Musicians* (1980).

SUSANA SALGADO

SEREGNI, LÍBER (1917–2004). Líber Seregni (*b.* 3 December 1917; *d.* July 2004), Uruguayan military leader and politician. The son of an anarchist father, Seregni opted paradoxically for a military career and achieved the rank of general.

Toward the end of his military career, he was known to be sympathetic to progressive elements in the Colorado Party. By 1971 he had distanced himself from this position to become a founding member and presidential candidate of the Frente Amplio, receiving 18 percent of the national vote. With the coup d'état of 1973, the leftist coalition and its political leaders were outlawed. Seregni was imprisoned until 1984.

Both in freedom and from prison, Seregni was a central proponent of democratization. He defended the blank ballot in the internal elections of 1982, which left the Frente outlawed. He later promoted and supported the strategy of negotiation that led to the legalization of many of the Frente's political forces and from which came the final formula for the democratic movement. Prevented from running for president in the November 1984 elections, Seregni assumed the presidency of the Frente Amplio. He did run for president of Uruguay again in 1989 and received 21 percent of the vote. In February 1996 he resigned his presidency of the Frente Amplio in the wake of a controversy over party reforms. He also founded the Center for Strategic Studies in 1815. The center, which he dissolved in 2004, was meant to study government activities and programs. He died in Montevideo in July 2004.

See also **Uruguay, Political Parties: Colorado Party.**

BIBLIOGRAPHY

Aguirre, Miguel. *El Frente Amplio* (1985).

Barros Lemes, Alvaro. *Seregni* (1989).

Butazzoni, Fernando. *Seregni–Rosencof: Mano a mano.* Montevideo, Uruguay: Aguilar, 2002.

Caetano, Gerardo. *Colección Líber Seregni.* 2 Vols. Montevideo, Uruguay: Taurus, 2005–2006.

Seregni, Liber, and Blanca Rodríguez. *El correo del General: Correspondencia de Gral. Líber Seregni a su esposa, Lily Lerena, escrita en su primera prisión (9/7/73 a 2/11/74).* Montevideo, Uruguay: Aguilar, 2004.

FERNANDO FILGUEIRA

SERGIPE. Sergipe (formerly Sergipe Rei), one of Brazil's easternmost states, whose capital is Aracaju. With an area of 8,490 square miles, roughly half of which is classified as Caatinga, Sergipe is the smallest Brazilian state. According to the Fundação Instituto Brasileiro de Geografia e Estatística (Brazilian Institute of Geography and Statistics), approximately 75 percent of its 2004 population of 1,712,786 people are of mixed racial origin. About 50 percent of the total population are urban dwellers, but agricultural products (including tobacco, cotton, rice, sugar, beans, coconut, and livestock), nevertheless, dominate the economy. The state possesses some mineral and oil reserves.

Indigenous peoples occupied the region that is now Sergipe until well beyond the mid-1500s, but the Portuguese, plagued by a risky sea route and by a strong French presence along the Brazilian coast, needed a secure hold over the Rio São Francisco and the surrounding area. Portuguese conquest commenced in 1589 when the crown, temporarily abrogating a 1587 law forbidding attacks on Indian populations, granted permission to wage a "just" war. By early 1590, the Portuguese controlled most of the territory.

In the 1700s, Bahian cattle ranchers and sugar planters settled the region. Originally a dependency of Bahia, Sergipe became an independent captaincy in 1821, a province of the empire (provincial capital São Cristovão) in 1824, and a state of the republic in 1889. The state continues to fall under Bahia's influence politically and economically.

As with other states in the northeast, Sergipe was invaded numerous times by the Dutch and frequently raided by French buccaneers. During the 1600s the state was known throughout the Americas for its kingwood, a prized commodity that was the primary attraction in the buccaneer raids and probably a factor in Dutch military expeditions. By the 1700s the Portuguese military had driven off the pirates permanently.

In the 1930s Sergipe became infamous for its outlaws, one of whom was Virgolino Ferreira da Silva, better known as Lampião, the "King of Bandits." He terrorized Sergipe for nearly a decade before he was beheaded by the Brazilian police in 1938. Subsequently, his head was placed on a pole in a village square.

See also **Brazil, Geography.**

BIBLIOGRAPHY

Luiz R. B. Mott, *Sergipe del Rey: População, economia e sociedade* (1986).

Additional Bibliography

Alves, Amy A. C. Faria. *De gente a gente só tem o nome: A mulher no sistema penitenciário em Sergipe*. São Cristóvão, Brazil: Editora Universidade Federal de Sergipe, 2001.

Dantas, José Ibarê Costa. *História de Sergipe: República (1889–2000)*. Rio de Janeiro: Tempo Brasileiro, 2004.

Jan Hoffman, French. "A Tale of Two Priests and Two Struggles: Liberation Theology from Dictatorship to Democracy in the Brazilian Northeast." *The Americas* 63, no.3 (January 2007): 409–443.

Milliet de Saint-Adolphe, J. C. R. *Dicionário da província de Sergipe*. São Cristóvão, Brazil: Editora UFS, 2001.

Monteiro, John M. *Guia de fontes para a história indígena e do indigenismo em arquivos brasileiros: Acervos das capitais*. São Paulo, Brazil: Núcleo de História Indígena e do Indigenismo, 1994.

Santos, Fábio Alves dos. *Começo de mundo novo: Sofrimento, luta e vitória dos posseiros de Santana dos Frades, Sergipe*. Petrópolis, Brazil: Vozes, 1990.

CARA SHELLY

SERINGAL.

A *seringal*, or rubber estate, is a large tract of Amazonian rain forest usually located on a river to facilitate the transport of rubber to market. Although land titles were easy to come by after the rubber boom began in the 1840s, they were often ill-defined, and battles were often fought over ownership of the *seringal*. The owner, or *seringalista*, often lived in Manaus, while agents or lessees (usually in debt to the rubber baron) ran their vast estates. Rubber barons kept gatherers on their *seringais* through a system of debt peonage. After World War II, the large rubber estates began to break up, and many *seringalistas* abandoned or sold their estates. Many rubber gatherers have remained on the land and continue to collect rubber from the trees.

See also **Rubber Industry.**

BIBLIOGRAPHY

Barbara Weinstein, *The Amazon Rubber Boom, 1850–1920* (1983).

Austin Coates, *The Commerce in Rubber: The First 250 Years* (1987).

Warren Dean, *Brazil and the Struggle for Rubber* (1987).

Additional Bibliography

Costa, Francisco de Assis. *Grande capital e agricultura na Amazonia: A experiencia Ford no Tapajós*. Belém: Editorial Universitaria UFPA, 2003.

Ferreira, Maria Liege Frietas. *O poder de arregimentaçao do estado: A utopia nos seringais amazonicos (1940-1945.)* Curitiba: Aos Quatro Ventos, 2003.

Rodrigues, Gomercindo and Linda Rabben. *Walking the Forest with Chico Mendes: Struggle for Justice in the Amazon*. Austin: University of Texas Press, 2007.

CAROLYN JOSTOCK

SERINGUEIROS.

The Industrial Revolution created the demand, and the process of vulcanization the means, to exploit Brazil's unique Amazonian seringueiras (rubber trees). For centuries, indigenous Amazonians had collected rubber from the trees to make items such as water bags. But the rubber boom that began in the 1880s created an extractive industry in which seringalistas (rubber barons) achieved control of the forest through the forced labor of indigenous people, local mestiços and poverty-stricken migrants.

Each *seringueiro* (rubber tapper) family received up to 200 trees to tend. They carved trails in the forest to reach distant trees and tap the latex, the white sap that dipped from shallow cuts in the bark into cups hung below. Collecting the liquid, they formed it into large balls using the heat of wood fires. The balls became currency used to pay the *seringalistas,* at inflated prices, for housing, food, and fuel. Most fell into a cycle of debt designed to tie them to the *seringalistas.* Despite abuse and debt-peonage, rubber-tapping provided a livelihood that was relatively secure for the *seringueiros* given the lack of alternative employment in Brazil's northern and northeastern regions.

By World War I the Brazilian rubber market had collapsed and many *seringueiros* fled the rubber estates. During World War II, however, the demand for Brazilian rubber surged and the government impressed into service more than 54,000 "rubber soldiers," receiving payment for each from the U.S. government. When the war boom subsided, some *seringueiros* stayed on to control their own rubber trails and produce at a subsistence level for existing markets.

In the 1970s the *seringueiros* organized unions to defend themselves against government colonization schemes and investors from the south. Unionized *seringueiros* attracted international attention as defenders of a forest endangered by destructive development projects designed to reap quick profits through exotic wood extraction, gold mining, cattle grazing, and soybean cultivation.

To preserve their environmentally sustainable way of life, *seringueiros* joined ranks with indigenous people and ecologists to establish extractive reserves. The first was named in 1990 to honor Chico Mendes, a second-generation rubber tapper who personified the *seringueiro* struggle internationally until murdered by a cattle rancher in 1988. Studies have concluded that the extractive reserves have worked to raise *seringueiro* income and preserve portions of the Amazon rain forest.

See also **Mendes Filho, Francisco "Chico" Alves; Rubber Gatherers' Unions; Rubber Industry.**

BIBLIOGRAPHY

Dean, Warren. *Brazil and the Struggle for Rubber: A Study in Environmental History.* Cambridge, U.K., and New York: Cambridge University Press, 1987.

Revkin, Andrew. *The Burning Season: The Murder of Chico Mendes and the Fight for the Amazon Rain Forest.* Washington, DC: Island Press, 2004.

Weinstein, Barbara. *The Amazon Rubber Boom, 1850-1920.* Stanford, CA: Stanford University Press, 1983.

CLIFF WELCH

SERRA, JUNÍPERO (1713–1784). Junípero Serra (*b.* 24 November 1713; *d.* 28 August 1784), Franciscan missionary in New Spain. The founder of Mission San Diego de Alcalá, Serra was born in Petra, on the Spanish island of Mallorca, to Antonio and Margarita Ferrer de Serra. Christened Miguel José, he attended a Franciscan primary school in Petra until age fifteen, when he traveled to Palma, the capital of Mallorca, to study theology. Serra took the name Junípero upon joining the Order of Friars Minor (Franciscans) in 1730; he was ordained a priest in 1738. Serra received a doctorate in theology in 1742 and served as a professor of philosophy at Palma's Lullian University until 1749, when he decided to leave Spain and become a missionary among the Indians in the Americas.

Serra began his new career in 1750, working among the natives in the Sierra Gorda region north of Mexico City until 1758. He then returned to the Mexican capital and, although suffering at times from asthma and a painful leg injury, assumed the duties of a traveling missionary priest. In 1768 Serra was placed in charge of former Jesuit missions in Baja (Lower) California, and from there helped plan the occupation of Alta (Upper) California.

Serra, at age fifty-six, accompanied a Spanish overland expedition led by Gaspar de Portolá that reached San Diego in the summer of 1769 and founded the first mission there on 16 July. His second mission, San Carlos Borromeo, founded at Monterey on 3 June 1770, served, with the adjoining presidio, as capital of California. The Franciscans, under Serra's direction as father president for the next fourteen years, founded nine missions; taught the Indians Christian doctrine, agricultural techniques, pottery making, and other useful arts; and helped in the settlement of California.

Serra served and protected the Indians until his death at Mission San Carlos Borromeo, by then located on the Carmel River. Because of his accomplishments and exemplary life, he is known as "the Apostle of California." He was declared venerable by Pope John Paul II in May 1986, beatified in Rome on 25 September 1988, and is under consideration for canonization as a saint.

Serra's treatment of his Indian charges is a topic that has aroused much debate. Native Americans claim he enslaved their ancestors. It must be admitted that the mission system did at times result in harsh treatment of Native Americans. Attracted to the missions with offerings of food and gifts, they were given religious instruction, but they also were often pressed into arduous work in the fields. Unmarried Indians were housed separately by sex and punished for attempting to leave the mission or for other infractions. Punishments included whipping and shackling—common disciplinary measures in the eighteenth century. European diseases spread through the confined areas and killed many Native Americans. The natural hunting-and-gathering economy and loose social organization of the Indians were replaced by a more structured, paternalistic administration. Serra's defenders claim that despite its failings, the Spanish mission system was humanitarian in its intent and sought to prepare Indians to live a settled, church-oriented, European way of life. Serra followed the teachings of his order and the goals of Catholic Spain. The California missions prospered and paved the way for a lasting agricultural economy on the Pacific Coast.

See also **Missions: Spanish America.**

BIBLIOGRAPHY

Francisco Palóu, O.F.M., *Palóu's Life of Fray Junípero Serra,* translated and edited by Maynard J. Geiger, O.F.M. (1945).

Junípero Serra, O.F.M., *Writings,* 4 vols. edited by Antonine Tibesar, O.F.M. (1955–1966).

Maynard Geiger, O.F.M., *The Life and Times of Fray Junípero Serra,* 2 vols. (1959).

Francis J. Weber, "California's Serrana Literature," in *Southern California Quarterly* 51 (1969): 325–342.

Iris H. W. Engstrand, *Serra's San Diego* (1982).

Don De Nevi and Noel Francis Moholy, O.F.M., *Junípero Serra* (1985).

Martin J. Morgado, *Junípero Serra: A Pictorial Biography* (1991).

Additional Bibliography

Oltra Perales, Enrique. *El beato fray Junípero Serra: Misiones y misioneros en la Alta California (1769–1823).* Valencia: Unión Misional Franciscana, 2004.

Sandos, James A. *Converting California: Indians and Franciscans in the Missions.* New Haven, CT: Yale University Press, 2004.

IRIS H. W. ENGSTRAND

SERRA DO MAR. Serra Do Mar, a thousand-mile escarpment that runs from northern Río Grande do Sul into Espírito Santo. In many places the Serra do Mar rises straight from the sea, itself forming the coastline. The sharpness of its peaks and the dense rain forest combine to form an almost impenetrable barrier from the Brazilian plateau to the sea. During the early colonial period it was a great obstacle to trade and commerce between the coast and São Paulo. The highest peak is the Pedra do Sino, which reaches 7,323 feet. The greatest rainfall in the country occurs on the escarpment near São Paulo.

Amerindians had long known about passages through the Serra do Mar and taught the European colonists about them. In 1790 a stone road was built across the Serra, but it was not kept in repair and eventually deteriorated until unsafe for use. A franchise was granted in 1840 to Thomas Cochrane, an Englishman, to build a railroad across the escarpment, but difficulties in financing and engineering delayed completion of the project until 1863. The abundant waters along the Serra do Mar contributed to the industrialization of Rio de Janeiro and São Paulo during the late nineteenth century.

See also **Brazil, Geography.**

BIBLIOGRAPHY

Sergio Buarque De Holanda, *História geral da civilização brasileira* (1967).

Additional Bibliography

Gallindo Leal, Carlos and Ibsen de Gusmão Camara. *The Atlantic Forest of South America: Biodiversity Status, Threats, and Outlook.* Washington, DC: Island Press, 2003.

The Rainforest of the Serra do Mar: Degradation and Reconstitution. São Paulo: The Secretariat, 1990.

SHEILA L. HOOKER

SERRANO, JOSÉ (1634–1713). José Serrano (*b.* 1634; *d.* 1713), Spanish missionary and translator. Serrano, born in Andalusia, entered the Society of Jesus and arrived in the Río de la Plata in 1658. In order to be appointed parish priest in the reductions, he had to take an examination in the Guaraní language. He passed the examination, and began mission work in 1665. Serrano is credited with the translation of two Spanish books into the Guaraní language: *De la diferencia entre lo temporal y eternal,* by Jesuit Juan Eusebio Nieremberg, and *Flos sanctorum.* The former was subsequently published and printed with illustrations in 1705, the first book printed in Argentina. Serrano was the rector of the Jesuit college in Buenos Aires in 1696. He died in the Guaraní mission town of Loreto.

See also **Jesuits; Missions: Jesuit Missions (Reducciones).**

BIBLIOGRAPHY

Santos Hernández, Angel. *Los Jesuitas en América.* Madrid: Editorial MAPFRE, 1992.

NICHOLAS P. CUSHNER

SERRANO ELÍAS, JORGE ANTONIO

(1945–). Jorge Antonio Serrano Elías (*b.* 26 April 1945), president of Guatemala (1991–1993), the first active Protestant to be elected president of a Latin American nation. Born in Guatemala City and educated at the University of San Carlos and at Stanford, Serrano became an evangelical Protestant in 1975. He served as president of the Council of State under the administration of General Efraín Ríos Montt (1982–1983). Serrano then formed the Solidary Action Movement (MAS) and placed third among eight candidates in the 1985 presidential election. In 1990, after the Court of Constitutionality ruled Ríos Montt ineligible for another term, most of his electoral support switched to Serrano. This propelled Serrano into the January 1991 runoff election in which he defeated National Center Union (UCN) candidate Jorge Carpio in a landslide. Serrano's administration was neoliberal and private-sector oriented. With army support, he suspended the Constitution on 25 May 1993 to quell rising social unrest. In the face of widespread domestic and international pressure, however, the military removed Serrano on 1 June 1993 and allowed the Congress to elect a successor, Ramiro de León Carpio. He now lives in Panama with his family. The Guatemalan government has made several unsuccessful attempts to have him extradited. He was linked with the 2001 Enron scandal in the United States, as investigators found that Enron made suspect payments of $17 million to a Panamanian company with close ties to Serrano.

BIBLIOGRAPHY

For a more detailed biographical sketch of Serrano, see the entry by Ralph Lee Woodward, Jr., in the *Encyclopedia of World Biography*, vol. 18, edited by David Eggenberger (1994). For a detailed overview of recent Guatemalan political history, see James Dunkerley, *Power in the Isthmus: A Political History of Modern Central America* (1988). Details of Serrano's presidential administration may be found in Howard H. Lentner, *State Formation in Central America: The Struggle for Autonomy, Development, and Democracy* (1993). For an excellent summary and analysis of Serrano's religious background, see David Stoll, "Guatemala Elects a Born-Again President," in *Christian Century* 108, no. 6 (20 February 1991): 189–190. For a perceptive interpretation of Guatemalan society and politics prior to and during the administration of Serrano, see Víctor Perera, *Unfinished Conquest: The Guatemalan Tragedy* (1993).

Dosal, Paul J. *Power in Transition: The Rise of Guatemala's Industrial Oligarchy, 1871–1994.* Westport, CT: Praeger, 1995.

García Laguardia, Jorge Mario, and Adolfo González Rodas. *Democracia y defensa constitucional.* Guatemala: Serviprensa, 1992.

McCleary, Rachel M. *Dictating Democracy: Guatemala and the End of Violent Revolution.* Gainesville: University Press of Florida, 1999.

RALPH LEE WOODWARD JR.

SERTANISTA.

Sertanista (backwoodsman), a specialist in the ways of the Sertão (undeveloped interior) of Portuguese America. Often Mamelucos (mixed bloods), these hardy backwoodsmen were fluent in the *língua geral* (vulgar Tupi-Guarani), well versed in indigenous forest lore, and indispensable to Portuguese military, slaving, and prospecting expeditions. During the seventeenth century, *sertanistas* from São Paulo gained significant notoriety for their frequent slave raids on native villages, as royal authorities, sugar planters, and cattle ranchers in the Northeast recruited them to combat recalcitrant tribes and runaway slave communities. In the northern colonies of Maranhão and Pará, *sertanistas* plied the Amazon region for Indian slaves and forest products throughout the seventeenth and eighteenth centuries.

See also **Slavery: Brazil.**

BIBLIOGRAPHY

John Hemming, *Red Gold* (1978), describes the *sertanistas'* activities in detail. Specifically on the backwoodsmen of São Paulo, Richard Morse, ed., *The Bandeirantes* (1965), provides an excellent introduction. A beautifully written Brazilian account is Sergio Buarque De Holanda, *Caminhos e fronteiras* (1957).

JOHN M. MONTEIRO

SERTÃO, SERTANEJO.

Sertanejo Sertão. Except during periodic droughts, average annual rainfall in the *sertão*—the semiarid region of Brazil extending from the interior of Minas Gerais and Bahia to the interior of Piauí and Maranhão—differs little from that of other areas; but rain tends to come in violent downpours punctuating prolonged dry spells. *Sertanejos* (inhabitants of the *sertão*), predominantly people of mixed European, Indian, and African ancestry, live as subsistence farmers, cotton sharecroppers, or ranch hands. In some contexts, *sertanejo* connotes uncouthness.

During the 1600s, the decline of coastal Indian populations and rumors of riches in the interior fueled exploration of the *sertão* by Bandeiras (armed expeditions privately organized by coastal settlements) and other *sertanistas* (backlands explorers). Cattle ranchers spearheaded settlement of the backlands in the late seventeenth and eighteenth centuries, and in the 1800s, cotton became a significant *sertão* crop.

Fazendeiros (owners of great estates) exercised broad economic, social, and political power over the majority of *sertanejos*. Among some *sertanejos,* such domination—together with poverty and weak policing mechanisms—fostered a tradition of banditry (*cangaço*) lasting until the late 1930s, when federal troops subdued the Cangaceiros. Occasionally, rebellions or movements superseded banditry, notably the followers of Antônio Conselheiro (suppressed at Canudos in 1896–1897) and the movement (ca. 1891–1934) headed by Padre Cícero Romão Batista of Joaseiro in Ceará.

In the twentieth century, leftist appeals seemed potential sparks of popular unrest; but despite the Prestes Column (1924–1927), popular-front propaganda, and the example of the Cuban Revolution, Communism failed to attract a large following in the Brazilian hinterlands.

In normal years, the *sertanejos* raise livestock and crops sufficient to feed themselves. Drought, however, leads quickly to hunger, driving tens of thousands of *flagelados* (literally, "the flagellated") or *retirantes* from the *sertão* to commercial and industrial centers and to the Amazon Basin. Government efforts to improve conditions in the *sertão* by encouraging industrial development, undertaking irrigation projects, and providing medical, educational, and other services progress slowly.

See also **Messianic Movements: Brazil.**

BIBLIOGRAPHY

Euclides Da Cunha, *Os Sertões* (1902), translated by Samuel Putnam as *Rebellion in the Backlands* (1944).

João Capistrano De Abreu, *Caminhos Antigos e o Povoamento do Brasil* (1930).

Allen W. Johnson, *Sharecroppers of the Sertão: Economics and Dependence on a Brazilian Plantation* (1971).

Joseph A. Page, *The Revolution That Never Was: Northeast Brazil, 1955–1964 (1972)*; Edinaldo G. Bastos, *Farming in the Brazilian Sertão: Social Organization and Economic Behavior* (1980).

Thomas E. Skidmore, *The Politics of Military Rule in Brazil, 1964–85* (1988).

Additional Bibliography

Caldeira, Jorge. *O banqueiro do sertão.* São Paulo: Mameluco, 2006.

Langfur, Hal. *The Forbidden Lands: Colonial Identity, Frontier Violence, and the Persistence of Brazil's Eastern Indians, 1750–1830.* Stanford, CA: Stanford University Press, 2006.

Silva, Tania Elias da, and Eliano Lopez. *Múlitplos olhares sobre o semi-arido nordestino: Sociedade, desenvolvimiento, políticas públicas.* Aracaju: Fundação de Amparo à Pesquisa do Estado de Sergipe, FAP, 2003.

CARA SHELLY

SERVICE FOR PEACE AND JUSTICE (SERPAJ).

Service for Peace and Justice (SERPAJ), international organization dedicated to promoting justice through active nonviolence. Founded in 1974 in Buenos Aires, by a group of Catholic activists, the goals of the Servicio de Paz y Justicia include education in nonviolent strategies to promote human rights, disarmament and demilitarization, alternative modes of economic development, effective political participation for all, and communal approaches to societal problems. Strongly influenced by the examples of Mohandas Gandhi and Martin Luther King Jr., SERPAJ emerged in a period of increasing violence by both the Right and the Left in Latin America.

Seeking to bring together groups experimenting with nonviolence and to increase knowledge of such strategies, the organization emphasized popular education, training, and networking. SERPAJ spread throughout Latin America in the 1970s with an international headquarters established in 1974 in Buenos Aires under the direction of Adolfo Pérez Esquivel, a sculptor and peace activist.

National units of international bodies tend to reflect the particular needs of specific countries and hence there is some variety in their programmatic emphases. In Uruguay, SERPAJ emerged as the principal human rights organization engaged in the documentation and denunciation of civil and political violations, particularly during the 1973–1985 military regime; in Ecuador and Paraguay the emphasis was on organizing for greater economic self-sufficiency among the rural poor. SERPAJ also works closely with Christian Base Communities to promote socioeconomic justice. In 1980 its general coordinator, Pérez Esquivel, was awarded the Nobel Peace Prize. In the late 1980s and 1990s democracy returned to Latin America, but SERPAJ has continued to investigate past human rights crimes under military rule. Moreover, SERPAJ through the early twenty–first century maintains its focus on economic and social injustice, by aiding, for instance, homeless children in Argentina.

See also **Christian Base Communities; Human Rights; Pérez Esquivel, Adolfo.**

BIBLIOGRAPHY

Basombrío Iglesias, Carlos. *Y ahora qué?: Desafíos para el trabajo por los derechos humanos en América Latina.* La Paz, Bolivia: Diakonía Acción Ecuménica Sueca, 1996.

Harper, Charles R. *O acompanhamento: Ecumenical Action for Human Rights in Latin America, 1970–1990.* Geneva, Switzerland: WCC Publications, 2006.

Servicio Paz y Justicia, Uruguay, *Uruguay, Nunca Más: Human Rights Violations, 1972–1985* (1992).

Weschter, Lawrence. *A Miracle, a Universe: Settling Accounts with Torturers* (1990).

MARGARET E. CRAHAN

SERVICE SECTOR. The term "service sector" refers to an economic sector that, unlike agriculture and industry, produces no goods, but provides a service that satisfies a need. Education, health, finance, government, transportation, and trade are service sectors. Since independence, services have been at least as vital in shaping the historical evolution of Latin America as either agriculture or industry. Often they have generated more income and employment than either or both.

Based on the United Nations' *International Standard Industrial Classification of All Economic*

Percentage of income generated in services in Latin America and the Caribbean, 1970, 1992[a]

	Distribution of gross domestic product (%)	
	1970	1992
Argentina	47	63
Bolivia[b]	48	—
Brazil	49	52
Chile[b]	52	—
Colombia	47	49
Costa Rica[b]	53	55
Dominican Republic[b]	51	56
Ecuador[b]	51	48
El Salvador[b]	48	66
Guatemala[b]	—	55
Honduras	45	49
Jamaica[b]	51	51
Mexico[b]	59	63
Nicaragua[b]	49	50
Panama[b]	66	76
Paraguay[b]	47	52
Peru[c]	50	—
Puerto Rico[b]	62	58
Trinidad and Tobago	51	61
Uruguay[b]	53	61
Venezuela[b]	54	53
Latin America & Caribbean	52[c]	—
World	54[c]	—

[a]Services includes value added in all branches of economic activities outside agriculture and industry (mining; manufacturing; construction; and electricity, water, and gas). It includes imputed bank service charges, import duties, any statistical discrepancies noted by national compilers, and unallocated items.
[b]The service component is at purchaser values.
[c]Weighted average.

SOURCE: World Bank, *World Development Report 1994: Infrastructure for Development* (1994), table 3, pp. 166–167.

Table 1

Activities, service activities include: (1) wholesale and retail trade; repair of motor vehicles, motorcycles, and personal and household goods; (2) hotels and restaurants; (3) transport, storage, and communications; (4) financial intermediation; (5) real estate, renting, and business activities; (6) public administration and defense; compulsory social security; (7) education; (8) health and social work; and (9) other community, social, and personal-service activities.

Services are classified as individual, semipublic, or collective, depending on which needs they satisfy. Individual (rival and excludable; a service is rival if its consumption by one individual reduces the amount of the service available for consumption by others and it is excludable if its consumption by one individual effectively excludes all other individuals from consuming it) services satisfy individual needs and are consumed by one person only. They are generally produced by private or state-owned enterprises for sale in a market. Examples include transportation (taxi rides), financial intermediation (lending), housing (renting), and retail trade (selling fruit in a supermarket).

Semipublic (partly rival, and partly excludable) services satisfy semipublic needs and are consumed by one or more persons. (A partially excludable service is one whose consumption by one person does not exclude its consumption by members of a group but excludes its consumption by all individuals outside the group.) For example, attendance at a class lecture by one student does not preclude attendance (that is, consumption of the educational service) by other students. It excludes however all individuals who do not belong to the class. Semipublic services are produced by nonprofit institutions, the state, and private enterprise. Education, health, and welfare are semipublic services.

Collective, or public, services (nonrival and nonexcludable) satisfy collective, or public, needs. (A nonexcludable service is one whose consumption by one person does not exclude its consumption by someone else. Once the service is provided, the additional cost of its consumption by another person is zero.) Public administration and the defense agencies of government are typically expected to produce the services that will satisfy the collective needs for political and economic freedom, safety, security and protection of life and private property (law and order), equal treatment by government, social harmony, and environmental protection. Collective services can be provided by the state or in some instances by private enterprise.

THE YEARS 1820 TO 1930
During the period 1820 to 1930, the years between the beginning of Latin American independence and the Great Depression, services may have created as much as 50 percent of income in some countries and employed between 20 and 30 percent of the labor force.

Individual Services. Individual services grew rapidly between 1820 and 1930. Their expansion largely reflected the powerful market forces unleashed by the entrance of Latin America into the international trading system. Phenomenal increases in exports and imports created an unprecedented demand for trade, transport, storage, communications, and financial

Percentage of labor force in services in Latin America and the Caribbean, 1965, 1981

	Percentage of labor force in services	
	1965	1981
Argentina	48	59
Bolivia	22	26
Brazil	34	46
Chile	53	62
Colombia	35	53
Costa Rica	33	48
Cuba	41	46
Dominican Republic	23	33
Ecuador	25	31
El Salvador	23	28
Guatemala	20	24
Haiti	16	19
Honduras	20	17
Jamaica	41	47
Mexico	29	38
Nicaragua	27	47
Panama	39	49
Paraguay	26	32
Peru	31	41
Trinidad and Tobago	42	51
Uruguay	52	57
Venezuela	46	55

SOURCE: World Bank, *World Development Report 1985, International Capital and Economic Development* (1985), table 21, pp. 214–215.

Table 2

services. Prosperous trading houses were established throughout Latin America. Railroads linked rural agricultural regions and distant mining centers with ports and major urban centers. Foreign (British, German, French, Italian, and U.S.) and national banks, which served the needs of producers, governments, and consumers, proliferated. Money and capital markets grew rapidly and became closely integrated with those of Europe, especially London, and New York. These services provided vital income components for the composite commodities being traded. In many instances, as much as 50 percent of the price of exports and imports reflected value added (markups) by trade, transport, finance, insurance, and related service activities. The agricultural staples bonanzas of Argentina, Uruguay, Brazil, and Colombia, and the mineral wealth of Chile, Venezuela, Peru, Bolivia, and Mexico, gave rise to corresponding production booms in individual business, personal, and social services. Demand for individual services gained additional momentum as a consequence of rising domestic incomes, urbanization, and industrialization.

In response to these rapid rises in demand by producers, households, and governments, Latin America experienced sharp supply increases, modernization, and turmoil in all individual service activities. Service output increased through domestic production, being supplemented, whenever shortages arose, by imported services. Financial, transport, trade, insurance, and other services were mostly produced locally by private (national and foreign) enterprises and banks. Output increases, including output through import substitution (i.e., domestic production of previously imported services) were largely a result of free market forces. Although often cyclical and precarious, prosperity in service activities was widespread in Argentina, Uruguay, Brazil, Mexico, Chile, and most urban and export centers in the rest of Latin America. Foreigners and immigrants made significant contributions to the development of modern individual services as entrepreneurs, capitalists, managers, professionals, and skilled workers. In few countries, however, did foreigners and immigrants play as important a role as in Argentina and Uruguay—the countries of new settlement.

Incomes in these modern, rapidly growing service activities often matched or even exceeded those of their European and North American counterparts. Socioeconomic inequality inherited from the colonial period was reinforced in much of Latin America as foreigners, immigrants, and skilled nationals earned incomes that greatly exceeded those of indigenous and other populations with limited skills and political power. The parallel existence of very rich, middle-class, poor, and indigent workers and households resulted from plural (i.e., highly differentiated in terms of income and productivity) labor markets in service activities. In Argentina and Uruguay almost all socioeconomic groups benefited from the agricultural, industrial, and service prosperity between independence and the Great Depression. In Brazil, Mexico, Peru, Chile, Guatemala, Bolivia, and Honduras, however, the benefits from the expansion of services, industry, agriculture, and mining accrued primarily to the upper socioeconomic groups.

Semipublic Services. The semipublic services of education, health, and welfare also experienced significant growth between independence and the Great Depression. The degree of illiteracy declined, especially in the cities, as primary education gradually became compulsory. Secondary education also improved, with immigrants and foreigners creating first-rate secondary

schools for their children. Furthermore, almost all Latin American countries had established internationally recognized universities by 1930. In many countries, universities, which often received disproportionate shares of governmental expenditures on education, catered almost exclusively to the middle- and upper-income strata. In Brazil, Mexico, Peru, Bolivia, Ecuador, Central America, and Paraguay, indigenous populations, women, and the poor frequently had no access to public education. Furthermore, even though health services improved significantly, mortality rates, especially of infants, remained especially high in rural areas and among the urban poor and the indigenous populations. Welfare services also grew but they covered almost exclusively organized labor, the politically powerful middle classes, and the rich. In Argentina and Uruguay, governments, to use modern terminology, invested heavily in human capital by providing educational, health, nutrition, and other services to all population segments, although not always to the same degree. In much of the rest of Latin America, semipublic services offered by the state to the poor, indigenous, and rural populations, especially women, were minimal, often nonexistent. Almost everywhere in Latin America, the relative distribution of government (and privately) produced semipublic educational, health, and welfare services suffered from extreme inequality. The 40 to 60 percent of households experiencing severe underinvestment in human capital—poor health, inadequate nutrition, illiteracy—neither contributed to nor shared much in the fruits of semipublic service development.

Collective Services. The collective services satisfying the collective needs for political and economic freedom, safety, security and protection of life and private property, equal treatment by government, social harmony and environmental protection, which were produced by public administration and defense agencies, also improved significantly, but by no means sufficiently or equally, between 1820 and 1930. Democratic governments, such as those of Chile and Costa Rica, were the exception rather than the rule. The bundle of political, economic, human, and social rights delivered by governments before 1930 was, in most countries, grossly inadequate. Far too often vast governmental incomes and riches created by the guano, wheat, coffee, tin, copper, and other agricultural and mineral export bonanzas were

Structure of consumption of services in Latin America and the Caribbean

	Percentage share of total household consumption[a]		
	Medical care	Education	Transport and communication
Argentina	4	6	13
Bolivia	5	7	12
Brazil	6	5	8
Chile	5	6	11
Colombia	7	6	13
Costa Rica	7	8	8
Dominican Republic	8	3	4
Ecuador	5	6[b]	12[c]
El Salvador	8	5	10
Guatemala	13	4	3
Honduras	8	5[b]	3
Jamaica	5	5	16
Mexico	5	5	12
Panama	8	9	7
Paraguay	2	3	10
Peru	4	6	10
Trinidad and Tobago	8	8	12
Uruguay	6	4	13
Venezuela	8	5[b]	11

[a]Data refer to either 1980 or 1985.
[b]Refers to government expenditure.
[c]Includes fuel.

SOURCE: World Bank, *World Development Report 1993: Investing in Health* (1993), table 10, pp. 256–257.

Table 3

not invested in either physical (buildings, roads, ports), human (education, health) or civil (political, economic, social capital to the extent necessary to achieve sustainable democracy and economic growth, reduce inequality, and remove poverty.

THE YEARS 1930 TO 1973

Latin America continued to experience a significant increase in the quantity and quality of privately and state produced services between 1930 and 1973. The role of government in the production of services increased. Neither the quantity nor the quality of services produced, however, attained the level required to bring about sustainable democracy and growth.

Income and Employment in Services. Total services continued to grow after 1930. Employment in services increased both in absolute and relative terms. At least in part, service employment growth reflected the inability of manufacturing to absorb the increase in the labor force caused by the post-1940 population explosion and persistent migration of labor from agricultural rural to urban areas. In contrast to the past, labor released by agriculture moved directly into services, as industrial employment growth was slow. In some activities, such as finance, government, health, and education, labor found employment in average- and high-paying service jobs. To a large extent, however, service employment increases materialized in low-paying, often marginally productive, informal activities in transportation (driving taxis and minibuses), trade (selling retail), and personal services (working as household servants or in repair shops). Especially in urban areas, much poverty and deprivation have been associated with the expansion of informal employment in services. The rural poor and destitute who migrated into the cities often joined the ranks of the urban poor and destitute in informal services.

Services' Shares of Income and Employment. As early as 1950, more than half of total income, or gross domestic product (GDP), was being generated in services in Chile (52.2 percent) and Uruguay (57.5 percent). By 1965 services were also creating more than half of income in Brazil (54.6 percent), the Dominican Republic (51.9 percent), El Salvador (50.6 percent), Guatemala (51.1 percent), Mexico (54.0 percent), and Panama (51.9 percent). Services also played important roles as employers. By 1965, they employed more than 40 percent of the labor force in Argentina (48.7 percent), Chile (41.3 percent), Uruguay (52.6 percent), and Venezuela (46.7 percent). Sharp increases in service employment, in relative terms, occurred in all Latin American countries.

Services displayed some new features from 1930 to 1973. Increasingly, individual services in transportation, finance, storage, and trade were provided by state corporations that often competed with or replaced private national or foreign enterprises. Furthermore, as a result of protectionism and nationalism, previously imported services were now produced locally. At least in part, therefore, the growth of services during this period was "artificial"; that is, it was determined by policies of government intervention rather than free market forces. Informal services also acted as a sector of employment of last resort, absorbing labor that was unable to enter the state- or privately-owned formal economy.

In some activities, government intervention and protectionism reduced employment growth, at least

Public expenditure on education

	Total expenditures (% of GDP)			Total expenditures (% of total govt. expenditure)			Total expenditure per pupil (% of per capita GDP)		
	2000	2001	2002	2000	2001	2002	2000	2001	2002
Caribbean									
Anguilla	—	—	—	—	—	10.4	—	—	—
Antigua and Barbuda	—	—	3.8	—	—	—	—	—	—
Aruba	4.8	4.8	5.1	16.0	17.2	15.6	16.5	16.6	17.6
Barbados	7.1	7.0	7.6	18.5	16.7	17.3	32.9	—	—
Belize	5.8	5.6	5.2	20.9	20.0	18.1	—	—	16.7
British Virgin Islands	—	—	—	—	9.0	—	—	—	—
Dominican Republic	—	2.3	2.3	—	13.2	12.4	—	—	—
Grenada	—	—	5.1	—	—	12.9	—	—	13.5
Guyana	8.5	8.4	8.4	18.2	18.4	18.4	—	—	24.7
Jamaica	6.1	6.1	4.9	11.1	12.3	9.5	22.9	22.2	19.8
Montserrat	—	—	—	6.6	3.5	—	—	—	—
Netherlands Antilles	—	—	—	13.6	12.8	—	—	—	—
St. Kitts and Nevis	6.4	7.6	3.2	14.7	19.0	7.9	—	15.0	8.6
St. Lucia	7.5	7.8	7.7	—	—	—	—	—	—
St. Vincent and Grenadines	9.3	9.5	10.0	13.4	17.7	20.3	30.1	—	32.0
Trinidad and Tobago	3.8	4.2	4.3	12.5	13.4	—	—	19.0	—
Turks and Caicos Islands	—	—	—	16.8	16.0	16.5	—	—	—
Central America									
Costa Rica	4.4	4.7	5.1	20.0	21.1	22.4	18.7	—	21.2
El Salvador	2.5	2.5	2.9	18.6	19.4	20.0	8.6	—	9.9
Nicaragua	3.9	3.7	3.1	13.8	13.0	15.0	—	—	11.7
Panama	5.0	4.3	4.5	7.4	7.3	7.7	19.1	14.6	15.5
South America									
Argentina	4.6	4.8	4.0	13.7	13.5	13.8	14.5	15.4	12.9
Bolivia	5.5	6.0	6.3	23.1	18.4	19.7	—	15.0	17.7
Brazil	4.3	4.2	—	12.0	12.0	—	13.8	13.7	—
Chile	3.9	—	4.2	17.5	—	18.7	15.1	—	16.0
Colombia	4.3	4.5	5.2	17.7	18.0	15.6	18.1	19.6	18.1
Ecuador	1.3	1.0	—	8.0	8.0	—	—	—	—
Paraguay	4.9	4.8	4.4	11.2	9.7	11.4	16.5	15.9	14.2
Peru	—	2.9	3.0	—	23.5	17.1	—	9.3	8.0
Uruguay	2.8	3.2	2.6	11.8	12.8	9.6	11.0	12.5	9.7
LAC									
Mexico	—	5.2	5.3	—	24.3	—	—	17.2	17.3

SOURCE: USAID, *LAC Databook 2006*, table 4.2, p. 49.

Table 4

temporarily, while permitting rapid expansion of income. Such a pattern, which coincided with high income but low employment shares, characterized trade and banking services, whose contribution to total income (GDP) by 1965 exceeded 20 percent in Argentina (20.8 percent), Brazil (22.0 percent), Chile (25.1 percent), El Salvador (28.3 percent), Guatemala (30.2 percent), Mexico (32.5 percent), and Paraguay (22.6 percent). In contrast, trade and banking services absorbed less than 10 percent of employment in all countries in 1965 except Argentina (15.5 percent), Peru (10.0 percent), and Venezuela (13.6 percent).

Employment in government services in the period 1950 to 1965 was 3 percent or less of total employment in Brazil, Colombia, Costa Rica, El Salvador, Guatemala, Haiti, Honduras, Nicaragua, and Paraguay. It exceeded 5 percent in Argentina (10.3 percent in 1960), Chile (5.6 percent in 1965), and Peru (6.0 percent in 1965). Income generated by government services, which consists of wages and salaries of government employees, regularly exceeded 5 percent of GDP in all of Latin America except Colombia, Guatemala, Honduras, Nicaragua, Panama, and Paraguay.

Individual Services. Individual services, which played a key role as a sector of employment of last resort, experienced a growth in employment that exceeded income growth. By 1965 individual services absorbed at least 15 percent of total employment

Gross and net enrollment ratios

(percentage of relevant age group)

	Pre-primary (gross)		Primary (gross)		Secondary (gross)		Tertiary (gross)		Primary (net)		Secondary (net)	
	2002	2004	2002	2004	2002	2004	2002	2004	2002	2004	2002	2004
Caribbean												
Aruba	100	100	114	114	101	98	28	29	98	98	78	74
Bahamas	31	—	93	93	93	80	—	—	87	84	77	74
Barbados	89	89	108	107	103	110	—	—	100	100	87	95
Belize	28	28	120	124	73	85	—	3	97	99	64	71
Bermuda	52	—	102	—	86	—	62	—	—	—	86	—
Cayman Islands	48	44	105	93	89	97	—	—	94	87	83	91
Dominica	—	65	—	95	—	107	—	—	—	88	—	90
Dominican Republic	34	32	122	112	66	68	—	33	99	86	40	49
Guyana	116	108	124	126	93	—	—	9	—	99	—	—
Jamaica	82	—	95	—	84	—	19	—	90	—	76	—
Netherlands Antilles	113	—	124	—	88	—	24	—		—	78	—
St. Lucia	73	71	103	106	76	74	—	14	96	98	62	63
St. Vincent and Grenadines	—	86	103	106	69	78	—	—	94	94	53	62
Suriname	91	—	119	—	74	—	12	—	92	—	63	—
Trinidad and Tobacco	63	86	96	102	80	84	7	12	—	92	70	72
Central America												
Cost Rica	61	64	108	112	66	68	19	—	90	92	52	50
El Salvador	48	50	111	113	58	60	17	18	89	91	47	—
Guatemala	27	28	108	113	44	49	10	—	89	93	31	34
Honduras	—	33	—	118	—	—	—	16	—	91	—	—
Nicaragua	31	35	112	112	60	64	18	—	88	83	38	41
Panama	55	55	112	112	71	70	43	46	100	100	63	64
South America												
Argentina	62	—	118	—	99	—	61	—		—	81	—
Bolivia	48	48	116	113	86	89	38	41	95	95	71	74
Brazil	55	—	145	—	110	—	20	—	97	—	75	—
Chile	53	—	100	—	86	—	41	—	86	—	76	—
Colombia	37	38	110	111	71	75	24	27	87	83	55	55
Ecuador	74	77	118	117	60	61	—		99	99	50	52
Paraguay	30	—	110	—	65	—	26	—	89	—	51	—
Peru	58	—	118	—	90	—	—	—	100	—	69	—
Uruguay	64	—	109	—	106	—	38	—	90	—	73	—
Venezuela	52	55	107	105	68	72	38	—	93	92	57	61
LAC												
Mexico	76	—	109	—	76	—	22	—	100	—	60	—

SOURCE: USAID, *LAC Databook 2006*, table 4.3, p. 30.

Table 5

in Argentina, Chile, Colombia, Costa Rica, and Panama. In Panama personal services created at least 25 percent of total income from 1950 to 1965. Elsewhere, their income share was below their employment share, suggesting low income and productivity, poverty, and possibly indigence.

The transportation sector was also significant in Latin America, employing more than 5 percent of the labor force in Argentina (6.7 percent in 1960), Chile (6.0 percent in 1965), and Venezuela (6.0 percent in 1965). Its income share from 1950 to 1965 was above 5 percent of GDP in Argentina, Bolivia, Chile, Guatemala (1965), Honduras, Nicaragua (1965), Panama

(1960, 1965), and Venezuela (1950). Production and private ownership of automobiles also increased the supply of transport services by households. Use of private automobiles manifested itself in large household expenditures on transportation, including the purchase of automobiles. These, however, do not form part of the statistics of employment and income generated by the transportation sector and enterprises.

According to the World Bank, as early as 1965, 50 percent of the regional GDP originated in service activities. By 1990, services generated 54 percent of GDP, much the same as in the whole world. Thus, at least since 1965, Latin America can be

Latin America and the Caribbean: gross domestic product, by kind of economic activity, at constant market prices, 1995–2005

(millions of dollars at constant 2000 prices)

	1995	2000	2002	2003	2004	2005
Agriculture, hunting, forestry and fishing	107,062.8	119,570.2	127,091.1	132,284 6	136,966.3	140,045.3
Mining and quarrying	56,507.7	70,397.8	70,499.9	73,846.5	78,332.8	81,373.7
Manufacturing	310,345.2	355,813.2	345,500.4	351,580.8	378,745.8	391,162.9
Construction	105,150.8	119,334.4	111,985.9	110,307.7	120,377.5	128,445.7
Electricity, gas and water	35,711.9	44,850.1	45,232.2	46,534.8	48,584.6	50,547.8
Transport, storage and communications	112,300.4	151,201.8	157,739.8	164,291.0	178,432.0	192,149.3
Wholesale and retail trade, restaurants and hotels	219,188.6	263,790.4	252,651.8	258,582.9	278,095.4	293,394.2
Finance, insurance, real estate and business services	251,229.4	293,678.8	299,123.7	302,693.8	314,221.3	329,310.7
Community, social and personal services	380,831.5	422,420.0	425,891.6	430,489.1	441,600.9	454,405.9
Computed commission for banking services	46,746.6	46,981.9	48,246.6	48,449.8	50,909.2	54,497.2
Value added tax and import duties	155,293.1	177,784.6	173,788.5	172,731.5	188,719.4	200,742.0
Gross domestic product[a]	1,683,150.4	1,972,014.9	1,962,251.5	2,001,018.6	2,119,739.2	2,215,472.1
Difference	−3,724.5	155.5	993.1	6,125.9	6,572.5	8,391.8

[a]Does not include Cuba.

SOURCE: ECLAC, *Statistical Yearbook for Latin America and the Caribbean* 2006, table 2.1.1.7, p. 91.

Table 6

characterized economically as a service region. Service production, as measured by the percentage contribution of service activities to GDP, was equal to or exceeded agricultural, industrial, and all goods sectors combined. The increase in regional relative income generated by services coincided with a decrease in relative income generated by agriculture, which was offset only partially (one third) by an increase in relative income generated by industry. Statistics on the percentage of income generated in services in Latin America and the Caribbean in 1970 and 1992 are presented in Table 1.

According to the figures of the percentage distribution of the labor force in Latin America and the Caribbean in 1965 and 1981 presented in Table 2, the size of the total service sector, as measured by its share in the labor force, differed significantly between countries of the region. It was generally larger in richer than in poorer countries, and, with rare exceptions, increased, often significantly, between 1965 and 1981. In the larger and richer countries, services were by far the largest and most rapidly growing economic activity, in terms of labor-force share. In 1981 they accounted for more than half of the labor force in Venezuela, Uruguay, Chile, and Colombia. By 1993 probably at least half of the region's labor force was employed in service activities. Thus, Latin America can be described as a service region, and the largest and medium-size countries as service economies, whether the criterion used is contribution to income (GDP) or share in the labor force.

Semipublic Services. As the provision of educational services improved, most Latin American countries experienced large increases in the levels of educational attainment of the population. Schooling levels have been lower, however, in rural areas, in poorer regions, and among the 30 million indigenous peoples. Improvements in health services have led to significant increases in life expectancy and declines in mortality rates, especially of infants. Welfare services also improved, but rarely have they adequately covered the poorest 40 percent of households operating in the informal economy.

Collective Services. Collective services were guided from 1930 to 1973 by philosophies of intervention, protectionism, redistribution, central planning, and pervasive distrust of private ownership, free markets, and open trade. The proportion of private ownership of productive enterprises declined as both national and foreign properties in agriculture, mining, finance and banking, industry, utilities, and industry were expropriated and state-owned enterprises were created in most economic sectors. In addition, almost all governments in Latin America restricted free internal and external exchange in commodity, labor, capital, and land factor services markets.

Structure of the total employed population, by sector of economic activity[a]

(percentage of total employed population[b])

Country	Agriculture				Industry				Services			
	1990[c]	1995	2000	2005	1990	1995	2000	2005	1990	1995	2000	2005
Argentina	0.4[d]	0.4[e]	0.6[f]	1.1[g]	31.6[d]	27.3[e]	22.5[f]	23.5[g]	68.0[d]	72.3[e]	76.9[f]	75.4[g]
Bolivia	—	—	36.8	32.3	—	—	19.5	21.6	—	—	43.7	46.0
Brazil	19.8	24.4	22.8	19.6	23.4	19.8	19.4	21.6	56.8	55.8	57.8	58.8
Chile	17.0	14.9	13.0	13.1	27.5	26.2	24.5	23.9	55.5	58.9	62.5	62.9
Colombia	25.9	22.1	22.0	20.9[h]	21.6	23.1	19.0	19.8[h]	52.6	54.8	59.0	59.4[h]
Costa Rica	25.4	21.0	16.9	15.0	25.9	24.3	22.6	21.6	48.7	54.7	60.5	63.4
Dominican Republic	20.2	15.9	15.9	14.7	21.5	24.3	23.8	22.5	58.4	59.8	60.2	62.8
Ecuador	—	—	28.5	30.3	—	—	20.1	17.6	—	—	51.4	52.1
El Salvador	—	25.6	20.7	18.4	—	26.7	24.4	23.9	—	47.7	54.9	57.7
Guatemala	48.0	37.6	36.5	36.2	18.9	23.2	20.5	20.2	33.2	39.2	43.0	43.7
Honduras	42.0	38.2	34.0	36.3	19.7	22.6	22.4	21.8	38.2	39.1	43.6	41.9
Mexico	25.3	20.3	17.5	13.9	24.7	25.6	28.3	25.7	49.9	54.1	54.2	60.4
Nicaragua	30.6	33.7	32.4	29.0	16.8	16.1	18.3	18.4	52.6	50.3	49.3	52.6
Panama	26.6	20.8	17.0	19.3	14.6	18.1	17.4	17.0	58.8	61.1	65.7	63.7
Paraguay	—	37.3	30.8	31.1	—	17.7	17.4	16.1	—	45.0	51.9	52.8
Peru	—	31.4	32.0	37.5	—	15.8	14.0	13.4	—	52.8	54.0	49.1
Uruguay[h]	3.3	4.7	3.9	4.6	29.2	26.7	24.6	22.0	67.5	68.6	71.5	73.4
Venezuela	13.1	13.4	10.6	9.7	24.6	23.2	22.8	20.8	62.3	63.4	66.6	69.5

[a]Refers to employed population aged 15 years and over.
[b]In accordance with the International Standard Industrial Classification of All Economic Activities (ISIC), Rev. 2.
[c]For all columns, data refers to the year nearest to the one heading the column.
[d]Metropolitan area.
[e]Greater Buenos Aires.
[f]Twenty-nine urban agglomerations.
[g]Twenty-eight urban agglomerations.
[h]Urban areas

SOURCE: ECLAC, *Statistical Yearbook for Latin America and the Caribbean,* 2006, table 1.2.5, p. 42.

Table 7

By the 1960s, Latin America had started displaying symptoms of acute fatigue with government intervention in the production of individual and semipublic services and goods. State ownership and intervention in the financial sector, which had created a privileged class of bank employees, had contributed to a sharp decline in financial services and private saving, acceleration of inflation, disintegration of money and capital markets, capital flight, and speculation. International and interregional trade had been victimized by excessive protectionism. Rarely did governments assign priority to delivering collective services that would have promoted basic human, political, social, and economic rights and freedoms.

THE YEARS SINCE 1973

Responding to this fatigue with state interventionism, attitudes toward and delivery of services experienced phenomenal, almost revolutionary, changes, beginning with Chile in 1973. (However, in numerous instances, and especially in Chile during the Pinochet dictatorship, satisfaction of the collective needs for economic freedom and private property coincided with the satisfaction of the immoral collective needs for violation of safety, security and protection of life, political freedom, and equal treatment by government.) Governments began actively to promote free markets, private ownership, and trade liberalization. Governments in Chile, Argentina, Mexico, Peru, Colombia, Venezuela, and elsewhere withdrew from the production of individual services and goods through privatization of banks, airlines, railroads, telephone companies, and other state-owned enterprises. The quantity and quality of individual services in finance, transport, storage, communications, and trade improved. Public-sector deficits were reduced or eliminated. Price stability was largely restored, except in Brazil. Money and capital markets gained impressive dynamism. Financial capital returned. Both international and interregional trade recovered some of their dynamism as barriers to trade

Latin America and the Caribbean: growth rates of gross domestic product, by kind of economic activity, 1995–2005

(annual rate of variation)

	1995	2000	2002	2003	2004	2005
Agriculture, hunting, forestry and fishing	3.9	1.8	2.3	4.1	3.5	2.2
Mining and quarrying	5.9	4.0	−2.4	4.7	6.1	3.9
Manufacturing	−0.3	4.2	−1.0	1.8	7.7	3.3
Construction	−6.3	0.7	−3.8	−1.5	9.1	6.7
Electricity, gas and water	5.7	4.8	1.8	2.9	4.4	4.0
Transport, storage and communications	2.6	7.0	1.4	4.2	8.6	7.7
Wholesale and retail trade, restaurants and hotels	−5.2	6.2	−3.0	2.3	7.5	5.5
Finance, insurance, real estate and business services	0.1	3.8	0.5	1.2	3.8	4.8
Community, social and personal services	0.4	2.1	0.3	1.1	2.6	2.9
Computed commission for banking services	−12.5	3.1	−1.0	0.4	5.1	7.0
Value added tax and import duties	1.0	4.9	−3.7	−0.6	9.3	6.4
Gross domestic product[a]	0.5	3.9	−0.8	2.0	5.9	4.5

[a]Does not include Cuba.

SOURCE: ECLAC, *Statistical Yearbook for Latin America and the Caribbean,* 2006, table 2.1.1.8, p. 91.

Table 8

were reduced or eliminated. Because of improved (liberalized) trade (transport, storage, communications, financial intermediation) services, exports originating in manufacturing increased rapidly, especially in Mexico and Brazil.

Major changes also affected the semipublic services of education, health, and welfare. A consensus emerged that the intractable problems of poverty and inequality could not be solved unless people, in particular the rural poor, women, and indigenous populations, were "put first." Increased emphasis was placed on investment in human capital (education, health, nutrition, and welfare) for the needy. However, even though health, education, nutrition, and welfare standards have improved markedly, according to World Bank statistics, in 1989, 130.9 million people, or 31.0 percent of Latin America's population, lived in poverty. Inequality has also persisted. In the 1970s the poorest 20 percent of households received only 4.0 percent of income. A minor reduction in inequality in income distribution may have occurred in the 1990s. The need for change in public policy was increasingly documented by international organizations, academia, and even Latin American governments themselves.

It has been increasingly recognized that public expenditures on services do not by themselves reveal whether the beneficiaries have been the rich, the middle classes, or the poor. Recent studies have offered ample evidence that throughout the post-independence period, public expenditures on services, which have often been both absolutely and relatively high, have benefited primarily, if not exclusively, high- and middle-income groups. The evidence for recent years on this matter, which is presented below, has been obtained from the World Bank's *Poverty Reduction Handbook* (1993).

According to a 1988 World Bank analysis of the incidence of major social-service expenditures in Brazil (which include social security, education, health, nutrition, housing, water, sanitation, and other urban services), "19 percent of the population, with per capita annual income below U.S. $180, benefits from 6 percent of social expenditures: whereas the top 16 percent receive 34 percent of social expenditures" (59). In Bolivia, as a consequence of the urban concentration of public services and infrastructure, the very poor had little or no access in the 1980s to health care, education, and training, thus deriving few benefits from public expenditures. Similarly, in Guatemala in the late 1980s, the urban areas and the nonpoor benefited disproportionately from spending on health and education. In Honduras most social programs in 1988 benefited primarily middle- and upper-income groups through spending on curative hospital care, pension benefits, and university education. In Venezuela, Peru, Paraguay, Ecuador, Central America, and Chile, the poorest 40 percent of households received limited or few benefits from social spending by government. With few exceptions,

Structure of the total urban employed population, by sector of economic activity, 2005[a]

(percentage of total urban employed population[b])

Country	Agriculture	Mining	Manufacturing	Electricity, gas and water	Construction	Commerce	Transport	Financial services	Other services	Unspecified
Argentina[d]	1.1	0.3	14.1	0.5	8.5	23.4	7.8	8.4	35.5	0.3
Bolivia	6.0	2.4	16.1	0.5	9.6	31.6	7.7	4.7	21.4	—
Brazil	7.4	0.3	15.9	0.5	7.5	21.0	5.4	8.4	33.3	0.3
Chile	6.4	1.6	14.2	0.6	9.1	21.4	8.4	7.7	30.3	0.3
Colombia[e]	5.9	0.6	16.1	0.6	5.5	29.2	8.5	7.6	25.9	—
Costa Rica	3.8	0.1	15.4	1.1	6.0	26.9	7.2	10.5	28.4	0.5
Ecuador	8.3	0.3	13.8	0.5	6.7	32.7	7.3	6.6	23.8	—
El Salvador	5.1	—	19.6	0.5	5.9	35.4	6.3	5.1	22.2	—
Guatemala	12.4	0.1	17.9	0.3	6.8	32.2	4.3	4.3	21.7	—
Honduras	8.4	0.3	21.1	0.7	7.1	29.0	5.4	5.5	22.6	—
Mexico	2.1	0.4	18.5	0.5	7.8	21.7	5.5	2.0	41.5	—
Nicaragua	6.6	0.3	18.2	0.9	4.9	31.2	5.6	3.9	28.4	—
Panama	2.6	—	9.0	0.8	8.7	28.6	9.3	9.7	31.5	—
Paraguay	5.6	0.1	12.6	1.1	7.3	30.9	5.0	6.4	31.1	—
Peru	11.6	0.9	11.8	0.3	5.2	34.0	8.0	5.7	22.6	—
Dominican Republic	5.1	0.2	16.4	0.9	6.5	29.6	7.7	6.4	27.2	—
Uruguay	4.6	0.1	14.3	0.9	6.7	22.9	5.5	9.2	35.8	—
Venezuela[f]	9.7	0.7	11.6	0.5	8.0	24.4	8.1	4.8	31.3	0.9

[a]Data refers to years nearest to 2005.
[b]Refers to employed population aged 15 years and over.
[c]In accordance with the International Standard Industrial Classification of All Economic Activities (ISIC). Rev. 3.
[d]Twenty-eight urban agglomerations.
[e]Municipality capitals.
[f]National.

SOURCE: ECLAC, *Statistical Yearbook for Latin America and the Caribbean*, 2006, table 1.2.8, p. 45.

Table 9

social-services spending by governments in Latin America has been characterized by inequality involving neglect and ostracism of the poorest households. A major effort is underway in much of the region to establish a more equitable distribution of semipublic and collective services.

Household expenditures on individual medical, education, transport, and communication services, the structure of which is presented in Table 3, have also been significant. Expenditures on transport, including automobiles, have been the largest in most countries.

As can be seen from Tables 4 and 5, public expenditure on education and gross and net enrollment ratios have differed widely during the period 2000 to 2004 among Latin American and Caribbean countries.

As can be observed in Tables 6, 7, 8, and 9, Latin America can be considered from 1990 to 2005 to have been a service economy continent in the sense that, in the great majority of the countries, and in the continent as a whole, more people are employed in, and more income is generated by, service activities than in agricultural and industrial goods production activities combined. No Latin American country has as yet recognized and satisfied the moral collective needs for political freedom (the pillar of procedural democracy) and for economic freedom, equal treatment by government, social harmony, safety, security and protection of life and private property, and environmental protection (the pillars of civil society), through the production of the respective collective services, to the extent necessary to attain sustainable democracy and economic growth. Thus, the unfortunate lack of economic convergence of incomes of the continent (reduction of the income gap) to those of the developed countries, as well as the persistent internal inequalities, poverty and indigence, are largely the result of the failure of all participants, and especially of government, in, and of, the collective markets to produce the required quantity and quality of the aforementioned moral collective services.

It is increasingly recognized that achievement of sustained growth, reduction of poverty and inequality, environmental protection, and stable democracy require continued quantitative expansion, qualitative improvement, and a fair distribution of individual, semipublic, and collective services.

See also **Agriculture; Chicago Boys; Cities and Urbanization; Foreign Trade; Industrialization; Neoliberalism.**

BIBLIOGRAPHY

Cole, Harold L., Lee E. Ohanian, Alvaro Riascos, and James A Schmitz, Jr. "Latin America in the Rearview Mirror." *Journal of Monetary Economics* 52, no. 1 (2005), 69–107.

International Standard Industrial Classification of All Economic Activities, 3rd revision. New York: United Nations, 1990.

Latin America and the Caribbean: Selected Economic and Social Data. Washington, DC: United States Agency for International Development (USAID), 2006.

Mamalakis, Markos. "Urbanization and Sectoral Transformation in Latin America, 1950–65." In *Actas y Memorias del XXXIX Congreso Internacional de Americanistas (Lima, 2–9 de agosto 1970)*, Vol. 2: *El proceso de urbanización en América desde sus orígenes hasta nuestros días*. Lima: Instituto de Estudios Peruanos, 1972.

Mamalakis, Markos. *The Growth and Structure of the Chilean Economy: From Independence to Allende*. New Haven, CT: Yale University Press, 1976.

Mamalakis, Markos. "Urbanización y transformaciones sectoriales en Latinoamérica (1950–1970): Antecedentes e implicaciones para una reforma urbana." In *Asentamientos urbanos y organización socioproductiva en la historia de América Latina*, ed. Jorge E. Hardoy and Richard P. Schaedel. Buenos Aires: Ediciones SIAP, 1977.

Mamalakis, Markos. "The Treatment of Interest and Financial Intermediaries in the National Accounts: The Old 'Bundle' versus the New 'Unbundle' Approach." *Review of Income and Wealth* 33, no. 2 (June 1987): 169–192.

Mamalakis, Markos J. "Social Justice in a Global Environment: A Theory of Natural Law and Social Justice." In *The Quest for Social Justice III: The Morris Fromkin Memorial Lectures 1992–2002*, ed. Peter G. Watson-Boone. Milwaukee: UWM Libraries, University of Wisconsin–Milwaukee, 2005.

Mamalakis, Markos J. "Sustainable Democracy and the Golden Rules." *Global Currents*, Center for International Education, University of Wisconsin–Milwaukee, 1, no. 2 (Spring 2005), 18–19.

Mamalakis, Markos, ed. *Historical Statistics of Chile*. Vol. 4: *Money, Prices, and Credit Services*. Westport, CT: Greenwood Press, 1983.

Mamalakis, Markos, ed. *Historical Statistics of Chile*. Vol. 5: *Money, Banking, and Financial Services*. Westport, CT: Greenwood Press, 1985.

Mamalakis, Markos, ed. *Historical Statistics of Chile*. Vol. 6: *Government Services and Public Sector and a Theory of Services*. Westport, CT: Greenwood Press, 1989.

Mesa-Lago, Carmelo. *Social Security in Latin America: Pressure Groups, Stratification, and Inequality*. Pittsburgh, PA: University of Pittsburgh Press, 1978.

Mesa-Lago, Carmelo. *Social Security and Prospects for Equity in Latin America*. Washington, DC: World Bank, 1991.

Mesa-Lago, Carmelo. "Social Security in Latin America Pension and Health Care Reforms in the Last Quarter Century." *Latin American Research Review* 42, no. 2 (June 2007), 180–201.

Patrinos, Harry A., Emmanuel Skoufias, and Trine Lunde. "Indigenous Peoples in Latin America: Economic Opportunities and Social Networks (May 1, 2007)." World Bank Policy Research Working Paper No. 4227, 81–201. Available from http://ssrn.com/abstract=984619.

Poverty Reduction Handbook. Washington, DC: World Bank, 1993.

Psacharopoulos, George, and Harry A. Patrinos. *Indigenous People and Poverty in Latin America: An Empirical Analysis*. Washington, DC: World Bank, 1994.

Statistical Yearbook for Latin America and the Caribbean. Santiago: United Nations Commission for Latin America and Caribbean (ECLAC), 2006.

World Development Report. New York: Oxford University Press for the World Bank, 1978– .

World Development Report 1989: Financial Systems and Development, World Development Indicators. New York: Oxford University Press for the World Bank, 1989.

World Development Report 1991: The Challenge of Development. New York: Oxford University Press for the World Bank, 1991.

World Development Report 1993: Investing in Health. New York: Oxford University Press for the World Bank, 1993.

MARKOS J. MAMALAKIS

SERVICIO DE PAZ Y JUSTICIA. *See* **Service for Peace and Justice (SERPAJ).**

SESMARIA. Sesmaria, plot of land of varied size granted to petitioners in colonial Brazil by the Portuguese monarchy in recognition of service to the crown. The *sesmaria* was the principal form of land distribution implemented by Portuguese colonizers, although purchase and inheritance were also legitimate forms of land acquisition.

Land was the domain of the crown and the personal patrimony of the king or queen. Personal contacts at court often influenced the granting of land in Brazil to persons of "quality." In keeping with the objectives of colonization, crown grants were subject to strict, selective regulation, defined by law and aimed at assuring effective settlement and exploration as well. The laws governing the granting of *sesmarias* restricted the amount of land assigned to any one grantee, regulated the exploration of the land, and did not confer private ownership of the *sesmaria*. By the eighteenth century it was necessary to confirm *sesmarias* in Lisbon.

Despite numerous abuses, including the sale and exchange of grants, the distribution of land in this form permitted the crown control over the effective settlement of Brazil and fixed on that country an archaic, long-lasting system of Land Tenure dominated by powerful sugar and coffee planters and cattle ranchers.

When Brazil became independent in 1822, the granting of *sesmarias* was suspended. Henceforth, they were officially recognized, but until 1850 effective occupation was the only form of legal acquisition of public lands. Until passage of the Land Law of 1850 there was unregulated occupancy of both small holdings and vast expanses of unclaimed public lands.

See also **Portuguese Empire.**

BIBLIOGRAPHY

Warren Dean, *Rio Claro: A Brazilian Plantation System, 1820–1920* (1975).

Jacob Gorender, *O escravismo colonial* (1980).

Emília Viotti Da Costa, *The Brazilian Empire: Myths and Histories* (1985).

Additional Bibliography

Bueno, Eduardo. *A coroa, a cruz, e a espada: Lei, ordem e corrupçao no Brasil colonia, 1548–1558.* Rio de Janeiro: Objetiva, 2006.

Diffie, Bailey W. *A History of Colonial Brazil, 1500–1792.* Malabar, Florida: R.E. Krieger Pub. Co., 1987.

Metcalf, Alida C. *Family and Frontier in Colonial Brazil: Santana de Paranaíba, 1580–1822.* Berkeley: University of California Press, 1992.

Metcalf, Alida C. *Go-betweens and the Colonization of Brazil, 1500–1600.* Austin: University of Texas Press, 2005.

NANCY PRISCILLA SMITH NARO

SEVEN CITIES OF CÍBOLA. Seven Cities of Cíbola, the first name given to New Mexico. The reference to Cíbola dates back to the medieval legend of the seven bishops who fled the Iberian Peninsula and founded the Seven Cities of Cíbola, noted for their gold, on the island of Antillia in 734, after Don Rodrigo of Spain lost his kingdom to the Moors in 714 CE. In 1539 Fray Marcos de Niza set out from Mexico City to seek the Seven Cities in the northern territories that Cabeza De Vaca had visited. Estevanico, the African slave in Cabeza de Vaca's party, led the expedition and was instructed to send back crosses whose size would indicate the significance of the towns. Estevanico was killed when he insisted on entering the Zuni village of Hawikuh. On his return, Fray Marcos described a kingdom that exceeded Mexico and Peru in size and wealth. This news prompted Viceroy Antonio de Mendoza to send Francisco Vásquez de Coronado to conquer Cíbola in April 1540.

See also **New Mexico.**

BIBLIOGRAPHY

Carl O. Sauer, *The Road to Cibola* (1932).

Stephen Clissold, *The Seven Cities of Cibola* (1962).

John Upton Terrell, *Estevanico the Black* (1968).

Maureen Ahern, "The Cross and the Gourd: The Appropriation of Ritual Signs in the *Relaciones* of Alvar Núñez and Fray Marcos de Niza," in *Early Images of the Americas: Transfer and Invention,* edited by Jerry M. Williams and Robert E. Lewis (1993).

Additional Bibliography

Verdugo Montoya, Laura Beatriz. *El país del más allá: Las siete ciudades de Cibola y Quivira.* Culiacán Rosales: Colegio de Bachilleres del Estado de Sinaloa, 1995.

JOSÉ RABASA

SEVEN YEARS' WAR.

SEVEN YEARS' WAR. Seven Years' War, conflict (1756–1763) also known in North America as the French and Indian War. The Seven Years' War aligned Prussia and England against France, Austria, and Russia in Europe and England against France in North America. It began when Frederick II the Great (1712–1786) of Prussia invaded Saxony and then Austria and ended after Great Britain, with the strongest navy, conquered all of Canada and took the French sugar islands. The final settlement, the Peace of Paris (10 February 1763) was favorable to Great Britain, which received all of Canada and land east of the Mississippi. Although unprepared to challenge British naval power, Spain entered the war after making the third (Bourbon) Family Compact with France on 15 August 1761. Britain captured Havana in 1762, but returned the port to Spain in 1763. Spain ceded Florida and all Spanish territory in North America to Great Britain. Spain's only victory in the war was taking Colônia Do Sacramento from Portugal, Britain's ally, but the peace terms required that Spain return the Río de la Plata colony. The war exposed Spain's colonial vulnerability and subsequently Charles III (1716–1788) instituted a variety of reforms to strengthen the ties between the colonies and Spain and improve military defense.

See also **Colonialism.**

BIBLIOGRAPHY

Richard Pares, *War and Trade in the West Indies, 1739–1763* (1963).

Max Savelle, *Empires to Nations: Expansion in America, 1713–1824* (1974).

Additional Bibliography

Anderson, Fred. *Crucible of War: The Seven Years' War and the Fate of Empire in British North America, 1754-1766.* New York: Alfred A. Knopf, 2000.

SUZANNE HILES BURKHOLDER

SEXAGENARIAN LAW.

SEXAGENARIAN LAW. Sexagenarian Law, or the Saraiva–Cotegipe Law (named for its principal sponsors), an 1885 decree that freed all Brazilian slaves when they reached age sixty. Proponents recognized that planters who had lied about the ages of African-born slaves—listing them as older than they were in order to subvert the 1831 law that prohibited the importation of African slaves into Brazil after that date—were now caught with slaves who would be eligible for freedom even though they were actually younger than sixty. The law stipulated that slaves thus freed would continue to work for an additional three years or until age sixty-five (whichever came first) as compensation to their owners. The ambiguously "freed" slaves, moreover, were to perform their work in the countries in which they were freed; elsewhere they would be regarded as vagabonds, arrested, and put to work on state projects. Unless they found work they would be imprisoned. In these ways planters could keep tight rein on former slaves, who they feared would become troublesome drifters. If the law largely favored planters, at least one provision satisfied abolitionists: not only did the law abolish the trading of slaves across provincial boundaries, but to penalize their owners, it also declared such slaves freed.

See also **Free Birth Law; Golden Law; Queirós Law; Slave Trade.**

BIBLIOGRAPHY

Robert Conrad, *The Destruction of Brazilian Slavery, 1850–1888* (1972), esp. pp. 210–237.

Additional Bibliography

Butler, Kim D. *Freedoms Given, Freedoms Won: Afro-Brazilians in Post-Abolition São Paulo and Salvador.* New Brunswick: Rutgers University Press, 1998.

Graden, Dale Torston. *From Slavery to Freedom in Brazil: Bahia, 1835-1900.* Albuquerque: University of New Mexico Press, 2006.

Mendonça, Joseli Maria Nunes. *Entre a mão e os anéis: A lei dos sexagenários e os caminhos da abolição no Brasil.* Campinas: Editora da UNICAMP: CECULT, 1999.

SANDRA LAUDERDALE GRAHAM

SEXUALITY

This entry includes the following articles:
GENDER AND SEXUALITY
SAME-SEX BEHAVIOR IN LATIN AMERICA, PRE-CONQUEST TO INDEPENDENCE
SAME-SEX BEHAVIOR IN LATIN AMERICA, MODERN PERIOD

GENDER AND SEXUALITY

In Latin America gender-laden terms designated the social worth and status of women and men. *Hembrismo, machismo, marianismo, feminismo,* and *patria potestad* describe and prescribe gender relations. As *hembra,* for example, women are identified by their biological nature and reproductive capacity. *Hembrismo* implies that women are physically vulnerable, pregnancy proves the virility of men, and sex is the medium of communication and the functional link between women and men.

Machismo is a convention that affords men respect and power. Manliness is measured by men's ability to head traditional families, produce children, protect the virginity of female relatives, and defend against other men. The *machista* is brave, forceful, insubordinate, and sexually aggressive but never sensitive. To display soft or effeminate traits invites ridicule or harassment for homosexual behavior.

Women are, then, both objects and proof of men's power and authority. Yet female purity, *marianismo,* arrogates to women moral superiority that men cannot attain. Wives and mothers are expected to suffer the sexual infidelities of their husbands, and for their pain they earn respect from their communities. Their families, and especially their sons, esteem their chastity and emotional restraint. *Maternidad,* or motherhood, is essential to women's public and private images. With the Virgin Mary, the mother of Christ, as their symbol of perfect womanhood, faithful, all-suffering women may gain a modicum of power as men's moral superiors. These traditional patterns are changing in urban Latin America.

Under the *patria potestad,* men/fathers have power over females in their family. Brought to Spain by the Romans, the *patria potestad* laws of the thirteenth-century were codified in the Siete Partidas, introduced to the American colonies and adapted to local circumstances in the Recopilación De Leyes De Las Indias of 1681, and conservatively reformed in the Spanish Napoleonic Code. These laws deemed men responsible for the economic survival of the family unit and the civil authority over all family members. Within the church family, men were religious leaders whose authority over moral covenants and institutionalized belief systems enshrined a patriarchal faith. Empowered by both civil and canon law, men arrogated to themselves all formal positions of authority, and they created laws and sanctions to protect and preserve a patriarchal social order.

Traditionally women's places were within the home, where their primary functions were to have children and to ensure the survival of the young. Prescriptive separate spheres, male domination, and homophobic attitudes notwithstanding, gender roles have always been complex and transitional. Attitudes set by an aggressive, masculine Iberian conquest of the region, by tenets of Roman Catholicism, and by Amerindian and African cultures have been challenged by survival needs. From the colonial period onward, widows and spinsters have acquired and maintained wealth and sought their own liberation. Only marriage, not gender per se, limited women's legal authority. In the modern period, technology has allowed women and men to control the sizes of families, to share in the financial support of the family unit, and to compete in politics and work. While it is unclear whether the power of patriarchy has been affected significantly over time, it is certain that new theories of government, industrial work structures, individual rights, sexuality consciousness, and modern gender standards have offered alternatives to old social and gender orderings.

COLONIALIZATION (1492–1810)

Outnumbered by millions, Iberians of necessity carried out conquest and domination by brute force and absolute authority. Upon contact, Iberian men formed legitimate and illegitimate unions with native women. Both the church and crown encouraged sanctioned marriage, but Iberian obsession with *pureza de sangre* (racial purity) caused the crown to accept unsanctioned unions between Iberians and Indians. The church, however, faithfully defended marriage, even between people of different racial backgrounds. At the Council of Trent (1545–1563), the church passed legislation regularizing marital union and imposed European standards of Catholic morality on citizens of the New World.

Initially Spaniards married Amerindian women, but by 1550 they preferred marriage with immigrant Spanish women and concubinage with women of color. To arrest legal interbreeding among people of different races and social status, the crown in

1728 decreed that men in the military, members of nobility, and bureaucrats needed official permission to marry people outside their class and caste. In 1778, the church, too, limited mixed marriages in the Real Pragmática, giving parents the right to guide their children in the selection of mates. Beginning in 1805, interracial marriages could take place only with the dispensation of civil authorities. Despite concern with *pureza de sangre,* mestizos—often the issuance of unsanctioned unions—outnumbered Iberians and creoles. Their social positions, however, were ambiguous, since they were neither indigenous nor Iberian.

Slavery, too, had sexual and gendered dimensions that reflected the dominance of the Iberian. Almost immediately, Spaniards and Portuguese traders brought Africans to the Americas to work on sugar plantations. In Brazil and the Caribbean, where male slaves outnumbered females, black men toiled and died, many without marrying. African women worked in homes as well as in fields, and they were prey to sexual advances of Iberian males. Like Amerindian women, they could not expect to marry their Iberian masters, but they might attain improved living standards for themselves and their offspring, though even that was not guaranteed. The African male was often powerless to protect the women of his race, and thus slavery also meant sexual domination of African women and the emasculation of African men.

From sexual associations formed during the Conquest came the predominant social customs. Iberians dominated people of color, powerful men could be sexually aggressive and promiscuous, Iberian blood was preferred, mestizos and mulattoes composed a new race that was despised, and women of all races assumed a subordinate status to Iberian men and to men within their own classes and castes.

Religious rituals reinforced, instructed, and prescribed behavior and beliefs associated with gender roles. Catholic conversion of non-Europeans, an essential aspect of conquest and colonization, suppressed and subsumed Amerindian and African polytheisms, rendering them undercurrents and folkways in a prevailing Catholic society. Church ritual and advice from the confessional box taught parishioners chastity and monogamy. At the Council of Trent, the church took moral issue with free and unsanctioned unions common to some

native communities and practiced by Iberian colonists, despite church disapproval. At stake was preserving women's virginity until marriage. Those who deviated from church dictates were branded sinners. Furthermore, instruction in proper sexual conduct became a means of acculturating the masses to Iberian culture, since sex, marriage, and cultural mingling fell under the jurisdiction of the church.

Unlike Catholicism, practical Amerindian and African beliefs resolved everyday gender problems such as impotence, unfaithfulness, attracting a love partner, and unwanted pregnancies. Catholic discouragement of folk religions came in the form of persecuting offenders before inquisitional tribunals. The persistence of these belief systems suggests that Santería, Voodoo, Candomblé, and indigenous *curanderas* (healers) allowed people to assert control over their sexuality. Since women more than men practiced witchcraft, it might also be assumed that women sought surreptitious ways of protecting their sex from domination by men, the church, and the state.

Class and caste created deep divisions between people of the same gender, divisions that may have been more important than the rift between women and men. Spanish and creole women, for example, tended to marry later, have fewer children, and work within the home more often than indigenous or mestizo women. They also remained single and did not remarry when widowed with the same frequency as lower-class women of color did. Upper-class white women, when they worked, managed properties or loaned money. But for the most part, women clustered more at the unskilled-service levels, although some Spanish and creole women were moneylenders and estate managers. The remaining professions were left for women of color in the lower classes, who worked in the cottage textile industry and as domestics, street vendors, pieceworkers, midwives, healers, prostitutes, and slaves.

Men, too, had careers, professions, or jobs according to their social status, but they reached professional levels women could never attain. Mestizo and mulatto men were artisans and skilled laborers, even teachers. Amerindian and black men were unskilled and skilled laborers, farmers, and slaves.

The power of the patriarch extended to nearly all aspects of life, but it was curtailed somewhat in convents. Though priests confessed the nuns and saw to their religious purity, in some convents nuns such as Sor Juana Inés De La Cruz studied and wrote. Convents not only shielded women from worldly realities, they also served as lending institutions. In Brazil, for example, entering novices paid a dowry, which the convent invested. Families contributing dowries could borrow money as long as their relative remained in the nunnery. Asunción Lavrin reminds us, however, that most nuns were pious women who devoted their lives to poverty, charity, chastity, and prayer. Though their associations with men differed from those of women outside the convent, their vows were not an attempt at liberation from patriarchal rule, for they were ultimately subordinates in a patriarchal faith.

The Bourbon Reforms (1764–1804) placed particular emphasis upon efficient, systematic production and introduced new governmental agencies and scientific procedures to extract New World wealth. Imposed Bourbon trade regulations threatened some of the cottage industries, such as textile production, which had been run by women. The reforms also created new opportunities in teaching for women.

The Bourbon Reforms notwithstanding, the century of enlightenment in Latin America left most women with limited work opportunities and divided along class and caste lines. Only women of the well-to-do classes were no longer cloistered and condemned to lives of idleness in the same numbers as before. But all women benefited from an enhanced notion of motherhood: they were viewed as fundamental conduits of modern values to their children and as leaders in philanthropy, which gave their historic private occupations a public importance.

GENDER ASSOCIATIONS IN THE NINETEENTH CENTURY

Napoleon Bonaparte's removal of the Spanish kings (1808) provoked wars of independence beginning in 1810. Women of all classes were affected by war, with many fleeing—some in carriages and others on foot—before advancing armies. Before it was all over, gender lines had blurred, as the focus on victory overcame the restrictions of sex. Left to survive outside the walls of their homes and spurred on by their devotion to the men in their families and to ideals of national independence, women served as soldiers, conspirators, nurses, arms smugglers,

writers, and money solicitors. In most countries, especially after independence had been won early in the nineteenth century, women's efforts were all but forgotten in societies insensitive to gender inequities. An exception to this rule was Cuba (independent in 1898), where women's contributions were legendary and served to drive men to equal their sacrifices. José Martí remarked about *mambisa* bravery, "With women such as these, it is easy to be heroes."

Independence pitted ideals of greater individual freedom, federalist government, the separation of church and state, and laissez-faire capitalism against the more familiar corporate state with community allegiance, central government, the union of church and government, and a controlled economy. Nineteenth-century leaders fought civil wars over rules of government and over national boundaries. Women moved with the troops as soldiers, cooks, and nurses, and they entered professions vacated by men. Destruction caused economic decline in agriculture but opened up work in light industry for both women and men. Economic and political instability forced women into new roles, and as that happened, nationalism and motherhood became inextricably intertwined. Mothers sacrificing themselves and their children for independence became a symbol of militant patriotism.

The end of the nineteenth century brought relative peace, but as the troops returned, men replaced women at work. Decades of struggle toward modern statehood made some women want to redefine gender roles. In some countries, male politicians modernized legal codes, which subsequently opened the way for demands that democratic rights be extended to all citizens, including women and men from the dominated classes. Educated women from the elite and professional classes came forward with petitions for suffrage, equal education, and new civil legislation. In a few instances, such as in the Tobacco Stemmers' Guild in Cuba, working women organized in unions and guilds for protective legislation and equal rights. These early reform efforts, which were rooted in nineteenth-century liberal notions of democracy, universal suffrage, and scientific government fueled the nascent labor movement.

GENDER ASSOCIATIONS IN THE TWENTIETH CENTURY

The twentieth century brought ideals of class struggle that involved women and men in revolutionary, sometimes Marxist, movements against old forms of rule. In the nineteenth century, new values and nascent capitalism emphasized individualism. The closed family unit opened to the public as women and children became wage earners and members of the informal labor force. Women organized reform movements that focused on political authority, legal reforms, and access to education and jobs.

The promise of prosperity and order did not materialize for most Latin Americans. Women and men were pushed off the land. Men migrated from farm to city in search of work, often leaving women unwed mothers and heads of impoverished households. Women migrated, too, leaving their families behind and finding work primarily as domestic servants or prostitutes in urban centers.

Between 1880 and 1940 social activists, both feminist and Marxist, rallied to defend the poor. In Chile, Argentina, Uruguay, Brazil, and Cuba, women's movements formed and demanded new rights and protection for women and children. These early women's groups grew out of nineteenth-century philanthropic associations, but they broadened their goals by viewing patriarchy as an impediment to female self-determination. Yet these early activists were slow to attack *machismo* directly as the root of repression. Instead, Latin Americans attempted to empower women as mothers and as the creators of a new social order based on moral responsibility. When forced to confront misogyny, they chided men and even objected to men's right to kill adulterous wives, to commit adultery with impunity, and to ignore their illegitimate children.

That Latin American feminists were loath to confront total and arbitrary male authority could imply female weakness and the absence of committed feminism. It is also explained by the multiple fronts where issues of social justice were addressed. They joined revolutionary movements that opposed illegitimate governments, repressive police action, foreign intervention, poverty, and social injustice. Thus, women sided with men when men fought for changing the social order, and they were against men when men repressed women. They were never purely feminists in the U.S. sense.

Early women's organizations were diverse, some seeking only suffrage, others general social reform, and still others socialist feminism. Conservative women activists, such as members of the Liga Patriótica in Argentina, supported liberal reforms for women in their quest to shore up power for the Conservative Party. Moderates formed the majority in the feminist movement. They approved of extensive social and labor reforms under a capitalist regime. Cuba, Brazil, and Argentina were the three countries with strong socialist feminist groups whose members, unlike other feminists, looked to political centralization and community guarantees, not autonomy and individual rights, to aid poor women. As a result of women's activism, nations passed progressive legislation that improved gender equity. Ecuador granted women suffrage in 1929, and by 1933 Uruguay, Brazil, and Cuba had followed. Surprisingly, Argentina and Mexico, two nations where women had organized early, did not grant voting rights to women until 1947 and 1953, respectively.

To men, women's liberation was only a minor side effect of a larger effort to establish a new ruling order. The outcome of this effort was progressive labor, penal, and civil laws in Argentina, Chile, Uruguay, Brazil, and Cuba that granted women divorce rights, labor protection and equality, maternity codes, and civil equality. Some of these reforms granted individual women authority and independence vis à vis individual men, but ultimately authority lay with the state.

Latin American women joined international feminist movements as early as 1889. At the 1928 Pan-American Union (PAU) meeting in Havana, Cuban feminists from a variety of organizations marched with Doris Stevens and the U.S. National Women's Party, spoke at special meetings, and succeeded in forming the Inter-American Commission on Women within the PAU to oversee women's rights throughout the hemisphere. This was the first international feminist organization, out of a spirit of Pan-Americanism. This effort did not, however, draw support from socialist feminists who viewed North American involvement as another form of imperialism.

From 1940 to 1960, rebelliousness in Latin America either languished or was suppressed by dictatorships. With the Cuban Revolution of 1959, however, social nationalism sent rebels to arms to challenge internal colonialism and U.S. hegemony. Women, confident of their place in a new socialist world, fought alongside men. Many, however, were disenchanted by the unliberated attitudes of their *compañeros,* who, on the personal level, relegated them to secondary positions within the movement and dominated them sexually. Neofeminists, convinced by national revolution as well as by notions of gender equality coming from the radical feminist movement in the United States, inspired Latin American women to restate their own principles of liberation. The tone of Latin American feminism became more militant than forty years earlier. Activists attacked the patriarchy directly but resisted lesbian feminism, which they associated with the North American movement. Latin American feminists sought ways to organize the poor, and to explain violence and sexual harassment. Theorists began deconstructing the language as a root cause of exaggerated gender separation and evaluation.

The split between North American and Latin American feminists was clearly articulated at the United Nations International Women's Year meeting in Mexico City in 1975. Mexican feminists, in particular, decried the irrelevance of the U.S. movement for Latin American women. They accused North Americans of concentrating on legal equality, redefinitions of gender, sexuality, political power, and birth control when Latin American women were intent on rescuing their families from poverty, military repression, and lack of economic development. Subsequently, many economic development projects in Latin America contained components for women, and in time notions of appropriate technology and appreciation for the social contributions of all members of communities informed development plans.

FORBIDDEN SEXUALITY
Prostitution, long considered a "necessary evil," was and is the logical consequence of female economic and educational destitution, the commercial value attached to sex, the social dominance of men, and strictly taught morals regarding the bonds of marriage. Men's presumed appetite for sex and women's presumed weaker physical drive have excused men's search for sexual satisfaction outside the home. Taboos placed on respectable women seeking sexual gratification have, on the surface,

discouraged expectations of sexual fulfillment between wives and husbands.

Prostitutes have been despised by society for selling themselves. Most prostitutes have been among the poorest and the most defiled members of society. More often than not, general condemnations of commercial sex have overwhelmed objective knowledge about the social and economic arrangements that have made prostitution a reasonable choice for some women. Male prostitution, often ignored by public authorities unless it included homosexual relations, has rarely incited the condemnations that female prostitution has.

During the colonial period, matters of prostitution were handled by ecclesiastical courts. In the eighteenth century, the church established *casas de corrección* or *casas de sanidad* (correctional houses) to rehabilitate women, usually nonwhites. Priests, bishops, and inquisitional tribunals heard accusations of prostitution, and all discouraged the practice. Most reprehensible was the offer by parents to sell their daughters to brothels and by husbands to prostitute their wives. Consenting adult women were reprimanded with increasing severity as connections between venereal disease and promiscuous sex became clear.

In the nineteenth century, prostitution came under the aegis of the state, and justifications for controlling it included deterring the spread of venereal disease and collecting taxes. During the second half of the nineteenth century, as governments began to stabilize and modernization challenged old moral codes, prostitution came to be understood as an economic, social, and political problem. Modern concepts of the state held that the family formed the basis of society. The values, belief systems, behavior, and relationships that were formed within the family projected patriotic images.

Argentina serves as an example of how and why the rules regarding prostitution changed. The government's legalization of prostitution by an 1875 ordinance was a means of controlling an already viable business. Under the ordinance, officials collected revenues, set up health clinics, and formally designated parts of the city for prostitution, thus isolating prostitutes from the rest of society. Moreover, in response to international and national accusations of white slavery (the importing of white prostitutes), the government increasingly limited the operations of brothels and passed antisolicitation laws.

In 1934, after 58 years of legalized prostitution, Argentine officials began outlawing bordellos, claiming that prostitutes did not register with health clinics, that venereal disease was spreading, and that prostitutes engaged in scandalous behavior. They were also responding to Buenos Aires's reputation as a center of white slave trade. Moreover, industrialization offered employment alternatives. Municipality after municipality abolished their licensed houses and incorporated new legislation, most notably the Law of Social Profilaxis (1936), that provided medical care, repatriation, and employment for reformed prostitutes.

With the advent of Juan Perón in 1944, governing values changed once again. Women had been working at respectable jobs in increased numbers since the turn of the century, and by 1947 they could vote. Women, thus, were supportive of the pro-labor administration. At the same time, homosexuals were beginning to demand a place in Argentina's moral ordering. Old sex-burdened folkways were disappearing. The tango, originally danced in bordellos between sexually commanding men and alluring women, was replaced by soccer (an all-male player and spectator sport) as the activity of national passion. Homosexuality was beginning to find some expression in literature and art, despite the fact that many Argentines were scandalized by gay relationships. In response Perón promised conservative morality and a return to family values. Part of his plan involved legalizing prostitution, and in 1954 the law was changed so that prostitutes again could practice their trade legally as part of a patriotic defense against illness and unspeakable perversion.

After the Cuban Revolution in 1959, Fidel Castro's government tried to end prostitution through rehabilitation programs, respectable jobs, and distribution of wealth. The Federation of Cuban Women, founded in 1960, educated women. Literacy programs were set up to rehabilitate former prostitutes, and vocational schools trained women to work in textile factories. The Cubans concentrated on the economic and political causes of prostitution, believing that by eliminating poverty and a sense of marginalization, prostitution would disappear.

Public soliciting was prohibited, but clandestine commerce continued. The source of inequality came from tourists, who were allowed to shop in "dollar stores" (where only foreign currency was accepted). Avoiding the surveillance of tourist police, young women approached tourists, exchanging sex for clothing and food bought in tourist and diplomatic stores. Until 1989 this sort of commerce was light, but the *período especial* (economic crisis caused by the dissolution of the Soviet Union) created such hardship in Cuba that prostitutes began plying their trade as openly as in the pre-1959 period.

Homosexual acts have been considered social aberrations and deviant behavior in every Latin American country. Yet the history of homosexuality in Latin America is complicated by the unification of Amerindian, Iberian, and African cultures, each of which has had a different perception of homosexuality.

According to some scholars, homosexuality was acceptable behavior among a few pre-contact groups. Archaeological evidence shows that Zunis in New Mexico, the Araucanians of Chile and southern Peru, and the Incas practiced male homosexuality. The most graphic evidence is in Peruvian Moche pottery, with its explicit depictions of men engaged in homosexual lovemaking. Furthermore, no source suggests that homosexual intercourse was punished or discouraged.

The Iberian conquerors, repulsed by native homosexual acts, called the mystified Indians sodomites, and the clergy condemned the accused to be eaten alive by dogs. Yet there is some evidence that the conquerors also practiced homosexual intercourse. During the colonial period, Iberian homosexuals were brought before inquisitional tribunals, where their sin was known as the "ultimate crime against morality" and the "abominable or unspeakable crime," and they were punished by the *auto-da-fé*. During periods of leniency or neglect, homosexuals in cities were forced to reside in the same poor areas where prostitutes lived. Individual freedoms did not extend to this marginalized group, as gay men could not belong to the military, seek public office, or hold government jobs. Their sexual behavior was also a crime for which individuals could be imprisoned.

Controlling vice proved increasingly difficult in the nineteenth century as Latin American ports opened to international trade and foreign immigration. Port cities were overpopulated with prostitutes. Police records note the arrests of purse snatchers who dressed as women, perhaps to disguise their criminal intent or, alternatively, to express their sexual preference.

Gays and lesbians have felt the greatest repression from authoritarian and totalitarian regimes, which direct police raids even against members of the ruling class. In post-1959 revolutionary Cuba, measures against homosexuals were especially repressive. Under liberal governments, homosexuals have been ignored and neglected but never accepted. Only in the middle- to late-twentieth century have homosexuals organized to protect themselves from arbitrary repression. As early as 1969 in Argentina, but generally in the early 1980s, gays and lesbians formed their own organizations. In 1983 the Fifth March for Gay Pride, which included thirteen homosexual groups, took place in Mexico City.

Venezuela, Colombia, Puerto Rico, and Brazil all have active gay movements. Formed in 1969, the Argentine El Grupo Nuestro Mundo attracted homosexuals with divergent political affiliations. In 1971, the organization renamed itself the Frente de Liberación Homosexual de la Argentina. What united members was a commitment to fighting *machismo,* the convention of male domination that affected all women and gay men. Members believed that by ending male domination, they would cause a profound revolution, a psychological transformation that would alter the fundamental tenets of Argentine culture.

Although the gay movement gathered force during a period of radical mobilization and revolt against military rule, gays found leftist groups as repressive as the right-wing military government. Only feminists appreciated the benefits to be gained by stopping male domination, but even they were often unwilling to support gay rights. Still, the Frente persisted and in 1973 published a manifesto that demanded the immediate cessation of police repression of homosexuals, the abrogation of an antihomosexual edict, and the freeing of homosexual prisoners. Homosexual activists, more than political dissidents, had to work clandestinely, which impeded the other great objective of creating a gay consciousness and identity. These early dissenters actively engaged in theoretical and cultural analyses that explained their social marginalization and planned confrontations with their oppressors.

Juan Perón's third presidency (1973–1974) proved as repressive of gays as the military government it replaced. Despite the fact that gay organizations had gone to the streets in support of Perón, the right wing of the Peronist Party assailed homosexuals while the party as a whole ignored their manifestos. Disillusioned gays found no comfort among the leftist Montoneros, who denied them membership in their organization. Still with no political home, homosexuals were despised and alone in their struggle. When gay activists declared their opposition to Perón in 1973, they became the victims of police repression. To survive, they had to go underground, where they remained until the fall of the military regime in 1982.

Since then, Argentine gay organizations have grown, especially as a result of their joining the chorus of protesters demanding information on the victims of the dirty war (1976–1981). Activists counted at least seventy of the missing from among their ranks. Under the new democratic governments of presidents Raúl Alfonsín, Carlos Menem, and Nestor Kirchner, gay organizations established official headquarters in downtown Buenos Aires, where they began publishing news journals and political pamphlets.

Although studies of gender and sexuality have often been assumed to concern only women, the field also offers a deepening scholarly understanding of masculinity and the experience of men. In addition, research considering the interactions between ethnicity, race, gender, and sexuality has made important strides.

See also **Feminism and Feminist Organizations; Inter-American Congress of Women; Women; Women in Paraguay.**

BIBLIOGRAPHY

Evelyn Stevens, *"Marianismo,* the Other Face of *Machismo* in Latin America," in *Female and Male in Latin America,* edited by Ann Pescatello (1973), pp. 89–101.

Verena Martínez Alier, *Marriage, Class, and Colour in Nineteenth-Century Cuba* (1974).

Jean G. Peristiany, *Honour and Shame: The Values of Mediterranean Society* (1974).

Asunción Lavrin, ed., *Latin American Women: Historical Perspectives* (1978).

Elsa Chaney, *Supermadre: Women in Politics in Latin America* (1979).

Doris M. Ladd, *Mexican Women in Anahuac and New Spain: Aztec Roles, Spanish Notary Revelations, Creole Genius* (1979).

Asunción Lavrin and Edith Couturier, "Dowries and Wills: A View of Women's Socio-Economic Role in Colonial Guadalajara and Puebla, 1640–1790," in *Hispanic American Historical Review* 59, no. 2 (May 1979): 280–304.

June Nash and Helen I. Safa, eds., *Sex and Class in Latin America: Women's Perspectives on Politics, Economics, and the Family in the Third World* (1980).

Susan Socolow, "Women and Crime: Buenos Aires, 1757–1797," in *Journal of Latin American Studies* 12 (May 1980): 39–54.

Susan Socolow, "Marriage, Birth, and Inheritance: The Merchants of Eighteenth-Century Buenos Aires," in *American Historical Review* 60, no. 3 (August 1980): 387–406.

Fondo De Cultura Económica, *Familia y sexualidad en Nueva España* (1982).

Maryssa Navarro, "Evita's Charismatic Leadership," in *Latin American Populism in Comparative Perspective*, edited by Michael L. Coniff (1982), pp. 47–66.

Maria Patricia Fernández Kelly, *For We Are Sold, I and My People: Women and Industry in Mexico's Frontier* (1983).

Luis Martin, *Daughters of the Conquistadores: Women of the Viceroyalty of Peru* (1983).

John Tutino, "Power, Class, and Family: Men and Women in the Mexican Elite, 1750–1810," in *The Americas* 39 (1983): 359–381.

Alejandro Jockl, *Ahora, los gay* (1984).

Sandra F. McGee, "Right-Wing Female Activists in Buenos Aires, 1900–1932," in *Women and the Structure of Society*, edited by Barbara J. Harris and Joann McNamara (1984), pp. 85–97.

Rigoberta Menchú, *I...Rigoberta Menchú: An Indian Woman in Guatemala* (1984).

Zelmar Acevedo, *Homosexualidad: Hacia la destrucción de mitos* (1985).

Silvia Arrom, *Women of Mexico City, 1790–1857* (1985).

Edith Couturier, "Women and the Family in Eighteenth-Century Mexico: Law and Practice," in *Journal of Family History* 10, no. 3 (Autumn 1985): 294–304.

Susan Kellogg, "Aztec Inheritance in Sixteenth-Century Mexico City: Colonial Patterns, Prehispanic Influences," in *Ethnohistory* 23, no. 3 (Summer 1986): 313–330.

Elizabeth Anne Kuznesof, *Household Economy and Urban Development: São Paulo, 1765 to 1836* (1986).

Eleanor L. Leacock and Helen I. Safa, eds., *Women's Work: Development and the Division of Labor by Gender* (1986).

Alida Metcalf, "Fathers and Sons: The Politics of Inheritance in a Colonial Brazilian Township," in *Hispanic American Historical Review* 66, no. 3 (August 1986): 455–484.

June Nash and Helen I. Safa, eds., *Women and Change in Latin America* (1986).

Ronaldo Vainfaz ed., *Historia e sexualidade no Brasil* (1986).

Ruth Behar, "Sex and Sin, Witchcraft and the Devil in Late-Colonial Mexico," in *American Ethnologist* 14, no. 1 (February 1987): 34–54.

Irene Silverblatt, *Moon, Sun, and Witches: Gender, Ideologies, and Class in Inca and Colonial Peru* (1987).

Susan Kellogg, "Households in Late Prehispanic and Early Colonial Mexico: Their Structure and Its Implications for the Study of Historical Demography," in *The Americas* 44 (April 1988): 483–494.

Daphne Patai, *Brazilian Women Speak: Contemporary Life Stories* (1988).

Octavio Paz, *Sor Juana: Or, the Traps of Faith*, translated by Margaret Peden (1988).

Patricia Seed, *To Love, Honor, and Obey in Colonial Mexico* (1988).

Electa Arenal and Stacey Schlau, *Untold Sisters: Hispanic Nuns in Their Own Works*, translated by Amanda Powell (1989).

Susan C. Bourque, "Gender and the State: Perspectives from Latin America," in *Women, the State, and Development*, edited by Sue Ellen Charlton, Jana Everett, and Kathleen Staudt (1989), pp. 114–129.

Jane S. Jaquette, ed., *The Women's Movement in Latin America: Feminism and the Transition to Democracy* (1989).

Alexandra Parma Cook and Nobel David Cook, *Good Faith and Truthful Ignorance: A Case of Transatlantic Bigamy* (1990).

Edith Couturier, " 'For the Greater Service of God': Opulent Foundations and Women's Philanthropy in Colonial Mexico," in *Lady Bountiful Revisited: Women, Philanthropy, and Power*, edited by Kathleen D. McCarthy (1990), pp. 119–141.

Elizabeth Salas, *Soldaderas in the Mexican Military: Myth and History* (1990).

Sandra Messinger Cypress, *La Malinche in Mexican Literature: From History to Myth* (1991).

David William Foster, *Gay and Lesbian Themes in Latin American Writing* (1991).

Ramón Gutiérrez, *When Jesus Came, the Corn Mothers Went Away: Marriage, Sexuality, and Power in New Mexico, 1500–1846* (1991).

Donna J. Guy, *Sex and Danger in Buenos Aires: Prostitution, Family, and Nation in Argentina* (1991).

Sandra F. McGee, "Gender and Sociopolitical Change in Twentieth-Century Latin America," in *Hispanic American Historical Review* 71 (1991): 259–306.

Francesca Miller, *Latin American Women and the Search for Social Justice* (1991).

Muriel Nazzari, *Disappearance of the Dowry: Women, Families, and Social Change in São Paulo, Brazil (1600–1900)* (1991).

Lynn Stephen, *Zapotec Women* (1991).

K. Lynn Stoner, *From the House to the Streets: The Cuban Woman's Movement for Legal Reform, 1898–1940* (1991).

K. Lynn Stoner, "On Men Reforming the Rights of Men: The Abrogation of the Cuban Adultery Law, 1930," in *Cuban Studies/Estudios Cubanos* 21 (1991): 83–99.

Additional Bibliography

Beattie, Peter M. *The Tribute of Blood: Army, Honor, Race, and Nation in Brazil, 1864–1945.* Durham, NC: Duke University Press, 2001.

Campuzano, Luisa. *Mujeres latinoamericanas del siglo XX: Historia y cultura.* Mexico: Universidad Autónoma Metropolitana, Unidad Iztapalapa, 1998.

Caulfield, Sueann. *In Defense of Honor: Sexual Morality, Modernity, and Nation in Early Twentieth-Century Brazil.* Durham, NC: Duke University Press, 1999.

Chambers, Sarah. *From Subjects to Citizens: Honor, Gender, and Politics in Arequipa, Peru, 1780–1854.* University Park: Pennsylvania State University Press, 1999.

Dias, Maria Odila Leite da Silva. *Power and Everyday Life: The Lives of Working Women in Nineteenth-Century Brazil.* Translated by Ann Frost. New Brunswick, NJ: Rutgers University Press, 1995.

Dore, Elizabeth, and Maxine Molyneux, eds. *Hidden Histories of Gender and the State in Latin America.* Durham, NC: Duke University Press, 2000.

French, John D., and Daniel James, eds. *The Gendered Worlds of Latin American Women Workers: From Household and Factory to the Union Hall and Ballot Box.* Durham, NC: Duke University Press, 1997.

French, William, and Katherine Elaine Bliss, eds. *Gender, Sexuality, and Power in Latin America since Independence.* Lanham, MD: Rowman and Littlefield, 2007.

Graham, Sandra Lauderdale. *Caetana Says No: Women's Stories from a Brazilian Slave Society.* Cambridge, U.K., and New York: Cambridge University Press, 2002.

Green, James Naylor. *Beyond Carnival: Male Homosexuality in Twentieth-Century Brazil.* Chicago: University of Chicago Press, 1999.

Higgins, Kathleen. *"Licentious Liberty" in a Brazilian Gold-Mining Region: Slavery, Gender, and Social Control in Eighteenth-Century Sabará, Minas Gerais.* University Park: Pennsylvania State University Press, 1999.

Hutchison, Elizabeth Quay. *Labors Appropriate to Their Sex: Gender, Labor, and Politics in Urban Chile, 1900–1930.* Durham, NC: Duke University Press, 2001.

Lavrin, Asunción. *Women, Feminism, and Social Change in Argentina, Chile, and Uruguay, 1890–1940.* Lincoln: University of Nebraska Press, 1995.

Lewis, Laura A. *Hall of Mirrors: Power, Witchcraft and Caste in Colonial Mexico.* Durham, NC: Duke University Press, 2003.

Morant Deusa, Isabel. *Historia de las mujeres en España y América Latina.* Madrid: Cátedra, 2005–2006.

Socolow, Susan Migden. *The Women of Colonial Latin America.* Cambridge, U.K., and New York: Cambridge University Press, 2000.

Tarrés, María Luisa, ed. *Género y cultura en América Latina: Cultura y participación política.* 2 vols. Mexico: Colegio de México, 1998–2003.

Tinsman, Heidi. *Partners in Conflict: The Politics of Gender, Sexuality, and Labor in the Chilean Agrarian Reform, 1950–1973.* Durham, NC: Duke University Press, 2003.

Twinam, Ann. *Public Lives, Private Secrets: Gender, Honor, Sexuality, and Illegitimacy in Colonial Spanish America.* Stanford, CA: Stanford University Press, 1999.

K. LYNN STONER

SAME-SEX BEHAVIOR IN LATIN AMERICA, PRE-CONQUEST TO INDEPENDENCE

Prior to the Spanish Conquest, same-sex behavior was present in indigenous societies and continued after the Conquest within different and changing contexts. The Spanish often pointed to same-sex behavior and transvestism as evidence of the fallen nature of the indigenous peoples and therefore as a justification for conquest and slaughter. Part of the colonial agenda was the denigration of an effeminate nobility; thus for the Spanish, portraying the indigenous societies as rife with sodomy, and the sexual desires of indigenous women as unsatisfied by their men, served to justify the colonial administration.

In certain tribes some men assumed the social role of women and married other men. Occasionally these men, considered to have special knowledge of both the male and the female, were treated with respect. In other instances these men were treated with disdain, either for choosing to live as women or for being so weak in the social hierarchy as to be forced to dress and behave as women. In their interpretations of the meaning of same-sex behavior and cross-dressing in the Americas prior to the Conquest, some scholars see this behavior as ritualized performance affirming the feminine, whereas others see it as an act of power that demonstrates the strength of certain groups and denigrates perceived inferiors.

Understandings and cultural constructions of same-sex behavior after the Conquest were in constant flux. Indigenous, Iberian, and African populations viewed same-sex desire and behavior in different ways, given their different sociohistorical contexts. Colonial mentions of same-sex behavior can be found in texts as varied as narratives of exploration (e.g., by Alvar Núñez Cabeza de Vaca) and Church liturgy (the Catechism of Peru, and companion sermons, Lima, 1583–1585). Other testimonies regarding same-sex behavior among all ethnic and class groups can be found in documents from the Inquisition, particularly from Brazil. There is also testimony of same-sex behavior in the slave communities, either as a choice or as a situational necessity. Research has also established the presence of male same-sex communities in the seventeenth and eighteenth centuries in Mexico and Brazil.

Although there is less documentation of same-sex behavior among women, evidence exists in Inquisition papers as well as references in sermons and catechisms. However, in a society in which women lacked sexual, as well as financial and familial, independence, lesbian activity has often gone unnoticed. There are notable exceptions: One is Sor Juana Inés de la Cruz (1651–1695), a nun from Mexico, known for her poetry and tracts in defense of women. Although there is no clear evidence of her sexual behavior, she has frequently been portrayed in modern times as both a protofeminist and protolesbian. Another is Henriette Faber (1791–?), a cross-dressing soldier and doctor in Napoleon's army who later, after immigrating to Cuba, married a woman; she was later exiled to New Orleans, after which point she disappears from the historical record. More research is needed to uncover evidence of female same-sex relationships.

See also **Cabeza de Vaca, Alvar Núñez; Homosexuality and Bisexuality in Literature; Juana Inés de la Cruz, Sor.**

BIBLIOGRAPHY

Bazán, Osvaldo. *Historia de la homosexualidad en la Argentina: De la conquista de América al siglo XXI.* Buenos Aires: Marea, 2004.

Benítez Rojo, Antonio. *Mujer en traje de batalla.* Madrid, Alfaguara, 2001.

Cevallos-Candau, Francisco Javier, et al., eds. *Coded Encounters: Writing, Gender, and Ethnicity in Colonial Latin America.* Amherst: University of Massachusetts Press, 1994.

Herren, Ricardo. *La conquista erótica de las Indias.* Barcelona: Planeta, 1992.

Mott, Luís R. B. *Escravidão, homossexualidade e demonología.* São Paulo: Ícone Editora, 1988.

Sigal, Peter Herman, ed. *Infamous Desire: Male Homosexuality in Colonial Latin America.* Chicago: University of Chicago Press, 2003.

Trevisan, João Silverio. *Perverts in Paradise,* translated by Martin Foreman. London: GMP, 1986.

Williams, Walter L. *The Spirit and the Flesh: Sexual Diversity in American Indian Culture.* Boston: Beacon Press, 1986, 1992.

RICHARD D. REITSMA

SAME-SEX BEHAVIOR IN LATIN AMERICA, MODERN PERIOD

Inquisitional accusations against individuals who allegedly had engaged in sodomy offer some insights into same-sex relationships in colonial Spanish and Portuguese America. Many more men than women were accused of the offense, and some received capital punishment for committing the "crime against nature."

Post independence constitutions and the reform of legal codes decriminalized sexual acts between men or between women in most countries of the region, making it more difficult for historians to trace social practices through the examination of criminal cases. Authorities controlled non-normative sexual behavior by policing public spaces where men gathered to meet others for sexual liaisons, charging those whom they suspected of "pederasty" with vagrancy or public indecency. Women were restricted from full access to public social spaces; nevertheless, those who desired sexual relations with other women maintained carefully guarded romances by taking advantage of acceptable

A gay couple celebrates after their civil union ceremony, Buenos Aires, Argentina, 2003. In December 2002, Buenos Aires passed the first ordinance in Latin America to allow civil unions to be contracted by same-sex couples. ALI BURAFI/AFP/GETTY IMAGES

patterns of female sociability. During the nineteenth century, the semi-clandestine world of same-sex erotic interaction developed in the capitals and large cities of almost all Latin American and Caribbean countries. Discreet social networks and semi-secret clubs and social gatherings provided some with opportunities for homoerotic relationships.

Throughout the nineteenth and twentieth centuries normative gender roles attributed effeminacy in men to sexual passivity and the assumption that they engaged exclusively in receptive anal intercourse. Given social restraints, exaggerated or somewhat feminine sartorial styles, meticulous grooming, and hints of makeup were used as markers by some men to attract male sexual partners. Men with traditionally masculine comportment who engaged in sexual intercourse with such effeminate men generally considered these escapades as sexual adventures that did not alter their masculine persona and

identity. Some women adopted masculine clothing and occupied public spaces as an assertion of their right to move freely about and as a means of attracting female sexual partners.

In the late nineteenth century, Latin American criminologists and physicians appropriated German, French, and to a lesser extent, British and U.S. medical and psychological theories that linked same-sex eroticism to criminality and perversion. The word *homosexuality* began to replace terms such as *sodomy* and *pederasty* to define same-sex sexuality. Although European and American authors attributed homosexuality to all people who engaged in same-sex eroticism, most Latin American intellectuals who wrote on the subject echoed notions pervasive in popular culture that associated homosexuality exclusively with effeminate men and masculine women. The common view persisted that the "active" masculine male who engaged in sex with a seemingly effeminate man had not lost his heterosexual status, and his masculinity remained intact. Likewise, masculinized women who "seduced" other women were considered homosexual, whereas their feminine partners were not. A vast lexicon of pejorative terms, many local or national but others shared across borders, described effeminate men and masculine women in negative ways and reinforced the idea that homosexuality merely mimicked traditional gendered relationships.

At the same time, urban centers and the semi-invisible spaces of homoerotic sociability served as magnets to attract men and women with non-normative sexual desires. By the turn of the twentieth century significant homoerotic worlds had formed in Havana, Mexico City, Lima, Buenos Aires, Montevideo, Rio de Janeiro, São Paulo, and Salvador, among other cities. Men, and to a lesser extent women, organized same-sex private parties and dances and used the more permissive moments of Carnival celebrations to cross-dress and publicly affirm their dissident gender personas and sexual proclivities. By the 1950s most capitals had bars or nightclubs that serviced a homosexual clientele, and certain restaurants and entertainment venues offered public spaces where men and women could congregate. Blurring the gender roles that developed in the 1960s in response to unisex clothing, the hippie and countercultural movements, rock music, and other international cultural expressions opened up new forms of individual performance and expanded possibilities to transgress traditional gender norms.

Parallel to the emergence of the gay and lesbian movements in the United States and Europe in the late 1960s and the early 1970s, small groups of politicized gay men and lesbians formed in Buenos Aires, Mexico City, and Puerto Rico. In 1971 several such groups in Buenos Aires formed the Frente de Liberación Homosexual de Argentina, which promoted a radical critique of sexual norms and a public debate about homosexuality. The organization collapsed in 1975 under the increasingly repressive political climate that ended in Argentina's military regime (1976–1983). Incipient gay and lesbian political groups in Brazil and Chile never came to fruition due to the dictatorships that dominated these countries in the 1970s.

In the early years of the Cuban Revolution (1953–1959), official state policy linked homosexuality to "bourgeois decadence," and homosexual men and women who did not conform to traditional gender roles were labeled counter-revolutionary and sent to forced labor camps, along with dissidents and others deemed undesirable by the revolutionary regime. Although these centers were dismantled in the late 1960s, official government policy barred homosexuals from educational and cultural institutions, though this ban was at times difficult to enforce.

The processes of democratization in the late 1970s and throughout the 1980s in countries that had been under military rule opened up new possibilities for political activism among gay men and lesbians. New social movements offered models for the organization of homosexuals. Concurrently, the expansion of feminist ideas and vibrant women's movements in most countries of Latin America offered opportunities for lesbians to challenge heteronormativity and forced activists to address discriminatory attitudes toward same-sex eroticism among women. Many leaders of gay and lesbian activist groups had been militants in left-wing or revolutionary organizations and had moved away from them because they persisted in their views that homosexuality reflected behavior inconsistent with working-class norms and values of the popular classes. These activists brought their experiences of organizing and mobilizing to gay and lesbian groups, bringing a political tone to many of the founding organizations in Argentina, Brazil, Chile, El Salvador, Mexico, Nicaragua, and Peru, among other countries. Some gay and lesbian leaders insisted on maintaining or forging strategic links with left-wing movements as part of a larger effort to develop progressive national agendas for social change in their countries.

The advent of AIDS in Latin America had a contradictory effect on gay men. At first, long-standing prejudices against homosexuality marginalized those who contracted the disease, and many died in the early years of the epidemic due to government indifference or inaction. At the same time, new activist groups lobbied public-health authorities to respond to AIDS with effective medical policies and sex-education campaigns. In Brazil, for example, the alliances formed by public-health experts and activists to develop creative responses to the disease have become international models for how to address AIDS. Gay and lesbian activists also used the need for effective AIDS education through the active participation of members of at-risk groups as a means to leverage state resources and sustain their ongoing operations. Many small consciousness-raising groups became institutionalized as nongovernment organizations through state and international financial support that provided resources to set up offices, hire staff members, and sustain an infrastructure that could be dedicated to political organizing.

Violence, murder, and everyday forms of aggression and discrimination persist throughout Latin America, especially targeting effeminate men, transvestites, and masculine women. The Catholic Church remains an outspoken opponent of the acceptance of same-sex sexuality. Television soap operas, public declarations by popular entertainers about their homosexuality, and news of increasing toleration of homosexuals in Europe and Canada (and to a certain extent in the United States) have mitigated persistent homophobic attitudes somewhat, and also have served as a means of encouraging local activism. Groups have lobbied legislatures in many cities and states throughout Latin America to enact antidiscrimination laws, and same-sex civil partnership legislation (and even the right to same-sex marriage) has been adopted in some localities. A rich and diverse literature by openly gay and lesbian authors has developed in recent decades and also has encouraged public debate about homosexuality.

In 1995 the International Lesbian and Gay Association held its seventeenth international conference in Rio de Janeiro, attracting activists from throughout Latin America. The meeting served as a catalyst for developing networks and regional organizations. This gathering and other national and regional efforts to coordinate activism also provided opportunities for transvestites to participate in the movement. In several Latin American countries, international gatherings of feminists, as well as meetings of lesbian activists and groups, have served to strengthen the autonomous organization of lesbians. Concurrently, annual gay and lesbian parades commemorating the 1969 Stonewall Rebellion in New York City, which symbolically marked the beginning of a militant rights movement, have become increasingly popular forms of public visibility and a means of promoting social tolerance. The Pride Parade in São Paulo has attracted three million people annually in recent years, becoming the largest such event in the world.

Although social discrimination still persists throughout Latin America and the Caribbean, and class and racial differences fragment social cohesion, in recent years the widespread assumption among activists is that the act of "coming out" to family, friends, employers, and to society as a whole is the most effective means of expanding social acceptance and encouraging legislation that will offer full rights to lesbians, transvestites, and gay men.

See also **Sexuality: Gender and Sexuality.**

BIBLIOGRAPHY

Bracamonte Allaín, Jorge. *De amores y luchas: Diversidad sexual, derechos humanos y ciudadanía.* Lima: Programa de Estudios de Género, 2001.

Drucker, Peter, ed. *Different Rainbows.* London: Gay Men's Press, 2000.

Green, James N. *Beyond Carnival: Male Homosexuality in Twentieth-Century Brazil.* Chicago: University of Chicago Press, 1999.

Ingenschay, Dieter. *Desde acera opuestas: Literatura-cultura gay y lesbiana en Latinoamérica.* Madrid: Iberoamericana, 2006.

JAMES N. GREEN

SHARP, BARTHOLOMEW Bartholomew Sharp (late 1600s), one of the last of the buccaneers. In 1679, Captain Bartholomew Sharp and other buccaneers from Jamaica raided the Caribbean ports of Honduras, plundering royal storehouses and carrying off some 500 chests of indigo, as well as cocoa, cochineal, tortoiseshell, money, and silver plate.

Later that year the same buccaneers, including Sharp and Captain John Coxon, set out upon a plan of much larger design. Six captains met at Point Morant, Jamaica, and on 7 January 1680, set sail for Porto Bello. They entered the town on 17 February. Meeting little resistance, they pillaged it, took prisoners and booty, and departed just after the arrival of Spanish troops. Then they captured two Spanish vessels headed for the port and divided their large haul of plunder. Finally, Sharp and the other buccaneers marched across the Isthmus of Darién to the coasts of Panama and the Pacific, wreaking havoc as they went.

In May 1680, Lord Charles Carlisle, governor of Jamaica, put out a warrant for the apprehension of Sharp and his associates. On 1 July, Henry Morgan issued a similar arrest order. Sharp eventually returned to England, where he was charged with committing piracy on the South Seas, but he was acquitted because of a reported lack of evidence.

See also **Piracy.**

BIBLIOGRAPHY

A. D. Exquemelin, *The Buccaneers of America* (1678, repr. 1972).

Philip Ayres, *The Voyages and Adventures of Captain Barth. Sharp and Others* (1684).

C. H. Haring, *The Buccaneers in the West Indies in the XVII Century* (1910).

N. M. Crouse, *The French Struggle for the West Indies, 1665–1713* (1943).

Additional Bibliography

Lane, Kris E. *Pillaging the Empire: Piracy in the Americas, 1500-1750.* Armonk, NY: M.E. Sharpe, 1998.

Lucena Salmoral, Manuel. *Piratas, bucaneros, filibusteros y corsarios en América: Perros, mendigos, y otros malditos del mar.* Madrid: Editorial MAPFRE, 1992.

Marley, David. *Pirates and Privateers of the Americas.* Santa Barbara: ABC-CLIO, 1994.

BLAKE D. PATTRIDGE

SHEEP. *See* **Livestock.**

SHIMOSE, PEDRO (1940–). Pedro Shimose (*b.* 1940), Bolivian poet. Shimose also sketches and composes popular music. Born in Riberalta del Beni, Bolivia, to Japanese immigrants, Shimose received a degree in communication sciences from the Universidad Complutense in Madrid. He worked as columnist and editor for the daily *Presencia* of La Paz and later taught literature at the Universidad Mayor de San Andrés in La Paz. In the early 1990s he was working at the Institute of Spanish-American Cooperation in Madrid. His poetry has received various prizes: Bolivia's National Poetry Prize in 1960 and 1966, Cuba's House of the Americas Prize in 1972, and Spain's Olive Prize in 1974 and Leopoldo Panero Prize in 1975.

Shimose's early poetry (*Triludio del exilio* [1961], *Sardonia* [1967], *Poemas para un pueblo* [1968], and *Quiero escribir, pero me sale espuma* [1972]) is characterized by a humanist social commitment of a mythico-religious nature, which evolves into a definitive denunciation of those who perpetuate the conditions causing misery and pain in Latin America. In *Caducidad del fuego* (1975), *Al pie de la letra* (1976), *Reflexiones maquiavélicas* (1980), and *Poemas* (1988), the tone changes. The violence is transformed into a bitter irony mixed with tenderness and humor. Shimose also published a book of stories, *El Coco se llama Drilo* (1976), and *Diccionario de autores iberoamericanos* (1982) He is a member of the Bolivian Academy of Language and the Spanish Association of Art Critics. In 1996 his *Riberalta y otros poemas* appeared, the first work of his published in Bolivia since 1971. In 2000 he received the National Culture Prize of Bolivia, and in subsequent years he directed the poetry collection of the Instituto de Cooperación Iberoamericana in Madrid.

See also **Asians in Latin America, Literature: Spanish America.**

BIBLIOGRAPHY

Ortega, José. *Letras bolivianas de hoy: Renato Prada y Pedro Shimose* (1973).

Salgado, María Antonia. *Modern Spanish American Poets: First Series.* Detroit, MI: Gale Group, 2003.

SILVIA M. NAGY

SHINING PATH. *See* **Peru, Revolutionary Movements: Shining Path.**

SHUAR. The Shuar are an indigenous people of the southeast Ecuadorian Amazon. Their native language is Shuar (the word *shuar* itself means "people"). Often referred to as Jívaro, a term that connotes "savage" and that the Shuar find insulting, they are historically famed as fierce warriors and headhunters. Previously semi-nomadic hunter-gatherers, they now raise cattle, practice slash-and-burn agriculture, fish, and hunt. There are about forty thousand Shuar living in a mountainous region of cloudforest with unnavigable rivers, covering approximately 25,000 square miles.

The Spanish first entered Shuar territory in 1549 seeking gold, but the Shuar revolted and expelled them just five years later. Protected from colonizing forces by their impassable locale and fierce reputation for resistance, Shuar remained almost totally isolated for the next three centuries. In the mid-nineteenth century, as Shuar increasingly lost land to colonists, they settled into more stable and centralized settlements called *centros*. Encouraged by missionaries, Shuar abandoned warfare, the production of *tsantas* (shrunken heads), and puberty rites and began to participate in the market economy, while still retaining traditional practices of shamanism and polygyny. With help from Salesian missionaries, in 1964 the Shuar founded the Federación Interprovincial de Centros Shuar-Achuar, the first indigenous governing federation of its kind in the Amazon. The federation continues to oversee land distribution, health, and education. A bilingual radio education system transmitted even to their most remote areas has made Shuar schooling and acculturation into a Spanish-speaking society possible. As one of the oldest and most successful organizations of indigenous resistance, the federation remains active, attracts foreign assistance, and serves as a model of self-governance to other indigenous peoples of the Amazon.

See also **Indianismo; Indigenous Peoples.**

BIBLIOGRAPHY

Descola, Philippe. *The Spears of Twilight: Life and Death in the Amazon Jungle*, trans. Janet Lloyd. New York: New Press, 1996.

Harner, Michael J. *The Jívaro: People of the Sacred Waterfalls*. Berkeley: University of California Press, 1984.

Hendricks, Janet Wall. *To Drink of Death: The Narrative of a Shuar Warrior*. Tucson: University of Arizona Press, 1993.

Rubenstein, Steven. *Alejandro Tsakimp: A Shuar Healer in the Margins of History*. Lincoln: University of Nebraska Press, 2002.

ERIC SCHNITER

SICÁN. Sicán, indigenous name in the Muchik language for an area in the lower La Leche Valley (the Poma district of Batán Grande) on the north coast of Peru. Literally, it means the house or temple of the moon. The term "Sicán" has been adopted to refer to the archaeological culture that emerged in the Batán Grande region following the demise of the Moche culture around 700–750 CE.

The chronology of the ancient Sicán culture is divided into three periods: Early Sicán lasted from 700–750 CE to 900 CE but is still poorly known. By 900 CE, the florescent middle period begins. The Middle Sicán often has been confused with the protohistoric Chimú Kingdom. Sicán was centered on the northern north coast and largely antecedent to the Chimú. The name "Lambayeque" is also sometimes applied to Middle Sicán. Usage of Lambayeque has been problematic as it was defined on the basis of looted ceramics (as a style) and its broader cultural significance built on a literal reading of the legend of Naymlap and his descendants, recorded early in the colonial era.

Middle Sicán cultural characteristics include: (1) a distinct religious art featuring the Sicán Deity and Sicán Lord, who represent the parallel natural and supernatural universes; (2) a powerful theocracy centered at the capital of Sicán, with its dozen monumental temples and rigid, hierarchical society; (3) production and use of arsenical copper (a type of bronze) and gold alloys on an unprecedented scale; and (4) control of an extensive trade in exotic luxury goods (such as gold nuggets, tropical shells, and emeralds) that reached as far as southern Colombia, the upper Amazon, and the Peru–Chile border area. Overall, the economic wealth, political clout, and religious prestige of the Middle Sicán culture were clearly unrivaled in Peru for its period and in some respects unprecedented within Andean civilization. Diffusion of its influence represented a major cultural horizon.

The culture's preeminence came to an end around 1050 CE. Temples at the capital of Sicán were burned and a new capital was established farther west at El Purgatorio, near Túcume, marking the onset of the Late Sicán (1100 to 1375 CE). Around 1375 CE, the Chimú Kingdom began its northward expansion toward Ecuador, conquering the Sicán people on its way. Within a hundred years, the expanding Inca defeated the Chimú, its coastal rival, and some seventy years later was in turn conquered by the Spaniards.

See also **Archaeology.**

BIBLIOGRAPHY

Izumi Shimada, "Cultural Continuities and Discontinuities on the Northern North Coast, Middle-Late Horizons," in *The Northern Dynasties: Kingship and Statecraft in Chimor,* edited by Michael E. Moseley and Alana Cordy-Collins (1990), pp. 297–392.

Izumi Shimada and John F. Merkel, "Copper-Alloy Metallurgy in Ancient Peru," in *Scientific American* 265, no. 1 (1991): 80–86.

Izumi Shimada, "The Regional States of the Coast during Late Intermediate Period: Archaeological Evidence, Ethnohistorical Record and Art Outline (in Italian), in *I Regni Preincaici e ll Mondo Inca* (Pre-Inca regional states and Inca empire), edited by Laura Laurencich-Minelli (1992), pp. 49–64, 97–110.

Izumi Shimada and Jo Ann Griffin, "Precious Metal Objects of the Middle Sicán," in *Scientific American* 270, no. 4 (1994): 82–89.

Additional Bibliography

Flórez Rocío, Suzanne Alfaro. *Primeros peruanos: Historia de las culturas prehispanicas.* Lima: Editora Nacional, 1999.

McEwan, Colin. *Precolumbian Gold: Technology, Style, and Iconography.* Chicago: Fitzroy Dearborn Publishers, 2000.

Sharpe, Colleen. *Ancient Peru Unearthed: Golden Treasures of a Lost Civilization.* Calgary: Nickle Arts Museum, 2006.

IZUMI SHIMADA

SICARIO.   *See* **Drugs and Drug Trade.**

SIERRA, STELLA (1917–1997). Stella Sierra (*b.* 5 July 1917; *d.* 1997), Panamanian poet. Sierra was born in Aguadulce, Panama. In 1936, she graduated from the Colegio Internacional de María Inmaculada, and in 1954 she received a degree in education with specialization in Spanish from the University of Panama.

Her first two books, *Sinfonía jubilosa en doce sonetos* (1942; Joyful Symphony in Twelve Sonnets) and *Canciones de mar y luna* (1944; Songs of Sea and Moon), confirmed her place in Panamanian letters. Her later publications, *Libre y cautiva* (1947; Free and Captive), *Cinco poemas* (1949; Five Poems), *Poesía* (1962; Poetry), and *Presencia del recuerdo* (1965; Presence of Memory) revealed her control over her poetic resources and the universality of her poetry.

Sierra has won many awards for both her poetry and her fiction. Among them the Demetrio H. Brid Prize for her short story *Con los pies descalzos* (1944; Barefooted), the Miró Prize for *Sinfonía jubilosa*, and a first prize from the Chancellery of Uruguay for her *Himno para la glorificación de Franklin D. Roosevelt* (1946; Hymn in Homage of Franklin D. Roosevelt). She has contributed to the weekly *Semanario Mundo Gráfico,* to *Correo Literario,* and to such literary magazines as *Poesía de América, Cultura,* and *Épocas.* Sierra has taught at the National Institute of Panama and at the University of Panama and has been a delegate at various international conferences. She died in Panama City in 1997. After her death, the Fundación Cultural Signos, the 9 Signos Grupo Editorial and her family members established the Stella Sierra Poetry Prize which is awarded Panamanian poets.

See also **Literature: Spanish America.**

BIBLIOGRAPHY

Enrique Jaramillo Levi, *Poesía erótica de Panamá* (1982).

Gloria Guardia, *Aproximación a Libre y Cautiva obra escogida de Stella Sierra* (1990).

Diane E. Marting, ed., *Women Writers of Spanish America* (1987).

David Foster, comp. *Handbook of Latin American Literature,* 2d ed. (1992), p. 461.

Additional Bibliography

Guardia, Gloria. *Aproximación a libre y cautiva, obra escogida de Stella Sierra.* Panamá: s.n., 1990.

Jiménez Faro, Luzmaría. *Brevario de los sentidos: Poesía erótica escrita por mujeres.* Madrid: Ediciones Torremozas, 2003.

Nathan, Viviane. *Mujer, prensa, y poesía.* Panamá: Dirección de Extensión Cultural, Universidad de Panamá, 1993.

ELBA D. BIRMINGHAM-POKORNY

SIERRA (ECUADOR).   Sierra (Ecuador) the mountain region, covering about 27,500 square miles, or about one quarter of the nation. Despite its location along the equator, the elevation of the sierra (often 9,000 feet and above) gives the region a temperate climate, what *serranos* call eternal springtime. Made up of two parallel branches of the Andes (375 miles north to south), the sierra has ten major basins, each formed by mountain spurs that connect the two main branches of the mountains. These verdant zones produce barley, corn, potatoes, wheat, fruit, and vegetables. Most Ecuadorian cities are set in these valleys, including Ibarra, Quito, Ambato, Riobamba, and Cuenca. Thickly populated by sedentary farming Indians, the sierra was the focus of Spanish colonizing efforts. In 1800 as much as 90 percent of the population of Ecuador lived in the sierra. By 1992 only about half did, as people fled overcrowding and exploitation by whites. Transportation difficulties have made the sierra a relatively isolated and culturally more traditional zone in Ecuador. The sierra corridor is sometimes known as the "Avenue of the Volcanoes," a name given by nineteenth-century naturalist Baron Alexander von Humboldt.

See also **Humboldt, Alexander von.**

BIBLIOGRAPHY

Details on Ecuador's geography can be found in Preston James, *Latin America* (1986). For information on the natives of Ecuador's sierra, see *Handbook of South American Indians,* vol. 2, *The Andean Civilizations,* edited by Julian H. Steward (1963).

Additional Bibliography

Gómez E., Nelson. *Transformación del espacio nacional: Pasado y presente del Ecuador.* Quito: EDICUIAS C., 1999.

Handelsman, Michael H. *Culture and Customs of Ecuador.* Westport, CT: Greenwood Press, 2000.

Helferich, Gerard. *Humboldt's Cosmos: Alexander von Humboldt and the Latin American Journey that Changed the Way We See the World.* New York: Gotham Books, 2004.

Hofstede, Robert Gerardus Maria, Johanna M. Lips, and Wibold Jongsma. *Geografía, ecología, y forestación de la sierra alta del Ecuador: Revisión de literatura.* Quito: Abya Yala, 1998.

RONN F. PINEO

SIERRA MADRE.

Sierra Madre, the principal mountain system of Mexico. It consists of the Sierra Madre Oriental, Sierra Madre Occidental, Sierra Madre del Sur, Sierra Madre de Oaxaca, and the Sierra Madre de Chiapas. The first four groups form the dissected edges of the vast central plateau of Mexico, while the Chiapas range lies east of the Isthmus of Tehuantepec. Extending the length of Mexico, from the United States to Guatemala, the mountains form a broad northwest-southeast arc. The average elevation of the range is 6,000 to 13,000 feet. Metals such as silver, gold, zinc, and iron first attracted Spanish settlers to the Sierra Madre, especially in the northern ranges. Although mining remained important, the exploitation of forest reserves and hydroelectric sites drew developers during the twentieth century. Throughout the Sierra Madre, isolated sections remain a refuge for small Amerindian groups maintaining their traditional ways of life.

The Occidental and Oriental mountains define the western and eastern edges of the central plateau and are similar in height. The Occidental range is volcanic and parallels the western coast of Mexico for 1,000 miles through the states of Chihuahua, Sonora, Sinaloa, Durango, and Nayarit. Vegetation on the steep lower slopes is poor, but the higher elevations contain some of the most important coniferous forest stands in the country. The deep canyons along the western slope support half a dozen major dams that provide water to the irrigated fields of Sonora and Sinaloa. Some agriculture exists within the intermontane valleys, but mining, especially of silver, has been the principal motive for settlement in the Sierra Madre Occidental.

The Sierra Madre Oriental is a series of elongated limestone ranges that parallel the Gulf of Mexico, crossing through Coahuila, Nuevo León, Tamaulipas, and San Luis Potosí states. From the central plateau, the Oriental range appears as a small lip, but from the Gulf, the peaks form an impressive escarpment. During the colonial era, the Veracruz-Jalapa road that crossed the sierra was the principal artery between the coast and the central plateau. The southern tip of the 700-mile-long chain is crowned by 18,760-foot Mount Orizaba (Citlaltépetl), the highest mountain in Mexico.

The Sierra Madre del Sur extends from Mount Orizaba toward the Pacific coast, ending at the Isthmus of Tehuantepec. This highly dissected upland area contains knife-edged ridges and steep valleys that cover Guerrero and Oaxaca states. Formed by ancient crystalline rock, the southern highlands average 7,000 feet in height and contain a few peaks over 10,000 feet. The eastern portion of this uplifted area is called the Sierra Madre de Oaxaca. Before the Conquest this area was inhabited by several important Indian groups, notably the Zapotecs and Mixtecs. Twentieth-century economic activities throughout the area have been limited to mining, forestry, coffee production, and subsistence farming.

The smaller Sierra Madre de Chiapas begins east of the Isthmus of Tehuantepec, crosses the state of Chipas, and reaches into western Guatemala. It is mostly crystalline rock with some volcanic activity. This area does not seem to have been very populated during pre-Hispanic times and is still sparsely populated. Forestry and coffee are the most important activities in this isolated area.

BIBLIOGRAPHY

David Henderson, "Land, Man, and Time," in *Six Faces of Mexico*, edited by Russell C. Ewing (1966), pp. 103–160.

Jorge L. Tamayo, *Geografía moderna de México*, 9th ed. (1980).

D. J. Fox, "Mexico," in *Latin America: Geographical Perspectives*, 2d ed., edited by Harold Blakemore and Clifford Smith (1983), pp. 25–76.

Robert C. West and John P. Augelli, *Middle America: Its Lands and Peoples*, 3d ed. (1989), pp. 24–31.

Additional Bibliography

Biggers, Jeff. *In the Sierra Madre*. Urbana: University of Illinois Press, 2006.

Cartron, Jean-Luc E. *Biodiversity, Ecosystems, and Conservation in Northern Mexico*. New York: Oxford University Press, 2005.

Finerty, Catherine Palmer. *In a Village far from Home: My Life among the Cora Indians of the Sierra Madre*. Tucson: University of Arizona Press, 2000.

Yetman, David. *The Guajiros of the Sierra Madre: Hidden People of Northwestern Mexico*. Albuquerque: University of New Mexico Press, 2002.

MARIE D. PRICE

SIERRA MAESTRA. Sierra Maestra, the coastal mountain chain in Cuba's southeast Oriente Province. Coastal swampland gives way to an inaccessible, rugged spine dividing the island. The Sierra Maestra is the highest Cuban range, with such local branches as Sierra Norte and Sierra Trinidad. It was the refuge of Cuba's rebels: runaway slaves, independence leaders José Martí and Máximo Gómez y Báez, Fidel Castro, and finally anti-Castro guerrillas in the 1960s.

In the Sierras, during the Ten Years' War (1868–1878), Carlos Manuel de Céspedes and Máximo Gómez y Báez developed a guerrilla strategy later used by Castro: using *guajiro* (mountain peasant) guerrillas in hit-and-run tactics, burning cane fields, and courting dissatisfied planters. In the War for Independence (1895–1899), Cuban literary figure and patriot José Martí died in a Sierras ambush.

In December 1956, Fidel Castro, a native of Oriente, repeated Martí's return from exile to a Sierra-based campaign. The climax was the Batista offensive "Fin de Fidel," from May to August 1958. The decisive battles were for the Sierra ridge, at Santo Domingo; and for Castro's headquarters, at El Jigüe.

The Sierra Maestra Manifesto and the agrarian reform law (Revolutionary Law 1) were symbolic measures to win middle-class support. However, Castro reached a secret alliance with the Communist Party, and Sierra "liberated zones" foreshadowed social revolution. Anti-Castro guerrillas were effectively eliminated from the Sierras only in the late 1960s.

See also **Castro Ruz, Fidel.**

BIBLIOGRAPHY

Tad Szulc, *Fidel: A Critical Portrait* (1986).

Additional Bibliography

Bethell, Leslie. *Cuba: A Short History*. New York: Cambridge University Press, 1993.

Fuente, Alejandro de la. *A Nation for All: Race, Inequality, and Politics in Twentieth-Century Cuba*. Chapel Hill: University of North Carolina Press, 2001.

Quevedo, José. *Misión en la Sierra*. Havana: Ediciones Verde Olivo, 1999.

Rodríguez Herrera, Mariano. *Las huellas del Che Guevara*. México: Plaza & Janés, 2002.

PAT KONRAD

SIERRA MÉNDEZ, JUSTO (1848–1912).

Justo Sierra Méndez (*b.* 26 January 1848; *d.* 13 September 1912), Mexican writer, political thinker, historian, and educational leader. Sierra was born in Campeche, the son of prominent Yucatecan politician, writer, and jurist Justo Sierra O'Reilly, and after 1861 lived and was educated in Mexico City, receiving a law degree in 1871 from the Escuela de Derecho. A protégé of Ignacio M. Altamirano, in 1868 Sierra began to write poetry, short stories, plays, and a novel. His career as a political journalist and thinker began in 1874 and reached a climax in the important newspaper *La Libertad* (1878–1884), which he directed until 1880, and which was an exponent of a "new" or transformed liberalism that called for a strong government and economic development. Of several histories, his most important was *Evolución política del pueblo mexicano,* first published under another title in 1900–1902. He was a deputy to Congress from 1880 until 1894, when he was appointed to the Supreme Court. As an educator, he taught at the National Preparatory School after 1877 and led the First and Second National Congresses of Public Instruction in 1889 and 1891, which established the principle of free obligatory primary education and reaffirmed the positivist preparatory curriculum. In 1901 he became subsecretary of public instruction, and then secretary from 1905 to 1911. He founded the National Autonomous University of Mexico (UNAM) in 1910. In 1912 he was appointed minister to Spain, where he died.

Sierra was the major Mexican intellectual of his era. His political and educational thought was characterized by a continuing tension between classic liberal principles, including French spiritualism, and positivism. Though an adherent of the regime of Porfirio Díaz (1877–1880, 1884–1911), Sierra led the effort (1892–1893) by the *científicos* to limit presidential authority.

See also **Altamirano, Ignacio Manuel; Díaz, Porfirio; Sierra O'Reilly, Justo.**

BIBLIOGRAPHY

Sierra's *Obras completas,* 15 vols. (1948), includes a biography by editor Agustín Yáñez. See also C. A. Hale, *The Transformation of Liberalism in Late Nineteenth-Century Mexico* (1989).

Additional Bibliography

Dumas, Claude. *Justo Sierra y el México de su tiempo, 1848–1912.* México: Universidad Nacional Autónoma de México, 1992.

Sáez Pueyo, Carmen. *Justo Sierra: Antecedentes del partido único en México.* Mexico, D.F.: Facultad de Ciencias Políticas y Sociales: M.A. Porrúa Grupo Editorial, 2002.

                                    CHARLES A. HALE

SIERRA O'REILLY, JUSTO (1814–1861).

Justo Sierra O'Reilly (*b.* 24 September 1814; *d.* 15 January 1861); Yucatecan jurist, journalist, novelist, and historian. The illegitimate son of a parish priest, Sierra grew up in Mérida and was educated first at the local seminary. Later he studied law in Mexico City (1838). After graduation he returned to Yucatán and practiced as a lawyer before turning to politics (serving as judge, ambassador, and congressman) and literary pursuits. He founded newspapers and wrote books on history and literature. He also composed fiction, his most famous novel probably being *La hija del judío* (The Jew's Daughter), a romance. He is the author of the Mexican republic's civil code (1860) and the father of Justo Sierra Méndez (1847–1912).

See also **Sierra Méndez, Justo.**

BIBLIOGRAPHY

Mary Wilhelmine Williams, "Secessionist Diplomacy of Yucatán," in *Hispanic American Historical Review* 9, no. 2 (1929): 132–143; *Enciclopedia yucatanense* (1944), vol. 5, pp. 623–631, and vol. 7, pp. 205–244.

Additional Bibliography

Cortés Campos, Rocío Leticia. *La novela histórica de Justo Sierra O'Reilly: La literatura y el poder.* Mérida: Ediciones de la Universidad Autónoma de Yucatán, 2004.

Quirarte, Martín. *Gabino Barreda, Justo Sierra y el Ateneo de la Juventud.* México: Universidad Nacional Autónoma de México, Escuela Nacional Preparatoria, Dirección General de Publicaciones, 1995.

                                    ROBERT W. PATCH

SIERRA (PERU).

Sierra (Peru), the Andean highland region where approximately half of the country's population lived in 1990. It is formed by three ranges of mountains with fertile river valleys, high plains, and deep canyons. The western Andean slopes lead to the desertic coastal region, while the easternmost slopes—the *ceja de selva* (jungle's eyebrow)—start the region of the Amazonian rain forest. By the time of the Spanish Conquest, the Andean people had developed a sophisticated system of vertical control that allowed access to a rich variety of crops at different altitudes as well as agrarian techniques such as terracing and irrigation. Under Spanish rule the Sierra became a highly productive mineral region.

See also **Agriculture.**

BIBLIOGRAPHY

Javier Pulgar Vidal, *Geografía del Perú: Las ocho regiones naturales del Perú* (1972).

Additional Bibliography

Klarén, Peter F. *Peru: Society and Nationhood in the Andes.* New York: Oxford University Press, 2000.

Reinhard, Johan. *The Ice Maiden: Inca Mummies, Mountain Gods, and Sacred Sites in the Andes.* Washington DC: National Geographic Society, 2005.

Stern, Steve J. *Shining and Other Paths: War and Society in Peru, 1980-1995.* Durham, NC: Duke University Press, 1998.

ALFONSO W. QUIROZ

SIETE DE MARZO.

SIETE DE MARZO. Siete de Marzo (1849), a divisive Colombian presidential selection. The tumultuous presidential selection of José Hilario López on the siete de marzo (7 March) signaled the Colombian Liberal Party's domination of the central government that lasted until 1885. The nascent Conservative Party, seriously divided by the reformist administration of the nominally conservative Tomás Cipriano de Mosquera, fielded several candidates in the 1848 contest. Splitting the vote in this manner enabled López to gain a plurality (López, 725; José Joaquín Gori, 384; Rufino Cuervo, 304; Mariano Ospina Rodríguez, 81; Joaquín María Barriga, 74; Florentino González, 71; and Eusebio Borrero, 52). The Congress, following its constitutional mandate to select the president, chose the Liberal López on 7 March 1849 in the face of severe intimidation by student and artisan militants in the congressional gallery. Conservatives claimed that crowd

pressures had made the selection process illegitimate. The López regime (1849–1853) initiated sweeping liberal reforms, which heightened the symbolism of the pivotal event.

See also **Colombia, Political Parties: Conservative Party; Colombia, Political Parties: Liberal Party.**

BIBLIOGRAPHY

José Manuel Restrepo, *Historia de la Nueva Granada: 1845–54,* vol. 2 (1963), pp. 103–106.

Helen Delpar, *Red Against Blue: The Liberal Party in Colombian Politics, 1863–1899* (1981), pp. 5–6.

David Bushnell and Neill Macaulay, *The Emergence of Latin America in the Nineteenth Century* (1988), pp. 209–220.

Additional Bibliography

Hylton, Forest. *Evil Hour in Colombia.* London: Verso, 2006.

Rojas, Cristina. *Civilization and Violence: Regimes of Representation in Nineteenth-Century Colombia.* Minneapolis: University of Minnesota Press, 2002.

Sanders, James E. *Contentious Republicans: Popular Politics, Race, and Class in Nineteenth-Century Colombia.* Durham, NC: Duke University Press, 2004.

DAVID SOWELL

SIETE PARTIDAS.

SIETE PARTIDAS. Siete Partidas, Castilian legal code influenced by principles of Roman law. The *Siete Partidas* (Seven Divisions of Law) (1265) was the greatest achievement of Alfonso X of Castile and León. Produced by jurists well-versed in Roman law, the compendium was meant to provide the Castilian monarch with a universal system of royal justice and absolute authority that would replace the jurisdictional privileges of the towns and noble estates of the realm. Because of strong opposition, the law was never put into effect and the *Siete Partidas,* written in the Castilian vernacular, merely served as a textbook or legal reference work to supplement previously existing laws.

Yet the *Siete Partidas* clearly influenced the outline and administration of the legal system in the Americas. For instance, scribes, *escribanos,* observed and recorded many steps of the judicial process in New Spain, introducing the idea of recording the judicial process. Also, the code provided a legal personality for slaves, a status that was implemented to varying degrees in the colonies. Furthermore, the *Siete Partidas* reserved town land for public use; this provision, as well, was implemented. Thus, more than a legal reference, the *Siete Partidas* affected many facets of life in Spanish American society.

See also **Judicial Systems: Spanish America.**

BIBLIOGRAPHY

Evelyn Stefanos Procter, *Alfonso X of Castile: Patron of Literature and Learning* (1951).

José Antonio Maravall, *Estudios de historia del pensamiento español* (1967).

Colin M. MacLachlan, *Criminal Justice in Eighteenth-Century Mexico* (1974).

Additional Bibliography

Aguirre, Carlos A., and Robert Buffington, eds. *Reconstructing Criminality in Latin America.* Wilmington, DE: Scholarly Resources, 2000.

Burns, Robert I., ed. *Las siete partidas.* Translated by Samuel Parsons Scott. Philadelphia: University of Pennsylvania Press, 2001.

Cutter, Charles R. *The Legal Culture of Northern New Spain, 1700–1810.* Albuquerque: University of New Mexico Press, 1995.

Klein, Herbert S. *African Slavery in Latin America and the Caribbean.* New York: Oxford University Press, 1986.

Mijares Ramírez, Ivonne. *Escribanos y escrituras públicas en el siglo XVI: El caso de la Cuidad de México.* México, D.F.: Universidad Nacional Autónoma de México, 1997.

Scardaville, Michael C. "Justice by Paperwork: A Day in the Life of a Court Scribe in Bourbon Mexico City." *Journal of Social History* 36, no. 4 (Summer 2003): 979–1007.

SUZANNE HILES BURKHOLDER

SIGAUD, EUGENIO DE PROENÇA
(1889–1979). Eugenio de Proença Sigaud (*b.* 1889; *d.* 1979) Brazilian architectural engineer and painter. Born in the interior of the state of Rio de Janeiro, Sigaud moved to Rio in the early 1920s to study architecture at the National School of Fine Arts. While there, the artist Modesto Brocos helped perfect Sigaud's drawing skills. In 1931 Sigaud joined Edson Mota, João Rescala, José Pancetti, Milton Dacosta, and other young artists to form the Núcleo Bernardelli, a group that sought

to counter the aesthetic traditionalism of the National School of Fine Arts. The Núcleo came to represent a moderate wing of the Brazilian modernist movement.

Sigaud's career consisted of two parallel aspects: he owned an architectural engineering and construction company, and he achieved prominence as a painter of social themes. His canvases and murals depict urban construction workers on scaffolding as well as rural coffee pickers. His most celebrated works include a painting entitled *Work Accident,* an architectural and interior design project for the church of São Jorge, and mural paintings for the cathedral of Jacarèzinho. He also dabbled in printing and book illustration.

See also **Rio de Janeiro (City).**

BIBLIOGRAPHY

Arte no Brasil, vol. 2 (1979), pp. 763–765.

Additional Bibliography

De Sá Rego, Stella, and Marguerite Itamar Harrison. *Modern Brazilian Painting.* Albuquerque: Latin American Institute, University of New Mexico, 1997.

CAREN A. MEGHREBLIAN

SIGÜENZA Y GÓNGORA, CARLOS DE
(1645–1700). Carlos de Sigüenza y Góngora (*b.* 20 August 1645; *d.* 22 August 1700), premier intellectual of seventeenth-century Mexico. Born in Mexico City, Sigüenza y Góngora was the son of a former tutor to the Spanish royal family; on his mother's side, he was distantly related to the poet Luís de Góngora. As a youth, he entered the Jesuit order, but curfew violations led to his expulsion in 1668. He then resumed theological and secular studies at the University of Mexico, where, in 1672, he gained the chair of mathematics and astrology. Over time, he accumulated several other important positions, including those of royal cosmographer of New Spain, chaplain of the Amor de Dios Hospital, and almoner to the archbishop of Mexico.

This talented polymath wrote extensively on a wide variety of subjects, but most of his works were not published. Despite his official capacity as an astrologer, Sigüenza y Góngora roundly belabored contemporary "superstitions." His scientific endeavors reached their summit with the *Libra astronómica y filosófica* (1690), an astronomical treatise in which he argued that comets were a natural phenomenon rather than an omen of divine displeasure; the work also attacked Aristotelian orthodoxy and upheld the validity of Mexican scholarship. In a more journalistic vein, Sigüenza y Góngora chronicled the triumph of Spanish arms in New Mexico and the Caribbean and wrote the finest eyewitness account of the Mexico City riot of 1692.

Sigüenza y Góngora devoted much scholarly energy to the study of Mexico's pre-Hispanic past. More important, he acquired and preserved the magnificent Ixtlilxochitl collection of codices and manuscripts. However, while he glorified the Aztec Empire, even claiming it as Mexico's version of classical antiquity, he despised the Indian masses of his own day. This contradiction ultimately proved fatal to his studies of indigenous peoples, which (along with a projected Indian museum) he abandoned after the 1692 riot.

His intellectual activities were further curtailed after 1694, when failing health forced him to resign his university post. Assailed by numerous ailments, he died in Mexico City. In retrospect, Sigüenza y Góngora appears as a precursor of both the Mexican Enlightenment and Mexican nationalism. Throughout his writings, he sought to delineate, praise, and defend the emerging creole *patria,* particularly as exemplified in its greatest center, Mexico City.

See also **Aztecs; Enlightenment, The; Mexico City; Nationalism.**

BIBLIOGRAPHY

Irving A. Leonard, *Don Carlos de Sigüenza y Góngora: A Mexican Savant of the Seventeenth Century* (1929).

Elías Trabulse, *Ciencia y religión en el siglo xvii* (1974).

Anthony Pagden, *Spanish Imperialism and the Political Imagination* (1990), pp. 90–116.

D. A. Brading, *The First America: The Spanish Monarchy, Creole Patriots, and the Liberal State, 1492–1867* (1991), pp. 363–371.

Additional Bibliography

Lorente Medina, Antonio. *La prosa de Sigüenza y Góngora y la formación de la conciencia criolla mexicana.* México, D.F.: Fondo de Cultura Económica, 1996.

Mayer, Alicia. *Carlos de Sigüenza y Góngora: Homenaje, 1700–2000.* México: Universidad Nacional Autónoma de México, Instituto de Investigaciones Históricas, 2002.

More, Anna Herron. "Colonial Baroque: Carlos de Sigüenza y Góngora and the Post-Colonization of New Spain." Ph.D. diss., University of California, Berkeley, 2003.

Poole, Stafford. *Our Lady of Guadalupe: The Origins and Sources of a Mexican National Symbol, 1531–1797.* Tucson: University of Arizona Press, 1995.

R. DOUGLAS COPE

SILES ZUAZO, HERNÁN (1914–1996). Hernán Siles Zuazo (*b.* 21 March 1914; *d.* August 1996), president of Bolivia (1956–1960, 1982–1985). Born in La Paz, the son of Hernando Siles Reyes, president of Bolivia (1926–1930), Siles Zuazo studied there at the American Institute and the National University. One of the founders of the Nationalist Revolutionary Movement (MNR) in 1941, he personally commanded the MNR forces in the April 1952 revolution. That year Siles became vice president of Bolivia, and in 1956 he was elected president. His principal task in office was to control the high inflation rate set off by the revolutionary process. Confronting organized labor, a faction of which supported the MNR, he was responsible for the implementation of an International Monetary Fund stabilization program. In 1960 he stepped down and was named Bolivian ambassador to Uruguay.

When the military overthrew the MNR in 1964, Siles became the consummate opponent of the authoritarian rulers, searching for ways to restore civilian rule. Unlike other founders of the MNR, Siles never allied himself with any faction of the military; instead he suffered imprisonment on several occasions and exile in Uruguay. In 1972 Siles founded a leftist offshoot of the MNR, which he called the MNR de Izquierda (MNRI). When the military convoked elections in the late 1970s, Siles led his MNRI into a coalition dubbed the Popular and Democratic Union (Unidad Democrática y Popular—UDP) that included the Communist Party and the young Movimiento de Izquierda Revolucionaria (MIR). As the UDP's presidential candidate, Siles won three consecutive elections in 1978, 1979, and 1980; each time he was denied victory either because his coalition did not achieve the 50 percent plus required or because the military prevented him from taking power.

In October 1982, Siles Zuazo was elected president of Bolivia by the Congress. Over the next three years, he presided over one of the most difficult periods in Bolivian history. His government faced the impossible task of both resolving the country's worst economic crisis, caused by years of military mismanagement, and responding to the pent-up demands of social groups. At the same time, Siles faced extreme pressure from international financial institutions to implement harsh austerity measures and from the United States to combat the booming cocaine industry. Governing Bolivia under these circumstances proved to be a daunting task. By late 1984, the economy had fallen to a historic low, reaching a yearly hyperinflation rate of 26,000 percent. Faced with tremendous pressure from every sector of Bolivian society, Siles was forced to convoke elections for July 1985 and step down one year before his term expired. Siles was largely responsible for launching Bolivia on the route to democracy.

Siles retired from politics in 1985 and returned to Uruguay. He died there in August 1996.

See also **Bolivia, Political Parties: Nationalist Revolutionary Movement (MNR); Drugs and Drug Trade.**

BIBLIOGRAPHY

James M. Malloy and Eduardo A. Gamarra, *Revolution and Reaction: Bolivia, 1964–1985* (1988).

Luis Anteza Ergueta, *Hernán Siles Zuazo: El estrategy y la contrarevolución* (1979).

Additional Bibliography

Andrade, Charles W. *Escenas y episodios de la historia: Estudios Bolivianos, 1953–1999.* La Paz: Editorial Los Amigos del Libro: Werner Guttentag, 2004.

Crespo, Alfonso. *Hernán Siles Zuazo: El hombre de abril.* La Paz, Bolivia: Plural Editores, 1997.

Klein, Herbert S. *Bolivia: The Evolution of a Multi-Ethnic Society, Second Edition.* New York: Oxford University Press, 1992.

EDUARDO A. GAMARRA

SILK INDUSTRY AND TRADE. Brazil never assumed an importance comparable to that of Mexico within the context of colonial trade with Asia.

Nevertheless, by the mid-seventeenth century, Portuguese East India merchantmen were calling at major Brazilian ports on their return voyages, in spite of official restraints regarding direct trade with the American colony. Silk ranked high among the products "illicitly" sold in Brazil, and studies based on estate inventories have demonstrated that fine textiles, including silk, were an important component of the possessions of wealthy Brazilians, as they were in Mexico. The discovery of gold in Minas Gerais led to an intensification of this direct trade in Asian goods during the eighteenth century. During the phase of Pombaline monopoly trade companies (1755–1777), silkworms and the cultivation of mulberry trees were successfully introduced to Maranhão, and Brazilian silk was actually exported to Lisbon. However, the experience was apparently short-lived. In the second quarter of the nineteenth century the provincial government of Minas Gerais attempted to promote silk production there, but these efforts resulted in failure. Similar efforts had been made in the province of Rio de Janeiro since 1811, and government subsidies were to prove vital to the success of a silk enterprise established at Itaguaí in the 1840s. Cloth produced by the Imperial Companhia Serapédica de Itaguahy figured at the Paris Exposition of 1851, but this vertically integrated "factory" did not survive beyond the last decade of the nineteenth century. Silk production was not taken up again until the 1920s, when a factory was established at Campinas in the state of São Paulo. The key to the success of this Paulista enterprise was the availability of Japanese immigrants who were familiar with the various phases of production. This immigrant element explains the near total concentration of the present-day Brazilian silk industry in São Paulo.

See also **Textile Industry: The Colonial Era; Textile Industry: Modern Textiles.**

BIBLIOGRAPHY

The silk trade is dealt with in C. R. Boxer, *The Portuguese Seaborne Empire, 1415–1825* (1973). For a brief account of silk production in Brazil see Andrée Mansuy-Diniz Silva, "Imperial Re-organization, 1750–1808," in *Colonial Brazil,* edited by Leslie Bethell (1987), p. 268.

Additional Bibliography

Maria y Campos, Teresa de, and Teresa Castelló Yturbide. *Historia y arte de la seda en México: Siglos XVI-XX.* Mexico City: Banamex, 1990.

DOUGLAS COLE LIBBY

SILVA, BARTOLOMEU BUENO DA.

See Bandeiras.

SILVA, BENEDITA DA

(1942–). Benedita da Silva (Benedita Souza da Silva; *b.* 11 March 1942), first Afro-Brazilian woman to be elected to Brazil's congress. Da Silva, known as Bené, was one of thirteen children born to a poor Rio de Janeiro family. Married at sixteen, she had five children in rapid succession, of whom only two survived. She was an early member of the newly formed Worker's Party (Partido dos Trabalhadores—PT), and in 1982 successfully ran on the PT ticket for Rio's city council. In 1986, having campaigned largely in Rio's *favelas* (slums), she was elected as a federal deputy to the Chamber of Deputies, Brazil's lower house, becoming one of only nine blacks and twenty-five women in Brazil's 559-member Congress. She was reelected in 1990.

An energetic supporter of the rights of the oppressed, da Silva has described herself as "three times a minority," stating: "As a black, a woman, and a *favelada* [slum dweller], I have a special responsibility to speak out on the subjects that I know about—against racial discrimination, against the unequal rights of women, and against the injustices suffered by the poor." An evangelical Christian, da Silva is a member of Brazil's rapidly growing Assembly of God Church. She ran unsuccessfully for mayor of Rio de Janeiro in 1992. In 1994 she was elected senator from Rio de Janeiro, becoming the first black woman to serve in the Senate. In 1997 her autobiography, *Benedita da Silva: An Afro–Brazilian Woman's Story of Politics and Love*, was published in English. In 1998, she was elected deputy governor of the state of Rio de Janeiro. In 2000, a documentary based on her life, *I Was Born a Black Woman* (directed by Maisa Mendonça and Vicente Franco), won the prize for best documentary at the Latino Film Festival of San Francisco, Marin, and Berkeley. In 2002, she became governor of the state of Rio de Janeiro when the standing governor resigned in order to run for president. From 2003 to 2004, she served as Brazil's minister of social action. In 2006, she ran the presidential campaign of Luiz Inácio da Silva in the state of Rio. In 2007, she became the secretary of human rights of Rio State.

See also **Brazil, Political Parties: Workers Party (PT); Women.**

BIBLIOGRAPHY

Crook, Larry, and Randal Johnson, eds. *Black Brazil: Culture, Identity, and Social Mobilization.* Los Angeles: UCLA Latin American Center Publications, University of California, Los Angeles, 1999.

Hanchard, Michael, ed. *Racial Politics in Contemporary Brazil.* Durham, NC: Duke University Press, 1999.

Langfur, Hal. "From Slums of Rio to Halls of Power," *Christian Science Monitor,* 24 September 1987, 1.

Marcom, John, Jr. "The Fire Down South," *Forbes,* 15 October 1990, 56.

McFarlane-Taylor, Joann. "Benedita da Silva Fighting for the Favelas," *Essence,* June 1991, 36.

Riding, Alan. "One Woman's Mission: To Make Brasília Sensitive," *New York Times,* 19 February 1987, 4.

DAPHNE PATAI

SILVA, CLARA

(1907–1976). Clara Silva (*b.* 1907; *d.* 1976), Uruguayan poet, novelist, and critic. Silva was born in Montevideo and began writing poetry early on. Her first book, *La cabellera oscura* (The Dark Mane, 1945), showed a mature writer. It was followed by *Memoria de la nada* (1948). A second phase in her work began with *Los delirios* (1954), a collection of sonnets on human and divine love. *Las bodas* (The Wedding, 1960) is a collection of poems that deal with religion, a preoccupation that continued in *Preludio indiano y otros poemas* (1960) and more pointedly in *Guitarra en sombra* (1964). *Juicio final* (1971) is her last book of poems. Her fiction included *El alma y los perros* (The Soul and the Dogs, 1962), *Aviso a la población* (Warning to the Population, 1964), *Habitación testigo* (A Room as Witness, 1967), *Prohibido pasar* (1969), a collection of short stories, and *Las furias del sueño* (The Furies of Dreaming, 1975).

An active participant in the cultural and literary life of Montevideo, she was married to Alberto Zum Felde, a prominent critic and writer. She wrote two books on the life and work of the modernist Uruguayan poet Delmira Agustini and elaborated an idealist vision of America through three universal themes: nature, love, and death. In 1976 she received the Grand National Prize of Literature of Uruguay. Silva died in Montevideo.

See also **Montevideo; Zum Felde, Alberto.**

BIBLIOGRAPHY

The Archive of Hispanic Literature on Tape: A Descriptive Guide, compiled by Francisco Aguilera and edited by Georgette Magassy Dorn (1974).

Sarah Bollo, *Literatura uruguaya, 1807–1975* (1976); and *Diccionario de literatura uruguaya* (1987).

Additional Bibliography

Pickenhayn, Jorge Oscar. *Voces Femeninas en La Poesia de Uruguay.* Buenos Aires: Editorial Plus Ultra, 1999.

MAGDALENA GARCÍA PINTO

SILVA, FRANCISCO MANUEL DA

(1795–1865). Francisco Manuel da Silva (*b.* 21 February 1795; *d.* 18 December 1865), Brazilian conductor, cellist, teacher, and composer. Silva studied at the music school in which Padre José Maurício Nunes Garcia taught children who were unable to pay for musical instruction. At the age of ten he began to study cello and shortly thereafter was accepted as a boy soprano in the Royal Chapel Choir. He studied counterpoint and composition with Sigismund Neukomm, the Austrian composer who had been lured to Brazil by the promises of Dom João VI, the reigning monarch intent on establishing a school of fine arts. Although Silva wrote considerable sacred music, several art songs, and some instrumental and piano music, he is remembered principally for his patriotic songs and especially for composing the Brazilian national anthem.

See also **Music: Art Music.**

BIBLIOGRAPHY

Ayres De Andrade, *Francisco Manuel da Silva e seu tempo, 1808–1865,* 2 vols. (1967).

Gérard Béhague, *Music in Latin America* (1979).

Additional Bibliography

Hazan, Marcelo Campos. "Francisco Manuel da Silva's Swan Song." *Inter-American Music Review* 16:2 (Spring–Summer 2000): 33–43.

DAVID P. APPLEBY

SILVA, JOSÉ ANTÔNIO DA (1909–

1996). José Antônio da Silva (*b.* 1909), Brazilian painter. Born in the interior of the state of São Paulo, Silva gave up his life as a rural agricultural laborer and at the age of thirty-seven, moved to São José do Rio Prêto, where he taught himself painting. Iconoclastic, with a contempt for art critics, Silva did a painting entitled *Hanging the Critics.* For his first three compositions, he won the first prize at a local exhibition whose jury, ironically, was composed of several important art critics.

While early works such as *Houses in the Rain* have an impressionistic look, later paintings were more radical and expressionistic. Examples of these latter include *Roundup, Crucifixion, Swimmers,* and *Demon Stampeding the Herd.* In his best-known work, *The Cotton Harvest,* for instance, painted in 1949, Silva attained dramatic effects by his unconventional use of color and bold composition. His paintings document his own life as well as that of the history of Brazil. He participated in a number of São Paulo biennials and exhibited his works outside of Brazil, including the 1954 Hispano-American Biennial in Havana and two Venice bienalles. In 1967 he founded a museum in São José do Rio Prêto in which he housed old baroque artwork from the local area, paintings of other artists, and those of his own. Silva is the author of *The Romance of My Life* (1949) and two novels, *Alice* and *Maria Clara.* In 1980, the Museu de Arte Primitivista 'Jose Antonio da Silva' was founded in Rio Prêto. From 1999 to 2001, many of his works of art were housed in the Teatro Municipal there. He died in São Paulo in 1996. In 2002, the Museo de Arte Primitivista opened a permanent exhibition of his works, entitled "Silva: Imagens e Meios."

See also **Art: The Twentieth Century.**

BIBLIOGRAPHY

Aquino, Flávio de. *Aspectos da pintura primitiva Brasileira.* New York: Alpine Fine Arts Collection, 1978.

Bach, Susan. *Imagens populares.* Rio de Janeiro: S. Bach, 1986.

Fundação Nacional De Arte, *Pinacoteca do Estado—São Paulo* (1982), pp. 138–139.

Rodman, Selden. *Genius in the Backlands: Popular Artists of Brazil* (1977), pp. 54–73; *Arte no Brasil,* vol. 2 (1979), pp. 828–829.

Silva, José Antonio da, et. al. *Silva: Pinturas, 1947–1995.* São Paulo: Pinacoteca, 1998.

CAREN A. MEGHREBLIAN

SILVA, JOSÉ ASUNCIÓN (1865–1896).

José Asunción Silva (*b.* 26 November 1865; *d.* 24 May 1896), Colombian poet and important precursor of Spanish modernism. Silva was born into wealth, but left school early due to difficulties with his fellow students. He continued to read the classics (French, English, and Spanish) with other young literati and traveled extensively in Europe (1884–1886), where he met Oscar Wilde and Stéphane Mallarmé. His family's ruin in the 1885 civil war forced his return. He attempted to establish a business career, but failed. His lack of success and his sister's death forced him to work as secretary of the Colombian Legation in Venezuela (1894). He lost his manuscripts in a shipwreck on his return trip to Colombia and committed suicide upon failing to rebuild his career a second time. Silva's works are the posthumous *De sobremesa* (1925), a partly autobiographical novel, and *Poesías* (1910). Despite their brevity, both are revolutionary in theme and technique. His poems rate among the most musical and rhythmic in the Spanish language. Most notable are "Nocturno III," on the death of his sister Elvira, "Día de difuntos," "Los maderos de San Juan," and "Vejeces."

See also **Literature: Spanish America.**

BIBLIOGRAPHY

Diccionario de la literatura latinoamericana: Colombia (1959).

Betty Tyree Osiek, *José Asunción Silva: Estudio estilístico de su poesía* (1968).

Héctor H. Orjuela, *"De sobremesa" y otros estudios sobre José Asunción Silva* (1976).

Betty Tyree Osiek, *José Asunción Silva* (1978).

Sonya A. Ingwersen, *Light and Longing: Silva and Darío: Modernism and Religious Heterodoxy* (1986).

Additional Bibliography

Dever, Aileen. *The Radical Insufficiency of Human Life: The Poetry of R. de Castro and J.A. Silva.* Jefferson: McFarland, 2000.

Jaramillo, María Dolores. *José Asunción Silva, poeta y lector moderno.* Bogotá: Universidad Nacional de Colombia, 2001.

Osorio, José Jesús. *José Asunción Silva y la ciudad letrada.* Lewiston: E. Mellen Press, 2006.

MARÍA A. SALGADO

SILVA, JOSÉ BARBOSA DA. *See* Sinhô.

SILVA, LINDOLFO (1924–).

Lindolfo Silva (*b.* 25 November 1924), rural labor spokesman of the Brazilian Communist Party (PCB). Born on a farm in Rio de Janeiro State, he worked as a tailor until hired by the PCB in 1952. In 1954, he helped found the semiclandestine Union of Farmers and Agricultural Laborers of Brazil (UL-TAB), becoming its first secretary. He traveled the nation to address farm workers, published regularly on rural labor matters, and led delegations of workers to lobby officials and attend Soviet-bloc conferences on peasants. Silva's 1963 election as president of the government-sanctioned National Confederation of Agricultural Laborers demonstrated PCB strength in the countryside and in national politics. With the coup d'état of 1964, the military suppressed the PCB, and Silva went into hiding. He did, however, remain a party bureaucrat into the 1990s.

See also **Brazil, Political Parties: Brazilian Communist Party (PCB).**

BIBLIOGRAPHY

Neale J. Pearson, *Small Farmer and Rural Worker Pressure Groups in Brazil* (1967).

Clodomir Moraes, "Peasant Leagues in Brazil," in *Agrarian Problems and Peasant Movements in Latin America,* edited by Rodolfo Stavenhagen (1970).

Additional Bibliography

Chilcote, Ronald H. *The Brazilian Communist Party: Conflict and Integration, 1922-1972.* New York: Oxford University Press, 1974.

Santana, Marco Aurélio. *Homens partidos: Comunistas e sindicatos no Brasil.* São Paulo: Boitempo Editorial, 2001.

Santos, Raimundo. *Política e agrarismo sindical no PCB.* Brasília, D.F.: Fundaçao Astrojildo Pereira, 2002.

CLIFF WELCH

SILVA, LUIS INÁCIO LULA DA

(1945–). Luis Inácio Lula da Silva became famous in the late 1970s as the leader of striking auto industry workers in the state of São Paulo, Brazil. As a union leader and founder of Brazil's radical Workers Party (Partido dos Trabalhadores, PT), he became an international symbol for leftist causes. On New Year's Day 2003, this poor migrant from the country's depressed northeastern region, commonly known by the childhood nickname Lula (Portuguese for "squid"), was inaugurated as Brazil's thirty-ninth president. Lula's personal journey from poverty to fame and power is among the country's most remarkable biographies.

Lula was born on October 27, 1945, to peasant parents in Caetés, a rural district in the poverty-stricken backlands of Pernambuco state. The seventh of eight children, Lula quit school early to help earn money for his family. In 1956 his mother moved the family to São Paulo city, attracted to the metropolitan area, as were tens of thousands of other northeasterners, by new industries and the promise of a better life. Job hungry, Lula sought work in the budding auto and steel industry, eventually becoming a journeyman lathe operator.

In the late 1960s Lula became involved in the labor movement by joining a group of dissident militants. By 1975 he had been elected president of the São Bernardo dos Campos and Diadema Metalworkers Union. Brazil had suffered a military coup d'etat in 1964, and Lula, as leader of a union in a strategic industry, played an important role in the regime's downfall in 1985. His career defined the "new unionism" that Brazilian workers supported with enthusiasm in the late 1970s. New leaders such as Lula arose from the grassroots to make the organizations more responsive to worker demands. In a series of innovative work stoppages in the late 1970s, Lula helped paralyze the industry and embarrass the regime. The military's attempts to repress the movement—Lula was jailed for a month—proved ineffective. In 1974 he married Marisa Letícia Rocco Casa (b. 1950); they raised five children (including one each from previous relationships).

In 1980 Lula was courted by leftist intellectuals and politicians who together founded the PT. In 1982, as the military relaxed its dictatorial grip on the nation, Lula ran for governor of São Paulo state; though he lost, his candidacy helped consolidate the PT. In 1983 he helped found an independent labor federation to coordinate the work of the new unionists, the Unique Labor Central (Central Única dos Trabalhadores, CUT). In 1986, following the military's withdrawal from power, Lula won a seat in the congress. As a delegate to the constituent assembly, he helped fashion Brazil's 1988 constitution to support broad workers' rights, including health care and land redistribution. The following year, the PT named Lula their presidential candidate. Running in 1990, 1994, and 1998, he placed second.

These campaigns helped build Lula's reputation and strategy. On the one hand, he sought to celebrate rather than negate his background as a poor, undereducated, northeastern migrant worker. He vigorously identified himself with social movements such as the Landless Workers Movement (Movimento dos Trabalhadores Rurais Sem Terra, MST) and a series of general strikes promoted by the CUT. He became a staunch critic of globalization, calling for fair, not free, trade. On the other hand, he learned to adapt to the corrupt realities of Brazilian politics, gathering around him a group of leftist advisers whose tactics reflected those of the Bolsheviks. While Lula's public appearances seemed to confirm a socialist agenda, his campaign built alliances with capitalists, reflecting values developed during his union career. The strategy guaranteed electoral victory in 2002.

Lula's overwhelming victory provoked ecstatic celebration. Finally, a true working-class leader had become president of a nation historically dominated by a ruling class little removed from the republic's slave-owning forefathers. His historic connection to radical social movements and antiglobalization campaigns encouraged many to believe that Lula's victory offered real change. However, once in office he proved to be a realist rather than the idealist many imagined him to be. He displayed more loyalty to his new allies than to his old comrades by pursuing policies and reforms consistent with neoliberal capitalism. He proudly outdid conservatives by enhancing Brazil's status abroad as a nation in good financial standing, free of International Monetary Fund restrictions for the first time in twenty years. Millions more were spent on industrial infrastructure and conventional agribusiness rather than on social development through education and land reform.

While gratifying the international left with globetrotting geared toward building a powerful coalition of Third World nations, Lula gradually alienated part of his popular base at home by proving more sensitive to the constant criticism of an insatiable bourgeoisie. The political tides, which had long carried Lula forward, seemed to turn in 2004 with allegations of his having paid bribes on a monthly basis to various politicians. The scandal forced the ouster of the apparatchiks who had crafted his campaign strategy but did not end his political career. Standing for reelection in 2006, Lula won a second term of office with more than 60 percent of the vote. By that time, however, many of his once ardent supporters were deeply disappointed with him.

Lula's political success owes much to welfare programs, such as Zero Hunger and the Family Grant, that have made a meaningful difference in the lives of millions of poor people. The stable economy has encouraged significant job growth, bringing real benefits to still more working-class people. These were the voters, statistics show, who overwhelmingly supported his reelection. Meanwhile, deep-seated class prejudice seemed to prevent the middle and upper classes from lending their support to Lula, despite his many efforts to please them.

See also **Brazil, Political Parties: Workers Party (PT); Brazil, Revolutions: Revolution of 1964.**

BIBLIOGRAPHY

Branford, Sue, and Bernardo Kucinski. *Lula and the Workers Party in Brazil*. New York: New Press, 2005.

Morel, Marío. *Lula: O início*, 3rd edition. Rio de Janeiro: Editora Nova Fronteira, 2006.

Parana, Denise. *Lula: Filho do Brasil*. São Paulo: Editora Perseu Abramo, 2002.

Power, Timothy J., and Wendy Hunter. "Rewarding Lula: Executive Power, Social Policy and the Brazilian Elections of 2006." *Latin American Politics and Society* 49, no. 1 (2007): 1–30.

Sader, Emir, and Ken Silverstein. *Without Fear of Being Happy: Lula, the Workers Party and Brazil*. London and New York: Verso, 1991.

CLIFF WELCH

SILVA, ORLANDO (1915–1978). Orlando Silva (Orlando Garcia da Silva; *b.* 3 October 1915; *d.* 1978), Brazilian singer and songwriter. As a youngster, Silva loved to sing, carrying leaflets of popular songs with him everywhere. Despite his lack of formal training either in music or voice, Silva received an invitation from Francisco Alves to sing in his program on Rádio Cajuti in 1934. That same year, Silva starred in radio shows under the pseudonym Orlando Navarro and made his first recordings, "Olha a baiana" (Look at the Girl of Bahia) and "Ondas curtas" (Short Waves). Throughout his career, Silva appeared in various films, including *Cidade-mulher* (City Woman, 1934), *Banana da terra* (Banana of the Earth, 1938), and *Segura essa mulher* (Hold That Woman, 1946). In 1936 he participated in the inauguration of Rádio Nacional, where he became the first singer to have his own show. The following year he recorded one of his greatest hits, "Lábios que beijei" (Lips That I Kissed). Silva was the first singer to interpret Pixinguinha's famous "Carinhoso" (Darling). In 1939, four of his productions received prizes: "A jardineira" (The Gardener), "Meu consolo é você" (You Are My Solace), "História antiga" (Ancient History), and "O homem sem mulher não vale nada" (A Man Is Worthless Without a Woman). In 1954, while broadcasting his midday radio program Doze Badaladas, which boasted a huge audience, Silva was awarded the title *rei do rádio* (king of radio). A few years later, he released the record *Carinhoso*, a recording of his greatest hits.

See also **Music: Popular Music and Dance; Radio and Television.**

BIBLIOGRAPHY

Marcos Antônio Marcondes, ed., *Enciclopédia da música brasileira: Erudita folclórica popular* (1977).

Additional Bibliography

McCann, Bryan. *Hello, Hello Brazil: Popular Music in the Making of Modern Brazil*. Durham, NC: Duke University Press, 2004.

Schreiner, Claus. *Música Brasileira: A History of Popular Music and the People of Brazil*. New York: Marion Boyars, 1993.

LISA MARÍC

SILVA, XICA DA (c. 1745–c. 1796).

Xica da Silva (*b.* ca. 1745; *d.* ca. 1796), mulatto mistress of the fantastically rich João Fernandes de Oliveira the younger, a diamond contractor in Minas Gerais from 1759 to 1771. Oliveira was so deeply in love with the slave Francisca (her baptismal name) that he convinced her owner to set her free. The story of Xica da Silva is a mixture of fact and legend. Apparently, Oliveira lavished a fortune on her, including building an artificial lake complete with sailing vessels.

Xica da Silva, the daughter of a Portuguese man and an African slave, has assumed an enduring place in the history of Brazil as a personification of the slave woman whose beauty and charms permit her to gain power over her master and lover. For some, her stature is a reflection of the cult of *mulata* beauty. For others, she represents a nationalist anti-imperialist statement. This latter perspective is evident in the film *Xica da Silva* (directed by Carlos Diegues, 1976; released in the United States, 1982), in which Xica da Silva uses her wiles to combat the Portuguese imperial authorities.

See also **Diegues, Carlos.**

BIBLIOGRAPHY

Joaquim Felicio Dos Santos, *Memórias do distrito diamantino*, 3d ed. (1956).

Charles R. Boxer, *The Golden Age of Brazil: 1695–1750* (1964).

Additional Bibliography

Abreu, Luis Alberto de. *Xica da Silva*. São Paulo: Martins Fontes, 1988.

Furico, Ze. *O arraial do Tijuco e a verdadeira historia de Chica da Silva*. São Paulo: Editora Ateniense, 1989.

Furtado, Junia Fereirra. *Chica da Silva e o contratador dos diamantes: O outro lado do mito*. São Paulo: Companhia das Letras, 2003.

DONALD RAMOS

SILVA HENRÍQUEZ, RAÚL (1907–1999).

Raúl Silva Henríquez (*b.* 27 September 1907; *d.* 1999), archbishop of Santiago, Chile (1961–1983), during a period of intensifying political struggle between the Left, Right, and Center, which culminated in the 1973 right-wing military coup that brought General Augusto Pinochet to power.

Unlike the majority of Chilean bishops, Silva was a member of the Salesians, a religious order dedicated primarily to missionary and educational work. Trained as a lawyer at the Catholic University in Santiago, Silva studied philosophy and theology in Italy, where he was ordained in 1938. Upon his return to Chile, he served as a professor and administrator in the Salesian major seminary and secondary schools. In the 1950s he became the director of Cáritas, a church-sponsored social welfare agency that focused on the urban and rural poor.

Silva was appointed to the archbishopric of Santiago in 1961 as a compromise between ostensibly more liberal and conservative candidates. The prelate soon became identified with the progressive sector and was particularly active in promoting workers' rights and agrarian reform, in part through divestment of some of the Catholic Church's own properties. He was made a cardinal in 1962.

Silva maintained courteous relations with the Socialist government of Salvador Allende (1970–1973), repeatedly serving as a mediator between it and the centrist Christian Democratic opposition. Eventually he came to accept military intervention as necessary in view of escalating public chaos and a deepening economic crisis. After the coup that ousted Allende, as the extent of assassinations, torture, and disappearances, as well as generalized repression became apparent, Silva helped organize the ecumenical Committee of Cooperation for Peace. When Pinochet forced that institution to close in 1975, the prelate created the Vicariate of Solidarity to provide legal, medical, and social services to victims of the Pinochet regime. He also supported the creation of the Academy of Christian Humanism to analyze public policy issues and assess government responses. By the time of his retirement in 1983, he had become one of the most outspoken critics of the military government. He was 91 years old when he died in the Salesian monastic order rest home in Chile in 1999. He was buried in the cathedral of Santiago.

See also **Catholic Church: The Modern Period; Salesians.**

BIBLIOGRAPHY

Hannah W. Stewart-Gambino, *The Church and Politics in the Chilean Countryside* (1992).

Additional Bibliography

Aguilar, Mario I. "Cardinal Raul Silva Henriquez, the Catholic Church, and the Pinochet Regime, 1973-1980: Public Responses to a National Security State." *The Catholic Historical Review*, 89 (Oct 2003): 712-731.

Reyes, Francisco. *El Cardenal: La batalla del humanismo cristiano: Crónicas de un alegato por la democracia.* Santiago, Chile: CESOC-Ediciones Nortemar, 1999.

Sapag Chain, Reinaldo. *Mi amigo, el Cardenal.* Santiago, Chile: Ediciones Copygraph, 1996.

MARGARET E. CRAHAN

SILVA HERZOG, JESÚS (1892–1985).

Jesús Silva Herzog (*b.* 14 November 1892; *d.* 14 March 1985), leading Mexican economist, author, intellectual, and public figure. Born in San Luis Potosí, he was the son of a German immigrant mother and Mexican engineer. Silva Herzog began his career as a teacher at the National Teachers School in 1919 and rose to prominence in the Secretariat of Education. After serving as ambassador to the Soviet Union, he managed Pemex, the national petroleum concern, for Lázaro Cárdenas in 1939. He served many years as a professor of economics at the National University, where he trained many disciples, and founded and directed *Cuadernos Americanos,* a leading interdisciplinary, intellectual journal. A recipient of the National Prize in Arts and Sciences (1962), Silva Herzog died in Mexico City.

See also **Petróleos Mexicanos (Pemex).**

BIBLIOGRAPHY

Jesús Silva Herzog, *Una vida en la vida de México* (1972) and *Mis últimas andanzas, 1947–1972* (1973).

Additional Bibliography

Babb, Sarah L. *Managing Mexico: Economists from Nationalism to Neoliberalism.* Princeton, NJ: Princeton University Press, 2001.

RODERIC AI CAMP

SILVA LISBOA, JOSÉ DA (1756–1835).

José da Silva Lisboa (Visconde de Cairú; *b.* 16 July 1756; *d.* 20 August 1835), Brazilian political economist and politician. Born in Brazil of a Portuguese father and Bahian mother, Silva Lisboa, completed his education at the University of Coimbra in Portugal, then taught Greek, Hebrew, and moral philosophy at Coimbra and in Bahia. Influenced especially by Adam Smith, he published *Princípios de direito mercantil* (1798, 1801) and *Princípios de economia política* (1804), the first major works in Portuguese about liberal political economic theory.

When the Portuguese court, fleeing Napoleon's invasion of the Iberian Peninsula, arrived in Bahia in 1808, Silva Lisboa inspired Emperor João VI's first decree in Brazil, which opened Brazilian ports to direct commerce with foreign nations. Serving as government spokesman, he argued in *Observações sobre o comércio franco do Brasil* (1808) that his free-trade measure would increase government revenues and revive Portuguese manufacturing by forcing it to compete with other nations' industries. Although it did not remove all monopolies and special privileges, the decree that opened Brazil's ports represented a major shift away from mercantilist colonial policies.

In the last years before independence, Silva Lisboa defended the idea of constitutional monarchy and opposed the reimposition of mercantilism but did not call for Brazil's separation from Portugal. After that separation came to pass, his loyalty to the first emperor of independent Brazil marked him as a political conservative. Through his career, Silva Lisboa held high political offices, including member of the 1823 Constituent Assembly and senator from Bahia (1826–1835).

See also **Brazil: 1808-1889; Brazil, The Empire (First).**

BIBLIOGRAPHY

João Soares Dutra, *Cairú* (1943, 1964).

Pinto De Aguiar, *A abertura dos portos: Cairú e os ingleses* (1960).

Emília Viotti Da Costa, "The Political Emancipation of Brazil," in *From Colony to Nation: Essays on the Independence of Brazil,* edited by A. J. R. Russell-Wood (1975), pp. 43–88.

Additional Bibliography

Barman, Roderick J. *Citizen Emperor: Pedro II and the Making of Brazil, 1825-9.* Stanford, CA: Stanford University Press, 1999.

Ramos, Luís A de Oliveira. *D. Pedro, imperador e rei: Experiências de um príncipe (1798–1834).* Lisboa: Edições Inapa, 2002.

Rocha, Antonio Penalves. *José da Silva Lisboa, Visconde de Cairu.* São Paulo: Editora 34, 2001.

Silva, Paulo Napoleão Nogueira da. *Pedro I, o português brasileiro.* Rio de Janeiro: Gryphus, 2000.

ROGER A. KITTLESON

SILVA XAVIER, JOAQUIM JOSÉ DA

(1746–1792). Joaquim José da Silva Xavier (Tirandentes; *b.* 1746; *d.* 21 April 1792), a participant in the Inconfidência Mineira. Silva Xavier was born near São João del Rei, Minas Gerais, Brazil. His father was a Portuguese-born gold miner important enough to be elected to the town council of São João del Rei; his mother was a native of Minas Gerais. Orphaned at an early age, Silva Xavier was raised by his brother, a priest. It is probable that his godfather, a dentist, provided Silva Xavier with the skills of what became his occasional trade and thus was the source of his nickname, Tiradentes (Toothpuller).

After an unsuccessful career as a muleteer and gold miner, Silva Xavier joined the royal dragoons as an *alferes* (ensign). He became the commander of the troops guarding a crucial portion of the Caminho Novo, the road between the mining district and Rio de Janeiro—an important post because gold and diamonds were shipped over this road.

Silva Xavier became involved in plotting independence after meeting José Álvares Maciel, newly returned from Portugal and England and imbued with the ideas of the French Enlightenment. The serious planning took shape in late 1788. Silva Xavier's motives for participating were probably a mixture of personal frustration at repeatedly being passed over for promotion and ideological commitment to ending Portuguese domination. Of the central group of plotters, Silva Xavier was the least important socially but perhaps was the most active in spreading their ideas. Under questioning he was unique in assuming sole responsibility for the plot. He was the only plotter to be executed by the state.

Silva Xavier has become one of the major heroic figures of Brazil's past—a symbol of opposition to Portuguese imperialism and of advocacy of Brazilian independence. While his role in the Inconfidência Mineira has often been controversial, he now is a significant symbol of Brazilian nationalism, reflecting the need for a national hero with strong republican roots.

See also **Brazil: The Colonial Era, 1500-1808; Brazil, Independence Movements.**

BIBLIOGRAPHY

Kenneth R. Maxwell, *Conflicts and Conspiracies: Brazil and Portugal, 1750–1808* (1973).

Additional Bibliography

Furtado, João Pinto. *O manto de Penélope: História, mito e memória da Inconfidência Mineira de 1788–9.* São Paulo: Companhia das Letras: Companhia das Letras, 2002.

DONALD RAMOS

SILVER MINING. *See* **Mining: Colonial Spanish America.**

SIMON, ANTOINE (1844–1923). Simon, Antoine (*b.* ca. 1844; *d.* ca 1923), president of Haiti (1908-1911). Simon overthrew Pierre Nord-Alexis and became the first black since Lysius Salomon to occupy the president's chair. From southern Haiti, uneducated, and with real sympathy for common folk and folk culture, Simon exhibited populist qualities. But overwhelming problems isolated him from those whom he might have served well.

Growing U.S. capitalist interests burdened his administration. The City Bank of New York extended its interests in the Bank Nationale d'Haiti and financed the McDonald contract—based on grants to James P. McDonald to build a railroad from Port-au-Prince to Cap Haitien. The McDonald contract especially irked rural *cacos* of northern

Haiti, who envisioned the confiscation of their small farms to build the hated American railroad. German and French capitalists also were active in the Haitian economy.

Simon's oppression of mulattoes, arbitrary arrests of protesting schoolteachers, and mass slaughter of a *caco* town in northeastern Haiti focused foreign scorn on him. In August 1911 he went into exile.

See also **Haiti; Nord, Pierre Alexis; Salomon, Louis Étienne Lysius Félicité.**

BIBLIOGRAPHY

James Leyburn, *The Haitian People* (1941); David Nicholls, *From Dessalines to Duvalier: Race, Colour, and National Independence in Haiti* (1979); Brenda Gayle Plummer, *Haiti and the Great Powers, 1902-1915* (1988).

Additional Bibliography

Dent, David W. *The Legacy of the Monroe Doctrine: A Reference Guide to U.S. Involvement in Latin America and the Caribbean.* Westport, CT: Greenwood Press, 1999.

Gaillard, Roger. *La république exterminatrice.* 6 v. Port-au-Prince: R. Gaillard, 1984.

THOMAS O. OTT

SIMONSEN, MÁRIO HENRIQUE

(1935–1997). Mário Henrique Simonsen (*b.* 19 February 1935; *d.* 9 February 1997), Brazilian minister of finance (1974–1979) and of planning (1979). Economist, professor, public official, and business administrator, Simonsen served as Brazil's principal economic minister following the high-growth period known as the Economic Miracle (1968–1974). Relatively orthodox in his economic thinking, Simonsen joined the faculty of the Instituto Brasileiro de Economia of the Fundação Getúlio Vargas in Rio de Janeiro in 1961, acted as director of the Graduate School of Economics (1965–1974), and became vice president of the institute (1979). In the mid-1960s, as a staff member in the planning ministry led by Roberto Campos, he designed the wage policy formula and participated in the creation of the housing finance system. In addition to his term as minister, he served as the president of the Brazilian Literacy Movement Foundation (Fundação Movimento Brasileiro de Alfabetização—MOBRAL) from 1970 to 1974

and as director of Citicorp (since 1979) and of other companies.

As minister of finance, Simonsen organized Brazil's response to the increase in world oil prices in 1973 and the adjustment to its spectacular growth in manufacturing capacity during the Economic Miracle. His program, reflected in the Second National Development Plan (Il Plano Nacional de Desenvolvimento), attempted to reduce dependence on external energy and other imports through large public investment projects in basic industry and infrastructure, including transportation and communications. Brazilian private and state companies as well as foreign firms participated in the program, which was financed in part with petrodollars. At the same time, to control inflation and to deal with recurring problems in Brazil's balance of payments and foreign reserves, Simonsen often resorted to restrictive macroeconomic policies in spite of their recessionary impact, although growth during the period was still substantial. In 1979, he resigned as planning minister in the new president's cabinet, owing to public resistance to the prospect of even harsher macroeconomic policies in response to rising inflation; he was replaced by Antônio Delfim Neto.

See also **Brazil, Economic Miracle (1968-1974); Economic Development.**

BIBLIOGRAPHY

Israel Beloch and Alzira Alves De Abreu, eds., *Dicionário histórico-biográfico brasileiro, 1930–1983,* vol. 4 (1984).

Werner Baer, *The Brazilian Economy: Growth and Development,* 3d ed. (1989).

Additional Bibliography

Aspe Armello, Pedro, and Rudiger Dornbusch. *Financial Policies and the World Capital Market: The Problem of Latin American Countries.* Chicago: University of Chicago Press, 1983.

Bruno, Michael. *Inflation Stabilization: The Experience of Israel, Argentina, Brazil, Bolivia, and Mexico.* Cambridge, MA: MIT Press, 1988.

Dornbusch, Rudiger, and Marío Henrique Simonsen. *Inflation, Debt, and Indexation.* Cambridge, MA: MIT Press, 1983.

RUSSELL E. SMITH

SIMONSEN, ROBERTO COCHRANE

(1889–1948). Roberto Cochrane Simonsen (*b.* 18 February 1889; *d.* 25 May 1948), Brazilian economist and industrialist. Raised in the port city of Santos, Simonsen studied engineering at São Paulo's Escola Politécnica. He graduated in 1909. In the 1910s, as director of a construction company in Santos, Simonsen experimented with methods of scientific management as well as with new forms of labor negotiation.

In the 1920s and 1930s, Simonsen became Brazil's most prominent advocate of industrialization, and emerged as the leading spokesman for São Paulo's powerful industrialist federation. In 1933 he founded the Escola Livre de Sociologia e Política; his appointment as professor of economic history at this institution for advanced study in the social sciences led him to compose his most famous work, *História econômica do Brasil, 1500–1820* (1937).

By the late 1930s Simonsen had become a supporter of the authoritarian regime of Getúlio Vargas, participating in several national economic commissions in which he called for protective tariffs, state intervention, and economic planning to promote industrial development. Simonsen energetically defended this position at the end of World War II, when Brazil faced intensified foreign competition and U.S. pressure for a return to liberal trade policies.

With the transition to electoral politics, Simonsen successfully ran for the federal senate in 1947. As senator he continued to promote the interests of industry, calling for the suppression of the newly legalized Communist Party, which he considered the chief threat to "social peace." Simonsen died while delivering an address to the Brazilian Academy of Letters, to which he had been elected in 1946.

See also **Vargas, Getúlio Dornelles.**

BIBLIOGRAPHY

The best collection of Simonsen's writings is *Evolução industrial do Brasil e outros estudos* (1973). A brief biography emphasizing Simonsen's professional accomplishments can be found in Heitor Ferreira Lima, *Três industrialistas brasileiros* (1976), especially pp. 141–185. On Simonsen's role in promoting industrialization, see Warren Dean, *The Industrialization of São Paulo, 1880–1945* (1969), and Marisa Saenz Leme, *A ideologia dos industriais brasileiros, 1919–1945* (1979).

Additional Bibliography

Carone, Edgard. *A evolução industrial de São Paulo, 1889–1930.* São Paulo: Editora SENAC São Paulo, 2000.

Weinstein, Barbara. *For Social Peace in Brazil: Industrialists and the Remaking of the Working Class in São Paulo, 1920–1964.* Chapel Hill: University of North Carolina Press, 1996.

                                                BARBARA WEINSTEIN

SINARQUISMO.

Sinarquismo, a movement of conservative, lay Mexican Catholics that originated in opposition to radical and liberal tendencies during the presidency of Lázaro Cárdenas (1934–1940). The term *sinarquismo* literally means "with order," the opposite of anarchism, but its advocates intended to counter not that ideology (peripheral in the 1930s) but both communism and capitalism by appeals to a traditional, hierarchical, Hispanic, corporate social order.

Allegedly founded at a clandestine meeting in León, Guanajuato, in May 1937, the National Sinarquist Union's (Unión Nacional Sinarquista) penchant for secrecy makes historical documentation difficult. The use of obscure gestures, code words, and a quasi-military structure has led some observers to overstate its ties with European fascism during World War II. The Sinarquistas claimed 900,000 members in 1944, but in view of its rapid decline soon thereafter, this figure seems inflated. Members were largely peasants from Guanajuato, Jalisco, and neighboring states where the Cristeros had arisen in the 1920s. Often left out of land reform and other government programs, these peasants turned to Sinarquismo as a form of political protest. After 1950 Sinarquistas maintained a marginal but outspoken opposition to the dominant National Revolutionary Party (by 1950 named the Institutional Revolutionary Party).

See also **Mexico, Political Parties: Institutional Revolutionary Party (PRI).**

BIBLIOGRAPHY

The historical and political context is explored in Donald J. Mabry, *Mexico's Acción Nacional: A Catholic Alternative to Revolution* (1973), esp. pp. 16–31, 43–44, 52–53, 193–194; and Jean Meyer, *El Sinarquismo: ¿Un fascismo mexicano?*, translated by Aurelio Garzón del Camino (1979). Nathan L. Whetten exaggerates Sinarquista influence in the 1940s but includes translations from several Sinarquista publications of that period in his *Rural Mexico* (1948), esp. pp. 454–522.

Additional Bibliography

Aguilar, Rubén, and Guillermo Zermeño P. *Religión, política y sociedad: El sinarquismo y la iglesia en México: Nueve ensayos.* Mexico: Universidad Iberoamericana, Departamento de Historia, 1992.

Hernández García de León, Héctor. *Historia política del sinarquismo, 1934–1944.* México: Universidad Iberoamericana; M.A. Porrúa, 2004.

Meyer, Jean A. *El sinarquismo, el cardenismo y la iglesia: 1937–1947.* México: Tusquets Editores, 2003.

Serrano Alvarez, Pablo. *La batalla del espíritu: El movimiento sinarquista en El Bajío, 1932–1951.* México, D.F.: Consejo Nacional para la Cultura y las Artes, 1992.

JOHN A. BRITTON

SINCLAIR, ALFREDO (1914–).

Alfredo Sinclair (*b.* 8 December 1914), Panamanian painter. After working as a neon sign technician, Sinclair studied under Humberto Ivaldi in Panama and then at the Escuela Superior de Bellas Artes E. de la Cárcova in Buenos Aires until 1950. Upon his return to Panama, he became an art professor at the Escuela Nacional de Artes Plásticas and later at the National University.

Initially a figurative painter, in the 1950s Sinclair was influenced by abstract expressionism, which led to the development of a personal style dominated by color and light. His paintings fluctuate from a semi-abstraction with references to the real world, as exemplified by his numerous collages and cityscapes like *La Ciudad* (1962), to a complete lyrical abstraction, as in his series *Movimientos de un río* (1981). In 1985, he participated in the prestigious "Arte Hispanoamericano de Hoy" exhibition in Miami's Galería de Armas. His daughter, Olga Sinclair, is also a famous artist.

See also **Art: The Twentieth Century.**

BIBLIOGRAPHY

Gilbert Chase, *Contemporary Art in Latin America* (1970).

P. Correa, "Sinclair o los mundos olvidados," in *Estrella de Panamá* (6 March 1975).

Mónica Kupfer, "Los cincuenta años de pintura de Alfredo Sinclair," in *Sinclair: El camino de un maestro* (1991).

Additional Bibliography

Sinclair, Alfredo. *Alfredo Sinclair: El camino de un maestro.* Panamá: Museo de Arte Contemporáneo, 1991.

MONICA E. KUPFER

SINHÔ (1888–1930).

Sinhô (José Barbosa da Silva; *b.* 18 September 1888; *d.* 4 August 1930), Brazilian songwriter. Born on Rua do Riachuelo, Rio de Janeiro, Sinhô was encouraged to study the flute by his father, who revered *chôro* performers. Sinhô (his family nickname) eventually abandoned the flute in favor of the piano and guitar. To earn a living, Sinhô played the piano at the society balls and in the dance clubs of Cidade Nova. At twenty-six, he was well regarded as a professional pianist.

His samba "Quem são eles?" (Who Are They?) of 1918 won immediate attention for its innovative rhythm and sparked a musical debate about the samba that soon became tradition in Rio de Janeiro. Organizing a group by the same name, Sinhô and his Quem São Eles? provoked traditional *sambistas,* who were devoted to their folkloric roots and resented Sinhô's urban melodies. He won tremendous success at Carnival in 1920 with "Fala, meu louro" (Speak, My Parrot), a parody of Rui Barbosa, and "O pé de anjo" (Angel's Foot). Persecuted by the police for his political satire, such as in "Fala baixo" (Speak Softly), a title alluding to government censorship, Sinhô was temporarily forced into hiding. He was named the *rei do samba* (king of the samba) in 1927 and reached the height of his popularity in 1928 with "Jura" (Promise) and "Gosto que me enrosco" (I Like to Swing), the latter coauthored by Heitor dos Prazeres. Although diagnosed with tuberculosis, Sinhô continued to write music intensively until his death in 1930. Numbering almost 150 published compositions, of which more than 100 have been recorded, Sinhô's music is remembered for its urban character, providing a chronicle of daily life and customs.

See also **Music: Popular Music and Dance; Samba.**

BIBLIOGRAPHY

Marcos Antônio Marcondes, ed., *Enciclopédia da música brasileira: Erudita folclórica popular* (1977).

Additional Bibliography

Gardel, André. *O encontro entre Bandeira e Sinhô*. Rio de Janeiro: Prefeitura da Cidade do Rio de Janeiro, Secretaria Municipal de Cultura, Departamento Geral de Documentação e Informação Cultural, Divisão de Editoração, 1996.

LISA MARÍC

SIPÁN. Sipán, a center of Peru's Moche culture, is an archaeological site discovered in the 1980s. In addition to pyramids, ramps, and platforms, several important tombs have been excavated. Archaeologists working at Sipán have been able to reconstruct part of America's pre-Hispanic past in terms of utensils, objects of the Moche culture, funeral ceremonies, power relationships, social stratification, and overall worldview. The Moche culture evolved on the northern coast of Peru between the first and seventh centuries CE. The Moche people's use of irrigation technology allowed them to produce agricultural surpluses out of the desert. Along with good management of resources from the sea, this gave them a sound economy that facilitated their development. The Moche experienced a flourishing copper era, as evidenced by copper ornaments, weapons, and tools found in the tomb of El Señor de Sipán.

The tomb of El Señor de Sipán, or the Lord of Sipán, dates back to about 300 CE. The find was of great importance to archaeologists because the main tomb had not been disturbed or looted. Due to his semidivine rank, this dignitary was buried with his offerings, worldly goods, provisions, and attendants. For the Moche, death was not the end; burial of the body along with a man's possessions reflected his status and position in society, thus allowing him to retain his position in the afterlife. The Lord of Sipán was buried with his headdress and several tunics, in which, according to Moche iconography, dignitaries like the Lord of Sipán presided over ritual ceremonies.

In the complex burial site, two llamas and a boy were found inside the burial chamber. There was a military chief on one side of the lord, a standard bearer on the other, and his young wife at his head. At his feet was his principal wife, holding a crown, and near his head a third woman. This entire arrangement was sealed, with the body of a guard for the chamber buried in the layer above.

See also **Archaeology; Moche.**

CARMEN ESCALANTE

SIQUEIROS, DAVID ALFARO. *See* **Alfaro Siqueiros, David.**

SIRIONÓ. The Sirionó are a seminomadic indigenous group living in the communities of Mató and Salvatierra in the tropical area of northeastern Bolivia's department of Beni. They call themselves the *mbla*, meaning "people" in their language, but since their first contact with outsiders they have been called the Sirionó. They belong to the Tupi-Guaraní language family. The Sirionó presently number 308, although in the past the number was much higher. Disease and mistreatment and exploitation by the mestizo populations of the region have led to their decline.

The social organization of Sirionó society is based on the nuclear family (for organizing animal hunting) and on the extended family. They practice polygamy, although they do so secretly to avoid sanctions from Christian society. Family relationships and descent are matrilineal, and marriage between cousins is preferred. Relationships between genders are equal, with women taking part in family and community decision making. Their simple social organization as a seminomadic band of hunters and gatherers, without any stratification other than a chief or leader for the entire group, contrasts with their wealth of knowledge about nature and their rich worldview.

Sirionó religion is a syncretism of Christian and indigenous beliefs. The Evangelical Church of Bolivia has been working in Sirionó territory since 1930. Christian ideas have melded with Sirionó polytheistic beliefs in the guardians of nature, the land, water, air, fauna, and flora. They also worship the hunted animal and rub themselves with the skins of animals or plants, hoping to take on their traits.

See also **Indigenous Peoples.**

BIBLIOGRAPHY

Ingham, John M. "Are the Sirionó Raw or Cooked?" *American Anthropologist*, New Series. 73:5 (October 1971), pp. 1092–1099.

CARMEN ESCALANTE

SITIO. *See* **Land Tenure, Brazil.**

SKÁRMETA, ANTONIO (1940–). Antonio Skármeta, the Chilean novelist and short story writer, was born November 7, 1940. An iconic literary figure for a generation of Chileans who lived under the military dictatorship of 1973–1990, Skármeta went into voluntary exile in 1975. He lived in Argentina and Germany and returned to Chile in 1989. Skármeta is the author of the short story collections *El entusiasmo* (1967), *Desnudo en el tejado* (1969), *El ciclista del San Cristóbal* (1973), *Tiro libre* (1973), *Novios y solitarios* (1975), and *La composición* (1998). His novel *Soñé que la nieve ardía* (1975; *I Dreamt the Snow Was Burning*, 1985) attests to the social and political aspirations and frustrations of the Salvador Allende years. *No pasó nada* (1980) is a short novel of the experience of exile; *Insurrección* (1982; *The Insurrection*, 1983) describes the Sandinista revolution in Nicaragua. *Ardiente paciencia* (1986; *Burning Patience*, 1987), a humorous novel portraying Pablo Neruda as matchmaker, was adapted as a drama, a video and a film, *Il Postino* (The Postman). (After the success of the film, the novel's title was changed to *El cartero de Neruda* in its editions published after 2000.) *Match Ball* (*Love-Fifteen*, 1989) is a satirical novel of the international world of professional tennis, whose title was also changed after 2003 to *La velocidad del amor*. A trilogy constituted by *La boda del poeta* (1999; The Poet's Wedding), *La chica del trombón* (2001; The Trombone Playgirl), and *El baile de la victoria* (2003; Victoria's Dance) is his most ambitious narrative work. Skármeta's narrative style mixes the nostalgia of a young generation's dream of social revolution with the experience of exile, parodying many literary genres from poetry to popular fiction to drama to journalism. Skármeta has also written a number of dramatic scripts in addition to *Ardiente paciencia*: *La victoria* (The Victory); *Reina la tranquilidad en todo el país* (The Entire Country Is in Peace); *La*

insurrección (The Insurrection); *Si viviéramos juntos* (If We Lived Together), and *Permiso de residencia* (Residence Permit).

See also **Allende Gossens, Salvador; Literature: Spanish America; Neruda, Pablo; Pinochet Ugarte, Augusto.**

BIBLIOGRAPHY

Lemaître, Monique J. *Skármeta, una narrativa de la liberación*. Santiago, Chile: Pehuén, 1991.

Lira, Constanza. *Skármeta: La inteligencia de los sentidos*. Santiago, Chile: Editorial Dante, 1985.

Rojo, Grinr. *Crítica del exilio: Ensayos sobre literature latinoamericana actual*. Santiago, Chile: Pehuén, 1989.

Rojo, Grinor. "Celebración de Antonio Skármeta." *Anales de Literatura Chilena* 3 (2002), 139–150.

Silva Cáceres, Raúl, ed. *Del cuerpo a las palabras: La narrativa de Antonio Skármeta*. Madrid: Literatura Americana Reunida, 1983.

CEDOMIL GOIC

SKINNER, GEORGE URE (1804–1867). George Ure Skinner (*b.* 18 March 1804; *d.* 9 January 1867), British merchant in Guatemala. The son of a Scottish Episcopal minister and great-grandson of an ecclesiastical historian of Scotland, Skinner worked in London and in Leeds before going to Guatemala in 1831. The company he formed with Charles Klée, a German merchant, linked Guatemalan commerce closely with Great Britain, via Belize, and became a major creditor of the Guatemalan government. In addition to building a large estate based on indigo and cochineal exports from Guatemala, Skinner became a noted naturalist; he was interested in insects, birds, and orchids, and shipped many of the latter to England. He died in Panama of yellow fever as he was returning from England.

See also **Cochineal; Indigo.**

BIBLIOGRAPHY

"The Late Mr. G. Ure Skinner," *Gardeners' Chronicle*, no. 8 (1867).

Merle A. Reinikka, *A History of the Orchid* (1972), pp. 169–173.

Ralph Lee Woodward, Jr., *Rafael Carrera and the Emergence of the Republic of Guatemala, 1821–1871* (1993).

Additional Bibliography

Pompejano, Daniele. *La crisis del antiguo régimen en Guatemala (1839–1871)*. Guatemala, Centroamérica: Editorial Universitaria, Universidad de San Carlos de Guatemala, 1997.

RALPH LEE WOODWARD JR.

SLAVE REVOLTS

This entry includes the following articles:
BRAZIL
SPANISH AMERICA

BRAZIL

Slave uprisings and the formation and defense of runaway slave communities (called *quilombos* or *mocambos* in Brazil) were common facts of Brazilian slavery. But whereas *quilombos* occurred throughout the history of slavery and throughout the vast territory of Brazil, slave revolts occurred primarily in certain areas and in certain periods. Over one hundred *quilombos* have been identified in the rich mining region of Minas Gerais in the seventeenth and eighteenth centuries, but there is no record of a slave uprising there except for three abortive conspiracies in 1711, 1719, and 1729. Most slave revolts happened in the plantation areas of the Northeast during the first half of the nineteenth century. Some of these were linked to or benefited from divisions that flourished among the free classes after the independence of Brazil in 1822. During the second half of the nineteenth century, the majority of the slave population was concentrated in the prosperous coffee regions to the south. There small but numerous rebellions took place independently of or in combination with the white-dominated abolitionist movement in the last decades of slavery, which was finally abolished in 1888.

The colonial era, however, did see one big slave movement: the large and long-lived Palmares *quilombo*, founded ca. 1630. Finally defeated in 1694 after having repelled many attacks, Palmares was a runaway community with the stature of an organized, independent state. Nothing like it would ever be allowed to happen again in Brazil.

Often, however, the history of smaller-scale *quilombos* and that of insurrection merged. Although many *quilombos* were begun peacefully by small groups of individual fugitives, there were cases in which they developed from slave insurrections. In 1838 in the parish of Pati do Alferes, in the province of Rio de Janeiro, more than 100 slave men and women, the majority from a large coffee plantation, rose and ran away under the leadership of Manuel Congo. Most of these slaves were southern and central Africans from Angola, Mozambique, and the Congo, but a few creoles also joined the movement. Possessing firearms and other weapons, they immediately tried to organize a *quilombo* in a nearby mountain range but were quickly dispersed, with seven killed and twenty-two arrested on the spot. Manuel Congo was sentenced to be hanged. Although most runaways later were returned to their masters, some managed to escape into the woods.

If there were insurrections that became *quilombos*, there were also *quilombos* behind insurrections. Some of the famous nineteenth-century Bahian revolts were initiated by groups of runaway slaves. In 1809 fugitives from the city of Salvador, Bahia's capital, and from plantations in the neighboring sugar zone, the Recôncavo, formed a *quilombo* on the banks of a river. From there they attacked and nearly took control of the village of Nazaré, a food-producing area. They were defeated by local militias and troops sent from the capital; many died, and eighty-three men and twelve women were arrested. The rebels were Hausa, jeje (Aja-Fon), and Nagô (Yoruba) slaves, some of whom escaped in small groups to live as highwaymen and raiders in the Recôncavo. Five years later, in 1814, a *quilombo* near Salvador was also involved in an insurrection of captives, mostly Hausas, who worked in whaling warehouses. It was a bloody affair in which perhaps fifty people were killed by the rebels, who were defeated with heavy losses, but only when they were already marching toward the plantation districts. Finally, there was the rebellion of the Urubu (Vulture) *quilombo* in 1826, which was strengthened by many new escapees in an attempt to occupy Salvador on Christmas eve. But the rebels were denounced and then overcome by militia and regular troops before they were able to begin acting on their plan. During the battle a valiant woman named Zeferina led the warriors, mainly Yoruba slaves.

Bahia was by far the region experiencing the greatest number and the most serious slave revolts.

There were more than twenty slave uprisings and conspiracies in Bahia between 1809 and 1835. Most of them were local affairs in the sugar plantation area of the Recôncavo, carried on by slaves protesting against local working or living conditions. At least two of the uprisings were led by Muslim slaves, the one in 1814 mentioned above and a more serious episode in 1835, often called the Malê revolt (from Imale, meaning Muslim in Yoruba). The latter occurred in Salvador. The result of long planning, it was led by Muslim religious preachers. The revolt was intended to begin on 25 January 1835, a Catholic holiday that fell at the end of the Muslim Ramadan. The police heard of the plot only hours before, which was time enough, however, to give them an advantage. But the uprising started anyway. For close to four hours, some 500 rebels fought in the streets and door-to-door, more than 70 dying before the uprising was defeated. The rebels were mostly Yoruba and Hausa slaves and freedmen, who later received punishments that varied from the death penalty (applied to four of them), whippings, prison with work, and deportation to Africa (for the freedmen).

As in other areas of the New World, slave revolts in Brazil, especially those in Bahia, have been explained by the high concentration of slaves in the population and by the fact that the majority were African-born and had common ethnic backgrounds. Thus, the revolts were in part ethnic rebellions. In the case of Bahia, scholars have added the role of Islam as a revolutionary religious ideology. Slave revolts may have been spurred by other ideological elements, such as the influence of the Haitian revolution (*haitianismo*), the liberal discourse peculiar to a time of decolonization, and after the mid-nineteenth century, abolitionist ideas. The creoles, however, were more in tune with these influences than the Africans.

In Bahia and other northern provinces, for instance, creole slaves joined several revolutionary movements of the free between 1823 and 1840. The movement known as the Balaiada exploded between 1838 and 1841 in the province of Maranhão. It mobilized thousands of poor country people under the leadership of liberal and federalist rebels who, like other rebels in this period, did not seek abolition. Slaves, however, took advantage of the rebellion to carry on their own movement guided by an extraordinary leader, Cosme Bento das Chagas, a black freedman who sought the destruction of slavery and the establishment of a color-blind republic. Faced with defeat, radical liberals eventually had to accept an alliance with slave forces that counted on hundreds of fugitives (*quilombolas*). But the very presence of slaves in the Balaiada pushed white supporters away. Thus weakened, both slave and free rebels became easy prey for the many troops sent from Rio de Janeiro to put down the rebellion. Chagas was captured and hanged, accused of murder and of leading a slave rebellion.

The 1870s and 1880s, especially the last years before abolition in 1888, saw a significant increase of tensions between slaves and masters, especially in the coffee-growing regions and suburbs of Rio de Janeiro and São Paulo. Recent studies have shown that individual flights and violent crimes against masters and overseers grew in the police statistics of this period, mostly accounted for by African slaves and captives imported from the declining sugar areas of the Northeast. The increasing unrest became a strong argument used by white politicians and ideologues in the abolitionist movement. As abolition approached, small slave uprisings, collective flights, and the formation of suburban *quilombos* multiplied by many times. Between 1885 and 1888, São Paulo alone witnessed more than two-dozen uprisings, although most were either small, localized, and hastily improvised or only potentially serious conspiracies that never materialized. In the same period, fires on several occasions destroyed plantations in the sugar districts of Campos in Rio de Janeiro. The radicalization of the slave movement radicalized the abolitionist movement, which often supported the former. The last country in the New World to abolish slavery, Brazil would surely have prolonged the system even longer had it not been for the struggle of the slaves themselves.

See also **Slavery: Brazil.**

BIBLIOGRAPHY

Raymond Kent, "African Revolt in Bahia: 24–25 January 1835," *Journal of Social History* 3, no. 4 (1970): 334–356.

Clovis Moura, *Rebeliões da senzala* (1972).

Lana Lage Gama Lima, *Rebeldia negra e abolicionismo* (1981).

Maria Januária Vilela Dos Santos, *A balaiada e a insurreição de escravos no Maranhão* (1983).

Julio Pinto Vallejos, "Slave Control and Slave Resistance in Colonial Minas Gerais, 1700–1750," *Journal of Latin American Studies* 17 (1985): 1–34.

Stuart B. Schwartz, *Sugar Plantations in the Formation of Brazilian Society: Bahia, 1550–1835* (1985), pp. 468–488.

João Luiz Pinaud et al, *Insurreição negra e justiça* (1987).

Luiz R. B. Mott, "Rebeliões escravas em Sergipe," *Estudos Econômicos* 17 (1987): 111–130.

João José Reis, *Slave Rebellion in Brazil: The Muslim Uprising of 1835 in Bahia* (1993).

Additional Bibliography

Gomes, Flávio dos Santos. *Palmares: Escravidão e liberdade no Atlântico Sul.* São Paulo: Contexto, 2005.

Reis, João José and Flávio dos Santos Gomes. *Liberdade por um fio: História dos quilombos no Brasil.* São Paulo: Companhia das Letras, 1996.

Soares, Carlos Eugênio Líbano. *A capoeira escrava e outras tradições rebeldes no Rio de Janeiro, 1808–1850.* Campinas: Editora da UNICAMP: CECULT, 2001.

JOÃO JOSÉ REIS

SPANISH AMERICA

Spanish America experienced many slave revolts during the more than three centuries of colonial rule and in some mainland countries during the first decades after Independence. Because the New Laws of 1542 forbade the enslavement of Indians except under narrow conditions, slave revolts in Spanish America quickly became the almost exclusive accomplishment of Africans and those of African descent. Some revolts displayed impressive size, intensity, and organization, and although sporadic and usually short-lived, they erupted with sufficient frequency to place rational masters in recurrent fear of what Simón Bolívar called "the volcano at their feet."

INCIDENCE OF REVOLT

Probably the first serious slave revolt by African slaves in the Americas broke out in 1522 in southeastern Hispaniola on a sugar estate owned by the son of Christopher Columbus. The revolt involved about forty slaves, most of them Wolofs from Senegambia in West Africa. Most of the principal slave revolts and conspiracies in Spanish America emerged from concentrations of slaves in plantation agriculture, mines, and urban services. For decades after the 1522 revolt, bands of runaway slaves preyed on Santo Domingo's sugar region. Although Maroon activity continued there for centuries, not until the end of the eighteenth century did planters witness slave revolts or conspiracies of any significance. The most violent revolt began near the city of Santo Domingo in 1796 on a large sugar estate called Boca Nigua.

Puerto Rico experienced few slave revolts or conspiracies before the expansion of sugar cultivation during the first half of the nineteenth century in the coastal districts of Ponce in the south and Vega Baja and Toa Baja in the north. Most instances occurred from 1820 to 1848 and were minor; the majority never reached the stage of open rebellion.

Cuba's first slave revolt seems to have been the 1533 rising of a few slave gold miners. In 1731 copper mines in roughly the same area of eastern Cuba gave rise to a larger revolt that embraced scores of slaves. During its nineteenth-century sugar boom western Cuba experienced one of the most intense periods of collective slave resistance in the history of Spanish America. The conspiracies of Aponte (1812) and La Escalera (1843–1844) involved extensive networks of people of color, slave and free, rural and urban, and rank among the largest slave resistance movements in the history of the Americas. The most destructive slave revolt in Cuban history occurred in 1825, when hundreds of slaves killed fifteen whites and ravaged more than twenty coffee and sugar estates in the western province of Matanzas.

In Spanish Louisiana the same district of tobacco and indigo plantations up-river from New Orleans served as a base for a preempted ethnic revolt of Mina slaves in 1791 and for a more broadly based and revolutionary conspiracy four years later that stands as one of the largest acts of collective slave resistance in the history of colonial North America.

Mexico developed sugar plantations and sizable slave holdings around the port of Veracruz soon after the Spanish conquest. By the end of the sixteenth century, Maroon raiders had created a battle zone comparable to that around the city of Santo Domingo a few decades earlier. In 1609, shortly after a slave conspiracy was wildly rumored in Mexico City, Spanish authorities decided to launch a military campaign against a mountain settlement of rebellious slaves led by an African named Ỹanga. An extraordinary sequence of five bloody slave rebellions afflicted the sugar heartland of Veracruz Province from 1725 to 1768; the largest, in 1735, lasted months and may have embraced 2,000 slaves. Mexico City suffered no large-scale slave revolts even though it had the largest slave population in New Spain, but extensive conspiracies were allegedly found in 1537, 1608, and 1612.

The seaboard provinces of Venezuela had slave revolts and conspiracies more serious than those of any other region in Spanish South America. A Ladino slave named Miguel, who ran away from the Buria gold mines near the Yaracuy River, became king of a large maroon enclave. In 1555 Spanish forces crushed his effort to unite Indians and slaves into an anti-Spanish rebellion. In the early 1730s a Zambo slave called Andresote proved more successful. With Dutch help, he joined Indians and people of color from the cacao-producing region of the Yaracuy River Valley in a great insurgency in which a slave rebellion conjoined with a popular outburst against the Caracas Company. Andresote's rebellion lasted several years and eventually took a government force of 1,500 men to put down. In 1795 a free *zambo,* José Leonardo Chirino, headed a destructive and bloody rebellion of slaves and free people of color in the western province of Coro. Slaves also combined with free people of color to hatch ambitious conspiracies in Caracas (1749) and Maracaibo (1799).

Conspicuous slave resistance in Colombia began with the razing by Africans of the Caribbean port of Santa Marta in 1529, four years after its founding. By the end of the sixteenth century gold mining had pulled thousands of African slaves into the region drained by the Cauca River. Several small revolts surfaced near the town of Popayán around mid-century; these paled by comparison to the great rising in 1598 by perhaps several thousand slaves from the gold mines near Zaragoza. An uprising of about forty slaves at a gold mine near the town of Tadó in 1728 quickly spread to other mines. Troops sent by the governor of Popayán finally drowned the threat in blood.

Cartagena, the central port through which slaves passed to the mines, seems to have had a number of slave conspiracies—in 1619, 1693, and 1799, for example—but no serious slave revolts. Neither did colonial Lima, although several haciendas in coastal Peru gave rise to minor slave revolts during the second half of the eighteenth century. Two larger, violent revolts, among the last in Spanish America, broke out in 1851 on sugar plantations in Peru's Chicama and Cañete valleys. The most notable act of collective slave resistance in colonial Argentina appears to have been some loose plotting in Buenos Aires in 1795 that was inspired by the French and St. Domingue revolutions.

CONTRIBUTING FACTORS
Conditions that favored slave revolt included high concentrations of slaves, master absenteeism, sharp reversals in working conditions, real or perceived weakening in the forces of control, divisions within the master class or between elite social groups, favorable terrain for establishing lines of communication and conducting subversive activity, and sufficient space within the slave system for the creation of a viable slave leadership. A strong tradition of resistance also mattered, whether carried from Africa by enslaved members of warrior societies or inherited in Spanish America by successive generations of unruly Creole slaves.

Few of Spanish America's revolts and conspiracies lacked privileged slaves in leadership roles. Drivers, for example, figure conspicuously as leaders in most of nineteenth-century Cuba's great acts of collective slave resistance. Domestic slaves appear centrally in plot after plot in Spanish American cities. The conspiracies of Aponte and La Escalera and the rebellions of Andresote and Coro attest to the complex relations and chains of command developed by slaves as arrangements were made and deals were struck between rural and urban slaves, mulatto and black slaves, African and creole slaves, and privileged and unprivileged slaves.

GOALS
The specific goals of collective resistance, whether expressed as personal liberation, extermination of whites, access to land, or the creation of a new society, could differ markedly from one rebel group to another or from the leadership to the soldiery. Ethnic tensions surfaced among African rebels, and intimacies existed with whites. Differences among slaves help to account for so many betrayed and failed revolts. In numerous cases slave rebels formed ties with other oppressed people or with foreign powers. Free people of color participated in and even led a number of the larger movements of slave resistance; Indians participated in some of the larger movements, particularly those on the mainland. Yet members of both groups also acted with whites as agents of repression.

Over time, patterns of slave resistance changed. The 1791 slave revolution in Saint Domingue was a turning point, for it marked the integration of American revolts into the Age of Democratic Revolution, a decisive shift away from restorationist revolts directed at withdrawal from the prevailing social arrangements to resistance directed at liberal-democratic restructuring of society. Evidence for this shift can be found after 1791 in slave conspiracies and revolts throughout Spanish America, especially those in Venezuela, Cuba, and Puerto Rico.

See also **Slavery: Spanish America.**

BIBLIOGRAPHY

José Antonio Saco, *História de la esclavitud de la raza africana* (1879).

Carlos Federico Guillot, *Negros rebeldes y negros cimarrones* (1961).

Leslie B. Rout, Jr., *The African Experience in Spanish America* (1976), chap. 4.

Eugene D. Genovese, *From Rebellion to Revolution* (1979).

Guillermo A. Baralt, *Esclavos rebeldes* (1982).

Robert L. Paquette, *Sugar Is Made with Blood* (1988).

Additional Bibliography

Andrés Gallego, José. *La esclavitud en la América española*. Madrid: Ediciones Encuentro; Fundación Ignacio Larramendi, 2005.

Landers, Jane and Barry Robinson. *Slaves, Subjects, and Subversives: Blacks in Colonial Latin America*. Albuquerque: University of New Mexico Press, 2006.

ROBERT L. PAQUETTE

SLAVERY

This entry includes the following articles:
BRAZIL
SPANISH AMERICA
INDIAN SLAVERY AND FORCED LABOR
ABOLITION

BRAZIL

The enslavement of Africans in Brazil had begun by 1550. The first enslaved Africans were introduced to Pernambuco and São Vicente, in the modern state of São Paulo. The centers of African slavery evolved not in colonial São Paulo, however, but in the Northeast of Brazil in the sixteenth and seventeenth centuries and in Minas Gerais, Goiás, and Mato Grosso in the eighteenth century. Only in the nineteenth century did African slavery supplant Indian slavery in São Paulo. African slavery also existed in the far north in Amazonia, as well as in the far south in Rio Grande do Sul. How many Africans were imported to be enslaved in Brazil over a little more than three centuries is uncertain; some estimates are 3.5 to 4 million. Nor do we know how many Africans served in Brazil, except for specific areas in which censuses were taken in the eighteenth and nineteenth centuries. Several censuses reveal that black and pardo slaves comprised 40 percent or more of the total population.

The Africans who journeyed to Brazil on the slave ships came from many parts of West and west-central Africa. Those traded from the Costa da Mina of what is now Ghana were known as Minas in Brazil, and by extension Mina often defined a person from West Africa, also known as Guinea. The second major region of export was the modern country of Angola, hence many Africans were known in Brazil as "Angolans," or "Congos" for the old kingdom of Kongo in northern Angola (and by extension all those exported from the mouth of the Congo River). A minority of Africans originated in East Africa, principally Mozambique.

African slavery was the foundation of the coastal Brazilian export economy until its abolition in 1888. The Africans provided the labor to produce the wealth based on plantation agriculture and gold mining. Those who aspired to wealth and status owned slaves, and slave ownership was dispersed among all strata of society throughout Brazil.

The conquest and settlement of coastal Brazil was a joint Luso-African project in the colonial period. The Portuguese first brought their African slaves from Portugal to assist them in the conquest of Brazil. Lacking enough Portuguese soldiers, the Portuguese employed soldier-slaves to protect themselves from Indian and French attacks or to wage offensive wars against the coastal Indians. Black troops termed "Henriques," in honor of Henrique Dias, the black hero in the Dutch wars of the seventeenth century, were essential thereafter to the defense of colonial Brazil.

Also introduced to Brazil in the sixteenth century was the sugar plantation (the *engenho*), which was worked by African slaves, and most of the

Slave labor in Brazil, mid-19th century. Slave ownership existed at all levels of society in Brazil. Plantations, small farmers, and industry of all kinds relied on the work of African slaves. © BETTMAN/CORBIS

Africans in Brazil labored as slaves on the *engenhos* in the sixteenth and seventeenth centuries or in support positions, such as food production, cattle raising, and transportation of sugar to the port cities, such as Salvador and Olinda. The first *engenhos* were established in São Vicente and Pernambuco in the 1530s and 1540s, and by 1570 an estimated 2,000 to 3,000 blacks lived in Brazil. As sugar became the dominant export, Africans grew in number, replacing Indian slaves who died or fled the plantations. In the last decades of the sixteenth century, Bahia and Pernambuco imported 30,000 Africans from the Guinea coast, but the dominant era of sugar cultivation was the seventeenth century, when a half million Africans were imported, mostly before 1640. They were forced to plant and harvest sugarcane for the great *senhores de engenho,* who owned large plantations, hundreds of slaves, and the sugar mills; or for the Lavradores De Cana, who owned or rented smaller plots of land, employed fewer slaves, and sent their cane to a nearby mill for processing. Because of the extraordinary labor demands of the sugar harvest,

slave mortality was high, leading to the importation of more Africans.

Africans also labored in other areas of agriculture, such as the production of staple crops, tobacco, cotton, rice, and coffee. Small farmers, often free people of color, employed their slaves in raising tropical fruits, beans, corn, manioc, and small animals for sale in nearby towns, while others worked patches of land near great plantations. Others cultivated tobacco in Bahia for export to Europe and Africa. Further inland, especially in the backlands of the Northeast and Goiás, slaves raised cotton, spun it into thread, and wove cloth on wooden looms and made lace. Africans also labored on rice plantations, utilizing methods familiar to them in West Africa.

Experiments with coffee plantations in the early nineteenth century soon led to the rapid expansion of coffee plantations worked by African slaves, first in the Paraíba Valley of Rio de Janeiro, with subsequent expansion into São Paulo, Minas Gerais, and Goiás. While slavery was being abolished elsewhere in Latin

America, African slavery actually expanded on the coffee plantations of the southeast in the nineteenth century. By the time of abolition in 1888, the majority of slaves labored in the coffee regions.

Although plantation labor dominated African lives in Brazil, some Africans escaped the harsh labor demands of plantations in pastoral activities, such as raising cattle, horses, and goats. Africans, familiar with such animals in their homelands, quickly took to animal husbandry in the Northeast, central Brazil, and the far south. From the interior, black and mulatto cowboys drove cattle for slaughter to the coastal cities to be converted into dried beef on *charqueadas,* especially in Rio Grande do Sul. As muleteers and drivers, slaves also conducted mule teams and oxcarts between cities and plantations.

African fishermen also transferred their skills to Brazil and went deep-sea fishing using rafts with triangular sails. They were also the whalers of colonial Rio and Bahia, returning to warehouses to cut up and process the whales, extracting whale oil. Their familiarity with the sea meant that many Africans were also put to work as slave sailors, boatmen, and oarsmen, who were essential to the coastal and river trade of Brazil.

The African tradition of head porterage was also important in Brazil, and slaves moved heavy loads on their heads, including jars of water from wells and rivers. They were also the stevedores in port cities and loaded Brazil's exports of sugar, tobacco, and coffee and imports of Asian textiles and English manufactures on and off ships in the harbors. In addition, slaves had to carry their owners in sedan chairs or in hammocks. In the absence of large animals, enslaved Africans served as "beasts of burden," being particularly important in the transportation infrastructure.

African slavery was also essential to the mining sector of the Brazilian economy, especially in the eighteenth century in the mining captaincies of Minas Gerais, Goiás, and Mato Grosso. Miners who aimed to strike it rich purchased young Africans in Rio and Bahia and led them to the gold-rush camps to work as *garimpeiros,* who panned for gold and diamonds in the rivers. Young women worked as the cooks of the mining gangs or as domestic servants as the camps evolved into towns. Although a few black women mined gold, most acquired gold through retail trades. With what they earned from the trade in foodstuffs, they purchased their freedom or that of their children.

The retail trades and domestic service were closely linked in Brazil, and female slaves usually did both. Not only did they care for customers, serving them food or drink, but they also prepared the meals for the household, did the cleaning, and took the laundry to wash in nearby rivers. In larger households there was more labor specialization, with ladies in waiting known as *mucamas,* a housekeeper, an *ama de leite* to nurse the children, cooks, buyers, seamstresses, and laundresses. Male slaves served as coachmen, footmen, uniformed sedan-chair porters, and stablemen. Additional slaves attached to large urban households were sent into the streets as *negros de ganho* (blacks for hire) to earn wages for their owners as tailors, shoemakers, carpenters, and street vendors.

Most African slaves, however, did not serve in luxurious houses as elegantly dressed domestic servants or as skilled craftsmen in the towns and cities. The vast majority of enslaved Africans, including the women, were forced to work in the fields or at hard menial labor as porters. They were the indispensable labor force of the Brazilian economy without which Brazil would not have developed as quickly as it did between 1532 and 1888. Most of this labor was not done willingly; it had to be coerced, and only fearful punishments forced the Africans to work against their wills, although some slaveowners used the promise of manumission to "persuade" their unwilling captives to labor for them. Thus, just as hard labor was one aspect of the history of African slavery in Brazil, the other side was implacable resistance to escape the slave status, symbolized by the great seventeenth-century quilombo of Palmares.

See also **Senzala; Slave Revolts: Brazil; Slavery: Indian Slavery and Forced Labor; Slave Trade.**

BIBLIOGRAPHY

Gilberto Freyre, *The Masters and the Slaves,* translated by Samuel Putnam (1946).

Stanley J. Stein, *Vassouras: A Brazilian Coffee County, 1850–1900* (1957).

Warren Dean, *Rio Claro: A Brazilian Plantation System, 1820–1920* (1976).

Gerald Cardoso, *Negro Slavery in the Sugar Plantations of Veracruz and Pernambuco, 1550–1680: A Comparative Study* (1983).

Robert E. Conrad, *Children of God's Fire* (1983).

Stuart B. Schwartz, *Sugar Plantations in the Formation of Brazilian Society: Bahia, 1550–1835* (1985).

Mary C. Karasch, "Suppliers, Sellers, Servants, and Slaves," in *Cities & Society in Colonial Latin America,* edited by Louisa Schell Hoberman and Susan Migden Socolow (1986), and *Slave Life in Rio de Janeiro, 1808–1850* (1987).

Katia M. De Queirós Mattoso, *To Be a Slave in Brazil, 1550–1888,* translated by Arthur Goldhammer (1986).

Additional Bibliography

Bergad, Laird W. *Slavery and the Demographic and Economic History of Minas Gerais, Brazil, 1720–1888.* New York: Cambridge University Press, 1999.

Carvalho, Marcus J M de. *Liberdade: Rotinas e rupturas do escravismo no Recife, 1822–1850.* Recife: Editora Universitária UFPE, 1998.

Graden, Dale Torston. *From Slavery to Freedom in Brazil: Bahia, 1835–1900.* Albuquerque: University of New Mexico Press, 2006.

Higgins, Kathleen J. *"Licentious Liberty" in a Brazilian Gold-mining Region: Slavery, Gender, and Social Control in Eighteenth-century Sabará, Minas Gerais.* University Park: Pennsylvania State University Press, 1999.

Klein, Herbert S. *The Atlantic Slave Trade.* Cambridge, U.K.: Cambridge University Press, 1999.

Lauderdale Graham, Sandra. *Caetana Says No: Women's Stories from a Brazilian Slave Society.* Cambridge, U.K.: Cambridge University Press, 2002.

Nishida, Mieko. *Slavery and Identity: Ethnicity, Gender, and Race in Salvador, Brazil, 1808–1888.* Bloomington: Indiana University Press, 2003.

Reis, João José and Flávio dos Santos Gomes. *Liberdade por um fio: História dos quilombos no Brasil.* São Paulo: Companhia das Letras, 1996.

Silva, Maria Beatriz Nizza da. *Brasil: Colonização e escravidão.* Rio de Janeiro: Nova Fronteira, 2000.

MARY KARASCH

SPANISH AMERICA

Spain enjoys the dubious distinction of having introduced the institution of African slavery to the Americas. In 1501 the Catholic monarchs, Ferdinand and Isabella, granted permission to Nicolás de Ovando, the governor of Hispaniola, to import Africans as slaves to that island. The first slaves arrived from Spain in 1502, thereby inaugurating a trade in human beings that would last until about 1870. Africans and their progeny helped change the human landscape of the Americas and contributed their energies to the making of the colonial societies.

Slavery was a feature of Spanish society prior to the colonization of the Americas. Black Africans, however, formed only one of several groups from which slaves were drawn. Spanish slaves also included Jews, Muslims, and other Spaniards. When the indigenous population of the Caribbean islands declined as a consequence of mistreatment and disease, the Iberian colonists introduced a form of labor exploitation with which they were already familiar. Although Indians were subjected to enslavement in the early years, slavery was increasingly confined to the peoples of African descent. Past practice, economic necessity, cultural chauvinism, and racist ideology all combined to legitimize slavery for Africans in the Spanish colonies.

Once slavery was established in Hispaniola, it soon spread to the other Spanish Caribbean colonies of Cuba, Puerto Rico, and Jamaica. Shortly after the defeat of the Aztecs, the colonists introduced the institution to Mexico. In time, African slaves served in Peru, Bolivia, Venezuela, Colombia, and Argentina; indeed they were present in all of the colonies. Their number varied, to be sure. Cuba, which experienced its heyday as a slave society during the nineteenth century, imported the largest number of Africans, probably around 700,000. Since Cuba lacked an indigenous population, the colonists came to depend on black slaves to perform a wide range of labor services. Mexico received about 200,000 slaves, Venezuela 121,000, Peru 95,000, and Puerto Rico about 80,000. The rest were divided among the remaining colonies, depending on the nature of their economies and the size of their native populations. Taken together, the Spanish colonies received from about 1.5 million to 2 million slaves. The aforementioned number does not include those who were born in the Americas and inherited their mother's slave status.

We will never know exactly how many Africans were actually enslaved, given the absence of regular and reliable census data. It is certain, nonetheless, that the life expectancy of the slave population everywhere was short. Most fell victim to overwork, poor diet, and disease. Consequently, the slaves in all of the societies generally experienced an annual rate of natural decrease.

Slavery was recognized in Spanish law, and slaves were accorded certain rights by the Siete Partidas, the body of laws that constituted the basis of Spanish jurisprudence. Drawing its inspiration from the law of ancient Rome, Spanish law granted slaves the right to marry, have a family, and be manumitted. Slaves were also protected from mistreatment by their masters. They could appeal to the authorities for redress of their grievances. Modern research has shown that in Spanish America, these rights were not always upheld. In fact, the laws that were enacted by the colonists themselves frequently contradicted the liberal spirit of the Siete Partidas. The colonists developed an extensive body of legislation that circumscribed the movement of the slaves, imposed harsh punishments for infractions, and regulated their public and private behavior.

Spanish American slaveowners used their human property in a variety of ways. Since slaves were acquired to help create wealth for the master class, it is not surprising that they constituted a significant share of the labor force in the silver mines of Mexico and Peru. Others were employed on the sugarcane plantations of Cuba, Puerto Rico, Mexico, and Peru. Some worked on cattle ranches in several societies, planted ginger in Puerto Rico and Hispaniola, coffee and tobacco in Cuba, and cacao in Venezuela. In the urban centers, particularly those of Mexico and Peru, they labored in the textile factories (*obrajes*) under very difficult physical conditions. Slaves who had specialized skills worked as carpenters, shoemakers, bakers and in a range of other trades. Many were domestic workers. There was not much gender differentiation in the assignment of tasks, although men tended to predominate in the artisanal trades, the mining industry, and the processing of sugar. The majority of the domestic workers were women; other women worked on the plantations.

There can be no doubt that slaves in Spanish America, in common with their peers elsewhere, experienced severe and sustained assaults on their personhood. Lacking liberty and occupying a subordinate place in society, African slaves and their progeny struggled to carve out a place for themselves in all of the societies of the Americas. It is impossible to measure their degree of success, but they were able, whenever and wherever their demographic structure permitted, to sustain families, practice their religions, and retain important aspects of their variegated African heritages.

While it is difficult to generalize about the content of the slaves' religious beliefs, one can say with some assurance that religion played a significant role in their lives. The Catholic Church made some attempt to catechize the slaves, but the results varied from colony to colony. Much depended on the size of the slave population, the energy of the priests, and the ratio of priests to slaves. Some Africans embraced aspects of Catholic dogma, went to confession, and received the sacraments of baptism, matrimony, and the Holy Eucharist. Many adopted the Catholic saints with a high degree of enthusiasm. But often these saints were Africanized and became symbolic representations of African deities. In fact, and in a larger sense, blacks Africanized Catholicism and imposed their own flavor upon its rituals and practices. African religious beliefs and practices were not usually abandoned, as slaves inhabited several spiritual worlds at once. In Mexico and Peru, the Holy Office of the Inquisition tried to ferret out and destroy surviving African religious beliefs, but to no avail.

The *Cofradía,* or religious brotherhood, was one of the institutions that attracted Christianized slaves. Essentially charitable and mutual aid organizations, the brotherhoods sponsored recreational activities and offered financial assistance to their members in times of difficulty. *Cofradías* appear to have been most prevalent in urban centers such as Lima, Mexico City, Caracas, and Havana, where slaves had greater opportunities for social interaction. Only a small minority of the black population, however, belonged to these organizations. They were the preserve of the elite slaves and to some extent reflected class and ethnic differences among the slave population.

Slaves also sought to establish some degree of family life. Yet their family life, it must be said, was precarious everywhere. Although slave marriages were protected by the Siete Partidas, in practice such unions could be broken up with impunity by the masters. The imbalance in the sex ratio that favored men almost everywhere complicated the difficulty of finding partners. Miscegenation became a characteristic feature of these societies as Africans, Spaniards, and Indians produced a variety of racially mixed children.

Slaves who applied for marriage licenses generally chose their partners from their own ethnic group. Similarly, creole slaves—those born in the Americas—tended to choose other creoles as their spouses. This should not be particularly surprising, since a shared ethnic heritage generally plays a role in spouse selection. The absence of a large number of formal Christian marriages, however, should not lead to the conclusion that family units did not exist or that men and women failed to establish enduring bonds. Slaves, as people, fell in love, reared children, and often created long-term unions without the sanction of the church or the state. They had to develop kinship ties and function as fully as they could within the boundaries set by those who owned them.

One of the important features of Spanish American slavery was the real possibility that slaves could be freed. The Siete Partidas encouraged the manumission of slaves, since it held that the institution was contrary to natural law and that there should be no legislation that would impede their inexorable march to freedom. Accordingly, Spanish laws and traditions had the effect of creating a climate favorable to manumission. Most slaves, to be sure, were never manumitted, and those who were so privileged consisted primarily of women and children, elderly slaves, and those whose freedom was purchased by themselves, a relative, or some other benefactor. The emergence of a significant free black population was due, in part, to the absence of laws prohibiting manumission. Panama, for example, boasted 33,000 free persons of African descent in 1778 to 3,500 slaves. Peru had 41,000 free persons in 1792 and 40,000 slaves. And in 1861 Cuba had 232,000 free persons and 371,000 slaves.

Many slaves rejected their condition by engaging in various forms of resistance. As early as 1522, the slaves in Hispaniola rose in rebellion, setting a precedent for their peers in other parts of Spain's empire. Thus Mexico, Peru, Cuba, Venezuela, and other colonies experienced challenges to the institution. Unlike their peers on the French island of Saint Domingue, however, Spanish American slaves were never able to achieve a successful revolution.

Some slaves, in spite of the obstacles they confronted, succeeded in claiming their freedom even while the institution continued to exist. These were the individuals who escaped and established sanctuaries, usually in very inaccessible parts of the colonies. Mexico, Cuba, Colombia, and Venezuela were topographically conducive to flight, and slaves were quick to exploit the advantages that the physical environment offered them. Known as *cimarrones* (Maroons), the runaways disturbed the colonists because of their frequent assaults on Hispanic settlements. They established their own settlements (Palenques) in several colonies and defended them against the frequent attacks of the masters and the authorities.

One of the most famous *palenques* existed in the area between Mount Orizaba and Veracruz, Mexico, in the early seventeenth century. Led by Ỹanga, an Angolan who had managed to maintain his freedom for thirty years, the community numbered about 500 inhabitants in 1608. After holding off the assaults of the Spaniards for some time, Ỹanga and his people eventually signed a truce recognizing their freedom and awarding them land upon which to build a pueblo. The town of San Lorenzo de los Negros was built by these *cimarrones* and received its charter in 1617. Runaway slaves signed similar treaties with the authorities elsewhere in the Americas, thereby demonstrating their extraordinary success in claiming and sustaining their freedom.

The institution of slavery ended at different times in the Spanish colonies. Many countries freed their slaves in the aftermath of their wars for independence. Only Chile, however, freed the slaves unconditionally and almost immediately after it won its independence. In the other societies, slavery ended gradually. By 1860, only Cuba and Puerto Rico held Africans in bondage. Puerto Rico freed all its slaves in 1873, and Cuba followed suit in 1886 after a period of gradual emancipation.

Africans and their children served as slaves in Spanish America for almost four centuries (1502–1886). They played important roles in building the economies of these New World societies and in helping shape their cultural life and institutions. In none of these societies were blacks accorded much personal worth. They had, perforce, to struggle to define themselves as human beings and to order their lives as best they could under the most difficult of circumstances.

See also **African-Latin American Religions: Overview; Africans in Hispanic America.**

BIBLIOGRAPHY

Franklin W. Knight, *Slave Society in Cuba During the Nineteenth Century* (1970).

John V. Lombardi, *The Decline and Abolition of Negro Slavery in Venezuela, 1820–1954* (1971).

Frederick P. Bowser, *The African Slave in Colonial Peru, 1524–1650* (1974).

Colin A. Palmer, *Slaves of the White Gold: Blacks in Mexico, 1570–1650* (1976).

Leslie B. Rout, Jr., *The African Experience in Spanish America, 1502 to the Present Day* (1976).

George Reid Andrews, *The Afro-Argentines of Buenos Aires, 1800–1900* (1980).

Herbert S. Klein, *African Slavery in Latin America and the Caribbean* (1986).

Additional Bibliography

Andrés Gallego, José. *La esclavitud en la América española.* Madrid: Ediciones Encuentro; Fundación Ignacio Larramendi, 2005.

Landers, Jane, and Barry Robinson. *Slaves, Subjects, and Subversives: Blacks in Colonial Latin America.* Albuquerque: University of New Mexico Press, 2006.

COLIN A. PALMER

INDIAN SLAVERY AND FORCED LABOR

During the colonial period in Brazil (1500–1822), Amerindian labor provided a fundamental source of manpower for Portuguese enterprises, particularly in areas peripheral to the Atlantic export economy. Early on, with the development of the sugar industry along the coast, settlers turned to the indigenous population in their search for labor. Though they attempted alternative forms of labor appropriation, the colonists ultimately favored native bondage. In a strictly legal sense, however, indigenous slavery failed to unfold on a large scale, since protective Portuguese legislation and Jesuit opposition to illegal slaving practices constrained its development. According to the law of 20 March 1570, slaves could be acquired legitimately only through the prosecution of "just wars" against tribes who had refused or renounced Christianity, or through the "ransom" of captives destined to be sacrificed in cannibalistic rituals. Colonists found many ways to circumvent legal restrictions, forging pretexts for "just wars," often with the collusion of corrupt authorities, and declaring that every captive taken had been "ransomed."

While native labor gradually was replaced by African slavery in the sugar zones, Amerindian slavery reached massive proportions in the southern colony of São Paulo and in the northern state of Maranhão, where the local economies revolved around the services of native agricultural laborers and porters. In seventeenth-century São Paulo, the colonists focused their attentions on the southern Guarani people, organizing several large-scale expeditions to assault their villages and the Jesuit missions, bringing thousands of captives back to the Portuguese settlements. Though treating the Indians as captives and disposing of them as property, the colonists did not consider them formally as slaves, always referring to them as *forros* (freedmen).

Claiming rights to the labor of the people they had extracted from the wilderness at great personal expense—feeding them, clothing them, and giving them Christian instruction—the colonists developed a parallel system of personal administration. In effect, though, the expansion and reproduction of this system depended less on its institutional contours than on objective demographic and economic variables. Subject to periodic epidemics and negative natural growth rates, the captive population had to be replenished by new expeditions. As a result, indigenous slavery flourished as long as the flow of new captives continued.

In Maranhão and Pará, the colonists also developed a labor-recruitment scheme based on slaving expeditions, though with peculiar regional characteristics. Throughout the seventeenth and eighteenth centuries, the basic organizational form was the *tropa de* Resgate (ransom expedition), canoe convoys that penetrated the many navigable rivers of the Amazon Valley in search of slaves and forest products. Though frequently contested by the Jesuits, many captives taken were judged legal slaves, even as late as the 1740s.

Though the Pombaline Reforms eradicated all forms of forced native labor in 1755, legal "Indian" slavery reemerged briefly after 1808, when the crown permitted the temporary bondage of war captives, especially among the Kaingang of São Paulo and the Botocudo of Minas Gerais and Espírito Santo. The province of Goiás and the cattle frontier of southern Maranhão also witnessed the reintroduction of Amerindian slavery during this period. Indigenous bondage was proscribed once again in 1831, though other forms of native forced labor, such as debt servitude in the Amazon, persisted into the twentieth century.

Generally indigenous slavery was prohibited in Spanish-speaking America, and therefore, unlike in

Brazil, the topic of Native-American slavery has not received much attention using this kind of terminology. Yet Pre-Columbian peoples held each other in slavery, not only with the *mit'a* in the Andes but also with parallel structures in Mesoamerica. The Nahua (Aztecs) held large quantities of peoples as slaves. Oftentimes when the Spanish arrived, they simply appropriated Amerindian practices in this regard. Cortés's *Cartas de relación* offer some insight. As Ward observes, every time Cortés arrived in a new town or city the local ruler would make gifts of slave women, called *esclavas* in Spanish. This usage can also be found in other chroniclers. Since the Amerindians did not generally have the concept of private property, later Iberian practices tended to reflect that and not view their indigenous slaves as chattel. Oftentimes in the Spanish-speaking world, indigenous servitude was hidden through institutions that seemed somewhat less sinister, such as with the *repartimiento* and the *encomienda*. Like in Brazil, native servitude in Spanish-speaking regions evolved into a form of debt peonage as early as the seventeenth century, chronicler Felipe Guaman Poma de Ayala reports. Debt peonage practices continue to the present day in Guatemala, Peru and other countries.

See also **Debt Peonage; Encomienda; Mita; Repartimiento; Slavery: Brazil; Slavery: Spanish America.**

BIBLIOGRAPHY

On early labor relations see Alexander Marchant, *From Barter to Slavery* (1942), which remains an important source. Stuart Schwartz, *Sugar Plantations in the Formation of Brazilian Society* (1985), provides an illuminating discussion of Indian labor in the northeast. John Monteiro, "From Indian to Slave," in *Slavery and Abolition* 9, no. 2 (1988): 105–127, examines the development of Indian slavery in São Paulo. Mathias Kiemen, *The Indian Policy of Portugal in the Amazon Region* (1954), deals with the legal dimensions of native labor in Maranhão, while Dauril Alden, "Indian versus Black Slavery in the State of Maranhão During the Seventeenth and Eighteenth Century," in *Bibliotheca Americana* 1 (1983): 91–142, offers a cogent summary of demographic and economic aspects. For a general treatment see John Hemming, *Red Gold* (1978) and *Amazon Frontier* (1987). For indigenous history, see Manuela Carneiro Da Cunha, ed., *Historia dos índios no Brasil* (1992).

Additional Bibliography

Metcalf, Alida C. *Go-betweens and the Colonization of Brazil, 1500–1600*. Austin: University of Texas Press, 2005.

Langfur, Hal. *The Forbidden Lands: Colonial Identity, Frontier Violence, and the Persistence of Brazil's Eastern Indians, 1750–1830*. Stanford, CA: Stanford University Press, 2006.

Ward, Thomas. "Expanding Ethnicity in Sixteenth-Century Anahuac: Ideologies of Ethnicity and Gender in the Nation-Building Process." *MLN* 116.2 (March 2001): 419–452; pp. 434–449.

JOHN M. MONTEIRO

ABOLITION

The abolition of slavery in the Americas occurred in fits and starts, some of them convulsive, between the outbreak of the Haitian Revolution in 1791 and the promulgation of the golden law of Brazil in 1888. Slavery was an institution entrenched both in economic life and in the social fabric of essentially hierarchical societies. The commodities produced by slave labor, particularly sugar, cotton, and coffee, were crucial to the expanding network of transatlantic trade. In Brazil and Cuba slaveholding was also widespread in the cities and in some food-producing regions. Thus while the ideological transformations accompanying the growth of capitalism in Great Britain set the stage for a general critique of chattel slavery and championing of "free labor," it took more than a changing intellectual climate to dislodge the institution. Abolitionism took on its greatest force when it coincided with economic change and domestic social upheaval, and particularly when it became an element in the defining of new nations or new colonial relationships.

It was often slaves themselves who forced the question to the center of the stage, threatening or carrying out revolt, and offering or withholding support for republican challenges to colonialism. Slaves seized upon moments of division within the free population to expand or redefine their customary rights, advance new claims, flee their owners, or join in the warfare that might finally bring slavery to an end. At times they found allies among free people of color, whose civil rights were in continual danger as long as slavery was recognized in law and in social practice.

Over the past decades scholars have moved from a chronicling of the political process of formal abolition to an examination of the dynamics of emancipation as a social and economic process, one intertwined with the politics of abolitionism but not simply derivative of it. While different studies vary in the weight given to slave initiatives and economic necessity, external pressures and internal conflicts, elite ideology and popular resistance, there is no necessary contradiction involved in recognizing the importance of each of these. As Robin Blackburn has argued, the key turning points in the campaign against slavery generally occurred when some combination of class conflict, war, and pressure for new forms of government brought into question the rights of property and encouraged a widening of the concepts of citizenship and national interest. Internal and external forces were thus inextricable.

In Latin America, the ending of slavery took place in three successive stages. The first was marked by emancipation in the context of and as a consequence of war. The Haitian Revolution opened the age of emancipation and helped to place abolition on the agenda when anticolonial rebellions erupted in Spanish America. This emancipationist phase was consolidated in Haiti, remained incomplete in most of the Spanish American republics, and was thwarted in Brazil and Cuba. The second stage was a more gradual one, marked by the slow breakdown and elimination of slavery through the nineteenth century in the mainland republics. But concurrent with this phase was the expansion of what one scholar has termed the "second slavery"—vigorous export economies based on slave labor in Cuba, Brazil, and the United States. The third and final phase of emancipation was initiated by the Civil War in the United States, the Liberal Revolution of 1868 in Spain, and the definitive suppression of the transatlantic slave trade. Nominal abolitionism finally became part of the Liberal creed in Spain, while a more militant opposition to slavery became central to Cuban anticolonial struggles. In Brazil a cautious abolitionism emerged as an element in the public moral stance of the imperial state. But in both cases the pace and character of emancipation were shaped by slave initiatives, including participation in insurgency in Cuba and widespread flight from plantations in Brazil.

EMANCIPATION IN THE CONTEXT OF WAR

The French colony of Saint Domingue (the western part of Hispaniola) was between 1791 and 1804 the site of the first successful large-scale slave revolt in the Americas, which established the second independent state in the hemisphere—one founded on a repudiation of slavery. The mobilization of rebellion rested on a longstanding tradition of slave resistance, combined with the cultural creations of a new, shared language (Creole, or Kreyol) and a vigorous popular religion (Vodun), as well as brilliant military leadership under Toussaint Louverture and Jean Jacques Dessalines. The opening for revolt was provided by an unparalleled international conjuncture, marked by the ideological innovations and ambiguities of the French Revolution, the fragmentation of colonial authority during that upheaval, and the military and political divisions with France itself. At the same time, events in Haiti illustrated the ambiguous role of free populations of color, torn between an isolated struggle for group privilege, allegiance to established authority in defense of property and order, or allegiance to slaves in revindication of broader rights. The insurgents were eventually able to achieve independence from France and establish the new nation of Haiti, while continuing to resist multiple efforts by both the French and British to recolonize them. Under Toussaint Louverture's leadership, the insurgents were also able to take over Spanish Santo Domingo (the eastern part of Hispaniola) and abolish slavery there in 1801, but this accomplishment was reversed one year later by a French military expedition.

The Haitian Revolution frightened slaveholders throughout the Americas and had an important direct effect on the course of the Spanish American wars of independence. After being thwarted in his initial revolutionary efforts, the "Liberator" Simón Bolívar went in 1815 to Jamaica and then to Haiti to seek assistance. President Alexandre Pétion of Haiti insisted on a commitment to emancipation as a condition for support, and Bolívar made such a commitment. Opposition to slavery became an element in a new Spanish American ideal of citizenship, expanding the possibility of recruiting among slaves and others opposed to the power of slaveholders. Material and strategic support from Pétion gave Bolívar's cause new life, but many of the leaders of the independence movement continued to temporize when faced with the choice between forthright abolitionism and the mobilization of slaves and free people of color on the one hand, and the continued protection of property rights as a means for obtaining or retaining elite support on the other.

It was thus not surprising that antislavery commitments were ratified by some of the early republican congresses, such as that of the Republic of Gran Colombia at Cúcuta in 1821, but encumbered with conditions and timetables that stalled the actual process of emancipation. The republicans of Peru were even more cautious, putting property rights and social stability first and not declaring emancipation, even as they sought to recruit among slaves and free people of color. In what was later to become the Dominican Republic, however, nationalists were overtaken by events, as Haitian forces under President Jean-Pierre Boyer invaded in 1822, declaring the freedom of all slaves for a second time, promising land to the freedmen, and enforcing these policies through a military occupation.

THE BREAKDOWN OF SLAVERY IN THE MAINLAND REPUBLICS

In the newly established mainland Spanish American republics, the question of slavery continued to be a contested one. Chile, where slaves were few in number and largely engaged in domestic service, was the first to make a definitive abolition of slavery, through a Senate decree in 1823. Abolition was declared in Central America in 1824. In Mexico, slavery, already in decline, was suppressed by decree during the presidency of Vicente Guerrero in 1829. In most of South America, however, there was sparring over the mode and timetable for conforming to this element of the republican credo. Estate owners and other slaveholding elites generally stalled, while some leaders, including Bolívar, argued for abolition as a matter of moral authority and nation building. Weak manumission laws and "free womb" legislation (declaring free the children of slave mothers) initiated very gradual processes of abolition, but final emancipation was delayed for decades in Venezuela, Colombia, Paraguay, and Argentina.

Around mid-century, as much of Latin America moved into a new and more externally oriented political economy, the aging slave populations of the remaining republics finally achieved juridical freedom. Slavery was legally abolished in Uruguay in 1846; in Colombia in 1850; in the Argentine Republic in 1853; in Venezuela and Peru in 1854; and, finally, in Paraguay in 1870. In each case formal abolition was essentially a coda to a longer process of gradual emancipation. The development of new economic sectors largely rested on modes of labor in which workers were nominally free—though the exaction of their labor might contain significant elements of coercion.

Chattel slavery, the holding of property rights in men and women, had become a relic.

Symbolically and to some extent juridically, emancipation in the Spanish American republics can be seen as an outgrowth of the independence struggles, in which many slaves and free people participated. The ideology of those struggles and the mobilization of so many persons of color during them made a full reimposition of slavery nearly impossible. In that sense, the independence movement brought the ending of slavery. In practical terms, however, slavery died a more lingering death. Juridically, drastic inequalities of power within the nation and within the slaveholding household blocked full revindication of the rights of slaves and their freeborn children, keeping gradual abolition to a slow pace and minimizing its social consequences. Economically, free labor gradually supplanted slave labor and diminished the vested interests of slaveholders in the institution.

EMANCIPATION IN CUBA AND BRAZIL

Resisting the tide of emancipation and republicanism, the elites of colonial Cuba and imperial Brazil constructed vigorous slave-based export economies in sugar and coffee. They purchased new slaves from Africa, oversaw the opening of new lands on the frontier, and developed new and expanded overseas markets. In Cuba, the most prosperous planters also purchased modern processing equipment, hired technicians from overseas, and established massive sugar factories. Into the 1870s, the work of Cuban sugar plantations continued to be done by slave men and women, as well as indentured Chinese immigrants and small numbers of free workers. In Brazil, the internal trade in slaves from north to south enabled coffee plantations to expand on the basis of slave labor, despite the attacks on the transatlantic trade.

Scholars differ in their opinions of the viability of this "second slavery." On one level, it was a great success for the planters, yielding numerous fortunes for Brazilian coffee "barons" and Cuban sugar "aristocrats." On another level, it was increasingly vulnerable, as the British campaign against the slave trade threatened its labor supply and increased labor costs. Some historians have argued that slave-based prosperity was founded on a central contradiction, and that rising slave prices, and a necessarily uneducated work force, would block the full modernization of the plantation complex. Slavery was a rapacious form of economic development, exploitative of those who labored and of the land they worked. Whether such rapaciousness had truly led to crisis, however, remains in dispute. One view is that slavery was essentially incompatible with the development of capitalism and that the resulting decline in profitability was leading unavoidably to abolition. Others argue, however, that planters were highly adaptable capitalists, preferring a gradual substitution of free laborers to taking substantive steps toward full emancipation.

Wherever one stands on the question of "internal contradictions," it is clear that by the late 1860s the slave economies of both Cuba and Brazil faced major challenges. The victory of the Union Forces in the Civil War in the United States was a major ideological blow to modernizing slaveholders in Cuba and Brazil. It cast doubt on the compatibility of slavery and sustained economic progress and removed a key example that proslavery apologists had cited in debates with proponents of free labor. Equally important, the transatlantic slave trade was definitively abolished by the 1860s. Since the slave populations of Cuba and Brazil did not, overall, sustain their numbers through natural reproduction, planters would have to find some alternative sources of labor. And many feared—correctly—that free immigrants would shun societies based on coerced labor.

In Cuba, these latent contradictions became an open crisis when the question of abolition was taken up by anticolonial insurgents. Spain, the colonial power, was placed on the defensive by the Cuban rebels who rose up in 1868. To try to undercut the appeal of the rebellion, and to bring Spain into belated conformity with liberal principles, a cautious law of gradual abolition, the Moret Law, freeing children and the elderly, was approved by the Spanish Cortes in 1870. It was enforced even more cautiously by the colonial authorities in Cuba. (In Puerto Rico, where the stakes were lower, it was followed by abolition in 1873.) By 1879, however, continued nationalist rebellion in the eastern end of Cuba, and resistance to work on the part of slaves, forced the issue. The Spanish Cortes declared all Cuban slaves free in 1880, though it imposed upon them an eight-year "apprenticeship" to their former masters. This apprenticeship was drastically undermined by multiple initiatives on the part of

the apprentices, many of whom achieved their own freedom through flight, self-purchase, and legal challenge, hastening the arrival of formal emancipation, finally declared in 1886.

In Brazil, the balance of forces within the elite was changing, particularly with the growth of urban professional sectors. Moreover, many believed that the future of agriculture lay with the attraction of immigrant labor. But Brazilian slaveholders remained very powerful and were able to help shape and control the cautious responses to abolitionist pressure. Although abolition was formally carried out through a series of parliamentary and executive maneuvers, much of the driving force came from slaves themselves. Legal abolition began with the Law of the Free Womb (Free Birth Law) in 1871, followed by municipal and provincial legislation in selected areas of the Northeast. In the final phase, slave initiatives accelerated what was intended to be a controlled process, and flights from the estates became widespread in the period just prior to the proclamation of final abolition in the *Lei Aurea,* or Golden Law, of 1888.

By 1888, almost a century after the Haitian Revolution, formal chattel slavery was gone from Latin America. In some areas, particularly Mexico and Argentina, the descendants of former slaves were absorbed, at least in theory, by a larger process of *mestizaje,* though death and social denial also figured in their apparent disappearance. In Colombia, the descendants of slaves remained regionally isolated, their presence viewed as anomalous within a nation defined by its elite as European and mestizo. In Cuba and Brazil, where the descendants of slaves constituted a large fraction of the population, class divisions continued to be marked by distinctions of "race." Though legal freedom made new forms of struggle possible, people of African descent generally faced discrimination and lack of access to productive resources, which together undermined the juridical equality that was the legacy of abolition.

See also **Debt Peonage; Slavery: Spanish America.**

BIBLIOGRAPHY

Emília Viotti Da Costa, *Da senzala à colônia* (1966).

Robert Conrad, *The Destruction of Brazilian Slavery, 1850–1888* (1972).

Robert Brent Toplin, *The Abolition of Slavery in Brazil* (1975).

Manuel Moreno Fraginals, *El ingenio: Complejo económico social cubano del azúcar* (1978).

George Reid Andrews, *The Afro-Argentines of Buenos Aires, 1800–1900* (1980).

Leslie Bethell, ed., *The Cambridge History of Latin America*, vol. 3 (1985), pp. 299–346.

Rebecca J. Scott, *Slave Emancipation in Cuba: The Transition to Free Labor, 1860–1899* (1985).

Herbert S. Klein, *African Slavery in Latin America and the Caribbean* (1986).

Robin Blackburn, *The Overthrow of Colonial Slavery, 1776–1848* (1988).

Rebecca J. Scott et al., *The Abolition of Slavery and the Aftermath of Emancipation in Brazil* (1988).

Dale W. Tomich, "The 'Second Slavery': Bonded Labor and the Transformation of the Nineteenth Century World Economy," in *Rethinking the Nineteenth Century: Movements and Contradictions,* edited by Francisco O. Ramirez (1988).

Peter Wade, *Blackness and Race Mixture: The Dynamics of Racial Identity in Colombia* (1993).

Additional Bibliography

Andrés Gallego, José. *La esclavitud en la América española.* Madrid: Ediciones Encuentro; Fundación Ignacio Larramendi, 2005.

Graden, Dale Torston. *From Slavery to Freedom in Brazil: Bahia, 1835–1900.* Albuquerque: University of New Mexico Press, 2006.

Landers, Jane, and Barry Robinson. *Slaves, Subjects, and Subversives: Blacks in Colonial Latin America.* Albuquerque: University of New Mexico Press, 2006.

Mendonça, Joseli Maria Nunes. *Entre a mão e os anéis: A lei dos sexagenários e os caminhos da abolição no Brasil.* Campinas: Editora da UNICAMP: CECULT, 1999.

Schmidt-Nowara, Christopher. *Empire and Antislavery Spain, Cuba, and Puerto Rico, 1833–1874.* Pittsburgh, PA: University of Pittsburgh Press, 1999.

Vila Vilar, Enriqueta and Luisa Vila Vilar. *Los abolicionistas españoles: Siglo XIX.* Madrid: Ediciones de Cultura Hispánica, 1996.

REBECCA J. SCOTT

SLAVE TRADE. Latin America, including the Caribbean region, received more than 85 percent of the 10 million or so Africans brought to the New World between 1494 and sometime in the 1860s. Brazil took about 35 percent of the total, the Caribbean (including the British islands) somewhat more, and the mainland colonies of Spain only about 10 percent.

The leading slavers of the fifteenth and sixteenth centuries were the Portuguese. The Dutch joined them during the seventeenth century, and the British and French transported the majority of the captive humans taken across the Atlantic in the 1700s. Among the Americans, only Brazilians at Rio de Janeiro and Salvador became prominent as slavers, accounting for a major part of the trade to those ports in the eighteenth century. As the British withdrew from slaving starting in 1807, Brazilians and Portuguese became the major nineteenth-century purveyors, with the Spaniards joined by a few North Americans and, intermittently, the French in providing African labor to Cuba.

OUTLINE HISTORY

The slave trade began as a minor component in Portugal's fifteenth-century attempts to buy gold and commodities in West Africa. Africans at first tended to sell products, not people. But droughts there threw the region into violent conflict. Warlords seized captives and thrived on selling them to other Africans and to Europeans. Also, in western Africa there was an older trans-Saharan trade to Muslim lands with which European Atlantic traders competed.

New African mercantile sectors arose to broker this trade in labor and to import textiles and commodity currencies (particularly shells, copper rods, iron bars, and beads), along with smaller quantities of spirits and wines, firearms, and consumer luxuries. The growing cohort of Africans committed to selling refugees from drought and captives taken in wars thrived on the Europeans' willingness to pay higher and higher prices for labor.

Gradually, the dominant African political interests in the most densely inhabited portions of the continent became dependent on selling slaves. Most came from the Lower Guinea Coast between modern Ghana and Cameroon or from Angola, a vaguely defined region along the west-central shores of Africa on either side of the mouth of the Zaire River.

Demand for African slaves arose out of long-term shortages in American colonies. There, low-cost virgin lands and accessible deposits of precious

Some estimates of numbers of slaves transported to Latin America, by destination

Period	Exports from Africa (1)	Imports in Americas (2)	Brazil (3)	Caribbean (4)	Spanish Main (5)
1450–1600	367,000	293,400	50,000	(??)	483,900[a]
1601–1700	1,868,000	1,494,500	560,000	463,500	
1701–1800	6,133,000	5,737,600	1,891,400	2,939,700	(??)
1811–1867[b]		2,294,400	1,478,200	789,300	8,700
Total[c]	11,863,000	9.6–10.8 million			

[a]Number for Spanish Main covers period 1450–1700.
[b]Data for 1811–1867 from David Eltis, "The Nineteenth-Century Transatlantic Slave Trade: An Annual Time Series of Imports into the Americas Broken Down by Region," in *Hispanic American Historical Review* 67, no. 1 (1987): 109–138.
[c]Total from Paul E. Lovejoy, "The Impact of the Atlantic Slave Trade on Africa: A Review of the Literature," in *Journal of African History* 30 (1989): 368; not modified by Dutch figures from Johannes Menne Postma, *The Dutch in the Atlantic Slave Trade, 1600–1815* (1990). Columns do not add to the revised totals given in this line.

SOURCE: Columns (1) and (2): Paul E. Lovejoy, "The Volume of the Atlantic Slave Trade: A Synthesis," in *Journal of African History* 23, no. 4 (1982): 473–501, Tables 1, 9; Column (3): Philip D. Curtin, *The Atlantic Slave Trade: A Census* (1969); Column (4): Interpolated from Philip D. Curtin, *The Atlantic Slave Trade: A Census* (1969).

Table 1

metal ores—principally silver in Mexico and Peru and gold in Minas Gerais, Brazil—generated rapid economic growth. Already sparse Native American populations declined under the onslaught of European diseases, while an expanding economy in Europe absorbed the local working population there. With the demographic stage thus set, American specie, multiplied by early modern banking techniques, financed merchants in buying the refugees and captives of Africa to fill the labor deficit. American land, African labor, and European capital formed an economic triangle that generated lethally explosive growth.

Slavers delivered human cargoes in large numbers, first to the expanding sugar captaincies of the Brazilian Northeast at the end of the sixteenth century through Recife, in Pernambuco, and Salvador da Bahia. The Dutch then invested in and supplied labor for English cane plantations in the Caribbean, the main magnet for slavers about 1640. By 1700, the English West Indies, principally Jamaica, and French Saint Domingue drove the West Africa–Caribbean branch of the trade, with Bahian sugar and tobacco planters adding a second major, southern Atlantic, sector. Gold and diamonds in south-central Brazil propelled the trade from Angola to Rio de Janeiro until about 1760. Thereafter, diversifying exports of sugar, cotton, and coffee led Brazilian economic expansion into the nineteenth century.

The African slaves headed to the New World thus formed one leg of an Atlantic commercial triangle completed by European manufactured goods sent to Africa and American minerals and agricultural commodities headed for Europe.

War in Europe from 1793 and British efforts at suppressing Atlantic slaving from 1807 gradually ended the trade from West Africa, with the Bahians among the last to give up there in the 1840s. Cuba, with Havana the main entry point, became the principal nineteenth-century Caribbean importer of African labor, increasingly from central Africa, to support the island's emergence as a major producer of sugar and, later, coffee. In southern Brazil, Rio slavers intensified their exploitation of Angola and expanded into Indian Ocean markets, particularly Mozambique. Brazil suppressed these last currents of slaving after 1850, and the Cuban trade finally died out in the 1860s. Thereafter, free immigrants from Europe replaced enslaved Africans in Brazil and Argentina, and indentured Asians supplemented French and British needs in the Caribbean region and the Guianas.

GOVERNMENT PARTICIPATION

The Spanish and Portuguese monarchies attempted to regulate and tax the trade in slaves to their American colonies, with decreasing success. Spain's famous Asiento contracts, begun in 1518, licensed royally favored Seville merchants to hire foreign traders to carry slaves to its mainland colonies, mostly through Cartagena and Buenos Aires, until the middle of the eighteenth century. These foreigners—Italians; then Portuguese; and eventually Dutch, French, and English, in a succession that reflected the rise of commercial bourgeoisies in Europe—exploited the privilege of delivering slaves by smuggling manufactured goods into the Spanish preserves and selling them there for silver.

The Portuguese concentrated their regulatory efforts on the Angolan coast, which they treated as a trading monopoly centered on a small colony at Luanda. They levied export taxes on slaves leaving the port and until 1769 subcontracted these duties out to Lisbon merchant interests, who dominated the trade financially. In Angola a community of resident colonials who intermarried with their African suppliers, along with exiled Portuguese criminals, Jews, and Gypsies, brought the slaves down to the coast, often owning them on through the point of sale in Brazil.

Brazil-based Portuguese merchants, who had married into American planting families, became the dominant shippers of slaves and supplied the sugarcane brandies that lubricated Angolan slaving and the sweetened tobacco that gave Bahians a secure niche in a separate "Mina" trade (named for a Portuguese post in Africa) between northeastern Brazil and the West African Lower Guinea coast. These varying commercial structures allowed Portuguese merchants to limit their involvement to the low-risk financial aspects of the trade until the late 1700s. Iberian merchants left the hazards of owning and carrying the slaves to foreigners within the Spanish sphere and, in Portugal's domains, to colonials.

COMMERCIAL ORGANIZATION

Private commercial interests gradually took over slaving, as early government-sponsored trade receded before the rising tides of mercantilism and, later, of liberal "free trade." In northern Europe only a few early ventures enjoyed royal patronage or participation. The precocious Dutch West India Company led Netherlands merchants in their assault on Iberian slaving beginning in the 1620s. By the 1670s and 1680s, companies of private merchants, though still aided by royal charters and grants of monopoly trading privileges, had emerged everywhere, even to buy up Spain's *asiento*—notably the Royal African Company and the South Sea Company in England, the Compagnie des Indes in France, and the Companhia da Guiné in Portugal. By 1700, smaller free traders that were intruding as smugglers or interlopers quickly overwhelmed the unwieldy corporate behemoths. The Brazilians in the southern Atlantic, British shipping interests from Bristol and Liverpool, French traders in Nantes and small Breton ports, private merchants in Holland, and Rhode Islanders from North America then pushed the trade to its eighteenth-century heights.

Portugal, which had lost the slave trade in its own empire to the colonials in Angola and Brazil, went against this tide of private entrepreneurship by floating two old-fashioned chartered companies of national merchants, active in the 1750s and 1760s. These commercial anachronisms, the Maranhão and Pernambuco companies, quickly failed. Spain finally loosened its antiquated restrictions on private trade in the empire during the 1780s, but too late. Its merchants had too small a market for slaves, too little capital, and only a toehold in Africa on the equatorial island of Fernando Po and so did not consolidate a Spanish slaving industry before American independence movements ended the mainland trade after 1810.

The nineteenth-century slave trade to Cuba and Brazil depended on colonial capital in Havana, Rio de Janeiro, and Bahia, supplemented by emigrant Portuguese merchants resident in Brazil. British manufacturers and merchants, though forbidden by Parliament from investing directly in slaving, drew profits from captive humans by financing the trade of the Iberians, safely protected by contracts from its primary risk—mortality. North Americans provided ships for the illegal trade of the 1840s. Thus, although the trade has sometimes been termed a "triangular" one because of the European goods, African slaves, and American commodities flowing clockwise with the winds of the North Atlantic, few individual ships or shippers completed all three of its legs. The institutions of slaving thus reflected the broad outlines of economic growth throughout the Atlantic economy, in Europe, America, and Africa.

Historians have inquired also into the economic contribution that slave trading may have made to the growth and transformation of the European economy, some claiming that it directly financed industrialization in Britain. Though exceptionally profitable voyages inspired many hopes, average returns did not exceed those common in other sectors of the economy. Slaving was a small component of all international trade flows and was minor in relation to domestic economies everywhere—including Africa and Brazil—except in the specialized sugar islands of the Caribbean.

On the other hand, slaving allowed new and still-fragile munitions and other manufacturing sectors in England and France to reach captive colonial and some African markets for their early, crude products. In Brazil the Africa trade sustained indebted planters unable otherwise to support the burden of Portuguese mercantilist taxes and monopolies. It restored the fortunes of a few of the Portuguese exiled and condemned to Angola and enabled even weak Portuguese merchants to compete with British-backed competitors in Brazil. For Portugal, too, it delayed the decline of national munitions and textile makers, as the country's economy fell steadily behind that of the rest of the continent. It animated commerce in the outports of northern Europe at a time when Amsterdam, London, Paris, and Rouen were moving ahead in finance and in continental trade. As trans-Atlantic economic diversification and specialization accelerated, Europe's weaker economic sectors, and disadvantaged colonial subjects, found markets in Africa and used the slaves acquired there to buy the American gold, silver, sugar, cotton, and coffee that they would otherwise have had to concede to stronger competitors.

DEMOGRAPHY

Slavers purchased enslaved Africans in ratios of about two males to each female, although sex ratios varied somewhat from one part of the African coast to another. American planters and miners may have preferred males because they found the costs of raising slave children—including high infant and child mortality—high so long as the price of African labor remained low. On the other hand, Africans may have preferred to retain women for themselves, to bear replacements for the people they lost to drought, war, disease, and enslaved exile abroad.

Women worked in the fields on both continents, alone in Africa but alongside male slaves on American plantations. The high cost of raising children to an age of productivity reduced the number of youngsters in the trade to a small fraction. Slave prices rose steadily into the 1790s, however, and the differential between buying and training youngsters decreased so that the average age of the slaves carried across the Atlantic tended to fall through time. By the nineteenth century, the typical enslaved individual was an adolescent boy.

The European slavers refined their techniques over the centuries so that more slaves survived, at lower transport cost, though without significantly relieving the extreme discomfort of their captives. The earliest human cargoes rode in the holds of ships built for carrying commodities rather than people, with no special accommodation. Provision for food and, in particular, water while at sea was minimal. Slaves died in numbers averaging as much as 25 percent during crossings that ranged from 40 or 50 days in the South Atlantic upward toward 80 to 120 days between West Africa and the Caribbean. By the early eighteenth century, slavers had developed specialized vessels carrying 300 to 400 passengers, though smaller operators, particularly Americans, still used general cargo vessels of lesser capacity.

On African coasts, slavers established commercial contacts that reduced the highly lethal time spent loading slaves, and they could estimate the water and food requirements of their captives closely enough that mortality at sea dropped toward 10 percent. Captains under pressure from their employers, or novice sailors, still sometimes dangerously overloaded their ships. Calms or storms at sea, pirates, war, equipment failure, or other accidents could always strike the slaves with catastrophic losses. However, on balance slaving in the high-volume decades of the 1700s tended toward business as usual, risky but bearable—for the slavers.

As the British navy gradually drove the slavers from the seas after 1811, the traders dispersed to remote and concealed ports in both Africa and the Americas. Although abolition raised the costs and risks of slaving, African and European traders survived the challenge. Africans held slaves safely near the coast and Europeans loaded ships in shorter periods of time when they arrived. The ships themselves became faster, some of them adding copper plating on their hulls. The slaves, packed more closely than ever below decks, bore the burden of other cost efficiencies, such as reduced rations of water and food, but gross neglect was less common in the furtive, highly professional, last, illegal years of slaving. As a result mortality among the slaves dropped further toward 5 percent on average, and catastrophes occurred less often.

Medical conditions, though always deadly, moderated over time. Throughout the long years of the trade, most slaves entered the holds of the ships in marginal nutritional condition. Many boarded after weeks and months of forced and underfed marches over long distances to the coast and after lengthy confinement with inadequate food or water in overcrowded shoreside barracoons. Spoiled foodstuffs, contaminated water, and illnesses acquired in unfamiliar disease environments left many with uncontrollable diarrheas. The stench added horribly to the miseries of those confined below decks, and ships carrying slaves trailed their malodorous stigma for hundreds of meters downwind.

Slaves from the higher African elevations also suffered from fevers picked up on the low-lying coast, particularly malaria. Contagious afflictions, especially smallpox, surged through some vessels in waves that, from Angola at least, rose after extended periods of drought in Africa. Emotional trauma was severe. Slaves experienced the loss of family and home, extreme isolation and dependency, and utter terror at an experience many believed had delivered them into the hands of red cannibals from beyond unending waters of death. Diarrheas, the nausea of seasickness, and profuse sweating in the holds must have depleted the body fluids faster than scarce supplies of drinking water could replace them. Slaves appeared to grow despondent and die, and these morbid melancholies, or *banzos,* may have been symptoms of terminal dehydration and mineral imbalances as well as of the profound psychological shock of captivity. The multiple afflictions of the slaves are almost impossible to translate into precise modern medical diagnoses.

Slavers gradually stumbled into remedies for starvation, dehydration, and salt depletion. From the early eighteenth century, the British occasionally inoculated slaves against smallpox, and slavers in the nineteenth century sometimes used Jennerian vaccine to prevent epidemic outbreaks of the disease in Africa from coming on board the slave ships. However, European medical technology never became widely efficacious under the extreme conditions of the trade. Better care for slaves before they boarded the ships, faster crossings, and adequate water and food probably contributed more to the falling death rates over the long history of the trade.

Most slave males spent the passage crammed below decks, lying beneath low ceilings on rough planks in darkness, chained to hull, deck, or bulkhead, so close to companions that they could not move. Some captains brought small, heavily guarded groups of their captive passengers onto the deck once or twice a day to get a breath of fresh air, exercise a bit, and eat a ration of manioc or rice or other starchy porridge flavored with small quantities of cooking oil, peppers, or dried meat or fish. On some ships, women, some with infants, occupied cabins, where the crew surely subjected many to sexual assault.

In a tragic irony, the slaves' human frailty, their very susceptibility to death, gave them their principal—albeit passive—influence over the organization and history of the trade. Monetary investments in people led the slavers to adopt technological and financial refinements that gradually enhanced the chances of their human cargoes for survival. The presence of hundreds of resentful captives bound below decks, ill and weakened as they were, frightened crews into designing specialized slaving ships for security, with heavy bars and barriers, chains and irons. Some slaves somehow occasionally overcame these obstacles to seize or scuttle ships, though recorded instances of revolt at sea number only in the dozens out of tens of thousands of voyages.

See also **Coffee Industry; Cotton; Sugar Industry; Tobacco Industry.**

BIBLIOGRAPHY

For bibliographic information, see the bibliography supplements in the historical journal *Slavery and Abolition* (1983–) and Joseph C. Miller, *Slavery: A Worldwide Bibliography, 1900–1982* (1985).

See also Eric Williams, *Capitalism and Slavery* (1944); Philip D. Curtin, *The Atlantic Slave Trade: A Census* (1969); Robert Louis Stein, *The French Slave Trade in the Eighteenth Century: An Old Regime Business* (1979); Edward Reynolds, *Stand the Storm: A History of the Atlantic Slave Trade* (1985); Herbert S. Klein,

African Slavery in Latin America and the Caribbean (1986); David Eltis, *Economic Growth and the Ending of the Transatlantic Slave Trade* (1987); Barbara L. Solow and Stanley L. Engerman, *British Capitalism and Caribbean Slavery: The Legacy of Eric Williams* (1987); Joseph C. Miller, *Way of Death: Merchant Capitalism and the Angolan Slave Trade, 1730–1830* (1988); Paul E. Lovejoy, "The Impact of the Atlantic Slave Trade on Africa: A Review of the Literature," in *Journal of African History* 30 (1989): 365–394; Philip D. Curtain, *The Rise and Fall of the Plantation Complex: Essays in Atlantic History* (1990); Patrick Manning, *Slavery and African Life: Oriental, Occidental, and African Slave Trades* (1990); and Johannes Menne Postma, *The Dutch in the Atlantic Slave Trade, 1600–1815* (1990).

Additional Bibliography

Andrés Gallego, José. *La esclavitud en la América española*. Madrid: Ediciones Encuentro; Fundación Ignacio Larramendi, 2005.

Cáceres Gómez, Rina. *Rutas de la esclavitud en Africa y América Latina*. San José, Costa Rica: Editorial de la Universidad de Costa Rica, 2001.

Vila Vilar, Enriqueta. *Aspectos sociales en América colonial: De extranjeros, contrabando y esclavos*. Bogotá: Instituto Caro y Cuervo: Universidad de Bogotá "Jorge Tadeo Lozano," 2001.

JOSEPH C. MILLER

SLAVE TRADE, ABOLITION OF

This entry includes the following articles:
BRAZIL
SPANISH AMERICA

BRAZIL

The struggle to end the Brazilian slave trade lasted more than forty years and was essentially a conflict between Britain on the one hand and Portugal and Brazil on the other. For hundreds of years prior to the nineteenth century, transporting the enslaved blacks from Africa to Brazil was considered essential in the Luso-Brazilian world because of the great importance of slave labor to the Brazilian economy and the inability of the slave population in that country to increase or even maintain itself through natural reproduction. The essentiality of the Brazilian slave trade is revealed by its long duration and the huge numbers of slaves involved. No precise figures exist,

but it is certain that the volume of this forced migration was much larger than that to any other American colony or country, including the United States. According to recent estimates, perhaps 100,000 slaves arrived in Brazil from Africa in the sixteenth century, 2 million in the seventeenth, another 2 million in the eighteenth, and about 1.5 million in the last fifty years of the slave trade, which finally ended in 1852. This total of well over 5 million persons does not include the hundreds of thousands who died en route.

In the early years of the nineteenth century, when the British campaign against the Brazilian slave trade began, the demand for slaves in Brazil was as large as it had ever been, so it is not surprising that Portuguese governments in Rio de Janeiro (and later those of independent Brazil) resisted British interference in this basic enterprise. However, for many complex economic and humanitarian reasons, including the cost advantage that the slave trade gave Brazilian producers over British competitors in the world sugar markets, British governments persisted in their crusade for nearly half a century, forcing the rulers of Brazil outwardly to restrict, then outlaw, the traffic while in fact they continued to tolerate and even encourage it on a vast scale.

The following key events in this long struggle suggest the high level of determination on both sides. In 1810, following the transfer of the Portuguese royal government from Lisbon to Rio de Janeiro, the prince regent of Portugal, Dom João, reluctantly agreed to ban participation by Portuguese subjects in slave trading in the non-Portuguese territories of Africa. In two agreements reached in 1815 and 1817, Portugal yielded to British demands to outlaw Portuguese slave trading north of the equator and to establish measures to enforce certain restrictions. These included the British right to board and search Portuguese ships at sea, to detain vessels involved in illegal trafficking, and to deliver those ships to special tribunals or "mixed commissions" in Brazil and Africa. Finally, in 1826, four years after Brazil became independent, the imperial government grudgingly agreed to a total ban on the slave trade, to take effect three years from the date of the treaty's ratification, such trading in slaves henceforth to be "deemed and treated as piracy." Thus, after nearly twenty years of unrelenting British effort and almost equally adamant

Luso-Brazilian resistance, the Brazilian slave trade became illegal on 13 March 1830. Less than two years later, on 7 November 1831, a Liberal government in Rio de Janeiro confirmed this commitment with legislation declaring the freedom of slaves entering the country from that day forth.

These extraordinary British efforts did not, however, end the slave trade. For seven years after the legal prohibition, Liberal governments made serious efforts to enforce the law, and the number of Africans entering Brazil, therefore, remained comparatively small. In 1837, however, with the rise to power of a proslavery Conservative government, attempts to prevent slave landings or otherwise to control the traffic all but ceased, and an illegal slave trade involving ships and citizens of many countries developed on a large scale that continued for another fifteen years. During those years the energies of Brazilian governments were in fact more often directed toward deceiving British diplomats and protecting slave importers and their illegal property than toward complying with treaties and enforcing laws. To cite one of the most egregious examples, under the first article of the anti-slave-trade law of 7 November 1831, the many hundreds of thousands of slaves who entered Brazil after that date were legally free, but most were in fact condemned along with their children to live out their lives in a state of de facto slavery.

In the 1840s, Britain persisted in its efforts to end the slave trade, seizing hundreds of ships at sea and on the African coast, and even encouraging a wave of public opposition within Brazil in the late 1840s. However, it was not until 1850, when the British government forcefully extended its naval campaign to the Brazilian coast itself, that the imperial government was at last persuaded to adopt more serious measures. Humiliated by British seizures of slave ships in Brazilian harbors and territorial waters, and fearing a British blockade of legitimate shipping and even war, the Brazilian government legislated the Queirós Law of 4 September 1850, which provided severe penalties for slave traders and permitted Brazilian authorities to seize ships known to be involved in the traffic, even when no slaves were found on board. Even then, however, Brazilian efforts were piecemeal and selective, and all but nonexistent at the port of Bahia. Thus another British threat to send warships into Brazilian territorial waters was made in January 1851. From then on, the Brazilian campaign against the slave trade was serious and effective, all but suppressing it by 1852.

The ending of the African slave trade generated an unprecedented internal commerce in slaves between the northern and southern provinces and a rapid decline of the slave population in the country as a whole, both of which were significant causes of outright abolition of slavery in 1888, less than forty years later.

See also **Slavery: Brazil.**

BIBLIOGRAPHY

Emília Viotti Da Costa, *Da senzala à colônia* (1966).

Philip D. Curtin, *The Atlantic Slave Trade: A Census* (1970).

Stanley J. Stein, *Vassouras, a Brazilian Coffee Country, 1850–1900* (1970).

Leslie Bethell, *The Abolition of the Brazilian Slave Trade* (1976).

Joaquim Nabuco, *Abolitionism: The Brazilian Antislavery Struggle,* edited and translated by Robert Edgar Conrad (1977).

Jacob Gorender, *O escravismo colonial* (1978).

Robert Edgar Conrad, *Children of God's Fire: A Documentary History of Black Slavery in Brazil* (1983), and *World of Sorrow: The African Slave Trade to Brazil* (1986).

Mary C. Karasch, *Slave Life in Rio de Janeiro, 1808–1850* (1987).

Joseph Calder Miller, *Way of Death: Merchant Capitalism and the Angolan Slave Trade, 1730–1830* (1988).

Additional Bibliography

Butler, Kim D. *Freedoms Given, Freedoms Won: Afro-Brazilians in Post-abolition, São Paulo and Salvador.* New Brunswick, NJ: Rutgers University Press, 1998.

Graden, Dale Torston. *From Slavery to Freedom in Brazil: Bahia, 1835–1900.* Albuquerque: University of New Mexico Press, 2006.

Mendonça, Joseli Maria Nunes. *Entre a mão e os anéis: A lei dos sexagenários e os caminhos da abolição no Brasil.* Campinas: Editora da UNICAMP: CECULT, 1999.

ROBERT EDGAR CONRAD

SPANISH AMERICA

The ending of the slave trade to the Spanish Americas is replete with paradoxes. More African slaves arrived in the region during the abolition era than in the long preceding period when the transatlantic traffic in people was never questioned. Indeed, many of the factors that explain the ending of the traffic are also vital to understanding its last rapid expansion. To make sense of these developments it is first necessary to look beyond Latin America.

Before the mid-nineteenth century, transatlantic migrants—whatever the labor regime under which they traveled—went in largest numbers to those areas that had the strongest export-based economies. After the early boom in gold and silver, Spanish America lagged behind the rest of European America in producing commodities that would sell in world markets. Thus in 1770, despite a nascent sugar and tobacco economy, the Spanish Caribbean accounted for less than 3 percent of all Caribbean exports. The English, French, and Portuguese colonies accounted for almost all slaves and free migrants that left the Old World between 1650 and 1800. During this period the natural advantages of Cuba and Puerto Rico in the growing and processing of a range of plantation products were held in check by the restrictive polices of the Spanish crown and premodern attitudes on private ownership of land.

Three factors transformed Spanish America in the century after 1770 and, at the same time, ensured in the long run that the slave trade would end. The first was a policy shift by the Spanish crown that liberalized colonial trade and encouraged the development of plantation agriculture. But while the tension this liberalization created was not immediately apparent, the so-called Bourbon Reforms of Charles III also drew on a worldview—espoused by Adam Smith and the philosophes, and certainly mistaken—that saw slavery as inefficient. The second was the impact of industrialization in the North Atlantic. This greatly increased the demand for commodities of all types, and at the same time increased production and facilitated technological changes in transportation, agriculture, and primary processing that greatly cheapened their production. Industrialization also reinforced the ideological commitment to free labor—especially in Great Britain and the United States. The third factor was the disappearance of competitors to the Spanish plantation system. Between 1791, when the Saint-Domingue slave revolt broke out, and 1865, the end of the Civil War in the United States, the British, French, Dutch, Brazilians, and Americans all saw the ending of either the slave trade or slavery itself in their territories. Only in Cuba and Puerto Rico was the slave trade and slavery allowed to continue virtually unchecked. But the other countries that were in the vanguard of abolition (also erstwhile competitors) were not likely to allow this situation to continue. British and U.S. diplomatic pressure against an open transatlantic slave trade escalated steadily throughout this period.

There was thus a pattern of an expanding system of coercion and increasing efforts to suppress that system, the contradiction lying in the fact that the same forces drove both. The Spanish had never been major slave traders, preferring to buy from other Europeans. But as the British and Americans withdrew from direct participation after 1807, the Spanish filled the void at least in the branch of the trade to Cuba and Puerto Rico. British capital, or at least credit, however, remained very important. So too did British goods used to obtain slaves and insurance. Americans supplied ships and a flag that the British navy would be hesitant to challenge in peacetime. Attempts to suppress the traffic at sea foundered on the rights of merchants to sail without interference from other nationals. Slave trading never became piracy, and while the British probably had the naval power to suppress most of the traffic, they could have done so only by ignoring international law. When the British obtained the right to challenge a flag, the slave trader simply changed registration. Thus the Anglo-Spanish conventions of 1817 and 1835, which gave the British some legal rights over those carrying slaves to the Spanish Americas, were largely ineffective.

On the surface, the key initiatives were within the Spanish rather than the British domain. The 1845 Spanish penal law and efforts by Spanish governors of the early 1860s, such as Francisco Serrano y Domínguez, had the effect of raising the costs of slave traders after they had run the British gauntlet at sea. The new Spanish law of 1867, which greatly increased penalties and widened the definition of slave trading, was probably unnecessary, yet the important point is that all these internal moves were taken at the behest of the British, and after 1861, the Americans. In a very real sense early Spanish attempts to restrict the slave trade and slavery must be seen as attempts to win time for the institution of coerced labor. By conceding something to international pressures, the ending of the institution itself could be delayed until an alternative source of labor, such as Chinese contract labor or free migration from Spain and the Canary Islands, became available. In this, the Spanish were very successful. At the very least, however, these developments cannot be understood without the international backdrop.

By 1850 Cuba and Puerto Rico, which together in 1770 had accounted for 3 percent of Caribbean export output by value, now generated close to 60 percent. Yet the system that made this possible—slavery and the slave trade—was subject to strangulation at the very time that this hegemony was being established. Nearly three-quarters of a million Africans arrived in the Spanish Caribbean and the Rio de la Plata after 1800. The last slaves from Africa landed in Puerto Rico in the mid-1840s (other than victims of shipwrecks) and in Cuba in 1867. Like slavery itself shortly afterwards, the slave trade was suppressed. It did not die a "natural" economic death.

See also **Debt Peonage; Repartimiento; Slavery: Spanish America.**

BIBLIOGRAPHY

David Murray, *Odious Commerce: Britain, Spain, and the Abolition of the Cuban Slave Trade* (1980).

David Eltis, *Economic Growth and the Ending of the Trans-Atlantic Slave Trade* (1987).

Additional Bibliography

Andrés Gallego, José. *La esclavitud en la América española.* Madrid: Ediciones Encuentro; Fundación Ignacio Larramendi, 2005.

Landers, Jane, and Barry Robinson. *Slaves, Subjects, and Subversives: Blacks in Colonial Latin America.* Albuquerque: University of New Mexico Press, 2006.

Schmidt-Nowara, Christopher. *Empire and Antislavery Spain, Cuba, and Puerto Rico, 1833–1874.* Pittsburgh, PA: University of Pittsburgh Press, 1999.

Vila Vilar, Enriqueta and Luisa Vila Vilar. *Los abolicionistas españoles: Siglo XIX.* Madrid: Ediciones de Cultura Hispánica, 1996.

DAVID ELTIS

SLIM HELÚ, CARLOS (1940–). A Mexican entrepreneur of Lebanese descent, Carlos Slim became one of the richest individuals in the world at the turn of the twenty-first century. His family came to Mexico during the first decade of the twentieth century from Lebanon. Son of Julián Slim Haddad, who died when Carlos was only thirteen years old, and Linda Helú, Carlos was the fifth among six siblings. He was born in Mexico City on January 28, 1940. In 1965 he married Soumaya Domit Gemayel (d. 1999), also of Lebanese descent; the couple had six children.

At age nineteen Carlos Slim began engineering studies at the Universidad Nacional Autonóma de Mexico, earning his degree in 1962. In 1966 he launched his entrepreneurial activities by incorporating Immobiliaria Carso, with operations in real estate and construction. He worked at the Mexican stock market and in 1965 founded Inversora Bursátil, where he worked with his cousin Alfredo Harp Helú, now a well-recognized banker in Mexico.

In the 1980s Slim bought a number of large enterprises, taking advantage of the fact that many investors wanted to take their money out of Mexico. In 1990 Slim, together with a group of investors, acquired the formerly public company Teléfonos de México (Telmex). Control of Telmex brought Slim wide public attention and, together with his investment in the wireless carrier América Móvil and other telecom businesses, vastly increased his wealth by the early years of the twenty-first century.

According to *Forbes*, by 2007 Slim's businesses included Impulsora del Desarrollo y el Empleo de América Latina (IDEAL), a share in Volaris (a Mexican budget airline), and a fortified position in Saks Inc. In 2007 the same magazine considered him the second-richest person in the world, behind only Bill Gates.

See also **Mexico: Since 1910.**

BIBLIOGRAPHY

Billionaries List. Available from http://www.forbes.com/lists/2007/10/07billionaires_Carlos-Slim-Helu_WYDJ.html.

Martínez, José Martínez. *Carlos Slim: Retrato inédito.* Mexico: Océano, 2002.

SERGIO SILVA-CASTAÑEDA

SLOTH. Sloths are slow-moving edentate mammals found in Central and South America. The sloth's slow movements help protect it from its principal enemy, the jaguar, and the blue–green algae that grow on the sloth's hair allow the animal to blend well with the tree foliage where it spends its time hanging upside down.

The five species of sloths are strictly neotropical in their range. The three species of three–toed sloths (family Bradypodidae) are found throughout much of Central America and the northern two–thirds of South America. Two–toed sloths (family Choloepidae) have a far more limited range, covering most of Central America but only a small part of northwestern South America. The pygmy sloth (*Bradypus pygmaeus*), found only on a small island off the Panama coast, has been listed since 2006 on the IUCN Red List of Threatened Species as critically endangered. Other sloth species are not considered threatened or endangered, though they face the same pressures as other animals in the face of humanity's extensive assault on the world's forests.

See also **Environmental Movements.**

BIBLIOGRAPHY

Bernard Grzimek, *Grzimek's Encyclopedia of Mammals* (1990).

SHEILA L. HOOKER

SMALLPOX. *See* **Diseases.**

SMUGGLING. *See* **Contraband (Colonial Spanish America).**

SOBREMONTE, RAFAEL DE (1745–1827). Rafael de Sobremonte (*b.* 27 November 1745; *d.* 14 January 1827), intendant of Córdoba (1783–1797), viceroy of Río de la Plata (1804–1807). Born in Seville to a noble family, Sobremonte trained for a military career. After service in Ceuta and Puerto Rico, he arrived in Buenos Aires in 1779 as viceregal secretary under Viceroy Vértiz. Three years later he married Juana María de Larrazábal, the daughter of a prominent local family. With Vértiz's patronage, he secured the post of intendant of Córdoba (1783), where he served as a dynamic, model administrator. In 1797 Sobremonte was promoted to subinspector general of the military within the viceroyalty, and seven years later was named viceroy.

Although he was well-known and respected throughout the region, Sobremonte's tenure as viceroy proved to be deeply disappointing. He is best remembered for his ignominious flight to Córdoba (ostensibly to raise fresh troops) during the English invasion of 1806, leaving the city of Buenos Aires to defend itself as best it could. Sobremonte was deposed by the Buenos Aires *cabildo* in 1807 and arrested shortly thereafter. He was allowed to return to Spain in 1809. Exonerated of any wrongdoing in 1813, he was allowed to continue his military career. Named to the Council of the Indies in 1814, he retired the next year, dying in Cádiz after a long illness.

See also **Brazil: The Colonial Era, 1500-1808; Brazil: 1808-1889; Brazil, Viceroys of.**

BIBLIOGRAPHY

Enrique Udaondo, *Diccionario biográfico colonial argentino* (1945), pp. 845–847.

John Lynch, *Spanish Colonial Administration, 1782–1810: The Intendant System in the Viceroyalty of the Río de la Plata* (1969).

Additional Bibliography

Aspell, Marcela. *Sobre Monte: El gobernador olvidado.* Córdoba: Junta Provincial de Historia de Córdoba, 2001.

Garzón, Rafael. *Sobre Monte y Córdoba en las invasiones inglesas.* Córdoba: Ediciones del Corredor Austral, 2000.

SUSAN M. SOCOLOW

SOCCER. *See* **Sports.**

SOCCER WAR. *See* **Football War.**

SOCIOLOGY.

Sociology as a discipline emerged in Latin America during the mid-twentieth century, but contributions to sociological issues and concerns are as old as Latin American civilizations. The writings of some pre-Conquest thinkers, many Catholic priests, and post-Conquest native scholars deal with problems of culture, inequality, and government. Sociologically significant ideas about domination, divided societies, culture, and intersocietal dynamics were developed between Independence and World War II. However, no disciplinary identity or institutional support was present. Between the war and 1980, sociology emerged as a discipline in universities, government agencies, and multigovernmental agencies such as the United Nations Economic Commission for Latin America and the Caribbean. Many Spanish and Portuguese language journals emerged in this period. Most of the sociological research and writing was viewed as being of interest only to other Latin American sociologists with the findings applying only to Latin America. However, Gino Germani, Pablo Casanova, and Enrique Cardoso were exceptions, making major contributions to sociological perspectives through their theories of modernity, dependency, internal colonialism, marginality, and democratic processes. Since the early 1980s sociology has made significant contributions to the understanding of Latin America and society in general. The theories and research focus on issues and problems in Latin America, but the results are applicable well beyond the region. Contributions have been made to knowledge of postmodernity, postcolonialism, subalternity, cultural hybridity, and indigenous peoples.

Sociology is a discipline with a tradition of active involvement in reform movements and social justice. Most Latin American sociologists are socially and politically active in efforts to criticize current conditions and remedy inequality, domination, and exploitation by seeking to reform societies through involvement in democratic action and resistance to governmental oppression.

Two major features characterize Latin American sociology in the early twenty-first century. First, it is closely related and responsive to issues in sociology in the United States and Europe. It has become a meeting ground for sociologists who were trained in the United States, Europe, and Latin America as a hybridization of diverse ideas and experiences from the three regions. Many Latin American sociologists contribute to understandings of internationally important processes such as inequality, stratification, consumerism, globalization, modernization, and gender. They employ concepts that are widely accepted such as social and human capital, postmodernity, and globalization, but they are not simply borrowers of the ideas. They have provided significant amplifications. Some of the unique features of Latin American sociology focus on issues of democracy, liberation, and socialism. Issues of the deepening of democracy to include the poor and native peoples are crucial.

Second, these same sociologists reflect the national and local issues they encounter. This leads to sociologies that are national as well as global. Poverty is present worldwide, but it has unique characteristics as an Argentine or Mexican problem. Local definitions and efforts to deal with it vary. Brazilian, Argentine, and Mexican sociologists deal with the problems of emerging democracy and globalization. Bolivian sociologists focus on the problems of democracy in a country where a large part of the population is indigenous and becoming politically active. Studies of the Caribbean, the Southern Cone, the Andes, and indigenous Mexico contain elements that seek to account for the enormous diversity in experience and problems. These sociologists offer an important view of sociology from the periphery with insights often missed by sociologists from the United States and Europe.

See also **Class Structure in Modern Latin America; Democracy; Globalization; Race and Ethnicity; Sexuality: Gender and Sexuality.**

BIBLIOGRAPHY

Cardoso, Fernando. *Dependencia y desarrollo en América Latina: Ensayos de interpretatión sociologica.* Mexico: Siglo XXI Editores, 1984.

García Canclini, Néstor. *Consumers and Citizens: Globalization and Multicultural Conflicts.* Minneapolis: University of Minnesota Press, 2001.

Germani, Gino. *Marginality.* New Brunswick, NJ: Transaction Books, 1980.

Germani, Gino. *The Sociology of Modernization: Studies on Its Historical and Theoretical Aspects with Special Regard to the Latin American Case.* New Brunswick, NJ: Transaction Books, 1981.

González Casanova, Pablo, and Marcos Roitman Rosenmann, eds. *Democracia y estado multiétnico en América Latina.* Mexico: Jornada Ediciones UNAM, 1996.

Kahl, Joseph. *Modernization, Exploitation, and Dependency in Latin America: Germani, Gonzalez Casanova, and Cardoso.* New Brunswick, NJ: Transaction Books, 1976.

Mires, Fernando. *El discurso de la Indianidad: La cuestion indigena en America Latina.* Quito: Ediciones Abya-Yala, 1992.

LYNN ENGLAND

SOCONUSCO. Soconusco, a rich agricultural region on the narrow, Pacific coastal plain of Chiapas, Mexico. The area was famous in prehistoric and colonial times for its high-quality cacao and later for its coffee. Today agriculture and ranching are major economic activities. In late prehistoric times (and probably much earlier) the native population of Soconusco spoke a Mixe-Zoquean language, but today residents speak Spanish and are culturally Ladino.

Archaeologists have uncovered evidence of human occupation in Soconusco as early as 3000 BCE, when small groups living in the estuaries subsisted primarily on shellfish. Pottery, some of the earliest in Mesoamerica, was used by ancient Soconuscans by around 2000 BCE Izapa, an archaeological site near Tapachula, is well known for its more than 250 carved stone monuments erected between ca. 300 BCE and 50 BCE. In the late 1490s Soconusco came under Aztec control.

In 1524 Soconusco was conquered by the Spanish, and for most of the colonial period it was part of the Audiencia of Guatemala. The introduction of Old World diseases reduced its Indian population by over 90 percent in the first fifty years after contact. Spanish presence in the area consisted largely of merchants involved in the cacao trade. Throughout the colonial period the cacao plantations were controlled primarily by the native population.

Following Mexican independence, Soconusco declared itself an independent state (1824), but by 1842 it was annexed by Mexico. In the late nineteenth century, foreign investors and colonists became active in Soconusco, and large coffee, rubber, and banana plantations were established.

Following the Mexican Revolution many of the large plantations were broken up and became part of the *ejido* system. Today much of the population has access to land and engages in subsistence agriculture, but increasingly larger portions live in urban settings or work as wage laborers on large plantations and ranches.

See also **Archaeology.**

BIBLIOGRAPHY

Peter Gerhard, *The Southeast Frontier of New Spain,* rev. ed. (1991), esp. pp. 165–172.

Gareth W. Lowe, Thomas A. Lee, Jr., and Eduardo Martínez Espinosa, *Izapa: An Introduction to the Ruins and Monuments* (1982).

Daniela Spenser, "Soconusco: The Formation of a Coffee Economy in Chiapas," in *Other Mexicos: Essays on Regional Mexican History, 1876–1911,* edited by Thomas Benjamin and William McNellie (1984).

Barbara Voorhies, ed., *Ancient Trade and Tribute: Economies of the Soconusco Region of Mesoamerica* (1989).

Additional Bibliography

Alvarez Simán, Fernando. *Capitalismo, el estado y el campesino en México: Un estudio sobre la región del Soconusco en Chiapas.* México: Universidad Autónoma de Chiapas, 1996.

Voorhies, Barbara, and Janine Gasco. *Postclassic Soconusco Society: The Late Prehistory of the Coast of Chiapas, Mexico.* Albany, NY: Institute for Mesoamerican Studies, University at Albany, 2004.

JANINE GASCO

SOCORRO. Socorro, a town in northeastern Colombia, 172 miles north-northeast of Bogotá, 2005 estimated population 22,807. Settled in the mid-1600s and formally founded in 1683, Socorro became an important commercial and textile-producing center by 1750, a status it partially lost over the nineteenth century. The town led the Comunero Revolt against colonial taxation in 1781, and played an active role on the patriot side in the Independence struggle, for which it suffered the rigors of the Spanish *reconquista* of 1816–1819. From 1821 to 1857 Socorro was capital of a province of the same name (1851 population 157,000), and from 1862 to 1885 it was capital of the much larger state of Santander. Socorro has historically been a Liberal Party bastion; in the nineteenth century it produced such notable political figures as Vicente Azuero (1787–1844) and Gonzalo A. Távera. Since the late 1800s the town has been surpassed in size and economic importance by its perennial rival San Gil, fourteen miles to the northeast.

See also **Colombia, Political Parties: Liberal Party.**

BIBLIOGRAPHY

Horacio Rodríguez Plata, *La antigua provincia del Socorro y la independencia* (1963).

John L. Phelan, *The People and the King* (1978).

Additional Bibliography

Palacios, Marco. *Between Legitimacy and Violence: A History of Colombia, 1875-2002.* Durham, NC: Duke University Press, 2006.

RICHARD J. STOLLER

SODRÉ, NELSON WERNECK (1911–1999).

Nelson Werneck Sodré (*b.* 27 April 1911; *d.* 13 January 1999), Brazilian army officer, historian, and intellectual. Son of a lawyer-businessman, Sodré, a native of Rio de Janeiro, attended the Colegio Militar (1924–1930) and the Escola Militar in Rio de Janeiro (1931–1934). He was a career army officer until his retirement in 1961. He was a professor of military history at the Escola do Estado Maior do Exército (Army General Staff School) from 1948 to 1950. In 1955 and 1956 Sodré was editorial editor at the center-left Rio newspaper *Última Hora.* In 1954 he became chairman of the history department at the Instituto Superior de Estudos Brasileiros (ISEB), a position he held until the military government closed the ISEB in the immediate aftermath of the coup in 1964. Beginning in 1964 he lived in Rio de Janeiro, devoting himself to intellectual pursuits.

Sodré participated in the Brazilian nationalist movement of the 1950s and early 1960s. During the 1950s he was influential in the Military Club, a group that generally sought to represent the interests of army officers, and played a role in the successful campaign to nationalize Brazilian oil. He also participated in ISEB's efforts to articulate a "national-developmentalist" ideology, which sought to overcome Brazil's colonial economic structure through national capitalist development.

Though never a political militant, Sodré was a lifelong Marxist, and in addition to his other works,

he wrote texts on Marxist theory. He was imprisoned for several months after the coup of 1964 and for a time thereafter was prohibited from public speaking and writing in the press. In 1995, he gave the National Library of Brazil a collection of many of his personal documents, including correspondence with historian Caio Prado, Jr. and Cuban president Fidel Castro.

See also **Brazil, Organizations: Advanced Institute of Brazilian Studies (ISEB); Nationalism.**

BIBLIOGRAPHY

Sodré's works include *Formação da sociedade brasileira* (1944); *História da burguesia brasileira* (1964); *História militar do Brasil* (1965); *História da imprensa no Brasil* (1966); *Memorias de um soldado* (1967); *Memorias de um escritor* (1970); *Síntese de história da cultura brasileira* (1970); *Que se dove ler para conhecer o Brasil* (1973); *Formação histórica do Brasil,* 9th ed. (1976); *História da história nova* (1986), a history of ISEB. See also E. Bradford Burns, *Nationalism in Brazil: A Historical Survey* (1968); and Simon Schwartzman, ed., *O pensamento nacionalista e os "Cadernos de Nosso Tempo"* (1981).

Additional Bibliography

Andrade, Manuel Correia de, and Maria Cecília Cysneiros. *Redescobrindo o Brasil seminário nacional.* Olinda, Brazil: Editora Livro Rápido, 2006.

Cunha, Paulo Ribero da, and Fátima Cabral. *Nelson Werneck Sodré: Entre o sabre e a pena.* São Paulo: Editora UNESP, 2006.

Toledo, Caio Navarro de. *Intelectuais e política no Brasil: A experiencia do ISEB.* Rio de Janeiro: Editora Revan, 2005.

BRIAN OWENSBY

SOJO, FELIPE (?–1869).

Felipe Sojo (*d.* 1869), Mexican sculptor. At the Academy of San Carlos in Mexico City, Sojo was a part of the first generation of students to leave behind the colonial technique of sculpture in wood and color, replacing it with white marble. In 1853 students under the Catalán master Manuel Vilar presented a biennial exhibition of their work. Sojo's contributions, a relief entitled *La degollación de San Juan Bautista* and the portrait *Señorita Barreiro,* are representative of two of the most common forms of sculpture at the time: the religious theme and the portrait. Sojo later took up another theme in sculpture: allegory. After the death of Manuel Vilar in 1860, Sojo was named director of sculpture at the academy.

The variety of patrons with whom Sojo became connected is notable. In 1853 he sculpted an industrial allegory for the Spanish architect Don Lorenzo de la Hidalga's private residence. As director at the academy during the reign of Maximilian, he undertook two projects commissioned by the emperor himself: a sarcophagus for the emperor Agustín de Iturbide, which was never completed, and whose plaster model was destroyed by the new republican regime after its triumph over the French, and a portrait in marble of Maximilian, which resides at the Mexican Museum of National History.

See also **Academia de San Carlos; Art: The Nineteenth Century.**

BIBLIOGRAPHY

Fausto Ramírez, *La plástica del siglo de la independencia* (1985).

Eloísa Uribe, ed., *Υ todo ... por una nación: Historia social de la producción plástica de la Ciudad de México, 1781–1910,* 2d ed. (1987).

ESTHER ACEVEDO

SOLANAS, FERNANDO E. (1936–).

Fernando "Pino" Solanas is an Argentine film director, screenwriter, and producer whose films focus on the politics and contemporary history of his country. Born on February 16, 1936, in Olivos, Buenos Aires, Solanas received his training in theater at the National Conservatory of Dramatic Art and then went into film in 1962. While working as a cartoon scriptwriter, he filmed his first short movies, *Seguir andando* (1962; Continue Walking) and *Reflexión ciudadana* (1963; Citizen Reflection). He also had great success in composing music for advertising jingles and founded a production company. In 1966, along with Octavio Getino, he began production on the film *La hora de los hornos: Notas y testimonios sobre el neocolonialismo, la violencia y la liberación* (*The Hour of the Furnaces*, 1968), which was filmed in secret because of the political situation in Argentina at the time. He worked for more than two years filming, in 16mm and without sound, this key work of liberation film, which was acclaimed for

both its formal freedom and its political content. After completion of this film, he formed, along with Gerardo Vallejo, Octavio Getino, and Edgardo Pallero, the Liberation Film Group, which prepared a manifesto entitled *Hacia un tercer cine* (Toward a Third Cinema), which analyzed the relationships between film and politics. The group produced two documentaries on the life and political career of Juan Domingo Perón: *Perón: Actualización política y doctrinaria para la toma del poder* (1971; Perón: Political and Doctrine Update for the Taking of the Power) and *Perón: La Revolución justicialista* (1971).

Solanas later adapted José Hernández's literary work, *Martín Fierro*, for film, under the title *Los hijos de Fierro* (Fierro's Brothers, 1975). The 1976 military coup against the presidency of Isabel Perón forced him into exile in Europe. In 1985 he premiered his most critically acclaimed film, *El exilio de Gardel* (*The Exile of Gardel*, also known as *Tangos*), a French-Argentine co-production that recounts the story of a group of Argentines exiled in Paris. The film was praised for its free structure and its use of different narrative registers. Solanas later made the film *Sur* (*The South*, 1987), a metaphor on the return of democracy to Argentina. His political activity intensified during the presidency of Carlos Menem, whom he criticized harshly for his privatization plan. On May 22, 1991, Solanas was shot in the legs, presumably for his accusations against the government. In 1993 he was elected deputy for the province of Buenos Aires. His films *El viaje* (*The Journey*, 1990) and *La nube* (*Clouds*, 1998) offer different visions of the country and its return to constitutional governance. *Memoria del saqueo* (*Social Genocide*, 2003), in which he returns to the documentary genre, recounts the experiences of Argentines living in deep poverty and reflects the atmosphere of the country during the political, social, and economic crisis of December 2001 and during 2002.

In 2003 Solanas was awarded the Golden Bear for Lifetime Achievement at the Berlin Film Festival. He continued to work in the documentary genre with *La dignidad de los nadies* (*The Dignity of the Nobodies*, 2005), about social activists striving to maintain solidarity in their acts of resistance. The film received four awards at the Venice Film Festival: the UNESCO award, Best Latin Film, Best Documentary, and the Human Rights Prize. He also wrote and directed the documentary *Argentina latente* (2007).

See also **Argentina: The Twentieth Century; Cinema: From the Silent Film to 1990; Cinema: Since 1990; Menem, Carlos Saúl; Perón, Juan Domingo.**

BIBLIOGRAPHY

Solanas, Fernando, and Octavio Getino. "Towards a Third Cinema." In *Movies and Methods: An Anthology*, ed. Bill Nichols. Tuscon: University of Arizona Press, 1976.

Solanas, Fernando, et al. "Round Table Discussion: Latin American Cinema." *Framework* 11 (Fall 1979):10–15.

ELENA MOREIRA

SOLANO, FRANCISCO (1549–1610).

Francisco Solano (*b.* March 1549; *d.* 14 July 1610), Franciscan missionary. Born in Montilla, Spain, Solano studied at the Jesuit college in that country, took minor orders, and was professed as a Franciscan in 1570. For twenty years he worked in Spain as a preacher and a novice master. In 1589 he arrived in America, where he worked principally with the Calchaquí Indians of central Argentina. Solano was the superior of all Franciscan houses and missions in the area and established houses and missions throughout Tucumán. He was noted for his compassion, patience, and love of the Indians. Solano died in Lima and was buried in the Franciscan church there. He was beatified in 1675 and canonized in 1726.

See also **Franciscans.**

BIBLIOGRAPHY

Claude Maimbourg, *The Lives of St. Thomas of Villanova, Archbishop of Valentia, and Augustinian Friar; and of St. Francis Solano, Apostle of Peru, of the Order of St. Francis* (1847).

José Pacífico Otero, *Dos heroes de la conquista, la Orden franciscana en el Tucumán y en el Plata* (1905).

Luis Julián Plandolit, *El apóstol de América, San Francisco solano* (1963).

Additional Bibliography

Oré, Luis Jerónimo de, and Noble David Cook. *Relación de la vida y milagros de San Francisco Solano.* Lima: Pontificia Universidad Católica del Perú, Fondo Editorial, 1998.

NICHOLAS P. CUSHNER

SOLÁS, HUMBERTO (1941–). Hum-

berto Solás is one of the great filmmakers of Cuban cinema. Born in Havana on December 14, 1941, he became politically aware from a young age, fighting in the Cuban resistance against President Fulgencio Batista when he was only fourteen years old. In 1959, at the age of seventeen, he joined the Instituto Cubano de Arte e Industria Cinematográfico, the Cuban Film Institute. Through his work there, he became a key part of the New Latin American Cinema movement of the 1960s, a generation of filmmakers whose work wedded art and politics. His 1968 release *Lucía* is generally considered one of the most important works of Latin American cinema. It follows the stories of three women named Lucía, each of whom lives in a different revolutionary period in Cuba's history: the fight for independence from Spain, the failed attempts at resistance against President Gerardo Machado in the 1930s, and the early period of the Cuban Revolution. *Lucía* won a Golden Prize at the 1969 Moscow Film Festival.

Despite this success, Solás was targeted during the Cuban government's crackdown on homosexuals, artists, and others thought to be "antirevolutionary" during the early 1970s and prohibited from making films about controversial topics. Nevertheless, he continued to work, and in 1982 his film *Cecilia* was nominated for a Golden Palm Award at the Cannes Film Festival. *Cecilia* was less controversial in the eyes of the Cuban authorities: It deals with a nineteenth-century slave rebellion. The next film, 1984's *Amada*, was also a period drama set in the late nineteenth century, about a love affair between an older woman and a younger man. The following year, *Un Hombre de éxito* (*A Successful Man*, 1985) also met with critical acclaim. This also was likely not viewed as controversial by the Cuban Revolution authorities as it deals with the pre-Revolutionary period and Castro's early rise to power.

Throughout his career Solás has received numerous awards, including the 2002 Silver Ariel from Mexico for his 2001 film *Miel para Oshún* (*Honey for Oshun*), which was the first Cuban full-length film shot entirely in digital video. In 2005 he released two films, a short, *Adela*, and *Barrio Cuba*, a comedy drama about finding love in Havana.

See also **Cinema: From the Silent Film to 1990; Cinema: Since 1990; Machado y Morales, Gerardo.**

BIBLIOGRAPHY

Chanan, Michael. *Cuban Cinema.* Minneapolis: University of Minnesota Press, 2004.

Flores González, Luis Ernesto. *Tras la huella de Solás: Bibliografía anotada.* Havana, Cuba: Ediciones ICAIC, 2000.

Noriega, Chon A., ed. *Visible Nations: Latin American Cinema and Video.* Minneapolis: University of Minnesota Press, 2000.

EMILY BERQUIST

SOLDADERAS.

Soldaderas, women warriors, camp followers, also known as "Juanas," "Adelitas," *viejas* (old ladies), *galletas* (cookies), *cucarachas* (cockroaches), *soldadas, capitanas,* and *coronelas. Soldaderas* are Mexican women who served in armies as camp followers and soldiers during wars. The custom of women fighting in wars, defending their tribes, or accompanying warriors also goes back to Mesoamerican practices. The Spanish origin of the word is *soldada,* which means "the pay of the soldier." A *soldadera* is a female servant who takes the *soldada* of the soldier and buys him food and other essentials.

Soldaderas functioned as foragers, cooks, nurses, laundresses, baggage carriers, sentinels, spies, gunrunners, prostitutes, and front-line soldiers. Because of the variety of roles and their semiofficial acceptance in the military until 1925, the *soldaderas* have an ambivalent position in Mexican society and popular culture. They are considered variously as silent bystanders, self-abnegating patriots, loose women, or valiant fighters for justice.

See also **Women.**

BIBLIOGRAPHY

A comprehensive study is Elizabeth Salas, *Soldaderas in the Mexican Military: Myth and History* (1990). See also María De Los Ángeles Mendieta Alatorre, *La mujer en la revolución mexicana* (1961).

Additional Bibliography

Lau J., Ana, and Carmen Ramos-Escandón. *Mujeres y revolución, 1900-1917.* México, D.F.: Instituto Nacional de Estudios Históricos de la Revolución Mexicana, 1993.

Mitchell, S. E., and Patience A. Schell. *The Women's Revolution in Mexico, 1910-1953.* Lanham, MD: Rowman & Littlefield, 2007.

ELIZABETH SALAS

SOLDADOS DE CUERA.

Soldados de Cuera, leather-armored cavalrymen of late-eighteenth-century presidios in northern New Spain. The *Regulation and Instruction for the Presidios of New Spain* of 1772 established a fortified line of fifteen forts, approximately 100 miles apart, from the Gulf of California to the Gulf of Mexico. To man these isolated posts with minimal troops, "flying companies" (*compañías volantes*) of cavalry patrolling between forts were formed to defend against possible foreign encroachment and hostile Indians. Armed with lances, short swords, muskets, and shields of two or three thicknesses of bullhide, the men wore knee-length, sleeveless leather coats, which gave them their name, cloth trousers, and high cowhide boots. As protection against attack and the thorny brush, horses wore leather "armor."

See also **Armed Forces.**

BIBLIOGRAPHY

Sidney B. Brinckerhoff and Odie B. Faulk, *Lancers for the King* (1965).

Odie B. Faulk, *The Leather Jacket Soldier* (1971).

Additional Bibliography

Anderson, Gary Clayton. *The Indian Southwest, 1580–1830. Ethnogenesis and Reinvention.* Norman: University of Oklahoma Press, 1999.

Griffin-Pierce, Trudy. *Native Peoples of the Southwest.* Albuquerque: University of New Mexico Press, 2002.

Weber, David J. *Bárbaros: Spaniards and Their Savages in the Age of Enlightenment.* New Haven, CT: Yale University Press, 2005.

W. MICHAEL MATHES

SOLDI, RAÚL

(1905–1994). Raúl Soldi (*b.* 27 March 1905; *d.* 21 April 1994), Argentine painter, printmaker, and muralist. Soldi was born in Buenos Aires and studied there, at the National Academy of Fine Arts, as well as at the Brera Royal Academy in Milan. He had a strict figurative training in drawing; later, in contact with the school of light devotees (Chiaristi), he developed his own technique and style. In 1938–1939 he worked in theater design and on numerous films. In 1953 he began painting murals in the chapel of Santa Ana in Glew, a small village in the province of Buenos Aires. Working there only in the summer, he finished in 1976. He painted the dome of the Teatro Colón in Buenos Aires in 1966 and a mural at the basilica of the Annunciation in Nazareth, Israel, in 1968. Soldi received numerous awards, including the Palanza Prize from the National Academy of Fine Arts (1952). In 1993 he had a retrospective of his work at the Salas Nacionales de Exposición.

See also **Art: The Twentieth Century; Teatro Colón; Theater.**

BIBLIOGRAPHY

Vicente Gesualdo, Aldo Biglione, and Rodolfo Santos, *Diccionario de artistas plásticos en la Argentina* (1988).

Additional Bibliography

Gutiérrez Zaldívar, Ignacio. *Soldi, 1905–1994: Su vida y su obra.* Buenos Aires: Zurbarán Ediciones, 2002.

AMALIA CORTINA ARAVENA

SOLER, ANDRÉS, DOMINGO, AND FERNANDO.

Andrés, Domingo, and Fernando Soler (*b.* 1899, 1902, 24 May 1900; *d.* 1969, 1961, 25 October 1979), Mexican film and stage actors. Three pillars of Mexican theater, altogether, the Soler brothers starred in over 200 films. They were key players in the "golden age" of Mexican cinema. Andrés and Domingo Soler served as character and secondary actors in such films as *Doña Bárbara* (1943), *Historia de un gran amor* (1942), *La barraca* (1944), and *Si yo fuera diputado* (1951). Fernando Soler had leading roles in the films *Rosenda* (1948), *La oveja negra* (1949), *México de mis recuerdos* (1943), *Una familia de tantas* (1948), and *Sensualidad* (1950), and received the Ariel from the Mexican film academy in 1951 for best performance by an actor. The Solers constitute one of the few family dynasties of Mexican cinema.

See also **Cinema: From the Silent Film to 1990.**

BIBLIOGRAPHY

Luis Reyes De La Maza, *El cine sonoro en México* (1973).

E. Bradford Burns, *Latin American Cinema: Film and History* (1975).

Carl J. Mora, *Mexican Cinema: Reflections of a Society: 1896–1980* (1982).

John King, *Magical Reels: A History of Cinema in Latin America* (1990).

Additional Bibliography

Coerver, Don M. Robert Buffington, and Suzanne B. Pastor. *Mexico: An Encyclopedia of Contemporary Culture and History.* Santa Barbara, CA: ABC-CLIO, 2004.

Hershfeld, Joanne, and David Maciel. *Mexico's Cinema: A Century of Film and Filmmakers.* Wilmington, DE: Scholarly Resources, 1999.

Mora, Carl J. *Mexican Cinema: Reflections of a Society, 1896-2004.* Jefferson, NC: McFarland & Co., 2005.

Paranaguá, Paulo Antonio. *Mexican Cinema.* London: British Film Institute, 1995.

DAVID MACIEL

SOLÍS, JUAN DÍAZ DE

(c. 1400–1516). Juan Díaz de Solís (*b.* mid-1400s; *d.* 1516), navigator who explored the Río de la Plata estuary. The birthplace of Díaz is unclear. Some think it was Lebrija (Seville); others argue that his family migrated from Asturias to Portugal, where he was born. He voyaged to India for Portugal several times, served French corsairs, then moved to Spain in late 1505. He met Juan de la Cosa and Amerigo Vespucci at a conference summoned by King Ferdinand in Burgos in 1508, and was commissioned on 23 March 1508 to search for a passage to the Orient along with Vicente Yáñez Pinzón. The exact itinerary is debated; it seems there was a coastal reconnaissance from central America north to the Yucatán, then Mexico's central Gulf coast.

Díaz de Solís returned to Spain and was serving in the Casa de Contratación in Seville in the late summer of 1509. When Amerigo Vespucci died (22 February 1512), Díaz de Solís was named *piloto mayor* (chief pilot) and commissioned to head two voyages, both of which came to naught. He was encharged with another expedition, which left Sanlúcar on 8 October 1515. This group explored the Río de la Plata estuary in early 1516. When Solís and his party disembarked to take possession of the left bank of the estuary, at a place before the confluence of the Uruguay and Paraná rivers, they were attacked. Indians wielding bows and arrows killed Solís and several companions.

See also **Explorers and Exploration: Spanish America; Vespucci, Amerigo.**

BIBLIOGRAPHY

Juan Manzano Manzano, *Los Pinzones y el descubrimiento de América* (1988).

NOBLE DAVID COOK

SOLÍS FOLCH DE CARDONA, JOSÉ

(1716–1770). José Solís Folch de Cardona (*b.* 4 February 1716; *d.* 27 April 1770), viceroy of the New Kingdom of Granada (1753–1761). Born in Madrid into a prestigious and noble family, Solís arrived in New Granada as one of the youngest American viceroys yet appointed. He was accused by contemporaries and modern historians of having a youthful and dissipate moral character, as evidenced by the notorious Marichuela liaison, which created a scandal in Bogotá. But his political administration has generally been judged one of the best in the eighteenth century. Solís is especially known for his promotion of transportation improvements throughout the viceroyalty.

As with his predecessors, complaints of poor health led him in 1757 to request a replacement. Two years later Ferdinand VI tapped Pedro Messía De La Cerda (1761–1772) as the next viceroy. Surprisingly, after he stepped down, Solís entered the Franciscan order and gave much of his personal fortune to the church. He remained in a Santa Fe de Bogotá monastery until his death.

See also **Franciscans; Messía de la Cerda, Pedro de.**

BIBLIOGRAPHY

Solís is the subject of a biography by Daniel Samper Ortega, *Don José Solís, virrey del Nuevo Reino de Granada* (1953). See also the discussion in Sergio Elías Ortiz, *Nuevo Reino de Granada: El virreynato,* pt. 2: *1753–1810,* in *Historia extensa de Colombia,* vol. 4 (1970); and Solís's own report of his administration in

Germán Colmenares, ed., *Relaciones e informes de los gobernantes de la Nueva Granada,* vol. 1 (1989).

Additional Bibliography

Domínguez Ortega, Montserrat. "Política económica del virrey Solís, 1753–1761." *Boletín de Historia y Antigüedades* 92, no. 830 (July–Sept. 2005): 515–574.

Mantilla Ruiz, Luis Carlos. "Una nueva imagen del virrey Solís: Ni leyenda ni apología." *Boletín de Historia y Antigüedades* 78, no. 773 (Apr.–June 1991): 389–395.

LANCE R. GRAHN

SOLOGUREN, JAVIER (1921–2004).

Javier Sologuren (*b.* 19 January 1921; *d.* 2004), Peruvian poet, publisher, and essayist. His father was the cousin of the poets Ricardo and Enrique Peña Barrenechea. Javier Sologuren studied literature and humanities in Peru, Mexico, and Belgium. He began publishing in the 1940s. In the 1950s, he lived in Sweden for seven years. Upon returning to Peru, Sologuren undertook the publication of his Ediciones de La Rama Florida, printing Peruvian and foreign literatures on a manual press. In 1960, he received the National Poetry Award. Later, Sologuren organized his poetry architectonically under the title *Vida continua* (1944, 1971, 1980, 1989, 1992). In 1990, he published *La Hora,* in English and in Spanish.

Sologuren's essays on pre-Columbian and contemporary Peruvian arts, crafts, and literature, reformulating national Andean tradition, link him to such writers as Emilio Adolfo Westphalen, José María Arguedas, and Jorge Eduardo Eielson, and to the painter Fernando de Szyszlo. He also worked with European and Asian literatures, translating Swedish, French, Italian, and Brazilian poetry into Spanish and collaborating in the translation of classical Japanese works. In 2004–2005, the Pontifica Universidad Católica in Peru published his *Obras Completas.*

See also **Literature: Spanish America.**

BIBLIOGRAPHY

Anna Soncini, ed., *Javier Sologuren, Vita continua: Poesie (1947–1987),* Italian translation, 1988, pp. 9–14.

Ana María Gazzolo, "Javier Sologuren: Poesía, razón de vida," in *Lienzo* 9 (1989): 219–278.

Additional Bibliography

Cornejo Polar, José. *Estudios de la literatura peruana.* Lima, Peru: Universidad de Lima, Fondo de Desarrollo Editorial, 1998.

Pollarolo, Giovanna, and Mauricio Novoa. "Fragmentos de una confesión incesante: Entrevista a Javier Sologuren." *Debate,* 17 (Nov–Dec 1995): 69–71.

LUIS REBAZA-SORALUZ

SOLÓRZANO, CARLOS (1922–). Car-

los Solórzano (*b.* 1 May 1922), Mexican playwright, director, professor, critic, historian, and governmental impresario. Born in Guatemala City, Solórzano moved to Mexico in 1939 to pursue studies in architecture and literature. In 1948 he received a degree from the National Autonomous University of Mexico. He studied dramatic art in Paris until 1951. Solórzano's exposure to French existentialism resulted in a successful three-act play, *Las manos de Dios* (1956), in which the protagonist chooses personal freedom and metaphorically the freedom of humanity over the repressive forces of church and state. Two earlier full-length plays and several one-act works deal with similar issues. Solórzano was the first critic to deal with twentieth-century Latin American theater on a hemispheric scale; his two books present overviews of major currents and comparative views by country. For years Solórzano was artistic director of the University Theater, taught classes, and wrote reviews and criticism; during the presidency of José López Portillo, he promoted theater under a project called Teatro de la Nación (1977–1981). In 1985 he became a professor emeritus at the Universidad Nacional Autónoma de México, or UNAM. In 1989 he was awarded the Premio Universidad Nacional and the Premio Nacional de Literatura Miguel Angel Asturias in Mexico, and he also won the Premio Nacional de Literatura de Guatemala in that same year. In 1993 his *Crossroads, and Other Plays* was published in English. Five years later he was awarded an honorary doctorate from the Universidad Nacional de Guatemala. He is married to Beatriz Caso de Solórzano, a sculptor and artist.

See also **Theater.**

BIBLIOGRAPHY

Careaga, Gabriel. *Sociedad y teatro moderno en México.* México, DF: Editorial Joaquín Moritz, 1994.

El teatro hispanoamericano del siglo XX (1961 and 1964).

Feliciano, Wilma. "Myth and Theatricality in Three Plays by Carlos Solórzano," in *Latin American Theatre Review* 25, no. 1 (Fall 1991): 123–133.

Feliciano, Wilma. *El teatro mítico de Carlos Solórzano.* México, DF: Facultad de Filosofía y Letras, Universidad Nacional Autónoma de México, 1995.

Radcliff-Umstead, Douglas. "Solórzano's Tormented Puppets," in *Latin American Theatre Review* 4, no. 2 (Spring 1971): 5–11.

Rivas, Esteban. *Carlos Solórzano y el teatro hispanoamericano.* México, 1970.

Rosenberg, John. "The Ritual of Solórzano's *Las manos de Dios,*" in *Latin American Theatre Review* 17, no. 2 (Spring 1984): 39–48.

GEORGE WOODYARD

SOLÓRZANO PEREIRA, JUAN DE

(1575–1655). Juan de Solórzano Pereira (*b.* 1575; *d.* 1655), Spanish jurist and author. Solórzano studied civil and canon law at the University of Salamanca and taught there before being named oidor of the Audiencia of Lima in 1609. In Peru he oversaw the rehabilitation of the Huancavelica mercury mine, married a creole woman from Cuzco, and mastered legislation related to the Indies. By the time he returned from what he considered exile in the New World as *fiscal* of the Council of the Indies in 1627, he was the foremost authority on the laws of the Indies. He published *De Indiarum iure* from 1629 to 1639 and, in 1647, a modified five-volume version, *Política indiana,* for readers of Spanish. Solórzano also was a major contributor, in 1636, to the final draft of the *Recopilación de leyes de los reynos de las Indias,* which was finally published in 1681. Unlike many of his contemporaries, Solórzano considered public office to be a public trust rather than a piece of property.

See also **Council of the Indies; Huancavelica.**

BIBLIOGRAPHY

D. A. Brading, *The First America: The Spanish Monarchy, Creole Patriots, and the Liberal State 1492–1867* (1991), chap. 10.

John Leddy Phelan, *The Kingdom of Quito in the Seventeenth Century: Bureaucratic Politics in the Spanish Empire* (1967).

Additional Bibliography

Muldoon, James. *The Americas in the Spanish World Order: The Justification for Conquest in the Seventeenth Century.* Philadelphia: University of Pennsylvania Press, 1994.

MARK A. BURKHOLDER

SOMERS, ARMONÍA

SOMERS, ARMONÍA (1914–1994). Armonía Somers (Armonía Etchepare de Henestrosa; b. 1914; d. 1994), Uruguayan writer, educator, and critic. Born in Montevideo, Somers taught elementary school for many years and served in various capacities in the Montevideo school system. She has written on subjects related to the education of adolescents. Her literary career began in 1950 with the publication of her first novel, *La mujer desnuda.*

From the beginning, Somers has been considered one of the major fiction writers of Uruguay, together with Juan Carlos Onetti and Felisberto Hernández. She is known for the innovative narrative style that she incorporates in her novels, considered by many as a fundamental break with the Uruguayan novel of the 1950s. In 1953 she published her first collection of short stories, in which a nightmarish and erotic atmosphere becomes almost unbearable to the alienated characters. *La calle del viento norte y otros cuentos* (The North Wind Street and Other Stories, 1963), her second collection of short stories, shows a more mature writer in style and depth, one who works slowly and patiently on the margins of literary circles.

Two novels followed, *De miedo en miedo* (From Fear to Fear, 1965) and *Un retrato para Dickens* (1969). *Todos los cuentos* (1967) included the two earlier collections of stories plus two unpublished ones. In these works Somers continued to elaborate the fictional world created in her previous works, emphasizing cruelty and loneliness as central elements that shape the lives of her protagonists.

After a silence of nine years, Somers published a second edition of her short stories. By that time her work had begun to be noticed by critics and readers

in several countries. In 1986 she published *Viaje al corazón del dia* and *Sólo los elefantes encuentran mandrágora* (Only Elephants Encounter Mandragora), the latter being her most ambitious and difficult text. She also published two additional anthologies of her work, *Muerte por alacrán* (1979; Death by Scorpion) and *La rebelión de la flor* (1988).

See also **Literature: Spanish America.**

BIBLIOGRAPHY

Armonía Somers: Papeles críticos. Cuarenta años de literatura, edited by R. Cosse (1990).

Ana María Rodríguez-Villaml, *Elementos fantásticos en la narrativa de Armonía Somers* (1990).

Additional Bibliography

Cosse, Rómulo, and Arturo Sergio Visca. *Armonía Somers, papeles críticos: Cuarenta años de literatura.* Montevideo: Librería Linardi y Riss, 1990.

Fitts, Alexandra. "Reading the Body, Writing the Body: Constructions of the Female Body in the Work of Latin American Women Writers." Ph.D. diss., Duke University, 1995.

MAGDALENA GARCÍA PINTO

SOMOZA DEBAYLE, ANASTASIO

SOMOZA DEBAYLE, ANASTASIO (1925–1980). Anastasio Somoza Debayle (b. 5 December 1925; d. 17 September 1980), president and dictator of Nicaragua (1967–1979). "Tachito" Somoza was the younger son of Anastasio Somoza García. Unlike his older brother, Luis, Tachito rose to power through the Nicaraguan military. A graduate of West Point (1948), he returned to Nicaragua to take on a number of high-ranking positions in the National Guard. His father, while president, made him commander of the Guard. Like his father, Tachito believed the National Guard was the only reliable constituency of support for the Somoza family. While Luis, as president, implemented liberal policies and moderate social reform, Anastasio provided the muscle to maintain control over Nicaraguan society. He used the National Guard to quell minor outbreaks of social unrest. During his brother's presidency (1956–1963), Tachito increasingly came into conflict with Luis on the issue of his own presidential ambitions. His brother's death in 1967 removed a restraining influence over Tachito, who engineered his temporary resignation from the National Guard to be eligible constitutionally to run for president. In 1967, the third Somoza was "elected" to the presidency of Nicaragua.

Tachito proved to be much more his father's son than did his older brother. He has been characterized as greedy, cruel, repressive, and inhuman. He continued his father's methods in maintaining Conservative compliance by raising the party's congressional seat allocation to 40 percent. He continued the pro-U.S. policy of his father and brother (his father had allowed the CIA to use the Managua airport in 1954 for bombing raids against the Arbenz government in Guatemala) and even offered Nicaraguan troops for Vietnam. Strict and repressive control kept him in power, and the stable economy initially kept discontent in check. The middle sectors of Nicaraguan society were weak and divided, and Somoza still represented order in a country where a small guerrilla group, the Sandinista National Liberation Front (FSLN), was beginning to cause political concern.

On 23 December 1972 a massive earthquake hit Managua and Somoza reclaimed the presidency under the auspices of a state of emergency. The corruption that characterized this period included the diversion of international relief funds and the private access to relief supplies of Somoza, his cronies, and the National Guard. Such behavior alienated the Nicaraguan upper classes and resulted in the formation of a broad opposition front, which was formed to challenge Somoza in the 1974 elections and led by *La Prensa* editor Pedro Joaquín Chamorro Cardenal. Increasing numbers of young Nicaraguans from all classes were joining the FSLN in its struggle against the Somoza dictatorship. As the success of FSLN attacks increased, Somoza used the National Guard to repress violently any form of perceived opposition. The human-rights abuses caused U.S. President Jimmy Carter to cool relations with the once favorite son.

In 1977 Somoza suffered a heart attack but did not relinquish power. In 1978 Chamorro was assassinated. Somoza and the guard were blamed, and Somoza's violent repression of the ensuing demonstrations solidified opposition forces on the left and the right. Washington attempted to negotiate, offering "Somocismo without Somoza," but with

Somoza's own intransigence and the opposition's strength, the mediation was rejected. An Organization of American States resolution demanded his resignation, and Tachito was forced to leave Nicaragua on 17 July 1979.

On the invitation of President General Alfredo Stroessner, Somoza ultimately went into exile to Paraguay. On 17 September 1980 he was killed in Asunción when a bomb exploded in the car he was driving. An Argentine guerrilla organization was initially held responsible, but subsequently the FSLN military was connected to the assassination.

See also **Chamorro Cardenal, Pedro Joaquín; Nicaragua; Nicaragua, Sandinista National Liberation Front (FSLN); Somoza Debayle, Luis; Somoza García, Anastasio.**

BIBLIOGRAPHY

Richard Millet, *Guardians of the Dynasty* (1977).

Eduardo Crawley, *Dictators Never Die* (1979).

Anastasio Somoza Debayle and Jack Cox, *Nicaragua Betrayed* (1980).

Bernard Diedrich, *Somoza and the Legacy of U.S. Involvement in Central America* (1981) and *Somoza* (1982).

Thomas Walker, *Nicaragua: The Land of Sandino* (1986).

David Close, *Nicaragua: Politics, Economics, and Society* (1988).

Dennis Gilbert, *Sandinistas* (1988).

Anthony Lake, *Somoza Falling* (1989).

Additional Bibliography

Everingham, Mark. *Revolution and the Multiclass Coalition in Nicaragua.* Pittsburgh, PA: University of Pittsburgh Press, 2002.

Morley, Morris H. *Washington, Somoza, and the Sandinistas: State and Regime in U.S. Policy toward Nicaragua, 1969–1981.* Cambridge; New York: Cambridge University Press, 2002.

Solaún, Mauricio. *U.S. Intervention and Regime Change in Nicaragua.* Lincoln: University of Nebraska Press, 2005.

HEATHER K. THIESSEN

SOMOZA DEBAYLE, LUIS (1922–1967). Luis Somoza Debayle (*b.* 18 November 1922; *d.* 13 April 1967), president of Nicaragua

(1956–1963). Son of Nicaraguan dictator Anastasio Somoza García, Luis Somoza was the elder and more liberal brother of Anastasio Somoza Debayle. He attended a number of universities in the United States and returned to Nicaragua to sit as a member of the Nationalist Liberal Party (PLN) in Congress while his father was president. Although Luis had an officer's commission in the National Guard, he chose the path of politics and became the president of the PLN, the president of Congress, and the first designate to the Nicaraguan presidency. Upon his father's assassination, Luis assumed the presidency. He served out his father's term and then was elected to the presidency in his own right.

Luis Somoza is best known for relaxing the political repression that characterized his father's time in power. Social reforms of his term included housing development, social-security legislation, limited land reform, and university autonomy. He allowed some measure of freedom of the press and released political detainees, measures that were aimed at improving the regime's image. His liberal social policy notwithstanding, four out of his seven years in office were conducted under martial law, and a number of abortive uprisings were repressed. His goal in liberalizing Nicaragua's political environment was the removal of the Somoza family from obvious political power, making them less vulnerable to attack and opposition. It has been suggested that Luis Somoza envisioned a role for the PLN based on the corporate political model of Mexico. Moreover, he sought a way for his family to exercise "discreet control" through the PLN, a plan that brought him into direct conflict with his younger brother, Anastasio ("Tachito"), who had assumed control of the National Guard under their father's last term in office. Luis's moderate approach was rejected by Tachito, who, like his father, felt control could be maintained only through the National Guard and a hard-line military style. Luis restored the constitutional articles banning the immediate reelection or succession to the presidency by any relative of the incumbent or by the incumbent himself. He reinforced this legislation by stepping down at the end of his term. Luis did not intend to remove the Somozas from power, however, and engineered the selection and election of PLN candidate René Schick Gutiérrez, a close Somoza associate, in 1963.

During his time in office, Luis attempted to reestablish friendly relations with Nicaragua's neighbors and supported the establishment of the Central American Common Market (CACM). Despite the variance in political style, Luis maintained the strong pro–United States stance of his father, allowing the ill-fated Bay of Pigs Invasion to be launched from Nicaragua's eastern coast. His last years were spent in conflict with his younger brother over the latter's aspirations to the presidency. Luis's death from a heart attack in 1967 removed a moderating influence from the Somoza family.

See also **Central American Common Market (CACM); Nicaragua; Schick Gutiérrez, René; Somoza Debayle, Anastasio; Somoza García, Anastasio.**

BIBLIOGRAPHY

Richard Millet, *Guardians of the Dynasty* (1977).

Eduardo Crawley, *Dictators Never Die* (1979).

Bernard Diedrich, *Somoza and the Legacy of U.S. Involvement in Central America* (1981), and *Somoza* (1982).

Thomas Walker, *Nicaragua: The Land of Sandino* (1986).

David Close, *Nicaragua: Politics, Economics, and Society* (1988).

Anthony Lake, *Somoza Falling* (1989).

Dennis Gilbert, *Sandinistas* (1990).

Additional Bibliography

Gambone, Michael D. *Eisenhower, Somoza, and the Cold War in Nicaragua, 1953–1961*. Westport, CT: Praeger, 1997.

HEATHER K. THIESSEN

SOMOZA GARCÍA, ANASTASIO (1896–1956).

Anastasio Somoza García (*b.* 1 February 1896; *d.* 29 September 1956), Nicaraguan dictator (1936–1956) and patriarch of the Somoza dynasty. Born in San Marcos, "Tacho" Somoza dominated Nicaragua from 1930 to 1956. Born in Carazo, department of San Marcos, Tacho was the grandnephew of Bernabé Somoza, Nicaragua's most notorious outlaw. He attended school in Philadelphia, where he gained an excellent command of English. Upon returning to Nicaragua, Somoza embarked upon a military career that would result, with the support of the U.S. representatives in Nicaragua, in his meteoric and violent rise to the presidency. He married Salvadora Debayle, the niece of leading Liberal and president Juan Bautista Sacasa, and gained entrance to the upper circles of Nicaraguan society and politics. During the 1927–1933 U.S. military occupation of Nicaragua, Somoza came to the attention of U.S. Secretary of State Henry Stimson. Based on his command of English and charismatic enthusiasm for the United States, he was named Stimson's envoy and also nicknamed "el yanqui." In 1927 the United States gave him command of the newly created National Guard. The guard was created to maintain order in the violent world of Nicaraguan politics, thus allowing the withdrawal of the U.S. Marines.

Under Somoza's tutelage, the guard became increasingly powerful, placing him in a position to challenge and surpass even the political and legal authority of the Nicaraguan president. Not surprisingly, he became embroiled in a struggle for political power with President Sacasa, his uncle-in-law, and increasingly used the guard to exert his influence and control over Nicaragua. In 1934, after Sacasa had completed peace negotiations with the guerrilla commander Augusto César Sandino, Somoza arranged for Sandino's murder. It has been suggested that he was forced into the plot to maintain his control over the guard. Somoza's authorization for the murder, however, was representative of his methods. Using the guard as a power base, Somoza ousted Sacasa from the presidency in 1936.

Backed by the guard, Somoza came to the presidency with more personal power than any other president in Nicaraguan history. Despite legal blocks to his becoming president—he was barred from the position as a relation of Sacasa and as commander of the National Guard—Somoza was "elected" to the presidency in December 1936. Although described as charming, astute, and ambitious, Tacho Somoza used guile, opportunism, and ruthlessness to maintain and build a political and economic dynasty. As president he maintained supreme command of the National Guard. He reestablished the Nationalist Liberal Party as a personal political machine, dusted off at election time to ensure his candidacy. The Conservative opposition was bought off with the 1948 and 1950 political pacts that guaranteed them one-third of congressional seats and a place on the Supreme Court while ensuring their compliance with Somoza's domination of Nicaragua.

His economic control of the country increased steadily. He came to power with the proverbial "ruined coffee finca," and died leaving personal wealth estimated between $100 and $150 million. His attitude toward Nicaragua was summed up in a single line, "Nicaragua es mi finca" (Nicaragua is my farm). His exploitation of foreign aid and technical assistance (a substantial amount due to his very pro-U.S. stance) and his opportunism during World War II increased his private holdings dramatically. Under the pretext of combating Nazism, he confiscated German and Italian-owned properties. By 1944 Somoza was the largest private landowner and the leading producer of sugar in the country. His holdings soon expanded to include meat and mining companies, cement works, textile mills, milk processing, and state transport facilities, many of which were monopolies. There were also the "dirty" businesses of gambling, brothels, racketeering, illegal alcohol production, and monopoly control of export-import licensing, much of which occurred with National Guard participation.

Somoza's ability to stay in power stemmed from his control over the National Guard but also from political astuteness. When the winds of political change began to favor prodemocracy movements and rising discontent resulted in democratically elected governments in Guatemala and El Salvador in the 1940s, Somoza enacted a new labor code in 1944 and an income tax law in 1952, and established a development institute in 1953. This "social progress" coincided with an economic boom from the expansion of the cotton industry. Somoza's support was also bolstered by Washington. His pro-U.S. line brought funding for infrastructure development. Despite increasing discontent with his economic and political domination and repressive tactics, the United States saw him as a staunch ally in a region that was fast becoming a concern for U.S. policy. His heavy-handed methods were cause for President Franklin D. Roosevelt's famous description of Somoza as "a son of a bitch, but our son of a bitch." Other Central American leaders became increasingly concerned with his power. In 1954 the Organization of American States (OAS) had to intervene to prevent Somoza from supporting Costa Rican exiles in

General Anastasio Somoza García with reporter, Managua, Nicaragua, 1955. Somoza's ability to converse in English with representatives of the United States helped earn him the leadership of the Nicaraguan National Guard, a move that allowed the withdrawal of U.S. Marines from the country. Eventually, Somoza would use this position of power to become president of Nicaragua, plundering great wealth during his dictatorship. © BETTMANN/CORBIS

launching a coup attempt on President José Figueres Ferrer from Nicaraguan soil.

Ultimately, the repressive nature of Somoza's economic, political, and military dictatorship resulted in his assassination. On 21 September 1956, a young Nicaraguan poet, Rigoberto López Pérez, shot Somoza in León. Somoza had been in the city to receive the presidential nomination from the Nationalist Liberal Party. U.S. Ambassador Thomas Wheaton, with support from President Dwight D. Eisenhower, airlifted Somoza to the American military hospital in Panama, where he died. He was survived by his wife, a daughter, and three sons (one illegitimate). Two of his sons, Luis

and Anastasio, would continue the dynasty for another twenty-three years.

See also **Nicaragua; Sacasa, Juan Batista; Sandino, Augusto César; Somoza Debayle, Anastasio; Somoza Debayle, Luis.**

BIBLIOGRAPHY

Richard Millet, *Guardians of the Dynasty* (1977).

Eduardo Crawley, *Dictators Never Die* (1979).

Anastasio Somoza and Jack Cox, *Nicaragua Betrayed* (1980).

Bernard Diedrich, *Somoza and the Legacy of U.S. Involvement in Central America* (1981) and *Somoza (1982);* Thomas Walker, *Nicaragua: The Land of Sandino* (1986).

David Close, *Nicaragua: Politics, Economics, and Society* (1988).

Anthony Lake, *Somoza Falling* (1989).

Additional Bibliography

Clark, Paul Coe. *The United States and Somoza, 1933–1956: A Revisionist Look*. Westport, CT: Praeger, 1992.

Crawley, Andrew. *Somoza and Roosevelt: Good Neighbor Diplomacy in Nicaragua, 1933–1945*. New York: Oxford University Press, 2007.

Walter, Knut. *The Regime of Anastasio Somoza, 1936–1956*. Chapel Hill: University of North Carolina Press, 1993.

HEATHER K. THIESSEN

SON.   The Cuban *son* is a musical and dance genre whose emergence as a nationally popular expressive form dates back to the 1910s. With roots in the eastern part of the island, *son* attracted the attention of not only musicians and dancers, but eventually poets, artists, and political leaders in Havana from the 1920s on. It surpassed the popularity of *danzón*, becoming the symbolic expression of Cuban national identity. Specifically, writers have identified *son*'s syncretization of African and Spanish musical structures as symbolic of the nation's *mestizaje*, or racially mixed essence.

From its earliest history *son* music has been stylistically vibrant, spawning several closely related styles of Cuban and Latin popular music and dance. Ignacio Piñeiro of the internationally popular Septeto Nacional was the genre's first commercially prolific composer and innovative stylist. Piñeiro was followed by Arsenio Rodríguez, who standardized the use of the congas, piano, and trumpet section in *son*'s original instrumental format. These and other innovations in *son* music led directly to the development of mambo in the 1940s and salsa music in the 1960s. Cuban and other musicians have continued to use *son* and other related Cuban forms as a source from which to develop new styles, including *songo* and, since the 1990s, *timba*.

See also **Mambo; Music: Popular Music and Dance.**

BIBLIOGRAPHY

Garcia, David. *Arsenio Rodriguez and the Transnational Flows of Latin Popular Music*. Philadelphia, PA: Temple University Press, 2006.

Moore, Robin. *Nationalizing Blackness: Afrocubanismo and Artistic Revolution in Havana, 1920–1940*. Pittsburgh, PA: University of Pittsburgh Press, 1997.

DAVID F. GARCIA

SON JAROCHO.   Son jarocho is a folkloric music and dance form from the southern coastal area of Vera Cruz state, Mexico. (The term *jarocho* itself refers to people and things associated with southern Vera Cruz.) Its development has been traced to the seventeenth and eighteenth centuries and is generally seen as a synthesis of the colonial-era Spanish, indigenous, and African cultures of the region. Such well known son jarochos as "La Bamba" and "El Besuquito" date back to the colonial period. While the instrumentation varies, the most common ensemble consists of an *arpa veracruzana* (a 32- to 36-string diatonic harp), a *requinto* (a small four-string guitar played with a large plectrum), and a small eight-string guitar known as a *jarana*.

Most songs feature short, repetitive harmonic cycles with alternating vocal and instrumental sections and, as dance music, tend to be fast and rhythmically complex. Meters of 3/4 or 6/8 are common, though tunes in duple meter exist. Song texts generally conform to traditional poetic forms such as the copla and décima and are frequently improvised; vocalists often make skillful use of metaphors and double entendres to comment on current social and political issues. The Son Jarocho form has proved to be both resilient and flexible, as demonstrated in its continual reinvention and reinterpretation in the hands of contemporary artists such as the Los Angeles-based band Los Lobos.

See also **Music: Popular Music and Dance.**

BIBLIOGRAPHY

Olsen, Dale A., and Daniel E. Sheehy, eds. *The Garland Handbook of Latin American Music*. New York: Garland, 2000.

Loza, Steven. "From Veracruz to Los Angeles: The Reinterpretation of the 'Son Jarocho.'" *Latin American Music Review* 13:2 (Autumn–Winter 1992), 179–194.

ANDREW M. CONNELL

SONORA.

Sonora, a state in northwest Mexico covering 110,000 square miles. Located between 108 degrees and 115 degrees west longitude and 26 degrees and 32 degrees north latitude, Sonora borders Arizona, the Gulf of California, Chihuahua, and Sinaloa. The Yaqui, Mayo, Sonora, and Concepción drainages constitute its principal river systems, flowing westward from the highlands to the Gulf of California. The Santa Cruz River flows northward to the Gila River; the Colorado River forms the boundary between Sonora and Baja California.

The Sierra Madre Occidental and the Sonoran Desert define its geographic features. Characteristic desert vegetation includes mesquite, paloverde, *palofierro* (ironwood), *gobernadora* (creosote), saguaro, *pitahaya* (a cactus), jojoba, and chollas. The mountains bear varieties of agaves, *encina,* and pine forests. Native fauna include bear, coyote, deer, mountain lion, wild boar, wild turkey, and the protected species of *bura* deer and long-horned sheep.

Firm archaeological evidence of human presence in Sonora can be dated from 10,000 to 15,000 years ago. Nomadic bands of lithic toolmakers hunted mammoths, mastodons, bison, and some animals that have survived to the present. These people left enduring remains in geoglyphs, petroglyphs, and stone artifacts, including the highly crafted Clovis point. Sedentary villagers have practiced agriculture in Sonora at least since the beginning of the common era. Lowland cultivation dependent on flows in ephemeral arroyos specialized in drought-resistant plants like cotton, *quelites* (wild greens), calabashes, and beans. More abundant rainfall and permanent streams sustained several varieties of maize, beans, squash, and gourds in the highlands, where agriculturalists developed irrigation systems and built permanent settlements.

On the eve of the Spanish Conquest, Sonoran peoples comprised many tribes and dialects grouped in two major linguistic families: Hokan and Uto-Aztecan. Highland villagers traveled long-distance trade routes extending from Mesoamerica to the Rio Grande pueblos. European exploration of Sonora began in the 1530s, but no permanent settlements were established until after 1610, when Jesuit missionaries brought riverine farmers under Spanish rule. Missions and presidios formed the nuclei of Sonoran rural towns, which have endured to the present. Mining strikes attracted private settlers to Sonora by the mid-seventeenth century. The mature colonial society of the late eighteenth century relied on a mining and ranching economy that was integrated into regional marketing networks, even as the Bourbon Reforms joined the separate provinces of Sinaloa, Ostimuri, and Sonora in the Intendancy of Arizpe.

The frontier quality of life persisted after Mexican independence, as Sonoran ranchers and townsmen fought against Apache bands who roamed the sierra and raided both white and Amerindian settlements. Moreover, Yaqui and Mayo villagers tenaciously defended their fertile lands against expanding private landholdings. The market economy grew: by the mid-nineteenth century Sonorans exported wheat to California and received increasing European trade through the port of Guaymas. The state capital moved from Arizpe to Ures and Hermosillo, as the leading landed and commercial families established their power base along the Hermosillo-Guaymas axis.

The U.S. invasion of Mexico (1846–1848) and the Treaty of Mesillas (1854), followed by the War of the Reform (1857–1860) and the French Intervention (1864–1867) were important political events for Sonora that redrew its territorial boundaries and redefined its relations with the central government. After 1880, the politics stemming from the presidency of Porfirio Díaz brought a new elite to power in the state and accelerated capitalist development through commercial agriculture and industrial mining. Sonoran leaders played a major role in the Revolution of 1910 and with their military strength brought the Constitutionalists to power. During the 1920s, Sonorans dominated the presidency, reshaping Mexico's political structures.

See also **Gadsden Purchase; Mexico, Wars and Revolutions: Mexican-American War.**

BIBLIOGRAPHY

Peter Gerhard, *The North Frontier of New Spain* (1982), provides a masterful overview of history and political geography for northern colonial Mexico. Armando Hopkins Durazo, gen. coord., *Historia general de Sonora*, 5 vols. (1985), is a summary of geographic, anthropological, and historical research to date. Principal published sources include Andrés Pérez De Ribas, *Los Triunfos de nuestra Santa Fé*, 3 vols. (1645; published in Mexico, 1944, 1985); Juan Nentvig, *Descripción geográfica,* natural, y curiosa de la Provincia de Sonora, edited by Germán Viveros (1971), also in English as *Rudo Ensayo, a Description of Sonora and Arizona in 1764,* edited by Alberto Francisco Pradeau (1980); Ignaz Pfefferkorn, *Beschreibung der Landschaft Sonora* (1795), also in English as *Sonora: A Description of the Province,* edited by Theodore Treutlein (1949). The Documentary Relations of the Southwest, University of Arizona, has compiled a computerized index to microfilmed documents in various archives and has published a number of annotated texts in translation, with introductions. Outstanding examples include Charles W. Polzer, *Rules and Precepts of the Jesuit Missions of Northwestern New Spain* (1976); Thomas H. Naylor and Charles W. Polzer, eds., *The Presidio and Militia on the Northern Frontier of New Spain: A Documentary History, 1570–1700* (1986); and *Pedro de Rivera and the Military Regulations for Northern New Spain, 1724–1729* (1988). Edward H. Spicer, *Cycles of Conquest* (1962) and *The Yaquis: A Cultural History* (1980), are classic ethnohistorical works. Stuart F. Voss, *On the Periphery of Nineteenth-Century Mexico: Sonora and Sinaloa, 1810–1877* (1982); and Evelyn Hu-dehart, *Yaqui Resistance and Survival: The Struggle for Land and Autonomy, 1821–1910* (1984), are two outstanding histories of nineteenth-century Sonora. Steven E. Sanderson, *Agrarian Populism and the Mexican State: The Struggle for Land in Sonora* (1981) provides an analysis of twentieth-century Sonora.

Additional Bibliography

Castro Luque, Ana Lucía, Jaime Olea Miranda, and Blanca E. Zepeda Bracamonte. *Cruzando el desierto: Construcción de una tipología para el análisis de la migración en Sonora.* Hermosillo, Mexico: Colegio de Sonora, 2006.

Radding Murrieta, Cynthia. *Landscapes of Power and Identity: Comparative Histories in the Sonoran Desert and the Forests of Amazonia from Colony to Republic.* Durham, NC: Duke University Press, 2006.

Teja, Jesús F. de la, and Ross Frank. *Choice, Persuasion, and Coercion: Social Control on Spain's North American Frontiers.* Albuquerque: University of New Mexico Press, 2005.

Tellman, Barbara, and Diana Hadley. *Crossing Boundaries: An Environmental History of the Upper San Pedro River Watershed, Arizona and Sonora.* Arizona: s.n., 2006.

CYNTHIA RADDING

SONSONATE. Sonsonate, one of fourteen departments of El Salvador (2006 estimated pop. 530,988). It was part of the territory of the colonial region of Izalcos, which later became the *alcaldía mayor* of Sonsonate, a colonial subdivision incorporated into the state of San Salvador in 1824. Economic activities include port services (at Acajutla), oil refining, and production of dairy products, cereals, coffee, cotton, and sugar. The capital city of the department, also named Sonsonate (2005 est. pop. 66, 201), is 37.8 miles west of San Salvador. Founded in 1552 with the name of Santísima Trinidad de Sonsonate, it was one of the first Spanish settlements in present-day El Salvador. It owed its early prosperity to the production of cacao and to the proximity of the Pacific port of Acajutla. Sonsonate means "Place of 400 Rivers" or "Place of Many Waters," as it receives well over 2,000 millimeters (79 inches) of rain per year.

See also **El Salvador.**

BIBLIOGRAPHY

Anderson, Thomas P. *Matanza: The 1932 "Slaughter" that Traumatized a Nation, Shaping US–Salvadoran Policy to This Day,* 2nd edition. Willimatic, CT: Curbstone Press, 1992.

Dym, Jordana, and Christophe Belaubre. *Politics, Economy, and Society in Bourbon Central America, 1759–1821.* Boulder, CO: University Press of Colorado, 2007.

Instituto Salvadoreño De Administración Municipal. *Prontuario municipal, departamento de Sonsonate.* Author, 1987.

Castro, Rodolfo Barón. *La población de El Salvador.* Madrid: Instituto Gonzalo Fernández de Oviedo, 1942.

HÉCTOR LINDO-FUENTES

SONTHONAX, LÉGER FÉLICITÉ

(1763–1813). Léger Félicité Sonthonax (*b.* 17 March 1763; *d.* 28 July 1813), French politician and lawyer. Sonthonax, a native of Oyonnax, France, was a controversial figure whose actions led to profoundly important but unintended results. Appointed commissioner of Saint-Domingue by Louis XVI in June 1792, with the mandate to halt revolutionary activity in the French colony, he implemented the 1792 decree that gave civil rights to coloreds (persons of mixed black and white heritage) and outlawed slavery. The decree had been designed to quell the frustration of blacks and win their support against the British. Instead, revolutionary momentum continued to increase. In 1794 irate white landowners and the revolutionary leader Toussaint L'ouverture forced Sonthonax out of Saint-Domingue and into the hands of the British. He returned to France but two years later was sent back to Haiti, where he undertook an unsuccessful campaign to eradicate voodoo (*vodun*) culture. Sonthonax retired to France in 1797 and died at Oyonnax.

See also **Haiti.**

BIBLIOGRAPHY

Gérard Mentor Laurent, *Le commissaire Sonthonax à Saint-Domingue*, 4 vols. (1965–1974).

Robert Louis Stein, *Léger Félicité Sonthonax: The Lost Sentinel of the Republic* (1985).

Michel Laguerre, *Voodoo and Politics in Haiti* (1989).

Additional Bibliography

Dorigny, Marcel. *Léger-Félicité Sonthonax: La premiére abolition de l'esclavage: La Révolution française et la Révolution de Saint-Domingue.* Saint-Denis: Société française d'histoire d'outre-mer; Paris: Association pour l'étude de la colonisation européenne, 1997.

ANNE GREENE

SORBONNE GROUP. Sorbonne Group, Brazilian reformist-nationalist army officers trained by the French Military Mission of 1919–1940. Instructed by battle-tested veterans under Chief of Mission General Maurice Gamelin (1919–1925), these junior officers, called *Tenentes* (literally, "lieutenants"), graduated from the General Staff School, the Advanced Officers Training School, and their Realengo Military Academy better trained than their superiors. Some Tenentes led a series of mutinies during the 1920s; others joined the Getúlio Vargas Revolution of 1930; and many fought in Italy in 1944–1945 with the Brazilian Expeditionary Force (*Força Expedicionária Brasileira—FEB*).

In 1949 these Tenentes and the World War II veterans known as Febianos took the lead in founding the Escola Superior Da Guerra (ESG), or Superior War College. Since the staff of this school, Brazil's highest-ranking military institution, either had been French-trained or had undertaken advanced studies in Paris, civilian politicians tended to view the ESG with suspicion, scornfully dubbing it the Sorbonne Group.

Not without reason did they distrust this group. As Tenentes ESG generals Oswaldo Cordeiro de Farias and Juarez Távora had called for a temporary military dictatorship to initiate social, economic, and political reforms. Febiano general Humberto de Castello Branco served as Távora's assistant. The Sorbonne Group, made up of Tenentes and Febianos, took the lead in overthrowing President João Goulart in 1964. Many members of the group served in subsequent military administrations.

See also **Tenentismo.**

BIBLIOGRAPHY

Nelson Werneck Sodré, *História militar do Brasil* (1965).

John W. F. Dulles, *Unrest in Brazil: Political-Military Crises, 1955–1964* (1970).

Raymond Estep, *The Military in Brazilian Politics, 1821–1970* (1971).

Lewis A. Tambs, "Five Times Against the System," in *Perspectives on Armed Politics in Brazil*, edited by Henry H. Keith and Robert A. Hayes (1976), pp. 177–206.

Additional Bibliography

Carvalho, José Murilo de. *Forças armadas e política no Brasil.* Rio de Janeiro: Jorge Zahar Editor, 2005.

LEWIS A. TAMBS

SORIANO, JUAN (1920–2006). Juan Soriano (*b.* 18 August 1920; *d.* February 2006), Mexican painter and sculptor. Born in Guadalajara, Jalisco, Mexico, he studied with Roberto Montenegro and Jesús (Chucho) Reyes Ferreira. In 1934, Soriano participated in the first one-person show of his paintings in the Guadalajara Museum. He left Guadalajara for Mexico City in 1935 and became affiliated with the Primary School of Art, where he later taught, and the Group of Revolutionary Writers and Artists (LEAR). In the 1950s, Soriano was at the forefront of the Mexican avant-garde movement. He lived for several periods in Rome: 1951–1952, 1956, and 1970–1974. Beginning in 1975 he lived in both Paris and Mexico City.

While Soriano has, throughout his career, associated with all of the great Latin American artists of his time, he has never been identified as a member of a particular group or school. His lyrical and idiosyncratic style does not lend itself easily to classification.

He possesses a distinct quality of "Mexican-ness," which is graphically reflected in his works of the 1940s. Since the 1950s his work has reflected a more international scope. With Rufino Tamayo, Soriano has had a major impact on the internationalization of Mexican art, and his own work has been exhibited internationally since the 1970s. In 1991, the Museum of Modern Art in Mexico City presented a major retrospective exhibition of his work. In 1994, he was commissioned to create the sculpture centerpiece for Mexico City's Plaza Loreto. That same year, a retrospective of his photographs traveled throughout the United States, with stops in Austin, Chicago, Washington, D.C., and elsewhere. In 1997, the Reina Sofia museum in Madrid mounted a major retrospective of his work. In 2000, in honor of his eightieth birthday, he created ten sculptures for the Plaza de la Constitución in Mexico City. In 2004, the French government awarded him membership in the Legion of Honor. He was eighty–five years old when he died in February 2006 in Mexico City.

See also **Art: The Twentieth Century.**

BIBLIOGRAPHY

Billeter, Erika, ed. *Images of Mexico* (1988).

Fernández, Justino, and Diego de Mesa. *Juan Soriano.* México: Universidad Nacional Autónoma de México, 1976.

Fuentes, Carlos, and Teresa Del Conde. *Juan Soriano y su obra* (1984).

González-Esteva, Orlando, Juan Soriano, and Pierre Schnieder. *Enigma, Old Friend: The Drawings of Juan Soriano.* Madrid: Ave de Paraíso Ediciones, 2000.

Paz, Octavio, and Edward J. Sullivan. *Juan Soriano: Retratos y esculturas* (1991).

Poniatowska, Elena. *Juan Soriano, niño de mil años.* México: Plaza Janes, 1998.

CLAYTON KIRKING

SORIANO, OSVALDO (1943–1997).
Osvaldo Soriano (*b.* 1943; *d.* 29 January 1997), Argentine writer. Born in Mar del Plata, Soriano is perhaps best known for the film adaptations of several of his novels, especially *No habrá más penas ni olvido* (1980; *A Funny Dirty Little War,* 1986), which uses the microcosm of a small town in the province of Buenos Aires as the arena for the bloody internal conflicts within the Peronist Party during its brief return to power (1973–1976). The events described in the novel become an allegory of Argentine sociopolitical violence and the irrational yet deadly forces it unleashes. *Cuarteles de invierno* (1982)—the film version starred the actor, psychiatrist, and dramatist Eduardo Pavlovsky, whose own works constitute a prominent entry in contemporary Argentine culture—focuses on the arbitrary exercise of violent power as yet another microcosmic example (it too takes place in a small town on the pampas) of a constant in Argentine history and life.

Soriano, as a significant example of the generation of writers in Argentina to emerge during the neofascist tyranny of the 1976–1983 period, has shown a particular talent for using a narrative voice colored by an intense black humor to describe common men (his narrative world is resolutely sexist) enmeshed in a horrendously violent political process. In his first novel, *Triste, solitario y final* (1976), an acerbic attack on U.S. culture is an oblique condemnation of Argentine cultural dependency.

See also **Cinema: From the Silent Film to 1990; Literature: Spanish America.**

BIBLIOGRAPHY

Nora Catelli, "Ni penas ni olvido: Entrevista con Osvaldo Soriano," in *Quimera,* no. 29 (1983): 26–31.

Lois Baer Barr, "*Cuarteles de invierno:* The Reign of the Unrighteous," in *Revista de Estudios Hispánicos* 19, no. 3 (1985): 49–59.

Corina S. Mathieu, "La realidad tragicómica de Osvaldo Soriano," in *Chasqui* 17, no. 1 (1988): 85–91.

Marta Giacomimo, "Espacios de soledad: Entrevista con Osvaldo Soriano," in *Quimera,* no. 89 (1989): 45–51.

Additional Bibliography

Berger, Silvia. *Cuatro textos autobiográficos latinoamericanos: Yo, historia e identidad nacional en A. Gerchunoff, M. Agosín, A. Bioy Casares y O. Soriano.* New York: P. Lang, 2004.

Croce, Marcela. *Osvaldo Soriano: El mercado complaciente.* Buenos Aires: América Libre, 1998.

Montes-Bradley, Eduardo. *Osvaldo Soriano: Un retrato.* Buenos Aires: Grupo Editorial Norma, 2000.

Spahr, Adriana. *La sonrisa de la amargura: 1973–1982: La historia argentina a través de tres novelas de Osvaldo Soriano.* Buenos Aires: Corregidor, 2006.

DAVID WILLIAM FOSTER

SOROCHE.

Soroche, the South American word for the "mountain sickness" experienced by people entering high altitude regions such as the Andes or the Sierra Madre in Mexico. The Spanish conquistadores were the first in the New World to write about it. Symptoms include fatigue, headache, forgetfulness, extreme thirst, nausea, and a propensity to frostbite and respiratory infection. Although the percentage of oxygen in the air remains constant, air pressure decreases at high altitudes; thus there is decreased pressure driving oxygen from the lungs into the bloodstream, resulting in hypoxia, or a deficient level of oxygen. Indigenous peoples have adapted with increased lung capacity and higher numbers of red blood cells; newcomers can successfully adapt over time. Traditionally, coca leaves have been used as a remedy. Some scholars believe *soroche* has had a historical impact, in that, for example, it decreases fertility and may have helped slow the increase of the European population in the Andes.

See also **Diseases.**

BIBLIOGRAPHY

Paul T. Baker and Michael A. Little, eds., *Man in the Andes* (1976).

Additional Bibliography

León Velarde, F., and A. Arregui. *Desadaptación a la vida en las grandes Alturas.* Lima: Instituto Francés de Estudios Andinos: Universidad Peruana Cayetano Heredia, 1994.

CAMILLA TOWNSEND

SOSA, MERCEDES

(1935–). Regarded as one of the foremost Latin American folksingers, Sosa was born in San Miguel de Tucumán, Argentina, on July 9, 1935. She began her professional singing career when she was fourteen years old, first performing popular songs on a local radio station under the pseudonym Gladys Osorio. Although exposed early in life to a variety of Latin American popular music styles, she identified most with the folkloric music of her own country, learning to accompany herself on the *bombo* drum and teaching folkloric dance classes in Tucumán while still a teenager.

In 1957 she married the guitarist Manuel Oscar Matus and moved soon thereafter to Mendoza, where they became an integral part of the political and artistic circle that founded the *nuevo cancionero*, a folkloric musical movement promoting the rights and concerns of the poor. Sosa's fame grew substantially after her performance at the 1965 Folklore Festival in Cosquín, Argentina's most important such festival, and by the end of the decade she was touring and recording internationally to great acclaim. Two projects from the early 1970s, *Cantata Sudamericana* and *Mujeres Argentinas*, created with the composer Ariel Ramírez and the lyricist Félix Luna, are regarded as seminal works.

In the mid-1970s Sosa came under increased scrutiny by the Argentine government for her political views. In 1978, with the country under military rule, she and more than three hundred members of her audience were arrested at a concert in La Plata. Forced into exile in Spain the following year, she remained an outspoken opponent of the military regime until its demise in 1982. Upon her return to Argentina, Sosa began a new chapter in her musical career by collaborating with rock musicians, particularly Charly Garcia, whose *rock nacional* had constituted the most significant voice of musical resistance to the military government. Though never becoming a songwriter herself, Sosa has continued to broaden her repertoire over her long career, including many songs from other countries in Latin America and collaborations with other popular musicians.

Since the mid-1980s Sosa has continued to record and tour, arguably becoming Argentina's most famous and frequently honored musician. Her concert in New York's Carnegie Hall in 1987 ended with a ten-minute standing ovation. Though reportedly battling illness in the mid-1990s, she returned to a full touring and recording schedule in subsequent years, winning Latin Grammy Awards for Best Folk Album in 2000, 2003, and 2006. In addition to these works, many of her most important recordings are anthologized on the album *30 Años* (Polygram, 1994).

See also **Music: Popular Music and Dance.**

BIBLIOGRAPHY

Bernstein, Jane. "Thanks for My Weapons in Battle: My Voice and the Desire to Use It." In *Women's Voices across Musical Worlds*, edited by Jane Bernstein. Boston: Northeastern University Press, 2003.

Braceli, Rodolfo. *Mercedes Sosa: La Negra*. Buenos Aires: Editorial Sudamericana, 2003.

Brizuela, Leopoldo. *Cantar la vida: Reportajes a cinco cantantes argentinas: Gerónima Sequeida, Leda Valladares, Mercedes Sosa, Aimé Painé, Teresa Parodi*. Buenos Aires: Libreria El Ateneo Editorial, 1992.

JONATHAN RITTER

SOSA, SAMMY (1968–). The baseball slugger and right fielder Samuel "Sammy" Peralta Sosa grew up in the baseball hotbed of San Pedro de Macorís, Dominican Republic. After dropping his dreams of being a boxer, Sosa developed his youthful baseball skills on the edge of poverty, shining shoes and playing with makeshift equipment on unkempt fields. He made his major-league debut with the Texas Rangers in 1989, finished that season and two more with the Chicago White Sox, then was traded across town to the Chicago Cubs, where he set records and achieved celebrity status. In 1998 he won the National League Most Valuable Player Award and, with St. Louis Cardinal Mark McGwire, shared the *Sports Illustrated* Sportsmen of the Year award. His friendly competitions with McGwire for the most home runs caught national attention in 1998 and 1999. In those two years and in 2001, Sosa was the only player ever to hit sixty or more homers in three seasons. Though his strikeout totals remained high in those peak seasons, his batting average never dropped below .288 between 1998 and 2002. In August 2007 his sixteen-year career average was .273 and his home run total 604, which made him only the fifth baseball player in the history of the sport to have hit 600 or more homers.

Each year between 2001 and 2004 Sosa's batting average, runs, hits, home runs, runs batted in, and slugging percentage all declined. Those falling numbers, combined with his eight-game suspension in 2003 for using a corked bat in a regulation game, his sometimes inconsiderate treatment of his teammates, his violations of team rules, and frequent yet unproven charges of steroid use, led the Cubs to trade him to the Baltimore Orioles in 2005. That season—probably Sammy's worst since 1992—was a disappointment for both parties, and the Orioles cut him loose. After sitting out a season, Sosa signed a minor-league contract with the Texas Rangers before spring training in 2007, then made the parent club as the regular designated hitter. He remains a beloved hero in the Dominican Republic.

See also **Hispanics in the United States; Sports.**

BIBLIOGRAPHY

Ballard, Chris. "Is There Any Whammy Left in Sammy?" *Sports Illustrated* (March 5, 2007): 44–47.

Duncan, P. J. *Sosa! Baseball's Home Run Hero*, bilingual edition. New York: Simon and Schuster, 1998.

Gutman, Bill. *Sammy Sosa: A Biography*, bilingual edition. New York: Pocket Books, 1998.

Morris, Timothy. "Home-Run Race of 1998." In *Sport in American Culture: From Ali to X-Games*, edited by Joyce D. Duncan. Santa Barbara, CA: ABC-CLIO, 2004.

Morrison, John. *Sammy Sosa*. New York: Chelsea House, 2006.

Olmstead, Frank J. "Sammy Sosa." In *Latino and African American Athletes Today: A Biographical Dictionary*, edited by David L. Porter. Westport, CT: Greenwood Press, 2004.

Sosa, Sammy, with Marcos Bretón. *Sosa: An Autobiography*. New York: Warner Books, 2000.

JOSEPH L. ARBENA

SOSÚA. Sosúa, a Jewish agricultural settlement founded in 1940 on the north coast of the Dominican Republic. At the invitation of President Rafael Leonidas Trujillo, approximately one thousand European Jews, mostly Germans and Austrians, fled to the Dominican Republic to escape Nazi persecution. Trujillo hoped their presence would counteract the Haitian influence in his country and improve relations with the United States. The colony at Sosúa received funding from the U.S.-based Dominican Republic Settlement Association (DORSA) and became famous for the manufacture of cheese. However, the Jewish colonists failed to integrate successfully into Dominican life, and Sosúa has suffered from the emigration of second- and third-generation inhabitants to the United States. As of 2007 their numbers had dwindled to 25 families from a high of 125 in 1947.

See also **Jews.**

BIBLIOGRAPHY

Josef David Eichen, *Sosúa: Una colonia hebrea en la República Dominicana* (1980).

Judith Laikin Elkin, *Jews of the Latin American Republics* (1980).

Frances Henry, "Strangers in Paradise: The Jewish Enclave at Sosúa," and Kai P. Schoenhals, "An Extraordinary Migration: Jews in the Dominican Republic," in *Caribbean Review* 14, no. 4 (Fall 1985).

Additional Bibliography

Castanos Morales, Juan Luis. *Sosúa: Origen, fundacion y desarrollo.* Santo Domingo: Editora Buho, 2002.

KAREN RACINE

SOTO, HERNANDO DE (c. 1497–1542).

Hernando de Soto (*b.* c. 1496/1497; *d.* 21 May 1542), Spanish explorer and conquistador. Born in Villanveva de Barcarrota, Soto came to America in 1514 as a member of the Pedro Arias de Ávila expedition to Darién. By 1520, Soto had acquired substantial wealth from the slave trade in Central America. In 1532, he joined Francisco Pizarro in the conquest of Peru, and after accumulating significant wealth from the spoliation of Peru, returned to Spain in 1536. Soto had been present at the capture of Atahualpa at Cajamarca and afterward had taken Cuzco. Although Soto was at this time one of the richest conquistadores, on his return he sought the governorship of Florida. His expedition landed in Florida near modern Tampa in May 1539. Soto's search for a kingdom as wealthy as Tenochtitlán and Cuzco led his group from Tampa Bay to the modern states of Tennessee and Arkansas. The armada then moved to northwest Texas, and after traveling east to modern Georgia, marched west again to the Mississippi River, reaching Pánuco after crossing the Gulf of Mexico in makeshift boats. Soto died in Guachoya in present-day Louisiana. His corpse was thrown into the Mississippi River to keep the Indians from learning that he had died. Only his cruelty toward Indians compares with his foolhardy pursuit of the mirage of a flourishing city in the hinterland.

See also **Explorers and Exploration: Spanish America; Pizarro, Francisco.**

BIBLIOGRAPHY

The major Soto narratives are available in English: *Narratives of the Career of Hernando de Soto in the Conquest of Florida,* edited by Edward Gaylord Bourne, 2 vols. (1922); Garcilaso De La Vega's masterpiece, *La Florida del Inca* (1605) also in English as *The Florida of the Inca,* translated and edited by John Grier Varner and Jeannette Johnson Varner (1951); and *The Soto Chronicles: The Expedition of Hernando de Soto to North America in 1539–1543,* edited by Lawrence A. Clayton, Vernon James Knight, Jr., and Edward C. Moore (1993). For romanticized profiles of Soto, see Robert B. Cunninghame Graham, *Hernando de Soto* (1912); and Miguel Albornoz, *Hernando de Soto: Knight of the Americas,* translated by Bruce Boeglin (1986). On Soto's violence see "Hernando de Soto: Scourge of the Southeast," special section of *Archaeology* 42, no. 3 (May/June 1989): 26–39.

Additional Bibliography

Duncan, David Ewing. *Hernando de Soto: A Savage Quest in the Americas.* New York: Crown Publishers, 1995.

Galloway, Patricia Kay. *The Hernando de Soto Expedition: History, Historiography, and "Discovery" in the Southeast.* Lincoln: University of Nebraska Press, 2005.

JOSÉ RABASA

SOTO, JESÚS RAFAEL (1923–2005).

Jesús Rafael Soto (*b.* 5 June 1923; *d.* 14 January 2005), Venezuelan artist. Born in Ciudad Bolívar to a peasant family living on the edge of the Orinoco River, Soto spent his youth in the countryside with Indian companions. He began his career by painting posters for the local movie house. At age nineteen he won a scholarship to study at the Cristóbal Rojas School of Fine and Applied Arts in Caracas, where he met Alejandro Otero and Carlos Cruz Diez. He became interested in synthetic and geometric forms in the manner of Cézanne and the cubists. In 1947 he was named director of the School of Fine Arts in Maracaibo and held his first exhibition two years later at the Taller Libre de Arte in Caracas. In 1950 he traveled to Paris, where he became friendly with Vasarely, Duchamp, and Calder and exhibited at the Salon des Réalités Nouvelles in 1951 and 1954. In 1955 his relief *Spiral* (composed of a sheet of plexiglass separated from the background, which by repeating the same thumblike fingerprint pattern produced visual movement) was included in the exhibition *The Movement*, which officially launched the kinetic art movement. In 1958 he launched his *Vibration* series (formed by a black and white thin-striped surface in which twisted wires or squares were hung in front, producing a visual vibration whenever the viewer moved in front of them). That same year he created two kinetic murals for the Venezuelan Pavilion at the Brussels International Exposition.

In 1963 Soto's work in the São Paulo Bienal was awarded the Grand Wolf Prize. The following year he won the David Bright Prize at the Venice Biennale and the second place at the American Bienal in Córdoba, Argentina. In 1965 he received the first prize at the first Salón Pan-Americano of Painting in Cali, Colombia. He had major retrospectives at the Stedelijk Museum, Amsterdam (1968), and at the Museum of Modern Art of Paris, where he presented his *Penetrable* (1969), an environment constructed out of plastic wires in which the viewer could play.

In 1969 the Venezuelan government created the Jesús Soto Foundation. Four years later the Museum of Modern Art Jesús Soto opened in Ciudad Bolívar filled with Soto's own private collection, which he had donated to his native city. Soto also completed many public commissions, including kinetic murals for UNESCO in Paris (1970), and the *Esfera Virtual* for the Hilton Hotel in Caracas and the Olympic Sculpture Park in Seoul, South Korea (1988). In 1990 he became the fifth person ever to receive the UNESCO Picasso Medal, given to individuals whose work symbolizes improved relationships between countries. In 1995 he completed one of his most impressive installations, "Welcoming Flag," on the facade of the Phoenix Tower in Osaka, Japan. In 1996 he represented Venezuela at the twenty-third biennial of contemporary art in São Paulo, Brazil. In 2004 he took part in the "Inverted Utopias: Avant-Garde Art in Latin America" exhibition at the Houston Museum of Fine Arts. He died in Paris on January 14, 2005. Ten days later the first Brazilian retrospective of his work opened at the Centro Cultural Banco do Brasil in Rio de Janeiro.

See also **Art: The Twentieth Century.**

BIBLIOGRAPHY

Basilio, Miriam, et al., eds. *Latin American & Caribbean Art: MoMA at El Museo.* New York: El Museo del Barrio and the Museum of Modern Art, Distributed by D.A.P/Distributed Art Publishers, 2004.

Jiménez, Ariel. *Conversaciones con Jesús Soto.* Caracas: Fundación Cisneros, 2005.

Museo De Arte Contemporáneo De Caracas, *Soto: Cuarenta años de creación* (1983).

Rodríguez, Bélgica. *La pintura abstracta en Venezuela, 1945–1965* (1980).

Soto, Jesús Rafael. *Soto: A Retrospective Exhibition: The Solomon R. Guggenheim Museum, New York.* New York: Solomon R. Guggenheim Foundation, 1974.

BÉLGICA RODRÍGUEZ

SOTO, MARCO AURELIO (1846–1908).

Marco Aurelio Soto (*b.* 13 November 1846; *d.* 25 February 1908), president of Honduras (1876–1883). Born in Tegucigalpa, the son of Máximo Soto and Francisca Martínez, Soto studied at universities in Honduras and Guatemala. Soto represented the best of the second generation of Liberal politicians who governed in Central America beginning in the 1870s. The Soto administration was characterized by an emphasis on scientific progress, education, foreign investment, and infrastructural development typical of the positivist governments that came to power after overthrowing Conservative regimes.

Soto had very strong connections to the Liberal Guatemalan government of Justo Rufino Barrios, whom he served at the cabinet level as minister of foreign affairs in the mid-1870s. In addition, he and Ramón Rosa had studied together with Barrios at the University of San Carlos in Guatemala. It was natural for Barrios to support Soto in his efforts to remove Ponciano Leiva and José María Medina as contenders for the presidency of Honduras, and at the second Conference of Chingo on 17 February 1876, Barrios and Andrés Valle of El Salvador signed a pact to do so. Meanwhile, Medina defeated Leiva at the Battle of El Naranjo on 22 February 1876, and on 8 June 1876 Medina and Soto signed the Convenio de Cedros, agreeing to name General Marcelino Mejía interim president. (Mejía served as president one week.) Soto followed as provisional president on 27 August 1876 and became constitutional president on 30 May 1877. He remained in power until 9 May 1883, when he resigned because of differences with Barrios.

Soto's administration dedicated itself to the economic progress and developmental goals espoused by Comtian positivism. The political and philosophical strength of the Liberal regime was sufficient to allow Soto to be relatively lenient with his former Conservative enemies. He was politically tolerant as a statesman, yet he did not apply this tolerance to people belonging to the lower sector of society, whom he considered lazy and without motivation. He did open a national library and initiate free public education, which had been previously decreed several times but never implemented. At the same time, Soto lamented the military interventionism in Central American civilian governments and institutionalized the armed forces on 21 December 1876 in an effort to check the military's power while defining its social and political role. These and other policies culminated in a new Liberal constitution in 1880 and the establishment of Liberal Tegucigalpa as the permanent national capital the same year.

There was also substantial economic progress during Soto's presidency. He personally helped revive the declining silver-mining industry of Tegucigalpa, particularly the El Rosario mine (Rosario Mining Co.). The government also founded a mint (Casa de la Moneda), which acted as a central bank. Soto opened up the country to foreign investment as a matter of policy, a liberal practice that paved the way for the banana boom of the early twentieth century. Infrastructural improvements accompanied economic reforms, and Soto's regime created a national postal service and a national telegraph service that provided relatively rapid and often instant communication in a country known for its regional isolation. Soto resigned in 1883, having asserted both Tegucigalpa's primacy over Comayagua and the Liberal Party's agenda as national policy. His chosen successor, Luis Bográn Baraona, continued to support Liberal oligarchical interests.

See also **Barrios, Justo Rufino; Honduras; Rosa, Ramón.**

BIBLIOGRAPHY

Rómulo E. Durón y Gamero, *Biografía del Doctor Marco Aurelio Soto* (1944).

Charles Abbey Brand, *The Background of Capitalist Underdevelopment: Honduras to 1913* (1972).

Kenneth V. Finney, *Precious Metal Mining and the Modernization of Honduras: In Quest of El Dorado, 1880–1900* (1973).

Gene S. Yeager, *The Honduran Foreign Debt, 1825–1953* (1975).

Luis Mariñas Otero, *Honduras* (1983).

Additional Bibliography

Zelaya, Gustavo. *El legado de la Reforma Liberal.* Tegucigalpa: Editorial Guaymuras, 1996.

JEFFREY D. SAMUELS

SOTO ALFARO, BERNARDO (1854–1931).

Bernardo Soto Alfaro (*b.* 12 February 1854; *d.* 28 January 1931), president of Costa Rica (1885–1889). As first designate, Soto assumed the presidency in 1885 following the death of Próspero Fernández, and a year later he was elected to a full four-year term. Continuing the liberal policies of his two immediate predecessors, Fernández and Tomás Guardia, Soto emphasized educational and social reforms. His Fundamental Law of Public Instruction (1886) committed the nation to free, compulsory, and secular education. The education budget was tripled during his administration. Other notable achievements included the construction of the National Library and the Asilo Chapuí mental hospital. Soto demanded complete separation of church and state, which resulted in the closing of the Jesuit University of Santo Tomás.

See also **Costa Rica; Guardia Gutiérrez, Tomás.**

BIBLIOGRAPHY

Dana G. Munro, *The Five Republics of Central America* (1918).

Chester Lloyd Jones, *Costa Rica and Civilization in the Caribbean* (1935; 2d ed., 1941).

John Hale Et Al., *Costa Rica en el siglo XIX* (1972).

Additional Bibliography

Díaz Arias, David. *Construcción de un estado moderno: Política, estado e identidad nacional en Costa Rica, 1821–1914.* San José: Editorial de la Universidad de Costa Rica, 2005.

Yashar, Deborah J. *Demanding Democracy: Reform and Reaction in Costa Rica and Guatemala, 1870s–1950s.* Stanford, CA: Stanford University Press, 1997.

THOMAS M. LEONARD

SOTOMAYOR VALDÉS, RAMÓN

(1830–1903). Ramón Sotomayor Valdés (April 3, 1830–July 14, 1903) was a highly regarded journalist, diplomat, and historian in nineteenth-century Chile. Sotomayor was born in the year Diego Portales established Chile's famous conservative republic, and his public life was heavily influenced by his country's early republican history. Like many of his generation of statesmen (often referred to as the Chilean Generation of 1842), and his was a graduate of both the Instituto Nacional (National Institute) and the Universidad de Chile (University of Chile). Unlike most of his generational peers, however, Sotomayor was a staunch conservative and defender of Portales.

In the 1850s he wrote for and edited several newspapers in Santiago and Valparaíso, including *El Conservador*, which in 1857 broke with fellow conservative President Manuel Montt over the question of church-state relations. During the 1859 civil war that followed, Sotomayor helped organize the *montoneras* (rural bands of mounted militia) that rose unsuccessfully against Montt's government. In the more relaxed political atmosphere of the 1860s Sotomayor was tapped for diplomatic service, serving as Chile's Ambassador to Mexico (1863–1866) and Bolivia (1867–1871). As a historian Sotomayor is best known for his *Historia de Chile, bajo el gobierno del Jeneral Don Joaquín Prieto* (Santiago de Chile: Imprenta Esmeralda, 1900–1903), which is recognized as a classic example of conservative historiography in Chile.

See also **Chile: The Nineteenth Century; Montt Torres, Manuel; Portales Palazuelos, Diego José Pedro Víctor.**

BIBLIOGRAPHY

Works by Ramón Sotomayor Valdés

Campaña del ejército chileno contra la Confederación Perú-Boliviana en 1837. Santiago de Chile: Imprenta Cervantes, 1896.

Estudio histórico de Bolivia bajo la administración del jeneral Don José María de Achá. Santiago de Chile: Imprenta Andrés Bello, 1874.

La legación de Chile en Bolivia desde septiembre de 1867 hasta principios de 1871, 2nd edition. Santiago de Chile: Imprenta de San José, 1912.

JAMES A. WOOD

SOUBLETTE, CARLOS (1789–1870).

Carlos Soublette (*b.* 15 December 1789; *d.* 11 February 1870), president of Venezuela (1837–1839, 1843–1847). Between 1810 and 1869, Soublette served Venezuelan governments as a soldier and a civilian. Perhaps no other military officer of his generation equaled his reputation for honesty and efficiency. Soublette served twice as president, between 1837 and 1839, following the resignation of José María Vargas, and between 1843 and 1847. A staunch ally of José Antonio Páez and a Conservative oligarch, he earned a reputation as a cautious but able administrator. His career as a politician included other important positions: vice president (1821, 1836–1837, 1839–1841), minister of war and marine (1825–1827, 1841–1842), and minister plenipotentiary to Europe (1835–1836). Forced into exile in 1848 as a result of the collapse of the Páez faction, Soublette returned in 1858, after the downfall of the Monagas regime, and served in various capacities as a military officer and as a senator, deputy, and minister between 1859 and 1869.

See also **Páez, José Antonio; Vargas, José María.**

BIBLIOGRAPHY

Francisco González Guinán, *Historia contemporánea de Venezuela*, vol. 3 (1954).

Juan Bautista Querales D., comp., *Estudios sobre el General Carlos Soublette* (1977) and *Soublette y la prensa de su época* (1980).

Ligia Delgado and Magaly Burguera, comps., *Carlos Soublette, correspondencia*, 3 vols. (1981).

Additional Bibliography

Carvallo, Gastón. *Próceres, caudillos y rebeldes: Crisis del sistema de dominación en Venezuela, 1830–1908.* Caracas: Grijalbo, 1994.

Zahler, Reuben. "Honor, Corruption, and Legitimacy: Liberal Projects in the Early Venezualan Republic, 1821–50." Ph.D. diss., University of Chicago, 2005.

WINTHROP R. WRIGHT

SOULOUQUE, FAUSTIN ÉLIE

(1785–1867). Faustin Élie Soulouque (*b.* 1785; *d.* 1867), president of Haiti (1 March 1847–28 August 1849), emperor of Haiti (29 August 1849–15 January 1859). Faustin Soulouque was the fourth president selected to govern by the Haitian army between 1844 and 1859. Faustin, an illiterate, conducted an extremely incompetent administration. In 1847 he was elected by the Assembly to succeed President Jean-Baptiste Riché because he was perceived as being docile, and thus easily manipulated. Once in power, however, he began a twelve-year regime of terror conducted by his secret police.

A plot to eliminate him in his first year in office failed. Following the example of Jean Jacques Dessalines, in his second year in office, Soulouque named himself Emperor Faustin I and created a peerage drawn from black generals that included 4 princes, 59 dukes, 90 counts, 215 barons and 30 knights. These men had no governmental or bureaucratic functions to perform; they were merely reflections of Soulouque's desire for grandeur.

To legitimate his empire, in 1849 Soulouque created his own constitution. Under Soulouque, the Haitian economy was completely destroyed. He lived like an over-indulgent aristocrat, defaulting on the national debt and increasing the deficit of the Haitian government. Soulouque's desire for more power motivated him to lead costly wars against the Dominican Republic, which resulted in the intermittent occupation of Dominican territory. During his reign, Soulouque openly practiced and encouraged voodoo (*vodun*). It was the first time in Haitian history that voodoo flourished openly, with official approval. Nevertheless, his unpopularity and the opposition to his regime increased until the end of 1858. In January 1859 he fled Haiti to escape the forces of General Nicolas Geffrard, who became his successor.

See also **Dessalines, Jean Jacques; Geffrard, Fabre Nicolas; Haiti.**

BIBLIOGRAPHY

Selden Rodman, *Haiti: The Black Republic* (1955).

Cyril L. R. James, *The Black Jacobins,* 2d ed. (1963).

James G. Leyburn, *The Haitian People* (1966). A more recent work is Michel-Rolph Trouillot, *Haiti: State Against Nation* (1990).

Additional Bibliography

Dorigny, Marcel. *Haïti, première république noire.* Saint-Denis, France: Société Française d'Histoire d'Outre-Mer, 2003.

DARIÉN DAVIS

SOUSA, GABRIEL SOARES DE

(c. 1540–1592). Gabriel Soares de Sousa (*b.* c. 1540s; *d.* 1592), Brazilian colonist. Nineteenth-century historian Francisco Adolfo de Varnhagen (1816–1878) determined that Sousa was the author of the seminal work *Tratado descriptivo do Brasil em 1587.* The original manuscript was lost, but with more than twenty copies, Varnhagen was able to establish the text and the identity of its author. In 1569, Sousa went to Bahia, where he acquired ownership of a sugar mill as well as several other rural estates. He lived in Brazil for seventeen years, during which he took note of everything he thought worth remembering. While in Madrid in March 1587, Sousa offered his work to Cristóvão de Moura. This manuscript was known in Portugal as early as 1589, when Pedro de Mariz (*d.* 1615) quoted it in the second edition of his *Diálogos de varia historia.*

Sousa's treatise is divided into two parts. In the first one, *Roteiro geral da costa brasílica,* he describes the Brazilian coast from the Amazon to the Río de la Plata; in the second part, *Memorial e declaração das grandezas da Bahia,* he analyzes the Government General in Salvador. This second part, the most frequently quoted by historians, documents the establishment of the colonial government by Tomé de Sousa, describes the city of Salvador, and enumerates all the sugar mills located in the Bahian Reconcavo.

See also **Brazil: The Colonial Era, 1500-1808; Sousa, Tomé de.**

BIBLIOGRAPHY

Francisco Adolfo De Varnhagen, *Historia geral do Brasil,* 5 vols. 8th ed. (1975).

Massaud Moisés, *História da literatura brasileira,* vol. 1, *Origens, barroco, arcadismo* (1983).

Additional Bibliography

Amado, Janaina. "Mythic Origins: Caramuru and the Founding of Brazil." *Hispanic American Historical Review* 80, no.4 (Nov. 2000): 783–811.

MARIA BEATRIZ NIZZA DA SILVA

Additional Bibliography

Neves, Cylaine Maria das. "A vila de São Paulo de Piratininga: fundação e representação." Ph.D. Thesis. Universidade de São Paulo, 2004.

MARIA BEATRIZ NIZZA DA SILVA

SOUSA, IRINEU EVANGELISTA DE.

See **Mauá, Visconde de.**

SOUSA, MARTIM AFONSO DE

(1500–1564). Martim Afonso de Sousa (*b.* 1500; *d.* 1564), Portuguese navigator and explorer. In 1531 he was the commander in chief of a naval and military expedition to Brazil whose purpose was fighting the French who were trying to settle along the Brazilian coast. Sousa also intended to explore the rivers and the hinterland and to create Portuguese settlements. He was given full jurisdiction: power to appoint governors, to choose notaries and justice officials, and to grant land under the Portuguese formula of *sesmarias*. He left Lisbon with five ships and approximately five hundred men (sailors, troops, and settlers). He fought the French on the Pernambuco coast and, sailing south, stayed three months in Rio de Janeiro Bay in order to acquire food supplies and two more ships. The expedition went as far as Río de la Plata. Pero de Sousa (c. 1500–c. 1539), Martim's brother, went up this river with thirty men to take possession of the territory for the Portuguese crown.

Returning to São Vicente, Pero de Sousa was sent to Portugal with news for King João III. Martim Afonso returned to Portugal later in July or August 1533, after having created the first *vila* of São Vicente, where the sugar enterprise was begun. Sousa received a donation from the king of one hundred leagues on the Brazilian coast.

See also **Explorers and Exploration: Brazil.**

BIBLIOGRAPHY

Carlos Malheiro Dias, ed., *História da colonização portuguesa no Brasil* (1921–1924).

Leslie Bethell, ed., *Colonial Brazil* (1987).

SOUSA, OTÁVIO TARQÜÍNIO DE

(1889–1959). Otávio Tarqüínio de Sousa (*b.* 7 September 1889; *d.* 22 December 1959), Brazilian historian. Born in Rio de Janeiro, Sousa graduated from Rio's Faculdade de Ciências Jurídicas e Sociais in 1907. He held high positions in public bureaucracies from the 1910s to 1932, after which he turned earlier interests into a career in literary journalism, publishing, and historiography, achieving his reputation in the latter two. He succeeded Gilberto de Mello Freyre and preceded Afonso Arinos de Melo Franco in the direction (1939–1959) of the Coleção Documentos Brasileiros, the pivotal nationalist series published by José Olympio. He also edited the *Revista do Brasil* (1938–1943).

Sousa's own works, devoted to the key statesmen of the era from 1822 to 1850, suggest the preoccupation with the nation-state common to the period. During his Coleção stewardship over ninety volumes were published by such figures as Freyre, Jõao Camilo de Oliveira Torres, Cassiano Ricardo, Luís Viana Filho, Nelson Werneck Sodré, Luís da Câmara Cascudo, Afonso de E. Taunay, Afonso Arinos de Melo Franco, and Sérgio Buarque de Holanda. Sousa's role in the nationalist milieu was central to the reconstruction and rehabilitation of Brazilian studies from the 1930s through the 1950s.

See also **Brazil: Since 1889; Freyre, Gilberto (de Mello); Melo Franco, Afonso Arinos de; Sodré, Nelson Werneck.**

BIBLIOGRAPHY

Otávio Tarqüínio De Sousa's works include *Bernardo Pereira de Vasconcellos e seu tempo* (1933), *Evaristo da Veiga* (1939), *História de dois golpes de estado* (1939), *Diogo Antônio Feijó* (1942), *José Bonifacio, 1763–1838* (1945), *A vida de D. Pedro I*, 3 vols. (1952), and *História dos fundadores do império do Brasil*, 10 vols. (1957–1958). Another helpful source is José Honório Rodrigues, "Otávio Tarqüínio de Sousa," in *Hispanic American Historical Review* 40, no. 3 (August 1960): 431–434.

Additional Bibliography

Iglésias, Francisco. *Historiadores do Brasil: Capítulos de historiografia brasileira.* Rio de Janeiro: Editora Nova Fronteira, 2000.

JEFFREY D. NEEDELL

SOUSA, PAULINO JOSÉ SOARES DE. *See* Uruguai, Visconde do.

SOUSA, TOMÉ DE (c. 1502–1579).

Tomé de Sousa (*b.* c. 1502; *d.* 1579) first governor-general of Brazil. Of noble birth, Sousa was the illegitimate son of a prior. A descendant of King Afonso III, he spent his youth at the royal court under the patronage of his cousin, the count of Castenheira, Antônio de Ataíde. As a soldier he fought in Morocco and participated in the spice trade with India. Appointed the first governor-general of Brazil, he arrived in Brazil in 1549 with six ships and one thousand settlers, including sailors, soldiers, six Jesuit missionaries, artisans, carpenters, stone masons, and criminals. His job was to centralize royal control over Brazil, defend the territory from French pirates, and pacify and Christianize the Indians. The Portuguese settler Caramurú met the new governor and promised an Indian alliance.

Sousa purchased land from the heirs of Francisco Pereira Coutinho, the Donatário of Bahia for the seat of a new capital and center of royal government in Brazil. Salvador, the new capital, was built on a location more suitable for defense. The governor provided a good example by helping personally with the construction. He then sent the chief justice and treasurer to the other captaincies to check on abuses and regularize administration, but he also went on an inspection tour of all the captaincies except Pernambuco. The new governor made land grants to settlers and expelled hostile Indians to make the settlement more attractive for European colonization. Livestock was introduced from the Atlantic islands, while *engenhos* (sugar mills) were built and fortified. Market days were established to facilitate trade with the Indians. A customhouse was erected in Salvador. Sousa fortified unprotected towns and patrolled the coastal waters to keep them free of foreign interlopers.

Tomé de Sousa had a close relationship with Manuel da Nóbrega and the Jesuits. He relied on Jesuit reports for information and sent Jesuits on inspection tours of the captaincies. During his governorship, forts and courts were established, new towns were laid out, and missions, churches, and schools were founded.

See also **Brazil: The Colonial Era, 1500–1808; Caramurú; Jesuits; Nóbrega, Manuel da.**

BIBLIOGRAPHY

Pedro De Azevedo, "Documentos para a história do Brasil—Thomé de Sousa e sua família," *Revista de historia* 3–4 (1914–1915): 68–81.

Ruth Laphan Butler, "Thomé de Sousa, First Governor General of Brazil, 1549–1553," *Mid-America* 24, no. 4 (1942): 229–251.

E. Bradford Burns, *A History of Brazil* (1980).

Bailey W. Diffie, *A History of Colonial Brazil, 1500–1792* (1987).

Additional Bibliography

Mariz de Moraes, José. *Nóbrega: O primeiro jesuita do Brasil.* Rio de Janeiro: Relume Dumará, 2000.

PATRICIA MULVEY

SOUSA, WASHINGTON LUÍS PEREIRA DE. *See* Luís Pereira de Sousa, Washington.

SOUTHERN CONE. Southern Cone, a term

applied to the three southernmost nations of Latin America: Argentina, Chile, and Uruguay. The expression "Southern Cone" has its source in the appearance of the southern tip of Latin America as seen on a map, but the bond between the three nations that comprise this region extends beyond cartography. Argentina, Chile, and Uruguay share similarly temperate climates and geographic features, as well as a rich supply of natural resources. These features, along with the presence of a population that was unique among the Latin American nations in being predominantly of European origin, contributed to the emergence of the Southern Cone nations as social and economic powers in the late nineteenth century.

For the first half of the twentieth century, the Southern Cone countries consistently led the turbulent continent of Latin America in economic growth and democratic development. The United States and the European powers viewed Argentina, Chile, and Uruguay as their most profitable and reliable economic and political allies, and other Latin American nations envied the level of modernization of these three nations.

This condition changed abruptly, however, with the onset of economic difficulties after World War II and particularly with the violent upheavals of the 1970s, which brought to power repressive and undemocratic regimes. Growing nationalism and political volatility isolated the Southern Cone culturally, politically, and economically from its traditional partners. In the 1990s Argentina was hit by a dire economic crisis due to hyperinflation and international debt, leading to riots and chaos by the early years of the twenty-first century. With the election of President Néstor Kirchner (b. 1950) in 2003, Argentina restructured its international debt and its economy slowly began to improve. In Chile, the late 1980s and early 1990s brought more freedom to the people, and this continues under the rule of Chile's first female president, Michelle Bachelet (b. 1951), who was elected in 2006. Uruguay's economy was adversely affected by the Argentinean crisis in the 1990s, yet its overall financial situation remained relatively stable. Its government also leaned toward the Left, especially in the 2004 elections, which were dominated by former socialists, communists, and various left-wing politicians.

See also **Argentina: Geography.**

BIBLIOGRAPHY

Arceneaux, Craig L. *Bounded Missions: Military Regimes and Democratization in the Southern Cone and Brazil.* University Park: Pennsylvania State University Press, 2001.

Roniger, Luis, and Mario Sznajder. *The Legacy of Human Rights Violations in the Southern Cone: Argentina, Chile, and Uruguay.* New York: Oxford University Press, 1999.

Sater, William F. *The Southern Cone Nations* (1984).

Silva, Hernán A. *Historia de las migraciones limítrofes en el Cono Sur de América: Argentina, Bolivia, Brasil, Chile, Paraguay, y Uruguay.* Mexico: Instituto Panamericano de Geografía e Historia, 2002.

Whitaker, Arthur Preston. *The United States and the Southern Cone: Argentina, Chile, and Uruguay.* (1976).

JOHN DUDLEY

SOUTHERN PERU COPPER CORPORATION.

Southern Peru Copper Corporation, a joint venture of the American Smelting and Refining Company, Cerro de Pasco, and other U.S. corporations that commenced mining operations in Peru in 1952. Over the next two decades Southern gained rights to and developed three great copper mines: Quellaveco, Toquepala, and Cuajone. Located in the southern departments of Moquegua and Tacna, these mines made Southern one of the largest and most profitable mining and smelting firms in the world.

Southern financial's gains evoked considerable nationalist resentment in Peru. In the 1960s and 1970s the civilian government of Fernando Belaúnde Terry and the revolutionary military government of Juan Velasco Alvarado criticized the company for its repatriation of profits, investment policy, and low tax rate. By reaching an accord with the Velasco regime, Southern, unlike other foreign mining firms in Peru, avoided expropriation.

See also **Mining: Modern.**

BIBLIOGRAPHY

Charles T. Goodsell, *American Corporations and Peruvian Politics* (1974).

David G. Becker, *The New Bourgeoisie and the Limits of Dependency: Mining, Class, and Power in "Revolutionary" Peru* (1983).

Elizabeth Dore, *The Peruvian Mining Industry: Growth, Stagnation, and Crisis* (1988).

Additional Bibliography

Balvín Díaz, Doris, Juan Tejedo Huamán, and Humberto Lozada Castro. *Agua, minería y contaminación: El caso Southern Perú.* Ilo: Ediciones Labor, 1995.

Martín Sánchez, Juan. *La revolución peruana: Ideología y práctica política de un gobierno militar, 1968-1975.* Sevilla: Consejo Superior de Investigaciones Científicas, Escuela de Estudios Hispano-Americanos: Universidad de Sevilla: Diputación de Sevilla, 2002.

STEVEN J. HIRSCH

SOUTHEY, ROBERT

SOUTHEY, ROBERT (1774–1843). Robert Southey (*b.* 12 August 1774; *d.* 21 March 1843), British poet laureate, epic poet, playwright, and historian who wrote a three-volume *History of Brazil*.

Southey was born in Bristol, England, to a family of farmers and tradesmen and educated at Oxford. In 1800, he spent the first of two extended visits with his uncle, the Reverend Herbert Hill, in Portugal. Hill had begun to amass a collection of manuscripts and notes on Portugal and its colonies. Southey became interested in writing a history of Brazil as part of a set of historical volumes on Portugal, Spain, the Portuguese Empire in Asia, the Jesuits in Japan, and monasticism. Begun in 1807, the *History of Brazil* was the only work completed in the set.

Detailing Brazilian history from 1500 to 1808, the three volumes of the *History of Brazil* were published in 1810, 1817, and 1819. Criticized for incorporating too much detail and too little interpretation, Southey was nonetheless recognized for the tremendous scope of his work by the queen of Portugal, who honored him in 1839 by naming him knight of the Order of the Tower and Sword.

See also **Brazil: The Colonial Era, 1500–1808.**

BIBLIOGRAPHY

Geoffrey Carnall, *Robert Southey* (1964).

Jack Simmons, *Southey* (1968).

Robert Southey, *The History of Brazil*, 3 vols., edited by Herbert Cahn (1971).

Lionel Madden, *Robert Southey: The Critical Heritage* (1972).

Kenneth Curry, *Southey* (1975).

Additional Bibliography

Fulford, Tim. *Romanticism and Millenarianism*. New York: Palgrave, 2002.

Storey, Mark. *Robert Southey: A Life*. Oxford: Oxford University Press, 1997.

MARY JO MILES

SOUZA, LUIZA ERUNDINA DE

SOUZA, LUIZA ERUNDINA DE (1934–). Luiza Erundina de Souza (*b.* 30 November 1934), Brazilian political figure and first woman mayor of South America's largest city, São Paulo, which has a population of 12 million (1989) and provides one-third of Brazil's GNP. Born in the small town of Uiraúna, in the backlands of the northeastern state of Paraíba, Erundina, as she is known, was one of ten children. An unmarried Catholic who considered becoming a nun, she trained as a social worker and in 1971 moved to São Paulo (which, despite its location in the southeast of Brazil, has the largest concentration of Northeasterners of any Brazilian city, the result of migration due to drought and unemployment in the Northeast). Politically active first in the struggle to unionize social workers, in 1979 she became a founding member of the opposition Worker's Party (Partido dos Trabalhadores—PT), which she later represented on the São Paulo City Council and then as a state assemblywoman. A self-proclaimed Marxist who has described capitalism as "unjust and inhuman by nature," Erundina successfully ran for mayor of São Paulo in 1988 on a platform defending the rights of the landless, the working class, and the poor. She held office until 1992, when she served briefly in the cabinet of President Itamar Franco but experienced constant conflict with her own party, the PT. Always outspoken, she denounced corruption within the government. In 1994 she ran for a Senate seat, once again without proper support of her party, and was not elected. In 1998 she decided to ally herself with the PSB (Brazilian Socialist Party), and with this party she was elected in 2000 as a federal deputy from São Paulo, a position that she won again in 2002 and again in 2006. In 2006 she was also an outspoken opponent of a proposed 91 percent pay raise for members of parliament.

See also **Brazil, Political Parties: Workers Party (PT).**

BIBLIOGRAPHY

Hanchard, Michael George. *Racial Politics in Contemporary Brazil*. Durham, NC: Duke University Press, 1999.

House, Richard. "São Paulo's Marxist Mayor Adjusts Her Tactics," *Washington Post*, 10 January 1989, A20.

Margolis, Mac. "Brazilians Turning Out Ruling Party's Mayors," *Washington Post*, 17 November 1988, A27.

Nêumanne, José. *Erundina: A mulher que veio com a chuva* (1989).

Patarra, Ivo. *O governo Luiza Erundina: Cronologia de quatro anos de administração do PT na Cidade de São Paulo, de 1989 a 1992*. São Paulo: Gereçao Editorial, 1996.

Riding, Alan. "A Mayor Bent on Inverting Priorities," *New York Times*, 18 March 1989, 4.

Singer, Paul. *Um governo de esquerda para todos: Luiza Erundina na prefeitura de São Paulo, 1989–1992.* São Paulo: Editora Brasilense, 1996.

DAPHNE PATAI

Maligo, Pedro. "Márcio Souza and His Predecessors," in *Tropical Paths: Essays on Modern Brazilian Literature,* edited by Randall Johnson (1993), pp. 53–75.

Stern, Irwin, ed. *Dictionary of Brazilian Literature.* New York: Greenwood Press, 1998.

PEDRO MALIGO

SOUZA, MÁRCIO GONÇALVES BENTES

(1946–). Márcio Gonçalves Bentes Souza (*b.* March 1946), Brazilian writer. A native of the state of Amazonas, Souza has been one of the most influential Brazilian writers since 1977, when his best-selling *Galvez, imperador do Acre* (*The Emperor of the Amazon,* 1980) was first published. Before then he had been a movie critic in his hometown of Manaus (early 1960s), a journalist in São Paulo (1965–1973), and a filmmaker, theater director, and playwright again in Manaus in the mid-1970s. A highly politicized author, Souza belongs to the generation of Brazilian artists who struggled under the constraints imposed by the military dictatorship between 1964 and the early 1980s. Although his reputation is due mostly to the sarcastic tone of his novels of Amazonian inspiration, including *Mad Maria* (1980; Eng. transl. 1985) and *A resistível ascensão do Boto Tucuxi* (1982), the core of his ideological and aesthetic beliefs can be found in *A expressão amazonense: Do colonialismo ao neocolonialismo* (1978). In this history of the literature of his native state, Souza develops the concept of cultural extractivism, according to which Amazonia has always been exploited aesthetically by authors in search of the exotic for its own sake, without any commitment to the region's social or political realities. He has served in several public administrative positions, including director of planning for the Cultural Foundation of Amazonas and, from 1995 to 2002, president of the Brazilian National Foundation of Art. In 1997 the first part of his *Cronicas do Grão-Pará e Rio Negro* was published; it includes *Lealdade* (1997), *Desordem* (2001), and *Revolta* (2005).

See also **Literature: Brazil.**

BIBLIOGRAPHY

Gondim, Neide. *Sima, Beirado e Galvez, imperador do Acre: Ficção e história.* Manaus, Brazil: Editora da Universidade do Amazonas, 1996.

SOUZA PRATA, SEBASTIÃO BERNARDES DE.   *See* **Grande Otelo.**

SOVIET–LATIN AMERICAN RELATIONS.

Soviet–Latin American relations often commanded the world's attention during the cold war because of the competitive relationship between the United States and the Soviet Union. From the 1960s until the 1980s, the Soviet Union expanded its diplomatic, political, and military presence in Latin America in spite of the huge distance that separated the two regions and the limited common interests throughout their histories.

Tsarist Russia's relations with Latin America began through the visits to the region of famous writers and scientists, including G. I. Langsdorf and F. P. Vrangel, when there were no official relations. Russia did not establish diplomatic relations with Latin America until late in the nineteenth century, and then only with Argentina (1885), Uruguay (1887), and Mexico (1890). Russia's principal immigration into Latin America was to Argentina and Brazil.

After the Russian Revolution only two states recognized the USSR before World War II: Mexico and Uruguay, and only Mexico exchanged diplomatic representatives with the USSR (from 1924 to 1930). From the beginning, Soviet governments capitalized on two political issues in the region: capitalist exploitation and foreign domination. Soviet-sponsored Communist parties attempted to mobilize industrial and agricultural workers against the "exploitation" imposed by the "ruling classes," and they rallied support against "foreign domination," usually by the United States.

The USSR's most important relations with Latin America in the interwar period were through the Communist International (Comintern), which was dissolved in 1943 as a concession to Stalin's Western allies in World War II. During the Comintern's lifetime Soviet leaders made the unconvincing argument that it was an independent international organization although it was, in fact, run by the executive organs of the Communist Party of the Soviet Union (CPSU). By the late 1930s, Communist parties, which had been established in most countries in Latin America, controlled trade unions in Chile, Cuba, and a few other countries but had limited electoral support, usually far less than 15 percent. Following Moscow's lead, the local parties sometimes favored overthrowing local governments, but mostly they participated in elections. The latter strategy was most prominent during the Popular Front period in the late 1930s in Chile and a little later in Cuba. Soviet foreign policies and the foreign policies of the Communist parties were virtually identical.

Toward the end of World War II most governments in the region recognized the USSR for the first time. At that time Argentina and Uruguay established relations, and Mexico resumed them; these three countries alone maintained relations during the cold war that began in the late 1940s. Although the Comintern no longer existed, Moscow and the Latin American Communist parties continued to maintain close ties. They included contacts with the radical nationalist revolution in Guatemala (1954), in which the Communists participated as a minority force, that was put down with U.S. support.

The Cuban Revolution of 1959 was a watershed in Soviet relations with Latin America. Fidel Castro was competing with the local Communist Party, most of whose members did not support him in his successful overthrow of Fulgencio Batista. When the United States imposed economic sanctions on the Cuban revolutionary regime, Moscow purchased Cuban sugar and provided oil and arms to Castro in 1960, permitting him to survive. Castro and the USSR disagreed over Cuban domestic policy and revolutionary tactics in Latin America, but by early 1970 Castro had adopted the Soviet political model and consistently backed Soviet foreign policy with regard to China and armed interventions in Africa, and through Cuba's leadership of the nonaligned movement. Soviet assistance mounted to billions of rubles in subsidies for Cuban sugar and nickel and provision of Soviet oil, trade-deficit financing, and technical assistance, as well as almost all of Cuba's military equipment and arms.

The Soviet effort to establish medium-range nuclear missiles in Cuba created the threat of a global nuclear war in October 1962. As became public only many years later, the Soviet commanding general had authority to use tactical nuclear weapons in the event of a U.S. invasion. President John F. Kennedy forced Soviet chairman Nikita Khrushchev to remove the missiles under threat of military action in exchange for a U.S. commitment not to invade Cuba.

Perhaps the Communists' greatest electoral success in Latin America was in Chile; in 1970, the party helped elect Salvador Allende Gossens, a socialist, to the presidency and was the second party in the government. The USSR gave strong moral support to Allende but was unwilling to provide the hard-currency grants he needed to survive. Fearful of a coup, the Chilean Communists tried to restrain Allende's most radical followers. The latter's leftist policies alienated the large Chilean middle class and facilitated the military's takeover and Allende's death in 1973.

In 1979 the Sandinistas, a radical nationalist revolutionary movement, overthrew the dictatorial Somoza regime in Nicaragua while the Nicaraguan Communists stood by and watched. Soviet General Secretary Leonid Brezhnev agilely shifted support to the Sandinistas. When the latter's relations with the United States deteriorated and civil conflict fueled by the Reagan administration began, Moscow provided economic and military assistance of more than $1 billion a year, an important sum but far less than Cuba received.

Moscow also backed the Farabundo Martí Front for National Liberation (FMLN), a radical political movement in El Salvador whose main foreign support came from Cuba and other leftist third-world governments. The Communist Party joined the Front late, as one of five guerrilla formations in an inconclusive armed struggle that continued into the early 1990s.

Radical nationalists took over the island of Grenada in 1979. They wooed Moscow ardently and won material support for their Marxist-oriented party, the New Jewel Movement, as well as arms, presumably to defend the movement from domestic or foreign enemies. After the popular leader Maurice Bishop was assassinated (1983) and some of his authoritarian lieutenants took over, President

Fidel Castro greets Mikhail Gorbachev on an official visit to Cuba, 1989. Cuba suffered from the withdrawal of Soviet aid, which had long supported the Cuban economy, after the collapse of the Soviet Union in 1991. © SYGMA/CORBIS

Ronald Reagan ordered an invasion of the island, which ended the New Jewel Movement and its relations with the Soviet Union.

Soviet trade with Latin America was minuscule before the 1960s. Prior to that time most Soviet interest was expressed in attempts to develop trade with the Río de la Plata countries (Argentina, Paraguay, and Uruguay) and Brazil, seeking to purchase grain, coffee, cocoa, wool, hides, and the like. When many Latin American nations established diplomatic relations with Moscow beginning in the late 1960s, Soviet buyers began to show interest in nonferrous metals from Peru and Bolivia. The difficulty was that none of the Latin American countries, except Cuba and Nicaragua, where trade was subsidized, were interested in Soviet exports. The USSR has never been able to develop a consistently favorable trade

balance with Latin America. Most Soviet trade with the area's market economies has consisted of Soviet purchases.

Moscow's political efforts have had limited results. Its one triumph was the establishment of a Marxist-Leninist regime in Cuba, unexpectedly achieved through the July 26 Movement, not the Cuban Communists. That victory was achieved and maintained at huge cost to the Soviet economy.

The establishment of a network of Communist parties throughout the Western hemisphere is an unprecedented achievement, but no Communist party has seized control of a Latin American government by force. The revolutionary parties that have taken power have been radical nationalist, not Marxist-Leninist, in their origins, and except in Cuba, all have been swept away. Linked closely and publicly to Moscow, most Communist parties have never been able to shake the image that they were serving Moscow's interests rather than those of their own country.

Soviet priorities changed rapidly after 1985. *Perestroika* and domestic problems meant that less attention could be devoted to low-priority areas like Latin America, and the USSR could not afford to continue its assistance at the former high levels. The December 1990 agreement with Cuba reduced Soviet aid and sought to put commercial relations on a business basis. The Cuban economy, cut off from its natural partners in the West, had been unable to stand firmly on its feet even with Soviet economic assistance. These developments portended a grim future for the Cuban economy and the Castro regime.

The emphasis on self-determination in Eastern Europe and inside the Soviet Union itself, which accelerated after the failed coup of August 1991, made the formerly Moscow-dominated Communist parties in Latin America an anachronism. Moreover, the Soviet Union, usually perceived as the main enemy of the United States in Latin America, sought arms agreements, closer commercial arrangements, and aid from the United States. Such arrangements were inconsistent with the support of national Communist parties, which the United States regarded as anti-American and destabilizing. In any case, Moscow set these parties loose. As a result, many were split by factionalism, and domestic and world events caused them to lose much of their popular support.

As the cold war ended in Latin America, and the political geography of Eastern Europe and the Soviet Union was being redrawn, there were new trends in Soviet relations with Latin America: Soviet aid to Cuba was rapidly ending; Soviet support for Communist parties, revolutionary movements, and radical governments was disappearing; Soviet trade, always low with most of the area, declined even more, due partly to economic turmoil in the USSR; and normal, often friendly diplomatic relations were being conducted with many governments. After the breakup of the Soviet Union, individual new republics had to decide whether to forge relations with Latin America. In the twenty–first century, the Russian economy has recouped, and in 2006 representatives from Russia signed a memorandum to discuss tighter economic relations with the South American countries in the Mercosur trading pact. Also, in the post–Soviet era

many archives have been made accessible to historians, allowing them to begin new research on the USSR's former relations with Latin America.

See also **Communism; Cuban Missile Crisis.**

BIBLIOGRAPHY

The most convenient sources of information on this subject are Russell H. Bartley, ed., *Soviet Historians on Latin America: Recent Scholarly Contributions* (1978); Cole Blasier, *The Giant's Rival: The USSR and Latin America,* rev. ed. (1987), pp. 91ff.; Augusto Varas, *Soviet–Latin American Relations in the 1980's* (1987); Nicola Miller, *Soviet Relations with Latin America, 1959–1987* (1989), pp. 226ff.; Eusebio Mujal-león, ed., *The USSR and Latin America* (1989); and the biannual *Latinskaia Amerika v Sovetskoi pechati.*

Ching, Erik, and Jussi Pakkasvirta. "Latin American Materials in the Comintern Archive." *Latin American Research Review* 35, no. 1 (2000): 138–149.

Grandin, Greg. *The Last Colonial Massacre: Latin America in the Cold War.* Chicago: University of Chicago Press, 2004.

Spenser, Daniela. *The Impossible Triangle: Mexico, Soviet Russia, and the United States in the 1920s.* Durham, NC: Duke University Press, 1999.

COLE BLASIER

SOYBEANS.

Soybeans are the battleship of agribusiness growth in Latin America. The crop is the most aggressive and damaging of commercial crops in Argentina and Brazil, and has expanded its territory dramatically in Bolivia, Paraguay, and Uruguay. The victims of the crop's destructiveness include family farmers, food supplies, biodiversity, soil quality, and clean water supplies; its beneficiaries are multinational corporations such as Cargill and Bunge, genetically modified seed manufacturers such as Monsanto, Chinese consumers, and a handful of Latin American agribusiness men, especially those in the meat industry.

By 1989 Brazil and Argentina supplied nearly two-thirds the total exports of world soybean meal. In response to growth of the Chinese market, soybean cultivation expanded dramatically during the 1990s in Latin America. By 2005, Brazil alone produced 30 percent of world supplies, second only to the United States.

Soybeans originated in Asia, and therefore many credit Japanese immigrants with introducing the beans to Latin America. But in 1882, before significant numbers of Asians immigrated to South America, the botanist Gustave Dutra reported experimenting with soybean crops in the state of Bahia, Brazil. Experiments were also conducted in Argentina before World War I. Scientists noted the special properties of the legume: One of the richest foods known, soybeans contain 38 percent protein and 18 percent oils and fats. They can be cooked and eaten in hundreds of different ways, used industrially to make everything from soaps to glue, and ground into a meal to make an excellent feed for hogs and chickens. Demand for soybeans did not begin to grow in the west until after World War II, and the Green Revolution brought great expansion of soybean agriculture came to Argentina and Brazil only after 1970.

Government policy has figured prominently in the growth of soybean agriculture in Latin America. In Brazil, the state encouraged its cultivation in the grasslands of the southernmost state of Rio Grande do Sul when climatic conditions weakened wheat crop yields. Much the same pattern developed in the state of Paraná in the early 1960s, when the government sponsored the eradication of coffee trees and the planting of soybeans and wheat. By the 1980s these two states yielded more than two-thirds the national total. State-sponsored experimentation produced soybean strains that would grow in the tropical, central plateau of Brazil. By 2000 soybeans were grown in seventeen of Brazil's twenty-six states. The introduction of genetically modified seed made it possible to better control damaging weeds and pests in humid zones, and the crop invaded hundreds of thousands of acres every year. In the early twenty-first century the government invested in roads, railroads, ports, and waterways to encourage its expansion into the Amazon region, greatly damaging biodiversity. In Argentina, Brazil, and Paraguay, the crop occupied more than 20 percent of agricultural land. In order to work the 500- to 2,500-acre fields of this highly mechanized crop, landowners and tenants relied on substantial government credit.

As an especially nutritious food, the soybean has been sold to the public as a means for ending starvation in Latin America. Most production, however, is geared toward export surpluses, cooking oil, derivatives for industrial use, and animal feed. Soy cooking oil now dominates the marketplace but critics note that fattened pig and poultry are too expensive for the poor. As an export crop grown most efficiently on large estates, the expansion of soybeans has forced millions of peasants off the land, further reducing the production of nutritious beans, vegetables, and fruits. Thus, rather than alleviating nutritional problems, soybean agriculture has tended to aggravate them. Moreover, without rotation, soybeans quickly exhaust soils, and the chemical fertilizers and pesticides required to sustain genetically modified soybeans pollute waterways. Supporters point to the tremendous foreign exchange earned by soybean exports and the thousands of jobs created by the soybean processing industry. They do not note, however, that for every job created by soybeans, eleven are eliminated.

See also **Beans.**

BIBLIOGRAPHY

Altieri, Miguel, and Walter Pengue. "GM Soybean: Latin America's New Colonizer." *Seedling* (January 2006): 13–17.

Girardi, Eduardo Paulon. "O Atlas da Questão Agrária Brasileira." Ph.D. diss., Universidade Estadual Paulista, Presidente Prudente, 2008.

Hinson, K., E. E. Hartwig, and Harry Minor. *Soybean Production in the Tropics.* Rome: Food and Agriculture Organization, 1982.

Morgan, Dan. *Merchants of Grain.* New York: Penguin, 1980.

Welch, Cliff. "Globalization and the Transformation of Work in Rural Brazil: Agribusiness, Rural Labor Unions, and Peasant Mobilization." *International Labor and Working Class History* 70, no. 1 (2007): 1–26.

CLIFF WELCH

SPAIN.

Contemporary Spain occupies approximately 195,000 square miles of the Iberian Peninsula. Its land connection to continental Europe is in the northeast quadrant, where the Pyrenees span the border with France. The Mediterranean Sea forms its eastern and southern boundaries, extending to the Strait of Gibraltar. Most of its western boundary is shared with Portugal, and the remainder is bounded by the Atlantic Ocean (Bay of Biscay). Mountains dominate the Spanish landscape, and there are few navigable rivers.

From the voyages of Columbus to the nineteenth century, Spain was committed to the exploration, settlement, development, administration, defense, and exploitation of its colonies in the Americas. It emerged as a major European power in the 1490s, declined in the seventeenth century, reemerged in the eighteenth century, and then fell to the rank of a minor power in the nineteenth century.

In the mid-fifteenth century, "Spain" did not exist as a political entity. The term simply referred to the Iberian Peninsula and included several kingdoms. The marriage of Isabella I of Castile and Ferdinand II of Aragon in 1469 and the couple's succession to their respective thrones in 1474 and 1479 brought about a union of crowns, but each realm retained its distinctive institutions, language, customs barriers, and other pre-union features. Each considered itself in a separate, patrimonial relationship to the monarch rather than part of a political entity known as Spain.

When Charles I (1516–1556), who later became Holy Roman Emperor Charles V (1519–1556), ascended the throne in 1516, Spain had a population of just under five million. Castilian society was stratified, with relatively few titled nobles who controlled most of the land, a larger group of untitled nobles, a few professionals, some merchants, and a large over-taxed peasantry.

New World bullion, which began to arrive in significant quantities late in Charles's reign, provided substantial revenues to his successor, Philip II (1556–1598), in some years furnishing as much as a quarter of the crown's income. Military expenses, especially in the Low Countries following the revolt of the Netherlands in 1566, however, constantly drained state finances. The government was always in debt and periodically, beginning in 1557, was forced into bankruptcy. Although the population rose in the sixteenth century, inflation adversely affected the economy and trade.

The following Hapsburg monarchs—Philip III (1598–1621), Philip IV (1621–1665), and Charles II (1665–1700)—struggled against a decline in population, a weak economy, an ongoing fiscal crisis, and, by the 1620s, a trade system with the New World colonies that was rapidly disintegrating as a result of extensive contraband trade. The revolt of Catalonia and Portugal that began in 1640 further strained the crown's coffers, and military defeat at the hands of the French in 1643 put a definitive end to Spain's era of glory. Fiscal crisis followed fiscal crisis until a deflationary policy implemented in the mid-1680s provided a base that made subsequent economic recovery possible.

Charles II's designation of Philip, duke of Anjou and a grandson of Louis XIV, as his heir provoked the War of the Spanish Succession. In the end, the Bourbon Philip V (1700–1746) gained the Spanish throne. Philip strengthened royal administration in Spain. Population rose in the eighteenth century and the economy improved. Philip's successors—Ferdinand VI (1746–1759), Charles III (1759–1788), and Charles IV (1788–1808), paid increased attention to reestablishing control over the colonies and securing for Spain the economic benefits of empire. Efforts at reform, especially during the reign of Charles III, paid dividends. Registered bullion production from Mexico, Peru, and Upper Peru almost quadrupled during the eighteenth century, and significant amounts entered the royal treasury. Trading restrictions were loosened and legal trade expanded rapidly between the late 1770s and the mid-1790s.

The outbreak of the French Revolution and Spain's almost constant involvement in European wars beginning in 1793 ended an era of relative prosperity. After Napoleon forced the abdications of Charles IV and Ferdinand VII (1808, 1814–1833), Spain was occupied by French troops and was the site of the bloody Peninsular War. The constitutional crisis provoked by the abdications led both Spaniards and Americans to proclaim that sovereignty had reverted to the people and they, through their juntas, would exercise it until Ferdinand returned. The crisis, war on the peninsula, the promulgation of a liberal constitution in 1812 that established constitutional monarchy, and the emergence of autonomist and independence movements on the American mainlands presaged the end of empire. By 1826 all of the mainland colonies were independent and Spain was left with only Cuba, Puerto Rico, and the Philippines. Political stability was gone as well, both in Spain and in its erstwhile colonies.

SPANISH MONARCHS FROM 1474

Isabella I of Castile, 1474–1504
Ferdinand II of Aragon, 1479–1516

Charles I, 1516–1556 (Holy Roman Emperor as Charles V, 1519–1556)

Philip II, 1556–1598

Philip III, 1598–1621

Philip IV, 1621–1665

Charles II, 1665–1700

Philip V, 1700–1746

Ferdinand VI, 1746–1759

Charles III, 1759–1788

Charles IV, 1788–1808

Ferdinand VII, 1808, 1814–1833

Isabella II, 1833–1868

Alfonso XII, 1874–1885

María de las Mercedes, 1885–1886

Alfonso XIII, 1886–1931

María Cristina, queen regent, 1885–1902

Juan Carlos I, 1975–present

See also **Spanish Empire.**

BIBLIOGRAPHY

John Huxtable Elliott, *Imperial Spain 1469–1716* (1964).

John Lynch, *Bourbon Spain 1700–1808* (1989).

Henry Kamen, *Spain 1469–1714: A Society of Conflict,* 2d ed. (1991).

John Lynch, *Spain 1516–1598: From Nation State to World Empire* (1991) and *The Hispanic World in Crisis and Change 1598–1700* (1992).

Additional Bibliography

Cañizares-Esguerra, Jorge. *How to Write the History of the New World: Histories, Epistemologies, and Identities in the Eighteenth-Century Atlantic World.* Stanford, CA: Stanford University Press, 2001.

Elliott, Jorge. *Empires of the Atlantic World: Britain and Spain in America, 1492-1830.* Stanford, CA: Stanford University Press, 2001.

Morales Folguera, José Miguel. *La construcción de la utopía: El proyecto de Felipe II (1556-1598) para Hispanoamérica.* Madrid: Biblioteca Nueva: Universidad de Málaga, 2001.

Ramos Pérez, Demetrio. *La formación de las sociedades iberoamericanas (1568-1700).* Madrid: Espasa Calpe, 1999.

Romano, Ruggiero. *Mecanismo y elementos del sistema económico colonial americano, siglos XVI-XVIII.* México: El Colegio de México, Fideicomiso Historia de las Americas: Fondo de Cultura Económica, 2004.

Stein, Stanley J. and Barbara H Stein. *Apogee of Empire: Spain and New Spain in the Age of Charles III, 1759-1789.* Baltimore: Johns Hopkins University Press, 2003.

Stein, Stanley J. and Barbara H Stein. *Silver, Trade, and War: Spain and America in the Making of Early Modern Europe.* Baltimore: Johns Hopkins University Press, 2000.

SUZANNE HILES BURKHOLDER

SPAIN, CONSTITUTION OF 1812.

The Political Constitution of the Spanish Monarchy, promulgated on 18 March 1812 by the Cortes of Cádiz, defined Spanish and Spanish-American liberalism for the early nineteenth century. It was a response to the constitutional crisis caused by the forced abdication and exile of Spain's legitimate monarch, Ferdinand VII, in 1808. Spanish liberals hoped to regenerate Spain through the adoption of a modern constitution influenced by Enlightenment principles and concepts stemming from the French and American revolutions. Although liberals dominated the Cortes, the resulting constitution was a blend of modern and traditional elements. Its controversial restriction of aristocratic and clerical privileges encouraged and strengthened liberal political arguments and emphasized the function and rights of local and provincial governments in making decisions for themselves, opposing traditional elites. The central idea behind the constitution was that sovereignty resided in the nation, which alone had the right to establish fundamental laws. Its makers hoped to correct the abuses of absolute monarchy without rejecting traditional features of Spanish law. Five American delegates sat on the committee in charge of drafting the document for debate.

The Constitution of 1812 essentially established a constitutional monarchy. Although it retained Roman Catholicism as the established church, it abolished the Inquisition, aristocratic privileges, feudal obligations, and seignorial levies. It provided for elections of deputies to future Cortes, representation without class distinctions, and the abolition of entailed estates. The Cortes were to convene on 1 March each year, for three months. Deputies were chosen every two years and sat for two consecutive sessions. Although not rejecting the monarchy, the constitution did moderate the power of the crown to ensure constitutional government. The crown retained only those functions that the Cortes could not exert, royal control over the administration was subjugated to an elected, unicameral assembly that met annually. A council of state watched over the crown's actions, although its members were chosen by the crown from a list compiled by the Cortes. Such restrictions on the monarch's powers, not surprisingly, caused great friction when Ferdinand VII returned to the Spanish throne in 1814.

The Constitution of 1812 extended universal suffrage to all free males under a deliberately indirect representative electoral system. Colonial representation in the Cortes provided political definition and substance to the demands of the creole liberal delegates. Although the American colonies gained full political rights within a unified Spanish empire, the Constitution did not allow the American dominions full self-rule. On the issue of free trade, for which the colonial delegates pressed, the constitution encouraged freer trade, but not to the full extent the colonies wished.

The document also provided for elected city councils and for representative provincial bodies (*diputaciones provinciales*). It proclaimed freedom of the press and threatened traditional fueros and monopolies. To encourage agrarian production, the constitution established clear and absolute property rights. True to liberal principles, individual property rights took precedence over corporate or collective rights. The constitution assured the individual's right to enclose, sell, or rent his land, paving the way for alienation of indigenous communal lands in some areas of Spanish America.

Although the conservatives tried to present the constitution of 1812 as the work of a radical minority—"a criminal conspiracy of a handful of *facciosos* [agitators]"—in reality the constitution had widespread support. Even the most radical of the clauses passed without effective opposition in the Cortes. What opposition to the constitution did exist was presented by the ecclesiastical orders and institutions whose petitions and privileges had been curtailed by the liberal clauses. The attack on church privilege, however, excited greater disapproval of the document outside the Cortes. In general, the Constitution of 1812 provided for a division of governmental powers, consolidated and updated the Spanish legal system, ensured civil equality, and curtailed corporate privilege.

Its restriction of monarchical power, however, led to open conflict upon Ferdinand VII's return to power. The king dissolved the Cortes and abrogated the constitution on 4 May 1814, restoring the unrestricted monarchy that had existed prior to 1808. Liberal opposition to Ferdinand's repressive power and to the war in the colonies led to the Riego Revolt of 1 January 1820, which reestablished the Constitution of 1812. In 1823, however, with the assistance of Bourbon troops from France, Ferdinand recovered his full authority and once more suppressed the constitution. The Constitution of 1812, however, both in Spain and in Spanish America, served as the initial model for the early nineteenth-century liberals. It is reflected strongly, for example, in the Mexican constitutions of 1814 (Apatzingán) and 1824, the Central American Constitution of 1824, and several early South American Republican constitutions.

See also **Ferdinand VII of Spain; Mexico, Constitutions: Constitutions Prior to 1917.**

BIBLIOGRAPHY

The Constitution of 1812 was published as *Constitución política de la monarquía española, promulgada en Cádiz a 19 de marzo de 1812* (1820). Secondary works dealing with the constitution and its influence include Luis Alayza Paz Soldán, *La Constitución de Cádiz, 1812: El egregio limeño Morales y Duárez* (1946); Rafael De Alba and Manuel Puga y Acal, eds., *La Constitución de 1812 en la Nueva España* (1912); Cesareo De Armellada, *La causa indígena americana en las Cortes de Cádiz* (1959); Nettie Lee Benson, ed., *Mexico and the Spanish Cortes, 1810–1822* (1966); Raymond Carr, *Spain 1808–1978* (1982); María Teresa Berruezo, *La participación americana en las Cortes de Cádiz, 1810–1814* (1986); Jorge Mario García La Guardia, *La Constitución de Cádiz y su influencia en América: Años 1812–1987* (1987); Daniel A. Moreno, *Las Cortes de Cádiz y la Constitución de 1812* (1964); and Mario Rodríguez, *The Cádiz Experiment in Central America, 1808 to 1826* (1978).

Additional Bibliography

Chust Calero, Manuel. *La cuestión nacional americana en las Cortes de Cádiz (1810–1814)*. Valencia: Centro Francisco Tomás y Valiente UNED Alzira-Valencia, Fundación Instituto Historia Social, 1999.

HEATHER THIESSEN

SPANISH–AMERICAN WAR.
Spanish–American War, a short and decisive conflict fought in 1898 that assured the final expulsion of Spain from the New World and the emergence of the

Lithograph of the Battle of San Juan Hill. An American interpretation of the bloodiest battle of the Spanish-American War. From *Harper's Weekly*, 1898. HARPER'S WEEKLY

United States as the dominant Caribbean power. Public opinion and the media in the United States had been urging intervention since the beginning of the Cuban rebellion against Spain in 1895. Many of the Cuban landowning elite had also been calling for U.S. intervention to restore order to the island. The pretext for the U.S. to enter the war was provided on 15 February 1898, when the *U.S.S Maine,* sent to Havana harbor to protect U.S. citizens, exploded and sank, killing 260 officers and enlisted men. No agreement was reached as to the cause of the explosion, but the United States concluded that it had been perpetrated from outside the ship. Since no accord for reparations was reached with Spain, the U.S. Congress declared war against Spain on 25 April. In the Teller Amendment to the war declaration, the United States asserted that it would make no attempt to establish control over the island.

The first battle of the war was fought in the Philippine islands, where the U.S. Navy destroyed the Spanish fleet in Manila Bay on 1 May 1898. The Spanish quickly surrendered possession of the Philippines to the United States. In June, 17,000 troops landed at Siboney and Daiquirí, east of Santiago de Cuba. On 3 July the U.S. Navy destroyed the Spanish fleet, and subsequent land victories by Cuban and U.S. forces prompted

the final surrender of the Spanish troops on 12 August.

The Cuban struggle for independence played a key role in Spain's defeat. The conflict had been consuming the crown's resources for several decades. From the outset of the rebellion in 1895, the Cuban Army of Liberation had controlled the rural areas, although not Havana or Santiago, the major cities. By the end of 1897, Cuban victory was all but complete. Yet although the war was fought between Cuban revolutionaries, the Spanish army, and the U.S. forces, Cuba was excluded from the peace negotiations that resulted in the Treaty of Paris. The independence movement of 1895–1898 had lost its most vital, younger leaders in the struggle, leaving older men and a weary liberation army to accept the compromise of its independence that was demanded by the U.S.

The Treaty of Paris, signed on 10 December 1898, involved more than just Spain's withdrawal from Cuba. In addition Spain lost Puerto Rico, the Philippine islands, and other islands in the Pacific and the West Indies. It terminated Spain's overseas empire. On 1 January 1899, when Spanish government officials retired from Cuba, General John R. Brooke established the U.S. military occupation of the island. Advocates of Manifest Destiny were vindicated by a relatively easy and inexpensive war. The United States assumed formal possession of Cuba and the right to supervise its national government by claiming responsibility for ending Spanish colonial government and unilaterally negotiating the peace terms.

See also **Cuba, War of Independence.**

BIBLIOGRAPHY

French E. Chadwick, *The Relations of the United States and Spain: The Spanish-American War*, 2 vols. (1911).

Walter Millis, *The Martial Spirit* (1931).

Joseph E. Wisan, *The Cuban Crisis as Reflected in the New York Press, 1895–1898* (1934).

Julius W. Pratt, *Expansionists of 1898: The Acquisition of Hawaii and the Spanish Islands* (1936).

Cosme De La Torriente y Peraza, *Fin de la dominación de España en Cuba* (1948), and *Calixto Garcia: Cooperó con las fuerzas armados de los Estados Unidos en 1898, cumpliendo órdenes del gobernio cubano* (1950).

Ramiro Guerra y Sánchez, et al., eds., *Historia de la nación cubana*, 10 vols. (1952).

Frank Freidel, *The Splendid Little War* (1958).

Hugh Thomas, *Cuba; or, the Pursuit of Freedom* (1971).

James D. Rudolph, *Cuba: A Country Study* (1985).

Louis A. Pérez, Jr., *Cuba: Between Reform and Revolution* (1988).

Additional Bibliography

Carrasco García, Antonio. *En guerra con Estados Unidos: Cuba 1898*. Madrid: Almena Ediciones, 1998.

Pérez, Louis A. *The War of 1898: The United States and Cuba in History and Historiography*. Chapel Hill: University of North Carolina Press, 1998.

DAVID CAREY JR.

SPANISH EMPIRE. The Spanish Empire unofficially began in 1402 when French explorer Jean de Béthencourt claimed the Canary Islands for Henry III of Castile. In 1462 the Crown of Castile took Gibraltar as part of its war against the Moors. Spain was accorded official possession of the Canary Islands by the Treaty of Alcaçovas in 1479, although it did not conquer the three major islands of Grand Canary (1478–1483), La Palma (1492–1493), and Tenerife (1494–1496) until the end of the century. Christopher Columbus used the Canaries as a fueling stop on his way to what would come to be known as the New World. While he was sailing in 1497, the Spanish seized the North African town of Melilla. After Columbus's initial coasting among the Caribbean islands, Spanish explorers began sailing along the coasts of North and South America in pursuit of the mythical Strait of Anián that would lead across the mainland. By the early 1500s, Spaniards had established themselves in Hispaniola, Puerto Rico, and Cuba, venturing out from there to new destinations. Their voyages led them to Florida in 1513, the estuary of the Río De La Plata in 1515–1516 and, by the early 1530s, as far north as Nova Scotia. Unsuccessful expeditions beginning about 1500 on the northern coast of Venezuela (Tierra Firme) and to Panama were followed by Vasco Núñez de Balboa's crossing the Isthmus of Panama and sighting the Pacific (South Sea) in 1513. The fall of Tenochtitlán in 1521 opened Mexico up for exploration, conquest, and settlement; the capture of Atahualpa in 1533 did the same for Peru.

The lure of finding "another Mexico" or "another Peru" stimulated rapid exploration of what became the viceroyalties of New Spain and Peru. The discovery of silver, notably in Potosí (Bolivia) and Zacatecas (Mexico); the presence of readily available native labor; and administrative and commercial needs determined the principal settlements of the Spanish Empire. Outlying regions lacking significant mineral wealth grew more slowly, but defensive needs and the development of nonmineral exports such as hides, cacao, tobacco, dyes, and sugar brought permanent settlement and expansion over a vast territory. At its apogee, the Spanish Empire stretched from the Pacific Northwest and California to Florida and from the northern border of the Louisiana Territory south through Central America. In South America it encompassed roughly present–day Venezuela, Colombia, Ecuador, Peru, Bolivia, Chile, Argentina, Uruguay, and Paraguay. Island holding in the Caribbean rounded out the New World possessions. Far west in the Pacific lay the Philippine Islands, a valuable entrepôt for the East Asian trade and an integral part of the Viceroyalty of New Spain, as well as the Caroline, Marshall, and Mariana Islands (including Guam) in Micronesia.

Spain's extensive territorial claims first suffered erosion in the seventeenth century, when English, Dutch, and French settled on a number of Caribbean islands, including Jamaica. Portuguese expansion extended the boundary of Brazil far beyond the line established by the Treaty of Tordesillas in 1494, but the border conflict was not resolved until 1777 with the Treaty of San Ildefonso, when Spain recognized the Portuguese claim to the Côlonia do Sacramento (present–day Uruguay) in exchange for the area now known as the Republic of Equatorial Guinea. In the meantime Spain gained the Mediterranean port of Ceuta from the Portuguese in the Treaty of Lisbon in 1668, but lost Gibraltar to Great Britain in 1704 as part of the War of Spanish Succession. By the Treaty of San Lorenzo del Escorial (Pinckney's Treaty) of 1795, Spain bowed to U.S. claims to the Ohio Valley and land below the Yazoo River. In 1800 it agreed to return the Louisiana Territory to France. In 1803 the United States purchased Louisiana and in 1819 gained Florida by treaty. The Wars of Independence (1810–1826) ended Spain's mainland empire in Latin America; at their conclusion the once great imperial presence was reduced to Cuba and Puerto Rico in North America; the Philippines and Micronesian islands in Asia, and Melilla and Ceuta in North Africa.

However, in 1860 Spain gained control over the Atlantic coast town of Ifni, 200 miles southwest of Marrakech and declared it a protectorate in 1884. The Cuban wars for independence began in 1868 and continued sporadically until 1898 when the United States intervened and defeated Spain. The empire lost its North American holdings as well as Guam and Puerto Rico and it sold the remaining Mariana and the Marshall islands to Germany the following year. As the twentieth century began, the Spanish Empire consisted solely of its few African possessions. The Treaty of Paris of 1898 recognized Spanish claims to Equatorial Guinea and the Franco–Spanish Convention in 1912 formalized Spain's claims to Spanish Morocco, divided into Northern (south of Larache on the Atlantic coast to the Moulouya River and north to the Mediterranean) and Southern Zones (from the northern boundary of Spanish Sahara to the Qued Draa and 150 miles into the African mainland). In 1934 Ifni and the Northern Zone began to be governed with Spanish Sahara; in 1946 this arrangement incorporated the Southern Zone and was renamed Western Sahara. The Northern Zone was given to Morocco in 1956, the Southern Zone in 1958, and Ifni in 1969. Spanish Equatorial Guinea achieved independence as the Republic of Equatorial Guinea in 1968 and in 1975 Spanish Sahara was divided between Morocco and Mauritania. After that time all that remained of the empire was Ceuta, Melilla, and Spanish claims to Gibraltar.

See also **San Ildefonso, Treaty of (1777); Spanish-American War; War of the Spanish Succession.**

BIBLIOGRAPHY

Davril Alden, *Royal Government in Colonial Brazil* (1968).

John Horace Parry, *The Discovery of South America* (1979).

James S. Olson, ed., *Historical Dictionary of the Spanish Empire, 1402–1975* (1992).

David J. Weber, *The Spanish Frontier in North America* (1992).

Additional Bibliography

Barrera–Osorio, Antonio. *Experiencing Nature: The Spanish American Empire and the Early Scientific Revolution.* Austin: University of Texas Press, 2006.

Cañizares–Esguerra, Jorge. *Puritan Conquistadors: Iberianizing the Atlantic, 1550–1700.* Stanford, CA: Stanford University Press, 2006.

Elliott, John Huxtable. *Empires of the Atlantic World: Britain and Spain in America, 1492–1830.* New Haven, CT: Yale University Press, 2006.

Fernández–Armesto, Felipe. *The Americas: A Hemispheric History.* New York: Modern Library, 2003.

Fisher, John Robert. *The Economic Aspects of Spanish Imperialism in America, 1492–1810.* Liverpool: Liverpool University Press, 1997.

Halperín Donghi, Tulio. *Reforma y disolución de los imperios ibéricos, 1750–1850.* Madrid: Alianza Editorial, 1985.

Kamen, Henry. *Empire: How Spain Became a World Power, 1492–1763.* New York: HarperCollins, 2003.

Stein, Stanley J., and Barbara H. Stein. *Apogee of Empire: Spain and New Spain in the Age of Charles III, 1759–1789.* Baltimore: Johns Hopkins University Press, 2003.

MARK A. BURKHOLDER

SPANISH LANGUAGE.

Spanish is spoken by upwards of 300 million people in Latin America, where it is the official language of eighteen countries and the Commonwealth of Puerto Rico. In spite of the fact that it has been the first language of far-flung communities ranging over thousands of miles for some five centuries, Latin American Spanish is remarkably homogeneous—especially in its morphology and syntax—and all varieties are mutually intelligible.

Carried bodily into southern Spain with the Reconquest, the language of fifteenth-century Castile continued on to the New World during a period of intense intercultural contact and internal linguistic change. Many of the features shared by Andalusian, Canarian, and Latin American varieties are undoubtedly the result of "dialect leveling," whereby tenuous linguistic distinctions tend to be lost. Thus, for example, American Spanish is characterized by *seseo* (one sound for orthographic *s* and *z* where Castilian has two).

Although prestige norms of urban centers (especially national capitals) are more influential than ever thanks to centralized education and media, it remains the case that dialect boundaries do not, by and large, follow political ones. Features may be shared across countries while varying considerably within them. In the Latin American context, the importance of the demographic explosion and rapid urbanization since the mid-1950s cannot be underestimated: What was once an urban vs. rural distinction has given way to marked sociolinguistic differentiation within cities, and speakers from a range of social strata contribute to the national standard.

In phonology, a useful dichotomy can be drawn between the consonant-heavy dialects of highland Mexico and the Andes versus the consonant-weak varieties of the coasts, lowland South America, and the Southern Cone. The latter are characterized by the effacement of syllable-final consonants, most notoriously the aspiration or deletion of *s*. The so-called trilled *r* provides another Latin American shibboleth; several regional variants are not trills at all, and these represent some of the few widespread phonological phenomena unrelated to developments in Spain.

Perhaps the most exclusively Latin American morphosyntactic phenomenon is the *voseo*, or use of the pronoun *vos* in place of *tú* for the second person familiar singular—together with its corresponding verb forms. Particularly robust in Argentina, Paraguay, Uruguay, and Central America, some vestige of the *voseo* is familiar to most speakers outside of Mexico, Peru, and the Antilles.

The Latin American Spanish vocabulary has borrowed heavily from indigenous languages, with names for fauna, food, and places most likely to be of local or regional character. Typical are lexical items from Nahuatl (*elote, cacahuate, aguacate, ejote*), Taino (*maíz, maní, batey*), and Quechua (*choclo, palta, poroto*), some of which have spread pan-Hispanically and beyond. Spanish has displaced indigenous languages almost everywhere except in Mesoamerica, the Andes, and Paraguay, and it is fast encroaching upon them there (perhaps less rapidly in Paraguay). Still, in the early twenty-first century, far less than half of the Paraguayan population speaks fluent Spanish, and probably just over half of the Bolivian and Guatemalan people claim it as a first language. In these places, as well as in Peru, Ecuador, and Mexico, as the work of Carol Klee (2008) shows, there are contact-induced features in the phonology and syntax of local Spanish varieties, but these are most apparent in the speech of adult second-language learners, and most tend to dissipate over successive generations.

Extra-Hispanic influence has also come from African languages, especially in the Caribbean basin where lexical borrowings abound and where arguments have been made for some African contribution to, say, consonant loss in Dominican Spanish. The greatest force in the foreseeable future, however, is undeniably English, due not to any large-scale bilingualism in Latin America but rather to its status as a world language of commerce and technology. Contact with English is constant and unstoppable throughout the hemisphere; even so, its effects, though significant, are largely limited to expansion of the lexicon.

National affiliates of the Real Academia Española exist in all nineteen of the Spanish-speaking territories mentioned above, where together they advocate for "*el cuidado y defensa del idioma común.*" The region's largest professional association of linguists is the Asociación de Lingüística y Filología de América Latina. The collection and documentation of dialect data has been the ongoing objective of the "Norma Culta" project, headed by Juan Lope Blanch (1986), and two online corpora with video dialect samples include sites managed by Terrell Morgan (2007) and Carlos-Eduardo Piñeros (2007).

See also **Hispanics in the United States; Indigenous Languages.**

BIBLIOGRAPHY

Gordon, Raymond G., Jr., ed. *Ethnologue: Languages of the World*, 15th edition. Dallas: SIL, 2005. Also available from http://www.ethnologue.org.

Hidalgo, Margarita. "The Emergence of Standard Spanish in the American Continent: Implications for Latin American Dialectology." *Language Problems and Language Planning* 14 (1990): 47–63.

Klee, Carol. "Migrations and Globalization: Their Effects on Contact Varieties of Latin American Spanish." In *Español en los Estados Unidos y en otros contextos: Cuestiones sociolingüísticas, políticas y pedagógicas*, ed. Manel Lacorte and Jennifer Leeman. Madrid: Vervuert/Iberoamericana, 2008.

Lipski, John M. *Latin American Spanish*. London and New York: Longman, 1994.

Lope Blanch, Juan. *El estudio del español hablado culto: Historia de un proyecto*. Mexico City: UNAM, 1986.

Morgan, Terrell A. *Digital Catalog of the Sounds of Spanish*. 2007. Online video corpus available from http://dialectos.osu.edu.

Piñeros, Carlos-Eduardo. *Dialectoteca del español*. 2007. Available from http://www.uiowa.edu/~acadtech/dialects.

TERRELL A. MORGAN

SPICES AND HERBS.

Native populations in America used plants for flavoring their foods before the arrival of Europeans, but the importance and varieties of these plants are poorly known. The most popular species that originated in present-day Latin America are discussed below.

Vanilla. Comes from the cured seedpod of an orchid vine that grows in tropical forests. In pre-Columbian times, the Aztec nobility used vanilla to flavor their chocolate drinks; several South American tribes considered it a desirable body perfume, wearing the pods in strings around the neck; medicinal properties were also attributed to it. The pod arrived in Spain aboard the first ships returning from America; it was used by priests and nuns to flavor their chocolate beverages. The aristocracy followed, then the French court in the seventeenth century. In colonial Latin America, vanilla was favored by the elites as an addition to chocolate drinks and sweet confections. During the seventeenth and eighteenth centuries, the Dutch, French, and British tried to start large-scale production of vanilla in their colonies in Africa and Asia; frequently they smuggled plants from the Spanish and Portuguese colonies in America for that purpose, but plants never produced seedpods outside their native habitats. It was not known then that a small bee found only in the American tropics is needed to pollinate the flowers. In the 1840s a former French slave developed a technique of hand-pollination; it proved so effective that later Mexico adopted it for large-scale production. Today vanilla is produced in tropical America, some Pacific islands, and Asia.

Chili peppers. Many varieties of chili peppers were widely cultivated throughout Mesoamerica and South America, and some of their ancient names are still in use: *chile* (Mexico), *ají* (the Caribbean), *huayka* (Peru, Bolivia). Chilies were so important in the diets of South American tribes that going without them was considered similar to fasting. Employed in initiations of young men and for protection in war, they were also used as medicines and insect repellents; the hottest varieties, macerated and mixed with water, served occasionally as weapons against the Spaniards. The Portuguese took hot peppers from Brazil around the world in the early 1600s; by the end of the century several varieties were grown in Africa, India, China, and some of the Pacific Islands, becoming important ingredients in their cuisines. The origins of the spicy malagueta pepper, African or Brazilian, has generated debate yet it remains a central ingredient to Bahian cooking in Brazil. The Ottoman Turkish armies brought hot peppers with them from India to Hungary, where it became established as paprika. Chilies entered colonial Anglo-America with the African slaves. Today chilies lend their fiery grace to foods from all over the world. All Latin American countries use hot peppers in their cuisine to a greater or lesser extent, either in sauces or as condiments for various dishes.

Achiote. Achiote (annato) is a seed that serves as both a red colorant and a spice. Native populations painted their bodies with *achiote* for ceremonial occasions and war. In Nicaragua it was added to chocolate to give the beverage a bloodlike color. Spanish colonists accepted it as a substitute for saffron. Today it flavors and colors dishes like *pollo pibil* (Yucatán), *corvina a la chorrillana* (Peru), and the ever-prevalent *arroz con pollo*.

Allspice. This Caribbean seed, used also by the Aztecs, was exported to Europe in 1601 as a substitute for cardamom and became popular in German, Italian, and Scandinavian sausages and other dishes. Most of the world's production comes from Jamaica, Honduras, Guatemala, and Mexico.

Between the twelfth and seventeenth centuries, the spice trade had enormous economic importance in Europe, comparable to that of oil today; in fact, it was in search of a spice route that Europeans first reached America. However, once established as a colonial power, Spain abandoned its interest in the spice trade: the exploitation of American precious stones and metals prevailed. Portugal, and later the Netherlands, France, and Britain, monopolized the spice trade in fierce competition. Oriental spices favored in Europe were traded with the colonies; black pepper, cinnamon and cloves, still popular in Latin America today, are often imported. Some herbaceous spices of Asian origin that rooted well in American soil have been staple flavorings since early colonial times: the ever-popular cilantro, mostly as an herb; cumin seeds, for *sofrito* and *guisado* preparations; gingerroot, for drinks and as medicine; anise, to flavor alcoholic beverages like *aguardiente;* and cardamom. The last, once more valuable than gold to Arabs, is cultivated today in Central America, Guatemala being the world's first producer. Plants of European origin like onion, garlic, parsley, and oregano, also introduced in the sixteenth century, are today essential flavorings in Latin American cooking.

See also **Food and Cookery.**

BIBLIOGRAPHY

A scholarly and well-documented ethnobotanical history of equatorial America and Central America is Victor Manuel Patiño, *Plantas cultivadas y animales domésticos en América equinoccial* vols. 2 (*Plantas alimenticias*) and 4 (*Plantas introducidas*) (1962). Good information on the origin and present situation of individual spices is Kenneth Farrell, *Spices, Condiments, and Seasonings* (1990). A fascinating introduction to the general history of spices is Wolfgang Schivelbush, *Tastes of Paradise: A Social History of Spices, Stimulants, and Intoxicants,* translated by David Jacobson (1992), chap. 1. Also useful are introductory chapters of Latin American cookbooks such as Barbara Karoff, *South American Cooking* (1989) and Elizabeth Lambert De Ortíz, *The Book of Latin American Cooking* (1979). See also Amal Naj, *Peppers: A Story of Hot Pursuits* (1992); and Larry Luxner, "A Spicy Tale," in *Américas* 44, no. 1 (1992): 2–3, on cardamom.

Additional Bibliography

Andrews, Jean. *The Pepper Trail: History and Recipes from around the World.* Denton: University of North Texas Press, 1999.

Cascudo, Luís da Câmara. *História da alimentação no Brasil.* São Paulo: Companhia Editora Nacional, 1967.

Dalby, Andrew. *Dangerous Tastes: The Story of Spices.* Berkeley: University of California Press, 2000.

Rain, Patricia. *Vanilla: The Cultural History of the World's Most Popular Flavor and Fragrance.* New York: J.P. Tarcher/Penguin, 2004.

                                     CARMENZA OLAYA FONSTAD

SPIRITISM. In everyday Spanish and Portuguese, the word *espiritismo* refers to a wide range of beliefs—including African, Native American, and Western—that have to do with spirits and mediums (people who claim they can communicate with spirits). However, for people more versed in the distinctions among the various spirit-oriented religious and philosophical systems in Latin America, "spiritism" usually refers to the movement founded by the French educator Allan Kardec (born Hippolyte Léon Denizard Rivail).

In the 1850s, Kardec began to attend sittings with mediums, and eventually he codified the spirits' teachings into a multivolume spiritist doctrine that began with his *Le livre des esprits* (1857; first translated into English as *Spiritualist Philosophy; The Spirits' Book*). In addition to supporting the idea of communication with the dead via mediums, Kardec also argued in favor of spiritual illnesses, reincarnation, and the existence of a spiritual body (perispirit). He saw spiritism not as a religion but as a philosophy rooted in observation and having moral implications. Kardec embraced Christian morality, but he did not accept key Christian dogmas such as the Trinity and the reality of heaven and hell.

The spiritist movement grew rapidly in France in the mid-nineteenth century, as did its nonreincarnationist sibling spiritualism in the English-speaking countries, and both were propagated in Latin America as well. In Europe and North America, spiritism and spiritualism soon faded into minor sects, whereas in Latin America they encountered a warm reception that was due in large part to the affinities between spiritism and African, Native American, and Iberian folk

Catholic magic and religion. The result was, in many places, a Syncretism, or blending of spiritist beliefs and practices with those of the local religions, such as the African religions of the Caribbean and coastal Brazil.

There are many today who follow Kardec's spiritism in a fairly pure form, especially in Brazil, where the spiritist population was estimated at 7 million in 1990. At one extreme of this diverse movement are the intellectuals: doctors, engineers, and lawyers who are more interested in psychical research and alternative medicine. At the other extreme are those who regard Kardec's doctrine as one element in a syncretic religious and healing system. In between are a large number of spiritists who have a frankly evangelical style; they tend to study closely Kardec's *The Gospel According to Spiritism,* and many view themselves as Christians.

In most countries, there are spiritist magazines and books, and in Brazil there is a huge network of bookstores to support the spiritist press. Spiritist publications include "psychographed" books, that is, texts that the spirits write via mediums in trance states. In Brazil, some of the medium-authors, such as Francisco Cãndido ("Chico") Xavier, have best-seller status.

Spiritists meet in spiritist centers, where they study the works of Kardec and other spiritists, develop their skills as mediums (although not all spiritists are mediums), and provide charitable services. In Brazil, spiritists run outpatient clinics, dental services, psychiatric hospitals, orphanages, pharmacies (sometimes homeopathic), and a number of other free services to the poor.

Spiritist centers also offer spiritual healing, which most frequently involves "passes" (roughly, the laying on of hands) and a type of exorcism known as "disobsession." Spiritists believe that one cause of illness is affliction from earthbound spirits, which attach themselves to people and cause them mental distress and physical illness.

Some mediums have also been known to practice "psychic" or "spirit surgery." One type involves pantomime-like operations over the body of the patient; spiritists operate on the spiritual body without actually touching the patient. Another type involves cutting into the skin with a scalpel or other instrument, usually to remove minor tumors such as lipomas. The latter type is extremely controversial, and in Brazil the practice has been condemned by an association of spiritists who are also practicing medical doctors. They

prefer conventional "passes" and "disobsession," as well as alternative psychotherapies such as "past-lives" therapy and neurolinguistic programming.

Spiritists occupy a position of mediation in the religious and class structure (between Roman Catholicism and Native American/African religions), but it is difficult to generalize about their politics and political ideology. Historically, they have suffered persecution by church and state, such as in Puerto Rico before the American occupation and in Brazil during the Getúlio Vargas years. Spiritists defend freedom of religion, rights for religious healers, and various other sorts of liberal freedoms. Spiritist doctrine also maintains that spirits have no sex and that the sex (and sexuality) of "incarnate" humans is a result of the karmic processes of past lives. Because at the spiritual level there are no sexual differences (and the same would apply to race or other biological differences), spiritists believe in human equality.

However, in practice spiritism tends to reveal the patriarchical and Eurocentric values of Latin American elite culture. Most of the positions of high prestige (psychographer mediums and organizational presidencies) are occupied by men, although women occasionally rise to power and prominence as well. In Brazil, spiritist mediums tend not to receive the *pretos velhos* (old black slave) and Caboclo (Native American) spirits of the more syncretic Umbanda centers, and while spiritists support birth control, they are often adamantly opposed to abortion. However, while older spiritists are often quite conservative, younger and university-educated spiritists tend to be more progressive. Thus, any discussion of spiritism should always keep in mind its tremendous variation across cultures and social strata, as well as its ongoing historical development.

See also **African-Latin American Religions: Brazil; Candomblé; Syncretism; Vodun, Voodoo, Vaudun.**

BIBLIOGRAPHY

For Brazil, see David J. Hess, *Spirits and Scientists* (1991). For Puerto Rico, see Alan Harwood, *Rx: Spiritist as Needed* (1977); Vivian Garrison, "The Puerto Rican Syndrome in Psychiatry and *Espiritismo,*" in *Case Studies in Spirit Possession,* edited by Vincent Crapanzano and Vivian Garrison (1977), pp. 383–449; and appendix 3 of David J. Hess, *Spirits and Scientists* (1991). For Mexico, see June Macklin, "Belief, Ritual, and Healing: New England Spiritualism and Mexican-American Spiritism Compared," in *Religious Movements in Contemporary America,* edited by Irving

Zaretsky and Mark P. Leone (1974), pp. 383–417. On the spiritualist movement in Mexico, see Kaja Finkler, *Spiritualist Healers in Mexico* (1985).

Additional Bibliography

Fernández Olmos, Margarite, and Lizabeth Paravisini-Gebert. *Creole Religions of the Caribbean: An Introduction from Vodou and Santería to Obeah and Espiritismo.* New York: New York University Press, 2003.

Ferrándiz Martín, Francisco. *Escenarios del cuerpo: Espiritismo y sociedad en Venezuela.* Bilbao: Universidad de Deusto, 2004.

Giumbelli, Emerson. *O cuidado dos mortos: Uma história da condenação e legitimação do espiritismo.* Rio de Janeiro: Ministério da Justicia, Arquivo Nacional, 1997.

Herzig Shannon, Nancy. *El iris de paz: El espiritismo y la mujer en Puerto Rico, 1900–1905.* Río Piedras: Ediciones Huracán, 2001.

Hess, David J. *Samba in the Night: Spiritism in Brazil.* New York: Columbia University Press, 1994.

Hodge Limonta, Ileana, and Minerva Rodríguez Delgado. *El espiritismo en Cuba: Percepción y exteriorización.* La Habana: Editorial Academia, 1997.

Santamaría, Daniel J. *Ocultismo y espiritismo en la Argentina.* Buenos Aires: Centro Editor de América Latina, 1992.

Silva, Fábio Luiz da. *Espiritismo: História e poder (1938–1949).* Londrina: Eduel, 2005.

Stoll, Sandra Jacqueline. *Espiritismo à Brasileira.* São Paulo: EDUSP: Curitiba: Orion, 2003.

DAVID J. HESS

SPOONER ACT. Spooner Act, a decree that authorized the president of the United States to conduct negotiations for the Panama Canal route. In early 1902, when the U.S. government appeared ready to select a transisthmian route in Nicaragua, the French-owned New Panama Canal Company lowered the asking price for its Panamanian rights to $40 million, an act that persuaded the Interoceanic Canal Commission (popularly known as the Walker Commission) to reverse its original recommendation and favor the Panama route. This action prompted the Senate to amend the Hepburn Bill, which had authorized the Nicaraguan site, with a proposal made by John C. Spooner (Republican of Wisconsin) that directed President Theodore Roosevelt to first pursue the Panamanian option. Roosevelt signed the revised bill on 28 June 1902.

See also **Panama Canal.**

BIBLIOGRAPHY

Dwight Carroll Miner, *The Fight for the Panama Route: The Story of the Spooner Act and the Hay–Herrán Treaty* (1940).

Charles D. Ameringer, "The Panama Canal Lobby of Philippe Bunau-Varilla and William Nelson Cromwell," in *American Historical Review* 68 (1963): 346–363.

David McCullough, *The Path Between the Seas: The Creation of the Panama Canal, 1870–1914* (1977).

Additional Bibliography

Diaz Espino, Ovidio. *How Wall Street Created a Nation: J.P. Morgan, Teddy Roosevelt, and the Panama Canal.* New York: Four Walls Eight Windows, 2001.

Tack, Juan Antonio. *El Canal de Panamá.* Panamá: Universidad de Panamá: Editorial Universitaria Carlos Manuel Gasteazoro: Instituto del Canal de la Universidad de Panamá, 1999.

THOMAS M. LEONARD

SPORTS. The history of sports in Latin America (including recreation and physical education) has been marked by great variety, both socially and geographically, and a recognition that sports are an integral part of society and an interactive dimension of larger historical processes. After the Conquest the Spanish, and less vigorously the Portuguese, sought to suppress indigenous games and sports as part of their pursuit of political and cultural domination and religious purification. Few Europeans participated in the remnants of Mesoamerican ball games, *chueca* (resembling field hockey and played by indigenous groups in Argentina and Chile), or other athletic activities surviving in isolated communities.

Simultaneously, the colonial era saw the emergence of various competitive and recreational physical activities derived mainly from older Iberian traditions, often linked to rural equestrian practices or other animal sports, and of numerous games of chance. Whites and mixed ethnic groups derived pleasure from hunting, bullfighting, horse racing (straight-line), cockfighting, and card games. Also important were work-related festivals and competitions that evolved into the "cowboy" cultures of the Mexican *charro*, Argentine *gaucho*, Chilean *huaso*, and Venezuelan *llanero*. From the Basque region came related ball games (*pelota vasca*) that evolved into squash, handball, and jai alai, especially popular in the Southern Cone and areas in and around the Caribbean, including Mexico.

By the mid-1800s sport was increasingly tied to the spread of so-called modern, European culture and its evolving recreational practices. These practices came to Latin America mainly with British, French, and, later (mostly around the Caribbean), North American businessmen, diplomats, missionaries, teachers, soldiers, sailors, and others, as well as with Latin Americans who studied on either side of the North Atlantic. They became part of the schools and the social and athletic clubs opened by foreigners and of similar institutions built by progressive locals who gradually displaced the foreigners as leaders of the sporting community. These newer, imported sports spread from capital cities and major ports into secondary cities and eventually rural areas. Consequently, most popular sports in Latin America in the early twenty-first century have little connection with traditional or colonial society, and even less with pre-Columbian civilizations.

Modernization altered the recreational landscape: *patolli* (a Mexican indigenous board game similar to Parcheesi), *pato* (an Argentine gaucho sport best described as basketball on horseback), cockfighting, *tejo* (stones are tossed underhand to explode blasting caps set on a target at the end of a measured path—played mostly in Colombia), *sortija* (riders on horseback try to place a needle through a hanging ring—seen in Argentina), and other preindustrial games and sports either disappeared or survived regionally in modified forms. *Patolli* has become virtually nonexistent; *tejo*, often accompanied by heavy drinking, is a game of lower-class mestizos; *pato* has moved from the rural pampa to enclaves of upper-class urban whites. Cockfighting, legal in some countries, remains popular in the entire circum-Caribbean area, less so farther south.

PROFESSIONALIZATION

The British amateur ideal did not prevail for long in Latin America, as the desire to improve performance led to longer practice sessions, salaries, and the acceptance of lower-class and darker-skinned players. Also, the increase in free time enabled workers to become recreational athletes and spectators, and paid admission, souvenir sales, and broadcasting rights boosted profits. Soccer, for example, allowed partial salaries—often paid under the table and labeled "brown money"—for about three decades before embracing full professionalization in the early 1930s, a move that caused major conflict between those administrators who favored the change and those who wished to keep the sport amateur. In the early twenty-first century, soccer and auto racing are highly professional, baseball and cycling are both amateur and professional, basketball and tennis are slightly but increasingly professional, and volleyball and swimming remain entirely amateur. Yet even amateur sports require structure and capital investment and carry with them the concomitant features of modern sports: rationalization, standardization, specialization, bureaucratization, and internationalization. They also enhance the sales of equipment.

Professionalization also encouraged unionization, codification of contract law, and welfare legislation for players. In truth, despite higher selective player incomes, at least in soccer, baseball, and boxing, such efforts protect few athletes from exploitation, and confrontations such as Argentina's soccer strike of 1948 and the Mexican baseball players' protest of the early 1980s have tended to end in failure for the athletes.

SOCCER

By the twentieth century, soccer (Spanish: *fútbol*; Portuguese: *futebol*) had become the preferred participant and spectator sport, a reflection of its intrinsic sportive qualities and its ties with British society and the values that it represented. As Cubans have done with baseball and West Indians with cricket, some Latin Americans adapted soccer, a sport of white foreigners, turning it into an anticolonial force to establish their dominion, if only symbolic, over those who previously (or continually) dominated them. Through 2006, Latin Americans have won the World Cup nine times: Uruguay in 1930 and 1950; Brazil in 1958, 1962, 1970, 1994, and 2002; and Argentina in 1978 and 1986. Brazil is the only country to have played in all eighteen Cups between 1930 and 2006. In addition, Latin Americans support regional tournaments such as the Copa América (played since 1917) for national teams and the Copa Libertadores de América (created in 1960) for club champions, the winner of which each year plays the European club champion in Tokyo's Toyota Cup. They also participate in world and inter-American competitions for youth teams. Success in soccer enhances, however briefly, national pride and identification. Unfortunately, soccer has not escaped the illegal narcotics scourge, as half of Colombia's clubs are reported to be owned by persons with drug connections; drug money is laundered through soccer deals and salaries, and individuals such as Argentina's heralded soccer hero of the 1986 World Cup, Diego Maradona, have fallen victim to drug usage.

BASEBALL

Soccer's popularity is not unchallenged, however. In the Spanish-speaking circum-Caribbean, including Mexico's Yucatán, baseball (*béisbol*) has been the "king of sports" for almost a century because of its leisurely pace, low cost, and association with more powerful societies. As early as the 1870s, baseball had numerous Cuban enthusiasts who joined North Americans in spreading the diamond game among their neighbors. Eventually Puerto Rico, the Dominican Republic, Mexico, Nicaragua, Venezuela, Panama, and Colombia became at least partial supporters of the Yankee pastime, all of them leaping into international competitions and exporting stars to northern professional leagues. Cuba, the Dominican Republic, Nicaragua, and Venezuela have each won the world series of amateur baseball at least once. After 1959 Puerto Rico, the Dominican Republic, and Venezuela replaced Cuba as the primary sources of Latin American talent in the majors. San Pedro de Macorís, on the southeastern coast of the Dominican Republic, has supplied more players per capita to the major leagues than any city in the world. Because of its own legal code, Mexico has not exported a substantial number of players, despite the stardom of Fernando Valenzuela in the 1980s. (At the age of forty-five, Valenzuela, "El Toro," played in 2006 with his son, Fernando Jr., "El Torito," on the Mexicali Eagles of the Mexican Pacific League.)

Since Branch Rickey and Jackie Robinson reintegrated U.S. Major League Baseball (MLB) in the mid-1940s, the American pastime has been progressively Latinized. On opening day in 2006, 190 (23.4 percent) of the 813 players on MLB rosters were born in Latin America: 85 Dominicans, 43 Venezuelans, 33 Puerto Ricans, 14 Mexicans, 6 Cubans, 4 Panamanians, 2 Colombians, and 1 each from Nicaragua, Aruba, and Curaçao; even more were under contract

Young Venezuelan baseball player. Introduced by U.S. oil workers in the 1920s, baseball is now Venezuela's most popular sport. © 1997 BY HENRY HORENSTEIN. REPRODUCED BY PERMISSION OF HARCOURT, INC.

in the minors. Surely this trend would be enhanced if U.S.-Cuban relations became normalized, though it might be somewhat tempered by the expanding pool of Asian talent. Surely the stardom and wealth gained by a few Latinos raises the national pride of their countrymen. But some American academics, such as Alan Klein and Milton Jamail, ask if this benefits or exploits the marginal societies that see another of their resources depleted by the capitalist center. Similar questions have been raised about the out-migration of soccer, cricket, and basketball talent.

BOXING

Latin America has produced numerous world champions in boxing, especially in the lighter weight divisions. The best known include Kid Chocolate, Kid Gavilán, and "Mantequilla" Nápoles (Cuba); Rodrigo Valdés and Kid Pambelé (Colombia); Carlos Monzón and Pascual Pérez (Argentina); Alexis Argüello (Nicaragua); Al Brown, Luis Ibarra, and Roberto Durán (Panama); Félix Trinidad (Puerto Rico); Juan Guzmán (Dominican Republic); Vicente Rondón (Venezuela); and Julio César Chávez (Mexico), who in 1994, after ninety fights and three world titles, was knocked out and defeated, both for the first time. In the early twenty-first century Cuba rules the amateur sphere at the Pan-American Games, Olympics, world boxing tournaments, and binational competitions with the United States. Individually best known has been heavyweight Teófilo Stevenson, who dominated the Olympics in the 1970s and later successfully coached his national team; less idolized internationally has been Félix Savón, who built a record similar to Stevenson's.

A new generation of boxing champions includes Brazilian light heavyweight Acelino "Popo" Freitas, Mexicans Marco Antonio Barrera and Erik Morales, and Nicaraguan welterweight Ricardo "El Matador" Mayorga, though in 2006–2007 he had numerous run-ins with the law. Also rising to prominence in the sport are Puerto Rican welterweight Miguel Cotto, Colombian junior welterweight Ricardo Torres, Panamanian super bantamweight Celestino "Pelechín" Caballero, Puerto Rican strawweight Ivan Calderón, and Argentine flyweight Omar Andrés Narváez. The list goes on, especially considering that there are at least five sanctioning bodies declaring champions in seventeen weight divisions.

BASKETBALL

Basketball spread initially via teachers and students, although more recently it has benefited from the televising of National Basketball Association games and high-level international competitions. Goodwill tours by such U.S. stars as Earvin (Magic) Johnson have raised interest and skills. In most countries basketball is an important part of the school physical education and recreation programs, and Argentina, Brazil, Cuba, and Puerto Rico have developed strong national teams. Uruguay has a limited professional league. Argentina hosted and won basketball's first world championship in 1950.

That the quality of basketball in some parts of Latin America has risen substantially since the mid-

Basketball match at the FIBA World Champtionship games between the Brazilian and United States women's teams, Sydney, Australia, 1994. Though soccer and baseball dominate, the sport of basketball in Latin America has won new fans and players. At the 2004 Olympics, Puerto Rico and Argentina beat the highly acclaimed U.S. team. The U.S. NBA continues to draw from the region's talented tool of players. KENNY RODGER/ARCHIVE PHOTOS/GETTY IMAGES

1990s or earlier or more is seen in two developments. First, men's teams have been increasingly successful in international competition. Argentina finished second at the World Championship in 2002 and fourth in 2006. In between they won the Olympic gold medal at Athens in 2004. At the end of 2006 the International Basketball Federation (FIBA) ranked Argentina fourth in the world; Brazil ranked seventeenth and Panama twenty-first. Puerto Rico remained highly competitive in all contests in the Western Hemisphere.

A second indicator of Latin America's rising basketball status is the success of the region's players in foreign countries at the highest professional levels. Arguably the brightest Latino star of the new millennium is Emanuel "Manu" Ginóbili, a native of Bahía Blanca, Argentina, who led his national team to those international triumphs, but was also an integral part of the San Antonio Spurs, who with Ginóbili won the NBA title in 2003, 2005, and 2007. Other prominent Latin Americans in the NBA have been Mexican Eduardo Nájera, who played college ball at Oklahoma and has been backup with three professional teams; St. Vincent and the Grenadines native Adonal Foyle, who graduated from Colgate University and has played center for the Golden State Warriors; Argentine Andrés Nocioni, who made an early impact on the Chicago Bulls; Brazilian Maybyner Rodney Hilário, who made the NBA All-Rookie first team after his first season with the Denver Nuggets; and Fabricio Oberto, Ginóbili's teammate on the Argentine national team and the 2007 Spurs championship squad. At least since "Butch" Lee left Marquette University for the NBA in the late 1970s, numerous Puerto Ricans have contributed to U.S. professional ball.

VOLLEYBALL, BULLFIGHTING, TENNIS

Volleyball, carried worldwide by YMCA workers, has gained less acceptance, although Brazil and Cuba have done well internationally, as have the Peruvian women, and beach varieties of the game have won adherents in some places. The beaches of Rio de Janeiro are daily the venue for a lively, coeducational game that combines the ball and some rules from soccer with the net and rules of volleyball.

Bullfighting and other Iberian sports remain most viable in countries where the European colonial presence was strongest and later immigration did less to alter the inherited traditions. Thus Mexico, Colombia, Peru, and Venezuela have the leading taurine establishments. Mexico, some Andean countries, and Cuba have long promoted jai alai; as in Florida, it is usually accompanied by vigorous gambling.

Latin American tennis stars have increasingly populated world rankings since the late 1950s and early 1960s, the glory days of Anita Linzana (Chile), Pancho Segura (Ecuador), Pancho González (Mexican American), Rafael Osuna (Mexico), and Maria Bueno (Brazil). Beginning in the 1970s such stars as Guillermo Vilas (Argentina), Alex Olmedo (Peru), Andrés Gómez (Ecuador), and Gabriela Sabatini (Argentina) emerged, and their successes promoted tennis as a recreational activity

Shelda Bede, Brazilian beach volleyball player diving to return ball in a 2004 semifinal match, Rio de Janeiro. Volleyball, a more recent sport in Latin America, continues to grow in popularity and strength. Brazil's women's team won a silver medal at the 2004 Olympic games and the men won gold. Argentina finished fifth. As of late 2007, the Brazilan men's volleyball team was ranked #1 internationally. ANTONIO SCORZA/GETTY IMAGES

for a limited middle class in their home countries. Bridging the turn of the century, several younger South Americans have entered the spotlight. The often moody and erratic Chilean Marcelo Ríos never won a Grand Slam, but in 1998 he became the first Latino male to be ranked number one. At Athens in 2004 his countrymen Nicolás Massú and Fernando González teamed up to win the doubles gold; in addition Massú won the singles gold, his partner the bronze. In December 2006 the

Venezuelan tennis player Maria Vento-Kabchi at the Central American and Caribbean Games, Maracaibo, Venezuela, 1998. AP IMAGES

Argentines, led by eleventh-ranked David Nalbandian, lost 3-2 to the Russians in the Davis Cup finals, after trouncing Australia 5-0 in the semis. González reemerged to finish second at the 2007 Australian Open.

GOLF

Despite the long careers and celebrity in the United States of Roberto De Vincenzo (Argentina), Juan "Chi-Chi" Rodrígues (Puerto Rico), and Tex-Mex Lee Treviño, golf sparked minimal interest in Latin America, and few from the region earned international recognition. Even after 2000 no males had premier global status until Argentine Angel Cabrera won the 2007 U.S. Open Championship. The surprising achievements of several females, however, are changing the environment: Colombian María Isabel Baena earned a scholarship to the University of Arizona, where she won ten matches and the NCAA individual championship in 1996. In 2005 she won the HSBC World Match Play Championship on the LPGA tour and gained national recognition back home. In November 2006 the twenty-year-old Paraguayan Julieta Granada entered golf's history books, winning the ADT Championship, played under an unusual format, and $1 million.

Two strokes behind Granada that day was the real star of 2006, Mexican Lorena Ochoa, the LPGA Player of the Year and the Associated Press Female Athlete of the Year. Another University of Arizona scholarship player and twice NCAA champion, Ochoa in 2006 won six titles, nearly $2.6 million, and the Vare Trophy for lowest average scores (69.24). She also led the tour in eagles, birdies, rounds in the 60s, and times in top ten. By June 2007 Ochoa was ranked number one on the LPGA Tour. She has made a few Mexicans at least think outside the soccer stadium.

In addition, countries such as Mexico, Puerto Rico, and the Cayman Islands are courting big-spending foreign tourists with designer links and upscale resorts. In the Los Cabos region of Mexico's southern Baja California, exclusive courses, some designed by players Jack Nicklaus and Robert Trent Jones, charge green fees of U.S. $250–300 and host PGA players needing practice time. In several countries gated communities and middle-class country clubs now include golf courses for an expanding professional sector. Thanks to these developments there is available in 2007, at least in Mexico, access to the Golf Channel and a large, slick monthly golf magazine, *Caras Golf*, which began publication in late 2005.

AUTO RACING

Perhaps because of their early industrialization, Argentina and Brazil embraced auto racing, both track and open-road, and produced international champions such as Argentina's Juan Manuel Fangio and Oscar Gálvez and Brazil's Emerson Fittipaldi, Nelson Piquet, and Ayrton Senna. Colombia's Roberto Guerrero joined the Indianapolis car circuit in the 1980s. Another successful Colombian, Juan Pablo Montoya, switched from Formula One to NASCAR's Nextel Cup competition in 2006–2007 and gained stature when he drove with his Chip Ganassi Racing team to victory in the January 2007 Rolex 24 Daytona sports car endurance race and later won a USA Busch Series road race in Mexico City and his first NEXTEL Cup triumph at California's Infineon Raceway in June. NASCAR's Busch Series has established a separate Mexican operation that includes the fourteen-race Desafío Corona and extensive broadcasting and marketing of NASCAR events and products. And Mexico's Baja, since 1967, has been home of the granddaddy of desert races, run normally in November out of Ensenada. Even women, such as Colombians Juliana González and María Isabel Cajiao, have entered competitive racing from Go Kart through street vehicles to Formula Ford.

OTHER SPORTS AND RECREATIONAL ACTIVITIES

Cycling, an early import from Europe because of its ties with technology, exercise, and French leisure, has been more prominent in mountainous countries such as Colombia, Costa Rica, and Mexico. Premier national events in their respective countries are La Vuelta a Colombia (begun in 1951 and now named for Pilsen, its principal sponsor), La Vuelta a Costa Rica (begun in 1965), and La Vuelta a Venezuela (run over forty times). Several Latin Americans, especially Colombians, have gained recognition on the European circuit, including the three grand tours, but none has ever dominated.

Latin Americans also support track and field, horse racing (in areas under British influence, horses run clockwise on grass), field hockey, swimming, handball and related court ball games (many derived from those various old Basque sports or *pelota vasca*), and chess (which is considered a sport

in the region and was led for years by the Cuban grandmaster José Raúl Capablanca). In the Southern Cone, thanks again to British influence, rugby is a notable scholastic and recreational sport, especially in Argentina, whose national squad, the Pumas, have gained midlevel international status. Polo, an elitist sport, long ago took root in the Argentine pampa, where it has produced the world's most dominant teams for more than half a century.

Recreational activities such as hiking, camping, jogging, survivalism, boating, and sport fishing have become popular. Yacht and powerboat racing are found along many coasts and on large lakes, as are surfboarding and waterskiing. A similar spread of the martial arts was witnessed at the XV Panamerican Taekwando Championship held in Buenos Aires in late 2006; leading medal winners among the Latin Americans were the Mexicans, Brazilians, and Argentines. Professional wrestling (*lucha libre*) has achieved popularity, especially among Mexico's working classes; "good guys" and "bad guys" appear publicly and wrestle in colorful full-body, masked costumes (as can be seen in the 2006 Jack Black film *Nacho Libre*).

From the above mix, the one with the greatest international spectator and economic appeal may be horse racing. Building on the legacies of Puerto Rican Angel Cordero and Panamanian Laffit Pincay, both members of the racing Hall of Fame, a younger generation of Latino turf stars has entered the scene. Peruvian Edgar Prado (b. 1967) in 1997 became the fourth rider to win five hundred races in one year and has since won two Belmont Stakes and one Kentucky Derby (on the horse Barbaro in 2006). Panamanian Fernando Jara (b. 1987) in 2006 won both the Belmont and America's richest race, the Breeders' Cup Classic, the latter on Invasor, a four-year-old bred in Argentina but trained mainly in Uruguay, where he was named 2006 Horse of the Year; Invasor has won nine of ten career starts. In the United States he is surely the best known Latin American horse since Cañonero II, bred in Kentucky but raised and initially raced in Venezuela, won two-thirds of the Triple Crown in 1971. Puerto Rican Johnny Velázquez (b. 1971) rode Rags to Riches, the first filly ever to win the Belmont Stakes (2007).

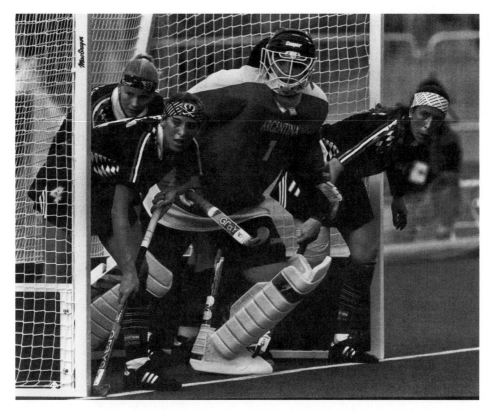

Argentina's national women's field hockey team, 1996. The Argentine team is one of the world's best field hockey teams, winning a silver medal at the 2000 Olympic Games and a bronze in 2004. KARL-HEINZ KREIFELTZ/AP IMAGES

AMERICAN FOOTBALL

American football has gained greater spectator interest with the spread of cable and satellite television, as has the Super Bowl as an excuse to party even among people who neither understand nor like the sport. Only in Mexico (and in the former Panama Canal Zone), however, has it recruited a noticeable number of scholastic participants, beginning as early as the 1930s. National Football League (NFL) games are widely televised in Mexico and covered in the local press; the NFL has scheduled several preseason games there since the 1980s. This interest reflects the fact that several Mexican Americans and Mexicans have played and coached successfully in the United States. Fans in earlier decades applauded the work of place kickers Rafael Septién and Raúl Allegre, quarterback Jim Plunkett, and coach Tom Flores.

In the new century the NFL features several former stars at Monterrey Tech, for several years the best team in Mexico's top American football league. Rolando Cantú is an offensive guard with the Arizona Cardinals; Luis Berlanga kicked briefly in 2006 for the San Francisco 49ers. In January 2007 the Kansas City Chiefs signed Monterrey native Ramiro Pruneda, a massive offensive lineman, to a two-year contract in hopes of developing him into a standout player.

A few non-Mexican Latinos have played college ball in the United States and connected with the NFL: José Cortez (El Salvador), kicker for several teams, and defensive lineman Luis Castillo of Dominican origin, starter for San Diego. Ron Rivera, his father a Puerto Rican career military officer, his mother Mexican, won a Super Bowl ring with the Chicago Bears in 1985 and as defensive coordinator helped them return to Super Bowl XLI. At least three other Puerto Ricans have played in the NFL.

THE USES OF SPORTS

Participants and spectators alike have been increasingly influenced by forces directed by private and public agencies seeking to use sport and recreation, including physical culture and education, for larger economic and political objectives: to teach constructive values, improve health and morality, increase labor productivity, reduce vice and crime, develop a sense of community and cooperation, promote patriotism and nationalism, attract foreign investment, and improve a nation's image abroad—objectives often aimed at social control as much as social development. These goals have been pursued by (1) the establishment of domestic physical education programs, sports competitions, and permanent institutions necessary to oversee athletic programs; (2) the preparation of individuals and teams capable of competing successfully at the international level; and (3) the hosting of international sporting events.

Examples of the overt use or abuse of sports for political reasons include the Guatemalan government's promotion of the Sixth Central American and Caribbean Games (1950) to enhance the Arévalo-Arbenz revolutionary program; in Chile, the efforts of the Augusto Pinochet dictatorship after September 1973 to suppress all sports clubs and events that might give voice to suspected critics and protesters; and the attempt by the ruling Brazilian military in 1970 to exploit their country's third soccer World Cup victory to strengthen its authoritarian rule and similar actions by the Argentine military in hosting and winning the 1978 Mundial.

ORGANIZATIONS AND EVENTS

All Latin American countries have, however ineffective and poorly funded, some version of an integrated national sports federation (such as Chile's Digeder, Colombia's Coldeportes, Cuba's Inder, and Mexico's Conade), national associations for most sports, Olympic organizing committees, a physical education institute, and periodic "national games" at different age levels. The professional leagues are usually separate entities. Overlapping these organizations are expanding linkages to international networks. Latin Americans began to join Olympic competitions in 1900, and FIFA, soccer's governing body founded in 1904, in 1913. In 1922, on the centenary of its independence, Brazil organized the now defunct South American Games; in 1926, encouraged by the Olympic leadership in Paris in 1924, Mexico hosted the first

Central American and Caribbean Games; the more limited Central American Games started in Guatemala in 1973; in 1938, on the four-hundredth anniversary of the founding of its capital, Colombia initiated the Bolivarian Games. In 1951 Juan Perón's Argentina inaugurated the Pan-American Games, a competition likewise encouraged by the Olympic leadership as early as the 1932 Los Angeles Olympics and originally scheduled for Buenos Aires in 1942. A smaller winter version of the Pan-American Games was launched in 1990 but, because of the lack of snow and support, soon faltered.

Uruguay hosted and won the first soccer World Cup (Mundial) in 1930, after winning the previous two Olympic gold medals in that sport. Brazil (1950), Chile (1962), Mexico (1970, 1986), and Argentina (1978) have also hosted the World Cup, which is the largest sporting event in the world other than the Olympics. Brazil is a strong favorite to host again in 2014. Mexico was the first developing country to sponsor the Summer Olympics (1968), an event marred by domestic political violence and the death and disappearance of numerous students and workers shortly before the torch arrived, but which the government cited as proof of Mexico's progress and international acceptance.

In addition to the competitive encounters and organizational ties, the growing internationalization of sports has generated increased migration of players and coaches within Latin America and to and from Europe and North America, as well as sales of foreign sporting equipment and televised sporting events. Building on a tradition that dates back to the 1930s, for example, more than four hundred Argentine soccer players were estimated to be playing in other countries in 1992. (Some of the better Argentine basketball players are also now spending time in European, especially Italian, leagues.) This is part of a larger global pattern that sees athletic talent follow the money from marginal areas and clubs to wealthier and more powerful centers in the larger cities of the richer countries, eventually, in the early twenty-first century, arriving in Western Europe or North America.

CUBA

Prior to 1959 Cuba had won numerous Olympic medals (the first in 1900), produced skilled professional boxers such as Kid Tunero and Kid Chocolate, and sent more baseball players to the U.S. major leagues than any foreign country. But critics then and since have contended that the Cuban sports structure, like that of other Latin American countries, was elitist, sexist, and too responsive to external monetary pressures. Following the revolution, Cuba eliminated open professionalism, increased its Olympic medal count (to thirty-one at Barcelona in 1992, for example), and built a balanced program of mass physical culture superior to any other in Latin America. However, some forty Cuban athletes defected during the Central American and Caribbean Games in Puerto Rico in 1993, suggesting that dissatisfaction runs high even among the privileged, a conviction reaffirmed by the similar flight of an increasing number of players from Cuba's Pan-American, world amateur, and Olympic championship baseball team, many of whom—including brothers Liván and Orlando "El Duque" Hernández—have signed professional contracts in North America. A number of these received help in defecting to the United States and in signing those contracts from the controversial agent Joe Cubas.

Before Barcelona, probably Cuba's greatest international sporting achievement occurred at the eleventh Pan American Games (1991), hosted by the island nation. Under severe economic and political difficulties, the Cubans provided the facilities for 4,519 athletes from thirty-nine countries and won ten more gold medals than did the United States (140 to the U.S.'s 130), although the total medal count favored the United States (352 to Cuba's 265). Since 1991–1992 Cuba has continued to be among the top three medal winners at the Pan American Games and among the top eleven at the Olympics; relative to population it is almost certainly number one in the world.

From the 2003 Pan American Games (Dominican Republic), Cubans carried home 270 total medals, 117 of them gold; that was second only to the United States, with 152 and 72. As a result, through the fourteen Pan Am Games, Cuba, with 1,658 total medals, of these 309 gold, ranks behind only the Americans with 3,679 and 1,651.

At the 2004 Summer Olympics (Greece), Cubans captured 27 total medals, 9 of them gold. At the 2006 Central American and Caribbean

Games (Colombia), they won the most total medals (285) and the most gold (138); Mexico, with seven times or more the population of Cuba, was a respectable second with 275 and 107.

WOMEN IN SPORTS

Cuba has been nearly as successful in developing female champions as male, although critics of the Castro system still identify sexist, as well as racist, qualities in the Cuban sports system. Women from other Latin American countries have achieved somewhat less than the Cubans, in part because their societies value women athletes less and provide less support, though those attitudes are changing in the new century. Earlier exceptions included Neomí Simonetto (long jump, Argentina), Marlene Ahrens (javelin throw, Chile), Silvia Poll (swimming, Costa Rica), and the tennis stars cited above. The 1988 Olympic Games displayed the continuing prowess of the Peruvian women's volleyball team, which took the silver medal.

In addition to the women golfers discussed above, competitive international athletes have emerged in unusual places. At the Sydney Olympics (2000) Colombian María Isabel Urrutia and Mexican Soraya Jiménez won gold in weightlifting. The latter's retirement has brought forth Carolina Valencia, who won three gold medals at the 2006 Central American and Caribbean Games. Gold from the 1991 World Championships and silver from the Athens Olympics belong to multiple-champion Ana Gabriela Guevara (Mexico), who specializes in the 400-meter and 4 x 400 relay. Women throughout the region are playing soccer, though as of 2006 only the Brazilians were close to world class. Cuban and Brazilian women are superior in beach volleyball.

SPORTS AND SOCIETY

Sports' importance in Latin American society is reflected in the use of sport jargon in the ordinary language and of sport themes in artistic expressions. Politicians often "move pieces on the board" in hopes of "getting to the head of the pack" in order to "score more goals," whereas great writers have long used play and game settings to convey their ideas—for example, Argentina's Julio Cortázar (boxing) and Chile's Antonio Skármeta (cycling, soccer, and tennis). Increasingly authors depict sport as physical activity rather than spectacle, thus providing a means to represent social and psychological conflicts among literary characters. This is evident in the boxing plays of Eduardo Pavlosky (Argentina) and Vicente Leñero (Mexico) and the novels of Isaac Goldemberg (soccer, Peru) and José Agustín (baseball, Mexico). An introduction to the extensive repertoire of sports-related short stories is found in the volumes edited by Jorge Valdano, who himself played with Argentina's World Cup victors in 1986.

Although originally the language of many sports was built on the Latinized pronunciation of imported, usually English terms ("golf," "round," "football," "fly"), Spanish and Portuguese linguistic inventions have been replacing many foreign words (boxeo for "boxing"; gol for "goal"; arquero for "goalie"), or reasonable translations have been identified (*fuera de lugar* for "offside"; *tiro de esquina* for "corner"; *lanzador* for "pitcher"; *el cuarto bate* for "cleanup hitter"; *árbitro* for "referee"; *baloncesto* for "basquet ball"). The importance of games and sports in the lives of Latin Americans is further evident in the success of sports periodicals of the quality of *El Gráfico* (Argentina), *Placar* (Brazil), the extensive sports sections in the daily newspapers, and the explosion of weekly and monthly specialized magazines aimed at both players of all levels and spectators.

See also **Capablanca, José Raúl; Fangio, Juan Manuel; Ginobili, Manu; Maradona, Diego; Ochoa Reyes, Lorena; Sabatini, Gabriela; Sosa, Sammy; Valenzuela, Fernando.**

BIBLIOGRAPHY

Arbena, Joseph L., comp. *An Annotated Bibliography of Latin American Sport: Pre-Conquest to the Present.* Westport, CT: Greenwood Press, 1989.

Arbena, Joseph L., comp. *Latin American Sport: An Annotated Bibliography, 1988–1998.* Westport, CT: Greenwood Press, 1999.

Arbena, Joseph L., and David G. La France, eds. *Sport in Latin America and the Caribbean.* Wilmington, DE: Scholarly Resources, 2002.

Beezley, William H. *Judas at the Jockey Club and Other Episodes of Porfirian Mexico*, 2nd edition. Lincoln: University of Nebraska Press, 2004.

Bellos, Alex. *Futebol: The Brazilian Way of Life.* New York: Bloomsbury, 2002.

Bjarkman, Peter C. *Baseball with a Latin Beat: A History of the Latin American Game.* Jefferson, NC: McFarland, 1994.

Bjarkman, Peter C. *A History of Cuban Baseball, 1864–2006.* Jefferson, NC: McFarland, 2007.

Galeano, Eduardo. *Soccer in Sun and Shadow*, 2nd edition, translated by Mark Fried. New York: Verso, 2003.

González Echevarría, Roberto. *The Pride of Havana: A History of Cuban Baseball.* New York: Oxford University Press, 1999.

Klein, Alan M. *Sugarball: The American Game, the Dominican Dream.* New Haven, CT: Yale University Press, 1991.

Mangan, J. A., and Lamartine, P. DaCosta, eds. *Sport in Latin American Society: Past and Present.* London and Portland, OR: Frank Cass, 2002.

Mason, Tony. *Passion of the People? Football in South America.* London and New York: Verso, 1995.

Morelli, Liliana. *Mujeres deportistas.* Buenos Aires: Planeta, 1990.

Murray, Bill. *The World's Game: A History of Soccer.* Urbana: University of Illinois Press, 1996.

Regalado, Samuel O. *Viva Baseball! Latin Major Leaguers and Their Special Hunger.* Urbana: University of Illinois Press, 1998.

JOSEPH L. ARBENA

SQUIER, EPHRAIM GEORGE (1821–1888).

Ephraim George Squier (*b.* 17 June 1821; *d.* 17 April 1888), U.S. diplomat and writer. Squier was one of the most important diplomats to represent the United States in Central America in the nineteenth century. Appointed in 1849, Squier was in Central America only one year. In that short period he energetically assisted agents of Cornelius Vanderbilt in negotiating a contract to build a transisthmian canal, signed a treaty with Nicaragua guaranteeing U.S. protection of the canal route, and persuaded Honduran authorities to cede territory in the Gulf of Fonseca to the United States. These actions, which exceeded his instructions, provoked a dispute with Great Britain that led to the negotiation of the Clayton-Bulwer Treaty. The treaty declared that neither country would attempt to colonize Central America or control any isthmian transportation facility. Although Squier thought that the treaty signaled a defeat for the United States, in reality it marked the beginning of the replacement of British influence in Central America with that of the United States.

The brief visit to Central America turned Squier into a publicist for Central America and an entrepreneur. He wrote extensively about Central American topics, ranging from archaeology to contemporary foreign relations, and was recognized in mid-century as the leading authority on the region. As an entrepreneur he was unsuccessful in his attempts to build a railway across Honduras.

See also **Honduras; Nicaragua; Panama Canal.**

BIBLIOGRAPHY

The following studies by Charles L. Stansifer cover differing aspects of Squier's career: "The Central American Writings of E. George Squier," in *Inter-American Review of Bibliography* 16, no. 2 (1966): 144–160; "E. George Squier and the Honduras Interoceanic Railroad Project," in *Hispanic American Historical Review* 46, no. 1 (1966): 1–27; *E. George Squier: Diversos aspectos de su carrera en Centro América* (1968).

Additional Bibliography

Barnhart, Terry A. *Ephraim George Squier and the Development of American Anthropology.* Lincoln: University of Nebraska Press, 2005.

CHARLES L. STANSIFER

STADEN, HANS (1525–1579).

Hans Staden was a German gunner in the service of the Portuguese. He traveled to Pernambuco in January 1548, then returned to Portugal the following October, but sailed again in March 1549 on a Spanish vessel that was part of a new expedition to Rio de la Plata. Unfavorable weather broke up the fleet, which was reunited at the Portuguese colony of São Vicente. Here the Portuguese were allied with the Tupiniquin, which meant that the Tupinambá to the north, who were allied with the French, were hostile to their settlement. Staden was persuaded to stay in Portuguese service for another two years, acting as a gunner in a Portuguese fort on the island of São Amaro. It was during this period that he was captured by the Tupinambá. *Warhaftige Historia*, the famous account of his captivity and the anthropophagic rituals of his captors, was published in 1557 and is a key work in the discovery literature about Brazil. Notably, his account contained numerous woodcuts depicting the Tupinambá, which became the basis for a chapter in the widely circulated compendium of early voyages to America by Theodor de Bry.

See also **Brazil: The Colonial Era, 1500–1808.**

BIBLIOGRAPHY

Whitehead, Neil L., and Michael Harbsmeier, eds. *Hans Staden's True History: An Account of Cannibal Captivity.* Durham, NC, and London: Duke University Press, 2008.

NEIL L. WHITEHEAD

STANDARD FRUIT AND STEAMSHIP COMPANY.

Standard Fruit and Steamship Company, a firm that grew out of Vaccaro Brothers and Company. The conversion of the latter to a public corporation—Standard Fruit and Steamship Company—in 1925, plus consistently high profits, provided sufficient capital for the firm to expand beyond Honduras, and to grow fruit or buy from producers in much of tropical America, including Mexico, Nicaragua, Guatemala, Costa Rica, Panama, Haiti, Cuba, and Ecuador. Most of its banana production was sold in the United States.

Honduras, the company's most reliable producer, originally lacked the infrastructure to support Standard's growth. Hence Standard pioneered in many related businesses, such as the manufacturing of paper, boxes, and beer; as Vaccaro Brothers, it built the first railroad, bank, and hospital in the land.

Although it was a public corporation, Standard continued to be managed by the Vaccaro and D'Antoni families until 1964. Family representatives always made their home in La Ceiba, Honduras, close to the banana farms; this personal stake meant that the company regularly directed much money and energy into research, seeking better soils and varieties of fruit, and new methods of combating the omnipresent and destructive Panama and Sigatoka diseases. Standard accomplished its greatest gain on the competition in the 1960s with the invention of a cardboard carton that could protect and keep cool a new variety of disease-resistant but easily bruised banana. This simple development thrust Standard into a position of marketing leadership and in time saved the entire industry from having to leave Central America.

From time to time Standard has owned and operated a fleet of banana freighters capable of carrying passengers on cruises. Since the 1960s economic conditions have dictated the leasing of ships and an end to the cruise business.

Standard has attempted to avoid involvement with local factions. Management has found it profitable to stay out of political affairs rather than attempt to manipulate them for the company's benefit.

The most serious business mistakes were the expensive and repeated efforts to grow bananas in the unsuitable soil found in much of Nicaragua; attempting to do business as usual in Mexico following the 1917 revolution; and battling (unsuccessfully) Haiti's preposterously small landholding patterns, thereby wiping out one of that nation's few viable industries.

Heirs of the Vaccaro and D'Antoni families eventually lost interest in the banana business; the last family chairman of the board, Joseph D'Antoni, was a physician who wanted to return to medical research and teaching. In 1964 the company was sold to Castle & Cooke, vast landowners in Hawaii and distributors of the best-selling brand of pineapple. Castle & Cooke poured millions into the merger and placed the Dole label on Standard's products.

See also **Banana Industry; United Fruit Company.**

BIBLIOGRAPHY

New Orleans Daily Picayune (1899–1913).

Claude W. Wardlaw and Laurence P. McGuire, *Panama Disease of Bananas* (1929).

Charles D. Kepner, Jr., and Jay H. Soothill, *The Banana Empire* (1935), esp. pp. 102, 112.

Standard Fruit and Steamship Company, *Annual Reports*; Thomas L. Karnes, *Tropical Enterprise: The Standard Fruit and Steamship Company in Latin America* (1978).

Tom Barry and Deb Preusch, *The Central American Fact Book* (1986), pp. 148–152.

Additional Bibliography

García Buchard, Ethel. *Poder político, interés bananero e identidad nacional en Centro América: Un estudio comparativo: Costa Rica (1884-1938) y Honduras (1902-1958)*. Tegucigalpa: Editorial Universitaria, 1997.

Soluri, John. *Banana Cultures: Agriculture, Consumption, and Environmental Change in Honduras and the United States.* Austin: University of Texas Press, 2005.

Striffler, Steve, and Mark Moberg. *Banana Wars: Power, Production, and History in the Americas.* Durham, NC: Duke University Press, 2003.

                                    THOMAS L. KARNES

STATE CORPORATIONS. The origins of state corporations, variously known as state-owned enterprises (SOEs), parastatal companies, and government-linked companies (GLCs), are found in economic nationalism. They symbolize national economic sovereignty in Latin America, East Asia, sub-Saharan Africa, the Middle East and North Africa, and even Europe. In developing parts of the world, SOEs have emerged as newly independent states (many of them former colonies), lacking domestic private capital, technology, and managerial know-how, have endeavored to develop their economies without allowing European firms to take control of their economies. This position dictates that the state-held enterprises become the principal instruments of national development, and that the state therefore is responsible for financing, production, management, distribution, and sale.

Typically state corporations dominate in natural resources, heavy industries, banking and finance, utilities, telecommunications, transport, and other infrastructure areas. SOEs were often created out of necessity, when a new type of political regime was instituted or when a government nationalized foreign-owned assets or private properties belonging to enemies of the new state. In Cuba under Fidel and Raúl Castro (1959–), Chile under Salvador Allende (1970–1973), and Nicaragua under the Sandinistas (1979–1989), Marxist governments established *compañías estatales* including banks, airlines, and energy, utility, and manufacturing companies. In Brazil, they are known as *companhias estatais*. In Africa, the wave of anticolonialism and post-independence socialism led to the creation of a host of parastatals. In noncommunist East Asia (Japan, Korea, Taiwan) and Southeast Asia, government-linked companies (GLCs) were built in the early stages of export-promoting industrialization, but once the economic sectors matured, they were privatized. Except for China, there are now few SOEs in East Asian countries. In Southeast Asia, GLCs play a prominent economic role. Petronas (Malaysia's state-owned and run oil company), SingTel (Singapore's telecommunications firm), and Pertaminas (Indonesia's oil and mining giant) are a few examples of the region's major state corporations.

In the past, the typical state corporations were the tools of import-substitution industrialization (ISI), drawing factors of production internally. The desire to become self-sufficient in industrial goods became the principal driver for Latin American ISI. The state owned, planned, financed, managed, distributed, and sold what it produced. Citizens regardless of their social station were given access to state products and services. The other side of this egalitarian economic philosophy is political populism. In Latin America, SOEs were founded on an ideology of populist consumption, a vital tool of social development. Economic nationalism, with its need to keep out and even compete against foreign firms, also played a major role in the creation and maintenance of SOEs, especially in energy, telecoms, transport, and banking.

There are three types of SOEs currently in operation throughout Latin America: production-oriented, service-providing, and financial and banking. Latin America's oldest state corporation still in operation, the Bank of Brazil, dates to 1808, but the continent began to establish state corporations only after the dawn of its populist age, around 1930. And the proliferation of today's major state-owned enterprises occurred during and after World War II. By the mid-1980s states in Latin America began to operate in such nonessential sectors as hotels, resorts, farms, bakeries, bookstores, and even beauty shops. State corporations became a fiscal burden to the public coffers, wrecking finances but remaining the countries' biggest employers. Employees were badly paid, productivity declined, and inefficiency grew. Brazil's SOEs hired four million employees, equivalent to the population of Norway. Of the 12,000 SOEs in Latin America, Mexico claimed 1,200, Argentina and Brazil 800 each, and Chile 400. As losses mounted under mismanagement, states covered them with taxpayers' money and money borrowed in international financial markets. As states ran out of money, international bankers refused to loan and Latin America led the Third World external debt crisis. In September 1982, Mexico became the first Latin American country to default. Soon others followed. Latin American states owed closed to $300 billion, 60 percent of Third World debt. As much as 80 percent of all Latin debt was held by SOEs. State corporations became ripe targets for public criticism, refuges for hard-to-place retired military officers, and growing nests of political nepotism. Savvy private businessmen exploited major state companies as contractors and suppliers who regularly overcharged for their goods and services; the result was the socialization of the costs and the privatization of the profits.

The World Bank, the International Monetary Fund, and the U.S. Treasury championed the now widely resented "Washington Consensus," which promoted privatizing the state sector, liberalizing international trade, and deregulating domestic markets. Although this neoliberal recipe has had global significance, the policy was more directed to Latin America's political economy. In East Asia, privatization occurred slowly, expanding the private sector's share of the national economies. By the mid-1980s, as the crisis worsened, international bankers refused to renegotiate debt until debtor countries adopted the Washington Consensus reform agenda.

In Chile, where neoliberalism was forced upon the country by the military coup after 1973, properties seized by the Allende government were either returned to the original owners or auctioned off. One ingenious approach Chile employed was "debt swap." One debt dollar held by the state was valued at as low as 18 cents in the international financial market. The government of Chile was willing to pay up to 87 cents per debt dollar. Many mining properties, public transportation, utilities, airlines, and other state firms were sold off to international and Chilean buyers. Although each dollar bought 87 cents worth of state assets, it actually cost the buyer 18 cents, a rate of discount that, one minister of mining observed, had the Chilean state playing the role of Santa Claus to international capital. The government justified the policy by insisting that the swap reduced the country's external debt. The debt swap was one of a host of neoliberal measures introduced by the dictatorship, among them the privatization of the national pension fund (akin to the American Social Security system). In spite of the zeal for privatization, the Chilean government kept the country's biggest copper mining SOE, Codelco, off the auction block, and it continues to this day as state corporation.

The great transformation of Latin America's economy from the populist, statist capitalism to the neoliberal market system has produced a mixed result. Chile is a success story, but not all Latin American economies are like Chile's. Many buyers of state assets expected to create private monopolies through privatization. To make the project work, the state often conceded monopoly rights for a fixed duration. Often old habits continued, of privatizing profits and socializing losses. Many privatized firms collapsed when the protection ran out. The governments of Argentina, Brazil, Mexico, and even Chile had to take back bankrupt firms in order to save jobs. And there were SOEs that proved unsaleable—national railroads, state-owned shipping lines, and airports. Except for Argentina, Latin American governments did not privatize oil companies. Pemex (Mexico), Petrobrás (Brazil), and PDVSA (Venezuela), among others, remain state-owned, although they compete in the neoliberal environment of the domestic and international markets.

The current trend is that the state must retain control over its domestic economy and external trade relations. Ever-expanding neoliberal globalization has made countries vulnerable to international competition. The Washington Consensus of neoliberal markets implemented throughout the hemisphere has not produced prosperity for all. Since the 1970s Latin America's economies have grown, but income distribution has for the most part retrogressed, and mass poverty has not been eradicated, seemingly confirming the popular belief that the rich get richer and the poor get poorer. Populism has returned and spread throughout the continent, with Hugo Chávez in Venezuela and Evo Moráles in Bolivia swept into office with mandates to reverse neoliberal economic policies. The return of SOEs has been one outcome.

In countries in which SOEs have been strengthened, much of state revenue comes from oil and gas. In Venezuela, state revenues are used to fund social programs intended to alleviate poverty, improve housing, make education accessible, and provide health care to a previously neglected population, reinforcing the regime's popularity. Rising anti-Americanism has turned oil into an important weapon for many states to challenge and resist current U.S. foreign and security policies. More importantly, SOEs are seen as a proper instrument to protect the national interest in the era of globalization, when many developing and developed countries fail to benefit from the global market.

See also **Dependency Theory; Economic Development; Foreign Trade; Globalization; International Monetary Fund (IMF); Neoliberalism; Privatization; Public Sector and Taxation; World Bank.**

BIBLIOGRAPHY

Abranches, Sérgio Henrique, et al. *A empresa pública no Brasil: Uma abordagem multidisciplinar: Coletânea de monografias.* Brasília: Instituto de Planejamento Econômico e Social, Secretaria de Modernização e Reforma Administrativa, 1980.

Castro, Paulo Rabello de, ed. *A crise do "bom patrão."* Rio de Janeiro: CEDES: APEC (1982).

Dornbusch, Rudiger, and Sebastian Edwards, eds. *The Macroeconomics of Populism in Latin America.* Chicago: University of Chicago Press, 1991.

Glade, William P., ed. *State Shrinking: A Comparative Inquiry into Privatization.* Austin: Institute of Latin American Studies, University of Texas at Austin, 1986.

Kelly Escobar, Janet. "The Comparison of State Enterprises across International Boundaries: The Corporación Venezolana de Guayana and the Companhia Vale do Rio Doce." In *Public Enterprise in Less-Developed Countries,* ed. Leroy P. Jones. Cambridge, U.K. and New York: Cambridge University Press, 1982.

Kuczynski, Pedro-Pablo, and John Williamson, eds. *After the Washington Consensus: Restarting Growth and Reform in Latin America.* Washington, DC: Institute for International Economics, 2003.

Lora, Eduardo, ed. *The State of State Reform in Latin America.* Stanford, CA: Stanford University Press; Washington, DC: World Bank, 2007.

Pang, Eul-Soo. *The International Political Economy of Transformation in Argentina, Brazil, and Chile since 1960.* Basingstoke, Hampshire, U.K. and New York: Palgrave Macmillan, 2002.

Toninelli, Pier Angelo, ed. *The Rise and Fall of State-Owned Enterprise in the Western World.* Cambridge, U.K. and New York: Cambridge University Press, 2000.

Trebat, Thomas J. *Brazil's State-Owned Enterprises: A Case Study of the State as Entrepreneur.* Cambridge, U.K., and New York: Cambridge University Press, 1983.

Williamson, John, ed. *The Political Economy of Policy Reform*. Washington, DC: Institute for International Economics, 1994.

EUL-SOO PANG

STATE OF SIEGE.
State of siege, a situation in which constitutional guarantees in a country are suspended and emergency powers of government are granted to the president. The provision of *estado de sitio* (*estado do sítio* in Portuguese) is put into action to deal with emergencies caused by invasion by a foreign power or major social disturbance. Usually such situations are declared by the legislature. Most Latin American constitutions contain the provision for the implementation of state of siege, usually with some restrictions. The president is granted the authority for all executive and legislative powers and can suspend judicial prerogative.

In most cases, a state of siege has been implemented for domestic crises. Abuse of the condition has been common in the region as dictators and military governments have used it as a legal pretext to act against political opponents or against perceived opposition. Indeed, such governments often keep the country under state of siege long after the initial crisis has subsided. Attempts to limit or restrict the implementation of state of siege have been successful only in those countries that have been able to attain some level of political stability or legislative strength.

See also **Golpe de Estado (coup d'état).**

BIBLIOGRAPHY

Clusellas, Eduardo L. Gregorini. *Estado de sitio y la armonía en la relación individuo-estado*. Argentina: Depalma, 1987.

HEATHER K. THIESSEN

STEDMAN, JOHN G. (1744–1779).
The military officer and author John G. Stedman participated during the 1770s in the Suriname colonial counterinsurgency campaigns against runaway slaves (Maroons). The son of a Scottish father who was an officer of the Scottish brigade within the Dutch army, at age twenty-nine Stedman joined an expedition to suppress a rebellion of Maroons in eastern Suriname (formerly Dutch Guiana). Five hundred Maroons, headed by the legendary guerrilla leader Boni, had resisted the attacks of the planters and their army of mercenaries and slave soldiers. After the arrival of 1,200 European enforcements in 1773 the colonial army took the initiative. After a lengthy guerrilla war of more than four years, the Boni-Maroons fled in 1777 to French Guiana. Afterwards, a kind of agreement was reached, paving the way for a series of peace agreement with the various Maroon clans.

Stedman kept a diary and painted more than 100 watercolor sketches during the antiguerrilla campaign. The diary was transformed into his memoirs, published to success—after a heavy redrafting by his editor—in 1796 with sixteen engravings by William Blake. In 1988 the American anthropologists Richard and Sally Price republished the original version of Stedman's manuscript. Stedman's memoirs are highly critical of the Surinamese administration: Although he was not an abolitionist, he criticized the slavery system considerably and pleaded for reforms.

See also **Maroons (Cimarrones); Suriname and the Dutch in the Caribbean.**

BIBLIOGRAPHY

Stedman, John Gabriel. *Narrative of a Five Years Expedition against the Revolted Negroes of Surinam*. Edited by Richared Price and Sally Price. Baltimore, MD: Johns Hopkins University Press, 1988.

Hoogbergen, Wim. *The Boni-Maroon Wars in Suriname*. Leiden: E. J. Brill, 1991.

DIRK KRUIJT

STEFANICH, JUAN (1889–1975).
Juan Stefanich (*b.* 3 May 1889; *d.* 1975), Paraguayan politician. Born in Asunción, Stefanich first came to public notice during the 1910s, when, as a brilliant law student, he won a series of prizes in literature and philosophy. Awarded a doctorate in law in 1920, he had already become a well-known professor, author, and political commentator.

In 1928 Stefanich helped found the National Independence League, a radical pressure group that offered a strong nationalist response to

Bolivian incursions in the Gran Chaco region. After full-fledged war with Bolivia became a reality in 1932, Stefanich pushed for the strongest possible territorial gains for Paraguay, becoming disappointed when his country had to settle for less.

The fall of the Liberal government in 1936 gave Stefanich an opportunity to try to transform these attitudes into reality. Allying himself with Colonel Rafael Franco and the military insurgents who had seized power, he became the main spokesman for their quasi-authoritarian ideology of *febrerismo*. In this, he drew his inspiration from an eclectic mix of Italian and Spanish fascism, German nazism, Soviet communism, and individualist democracy. He argued that the new Paraguay presented the chance for a new kind of democracy (*democracia solidarista*) in which all class conflicts would cease and be replaced by a dynamic sense of community. Some elements of *febrerista* thinking, especially those that stressed firm executive power, found their way into the 1940 constitution.

Stefanich himself became foreign minister in the Franco government, but when the latter regime was overthrown in 1937, he fled into exile. He continued to participate in party politics and publish *febrerista* tracts and philosophical works from exile, and periodically reappeared in Asunción. He later came to repudiate his earlier extremism, however, in favor of a social-democratic model.

See also **Franco, Rafael; Paraguay: The Twentieth Century.**

BIBLIOGRAPHY

William Belmont Parker, *Paraguayans of To-Day* (1921), pp. 81–82.

Paul H. Lewis, *The Politics of Exile* (1965), *passim*.

Additional Bibliography

Farcau, Bruce W. *The Chaco War: Bolivia and Paraguay, 1932–1935.* Westport, CT: Praeger, 1996.

Rahi, Arturo. *Franco y la revolución de febrero.* Asunción: Augusto Gallegos, 2001.

                                    THOMAS L. WHIGHAM

STEIMBERG, ALICIA (1933–). Alicia Steimberg (*b.* 1933), Argentine fiction writer, born in Buenos Aires. Her first novel, *Músicos y relojeros* (Musicians and Watchmakers, 1971), was a finalist in two major literary contests. Her second novel, *La loca 101* (Insane Prisoner 101, 1973), won the Satiricón de Oro Award from Argentina. In the 1980s she published several novels and a collection of short stories. The short stories are in *Como todas las mañanas* (1983), and the novels are *Su espíritu inocente* (1981), which is set in the Buenos Aires of the 1940s, *El árbol del placer* (1986; The Tree of Pleasures), and *Amatista* (1989), a humorous erotic novel that portrays the apprenticeship of a serious gentleman in the practice of erotic games. This book came out in the series La Sonrisa Vertical by Tusquets of Barcelona as the result of winning an award as the best erotic novel of the year. That same year she also published *Salirse de madre*. In 1991 she published a "gastronomic novel" for adolescents, *El mundo no es polenta* (The World Is Not Humor).

The humor and wit of the female protagonists is an important feature of Steimberg's fiction. Her novel *Cuando digo Magdalena* (1992; When I Pronounce Magdalena) won the distinguished Premio Planeta Biblioteca del Sur for 1992. It describes the daily life of a group of people confined on a ranch while practicing "mental control," a technique that became popular in Argentina in the 1990s. In 2001, her book *Call Me Magdalena* was published in English. This was followed by a translation of *The Rainforest* in 2006.

See also **Literature: Spanish America.**

BIBLIOGRAPHY

Saúl Sosnowski, "Alicia Steimberg: Enhebrando pequeñas historias," in *Folio: Essays on Foreign Languages and Literatures* (1987).

Monica Flori, "Alicia Steimberg and Cecilia Absatz: Dos narradores argentinas" in *Chasqui* 17 (November 1988): 2, 83–92.

Additional Bibliography

Ferrero, Adrián. "'Creo que segrego feminismo automática porque soy mujer': Entrevista a la narradora Argentina, Alicia Steimberg." *Chasqui* 34: (May 2005): 65–73.

Flori, Mónica Roy. *Streams of Silver: Six Contemporary Women Writers from Argentina.* Lewisburg, PA: Bucknell University Press, 1995.

                              MAGDALENA GARCÍA PINTO

STEIN, EDUARDO

STEIN, EDUARDO (1945–). Eduardo Stein was elected vice president of Guatemala, serving with President Oscar Berger, the leader of a center-right political coalition, in 2004. From 1996 to 2000, Stein was the foreign minister in the administration of President Álvaro Arzú. At the Organization of American States (OAS), the United Nations, and the International Organization for Migration, Stein worked to promote regional agreements for the solution of internal problems. In Peru in 2000 he led the OAS election-observation delegation, which became the first in OAS history to judge an election to have failed to meet international standards.

See also **Organization of American States (OAS).**

BIBLIOGRAPHY

Fund for Peace. "Building Peace in the 21st Century." *Reality Check* no. 5, June 2002. Available from http://www.fundforpeace.org.

Gobierno de Guatemala. Available from http://www.guatemala.gob.gt (see Gobierno/Vicepresidente).

McClintock, Cynthia, and Fabián Vallas. *The United States and Peru: Cooperation at a Cost.* New York: Routledge, 2003.

CYNTHIA McCLINTOCK

STEPHENS, JOHN LLOYD

STEPHENS, JOHN LLOYD (1805–1852). John Lloyd Stephens (*b.* 28 November 1805; *d.* 12 October 1852), U.S. diplomat, author, and president of the Panama Railroad Company (1849–1852). Stephens served as U.S. minister to Central America in 1839 and 1840. His diplomatic mission—to renew a treaty of commerce and seek trans-isthmian railroad and canal routes—failed due to the collapse of the Central American Federation. Stephens proved more interested in archaeology than diplomacy. He visited a number of Maya ruins during his first and second (1841) trips to Central America and Mexico. Stephens's *Incidents of Travel in Central America, Chiapas, and Yucatán* (1841) is probably the most interesting and useful nineteenth-century traveler's account of Central America.

Stephens played a pivotal role in building the first trans-isthmian railroad. He helped William H. Aspinwall secure a concession for the Panama route from the Colombian government in 1848 and later became president of Aspinwall's Panama Railroad Company. Stephens spent a great deal of time in Panama during the railway's construction. He contracted a fever there and died in New York City before the railroad began operation in 1855.

See also **Panama Railroad; Travel Literature.**

BIBLIOGRAPHY

John Lloyd Stephens, *Incidents of Travel in Central America, Chiapas, and Yucatán* (1841).

John Haskell Kemble, *The Panama Route, 1848–1869* (1943).

Joseph L. Schott, *Rails Across Panama: The Story of the Building of the Panama Railroad, 1849–1855* (1967).

Victor Wolfgang Von Hagen, *Search for the Maya: The Story of Stephens and Catherwood* (1973).

Additional Bibliography

Evans, R. Tripp. *Romancing the Maya: Mexican Antiquity in the American Imagination, 1820–1915.* Austin: University of Texas Press, 2004.

Glassman, Steve. *On the Trail of the Maya Explorer: Tracing the Epic Journey of John Lloyd Stephens.* Tuscaloosa: University of Alabama Press, 2003.

STEVEN S. GILLICK

STORM, RICARDO

STORM, RICARDO (1930–2000). Ricardo Storm (*b.* 14 March 1930; *d.* 26 March 2000), Uruguayan composer. Storm was born in Montevideo and began his musical education while very young. He studied piano under Wilhelm Kolischer and composition with the Spanish composer Enrique Casal Chapí, who was living in Montevideo at that time. Storm's initial works, dating from the early 1950s, already showed the composer's preferred style: vocal pieces in the form of songs, lieder and opera. His compositions for piano include a suite (1949), *Fantasía* (1950), several fugues (1950–1951), and a Sonata (1963). *Introducción y allegro,* Storm's first orchestral work, was premiered in 1954 by the OSSODRE (national public broadcast symphony orchestra) under Juan Protasi. His opera *El regreso* is an intensive work, substantial in scope, based on Aeschylus's *Choephoroi,* with a libretto written by the composer. It premiered at the SODRE theater on 17 April 1958. The music is in universalist style, sober in its musical language but distinctly Italian in its dramatic vocal treatment. Among Storm's vocal and choral productions is *Tres canciones para mezzosoprano y orquesta,* on texts by the Nicaraguan poet Rubén Darío, performed by Matilde Siano and the OSSODRE under Antonio Pereira Arias in February 1963. Other works of his include *Música para cuerdas, piano y timbales* (1959) and a symphony (1989), both premiered by the OSSODRE. He died in Montevideo on March 26, 2000. On August 19 of that year, a concert was staged to pay honor to his memory. It included a performance of Dvorak's Ninth Symphony.

See also **Music: Art Music.**

BIBLIOGRAPHY

Composers of the Americas, vol. 16 (1970), pp. 149–153.

Susana Salgado, *Breve historia de la música culta en el Uruguay,* 2d ed. (1980); *Diccionario de la música española e hispanoamericana* (1993).

Additional Bibliography

Ficher, Miguel. *Latin American Classical Composers: A Biographical Dictionary.* Lanham, MD: Scarecrow Press, 1996.

Salgado, Susana. *The Teatro Solís: 150 Years of Opera, Concert, and Ballet in Montevideo.* Middletown, CT: Wesleyan University Press, 2003.

SUSANA SALGADO

STORNI, ALFONSINA (1892–1938).

Alfonsina Storni (*b.* 29 May 1892; *d.* 25 October 1938), Argentine poet, teacher, and journalist. Born in Switzerland, Storni emigrated to Argentina with her prosperous Italian Swiss family when she was four. Losing most of their possessions shortly thereafter owing to bad management, they lived in San Juan Province until 1901, when they moved to Rosario, in Santa Fe Province. Storni went to work when she was ten, washing dishes and serving tables in a short-lived family restaurant, helping her mother with sewing, and taking care of her youngest brother. Her father died young in 1906, and his death changed the family's fate. Storni began to work in a factory and became interested

in anarchist ideas. This background gave her the knowledge and motivation for her later work as a journalist and a feminist.

Storni joined a theatrical company that performed around the country and then taught in a rural school for two years. In 1910 she completed her degree and began a new teaching career in Rosario. She also began to write steadily. In Rosario she met a married man with whom she had a child in April 1912. She remained a single mother for the rest of her life, thus confronting the code of moral behavior of her time.

In 1912 Storni arrived in Buenos Aires, then a city of 1.5 million people. It was a booming city built after the image of Paris. At first she held small jobs and had to compete with male workers until she found a teaching position. In 1916 she published her first collection of poems, *La inquietud del rosal* (The Disquiet of the Rosebush). She also began to write articles for the magazine *Caras y Caretas.* Being a single woman, the self-supporting mother of a child, and a published poet made Storni a symbol of the rebel, the revolutionary, the feminist, and the fighter against a male-dominated society. She published *El dulce daño* (Sweet Harm) in 1918 and *Irremediablemente* the following year.

Storni began writing articles for the daily *La Nación* with the pen name of Tao-Lao. *Languidez* (1920; Languor) was received with great acclaim and won two important literary awards. That same year she was invited to Montevideo to speak about the Uruguayan poet Delmira Agustini. She published *Ocre,* her major collection of poems, in 1925, and the following year *Poemas de amor* appeared in the journal *Nosotros.* She also wrote for children's theater and the play *El amo del mundo* (1927).

In 1930 Storni traveled to Europe where she met many writers, including Federico García Lorca and Ramón Gómez de la Serna. She underwent surgery for breast cancer in 1935, from which she recovered only partially. In 1938 she was honored in a ceremony along with Gabriela Mistral of Chile and Juana de Ibarbourou of Uruguay. That fateful year she published her last book of poems, *Mascarilla y trébol,* and she took her life in Mar del Plata.

See also **Argentina: The Twentieth Century; Feminism and Feminist Organizations; Ibarbourou, Juana de; Journalism; Mistral, Gabriela.**

BIBLIOGRAPHY

Conrado Nalé Roxlo, *Genio y figura de Alfonsina Storni* (1964).

Rachel Phillips, *Alfonsina Storni: From Poetess to Poet* (1975).

Isabel Cuchí Coll, *La poetisa de los tristes destinos* (1979).

Miriam Figueras, *Alfonsina Storni, análisis de poemas y antología* (1979).

Sonia Jones, *Alfonsina Storni* (1979).

Gabriella Verna, *Alfonsina* (1985).

Additional Bibliography

Delgado, Josefina. *Alfonsina Storni: Una biografía esencial.* Buenos Aires: Planeta, 2001.

Gociol, Judith. *Alfonsina Storni con-textos.* Buenos Aires: Ediciones Biblioteca Nacional, 1998.

Pleitez, Tania. *Alfonsina Storni: Mi casa es el mar.* Madrid: Espasa, 2003.

MAGDALENA GARCÍA PINTO

STRANGFORD TREATIES (1810).

The Strangford Treaties (1810) comprised a series of agreements between Portugal and Great Britain that granted the British special commercial privileges in exchange for their defense of Portugal and its colonies during the Napoleonic War. Earlier, in 1807, Britain had threatened to destroy Portuguese naval forces and merchant fleets and to seize Portugal's colonies if Portugal acceded to Napoleon's demand and closed its ports to British ships. At that time, the Portuguese royal family agreed to British demands in exchange for protection during a forced retreat resulting in an imminent invasion by the French army. The English envoy to Lisbon, Percy Clinton Sydney Smythe, Viscount Strangford, negotiated the evacuation of the Portuguese royal family and followed them to Brazil, where in 1810 he negotiated the Treaty of Commerce and Navigation and the Treaty of Alliance and Friendship. These agreements, known as the Strangford Treaties, set preferential tariffs of 15 percent on British goods imported into Brazil and effectively undermined Brazilian industrialization. British merchants were granted the right to live in Brazil while they sold British products in both wholesale and retail establishments, but they were subject only to British-appointed magistrates when accused of wrongdoing. Portugal also agreed to restrict the importation of African slaves and to consider the abolition of such trade.

Brazilians were angered over the preferential treatment the Strangford Treaties gave to the British and considered them another example of Portuguese interests taking priority over colonial concerns. For example, British duties on Brazilian sugar and coffee imports were not reduced. Furthermore, Great Britain established itself as a major economic force in Brazil, and the British navy patrolled the coastal waters as a protective force for British commerce and a deterrent to the African slave trade.

See also **Commercial Policy: Colonial Brazil; Trade, Colonial Brazil.**

BIBLIOGRAPHY

Barman, Roderick. Brazil: The Forging of a Nation, 1798–1852. Stanford University Press, 1994. See pp. 257, 263.

Bethell, Leslie. *The Cambridge History of Latin America.* New York: Cambridge University Press, 1995. See pp. 168–177, 203–204

Burns, E. Bradford. A History of Brazil. Columbia University Press, 1993, pp. 111–113

Clarence-Smith, Gervase. *The Third Portuguese Empire, 1825–1975: A Study in Economic Imperialism* Manchester, U.K.: Manchester University Press, 1985.

Graham, Richard. *Britain and the Onset of Modernization in Brazil, 1850–1914* Cambridge, U.K.: Cambridge University Press, 1968.

Miller, Joseph C. *Way of Death: Merchant Capitalism and the Angolan Slave Trade 1730–1830.* Madison: University of Wisconsin Press, 1996.

Seckinger, Ron. *The Brazilian Monarchy and the South American Republics, 1822–1831: Diplomacy and State Building.* Baton Rouge: Louisiana State University Press, 1984.

LESLEY R. LUSTER

STROESSNER, ALFREDO (1912–2006).
Alfredo Stroessner (*b.* 3 November 1912, *d.* 16 August 2006), president of Paraguay (1954–1989).

Alfredo Stroessner ruled Paraguay for thirty-five years, becoming thereby the most durable dictator in Latin America's history. The secret of his success was not to be found in any personal charisma, for he had none, nor in the support of a mass revolutionary movement, because he ruled in favor of the status quo. Nevertheless, he was more than a mere army strongman. Stroessner's longevity in power was due to an extraordinary capacity for work, an attention to detail, and a genius for organization. Behind a dull, plodding appearance he created a system of rule that approached totalitarian thoroughness, reaching into every corner of the republic and tying every significant social group to his political machine.

Little is known of his early life except that he was born in Encarnación, a southern border town on the Paraná River, to a German immigrant father and a Paraguayan mother. In 1929, at the age of sixteen he entered the Military Academy in Asunción. Three years later the Chaco War broke out and, even though his studies were not completed, Stroessner was sent to the front. Decorated for bravery at the battle of Boquerón (1932), he was awarded his commission as a second lieutenant and given an artillery command. He won a second medal after the battle of El Carmen (1934). By the end of the war (1935) he was a first lieutenant.

After the war Stroessner continued to receive favorable notice from his commanding officers, rising to captain in 1936 and major in 1940. In October 1940 he was selected as one of a group of junior officers to go to Brazil for special artillery training. After returning to Paraguay, Stroessner continued to rise in the military hierarchy. President Higínio Morínigo rewarded him for staying loyal during an abortive coup in 1943 by sending him to the Superior War School; upon graduating he was appointed commander of Paraguay's main artillery unit. In 1946 Stroessner was assigned to the army's General Staff Headquarters.

The civil war of 1947 brought Stroessner to real prominence because he was one of the few officers who remained loyal to the government. Morínigo ordered him to use his artillery to smash a revolt by the navy, which had taken over the Asunción shipyards in the name of the rebel cause. Next, Stroessner took command of the southern front and successfully prevented two heavily armed rebel gunboats from ascending the Paraguay River to bombard the capital. When the rebels were finally defeated, in August 1947, he was one of a handful of officers heading a purged and reorganized army.

Post-civil war Paraguay was dominated by the Colorado Party, one of Paraguay's two traditional parties, which had provided mass support for Morínigo. With their rivals eliminated, the Colorados had a clear political field, which they took advantage of by removing Morínigo in 1948 and seizing power for themselves. Soon afterward, however, the Colorados divided into factions whose leaders struggled for the presidency. From the end of the civil war until May 1954, Paraguay had five different presidents. Stroessner was deeply involved in all the plotting. On 25 October 1948 he backed the wrong side in a coup and had to escape the country hidden in the trunk of a car; three months later he slipped back into Paraguay and rallied his artillery regiment to support the winning side in a new coup. After that he rose rapidly to the top, becoming army commander in chief in April 1951. In May 1954 he ousted the Colorados' Federico Chaves, who still headed a faction-ridden administration, and seized the presidency for himself.

Stroessner based his government on two pillars: the army and the Colorado Party. As a much-decorated veteran of two wars he enjoyed great prestige among the soldiers. The few officers who opposed him were soon eliminated, with major purges taking place in February 1955 and June 1959. Those coincided with upheavals inside the Colorado Party, for Stroessner encouraged party bickering that allowed him to play the factions off against each other. By mid-1959 factional purges had eliminated all independent spirits among the Colorados, leaving Stroessner with a docile organization that he could dominate.

The control of a political party with a mass following made Stroessner's right-wing military dictatorship unique. By manipulating party symbols and patronage he was able to generate mass demonstrations in support of his policies. Businessmen, professionals, youth, women, veterans, and peasants were tied to the regime through the Colorados' ancillary organizations, and party cells (*seccionales*) reached into every village and every city block. Though his economic policies tended to favor large landowners and foreign investors, Stroessner was able to reward his followers through public works projects that generated jobs and contracts. Up to about 1981 steady economic growth and material improvements made the regime popular. Stroessner also permitted widespread smuggling and racketeering among top military and Colorado Party officials, with benefits trickling down through the clientele system. Those who refused to conform, however, such as the opposition Liberal and Febrerista parties and the Catholic church, were ruthlessly persecuted.

Stroessner's regime began to crumble during the 1980s. Inflation became unmanageable, capital dried up for new public works projects, and the emergence of a new middle class—the fruit of previous economic growth—challenged the regime's rigid structure. Above all, Stroessner was aging, and those around him began jockeying over the question of succession. Some of his cabinet ministers and presidential aides, calling themselves "the militants," wanted to name Stroessner's son, Gustavo, as his successor; but opposing them were the Colorado "traditionalists," who saw their chance to regain the party's independence. The feud split the military as well. When Stroessner backed the "militants" and plotted to remove General Andrés Rodríguez as army commander, the latter struck first. During the night of 2 February 1989 Rodríguez's tanks forced Stroessner to relinquish power and leave the country for Brazilian exile. After he left office, historians and activists discovered archives with evidence confirming the ways in which the Stroessner regime engaged in torture, kidnappings, and corruption. In 2006, Stroessner died in Brasília. Even though Stroessner still has defenders, the Paraguayan government decisively stated that there would be no official honors for him.

See also **Paraguay, Political Parties: Colorado Party.**

BIBLIOGRAPHY

Bourne, Richard. *Political Leaders of Latin America* (1969).

Lewis, Paul H. *Paraguay Under Stroessner* (1980).

Lewis, Paul H. *Socialism, Liberalism, and Dictatorship in Paraguay* (1982).

Miranda, Carlos. *The Stroessner Era* (1990).

Paredes, Roberto. *Stroessner y el stronismo.* Asunción, Paraguay: Servilibro, 2004.

PAUL H. LEWIS

SUÁREZ, INÉS DE (1512?–1580?). Inés de Suárez (*b.* 1512?; *d.* 1580?), Spanish woman who played a forceful and colorful part in the conquest of Chile. In her twenties she went to America, where she became the mistress of Pedro de Valdivia (1500–1553). She accompanied him on his expedition to Chile in 1540, and was well liked by the conquistadores. In September 1541, during Valdivia's temporary absence, the newly founded settlement at Santiago was attacked by large numbers of natives. With the inadequate Spanish force facing total defeat, Inés de Suárez suggested the murder of seven captive caciques (chiefs) as a means of instilling terror among the natives. It is generally accepted that she did (or helped with) the killing herself. After the heads (or possibly the corpses) of the dead caciques were thrown into the crowd of attackers, Suárez donned a coat of mail and led the fighting during the remainder of the battle. The only Spanish woman in the settlement, she devoted herself to caring for the wounded and supervising food supplies.

In recognition of her contributions, Valdivia granted her an *encomienda*. When the king's representative in Lima, Pedro de la Gasca, heard charges against Valdivia in November 1548, he advised him to terminate his liaison with Suárez. (Valdivia's wife, who was in Spain, traveled to Chile soon afterward, but arrived there only after his death.) Valdivia complied with La Gasca's suggestion, and married Suárez off to one of his most trusted lieutenants, Rodrigo de Quiroga, who himself later became governor of Chile (1565–1567 and 1575–1580). As an act of penitence, Suárez maintained a small church on the Cerro Blanco in Santiago. In 1553 she and Quiroga presented it to the Dominican order. The present church near the site dates from the 1830s. In 2006, novelist Isabel Allende published a novel, *Inés of My Soul*, based on the life of Suárez.

See also **Chile: Foundations Through Independence.**

BIBLIOGRAPHY

Stella (Burke) May, *The Conqueror's Lady* (1930).

Additional Bibliography

Allende, Isabel. *Inés of My Soul.* New York: Harper Collins, 2006.

SIMON COLLIER

SUÁREZ, MARCO FIDEL (1855–1927).

Marco Fidel Suárez (*b.* 23 April 1855; *d.* 3 April 1927), Colombian man of letters and president (1918–1921). Suárez was born out of wedlock in Hatoviejo (now Bello), Antioquia. Although his mother, a washerwoman, was very poor, a visiting priest recognized his intellectual ability and secured his admission to the seminary in Medellín. Suárez left the seminary in 1877 before ordination and found employment as a teacher in Antioquia and Bogotá. He first gained notice in 1881, when he won a contest sponsored by the Colombian Academy to commemorate the centenary of the birth of philologist Andrés Bello. His winning essay, *Ensayo sobre la "Gramática castellana de D. Andrés Bello,"* was published, and he became a member of the academy in 1883.

In the 1880s and 1890s Suárez held increasingly important government positions and was an articulate spokesman for the Nationalist wing of the Conservative Party. As a cabinet member under President Manuel A. Sanclemente, he protested the latter's removal on 31 July 1900. Returning to public life in 1910, Suárez defeated two other candidates in the presidential election of 1917. Critics charged that his victory was fraudulent, and he had to contend with bitter opposition during his administration.

In 1919 workers who erroneously believed that the government planned to buy army uniforms abroad staged a demonstration in Bogotá. When the crowd prevented Suárez from speaking, there was an outbreak of violence in which seven persons were killed. There was also controversy over ratification of the Thomson-Urrutia Treaty, which aimed at restoring harmonious relations between Colombia and the United States. On 26 October 1921 Laureano Gómez, then a Conservative deputy, directed a vitriolic attack at Suárez, accusing him of various financial improprieties. Suárez denied any misconduct but resigned the following month. He spent his remaining years writing his memoirs in dialogue form. These were published in twelve volumes as *Sueños de Luciano Pulgar* (1925–1940).

See also **Colombia: Since Independence; Colombia, Political Parties: Conservative Party.**

BIBLIOGRAPHY

Fernando Galvis Salazar, *Don Marco Fidel Suárez* (1974).

Charles W. Bergquist, *Coffee and Conflict in Colombia, 1886–1910* (1978).

Additional Bibliography

Morales Benítez, Otto. *Sanclemente, Marroquín: El liberalismo y Panamá.* Bogotá: Stamato Editores, 1998.

HELEN DELPAR

SUASSUNA, ARIANO VILAR (1927–).

Ariano Vilar Suassuna (*b.* 16 June 1927), poet, playwright, and novelist from João Pessoa, Paraíba, in northeastern Brazil. Suassuna received an informal education during the years he lived in the *sertão* among ballad singers, puppeteers, and storytellers whose themes, poetic forms, and language would be the substance of his writing. In 1946 Suassuna enrolled at the university in Recife, Pernambuco. With Hermilo Borba Filho and others, he founded in 1948 the Teatro do Estudante de Pernambuco, whose purpose was to bring literature to the masses through theater. Performances were given in parks, factories, churches, and squares. The same year, Suassuna received the prestigious Carlo Magno Prize for *Uma mulher vestida de sol,* a play written in 1947.

His next important work for the theater was *O auto da compadecida* (1957). No other Brazilian play has become as nationally and internationally well known as *The Rogue's Trial,* first presented in Recife. Its novelty was in the revelation of Northeastern Brazil's harsh reality, with its social problems and cultural values. The author incorporates this reality into the traditions of European theater, medieval liturgical drama, and the religious theater of the Golden Age. Suassuna was inspired by the *romanceiro popular do nordeste,* as he called the literature of the cordel.

Suassuna dedicated himself to the theater until 1971. Not only *O auto da compadecida* but *O casamento suspeitoso, O santo e a porca,* and *A pena e a lei* were awarded prizes in Brazil and abroad. From 1971 to 1977 he wrote a novel in two parts, *Romance d'a pedra do reino,* based on ten years of historical and literary research and announced as the first volume of a trilogy. Enthusiastically received, it is an extremely ambitious work in which Suassuna, through a main character representing earlier real or fictional heroes, attempts to create an epic according to armorial or formulaic patterns. After 1977, Suassuna abandoned the theater and the novel, and returned to writing poetry. He also took up painting, illustrating *A pedra do reino,* and taught at the Federal University of Pernambuco. Since 1990, he has held a position on the Brazilian Academy of Letters. In 1993, he was elected to the Pernambuco Academy of Letters as well. From 1995 to 1998, he served as Secretary of Culture of Pernambuco.

See also **Literature: Brazil.**

BIBLIOGRAPHY

Richard A. Mazzara, "Poetic Humor and Universality of Ariano Suassuna's *Compadecida,*" in *Ball State University Forum* 10 (1969): 25–30.

Additional Bibliography

Dineen, Mark. *Listening to the People's Voice: Erudite and Popular Literature in North East Brazil.* London: Kegan Paul International, 1996.

Santos, Idelette Fonseca dos. *Em demanda da poética popular: Ariana Suassana e o Movimento Armorial.* Campinas, Brasil: Editora da Unicamp, 1999.

Suassuna, Ariano. *Fernando e Isaura.* Recife, Brazil: Edicões Bagaco, 1994.

RICHARD A. MAZZARA

SUAZO CÓRDOVA, ROBERTO

(1927–). Roberto Suazo Córdova (*b.* 17 March 1927), president of Honduras (1982–1986). Suazo was born in the small town of La Paz, where he practiced medicine for twenty-five years. Active in the Liberal Party for a number of years, Suazo succeeded Modesto Rodas Alvarado in 1979 as general coordinator of the Liberal Party and leader of its conservative Rodista wing. After the military rulers agreed in 1980 to restore civilian government, Suazo was elected president in November 1981 and took office on 27 January 1982. He promoted the democratic process and moderate economic reform while cooperating with a U.S. military buildup in response to the Sandinista rise in Nicaragua, which included a substantial increase in the Honduran military as well as support of the Nicaraguan contras in Honduras. In collaboration with U.S. ambassador John Negroponte, the Honduran military, led by Colonel Gustavo Álvarez Martínez, retained much power, thereby creating considerable anti-Americanism and internal criticism of Suazo. Suazo, however, successfully reasserted civilian authority when he dismissed Álvarez in March 1984 and replaced him with Air Force General Walter López Reyes as commander in chief of the armed forces. The FBI arrested Álvarez in Miami in November 1984 in connection with a plot to murder Suazo. Despite this shakeup in the military, there was no reversal of the trend toward greater militarization of Honduras. In 1989 Souza and Honduras became involved in the Iran-Contra affair. It was alleged that Vice President George H. W. Bush had met with Souza and offered increased aid to Honduras in return for its assistance to the Nicaraguan Contras, the rebel group the United States opposed. This was later proved to be untrue. Nevertheless, the election of 1989 in Nicaragua did not turn out favorably for Souza's Liberal Party.

See also **Honduras.**

BIBLIOGRAPHY

James A. Morris, *Honduras: Caudillo Politics and Military Rulers* (1984).

Ralph Lee Woodward, Jr., "Suazo Córdova," in *Encyclopedia of World Biography,* vol. 15 (1987), pp. 378–379.

Additional Bibliography

Martínez, Juan Ramón. *La transición política: Del autoritarismo militar a la democracia electoral.* Tegucigalpa, Honduras: Ediciones 18 Conejo, 2004.

Meza, Victor, Leticia Salomón, and Mirna Flores. *Democracia y partidos políticos en Honduras.* Tegucigalpa: Centro de Documentación de Honduras, 2004.

Salomón, Leticia, Julieta Castellanos, and Mirna Flores. *Ciudadanía y participación en Honduras.* Tegucigalpa: Centro de Documentación de Honduras, 1996.

RALPH LEE WOODWARD JR.

SUBCOMANDANTE MARCOS (1957–).

Hiding his face behind a dark balaclava, Subcomandante Marcos headed the indigenous uprising in Chiapas that shocked Mexico on the morning of January 1, 1994, when the North American Trade Agreement (NAFTA) went into effect. As the spokesperson of the Ejército Zapatista de Liberación Nacional (EZLN; Zapatista Army of National Liberation), Marcos communicated the critical situation of Chiapas indigenous people to Mexico and the world. By means of widely published political and literary writings and appealing oratory, Marcos gained worldwide attention and sympathy toward the movement. His inflammatory rhetoric against neoliberalism addressed the profound injustices, inequalities, and discrimination suffered by Chiapas indigenous people. International support from European and U.S. representatives of important NGOs boosted Marcos and the EZLN's influential presence in Mexico. In such a context, the Mexican government chose to limit its repressive action and sought negotiation with the rebels. However, concrete gains for the EZLN and Chiapas indigenous people have proved narrow, since most of the 1996 Acuerdos de San Andrés—signed between the government and the EZLN—became a dead letter, and only limited reform, granting some cultural rights to the Mexican indigenous people, was incorporated into the national Constitution in 2001.

Even though Marcos has remained an enigmatic figure, his true identity was allegedly revealed by government investigations, which in early 1995 concluded that he was Rafael Sebastián Guillén Vicente, born in Tamaulipus on June 19, 1957, a professor of graphic arts at the Universidad Autónoma Metropolitana (Metropolitan Autonomous University) in Mexico City (La Grange and Rico 1995, pp. 33–37). His identity as an urban and white/mestizo intellectual, an outsider from indigenous reality, has been used by his detractors to brand him as a manipulator and opportunist. Others, however, have considered him as the ultimate realization of Antonio Gramsci's organic intellectual, because Marcos seemingly translated Chiapas indigenous people's demands into concrete revolutionary action.

See also **Chiapas.**

BIBLIOGRAPHY

Works by Subcomandante Marcos

Yo Marcos. Mexico: Ediciones del Milenio, 1994.

With Adolfo Gilly and Carlo Ginzburg. *Discusión sobre la historia.* Mexico: Taurus, 1995.

Shadows of Tender Fury: The Letters and Communiqués of Subcomandante Marcos and the Zapatista Army of National Liberation, trans. Frank Bardacke and Leslie López. New York: Monthly Review Press, 1995.

Cuentos para una soledad desvelada. Mexico: Ekosol-EZLN, 1997.

The Story of Colors. El Paso, TX: Cinco Puntos Press, 1999.

Detrás de nosotros estamos ustedes. Mexico: Plaza y Janés, 2000.

Siete piezas del rompecabezas mundial. Mexico: Editorial del Frente Zapatista de Liberación Nacional, 2000.

Comunicados del EZLN. San Cristóbal de las Casas, Mexico: Ediciones Pirata, 2001.

El correo de la selva (cartas y comunicados del EZLN durante el año 2000). Buenos Aires: Retórica Ediciones, 2001.

With Paco Ignacio Taibo II. *Muertos incómodos: Falta lo que falta.* Mexico: Joaquín Mórtiz, 2005.

The Other Campaign = La otra campaña. San Francisco: City Lights, 2006.

Secondary Sources

Chiapas: La rebelión de los pobres. Donosita, Spain: Tercera Prensa, 1994.

Durán de la Huerta, Martha. *El tejido del pasamontañas: Una conversación con el Subcomandante Marcos.* Mexico: Time, 1999.

Estrada Saavedra, Marco. *La comunidad armada rebelde y el EZLN.* Mexico: El Colegio de México, 2007.

Gosner, Kevin, and Arij Ouweneel, eds. *Indigenous Revolts in Chiapas and the Andean Highlands.* Amsterdam: Centro de Estudios y Documentación Latinoamericanos, 1996.

Hernández Navarro, Luis, and Ramón Vera Herrera, eds. *Acuerdos de San Andrés.* Mexico: Era, 1998.

Katzenberger, Elaine, ed. *First World, Ha Ha Ha!: The Zapatista Challenge.* San Francisco: City Light Books, 1995.

La Grange, Bertrand de, and Maite Rico. *Subcomandante Marcos, la genial impostura.* Mexico: Cal y Arena, 1998.

Montemayor, Carlos. *Chiapas: La rebelión indígena de México.* Mexico: Joaquín Motriz, 1997.

Vanden Berghe, Kristine. *Narrativa de la rebelión zapatista: Los relatos del subcomandante Marcos.* Madrid and Frankfurt: Editorial Iberoamericana, 2005.

Vázquez Montalbán, Manuel. *Marcos: El señor de los espejos.* Madrid: Aguilar, 1999.

EMILIO CORAL

Otera Silva, Miguel, José Ramón Medina, Efraín Subero et al. *Casas muertas: Lope de Aguirre, príncipe de la libertad.* Caracas: Biblioteca Ayacucho, 1985.

MICHAEL J. DOUDOROFF

SUBERO, EFRAÍN (1931–2007).

Efraín Subero (*b.* 16 October 1931; *d.* 18 January 2007), Venezuelan scholar, critic, and poet. Professor of literature at the Universidad Católica Andrés Bello and the Universidad Simón Bolívar, Subero has been a prolific writer and an important scholar in the fields of literary history and criticism, cultural criticism, and folklore. His poetry, most of which was published between 1956 and 1974, reflects his interest in popular expression and his concern for accessibility even when his writing is of private or intimate content. *Matarile* (1968) is a charming collection of poetry, stories, and one Christmas play for children. *La décima popular en Venezuela* (1977; 2d ed. 1991) is a major contribution to folklore scholarship, an extensive study and presentation of texts of this ancient traditional Hispanic form. He is also noted for his editions and bibliographical work on such figures as Rómulo Gallegos, Miguel Otero Silva, Arturo Uslar Pietri, Teresa de la Parra, Aquiles Nazoa, Andrés Eloy Blanco, and Manuel Vicente Romero García. He had held faculty positions at the Universidad Central de Venezuela and the Universidad Católica Andres Bello, also in Venezuela. In 2002, he published *Memoria del Puerto.* He died in Caracas and the regional government of Nueva Esparta created a scholarship foundation for university students in his honor.

See also **Literature: Spanish America.**

BIBLIOGRAPHY

Collections of notes and essays are *Norte franco* (1961) and *La vida perdurable,* 2 vols. (1989). Representative books of poetry are *Todavía la noche* (1963), *En estos parajes* (1965), and *Razones* (1969). Other contributions in folklore and popular culture include *Poesía infantil venezolana* (1967), *Orígen y expansión de la quema de Judas* (1974), and *La navidad en la literatura venezolana* (1977).

Additional Bibliography

Martín, Rebecca. *Efraín Subero: Un hombre lejano entre los hombres.* Los Teques, Estado Miranda, Venezuela: R. Martín, 2001.

SUBIRANA, MANUEL DE JESÚS (1807–1864).

Manuel de Jesús Subirana (*b.* 1807; *d.* 27 November 1864), Spanish missionary in Cuba and Honduras. Born in Manresa and educated in the seminary in nearby Vich, Subirana was ordained in 1834. He left Spain in 1850 for Cuba, where he worked in El Cobre. In 1856 he was sent to Christianize the Indians of Honduras. Finding them exploited, he struggled to alleviate their misery while catechizing them. He won land and ownership titles for the Jicaque Indians of Yoro and the Paya Indians of Olancho. Subirana's protests to the central government succeeded in mitigating the widespread practices of debt peonage and forced labor. He ended the practice of paying lower prices to Indians for their sarsaparilla than was paid to ladinos. Such efforts won the trust of the Indians, enabling Subirana to baptize thousands. After his death his work passed on to less zealous priests, and past abuses were soon revived.

See also **Cuba: The Colonial Era (1492–1898); Honduras; Missions: Spanish America.**

BIBLIOGRAPHY

Ernesto Alvarado García, *El misionero español Manuel Subirana* (1964).

José María Tojeira, *Panorama histórico de la iglesia en Honduras* (1986), pp. 173–177; William V. Davidson, "El Padre Subirana y las tierras concedidas a los indios, hondureños en el siglo XIX," in *América Indígena* 44, no. 3 (1984): 447–459.

Donna Whitson Brett and Edward T. Brett, *Murdered in Central America: The Stories of Eleven U.S. Missionaries* (1988), pp. 6–7.

Additional Bibliography

Sierra Fonseca, Rolando. *Manuel Subirana y el movimiento mesiánico en Honduras, 1857–1864.* Tegucigalpa: Instituto Hondureño de Antropología e Historia, 1997.

EDWARD T. BRETT

SUCRE. Sucre is the judicial capital of Bolivia, with a population of 215,778 (2001 census). Called La Plata or Chuquisaca during the colonial period, the city was the seat of the Audiencia of Charcas and after independence the capital of Bolivia. Chuquisaca is also the name of the surrounding department, of which Sucre is the capital. Closely tied to the silver-mining center of Potosí, Sucre was the residence of many silver-mine owners throughout its history.

In 1538 or 1539 Pedro de Anzures founded La Plata on a site inhabited by the Yampara ethnic group. It quickly became the administrative center of the vast territories of the southern Andean region. At 8,500 feet, it boasted a temperate climate that made it an ideal site for haciendas producing foodstuffs for Potosí. In 1552 La Plata became the new Episcopal seat and in 1559 the seat of the Audiencia of Charcas, the highest colonial judicial body in the vast region south of Lake Titicaca to Paraguay and Argentina. This jurisdiction later became the basis for the territorial claims of the Republic of Bolivia.

The city reached its apogee during the seventeenth century, when most prosperous Potosí silvermine owners took up residence there. Pedro Ramírez del Aguila's seventeenth-century description reveals an urban center intent on the celebration of ostentatious religious rituals and other such luxuries. This wealth was not restricted to the city alone. Indeed, one eighteenth-century traveler compared the sumptuous haciendas of the nearby Cachimayo valley to the aristocratic manors of Spanish Cantabria. Farther south, the Cinti region provided warm valleys that produced wine and fruit for consumption in Potosí. However, only a few hundred kilometers east lay the dangerous Indian frontier. In the sixteenth century the Chiriguano Indians had attempted to conquer the Potosí mines. Although the Spanish later set up a series of fortress-towns in the eastern Tomina jurisdiction, warfare kept the Chuquisaca frontier in constant flux until the 1780s.

La Plata was one of the first cities in Spanish America to experience political unrest after Napoleon's 1808 invasion of Spain. When on May 25, 1809, the president of the audiencia imprisoned Jaime Zudáñez, a radical favoring independence, a popular revolt erupted. Spanish troops sent from Buenos Aires suppressed the uprising by December 1809. Clashes with guerrilla forces allied with the Chiriguano continued until 1818, which decimated the surrounding countryside.

The city became independent as a result of the invasion of the Colombian army under Antonio José de Sucre in 1825. La Plata (now renamed Sucre) became the capital of the new Republic of Bolivia. Despite its status as the capital, few Bolivian presidents resided in town, as they managed the country (and put down revolts) while moving from city to city.

Many mine owners remained in Sucre, but only an infusion of fresh capital and entrepreneurship from merchants-turned-miners helped revive the silver-mining industry in the 1860s. By the 1870s the mining elite had gathered much financial and political power, which they used in the aftermath of the War of the Pacific (1879–1884) to seize national control through the Conservative Party. The last four decades of the nineteenth century constituted the region's second boom period, during which Sucre elites remodeled their houses to imitate Parisian styles and built ostentatious hacienda houses in the Cachimayo valley. Prosperity was a double-edged sword for the surrounding Indian communities who lost their lands to the miners. In turn, the demand for cattle heightened by the silver boom brought about a period of intense frontier expansion to the east and the final subjugation of the Chiriguano.

The declining price of silver put an end to the boom in the late 1890s. In the wake of this loss of economic clout, the Conservative Party lost the Federalist War (1898–1899), and La Paz became the de facto capital, with Sucre keeping only the Supreme Court. Since then the Sucre economy has stagnated. A brief petroleum rush and an attempt by elites to form new mining companies in the early twentieth century failed because of a lack of capital. The last refuge of the Sucre elites, their haciendas, were confiscated and divided among estate workers after the 1953 agrarian reform.

In the early twenty-first century, Sucre and the surrounding region is one of the poorest areas in the country. The city is mainly service-oriented and survives in great part on the income brought by the many students who come to study. The only other regular source of income is that from oil wells in the former Chiriguano territory. Tourism has also expanded since UNESCO declared Sucre a World Heritage Site in 1991.

See also **Bolivia: Since 1825; Chiriguanos; Federalist War (1898–1899); Mining: Modern.**

BIBLIOGRAPHY

Barnadas, Josep. *Charcas: Orígenes históricos de una sociedad colonial.* La Paz: Centro de Investigacíon y Promoción del Campesinado, 1973.

Langer, Erick D. *Economic Change and Rural Resistance in Southern Bolivia, 1880–1930.* Stanford, CA: Stanford University Press, 1989.

Mendoza, Gunnar, et al. *Monografía de Bolivia*, vol. 1 . La Paz: Biblioteca del Sesquicentenario de la República, 1975.

Querejazu Calvo, Roberto. *Chuquisaca: 1539–1825.* Sucre: Impr. Universitaria, 1987.

Wolff, Inge. *Regierung und Verwaltung der kolonialspanischen Städte in Hochperu, 1538–1650.* Cologne, Germany: Böhlau, 1970.

ERNESTO CAPELLO

SUCRE ALCALÁ, ANTONIO JOSÉ DE

(1795–1830). Antonio José de Sucre Alcalá (*b.* 3 February 1795; *d.* 4 June 1830), Venezuelan military officer in the Wars of Independence, Simón Bolívar's trusted lieutenant, statesman, and the first constitutionally elected president of Bolivia. Sucre's parents were descended from well-to-do Europeans established in the coastal town of Cumaná. When news of the Napoleonic invasion of Spain reached Venezuela, Sucre was studying military engineering in Caracas. In July 1810 he joined the patriotic militia in Cumaná, launching a distinguished military career that culminated in the 9 December 1824 final victory of patriot forces over the Spanish at the battle of Ayacucho (Peru).

Sucre saw active service under the first and second Venezuelan republics but was forced to flee to the Antilles in 1814. After a brief effort to join patriot forces in New Granada (Colombia) at the end of 1815, he again went into exile. Aligning himself with Bolívar, who by 1816 was beginning to succeed in his campaign against loyalists in Venezuela, Sucre undertook a number of successful military assignments for the Liberator and by late

1820 had become his chief of staff. As such, Sucre undertook a delicate mission as head of an expeditionary force sent to Guayaquil (Ecuador) to aid local patriots following their October 1819 uprising against royal authority. Success in Guayaquil was followed by an expedition to liberate Quito, aided by auxiliary forces sent from Peru, which culminated in a patriot victory at the pivotal battle of Pichincha (24 May 1822) on the outskirts of Quito.

With virtually all of Gran Colombia liberated, Bolívar and Sucre turned their attention southward to Peru, where the army of José de San Martín and its Peruvian allies were engaged in a bitter struggle against the Spanish army and royalists for possession of Lima and the once-rich viceroyalty. After Bolívar's arrival in Lima, Sucre took charge of the military campaign in the Andean highlands, achieving a crucial victory at the battle of Junín (6 August 1824) and final victory at Ayacucho in December. Sucre was the author of a brilliant strategy that led to the humiliating defeat of the royalist forces, and dictated generous, humanitarian terms of surrender.

After Ayacucho the only serious obstacle to the liberation of Spanish South America was the ragtag army of royalist General Pedro de Olañeta in Upper Peru (today Bolivia). With Sucre in hot pursuit, Olañeta's forces melted away early in 1825, leaving the twenty-five-year-old Venezuelan with the responsibility for creating a republican form of government in the former Audiencia of Charcas. Two days after his triumphant arrival in La Paz, Upper Peru's largest and economically most important city, Sucre issued a decree (9 February 1825) convoking a constituent assembly of delegates from the audiencia's five former *intendencias* to decide whether they wished to ally themselves with the former viceroyalty of the Río de la Plata, with that of Lima, or to become an independent nation. Sucre, without explicit authorization from Bolívar (who had returned to Lima after the victory at Junín) pledged to respect the wishes of the Upper Peruvian delegates.

The assembly, which met during July and August 1825 in Chuquisaca (renamed Sucre in honor of the victor of Ayacucho), voted overwhelmingly to create an independent state. Anticipating Bolívar's unhappiness, the delegates also voted to call the new nation the "Republic of Bolívar" and to name the Liberator its first constitutional president. Reluctantly accepting this fait accompli, during his visit to Upper Peru (July–December 1825) Bolívar acted as president of the infant nation, but most of the routine details of government were left to Sucre. Sucre's presidency ended when he was seriously wounded in a barracks revolt in the Bolivian capital and was forced to delegate his powers (April 1828). He left Bolivia in August of the same year for Quito, to join the woman to whom he had been married by proxy while still in Chuquisaca, Mariana Carcelén y Larrea, the Marquesa de Solanda, one of the wealthiest women in the former Audiencia of Quito.

Sucre's tenure as president of Bolivia (December 1825–April 1828) was marked by a revolutionary effort to impose economic and social reform upon a racially divided, geographically dispersed, and economically weak society led by a traditionalist elite that was jealous of its prerogatives and in time became very resentful of outside political and military influence. This effort included a wholesale reform of the Upper Peruvian church and the liquidation of most of its assets in favor of public education. Sucre created and funded a network of public secondary schools, for which he dictated a modern curriculum, recruited teachers, and provided books and supplies. New primary schools, orphanages, and asylums for the destitute were part of this reform, as were efforts to provide the principal cities with better water supplies, new public markets, street lighting, and public cemeteries. Sucre created a new port for the infant nation at Cobija, on the Atacama coast, in territory that would eventually become part of Chile. He tried to revive silver mining, the traditional mainstay of the Upper Peruvian economy, by attracting European investment, employing new technology, and reforming colonial institutions. Finally, Sucre tried to impose a revolutionary new experiment in public financing, eliminating the Indian tribute and the tithe and creating in their stead a system of taxes on wealth and income, and a universal head tax. Financially, the experiment was a dismal failure. The negative reaction toward this radical reform effort and toward the continued presence in Bolivia of large numbers of Colombian troops, along with growing hostility from Peru, eventually provoked Sucre's downfall.

Returning to Quito in September 1828, Sucre hoped to dedicate himself to family life and the administration of his wife's estate. But with the outbreak of hostilities between Peru and Gran Colombia, his military services were again needed. In February 1829 an army under his command defeated Peruvian invaders at the battle of Tarqui, in what became southern Ecuador. Fresh from the victory at Tarqui, in 1830 Sucre served as president of the Congreso Admirable meeting in Bogotá, a last-ditch effort to preserve Gran Colombian unity. The Congreso failed, despite Sucre's prestige, and Bolívar's creation broke up into three independent republics. On his way back to Quito, Sucre was killed at Berruecos, near Pasto. The identity of the assassins remains the object of historical speculation.

See also **Bolívar, Simón; Bolivia: Since 1825; Venezuela: The Colonial Era.**

BIBLIOGRAPHY

Laureano Villanueva, *Vida de don Antonio José de Sucre, Gran Mariscal de Ayacucho* (1945).

Guillermo A. Sherwell, *Antonio José de Sucre (Gran Mariscal de Ayacucho), Hero and Martyr of American Independence: A Sketch of His Life* (1924).

Charles W. Arnade, *The Emergence of the Republic of Bolivia* (1957).

Alfonso Rumazo González, *Sucre, Gran Mariscal de Ayacucho* (1963).

William Lofstrom, *La presidencia de Sucre en Bolivia* (1987).

Thomas Millington, *Debt Politics after Independence: The Funding Conflict in Bolivia* (1992).

Additional Bibliography

Kieffer Guzmán, Fernando. *Antonio José de Sucre: Un estudio del guerrero y estadista.* La Paz: s.n., 1995.

Quintero Montiel, Inés Mercedes. *Antonio José de Sucre: Biografía política.* Caracas: Academia Nacional de la Historia, 1998.

WILLIAM LOFSTROM

SUGAR INDUSTRY. Carried to the New World from the Spanish Canary Islands by Columbus on his second voyage in 1493, sugar was first grown in the New World in Spanish Santo Domingo and was exported to Europe beginning around

African slaves working on a sugar plantation, Spanish West Indies, copper engraving by Theodore de Bry, 1596. THE GRANGER COLLECTION. REPRODUCED BY PERMISSION

1516. Santo Domingo's incipient sugar industry was worked by African slaves who were imported soon after the sugarcane itself. Thus, Spain pioneered growing sugarcane, making sugar, using African slaves as labor, and establishing the plantation form in the Americas.

Within the New World, however, the early achievements in Santo Domingo and the rest of the Caribbean were surpassed by developments on the mainland. By 1526 Brazil was shipping sugar to Lisbon in commercial quantities. In Mexico, Paraguay, the Pacific coast of South America, and in fertile valleys everywhere, sugarcane thrived. In the other Greater Antilles—Cuba, Puerto Rico, and Jamaica—Spanish settlers eventually imported sugarcane plants, the methods for their cultivation, the technology of water and animal-powered mills, enslaved labor, and the processes of grinding, boiling, and fabricating sugars, creating molasses from extracted sugar juice, and distilling rum from the molasses.

Portuguese planters in Brazil, with the assistance of Dutch capital and merchants, enormously expanded sugarcane cultivation throughout the Northeast. A typical plantation consisted of fifteen or twenty Portuguese workers and more than one hundred African and Indian slaves, a chapel, workshops, a processing plant, a *casa grande* (big house) for the owner and his family, and a *senzala* (slave quarters). The entire enterprise depended on its *engenho* (mill), a water- or oxen-powered grinder that used a three-roller mechanism to extract the cane's juices. By 1618 the larger mills could produce between 192,000 and 320,000 pounds of sugar annually (85.7 and 143 tons), of which they exported some 384 million pounds to Europe.

The productive capacity of Brazilian sugar plantations drew foreign invaders to Brazil: first the French fruitlessly tried to found their own colonies there, then the Dutch succeeded in capturing Brazil from 1630 to 1654. In the meantime the British and the French were themselves trying to establish a presence on other Caribbean islands and turn them into sugar factories as well. By the time the Brazilians under Mem da Sá finally drove the Dutch out of Brazil in 1654, they had lost their predominance over world markets to competition from a series of new Caribbean producers and the erection of tariff barriers in Europe, notably in France and England. Nevertheless, the lust for sugar profits resulted in the continuous populating of other Caribbean islands with masters and slaves and helped spur the settlement of areas of the present-day United States, like South Carolina.

Within a century the French and, even more so, the British became the New World's great sugar makers and exporters. Inseparably linked to this development was the emergence of the triangular trade and mercantilism in the latter half of the seventeenth century. Finished European goods were sold in Africa, where African slaves were bought and transported to the Americas for sale, and then the profits from the first two parts of the journey were used to buy American tropical commodities (especially sugar) to market in the mother country and her importing neighbors. In the eighteenth century, as the imperial relationship solidified between mother country and colony, the French and British slave-based plantations of the Caribbean reached their apogee.

The late eighteenth and early nineteenth centuries brought dramatic changes to the Caribbean sugar colonies. First, revolution destroyed France's most lucrative and profitable slave-based sugar economy, Haiti. Subsequently, the British moved to limit and then abolish the slave trade and slavery (1834–1838). In the wake of these developments, European demand for other sugar sources increased significantly in the early decades of the nineteenth century.

Although sugarcane was planted there in the sixteenth century, Cuba was the last Caribbean island to develop its industry. By the beginning of the nineteenth century, sugar had become Cuba's main export. In the late 1820s about 1,000 sugar plantations covered some 500,000 acres, largely in the western region of the island. Investments in sugar, including the mechanization of the industry, led to spectacular increases in production and the construction of a railroad system. Before the Ten Years' War for

independence (1868–1878), owners grew their own cane and milled it in their own mills. Massive destruction of property throughout the island coupled with the emancipation of the slaves, upon whom the industry had depended, led to bankruptcies and purchases by foreign investors, largely from the United States. After the war, the number of mills declined to 500 and the cultivation of sugarcane fell increasingly into the hands of Colonos, renters, or sharecroppers who depended on the mill. Some scholars have speculated that this investment played a role in U.S. involvement in Cuba's second war for independence (1895–1898) with Spain, which became the Spanish-American War. Furthermore, the production of beet sugar in Europe and the United States forced sugar prices down on the global market.

Technological innovations developed during the twentieth century led to even further mechanization and concentration within the industry: by the 1920s there were fewer than 200 mills working on the island, of which 40 to 50 percent were controlled by U.S. investors. During World War I, when Cuban sugar had to make up for losses of European beet sugar, cultivation expanded and prices skyrocketed. From the end of the war until 1920, a time known in Cuba as the Dance of the Millions, sugar reigned supreme. But then average prices per pound dropped from a high of 22.5 cents in May 1920 to a mere 3.75 cents by the end of the year, causing industry collapse and opening the door to greater U.S. takeover. Yet, the sugar industry continued to dominate Cuba throughout the first half of the twentieth century and affected all segments of its economy. By 1958, for example, it is estimated that the sugar industry alone generated one-quarter of national GNP.

After the success of the Cuban Revolution in 1959, Fidel Castro believed that agrarian reform measures would finally end the island's dependence on sugar cultivation. Yet, despite efforts to diversify agriculture and industrialize, Cuba soon found itself desperately trying to harvest 10 million metric tons of sugar in 1970. Meanwhile, international agricultural conglomerates rapidly developed sugar substitutes for use in food processing and as sweeteners for the diet-conscious, thus cutting the need for sugarcane even further. Cuba, more than any other economy in the Western Hemisphere, has dramatically demonstrated the risks and rewards that come from dependency on a monocultural crop like sugar.

Since the 1990s, sugar producers have principally complained about the levels of subsidies and import quotas that the United States provides to national producers. Without these subsidies, Latin American sugar could compete in the larger U.S. market. Moreover, U.S. intransigence on this issue has caused much skepticism within Latin America over trade pacts. Latin American sugar producers, as well as other agricultural producers, fear that free trade will still be stifled. Brazil has successfully turned sugar into ethanol on a wide scale, and it is frequently used in place of gasoline, confirming the increasing importance of this crop as a bio-fuel and renewable resource.

See also **Cuban American Sugar Company; Economic Development.**

BIBLIOGRAPHY

Bethell, Leslie, ed. *Cambridge History of Latin America,* vols. 1 and 2 (1984).

Bethell, Leslie. *Cuba: A Short History* (1993).

Knight, Franklin W. *Slave Society in Cuba During the Nineteenth Century* (1970).

Knight, Franklin W., and Colin A. Palmer, eds. *The Modern Caribbean* (1989).

Mintz, Sidney W. *Sweetness and Power: The Place of Sugar in Modern History* (1985).

Moreno Fraginals, Manuel. *El ingenio. El complejo económico social cubano del azúcar,* 3 vols. (1978).

Pérez, Louis A. *Cuba: Between Reform and Revolution* (1989).

Schwartz, Stuart B. *Sugar Plantations in the Formation of Brazilian Society* (1985).

Schwartz, Stuart B. *Tropical Babylons: Sugar and the Making of the Atlantic World, 1450–1680.* Chapel Hill: University of North Carolina Press, 2004.

Williams, Eric Eustace. *From Columbus to Castro: The History of the Caribbean, 1492–1969* (1970).

Wolford, Wendy. "Of Land and Labor: Agrarian Reform on the Sugarcane Plantations of Northeast Brazil." *Latin American Perspectives* 31, no. 2 (March 2004): 147–170.

WADE A. KIT

SUMAC, YMA (1927–). Yma Sumac (*b.* 10 September 1927), Peruvian-born singer, noted for the extraordinary range of her voice and her exotic stage presence. Sumac was born in Ichocan, a small mountain village in Peru. Her parents named her Emperatriz Chavarri, but she chose a variation of her mother's name when she began her singing career.

When she was little more than a child she was heard singing in a local festival by an official from Lima. He persuaded her parents to bring her to the capital, where she could be presented in concert while continuing her education at a convent school. In Lima Sumac met her husband, Moises Vivanco, a composer, musician, and the director of the Peruvian National Board of Broadcasting. He cast her as the star of his musical group, the Compania Peruana de Arte. After a successful career in Latin America, in 1946 Sumac and Vivanco moved to the United States. Sumac became a naturalized U.S. citizen in 1955.

Sumac struggled to advance her career in the United States. With the 1950 release of her first album for Capitol Records, *Voice of Xtabay* (a nonsense word coined by the recording company to underscore Sumac's Incan roots), she caught the public's attention. Her popularity reached its climax in the early 1950s. Her records sold over a million copies. She appeared on television, in a minor Broadway musical, and appeared in the films *Secret of the Incas* (1954) and *Omar Khayyam* (1957).

Sumac's music, much of it written by her husband, was based on ancient Peruvian folk music. It was adapted to showcase her remarkable four-octave voice, and her ability to evoke the sounds of jaguars and Andean birds. Sumac also performed in opera houses in Europe and South America, singing roles in *The Magic Flute, Lakmé,* and *La Traviata.* After a hiatus of several years, Sumac returned to American music clubs in the 1970s and 1980s. She received good reviews and a modest popularity that did not match her earlier acclaim. In 1992, she was the subject of a documentary by German filmmaker Günther Czernetsky, "Yma Sumac—Hollywood's Inca Princess." In July 1997, she performed in Montreal at the Montreal International Jazz Festival. In 2006, she was awarded the "Orden del Sol" by Peruvian President Alejandro Toledo, and the Jorge Basadre medal by the Universidad Mayor de San Marcos.

See also **Music: Popular Music and Dance.**

BIBLIOGRAPHY

Hayward, Philip. *Widening the Horizon: Exoticism in Post-War Popular Music.* Sydney, Australia: John Libbey, 1999.

Krause, Anna-Bianca. *Apropos Yma Sumac*. Frankfurt, Germany: Neue Kritik, 2001.

Schnabel, Tom. *Stolen Moments: Conversations with Contemporary Musicians*. Los Angeles: Acrobat Books, 1988.

SHEILA HOOKER

SUMAPAZ, REPUBLIC OF.

Republic of Sumapaz, Colombian peasant squatter colony located in portions of Cundinamarca, Tolima, Huila, Caquetá, and Meta departments. The site of numerous peasant–landlord conflicts since 1870, Sumapaz developed peasant leaders in Erasmo Valencia and Juan de la Cruz Varela in the 1920s and 1930s. Autonomous in many ways, the squatters' colony represented some 6,000 peasants. Liberal governments' efforts to mediate agrarian conflicts there in the later 1930s and early 1940s failed. After 1948, officially sponsored violence by the Conservative regimes of Mariano Ospina Pérez and Laureano Gómez Castro triggered the creation of the Communist-led Republic of Sumapaz in the later 1940s. The region was the site of three military campaigns (1948–1953, 1954–1957, 1958–1965) that, together with counterviolence, left its agricultural base in ruins. They also ended (by 1958) the Sumapaz Republic. With coffee growing partly replaced by cattle, the population has been beggared and dispersed.

See also **Violencia, La.**

BIBLIOGRAPHY

Catherine Le Grand, *Frontier Expansion and Peasant Protest in Colombia, 1830–1936* (1986), pp. 110ff.

Elsy Marulanda, *Colonización y conflicto: Las lecciones del Sumapaz* (1991).

Additional Bibliography

Ortiz Bernal, José Afranio. *El mundo campesino en Colombia, siglo XX: Historia agraria y rebelión social*. Ibagué: Fondo Mixto para la Promoción de la Cultura y las Artes del Tolima, 1999.

J. LEÓN HELGUERA

SUMMIT OF THE AMERICAS.

The Summit of the Americas, coordinated by the Organization of American States (OAS), is an inter-American conference that occurs every few years, bringing together the heads of government from thirty-four participating democratic nations of the Western Hemisphere to discuss areas of mutual concern and to advance dialogue on development in the region. In the years following the signing of the OAS Charter in 1948, inter-American conferences consisted of few participants and served as a system for developing inter-American law. These initial meetings laid the groundwork for multilateral cooperation and hemispheric integration and sought to reinforce the Alliance for Progress. During the cold war years they occurred infrequently, making consensus and cooperation difficult. By the first Summit of the Americas in 1994, a common understanding had developed that democracy and market economies require multilateral cooperation for regional development to be sustainable and equitable. To encourage this cooperation, representatives from each of the thirty-four countries meet prior to each summit to develop the agenda and final documents coordinating the declarations to be agreed upon by the participant countries during the summit. Each summit held since 1994 has addressed a unique set of initiatives and themes predetermined during the summit process. Included in the achievements of the summits are the drafting of the Declaration of Principles and the development of the Inter-American Democratic Charter.

See also **Organization of American States (OAS).**

BIBLIOGRAPHY

Summits of the Americas Secretariat, Organization of American States. "The Summit of the Americas Process." Available from http://www.summit-americas.org/eng-2002/summit-process.htm.

MAGGIE K. HUMMEL

SUR.

Sur, prestigious and influential cultural review published in Buenos Aires. Following the advice of the Spanish philosopher José Ortega y Gasset, and with his support as well as that of the American writer Waldo Frank and the Argentine novelist Eduardo Mallea, Victoria Ocampo founded *Sur* in 1931. It was financed out of Ocampo's personal fortune. *Sur* contained fiction, poetry, philosophy, criticism, and history. Distinguished men of letters, including Jorge Luis Borges, Pedro Henríquez Ureña, and Ortega y Gasset, served on the editorial board. Writer José Bianco was head of the editorial staff between 1938 and 1961, the most prosperous years for the journal. Highly controversial, *Sur* was considered elitist and Europeanized by nationalist and leftist writers, such as Pablo Neruda. Writers were not excluded for ideological reasons, however; literary excellence was the requisite for inclusion. Ocampo, a woman of strong opinions, did refuse to publish people she did not like. The journal became the best-known literary magazine in Latin America and served to introduce many foreign writers in translation, including T. S. Eliot, Ezra Pound, Henry Miller, Jacques Maritain, Aldous Huxley, André Gide, and Nathalie Sarraute.

Politically, *Sur* staunchly opposed every form of totalitarianism, both of the Right and the Left. In particular, the editors of *Sur* took a strong stance against anti-Semitism in Argentina after World War II. Also, the literary journal protested Juan Perón's presidency and celebrated his removal from power in 1955. It was published every month or two until 1971. Since then, special issues have appeared occasionally.

See also **Ocampo, Victoria.**

BIBLIOGRAPHY

Calomarde, Nancy. *Políticas y ficciones en Sur, 1945–1955: Las operaciones culturales en los contextos de "peronización."* Córdoba, Argentina: Facultad de Filosofía y Humanidades, Universidad Nacional de Córdoba, 2004.

King, John. *Sur: A Study of the Argentine Literary Journal and Its Role in the Development of a Culture* (1986).

Lafleur, H. R., et al. *Las revistas literarias argentinas, 1893–1967* (1968).

Ocampo, Victoria. "Vida de la revista *Sur:* 35 años de una labor," in *Sur,* no. 303–305 (November 1966–April 1967): 1–36 (this issue also contains an index for issues 1–302).

Pasternac, Nora. *Sur, una revista en la tormenta: Los años de formación, 1931–1944.* Buenos Aires: Paradiso, 2002.

ROLANDO COSTA PICAZO

SURINAME AND THE DUTCH IN THE CARIBBEAN.

During World War II the Dutch government and royal family sought refuge in England. In 1942 Japan occupied what was then the colonial Dutch East Indies, present-day Indonesia. Consequently the Dutch government's

authority was limited to the West Indies: Suriname and the six islands of the Dutch Antilles. To ensure the loyalty of her colonies, in late 1942 Queen Wilhelmina (1880–1962) announced a new political system of overseas "internal autonomy." In 1945, immediately before Japan surrendered to the Allies, it granted independence to Indonesia under a government headed by Sukarno (1901–1970). Holland attempted to reestablish its rule in the region by sending troops and occupying the large cities of Java, the main island, but under pressure from the United States, the government in The Hague opened negotiations for independence. Indonesia rejected the offer of a British-style commonwealth, and independence was declared in 1949.

Meanwhile, The Hague had begun negotiating with the remaining portions of its empire, Suriname and the Dutch Antilles. The negotiations ended with a statute establishing in 1954 the relationship between the three "autonomous nations" of the Kingdom of the Netherlands: European Holland, Suriname, and the Dutch Antilles. The relationship was gilded by cooperation funds. In 1969 a labor conflict in Willemstad, the capital of the Antilles, ended in a confrontation with the police. There were deaths and wounded, and the police forces requested aid from the Dutch Navy. In additional confrontations, the population burned part of the historical center of the capital city. In Holland a public debate arose, recalling the military intervention in Indonesia. The government appointed an investigative commission whose recommendations resulted in new, tripartite deliberations on future independence. Keeping colonies was expensive in terms of both finances and international prestige. A Dutch parliamentarian proposed sending a certificate of independence by certified mail when the colonies rejected independence.

In 1973 the prime minister of Suriname, Henck A. E. Arron, the leader of a coalition with a small electoral majority, announced Suriname's intention of becoming independent within two years. The government in The Hague immediately expressed its approval. Independence without a plebiscite was sweetened by an agreement for a financial donation of 3.5 billion florins (€1.6 billion). The government of the Antilles, in contrast, rejected independence. In 1986, the island of Aruba gained autonomy from the Antilles and in 2006, following a plebiscite, the population of the five remaining islands voted in

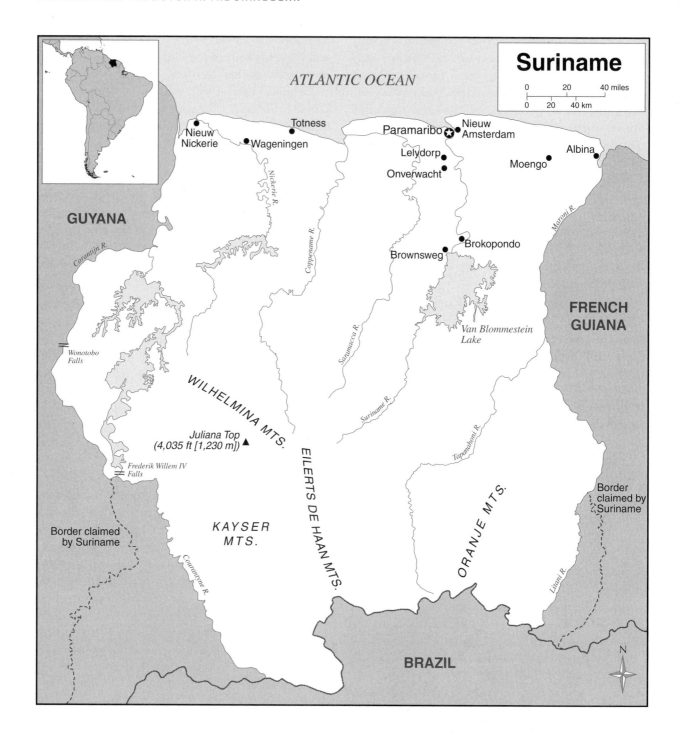

favor of dissolving the political structure of the Antilles as a nation whilst securing a bilateral relationship with Holland for each of the islands.

At the time of its independence in 1975, Suriname had the highest per capita income in Latin America. Exports of aluminum and aid funds from Holland seemed to ensure a stable nation. But many inhabitants left for Holland, opting for Dutch citizenship. The result of the population exodus was that, by 2005, Suriname had about 480,000 inhabitants, with another 325,000 Surinamese-Dutch living in Holland. Most families in Suriname have relatives in Holland, and the flow of capital towards Suriname averaged €100 million per year between 2000 and 2005. Dutch cooperation has always been a "reserve economy," but the funds committed in 1975 will be exhausted by 2008.

Suriname

Population:	470,784 (2007 est.)
Area:	63,039 sq. mi
Offical language:	Dutch
Languages:	English; Sranang Tongo (Surinamese, or Taki-Taki); Caribbean Hindustani (a dialect of Hindi); Javanese
National currency:	Surinam dollar
Principal religions:	Hindu 27%; Protestant 25% (predominantly Moravian); Roman Catholic 23%; Muslim 20%; indigenous beliefs 5%
Ethnicity:	Hindustani (or "East Indians") 37%; Creole (mixed white and black) 31%; Javanese 15%; "Maroons" (their African ancestors were brought to the country in the 17th and 18th centuries as slaves and escaped to the interior) 10%; Amerindian 2%; Chinese 2%; white 1%; other 2%
Capital:	Paramaribo
Annual rainfall:	Averages about 90 in on the coast
Economy:	*GDP per capita:* US$7,100 (2006)

With independence, a small Surinamese national army was created. A labor dispute by noncommissioned officers turned into a coup d'état in 1980. In its first twenty-five years of independence, Suriname experienced two government coups and several attempted palace coups, and had seven civilian government administrations and seven civilian-military administrations between 1975 and 2000. During the years of the military government headed by former sergeant-major (later colonel) Dési Bouterse, the nation's relations with Holland worsened, and a second population exodus followed. The economy worsened, partly due to the suspension of Dutch financial cooperation from 1980 to 1987. Democracy was reestablished in 1987. A second coup took place in 1990, and cooperation was again suspended. When a civilian government was reestablished, after consulting with civilian leaders in Suriname, Holland again offered to create a commonwealth, but Suriname later decided against it, partly due to a military veto. All this was aggravated by an internal conflict led by ex-sergeant Ronnie Brunswijk (b. 1962), formerly one of Bouterse's bodyguards. Lengthy negotiations resulted in a peace agreement in 1992, sponsored by the Organization of American States. Military influence on politics gradually disappeared after that, and as of 2007 country is governed by the three-time civilian president, Ronald Venetiaan (b. 1936).

See also **Arron, Henck A. E.; Bouterse, Desi; Dutch-Latin American Relations.**

BIBLIOGRAPHY

Hoogbergen, Wim, and Dirk Kruijt. *De oorlog der ser-geanten: Surinaamse militairen in de politiek, 1980–1992.* [The Sergeant's War: The Surinamese Military in National Politics]. Amsterdam: Bert Bakker, 2005.

Lier, Rudolf A. J. van. *Frontier Society: A Social Analysis of the History of Surinam.* The Hague: Martinus Nijhoff, 1971.

Oostindie, Gert, and Inge Klinkers. *Decolonising the Caribbean: Dutch Policies in a Comparative Perspective.* Amsterdam: Amsterdam University Press, 2003.

Organization of American States (OAS). *Peace and Democracy in Suriname: Final Report of the Special Mission to Suriname (1992–2000).* Washington, DC: OAS Unit for the Promotion of Democracy, 2001.

DIRK KRUIJT

SWAN ISLANDS. The Swan Islands—Great Swan, Little Swan, and Booby Cay—are located in the Caribbean Sea approximately ninety miles from the Honduran coast. Great Swan, approximately two miles in length, is separated by a narrow, shallow canal of coral reef from Little Swan, 1.5 miles in length; Booby Cay can be reached by foot from Great Swan during low tide. Named for the seventeenth-century privateer Captain Swan, under the Honduran constitution they are known as Islas Santanilla, replacing the colonial name Santa Ana, given by Christopher Columbus who came upon the islands on St. Anne Day, on his last voyage in 1502. The Swan Islands have a small population, mostly employees of the radio and meteorological installations. The islands boast a large population of birds as well as tortoises, iguanas, fish, shrimp, and lobster.

Privateers and revolutionaries fighting for independence in South America took refuge in the islands from 1815 to 1821. In the 1860s the Pacific Guano Company mined guano deposits there and exported guano to New England farmers. At one time claimed by the United States, the islands were rented to the United Fruit Company to establish the Tropical Wireless Company; several installations were built in 1908 and 1927. By 1923, in response to U.S. operations and civilian territorial claims, Honduras also began to claim the islands. The islands became key to U.S. military and political interests; in 1960 the United States sponsored Radio Swan, a Cuban-exile-run radio station that broadcasted from Great Swan into Cuba. The Swan Islands were recognized as part of the Honduran sovereign territory by 1971.

See also **Columbus, Christopher; Guano Industry; Honduras; United Fruit Company.**

BIBLIOGRAPHY

Ferro, Carlos A. 1972. *El Caso de las Islas Santanilla*. Tegucigalpa: Oficina de Relaciones Públicas, Presidencia de Honduras.

Swan Islands, Honduras. Donald E. Keith, Tarleton State University. Available from http://www.tarleton.edu/~dekeith/swanislands.html.

SUYAPA GRICELDA PORTILLO VILLEDA

SYNCRETISM. Syncretism, a process of assimilating different religious beliefs into a system different from its component parts. Strictly, this process does not include the retention of old beliefs or forms under a veneer of new ones, especially if the latter are imposed by force or represent merely the adoption of certain alien rituals. More widely, however, the term is used to signify the borrowing of beliefs and ritual of one religious system by another. In this latter sense, syncretism is as old as religion itself. Syncretic elements appear in the Bible, derived from Canaanite, Babylonian, and Greek sources. Almost from its origins, Christianity has incorporated features of other religions. The first part of the Roman Catholic Mass is based on the first-century Jewish synagogue service. Pagan feasts were freely borrowed, such as that of Sol Invictus (the Unconquered Sun), a Syrian solar god whose anniversary on 25 December, at the winter solstice, gives the date of modern Christmas, or the pagan seasonal celebrations that became the Ember Days. The bold experiment of the Jesuits in sixteenth-century China in adapting Catholicism to native customs and rites was eventually condemned by the papacy because it seemed to involve genuine syncretism.

Though Spanish Catholicism of the sixteenth century was often a folk religion mingled with superstition, the process of syncretism with pre-Christian elements had been so thorough that it is difficult to separate these syncretic elements from orthodox Catholicism. The syncretic process is seen more easily in the religion of the *conversos* (Jewish converts to Catholicism), who often retained Judaic practices that still can be found in New Mexico among present-day descendants of *conversos* who moved north from New Spain in the colonial period.

In pre-Conquest America, religious syncretism seems to have been common. The Mexica (Aztecs) commonly adopted the gods of conquered or tributary peoples, thus adding greatly to the complexity of their myths and deities. The southward movement of Mexican, or Toltec, influences from the central plateau had a strong impact on Maya religion of the post-Classical Period. Prominent among these was the acceptance of Quetzalcoatl under the name Kukulcan and the increased emphasis on human sacrifice. Because of the lack of clear evidence, it is difficult to draw definitive conclusions about pre-Conquest syncretism in Latin America.

The open-minded attitude of the Mexicas found difficulty with the exclusive demands of the Christian God preached by the early Spanish friars. There seems, however, to have been little active resistance, in part because of the wholesale disappearance of the native priesthood and temples during and after the Spanish Conquest. In the sixteenth century, cases were reported of relapses into idolatry and even of secret human sacrifice. More common were passive/aggressive techniques that involved external compliance without substantially altering the pre-Conquest religious viewpoint. In seventeenth-century Peru the church launched a major campaign against residual idolatry and syncretism.

Late twentieth-century research emphasized the subtle role played by the translation of religious concepts from one language to another. Europeans and Native Americans were separated by a vast cognitive and psychological gap. Basic Christian concepts, such as the afterlife as reward or punishment, hell, personal sin, and redemption, did not exist in the pre-Conquest New World. Translating these concepts and making them intelligible and acceptable to the Indians was one of the most daunting challenges faced by the early missionaries. The translation of western European religious terms into the native languages added nuances and were received by the Indians in terms of their own religious mentality and worldview. In Mexico this process has been called the "nahuatilization" of Christianity. The assertion that the early friars deliberately substituted Christian devotions or saints for pre-Conquest deities lacks any firm evidence. Most missionary friars were strongly opposed to any form of syncretism, which they regarded as neo- or crypto-idolatry.

The retention of native beliefs or their mingling with Christianity seems to have been strongest among Native Americans in those areas that were farthest from Spanish influence or those who held most tenaciously to traditional ways. The Mayas, in a special way, were resistant to change. In 1585, Pedro de Feria, the bishop of Chiapas, complained that Christianity was only a veneer among the Maya Indians of his diocese. The same thing was encountered among the Yaqui of northern Mexico, the Hopis of Arizona, and among the various Maya groups of Guatemala. In South America the old ways were reinforced by geographical isolation.

In the twentieth century some missionaries grew more tolerant and even accepting of syncretism, which they used as a missionary tool. The mingling of Christian and pre-Christian elements is regarded as inevitable and not subject to immediate change.

The term "syncretism" has become somewhat contested, and fallen into some disuse and is often replaced with terms such as "religious hybridity" and "religious creolization."

See also **African-Latin American Religions: Overview; Religion in Mexico, Catholic Church and Beyond.**

BIBLIOGRAPHY

Charles Gibson, *The Aztecs Under Spanish Rule* (1964).

Charles E. Dibble, "The Nahuatilization of Christianity," in *Sixteenth Century Mexico: The Work of Sahagún*, edited by Munro S. Edmonson (1974), pp. 225–233.

Mircea Eliade, *A History of Religious Ideas,* 3 vols. (1978–1985).

John M. Ingham, *Mary, Michael, and Lucifer: Folk Catholicism in Central Mexico* (1986).

Muriel Thayer Painter, *With Good Heart: Yaqui Beliefs and Ceremonies in Pascua Village,* edited by Edward H. Spicer and Wilma Kaemlein (1986).

Louise Burkhart, *The Slippery Earth: Nahua-Christian Moral Dialogue in Sixteenth-Century Mexico* (1989).

Additional Bibliography

Greenfield, Sidney M., and A. F. Droogers, eds. *Reinventing Religions: Syncretism and Transformation in Africa and the Americas.* Lanham, MD: Rowman & Littlefield, 2001.

Lockhart, James. *The Nahuas after the Conquest: A Social and Cultural History of the Indians of Central Mexico, Sixteenth through Eighteenth Centuries.* Stanford, CA: Stanford University Press, 1992.

Marzal, Manuel M. *The Indian Face of God in Latin America.* Trans. Penelope R. Hall. Maryknoll, NY: Orbis Books, 1996.

Mills, Kenneth. *Idolatry and Its Enemies: Colonial Andean Religion and Extirpation, 1640–1750.* Princeton, NJ: Princeton University Press, 1997.

Pereira, José Carlos. *Sincretismo religioso & ritos sacrificiais: Influências das religiões afro no catolicismo popular Brasileiro.* São Paulo: Zouk, 2004.

Rostworowski de Diez Canseco, María. *Pachacamac y el señor de los milagros: Una trayectoria milenaria.* Lima: Instituto de Estudios Peruanos, 1992.

STAFFORD POOLE C.M.

SYPHILIS. *See* **Diseases.**

SZYSZLO, FERNANDO DE (1925–). The Peruvian painter and sculptor Fernando de Szyszlo was born on July 5, 1925, in Lima. His father was a Polish botanist, zoologist, and geographer, and his mother was a native Peruvian, sister of the Peruvian poet Abraham Valdelomar. Mario Vargas Llosa has described Szyszlo's works as among the most original representations of Latin American Art, rooted in pre-Hispanic symbols and motifs in audacious alliance with cubism, abstract art, and surrealism (Vargas Llosa, p. 9). Szyszlo studied for three years (1944–1947) with the Austrian artist Adolfo Winternitz at the School of Fine Arts at Lima's Pontificia Universidad

Católica del Perú, where he then taught for twenty years (1956–1977). In 1948 he joined Espacio, a group of painters and architects who addressed nativism, seeking artistic renewal in the disciplines of indigenous pre-Hispanic cultures. Szyszlo's early paintings were figurative, but after his first trip to Europe in 1949 he turned to abstraction. He studied the lore, language, and arts of Peruvian pre-Conquest cultures, especially the Chancay culture (1200–1400 CE). He traveled to the United States in 1958 and remained in Washington, D.C., to serve as a visual arts unit consultant to the Organization of American States (1958–1960). He settled permanently in Lima in 1970.

In the 1960s Szyszlo worked on a series of thirteen paintings inspired by Quechua elegy *Apu Inka Atawallpaman*, on the death of Atahualpa, last ruling Inca. By the late 1960s Szyszlo had created a personal style called abstract nativism. He was artist in residence at Cornell in 1962 and a visiting lecturer at Yale University in 1966. He won the first national prize for paintings at the Esso Salon of young artists in Lima in 1964

In his abstract paintings of the 1970s he began to incorporate shapes suggestive of knives, ceremonial tables, and mummies wrapped in sacred gowns. In the 1980s he painted totemic forms in closed, three-dimensional spaces that suggest chambers. His oeuvre is mainly characterized by series of works with specific themes, most notably, in his later period, the seacoast series (the "Mar de Lurín," "Camino a Mendieta," and "Sol Negro").

Szyszlo has had a powerful influence on Peruvian painting and is the recipient of numerous honors. He became a member of the Academia Peruana de la Lengua in 1997, was named honorary professor of the Universidad de Lima in 1998, and *doctor honoris causa* of the Pontificia Universidad Católica del Perú in 2005. The French Ministry of Culture named him Officier de l'Ordre des Arts et des Lettres in 2001. He was awarded for the best engraving at the Feria de la Estampa in 2005 by the Asociación de Críticos de Arte de Madrid.

See also **Art: The Twentieth Century; Atahualpa; Chancay; Quechua.**

BIBLIOGRAPHY

Primary Work

Szyszlo, Fernando de. *Miradas furtivas*. México: Fondo de Cultura Económica, 1996.

Secondary Works

Ashton, Dore. *Szyszlo*. Barcelona: Ediciones Polígrafa S.A., 2003.

Balbi, Mariella. *Szyszlo: Travesía*. Lima: Universidad de Ciencias Aplicadas, 2001.

Chase, Gilbert. *Contemporary Art in Latin America: Painting, Graphic Art, Sculpture, Architecture*. New York and London: Free Press/Collier-Macmillan, 1970. See pp. 105–107.

Escallón, Ana María, Ricardo Pau-Llosa, and Mario Vargas Llosa. *Fernando de Szyszlo*. Santa Fé de Bogotá: Ediciones Alfred Wild, 1991.

Traba, Marta, curator. *Museum of Modern Art in Latin America*. Selections from the Permanent Collection. Washington, DC: Organization of American States, General Secretariat, 1985. Introductory essay by Marta Traba, p. 86.

Vargas Llosa, Mario. "Prólogo." In *Szyszlo: Travesía*, by Mariella Balbi. Lima: Universidad de Ciencias Aplicadas, 2001.

MARTA GARDS
ELISABETH. ACHA